AMERICAN KING JAMES BIBLE and FOUNDING DOCUMENTS

God's Holy Spirit was the Author of the Holy Bible in its original languages

Compiled by Eve Engelbrite

The American King James Version of the Bible was produced by Peter Engelbrite with assistance from Tye Rausch and Eve Engelbrite. This translation of the Bible based on the original 1611 King James Version. It substitutes modern words for archaic words of King James English (see Appendix). Syntax, semantics, and spellings have NOT been changed.

"I am hereby putting the American King James version of the Bible into the public domain on November 8, 1999. *Michael Peter Engelbrite*"
"You may use it in any manner you wish: copy it, sell it, modify it, etc. You can't copyright it or prevent others from using it, nor can you claim that you created it. Please be encouraged to share it with others. *Michael Peter Engelbrite*"

The American King James Version is available for free in various electronic formats: one of which is The Sword Project at http://www.crosswire.org/sword/index.jsp. Electronic formats do not include the many subsequent corrections in printed editions.

American King James Bible and Founding Documents © 2024 Eve Engelbrite

This printed, copyrighted compilation contains the following:

American King James Version of the Holy Bible, 6th revision July 28, 2018

The U. S. Declaration of Independence
The U. S. Constitution
The U. S. Bill of Rights
The United States Pledge of Allegiance

and Founders' documents and quotes

Library of Congress Control Number: 2024922979

ISBN 978-1-931203-37-1

Published by Inspired Idea in

Sacramento, CA, USA

www.kneelingmedia.org

CONTENTS

Old Testament of Holy Bible

Genesis	7	Second Chronicles	247	Daniel	450
Exodus	36	Ezra	268	Hosea	459
Leviticus	61	Nehemiah	274	Joel	463
Numbers	79	Esther	283	Amos	465
Deuteronomy	105	Job	288	Obadiah	469
Joshua	126	Psalms	302	Jonah	470
Judges	141	Proverbs	336	Micah	471
Ruth	156	Ecclesiastes	348	Nahum	474
First Samuel	158	Song of Solomon	353	Habakkuk	476
Second Samuel	177	Isaiah	356	Zephaniah	478
First Kings	193	Jeremiah	384	Haggai	480
Second Kings	212	Lamentations	417	Zechariah	481
First Chronicles	230	Ezekiel	420	Malachi	486

New Testament of Holy Bible

Matthew	489	First Timothy	609
Mark	508	Second Timothy	611
Luke	520	Titus	613
John	540	Philemon	614
Acts	555	Hebrews	615
Romans	575	James	621
First Corinthians	583	First Peter	623
Second Corinthians	591	Second Peter	625
Galatians	596	First John	627
Ephesians	599	Second John	629
Philippians	602	Third John	630
Colossians	604	Jude	631
First Thessalonians	606	Revelation	632
Second Thessalonians	608	Appendix	642

CONTENTS (continued)

Founding Documents

The U. S. Declaration of Independence	651
The U. S. Constitution	654
The U. S. Bill of Rights	661
The United States Pledge of Allegiance	662

Founders' Documents and Quotes

Sermons Sparked American Revolution	665
Patrick Henry and Samuel Adams	666
All Education is Religious	667
Deists or Not?	668
Bible's Importance	669
Presbyterian Minister John Witherspoon	670
John Adams	671
Was America Christian or Not?	672
James Madison	673
Virginia Statue of Religious Freedom	674
Jefferson's "Wall of Separation" letter	675
Signers from Northern Colonies/States	676
Signers from Middle Colonies/States	678
Signers from Southern Colonies/States	681
Washington's Thanksgiving Proclamation	684
Washington's Farewell Address	685
Franklin's motion for prayer	691

OLD TESTAMENT

Genesis

1 ¹In the beginning God created the heaven and the earth. ²And the earth was without form, and void; and darkness was on the face of the deep. And the Spirit of God moved on the face of the waters. ³And God said, Let there be light: and there was light. ⁴And God saw the light, that it was good: and God divided the light from the darkness. ⁵And God called the light Day, and the darkness he called Night. And the evening and the morning were the first day. ⁶And God said, Let there be a firmament in the middle of the waters, and let it divide the waters from the waters. ⁷And God made the firmament, and divided the waters which were under the firmament from the waters which were above the firmament: and it was so. ⁸And God called the firmament Heaven. And the evening and the morning were the second day. ⁹And God said, Let the waters under the heaven be gathered together to one place, and let the dry land appear: and it was so. ¹⁰And God called the dry land Earth; and the gathering together of the waters called he Seas: and God saw that it was good. ¹¹And God said, Let the earth bring forth grass, the herb yielding seed, and the fruit tree yielding fruit after his kind, whose seed is in itself, on the earth: and it was so. ¹²And the earth brought forth grass, and herb yielding seed after his kind, and the tree yielding fruit, whose seed was in itself, after his kind: and God saw that it was good. ¹³And the evening and the morning were the third day. ¹⁴And God said, Let there be lights in the firmament of the heaven to divide the day from the night; and let them be for signs, and for seasons, and for days, and years: ¹⁵And let them be for lights in the firmament of the heaven to give light on the earth: and it was so. ¹⁶And God made two great lights; the greater light to rule the day, and the lesser light to rule the night: he made the stars also. ¹⁷And God set them in the firmament of the heaven to give light on the earth, ¹⁸And to rule over the day and over the night, and to divide the light from the darkness: and God saw that it was good. ¹⁹And the evening and the morning were the fourth day. ²⁰And God said, Let the waters bring forth abundantly the moving creature that has life, and fowl that may fly above the earth in the open firmament of heaven. ²¹And God created great whales, and every living creature that moves, which the waters brought forth abundantly, after their kind, and every winged fowl after his kind: and God saw that it was good. ²²And God blessed them, saying, Be fruitful, and multiply, and fill the waters in the seas, and let fowl multiply in the earth. ²³And the evening and the morning were the fifth day. ²⁴And God said, Let the earth bring forth the living creature after his kind, cattle, and creeping thing, and beast of the earth after his kind: and it was so. ²⁵And God made the beast of the earth after his kind, and cattle after their kind, and every thing that creeps on the earth after his kind: and God saw that it was good. ²⁶And God said, Let us make man in our image, after our likeness: and let them have dominion over the fish of the sea, and over the fowl of the air, and over the cattle, and over all the earth, and over every creeping thing that creeps on the earth. ²⁷So God created man in his own image, in the image of God created he him; male and female created he them. ²⁸And God blessed them, and God said to them, Be fruitful, and multiply, and replenish the earth, and subdue it: and have dominion over the fish of the sea, and over the fowl of the air, and over every living thing that moves on the earth. ²⁹And God said, Behold, I have given you every herb bearing seed, which is on the face of all the earth, and every tree, in the which is the fruit of a tree yielding seed; to you it shall be for meat. ³⁰And to every beast of the earth, and to every fowl of the air, and to every thing that creeps on the earth, wherein there is life, I have given every green herb for meat: and it was so. ³¹And God saw every thing that he had made, and, behold, it was very good. And the evening and the morning were the sixth day.

2 ¹Thus the heavens and the earth were finished, and all the host of them. ²And on the seventh day God ended his work which he had made; and he rested on the seventh day from all his work which he had made. ³And God blessed the seventh day, and sanctified it: because that in it he had rested from all his work which God created and made. ⁴These are the generations of the heavens and of the earth when they were created, in the day that the LORD God made the earth and the heavens, ⁵And every plant of the field before it was in the earth, and every herb of the field before it grew: for the LORD God had not caused it to rain on the earth, and there was not a man to till the ground. ⁶But there went up a mist from the earth, and watered the whole face of the ground. ⁷And the LORD God formed man of the dust of the ground, and breathed into his nostrils the breath of life; and man became a living soul. ⁸And the LORD God planted a garden eastward in Eden; and there he put the man whom he had formed. ⁹And out of the ground made the LORD God to grow every tree that is pleasant to the sight, and good for food; the tree of life also in the middle of the garden, and the tree of knowledge of good and evil. ¹⁰And a river went out of Eden to water the garden; and from there it was parted, and became into four heads. ¹¹The name of the first is Pison: that is it which compasses the whole land of Havilah, where there is gold; ¹²And the gold of that land is good: there is bdellium and the onyx stone. ¹³And the name of the second river is Gihon: the same is it that compasses the whole land of Ethiopia. ¹⁴And the name of the third river is Hiddekel: that is it which goes toward the east of Assyria. And the fourth river is Euphrates. ¹⁵And the LORD God took the man, and put him into the garden of Eden to dress it and to keep it. ¹⁶And the LORD God commanded the man, saying, Of every tree of the garden you may freely eat: ¹⁷But of the tree of the knowledge of good and evil, you shall not eat of it: for in the day that you eat thereof you shall surely die. ¹⁸And the LORD God said, It is not good that the man should be alone; I will make him an help meet for him. ¹⁹And out of the ground the LORD God formed every beast of the field, and every fowl of the air; and brought them to Adam to see what he would call them: and whatever Adam called every living creature, that was the name thereof. ²⁰And Adam gave names to all cattle, and to the fowl of the air, and to every beast of the field; but for Adam there was not found an help meet for him. ²¹And the LORD God caused a deep sleep to fall on Adam, and he slept: and he took one of his ribs, and closed up the flesh instead thereof; ²²And the rib, which the LORD God had taken from man, made he a woman, and brought her to the man. ²³And Adam said, This is now bone of my bones, and flesh of my flesh: she shall be called Woman, because she was taken out of Man. ²⁴Therefore shall a man leave his father and his mother, and shall join to his wife: and they shall be one flesh. ²⁵And they were both naked, the man and his wife, and were not ashamed.

3 ¹Now the serpent was more subtle than any beast of the field which the LORD God had made. And he said to the woman, Yes, has God said, You shall not eat of every tree of the garden? ²And the woman said to the serpent, We may eat of the fruit of the trees of the garden: ³But of the fruit of the tree which is in the middle of the garden, God has said, You shall not eat of it, neither shall you touch it, lest you die. ⁴And the serpent said to the woman, You shall not surely die: ⁵For God does know that in the day you eat thereof, then your eyes shall be opened, and you shall be as gods, knowing good and evil. ⁶And when the woman saw that the tree was good for food, and that it was pleasant to the eyes, and a tree to be desired to make one wise, she took of the fruit thereof, and did eat, and gave also to her husband with her; and he did eat. ⁷And the eyes of them both were opened, and they knew that they were naked; and they sewed fig leaves together, and made themselves aprons. ⁸And they heard the voice of the LORD God walking in the garden in the cool of the day: and Adam and his wife hid themselves from the presence of the LORD God among the trees of the garden. ⁹And the LORD God called to Adam, and said to him, Where are you? ¹⁰And he said, I heard your voice in the garden, and I was afraid, because I was naked; and I hid myself. ¹¹And he said, Who told you that you were naked? Have you eaten of the tree, whereof I commanded you that you should not eat? ¹²And the man said, The woman whom you gave to be with me, she gave me of the tree, and I did eat. ¹³And the LORD God said to the woman, What is this that you have done? And the woman said, The serpent beguiled me, and I did eat. ¹⁴And the LORD God said to the serpent, Because you have done this, you are cursed above all cattle, and above every beast of the field; on your belly shall you go, and dust shall you eat all the days of your life: ¹⁵And I will put enmity between you and the woman, and between your seed and her seed; it shall bruise your head, and you shall bruise his heel. ¹⁶To the woman he said, I will greatly multiply your sorrow and your conception; in sorrow you shall bring forth children; and your desire shall be to your husband, and he shall rule over you. ¹⁷And to Adam he said, Because you have listened to the voice of your wife, and have eaten of the tree, of which I commanded you, saying, You shall not eat of it: cursed is the ground for your sake; in sorrow shall you eat of it all the days of your life; ¹⁸Thorns also and thistles shall it bring forth to you; and you shall eat the herb of the field; ¹⁹In the sweat of your face shall you eat bread, till you return to the ground; for out of it were you taken: for dust you are, and to dust shall you return. ²⁰And Adam called his wife's name Eve; because she was the mother of all living. ²¹To Adam also and to his wife did the LORD God make coats of skins, and clothed them. ²²And the LORD God said, Behold, the man is become as one of us, to know good and evil: and now, lest he put forth his hand, and take also of the tree of life, and eat, and live for ever: ²³Therefore the LORD God sent him forth from the garden of Eden, to till the ground from from where he was taken. ²⁴So he drove out the man; and he placed at the east of the garden of Eden Cherubim, and a flaming sword which turned every way, to keep the way of the tree of life.

4 ¹And Adam knew Eve his wife; and she conceived, and bore Cain, and said, I have gotten a man from the LORD. ²And she again bore his brother Abel. And Abel was a keeper of sheep, but Cain was a tiller of the ground. ³And in process of time it came to pass, that Cain brought of the fruit of the ground an offering to the LORD. ⁴And Abel, he also brought of the firstborn of his flock and of the fat thereof. And the LORD had respect to Abel and to his offering: ⁵But to Cain and to his offering he had not respect. And Cain was very wroth, and his countenance fell. ⁶And the LORD said to Cain, Why are you wroth? and why is your countenance fallen? ⁷If you do well, shall you not be accepted? and if you do not well, sin lies at the door. And to you shall be his desire, and you shall rule over him. ⁸And Cain talked with Abel his brother: and it came to pass, when they were in the field, that Cain rose up against Abel his brother, and slew him. ⁹And the LORD said to Cain, Where is Abel your brother? And he said, I know not: Am I my brother's keeper? ¹⁰And he said, What have you done? the voice of your brother's blood cries to me from the ground. ¹¹And now are you cursed from the earth, which has opened her mouth to receive your brother's blood from your hand; ¹²When you till the ground, it shall not from now on yield to you her strength; a fugitive and a vagabond shall you be in the earth. ¹³And Cain said to the LORD, My punishment is greater than I can bear. ¹⁴Behold, you have driven me out this day from the face of the earth; and from your face shall I be hid; and I shall be a fugitive and a vagabond in the earth; and it shall come to pass, that every one that finds me shall slay me. ¹⁵And the LORD said to him, Therefore whoever slays Cain, vengeance shall be taken on him sevenfold. And the LORD set a mark on Cain, lest any finding him should kill him. ¹⁶And Cain went out from the presence of the LORD, and dwelled in the land of Nod, on the east of Eden. ¹⁷And Cain knew his wife; and she conceived, and bore Enoch: and he built a city, and called the name of the city, after the name of his son, Enoch. ¹⁸And to Enoch was born Irad: and Irad begat Mehujael: and Mehujael begat Methusael: and Methusael begat Lamech. ¹⁹And Lamech took to him two wives: the name of the one was Adah, and the name of the other Zillah. ²⁰And Adah bore Jabal: he was the father of such as dwell in tents, and of such as have cattle. ²¹And his brother's name was Jubal: he was the father of all such as handle the harp and organ. ²²And Zillah, she also bore Tubalcain, an instructor of every artificer in brass and iron: and the sister of Tubalcain was Naamah. ²³And Lamech said to his wives, Adah and Zillah, Hear my voice; you wives of Lamech, listen to my speech: for I have slain a man to my wounding, and a young man to my hurt. ²⁴If Cain shall be avenged sevenfold, truly Lamech seventy and sevenfold. ²⁵And Adam knew his wife again; and she bore a son, and called his name Seth: For God, said she, has appointed me another seed instead of Abel, whom Cain slew. ²⁶And to Seth, to him also there was born a son; and he called his name Enos: then began men to call on the name of the LORD.

5 ¹This is the book of the generations of Adam. In the day that God created man, in the likeness of God made he him; ²Male and female created he them; and blessed them, and called their name Adam, in the day when they were created. ³And Adam lived an hundred and thirty years, and begat a son in his own likeness, and after his image; and called his name Seth: ⁴And the days of Adam after he had begotten Seth were eight hundred years: and he begat sons and daughters: ⁵And all the days that Adam lived were nine hundred and thirty years: and he died. ⁶And Seth lived an hundred and five years, and begat Enos: ⁷And Seth lived after he begat Enos eight hundred and seven years, and begat sons and daughters: ⁸And all the days of Seth were nine hundred and twelve years: and he died. ⁹And Enos lived ninety years, and begat Cainan: ¹⁰And Enos lived after he begat Cainan eight hundred and fifteen years, and begat sons and daughters: ¹¹And all the days of Enos were nine hundred and five years: and he died. ¹²And Cainan lived seventy years and begat Mahalaleel: ¹³And Cainan lived after he begat Mahalaleel eight hundred and forty years, and begat sons and daughters: ¹⁴And all the days of Cainan were nine hundred and ten years: and he died. ¹⁵And Mahalaleel lived sixty and five years, and begat Jared: ¹⁶And Mahalaleel lived after he begat Jared eight hundred and thirty years, and begat sons and daughters: ¹⁷And all the days of Mahalaleel were eight hundred ninety and five years: and he died. ¹⁸And Jared lived an hundred sixty and two years, and he begat Enoch: ¹⁹And Jared lived after he begat Enoch eight hundred years, and begat sons and daughters: ²⁰And all the days of Jared were nine hundred sixty and two years: and he died. ²¹And Enoch lived sixty and five years, and begat Methuselah: ²²And Enoch walked with God after he begat Methuselah three hundred years, and begat sons and daughters: ²³And all the days of Enoch were three hundred sixty and five years: ²⁴And Enoch walked with God: and he was not; for God took him. ²⁵And Methuselah lived an hundred eighty and seven years, and begat Lamech. ²⁶And Methuselah lived after he begat Lamech seven hundred eighty and two years, and begat sons and daughters: ²⁷And all the days of Methuselah were nine hundred sixty and nine years: and he died. ²⁸And Lamech lived an hundred eighty and two years, and begat a son: ²⁹And he called his name Noah, saying, This same shall comfort us concerning our work and toil of our hands, because of the ground which the LORD has cursed. ³⁰And Lamech lived after he begat Noah five hundred ninety and five years, and begat sons and daughters: ³¹And all the days of Lamech were seven hundred seventy and seven years: and he died. ³²And Noah was five hundred years old: and Noah begat Shem, Ham, and Japheth.

6 ¹And it came to pass, when men began to multiply on the face of the earth, and daughters were born to them, ²That the sons of God saw the daughters of men that they were fair; and they took them wives of all which they chose. ³And the LORD said, My spirit shall not always strive with man, for that he also is flesh: yet his days shall be an hundred and twenty years. ⁴There were giants in the earth in those days; and also after that, when the sons of God came in to the daughters of men, and they bore children to them, the same became mighty men which were of old, men of renown. ⁵And God saw that the wickedness of man was great in the earth, and that every imagination of the thoughts of his heart was only evil continually. ⁶And it repented the LORD that he had made man on the earth, and it grieved him at his heart. ⁷And the LORD said, I will destroy man whom I have created from the face of the earth; both man, and beast, and the creeping thing, and the fowls of the air; for it repents me that I have made them. ⁸But Noah found grace in the eyes of the LORD. ⁹These are the generations of Noah: Noah was a just man and perfect in his generations, and Noah walked with God. ¹⁰And Noah begat three sons, Shem, Ham, and Japheth. ¹¹The earth also was corrupt before God, and the earth was filled with violence. ¹²And God looked on the earth, and, behold, it was corrupt; for all flesh had corrupted his way on the earth. ¹³And God said to Noah, The end of all flesh is come before me; for the earth is filled with violence through them; and, behold, I will destroy them with the earth. ¹⁴Make you an ark of gopher wood; rooms shall you make in the ark, and shall pitch it within and without with pitch. ¹⁵And this is the fashion which you shall make it of: The length of the ark shall be three hundred cubits, the breadth of it fifty cubits, and the height of it thirty cubits. ¹⁶A window shall you make to the ark, and in a cubit shall you finish it above; and the door of the ark shall you set in the side thereof; with lower, second, and third stories shall you make it. ¹⁷And, behold, I, even I, do bring a flood of waters on the earth, to destroy all flesh, wherein is the breath of life, from under heaven; and every thing that is in the earth shall die. ¹⁸But with you will I establish my covenant; and you shall come into the ark, you, and your sons, and your wife, and your sons' wives with you. ¹⁹And of every living thing of all flesh, two of every sort shall you bring into the ark, to keep them alive with you; they shall be male and female. ²⁰Of fowls after their kind, and of cattle after their kind, of every creeping thing of the earth after his kind, two of every sort shall come to you, to keep them alive. ²¹And take you to you of all food that is eaten, and you shall gather it to you; and it shall be for food for you, and for them. ²²Thus did Noah; according to all that God commanded him, so did he.

7 ¹And the LORD said to Noah, Come you and all your house into the ark; for you have I seen righteous before me in this generation. ²Of every clean beast you shall take to you by sevens, the male and his female: and of beasts that are not clean by two, the male and his female. ³Of fowls also of the air by sevens, the male and the female; to keep seed alive on the face of all the earth. ⁴For yet seven days, and I will cause it to rain on the earth forty days and forty nights; and every living substance that I have made will I destroy

from off the face of the earth. ⁵And Noah did according to all that the LORD commanded him. ⁶And Noah was six hundred years old when the flood of waters was on the earth. ⁷And Noah went in, and his sons, and his wife, and his sons' wives with him, into the ark, because of the waters of the flood. ⁸Of clean beasts, and of beasts that are not clean, and of fowls, and of every thing that creeps on the earth, ⁹There went in two and two to Noah into the ark, the male and the female, as God had commanded Noah. ¹⁰And it came to pass after seven days, that the waters of the flood were on the earth. ¹¹In the six hundredth year of Noah's life, in the second month, the seventeenth day of the month, the same day were all the fountains of the great deep broken up, and the windows of heaven were opened. ¹²And the rain was on the earth forty days and forty nights. ¹³In the selfsame day entered Noah, and Shem, and Ham, and Japheth, the sons of Noah, and Noah's wife, and the three wives of his sons with them, into the ark; ¹⁴They, and every beast after his kind, and all the cattle after their kind, and every creeping thing that creeps on the earth after his kind, and every fowl after his kind, every bird of every sort. ¹⁵And they went in to Noah into the ark, two and two of all flesh, wherein is the breath of life. ¹⁶And they that went in, went in male and female of all flesh, as God had commanded him: and the LORD shut him in. ¹⁷And the flood was forty days on the earth; and the waters increased, and bore up the ark, and it was lift up above the earth. ¹⁸And the waters prevailed, and were increased greatly on the earth; and the ark went on the face of the waters. ¹⁹And the waters prevailed exceedingly on the earth; and all the high hills, that were under the whole heaven, were covered. ²⁰Fifteen cubits upward did the waters prevail; and the mountains were covered. ²¹And all flesh died that moved on the earth, both of fowl, and of cattle, and of beast, and of every creeping thing that creeps on the earth, and every man: ²²All in whose nostrils was the breath of life, of all that was in the dry land, died. ²³And every living substance was destroyed which was on the face of the ground, both man, and cattle, and the creeping things, and the fowl of the heaven; and they were destroyed from the earth: and Noah only remained alive, and they that were with him in the ark. ²⁴And the waters prevailed on the earth an hundred and fifty days.

8 ¹And God remembered Noah, and every living thing, and all the cattle that was with him in the ark: and God made a wind to pass over the earth, and the waters assuaged; ²The fountains also of the deep and the windows of heaven were stopped, and the rain from heaven was restrained; ³And the waters returned from off the earth continually: and after the end of the hundred and fifty days the waters were abated. ⁴And the ark rested in the seventh month, on the seventeenth day of the month, on the mountains of Ararat. ⁵And the waters decreased continually until the tenth month: in the tenth month, on the first day of the month, were the tops of the mountains seen. ⁶And it came to pass at the end of forty days, that Noah opened the window of the ark which he had made: ⁷And he sent forth a raven, which went forth to and fro, until the waters were dried up from off the earth. ⁸Also he sent forth a dove from him, to see if the waters were abated from off the face of the ground; ⁹But the dove found no rest for the sole of her foot, and she returned to him into the ark, for the waters were on the face of the whole earth: then he put forth his hand, and took her, and pulled her in to him into the ark. ¹⁰And he stayed yet other seven days; and again he sent forth the dove out of the ark; ¹¹And the dove came in to him in the evening; and, see, in her mouth was an olive leaf plucked off: so Noah knew that the waters were abated from off the earth. ¹²And he stayed yet other seven days; and sent forth the dove; which returned not again to him any more. ¹³And it came to pass in the six hundredth and first year, in the first month, the first day of the month, the waters were dried up from off the earth: and Noah removed the covering of the ark, and looked, and, behold, the face of the ground was dry. ¹⁴And in the second month, on the seven and twentieth day of the month, was the earth dried. ¹⁵And God spoke to Noah, saying, ¹⁶Go forth of the ark, you, and your wife, and your sons, and your sons' wives with you. ¹⁷Bring forth with you every living thing that is with you, of all flesh, both of fowl, and of cattle, and of every creeping thing that creeps on the earth; that they may breed abundantly in the earth, and be fruitful, and multiply on the earth. ¹⁸And Noah went forth, and his sons, and his wife, and his sons' wives with him: ¹⁹Every beast, every creeping thing, and every fowl, and whatever creeps on the earth, after their kinds, went forth out of the ark. ²⁰And Noah built an altar to the LORD; and took of every clean beast, and of every clean fowl, and offered burnt offerings on the altar. ²¹And the LORD smelled a sweet smell; and the LORD said in his heart, I will not again curse the ground any more for man's sake; for the imagination of man's heart is evil from his youth; neither will I again smite any more every thing living, as I have done. ²²While the earth remains, seedtime and harvest, and cold and heat, and summer and winter, and day and night shall not cease.

9 ¹And God blessed Noah and his sons, and said to them, Be fruitful, and multiply, and replenish the earth. ²And the fear of you and the dread of you shall be on every beast of the earth, and on every fowl of the air, on all that moves on the earth, and on all the fishes of the sea; into your hand are they delivered. ³Every moving thing that lives shall be meat for you; even as the green herb have I given you all things. ⁴But flesh with the life thereof, which is the blood thereof, shall you not eat. ⁵And surely your blood of your lives will I require; at the hand of every beast will I require it, and at the hand of man; at the hand of every man's brother will I require the life of man. ⁶Whoever sheds man's blood, by man shall his blood be shed: for in the image of God made he man. ⁷And you, be you fruitful, and multiply; bring forth abundantly in the earth, and multiply therein. ⁸And God spoke to Noah, and to his sons with him, saying, ⁹And I, behold, I establish my covenant with you, and with your seed after you; ¹⁰And with every living creature that is with you, of the fowl, of the cattle, and of every beast of the earth with you; from all that go out of the ark, to every beast of the earth. ¹¹And I will establish my covenant with you, neither shall all flesh be cut off any more by the waters of a flood; neither shall there any more be a flood to destroy the earth. ¹²And God said, This is the token of the covenant which I make between me and you and every living creature that is with you, for perpetual generations: ¹³I do set my bow in the cloud, and it shall be for a token of a covenant between me and the earth. ¹⁴And it shall come to pass, when I bring a cloud over the earth, that the bow shall be seen in the cloud: ¹⁵And I will remember my covenant, which is between me and you and every living creature of all flesh; and the waters shall no more become a flood to destroy all flesh. ¹⁶And the bow shall be in the cloud; and I will look on it, that I may remember the everlasting covenant between God and every living creature of all flesh that is on the earth. ¹⁷And God said to Noah, This is the token of the covenant, which I have established between me and all flesh that is on the earth. ¹⁸And the sons of Noah, that went forth of the ark, were Shem, and Ham, and Japheth: and Ham is the father of Canaan. ¹⁹These are the three sons of Noah: and of them was the whole earth covered. ²⁰And Noah began to be an farmer, and he planted a vineyard: ²¹And he drank of the wine, and was drunken; and he was uncovered within his tent. ²²And Ham, the father of Canaan, saw the nakedness of his father, and told his two brothers without. ²³And Shem and Japheth took a garment, and laid it on both their shoulders, and went backward, and covered the nakedness of their father; and their faces were backward, and they saw not their father's nakedness. ²⁴And Noah awoke from his wine, and knew what his younger son had done to him. ²⁵And he said, Cursed be Canaan; a servant of servants shall he be to his brothers. ²⁶And he said, Blessed be the LORD God of Shem; and Canaan shall be his servant. ²⁷God shall enlarge Japheth, and he shall dwell in the tents of Shem; and Canaan shall be his servant. ²⁸And Noah lived after the flood three hundred and fifty years. ²⁹And all the days of Noah were nine hundred and fifty years: and he died.

10

¹Now these are the generations of the sons of Noah, Shem, Ham, and Japheth: and to them were sons born after the flood. ²The sons of Japheth; Gomer, and Magog, and Madai, and Javan, and Tubal, and Meshech, and Tiras. ³And the sons of Gomer; Ashkenaz, and Riphath, and Togarmah. ⁴And the sons of Javan; Elishah, and Tarshish, Kittim, and Dodanim. ⁵By these were the isles of the Gentiles divided in their lands; every one after his tongue, after their families, in their nations. ⁶And the sons of Ham; Cush, and Mizraim, and Phut, and Canaan. ⁷And the sons of Cush; Seba, and Havilah, and Sabtah, and Raamah, and Sabtechah: and the sons of Raamah; Sheba, and Dedan. ⁸And Cush begat Nimrod: he began to be a mighty one in the earth. ⁹He was a mighty hunter before the LORD: why it is said, Even as Nimrod the mighty hunter before the LORD. ¹⁰And the beginning of his kingdom was Babel, and Erech, and Accad, and Calneh, in the land of Shinar. ¹¹Out of that land went forth Asshur, and built Nineveh, and the city Rehoboth, and Calah, ¹²And Resen between Nineveh and Calah: the same is a great city. ¹³And Mizraim begat Ludim, and Anamim, and Lehabim, and Naphtuhim, ¹⁴And Pathrusim, and Casluhim, (out of whom came Philistim,) and Caphtorim. ¹⁵And Canaan begat Sidon his first born, and Heth, ¹⁶And the Jebusite, and the Amorite, and the Girgasite, ¹⁷And the Hivite, and the Arkite, and the Sinite, ¹⁸And the Arvadite, and the Zemarite, and the Hamathite: and afterward were the families of the Canaanites spread abroad. ¹⁹And the border of the Canaanites was from Sidon, as you come to Gerar, to Gaza; as you go, to Sodom, and Gomorrah, and Admah, and Zeboim, even to Lasha. ²⁰These are the sons of Ham, after their families, after their tongues, in their countries, and in their nations. ²¹To Shem also, the father of all the children of Eber, the brother of Japheth the elder, even to him were children born. ²²The children of Shem; Elam, and Asshur, and Arphaxad, and Lud, and Aram. ²³And the children of Aram; Uz, and Hul, and Gether, and Mash. ²⁴And Arphaxad begat Salah; and Salah begat Eber. ²⁵And to Eber were born two sons: the name of one was Peleg; for in his days was the earth divided; and his brother's name was Joktan. ²⁶And Joktan begat Almodad, and Sheleph, and Hazarmaveth, and Jerah, ²⁷And Hadoram, and Uzal, and Diklah, ²⁸And Obal, and Abimael, and Sheba, ²⁹And Ophir, and Havilah, and Jobab: all these were the sons of Joktan. ³⁰And their dwelling was from Mesha, as you go to Sephar a mount of the east. ³¹These are the sons of Shem, after their families, after their tongues, in their lands, after their nations. ³²These are the families of the sons of Noah, after their generations, in their nations: and by these were the nations divided in the earth after the flood.

11

¹And the whole earth was of one language, and of one speech. ²And it came to pass, as they journeyed from the east, that they found a plain in the land of Shinar; and they dwelled there. ³And they said one to another, Go to, let us make brick, and burn them thoroughly. And they had brick for stone, and slime had they for mortar. ⁴And they said, Go to, let us build us a city and a tower, whose top may reach to heaven; and let us make us a name, lest we be scattered abroad on the face of the whole earth. ⁵And the LORD came down to see the city and the tower, which the children of men built. ⁶And the LORD said, Behold, the people is one, and they have all one language; and this they begin to do: and now nothing will be restrained from them, which they have imagined to do. ⁷Go to, let us go down, and there confound their language, that they may not understand one another's speech. ⁸So the LORD scattered them abroad from there on the face of all the earth: and they left off to build the city. ⁹Therefore is the name of it called Babel; because the LORD did there confound the language of all the earth: and from there did the LORD scatter them abroad on the face of all the earth. ¹⁰These are the generations of Shem: Shem was an hundred years old, and begat Arphaxad two years after the flood: ¹¹And Shem lived after he begat Arphaxad five hundred years, and begat sons and daughters. ¹²And Arphaxad lived five and thirty years, and begat Salah: ¹³And Arphaxad lived after he begat Salah four hundred and three years, and begat sons and daughters. ¹⁴And Salah lived thirty years, and begat Eber: ¹⁵And Salah lived after he begat Eber four hundred and three years, and begat sons and daughters. ¹⁶And Eber lived four and thirty years, and begat Peleg: ¹⁷And Eber lived after he begat Peleg four hundred and thirty years, and begat sons and daughters. ¹⁸And Peleg lived thirty years, and begat Reu: ¹⁹And Peleg lived after he begat Reu two hundred and nine years, and begat sons and daughters. ²⁰And Reu lived two and thirty years, and begat Serug: ²¹And Reu lived after he begat Serug two hundred

and seven years, and begat sons and daughters. ²²And Serug lived thirty years, and begat Nahor: ²³And Serug lived after he begat Nahor two hundred years, and begat sons and daughters. ²⁴And Nahor lived nine and twenty years, and begat Terah: ²⁵And Nahor lived after he begat Terah an hundred and nineteen years, and begat sons and daughters. ²⁶And Terah lived seventy years, and begat Abram, Nahor, and Haran. ²⁷Now these are the generations of Terah: Terah begat Abram, Nahor, and Haran; and Haran begat Lot. ²⁸And Haran died before his father Terah in the land of his nativity, in Ur of the Chaldees. ²⁹And Abram and Nahor took them wives: the name of Abram's wife was Sarai; and the name of Nahor's wife, Milcah, the daughter of Haran, the father of Milcah, and the father of Iscah. ³⁰But Sarai was barren; she had no child. ³¹And Terah took Abram his son, and Lot the son of Haran his son's son, and Sarai his daughter in law, his son Abram's wife; and they went forth with them from Ur of the Chaldees, to go into the land of Canaan; and they came to Haran, and dwelled there. ³²And the days of Terah were two hundred and five years: and Terah died in Haran.

12

¹Now the LORD had said to Abram, Get you out of your country, and from your kindred, and from your father's house, to a land that I will show you: ²And I will make of you a great nation, and I will bless you, and make your name great; and you shall be a blessing: ³And I will bless them that bless you, and curse him that curses you: and in you shall all families of the earth be blessed. ⁴So Abram departed, as the LORD had spoken to him; and Lot went with him: and Abram was seventy and five years old when he departed out of Haran. ⁵And Abram took Sarai his wife, and Lot his brother's son, and all their substance that they had gathered, and the souls that they had gotten in Haran; and they went forth to go into the land of Canaan; and into the land of Canaan they came. ⁶And Abram passed through the land to the place of Sichem, to the plain of Moreh. And the Canaanite was then in the land. ⁷And the LORD appeared to Abram, and said, To your seed will I give this land: and there built he an altar to the LORD, who appeared to him. ⁸And he removed from there to a mountain on the east of Bethel, and pitched his tent, having Bethel on the west, and Hai on the east: and there he built an altar to the LORD, and called on the name of the LORD. ⁹And Abram journeyed, going on still toward the south. ¹⁰And there was a famine in the land: and Abram went down into Egypt to sojourn there; for the famine was grievous in the land. ¹¹And it came to pass, when he was come near to enter into Egypt, that he said to Sarai his wife, Behold now, I know that you are a fair woman to look on: ¹²Therefore it shall come to pass, when the Egyptians shall see you, that they shall say, This is his wife: and they will kill me, but they will save you alive. ¹³Say, I pray you, you are my sister: that it may be well with me for your sake; and my soul shall live because of you. ¹⁴And it came to pass, that, when Abram was come into Egypt, the Egyptians beheld the woman that she was very fair. ¹⁵The princes also of Pharaoh saw her, and commended her before Pharaoh: and the woman was taken into Pharaoh's house. ¹⁶And he entreated Abram well for her sake: and he had sheep, and oxen, and he asses, and menservants, and maidservants, and she asses, and camels.

¹⁷And the LORD plagued Pharaoh and his house with great plagues because of Sarai Abram's wife. ¹⁸And Pharaoh called Abram and said, What is this that you have done to me? why did you not tell me that she was your wife? ¹⁹Why said you, She is my sister? so I might have taken her to me to wife: now therefore behold your wife, take her, and go your way. ²⁰And Pharaoh commanded his men concerning him: and they sent him away, and his wife, and all that he had.

13

¹And Abram went up out of Egypt, he, and his wife, and all that he had, and Lot with him, into the south. ²And Abram was very rich in cattle, in silver, and in gold. ³And he went on his journeys from the south even to Bethel, to the place where his tent had been at the beginning, between Bethel and Hai; ⁴To the place of the altar, which he had make there at the first: and there Abram called on the name of the LORD. ⁵And Lot also, which went with Abram, had flocks, and herds, and tents. ⁶And the land was not able to bear them, that they might dwell together: for their substance was great, so that they could not dwell together. ⁷And there was a strife between the herdsmen of Abram's cattle and the herdsmen of Lot's cattle: and the Canaanite and the Perizzite dwelled then in the land. ⁸And Abram said to Lot, Let there be no strife, I pray you, between me and you, and between my herdsmen and your herdsmen; for we be brothers. ⁹Is not the whole land before you? separate yourself, I pray you, from me: if you will take the left hand, then I will go to the right; or if you depart to the right hand, then I will go to the left. ¹⁰And Lot lifted up his eyes, and beheld all the plain of Jordan, that it was well watered every where, before the LORD destroyed Sodom and Gomorrah, even as the garden of the LORD, like the land of Egypt, as you come to Zoar. ¹¹Then Lot chose him all the plain of Jordan; and Lot journeyed east: and they separated themselves the one from the other. ¹²Abram dwelled in the land of Canaan, and Lot dwelled in the cities of the plain, and pitched his tent toward Sodom. ¹³But the men of Sodom were wicked and sinners before the LORD exceedingly. ¹⁴And the LORD said to Abram, after that Lot was separated from him, Lift up now your eyes, and look from the place where you are northward, and southward, and eastward, and westward: ¹⁵For all the land which you see, to you will I give it, and to your seed for ever. ¹⁶And I will make your seed as the dust of the earth: so that if a man can number the dust of the earth, then shall your seed also be numbered. ¹⁷Arise, walk through the land in the length of it and in the breadth of it; for I will give it to you. ¹⁸Then Abram removed his tent, and came and dwelled in the plain of Mamre, which is in Hebron, and built there an altar to the LORD.

14

¹And it came to pass in the days of Amraphel king of Shinar, Arioch king of Ellasar, Chedorlaomer king of Elam, and Tidal king of nations; ²That these made war with Bera king of Sodom, and with Birsha king of Gomorrah, Shinab king of Admah, and Shemeber king of Zeboiim, and the king of Bela, which is Zoar. ³All these were joined together in the vale of Siddim, which is the salt sea. ⁴Twelve years they served Chedorlaomer, and in the

thirteenth year they rebelled. ⁵And in the fourteenth year came Chedorlaomer, and the kings that were with him, and smote the Rephaims in Ashteroth Karnaim, and the Zuzims in Ham, and the Emins in Shaveh Kiriathaim, ⁶And the Horites in their mount Seir, to Elparan, which is by the wilderness. ⁷And they returned, and came to Enmishpat, which is Kadesh, and smote all the country of the Amalekites, and also the Amorites, that dwelled in Hazezontamar. ⁸And there went out the king of Sodom, and the king of Gomorrah, and the king of Admah, and the king of Zeboiim, and the king of Bela (the same is Zoar;) and they joined battle with them in the vale of Siddim; ⁹With Chedorlaomer the king of Elam, and with Tidal king of nations, and Amraphel king of Shinar, and Arioch king of Ellasar; four kings with five. ¹⁰And the vale of Siddim was full of slime pits; and the kings of Sodom and Gomorrah fled, and fell there; and they that remained fled to the mountain. ¹¹And they took all the goods of Sodom and Gomorrah, and all their victuals, and went their way. ¹²And they took Lot, Abram's brother's son, who dwelled in Sodom, and his goods, and departed. ¹³And there came one that had escaped, and told Abram the Hebrew; for he dwelled in the plain of Mamre the Amorite, brother of Eshcol, and brother of Aner: and these were confederate with Abram. ¹⁴And when Abram heard that his brother was taken captive, he armed his trained servants, born in his own house, three hundred and eighteen, and pursued them to Dan. ¹⁵And he divided himself against them, he and his servants, by night, and smote them, and pursued them to Hobah, which is on the left hand of Damascus. ¹⁶And he brought back all the goods, and also brought again his brother Lot, and his goods, and the women also, and the people. ¹⁷And the king of Sodom went out to meet him after his return from the slaughter of Chedorlaomer, and of the kings that were with him, at the valley of Shaveh, which is the king's dale. ¹⁸And Melchizedek king of Salem brought forth bread and wine: and he was the priest of the most high God. ¹⁹And he blessed him, and said, Blessed be Abram of the most high God, possessor of heaven and earth: ²⁰And blessed be the most high God, which has delivered your enemies into your hand. And he gave him tithes of all. ²¹And the king of Sodom said to Abram, Give me the persons, and take the goods to yourself. ²²And Abram said to the king of Sodom, I have lift up my hand to the LORD, the most high God, the possessor of heaven and earth, ²³That I will not take from a thread even to a shoelatchet, and that I will not take any thing that is yours, lest you should say, I have made Abram rich: ²⁴Save only that which the young men have eaten, and the portion of the men which went with me, Aner, Eshcol, and Mamre; let them take their portion.

15 ¹After these things the word of the LORD came to Abram in a vision, saying, Fear not, Abram: I am your shield, and your exceeding great reward. ²And Abram said, LORD God, what will you give me, seeing I go childless, and the steward of my house is this Eliezer of Damascus? ³And Abram said, Behold, to me you have given no seed: and, see, one born in my house is my heir. ⁴And, behold, the word of the LORD came to him, saying, This shall not be your heir; but he that shall come forth out of your own bowels shall be your heir. ⁵And he brought him forth abroad, and said, Look now toward heaven, and tell the stars, if you be able to number them: and he said to him, So shall your seed be. ⁶And he believed in the LORD; and he counted it to him for righteousness. ⁷And he said to him, I am the LORD that brought you out of Ur of the Chaldees, to give you this land to inherit it. ⁸And he said, LORD God, whereby shall I know that I shall inherit it? ⁹And he said to him, Take me an heifer of three years old, and a she goat of three years old, and a ram of three years old, and a turtledove, and a young pigeon. ¹⁰And he took to him all these, and divided them in the middle, and laid each piece one against another: but the birds divided he not. ¹¹And when the fowls came down on the carcasses, Abram drove them away. ¹²And when the sun was going down, a deep sleep fell on Abram; and, see, an horror of great darkness fell on him. ¹³And he said to Abram, Know of a surety that your seed shall be a stranger in a land that is not theirs, and shall serve them; and they shall afflict them four hundred years; ¹⁴And also that nation, whom they shall serve, will I judge: and afterward shall they come out with great substance. ¹⁵And you shall go to your fathers in peace; you shall be buried in a good old age. ¹⁶But in the fourth generation they shall come here again: for the iniquity of the Amorites is not yet full. ¹⁷And it came to pass, that, when the sun went down, and it was dark, behold a smoking furnace, and a burning lamp that passed between those pieces. ¹⁸In the same day the LORD made a covenant with Abram, saying, To your seed have I given this land, from the river of Egypt to the great river, the river Euphrates: ¹⁹The Kenites, and the Kenizzites, and the Kadmonites, ²⁰And the Hittites, and the Perizzites, and the Rephaims, ²¹And the Amorites, and the Canaanites, and the Girgashites, and the Jebusites.

16 ¹Now Sarai Abram's wife bore him no children: and she had an handmaid, an Egyptian, whose name was Hagar. ²And Sarai said to Abram, Behold now, the LORD has restrained me from bearing: I pray you, go in to my maid; it may be that I may obtain children by her. And Abram listened to the voice of Sarai. ³And Sarai Abram's wife took Hagar her maid the Egyptian, after Abram had dwelled ten years in the land of Canaan, and gave her to her husband Abram to be his wife. ⁴And he went in to Hagar, and she conceived: and when she saw that she had conceived, her mistress was despised in her eyes. ⁵And Sarai said to Abram, My wrong be on you: I have given my maid into your bosom; and when she saw that she had conceived, I was despised in her eyes: the LORD judge between me and you. ⁶But Abram said to Sarai, Behold, your maid is in your hand; do to her as it pleases you. And when Sarai dealt hardly with her, she fled from her face. ⁷And the angel of the LORD found her by a fountain of water in the wilderness, by the fountain in the way to Shur. ⁸And he said, Hagar, Sarai's maid, from where came you? and where will you go? And she said, I flee from the face of my mistress Sarai. ⁹And the angel of the LORD said to her, Return to your mistress, and submit yourself under her hands. ¹⁰And the angel of the LORD said to her, I will multiply your seed exceedingly, that it shall not be numbered for multitude. ¹¹And the angel of the LORD said to her, Behold, you are with child and shall bear a son, and shall call his name Ishmael; because the LORD has heard your affliction. ¹²And he will be a wild man; his hand will be against every man, and every man's hand against him; and he shall dwell in the presence of all his brothers. ¹³And she called the name of the LORD that spoke to her, You God see me: for she said, Have I also here looked after him that sees me? ¹⁴Why the well was called Beerlahairoi; behold, it is between Kadesh and Bered. ¹⁵And Hagar bore Abram a son: and Abram called his son's name, which Hagar bore, Ishmael. ¹⁶And Abram was fourscore and six years old, when Hagar bore Ishmael to Abram.

17 ¹And when Abram was ninety years old and nine, the LORD appeared to Abram, and said to him, I am the Almighty God; walk before me, and be you perfect. ²And I will make my covenant between me and you, and will multiply you exceedingly. ³And Abram fell on his face: and God talked with him, saying, ⁴As for me, behold, my covenant is with you, and you shall be a father of many nations. ⁵Neither shall your name any more be called Abram, but your name shall be Abraham; for a father of many nations have I made you. ⁶And I will make you exceeding fruitful, and I will make nations of you, and kings shall come out of you. ⁷And I will establish my covenant between me and you and your seed after you in their generations for an everlasting covenant, to be a God to you, and to your seed after you. ⁸And I will give to you, and to your seed after you, the land wherein you are a stranger, all the land of Canaan, for an everlasting possession; and I will be their God. ⁹And God said to Abraham, You shall keep my covenant therefore, you, and your seed after you in their generations. ¹⁰This is my covenant, which you shall keep, between me and you and your seed after you; Every man child among you shall be circumcised. ¹¹And you shall circumcise the flesh of your foreskin; and it shall be a token of the covenant between me and you. ¹²And he that is eight days old shall be circumcised among you, every man child in your generations, he that is born in the house, or bought with money of any stranger, which is not of your seed. ¹³He that is born in your house, and he that is bought with your money, must needs be circumcised: and my covenant shall be in your flesh for an everlasting covenant. ¹⁴And the uncircumcised man child whose flesh of his foreskin is not circumcised, that soul shall be cut off from his people; he has broken my covenant. ¹⁵And God said to Abraham, As for Sarai your wife, you shall not call her name Sarai, but Sarah shall her name be. ¹⁶And I will bless her, and give you a son also of her: yes, I will bless her, and she shall be a mother of nations; kings of people shall be of her. ¹⁷Then Abraham fell on his face, and laughed, and said in his heart, Shall a child be born to him that is an hundred years old? and shall Sarah, that is ninety years old, bear? ¹⁸And Abraham said to God, O that Ishmael might live before you! ¹⁹And God said, Sarah your wife shall bear you a son indeed; and you shall call his name Isaac: and I will establish my covenant with him for an everlasting covenant, and with his seed after him. ²⁰And as for Ishmael, I have heard you: Behold, I have blessed him, and will make him fruitful, and will multiply him exceedingly; twelve princes shall he beget, and I will make him a great nation. ²¹But my covenant will I establish with Isaac, which Sarah shall bear to you at this set time in the next year. ²²And he left off talking with him, and God went up from Abraham. ²³And Abraham took Ishmael his son, and all that were born in his house, and all that were bought with his money, every male among the men of Abraham's house; and circumcised the flesh of their foreskin in the selfsame day, as God had said to him. ²⁴And Abraham was ninety years old and nine, when he was circumcised in the flesh of his foreskin. ²⁵And Ishmael his son was thirteen years old, when he was circumcised in the flesh of his foreskin. ²⁶In the selfsame day was Abraham circumcised, and Ishmael his son. ²⁷And all the men of his house, born in the house, and bought with money of the stranger, were circumcised with him.

18 ¹And the LORD appeared to him in the plains of Mamre: and he sat in the tent door in the heat of the day; ²And he lift up his eyes and looked, and, see, three men stood by him: and when he saw them, he ran to meet them from the tent door, and bowed himself toward the ground, ³And said, My LORD, if now I have found favor in your sight, pass not away, I pray you, from your servant: ⁴Let a little water, I pray you, be fetched, and wash your feet, and rest yourselves under the tree: ⁵And I will fetch a morsel of bread, and comfort you your hearts; after that you shall pass on: for therefore are you come to your servant. And they said, So do, as you have said. ⁶And Abraham hastened into the tent to Sarah, and said, Make ready quickly three measures of fine meal, knead it, and make cakes on the hearth. ⁷And Abraham ran to the herd, and fetched a calf tender and good, and gave it to a young man; and he hurried to dress it. ⁸And he took butter, and milk, and the calf which he had dressed, and set it before them; and he stood by them under the tree, and they did eat. ⁹And they said to him, Where is Sarah your wife? And he said, Behold, in the tent. ¹⁰And he said, I will certainly return to you according to the time of life; and, see, Sarah your wife shall have a son. And Sarah heard it in the tent door, which was behind him. ¹¹Now Abraham and Sarah were old and well stricken in age; and it ceased to be with Sarah after the manner of women. ¹²Therefore Sarah laughed within herself, saying, After I am waxed old shall I have pleasure, my lord being old also? ¹³And the LORD said to Abraham, Why did Sarah laugh, saying, Shall I of a surety bear a child, which am old? ¹⁴Is any thing too hard for the LORD? At the time appointed I will return to you, according to the time of life, and Sarah shall have a son. ¹⁵Then Sarah denied, saying, I laughed not; for she was afraid. And he said, No; but you did laugh. ¹⁶And the men rose up from there, and looked toward Sodom: and Abraham went with them to bring them on the way. ¹⁷And the LORD said, Shall I hide from Abraham that thing which I do; ¹⁸Seeing that Abraham shall surely become a great and mighty nation, and all the nations of the earth shall be blessed in him? ¹⁹For I know him, that he will command his children and his household after him, and they shall keep the way of the LORD, to do justice and judgment; that the LORD may bring on Abraham that which he has spoken of him. ²⁰And the LORD said, Because the cry of Sodom and Gomorrah is great, and because their sin is very grievous; ²¹I will go down now, and see whether they have done altogether according to the cry of it, which is come to me; and if not, I will know. ²²And the men turned their faces from there, and went toward Sodom: but Abraham stood yet before the LORD. ²³And Abraham drew near, and said, Will you also destroy the righteous with the wicked? ²⁴Peradventure there be fifty righteous within the city: will you also destroy and not spare the place for the fifty righteous that are therein? ²⁵That be far from you to do after this manner, to slay the righteous with the wicked: and that the righteous should be as the wicked, that be far from you: Shall not the Judge of all the earth do right? ²⁶And the LORD said, If I find in Sodom fifty righteous within the city, then I will spare all the place for their sakes. ²⁷And Abraham answered and said, Behold now, I have taken on me to speak to the LORD, which am but dust and ashes: ²⁸Peradventure there shall lack five of the fifty righteous: will you destroy all the city for lack of five? And he said, If I find there forty and five, I will not destroy it. ²⁹And he spoke to him yet again, and said, Peradventure there shall be forty found there. And he said, I will not do it for forty's sake. ³⁰And he said to him, Oh let not the LORD be angry, and I will speak: Peradventure there shall thirty be found there. And he said, I will not do it, if I find thirty there. ³¹And he said, Behold now, I have taken on me to speak to the LORD: Peradventure there shall be twenty found there. And he said, I will not destroy it for twenty's sake. ³²And he said, Oh let not the LORD be angry, and I will speak yet but this once: Peradventure ten shall be found there. And he said, I will not destroy it for ten's sake. ³³And the LORD went his way, as soon as he had left communing with Abraham: and Abraham returned to his place.

19 ¹And there came two angels to Sodom at even; and Lot sat in the gate of Sodom: and Lot seeing them rose up to meet them; and he bowed himself with his face toward the ground; ²And he said, Behold now, my lords, turn in, I pray you, into your servant's house, and tarry all night, and wash your feet, and you shall rise up early, and go on your ways. And they said, No; but we will abide in the street all night. ³And he pressed on them greatly; and they turned in to him, and entered into his house; and he made them a feast, and did bake unleavened bread, and they did eat. ⁴But before they lay down, the men of the city, even the men of Sodom, compassed the house round, both old and young, all the people from every quarter: ⁵And they called to Lot, and said to him, Where are the men which came in to you this night? bring them out to us, that we may know them. ⁶And Lot went out at the door to them, and shut the door after him, ⁷And said, I pray you, brothers, do not so wickedly. ⁸Behold now, I have two daughters which have not known man; let me, I pray you, bring them out to you, and do you to them as is good in your eyes: only to these men do nothing; for therefore came they under the shadow of my roof. ⁹And they said, Stand back. And they said again, This one fellow came in to sojourn, and he will needs be a judge: now will we deal worse with you, than with them. And they pressed sore on the man, even Lot, and came near to break the door. ¹⁰But the men put forth their hand, and pulled Lot into the house to them, and shut to the door.

¹¹And they smote the men that were at the door of the house with blindness, both small and great: so that they wearied themselves to find the door. ¹²And the men said to Lot, Have you here any besides? son in law, and your sons, and your daughters, and whatever you have in the city, bring them out of this place: ¹³For we will destroy this place, because the cry of them is waxen great before the face of the LORD; and the LORD has sent us to destroy it. ¹⁴And Lot went out, and spoke to his sons in law, which married his daughters, and said, Up, get you out of this place; for the LORD will destroy this city. But he seemed as one that mocked to his sons in law. ¹⁵And when the morning arose, then the angels hastened Lot, saying, Arise, take your wife, and your two daughters, which are here; lest you be consumed in the iniquity of the city. ¹⁶And while he lingered, the men laid hold on his hand, and on the hand of his wife, and on the hand of his two daughters; the LORD being merciful to him: and they brought him forth, and set him without the city. ¹⁷And it came to pass, when they had brought them forth abroad, that he said, Escape for your life; look not behind you, neither stay you in all the plain; escape to the mountain, lest you be consumed. ¹⁸And Lot said to them, Oh, not so, my LORD: ¹⁹Behold now, your servant has found grace in your sight, and you have magnified your mercy, which you have showed to me in saving my life; and I cannot escape to the mountain, lest some evil take me, and I die: ²⁰Behold now, this city is near to flee to, and it is a little one: Oh, let me escape thither, (is it not a little one?) and my soul shall live. ²¹And he said to him, See, I have accepted you concerning this thing also, that I will not overthrow this city, for the which you have spoken. ²²Haste you, escape thither; for I cannot do anything till you be come thither. Therefore the name of the city was called Zoar. ²³The sun was risen on the earth when Lot entered into Zoar. ²⁴Then the LORD rained on Sodom and on Gomorrah brimstone and fire from the LORD out of heaven; ²⁵And he overthrew those cities, and all the plain, and all the inhabitants of the cities, and that which grew on the ground. ²⁶But his wife looked back from behind him, and she became a pillar of salt. ²⁷And Abraham got up early in the morning to the place where he stood before the LORD: ²⁸And he looked toward Sodom and Gomorrah, and toward all the land of the plain, and beheld, and, see, the smoke of the country went up as the smoke of a furnace. ²⁹And it came to pass, when God destroyed the cities of the plain, that God remembered Abraham, and sent Lot out of the middle of the overthrow, when he overthrew the cities in the which Lot dwelled. ³⁰And Lot went up out of Zoar, and dwelled in the mountain, and his two daughters with him; for he feared to dwell in Zoar: and he dwelled in a cave, he and his two daughters. ³¹And the firstborn said to the younger, Our father is old, and there is not a man in the earth to come in to us after the manner of all the earth: ³²Come, let us make our father drink wine, and we will lie with him, that we may preserve seed of our father. ³³And they made their father drink wine that night: and the firstborn went in, and lay with her father; and he perceived not when she lay down, nor when she arose. ³⁴And it came to pass on the morrow, that the firstborn said to the younger, Behold, I lay last night with my father: let us make him drink wine this night also; and go you in, and lie with him,

that we may preserve seed of our father. ³⁵And they made their father drink wine that night also: and the younger arose, and lay with him; and he perceived not when she lay down, nor when she arose. ³⁶Thus were both the daughters of Lot with child by their father. ³⁷And the first born bore a son, and called his name Moab: the same is the father of the Moabites to this day. ³⁸And the younger, she also bore a son, and called his name Benammi: the same is the father of the children of Ammon to this day.

20 ¹And Abraham journeyed from there toward the south country, and dwelled between Kadesh and Shur, and sojourned in Gerar. ²And Abraham said of Sarah his wife, She is my sister: and Abimelech king of Gerar sent, and took Sarah. ³But God came to Abimelech in a dream by night, and said to him, Behold, you are but a dead man, for the woman which you have taken; for she is a man's wife. ⁴But Abimelech had not come near her: and he said, LORD, will you slay also a righteous nation? ⁵Said he not to me, She is my sister? and she, even she herself said, He is my brother: in the integrity of my heart and innocence of my hands have I done this. ⁶And God said to him in a dream, Yes, I know that you did this in the integrity of your heart; for I also withheld you from sinning against me: therefore suffered I you not to touch her. ⁷Now therefore restore the man his wife; for he is a prophet, and he shall pray for you, and you shall live: and if you restore her not, know you that you shall surely die, you, and all that are yours. ⁸Therefore Abimelech rose early in the morning, and called all his servants, and told all these things in their ears: and the men were sore afraid. ⁹Then Abimelech called Abraham, and said to him, What have you done to us? and what have I offended you, that you have brought on me and on my kingdom a great sin? you have done deeds to me that should not to be done. ¹⁰And Abimelech said to Abraham, What saw you, that you have done this thing? ¹¹And Abraham said, Because I thought, Surely the fear of God is not in this place; and they will slay me for my wife's sake. ¹²And yet indeed she is my sister; she is the daughter of my father, but not the daughter of my mother; and she became my wife. ¹³And it came to pass, when God caused me to wander from my father's house, that I said to her, This is your kindness which you shall show to me; at every place where we shall come, say of me, He is my brother. ¹⁴And Abimelech took sheep, and oxen, and menservants, and womenservants, and gave them to Abraham, and restored him Sarah his wife. ¹⁵And Abimelech said, Behold, my land is before you: dwell where it pleases you. ¹⁶And to Sarah he said, Behold, I have given your brother a thousand pieces of silver: behold, he is to you a covering of the eyes, to all that are with you, and with all other: thus she was reproved. ¹⁷So Abraham prayed to God: and God healed Abimelech, and his wife, and his maidservants; and they bore children. ¹⁸For the LORD had fast closed up all the wombs of the house of Abimelech, because of Sarah Abraham's wife.

21 ¹And the LORD visited Sarah as he had said, and the LORD did to Sarah as he had spoken. ²For Sarah conceived, and bore Abraham a son in his old age, at the set time of which God had spoken to him. ³And Abraham called the name of his son that was born to him, whom Sarah bore to him, Isaac. ⁴And Abraham circumcised his son Isaac being eight days old, as God had commanded him. ⁵And Abraham was an hundred years old, when his son Isaac was born to him. ⁶And Sarah said, God has made me to laugh, so that all that hear will laugh with me. ⁷And she said, Who would have said to Abraham, that Sarah should have given children suck? for I have born him a son in his old age. ⁸And the child grew, and was weaned: and Abraham made a great feast the same day that Isaac was weaned. ⁹And Sarah saw the son of Hagar the Egyptian, which she had born to Abraham, mocking. ¹⁰Why she said to Abraham, Cast out this female slave and her son: for the son of this female slave shall not be heir with my son, even with Isaac. ¹¹And the thing was very grievous in Abraham's sight because of his son. ¹²And God said to Abraham, Let it not be grievous in your sight because of the lad, and because of your female slave; in all that Sarah has said to you, listen to her voice; for in Isaac shall your seed be called. ¹³And also of the son of the female slave will I make a nation, because he is your seed. ¹⁴And Abraham rose up early in the morning, and took bread, and a bottle of water, and gave it to Hagar, putting it on her shoulder, and the child, and sent her away: and she departed, and wandered in the wilderness of Beersheba. ¹⁵And the water was spent in the bottle, and she cast the child under one of the shrubs. ¹⁶And she went, and sat her down over against him a good way off, as it were a bow shot: for she said, Let me not see the death of the child. And she sat over against him, and lift up her voice, and wept. ¹⁷And God heard the voice of the lad; and the angel of God called to Hagar out of heaven, and said to her, What ails you, Hagar? fear not; for God has heard the voice of the lad where he is. ¹⁸Arise, lift up the lad, and hold him in your hand; for I will make him a great nation. ¹⁹And God opened her eyes, and she saw a well of water; and she went, and filled the bottle with water, and gave the lad drink. ²⁰And God was with the lad; and he grew, and dwelled in the wilderness, and became an archer. ²¹And he dwelled in the wilderness of Paran: and his mother took him a wife out of the land of Egypt. ²²And it came to pass at that time, that Abimelech and Phichol the chief captain of his host spoke to Abraham, saying, God is with you in all that you do: ²³Now therefore swear to me here by God that you will not deal falsely with me, nor with my son, nor with my son's son: but according to the kindness that I have done to you, you shall do to me, and to the land wherein you have sojourned. ²⁴And Abraham said, I will swear. ²⁵And Abraham reproved Abimelech because of a well of water, which Abimelech's servants had violently taken away. ²⁶And Abimelech said, I know not who has done this thing; neither did you tell me, neither yet heard I of it, but to day. ²⁷And Abraham took sheep and oxen, and gave them to Abimelech; and both of them made a covenant. ²⁸And Abraham set seven ewe lambs of the flock by themselves. ²⁹And Abimelech said to Abraham, What mean these seven ewe lambs which you have set by themselves? ³⁰And he said, For these seven ewe lambs shall you take of my hand, that they may be a witness to me, that I have dig this well. ³¹Why he called that place Beersheba; because there they swore both of them. ³²Thus they made a covenant at Beersheba: then Abimelech rose up, and Phichol the chief captain of his host, and they returned into the land of the Philistines. ³³And Abraham planted a grove in Beersheba, and called there on the name of the LORD, the everlasting God. ³⁴And Abraham sojourned in the Philistines' land many days.

22 ¹And it came to pass after these things, that God did tempt Abraham, and said to him, Abraham: and he said, Behold, here I am. ²And he said, Take now your son, your only son Isaac, whom you love, and get you into the land of Moriah; and offer him there for a burnt offering on one of the mountains which I will tell you of. ³And Abraham rose up early in the morning, and saddled his ass, and took two of his young men with him, and Isaac his son, and split the wood for the burnt offering, and rose up, and went to the place of which God had told him. ⁴Then on the third day Abraham lifted up his eyes, and saw the place afar off. ⁵And Abraham said to his young men, Abide you here with the ass; and I and the lad will go yonder and worship, and come again to you. ⁶And Abraham took the wood of the burnt offering, and laid it on Isaac his son; and he took the fire in his hand, and a knife; and they went both of them together. ⁷And Isaac spoke to Abraham his father, and said, My father: and he said, Here am I, my son. And he said, Behold the fire and the wood: but where is the lamb for a burnt offering? ⁸And Abraham said, My son, God will provide himself a lamb for a burnt offering: so they went both of them together. ⁹And they came to the place which God had told him of; and Abraham built an altar there, and laid the wood in order, and bound Isaac his son, and laid him on the altar on the wood. ¹⁰And Abraham stretched forth his hand, and took the knife to slay his son. ¹¹And the angel of the LORD called to him out of heaven, and said, Abraham, Abraham: and he said, Here am I. ¹²And he said, Lay not your hand on the lad, neither do you any thing to him: for now I know that you fear God, seeing you have not withheld your son, your only son from me. ¹³And Abraham lifted up his eyes, and looked, and behold behind him a ram caught in a thicket by his horns: and Abraham went and took the ram, and offered him up for a burnt offering in the stead of his son. ¹⁴And Abraham called the name of that place Jehovahjireh: as it is said to this day, In the mount of the LORD it shall be seen. ¹⁵And the angel of the LORD called to Abraham out of heaven the second time, ¹⁶And said, By myself have I sworn, says the LORD, for because you have done this thing, and have not withheld your son, your only son: ¹⁷That in blessing I will bless you, and in multiplying I will multiply your seed as the stars of the heaven, and as the sand which is on the sea shore; and your seed shall possess the gate of his enemies; ¹⁸And in your seed shall all the nations of the earth be blessed; because you have obeyed my voice. ¹⁹So Abraham returned to his young men, and they rose up and went together to Beersheba; and Abraham dwelled at Beersheba. ²⁰And it came to pass after these things, that it was told Abraham, saying, Behold, Milcah, she has also born children to your brother Nahor; ²¹Huz his firstborn, and Buz his brother, and Kemuel the father of Aram, ²²And Chesed, and Hazo, and Pildash, and Jidlaph, and Bethuel. ²³And Bethuel begat Rebekah: these eight Milcah did bear to Nahor, Abraham's brother. ²⁴And his concubine, whose name was Reumah, she bore also Tebah, and Gaham, and Thahash, and Maachah.

23 ¹And Sarah was an hundred and seven and twenty years old: these were the years of the life of Sarah. ²And Sarah died in Kirjatharba; the same is Hebron in the land of Canaan: and Abraham came to mourn for Sarah, and to weep for her. ³And Abraham stood up from before his dead, and spoke to the sons of Heth, saying, ⁴I am a stranger and a sojourner with you: give me a possession of a burial plot with you, that I may bury my dead out of my sight. ⁵And the children of Heth answered Abraham, saying to him, ⁶Hear us, my lord: you are a mighty prince among us: in the choice of our sepulchers bury your dead; none of us shall withhold from you his sepulcher, but that you may bury your dead. ⁷And Abraham stood up, and bowed himself to the people of the land, even to the children of Heth. ⁸And he communed with them, saying, If it be your mind that I should bury my dead out of my sight; hear me, and entreat for me to Ephron the son of Zohar, ⁹That he may give me the cave of Machpelah, which he has, which is in the end of his field; for as much money as it is worth he shall give it me for a possession of a burial plot among you. ¹⁰And Ephron dwelled among the children of Heth: and Ephron the Hittite answered Abraham in the audience of the children of Heth, even of all that went in at the gate of his city, saying, ¹¹No, my lord, hear me: the field give I you, and the cave that is therein, I give it you; in the presence of the sons of my people give I it you: bury your dead. ¹²And Abraham bowed down himself before the people of the land. ¹³And he spoke to Ephron in the audience of the people of the land, saying, But if you will give it, I pray you, hear me: I will give you money for the field; take it of me, and I will bury my dead there. ¹⁴And Ephron answered Abraham, saying to him, ¹⁵My lord, listen to me: the land is worth four hundred shekels of silver; what is that between me and you? bury therefore your dead. ¹⁶And Abraham listened to Ephron; and Abraham weighed to Ephron the silver, which he had named in the audience of the sons of Heth, four hundred shekels of silver, current money with the merchant. ¹⁷And the field of Ephron which was in Machpelah, which was before Mamre, the field, and the cave which was therein, and all the trees that were in the field, that were in all the borders round about, were made sure ¹⁸To Abraham for a possession in the presence of the children of Heth, before all that went in at the gate of his city. ¹⁹And after this, Abraham buried Sarah his wife in the cave of the field of Machpelah before Mamre: the same is Hebron in the land of Canaan. ²⁰And the field, and the cave that is therein, were made sure to Abraham for a possession of a burial plot by the sons of Heth.

24 ¹And Abraham was old, and well stricken in age: and the LORD had blessed Abraham in all things. ²And Abraham said to his oldest servant of his house, that ruled over all that he had, Put, I pray you, your hand under my thigh: ³And I will make you swear by the LORD, the God of heaven, and the God of the earth, that you shall not take a wife to my son of the daughters of the Canaanites, among whom I dwell: ⁴But you shall go to my country, and to my kindred, and take a wife to my son Isaac. ⁵And the servant said to him, Peradventure the woman will not be willing to follow me to this land: must I needs bring your son again to the land from from where you came? ⁶And Abraham said to him, Beware you that you bring not my son thither again. ⁷The LORD God of heaven, which took me from my father's house, and from the land of my kindred, and which spoke to me, and that swore to me, saying, To your seed will I give this land; he shall send his angel before you, and you shall take a wife to my son from there. ⁸And if the woman will not be willing to follow you, then you shall be clear from this my oath: only bring not my son thither again. ⁹And the servant put his hand under the thigh of Abraham his master, and swore to him concerning that matter. ¹⁰And the servant took ten camels of the camels of his master, and departed; for all the goods of his master were in his hand: and he arose, and went to Mesopotamia, to the city of Nahor. ¹¹And he made his camels to kneel down without the city by a well of water at the time of the evening, even the time that women go out to draw water. ¹²And he said O LORD God of my master Abraham, I pray you, send me good speed this day, and show kindness to my master Abraham. ¹³Behold, I stand here by the well of water; and the daughters of the men of the city come out to draw water: ¹⁴And let it come to pass, that the damsel to whom I shall say, Let down your pitcher, I pray you, that I may drink; and she shall say, Drink, and I will give your camels drink also: let the same be she that you have appointed for your servant Isaac; and thereby shall I know that you have showed kindness to my master. ¹⁵And it came to pass, before he had done speaking, that, behold, Rebekah came out, who was born to Bethuel, son of Milcah, the wife of Nahor, Abraham's brother, with her pitcher on her shoulder. ¹⁶And the damsel was very fair to look on, a virgin, neither had any man known her: and she went down to the well, and filled her pitcher, and came up. ¹⁷And the servant ran to meet her, and said, Let me, I pray you, drink a little water of your pitcher. ¹⁸And she said, Drink, my lord: and she hurried, and let down her pitcher on her hand, and gave him drink. ¹⁹And when she had done giving him drink, she said, I will draw water for your camels also, until they have done drinking. ²⁰And she hurried, and emptied her pitcher into the trough, and ran again to the well to draw water, and drew for all his camels. ²¹And the man wondering at her held his peace, to wit whether the LORD had made his journey prosperous or not. ²²And it came to pass, as the camels had done drinking, that the man took a golden earring of half a shekel weight, and two bracelets for her hands of ten shekels weight of gold; ²³And said, Whose daughter are you? tell me, I pray you: is there room in your father's house for us to lodge in? ²⁴And she said to him, I am the daughter of Bethuel the son of Milcah, which she bore to Nahor. ²⁵She said moreover to him, We have both straw and provender enough, and room to lodge in. ²⁶And the man bowed down his head, and worshipped the LORD. ²⁷And he said, Blessed be the LORD God of my master Abraham, who has not left destitute my master of his mercy and his truth: I being in the way, the LORD led me to the house of my master's brothers. ²⁸And the damsel ran, and told them of her mother's house these things. ²⁹And Rebekah had a brother, and his name was Laban: and Laban ran out to the man, to the well. ³⁰And it came to pass, when he saw the earring and bracelets on his sister's hands, and when he heard the words of Rebekah his sister, saying, Thus spoke the man to me; that he came to the man; and, behold, he stood by the camels at the well. ³¹And he said, Come in, you blessed of the LORD; why stand you without? for I have prepared the house, and room for the camels. ³²And the man came into the house: and he ungirded his camels, and gave straw and provender for the camels, and water to wash his feet, and the men's feet that were with him. ³³And there was set meat before him to eat: but he said, I will not eat, until I have told my errand. And he said, Speak on. ³⁴And he said, I am Abraham's servant. ³⁵And the LORD has blessed my master greatly; and he is become great: and he has given him flocks, and herds, and silver, and gold, and menservants, and maidservants, and camels, and asses. ³⁶And Sarah my master's wife bore a son to my master when she was old: and to him has he given all that he has. ³⁷And my master made me swear, saying, You shall not take a wife to my son of the daughters of the Canaanites, in whose land I dwell: ³⁸But you shall go to my father's house, and to my kindred, and take a wife to my son. ³⁹And I said to my master, Peradventure the woman will not follow me. ⁴⁰And he said to me, The LORD, before whom I walk, will send his angel with you, and prosper your way; and you shall take a wife for my son of my kindred, and of my father's house: ⁴¹Then shall you be clear from this my oath, when you come to my kindred; and if they give not you one, you shall be clear from my oath. ⁴²And I came this day to the well, and said, O LORD God of my master Abraham, if now you do prosper my way which I go: ⁴³Behold, I stand by the well of water; and it shall come to pass, that when the virgin comes forth to draw water, and I say to her, Give me, I pray you, a little water of your pitcher to drink; ⁴⁴And she say to me, Both drink you, and I will also draw for your camels: let the same be the woman whom the LORD has appointed out for my master's son. ⁴⁵And before I had done speaking in my heart, behold, Rebekah came forth with her pitcher on her shoulder; and she went down to the well, and drew water: and I said to her, Let me drink, I pray you. ⁴⁶And she made haste, and let down her pitcher from her shoulder, and said, Drink, and I will give your camels drink also: so I drank, and she made the camels drink also. ⁴⁷And I asked her, and said, Whose daughter are you? And she said, the daughter of Bethuel, Nahor's son, whom Milcah bore to him: and I put the earring on her face, and the bracelets on her hands. ⁴⁸And I bowed down my head, and worshipped the LORD, and blessed the LORD God of my master Abraham, which had led me in the right way to take my master's brother's daughter to his son. ⁴⁹And now if you will deal kindly and truly with my master, tell me: and if not, tell me; that I may turn to the right hand, or to the left. ⁵⁰Then Laban and Bethuel answered and said, The thing proceeds from the LORD: we cannot speak to you bad or good. ⁵¹Behold, Rebekah is before you, take her, and go, and let her be your master's son's wife, as the LORD has spoken. ⁵²And it came to pass, that, when Abraham's servant heard their words, he worshipped the LORD, bowing himself to the earth. ⁵³And the servant brought forth jewels of silver, and jewels of gold, and raiment, and gave them to Rebekah: he gave also to her brother and to her mother precious things. ⁵⁴And they did eat and drink, he and the men that were with him, and tarried all night; and they rose up in the morning, and he said, Send me away to my master. ⁵⁵And her brother and her mother said, Let the damsel abide with us a few days, at the least ten; after that she shall go. ⁵⁶And he said to them, Hinder me not, seeing the LORD has prospered my way; send me away that I may go to my master. ⁵⁷And they said, We will call the damsel, and inquire at her mouth. ⁵⁸And they called Rebekah, and said to her, Will you go with this man? And she said, I will go. ⁵⁹And they sent away Rebekah their sister, and her nurse, and Abraham's servant, and his men. ⁶⁰And they blessed Rebekah, and said to her, You are our sister, be you the mother of thousands of millions, and let your seed possess the gate of those which hate them. ⁶¹And Rebekah arose, and her damsels, and they rode on the camels, and followed the man: and the servant took Rebekah, and went his way. ⁶²And Isaac came from the way of the well Lahairoi; for he dwelled in the south country. ⁶³And Isaac went out to meditate in the field at the eventide: and he lifted up his eyes, and saw, and, behold, the camels were coming. ⁶⁴And Rebekah lifted up her eyes, and when she saw Isaac, she lighted off the camel. ⁶⁵For she had said to the servant, What man is this that walks in the field to meet us? And the servant had said, It is my master: therefore she took a veil, and covered herself. ⁶⁶And the servant told Isaac all things that he had done. ⁶⁷And Isaac brought her into his mother Sarah's tent, and took Rebekah, and she became his wife; and he loved her: and Isaac was comforted after his mother's death.

25 ¹Then again Abraham took a wife, and her name was Keturah. ²And she bore him Zimran, and Jokshan, and Medan, and Midian, and Ishbak, and Shuah. ³And Jokshan begat Sheba, and Dedan. And the sons of Dedan were Asshurim, and Letushim, and Leummim. ⁴And the sons of Midian; Ephah, and Epher, and Hanoch, and Abidah, and Eldaah. All these were the children of Keturah. ⁵And Abraham gave all that he had to Isaac. ⁶But to the sons of the concubines, which Abraham had, Abraham gave gifts, and sent them away from Isaac his son, while he yet lived, eastward, to the east country. ⁷And these are the days of the years of Abraham's life which he lived, an hundred three score and fifteen years. ⁸Then Abraham gave up the ghost, and died in a good old age, an old man, and full of years; and was gathered to his people. ⁹And his sons Isaac and Ishmael buried him in the cave of Machpelah, in the field of Ephron the son of Zohar the Hittite, which is before Mamre; ¹⁰The field which Abraham purchased of the sons of Heth: there was Abraham buried, and Sarah his wife. ¹¹And it came to pass after the death of Abraham, that God blessed his son Isaac; and Isaac dwelled by the well Lahairoi. ¹²Now these are the generations of Ishmael, Abraham's son, whom Hagar the Egyptian, Sarah's handmaid, bore to Abraham: ¹³And these are the names of the sons of Ishmael, by their names, according to their generations: the firstborn of Ishmael, Nebajoth; and Kedar, and Adbeel, and Mibsam, ¹⁴And Mishma, and Dumah, and Massa, ¹⁵Hadar, and Tema, Jetur, Naphish, and Kedemah: ¹⁶These are the sons of Ishmael, and these are their names, by their towns, and by their castles; twelve princes according to their nations. ¹⁷And these are the years of the life of Ishmael, an hundred and thirty and seven years: and he gave up the ghost and died; and was gathered to his people. ¹⁸And they dwelled from Havilah to Shur, that is before Egypt, as you go toward Assyria: and he died in the presence of all his brothers. ¹⁹And these are the generations of Isaac, Abraham's son: Abraham begat Isaac: ²⁰And Isaac was forty years old when he took Rebekah to wife, the daughter of Bethuel the Syrian of Padanaram, the sister to Laban the Syrian. ²¹And Isaac entreated the LORD for his wife, because she was barren: and the LORD was entreated of him, and Rebekah his wife conceived. ²²And the children struggled together within her; and she said, If it be so, why am I thus? And she went to inquire of the LORD. ²³And the LORD said to her, Two nations are in your womb, and two manner of people shall be separated from your bowels; and the one people shall be stronger than the other people; and the elder shall serve the younger. ²⁴And when her days to be delivered were fulfilled, behold, there were twins in her womb. ²⁵And the first came out red, all over like an hairy garment; and they called his name Esau. ²⁶And after that came his brother out, and his hand took hold on Esau's heel; and his name was called Jacob: and Isaac was three score years old when she bore them. ²⁷And the boys grew: and Esau was a cunning hunter, a man of the field; and Jacob was a plain man, dwelling in tents. ²⁸And Isaac loved Esau, because he did eat of his venison: but Rebekah loved Jacob. ²⁹And Jacob sod pottage: and Esau came from the field, and he was faint: ³⁰And Esau said to Jacob, Feed me, I pray you, with that same red pottage; for I am faint: therefore was his name called Edom. ³¹And Jacob said, Sell me this day your birthright. ³²And Esau said, Behold, I am at the point to die: and what profit shall this birthright do to me? ³³And Jacob said, Swear to me this day; and he swore to him: and he sold his birthright to Jacob. ³⁴Then Jacob gave Esau bread and pottage of lentils; and he did eat and drink, and rose up, and went his way: thus Esau despised his birthright.

26 ¹And there was a famine in the land, beside the first famine that was in the days of Abraham. And Isaac went to Abimelech king of the Philistines to Gerar. ²And the LORD appeared to him, and said, Go not down into Egypt; dwell in the land which I shall tell you of: ³Sojourn in this land, and I will be with you, and will bless you; for to you, and to your seed, I will give all these countries, and I will perform the oath which I swore to Abraham your father; ⁴And I will make your seed to multiply as the stars of heaven, and will give to your seed all these countries; and in your seed shall all the nations of the earth be blessed; ⁵Because that Abraham obeyed my voice, and kept my charge, my commandments, my statutes, and my laws. ⁶And Isaac dwelled in Gerar: ⁷And the men of the place asked him of his wife; and he said, She is my sister: for he feared to say, She is my wife; lest, said he, the men of the place should kill me for Rebekah; because she was fair to look on. ⁸And it came to pass, when he had been there a long time, that Abimelech king of the Philistines looked out at a window, and saw, and, behold, Isaac was sporting with Rebekah his wife. ⁹And Abimelech called Isaac, and said,

Behold, of a surety she is your wife; and how said you, She is my sister? And Isaac said to him, Because I said, Lest I die for her. ¹⁰And Abimelech said, What is this you have done to us? one of the people might lightly have lien with your wife, and you should have brought guiltiness on us. ¹¹And Abimelech charged all his people, saying, He that touches this man or his wife shall surely be put to death. ¹²Then Isaac sowed in that land, and received in the same year an hundred times: and the LORD blessed him. ¹³And the man waxed great, and went forward, and grew until he became very great: ¹⁴For he had possession of flocks, and possession of herds, and great store of servants: and the Philistines envied him. ¹⁵For all the wells which his father's servants had dig in the days of Abraham his father, the Philistines had stopped them, and filled them with earth. ¹⁶And Abimelech said to Isaac, Go from us; for you are much mightier than we. ¹⁷And Isaac departed there, and pitched his tent in the valley of Gerar, and dwelled there. ¹⁸And Isaac dig again the wells of water, which they had dig in the days of Abraham his father; for the Philistines had stopped them after the death of Abraham: and he called their names after the names by which his father had called them. ¹⁹And Isaac's servants dig in the valley, and found there a well of springing water. ²⁰And the herdsmen of Gerar did strive with Isaac's herdsmen, saying, The water is ours: and he called the name of the well Esek; because they strove with him. ²¹And they dig another well, and strove for that also: and he called the name of it Sitnah. ²²And he removed from there, and dig another well; and for that they strove not: and he called the name of it Rehoboth; and he said, For now the LORD has made room for us, and we shall be fruitful in the land. ²³And he went up from there to Beersheba. ²⁴And the LORD appeared to him the same night, and said, I am the God of Abraham your father: fear not, for I am with you, and will bless you, and multiply your seed for my servant Abraham's sake. ²⁵And he built an altar there, and called on the name of the LORD, and pitched his tent there: and there Isaac's servants dig a well. ²⁶Then Abimelech went to him from Gerar, and Ahuzzath one of his friends, and Phichol the chief captain of his army. ²⁷And Isaac said to them, Why come you to me, seeing you hate me, and have sent me away from you? ²⁸And they said, We saw certainly that the LORD was with you: and we said, Let there be now an oath between us, even between us and you, and let us make a covenant with you; ²⁹That you will do us no hurt, as we have not touched you, and as we have done to you nothing but good, and have sent you away in peace: you are now the blessed of the LORD. ³⁰And he made them a feast, and they did eat and drink. ³¹And they rose up betimes in the morning, and swore one to another: and Isaac sent them away, and they departed from him in peace. ³²And it came to pass the same day, that Isaac's servants came, and told him concerning the well which they had dig, and said to him, We have found water. ³³And he called it Shebah: therefore the name of the city is Beersheba to this day. ³⁴And Esau was forty years old when he took to wife Judith the daughter of Beeri the Hittite, and Bashemath the daughter of Elon the Hittite: ³⁵Which were a grief of mind to Isaac and to Rebekah.

27 ¹And it came to pass, that when Isaac was old, and his eyes were dim, so that he could not see, he called Esau his oldest son, and said to him, My son: and he said to him, Behold, here am I. ²And he said, Behold now, I am old, I know not the day of my death: ³Now therefore take, I pray you, your weapons, your quiver and your bow, and go out to the field, and take me some venison; ⁴And make me savoury meat, such as I love, and bring it to me, that I may eat; that my soul may bless you before I die. ⁵And Rebekah heard when Isaac spoke to Esau his son. And Esau went to the field to hunt for venison, and to bring it. ⁶And Rebekah spoke to Jacob her son, saying, Behold, I heard your father speak to Esau your brother, saying, ⁷Bring me venison, and make me savoury meat, that I may eat, and bless you before the LORD before my death. ⁸Now therefore, my son, obey my voice according to that which I command you. ⁹Go now to the flock, and fetch me from there two good kids of the goats; and I will make them savoury meat for your father, such as he loves: ¹⁰And you shall bring it to your father, that he may eat, and that he may bless you before his death. ¹¹And Jacob said to Rebekah his mother, Behold, Esau my brother is a hairy man, and I am a smooth man: ¹²My father peradventure will feel me, and I shall seem to him as a deceiver; and I shall bring a curse on me, and not a blessing. ¹³And his mother said to him, On me be your curse, my son: only obey my voice, and go fetch me them. ¹⁴And he went, and fetched, and brought them to his mother: and his mother made savoury meat, such as his father loved. ¹⁵And Rebekah took goodly raiment of her oldest son Esau, which were with her in the house, and put them on Jacob her younger son: ¹⁶And she put the skins of the kids of the goats on his hands, and on the smooth of his neck: ¹⁷And she gave the savoury meat and the bread, which she had prepared, into the hand of her son Jacob. ¹⁸And he came to his father, and said, My father: and he said, Here am I; who are you, my son? ¹⁹And Jacob said to his father, I am Esau your first born; I have done according as you bade me: arise, I pray you, sit and eat of my venison, that your soul may bless me. ²⁰And Isaac said to his son, How is it that you have found it so quickly, my son? And he said, Because the LORD your God brought it to me. ²¹And Isaac said to Jacob, Come near, I pray you, that I may feel you, my son, whether you be my very son Esau or not. ²²And Jacob went near to Isaac his father; and he felt him, and said, The voice is Jacob's voice, but the hands are the hands of Esau. ²³And he discerned him not, because his hands were hairy, as his brother Esau's hands: so he blessed him. ²⁴And he said, Are you my very son Esau? And he said, I am. ²⁵And he said, Bring it near to me, and I will eat of my son's venison, that my soul may bless you. And he brought it near to him, and he did eat: and he brought him wine and he drank. ²⁶And his father Isaac said to him, Come near now, and kiss me, my son. ²⁷And he came near, and kissed him: and he smelled the smell of his raiment, and blessed him, and said, See, the smell of my son is as the smell of a field which the LORD has blessed: ²⁸Therefore God give you of the dew of heaven, and the fatness of the earth, and plenty of corn and wine: ²⁹Let people serve you, and nations bow down to you: be lord over your brothers, and let your mother's sons bow down to you: cursed be every one that curses you, and blessed be he that blesses you. ³⁰And it came to pass, as soon as Isaac had made an end of blessing Jacob, and Jacob was yet scarce gone out from the presence of Isaac his father, that Esau his brother came in from his hunting. ³¹And he also had made savoury meat, and brought it to his father, and said to his father, Let my father arise, and eat of his son's venison, that your soul may bless me. ³²And Isaac his father said to him, Who are you? And he said, I am your son, your firstborn Esau. ³³And Isaac trembled very exceedingly, and said, Who? where is he that has taken venison, and brought it me, and I have eaten of all before you came, and have blessed him? yes, and he shall be blessed. ³⁴And when Esau heard the words of his father, he cried with a great and exceeding bitter cry, and said to his father, Bless me, even me also, O my father. ³⁵And he said, Your brother came with subtlety, and has taken away your blessing. ³⁶And he said, Is not he rightly named Jacob? for he has supplanted me these two times: he took away my birthright; and, behold, now he has taken away my blessing. And he said, Have you not reserved a blessing for me? ³⁷And Isaac answered and said to Esau, Behold, I have made him your lord, and all his brothers have I given to him for servants; and with corn and wine have I sustained him: and what shall I do now to you, my son? ³⁸And Esau said to his father, Have you but one blessing, my father? bless me, even me also, O my father. And Esau lifted up his voice, and wept. ³⁹And Isaac his father answered and said to him, Behold, your dwelling shall be the fatness of the earth, and of the dew of heaven from above; ⁴⁰And by your sword shall you live, and shall serve your brother; and it shall come to pass when you shall have the dominion, that you shall break his yoke from off your neck. ⁴¹And Esau hated Jacob because of the blessing with which his father blessed him: and Esau said in his heart, The days of mourning for my father are at hand; then will I slay my brother Jacob. ⁴²And these words of Esau her elder son were told to Rebekah: and she sent and called Jacob her younger son, and said to him, Behold, your brother Esau, as touching you, does comfort himself, purposing to kill you. ⁴³Now therefore, my son, obey my voice; arise, flee you to Laban my brother to Haran; ⁴⁴And tarry with him a few days, until your brother's fury turn away; ⁴⁵Until your brother's anger turn away from you, and he forget that which you have done to him: then I will send, and fetch you from there: why should I be deprived also of you both in one day? ⁴⁶And Rebekah said to Isaac, I am weary of my life because of the daughters of Heth: if Jacob take a wife of the daughters of Heth, such as these which are of the daughters of the land, what good shall my life do me?

28 ¹And Isaac called Jacob, and blessed him, and charged him, and said to him, You shall not take a wife of the daughters of Canaan. ²Arise, go to Padanaram, to the house of Bethuel your mother's father; and take you a wife from there of the daughters of Laban your mother's brother. ³And God Almighty bless you, and make you fruitful, and multiply you, that you may be a multitude of people; ⁴And give you the blessing of Abraham, to you, and to your seed with you; that you may inherit the land wherein you are a stranger, which God gave to Abraham. ⁵And Isaac sent away Jacob: and he went to Padanaram to Laban, son of Bethuel the Syrian, the brother of Rebekah, Jacob's and Esau's mother. ⁶When Esau saw that Isaac had blessed Jacob, and sent him away to Padanaram, to take him a wife from there; and that as he blessed him he gave him a charge, saying, You shall not take a wife of the daughters of Canaan; ⁷And that Jacob obeyed his father and his mother, and was gone to Padanaram; ⁸And Esau seeing that the daughters of Canaan pleased not Isaac his father; ⁹Then went Esau to Ishmael, and took to the wives which he had Mahalath the daughter of Ishmael Abraham's son, the sister of Nebajoth, to be his wife. ¹⁰And Jacob went out from Beersheba, and went toward Haran. ¹¹And he lighted on a certain place, and tarried there all night, because the sun was set; and he took of the stones of that place, and put them for his pillows, and lay down in that place to sleep. ¹²And he dreamed, and behold a ladder set up on the earth, and the top of it reached to heaven: and behold the angels of God ascending and descending on it. ¹³And, behold, the LORD stood above it, and said, I am the LORD God of Abraham your father, and the God of Isaac: the land where on you lie, to you will I give it, and to your seed; ¹⁴And your seed shall be as the dust of the earth, and you shall spread abroad to the west, and to the east, and to the north, and to the south: and in you and in your seed shall all the families of the earth be blessed. ¹⁵And, behold, I am with you, and will keep you in all places where you go, and will bring you again into this land; for I will not leave you, until I have done that which I have spoken to you of. ¹⁶And Jacob awaked out of his sleep, and he said, Surely the LORD is in this place; and I knew it not. ¹⁷And he was afraid, and said, How dreadful is this place! this is none other but the house of God, and this is the gate of heaven. ¹⁸And Jacob rose up early in the morning, and took the stone that he had put for his pillows, and set it up for a pillar, and poured oil on the top of it. ¹⁹And he called the name of that place Bethel: but the name of that city was called Luz at the first. ²⁰And Jacob vowed a vow, saying, If God will be with me, and will keep me in this way that I go, and will give me bread to eat, and raiment to put on, ²¹So that I come again to my father's house in peace; then shall the LORD be my God: ²²And this stone, which I have set for a pillar, shall be God's house: and of all that you shall give me I will surely give the tenth to you.

29 ¹Then Jacob went on his journey, and came into the land of the people of the east. ²And he looked, and behold a well in the field, and, see, there were three flocks of sheep lying by it; for out of that well they watered the flocks: and a great stone was on the well's mouth. ³And thither were all the flocks gathered: and they rolled the stone from the well's mouth, and watered the sheep, and put the stone again on the well's mouth in his place. ⁴And Jacob said to them, My brothers, from where be you? And they said, Of Haran are we. ⁵And he said to them, Know you Laban the son of Nahor? And they said, We know him. ⁶And he said to them, Is he well? And they said, He is well: and, behold, Rachel his daughter comes with the sheep. ⁷And he said, See, it is yet high day, neither is it time that the cattle should be gathered together: water you the sheep, and go and feed them. ⁸And they said, We cannot, until all the flocks be gathered together, and till they roll the stone from the well's mouth; then we water the sheep. ⁹And while he yet spoke with them, Rachel came with her father's sheep; for she kept them. ¹⁰And it came to pass, when Jacob saw Rachel the daughter of Laban his mother's brother, and the sheep of Laban his mother's brother, that Jacob went near, and rolled the stone from the well's mouth, and watered the flock of Laban his mother's brother. ¹¹And Jacob kissed Rachel, and lifted up his voice, and wept. ¹²And Jacob told Rachel that he was her father's brother, and that he was Rebekah's son: and she ran and told her father. ¹³And it came to pass, when Laban heard the tidings of Jacob his sister's son, that he ran to meet him, and embraced him, and kissed him, and brought him to his house. And he told Laban all these things. ¹⁴And Laban said to him, Surely you are my bone and my flesh. And he stayed with him the space of a month. ¹⁵And Laban said to Jacob, Because you are my brother, should you therefore serve me for nothing? tell me, what shall your wages be? ¹⁶And Laban had two daughters: the name of the elder was Leah, and the name of the younger was Rachel. ¹⁷Leah was tender eyed; but Rachel was beautiful and well favored. ¹⁸And Jacob loved Rachel; and said, I will serve you seven years for Rachel your younger daughter. ¹⁹And Laban said, It is better that I give her to you, than that I should give her to another man: abide with me. ²⁰And Jacob served seven years for Rachel; and they seemed to him but a few days, for the love he had to her. ²¹And Jacob said to Laban, Give me my wife, for my days are fulfilled, that I may go in to her. ²²And Laban gathered together all the men of the place, and made a feast. ²³And it came to pass in the evening, that he took Leah his daughter, and brought her to him; and he went in to her. ²⁴And Laban gave to his daughter Leah Zilpah his maid for an handmaid. ²⁵And it came to pass, that in the morning, behold, it was Leah: and he said to Laban, What is this you have done to me? did not I serve with you for Rachel? why then have you beguiled me? ²⁶And Laban said, It must not be so done in our country, to give the younger before the firstborn. ²⁷Fulfill her week, and we will give you this also for the service which you shall serve with me yet seven other years. ²⁸And Jacob did so, and fulfilled her week: and he gave him Rachel his daughter to wife also. ²⁹And Laban gave to Rachel his daughter Bilhah his handmaid to be her maid. ³⁰And he went in also to Rachel, and he loved also Rachel more than Leah, and served with him yet seven other years. ³¹And when the LORD saw that Leah was hated, he opened her womb: but Rachel was barren. ³²And Leah conceived, and bore a son, and she called his name Reuben: for she said, Surely the LORD has looked on my affliction; now therefore my husband will love me. ³³And she conceived again, and bore a son; and said, Because the LORD has heard I was hated, he has therefore given me this son also: and she called his name Simeon. ³⁴And she conceived again, and bore a son; and said, Now this time will my husband be joined to me, because I have born him three sons: therefore was his name called Levi. ³⁵And she conceived again, and bore a son: and she said, Now will I praise the LORD: therefore she called his name Judah; and left bearing.

30

¹And when Rachel saw that she bore Jacob no children, Rachel envied her sister; and said to Jacob, Give me children, or else I die. ²And Jacob's anger was kindled against Rachel: and he said, Am I in God's stead, who has withheld from you the fruit of the womb? ³And she said, Behold my maid Bilhah, go in to her; and she shall bear on my knees, that I may also have children by her. ⁴And she gave him Bilhah her handmaid to wife: and Jacob went in to her. ⁵And Bilhah conceived, and bore Jacob a son. ⁶And Rachel said, God has judged me, and has also heard my voice, and has given me a son: therefore called she his name Dan. ⁷And Bilhah Rachel's maid conceived again, and bore Jacob a second son. ⁸And Rachel said, With great wrestlings have I wrestled with my sister, and I have prevailed: and she called his name Naphtali. ⁹When Leah saw that she had left bearing, she took Zilpah her maid, and gave her Jacob to wife. ¹⁰And Zilpah Leah's maid bore Jacob a son. ¹¹And Leah said, A troop comes: and she called his name Gad. ¹²And Zilpah Leah's maid bore Jacob a second son. ¹³And Leah said, Happy am I, for the daughters will call me blessed: and she called his name Asher. ¹⁴And Reuben went in the days of wheat harvest, and found mandrakes in the field, and brought them to his mother Leah. Then Rachel said to Leah, Give me, I pray you, of your son's mandrakes. ¹⁵And she said to her, Is it a small matter that you have taken my husband? and would you take away my son's mandrakes also? And Rachel said, Therefore he shall lie with you to night for your son's mandrakes. ¹⁶And Jacob came out of the field in the evening, and Leah went out to meet him, and said, You must come in to me; for surely I have hired you with my son's mandrakes. And he lay with her that night. ¹⁷And God listened to Leah, and she conceived, and bore Jacob the fifth son. ¹⁸And Leah said, God has given me my hire, because I have given my maiden to my husband: and she called his name Issachar. ¹⁹And Leah conceived again, and bore Jacob the sixth son. ²⁰And Leah said, God has endued me with a good dowry; now will my husband dwell with me, because I have born him six sons: and she called his name Zebulun. ²¹And afterwards she bore a daughter, and called her name Dinah. ²²And God remembered Rachel, and God listened to her, and opened her womb. ²³And she conceived, and bore a son; and said, God has taken away my reproach: ²⁴And she called his name Joseph; and said, The LORD shall add to me another son. ²⁵And it came to pass, when Rachel had born Joseph, that Jacob said to Laban, Send me away, that I may go to my own place, and to my country. ²⁶Give me my wives and my children, for whom I have served you, and let me go: for you know my service which I have done you. ²⁷And Laban said to him, I pray you, if I have found favor in your eyes, tarry: for I have learned by experience that the LORD has blessed me for your sake. ²⁸And he said, Appoint me your wages, and I will give it. ²⁹And he said to him, You know how I have served you, and how your cattle was with me. ³⁰For it was little which you had before I came, and it is now increased to a multitude; and the LORD has blessed you since my coming: and now when shall I provide for my own house also? ³¹And he said, What shall I give you? And Jacob said, You shall not give me any thing: if you will do this thing for me, I will again feed and keep your flock. ³²I will pass through all your flock

to day, removing from there all the speckled and spotted cattle, and all the brown cattle among the sheep, and the spotted and speckled among the goats: and of such shall be my hire. ³³So shall my righteousness answer for me in time to come, when it shall come for my hire before your face: every one that is not speckled and spotted among the goats, and brown among the sheep, that shall be counted stolen with me. ³⁴And Laban said, Behold, I would it might be according to your word. ³⁵And he removed that day the he goats that were ringstraked and spotted, and all the she goats that were speckled and spotted, and every one that had some white in it, and all the brown among the sheep, and gave them into the hand of his sons. ³⁶And he set three days' journey between himself and Jacob: and Jacob fed the rest of Laban's flocks. ³⁷And Jacob took him rods of green poplar, and of the hazel and chesnut tree; and pilled white strakes in them, and made the white appear which was in the rods. ³⁸And he set the rods which he had pilled before the flocks in the gutters in the watering troughs when the flocks came to drink, that they should conceive when they came to drink. ³⁹And the flocks conceived before the rods, and brought forth cattle ringstraked, speckled, and spotted. ⁴⁰And Jacob did separate the lambs, and set the faces of the flocks toward the ringstraked, and all the brown in the flock of Laban; and he put his own flocks by themselves, and put them not to Laban's cattle. ⁴¹And it came to pass, whenever the stronger cattle did conceive, that Jacob laid the rods before the eyes of the cattle in the gutters, that they might conceive among the rods. ⁴²But when the cattle were feeble, he put them not in: so the feebler were Laban's, and the stronger Jacob's. ⁴³And the man increased exceedingly, and had much cattle, and maidservants, and menservants, and camels, and asses.

31

¹And he heard the words of Laban's sons, saying, Jacob has taken away all that was our father's; and of that which was our father's has he gotten all this glory. ²And Jacob beheld the countenance of Laban, and, behold, it was not toward him as before. ³And the LORD said to Jacob, Return to the land of your fathers, and to your kindred; and I will be with you. ⁴And Jacob sent and called Rachel and Leah to the field to his flock, ⁵And said to them, I see your father's countenance, that it is not toward me as before; but the God of my father has been with me. ⁶And you know that with all my power I have served your father. ⁷And your father has deceived me, and changed my wages ten times; but God suffered him not to hurt me. ⁸If he said thus, The speckled shall be your wages; then all the cattle bore speckled: and if he said thus, The ringstraked shall be your hire; then bore all the cattle ringstraked. ⁹Thus God has taken away the cattle of your father, and given them to me. ¹⁰And it came to pass at the time that the cattle conceived, that I lifted up my eyes, and saw in a dream, and, behold, the rams which leaped on the cattle were ringstraked, speckled, and spotted. ¹¹And the angel of God spoke to me in a dream, saying, Jacob: And I said, Here am I. ¹²And he said, Lift up now your eyes, and see, all the rams which leap on the cattle are ringstraked, speckled, and spotted: for I have seen all that Laban does to you. ¹³I am the God of Bethel, where you anointed the pillar, and where you vowed a vow to me: now arise, get you out from this land, and return to the land of your kindred. ¹⁴And Rachel and Leah answered and said to him, Is there yet any portion or inheritance for us in our father's house? ¹⁵Are we not counted of him strangers? for he has sold us, and has quite devoured also our money. ¹⁶For all the riches which God has taken from our father, that is ours, and our children's: now then, whatever God has said to you, do. ¹⁷Then Jacob rose up, and set his sons and his wives on camels; ¹⁸And he carried away all his cattle, and all his goods which he had gotten, the cattle of his getting, which he had gotten in Padanaram, for to go to Isaac his father in the land of Canaan. ¹⁹And Laban went to shear his sheep: and Rachel had stolen the images that were her father's. ²⁰And Jacob stole away unawares to Laban the Syrian, in that he told him not that he fled. ²¹So he fled with all that he had; and he rose up, and passed over the river, and set his face toward the mount Gilead. ²²And it was told Laban on the third day that Jacob was fled. ²³And he took his brothers with him, and pursued after him seven days' journey; and they overtook him in the mount Gilead. ²⁴And God came to Laban the Syrian in a dream by night, and said to him, Take heed that you speak not to Jacob either good or bad. ²⁵Then Laban overtook Jacob. Now Jacob had pitched his tent in the mount: and Laban with his brothers pitched in the mount of Gilead. ²⁶And Laban said to Jacob, What have you done, that you have stolen away unawares to me, and carried away my daughters, as captives taken with the sword? ²⁷Why did you flee away secretly, and steal away from me; and did not tell me, that I might have sent you away with mirth, and with songs, with tabret, and with harp? ²⁸And have not suffered me to kiss my sons and my daughters? you have now done foolishly in so doing. ²⁹It is in the power of my hand to do you hurt: but the God of your father spoke to me last night, saying, Take you heed that you speak not to Jacob either good or bad. ³⁰And now, though you would needs be gone, because you sore longed after your father's house, yet why have you stolen my gods? ³¹And Jacob answered and said to Laban, Because I was afraid: for I said, Peradventure you would take by force your daughters from me. ³²With whomsoever you find your gods, let him not live: before our brothers discern you what is your with me, and take it to you. For Jacob knew not that Rachel had stolen them. ³³And Laban went into Jacob's tent, and into Leah's tent, and into the two maidservants' tents; but he found them not. Then went he out of Leah's tent, and entered into Rachel's tent. ³⁴Now Rachel had taken the images, and put them in the camel's furniture, and sat on them. And Laban searched all the tent, but found them not. ³⁵And she said to her father, Let it not displease my lord that I cannot rise up before you; for the custom of women is on me. And he searched but found not the images. ³⁶And Jacob was wroth, and strived with Laban: and Jacob answered and said to Laban, What is my trespass? what is my sin, that you have so hotly pursued after me? ³⁷Whereas you have searched all my stuff, what have you found of all your household stuff? set it here before my brothers and your brothers, that they may judge between us both. ³⁸This twenty years have I been with you; your ewes and your she goats have not cast their young, and the rams of your flock have I not eaten. ³⁹That which was torn of beasts I brought not to you; I bore the loss of it; of

my hand did you require it, whether stolen by day, or stolen by night. ⁴⁰Thus I was; in the day the drought consumed me, and the frost by night; and my sleep departed from my eyes. ⁴¹Thus have I been twenty years in your house; I served you fourteen years for your two daughters, and six years for your cattle: and you have changed my wages ten times. ⁴²Except the God of my father, the God of Abraham, and the fear of Isaac, had been with me, surely you had sent me away now empty. God has seen my affliction and the labor of my hands, and rebuked you last night. ⁴³And Laban answered and said to Jacob, These daughters are my daughters, and these children are my children, and these cattle are my cattle, and all that you see is mine: and what can I do this day to these my daughters, or to their children which they have born? ⁴⁴Now therefore come you, let us make a covenant, I and you; and let it be for a witness between me and you. ⁴⁵And Jacob took a stone, and set it up for a pillar. ⁴⁶And Jacob said to his brothers, Gather stones; and they took stones, and made an heap: and they did eat there on the heap. ⁴⁷And Laban called it Jegarsahadutha: but Jacob called it Galeed. ⁴⁸And Laban said, This heap is a witness between me and you this day. Therefore was the name of it called Galeed; ⁴⁹And Mizpah; for he said, The LORD watch between me and you, when we are absent one from another. ⁵⁰If you shall afflict my daughters, or if you shall take other wives beside my daughters, no man is with us; see, God is witness between me and you. ⁵¹And Laban said to Jacob, Behold this heap, and behold this pillar, which I have cast between me and you: ⁵²This heap be witness, and this pillar be witness, that I will not pass over this heap to you, and that you shall not pass over this heap and this pillar to me, for harm. ⁵³The God of Abraham, and the God of Nahor, the God of their father, judge between us. And Jacob swore by the fear of his father Isaac. ⁵⁴Then Jacob offered sacrifice on the mount, and called his brothers to eat bread: and they did eat bread, and tarried all night in the mount. ⁵⁵And early in the morning Laban rose up, and kissed his sons and his daughters, and blessed them: and Laban departed, and returned to his place.

32

¹And Jacob went on his way, and the angels of God met him. ²And when Jacob saw them, he said, This is God's host: and he called the name of that place Mahanaim. ³And Jacob sent messengers before him to Esau his brother to the land of Seir, the country of Edom. ⁴And he commanded them, saying, Thus shall you speak to my lord Esau; Your servant Jacob says thus, I have sojourned with Laban, and stayed there until now: ⁵And I have oxen, and asses, flocks, and menservants, and womenservants: and I have sent to tell my lord, that I may find grace in your sight. ⁶And the messengers returned to Jacob, saying, We came to your brother Esau, and also he comes to meet you, and four hundred men with him. ⁷Then Jacob was greatly afraid and distressed: and he divided the people that was with him, and the flocks, and herds, and the camels, into two bands; ⁸And said, If Esau come to the one company, and smite it, then the other company which is left shall escape. ⁹And Jacob said, O God of my father Abraham, and God of my father Isaac, the LORD which said to me, Return to your country, and to your kindred, and I will deal well with you: ¹⁰I am not worthy of the least of all the mercies, and of all the truth, which you have showed to your servant; for with my staff I passed over this Jordan; and now I am become two bands. ¹¹Deliver me, I pray you, from the hand of my brother, from the hand of Esau: for I fear him, lest he will come and smite me, and the mother with the children. ¹²And you said, I will surely do you good, and make your seed as the sand of the sea, which cannot be numbered for multitude. ¹³And he lodged there that same night; and took of that which came to his hand a present for Esau his brother; ¹⁴Two hundred she goats, and twenty he goats, two hundred ewes, and twenty rams, ¹⁵Thirty milk camels with their colts, forty cows, and ten bulls, twenty she asses, and ten foals. ¹⁶And he delivered them into the hand of his servants, every drove by themselves; and said to his servants, Pass over before me, and put a space between drove and drove. ¹⁷And he commanded the foremost, saying, When Esau my brother meets you, and asks you, saying, Whose are you? and where go you? and whose are these before you? ¹⁸Then you shall say, They be your servant Jacob's; it is a present sent to my lord Esau: and, behold, also he is behind us. ¹⁹And so commanded he the second, and the third, and all that followed the droves, saying, On this manner shall you speak to Esau, when you find him. ²⁰And say you moreover, Behold, your servant Jacob is behind us. For he said, I will appease him with the present that goes before me, and afterward I will see his face; peradventure he will accept of me. ²¹So went the present over before him: and himself lodged that night in the company. ²²And he rose up that night, and took his two wives, and his two womenservants, and his eleven sons, and passed over the ford Jabbok. ²³And he took them, and sent them over the brook, and sent over that he had. ²⁴And Jacob was left alone; and there wrestled a man with him until the breaking of the day. ²⁵And when he saw that he prevailed not against him, he touched the hollow of his thigh; and the hollow of Jacob's thigh was out of joint, as he wrestled with him. ²⁶And he said, Let me go, for the day breaks. And he said, I will not let you go, except you bless me. ²⁷And he said to him, What is your name? And he said, Jacob. ²⁸And he said, Your name shall be called no more Jacob, but Israel: for as a prince have you power with God and with men, and have prevailed. ²⁹And Jacob asked him, and said, Tell me, I pray you, your name. And he said, Why is it that you do ask after my name? And he blessed him there. ³⁰And Jacob called the name of the place Peniel: for I have seen God face to face, and my life is preserved. ³¹And as he passed over Penuel the sun rose on him, and he halted on his thigh. ³²Therefore the children of Israel eat not of the sinew which shrank, which is on the hollow of the thigh, to this day: because he touched the hollow of Jacob's thigh in the sinew that shrank.

33

¹And Jacob lifted up his eyes, and looked, and, behold, Esau came, and with him four hundred men. And he divided the children to Leah, and to Rachel, and to the two handmaids. ²And he put the handmaids and their children foremost, and Leah and her children after, and Rachel and Joseph last. ³And he passed over before them, and bowed himself to the ground seven times, until he came near to his brother. ⁴And Esau ran to meet him, and

embraced him, and fell on his neck, and kissed him: and they wept. ⁵And he lifted up his eyes, and saw the women and the children; and said, Who are those with you? And he said, The children which God has graciously given your servant. ⁶Then the handmaidens came near, they and their children, and they bowed themselves. ⁷And Leah also with her children came near, and bowed themselves: and after came Joseph near and Rachel, and they bowed themselves. ⁸And he said, What mean you by all this drove which I met? And he said, These are to find grace in the sight of my lord. ⁹And Esau said, I have enough, my brother; keep that you have to yourself. ¹⁰And Jacob said, No, I pray you, if now I have found grace in your sight, then receive my present at my hand: for therefore I have seen your face, as though I had seen the face of God, and you were pleased with me. ¹¹Take, I pray you, my blessing that is brought to you; because God has dealt graciously with me, and because I have enough. And he urged him, and he took it. ¹²And he said, Let us take our journey, and let us go, and I will go before you. ¹³And he said to him, My lord knows that the children are tender, and the flocks and herds with young are with me: and if men should overdrive them one day, all the flock will die. ¹⁴Let my lord, I pray you, pass over before his servant: and I will lead on softly, according as the cattle that goes before me and the children be able to endure, until I come to my lord to Seir. ¹⁵And Esau said, Let me now leave with you some of the folk that are with me. And he said, What needs it? let me find grace in the sight of my lord. ¹⁶So Esau returned that day on his way to Seir. ¹⁷And Jacob journeyed to Succoth, and built him an house, and made booths for his cattle: therefore the name of the place is called Succoth. ¹⁸And Jacob came to Shalem, a city of Shechem, which is in the land of Canaan, when he came from Padanaram; and pitched his tent before the city. ¹⁹And he bought a parcel of a field, where he had spread his tent, at the hand of the children of Hamor, Shechem's father, for an hundred pieces of money. ²⁰And he erected there an altar, and called it EleloheIsrael.

34 ¹And Dinah the daughter of Leah, which she bore to Jacob, went out to see the daughters of the land. ²And when Shechem the son of Hamor the Hivite, prince of the country, saw her, he took her, and lay with her, and defiled her. ³And his soul joined to Dinah the daughter of Jacob, and he loved the damsel, and spoke kindly to the damsel. ⁴And Shechem spoke to his father Hamor, saying, Get me this damsel to wife. ⁵And Jacob heard that he had defiled Dinah his daughter: now his sons were with his cattle in the field: and Jacob held his peace until they were come. ⁶And Hamor the father of Shechem went out to Jacob to commune with him. ⁷And the sons of Jacob came out of the field when they heard it: and the men were grieved, and they were very wroth, because he had worked folly in Israel in lying with Jacob's daughter: which thing should not to be done. ⁸And Hamor communed with them, saying, The soul of my son Shechem longs for your daughter: I pray you give her to him to wife. ⁹And make you marriages with us, and give your daughters to us, and take our daughters to you. ¹⁰And you shall dwell with us: and the land shall be before you; dwell and trade you therein, and get you possessions therein.

¹¹And Shechem said to her father and to her brothers, Let me find grace in your eyes, and what you shall say to me I will give. ¹²Ask me never so much dowry and gift, and I will give according as you shall say to me: but give me the damsel to wife. ¹³And the sons of Jacob answered Shechem and Hamor his father deceitfully, and said, because he had defiled Dinah their sister: ¹⁴And they said to them, We cannot do this thing, to give our sister to one that is uncircumcised; for that were a reproach to us: ¹⁵But in this will we consent to you: If you will be as we be, that every male of you be circumcised; ¹⁶Then will we give our daughters to you, and we will take your daughters to us, and we will dwell with you, and we will become one people. ¹⁷But if you will not listen to us, to be circumcised; then will we take our daughter, and we will be gone. ¹⁸And their words pleased Hamor, and Shechem Hamor's son. ¹⁹And the young man deferred not to do the thing, because he had delight in Jacob's daughter: and he was more honorable than all the house of his father. ²⁰And Hamor and Shechem his son came to the gate of their city, and communed with the men of their city, saying, ²¹These men are peaceable with us; therefore let them dwell in the land, and trade therein; for the land, behold, it is large enough for them; let us take their daughters to us for wives, and let us give them our daughters. ²²Only herein will the men consent to us for to dwell with us, to be one people, if every male among us be circumcised, as they are circumcised. ²³Shall not their cattle and their substance and every beast of theirs be ours? only let us consent to them, and they will dwell with us. ²⁴And to Hamor and to Shechem his son listened all that went out of the gate of his city; and every male was circumcised, all that went out of the gate of his city. ²⁵And it came to pass on the third day, when they were sore, that two of the sons of Jacob, Simeon and Levi, Dinah's brothers, took each man his sword, and came on the city boldly, and slew all the males. ²⁶And they slew Hamor and Shechem his son with the edge of the sword, and took Dinah out of Shechem's house, and went out. ²⁷The sons of Jacob came on the slain, and spoiled the city, because they had defiled their sister. ²⁸They took their sheep, and their oxen, and their asses, and that which was in the city, and that which was in the field, ²⁹And all their wealth, and all their little ones, and their wives took they captive, and spoiled even all that was in the house. ³⁰And Jacob said to Simeon and Levi, You have troubled me to make me to stink among the inhabitants of the land, among the Canaanites and the Perizzites: and I being few in number, they shall gather themselves together against me, and slay me; and I shall be destroyed, I and my house. ³¹And they said, Should he deal with our sister as with an harlot?

35 ¹And God said to Jacob, Arise, go up to Bethel, and dwell there: and make there an altar to God, that appeared to you when you fled from the face of Esau your brother. ²Then Jacob said to his household, and to all that were with him, Put away the strange gods that are among you, and be clean, and change your garments: ³And let us arise, and go up to Bethel; and I will make there an altar to God, who answered me in the day of my distress, and was with me in the way which I went. ⁴And they gave to Jacob all the strange gods which were in their hand, and all their earrings which were in their ears; and Jacob hid them under the oak which was by Shechem. ⁵And they journeyed: and the terror of God was on the cities that were round about them, and they did not pursue after the sons of Jacob. ⁶So Jacob came to Luz, which is in the land of Canaan, that is, Bethel, he and all the people that were with him. ⁷And he built there an altar, and called the place Elbethel: because there God appeared to him, when he fled from the face of his brother. ⁸But Deborah Rebekah's nurse died, and she was buried beneath Bethel under an oak: and the name of it was called Allonbachuth. ⁹And God appeared to Jacob again, when he came out of Padanaram, and blessed him. ¹⁰And God said to him, Your name is Jacob: your name shall not be called any more Jacob, but Israel shall be your name: and he called his name Israel. ¹¹And God said to him, I am God Almighty: be fruitful and multiply; a nation and a company of nations shall be of you, and kings shall come out of your loins; ¹²And the land which I gave Abraham and Isaac, to you I will give it, and to your seed after you will I give the land. ¹³And God went up from him in the place where he talked with him. ¹⁴And Jacob set up a pillar in the place where he talked with him, even a pillar of stone: and he poured a drink offering thereon, and he poured oil thereon. ¹⁵And Jacob called the name of the place where God spoke with him, Bethel. ¹⁶And they journeyed from Bethel; and there was but a little way to come to Ephrath: and Rachel travailed, and she had hard labor. ¹⁷And it came to pass, when she was in hard labor, that the midwife said to her, Fear not; you shall have this son also. ¹⁸And it came to pass, as her soul was in departing, (for she died) that she called his name Benoni: but his father called him Benjamin. ¹⁹And Rachel died, and was buried in the way to Ephrath, which is Bethlehem. ²⁰And Jacob set a pillar on her grave: that is the pillar of Rachel's grave to this day. ²¹And Israel journeyed, and spread his tent beyond the tower of Edar. ²²And it came to pass, when Israel dwelled in that land, that Reuben went and lay with Bilhah his father's concubine: and Israel heard it. Now the sons of Jacob were twelve: ²³The sons of Leah; Reuben, Jacob's firstborn, and Simeon, and Levi, and Judah, and Issachar, and Zebulun: ²⁴The sons of Rachel; Joseph, and Benjamin: ²⁵And the sons of Bilhah, Rachel's handmaid; Dan, and Naphtali: ²⁶And the sons of Zilpah, Leah's handmaid: Gad, and Asher: these are the sons of Jacob, which were born to him in Padanaram. ²⁷And Jacob came to Isaac his father to Mamre, to the city of Arbah, which is Hebron, where Abraham and Isaac sojourned. ²⁸And the days of Isaac were an hundred and fourscore years. ²⁹And Isaac gave up the ghost, and died, and was gathered to his people, being old and full of days: and his sons Esau and Jacob buried him.

36

¹Now these are the generations of Esau, who is Edom. ²Esau took his wives of the daughters of Canaan; Adah the daughter of Elon the Hittite, and Aholibamah the daughter of Anah the daughter of Zibeon the Hivite; ³And Bashemath Ishmael's daughter, sister of Nebajoth. ⁴And Adah bore to Esau Eliphaz; and Bashemath bore Reuel; ⁵And Aholibamah bore Jeush, and Jaalam, and Korah: these are the sons of Esau, which were born to him in the land of Canaan. ⁶And Esau took his wives, and his sons, and his daughters, and all the persons of his house, and his cattle, and all his beasts, and all his substance, which he had got in the land of Canaan; and went into the country from the face of his brother Jacob. ⁷For their riches were more than that they might dwell together; and the land wherein they were strangers could not bear them because of their cattle. ⁸Thus dwelled Esau in mount Seir: Esau is Edom. ⁹And these are the generations of Esau the father of the Edomites in mount Seir: ¹⁰These are the names of Esau's sons; Eliphaz the son of Adah the wife of Esau, Reuel the son of Bashemath the wife of Esau. ¹¹And the sons of Eliphaz were Teman, Omar, Zepho, and Gatam, and Kenaz. ¹²And Timna was concubine to Eliphaz Esau's son; and she bore to Eliphaz Amalek: these were the sons of Adah Esau's wife. ¹³And these are the sons of Reuel; Nahath, and Zerah, Shammah, and Mizzah: these were the sons of Bashemath Esau's wife. ¹⁴And these were the sons of Aholibamah, the daughter of Anah the daughter of Zibeon, Esau's wife: and she bore to Esau Jeush, and Jaalam, and Korah. ¹⁵These were dukes of the sons of Esau: the sons of Eliphaz the firstborn son of Esau; duke Teman, duke Omar, duke Zepho, duke Kenaz, ¹⁶Duke Korah, duke Gatam, and duke Amalek: these are the dukes that came of Eliphaz in the land of Edom; these were the sons of Adah. ¹⁷And these are the sons of Reuel Esau's son; duke Nahath, duke Zerah, duke Shammah, duke Mizzah: these are the dukes that came of Reuel in the land of Edom; these are the sons of Bashemath Esau's wife. ¹⁸And these are the sons of Aholibamah Esau's wife; duke Jeush, duke Jaalam, duke Korah: these were the dukes that came of Aholibamah the daughter of Anah, Esau's wife. ¹⁹These are the sons of Esau, who is Edom, and these are their dukes. ²⁰These are the sons of Seir the Horite, who inhabited the land; Lotan, and Shobal, and Zibeon, and Anah, ²¹And Dishon, and Ezer, and Dishan: these are the dukes of the Horites, the children of Seir in the land of Edom. ²²And the children of Lotan were Hori and Hemam; and Lotan's sister was Timna. ²³And the children of Shobal were these; Alvan, and Manahath, and Ebal, Shepho, and Onam. ²⁴And these are the children of Zibeon; both Ajah, and Anah: this was that Anah that found the mules in the wilderness, as he fed the asses of Zibeon his father. ²⁵And the children of Anah were these; Dishon, and Aholibamah the daughter of Anah. ²⁶And these are the children of Dishon; Hemdan, and Eshban, and Ithran, and Cheran. ²⁷The children of Ezer are these; Bilhan, and Zaavan, and Akan. ²⁸The children of Dishan are these; Uz, and Aran. ²⁹These are the dukes that came of the Horites; duke Lotan, duke Shobal, duke Zibeon, duke Anah, ³⁰Duke Dishon, duke Ezer, duke Dishan: these are the dukes that came of Hori, among their dukes in the land of Seir. ³¹And these are the kings that reigned in the land of Edom, before there reigned any king over the children of Israel. ³²And Bela the son of Beor reigned in Edom: and the name of his city was Dinhabah. ³³And Bela died, and Jobab the son of Zerah of Bozrah reigned in his stead. ³⁴And Jobab died, and Husham of the land of Temani reigned in his stead. ³⁵And Husham died, and Hadad the son of Bedad, who smote Midian in the field of Moab, reigned in his stead: and the name of his city was Avith. ³⁶And Hadad died, and Samlah of Masrekah reigned

in his stead. ³⁷And Samlah died, and Saul of Rehoboth by the river reigned in his stead. ³⁸And Saul died, and Baalhanan the son of Achbor reigned in his stead. ³⁹And Baalhanan the son of Achbor died, and Hadar reigned in his stead: and the name of his city was Pau; and his wife's name was Mehetabel, the daughter of Matred, the daughter of Mezahab. ⁴⁰And these are the names of the dukes that came of Esau, according to their families, after their places, by their names; duke Timnah, duke Alvah, duke Jetheth, ⁴¹Duke Aholibamah, duke Elah, duke Pinon, ⁴²Duke Kenaz, duke Teman, duke Mibzar, ⁴³Duke Magdiel, duke Iram: these be the dukes of Edom, according to their habitations in the land of their possession: he is Esau the father of the Edomites.

37 ¹And Jacob dwelled in the land wherein his father was a stranger, in the land of Canaan. ²These are the generations of Jacob. Joseph, being seventeen years old, was feeding the flock with his brothers; and the lad was with the sons of Bilhah, and with the sons of Zilpah, his father's wives: and Joseph brought to his father their evil report. ³Now Israel loved Joseph more than all his children, because he was the son of his old age: and he made him a coat of many colors. ⁴And when his brothers saw that their father loved him more than all his brothers, they hated him, and could not speak peaceably to him. ⁵And Joseph dreamed a dream, and he told it his brothers: and they hated him yet the more. ⁶And he said to them, Hear, I pray you, this dream which I have dreamed: ⁷For, behold, we were binding sheaves in the field, and, see, my sheaf arose, and also stood upright; and, behold, your sheaves stood round about, and made obeisance to my sheaf. ⁸And his brothers said to him, Shall you indeed reign over us? or shall you indeed have dominion over us? And they hated him yet the more for his dreams, and for his words. ⁹And he dreamed yet another dream, and told it his brothers, and said, Behold, I have dreamed a dream more; and, behold, the sun and the moon and the eleven stars made obeisance to me. ¹⁰And he told it to his father, and to his brothers: and his father rebuked him, and said to him, What is this dream that you have dreamed? Shall I and your mother and your brothers indeed come to bow down ourselves to you to the earth? ¹¹And his brothers envied him; but his father observed the saying. ¹²And his brothers went to feed their father's flock in Shechem. ¹³And Israel said to Joseph, Do not your brothers feed the flock in Shechem? come, and I will send you to them. And he said to him, Here am I. ¹⁴And he said to him, Go, I pray you, see whether it be well with your brothers, and well with the flocks; and bring me word again. So he sent him out of the vale of Hebron, and he came to Shechem. ¹⁵And a certain man found him, and, behold, he was wandering in the field: and the man asked him, saying, What seek you? ¹⁶And he said, I seek my brothers: tell me, I pray you, where they feed their flocks. ¹⁷And the man said, They are departed hence; for I heard them say, Let us go to Dothan. And Joseph went after his brothers, and found them in Dothan. ¹⁸And when they saw him afar off, even before he came near to them, they conspired against him to slay him. ¹⁹And they said one to another, Behold, this dreamer comes. ²⁰Come now therefore, and let us slay him, and cast him into some pit, and we will say, Some evil beast has devoured him: and we shall see what will become of his dreams. ²¹And Reuben heard it, and he delivered him out of their hands; and said, Let us not kill him. ²²And Reuben said to them, Shed no blood, but cast him into this pit that is in the wilderness, and lay no hand on him; that he might rid him out of their hands, to deliver him to his father again. ²³And it came to pass, when Joseph was come to his brothers, that they stripped Joseph out of his coat, his coat of many colors that was on him; ²⁴And they took him, and cast him into a pit: and the pit was empty, there was no water in it. ²⁵And they sat down to eat bread: and they lifted up their eyes and looked, and, behold, a company of Ishmeelites came from Gilead with their camels bearing spices and balm and myrrh, going to carry it down to Egypt. ²⁶And Judah said to his brothers, What profit is it if we slay our brother, and conceal his blood? ²⁷Come, and let us sell him to the Ishmeelites, and let not our hand be on him; for he is our brother and our flesh. And his brothers were content. ²⁸Then there passed by Midianites merchants; and they drew and lifted up Joseph out of the pit, and sold Joseph to the Ishmeelites for twenty pieces of silver: and they brought Joseph into Egypt. ²⁹And Reuben returned to the pit; and, behold, Joseph was not in the pit; and he rent his clothes. ³⁰And he returned to his brothers, and said, The child is not; and I, where shall I go? ³¹And they took Joseph's coat, and killed a kid of the goats, and dipped the coat in the blood; ³²And they sent the coat of many colors, and they brought it to their father; and said, This have we found: know now whether it be your son's coat or no. ³³And he knew it, and said, It is my son's coat; an evil beast has devoured him; Joseph is without doubt rent in pieces. ³⁴And Jacob rent his clothes, and put sackcloth on his loins, and mourned for his son many days. ³⁵And all his sons and all his daughters rose up to comfort him; but he refused to be comforted; and he said, For I will go down into the grave to my son mourning. Thus his father wept for him. ³⁶And the Midianites sold him into Egypt to Potiphar, an officer of Pharaoh's, and captain of the guard.

38 ¹And it came to pass at that time, that Judah went down from his brothers, and turned in to a certain Adullamite, whose name was Hirah. ²And Judah saw there a daughter of a certain Canaanite, whose name was Shuah; and he took her, and went in to her. ³And she conceived, and bore a son; and he called his name Er. ⁴And she conceived again, and bore a son; and she called his name Onan. ⁵And she yet again conceived, and bore a son; and called his name Shelah: and he was at Chezib, when she bore him. ⁶And Judah took a wife for Er his firstborn, whose name was Tamar. ⁷And Er, Judah's firstborn, was wicked in the sight of the LORD; and the LORD slew him. ⁸And Judah said to Onan, Go in to your brother's wife, and marry her, and raise up seed to your brother. ⁹And Onan knew that the seed should not be his; and it came to pass, when he went in to his brother's wife, that he spilled it on the ground, lest that he should give seed to his brother. ¹⁰And the thing which he did displeased the LORD: why he slew him also. ¹¹Then said Judah to Tamar his daughter in law, Remain a widow at your father's house, till Shelah my son be grown: for he said, Lest peradventure he die also, as his brothers did. And

Tamar went and dwelled in her father's house. ¹²And in process of time the daughter of Shuah Judah's wife died; and Judah was comforted, and went up to his sheep shearers to Timnath, he and his friend Hirah the Adullamite. ¹³And it was told Tamar, saying, Behold your father in law goes up to Timnath to shear his sheep. ¹⁴And she put her widow's garments off from her, and covered her with a veil, and wrapped herself, and sat in an open place, which is by the way to Timnath; for she saw that Shelah was grown, and she was not given to him to wife. ¹⁵When Judah saw her, he thought her to be an harlot; because she had covered her face. ¹⁶And he turned to her by the way, and said, Go to, I pray you, let me come in to you; (for he knew not that she was his daughter in law.) And she said, What will you give me, that you may come in to me? ¹⁷And he said, I will send you a kid from the flock. And she said, Will you give me a pledge, till you send it? ¹⁸And he said, What pledge shall I give you? And she said, Your signet, and your bracelets, and your staff that is in your hand. And he gave it her, and came in to her, and she conceived by him. ¹⁹And she arose, and went away, and laid by her veil from her, and put on the garments of her widowhood. ²⁰And Judah sent the kid by the hand of his friend the Adullamite, to receive his pledge from the woman's hand: but he found her not. ²¹Then he asked the men of that place, saying, Where is the harlot, that was openly by the way side? And they said, There was no harlot in this place. ²²And he returned to Judah, and said, I cannot find her; and also the men of the place said, that there was no harlot in this place. ²³And Judah said, Let her take it to her, lest we be shamed: behold, I sent this kid, and you have not found her. ²⁴And it came to pass about three months after, that it was told Judah, saying, Tamar your daughter in law has played the harlot; and also, behold, she is with child by prostitution. And Judah said, Bring her forth, and let her be burnt. ²⁵When she was brought forth, she sent to her father in law, saying, By the man, whose these are, am I with child: and she said, Discern, I pray you, whose are these, the signet, and bracelets, and staff. ²⁶And Judah acknowledged them, and said, She has been more righteous than I; because that I gave her not to Shelah my son. And he knew her again no more. ²⁷And it came to pass in the time of her travail, that, behold, twins were in her womb. ²⁸And it came to pass, when she travailed, that the one put out his hand: and the midwife took and bound on his hand a scarlet thread, saying, This came out first. ²⁹And it came to pass, as he drew back his hand, that, behold, his brother came out: and she said, How have you broken forth? this breach be on you: therefore his name was called Pharez. ³⁰And afterward came out his brother, that had the scarlet thread on his hand: and his name was called Zarah.

39

¹And Joseph was brought down to Egypt; and Potiphar, an officer of Pharaoh, captain of the guard, an Egyptian, bought him of the hands of the Ishmeelites, which had brought him down thither. ²And the LORD was with Joseph, and he was a prosperous man; and he was in the house of his master the Egyptian. ³And his master saw that the LORD was with him, and that the LORD made all that he did to prosper in his hand. ⁴And Joseph found grace in his sight, and he served him: and he made him overseer over his house, and all that he had he put into his hand. ⁵And it came to pass from the time that he had made him overseer in his house, and over all that he had, that the LORD blessed the Egyptian's house for Joseph's sake; and the blessing of the LORD was on all that he had in the house, and in the field. ⁶And he left all that he had in Joseph's hand; and he knew not anything he had, save the bread which he did eat. And Joseph was a goodly person, and well favored. ⁷And it came to pass after these things, that his master's wife cast her eyes on Joseph; and she said, Lie with me. ⁸But he refused, and said to his master's wife, Behold, my master wotteth not what is with me in the house, and he has committed all that he has to my hand; ⁹There is none greater in this house than I; neither has he kept back any thing from me but you, because you are his wife: how then can I do this great wickedness, and sin against God? ¹⁰And it came to pass, as she spoke to Joseph day by day, that he listened not to her, to lie by her, or to be with her. ¹¹And it came to pass about this time, that Joseph went into the house to do his business; and there was none of the men of the house there within. ¹²And she caught him by his garment, saying, Lie with me: and he left his garment in her hand, and fled, and got him out. ¹³And it came to pass, when she saw that he had left his garment in her hand, and was fled forth, ¹⁴That she called to the men of her house, and spoke to them, saying, See, he has brought in an Hebrew to us to mock us; he came in to me to lie with me, and I cried with a loud voice: ¹⁵And it came to pass, when he heard that I lifted up my voice and cried, that he left his garment with me, and fled, and got him out. ¹⁶And she laid up his garment by her, until his lord came home. ¹⁷And she spoke to him according to these words, saying, The Hebrew servant, which you have brought to us, came in to me to mock me: ¹⁸And it came to pass, as I lifted up my voice and cried, that he left his garment with me, and fled out. ¹⁹And it came to pass, when his master heard the words of his wife, which she spoke to him, saying, After this manner did your servant to me; that his wrath was kindled. ²⁰And Joseph's master took him, and put him into the prison, a place where the king's prisoners were bound: and he was there in the prison. ²¹But the LORD was with Joseph, and showed him mercy, and gave him favor in the sight of the keeper of the prison. ²²And the keeper of the prison committed to Joseph's hand all the prisoners that were in the prison; and whatever they did there, he was the doer of it. ²³The keeper of the prison looked not to any thing that was under his hand; because the LORD was with him, and that which he did, the LORD made it to prosper.

40

¹And it came to pass after these things, that the butler of the king of Egypt and his baker had offended their lord the king of Egypt. ²And Pharaoh was wroth against two of his officers, against the chief of the butlers, and against the chief of the bakers. ³And he put them in ward in the house of the captain of the guard, into the prison, the place where Joseph was bound. ⁴And the captain of the guard charged Joseph with them, and he served them: and they continued a season in ward. ⁵And they dreamed a dream both of them, each man his dream in one night, each man according to the interpretation of his dream, the butler

and the baker of the king of Egypt, which were bound in the prison. ⁶And Joseph came in to them in the morning, and looked on them, and, behold, they were sad. ⁷And he asked Pharaoh's officers that were with him in the ward of his lord's house, saying, Why look you so sadly to day? ⁸And they said to him, We have dreamed a dream, and there is no interpreter of it. And Joseph said to them, Do not interpretations belong to God? tell me them, I pray you. ⁹And the chief butler told his dream to Joseph, and said to him, In my dream, behold, a vine was before me; ¹⁰And in the vine were three branches: and it was as though it budded, and her blossoms shot forth; and the clusters thereof brought forth ripe grapes: ¹¹And Pharaoh's cup was in my hand: and I took the grapes, and pressed them into Pharaoh's cup, and I gave the cup into Pharaoh's hand. ¹²And Joseph said to him, This is the interpretation of it: The three branches are three days: ¹³Yet within three days shall Pharaoh lift up your head, and restore you to your place: and you shall deliver Pharaoh's cup into his hand, after the former manner when you were his butler. ¹⁴But think on me when it shall be well with you, and show kindness, I pray you, to me, and make mention of me to Pharaoh, and bring me out of this house: ¹⁵For indeed I was stolen away out of the land of the Hebrews: and here also have I done nothing that they should put me into the dungeon. ¹⁶When the chief baker saw that the interpretation was good, he said to Joseph, I also was in my dream, and, behold, I had three white baskets on my head: ¹⁷And in the uppermost basket there was of all manner of bakemeats for Pharaoh; and the birds did eat them out of the basket on my head. ¹⁸And Joseph answered and said, This is the interpretation thereof: The three baskets are three days: ¹⁹Yet within three days shall Pharaoh lift up your head from off you, and shall hang you on a tree; and the birds shall eat your flesh from off you. ²⁰And it came to pass the third day, which was Pharaoh's birthday, that he made a feast to all his servants: and he lifted up the head of the chief butler and of the chief baker among his servants. ²¹And he restored the chief butler to his butlership again; and he gave the cup into Pharaoh's hand: ²²But he hanged the chief baker: as Joseph had interpreted to them. ²³Yet did not the chief butler remember Joseph, but forgot him.

41 ¹And it came to pass at the end of two full years, that Pharaoh dreamed: and, behold, he stood by the river. ²And, behold, there came up out of the river seven well favored cows and fat; and they fed in a meadow. ³And, behold, seven other cows came up after them out of the river, ill favored and skinney; and stood by the other cows on the brink of the river. ⁴And the ill favored and skinney cows did eat up the seven well favored and fat cows. So Pharaoh awoke. ⁵And he slept and dreamed the second time: and, behold, seven ears of corn came up on one stalk, rank and good. ⁶And, behold, seven thin ears and blasted with the east wind sprung up after them. ⁷And the seven thin ears devoured the seven rank and full ears. And Pharaoh awoke, and, behold, it was a dream. ⁸And it came to pass in the morning that his spirit was troubled; and he sent and called for all the magicians of Egypt, and all the wise men thereof: and Pharaoh told them his dream; but there was none that could interpret them to Pharaoh. ⁹Then spoke the chief butler to Pharaoh, saying, I do remember my faults this day: ¹⁰Pharaoh was wroth with his servants, and put me in ward in the captain of the guard's house, both me and the chief baker: ¹¹And we dreamed a dream in one night, I and he; we dreamed each man according to the interpretation of his dream. ¹²And there was there with us a young man, an Hebrew, servant to the captain of the guard; and we told him, and he interpreted to us our dreams; to each man according to his dream he did interpret. ¹³And it came to pass, as he interpreted to us, so it was; me he restored to my office, and him he hanged. ¹⁴Then Pharaoh sent and called Joseph, and they brought him hastily out of the dungeon: and he shaved himself, and changed his raiment, and came in to Pharaoh. ¹⁵And Pharaoh said to Joseph, I have dreamed a dream, and there is none that can interpret it: and I have heard say of you, that you can understand a dream to interpret it. ¹⁶And Joseph answered Pharaoh, saying, It is not in me: God shall give Pharaoh an answer of peace. ¹⁷And Pharaoh said to Joseph, In my dream, behold, I stood on the bank of the river: ¹⁸And, behold, there came up out of the river seven cows, fat and well favored; and they fed in a meadow: ¹⁹And, behold, seven other cows came up after them, poor and very ill favored and skinney, such as I never saw in all the land of Egypt for badness: ²⁰And the lean and the ill favored cows did eat up the first seven fat cows: ²¹And when they had eaten them up, it could not be known that they had eaten them; but they were still ill favored, as at the beginning. So I awoke. ²²And I saw in my dream, and, behold, seven ears came up in one stalk, full and good: ²³And, behold, seven ears, withered, thin, and blasted with the east wind, sprung up after them: ²⁴And the thin ears devoured the seven good ears: and I told this to the magicians; but there was none that could declare it to me. ²⁵And Joseph said to Pharaoh, The dream of Pharaoh is one: God has showed Pharaoh what he is about to do. ²⁶The seven good cows are seven years; and the seven good ears are seven years: the dream is one. ²⁷And the seven thin and ill favored cows that came up after them are seven years; and the seven empty ears blasted with the east wind shall be seven years of famine. ²⁸This is the thing which I have spoken to Pharaoh: What God is about to do he shows to Pharaoh. ²⁹Behold, there come seven years of great plenty throughout all the land of Egypt: ³⁰And there shall arise after them seven years of famine; and all the plenty shall be forgotten in the land of Egypt; and the famine shall consume the land; ³¹And the plenty shall not be known in the land by reason of that famine following; for it shall be very grievous. ³²And for that the dream was doubled to Pharaoh twice; it is because the thing is established by God, and God will shortly bring it to pass. ³³Now therefore let Pharaoh look out a man discreet and wise, and set him over the land of Egypt. ³⁴Let Pharaoh do this, and let him appoint officers over the land, and take up the fifth part of the land of Egypt in the seven plenteous years. ³⁵And let them gather all the food of those good years that come, and lay up corn under the hand of Pharaoh, and let them keep food in the cities. ³⁶And that food shall be for store to the land against the seven years of famine, which shall be in the land of Egypt; that the land perish not through the famine. ³⁷And the thing was good in the eyes of Pharaoh, and in the eyes of all his servants. ³⁸And Pharaoh said to his servants, Can we find such a one as this is, a man in whom the Spirit of God is? ³⁹And Pharaoh said to Joseph, For as much as God has showed you all this, there is none so discreet and wise as you are: ⁴⁰You shall be over my house, and according to your word shall all my people be ruled: only in the throne will I be greater than you. ⁴¹And Pharaoh said to Joseph, See, I have set you over all the land of Egypt. ⁴²And Pharaoh took off his ring from his hand, and put it on Joseph's hand, and arrayed him in clothing of fine linen, and put a gold chain about his neck; ⁴³And he made him to ride in the second chariot which he had; and they cried before him, Bow the knee: and he made him ruler over all the land of Egypt. ⁴⁴And Pharaoh said to Joseph, I am Pharaoh, and without you shall no man lift up his hand or foot in all the land of Egypt. ⁴⁵And Pharaoh called Joseph's name Zaphnathpaaneah; and he gave him to wife Asenath the daughter of Potipherah priest of On. And Joseph went out over all the land of Egypt. ⁴⁶And Joseph was thirty years old when he stood before Pharaoh king of Egypt. And Joseph went out from the presence of Pharaoh, and went throughout all the land of Egypt. ⁴⁷And in the seven plenteous years the earth brought forth by handfuls. ⁴⁸And he gathered up all the food of the seven years, which were in the land of Egypt, and laid up the food in the cities: the food of the field, which was round about every city, laid he up in the same. ⁴⁹And Joseph gathered corn as the sand of the sea, very much, until he left numbering; for it was without number. ⁵⁰And to Joseph were born two sons before the years of famine came, which Asenath the daughter of Potipherah priest of On bore to him. ⁵¹And Joseph called the name of the firstborn Manasseh: For God, said he, has made me forget all my toil, and all my father's house. ⁵²And the name of the second called he Ephraim: For God has caused me to be fruitful in the land of my affliction. ⁵³And the seven years of plenty, that was in the land of Egypt, were ended. ⁵⁴And the seven years of dearth began to come, according as Joseph had said: and the dearth was in all lands; but in all the land of Egypt there was bread. ⁵⁵And when all the land of Egypt was famished, the people cried to Pharaoh for bread: and Pharaoh said to all the Egyptians, Go to Joseph; what he says to you, do. ⁵⁶And the famine was over all the face of the earth: and Joseph opened all the storehouses, and sold to the Egyptians; and the famine waxed sore in the land of Egypt. ⁵⁷And all countries came into Egypt to Joseph for to buy corn; because that the famine was so sore in all lands.

42 ¹Now when Jacob saw that there was corn in Egypt, Jacob said to his sons, Why do you look one on another? ²And he said, Behold, I have heard that there is corn in Egypt: get you down thither, and buy for us from there; that we may live, and not die. ³And Joseph's ten brothers went down to buy corn in Egypt. ⁴But Benjamin, Joseph's brother, Jacob sent not with his brothers; for he said, Lest peradventure mischief befall him. ⁵And the sons of Israel came to buy corn among those that came: for the famine was in the land of Canaan. ⁶And Joseph was the governor over the land, and he it was that sold to all the people of the land: and Joseph's brothers came, and bowed down themselves before him with their faces to the earth. ⁷And Joseph saw his brothers, and he knew them, but made himself strange to them, and spoke roughly to them; and he said to them, From where come you? And they said, From the land of Canaan to buy food. ⁸And Joseph knew his brothers, but they knew not him. ⁹And Joseph remembered the dreams which he dreamed of them, and said to them, You are spies; to see the nakedness of the land you are come. ¹⁰And they said to him, No, my lord, but to buy food are your servants come. ¹¹We are all one man's sons; we are true men, your servants are no spies. ¹²And he said to them, No, but to see the nakedness of the land you are come. ¹³And they said, Your servants are twelve brothers, the sons of one man in the land of Canaan; and, behold, the youngest is this day with our father, and one is not. ¹⁴And Joseph said to them, That is it that I spoke to you, saying, You are spies: ¹⁵Hereby you shall be proved: By the life of Pharaoh you shall not go forth hence, except your youngest brother come here. ¹⁶Send one of you, and let him fetch your brother, and you shall be kept in prison, that your words may be proved, whether there be any truth in you: or else by the life of Pharaoh surely you are spies. ¹⁷And he put them all together into ward three days. ¹⁸And Joseph said to them the third day, This do, and live; for I fear God: ¹⁹If you be true men, let one of your brothers be bound in the house of your prison: go you, carry corn for the famine of your houses: ²⁰But bring your youngest brother to me; so shall your words be verified, and you shall not die. And they did so. ²¹And they said one to another, We are truly guilty concerning our brother, in that we saw the anguish of his soul, when he sought us, and we would not hear; therefore is this distress come on us. ²²And Reuben answered them, saying, Spoke I not to you, saying, Do not sin against the child; and you would not hear? therefore, behold, also his blood is required. ²³And they knew not that Joseph understood them; for he spoke to them by an interpreter. ²⁴And he turned himself about from them, and wept; and returned to them again, and communed with them, and took from them Simeon, and bound him before their eyes. ²⁵Then Joseph commanded to fill their sacks with corn, and to restore every man's money into his sack, and to give them provision for the way: and thus did he to them. ²⁶And they laded their asses with the corn, and departed there. ²⁷And as one of them opened his sack to give his ass provender in the inn, he espied his money; for, behold, it was in his sack's mouth. ²⁸And he said to his brothers, My money is restored; and, see, it is even in my sack: and their heart failed them, and they were afraid, saying one to another, What is this that God has done to us? ²⁹And they came to Jacob their father to the land of Canaan, and told him all that befell to them; saying, ³⁰The man, who is the lord of the land, spoke roughly to us, and took us for spies of the country. ³¹And we said to him, We are true men; we are no spies: ³²We be twelve brothers, sons of our father; one is not, and the youngest is this day with our father in the land of Canaan. ³³And the man, the lord of the country, said to us, Hereby shall I know that you are true men; leave one of your brothers here with me, and take food for the famine of your households, and be gone: ³⁴And bring your youngest brother to me: then shall I know that you are no spies, but that you are true men: so will I deliver you your brother, and you shall traffic in the land. ³⁵And it came to pass as they emptied their sacks, that, behold, every man's bundle of money was in his sack: and when both they and their father saw the bundles of money, they were afraid. ³⁶And Jacob their father said to them, Me have you bereaved of my children: Joseph is not, and Simeon is not, and you will take Benjamin away: all these things are against me. ³⁷And Reuben spoke to his father, saying, Slay my two sons, if I bring him not to you: deliver him into my hand, and I will bring him to you again. ³⁸And he said, My son shall not go down with you; for his brother is dead, and he is left alone: if mischief befall him by the way in the which you go, then shall you bring down my gray hairs with sorrow to the grave.

43 ¹And the famine was sore in the land. ²And it came to pass, when they had eaten up the corn which they had brought out of Egypt, their father said to them, Go again, buy us a little food. ³And Judah spoke to him, saying, The man did solemnly protest to us, saying, You shall not see my face, except your brother be with you. ⁴If you will send our brother with us, we will go down and buy you food: ⁵But if you will not send him, we will not go down: for the man said to us, You shall not see my face, except your brother be with you. ⁶And Israel said, Why dealt you so ill with me, as to tell the man whether you had yet a brother? ⁷And they said, The man asked us straightly of our state, and of our kindred, saying, Is your father yet alive? have you another brother? and we told him according to the tenor of these words: could we certainly know that he would say, Bring your brother down? ⁸And Judah said to Israel his father, Send the lad with me, and we will arise and go; that we may live, and not die, both we, and you, and also our little ones. ⁹I will be surety for him; of my hand shall you require him: if I bring him not to you, and set him before you, then let me bear the blame for ever: ¹⁰For except we had lingered, surely now we had returned this second time. ¹¹And their father Israel said to them, If it must be so now, do this; take of the best fruits in the land in your vessels, and carry down the man a present, a little balm, and a little honey, spices, and myrrh, nuts, and almonds: ¹²And take double money in your hand; and the money that was brought again in the mouth of your sacks, carry it again in your hand; peradventure it was an oversight: ¹³Take also your brother, and arise, go again to the man: ¹⁴And God Almighty give you mercy before the man, that he may send away your other brother, and Benjamin. If I be bereaved of my children, I am bereaved. ¹⁵And the men took that present, and they took double money in their hand and Benjamin; and rose up, and went down to Egypt, and stood before Joseph. ¹⁶And when Joseph saw Benjamin with them, he said to the ruler of his house, Bring these men home, and slay, and make ready; for these men shall dine with me at noon. ¹⁷And the man did as Joseph bade; and the man brought the men into Joseph's house. ¹⁸And the men were afraid, because they were brought into Joseph's house; and they said, Because of the money that was returned in our sacks at the first time are we brought in; that he may seek occasion against us, and fall on us, and take us for slaves, and our asses. ¹⁹And they came near to the steward of Joseph's house, and they communed with him at the door of the house, ²⁰And said, O sir, we came indeed down at the first time to buy food: ²¹And it came to pass, when we came to the inn, that we opened our sacks, and, behold, every man's money was in the mouth of his sack, our money in full weight: and we have brought it again in our hand. ²²And other money have we brought down in our hands to buy food: we cannot tell who put our money in our sacks. ²³And he said, Peace be to you, fear not: your God, and the God of your father, has given you treasure in your sacks: I had your money. And he brought Simeon out to them. ²⁴And the man brought the men into Joseph's house, and gave them water, and they washed their feet; and he gave their asses provender. ²⁵And they made ready the present against Joseph came at noon: for they heard that they should eat bread there. ²⁶And when Joseph came home, they brought him the present which was in their hand into the house, and bowed themselves to him to the earth. ²⁷And he asked them of their welfare, and said, Is your father well, the old man of whom you spoke? Is he yet alive? ²⁸And they answered, Your servant our father is in good health, he is yet alive. And they bowed down their heads, and made obeisance. ²⁹And he lifted up his eyes, and saw his brother Benjamin, his mother's son, and said, Is this your younger brother, of whom you spoke to me? And he said, God be gracious to you, my son. ³⁰And Joseph made haste; for his bowels did yearn on his brother: and he sought where to weep; and he entered into his chamber, and wept there. ³¹And he washed his face, and went out, and refrained himself, and said, Set on bread. ³²And they set on for him by himself, and for them by themselves, and for the Egyptians, which did eat with him, by themselves: because the Egyptians might not eat bread with the Hebrews; for that is an abomination to the Egyptians. ³³And they sat before him, the firstborn according to his birthright, and the youngest according to his youth: and the men marveled one at another. ³⁴And he took and sent messes to them from before him: but Benjamin's mess was five times so much as any of theirs. And they drank, and were merry with him.

44 ¹And he commanded the steward of his house, saying, Fill the men's sacks with food, as much as they can carry, and put every man's money in his sack's mouth. ²And put my cup, the silver cup, in the sack's mouth of the youngest, and his corn money. And he did according to the word that Joseph had spoken. ³As soon as the morning was light, the men were sent away, they and their asses. ⁴And when they were gone out of the city, and not yet far off, Joseph said to his steward, Up, follow after the men; and when you do overtake them, say to them, Why have you rewarded evil for good? ⁵Is not this it in which my lord drinks, and whereby indeed he divines? you have done evil in so doing. ⁶And he overtook them, and he spoke to them these same words. ⁷And they said to him, Why says my lord these words? God forbid that your servants should do according to this thing: ⁸Behold, the money, which we found in our sacks' mouths, we brought again to you out of the land of Canaan: how then should we steal out of your lord's house silver or gold? ⁹With whomsoever of your servants it be found, both let him die, and we also will be my lord's

slaves. ¹⁰And he said, Now also let it be according to your words: he with whom it is found shall be my servant; and you shall be blameless. ¹¹Then they speedily took down every man his sack to the ground, and opened every man his sack. ¹²And he searched, and began at the oldest, and left at the youngest: and the cup was found in Benjamin's sack. ¹³Then they rent their clothes, and laded every man his ass, and returned to the city. ¹⁴And Judah and his brothers came to Joseph's house; for he was yet there: and they fell before him on the ground. ¹⁵And Joseph said to them, What deed is this that you have done? know you not that such a man as I can certainly divine? ¹⁶And Judah said, What shall we say to my lord? what shall we speak? or how shall we clear ourselves? God has found out the iniquity of your servants: behold, we are my lord's servants, both we, and he also with whom the cup is found. ¹⁷And he said, God forbid that I should do so: but the man in whose hand the cup is found, he shall be my servant; and as for you, get you up in peace to your father. ¹⁸Then Judah came near to him, and said, Oh my lord, let your servant, I pray you, speak a word in my lord's ears, and let not your anger burn against your servant: for you are even as Pharaoh. ¹⁹My lord asked his servants, saying, Have you a father, or a brother? ²⁰And we said to my lord, We have a father, an old man, and a child of his old age, a little one; and his brother is dead, and he alone is left of his mother, and his father loves him. ²¹And you said to your servants, Bring him down to me, that I may set my eyes on him. ²²And we said to my lord, The lad cannot leave his father: for if he should leave his father, his father would die. ²³And you said to your servants, Except your youngest brother come down with you, you shall see my face no more. ²⁴And it came to pass when we came up to your servant my father, we told him the words of my lord. ²⁵And our father said, Go again, and buy us a little food. ²⁶And we said, We cannot go down: if our youngest brother be with us, then will we go down: for we may not see the man's face, except our youngest brother be with us. ²⁷And your servant my father said to us, You know that my wife bore me two sons: ²⁸And the one went out from me, and I said, Surely he is torn in pieces; and I saw him not since: ²⁹And if you take this also from me, and mischief befall him, you shall bring down my gray hairs with sorrow to the grave. ³⁰Now therefore when I come to your servant my father, and the lad be not with us; seeing that his life is bound up in the lad's life; ³¹It shall come to pass, when he sees that the lad is not with us, that he will die: and your servants shall bring down the gray hairs of your servant our father with sorrow to the grave. ³²For your servant became surety for the lad to my father, saying, If I bring him not to you, then I shall bear the blame to my father for ever. ³³Now therefore, I pray you, let your servant abide instead of the lad a slave to my lord; and let the lad go up with his brothers. ³⁴For how shall I go up to my father, and the lad be not with me? lest peradventure I see the evil that shall come on my father.

45

¹Then Joseph could not refrain himself before all them that stood by him; and he cried, Cause every man to go out from me. And there stood no man with him, while Joseph made himself known to his brothers. ²And he wept aloud: and the Egyptians and the house of Pharaoh heard. ³And Joseph said to his brothers, I am Joseph; does my father yet live? And his brothers could not answer him; for they were troubled at his presence. ⁴And Joseph said to his brothers, Come near to me, I pray you. And they came near. And he said, I am Joseph your brother, whom you sold into Egypt. ⁵Now therefore be not grieved, nor angry with yourselves, that you sold me here: for God did send me before you to preserve life. ⁶For these two years has the famine been in the land: and yet there are five years, in the which there shall neither be ripening nor harvest. ⁷And God sent me before you to preserve you a posterity in the earth, and to save your lives by a great deliverance. ⁸So now it was not you that sent me here, but God: and he has made me a father to Pharaoh, and lord of all his house, and a ruler throughout all the land of Egypt. ⁹Haste you, and go up to my father, and say to him, Thus says your son Joseph, God has made me lord of all Egypt: come down to me, tarry not: ¹⁰And you shall dwell in the land of Goshen, and you shall be near to me, you, and your children, and your children's children, and your flocks, and your herds, and all that you have: ¹¹And there will I nourish you; for yet there are five years of famine; lest you, and your household, and all that you have, come to poverty. ¹²And, behold, your eyes see, and the eyes of my brother Benjamin, that it is my mouth that speaks to you. ¹³And you shall tell my father of all my glory in Egypt, and of all that you have seen; and you shall haste and bring down my father here. ¹⁴And he fell on his brother Benjamin's neck, and wept; and Benjamin wept on his neck. ¹⁵Moreover he kissed all his brothers, and wept on them: and after that his brothers talked with him. ¹⁶And the fame thereof was heard in Pharaoh's house, saying, Joseph's brothers are come: and it pleased Pharaoh well, and his servants. ¹⁷And Pharaoh said to Joseph, Say to your brothers, This do you; lade your beasts, and go, get you to the land of Canaan; ¹⁸And take your father and your households, and come to me: and I will give you the good of the land of Egypt, and you shall eat the fat of the land. ¹⁹Now you are commanded, this do you; take you wagons out of the land of Egypt for your little ones, and for your wives, and bring your father, and come. ²⁰Also regard not your stuff; for the good of all the land of Egypt is yours. ²¹And the children of Israel did so: and Joseph gave them wagons, according to the commandment of Pharaoh, and gave them provision for the way. ²²To all of them he gave each man changes of raiment; but to Benjamin he gave three hundred pieces of silver, and five changes of raiment. ²³And to his father he sent after this manner; ten asses laden with the good things of Egypt, and ten she asses laden with corn and bread and meat for his father by the way. ²⁴So he sent his brothers away, and they departed: and he said to them, See that you fall not out by the way. ²⁵And they went up out of Egypt, and came into the land of Canaan to Jacob their father, ²⁶And told him, saying, Joseph is yet alive, and he is governor over all the land of Egypt. And Jacob's heart fainted, for he believed them not. ²⁷And they told him all the words of Joseph, which he had said to them: and when he saw the wagons which Joseph had sent to carry him, the spirit of Jacob their father revived: ²⁸And Israel said, It is enough; Joseph my son is yet alive: I will go and see him before I die.

46 ¹And Israel took his journey with all that he had, and came to Beersheba, and offered sacrifices to the God of his father Isaac. ²And God spoke to Israel in the visions of the night, and said, Jacob, Jacob. And he said, Here am I. ³And he said, I am God, the God of your father: fear not to go down into Egypt; for I will there make of you a great nation: ⁴I will go down with you into Egypt; and I will also surely bring you up again: and Joseph shall put his hand on your eyes. ⁵And Jacob rose up from Beersheba: and the sons of Israel carried Jacob their father, and their little ones, and their wives, in the wagons which Pharaoh had sent to carry him. ⁶And they took their cattle, and their goods, which they had gotten in the land of Canaan, and came into Egypt, Jacob, and all his seed with him: ⁷His sons, and his sons' sons with him, his daughters, and his sons' daughters, and all his seed brought he with him into Egypt. ⁸And these are the names of the children of Israel, which came into Egypt, Jacob and his sons: Reuben, Jacob's firstborn. ⁹And the sons of Reuben; Hanoch, and Phallu, and Hezron, and Carmi. ¹⁰And the sons of Simeon; Jemuel, and Jamin, and Ohad, and Jachin, and Zohar, and Shaul the son of a Canaanitish woman. ¹¹And the sons of Levi; Gershon, Kohath, and Merari. ¹²And the sons of Judah; Er, and Onan, and Shelah, and Pharez, and Zarah: but Er and Onan died in the land of Canaan. And the sons of Pharez were Hezron and Hamul. ¹³And the sons of Issachar; Tola, and Phuvah, and Job, and Shimron. ¹⁴And the sons of Zebulun; Sered, and Elon, and Jahleel. ¹⁵These be the sons of Leah, which she bore to Jacob in Padanaram, with his daughter Dinah: all the souls of his sons and his daughters were thirty and three. ¹⁶And the sons of Gad; Ziphion, and Haggi, Shuni, and Ezbon, Eri, and Arodi, and Areli. ¹⁷And the sons of Asher; Jimnah, and Ishuah, and Isui, and Beriah, and Serah their sister: and the sons of Beriah; Heber, and Malchiel. ¹⁸These are the sons of Zilpah, whom Laban gave to Leah his daughter, and these she bore to Jacob, even sixteen souls. ¹⁹The sons of Rachel Jacob's wife; Joseph, and Benjamin. ²⁰And to Joseph in the land of Egypt were born Manasseh and Ephraim, which Asenath the daughter of Potipherah priest of On bore to him. ²¹And the sons of Benjamin were Belah, and Becher, and Ashbel, Gera, and Naaman, Ehi, and Rosh, Muppim, and Huppim, and Ard. ²²These are the sons of Rachel, which were born to Jacob: all the souls were fourteen. ²³And the sons of Dan; Hushim. ²⁴And the sons of Naphtali; Jahzeel, and Guni, and Jezer, and Shillem. ²⁵These are the sons of Bilhah, which Laban gave to Rachel his daughter, and she bore these to Jacob: all the souls were seven. ²⁶All the souls that came with Jacob into Egypt, which came out of his loins, besides Jacob's sons' wives, all the souls were three score and six; ²⁷And the sons of Joseph, which were born him in Egypt, were two souls: all the souls of the house of Jacob, which came into Egypt, were three score and ten. ²⁸And he sent Judah before him to Joseph, to direct his face to Goshen; and they came into the land of Goshen. ²⁹And Joseph made ready his chariot, and went up to meet Israel his father, to Goshen, and presented himself to him; and he fell on his neck, and wept on his neck a good while. ³⁰And Israel said to Joseph, Now let me die, since I have seen your face, because you are yet alive. ³¹And Joseph said to his brothers, and to his father's house, I will go up, and show Pharaoh, and say to him, My brothers, and my father's house, which were in the land of Canaan, are come to me; ³²And the men are shepherds, for their trade has been to feed cattle; and they have brought their flocks, and their herds, and all that they have. ³³And it shall come to pass, when Pharaoh shall call you, and shall say, What is your occupation? ³⁴That you shall say, Your servants' trade has been about cattle from our youth even until now, both we, and also our fathers: that you may dwell in the land of Goshen; for every shepherd is an abomination to the Egyptians.

47 ¹Then Joseph came and told Pharaoh, and said, My father and my brothers, and their flocks, and their herds, and all that they have, are come out of the land of Canaan; and, behold, they are in the land of Goshen. ²And he took some of his brothers, even five men, and presented them to Pharaoh. ³And Pharaoh said to his brothers, What is your occupation? And they said to Pharaoh, Your servants are shepherds, both we, and also our fathers. ⁴They said morever to Pharaoh, For to sojourn in the land are we come; for your servants have no pasture for their flocks; for the famine is sore in the land of Canaan: now therefore, we pray you, let your servants dwell in the land of Goshen. ⁵And Pharaoh spoke to Joseph, saying, Your father and your brothers are come to you: ⁶The land of Egypt is before you; in the best of the land make your father and brothers to dwell; in the land of Goshen let them dwell: and if you know any men of activity among them, then make them rulers over my cattle. ⁷And Joseph brought in Jacob his father, and set him before Pharaoh: and Jacob blessed Pharaoh. ⁸And Pharaoh said to Jacob, How old are you? ⁹And Jacob said to Pharaoh, The days of the years of my pilgrimage are an hundred and thirty years: few and evil have the days of the years of my life been, and have not attained to the days of the years of the life of my fathers in the days of their pilgrimage. ¹⁰And Jacob blessed Pharaoh, and went out from before Pharaoh. ¹¹And Joseph placed his father and his brothers, and gave them a possession in the land of Egypt, in the best of the land, in the land of Rameses, as Pharaoh had commanded. ¹²And Joseph nourished his father, and his brothers, and all his father's household, with bread, according to their families. ¹³And there was no bread in all the land; for the famine was very sore, so that the land of Egypt and all the land of Canaan fainted by reason of the famine. ¹⁴And Joseph gathered up all the money that was found in the land of Egypt, and in the land of Canaan, for the corn which they bought: and Joseph brought the money into Pharaoh's house. ¹⁵And when money failed in the land of Egypt, and in the land of Canaan, all the Egyptians came to Joseph, and said, Give us bread: for why should we die in your presence? for the money fails. ¹⁶And Joseph said, Give your cattle; and I will give you for your cattle, if money fail. ¹⁷And they brought their cattle to Joseph: and Joseph gave them bread in exchange for horses, and for the flocks, and for the cattle of the herds, and for the asses: and he fed them with bread for all their cattle for that year. ¹⁸When that year was ended, they came to him the second year, and said to him, We will not hide it from my lord, how that our money is spent; my lord also has our herds of cattle; there is not anything left in the sight of my lord, but our bodies, and our lands: ¹⁹Why shall we die before your eyes, both we and our land? buy us and our land for bread, and we and our land will be servants to Pharaoh: and give us seed, that we may live, and not die, that the land be not desolate. ²⁰And Joseph bought all the land of Egypt for Pharaoh; for the Egyptians sold every man his field, because the famine prevailed over them: so the land became Pharaoh's. ²¹And as for the people, he removed them to cities from one end of the borders of Egypt even to the other end thereof. ²²Only the land of the priests bought he not; for the priests had a portion assigned them of Pharaoh, and did eat their portion which Pharaoh gave them: why they sold not their lands. ²³Then Joseph said to the people, Behold, I have bought you this day and your land for Pharaoh: see, here is seed for you, and you shall sow the land. ²⁴And it shall come to pass in the increase, that you shall give the fifth part to Pharaoh, and four parts shall be your own, for seed of the field, and for your food, and for them of your households, and for food for your little ones. ²⁵And they said, You have saved our lives: let us find grace in the sight of my lord, and we will be Pharaoh's servants. ²⁶And Joseph made it a law over the land of Egypt to this day, that Pharaoh should have the fifth part, except the land of the priests only, which became not Pharaoh's. ²⁷And Israel dwelled in the land of Egypt, in the country of Goshen; and they had possessions therein, and grew, and multiplied exceedingly. ²⁸And Jacob lived in the land of Egypt seventeen years: so the whole age of Jacob was an hundred forty and seven years. ²⁹And the time drew near that Israel must die: and he called his son Joseph, and said to him, If now I have found grace in your sight, put, I pray you, your hand under my thigh, and deal kindly and truly with me; bury me not, I pray you, in Egypt: ³⁰But I will lie with my fathers, and you shall carry me out of Egypt, and bury me in their burial plot. And he said, I will do as you have said. ³¹And he said, Swear to me. And he swore to him. And Israel bowed himself on the bed's head.

48

¹And it came to pass after these things, that one told Joseph, Behold, your father is sick: and he took with him his two sons, Manasseh and Ephraim. ²And one told Jacob, and said, Behold, your son Joseph comes to you: and Israel strengthened himself, and sat on the bed. ³And Jacob said to Joseph, God Almighty appeared to me at Luz in the land of Canaan, and blessed me, ⁴And said to me, Behold, I will make you fruitful, and multiply you, and I will make of you a multitude of people; and will give this land to your seed after you for an everlasting possession. ⁵And now your two sons, Ephraim and Manasseh, which were born to you in the land of Egypt before I came to you into Egypt, are mine; as Reuben and Simeon, they shall be mine. ⁶And your issue, which you beget after them, shall be yours, and shall be called after the name of their brothers in their inheritance. ⁷And as for me, when I came from Padan, Rachel died by me in the land of Canaan in the way, when yet there was but a little way to come to Ephrath: and I buried her there in the way of Ephrath; the same is Bethlehem. ⁸And Israel beheld Joseph's sons, and said, Who are these? ⁹And Joseph said to his father, They are my sons, whom God has given me in this place. And he said, Bring them, I pray you, to me, and I will bless them. ¹⁰Now the eyes of Israel were dim for age, so that he could not see. And he brought them near to him; and he kissed them, and embraced them. ¹¹And Israel said to Joseph, I had not thought to see your face: and, see, God has showed me also your seed. ¹²And Joseph brought them out from between his knees, and he bowed himself with his face to the earth. ¹³And Joseph took them both, Ephraim in his right hand toward Israel's left hand, and Manasseh in his left hand toward Israel's right hand, and brought them near to him. ¹⁴And Israel stretched out his right hand, and laid it on Ephraim's head, who was the younger, and his left hand on Manasseh's head, guiding his hands wittingly; for Manasseh was the firstborn. ¹⁵And he blessed Joseph, and said, God, before whom my fathers Abraham and Isaac did walk, the God which fed me all my life long to this day, ¹⁶The Angel which redeemed me from all evil, bless the lads; and let my name be named on them, and the name of my fathers Abraham and Isaac; and let them grow into a multitude in the middle of the earth. ¹⁷And when Joseph saw that his father laid his right hand on the head of Ephraim, it displeased him: and he held up his father's hand, to remove it from Ephraim's head to Manasseh's head. ¹⁸And Joseph said to his father, Not so, my father: for this is the firstborn; put your right hand on his head. ¹⁹And his father refused, and said, I know it, my son, I know it: he also shall become a people, and he also shall be great: but truly his younger brother shall be greater than he, and his seed shall become a multitude of nations. ²⁰And he blessed them that day, saying, In you shall Israel bless, saying, God make you as Ephraim and as Manasseh: and he set Ephraim before Manasseh. ²¹And Israel said to Joseph, Behold, I die: but God shall be with you, and bring you again to the land of your fathers. ²²Moreover I have given to you one portion above your brothers, which I took out of the hand of the Amorite with my sword and with my bow.

49

¹And Jacob called to his sons, and said, Gather yourselves together, that I may tell you that which shall befall you in the last days. ²Gather yourselves together, and hear, you sons of Jacob; and listen to Israel your father. ³Reuben, you are my firstborn, my might, and the beginning of my strength, the excellency of dignity, and the excellency of power: ⁴Unstable as water, you shall not excel; because you went up to your father's bed; then defiled you it: he went up to my couch. ⁵Simeon and Levi are brothers; instruments of cruelty are in their habitations. ⁶O my soul, come not you into their secret; to their assembly, my honor, be not you united: for in their anger they slew a man, and in their self-will they dig down a wall. ⁷Cursed be their anger, for it was fierce; and their wrath, for it was cruel: I will divide them in Jacob, and scatter them in Israel. ⁸Judah, you are he whom your brothers shall praise: your hand shall be in the neck of your enemies; your father's children shall bow down before you. ⁹Judah is a lion's whelp: from the prey, my son, you are gone up: he stooped down, he couched as a lion, and as an old lion; who shall rouse him up? ¹⁰The scepter shall not depart from Judah, nor a lawgiver from between his feet, until Shiloh come; and to him shall the

gathering of the people be. ¹¹Binding his foal to the vine, and his ass's colt to the choice vine; he washed his garments in wine, and his clothes in the blood of grapes: ¹²His eyes shall be red with wine, and his teeth white with milk. ¹³Zebulun shall dwell at the haven of the sea; and he shall be for an haven of ships; and his border shall be to Zidon. ¹⁴Issachar is a strong ass couching down between two burdens: ¹⁵And he saw that rest was good, and the land that it was pleasant; and bowed his shoulder to bear, and became a servant to tribute. ¹⁶Dan shall judge his people, as one of the tribes of Israel. ¹⁷Dan shall be a serpent by the way, an adder in the path, that bites the horse heels, so that his rider shall fall backward. ¹⁸I have waited for your salvation, O LORD. ¹⁹Gad, a troop shall overcome him: but he shall overcome at the last. ²⁰Out of Asher his bread shall be fat, and he shall yield royal dainties. ²¹Naphtali is a hind let loose: he gives goodly words. ²²Joseph is a fruitful bough, even a fruitful bough by a well; whose branches run over the wall: ²³The archers have sorely grieved him, and shot at him, and hated him: ²⁴But his bow stayed in strength, and the arms of his hands were made strong by the hands of the mighty God of Jacob; (from there is the shepherd, the stone of Israel:) ²⁵Even by the God of your father, who shall help you; and by the Almighty, who shall bless you with blessings of heaven above, blessings of the deep that lies under, blessings of the breasts, and of the womb: ²⁶The blessings of your father have prevailed above the blessings of my progenitors to the utmost bound of the everlasting hills: they shall be on the head of Joseph, and on the crown of the head of him that was separate from his brothers. ²⁷Benjamin shall shred as a wolf: in the morning he shall devour the prey, and at night he shall divide the spoil. ²⁸All these are the twelve tribes of Israel: and this is it that their father spoke to them, and blessed them; every one according to his blessing he blessed them. ²⁹And he charged them, and said to them, I am to be gathered to my people: bury me with my fathers in the cave that is in the field of Ephron the Hittite, ³⁰In the cave that is in the field of Machpelah, which is before Mamre, in the land of Canaan, which Abraham bought with the field of Ephron the Hittite for a possession of a burial plot. ³¹There they buried Abraham and Sarah his wife; there they buried Isaac and Rebekah his wife; and there I buried Leah. ³²The purchase of the field and of the cave that is therein was from the children of Heth. ³³And when Jacob had made an end of commanding his sons, he gathered up his feet into the bed, and yielded up the ghost, and was gathered to his people.

50 ¹And Joseph fell on his father's face, and wept on him, and kissed him. ²And Joseph commanded his servants the physicians to embalm his father: and the physicians embalmed Israel. ³And forty days were fulfilled for him; for so are fulfilled the days of those which are embalmed: and the Egyptians mourned for him three score and ten days. ⁴And when the days of his mourning were past, Joseph spoke to the house of Pharaoh, saying, If now I have found grace in your eyes, speak, I pray you, in the ears of Pharaoh, saying, ⁵My father made me swear, saying, See, I die: in my grave which I have dig for me in the land of Canaan, there shall you bury me. Now therefore let me go up, I pray you, and bury my father, and I will come again. ⁶And Pharaoh said, Go up, and bury your father, according as he made you swear. ⁷And Joseph went up to bury his father: and with him went up all the servants of Pharaoh, the elders of his house, and all the elders of the land of Egypt, ⁸And all the house of Joseph, and his brothers, and his father's house: only their little ones, and their flocks, and their herds, they left in the land of Goshen. ⁹And there went up with him both chariots and horsemen: and it was a very great company. ¹⁰And they came to the threshing floor of Atad, which is beyond Jordan, and there they mourned with a great and very sore lamentation: and he made a mourning for his father seven days. ¹¹And when the inhabitants of the land, the Canaanites, saw the mourning in the floor of Atad, they said, This is a grievous mourning to the Egyptians: why the name of it was called Abelmizraim, which is beyond Jordan. ¹²And his sons did to him according as he commanded them: ¹³For his sons carried him into the land of Canaan, and buried him in the cave of the field of Machpelah, which Abraham bought with the field for a possession of a burial plot of Ephron the Hittite, before Mamre. ¹⁴And Joseph returned into Egypt, he, and his brothers, and all that went up with him to bury his father, after he had buried his father. ¹⁵And when Joseph's brothers saw that their father was dead, they said, Joseph will peradventure hate us, and will certainly requite us all the evil which we did to him. ¹⁶And they sent a messenger to Joseph, saying, Your father did command before he died, saying, ¹⁷So shall you say to Joseph, Forgive, I pray you now, the trespass of your brothers, and their sin; for they did to you evil: and now, we pray you, forgive the trespass of the servants of the God of your father. And Joseph wept when they spoke to him. ¹⁸And his brothers also went and fell down before his face; and they said, Behold, we be your servants. ¹⁹And Joseph said to them, Fear not: for am I in the place of God? ²⁰But as for you, you thought evil against me; but God meant it to good, to bring to pass, as it is this day, to save much people alive. ²¹Now therefore fear you not: I will nourish you, and your little ones. And he comforted them, and spoke kindly to them. ²²And Joseph dwelled in Egypt, he, and his father's house: and Joseph lived an hundred and ten years. ²³And Joseph saw Ephraim's children of the third generation: the children also of Machir the son of Manasseh were brought up on Joseph's knees. ²⁴And Joseph said to his brothers, I die: and God will surely visit you, and bring you out of this land to the land which he swore to Abraham, to Isaac, and to Jacob. ²⁵And Joseph took an oath of the children of Israel, saying, God will surely visit you, and you shall carry up my bones from hence. ²⁶So Joseph died, being an hundred and ten years old: and they embalmed him, and he was put in a coffin in Egypt.

Exodus

1 ¹Now these are the names of the children of Israel, which came into Egypt; every man and his household came with Jacob. ²Reuben, Simeon, Levi, and Judah, ³Issachar, Zebulun, and Benjamin, ⁴Dan, and Naphtali, Gad, and Asher. ⁵And all the souls that came out of the loins of Jacob were seventy souls: for Joseph was in Egypt already. ⁶And Joseph died, and all his brothers, and all that generation. ⁷And the children of Israel were fruitful, and increased abundantly, and multiplied, and waxed exceeding mighty; and the land was filled with them. ⁸Now there arose up a new king over Egypt, which knew not Joseph. ⁹And he said to his people, Behold, the people of the children of Israel are more and mightier than we: ¹⁰Come on, let us deal wisely with them; lest they multiply, and it come to pass, that, when there falls out any war, they join also to our enemies, and fight against us, and so get them up out of the land. ¹¹Therefore they did set over them taskmasters to afflict them with their burdens. And they built for Pharaoh treasure cities, Pithom and Raamses. ¹²But the more they afflicted them, the more they multiplied and grew. And they were grieved because of the children of Israel. ¹³And the Egyptians made the children of Israel to serve with rigor: ¹⁴And they made their lives bitter with hard bondage, in mortar, and in brick, and in all manner of service in the field: all their service, wherein they made them serve, was with rigor. ¹⁵And the king of Egypt spoke to the Hebrew midwives, of which the name of the one was Shiphrah, and the name of the other Puah: ¹⁶And he said, When you do the office of a midwife to the Hebrew women, and see them on the stools; if it be a son, then you shall kill him: but if it be a daughter, then she shall live. ¹⁷But the midwives feared God, and did not as the king of Egypt commanded them, but saved the men children alive. ¹⁸And the king of Egypt called for the midwives, and said to them, Why have you done this thing, and have saved the men children alive? ¹⁹And the midwives said to Pharaoh, Because the Hebrew women are not as the Egyptian women; for they are lively, and are delivered before the midwives come in to them. ²⁰Therefore God dealt well with the midwives: and the people multiplied, and waxed very mighty. ²¹And it came to pass, because the midwives feared God, that he made them houses. ²²And Pharaoh charged all his people, saying, Every son that is born you shall cast into the river, and every daughter you shall save alive.

2 ¹And there went a man of the house of Levi, and took to wife a daughter of Levi. ²And the woman conceived, and bore a son: and when she saw him that he was a goodly child, she hid him three months. ³And when she could not longer hide him, she took for him an ark of bulrushes, and daubed it with slime and with pitch, and put the child therein; and she laid it in the flags by the river's brink. ⁴And his sister stood afar off, to wit what would be done to him. ⁵And the daughter of Pharaoh came down to wash herself at the river; and her maidens walked along by the river's side; and when she saw the ark among the flags, she sent her maid to fetch it. ⁶And when she had opened it, she saw the child: and, behold, the babe wept. And she had compassion on him, and said, This is one of the Hebrews' children. ⁷Then said his sister to Pharaoh's daughter, Shall I go and call to you a nurse of the Hebrew women, that she may nurse the child for you? ⁸And Pharaoh's daughter said to her, Go. And the maid went and called the child's mother. ⁹And Pharaoh's daughter said to her, Take this child away, and nurse it for me, and I will give you your wages. And the women took the child, and nursed it. ¹⁰And the child grew, and she brought him to Pharaoh's daughter, and he became her son. And she called his name Moses: and she said, Because I drew him out of the water. ¹¹And it came to pass in those days, when Moses was grown, that he went out to his brothers, and looked on their burdens: and he spied an Egyptian smiting an Hebrew, one of his brothers. ¹²And he looked this way and that way, and when he saw that there was no man, he slew the Egyptian, and hid him in the sand. ¹³And when he went out the second day, behold, two men of the Hebrews strove together: and he said to him that did the wrong, Why smite you your fellow? ¹⁴And he said, Who made you a prince and a judge over us? intend you to kill me, as you killed the Egyptian? And Moses feared, and said, Surely this thing is known. ¹⁵Now when Pharaoh heard this thing, he sought to slay Moses. But Moses fled from the face of Pharaoh, and dwelled in the land of Midian: and he sat down by a well. ¹⁶Now the priest of Midian had seven daughters: and they came and drew water, and filled the troughs to water their father's flock. ¹⁷And the shepherds came and drove them away: but Moses stood up and helped them, and watered their flock. ¹⁸And when they came to Reuel their father, he said, How is it that you are come so soon to day? ¹⁹And they said, An Egyptian delivered us out of the hand of the shepherds, and also drew water enough for us, and watered the flock. ²⁰And he said to his daughters, And where is he? why is it that you have left the man? call him, that he may eat bread. ²¹And Moses was content to dwell with the man: and he gave Moses Zipporah his daughter. ²²And she bore him a son, and he called his name Gershom: for he said, I have been a stranger in a strange land. ²³And it came to pass in process of time, that the king of Egypt died: and the children of Israel sighed by reason of the bondage, and they cried, and their cry came up to God by reason of the bondage. ²⁴And God heard their groaning, and God remembered his covenant with Abraham, with Isaac, and with Jacob. ²⁵And God looked on the children of Israel, and God had respect to them.

3 ¹Now Moses kept the flock of Jethro his father in law, the priest of Midian: and he led the flock to the backside of the desert, and came to the mountain of God, even to Horeb. ²And the angel of the LORD appeared to him in a flame of fire out of the middle of a bush: and he looked, and, behold, the bush burned with fire, and the bush was not consumed. ³And Moses said, I will now turn aside, and see this great sight, why the bush is not burnt. ⁴And when the LORD saw that he turned aside to see, God called to him out of the middle of the bush, and said, Moses, Moses. And he said, Here am I. ⁵And he said, Draw not near here: put off your shoes from off your feet, for the place where on you stand is holy ground. ⁶Moreover he said, I am the God of your father, the God of Abraham, the God of Isaac, and the

God of Jacob. And Moses hid his face; for he was afraid to look on God. ⁷And the LORD said, I have surely seen the affliction of my people which are in Egypt, and have heard their cry by reason of their taskmasters; for I know their sorrows; ⁸And I am come down to deliver them out of the hand of the Egyptians, and to bring them up out of that land to a good land and a large, to a land flowing with milk and honey; to the place of the Canaanites, and the Hittites, and the Amorites, and the Perizzites, and the Hivites, and the Jebusites. ⁹Now therefore, behold, the cry of the children of Israel is come to me: and I have also seen the oppression with which the Egyptians oppress them. ¹⁰Come now therefore, and I will send you to Pharaoh, that you may bring forth my people the children of Israel out of Egypt. ¹¹And Moses said to God, Who am I, that I should go to Pharaoh, and that I should bring forth the children of Israel out of Egypt? ¹²And he said, Certainly I will be with you; and this shall be a token to you, that I have sent you: When you have brought forth the people out of Egypt, you shall serve God on this mountain. ¹³And Moses said to God, Behold, when I come to the children of Israel, and shall say to them, The God of your fathers has sent me to you; and they shall say to me, What is his name? what shall I say to them? ¹⁴And God said to Moses, I AM THAT I AM: and he said, Thus shall you say to the children of Israel, I AM has sent me to you. ¹⁵And God said moreover to Moses, Thus shall you say to the children of Israel, the LORD God of your fathers, the God of Abraham, the God of Isaac, and the God of Jacob, has sent me to you: this is my name for ever, and this is my memorial to all generations. ¹⁶Go, and gather the elders of Israel together, and say to them, The LORD God of your fathers, the God of Abraham, of Isaac, and of Jacob, appeared to me, saying, I have surely visited you, and seen that which is done to you in Egypt: ¹⁷And I have said, I will bring you up out of the affliction of Egypt to the land of the Canaanites, and the Hittites, and the Amorites, and the Perizzites, and the Hivites, and the Jebusites, to a land flowing with milk and honey. ¹⁸And they shall listen to your voice: and you shall come, you and the elders of Israel, to the king of Egypt, and you shall say to him, The LORD God of the Hebrews has met with us: and now let us go, we beseech you, three days' journey into the wilderness, that we may sacrifice to the LORD our God. ¹⁹And I am sure that the king of Egypt will not let you go, no, not by a mighty hand. ²⁰And I will stretch out my hand, and smite Egypt with all my wonders which I will do in the middle thereof: and after that he will let you go. ²¹And I will give this people favor in the sight of the Egyptians: and it shall come to pass, that, when you go, you shall not go empty. ²²But every woman shall borrow of her neighbor, and of her that sojourns in her house, jewels of silver, and jewels of gold, and raiment: and you shall put them on your sons, and on your daughters; and you shall spoil the Egyptians.

4 ¹And Moses answered and said, But, behold, they will not believe me, nor listen to my voice: for they will say, The LORD has not appeared to you. ²And the LORD said to him, What is that in your hand? And he said, A rod. ³And he said, Cast it on the ground. And he cast it on the ground, and it became a serpent; and Moses fled from before it. ⁴And the LORD said to Moses, Put forth your hand, and take it by the tail. And he put forth his hand, and caught it, and it became a rod in his hand: ⁵That they may believe that the LORD God of their fathers, the God of Abraham, the God of Isaac, and the God of Jacob, has appeared to you. ⁶And the LORD said furthermore to him, Put now your hand into your bosom. And he put his hand into his bosom: and when he took it out, behold, his hand was leprous as snow. ⁷And he said, Put your hand into your bosom again. And he put his hand into his bosom again; and plucked it out of his bosom, and, behold, it was turned again as his other flesh. ⁸And it shall come to pass, if they will not believe you, neither listen to the voice of the first sign, that they will believe the voice of the latter sign. ⁹And it shall come to pass, if they will not believe also these two signs, neither listen to your voice, that you shall take of the water of the river, and pour it on the dry land: and the water which you take out of the river shall become blood on the dry land. ¹⁰And Moses said to the LORD, O my LORD, I am not eloquent, neither heretofore, nor since you have spoken to your servant: but I am slow of speech, and of a slow tongue. ¹¹And the LORD said to him, Who has made man's mouth? or who makes the dumb, or deaf, or the seeing, or the blind? have not I the LORD? ¹²Now therefore go, and I will be with your mouth, and teach you what you shall say. ¹³And he said, O my LORD, send, I pray you, by the hand of him whom you will send. ¹⁴And the anger of the LORD was kindled against Moses, and he said, Is not Aaron the Levite your brother? I know that he can speak well. And also, behold, he comes forth to meet you: and when he sees you, he will be glad in his heart. ¹⁵And you shall speak to him, and put words in his mouth: and I will be with your mouth, and with his mouth, and will teach you what you shall do. ¹⁶And he shall be your spokesman to the people: and he shall be, even he shall be to you instead of a mouth, and you shall be to him instead of God. ¹⁷And you shall take this rod in your hand, with which you shall do signs. ¹⁸And Moses went and returned to Jethro his father in law, and said to him, Let me go, I pray you, and return to my brothers which are in Egypt, and see whether they be yet alive. And Jethro said to Moses, Go in peace. ¹⁹And the LORD said to Moses in Midian, Go, return into Egypt: for all the men are dead which sought your life. ²⁰And Moses took his wife and his sons, and set them on an ass, and he returned to the land of Egypt: and Moses took the rod of God in his hand. ²¹And the LORD said to Moses, When you go to return into Egypt, see that you do all those wonders before Pharaoh, which I have put in your hand: but I will harden his heart, that he shall not let the people go. ²²And you shall say to Pharaoh, Thus says the LORD, Israel is my son, even my firstborn: ²³And I say to you, Let my son go, that he may serve me: and if you refuse to let him go, behold, I will slay your son, even your firstborn. ²⁴And it came to pass by the way in the inn, that the LORD met him, and sought to kill him. ²⁵Then Zipporah took a sharp stone, and cut off the foreskin of her son, and cast it at his feet, and said, Surely a bloody husband are you to me. ²⁶So he let him go: then she said, A bloody husband you are, because of the circumcision. ²⁷And the LORD said to Aaron, Go into the wilderness to meet Moses. And he went, and met him in the mount of God, and kissed him. ²⁸And Moses told Aaron all the words of the LORD who had sent him, and all the signs which he had commanded him.²⁹And Moses and Aaron went and gathered together all the elders of the children of Israel: ³⁰And Aaron spoke all the words which the LORD had spoken to Moses, and did the signs in the sight of the people. ³¹And the people believed: and when they heard that the LORD had visited the children of Israel, and that he had looked on their affliction, then they bowed their heads and worshipped.

5 ¹And afterward Moses and Aaron went in, and told Pharaoh, Thus says the LORD God of Israel, Let my people go, that they may hold a feast to me in the wilderness. ²And Pharaoh said, Who is the LORD, that I should obey his voice to let Israel go? I know not the LORD, neither will I let Israel go. ³And they said, The God of the Hebrews has met with us: let us go, we pray you, three days' journey into the desert, and sacrifice to the LORD our God; lest he fall on us with pestilence, or with the sword. ⁴And the king of Egypt said to them, Why do you, Moses and Aaron, let the people from their works? get you to your burdens. ⁵And Pharaoh said, Behold, the people of the land now are many, and you make them rest from their burdens. ⁶And Pharaoh commanded the same day the taskmasters of the people, and their officers, saying, ⁷You shall no more give the people straw to make brick, as heretofore: let them go and gather straw for themselves. ⁸And the tale of the bricks, which they did make heretofore, you shall lay on them; you shall not diminish any thereof: for they be idle; therefore they cry, saying, Let us go and sacrifice to our God. ⁹Let there more work be laid on the men, that they may labor therein; and let them not regard vain words. ¹⁰And the taskmasters of the people went out, and their officers, and they spoke to the people, saying, Thus says Pharaoh, I will not give you straw. ¹¹Go you, get you straw where you can find it: yet not any of your work shall be diminished. ¹²So the people were scattered abroad throughout all the land of Egypt to gather stubble instead of straw. ¹³And the taskmasters hurried them, saying, Fulfill your works, your daily tasks, as when there was straw. ¹⁴And the officers of the children of Israel, which Pharaoh's taskmasters had set over them, were beaten, and demanded, Why have you not fulfilled your task in making brick both yesterday and to day, as heretofore? ¹⁵Then the officers of the children of Israel came and cried to Pharaoh, saying, Why deal you thus with your servants? ¹⁶There is no straw given to your servants, and they say to us, Make brick: and, behold, your servants are beaten; but the fault is in your own people. ¹⁷But he said, You are idle, you are idle: therefore you say, Let us go and do sacrifice to the LORD. ¹⁸Go therefore now, and work; for there shall no straw be given you, yet shall you deliver the tale of bricks. ¹⁹And the officers of the children of Israel did see that they were in evil case, after it was said, You shall not diminish any from your bricks of your daily task. ²⁰And they met Moses and Aaron, who stood in the way, as they came forth from Pharaoh: ²¹And they said to them, The LORD look on you, and judge; because you have made our smell to be abhorred in the eyes of Pharaoh, and in the eyes of his servants, to put a sword in their hand to slay us. ²²And Moses returned to the LORD, and said, LORD, why have you so evil entreated this people? why is it that you have sent me? ²³For since I came to Pharaoh to speak in your name, he has done evil to this people; neither have you delivered your people at all.

6 ¹Then the LORD said to Moses, Now shall you see what I will do to Pharaoh: for with a strong hand shall he let them go, and with a strong hand shall he drive them out of his land. ²And God spoke to Moses, and said to him, I am the LORD: ³And I appeared to Abraham, to Isaac, and to Jacob, by the name of God Almighty, but by my name JEHOVAH was I not known to them. ⁴And I have also established my covenant with them, to give them the land of Canaan, the land of their pilgrimage, wherein they were strangers. ⁵And I have also heard the groaning of the children of Israel, whom the Egyptians keep in bondage; and I have remembered my covenant. ⁶Why say to the children of Israel, I am the LORD, and I will bring you out from under the burdens of the Egyptians, and I will rid you out of their bondage, and I will redeem you with a stretched out arm, and with great judgments: ⁷And I will take you to me for a people, and I will be to you a God: and you shall know that I am the LORD your God, which brings you out from under the burdens of the Egyptians. ⁸And I will bring you in to the land, concerning the which I did swear to give it to Abraham, to Isaac, and to Jacob; and I will give it you for an heritage: I am the LORD. ⁹And Moses spoke so to the children of Israel: but they listened not to Moses for anguish of spirit, and for cruel bondage. ¹⁰And the LORD spoke to Moses, saying, ¹¹Go in, speak to Pharaoh king of Egypt, that he let the children of Israel go out of his land. ¹²And Moses spoke before the LORD, saying, Behold, the children of Israel have not listened to me; how then shall Pharaoh hear me, who am of uncircumcised lips? ¹³And the LORD spoke to Moses and to Aaron, and gave them a charge to the children of Israel, and to Pharaoh king of Egypt, to bring the children of Israel out of the land of Egypt. ¹⁴These be the heads of their fathers' houses: The sons of Reuben the firstborn of Israel; Hanoch, and Pallu, Hezron, and Carmi: these be the families of Reuben. ¹⁵And the sons of Simeon; Jemuel, and Jamin, and Ohad, and Jachin, and Zohar, and Shaul the son of a Canaanitish woman: these are the families of Simeon. ¹⁶And these are the names of the sons of Levi according to their generations; Gershon, and Kohath, and Merari: and the years of the life of Levi were an hundred thirty and seven years. ¹⁷The sons of Gershon; Libni, and Shimi, according to their families. ¹⁸And the sons of Kohath; Amram, and Izhar, and Hebron, and Uzziel: and the years of the life of Kohath were an hundred thirty and three years. ¹⁹And the sons of Merari; Mahali and Mushi: these are the families of Levi according to their generations. ²⁰And Amram took him Jochebed his father's sister to wife; and she bore him Aaron and Moses: and the years of the life of Amram were an hundred and thirty and seven years. ²¹And the sons of Izhar; Korah, and Nepheg, and Zichri. ²²And the sons of Uzziel; Mishael, and Elzaphan, and Zithri. ²³And Aaron took him Elisheba, daughter of Amminadab, sister of Naashon, to wife; and she bore him Nadab, and Abihu, Eleazar, and Ithamar. ²⁴And the sons of Korah; Assir, and Elkanah, and Abiasaph: these are the families of the Korhites. ²⁵And Eleazar Aaron's son took him one of the daughters of Putiel to wife; and she bore him Phinehas: these are the heads of the fathers of the Levites according to

their families. ²⁶These are that Aaron and Moses, to whom the LORD said, Bring out the children of Israel from the land of Egypt according to their armies. ²⁷These are they which spoke to Pharaoh king of Egypt, to bring out the children of Israel from Egypt: these are that Moses and Aaron. ²⁸And it came to pass on the day when the LORD spoke to Moses in the land of Egypt, ²⁹That the LORD spoke to Moses, saying, I am the LORD: speak you to Pharaoh king of Egypt all that I say to you. ³⁰And Moses said before the LORD, Behold, I am of uncircumcised lips, and how shall Pharaoh listen to me?

7 ¹And the LORD said to Moses, See, I have made you a god to Pharaoh: and Aaron your brother shall be your prophet. ²You shall speak all that I command you: and Aaron your brother shall speak to Pharaoh, that he send the children of Israel out of his land. ³And I will harden Pharaoh's heart, and multiply my signs and my wonders in the land of Egypt. ⁴But Pharaoh shall not listen to you, that I may lay my hand on Egypt, and bring forth my armies, and my people the children of Israel, out of the land of Egypt by great judgments. ⁵And the Egyptians shall know that I am the LORD, when I stretch forth my hand on Egypt, and bring out the children of Israel from among them. ⁶And Moses and Aaron did as the LORD commanded them, so did they. ⁷And Moses was fourscore years old, and Aaron fourscore and three years old, when they spoke to Pharaoh. ⁸And the LORD spoke to Moses and to Aaron, saying, ⁹When Pharaoh shall speak to you, saying, Show a miracle for you: then you shall say to Aaron, Take your rod, and cast it before Pharaoh, and it shall become a serpent. ¹⁰And Moses and Aaron went in to Pharaoh, and they did so as the LORD had commanded: and Aaron cast down his rod before Pharaoh, and before his servants, and it became a serpent. ¹¹Then Pharaoh also called the wise men and the sorcerers: now the magicians of Egypt, they also did in like manner with their enchantments. ¹²For they cast down every man his rod, and they became serpents: but Aaron's rod swallowed up their rods. ¹³And he hardened Pharaoh's heart, that he listened not to them; as the LORD had said. ¹⁴And the LORD said to Moses, Pharaoh's heart is hardened, he refuses to let the people go. ¹⁵Get you to Pharaoh in the morning; see, he goes out to the water; and you shall stand by the river's brink against he come; and the rod which was turned to a serpent shall you take in your hand. ¹⁶And you shall say to him, The LORD God of the Hebrews has sent me to you, saying, Let my people go, that they may serve me in the wilderness: and, behold, till now you would not hear. ¹⁷Thus says the LORD, In this you shall know that I am the LORD: behold, I will smite with the rod that is in my hand on the waters which are in the river, and they shall be turned to blood. ¹⁸And the fish that is in the river shall die, and the river shall stink; and the Egyptians shall loathe to drink of the water of the river. ¹⁹And the LORD spoke to Moses, Say to Aaron, Take your rod, and stretch out your hand on the waters of Egypt, on their streams, on their rivers, and on their ponds, and on all their pools of water, that they may become blood; and that there may be blood throughout all the land of Egypt, both in vessels of wood, and in vessels of stone. ²⁰And Moses and Aaron did so, as the LORD commanded; and he lifted up the rod, and smote the waters that were in the river, in the sight of Pharaoh, and in the sight of his servants; and all the waters that were in the river were turned to blood. ²¹And the fish that was in the river died; and the river stank, and the Egyptians could not drink of the water of the river; and there was blood throughout all the land of Egypt. ²²And the magicians of Egypt did so with their enchantments: and Pharaoh's heart was hardened, neither did he listen to them; as the LORD had said. ²³And Pharaoh turned and went into his house, neither did he set his heart to this also. ²⁴And all the Egyptians dig round about the river for water to drink; for they could not drink of the water of the river. ²⁵And seven days were fulfilled, after that the LORD had smitten the river.

8 ¹And the LORD spoke to Moses, Go to Pharaoh, and say to him, Thus says the LORD, Let my people go, that they may serve me. ²And if you refuse to let them go, behold, I will smite all your borders with frogs: ³And the river shall bring forth frogs abundantly, which shall go up and come into your house, and into your bedchamber, and on your bed, and into the house of your servants, and on your people, and into your ovens, and into your kneading troughs: ⁴And the frogs shall come up both on you, and on your people, and on all your servants. ⁵And the LORD spoke to Moses, Say to Aaron, Stretch forth your hand with your rod over the streams, over the rivers, and over the ponds, and cause frogs to come up on the land of Egypt. ⁶And Aaron stretched out his hand over the waters of Egypt; and the frogs came up, and covered the land of Egypt. ⁷And the magicians did so with their enchantments, and brought up frogs on the land of Egypt. ⁸Then Pharaoh called for Moses and Aaron, and said, Entreat the LORD, that he may take away the frogs from me, and from my people; and I will let the people go, that they may do sacrifice to the LORD. ⁹And Moses said to Pharaoh, Glory over me: when shall I entreat for you, and for your servants, and for your people, to destroy the frogs from you and your houses, that they may remain in the river only? ¹⁰And he said, To morrow. And he said, Be it according to your word: that you may know that there is none like to the LORD our God. ¹¹And the frogs shall depart from you, and from your houses, and from your servants, and from your people; they shall remain in the river only. ¹²And Moses and Aaron went out from Pharaoh: and Moses cried to the LORD because of the frogs which he had brought against Pharaoh. ¹³And the LORD did according to the word of Moses; and the frogs died out of the houses, out of the villages, and out of the fields. ¹⁴And they gathered them together on heaps: and the land stank. ¹⁵But when Pharaoh saw that there was respite, he hardened his heart, and listened not to them; as the LORD had said. ¹⁶And the LORD said to Moses, Say to Aaron, Stretch out your rod, and smite the dust of the land, that it may become lice throughout all the land of Egypt. ¹⁷And they did so; for Aaron stretched out his hand with his rod, and smote the dust of the earth, and it became lice in man, and in beast; all the dust of the land became lice throughout all the land of Egypt. ¹⁸And the magicians did so with their enchantments to bring forth lice, but they could not: so there were lice on man, and on beast. ¹⁹Then the magicians said to Pharaoh, This is the finger of God: and Pharaoh's heart was hardened,

and he listened not to them; as the LORD had said. ²⁰And the LORD said to Moses, Rise up early in the morning, and stand before Pharaoh; see, he comes forth to the water; and say to him, Thus says the LORD, Let my people go, that they may serve me. ²¹Else, if you will not let my people go, behold, I will send swarms of flies on you, and on your servants, and on your people, and into your houses: and the houses of the Egyptians shall be full of swarms of flies, and also the ground where on they are. ²²And I will sever in that day the land of Goshen, in which my people dwell, that no swarms of flies shall be there; to the end you may know that I am the LORD in the middle of the earth. ²³And I will put a division between my people and your people: to morrow shall this sign be. ²⁴And the LORD did so; and there came a grievous swarm of flies into the house of Pharaoh, and into his servants' houses, and into all the land of Egypt: the land was corrupted by reason of the swarm of flies. ²⁵And Pharaoh called for Moses and for Aaron, and said, Go you, sacrifice to your God in the land. ²⁶And Moses said, It is not meet so to do; for we shall sacrifice the abomination of the Egyptians to the LORD our God: see, shall we sacrifice the abomination of the Egyptians before their eyes, and will they not stone us? ²⁷We will go three days' journey into the wilderness, and sacrifice to the LORD our God, as he shall command us. ²⁸And Pharaoh said, I will let you go, that you may sacrifice to the LORD your God in the wilderness; only you shall not go very far away: entreat for me. ²⁹And Moses said, Behold, I go out from you, and I will entreat the LORD that the swarms of flies may depart from Pharaoh, from his servants, and from his people, to morrow: but let not Pharaoh deal deceitfully any more in not letting the people go to sacrifice to the LORD. ³⁰And Moses went out from Pharaoh, and entreated the LORD. ³¹And the LORD did according to the word of Moses; and he removed the swarms of flies from Pharaoh, from his servants, and from his people; there remained not one. ³²And Pharaoh hardened his heart at this time also, neither would he let the people go.

9 ¹Then the LORD said to Moses, Go in to Pharaoh, and tell him, Thus says the LORD God of the Hebrews, Let my people go, that they may serve me. ²For if you refuse to let them go, and will hold them still, ³Behold, the hand of the LORD is on your cattle which is in the field, on the horses, on the asses, on the camels, on the oxen, and on the sheep: there shall be a very grievous murrain. ⁴And the LORD shall sever between the cattle of Israel and the cattle of Egypt: and there shall nothing die of all that is the children's of Israel. ⁵And the LORD appointed a set time, saying, To morrow the LORD shall do this thing in the land. ⁶And the LORD did that thing on the morrow, and all the cattle of Egypt died: but of the cattle of the children of Israel died not one. ⁷And Pharaoh sent, and, behold, there was not one of the cattle of the Israelites dead. And the heart of Pharaoh was hardened, and he did not let the people go. ⁸And the LORD said to Moses and to Aaron, Take to you handfuls of ashes of the furnace, and let Moses sprinkle it toward the heaven in the sight of Pharaoh. ⁹And it shall become small dust in all the land of Egypt, and shall be a boil breaking forth with blains on man, and on beast, throughout all the land of Egypt. ¹⁰And they took ashes of the furnace, and stood before Pharaoh; and Moses sprinkled it up toward heaven; and it became a boil breaking forth with blains on man, and on beast. ¹¹And the magicians could not stand before Moses because of the boils; for the boil was on the magicians, and on all the Egyptians. ¹²And the LORD hardened the heart of Pharaoh, and he listened not to them; as the LORD had spoken to Moses. ¹³And the LORD said to Moses, Rise up early in the morning, and stand before Pharaoh, and say to him, Thus says the LORD God of the Hebrews, Let my people go, that they may serve me. ¹⁴For I will at this time send all my plagues on your heart, and on your servants, and on your people; that you may know that there is none like me in all the earth. ¹⁵For now I will stretch out my hand, that I may smite you and your people with pestilence; and you shall be cut off from the earth. ¹⁶And in very deed for this cause have I raised you up, for to show in you my power; and that my name may be declared throughout all the earth. ¹⁷As yet exalt you yourself against my people, that you will not let them go? ¹⁸Behold, to morrow about this time I will cause it to rain a very grievous hail, such as has not been in Egypt since the foundation thereof even until now. ¹⁹Send therefore now, and gather your cattle, and all that you have in the field; for on every man and beast which shall be found in the field, and shall not be brought home, the hail shall come down on them, and they shall die. ²⁰He that feared the word of the LORD among the servants of Pharaoh made his servants and his cattle flee into the houses: ²¹And he that regarded not the word of the LORD left his servants and his cattle in the field. ²²And the LORD said to Moses, Stretch forth your hand toward heaven, that there may be hail in all the land of Egypt, on man, and on beast, and on every herb of the field, throughout the land of Egypt. ²³And Moses stretched forth his rod toward heaven: and the LORD sent thunder and hail, and the fire ran along on the ground; and the LORD rained hail on the land of Egypt. ²⁴So there was hail, and fire mingled with the hail, very grievous, such as there was none like it in all the land of Egypt since it became a nation. ²⁵And the hail smote throughout all the land of Egypt all that was in the field, both man and beast; and the hail smote every herb of the field, and broke every tree of the field. ²⁶Only in the land of Goshen, where the children of Israel were, was there no hail. ²⁷And Pharaoh sent, and called for Moses and Aaron, and said to them, I have sinned this time: the LORD is righteous, and I and my people are wicked. ²⁸Entreat the LORD (for it is enough) that there be no more mighty thunder and hail; and I will let you go, and you shall stay no longer. ²⁹And Moses said to him, As soon as I am gone out of the city, I will spread abroad my hands to the LORD; and the thunder shall cease, neither shall there be any more hail; that you may know how that the earth is the LORD's. ³⁰But as for you and your servants, I know that you will not yet fear the LORD God. ³¹And the flax and the barley was smitten: for the barley was in the ear, and the flax was in bloom. ³²But the wheat and the rye were not smitten: for they were not grown up. ³³And Moses went out of the city from Pharaoh, and spread abroad his hands to the LORD: and the thunders and hail ceased, and the rain was not poured on the earth. ³⁴And when Pharaoh saw that the rain and the hail and the thunders were ceased, he sinned yet more, and hardened his heart, he and his servants. ³⁵And the heart of Pharaoh was hardened, neither would he let the children of Israel go; as the LORD had spoken by Moses.

10 ¹And the LORD said to Moses, Go in to Pharaoh: for I have hardened his heart, and the heart of his servants, that I might show these my signs before him: ²And that you may tell in the ears of your son, and of your son's son, what things I have worked in Egypt, and my signs which I have done among them; that you may know how that I am the LORD. ³And Moses and Aaron came in to Pharaoh, and said to him, Thus says the LORD God of the Hebrews, How long will you refuse to humble yourself before me? let my people go, that they may serve me. ⁴Else, if you refuse to let my people go, behold, to morrow will I bring the locusts into your coast: ⁵And they shall cover the face of the earth, that one cannot be able to see the earth: and they shall eat the residue of that which is escaped, which remains to you from the hail, and shall eat every tree which grows for you out of the field: ⁶And they shall fill your houses, and the houses of all your servants, and the houses of all the Egyptians; which neither your fathers, nor your fathers' fathers have seen, since the day that they were on the earth to this day. And he turned himself, and went out from Pharaoh. ⁷And Pharaoh's servants said to him, How long shall this man be a snare to us? let the men go, that they may serve the LORD their God: know you not yet that Egypt is destroyed? ⁸And Moses and Aaron were brought again to Pharaoh: and he said to them, Go, serve the LORD your God: but who are they that shall go? ⁹And Moses said, We will go with our young and with our old, with our sons and with our daughters, with our flocks and with our herds will we go; for we must hold a feast to the LORD. ¹⁰And he said to them, Let the LORD be so with you, as I will let you go, and your little ones: look to it; for evil is before you. ¹¹Not so: go now you that are men, and serve the LORD; for that you did desire. And they were driven out from Pharaoh's presence. ¹²And the LORD said to Moses, Stretch out your hand over the land of Egypt for the locusts, that they may come up on the land of Egypt, and eat every herb of the land, even all that the hail has left. ¹³And Moses stretched forth his rod over the land of Egypt, and the LORD brought an east wind on the land all that day, and all that night; and when it was morning, the east wind brought the locusts. ¹⁴And the locust went up over all the land of Egypt, and rested in all the coasts of Egypt: very grievous were they; before them there were no such locusts as they, neither after them shall be such. ¹⁵For they covered the face of the whole earth, so that the land was darkened; and they did eat every herb of the land, and all the fruit of the trees which the hail had left: and there remained not any green thing in the trees, or in the herbs of the field, through all the land of Egypt. ¹⁶Then Pharaoh called for Moses and Aaron in haste; and he said, I have sinned against the LORD your God, and against you. ¹⁷Now therefore forgive, I pray you, my sin only this once, and entreat the LORD your God, that he may take away from me this death only. ¹⁸And he went out from Pharaoh, and entreated the LORD. ¹⁹And the LORD turned a mighty strong west wind, which took away the locusts, and cast them into the Red sea; there remained not one locust in all the coasts of Egypt. ²⁰But the LORD hardened Pharaoh's heart, so that he would not let the children of Israel go.

²¹And the LORD said to Moses, Stretch out your hand toward heaven, that there may be darkness over the land of Egypt, even darkness which may be felt. ²²And Moses stretched forth his hand toward heaven; and there was a thick darkness in all the land of Egypt three days: ²³They saw not one another, neither rose any from his place for three days: but all the children of Israel had light in their dwellings. ²⁴And Pharaoh called to Moses, and said, Go you, serve the LORD; only let your flocks and your herds be stayed: let your little ones also go with you. ²⁵And Moses said, You must give us also sacrifices and burnt offerings, that we may sacrifice to the LORD our God. ²⁶Our cattle also shall go with us; there shall not an hoof be left behind; for thereof must we take to serve the LORD our God; and we know not with what we must serve the LORD, until we come thither. ²⁷But the LORD hardened Pharaoh's heart, and he would not let them go. ²⁸And Pharaoh said to him, Get you from me, take heed to yourself, see my face no more; for in that day you see my face you shall die. ²⁹And Moses said, You have spoken well, I will see your face again no more.

11 ¹And the LORD said to Moses, Yet will I bring one plague more on Pharaoh, and on Egypt; afterwards he will let you go hence: when he shall let you go, he shall surely thrust you out hence altogether. ²Speak now in the ears of the people, and let every man borrow of his neighbor, and every woman of her neighbor, jewels of silver and jewels of gold. ³And the LORD gave the people favor in the sight of the Egyptians. Moreover the man Moses was very great in the land of Egypt, in the sight of Pharaoh's servants, and in the sight of the people. ⁴And Moses said, Thus says the LORD, About midnight will I go out into the middle of Egypt: ⁵And all the firstborn in the land of Egypt shall die, from the first born of Pharaoh that sits on his throne, even to the firstborn of the maidservant that is behind the mill; and all the firstborn of beasts. ⁶And there shall be a great cry throughout all the land of Egypt, such as there was none like it, nor shall be like it any more. ⁷But against any of the children of Israel shall not a dog move his tongue, against man or beast: that you may know how that the LORD does put a difference between the Egyptians and Israel. ⁸And all these your servants shall come down to me, and bow down themselves to me, saying, Get you out, and all the people that follow you: and after that I will go out. And he went out from Pharaoh in a great anger. ⁹And the LORD said to Moses, Pharaoh shall not listen to you; that my wonders may be multiplied in the land of Egypt. ¹⁰And Moses and Aaron did all these wonders before Pharaoh: and the LORD hardened Pharaoh's heart, so that he would not let the children of Israel go out of his land.

12 ¹And the LORD spoke to Moses and Aaron in the land of Egypt saying, ²This month shall be to you the beginning of months: it shall be the first month of the year to you. ³Speak you to all the congregation of Israel, saying, In the tenth day of this month they shall take to them every man a lamb, according to the house of their fathers, a lamb for an house: ⁴And if the household be too little for the lamb, let him and his neighbor next to his house take it according to the number of the souls; every man according to his eating shall make your count for the lamb. ⁵Your lamb shall be without blemish, a male of the first year: you shall take it out from the sheep, or from the goats: ⁶And you shall keep it up until the fourteenth day of the same month: and the whole assembly of the congregation of Israel shall kill it in the evening. ⁷And they shall take of the blood, and strike it on the two side posts and on the upper door post of the houses, wherein they shall eat it. ⁸And they shall eat the flesh in that night, roast with fire, and unleavened bread; and with bitter herbs they shall eat it. ⁹Eat not of it raw, nor sodden at all with water, but roast with fire; his head with his legs, and with the entrails thereof. ¹⁰And you shall let nothing of it remain until the morning; and that which remains of it until the morning you shall burn with fire. ¹¹And thus shall you eat it; with your loins girded, your shoes on your feet, and your staff in your hand; and you shall eat it in haste: it is the LORD's passover. ¹²For I will pass through the land of Egypt this night, and will smite all the firstborn in the land of Egypt, both man and beast; and against all the gods of Egypt I will execute judgment: I am the LORD. ¹³And the blood shall be to you for a token on the houses where you are: and when I see the blood, I will pass over you, and the plague shall not be on you to destroy you, when I smite the land of Egypt. ¹⁴And this day shall be to you for a memorial; and you shall keep it a feast to the LORD throughout your generations; you shall keep it a feast by an ordinance for ever. ¹⁵Seven days shall you eat unleavened bread; even the first day you shall put away leaven out of your houses: for whoever eats leavened bread from the first day until the seventh day, that soul shall be cut off from Israel. ¹⁶And in the first day there shall be an holy convocation, and in the seventh day there shall be an holy convocation to you; no manner of work shall be done in them, save that which every man must eat, that only may be done of you. ¹⁷And you shall observe the feast of unleavened bread; for in this selfsame day have I brought your armies out of the land of Egypt: therefore shall you observe this day in your generations by an ordinance for ever. ¹⁸In the first month, on the fourteenth day of the month at even, you shall eat unleavened bread, until the one and twentieth day of the month at even. ¹⁹Seven days shall there be no leaven found in your houses: for whoever eats that which is leavened, even that soul shall be cut off from the congregation of Israel, whether he be a stranger, or born in the land. ²⁰You shall eat nothing leavened; in all your habitations shall you eat unleavened bread. ²¹Then Moses called for all the elders of Israel, and said to them, Draw out and take you a lamb according to your families, and kill the passover. ²²And you shall take a bunch of hyssop, and dip it in the blood that is in the basin, and strike the lintel and the two side posts with the blood that is in the basin; and none of you shall go out at the door of his house until the morning. ²³For the LORD will pass through to smite the Egyptians; and when he sees the blood on the lintel, and on the two side posts, the LORD will pass over the door, and will not suffer the destroyer to come in to your houses to smite you. ²⁴And you shall observe this thing for an ordinance to you and to your sons for ever. ²⁵And it shall come to pass, when you be come to the land which the LORD will give you, according as he has promised, that you shall keep this service. ²⁶And it shall come to pass, when your children shall say to you, What mean you by this service? ²⁷That you shall say, It is the sacrifice of the LORD's passover, who passed over the houses of the children of Israel in Egypt, when he smote the Egyptians, and delivered our houses. And the people bowed the head and worshipped. ²⁸And the children of Israel went away, and did as the LORD had commanded Moses and Aaron, so did they. ²⁹And it came to pass, that at midnight the LORD smote all the firstborn in the land of Egypt, from the firstborn of Pharaoh that sat on his throne to the firstborn of the captive that was in the dungeon; and all the firstborn of cattle. ³⁰And Pharaoh rose up in the night, he, and all his servants, and all the Egyptians; and there was a great cry in Egypt; for there was not a house where there was not one dead. ³¹And he called for Moses and Aaron by night, and said, Rise up, and get you forth from among my people, both you and the children of Israel; and go, serve the LORD, as you have said. ³²Also take your flocks and your herds, as you have said, and be gone; and bless me also. ³³And the Egyptians were urgent on the people, that they might send them out of the land in haste; for they said, We be all dead men. ³⁴And the people took their dough before it was leavened, their kneading troughs being bound up in their clothes on their shoulders. ³⁵And the children of Israel did according to the word of Moses; and they borrowed of the Egyptians jewels of silver, and jewels of gold, and raiment: ³⁶And the LORD gave the people favor in the sight of the Egyptians, so that they lent to them such things as they required. And they spoiled the Egyptians. ³⁷And the children of Israel journeyed from Rameses to Succoth, about six hundred thousand on foot that were men, beside children. ³⁸And a mixed multitude went up also with them; and flocks, and herds, even very much cattle. ³⁹And they baked unleavened cakes of the dough which they brought forth out of Egypt, for it was not leavened; because they were thrust out of Egypt, and could not tarry, neither had they prepared for themselves any victual. ⁴⁰Now the sojourning of the children of Israel, who dwelled in Egypt, was four hundred and thirty years. ⁴¹And it came to pass at the end of the four hundred and thirty years, even the selfsame day it came to pass, that all the hosts of the LORD went out from the land of Egypt. ⁴²It is a night to be much observed to the LORD for bringing them out from the land of Egypt: this is that night of the LORD to be observed of all the children of Israel in their generations. ⁴³And the LORD said to Moses and Aaron, This is the ordinance of the passover: There shall no stranger eat thereof: ⁴⁴But every man's servant that is bought for money, when you have circumcised him, then shall he eat thereof. ⁴⁵A foreigner and an hired servant shall not eat thereof. ⁴⁶In one house shall it be eaten; you shall not carry forth any of the flesh abroad out of the house; neither shall you break a bone thereof. ⁴⁷All the congregation of Israel shall keep it. ⁴⁸And when a stranger shall sojourn with you, and will keep the passover to the LORD, let all his males be circumcised, and then let him come near and keep it; and he shall be as one that is born in the land: for no uncircumcised person shall eat thereof. ⁴⁹One law shall be to him that is home born, and to the stranger that sojourns among you. ⁵⁰Thus did all the children of Israel; as the LORD commanded Moses and Aaron, so did they. ⁵¹And it came to pass the selfsame day, that the LORD did bring the children of Israel out of the land of Egypt by their armies.

13 ¹And the LORD spoke to Moses, saying, ²Sanctify to me all the firstborn, whatever opens the womb among the children of Israel, both of man and of beast: it is mine. ³And Moses said to the people, Remember this day, in which you came out from Egypt, out of the house of bondage; for by strength of hand the LORD brought you out from this place: there shall no leavened bread be eaten. ⁴This day came you out in the month Abib. ⁵And it shall be when the LORD shall bring you into the land of the Canaanites, and the Hittites, and the Amorites, and the Hivites, and the Jebusites, which he swore to your fathers to give you, a land flowing with milk and honey, that you shall keep this service in this month. ⁶Seven days you shall eat unleavened bread, and in the seventh day shall be a feast to the LORD. ⁷Unleavened bread shall be eaten seven days; and there shall no leavened bread be seen with you, neither shall there be leaven seen with you in all your quarters. ⁸And you shall show your son in that day, saying, This is done because of that which the LORD did to me when I came forth out of Egypt. ⁹And it shall be for a sign to you on your hand, and for a memorial between your eyes, that the LORD's law may be in your mouth: for with a strong hand has the LORD brought you out of Egypt. ¹⁰You shall therefore keep this ordinance in his season from year to year. ¹¹And it shall be when the LORD shall bring you into the land of the Canaanites, as he swore to you and to your fathers, and shall give it you, ¹²That you shall set apart to the LORD all that opens the matrix, and every firstling that comes of a beast which you have; the males shall be the LORD's. ¹³And every firstling of an ass you shall redeem with a lamb; and if you will not redeem it, then you shall break his neck: and all the firstborn of man among your children shall you redeem. ¹⁴And it shall be when your son asks you in time to come, saying, What is this? that you shall say to him, By strength of hand the LORD brought us out from Egypt, from the house of bondage: ¹⁵And it came to pass, when Pharaoh would hardly let us go, that the LORD slew all the firstborn in the land of Egypt, both the firstborn of man, and the firstborn of beast: therefore I sacrifice to the LORD all that opens the matrix, being males; but all the firstborn of my children I redeem. ¹⁶And it shall be for a token on your hand, and for frontlets between your eyes: for by strength of hand the LORD brought us forth out of Egypt. ¹⁷And it came to pass, when Pharaoh had let the people go, that God led them not through the way of the land of the Philistines, although that was near; for God said, Lest peradventure the people repent when they see war, and they return to Egypt: ¹⁸But God led the people about, through the way of the wilderness of the Red sea: and the children of Israel went up harnessed out of the land of Egypt. ¹⁹And Moses took the bones of Joseph with him: for he had straightly sworn the children of Israel, saying, God will surely visit you; and you shall carry up my bones away hence with you. ²⁰And they took their journey from Succoth, and encamped in Etham, in the edge of the wilderness. ²¹And the LORD went before them by day in a pillar of a cloud, to lead them the way; and by night in a pillar of fire, to give them light; to go by day and night: ²²He took not away the pillar of the cloud by day, nor the pillar of fire by night, from before the people.

14 ¹And the LORD spoke to Moses, saying, ²Speak to the children of Israel, that they turn and encamp before Pihahiroth, between Migdol and the sea, over against Baalzephon: before it shall you encamp by the sea. ³For Pharaoh will say of the children of Israel, They are entangled in the land, the wilderness has shut them in. ⁴And I will harden Pharaoh's heart, that he shall follow after them; and I will be honored on Pharaoh, and on all his host; that the Egyptians may know that I am the LORD. And they did so. ⁵And it was told the king of Egypt that the people fled: and the heart of Pharaoh and of his servants was turned against the people, and they said, Why have we done this, that we have let Israel go from serving us? ⁶And he made ready his chariot, and took his people with him: ⁷And he took six hundred chosen chariots, and all the chariots of Egypt, and captains over every one of them. ⁸And the LORD hardened the heart of Pharaoh king of Egypt, and he pursued after the children of Israel: and the children of Israel went out with an high hand. ⁹But the Egyptians pursued after them, all the horses and chariots of Pharaoh, and his horsemen, and his army, and overtook them encamping by the sea, beside Pihahiroth, before Baalzephon. ¹⁰And when Pharaoh drew near, the children of Israel lifted up their eyes, and, behold, the Egyptians marched after them; and they were sore afraid: and the children of Israel cried out to the LORD. ¹¹And they said to Moses, Because there were no graves in Egypt, have you taken us away to die in the wilderness? why have you dealt thus with us, to carry us forth out of Egypt? ¹²Is not this the word that we did tell you in Egypt, saying, Let us alone, that we may serve the Egyptians? For it had been better for us to serve the Egyptians, than that we should die in the wilderness. ¹³And Moses said to the people, Fear you not, stand still, and see the salvation of the LORD, which he will show to you to day: for the Egyptians whom you have seen to day, you shall see them again no more for ever. ¹⁴The LORD shall fight for you, and you shall hold your peace. ¹⁵And the LORD said to Moses, Why cry you to me? speak to the children of Israel, that they go forward: ¹⁶But lift you up your rod, and stretch out your hand over the sea, and divide it: and the children of Israel shall go on dry ground through the middle of the sea. ¹⁷And I, behold, I will harden the hearts of the Egyptians, and they shall follow them: and I will get me honor on Pharaoh, and on all his host, on his chariots, and on his horsemen. ¹⁸And the Egyptians shall know that I am the LORD, when I have gotten me honor on Pharaoh, on his chariots, and on his horsemen. ¹⁹And the angel of God, which went before the camp of Israel, removed and went behind them; and the pillar of the cloud went from before their face, and stood behind them: ²⁰And it came between the camp of the Egyptians and the camp of Israel; and it was a cloud and darkness to them, but it gave light by night to these: so that the one came not near the other all the night. ²¹And Moses stretched out his hand over the sea; and the LORD caused the sea to go back by a strong east wind all that night, and made the sea dry land, and the waters were divided. ²²And the children of Israel went into the middle of the sea on the dry ground: and the waters were a wall to them on their right hand, and on their left. ²³And the Egyptians pursued, and went in after them to the middle of the sea, even all Pharaoh's horses, his chariots, and his horsemen. ²⁴And it came to pass, that in the morning watch the LORD looked to the host of the Egyptians through the pillar of fire and of the cloud, and troubled the host of the Egyptians, ²⁵And took off their chariot wheels, that they drove them heavily: so that the Egyptians said, Let us flee from the face of Israel; for the LORD fights for them against the Egyptians. ²⁶And the LORD said to Moses, Stretch out your hand over the sea, that the waters may come again on the Egyptians, on their chariots, and on their horsemen. ²⁷And Moses stretched forth his hand over the sea, and the sea returned to his strength when the morning appeared; and the Egyptians fled against it; and the LORD overthrew the Egyptians in the middle of the sea. ²⁸And the waters returned, and covered the chariots, and the horsemen, and all the host of Pharaoh that came into the sea after them; there remained not so much as one of them. ²⁹But the children of Israel walked on dry land in the middle of the sea; and the waters were a wall to them on their right hand, and on their left. ³⁰Thus the LORD saved Israel that day out of the hand of the Egyptians; and Israel saw the Egyptians dead on the sea shore. ³¹And Israel saw that great work which the LORD did on the Egyptians: and the people feared the LORD, and believed the LORD, and his servant Moses.

15 ¹Then sang Moses and the children of Israel this song to the LORD, and spoke, saying, I will sing to the LORD, for he has triumphed gloriously: the horse and his rider has he thrown into the sea. ²The LORD is my strength and song, and he is become my salvation: he is my God, and I will prepare him an habitation; my father's God, and I will exalt him. ³The LORD is a man of war: the LORD is his name. ⁴Pharaoh's chariots and his host has he cast into the sea: his chosen captains also are drowned in the Red sea. ⁵The depths have covered them: they sank into the bottom as a stone. ⁶Your right hand, O LORD, is become glorious in power: your right hand, O LORD, has dashed in pieces the enemy. ⁷And in the greatness of your excellency you have overthrown them that rose up against you: you sent forth your wrath, which consumed them as stubble. ⁸And with the blast of your nostrils the waters were gathered together, the floods stood upright as an heap, and the depths were congealed in the heart of the sea. ⁹The enemy said, I will pursue, I will overtake, I will divide the spoil; my lust shall be satisfied on them; I will draw my sword, my hand shall destroy them. ¹⁰You did blow with your wind, the sea covered them: they sank as lead in the mighty waters. ¹¹Who is like to you, O LORD, among the gods? who is like you, glorious in holiness, fearful in praises, doing wonders? ¹²You stretched out your right hand, the earth swallowed them. ¹³You in your mercy have led forth the people which you have redeemed: you have guided them in your strength to your holy habitation. ¹⁴The people shall hear, and be afraid: sorrow shall take hold on the inhabitants of Palestina. ¹⁵Then the dukes of Edom shall be amazed; the mighty men of Moab, trembling shall take hold on them; all the inhabitants of Canaan shall melt away. ¹⁶Fear and dread shall fall on them; by the greatness of your arm they shall be as still as a stone; till your people pass over, O LORD, till the people pass over, which you have purchased. ¹⁷You shall bring them in, and plant them in the mountain of your inheritance, in the place, O LORD, which you have made for you to dwell in, in the Sanctuary, O LORD, which your hands have established. ¹⁸The LORD shall reign for ever and ever. ¹⁹For the horse of Pharaoh went in with his chariots and with his horsemen into the sea, and the LORD brought again the waters of the sea on them; but the children of Israel went on dry land in the middle of the sea. ²⁰And Miriam the prophetess, the sister of Aaron, took a tambourine in her hand; and all the women went out after her with tambourines and with dances. ²¹And Miriam answered them, Sing you to the LORD, for he has triumphed gloriously; the horse and his rider has he thrown into the sea. ²²So Moses brought Israel from the Red sea, and they went out into the wilderness of Shur; and they went three days in the wilderness, and found no water. ²³And when they came to Marah, they could not drink of the waters of Marah, for they were bitter: therefore the name of it was called Marah. ²⁴And the people murmured against Moses, saying, What shall we drink? ²⁵And he cried to the LORD; and the LORD showed him a tree, which when he had cast into the waters, the waters were made sweet: there he made for them a statute and an ordinance, and there he proved them, ²⁶And said, If you will diligently listen to the voice of the LORD your God, and will do that which is right in his sight, and will give ear to his commandments, and keep all his statutes, I will put none of these diseases on you, which I have brought on the Egyptians: for I am the LORD that heals you. ²⁷And they came to Elim, where were twelve wells of water, and three score and ten palm trees: and they encamped there by the waters.

16 ¹And they took their journey from Elim, and all the congregation of the children of Israel came to the wilderness of Sin, which is between Elim and Sinai, on the fifteenth day of the second month after their departing out of the land of Egypt. ²And the whole congregation of the children of Israel murmured against Moses and Aaron in the wilderness: ³And the children of Israel said to them, Would to God we had died by the hand of the LORD in the land of Egypt, when we sat by the flesh pots, and when we did eat bread to the full; for you have brought us forth into this wilderness, to kill this whole assembly with hunger. ⁴Then said the LORD to Moses, Behold, I will rain bread from heaven for you; and the people shall go out and gather a certain rate every day, that I may prove them, whether they will walk in my law, or no. ⁵And it shall come to pass, that on the sixth day they shall prepare that which they bring in; and it shall be twice as much as they gather daily. ⁶And Moses and Aaron said to all the children of Israel, At even, then you shall know that the LORD has brought you out from the land of Egypt: ⁷And in the morning, then you shall see the glory of the LORD; for that he hears your murmurings against the LORD: and what are we, that you murmur against us? ⁸And Moses said, This shall be, when the LORD shall give you in the evening flesh to eat, and in the morning bread to the full; for that the LORD hears your murmurings which you murmur against him: and what are we? your murmurings are not against us, but against the LORD. ⁹And Moses spoke to Aaron, Say to all the congregation of the children of Israel, Come near before the LORD: for he has heard your murmurings. ⁱ⁰And it came to pass, as Aaron spoke to the whole congregation of the children of Israel, that they looked toward the wilderness, and, behold, the glory of the LORD appeared in the cloud. ¹¹And the LORD spoke to Moses, saying, ¹²I have heard the murmurings of the children of Israel: speak to them, saying, At even you shall eat flesh, and in the morning you shall be filled with bread; and you shall know that I am the LORD your God. ¹³And it came to pass, that at even the quails came up, and covered the camp: and in the morning the dew lay round about the host. ¹⁴And when the dew that lay was gone up, behold, on the face of the wilderness there lay a small round thing, as small as the hoar frost on the ground. ¹⁵And when the children of Israel saw it, they said one to another, It is manna: for they knew not what it was. And Moses said to them, This is the bread which the LORD has given you to eat. ¹⁶This is the thing which the LORD has commanded, Gather of it every man according to his eating, an omer for every man, according to the number of your persons; take you every man for them which are in his tents. ¹⁷And the children of Israel did so, and gathered, some more, some less. ¹⁸And when they did mete it with an omer, he that gathered much had nothing over, and he that gathered little had no lack; they gathered every man according to his eating. ¹⁹And Moses said, Let no man leave of it till the morning. ²⁰Notwithstanding they listened not to Moses; but some of them left of it until the morning, and it bred worms, and stank: and Moses was wroth with them. ²¹And they gathered it every morning, every man according to his eating: and when the sun waxed hot, it melted. ²²And it came to pass, that on the sixth day they gathered twice as much bread, two omers for one man: and all the rulers of the congregation came and told Moses. ²³And he said to them, This is that which the LORD has said, To morrow is the rest of the holy sabbath to the LORD: bake that which you will bake to day, and seethe that which you will seethe; and that which remains over lay up for you to be kept until the morning. ²⁴And they laid it up till the morning, as Moses bade: and it did not stink, neither was there any worm therein. ²⁵And Moses said, Eat that to day; for to day is a sabbath to the LORD: to day you shall not find it in the field. ²⁶Six days you shall gather it; but on the seventh day, which is the sabbath, in it there shall be none. ²⁷And it came to pass, that there went out some of the people on the seventh day for to gather, and they found none. ²⁸And the LORD said to Moses, How long refuse you to keep my commandments and my laws? ²⁹See, for that the LORD has given you the sabbath, therefore he gives you on the sixth day the bread of two days; abide you every man in his place, let no man go out of his place on the seventh day. ³⁰So the people rested on the seventh day. ³¹And the house of Israel called the name thereof Manna: and it was like coriander seed, white; and the taste of it was like wafers made with honey. ³²And Moses said, This is the thing which the LORD commands, Fill an omer of it to be kept for your generations; that they may see the bread with which I have fed you in the wilderness, when I brought you forth from the land of Egypt. ³³And Moses said to Aaron, Take a pot, and put an omer full of manna therein, and lay it up before the LORD, to be kept for your generations. ³⁴As the LORD commanded Moses, so Aaron laid it up before the Testimony, to be kept. ³⁵And the children of Israel did eat manna forty years, until they came to a land inhabited; they did eat manna, until they came to the borders of the land of Canaan. ³⁶Now an omer is the tenth part of an ephah.

17 ¹And all the congregation of the children of Israel journeyed from the wilderness of Sin, after their journeys, according to the commandment of the LORD, and pitched in Rephidim: and there was no water for the people to drink. ²Why the people did chide with Moses, and said, Give us water that we may drink. And Moses said to them, Why chide you with me? why do you tempt the LORD? ³And the people thirsted there for water; and the people murmured against Moses, and said, Why is this that you have brought us up out of Egypt, to kill us and our children and our cattle with thirst? ⁴And Moses cried to the LORD, saying, What shall I do to this people? they be almost ready to stone me. ⁵And the LORD said to Moses, Go on before the people, and take with you of the elders of Israel; and your rod, with which you smote the river, take in your hand, and go. ⁶Behold, I will stand before you there on the rock in Horeb; and you shall smite the rock, and there shall come water out of it, that the people may drink. And Moses did so in the sight of the elders of Israel. ⁷And he called the name of the place Massah, and Meribah, because of the chiding of the children of Israel, and because they tempted the LORD, saying, Is the LORD among us, or not? ⁸Then came Amalek, and fought with Israel in Rephidim. ⁹And Moses said to Joshua, Choose us out men, and go out, fight with Amalek: to morrow I will stand on the top of the hill with the rod of God in my hand. ¹⁰So Joshua did as Moses had said to him, and fought with Amalek: and Moses, Aaron, and Hur went up to the top of the hill. ¹¹And it came to pass, when Moses held up his hand, that Israel prevailed: and when he let down his hand, Amalek prevailed. ¹²But Moses hands were heavy; and they took a stone, and put it under him, and he sat thereon; and Aaron and Hur stayed up his hands, the one on the one side, and the other on the other side; and his hands were steady until the going down of the sun. ¹³And Joshua discomfited Amalek and his people with the edge of the sword. ¹⁴And the LORD said to Moses, Write this for a memorial in a book, and rehearse it in the ears of Joshua: for I will utterly put out the remembrance of Amalek from under heaven. ¹⁵And Moses built an altar, and called the name of it Jehovahnissi: ¹⁶For he said, Because the LORD has sworn that the LORD will have war with Amalek from generation to generation.

18 ¹When Jethro, the priest of Midian, Moses' father in law, heard of all that God had done for Moses, and for Israel his people, and that the LORD had brought Israel out of Egypt; ²Then Jethro, Moses' father in law, took Zipporah, Moses' wife, after he had sent her back, ³And her two sons; of which the name of the one was Gershom; for he said, I have been an alien in a strange land: ⁴And the name of the other was Eliezer; for the God of my father, said he, was my help, and delivered me from the sword of Pharaoh: ⁵And Jethro, Moses' father in law, came with his sons and his wife to Moses into the wilderness, where he encamped at the mount of God: ⁶And he said to Moses, I your father in law Jethro am come to you, and your wife, and her two sons with her. ⁷And Moses went out to meet his father in law, and did obeisance, and kissed him; and they asked each other of their welfare; and they came into the tent. ⁸And Moses told his father in law all that the LORD had done to Pharaoh and to the Egyptians for Israel's sake, and all the travail that had come on them by the way, and how the LORD delivered them. ⁹And Jethro rejoiced for all the goodness which the LORD had done to Israel, whom he had delivered out of the hand of the Egyptians. ¹⁰And Jethro said, Blessed be the LORD, who has delivered you out of the hand of the Egyptians, and out of the hand of Pharaoh, who has delivered the people from under the hand of the Egyptians. ¹¹Now I know that the LORD is greater than all gods: for in the thing wherein they dealt proudly he was above them. ¹²And Jethro, Moses' father in law, took a burnt offering and sacrifices for God: and Aaron came, and all the elders of Israel, to eat bread with Moses' father in law before God. ¹³And it came to pass on the morrow, that Moses sat to judge the people: and the people stood by Moses from the morning to the evening. ¹⁴And when Moses' father in law saw all that he did to the people, he said, What is this thing that you do to the people? why sit you yourself alone, and all the people stand by you from morning to even? ¹⁵And Moses said to his father in law, Because the people come to me to inquire of God: ¹⁶When they have a matter, they come to me; and I judge between one and another, and I do make them know the statutes of God, and his laws. ¹⁷And Moses' father in law said to him, The thing that you do is not good. ¹⁸You will surely wear away, both you, and this people that is with you: for this thing is too heavy for you; you are not able to perform it yourself alone. ¹⁹Listen now to my voice, I will give you counsel, and God shall be with you: Be you for the people to God-ward, that you may bring the causes to God: ²⁰And you shall teach them ordinances and laws, and shall show them the way wherein they must walk, and the work that they must do. ²¹Moreover you shall provide out of all the people able men, such as fear God, men of truth, hating covetousness; and place such over them, to be rulers of thousands, and rulers of hundreds, rulers of fifties, and rulers of tens: ²²And let them judge the people at all seasons: and it shall be, that every great matter they shall bring to you, but every small matter they shall judge: so shall it be easier for yourself, and they shall bear the burden with you. ²³If you shall do this thing, and God command you so, then you shall be able to endure, and all this people shall also go to their place in peace. ²⁴So Moses listened to the voice of his father in law, and did all that he had said. ²⁵And Moses chose able men out of all Israel, and made them heads over the people, rulers of thousands, rulers of hundreds, rulers of fifties, and rulers of tens. ²⁶And they judged the people at all seasons: the hard causes they brought to Moses, but every small matter they judged themselves. ²⁷And Moses let his father in law depart; and he went his way into his own land.

19 ¹In the third month, when the children of Israel were gone forth out of the land of Egypt, the same day came they into the wilderness of Sinai. ²For they were departed from Rephidim, and were come to the desert of Sinai, and had pitched in the wilderness; and there Israel camped before the mount. ³And Moses went up to God, and the LORD called to him out of the mountain, saying, Thus shall you say to the house of Jacob, and tell the children of Israel; ⁴You have seen what I did to the Egyptians, and how I bore you on eagles' wings, and brought you to myself. ⁵Now therefore, if you will obey my voice indeed, and keep my covenant, then you shall be a peculiar treasure to me above all people: for all the earth is mine: ⁶And you shall be to me a kingdom of priests, and an holy nation. These are the words which you shall speak to the children of Israel. ⁷And Moses came and called for the elders of the people, and laid before their faces all these words which the LORD commanded him. ⁸And all the people answered together, and said, All that the LORD has spoken we will do. And Moses returned the words of the people to the LORD. ⁹And the LORD said to Moses, See, I come to you in a thick cloud, that the people may hear when I speak with you, and believe you for ever. And Moses told the words of the people to the LORD. ¹⁰And the LORD said to Moses, Go to the people, and sanctify them to day and to morrow, and let them wash their clothes, ¹¹And be ready against the third day: for the third day the LORD will come down in the sight of all the people on mount Sinai. ¹²And you shall set bounds to the people round about, saying, Take heed to yourselves, that you go not up into the mount, or touch the border of it: whoever touches the mount shall be surely put to death: ¹³There shall not an hand touch it, but he shall surely be stoned, or shot through; whether it be beast or man, it shall not live: when the trumpet sounds long, they shall come up to the mount. ¹⁴And Moses went down from the mount to the people, and sanctified the people; and they washed their clothes. ¹⁵And he said to the people, Be ready against the third day: come not at your wives. ¹⁶And it came to pass on the third day in the morning, that there were thunders and lightning, and a thick cloud on the mount, and the voice of the trumpet exceeding loud; so that all the people that was in the camp trembled. ¹⁷And Moses brought forth the people out of the camp to meet with God; and they stood at the nether part of the mount. ¹⁸And mount Sinai was altogether on a smoke, because the LORD descended on it in fire: and the smoke thereof ascended as the smoke of a furnace, and the whole mount quaked greatly. ¹⁹And when the voice of the trumpet sounded long, and waxed louder and louder, Moses spoke, and God answered him by a voice. ²⁰And the LORD came down on mount Sinai, on the top of the mount: and the LORD called Moses up to the top of the mount; and Moses went up. ²¹And the LORD said to Moses, Go down, charge the people, lest they break through to the LORD to gaze, and many of them perish. ²²And let the priests also, which come near to the LORD, sanctify themselves, lest the LORD break forth on them. ²³And Moses said to the LORD, The people cannot come up to mount Sinai: for you charged us, saying, Set bounds about the mount, and sanctify it. ²⁴And the LORD said to him, Away, get you down, and you shall come up, you, and Aaron with you: but let not the priests and the people break through to come up to the LORD, lest he break forth on them. ²⁵So Moses went down to the people, and spoke to them.

20 ¹And God spoke all these words, saying, ²I am the LORD your God, which have brought you out of the land of Egypt, out of the house of bondage. ³You shall have no other gods before me. ⁴You shall not make to you any graven image, or any likeness of any thing that is in heaven above, or that is in the earth beneath, or that is in the water under the earth. ⁵You shall not bow down yourself to them, nor serve them: for I the LORD your God am a jealous God, visiting the iniquity of the fathers on the children to the third and fourth generation of them that hate me; ⁶And showing mercy to thousands of them that love me, and keep my commandments. ⁷You shall not take the name of the LORD your God in vain; for the LORD will not hold him guiltless that takes his name in vain. ⁸Remember the sabbath day, to keep it holy. ⁹Six days shall you labor, and do all your work: ¹⁰But the seventh day is the sabbath of the LORD your God: in it you shall not do any work, you, nor your son, nor your daughter, your manservant, nor your maidservant, nor your cattle, nor your stranger that is within your gates: ¹¹For in six days the LORD made heaven and earth, the sea, and all that in them is, and rested the seventh day: why the LORD blessed the sabbath day, and hallowed it. ¹²Honor your father and your mother: that your days may be long on the land which the LORD your God gives you. ¹³You shall not kill. ¹⁴You shall not commit adultery. ¹⁵You shall not steal. ¹⁶You shall not bear false witness against your neighbor. ¹⁷You shall not covet your neighbor's house, you shall not covet your neighbor's wife, nor his manservant, nor his maidservant, nor his ox, nor his ass, nor any thing that is your neighbor's. ¹⁸And all the people saw the thunder, and the lightning, and the noise of the trumpet, and the mountain smoking: and when the people saw it, they removed, and stood afar off. ¹⁹And they said to Moses, Speak you with us, and we will hear: but let not God speak with us, lest we die. ²⁰And Moses said to the people, Fear not: for God is come to prove you, and that his fear may be before your faces, that you sin not. ²¹And the people stood afar off, and Moses drew near to the thick darkness where God was. ²²And the LORD said to Moses, Thus you shall say to the children of Israel, You have seen that I have talked with you from heaven. ²³You shall not make with me gods of silver, neither shall you make to you gods of gold. ²⁴An altar of earth you shall make to me, and shall sacrifice thereon your burnt offerings, and your peace offerings, your sheep, and your oxen: in all places where I record my name I will come to you, and I will bless you. ²⁵And if you will make me an altar of stone, you shall not build it of hewn stone: for if you lift up your tool on it, you have polluted it. ²⁶Neither shall you go up by steps to my altar, that your nakedness be not discovered thereon.

21

¹Now these are the judgments which you shall set before them. ²If you buy an Hebrew servant, six years he shall serve: and in the seventh he shall go out free for nothing. ³If he came in by himself, he shall go out by himself: if he were married, then his wife shall go out with him. ⁴If his master have given him a wife, and she have born him sons or daughters; the wife and her children shall be her master's, and he shall go out by himself. ⁵And if the servant shall plainly say, I love my master, my wife, and my children; I will not go out free: ⁶Then his master shall bring him to the judges; he shall also bring him to the door, or to the door post; and his master shall bore his ear through with an awl; and he shall serve him for ever. ⁷And if a man sell his daughter to be a maidservant, she shall not go out as the menservants do. ⁸If she please not her master, who has betrothed her to himself, then shall he let her be redeemed: to sell her to a strange nation he shall have no power, seeing he has dealt deceitfully with her. ⁹And if he have betrothed her to his son, he shall deal with her after the manner of daughters. ¹⁰If he take him another wife; her food, her raiment, and her duty of marriage, shall he not diminish. ¹¹And if he do not these three to her, then shall she go out free without money. ¹²He that smites a man, so that he die, shall be surely put to death. ¹³And if a man lie not in wait, but God deliver him into his hand; then I will appoint you a place where he shall flee. ¹⁴But if a man come presumptuously on his neighbor, to slay him with guile; you shall take him from my altar, that he may die. ¹⁵And he that smites his father, or his mother, shall be surely put to death. ¹⁶And he that steals a man, and sells him, or if he be found in his hand, he shall surely be put to death. ¹⁷And he that curses his father, or his mother, shall surely be put to death. ¹⁸And if men strive together, and one smite another with a stone, or with his fist, and he die not, but keeps his bed: ¹⁹If he rise again, and walk abroad on his staff, then shall he that smote him be quit: only he shall pay for the loss of his time, and shall cause him to be thoroughly healed. ²⁰And if a man smite his servant, or his maid, with a rod, and he die under his hand; he shall be surely punished. ²¹Notwithstanding, if he continue a day or two, he shall not be punished: for he is his money. ²²If men strive, and hurt a woman with child, so that her fruit depart from her, and yet no mischief follow: he shall be surely punished, according as the woman's husband will lay on him; and he shall pay as the judges determine. ²³And if any mischief follow, then you shall give life for life, ²⁴Eye for eye, tooth for tooth, hand for hand, foot for foot, ²⁵Burning for burning, wound for wound, stripe for stripe. ²⁶And if a man smite the eye of his servant, or the eye of his maid, that it perish; he shall let him go free for his eye's sake. ²⁷And if he smite out his manservant's tooth, or his maidservant's tooth; he shall let him go free for his tooth's sake. ²⁸If an ox gore a man or a woman, that they die: then the ox shall be surely stoned, and his flesh shall not be eaten; but the owner of the ox shall be quit. ²⁹But if the ox were wont to push with his horn in time past, and it has been testified to his owner, and he has not kept him in, but that he has killed a man or a woman; the ox shall be stoned, and his owner also shall be put to death. ³⁰If there be laid on him a sum of money, then he shall give for the ransom of his life whatever is laid on him. ³¹Whether he have gored a son, or have gored a daughter, according to this judgment shall it be done to him. ³²If the ox shall push a manservant or a maidservant; he shall give to their master thirty shekels of silver, and the ox shall be stoned. ³³And if a man shall open a pit, or if a man shall dig a pit, and not cover it, and an ox or an ass fall therein; ³⁴The owner of the pit shall make it good, and give money to the owner of them; and the dead beast shall be his. ³⁵And if one man's ox hurt another's, that he die; then they shall sell the live ox, and divide the money of it; and the dead ox also they shall divide. ³⁶Or if it be known that the ox has used to push in time past, and his

owner has not kept him in; he shall surely pay ox for ox; and the dead shall be his own.

22 ¹If a man shall steal an ox, or a sheep, and kill it, or sell it; he shall restore five oxen for an ox, and four sheep for a sheep. ²If a thief be found breaking up, and be smitten that he die, there shall no blood be shed for him. ³If the sun be risen on him, there shall be blood shed for him; for he should make full restitution; if he have nothing, then he shall be sold for his theft. ⁴If the theft be certainly found in his hand alive, whether it be ox, or ass, or sheep; he shall restore double. ⁵If a man shall cause a field or vineyard to be eaten, and shall put in his beast, and shall feed in another man's field; of the best of his own field, and of the best of his own vineyard, shall he make restitution. ⁶If fire break out, and catch in thorns, so that the stacks of corn, or the standing corn, or the field, be consumed therewith; he that kindled the fire shall surely make restitution. ⁷If a man shall deliver to his neighbor money or stuff to keep, and it be stolen out of the man's house; if the thief be found, let him pay double. ⁸If the thief be not found, then the master of the house shall be brought to the judges, to see whether he have put his hand to his neighbor's goods. ⁹For all manner of trespass, whether it be for ox, for ass, for sheep, for raiment, or for any manner of lost thing which another challenges to be his, the cause of both parties shall come before the judges; and whom the judges shall condemn, he shall pay double to his neighbor. ¹⁰If a man deliver to his neighbor an ass, or an ox, or a sheep, or any beast, to keep; and it die, or be hurt, or driven away, no man seeing it: ¹¹Then shall an oath of the LORD be between them both, that he has not put his hand to his neighbor's goods; and the owner of it shall accept thereof, and he shall not make it good. ¹²And if it be stolen from him, he shall make restitution to the owner thereof. ¹³If it be torn in pieces, then let him bring it for witness, and he shall not make good that which was torn. ¹⁴And if a man borrow something of his neighbor, and it be hurt, or die, the owner thereof being not with it, he shall surely make it good. ¹⁵But if the owner thereof be with it, he shall not make it good: if it be an hired thing, it came for his hire. ¹⁶And if a man entice a maid that is not betrothed, and lie with her, he shall surely endow her to be his wife. ¹⁷If her father utterly refuse to give her to him, he shall pay money according to the dowry of virgins. ¹⁸You shall not suffer a witch to live. ¹⁹Whoever lies with a beast shall surely be put to death. ²⁰He that sacrifices to any god, save to the LORD only, he shall be utterly destroyed. ²¹You shall neither vex a stranger, nor oppress him: for you were strangers in the land of Egypt. ²²You shall not afflict any widow, or fatherless child. ²³If you afflict them in any wise, and they cry at all to me, I will surely hear their cry; ²⁴And my wrath shall wax hot, and I will kill you with the sword; and your wives shall be widows, and your children fatherless. ²⁵If you lend money to any of my people that is poor by you, you shall not be to him as an usurer, neither shall you lay on him usury. ²⁶If you at all take your neighbor's raiment to pledge, you shall deliver it to him by that the sun goes down: ²⁷For that is his covering only, it is his raiment for his skin: wherein shall he sleep? and it shall come to pass, when he cries to me, that I will hear; for I am gracious. ²⁸You shall not revile the gods, nor curse the ruler of your people. ²⁹You shall not delay to offer the first of your ripe fruits, and of your liquors: the firstborn of your sons shall you give to me. ³⁰Likewise shall you do with your oxen, and with your sheep: seven days it shall be with his dam; on the eighth day you shall give it me. ³¹And you shall be holy men to me: neither shall you eat any flesh that is torn of beasts in the field; you shall cast it to the dogs.

23 ¹You shall not raise a false report: put not your hand with the wicked to be an unrighteous witness. ²You shall not follow a multitude to do evil; neither shall you speak in a cause to decline after many to wrest judgment: ³Neither shall you countenance a poor man in his cause. ⁴If you meet your enemy's ox or his ass going astray, you shall surely bring it back to him again. ⁵If you see the ass of him that hates you lying under his burden, and would forbear to help him, you shall surely help with him. ⁶You shall not wrest the judgment of your poor in his cause. ⁷Keep you far from a false matter; and the innocent and righteous slay you not: for I will not justify the wicked. ⁸And you shall take no gift: for the gift blinds the wise, and perverts the words of the righteous. ⁹Also you shall not oppress a stranger: for you know the heart of a stranger, seeing you were strangers in the land of Egypt. ¹⁰And six years you shall sow your land, and shall gather in the fruits thereof: ¹¹But the seventh year you shall let it rest and lie still; that the poor of your people may eat: and what they leave the beasts of the field shall eat. In like manner you shall deal with your vineyard, and with your olive grove. ¹²Six days you shall do your work, and on the seventh day you shall rest: that your ox and your ass may rest, and the son of your handmaid, and the stranger, may be refreshed. ¹³And in all things that I have said to you be circumspect: and make no mention of the name of other gods, neither let it be heard out of your mouth. ¹⁴Three times you shall keep a feast to me in the year. ¹⁵You shall keep the feast of unleavened bread: (you shall eat unleavened bread seven days, as I commanded you, in the time appointed of the month Abib; for in it you came out from Egypt: and none shall appear before me empty:) ¹⁶And the feast of harvest, the first fruits of your labors, which you have sown in the field: and the feast of ingathering, which is in the end of the year, when you have gathered in your labors out of the field. ¹⁷Three items in the year all your males shall appear before the LORD God. ¹⁸You shall not offer the blood of my sacrifice with leavened bread; neither shall the fat of my sacrifice remain until the morning. ¹⁹The first of the first fruits of your land you shall bring into the house of the LORD your God. You shall not seethe a kid in his mother's milk. ²⁰Behold, I send an Angel before you, to keep you in the way, and to bring you into the place which I have prepared. ²¹Beware of him, and obey his voice, provoke him not; for he will not pardon your transgressions: for my name is in him. ²²But if you shall indeed obey his voice, and do all that I speak; then I will be an enemy to your enemies, and an adversary to your adversaries. ²³For my Angel shall go before you, and bring you in to the Amorites, and the Hittites, and the Perizzites, and the Canaanites, the Hivites, and the Jebusites: and I will cut them off. ²⁴You shall not bow down to their gods, nor serve them, nor do after their works: but you shall utterly overthrow them, and quite break down their images. ²⁵And you shall serve the LORD your

God, and he shall bless your bread, and your water; and I will take sickness away from the middle of you. ²⁶There shall nothing cast their young, nor be barren, in your land: the number of your days I will fulfill. ²⁷I will send my fear before you, and will destroy all the people to whom you shall come, and I will make all your enemies turn their backs to you. ²⁸And I will send hornets before you, which shall drive out the Hivite, the Canaanite, and the Hittite, from before you. ²⁹I will not drive them out from before you in one year; lest the land become desolate, and the beast of the field multiply against you. ³⁰By little and little I will drive them out from before you, until you be increased, and inherit the land. ³¹And I will set your bounds from the Red sea even to the sea of the Philistines, and from the desert to the river: for I will deliver the inhabitants of the land into your hand; and you shall drive them out before you. ³²You shall make no covenant with them, nor with their gods. ³³They shall not dwell in your land, lest they make you sin against me: for if you serve their gods, it will surely be a snare to you.

24 ¹And he said to Moses, Come up to the LORD, you, and Aaron, Nadab, and Abihu, and seventy of the elders of Israel; and worship you afar off. ²And Moses alone shall come near the LORD: but they shall not come near; neither shall the people go up with him. ³And Moses came and told the people all the words of the LORD, and all the judgments: and all the people answered with one voice, and said, All the words which the LORD has said will we do. ⁴And Moses wrote all the words of the LORD, and rose up early in the morning, and built an altar under the hill, and twelve pillars, according to the twelve tribes of Israel. ⁵And he sent young men of the children of Israel, which offered burnt offerings, and sacrificed peace offerings of oxen to the LORD. ⁶And Moses took half of the blood, and put it in basins; and half of the blood he sprinkled on the altar. ⁷And he took the book of the covenant, and read in the audience of the people: and they said, All that the LORD has said will we do, and be obedient. ⁸And Moses took the blood, and sprinkled it on the people, and said, Behold the blood of the covenant, which the LORD has made with you concerning all these words. ⁹Then went up Moses, and Aaron, Nadab, and Abihu, and seventy of the elders of Israel: ¹⁰And they saw the God of Israel: and there was under his feet as it were a paved work of a sapphire stone, and as it were the body of heaven in his clearness. ¹¹And on the nobles of the children of Israel he laid not his hand: also they saw God, and did eat and drink. ¹²And the LORD said to Moses, Come up to me into the mount, and be there: and I will give you tables of stone, and a law, and commandments which I have written; that you may teach them. ¹³And Moses rose up, and his minister Joshua: and Moses went up into the mount of God. ¹⁴And he said to the elders, Tarry you here for us, until we come again to you: and, behold, Aaron and Hur are with you: if any man have any matters to do, let him come to them. ¹⁵And Moses went up into the mount, and a cloud covered the mount. ¹⁶And the glory of the LORD stayed on mount Sinai, and the cloud covered it six days: and the seventh day he called to Moses out of the middle of the cloud. ¹⁷And the sight of the glory of the LORD was like devouring fire on the top of the mount in the eyes of the children of Israel. ¹⁸And Moses went into the middle of the cloud, and got him up into the mount: and Moses was in the mount forty days and forty nights.

25 ¹And the LORD spoke to Moses, saying, ²Speak to the children of Israel, that they bring me an offering: of every man that gives it willingly with his heart you shall take my offering. ³And this is the offering which you shall take of them; gold, and silver, and brass, ⁴And blue, and purple, and scarlet, and fine linen, and goats' hair, ⁵And rams' skins dyed red, and badgers' skins, and shittim wood, ⁶Oil for the light, spices for anointing oil, and for sweet incense, ⁷Onyx stones, and stones to be set in the ephod, and in the breastplate. ⁸And let them make me a sanctuary; that I may dwell among them. ⁹According to all that I show you, after the pattern of the tabernacle, and the pattern of all the instruments thereof, even so shall you make it. ¹⁰And they shall make an ark of shittim wood: two cubits and a half shall be the length thereof, and a cubit and a half the breadth thereof, and a cubit and a half the height thereof. ¹¹And you shall overlay it with pure gold, within and without shall you overlay it, and shall make on it a crown of gold round about. ¹²And you shall cast four rings of gold for it, and put them in the four corners thereof; and two rings shall be in the one side of it, and two rings in the other side of it. ¹³And you shall make staves of shittim wood, and overlay them with gold. ¹⁴And you shall put the staves into the rings by the sides of the ark, that the ark may be borne with them. ¹⁵The staves shall be in the rings of the ark: they shall not be taken from it. ¹⁶And you shall put into the ark the testimony which I shall give you. ¹⁷And you shall make a mercy seat of pure gold: two cubits and a half shall be the length thereof, and a cubit and a half the breadth thereof. ¹⁸And you shall make two cherubim of gold, of beaten work shall you make them, in the two ends of the mercy seat. ¹⁹And make one cherub on the one end, and the other cherub on the other end: even of the mercy seat shall you make the cherubim on the two ends thereof. ²⁰And the cherubim shall stretch forth their wings on high, covering the mercy seat with their wings, and their faces shall look one to another; toward the mercy seat shall the faces of the cherubim be. ²¹And you shall put the mercy seat above on the ark; and in the ark you shall put the testimony that I shall give you. ²²And there I will meet with you, and I will commune with you from above the mercy seat, from between the two cherubim which are on the ark of the testimony, of all things which I will give you in commandment to the children of Israel. ²³You shall also make a table of shittim wood: two cubits shall be the length thereof, and a cubit the breadth thereof, and a cubit and a half the height thereof. ²⁴And you shall overlay it with pure gold, and make thereto a crown of gold round about. ²⁵And you shall make to it a border of an hand breadth round about, and you shall make a golden crown to the border thereof round about. ²⁶And you shall make for it four rings of gold, and put the rings in the four corners that are on the four feet thereof. ²⁷Over against the border shall the rings be for places of the staves to bear the table. ²⁸And you shall make the staves of shittim wood, and overlay them with gold, that the table may be borne with them. ²⁹And you shall make the dishes thereof, and spoons thereof, and covers thereof, and bowls thereof, to cover with: of pure gold shall you make them. ³⁰And you shall set on the table show bread before me always. ³¹And you shall make a candlestick of pure gold: of beaten work shall the candlestick be made: his shaft, and his branches, his bowls, his knops, and his flowers, shall be of the same. ³²And six branches shall come out of the sides of it; three branches of the candlestick out of the one side, and three branches of the candlestick out of the other side: ³³Three bowls made like to almonds, with a bud and a flower in one branch; and three bowls made like almonds in the other branch, with a bud and a flower: so in the six branches that come out of the candlestick. ³⁴And in the candlesticks shall be four bowls made like to almonds, with their knops and their flowers. ³⁵And there shall be a bud under two branches of the same, and a bud under two branches of the same, and a bud under two branches of the same, according to the six branches that proceed out of the candlestick. ³⁶Their knops and their branches shall be of the same: all it shall be one beaten work of pure gold. ³⁷And you shall make the seven lamps thereof: and they shall light the lamps thereof, that they may give light over against it. ³⁸And the tongs thereof, and the firepans thereof, shall be of pure gold. ³⁹Of a talent of pure gold shall he make it, with all these vessels. ⁴⁰And look that you make them after their pattern, which was showed you in the mount.

26

¹Moreover you shall make the tabernacle with ten curtains of fine twined linen, and blue, and purple, and scarlet: with cherubim of cunning work shall you make them. ²The length of one curtain shall be eight and twenty cubits, and the breadth of one curtain four cubits: and every one of the curtains shall have one measure. ³The five curtains shall be coupled together one to another; and other five curtains shall be coupled one to another. ⁴And you shall make loops of blue on the edge of the one curtain from the selvedge in the coupling; and likewise shall you make in the uttermost edge of another curtain, in the coupling of the second. ⁵Fifty loops shall you make in the one curtain, and fifty loops shall you make in the edge of the curtain that is in the coupling of the second; that the loops may take hold one of another. ⁶And you shall make fifty clasps of gold, and couple the curtains together with the clasps: and it shall be one tabernacle. ⁷And you shall make curtains of goats' hair to be a covering on the tabernacle: eleven curtains shall you make. ⁸The length of one curtain shall be thirty cubits, and the breadth of one curtain four cubits: and the eleven curtains shall be all of one measure. ⁹And you shall couple five curtains by themselves, and six curtains by themselves, and shall double the sixth curtain in the forefront of the tabernacle. ¹⁰And you shall make fifty loops on the edge of the one curtain that is outmost in the coupling, and fifty loops in the edge of the curtain which couples the second. ¹¹And you shall make fifty clasps of brass, and put the clasps into the loops, and couple the tent together, that it may be one. ¹²And the remnant that remains of the curtains of the tent, the half curtain that remains, shall hang over the backside of the tabernacle. ¹³And a cubit on the one side, and a cubit on the other side of that which remains in the length of the curtains of the tent, it shall hang over the sides of the tabernacle on this side and on that side, to cover it. ¹⁴And you shall make a covering for the tent of rams' skins dyed red, and a covering above of badgers' skins. ¹⁵And you shall make boards for the tabernacle of shittim wood standing up. ¹⁶Ten cubits shall be the length of a board, and a cubit and a half shall be the breadth of one board. ¹⁷Two tenons shall there be in one board, set in order one against another: thus shall you make for all the boards of the tabernacle. ¹⁸And you shall make the boards for the tabernacle, twenty boards on the south side southward. ¹⁹And you shall make forty sockets of silver under the twenty boards; two sockets under one board for his two tenons, and two sockets under another board for his two tenons. ²⁰And for the second side of the tabernacle on the north side there shall be twenty boards: ²¹And their forty sockets of silver; two sockets under one board, and two sockets under another board. ²²And for the sides of the tabernacle westward you shall make six boards. ²³And two boards shall you make for the corners of the tabernacle in the two sides. ²⁴And they shall be coupled together beneath, and they shall be coupled together above the head of it to one ring: thus shall it be for them both; they shall be for the two corners. ²⁵And they shall be eight boards, and their sockets of silver, sixteen sockets; two sockets under one board, and two sockets under another board. ²⁶And you shall make bars of shittim wood; five for the boards of the one side of the tabernacle, ²⁷And five bars for the boards of the other side of the tabernacle, and five bars for the boards of the side of the tabernacle, for the two sides westward. ²⁸And the middle bar in the middle of the boards shall reach from end to end. ²⁹And you shall overlay the boards with gold, and make their rings of gold for places for the bars: and you shall overlay the bars with gold. ³⁰And you shall raise up the tabernacle according to the fashion thereof which was showed you in the mount. ³¹And you shall make a veil of blue, and purple, and scarlet, and fine twined linen of cunning work: with cherubim shall it be made: ³²And you shall hang it on four pillars of shittim wood overlaid with gold: their hooks shall be of gold, on the four sockets of silver. ³³And you shall hang up the veil under the clasps, that you may bring in thither within the veil the ark of the testimony: and the veil shall divide to you between the holy place and the most holy. ³⁴And you shall put the mercy seat on the ark of the testimony in the most holy place. ³⁵And you shall set the table without the veil, and the candlestick over against the table on the side of the tabernacle toward the south: and you shall put the table on the north side. ³⁶And you shall make an hanging for the door of the tent, of blue, and purple, and scarlet, and fine twined linen, worked with needlework. ³⁷And you shall make for the hanging five pillars of shittim wood, and overlay them with gold, and their hooks shall be of gold: and you shall cast five sockets of brass for them.

27

¹And you shall make an altar of shittim wood, five cubits long, and five cubits broad; the altar shall be foursquare: and the height thereof shall be three cubits. ²And you shall make the horns of it on the four corners thereof: his horns shall be of the same: and you shall overlay it with brass. ³And you shall make his pans to receive his ashes, and his shovels, and his basins, and his meat hooks, and his fire pans: all the vessels thereof you shall make of brass. ⁴And you shall make for it a grate of network of brass; and on the net shall you make four brazen rings in the four corners thereof. ⁵And you shall put it under the compass of the altar

beneath, that the net may be even to the middle of the altar. ⁶And you shall make staves for the altar, staves of shittim wood, and overlay them with brass. ⁷And the staves shall be put into the rings, and the staves shall be on the two sides of the altar, to bear it. ⁸Hollow with boards shall you make it: as it was showed you in the mount, so shall they make it. ⁹And you shall make the court of the tabernacle: for the south side southward there shall be hangings for the court of fine twined linen of an hundred cubits long for one side: ¹⁰And the twenty pillars thereof and their twenty sockets shall be of brass; the hooks of the pillars and their fillets shall be of silver. ¹¹And likewise for the north side in length there shall be hangings of an hundred cubits long, and his twenty pillars and their twenty sockets of brass; the hooks of the pillars and their fillets of silver. ¹²And for the breadth of the court on the west side shall be hangings of fifty cubits: their pillars ten, and their sockets ten. ¹³And the breadth of the court on the east side eastward shall be fifty cubits. ¹⁴The hangings of one side of the gate shall be fifteen cubits: their pillars three, and their sockets three. ¹⁵And on the other side shall be hangings fifteen cubits: their pillars three, and their sockets three. ¹⁶And for the gate of the court shall be an hanging of twenty cubits, of blue, and purple, and scarlet, and fine twined linen, worked with needlework: and their pillars shall be four, and their sockets four. ¹⁷All the pillars round about the court shall be filleted with silver; their hooks shall be of silver, and their sockets of brass. ¹⁸The length of the court shall be an hundred cubits, and the breadth fifty every where, and the height five cubits of fine twined linen, and their sockets of brass. ¹⁹All the vessels of the tabernacle in all the service thereof, and all the pins thereof, and all the pins of the court, shall be of brass. ²⁰And you shall command the children of Israel, that they bring you pure oil olive beaten for the light, to cause the lamp to burn always. ²¹In the tabernacle of the congregation without the veil, which is before the testimony, Aaron and his sons shall order it from evening to morning before the LORD: it shall be a statute for ever to their generations on the behalf of the children of Israel.

28 ¹And take you to you Aaron your brother, and his sons with him, from among the children of Israel, that he may minister to me in the priest's office, even Aaron, Nadab and Abihu, Eleazar and Ithamar, Aaron's sons. ²And you shall make holy garments for Aaron your brother for glory and for beauty. ³And you shall speak to all that are wise hearted, whom I have filled with the spirit of wisdom, that they may make Aaron's garments to consecrate him, that he may minister to me in the priest's office. ⁴And these are the garments which they shall make; a breastplate, and an ephod, and a robe, and a broidered coat, a turban, and a girdle: and they shall make holy garments for Aaron your brother, and his sons, that he may minister to me in the priest's office. ⁵And they shall take gold, and blue, and purple, and scarlet, and fine linen. ⁶And they shall make the ephod of gold, of blue, and of purple, of scarlet, and fine twined linen, with cunning work. ⁷It shall have the two shoulder pieces thereof joined at the two edges thereof; and so it shall be joined together. ⁸And the curious girdle of the ephod, which is on it, shall be of the same, according to the work thereof; even of gold, of blue, and purple, and scarlet, and fine twined linen. ⁹And you shall take two onyx stones, and grave on them the names of the children of Israel: ¹⁰Six of their names on one stone, and the other six names of the rest on the other stone, according to their birth. ¹¹With the work of an engraver in stone, like the engravings of a signet, shall you engrave the two stones with the names of the children of Israel: you shall make them to be set in ouches of gold. ¹²And you shall put the two stones on the shoulders of the ephod for stones of memorial to the children of Israel: and Aaron shall bear their names before the LORD on his two shoulders for a memorial. ¹³And you shall make ouches of gold; ¹⁴And two chains of pure gold at the ends; of wreathen work shall you make them, and fasten the wreathen chains to the ouches. ¹⁵And you shall make the breastplate of judgment with cunning work; after the work of the ephod you shall make it; of gold, of blue, and of purple, and of scarlet, and of fine twined linen, shall you make it. ¹⁶Foursquare it shall be being doubled; a span shall be the length thereof, and a span shall be the breadth thereof. ¹⁷And you shall set in it settings of stones, even four rows of stones: the first row shall be a sardius, a topaz, and a carbuncle: this shall be the first row. ¹⁸And the second row shall be an emerald, a sapphire, and a diamond. ¹⁹And the third row a ligure, an agate, and an amethyst. ²⁰And the fourth row a beryl, and an onyx, and a jasper: they shall be set in gold in their settings. ²¹And the stones shall be with the names of the children of Israel, twelve, according to their names, like the engravings of a signet; every one with his name shall they be according to the twelve tribes. ²²And you shall make on the breastplate chains at the ends of wreathen work of pure gold. ²³And you shall make on the breastplate two rings of gold, and shall put the two rings on the two ends of the breastplate. ²⁴And you shall put the two wreathen chains of gold in the two rings which are on the ends of the breastplate. ²⁵And the other two ends of the two wreathen chains you shall fasten in the two ouches, and put them on the shoulder pieces of the ephod before it. ²⁶And you shall make two rings of gold, and you shall put them on the two ends of the breastplate in the border thereof, which is in the side of the ephod inward. ²⁷And two other rings of gold you shall make, and shall put them on the two sides of the ephod underneath, toward the forepart thereof, over against the other coupling thereof, above the curious girdle of the ephod. ²⁸And they shall bind the breastplate by the rings thereof to the rings of the ephod with a lace of blue, that it may be above the curious girdle of the ephod, and that the breastplate be not loosed from the ephod. ²⁹And Aaron shall bear the names of the children of Israel in the breastplate of judgment on his heart, when he goes in to the holy place, for a memorial before the LORD continually. ³⁰And you shall put in the breastplate of judgment the Urim and the Thummim; and they shall be on Aaron's heart, when he goes in before the LORD: and Aaron shall bear the judgment of the children of Israel on his heart before the LORD continually. ³¹And you shall make the robe of the ephod all of blue. ³²And there shall be an hole in the top of it, in the middle thereof: it shall have a binding of woven work round about the hole of it, as it were the hole of an habergeon, that it be not rent. ³³And beneath on the hem of it you shall make pomegranates of blue, and of purple, and of scarlet, round about the hem thereof; and bells of gold between them round about: ³⁴A golden bell and a pomegranate, a golden bell and a pomegranate, on the hem of the robe round about. ³⁵And it shall be on Aaron to minister: and his sound shall be heard when he goes in to the holy place before the LORD, and when he comes out, that he die not. ³⁶And you shall make a plate of pure gold, and grave on it, like the engravings of a signet, HOLINESS TO THE LORD. ³⁷And you shall put it on a blue lace, that it may be on the turban; on the forefront of the turban it shall be. ³⁸And it shall be on Aaron's forehead, that Aaron may bear the iniquity of the holy things, which the children of Israel shall hallow in all their holy gifts; and it shall be always on his forehead, that they may be accepted before the LORD. ³⁹And you shall embroider the coat of fine linen, and you shall make the turban of fine linen, and you shall make the girdle of needlework. ⁴⁰And for Aaron's sons you shall make coats, and you shall make for them girdles, and bonnets shall you make for them, for glory and for beauty. ⁴¹And you shall put them on Aaron your brother, and his sons with him; and shall anoint them, and consecrate them, and sanctify them, that they may minister to me in the priest's office. ⁴²And you shall make them linen breeches to cover their nakedness; from the loins even to the thighs they shall reach: ⁴³And they shall be on Aaron, and on his sons, when they come in to the tabernacle of the congregation, or when they come near to the altar to minister in the holy place; that they bear not iniquity, and die: it shall be a statute for ever to him and his seed after him.

29

¹And this is the thing that you shall do to them to hallow them, to minister to me in the priest's office: Take one young bullock, and two rams without blemish, ²And unleavened bread, and cakes unleavened tempered with oil, and wafers unleavened anointed with oil: of wheaten flour shall you make them. ³And you shall put them into one basket, and bring them in the basket, with the bullock and the two rams. ⁴And Aaron and his sons you shall bring to the door of the tabernacle of the congregation, and shall wash them with water. ⁵And you shall take the garments, and put on Aaron the coat, and the robe of the ephod, and the ephod, and the breastplate, and gird him with the curious girdle of the ephod: ⁶And you shall put the turban on his head, and put the holy crown on the turban. ⁷Then shall you take the anointing oil, and pour it on his head, and anoint him. ⁸And you shall bring his sons, and put coats on them. ⁹And you shall gird them with girdles, Aaron and his sons, and put the bonnets on them: and the priest's office shall be theirs for a perpetual statute: and you shall consecrate Aaron and his sons. ¹⁰And you shall cause a bullock to be brought before the tabernacle of the congregation: and Aaron and his sons shall put their hands on the head of the bullock. ¹¹And you shall kill the bullock before the LORD, by the door of the tabernacle of the congregation. ¹²And you shall take of the blood of the bullock, and put it on the horns of the altar with your finger, and pour all the blood beside the bottom of the altar. ¹³And you shall take all the fat that covers the inwards, and the lobe that is above the liver, and the two kidneys, and the fat that is on them, and burn them on the altar. ¹⁴But the flesh of the bullock, and his skin, and his dung, shall you burn with fire without the camp: it is a sin offering. ¹⁵You shall also take one ram; and Aaron and his sons shall put their hands on the head of the ram. ¹⁶And you shall slay the ram, and you shall take his blood, and sprinkle it round about on the altar. ¹⁷And you shall cut the ram in pieces, and wash the inwards of him, and his legs, and put them to his pieces, and to his head. ¹⁸And you shall burn the whole ram on the altar: it is a burnt offering to the LORD: it is a sweet smell, an offering made by fire to the LORD. ¹⁹And you shall take the other ram; and Aaron and his sons shall put their hands on the head of the ram. ²⁰Then shall you kill the ram, and take of his blood, and put it on the tip of the right ear of Aaron, and on the tip of the right ear of his sons, and on the thumb of their right hand, and on the great toe of their right foot, and sprinkle the blood on the altar round about. ²¹And you shall take of the blood that is on the altar, and of the anointing oil, and sprinkle it on Aaron, and on his garments, and on his sons, and on the garments of his sons with him: and he shall be hallowed, and his garments, and his sons, and his sons' garments with him. ²²Also you shall take of the ram the fat and the rump, and the fat that covers the inwards, and the lobe above the liver, and the two kidneys, and the fat that is on them, and the right shoulder; for it is a ram of consecration: ²³And one loaf of bread, and one cake of oiled bread, and one wafer out of the basket of the unleavened bread that is before the LORD: ²⁴And you shall put all in the hands of Aaron, and in the hands of his sons; and shall wave them for a wave offering before the LORD. ²⁵And you shall receive them of their hands, and burn them on the altar for a burnt offering, for a sweet smell before the LORD: it is an offering made by fire to the LORD. ²⁶And you shall take the breast of the ram of Aaron's consecration, and wave it for a wave offering before the LORD: and it shall be your part. ²⁷And you shall sanctify the breast of the wave offering, and the shoulder of the heave offering, which is waved, and which is heaved up, of the ram of the consecration, even of that which is for Aaron, and of that which is for his sons: ²⁸And it shall be Aaron's and his sons' by a statute for ever from the children of Israel: for it is an heave offering: and it shall be an heave offering from the children of Israel of the sacrifice of their peace offerings, even their heave offering to the LORD. ²⁹And the holy garments of Aaron shall be his sons' after him, to be anointed therein, and to be consecrated in them. ³⁰And that son that is priest in his stead shall put them on seven days, when he comes into the tabernacle of the congregation to minister in the holy place. ³¹And you shall take the ram of the consecration, and seethe his flesh in the holy place. ³²And Aaron and his sons shall eat the flesh of the ram, and the bread that is in the basket by the door of the tabernacle of the congregation. ³³And they shall eat those things with which the atonement was made, to consecrate and to sanctify them: but a stranger shall not eat thereof, because they are holy. ³⁴And if any of the flesh of the consecrations, or of the bread, remain to the morning, then you shall burn the remainder with fire: it shall not be eaten, because it is holy. ³⁵And thus shall you do to Aaron, and to his sons, according to all things which I have commanded you: seven days shall you consecrate them. ³⁶And you shall offer every day a bullock for a sin offering for atonement: and you shall cleanse the altar, when you have made an

atonement for it, and you shall anoint it, to sanctify it. ³⁷Seven days you shall make an atonement for the altar, and sanctify it; and it shall be an altar most holy: whatever touches the altar shall be holy. ³⁸Now this is that which you shall offer on the altar; two lambs of the first year day by day continually. ³⁹The one lamb you shall offer in the morning; and the other lamb you shall offer at even: ⁴⁰And with the one lamb a tenth deal of flour mingled with the fourth part of an hin of beaten oil; and the fourth part of an hin of wine for a drink offering. ⁴¹And the other lamb you shall offer at even, and shall do thereto according to the meat offering of the morning, and according to the drink offering thereof, for a sweet smell, an offering made by fire to the LORD. ⁴²This shall be a continual burnt offering throughout your generations at the door of the tabernacle of the congregation before the LORD: where I will meet you, to speak there to you. ⁴³And there I will meet with the children of Israel, and the tabernacle shall be sanctified by my glory. ⁴⁴And I will sanctify the tabernacle of the congregation, and the altar: I will sanctify also both Aaron and his sons, to minister to me in the priest's office. ⁴⁵And I will dwell among the children of Israel, and will be their God. ⁴⁶And they shall know that I am the LORD their God, that brought them forth out of the land of Egypt, that I may dwell among them: I am the LORD their God.

30 ¹And you shall make an altar to burn incense on: of shittim wood shall you make it. ²A cubit shall be the length thereof, and a cubit the breadth thereof; foursquare shall it be: and two cubits shall be the height thereof: the horns thereof shall be of the same. ³And you shall overlay it with pure gold, the top thereof, and the sides thereof round about, and the horns thereof; and you shall make to it a crown of gold round about. ⁴And two golden rings shall you make to it under the crown of it, by the two corners thereof, on the two sides of it shall you make it; and they shall be for places for the staves to bear it with. ⁵And you shall make the staves of shittim wood, and overlay them with gold. ⁶And you shall put it before the veil that is by the ark of the testimony, before the mercy seat that is over the testimony, where I will meet with you. ⁷And Aaron shall burn thereon sweet incense every morning: when he dresses the lamps, he shall burn incense on it. ⁸And when Aaron lights the lamps at even, he shall burn incense on it, a perpetual incense before the LORD throughout your generations. ⁹You shall offer no strange incense thereon, nor burnt sacrifice, nor meat offering; neither shall you pour drink offering thereon. ¹⁰And Aaron shall make an atonement on the horns of it once in a year with the blood of the sin offering of atonements: once in the year shall he make atonement on it throughout your generations: it is most holy to the LORD. ¹¹And the LORD spoke to Moses, saying, ¹²When you take the sum of the children of Israel after their number, then shall they give every man a ransom for his soul to the LORD, when you number them; that there be no plague among them, when you number them. ¹³This they shall give, every one that passes among them that are numbered, half a shekel after the shekel of the sanctuary: (a shekel is twenty gerahs:) an half shekel shall be the offering of the LORD. ¹⁴Every one that passes among them that are numbered, from twenty years old and above, shall give an offering to the LORD. ¹⁵The rich shall not give more, and the poor shall not give less than half a shekel, when they give an offering to the LORD, to make an atonement for your souls. ¹⁶And you shall take the atonement money of the children of Israel, and shall appoint it for the service of the tabernacle of the congregation; that it may be a memorial to the children of Israel before the LORD, to make an atonement for your souls. ¹⁷And the LORD spoke to Moses, saying, ¹⁸You shall also make a laver of brass, and his foot also of brass, to wash with: and you shall put it between the tabernacle of the congregation and the altar, and you shall put water therein. ¹⁹For Aaron and his sons shall wash their hands and their feet thereat: ²⁰When they go into the tabernacle of the congregation, they shall wash with water, that they die not; or when they come near to the altar to minister, to burn offering made by fire to the LORD: ²¹So they shall wash their hands and their feet, that they die not: and it shall be a statute for ever to them, even to him and to his seed throughout their generations. ²²Moreover the LORD spoke to Moses, saying, ²³Take you also to you principal spices, of pure myrrh five hundred shekels, and of sweet cinnamon half so much, even two hundred and fifty shekels, and of sweet calamus two hundred and fifty shekels, ²⁴And of cassia five hundred shekels, after the shekel of the sanctuary, and of oil olive an hin: ²⁵And you shall make it an oil of holy ointment, an ointment compound after the are of the apothecary: it shall be an holy anointing oil. ²⁶And you shall anoint the tabernacle of the congregation therewith, and the ark of the testimony, ²⁷And the table and all his vessels, and the candlestick and his vessels, and the altar of incense, ²⁸And the altar of burnt offering with all his vessels, and the laver and his foot. ²⁹And you shall sanctify them, that they may be most holy: whatever touches them shall be holy. ³⁰And you shall anoint Aaron and his sons, and consecrate them, that they may minister to me in the priest's office. ³¹And you shall speak to the children of Israel, saying, This shall be an holy anointing oil to me throughout your generations. ³²On man's flesh shall it not be poured, neither shall you make any other like it, after the composition of it: it is holy, and it shall be holy to you. ³³Whoever compounds any like it, or whoever puts any of it on a stranger, shall even be cut off from his people. ³⁴And the LORD said to Moses, Take to you sweet spices, stacte, and onycha, and galbanum; these sweet spices with pure frankincense: of each shall there be a like weight: ³⁵And you shall make it a perfume, a confection after the are of the apothecary, tempered together, pure and holy: ³⁶And you shall beat some of it very small, and put of it before the testimony in the tabernacle of the congregation, where I will meet with you: it shall be to you most holy. ³⁷And as for the perfume which you shall make, you shall not make to yourselves according to the composition thereof: it shall be to you holy for the LORD. ³⁸Whoever shall make like to that, to smell thereto, shall even be cut off from his people.

31 ¹And the LORD spoke to Moses, saying, ²See, I have called by name Bezaleel the son of Uri, the son of Hur, of the tribe of Judah: ³And I have filled him with the spirit of God, in wisdom, and in understanding, and in knowledge, and in all manner of workmanship, ⁴To devise cunning works, to work in gold, and in silver, and in brass,

⁵And in cutting of stones, to set them, and in carving of timber, to work in all manner of workmanship. ⁶And I, behold, I have given with him Aholiab, the son of Ahisamach, of the tribe of Dan: and in the hearts of all that are wise hearted I have put wisdom, that they may make all that I have commanded you; ⁷The tabernacle of the congregation, and the ark of the testimony, and the mercy seat that is thereupon, and all the furniture of the tabernacle, ⁸And the table and his furniture, and the pure candlestick with all his furniture, and the altar of incense, ⁹And the altar of burnt offering with all his furniture, and the laver and his foot, ¹⁰And the cloths of service, and the holy garments for Aaron the priest, and the garments of his sons, to minister in the priest's office, ¹¹And the anointing oil, and sweet incense for the holy place: according to all that I have commanded you shall they do. ¹²And the LORD spoke to Moses, saying, ¹³Speak you also to the children of Israel, saying, Truly my sabbaths you shall keep: for it is a sign between me and you throughout your generations; that you may know that I am the LORD that does sanctify you. ¹⁴You shall keep the sabbath therefore; for it is holy to you: every one that defiles it shall surely be put to death: for whoever does any work therein, that soul shall be cut off from among his people. ¹⁵Six days may work be done; but in the seventh is the sabbath of rest, holy to the LORD: whoever does any work in the sabbath day, he shall surely be put to death. ¹⁶Why the children of Israel shall keep the sabbath, to observe the sabbath throughout their generations, for a perpetual covenant. ¹⁷It is a sign between me and the children of Israel for ever: for in six days the LORD made heaven and earth, and on the seventh day he rested, and was refreshed. ¹⁸And he gave to Moses, when he had made an end of communing with him on mount Sinai, two tables of testimony, tables of stone, written with the finger of God.

32 ¹And when the people saw that Moses delayed to come down out of the mount, the people gathered themselves together to Aaron, and said to him, Up, make us gods, which shall go before us; for as for this Moses, the man that brought us up out of the land of Egypt, we know not what is become of him. ²And Aaron said to them, Break off the golden earrings, which are in the ears of your wives, of your sons, and of your daughters, and bring them to me. ³And all the people broke off the golden earrings which were in their ears, and brought them to Aaron. ⁴And he received them at their hand, and fashioned it with a engraving tool, after he had made it a molten calf: and they said, These be your gods, O Israel, which brought you up out of the land of Egypt. ⁵And when Aaron saw it, he built an altar before it; and Aaron made proclamation, and said, To morrow is a feast to the LORD. ⁶And they rose up early on the morrow, and offered burnt offerings, and brought peace offerings; and the people sat down to eat and to drink, and rose up to play. ⁷And the LORD said to Moses, Go, get you down; for your people, which you brought out of the land of Egypt, have corrupted themselves: ⁸They have turned aside quickly out of the way which I commanded them: they have made them a molten calf, and have worshiped it, and have sacrificed thereunto, and said, These be your gods, O Israel, which have brought you up out of the land of Egypt. ⁹And the LORD said to Moses, I have seen this people, and, behold, it is a stiff necked people: ¹⁰Now therefore let me alone, that my wrath may wax hot against them, and that I may consume them: and I will make of you a great nation. ¹¹And Moses sought the LORD his God, and said, LORD, why does your wrath wax hot against your people, which you have brought forth out of the land of Egypt with great power, and with a mighty hand? ¹²Why should the Egyptians speak, and say, For mischief did he bring them out, to slay them in the mountains, and to consume them from the face of the earth? Turn from your fierce wrath, and repent of this evil against your people. ¹³Remember Abraham, Isaac, and Israel, your servants, to whom you swore by your own self, and said to them, I will multiply your seed as the stars of heaven, and all this land that I have spoken of will I give to your seed, and they shall inherit it for ever. ¹⁴And the LORD repented of the evil which he thought to do to his people. ¹⁵And Moses turned, and went down from the mount, and the two tables of the testimony were in his hand: the tables were written on both their sides; on the one side and on the other were they written. ¹⁶And the tables were the work of God, and the writing was the writing of God, graven on the tables. ¹⁷And when Joshua heard the noise of the people as they shouted, he said to Moses, There is a noise of war in the camp. ¹⁸And he said, It is not the voice of them that shout for mastery, neither is it the voice of them that cry for being overcome: but the noise of them that sing do I hear. ¹⁹And it came to pass, as soon as he came near to the camp, that he saw the calf, and the dancing: and Moses' anger waxed hot, and he cast the tables out of his hands, and broke them beneath the mount. ²⁰And he took the calf which they had made, and burnt it in the fire, and ground it to powder, and strewed it on the water, and made the children of Israel drink of it. ²¹And Moses said to Aaron, What did this people to you, that you have brought so great a sin on them? ²²And Aaron said, Let not the anger of my lord wax hot: you know the people, that they are set on mischief. ²³For they said to me, Make us gods, which shall go before us: for as for this Moses, the man that brought us up out of the land of Egypt, we know not what is become of him. ²⁴And I said to them, Whoever has any gold, let them break it off. So they gave it me: then I cast it into the fire, and there came out this calf. ²⁵And when Moses saw that the people were naked; (for Aaron had made them naked to their shame among their enemies:) ²⁶Then Moses stood in the gate of the camp, and said, Who is on the LORD's side? let him come to me. And all the sons of Levi gathered themselves together to him. ²⁷And he said to them, Thus says the LORD God of Israel, Put every man his sword by his side, and go in and out from gate to gate throughout the camp, and slay every man his brother, and every man his companion, and every man his neighbor. ²⁸And the children of Levi did according to the word of Moses: and there fell of the people that day about three thousand men. ²⁹For Moses had said, Consecrate yourselves today to the LORD, even every man on his son, and on his brother; that he may bestow on you a blessing this day. ³⁰And it came to pass on the morrow, that Moses said to the people, You have sinned a great sin: and now I will go up to the LORD; peradventure I shall make an atonement for your sin. ³¹And Moses returned to the LORD, and said, Oh, this people have sinned a great sin, and have made them gods of gold. ³²Yet now, if you will forgive their sin--; and if not, blot me, I pray you, out of your book which you have written. ³³And the LORD said to Moses, Whoever has sinned against me, him will I blot out of my book. ³⁴Therefore now go, lead the people to the place of which I have spoken to you: behold, my Angel shall go before you: nevertheless in the day when I visit I will visit their sin on them. ³⁵And the LORD plagued the people, because they made the calf, which Aaron made.

33 ¹And the LORD said to Moses, Depart, and go up hence, you and the people which you have brought up out of the land of Egypt, to the land which I swore to Abraham, to Isaac, and to Jacob, saying, To your seed will I give it: ²And I will send an angel before you; and I will drive out the Canaanite, the Amorite, and the Hittite, and the Perizzite, the Hivite, and the Jebusite: ³To a land flowing with milk and honey: for I will not go up in the middle of you; for you are a stiff necked people: lest I consume you in the way. ⁴And when the people heard these evil tidings, they mourned: and no man did put on him his ornaments. ⁵For the LORD had said to Moses, Say to the children of Israel, You are a stiff necked people: I will come up into the middle of you in a moment, and consume you: therefore now put off your ornaments from you, that I may know what to do to you. ⁶And the children of Israel stripped themselves of their ornaments by the mount Horeb. ⁷And Moses took the tabernacle, and pitched it without the camp, afar off from the camp, and called it the Tabernacle of the congregation. And it came to pass, that every one which sought the LORD went out to the tabernacle of the congregation, which was without the camp. ⁸And it came to pass, when Moses went out to the tabernacle, that all the people rose up, and stood every man at his tent door, and looked after Moses, until he was gone into the tabernacle. ⁹And it came to pass, as Moses entered into the tabernacle, the cloudy pillar descended, and stood at the door of the tabernacle, and the Lord talked with Moses. ¹⁰And all the people saw the cloudy pillar stand at the tabernacle door: and all the people rose up and worshipped, every man in his tent door. ¹¹And the LORD spoke to Moses face to face, as a man speaks to his friend. And he turned again into the camp: but his servant Joshua, the son of Nun, a young man, departed not out of the tabernacle. ¹²And Moses said to the LORD, See, you say to me, Bring up this people: and you have not let me know whom you will send with me. Yet you have said, I know you by name, and you have also found grace in my sight. ¹³Now therefore, I pray you, if I have found grace in your sight, show me now your way, that I may know you, that I may find grace in your sight: and consider that this nation is your people. ¹⁴And he said, My presence shall go with you, and I will give you rest. ¹⁵And he said to him, If your presence go not with me, carry us not up hence. ¹⁶For wherein shall it be known here that I and your people have found grace in your sight? is it not in that you go with us? so shall we be separated, I and your people, from all the people that are on the face of the earth. ¹⁷And the LORD said to Moses, I will do this thing also that you have spoken: for you have found grace in my sight, and I know you by name. ¹⁸And he said, I beseech you, show me your glory. ¹⁹And he said, I will make all my goodness pass before you, and I will proclaim the name of the LORD before you; and will be gracious to whom I will be gracious, and will show mercy on whom I will show mercy. ²⁰And he said, You can not see my face: for there shall no man see me, and live. ²¹And the LORD said, Behold, there is a place by me, and you shall stand on a rock: ²²And it shall come to pass, while my glory passes by, that I will put you in a cleft of the rock, and will cover you with my hand while I pass by: ²³And I will take away my hand, and you shall see my back parts: but my face shall not be seen.

34 ¹And the LORD said to Moses, Hew you two tables of stone like to the first: and I will write on these tables the words that were in the first tables, which you brake. ²And be ready in the morning, and come up in the morning to mount Sinai, and present yourself there to me in the top of the mount. ³And no man shall come up with you, neither let any man be seen throughout all the mount; neither let the flocks nor herds feed before that mount. ⁴And he hewed two tables of stone like to the first; and Moses rose up early in the morning, and went up to mount Sinai, as the LORD had commanded him, and took in his hand the two tables of stone. ⁵And the LORD descended in the cloud, and stood with him there, and proclaimed the name of the LORD. ⁶And the LORD passed by before him, and proclaimed, The LORD, The LORD God, merciful and gracious, long-suffering, and abundant in goodness and truth, ⁷Keeping mercy for thousands, forgiving iniquity and transgression and sin, and that will by no means clear the guilty; visiting the iniquity of the fathers on the children, and on the children's children, to the third and to the fourth generation. ⁸And Moses made haste, and bowed his head toward the earth, and worshipped. ⁹And he said, If now I have found grace in your sight, O LORD, let my LORD, I pray you, go among us; for it is a stiff necked people; and pardon our iniquity and our sin, and take us for your inheritance. ¹⁰And he said, Behold, I make a covenant: before all your people I will do marvels, such as have not been done in all the earth, nor in any nation: and all the people among which you are shall see the work of the LORD: for it is a terrible thing that I will do with you. ¹¹Observe you that which I command you this day: behold, I drive out before you the Amorite, and the Canaanite, and the Hittite, and the Perizzite, and the Hivite, and the Jebusite. ¹²Take heed to yourself, lest you make a covenant with the inhabitants of the land where you go, lest it be for a snare in the middle of you: ¹³But you shall destroy their altars, break their images, and cut down their groves: ¹⁴For you shall worship no other god: for the LORD, whose name is Jealous, is a jealous God: ¹⁵Lest you make a covenant with the inhabitants of the land, and they go a whoring after their gods, and do sacrifice to their gods, and one call you, and you eat of his sacrifice; ¹⁶And you take of their daughters to your sons, and their daughters go a whoring after their gods, and make your sons go a whoring after their gods. ¹⁷You shall make you no molten gods. ¹⁸The feast of unleavened bread shall you keep. Seven days you shall eat unleavened bread, as I commanded you, in the time of the month Abib: for in the month Abib you came out from Egypt. ¹⁹All that opens the matrix is mine; and every firstling among your cattle, whether ox or sheep, that is male. ²⁰But the firstling of an ass you shall redeem with a lamb: and if you redeem him not, then shall you break his neck. All the firstborn of your sons you shall redeem. And none shall appear before me empty. ^{21}Six days you shall work, but on the seventh day you shall rest: in ripening time and in harvest you shall rest. ^{22}And you shall observe the feast of weeks, of the first fruits of wheat harvest, and the feast of ingathering at the year's end. ^{23}Thrice in the year shall all your male children appear before the LORD God, the God of Israel. ^{24}For I will cast out the nations before you, and enlarge your borders: neither shall any man desire your land, when you shall go up to appear before the LORD your God thrice in the year. ^{25}You shall not offer the blood of my sacrifice with leaven; neither shall the sacrifice of the feast of the passover be left to the morning. ^{26}The first of the first fruits of your land you shall bring to the house of the LORD your God. You shall not seethe a kid in his mother's milk. ^{27}And the LORD said to Moses, Write you these words: for after the tenor of these words I have made a covenant with you and with Israel. ^{28}And he was there with the LORD forty days and forty nights; he did neither eat bread, nor drink water. And he wrote on the tables the words of the covenant, the ten commandments. ^{29}And it came to pass, when Moses came down from mount Sinai with the two tables of testimony in Moses' hand, when he came down from the mount, that Moses knew not that the skin of his face shone while he talked with him. ^{30}And when Aaron and all the children of Israel saw Moses, behold, the skin of his face shone; and they were afraid to come near him. ^{31}And Moses called to them; and Aaron and all the rulers of the congregation returned to him: and Moses talked with them. ^{32}And afterward all the children of Israel came near: and he gave them in commandment all that the LORD had spoken with him in mount Sinai. ^{33}And till Moses had done speaking with them, he put a veil on his face. ^{34}But when Moses went in before the LORD to speak with him, he took the veil off, until he came out. And he came out, and spoke to the children of Israel that which he was commanded. ^{35}And the children of Israel saw the face of Moses, that the skin of Moses' face shone: and Moses put the veil on his face again, until he went in to speak with him.

35 ^{1}And Moses gathered all the congregation of the children of Israel together, and said to them, These are the words which the LORD has commanded, that you should do them. ^{2}Six days shall work be done, but on the seventh day there shall be to you an holy day, a sabbath of rest to the LORD: whoever does work therein shall be put to death. ^{3}You shall kindle no fire throughout your habitations on the sabbath day. ^{4}And Moses spoke to all the congregation of the children of Israel, saying, This is the thing which the LORD commanded, saying, ^{5}Take you from among you an offering to the LORD: whoever is of a willing heart, let him bring it, an offering of the LORD; gold, and silver, and brass, ^{6}And blue, and purple, and scarlet, and fine linen, and goats' hair, ^{7}And rams' skins dyed red, and badgers' skins, and shittim wood, ^{8}And oil for the light, and spices for anointing oil, and for the sweet incense, ^{9}And onyx stones, and stones to be set for the ephod, and for the breastplate. ^{10}And every wise hearted among you shall come, and make all that the LORD has commanded; ^{11}The tabernacle, his tent, and his covering, his clasps, and his boards, his bars, his pillars, and his sockets, ^{12}The ark, and the staves thereof, with the mercy seat, and the veil of the covering, ^{13}The table, and his staves, and all his vessels, and the show bread, ^{14}The candlestick also for the light, and his furniture, and his lamps, with the oil for the light, ^{15}And the incense altar, and his staves, and the anointing oil, and the sweet incense, and the hanging for the door at the entering in of the tabernacle, ^{16}The altar of burnt offering, with his brazen grate, his staves, and all his vessels, the laver and his foot, ^{17}The hangings of the court, his pillars, and their sockets, and the hanging for the door of the court, ^{18}The pins of the tabernacle, and the pins of the court, and their cords, ^{19}The cloths of service, to do service in the holy place, the holy garments for Aaron the priest, and the garments of his sons, to minister in the priest's office. ^{20}And all the congregation of the children of Israel departed from the presence of Moses. ^{21}And they came, every one whose heart stirred him up, and every one whom his spirit made willing, and they brought the LORD's offering to the work of the tabernacle of the congregation, and for all his service, and for the holy garments. ^{22}And they came, both men and women, as many as were willing hearted, and brought bracelets, and earrings, and rings, and tablets, all jewels of gold: and every man that offered offered an offering of gold to the LORD. ^{23}And every man, with whom was found blue, and purple, and scarlet, and fine linen, and goats' hair, and red skins of rams, and badgers' skins, brought them. ^{24}Every one that did offer an offering of silver and brass brought the LORD's offering: and every man, with whom was found shittim wood for any work of the service, brought it. ^{25}And all the women that were wise hearted did spin with their hands, and brought that which they had spun, both of blue, and of purple, and of scarlet, and of fine linen. ^{26}And all the women whose heart stirred them up in wisdom spun goats' hair. ^{27}And the rulers brought onyx stones, and stones to be set, for the ephod, and for the breastplate; ^{28}And spice, and oil for the light, and for the anointing oil, and for the sweet incense. ^{29}The children of Israel brought a willing offering to the LORD, every man and woman, whose heart made them willing to bring for all manner of work, which the LORD had commanded to be made by the hand of Moses. ^{30}And Moses said to the children of Israel, See, the LORD has called by name Bezaleel the son of Uri, the son of Hur, of the tribe of Judah; ^{31}And he has filled him with the spirit of God, in wisdom, in understanding, and in knowledge, and in all manner of workmanship; ^{32}And to devise curious works, to work in gold, and in silver, and in brass, ^{33}And in the cutting of stones, to set them, and in carving of wood, to make any manner of cunning work. ^{34}And he has put in his heart that he may teach, both he, and Aholiab, the son of Ahisamach, of the tribe of Dan. ^{35}Them has he filled with wisdom of heart, to work all manner of work, of the engraver, and of the cunning workman, and of the embroiderer, in blue, and in purple, in scarlet, and in fine linen, and of the weaver, even of them that do any work, and of those that devise cunning work.

36 ^{1}Then worked Bezaleel and Aholiab, and every wise hearted man, in whom the LORD put wisdom and understanding to know how to work all manner of work for the service of the sanctuary, according to all that the LORD had commanded. ²And Moses called Bezaleel and Aholiab, and every wise hearted man, in whose heart the LORD had put wisdom, even every one whose heart stirred him up to come to the work to do it: ³And they received of Moses all the offering, which the children of Israel had brought for the work of the service of the sanctuary, to make it with. And they brought yet to him free offerings every morning. ⁴And all the wise men, that worked all the work of the sanctuary, came every man from his work which they made; ⁵And they spoke to Moses, saying, The people bring much more than enough for the service of the work, which the LORD commanded to make. ⁶And Moses gave commandment, and they caused it to be proclaimed throughout the camp, saying, Let neither man nor woman make any more work for the offering of the sanctuary. So the people were restrained from bringing. ⁷For the stuff they had was sufficient for all the work to make it, and too much. ⁸And every wise hearted man among them that worked the work of the tabernacle made ten curtains of fine twined linen, and blue, and purple, and scarlet: with cherubim of cunning work made he them. ⁹The length of one curtain was twenty and eight cubits, and the breadth of one curtain four cubits: the curtains were all of one size. ¹⁰And he coupled the five curtains one to another: and the other five curtains he coupled one to another. ¹¹And he made loops of blue on the edge of one curtain from the selvedge in the coupling: likewise he made in the uttermost side of another curtain, in the coupling of the second. ¹²Fifty loops made he in one curtain, and fifty loops made he in the edge of the curtain which was in the coupling of the second: the loops held one curtain to another. ¹³And he made fifty clasps of gold, and coupled the curtains one to another with the clasps: so it became one tabernacle. ¹⁴And he made curtains of goats' hair for the tent over the tabernacle: eleven curtains he made them. ¹⁵The length of one curtain was thirty cubits, and four cubits was the breadth of one curtain: the eleven curtains were of one size. ¹⁶And he coupled five curtains by themselves, and six curtains by themselves. ¹⁷And he made fifty loops on the uttermost edge of the curtain in the coupling, and fifty loops made he on the edge of the curtain which couples the second. ¹⁸And he made fifty clasps of brass to couple the tent together, that it might be one. ¹⁹And he made a covering for the tent of rams' skins dyed red, and a covering of badgers' skins above that. ²⁰And he made boards for the tabernacle of shittim wood, standing up. ²¹The length of a board was ten cubits, and the breadth of a board one cubit and a half. ²²One board had two tenons, equally distant one from another: thus did he make for all the boards of the tabernacle. ²³And he made boards for the tabernacle; twenty boards for the south side southward: ²⁴And forty sockets of silver he made under the twenty boards; two sockets under one board for his two tenons, and two sockets under another board for his two tenons. ²⁵And for the other side of the tabernacle, which is toward the north corner, he made twenty boards, ²⁶And their forty sockets of silver; two sockets under one board, and two sockets under another board. ²⁷And for the sides of the tabernacle westward he made six boards. ²⁸And two boards made he for the corners of the tabernacle in the two sides. ²⁹And they were coupled beneath, and coupled together at the head thereof, to one ring: thus he did to both of them in both the corners. ³⁰And there were eight boards; and their sockets were sixteen sockets of silver, under every board two sockets. ³¹And he made bars of shittim wood; five for the boards of the one side of the tabernacle, ³²And five bars for the boards of the other side of the tabernacle, and five bars for the boards of the tabernacle for the sides westward. ³³And he made the middle bar to shoot through the boards from the one end to the other. ³⁴And he overlaid the boards with gold, and made their rings of gold to be places for the bars, and overlaid the bars with gold. ³⁵And he made a veil of blue, and purple, and scarlet, and fine twined linen: with cherubim made he it of cunning work. ³⁶And he made thereunto four pillars of shittim wood, and overlaid them with gold: their hooks were of gold; and he cast for them four sockets of silver. ³⁷And he made an hanging for the tabernacle door of blue, and purple, and scarlet, and fine twined linen, of needlework; ³⁸And the five pillars of it with their hooks: and he overlaid their capitals and their fillets with gold: but their five sockets were of brass.

37 ¹And Bezaleel made the ark of shittim wood: two cubits and a half was the length of it, and a cubit and a half the breadth of it, and a cubit and a half the height of it: ²And he overlaid it with pure gold within and without, and made a crown of gold to it round about. ³And he cast for it four rings of gold, to be set by the four corners of it; even two rings on the one side of it, and two rings on the other side of it. ⁴And he made staves of shittim wood, and overlaid them with gold. ⁵And he put the staves into the rings by the sides of the ark, to bear the ark. ⁶And he made the mercy seat of pure gold: two cubits and a half was the length thereof, and one cubit and a half the breadth thereof. ⁷And he made two cherubim of gold, beaten out of one piece made he them, on the two ends of the mercy seat; ⁸One cherub on the end on this side, and another cherub on the other end on that side: out of the mercy seat made he the cherubim on the two ends thereof. ⁹And the cherubim spread out their wings on high, and covered with their wings over the mercy seat, with their faces one to another; even to the mercy seat were the faces of the cherubim. ¹⁰And he made the table of shittim wood: two cubits was the length thereof, and a cubit the breadth thereof, and a cubit and a half the height thereof: ¹¹And he overlaid it with pure gold, and made thereunto a crown of gold round about. ¹²Also he made thereunto a border of an handbreadth round about; and made a crown of gold for the border thereof round about. ¹³And he cast for it four rings of gold, and put the rings on the four corners that were in the four feet thereof. ¹⁴Over against the border were the rings, the places for the staves to bear the table. ¹⁵And he made the staves of shittim wood, and overlaid them with gold, to bear the table. ¹⁶And he made the vessels which were on the table, his dishes, and his spoons, and his bowls, and his covers to cover with, of pure gold. ¹⁷And he made the candlestick of pure gold: of beaten work made he the candlestick; his shaft, and his branch, his bowls, his knops, and his flowers, were of the same: ¹⁸And six branches going out of the sides thereof; three branches of the candlestick out of the one side thereof, and three branches of the candlestick out of the other side thereof: ¹⁹Three bowls

made after the fashion of almonds in one branch, a bud and a flower; and three bowls made like almonds in another branch, a bud and a flower: so throughout the six branches going out of the candlestick. ²⁰And in the candlestick were four bowls made like almonds, his knops, and his flowers: ²¹And a bud under two branches of the same, and a bud under two branches of the same, and a bud under two branches of the same, according to the six branches going out of it. ²²Their knops and their branches were of the same: all of it was one beaten work of pure gold. ²³And he made his seven lamps, and his snuffers, and his firepans, of pure gold. ²⁴Of a talent of pure gold made he it, and all the vessels thereof. ²⁵And he made the incense altar of shittim wood: the length of it was a cubit, and the breadth of it a cubit; it was foursquare; and two cubits was the height of it; the horns thereof were of the same. ²⁶And he overlaid it with pure gold, both the top of it, and the sides thereof round about, and the horns of it: also he made to it a crown of gold round about. ²⁷And he made two rings of gold for it under the crown thereof, by the two corners of it, on the two sides thereof, to be places for the staves to bear it with. ²⁸And he made the staves of shittim wood, and overlaid them with gold. ²⁹And he made the holy anointing oil, and the pure incense of sweet spices, according to the work of the apothecary.

38 ¹And he made the altar of burnt offering of shittim wood: five cubits was the length thereof, and five cubits the breadth thereof; it was foursquare; and three cubits the height thereof. ²And he made the horns thereof on the four corners of it; the horns thereof were of the same: and he overlaid it with brass. ³And he made all the vessels of the altar, the pots, and the shovels, and the basins, and the meat hooks, and the fire pans: all the vessels thereof made he of brass. ⁴And he made for the altar a brazen grate of network under the compass thereof beneath to the middle of it. ⁵And he cast four rings for the four ends of the grate of brass, to be places for the staves. ⁶And he made the staves of shittim wood, and overlaid them with brass. ⁷And he put the staves into the rings on the sides of the altar, to bear it with; he made the altar hollow with boards. ⁸And he made the laver of brass, and the foot of it of brass, of the mirrors of the women assembling, which assembled at the door of the tabernacle of the congregation. ⁹And he made the court: on the south side southward the hangings of the court were of fine twined linen, an hundred cubits: ¹⁰Their pillars were twenty, and their brazen sockets twenty; the hooks of the pillars and their fillets were of silver. ¹¹And for the north side the hangings were an hundred cubits, their pillars were twenty, and their sockets of brass twenty; the hooks of the pillars and their fillets of silver. ¹²And for the west side were hangings of fifty cubits, their pillars ten, and their sockets ten; the hooks of the pillars and their fillets of silver. ¹³And for the east side eastward fifty cubits. ¹⁴The hangings of the one side of the gate were fifteen cubits; their pillars three, and their sockets three. ¹⁵And for the other side of the court gate, on this hand and that hand, were hangings of fifteen cubits; their pillars three, and their sockets three. ¹⁶All the hangings of the court round about were of fine twined linen. ¹⁷And the sockets for the pillars were of brass; the hooks of the pillars and their fillets of silver; and the overlaying of their capitals of silver; and all the pillars of the court were filleted with silver. ¹⁸And the hanging for the gate of the court was needlework, of blue, and purple, and scarlet, and fine twined linen: and twenty cubits was the length, and the height in the breadth was five cubits, answerable to the hangings of the court. ¹⁹And their pillars were four, and their sockets of brass four; their hooks of silver, and the overlaying of their capitals and their fillets of silver. ²⁰And all the pins of the tabernacle, and of the court round about, were of brass. ²¹This is the sum of the tabernacle, even of the tabernacle of testimony, as it was counted, according to the commandment of Moses, for the service of the Levites, by the hand of Ithamar, son to Aaron the priest. ²²And Bezaleel the son Uri, the son of Hur, of the tribe of Judah, made all that the LORD commanded Moses. ²³And with him was Aholiab, son of Ahisamach, of the tribe of Dan, an engraver, and a cunning workman, and an embroiderer in blue, and in purple, and in scarlet, and fine linen. ²⁴All the gold that was occupied for the work in all the work of the holy place, even the gold of the offering, was twenty and nine talents, and seven hundred and thirty shekels, after the shekel of the sanctuary. ²⁵And the silver of them that were numbered of the congregation was an hundred talents, and a thousand seven hundred and three score and fifteen shekels, after the shekel of the sanctuary: ²⁶A bekah for every man, that is, half a shekel, after the shekel of the sanctuary, for every one that went to be numbered, from twenty years old and upward, for six hundred thousand and three thousand and five hundred and fifty men. ²⁷And of the hundred talents of silver were cast the sockets of the sanctuary, and the sockets of the veil; an hundred sockets of the hundred talents, a talent for a socket. ²⁸And of the thousand seven hundred seventy and five shekels he made hooks for the pillars, and overlaid their capitals, and filleted them. ²⁹And the brass of the offering was seventy talents, and two thousand and four hundred shekels. ³⁰And therewith he made the sockets to the door of the tabernacle of the congregation, and the brazen altar, and the brazen grate for it, and all the vessels of the altar, ³¹And the sockets of the court round about, and the sockets of the court gate, and all the pins of the tabernacle, and all the pins of the court round about.

39 ¹And of the blue, and purple, and scarlet, they made cloths of service, to do service in the holy place, and made the holy garments for Aaron; as the LORD commanded Moses. ²And he made the ephod of gold, blue, and purple, and scarlet, and fine twined linen. ³And they did beat the gold into thin plates, and cut it into wires, to work it in the blue, and in the purple, and in the scarlet, and in the fine linen, with cunning work. ⁴They made shoulder pieces for it, to couple it together: by the two edges was it coupled together. ⁵And the curious girdle of his ephod, that was on it, was of the same, according to the work thereof; of gold, blue, and purple, and scarlet, and fine twined linen; as the LORD commanded Moses. ⁶And they worked onyx stones enclosed in ouches of gold, graven, as signets are graven, with the names of the children of Israel. ⁷And he put them on the shoulders of the ephod, that they should be stones for a memorial to the children of Israel; as the LORD commanded Moses. ⁸And he made the breastplate of cunning work, like the work of the ephod; of gold, blue, and purple, and scarlet, and fine twined linen. ⁹It was foursquare; they made the breastplate double: a span was the length thereof, and a span the breadth thereof, being doubled. ¹⁰And they set in it four rows of stones: the first row was a sardius, a topaz, and a carbuncle: this was the first row. ¹¹And the second row, an emerald, a sapphire, and a diamond. ¹²And the third row, a ligure, an agate, and an amethyst. ¹³And the fourth row, a beryl, an onyx, and a jasper: they were enclosed in ouches of gold in their settings. ¹⁴And the stones were according to the names of the children of Israel, twelve, according to their names, like the engravings of a signet, every one with his name, according to the twelve tribes. ¹⁵And they made on the breastplate chains at the ends, of wreathen work of pure gold. ¹⁶And they made two ouches of gold, and two gold rings; and put the two rings in the two ends of the breastplate. ¹⁷And they put the two wreathen chains of gold in the two rings on the ends of the breastplate. ¹⁸And the two ends of the two wreathen chains they fastened in the two ouches, and put them on the shoulder pieces of the ephod, before it. ¹⁹And they made two rings of gold, and put them on the two ends of the breastplate, on the border of it, which was on the side of the ephod inward. ²⁰And they made two other golden rings, and put them on the two sides of the ephod underneath, toward the forepart of it, over against the other coupling thereof, above the curious girdle of the ephod. ²¹And they did bind the breastplate by his rings to the rings of the ephod with a lace of blue, that it might be above the curious girdle of the ephod, and that the breastplate might not be loosed from the ephod; as the LORD commanded Moses. ²²And he made the robe of the ephod of woven work, all of blue. ²³And there was an hole in the middle of the robe, as the hole of an habergeon, with a band round about the hole, that it should not rend. ²⁴And they made on the hems of the robe pomegranates of blue, and purple, and scarlet, and twined linen. ²⁵And they made bells of pure gold, and put the bells between the pomegranates on the hem of the robe, round about between the pomegranates; ²⁶A bell and a pomegranate, a bell and a pomegranate, round about the hem of the robe to minister in; as the LORD commanded Moses. ²⁷And they made coats of fine linen of woven work for Aaron, and for his sons, ²⁸And a turban of fine linen, and goodly bonnets of fine linen, and linen breeches of fine twined linen, ²⁹And a girdle of fine twined linen, and blue, and purple, and scarlet, of needlework; as the LORD commanded Moses. ³⁰And they made the plate of the holy crown of pure gold, and wrote on it a writing, like to the engravings of a signet, HOLINESS TO THE LORD. ³¹And they tied to it a lace of blue, to fasten it on high on the turban; as the LORD commanded Moses. ³²Thus was all the work of the tabernacle of the tent of the congregation finished: and the children of Israel did according to all that the LORD commanded Moses, so did they. ³³And they brought the tabernacle to Moses, the tent, and all his furniture, his clasps, his boards, his bars, and his pillars, and his sockets, ³⁴And the covering of rams' skins dyed red, and the covering of badgers' skins, and the veil of the covering, ³⁵The ark of the testimony, and the staves thereof, and the mercy seat, ³⁶The table, and all the vessels thereof, and the show bread, ³⁷The pure candlestick, with the lamps thereof, even with the lamps to be set in order, and all the vessels thereof, and the oil for light, ³⁸And the golden altar, and the anointing oil, and the sweet incense, and the hanging for the tabernacle door, ³⁹The brazen altar, and his grate of brass, his staves, and all his vessels, the laver and his foot, ⁴⁰The hangings of the court, his pillars, and his sockets, and the hanging for the court gate, his cords, and his pins, and all the vessels of the service of the tabernacle, for the tent of the congregation, ⁴¹The cloths of service to do service in the holy place, and the holy garments for Aaron the priest, and his sons' garments, to minister in the priest's office. ⁴²According to all that the LORD commanded Moses, so the children of Israel made all the work. ⁴³And Moses did look on all the work, and, behold, they had done it as the LORD had commanded, even so had they done it: and Moses blessed them.

40 ¹And the LORD spoke to Moses, saying, ²On the first day of the first month shall you set up the tabernacle of the tent of the congregation. ³And you shall put therein the ark of the testimony, and cover the ark with the veil. ⁴And you shall bring in the table, and set in order the things that are to be set in order on it; and you shall bring in the candlestick, and light the lamps thereof. ⁵And you shall set the altar of gold for the incense before the ark of the testimony, and put the hanging of the door to the tabernacle. ⁶And you shall set the altar of the burnt offering before the door of the tabernacle of the tent of the congregation. ⁷And you shall set the laver between the tent of the congregation and the altar, and shall put water therein. ⁸And you shall set up the court round about, and hang up the hanging at the court gate. ⁹And you shall take the anointing oil, and anoint the tabernacle, and all that is therein, and shall hallow it, and all the vessels thereof: and it shall be holy. ¹⁰And you shall anoint the altar of the burnt offering, and all his vessels, and sanctify the altar: and it shall be an altar most holy. ¹¹And you shall anoint the laver and his foot, and sanctify it. ¹²And you shall bring Aaron and his sons to the door of the tabernacle of the congregation, and wash them with water. ¹³And you shall put on Aaron the holy garments, and anoint him, and sanctify him; that he may minister to me in the priest's office. ¹⁴And you shall bring his sons, and clothe them with coats: ¹⁵And you shall anoint them, as you did anoint their father, that they may minister to me in the priest's office: for their anointing shall surely be an everlasting priesthood throughout their generations. ¹⁶Thus did Moses: according to all that the LORD commanded him, so did he. ¹⁷And it came to pass in the first month in the second year, on the first day of the month, that the tabernacle was reared up. ¹⁸And Moses reared up the tabernacle, and fastened his sockets, and set up the boards thereof, and put in the bars thereof, and reared up his pillars. ¹⁹And he spread abroad the tent over the tabernacle, and put the covering of the tent above on it; as the LORD commanded Moses. ²⁰And he took and put the testimony into the ark, and set the staves on the ark, and put the mercy seat above on the ark: ²¹And he brought the ark into the tabernacle, and set up the veil of the covering, and covered the ark of the testimony; as the LORD commanded Moses. ²²And he put the table in the tent of the congregation, on the side of the tabernacle northward, without the veil. ²³And he set the bread in order on it before the LORD; as the LORD had commanded Moses. ²⁴And he put the candlestick in the tent of the congregation, over against the table, on the side of the tabernacle southward. ²⁵And he lighted the lamps before the LORD; as the LORD commanded Moses. ²⁶And he put the golden altar in the tent of the congregation before the veil: ²⁷And he burnt sweet incense thereon; as the LORD commanded Moses. ²⁸And he set up the hanging at the door of the tabernacle. ²⁹And he put the altar of burnt offering by the door of the tabernacle of the tent of the congregation, and offered on it the burnt offering and the meat offering; as the LORD commanded Moses. ³⁰And he set the laver between the tent of the congregation and the altar, and put water there, to wash with. ³¹And Moses and Aaron and his sons washed their hands and their feet thereat: ³²When they went into the tent of the congregation, and when they came near to the altar, they washed; as the LORD commanded Moses. ³³And he reared up the court round about the tabernacle and the altar, and set up the hanging of the court gate. So Moses finished the work. ³⁴Then a cloud covered the tent of the congregation, and the glory of the LORD filled the tabernacle. ³⁵And Moses was not able to enter into the tent of the congregation, because the cloud stayed thereon, and the glory of the LORD filled the tabernacle. ³⁶And when the cloud was taken up from over the tabernacle, the children of Israel went onward in all their journeys: ³⁷But if the cloud were not taken up, then they journeyed not till the day that it was taken up. ³⁸For the cloud of the LORD was on the tabernacle by day, and fire was on it by night, in the sight of all the house of Israel, throughout all their journeys.

Leviticus

1 ¹And the LORD called to Moses, and spoke to him out of the tabernacle of the congregation, saying, ²Speak to the children of Israel, and say to them, If any man of you bring an offering to the LORD, you shall bring your offering of the cattle, even of the herd, and of the flock. ³If his offering be a burnt sacrifice of the herd, let him offer a male without blemish: he shall offer it of his own voluntary will at the door of the tabernacle of the congregation before the LORD. ⁴And he shall put his hand on the head of the burnt offering; and it shall be accepted for him to make atonement for him. ⁵And he shall kill the bullock before the LORD: and the priests, Aaron's sons, shall bring the blood, and sprinkle the blood round about on the altar that is by the door of the tabernacle of the congregation. ⁶And he shall flay the burnt offering, and cut it into his pieces. ⁷And the sons of Aaron the priest shall put fire on the altar, and lay the wood in order on the fire: ⁸And the priests, Aaron's sons, shall lay the parts, the head, and the fat, in order on the wood that is on the fire which is on the altar: ⁹But his inwards and his legs shall he wash in water: and the priest shall burn all on the altar, to be a burnt sacrifice, an offering made by fire, of a sweet smell to the LORD. ¹⁰And if his offering be of the flocks, namely, of the sheep, or of the goats, for a burnt sacrifice; he shall bring it a male without blemish. ¹¹And he shall kill it on the side of the altar northward before the LORD: and the priests, Aaron's sons, shall sprinkle his blood round about on the altar. ¹²And he shall cut it into his pieces, with his head and his fat: and the priest shall lay them in order on the wood that is on the fire which is on the altar: ¹³But he shall wash the inwards and the legs with water: and the priest shall bring it all, and burn it on the altar: it is a burnt sacrifice, an offering made by fire, of a sweet smell to the LORD. ¹⁴And if the burnt sacrifice for his offering to the LORD be of fowls, then he shall bring his offering of turtledoves, or of young pigeons. ¹⁵And the priest shall bring it to the altar, and wring off his head, and burn it on the altar; and the blood thereof shall be wrung out at the side of the altar: ¹⁶And he shall pluck away his crop with his feathers, and cast it beside the altar on the east part, by the place of the ashes: ¹⁷And he shall split it with the wings thereof, but shall not divide it asunder: and the priest shall burn it on the altar, on the wood that is on the fire: it is a burnt sacrifice, an offering made by fire, of a sweet smell to the LORD.

2 ¹And when any will offer a meat offering to the LORD, his offering shall be of fine flour; and he shall pour oil on it, and put frankincense thereon: ²And he shall bring it to Aaron's sons the priests: and he shall take out of there his handful of the flour thereof, and of the oil thereof, with all the frankincense thereof; and the priest shall burn the memorial of it on the altar, to be an offering made by fire, of a sweet smell to the LORD: ³And the remnant of the meat offering shall be Aaron's and his sons': it is a thing most holy of the offerings of the LORD made by fire. ⁴And if you bring an oblation of a meat offering baked in the oven, it shall be unleavened cakes of fine flour mingled with oil, or unleavened wafers anointed with oil. ⁵And if your oblation be a meat offering baked in a pan, it shall be of fine flour unleavened, mingled with oil. ⁶You shall part it in pieces, and pour oil thereon: it is a meat offering. ⁷And if your oblation be a meat offering baked in the frying pan, it shall be made of fine flour with oil. ⁸And you shall bring the meat offering that is made of these things to the LORD: and when it is presented to the priest, he shall bring it to the altar. ⁹And the priest shall take from the meat offering a memorial thereof, and shall burn it on the altar: it is an offering made by fire, of a sweet smell to the LORD. ¹⁰And that which is left of the meat offering shall be Aaron's and his sons': it is a thing most holy of the offerings of the LORD made by fire. ¹¹No meat offering, which you shall bring to the LORD, shall be made with leaven: for you shall burn no leaven, nor any honey, in any offering of the LORD made by fire. ¹²As for the oblation of the first fruits, you shall offer them to the LORD: but they shall not be burnt on the altar for a sweet smell. ¹³And every oblation of your meat offering shall you season with salt; neither shall you suffer the salt of the covenant of your God to be lacking from your meat offering: with all your offerings you shall offer salt. ¹⁴And if you offer a meat offering of your first fruits to the LORD, you shall offer for the meat offering of your first fruits green ears of corn dried by the fire, even corn beaten out of full ears. ¹⁵And you shall put oil on it, and lay frankincense thereon: it is a meat offering. ¹⁶And the priest shall burn the memorial of it, part of the beaten corn thereof, and part of the oil thereof, with all the frankincense thereof: it is an offering made by fire to the LORD.

3 ¹And if his oblation be a sacrifice of peace offering, if he offer it of the herd; whether it be a male or female, he shall offer it without blemish before the LORD. ²And he shall lay his hand on the head of his offering, and kill it at the door of the tabernacle of the congregation: and Aaron's sons the priests shall sprinkle the blood on the altar round about. ³And he shall offer of the sacrifice of the peace offering an offering made by fire to the LORD; the fat that covers the inwards, and all the fat that is on the inwards, ⁴And the two kidneys, and the fat that is on them, which is by the flanks, and the lobe above the liver, with the kidneys, it shall he take away. ⁵And Aaron's sons shall burn it on the altar on the burnt sacrifice, which is on the wood that is on the fire: it is an offering made by fire, of a sweet smell to the LORD. ⁶And if his offering for a sacrifice of peace offering to the LORD be of the flock; male or female, he shall offer it without blemish. ⁷If he offer a lamb for his offering, then shall he offer it before the LORD. ⁸And he shall lay his hand on the head of his offering, and kill it before the tabernacle of the congregation: and Aaron's sons shall sprinkle the blood thereof round about on the altar. ⁹And he shall offer of the sacrifice of the peace offering an offering made by fire to the LORD; the fat thereof, and the whole rump, it shall he take off hard by the backbone; and the fat that covers the inwards, and all the fat that is on the inwards, ¹⁰And the two kidneys, and the fat that is on them, which is by the flanks,

and the lobe above the liver, with the kidneys, it shall he take away. ¹¹And the priest shall burn it on the altar: it is the food of the offering made by fire to the LORD. ¹²And if his offering be a goat, then he shall offer it before the LORD. ¹³And he shall lay his hand on the head of it, and kill it before the tabernacle of the congregation: and the sons of Aaron shall sprinkle the blood thereof on the altar round about. ¹⁴And he shall offer thereof his offering, even an offering made by fire to the LORD; the fat that covers the inwards, and all the fat that is on the inwards, ¹⁵And the two kidneys, and the fat that is on them, which is by the flanks, and the lobe above the liver, with the kidneys, it shall he take away. ¹⁶And the priest shall burn them on the altar: it is the food of the offering made by fire for a sweet smell: all the fat is the LORD's. ¹⁷It shall be a perpetual statute for your generations throughout all your dwellings, that you eat neither fat nor blood.

4 ¹And the LORD spoke to Moses, saying, ²Speak to the children of Israel, saying, If a soul shall sin through ignorance against any of the commandments of the LORD concerning things which should not to be done, and shall do against any of them: ³If the priest that is anointed do sin according to the sin of the people; then let him bring for his sin, which he has sinned, a young bullock without blemish to the LORD for a sin offering. ⁴And he shall bring the bullock to the door of the tabernacle of the congregation before the LORD; and shall lay his hand on the bullock's head, and kill the bullock before the LORD. ⁵And the priest that is anointed shall take of the bullock's blood, and bring it to the tabernacle of the congregation: ⁶And the priest shall dip his finger in the blood, and sprinkle of the blood seven times before the LORD, before the veil of the sanctuary. ⁷And the priest shall put some of the blood on the horns of the altar of sweet incense before the LORD, which is in the tabernacle of the congregation; and shall pour all the blood of the bullock at the bottom of the altar of the burnt offering, which is at the door of the tabernacle of the congregation. ⁸And he shall take off from it all the fat of the bullock for the sin offering; the fat that covers the inwards, and all the fat that is on the inwards, ⁹And the two kidneys, and the fat that is on them, which is by the flanks, and the lobe above the liver, with the kidneys, it shall he take away, ¹⁰As it was taken off from the bullock of the sacrifice of peace offerings: and the priest shall burn them on the altar of the burnt offering. ¹¹And the skin of the bullock, and all his flesh, with his head, and with his legs, and his inwards, and his dung, ¹²Even the whole bullock shall he carry forth without the camp to a clean place, where the ashes are poured out, and burn him on the wood with fire: where the ashes are poured out shall he be burnt. ¹³And if the whole congregation of Israel sin through ignorance, and the thing be hid from the eyes of the assembly, and they have done somewhat against any of the commandments of the LORD concerning things which should not be done, and are guilty; ¹⁴When the sin, which they have sinned against it, is known, then the congregation shall offer a young bullock for the sin, and bring him before the tabernacle of the congregation. ¹⁵And the elders of the congregation shall lay their hands on the head of the bullock before the LORD: and the bullock shall be killed before the LORD. ¹⁶And the priest that is anointed shall bring of the bullock's blood to the tabernacle of the congregation: ¹⁷And the priest shall dip his finger in some of the blood, and sprinkle it seven times before the LORD, even before the veil. ¹⁸And he shall put some of the blood on the horns of the altar which is before the LORD, that is in the tabernacle of the congregation, and shall pour out all the blood at the bottom of the altar of the burnt offering, which is at the door of the tabernacle of the congregation. ¹⁹And he shall take all his fat from him, and burn it on the altar. ²⁰And he shall do with the bullock as he did with the bullock for a sin offering, so shall he do with this: and the priest shall make an atonement for them, and it shall be forgiven them. ²¹And he shall carry forth the bullock without the camp, and burn him as he burned the first bullock: it is a sin offering for the congregation. ²²When a ruler has sinned, and done somewhat through ignorance against any of the commandments of the LORD his God concerning things which should not be done, and is guilty; ²³Or if his sin, wherein he has sinned, come to his knowledge; he shall bring his offering, a kid of the goats, a male without blemish: ²⁴And he shall lay his hand on the head of the goat, and kill it in the place where they kill the burnt offering before the LORD: it is a sin offering. ²⁵And the priest shall take of the blood of the sin offering with his finger, and put it on the horns of the altar of burnt offering, and shall pour out his blood at the bottom of the altar of burnt offering. ²⁶And he shall burn all his fat on the altar, as the fat of the sacrifice of peace offerings: and the priest shall make an atonement for him as concerning his sin, and it shall be forgiven him. ²⁷And if any one of the common people sin through ignorance, while he does somewhat against any of the commandments of the LORD concerning things which should not to be done, and be guilty; ²⁸Or if his sin, which he has sinned, come to his knowledge: then he shall bring his offering, a kid of the goats, a female without blemish, for his sin which he has sinned. ²⁹And he shall lay his hand on the head of the sin offering, and slay the sin offering in the place of the burnt offering. ³⁰And the priest shall take of the blood thereof with his finger, and put it on the horns of the altar of burnt offering, and shall pour out all the blood thereof at the bottom of the altar. ³¹And he shall take away all the fat thereof, as the fat is taken away from off the sacrifice of peace offerings; and the priest shall burn it on the altar for a sweet smell to the LORD; and the priest shall make an atonement for him, and it shall be forgiven him. ³²And if he bring a lamb for a sin offering, he shall bring it a female without blemish. ³³And he shall lay his hand on the head of the sin offering, and slay it for a sin offering in the place where they kill the burnt offering. ³⁴And the priest shall take of the blood of the sin offering with his finger, and put it on the horns of the altar of burnt offering, and shall pour out all the blood thereof at the bottom of the altar: ³⁵And he shall take away all the fat thereof, as the fat of the lamb is taken away from the sacrifice of the peace offerings; and the priest shall burn them on the altar, according to the offerings made by fire to the LORD: and the priest shall make an atonement for his sin that he has committed, and it shall be forgiven him.

5 ¹And if a soul sin, and hear the voice of swearing, and is a witness, whether he has seen or known of it; if he do

not utter it, then he shall bear his iniquity. ²Or if a soul touch any unclean thing, whether it be a carcass of an unclean beast, or a carcass of unclean cattle, or the carcass of unclean creeping things, and if it be hidden from him; he also shall be unclean, and guilty. ³Or if he touch the uncleanness of man, whatever uncleanness it be that a man shall be defiled with, and it be hid from him; when he knows of it, then he shall be guilty. ⁴Or if a soul swear, pronouncing with his lips to do evil, or to do good, whatever it be that a man shall pronounce with an oath, and it be hid from him; when he knows of it, then he shall be guilty in one of these. ⁵And it shall be, when he shall be guilty in one of these things, that he shall confess that he has sinned in that thing: ⁶And he shall bring his trespass offering to the LORD for his sin which he has sinned, a female from the flock, a lamb or a kid of the goats, for a sin offering; and the priest shall make an atonement for him concerning his sin. ⁷And if he be not able to bring a lamb, then he shall bring for his trespass, which he has committed, two turtledoves, or two young pigeons, to the LORD; one for a sin offering, and the other for a burnt offering. ⁸And he shall bring them to the priest, who shall offer that which is for the sin offering first, and wring off his head from his neck, but shall not divide it asunder: ⁹And he shall sprinkle of the blood of the sin offering on the side of the altar; and the rest of the blood shall be wrung out at the bottom of the altar: it is a sin offering. ¹⁰And he shall offer the second for a burnt offering, according to the manner: and the priest shall make an atonement for him for his sin which he has sinned, and it shall be forgiven him. ¹¹But if he be not able to bring two turtledoves, or two young pigeons, then he that sinned shall bring for his offering the tenth part of an ephah of fine flour for a sin offering; he shall put no oil on it, neither shall he put any frankincense thereon: for it is a sin offering. ¹²Then shall he bring it to the priest, and the priest shall take his handful of it, even a memorial thereof, and burn it on the altar, according to the offerings made by fire to the LORD: it is a sin offering. ¹³And the priest shall make an atonement for him as touching his sin that he has sinned in one of these, and it shall be forgiven him: and the remnant shall be the priest's, as a meat offering. ¹⁴And the LORD spoke to Moses, saying, ¹⁵If a soul commit a trespass, and sin through ignorance, in the holy things of the LORD; then he shall bring for his trespass to the LORD a ram without blemish out of the flocks, with your estimation by shekels of silver, after the shekel of the sanctuary, for a trespass offering. ¹⁶And he shall make amends for the harm that he has done in the holy thing, and shall add the fifth part thereto, and give it to the priest: and the priest shall make an atonement for him with the ram of the trespass offering, and it shall be forgiven him. ¹⁷And if a soul sin, and commit any of these things which are forbidden to be done by the commandments of the LORD; though he knew it not, yet is he guilty, and shall bear his iniquity. ¹⁸And he shall bring a ram without blemish out of the flock, with your estimation, for a trespass offering, to the priest: and the priest shall make an atonement for him concerning his ignorance wherein he erred and knew it not, and it shall be forgiven him. ¹⁹It is a trespass offering: he has certainly trespassed against the LORD.

6 ¹And the LORD spoke to Moses, saying, ²If a soul sin, and commit a trespass against the LORD, and lie to his neighbor in that which was delivered him to keep, or in fellowship, or in a thing taken away by violence, or has deceived his neighbor; ³Or have found that which was lost, and lies concerning it, and swears falsely; in any of all these that a man does, sinning therein: ⁴Then it shall be, because he has sinned, and is guilty, that he shall restore that which he took violently away, or the thing which he has deceitfully gotten, or that which was delivered him to keep, or the lost thing which he found, ⁵Or all that about which he has sworn falsely; he shall even restore it in the principal, and shall add the fifth part more thereto, and give it to him to whom it appertains, in the day of his trespass offering. ⁶And he shall bring his trespass offering to the LORD, a ram without blemish out of the flock, with your estimation, for a trespass offering, to the priest: ⁷And the priest shall make an atonement for him before the LORD: and it shall be forgiven him for any thing of all that he has done in trespassing therein. ⁸And the LORD spoke to Moses, saying, ⁹Command Aaron and his sons, saying, This is the law of the burnt offering: It is the burnt offering, because of the burning on the altar all night to the morning, and the fire of the altar shall be burning in it. ¹⁰And the priest shall put on his linen garment, and his linen breeches shall he put on his flesh, and take up the ashes which the fire has consumed with the burnt offering on the altar, and he shall put them beside the altar. ¹¹And he shall put off his garments, and put on other garments, and carry forth the ashes without the camp to a clean place. ¹²And the fire on the altar shall be burning in it; it shall not be put out: and the priest shall burn wood on it every morning, and lay the burnt offering in order on it; and he shall burn thereon the fat of the peace offerings. ¹³The fire shall ever be burning on the altar; it shall never go out. ¹⁴And this is the law of the meat offering: the sons of Aaron shall offer it before the LORD, before the altar. ¹⁵And he shall take of it his handful, of the flour of the meat offering, and of the oil thereof, and all the frankincense which is on the meat offering, and shall burn it on the altar for a sweet smell, even the memorial of it, to the LORD. ¹⁶And the remainder thereof shall Aaron and his sons eat: with unleavened bread shall it be eaten in the holy place; in the court of the tabernacle of the congregation they shall eat it. ¹⁷It shall not be baked with leaven. I have given it to them for their portion of my offerings made by fire; it is most holy, as is the sin offering, and as the trespass offering. ¹⁸All the males among the children of Aaron shall eat of it. It shall be a statute for ever in your generations concerning the offerings of the LORD made by fire: every one that touches them shall be holy. ¹⁹And the LORD spoke to Moses, saying, ²⁰This is the offering of Aaron and of his sons, which they shall offer to the LORD in the day when he is anointed; the tenth part of an ephah of fine flour for a meat offering perpetual, half of it in the morning, and half thereof at night. ²¹In a pan it shall be made with oil; and when it is baked, you shall bring it in: and the baked pieces of the meat offering shall you offer for a sweet smell to the LORD. ²²And the priest of his sons that is anointed in his stead shall offer it: it is a statute for ever to the LORD; it shall be wholly burnt. ²³For every meat offering for the priest shall be wholly burnt: it shall not be eaten. ²⁴And the LORD spoke to Moses, saying, ²⁵Speak to Aaron and to his sons, saying, This is the law of the sin offering: In the place where the burnt offering is killed shall the sin offering be killed before the LORD: it is most holy. ²⁶The priest that offers it for sin shall eat it: in the holy place shall it be eaten, in the court of the tabernacle of the congregation. ²⁷Whatever shall touch the flesh thereof shall be holy: and when there is sprinkled of the blood thereof on any garment, you shall wash that where on it was sprinkled in the holy place. ²⁸But the earthen vessel wherein it is sodden shall be broken: and if it be sodden in a brazen pot, it shall be both scoured, and rinsed in water. ²⁹All the males among the priests shall eat thereof: it is most holy. ³⁰And no sin offering, whereof any of the blood is brought into the tabernacle of the congregation to reconcile with in the holy place, shall be eaten: it shall be burnt in the fire.

7 ¹Likewise this is the law of the trespass offering: it is most holy. ²In the place where they kill the burnt offering shall they kill the trespass offering: and the blood thereof shall he sprinkle round about on the altar. ³And he shall offer of it all the fat thereof; the rump, and the fat that covers the inwards, ⁴And the two kidneys, and the fat that is on them, which is by the flanks, and the lobe that is above the liver, with the kidneys, it shall he take away: ⁵And the priest shall burn them on the altar for an offering made by fire to the LORD: it is a trespass offering. ⁶Every male among the priests shall eat thereof: it shall be eaten in the holy place: it is most holy. ⁷As the sin offering is, so is the trespass offering: there is one law for them: the priest that makes atonement therewith shall have it. ⁸And the priest that offers any man's burnt offering, even the priest shall have to himself the skin of the burnt offering which he has offered. ⁹And all the meat offering that is baked in the oven, and all that is dressed in the frying pan, and in the pan, shall be the priest's that offers it. ¹⁰And every meat offering, mingled with oil, and dry, shall all the sons of Aaron have, one as much as another. ¹¹And this is the law of the sacrifice of peace offerings, which he shall offer to the LORD. ¹²If he offer it for a thanksgiving, then he shall offer with the sacrifice of thanksgiving unleavened cakes mingled with oil, and unleavened wafers anointed with oil, and cakes mingled with oil, of fine flour, fried. ¹³Besides the cakes, he shall offer for his offering leavened bread with the sacrifice of thanksgiving of his peace offerings. ¹⁴And of it he shall offer one out of the whole oblation for an heave offering to the LORD, and it shall be the priest's that sprinkles the blood of the peace offerings. ¹⁵And the flesh of the sacrifice of his peace offerings for thanksgiving shall be eaten the same day that it is offered; he shall not leave any of it until the morning. ¹⁶But if the sacrifice of his offering be a vow, or a voluntary offering, it shall be eaten the same day that he offers his sacrifice: and on the morrow also the remainder of it shall be eaten: ¹⁷But the remainder of the flesh of the sacrifice on the third day shall be burnt with fire. ¹⁸And if any of the flesh of the sacrifice of his peace offerings be eaten at all on the third day, it shall not be accepted, neither shall it be imputed to him that offers it: it shall be an abomination, and the soul that eats of it shall bear his iniquity. ¹⁹And the flesh that touches any unclean thing shall not be eaten; it shall be burnt with fire: and as for the flesh, all that be clean shall eat thereof. ²⁰But the soul that eats of the flesh of the sacrifice of peace offerings, that pertain to the LORD, having his uncleanness on him, even that soul shall be cut off from his people. ²¹Moreover the soul that shall touch any unclean thing, as the uncleanness of man, or any unclean beast, or any abominable unclean thing, and eat of the flesh of the sacrifice of peace offerings, which pertain to the LORD, even that soul shall be cut off from his people. ²²And the LORD spoke to Moses, saying, ²³Speak to the children of Israel, saying, You shall eat no manner of fat, of ox, or of sheep, or of goat. ²⁴And the fat of the beast that dies of itself, and the fat of that which is torn with beasts, may be used in any other use: but you shall in no wise eat of it. ²⁵For whoever eats the fat of the beast, of which men offer an offering made by fire to the LORD, even the soul that eats it shall be cut off from his people. ²⁶Moreover you shall eat no manner of blood, whether it be of fowl or of beast, in any of your dwellings. ²⁷Whatever soul it be that eats any manner of blood, even that soul shall be cut off from his people. ²⁸And the LORD spoke to Moses, saying, ²⁹Speak to the children of Israel, saying, He that offers the sacrifice of his peace offerings to the LORD shall bring his oblation to the LORD of the sacrifice of his peace offerings. ³⁰His own hands shall bring the offerings of the LORD made by fire, the fat with the breast, it shall he bring, that the breast may be waved for a wave offering before the LORD. ³¹And the priest shall burn the fat on the altar: but the breast shall be Aaron's and his sons'. ³²And the right shoulder shall you give to the priest for an heave offering of the sacrifices of your peace offerings. ³³He among the sons of Aaron, that offers the blood of the peace offerings, and the fat, shall have the right shoulder for his part. ³⁴For the wave breast and the heave shoulder have I taken of the children of Israel from off the sacrifices of their peace offerings, and have given them to Aaron the priest and to his sons by a statute for ever from among the children of Israel. ³⁵This is the portion of the anointing of Aaron, and of the anointing of his sons, out of the offerings of the LORD made by fire, in the day when he presented them to minister to the LORD in the priest's office; ³⁶Which the LORD commanded to be given them of the children of Israel, in the day that he anointed them, by a statute for ever throughout their generations. ³⁷This is the law of the burnt offering, of the meat offering, and of the sin offering, and of the trespass offering, and of the consecrations, and of the sacrifice of the peace offerings; ³⁸Which the LORD commanded Moses in mount Sinai, in the day that he commanded the children of Israel to offer their oblations to the LORD, in the wilderness of Sinai.

8 ¹And the LORD spoke to Moses, saying, ²Take Aaron and his sons with him, and the garments, and the anointing oil, and a bullock for the sin offering, and two rams, and a basket of unleavened bread; ³And gather you all the congregation together to the door of the tabernacle of the congregation. ⁴And Moses did as the LORD commanded him; and the assembly was gathered together to the door of the tabernacle of the congregation. ⁵And Moses said to the congregation, This is the thing which the LORD commanded to be done. ⁶And Moses brought Aaron and his sons, and washed them with water. ⁷And he put on him the

coat, and girded him with the girdle, and clothed him with the robe, and put the ephod on him, and he girded him with the curious girdle of the ephod, and bound it to him therewith. ⁸And he put the breastplate on him: also he put in the breastplate the Urim and the Thummim. ⁹And he put the turban on his head; also on the turban, even on his forefront, did he put the golden plate, the holy crown; as the LORD commanded Moses. ¹⁰And Moses took the anointing oil, and anointed the tabernacle and all that was therein, and sanctified them. ¹¹And he sprinkled thereof on the altar seven times, and anointed the altar and all his vessels, both the laver and his foot, to sanctify them. ¹²And he poured of the anointing oil on Aaron's head, and anointed him, to sanctify him. ¹³And Moses brought Aaron's sons, and put coats on them, and girded them with girdles, and put bonnets on them; as the LORD commanded Moses. ¹⁴And he brought the bullock for the sin offering: and Aaron and his sons laid their hands on the head of the bullock for the sin offering. ¹⁵And he slew it; and Moses took the blood, and put it on the horns of the altar round about with his finger, and purified the altar, and poured the blood at the bottom of the altar, and sanctified it, to make reconciliation on it. ¹⁶And he took all the fat that was on the inwards, and the lobe above the liver, and the two kidneys, and their fat, and Moses burned it on the altar. ¹⁷But the bullock, and his hide, his flesh, and his dung, he burnt with fire without the camp; as the LORD commanded Moses. ¹⁸And he brought the ram for the burnt offering: and Aaron and his sons laid their hands on the head of the ram. ¹⁹And he killed it; and Moses sprinkled the blood on the altar round about. ²⁰And he cut the ram into pieces; and Moses burnt the head, and the pieces, and the fat. ²¹And he washed the inwards and the legs in water; and Moses burnt the whole ram on the altar: it was a burnt sacrifice for a sweet smell, and an offering made by fire to the LORD; as the LORD commanded Moses. ²²And he brought the other ram, the ram of consecration: and Aaron and his sons laid their hands on the head of the ram. ²³And he slew it; and Moses took of the blood of it, and put it on the tip of Aaron's right ear, and on the thumb of his right hand, and on the great toe of his right foot. ²⁴And he brought Aaron's sons, and Moses put of the blood on the tip of their right ear, and on the thumbs of their right hands, and on the great toes of their right feet: and Moses sprinkled the blood on the altar round about. ²⁵And he took the fat, and the rump, and all the fat that was on the inwards, and the lobe above the liver, and the two kidneys, and their fat, and the right shoulder: ²⁶And out of the basket of unleavened bread, that was before the LORD, he took one unleavened cake, and a cake of oiled bread, and one wafer, and put them on the fat, and on the right shoulder: ²⁷And he put all on Aaron's hands, and on his sons' hands, and waved them for a wave offering before the LORD. ²⁸And Moses took them from off their hands, and burnt them on the altar on the burnt offering: they were consecrations for a sweet smell: it is an offering made by fire to the LORD. ²⁹And Moses took the breast, and waved it for a wave offering before the LORD: for of the ram of consecration it was Moses' part; as the LORD commanded Moses. ³⁰And Moses took of the anointing oil, and of the blood which was on the altar, and sprinkled it on Aaron, and on his garments, and on his sons, and on his sons' garments with him; and sanctified Aaron, and his garments, and his sons, and his sons' garments with him. ³¹And Moses said to Aaron and to his sons, Boil the flesh at the door of the tabernacle of the congregation: and there eat it with the bread that is in the basket of consecrations, as I commanded, saying, Aaron and his sons shall eat it. ³²And that which remains of the flesh and of the bread shall you burn with fire. ³³And you shall not go out of the door of the tabernacle of the congregation in seven days, until the days of your consecration be at an end: for seven days shall he consecrate you. ³⁴As he has done this day, so the LORD has commanded to do, to make an atonement for you. ³⁵Therefore shall you abide at the door of the tabernacle of the congregation day and night seven days, and keep the charge of the LORD, that you die not: for so I am commanded. ³⁶So Aaron and his sons did all things which the LORD commanded by the hand of Moses.

9 ¹And it came to pass on the eighth day, that Moses called Aaron and his sons, and the elders of Israel; ²And he said to Aaron, Take you a young calf for a sin offering, and a ram for a burnt offering, without blemish, and offer them before the LORD. ³And to the children of Israel you shall speak, saying, Take you a kid of the goats for a sin offering; and a calf and a lamb, both of the first year, without blemish, for a burnt offering; ⁴Also a bullock and a ram for peace offerings, to sacrifice before the LORD; and a meat offering mingled with oil: for to day the LORD will appear to you. ⁵And they brought that which Moses commanded before the tabernacle of the congregation: and all the congregation drew near and stood before the LORD. ⁶And Moses said, This is the thing which the LORD commanded that you should do: and the glory of the LORD shall appear to you. ⁷And Moses said to Aaron, Go to the altar, and offer your sin offering, and your burnt offering, and make an atonement for yourself, and for the people: and offer the offering of the people, and make an atonement for them; as the LORD commanded. ⁸Aaron therefore went to the altar, and slew the calf of the sin offering, which was for himself. ⁹And the sons of Aaron brought the blood to him: and he dipped his finger in the blood, and put it on the horns of the altar, and poured out the blood at the bottom of the altar: ¹⁰But the fat, and the kidneys, and the lobe above the liver of the sin offering, he burnt on the altar; as the LORD commanded Moses. ¹¹And the flesh and the hide he burnt with fire without the camp. ¹²And he slew the burnt offering; and Aaron's sons presented to him the blood, which he sprinkled round about on the altar. ¹³And they presented the burnt offering to him, with the pieces thereof, and the head: and he burnt them on the altar. ¹⁴And he did wash the inwards and the legs, and burnt them on the burnt offering on the altar. ¹⁵And he brought the people's offering, and took the goat, which was the sin offering for the people, and slew it, and offered it for sin, as the first. ¹⁶And he brought the burnt offering, and offered it according to the manner. ¹⁷And he brought the meat offering, and took an handful thereof, and burnt it on the altar, beside the burnt sacrifice of the morning. ¹⁸He slew also the bullock and the ram for a sacrifice of peace offerings, which was for the people: and Aaron's sons presented to him the blood, which he sprinkled on the altar round about, ¹⁹And the fat of the bullock and of the ram, the rump, and that which covers the inwards, and the kidneys, and the lobe above the liver: ²⁰And they put the fat on the breasts, and he burnt the fat on the altar: ²¹And the breasts and the right shoulder Aaron waved for a wave offering before the LORD; as Moses commanded. ²²And Aaron lifted up his hand toward the people, and blessed them, and came down from offering of the sin offering, and the burnt offering, and peace offerings. ²³And Moses and Aaron went into the tabernacle of the congregation, and came out, and blessed the people: and the glory of the LORD appeared to all the people. ²⁴And there came a fire out from before the LORD, and consumed on the altar the burnt offering and the fat: which when all the people saw, they shouted, and fell on their faces.

10 ¹And Nadab and Abihu, the sons of Aaron, took either of them his censer, and put fire therein, and put incense thereon, and offered strange fire before the LORD, which he commanded them not. ²And there went out fire from the LORD, and devoured them, and they died before the LORD. ³Then Moses said to Aaron, This is it that the LORD spoke, saying, I will be sanctified in them that come near me, and before all the people I will be glorified. And Aaron held his peace. ⁴And Moses called Mishael and Elzaphan, the sons of Uzziel the uncle of Aaron, and said to them, Come near, carry your brothers from before the sanctuary out of the camp. ⁵So they went near, and carried them in their coats out of the camp; as Moses had said. ⁶And Moses said to Aaron, and to Eleazar and to Ithamar, his sons, Uncover not your heads, neither rend your clothes; lest you die, and lest wrath come on all the people: but let your brothers, the whole house of Israel, mourn the burning which the LORD has kindled. ⁷And you shall not go out from the door of the tabernacle of the congregation, lest you die: for the anointing oil of the LORD is on you. And they did according to the word of Moses. ⁸And the LORD spoke to Aaron, saying, ⁹Do not drink wine nor strong drink, you, nor your sons with you, when you go into the tabernacle of the congregation, lest you die: it shall be a statute for ever throughout your generations: ¹⁰And that you may put difference between holy and unholy, and between unclean and clean; ¹¹And that you may teach the children of Israel all the statutes which the LORD has spoken to them by the hand of Moses. ¹²And Moses spoke to Aaron, and to Eleazar and to Ithamar, his sons that were left, Take the meat offering that remains of the offerings of the LORD made by fire, and eat it without leaven beside the altar: for it is most holy: ¹³And you shall eat it in the holy place, because it is your due, and your sons' due, of the sacrifices of the LORD made by fire: for so I am commanded. ¹⁴And the wave breast and heave shoulder shall you eat in a clean place; you, and your sons, and your daughters with you: for they be your due, and your sons' due, which are given out of the sacrifices of peace offerings of the children of Israel. ¹⁵The heave shoulder and the wave breast shall they bring with the offerings made by fire of the fat, to wave it for a wave offering before the LORD; and it shall be yours, and your sons' with you, by a statute for ever; as the LORD has commanded. ¹⁶And Moses diligently sought the goat of the sin offering, and, behold, it was burnt: and he was angry with Eleazar and Ithamar, the sons of Aaron which were left alive, saying, ¹⁷Why have you not eaten the sin offering in the holy place, seeing it is most holy, and God has given it you to bear the iniquity of the congregation, to make atonement for them before the LORD? ¹⁸Behold, the blood of it was not brought in within the holy place: you should indeed have eaten it in the holy place, as I commanded. ¹⁹And Aaron said to Moses, Behold, this day have they offered their sin offering and their burnt offering before the LORD; and such things have befallen me: and if I had eaten the sin offering to day, should it have been accepted in the sight of the LORD? ²⁰And when Moses heard that, he was content.

11 ¹And the LORD spoke to Moses and to Aaron, saying to them, ²Speak to the children of Israel, saying, These are the beasts which you shall eat among all the beasts that are on the earth. ³Whatever parts the hoof, and is cloven footed, and chews the cud, among the beasts, that shall you eat. ⁴Nevertheless these shall you not eat of them that chew the cud, or of them that divide the hoof: as the camel, because he chews the cud, but divides not the hoof; he is unclean to you. ⁵And the coney, because he chews the cud, but divides not the hoof; he is unclean to you. ⁶And the hare, because he chews the cud, but divides not the hoof; he is unclean to you. ⁷And the swine, though he divide the hoof, and be cloven footed, yet he chews not the cud; he is unclean to you. ⁸Of their flesh shall you not eat, and their carcass shall you not touch; they are unclean to you. ⁹These shall you eat of all that are in the waters: whatever has fins and scales in the waters, in the seas, and in the rivers, them shall you eat. ¹⁰And all that have not fins and scales in the seas, and in the rivers, of all that move in the waters, and of any living thing which is in the waters, they shall be an abomination to you: ¹¹They shall be even an abomination to you; you shall not eat of their flesh, but you shall have their carcasses in abomination. ¹²Whatever has no fins nor scales in the waters, that shall be an abomination to you. ¹³And these are they which you shall have in abomination among the fowls; they shall not be eaten, they are an abomination: the eagle, and the ossifrage, and the ospray, ¹⁴And the vulture, and the kite after his kind; ¹⁵Every raven after his kind; ¹⁶And the owl, and the night hawk, and the cuckow, and the hawk after his kind, ¹⁷And the little owl, and the cormorant, and the great owl, ¹⁸And the swan, and the pelican, and the gier eagle, ¹⁹And the stork, the heron after her kind, and the lapwing, and the bat. ²⁰All fowls that creep, going on all four, shall be an abomination to you. ²¹Yet these may you eat of every flying creeping thing that goes on all four, which have legs above their feet, to leap with on the earth; ²²Even these of them you may eat; the locust after his kind, and the bald locust after his kind, and the beetle after his kind, and the grasshopper after his kind. ²³But all other flying creeping things, which have four feet, shall be an abomination to you. ²⁴And for these you shall be unclean: whoever touches the carcass of them shall be unclean until the even. ²⁵And whoever bears any of the carcass of them shall wash his clothes, and be unclean until the even. ²⁶The carcasses of every beast which divides the hoof, and is not cloven footed, nor chews the cud, are unclean to you: every one that touches them shall be unclean. ²⁷And whatever goes on his paws, among all

manner of beasts that go on all four, those are unclean to you: whoever touches their carcass shall be unclean until the even. ²⁸And he that bears the carcass of them shall wash his clothes, and be unclean until the even: they are unclean to you. ²⁹These also shall be unclean to you among the creeping things that creep on the earth; the weasel, and the mouse, and the tortoise after his kind, ³⁰And the ferret, and the chameleon, and the lizard, and the snail, and the mole. ³¹These are unclean to you among all that creep: whoever does touch them, when they be dead, shall be unclean until the even. ³²And on whatever any of them, when they are dead, does fall, it shall be unclean; whether it be any vessel of wood, or raiment, or skin, or sack, whatever vessel it be, wherein any work is done, it must be put into water, and it shall be unclean until the even; so it shall be cleansed. ³³And every earthen vessel, into where any of them falls, whatever is in it shall be unclean; and you shall break it. ³⁴Of all meat which may be eaten, that on which such water comes shall be unclean: and all drink that may be drunk in every such vessel shall be unclean. ³⁵And every thing whereupon any part of their carcass falls shall be unclean; whether it be oven, or ranges for pots, they shall be broken down: for they are unclean and shall be unclean to you. ³⁶Nevertheless a fountain or pit, wherein there is plenty of water, shall be clean: but that which touches their carcass shall be unclean. ³⁷And if any part of their carcass fall on any sowing seed which is to be sown, it shall be clean. ³⁸But if any water be put on the seed, and any part of their carcass fall thereon, it shall be unclean to you. ³⁹And if any beast, of which you may eat, die; he that touches the carcass thereof shall be unclean until the even. ⁴⁰And he that eats of the carcass of it shall wash his clothes, and be unclean until the even: he also that bears the carcass of it shall wash his clothes, and be unclean until the even. ⁴¹And every creeping thing that creeps on the earth shall be an abomination; it shall not be eaten. ⁴²Whatever goes on the belly, and whatever goes on all four, or whatever has more feet among all creeping things that creep on the earth, them you shall not eat; for they are an abomination. ⁴³You shall not make yourselves abominable with any creeping thing that creeps, neither shall you make yourselves unclean with them, that you should be defiled thereby. ⁴⁴For I am the LORD your God: you shall therefore sanctify yourselves, and you shall be holy; for I am holy: neither shall you defile yourselves with any manner of creeping thing that creeps on the earth. ⁴⁵For I am the LORD that brings you up out of the land of Egypt, to be your God: you shall therefore be holy, for I am holy. ⁴⁶This is the law of the beasts, and of the fowl, and of every living creature that moves in the waters, and of every creature that creeps on the earth: ⁴⁷To make a difference between the unclean and the clean, and between the beast that may be eaten and the beast that may not be eaten.

12 ¹And the LORD spoke to Moses, saying, ²Speak to the children of Israel, saying, If a woman have conceived seed, and born a man child: then she shall be unclean seven days; according to the days of the separation for her infirmity shall she be unclean. ³And in the eighth day the flesh of his foreskin shall be circumcised. ⁴And she shall then continue in the blood of her purifying three and thirty days; she shall touch no hallowed thing, nor come into the sanctuary, until the days of her purifying be fulfilled. ⁵But if she bear a maid child, then she shall be unclean two weeks, as in her separation: and she shall continue in the blood of her purifying three score and six days. ⁶And when the days of her purifying are fulfilled, for a son, or for a daughter, she shall bring a lamb of the first year for a burnt offering, and a young pigeon, or a turtledove, for a sin offering, to the door of the tabernacle of the congregation, to the priest: ⁷Who shall offer it before the LORD, and make an atonement for her; and she shall be cleansed from the issue of her blood. This is the law for her that has born a male or a female. ⁸And if she be not able to bring a lamb, then she shall bring two turtles, or two young pigeons; the one for the burnt offering, and the other for a sin offering: and the priest shall make an atonement for her, and she shall be clean.

13 ¹And the LORD spoke to Moses and Aaron, saying, ²When a man shall have in the skin of his flesh a rising, a scab, or bright spot, and it be in the skin of his flesh like the plague of leprosy; then he shall be brought to Aaron the priest, or to one of his sons the priests: ³And the priest shall look on the plague in the skin of the flesh: and when the hair in the plague is turned white, and the plague in sight be deeper than the skin of his flesh, it is a plague of leprosy: and the priest shall look on him, and pronounce him unclean. ⁴If the bright spot be white in the skin of his flesh, and in sight be not deeper than the skin, and the hair thereof be not turned white; then the priest shall shut up him that has the plague seven days: ⁵And the priest shall look on him the seventh day: and, behold, if the plague in his sight be at a stay, and the plague spread not in the skin; then the priest shall shut him up seven days more: ⁶And the priest shall look on him again the seventh day: and, behold, if the plague be somewhat dark, and the plague spread not in the skin, the priest shall pronounce him clean: it is but a scab: and he shall wash his clothes, and be clean. ⁷But if the scab spread much abroad in the skin, after that he has been seen of the priest for his cleansing, he shall be seen of the priest again. ⁸And if the priest see that, behold, the scab spreads in the skin, then the priest shall pronounce him unclean: it is a leprosy. ⁹When the plague of leprosy is in a man, then he shall be brought to the priest; ¹⁰And the priest shall see him: and, behold, if the rising be white in the skin, and it have turned the hair white, and there be quick raw flesh in the rising; ¹¹It is an old leprosy in the skin of his flesh, and the priest shall pronounce him unclean, and shall not shut him up: for he is unclean. ¹²And if a leprosy break out abroad in the skin, and the leprosy cover all the skin of him that has the plague from his head even to his foot, wherever the priest looks; ¹³Then the priest shall consider: and, behold, if the leprosy have covered all his flesh, he shall pronounce him clean that has the plague: it is all turned white: he is clean. ¹⁴But when raw flesh appears in him, he shall be unclean. ¹⁵And the priest shall see the raw flesh, and pronounce him to be unclean: for the raw flesh is unclean: it is a leprosy. ¹⁶Or if the raw flesh turn again, and be changed to white, he shall come to the priest; ¹⁷And the priest shall see him: and, behold, if the plague be turned into white; then the priest shall pronounce him clean that has the plague: he is clean. ¹⁸The flesh also, in which, even in the skin thereof, was a boil, and is healed, ¹⁹And in the place of the boil there be a white rising, or a bright spot, white, and somewhat reddish, and it be showed to the priest; ²⁰And if, when the priest sees it, behold, it be in sight lower than the skin, and the hair thereof be turned white; the priest shall pronounce him unclean: it is a plague of leprosy broken out of the boil. ²¹But if the priest look on it, and, behold, there be no white hairs therein, and if it be not lower than the skin, but be somewhat dark; then the priest shall shut him up seven days: ²²And if it spread much abroad in the skin, then the priest shall pronounce him unclean: it is a plague. ²³But if the bright spot stay in his place, and spread not, it is a burning boil; and the priest shall pronounce him clean. ²⁴Or if there be any flesh, in the skin whereof there is a hot burning, and the quick flesh that burns have a white bright spot, somewhat reddish, or white; ²⁵Then the priest shall look on it: and, behold, if the hair in the bright spot be turned white, and it be in sight deeper than the skin; it is a leprosy broken out of the burning: why the priest shall pronounce him unclean: it is the plague of leprosy. ²⁶But if the priest look on it, and, behold, there be no white hair in the bright spot, and it be no lower than the other skin, but be somewhat dark; then the priest shall shut him up seven days: ²⁷And the priest shall look on him the seventh day: and if it be spread much abroad in the skin, then the priest shall pronounce him unclean: it is the plague of leprosy. ²⁸And if the bright spot stay in his place, and spread not in the skin, but it be somewhat dark; it is a rising of the burning, and the priest shall pronounce him clean: for it is an inflammation of the burning. ²⁹If a man or woman have a plague on the head or the beard; ³⁰Then the priest shall see the plague: and, behold, if it be in sight deeper than the skin; and there be in it a yellow thin hair; then the priest shall pronounce him unclean: it is a dry scale, even a leprosy on the head or beard. ³¹And if the priest look on the plague of the scale, and, behold, it be not in sight deeper than the skin, and that there is no black hair in it; then the priest shall shut up him that has the plague of the scale seven days: ³²And in the seventh day the priest shall look on the plague: and, behold, if the scale spread not, and there be in it no yellow hair, and the scale be not in sight deeper than the skin; ³³He shall be shaven, but the scale shall he not shave; and the priest shall shut up him that has the scale seven days more: ³⁴And in the seventh day the priest shall look on the scale: and, behold, if the scale be not spread in the skin, nor be in sight deeper than the skin; then the priest shall pronounce him clean: and he shall wash his clothes, and be clean. ³⁵But if the scale spread much in the skin after his cleansing; ³⁶Then the priest shall look on him: and, behold, if the scale be spread in the skin, the priest shall not seek for yellow hair; he is unclean. ³⁷But if the scale be in his sight at a stay, and that there is black hair grown up therein; the scale is healed, he is clean: and the priest shall pronounce him clean. ³⁸If a man also or a woman have in the skin of their flesh bright spots, even white bright spots; ³⁹Then the priest shall look: and, behold, if the bright spots in the skin of their flesh be darkish white; it is a freckled spot that grows in the skin; he is clean. ⁴⁰And the man whose hair is fallen off his head, he is bald; yet is he clean. ⁴¹And he that has his hair fallen off from the part of his head toward his face, he is forehead bald: yet is he clean. ⁴²And if there be in the bald head, or bald forehead, a white reddish sore; it is a leprosy sprung up in his bald head, or his bald forehead. ⁴³Then the priest shall look on it: and, behold, if the rising of the sore be white reddish in his bald head, or in his bald forehead, as the leprosy appears in the skin of the flesh; ⁴⁴He is a leprous man, he is unclean: the priest shall pronounce him utterly unclean; his plague is in his head. ⁴⁵And the leper in whom the plague is, his clothes shall be rent, and his head bore, and he shall put a covering on his upper lip, and shall cry, Unclean, unclean. ⁴⁶All the days wherein the plague shall be in him he shall be defiled; he is unclean: he shall dwell alone; without the camp shall his habitation be. ⁴⁷The garment also that the plague of leprosy is in, whether it be a woolen garment, or a linen garment; ⁴⁸Whether it be in the warp, or woof; of linen, or of woolen; whether in a skin, or in any thing made of skin; ⁴⁹And if the plague be greenish or reddish in the garment, or in the skin, either in the warp, or in the woof, or in any thing of skin; it is a plague of leprosy, and shall be showed to the priest: ⁵⁰And the priest shall look on the plague, and shut up it that has the plague seven days: ⁵¹And he shall look on the plague on the seventh day: if the plague be spread in the garment, either in the warp, or in the woof, or in a skin, or in any work that is made of skin; the plague is a fretting leprosy; it is unclean. ⁵²He shall therefore burn that garment, whether warp or woof, in woolen or in linen, or any thing of skin, wherein the plague is: for it is a fretting leprosy; it shall be burnt in the fire. ⁵³And if the priest shall look, and, behold, the plague be not spread in the garment, either in the warp, or in the woof, or in any thing of skin; ⁵⁴Then the priest shall command that they wash the thing wherein the plague is, and he shall shut it up seven days more: ⁵⁵And the priest shall look on the plague, after that it is washed: and, behold, if the plague have not changed his color, and the plague be not spread; it is unclean; you shall burn it in the fire; it is fret inward, whether it be bore within or without. ⁵⁶And if the priest look, and, behold, the plague be somewhat dark after the washing of it; then he shall rend it out of the garment, or out of the skin, or out of the warp, or out of the woof: ⁵⁷And if it appear still in the garment, either in the warp, or in the woof, or in any thing of skin; it is a spreading plague: you shall burn that wherein the plague is with fire. ⁵⁸And the garment, either warp, or woof, or whatever thing of skin it be, which you shall wash, if the plague be departed from them, then it shall be washed the second time, and shall be clean. ⁵⁹This is the law of the plague of leprosy in a garment of woolen or linen, either in the warp, or woof, or any thing of skins, to pronounce it clean, or to pronounce it unclean.

14 ¹And the LORD spoke to Moses, saying, ²This shall be the law of the leper in the day of his cleansing: He shall be brought to the priest: ³And the priest shall go forth out of the camp; and the priest shall look, and, behold, if the plague of leprosy be healed in the leper; ⁴Then shall the priest command to take for him that is to be cleansed two birds alive and clean, and cedar wood, and scarlet, and hyssop: ⁵And the priest shall command that one of the birds be killed in an earthen vessel over running water: ⁶As for the living bird, he shall take it, and the cedar wood, and the scarlet, and the hyssop, and shall dip them and the living bird in the blood of the bird that was killed over the running water: ⁷And he shall sprinkle on him that is to be cleansed from the leprosy seven times, and shall pronounce him clean, and shall let the living bird loose into the open field. ⁸And he that is to be cleansed shall wash his clothes, and shave off all his hair, and wash himself in water, that he may be clean: and after that he shall come into the camp, and shall tarry abroad out of his tent seven days. ⁹But it shall be on the seventh day, that he shall shave all his hair off his head and his beard and his eyebrows, even all his hair he shall shave off: and he shall wash his clothes, also he shall wash his flesh in water, and he shall be clean. ¹⁰And on the eighth day he shall take two he lambs without blemish, and one ewe lamb of the first year without blemish, and three tenth deals of fine flour for a meat offering, mingled with oil, and one log of oil. ¹¹And the priest that makes him clean shall present the man that is to be made clean, and those things, before the LORD, at the door of the tabernacle of the congregation: ¹²And the priest shall take one he lamb, and offer him for a trespass offering, and the log of oil, and wave them for a wave offering before the LORD: ¹³And he shall slay the lamb in the place where he shall kill the sin offering and the burnt offering, in the holy place: for as the sin offering is the priest's, so is the trespass offering: it is most holy: ¹⁴And the priest shall take some of the blood of the trespass offering, and the priest shall put it on the tip of the right ear of him that is to be cleansed, and on the thumb of his right hand, and on the great toe of his right foot: ¹⁵And the priest shall take some of the log of oil, and pour it into the palm of his own left hand: ¹⁶And the priest shall dip his right finger in the oil that is in his left hand, and shall sprinkle of the oil with his finger seven times before the LORD: ¹⁷And of the rest of the oil that is in his hand shall the priest put on the tip of the right ear of him that is to be cleansed, and on the thumb of his right hand, and on the great toe of his right foot, on the blood of the trespass offering: ¹⁸And the remnant of the oil that is in the priest's hand he shall pour on the head of him that is to be cleansed: and the priest shall make an atonement for him before the LORD. ¹⁹And the priest shall offer the sin offering, and make an atonement for him that is to be cleansed from his uncleanness; and afterward he shall kill the burnt offering: ²⁰And the priest shall offer the burnt offering and the meat offering on the altar: and the priest shall make an atonement for him, and he shall be clean. ²¹And if he be poor, and cannot get so much; then he shall take one lamb for a trespass offering to be waved, to make an atonement for him, and one tenth deal of fine flour mingled with oil for a meat offering, and a log of oil; ²²And two turtledoves, or two young pigeons, such as he is able to get; and the one shall be a sin offering, and the other a burnt offering. ²³And he shall bring them on the eighth day for his cleansing to the priest, to the door of the tabernacle of the congregation, before the LORD. ²⁴And the priest shall take the lamb of the trespass offering, and the log of oil, and the priest shall wave them for a wave offering before the LORD: ²⁵And he shall kill the lamb of the trespass offering, and the priest shall take some of the blood of the trespass offering, and put it on the tip of the right ear of him that is to be cleansed, and on the thumb of his right hand, and on the great toe of his right foot: ²⁶And the priest shall pour of the oil into the palm of his own left hand: ²⁷And the priest shall sprinkle with his right finger some of the oil that is in his left hand seven times before the LORD: ²⁸And the priest shall put of the oil that is in his hand on the tip of the right ear of him that is to be cleansed, and on the thumb of his right hand, and on the great toe of his right foot, on the place of the blood of the trespass offering: ²⁹And the rest of the oil that is in the priest's hand he shall put on the head of him that is to be cleansed, to make an atonement for him before the LORD. ³⁰And he shall offer the one of the turtledoves, or of the young pigeons, such as he can get; ³¹Even such as he is able to get, the one for a sin offering, and the other for a burnt offering, with the meat offering: and the priest shall make an atonement for him that is to be cleansed before the LORD. ³²This is the law of him in whom is the plague of leprosy, whose hand is not able to get that which pertains to his cleansing. ³³And the LORD spoke to Moses and to Aaron, saying, ³⁴When you be come into the land of Canaan, which I give to you for a possession, and I put the plague of leprosy in a house of the land of your possession; ³⁵And he that owns the house shall come and tell the priest, saying, It seems to me there is as it were a plague in the house: ³⁶Then the priest shall command that they empty the house, before the priest go into it to see the plague, that all that is in the house be not made unclean: and afterward the priest shall go in to see the house: ³⁷And he shall look on the plague, and, behold, if the plague be in the walls of the house with hollow strakes, greenish or reddish, which in sight are lower than the wall; ³⁸Then the priest shall go out of the house to the door of the house, and shut up the house seven days: ³⁹And the priest shall come again the seventh day, and shall look: and, behold, if the plague be spread in the walls of the house; ⁴⁰Then the priest shall command that they take away the stones in which the plague is, and they shall cast them into an unclean place without the city: ⁴¹And he shall cause the house to be scraped within round about, and they shall pour out the dust that they scrape off without the city into an unclean place: ⁴²And they shall take other stones, and put them in the place of those stones; and he shall take other mortar, and shall plaster the house. ⁴³And if the plague come again, and break out in the house, after that he has taken away the stones, and after he has scraped the house, and after it is plastered; ⁴⁴Then the priest shall come and look, and, behold, if the plague be spread in the house, it is a fretting leprosy in the house; it is unclean. ⁴⁵And he shall break down the house, the stones of it, and the timber thereof, and all the mortar of the house; and he shall carry them forth out of the city into an unclean place. ⁴⁶Moreover he that goes into the house all the while that it is shut up shall be unclean until the even. ⁴⁷And he that lies in the house shall wash his clothes; and he that eats in the house shall wash his clothes. ⁴⁸And if the priest shall come in, and look on it, and, behold, the plague has not spread in the house, after the house was plastered: then the priest shall pronounce the house clean, because the plague is healed. ⁴⁹And he shall take to cleanse the house two birds, and cedar wood, and scarlet, and hyssop: ⁵⁰And he shall kill the one of the birds in an earthen vessel over running water: ⁵¹And he shall take the cedar wood, and the hyssop, and the scarlet, and the living bird, and dip them in the blood of the slain bird, and in the running water, and sprinkle the house seven times: ⁵²And he shall cleanse the house with the blood of the bird, and with the running water, and with the living bird, and with the cedar wood, and with the hyssop, and with the scarlet: ⁵³But he shall let go the living bird out of the city into the open fields, and make an atonement for the house: and it shall be clean. ⁵⁴This is the law for all manner of plague of leprosy, and scale, ⁵⁵And for the leprosy of a garment, and of a house, ⁵⁶And for a rising, and for a scab, and for a bright spot: ⁵⁷To teach when it is unclean, and when it is clean: this is the law of leprosy.

15 ¹And the LORD spoke to Moses and to Aaron, saying, ²Speak to the children of Israel, and say to them, When any man has a running issue out of his flesh, because of his issue he is unclean. ³And this shall be his uncleanness in his issue: whether his flesh run with his issue, or his flesh be stopped from his issue, it is his uncleanness. ⁴Every bed, where on he lies that has the issue, is unclean: and every thing, where on he sits, shall be unclean. ⁵And whoever touches his bed shall wash his clothes, and bathe himself in water, and be unclean until the even. ⁶And he that sits on any thing where on he sat that has the issue shall wash his clothes, and bathe himself in water, and be unclean until the even. ⁷And he that touches the flesh of him that has the issue shall wash his clothes, and bathe himself in water, and be unclean until the even. ⁸And if he that has the issue spit on him that is clean; then he shall wash his clothes, and bathe himself in water, and be unclean until the even. ⁹And what saddle soever he rides on that has the issue shall be unclean. ¹⁰And whoever touches any thing that was under him shall be unclean until the even: and he that bears any of those things shall wash his clothes, and bathe himself in water, and be unclean until the even. ¹¹And whomsoever he touches that has the issue, and has not rinsed his hands in water, he shall wash his clothes, and bathe himself in water, and be unclean until the even. ¹²And the vessel of earth, that he touches which has the issue, shall be broken: and every vessel of wood shall be rinsed in water. ¹³And when he that has an issue is cleansed of his issue; then he shall number to himself seven days for his cleansing, and wash his clothes, and bathe his flesh in running water, and shall be clean. ¹⁴And on the eighth day he shall take to him two turtledoves, or two young pigeons, and come before the LORD to the door of the tabernacle of the congregation, and give them to the priest: ¹⁵And the priest shall offer them, the one for a sin offering, and the other for a burnt offering; and the priest shall make an atonement for him before the LORD for his issue. ¹⁶And if any man's seed of copulation go out from him, then he shall wash all his flesh in water, and be unclean until the even. ¹⁷And every garment, and every skin, where on is the seed of copulation, shall be washed with water, and be unclean until the even. ¹⁸The woman also with whom man shall lie with seed of copulation, they shall both bathe themselves in water, and be unclean until the even. ¹⁹And if a woman have an issue, and her issue in her flesh be blood, she shall be put apart seven days: and whoever touches her shall be unclean until the even. ²⁰And every thing that she lies on in her separation shall be unclean: every thing also that she sits on shall be unclean. ²¹And whoever touches her bed shall wash his clothes, and bathe himself in water, and be unclean until the even. ²²And whoever touches any thing that she sat on shall wash his clothes, and bathe himself in water, and be unclean until the even. ²³And if it be on her bed, or on any thing where on she sits, when he touches it, he shall be unclean until the even. ²⁴And if any man lie with her at all, and her flowers be on him, he shall be unclean seven days; and all the bed where on he lies shall be unclean. ²⁵And if a woman have an issue of her blood many days out of the time of her separation, or if it run beyond the time of her separation; all the days of the issue of her uncleanness shall be as the days of her separation: she shall be unclean. ²⁶Every bed where on she lies all the days of her issue shall be to her as the bed of her separation: and whatever she sits on shall be unclean, as the uncleanness of her separation. ²⁷And whoever touches those things shall be unclean, and shall wash his clothes, and bathe himself in water, and be unclean until the even. ²⁸But if she be cleansed of her issue, then she shall number to herself seven days, and after that she shall be clean. ²⁹And on the eighth day she shall take to her two turtles, or two young pigeons, and bring them to the priest, to the door of the tabernacle of the congregation. ³⁰And the priest shall offer the one for a sin offering, and the other for a burnt offering; and the priest shall make an atonement for her before the LORD for the issue of her uncleanness. ³¹Thus shall you separate the children of Israel from their uncleanness; that they die not in their uncleanness, when they defile my tabernacle that is among them. ³²This is the law of him that has an issue, and of him whose seed goes from him, and is defiled therewith; ³³And of her that is sick of her flowers, and of him that has an issue, of the man, and of the woman, and of him that lies with her that is unclean.

16 ¹And the LORD spoke to Moses after the death of the two sons of Aaron, when they offered before the LORD, and died; ²And the LORD said to Moses, Speak to Aaron your brother, that he come not at all times into the holy place within the veil before the mercy seat, which is on the ark; that he die not: for I will appear in the cloud on the mercy seat. ³Thus shall Aaron come into the holy place: with a young bullock for a sin offering, and a ram for a burnt offering. ⁴He shall put on the holy linen coat, and he shall have the linen breeches on his flesh, and shall be girded with a linen girdle, and with the linen turban shall he be attired: these are holy garments; therefore shall he wash his flesh in water, and so put them on. ⁵And he shall take of the congregation of the children of Israel two kids of the goats for a sin offering, and one ram for a burnt offering. ⁶And Aaron shall offer his bullock of the sin offering, which is for himself, and make an atonement for himself, and for his house. ⁷And he shall take the two goats, and present them before the LORD at the door of the tabernacle of the congregation. ⁸And Aaron shall cast lots on the two goats; one lot for the LORD, and the other lot for the scapegoat. ⁹And Aaron shall bring the goat on which the LORD's lot fell, and offer him for a sin offering. ¹⁰But the goat, on which the lot fell to be the scapegoat, shall be presented alive before the LORD, to make an atonement with him, and to let him go for a scapegoat into the wilderness. ¹¹And Aaron shall bring the bullock of the sin offering, which is for himself, and shall make an atonement for himself, and for his house, and shall kill the bullock of the sin offering which is for himself: ¹²And he shall take a censer full of burning coals of fire from off the altar before the LORD, and his hands full of sweet incense beaten small, and bring it within the veil: ¹³And he shall put the incense on the fire before the LORD, that the cloud of the incense may cover the mercy seat that is on the testimony, that he die not: ¹⁴And he shall take of the blood of the bullock, and sprinkle it with his finger on the mercy seat eastward; and before the mercy seat shall he sprinkle of the blood with his finger seven times. ¹⁵Then shall he kill the goat of the sin offering, that is for the people, and bring his blood within the veil, and do with that blood as he did with the blood of the bullock, and sprinkle it on the mercy seat, and before the mercy seat: ¹⁶And he shall make an atonement for the holy place, because of the uncleanness of the children of Israel, and because of their transgressions in all their sins: and so shall he do for the tabernacle of the congregation, that remains among them in the middle of their uncleanness. ¹⁷And there shall be no man in the tabernacle of the congregation when he goes in to make an atonement in the holy place, until he come out, and have made an atonement for himself, and for his household, and for all the congregation of Israel. ¹⁸And he shall go out to the altar that is before the LORD, and make an atonement for it; and shall take of the blood of the bullock, and of the blood of the goat, and put it on the horns of the altar round about. ¹⁹And he shall sprinkle of the blood on it with his finger seven times, and cleanse it, and hallow it from the uncleanness of the children of Israel. ²⁰And when he has made an end of reconciling the holy place, and the tabernacle of the congregation, and the altar, he shall bring the live goat: ²¹And Aaron shall lay both his hands on the head of the live goat, and confess over him all the iniquities of the children of Israel, and all their transgressions in all their sins, putting them on the head of the goat, and shall send him away by the hand of a fit man into the wilderness: ²²And the goat shall bear on him all their iniquities to a land not inhabited: and he shall let go the goat in the wilderness. ²³And Aaron shall come into the tabernacle of the congregation, and shall put off the linen garments, which he put on when he went into the holy place, and shall leave them there: ²⁴And he shall wash his flesh with water in the holy place, and put on his garments, and come forth, and offer his burnt offering, and the burnt offering of the people, and make an atonement for himself, and for the people. ²⁵And the fat of the sin offering shall he burn on the altar. ²⁶And he that let go the goat for the scapegoat shall wash his clothes, and bathe his flesh in water, and afterward come into the camp. ²⁷And the bullock for the sin offering, and the goat for the sin offering, whose blood was brought in to make atonement in the holy place, shall one carry forth without the camp; and they shall burn in the fire their skins, and their flesh, and their dung. ²⁸And he that burns them shall wash his clothes, and bathe his flesh in water, and afterward he shall come into the camp. ²⁹And this shall be a statute for ever to you: that in the seventh month, on the tenth day of the month, you shall afflict your souls, and do no work at all, whether it be one of your own country, or a stranger that sojourns among you: ³⁰For on that day shall the priest make an atonement for you, to cleanse you, that you may be clean from all your sins before the LORD. ³¹It shall be a sabbath of rest to you, and you shall afflict your souls, by a statute for ever. ³²And the priest, whom he shall anoint, and whom he shall consecrate to minister in the priest's office in his father's stead, shall make the atonement, and shall put on the linen clothes, even the holy garments: ³³And he shall make an atonement for the holy sanctuary, and he shall make an atonement for the tabernacle of the congregation, and for the altar, and he shall make an atonement for the priests, and for all the people of the congregation. ³⁴And this shall be an everlasting statute to you, to make an atonement for the children of Israel for all their sins once a year. And he did as the LORD commanded Moses.

17 ¹And the LORD spoke to Moses, saying, ²Speak to Aaron, and to his sons, and to all the children of Israel, and say to them; This is the thing which the LORD has commanded, saying, ³What man soever there be of the house of Israel, that kills an ox, or lamb, or goat, in the camp, or that kills it out of the camp, ⁴And brings it not to the door of the tabernacle of the congregation, to offer an offering to the LORD before the tabernacle of the LORD; blood shall be imputed to that man; he has shed blood; and that man shall be cut off from among his people: ⁵To the end that the children of Israel may bring their sacrifices, which they offer in the open field, even that they may bring them to the LORD, to the door of the tabernacle of the congregation, to the priest, and offer them for peace offerings to the LORD. ⁶And the priest shall sprinkle the blood on the altar of the LORD at the door of the tabernacle of the congregation, and burn the fat for a sweet smell to the LORD. ⁷And they shall no more offer their sacrifices to devils, after whom they have gone a whoring. This shall be a statute for ever to them throughout their generations. ⁸And you shall say to them, Whatever man there be of the house of Israel, or of the strangers which sojourn among you, that offers a burnt offering or sacrifice, ⁹And brings it not to the door of the tabernacle of the congregation, to offer it to the LORD; even that man shall be cut off from among his people. ¹⁰And whatever man there be of the house of Israel, or of the strangers that sojourn among you, that eats any manner of blood; I will even set my face against that soul that eats blood, and will cut him off from among his people. ¹¹For the life of the flesh is in the blood: and I have given it to you on the altar to make an atonement for your souls: for it is the blood that makes an atonement for the soul. ¹²Therefore I said to the children of Israel, No soul of you shall eat blood, neither shall any stranger that sojourns among you eat blood. ¹³And whatever man there be of the children of Israel, or of the strangers that sojourn among you, which hunts and catches any beast or fowl that may be eaten; he shall even pour out the blood thereof, and cover it with dust. ¹⁴For it is the life of all flesh; the blood of it is for the life thereof: therefore I said to the children of Israel, You shall eat the blood of no manner of flesh: for the life of all flesh is the blood thereof: whoever eats it shall be cut off. ¹⁵And every soul that eats that which died of itself, or that which was torn with beasts, whether it be one of your own country, or a stranger, he shall both wash his clothes, and bathe himself in water, and be unclean until the even: then shall he be clean. ¹⁶But if he wash them not, nor bathe his flesh; then he shall bear his iniquity.

18 ¹And the LORD spoke to Moses, saying, ²Speak to the children of Israel, and say to them, I am the LORD your God. ³After the doings of the land of Egypt, wherein you dwelled, shall you not do: and after the doings of the land of Canaan, where I bring you, shall you not do: neither shall you walk in their ordinances. ⁴You shall do my judgments, and keep my ordinances, to walk therein: I am the LORD your God. ⁵You shall therefore keep my statutes, and my judgments: which if a man do, he shall live in them: I am the LORD. ⁶None of you shall approach to any that is near of kin to him, to uncover their nakedness: I am the LORD. ⁷The nakedness of your father, or the nakedness of your mother, shall you not uncover: she is your mother; you shall not uncover her nakedness. ⁸The nakedness of your father's wife shall you not uncover: it is your father's nakedness. ⁹The nakedness of your sister, the daughter of your father, or daughter of your mother, whether she be born at home, or born abroad, even their nakedness you shall not uncover. ¹⁰The nakedness of your son's daughter, or of your daughter's daughter, even their nakedness you shall not uncover: for theirs is your own nakedness. ¹¹The nakedness of your father's wife's daughter, begotten of your father, she is your sister, you shall not uncover her nakedness. ¹²You shall not uncover the nakedness of your father's sister: she is your father's near kinswoman. ¹³You shall not uncover the nakedness of your mother's sister: for she is your mother's near kinswoman. ¹⁴You shall not uncover the nakedness of your father's brother, you shall not approach to his wife: she is your aunt. ¹⁵You shall not uncover the nakedness of your daughter in law: she is your son's wife; you shall not uncover her nakedness. ¹⁶You shall not uncover the nakedness of your brother's wife: it is your brother's nakedness. ¹⁷You shall not uncover the nakedness of a woman and her daughter, neither shall you take her son's daughter, or her daughter's daughter, to uncover her nakedness; for they are her near kinswomen: it is wickedness. ¹⁸Neither shall you take a wife to her sister, to vex her, to uncover her nakedness, beside the other in her life time. ¹⁹Also you shall not approach to a woman to uncover her nakedness, as long as she is put apart for her uncleanness. ²⁰Moreover you shall not lie carnally with your neighbor's wife, to defile yourself with her. ²¹And you shall not let any of your seed pass through the fire to Molech, neither shall you profane the name of your God: I am the LORD. ²²You shall not lie with mankind, as with womankind: it is abomination. ²³Neither shall you lie with any beast to defile yourself therewith: neither shall any woman stand before a beast to lie down thereto: it is confusion. ²⁴Defile not you yourselves in any of these things: for in all these the nations are defiled which I cast out before you: ²⁵And the land is defiled: therefore I do visit the iniquity thereof on it, and the land itself vomits out her inhabitants. ²⁶You shall therefore keep my statutes and my judgments, and shall not commit any of these abominations; neither any of your own nation, nor any stranger that sojourns among you: ²⁷(For all these abominations have the men of the land done, which were before you, and the land is defiled;) ²⁸That the land spew not you out also, when you defile it, as it spewed out the nations that were before you. ²⁹For whoever shall commit any of these abominations, even the souls that commit them shall be cut off from among their people. ³⁰Therefore shall you keep my ordinance, that you commit not any one of these abominable customs, which were committed before you, and that you defile not yourselves therein: I am the LORD your God.

19 ¹And the LORD spoke to Moses, saying, ²Speak to all the congregation of the children of Israel, and say to them, You shall be holy: for I the LORD your God am holy. ³You shall fear every man his mother, and his father, and keep my sabbaths: I am the LORD your God. ⁴Turn you not to idols, nor make to yourselves molten gods: I am the LORD your God. ⁵And if you offer a sacrifice of peace offerings to the LORD, you shall offer it at your own will. ⁶It shall be eaten the same day you offer it, and on the morrow: and if any remain until the third day, it shall be burnt in the fire. ⁷And if it be eaten at all on the third day, it is abominable; it shall not be accepted. ⁸Therefore every one that eats it shall bear his iniquity, because he has profaned the hallowed thing of the LORD: and that soul shall be cut off from among his people. ⁹And when you reap the harvest of your land, you shall not wholly reap the corners of your field, neither shall you gather the gleanings of your harvest. ¹⁰And you shall not glean your vineyard, neither shall you gather every grape of your vineyard; you shall leave them for the poor and stranger: I am the LORD your God. ¹¹You shall not steal, neither deal falsely, neither lie one to another. ¹²And you shall not swear by my name falsely, neither shall you profane the name of your God: I am the LORD. ¹³You shall not defraud your neighbor, neither rob him: the wages of him that is hired shall not abide with you all night until the morning. ¹⁴You shall not curse the deaf, nor put a stumbling block before the blind, but shall fear your God: I am the LORD. ¹⁵You shall do no unrighteousness in judgment: you shall not respect the person of the poor, nor honor the person of the mighty: but in righteousness shall you judge your neighbor. ¹⁶You shall not go up and down as a talebearer among your people: neither shall you stand against the blood of your neighbor; I am the LORD. ¹⁷You shall not hate your brother in your heart: you shall in any wise rebuke your neighbor, and not suffer sin on him. ¹⁸You shall not avenge, nor bear any grudge against the children of your people, but you shall love your neighbor as yourself: I am the LORD. ¹⁹You shall keep my statutes. You shall not let your cattle engender with a diverse kind: you shall not sow your field with mingled seed: neither shall a garment mingled of linen and woolen come on you. ²⁰And whoever lies carnally with a woman, that is a female slave, betrothed to an husband, and not at all redeemed, nor freedom given her; she shall be scourged; they shall not be put to death, because she was not free. ²¹And he shall bring his trespass offering to the LORD, to the door of the tabernacle of the congregation, even a ram for a trespass offering. ²²And the priest shall make an atonement for him with the ram of the trespass offering before the LORD for his sin which he has done: and the sin which he has done shall be forgiven him. ²³And when you shall come into the land, and shall have planted all manner of trees for food, then you shall count the fruit thereof as uncircumcised: three years shall it be as uncircumcised to you: it shall not be eaten of. ²⁴But in the fourth year all the fruit thereof shall be holy to praise the

LORD with. ²⁵And in the fifth year shall you eat of the fruit thereof, that it may yield to you the increase thereof: I am the LORD your God. ²⁶You shall not eat any thing with the blood: neither shall you use enchantment, nor observe times. ²⁷You shall not round the corners of your heads, neither shall you mar the corners of your beard. ²⁸You shall not make any cuttings in your flesh for the dead, nor print any marks on you: I am the LORD. ²⁹Do not prostitute your daughter, to cause her to be a whore; lest the land fall to prostitution, and the land become full of wickedness. ³⁰You shall keep my sabbaths, and reverence my sanctuary: I am the LORD. ³¹Regard not them that have familiar spirits, neither seek after wizards, to be defiled by them: I am the LORD your God. ³²You shall rise up before the hoary head, and honor the face of the old man, and fear your God: I am the LORD. ³³And if a stranger sojourn with you in your land, you shall not vex him. ³⁴But the stranger that dwells with you shall be to you as one born among you, and you shall love him as yourself; for you were strangers in the land of Egypt: I am the LORD your God. ³⁵You shall do no unrighteousness in judgment, in length, in weight, or in measure. ³⁶Just balances, just weights, a just ephah, and a just hin, shall you have: I am the LORD your God, which brought you out of the land of Egypt. ³⁷Therefore shall you observe all my statutes, and all my judgments, and do them: I am the LORD.

20 ¹And the LORD spoke to Moses, saying, ²Again, you shall say to the children of Israel, Whoever he be of the children of Israel, or of the strangers that sojourn in Israel, that gives any of his seed to Molech; he shall surely be put to death: the people of the land shall stone him with stones. ³And I will set my face against that man, and will cut him off from among his people; because he has given of his seed to Molech, to defile my sanctuary, and to profane my holy name. ⁴And if the people of the land do any ways hide their eyes from the man, when he gives of his seed to Molech, and kill him not: ⁵Then I will set my face against that man, and against his family, and will cut him off, and all that go a whoring after him, to commit prostitution with Molech, from among their people. ⁶And the soul that turns after such as have familiar spirits, and after wizards, to go a whoring after them, I will even set my face against that soul, and will cut him off from among his people. ⁷Sanctify yourselves therefore, and be you holy: for I am the LORD your God. ⁸And you shall keep my statutes, and do them: I am the LORD which sanctify you. ⁹For every one that curses his father or his mother shall be surely put to death: he has cursed his father or his mother; his blood shall be on him. ¹⁰And the man that commits adultery with another man's wife, even he that commits adultery with his neighbor's wife, the adulterer and the adulteress shall surely be put to death. ¹¹And the man that lies with his father's wife has uncovered his father's nakedness: both of them shall surely be put to death; their blood shall be on them. ¹²And if a man lie with his daughter in law, both of them shall surely be put to death: they have worked confusion; their blood shall be on them. ¹³If a man also lie with mankind, as he lies with a woman, both of them have committed an abomination: they shall surely be put to death; their blood shall be on them. ¹⁴And if a man take a wife and her mother, it is wickedness: they shall be burnt with fire, both he and they; that there be no wickedness among you. ¹⁵And if a man lie with a beast, he shall surely be put to death: and you shall slay the beast. ¹⁶And if a woman approach to any beast, and lie down thereto, you shall kill the woman, and the beast: they shall surely be put to death; their blood shall be on them. ¹⁷And if a man shall take his sister, his father's daughter, or his mother's daughter, and see her nakedness, and she see his nakedness; it is a wicked thing; and they shall be cut off in the sight of their people: he has uncovered his sister's nakedness; he shall bear his iniquity. ¹⁸And if a man shall lie with a woman having her sickness, and shall uncover her nakedness; he has discovered her fountain, and she has uncovered the fountain of her blood: and both of them shall be cut off from among their people. ¹⁹And you shall not uncover the nakedness of your mother's sister, nor of your father's sister: for he uncovers his near kin: they shall bear their iniquity. ²⁰And if a man shall lie with his uncle's wife, he has uncovered his uncle's nakedness: they shall bear their sin; they shall die childless. ²¹And if a man shall take his brother's wife, it is an unclean thing: he has uncovered his brother's nakedness; they shall be childless. ²²You shall therefore keep all my statutes, and all my judgments, and do them: that the land, where I bring you to dwell therein, spew you not out. ²³And you shall not walk in the manners of the nation, which I cast out before you: for they committed all these things, and therefore I abhorred them. ²⁴But I have said to you, You shall inherit their land, and I will give it to you to possess it, a land that flows with milk and honey: I am the LORD your God, which have separated you from other people. ²⁵You shall therefore put difference between clean beasts and unclean, and between unclean fowls and clean: and you shall not make your souls abominable by beast, or by fowl, or by any manner of living thing that creeps on the ground, which I have separated from you as unclean. ²⁶And you shall be holy to me: for I the LORD am holy, and have severed you from other people, that you should be mine. ²⁷A man also or woman that has a familiar spirit, or that is a wizard, shall surely be put to death: they shall stone them with stones: their blood shall be on them.

21 ¹And the LORD said to Moses, Speak to the priests the sons of Aaron, and say to them, There shall none be defiled for the dead among his people: ²But for his kin, that is near to him, that is, for his mother, and for his father, and for his son, and for his daughter, and for his brother. ³And for his sister a virgin, that is near to him, which has had no husband; for her may he be defiled. ⁴But he shall not defile himself, being a chief man among his people, to profane himself. ⁵They shall not make baldness on their head, neither shall they shave off the corner of their beard, nor make any cuttings in their flesh. ⁶They shall be holy to their God, and not profane the name of their God: for the offerings of the LORD made by fire, and the bread of their God, they do offer: therefore they shall be holy. ⁷They shall not take a wife that is a whore, or profane; neither shall they take a woman put away from her husband: for he is holy to his God. ⁸You shall sanctify him therefore; for he offers the bread of your God: he shall be holy to you: for I the LORD, which sanctify you, am holy. ⁹And the daughter of any priest, if she profane herself by playing the whore, she profanes her father: she shall be burnt with fire. ¹⁰And he that is the high priest among his brothers, on whose head the anointing oil was poured, and that is consecrated to put on the garments, shall not uncover his head, nor rend his clothes; ¹¹Neither shall he go in to any dead body, nor defile himself for his father, or for his mother; ¹²Neither shall he go out of the sanctuary, nor profane the sanctuary of his God; for the crown of the anointing oil of his God is on him: I am the LORD. ¹³And he shall take a wife in her virginity. ¹⁴A widow, or a divorced woman, or profane, or an harlot, these shall he not take: but he shall take a virgin of his own people to wife. ¹⁵Neither shall he profane his seed among his people: for I the LORD do sanctify him. ¹⁶And the LORD spoke to Moses, saying, ¹⁷Speak to Aaron, saying, Whoever he be of your seed in their generations that has any blemish, let him not approach to offer the bread of his God. ¹⁸For whatever man he be that has a blemish, he shall not approach: a blind man, or a lame, or he that has a flat nose, or any thing superfluous, ¹⁹Or a man that is broken footed, or broken handed, ²⁰Or hunch back, or a dwarf, or that has a blemish in his eye, or be scurvy, or scabbed, or has his stones broken; ²¹No man that has a blemish of the seed of Aaron the priest shall come near to offer the offerings of the LORD made by fire: he has a blemish; he shall not come near to offer the bread of his God. ²²He shall eat the bread of his God, both of the most holy, and of the holy. ²³Only he shall not go in to the veil, nor come near to the altar, because he has a blemish; that he profane not my sanctuaries: for I the LORD do sanctify them. ²⁴And Moses told it to Aaron, and to his sons, and to all the children of Israel.

22 ¹And the LORD spoke to Moses, saying, ²Speak to Aaron and to his sons, that they separate themselves from the holy things of the children of Israel, and that they profane not my holy name in those things which they hallow to me: I am the LORD. ³Say to them, Whoever he be of all your seed among your generations, that goes to the holy things, which the children of Israel hallow to the LORD, having his uncleanness on him, that soul shall be cut off from my presence: I am the LORD. ⁴What man soever of the seed of Aaron is a leper, or has a running issue; he shall not eat of the holy things, until he be clean. And whoever touches any thing that is unclean by the dead, or a man whose seed goes from him; ⁵Or whoever touches any creeping thing, whereby he may be made unclean, or a man of whom he may take uncleanness, whatever uncleanness he has; ⁶The soul which has touched any such shall be unclean until even, and shall not eat of the holy things, unless he wash his flesh with water. ⁷And when the sun is down, he shall be clean, and shall afterward eat of the holy things; because it is his food. ⁸That which dies of itself, or is torn with beasts, he shall not eat to defile himself therewith; I am the LORD. ⁹They shall therefore keep my ordinance, lest they bear sin for it, and die therefore, if they profane it: I the LORD do sanctify them. ¹⁰There shall no stranger eat of the holy thing: a sojourner of the priest, or an hired servant, shall not eat of the holy thing. ¹¹But if the priest buy any soul with his money, he shall eat of it, and he that is born in his house: they shall eat of his meat. ¹²If the priest's daughter also be married to a stranger, she may not eat of an offering of the holy things. ¹³But if the priest's daughter be a widow, or divorced, and have no child, and is returned to her father's house, as in her youth, she shall eat of her father's meat: but there shall be no stranger eat thereof. ¹⁴And if a man eat of the holy thing unwittingly, then he shall put the fifth part thereof to it, and shall give it to the priest with the holy thing. ¹⁵And they shall not profane the holy things of the children of Israel, which they offer to the LORD; ¹⁶Or suffer them to bear the iniquity of trespass, when they eat their holy things: for I the LORD do sanctify them. ¹⁷And the LORD spoke to Moses, saying, ¹⁸Speak to Aaron, and to his sons, and to all the children of Israel, and say to them, Whatever he be of the house of Israel, or of the strangers in Israel, that will offer his oblation for all his vows, and for all his freewill offerings, which they will offer to the LORD for a burnt offering; ¹⁹You shall offer at your own will a male without blemish, of the beeves, of the sheep, or of the goats. ²⁰But whatever has a blemish, that shall you not offer: for it shall not be acceptable for you. ²¹And whoever offers a sacrifice of peace offerings to the LORD to accomplish his vow, or a freewill offering in beeves or sheep, it shall be perfect to be accepted; there shall be no blemish therein. ²²Blind, or broken, or maimed, or having a running sore, or scurvy, or scabbed, you shall not offer these to the LORD, nor make an offering by fire of them on the altar to the LORD. ²³Either a bullock or a lamb that has any thing superfluous or lacking in his parts, that may you offer for a freewill offering; but for a vow it shall not be accepted. ²⁴You shall not offer to the LORD that which is bruised, or crushed, or broken, or cut; neither shall you make any offering thereof in your land. ²⁵Neither from a stranger's hand shall you offer the bread of your God of any of these; because their corruption is in them, and blemishes be in them: they shall not be accepted for you. ²⁶And the LORD spoke to Moses, saying, ²⁷When a bullock, or a sheep, or a goat, is brought forth, then it shall be seven days under the dam; and from the eighth day and thereafter it shall be accepted for an offering made by fire to the LORD. ²⁸And whether it be cow, or ewe, you shall not kill it and her young both in one day. ²⁹And when you will offer a sacrifice of thanksgiving to the LORD, offer it at your own will. ³⁰On the same day it shall be eaten up; you shall leave none of it until the morrow: I am the LORD. ³¹Therefore shall you keep my commandments, and do them: I am the LORD. ³²Neither shall you profane my holy name; but I will be hallowed among the children of Israel: I am the LORD which hallow you, ³³That brought you out of the land of Egypt, to be your God: I am the LORD.

23 ¹And the LORD spoke to Moses, saying, ²Speak to the children of Israel, and say to them, Concerning the feasts of the LORD, which you shall proclaim to be holy convocations, even these are my feasts. ³Six days shall work be done: but the seventh day is the sabbath of rest, an holy convocation; you shall do no work therein: it is the sabbath of the LORD in all your dwellings. ⁴These are the feasts of the LORD, even holy convocations, which you shall proclaim in their seasons. ⁵In the fourteenth day of the first month at even is the LORD's passover. ⁶And on the fifteenth day of the same month is the feast of unleavened bread to the LORD: seven days you must eat unleavened bread. ⁷In the first day you shall have an holy convocation: you shall do no servile work therein. ⁸But you shall offer an offering made by fire to the LORD seven days: in the seventh day is an holy convocation: you shall do no servile work therein. ⁹And the LORD spoke to Moses, saying, ¹⁰Speak to the children of Israel, and say to them, When you be come into the land which I give to you, and shall reap the harvest thereof, then you shall bring a sheaf of the first fruits of your harvest to the priest: ¹¹And he shall wave the sheaf before the LORD, to be accepted for you: on the morrow after the sabbath the priest shall wave it. ¹²And you shall offer that day when you wave the sheaf an he lamb without blemish of the first year for a burnt offering to the LORD. ¹³And the meat offering thereof shall be two tenth deals of fine flour mingled with oil, an offering made by fire to the LORD for a sweet smell: and the drink offering thereof shall be of wine, the fourth part of an hin. ¹⁴And you shall eat neither bread, nor parched corn, nor green ears, until the selfsame day that you have brought an offering to your God: it shall be a statute for ever throughout your generations in all your dwellings. ¹⁵And you shall count to you from the morrow after the sabbath, from the day that you brought the sheaf of the wave offering; seven sabbaths shall be complete: ¹⁶Even to the morrow after the seventh sabbath shall you number fifty days; and you shall offer a new meat offering to the LORD. ¹⁷You shall bring out of your habitations two wave loaves of two tenth deals; they shall be of fine flour; they shall be baked with leaven; they are the first fruits to the LORD. ¹⁸And you shall offer with the bread seven lambs without blemish of the first year, and one young bullock, and two rams: they shall be for a burnt offering to the LORD, with their meat offering, and their drink offerings, even an offering made by fire, of sweet smell to the LORD. ¹⁹Then you shall sacrifice one kid of the goats for a sin offering, and two lambs of the first year for a sacrifice of peace offerings. ²⁰And the priest shall wave them with the bread of the first fruits for a wave offering before the LORD, with the two lambs: they shall be holy to the LORD for the priest. ²¹And you shall proclaim on the selfsame day, that it may be an holy convocation to you: you shall do no servile work therein: it shall be a statute for ever in all your dwellings throughout your generations. ²²And when you reap the harvest of your land, you shall not make clean riddance of the corners of your field when you reap, neither shall you gather any gleaning of your harvest: you shall leave them to the poor, and to the stranger: I am the LORD your God. ²³And the LORD spoke to Moses, saying, ²⁴Speak to the children of Israel, saying, In the seventh month, in the first day of the month, shall you have a sabbath, a memorial of blowing of trumpets, an holy convocation. ²⁵You shall do no servile work therein: but you shall offer an offering made by fire to the LORD. ²⁶And the LORD spoke to Moses, saying, ²⁷Also on the tenth day of this seventh month there shall be a day of atonement: it shall be an holy convocation to you; and you shall afflict your souls, and offer an offering made by fire to the LORD. ²⁸And you shall do no work in that same day: for it is a day of atonement, to make an atonement for you before the LORD your God. ²⁹For whatever soul it be that shall not be afflicted in that same day, he shall be cut off from among his people. ³⁰And whatever soul it be that does any work in that same day, the same soul will I destroy from among his people. ³¹You shall do no manner of work: it shall be a statute for ever throughout your generations in all your dwellings. ³²It shall be to you a sabbath of rest, and you shall afflict your souls: in the ninth day of the month at even, from even to even, shall you celebrate your sabbath. ³³And the LORD spoke to Moses, saying, ³⁴Speak to the children of Israel, saying, The fifteenth day of this seventh month shall be the feast of tabernacles for seven days to the LORD. ³⁵On the first day shall be an holy convocation: you shall do no servile work therein. ³⁶Seven days you shall offer an offering made by fire to the LORD: on the eighth day shall be an holy convocation to you; and you shall offer an offering made by fire to the LORD: it is a solemn assembly; and you shall do no servile work therein. ³⁷These are the feasts of the LORD, which you shall proclaim to be holy convocations, to offer an offering made by fire to the LORD, a burnt offering, and a meat offering, a sacrifice, and drink offerings, every thing on his day: ³⁸Beside the sabbaths of the LORD, and beside your gifts, and beside all your vows, and beside all your freewill offerings, which you give to the LORD. ³⁹Also in the fifteenth day of the seventh month, when you have gathered in the fruit of the land, you shall keep a feast to the LORD seven days: on the first day shall be a sabbath, and on the eighth day shall be a sabbath. ⁴⁰And you shall take you on the first day the boughs of goodly trees, branches of palm trees, and the boughs of thick trees, and willows of the brook; and you shall rejoice before the LORD your God seven days. ⁴¹And you shall keep it a feast to the LORD seven days in the year. It shall be a statute for ever in your generations: you shall celebrate it in the seventh month. ⁴²You shall dwell in booths seven days; all that are Israelites born shall dwell in booths: ⁴³That your generations may know that I made the children of Israel to dwell in booths, when I brought them out of the land of Egypt: I am the LORD your God. ⁴⁴And Moses declared to the children of Israel the feasts of the LORD.

24 ¹And the LORD spoke to Moses, saying, ²Command the children of Israel, that they bring to you pure oil olive beaten for the light, to cause the lamps to burn continually. ³Without the veil of the testimony, in the tabernacle of the congregation, shall Aaron order it from the evening to the morning before the LORD continually: it shall be a statute for ever in your generations. ⁴He shall order the lamps on the pure candlestick before the LORD continually. ⁵And you shall take fine flour, and bake twelve cakes thereof: two tenth deals shall be in one cake. ⁶And you shall set them in two rows, six on a row, on the pure table before the LORD. ⁷And you shall put pure frankincense on each row, that it may be on the bread for a memorial, even an offering made by fire to the LORD. ⁸Every sabbath he shall set it in order before the LORD continually, being taken from the children of Israel by an everlasting covenant. ⁹And it shall be Aaron's and his sons'; and they shall eat it in the holy place: for it is most holy to him of the offerings of the LORD made by fire by a perpetual statute. ¹⁰And the son of an Israelitish woman, whose father was an Egyptian, went out among the children of Israel: and this son of the Israelitish woman and a man of Israel strove together in the camp; ¹¹And the Israelitish woman's son blasphemed the name of the Lord, and cursed. And they brought him to Moses: (and his mother's name was Shelomith, the daughter of Dibri, of the tribe of Dan:) ¹²And they put him in ward, that the mind of the LORD might be showed them. ¹³And the LORD spoke to Moses, saying, ¹⁴Bring forth him that has cursed without the camp; and let all that heard him lay their hands on his head, and let all the congregation stone him. ¹⁵And you shall speak to the children of Israel, saying, Whoever curses his God shall bear his sin. ¹⁶And he that blasphemes the name of the LORD, he shall surely be put to death, and all the congregation shall certainly stone him: as well the stranger, as he that is born in the land, when he blasphemes the name of the Lord, shall be put to death. ¹⁷And he that kills any man shall surely be put to death. ¹⁸And he that kills a beast shall make it good; beast for beast. ¹⁹And if a man cause a blemish in his neighbor; as he has done, so shall it be done to him; ²⁰Breach for breach, eye for eye, tooth for tooth: as he has caused a blemish in a man, so shall it be done to him again. ²¹And he that kills a beast, he shall restore it: and he that kills a man, he shall be put to death. ²²You shall have one manner of law, as well for the stranger, as for one of your own country: for I am the LORD your God. ²³And Moses spoke to the children of Israel, that they should bring forth him that had cursed out of the camp, and stone him with stones. And the children of Israel did as the LORD commanded Moses.

25 ¹And the LORD spoke to Moses in mount Sinai, saying, ²Speak to the children of Israel, and say to them, When you come into the land which I give you, then shall the land keep a sabbath to the LORD. ³Six years you shall sow your field, and six years you shall prune your vineyard, and gather in the fruit thereof; ⁴But in the seventh year shall be a sabbath of rest to the land, a sabbath for the LORD: you shall neither sow your field, nor prune your vineyard. ⁵That which grows of its own accord of your harvest you shall not reap, neither gather the grapes of your vine undressed: for it is a year of rest to the land. ⁶And the sabbath of the land shall be meat for you; for you, and for your servant, and for your maid, and for your hired servant, and for your stranger that sojourns with you. ⁷And for your cattle, and for the beast that are in your land, shall all the increase thereof be meat. ⁸And you shall number seven sabbaths of years to you, seven times seven years; and the space of the seven sabbaths of years shall be to you forty and nine years. ⁹Then shall you cause the trumpet of the jubilee to sound on the tenth day of the seventh month, in the day of atonement shall you make the trumpet sound throughout all your land. ¹⁰And you shall hallow the fiftieth year, and proclaim liberty throughout all the land to all the inhabitants thereof: it shall be a jubilee to you; and you shall return every man to his possession, and you shall return every man to his family. ¹¹A jubilee shall that fiftieth year be to you: you shall not sow, neither reap that which grows of itself in it, nor gather the grapes in it of your vine undressed. ¹²For it is the jubilee; it shall be holy to you: you shall eat the increase thereof out of the field. ¹³In the year of this jubilee you shall return every man to his possession. ¹⁴And if you sell something to your neighbor, or buy something of your neighbor's hand, you shall not oppress one another: ¹⁵According to the number of years after the jubilee you shall buy of your neighbor, and according to the number of years of the fruits he shall sell to you: ¹⁶According to the multitude of years you shall increase the price thereof, and according to the fewness of years you shall diminish the price of it: for according to the number of the years of the fruits does he sell to you. ¹⁷You shall not therefore oppress one another; but you shall fear your God: for I am the LORD your God. ¹⁸Why you shall do my statutes, and keep my judgments, and do them; and you shall dwell in the land in safety. ¹⁹And the land shall yield her fruit, and you shall eat your fill, and dwell therein in safety. ²⁰And if you shall say, What shall we eat the seventh year? behold, we shall not sow, nor gather in our increase: ²¹Then I will command my blessing on you in the sixth year, and it shall bring forth fruit for three years. ²²And you shall sow the eighth year, and eat yet of old fruit until the ninth year; until her fruits come in you shall eat of the old store. ²³The land shall not be sold for ever: for the land is mine, for you are strangers and sojourners with me. ²⁴And in all the land of your possession you shall grant a redemption for the land. ²⁵If your brother be waxen poor, and has sold away some of his possession, and if any of his kin come to redeem it, then shall he redeem that which his brother sold. ²⁶And if the man have none to redeem it, and himself be able to redeem it; ²⁷Then let him count the years of the sale thereof, and restore the remainder to the man to whom he sold it; that he may return to his possession. ²⁸But if he be not able to restore it to him, then that which is sold shall remain in the hand of him that has bought it until the year of jubilee: and in the jubilee it shall go out, and he shall return to his possession. ²⁹And if a man sell a dwelling house in a walled city, then he may redeem it within a whole year after it is sold; within a full year may he redeem it. ³⁰And if it be not redeemed within the space of a full year, then the house that is in the walled city shall be established for ever to him that bought it throughout his generations: it shall not go out in the jubilee. ³¹But the houses of the villages which have no wall round about them shall be counted as the fields of the country: they may be redeemed, and they shall go out in the jubilee. ³²Notwithstanding the cities of the Levites, and the houses of the cities of their possession, may the Levites redeem at any time. ³³And if a man purchase of the Levites, then the house that was sold, and the city of his possession, shall go out in the year of jubilee: for the houses of the cities of the Levites are their possession among the children of Israel. ³⁴But the field of the suburbs of their cities may not be sold; for it is their perpetual possession. ³⁵And if your brother be waxen poor, and fallen in decay with you; then you shall relieve him: yes, though he be a stranger, or a sojourner; that he may live with you. ³⁶Take you no usury of him, or increase: but fear your God; that your brother may live with you. ³⁷You shall not give him your money on usury, nor lend him your victuals for increase. ³⁸I am the LORD your God, which brought you forth out of the land of Egypt, to give you the land of Canaan, and to be your God. ³⁹And if your brother that dwells by you be waxen poor, and be sold to you; you shall not compel him to serve as a bondservant: ⁴⁰But as an hired servant, and as a sojourner, he shall be with you, and shall serve you to the year of jubilee. ⁴¹And then shall he depart from you, both he and his children with him, and shall return to his own family, and to the possession of his fathers shall he return. ⁴²For they are my servants, which I brought forth out of the land of Egypt: they shall not be sold as slaves. ⁴³You shall not rule over him with rigor; but shall fear your God. ⁴⁴Both your slaves, and your bondmaids, which you shall have, shall be of the heathen that are round about you; of them shall you buy slaves and bondmaids. ⁴⁵Moreover of the children of the strangers that do sojourn among you, of them shall you buy, and of their families that are with you, which they begat in your land: and they shall be your possession. ⁴⁶And you shall take them as an inheritance for your children after you, to inherit them for a possession; they shall be your slaves for ever: but over your brothers the children of Israel, you shall not rule one over another with rigor. ⁴⁷And if a sojourner or stranger wax rich by you, and your brother that dwells by him wax poor, and sell himself to the stranger or sojourner by you, or to the stock of the stranger's family: ⁴⁸After that he is sold he may be redeemed again; one of his brothers may redeem him: ⁴⁹Either his uncle, or his uncle's son, may redeem him, or any that is near of kin to him of his family may redeem him; or if he be able, he may redeem himself. ⁵⁰And he shall reckon with him that bought him from the year that he was sold to him to the year of jubilee: and the price of his sale shall be according to the number of years, according to the time of an hired servant shall it be with him. ⁵¹If there be yet many years behind, according to them he shall give again the price of his redemption out of the money that he was bought for. ⁵²And if there remain but few years to the year of jubilee, then he shall count with him, and according to his years shall he give him again the price of his redemption. ⁵³And as a yearly hired servant shall he be with him: and the other shall not rule with rigor over him in your sight. ⁵⁴And if he be not redeemed in these years, then he shall go out in the year of jubilee, both he, and his children with him. ⁵⁵For to me the children of Israel are servants; they are my servants whom I brought forth out of the land of Egypt: I am the LORD your God.

26 ¹You shall make you no idols nor graven image, neither raise you up a standing image, neither shall you set up any image of stone in your land, to bow down to it: for I am the LORD your God. ²You shall keep my sabbaths, and reverence my sanctuary: I am the LORD. ³If you walk in my statutes, and keep my commandments, and do them; ⁴Then I will give you rain in due season, and the land shall yield her increase, and the trees of the field shall yield their fruit. ⁵And your threshing shall reach to the vintage, and the vintage shall reach to the sowing time: and you shall eat your bread to the full, and dwell in your land safely. ⁶And I will give peace in the land, and you shall lie down, and none shall make you afraid: and I will rid evil beasts out of the land, neither shall the sword go through your land. ⁷And you shall chase your enemies, and they shall fall before you by the sword. ⁸And five of you shall chase an hundred, and an hundred of you shall put ten thousand to flight: and your enemies shall fall before you by the sword. ⁹For I will have respect to you, and make you fruitful, and multiply you, and establish my covenant with you. ¹⁰And you shall eat old store, and bring forth the old because of the new. ¹¹And I set my tabernacle among you: and my soul shall not abhor you. ¹²And I will walk among you, and will be your God, and you shall be my people. ¹³I am the LORD your God, which brought you forth out of the land of Egypt, that you should not be their slaves; and I have broken the bands of your yoke, and made you go upright. ¹⁴But if you will not listen to me, and will not do all these commandments; ¹⁵And if you shall despise my statutes, or if your soul abhor my judgments, so that you will not do all my commandments, but that you break my covenant: ¹⁶I also will do this to you; I will even appoint over you terror, consumption, and the burning ague, that shall consume the eyes, and cause sorrow of heart: and you shall sow your seed in vain, for your enemies shall eat it. ¹⁷And I will set my face against you, and you shall be slain before your enemies: they that hate you shall reign over you; and you shall flee when none pursues you. ¹⁸And if you will not yet for all this listen to me, then I will punish you seven times more for your sins. ¹⁹And I will break the pride of your power; and I will make your heaven as iron, and your earth as brass: ²⁰And your strength shall be spent in vain: for your land shall not yield her increase, neither shall the trees of the land yield their fruits. ²¹And if you walk contrary to me, and will not listen to me; I will bring seven times more plagues on you according to your sins. ²²I will also send wild beasts among you, which shall rob you of your children, and destroy your cattle, and make you few in number; and your high ways shall be desolate. ²³And if you will not be reformed by me by these things, but will walk contrary to me; ²⁴Then will I also walk contrary to you, and will punish you yet seven times for your sins. ²⁵And I will bring a sword on you, that shall avenge the quarrel of my covenant: and when you are gathered together within your cities, I will send the pestilence among you; and you shall be delivered into the hand of the enemy. ²⁶And when I have broken the staff of your bread, ten women shall bake your bread in one oven, and they shall deliver you your bread again by weight: and you shall eat, and not be satisfied. ²⁷And if you will not for all this listen to me, but walk contrary to me; ²⁸Then I will walk contrary to you also in fury; and I, even I, will chastise you seven times for your sins. ²⁹And you shall eat the flesh of your sons, and the flesh of your daughters shall you eat. ³⁰And I will destroy your high places, and cut down your images, and cast your carcasses on the carcasses of your idols, and my soul shall abhor you. ³¹And I will make your cities waste, and bring your sanctuaries to desolation, and I will not smell the smell of your sweet odors. ³²And I will bring the land into desolation: and your enemies which dwell therein shall be astonished at it. ³³And I will scatter you among the heathen, and will draw out a sword after you: and your land shall be desolate, and your cities waste. ³⁴Then shall the land enjoy her sabbaths, as long as it lies desolate, and you be in your enemies' land; even then shall the land rest, and enjoy her sabbaths. ³⁵As long as it lies desolate it shall rest; because it did not rest in your sabbaths, when you dwelled on it. ³⁶And on them that are left alive of you I will send a faintness into their hearts in the lands of their enemies; and the sound of a shaken leaf shall chase them; and they shall flee, as fleeing from a sword; and they shall fall when none pursues. ³⁷And they shall fall one on another, as it were before a sword, when none pursues: and you shall have no power to stand before your enemies. ³⁸And you shall perish among the heathen, and the land of your enemies shall eat you up. ³⁹And they that are left of you shall pine away in their iniquity in your enemies' lands; and also in the iniquities of their fathers shall they pine away with them. ⁴⁰If they shall confess their iniquity, and the iniquity of their fathers, with their trespass which they trespassed against me, and that also they have walked contrary to me; ⁴¹And that I also have walked contrary to them, and have brought them into the land of their enemies; if then their uncircumcised hearts be humbled, and they then accept of the punishment of their iniquity: ⁴²Then will I remember my covenant with Jacob, and also my covenant with Isaac, and also my covenant with Abraham will I remember; and I will remember the land. ⁴³The land also shall be left of them, and shall enjoy her sabbaths, while she lies desolate without them: and they shall accept of the punishment of their iniquity: because, even because they despised my judgments, and because their soul abhorred my statutes. ⁴⁴And yet for all that, when they be in the land of their enemies, I will not cast them away, neither will I abhor them, to destroy them utterly, and to break my covenant with them: for I am the LORD their God. ⁴⁵But I will for their sakes remember the covenant of their ancestors, whom I brought forth out of the land of Egypt in the sight of the heathen, that I might be their God: I am the LORD. ⁴⁶These are the statutes and judgments and laws, which the LORD made between him and the children of Israel in mount Sinai by the hand of Moses.

27 ¹And the LORD spoke to Moses, saying, ²Speak to the children of Israel, and say to them, When a man shall make a singular vow, the persons shall be for the LORD by your estimation. ³And your estimation shall be of the male from twenty years old even to sixty years old, even your estimation shall be fifty shekels of silver, after the shekel of the sanctuary. ⁴And if it be a female, then your estimation shall be thirty shekels. ⁵And if it be from five years old even to twenty years old, then your estimation shall be of the male twenty shekels, and for the female ten shekels. ⁶And if it be from a month old even to five years old, then your estimation shall be of the male five shekels of silver, and for the female your estimation shall be three shekels of silver. ⁷And if it be from sixty years old and above; if it be a male, then your estimation shall be fifteen shekels, and for the female ten shekels. ⁸But if he be poorer than your estimation, then he shall present himself before the priest, and the priest shall value him; according to his ability that vowed shall the priest value him. ⁹And if it be a beast, whereof men bring an offering to the LORD, all that any man gives of such to the LORD shall be holy. ¹⁰He shall not alter it, nor change it, a good for a bad, or a bad for a good: and if he shall at all change beast for beast, then it and the exchange thereof shall be holy. ¹¹And if it be any unclean beast, of which they do not offer a sacrifice to the LORD, then he shall present the beast before the priest: ¹²And the priest shall value it, whether it be good or bad: as you value it, who are the priest, so shall it be. ¹³But if he will at all redeem it, then he shall add a fifth part thereof to your estimation. ¹⁴And when a man shall sanctify his house to be holy to the LORD, then the priest shall estimate it, whether it be good or bad: as the priest shall estimate it, so shall it stand. ¹⁵And if he that sanctified it will redeem his house, then he shall add the fifth part of the money of your estimation to it, and it shall be his. ¹⁶And if a man shall sanctify to the LORD some part of a field of his possession, then your estimation shall be according to the seed thereof: an homer of barley seed shall be valued at fifty shekels of silver. ¹⁷If he sanctify his field from the year of jubilee, according to your estimation it shall stand. ¹⁸But if he sanctify his field after the jubilee, then the priest shall reckon to him the money according to the years that remain, even to the year of the jubilee, and it shall be abated from your estimation. ¹⁹And if he that sanctified the field will in any wise redeem it, then he shall add the fifth part of the money of your estimation to it, and it shall be assured to him. ²⁰And if he will not redeem the field, or if he have sold the field to another man, it shall not be redeemed any more. ²¹But the field, when it goes out in the jubilee, shall be holy to the LORD, as a field devoted; the possession thereof shall be the priest's. ²²And if a man sanctify to the LORD a field which he has bought, which is not of the fields of his possession; ²³Then the priest shall reckon to him the worth of your estimation, even to the year of the jubilee: and he shall give your estimation in that day, as a holy thing to the LORD. ²⁴In the year of the jubilee the field shall return to him of whom it was bought, even to him to whom the possession of the land did belong. ²⁵And all your estimations shall be according to the shekel of the sanctuary: twenty gerahs shall be the shekel. ²⁶Only the firstling of the beasts, which should be the LORD's firstling, no man shall sanctify it; whether it be ox, or sheep: it is the LORD's. ²⁷And if it be of an unclean beast, then he shall redeem it according to your estimation, and shall add a fifth part of it thereto: or if it be not redeemed, then it shall be sold according to your estimation. ²⁸Notwithstanding no devoted thing, that a man shall devote to the LORD of all that he has, both of man and beast, and of the field of his possession, shall be sold or redeemed: every devoted thing is most holy to the LORD. ²⁹None devoted, which shall be devoted of men, shall be redeemed; but shall surely be put to death. ³⁰And all the tithe of the land, whether of the seed of the land, or of the fruit of the tree, is the LORD's: it is holy to the LORD. ³¹And if a man will at all redeem some of his tithes, he shall add thereto the fifth part thereof. ³²And concerning the tithe of the herd, or of the flock, even of whatever passes under the rod, the tenth shall be holy to the LORD. ³³He shall not search whether it be good or bad, neither shall he change it: and if he change it at all, then both it and the change thereof shall be holy; it shall not be redeemed. ³⁴These are the commandments, which the LORD commanded Moses for the children of Israel in mount Sinai.

Numbers

1 ¹And the LORD spoke to Moses in the wilderness of Sinai, in the tabernacle of the congregation, on the first day of the second month, in the second year after they were come out of the land of Egypt, saying, ²Take you the sum of all the congregation of the children of Israel, after their families, by the house of their fathers, with the number of their names, every male by their polls; ³From twenty years old and upward, all that are able to go forth to war in Israel: you and Aaron shall number them by their armies. ⁴And with you there shall be a man of every tribe; every one head of the house of his fathers. ⁵And these are the names of the men that shall stand with you: of the tribe of Reuben; Elizur the son of Shedeur. ⁶Of Simeon; Shelumiel the son of Zurishaddai. ⁷Of Judah; Nahshon the son of Amminadab. ⁸Of Issachar; Nethaneel the son of Zuar. ⁹Of Zebulun; Eliab the son of Helon. ¹⁰Of the children of Joseph: of Ephraim; Elishama the son of Ammihud: of Manasseh; Gamaliel the son of Pedahzur. ¹¹Of Benjamin; Abidan the son of Gideoni. ¹²Of Dan; Ahiezer the son of Ammishaddai. ¹³Of Asher; Pagiel the son of Ocran. ¹⁴Of Gad; Eliasaph the son of Deuel. ¹⁵Of Naphtali; Ahira the son of Enan. ¹⁶These were the renowned of the congregation, princes of the tribes of their fathers, heads of thousands in Israel. ¹⁷And Moses and Aaron took these men which are expressed by their names: ¹⁸And they assembled all the congregation together on the first day of the second month, and they declared their pedigrees after their families, by the house of their fathers, according to the number of the names, from twenty years old and upward, by their polls. ¹⁹As the LORD commanded Moses, so he numbered them in the wilderness of Sinai. ²⁰And the children of Reuben, Israel's oldest son, by their generations, after their families, by the house of their fathers, according to the number of the names, by their polls, every male from twenty years old and upward, all that were able to go forth to war; ²¹Those that were numbered of them, even of the tribe of Reuben, were forty and six thousand and five hundred. ²²Of the children of Simeon, by their generations, after their families, by the house of their fathers, those that were numbered of them, according to the number of the names, by their polls, every male from twenty years old and upward, all that were able to go forth to war; ²³Those that were numbered of them, even of the tribe of Simeon, were fifty and nine thousand and three hundred. ²⁴Of the children of Gad, by their generations, after their families, by the house of their fathers, according to the number of the names, from twenty years old and upward, all that were able to go forth to war; ²⁵Those that were numbered of them, even of the tribe of Gad, were forty and five thousand six hundred and fifty. ²⁶Of the children of Judah, by their generations, after their families, by the house of their fathers, according to the number of the names, from twenty years old and upward, all that were able to go forth to war; ²⁷Those that were numbered of them, even of the tribe of Judah, were three score and fourteen thousand and six hundred. ²⁸Of the children of Issachar, by their generations, after their families, by the house of their fathers, according to the number of the names, from twenty years old and upward, all that were able to go forth to war; ²⁹Those that were numbered of them, even of the tribe of Issachar, were fifty and four thousand and four hundred. ³⁰Of the children of Zebulun, by their generations, after their families, by the house of their fathers, according to the number of the names, from twenty years old and upward, all that were able to go forth to war; ³¹Those that were numbered of them, even of the tribe of Zebulun, were fifty and seven thousand and four hundred. ³²Of the children of Joseph, namely, of the children of Ephraim, by their generations, after their families, by the house of their fathers, according to the number of the names, from twenty years old and upward, all that were able to go forth to war; ³³Those that were numbered of them, even of the tribe of Ephraim, were forty thousand and five hundred. ³⁴Of the children of Manasseh, by their generations, after their families, by the house of their fathers, according to the number of the names, from twenty years old and upward, all that were able to go forth to war; ³⁵Those that were numbered of them, even of the tribe of Manasseh, were thirty and two thousand and two hundred. ³⁶Of the children of Benjamin, by their generations, after their families, by the house of their fathers, according to the number of the names, from twenty years old and upward, all that were able to go forth to war; ³⁷Those that were numbered of them, even of the tribe of Benjamin, were thirty and five thousand and four hundred. ³⁸Of the children of Dan, by their generations, after their families, by the house of their fathers, according to the number of the names, from twenty years old and upward, all that were able to go forth to war; ³⁹Those that were numbered of them, even of the tribe of Dan, were three score and two thousand and seven hundred. ⁴⁰Of the children of Asher, by their generations, after their families, by the house of their fathers, according to the number of the names, from twenty years old and upward, all that were able to go forth to war; ⁴¹Those that were numbered of them, even of the tribe of Asher, were forty and one thousand and five hundred. ⁴²Of the children of Naphtali, throughout their generations, after their families, by the house of their fathers, according to the number of the names, from twenty years old and upward, all that were able to go forth to war; ⁴³Those that were numbered of them, even of the tribe of Naphtali, were fifty and three thousand and four hundred. ⁴⁴These are those that were numbered, which Moses and Aaron numbered, and the princes of Israel, being twelve men: each one was for the house of his fathers. ⁴⁵So were all those that were numbered of the children of Israel, by the house of their fathers, from twenty years old and upward, all that were able to go forth to war in Israel; ⁴⁶Even all they that were numbered were six hundred thousand and three thousand and five hundred and fifty. ⁴⁷But the Levites after the tribe of their fathers were not numbered among them. ⁴⁸For the LORD had spoken to Moses, saying, ⁴⁹Only you shall not number the tribe of Levi, neither take the sum of them among the children of Israel: ⁵⁰But you shall appoint the Levites over the tabernacle of testimony, and over all the vessels thereof, and over all things that belong to it: they shall bear the tabernacle, and all the vessels thereof; and

they shall minister to it, and shall encamp round about the tabernacle. ⁵¹And when the tabernacle sets forward, the Levites shall take it down: and when the tabernacle is to be pitched, the Levites shall set it up: and the stranger that comes near shall be put to death. ⁵²And the children of Israel shall pitch their tents, every man by his own camp, and every man by his own standard, throughout their hosts. ⁵³But the Levites shall pitch round about the tabernacle of testimony, that there be no wrath on the congregation of the children of Israel: and the Levites shall keep the charge of the tabernacle of testimony. ⁵⁴And the children of Israel did according to all that the LORD commanded Moses, so did they.

2 ¹And the LORD spoke to Moses and to Aaron, saying, ²Every man of the children of Israel shall pitch by his own standard, with the ensign of their father's house: far off about the tabernacle of the congregation shall they pitch. ³And on the east side toward the rising of the sun shall they of the standard of the camp of Judah pitch throughout their armies: and Nahshon the son of Amminadab shall be captain of the children of Judah. ⁴And his host, and those that were numbered of them, were three score and fourteen thousand and six hundred. ⁵And those that do pitch next to him shall be the tribe of Issachar: and Nethaneel the son of Zuar shall be captain of the children of Issachar. ⁶And his host, and those that were numbered thereof, were fifty and four thousand and four hundred. ⁷Then the tribe of Zebulun: and Eliab the son of Helon shall be captain of the children of Zebulun. ⁸And his host, and those that were numbered thereof, were fifty and seven thousand and four hundred. ⁹All that were numbered in the camp of Judah were an hundred thousand and fourscore thousand and six thousand and four hundred, throughout their armies. These shall first set forth. ¹⁰On the south side shall be the standard of the camp of Reuben according to their armies: and the captain of the children of Reuben shall be Elizur the son of Shedeur. ¹¹And his host, and those that were numbered thereof, were forty and six thousand and five hundred. ¹²And those which pitch by him shall be the tribe of Simeon: and the captain of the children of Simeon shall be Shelumiel the son of Zurishaddai. ¹³And his host, and those that were numbered of them, were fifty and nine thousand and three hundred. ¹⁴Then the tribe of Gad: and the captain of the sons of Gad shall be Eliasaph the son of Reuel. ¹⁵And his host, and those that were numbered of them, were forty and five thousand and six hundred and fifty. ¹⁶All that were numbered in the camp of Reuben were an hundred thousand and fifty and one thousand and four hundred and fifty, throughout their armies. And they shall set forth in the second rank. ¹⁷Then the tabernacle of the congregation shall set forward with the camp of the Levites in the middle of the camp: as they encamp, so shall they set forward, every man in his place by their standards. ¹⁸On the west side shall be the standard of the camp of Ephraim according to their armies: and the captain of the sons of Ephraim shall be Elishama the son of Ammihud. ¹⁹And his host, and those that were numbered of them, were forty thousand and five hundred. ²⁰And by him shall be the tribe of Manasseh: and the captain of the children of Manasseh shall be Gamaliel the son of Pedahzur. ²¹And his host, and those that were numbered of them, were thirty and two thousand and two hundred. ²²Then the tribe of Benjamin: and the captain of the sons of Benjamin shall be Abidan the son of Gideoni. ²³And his host, and those that were numbered of them, were thirty and five thousand and four hundred. ²⁴All that were numbered of the camp of Ephraim were an hundred thousand and eight thousand and an hundred, throughout their armies. And they shall go forward in the third rank. ²⁵The standard of the camp of Dan shall be on the north side by their armies: and the captain of the children of Dan shall be Ahiezer the son of Ammishaddai. ²⁶And his host, and those that were numbered of them, were three score and two thousand and seven hundred. ²⁷And those that encamp by him shall be the tribe of Asher: and the captain of the children of Asher shall be Pagiel the son of Ocran. ²⁸And his host, and those that were numbered of them, were forty and one thousand and five hundred. ²⁹Then the tribe of Naphtali: and the captain of the children of Naphtali shall be Ahira the son of Enan. ³⁰And his host, and those that were numbered of them, were fifty and three thousand and four hundred. ³¹All they that were numbered in the camp of Dan were an hundred thousand and fifty and seven thousand and six hundred. They shall go hindmost with their standards. ³²These are those which were numbered of the children of Israel by the house of their fathers: all those that were numbered of the camps throughout their hosts were six hundred thousand and three thousand and five hundred and fifty. ³³But the Levites were not numbered among the children of Israel; as the LORD commanded Moses. ³⁴And the children of Israel did according to all that the LORD commanded Moses: so they pitched by their standards, and so they set forward, every one after their families, according to the house of their fathers.

3 ¹These also are the generations of Aaron and Moses in the day that the LORD spoke with Moses in mount Sinai. ²And these are the names of the sons of Aaron; Nadab the firstborn, and Abihu, Eleazar, and Ithamar. ³These are the names of the sons of Aaron, the priests which were anointed, whom he consecrated to minister in the priest's office. ⁴And Nadab and Abihu died before the LORD, when they offered strange fire before the LORD, in the wilderness of Sinai, and they had no children: and Eleazar and Ithamar ministered in the priest's office in the sight of Aaron their father. ⁵And the LORD spoke to Moses, saying, ⁶Bring the tribe of Levi near, and present them before Aaron the priest, that they may minister to him. ⁷And they shall keep his charge, and the charge of the whole congregation before the tabernacle of the congregation, to do the service of the tabernacle. ⁸And they shall keep all the instruments of the tabernacle of the congregation, and the charge of the children of Israel, to do the service of the tabernacle. ⁹And you shall give the Levites to Aaron and to his sons: they are wholly given to him out of the children of Israel. ¹⁰And you shall appoint Aaron and his sons, and they shall wait on their priest's office: and the stranger that comes near shall be put to death. ¹¹And the LORD spoke to Moses, saying, ¹²And I, behold, I have taken the Levites from among the children of Israel instead of all the firstborn that opens the matrix among the children of Israel: therefore the Levites shall be mine; ¹³Because all the firstborn are mine; for on the day

that I smote all the firstborn in the land of Egypt I hallowed to me all the firstborn in Israel, both man and beast: my shall they be: I am the LORD. ¹⁴And the LORD spoke to Moses in the wilderness of Sinai, saying, ¹⁵Number the children of Levi after the house of their fathers, by their families: every male from a month old and upward shall you number them. ¹⁶And Moses numbered them according to the word of the LORD, as he was commanded. ¹⁷And these were the sons of Levi by their names; Gershon, and Kohath, and Merari. ¹⁸And these are the names of the sons of Gershon by their families; Libni, and Shimei. ¹⁹And the sons of Kohath by their families; Amram, and Izehar, Hebron, and Uzziel. ²⁰And the sons of Merari by their families; Mahli, and Mushi. These are the families of the Levites according to the house of their fathers. ²¹Of Gershon was the family of the Libnites, and the family of the Shimites: these are the families of the Gershonites. ²²Those that were numbered of them, according to the number of all the males, from a month old and upward, even those that were numbered of them were seven thousand and five hundred. ²³The families of the Gershonites shall pitch behind the tabernacle westward. ²⁴And the chief of the house of the father of the Gershonites shall be Eliasaph the son of Lael. ²⁵And the charge of the sons of Gershon in the tabernacle of the congregation shall be the tabernacle, and the tent, the covering thereof, and the hanging for the door of the tabernacle of the congregation, ²⁶And the hangings of the court, and the curtain for the door of the court, which is by the tabernacle, and by the altar round about, and the cords of it for all the service thereof. ²⁷And of Kohath was the family of the Amramites, and the family of the Izeharites, and the family of the Hebronites, and the family of the Uzzielites: these are the families of the Kohathites. ²⁸In the number of all the males, from a month old and upward, were eight thousand and six hundred, keeping the charge of the sanctuary. ²⁹The families of the sons of Kohath shall pitch on the side of the tabernacle southward. ³⁰And the chief of the house of the father of the families of the Kohathites shall be Elizaphan the son of Uzziel. ³¹And their charge shall be the ark, and the table, and the candlestick, and the altars, and the vessels of the sanctuary with which they minister, and the hanging, and all the service thereof. ³²And Eleazar the son of Aaron the priest shall be chief over the chief of the Levites, and have the oversight of them that keep the charge of the sanctuary. ³³Of Merari was the family of the Mahlites, and the family of the Mushites: these are the families of Merari. ³⁴And those that were numbered of them, according to the number of all the males, from a month old and upward, were six thousand and two hundred. ³⁵And the chief of the house of the father of the families of Merari was Zuriel the son of Abihail: these shall pitch on the side of the tabernacle northward. ³⁶And under the custody and charge of the sons of Merari shall be the boards of the tabernacle, and the bars thereof, and the pillars thereof, and the sockets thereof, and all the vessels thereof, and all that serves thereto, ³⁷And the pillars of the court round about, and their sockets, and their pins, and their cords. ³⁸But those that encamp before the tabernacle toward the east, even before the tabernacle of the congregation eastward, shall be Moses, and Aaron and his sons, keeping the charge of the sanctuary for the charge of the children of Israel; and the stranger that comes near shall be put to death. ³⁹All that were numbered of the Levites, which Moses and Aaron numbered at the commandment of the LORD, throughout their families, all the males from a month old and upward, were twenty and two thousand. ⁴⁰And the LORD said to Moses, Number all the firstborn of the males of the children of Israel from a month old and upward, and take the number of their names. ⁴¹And you shall take the Levites for me (I am the LORD) instead of all the firstborn among the children of Israel; and the cattle of the Levites instead of all the firstborn among the cattle of the children of Israel. ⁴²And Moses numbered, as the LORD commanded him, all the firstborn among the children of Israel. ⁴³And all the firstborn males by the number of names, from a month old and upward, of those that were numbered of them, were twenty and two thousand two hundred and three score and thirteen. ⁴⁴And the LORD spoke to Moses, saying, ⁴⁵Take the Levites instead of all the firstborn among the children of Israel, and the cattle of the Levites instead of their cattle; and the Levites shall be mine: I am the LORD. ⁴⁶And for those that are to be redeemed of the two hundred and three score and thirteen of the firstborn of the children of Israel, which are more than the Levites; ⁴⁷You shall even take five shekels apiece by the poll, after the shekel of the sanctuary shall you take them: (the shekel is twenty gerahs:) ⁴⁸And you shall give the money, with which the odd number of them is to be redeemed, to Aaron and to his sons. ⁴⁹And Moses took the redemption money of them that were over and above them that were redeemed by the Levites: ⁵⁰Of the firstborn of the children of Israel took he the money; a thousand three hundred and three score and five shekels, after the shekel of the sanctuary: ⁵¹And Moses gave the money of them that were redeemed to Aaron and to his sons, according to the word of the LORD, as the LORD commanded Moses.

4 ¹And the LORD spoke to Moses and to Aaron, saying, ²Take the sum of the sons of Kohath from among the sons of Levi, after their families, by the house of their fathers, ³From thirty years old and upward even until fifty years old, all that enter into the host, to do the work in the tabernacle of the congregation. ⁴This shall be the service of the sons of Kohath in the tabernacle of the congregation, about the most holy things: ⁵And when the camp sets forward, Aaron shall come, and his sons, and they shall take down the covering veil, and cover the ark of testimony with it: ⁶And shall put thereon the covering of badgers' skins, and shall spread over it a cloth wholly of blue, and shall put in the staves thereof. ⁷And on the table of show bread they shall spread a cloth of blue, and put thereon the dishes, and the spoons, and the bowls, and covers to cover with: and the continual bread shall be thereon: ⁸And they shall spread on them a cloth of scarlet, and cover the same with a covering of badgers' skins, and shall put in the staves thereof. ⁹And they shall take a cloth of blue, and cover the candlestick of the light, and his lamps, and his tongs, and his firepans, and all the oil vessels thereof, with which they minister to it: ¹⁰And they shall put it and all the vessels thereof within a covering of badgers' skins, and shall put it on a bar. ¹¹And on the golden altar they shall spread a cloth of blue, and cover it with a covering of badgers' skins, and shall put to the

staves thereof: ¹²And they shall take all the instruments of ministry, with which they minister in the sanctuary, and put them in a cloth of blue, and cover them with a covering of badgers' skins, and shall put them on a bar: ¹³And they shall take away the ashes from the altar, and spread a purple cloth thereon: ¹⁴And they shall put on it all the vessels thereof, with which they minister about it, even the censers, the meat hooks, and the shovels, and the basins, all the vessels of the altar; and they shall spread on it a covering of badgers' skins, and put to the staves of it. ¹⁵And when Aaron and his sons have made an end of covering the sanctuary, and all the vessels of the sanctuary, as the camp is to set forward; after that, the sons of Kohath shall come to bear it: but they shall not touch any holy thing, lest they die. These things are the burden of the sons of Kohath in the tabernacle of the congregation. ¹⁶And to the office of Eleazar the son of Aaron the priest pertains the oil for the light, and the sweet incense, and the daily meat offering, and the anointing oil, and the oversight of all the tabernacle, and of all that therein is, in the sanctuary, and in the vessels thereof. ¹⁷And the LORD spoke to Moses and to Aaron saying, ¹⁸Cut you not off the tribe of the families of the Kohathites from among the Levites: ¹⁹But thus do to them, that they may live, and not die, when they approach to the most holy things: Aaron and his sons shall go in, and appoint them every one to his service and to his burden: ²⁰But they shall not go in to see when the holy things are covered, lest they die. ²¹And the LORD spoke to Moses, saying, ²²Take also the sum of the sons of Gershon, throughout the houses of their fathers, by their families; ²³From thirty years old and upward until fifty years old shall you number them; all that enter in to perform the service, to do the work in the tabernacle of the congregation. ²⁴This is the service of the families of the Gershonites, to serve, and for burdens: ²⁵And they shall bear the curtains of the tabernacle, and the tabernacle of the congregation, his covering, and the covering of the badgers' skins that is above on it, and the hanging for the door of the tabernacle of the congregation, ²⁶And the hangings of the court, and the hanging for the door of the gate of the court, which is by the tabernacle and by the altar round about, and their cords, and all the instruments of their service, and all that is made for them: so shall they serve. ²⁷At the appointment of Aaron and his sons shall be all the service of the sons of the Gershonites, in all their burdens, and in all their service: and you shall appoint to them in charge all their burdens. ²⁸This is the service of the families of the sons of Gershon in the tabernacle of the congregation: and their charge shall be under the hand of Ithamar the son of Aaron the priest. ²⁹As for the sons of Merari, you shall number them after their families, by the house of their fathers; ³⁰From thirty years old and upward even to fifty years old shall you number them, every one that enters into the service, to do the work of the tabernacle of the congregation. ³¹And this is the charge of their burden, according to all their service in the tabernacle of the congregation; the boards of the tabernacle, and the bars thereof, and the pillars thereof, and sockets thereof, ³²And the pillars of the court round about, and their sockets, and their pins, and their cords, with all their instruments, and with all their service: and by name you shall reckon the instruments of the charge of their burden. ³³This is the service of the families of the sons of Merari, according to all their service, in the tabernacle of the congregation, under the hand of Ithamar the son of Aaron the priest. ³⁴And Moses and Aaron and the chief of the congregation numbered the sons of the Kohathites after their families, and after the house of their fathers, ³⁵From thirty years old and upward even to fifty years old, every one that enters into the service, for the work in the tabernacle of the congregation: ³⁶And those that were numbered of them by their families were two thousand seven hundred and fifty. ³⁷These were they that were numbered of the families of the Kohathites, all that might do service in the tabernacle of the congregation, which Moses and Aaron did number according to the commandment of the LORD by the hand of Moses. ³⁸And those that were numbered of the sons of Gershon, throughout their families, and by the house of their fathers, ³⁹From thirty years old and upward even to fifty years old, every one that enters into the service, for the work in the tabernacle of the congregation, ⁴⁰Even those that were numbered of them, throughout their families, by the house of their fathers, were two thousand and six hundred and thirty. ⁴¹These are they that were numbered of the families of the sons of Gershon, of all that might do service in the tabernacle of the congregation, whom Moses and Aaron did number according to the commandment of the LORD. ⁴²And those that were numbered of the families of the sons of Merari, throughout their families, by the house of their fathers, ⁴³From thirty years old and upward even to fifty years old, every one that enters into the service, for the work in the tabernacle of the congregation, ⁴⁴Even those that were numbered of them after their families, were three thousand and two hundred. ⁴⁵These be those that were numbered of the families of the sons of Merari, whom Moses and Aaron numbered according to the word of the LORD by the hand of Moses. ⁴⁶All those that were numbered of the Levites, whom Moses and Aaron and the chief of Israel numbered, after their families, and after the house of their fathers, ⁴⁷From thirty years old and upward even to fifty years old, every one that came to do the service of the ministry, and the service of the burden in the tabernacle of the congregation. ⁴⁸Even those that were numbered of them, were eight thousand and five hundred and fourscore, ⁴⁹According to the commandment of the LORD they were numbered by the hand of Moses, every one according to his service, and according to his burden: thus were they numbered of him, as the LORD commanded Moses.

5 ¹And the LORD spoke to Moses, saying, ²Command the children of Israel, that they put out of the camp every leper, and every one that has an issue, and whoever is defiled by the dead: ³Both male and female shall you put out, without the camp shall you put them; that they defile not their camps, in the middle whereof I dwell. ⁴And the children of Israel did so, and put them out without the camp: as the LORD spoke to Moses, so did the children of Israel. ⁵And the LORD spoke to Moses, saying, ⁶Speak to the children of Israel, When a man or woman shall commit any sin that men commit, to do a trespass against the LORD, and that person be guilty; ⁷Then they shall confess their sin which they have done: and he shall recompense his trespass with the principal thereof, and add to it the fifth part thereof,

and give it to him against whom he has trespassed. ⁸But if the man have no kinsman to recompense the trespass to, let the trespass be recompensed to the LORD, even to the priest; beside the ram of the atonement, whereby an atonement shall be made for him. ⁹And every offering of all the holy things of the children of Israel, which they bring to the priest, shall be his. ¹⁰And every man's hallowed things shall be his: whatever any man gives the priest, it shall be his. ¹¹And the LORD spoke to Moses, saying, ¹²Speak to the children of Israel, and say to them, If any man's wife go aside, and commit a trespass against him, ¹³And a man lie with her carnally, and it be hid from the eyes of her husband, and be kept close, and she be defiled, and there be no witness against her, neither she be taken with the manner; ¹⁴And the spirit of jealousy come on him, and he be jealous of his wife, and she be defiled: or if the spirit of jealousy come on him, and he be jealous of his wife, and she be not defiled: ¹⁵Then shall the man bring his wife to the priest, and he shall bring her offering for her, the tenth part of an ephah of barley meal; he shall pour no oil on it, nor put frankincense thereon; for it is an offering of jealousy, an offering of memorial, bringing iniquity to remembrance. ¹⁶And the priest shall bring her near, and set her before the LORD: ¹⁷And the priest shall take holy water in an earthen vessel; and of the dust that is in the floor of the tabernacle the priest shall take, and put it into the water: ¹⁸And the priest shall set the woman before the LORD, and uncover the woman's head, and put the offering of memorial in her hands, which is the jealousy offering: and the priest shall have in his hand the bitter water that causes the curse: ¹⁹And the priest shall charge her by an oath, and say to the woman, If no man have lain with you, and if you have not gone aside to uncleanness with another instead of your husband, be you free from this bitter water that causes the curse: ²⁰But if you have gone aside to another instead of your husband, and if you be defiled, and some man have lain with you beside your husband: ²¹Then the priest shall charge the woman with an oath of cursing, and the priest shall say to the woman, The LORD make you a curse and an oath among your people, when the LORD does make your thigh to rot, and your belly to swell; ²²And this water that causes the curse shall go into your bowels, to make your belly to swell, and your thigh to rot: And the woman shall say, Amen, amen. ²³And the priest shall write these curses in a book, and he shall blot them out with the bitter water: ²⁴And he shall cause the woman to drink the bitter water that causes the curse: and the water that causes the curse shall enter into her, and become bitter. ²⁵Then the priest shall take the jealousy offering out of the woman's hand, and shall wave the offering before the LORD, and offer it on the altar: ²⁶And the priest shall take an handful of the offering, even the memorial thereof, and burn it on the altar, and afterward shall cause the woman to drink the water. ²⁷And when he has made her to drink the water, then it shall come to pass, that, if she be defiled, and have done trespass against her husband, that the water that causes the curse shall enter into her, and become bitter, and her belly shall swell, and her thigh shall rot: and the woman shall be a curse among her people. ²⁸And if the woman be not defiled, but be clean; then she shall be free, and shall conceive seed. ²⁹This is the law of jealousies, when a wife goes aside to another instead of her husband, and is defiled; ³⁰Or when the spirit of jealousy comes on him, and he be jealous over his wife, and shall set the woman before the LORD, and the priest shall execute on her all this law. ³¹Then shall the man be guiltless from iniquity, and this woman shall bear her iniquity.

6 ¹And the LORD spoke to Moses, saying, ²Speak to the children of Israel, and say to them, When either man or woman shall separate themselves to vow a vow of a Nazarite, to separate themselves to the LORD: ³He shall separate himself from wine and strong drink, and shall drink no vinegar of wine, or vinegar of strong drink, neither shall he drink any liquor of grapes, nor eat moist grapes, or dried. ⁴All the days of his separation shall he eat nothing that is made of the vine tree, from the kernels even to the husk. ⁵All the days of the vow of his separation there shall no razor come on his head: until the days be fulfilled, in the which he separates himself to the LORD, he shall be holy, and shall let the locks of the hair of his head grow. ⁶All the days that he separates himself to the LORD he shall come at no dead body. ⁷He shall not make himself unclean for his father, or for his mother, for his brother, or for his sister, when they die: because the consecration of his God is on his head. ⁸All the days of his separation he is holy to the LORD. ⁹And if any man die very suddenly by him, and he has defiled the head of his consecration; then he shall shave his head in the day of his cleansing, on the seventh day shall he shave it. ¹⁰And on the eighth day he shall bring two turtles, or two young pigeons, to the priest, to the door of the tabernacle of the congregation: ¹¹And the priest shall offer the one for a sin offering, and the other for a burnt offering, and make an atonement for him, for that he sinned by the dead, and shall hallow his head that same day. ¹²And he shall consecrate to the LORD the days of his separation, and shall bring a lamb of the first year for a trespass offering: but the days that were before shall be lost, because his separation was defiled. ¹³And this is the law of the Nazarite, when the days of his separation are fulfilled: he shall be brought to the door of the tabernacle of the congregation: ¹⁴And he shall offer his offering to the LORD, one he lamb of the first year without blemish for a burnt offering, and one ewe lamb of the first year without blemish for a sin offering, and one ram without blemish for peace offerings, ¹⁵And a basket of unleavened bread, cakes of fine flour mingled with oil, and wafers of unleavened bread anointed with oil, and their meat offering, and their drink offerings. ¹⁶And the priest shall bring them before the LORD, and shall offer his sin offering, and his burnt offering: ¹⁷And he shall offer the ram for a sacrifice of peace offerings to the LORD, with the basket of unleavened bread: the priest shall offer also his meat offering, and his drink offering. ¹⁸And the Nazarite shall shave the head of his separation at the door of the tabernacle of the congregation, and shall take the hair of the head of his separation, and put it in the fire which is under the sacrifice of the peace offerings. ¹⁹And the priest shall take the sodden shoulder of the ram, and one unleavened cake out of the basket, and one unleavened wafer, and shall put them on the hands of the Nazarite, after the hair of his separation is shaven: ²⁰And the priest shall wave them for a wave offering before the LORD: this is holy for the priest, with the wave breast and

heave shoulder: and after that the Nazarite may drink wine. ²¹This is the law of the Nazarite who has vowed, and of his offering to the LORD for his separation, beside that that his hand shall get: according to the vow which he vowed, so he must do after the law of his separation. ²²And the LORD spoke to Moses, saying, ²³Speak to Aaron and to his sons, saying, On this wise you shall bless the children of Israel, saying to them, ²⁴The LORD bless you, and keep you: ²⁵The LORD make his face shine on you, and be gracious to you: ²⁶The LORD lift up his countenance on you, and give you peace. ²⁷And they shall put my name on the children of Israel, and I will bless them.

7

¹And it came to pass on the day that Moses had fully set up the tabernacle, and had anointed it, and sanctified it, and all the instruments thereof, both the altar and all the vessels thereof, and had anointed them, and sanctified them; ²That the princes of Israel, heads of the house of their fathers, who were the princes of the tribes, and were over them that were numbered, offered: ³And they brought their offering before the LORD, six covered wagons, and twelve oxen; a wagon for two of the princes, and for each one an ox: and they brought them before the tabernacle. ⁴And the LORD spoke to Moses, saying, ⁵Take it of them, that they may be to do the service of the tabernacle of the congregation; and you shall give them to the Levites, to every man according to his service. ⁶And Moses took the wagons and the oxen, and gave them to the Levites. ⁷Two wagons and four oxen he gave to the sons of Gershon, according to their service: ⁸And four wagons and eight oxen he gave to the sons of Merari, according to their service, under the hand of Ithamar the son of Aaron the priest. ⁹But to the sons of Kohath he gave none: because the service of the sanctuary belonging to them was that they should bear on their shoulders. ¹⁰And the princes offered for dedicating of the altar in the day that it was anointed, even the princes offered their offering before the altar. ¹¹And the LORD said to Moses, They shall offer their offering, each prince on his day, for the dedicating of the altar. ¹²And he that offered his offering the first day was Nahshon the son of Amminadab, of the tribe of Judah: ¹³And his offering was one silver charger, the weight thereof was an hundred and thirty shekels, one silver bowl of seventy shekels, after the shekel of the sanctuary; both of them were full of fine flour mingled with oil for a meat offering: ¹⁴One spoon of ten shekels of gold, full of incense: ¹⁵One young bullock, one ram, one lamb of the first year, for a burnt offering: ¹⁶One kid of the goats for a sin offering: ¹⁷And for a sacrifice of peace offerings, two oxen, five rams, five he goats, five lambs of the first year: this was the offering of Nahshon the son of Amminadab. ¹⁸On the second day Nethaneel the son of Zuar, prince of Issachar, did offer: ¹⁹He offered for his offering one silver charger, the weight whereof was an hundred and thirty shekels, one silver bowl of seventy shekels, after the shekel of the sanctuary; both of them full of fine flour mingled with oil for a meat offering: ²⁰One spoon of gold of ten shekels, full of incense: ²¹One young bullock, one ram, one lamb of the first year, for a burnt offering: ²²One kid of the goats for a sin offering: ²³And for a sacrifice of peace offerings, two oxen, five rams, five he goats, five lambs of the first year: this was the offering of Nethaneel the son of Zuar. ²⁴On the third day Eliab the son of Helon, prince of the children of Zebulun, did offer: ²⁵His offering was one silver charger, the weight whereof was an hundred and thirty shekels, one silver bowl of seventy shekels, after the shekel of the sanctuary; both of them full of fine flour mingled with oil for a meat offering: ²⁶One golden spoon of ten shekels, full of incense: ²⁷One young bullock, one ram, one lamb of the first year, for a burnt offering: ²⁸One kid of the goats for a sin offering: ²⁹And for a sacrifice of peace offerings, two oxen, five rams, five he goats, five lambs of the first year: this was the offering of Eliab the son of Helon. ³⁰On the fourth day Elizur the son of Shedeur, prince of the children of Reuben, did offer: ³¹His offering was one silver charger of the weight of an hundred and thirty shekels, one silver bowl of seventy shekels, after the shekel of the sanctuary; both of them full of fine flour mingled with oil for a meat offering: ³²One golden spoon of ten shekels, full of incense: ³³One young bullock, one ram, one lamb of the first year, for a burnt offering: ³⁴One kid of the goats for a sin offering: ³⁵And for a sacrifice of peace offerings, two oxen, five rams, five he goats, five lambs of the first year: this was the offering of Elizur the son of Shedeur. ³⁶On the fifth day Shelumiel the son of Zurishaddai, prince of the children of Simeon, did offer: ³⁷His offering was one silver charger, the weight whereof was an hundred and thirty shekels, one silver bowl of seventy shekels, after the shekel of the sanctuary; both of them full of fine flour mingled with oil for a meat offering: ³⁸One golden spoon of ten shekels, full of incense: ³⁹One young bullock, one ram, one lamb of the first year, for a burnt offering: ⁴⁰One kid of the goats for a sin offering: ⁴¹And for a sacrifice of peace offerings, two oxen, five rams, five he goats, five lambs of the first year: this was the offering of Shelumiel the son of Zurishaddai. ⁴²On the sixth day Eliasaph the son of Deuel, prince of the children of Gad, offered: ⁴³His offering was one silver charger of the weight of an hundred and thirty shekels, a silver bowl of seventy shekels, after the shekel of the sanctuary; both of them full of fine flour mingled with oil for a meat offering: ⁴⁴One golden spoon of ten shekels, full of incense: ⁴⁵One young bullock, one ram, one lamb of the first year, for a burnt offering: ⁴⁶One kid of the goats for a sin offering: ⁴⁷And for a sacrifice of peace offerings, two oxen, five rams, five he goats, five lambs of the first year: this was the offering of Eliasaph the son of Deuel. ⁴⁸On the seventh day Elishama the son of Ammihud, prince of the children of Ephraim, offered: ⁴⁹His offering was one silver charger, the weight whereof was an hundred and thirty shekels, one silver bowl of seventy shekels, after the shekel of the sanctuary; both of them full of fine flour mingled with oil for a meat offering: ⁵⁰One golden spoon of ten shekels, full of incense: ⁵¹One young bullock, one ram, one lamb of the first year, for a burnt offering: ⁵²One kid of the goats for a sin offering: ⁵³And for a sacrifice of peace offerings, two oxen, five rams, five he goats, five lambs of the first year: this was the offering of Elishama the son of Ammihud. ⁵⁴On the eighth day offered Gamaliel the son of Pedahzur, prince of the children of Manasseh: ⁵⁵His offering was one silver charger of the weight of an hundred and thirty shekels, one silver bowl of seventy shekels, after the shekel of the sanctuary;

both of them full of fine flour mingled with oil for a meat offering: ⁵⁶One golden spoon of ten shekels, full of incense: ⁵⁷One young bullock, one ram, one lamb of the first year, for a burnt offering: ⁵⁸One kid of the goats for a sin offering: ⁵⁹And for a sacrifice of peace offerings, two oxen, five rams, five he goats, five lambs of the first year: this was the offering of Gamaliel the son of Pedahzur. ⁶⁰On the ninth day Abidan the son of Gideoni, prince of the children of Benjamin, offered: ⁶¹His offering was one silver charger, the weight whereof was an hundred and thirty shekels, one silver bowl of seventy shekels, after the shekel of the sanctuary; both of them full of fine flour mingled with oil for a meat offering: ⁶²One golden spoon of ten shekels, full of incense: ⁶³One young bullock, one ram, one lamb of the first year, for a burnt offering: ⁶⁴One kid of the goats for a sin offering: ⁶⁵And for a sacrifice of peace offerings, two oxen, five rams, five he goats, five lambs of the first year: this was the offering of Abidan the son of Gideoni. ⁶⁶On the tenth day Ahiezer the son of Ammishaddai, prince of the children of Dan, offered: ⁶⁷His offering was one silver charger, the weight whereof was an hundred and thirty shekels, one silver bowl of seventy shekels, after the shekel of the sanctuary; both of them full of fine flour mingled with oil for a meat offering: ⁶⁸One golden spoon of ten shekels, full of incense: ⁶⁹One young bullock, one ram, one lamb of the first year, for a burnt offering: ⁷⁰One kid of the goats for a sin offering: ⁷¹And for a sacrifice of peace offerings, two oxen, five rams, five he goats, five lambs of the first year: this was the offering of Ahiezer the son of Ammishaddai. ⁷²On the eleventh day Pagiel the son of Ocran, prince of the children of Asher, offered: ⁷³His offering was one silver charger, the weight whereof was an hundred and thirty shekels, one silver bowl of seventy shekels, after the shekel of the sanctuary; both of them full of fine flour mingled with oil for a meat offering: ⁷⁴One golden spoon of ten shekels, full of incense: ⁷⁵One young bullock, one ram, one lamb of the first year, for a burnt offering: ⁷⁶One kid of the goats for a sin offering: ⁷⁷And for a sacrifice of peace offerings, two oxen, five rams, five he goats, five lambs of the first year: this was the offering of Pagiel the son of Ocran. ⁷⁸On the twelfth day Ahira the son of Enan, prince of the children of Naphtali, offered: ⁷⁹His offering was one silver charger, the weight whereof was an hundred and thirty shekels, one silver bowl of seventy shekels, after the shekel of the sanctuary; both of them full of fine flour mingled with oil for a meat offering: ⁸⁰One golden spoon of ten shekels, full of incense: ⁸¹One young bullock, one ram, one lamb of the first year, for a burnt offering: ⁸²One kid of the goats for a sin offering: ⁸³And for a sacrifice of peace offerings, two oxen, five rams, five he goats, five lambs of the first year: this was the offering of Ahira the son of Enan. ⁸⁴This was the dedication of the altar, in the day when it was anointed, by the princes of Israel: twelve chargers of silver, twelve silver bowls, twelve spoons of gold: ⁸⁵Each charger of silver weighing an hundred and thirty shekels, each bowl seventy: all the silver vessels weighed two thousand and four hundred shekels, after the shekel of the sanctuary: ⁸⁶The golden spoons were twelve, full of incense, weighing ten shekels apiece, after the shekel of the sanctuary: all the gold of the spoons was an hundred and twenty shekels. ⁸⁷All the oxen for the burnt offering were twelve bullocks, the rams twelve, the lambs of the first year twelve, with their meat offering: and the kids of the goats for sin offering twelve. ⁸⁸And all the oxen for the sacrifice of the peace offerings were twenty and four bullocks, the rams sixty, the he goats sixty, the lambs of the first year sixty. This was the dedication of the altar, after that it was anointed. ⁸⁹And when Moses was gone into the tabernacle of the congregation to speak with him, then he heard the voice of one speaking to him from off the mercy seat that was on the ark of testimony, from between the two cherubim: and he spoke to him.

8 ¹And the LORD spoke to Moses, saying, ²Speak to Aaron and say to him, When you light the lamps, the seven lamps shall give light over against the candlestick. ³And Aaron did so; he lighted the lamps thereof over against the candlestick, as the LORD commanded Moses. ⁴And this work of the candlestick was of beaten gold, to the shaft thereof, to the flowers thereof, was beaten work: according to the pattern which the LORD had showed Moses, so he made the candlestick. ⁵And the LORD spoke to Moses, saying, ⁶Take the Levites from among the children of Israel, and cleanse them. ⁷And thus shall you do to them, to cleanse them: Sprinkle water of purifying on them, and let them shave all their flesh, and let them wash their clothes, and so make themselves clean. ⁸Then let them take a young bullock with his meat offering, even fine flour mingled with oil, and another young bullock shall you take for a sin offering. ⁹And you shall bring the Levites before the tabernacle of the congregation: and you shall gather the whole assembly of the children of Israel together: ¹⁰And you shall bring the Levites before the LORD: and the children of Israel shall put their hands on the Levites: ¹¹And Aaron shall offer the Levites before the LORD for an offering of the children of Israel, that they may execute the service of the LORD. ¹²And the Levites shall lay their hands on the heads of the bullocks: and you shall offer the one for a sin offering, and the other for a burnt offering, to the LORD, to make an atonement for the Levites. ¹³And you shall set the Levites before Aaron, and before his sons, and offer them for an offering to the LORD. ¹⁴Thus shall you separate the Levites from among the children of Israel: and the Levites shall be mine. ¹⁵And after that shall the Levites go in to do the service of the tabernacle of the congregation: and you shall cleanse them, and offer them for an offering. ¹⁶For they are wholly given to me from among the children of Israel; instead of such as open every womb, even instead of the firstborn of all the children of Israel, have I taken them to me. ¹⁷For all the firstborn of the children of Israel are mine, both man and beast: on the day that I smote every firstborn in the land of Egypt I sanctified them for myself. ¹⁸And I have taken the Levites for all the firstborn of the children of Israel. ¹⁹And I have given the Levites as a gift to Aaron and to his sons from among the children of Israel, to do the service of the children of Israel in the tabernacle of the congregation, and to make an atonement for the children of Israel: that there be no plague among the children of Israel, when the children of Israel come near to the sanctuary. ²⁰And Moses, and Aaron, and all the congregation of the children of Israel, did to the Levites according to all that the

LORD commanded Moses concerning the Levites, so did the children of Israel to them. ²¹And the Levites were purified, and they washed their clothes; and Aaron offered them as an offering before the LORD; and Aaron made an atonement for them to cleanse them. ²²And after that went the Levites in to do their service in the tabernacle of the congregation before Aaron, and before his sons: as the LORD had commanded Moses concerning the Levites, so did they to them. ²³And the LORD spoke to Moses, saying, ²⁴This is it that belongs to the Levites: from twenty and five years old and upward they shall go in to wait on the service of the tabernacle of the congregation: ²⁵And from the age of fifty years they shall cease waiting on the service thereof, and shall serve no more: ²⁶But shall minister with their brothers in the tabernacle of the congregation, to keep the charge, and shall do no service. Thus shall you do to the Levites touching their charge.

9 ¹And the LORD spoke to Moses in the wilderness of Sinai, in the first month of the second year after they were come out of the land of Egypt, saying, ²Let the children of Israel also keep the passover at his appointed season. ³In the fourteenth day of this month, at even, you shall keep it in his appointed season: according to all the rites of it, and according to all the ceremonies thereof, shall you keep it. ⁴And Moses spoke to the children of Israel, that they should keep the passover. ⁵And they kept the passover on the fourteenth day of the first month at even in the wilderness of Sinai: according to all that the LORD commanded Moses, so did the children of Israel. ⁶And there were certain men, who were defiled by the dead body of a man, that they could not keep the passover on that day: and they came before Moses and before Aaron on that day: ⁷And those men said to him, We are defiled by the dead body of a man: why are we kept back, that we may not offer an offering of the LORD in his appointed season among the children of Israel? ⁸And Moses said to them, Stand still, and I will hear what the LORD will command concerning you. ⁹And the LORD spoke to Moses, saying, ¹⁰Speak to the children of Israel, saying, If any man of you or of your posterity shall be unclean by reason of a dead body, or be in a journey afar off, yet he shall keep the passover to the LORD. ¹¹The fourteenth day of the second month at even they shall keep it, and eat it with unleavened bread and bitter herbs. ¹²They shall leave none of it to the morning, nor break any bone of it: according to all the ordinances of the passover they shall keep it. ¹³But the man that is clean, and is not in a journey, and declines to keep the passover, even the same soul shall be cut off from among his people: because he brought not the offering of the LORD in his appointed season, that man shall bear his sin. ¹⁴And if a stranger shall sojourn among you, and will keep the passover to the LORD; according to the ordinance of the passover, and according to the manner thereof, so shall he do: you shall have one ordinance, both for the stranger, and for him that was born in the land. ¹⁵And on the day that the tabernacle was reared up the cloud covered the tabernacle, namely, the tent of the testimony: and at even there was on the tabernacle as it were the appearance of fire, until the morning. ¹⁶So it was always: the cloud covered it by day, and the appearance of fire by night. ¹⁷And when the cloud was taken up from the tabernacle, then after that the children of Israel journeyed: and in the place where the cloud stayed, there the children of Israel pitched their tents. ¹⁸At the commandment of the LORD the children of Israel journeyed, and at the commandment of the LORD they pitched: as long as the cloud stayed on the tabernacle they rested in their tents. ¹⁹And when the cloud tarried long on the tabernacle many days, then the children of Israel kept the charge of the LORD, and journeyed not. ²⁰And so it was, when the cloud was a few days on the tabernacle; according to the commandment of the LORD they stayed in their tents, and according to the commandment of the LORD they journeyed. ²¹And so it was, when the cloud stayed from even to the morning, and that the cloud was taken up in the morning, then they journeyed: whether it was by day or by night that the cloud was taken up, they journeyed. ²²Or whether it were two days, or a month, or a year, that the cloud tarried on the tabernacle, remaining thereon, the children of Israel stayed in their tents, and journeyed not: but when it was taken up, they journeyed. ²³At the commandment of the LORD they rested in the tents, and at the commandment of the LORD they journeyed: they kept the charge of the LORD, at the commandment of the LORD by the hand of Moses.

10 ¹And the LORD spoke to Moses, saying, ²Make you two trumpets of silver; of a whole piece shall you make them: that you may use them for the calling of the assembly, and for the journeying of the camps. ³And when they shall blow with them, all the assembly shall assemble themselves to you at the door of the tabernacle of the congregation. ⁴And if they blow but with one trumpet, then the princes, which are heads of the thousands of Israel, shall gather themselves to you. ⁵When you blow an alarm, then the camps that lie on the east parts shall go forward. ⁶When you blow an alarm the second time, then the camps that lie on the south side shall take their journey: they shall blow an alarm for their journeys. ⁷But when the congregation is to be gathered together, you shall blow, but you shall not sound an alarm. ⁸And the sons of Aaron, the priests, shall blow with the trumpets; and they shall be to you for an ordinance for ever throughout your generations. ⁹And if you go to war in your land against the enemy that oppresses you, then you shall blow an alarm with the trumpets; and you shall be remembered before the LORD your God, and you shall be saved from your enemies. ¹⁰Also in the day of your gladness, and in your solemn days, and in the beginnings of your months, you shall blow with the trumpets over your burnt offerings, and over the sacrifices of your peace offerings; that they may be to you for a memorial before your God: I am the LORD your God. ¹¹And it came to pass on the twentieth day of the second month, in the second year, that the cloud was taken up from off the tabernacle of the testimony. ¹²And the children of Israel took their journeys out of the wilderness of Sinai; and the cloud rested in the wilderness of Paran. ¹³And they first took their journey according to the commandment of the LORD by the hand of Moses. ¹⁴In the first place went the standard of the camp of the children of Judah according to their armies: and over his host was Nahshon the son of Amminadab. ¹⁵And over the host of the tribe of the children of Issachar was Nethaneel the son of Zuar. ¹⁶And over the host of the tribe of the children of Zebulun was Eliab the son of Helon. ¹⁷And the tabernacle was taken down; and the sons of Gershon and the sons of Merari set forward, bearing the tabernacle. ¹⁸And the standard of the camp of Reuben set forward according to their armies: and over his host was Elizur the son of Shedeur. ¹⁹And over the host of the tribe of the children of Simeon was Shelumiel the son of Zurishaddai. ²⁰And over the host of the tribe of the children of Gad was Eliasaph the son of Deuel. ²¹And the Kohathites set forward, bearing the sanctuary: and the other did set up the tabernacle against they came. ²²And the standard of the camp of the children of Ephraim set forward according to their armies: and over his host was Elishama the son of Ammihud. ²³And over the host of the tribe of the children of Manasseh was Gamaliel the son of Pedahzur. ²⁴And over the host of the tribe of the children of Benjamin was Abidan the son of Gideoni. ²⁵And the standard of the camp of the children of Dan set forward, which was the rear guard of all the camps throughout their hosts: and over his host was Ahiezer the son of Ammishaddai. ²⁶And over the host of the tribe of the children of Asher was Pagiel the son of Ocran. ²⁷And over the host of the tribe of the children of Naphtali was Ahira the son of Enan. ²⁸Thus were the journeys of the children of Israel according to their armies, when they set forward. ²⁹And Moses said to Hobab, the son of Raguel the Midianite, Moses' father in law, We are journeying to the place of which the LORD said, I will give it you: come you with us, and we will do you good: for the LORD has spoken good concerning Israel. ³⁰And he said to him, I will not go; but I will depart to my own land, and to my kindred. ³¹And he said, Leave us not, I pray you; for as much as you know how we are to encamp in the wilderness, and you may be to us instead of eyes. ³²And it shall be, if you go with us, yes, it shall be, that what goodness the LORD shall do to us, the same will we do to you. ³³And they departed from the mount of the LORD three days' journey: and the ark of the covenant of the LORD went before them in the three days' journey, to search out a resting place for them. ³⁴And the cloud of the LORD was on them by day, when they went out of the camp. ³⁵And it came to pass, when the ark set forward, that Moses said, Rise up, LORD, and let your enemies be scattered; and let them that hate you flee before you. ³⁶And when it rested, he said, Return, O LORD, to the many thousands of Israel.

11 ¹And when the people complained, it displeased the LORD: and the LORD heard it; and his anger was kindled; and the fire of the LORD burnt among them, and consumed them that were in the uttermost parts of the camp. ²And the people cried to Moses; and when Moses prayed to the LORD, the fire was quenched. ³And he called the name of the place Taberah: because the fire of the LORD burnt among them. ⁴And the mixed multitude that was among them fell a lusting: and the children of Israel also wept again, and said, Who shall give us flesh to eat? ⁵We remember the fish, which we did eat in Egypt freely; the cucumbers, and the melons, and the leeks, and the onions, and the garlic: ⁶But now our soul is dried away: there is nothing at all, beside this manna, before our eyes. ⁷And the manna was as coriander seed, and the color thereof as the color of bdellium. ⁸And the people went about, and gathered it, and ground it in mills, or beat it in a mortar, and baked it in pans, and made cakes of it: and the taste of it was as the taste of fresh oil. ⁹And when the dew fell on the camp in the night, the manna fell on it. ¹⁰Then Moses heard the people weep throughout their families, every man in the door of his tent: and the anger of the LORD was kindled greatly; Moses also was displeased. ¹¹And Moses said to the LORD, Why have you afflicted your servant? and why have I not found favor in your sight, that you lay the burden of all this people on me? ¹²Have I conceived all this people? have I begotten them, that you should say to me, Carry them in your bosom, as a nursing father bears the sucking child, to the land which you swore to their fathers? ¹³From where should I have flesh to give to all this people? for they weep to me, saying, Give us flesh, that we may eat. ¹⁴I am not able to bear all this people alone, because it is too heavy for me. ¹⁵And if you deal thus with me, kill me, I pray you, out of hand, if I have found favor in your sight; and let me not see my wretchedness. ¹⁶And the LORD said to Moses, Gather to me seventy men of the elders of Israel, whom you know to be the elders of the people, and officers over them; and bring them to the tabernacle of the congregation, that they may stand there with you. ¹⁷And I will come down and talk with you there: and I will take of the spirit which is on you, and will put it on them; and they shall bear the burden of the people with you, that you bear it not yourself alone. ¹⁸And say you to the people, Sanctify yourselves against to morrow, and you shall eat flesh: for you have wept in the ears of the LORD, saying, Who shall give us flesh to eat? for it was well with us in Egypt: therefore the LORD will give you flesh, and you shall eat. ¹⁹You shall not eat one day, nor two days, nor five days, neither ten days, nor twenty days; ²⁰But even a whole month, until it come out at your nostrils, and it be loathsome to you: because that you have despised the LORD which is among you, and have wept before him, saying, Why came we forth out of Egypt? ²¹And Moses said, The people, among whom I am, are six hundred thousand footmen; and you have said, I will give them flesh, that they may eat a whole month. ²²Shall the flocks and the herds be slain for them, to suffice them? or shall all the fish of the sea be gathered together for them, to suffice them? ²³And the LORD said to Moses, Is the LORD's hand waxed short? you shall see now whether my word shall come to pass to you or not. ²⁴And Moses went out, and told the people the words of the LORD, and gathered the seventy men of the elders of the people, and set them round about the tabernacle. ²⁵And the LORD came down in a cloud, and spoke to him, and took of the spirit that was on him, and gave it to the seventy elders: and it came to pass, that, when the spirit rested on them, they prophesied, and did not cease. ²⁶But there remained two of the men in the camp, the name of the one was Eldad, and the name of the other Medad: and the spirit rested on them; and they were of them that were written, but went not out to the tabernacle: and they prophesied in the camp. ²⁷And there ran a young man, and told Moses, and said, Eldad and Medad do prophesy in the camp. ²⁸And Joshua the son of Nun, the servant of Moses, one of his young men, answered and said, My lord Moses, forbid them. ²⁹And Moses said to him, Envy you for my sake? would God that all the LORD's people were prophets, and that the LORD would put his spirit on them! ³⁰And Moses got him into the camp, he and the elders of Israel. ³¹And there went forth a wind from the LORD, and brought quails from the sea, and let them fall by the camp, as it were a day's journey on this side, and as it were a day's journey on the other side, round about the camp, and as it were two cubits high on the face of the earth. ³²And the people stood up all that day, and all that night, and all the next day, and they gathered the quails: he that gathered least gathered ten homers: and they spread them all abroad for themselves round about the camp. ³³And while the flesh was yet between their teeth, before it was chewed, the wrath of the LORD was kindled against the people, and the LORD smote the people with a very great plague. ³⁴And he called the name of that place Kibrothhattaavah: because there they buried the people that lusted. ³⁵And the people journeyed from Kibrothhattaavah to Hazeroth; and stayed at Hazeroth.

12

¹And Miriam and Aaron spoke against Moses because of the Ethiopian woman whom he had married: for he had married an Ethiopian woman. ²And they said, Has the LORD indeed spoken only by Moses? has he not spoken also by us? And the LORD heard it. ³(Now the man Moses was very meek, above all the men which were on the face of the earth.) ⁴And the LORD spoke suddenly to Moses, and to Aaron, and to Miriam, Come out you three to the tabernacle of the congregation. And they three came out. ⁵And the LORD came down in the pillar of the cloud, and stood in the door of the tabernacle, and called Aaron and Miriam: and they both came forth. ⁶And he said, Hear now my words: If there be a prophet among you, I the LORD will make myself known to him in a vision, and will speak to him in a dream. ⁷My servant Moses is not so, who is faithful in all my house. ⁸With him will I speak mouth to mouth, even apparently, and not in dark speeches; and the similitude of the LORD shall he behold: why then were you not afraid to speak against my servant Moses? ⁹And the anger of the LORD was kindled against them; and he departed. ¹⁰And the cloud departed from off the tabernacle; and, behold, Miriam became leprous, white as snow: and Aaron looked on Miriam, and, behold, she was leprous. ¹¹And Aaron said to Moses, Alas, my lord, I beseech you, lay not the sin on us, wherein we have done foolishly, and wherein we have sinned. ¹²Let her not be as one dead, of whom the flesh is half consumed when he comes out of his mother's womb. ¹³And Moses cried to the LORD, saying, Heal her now, O God, I beseech you. ¹⁴And the LORD said to Moses, If her father had but spit in her face, should she not be ashamed seven days? let her be shut out from the camp seven days, and after that let her be received in again. ¹⁵And Miriam was shut out from the camp seven days: and the people journeyed not till Miriam was brought in again. ¹⁶And afterward the people removed from Hazeroth, and pitched in the wilderness of Paran.

13

¹And the LORD spoke to Moses, saying, ²Send you men, that they may search the land of Canaan, which I give to the children of Israel: of every tribe of their fathers shall you send a man, every one a ruler among them. ³And Moses by the commandment of the LORD sent them from the wilderness of Paran: all those men were heads of the children of Israel. ⁴And these were their names: of the tribe of Reuben, Shammua the son of Zaccur. ⁵Of the tribe of Simeon, Shaphat the son of Hori. ⁶Of the tribe of Judah, Caleb the son of Jephunneh. ⁷Of the tribe of Issachar, Igal the son of Joseph. ⁸Of the tribe of Ephraim, Oshea the son of Nun. ⁹Of the tribe of Benjamin, Palti the son of Raphu. ¹⁰Of the tribe of Zebulun, Gaddiel the son of Sodi. ¹¹Of the tribe of Joseph, namely, of the tribe of Manasseh, Gaddi the son of Susi. ¹²Of the tribe of Dan, Ammiel the son of Gemalli. ¹³Of the tribe of Asher, Sethur the son of Michael. ¹⁴Of the tribe of Naphtali, Nahbi the son of Vophsi. ¹⁵Of the tribe of Gad, Geuel the son of Machi. ¹⁶These are the names of the men which Moses sent to spy out the land. And Moses called Oshea the son of Nun Jehoshua. ¹⁷And Moses sent them to spy out the land of Canaan, and said to them, Get you up this way southward, and go up into the mountain: ¹⁸And see the land, what it is, and the people that dwells therein, whether they be strong or weak, few or many; ¹⁹And what the land is that they dwell in, whether it be good or bad; and what cities they be that they dwell in, whether in tents, or in strong holds; ²⁰And what the land is, whether it be fat or lean, whether there be wood therein, or not. And be you of good courage, and bring of the fruit of the land. Now the time was the time of the first ripe grapes. ²¹So they went up, and searched the land from the wilderness of Zin to Rehob, as men come to Hamath. ²²And they ascended by the south, and came to Hebron; where Ahiman, Sheshai, and Talmai, the children of Anak, were. (Now Hebron was built seven years before Zoan in Egypt.) ²³And they came to the brook of Eshcol, and cut down from there a branch with one cluster of grapes, and they bore it between two on a staff; and they brought of the pomegranates, and of the figs. ²⁴The place was called the brook Eshcol, because of the cluster of grapes which the children of Israel cut down from there. ²⁵And they returned from searching of the land after forty days. ²⁶And they went and came to Moses, and to Aaron, and to all the congregation of the children of Israel, to the wilderness of Paran, to Kadesh; and brought back word to them, and to all the congregation, and showed them the fruit of the land. ²⁷And they told him, and said, We came to the land where you sent us, and surely it flows with milk and honey; and this is the fruit of it. ²⁸Nevertheless the people be strong that dwell in the land, and the cities are walled, and very great: and moreover we saw the children of Anak there. ²⁹The Amalekites dwell in the land of the south: and the Hittites, and the Jebusites, and the Amorites, dwell in the mountains: and the Canaanites dwell by the sea, and by the coast of Jordan. ³⁰And Caleb stilled the people before Moses, and said, Let us go up at once, and possess it; for we are well able to overcome it. ³¹But the men that went up with him said, We be not able to go up against the people; for they are stronger than we. ³²And they brought up an evil report of the land which they had searched to the children of Israel, saying, The land, through which we have gone to search it, is a land that eats up the inhabitants thereof; and all the people that we saw in it are men of a great stature. ³³And there we saw the giants, the sons of Anak, which come of the giants: and we were in our own sight as grasshoppers, and so we were in their sight.

14 ¹And all the congregation lifted up their voice, and cried; and the people wept that night. ²And all the children of Israel murmured against Moses and against Aaron: and the whole congregation said to them, Would God that we had died in the land of Egypt! or would God we had died in this wilderness! ³And why has the LORD brought us to this land, to fall by the sword, that our wives and our children should be a prey? were it not better for us to return into Egypt? ⁴And they said one to another, Let us make a captain, and let us return into Egypt. ⁵Then Moses and Aaron fell on their faces before all the assembly of the congregation of the children of Israel. ⁶And Joshua the son of Nun, and Caleb the son of Jephunneh, which were of them that searched the land, rent their clothes: ⁷And they spoke to all the company of the children of Israel, saying, The land, which we passed through to search it, is an exceeding good land. ⁸If the LORD delight in us, then he will bring us into this land, and give it us; a land which flows with milk and honey. ⁹Only rebel not you against the LORD, neither fear you the people of the land; for they are bread for us: their defense is departed from them, and the LORD is with us: fear them not. ¹⁰But all the congregation bade stone them with stones. And the glory of the LORD appeared in the tabernacle of the congregation before all the children of Israel. ¹¹And the LORD said to Moses, How long will this people provoke me? and how long will it be before they believe me, for all the signs which I have showed among them? ¹²I will smite them with the pestilence, and disinherit them, and will make of you a greater nation and mightier than they. ¹³And Moses said to the LORD, Then the Egyptians shall hear it, (for you brought up this people in your might from among them;) ¹⁴And they will tell it to the inhabitants of this land: for they have heard that you LORD are among this people, that you LORD are seen face to face, and that your cloud stands over them, and that you go before them, by day time in a pillar of a cloud, and in a pillar of fire by night. ¹⁵Now if you shall kill all this people as one man, then the nations which have heard the fame of you will speak, saying, ¹⁶Because the LORD was not able to bring this people into the land which he swore to them, therefore he has slain them in the wilderness. ¹⁷And now, I beseech you, let the power of my LORD be great, according as you have spoken, saying, ¹⁸The LORD is long-suffering, and of great mercy, forgiving iniquity and transgression, and by no means clearing the guilty, visiting the iniquity of the fathers on the children to the third and fourth generation. ¹⁹Pardon, I beseech you, the iniquity of this people according to the greatness of your mercy, and as you have forgiven this people, from Egypt even until now. ²⁰And the LORD said, I have pardoned according to your word: ²¹But as truly as I live, all the earth shall be filled with the glory of the LORD. ²²Because all those men which have seen my glory, and my miracles, which I did in Egypt and in the wilderness, and have tempted me now these ten times, and have not listened to my voice; ²³Surely they shall not see the land which I swore to their fathers, neither shall any of them that provoked me see it: ²⁴But my servant Caleb, because he had another spirit with him, and has followed me fully, him will I bring into the land into where he went; and his seed shall possess it. ²⁵(Now the Amalekites and the Canaanites dwelled in the valley.) Tomorrow turn you, and get you into the wilderness by the way of the Red sea. ²⁶And the LORD spoke to Moses and to Aaron, saying, ²⁷How long shall I bear with this evil congregation, which murmur against me? I have heard the murmurings of the children of Israel, which they murmur against me. ²⁸Say to them, As truly as I live, says the LORD, as you have spoken in my ears, so will I do to you: ²⁹Your carcasses shall fall in this wilderness; and all that were numbered of you, according to your whole number, from twenty years old and upward which have murmured against me. ³⁰Doubtless you shall not come into the land, concerning which I swore to make you dwell therein, save Caleb the son of Jephunneh, and Joshua the son of Nun. ³¹But your little ones, which you said should be a prey, them will I bring in, and they shall know the land which you have despised. ³²But as for you, your carcasses, they shall fall in this wilderness. ³³And your children shall wander in the wilderness forty years, and bear your prostitutions, until your carcasses be wasted in the wilderness. ³⁴After the number of the days in which you searched the land, even forty days, each day for a year, shall you bear your iniquities, even forty years, and you shall know my breach of promise. ³⁵I the LORD have said, I will surely do it to all this evil congregation, that are gathered together against me: in this wilderness they shall be consumed, and there they shall die. ³⁶And the men, which Moses sent to search the land, who returned, and made all the congregation to murmur against him, by bringing up a slander on the land, ³⁷Even those men that did bring up the evil report on the land, died by the plague before the LORD. ³⁸But Joshua the son of Nun, and Caleb the son of Jephunneh, which were of the men that went to search the land, lived still. ³⁹And Moses told these sayings to all the children of Israel: and the people mourned greatly. ⁴⁰And they rose up early in the morning, and got them up into the top of the mountain, saying, See, we be here, and will go up to the place which the LORD has promised: for we have sinned. ⁴¹And Moses said, Why now do you transgress the commandment of the LORD? but it shall not prosper. ⁴²Go not up, for the LORD is not among you; that you be not smitten before your enemies. ⁴³For the Amalekites and the Canaanites are there before you, and you shall fall by the sword: because you are turned away from the LORD, therefore the LORD will not be with you. ⁴⁴But they presumed to go up to the hill top: nevertheless the ark of the covenant of the LORD, and Moses, departed not out of the camp. ⁴⁵Then the Amalekites came down, and the Canaanites which dwelled in that hill, and smote them, and discomfited them, even to Hormah.

15 ¹And the LORD spoke to Moses, saying, ²Speak to the children of Israel, and say to them, When you be come into the land of your habitations, which I give to you, ³And will make an offering by fire to the LORD, a burnt offering, or a sacrifice in performing a vow, or in a freewill offering, or in your solemn feasts, to make a sweet smell to the LORD, of the herd or of the flock: ⁴Then shall he that offers his offering to the LORD bring a meat offering of a tenth deal of flour mingled with the fourth part of an hin of oil. ⁵And the fourth part of an hin of wine for a drink offering shall you prepare with the burnt offering or sacrifice, for one lamb. ⁶Or for a ram, you shall prepare for a meat offering two tenth deals of flour mingled with the third part of an hin of oil. ⁷And for a drink offering you shall offer the third part of an hin of wine, for a sweet smell to the LORD. ⁸And when you prepare a bullock for a burnt offering, or for a sacrifice in performing a vow, or peace offerings to the LORD: ⁹Then shall he bring with a bullock a meat offering of three tenth deals of flour mingled with half an hin of oil. ¹⁰And you shall bring for a drink offering half an hin of wine, for an offering made by fire, of a sweet smell to the LORD. ¹¹Thus shall it be done for one bullock, or for one ram, or for a lamb, or a kid. ¹²According to the number that you shall prepare, so shall you do to every one according to their number. ¹³All that are born of the country shall do these things after this manner, in offering an offering made by fire, of a sweet smell to the LORD. ¹⁴And if a stranger sojourn with you, or whoever be among you in your generations, and will offer an offering made by fire, of a sweet smell to the LORD; as you do, so he shall do. ¹⁵One ordinance shall be both for you of the congregation, and also for the stranger that sojourns with you, an ordinance for ever in your generations: as you are, so shall the stranger be before the LORD. ¹⁶One law and one manner shall be for you, and for the stranger that sojourns with you. ¹⁷And the LORD spoke to Moses, saying, ¹⁸Speak to the children of Israel, and say to them, When you come into the land where I bring you, ¹⁹Then it shall be, that, when you eat of the bread of the land, you shall offer up an heave offering to the LORD. ²⁰You shall offer up a cake of the first of your dough for an heave offering: as you do the heave offering of the threshing floor, so shall you heave it. ²¹Of the first of your dough you shall give to the LORD an heave offering in your generations. ²²And if you have erred, and not observed all these commandments, which the LORD has spoken to Moses, ²³Even all that the LORD has commanded you by the hand of Moses, from the day that the LORD commanded Moses, and henceforward among your generations; ²⁴Then it shall be, if something be committed by ignorance without the knowledge of the congregation, that all the congregation shall offer one young bullock for a burnt offering, for a sweet smell to the LORD, with his meat offering, and his drink offering, according to the manner, and one kid of the goats for a sin offering. ²⁵And the priest shall make an atonement for all the congregation of the children of Israel, and it shall be forgiven them; for it is ignorance: and they shall bring their offering, a sacrifice made by fire to the LORD, and their sin offering before the LORD, for their ignorance: ²⁶And it shall be forgiven all the congregation of the children of Israel, and the stranger that sojourns among them; seeing all the people were in ignorance. ²⁷And if any soul sin through ignorance, then he shall bring a she goat of the first year for a sin offering. ²⁸And the priest shall make an atonement for the soul that sins ignorantly, when he sins by ignorance before the LORD, to make an atonement for him; and it shall be forgiven him. ²⁹You shall have one law for him that sins through ignorance, both for him that is born among the children of Israel, and for the stranger that sojourns among them. ³⁰But the soul that does something presumptuously, whether he be born in the land, or a stranger, the same reproaches the LORD; and that soul shall be cut off from among his people. ³¹Because he has despised the word of the LORD, and has broken his commandment, that soul shall utterly be cut off; his iniquity shall be on him. ³²And while the children of Israel were in the wilderness, they found a man that gathered sticks on the sabbath day. ³³And they that found him gathering sticks brought him to Moses and Aaron, and to all the congregation. ³⁴And they put him in ward, because it was not declared what should be done to him. ³⁵And the LORD said to Moses, The man shall be surely put to death: all the congregation shall stone him with stones without the camp. ³⁶And all the congregation brought him without the camp, and stoned him with stones, and he died; as the LORD commanded Moses. ³⁷And the LORD spoke to Moses, saying, ³⁸Speak to the children of Israel, and bid them that they make them fringes in the borders of their garments throughout their generations, and that they put on the fringe of the borders a ribbon of blue: ³⁹And it shall be to you for a fringe, that you may look on it, and remember all the commandments of the LORD, and do them; and that you seek not after your own heart and your own eyes, after which you use to go a whoring: ⁴⁰That you may remember, and do all my commandments, and be holy to your God. ⁴¹I am the LORD your God, which brought you out of the land of Egypt, to be your God: I am the LORD your God.

16

¹Now Korah, the son of Izhar, the son of Kohath, the son of Levi, and Dathan and Abiram, the sons of Eliab, and On, the son of Peleth, sons of Reuben, took men: ²And they rose up before Moses, with certain of the children of Israel, two hundred and fifty princes of the assembly, famous in the congregation, men of renown: ³And they gathered themselves together against Moses and against Aaron, and said to them, You take too much on you, seeing all the congregation are holy, every one of them, and the LORD is among them: why then lift you up yourselves above the congregation of the LORD? ⁴And when Moses heard it, he fell on his face: ⁵And he spoke to Korah and to all his company, saying, Even to morrow the LORD will show who are his, and who is holy; and will cause him to come near to him: even him whom he has chosen will he cause to come near to him. ⁶This do; Take you censers, Korah, and all his company; ⁷And put fire therein, and put incense in them before the LORD to morrow: and it shall be that the man whom the LORD does choose, he shall be holy: you take too much on you, you sons of Levi. ⁸And Moses said to Korah, Hear, I pray you, you sons of Levi: ⁹Seems it but a small thing to you, that the God of Israel has separated you from the congregation of Israel, to bring you near to himself to do the service of the tabernacle of the LORD, and to stand before the congregation to minister to them? ¹⁰And he has brought you near to him, and all your brothers the sons of Levi with you: and seek you the priesthood also? ¹¹For which cause both you and all your company are gathered together against the LORD: and what is Aaron, that you murmur against him? ¹²And Moses sent to call Dathan and Abiram, the sons of Eliab: which said, We will not come up: ¹³Is it a small thing that you have brought us up out of a land that flows with milk and honey, to kill us in the wilderness, except you make yourself altogether a prince over us? ¹⁴Moreover you have not brought us into a land that

flows with milk and honey, or given us inheritance of fields and vineyards: will you put out the eyes of these men? we will not come up. ¹⁵And Moses was very wroth, and said to the LORD, Respect not you their offering: I have not taken one ass from them, neither have I hurt one of them. ¹⁶And Moses said to Korah, Be you and all your company before the LORD, you, and they, and Aaron, to morrow: ¹⁷And take every man his censer, and put incense in them, and bring you before the LORD every man his censer, two hundred and fifty censers; you also, and Aaron, each of you his censer. ¹⁸And they took every man his censer, and put fire in them, and laid incense thereon, and stood in the door of the tabernacle of the congregation with Moses and Aaron. ¹⁹And Korah gathered all the congregation against them to the door of the tabernacle of the congregation: and the glory of the LORD appeared to all the congregation. ²⁰And the LORD spoke to Moses and to Aaron, saying, ²¹Separate yourselves from among this congregation, that I may consume them in a moment. ²²And they fell on their faces, and said, O God, the God of the spirits of all flesh, shall one man sin, and will you be wroth with all the congregation? ²³And the LORD spoke to Moses, saying, ²⁴Speak to the congregation, saying, Get you up from about the tabernacle of Korah, Dathan, and Abiram. ²⁵And Moses rose up and went to Dathan and Abiram; and the elders of Israel followed him. ²⁶And he spoke to the congregation, saying, Depart, I pray you, from the tents of these wicked men, and touch nothing of theirs, lest you be consumed in all their sins. ²⁷So they got up from the tabernacle of Korah, Dathan, and Abiram, on every side: and Dathan and Abiram came out, and stood in the door of their tents, and their wives, and their sons, and their little children. ²⁸And Moses said, Hereby you shall know that the LORD has sent me to do all these works; for I have not done them of my own mind. ²⁹If these men die the common death of all men, or if they be visited after the visitation of all men; then the LORD has not sent me. ³⁰But if the LORD make a new thing, and the earth open her mouth, and swallow them up, with all that appertain to them, and they go down quick into the pit; then you shall understand that these men have provoked the LORD. ³¹And it came to pass, as he had made an end of speaking all these words, that the ground split asunder that was under them: ³²And the earth opened her mouth, and swallowed them up, and their houses, and all the men that appertained to Korah, and all their goods. ³³They, and all that appertained to them, went down alive into the pit, and the earth closed on them: and they perished from among the congregation. ³⁴And all Israel that were round about them fled at the cry of them: for they said, Lest the earth swallow us up also. ³⁵And there came out a fire from the LORD, and consumed the two hundred and fifty men that offered incense. ³⁶And the LORD spoke to Moses, saying, ³⁷Speak to Eleazar the son of Aaron the priest, that he take up the censers out of the burning, and scatter you the fire yonder; for they are hallowed. ³⁸The censers of these sinners against their own souls, let them make them broad plates for a covering of the altar: for they offered them before the LORD, therefore they are hallowed: and they shall be a sign to the children of Israel. ³⁹And Eleazar the priest took the brazen censers, with which they that were burnt had offered; and they were made broad plates for a covering of the altar: ⁴⁰To be a memorial to the children of Israel, that no stranger, which is not of the seed of Aaron, come near to offer incense before the LORD; that he be not as Korah, and as his company: as the LORD said to him by the hand of Moses. ⁴¹But on the morrow all the congregation of the children of Israel murmured against Moses and against Aaron, saying, You have killed the people of the LORD. ⁴²And it came to pass, when the congregation was gathered against Moses and against Aaron, that they looked toward the tabernacle of the congregation: and, behold, the cloud covered it, and the glory of the LORD appeared. ⁴³And Moses and Aaron came before the tabernacle of the congregation. ⁴⁴And the LORD spoke to Moses, saying, ⁴⁵Get you up from among this congregation, that I may consume them as in a moment. And they fell on their faces. ⁴⁶And Moses said to Aaron, Take a censer, and put fire therein from off the altar, and put on incense, and go quickly to the congregation, and make an atonement for them: for there is wrath gone out from the LORD; the plague is begun. ⁴⁷And Aaron took as Moses commanded, and ran into the middle of the congregation; and, behold, the plague was begun among the people: and he put on incense, and made an atonement for the people. ⁴⁸And he stood between the dead and the living; and the plague was stayed. ⁴⁹Now they that died in the plague were fourteen thousand and seven hundred, beside them that died about the matter of Korah. ⁵⁰And Aaron returned to Moses to the door of the tabernacle of the congregation: and the plague was stayed.

17 ¹And the LORD spoke to Moses, saying, ²Speak to the children of Israel, and take of every one of them a rod according to the house of their fathers, of all their princes according to the house of their fathers twelve rods: write you every man's name on his rod. ³And you shall write Aaron's name on the rod of Levi: for one rod shall be for the head of the house of their fathers. ⁴And you shall lay them up in the tabernacle of the congregation before the testimony, where I will meet with you. ⁵And it shall come to pass, that the man's rod, whom I shall choose, shall blossom: and I will make to cease from me the murmurings of the children of Israel, whereby they murmur against you. ⁶And Moses spoke to the children of Israel, and every one of their princes gave him a rod apiece, for each prince one, according to their fathers' houses, even twelve rods: and the rod of Aaron was among their rods. ⁷And Moses laid up the rods before the LORD in the tabernacle of witness. ⁸And it came to pass, that on the morrow Moses went into the tabernacle of witness; and, behold, the rod of Aaron for the house of Levi was budded, and brought forth buds, and bloomed blossoms, and yielded almonds. ⁹And Moses brought out all the rods from before the LORD to all the children of Israel: and they looked, and took every man his rod. ¹⁰And the LORD said to Moses, Bring Aaron's rod again before the testimony, to be kept for a token against the rebels; and you shall quite take away their murmurings from me, that they die not. ¹¹And Moses did so: as the LORD commanded him, so did he. ¹²And the children of Israel spoke to Moses, saying, Behold, we die, we perish, we all perish. ¹³Whoever comes any thing near to the tabernacle of the LORD shall die: shall we be consumed with dying?

18 ¹And the LORD said to Aaron, You and your sons and your father's house with you shall bear the iniquity of the sanctuary: and you and your sons with you shall bear the iniquity of your priesthood. ²And your brothers also of the tribe of Levi, the tribe of your father, bring you with you, that they may be joined to you, and minister to you: but you and your sons with you shall minister before the tabernacle of witness. ³And they shall keep your charge, and the charge of all the tabernacle: only they shall not come near the vessels of the sanctuary and the altar, that neither they, nor you also, die. ⁴And they shall be joined to you, and keep the charge of the tabernacle of the congregation, for all the service of the tabernacle: and a stranger shall not come near to you. ⁵And you shall keep the charge of the sanctuary, and the charge of the altar: that there be no wrath any more on the children of Israel. ⁶And I, behold, I have taken your brothers the Levites from among the children of Israel: to you they are given as a gift for the LORD, to do the service of the tabernacle of the congregation. ⁷Therefore you and your sons with you shall keep your priest's office for everything of the altar, and within the veil; and you shall serve: I have given your priest's office to you as a service of gift: and the stranger that comes near shall be put to death. ⁸And the LORD spoke to Aaron, Behold, I also have given you the charge of my heave offerings of all the hallowed things of the children of Israel; to you have I given them by reason of the anointing, and to your sons, by an ordinance for ever. ⁹This shall be your of the most holy things, reserved from the fire: every oblation of theirs, every meat offering of theirs, and every sin offering of theirs, and every trespass offering of theirs which they shall render to me, shall be most holy for you and for your sons. ¹⁰In the most holy place shall you eat it; every male shall eat it: it shall be holy to you. ¹¹And this is yours; the heave offering of their gift, with all the wave offerings of the children of Israel: I have given them to you, and to your sons and to your daughters with you, by a statute for ever: every one that is clean in your house shall eat of it. ¹²All the best of the oil, and all the best of the wine, and of the wheat, the first fruits of them which they shall offer to the LORD, them have I given you. ¹³And whatever is first ripe in the land, which they shall bring to the LORD, shall be yours; every one that is clean in your house shall eat of it. ¹⁴Every thing devoted in Israel shall be yours. ¹⁵Every thing that opens the matrix in all flesh, which they bring to the LORD, whether it be of men or beasts, shall be yours: nevertheless the firstborn of man shall you surely redeem, and the firstling of unclean beasts shall you redeem. ¹⁶And those that are to be redeemed from a month old shall you redeem, according to your estimation, for the money of five shekels, after the shekel of the sanctuary, which is twenty gerahs. ¹⁷But the firstling of a cow, or the firstling of a sheep, or the firstling of a goat, you shall not redeem; they are holy: you shall sprinkle their blood on the altar, and shall burn their fat for an offering made by fire, for a sweet smell to the LORD. ¹⁸And the flesh of them shall be yours, as the wave breast and as the right shoulder are yours. ¹⁹All the heave offerings of the holy things, which the children of Israel offer to the LORD, have I given you, and your sons and your daughters with you, by a statute for ever: it is a covenant of salt for ever before the LORD to you and to your seed with you. ²⁰And the LORD spoke to Aaron, You shall have no inheritance in their land, neither shall you have any part among them: I am your part and your inheritance among the children of Israel. ²¹And, behold, I have given the children of Levi all the tenth in Israel for an inheritance, for their service which they serve, even the service of the tabernacle of the congregation. ²²Neither must the children of Israel from now on come near the tabernacle of the congregation, lest they bear sin, and die. ²³But the Levites shall do the service of the tabernacle of the congregation, and they shall bear their iniquity: it shall be a statute for ever throughout your generations, that among the children of Israel they have no inheritance. ²⁴But the tithes of the children of Israel, which they offer as an heave offering to the LORD, I have given to the Levites to inherit: therefore I have said to them, Among the children of Israel they shall have no inheritance. ²⁵And the LORD spoke to Moses, saying, ²⁶Thus speak to the Levites, and say to them, When you take of the children of Israel the tithes which I have given you from them for your inheritance, then you shall offer up an heave offering of it for the LORD, even a tenth part of the tithe. ²⁷And this your heave offering shall be reckoned to you, as though it were the corn of the threshing floor, and as the fullness of the wine press. ²⁸Thus you also shall offer an heave offering to the LORD of all your tithes, which you receive of the children of Israel; and you shall give thereof the LORD's heave offering to Aaron the priest. ²⁹Out of all your gifts you shall offer every heave offering of the LORD, of all the best thereof, even the hallowed part thereof out of it. ³⁰Therefore you shall say to them, When you have heaved the best thereof from it, then it shall be counted to the Levites as the increase of the threshing floor, and as the increase of the wine press. ³¹And you shall eat it in every place, you and your households: for it is your reward for your service in the tabernacle of the congregation. ³²And you shall bear no sin by reason of it, when you have heaved from it the best of it: neither shall you pollute the holy things of the children of Israel, lest you die.

19 ¹And the LORD spoke to Moses and to Aaron, saying, ²This is the ordinance of the law which the LORD has commanded, saying, Speak to the children of Israel, that they bring you a red heifer without spot, wherein is no blemish, and on which never came yoke: ³And you shall give her to Eleazar the priest, that he may bring her forth without the camp, and one shall slay her before his face: ⁴And Eleazar the priest shall take of her blood with his finger, and sprinkle of her blood directly before the tabernacle of the congregation seven times: ⁵And one shall burn the heifer in his sight; her skin, and her flesh, and her blood, with her dung, shall he burn: ⁶And the priest shall take cedar wood, and hyssop, and scarlet, and cast it into the middle of the burning of the heifer. ⁷Then the priest shall wash his clothes, and he shall bathe his flesh in water, and afterward he shall come into the camp, and the priest shall be unclean until the even. ⁸And he that burns her shall wash his clothes in water, and bathe his flesh in water, and shall be unclean until the even. ⁹And a man that is clean shall gather up the ashes of the heifer, and lay them up without the camp in a clean place, and it shall be kept for the congregation of the children of Israel for a water of separation: it is a purification for sin. [10]And he that gathers the ashes of the heifer shall wash his clothes, and be unclean until the even: and it shall be to the children of Israel, and to the stranger that sojourns among them, for a statute for ever. [11]He that touches the dead body of any man shall be unclean seven days. [12]He shall purify himself with it on the third day, and on the seventh day he shall be clean: but if he purify not himself the third day, then the seventh day he shall not be clean. [13]Whoever touches the dead body of any man that is dead, and purifies not himself, defiles the tabernacle of the LORD; and that soul shall be cut off from Israel: because the water of separation was not sprinkled on him, he shall be unclean; his uncleanness is yet on him. [14]This is the law, when a man dies in a tent: all that come into the tent, and all that is in the tent, shall be unclean seven days. [15]And every open vessel, which has no covering bound on it, is unclean. [16]And whoever touches one that is slain with a sword in the open fields, or a dead body, or a bone of a man, or a grave, shall be unclean seven days. [17]And for an unclean person they shall take of the ashes of the burnt heifer of purification for sin, and running water shall be put thereto in a vessel: [18]And a clean person shall take hyssop, and dip it in the water, and sprinkle it on the tent, and on all the vessels, and on the persons that were there, and on him that touched a bone, or one slain, or one dead, or a grave: [19]And the clean person shall sprinkle on the unclean on the third day, and on the seventh day: and on the seventh day he shall purify himself, and wash his clothes, and bathe himself in water, and shall be clean at even. [20]But the man that shall be unclean, and shall not purify himself, that soul shall be cut off from among the congregation, because he has defiled the sanctuary of the LORD: the water of separation has not been sprinkled on him; he is unclean. [21]And it shall be a perpetual statute to them, that he that sprinkles the water of separation shall wash his clothes; and he that touches the water of separation shall be unclean until even. [22]And whatever the unclean person touches shall be unclean; and the soul that touches it shall be unclean until even.

20 [1]Then came the children of Israel, even the whole congregation, into the desert of Zin in the first month: and the people stayed in Kadesh; and Miriam died there, and was buried there. [2]And there was no water for the congregation: and they gathered themselves together against Moses and against Aaron. [3]And the people strived with Moses, and spoke, saying, Would God that we had died when our brothers died before the LORD! [4]And why have you brought up the congregation of the LORD into this wilderness, that we and our cattle should die there? [5]And why have you made us to come up out of Egypt, to bring us in to this evil place? it is no place of seed, or of figs, or of vines, or of pomegranates; neither is there any water to drink. [6]And Moses and Aaron went from the presence of the assembly to the door of the tabernacle of the congregation, and they fell on their faces: and the glory of the LORD appeared to them. [7]And the LORD spoke to Moses, saying, [8]Take the rod, and gather you the assembly together, you, and Aaron your brother, and speak you to the rock before their eyes; and it shall give forth his water, and you shall bring forth to them water out of the rock: so you shall give the congregation and their beasts drink. [9]And Moses took the rod from before the LORD, as he commanded him. [10]And Moses and Aaron gathered the congregation together before the rock, and he said to them, Hear now, you rebels; must we fetch you water out of this rock? [11]And Moses lifted up his hand, and with his rod he smote the rock twice: and the water came out abundantly, and the congregation drank, and their beasts also. [12]And the LORD spoke to Moses and Aaron, Because you believed me not, to sanctify me in the eyes of the children of Israel, therefore you shall not bring this congregation into the land which I have given them. [13]This is the water of Meribah; because the children of Israel strove with the LORD, and he was sanctified in them. [14]And Moses sent messengers from Kadesh to the king of Edom, Thus says your brother Israel, You know all the travail that has befallen us: [15]How our fathers went down into Egypt, and we have dwelled in Egypt a long time; and the Egyptians vexed us, and our fathers: [16]And when we cried to the LORD, he heard our voice, and sent an angel, and has brought us forth out of Egypt: and, behold, we are in Kadesh, a city in the uttermost of your border: [17]Let us pass, I pray you, through your country: we will not pass through the fields, or through the vineyards, neither will we drink of the water of the wells: we will go by the king's high way, we will not turn to the right hand nor to the left, until we have passed your borders. [18]And Edom said to him, You shall not pass by me, lest I come out against you with the sword. [19]And the children of Israel said to him, We will go by the high way: and if I and my cattle drink of your water, then I will pay for it: I will only, without doing anything else, go through on my feet. [20]And he said, You shall not go through. And Edom came out against him with much people, and with a strong hand. [21]Thus Edom refused to give Israel passage through his border: why Israel turned away from him. [22]And the children of Israel, even the whole congregation, journeyed from Kadesh, and came to mount Hor. [23]And the LORD spoke to Moses and Aaron in mount Hor, by the coast of the land of Edom, saying, [24]Aaron shall be gathered to his people: for he shall not enter into the land which I have given to the children of Israel, because you rebelled against my word at the water of Meribah. [25]Take Aaron and Eleazar his son, and bring them up to mount Hor: [26]And strip Aaron of his garments, and put them on Eleazar his son: and Aaron shall be gathered to his people, and shall die there. [27]And Moses did as the LORD commanded: and they went up into mount Hor in the sight of all the congregation. [28]And Moses stripped Aaron of his garments, and put them on Eleazar his son; and Aaron died there in the top of the mount: and Moses and Eleazar came down from the mount. [29]And when all the congregation saw that Aaron was dead, they mourned for Aaron thirty days, even all the house of Israel.

21 [1]And when king Arad the Canaanite, which dwelled in the south, heard tell that Israel came by the way of the spies; then he fought against Israel, and took some of them prisoners. [2]And Israel vowed a vow to the LORD, and said, If you will indeed deliver this people into my hand, then I will utterly destroy their cities. [3]And the LORD listened to the voice of Israel, and delivered up the

Canaanites; and they utterly destroyed them and their cities: and he called the name of the place Hormah. ⁴And they journeyed from mount Hor by the way of the Red sea, to compass the land of Edom: and the soul of the people was much discouraged because of the way. ⁵And the people spoke against God, and against Moses, Why have you brought us up out of Egypt to die in the wilderness? for there is no bread, neither is there any water; and our soul loathes this light bread. ⁶And the LORD sent fiery serpents among the people, and they bit the people; and much people of Israel died. ⁷Therefore the people came to Moses, and said, We have sinned, for we have spoken against the LORD, and against you; pray to the LORD, that he take away the serpents from us. And Moses prayed for the people. ⁸And the LORD said to Moses, Make you a fiery serpent, and set it on a pole: and it shall come to pass, that every one that is bitten, when he looks on it, shall live. ⁹And Moses made a serpent of brass, and put it on a pole, and it came to pass, that if a serpent had bitten any man, when he beheld the serpent of brass, he lived. ¹⁰And the children of Israel set forward, and pitched in Oboth. ¹¹And they journeyed from Oboth, and pitched at Ijeabarim, in the wilderness which is before Moab, toward the sun rise. ¹²From there they removed, and pitched in the valley of Zared. ¹³From there they removed, and pitched on the other side of Arnon, which is in the wilderness that comes out of the coasts of the Amorites: for Arnon is the border of Moab, between Moab and the Amorites. ¹⁴Why it is said in the book of the wars of the LORD, What he did in the Red sea, and in the brooks of Arnon, ¹⁵And at the stream of the brooks that goes down to the dwelling of Ar, and lies on the border of Moab. ¹⁶And from there they went to Beer: that is the well whereof the LORD spoke to Moses, Gather the people together, and I will give them water. ¹⁷Then Israel sang this song, Spring up, O well; sing you to it: ¹⁸The princes dig the well, the nobles of the people dig it, by the direction of the lawgiver, with their staves. And from the wilderness they went to Mattanah: ¹⁹And from Mattanah to Nahaliel: and from Nahaliel to Bamoth: ²⁰And from Bamoth in the valley, that is in the country of Moab, to the top of Pisgah, which looks toward Jeshimon. ²¹And Israel sent messengers to Sihon king of the Amorites, saying, ²²Let me pass through your land: we will not turn into the fields, or into the vineyards; we will not drink of the waters of the well: but we will go along by the king's high way, until we be past your borders. ²³And Sihon would not suffer Israel to pass through his border: but Sihon gathered all his people together, and went out against Israel into the wilderness: and he came to Jahaz, and fought against Israel. ²⁴And Israel smote him with the edge of the sword, and possessed his land from Arnon to Jabbok, even to the children of Ammon: for the border of the children of Ammon was strong. ²⁵And Israel took all these cities: and Israel dwelled in all the cities of the Amorites, in Heshbon, and in all the villages thereof. ²⁶For Heshbon was the city of Sihon the king of the Amorites, who had fought against the former king of Moab, and taken all his land out of his hand, even to Arnon. ²⁷Why they that speak in proverbs say, Come into Heshbon, let the city of Sihon be built and prepared: ²⁸For there is a fire gone out of Heshbon, a flame from the city of Sihon: it has consumed Ar of Moab, and the lords of the high places of Arnon. ²⁹Woe to you, Moab! you are undone, O people of Chemosh: he has given his sons that escaped, and his daughters, into captivity to Sihon king of the Amorites. ³⁰We have shot at them; Heshbon is perished even to Dibon, and we have laid them waste even to Nophah, which reaches to Medeba. ³¹Thus Israel dwelled in the land of the Amorites. ³²And Moses sent to spy out Jaazer, and they took the villages thereof, and drove out the Amorites that were there. ³³And they turned and went up by the way of Bashan: and Og the king of Bashan went out against them, he, and all his people, to the battle at Edrei. ³⁴And the LORD said to Moses, Fear him not: for I have delivered him into your hand, and all his people, and his land; and you shall do to him as you did to Sihon king of the Amorites, which dwelled at Heshbon. ³⁵So they smote him, and his sons, and all his people, until there was none left him alive: and they possessed his land.

22 ¹And the children of Israel set forward, and pitched in the plains of Moab on this side Jordan by Jericho. ²And Balak the son of Zippor saw all that Israel had done to the Amorites. ³And Moab was sore afraid of the people, because they were many: and Moab was distressed because of the children of Israel. ⁴And Moab said to the elders of Midian, Now shall this company lick up all that are round about us, as the ox licks up the grass of the field. And Balak the son of Zippor was king of the Moabites at that time. ⁵He sent messengers therefore to Balaam the son of Beor to Pethor, which is by the river of the land of the children of his people, to call him, saying, Behold, there is a people come out from Egypt: behold, they cover the face of the earth, and they abide over against me: ⁶Come now therefore, I pray you, curse me this people; for they are too mighty for me: peradventure I shall prevail, that we may smite them, and that I may drive them out of the land: for I know that he whom you bless is blessed, and he whom you curse is cursed. ⁷And the elders of Moab and the elders of Midian departed with the rewards of divination in their hand; and they came to Balaam, and spoke to him the words of Balak. ⁸And he said to them, Lodge here this night, and I will bring you word again, as the LORD shall speak to me: and the princes of Moab stayed with Balaam. ⁹And God came to Balaam, and said, What men are these with you? ¹⁰And Balaam said to God, Balak the son of Zippor, king of Moab, has sent to me, saying, ¹¹Behold, there is a people come out of Egypt, which covers the face of the earth: come now, curse me them; peradventure I shall be able to overcome them, and drive them out. ¹²And God said to Balaam, You shall not go with them; you shall not curse the people: for they are blessed. ¹³And Balaam rose up in the morning, and said to the princes of Balak, Get you into your land: for the LORD refuses to give me leave to go with you. ¹⁴And the princes of Moab rose up, and they went to Balak, and said, Balaam refuses to come with us. ¹⁵And Balak sent yet again princes, more, and more honorable than they. ¹⁶And they came to Balaam, and said to him, Thus says Balak the son of Zippor, Let nothing, I pray you, hinder you from coming to me: ¹⁷For I will promote you to very great honor, and I will do whatever you say to me: come therefore, I pray you, curse me this people. ¹⁸And Balaam answered and said to the servants of Balak, If Balak would give me his house full of silver and gold, I cannot go beyond the word of the LORD my God, to do less or more. ¹⁹Now therefore, I pray you, tarry you also here this night, that I may know what the LORD will say to me more. ²⁰And God came to Balaam at night, and said to him, If the men come to call you, rise up, and go with them; but yet the word which I shall say to you, that shall you do. ²¹And Balaam rose up in the morning, and saddled his ass, and went with the princes of Moab. ²²And God's anger was kindled because he went: and the angel of the LORD stood in the way for an adversary against him. Now he was riding on his ass, and his two servants were with him. ²³And the ass saw the angel of the LORD standing in the way, and his sword drawn in his hand: and the ass turned aside out of the way, and went into the field: and Balaam smote the ass, to turn her into the way. ²⁴But the angel of the LORD stood in a path of the vineyards, a wall being on this side, and a wall on that side. ²⁵And when the ass saw the angel of the LORD, she thrust herself to the wall, and crushed Balaam's foot against the wall: and he smote her again. ²⁶And the angel of the LORD went further, and stood in a narrow place, where was no way to turn either to the right hand or to the left. ²⁷And when the ass saw the angel of the LORD, she fell down under Balaam: and Balaam's anger was kindled, and he smote the ass with a staff. ²⁸And the LORD opened the mouth of the ass, and she said to Balaam, What have I done to you, that you have smitten me these three times? ²⁹And Balaam said to the ass, Because you have mocked me: I would there were a sword in my hand, for now would I kill you. ³⁰And the ass said to Balaam, Am not I your ass, on which you have ridden ever since I was yours to this day? was I ever wont to do so to you? And he said, No. ³¹Then the LORD opened the eyes of Balaam, and he saw the angel of the LORD standing in the way, and his sword drawn in his hand: and he bowed down his head, and fell flat on his face. ³²And the angel of the LORD said to him, Why have you smitten your ass these three times? behold, I went out to withstand you, because your way is perverse before me: ³³And the ass saw me, and turned from me these three times: unless she had turned from me, surely now also I had slain you, and saved her alive. ³⁴And Balaam said to the angel of the LORD, I have sinned; for I knew not that you stood in the way against me: now therefore, if it displease you, I will get me back again. ³⁵And the angel of the LORD said to Balaam, Go with the men: but only the word that I shall speak to you, that you shall speak. So Balaam went with the princes of Balak. ³⁶And when Balak heard that Balaam was come, he went out to meet him to a city of Moab, which is in the border of Arnon, which is in the utmost coast. ³⁷And Balak said to Balaam, Did I not earnestly send to you to call you? why came you not to me? am I not able indeed to promote you to honor? ³⁸And Balaam said to Balak, See, I am come to you: have I now any power at all to say any thing? the word that God puts in my mouth, that shall I speak. ³⁹And Balaam went with Balak, and they came to Kirjathhuzoth. ⁴⁰And Balak offered oxen and sheep, and sent to Balaam, and to the princes that were with him. ⁴¹And it came to pass on the morrow, that Balak took Balaam, and brought him up into the high places of Baal, that there he might see the utmost part of the people.

23 ¹And Balaam said to Balak, Build me here seven altars, and prepare me here seven oxen and seven rams. ²And Balak did as Balaam had spoken; and Balak and Balaam offered on every altar a bullock and a ram. ³And Balaam said to Balak, Stand by your burnt offering, and I will go: peradventure the LORD will come to meet me: and whatever he shows me I will tell you. And he went to an high place. ⁴And God met Balaam: and he said to him, I have prepared seven altars, and I have offered on every altar a bullock and a ram. ⁵And the LORD put a word in Balaam's mouth, and said, Return to Balak, and thus you shall speak. ⁶And he returned to him, and, see, he stood by his burnt sacrifice, he, and all the princes of Moab. ⁷And he took up his parable, and said, Balak the king of Moab has brought me from Aram, out of the mountains of the east, saying, Come, curse me Jacob, and come, defy Israel. ⁸How shall I curse, whom God has not cursed? or how shall I defy, whom the LORD has not defied? ⁹For from the top of the rocks I see him, and from the hills I behold him: see, the people shall dwell alone, and shall not be reckoned among the nations. ¹⁰Who can count the dust of Jacob, and the number of the fourth part of Israel? Let me die the death of the righteous, and let my last end be like his! ¹¹And Balak said to Balaam, What have you done to me? I took you to curse my enemies, and, behold, you have blessed them altogether. ¹²And he answered and said, Must I not take heed to speak that which the LORD has put in my mouth? ¹³And Balak said to him, Come, I pray you, with me to another place, from from where you may see them: you shall see but the utmost part of them, and shall not see them all: and curse me them from there. ¹⁴And he brought him into the field of Zophim, to the top of Pisgah, and built seven altars, and offered a bullock and a ram on every altar. ¹⁵And he said to Balak, Stand here by your burnt offering, while I meet the LORD yonder. ¹⁶And the LORD met Balaam, and put a word in his mouth, and said, Go again to Balak, and say thus. ¹⁷And when he came to him, behold, he stood by his burnt offering, and the princes of Moab with him. And Balak said to him, What has the LORD spoken? ¹⁸And he took up his parable, and said, Rise up, Balak, and hear; listen to me, you son of Zippor: ¹⁹God is not a man, that he should lie; neither the son of man, that he should repent: has he said, and shall he not do it? or has he spoken, and shall he not make it good? ²⁰Behold, I have received commandment to bless: and he has blessed; and I cannot reverse it. ²¹He has not beheld iniquity in Jacob, neither has he seen perverseness in Israel: the LORD his God is with him, and the shout of a king is among them. ²²God brought them out of Egypt; he has as it were the strength of an unicorn. ²³Surely there is no enchantment against Jacob, neither is there any divination against Israel: according to this time it shall be said of Jacob and of Israel, What has God worked! ²⁴Behold, the people shall rise up as a great lion, and lift up himself as a young lion: he shall not lie down until he eat of the prey, and drink the blood of the slain. ²⁵And Balak said to Balaam, Neither curse them at all, nor bless them at all. ²⁶But Balaam answered and said to Balak, Told not I you, saying, All that the LORD speaks, that I must do? ²⁷And Balak said to Balaam, Come, I pray you, I will bring you to another place; peradventure it will please God that you may curse me them from there. ²⁸And Balak brought Balaam to the top of Peor, that looks toward Jeshimon. ²⁹And Balaam said to Balak, Build me here seven altars, and prepare me here seven bullocks and seven rams. ³⁰And Balak did as Balaam had said, and offered a bullock and a ram on every altar.

24 ¹And when Balaam saw that it pleased the LORD to bless Israel, he went not, as at other times, to seek for enchantments, but he set his face toward the wilderness. ²And Balaam lifted up his eyes, and he saw Israel abiding in his tents according to their tribes; and the spirit of God came on him. ³And he took up his parable, and said, Balaam the son of Beor has said, and the man whose eyes are open has said: ⁴He has said, which heard the words of God, which saw the vision of the Almighty, falling into a trance, but having his eyes open: ⁵How goodly are your tents, O Jacob, and your tabernacles, O Israel! ⁶As the valleys are they spread forth, as gardens by the river's side, as the trees of lign aloes which the LORD has planted, and as cedar trees beside the waters. ⁷He shall pour the water out of his buckets, and his seed shall be in many waters, and his king shall be higher than Agag, and his kingdom shall be exalted. ⁸God brought him forth out of Egypt; he has as it were the strength of an unicorn: he shall eat up the nations his enemies, and shall break their bones, and pierce them through with his arrows. ⁹He couched, he lay down as a lion, and as a great lion: who shall stir him up? Blessed is he that blesses you, and cursed is he that curses you. ¹⁰And Balak's anger was kindled against Balaam, and he smote his hands together: and Balak said to Balaam, I called you to curse my enemies, and, behold, you have altogether blessed them these three times. ¹¹Therefore now flee you to your place: I thought to promote you to great honor; but, see, the LORD has kept you back from honor. ¹²And Balaam said to Balak, Spoke I not also to your messengers which you sent to me, saying, ¹³If Balak would give me his house full of silver and gold, I cannot go beyond the commandment of the LORD, to do either good or bad of my own mind; but what the LORD says, that will I speak? ¹⁴And now, behold, I go to my people: come therefore, and I will advertise you what this people shall do to your people in the latter days. ¹⁵And he took up his parable, and said, Balaam the son of Beor has said, and the man whose eyes are open has said: ¹⁶He has said, which heard the words of God, and knew the knowledge of the most High, which saw the vision of the Almighty, falling into a trance, but having his eyes open: ¹⁷I shall see him, but not now: I shall behold him, but not near: there shall come a Star out of Jacob, and a Scepter shall rise out of Israel, and shall smite the corners of Moab, and destroy all the children of Sheth. ¹⁸And Edom shall be a possession, Seir also shall be a possession for his enemies; and Israel shall do valiantly. ¹⁹Out of Jacob shall come he that shall have dominion, and shall destroy him that remains of the city. ²⁰And when he looked on Amalek, he took up his parable, and said, Amalek was the first of the nations; but his latter end shall be that he perish for ever. ²¹And he looked on the Kenites, and took up his parable, and said, Strong is your dwelling place, and you put your nest in a rock. ²²Nevertheless the Kenite shall be wasted, until Asshur shall carry you away captive. ²³And he took up his parable, and said, Alas, who shall live when God does this! ²⁴And ships shall come from the coast of Chittim, and shall afflict Asshur, and shall afflict Eber, and he also shall perish for ever. ²⁵And Balaam rose up, and went and returned to his place: and Balak also went his way.

25 ¹And Israel stayed in Shittim, and the people began to commit prostitution with the daughters of Moab. ²And they called the people to the sacrifices of their gods: and the people did eat, and bowed down to their gods. ³And Israel joined himself to Baalpeor: and the anger of the LORD was kindled against Israel. ⁴And the LORD said to Moses, Take all the heads of the people, and hang them up before the LORD against the sun, that the fierce anger of the LORD may be turned away from Israel. ⁵And Moses said to the judges of Israel, Slay you every one his men that were joined to Baalpeor. ⁶And, behold, one of the children of Israel came and brought to his brothers a Midianitish woman in the sight of Moses, and in the sight of all the congregation of the children of Israel, who were weeping before the door of the tabernacle of the congregation. ⁷And when Phinehas, the son of Eleazar, the son of Aaron the priest, saw it, he rose up from among the congregation, and took a javelin in his hand; ⁸And he went after the man of Israel into the tent, and thrust both of them through, the man of Israel, and the woman through her belly. So the plague was stayed from the children of Israel. ⁹And those that died in the plague were twenty and four thousand. ¹⁰And the LORD spoke to Moses, saying, ¹¹Phinehas, the son of Eleazar, the son of Aaron the priest, has turned my wrath away from the children of Israel, while he was zealous for my sake among them, that I consumed not the children of Israel in my jealousy. ¹²Why say, Behold, I give to him my covenant of peace: ¹³And he shall have it, and his seed after him, even the covenant of an everlasting priesthood; because he was zealous for his God, and made an atonement for the children of Israel. ¹⁴Now the name of the Israelite that was slain, even that was slain with the Midianitish woman, was Zimri, the son of Salu, a prince of a chief house among the Simeonites. ¹⁵And the name of the Midianitish woman that was slain was Cozbi, the daughter of Zur; he was head over a people, and of a chief house in Midian. ¹⁶And the LORD spoke to Moses, saying, ¹⁷Vex the Midianites, and smite them: ¹⁸For they vex you with their wiles, with which they have beguiled you in the matter of Peor, and in the matter of Cozbi, the daughter of a prince of Midian, their sister, which was slain in the day of the plague for Peor's sake.

26 ¹And it came to pass after the plague, that the LORD spoke to Moses and to Eleazar the son of Aaron the priest, saying, ²Take the sum of all the congregation of the children of Israel, from twenty years old and upward, throughout their fathers' house, all that are able to go to war in Israel. ³And Moses and Eleazar the priest spoke with them in the plains of Moab by Jordan near Jericho, saying, ⁴Take the sum of the people, from twenty years old and upward; as the LORD commanded Moses and the children of Israel, which went forth out of the land of Egypt. ⁵Reuben, the oldest son of Israel: the children of Reuben; Hanoch, of whom comes the family of the Hanochites: of Pallu, the family of the Palluites: ⁶Of Hezron,

the family of the Hezronites: of Carmi, the family of the Carmites. ⁷These are the families of the Reubenites: and they that were numbered of them were forty and three thousand and seven hundred and thirty. ⁸And the sons of Pallu; Eliab. ⁹And the sons of Eliab; Nemuel, and Dathan, and Abiram. This is that Dathan and Abiram, which were famous in the congregation, who strove against Moses and against Aaron in the company of Korah, when they strove against the LORD: ¹⁰And the earth opened her mouth, and swallowed them up together with Korah, when that company died, what time the fire devoured two hundred and fifty men: and they became a sign. ¹¹Notwithstanding the children of Korah died not. ¹²The sons of Simeon after their families: of Nemuel, the family of the Nemuelites: of Jamin, the family of the Jaminites: of Jachin, the family of the Jachinites: ¹³Of Zerah, the family of the Zarhites: of Shaul, the family of the Shaulites. ¹⁴These are the families of the Simeonites, twenty and two thousand and two hundred. ¹⁵The children of Gad after their families: of Zephon, the family of the Zephonites: of Haggi, the family of the Haggites: of Shuni, the family of the Shunites: ¹⁶Of Ozni, the family of the Oznites: of Eri, the family of the Erites: ¹⁷Of Arod, the family of the Arodites: of Areli, the family of the Arelites. ¹⁸These are the families of the children of Gad according to those that were numbered of them, forty thousand and five hundred. ¹⁹The sons of Judah were Er and Onan: and Er and Onan died in the land of Canaan. ²⁰And the sons of Judah after their families were; of Shelah, the family of the Shelanites: of Pharez, the family of the Pharzites: of Zerah, the family of the Zarhites. ²¹And the sons of Pharez were; of Hezron, the family of the Hezronites: of Hamul, the family of the Hamulites. ²²These are the families of Judah according to those that were numbered of them, three score and sixteen thousand and five hundred. ²³Of the sons of Issachar after their families: of Tola, the family of the Tolaites: of Pua, the family of the Punites: ²⁴Of Jashub, the family of the Jashubites: of Shimron, the family of the Shimronites. ²⁵These are the families of Issachar according to those that were numbered of them, three score and four thousand and three hundred. ²⁶Of the sons of Zebulun after their families: of Sered, the family of the Sardites: of Elon, the family of the Elonites: of Jahleel, the family of the Jahleelites. ²⁷These are the families of the Zebulunites according to those that were numbered of them, three score thousand and five hundred. ²⁸The sons of Joseph after their families were Manasseh and Ephraim. ²⁹Of the sons of Manasseh: of Machir, the family of the Machirites: and Machir begat Gilead: of Gilead come the family of the Gileadites. ³⁰These are the sons of Gilead: of Jeezer, the family of the Jeezerites: of Helek, the family of the Helekites: ³¹And of Asriel, the family of the Asrielites: and of Shechem, the family of the Shechemites: ³²And of Shemida, the family of the Shemidaites: and of Hepher, the family of the Hepherites. ³³And Zelophehad the son of Hepher had no sons, but daughters: and the names of the daughters of Zelophehad were Mahlah, and Noah, Hoglah, Milcah, and Tirzah. ³⁴These are the families of Manasseh, and those that numbered of them, fifty and two thousand and seven hundred. ³⁵These are the sons of Ephraim after their families: of Shuthelah, the family of the Shuthalhites: of Becher, the family of the Bachrites: of Tahan, the family of the Tahanites. ³⁶And these are the sons of Shuthelah: of Eran, the family of the Eranites. ³⁷These are the families of the sons of Ephraim according to those that were numbered of them, thirty and two thousand and five hundred. These are the sons of Joseph after their families. ³⁸The sons of Benjamin after their families: of Bela, the family of the Belaites: of Ashbel, the family of the Ashbelites: of Ahiram, the family of the Ahiramites: ³⁹Of Shupham, the family of the Shuphamites: of Hupham, the family of the Huphamites. ⁴⁰And the sons of Bela were Ard and Naaman: of Ard, the family of the Ardites: and of Naaman, the family of the Naamites. ⁴¹These are the sons of Benjamin after their families: and they that were numbered of them were forty and five thousand and six hundred. ⁴²These are the sons of Dan after their families: of Shuham, the family of the Shuhamites. These are the families of Dan after their families. ⁴³All the families of the Shuhamites, according to those that were numbered of them, were three score and four thousand and four hundred. ⁴⁴Of the children of Asher after their families: of Jimna, the family of the Jimnites: of Jesui, the family of the Jesuites: of Beriah, the family of the Beriites. ⁴⁵Of the sons of Beriah: of Heber, the family of the Heberites: of Malchiel, the family of the Malchielites. ⁴⁶And the name of the daughter of Asher was Sarah. ⁴⁷These are the families of the sons of Asher according to those that were numbered of them; who were fifty and three thousand and four hundred. ⁴⁸Of the sons of Naphtali after their families: of Jahzeel, the family of the Jahzeelites: of Guni, the family of the Gunites: ⁴⁹Of Jezer, the family of the Jezerites: of Shillem, the family of the Shillemites. ⁵⁰These are the families of Naphtali according to their families: and they that were numbered of them were forty and five thousand and four hundred. ⁵¹These were the numbered of the children of Israel, six hundred thousand and a thousand seven hundred and thirty. ⁵²And the LORD spoke to Moses, saying, ⁵³To these the land shall be divided for an inheritance according to the number of names. ⁵⁴To many you shall give the more inheritance, and to few you shall give the less inheritance: to every one shall his inheritance be given according to those that were numbered of him. ⁵⁵Notwithstanding the land shall be divided by lot: according to the names of the tribes of their fathers they shall inherit. ⁵⁶According to the lot shall the possession thereof be divided between many and few. ⁵⁷And these are they that were numbered of the Levites after their families: of Gershon, the family of the Gershonites: of Kohath, the family of the Kohathites: of Merari, the family of the Merarites. ⁵⁸These are the families of the Levites: the family of the Libnites, the family of the Hebronites, the family of the Mahlites, the family of the Mushites, the family of the Korathites. And Kohath begat Amram. ⁵⁹And the name of Amram's wife was Jochebed, the daughter of Levi, whom her mother bore to Levi in Egypt: and she bore to Amram Aaron and Moses, and Miriam their sister. ⁶⁰And to Aaron was born Nadab, and Abihu, Eleazar, and Ithamar. ⁶¹And Nadab and Abihu died, when they offered strange fire before the LORD. ⁶²And those that were numbered of them were twenty and three thousand, all males from a month old and upward: for they were not numbered among the children of Israel, because there was no inheritance given them among the children of Israel. ⁶³These are they that were numbered by Moses and Eleazar the priest, who numbered the children of Israel in the plains of Moab by Jordan near Jericho. ⁶⁴But among these there was not a man of them whom Moses and Aaron the priest numbered, when they numbered the children of Israel in the wilderness of Sinai. ⁶⁵For the LORD had said of them, They shall surely die in the wilderness. And there was not left a man of them, save Caleb the son of Jephunneh, and Joshua the son of Nun.

27 ¹Then came the daughters of Zelophehad, the son of Hepher, the son of Gilead, the son of Machir, the son of Manasseh, of the families of Manasseh the son of Joseph: and these are the names of his daughters; Mahlah, Noah, and Hoglah, and Milcah, and Tirzah. ²And they stood before Moses, and before Eleazar the priest, and before the princes and all the congregation, by the door of the tabernacle of the congregation, saying, ³Our father died in the wilderness, and he was not in the company of them that gathered themselves together against the LORD in the company of Korah; but died in his own sin, and had no sons. ⁴Why should the name of our father be done away from among his family, because he has no son? Give to us therefore a possession among the brothers of our father. ⁵And Moses brought their cause before the LORD. ⁶And the LORD spoke to Moses, saying, ⁷The daughters of Zelophehad speak right: you shall surely give them a possession of an inheritance among their father's brothers; and you shall cause the inheritance of their father to pass to them. ⁸And you shall speak to the children of Israel, saying, If a man die, and have no son, then you shall cause his inheritance to pass to his daughter. ⁹And if he have no daughter, then you shall give his inheritance to his brothers. ¹⁰And if he have no brothers, then you shall give his inheritance to his father's brothers. ¹¹And if his father have no brothers, then you shall give his inheritance to his kinsman that is next to him of his family, and he shall possess it: and it shall be to the children of Israel a statute of judgment, as the LORD commanded Moses. ¹²And the LORD said to Moses, Get you up into this mount Abarim, and see the land which I have given to the children of Israel. ¹³And when you have seen it, you also shall be gathered to your people, as Aaron your brother was gathered. ¹⁴For you rebelled against my commandment in the desert of Zin, in the strife of the congregation, to sanctify me at the water before their eyes: that is the water of Meribah in Kadesh in the wilderness of Zin. ¹⁵And Moses spoke to the LORD, saying, ¹⁶Let the LORD, the God of the spirits of all flesh, set a man over the congregation, ¹⁷Which may go out before them, and which may go in before them, and which may lead them out, and which may bring them in; that the congregation of the LORD be not as sheep which have no shepherd. ¹⁸And the LORD said to Moses, Take you Joshua the son of Nun, a man in whom is the spirit, and lay your hand on him; ¹⁹And set him before Eleazar the priest, and before all the congregation; and give him a charge in their sight. ²⁰And you shall put some of your honor on him, that all the congregation of the children of Israel may be obedient. ²¹And he shall stand before Eleazar the priest, who shall ask counsel for him after the judgment of Urim before the LORD: at his word shall they go out, and at his word they shall come in, both he, and all the children of Israel with him, even all the congregation. ²²And Moses did as the LORD commanded him: and he took Joshua, and set him before Eleazar the priest, and before all the congregation: ²³And he laid his hands on him, and gave him a charge, as the LORD commanded by the hand of Moses.

28 ¹And the LORD spoke to Moses, saying, ²Command the children of Israel, and say to them, My offering, and my bread for my sacrifices made by fire, for a sweet smell to me, shall you observe to offer to me in their due season. ³And you shall say to them, This is the offering made by fire which you shall offer to the LORD; two lambs of the first year without spot day by day, for a continual burnt offering. ⁴The one lamb shall you offer in the morning, and the other lamb shall you offer at even; ⁵And a tenth part of an ephah of flour for a meat offering, mingled with the fourth part of an hin of beaten oil. ⁶It is a continual burnt offering, which was ordained in mount Sinai for a sweet smell, a sacrifice made by fire to the LORD. ⁷And the drink offering thereof shall be the fourth part of an hin for the one lamb: in the holy place shall you cause the strong wine to be poured to the LORD for a drink offering. ⁸And the other lamb shall you offer at even: as the meat offering of the morning, and as the drink offering thereof, you shall offer it, a sacrifice made by fire, of a sweet smell to the LORD. ⁹And on the sabbath day two lambs of the first year without spot, and two tenth deals of flour for a meat offering, mingled with oil, and the drink offering thereof: ¹⁰This is the burnt offering of every sabbath, beside the continual burnt offering, and his drink offering. ¹¹And in the beginnings of your months you shall offer a burnt offering to the LORD; two young bullocks, and one ram, seven lambs of the first year without spot; ¹²And three tenth deals of flour for a meat offering, mingled with oil, for one bullock; and two tenth deals of flour for a meat offering, mingled with oil, for one ram; ¹³And a several tenth deal of flour mingled with oil for a meat offering to one lamb; for a burnt offering of a sweet smell, a sacrifice made by fire to the LORD. ¹⁴And their drink offerings shall be half an hin of wine to a bullock, and the third part of an hin to a ram, and a fourth part of an hin to a lamb: this is the burnt offering of every month throughout the months of the year. ¹⁵And one kid of the goats for a sin offering to the LORD shall be offered, beside the continual burnt offering, and his drink offering. ¹⁶And in the fourteenth day of the first month is the passover of the LORD. ¹⁷And in the fifteenth day of this month is the feast: seven days shall unleavened bread be eaten. ¹⁸In the first day shall be an holy convocation; you shall do no manner of servile work therein: ¹⁹But you shall offer a sacrifice made by fire for a burnt offering to the LORD; two young bullocks, and one ram, and seven lambs of the first year: they shall be to you without blemish: ²⁰And their meat offering shall be of flour mingled with oil: three tenth deals shall you offer for a bullock, and two tenth deals for a ram; ²¹A several tenth deal shall you offer for every lamb, throughout the seven lambs: ²²And one goat for a sin offering, to make an atonement for you. ²³You shall offer these beside the burnt offering in the morning, which is for a continual burnt offering. ²⁴After this manner you shall offer daily, throughout the seven days, the meat of the sacrifice made by fire, of a sweet smell to the LORD: it shall be offered beside the continual burnt offering, and his drink offering. ²⁵And on the seventh day you shall have an holy convocation; you shall do no servile work. ²⁶Also in the day of the first fruits, when you bring a new meat offering to the LORD, after your weeks be out, you shall have an holy convocation; you shall do no servile work: ²⁷But you shall offer the burnt offering for a sweet smell to the LORD; two young bullocks, one ram, seven lambs of the first year; ²⁸And their meat offering of flour mingled with oil, three tenth deals to one bullock, two tenth deals to one ram, ²⁹A several tenth deal to one lamb, throughout the seven lambs; ³⁰And one kid of the goats, to make an atonement for you. ³¹You shall offer them beside the continual burnt offering, and his meat offering, (they shall be to you without blemish) and their drink offerings.

29 ¹And in the seventh month, on the first day of the month, you shall have an holy convocation; you shall do no servile work: it is a day of blowing the trumpets to you. ²And you shall offer a burnt offering for a sweet smell to the LORD; one young bullock, one ram, and seven lambs of the first year without blemish: ³And their meat offering shall be of flour mingled with oil, three tenth deals for a bullock, and two tenth deals for a ram, ⁴And one tenth deal for one lamb, throughout the seven lambs: ⁵And one kid of the goats for a sin offering, to make an atonement for you: ⁶Beside the burnt offering of the month, and his meat offering, and the daily burnt offering, and his meat offering, and their drink offerings, according to their manner, for a sweet smell, a sacrifice made by fire to the LORD. ⁷And you shall have on the tenth day of this seventh month an holy convocation; and you shall afflict your souls: you shall not do any work therein: ⁸But you shall offer a burnt offering to the LORD for a sweet smell; one young bullock, one ram, and seven lambs of the first year; they shall be to you without blemish: ⁹And their meat offering shall be of flour mingled with oil, three tenth deals to a bullock, and two tenth deals to one ram, ¹⁰A several tenth deal for one lamb, throughout the seven lambs; ¹¹One kid of the goats for a sin offering; beside the sin offering of atonement, and the continual burnt offering, and the meat offering of it, and their drink offerings. ¹²And on the fifteenth day of the seventh month you shall have an holy convocation; you shall do no servile work, and you shall keep a feast to the LORD seven days: ¹³And you shall offer a burnt offering, a sacrifice made by fire, of a sweet smell to the LORD; thirteen young bullocks, two rams, and fourteen lambs of the first year; they shall be without blemish: ¹⁴And their meat offering shall be of flour mingled with oil, three tenth deals to every bullock of the thirteen bullocks, two tenth deals to each ram of the two rams, ¹⁵And a several tenth deal to each lamb of the fourteen lambs: ¹⁶And one kid of the goats for a sin offering; beside the continual burnt offering, his meat offering, and his drink offering. ¹⁷And on the second day you shall offer twelve young bullocks, two rams, fourteen lambs of the first year without spot: ¹⁸And their meat offering and their drink offerings for the bullocks, for the rams, and for the lambs, shall be according to their number, after the manner: ¹⁹And one kid of the goats for a sin offering; beside the continual burnt offering, and the meat offering thereof, and their drink offerings. ²⁰And on the third day eleven bullocks, two rams, fourteen lambs of the first year without blemish; ²¹And their meat offering and their drink offerings for the bullocks, for the rams, and for the lambs, shall be according to their number, after the manner: ²²And one goat for a sin offering; beside the continual burnt offering, and his meat offering, and his drink offering. ²³And on the fourth day ten bullocks, two rams, and fourteen lambs of the first year without blemish: ²⁴Their meat offering and their drink offerings for the bullocks, for the rams, and for the lambs, shall be according to their number, after the manner: ²⁵And one kid of the goats for a sin offering; beside the continual burnt offering, his meat offering, and his drink offering. ²⁶And on the fifth day nine bullocks, two rams, and fourteen lambs of the first year without spot: ²⁷And their meat offering and their drink offerings for the bullocks, for the rams, and for the lambs, shall be according to their number, after the manner: ²⁸And one goat for a sin offering; beside the continual burnt offering, and his meat offering, and his drink offering. ²⁹And on the sixth day eight bullocks, two rams, and fourteen lambs of the first year without blemish: ³⁰And their meat offering and their drink offerings for the bullocks, for the rams, and for the lambs, shall be according to their number, after the manner: ³¹And one goat for a sin offering; beside the continual burnt offering, his meat offering, and his drink offering. ³²And on the seventh day seven bullocks, two rams, and fourteen lambs of the first year without blemish: ³³And their meat offering and their drink offerings for the bullocks, for the rams, and for the lambs, shall be according to their number, after the manner: ³⁴And one goat for a sin offering; beside the continual burnt offering, his meat offering, and his drink offering. ³⁵On the eighth day you shall have a solemn assembly: you shall do no servile work therein: ³⁶But you shall offer a burnt offering, a sacrifice made by fire, of a sweet smell to the LORD: one bullock, one ram, seven lambs of the first year without blemish: ³⁷Their meat offering and their drink offerings for the bullock, for the ram, and for the lambs, shall be according to their number, after the manner: ³⁸And one goat for a sin offering; beside the continual burnt offering, and his meat offering, and his drink offering. ³⁹These things you shall do to the LORD in your set feasts, beside your vows, and your freewill offerings, for your burnt offerings, and for your meat offerings, and for your drink offerings, and for your peace offerings. ⁴⁰And Moses told the children of Israel according to all that the LORD commanded Moses.

30 ¹And Moses spoke to the heads of the tribes concerning the children of Israel, saying, This is the thing which the LORD has commanded. ²If a man vow a vow to the LORD, or swear an oath to bind his soul with a bond; he shall not break his word, he shall do according to all that proceeds out of his mouth. ³If a woman also vow a vow to the LORD, and bind herself by a bond, being in her father's house in her youth; ⁴And her father hear her vow, and her bond with which she has bound her soul, and her father shall hold his peace at her; then all her vows shall stand, and every bond with which she has bound her soul shall stand. ⁵But if her father disallow her in the day that he hears; not any of her vows, or of her bonds with which she has bound her soul, shall stand: and the LORD shall forgive her, because her father disallowed her. ⁶And if she had at all an husband, when she vowed, or uttered something out of her lips, with which she bound her soul; ⁷And her husband heard it, and held his peace at her in the day that he heard it: then her vows shall stand, and her bonds with which she bound her soul shall stand. ⁸But if her husband disallowed her on the day that he heard it; then he shall make her vow which she vowed, and that which she uttered with her lips, with which she bound her soul, of none effect: and the LORD shall forgive her. ⁹But every vow of a widow, and of her that is divorced, with which they have bound their souls, shall stand against her. ¹⁰And if she vowed in her husband's house, or bound her soul by a bond with an oath; ¹¹And her husband heard it, and held his peace at her, and disallowed her not: then all her vows shall stand, and every bond with which she bound her soul shall stand. ¹²But if her husband has utterly made them void on the day he heard them; then whatever proceeded out of her lips concerning her vows, or concerning the bond of her soul, shall not stand: her husband has made them void; and the LORD shall forgive her. ¹³Every vow, and every binding oath to afflict the soul, her husband may establish it, or her husband may make it void. ¹⁴But if her husband altogether hold his peace at her from day to day; then he establishes all her vows, or all her bonds, which are on her: he confirms them, because he held his peace at her in the day that he heard them. ¹⁵But if he shall any ways make them void after that he has heard them; then he shall bear her iniquity. ¹⁶These are the statutes, which the LORD commanded Moses, between a man and his wife, between the father and his daughter, being yet in her youth in her father's house.

31 ¹And the LORD spoke to Moses, saying, ²Avenge the children of Israel of the Midianites: afterward shall you be gathered to your people. ³And Moses spoke to the people, saying, Arm some of yourselves to the war, and let them go against the Midianites, and avenge the LORD of Midian. ⁴Of every tribe a thousand, throughout all the tribes of Israel, shall you send to the war. ⁵So there were delivered out of the thousands of Israel, a thousand of every tribe, twelve thousand armed for war. ⁶And Moses sent them to the war, a thousand of every tribe, them and Phinehas the son of Eleazar the priest, to the war, with the holy instruments, and the trumpets to blow in his hand. ⁷And they warred against the Midianites, as the LORD commanded Moses; and they slew all the males. ⁸And they slew the kings of Midian, beside the rest of them that were slain; namely, Evi, and Rekem, and Zur, and Hur, and Reba, five kings of Midian: Balaam also the son of Beor they slew with the sword. ⁹And the children of Israel took all the women of Midian captives, and their little ones, and took the spoil of all their cattle, and all their flocks, and all their goods. ¹⁰And they burnt all their cities wherein they dwelled, and all their goodly castles, with fire. ¹¹And they took all the spoil, and all the prey, both of men and of beasts. ¹²And they brought the captives, and the prey, and the spoil, to Moses, and Eleazar the priest, and to the congregation of the children of Israel, to the camp at the plains of Moab, which are by Jordan near Jericho. ¹³And Moses, and Eleazar the priest, and all the princes of the congregation, went forth to meet them without the camp. ¹⁴And Moses was wroth with the officers of the host, with the captains over thousands, and captains over hundreds, which came from the battle. ¹⁵And Moses said to them, Have you saved all the women alive? ¹⁶Behold, these caused the children of Israel, through the counsel of Balaam, to commit trespass against the LORD in the matter of Peor, and there was a plague among the congregation of the LORD. ¹⁷Now therefore kill every male among the little ones, and kill every woman that has known man by lying with him. ¹⁸But all the women children, that have not known a man by lying with him, keep alive for yourselves. ¹⁹And do you abide without the camp seven days: whoever has killed any person, and whoever has touched any slain, purify both yourselves and your captives on the third day, and on the seventh day. ²⁰And purify all your raiment, and all that is made of skins, and all work of goats' hair, and all things made of wood. ²¹And Eleazar the priest said to the men of war which went to the battle, This is the ordinance of the law which the LORD commanded Moses; ²²Only the gold, and the silver, the brass, the iron, the tin, and the lead, ²³Every thing that may abide the fire, you shall make it go through the fire, and it shall be clean: nevertheless it shall be purified with the water of separation: and all that stays not the fire you shall make go through the water. ²⁴And you shall wash your clothes on the seventh day, and you shall be clean, and afterward you shall come into the camp. ²⁵And the LORD spoke to Moses, saying, ²⁶Take the sum of the prey that was taken, both of man and of beast, you, and Eleazar the priest, and the chief fathers of the congregation: ²⁷And divide the prey into two parts; between them that took the war on them, who went out to battle, and between all the congregation: ²⁸And levy a tribute to the Lord of the men of war which went out to battle: one soul of five hundred, both of the persons, and of the beeves, and of the asses, and of the sheep: ²⁹Take it of their half, and give it to Eleazar the priest, for an heave offering of the LORD. ³⁰And of the children of Israel's half, you shall take one portion of fifty, of the persons, of the beeves, of the asses, and of the flocks, of all manner of beasts, and give them to the Levites, which keep the charge of the tabernacle of the LORD. ³¹And Moses and Eleazar the priest did as the LORD commanded Moses. ³²And the booty, being the rest of the prey which the men of war had caught, was six hundred thousand and seventy thousand and five thousand sheep, ³³And three score and twelve thousand beeves, ³⁴And three score and one thousand asses, ³⁵And thirty and two thousand persons in all, of women that had not known man by lying with him. ³⁶And the half, which was the portion of them that went out to war, was in number three hundred thousand and seven and thirty thousand and five hundred sheep: ³⁷And the LORD's tribute of the sheep was six hundred and three score and fifteen. ³⁸And the beeves were thirty and six thousand; of which the LORD's tribute was three score and twelve. ³⁹And the asses were thirty thousand and five hundred; of which the LORD's tribute was three score and one. ⁴⁰And the persons were sixteen thousand; of which the LORD's tribute was thirty and two persons. ⁴¹And Moses gave the tribute, which was the LORD's heave offering, to Eleazar the priest, as the LORD commanded Moses. ⁴²And of the children of

Israel's half, which Moses divided from the men that warred, ⁴³(Now the half that pertained to the congregation was three hundred thousand and thirty thousand and seven thousand and five hundred sheep, ⁴⁴And thirty and six thousand beeves, ⁴⁵And thirty thousand asses and five hundred, ⁴⁶And sixteen thousand persons;) ⁴⁷Even of the children of Israel's half, Moses took one portion of fifty, both of man and of beast, and gave them to the Levites, which kept the charge of the tabernacle of the LORD; as the LORD commanded Moses. ⁴⁸And the officers which were over thousands of the host, the captains of thousands, and captains of hundreds, came near to Moses: ⁴⁹And they said to Moses, Your servants have taken the sum of the men of war which are under our charge, and there lacks not one man of us. ⁵⁰We have therefore brought an oblation for the LORD, what every man has gotten, of jewels of gold, chains, and bracelets, rings, earrings, and tablets, to make an atonement for our souls before the LORD. ⁵¹And Moses and Eleazar the priest took the gold of them, even all worked jewels. ⁵²And all the gold of the offering that they offered up to the LORD, of the captains of thousands, and of the captains of hundreds, was sixteen thousand seven hundred and fifty shekels. ⁵³(For the men of war had taken spoil, every man for himself.) ⁵⁴And Moses and Eleazar the priest took the gold of the captains of thousands and of hundreds, and brought it into the tabernacle of the congregation, for a memorial for the children of Israel before the LORD.

32

¹Now the children of Reuben and the children of Gad had a very great multitude of cattle: and when they saw the land of Jazer, and the land of Gilead, that, behold, the place was a place for cattle; ²The children of Gad and the children of Reuben came and spoke to Moses, and to Eleazar the priest, and to the princes of the congregation, saying, ³Ataroth, and Dibon, and Jazer, and Nimrah, and Heshbon, and Elealeh, and Shebam, and Nebo, and Beon, ⁴Even the country which the LORD smote before the congregation of Israel, is a land for cattle, and your servants have cattle: ⁵Why, said they, if we have found grace in your sight, let this land be given to your servants for a possession, and bring us not over Jordan. ⁶And Moses said to the children of Gad and to the children of Reuben, Shall your brothers go to war, and shall you sit here? ⁷And why discourage you the heart of the children of Israel from going over into the land which the LORD has given them? ⁸Thus did your fathers, when I sent them from Kadeshbarnea to see the land. ⁹For when they went up to the valley of Eshcol, and saw the land, they discouraged the heart of the children of Israel, that they should not go into the land which the LORD had given them. ¹⁰And the LORD's anger was kindled the same time, and he swore, saying, ¹¹Surely none of the men that came up out of Egypt, from twenty years old and upward, shall see the land which I swore to Abraham, to Isaac, and to Jacob; because they have not wholly followed me: ¹²Save Caleb the son of Jephunneh the Kenezite, and Joshua the son of Nun: for they have wholly followed the LORD. ¹³And the LORD's anger was kindled against Israel, and he made them wander in the wilderness forty years, until all the generation, that had done evil in the sight of the LORD, was consumed. ¹⁴And, behold, you are risen up in your fathers' stead, an increase of sinful men, to augment yet the fierce anger of the LORD toward Israel. ¹⁵For if you turn away from after him, he will yet again leave them in the wilderness; and you shall destroy all this people. ¹⁶And they came near to him, and said, We will build sheepfolds here for our cattle, and cities for our little ones: ¹⁷But we ourselves will go ready armed before the children of Israel, until we have brought them to their place: and our little ones shall dwell in the fenced cities because of the inhabitants of the land. ¹⁸We will not return to our houses, until the children of Israel have inherited every man his inheritance. ¹⁹For we will not inherit with them on yonder side Jordan, or forward; because our inheritance is fallen to us on this side Jordan eastward. ²⁰And Moses said to them, If you will do this thing, if you will go armed before the LORD to war, ²¹And will go all of you armed over Jordan before the LORD, until he has driven out his enemies from before him, ²²And the land be subdued before the LORD: then afterward you shall return, and be guiltless before the LORD, and before Israel; and this land shall be your possession before the LORD. ²³But if you will not do so, behold, you have sinned against the LORD: and be sure your sin will find you out. ²⁴Build you cities for your little ones, and folds for your sheep; and do that which has proceeded out of your mouth. ²⁵And the children of Gad and the children of Reuben spoke to Moses, saying, Your servants will do as my lord commands. ²⁶Our little ones, our wives, our flocks, and all our cattle, shall be there in the cities of Gilead: ²⁷But your servants will pass over, every man armed for war, before the LORD to battle, as my lord says. ²⁸So concerning them Moses commanded Eleazar the priest, and Joshua the son of Nun, and the chief fathers of the tribes of the children of Israel: ²⁹And Moses said to them, If the children of Gad and the children of Reuben will pass with you over Jordan, every man armed to battle, before the LORD, and the land shall be subdued before you; then you shall give them the land of Gilead for a possession: ³⁰But if they will not pass over with you armed, they shall have possessions among you in the land of Canaan. ³¹And the children of Gad and the children of Reuben answered, saying, As the LORD has said to your servants, so will we do. ³²We will pass over armed before the LORD into the land of Canaan, that the possession of our inheritance on this side Jordan may be ours. ³³And Moses gave to them, even to the children of Gad, and to the children of Reuben, and to half the tribe of Manasseh the son of Joseph, the kingdom of Sihon king of the Amorites, and the kingdom of Og king of Bashan, the land, with the cities thereof in the coasts, even the cities of the country round about. ³⁴And the children of Gad built Dibon, and Ataroth, and Aroer, ³⁵And Atroth, Shophan, and Jaazer, and Jogbehah, ³⁶And Bethnimrah, and Bethharan, fenced cities: and folds for sheep. ³⁷And the children of Reuben built Heshbon, and Elealeh, and Kirjathaim, ³⁸And Nebo, and Baalmeon, (their names being changed,) and Shibmah: and gave other names to the cities which they built. ³⁹And the children of Machir the son of Manasseh went to Gilead, and took it, and dispossessed the Amorite which was in it. ⁴⁰And Moses gave Gilead to Machir the son of Manasseh; and he dwelled therein. ⁴¹And Jair the son of Manasseh went and took the small towns thereof, and called them Havothjair.

⁴²And Nobah went and took Kenath, and the villages thereof, and called it Nobah, after his own name.

33

¹These are the journeys of the children of Israel, which went forth out of the land of Egypt with their armies under the hand of Moses and Aaron. ²And Moses wrote their goings out according to their journeys by the commandment of the LORD: and these are their journeys according to their goings out. ³And they departed from Rameses in the first month, on the fifteenth day of the first month; on the morrow after the passover the children of Israel went out with an high hand in the sight of all the Egyptians. ⁴For the Egyptians buried all their firstborn, which the LORD had smitten among them: on their gods also the LORD executed judgments. ⁵And the children of Israel removed from Rameses, and pitched in Succoth. ⁶And they departed from Succoth, and pitched in Etham, which is in the edge of the wilderness. ⁷And they removed from Etham, and turned again to Pihahiroth, which is before Baalzephon: and they pitched before Migdol. ⁸And they departed from before Pihahiroth, and passed through the middle of the sea into the wilderness, and went three days' journey in the wilderness of Etham, and pitched in Marah. ⁹And they removed from Marah, and came to Elim: and in Elim were twelve fountains of water, and three score and ten palm trees; and they pitched there. ¹⁰And they removed from Elim, and encamped by the Red sea. ¹¹And they removed from the Red sea, and encamped in the wilderness of Sin. ¹²And they took their journey out of the wilderness of Sin, and encamped in Dophkah. ¹³And they departed from Dophkah, and encamped in Alush. ¹⁴And they removed from Alush, and encamped at Rephidim, where was no water for the people to drink. ¹⁵And they departed from Rephidim, and pitched in the wilderness of Sinai. ¹⁶And they removed from the desert of Sinai, and pitched at Kibrothhattaavah. ¹⁷And they departed from Kibrothhattaavah, and encamped at Hazeroth. ¹⁸And they departed from Hazeroth, and pitched in Rithmah. ¹⁹And they departed from Rithmah, and pitched at Rimmonparez. ²⁰And they departed from Rimmonparez, and pitched in Libnah. ²¹And they removed from Libnah, and pitched at Rissah. ²²And they journeyed from Rissah, and pitched in Kehelathah. ²³And they went from Kehelathah, and pitched in mount Shapher. ²⁴And they removed from mount Shapher, and encamped in Haradah. ²⁵And they removed from Haradah, and pitched in Makheloth. ²⁶And they removed from Makheloth, and encamped at Tahath. ²⁷And they departed from Tahath, and pitched at Tarah. ²⁸And they removed from Tarah, and pitched in Mithcah. ²⁹And they went from Mithcah, and pitched in Hashmonah. ³⁰And they departed from Hashmonah, and encamped at Moseroth. ³¹And they departed from Moseroth, and pitched in Benejaakan. ³²And they removed from Benejaakan, and encamped at Horhagidgad. ³³And they went from Horhagidgad, and pitched in Jotbathah. ³⁴And they removed from Jotbathah, and encamped at Ebronah. ³⁵And they departed from Ebronah, and encamped at Eziongaber. ³⁶And they removed from Eziongaber, and pitched in the wilderness of Zin, which is Kadesh. ³⁷And they removed from Kadesh, and pitched in mount Hor, in the edge of the land of Edom. ³⁸And Aaron the priest went up into mount Hor at the commandment of the LORD, and died there, in the fortieth year after the children of Israel were come out of the land of Egypt, in the first day of the fifth month. ³⁹And Aaron was an hundred and twenty and three years old when he died in mount Hor. ⁴⁰And king Arad the Canaanite, which dwelled in the south in the land of Canaan, heard of the coming of the children of Israel. ⁴¹And they departed from mount Hor, and pitched in Zalmonah. ⁴²And they departed from Zalmonah, and pitched in Punon. ⁴³And they departed from Punon, and pitched in Oboth. ⁴⁴And they departed from Oboth, and pitched in Ijeabarim, in the border of Moab. ⁴⁵And they departed from Iim, and pitched in Dibongad. ⁴⁶And they removed from Dibongad, and encamped in Almondiblathaim. ⁴⁷And they removed from Almondiblathaim, and pitched in the mountains of Abarim, before Nebo. ⁴⁸And they departed from the mountains of Abarim, and pitched in the plains of Moab by Jordan near Jericho. ⁴⁹And they pitched by Jordan, from Bethjesimoth even to Abelshittim in the plains of Moab. ⁵⁰And the LORD spoke to Moses in the plains of Moab by Jordan near Jericho, saying, ⁵¹Speak to the children of Israel, and say to them, When you are passed over Jordan into the land of Canaan; ⁵²Then you shall drive out all the inhabitants of the land from before you, and destroy all their pictures, and destroy all their molten images, and quite pluck down all their high places: ⁵³And you shall dispossess the inhabitants of the land, and dwell therein: for I have given you the land to possess it. ⁵⁴And you shall divide the land by lot for an inheritance among your families: and to the more you shall give the more inheritance, and to the fewer you shall give the less inheritance: every man's inheritance shall be in the place where his lot falls; according to the tribes of your fathers you shall inherit. ⁵⁵But if you will not drive out the inhabitants of the land from before you; then it shall come to pass, that those which you let remain of them shall be pricks in your eyes, and thorns in your sides, and shall vex you in the land wherein you dwell. ⁵⁶Moreover it shall come to pass, that I shall do to you, as I thought to do to them.

34

¹And the LORD spoke to Moses, saying, ²Command the children of Israel, and say to them, When you come into the land of Canaan; (this is the land that shall fall to you for an inheritance, even the land of Canaan with the coasts thereof:) ³Then your south quarter shall be from the wilderness of Zin along by the coast of Edom, and your south border shall be the outmost coast of the salt sea eastward: ⁴And your border shall turn from the south to the ascent of Akrabbim, and pass on to Zin: and the going forth thereof shall be from the south to Kadeshbarnea, and shall go on to Hazaraddar, and pass on to Azmon: ⁵And the border shall fetch a compass from Azmon to the river of Egypt, and the goings out of it shall be at the sea. ⁶And as for the western border, you shall even have the great sea for a border: this shall be your west border. ⁷And this shall be your north border: from the great sea you shall point out for you mount Hor: ⁸From mount Hor you shall point out your border to the entrance of Hamath; and the goings forth of the border shall be to Zedad: ⁹And the border shall go on to Ziphron, and the goings out of it shall be at Hazarenan: this shall be your north border. ¹⁰And you shall point out your east border from Hazarenan to Shepham: ¹¹And the coast

shall go down from Shepham to Riblah, on the east side of Ain; and the border shall descend, and shall reach to the side of the sea of Chinnereth eastward: ¹²And the border shall go down to Jordan, and the goings out of it shall be at the salt sea: this shall be your land with the coasts thereof round about. ¹³And Moses commanded the children of Israel, saying, This is the land which you shall inherit by lot, which the LORD commanded to give to the nine tribes, and to the half tribe: ¹⁴For the tribe of the children of Reuben according to the house of their fathers, and the tribe of the children of Gad according to the house of their fathers, have received their inheritance; and half the tribe of Manasseh have received their inheritance: ¹⁵The two tribes and the half tribe have received their inheritance on this side Jordan near Jericho eastward, toward the sun rise. ¹⁶And the LORD spoke to Moses, saying, ¹⁷These are the names of the men which shall divide the land to you: Eleazar the priest, and Joshua the son of Nun. ¹⁸And you shall take one prince of every tribe, to divide the land by inheritance. ¹⁹And the names of the men are these: Of the tribe of Judah, Caleb the son of Jephunneh. ²⁰And of the tribe of the children of Simeon, Shemuel the son of Ammihud. ²¹Of the tribe of Benjamin, Elidad the son of Chislon. ²²And the prince of the tribe of the children of Dan, Bukki the son of Jogli. ²³The prince of the children of Joseph, for the tribe of the children of Manasseh, Hanniel the son of Ephod. ²⁴And the prince of the tribe of the children of Ephraim, Kemuel the son of Shiphtan. ²⁵And the prince of the tribe of the children of Zebulun, Elizaphan the son of Parnach. ²⁶And the prince of the tribe of the children of Issachar, Paltiel the son of Azzan. ²⁷And the prince of the tribe of the children of Asher, Ahihud the son of Shelomi. ²⁸And the prince of the tribe of the children of Naphtali, Pedahel the son of Ammihud. ²⁹These are they whom the LORD commanded to divide the inheritance to the children of Israel in the land of Canaan.

35 ¹And the LORD spoke to Moses in the plains of Moab by Jordan near Jericho, saying, ²Command the children of Israel, that they give to the Levites of the inheritance of their possession cities to dwell in; and you shall give also to the Levites suburbs for the cities round about them. ³And the cities shall they have to dwell in; and the suburbs of them shall be for their cattle, and for their goods, and for all their beasts. ⁴And the suburbs of the cities, which you shall give to the Levites, shall reach from the wall of the city and outward a thousand cubits round about. ⁵And you shall measure from without the city on the east side two thousand cubits, and on the south side two thousand cubits, and on the west side two thousand cubits, and on the north side two thousand cubits; and the city shall be in the middle: this shall be to them the suburbs of the cities. ⁶And among the cities which you shall give to the Levites there shall be six cities for refuge, which you shall appoint for the manslayer, that he may flee thither: and to them you shall add forty and two cities. ⁷So all the cities which you shall give to the Levites shall be forty and eight cities: them shall you give with their suburbs. ⁸And the cities which you shall give shall be of the possession of the children of Israel: from them that have many you shall give many; but from them that have few you shall give few: every one shall give of his cities to the Levites according to his inheritance which he inherits. ⁹And the LORD spoke to Moses, saying, ¹⁰Speak to the children of Israel, and say to them, When you be come over Jordan into the land of Canaan; ¹¹Then you shall appoint you cities to be cities of refuge for you; that the slayer may flee thither, which kills any person at unawares. ¹²And they shall be to you cities for refuge from the avenger; that the manslayer die not, until he stand before the congregation in judgment. ¹³And of these cities which you shall give six cities shall you have for refuge. ¹⁴You shall give three cities on this side Jordan, and three cities shall you give in the land of Canaan, which shall be cities of refuge. ¹⁵These six cities shall be a refuge, both for the children of Israel, and for the stranger, and for the sojourner among them: that every one that kills any person unawares may flee thither. ¹⁶And if he smite him with an instrument of iron, so that he die, he is a murderer: the murderer shall surely be put to death. ¹⁷And if he smite him with throwing a stone, with which he may die, and he die, he is a murderer: the murderer shall surely be put to death. ¹⁸Or if he smite him with an hand weapon of wood, with which he may die, and he die, he is a murderer: the murderer shall surely be put to death. ¹⁹The revenger of blood himself shall slay the murderer: when he meets him, he shall slay him. ²⁰But if he thrust him of hatred, or hurl at him by laying of wait, that he die; ²¹Or in enmity smite him with his hand, that he die: he that smote him shall surely be put to death; for he is a murderer: the revenger of blood shall slay the murderer, when he meets him. ²²But if he thrust him suddenly without enmity, or have cast on him any thing without laying of wait, ²³Or with any stone, with which a man may die, seeing him not, and cast it on him, that he die, and was not his enemy, neither sought his harm: ²⁴Then the congregation shall judge between the slayer and the revenger of blood according to these judgments: ²⁵And the congregation shall deliver the slayer out of the hand of the revenger of blood, and the congregation shall restore him to the city of his refuge, where he was fled: and he shall abide in it to the death of the high priest, which was anointed with the holy oil. ²⁶But if the slayer shall at any time come without the border of the city of his refuge, where he was fled; ²⁷And the revenger of blood find him without the borders of the city of his refuge, and the revenger of blood kill the slayer; he shall not be guilty of blood: ²⁸Because he should have remained in the city of his refuge until the death of the high priest: but after the death of the high priest the slayer shall return into the land of his possession. ²⁹So these things shall be for a statute of judgment to you throughout your generations in all your dwellings. ³⁰Whoever kills any person, the murderer shall be put to death by the mouth of witnesses: but one witness shall not testify against any person to cause him to die. ³¹Moreover you shall take no satisfaction for the life of a murderer, which is guilty of death: but he shall be surely put to death. ³²And you shall take no satisfaction for him that is fled to the city of his refuge, that he should come again to dwell in the land, until the death of the priest. ³³So you shall not pollute the land wherein you are: for blood it defiles the land: and the land cannot be cleansed of the blood that is shed therein, but by the blood of him that shed it. ³⁴Defile not therefore the land which you shall inhabit, wherein I dwell: for I the LORD dwell among the children of Israel.

36

¹And the chief fathers of the families of the children of Gilead, the son of Machir, the son of Manasseh, of the families of the sons of Joseph, came near, and spoke before Moses, and before the princes, the chief fathers of the children of Israel: ²And they said, The LORD commanded my lord to give the land for an inheritance by lot to the children of Israel: and my lord was commanded by the LORD to give the inheritance of Zelophehad our brother to his daughters. ³And if they be married to any of the sons of the other tribes of the children of Israel, then shall their inheritance be taken from the inheritance of our fathers, and shall be put to the inheritance of the tribe which they are received: so shall it be taken from the lot of our inheritance. ⁴And when the jubilee of the children of Israel shall be, then shall their inheritance be put to the inheritance of the tribe which they are received: so shall their inheritance be taken away from the inheritance of the tribe of our fathers. ⁵And Moses commanded the children of Israel according to the word of the LORD, saying, The tribe of the sons of Joseph has said well. ⁶This is the thing which the LORD does command concerning the daughters of Zelophehad, saying, Let them marry to whom they think best; only to the family of the tribe of their father shall they marry. ⁷So shall not the inheritance of the children of Israel remove from tribe to tribe: for every one of the children of Israel shall keep himself to the inheritance of the tribe of his fathers. ⁸And every daughter, that possesses an inheritance in any tribe of the children of Israel, shall be wife to one of the family of the tribe of her father, that the children of Israel may enjoy every man the inheritance of his fathers. ⁹Neither shall the inheritance remove from one tribe to another tribe; but every one of the tribes of the children of Israel shall keep himself to his own inheritance. ¹⁰Even as the LORD commanded Moses, so did the daughters of Zelophehad: ¹¹For Mahlah, Tirzah, and Hoglah, and Milcah, and Noah, the daughters of Zelophehad, were married to their father's brothers' sons: ¹²And they were married into the families of the sons of Manasseh the son of Joseph, and their inheritance remained in the tribe of the family of their father. ¹³These are the commandments and the judgments, which the LORD commanded by the hand of Moses to the children of Israel in the plains of Moab by Jordan near Jericho.

Deuteronomy

1 ¹These be the words which Moses spoke to all Israel on this side Jordan in the wilderness, in the plain over against the Red sea, between Paran, and Tophel, and Laban, and Hazeroth, and Dizahab. ²(There are eleven days' journey from Horeb by the way of mount Seir to Kadeshbarnea.) ³And it came to pass in the fortieth year, in the eleventh month, on the first day of the month, that Moses spoke to the children of Israel, according to all that the LORD had given him in commandment to them; ⁴After he had slain Sihon the king of the Amorites, which dwelled in Heshbon, and Og the king of Bashan, which dwelled at Astaroth in Edrei: ⁵On this side Jordan, in the land of Moab, began Moses to declare this law, saying, ⁶The LORD our God spoke to us in Horeb, saying, You have dwelled long enough in this mount: ⁷Turn you, and take your journey, and go to the mount of the Amorites, and to all the places near thereunto, in the plain, in the hills, and in the vale, and in the south, and by the sea side, to the land of the Canaanites, and to Lebanon, to the great river, the river Euphrates. ⁸Behold, I have set the land before you: go in and possess the land which the LORD swore to your fathers, Abraham, Isaac, and Jacob, to give to them and to their seed after them. ⁹And I spoke to you at that time, saying, I am not able to bear you myself alone: ¹⁰The LORD your God has multiplied you, and, behold, you are this day as the stars of heaven for multitude. ¹¹(The LORD God of your fathers make you a thousand times so many more as you are, and bless you, as he has promised you!) ¹²How can I myself alone bear your cumbrance, and your burden, and your strife? ¹³Take you wise men, and understanding, and known among your tribes, and I will make them rulers over you. ¹⁴And you answered me, and said, The thing which you have spoken is good for us to do. ¹⁵So I took the chief of your tribes, wise men, and known, and made them heads over you, captains over thousands, and captains over hundreds, and captains over fifties, and captains over tens, and officers among your tribes. ¹⁶And I charged your judges at that time, saying, Hear the causes between your brothers, and judge righteously between every man and his brother, and the stranger that is with him. ¹⁷You shall not respect persons in judgment; but you shall hear the small as well as the great; you shall not be afraid of the face of man; for the judgment is God's: and the cause that is too hard for you, bring it to me, and I will hear it. ¹⁸And I commanded you at that time all the things which you should do. ¹⁹And when we departed from Horeb, we went through all that great and terrible wilderness, which you saw by the way of the mountain of the Amorites, as the LORD our God commanded us; and we came to Kadeshbarnea. ²⁰And I said to you, You are come to the mountain of the Amorites, which the LORD our God does give to us. ²¹Behold, the LORD your God has set the land before you: go up and possess it, as the LORD God of your fathers has said to you; fear not, neither be discouraged. ²²And you came near to me every one of you, and said, We will send men before us, and they shall search us out the land, and bring us word again by what way we must go up, and into what cities we shall come. ²³And the saying pleased me well: and I took twelve men of you, one of a tribe: ²⁴And they turned and went up into the mountain, and came to the valley of Eshcol, and searched it out. ²⁵And they took of the fruit of the land in their hands, and brought it down to us, and brought us word again, and said, It is a good land which the LORD our God does give us. ²⁶Notwithstanding you would not go up, but rebelled against the commandment of the LORD your God: ²⁷And you murmured in your tents, and said, Because the LORD hated us, he has brought us forth out of the land of Egypt, to deliver us into the hand of the Amorites, to destroy us. ²⁸Where shall we go up? our brothers have discouraged our heart, saying, The people is greater and taller than we; the cities are great and walled up to heaven; and moreover we have seen the sons of the Anakims there. ²⁹Then I said to you, Dread not, neither be afraid of them. ³⁰The LORD your God which goes before you, he shall fight for you, according to all that he did for you in Egypt before your eyes; ³¹And in the wilderness, where you have seen how that the LORD your God bore you, as a man does bear his son, in all the way that you went, until you came into this place. ³²Yet in this thing you did not believe the LORD your God, ³³Who went in the way before you, to search you out a place to pitch your tents in, in fire by night, to show you by what way you should go, and in a cloud by day. ³⁴And the LORD heard the voice of your words, and was wroth, and swore, saying, ³⁵Surely there shall not one of these men of this evil generation see that good land, which I swore to give to your fathers. ³⁶Save Caleb the son of Jephunneh; he shall see it, and to him will I give the land that he has trodden on, and to his children, because he has wholly followed the LORD. ³⁷Also the LORD was angry with me for your sakes, saying, You also shall not go in thither. ³⁸But Joshua the son of Nun, which stands before you, he shall go in thither: encourage him: for he shall cause Israel to inherit it. ³⁹Moreover your little ones, which you said should be a prey, and your children, which in that day had no knowledge between good and evil, they shall go in thither, and to them will I give it, and they shall possess it. ⁴⁰But as for you, turn you, and take your journey into the wilderness by the way of the Red sea. ⁴¹Then you answered and said to me, We have sinned against the LORD, we will go up and fight, according to all that the LORD our God commanded us. And when you had girded on every man his weapons of war, you were ready to go up into the hill. ⁴²And the LORD said to me, Say to them. Go not up, neither fight; for I am not among you; lest you be smitten before your enemies. ⁴³So I spoke to you; and you would not hear, but rebelled against the commandment of the LORD, and went presumptuously up into the hill. ⁴⁴And the Amorites, which dwelled in that mountain, came out against you, and chased you, as bees do, and destroyed you in Seir, even to Hormah. ⁴⁵And you returned and wept before the LORD; but the LORD would not listen to your voice, nor give ear to you. ⁴⁶So you stayed in Kadesh many days, according to the days that you stayed there.

2 ¹Then we turned, and took our journey into the wilderness by the way of the Red sea, as the LORD spoke to me: and we compassed mount Seir many days. ²And the LORD spoke to me, saying, ³You have compassed

this mountain long enough: turn you northward. ⁴And command you the people, saying, You are to pass through the coast of your brothers the children of Esau, which dwell in Seir; and they shall be afraid of you: take you good heed to yourselves therefore: ⁵Meddle not with them; for I will not give you of their land, no, not so much as a foot breadth; because I have given mount Seir to Esau for a possession. ⁶You shall buy meat of them for money, that you may eat; and you shall also buy water of them for money, that you may drink. ⁷For the LORD your God has blessed you in all the works of your hand: he knows your walking through this great wilderness: these forty years the LORD your God has been with you; you have lacked nothing. ⁸And when we passed by from our brothers the children of Esau, which dwelled in Seir, through the way of the plain from Elath, and from Eziongaber, we turned and passed by the way of the wilderness of Moab. ⁹And the LORD said to me, Distress not the Moabites, neither contend with them in battle: for I will not give you of their land for a possession; because I have given Ar to the children of Lot for a possession. ¹⁰The Emims dwelled therein in times past, a people great, and many, and tall, as the Anakims; ¹¹Which also were accounted giants, as the Anakims; but the Moabites called them Emims. ¹²The Horims also dwelled in Seir beforetime; but the children of Esau succeeded them, when they had destroyed them from before them, and dwelled in their stead; as Israel did to the land of his possession, which the LORD gave to them. ¹³Now rise up, said I, and get you over the brook Zered. And we went over the brook Zered. ¹⁴And the space in which we came from Kadeshbarnea, until we were come over the brook Zered, was thirty and eight years; until all the generation of the men of war were wasted out from among the host, as the LORD swore to them. ¹⁵For indeed the hand of the LORD was against them, to destroy them from among the host, until they were consumed. ¹⁶So it came to pass, when all the men of war were consumed and dead from among the people, ¹⁷That the LORD spoke to me, saying, ¹⁸You are to pass over through Ar, the coast of Moab, this day: ¹⁹And when you come near over against the children of Ammon, distress them not, nor meddle with them: for I will not give you of the land of the children of Ammon any possession; because I have given it to the children of Lot for a possession. ²⁰(That also was accounted a land of giants: giants dwelled therein in old time; and the Ammonites call them Zamzummims; ²¹A people great, and many, and tall, as the Anakims; but the LORD destroyed them before them; and they succeeded them, and dwelled in their stead: ²²As he did to the children of Esau, which dwelled in Seir, when he destroyed the Horims from before them; and they succeeded them, and dwelled in their stead even to this day: ²³And the Avims which dwelled in Hazerim, even to Azzah, the Caphtorims, which came forth out of Caphtor, destroyed them, and dwelled in their stead.) ²⁴Rise you up, take your journey, and pass over the river Arnon: behold, I have given into your hand Sihon the Amorite, king of Heshbon, and his land: begin to possess it, and contend with him in battle. ²⁵This day will I begin to put the dread of you and the fear of you on the nations that are under the whole heaven, who shall hear report of you, and shall tremble, and be in anguish because of you. ²⁶And I sent messengers out of the wilderness of Kedemoth to Sihon king of Heshbon with words of peace, saying, ²⁷Let me pass through your land: I will go along by the high way, I will neither turn to the right hand nor to the left. ²⁸You shall sell me meat for money, that I may eat; and give me water for money, that I may drink: only I will pass through on my feet; ²⁹(As the children of Esau which dwell in Seir, and the Moabites which dwell in Ar, did to me;) until I shall pass over Jordan into the land which the LORD our God gives us. ³⁰But Sihon king of Heshbon would not let us pass by him: for the LORD your God hardened his spirit, and made his heart obstinate, that he might deliver him into your hand, as appears this day. ³¹And the LORD said to me, Behold, I have begun to give Sihon and his land before you: begin to possess, that you may inherit his land. ³²Then Sihon came out against us, he and all his people, to fight at Jahaz. ³³And the LORD our God delivered him before us; and we smote him, and his sons, and all his people. ³⁴And we took all his cities at that time, and utterly destroyed the men, and the women, and the little ones, of every city, we left none to remain: ³⁵Only the cattle we took for a prey to ourselves, and the spoil of the cities which we took. ³⁶From Aroer, which is by the brink of the river of Arnon, and from the city that is by the river, even to Gilead, there was not one city too strong for us: the LORD our God delivered all to us: ³⁷Only to the land of the children of Ammon you came not, nor to any place of the river Jabbok, nor to the cities in the mountains, nor to whatever the LORD our God forbade us.

3 ¹Then we turned, and went up the way to Bashan: and Og the king of Bashan came out against us, he and all his people, to battle at Edrei. ²And the LORD said to me, Fear him not: for I will deliver him, and all his people, and his land, into your hand; and you shall do to him as you did to Sihon king of the Amorites, which dwelled at Heshbon. ³So the LORD our God delivered into our hands Og also, the king of Bashan, and all his people: and we smote him until none was left to him remaining. ⁴And we took all his cities at that time, there was not a city which we took not from them, three score cities, all the region of Argob, the kingdom of Og in Bashan. ⁵All these cities were fenced with high walls, gates, and bars; beside unwalled towns a great many. ⁶And we utterly destroyed them, as we did to Sihon king of Heshbon, utterly destroying the men, women, and children, of every city. ⁷But all the cattle, and the spoil of the cities, we took for a prey to ourselves. ⁸And we took at that time out of the hand of the two kings of the Amorites the land that was on this side Jordan, from the river of Arnon to mount Hermon; ⁹(Which Hermon the Sidonians call Sirion; and the Amorites call it Shenir;) ¹⁰All the cities of the plain, and all Gilead, and all Bashan, to Salchah and Edrei, cities of the kingdom of Og in Bashan. ¹¹For only Og king of Bashan remained of the remnant of giants; behold his bedstead was a bedstead of iron; is it not in Rabbath of the children of Ammon? nine cubits was the length thereof, and four cubits the breadth of it, after the cubit of a man. ¹²And this land, which we possessed at that time, from Aroer, which is by the river Arnon, and half mount Gilead, and cities thereof, gave I to the Reubenites and to the Gadites. ¹³And the rest of Gilead, and all Bashan, being the kingdom of Og, gave I to the half tribe of Manasseh; all the region of

Argob, with all Bashan, which was called the land of giants. ¹⁴Jair the son of Manasseh took all the country of Argob to the coasts of Geshuri and Maachathi; and called them after his own name, Bashanhavothjair, to this day. ¹⁵And I gave Gilead to Machir. ¹⁶And to the Reubenites and to the Gadites I gave from Gilead even to the river Arnon half the valley, and the border even to the river Jabbok, which is the border of the children of Ammon; ¹⁷The plain also, and Jordan, and the coast thereof, from Chinnereth even to the sea of the plain, even the salt sea, under Ashdothpisgah eastward. ¹⁸And I commanded you at that time, saying, The LORD your God has given you this land to possess it: you shall pass over armed before your brothers the children of Israel, all that are meet for the war. ¹⁹But your wives, and your little ones, and your cattle, (for I know that you have much cattle,) shall abide in your cities which I have given you; ²⁰Until the LORD have given rest to your brothers, as well as to you, and until they also possess the land which the LORD your God has given them beyond Jordan: and then shall you return every man to his possession, which I have given you. ²¹And I commanded Joshua at that time, saying, Your eyes have seen all that the LORD your God has done to these two kings: so shall the LORD do to all the kingdoms where you pass. ²²You shall not fear them: for the LORD your God he shall fight for you. ²³And I sought the LORD at that time, saying, ²⁴O Lord GOD, you have begun to show your servant your greatness, and your mighty hand: for what God is there in heaven or in earth, that can do according to your works, and according to your might? ²⁵I pray you, let me go over, and see the good land that is beyond Jordan, that goodly mountain, and Lebanon. ²⁶But the LORD was wroth with me for your sakes, and would not hear me: and the LORD said to me, Let it suffice you; speak no more to me of this matter. ²⁷Get you up into the top of Pisgah, and lift up your eyes westward, and northward, and southward, and eastward, and behold it with your eyes: for you shall not go over this Jordan. ²⁸But charge Joshua, and encourage him, and strengthen him: for he shall go over before this people, and he shall cause them to inherit the land which you shall see. ²⁹So we stayed in the valley over against Bethpeor.

4 ¹Now therefore listen, O Israel, to the statutes and to the judgments, which I teach you, for to do them, that you may live, and go in and possess the land which the LORD God of your fathers gives you. ²You shall not add to the word which I command you, neither shall you diminish anything from it, that you may keep the commandments of the LORD your God which I command you. ³Your eyes have seen what the LORD did because of Baalpeor: for all the men that followed Baalpeor, the LORD your God has destroyed them from among you. ⁴But you that did join to the LORD your God are alive every one of you this day. ⁵Behold, I have taught you statutes and judgments, even as the LORD my God commanded me, that you should do so in the land where you go to possess it. ⁶Keep therefore and do them; for this is your wisdom and your understanding in the sight of the nations, which shall hear all these statutes, and say, Surely this great nation is a wise and understanding people. ⁷For what nation is there so great, who has God so near to them, as the LORD our God is in all things that we call on him for? ⁸And what nation is there so great, that has statutes and judgments so righteous as all this law, which I set before you this day? ⁹Only take heed to yourself, and keep your soul diligently, lest you forget the things which your eyes have seen, and lest they depart from your heart all the days of your life: but teach them your sons, and your sons' sons; ¹⁰Specially the day that you stood before the LORD your God in Horeb, when the LORD said to me, Gather me the people together, and I will make them hear my words, that they may learn to fear me all the days that they shall live on the earth, and that they may teach their children. ¹¹And you came near and stood under the mountain; and the mountain burned with fire to the middle of heaven, with darkness, clouds, and thick darkness. ¹²And the LORD spoke to you out of the middle of the fire: you heard the voice of the words, but saw no similitude; only you heard a voice. ¹³And he declared to you his covenant, which he commanded you to perform, even ten commandments; and he wrote them on two tables of stone. ¹⁴And the LORD commanded me at that time to teach you statutes and judgments, that you might do them in the land where you go over to possess it. ¹⁵Take you therefore good heed to yourselves; for you saw no manner of similitude on the day that the LORD spoke to you in Horeb out of the middle of the fire: ¹⁶Lest you corrupt yourselves, and make you a graven image, the similitude of any figure, the likeness of male or female, ¹⁷The likeness of any beast that is on the earth, the likeness of any winged fowl that flies in the air, ¹⁸The likeness of any thing that creeps on the ground, the likeness of any fish that is in the waters beneath the earth: ¹⁹And lest you lift up your eyes to heaven, and when you see the sun, and the moon, and the stars, even all the host of heaven, should be driven to worship them, and serve them, which the LORD your God has divided to all nations under the whole heaven. ²⁰But the LORD has taken you, and brought you forth out of the iron furnace, even out of Egypt, to be to him a people of inheritance, as you are this day. ²¹Furthermore the LORD was angry with me for your sakes, and swore that I should not go over Jordan, and that I should not go in to that good land, which the LORD your God gives you for an inheritance: ²²But I must die in this land, I must not go over Jordan: but you shall go over, and possess that good land. ²³Take heed to yourselves, lest you forget the covenant of the LORD your God, which he made with you, and make you a graven image, or the likeness of any thing, which the LORD your God has forbidden you. ²⁴For the LORD your God is a consuming fire, even a jealous God. ²⁵When you shall beget children, and children's children, and you shall have remained long in the land, and shall corrupt yourselves, and make a graven image, or the likeness of any thing, and shall do evil in the sight of the LORD your God, to provoke him to anger: ²⁶I call heaven and earth to witness against you this day, that you shall soon utterly perish from off the land where you go over Jordan to possess it; you shall not prolong your days on it, but shall utterly be destroyed. ²⁷And the LORD shall scatter you among the nations, and you shall be left few in number among the heathen, where the LORD shall lead you. ²⁸And there you shall serve gods, the work of men's hands, wood and stone, which neither see, nor hear, nor eat, nor smell. ²⁹But if from

there you shall seek the LORD your God, you shall find him, if you seek him with all your heart and with all your soul. ³⁰When you are in tribulation, and all these things are come on you, even in the latter days, if you turn to the LORD your God, and shall be obedient to his voice; ³¹(For the LORD your God is a merciful God;) he will not forsake you, neither destroy you, nor forget the covenant of your fathers which he swore to them. ³²For ask now of the days that are past, which were before you, since the day that God created man on the earth, and ask from the one side of heaven to the other, whether there has been any such thing as this great thing is, or has been heard like it? ³³Did ever people hear the voice of God speaking out of the middle of the fire, as you have heard, and live? ³⁴Or has God assayed to go and take him a nation from the middle of another nation, by temptations, by signs, and by wonders, and by war, and by a mighty hand, and by a stretched out arm, and by great terrors, according to all that the LORD your God did for you in Egypt before your eyes? ³⁵To you it was showed, that you might know that the LORD he is God; there is none else beside him. ³⁶Out of heaven he made you to hear his voice, that he might instruct you: and on earth he showed you his great fire; and you heard his words out of the middle of the fire. ³⁷And because he loved your fathers, therefore he chose their seed after them, and brought you out in his sight with his mighty power out of Egypt; ³⁸To drive out nations from before you greater and mightier than you are, to bring you in, to give you their land for an inheritance, as it is this day. ³⁹Know therefore this day, and consider it in your heart, that the LORD he is God in heaven above, and on the earth beneath: there is none else. ⁴⁰You shall keep therefore his statutes, and his commandments, which I command you this day, that it may go well with you, and with your children after you, and that you may prolong your days on the earth, which the LORD your God gives you, for ever. ⁴¹Then Moses severed three cities on this side Jordan toward the sun rise; ⁴²That the slayer might flee thither, which should kill his neighbor unawares, and hated him not in times past; and that fleeing to one of these cities he might live: ⁴³Namely, Bezer in the wilderness, in the plain country, of the Reubenites; and Ramoth in Gilead, of the Gadites; and Golan in Bashan, of the Manassites. ⁴⁴And this is the law which Moses set before the children of Israel: ⁴⁵These are the testimonies, and the statutes, and the judgments, which Moses spoke to the children of Israel, after they came forth out of Egypt. ⁴⁶On this side Jordan, in the valley over against Bethpeor, in the land of Sihon king of the Amorites, who dwelled at Heshbon, whom Moses and the children of Israel smote, after they were come forth out of Egypt: ⁴⁷And they possessed his land, and the land of Og king of Bashan, two kings of the Amorites, which were on this side Jordan toward the sun rise; ⁴⁸From Aroer, which is by the bank of the river Arnon, even to mount Sion, which is Hermon, ⁴⁹And all the plain on this side Jordan eastward, even to the sea of the plain, under the springs of Pisgah.

5 ¹And Moses called all Israel, and said to them, Hear, O Israel, the statutes and judgments which I speak in your ears this day, that you may learn them, and keep, and do them. ²The LORD our God made a covenant with us in Horeb. ³The LORD made not this covenant with our fathers, but with us, even us, who are all of us here alive this day. ⁴The LORD talked with you face to face in the mount out of the middle of the fire, ⁵(I stood between the LORD and you at that time, to show you the word of the LORD: for you were afraid by reason of the fire, and went not up into the mount;) saying, ⁶I am the LORD your God, which brought you out of the land of Egypt, from the house of bondage. ⁷You shall have none other gods before me. ⁸You shall not make you any graven image, or any likeness of any thing that is in heaven above, or that is in the earth beneath, or that is in the waters beneath the earth: ⁹You shall not bow down yourself to them, nor serve them: for I the LORD your God am a jealous God, visiting the iniquity of the fathers on the children to the third and fourth generation of them that hate me, ¹⁰And showing mercy to thousands of them that love me and keep my commandments. ¹¹You shall not take the name of the LORD your God in vain: for the LORD will not hold him guiltless that takes his name in vain. ¹²Keep the sabbath day to sanctify it, as the LORD your God has commanded you. ¹³Six days you shall labor, and do all your work: ¹⁴But the seventh day is the sabbath of the LORD your God: in it you shall not do any work, you, nor your son, nor your daughter, nor your manservant, nor your maidservant, nor your ox, nor your ass, nor any of your cattle, nor your stranger that is within your gates; that your manservant and your maidservant may rest as well as you. ¹⁵And remember that you were a servant in the land of Egypt, and that the LORD your God brought you out there through a mighty hand and by a stretched out arm: therefore the LORD your God commanded you to keep the sabbath day. ¹⁶Honor your father and your mother, as the LORD your God has commanded you; that your days may be prolonged, and that it may go well with you, in the land which the LORD your God gives you. ¹⁷You shall not kill. ¹⁸Neither shall you commit adultery. ¹⁹Neither shall you steal. ²⁰Neither shall you bear false witness against your neighbor. ²¹Neither shall you desire your neighbor's wife, neither shall you covet your neighbor's house, his field, or his manservant, or his maidservant, his ox, or his ass, or any thing that is your neighbor's. ²²These words the LORD spoke to all your assembly in the mount out of the middle of the fire, of the cloud, and of the thick darkness, with a great voice: and he added no more. And he wrote them in two tables of stone, and delivered them to me. ²³And it came to pass, when you heard the voice out of the middle of the darkness, (for the mountain did burn with fire,) that you came near to me, even all the heads of your tribes, and your elders; ²⁴And you said, Behold, the LORD our God has showed us his glory and his greatness, and we have heard his voice out of the middle of the fire: we have seen this day that God does talk with man, and he lives. ²⁵Now therefore why should we die? for this great fire will consume us: if we hear the voice of the LORD our God any more, then we shall die. ²⁶For who is there of all flesh, that has heard the voice of the living God speaking out of the middle of the fire, as we have, and lived? ²⁷Go you near, and hear all that the LORD our God shall say: and speak you to us all that the LORD our God shall speak to you; and we will hear it, and do it. ²⁸And the LORD heard the voice of your words, when you spoke to me; and the LORD said to me, I have heard the voice of the words of this people, which they have spoken to you: they have well said all that they have spoken. ²⁹O that there were such an heart in them, that they would fear me, and keep all my commandments always, that it might be well with them, and with their children for ever! ³⁰Go say to them, Get you into your tents again. ³¹But as for you, stand you here by me, and I will speak to you all the commandments, and the statutes, and the judgments, which you shall teach them, that they may do them in the land which I give them to possess it. ³²You shall observe to do therefore as the LORD your God has commanded you: you shall not turn aside to the right hand or to the left. ³³You shall walk in all the ways which the LORD your God has commanded you, that you may live, and that it may be well with you, and that you may prolong your days in the land which you shall possess.

6 ¹Now these are the commandments, the statutes, and the judgments, which the LORD your God commanded to teach you, that you might do them in the land where you go to possess it: ²That you might fear the LORD your God, to keep all his statutes and his commandments, which I command you, you, and your son, and your son's son, all the days of your life; and that your days may be prolonged. ³Hear therefore, O Israel, and observe to do it; that it may be well with you, and that you may increase mightily, as the LORD God of your fathers has promised you, in the land that flows with milk and honey. ⁴Hear, O Israel: The LORD our God is one LORD: ⁵And you shall love the LORD your God with all your heart, and with all your soul, and with all your might. ⁶And these words, which I command you this day, shall be in your heart: ⁷And you shall teach them diligently to your children, and shall talk of them when you sit in your house, and when you walk by the way, and when you lie down, and when you rise up. ⁸And you shall bind them for a sign on your hand, and they shall be as frontlets between your eyes. ⁹And you shall write them on the posts of your house, and on your gates. ¹⁰And it shall be, when the LORD your God shall have brought you into the land which he swore to your fathers, to Abraham, to Isaac, and to Jacob, to give you great and goodly cities, which you built not, ¹¹And houses full of all good things, which you filled not, and wells dig, which you digged not, vineyards and olive trees, which you planted not; when you shall have eaten and be full; ¹²Then beware lest you forget the LORD, which brought you forth out of the land of Egypt, from the house of bondage. ¹³You shall fear the LORD your God, and serve him, and shall swear by his name. ¹⁴You shall not go after other gods, of the gods of the people which are round about you; ¹⁵(For the LORD your God is a jealous God among you) lest the anger of the LORD your God be kindled against you, and destroy you from off the face of the earth. ¹⁶You shall not tempt the LORD your God, as you tempted him in Massah. ¹⁷You shall diligently keep the commandments of the LORD your God, and his testimonies, and his statutes, which he has commanded you. ¹⁸And you shall do that which is right and good in the sight of the LORD: that it may be well with you, and that you may go in and possess the good land which the LORD swore to your fathers. ¹⁹To cast out all your enemies from before you, as the LORD has spoken. ²⁰And when your son asks you in time to come, saying, What mean the testimonies, and the statutes, and the judgments, which the LORD our God has commanded you? ²¹Then you shall say to your son, We were Pharaoh's slaves in Egypt; and the LORD brought us out of Egypt with a mighty hand: ²²And the LORD showed signs and wonders, great and sore, on Egypt, on Pharaoh, and on all his household, before our eyes: ²³And he brought us out from there, that he might bring us in, to give us the land which he swore to our fathers. ²⁴And the LORD commanded us to do all these statutes, to fear the LORD our God, for our good always, that he might preserve us alive, as it is at this day. ²⁵And it shall be our righteousness, if we observe to do all these commandments before the LORD our God, as he has commanded us.

7 ¹When the LORD your God shall bring you into the land where you go to possess it, and has cast out many nations before you, the Hittites, and the Girgashites, and the Amorites, and the Canaanites, and the Perizzites, and the Hivites, and the Jebusites, seven nations greater and mightier than you; ²And when the LORD your God shall deliver them before you; you shall smite them, and utterly destroy them; you shall make no covenant with them, nor show mercy to them: ³Neither shall you make marriages with them; your daughter you shall not give to his son, nor his daughter shall you take to your son. ⁴For they will turn away your son from following me, that they may serve other gods: so will the anger of the LORD be kindled against you, and destroy you suddenly. ⁵But thus shall you deal with them; you shall destroy their altars, and break down their images, and cut down their groves, and burn their graven images with fire. ⁶For you are an holy people to the LORD your God: the LORD your God has chosen you to be a special people to himself, above all people that are on the face of the earth. ⁷The LORD did not set his love on you, nor choose you, because you were more in number than any people; for you were the fewest of all people: ⁸But because the LORD loved you, and because he would keep the oath which he had sworn to your fathers, has the LORD brought you out with a mighty hand, and redeemed you out of the house of slaves, from the hand of Pharaoh king of Egypt. ⁹Know therefore that the LORD your God, he is God, the faithful God, which keeps covenant and mercy with them that love him and keep his commandments to a thousand generations; ¹⁰And repays them that hate him to their face, to destroy them: he will not be slack to him that hates him, he will repay him to his face. ¹¹You shall therefore keep the commandments, and the statutes, and the judgments, which I command you this day, to do them. ¹²Why it shall come to pass, if you listen to these judgments, and keep, and do them, that the LORD your God shall keep to you the covenant and the mercy which he swore to your fathers: ¹³And he will love you, and bless you, and multiply you: he will also bless the fruit of your womb, and the fruit of your land, your corn, and your wine, and your oil, the increase of your cows, and the flocks of your sheep, in the land which he swore to your fathers to give you. ¹⁴You shall be blessed above all people: there shall not be male or female barren among you, or among your cattle. ¹⁵And the LORD will take away from you all sickness, and will put none of the evil diseases of Egypt, which you know, on you; but will lay them on all them that hate you. ¹⁶And you shall consume all

the people which the LORD your God shall deliver you; your eye shall have no pity on them: neither shall you serve their gods; for that will be a snare to you. ¹⁷If you shall say in your heart, These nations are more than I; how can I dispossess them? ¹⁸You shall not be afraid of them: but shall well remember what the LORD your God did to Pharaoh, and to all Egypt; ¹⁹The great temptations which your eyes saw, and the signs, and the wonders, and the mighty hand, and the stretched out arm, whereby the LORD your God brought you out: so shall the LORD your God do to all the people of whom you are afraid. ²⁰Moreover the LORD your God will send the hornet among them, until they that are left, and hide themselves from you, be destroyed. ²¹You shall not be affrighted at them: for the LORD your God is among you, a mighty God and terrible. ²²And the LORD your God will put out those nations before you by little and little: you may not consume them at once, lest the beasts of the field increase on you. ²³But the LORD your God shall deliver them to you, and shall destroy them with a mighty destruction, until they be destroyed. ²⁴And he shall deliver their kings into your hand, and you shall destroy their name from under heaven: there shall no man be able to stand before you, until you have destroyed them. ²⁵The graven images of their gods shall you burn with fire: you shall not desire the silver or gold that is on them, nor take it to you, lest you be snared therein: for it is an abomination to the LORD your God. ²⁶Neither shall you bring an abomination into your house, lest you be a cursed thing like it: but you shall utterly detest it, and you shall utterly abhor it; for it is a cursed thing.

8 ¹All the commandments which I command you this day shall you observe to do, that you may live, and multiply, and go in and possess the land which the LORD swore to your fathers. ²And you shall remember all the way which the LORD your God led you these forty years in the wilderness, to humble you, and to prove you, to know what was in your heart, whether you would keep his commandments, or no. ³And he humbled you, and suffered you to hunger, and fed you with manna, which you knew not, neither did your fathers know; that he might make you know that man does not live by bread only, but by every word that proceeds out of the mouth of the LORD does man live. ⁴Your raiment waxed not old on you, neither did your foot swell, these forty years. ⁵You shall also consider in your heart, that, as a man chastens his son, so the LORD your God chastens you. ⁶Therefore you shall keep the commandments of the LORD your God, to walk in his ways, and to fear him. ⁷For the LORD your God brings you into a good land, a land of brooks of water, of fountains and depths that spring out of valleys and hills; ⁸A land of wheat, and barley, and vines, and fig trees, and pomegranates; a land of oil olive, and honey; ⁹A land wherein you shall eat bread without scarceness, you shall not lack any thing in it; a land whose stones are iron, and out of whose hills you may dig brass. ¹⁰When you have eaten and are full, then you shall bless the LORD your God for the good land which he has given you. ¹¹Beware that you forget not the LORD your God, in not keeping his commandments, and his judgments, and his statutes, which I command you this day: ¹²Lest when you have eaten and are full, and have built goodly houses, and dwelled therein; ¹³And when your herds and your flocks multiply, and your silver and your gold is multiplied, and all that you have is multiplied; ¹⁴Then your heart be lifted up, and you forget the LORD your God, which brought you forth out of the land of Egypt, from the house of bondage; ¹⁵Who led you through that great and terrible wilderness, wherein were fiery serpents, and scorpions, and drought, where there was no water; who brought you forth water out of the rock of flint; ¹⁶Who fed you in the wilderness with manna, which your fathers knew not, that he might humble you, and that he might prove you, to do you good at your latter end; ¹⁷And you say in your heart, My power and the might of my hand has gotten me this wealth. ¹⁸But you shall remember the LORD your God: for it is he that gives you power to get wealth, that he may establish his covenant which he swore to your fathers, as it is this day. ¹⁹And it shall be, if you do at all forget the LORD your God, and walk after other gods, and serve them, and worship them, I testify against you this day that you shall surely perish. ²⁰As the nations which the LORD destroys before your face, so shall you perish; because you would not be obedient to the voice of the LORD your God.

9 ¹Hear, O Israel: You are to pass over Jordan this day, to go in to possess nations greater and mightier than yourself, cities great and fenced up to heaven, ²A people great and tall, the children of the Anakims, whom you know, and of whom you have heard say, Who can stand before the children of Anak! ³Understand therefore this day, that the LORD your God is he which goes over before you; as a consuming fire he shall destroy them, and he shall bring them down before your face: so shall you drive them out, and destroy them quickly, as the LORD has said to you. ⁴Speak not you in your heart, after that the LORD your God has cast them out from before you, saying, For my righteousness the LORD has brought me in to possess this land: but for the wickedness of these nations the LORD does drive them out from before you. ⁵Not for your righteousness, or for the uprightness of your heart, do you go to possess their land: but for the wickedness of these nations the LORD your God does drive them out from before you, and that he may perform the word which the LORD swore to your fathers, Abraham, Isaac, and Jacob. ⁶Understand therefore, that the LORD your God gives you not this good land to possess it for your righteousness; for you are a stiff necked people. ⁷Remember, and forget not, how you provoked the LORD your God to wrath in the wilderness: from the day that you did depart out of the land of Egypt, until you came to this place, you have been rebellious against the LORD. ⁸Also in Horeb you provoked the LORD to wrath, so that the LORD was angry with you to have destroyed you. ⁹When I was gone up into the mount to receive the tables of stone, even the tables of the covenant which the LORD made with you, then I stayed in the mount forty days and forty nights, I neither did eat bread nor drink water: ¹⁰And the LORD delivered to me two tables of stone written with the finger of God; and on them was written according to all the words, which the LORD spoke with you in the mount out of the middle of the fire in the day of the assembly. ¹¹And it came to pass at the end of forty days and forty nights, that the LORD gave me the two tables of stone, even the tables of

the covenant. ¹²And the LORD said to me, Arise, get you down quickly from hence; for your people which you have brought forth out of Egypt have corrupted themselves; they are quickly turned aside out of the way which I commanded them; they have made them a molten image. ¹³Furthermore the LORD spoke to me, saying, I have seen this people, and, behold, it is a stiff necked people: ¹⁴Let me alone, that I may destroy them, and blot out their name from under heaven: and I will make of you a nation mightier and greater than they. ¹⁵So I turned and came down from the mount, and the mount burned with fire: and the two tables of the covenant were in my two hands. ¹⁶And I looked, and, behold, you had sinned against the LORD your God, and had made you a molten calf: you had turned aside quickly out of the way which the LORD had commanded you. ¹⁷And I took the two tables, and cast them out of my two hands, and broke them before your eyes. ¹⁸And I fell down before the LORD, as at the first, forty days and forty nights: I did neither eat bread, nor drink water, because of all your sins which you sinned, in doing wickedly in the sight of the LORD, to provoke him to anger. ¹⁹For I was afraid of the anger and hot displeasure, with which the LORD was wroth against you to destroy you. But the LORD listened to me at that time also. ²⁰And the LORD was very angry with Aaron to have destroyed him: and I prayed for Aaron also the same time. ²¹And I took your sin, the calf which you had made, and burnt it with fire, and stamped it, and ground it very small, even until it was as small as dust: and I cast the dust thereof into the brook that descended out of the mount. ²²And at Taberah, and at Massah, and at Kibrothhattaavah, you provoked the LORD to wrath. ²³Likewise when the LORD sent you from Kadeshbarnea, saying, Go up and possess the land which I have given you; then you rebelled against the commandment of the LORD your God, and you believed him not, nor listened to his voice. ²⁴You have been rebellious against the LORD from the day that I knew you. ²⁵Thus I fell down before the LORD forty days and forty nights, as I fell down at the first; because the LORD had said he would destroy you. ²⁶I prayed therefore to the LORD, and said, O Lord GOD, destroy not your people and your inheritance, which you have redeemed through your greatness, which you have brought forth out of Egypt with a mighty hand. ²⁷Remember your servants, Abraham, Isaac, and Jacob; look not to the stubbornness of this people, nor to their wickedness, nor to their sin: ²⁸Lest the land from where you brought us out say, Because the LORD was not able to bring them into the land which he promised them, and because he hated them, he has brought them out to slay them in the wilderness. ²⁹Yet they are your people and your inheritance, which you brought out by your mighty power and by your stretched out arm.

10 ¹At that time the LORD said to me, Hew you two tables of stone like to the first, and come up to me into the mount, and make you an ark of wood. ²And I will write on the tables the words that were in the first tables which you brake, and you shall put them in the ark. ³And I made an ark of shittim wood, and hewed two tables of stone like to the first, and went up into the mount, having the two tables in my hand. ⁴And he wrote on the tables, according to the first writing, the ten commandments, which the LORD spoke to you in the mount out of the middle of the fire in the day of the assembly: and the LORD gave them to me. ⁵And I turned myself and came down from the mount, and put the tables in the ark which I had made; and there they be, as the LORD commanded me. ⁶And the children of Israel took their journey from Beeroth of the children of Jaakan to Mosera: there Aaron died, and there he was buried; and Eleazar his son ministered in the priest's office in his stead. ⁷From there they journeyed to Gudgodah; and from Gudgodah to Jotbath, a land of rivers of waters. ⁸At that time the LORD separated the tribe of Levi, to bear the ark of the covenant of the LORD, to stand before the LORD to minister to him, and to bless in his name, to this day. ⁹Why Levi has no part nor inheritance with his brothers; the LORD is his inheritance, according as the LORD your God promised him. ¹⁰And I stayed in the mount, according to the first time, forty days and forty nights; and the LORD listened to me at that time also, and the LORD would not destroy you. ¹¹And the LORD said to me, Arise, take your journey before the people, that they may go in and possess the land, which I swore to their fathers to give to them. ¹²And now, Israel, what does the LORD your God require of you, but to fear the LORD your God, to walk in all his ways, and to love him, and to serve the LORD your God with all your heart and with all your soul, ¹³To keep the commandments of the LORD, and his statutes, which I command you this day for your good? ¹⁴Behold, the heaven and the heaven of heavens is the LORD's your God, the earth also, with all that therein is. ¹⁵Only the LORD had a delight in your fathers to love them, and he chose their seed after them, even you above all people, as it is this day. ¹⁶Circumcise therefore the foreskin of your heart, and be no more stiff necked. ¹⁷For the LORD your God is God of gods, and Lord of lords, a great God, a mighty, and a terrible, which regards not persons, nor takes reward: ¹⁸He does execute the judgment of the fatherless and widow, and loves the stranger, in giving him food and raiment. ¹⁹Love you therefore the stranger: for you were strangers in the land of Egypt. ²⁰You shall fear the LORD your God; him shall you serve, and to him shall you hold, and swear by his name. ²¹He is your praise, and he is your God, that has done for you these great and terrible things, which your eyes have seen. ²²Your fathers went down into Egypt with three score and ten persons; and now the LORD your God has made you as the stars of heaven for multitude.

11 ¹Therefore you shall love the LORD your God, and keep his charge, and his statutes, and his judgments, and his commandments, always. ²And know you this day: for I speak not with your children which have not known, and which have not seen the chastisement of the LORD your God, his greatness, his mighty hand, and his stretched out arm, ³And his miracles, and his acts, which he did in the middle of Egypt to Pharaoh the king of Egypt, and to all his land; ⁴And what he did to the army of Egypt, to their horses, and to their chariots; how he made the water of the Red sea to overflow them as they pursued after you, and how the LORD has destroyed them to this day; ⁵And what he did to you in the wilderness, until you came into this place; ⁶And what he did to Dathan and Abiram, the sons of Eliab, the son of Reuben: how the earth opened her mouth, and swallowed them up, and their households, and their tents, and all the substance that was in their possession, in the middle of all Israel: ⁷But your eyes have seen all the great acts of the LORD which he did. ⁸Therefore shall you keep all the commandments which I command you this day, that you may be strong, and go in and possess the land, where you go to possess it; ⁹And that you may prolong your days in the land, which the LORD swore to your fathers to give to them and to their seed, a land that flows with milk and honey. ¹⁰For the land, where you go in to possess it, is not as the land of Egypt, from from where you came out, where you sowed your seed, and watered it with your foot, as a garden of herbs: ¹¹But the land, where you go to possess it, is a land of hills and valleys, and drinks water of the rain of heaven: ¹²A land which the LORD your God cares for: the eyes of the LORD your God are always on it, from the beginning of the year even to the end of the year. ¹³And it shall come to pass, if you shall listen diligently to my commandments which I command you this day, to love the LORD your God, and to serve him with all your heart and with all your soul, ¹⁴That I will give you the rain of your land in his due season, the first rain and the latter rain, that you may gather in your corn, and your wine, and your oil. ¹⁵And I will send grass in your fields for your cattle, that you may eat and be full. ¹⁶Take heed to yourselves, that your heart be not deceived, and you turn aside, and serve other gods, and worship them; ¹⁷And then the LORD's wrath be kindled against you, and he shut up the heaven, that there be no rain, and that the land yield not her fruit; and lest you perish quickly from off the good land which the LORD gives you. ¹⁸Therefore shall you lay up these my words in your heart and in your soul, and bind them for a sign on your hand, that they may be as frontlets between your eyes. ¹⁹And you shall teach them your children, speaking of them when you sit in your house, and when you walk by the way, when you lie down, and when you rise up. ²⁰And you shall write them on the door posts of your house, and on your gates: ²¹That your days may be multiplied, and the days of your children, in the land which the LORD swore to your fathers to give them, as the days of heaven on the earth. ²²For if you shall diligently keep all these commandments which I command you, to do them, to love the LORD your God, to walk in all his ways, and to join to him; ²³Then will the LORD drive out all these nations from before you, and you shall possess greater nations and mightier than yourselves. ²⁴Every place where on the soles of your feet shall tread shall be yours: from the wilderness and Lebanon, from the river, the river Euphrates, even to the uttermost sea shall your coast be. ²⁵There shall no man be able to stand before you: for the LORD your God shall lay the fear of you and the dread of you on all the land that you shall tread on, as he has said to you. ²⁶Behold, I set before you this day a blessing and a curse; ²⁷A blessing, if you obey the commandments of the LORD your God, which I command you this day: ²⁸And a curse, if you will not obey the commandments of the LORD your God, but turn aside out of the way which I command you this day, to go after other gods, which you have not known. ²⁹And it shall come to pass, when the LORD your God has brought you in to the land where you go to possess it, that you shall put the blessing on mount Gerizim, and the curse on mount Ebal. ³⁰Are they not on the other side Jordan, by the way where the sun goes down, in the land of the Canaanites, which dwell in the desert over against Gilgal, beside the plains of Moreh? ³¹For you shall pass over Jordan to go in to possess the land which the LORD your God gives you, and you shall possess it, and dwell therein. ³²And you shall observe to do all the statutes and judgments which I set before you this day.

12

¹These are the statutes and judgments, which you shall observe to do in the land, which the LORD God of your fathers gives you to possess it, all the days that you live on the earth. ²You shall utterly destroy all the places, wherein the nations which you shall possess served their gods, on the high mountains, and on the hills, and under every green tree: ³And you shall overthrow their altars, and break their pillars, and burn their groves with fire; and you shall hew down the graven images of their gods, and destroy the names of them out of that place. ⁴You shall not do so to the LORD your God. ⁵But to the place which the LORD your God shall choose out of all your tribes to put his name there, even to his habitation shall you seek, and thither you shall come: ⁶And thither you shall bring your burnt offerings, and your sacrifices, and your tithes, and heave offerings of your hand, and your vows, and your freewill offerings, and the firstborn of your herds and of your flocks: ⁷And there you shall eat before the LORD your God, and you shall rejoice in all that you put your hand to, you and your households, wherein the LORD your God has blessed you. ⁸You shall not do after all the things that we do here this day, every man whatever is right in his own eyes. ⁹For you are not as yet come to the rest and to the inheritance, which the LORD your God gives you. ¹⁰But when you go over Jordan, and dwell in the land which the LORD your God gives you to inherit, and when he gives you rest from all your enemies round about, so that you dwell in safety; ¹¹Then there shall be a place which the LORD your God shall choose to cause his name to dwell there; thither shall you bring all that I command you; your burnt offerings, and your sacrifices, your tithes, and the heave offering of your hand, and all your choice vows which you vow to the LORD: ¹²And you shall rejoice before the LORD your God, you, and your sons, and your daughters, and your menservants, and your maidservants, and the Levite that is within your gates; for as much as he has no part nor inheritance with you. ¹³Take heed to yourself that you offer not your burnt offerings in every place that you see: ¹⁴But in the place which the LORD shall choose in one of your tribes, there you shall offer your burnt offerings, and there you shall do all that I command you. ¹⁵Notwithstanding you may kill and eat flesh in all your gates, whatever your soul lusts after, according to the blessing of the LORD your God which he has given you: the unclean and the clean may eat thereof, as of the roebuck, and as of the hart. ¹⁶Only you shall not eat the blood; you shall pour it on the earth as water. ¹⁷You may not eat within your gates the tithe of your corn, or of your wine, or of your oil, or the firstborn of your herds or of your flock, nor any of your vows which you vow, nor your freewill offerings, or heave offering of your hand: ¹⁸But you must eat them before the LORD your God in the place which the LORD your God shall choose, you, and your son, and your daughter, and your

manservant, and your maidservant, and the Levite that is within your gates: and you shall rejoice before the LORD your God in all that you put your hands to. ¹⁹Take heed to yourself that you forsake not the Levite as long as you live on the earth. ²⁰When the LORD your God shall enlarge your border, as he has promised you, and you shall say, I will eat flesh, because your soul longs to eat flesh; you may eat flesh, whatever your soul lusts after. ²¹If the place which the LORD your God has chosen to put his name there be too far from you, then you shall kill of your herd and of your flock, which the LORD has given you, as I have commanded you, and you shall eat in your gates whatever your soul lusts after. ²²Even as the roebuck and the hart is eaten, so you shall eat them: the unclean and the clean shall eat of them alike. ²³Only be sure that you eat not the blood: for the blood is the life; and you may not eat the life with the flesh. ²⁴You shall not eat it; you shall pour it on the earth as water. ²⁵You shall not eat it; that it may go well with you, and with your children after you, when you shall do that which is right in the sight of the LORD. ²⁶Only your holy things which you have, and your vows, you shall take, and go to the place which the LORD shall choose: ²⁷And you shall offer your burnt offerings, the flesh and the blood, on the altar of the LORD your God: and the blood of your sacrifices shall be poured out on the altar of the LORD your God, and you shall eat the flesh. ²⁸Observe and hear all these words which I command you, that it may go well with you, and with your children after you for ever, when you do that which is good and right in the sight of the LORD your God. ²⁹When the LORD your God shall cut off the nations from before you, where you go to possess them, and you succeed them, and dwell in their land; ³⁰Take heed to yourself that you be not snared by following them, after that they be destroyed from before you; and that you inquire not after their gods, saying, How did these nations serve their gods? even so will I do likewise. ³¹You shall not do so to the LORD your God: for every abomination to the LORD, which he hates, have they done to their gods; for even their sons and their daughters they have burnt in the fire to their gods. ³²What thing soever I command you, observe to do it: you shall not add thereto, nor diminish from it.

13 ¹If there arise among you a prophet, or a dreamer of dreams, and gives you a sign or a wonder, ²And the sign or the wonder come to pass, whereof he spoke to you, saying, Let us go after other gods, which you have not known, and let us serve them; ³You shall not listen to the words of that prophet, or that dreamer of dreams: for the LORD your God proves you, to know whether you love the LORD your God with all your heart and with all your soul. ⁴You shall walk after the LORD your God, and fear him, and keep his commandments, and obey his voice, and you shall serve him, and join to him. ⁵And that prophet, or that dreamer of dreams, shall be put to death; because he has spoken to turn you away from the LORD your God, which brought you out of the land of Egypt, and redeemed you out of the house of bondage, to thrust you out of the way which the LORD your God commanded you to walk in. So shall you put the evil away from the middle of you. ⁶If your brother, the son of your mother, or your son, or your daughter, or the wife of your bosom, or your friend, which is as your own soul, entice you secretly, saying, Let us go and serve other gods, which you have not known, you, nor your fathers; ⁷Namely, of the gods of the people which are round about you, near to you, or far off from you, from the one end of the earth even to the other end of the earth; ⁸You shall not consent to him, nor listen to him; neither shall your eye pity him, neither shall you spare, neither shall you conceal him: ⁹But you shall surely kill him; your hand shall be first on him to put him to death, and afterwards the hand of all the people. ¹⁰And you shall stone him with stones, that he die; because he has sought to thrust you away from the LORD your God, which brought you out of the land of Egypt, from the house of bondage. ¹¹And all Israel shall hear, and fear, and shall do no more any such wickedness as this is among you. ¹²If you shall hear say in one of your cities, which the LORD your God has given you to dwell there, saying, ¹³Certain men, the children of Belial, are gone out from among you, and have withdrawn the inhabitants of their city, saying, Let us go and serve other gods, which you have not known; ¹⁴Then shall you inquire, and make search, and ask diligently; and, behold, if it be truth, and the thing certain, that such abomination is worked among you; ¹⁵You shall surely smite the inhabitants of that city with the edge of the sword, destroying it utterly, and all that is therein, and the cattle thereof, with the edge of the sword. ¹⁶And you shall gather all the spoil of it into the middle of the street thereof, and shall burn with fire the city, and all the spoil thereof every whit, for the LORD your God: and it shall be an heap for ever; it shall not be built again. ¹⁷And there shall stick nothing of the cursed thing to your hand: that the LORD may turn from the fierceness of his anger, and show you mercy, and have compassion on you, and multiply you, as he has sworn to your fathers; ¹⁸When you shall listen to the voice of the LORD your God, to keep all his commandments which I command you this day, to do that which is right in the eyes of the LORD your God.

14 ¹You are the children of the LORD your God: you shall not cut yourselves, nor make any baldness between your eyes for the dead. ²For you are an holy people to the LORD your God, and the LORD has chosen you to be a peculiar people to himself, above all the nations that are on the earth. ³You shall not eat any abominable thing. ⁴These are the beasts which you shall eat: the ox, the sheep, and the goat, ⁵The hart, and the roebuck, and the fallow deer, and the wild goat, and the pygarg, and the wild ox, and the chamois. ⁶And every beast that parts the hoof, and separates the cleft into two claws, and chews the cud among the beasts, that you shall eat. ⁷Nevertheless these you shall not eat of them that chew the cud, or of them that divide the cloven hoof; as the camel, and the hare, and the coney: for they chew the cud, but divide not the hoof; therefore they are unclean to you. ⁸And the swine, because it divides the hoof, yet chews not the cud, it is unclean to you: you shall not eat of their flesh, nor touch their dead carcass. ⁹These you shall eat of all that are in the waters: all that have fins and scales shall you eat: ¹⁰And whatever has not fins and scales you may not eat; it is unclean to you. ¹¹Of all clean birds you shall eat. ¹²But these are they of which you shall not eat: the eagle, and the ossifrage, and the ospray, ¹³And the glede, and the kite, and the vulture after his kind, ¹⁴And every raven after his kind, ¹⁵And the owl, and the night hawk, and the cuckow, and the hawk after his kind, ¹⁶The little owl, and the great owl, and the swan, ¹⁷And the pelican, and the gier eagle, and the cormorant, ¹⁸And the stork, and the heron after her kind, and the lapwing, and the bat. ¹⁹And every creeping thing that flies is unclean to you: they shall not be eaten. ²⁰But of all clean fowls you may eat. ²¹You shall not eat of anything that dies of itself: you shall give it to the stranger that is in your gates, that he may eat it; or you may sell it to an alien: for you are an holy people to the LORD your God. You shall not seethe a kid in his mother's milk. ²²You shall truly tithe all the increase of your seed, that the field brings forth year by year. ²³And you shall eat before the LORD your God, in the place which he shall choose to place his name there, the tithe of your corn, of your wine, and of your oil, and the firstborn of your herds and of your flocks; that you may learn to fear the LORD your God always. ²⁴And if the way be too long for you, so that you are not able to carry it; or if the place be too far from you, which the LORD your God shall choose to set his name there, when the LORD your God has blessed you: ²⁵Then shall you turn it into money, and bind up the money in your hand, and shall go to the place which the LORD your God shall choose: ²⁶And you shall bestow that money for whatever your soul lusts after, for oxen, or for sheep, or for wine, or for strong drink, or for whatever your soul desires: and you shall eat there before the LORD your God, and you shall rejoice, you, and your household, ²⁷And the Levite that is within your gates; you shall not forsake him; for he has no part nor inheritance with you. ²⁸At the end of three years you shall bring forth all the tithe of your increase the same year, and shall lay it up within your gates: ²⁹And the Levite, (because he has no part nor inheritance with you,) and the stranger, and the fatherless, and the widow, which are within your gates, shall come, and shall eat and be satisfied; that the LORD your God may bless you in all the work of your hand which you do.

15 ¹At the end of every seven years you shall make a release. ²And this is the manner of the release: Every creditor that lends something to his neighbor shall release it; he shall not exact it of his neighbor, or of his brother; because it is called the LORD's release. ³Of a foreigner you may exact it again: but that which is your with your brother your hand shall release; ⁴Save when there shall be no poor among you; for the LORD shall greatly bless you in the land which the LORD your God gives you for an inheritance to possess it: ⁵Only if you carefully listen to the voice of the LORD your God, to observe to do all these commandments which I command you this day. ⁶For the LORD your God blesses you, as he promised you: and you shall lend to many nations, but you shall not borrow; and you shall reign over many nations, but they shall not reign over you. ⁷If there be among you a poor man of one of your brothers within any of your gates in your land which the LORD your God gives you, you shall not harden your heart, nor shut your hand from your poor brother: ⁸But you shall open your hand wide to him, and shall surely lend him sufficient for his need, in that which he wants. ⁹Beware that there be not a thought in your wicked heart, saying, The seventh year, the year of release, is at hand; and your eye be evil against your poor brother, and you give him nothing; and he cry to the LORD against you, and it be sin to you. ¹⁰You shall surely give him, and your heart shall not be grieved when you give to him: because that for this thing the LORD your God shall bless you in all your works, and in all that you put your hand to. ¹¹For the poor shall never cease out of the land: therefore I command you, saying, You shall open your hand wide to your brother, to your poor, and to your needy, in your land. ¹²And if your brother, an Hebrew man, or an Hebrew woman, be sold to you, and serve you six years; then in the seventh year you shall let him go free from you. ¹³And when you send him out free from you, you shall not let him go away empty: ¹⁴You shall furnish him liberally out of your flock, and out of your floor, and out of your wine press: of that with which the LORD your God has blessed you you shall give to him. ¹⁵And you shall remember that you were a slave in the land of Egypt, and the LORD your God redeemed you: therefore I command you this thing to day. ¹⁶And it shall be, if he say to you, I will not go away from you; because he loves you and your house, because he is well with you; ¹⁷Then you shall take an awl, and thrust it through his ear to the door, and he shall be your servant for ever. And also to your maidservant you shall do likewise. ¹⁸It shall not seem hard to you, when you send him away free from you; for he has been worth a double hired servant to you, in serving you six years: and the LORD your God shall bless you in all that you do. ¹⁹All the firstling males that come of your herd and of your flock you shall sanctify to the LORD your God: you shall do no work with the firstling of your bullock, nor shear the firstling of your sheep. ²⁰You shall eat it before the LORD your God year by year in the place which the LORD shall choose, you and your household. ²¹And if there be any blemish therein, as if it be lame, or blind, or have any ill blemish, you shall not sacrifice it to the LORD your God. ²²You shall eat it within your gates: the unclean and the clean person shall eat it alike, as the roebuck, and as the hart. ²³Only you shall not eat the blood thereof; you shall pour it on the ground as water.

16 ¹Observe the month of Abib, and keep the passover to the LORD your God: for in the month of Abib the LORD your God brought you forth out of Egypt by night. ²You shall therefore sacrifice the passover to the LORD your God, of the flock and the herd, in the place which the LORD shall choose to place his name there. ³You shall eat no leavened bread with it; seven days shall you eat unleavened bread therewith, even the bread of affliction; for you came forth out of the land of Egypt in haste: that you may remember the day when you came forth out of the land of Egypt all the days of your life. ⁴And there shall be no leavened bread seen with you in all your coast seven days; neither shall there any thing of the flesh, which you sacrificed the first day at even, remain all night until the morning. ⁵You may not sacrifice the passover within any of your gates, which the LORD your God gives you: ⁶But at the place which the LORD your God shall choose to place his name in, there you shall sacrifice the passover at even, at the going down of the sun, at the season that you came forth out of Egypt. ⁷And you shall roast and eat it in the place which the LORD your God shall choose: and you shall turn in the morning, and go to your tents. ⁸Six days you shall eat unleavened bread: and on the seventh day shall be a solemn assembly to the LORD your God: you shall do no work therein. ⁹Seven weeks shall you number to you: begin to number the seven weeks from such time as you begin to put the sickle to the corn. ¹⁰And you shall keep the feast of weeks to the LORD your God with a tribute of a freewill offering of your hand, which you shall give to the LORD your God, according as the LORD your God has blessed you: ¹¹And you shall rejoice before the LORD your God, you, and your son, and your daughter, and your manservant, and your maidservant, and the Levite that is within your gates, and the stranger, and the fatherless, and the widow, that are among you, in the place which the LORD your God has chosen to place his name there. ¹²And you shall remember that you were a slave in Egypt: and you shall observe and do these statutes. ¹³You shall observe the feast of tabernacles seven days, after that you have gathered in your corn and your wine: ¹⁴And you shall rejoice in your feast, you, and your son, and your daughter, and your manservant, and your maidservant, and the Levite, the stranger, and the fatherless, and the widow, that are within your gates. ¹⁵Seven days shall you keep a solemn feast to the LORD your God in the place which the LORD shall choose: because the LORD your God shall bless you in all your increase, and in all the works of your hands, therefore you shall surely rejoice. ¹⁶Three times in a year shall all your males appear before the LORD your God in the place which he shall choose; in the feast of unleavened bread, and in the feast of weeks, and in the feast of tabernacles: and they shall not appear before the LORD empty: ¹⁷Every man shall give as he is able, according to the blessing of the LORD your God which he has given you. ¹⁸Judges and officers shall you make you in all your gates, which the LORD your God gives you, throughout your tribes: and they shall judge the people with just judgment. ¹⁹You shall not wrest judgment; you shall not respect persons, neither take a gift: for a gift does blind the eyes of the wise, and pervert the words of the righteous. ²⁰That which is altogether just shall you follow, that you may live, and inherit the land which the LORD your God gives you. ²¹You shall not plant you a grove of any trees near to the altar of the LORD your God, which you shall make you. ²²Neither shall you set you up any image; which the LORD your God hates.

17 ¹You shall not sacrifice to the LORD your God any bullock, or sheep, wherein is blemish, or any bad reputation: for that is an abomination to the LORD your God. ²If there be found among you, within any of your gates which the LORD your God gives you, man or woman, that has worked wickedness in the sight of the LORD your God, in transgressing his covenant, ³And has gone and served other gods, and worshipped them, either the sun, or moon, or any of the host of heaven, which I have not commanded; ⁴And it be told you, and you have heard of it, and inquired diligently, and, behold, it be true, and the thing certain, that such abomination is worked in Israel: ⁵Then shall you bring forth that man or that woman, which have committed that wicked thing, to your gates, even that man or that woman, and shall stone them with stones, till they die. ⁶At the mouth of two witnesses, or three witnesses, shall he that is worthy of death be put to death; but at the mouth of one witness he shall not be put to death. ⁷The hands of the witnesses shall be first on him to put him to death, and afterward the hands of all the people. So you shall put the evil away from among you. ⁸If there arise a matter too hard for you in judgment, between blood and blood, between plea and plea, and between stroke and stroke, being matters of controversy within your gates: then shall you arise, and get you up into the place which the LORD your God shall choose; ⁹And you shall come to the priests the Levites, and to the judge that shall be in those days, and inquire; and they shall show you the sentence of judgment: ¹⁰And you shall do according to the sentence, which they of that place which the LORD shall choose shall show you; and you shall observe to do according to all that they inform you: ¹¹According to the sentence of the law which they shall teach you, and according to the judgment which they shall tell you, you shall do: you shall not decline from the sentence which they shall show you, to the right hand, nor to the left. ¹²And the man that will do presumptuously, and will not listen to the priest that stands to minister there before the LORD your God, or to the judge, even that man shall die: and you shall put away the evil from Israel. ¹³And all the people shall hear, and fear, and do no more presumptuously. ¹⁴When you are come to the land which the LORD your God gives you, and shall possess it, and shall dwell therein, and shall say, I will set a king over me, like as all the nations that are about me; ¹⁵You shall in any wise set him king over you, whom the LORD your God shall choose: one from among your brothers shall you set king over you: you may not set a stranger over you, which is not your brother. ¹⁶But he shall not multiply horses to himself, nor cause the people to return to Egypt, to the end that he should multiply horses: for as much as the LORD has said to you, You shall from now on return no more that way. ¹⁷Neither shall he multiply wives to himself, that his heart turn not away: neither shall he greatly multiply to himself silver and gold. ¹⁸And it shall be, when he sits on the throne of his kingdom, that he shall write him a copy of this law in a book out of that which is before the priests the Levites: ¹⁹And it shall be with him, and he shall read therein all the days of his life: that he may learn to fear the LORD his God, to keep all the words of this law and these statutes, to do them: ²⁰That his heart be not lifted up above his brothers, and that he turn not aside from the commandment, to the right hand, or to the left: to the end that he may prolong his days in his kingdom, he, and his children, in the middle of Israel.

18 ¹The priests the Levites, and all the tribe of Levi, shall have no part nor inheritance with Israel: they shall eat the offerings of the LORD made by fire, and his inheritance. ²Therefore shall they have no inheritance among their brothers: the LORD is their inheritance, as he has said to them. ³And this shall be the priest's due from the people, from them that offer a sacrifice, whether it be ox or sheep; and they shall give to the priest the shoulder, and the two cheeks, and the maw. ⁴The first fruit also of your corn, of your wine, and of your oil, and the first of the fleece of your sheep, shall you give him. ⁵For the LORD your God has chosen him out of all your tribes, to stand to minister in the name of the LORD, him and his sons for ever. ⁶And if a

Levite come from any of your gates out of all Israel, where he sojourned, and come with all the desire of his mind to the place which the LORD shall choose; ⁷Then he shall minister in the name of the LORD his God, as all his brothers the Levites do, which stand there before the LORD. ⁸They shall have like portions to eat, beside that which comes of the sale of his patrimony. ⁹When you are come into the land which the LORD your God gives you, you shall not learn to do after the abominations of those nations. ¹⁰There shall not be found among you any one that makes his son or his daughter to pass through the fire, or that uses divination, or an observer of times, or an enchanter, or a witch. ¹¹Or a charmer, or a consulter with familiar spirits, or a wizard, or a necromancer. ¹²For all that do these things are an abomination to the LORD: and because of these abominations the LORD your God does drive them out from before you. ¹³You shall be perfect with the LORD your God. ¹⁴For these nations, which you shall possess, listened to observers of times, and to diviners: but as for you, the LORD your God has not suffered you so to do. ¹⁵The LORD your God will raise up to you a Prophet from the middle of you, of your brothers, like to me; to him you shall listen; ¹⁶According to all that you desired of the LORD your God in Horeb in the day of the assembly, saying, Let me not hear again the voice of the LORD my God, neither let me see this great fire any more, that I die not. ¹⁷And the LORD said to me, They have well spoken that which they have spoken. ¹⁸I will raise them up a Prophet from among their brothers, like to you, and will put my words in his mouth; and he shall speak to them all that I shall command him. ¹⁹And it shall come to pass, that whoever will not listen to my words which he shall speak in my name, I will require it of him. ²⁰But the prophet, which shall presume to speak a word in my name, which I have not commanded him to speak, or that shall speak in the name of other gods, even that prophet shall die. ²¹And if you say in your heart, How shall we know the word which the LORD has not spoken? ²²When a prophet speaks in the name of the LORD, if the thing follow not, nor come to pass, that is the thing which the LORD has not spoken, but the prophet has spoken it presumptuously: you shall not be afraid of him.

19 ¹When the LORD your God has cut off the nations, whose land the LORD your God gives you, and you succeed them, and dwell in their cities, and in their houses; ²You shall separate three cities for you in the middle of your land, which the LORD your God gives you to possess it. ³You shall prepare you a way, and divide the coasts of your land, which the LORD your God gives you to inherit, into three parts, that every slayer may flee thither. ⁴And this is the case of the slayer, which shall flee thither, that he may live: Whoever kills his neighbor ignorantly, whom he hated not in time past; ⁵As when a man goes into the wood with his neighbor to hew wood, and his hand fetches a stroke with the ax to cut down the tree, and the head slips from the helve, and lights on his neighbor, that he die; he shall flee to one of those cities, and live: ⁶Lest the avenger of the blood pursue the slayer, while his heart is hot, and overtake him, because the way is long, and slay him; whereas he was not worthy of death, inasmuch as he hated him not in time past. ⁷Why I command you, saying, You shall separate three cities for you. ⁸And if the LORD your God enlarge your coast, as he has sworn to your fathers, and give you all the land which he promised to give to your fathers; ⁹If you shall keep all these commandments to do them, which I command you this day, to love the LORD your God, and to walk ever in his ways; then shall you add three cities more for you, beside these three: ¹⁰That innocent blood be not shed in your land, which the LORD your God gives you for an inheritance, and so blood be on you. ¹¹But if any man hate his neighbor, and lie in wait for him, and rise up against him, and smite him mortally that he die, and flees into one of these cities: ¹²Then the elders of his city shall send and fetch him there, and deliver him into the hand of the avenger of blood, that he may die. ¹³Your eye shall not pity him, but you shall put away the guilt of innocent blood from Israel, that it may go well with you. ¹⁴You shall not remove your neighbor's landmark, which they of old time have set in your inheritance, which you shall inherit in the land that the LORD your God gives you to possess it. ¹⁵One witness shall not rise up against a man for any iniquity, or for any sin, in any sin that he sins: at the mouth of two witnesses, or at the mouth of three witnesses, shall the matter be established. ¹⁶If a false witness rise up against any man to testify against him that which is wrong; ¹⁷Then both the men, between whom the controversy is, shall stand before the LORD, before the priests and the judges, which shall be in those days; ¹⁸And the judges shall make diligent inquisition: and, behold, if the witness be a false witness, and has testified falsely against his brother; ¹⁹Then shall you do to him, as he had thought to have done to his brother: so shall you put the evil away from among you. ²⁰And those which remain shall hear, and fear, and shall from now on commit no more any such evil among you. ²¹And your eye shall not pity; but life shall go for life, eye for eye, tooth for tooth, hand for hand, foot for foot.

20 ¹When you go out to battle against your enemies, and see horses, and chariots, and a people more than you, be not afraid of them: for the LORD your God is with you, which brought you up out of the land of Egypt. ²And it shall be, when you are come near to the battle, that the priest shall approach and speak to the people, ³And shall say to them, Hear, O Israel, you approach this day to battle against your enemies: let not your hearts faint, fear not, and do not tremble, neither be you terrified because of them; ⁴For the LORD your God is he that goes with you, to fight for you against your enemies, to save you. ⁵And the officers shall speak to the people, saying, What man is there that has built a new house, and has not dedicated it? let him go and return to his house, lest he die in the battle, and another man dedicate it. ⁶And what man is he that has planted a vineyard, and has not yet eaten of it? let him also go and return to his house, lest he die in the battle, and another man eat of it. ⁷And what man is there that has betrothed a wife, and has not taken her? let him go and return to his house, lest he die in the battle, and another man take her. ⁸And the officers shall speak further to the people, and they shall say, What man is there that is fearful and fainthearted? let him go and return to his house, lest his brethren's heart faint as well as his heart. ⁹And it shall be, when the officers have made an end of speaking to the people that they shall make captains of the armies to lead the people. ¹⁰When you come near to a city to fight against it, then proclaim peace to it. ¹¹And it shall be, if it make you answer of peace, and open to you, then it shall be, that all the people that is found therein shall be tributaries to you, and they shall serve you. ¹²And if it will make no peace with you, but will make war against you, then you shall besiege it: ¹³And when the LORD your God has delivered it into your hands, you shall smite every male thereof with the edge of the sword: ¹⁴But the women, and the little ones, and the cattle, and all that is in the city, even all the spoil thereof, shall you take to yourself; and you shall eat the spoil of your enemies, which the LORD your God has given you. ¹⁵Thus shall you do to all the cities which are very far off from you, which are not of the cities of these nations. ¹⁶But of the cities of these people, which the LORD your God does give you for an inheritance, you shall save alive nothing that breathes: ¹⁷But you shall utterly destroy them; namely, the Hittites, and the Amorites, the Canaanites, and the Perizzites, the Hivites, and the Jebusites; as the LORD your God has commanded you: ¹⁸That they teach you not to do after all their abominations, which they have done to their gods; so should you sin against the LORD your God. ¹⁹When you shall besiege a city a long time, in making war against it to take it, you shall not destroy the trees thereof by forcing an ax against them: for you may eat of them, and you shall not cut them down (for the tree of the field is man's life) to employ them in the siege: ²⁰Only the trees which you know that they be not trees for meat, you shall destroy and cut them down; and you shall build bulwarks against the city that makes war with you, until it be subdued.

21

¹If one be found slain in the land which the LORD your God gives you to possess it, lying in the field, and it be not known who has slain him: ²Then your elders and your judges shall come forth, and they shall measure to the cities which are round about him that is slain: ³And it shall be, that the city which is next to the slain man, even the elders of that city shall take an heifer, which has not been worked with, and which has not drawn in the yoke; ⁴And the elders of that city shall bring down the heifer to a rough valley, which is neither eared nor sown, and shall strike off the heifer's neck there in the valley: ⁵And the priests the sons of Levi shall come near; for them the LORD your God has chosen to minister to him, and to bless in the name of the LORD; and by their word shall every controversy and every stroke be tried: ⁶And all the elders of that city, that are next to the slain man, shall wash their hands over the heifer that is beheaded in the valley: ⁷And they shall answer and say, Our hands have not shed this blood, neither have our eyes seen it. ⁸Be merciful, O LORD, to your people Israel, whom you have redeemed, and lay not innocent blood to your people of Israel's charge. And the blood shall be forgiven them. ⁹So shall you put away the guilt of innocent blood from among you, when you shall do that which is right in the sight of the LORD. ¹⁰When you go forth to war against your enemies, and the LORD your God has delivered them into your hands, and you have taken them captive, ¹¹And see among the captives a beautiful woman, and have a desire to her, that you would have her to your wife; ¹²Then you shall bring her home to your house, and she shall shave her head, and pare her nails; ¹³And she shall put the raiment of her captivity from off her, and shall remain in your house, and mourn her father and her mother a full month: and after that you shall go in to her, and be her husband, and she shall be your wife. ¹⁴And it shall be, if you have no delight in her, then you shall let her go where she will; but you shall not sell her at all for money, you shall not make merchandise of her, because you have humbled her. ¹⁵If a man have two wives, one beloved, and another hated, and they have born him children, both the beloved and the hated; and if the firstborn son be hers that was hated: ¹⁶Then it shall be, when he makes his sons to inherit that which he has, that he may not make the son of the beloved firstborn before the son of the hated, which is indeed the firstborn: ¹⁷But he shall acknowledge the son of the hated for the firstborn, by giving him a double portion of all that he has: for he is the beginning of his strength; the right of the firstborn is his. ¹⁸If a man have a stubborn and rebellious son, which will not obey the voice of his father, or the voice of his mother, and that, when they have chastened him, will not listen to them: ¹⁹Then shall his father and his mother lay hold on him, and bring him out to the elders of his city, and to the gate of his place; ²⁰And they shall say to the elders of his city, This our son is stubborn and rebellious, he will not obey our voice; he is a glutton, and a drunkard. ²¹And all the men of his city shall stone him with stones, that he die: so shall you put evil away from among you; and all Israel shall hear, and fear. ²²And if a man have committed a sin worthy of death, and he be to be put to death, and you hang him on a tree: ²³His body shall not remain all night on the tree, but you shall in any wise bury him that day; (for he that is hanged is accursed of God;) that your land be not defiled, which the LORD your God gives you for an inheritance.

22

¹You shall not see your brother's ox or his sheep go astray, and hide yourself from them: you shall in any case bring them again to your brother. ²And if your brother be not near to you, or if you know him not, then you shall bring it to your own house, and it shall be with you until your brother seek after it, and you shall restore it to him again. ³In like manner shall you do with his ass; and so shall you do with his raiment; and with all lost thing of your brother's, which he has lost, and you have found, shall you do likewise: you may not hide yourself. ⁴You shall not see your brother's ass or his ox fall down by the way, and hide yourself from them: you shall surely help him to lift them up again. ⁵The woman shall not wear that which pertains to a man, neither shall a man put on a woman's garment: for all that do so are abomination to the LORD your God. ⁶If a bird's nest chance to be before you in the way in any tree, or on the ground, whether they be young ones, or eggs, and the dam sitting on the young, or on the eggs, you shall not take the dam with the young: ⁷But you shall in any wise let the dam go, and take the young to you; that it may be well with you, and that you may prolong your days. ⁸When you build a new house, then you shall make a battlement for your roof, that you bring not blood on your house, if any man fall from there. ⁹You shall not sow your vineyard with divers seeds: lest the fruit of your seed which you have sown, and the fruit of your vineyard, be defiled. ¹⁰You shall not plow with an ox and an ass together. ¹¹You shall not wear a garment of divers sorts, as of woolen and linen together. ¹²You shall make you fringes on the four quarters of your clothing, with which you

cover yourself. ¹³If any man take a wife, and go in to her, and hate her, ¹⁴And give occasions of speech against her, and bring up an evil name on her, and say, I took this woman, and when I came to her, I found her not a maid: ¹⁵Then shall the father of the damsel, and her mother, take and bring forth the tokens of the damsel's virginity to the elders of the city in the gate: ¹⁶And the damsel's father shall say to the elders, I gave my daughter to this man to wife, and he hates her; ¹⁷And, see, he has given occasions of speech against her, saying, I found not your daughter a maid; and yet these are the tokens of my daughter's virginity. And they shall spread the cloth before the elders of the city. ¹⁸And the elders of that city shall take that man and chastise him; ¹⁹And they shall amerce him in an hundred shekels of silver, and give them to the father of the damsel, because he has brought up an evil name on a virgin of Israel: and she shall be his wife; he may not put her away all his days. ²⁰But if this thing be true, and the tokens of virginity be not found for the damsel: ²¹Then they shall bring out the damsel to the door of her father's house, and the men of her city shall stone her with stones that she die: because she has worked folly in Israel, to play the whore in her father's house: so shall you put evil away from among you. ²²If a man be found lying with a woman married to an husband, then they shall both of them die, both the man that lay with the woman, and the woman: so shall you put away evil from Israel. ²³If a damsel that is a virgin be betrothed to an husband, and a man find her in the city, and lie with her; ²⁴Then you shall bring them both out to the gate of that city, and you shall stone them with stones that they die; the damsel, because she cried not, being in the city; and the man, because he has humbled his neighbor's wife: so you shall put away evil from among you. ²⁵But if a man find a betrothed damsel in the field, and the man force her, and lie with her: then the man only that lay with her shall die. ²⁶But to the damsel you shall do nothing; there is in the damsel no sin worthy of death: for as when a man rises against his neighbor, and slays him, even so is this matter: ²⁷For he found her in the field, and the betrothed damsel cried, and there was none to save her. ²⁸If a man find a damsel that is a virgin, which is not betrothed, and lay hold on her, and lie with her, and they be found; ²⁹Then the man that lay with her shall give to the damsel's father fifty shekels of silver, and she shall be his wife; because he has humbled her, he may not put her away all his days. ³⁰A man shall not take his father's wife, nor discover his father's skirt.

23

¹He that is wounded in the stones, or has his privy member cut off, shall not enter into the congregation of the LORD. ²A bastard shall not enter into the congregation of the LORD; even to his tenth generation shall he not enter into the congregation of the LORD. ³An Ammonite or Moabite shall not enter into the congregation of the LORD; even to their tenth generation shall they not enter into the congregation of the LORD for ever: ⁴Because they met you not with bread and with water in the way, when you came forth out of Egypt; and because they hired against you Balaam the son of Beor of Pethor of Mesopotamia, to curse you. ⁵Nevertheless the LORD your God would not listen to Balaam; but the LORD your God turned the curse into a blessing to you, because the LORD your God loved you. ⁶You shall not seek their peace nor their prosperity all your days for ever. ⁷You shall not abhor an Edomite; for he is your brother: you shall not abhor an Egyptian; because you were a stranger in his land. ⁸The children that are begotten of them shall enter into the congregation of the LORD in their third generation. ⁹When the host goes forth against your enemies, then keep you from every wicked thing. ¹⁰If there be among you any man, that is not clean by reason of uncleanness that chances him by night, then shall he go abroad out of the camp, he shall not come within the camp: ¹¹But it shall be, when evening comes on, he shall wash himself with water: and when the sun is down, he shall come into the camp again. ¹²You shall have a place also without the camp, where you shall go forth abroad: ¹³And you shall have a paddle on your weapon; and it shall be, when you will ease yourself abroad, you shall dig therewith, and shall turn back and cover that which comes from you: ¹⁴For the LORD your God walks in the middle of your camp, to deliver you, and to give up your enemies before you; therefore shall your camp be holy: that he see no unclean thing in you, and turn away from you. ¹⁵You shall not deliver to his master the servant which is escaped from his master to you: ¹⁶He shall dwell with you, even among you, in that place which he shall choose in one of your gates, where it likes him best: you shall not oppress him. ¹⁷There shall be no whore of the daughters of Israel, nor a sodomite of the sons of Israel. ¹⁸You shall not bring the hire of a whore, or the price of a dog, into the house of the LORD your God for any vow: for even both these are abomination to the LORD your God. ¹⁹You shall not lend on usury to your brother; usury of money, usury of victuals, usury of any thing that is lent on usury: ²⁰To a stranger you may lend on usury; but to your brother you shall not lend on usury: that the LORD your God may bless you in all that you set your hand to in the land where you go to possess it. ²¹When you shall vow a vow to the LORD your God, you shall not slack to pay it: for the LORD your God will surely require it of you; and it would be sin in you. ²²But if you shall forbear to vow, it shall be no sin in you. ²³That which is gone out of your lips you shall keep and perform; even a freewill offering, according as you have vowed to the LORD your God, which you have promised with your mouth. ²⁴When you come into your neighbor's vineyard, then you may eat grapes your fill at your own pleasure; but you shall not put any in your vessel. ²⁵When you come into the standing corn of your neighbor, then you may pluck the ears with your hand; but you shall not move a sickle to your neighbor's standing corn.

24

¹When a man has taken a wife, and married her, and it come to pass that she find no favor in his eyes, because he has found some uncleanness in her: then let him write her a bill of divorce, and give it in her hand, and send her out of his house. ²And when she is departed out of his house, she may go and be another man's wife. ³And if the latter husband hate her, and write her a bill of divorce, and gives it in her hand, and sends her out of his house; or if the latter husband die, which took her to be his wife; ⁴Her former husband, which sent her away, may not take her again to be his wife, after that she is defiled; for that is abomination before the LORD: and you shall not cause the

land to sin, which the LORD your God gives you for an inheritance. ⁵When a man has taken a new wife, he shall not go out to war, neither shall he be charged with any business: but he shall be free at home one year, and shall cheer up his wife which he has taken. ⁶No man shall take the nether or the upper millstone to pledge: for he takes a man's life to pledge. ⁷If a man be found stealing any of his brothers of the children of Israel, and makes merchandise of him, or sells him; then that thief shall die; and you shall put evil away from among you. ⁸Take heed in the plague of leprosy, that you observe diligently, and do according to all that the priests the Levites shall teach you: as I commanded them, so you shall observe to do. ⁹Remember what the LORD your God did to Miriam by the way, after that you were come forth out of Egypt. ¹⁰When you do lend your brother any thing, you shall not go into his house to fetch his pledge. ¹¹You shall stand abroad, and the man to whom you do lend shall bring out the pledge abroad to you. ¹²And if the man be poor, you shall not sleep with his pledge: ¹³In any case you shall deliver him the pledge again when the sun goes down, that he may sleep in his own raiment, and bless you: and it shall be righteousness to you before the LORD your God. ¹⁴You shall not oppress an hired servant that is poor and needy, whether he be of your brothers, or of your strangers that are in your land within your gates: ¹⁵At his day you shall give him his hire, neither shall the sun go down on it; for he is poor, and sets his heart on it: lest he cry against you to the LORD, and it be sin to you. ¹⁶The fathers shall not be put to death for the children, neither shall the children be put to death for the fathers: every man shall be put to death for his own sin. ¹⁷You shall not pervert the judgment of the stranger, nor of the fatherless; nor take a widow's raiment to pledge: ¹⁸But you shall remember that you were a slave in Egypt, and the LORD your God redeemed you there: therefore I command you to do this thing. ¹⁹When you cut down your harvest in your field, and have forgot a sheaf in the field, you shall not go again to fetch it: it shall be for the stranger, for the fatherless, and for the widow: that the LORD your God may bless you in all the work of your hands. ²⁰When you beat your olive tree, you shall not go over the boughs again: it shall be for the stranger, for the fatherless, and for the widow. ²¹When you gather the grapes of your vineyard, you shall not glean it afterward: it shall be for the stranger, for the fatherless, and for the widow. ²²And you shall remember that you were a slave in the land of Egypt: therefore I command you to do this thing.

25 ¹If there be a controversy between men, and they come to judgment, that the judges may judge them; then they shall justify the righteous, and condemn the wicked. ²And it shall be, if the wicked man be worthy to be beaten, that the judge shall cause him to lie down, and to be beaten before his face, according to his fault, by a certain number. ³Forty stripes he may give him, and not exceed: lest, if he should exceed, and beat him above these with many stripes, then your brother should seem vile to you. ⁴You shall not muzzle the ox when he treads out the corn. ⁵If brothers dwell together, and one of them die, and have no child, the wife of the dead shall not marry without to a stranger: her husband's brother shall go in to her, and take her to him to wife, and perform the duty of an husband's brother to her. ⁶And it shall be, that the firstborn which she bears shall succeed in the name of his brother which is dead, that his name be not put out of Israel. ⁷And if the man like not to take his brother's wife, then let his brother's wife go up to the gate to the elders, and say, My husband's brother refuses to raise up to his brother a name in Israel, he will not perform the duty of my husband's brother. ⁸Then the elders of his city shall call him, and speak to him: and if he stand to it, and say, I like not to take her; ⁹Then shall his brother's wife come to him in the presence of the elders, and loose his shoe from off his foot, and spit in his face, and shall answer and say, So shall it be done to that man that will not build up his brother's house. ¹⁰And his name shall be called in Israel, The house of him that has his shoe loosed. ¹¹When men strive together one with another, and the wife of the one draws near for to deliver her husband out of the hand of him that smites him, and puts forth her hand, and takes him by the secrets: ¹²Then you shall cut off her hand, your eye shall not pity her. ¹³You shall not have in your bag divers weights, a great and a small. ¹⁴You shall not have in your house divers measures, a great and a small. ¹⁵But you shall have a perfect and just weight, a perfect and just measure shall you have: that your days may be lengthened in the land which the LORD your God gives you. ¹⁶For all that do such things, and all that do unrighteously, are an abomination to the LORD your God. ¹⁷Remember what Amalek did to you by the way, when you were come forth out of Egypt; ¹⁸How he met you by the way, and smote the hindmost of you, even all that were feeble behind you, when you were faint and weary; and he feared not God. ¹⁹Therefore it shall be, when the LORD your God has given you rest from all your enemies round about, in the land which the LORD your God gives you for an inheritance to possess it, that you shall blot out the remembrance of Amalek from under heaven; you shall not forget it.

26 ¹And it shall be, when you are come in to the land which the LORD your God gives you for an inheritance, and possess it, and dwell therein; ²That you shall take of the first of all the fruit of the earth, which you shall bring of your land that the LORD your God gives you, and shall put it in a basket, and shall go to the place which the LORD your God shall choose to place his name there. ³And you shall go to the priest that shall be in those days, and say to him, I profess this day to the LORD your God, that I am come to the country which the LORD swore to our fathers for to give us. ⁴And the priest shall take the basket out of your hand, and set it down before the altar of the LORD your God. ⁵And you shall speak and say before the LORD your God, A Syrian ready to perish was my father, and he went down into Egypt, and sojourned there with a few, and became there a nation, great, mighty, and populous: ⁶And the Egyptians evil entreated us, and afflicted us, and laid on us hard bondage: ⁷And when we cried to the LORD God of our fathers, the LORD heard our voice, and looked on our affliction, and our labor, and our oppression: ⁸And the LORD brought us forth out of Egypt with a mighty hand, and with an outstretched arm, and with great terribleness, and with signs, and with wonders: ⁹And he has brought us into this place, and has given us this land, even a land that flows with milk and honey. ¹⁰And now, behold, I have brought the first fruits of the land, which you, O LORD, have given me. And you shall set it before the LORD your God, and worship before the LORD your God: [11]And you shall rejoice in every good thing which the LORD your God has given to you, and to your house, you, and the Levite, and the stranger that is among you. [12]When you have made an end of tithing all the tithes of your increase the third year, which is the year of tithing, and have given it to the Levite, the stranger, the fatherless, and the widow, that they may eat within your gates, and be filled; [13]Then you shall say before the LORD your God, I have brought away the hallowed things out of my house, and also have given them to the Levite, and to the stranger, to the fatherless, and to the widow, according to all your commandments which you have commanded me: I have not transgressed your commandments, neither have I forgotten them. [14]I have not eaten thereof in my mourning, neither have I taken away anything thereof for any unclean use, nor given anything thereof for the dead: but I have listened to the voice of the LORD my God, and have done according to all that you have commanded me. [15]Look down from your holy habitation, from heaven, and bless your people Israel, and the land which you have given us, as you swore to our fathers, a land that flows with milk and honey. [16]This day the LORD your God has commanded you to do these statutes and judgments: you shall therefore keep and do them with all your heart, and with all your soul. [17]You have avouched the LORD this day to be your God, and to walk in his ways, and to keep his statutes, and his commandments, and his judgments, and to listen to his voice: [18]And the LORD has avouched you this day to be his peculiar people, as he has promised you, and that you should keep all his commandments; [19]And to make you high above all nations which he has made, in praise, and in name, and in honor; and that you may be an holy people to the LORD your God, as he has spoken.

27 [1]And Moses with the elders of Israel commanded the people, saying, Keep all the commandments which I command you this day. [2]And it shall be on the day when you shall pass over Jordan to the land which the LORD your God gives you, that you shall set you up great stones, and plaster them with plaster: [3]And you shall write on them all the words of this law, when you are passed over, that you may go in to the land which the LORD your God gives you, a land that flows with milk and honey; as the LORD God of your fathers has promised you. [4]Therefore it shall be when you be gone over Jordan, that you shall set up these stones, which I command you this day, in mount Ebal, and you shall plaster them with plaster. [5]And there shall you build an altar to the LORD your God, an altar of stones: you shall not lift up any iron tool on them. [6]You shall build the altar of the LORD your God of whole stones: and you shall offer burnt offerings thereon to the LORD your God: [7]And you shall offer peace offerings, and shall eat there, and rejoice before the LORD your God. [8]And you shall write on the stones all the words of this law very plainly. [9]And Moses and the priests the Levites spoke to all Israel, saying, Take heed, and listen, O Israel; this day you are become the people of the LORD your God. [10]You shall therefore obey the voice of the LORD your God, and do his commandments and his statutes, which I command you this day. [11]And Moses charged the people the same day, saying, [12]These shall stand on mount Gerizim to bless the people, when you are come over Jordan; Simeon, and Levi, and Judah, and Issachar, and Joseph, and Benjamin: [13]And these shall stand on mount Ebal to curse; Reuben, Gad, and Asher, and Zebulun, Dan, and Naphtali. [14]And the Levites shall speak, and say to all the men of Israel with a loud voice, [15]Cursed be the man that makes any graven or molten image, an abomination to the LORD, the work of the hands of the craftsman, and puts it in a secret place. And all the people shall answer and say, Amen. [16]Cursed be he that sets light by his father or his mother. And all the people shall say, Amen. [17]Cursed be he that removes his neighbor's landmark. And all the people shall say, Amen. [18]Cursed be he that makes the blind to wander out of the way. And all the people shall say, Amen. [19]Cursed be he that perverts the judgment of the stranger, fatherless, and widow. And all the people shall say, Amen. [20]Cursed be he that lies with his father's wife; because he uncovers his father's skirt. And all the people shall say, Amen. [21]Cursed be he that lies with any manner of beast. And all the people shall say, Amen. [22]Cursed be he that lies with his sister, the daughter of his father, or the daughter of his mother. And all the people shall say, Amen. [23]Cursed be he that lies with his mother in law. And all the people shall say, Amen. [24]Cursed be he that smites his neighbor secretly. And all the people shall say, Amen. [25]Cursed be he that takes reward to slay an innocent person. And all the people shall say, Amen. [26]Cursed be he that confirms not all the words of this law to do them. And all the people shall say, Amen.

28 [1]And it shall come to pass, if you shall listen diligently to the voice of the LORD your God, to observe and to do all his commandments which I command you this day, that the LORD your God will set you on high above all nations of the earth: [2]And all these blessings shall come on you, and overtake you, if you shall listen to the voice of the LORD your God. [3]Blessed shall you be in the city, and blessed shall you be in the field. [4]Blessed shall be the fruit of your body, and the fruit of your ground, and the fruit of your cattle, the increase of your cows, and the flocks of your sheep. [5]Blessed shall be your basket and your store. [6]Blessed shall you be when you come in, and blessed shall you be when you go out. [7]The LORD shall cause your enemies that rise up against you to be smitten before your face: they shall come out against you one way, and flee before you seven ways. [8]The LORD shall command the blessing on you in your storehouses, and in all that you set your hand to; and he shall bless you in the land which the LORD your God gives you. [9]The LORD shall establish you an holy people to himself, as he has sworn to you, if you shall keep the commandments of the LORD your God, and walk in his ways. [10]And all people of the earth shall see that you are called by the name of the LORD; and they shall be afraid of you. [11]And the LORD shall make you plenteous in goods, in the fruit of your body, and in the fruit of your cattle, and in the fruit of your ground, in the land which the LORD swore to your fathers to give you. [12]The LORD shall open to you his good treasure, the heaven to give the rain to your land in his season, and to bless all the work of your hand: and you shall lend to many nations, and you shall not borrow. ¹³And the LORD shall make you the head, and not the tail; and you shall be above only, and you shall not be beneath; if that you listen to the commandments of the LORD your God, which I command you this day, to observe and to do them: ¹⁴And you shall not go aside from any of the words which I command you this day, to the right hand, or to the left, to go after other gods to serve them. ¹⁵But it shall come to pass, if you will not listen to the voice of the LORD your God, to observe to do all his commandments and his statutes which I command you this day; that all these curses shall come on you, and overtake you: ¹⁶Cursed shall you be in the city, and cursed shall you be in the field. ¹⁷Cursed shall be your basket and your store. ¹⁸Cursed shall be the fruit of your body, and the fruit of your land, the increase of your cows, and the flocks of your sheep. ¹⁹Cursed shall you be when you come in, and cursed shall you be when you go out. ²⁰The LORD shall send on you cursing, vexation, and rebuke, in all that you set your hand to for to do, until you be destroyed, and until you perish quickly; because of the wickedness of your doings, whereby you have forsaken me. ²¹The LORD shall make the pestilence stick to you, until he have consumed you from off the land, where you go to possess it. ²²The LORD shall smite you with a consumption, and with a fever, and with an inflammation, and with an extreme burning, and with the sword, and with blasting, and with mildew; and they shall pursue you until you perish. ²³And your heaven that is over your head shall be brass, and the earth that is under you shall be iron. ²⁴The LORD shall make the rain of your land powder and dust: from heaven shall it come down on you, until you be destroyed. ²⁵The LORD shall cause you to be smitten before your enemies: you shall go out one way against them, and flee seven ways before them: and shall be removed into all the kingdoms of the earth. ²⁶And your carcass shall be meat to all fowls of the air, and to the beasts of the earth, and no man shall fray them away. ²⁷The LORD will smite you with the botch of Egypt, and with the tumors, and with the scab, and with the itch, whereof you can not be healed. ²⁸The LORD shall smite you with madness, and blindness, and astonishment of heart: ²⁹And you shall grope at noonday, as the blind gropes in darkness, and you shall not prosper in your ways: and you shall be only oppressed and spoiled ever more, and no man shall save you. ³⁰You shall betroth a wife, and another man shall lie with her: you shall build an house, and you shall not dwell therein: you shall plant a vineyard, and shall not gather the grapes thereof. ³¹Your ox shall be slain before your eyes, and you shall not eat thereof: your ass shall be violently taken away from before your face, and shall not be restored to you: your sheep shall be given to your enemies, and you shall have none to rescue them. ³²Your sons and your daughters shall be given to another people, and your eyes shall look, and fail with longing for them all the day long; and there shall be no might in your hand. ³³The fruit of your land, and all your labors, shall a nation which you know not eat up; and you shall be only oppressed and crushed always: ³⁴So that you shall be mad for the sight of your eyes which you shall see. ³⁵The LORD shall smite you in the knees, and in the legs, with a sore botch that cannot be healed, from the sole of your foot to the top of your head.

³⁶The LORD shall bring you, and your king which you shall set over you, to a nation which neither you nor your fathers have known; and there shall you serve other gods, wood and stone. ³⁷And you shall become an astonishment, a proverb, and a byword, among all nations where the LORD shall lead you. ³⁸You shall carry much seed out into the field, and shall gather but little in; for the locust shall consume it. ³⁹You shall plant vineyards, and dress them, but shall neither drink of the wine, nor gather the grapes; for the worms shall eat them. ⁴⁰You shall have olive trees throughout all your coasts, but you shall not anoint yourself with the oil; for your olive shall cast his fruit. ⁴¹You shall beget sons and daughters, but you shall not enjoy them; for they shall go into captivity. ⁴²All your trees and fruit of your land shall the locust consume. ⁴³The stranger that is within you shall get up above you very high; and you shall come down very low. ⁴⁴He shall lend to you, and you shall not lend to him: he shall be the head, and you shall be the tail. ⁴⁵Moreover all these curses shall come on you, and shall pursue you, and overtake you, till you be destroyed; because you listened not to the voice of the LORD your God, to keep his commandments and his statutes which he commanded you: ⁴⁶And they shall be on you for a sign and for a wonder, and on your seed for ever. ⁴⁷Because you served not the LORD your God with joyfulness, and with gladness of heart, for the abundance of all things; ⁴⁸Therefore shall you serve your enemies which the LORD shall send against you, in hunger, and in thirst, and in nakedness, and in want of all things: and he shall put a yoke of iron on your neck, until he have destroyed you. ⁴⁹The LORD shall bring a nation against you from far, from the end of the earth, as swift as the eagle flies; a nation whose tongue you shall not understand; ⁵⁰A nation of fierce countenance, which shall not regard the person of the old, nor show favor to the young: ⁵¹And he shall eat the fruit of your cattle, and the fruit of your land, until you be destroyed: which also shall not leave you either corn, wine, or oil, or the increase of your cows, or flocks of your sheep, until he have destroyed you. ⁵²And he shall besiege you in all your gates, until your high and fenced walls come down, wherein you trusted, throughout all your land: and he shall besiege you in all your gates throughout all your land, which the LORD your God has given you. ⁵³And you shall eat the fruit of your own body, the flesh of your sons and of your daughters, which the LORD your God has given you, in the siege, and in the narrow place, with which your enemies shall distress you: ⁵⁴So that the man that is tender among you, and very delicate, his eye shall be evil toward his brother, and toward the wife of his bosom, and toward the remnant of his children which he shall leave: ⁵⁵So that he will not give to any of them of the flesh of his children whom he shall eat: because he has nothing left him in the siege, and in the narrow place, with which your enemies shall distress you in all your gates. ⁵⁶The tender and delicate woman among you, which would not adventure to set the sole of her foot on the ground for delicateness and tenderness, her eye shall be evil toward the husband of her bosom, and toward her son, and toward her daughter, ⁵⁷And toward her young one that comes out from between her feet, and toward her children which she shall bear: for she shall eat them for want of all things secretly in the siege and

narrow place, with which your enemy shall distress you in your gates. ⁵⁸If you will not observe to do all the words of this law that are written in this book, that you may fear this glorious and fearful name, THE LORD THY GOD; ⁵⁹Then the LORD will make your plagues wonderful, and the plagues of your seed, even great plagues, and of long continuance, and sore sicknesses, and of long continuance. ⁶⁰Moreover he will bring on you all the diseases of Egypt, which you were afraid of; and they shall stick to you. ⁶¹Also every sickness, and every plague, which is not written in the book of this law, them will the LORD bring on you, until you be destroyed. ⁶²And you shall be left few in number, whereas you were as the stars of heaven for multitude; because you would not obey the voice of the LORD your God. ⁶³And it shall come to pass, that as the LORD rejoiced over you to do you good, and to multiply you; so the LORD will rejoice over you to destroy you, and to bring you to nothing; and you shall be plucked from off the land where you go to possess it. ⁶⁴And the LORD shall scatter you among all people, from the one end of the earth even to the other; and there you shall serve other gods, which neither you nor your fathers have known, even wood and stone. ⁶⁵And among these nations shall you find no ease, neither shall the sole of your foot have rest: but the LORD shall give you there a trembling heart, and failing of eyes, and sorrow of mind: ⁶⁶And your life shall hang in doubt before you; and you shall fear day and night, and shall have none assurance of your life: ⁶⁷In the morning you shall say, Would God it were even! and at even you shall say, Would God it were morning! for the fear of your heart with which you shall fear, and for the sight of your eyes which you shall see. ⁶⁸And the LORD shall bring you into Egypt again with ships, by the way whereof I spoke to you, You shall see it no more again: and there you shall be sold to your enemies for slaves and bondwomen, and no man shall buy you.

29 ¹These are the words of the covenant, which the LORD commanded Moses to make with the children of Israel in the land of Moab, beside the covenant which he made with them in Horeb. ²And Moses called to all Israel, and said to them, You have seen all that the LORD did before your eyes in the land of Egypt to Pharaoh, and to all his servants, and to all his land; ³The great temptations which your eyes have seen, the signs, and those great miracles: ⁴Yet the LORD has not given you an heart to perceive, and eyes to see, and ears to hear, to this day. ⁵And I have led you forty years in the wilderness: your clothes are not waxen old on you, and your shoe is not waxen old on your foot. ⁶You have not eaten bread, neither have you drunk wine or strong drink: that you might know that I am the LORD your God. ⁷And when you came to this place, Sihon the king of Heshbon, and Og the king of Bashan, came out against us to battle, and we smote them: ⁸And we took their land, and gave it for an inheritance to the Reubenites, and to the Gadites, and to the half tribe of Manasseh. ⁹Keep therefore the words of this covenant, and do them, that you may prosper in all that you do. ¹⁰You stand this day all of you before the LORD your God; your captains of your tribes, your elders, and your officers, with all the men of Israel, ¹¹Your little ones, your wives, and your stranger that is in your camp, from the hewer of your wood to the drawer of your water: ¹²That you should enter into covenant with the LORD your God, and into his oath, which the LORD your God makes with you this day: ¹³That he may establish you to day for a people to himself, and that he may be to you a God, as he has said to you, and as he has sworn to your fathers, to Abraham, to Isaac, and to Jacob. ¹⁴Neither with you only do I make this covenant and this oath; ¹⁵But with him that stands here with us this day before the LORD our God, and also with him that is not here with us this day: ¹⁶(For you know how we have dwelled in the land of Egypt; and how we came through the nations which you passed by; ¹⁷And you have seen their abominations, and their idols, wood and stone, silver and gold, which were among them:) ¹⁸Lest there should be among you man, or woman, or family, or tribe, whose heart turns away this day from the LORD our God, to go and serve the gods of these nations; lest there should be among you a root that bears gall and wormwood; ¹⁹And it come to pass, when he hears the words of this curse, that he bless himself in his heart, saying, I shall have peace, though I walk in the imagination of my heart, to add drunkenness to thirst: ²⁰The LORD will not spare him, but then the anger of the LORD and his jealousy shall smoke against that man, and all the curses that are written in this book shall lie on him, and the LORD shall blot out his name from under heaven. ²¹And the LORD shall separate him to evil out of all the tribes of Israel, according to all the curses of the covenant that are written in this book of the law: ²²So that the generation to come of your children that shall rise up after you, and the stranger that shall come from a far land, shall say, when they see the plagues of that land, and the sicknesses which the LORD has laid on it; ²³And that the whole land thereof is brimstone, and salt, and burning, that it is not sown, nor bears, nor any grass grows therein, like the overthrow of Sodom, and Gomorrah, Admah, and Zeboim, which the LORD overthrew in his anger, and in his wrath: ²⁴Even all nations shall say, Why has the LORD done thus to this land? what means the heat of this great anger? ²⁵Then men shall say, Because they have forsaken the covenant of the LORD God of their fathers, which he made with them when he brought them forth out of the land of Egypt: ²⁶For they went and served other gods, and worshipped them, gods whom they knew not, and whom he had not given to them: ²⁷And the anger of the LORD was kindled against this land, to bring on it all the curses that are written in this book: ²⁸And the LORD rooted them out of their land in anger, and in wrath, and in great indignation, and cast them into another land, as it is this day. ²⁹The secret things belong to the LORD our God: but those things which are revealed belong to us and to our children for ever, that we may do all the words of this law.

30 ¹And it shall come to pass, when all these things are come on you, the blessing and the curse, which I have set before you, and you shall call them to mind among all the nations, where the LORD your God has driven you, ²And shall return to the LORD your God, and shall obey his voice according to all that I command you this day, you and your children, with all your heart, and with all your soul; ³That then the LORD your God will turn your captivity, and have compassion on you, and will return and gather you from all the nations, where the LORD your God has scattered you. ⁴If any of your be driven out to the outmost parts of heaven, from there will the LORD your God gather you, and from there will he fetch you: ⁵And the LORD your God will bring you into the land which your fathers possessed, and you shall possess it; and he will do you good, and multiply you above your fathers. ⁶And the LORD your God will circumcise your heart, and the heart of your seed, to love the LORD your God with all your heart, and with all your soul, that you may live. ⁷And the LORD your God will put all these curses on your enemies, and on them that hate you, which persecuted you. ⁸And you shall return and obey the voice of the LORD, and do all his commandments which I command you this day. ⁹And the LORD your God will make you plenteous in every work of your hand, in the fruit of your body, and in the fruit of your cattle, and in the fruit of your land, for good: for the LORD will again rejoice over you for good, as he rejoiced over your fathers: ¹⁰If you shall listen to the voice of the LORD your God, to keep his commandments and his statutes which are written in this book of the law, and if you turn to the LORD your God with all your heart, and with all your soul. ¹¹For this commandment which I command you this day, it is not hidden from you, neither is it far off. ¹²It is not in heaven, that you should say, Who shall go up for us to heaven, and bring it to us, that we may hear it, and do it? ¹³Neither is it beyond the sea, that you should say, Who shall go over the sea for us, and bring it to us, that we may hear it, and do it? ¹⁴But the word is very near to you, in your mouth, and in your heart, that you may do it. ¹⁵See, I have set before you this day life and good, and death and evil; ¹⁶In that I command you this day to love the LORD your God, to walk in his ways, and to keep his commandments and his statutes and his judgments, that you may live and multiply: and the LORD your God shall bless you in the land where you go to possess it. ¹⁷But if your heart turn away, so that you will not hear, but shall be drawn away, and worship other gods, and serve them; ¹⁸I denounce to you this day, that you shall surely perish, and that you shall not prolong your days on the land, where you pass over Jordan to go to possess it. ¹⁹I call heaven and earth to record this day against you, that I have set before you life and death, blessing and cursing: therefore choose life, that both you and your seed may live: ²⁰That you may love the LORD your God, and that you may obey his voice, and that you may hold to him: for he is your life, and the length of your days: that you may dwell in the land which the LORD swore to your fathers, to Abraham, to Isaac, and to Jacob, to give them.

31

¹And Moses went and spoke these words to all Israel. ²And he said to them, I am an hundred and twenty years old this day; I can no more go out and come in: also the LORD has said to me, You shall not go over this Jordan. ³The LORD your God, he will go over before you, and he will destroy these nations from before you, and you shall possess them: and Joshua, he shall go over before you, as the LORD has said. ⁴And the LORD shall do to them as he did to Sihon and to Og, kings of the Amorites, and to the land of them, whom he destroyed. ⁵And the LORD shall give them up before your face, that you may do to them according to all the commandments which I have commanded you. ⁶Be strong and of a good courage, fear not, nor be afraid of them: for the LORD your God, he it is that does go with you; he will not fail you, nor forsake you. ⁷And Moses called to Joshua, and said to him in the sight of all Israel, Be strong and of a good courage: for you must go with this people to the land which the LORD has sworn to their fathers to give them; and you shall cause them to inherit it. ⁸And the LORD, he it is that does go before you; he will be with you, he will not fail you, neither forsake you: fear not, neither be dismayed. ⁹And Moses wrote this law, and delivered it to the priests the sons of Levi, which bore the ark of the covenant of the LORD, and to all the elders of Israel. ¹⁰And Moses commanded them, saying, At the end of every seven years, in the solemnity of the year of release, in the feast of tabernacles, ¹¹When all Israel is come to appear before the LORD your God in the place which he shall choose, you shall read this law before all Israel in their hearing. ¹²Gather the people together, men and women, and children, and your stranger that is within your gates, that they may hear, and that they may learn, and fear the LORD your God, and observe to do all the words of this law: ¹³And that their children, which have not known any thing, may hear, and learn to fear the LORD your God, as long as you live in the land where you go over Jordan to possess it. ¹⁴And the LORD said to Moses, Behold, your days approach that you must die: call Joshua, and present yourselves in the tabernacle of the congregation, that I may give him a charge. And Moses and Joshua went, and presented themselves in the tabernacle of the congregation. ¹⁵And the LORD appeared in the tabernacle in a pillar of a cloud: and the pillar of the cloud stood over the door of the tabernacle. ¹⁶And the LORD said to Moses, Behold, you shall sleep with your fathers; and this people will rise up, and go a whoring after the gods of the strangers of the land, where they go to be among them, and will forsake me, and break my covenant which I have made with them. ¹⁷Then my anger shall be kindled against them in that day, and I will forsake them, and I will hide my face from them, and they shall be devoured, and many evils and troubles shall befall them; so that they will say in that day, Are not these evils come on us, because our God is not among us? ¹⁸And I will surely hide my face in that day for all the evils which they shall have worked, in that they are turned to other gods. ¹⁹Now therefore write you this song for you, and teach it the children of Israel: put it in their mouths, that this song may be a witness for me against the children of Israel. ²⁰For when I shall have brought them into the land which I swore to their fathers, that flows with milk and honey; and they shall have eaten and filled themselves, and waxen fat; then will they turn to other gods, and serve them, and provoke me, and break my covenant. ²¹And it shall come to pass, when many evils and troubles are befallen them, that this song shall testify against them as a witness; for it shall not be forgotten out of the mouths of their seed: for I know their imagination which they go about, even now, before I have brought them into the land which I swore. ²²Moses therefore wrote this song the same day, and taught it the children of Israel. ²³And he gave Joshua the son of Nun a charge, and said, Be strong and of a good courage: for you shall bring the children of Israel into the land which I swore to them: and I will be with you. ²⁴And it came to pass, when Moses

had made an end of writing the words of this law in a book, until they were finished, ²⁵That Moses commanded the Levites, which bore the ark of the covenant of the LORD, saying, ²⁶Take this book of the law, and put it in the side of the ark of the covenant of the LORD your God, that it may be there for a witness against you. ²⁷For I know your rebellion, and your stiff neck: behold, while I am yet alive with you this day, you have been rebellious against the LORD; and how much more after my death? ²⁸Gather to me all the elders of your tribes, and your officers, that I may speak these words in their ears, and call heaven and earth to record against them. ²⁹For I know that after my death you will utterly corrupt yourselves, and turn aside from the way which I have commanded you; and evil will befall you in the latter days; because you will do evil in the sight of the LORD, to provoke him to anger through the work of your hands. ³⁰And Moses spoke in the ears of all the congregation of Israel the words of this song, until they were ended.

32 ¹Give ear, O you heavens, and I will speak; and hear, O earth, the words of my mouth. ²My doctrine shall drop as the rain, my speech shall distil as the dew, as the small rain on the tender herb, and as the showers on the grass: ³Because I will publish the name of the LORD: ascribe you greatness to our God. ⁴He is the Rock, his work is perfect: for all his ways are judgment: a God of truth and without iniquity, just and right is he. ⁵They have corrupted themselves, their spot is not the spot of his children: they are a perverse and crooked generation. ⁶Do you thus requite the LORD, O foolish people and unwise? is not he your father that has bought you? has he not made you, and established you? ⁷Remember the days of old, consider the years of many generations: ask your father, and he will show you; your elders, and they will tell you. ⁸When the Most High divided to the nations their inheritance, when he separated the sons of Adam, he set the bounds of the people according to the number of the children of Israel. ⁹For the LORD's portion is his people; Jacob is the lot of his inheritance. ¹⁰He found him in a desert land, and in the waste howling wilderness; he led him about, he instructed him, he kept him as the apple of his eye. ¹¹As an eagle stirs up her nest, flutters over her young, spreads abroad her wings, takes them, bears them on her wings; ¹²So the LORD alone did lead him, and there was no strange god with him. ¹³He made him ride on the high places of the earth, that he might eat the increase of the fields; and he made him to suck honey out of the rock, and oil out of the flinty rock; ¹⁴Butter of cows, and milk of sheep, with fat of lambs, and rams of the breed of Bashan, and goats, with the fat of kidneys of wheat; and you did drink the pure blood of the grape. ¹⁵But Jeshurun waxed fat, and kicked: you are waxen fat, you are grown thick, you are covered with fatness; then he forsook God which made him, and lightly esteemed the Rock of his salvation. ¹⁶They provoked him to jealousy with strange gods, with abominations provoked they him to anger. ¹⁷They sacrificed to devils, not to God; to gods whom they knew not, to new gods that came newly up, whom your fathers feared not. ¹⁸Of the Rock that begat you you are unmindful, and have forgotten God that formed you. ¹⁹And when the LORD saw it, he abhorred them, because of the provoking of his sons, and of his daughters. ²⁰And he said, I will hide my face from them, I will see what their end shall be: for they are a very fraudulent generation, children in whom is no faith. ²¹They have moved me to jealousy with that which is not God; they have provoked me to anger with their vanities: and I will move them to jealousy with those which are not a people; I will provoke them to anger with a foolish nation. ²²For a fire is kindled in my anger, and shall burn to the lowest hell, and shall consume the earth with her increase, and set on fire the foundations of the mountains. ²³I will heap mischiefs on them; I will spend my arrows on them. ²⁴They shall be burnt with hunger, and devoured with burning heat, and with bitter destruction: I will also send the teeth of beasts on them, with the poison of serpents of the dust. ²⁵The sword without, and terror within, shall destroy both the young man and the virgin, the suckling also with the man of gray hairs. ²⁶I said, I would scatter them into corners, I would make the remembrance of them to cease from among men: ²⁷Were it not that I feared the wrath of the enemy, lest their adversaries should behave themselves strangely, and lest they should say, Our hand is high, and the LORD has not done all this. ²⁸For they are a nation void of counsel, neither is there any understanding in them. ²⁹O that they were wise, that they understood this, that they would consider their latter end! ³⁰How should one chase a thousand, and two put ten thousand to flight, except their Rock had sold them, and the LORD had shut them up? ³¹For their rock is not as our Rock, even our enemies themselves being judges. ³²For their vine is of the vine of Sodom, and of the fields of Gomorrah: their grapes are grapes of gall, their clusters are bitter: ³³Their wine is the poison of dragons, and the cruel venom of asps. ³⁴Is not this laid up in store with me, and sealed up among my treasures? ³⁵To me belongs vengeance and recompense; their foot shall slide in due time: for the day of their calamity is at hand, and the things that shall come on them make haste. ³⁶For the LORD shall judge his people, and repent himself for his servants, when he sees that their power is gone, and there is none shut up, or left. ³⁷And he shall say, Where are their gods, their rock in whom they trusted, ³⁸Which did eat the fat of their sacrifices, and drank the wine of their drink offerings? let them rise up and help you, and be your protection. ³⁹See now that I, even I, am he, and there is no god with me: I kill, and I make alive; I wound, and I heal: neither is there any that can deliver out of my hand. ⁴⁰For I lift up my hand to heaven, and say, I live for ever. ⁴¹If I whet my glittering sword, and my hand take hold on judgment; I will render vengeance to my enemies, and will reward them that hate me. ⁴²I will make my arrows drunk with blood, and my sword shall devour flesh; and that with the blood of the slain and of the captives, from the beginning of revenges on the enemy. ⁴³Rejoice, O you nations, with his people: for he will avenge the blood of his servants, and will render vengeance to his adversaries, and will be merciful to his land, and to his people. ⁴⁴And Moses came and spoke all the words of this song in the ears of the people, he, and Hoshea the son of Nun. ⁴⁵And Moses made an end of speaking all these words to all Israel: ⁴⁶And he said to them, Set your hearts to all the words which I testify among you this day, which you shall command your children to observe to do, all the words of this law. ⁴⁷For it is not a vain thing for you; because it is your life: and through this thing you shall prolong your days in the land, where you go over Jordan to possess it. ⁴⁸And the LORD spoke to Moses that selfsame day, saying, ⁴⁹Get you up into this mountain Abarim, to mount Nebo, which is in the land of Moab, that is over against Jericho; and behold the land of Canaan, which I give to the children of Israel for a possession: ⁵⁰And die in the mount where you go up, and be gathered to your people; as Aaron your brother died in mount Hor, and was gathered to his people: ⁵¹Because you trespassed against me among the children of Israel at the waters of MeribahKadesh, in the wilderness of Zin; because you sanctified me not in the middle of the children of Israel. ⁵²Yet you shall see the land before you; but you shall not go thither to the land which I give the children of Israel.

33

¹And this is the blessing, with which Moses the man of God blessed the children of Israel before his death. ²And he said, The LORD came from Sinai, and rose up from Seir to them; he shined forth from mount Paran, and he came with ten thousands of saints: from his right hand went a fiery law for them. ³Yes, he loved the people; all his saints are in your hand: and they sat down at your feet; every one shall receive of your words. ⁴Moses commanded us a law, even the inheritance of the congregation of Jacob. ⁵And he was king in Jeshurun, when the heads of the people and the tribes of Israel were gathered together. ⁶Let Reuben live, and not die; and let not his men be few. ⁷And this is the blessing of Judah: and he said, Hear, LORD, the voice of Judah, and bring him to his people: let his hands be sufficient for him; and be you an help to him from his enemies. ⁸And of Levi he said, Let your Thummim and your Urim be with your holy one, whom you did prove at Massah, and with whom you did strive at the waters of Meribah; ⁹Who said to his father and to his mother, I have not seen him; neither did he acknowledge his brothers, nor knew his own children: for they have observed your word, and kept your covenant. ¹⁰They shall teach Jacob your judgments, and Israel your law: they shall put incense before you, and whole burnt sacrifice on your altar. ¹¹Bless, LORD, his substance, and accept the work of his hands; smite through the loins of them that rise against him, and of them that hate him, that they rise not again. ¹²And of Benjamin he said, The beloved of the LORD shall dwell in safety by him; and the Lord shall cover him all the day long, and he shall dwell between his shoulders. ¹³And of Joseph he said, Blessed of the LORD be his land, for the precious things of heaven, for the dew, and for the deep that coucheth beneath, ¹⁴And for the precious fruits brought forth by the sun, and for the precious things put forth by the moon, ¹⁵And for the chief things of the ancient mountains, and for the precious things of the lasting hills, ¹⁶And for the precious things of the earth and fullness thereof, and for the good will of him that dwelled in the bush: let the blessing come on the head of Joseph, and on the top of the head of him that was separated from his brothers. ¹⁷His glory is like the firstling of his bullock, and his horns are like the horns of unicorns: with them he shall push the people together to the ends of the earth: and they are the ten thousands of Ephraim, and they are the thousands of Manasseh. ¹⁸And of Zebulun he said, Rejoice, Zebulun, in your going out; and, Issachar, in your tents. ¹⁹They shall call the people to the mountain; there they shall offer sacrifices of righteousness: for they shall suck of the abundance of the seas, and of treasures hid in the sand. ²⁰And of Gad he said, Blessed be he that enlarges Gad: he dwells as a lion, and tears the arm with the crown of the head. ²¹And he provided the first part for himself, because there, in a portion of the lawgiver, was he seated; and he came with the heads of the people, he executed the justice of the LORD, and his judgments with Israel. ²²And of Dan he said, Dan is a lion's whelp: he shall leap from Bashan. ²³And of Naphtali he said, O Naphtali, satisfied with favor, and full with the blessing of the LORD: possess you the west and the south. ²⁴And of Asher he said, Let Asher be blessed with children; let him be acceptable to his brothers, and let him dip his foot in oil. ²⁵Your shoes shall be iron and brass; and as your days, so shall your strength be. ²⁶There is none like to the God of Jeshurun, who rides on the heaven in your help, and in his excellency on the sky. ²⁷The eternal God is your refuge, and underneath are the everlasting arms: and he shall thrust out the enemy from before you; and shall say, Destroy them. ²⁸Israel then shall dwell in safety alone: the fountain of Jacob shall be on a land of corn and wine; also his heavens shall drop down dew. ²⁹Happy are you, O Israel: who is like to you, O people saved by the LORD, the shield of your help, and who is the sword of your excellency! and your enemies shall be found liars to you; and you shall tread on their high places.

34

¹And Moses went up from the plains of Moab to the mountain of Nebo, to the top of Pisgah, that is over against Jericho. And the LORD showed him all the land of Gilead, to Dan, ²And all Naphtali, and the land of Ephraim, and Manasseh, and all the land of Judah, to the utmost sea, ³And the south, and the plain of the valley of Jericho, the city of palm trees, to Zoar. ⁴And the LORD said to him, This is the land which I swore to Abraham, to Isaac, and to Jacob, saying, I will give it to your seed: I have caused you to see it with your eyes, but you shall not go over thither. ⁵So Moses the servant of the LORD died there in the land of Moab, according to the word of the LORD. ⁶And he buried him in a valley in the land of Moab, over against Bethpeor: but no man knows of his sepulcher to this day. ⁷And Moses was an hundred and twenty years old when he died: his eye was not dim, nor his natural force abated. ⁸And the children of Israel wept for Moses in the plains of Moab thirty days: so the days of weeping and mourning for Moses were ended. ⁹And Joshua the son of Nun was full of the spirit of wisdom; for Moses had laid his hands on him: and the children of Israel listened to him, and did as the LORD commanded Moses. ¹⁰And there arose not a prophet since in Israel like to Moses, whom the LORD knew face to face, ¹¹In all the signs and the wonders, which the LORD sent him to do in the land of Egypt to Pharaoh, and to all his servants, and to all his land, ¹²And in all that mighty hand, and in all the great terror which Moses showed in the sight of all Israel.

Joshua

1 ¹Now after the death of Moses the servant of the LORD it came to pass, that the LORD spoke to Joshua the son of Nun, Moses' minister, saying, ²Moses my servant is dead; now therefore arise, go over this Jordan, you, and all this people, to the land which I do give to them, even to the children of Israel. ³Every place that the sole of your foot shall tread on, that have I given to you, as I said to Moses. ⁴From the wilderness and this Lebanon even to the great river, the river Euphrates, all the land of the Hittites, and to the great sea toward the going down of the sun, shall be your coast. ⁵There shall not any man be able to stand before you all the days of your life: as I was with Moses, so I will be with you: I will not fail you, nor forsake you. ⁶Be strong and of a good courage: for to this people shall you divide for an inheritance the land, which I swore to their fathers to give them. ⁷Only be you strong and very courageous, that you may observe to do according to all the law, which Moses my servant commanded you: turn not from it to the right hand or to the left, that you may prosper wherever you go. ⁸This book of the law shall not depart out of your mouth; but you shall meditate therein day and night, that you may observe to do according to all that is written therein: for then you shall make your way prosperous, and then you shall have good success. ⁹Have not I commanded you? Be strong and of a good courage; be not afraid, neither be you dismayed: for the LORD your God is with you wherever you go. ¹⁰Then Joshua commanded the officers of the people, saying, ¹¹Pass through the host, and command the people, saying, Prepare you victuals; for within three days you shall pass over this Jordan, to go in to possess the land, which the LORD your God gives you to possess it. ¹²And to the Reubenites, and to the Gadites, and to half the tribe of Manasseh, spoke Joshua, saying, ¹³Remember the word which Moses the servant of the LORD commanded you, saying, The LORD your God has given you rest, and has given you this land. ¹⁴Your wives, your little ones, and your cattle, shall remain in the land which Moses gave you on this side Jordan; but you shall pass before your brothers armed, all the mighty men of valor, and help them; ¹⁵Until the LORD have given your brothers rest, as he has given you, and they also have possessed the land which the LORD your God gives them: then you shall return to the land of your possession, and enjoy it, which Moses the LORD's servant gave you on this side Jordan toward the sun rise. ¹⁶And they answered Joshua, saying, All that you command us we will do, and wherever you send us, we will go. ¹⁷According as we listened to Moses in all things, so will we listen to you: only the LORD your God be with you, as he was with Moses. ¹⁸Whoever he be that does rebel against your commandment, and will not listen to your words in all that you command him, he shall be put to death: only be strong and of a good courage.

2 ¹And Joshua the son of Nun sent out of Shittim two men to spy secretly, saying, Go view the land, even Jericho. And they went, and came into an harlot's house, named Rahab, and lodged there. ²And it was told the king of Jericho, saying, Behold, there came men in here to night of the children of Israel to search out the country. ³And the king of Jericho sent to Rahab, saying, Bring forth the men that are come to you, which are entered into your house: for they be come to search out all the country. ⁴And the woman took the two men, and hid them, and said thus, There came men to me, but I knew not from where they were: ⁵And it came to pass about the time of shutting of the gate, when it was dark, that the men went out: where the men went I know not: pursue after them quickly; for you shall overtake them. ⁶But she had brought them up to the roof of the house, and hid them with the stalks of flax, which she had laid in order on the roof. ⁷And the men pursued after them the way to Jordan to the fords: and as soon as they which pursued after them were gone out, they shut the gate. ⁸And before they were laid down, she came up to them on the roof; ⁹And she said to the men, I know that the LORD has given you the land, and that your terror is fallen on us, and that all the inhabitants of the land faint because of you. ¹⁰For we have heard how the LORD dried up the water of the Red sea for you, when you came out of Egypt; and what you did to the two kings of the Amorites, that were on the other side Jordan, Sihon and Og, whom you utterly destroyed. ¹¹And as soon as we had heard these things, our hearts did melt, neither did there remain any more courage in any man, because of you: for the LORD your God, he is God in heaven above, and in earth beneath. ¹²Now therefore, I pray you, swear to me by the LORD, since I have showed you kindness, that you will also show kindness to my father's house, and give me a true token: ¹³And that you will save alive my father, and my mother, and my brothers, and my sisters, and all that they have, and deliver our lives from death. ¹⁴And the men answered her, Our life for yours, if you utter not this our business. And it shall be, when the LORD has given us the land, that we will deal kindly and truly with you. ¹⁵Then she let them down by a cord through the window: for her house was on the town wall, and she dwelled on the wall. ¹⁶And she said to them, Get you to the mountain, lest the pursuers meet you; and hide yourselves there three days, until the pursuers be returned: and afterward may you go your way. ¹⁷And the men said to her, We will be blameless of this your oath which you have made us swear. ¹⁸Behold, when we come into the land, you shall bind this line of scarlet thread in the window which you did let us down by: and you shall bring your father, and your mother, and your brothers, and all your father's household, home to you. ¹⁹And it shall be, that whoever shall go out of the doors of your house into the street, his blood shall be on his head, and we will be guiltless: and whoever shall be with you in the house, his blood shall be on our head, if any hand be on him. ²⁰And if you utter this our business, then we will be quit of your oath which you have made us to swear. ²¹And she said, According to your words, so be it. And she sent them away, and they departed: and she bound the scarlet line in the window. ²²And they went, and came to the mountain, and stayed there three days, until the pursuers were returned: and the pursuers sought them throughout all the way, but found them not. ²³So the two men returned, and descended from the mountain, and passed over, and came to Joshua the son of Nun, and told him all things that befell them: ²⁴And they said to Joshua, Truly the LORD has delivered into our hands all the land; for even all the inhabitants of the country do faint because of us.

3 ¹And Joshua rose early in the morning; and they removed from Shittim, and came to Jordan, he and all the children of Israel, and lodged there before they passed over. ²And it came to pass after three days, that the officers went through the host; ³And they commanded the people, saying, When you see the ark of the covenant of the LORD your God, and the priests the Levites bearing it, then you shall remove from your place, and go after it. ⁴Yet there shall be a space between you and it, about two thousand cubits by measure: come not near to it, that you may know the way by which you must go: for you have not passed this way heretofore. ⁵And Joshua said to the people, Sanctify yourselves: for to morrow the LORD will do wonders among you. ⁶And Joshua spoke to the priests, saying, Take up the ark of the covenant, and pass over before the people. And they took up the ark of the covenant, and went before the people. ⁷And the LORD said to Joshua, This day will I begin to magnify you in the sight of all Israel, that they may know that, as I was with Moses, so I will be with you. ⁸And you shall command the priests that bear the ark of the covenant, saying, When you are come to the brink of the water of Jordan, you shall stand still in Jordan. ⁹And Joshua said to the children of Israel, Come here, and hear the words of the LORD your God. ¹⁰And Joshua said, Hereby you shall know that the living God is among you, and that he will without fail drive out from before you the Canaanites, and the Hittites, and the Hivites, and the Perizzites, and the Girgashites, and the Amorites, and the Jebusites. ¹¹Behold, the ark of the covenant of the LORD of all the earth passes over before you into Jordan. ¹²Now therefore take you twelve men out of the tribes of Israel, out of every tribe a man. ¹³And it shall come to pass, as soon as the soles of the feet of the priests that bear the ark of the LORD, the LORD of all the earth, shall rest in the waters of Jordan, that the waters of Jordan shall be cut off from the waters that come down from above; and they shall stand on an heap. ¹⁴And it came to pass, when the people removed from their tents, to pass over Jordan, and the priests bearing the ark of the covenant before the people; ¹⁵And as they that bore the ark were come to Jordan, and the feet of the priests that bore the ark were dipped in the brim of the water, (for Jordan overflows all his banks all the time of harvest,) ¹⁶That the waters which came down from above stood and rose up on an heap very far from the city Adam, that is beside Zaretan: and those that came down toward the sea of the plain, even the salt sea, failed, and were cut off: and the people passed over right against Jericho. ¹⁷And the priests that bore the ark of the covenant of the LORD stood firm on dry ground in the middle of Jordan, and all the Israelites passed over on dry ground, until all the people were passed clean over Jordan.

4 ¹And it came to pass, when all the people were clean passed over Jordan, that the LORD spoke to Joshua, saying, ²Take you twelve men out of the people, out of every tribe a man, ³And command you them, saying, Take you hence out of the middle of Jordan, out of the place where the priests' feet stood firm, twelve stones, and you shall carry them over with you, and leave them in the lodging place, where you shall lodge this night. ⁴Then Joshua called the twelve men, whom he had prepared of the children of Israel, out of every tribe a man: ⁵And Joshua said to them, Pass over before the ark of the LORD your God into the middle of Jordan, and take you up every man of you a stone on his shoulder, according to the number of the tribes of the children of Israel: ⁶That this may be a sign among you, that when your children ask their fathers in time to come, saying, What mean you by these stones? ⁷Then you shall answer them, That the waters of Jordan were cut off before the ark of the covenant of the LORD; when it passed over Jordan, the waters of Jordan were cut off: and these stones shall be for a memorial to the children of Israel for ever. ⁸And the children of Israel did so as Joshua commanded, and took up twelve stones out of the middle of Jordan, as the LORD spoke to Joshua, according to the number of the tribes of the children of Israel, and carried them over with them to the place where they lodged, and laid them down there. ⁹And Joshua set up twelve stones in the middle of Jordan, in the place where the feet of the priests which bore the ark of the covenant stood: and they are there to this day. ¹⁰For the priests which bore the ark stood in the middle of Jordan, until everything was finished that the LORD commanded Joshua to speak to the people, according to all that Moses commanded Joshua: and the people hurried and passed over. ¹¹And it came to pass, when all the people were clean passed over, that the ark of the LORD passed over, and the priests, in the presence of the people. ¹²And the children of Reuben, and the children of Gad, and half the tribe of Manasseh, passed over armed before the children of Israel, as Moses spoke to them: ¹³About forty thousand prepared for war passed over before the LORD to battle, to the plains of Jericho. ¹⁴On that day the LORD magnified Joshua in the sight of all Israel; and they feared him, as they feared Moses, all the days of his life. ¹⁵And the LORD spoke to Joshua, saying, ¹⁶Command the priests that bear the ark of the testimony, that they come up out of Jordan. ¹⁷Joshua therefore commanded the priests, saying, Come you up out of Jordan. ¹⁸And it came to pass, when the priests that bore the ark of the covenant of the LORD were come up out of the middle of Jordan, and the soles of the priests' feet were lifted up to the dry land, that the waters of Jordan returned to their place, and flowed over all his banks, as they did before. ¹⁹And the people came up out of Jordan on the tenth day of the first month, and encamped in Gilgal, in the east border of Jericho. ²⁰And those twelve stones, which they took out of Jordan, did Joshua pitch in Gilgal. ²¹And he spoke to the children of Israel, saying, When your children shall ask their fathers in time to come, saying, What mean these stones? ²²Then you shall let your children know, saying, Israel came over this Jordan on dry land. ²³For the LORD your God dried up the waters of Jordan from before you, until you were passed over, as the LORD your God did to the Red sea, which he dried up from before us, until we were gone over: ²⁴That all the people of the earth might know the hand of the LORD, that it is mighty: that you might fear the LORD your God for ever.

5 ¹And it came to pass, when all the kings of the Amorites, which were on the side of Jordan westward, and all the kings of the Canaanites, which were by the sea, heard that the LORD had dried up the waters of Jordan from before the children of Israel, until we were passed over, that their heart melted, neither was there spirit in them any more, because of the children of Israel. ²At that time the LORD said to Joshua, Make you sharp knives, and circumcise again the children of Israel the second time. ³And Joshua made him sharp knives, and circumcised the children of Israel at the hill of the foreskins. ⁴And this is the cause why Joshua did circumcise: All the people that came out of Egypt, that were males, even all the men of war, died in the wilderness by the way, after they came out of Egypt. ⁵Now all the people that came out were circumcised: but all the people that were born in the wilderness by the way as they came forth out of Egypt, them they had not circumcised. ⁶For the children of Israel walked forty years in the wilderness, till all the people that were men of war, which came out of Egypt, were consumed, because they obeyed not the voice of the LORD: to whom the LORD swore that he would not show them the land, which the LORD swore to their fathers that he would give us, a land that flows with milk and honey. ⁷And their children, whom he raised up in their stead, them Joshua circumcised: for they were uncircumcised, because they had not circumcised them by the way. ⁸And it came to pass, when they had done circumcising all the people, that they stayed in their places in the camp, till they were whole. ⁹And the LORD said to Joshua, This day have I rolled away the reproach of Egypt from off you. Why the name of the place is called Gilgal to this day. ¹⁰And the children of Israel encamped in Gilgal, and kept the passover on the fourteenth day of the month at even in the plains of Jericho. ¹¹And they did eat of the old corn of the land on the morrow after the passover, unleavened cakes, and parched corn in the selfsame day. ¹²And the manna ceased on the morrow after they had eaten of the old corn of the land; neither had the children of Israel manna any more; but they did eat of the fruit of the land of Canaan that year. ¹³And it came to pass, when Joshua was by Jericho, that he lifted up his eyes and looked, and, behold, there stood a man over against him with his sword drawn in his hand: and Joshua went to him, and said to him, Are you for us, or for our adversaries? ¹⁴And he said, No; but as captain of the host of the LORD am I now come. And Joshua fell on his face to the earth, and did worship, and said to him, What says my Lord to his servant? ¹⁵And the captain of the LORD's host said to Joshua, Loose your shoe from off your foot; for the place where on you stand is holy. And Joshua did so.

6 ¹Now Jericho was straightly shut up because of the children of Israel: none went out, and none came in. ²And the LORD said to Joshua, See, I have given into your hand Jericho, and the king thereof, and the mighty men of valor. ³And you shall compass the city, all you men of war, and go round about the city once. Thus shall you do six days. ⁴And seven priests shall bear before the ark seven trumpets of rams' horns: and the seventh day you shall compass the city seven times, and the priests shall blow with the trumpets. ⁵And it shall come to pass, that when they make a long blast with the ram's horn, and when you hear the sound of the trumpet, all the people shall shout with a great shout; and the wall of the city shall fall down flat, and the people shall ascend up every man straight before him. ⁶And Joshua the son of Nun called the priests, and said to them, Take up the ark of the covenant, and let seven priests bear seven trumpets of rams' horns before the ark of the LORD. ⁷And he said to the people, Pass on, and compass the city, and let him that is armed pass on before the ark of the LORD. ⁸And it came to pass, when Joshua had spoken to the people, that the seven priests bearing the seven trumpets of rams' horns passed on before the LORD, and blew with the trumpets: and the ark of the covenant of the LORD followed them. ⁹And the armed men went before the priests that blew with the trumpets, and the rear guard came after the ark, the priests going on, and blowing with the trumpets. ¹⁰And Joshua had commanded the people, saying, You shall not shout, nor make any noise with your voice, neither shall any word proceed out of your mouth, until the day I bid you shout; then shall you shout. ¹¹So the ark of the LORD compassed the city, going about it once: and they came into the camp, and lodged in the camp. ¹²And Joshua rose early in the morning, and the priests took up the ark of the LORD. ¹³And seven priests bearing seven trumpets of rams' horns before the ark of the LORD went on continually, and blew with the trumpets: and the armed men went before them; but the rear guard came after the ark of the LORD, the priests going on, and blowing with the trumpets. ¹⁴And the second day they compassed the city once, and returned into the camp: so they did six days. ¹⁵And it came to pass on the seventh day, that they rose early about the dawning of the day, and compassed the city after the same manner seven times: only on that day they compassed the city seven times. ¹⁶And it came to pass at the seventh time, when the priests blew with the trumpets, Joshua said to the people, Shout; for the LORD has given you the city. ¹⁷And the city shall be accursed, even it, and all that are therein, to the LORD: only Rahab the harlot shall live, she and all that are with her in the house, because she hid the messengers that we sent. ¹⁸And you, in any wise keep yourselves from the accursed thing, lest you make yourselves accursed, when you take of the accursed thing, and make the camp of Israel a curse, and trouble it. ¹⁹But all the silver, and gold, and vessels of brass and iron, are consecrated to the LORD: they shall come into the treasury of the LORD. ²⁰So the people shouted when the priests blew with the trumpets: and it came to pass, when the people heard the sound of the trumpet, and the people shouted with a great shout, that the wall fell down flat, so that the people went up into the city, every man straight before him, and they took the city. ²¹And they utterly destroyed all that was in the city, both man and woman, young and old, and ox, and sheep, and ass, with the edge of the sword. ²²But Joshua had said to the two men that had spied out the country, Go into the harlot's house, and bring out there the woman, and all that she has, as you swore to her. ²³And the young men that were spies went in, and brought out Rahab, and her father, and her mother, and her brothers, and all that she had; and they brought out all her kindred, and left them without the camp of Israel. ²⁴And they burnt the city with fire, and all that was therein: only the silver, and the gold, and the vessels of brass and of iron, they put into the treasury of the house of the LORD. ²⁵And Joshua saved Rahab the harlot alive, and her father's household, and all that she had; and she dwells in Israel even to this day; because she hid the messengers, which Joshua sent to spy out Jericho. ²⁶And Joshua adjured them at that time, saying, Cursed be the man before the LORD, that rises up and builds this city Jericho: he shall lay the foundation thereof in his firstborn, and in his youngest son shall he set up the gates of it. ²⁷So the LORD was with Joshua; and his fame was noised throughout all the country.

7 ¹But the children of Israel committed a trespass in the accursed thing: for Achan, the son of Carmi, the son of Zabdi, the son of Zerah, of the tribe of Judah, took of the accursed thing: and the anger of the LORD was kindled against the children of Israel. ²And Joshua sent men from Jericho to Ai, which is beside Bethaven, on the east of Bethel, and spoke to them, saying, Go up and view the country. And the men went up and viewed Ai. ³And they returned to Joshua, and said to him, Let not all the people go up; but let about two or three thousand men go up and smite Ai; and make not all the people to labor thither; for they are but few. ⁴So there went up thither of the people about three thousand men: and they fled before the men of Ai. ⁵And the men of Ai smote of them about thirty and six men: for they chased them from before the gate even to Shebarim, and smote them in the going down: why the hearts of the people melted, and became as water. ⁶And Joshua rent his clothes, and fell to the earth on his face before the ark of the LORD until the eventide, he and the elders of Israel, and put dust on their heads. ⁷And Joshua said, Alas, O LORD God, why have you at all brought this people over Jordan, to deliver us into the hand of the Amorites, to destroy us? would to God we had been content, and dwelled on the other side Jordan! ⁸O LORD, what shall I say, when Israel turns their backs before their enemies! ⁹For the Canaanites and all the inhabitants of the land shall hear of it, and shall environ us round, and cut off our name from the earth: and what will you do to your great name? ¹⁰And the LORD said to Joshua, Get you up; why lie you thus on your face? ¹¹Israel has sinned, and they have also transgressed my covenant which I commanded them: for they have even taken of the accursed thing, and have also stolen, and dissembled also, and they have put it even among their own stuff. ¹²Therefore the children of Israel could not stand before their enemies, but turned their backs before their enemies, because they were accursed: neither will I be with you any more, except you destroy the accursed from among you. ¹³Up, sanctify the people, and say, Sanctify yourselves against to morrow: for thus says the LORD God of Israel, There is an accursed thing in the middle of you, O Israel: you can not stand before your enemies, until you take away the accursed thing from among you. ¹⁴In the morning therefore you shall be brought according to your tribes: and it shall be, that the tribe which the LORD takes shall come according to the families thereof; and the family which the LORD shall take shall come by households; and the household which the LORD shall take shall come man by man. ¹⁵And it shall be, that he that is taken with the accursed thing shall be burnt with fire, he and all that he has: because he has transgressed the covenant of the LORD, and because he has worked folly in Israel. ¹⁶So Joshua rose up early in the morning, and brought Israel by their tribes; and the tribe of Judah was taken: ¹⁷And he brought the family of Judah; and he took the family of the Zarhites: and he brought the family of the Zarhites man by man; and Zabdi was taken: ¹⁸And he brought his household man by man; and Achan, the son of Carmi, the son of Zabdi, the son of Zerah, of the tribe of Judah, was taken. ¹⁹And Joshua said to Achan, My son, give, I pray you, glory to the LORD God of Israel, and make confession to him; and tell me now what you have done; hide it not from me. ²⁰And Achan answered Joshua, and said, Indeed I have sinned against the LORD God of Israel, and thus and thus have I done: ²¹When I saw among the spoils a goodly Babylonish garment, and two hundred shekels of silver, and a wedge of gold of fifty shekels weight, then I coveted them, and took them; and, behold, they are hid in the earth in the middle of my tent, and the silver under it. ²²So Joshua sent messengers, and they ran to the tent; and, behold, it was hid in his tent, and the silver under it. ²³And they took them out of the middle of the tent, and brought them to Joshua, and to all the children of Israel, and laid them out before the LORD. ²⁴And Joshua, and all Israel with him, took Achan the son of Zerah, and the silver, and the garment, and the wedge of gold, and his sons, and his daughters, and his oxen, and his asses, and his sheep, and his tent, and all that he had: and they brought them to the valley of Achor. ²⁵And Joshua said, Why have you troubled us? the LORD shall trouble you this day. And all Israel stoned him with stones, and burned them with fire, after they had stoned them with stones. ²⁶And they raised over him a great heap of stones to this day. So the LORD turned from the fierceness of his anger. Why the name of that place was called, The valley of Achor, to this day.

8 ¹And the LORD said to Joshua, Fear not, neither be you dismayed: take all the people of war with you, and arise, go up to Ai: see, I have given into your hand the king of Ai, and his people, and his city, and his land: ²And you shall do to Ai and her king as you did to Jericho and her king: only the spoil thereof, and the cattle thereof, shall you take for a prey to yourselves: lay you an ambush for the city behind it. ³So Joshua arose, and all the people of war, to go up against Ai: and Joshua chose out thirty thousand mighty men of valor, and sent them away by night. ⁴And he commanded them, saying, Behold, you shall lie in wait against the city, even behind the city: go not very far from the city, but be you all ready: ⁵And I, and all the people that are with me, will approach to the city: and it shall come to pass, when they come out against us, as at the first, that we will flee before them, ⁶(For they will come out after us) till we have drawn them from the city; for they will say, They flee before us, as at the first: therefore we will flee before them. ⁷Then you shall rise up from the ambush, and seize on the city: for the LORD your God will deliver it into your hand. ⁸And it shall be, when you have taken the city, that you shall set the city on fire: according to the commandment of the LORD shall you do. See, I have commanded you. ⁹Joshua therefore sent them forth: and they went to lie in ambush, and stayed between Bethel and Ai, on the west side of Ai: but Joshua lodged that night among the people. ¹⁰And Joshua rose up early in the morning, and numbered the people, and went up, he and the elders of Israel, before the people to Ai. ¹¹And all the people, even the people of war that were with him, went up, and drew near, and came before the city, and pitched on the north side of Ai: now there was a valley between them and Ai. ¹²And he took about five thousand men, and set them to lie in ambush between Bethel and Ai, on the west side of the city. ¹³And when they had set the people, even all the host that was on the north of the city, and their liers in wait on the west of the city, Joshua went that night into the middle of the valley. ¹⁴And it came to pass, when the king of Ai saw it, that they hurried and rose up early, and the men of the city went out against Israel to battle, he and all his people, at a time appointed, before the plain; but he knew not that there were liers in ambush against him behind the city. ¹⁵And Joshua and all Israel made as if they were beaten before them, and fled by the way of the wilderness. ¹⁶And all the people that were in Ai were called together to pursue after them: and they pursued after Joshua, and were drawn away from the city. ¹⁷And there was not a man left in Ai or Bethel, that went not out after Israel: and they left the city open, and pursued after Israel. ¹⁸And the LORD said to Joshua, Stretch out the spear that is in your hand toward Ai; for I will give it into your hand. And Joshua stretched out the spear that he had in his hand toward the city. ¹⁹And the ambush arose quickly out of their place, and they ran as soon as he had stretched out his hand: and they entered into the city, and took it, and hurried and set the city on fire. ²⁰And when the men of Ai looked behind them, they saw, and, behold, the smoke of the city ascended up to heaven, and they had no power to flee this way or that way: and the people that fled to the wilderness turned back on the pursuers. ²¹And when Joshua and all Israel saw that the ambush had taken the city, and that the smoke of the city ascended, then they turned again, and slew the men of Ai. ²²And the other issued out of the city against them; so they were in the middle of Israel, some on this side, and some on that side: and they smote them, so that they let none of them remain or escape. ²³And the king of Ai they took alive, and brought him to Joshua. ²⁴And it came to pass, when Israel had made an end of slaying all the inhabitants of Ai in the field, in the wilderness wherein they chased them, and when they were all fallen on the edge of the sword, until they were consumed, that all the Israelites returned to Ai, and smote it with the edge of the sword. ²⁵And so it was, that all that fell that day, both of men and women, were twelve thousand, even all the men of Ai. ²⁶For Joshua drew not his hand back, with which he stretched out the spear, until he had utterly destroyed all the inhabitants of Ai. ²⁷Only the cattle and the spoil of that city Israel took for a prey to themselves, according to the word of the LORD which he commanded Joshua. ²⁸And Joshua burnt Ai, and made it an heap for ever, even a desolation to this day. ²⁹And the king of Ai he hanged on a tree until eventide: and as soon as the sun was down, Joshua commanded that they should take his carcass down from the tree, and cast it at the entering of the gate of the city, and raise thereon a great heap of stones, that remains to this day. ³⁰Then Joshua built an altar to the LORD God of Israel in mount Ebal, ³¹As Moses the servant of the LORD commanded the children of Israel, as it is written in the book of the law of Moses, an altar of whole stones, over which no man has lift up any iron: and they offered thereon burnt offerings to the LORD, and sacrificed peace offerings. ³²And he wrote there on the stones a copy of the law of Moses, which he wrote in the presence of the children of Israel. ³³And all Israel, and their elders, and officers, and their judges, stood on this side the ark and on that side before the priests the Levites, which bore the ark of the covenant of the LORD, as well the stranger, as he that was born among them; half of them over against mount Gerizim, and half of them over against mount Ebal; as Moses the servant of the LORD had commanded before, that they should bless the people of Israel. ³⁴And afterward he read all the words of the law, the blessings and cursings, according to all that is written in the book of the law. ³⁵There was not a word of all that Moses commanded, which Joshua read not before all the congregation of Israel, with the women, and the little ones, and the strangers that were conversant among them.

9 ¹And it came to pass, when all the kings which were on this side Jordan, in the hills, and in the valleys, and in all the coasts of the great sea over against Lebanon, the Hittite, and the Amorite, the Canaanite, the Perizzite, the Hivite, and the Jebusite, heard thereof; ²That they gathered themselves together, to fight with Joshua and with Israel, with one accord. ³And when the inhabitants of Gibeon heard what Joshua had done to Jericho and to Ai, ⁴They did work wilily, and went and made as if they had been ambassadors, and took old sacks on their asses, and wine bottles, old, and rent, and bound up; ⁵And old shoes and clouted on their feet, and old garments on them; and all the bread of their provision was dry and moldy. ⁶And they went to Joshua to the camp at Gilgal, and said to him, and to the men of Israel, We be come from a far country: now therefore make you a league with us. ⁷And the men of Israel said to the Hivites, Peradventure you dwell among us; and how shall we make a league with you? ⁸And they said to Joshua, We are your servants. And Joshua said to them, Who are you? and from from where come you? ⁹And they said to him, From a very far country your servants are come because of the name of the LORD your God: for we have heard the fame of him, and all that he did in Egypt, ¹⁰And all that he did to the two kings of the Amorites, that were beyond Jordan, to Sihon king of Heshbon, and to Og king of Bashan, which was at Ashtaroth. ¹¹Why our elders and all the inhabitants of our country spoke to us, saying, Take victuals with you for the journey, and go to meet them, and say to them, We are your servants: therefore now make you a league with us. ¹²This our bread we took hot for our provision out of our houses on the day we came forth to go to you; but now, behold, it is dry, and it is moldy: ¹³And these bottles of wine, which we filled, were new; and, behold, they be rent: and these our garments and our shoes are become old by reason of the very long journey. ¹⁴And the men took of their victuals, and asked not counsel at the mouth of the LORD. ¹⁵And Joshua made peace with them, and made a league with them, to let them live: and the princes of the congregation swore to them. ¹⁶And it came to pass at the end of three days after they had made a league with them, that they heard that they were their neighbors, and that they dwelled among them. ¹⁷And the children of Israel journeyed, and came to their cities on the third day. Now their cities were Gibeon, and Chephirah, and Beeroth, and Kirjathjearim. ¹⁸And the children of Israel smote them not, because the princes of the congregation had sworn to them by the LORD God of Israel.

And all the congregation murmured against the princes. ¹⁹But all the princes said to all the congregation, We have sworn to them by the LORD God of Israel: now therefore we may not touch them. ²⁰This we will do to them; we will even let them live, lest wrath be on us, because of the oath which we swore to them. ²¹And the princes said to them, Let them live; but let them be hewers of wood and drawers of water to all the congregation; as the princes had promised them. ²²And Joshua called for them, and he spoke to them, saying, Why have you beguiled us, saying, We are very far from you; when you dwell among us? ²³Now therefore you are cursed, and there shall none of you be freed from being slaves, and hewers of wood and drawers of water for the house of my God. ²⁴And they answered Joshua, and said, Because it was certainly told your servants, how that the LORD your God commanded his servant Moses to give you all the land, and to destroy all the inhabitants of the land from before you, therefore we were sore afraid of our lives because of you, and have done this thing. ²⁵And now, behold, we are in your hand: as it seems good and right to you to do to us, do. ²⁶And so did he to them, and delivered them out of the hand of the children of Israel, that they slew them not. ²⁷And Joshua made them that day hewers of wood and drawers of water for the congregation, and for the altar of the LORD, even to this day, in the place which he should choose.

10

¹Now it came to pass, when Adonizedec king of Jerusalem had heard how Joshua had taken Ai, and had utterly destroyed it; as he had done to Jericho and her king, so he had done to Ai and her king; and how the inhabitants of Gibeon had made peace with Israel, and were among them; ²That they feared greatly, because Gibeon was a great city, as one of the royal cities, and because it was greater than Ai, and all the men thereof were mighty. ³Why Adonizedec king of Jerusalem, sent to Hoham king of Hebron, and to Piram king of Jarmuth, and to Japhia king of Lachish, and to Debir king of Eglon, saying, ⁴Come up to me, and help me, that we may smite Gibeon: for it has made peace with Joshua and with the children of Israel. ⁵Therefore the five kings of the Amorites, the king of Jerusalem, the king of Hebron, the king of Jarmuth, the king of Lachish, the king of Eglon, gathered themselves together, and went up, they and all their hosts, and encamped before Gibeon, and made war against it. ⁶And the men of Gibeon sent to Joshua to the camp to Gilgal, saying, Slack not your hand from your servants; come up to us quickly, and save us, and help us: for all the kings of the Amorites that dwell in the mountains are gathered together against us. ⁷So Joshua ascended from Gilgal, he, and all the people of war with him, and all the mighty men of valor. ⁸And the LORD said to Joshua, Fear them not: for I have delivered them into your hand; there shall not a man of them stand before you. ⁹Joshua therefore came to them suddenly, and went up from Gilgal all night. ¹⁰And the LORD discomfited them before Israel, and slew them with a great slaughter at Gibeon, and chased them along the way that goes up to Bethhoron, and smote them to Azekah, and to Makkedah. ¹¹And it came to pass, as they fled from before Israel, and were in the going down to Bethhoron, that the LORD cast down great stones from heaven on them to Azekah, and they died: they were more which died with hailstones than they whom the children of Israel slew with the sword. ¹²Then spoke Joshua to the LORD in the day when the LORD delivered up the Amorites before the children of Israel, and he said in the sight of Israel, Sun, stand you still on Gibeon; and you, Moon, in the valley of Ajalon. ¹³And the sun stood still, and the moon stayed, until the people had avenged themselves on their enemies. Is not this written in the book of Jasher? So the sun stood still in the middle of heaven, and hurried not to go down about a whole day. ¹⁴And there was no day like that before it or after it, that the LORD listened to the voice of a man: for the LORD fought for Israel. ¹⁵And Joshua returned, and all Israel with him, to the camp to Gilgal. ¹⁶But these five kings fled, and hid themselves in a cave at Makkedah. ¹⁷And it was told Joshua, saying, The five kings are found hid in a cave at Makkedah. ¹⁸And Joshua said, Roll great stones on the mouth of the cave, and set men by it for to keep them: ¹⁹And stay you not, but pursue after your enemies, and smite the hindmost of them; suffer them not to enter into their cities: for the LORD your God has delivered them into your hand. ²⁰And it came to pass, when Joshua and the children of Israel had made an end of slaying them with a very great slaughter, till they were consumed, that the rest which remained of them entered into fenced cities. ²¹And all the people returned to the camp to Joshua at Makkedah in peace: none moved his tongue against any of the children of Israel. ²²Then said Joshua, Open the mouth of the cave, and bring out those five kings to me out of the cave. ²³And they did so, and brought forth those five kings to him out of the cave, the king of Jerusalem, the king of Hebron, the king of Jarmuth, the king of Lachish, and the king of Eglon. ²⁴And it came to pass, when they brought out those kings to Joshua, that Joshua called for all the men of Israel, and said to the captains of the men of war which went with him, Come near, put your feet on the necks of these kings. And they came near, and put their feet on the necks of them. ²⁵And Joshua said to them, Fear not, nor be dismayed, be strong and of good courage: for thus shall the LORD do to all your enemies against whom you fight. ²⁶And afterward Joshua smote them, and slew them, and hanged them on five trees: and they were hanging on the trees until the evening. ²⁷And it came to pass at the time of the going down of the sun, that Joshua commanded, and they took them down off the trees, and cast them into the cave wherein they had been hid, and laid great stones in the cave's mouth, which remain until this very day. ²⁸And that day Joshua took Makkedah, and smote it with the edge of the sword, and the king thereof he utterly destroyed, them, and all the souls that were therein; he let none remain: and he did to the king of Makkedah as he did to the king of Jericho. ²⁹Then Joshua passed from Makkedah, and all Israel with him, to Libnah, and fought against Libnah: ³⁰And the LORD delivered it also, and the king thereof, into the hand of Israel; and he smote it with the edge of the sword, and all the souls that were therein; he let none remain in it; but did to the king thereof as he did to the king of Jericho. ³¹And Joshua passed from Libnah, and all Israel with him, to Lachish, and encamped against it, and fought against it: ³²And the LORD delivered Lachish into the hand of Israel, which took it on the second day, and smote it with the edge of the sword, and

all the souls that were therein, according to all that he had done to Libnah. ³³Then Horam king of Gezer came up to help Lachish; and Joshua smote him and his people, until he had left him none remaining. ³⁴And from Lachish Joshua passed to Eglon, and all Israel with him; and they encamped against it, and fought against it: ³⁵And they took it on that day, and smote it with the edge of the sword, and all the souls that were therein he utterly destroyed that day, according to all that he had done to Lachish. ³⁶And Joshua went up from Eglon, and all Israel with him, to Hebron; and they fought against it: ³⁷And they took it, and smote it with the edge of the sword, and the king thereof, and all the cities thereof, and all the souls that were therein; he left none remaining, according to all that he had done to Eglon; but destroyed it utterly, and all the souls that were therein. ³⁸And Joshua returned, and all Israel with him, to Debir; and fought against it: ³⁹And he took it, and the king thereof, and all the cities thereof; and they smote them with the edge of the sword, and utterly destroyed all the souls that were therein; he left none remaining: as he had done to Hebron, so he did to Debir, and to the king thereof; as he had done also to Libnah, and to her king. ⁴⁰So Joshua smote all the country of the hills, and of the south, and of the vale, and of the springs, and all their kings: he left none remaining, but utterly destroyed all that breathed, as the LORD God of Israel commanded. ⁴¹And Joshua smote them from Kadeshbarnea even to Gaza, and all the country of Goshen, even to Gibeon. ⁴²And all these kings and their land did Joshua take at one time, because the LORD God of Israel fought for Israel. ⁴³And Joshua returned, and all Israel with him, to the camp to Gilgal.

11

¹And it came to pass, when Jabin king of Hazor had heard those things, that he sent to Jobab king of Madon, and to the king of Shimron, and to the king of Achshaph, ²And to the kings that were on the north of the mountains, and of the plains south of Chinneroth, and in the valley, and in the borders of Dor on the west, ³And to the Canaanite on the east and on the west, and to the Amorite, and the Hittite, and the Perizzite, and the Jebusite in the mountains, and to the Hivite under Hermon in the land of Mizpeh. ⁴And they went out, they and all their hosts with them, much people, even as the sand that is on the sea shore in multitude, with horses and chariots very many. ⁵And when all these kings were met together, they came and pitched together at the waters of Merom, to fight against Israel. ⁶And the LORD said to Joshua, Be not afraid because of them: for to morrow about this time will I deliver them up all slain before Israel: you shall hamstring their horses, and burn their chariots with fire. ⁷So Joshua came, and all the people of war with him, against them by the waters of Merom suddenly; and they fell on them. ⁸And the LORD delivered them into the hand of Israel, who smote them, and chased them to great Zidon, and to Misrephothmaim, and to the valley of Mizpeh eastward; and they smote them, until they left them none remaining. ⁹And Joshua did to them as the LORD bade him: he hamstrung their horses, and burnt their chariots with fire. ¹⁰And Joshua at that time turned back, and took Hazor, and smote the king thereof with the sword: for Hazor beforetime was the head of all those kingdoms. ¹¹And they smote all the souls that were therein with the edge of the sword, utterly destroying them: there was not any left to breathe: and he burnt Hazor with fire. ¹²And all the cities of those kings, and all the kings of them, did Joshua take, and smote them with the edge of the sword, and he utterly destroyed them, as Moses the servant of the LORD commanded. ¹³But as for the cities that stood still in their strength, Israel burned none of them, save Hazor only; that did Joshua burn. ¹⁴And all the spoil of these cities, and the cattle, the children of Israel took for a prey to themselves; but every man they smote with the edge of the sword, until they had destroyed them, neither left they any to breathe. ¹⁵As the LORD commanded Moses his servant, so did Moses command Joshua, and so did Joshua; he left nothing undone of all that the LORD commanded Moses. ¹⁶So Joshua took all that land, the hills, and all the south country, and all the land of Goshen, and the valley, and the plain, and the mountain of Israel, and the valley of the same; ¹⁷Even from the mount Halak, that goes up to Seir, even to Baalgad in the valley of Lebanon under mount Hermon: and all their kings he took, and smote them, and slew them. ¹⁸Joshua made war a long time with all those kings. ¹⁹There was not a city that made peace with the children of Israel, save the Hivites the inhabitants of Gibeon: all other they took in battle. ²⁰For it was of the LORD to harden their hearts, that they should come against Israel in battle, that he might destroy them utterly, and that they might have no favor, but that he might destroy them, as the LORD commanded Moses. ²¹And at that time came Joshua, and cut off the Anakims from the mountains, from Hebron, from Debir, from Anab, and from all the mountains of Judah, and from all the mountains of Israel: Joshua destroyed them utterly with their cities. ²²There was none of the Anakims left in the land of the children of Israel: only in Gaza, in Gath, and in Ashdod, there remained. ²³So Joshua took the whole land, according to all that the LORD said to Moses; and Joshua gave it for an inheritance to Israel according to their divisions by their tribes. And the land rested from war.

12

¹Now these are the kings of the land, which the children of Israel smote, and possessed their land on the other side Jordan toward the rising of the sun, from the river Arnon to mount Hermon, and all the plain on the east: ²Sihon king of the Amorites, who dwelled in Heshbon, and ruled from Aroer, which is on the bank of the river Arnon, and from the middle of the river, and from half Gilead, even to the river Jabbok, which is the border of the children of Ammon; ³And from the plain to the sea of Chinneroth on the east, and to the sea of the plain, even the salt sea on the east, the way to Bethjeshimoth; and from the south, under Ashdothpisgah: ⁴And the coast of Og king of Bashan, which was of the remnant of the giants, that dwelled at Ashtaroth and at Edrei, ⁵And reigned in mount Hermon, and in Salcah, and in all Bashan, to the border of the Geshurites and the Maachathites, and half Gilead, the border of Sihon king of Heshbon. ⁶Them did Moses the servant of the LORD and the children of Israel smite: and Moses the servant of the LORD gave it for a possession to the Reubenites, and the Gadites, and the half tribe of Manasseh. ⁷And these are the kings of the country which Joshua and the children of Israel smote on this side Jordan on the west, from Baalgad in the valley of Lebanon even to the mount Halak, that goes up to Seir;

which Joshua gave to the tribes of Israel for a possession according to their divisions; ⁸In the mountains, and in the valleys, and in the plains, and in the springs, and in the wilderness, and in the south country; the Hittites, the Amorites, and the Canaanites, the Perizzites, the Hivites, and the Jebusites: ⁹The king of Jericho, one; the king of Ai, which is beside Bethel, one; ¹⁰The king of Jerusalem, one; the king of Hebron, one; ¹¹The king of Jarmuth, one; the king of Lachish, one; ¹²The king of Eglon, one; the king of Gezer, one; ¹³The king of Debir, one; the king of Geder, one; ¹⁴The king of Hormah, one; the king of Arad, one; ¹⁵The king of Libnah, one; the king of Adullam, one; ¹⁶The king of Makkedah, one; the king of Bethel, one; ¹⁷The king of Tappuah, one; the king of Hepher, one; ¹⁸The king of Aphek, one; the king of Lasharon, one; ¹⁹The king of Madon, one; the king of Hazor, one; ²⁰The king of Shimronmeron, one; the king of Achshaph, one; ²¹The king of Taanach, one; the king of Megiddo, one; ²²The king of Kedesh, one; the king of Jokneam of Carmel, one; ²³The king of Dor in the coast of Dor, one; the king of the nations of Gilgal, one; ²⁴The king of Tirzah, one: all the kings thirty and one.

13 ¹Now Joshua was old and stricken in years; and the LORD said to him, You are old and stricken in years, and there remains yet very much land to be possessed. ²This is the land that yet remains: all the borders of the Philistines, and all Geshuri, ³From Sihor, which is before Egypt, even to the borders of Ekron northward, which is counted to the Canaanite: five lords of the Philistines; the Gazathites, and the Ashdothites, the Eshkalonites, the Gittites, and the Ekronites; also the Avites: ⁴From the south, all the land of the Canaanites, and Mearah that is beside the Sidonians to Aphek, to the borders of the Amorites: ⁵And the land of the Giblites, and all Lebanon, toward the sun rise, from Baalgad under mount Hermon to the entering into Hamath. ⁶All the inhabitants of the hill country from Lebanon to Misrephothmaim, and all the Sidonians, them will I drive out from before the children of Israel: only divide you it by lot to the Israelites for an inheritance, as I have commanded you. ⁷Now therefore divide this land for an inheritance to the nine tribes, and the half tribe of Manasseh, ⁸With whom the Reubenites and the Gadites have received their inheritance, which Moses gave them, beyond Jordan eastward, even as Moses the servant of the LORD gave them; ⁹From Aroer, that is on the bank of the river Arnon, and the city that is in the middle of the river, and all the plain of Medeba to Dibon; ¹⁰And all the cities of Sihon king of the Amorites, which reigned in Heshbon, to the border of the children of Ammon; ¹¹And Gilead, and the border of the Geshurites and Maachathites, and all mount Hermon, and all Bashan to Salcah; ¹²All the kingdom of Og in Bashan, which reigned in Ashtaroth and in Edrei, who remained of the remnant of the giants: for these did Moses smite, and cast them out. ¹³Nevertheless the children of Israel expelled not the Geshurites, nor the Maachathites: but the Geshurites and the Maachathites dwell among the Israelites until this day. ¹⁴Only to the tribes of Levi he gave none inheritance; the sacrifices of the LORD God of Israel made by fire are their inheritance, as he said to them. ¹⁵And Moses gave to the tribe of the children of Reuben inheritance according to their families. ¹⁶And their coast was from Aroer, that is on the bank of the river Arnon, and the city that is in the middle of the river, and all the plain by Medeba; ¹⁷Heshbon, and all her cities that are in the plain; Dibon, and Bamothbaal, and Bethbaalmeon, ¹⁸And Jahaza, and Kedemoth, and Mephaath, ¹⁹And Kirjathaim, and Sibmah, and Zarethshahar in the mount of the valley, ²⁰And Bethpeor, and Ashdothpisgah, and Bethjeshimoth, ²¹And all the cities of the plain, and all the kingdom of Sihon king of the Amorites, which reigned in Heshbon, whom Moses smote with the princes of Midian, Evi, and Rekem, and Zur, and Hur, and Reba, which were dukes of Sihon, dwelling in the country. ²²Balaam also the son of Beor, the soothsayer, did the children of Israel slay with the sword among them that were slain by them. ²³And the border of the children of Reuben was Jordan, and the border thereof. This was the inheritance of the children of Reuben after their families, the cities and the villages thereof. ²⁴And Moses gave inheritance to the tribe of Gad, even to the children of Gad according to their families. ²⁵And their coast was Jazer, and all the cities of Gilead, and half the land of the children of Ammon, to Aroer that is before Rabbah; ²⁶And from Heshbon to Ramathmizpeh, and Betonim; and from Mahanaim to the border of Debir; ²⁷And in the valley, Betharam, and Bethnimrah, and Succoth, and Zaphon, the rest of the kingdom of Sihon king of Heshbon, Jordan and his border, even to the edge of the sea of Chinnereth on the other side Jordan eastward. ²⁸This is the inheritance of the children of Gad after their families, the cities, and their villages. ²⁹And Moses gave inheritance to the half tribe of Manasseh: and this was the possession of the half tribe of the children of Manasseh by their families. ³⁰And their coast was from Mahanaim, all Bashan, all the kingdom of Og king of Bashan, and all the towns of Jair, which are in Bashan, three score cities: ³¹And half Gilead, and Ashtaroth, and Edrei, cities of the kingdom of Og in Bashan, were pertaining to the children of Machir the son of Manasseh, even to the one half of the children of Machir by their families. ³²These are the countries which Moses did distribute for inheritance in the plains of Moab, on the other side Jordan, by Jericho, eastward. ³³But to the tribe of Levi Moses gave not any inheritance: the LORD God of Israel was their inheritance, as he said to them.

14 ¹And these are the countries which the children of Israel inherited in the land of Canaan, which Eleazar the priest, and Joshua the son of Nun, and the heads of the fathers of the tribes of the children of Israel, distributed for inheritance to them. ²By lot was their inheritance, as the LORD commanded by the hand of Moses, for the nine tribes, and for the half tribe. ³For Moses had given the inheritance of two tribes and an half tribe on the other side Jordan: but to the Levites he gave none inheritance among them. ⁴For the children of Joseph were two tribes, Manasseh and Ephraim: therefore they gave no part to the Levites in the land, save cities to dwell in, with their suburbs for their cattle and for their substance. ⁵As the LORD commanded Moses, so the children of Israel did, and they divided the land. ⁶Then the children of Judah came to Joshua in Gilgal: and Caleb the son of Jephunneh the Kenezite said to him, You know the thing that the LORD said to Moses the man of God concerning me and you in Kadeshbarnea. ⁷Forty years old was I when Moses the servant of the LORD sent me from Kadeshbarnea to espy out the land; and I brought him word again as it was in my heart. ⁸Nevertheless my brothers that went up with me made the heart of the people melt: but I wholly followed the LORD my God. ⁹And Moses swore on that day, saying, Surely the land where on your feet have trodden shall be your inheritance, and your children's for ever, because you have wholly followed the LORD my God. ¹⁰And now, behold, the LORD has kept me alive, as he said, these forty and five years, even since the LORD spoke this word to Moses, while the children of Israel wandered in the wilderness: and now, see, I am this day fourscore and five years old. ¹¹As yet I am as strong this day as I was in the day that Moses sent me: as my strength was then, even so is my strength now, for war, both to go out, and to come in. ¹²Now therefore give me this mountain, whereof the LORD spoke in that day; for you heard in that day how the Anakims were there, and that the cities were great and fenced: if so be the LORD will be with me, then I shall be able to drive them out, as the LORD said. ¹³And Joshua blessed him, and gave to Caleb the son of Jephunneh Hebron for an inheritance. ¹⁴Hebron therefore became the inheritance of Caleb the son of Jephunneh the Kenezite to this day, because that he wholly followed the LORD God of Israel. ¹⁵And the name of Hebron before was Kirjatharba; which Arba was a great man among the Anakims. And the land had rest from war.

15 ¹This then was the lot of the tribe of the children of Judah by their families; even to the border of Edom the wilderness of Zin southward was the uttermost part of the south coast. ²And their south border was from the shore of the salt sea, from the bay that looks southward: ³And it went out to the south side to Maalehacrabbim, and passed along to Zin, and ascended up on the south side to Kadeshbarnea, and passed along to Hezron, and went up to Adar, and fetched a compass to Karkaa: ⁴From there it passed toward Azmon, and went out to the river of Egypt; and the goings out of that coast were at the sea: this shall be your south coast. ⁵And the east border was the salt sea, even to the end of Jordan. And their border in the north quarter was from the bay of the sea at the uttermost part of Jordan: ⁶And the border went up to Bethhogla, and passed along by the north of Betharabah; and the border went up to the stone of Bohan the son of Reuben: ⁷And the border went up toward Debir from the valley of Achor, and so northward, looking toward Gilgal, that is before the going up to Adummim, which is on the south side of the river: and the border passed toward the waters of Enshemesh, and the goings out thereof were at Enrogel: ⁸And the border went up by the valley of the son of Hinnom to the south side of the Jebusite; the same is Jerusalem: and the border went up to the top of the mountain that lies before the valley of Hinnom westward, which is at the end of the valley of the giants northward: ⁹And the border was drawn from the top of the hill to the fountain of the water of Nephtoah, and went out to the cities of mount Ephron; and the border was drawn to Baalah, which is Kirjathjearim: ¹⁰And the border compassed from Baalah westward to mount Seir, and passed along to the side of mount Jearim, which is Chesalon, on the north side, and went down to Bethshemesh, and passed on to Timnah: ¹¹And the border went out to the side of Ekron northward: and the border was drawn to Shicron, and passed along to mount Baalah, and went out to Jabneel; and the goings out of the border were at the sea. ¹²And the west border was to the great sea, and the coast thereof. This is the coast of the children of Judah round about according to their families. ¹³And to Caleb the son of Jephunneh he gave a part among the children of Judah, according to the commandment of the LORD to Joshua, even the city of Arba the father of Anak, which city is Hebron. ¹⁴And Caleb drove there the three sons of Anak, Sheshai, and Ahiman, and Talmai, the children of Anak. ¹⁵And he went up there to the inhabitants of Debir: and the name of Debir before was Kirjathsepher. ¹⁶And Caleb said, He that smites Kirjathsepher, and takes it, to him will I give Achsah my daughter to wife. ¹⁷And Othniel the son of Kenaz, the brother of Caleb, took it: and he gave him Achsah his daughter to wife. ¹⁸And it came to pass, as she came to him, that she moved him to ask of her father a field: and she lighted off her ass; and Caleb said to her, What would you? ¹⁹Who answered, Give me a blessing; for you have given me a south land; give me also springs of water. And he gave her the upper springs, and the nether springs. ²⁰This is the inheritance of the tribe of the children of Judah according to their families. ²¹And the uttermost cities of the tribe of the children of Judah toward the coast of Edom southward were Kabzeel, and Eder, and Jagur, ²²And Kinah, and Dimonah, and Adadah, ²³And Kedesh, and Hazor, and Ithnan, ²⁴Ziph, and Telem, and Bealoth, ²⁵And Hazor, Hadattah, and Kerioth, and Hezron, which is Hazor, ²⁶Amam, and Shema, and Moladah, ²⁷And Hazargaddah, and Heshmon, and Bethpalet, ²⁸And Hazarshual, and Beersheba, and Bizjothjah, ²⁹Baalah, and Iim, and Azem, ³⁰And Eltolad, and Chesil, and Hormah, ³¹And Ziklag, and Madmannah, and Sansannah, ³²And Lebaoth, and Shilhim, and Ain, and Rimmon: all the cities are twenty and nine, with their villages: ³³And in the valley, Eshtaol, and Zoreah, and Ashnah, ³⁴And Zanoah, and Engannim, Tappuah, and Enam, ³⁵Jarmuth, and Adullam, Socoh, and Azekah, ³⁶And Sharaim, and Adithaim, and Gederah, and Gederothaim; fourteen cities with their villages: ³⁷Zenan, and Hadashah, and Migdalgad, ³⁸And Dilean, and Mizpeh, and Joktheel, ³⁹Lachish, and Bozkath, and Eglon, ⁴⁰And Cabbon, and Lahmam, and Kithlish, ⁴¹And Gederoth, Bethdagon, and Naamah, and Makkedah; sixteen cities with their villages: ⁴²Libnah, and Ether, and Ashan, ⁴³And Jiphtah, and Ashnah, and Nezib, ⁴⁴And Keilah, and Achzib, and Mareshah; nine cities with their villages: ⁴⁵Ekron, with her towns and her villages: ⁴⁶From Ekron even to the sea, all that lay near Ashdod, with their villages: ⁴⁷Ashdod with her towns and her villages, Gaza with her towns and her villages, to the river of Egypt, and the great sea, and the border thereof: ⁴⁸And in the mountains, Shamir, and Jattir, and Socoh, ⁴⁹And Dannah, and Kirjathsannah, which is Debir, ⁵⁰And Anab, and Eshtemoh, and Anim, ⁵¹And Goshen, and Holon, and Giloh; eleven cities with their villages: ⁵²Arab, and Dumah, and Eshean, ⁵³And Janum, and Bethtappuah, and Aphekah, ⁵⁴And Humtah, and Kirjatharba, which is Hebron, and Zior; nine cities with their villages: ⁵⁵Maon, Carmel, and Ziph, and Juttah, ⁵⁶And Jezreel, and Jokdeam, and Zanoah, ⁵⁷Cain, Gibeah, and Timnah; ten cities with their villages: ⁵⁸Halhul, Bethzur, and Gedor, ⁵⁹And

Maarath, and Bethanoth, and Eltekon; six cities with their villages: ⁶⁰Kirjathbaal, which is Kirjathjearim, and Rabbah; two cities with their villages: ⁶¹In the wilderness, Betharabah, Middin, and Secacah, ⁶²And Nibshan, and the city of Salt, and Engedi; six cities with their villages. ⁶³As for the Jebusites the inhabitants of Jerusalem, the children of Judah could not drive them out; but the Jebusites dwell with the children of Judah at Jerusalem to this day.

16

¹And the lot of the children of Joseph fell from Jordan by Jericho, to the water of Jericho on the east, to the wilderness that goes up from Jericho throughout mount Bethel, ²And goes out from Bethel to Luz, and passes along to the borders of Archi to Ataroth, ³And goes down westward to the coast of Japhleti, to the coast of Bethhoron the nether, and to Gezer; and the goings out thereof are at the sea. ⁴So the children of Joseph, Manasseh and Ephraim, took their inheritance. ⁵And the border of the children of Ephraim according to their families was thus: even the border of their inheritance on the east side was Atarothaddar, to Bethhoron the upper; ⁶And the border went out toward the sea to Michmethah on the north side; and the border went about eastward to Taanathshiloh, and passed by it on the east to Janohah; ⁷And it went down from Janohah to Ataroth, and to Naarath, and came to Jericho, and went out at Jordan. ⁸The border went out from Tappuah westward to the river Kanah; and the goings out thereof were at the sea. This is the inheritance of the tribe of the children of Ephraim by their families. ⁹And the separate cities for the children of Ephraim were among the inheritance of the children of Manasseh, all the cities with their villages. ¹⁰And they drove not out the Canaanites that dwelled in Gezer: but the Canaanites dwell among the Ephraimites to this day, and serve under tribute.

17

¹There was also a lot for the tribe of Manasseh; for he was the firstborn of Joseph; to wit, for Machir the firstborn of Manasseh, the father of Gilead: because he was a man of war, therefore he had Gilead and Bashan. ²There was also a lot for the rest of the children of Manasseh by their families; for the children of Abiezer, and for the children of Helek, and for the children of Asriel, and for the children of Shechem, and for the children of Hepher, and for the children of Shemida: these were the male children of Manasseh the son of Joseph by their families. ³But Zelophehad, the son of Hepher, the son of Gilead, the son of Machir, the son of Manasseh, had no sons, but daughters: and these are the names of his daughters, Mahlah, and Noah, Hoglah, Milcah, and Tirzah. ⁴And they came near before Eleazar the priest, and before Joshua the son of Nun, and before the princes, saying, The LORD commanded Moses to give us an inheritance among our brothers. Therefore according to the commandment of the LORD he gave them an inheritance among the brothers of their father. ⁵And there fell ten portions to Manasseh, beside the land of Gilead and Bashan, which were on the other side Jordan; ⁶Because the daughters of Manasseh had an inheritance among his sons: and the rest of Manasseh's sons had the land of Gilead. ⁷And the coast of Manasseh was from Asher to Michmethah, that lies before Shechem; and the border went along on the right hand to the inhabitants of Entappuah. ⁸Now Manasseh had the land of Tappuah: but Tappuah on the border of Manasseh belonged to the children of Ephraim; ⁹And the coast descended to the river Kanah, southward of the river: these cities of Ephraim are among the cities of Manasseh: the coast of Manasseh also was on the north side of the river, and the outgoings of it were at the sea: ¹⁰Southward it was Ephraim's, and northward it was Manasseh's, and the sea is his border; and they met together in Asher on the north, and in Issachar on the east. ¹¹And Manasseh had in Issachar and in Asher Bethshean and her towns, and Ibleam and her towns, and the inhabitants of Dor and her towns, and the inhabitants of Endor and her towns, and the inhabitants of Taanach and her towns, and the inhabitants of Megiddo and her towns, even three countries. ¹²Yet the children of Manasseh could not drive out the inhabitants of those cities; but the Canaanites would dwell in that land. ¹³Yet it came to pass, when the children of Israel were waxen strong, that they put the Canaanites to tribute, but did not utterly drive them out. ¹⁴And the children of Joseph spoke to Joshua, saying, Why have you given me but one lot and one portion to inherit, seeing I am a great people, for as much as the LORD has blessed me till now? ¹⁵And Joshua answered them, If you be a great people, then get you up to the wood country, and cut down for yourself there in the land of the Perizzites and of the giants, if mount Ephraim be too narrow for you. ¹⁶And the children of Joseph said, The hill is not enough for us: and all the Canaanites that dwell in the land of the valley have chariots of iron, both they who are of Bethshean and her towns, and they who are of the valley of Jezreel. ¹⁷And Joshua spoke to the house of Joseph, even to Ephraim and to Manasseh, saying, You are a great people, and have great power: you shall not have one lot only: ¹⁸But the mountain shall be yours; for it is a wood, and you shall cut it down: and the outgoings of it shall be yours: for you shall drive out the Canaanites, though they have iron chariots, and though they be strong.

18

¹And the whole congregation of the children of Israel assembled together at Shiloh, and set up the tabernacle of the congregation there. And the land was subdued before them. ²And there remained among the children of Israel seven tribes, which had not yet received their inheritance. ³And Joshua said to the children of Israel, How long are you slack to go to possess the land, which the LORD God of your fathers has given you? ⁴Give out from among you three men for each tribe: and I will send them, and they shall rise, and go through the land, and describe it according to the inheritance of them; and they shall come again to me. ⁵And they shall divide it into seven parts: Judah shall abide in their coast on the south, and the house of Joseph shall abide in their coasts on the north. ⁶You shall therefore describe the land into seven parts, and bring the description here to me, that I may cast lots for you here before the LORD our God. ⁷But the Levites have no part among you; for the priesthood of the LORD is their inheritance: and Gad, and Reuben, and half the tribe of Manasseh, have received their inheritance beyond Jordan on the east, which Moses the servant of the LORD gave them. ⁸And the men arose, and went away: and Joshua charged them that went to describe the land, saying, Go and walk through the land, and describe it, and come again to me, that

I may here cast lots for you before the LORD in Shiloh. ⁹And the men went and passed through the land, and described it by cities into seven parts in a book, and came again to Joshua to the host at Shiloh. ¹⁰And Joshua cast lots for them in Shiloh before the LORD: and there Joshua divided the land to the children of Israel according to their divisions. ¹¹And the lot of the tribe of the children of Benjamin came up according to their families: and the coast of their lot came forth between the children of Judah and the children of Joseph. ¹²And their border on the north side was from Jordan; and the border went up to the side of Jericho on the north side, and went up through the mountains westward; and the goings out thereof were at the wilderness of Bethaven. ¹³And the border went over from there toward Luz, to the side of Luz, which is Bethel, southward; and the border descended to Atarothadar, near the hill that lies on the south side of the nether Bethhoron. ¹⁴And the border was drawn there, and compassed the corner of the sea southward, from the hill that lies before Bethhoron southward; and the goings out thereof were at Kirjathbaal, which is Kirjathjearim, a city of the children of Judah: this was the west quarter. ¹⁵And the south quarter was from the end of Kirjathjearim, and the border went out on the west, and went out to the well of waters of Nephtoah: ¹⁶And the border came down to the end of the mountain that lies before the valley of the son of Hinnom, and which is in the valley of the giants on the north, and descended to the valley of Hinnom, to the side of Jebusi on the south, and descended to Enrogel, ¹⁷And was drawn from the north, and went forth to Enshemesh, and went forth toward Geliloth, which is over against the going up of Adummim, and descended to the stone of Bohan the son of Reuben, ¹⁸And passed along toward the side over against Arabah northward, and went down to Arabah: ¹⁹And the border passed along to the side of Bethhoglah northward: and the outgoings of the border were at the north bay of the salt sea at the south end of Jordan: this was the south coast. ²⁰And Jordan was the border of it on the east side. This was the inheritance of the children of Benjamin, by the coasts thereof round about, according to their families. ²¹Now the cities of the tribe of the children of Benjamin according to their families were Jericho, and Bethhoglah, and the valley of Keziz, ²²And Betharabah, and Zemaraim, and Bethel, ²³And Avim, and Pharah, and Ophrah, ²⁴And Chepharhaammonai, and Ophni, and Gaba; twelve cities with their villages: ²⁵Gibeon, and Ramah, and Beeroth, ²⁶And Mizpeh, and Chephirah, and Mozah, ²⁷And Rekem, and Irpeel, and Taralah, ²⁸And Zelah, Eleph, and Jebusi, which is Jerusalem, Gibeath, and Kirjath; fourteen cities with their villages. This is the inheritance of the children of Benjamin according to their families.

19

¹And the second lot came forth to Simeon, even for the tribe of the children of Simeon according to their families: and their inheritance was within the inheritance of the children of Judah. ²And they had in their inheritance Beersheba, and Sheba, and Moladah, ³And Hazarshual, and Balah, and Azem, ⁴And Eltolad, and Bethul, and Hormah, ⁵And Ziklag, and Bethmarcaboth, and Hazarsusah, ⁶And Bethlebaoth, and Sharuhen; thirteen cities and their villages: ⁷Ain, Remmon, and Ether, and Ashan; four cities and their villages: ⁸And all the villages that were round about these cities to Baalathbeer, Ramath of the south. This is the inheritance of the tribe of the children of Simeon according to their families. ⁹Out of the portion of the children of Judah was the inheritance of the children of Simeon: for the part of the children of Judah was too much for them: therefore the children of Simeon had their inheritance within the inheritance of them. ¹⁰And the third lot came up for the children of Zebulun according to their families: and the border of their inheritance was to Sarid: ¹¹And their border went up toward the sea, and Maralah, and reached to Dabbasheth, and reached to the river that is before Jokneam; ¹²And turned from Sarid eastward toward the sun rise to the border of Chislothtabor, and then goes out to Daberath, and goes up to Japhia, ¹³And from there passes on along on the east to Gittahhepher, to Ittahkazin, and goes out to Remmonmethoar to Neah; ¹⁴And the border compasses it on the north side to Hannathon: and the outgoings thereof are in the valley of Jiphthahel: ¹⁵And Kattath, and Nahallal, and Shimron, and Idalah, and Bethlehem: twelve cities with their villages. ¹⁶This is the inheritance of the children of Zebulun according to their families, these cities with their villages. ¹⁷And the fourth lot came out to Issachar, for the children of Issachar according to their families. ¹⁸And their border was toward Jezreel, and Chesulloth, and Shunem, ¹⁹And Haphraim, and Shihon, and Anaharath, ²⁰And Rabbith, and Kishion, and Abez, ²¹And Remeth, and Engannim, and Enhaddah, and Bethpazzez; ²²And the coast reaches to Tabor, and Shahazimah, and Bethshemesh; and the outgoings of their border were at Jordan: sixteen cities with their villages. ²³This is the inheritance of the tribe of the children of Issachar according to their families, the cities and their villages. ²⁴And the fifth lot came out for the tribe of the children of Asher according to their families. ²⁵And their border was Helkath, and Hali, and Beten, and Achshaph, ²⁶And Alammelech, and Amad, and Misheal; and reaches to Carmel westward, and to Shihorlibnath; ²⁷And turns toward the sun rise to Bethdagon, and reaches to Zebulun, and to the valley of Jiphthahel toward the north side of Bethemek, and Neiel, and goes out to Cabul on the left hand, ²⁸And Hebron, and Rehob, and Hammon, and Kanah, even to great Zidon; ²⁹And then the coast turns to Ramah, and to the strong city Tyre; and the coast turns to Hosah; and the outgoings thereof are at the sea from the coast to Achzib: ³⁰Ummah also, and Aphek, and Rehob: twenty and two cities with their villages. ³¹This is the inheritance of the tribe of the children of Asher according to their families, these cities with their villages. ³²The sixth lot came out to the children of Naphtali, even for the children of Naphtali according to their families. ³³And their coast was from Heleph, from Allon to Zaanannim, and Adami, Nekeb, and Jabneel, to Lakum; and the outgoings thereof were at Jordan: ³⁴And then the coast turns westward to Aznothtabor, and goes out from there to Hukkok, and reaches to Zebulun on the south side, and reaches to Asher on the west side, and to Judah on Jordan toward the sun rise. ³⁵And the fenced cities are Ziddim, Zer, and Hammath, Rakkath, and Chinnereth, ³⁶And Adamah, and Ramah, and Hazor, ³⁷And Kedesh, and Edrei, and Enhazor, ³⁸And Iron, and Migdalel, Horem, and Bethanath, and Bethshemesh; nineteen cities with their villages. ³⁹This is the inheritance of the tribe of the

children of Naphtali according to their families, the cities and their villages. ⁴⁰And the seventh lot came out for the tribe of the children of Dan according to their families. ⁴¹And the coast of their inheritance was Zorah, and Eshtaol, and Irshemesh, ⁴²And Shaalabbin, and Ajalon, and Jethlah, ⁴³And Elon, and Thimnathah, and Ekron, ⁴⁴And Eltekeh, and Gibbethon, and Baalath, ⁴⁵And Jehud, and Beneberak, and Gathrimmon, ⁴⁶And Mejarkon, and Rakkon, with the border before Japho. ⁴⁷And the coast of the children of Dan went out too little for them: therefore the children of Dan went up to fight against Leshem, and took it, and smote it with the edge of the sword, and possessed it, and dwelled therein, and called Leshem, Dan, after the name of Dan their father. ⁴⁸This is the inheritance of the tribe of the children of Dan according to their families, these cities with their villages. ⁴⁹When they had made an end of dividing the land for inheritance by their coasts, the children of Israel gave an inheritance to Joshua the son of Nun among them: ⁵⁰According to the word of the LORD they gave him the city which he asked, even Timnathserah in mount Ephraim: and he built the city, and dwelled therein. ⁵¹These are the inheritances, which Eleazar the priest, and Joshua the son of Nun, and the heads of the fathers of the tribes of the children of Israel, divided for an inheritance by lot in Shiloh before the LORD, at the door of the tabernacle of the congregation. So they made an end of dividing the country.

20 ¹The LORD also spoke to Joshua, saying, ²Speak to the children of Israel, saying, Appoint out for you cities of refuge, whereof I spoke to you by the hand of Moses: ³That the slayer that kills any person unawares and unwittingly may flee thither: and they shall be your refuge from the avenger of blood. ⁴And when he that does flee to one of those cities shall stand at the entering of the gate of the city, and shall declare his cause in the ears of the elders of that city, they shall take him into the city to them, and give him a place, that he may dwell among them. ⁵And if the avenger of blood pursue after him, then they shall not deliver the slayer up into his hand; because he smote his neighbor unwittingly, and hated him not beforetime. ⁶And he shall dwell in that city, until he stand before the congregation for judgment, and until the death of the high priest that shall be in those days: then shall the slayer return, and come to his own city, and to his own house, to the city from from where he fled. ⁷And they appointed Kedesh in Galilee in mount Naphtali, and Shechem in mount Ephraim, and Kirjatharba, which is Hebron, in the mountain of Judah. ⁸And on the other side Jordan by Jericho eastward, they assigned Bezer in the wilderness on the plain out of the tribe of Reuben, and Ramoth in Gilead out of the tribe of Gad, and Golan in Bashan out of the tribe of Manasseh. ⁹These were the cities appointed for all the children of Israel, and for the stranger that sojourns among them, that whoever kills any person at unawares might flee thither, and not die by the hand of the avenger of blood, until he stood before the congregation.

21 ¹Then came near the heads of the fathers of the Levites to Eleazar the priest, and to Joshua the son of Nun, and to the heads of the fathers of the tribes of the children of Israel; ²And they spoke to them at Shiloh in the land of Canaan, saying, The LORD commanded by the hand of Moses to give us cities to dwell in, with the suburbs thereof for our cattle. ³And the children of Israel gave to the Levites out of their inheritance, at the commandment of the LORD, these cities and their suburbs. ⁴And the lot came out for the families of the Kohathites: and the children of Aaron the priest, which were of the Levites, had by lot out of the tribe of Judah, and out of the tribe of Simeon, and out of the tribe of Benjamin, thirteen cities. ⁵And the rest of the children of Kohath had by lot out of the families of the tribe of Ephraim, and out of the tribe of Dan, and out of the half tribe of Manasseh, ten cities. ⁶And the children of Gershon had by lot out of the families of the tribe of Issachar, and out of the tribe of Asher, and out of the tribe of Naphtali, and out of the half tribe of Manasseh in Bashan, thirteen cities. ⁷The children of Merari by their families had out of the tribe of Reuben, and out of the tribe of Gad, and out of the tribe of Zebulun, twelve cities. ⁸And the children of Israel gave by lot to the Levites these cities with their suburbs, as the LORD commanded by the hand of Moses. ⁹And they gave out of the tribe of the children of Judah, and out of the tribe of the children of Simeon, these cities which are here mentioned by name. ¹⁰Which the children of Aaron, being of the families of the Kohathites, who were of the children of Levi, had: for theirs was the first lot. ¹¹And they gave them the city of Arba the father of Anak, which city is Hebron, in the hill country of Judah, with the suburbs thereof round about it. ¹²But the fields of the city, and the villages thereof, gave they to Caleb the son of Jephunneh for his possession. ¹³Thus they gave to the children of Aaron the priest Hebron with her suburbs, to be a city of refuge for the slayer; and Libnah with her suburbs, ¹⁴And Jattir with her suburbs, and Eshtemoa with her suburbs, ¹⁵And Holon with her suburbs, and Debir with her suburbs, ¹⁶And Ain with her suburbs, and Juttah with her suburbs, and Bethshemesh with her suburbs; nine cities out of those two tribes. ¹⁷And out of the tribe of Benjamin, Gibeon with her suburbs, Geba with her suburbs, ¹⁸Anathoth with her suburbs, and Almon with her suburbs; four cities. ¹⁹All the cities of the children of Aaron, the priests, were thirteen cities with their suburbs. ²⁰And the families of the children of Kohath, the Levites which remained of the children of Kohath, even they had the cities of their lot out of the tribe of Ephraim. ²¹For they gave them Shechem with her suburbs in mount Ephraim, to be a city of refuge for the slayer; and Gezer with her suburbs, ²²And Kibzaim with her suburbs, and Bethhoron with her suburbs; four cities. ²³And out of the tribe of Dan, Eltekeh with her suburbs, Gibbethon with her suburbs, ²⁴Aijalon with her suburbs, Gathrimmon with her suburbs; four cities. ²⁵And out of the half tribe of Manasseh, Tanach with her suburbs, and Gathrimmon with her suburbs; two cities. ²⁶All the cities were ten with their suburbs for the families of the children of Kohath that remained. ²⁷And to the children of Gershon, of the families of the Levites, out of the other half tribe of Manasseh they gave Golan in Bashan with her suburbs, to be a city of refuge for the slayer; and Beeshterah with her suburbs; two cities. ²⁸And out of the tribe of Issachar, Kishon with her suburbs, Dabareh with her suburbs, ²⁹Jarmuth with her suburbs, Engannim with her suburbs; four cities. ³⁰And out of the tribe of Asher, Mishal with her suburbs, Abdon with her suburbs, ³¹Helkath with her suburbs, and Rehob with her suburbs; four cities. ³²And out of the tribe of Naphtali, Kedesh in Galilee with her suburbs, to be a city of refuge for the slayer; and Hammothdor with her suburbs, and Kartan with her suburbs; three cities. ³³All the cities of the Gershonites according to their families were thirteen cities with their suburbs. ³⁴And to the families of the children of Merari, the rest of the Levites, out of the tribe of Zebulun, Jokneam with her suburbs, and Kartah with her suburbs, ³⁵Dimnah with her suburbs, Nahalal with her suburbs; four cities. ³⁶And out of the tribe of Reuben, Bezer with her suburbs, and Jahazah with her suburbs, ³⁷Kedemoth with her suburbs, and Mephaath with her suburbs; four cities. ³⁸And out of the tribe of Gad, Ramoth in Gilead with her suburbs, to be a city of refuge for the slayer; and Mahanaim with her suburbs, ³⁹Heshbon with her suburbs, Jazer with her suburbs; four cities in all. ⁴⁰So all the cities for the children of Merari by their families, which were remaining of the families of the Levites, were by their lot twelve cities. ⁴¹All the cities of the Levites within the possession of the children of Israel were forty and eight cities with their suburbs. ⁴²These cities were every one with their suburbs round about them: thus were all these cities. ⁴³And the LORD gave to Israel all the land which he swore to give to their fathers; and they possessed it, and dwelled therein. ⁴⁴And the LORD gave them rest round about, according to all that he swore to their fathers: and there stood not a man of all their enemies before them; the LORD delivered all their enemies into their hand. ⁴⁵There failed not anything of any good thing which the LORD had spoken to the house of Israel; all came to pass.

22 ¹Then Joshua called the Reubenites, and the Gadites, and the half tribe of Manasseh, ²And said to them, You have kept all that Moses the servant of the LORD commanded you, and have obeyed my voice in all that I commanded you: ³You have not left your brothers these many days to this day, but have kept the charge of the commandment of the LORD your God. ⁴And now the LORD your God has given rest to your brothers, as he promised them: therefore now return you, and get you to your tents, and to the land of your possession, which Moses the servant of the LORD gave you on the other side Jordan. ⁵But take diligent heed to do the commandment and the law, which Moses the servant of the LORD charged you, to love the LORD your God, and to walk in all his ways, and to keep his commandments, and to hold to him, and to serve him with all your heart and with all your soul. ⁶So Joshua blessed them, and sent them away: and they went to their tents. ⁷Now to the one half of the tribe of Manasseh Moses had given possession in Bashan: but to the other half thereof gave Joshua among their brothers on this side Jordan westward. And when Joshua sent them away also to their tents, then he blessed them, ⁸And he spoke to them, saying, Return with much riches to your tents, and with very much cattle, with silver, and with gold, and with brass, and with iron, and with very much raiment: divide the spoil of your enemies with your brothers. ⁹And the children of Reuben and the children of Gad and the half tribe of Manasseh returned, and departed from the children of Israel out of Shiloh, which is in the land of Canaan, to go to the country of Gilead, to the land of their possession, whereof they were possessed, according to the word of the LORD by the hand of Moses. ¹⁰And when they came to the borders of Jordan, that are in the land of Canaan, the children of Reuben and the children of Gad and the half tribe of Manasseh built there an altar by Jordan, a great altar to see to. ¹¹And the children of Israel heard say, Behold, the children of Reuben and the children of Gad and the half tribe of Manasseh have built an altar over against the land of Canaan, in the borders of Jordan, at the passage of the children of Israel. ¹²And when the children of Israel heard of it, the whole congregation of the children of Israel gathered themselves together at Shiloh, to go up to war against them. ¹³And the children of Israel sent to the children of Reuben, and to the children of Gad, and to the half tribe of Manasseh, into the land of Gilead, Phinehas the son of Eleazar the priest, ¹⁴And with him ten princes, of each chief house a prince throughout all the tribes of Israel; and each one was an head of the house of their fathers among the thousands of Israel. ¹⁵And they came to the children of Reuben, and to the children of Gad, and to the half tribe of Manasseh, to the land of Gilead, and they spoke with them, saying, ¹⁶Thus says the whole congregation of the LORD, What trespass is this that you have committed against the God of Israel, to turn away this day from following the LORD, in that you have built you an altar, that you might rebel this day against the LORD? ¹⁷Is the iniquity of Peor too little for us, from which we are not cleansed until this day, although there was a plague in the congregation of the LORD, ¹⁸But that you must turn away this day from following the LORD? and it will be, seeing you rebel to day against the LORD, that to morrow he will be wroth with the whole congregation of Israel. ¹⁹Notwithstanding, if the land of your possession be unclean, then pass you over to the land of the possession of the LORD, wherein the LORD's tabernacle dwells, and take possession among us: but rebel not against the LORD, nor rebel against us, in building you an altar beside the altar of the LORD our God. ²⁰Did not Achan the son of Zerah commit a trespass in the accursed thing, and wrath fell on all the congregation of Israel? and that man perished not alone in his iniquity. ²¹Then the children of Reuben and the children of Gad and the half tribe of Manasseh answered, and said to the heads of the thousands of Israel, ²²The LORD God of gods, the LORD God of gods, he knows, and Israel he shall know; if it be in rebellion, or if in transgression against the LORD, (save us not this day,) ²³That we have built us an altar to turn from following the LORD, or if to offer thereon burnt offering or meat offering, or if to offer peace offerings thereon, let the LORD himself require it; ²⁴And if we have not rather done it for fear of this thing, saying, In time to come your children might speak to our children, saying, What have you to do with the LORD God of Israel? ²⁵For the LORD has made Jordan a border between us and you, you children of Reuben and children of Gad; you have no part in the LORD: so shall your children make our children cease from fearing the LORD. ²⁶Therefore we said, Let us now prepare to build us an altar, not for burnt offering, nor for sacrifice: ²⁷But that it may be a witness between us, and you, and our generations after us, that we might do the service of the LORD before him with our burnt offerings, and with our sacrifices, and with our peace offerings; that your children may not say to our children in time to come, You have no part in the LORD. ²⁸Therefore said we, that it shall be, when they should so say to us or to our generations in time to come, that we may say again, Behold the pattern of the altar of the LORD, which our fathers made, not for burnt offerings, nor for sacrifices; but it is a witness between us and you. ²⁹God forbid that we should rebel against the LORD, and turn this day from following the LORD, to build an altar for burnt offerings, for meat offerings, or for sacrifices, beside the altar of the LORD our God that is before his tabernacle. ³⁰And when Phinehas the priest, and the princes of the congregation and heads of the thousands of Israel which were with him, heard the words that the children of Reuben and the children of Gad and the children of Manasseh spoke, it pleased them. ³¹And Phinehas the son of Eleazar the priest said to the children of Reuben, and to the children of Gad, and to the children of Manasseh, This day we perceive that the LORD is among us, because you have not committed this trespass against the LORD: now you have delivered the children of Israel out of the hand of the LORD. ³²And Phinehas the son of Eleazar the priest, and the princes, returned from the children of Reuben, and from the children of Gad, out of the land of Gilead, to the land of Canaan, to the children of Israel, and brought them word again. ³³And the thing pleased the children of Israel; and the children of Israel blessed God, and did not intend to go up against them in battle, to destroy the land wherein the children of Reuben and Gad dwelled. ³⁴And the children of Reuben and the children of Gad called the altar Ed: for it shall be a witness between us that the LORD is God.

23 ¹And it came to pass a long time after that the LORD had given rest to Israel from all their enemies round about, that Joshua waxed old and stricken in age. ²And Joshua called for all Israel, and for their elders, and for their heads, and for their judges, and for their officers, and said to them, I am old and stricken in age: ³And you have seen all that the LORD your God has done to all these nations because of you; for the LORD your God is he that has fought for you. ⁴Behold, I have divided to you by lot these nations that remain, to be an inheritance for your tribes, from Jordan, with all the nations that I have cut off, even to the great sea westward. ⁵And the LORD your God, he shall expel them from before you, and drive them from out of your sight; and you shall possess their land, as the LORD your God has promised to you. ⁶Be you therefore very courageous to keep and to do all that is written in the book of the law of Moses, that you turn not aside therefrom to the right hand or to the left; ⁷That you come not among these nations, these that remain among you; neither make mention of the name of their gods, nor cause to swear by them, neither serve them, nor bow yourselves to them: ⁸But hold to the LORD your God, as you have done to this day. ⁹For the LORD has driven out from before you great nations and strong: but as for you, no man has been able to stand before you to this day. ¹⁰One man of you shall chase a thousand: for the LORD your God, he it is that fights for you, as he has promised you. ¹¹Take good heed therefore to yourselves, that you love the LORD your God. ¹²Else if you do in any wise go back, and join to the remnant of these nations, even these that remain among you, and shall make marriages with them, and go in to them, and they to you: ¹³Know for a certainty that the LORD your God will no more drive out any of these nations from before you; but they shall be snares and traps to you, and scourges in your sides, and thorns in your eyes, until you perish from off this good land which the LORD your God has given you. ¹⁴And, behold, this day I am going the way of all the earth: and you know in all your hearts and in all your souls, that not one thing has failed of all the good things which the LORD your God spoke concerning you; all are come to pass to you, and not one thing has failed thereof. ¹⁵Therefore it shall come to pass, that as all good things are come on you, which the LORD your God promised you; so shall the LORD bring on you all evil things, until he have destroyed you from off this good land which the LORD your God has given you. ¹⁶When you have transgressed the covenant of the LORD your God, which he commanded you, and have gone and served other gods, and bowed yourselves to them; then shall the anger of the LORD be kindled against you, and you shall perish quickly from off the good land which he has given to you.

24 ¹And Joshua gathered all the tribes of Israel to Shechem, and called for the elders of Israel, and for their heads, and for their judges, and for their officers; and they presented themselves before God. ²And Joshua said to all the people, Thus says the LORD God of Israel, Your fathers dwelled on the other side of the flood in old time, even Terah, the father of Abraham, and the father of Nachor: and they served other gods. ³And I took your father Abraham from the other side of the flood, and led him throughout all the land of Canaan, and multiplied his seed, and gave him Isaac. ⁴And I gave to Isaac Jacob and Esau: and I gave to Esau mount Seir, to possess it; but Jacob and his children went down into Egypt. ⁵I sent Moses also and Aaron, and I plagued Egypt, according to that which I did among them: and afterward I brought you out. ⁶And I brought your fathers out of Egypt: and you came to the sea; and the Egyptians pursued after your fathers with chariots and horsemen to the Red sea. ⁷And when they cried to the LORD, he put darkness between you and the Egyptians, and brought the sea on them, and covered them; and your eyes have seen what I have done in Egypt: and you dwelled in the wilderness a long season. ⁸And I brought you into the land of the Amorites, which dwelled on the other side Jordan; and they fought with you: and I gave them into your hand, that you might possess their land; and I destroyed them from before you. ⁹Then Balak the son of Zippor, king of Moab, arose and warred against Israel, and sent and called Balaam the son of Beor to curse you: ¹⁰But I would not listen to Balaam; therefore he blessed you still: so I delivered you out of his hand. ¹¹And you went over Jordan, and came to Jericho: and the men of Jericho fought against you, the Amorites, and the Perizzites, and the Canaanites, and the Hittites, and the Girgashites, the Hivites, and the Jebusites; and I delivered them into your hand. ¹²And I sent the hornet before you, which drove them out from before you, even the two kings of the Amorites; but not with your sword, nor with your bow. ¹³And I have given you a land for which you did not labor, and cities which you built not, and you dwell in them; of the vineyards and olive groves which you planted not do you eat. ¹⁴Now therefore fear the LORD, and serve him in sincerity and in truth: and put away the gods which your fathers served on the other side of the flood, and in Egypt; and serve you the LORD. ¹⁵And if it seem evil to you to serve the LORD, choose you this day whom you will serve; whether the gods which your fathers served that were on the other side of the flood, or the gods of the Amorites, in whose land you dwell: but as for me and my house, we will serve the LORD. ¹⁶And the people answered and said, God forbid that we should forsake the LORD, to serve other gods; ¹⁷For the LORD our God, he it is that brought us up and our fathers out of the land of Egypt, from the house of bondage, and which did those great signs in our sight, and preserved us in all the way wherein we went, and among all the people through whom we passed: ¹⁸And the LORD drove out from before us all the people, even the Amorites which dwelled in the land: therefore will we also serve the LORD; for he is our God. ¹⁹And Joshua said to the people, You cannot serve the LORD: for he is an holy God; he is a jealous God; he will not forgive your transgressions nor your sins. ²⁰If you forsake the LORD, and serve strange gods, then he will turn and do you hurt, and consume you, after that he has done you good. ²¹And the people said to Joshua, No; but we will serve the LORD. ²²And Joshua said to the people, You are witnesses against yourselves that you have chosen you the LORD, to serve him. And they said, We are witnesses. ²³Now therefore put away, said he, the strange gods which are among you, and incline your heart to the LORD God of Israel. ²⁴And the people said to Joshua, The LORD our God will we serve, and his voice will we obey. ²⁵So Joshua made a covenant with the people that day, and set them a statute and an ordinance in Shechem. ²⁶And Joshua wrote these words in the book of the law of God, and took a great stone, and set it up there under an oak, that was by the sanctuary of the LORD. ²⁷And Joshua said to all the people, Behold, this stone shall be a witness to us; for it has heard all the words of the LORD which he spoke to us: it shall be therefore a witness to you, lest you deny your God. ²⁸So Joshua let the people depart, every man to his inheritance. ²⁹And it came to pass after these things, that Joshua the son of Nun, the servant of the LORD, died, being an hundred and ten years old. ³⁰And they buried him in the border of his inheritance in Timnathserah, which is in mount Ephraim, on the north side of the hill of Gaash. ³¹And Israel served the LORD all the days of Joshua, and all the days of the elders that outlived Joshua, and which had known all the works of the LORD, that he had done for Israel. ³²And the bones of Joseph, which the children of Israel brought up out of Egypt, buried they in Shechem, in a parcel of ground which Jacob bought of the sons of Hamor the father of Shechem for an hundred pieces of silver: and it became the inheritance of the children of Joseph. ³³And Eleazar the son of Aaron died; and they buried him in a hill that pertained to Phinehas his son, which was given him in mount Ephraim.

Judges

1 ¹Now after the death of Joshua it came to pass, that the children of Israel asked the LORD, saying, Who shall go up for us against the Canaanites first, to fight against them? ²And the LORD said, Judah shall go up: behold, I have delivered the land into his hand. ³And Judah said to Simeon his brother, Come up with me into my lot, that we may fight against the Canaanites; and I likewise will go with you into your lot. So Simeon went with him. ⁴And Judah went up; and the LORD delivered the Canaanites and the Perizzites into their hand: and they slew of them in Bezek ten thousand men. ⁵And they found Adonibezek in Bezek: and they fought against him, and they slew the Canaanites and the Perizzites. ⁶But Adonibezek fled; and they pursued after him, and caught him, and cut off his thumbs and his great toes. ⁷And Adonibezek said, Three score and ten kings, having their thumbs and their great toes cut off, gathered their meat under my table: as I have done, so God has requited me. And they brought him to Jerusalem, and there he died. ⁸Now the children of Judah had fought against Jerusalem, and had taken it, and smitten it with the edge of the sword, and set the city on fire. ⁹And afterward the children of Judah went down to fight against the Canaanites, that dwelled in the mountain, and in the south, and in the valley. ¹⁰And Judah went against the Canaanites that dwelled in Hebron: (now the name of Hebron before was Kirjatharba:) and they slew Sheshai, and Ahiman, and Talmai. ¹¹And from there he went against the inhabitants of Debir: and the name of Debir before was Kirjathsepher: ¹²And Caleb said, He that smites Kirjathsepher, and takes it, to him will I give Achsah my daughter to wife. ¹³And Othniel the son of Kenaz, Caleb's younger brother, took it: and he gave him Achsah his daughter to wife. ¹⁴And it came to pass, when she came to him, that she moved him to ask of her father a field: and she lighted from off her ass; and Caleb said to her, What will you? ¹⁵And she said to him, Give me a blessing: for you have given me a south land; give me also springs of water. And Caleb gave her the upper springs and the nether springs. ¹⁶And the children of the Kenite, Moses' father in law, went up out of the city of palm trees with the children of Judah into the wilderness of Judah, which lies in the south of Arad; and they went and dwelled among the people. ¹⁷And Judah went with Simeon his brother, and they slew the Canaanites that inhabited Zephath, and utterly destroyed it. And the name of the city was called Hormah. ¹⁸Also Judah took Gaza with the coast thereof, and Askelon with the coast thereof, and Ekron with the coast thereof. ¹⁹And the LORD was with Judah; and he drove out the inhabitants of the mountain; but could not drive out the inhabitants of the valley, because they had chariots of iron. ²⁰And they gave Hebron to Caleb, as Moses said: and he expelled there the three sons of Anak. ²¹And the children of Benjamin did not drive out the Jebusites that inhabited Jerusalem; but the Jebusites dwell with the children of Benjamin in Jerusalem to this day. ²²And the house of Joseph, they also went up against Bethel: and the LORD was with them. ²³And the house of Joseph sent to descry Bethel. (Now the name of the city before was Luz.) ²⁴And the spies saw a man come forth out of the city, and they said to him, Show us, we pray you, the entrance into the city, and we will show you mercy. ²⁵And when he showed them the entrance into the city, they smote the city with the edge of the sword; but they let go the man and all his family. ²⁶And the man went into the land of the Hittites, and built a city, and called the name thereof Luz: which is the name thereof to this day. ²⁷Neither did Manasseh drive out the inhabitants of Bethshean and her towns, nor Taanach and her towns, nor the inhabitants of Dor and her towns, nor the inhabitants of Ibleam and her towns, nor the inhabitants of Megiddo and her towns: but the Canaanites would dwell in that land. ²⁸And it came to pass, when Israel was strong, that they put the Canaanites to tribute, and did not utterly drive them out. ²⁹Neither did Ephraim drive out the Canaanites that dwelled in Gezer; but the Canaanites dwelled in Gezer among them. ³⁰Neither did Zebulun drive out the inhabitants of Kitron, nor the inhabitants of Nahalol; but the Canaanites dwelled among them, and became tributaries. ³¹Neither did Asher drive out the inhabitants of Accho, nor the inhabitants of Zidon, nor of Ahlab, nor of Achzib, nor of Helbah, nor of Aphik, nor of Rehob: ³²But the Asherites dwelled among the Canaanites, the inhabitants of the land: for they did not drive them out. ³³Neither did Naphtali drive out the inhabitants of Bethshemesh, nor the inhabitants of Bethanath; but he dwelled among the Canaanites, the inhabitants of the land: nevertheless the inhabitants of Bethshemesh and of Bethanath became tributaries to them. ³⁴And the Amorites forced the children of Dan into the mountain: for they would not suffer them to come down to the valley: ³⁵But the Amorites would dwell in mount Heres in Aijalon, and in Shaalbim: yet the hand of the house of Joseph prevailed, so that they became tributaries. ³⁶And the coast of the Amorites was from the going up to Akrabbim, from the rock, and upward.

2 ¹And an angel of the LORD came up from Gilgal to Bochim, and said, I made you to go up out of Egypt, and have brought you to the land which I swore to your fathers; and I said, I will never break my covenant with you. ²And you shall make no league with the inhabitants of this land; you shall throw down their altars: but you have not obeyed my voice: why have you done this? ³Why I also said, I will not drive them out from before you; but they shall be as thorns in your sides, and their gods shall be a snare to you. ⁴And it came to pass, when the angel of the LORD spoke these words to all the children of Israel, that the people lifted up their voice, and wept. ⁵And they called the name of that place Bochim: and they sacrificed there to the LORD. ⁶And when Joshua had let the people go, the children of Israel went every man to his inheritance to possess the land. ⁷And the people served the LORD all the days of Joshua, and all the days of the elders that outlived Joshua, who had seen all the great works of the LORD, that he did for Israel. ⁸And Joshua the son of Nun, the servant of the LORD, died, being an hundred and ten years old. ⁹And they buried him in the border of his inheritance in Timnathheres, in the mount of Ephraim, on the north side of the hill Gaash. ¹⁰And also all that generation were gathered to their fathers: and there arose another generation after them, which knew not the LORD, nor yet the works which he had done for Israel. ¹¹And the children of Israel did evil in the sight of the LORD, and served Baalim: ¹²And they forsook the LORD God of their fathers, which brought them out of the land of Egypt, and followed other gods, of the gods of the people that were round about them, and bowed themselves to them, and provoked the LORD to anger. ¹³And they forsook the LORD, and served Baal and Ashtaroth. ¹⁴And the anger of the LORD was hot against Israel, and he delivered them into the hands of spoilers that spoiled them, and he sold them into the hands of their enemies round about, so that they could not any longer stand before their enemies. ¹⁵Wherever they went out, the hand of the LORD was against them for evil, as the LORD had said, and as the LORD had sworn to them: and they were greatly distressed. ¹⁶Nevertheless the LORD raised up judges, which delivered them out of the hand of those that spoiled them. ¹⁷And yet they would not listen to their judges, but they went a whoring after other gods, and bowed themselves to them: they turned quickly out of the way which their fathers walked in, obeying the commandments of the LORD; but they did not so. ¹⁸And when the LORD raised them up judges, then the LORD was with the judge, and delivered them out of the hand of their enemies all the days of the judge: for it repented the LORD because of their groanings by reason of them that oppressed them and vexed them. ¹⁹And it came to pass, when the judge was dead, that they returned, and corrupted themselves more than their fathers, in following other gods to serve them, and to bow down to them; they ceased not from their own doings, nor from their stubborn way. ²⁰And the anger of the LORD was hot against Israel; and he said, Because that this people has transgressed my covenant which I commanded their fathers, and have not listened to my voice; ²¹I also will not from now on drive out any from before them of the nations which Joshua left when he died: ²²That through them I may prove Israel, whether they will keep the way of the LORD to walk therein, as their fathers did keep it, or not. ²³Therefore the LORD left those nations, without driving them out hastily; neither delivered he them into the hand of Joshua.

3 ¹Now these are the nations which the LORD left, to prove Israel by them, even as many of Israel as had not known all the wars of Canaan; ²Only that the generations of the children of Israel might know, to teach them war, at the least such as before knew nothing thereof; ³Namely, five lords of the Philistines, and all the Canaanites, and the Sidonians, and the Hivites that dwelled in mount Lebanon, from mount Baalhermon to the entering in of Hamath. ⁴And they were to prove Israel by them, to know whether they would listen to the commandments of the LORD, which he commanded their fathers by the hand of Moses. ⁵And the children of Israel dwelled among the Canaanites, Hittites, and Amorites, and Perizzites, and Hivites, and Jebusites: ⁶And they took their daughters to be their wives, and gave their daughters to their sons, and served their gods. ⁷And the children of Israel did evil in the sight of the LORD, and forgot the LORD their God, and served Baalim and the groves. ⁸Therefore the anger of the LORD was hot against Israel, and he sold them into the hand of Chushanrishathaim king of Mesopotamia: and the children of Israel served Chushanrishathaim eight years. ⁹And when the children of Israel cried to the LORD, the LORD raised up a deliverer to the children of Israel, who delivered them, even Othniel the son of Kenaz, Caleb's younger brother. ¹⁰And the Spirit of the LORD came on him, and he judged Israel, and went out to war: and the LORD delivered Chushanrishathaim king of Mesopotamia into his hand; and his hand prevailed against Chushanrishathaim. ¹¹And the land had rest forty years. And Othniel the son of Kenaz died. ¹²And the children of Israel did evil again in the sight of the LORD: and the LORD strengthened Eglon the king of Moab against Israel, because they had done evil in the sight of the LORD. ¹³And he gathered to him the children of Ammon and Amalek, and went and smote Israel, and possessed the city of palm trees. ¹⁴So the children of Israel served Eglon the king of Moab eighteen years. ¹⁵But when the children of Israel cried to the LORD, the LORD raised them up a deliverer, Ehud the son of Gera, a Benjamite, a man left handed: and by him the children of Israel sent a present to Eglon the king of Moab. ¹⁶But Ehud made him a dagger which had two edges, of a cubit length; and he did gird it under his raiment on his right thigh. ¹⁷And he brought the present to Eglon king of Moab: and Eglon was a very fat man. ¹⁸And when he had made an end to offer the present, he sent away the people that bore the present. ¹⁹But he himself turned again from the quarries that were by Gilgal, and said, I have a secret errand to you, O king: who said, Keep silence. And all that stood by him went out from him. ²⁰And Ehud came to him; and he was sitting in a summer parlor, which he had for himself alone. And Ehud said, I have a message from God to you. And he arose out of his seat. ²¹And Ehud put forth his left hand, and took the dagger from his right thigh, and thrust it into his belly: ²²And the haft also went in after the blade; and the fat closed on the blade, so that he could not draw the dagger out of his belly; and the dirt came out. ²³Then Ehud went forth through the porch, and shut the doors of the parlor on him, and locked them. ²⁴When he was gone out, his servants came; and when they saw that, behold, the doors of the parlor were locked, they said, Surely he covers his feet in his summer chamber. ²⁵And they tarried till they were ashamed: and, behold, he opened not the doors of the parlor; therefore they took a key, and opened them: and, behold, their lord was fallen down dead on the earth. ²⁶And Ehud escaped while they tarried, and passed beyond the quarries, and escaped to Seirath. ²⁷And it came to pass, when he was come, that he blew a trumpet in the mountain of Ephraim, and the children of Israel went down with him from the mount, and he before them. ²⁸And he said to them, Follow after me: for the LORD has delivered your enemies the Moabites into your hand. And they went down after him, and took the fords of Jordan toward Moab, and suffered not a man to pass over. ²⁹And they slew of Moab at that time about ten thousand men, all lusty, and all men of valor; and there escaped not a man. ³⁰So Moab was subdued that day under the hand of Israel. And the land had rest fourscore years. ³¹And after him was Shamgar the son of Anath, which slew of the Philistines six hundred men with an ox goad: and he also delivered Israel.

4 ¹And the children of Israel again did evil in the sight of the LORD, when Ehud was dead. ²And the LORD sold them into the hand of Jabin king of Canaan, that reigned in Hazor; the captain of whose host was Sisera, which dwelled in Harosheth of the Gentiles. ³And the children of Israel cried to the LORD: for he had nine hundred chariots of iron; and twenty years he mightily oppressed the children of Israel. ⁴And Deborah, a prophetess, the wife of Lapidoth, she judged Israel at that time. ⁵And she dwelled under the palm tree of Deborah between Ramah and Bethel in mount Ephraim: and the children of Israel came up to her for judgment. ⁶And she sent and called Barak the son of Abinoam out of Kedeshnaphtali, and said to him, Has not the LORD God of Israel commanded, saying, Go and draw toward mount Tabor, and take with you ten thousand men of the children of Naphtali and of the children of Zebulun? ⁷And I will draw to you to the river Kishon Sisera, the captain of Jabin's army, with his chariots and his multitude; and I will deliver him into your hand. ⁸And Barak said to her, If you will go with me, then I will go: but if you will not go with me, then I will not go. ⁹And she said, I will surely go with you: notwithstanding the journey that you take shall not be for your honor; for the LORD shall sell Sisera into the hand of a woman. And Deborah arose, and went with Barak to Kedesh. ¹⁰And Barak called Zebulun and Naphtali to Kedesh; and he went up with ten thousand men at his feet: and Deborah went up with him. ¹¹Now Heber the Kenite, which was of the children of Hobab the father in law of Moses, had severed himself from the Kenites, and pitched his tent to the plain of Zaanaim, which is by Kedesh. ¹²And they showed Sisera that Barak the son of Abinoam was gone up to mount Tabor. ¹³And Sisera gathered together all his chariots, even nine hundred chariots of iron, and all the people that were with him, from Harosheth of the Gentiles to the river of Kishon. ¹⁴And Deborah said to Barak, Up; for this is the day in which the LORD has delivered Sisera into your hand: is not the LORD gone out before you? So Barak went down from mount Tabor, and ten thousand men after him. ¹⁵And the LORD discomfited Sisera, and all his chariots, and all his host, with the edge of the sword before Barak; so that Sisera lighted down off his chariot, and fled away on his feet. ¹⁶But Barak pursued after the chariots, and after the host, to Harosheth of the Gentiles: and all the host of Sisera fell on the edge of the sword; and there was not a man left. ¹⁷However, Sisera fled away on his feet to the tent of Jael the wife of Heber the Kenite: for there was peace between Jabin the king of Hazor and the house of Heber the Kenite. ¹⁸And Jael went out to meet Sisera, and said to him, Turn in, my lord, turn in to me; fear not. And when he had turned in to her into the tent, she covered him with a mantle. ¹⁹And he said to her, Give me, I pray you, a little water to drink; for I am thirsty. And she opened a bottle of milk, and gave him drink, and covered him. ²⁰Again he said to her, Stand in the door of the tent, and it shall be, when any man does come and inquire of you, and say, Is there any man here? that you shall say, No. ²¹Then Jael Heber's wife took a nail of the tent, and took an hammer in her hand, and went softly to him, and smote the nail into his temples, and fastened it into the ground: for he was fast asleep and weary. So he died. ²²And, behold, as Barak pursued Sisera, Jael came out to meet him, and said to him, Come, and I will show you the man whom you seek. And when he came into her tent, behold, Sisera lay dead, and the nail was in his temples. ²³So God subdued on that day Jabin the king of Canaan before the children of Israel. ²⁴And the hand of the children of Israel prospered, and prevailed against Jabin the king of Canaan, until they had destroyed Jabin king of Canaan.

5 ¹Then sang Deborah and Barak the son of Abinoam on that day, saying, ²Praise you the LORD for the avenging of Israel, when the people willingly offered themselves. ³Hear, O you kings; give ear, O you princes; I, even I, will sing to the LORD; I will sing praise to the LORD God of Israel. ⁴LORD, when you went out of Seir, when you marched out of the field of Edom, the earth trembled, and the heavens dropped, the clouds also dropped water. ⁵The mountains melted from before the LORD, even that Sinai from before the LORD God of Israel. ⁶In the days of Shamgar the son of Anath, in the days of Jael, the highways were unoccupied, and the travelers walked through byways. ⁷The inhabitants of the villages ceased, they ceased in Israel, until that I Deborah arose, that I arose a mother in Israel. ⁸They chose new gods; then was war in the gates: was there a shield or spear seen among forty thousand in Israel? ⁹My heart is toward the governors of Israel, that offered themselves willingly among the people. Bless you the LORD. ¹⁰Speak, you that ride on white asses, you that sit in judgment, and walk by the way. ¹¹They that are delivered from the noise of archers in the places of drawing water, there shall they rehearse the righteous acts of the LORD, even the righteous acts toward the inhabitants of his villages in Israel: then shall the people of the LORD go down to the gates. ¹²Awake, awake, Deborah: awake, awake, utter a song: arise, Barak, and lead your captivity captive, you son of Abinoam. ¹³Then he made him that remains have dominion over the nobles among the people: the LORD made me have dominion over the mighty. ¹⁴Out of Ephraim was there a root of them against Amalek; after you, Benjamin, among your people; out of Machir came down governors, and out of Zebulun they that handle the pen of the writer. ¹⁵And the princes of Issachar were with Deborah; even Issachar, and also Barak: he was sent on foot into the valley. For the divisions of Reuben there were great thoughts of heart. ¹⁶Why stayed you among the sheepfolds, to hear the bleatings of the flocks? For the divisions of Reuben there were great searchings of heart. ¹⁷Gilead stayed beyond Jordan: and why did Dan remain in ships? Asher continued on the sea shore, and stayed in his breaches. ¹⁸Zebulun and Naphtali were a people that risked their lives to the death in the high places of the field. ¹⁹The kings came and fought, then fought the kings of Canaan in Taanach by the waters of Megiddo; they took no gain of money. ²⁰They fought from heaven; the stars in their courses fought against Sisera. ²¹The river of Kishon swept them away, that ancient river, the river Kishon. O my soul, you have trodden down strength. ²²Then were the horse hoofs broken by the means of the prancings, the prancings of their mighty ones. ²³Curse you Meroz, said the angel of the LORD, curse you bitterly the inhabitants thereof; because they came not to the help of the LORD, to the help of the LORD against the mighty.

²⁴Blessed above women shall Jael the wife of Heber the Kenite be, blessed shall she be above women in the tent. ²⁵He asked water, and she gave him milk; she brought forth butter in a lordly dish. ²⁶She put her hand to the nail, and her right hand to the workmen's hammer; and with the hammer she smote Sisera, she smote off his head, when she had pierced and stricken through his temples. ²⁷At her feet he bowed, he fell, he lay down: at her feet he bowed, he fell: where he bowed, there he fell down dead. ²⁸The mother of Sisera looked out at a window, and cried through the lattice, Why is his chariot so long in coming? why tarry the wheels of his chariots? ²⁹Her wise ladies answered her, yes, she returned answer to herself, ³⁰Have they not sped? have they not divided the prey; to every man a damsel or two; to Sisera a prey of divers colors, a prey of divers colors of needlework, of divers colors of needlework on both sides, meet for the necks of them that take the spoil? ³¹So let all your enemies perish, O LORD: but let them that love him be as the sun when he goes forth in his might. And the land had rest forty years.

6 ¹And the children of Israel did evil in the sight of the LORD: and the LORD delivered them into the hand of Midian seven years. ²And the hand of Midian prevailed against Israel: and because of the Midianites the children of Israel made them the dens which are in the mountains, and caves, and strong holds. ³And so it was, when Israel had sown, that the Midianites came up, and the Amalekites, and the children of the east, even they came up against them; ⁴And they encamped against them, and destroyed the increase of the earth, till you come to Gaza, and left no sustenance for Israel, neither sheep, nor ox, nor ass. ⁵For they came up with their cattle and their tents, and they came as grasshoppers for multitude; for both they and their camels were without number: and they entered into the land to destroy it. ⁶And Israel was greatly impoverished because of the Midianites; and the children of Israel cried to the LORD. ⁷And it came to pass, when the children of Israel cried to the LORD because of the Midianites, ⁸That the LORD sent a prophet to the children of Israel, which said to them, Thus says the LORD God of Israel, I brought you up from Egypt, and brought you forth out of the house of bondage; ⁹And I delivered you out of the hand of the Egyptians, and out of the hand of all that oppressed you, and drove them out from before you, and gave you their land; ¹⁰And I said to you, I am the LORD your God; fear not the gods of the Amorites, in whose land you dwell: but you have not obeyed my voice. ¹¹And there came an angel of the LORD, and sat under an oak which was in Ophrah, that pertained to Joash the Abiezrite: and his son Gideon threshed wheat by the wine press, to hide it from the Midianites. ¹²And the angel of the LORD appeared to him, and said to him, The LORD is with you, you mighty man of valor. ¹³And Gideon said to him, Oh my Lord, if the LORD be with us, why then is all this befallen us? and where be all his miracles which our fathers told us of, saying, Did not the LORD bring us up from Egypt? but now the LORD has forsaken us, and delivered us into the hands of the Midianites. ¹⁴And the LORD looked on him, and said, Go in this your might, and you shall save Israel from the hand of the Midianites: have not I sent you? ¹⁵And he said to him, Oh my Lord, with which shall I save Israel? behold, my family is poor in Manasseh, and I am the least in my father's house. ¹⁶And the LORD said to him, Surely I will be with you, and you shall smite the Midianites as one man. ¹⁷And he said to him, If now I have found grace in your sight, then show me a sign that you talk with me. ¹⁸Depart not hence, I pray you, until I come to you, and bring forth my present, and set it before you. And he said, I will tarry until you come again. ¹⁹And Gideon went in, and made ready a kid, and unleavened cakes of an ephah of flour: the flesh he put in a basket, and he put the broth in a pot, and brought it out to him under the oak, and presented it. ²⁰And the angel of God said to him, Take the flesh and the unleavened cakes, and lay them on this rock, and pour out the broth. And he did so. ²¹Then the angel of the LORD put forth the end of the staff that was in his hand, and touched the flesh and the unleavened cakes; and there rose up fire out of the rock, and consumed the flesh and the unleavened cakes. Then the angel of the LORD departed out of his sight. ²²And when Gideon perceived that he was an angel of the LORD, Gideon said, Alas, O LORD God! for because I have seen an angel of the LORD face to face. ²³And the LORD said to him, Peace be to you; fear not: you shall not die. ²⁴Then Gideon built an altar there to the LORD, and called it Jehovahshalom: to this day it is yet in Ophrah of the Abiezrites. ²⁵And it came to pass the same night, that the LORD said to him, Take your father's young bullock, even the second bullock of seven years old, and throw down the altar of Baal that your father has, and cut down the grove that is by it: ²⁶And build an altar to the LORD your God on the top of this rock, in the ordered place, and take the second bullock, and offer a burnt sacrifice with the wood of the grove which you shall cut down. ²⁷Then Gideon took ten men of his servants, and did as the LORD had said to him: and so it was, because he feared his father's household, and the men of the city, that he could not do it by day, that he did it by night. ²⁸And when the men of the city arose early in the morning, behold, the altar of Baal was cast down, and the grove was cut down that was by it, and the second bullock was offered on the altar that was built. ²⁹And they said one to another, Who has done this thing? And when they inquired and asked, they said, Gideon the son of Joash has done this thing. ³⁰Then the men of the city said to Joash, Bring out your son, that he may die: because he has cast down the altar of Baal, and because he has cut down the grove that was by it. ³¹And Joash said to all that stood against him, Will you plead for Baal? will you save him? he that will plead for him, let him be put to death whilst it is yet morning: if he be a god, let him plead for himself, because one has cast down his altar. ³²Therefore on that day he called him Jerubbaal, saying, Let Baal plead against him, because he has thrown down his altar. ³³Then all the Midianites and the Amalekites and the children of the east were gathered together, and went over, and pitched in the valley of Jezreel. ³⁴But the Spirit of the LORD came on Gideon, and he blew a trumpet; and Abiezer was gathered after him. ³⁵And he sent messengers throughout all Manasseh; who also was gathered after him: and he sent messengers to Asher, and to Zebulun, and to Naphtali; and they came up to meet them. ³⁶And Gideon said to God, If

you will save Israel by my hand, as you have said, ³⁷Behold, I will put a fleece of wool in the floor; and if the dew be on the fleece only, and it be dry on all the earth beside, then shall I know that you will save Israel by my hand, as you have said. ³⁸And it was so: for he rose up early on the morrow, and thrust the fleece together, and wringed the dew out of the fleece, a bowl full of water. ³⁹And Gideon said to God, Let not your anger be hot against me, and I will speak but this once: let me prove, I pray you, but this once with the fleece; let it now be dry only on the fleece, and on all the ground let there be dew. ⁴⁰And God did so that night: for it was dry on the fleece only, and there was dew on all the ground.

7 ¹Then Jerubbaal, who is Gideon, and all the people that were with him, rose up early, and pitched beside the well of Harod: so that the host of the Midianites were on the north side of them, by the hill of Moreh, in the valley. ²And the LORD said to Gideon, The people that are with you are too many for me to give the Midianites into their hands, lest Israel vaunt themselves against me, saying, My own hand has saved me. ³Now therefore go to, proclaim in the ears of the people, saying, Whoever is fearful and afraid, let him return and depart early from mount Gilead. And there returned of the people twenty and two thousand; and there remained ten thousand. ⁴And the LORD said to Gideon, The people are yet too many; bring them down to the water, and I will try them for you there: and it shall be, that of whom I say to you, This shall go with you, the same shall go with you; and of whomsoever I say to you, This shall not go with you, the same shall not go. ⁵So he brought down the people to the water: and the LORD said to Gideon, Every one that laps of the water with his tongue, as a dog laps, him shall you set by himself; likewise every one that bows down on his knees to drink. ⁶And the number of them that lapped, putting their hand to their mouth, were three hundred men: but all the rest of the people bowed down on their knees to drink water. ⁷And the LORD said to Gideon, By the three hundred men that lapped will I save you, and deliver the Midianites into your hand: and let all the other people go every man to his place. ⁸So the people took victuals in their hand, and their trumpets: and he sent all the rest of Israel every man to his tent, and retained those three hundred men: and the host of Midian was beneath him in the valley. ⁹And it came to pass the same night, that the LORD said to him, Arise, get you down to the host; for I have delivered it into your hand. ¹⁰But if you fear to go down, go you with Phurah your servant down to the host: ¹¹And you shall hear what they say; and afterward shall your hands be strengthened to go down to the host. Then went he down with Phurah his servant to the outside of the armed men that were in the host. ¹²And the Midianites and the Amalekites and all the children of the east lay along in the valley like grasshoppers for multitude; and their camels were without number, as the sand by the sea side for multitude. ¹³And when Gideon was come, behold, there was a man that told a dream to his fellow, and said, Behold, I dreamed a dream, and, see, a cake of barley bread tumbled into the host of Midian, and came to a tent, and smote it that it fell, and overturned it, that the tent lay along. ¹⁴And his fellow answered and said, This is nothing else save the sword of Gideon the son of Joash, a man of Israel: for into his hand has God delivered Midian, and all the host. ¹⁵And it was so, when Gideon heard the telling of the dream, and the interpretation thereof, that he worshipped, and returned into the host of Israel, and said, Arise; for the LORD has delivered into your hand the host of Midian. ¹⁶And he divided the three hundred men into three companies, and he put a trumpet in every man's hand, with empty pitchers, and lamps within the pitchers. ¹⁷And he said to them, Look on me, and do likewise: and, behold, when I come to the outside of the camp, it shall be that, as I do, so shall you do. ¹⁸When I blow with a trumpet, I and all that are with me, then blow you the trumpets also on every side of all the camp, and say, The sword of the LORD, and of Gideon. ¹⁹So Gideon, and the hundred men that were with him, came to the outside of the camp in the beginning of the middle watch; and they had but newly set the watch: and they blew the trumpets, and broke the pitchers that were in their hands. ²⁰And the three companies blew the trumpets, and broke the pitchers, and held the lamps in their left hands, and the trumpets in their right hands to blow with: and they cried, The sword of the LORD, and of Gideon. ²¹And they stood every man in his place round about the camp; and all the host ran, and cried, and fled. ²²And the three hundred blew the trumpets, and the LORD set every man's sword against his fellow, even throughout all the host: and the host fled to Bethshittah in Zererath, and to the border of Abelmeholah, to Tabbath. ²³And the men of Israel gathered themselves together out of Naphtali, and out of Asher, and out of all Manasseh, and pursued after the Midianites. ²⁴And Gideon sent messengers throughout all mount Ephraim, saying, come down against the Midianites, and take before them the waters to Bethbarah and Jordan. Then all the men of Ephraim gathered themselves together, and took the waters to Bethbarah and Jordan. ²⁵And they took two princes of the Midianites, Oreb and Zeeb; and they slew Oreb on the rock Oreb, and Zeeb they slew at the wine press of Zeeb, and pursued Midian, and brought the heads of Oreb and Zeeb to Gideon on the other side Jordan.

8 ¹And the men of Ephraim said to him, Why have you served us thus, that you called us not, when you went to fight with the Midianites? And they did chide with him sharply. ²And he said to them, What have I done now in comparison of you? Is not the gleaning of the grapes of Ephraim better than the vintage of Abiezer? ³God has delivered into your hands the princes of Midian, Oreb and Zeeb: and what was I able to do in comparison of you? Then their anger was abated toward him, when he had said that. ⁴And Gideon came to Jordan, and passed over, he, and the three hundred men that were with him, faint, yet pursuing them. ⁵And he said to the men of Succoth, Give, I pray you, loaves of bread to the people that follow me; for they be faint, and I am pursuing after Zebah and Zalmunna, kings of Midian. ⁶And the princes of Succoth said, Are the hands of Zebah and Zalmunna now in your hand, that we should give bread to your army? ⁷And Gideon said, Therefore when the LORD has delivered Zebah and Zalmunna into my hand, then I will tear your flesh with the thorns of the wilderness and with briers. ⁸And he went up there to Penuel, and spoke to them likewise: and the men of

Penuel answered him as the men of Succoth had answered him. ⁹And he spoke also to the men of Penuel, saying, When I come again in peace, I will break down this tower. ¹⁰Now Zebah and Zalmunna were in Karkor, and their hosts with them, about fifteen thousand men, all that were left of all the hosts of the children of the east: for there fell an hundred and twenty thousand men that drew sword. ¹¹And Gideon went up by the way of them that dwelled in tents on the east of Nobah and Jogbehah, and smote the host; for the host was secure. ¹²And when Zebah and Zalmunna fled, he pursued after them, and took the two kings of Midian, Zebah and Zalmunna, and discomfited all the host. ¹³And Gideon the son of Joash returned from battle before the sun was up, ¹⁴And caught a young man of the men of Succoth, and inquired of him: and he described to him the princes of Succoth, and the elders thereof, even three score and seventeen men. ¹⁵And he came to the men of Succoth, and said, Behold Zebah and Zalmunna, with whom you did upbraid me, saying, Are the hands of Zebah and Zalmunna now in your hand, that we should give bread to your men that are weary? ¹⁶And he took the elders of the city, and thorns of the wilderness and briers, and with them he taught the men of Succoth. ¹⁷And he beat down the tower of Penuel, and slew the men of the city. ¹⁸Then said he to Zebah and Zalmunna, What manner of men were they whom you slew at Tabor? And they answered, As you are, so were they; each one resembled the children of a king. ¹⁹And he said, They were my brothers, even the sons of my mother: as the LORD lives, if you had saved them alive, I would not slay you. ²⁰And he said to Jether his firstborn, Up, and slay them. But the youth drew not his sword: for he feared, because he was yet a youth. ²¹Then Zebah and Zalmunna said, Rise you, and fall on us: for as the man is, so is his strength. And Gideon arose, and slew Zebah and Zalmunna, and took away the ornaments that were on their camels' necks. ²²Then the men of Israel said to Gideon, Rule you over us, both you, and your son, and your son's son also: for you have delivered us from the hand of Midian. ²³And Gideon said to them, I will not rule over you, neither shall my son rule over you: the LORD shall rule over you. ²⁴And Gideon said to them, I would desire a request of you, that you would give me every man the earrings of his prey. (For they had golden earrings, because they were Ishmaelites.) ²⁵And they answered, We will willingly give them. And they spread a garment, and did cast therein every man the earrings of his prey. ²⁶And the weight of the golden earrings that he requested was a thousand and seven hundred shekels of gold; beside ornaments, and collars, and purple raiment that was on the kings of Midian, and beside the chains that were about their camels' necks. ²⁷And Gideon made an ephod thereof, and put it in his city, even in Ophrah: and all Israel went thither a whoring after it: which thing became a snare to Gideon, and to his house. ²⁸Thus was Midian subdued before the children of Israel, so that they lifted up their heads no more. And the country was in quietness forty years in the days of Gideon. ²⁹And Jerubbaal the son of Joash went and dwelled in his own house. ³⁰And Gideon had three score and ten sons of his body begotten: for he had many wives. ³¹And his concubine that was in Shechem, she also bore him a son, whose name he called Abimelech. ³²And Gideon the son of Joash died in a good old age, and was buried in the sepulcher of Joash his father, in Ophrah of the Abiezrites. ³³And it came to pass, as soon as Gideon was dead, that the children of Israel turned again, and went a whoring after Baalim, and made Baalberith their god. ³⁴And the children of Israel remembered not the LORD their God, who had delivered them out of the hands of all their enemies on every side: ³⁵Neither showed they kindness to the house of Jerubbaal, namely, Gideon, according to all the goodness which he had showed to Israel.

9 ¹And Abimelech the son of Jerubbaal went to Shechem to his mother's brothers, and communed with them, and with all the family of the house of his mother's father, saying, ²Speak, I pray you, in the ears of all the men of Shechem, Whether is better for you, either that all the sons of Jerubbaal, which are three score and ten persons, reign over you, or that one reign over you? remember also that I am your bone and your flesh. ³And his mother's brothers spoke of him in the ears of all the men of Shechem all these words: and their hearts inclined to follow Abimelech; for they said, He is our brother. ⁴And they gave him three score and ten pieces of silver out of the house of Baalberith, with which Abimelech hired vain and light persons, which followed him. ⁵And he went to his father's house at Ophrah, and slew his brothers the sons of Jerubbaal, being three score and ten persons, on one stone: notwithstanding yet Jotham the youngest son of Jerubbaal was left; for he hid himself. ⁶And all the men of Shechem gathered together, and all the house of Millo, and went, and made Abimelech king, by the plain of the pillar that was in Shechem. ⁷And when they told it to Jotham, he went and stood in the top of mount Gerizim, and lifted up his voice, and cried, and said to them, Listen to me, you men of Shechem, that God may listen to you. ⁸The trees went forth on a time to anoint a king over them; and they said to the olive tree, Reign you over us. ⁹But the olive tree said to them, Should I leave my fatness, with which by me they honor God and man, and go to be promoted over the trees? ¹⁰And the trees said to the fig tree, Come you, and reign over us. ¹¹But the fig tree said to them, Should I forsake my sweetness, and my good fruit, and go to be promoted over the trees? ¹²Then said the trees to the vine, Come you, and reign over us. ¹³And the vine said to them, Should I leave my wine, which cheers God and man, and go to be promoted over the trees? ¹⁴Then said all the trees to the bramble, Come you, and reign over us. ¹⁵And the bramble said to the trees, If in truth you anoint me king over you, then come and put your trust in my shadow: and if not, let fire come out of the bramble, and devour the cedars of Lebanon. ¹⁶Now therefore, if you have done truly and sincerely, in that you have made Abimelech king, and if you have dealt well with Jerubbaal and his house, and have done to him according to the deserving of his hands; ¹⁷(For my father fought for you, and adventured his life far, and delivered you out of the hand of Midian: ¹⁸And you are risen up against my father's house this day, and have slain his sons, three score and ten persons, on one stone, and have made Abimelech, the son of his maidservant, king over the men of Shechem, because he is your brother;) ¹⁹If you then have dealt truly and sincerely with Jerubbaal and with his house this day, then rejoice you in Abimelech, and let him also rejoice in you: ²⁰But if not, let fire come out from Abimelech, and devour the men of Shechem, and the house of Millo; and let fire come out from the men of Shechem, and from the house of Millo, and devour Abimelech. ²¹And Jotham ran away, and fled, and went to Beer, and dwelled there, for fear of Abimelech his brother. ²²When Abimelech had reigned three years over Israel, ²³Then God sent an evil spirit between Abimelech and the men of Shechem; and the men of Shechem dealt treacherously with Abimelech: ²⁴That the cruelty done to the three score and ten sons of Jerubbaal might come, and their blood be laid on Abimelech their brother, which slew them; and on the men of Shechem, which aided him in the killing of his brothers. ²⁵And the men of Shechem set liers in wait for him in the top of the mountains, and they robbed all that came along that way by them: and it was told Abimelech. ²⁶And Gaal the son of Ebed came with his brothers, and went over to Shechem: and the men of Shechem put their confidence in him. ²⁷And they went out into the fields, and gathered their vineyards, and stepped the grapes, and made merry, and went into the house of their god, and did eat and drink, and cursed Abimelech. ²⁸And Gaal the son of Ebed said, Who is Abimelech, and who is Shechem, that we should serve him? is not he the son of Jerubbaal? and Zebul his officer? serve the men of Hamor the father of Shechem: for why should we serve him? ²⁹And would to God this people were under my hand! then would I remove Abimelech. And he said to Abimelech, Increase your army, and come out. ³⁰And when Zebul the ruler of the city heard the words of Gaal the son of Ebed, his anger was kindled. ³¹And he sent messengers to Abimelech privately, saying, Behold, Gaal the son of Ebed and his brothers be come to Shechem; and, behold, they fortify the city against you. ³²Now therefore up by night, you and the people that is with you, and lie in wait in the field: ³³And it shall be, that in the morning, as soon as the sun is up, you shall rise early, and set on the city: and, behold, when he and the people that is with him come out against you, then may you do to them as you shall find occasion. ³⁴And Abimelech rose up, and all the people that were with him, by night, and they laid wait against Shechem in four companies. ³⁵And Gaal the son of Ebed went out, and stood in the entering of the gate of the city: and Abimelech rose up, and the people that were with him, from lying in wait. ³⁶And when Gaal saw the people, he said to Zebul, Behold, there come people down from the top of the mountains. And Zebul said to him, You see the shadow of the mountains as if they were men. ³⁷And Gaal spoke again, and said, See there come people down by the middle of the land, and another company come along by the plain of Meonenim. ³⁸Then said Zebul to him, Where is now your mouth, with which you said, Who is Abimelech, that we should serve him? is not this the people that you have despised? go out, I pray now, and fight with them. ³⁹And Gaal went out before the men of Shechem, and fought with Abimelech. ⁴⁰And Abimelech chased him, and he fled before him, and many were overthrown and wounded, even to the entering of the gate. ⁴¹And Abimelech dwelled at Arumah: and Zebul thrust out Gaal and his brothers, that they should not dwell in Shechem. ⁴²And it came to pass on the morrow, that the people went out into the field; and they told Abimelech. ⁴³And he took the people, and divided them into three companies, and laid wait in the field, and looked, and, behold, the people were come forth out of the city; and he rose up against them, and smote them. ⁴⁴And Abimelech, and the company that was with him, rushed forward, and stood in the entering of the gate of the city: and the two other companies ran on all the people that were in the fields, and slew them. ⁴⁵And Abimelech fought against the city all that day; and he took the city, and slew the people that was therein, and beat down the city, and sowed it with salt. ⁴⁶And when all the men of the tower of Shechem heard that, they entered into an hold of the house of the god Berith. ⁴⁷And it was told Abimelech, that all the men of the tower of Shechem were gathered together. ⁴⁸And Abimelech got him up to mount Zalmon, he and all the people that were with him; and Abimelech took an ax in his hand, and cut down a bough from the trees, and took it, and laid it on his shoulder, and said to the people that were with him, What you have seen me do, make haste, and do as I have done. ⁴⁹And all the people likewise cut down every man his bough, and followed Abimelech, and put them to the hold, and set the hold on fire on them; so that all the men of the tower of Shechem died also, about a thousand men and women. ⁵⁰Then went Abimelech to Thebez, and encamped against Thebez, and took it. ⁵¹But there was a strong tower within the city, and thither fled all the men and women, and all they of the city, and shut it to them, and got them up to the top of the tower. ⁵²And Abimelech came to the tower, and fought against it, and went hard to the door of the tower to burn it with fire. ⁵³And a certain woman cast a piece of a millstone on Abimelech's head, and all to broke his skull. ⁵⁴Then he called hastily to the young man his armor bearer, and said to him, Draw your sword, and slay me, that men say not of me, A women slew him. And his young man thrust him through, and he died. ⁵⁵And when the men of Israel saw that Abimelech was dead, they departed every man to his place. ⁵⁶Thus God rendered the wickedness of Abimelech, which he did to his father, in slaying his seventy brothers: ⁵⁷And all the evil of the men of Shechem did God render on their heads: and on them came the curse of Jotham the son of Jerubbaal.

10 ¹And after Abimelech there arose to defend Israel Tola the son of Puah, the son of Dodo, a man of Issachar; and he dwelled in Shamir in mount Ephraim. ²And he judged Israel twenty and three years, and died, and was buried in Shamir. ³And after him arose Jair, a Gileadite, and judged Israel twenty and two years. ⁴And he had thirty sons that rode on thirty ass colts, and they had thirty cities, which are called Havothjair to this day, which are in the land of Gilead. ⁵And Jair died, and was buried in Camon. ⁶And the children of Israel did evil again in the sight of the LORD, and served Baalim, and Ashtaroth, and the gods of Syria, and the gods of Zidon, and the gods of Moab, and the gods of the children of Ammon, and the gods of the Philistines, and forsook the LORD, and served not him. ⁷And the anger of the LORD was hot against Israel, and he sold them into the hands of the Philistines, and into the hands of the children of Ammon. ⁸And that year they vexed and oppressed the children of Israel: eighteen years, all the children of Israel that were on the other side Jordan in the land of the Amorites, which is in Gilead. ⁹Moreover the children of Ammon passed over Jordan to fight also against Judah, and against Benjamin, and against the house of Ephraim; so that Israel was sore distressed. ¹⁰And the children of Israel cried to the LORD, saying, We have sinned against you, both because we have forsaken our God, and also served Baalim. ¹¹And the LORD said to the children of Israel, Did not I deliver you from the Egyptians, and from the Amorites, from the children of Ammon, and from the Philistines? ¹²The Zidonians also, and the Amalekites, and the Maonites, did oppress you; and you cried to me, and I delivered you out of their hand. ¹³Yet you have forsaken me, and served other gods: why I will deliver you no more. ¹⁴Go and cry to the gods which you have chosen; let them deliver you in the time of your tribulation. ¹⁵And the children of Israel said to the LORD, We have sinned: do you to us whatever seems good to you; deliver us only, we pray you, this day. ¹⁶And they put away the strange gods from among them, and served the LORD: and his soul was grieved for the misery of Israel. ¹⁷Then the children of Ammon were gathered together, and encamped in Gilead. And the children of Israel assembled themselves together, and encamped in Mizpeh. ¹⁸And the people and princes of Gilead said one to another, What man is he that will begin to fight against the children of Ammon? he shall be head over all the inhabitants of Gilead.

11 ¹Now Jephthah the Gileadite was a mighty man of valor, and he was the son of an harlot: and Gilead begat Jephthah. ²And Gilead's wife bore him sons; and his wife's sons grew up, and they thrust out Jephthah, and said to him, You shall not inherit in our father's house; for you are the son of a strange woman. ³Then Jephthah fled from his brothers, and dwelled in the land of Tob: and there were gathered vain men to Jephthah, and went out with him. ⁴And it came to pass in process of time, that the children of Ammon made war against Israel. ⁵And it was so, that when the children of Ammon made war against Israel, the elders of Gilead went to fetch Jephthah out of the land of Tob: ⁶And they said to Jephthah, Come, and be our captain, that we may fight with the children of Ammon. ⁷And Jephthah said to the elders of Gilead, Did not you hate me, and expel me out of my father's house? and why are you come to me now when you are in distress? ⁸And the elders of Gilead said to Jephthah, Therefore we turn again to you now, that you may go with us, and fight against the children of Ammon, and be our head over all the inhabitants of Gilead. ⁹And Jephthah said to the elders of Gilead, If you bring me home again to fight against the children of Ammon, and the LORD deliver them before me, shall I be your head? ¹⁰And the elders of Gilead said to Jephthah, The LORD be witness between us, if we do not so according to your words. ¹¹Then Jephthah went with the elders of Gilead, and the people made him head and captain over them: and Jephthah uttered all his words before the LORD in Mizpeh. ¹²And Jephthah sent messengers to the king of the children of Ammon, saying, What have you to do with me, that you are come against me to fight in my land? ¹³And the king of the children of Ammon answered to the messengers of Jephthah, Because Israel took away my land, when they came up out of Egypt, from Arnon even to Jabbok, and to Jordan: now therefore restore those lands again peaceably. ¹⁴And Jephthah sent messengers again to the king of the children of Ammon: ¹⁵And said to him, Thus says Jephthah, Israel took not away the land of Moab, nor the land of the children of Ammon: ¹⁶But when Israel came up from Egypt, and walked through the wilderness to the Red sea, and came to Kadesh; ¹⁷Then Israel sent messengers to the king of Edom, saying, Let me, I pray you, pass through your land: but the king of Edom would not listen thereto. And in like manner they sent to the king of Moab: but he would not consent: and Israel stayed in Kadesh. ¹⁸Then they went along through the wilderness, and compassed the land of Edom, and the land of Moab, and came by the east side of the land of Moab, and pitched on the other side of Arnon, but came not within the border of Moab: for Arnon was the border of Moab. ¹⁹And Israel sent messengers to Sihon king of the Amorites, the king of Heshbon; and Israel said to him, Let us pass, we pray you, through your land into my place. ²⁰But Sihon trusted not Israel to pass through his coast: but Sihon gathered all his people together, and pitched in Jahaz, and fought against Israel. ²¹And the LORD God of Israel delivered Sihon and all his people into the hand of Israel, and they smote them: so Israel possessed all the land of the Amorites, the inhabitants of that country. ²²And they possessed all the coasts of the Amorites, from Arnon even to Jabbok, and from the wilderness even to Jordan. ²³So now the LORD God of Israel has dispossessed the Amorites from before his people Israel, and should you possess it? ²⁴Will not you possess that which Chemosh your god gives you to possess? So whomsoever the LORD our God shall drive out from before us, them will we possess. ²⁵And now are you any thing better than Balak the son of Zippor, king of Moab? did he ever strive against Israel, or did he ever fight against them, ²⁶While Israel dwelled in Heshbon and her towns, and in Aroer and her towns, and in all the cities that be along by the coasts of Arnon, three hundred years? why therefore did you not recover them within that time? ²⁷Why I have not sinned against you, but you do me wrong to war against me: the LORD the Judge be judge this day between the children of Israel and the children of Ammon. ²⁸However, the king of the children of Ammon listened not to the words of Jephthah which he sent him. ²⁹Then the Spirit of the LORD came on Jephthah, and he passed over Gilead, and Manasseh, and passed over Mizpeh of Gilead, and from Mizpeh of Gilead he passed over to the children of Ammon. ³⁰And Jephthah vowed a vow to the LORD, and said, If you shall without fail deliver the children of Ammon into my hands, ³¹Then it shall be, that whatever comes forth of the doors of my house to meet me, when I return in peace from the children of Ammon, shall surely be the LORD's, and I will offer it up for a burnt offering. ³²So Jephthah passed over to the children of Ammon to fight against them; and the LORD delivered them into his hands. ³³And he smote them from Aroer, even till you come to Minnith, even twenty cities, and to the plain of the vineyards, with a very great slaughter. Thus the children of Ammon were subdued before the children of Israel. ³⁴And Jephthah came to Mizpeh to his house, and, behold, his daughter came out to meet him with tambourines and with dances: and she was his only child; beside her he had neither son nor daughter. ³⁵And it came to pass, when he saw her, that he rent his clothes, and said, Alas, my daughter! you have brought me very low, and you are one of them that trouble me: for I have opened my mouth to the LORD, and I cannot go back. ³⁶And she said to him, My father, if you have opened your mouth to the LORD, do to me according to that which has proceeded out of your mouth; for as much as the LORD has taken vengeance for you of your enemies, even of the children of Ammon. ³⁷And she said to her father, Let this thing be done for me: let me alone two months, that I may go up and down on the mountains, and mourn my virginity, I and my fellows. ³⁸And he said, Go. And he sent her away for two months: and she went with her companions, and bewailed her virginity on the mountains. ³⁹And it came to pass at the end of two months, that she returned to her father, who did with her according to his vow which he had vowed: and she knew no man. And it was a custom in Israel, ⁴⁰That the daughters of Israel went yearly to lament the daughter of Jephthah the Gileadite four days in a year.

12 ¹And the men of Ephraim gathered themselves together, and went northward, and said to Jephthah, Why passed you over to fight against the children of Ammon, and did not call us to go with you? we will burn your house on you with fire. ²And Jephthah said to them, I and my people were at great strife with the children of Ammon; and when I called you, you delivered me not out of their hands. ³And when I saw that you delivered me not, I put my life in my hands, and passed over against the children of Ammon, and the LORD delivered them into my hand: why then are you come up to me this day, to fight against me? ⁴Then Jephthah gathered together all the men of Gilead, and fought with Ephraim: and the men of Gilead smote Ephraim, because they said, You Gileadites are fugitives of Ephraim among the Ephraimites, and among the Manassites. ⁵And the Gileadites took the passages of Jordan before the Ephraimites: and it was so, that when those Ephraimites which were escaped said, Let me go over; that the men of Gilead said to him, Are you an Ephraimite? If he said, No; ⁶Then said they to him, Say now Shibboleth: and he said Sibboleth: for he could not frame to pronounce it right. Then they took him, and slew him at the passages of Jordan: and there fell at that time of the Ephraimites forty and two thousand. ⁷And Jephthah judged Israel six years. Then died Jephthah the Gileadite, and was buried in one of the cities of Gilead. ⁸And after him Ibzan of Bethlehem judged Israel. ⁹And he had thirty sons, and thirty daughters, whom he sent abroad, and took in thirty daughters from abroad for his sons. And he judged Israel seven years. ¹⁰Then died Ibzan, and was buried at Bethlehem. ¹¹And after him Elon, a Zebulonite, judged Israel; and he judged Israel ten years. ¹²And Elon the Zebulonite died, and was buried in Aijalon in the country of Zebulun. ¹³And after him Abdon the son of Hillel, a Pirathonite, judged Israel. ¹⁴And he had forty sons and thirty nephews, that rode on three score and ten ass colts: and he judged Israel eight years. ¹⁵And Abdon the son of Hillel the Pirathonite died, and was buried in Pirathon in the land of Ephraim, in the mount of the Amalekites.

13 ¹And the men of Ephraim gathered themselves together, and went northward, and said to Jephthah, Why passed you over to fight against the children of Ammon, and did not call us to go with you? we will burn your house on you with fire. ²And Jephthah said to them, I and my people were at great strife with the children of Ammon; and when I called you, you delivered me not out of their hands. ³And when I saw that you delivered me not, I put my life in my hands, and passed over against the children of Ammon, and the LORD delivered them into my hand: why then are you come up to me this day, to fight against me? ⁴Then Jephthah gathered together all the men of Gilead, and fought with Ephraim: and the men of Gilead smote Ephraim, because they said, You Gileadites are fugitives of Ephraim among the Ephraimites, and among the Manassites. ⁵And the Gileadites took the passages of Jordan before the Ephraimites: and it was so, that when those Ephraimites which were escaped said, Let me go over; that the men of Gilead said to him, Are you an Ephraimite? If he said, No; ⁶Then said they to him, Say now Shibboleth: and he said Sibboleth: for he could not frame to pronounce it right. Then they took him, and slew him at the passages of Jordan: and there fell at that time of the Ephraimites forty and two thousand. ⁷And Jephthah judged Israel six years. Then died Jephthah the Gileadite, and was buried in one of the cities of Gilead. ⁸And after him Ibzan of Bethlehem judged Israel. ⁹And he had thirty sons, and thirty daughters, whom he sent abroad, and took in thirty daughters from abroad for his sons. And he judged Israel seven years. ¹⁰Then died Ibzan, and was buried at Bethlehem. ¹¹And after him Elon, a Zebulonite, judged Israel; and he judged Israel ten years. ¹²And Elon the Zebulonite died, and was buried in Aijalon in the country of Zebulun. ¹³And after him Abdon the son of Hillel, a Pirathonite, judged Israel. ¹⁴And he had forty sons and thirty nephews, that rode on three score and ten ass colts: and he judged Israel eight years. ¹⁵And Abdon the son of Hillel the Pirathonite died, and was buried in Pirathon in the land of Ephraim, in the mount of the Amalekites.

14 ¹And Samson went down to Timnath, and saw a woman in Timnath of the daughters of the Philistines. ²And he came up, and told his father and his mother, and said, I have seen a woman in Timnath of the daughters of the Philistines: now therefore get her for me to wife. ³Then his father and his mother said to him, Is there never a woman among the daughters of your brothers, or among all my people, that you go to take a wife of the uncircumcised Philistines? And Samson said to his father, Get her for me; for she pleases me well. ⁴But his father and his mother knew not that it was of the LORD, that he sought an occasion against the Philistines: for at that time the Philistines had dominion over Israel. ⁵Then went Samson down, and his father and his mother, to Timnath, and came to the vineyards of Timnath: and, behold, a young lion roared against him. ⁶And the Spirit of the LORD came mightily on him, and he rent him as he would have rent a kid, and he had nothing in his hand: but he told not his father or his mother what he had done. ⁷And he went down, and talked with the woman; and she pleased Samson well. ⁸And after a time he returned to take her, and he turned

aside to see the carcass of the lion: and, behold, there was a swarm of bees and honey in the carcass of the lion. ⁹And he took thereof in his hands, and went on eating, and came to his father and mother, and he gave them, and they did eat: but he told not them that he had taken the honey out of the carcass of the lion. ¹⁰So his father went down to the woman: and Samson made there a feast; for so used the young men to do. ¹¹And it came to pass, when they saw him, that they brought thirty companions to be with him. ¹²And Samson said to them, I will now put forth a riddle to you: if you can certainly declare it me within the seven days of the feast, and find it out, then I will give you thirty sheets and thirty change of garments: ¹³But if you cannot declare it me, then shall you give me thirty sheets and thirty change of garments. And they said to him, Put forth your riddle, that we may hear it. ¹⁴And he said to them, Out of the eater came forth meat, and out of the strong came forth sweetness. And they could not in three days expound the riddle. ¹⁵And it came to pass on the seventh day, that they said to Samson's wife, Entice your husband, that he may declare to us the riddle, lest we burn you and your father's house with fire: have you called us to take that we have? is it not so? ¹⁶And Samson's wife wept before him, and said, You do but hate me, and love me not: you have put forth a riddle to the children of my people, and have not told it me. And he said to her, Behold, I have not told it my father nor my mother, and shall I tell it you? ¹⁷And she wept before him the seven days, while their feast lasted: and it came to pass on the seventh day, that he told her, because she lay sore on him: and she told the riddle to the children of her people. ¹⁸And the men of the city said to him on the seventh day before the sun went down, What is sweeter than honey? And what is stronger than a lion? and he said to them, If you had not plowed with my heifer, you had not found out my riddle. ¹⁹And the Spirit of the LORD came on him, and he went down to Ashkelon, and slew thirty men of them, and took their spoil, and gave change of garments to them which expounded the riddle. And his anger was kindled, and he went up to his father's house. ²⁰But Samson's wife was given to his companion, whom he had used as his friend.

15 ¹But it came to pass within a while after, in the time of wheat harvest, that Samson visited his wife with a kid; and he said, I will go in to my wife into the chamber. But her father would not suffer him to go in. ²And her father said, I truly thought that you had utterly hated her; therefore I gave her to your companion: is not her younger sister fairer than she? take her, I pray you, instead of her. ³And Samson said concerning them, Now shall I be more blameless than the Philistines, though I do them a displeasure. ⁴And Samson went and caught three hundred foxes, and took firebrands, and turned tail to tail, and put a firebrand in the middle between two tails. ⁵And when he had set the brands on fire, he let them go into the standing corn of the Philistines, and burnt up both the shocks, and also the standing corn, with the vineyards and olives. ⁶Then the Philistines said, Who has done this? And they answered, Samson, the son in law of the Timnite, because he had taken his wife, and given her to his companion. And the Philistines came up, and burnt her and her father with fire. ⁷And Samson said to them, Though you have done this, yet will I be avenged of you, and after that I will cease. ⁸And he smote them hip and thigh with a great slaughter: and he went down and dwelled in the top of the rock Etam. ⁹Then the Philistines went up, and pitched in Judah, and spread themselves in Lehi. ¹⁰And the men of Judah said, Why are you come up against us? And they answered, To bind Samson are we come up, to do to him as he has done to us. ¹¹Then three thousand men of Judah went to the top of the rock Etam, and said to Samson, Know you not that the Philistines are rulers over us? what is this that you have done to us? And he said to them, As they did to me, so have I done to them. ¹²And they said to him, We are come down to bind you, that we may deliver you into the hand of the Philistines. And Samson said to them, Swear to me, that you will not fall on me yourselves. ¹³And they spoke to him, saying, No; but we will bind you fast, and deliver you into their hand: but surely we will not kill you. And they bound him with two new cords, and brought him up from the rock. ¹⁴And when he came to Lehi, the Philistines shouted against him: and the Spirit of the LORD came mightily on him, and the cords that were on his arms became as flax that was burnt with fire, and his bands loosed from off his hands. ¹⁵And he found a new jawbone of an ass, and put forth his hand, and took it, and slew a thousand men therewith. ¹⁶And Samson said, With the jawbone of an ass, heaps on heaps, with the jaw of an ass have I slain a thousand men. ¹⁷And it came to pass, when he had made an end of speaking, that he cast away the jawbone out of his hand, and called that place Ramathlehi. ¹⁸And he was sore thirsty, and called on the LORD, and said, You have given this great deliverance into the hand of your servant: and now shall I die for thirst, and fall into the hand of the uncircumcised? ¹⁹But God split an hollow place that was in the jaw, and there came water out of there; and when he had drunk, his spirit came again, and he revived: why he called the name thereof Enhakkore, which is in Lehi to this day. ²⁰And he judged Israel in the days of the Philistines twenty years.

16 ¹Then went Samson to Gaza, and saw there an harlot, and went in to her. ²And it was told the Gazites, saying, Samson is come here. And they compassed him in, and laid wait for him all night in the gate of the city, and were quiet all the night, saying, In the morning, when it is day, we shall kill him. ³And Samson lay till midnight, and arose at midnight, and took the doors of the gate of the city, and the two posts, and went away with them, bar and all, and put them on his shoulders, and carried them up to the top of an hill that is before Hebron. ⁴And it came to pass afterward, that he loved a woman in the valley of Sorek, whose name was Delilah. ⁵And the lords of the Philistines came up to her, and said to her, Entice him, and see wherein his great strength lies, and by what means we may prevail against him, that we may bind him to afflict him; and we will give you every one of us eleven hundred pieces of silver. ⁶And Delilah said to Samson, Tell me, I pray you, wherein your great strength lies, and with which you might be bound to afflict you. ⁷And Samson said to her, If they bind me with seven green thongs that were never dried, then shall I be weak, and be as another man. ⁸Then the lords of the Philistines brought up to her seven green thongs which had not been dried, and she bound him with them.

⁹Now there were men lying in wait, abiding with her in the chamber. And she said to him, The Philistines be on you, Samson. And he broke the thongs, as a thread of wick is broken when it touches the fire. So his strength was not known. ¹⁰And Delilah said to Samson, Behold, you have mocked me, and told me lies: now tell me, I pray you, with which you might be bound. ¹¹And he said to her, If they bind me fast with new ropes that never were occupied, then shall I be weak, and be as another man. ¹²Delilah therefore took new ropes, and bound him therewith, and said to him, The Philistines be on you, Samson. And there were liers in wait abiding in the chamber. And he broke them from off his arms like a thread. ¹³And Delilah said to Samson, Till now you have mocked me, and told me lies: tell me with which you might be bound. And he said to her, If you weave the seven locks of my head with the web. ¹⁴And she fastened it with the pin, and said to him, The Philistines be on you, Samson. And he awaked out of his sleep, and went away with the pin of the beam, and with the web. ¹⁵And she said to him, How can you say, I love you, when your heart is not with me? you have mocked me these three times, and have not told me wherein your great strength lies. ¹⁶And it came to pass, when she pressed him daily with her words, and urged him, so that his soul was vexed to death; ¹⁷That he told her all his heart, and said to her, There has not come a razor on my head; for I have been a Nazarite to God from my mother's womb: if I be shaven, then my strength will go from me, and I shall become weak, and be like any other man. ¹⁸And when Delilah saw that he had told her all his heart, she sent and called for the lords of the Philistines, saying, Come up this once, for he has showed me all his heart. Then the lords of the Philistines came up to her, and brought money in their hand. ¹⁹And she made him sleep on her knees; and she called for a man, and she caused him to shave off the seven locks of his head; and she began to afflict him, and his strength went from him. ²⁰And she said, The Philistines be on you, Samson. And he awoke out of his sleep, and said, I will go out as at other times before, and shake myself. And he knew not that the LORD was departed from him. ²¹But the Philistines took him, and put out his eyes, and brought him down to Gaza, and bound him with fetters of brass; and he did grind in the prison house. ²²However, the hair of his head began to grow again after he was shaven. ²³Then the lords of the Philistines gathered them together for to offer a great sacrifice to Dagon their god, and to rejoice: for they said, Our god has delivered Samson our enemy into our hand. ²⁴And when the people saw him, they praised their god: for they said, Our god has delivered into our hands our enemy, and the destroyer of our country, which slew many of us. ²⁵And it came to pass, when their hearts were merry, that they said, Call for Samson, that he may make us sport. And they called for Samson out of the prison house; and he made them sport: and they set him between the pillars. ²⁶And Samson said to the lad that held him by the hand, Suffer me that I may feel the pillars whereupon the house stands, that I may lean on them. ²⁷Now the house was full of men and women; and all the lords of the Philistines were there; and there were on the roof about three thousand men and women, that beheld while Samson made sport. ²⁸And Samson called to the LORD, and said, O Lord God, remember me, I pray you, and strengthen me, I pray you, only this once, O God, that I may be at once avenged of the Philistines for my two eyes. ²⁹And Samson took hold of the two middle pillars on which the house stood, and on which it was borne up, of the one with his right hand, and of the other with his left. ³⁰And Samson said, Let me die with the Philistines. And he bowed himself with all his might; and the house fell on the lords, and on all the people that were therein. So the dead which he slew at his death were more than they which he slew in his life. ³¹Then his brothers and all the house of his father came down, and took him, and brought him up, and buried him between Zorah and Eshtaol in the burial plot of Manoah his father. And he judged Israel twenty years.

17

¹And there was a man of mount Ephraim, whose name was Micah. ²And he said to his mother, The eleven hundred shekels of silver that were taken from you, about which you cursed, and spoke of also in my ears, behold, the silver is with me; I took it. And his mother said, Blessed be you of the LORD, my son. ³And when he had restored the eleven hundred shekels of silver to his mother, his mother said, I had wholly dedicated the silver to the LORD from my hand for my son, to make a graven image and a molten image: now therefore I will restore it to you. ⁴Yet he restored the money to his mother; and his mother took two hundred shekels of silver, and gave them to the founder, who made thereof a graven image and a molten image: and they were in the house of Micah. ⁵And the man Micah had an house of gods, and made an ephod, and teraphim, and consecrated one of his sons, who became his priest. ⁶In those days there was no king in Israel, but every man did that which was right in his own eyes. ⁷And there was a young man out of Bethlehemjudah of the family of Judah, who was a Levite, and he sojourned there. ⁸And the man departed out of the city from Bethlehemjudah to sojourn where he could find a place: and he came to mount Ephraim to the house of Micah, as he journeyed. ⁹And Micah said to him, From where come you? And he said to him, I am a Levite of Bethlehemjudah, and I go to sojourn where I may find a place. ¹⁰And Micah said to him, Dwell with me, and be to me a father and a priest, and I will give you ten shekels of silver by the year, and a suit of apparel, and your victuals. So the Levite went in. ¹¹And the Levite was content to dwell with the man; and the young man was to him as one of his sons. ¹²And Micah consecrated the Levite; and the young man became his priest, and was in the house of Micah. ¹³Then said Micah, Now know I that the LORD will do me good, seeing I have a Levite to my priest.

18

¹In those days there was no king in Israel: and in those days the tribe of the Danites sought them an inheritance to dwell in; for to that day all their inheritance had not fallen to them among the tribes of Israel. ²And the children of Dan sent of their family five men from their coasts, men of valor, from Zorah, and from Eshtaol, to spy out the land, and to search it; and they said to them, Go, search the land: who when they came to mount Ephraim, to the house of Micah, they lodged there. ³When they were by the house of Micah, they knew the voice of the young man

the Levite: and they turned in thither, and said to him, Who brought you here? and what make you in this place? and what have you here? ⁴And he said to them, Thus and thus deals Micah with me, and has hired me, and I am his priest. ⁵And they said to him, Ask counsel, we pray you, of God, that we may know whether our way which we go shall be prosperous. ⁶And the priest said to them, Go in peace: before the LORD is your way wherein you go. ⁷Then the five men departed, and came to Laish, and saw the people that were therein, how they dwelled careless, after the manner of the Zidonians, quiet and secure; and there was no magistrate in the land, that might put them to shame in any thing; and they were far from the Zidonians, and had no business with any man. ⁸And they came to their brothers to Zorah and Eshtaol: and their brothers said to them, What say you? ⁹And they said, Arise, that we may go up against them: for we have seen the land, and, behold, it is very good: and are you still? be not slothful to go, and to enter to possess the land. ¹⁰When you go, you shall come to a people secure, and to a large land: for God has given it into your hands; a place where there is no want of any thing that is in the earth. ¹¹And there went from there of the family of the Danites, out of Zorah and out of Eshtaol, six hundred men appointed with weapons of war. ¹²And they went up, and pitched in Kirjathjearim, in Judah: why they called that place Mahanehdan to this day: behold, it is behind Kirjathjearim. ¹³And they passed there to mount Ephraim, and came to the house of Micah. ¹⁴Then answered the five men that went to spy out the country of Laish, and said to their brothers, Do you know that there is in these houses an ephod, and teraphim, and a graven image, and a molten image? now therefore consider what you have to do. ¹⁵And they turned thitherward, and came to the house of the young man the Levite, even to the house of Micah, and saluted him. ¹⁶And the six hundred men appointed with their weapons of war, which were of the children of Dan, stood by the entering of the gate. ¹⁷And the five men that went to spy out the land went up, and came in thither, and took the graven image, and the ephod, and the teraphim, and the molten image: and the priest stood in the entering of the gate with the six hundred men that were appointed with weapons of war. ¹⁸And these went into Micah's house, and fetched the carved image, the ephod, and the teraphim, and the molten image. Then said the priest to them, What do you? ¹⁹And they said to him, Hold your peace, lay your hand on your mouth, and go with us, and be to us a father and a priest: is it better for you to be a priest to the house of one man, or that you be a priest to a tribe and a family in Israel? ²⁰And the priest's heart was glad, and he took the ephod, and the teraphim, and the graven image, and went in the middle of the people. ²¹So they turned and departed, and put the little ones and the cattle and the carriage before them. ²²And when they were a good way from the house of Micah, the men that were in the houses near to Micah's house were gathered together, and overtook the children of Dan. ²³And they cried to the children of Dan. And they turned their faces, and said to Micah, What ails you, that you come with such a company? ²⁴And he said, You have taken away my gods which I made, and the priest, and you are gone away: and what have I more? and what is this that you say to me, What ails you? ²⁵And the children of Dan said to him, Let not your voice be heard among us, lest angry fellows run on you, and you lose your life, with the lives of your household. ²⁶And the children of Dan went their way: and when Micah saw that they were too strong for him, he turned and went back to his house. ²⁷And they took the things which Micah had made, and the priest which he had, and came to Laish, to a people that were at quiet and secure: and they smote them with the edge of the sword, and burnt the city with fire. ²⁸And there was no deliverer, because it was far from Zidon, and they had no business with any man; and it was in the valley that lies by Bethrehob. And they built a city, and dwelled therein. ²⁹And they called the name of the city Dan, after the name of Dan their father, who was born to Israel: however, the name of the city was Laish at the first. ³⁰And the children of Dan set up the graven image: and Jonathan, the son of Gershom, the son of Manasseh, he and his sons were priests to the tribe of Dan until the day of the captivity of the land. ³¹And they set them up Micah's graven image, which he made, all the time that the house of God was in Shiloh.

19

¹And it came to pass in those days, when there was no king in Israel, that there was a certain Levite sojourning on the side of mount Ephraim, who took to him a concubine out of Bethlehemjudah. ²And his concubine played the whore against him, and went away from him to her father's house to Bethlehemjudah, and was there four whole months. ³And her husband arose, and went after her, to speak friendly to her, and to bring her again, having his servant with him, and a couple of asses: and she brought him into her father's house: and when the father of the damsel saw him, he rejoiced to meet him. ⁴And his father in law, the damsel's father, retained him; and he stayed with him three days: so they did eat and drink, and lodged there. ⁵And it came to pass on the fourth day, when they arose early in the morning, that he rose up to depart: and the damsel's father said to his son in law, Comfort your heart with a morsel of bread, and afterward go your way. ⁶And they sat down, and did eat and drink both of them together: for the damsel's father had said to the man, Be content, I pray you, and tarry all night, and let your heart be merry. ⁷And when the man rose up to depart, his father in law urged him: therefore he lodged there again. ⁸And he arose early in the morning on the fifth day to depart; and the damsel's father said, Comfort your heart, I pray you. And they tarried until afternoon, and they did eat both of them. ⁹And when the man rose up to depart, he, and his concubine, and his servant, his father in law, the damsel's father, said to him, Behold, now the day draws toward evening, I pray you tarry all night: behold, the day grows to an end, lodge here, that your heart may be merry; and to morrow get you early on your way, that you may go home. ¹⁰But the man would not tarry that night, but he rose up and departed, and came over against Jebus, which is Jerusalem; and there were with him two asses saddled, his concubine also was with him. ¹¹And when they were by Jebus, the day was far spent; and the servant said to his master, Come, I pray you, and let us turn in into this city of the Jebusites, and lodge in it. ¹²And his master said to him, We will not turn aside here into the city of a stranger, that is not of the

children of Israel; we will pass over to Gibeah. ¹³And he said to his servant, Come, and let us draw near to one of these places to lodge all night, in Gibeah, or in Ramah. ¹⁴And they passed on and went their way; and the sun went down on them when they were by Gibeah, which belongs to Benjamin. ¹⁵And they turned aside thither, to go in and to lodge in Gibeah: and when he went in, he sat him down in a street of the city: for there was no man that took them into his house to lodging. ¹⁶And, behold, there came an old man from his work out of the field at even, which was also of mount Ephraim; and he sojourned in Gibeah: but the men of the place were Benjamites. ¹⁷And when he had lifted up his eyes, he saw a wayfaring man in the street of the city: and the old man said, Where go you? and from where come you? ¹⁸And he said to him, We are passing from Bethlehemjudah toward the side of mount Ephraim; from there am I: and I went to Bethlehemjudah, but I am now going to the house of the LORD; and there is no man that receives me to house. ¹⁹Yet there is both straw and provender for our asses; and there is bread and wine also for me, and for your handmaid, and for the young man which is with your servants: there is no want of any thing. ²⁰And the old man said, Peace be with you; howsoever let all your wants lie on me; only lodge not in the street. ²¹So he brought him into his house, and gave provender to the asses: and they washed their feet, and did eat and drink. ²²Now as they were making their hearts merry, behold, the men of the city, certain sons of Belial, beset the house round about, and beat at the door, and spoke to the master of the house, the old man, saying, Bring forth the man that came into your house, that we may know him. ²³And the man, the master of the house, went out to them, and said to them, No, my brothers, no, I pray you, do not so wickedly; seeing that this man is come into my house, do not this folly. ²⁴Behold, here is my daughter a maiden, and his concubine; them I will bring out now, and humble you them, and do with them what seems good to you: but to this man do not so vile a thing. ²⁵But the men would not listen to him: so the man took his concubine, and brought her forth to them; and they knew her, and abused her all the night until the morning: and when the day began to spring, they let her go. ²⁶Then came the woman in the dawning of the day, and fell down at the door of the man's house where her lord was, till it was light. ²⁷And her lord rose up in the morning, and opened the doors of the house, and went out to go his way: and, behold, the woman his concubine was fallen down at the door of the house, and her hands were on the threshold. ²⁸And he said to her, Up, and let us be going. But none answered. Then the man took her up on an ass, and the man rose up, and got him to his place. ²⁹And when he was come into his house, he took a knife, and laid hold on his concubine, and divided her, together with her bones, into twelve pieces, and sent her into all the coasts of Israel. ³⁰And it was so, that all that saw it said, There was no such deed done nor seen from the day that the children of Israel came up out of the land of Egypt to this day: consider of it, take advice, and speak your minds.

20 ¹Then all the children of Israel went out, and the congregation was gathered together as one man, from Dan even to Beersheba, with the land of Gilead, to the LORD in Mizpeh. ²And the chief of all the people, even of all the tribes of Israel, presented themselves in the assembly of the people of God, four hundred thousand footmen that drew sword. ³(Now the children of Benjamin heard that the children of Israel were gone up to Mizpeh.) Then said the children of Israel, Tell us, how was this wickedness? ⁴And the Levite, the husband of the woman that was slain, answered and said, I came into Gibeah that belongs to Benjamin, I and my concubine, to lodge. ⁵And the men of Gibeah rose against me, and beset the house round about on me by night, and thought to have slain me: and my concubine have they forced, that she is dead. ⁶And I took my concubine, and cut her in pieces, and sent her throughout all the country of the inheritance of Israel: for they have committed lewdness and folly in Israel. ⁷Behold, you are all children of Israel; give here your advice and counsel. ⁸And all the people arose as one man, saying, We will not any of us go to his tent, neither will we any of us turn into his house. ⁹But now this shall be the thing which we will do to Gibeah; we will go up by lot against it; ¹⁰And we will take ten men of an hundred throughout all the tribes of Israel, and an hundred of a thousand, and a thousand out of ten thousand, to fetch victual for the people, that they may do, when they come to Gibeah of Benjamin, according to all the folly that they have worked in Israel. ¹¹So all the men of Israel were gathered against the city, knit together as one man. ¹²And the tribes of Israel sent men through all the tribe of Benjamin, saying, What wickedness is this that is done among you? ¹³Now therefore deliver us the men, the children of Belial, which are in Gibeah, that we may put them to death, and put away evil from Israel. But the children of Benjamin would not listen to the voice of their brothers the children of Israel. ¹⁴But the children of Benjamin gathered themselves together out of the cities to Gibeah, to go out to battle against the children of Israel. ¹⁵And the children of Benjamin were numbered at that time out of the cities twenty and six thousand men that drew sword, beside the inhabitants of Gibeah, which were numbered seven hundred chosen men. ¹⁶Among all this people there were seven hundred chosen men left handed; every one could sling stones at an hair breadth, and not miss. ¹⁷And the men of Israel, beside Benjamin, were numbered four hundred thousand men that drew sword: all these were men of war. ¹⁸And the children of Israel arose, and went up to the house of God, and asked counsel of God, and said, Which of us shall go up first to the battle against the children of Benjamin? And the LORD said, Judah shall go up first. ¹⁹And the children of Israel rose up in the morning, and encamped against Gibeah. ²⁰And the men of Israel went out to battle against Benjamin; and the men of Israel put themselves in array to fight against them at Gibeah. ²¹And the children of Benjamin came forth out of Gibeah, and destroyed down to the ground of the Israelites that day twenty and two thousand men. ²²And the people the men of Israel encouraged themselves, and set their battle again in array in the place where they put themselves in array the first day. ²³(And the children of Israel went up and wept before the LORD until even, and asked counsel of the LORD, saying, Shall I go up again to battle against the children of Benjamin my brother? And the LORD said, Go up against him.) ²⁴And the children of Israel came near against the children of Benjamin the second day. ²⁵And Benjamin went forth against them out of Gibeah the second day, and destroyed down to the ground of the children of Israel again eighteen thousand men; all these drew the sword. ²⁶Then all the children of Israel, and all the people, went up, and came to the house of God, and wept, and sat there before the LORD, and fasted that day until even, and offered burnt offerings and peace offerings before the LORD. ²⁷And the children of Israel inquired of the LORD, (for the ark of the covenant of God was there in those days, ²⁸And Phinehas, the son of Eleazar, the son of Aaron, stood before it in those days,) saying, Shall I yet again go out to battle against the children of Benjamin my brother, or shall I cease? And the LORD said, Go up; for to morrow I will deliver them into your hand. ²⁹And Israel set liers in wait round about Gibeah. ³⁰And the children of Israel went up against the children of Benjamin on the third day, and put themselves in array against Gibeah, as at other times. ³¹And the children of Benjamin went out against the people, and were drawn away from the city; and they began to smite of the people, and kill, as at other times, in the highways, of which one goes up to the house of God, and the other to Gibeah in the field, about thirty men of Israel. ³²And the children of Benjamin said, They are smitten down before us, as at the first. But the children of Israel said, Let us flee, and draw them from the city to the highways. ³³And all the men of Israel rose up out of their place, and put themselves in array at Baaltamar: and the liers in wait of Israel came forth out of their places, even out of the meadows of Gibeah. ³⁴And there came against Gibeah ten thousand chosen men out of all Israel, and the battle was sore: but they knew not that evil was near them. ³⁵And the LORD smote Benjamin before Israel: and the children of Israel destroyed of the Benjamites that day twenty and five thousand and an hundred men: all these drew the sword. ³⁶So the children of Benjamin saw that they were smitten: for the men of Israel gave place to the Benjamites, because they trusted to the liers in wait which they had set beside Gibeah. ³⁷And the liers in wait hurried, and rushed on Gibeah; and the liers in wait drew themselves along, and smote all the city with the edge of the sword. ³⁸Now there was an appointed sign between the men of Israel and the liers in wait, that they should make a great flame with smoke rise up out of the city. ³⁹And when the men of Israel retired in the battle, Benjamin began to smite and kill of the men of Israel about thirty persons: for they said, Surely they are smitten down before us, as in the first battle. ⁴⁰But when the flame began to arise up out of the city with a pillar of smoke, the Benjamites looked behind them, and, behold, the flame of the city ascended up to heaven. ⁴¹And when the men of Israel turned again, the men of Benjamin were amazed: for they saw that evil was come on them. ⁴²Therefore they turned their backs before the men of Israel to the way of the wilderness; but the battle overtook them; and them which came out of the cities they destroyed in the middle of them. ⁴³Thus they enclosed the Benjamites round about, and chased them, and stepped them down with ease over against Gibeah toward the sun rise. ⁴⁴And there fell of Benjamin eighteen thousand men; all these were men of valor. ⁴⁵And they turned and fled toward the wilderness to the rock of Rimmon: and they gleaned of them in the highways five thousand men; and pursued hard after them to Gidom, and slew two thousand men of them. ⁴⁶So that all which fell that day of Benjamin were twenty and five thousand men that drew the sword; all these were men of valor. ⁴⁷But six hundred men turned and fled to the wilderness to the rock Rimmon, and stayed in the rock Rimmon four months. ⁴⁸And the men of Israel turned again on the children of Benjamin, and smote them with the edge of the sword, as well the men of every city, as the beast, and all that came to hand: also they set on fire all the cities that they came to.

21

¹Now the men of Israel had sworn in Mizpeh, saying, There shall not any of us give his daughter to Benjamin to wife. ²And the people came to the house of God, and stayed there till even before God, and lifted up their voices, and wept sore; ³And said, O LORD God of Israel, why is this come to pass in Israel, that there should be to day one tribe lacking in Israel? ⁴And it came to pass on the morrow, that the people rose early, and built there an altar, and offered burnt offerings and peace offerings. ⁵And the children of Israel said, Who is there among all the tribes of Israel that came not up with the congregation to the LORD? For they had made a great oath concerning him that came not up to the LORD to Mizpeh, saying, He shall surely be put to death. ⁶And the children of Israel repented them for Benjamin their brother, and said, There is one tribe cut off from Israel this day. ⁷How shall we do for wives for them that remain, seeing we have sworn by the LORD that we will not give them of our daughters to wives? ⁸And they said, What one is there of the tribes of Israel that came not up to Mizpeh to the LORD? And, behold, there came none to the camp from Jabeshgilead to the assembly. ⁹For the people were numbered, and, behold, there were none of the inhabitants of Jabeshgilead there. ¹⁰And the congregation sent thither twelve thousand men of the most valiant, and commanded them, saying, Go and smite the inhabitants of Jabeshgilead with the edge of the sword, with the women and the children. ¹¹And this is the thing that you shall do, You shall utterly destroy every male, and every woman that has lain by man. ¹²And they found among the inhabitants of Jabeshgilead four hundred young virgins, that had known no man by lying with any male: and they brought them to the camp to Shiloh, which is in the land of Canaan. ¹³And the whole congregation sent some to speak to the children of Benjamin that were in the rock Rimmon, and to call peaceably to them. ¹⁴And Benjamin came again at that time; and they gave them wives which they had saved alive of the women of Jabeshgilead: and yet so they sufficed them not. ¹⁵And the people repented them for Benjamin, because that the LORD had made a breach in the tribes of Israel. ¹⁶Then the elders of the congregation said, How shall we do for wives for them that remain, seeing the women are destroyed out of Benjamin? ¹⁷And they said, There must be an inheritance for them that be escaped of Benjamin, that a tribe be not destroyed out of Israel. ¹⁸However, we may not give them wives of our daughters: for the children of Israel have sworn, saying, Cursed be he that gives a wife to Benjamin.

¹⁹Then they said, Behold, there is a feast of the LORD in Shiloh yearly in a place which is on the north side of Bethel, on the east side of the highway that goes up from Bethel to Shechem, and on the south of Lebonah. ²⁰Therefore they commanded the children of Benjamin, saying, Go and lie in wait in the vineyards; ²¹And see, and, behold, if the daughters of Shiloh come out to dance in dances, then come you out of the vineyards, and catch you every man his wife of the daughters of Shiloh, and go to the land of Benjamin. ²²And it shall be, when their fathers or their brothers come to us to complain, that we will say to them, Be favorable to them for our sakes: because we reserved not to each man his wife in the war: for you did not give to them at this time, that you should be guilty. ²³And the children of Benjamin did so, and took them wives, according to their number, of them that danced, whom they caught: and they went and returned to their inheritance, and repaired the cities, and dwelled in them. ²⁴And the children of Israel departed there at that time, every man to his tribe and to his family, and they went out from there every man to his inheritance. ²⁵In those days there was no king in Israel: every man did that which was right in his own eyes.

Ruth

1 ¹Now it came to pass in the days when the judges ruled, that there was a famine in the land. And a certain man of Bethlehemjudah went to sojourn in the country of Moab, he, and his wife, and his two sons. ²And the name of the man was Elimelech, and the name of his wife Naomi, and the name of his two sons Mahlon and Chilion, Ephrathites of Bethlehemjudah. And they came into the country of Moab, and continued there. ³And Elimelech Naomi's husband died; and she was left, and her two sons. ⁴And they took them wives of the women of Moab; the name of the one was Orpah, and the name of the other Ruth: and they dwelled there about ten years. ⁵And Mahlon and Chilion died also both of them; and the woman was left of her two sons and her husband. ⁶Then she arose with her daughters in law, that she might return from the country of Moab: for she had heard in the country of Moab how that the LORD had visited his people in giving them bread. ⁷Why she went forth out of the place where she was, and her two daughters in law with her; and they went on the way to return to the land of Judah. ⁸And Naomi said to her two daughters in law, Go, return each to her mother's house: the LORD deal kindly with you, as you have dealt with the dead, and with me. ⁹The LORD grant you that you may find rest, each of you in the house of her husband. Then she kissed them; and they lifted up their voice, and wept. ¹⁰And they said to her, Surely we will return with you to your people. ¹¹And Naomi said, Turn again, my daughters: why will you go with me? are there yet any more sons in my womb, that they may be your husbands? ¹²Turn again, my daughters, go your way; for I am too old to have an husband. If I should say, I have hope, if I should have an husband also to night, and should also bear sons; ¹³Would you tarry for them till they were grown? would you stay for them from having husbands? no, my daughters; for it grieves me much for your sakes that the hand of the LORD is gone out against me. ¹⁴And they lifted up their voice, and wept again: and Orpah kissed her mother in law; but Ruth joined to her. ¹⁵And she said, Behold, your sister in law is gone back to her people, and to her gods: return you after your sister in law. ¹⁶And Ruth said, Entreat me not to leave you, or to return from following after you: for where you go, I will go; and where you lodge, I will lodge: your people shall be my people, and your God my God; ¹⁷Where you die, will I die, and there will I be buried: the LORD do so to me, and more also, if anything but death part you and me. ¹⁸When she saw that she was steadfastly minded to go with her, then she left speaking to her. ¹⁹So they two went until they came to Bethlehem. And it came to pass, when they were come to Bethlehem, that all the city was moved about them, and they said, Is this Naomi? ²⁰And she said to them, Call me not Naomi, call me Mara: for the Almighty has dealt very bitterly with me. ²¹I went out full and the LORD has brought me home again empty: why then call you me Naomi, seeing the LORD has testified against me, and the Almighty has afflicted me? ²²So Naomi returned, and Ruth the Moabitess, her daughter in law, with her, which returned out of the country of Moab: and they came to Bethlehem in the beginning of barley harvest.

2 ¹And Naomi had a kinsman of her husband's, a mighty man of wealth, of the family of Elimelech; and his name was Boaz. ²And Ruth the Moabitess said to Naomi, Let me now go to the field, and glean ears of corn after him in whose sight I shall find grace. And she said to her, Go, my daughter. ³And she went, and came, and gleaned in the field after the reapers: and her hap was to light on a part of the field belonging to Boaz, who was of the kindred of Elimelech. ⁴And, behold, Boaz came from Bethlehem, and said to the reapers, The LORD be with you. And they answered him, The LORD bless you. ⁵Then said Boaz to his servant that was set over the reapers, Whose damsel is this? ⁶And the servant that was set over the reapers answered and said, It is the Moabitish damsel that came back with Naomi out of the country of Moab: ⁷And she said, I pray you, let me glean and gather after the reapers among the sheaves: so she came, and has continued even from the morning until now, that she tarried a little in the house. ⁸Then said Boaz to Ruth, Hear you not, my daughter? Go not to glean in another field, neither go from hence, but abide here fast by my maidens: ⁹Let your eyes be on the field that they do reap, and go you after them: have I not charged the young men that they shall not touch you? and when you are thirsty, go to the vessels, and drink of that which the young men have drawn. ¹⁰Then she fell on her face, and bowed herself to the ground, and said to him, Why have I found grace in your eyes, that you should take knowledge of me, seeing I am a stranger? ¹¹And Boaz answered and said to her, It has fully been showed me, all that you have done to your mother in law since the death of your husband: and how you have left your father and your mother, and the land of your nativity, and are come to a people which you knew not heretofore. ¹²The LORD recompense your work, and a full reward be given you of the LORD God of Israel, under whose wings you are come to trust. ¹³Then she said, Let me find favor in your sight, my lord; for that you have comforted me, and for that you have spoken friendly to your handmaid, though I be not like to one of your handmaidens. ¹⁴And Boaz said to her, At mealtime come you here, and eat of the bread, and dip your morsel in the vinegar. And she sat beside the reapers: and he reached her parched corn, and she did eat, and was sufficed, and left. ¹⁵And when she was risen up to glean, Boaz commanded his young men, saying, Let her glean even among the sheaves, and reproach her not: ¹⁶And let fall also some of the handfuls of purpose for her, and leave them, that she may glean them, and rebuke her not. ¹⁷So she gleaned in the field until even, and beat out that she had gleaned: and it was about an ephah of barley. ¹⁸And she took it up, and went into the city: and her mother in law saw what she had gleaned: and she brought forth, and gave to her that she had reserved after she was sufficed. ¹⁹And her mother in law said to her, Where have you gleaned to day? and where worked you? blessed be he that did take knowledge of you. And she showed her mother in law with whom she had worked, and said, The man's name with whom I worked to day is Boaz. ²⁰And Naomi said to her daughter in law, Blessed be he of the LORD, who has not left off his kindness to the living and to the dead. And Naomi said to her, The man is near of kin to us, one of our next kinsmen. ²¹And Ruth the Moabitess said, He said to me also, You shall keep fast by my young men, until they have ended all my harvest. ²²And Naomi said to Ruth her daughter in law, It is good, my daughter, that you go out with his maidens, that they meet you not in any other field. ²³So she kept fast by the maidens of Boaz to glean to the end of barley harvest and of wheat harvest; and dwelled with her mother in law.

3 ¹Then Naomi her mother in law said to her, My daughter, shall I not seek rest for you, that it may be well with you? ²And now is not Boaz of our kindred, with whose maidens you were? Behold, he winnows barley to night in the threshing floor. ³Wash yourself therefore, and anoint you, and put your raiment on you, and get you down to the floor: but make not yourself known to the man, until he shall have done eating and drinking. ⁴And it shall be, when he lies down, that you shall mark the place where he shall lie, and you shall go in, and uncover his feet, and lay you down; and he will tell you what you shall do. ⁵And she said to her, All that you say to me I will do. ⁶And she went down to the floor, and did according to all that her mother in law bade her. ⁷And when Boaz had eaten and drunk, and his heart was merry, he went to lie down at the end of the heap of corn: and she came softly, and uncovered his feet, and laid her down. ⁸And it came to pass at midnight, that the man was afraid, and turned himself: and, behold, a woman lay at his feet. ⁹And he said, Who are you? And she answered, I am Ruth your handmaid: spread therefore your skirt over your handmaid; for you are a near kinsman. ¹⁰And he said, Blessed be you of the LORD, my daughter: for you have showed more kindness in the latter end than at the beginning, inasmuch as you followed not young men, whether poor or rich. ¹¹And now, my daughter, fear not; I will do to you all that you require: for all the city of my people does know that you are a virtuous woman. ¹²And now it is true that I am your near kinsman: however, there is a kinsman nearer than I. ¹³Tarry this night, and it shall be in the morning, that if he will perform to you the part of a kinsman, well; let him do the kinsman's part: but if he will not do the part of a kinsman to you, then will I do the part of a kinsman to you, as the LORD lives: lie down until the morning. ¹⁴And she lay at his feet until the morning: and she rose up before one could know another. And he said, Let it not be known that a woman came into the floor. ¹⁵Also he said, Bring the veil that you have on you, and hold it. And when she held it, he measured six measures of barley, and laid it on her: and she went into the city. ¹⁶And when she came to her mother in law, she said, Who are you, my daughter? And she told her all that the man had done to her. ¹⁷And she said, These six measures of barley gave he me; for he said to me, Go not empty to your mother in law. ¹⁸Then said she, Sit still, my daughter, until you know how the matter will fall: for the man will not be in rest, until he have finished the thing this day.

4 ¹Then went Boaz up to the gate, and sat him down there: and, behold, the kinsman of whom Boaz spoke came by; to whom he said, Ho, such a one! turn aside, sit down here. And he turned aside, and sat down. ²And he took ten men of the elders of the city, and said, Sit you down here. And they sat down. ³And he said to the kinsman, Naomi, that is come again out of the country of Moab, sells a parcel of land, which was our brother Elimelech's: ⁴And I thought to advertise you, saying, Buy it before the inhabitants, and before the elders of my people. If you will redeem it, redeem it: but if you will not redeem it, then tell me, that I may know: for there is none to redeem it beside you; and I am after you. And he said, I will redeem it. ⁵Then said Boaz, What day you buy the field of the hand of Naomi, you must buy it also of Ruth the Moabitess, the wife of the dead, to raise up the name of the dead on his inheritance. ⁶And the kinsman said, I cannot redeem it for myself, lest I mar my own inheritance: redeem you my right to yourself; for I cannot redeem it. ⁷Now this was the manner in former time in Israel concerning redeeming and concerning changing, for to confirm all things; a man plucked off his shoe, and gave it to his neighbor: and this was a testimony in Israel. ⁸Therefore the kinsman said to Boaz, Buy it for you. So he drew off his shoe. ⁹And Boaz said to the elders, and to all the people, You are witnesses this day, that I have bought all that was Elimelech's, and all that was Chilion's and Mahlon's, of the hand of Naomi. ¹⁰Moreover Ruth the Moabitess, the wife of Mahlon, have I purchased to be my wife, to raise up the name of the dead on his inheritance, that the name of the dead be not cut off from among his brothers, and from the gate of his place: you are witnesses this day. ¹¹And all the people that were in the gate, and the elders, said, We are witnesses. The LORD make the woman that is come into your house like Rachel and like Leah, which two did build the house of Israel: and do you worthily in Ephratah, and be famous in Bethlehem: ¹²And let your house be like the house of Pharez, whom Tamar bore to Judah, of the seed which the LORD shall give you of this young woman. ¹³So Boaz took Ruth, and she was his wife: and when he went in to her, the LORD gave her conception, and she bore a son. ¹⁴And the women said to Naomi, Blessed be the LORD, which has not left you this day without a kinsman, that his name may be famous in Israel. ¹⁵And he shall be to you a restorer of your life, and a nourisher of your old age: for your daughter in law, which loves you, which is better to you than seven sons, has born him. ¹⁶And Naomi took the child, and laid it in her bosom, and became nurse to it. ¹⁷And the women her neighbors gave it a name, saying, There is a son born to Naomi; and they called his name Obed: he is the father of Jesse, the father of David. ¹⁸Now these are the generations of Pharez: Pharez begat Hezron, ¹⁹And Hezron begat Ram, and Ram begat Amminadab, ²⁰And Amminadab begat Nahshon, and Nahshon begat Salmon, ²¹And Salmon begat Boaz, and Boaz begat Obed, ²²And Obed begat Jesse, and Jesse begat David.

First Samuel

1 ¹Now there was a certain man of Ramathaimzophim, of mount Ephraim, and his name was Elkanah, the son of Jeroham, the son of Elihu, the son of Tohu, the son of Zuph, an Ephrathite: ²And he had two wives; the name of the one was Hannah, and the name of the other Peninnah: and Peninnah had children, but Hannah had no children. ³And this man went up out of his city yearly to worship and to sacrifice to the LORD of hosts in Shiloh. And the two sons of Eli, Hophni and Phinehas, the priests of the LORD, were there. ⁴And when the time was that Elkanah offered, he gave to Peninnah his wife, and to all her sons and her daughters, portions: ⁵But to Hannah he gave a worthy portion; for he loved Hannah: but the LORD had shut up her womb. ⁶And her adversary also provoked her sore, for to make her fret, because the LORD had shut up her womb. ⁷And as he did so year by year, when she went up to the house of the LORD, so she provoked her; therefore she wept, and did not eat. ⁸Then said Elkanah her husband to her, Hannah, why weep you? and why eat you not? and why is your heart grieved? am not I better to you than ten sons? ⁹So Hannah rose up after they had eaten in Shiloh, and after they had drunk. Now Eli the priest sat on a seat by a post of the temple of the LORD. ¹⁰And she was in bitterness of soul, and prayed to the LORD, and wept sore. ¹¹And she vowed a vow, and said, O LORD of hosts, if you will indeed look on the affliction of your handmaid, and remember me, and not forget your handmaid, but will give to your handmaid a man child, then I will give him to the LORD all the days of his life, and there shall no razor come on his head. ¹²And it came to pass, as she continued praying before the LORD, that Eli marked her mouth. ¹³Now Hannah, she spoke in her heart; only her lips moved, but her voice was not heard: therefore Eli thought she had been drunken. ¹⁴And Eli said to her, How long will you be drunken? put away your wine from you. ¹⁵And Hannah answered and said, No, my lord, I am a woman of a sorrowful spirit: I have drunk neither wine nor strong drink, but have poured out my soul before the LORD. ¹⁶Count not your handmaid for a daughter of Belial: for out of the abundance of my complaint and grief have I spoken till now. ¹⁷Then Eli answered and said, Go in peace: and the God of Israel grant you your petition that you have asked of him. ¹⁸And she said, Let your handmaid find grace in your sight. So the woman went her way, and did eat, and her countenance was no more sad. ¹⁹And they rose up in the morning early, and worshipped before the LORD, and returned, and came to their house to Ramah: and Elkanah knew Hannah his wife; and the LORD remembered her. ²⁰Why it came to pass, when the time was come about after Hannah had conceived, that she bore a son, and called his name Samuel, saying, Because I have asked him of the LORD. ²¹And the man Elkanah, and all his house, went up to offer to the LORD the yearly sacrifice, and his vow. ²²But Hannah went not up; for she said to her husband, I will not go up until the child be weaned, and then I will bring him, that he may appear before the LORD, and there abide for ever. ²³And Elkanah her husband said to her, Do what seems you good; tarry until you have weaned him; only the LORD establish his word. So the woman stayed, and gave her son suck until she weaned him. ²⁴And when she had weaned him, she took him up with her, with three bullocks, and one ephah of flour, and a bottle of wine, and brought him to the house of the LORD in Shiloh: and the child was young. ²⁵And they slew a bullock, and brought the child to Eli. ²⁶And she said, Oh my lord, as your soul lives, my lord, I am the woman that stood by you here, praying to the LORD. ²⁷For this child I prayed; and the LORD has given me my petition which I asked of him: ²⁸Therefore also I have lent him to the LORD; as long as he lives he shall be lent to the LORD. And he worshipped the LORD there.

2 ¹And Hannah prayed, and said, My heart rejoices in the LORD, my horn is exalted in the LORD: my mouth is enlarged over my enemies; because I rejoice in your salvation. ²There is none holy as the LORD: for there is none beside you: neither is there any rock like our God. ³Talk no more so exceeding proudly; let not arrogance come out of your mouth: for the LORD is a God of knowledge, and by him actions are weighed. ⁴The bows of the mighty men are broken, and they that stumbled are girded with strength. ⁵They that were full have hired out themselves for bread; and they that were hungry ceased: so that the barren has born seven; and she that has many children is waxed feeble. ⁶The LORD kills, and makes alive: he brings down to the grave, and brings up. ⁷The LORD makes poor, and makes rich: he brings low, and lifts up. ⁸He raises up the poor out of the dust, and lifts up the beggar from the dunghill, to set them among princes, and to make them inherit the throne of glory: for the pillars of the earth are the LORD's, and he has set the world on them. ⁹He will keep the feet of his saints, and the wicked shall be silent in darkness; for by strength shall no man prevail. ¹⁰The adversaries of the LORD shall be broken to pieces; out of heaven shall he thunder on them: the LORD shall judge the ends of the earth; and he shall give strength to his king, and exalt the horn of his anointed. ¹¹And Elkanah went to Ramah to his house. And the child did minister to the LORD before Eli the priest. ¹²Now the sons of Eli were sons of Belial; they knew not the LORD. ¹³And the priest's custom with the people was, that, when any man offered sacrifice, the priest's servant came, while the flesh was in seething, with a meat hook of three teeth in his hand; ¹⁴And he struck it into the pan, or kettle, or caldron, or pot; all that the meat hook brought up the priest took for himself. So they did in Shiloh to all the Israelites that came thither. ¹⁵Also before they burnt the fat, the priest's servant came, and said to the man that sacrificed, Give flesh to roast for the priest; for he will not have sodden flesh of you, but raw. ¹⁶And if any man said to him, Let them not fail to burn the fat presently, and then take as much as your soul desires; then he would answer him, No; but you shall give it me now: and if not, I will take it by force. ¹⁷Why the sin of the young men was very great before the LORD: for men abhorred the offering of the LORD. ¹⁸But Samuel ministered before the LORD, being a child, girded with a linen ephod. ¹⁹Moreover his mother made him a little coat, and brought it to him from year to year, when she came up with her husband to offer the yearly sacrifice. ²⁰And Eli blessed Elkanah and his wife, and said, The LORD give you seed of this woman for the loan which is lent to the LORD. And they went to their own home. ²¹And the LORD visited Hannah, so that she conceived, and bore three sons and two daughters. And the child Samuel grew before the LORD. ²²Now Eli was very old, and heard all that his sons did to all Israel; and how they lay with the women that assembled at the door of the tabernacle of the congregation. ²³And he said to them, Why do you such things? for I hear of your evil dealings by all this people. ²⁴No, my sons; for it is no good report that I hear: you make the LORD's people to transgress. ²⁵If one man sin against another, the judge shall judge him: but if a man sin against the LORD, who shall entreat for him? Notwithstanding they listened not to the voice of their father, because the LORD would slay them. ²⁶And the child Samuel grew on, and was in favor both with the LORD, and also with men. ²⁷And there came a man of God to Eli, and said to him, Thus says the LORD, Did I plainly appear to the house of your father, when they were in Egypt in Pharaoh's house? ²⁸And did I choose him out of all the tribes of Israel to be my priest, to offer on my altar, to burn incense, to wear an ephod before me? and did I give to the house of your father all the offerings made by fire of the children of Israel? ²⁹Why kick you at my sacrifice and at my offering, which I have commanded in my habitation; and honor your sons above me, to make yourselves fat with the most chief of all the offerings of Israel my people? ³⁰Why the LORD God of Israel said, I said indeed that your house, and the house of your father, should walk before me for ever: but now the LORD says, Be it far from me; for them that honor me I will honor, and they that despise me shall be lightly esteemed. ³¹Behold, the days come, that I will cut off your arm, and the arm of your father's house, that there shall not be an old man in your house. ³²And you shall see an enemy in my habitation, in all the wealth which God shall give Israel: and there shall not be an old man in your house for ever. ³³And the man of yours, whom I shall not cut off from my altar, shall be to consume your eyes, and to grieve your heart: and all the increase of your house shall die in the flower of their age. ³⁴And this shall be a sign to you, that shall come on your two sons, on Hophni and Phinehas; in one day they shall die both of them. ³⁵And I will raise me up a faithful priest, that shall do according to that which is in my heart and in my mind: and I will build him a sure house; and he shall walk before my anointed for ever. ³⁶And it shall come to pass, that every one that is left in your house shall come and crouch to him for a piece of silver and a morsel of bread, and shall say, Put me, I pray you, into one of the priests' offices, that I may eat a piece of bread.

3 ¹And the child Samuel ministered to the LORD before Eli. And the word of the LORD was precious in those days; there was no open vision. ²And it came to pass at that time, when Eli was laid down in his place, and his eyes began to wax dim, that he could not see; ³And before the lamp of God went out in the temple of the LORD, where the ark of God was, and Samuel was laid down to sleep; ⁴That the LORD called Samuel: and he answered, Here am I. ⁵And he ran to Eli, and said, Here am I; for you called me. And he said, I called not; lie down again. And he went and lay down. ⁶And the LORD called yet again, Samuel. And Samuel arose and went to Eli, and said, Here am I; for you did call me. And he answered, I called not, my son; lie down again. ⁷Now Samuel did not yet know the LORD, neither was the word of the LORD yet revealed to him. ⁸And the LORD called Samuel again the third time. And he arose and went to Eli, and said, Here am I; for you did call me. And Eli perceived that the LORD had called the child. ⁹Therefore Eli said to Samuel, Go, lie down: and it shall be, if he call you, that you shall say, Speak, LORD; for your servant hears. So Samuel went and lay down in his place. ¹⁰And the LORD came, and stood, and called as at other times, Samuel, Samuel. Then Samuel answered, Speak; for your servant hears. ¹¹And the LORD said to Samuel, Behold, I will do a thing in Israel, at which both the ears of every one that hears it shall tingle. ¹²In that day I will perform against Eli all things which I have spoken concerning his house: when I begin, I will also make an end. ¹³For I have told him that I will judge his house for ever for the iniquity which he knows; because his sons made themselves vile, and he restrained them not. ¹⁴And therefore I have sworn to the house of Eli, that the iniquity of Eli's house shall not be purged with sacrifice nor offering for ever. ¹⁵And Samuel lay until the morning, and opened the doors of the house of the LORD. And Samuel feared to show Eli the vision. ¹⁶Then Eli called Samuel, and said, Samuel, my son. And he answered, Here am I. ¹⁷And he said, What is the thing that the LORD has said to you? I pray you hide it not from me: God do so to you, and more also, if you hide any thing from me of all the things that he said to you. ¹⁸And Samuel told him every whit, and hid nothing from him. And he said, It is the LORD: let him do what seems him good. ¹⁹And Samuel grew, and the LORD was with him, and did let none of his words fall to the ground. ²⁰And all Israel from Dan even to Beersheba knew that Samuel was established to be a prophet of the LORD. ²¹And the LORD appeared again in Shiloh: for the LORD revealed himself to Samuel in Shiloh by the word of the LORD.

4 ¹And the word of Samuel came to all Israel. Now Israel went out against the Philistines to battle, and pitched beside Ebenezer: and the Philistines pitched in Aphek. ²And the Philistines put themselves in array against Israel: and when they joined battle, Israel was smitten before the Philistines: and they slew of the army in the field about four thousand men. ³And when the people were come into the camp, the elders of Israel said, Why has the LORD smitten us to day before the Philistines? Let us fetch the ark of the covenant of the LORD out of Shiloh to us, that, when it comes among us, it may save us out of the hand of our enemies. ⁴So the people sent to Shiloh, that they might bring from there the ark of the covenant of the LORD of hosts, which dwells between the cherubim: and the two sons of Eli, Hophni and Phinehas, were there with the ark of the covenant of God. ⁵And when the ark of the covenant of the LORD came into the camp, all Israel shouted with a great shout, so that the earth rang again. ⁶And when the Philistines heard the noise of the shout, they said, What means the noise of this great shout in the camp of the Hebrews? And they understood that the ark of the LORD was come into the camp. ⁷And the Philistines were afraid, for they said, God is come into the camp. And they said, Woe to us! for there has not been such a thing heretofore. ⁸Woe to us! who shall deliver us out of the hand of these mighty Gods? these are the Gods that smote the Egyptians with all the plagues in the wilderness. ⁹Be strong and quit yourselves like men, O you Philistines, that you be not servants to the Hebrews, as they have been to you: quit yourselves like men, and fight. ¹⁰And the Philistines fought, and Israel was smitten, and they fled every man into his tent: and there was a very great slaughter; for there fell of Israel thirty thousand footmen. ¹¹And the ark of God was taken; and the two sons of Eli, Hophni and Phinehas, were slain. ¹²And there ran a man of Benjamin out of the army, and came to Shiloh the same day with his clothes rent, and with earth on his head. ¹³And when he came, see, Eli sat on a seat by the wayside watching: for his heart trembled for the ark of God. And when the man came into the city, and told it, all the city cried out. ¹⁴And when Eli heard the noise of the crying, he said, What means the noise of this tumult? And the man came in hastily, and told Eli. ¹⁵Now Eli was ninety and eight years old; and his eyes were dim, that he could not see. ¹⁶And the man said to Eli, I am he that came out of the army, and I fled to day out of the army. And he said, What is there done, my son? ¹⁷And the messenger answered and said, Israel is fled before the Philistines, and there has been also a great slaughter among the people, and your two sons also, Hophni and Phinehas, are dead, and the ark of God is taken. ¹⁸And it came to pass, when he made mention of the ark of God, that he fell from off the seat backward by the side of the gate, and his neck broke, and he died: for he was an old man, and heavy. And he had judged Israel forty years. ¹⁹And his daughter in law, Phinehas' wife, was with child, near to be delivered: and when she heard the tidings that the ark of God was taken, and that her father in law and her husband were dead, she bowed herself and travailed; for her pains came on her. ²⁰And about the time of her death the women that stood by her said to her, Fear not; for you have born a son. But she answered not, neither did she regard it. ²¹And she named the child Ichabod, saying, The glory is departed from Israel: because the ark of God was taken, and because of her father in law and her husband. ²²And she said, The glory is departed from Israel: for the ark of God is taken.

5 ¹And the Philistines took the ark of God, and brought it from Ebenezer to Ashdod. ²When the Philistines took the ark of God, they brought it into the house of Dagon, and set it by Dagon. ³And when they of Ashdod arose early on the morrow, behold, Dagon was fallen on his face to the earth before the ark of the LORD. And they took Dagon, and set him in his place again. ⁴And when they arose early on the morrow morning, behold, Dagon was fallen on his face to the ground before the ark of the LORD; and the head of Dagon and both the palms of his hands were cut off on the threshold; only the stump of Dagon was left to him. ⁵Therefore neither the priests of Dagon, nor any that come into Dagon's house, tread on the threshold of Dagon in Ashdod to this day. ⁶But the hand of the LORD was heavy on them of Ashdod, and he destroyed them, and smote them with tumors, even Ashdod and the coasts thereof. ⁷And when the men of Ashdod saw that it was so, they said, The ark of the God of Israel shall not abide with us: for his hand is sore on us, and on Dagon our god. ⁸They sent therefore and gathered all the lords of the Philistines to them, and said, What shall we do with the ark of the God of Israel? And they answered, Let the ark of the God of Israel be carried about to Gath. And they carried the ark of the God of Israel about thither. ⁹And it was so, that, after they had carried it about, the hand of the LORD was against the city with a very great destruction: and he smote the men of the city, both small and great, and they had tumors in their secret parts. ¹⁰Therefore they sent the ark of God to Ekron. And it came to pass, as the ark of God came to Ekron, that the Ekronites cried out, saying, They have brought about the ark of the God of Israel to us, to slay us and our people. ¹¹So they sent and gathered together all the lords of the Philistines, and said, Send away the ark of the God of Israel, and let it go again to his own place, that it slay us not, and our people: for there was a deadly destruction throughout all the city; the hand of God was very heavy there. ¹²And the men that died not were smitten with the tumors: and the cry of the city went up to heaven.

6 ¹And the ark of the LORD was in the country of the Philistines seven months. ²And the Philistines called for the priests and the diviners, saying, What shall we do to the ark of the LORD? tell us with which we shall send it to his place. ³And they said, If you send away the ark of the God of Israel, send it not empty; but in any wise return him a trespass offering: then you shall be healed, and it shall be known to you why his hand is not removed from you. ⁴Then said they, What shall be the trespass offering which we shall return to him? They answered, Five golden tumors, and five golden mice, according to the number of the lords of the Philistines: for one plague was on you all, and on your lords. ⁵Why you shall make images of your tumors, and images of your mice that mar the land; and you shall give glory to the God of Israel: peradventure he will lighten his hand from off you, and from off your gods, and from off your land. ⁶Why then do you harden your hearts, as the Egyptians and Pharaoh hardened their hearts? when he had worked wonderfully among them, did they not let the people go, and they departed? ⁷Now therefore make a new cart, and take two milk cows, on which there has come no yoke, and tie the cows to the cart, and bring their calves home from them: ⁸And take the ark of the LORD, and lay it on the cart; and put the jewels of gold, which you return him for a trespass offering, in a coffer by the side thereof; and send it away, that it may go. ⁹And see, if it goes up by the way of his own coast to Bethshemesh, then he has done us this great evil: but if not, then we shall know that it is not his hand that smote us: it was a chance that happened to us. ¹⁰And the men did so; and took two milk cows, and tied them to the cart, and shut up their calves at home: ¹¹And they laid the ark of the LORD on the cart, and the coffer with the mice of gold and the images of their tumors. ¹²And the cows took the straight way to the way of Bethshemesh, and went along the highway, lowing as they went, and turned not aside to the right hand or to the left; and the lords of the Philistines went after them to the border of Bethshemesh. ¹³And they of Bethshemesh were reaping their wheat harvest in the valley: and they lifted up their eyes, and saw the ark, and rejoiced to see it. ¹⁴And the cart came into the field of Joshua, a Bethshemite, and stood there, where there was a great stone: and they split the wood of the cart, and offered the cows a burnt offering to the LORD. ¹⁵And the Levites took down the ark of the LORD, and the coffer that was with it, wherein the jewels of gold were, and put them on the great stone: and the men of Bethshemesh offered burnt offerings and sacrificed sacrifices the same day to the LORD. ¹⁶And when the five lords of the Philistines had seen it, they returned to Ekron the same day. ¹⁷And these are the golden tumors which the Philistines returned for a trespass offering to the LORD; for Ashdod one, for Gaza one, for Askelon one, for Gath one, for Ekron one; ¹⁸And the golden mice, according to the number of all the cities of the Philistines belonging to the five lords, both of fenced cities, and of country villages, even to the great stone of Abel, where on they set down the ark of the LORD: which stone remains to this day in the field of Joshua, the Bethshemite. ¹⁹And he smote the men of Bethshemesh, because they had looked into the ark of the LORD, even he smote of the people fifty thousand and three score and ten men: and the people lamented, because the LORD had smitten many of the people with a great slaughter. ²⁰And the men of Bethshemesh said, Who is able to stand before this holy LORD God? and to whom shall he go up from us? ²¹And they sent messengers to the inhabitants of Kirjathjearim, saying, The Philistines have brought again the ark of the LORD; come you down, and fetch it up to you.

7 ¹And the men of Kirjathjearim came, and fetched up the ark of the LORD, and brought it into the house of Abinadab in the hill, and sanctified Eleazar his son to keep the ark of the LORD. ²And it came to pass, while the ark stayed in Kirjathjearim, that the time was long; for it was twenty years: and all the house of Israel lamented after the LORD. ³And Samuel spoke to all the house of Israel, saying, If you do return to the LORD with all your hearts, then put away the strange gods and Ashtaroth from among you, and prepare your hearts to the LORD, and serve him only: and he will deliver you out of the hand of the Philistines. ⁴Then the children of Israel did put away Baalim and Ashtaroth, and served the LORD only. ⁵And Samuel said, Gather all Israel to Mizpeh, and I will pray for you to the LORD. ⁶And they gathered together to Mizpeh, and drew water, and poured it out before the LORD, and fasted on that day, and said there, We have sinned against the LORD. And Samuel judged the children of Israel in Mizpeh. ⁷And when the Philistines heard that the children of Israel were gathered together to Mizpeh, the lords of the Philistines went up against Israel. And when the children of Israel heard it, they were afraid of the Philistines. ⁸And the children of Israel said to Samuel, Cease not to cry to the LORD our God for us, that he will save us out of the hand of the Philistines. ⁹And Samuel took a sucking lamb, and offered it for a burnt offering wholly to the LORD: and Samuel cried to the LORD for Israel; and the LORD heard him. ¹⁰And as Samuel was offering up the burnt offering, the Philistines drew near to battle against Israel: but the LORD thundered with a great thunder on that day on the Philistines, and discomfited them; and they were smitten before Israel. ¹¹And the men of Israel went out of Mizpeh, and pursued the Philistines, and smote them, until they came under Bethcar. ¹²Then Samuel took a stone, and set it between Mizpeh and Shen, and called the name of it Ebenezer, saying, Till now has the LORD helped us. ¹³So the Philistines were subdued, and they came no more into the coast of Israel: and the hand of the LORD was against the Philistines all the days of Samuel. ¹⁴And the cities which the Philistines had taken from Israel were restored to Israel, from Ekron even to Gath; and the coasts thereof did Israel deliver out of the hands of the Philistines. And there was peace between Israel and the Amorites. ¹⁵And Samuel judged Israel all the days of his life. ¹⁶And he went from year to year in circuit to Bethel, and Gilgal, and Mizpeh, and judged Israel in all those places. ¹⁷And his return was to Ramah; for there was his house; and there he judged Israel; and there he built an altar to the LORD.

8 ¹And it came to pass, when Samuel was old, that he made his sons judges over Israel. ²Now the name of his firstborn was Joel; and the name of his second, Abiah: they were judges in Beersheba. ³And his sons walked not in his ways, but turned aside after lucre, and took bribes, and perverted judgment. ⁴Then all the elders of Israel gathered themselves together, and came to Samuel to Ramah, ⁵And said to him, Behold, you are old, and your sons walk not in your ways: now make us a king to judge us like all the nations. ⁶But the thing displeased Samuel, when they said, Give us a king to judge us. And Samuel prayed to the LORD. ⁷And the LORD said to Samuel, Listen to the voice of the people in all that they say to you: for they have not rejected you, but they have rejected me, that I should not reign over them. ⁸According to all the works which they have done since the day that I brought them up out of Egypt even to this day, with which they have forsaken me, and served other gods, so do they also to you. ⁹Now therefore listen to their voice: however, yet protest solemnly to them, and show them the manner of the king that shall reign over them. ¹⁰And Samuel told all the words of the LORD to the people that asked of him a king. ¹¹And he said, This will be the manner of the king that shall reign over you: He will take your sons, and appoint them for himself, for his chariots, and to be his horsemen; and some shall run before his chariots. ¹²And he will appoint him captains over thousands, and captains over fifties; and will set them to ear his ground, and to reap his harvest, and to make his instruments of war, and instruments of his chariots. ¹³And he will take your daughters to be confectionaries, and to be cooks, and to be bakers. ¹⁴And he will take your fields, and your vineyards, and your olive groves, even the best of them, and give them to his servants. ¹⁵And he will take the tenth of your seed, and of your vineyards, and give to his officers, and to his servants. ¹⁶And he will take your menservants, and your maidservants, and your best young men, and your asses, and put them to his work. ¹⁷He will take the tenth of your sheep: and you shall be his servants. ¹⁸And you shall cry out in that day because of your king which you shall have chosen you; and the LORD will not hear you in that day. ¹⁹Nevertheless the people refused to obey the voice of Samuel; and they said, No; but we will have a king over us; ²⁰That we also may be like all the nations; and that our king may judge us, and go out before us, and fight our battles. ²¹And Samuel heard all the words of the people, and he rehearsed them in the ears of the LORD. ²²And the LORD said to Samuel, Listen to their voice, and make them a king.

And Samuel said to the men of Israel, Go you every man to his city.

9 ¹Now there was a man of Benjamin, whose name was Kish, the son of Abiel, the son of Zeror, the son of Bechorath, the son of Aphiah, a Benjamite, a mighty man of power. ²And he had a son, whose name was Saul, a choice young man, and a goodly: and there was not among the children of Israel a goodlier person than he: from his shoulders and upward he was higher than any of the people. ³And the asses of Kish Saul's father were lost. And Kish said to Saul his son, Take now one of the servants with you, and arise, go seek the asses. ⁴And he passed through mount Ephraim, and passed through the land of Shalisha, but they found them not: then they passed through the land of Shalim, and there they were not: and he passed through the land of the Benjamites, but they found them not. ⁵And when they were come to the land of Zuph, Saul said to his servant that was with him, Come, and let us return; lest my father leave caring for the asses, and take thought for us. ⁶And he said to him, Behold now, there is in this city a man of God, and he is an honorable man; all that he says comes surely to pass: now let us go thither; peradventure he can show us our way that we should go. ⁷Then said Saul to his servant, But, behold, if we go, what shall we bring the man? for the bread is spent in our vessels, and there is not a present to bring to the man of God: what have we? ⁸And the servant answered Saul again, and said, Behold, I have here at hand the fourth part of a shekel of silver: that will I give to the man of God, to tell us our way. ⁹(Beforetime in Israel, when a man went to inquire of God, thus he spoke, Come, and let us go to the seer: for he that is now called a Prophet was beforetime called a Seer.) ¹⁰Then said Saul to his servant, Well said; come, let us go. So they went to the city where the man of God was. ¹¹And as they went up the hill to the city, they found young maidens going out to draw water, and said to them, Is the seer here? ¹²And they answered them, and said, He is; behold, he is before you: make haste now, for he came to day to the city; for there is a sacrifice of the people to day in the high place: ¹³As soon as you be come into the city, you shall straightway find him, before he go up to the high place to eat: for the people will not eat until he come, because he does bless the sacrifice; and afterwards they eat that be bidden. Now therefore get you up; for about this time you shall find him. ¹⁴And they went up into the city: and when they were come into the city, behold, Samuel came out against them, for to go up to the high place. ¹⁵Now the LORD had told Samuel in his ear a day before Saul came, saying, ¹⁶To morrow about this time I will send you a man out of the land of Benjamin, and you shall anoint him to be captain over my people Israel, that he may save my people out of the hand of the Philistines: for I have looked on my people, because their cry is come to me. ¹⁷And when Samuel saw Saul, the LORD said to him, Behold the man whom I spoke to you of! this same shall reign over my people. ¹⁸Then Saul drew near to Samuel in the gate, and said, Tell me, I pray you, where the seer's house is. ¹⁹And Samuel answered Saul, and said, I am the seer: go up before me to the high place; for you shall eat with me to day, and to morrow I will let you go, and will tell you all that is in your heart. ²⁰And as for your asses that were lost three days ago, set not your mind on them; for they are found. And on whom is all the desire of Israel? Is it not on you, and on all your father's house? ²¹And Saul answered and said, Am not I a Benjamite, of the smallest of the tribes of Israel? and my family the least of all the families of the tribe of Benjamin? why then speak you so to me? ²²And Samuel took Saul and his servant, and brought them into the parlor, and made them sit in the most chief place among them that were bidden, which were about thirty persons. ²³And Samuel said to the cook, Bring the portion which I gave you, of which I said to you, Set it by you. ²⁴And the cook took up the shoulder, and that which was on it, and set it before Saul. And Samuel said, Behold that which is left! set it before you, and eat: for to this time has it been kept for you since I said, I have invited the people. So Saul did eat with Samuel that day. ²⁵And when they were come down from the high place into the city, Samuel communed with Saul on the top of the house. ²⁶And they arose early: and it came to pass about the spring of the day, that Samuel called Saul to the top of the house, saying, Up, that I may send you away. And Saul arose, and they went out both of them, he and Samuel, abroad. ²⁷And as they were going down to the end of the city, Samuel said to Saul, Bid the servant pass on before us, (and he passed on), but stand you still a while, that I may show you the word of God.

10 ¹Then Samuel took a vial of oil, and poured it on his head, and kissed him, and said, Is it not because the LORD has anointed you to be captain over his inheritance? ²When you are departed from me to day, then you shall find two men by Rachel's sepulcher in the border of Benjamin at Zelzah; and they will say to you, The asses which you went to seek are found: and, see, your father has left the care of the asses, and sorrows for you, saying, What shall I do for my son? ³Then shall you go on forward from there, and you shall come to the plain of Tabor, and there shall meet you three men going up to God to Bethel, one carrying three kids, and another carrying three loaves of bread, and another carrying a bottle of wine: ⁴And they will salute you, and give you two loaves of bread; which you shall receive of their hands. ⁵After that you shall come to the hill of God, where is the garrison of the Philistines: and it shall come to pass, when you are come thither to the city, that you shall meet a company of prophets coming down from the high place with a psaltery, and a tabret, and a pipe, and a harp, before them; and they shall prophesy: ⁶And the Spirit of the LORD will come on you, and you shall prophesy with them, and shall be turned into another man. ⁷And let it be, when these signs are come to you, that you do as occasion serve you; for God is with you. ⁸And you shall go down before me to Gilgal; and, behold, I will come down to you, to offer burnt offerings, and to sacrifice sacrifices of peace offerings: seven days shall you tarry, till I come to you, and show you what you shall do. ⁹And it was so, that when he had turned his back to go from Samuel, God gave him another heart: and all those signs came to pass that day. ¹⁰And when they came thither to the hill, behold, a company of prophets met him; and the Spirit of God came on him, and he prophesied among them. ¹¹And it came to pass, when all that knew him beforetime saw that, behold, he prophesied among the prophets, then the people said one to another, What is this that is come to the son of Kish? Is Saul also among the prophets? ¹²And one of the same place answered and said, But who is their father? Therefore it became a proverb, Is Saul also among the prophets? ¹³And when he had made an end of prophesying, he came to the high place. ¹⁴And Saul's uncle said to him and to his servant, Where went you? And he said, To seek the asses: and when we saw that they were no where, we came to Samuel. ¹⁵And Saul's uncle said, Tell me, I pray you, what Samuel said to you. ¹⁶And Saul said to his uncle, He told us plainly that the asses were found. But of the matter of the kingdom, whereof Samuel spoke, he told him not. ¹⁷And Samuel called the people together to the LORD to Mizpeh; ¹⁸And said to the children of Israel, Thus says the LORD God of Israel, I brought up Israel out of Egypt, and delivered you out of the hand of the Egyptians, and out of the hand of all kingdoms, and of them that oppressed you: ¹⁹And you have this day rejected your God, who himself saved you out of all your adversities and your tribulations; and you have said to him, No, but set a king over us. Now therefore present yourselves before the LORD by your tribes, and by your thousands. ²⁰And when Samuel had caused all the tribes of Israel to come near, the tribe of Benjamin was taken. ²¹When he had caused the tribe of Benjamin to come near by their families, the family of Matri was taken, and Saul the son of Kish was taken: and when they sought him, he could not be found. ²²Therefore they inquired of the LORD further, if the man should yet come thither. And the LORD answered, Behold he has hid himself among the stuff. ²³And they ran and fetched him there: and when he stood among the people, he was higher than any of the people from his shoulders and upward. ²⁴And Samuel said to all the people, See you him whom the LORD has chosen, that there is none like him among all the people? And all the people shouted, and said, God save the king. ²⁵Then Samuel told the people the manner of the kingdom, and wrote it in a book, and laid it up before the LORD. And Samuel sent all the people away, every man to his house. ²⁶And Saul also went home to Gibeah; and there went with him a band of men, whose hearts God had touched. ²⁷But the children of Belial said, How shall this man save us? And they despised him, and brought no presents. But he held his peace.

11 ¹Then Nahash the Ammonite came up, and encamped against Jabeshgilead: and all the men of Jabesh said to Nahash, Make a covenant with us, and we will serve you. ²And Nahash the Ammonite answered them, On this condition will I make a covenant with you, that I may thrust out all your right eyes, and lay it for a reproach on all Israel. ³And the elders of Jabesh said to him, Give us seven days' respite, that we may send messengers to all the coasts of Israel: and then, if there be no man to save us, we will come out to you. ⁴Then came the messengers to Gibeah of Saul, and told the tidings in the ears of the people: and all the people lifted up their voices, and wept. ⁵And, behold, Saul came after the herd out of the field; and Saul said, What ails the people that they weep? And they told him the tidings of the men of Jabesh. ⁶And the Spirit of God came on Saul when he heard those tidings, and his anger was kindled greatly. ⁷And he took a yoke of oxen, and hewed them in pieces, and sent them throughout all the coasts of Israel by the hands of messengers, saying, Whoever comes not forth after Saul and after Samuel, so shall it be done to his oxen. And the fear of the LORD fell on the people, and they came out with one consent. ⁸And when he numbered them in Bezek, the children of Israel were three hundred thousand, and the men of Judah thirty thousand. ⁹And they said to the messengers that came, Thus shall you say to the men of Jabeshgilead, To morrow, by that time the sun be hot, you shall have help. And the messengers came and showed it to the men of Jabesh; and they were glad. ¹⁰Therefore the men of Jabesh said, To morrow we will come out to you, and you shall do with us all that seems good to you. ¹¹And it was so on the morrow, that Saul put the people in three companies; and they came into the middle of the host in the morning watch, and slew the Ammonites until the heat of the day: and it came to pass, that they which remained were scattered, so that two of them were not left together. ¹²And the people said to Samuel, Who is he that said, Shall Saul reign over us? bring the men, that we may put them to death. ¹³And Saul said, There shall not a man be put to death this day: for to day the LORD has worked salvation in Israel. ¹⁴Then said Samuel to the people, Come, and let us go to Gilgal, and renew the kingdom there. ¹⁵And all the people went to Gilgal; and there they made Saul king before the LORD in Gilgal; and there they sacrificed sacrifices of peace offerings before the LORD; and there Saul and all the men of Israel rejoiced greatly.

12 ¹And Samuel said to all Israel, Behold, I have listened to your voice in all that you said to me, and have made a king over you. ²And now, behold, the king walks before you: and I am old and gray headed; and, behold, my sons are with you: and I have walked before you from my childhood to this day. ³Behold, here I am: witness against me before the LORD, and before his anointed: whose ox have I taken? or whose ass have I taken? or whom have I defrauded? whom have I oppressed? or of whose hand have I received any bribe to blind my eyes therewith? and I will restore it you. ⁴And they said, You have not defrauded us, nor oppressed us, neither have you taken anything of any man's hand. ⁵And he said to them, The LORD is witness against you, and his anointed is witness this day, that you have not found anything in my hand. And they answered, He is witness. ⁶And Samuel said to the people, It is the LORD that advanced Moses and Aaron, and that brought your fathers up out of the land of Egypt. ⁷Now therefore stand still, that I may reason with you before the LORD of all the righteous acts of the LORD, which he did to you and to your fathers. ⁸When Jacob was come into Egypt, and your fathers cried to the LORD, then the LORD sent Moses and Aaron, which brought forth your fathers out of Egypt, and made them dwell in this place. ⁹And when they forgot the LORD their God, he sold them into the hand of Sisera, captain of the host of Hazor, and into the hand of the Philistines, and into the hand of the king of Moab, and they fought against them. ¹⁰And they cried to the LORD, and said, We have sinned, because we have forsaken the LORD, and have served Baalim and Ashtaroth: but now deliver us out of the hand of our enemies, and we will serve you. ¹¹And the LORD sent Jerubbaal, and Bedan, and Jephthah, and Samuel, and delivered you out of the hand of your enemies on every side, and you dwelled safe. ¹²And when you saw that Nahash the king of the children of Ammon came against you, you said to me, No; but a king shall reign over us: when the LORD your God was your king. ¹³Now therefore behold the king whom you have chosen, and whom you have desired! and, behold, the LORD has set a king over you. ¹⁴If you will fear the LORD, and serve him, and obey his voice, and not rebel against the commandment of the LORD, then shall both you and also the king that reigns over you continue following the LORD your God: ¹⁵But if you will not obey the voice of the LORD, but rebel against the commandment of the LORD, then shall the hand of the LORD be against you, as it was against your fathers. ¹⁶Now therefore stand and see this great thing, which the LORD will do before your eyes. ¹⁷Is it not wheat harvest to day? I will call to the LORD, and he shall send thunder and rain; that you may perceive and see that your wickedness is great, which you have done in the sight of the LORD, in asking you a king. ¹⁸So Samuel called to the LORD; and the LORD sent thunder and rain that day: and all the people greatly feared the LORD and Samuel. ¹⁹And all the people said to Samuel, Pray for your servants to the LORD your God, that we die not: for we have added to all our sins this evil, to ask us a king. ²⁰And Samuel said to the people, Fear not: you have done all this wickedness: yet turn not aside from following the LORD, but serve the LORD with all your heart; ²¹And turn you not aside: for then should you go after vain things, which cannot profit nor deliver; for they are vain. ²²For the LORD will not forsake his people for his great name's sake: because it has pleased the LORD to make you his people. ²³Moreover as for me, God forbid that I should sin against the LORD in ceasing to pray for you: but I will teach you the good and the right way: ²⁴Only fear the LORD, and serve him in truth with all your heart: for consider how great things he has done for you. ²⁵But if you shall still do wickedly, you shall be consumed, both you and your king.

13

¹Saul reigned one year; and when he had reigned two years over Israel, ²Saul chose him three thousand men of Israel; whereof two thousand were with Saul in Michmash and in mount Bethel, and a thousand were with Jonathan in Gibeah of Benjamin: and the rest of the people he sent every man to his tent. ³And Jonathan smote the garrison of the Philistines that was in Geba, and the Philistines heard of it. And Saul blew the trumpet throughout all the land, saying, Let the Hebrews hear. ⁴And all Israel heard say that Saul had smitten a garrison of the Philistines, and that Israel also was had in abomination with the Philistines. And the people were called together after Saul to Gilgal. ⁵And the Philistines gathered themselves together to fight with Israel, thirty thousand chariots, and six thousand horsemen, and people as the sand which is on the sea shore in multitude: and they came up, and pitched in Michmash, eastward from Bethaven. ⁶When the men of Israel saw that they were in a strait, (for the people were distressed,) then the people did hide themselves in caves, and in thickets, and in rocks, and in high places, and in pits. ⁷And some of the Hebrews went over Jordan to the land of Gad and Gilead. As for Saul, he was yet in Gilgal, and all the people followed him trembling. ⁸And he tarried seven days, according to the set time that Samuel had appointed: but Samuel came not to Gilgal; and the people were scattered from him. ⁹And Saul said, Bring here a burnt offering to me, and peace offerings. And he offered the burnt offering. ¹⁰And it came to pass, that as soon as he had made an end of offering the burnt offering, behold, Samuel came; and Saul went out to meet him, that he might salute him. ¹¹And Samuel said, What have you done? And Saul said, Because I saw that the people were scattered from me, and that you came not within the days appointed, and that the Philistines gathered themselves together at Michmash; ¹²Therefore said I, The Philistines will come down now on me to Gilgal, and I have not made supplication to the LORD: I forced myself therefore, and offered a burnt offering. ¹³And Samuel said to Saul, You have done foolishly: you have not kept the commandment of the LORD your God, which he commanded you: for now would the LORD have established your kingdom on Israel for ever. ¹⁴But now your kingdom shall not continue: the LORD has sought him a man after his own heart, and the LORD has commanded him to be captain over his people, because you have not kept that which the LORD commanded you. ¹⁵And Samuel arose, and got him up from Gilgal to Gibeah of Benjamin. And Saul numbered the people that were present with him, about six hundred men. ¹⁶And Saul, and Jonathan his son, and the people that were present with them, stayed in Gibeah of Benjamin: but the Philistines encamped in Michmash. ¹⁷And the spoilers came out of the camp of the Philistines in three companies: one company turned to the way that leads to Ophrah, to the land of Shual: ¹⁸And another company turned the way to Bethhoron: and another company turned to the way of the border that looks to the valley of Zeboim toward the wilderness. ¹⁹Now there was no smith found throughout all the land of Israel: for the Philistines said, Lest the Hebrews make them swords or spears: ²⁰But all the Israelites went down to the Philistines, to sharpen every man his share, and his coulter, and his ax, and his mattock. ²¹Yet they had a file for the mattocks, and for the coulters, and for the forks, and for the axes, and to sharpen the goads. ²²So it came to pass in the day of battle, that there was neither sword nor spear found in the hand of any of the people that were with Saul and Jonathan: but with Saul and with Jonathan his son was there found. ²³And the garrison of the Philistines went out to the passage of Michmash.

14

¹Now it came to pass on a day, that Jonathan the son of Saul said to the young man that bore his armor, Come, and let us go over to the Philistines' garrison, that is on the other side. But he told not his father. ²And Saul tarried in the uttermost part of Gibeah under a pomegranate tree which is in Migron: and the people that were with him were about six hundred men; ³And Ahiah, the son of Ahitub, Ichabod's brother, the son of Phinehas, the son of Eli, the LORD's priest in Shiloh, wearing an ephod. And the people knew not that Jonathan was gone. ⁴And between the passages, by which Jonathan sought to go over to the Philistines' garrison, there was a sharp rock on the one side, and a sharp rock on the other side: and the name of the one was Bozez, and the name of the other Seneh. ⁵The forefront of the one was situate northward over against Michmash,

and the other southward over against Gibeah. ⁶And Jonathan said to the young man that bore his armor, Come, and let us go over to the garrison of these uncircumcised: it may be that the LORD will work for us: for there is no restraint to the LORD to save by many or by few. ⁷And his armor bearer said to him, Do all that is in your heart: turn you; behold, I am with you according to your heart. ⁸Then said Jonathan, Behold, we will pass over to these men, and we will discover ourselves to them. ⁹If they say thus to us, Tarry until we come to you; then we will stand still in our place, and will not go up to them. ¹⁰But if they say thus, Come up to us; then we will go up: for the LORD has delivered them into our hand: and this shall be a sign to us. ¹¹And both of them discovered themselves to the garrison of the Philistines: and the Philistines said, Behold, the Hebrews come forth out of the holes where they had hid themselves. ¹²And the men of the garrison answered Jonathan and his armor bearer, and said, Come up to us, and we will show you a thing. And Jonathan said to his armor bearer, Come up after me: for the LORD has delivered them into the hand of Israel. ¹³And Jonathan climbed up on his hands and on his feet, and his armor bearer after him: and they fell before Jonathan; and his armor bearer slew after him. ¹⁴And that first slaughter, which Jonathan and his armor bearer made, was about twenty men, within as it were an half acre of land, which a yoke of oxen might plow. ¹⁵And there was trembling in the host, in the field, and among all the people: the garrison, and the spoilers, they also trembled, and the earth quaked: so it was a very great trembling. ¹⁶And the watchmen of Saul in Gibeah of Benjamin looked; and, behold, the multitude melted away, and they went on beating down one another. ¹⁷Then said Saul to the people that were with him, Number now, and see who is gone from us. And when they had numbered, behold, Jonathan and his armor bearer were not there. ¹⁸And Saul said to Ahiah, Bring here the ark of God. For the ark of God was at that time with the children of Israel. ¹⁹And it came to pass, while Saul talked to the priest, that the noise that was in the host of the Philistines went on and increased: and Saul said to the priest, Withdraw your hand. ²⁰And Saul and all the people that were with him assembled themselves, and they came to the battle: and, behold, every man's sword was against his fellow, and there was a very great discomfiture. ²¹Moreover the Hebrews that were with the Philistines before that time, which went up with them into the camp from the country round about, even they also turned to be with the Israelites that were with Saul and Jonathan. ²²Likewise all the men of Israel which had hid themselves in mount Ephraim, when they heard that the Philistines fled, even they also followed hard after them in the battle. ²³So the LORD saved Israel that day: and the battle passed over to Bethaven. ²⁴And the men of Israel were distressed that day: for Saul had adjured the people, saying, Cursed be the man that eats any food until evening, that I may be avenged on my enemies. So none of the people tasted any food. ²⁵And all they of the land came to a wood; and there was honey on the ground. ²⁶And when the people were come into the wood, behold, the honey dropped; but no man put his hand to his mouth: for the people feared the oath. ²⁷But Jonathan heard not when his father charged the people with the oath: why he put forth the end of the rod that was in his hand, and dipped it in an honeycomb, and put his hand to his mouth; and his eyes were enlightened. ²⁸Then answered one of the people, and said, Your father straightly charged the people with an oath, saying, Cursed be the man that eats any food this day. And the people were faint. ²⁹Then said Jonathan, My father has troubled the land: see, I pray you, how my eyes have been enlightened, because I tasted a little of this honey. ³⁰How much more, if haply the people had eaten freely to day of the spoil of their enemies which they found? for had there not been now a much greater slaughter among the Philistines? ³¹And they smote the Philistines that day from Michmash to Aijalon: and the people were very faint. ³²And the people flew on the spoil, and took sheep, and oxen, and calves, and slew them on the ground: and the people did eat them with the blood. ³³Then they told Saul, saying, Behold, the people sin against the LORD, in that they eat with the blood. And he said, You have transgressed: roll a great stone to me this day. ³⁴And Saul said, Disperse yourselves among the people, and say to them, Bring me here every man his ox, and every man his sheep, and slay them here, and eat; and sin not against the LORD in eating with the blood. And all the people brought every man his ox with him that night, and slew them there. ³⁵And Saul built an altar to the LORD: the same was the first altar that he built to the LORD. ³⁶And Saul said, Let us go down after the Philistines by night, and spoil them until the morning light, and let us not leave a man of them. And they said, Do whatever seems good to you. Then said the priest, Let us draw near here to God. ³⁷And Saul asked counsel of God, Shall I go down after the Philistines? will you deliver them into the hand of Israel? But he answered him not that day. ³⁸And Saul said, Draw you near here, all the chief of the people: and know and see wherein this sin has been this day. ³⁹For, as the LORD lives, which saves Israel, though it be in Jonathan my son, he shall surely die. But there was not a man among all the people that answered him. ⁴⁰Then said he to all Israel, Be you on one side, and I and Jonathan my son will be on the other side. And the people said to Saul, Do what seems good to you. ⁴¹Therefore Saul said to the LORD God of Israel, Give a perfect lot. And Saul and Jonathan were taken: but the people escaped. ⁴²And Saul said, Cast lots between me and Jonathan my son. And Jonathan was taken. ⁴³Then Saul said to Jonathan, Tell me what you have done. And Jonathan told him, and said, I did but taste a little honey with the end of the rod that was in my hand, and, see, I must die. ⁴⁴And Saul answered, God do so and more also: for you shall surely die, Jonathan. ⁴⁵And the people said to Saul, Shall Jonathan die, who has worked this great salvation in Israel? God forbid: as the LORD lives, there shall not one hair of his head fall to the ground; for he has worked with God this day. So the people rescued Jonathan, that he died not. ⁴⁶Then Saul went up from following the Philistines: and the Philistines went to their own place. ⁴⁷So Saul took the kingdom over Israel, and fought against all his enemies on every side, against Moab, and against the children of Ammon, and against Edom, and against the kings of Zobah, and against the Philistines: and wherever he turned himself, he vexed them. ⁴⁸And he gathered an host, and smote the Amalekites, and delivered Israel out of the hands of them that spoiled them. ⁴⁹Now the sons of Saul were Jonathan, and Ishui, and Melchishua: and the names of his two daughters were these; the name of the firstborn Merab, and the name of the younger Michal: ⁵⁰And the name of Saul's wife was Ahinoam, the daughter of Ahimaaz: and the name of the captain of his host was Abner, the son of Ner, Saul's uncle. ⁵¹And Kish was the father of Saul; and Ner the father of Abner was the son of Abiel. ⁵²And there was sore war against the Philistines all the days of Saul: and when Saul saw any strong man, or any valiant man, he took him to him.

15 ¹Samuel also said to Saul, The LORD sent me to anoint you to be king over his people, over Israel: now therefore listen you to the voice of the words of the LORD. ²Thus says the LORD of hosts, I remember that which Amalek did to Israel, how he laid wait for him in the way, when he came up from Egypt. ³Now go and smite Amalek, and utterly destroy all that they have, and spare them not; but slay both man and woman, infant and suckling, ox and sheep, camel and ass. ⁴And Saul gathered the people together, and numbered them in Telaim, two hundred thousand footmen, and ten thousand men of Judah. ⁵And Saul came to a city of Amalek, and laid wait in the valley. ⁶And Saul said to the Kenites, Go, depart, get you down from among the Amalekites, lest I destroy you with them: for you showed kindness to all the children of Israel, when they came up out of Egypt. So the Kenites departed from among the Amalekites. ⁷And Saul smote the Amalekites from Havilah until you come to Shur, that is over against Egypt. ⁸And he took Agag the king of the Amalekites alive, and utterly destroyed all the people with the edge of the sword. ⁹But Saul and the people spared Agag, and the best of the sheep, and of the oxen, and of the fatted calves, and the lambs, and all that was good, and would not utterly destroy them: but every thing that was vile and refuse, that they destroyed utterly. ¹⁰Then came the word of the LORD to Samuel, saying, ¹¹It repents me that I have set up Saul to be king: for he is turned back from following me, and has not performed my commandments. And it grieved Samuel; and he cried to the LORD all night. ¹²And when Samuel rose early to meet Saul in the morning, it was told Samuel, saying, Saul came to Carmel, and, behold, he set him up a place, and is gone about, and passed on, and gone down to Gilgal. ¹³And Samuel came to Saul: and Saul said to him, Blessed be you of the LORD: I have performed the commandment of the LORD. ¹⁴And Samuel said, What means then this bleating of the sheep in my ears, and the lowing of the oxen which I hear? ¹⁵And Saul said, They have brought them from the Amalekites: for the people spared the best of the sheep and of the oxen, to sacrifice to the LORD your God; and the rest we have utterly destroyed. ¹⁶Then Samuel said to Saul, Stay, and I will tell you what the LORD has said to me this night. And he said to him, Say on. ¹⁷And Samuel said, When you were little in your own sight, were you not made the head of the tribes of Israel, and the LORD anointed you king over Israel? ¹⁸And the LORD sent you on a journey, and said, Go and utterly destroy the sinners the Amalekites, and fight against them until they be consumed. ¹⁹Why then did you not obey the voice of the LORD, but did fly on the spoil, and did evil in the sight of the LORD? ²⁰And Saul said to Samuel, Yes, I have obeyed the voice of the LORD, and have gone the way which the LORD sent me, and have brought Agag the king of Amalek, and have utterly destroyed the Amalekites. ²¹But the people took of the spoil, sheep and oxen, the chief of the things which should have been utterly destroyed, to sacrifice to the LORD your God in Gilgal. ²²And Samuel said, Has the LORD as great delight in burnt offerings and sacrifices, as in obeying the voice of the LORD? Behold, to obey is better than sacrifice, and to listen than the fat of rams. ²³For rebellion is as the sin of witchcraft, and stubbornness is as iniquity and idolatry. Because you have rejected the word of the LORD, he has also rejected you from being king. ²⁴And Saul said to Samuel, I have sinned: for I have transgressed the commandment of the LORD, and your words: because I feared the people, and obeyed their voice. ²⁵Now therefore, I pray you, pardon my sin, and turn again with me, that I may worship the LORD. ²⁶And Samuel said to Saul, I will not return with you: for you have rejected the word of the LORD, and the LORD has rejected you from being king over Israel. ²⁷And as Samuel turned about to go away, he laid hold on the skirt of his mantle, and it rent. ²⁸And Samuel said to him, The LORD has rent the kingdom of Israel from you this day, and has given it to a neighbor of yours, that is better than you. ²⁹And also the Strength of Israel will not lie nor repent: for he is not a man, that he should repent. ³⁰Then he said, I have sinned: yet honor me now, I pray you, before the elders of my people, and before Israel, and turn again with me, that I may worship the LORD your God. ³¹So Samuel turned again after Saul; and Saul worshipped the LORD. ³²Then said Samuel, Bring you here to me Agag the king of the Amalekites. And Agag came to him delicately. And Agag said, Surely the bitterness of death is past. ³³And Samuel said, As the sword has made women childless, so shall your mother be childless among women. And Samuel hewed Agag in pieces before the LORD in Gilgal. ³⁴Then Samuel went to Ramah; and Saul went up to his house to Gibeah of Saul. ³⁵And Samuel came no more to see Saul until the day of his death: nevertheless Samuel mourned for Saul: and the LORD repented that he had made Saul king over Israel.

16 ¹And the LORD said to Samuel, How long will you mourn for Saul, seeing I have rejected him from reigning over Israel? fill your horn with oil, and go, I will send you to Jesse the Bethlehemite: for I have provided me a king among his sons. ²And Samuel said, How can I go? if Saul hear it, he will kill me. And the LORD said, Take an heifer with you, and say, I am come to sacrifice to the LORD. ³And call Jesse to the sacrifice, and I will show you what you shall do: and you shall anoint to me him whom I name to you. ⁴And Samuel did that which the LORD spoke, and came to Bethlehem. And the elders of the town trembled at his coming, and said, Come you peaceably? ⁵And he said, Peaceably: I am come to sacrifice to the LORD: sanctify yourselves, and come with me to the sacrifice. And he sanctified Jesse and his sons, and called them to the sacrifice. ⁶And it came to pass, when they were come, that he looked on Eliab, and said, Surely the LORD's anointed is before him. ⁷But the LORD said to Samuel, Look not on his countenance, or on the height of his stature; because I have refused him: for the LORD sees not as man sees; for man looks on the outward appearance, but the LORD looks on the heart. ⁸Then Jesse called Abinadab, and made him pass before Samuel. And he said, Neither has the LORD chosen this. ⁹Then Jesse made Shammah to pass by. And he said, Neither has the LORD chosen this. ¹⁰Again, Jesse made seven of his sons to pass before Samuel. And Samuel said to Jesse, The LORD has not chosen these. ¹¹And Samuel said to Jesse, Are here all your children? And he said, There remains yet the youngest, and, behold, he keeps the sheep. And Samuel said to Jesse, Send and fetch him: for we will not sit down till he come here. ¹²And he sent, and brought him in. Now he was ruddy, and with of a beautiful countenance, and goodly to look to. And the LORD said, Arise, anoint him: for this is he. ¹³Then Samuel took the horn of oil, and anointed him in the middle of his brothers: and the Spirit of the LORD came on David from that day forward. So Samuel rose up, and went to Ramah. ¹⁴But the Spirit of the LORD departed from Saul, and an evil spirit from the LORD troubled him. ¹⁵And Saul's servants said to him, Behold now, an evil spirit from God troubles you. ¹⁶Let our lord now command your servants, which are before you, to seek out a man, who is a cunning player on an harp: and it shall come to pass, when the evil spirit from God is on you, that he shall play with his hand, and you shall be well. ¹⁷And Saul said to his servants, Provide me now a man that can play well, and bring him to me. ¹⁸Then answered one of the servants, and said, Behold, I have seen a son of Jesse the Bethlehemite, that is cunning in playing, and a mighty valiant man, and a man of war, and prudent in matters, and a comely person, and the LORD is with him. ¹⁹Why Saul sent messengers to Jesse, and said, Send me David your son, which is with the sheep. ²⁰And Jesse took an ass laden with bread, and a bottle of wine, and a kid, and sent them by David his son to Saul. ²¹And David came to Saul, and stood before him: and he loved him greatly; and he became his armor bearer. ²²And Saul sent to Jesse, saying, Let David, I pray you, stand before me; for he has found favor in my sight. ²³And it came to pass, when the evil spirit from God was on Saul, that David took an harp, and played with his hand: so Saul was refreshed, and was well, and the evil spirit departed from him.

17 ¹Now the Philistines gathered together their armies to battle, and were gathered together at Shochoh, which belongs to Judah, and pitched between Shochoh and Azekah, in Ephesdammim. ²And Saul and the men of Israel were gathered together, and pitched by the valley of Elah, and set the battle in array against the Philistines. ³And the Philistines stood on a mountain on the one side, and Israel stood on a mountain on the other side: and there was a valley between them. ⁴And there went out a champion out of the camp of the Philistines, named Goliath, of Gath, whose height was six cubits and a span. ⁵And he had an helmet of brass on his head, and he was armed with a coat of mail; and the weight of the coat was five thousand shekels of brass. ⁶And he had greaves of brass on his legs, and a target of brass between his shoulders. ⁷And the staff of his spear was like a weaver's beam; and his spear's head weighed six hundred shekels of iron: and one bearing a shield went before him. ⁸And he stood and cried to the armies of Israel, and said to them, Why are you come out to set your battle in array? am not I a Philistine, and you servants to Saul? choose you a man for you, and let him come down to me. ⁹If he be able to fight with me, and to kill me, then will we be your servants: but if I prevail against him, and kill him, then shall you be our servants, and serve us. ¹⁰And the Philistine said, I defy the armies of Israel this day; give me a man, that we may fight together. ¹¹When Saul and all Israel heard those words of the Philistine, they were dismayed, and greatly afraid. ¹²Now David was the son of that Ephrathite of Bethlehemjudah, whose name was Jesse; and he had eight sons: and the man went among men for an old man in the days of Saul. ¹³And the three oldest sons of Jesse went and followed Saul to the battle: and the names of his three sons that went to the battle were Eliab the firstborn, and next to him Abinadab, and the third Shammah. ¹⁴And David was the youngest: and the three oldest followed Saul. ¹⁵But David went and returned from Saul to feed his father's sheep at Bethlehem. ¹⁶And the Philistine drew near morning and evening, and presented himself forty days. ¹⁷And Jesse said to David his son, Take now for your brothers an ephah of this parched corn, and these ten loaves, and run to the camp of your brothers; ¹⁸And carry these ten cheeses to the captain of their thousand, and look how your brothers fare, and take their pledge. ¹⁹Now Saul, and they, and all the men of Israel, were in the valley of Elah, fighting with the Philistines. ²⁰And David rose up early in the morning, and left the sheep with a keeper, and took, and went, as Jesse had commanded him; and he came to the trench, as the host was going forth to the fight, and shouted for the battle. ²¹For Israel and the Philistines had put the battle in array, army against army. ²²And David left his carriage in the hand of the keeper of the carriage, and ran into the army, and came and saluted his brothers. ²³And as he talked with them, behold, there came up the champion, the Philistine of Gath, Goliath by name, out of the armies of the Philistines, and spoke according to the same words: and David heard them. ²⁴And all the men of Israel, when they saw the man, fled from him, and were sore afraid. ²⁵And the men of Israel said, Have you seen this man that is come up? surely to defy Israel is he come up: and it shall be, that the man who kills him, the king will enrich him with great riches, and will give him his daughter, and make his father's house free in Israel. ²⁶And David spoke to the men that stood by him, saying, What shall be done to the man that kills this Philistine, and takes away the reproach from Israel? for who is this uncircumcised Philistine, that he should defy the armies of the living God? ²⁷And the people answered him after this manner, saying, So shall it be done to the man that kills him. ²⁸And Eliab his oldest brother heard when he spoke to the men; and Eliab's anger was kindled against David, and he said, Why came you down here? and with whom have you left those few sheep in the wilderness? I know your pride, and the naughtiness of your heart; for you are come down that you might see the battle. ²⁹And David said, What have I now done? Is there not a cause? ³⁰And he turned from him toward another, and spoke after the same manner: and the people answered him again after the former manner. ³¹And when the words were heard which David spoke, they rehearsed them before Saul: and he sent for him. ³²And David said to Saul, Let no man's heart fail because of him; your servant will go and fight with this

Philistine. ³³And Saul said to David, You are not able to go against this Philistine to fight with him: for you are but a youth, and he a man of war from his youth. ³⁴And David said to Saul, Your servant kept his father's sheep, and there came a lion, and a bear, and took a lamb out of the flock: ³⁵And I went out after him, and smote him, and delivered it out of his mouth: and when he arose against me, I caught him by his beard, and smote him, and slew him. ³⁶Your servant slew both the lion and the bear: and this uncircumcised Philistine shall be as one of them, seeing he has defied the armies of the living God. ³⁷David said moreover, The LORD that delivered me out of the paw of the lion, and out of the paw of the bear, he will deliver me out of the hand of this Philistine. And Saul said to David, Go, and the LORD be with you. ³⁸And Saul armed David with his armor, and he put an helmet of brass on his head; also he armed him with a coat of mail. ³⁹And David girded his sword on his armor, and he assayed to go; for he had not proved it. And David said to Saul, I cannot go with these; for I have not proved them. And David put them off him. ⁴⁰And he took his staff in his hand, and chose him five smooth stones out of the brook, and put them in a shepherd's bag which he had, even in a money; and his sling was in his hand: and he drew near to the Philistine. ⁴¹And the Philistine came on and drew near to David; and the man that bore the shield went before him. ⁴²And when the Philistine looked about, and saw David, he disdained him: for he was but a youth, and ruddy, and of a fair countenance. ⁴³And the Philistine said to David, Am I a dog, that you come to me with staves? And the Philistine cursed David by his gods. ⁴⁴And the Philistine said to David, Come to me, and I will give your flesh to the fowls of the air, and to the beasts of the field. ⁴⁵Then said David to the Philistine, You come to me with a sword, and with a spear, and with a shield: but I come to you in the name of the LORD of hosts, the God of the armies of Israel, whom you have defied. ⁴⁶This day will the LORD deliver you into my hand; and I will smite you, and take your head from you; and I will give the carcasses of the host of the Philistines this day to the fowls of the air, and to the wild beasts of the earth; that all the earth may know that there is a God in Israel. ⁴⁷And all this assembly shall know that the LORD saves not with sword and spear: for the battle is the LORD's, and he will give you into our hands. ⁴⁸And it came to pass, when the Philistine arose, and came, and drew near to meet David, that David hastened, and ran toward the army to meet the Philistine. ⁴⁹And David put his hand in his bag, and took there a stone, and slang it, and smote the Philistine in his forehead, that the stone sunk into his forehead; and he fell on his face to the earth. ⁵⁰So David prevailed over the Philistine with a sling and with a stone, and smote the Philistine, and slew him; but there was no sword in the hand of David. ⁵¹Therefore David ran, and stood on the Philistine, and took his sword, and drew it out of the sheath thereof, and slew him, and cut off his head therewith. And when the Philistines saw their champion was dead, they fled. ⁵²And the men of Israel and of Judah arose, and shouted, and pursued the Philistines, until you come to the valley, and to the gates of Ekron. And the wounded of the Philistines fell down by the way to Shaaraim, even to Gath, and to Ekron. ⁵³And the children of Israel returned from chasing after the Philistines, and they spoiled their tents. ⁵⁴And David took the head of the Philistine, and brought it to Jerusalem; but he put his armor in his tent. ⁵⁵And when Saul saw David go forth against the Philistine, he said to Abner, the captain of the host, Abner, whose son is this youth? And Abner said, As your soul lives, O king, I cannot tell. ⁵⁶And the king said, Inquire you whose son the stripling is. ⁵⁷And as David returned from the slaughter of the Philistine, Abner took him, and brought him before Saul with the head of the Philistine in his hand. ⁵⁸And Saul said to him, Whose son are you, you young man? And David answered, I am the son of your servant Jesse the Bethlehemite.

18

¹And it came to pass, when he had made an end of speaking to Saul, that the soul of Jonathan was knit with the soul of David, and Jonathan loved him as his own soul. ²And Saul took him that day, and would let him go no more home to his father's house. ³Then Jonathan and David made a covenant, because he loved him as his own soul. ⁴And Jonathan stripped himself of the robe that was on him, and gave it to David, and his garments, even to his sword, and to his bow, and to his girdle. ⁵And David went out wherever Saul sent him, and behaved himself wisely: and Saul set him over the men of war, and he was accepted in the sight of all the people, and also in the sight of Saul's servants. ⁶And it came to pass as they came, when David was returned from the slaughter of the Philistine, that the women came out of all cities of Israel, singing and dancing, to meet king Saul, with tabrets, with joy, and with instruments of music. ⁷And the women answered one another as they played, and said, Saul has slain his thousands, and David his ten thousands. ⁸And Saul was very wroth, and the saying displeased him; and he said, They have ascribed to David ten thousands, and to me they have ascribed but thousands: and what can he have more but the kingdom? ⁹And Saul eyed David from that day and forward. ¹⁰And it came to pass on the morrow, that the evil spirit from God came on Saul, and he prophesied in the middle of the house: and David played with his hand, as at other times: and there was a javelin in Saul's hand. ¹¹And Saul cast the javelin; for he said, I will smite David even to the wall with it. And David avoided out of his presence twice. ¹²And Saul was afraid of David, because the LORD was with him, and was departed from Saul. ¹³Therefore Saul removed him from him, and made him his captain over a thousand; and he went out and came in before the people. ¹⁴And David behaved himself wisely in all his ways; and the LORD was with him. ¹⁵Why when Saul saw that he behaved himself very wisely, he was afraid of him. ¹⁶But all Israel and Judah loved David, because he went out and came in before them. ¹⁷And Saul said to David, Behold my elder daughter Merab, her will I give you to wife: only be you valiant for me, and fight the LORD's battles. For Saul said, Let not my hand be on him, but let the hand of the Philistines be on him. ¹⁸And David said to Saul, Who am I? and what is my life, or my father's family in Israel, that I should be son in law to the king? ¹⁹But it came to pass at the time when Merab Saul's daughter should have been given to David, that she was given to Adriel the Meholathite to wife. ²⁰And Michal Saul's daughter loved David: and they told Saul, and the thing pleased him. ²¹And Saul said, I will give him her, that she may be a snare

to him, and that the hand of the Philistines may be against him. Why Saul said to David, You shall this day be my son in law in the one of the two. ²²And Saul commanded his servants, saying, Commune with David secretly, and say, Behold, the king has delight in you, and all his servants love you: now therefore be the king's son in law. ²³And Saul's servants spoke those words in the ears of David. And David said, Seems it to you a light thing to be a king's son in law, seeing that I am a poor man, and lightly esteemed? ²⁴And the servants of Saul told him, saying, On this manner spoke David. ²⁵And Saul said, Thus shall you say to David, The king desires not any dowry, but an hundred foreskins of the Philistines, to be avenged of the king's enemies. But Saul thought to make David fall by the hand of the Philistines. ²⁶And when his servants told David these words, it pleased David well to be the king's son in law: and the days were not expired. ²⁷Why David arose and went, he and his men, and slew of the Philistines two hundred men; and David brought their foreskins, and they gave them in full tale to the king, that he might be the king's son in law. And Saul gave him Michal his daughter to wife. ²⁸And Saul saw and knew that the LORD was with David, and that Michal Saul's daughter loved him. ²⁹And Saul was yet the more afraid of David; and Saul became David's enemy continually. ³⁰Then the princes of the Philistines went forth: and it came to pass, after they went forth, that David behaved himself more wisely than all the servants of Saul; so that his name was much set by.

19 ¹And Saul spoke to Jonathan his son, and to all his servants, that they should kill David. ²But Jonathan Saul's son delighted much in David: and Jonathan told David, saying, Saul my father seeks to kill you: now therefore, I pray you, take heed to yourself until the morning, and abide in a secret place, and hide yourself: ³And I will go out and stand beside my father in the field where you are, and I will commune with my father of you; and what I see, that I will tell you. ⁴And Jonathan spoke good of David to Saul his father, and said to him, Let not the king sin against his servant, against David; because he has not sinned against you, and because his works have been to youward very good: ⁵For he did put his life in his hand, and slew the Philistine, and the LORD worked a great salvation for all Israel: you saw it, and did rejoice: why then will you sin against innocent blood, to slay David without a cause? ⁶And Saul listened to the voice of Jonathan: and Saul swore, As the LORD lives, he shall not be slain. ⁷And Jonathan called David, and Jonathan showed him all those things. And Jonathan brought David to Saul, and he was in his presence, as in times past. ⁸And there was war again: and David went out, and fought with the Philistines, and slew them with a great slaughter; and they fled from him. ⁹And the evil spirit from the LORD was on Saul, as he sat in his house with his javelin in his hand: and David played with his hand. ¹⁰And Saul sought to smite David even to the wall with the javelin: but he slipped away out of Saul's presence, and he smote the javelin into the wall: and David fled, and escaped that night. ¹¹Saul also sent messengers to David's house, to watch him, and to slay him in the morning: and Michal David's wife told him, saying, If you save not your life to night, to morrow you shall be slain. ¹²So Michal let David down through a window: and he went, and fled, and escaped. ¹³And Michal took an image, and laid it in the bed, and put a pillow of goats' hair for his bolster, and covered it with a cloth. ¹⁴And when Saul sent messengers to take David, she said, He is sick. ¹⁵And Saul sent the messengers again to see David, saying, Bring him up to me in the bed, that I may slay him. ¹⁶And when the messengers were come in, behold, there was an image in the bed, with a pillow of goats' hair for his bolster. ¹⁷And Saul said to Michal, Why have you deceived me so, and sent away my enemy, that he is escaped? And Michal answered Saul, He said to me, Let me go; why should I kill you? ¹⁸So David fled, and escaped, and came to Samuel to Ramah, and told him all that Saul had done to him. And he and Samuel went and dwelled in Naioth. ¹⁹And it was told Saul, saying, Behold, David is at Naioth in Ramah. ²⁰And Saul sent messengers to take David: and when they saw the company of the prophets prophesying, and Samuel standing as appointed over them, the Spirit of God was on the messengers of Saul, and they also prophesied. ²¹And when it was told Saul, he sent other messengers, and they prophesied likewise. And Saul sent messengers again the third time, and they prophesied also. ²²Then went he also to Ramah, and came to a great well that is in Sechu: and he asked and said, Where are Samuel and David? And one said, Behold, they be at Naioth in Ramah. ²³And he went thither to Naioth in Ramah: and the Spirit of God was on him also, and he went on, and prophesied, until he came to Naioth in Ramah. ²⁴And he stripped off his clothes also, and prophesied before Samuel in like manner, and lay down naked all that day and all that night. Why they say, Is Saul also among the prophets?

20 ¹And David fled from Naioth in Ramah, and came and said before Jonathan, What have I done? what is my iniquity? and what is my sin before your father, that he seeks my life? ²And he said to him, God forbid; you shall not die: behold, my father will do nothing either great or small, but that he will show it me: and why should my father hide this thing from me? it is not so. ³And David swore moreover, and said, Your father certainly knows that I have found grace in your eyes; and he says, Let not Jonathan know this, lest he be grieved: but truly as the LORD lives, and as your soul lives, there is but a step between me and death. ⁴Then said Jonathan to David, Whatever your soul desires, I will even do it for you. ⁵And David said to Jonathan, Behold, to morrow is the new moon, and I should not fail to sit with the king at meat: but let me go, that I may hide myself in the field to the third day at even. ⁶If your father at all miss me, then say, David earnestly asked leave of me that he might run to Bethlehem his city: for there is a yearly sacrifice there for all the family. ⁷If he say thus, It is well; your servant shall have peace: but if he be very wroth, then be sure that evil is determined by him. ⁸Therefore you shall deal kindly with your servant; for you have brought your servant into a covenant of the LORD with you: notwithstanding, if there be in me iniquity, slay me yourself; for why should you bring me to your father? ⁹And Jonathan said, Far be it from you: for if I knew certainly that evil were determined by my father to come on you, then would not I tell it you? ¹⁰Then said David to Jonathan, Who shall tell me? or what if your father answer you roughly? ¹¹And Jonathan said to David, Come, and let us go out into the field. And they went out both of them into the field. ¹²And Jonathan said to David, O LORD God of Israel, when I have sounded my father about to morrow any time, or the third day, and, behold, if there be good toward David, and I then send not to you, and show it you; ¹³The LORD do so and much more to Jonathan: but if it please my father to do you evil, then I will show it you, and send you away, that you may go in peace: and the LORD be with you, as he has been with my father. ¹⁴And you shall not only while yet I live show me the kindness of the LORD, that I die not: ¹⁵But also you shall not cut off your kindness from my house for ever: no, not when the LORD has cut off the enemies of David every one from the face of the earth. ¹⁶So Jonathan made a covenant with the house of David, saying, Let the LORD even require it at the hand of David's enemies. ¹⁷And Jonathan caused David to swear again, because he loved him: for he loved him as he loved his own soul. ¹⁸Then Jonathan said to David, To morrow is the new moon: and you shall be missed, because your seat will be empty. ¹⁹And when you have stayed three days, then you shall go down quickly, and come to the place where you did hide yourself when the business was in hand, and shall remain by the stone Ezel. ²⁰And I will shoot three arrows on the side thereof, as though I shot at a mark. ²¹And, behold, I will send a lad, saying, Go, find out the arrows. If I expressly say to the lad, Behold, the arrows are on this side of you, take them; then come you: for there is peace to you, and no hurt; as the LORD lives. ²²But if I say thus to the young man, Behold, the arrows are beyond you; go your way: for the LORD has sent you away. ²³And as touching the matter which you and I have spoken of, behold, the LORD be between you and me for ever. ²⁴So David hid himself in the field: and when the new moon was come, the king sat him down to eat meat. ²⁵And the king sat on his seat, as at other times, even on a seat by the wall: and Jonathan arose, and Abner sat by Saul's side, and David's place was empty. ²⁶Nevertheless Saul spoke not any thing that day: for he thought, Something has befallen him, he is not clean; surely he is not clean. ²⁷And it came to pass on the morrow, which was the second day of the month, that David's place was empty: and Saul said to Jonathan his son, Why comes not the son of Jesse to meat, neither yesterday, nor to day? ²⁸And Jonathan answered Saul, David earnestly asked leave of me to go to Bethlehem: ²⁹And he said, Let me go, I pray you; for our family has a sacrifice in the city; and my brother, he has commanded me to be there: and now, if I have found favor in your eyes, let me get away, I pray you, and see my brothers. Therefore he comes not to the king's table. ³⁰Then Saul's anger was kindled against Jonathan, and he said to him, You son of the perverse rebellious woman, do not I know that you have chosen the son of Jesse to your own confusion, and to the confusion of your mother's nakedness? ³¹For as long as the son of Jesse lives on the ground, you shall not be established, nor your kingdom. Why now send and fetch him to me, for he shall surely die. ³²And Jonathan answered Saul his father, and said to him, Why shall he be slain? what has he done? ³³And Saul cast a javelin at him to smite him: whereby Jonathan knew that it was determined of his father to slay David. ³⁴So Jonathan arose from the table in fierce anger, and did eat no meat the second day of the month: for he was grieved for David, because his father had done him shame. ³⁵And it came to pass in the morning, that Jonathan went out into the field at the time appointed with David, and a little lad with him. ³⁶And he said to his lad, Run, find out now the arrows which I shoot. And as the lad ran, he shot an arrow beyond him. ³⁷And when the lad was come to the place of the arrow which Jonathan had shot, Jonathan cried after the lad, and said, Is not the arrow beyond you? ³⁸And Jonathan cried after the lad, Make speed, haste, stay not. And Jonathan's lad gathered up the arrows, and came to his master. ³⁹But the lad knew not any thing: only Jonathan and David knew the matter. ⁴⁰And Jonathan gave his artillery to his lad, and said to him, Go, carry them to the city. ⁴¹And as soon as the lad was gone, David arose out of a place toward the south, and fell on his face to the ground, and bowed himself three times: and they kissed one another, and wept one with another, until David exceeded. ⁴²And Jonathan said to David, Go in peace, for as much as we have sworn both of us in the name of the LORD, saying, The LORD be between me and you, and between my seed and your seed for ever. And he arose and departed: and Jonathan went into the city.

21

¹Then came David to Nob to Ahimelech the priest: and Ahimelech was afraid at the meeting of David, and said to him, Why are you alone, and no man with you? ²And David said to Ahimelech the priest, The king has commanded me a business, and has said to me, Let no man know any thing of the business about which I send you, and what I have commanded you: and I have appointed my servants to such and such a place. ³Now therefore what is under your hand? give me five loaves of bread in my hand, or what there is present. ⁴And the priest answered David, and said, There is no common bread under my hand, but there is hallowed bread; if the young men have kept themselves at least from women. ⁵And David answered the priest, and said to him, Of a truth women have been kept from us about these three days, since I came out, and the vessels of the young men are holy, and the bread is in a manner common, yes, though it were sanctified this day in the vessel. ⁶So the priest gave him hallowed bread: for there was no bread there but the show bread, that was taken from before the LORD, to put hot bread in the day when it was taken away. ⁷Now a certain man of the servants of Saul was there that day, detained before the LORD; and his name was Doeg, an Edomite, the most chief of the herdsmen that belonged to Saul. ⁸And David said to Ahimelech, And is there not here under your hand spear or sword? for I have neither brought my sword nor my weapons with me, because the king's business required haste. ⁹And the priest said, The sword of Goliath the Philistine, whom you slew in the valley of Elah, behold, it is here wrapped in a cloth behind the ephod: if you will take that, take it: for there is no other save that here. And David said, There is none like that; give it me. ¹⁰And David arose and fled that day for fear of Saul, and went to Achish the king of Gath. ¹¹And the servants of Achish said to him, Is not this David the king of the land? did they not sing one to another of him in dances, saying, Saul has slain his thousands, and David his ten thousands? ¹²And David laid up these words in his heart, and was sore afraid of Achish the king of Gath. ¹³And he changed his behavior before them,

and feigned himself mad in their hands, and scrabbled on the doors of the gate, and let his spittle fall down on his beard. ¹⁴Then said Achish to his servants, See, you see the man is mad: why then have you brought him to me? ¹⁵Have I need of mad men, that you have brought this fellow to play the mad man in my presence? shall this fellow come into my house?

22 ¹David therefore departed there, and escaped to the cave Adullam: and when his brothers and all his father's house heard it, they went down thither to him. ²And every one that was in distress, and every one that was in debt, and every one that was discontented, gathered themselves to him; and he became a captain over them: and there were with him about four hundred men. ³And David went there to Mizpeh of Moab: and he said to the king of Moab, Let my father and my mother, I pray you, come forth, and be with you, till I know what God will do for me. ⁴And he brought them before the king of Moab: and they dwelled with him all the while that David was in the hold. ⁵And the prophet Gad said to David, Abide not in the hold; depart, and get you into the land of Judah. Then David departed, and came into the forest of Hareth. ⁶When Saul heard that David was discovered, and the men that were with him, (now Saul stayed in Gibeah under a tree in Ramah, having his spear in his hand, and all his servants were standing about him;) ⁷Then Saul said to his servants that stood about him, Hear now, you Benjamites; will the son of Jesse give every one of you fields and vineyards, and make you all captains of thousands, and captains of hundreds; ⁸That all of you have conspired against me, and there is none that shows me that my son has made a league with the son of Jesse, and there is none of you that is sorry for me, or shows to me that my son has stirred up my servant against me, to lie in wait, as at this day? ⁹Then answered Doeg the Edomite, which was set over the servants of Saul, and said, I saw the son of Jesse coming to Nob, to Ahimelech the son of Ahitub. ¹⁰And he inquired of the LORD for him, and gave him victuals, and gave him the sword of Goliath the Philistine. ¹¹Then the king sent to call Ahimelech the priest, the son of Ahitub, and all his father's house, the priests that were in Nob: and they came all of them to the king. ¹²And Saul said, Hear now, you son of Ahitub. And he answered, Here I am, my lord. ¹³And Saul said to him, Why have you conspired against me, you and the son of Jesse, in that you have given him bread, and a sword, and have inquired of God for him, that he should rise against me, to lie in wait, as at this day? ¹⁴Then Ahimelech answered the king, and said, And who is so faithful among all your servants as David, which is the king's son in law, and goes at your bidding, and is honorable in your house? ¹⁵Did I then begin to inquire of God for him? be it far from me: let not the king impute any thing to his servant, nor to all the house of my father: for your servant knew nothing of all this, less or more. ¹⁶And the king said, You shall surely die, Ahimelech, you, and all your father's house. ¹⁷And the king said to the footmen that stood about him, Turn, and slay the priests of the LORD: because their hand also is with David, and because they knew when he fled, and did not show it to me. But the servants of the king would not put forth their hand to fall on the priests of the LORD. ¹⁸And the king said to Doeg, Turn you, and fall on the priests. And Doeg the Edomite turned, and he fell on the priests, and slew on that day fourscore and five persons that did wear a linen ephod. ¹⁹And Nob, the city of the priests, smote he with the edge of the sword, both men and women, children and sucklings, and oxen, and asses, and sheep, with the edge of the sword. ²⁰And one of the sons of Ahimelech the son of Ahitub, named Abiathar, escaped, and fled after David. ²¹And Abiathar showed David that Saul had slain the LORD's priests. ²²And David said to Abiathar, I knew it that day, when Doeg the Edomite was there, that he would surely tell Saul: I have occasioned the death of all the persons of your father's house. ²³Abide you with me, fear not: for he that seeks my life seeks your life: but with me you shall be in safeguard.

23 ¹Then they told David, saying, Behold, the Philistines fight against Keilah, and they rob the threshing floors. ²Therefore David inquired of the LORD, saying, Shall I go and smite these Philistines? And the LORD said to David, Go, and smite the Philistines, and save Keilah. ³And David's men said to him, Behold, we be afraid here in Judah: how much more then if we come to Keilah against the armies of the Philistines? ⁴Then David inquired of the LORD yet again. And the LORD answered him and said, Arise, go down to Keilah; for I will deliver the Philistines into your hand. ⁵So David and his men went to Keilah, and fought with the Philistines, and brought away their cattle, and smote them with a great slaughter. So David saved the inhabitants of Keilah. ⁶And it came to pass, when Abiathar the son of Ahimelech fled to David to Keilah, that he came down with an ephod in his hand. ⁷And it was told Saul that David was come to Keilah. And Saul said, God has delivered him into my hand; for he is shut in, by entering into a town that has gates and bars. ⁸And Saul called all the people together to war, to go down to Keilah, to besiege David and his men. ⁹And David knew that Saul secretly practiced mischief against him; and he said to Abiathar the priest, Bring here the ephod. ¹⁰Then said David, O LORD God of Israel, your servant has certainly heard that Saul seeks to come to Keilah, to destroy the city for my sake. ¹¹Will the men of Keilah deliver me up into his hand? will Saul come down, as your servant has heard? O LORD God of Israel, I beseech you, tell your servant. And the LORD said, He will come down. ¹²Then said David, Will the men of Keilah deliver me and my men into the hand of Saul? And the LORD said, They will deliver you up. ¹³Then David and his men, which were about six hundred, arose and departed out of Keilah, and went wherever they could go. And it was told Saul that David was escaped from Keilah; and he declined to go forth. ¹⁴And David stayed in the wilderness in strong holds, and remained in a mountain in the wilderness of Ziph. And Saul sought him every day, but God delivered him not into his hand. ¹⁵And David saw that Saul was come out to seek his life: and David was in the wilderness of Ziph in a wood. ¹⁶And Jonathan Saul's son arose, and went to David into the wood, and strengthened his hand in God. ¹⁷And he said to him, Fear not: for the hand of Saul my father shall not find you; and you shall be king over Israel, and I shall be next to you; and that also Saul my father knows. ¹⁸And they two made a covenant before the LORD: and David stayed in the wood, and Jonathan went to his house. ¹⁹Then came up the Ziphites to Saul to Gibeah, saying, Does not David hide himself with us in strong holds in the wood, in the hill of Hachilah, which is on the south of Jeshimon? ²⁰Now therefore, O king, come down according to all the desire of your soul to come down; and our part shall be to deliver him into the king's hand. ²¹And Saul said, Blessed be you of the LORD; for you have compassion on me. ²²Go, I pray you, prepare yet, and know and see his place where his haunt is, and who has seen him there: for it is told me that he deals very subtly. ²³See therefore, and take knowledge of all the lurking places where he hides himself, and come you again to me with the certainty, and I will go with you: and it shall come to pass, if he be in the land, that I will search him out throughout all the thousands of Judah. ²⁴And they arose, and went to Ziph before Saul: but David and his men were in the wilderness of Maon, in the plain on the south of Jeshimon. ²⁵Saul also and his men went to seek him. And they told David; why he came down into a rock, and stayed in the wilderness of Maon. And when Saul heard that, he pursued after David in the wilderness of Maon. ²⁶And Saul went on this side of the mountain, and David and his men on that side of the mountain: and David made haste to get away for fear of Saul; for Saul and his men compassed David and his men round about to take them. ²⁷But there came a messenger to Saul, saying, Haste you, and come; for the Philistines have invaded the land. ²⁸Why Saul returned from pursuing after David, and went against the Philistines: therefore they called that place Selahammahlekoth. ²⁹And David went up from there, and dwelled in strong holds at Engedi.

24 ¹And it came to pass, when Saul was returned from following the Philistines, that it was told him, saying, Behold, David is in the wilderness of Engedi. ²Then Saul took three thousand chosen men out of all Israel, and went to seek David and his men on the rocks of the wild goats. ³And he came to the sheepcotes by the way, where was a cave; and Saul went in to cover his feet: and David and his men remained in the sides of the cave. ⁴And the men of David said to him, Behold the day of which the LORD said to you, Behold, I will deliver your enemy into your hand, that you may do to him as it shall seem good to you. Then David arose, and cut off the skirt of Saul's robe privately. ⁵And it came to pass afterward, that David's heart smote him, because he had cut off Saul's skirt. ⁶And he said to his men, The LORD forbid that I should do this thing to my master, the LORD's anointed, to stretch forth my hand against him, seeing he is the anointed of the LORD. ⁷So David stayed his servants with these words, and suffered them not to rise against Saul. But Saul rose up out of the cave, and went on his way. ⁸David also arose afterward, and went out of the cave, and cried after Saul, saying, My lord the king. And when Saul looked behind him, David stooped with his face to the earth, and bowed himself. ⁹And David said to Saul, Why hear you men's words, saying, Behold, David seeks your hurt? ¹⁰Behold, this day your eyes have seen how that the LORD had delivered you to day into my hand in the cave: and some bade me kill you: but my eye spared you; and I said, I will not put forth my hand against my lord; for he is the LORD's anointed. ¹¹Moreover, my father, see, yes, see the skirt of your robe in my hand: for in that I cut off the skirt of your robe, and killed you not, know you and see that there is neither evil nor transgression in my hand, and I have not sinned against you; yet you hunt my soul to take it. ¹²The LORD judge between me and you, and the LORD avenge me of you: but my hand shall not be on you. ¹³As says the proverb of the ancients, Wickedness proceeds from the wicked: but my hand shall not be on you. ¹⁴After whom is the king of Israel come out? after whom do you pursue? after a dead dog, after a flea. ¹⁵The LORD therefore be judge, and judge between me and you, and see, and plead my cause, and deliver me out of your hand. ¹⁶And it came to pass, when David had made an end of speaking these words to Saul, that Saul said, Is this your voice, my son David? And Saul lifted up his voice, and wept. ¹⁷And he said to David, You are more righteous than I: for you have rewarded me good, whereas I have rewarded you evil. ¹⁸And you have showed this day how that you have dealt well with me: for as much as when the LORD had delivered me into your hand, you killed me not. ¹⁹For if a man find his enemy, will he let him go well away? why the LORD reward you good for that you have done to me this day. ²⁰And now, behold, I know well that you shall surely be king, and that the kingdom of Israel shall be established in your hand. ²¹Swear now therefore to me by the LORD, that you will not cut off my seed after me, and that you will not destroy my name out of my father's house. ²²And David swore to Saul. And Saul went home; but David and his men got them up to the hold.

25 ¹And Samuel died; and all the Israelites were gathered together, and lamented him, and buried him in his house at Ramah. And David arose, and went down to the wilderness of Paran. ²And there was a man in Maon, whose possessions were in Carmel; and the man was very great, and he had three thousand sheep, and a thousand goats: and he was shearing his sheep in Carmel. ³Now the name of the man was Nabal; and the name of his wife Abigail: and she was a woman of good understanding, and of a beautiful countenance: but the man was churlish and evil in his doings; and he was of the house of Caleb. ⁴And David heard in the wilderness that Nabal did shear his sheep. ⁵And David sent out ten young men, and David said to the young men, Get you up to Carmel, and go to Nabal, and greet him in my name: ⁶And thus shall you say to him that lives in prosperity, Peace be both to you, and peace be to your house, and peace be to all that you have. ⁷And now I have heard that you have shearers: now your shepherds which were with us, we hurt them not, neither was there anything missing to them, all the while they were in Carmel. ⁸Ask your young men, and they will show you. Why let the young men find favor in your eyes: for we come in a good day: give, I pray you, whatever comes to your hand to your servants, and to your son David. ⁹And when David's young men came, they spoke to Nabal according to all those words in the name of David, and ceased. ¹⁰And Nabal answered David's servants, and said, Who is David? and who is the son of Jesse? there be many servants now a days that break away every man from his master. ¹¹Shall I then take my bread, and my water, and my flesh that I have killed for my shearers, and give it to men, whom I know not from where they be? ¹²So David's young men turned their way, and went again, and came and told him all those sayings. ¹³And David said to his men, Gird you on every man his sword. And they girded on every man his sword; and David also girded on his sword: and there went up after David about four hundred men; and two hundred stayed by the stuff. ¹⁴But one of the young men told Abigail, Nabal's wife, saying, Behold, David sent messengers out of the wilderness to salute our master; and he railed on them. ¹⁵But the men were very good to us, and we were not hurt, neither missed we any thing, as long as we were conversant with them, when we were in the fields: ¹⁶They were a wall to us both by night and day, all the while we were with them keeping the sheep. ¹⁷Now therefore know and consider what you will do; for evil is determined against our master, and against all his household: for he is such a son of Belial, that a man cannot speak to him. ¹⁸Then Abigail made haste, and took two hundred loaves, and two bottles of wine, and five sheep ready dressed, and five measures of parched corn, and an hundred clusters of raisins, and two hundred cakes of figs, and laid them on asses. ¹⁹And she said to her servants, Go on before me; behold, I come after you. But she told not her husband Nabal. ²⁰And it was so, as she rode on the ass, that she came down by the covert on the hill, and, behold, David and his men came down against her; and she met them. ²¹Now David had said, Surely in vain have I kept all that this fellow has in the wilderness, so that nothing was missed of all that pertained to him: and he has requited me evil for good. ²²So and more also do God to the enemies of David, if I leave of all that pertain to him by the morning light any that urinates against the wall. ²³And when Abigail saw David, she hurried, and lighted off the ass, and fell before David on her face, and bowed herself to the ground, ²⁴And fell at his feet, and said, On me, my lord, on me let this iniquity be: and let your handmaid, I pray you, speak in your audience, and hear the words of your handmaid. ²⁵Let not my lord, I pray you, regard this man of Belial, even Nabal: for as his name is, so is he; Nabal is his name, and folly is with him: but I your handmaid saw not the young men of my lord, whom you did send. ²⁶Now therefore, my lord, as the LORD lives, and as your soul lives, seeing the LORD has withheld you from coming to shed blood, and from avenging yourself with your own hand, now let your enemies, and they that seek evil to my lord, be as Nabal. ²⁷And now this blessing which your handmaid has brought to my lord, let it even be given to the young men that follow my lord. ²⁸I pray you, forgive the trespass of your handmaid: for the LORD will certainly make my lord a sure house; because my lord fights the battles of the LORD, and evil has not been found in you all your days. ²⁹Yet a man is risen to pursue you, and to seek your soul: but the soul of my lord shall be bound in the bundle of life with the LORD your God; and the souls of your enemies, them shall he sling out, as out of the middle of a sling. ³⁰And it shall come to pass, when the LORD shall have done to my lord according to all the good that he has spoken concerning you, and shall have appointed you ruler over Israel; ³¹That this shall be no grief to you, nor offense of heart to my lord, either that you have shed blood causeless, or that my lord has avenged himself: but when the LORD shall have dealt well with my lord, then remember your handmaid. ³²And David said to Abigail, Blessed be the LORD God of Israel, which sent you this day to meet me: ³³And blessed be your advice, and blessed be you, which have kept me this day from coming to shed blood, and from avenging myself with my own hand. ³⁴For in very deed, as the LORD God of Israel lives, which has kept me back from hurting you, except you had hurried and come to meet me, surely there had not been left to Nabal by the morning light any that urinates against the wall. ³⁵So David received of her hand that which she had brought him, and said to her, Go up in peace to your house; see, I have listened to your voice, and have accepted your person. ³⁶And Abigail came to Nabal; and, behold, he held a feast in his house, like the feast of a king; and Nabal's heart was merry within him, for he was very drunken: why she told him nothing, less or more, until the morning light. ³⁷But it came to pass in the morning, when the wine was gone out of Nabal, and his wife had told him these things, that his heart died within him, and he became as a stone. ³⁸And it came to pass about ten days after, that the LORD smote Nabal, that he died. ³⁹And when David heard that Nabal was dead, he said, Blessed be the LORD, that has pleaded the cause of my reproach from the hand of Nabal, and has kept his servant from evil: for the LORD has returned the wickedness of Nabal on his own head. And David sent and communed with Abigail, to take her to him to wife. ⁴⁰And when the servants of David were come to Abigail to Carmel, they spoke to her, saying, David sent us to you, to take you to him to wife. ⁴¹And she arose, and bowed herself on her face to the earth, and said, Behold, let your handmaid be a servant to wash the feet of the servants of my lord. ⁴²And Abigail hurried, and arose and rode on an ass, with five damsels of hers that went after her; and she went after the messengers of David, and became his wife. ⁴³David also took Ahinoam of Jezreel; and they were also both of them his wives. ⁴⁴But Saul had given Michal his daughter, David's wife, to Phalti the son of Laish, which was of Gallim.

26 ¹And the Ziphites came to Saul to Gibeah, saying, Does not David hide himself in the hill of Hachilah, which is before Jeshimon? ²Then Saul arose, and went down to the wilderness of Ziph, having three thousand chosen men of Israel with him, to seek David in the wilderness of Ziph. ³And Saul pitched in the hill of Hachilah, which is before Jeshimon, by the way. But David stayed in the wilderness, and he saw that Saul came after him into the wilderness. ⁴David therefore sent out spies, and understood that Saul was come in very deed. ⁵And David arose, and came to the place where Saul had pitched: and David beheld the place where Saul lay, and Abner the son of Ner, the captain of his host: and Saul lay in the trench, and the people pitched round about him. ⁶Then answered David and said to Ahimelech the Hittite, and to Abishai the son of Zeruiah, brother to Joab, saying, Who will go down with me to Saul to the camp? And Abishai said, I will go down with you. ⁷So David and Abishai came to the people by night: and, behold, Saul lay sleeping within the trench, and his spear stuck in the ground at his bolster: but Abner and the people lay round about him. ⁸Then said Abishai to David, God has delivered your enemy into your hand this day: now therefore let me smite him, I pray you, with the spear even to the earth at once, and I will not smite him the second time. ⁹And David said to Abishai,

Destroy him not: for who can stretch forth his hand against the LORD's anointed, and be guiltless? ¹⁰David said furthermore, As the LORD lives, the LORD shall smite him; or his day shall come to die; or he shall descend into battle, and perish. ¹¹The LORD forbid that I should stretch forth my hand against the LORD's anointed: but, I pray you, take you now the spear that is at his bolster, and the cruse of water, and let us go. ¹²So David took the spear and the cruse of water from Saul's bolster; and they got them away, and no man saw it, nor knew it, neither awaked: for they were all asleep; because a deep sleep from the LORD was fallen on them. ¹³Then David went over to the other side, and stood on the top of an hill afar off; a great space being between them: ¹⁴And David cried to the people, and to Abner the son of Ner, saying, Answer you not, Abner? Then Abner answered and said, Who are you that cry to the king? ¹⁵And David said to Abner, Are not you a valiant man? and who is like to you in Israel? why then have you not kept your lord the king? for there came one of the people in to destroy the king your lord. ¹⁶This thing is not good that you have done. As the LORD lives, you are worthy to die, because you have not kept your master, the LORD's anointed. And now see where the king's spear is, and the cruse of water that was at his bolster. ¹⁷And Saul knew David's voice, and said, Is this your voice, my son David? And David said, It is my voice, my lord, O king. ¹⁸And he said, Why does my lord thus pursue after his servant? for what have I done? or what evil is in my hand? ¹⁹Now therefore, I pray you, let my lord the king hear the words of his servant. If the LORD have stirred you up against me, let him accept an offering: but if they be the children of men, cursed be they before the LORD; for they have driven me out this day from abiding in the inheritance of the LORD, saying, Go, serve other gods. ²⁰Now therefore, let not my blood fall to the earth before the face of the LORD: for the king of Israel is come out to seek a flea, as when one does hunt a partridge in the mountains. ²¹Then said Saul, I have sinned: return, my son David: for I will no more do you harm, because my soul was precious in your eyes this day: behold, I have played the fool, and have erred exceedingly. ²²And David answered and said, Behold the king's spear! and let one of the young men come over and fetch it. ²³The LORD render to every man his righteousness and his faithfulness; for the LORD delivered you into my hand to day, but I would not stretch forth my hand against the LORD's anointed. ²⁴And, behold, as your life was much set by this day in my eyes, so let my life be much set by in the eyes of the LORD, and let him deliver me out of all tribulation. ²⁵Then Saul said to David, Blessed be you, my son David: you shall both do great things, and also shall still prevail. So David went on his way, and Saul returned to his place.

27 ¹And David said in his heart, I shall now perish one day by the hand of Saul: there is nothing better for me than that I should speedily escape into the land of the Philistines; and Saul shall despair of me, to seek me any more in any coast of Israel: so shall I escape out of his hand. ²And David arose, and he passed over with the six hundred men that were with him to Achish, the son of Maoch, king of Gath. ³And David dwelled with Achish at Gath, he and his men, every man with his household, even David with his two wives, Ahinoam the Jezreelitess, and Abigail the Carmelitess, Nabal's wife. ⁴And it was told Saul that David was fled to Gath: and he sought no more again for him. ⁵And David said to Achish, If I have now found grace in your eyes, let them give me a place in some town in the country, that I may dwell there: for why should your servant dwell in the royal city with you? ⁶Then Achish gave him Ziklag that day: why Ziklag pertains to the kings of Judah to this day. ⁷And the time that David dwelled in the country of the Philistines was a full year and four months. ⁸And David and his men went up, and invaded the Geshurites, and the Gezrites, and the Amalekites: for those nations were of old the inhabitants of the land, as you go to Shur, even to the land of Egypt. ⁹And David smote the land, and left neither man nor woman alive, and took away the sheep, and the oxen, and the asses, and the camels, and the apparel, and returned, and came to Achish. ¹⁰And Achish said, Where have you made a road to day? And David said, Against the south of Judah, and against the south of the Jerahmeelites, and against the south of the Kenites. ¹¹And David saved neither man nor woman alive, to bring tidings to Gath, saying, Lest they should tell on us, saying, So did David, and so will be his manner all the while he dwells in the country of the Philistines. ¹²And Achish believed David, saying, He has made his people Israel utterly to abhor him; therefore he shall be my servant for ever.

28 ¹And it came to pass in those days, that the Philistines gathered their armies together for warfare, to fight with Israel. And Achish said to David, Know you assuredly, that you shall go out with me to battle, you and your men. ²And David said to Achish, Surely you shall know what your servant can do. And Achish said to David, Therefore will I make you keeper of my head for ever. ³Now Samuel was dead, and all Israel had lamented him, and buried him in Ramah, even in his own city. And Saul had put away those that had familiar spirits, and the wizards, out of the land. ⁴And the Philistines gathered themselves together, and came and pitched in Shunem: and Saul gathered all Israel together, and they pitched in Gilboa. ⁵And when Saul saw the host of the Philistines, he was afraid, and his heart greatly trembled. ⁶And when Saul inquired of the LORD, the LORD answered him not, neither by dreams, nor by Urim, nor by prophets. ⁷Then said Saul to his servants, Seek me a woman that has a familiar spirit, that I may go to her, and inquire of her. And his servants said to him, Behold, there is a woman that has a familiar spirit at Endor. ⁸And Saul disguised himself, and put on other raiment, and he went, and two men with him, and they came to the woman by night: and he said, I pray you, divine to me by the familiar spirit, and bring me him up, whom I shall name to you. ⁹And the woman said to him, Behold, you know what Saul has done, how he has cut off those that have familiar spirits, and the wizards, out of the land: why then lay you a snare for my life, to cause me to die? ¹⁰And Saul swore to her by the LORD, saying, As the LORD lives, there shall no punishment happen to you for this thing. ¹¹Then said the woman, Whom shall I bring up to you? And he said, Bring me up Samuel. ¹²And when the woman saw Samuel, she cried with a loud voice: and the woman spoke to Saul, saying, Why have you deceived me? for you are

Saul. ¹³And the king said to her, Be not afraid: for what saw you? And the woman said to Saul, I saw gods ascending out of the earth. ¹⁴And he said to her, What form is he of? And she said, An old man comes up; and he is covered with a mantle. And Saul perceived that it was Samuel, and he stooped with his face to the ground, and bowed himself. ¹⁵And Samuel said to Saul, Why have you disquieted me, to bring me up? And Saul answered, I am sore distressed; for the Philistines make war against me, and God is departed from me, and answers me no more, neither by prophets, nor by dreams: therefore I have called you, that you may make known to me what I shall do. ¹⁶Then said Samuel, Why then do you ask of me, seeing the LORD is departed from you, and is become your enemy? ¹⁷And the LORD has done to him, as he spoke by me: for the LORD has rent the kingdom out of your hand, and given it to your neighbor, even to David: ¹⁸Because you obeyed not the voice of the LORD, nor executed his fierce wrath on Amalek, therefore has the LORD done this thing to you this day. ¹⁹Moreover the LORD will also deliver Israel with you into the hand of the Philistines: and to morrow shall you and your sons be with me: the LORD also shall deliver the host of Israel into the hand of the Philistines. ²⁰Then Saul fell straightway all along on the earth, and was sore afraid, because of the words of Samuel: and there was no strength in him; for he had eaten no bread all the day, nor all the night. ²¹And the woman came to Saul, and saw that he was sore troubled, and said to him, Behold, your handmaid has obeyed your voice, and I have put my life in my hand, and have listened to your words which you spoke to me. ²²Now therefore, I pray you, listen you also to the voice of your handmaid, and let me set a morsel of bread before you; and eat, that you may have strength, when you go on your way. ²³But he refused, and said, I will not eat. But his servants, together with the woman, compelled him; and he listened to their voice. So he arose from the earth, and sat on the bed. ²⁴And the woman had a fat calf in the house; and she hurried, and killed it, and took flour, and kneaded it, and did bake unleavened bread thereof: ²⁵And she brought it before Saul, and before his servants; and they did eat. Then they rose up, and went away that night.

29 ¹Now the Philistines gathered together all their armies to Aphek: and the Israelites pitched by a fountain which is in Jezreel. ²And the lords of the Philistines passed on by hundreds, and by thousands: but David and his men passed on in the rear guard with Achish. ³Then said the princes of the Philistines, What do these Hebrews here? And Achish said to the princes of the Philistines, Is not this David, the servant of Saul the king of Israel, which has been with me these days, or these years, and I have found no fault in him since he fell to me to this day? ⁴And the princes of the Philistines were wroth with him; and the princes of the Philistines said to him, Make this fellow return, that he may go again to his place which you have appointed him, and let him not go down with us to battle, lest in the battle he be an adversary to us: for with which should he reconcile himself to his master? should it not be with the heads of these men? ⁵Is not this David, of whom they sang one to another in dances, saying, Saul slew his thousands, and David his ten thousands? ⁶Then Achish called David, and said to him,

Surely, as the LORD lives, you have been upright, and your going out and your coming in with me in the host is good in my sight: for I have not found evil in you since the day of your coming to me to this day: nevertheless the lords favor you not. ⁷Why now return, and go in peace, that you displease not the lords of the Philistines. ⁸And David said to Achish, But what have I done? and what have you found in your servant so long as I have been with you to this day, that I may not go fight against the enemies of my lord the king? ⁹And Achish answered and said to David, I know that you are good in my sight, as an angel of God: notwithstanding the princes of the Philistines have said, He shall not go up with us to the battle. ¹⁰Why now rise up early in the morning with your master's servants that are come with you: and as soon as you be up early in the morning, and have light, depart. ¹¹So David and his men rose up early to depart in the morning, to return into the land of the Philistines. And the Philistines went up to Jezreel.

30 ¹And it came to pass, when David and his men were come to Ziklag on the third day, that the Amalekites had invaded the south, and Ziklag, and smitten Ziklag, and burned it with fire; ²And had taken the women captives, that were therein: they slew not any, either great or small, but carried them away, and went on their way. ³So David and his men came to the city, and, behold, it was burned with fire; and their wives, and their sons, and their daughters, were taken captives. ⁴Then David and the people that were with him lifted up their voice and wept, until they had no more power to weep. ⁵And David's two wives were taken captives, Ahinoam the Jezreelitess, and Abigail the wife of Nabal the Carmelite. ⁶And David was greatly distressed; for the people spoke of stoning him, because the soul of all the people was grieved, every man for his sons and for his daughters: but David encouraged himself in the LORD his God. ⁷And David said to Abiathar the priest, Ahimelech's son, I pray you, bring me here the ephod. And Abiathar brought thither the ephod to David. ⁸And David inquired at the LORD, saying, Shall I pursue after this troop? shall I overtake them? And he answered him, Pursue: for you shall surely overtake them, and without fail recover all. ⁹So David went, he and the six hundred men that were with him, and came to the brook Besor, where those that were left behind stayed. ¹⁰But David pursued, he and four hundred men: for two hundred stayed behind, which were so faint that they could not go over the brook Besor. ¹¹And they found an Egyptian in the field, and brought him to David, and gave him bread, and he did eat; and they made him drink water; ¹²And they gave him a piece of a cake of figs, and two clusters of raisins: and when he had eaten, his spirit came again to him: for he had eaten no bread, nor drunk any water, three days and three nights. ¹³And David said to him, To whom belong you? and from where are you? And he said, I am a young man of Egypt, servant to an Amalekite; and my master left me, because three days ago I fell sick. ¹⁴We made an invasion on the south of the Cherethites, and on the coast which belongs to Judah, and on the south of Caleb; and we burned Ziklag with fire. ¹⁵And David said to him, Can you bring me down to this company? And he said, Swear to me by God, that you will neither kill me, nor deliver me into the hands of my master, and I will bring you down to this company. ¹⁶And when he had brought him down, behold, they were spread abroad on all the earth, eating and drinking, and dancing, because of all the great spoil that they had taken out of the land of the Philistines, and out of the land of Judah. ¹⁷And David smote them from the twilight even to the evening of the next day: and there escaped not a man of them, save four hundred young men, which rode on camels, and fled. ¹⁸And David recovered all that the Amalekites had carried away: and David rescued his two wives. ¹⁹And there was nothing lacking to them, neither small nor great, neither sons nor daughters, neither spoil, nor any thing that they had taken to them: David recovered all. ²⁰And David took all the flocks and the herds, which they drove before those other cattle, and said, This is David's spoil. ²¹And David came to the two hundred men, which were so faint that they could not follow David, whom they had made also to abide at the brook Besor: and they went forth to meet David, and to meet the people that were with him: and when David came near to the people, he saluted them. ²²Then answered all the wicked men and men of Belial, of those that went with David, and said, Because they went not with us, we will not give them any of the spoil that we have recovered, save to every man his wife and his children, that they may lead them away, and depart. ²³Then said David, You shall not do so, my brothers, with that which the LORD has given us, who has preserved us, and delivered the company that came against us into our hand. ²⁴For who will listen to you in this matter? but as his part is that goes down to the battle, so shall his part be that tarries by the stuff: they shall part alike. ²⁵And it was so from that day forward, that he made it a statute and an ordinance for Israel to this day. ²⁶And when David came to Ziklag, he sent of the spoil to the elders of Judah, even to his friends, saying, Behold a present for you of the spoil of the enemies of the LORD; ²⁷To them which were in Bethel, and to them which were in south Ramoth, and to them which were in Jattir, ²⁸And to them which were in Aroer, and to them which were in Siphmoth, and to them which were in Eshtemoa, ²⁹And to them which were in Rachal, and to them which were in the cities of the Jerahmeelites, and to them which were in the cities of the Kenites, ³⁰And to them which were in Hormah, and to them which were in Chorashan, and to them which were in Athach, ³¹And to them which were in Hebron, and to all the places where David himself and his men were wont to haunt.

31

¹Now the Philistines fought against Israel: and the men of Israel fled from before the Philistines, and fell down slain in mount Gilboa. ²And the Philistines followed hard on Saul and on his sons; and the Philistines slew Jonathan, and Abinadab, and Melchishua, Saul's sons. ³And the battle went sore against Saul, and the archers hit him; and he was sore wounded of the archers. ⁴Then said Saul to his armor bearer, Draw your sword, and thrust me through therewith; lest these uncircumcised come and thrust me through, and abuse me. But his armor bearer would not; for he was sore afraid. Therefore Saul took a sword, and fell on it. ⁵And when his armor bearer saw that Saul was dead, he fell likewise on his sword, and died with him. ⁶So Saul died, and his three sons, and his armor bearer, and all his men, that same day together. ⁷And when the men of Israel that were on the other side of the valley, and they that were on the other side Jordan, saw that the men of Israel fled, and that Saul and his sons were dead, they forsook the cities, and fled; and the Philistines came and dwelled in them. ⁸And it came to pass on the morrow, when the Philistines came to strip the slain, that they found Saul and his three sons fallen in mount Gilboa. ⁹And they cut off his head, and stripped off his armor, and sent into the land of the Philistines round about, to publish it in the house of their idols, and among the people. ¹⁰And they put his armor in the house of Ashtaroth: and they fastened his body to the wall of Bethshan. ¹¹And when the inhabitants of Jabeshgilead heard of that which the Philistines had done to Saul; ¹²All the valiant men arose, and went all night, and took the body of Saul and the bodies of his sons from the wall of Bethshan, and came to Jabesh, and burnt them there. ¹³And they took their bones, and buried them under a tree at Jabesh, and fasted seven days.

Second Samuel

1 ¹Now it came to pass after the death of Saul, when David was returned from the slaughter of the Amalekites, and David had stayed two days in Ziklag; ²It came even to pass on the third day, that, behold, a man came out of the camp from Saul with his clothes rent, and earth on his head: and so it was, when he came to David, that he fell to the earth, and did obeisance. ³And David said to him, From where come you? And he said to him, Out of the camp of Israel am I escaped. ⁴And David said to him, How went the matter? I pray you, tell me. And he answered, That the people are fled from the battle, and many of the people also are fallen and dead; and Saul and Jonathan his son are dead also. ⁵And David said to the young man that told him, How know you that Saul and Jonathan his son be dead? ⁶And the young man that told him said, As I happened by chance on mount Gilboa, behold, Saul leaned on his spear; and, see, the chariots and horsemen followed hard after him. ⁷And when he looked behind him, he saw me, and called to me. And I answered, Here am I. ⁸And he said to me, Who are you? And I answered him, I am an Amalekite. ⁹He said to me again, Stand, I pray you, on me, and slay me: for anguish is come on me, because my life is yet whole in me. ¹⁰So I stood on him, and slew him, because I was sure that he could not live after that he was fallen: and I took the crown that was on his head, and the bracelet that was on his arm, and have brought them here to my lord. ¹¹Then David took hold on his clothes, and rent them; and likewise all the men that were with him: ¹²And they mourned, and wept, and fasted until even, for Saul, and for Jonathan his son, and for the people of the LORD, and for the house of Israel; because they were fallen by the sword. ¹³And David said to the young man that told him, From where are you? And he answered, I am the son of a stranger, an Amalekite. ¹⁴And David said to him, How were you not afraid to stretch forth your hand to destroy the LORD's anointed? ¹⁵And David called one of the young men, and said, Go near, and fall on him. And he smote him that he died. ¹⁶And David said to him, Your blood be on your head; for your mouth has testified against you, saying, I have slain the LORD's anointed. ¹⁷And David lamented with this lamentation over Saul and over Jonathan his son: ¹⁸(Also he bade them teach the children of Judah the use of the bow: behold, it is written in the book of Jasher.) ¹⁹The beauty of Israel is slain on your high places: how are the mighty fallen! ²⁰Tell it not in Gath, publish it not in the streets of Askelon; lest the daughters of the Philistines rejoice, lest the daughters of the uncircumcised triumph. ²¹You mountains of Gilboa, let there be no dew, neither let there be rain, on you, nor fields of offerings: for there the shield of the mighty is vilely cast away, the shield of Saul, as though he had not been anointed with oil. ²²From the blood of the slain, from the fat of the mighty, the bow of Jonathan turned not back, and the sword of Saul returned not empty. ²³Saul and Jonathan were lovely and pleasant in their lives, and in their death they were not divided: they were swifter than eagles, they were stronger than lions. ²⁴You daughters of Israel, weep over Saul, who clothed you in scarlet, with other delights, who put on ornaments of gold on your apparel. ²⁵How are the mighty fallen in the middle of the battle! O Jonathan, you were slain in your high places. ²⁶I am distressed for you, my brother Jonathan: very pleasant have you been to me: your love to me was wonderful, passing the love of women. ²⁷How are the mighty fallen, and the weapons of war perished!

2 ¹And it came to pass after this, that David inquired of the LORD, saying, Shall I go up into any of the cities of Judah? And the LORD said to him, Go up. And David said, Where shall I go up? And he said, To Hebron. ²So David went up thither, and his two wives also, Ahinoam the Jezreelitess, and Abigail Nabal's wife the Carmelite. ³And his men that were with him did David bring up, every man with his household: and they dwelled in the cities of Hebron. ⁴And the men of Judah came, and there they anointed David king over the house of Judah. And they told David, saying, That the men of Jabeshgilead were they that buried Saul. ⁵And David sent messengers to the men of Jabeshgilead, and said to them, Blessed be you of the LORD, that you have showed this kindness to your lord, even to Saul, and have buried him. ⁶And now the LORD show kindness and truth to you: and I also will requite you this kindness, because you have done this thing. ⁷Therefore now let your hands be strengthened, and be you valiant: for your master Saul is dead, and also the house of Judah have anointed me king over them. ⁸But Abner the son of Ner, captain of Saul's host, took Ishbosheth the son of Saul, and brought him over to Mahanaim; ⁹And made him king over Gilead, and over the Ashurites, and over Jezreel, and over Ephraim, and over Benjamin, and over all Israel. ¹⁰Ishbosheth Saul's son was forty years old when he began to reign over Israel, and reigned two years. But the house of Judah followed David. ¹¹And the time that David was king in Hebron over the house of Judah was seven years and six months. ¹²And Abner the son of Ner, and the servants of Ishbosheth the son of Saul, went out from Mahanaim to Gibeon. ¹³And Joab the son of Zeruiah, and the servants of David, went out, and met together by the pool of Gibeon: and they sat down, the one on the one side of the pool, and the other on the other side of the pool. ¹⁴And Abner said to Joab, Let the young men now arise, and play before us. And Joab said, Let them arise. ¹⁵Then there arose and went over by number twelve of Benjamin, which pertained to Ishbosheth the son of Saul, and twelve of the servants of David. ¹⁶And they caught every one his fellow by the head, and thrust his sword in his fellow's side; so they fell down together: why that place was called Helkathhazzurim, which is in Gibeon. ¹⁷And there was a very sore battle that day; and Abner was beaten, and the men of Israel, before the servants of David. ¹⁸And there were three sons of Zeruiah there, Joab, and Abishai, and Asahel: and Asahel was as light of foot as a wild roe. ¹⁹And Asahel pursued after Abner; and in going he turned not to the right hand nor to the left from following Abner. ²⁰Then Abner looked behind him, and said, Are you Asahel? And he answered, I am. ²¹And Abner said to him, Turn you aside to your right hand or to your left, and lay you hold on one of the young men, and take you his armor. But Asahel would not turn aside from following of him. ²²And Abner said again to Asahel, Turn you aside from following me: why should I

smite you to the ground? how then should I hold up my face to Joab your brother? ²³However, he refused to turn aside: why Abner with the hinder end of the spear smote him under the fifth rib, that the spear came out behind him; and he fell down there, and died in the same place: and it came to pass, that as many as came to the place where Asahel fell down and died stood still. ²⁴Joab also and Abishai pursued after Abner: and the sun went down when they were come to the hill of Ammah, that lies before Giah by the way of the wilderness of Gibeon. ²⁵And the children of Benjamin gathered themselves together after Abner, and became one troop, and stood on the top of an hill. ²⁶Then Abner called to Joab, and said, Shall the sword devour for ever? know you not that it will be bitterness in the latter end? how long shall it be then, before you bid the people return from following their brothers? ²⁷And Joab said, As God lives, unless you had spoken, surely then in the morning the people had gone up every one from following his brother. ²⁸So Joab blew a trumpet, and all the people stood still, and pursued after Israel no more, neither fought they any more. ²⁹And Abner and his men walked all that night through the plain, and passed over Jordan, and went through all Bithron, and they came to Mahanaim. ³⁰And Joab returned from following Abner: and when he had gathered all the people together, there lacked of David's servants nineteen men and Asahel. ³¹But the servants of David had smitten of Benjamin, and of Abner's men, so that three hundred and three score men died. ³²And they took up Asahel, and buried him in the sepulcher of his father, which was in Bethlehem. And Joab and his men went all night, and they came to Hebron at break of day.

3 ¹Now there was long war between the house of Saul and the house of David: but David waxed stronger and stronger, and the house of Saul waxed weaker and weaker. ²And to David were sons born in Hebron: and his firstborn was Amnon, of Ahinoam the Jezreelitess; ³And his second, Chileab, of Abigail the wife of Nabal the Carmelite; and the third, Absalom the son of Maacah the daughter of Talmai king of Geshur; ⁴And the fourth, Adonijah the son of Haggith; and the fifth, Shephatiah the son of Abital; ⁵And the sixth, Ithream, by Eglah David's wife. These were born to David in Hebron. ⁶And it came to pass, while there was war between the house of Saul and the house of David, that Abner made himself strong for the house of Saul. ⁷And Saul had a concubine, whose name was Rizpah, the daughter of Aiah: and Ishbosheth said to Abner, Why have you gone in to my father's concubine? ⁸Then was Abner very wroth for the words of Ishbosheth, and said, Am I a dog's head, which against Judah do show kindness this day to the house of Saul your father, to his brothers, and to his friends, and have not delivered you into the hand of David, that you charge me to day with a fault concerning this woman? ⁹So do God to Abner, and more also, except, as the LORD has sworn to David, even so I do to him; ¹⁰To translate the kingdom from the house of Saul, and to set up the throne of David over Israel and over Judah, from Dan even to Beersheba. ¹¹And he could not answer Abner a word again, because he feared him. ¹²And Abner sent messengers to David on his behalf, saying, Whose is the land? saying also, Make your league with me, and, behold, my hand shall be with you, to bring about all Israel to you. ¹³And he said, Well; I will make a league with you: but one thing I require of you, that is, You shall not see my face, except you first bring Michal Saul's daughter, when you come to see my face. ¹⁴And David sent messengers to Ishbosheth Saul's son, saying, Deliver me my wife Michal, which I espoused to me for an hundred foreskins of the Philistines. ¹⁵And Ishbosheth sent, and took her from her husband, even from Phaltiel the son of Laish. ¹⁶And her husband went with her along weeping behind her to Bahurim. Then said Abner to him, Go, return. And he returned. ¹⁷And Abner had communication with the elders of Israel, saying, You sought for David in times past to be king over you: ¹⁸Now then do it: for the LORD has spoken of David, saying, By the hand of my servant David I will save my people Israel out of the hand of the Philistines, and out of the hand of all their enemies. ¹⁹And Abner also spoke in the ears of Benjamin: and Abner went also to speak in the ears of David in Hebron all that seemed good to Israel, and that seemed good to the whole house of Benjamin. ²⁰So Abner came to David to Hebron, and twenty men with him. And David made Abner and the men that were with him a feast. ²¹And Abner said to David, I will arise and go, and will gather all Israel to my lord the king, that they may make a league with you, and that you may reign over all that your heart desires. And David sent Abner away; and he went in peace. ²²And, behold, the servants of David and Joab came from pursuing a troop, and brought in a great spoil with them: but Abner was not with David in Hebron; for he had sent him away, and he was gone in peace. ²³When Joab and all the host that was with him were come, they told Joab, saying, Abner the son of Ner came to the king, and he has sent him away, and he is gone in peace. ²⁴Then Joab came to the king, and said, What have you done? behold, Abner came to you; why is it that you have sent him away, and he is quite gone? ²⁵You know Abner the son of Ner, that he came to deceive you, and to know your going out and your coming in, and to know all that you do. ²⁶And when Joab was come out from David, he sent messengers after Abner, which brought him again from the well of Sirah: but David knew it not. ²⁷And when Abner was returned to Hebron, Joab took him aside in the gate to speak with him quietly, and smote him there under the fifth rib, that he died, for the blood of Asahel his brother. ²⁸And afterward when David heard it, he said, I and my kingdom are guiltless before the LORD for ever from the blood of Abner the son of Ner: ²⁹Let it rest on the head of Joab, and on all his father's house; and let there not fail from the house of Joab one that has an issue, or that is a leper, or that leans on a staff, or that falls on the sword, or that lacks bread. ³⁰So Joab, and Abishai his brother slew Abner, because he had slain their brother Asahel at Gibeon in the battle. ³¹And David said to Joab, and to all the people that were with him, Rend your clothes, and gird you with sackcloth, and mourn before Abner. And king David himself followed the bier. ³²And they buried Abner in Hebron: and the king lifted up his voice, and wept at the grave of Abner; and all the people wept. ³³And the king lamented over Abner, and said, Died Abner as a fool dies? ³⁴Your hands were not bound, nor your feet put into fetters: as a man falls before wicked men, so fell you. And all the people wept again over him. ³⁵And when all the people came to cause David to eat meat while it was yet day, David swore, saying, So do God to me, and more also, if I taste bread, or anything else, till the sun be down. ³⁶And all the people took notice of it, and it pleased them: as whatever the king did pleased all the people. ³⁷For all the people and all Israel understood that day that it was not of the king to slay Abner the son of Ner. ³⁸And the king said to his servants, Know you not that there is a prince and a great man fallen this day in Israel? ³⁹And I am this day weak, though anointed king; and these men the sons of Zeruiah be too hard for me: the LORD shall reward the doer of evil according to his wickedness.

4 ¹And when Saul's son heard that Abner was dead in Hebron, his hands were feeble, and all the Israelites were troubled. ²And Saul's son had two men that were captains of bands: the name of the one was Baanah, and the name of the other Rechab, the sons of Rimmon a Beerothite, of the children of Benjamin: (for Beeroth also was reckoned to Benjamin. ³And the Beerothites fled to Gittaim, and were sojourners there until this day.) ⁴And Jonathan, Saul's son, had a son that was lame of his feet. He was five years old when the tidings came of Saul and Jonathan out of Jezreel, and his nurse took him up, and fled: and it came to pass, as she made haste to flee, that he fell, and became lame. And his name was Mephibosheth. ⁵And the sons of Rimmon the Beerothite, Rechab and Baanah, went, and came about the heat of the day to the house of Ishbosheth, who lay on a bed at noon. ⁶And they came thither into the middle of the house, as though they would have fetched wheat; and they smote him under the fifth rib: and Rechab and Baanah his brother escaped. ⁷For when they came into the house, he lay on his bed in his bedchamber, and they smote him, and slew him, and beheaded him, and took his head, and got them away through the plain all night. ⁸And they brought the head of Ishbosheth to David to Hebron, and said to the king, Behold the head of Ishbosheth the son of Saul your enemy, which sought your life; and the LORD has avenged my lord the king this day of Saul, and of his seed. ⁹And David answered Rechab and Baanah his brother, the sons of Rimmon the Beerothite, and said to them, As the LORD lives, who has redeemed my soul out of all adversity, ¹⁰When one told me, saying, Behold, Saul is dead, thinking to have brought good tidings, I took hold of him, and slew him in Ziklag, who thought that I would have given him a reward for his tidings: ¹¹How much more, when wicked men have slain a righteous person in his own house on his bed? shall I not therefore now require his blood of your hand, and take you away from the earth? ¹²And David commanded his young men, and they slew them, and cut off their hands and their feet, and hanged them up over the pool in Hebron. But they took the head of Ishbosheth, and buried it in the sepulcher of Abner in Hebron.

5 ¹Then came all the tribes of Israel to David to Hebron, and spoke, saying, Behold, we are your bone and your flesh. ²Also in time past, when Saul was king over us, you were he that led out and brought in Israel: and the LORD said to you, You shall feed my people Israel, and you shall be a captain over Israel. ³So all the elders of Israel came to the king to Hebron; and king David made a league with them in Hebron before the LORD: and they anointed David king over Israel. ⁴David was thirty years old when he began to reign, and he reigned forty years. ⁵In Hebron he reigned over Judah seven years and six months: and in Jerusalem he reigned thirty and three years over all Israel and Judah. ⁶And the king and his men went to Jerusalem to the Jebusites, the inhabitants of the land: which spoke to David, saying, Except you take away the blind and the lame, you shall not come in here: thinking, David cannot come in here. ⁷Nevertheless David took the strong hold of Zion: the same is the city of David. ⁸And David said on that day, Whoever gets up to the gutter, and smites the Jebusites, and the lame and the blind that are hated of David's soul, he shall be chief and captain. Why they said, The blind and the lame shall not come into the house. ⁹So David dwelled in the fort, and called it the city of David. And David built round about from Millo and inward. ¹⁰And David went on, and grew great, and the LORD God of hosts was with him. ¹¹And Hiram king of Tyre sent messengers to David, and cedar trees, and carpenters, and masons: and they built David an house. ¹²And David perceived that the LORD had established him king over Israel, and that he had exalted his kingdom for his people Israel's sake. ¹³And David took him more concubines and wives out of Jerusalem, after he was come from Hebron: and there were yet sons and daughters born to David. ¹⁴And these be the names of those that were born to him in Jerusalem; Shammuah, and Shobab, and Nathan, and Solomon, ¹⁵Ibhar also, and Elishua, and Nepheg, and Japhia, ¹⁶And Elishama, and Eliada, and Eliphalet. ¹⁷But when the Philistines heard that they had anointed David king over Israel, all the Philistines came up to seek David; and David heard of it, and went down to the hold. ¹⁸The Philistines also came and spread themselves in the valley of Rephaim. ¹⁹And David inquired of the LORD, saying, Shall I go up to the Philistines? will you deliver them into my hand? And the LORD said to David, Go up: for I will doubtless deliver the Philistines into your hand. ²⁰And David came to Baalperazim, and David smote them there, and said, The LORD has broken forth on my enemies before me, as the breach of waters. Therefore he called the name of that place Baalperazim. ²¹And there they left their images, and David and his men burned them. ²²And the Philistines came up yet again, and spread themselves in the valley of Rephaim. ²³And when David inquired of the LORD, he said, You shall not go up; but fetch a compass behind them, and come on them over against the mulberry trees. ²⁴And let it be, when you hear the sound of a going in the tops of the mulberry trees, that then you shall bestir yourself: for then shall the LORD go out before you, to smite the host of the Philistines. ²⁵And David did so, as the LORD had commanded him; and smote the Philistines from Geba until you come to Gazer.

6 ¹Again, David gathered together all the chosen men of Israel, thirty thousand. ²And David arose, and went with all the people that were with him from Baale of Judah, to bring up from there the ark of God, whose name is called by the name of the LORD of hosts that dwells between the cherubim. ³And they set the ark of God on a new cart, and brought it out of the house of Abinadab that was in Gibeah: and Uzzah and Ahio, the sons of Abinadab, drove the new

cart. ⁴And they brought it out of the house of Abinadab which was at Gibeah, accompanying the ark of God: and Ahio went before the ark. ⁵And David and all the house of Israel played before the LORD on all manner of instruments made of fir wood, even on harps, and on psalteries, and on tambourines, and on cornets, and on cymbals. ⁶And when they came to Nachon's threshing floor, Uzzah put forth his hand to the ark of God, and took hold of it; for the oxen shook it. ⁷And the anger of the LORD was kindled against Uzzah; and God smote him there for his error; and there he died by the ark of God. ⁸And David was displeased, because the LORD had made a breach on Uzzah: and he called the name of the place Perezuzzah to this day. ⁹And David was afraid of the LORD that day, and said, How shall the ark of the LORD come to me? ¹⁰So David would not remove the ark of the LORD to him into the city of David: but David carried it aside into the house of Obededom the Gittite. ¹¹And the ark of the LORD continued in the house of Obededom the Gittite three months: and the LORD blessed Obededom, and all his household. ¹²And it was told king David, saying, The LORD has blessed the house of Obededom, and all that pertains to him, because of the ark of God. So David went and brought up the ark of God from the house of Obededom into the city of David with gladness. ¹³And it was so, that when they that bore the ark of the LORD had gone six paces, he sacrificed oxen and fatted calves. ¹⁴And David danced before the LORD with all his might; and David was girded with a linen ephod. ¹⁵So David and all the house of Israel brought up the ark of the LORD with shouting, and with the sound of the trumpet. ¹⁶And as the ark of the LORD came into the city of David, Michal Saul's daughter looked through a window, and saw king David leaping and dancing before the LORD; and she despised him in her heart. ¹⁷And they brought in the ark of the LORD, and set it in his place, in the middle of the tabernacle that David had pitched for it: and David offered burnt offerings and peace offerings before the LORD. ¹⁸And as soon as David had made an end of offering burnt offerings and peace offerings, he blessed the people in the name of the LORD of hosts. ¹⁹And he dealt among all the people, even among the whole multitude of Israel, as well to the women as men, to every one a cake of bread, and a good piece of flesh, and a flagon of wine. So all the people departed every one to his house. ²⁰Then David returned to bless his household. And Michal the daughter of Saul came out to meet David, and said, How glorious was the king of Israel to day, who uncovered himself to day in the eyes of the handmaids of his servants, as one of the vain fellows shamelessly uncovers himself! ²¹And David said to Michal, It was before the LORD, which chose me before your father, and before all his house, to appoint me ruler over the people of the LORD, over Israel: therefore will I play before the LORD. ²²And I will yet be more vile than thus, and will be base in my own sight: and of the maidservants which you have spoken of, of them shall I be had in honor. ²³Therefore Michal the daughter of Saul had no child to the day of her death.

7 ¹And it came to pass, when the king sat in his house, and the LORD had given him rest round about from all his enemies; ²That the king said to Nathan the prophet, See now, I dwell in an house of cedar, but the ark of God dwells within curtains. ³And Nathan said to the king, Go, do all that is in your heart; for the LORD is with you. ⁴And it came to pass that night, that the word of the LORD came to Nathan, saying, ⁵Go and tell my servant David, Thus says the LORD, Shall you build me an house for me to dwell in? ⁶Whereas I have not dwelled in any house since the time that I brought up the children of Israel out of Egypt, even to this day, but have walked in a tent and in a tabernacle. ⁷In all the places wherein I have walked with all the children of Israel spoke I a word with any of the tribes of Israel, whom I commanded to feed my people Israel, saying, Why build you not me an house of cedar? ⁸Now therefore so shall you say to my servant David, Thus says the LORD of hosts, I took you from the sheepcote, from following the sheep, to be ruler over my people, over Israel: ⁹And I was with you wherever you went, and have cut off all your enemies out of your sight, and have made you a great name, like to the name of the great men that are in the earth. ¹⁰Moreover I will appoint a place for my people Israel, and will plant them, that they may dwell in a place of their own, and move no more; neither shall the children of wickedness afflict them any more, as beforetime, ¹¹And as since the time that I commanded judges to be over my people Israel, and have caused you to rest from all your enemies. Also the LORD tells you that he will make you an house. ¹²And when your days be fulfilled, and you shall sleep with your fathers, I will set up your seed after you, which shall proceed out of your bowels, and I will establish his kingdom. ¹³He shall build an house for my name, and I will establish the throne of his kingdom for ever. ¹⁴I will be his father, and he shall be my son. If he commit iniquity, I will chasten him with the rod of men, and with the stripes of the children of men: ¹⁵But my mercy shall not depart away from him, as I took it from Saul, whom I put away before you. ¹⁶And your house and your kingdom shall be established for ever before you: your throne shall be established for ever. ¹⁷According to all these words, and according to all this vision, so did Nathan speak to David. ¹⁸Then went king David in, and sat before the LORD, and he said, Who am I, O Lord GOD? and what is my house, that you have brought me till now? ¹⁹And this was yet a small thing in your sight, O Lord GOD; but you have spoken also of your servant's house for a great while to come. And is this the manner of man, O Lord GOD? ²⁰And what can David say more to you? for you, Lord GOD, know your servant. ²¹For your word's sake, and according to your own heart, have you done all these great things, to make your servant know them. ²²Why you are great, O LORD God: for there is none like you, neither is there any God beside you, according to all that we have heard with our ears. ²³And what one nation in the earth is like your people, even like Israel, whom God went to redeem for a people to himself, and to make him a name, and to do for you great things and terrible, for your land, before your people, which you redeemed to you from Egypt, from the nations and their gods? ²⁴For you have confirmed to yourself your people Israel to be a people to you for ever: and you, LORD, are become their God. ²⁵And now, O LORD God, the word that you have spoken concerning your servant, and concerning his house, establish it for ever, and do as you have said.

²⁶And let your name be magnified for ever, saying, The LORD of hosts is the God over Israel: and let the house of your servant David be established before you. ²⁷For you, O LORD of hosts, God of Israel, have revealed to your servant, saying, I will build you an house: therefore has your servant found in his heart to pray this prayer to you. ²⁸And now, O Lord GOD, you are that God, and your words be true, and you have promised this goodness to your servant: ²⁹Therefore now let it please you to bless the house of your servant, that it may continue for ever before you: for you, O Lord GOD, have spoken it: and with your blessing let the house of your servant be blessed for ever.

8 ¹And after this it came to pass that David smote the Philistines, and subdued them: and David took Methegammah out of the hand of the Philistines. ²And he smote Moab, and measured them with a line, casting them down to the ground; even with two lines measured he to put to death, and with one full line to keep alive. And so the Moabites became David's servants, and brought gifts. ³David smote also Hadadezer, the son of Rehob, king of Zobah, as he went to recover his border at the river Euphrates. ⁴And David took from him a thousand chariots, and seven hundred horsemen, and twenty thousand footmen: and David hamstrung all the chariot horses, but reserved of them for an hundred chariots. ⁵And when the Syrians of Damascus came to succor Hadadezer king of Zobah, David slew of the Syrians two and twenty thousand men. ⁶Then David put garrisons in Syria of Damascus: and the Syrians became servants to David, and brought gifts. And the LORD preserved David wherever he went. ⁷And David took the shields of gold that were on the servants of Hadadezer, and brought them to Jerusalem. ⁸And from Betah, and from Berothai, cities of Hadadezer, king David took exceeding much brass. ⁹When Toi king of Hamath heard that David had smitten all the host of Hadadezer, ¹⁰Then Toi sent Joram his son to king David, to salute him, and to bless him, because he had fought against Hadadezer, and smitten him: for Hadadezer had wars with Toi. And Joram brought with him vessels of silver, and vessels of gold, and vessels of brass: ¹¹Which also king David did dedicate to the LORD, with the silver and gold that he had dedicated of all nations which he subdued; ¹²Of Syria, and of Moab, and of the children of Ammon, and of the Philistines, and of Amalek, and of the spoil of Hadadezer, son of Rehob, king of Zobah. ¹³And David got him a name when he returned from smiting of the Syrians in the valley of salt, being eighteen thousand men. ¹⁴And he put garrisons in Edom; throughout all Edom put he garrisons, and all they of Edom became David's servants. And the LORD preserved David wherever he went. ¹⁵And David reigned over all Israel; and David executed judgment and justice to all his people. ¹⁶And Joab the son of Zeruiah was over the host; and Jehoshaphat the son of Ahilud was recorder; ¹⁷And Zadok the son of Ahitub, and Ahimelech the son of Abiathar, were the priests; and Seraiah was the scribe; ¹⁸And Benaiah the son of Jehoiada was over both the Cherethites and the Pelethites; and David's sons were chief rulers.

9 ¹And David said, Is there yet any that is left of the house of Saul, that I may show him kindness for Jonathan's sake? ²And there was of the house of Saul a servant whose name was Ziba. And when they had called him to David, the king said to him, Are you Ziba? And he said, Your servant is he. ³And the king said, Is there not yet any of the house of Saul, that I may show the kindness of God to him? And Ziba said to the king, Jonathan has yet a son, which is lame on his feet. ⁴And the king said to him, Where is he? And Ziba said to the king, Behold, he is in the house of Machir, the son of Ammiel, in Lodebar. ⁵Then king David sent, and fetched him out of the house of Machir, the son of Ammiel, from Lodebar. ⁶Now when Mephibosheth, the son of Jonathan, the son of Saul, was come to David, he fell on his face, and did reverence. And David said, Mephibosheth. And he answered, Behold your servant! ⁷And David said to him, Fear not: for I will surely show you kindness for Jonathan your father's sake, and will restore you all the land of Saul your father; and you shall eat bread at my table continually. ⁸And he bowed himself, and said, What is your servant, that you should look on such a dead dog as I am? ⁹Then the king called to Ziba, Saul's servant, and said to him, I have given to your master's son all that pertained to Saul and to all his house. ¹⁰You therefore, and your sons, and your servants, shall till the land for him, and you shall bring in the fruits, that your master's son may have food to eat: but Mephibosheth your master's son shall eat bread always at my table. Now Ziba had fifteen sons and twenty servants. ¹¹Then said Ziba to the king, According to all that my lord the king has commanded his servant, so shall your servant do. As for Mephibosheth, said the king, he shall eat at my table, as one of the king's sons. ¹²And Mephibosheth had a young son, whose name was Micha. And all that dwelled in the house of Ziba were servants to Mephibosheth. ¹³So Mephibosheth dwelled in Jerusalem: for he did eat continually at the king's table; and was lame on both his feet.

10 ¹And it came to pass after this, that the king of the children of Ammon died, and Hanun his son reigned in his stead. ²Then said David, I will show kindness to Hanun the son of Nahash, as his father showed kindness to me. And David sent to comfort him by the hand of his servants for his father. And David's servants came into the land of the children of Ammon. ³And the princes of the children of Ammon said to Hanun their lord, Think you that David does honor your father, that he has sent comforters to you? has not David rather sent his servants to you, to search the city, and to spy it out, and to overthrow it? ⁴Why Hanun took David's servants, and shaved off the one half of their beards, and cut off their garments in the middle, even to their buttocks, and sent them away. ⁵When they told it to David, he sent to meet them, because the men were greatly ashamed: and the king said, Tarry at Jericho until your beards be grown, and then return. ⁶And when the children of Ammon saw that they stank before David, the children of Ammon sent and hired the Syrians of Bethrehob and the Syrians of Zoba, twenty thousand footmen, and of king Maacah a thousand men, and of Ishtob twelve thousand men. ⁷And when David heard of it, he sent Joab, and all the host of the mighty men. ⁸And the children of Ammon came out, and put the battle in array at the entering in of the gate: and the Syrians of Zoba, and of Rehob, and Ishtob, and Maacah, were by themselves in the field. ⁹When Joab saw

that the front of the battle was against him before and behind, he chose of all the choice men of Israel, and put them in array against the Syrians: ¹⁰And the rest of the people he delivered into the hand of Abishai his brother, that he might put them in array against the children of Ammon. ¹¹And he said, If the Syrians be too strong for me, then you shall help me: but if the children of Ammon be too strong for you, then I will come and help you. ¹²Be of good courage, and let us play the men for our people, and for the cities of our God: and the LORD do that which seems him good. ¹³And Joab drew near, and the people that were with him, to the battle against the Syrians: and they fled before him. ¹⁴And when the children of Ammon saw that the Syrians were fled, then fled they also before Abishai, and entered into the city. So Joab returned from the children of Ammon, and came to Jerusalem. ¹⁵And when the Syrians saw that they were smitten before Israel, they gathered themselves together. ¹⁶And Hadarezer sent, and brought out the Syrians that were beyond the river: and they came to Helam; and Shobach the captain of the host of Hadarezer went before them. ¹⁷And when it was told David, he gathered all Israel together, and passed over Jordan, and came to Helam. And the Syrians set themselves in array against David, and fought with him. ¹⁸And the Syrians fled before Israel; and David slew the men of seven hundred chariots of the Syrians, and forty thousand horsemen, and smote Shobach the captain of their host, who died there. ¹⁹And when all the kings that were servants to Hadarezer saw that they were smitten before Israel, they made peace with Israel, and served them. So the Syrians feared to help the children of Ammon any more.

11 ¹And it came to pass, after the year was expired, at the time when kings go forth to battle, that David sent Joab, and his servants with him, and all Israel; and they destroyed the children of Ammon, and besieged Rabbah. But David tarried still at Jerusalem. ²And it came to pass in an evening, that David arose from off his bed, and walked on the roof of the king's house: and from the roof he saw a woman washing herself; and the woman was very beautiful to look on. ³And David sent and inquired after the woman. And one said, Is not this Bathsheba, the daughter of Eliam, the wife of Uriah the Hittite? ⁴And David sent messengers, and took her; and she came in to him, and he lay with her; for she was purified from her uncleanness: and she returned to her house. ⁵And the woman conceived, and sent and told David, and said, I am with child. ⁶And David sent to Joab, saying, Send me Uriah the Hittite. And Joab sent Uriah to David. ⁷And when Uriah was come to him, David demanded of him how Joab did, and how the people did, and how the war prospered. ⁸And David said to Uriah, Go down to your house, and wash your feet. And Uriah departed out of the king's house, and there followed him a mess of meat from the king. ⁹But Uriah slept at the door of the king's house with all the servants of his lord, and went not down to his house. ¹⁰And when they had told David, saying, Uriah went not down to his house, David said to Uriah, Came you not from your journey? why then did you not go down to your house? ¹¹And Uriah said to David, The ark, and Israel, and Judah, abide in tents; and my lord Joab, and the servants of my lord, are encamped in the open fields; shall I then go into my house, to eat and to drink, and to lie with my wife? as you live, and as your soul lives, I will not do this thing. ¹²And David said to Uriah, Tarry here to day also, and to morrow I will let you depart. So Uriah stayed in Jerusalem that day, and the morrow. ¹³And when David had called him, he did eat and drink before him; and he made him drunk: and at even he went out to lie on his bed with the servants of his lord, but went not down to his house. ¹⁴And it came to pass in the morning, that David wrote a letter to Joab, and sent it by the hand of Uriah. ¹⁵And he wrote in the letter, saying, Set you Uriah in the forefront of the hottest battle, and retire you from him, that he may be smitten, and die. ¹⁶And it came to pass, when Joab observed the city, that he assigned Uriah to a place where he knew that valiant men were. ¹⁷And the men of the city went out, and fought with Joab: and there fell some of the people of the servants of David; and Uriah the Hittite died also. ¹⁸Then Joab sent and told David all the things concerning the war; ¹⁹And charged the messenger, saying, When you have made an end of telling the matters of the war to the king, ²⁰And if so be that the king's wrath arise, and he say to you, Why approached you so near to the city when you did fight? knew you not that they would shoot from the wall? ²¹Who smote Abimelech the son of Jerubbesheth? did not a woman cast a piece of a millstone on him from the wall, that he died in Thebez? why went you near the wall? then say you, Your servant Uriah the Hittite is dead also. ²²So the messenger went, and came and showed David all that Joab had sent him for. ²³And the messenger said to David, Surely the men prevailed against us, and came out to us into the field, and we were on them even to the entering of the gate. ²⁴And the shooters shot from off the wall on your servants; and some of the king's servants be dead, and your servant Uriah the Hittite is dead also. ²⁵Then David said to the messenger, Thus shall you say to Joab, Let not this thing displease you, for the sword devours one as well as another: make your battle more strong against the city, and overthrow it: and encourage you him. ²⁶And when the wife of Uriah heard that Uriah her husband was dead, she mourned for her husband. ²⁷And when the mourning was past, David sent and fetched her to his house, and she became his wife, and bore him a son. But the thing that David had done displeased the LORD.

12 ¹And the LORD sent Nathan to David. And he came to him, and said to him, There were two men in one city; the one rich, and the other poor. ²The rich man had exceeding many flocks and herds: ³But the poor man had nothing, save one little ewe lamb, which he had bought and nourished up: and it grew up together with him, and with his children; it did eat of his own meat, and drank of his own cup, and lay in his bosom, and was to him as a daughter. ⁴And there came a travelers to the rich man, and he spared to take of his own flock and of his own herd, to dress for the wayfaring man that was come to him; but took the poor man's lamb, and dressed it for the man that was come to him. ⁵And David's anger was greatly kindled against the man; and he said to Nathan, As the LORD lives, the man that has done this thing shall surely die: ⁶And he shall restore the lamb fourfold, because he did this thing, and because he had no pity. ⁷And Nathan said to David, You are the man. Thus says the LORD God of Israel, I anointed you king over

Israel, and I delivered you out of the hand of Saul; ⁸And I gave you your master's house, and your master's wives into your bosom, and gave you the house of Israel and of Judah; and if that had been too little, I would moreover have given to you such and such things. ⁹Why have you despised the commandment of the LORD, to do evil in his sight? you have killed Uriah the Hittite with the sword, and have taken his wife to be your wife, and have slain him with the sword of the children of Ammon. ¹⁰Now therefore the sword shall never depart from your house; because you have despised me, and have taken the wife of Uriah the Hittite to be your wife. ¹¹Thus says the LORD, Behold, I will raise up evil against you out of your own house, and I will take your wives before your eyes, and give them to your neighbor, and he shall lie with your wives in the sight of this sun. ¹²For you did it secretly: but I will do this thing before all Israel, and before the sun. ¹³And David said to Nathan, I have sinned against the LORD. And Nathan said to David, The LORD also has put away your sin; you shall not die. ¹⁴However,, because by this deed you have given great occasion to the enemies of the LORD to blaspheme, the child also that is born to you shall surely die. ¹⁵And Nathan departed to his house. And the LORD struck the child that Uriah's wife bore to David, and it was very sick. ¹⁶David therefore sought God for the child; and David fasted, and went in, and lay all night on the earth. ¹⁷And the elders of his house arose, and went to him, to raise him up from the earth: but he would not, neither did he eat bread with them. ¹⁸And it came to pass on the seventh day, that the child died. And the servants of David feared to tell him that the child was dead: for they said, Behold, while the child was yet alive, we spoke to him, and he would not listen to our voice: how will he then vex himself, if we tell him that the child is dead? ¹⁹But when David saw that his servants whispered, David perceived that the child was dead: therefore David said to his servants, Is the child dead? And they said, He is dead. ²⁰Then David arose from the earth, and washed, and anointed himself, and changed his apparel, and came into the house of the LORD, and worshipped: then he came to his own house; and when he required, they set bread before him, and he did eat. ²¹Then said his servants to him, What thing is this that you have done? you did fast and weep for the child, while it was alive; but when the child was dead, you did rise and eat bread. ²²And he said, While the child was yet alive, I fasted and wept: for I said, Who can tell whether GOD will be gracious to me, that the child may live? ²³But now he is dead, why should I fast? can I bring him back again? I shall go to him, but he shall not return to me. ²⁴And David comforted Bathsheba his wife, and went in to her, and lay with her: and she bore a son, and he called his name Solomon: and the LORD loved him. ²⁵And he sent by the hand of Nathan the prophet; and he called his name Jedidiah, because of the LORD. ²⁶And Joab fought against Rabbah of the children of Ammon, and took the royal city. ²⁷And Joab sent messengers to David, and said, I have fought against Rabbah, and have taken the city of waters. ²⁸Now therefore gather the rest of the people together, and encamp against the city, and take it: lest I take the city, and it be called after my name. ²⁹And David gathered all the people together, and went to Rabbah, and fought against it, and took it. ³⁰And he took their king's crown from off his head, the weight whereof was a talent of gold with the precious stones: and it was set on David's head. And he brought forth the spoil of the city in great abundance. ³¹And he brought forth the people that were therein, and put them under saws, and under harrows of iron, and under axes of iron, and made them pass through the brick-kiln: and thus did he to all the cities of the children of Ammon. So David and all the people returned to Jerusalem.

13

¹And it came to pass after this, that Absalom the son of David had a fair sister, whose name was Tamar; and Amnon the son of David loved her. ²And Amnon was so vexed, that he fell sick for his sister Tamar; for she was a virgin; and Amnon thought it hard for him to do anything to her. ³But Amnon had a friend, whose name was Jonadab, the son of Shimeah David's brother: and Jonadab was a very subtle man. ⁴And he said to him, Why are you, being the king's son, lean from day to day? will you not tell me? And Amnon said to him, I love Tamar, my brother Absalom's sister. ⁵And Jonadab said to him, Lay you down on your bed, and make yourself sick: and when your father comes to see you, say to him, I pray you, let my sister Tamar come, and give me meat, and dress the meat in my sight, that I may see it, and eat it at her hand. ⁶So Amnon lay down, and made himself sick: and when the king was come to see him, Amnon said to the king, I pray you, let Tamar my sister come, and make me a couple of cakes in my sight, that I may eat at her hand. ⁷Then David sent home to Tamar, saying, Go now to your brother Amnon's house, and dress him meat. ⁸So Tamar went to her brother Amnon's house; and he was laid down. And she took flour, and kneaded it, and made cakes in his sight, and did bake the cakes. ⁹And she took a pan, and poured them out before him; but he refused to eat. And Amnon said, Have out all men from me. And they went out every man from him. ¹⁰And Amnon said to Tamar, Bring the meat into the chamber, that I may eat of your hand. And Tamar took the cakes which she had made, and brought them into the chamber to Amnon her brother. ¹¹And when she had brought them to him to eat, he took hold of her, and said to her, Come lie with me, my sister. ¹²And she answered him, No, my brother, do not force me; for no such thing should to be done in Israel: do not you this folly. ¹³And I, where shall I cause my shame to go? and as for you, you shall be as one of the fools in Israel. Now therefore, I pray you, speak to the king; for he will not withhold me from you. ¹⁴However, he would not listen to her voice: but, being stronger than she, forced her, and lay with her. ¹⁵Then Amnon hated her exceedingly; so that the hatred with which he hated her was greater than the love with which he had loved her. And Amnon said to her, Arise, be gone. ¹⁶And she said to him, There is no cause: this evil in sending me away is greater than the other that you did to me. But he would not listen to her. ¹⁷Then he called his servant that ministered to him, and said, Put now this woman out from me, and bolt the door after her. ¹⁸And she had a garment of divers colors on her: for with such robes were the king's daughters that were virgins appareled. Then his servant brought her out, and bolted the door after her. ¹⁹And Tamar put ashes on her head, and rent her garment of divers colors that was on her, and laid her hand on her head, and went on crying. ²⁰And Absalom her brother said to her, Has Amnon your brother

been with you? but hold now your peace, my sister: he is your brother; regard not this thing. So Tamar remained desolate in her brother Absalom's house. ²¹But when king David heard of all these things, he was very wroth. ²²And Absalom spoke to his brother Amnon neither good nor bad: for Absalom hated Amnon, because he had forced his sister Tamar. ²³And it came to pass after two full years, that Absalom had sheep shearers in Baalhazor, which is beside Ephraim: and Absalom invited all the king's sons. ²⁴And Absalom came to the king, and said, Behold now, your servant has sheep shearers; let the king, I beseech you, and his servants go with your servant. ²⁵And the king said to Absalom, No, my son, let us not all now go, lest we be chargeable to you. And he pressed him: however, he would not go, but blessed him. ²⁶Then said Absalom, If not, I pray you, let my brother Amnon go with us. And the king said to him, Why should he go with you? ²⁷But Absalom pressed him, that he let Amnon and all the king's sons go with him. ²⁸Now Absalom had commanded his servants, saying, Mark you now when Amnon's heart is merry with wine, and when I say to you, Smite Amnon; then kill him, fear not: have not I commanded you? be courageous, and be valiant. ²⁹And the servants of Absalom did to Amnon as Absalom had commanded. Then all the king's sons arose, and every man got him up on his mule, and fled. ³⁰And it came to pass, while they were in the way, that tidings came to David, saying, Absalom has slain all the king's sons, and there is not one of them left. ³¹Then the king arose, and tare his garments, and lay on the earth; and all his servants stood by with their clothes rent. ³²And Jonadab, the son of Shimeah David's brother, answered and said, Let not my lord suppose that they have slain all the young men the king's sons; for Amnon only is dead: for by the appointment of Absalom this has been determined from the day that he forced his sister Tamar. ³³Now therefore let not my lord the king take the thing to his heart, to think that all the king's sons are dead: for Amnon only is dead. ³⁴But Absalom fled. And the young man that kept the watch lifted up his eyes, and looked, and, behold, there came much people by the way of the hill side behind him. ³⁵And Jonadab said to the king, Behold, the king's sons come: as your servant said, so it is. ³⁶And it came to pass, as soon as he had made an end of speaking, that, behold, the king's sons came, and lifted up their voice and wept: and the king also and all his servants wept very sore. ³⁷But Absalom fled, and went to Talmai, the son of Ammihud, king of Geshur. And David mourned for his son every day. ³⁸So Absalom fled, and went to Geshur, and was there three years. ³⁹And the soul of king David longed to go forth to Absalom: for he was comforted concerning Amnon, seeing he was dead.

14 ¹Now Joab the son of Zeruiah perceived that the king's heart was toward Absalom. ²And Joab sent to Tekoah, and fetched there a wise woman, and said to her, I pray you, feign yourself to be a mourner, and put on now mourning apparel, and anoint not yourself with oil, but be as a woman that had a long time mourned for the dead: ³And come to the king, and speak on this manner to him. So Joab put the words in her mouth. ⁴And when the woman of Tekoah spoke to the king, she fell on her face to the ground, and did obeisance, and said, Help, O king. ⁵And the king said to her, What ails you? And she answered, I am indeed a widow woman, and my husband is dead. ⁶And your handmaid had two sons, and they two strove together in the field, and there was none to part them, but the one smote the other, and slew him. ⁷And, behold, the whole family is risen against your handmaid, and they said, Deliver him that smote his brother, that we may kill him, for the life of his brother whom he slew; and we will destroy the heir also: and so they shall quench my coal which is left, and shall not leave to my husband neither name nor remainder on the earth. ⁸And the king said to the woman, Go to your house, and I will give charge concerning you. ⁹And the woman of Tekoah said to the king, My lord, O king, the iniquity be on me, and on my father's house: and the king and his throne be guiltless. ¹⁰And the king said, Whoever says anything to you, bring him to me, and he shall not touch you any more. ¹¹Then said she, I pray you, let the king remember the LORD your God, that you would not suffer the revengers of blood to destroy any more, lest they destroy my son. And he said, As the LORD lives, there shall not one hair of your son fall to the earth. ¹²Then the woman said, Let your handmaid, I pray you, speak one word to my lord the king. And he said, Say on. ¹³And the woman said, Why then have you thought such a thing against the people of God? for the king does speak this thing as one which is faulty, in that the king does not fetch home again his banished. ¹⁴For we must needs die, and are as water spilt on the ground, which cannot be gathered up again; neither does God respect any person: yet does he devise means, that his banished be not expelled from him. ¹⁵Now therefore that I am come to speak of this thing to my lord the king, it is because the people have made me afraid: and your handmaid said, I will now speak to the king; it may be that the king will perform the request of his handmaid. ¹⁶For the king will hear, to deliver his handmaid out of the hand of the man that would destroy me and my son together out of the inheritance of God. ¹⁷Then your handmaid said, The word of my lord the king shall now be comfortable: for as an angel of God, so is my lord the king to discern good and bad: therefore the LORD your God will be with you. ¹⁸Then the king answered and said to the woman, Hide not from me, I pray you, the thing that I shall ask you. And the woman said, Let my lord the king now speak. ¹⁹And the king said, Is not the hand of Joab with you in all this? And the woman answered and said, As your soul lives, my lord the king, none can turn to the right hand or to the left from anything that my lord the king has spoken: for your servant Joab, he bade me, and he put all these words in the mouth of your handmaid: ²⁰To fetch about this form of speech has your servant Joab done this thing: and my lord is wise, according to the wisdom of an angel of God, to know all things that are in the earth. ²¹And the king said to Joab, Behold now, I have done this thing: go therefore, bring the young man Absalom again. ²²And Joab fell to the ground on his face, and bowed himself, and thanked the king: and Joab said, To day your servant knows that I have found grace in your sight, my lord, O king, in that the king has fulfilled the request of his servant. ²³So Joab arose and went to Geshur, and brought Absalom to Jerusalem. ²⁴And the king said, Let him turn to his own house, and let him not see my face. So Absalom returned to his own house, and saw not the king's face. ²⁵But in all Israel there was none to be so much praised as Absalom for his beauty: from the sole of his foot even to the crown of his head there was no blemish in him. ²⁶And when he polled his head, (for it was at every year's end that he polled it: because the hair was heavy on him, therefore he polled it:) he weighed the hair of his head at two hundred shekels after the king's weight. ²⁷And to Absalom there were born three sons, and one daughter, whose name was Tamar: she was a woman of a fair countenance. ²⁸So Absalom dwelled two full years in Jerusalem, and saw not the king's face. ²⁹Therefore Absalom sent for Joab, to have sent him to the king; but he would not come to him: and when he sent again the second time, he would not come. ³⁰Therefore he said to his servants, See, Joab's field is near mine, and he has barley there; go and set it on fire. And Absalom's servants set the field on fire. ³¹Then Joab arose, and came to Absalom to his house, and said to him, Why have your servants set my field on fire? ³²And Absalom answered Joab, Behold, I sent to you, saying, Come here, that I may send you to the king, to say, Why am I come from Geshur? it had been good for me to have been there still: now therefore let me see the king's face; and if there be any iniquity in me, let him kill me. ³³So Joab came to the king, and told him: and when he had called for Absalom, he came to the king, and bowed himself on his face to the ground before the king: and the king kissed Absalom.

15

¹And it came to pass after this, that Absalom prepared him chariots and horses, and fifty men to run before him. ²And Absalom rose up early, and stood beside the way of the gate: and it was so, that when any man that had a controversy came to the king for judgment, then Absalom called to him, and said, Of what city are you? And he said, Your servant is of one of the tribes of Israel. ³And Absalom said to him, See, your matters are good and right; but there is no man deputed of the king to hear you. ⁴Absalom said moreover, Oh that I were made judge in the land, that every man which has any suit or cause might come to me, and I would do him justice! ⁵And it was so, that when any man came near to him to do him obeisance, he put forth his hand, and took him, and kissed him. ⁶And on this manner did Absalom to all Israel that came to the king for judgment: so Absalom stole the hearts of the men of Israel. ⁷And it came to pass after forty years, that Absalom said to the king, I pray you, let me go and pay my vow, which I have vowed to the LORD, in Hebron. ⁸For your servant vowed a vow while I stayed at Geshur in Syria, saying, If the LORD shall bring me again indeed to Jerusalem, then I will serve the LORD. ⁹And the king said to him, Go in peace. So he arose, and went to Hebron. ¹⁰But Absalom sent spies throughout all the tribes of Israel, saying, As soon as you hear the sound of the trumpet, then you shall say, Absalom reigns in Hebron. ¹¹And with Absalom went two hundred men out of Jerusalem, that were called; and they went in their simplicity, and they knew not any thing. ¹²And Absalom sent for Ahithophel the Gilonite, David's counselor, from his city, even from Giloh, while he offered sacrifices. And the conspiracy was strong; for the people increased continually with Absalom. ¹³And there came a messenger to David, saying, The hearts of the men of Israel are after Absalom. ¹⁴And David said to all his servants that were with him at Jerusalem, Arise, and let us flee; for we shall not else escape from Absalom: make speed to depart, lest he overtake us suddenly, and bring evil on us, and smite the city with the edge of the sword. ¹⁵And the king's servants said to the king, Behold, your servants are ready to do whatever my lord the king shall appoint. ¹⁶And the king went forth, and all his household after him. And the king left ten women, which were concubines, to keep the house. ¹⁷And the king went forth, and all the people after him, and tarried in a place that was far off. ¹⁸And all his servants passed on beside him; and all the Cherethites, and all the Pelethites, and all the Gittites, six hundred men which came after him from Gath, passed on before the king. ¹⁹Then said the king to Ittai the Gittite, Why go you also with us? return to your place, and abide with the king: for you are a stranger, and also an exile. ²⁰Whereas you came but yesterday, should I this day make you go up and down with us? seeing I go where I may, return you, and take back your brothers: mercy and truth be with you. ²¹And Ittai answered the king, and said, As the LORD lives, and as my lord the king lives, surely in what place my lord the king shall be, whether in death or life, even there also will your servant be. ²²And David said to Ittai, Go and pass over. And Ittai the Gittite passed over, and all his men, and all the little ones that were with him. ²³And all the country wept with a loud voice, and all the people passed over: the king also himself passed over the brook Kidron, and all the people passed over, toward the way of the wilderness. ²⁴And see Zadok also, and all the Levites were with him, bearing the ark of the covenant of God: and they set down the ark of God; and Abiathar went up, until all the people had done passing out of the city. ²⁵And the king said to Zadok, Carry back the ark of God into the city: if I shall find favor in the eyes of the LORD, he will bring me again, and show me both it, and his habitation: ²⁶But if he thus say, I have no delight in you; behold, here am I, let him do to me as seems good to him. ²⁷The king said also to Zadok the priest, Are not you a seer? return into the city in peace, and your two sons with you, Ahimaaz your son, and Jonathan the son of Abiathar. ²⁸See, I will tarry in the plain of the wilderness, until there come word from you to certify me. ²⁹Zadok therefore and Abiathar carried the ark of God again to Jerusalem: and they tarried there. ³⁰And David went up by the ascent of mount Olivet, and wept as he went up, and had his head covered, and he went barefoot: and all the people that was with him covered every man his head, and they went up, weeping as they went up. ³¹And one told David, saying, Ahithophel is among the conspirators with Absalom. And David said, O LORD, I pray you, turn the counsel of Ahithophel into foolishness. ³²And it came to pass, that when David was come to the top of the mount, where he worshipped God, behold, Hushai the Archite came to meet him with his coat rent, and earth on his head: ³³To whom David said, If you pass on with me, then you shall be a burden to me: ³⁴But if you return to the city, and say to Absalom, I will be your servant, O king; as I have been your father's servant till now, so will I now also be your servant: then may you for me defeat the counsel of Ahithophel. ³⁵And have you not there with you Zadok and Abiathar the priests? therefore it shall be, that what thing soever you shall hear out of the king's house, you shall tell it to Zadok and

Abiathar the priests. ³⁶Behold, they have there with them their two sons, Ahimaaz Zadok's son, and Jonathan Abiathar's son; and by them you shall send to me every thing that you can hear. ³⁷So Hushai David's friend came into the city, and Absalom came into Jerusalem.

16 ¹And when David was a little past the top of the hill, behold, Ziba the servant of Mephibosheth met him, with a couple of asses saddled, and on them two hundred loaves of bread, and an hundred bunches of raisins, and an hundred of summer fruits, and a bottle of wine. ²And the king said to Ziba, What mean you by these? And Ziba said, The asses be for the king's household to ride on; and the bread and summer fruit for the young men to eat; and the wine, that such as be faint in the wilderness may drink. ³And the king said, And where is your master's son? And Ziba said to the king, Behold, he stays at Jerusalem: for he said, To day shall the house of Israel restore me the kingdom of my father. ⁴Then said the king to Ziba, Behold, your are all that pertained to Mephibosheth. And Ziba said, I humbly beseech you that I may find grace in your sight, my lord, O king. ⁵And when king David came to Bahurim, behold, there came out a man of the family of the house of Saul, whose name was Shimei, the son of Gera: he came forth, and cursed still as he came. ⁶And he cast stones at David, and at all the servants of king David: and all the people and all the mighty men were on his right hand and on his left. ⁷And thus said Shimei when he cursed, Come out, come out, you bloody man, and you man of Belial: ⁸The LORD has returned on you all the blood of the house of Saul, in whose stead you have reigned; and the LORD has delivered the kingdom into the hand of Absalom your son: and, behold, you are taken in your mischief, because you are a bloody man. ⁹Then said Abishai the son of Zeruiah to the king, Why should this dead dog curse my lord the king? let me go over, I pray you, and take off his head. ¹⁰And the king said, What have I to do with you, you sons of Zeruiah? so let him curse, because the LORD has said to him, Curse David. Who shall then say, Why have you done so? ¹¹And David said to Abishai, and to all his servants, Behold, my son, which came forth of my bowels, seeks my life: how much more now may this Benjamite do it? let him alone, and let him curse; for the LORD has bidden him. ¹²It may be that the LORD will look on my affliction, and that the LORD will requite me good for his cursing this day. ¹³And as David and his men went by the way, Shimei went along on the hill's side over against him, and cursed as he went, and threw stones at him, and cast dust. ¹⁴And the king, and all the people that were with him, came weary, and refreshed themselves there. ¹⁵And Absalom, and all the people the men of Israel, came to Jerusalem, and Ahithophel with him. ¹⁶And it came to pass, when Hushai the Archite, David's friend, was come to Absalom, that Hushai said to Absalom, God save the king, God save the king. ¹⁷And Absalom said to Hushai, Is this your kindness to your friend? why went you not with your friend? ¹⁸And Hushai said to Absalom, No; but whom the LORD, and this people, and all the men of Israel, choose, his will I be, and with him will I abide. ¹⁹And again, whom should I serve? should I not serve in the presence of his son? as I have served in your father's presence, so will I be in your presence. ²⁰Then said Absalom to Ahithophel, Give counsel among you what we shall do. ²¹And Ahithophel said to Absalom, Go in to your father's concubines, which he has left to keep the house; and all Israel shall hear that you are abhorred of your father: then shall the hands of all that are with you be strong. ²²So they spread Absalom a tent on the top of the house; and Absalom went in to his father's concubines in the sight of all Israel. ²³And the counsel of Ahithophel, which he counceled in those days, was as if a man had inquired at the oracle of God: so was all the counsel of Ahithophel both with David and with Absalom.

17 ¹Moreover Ahithophel said to Absalom, Let me now choose out twelve thousand men, and I will arise and pursue after David this night: ²And I will come on him while he is weary and weak handed, and will make him afraid: and all the people that are with him shall flee; and I will smite the king only: ³And I will bring back all the people to you: the man whom you seek is as if all returned: so all the people shall be in peace. ⁴And the saying pleased Absalom well, and all the elders of Israel. ⁵Then said Absalom, Call now Hushai the Archite also, and let us hear likewise what he says. ⁶And when Hushai was come to Absalom, Absalom spoke to him, saying, Ahithophel has spoken after this manner: shall we do after his saying? if not; speak you. ⁷And Hushai said to Absalom, The counsel that Ahithophel has given is not good at this time. ⁸For, said Hushai, you know your father and his men, that they be mighty men, and they be chafed in their minds, as a bear robbed of her whelps in the field: and your father is a man of war, and will not lodge with the people. ⁹Behold, he is hid now in some pit, or in some other place: and it will come to pass, when some of them be overthrown at the first, that whoever hears it will say, There is a slaughter among the people that follow Absalom. ¹⁰And he also that is valiant, whose heart is as the heart of a lion, shall utterly melt: for all Israel knows that your father is a mighty man, and they which be with him are valiant men. ¹¹Therefore I counsel that all Israel be generally gathered to you, from Dan even to Beersheba, as the sand that is by the sea for multitude; and that you go to battle in your own person. ¹²So shall we come on him in some place where he shall be found, and we will light on him as the dew falls on the ground: and of him and of all the men that are with him there shall not be left so much as one. ¹³Moreover, if he be gotten into a city, then shall all Israel bring ropes to that city, and we will draw it into the river, until there be not one small stone found there. ¹⁴And Absalom and all the men of Israel said, The counsel of Hushai the Archite is better than the counsel of Ahithophel. For the LORD had appointed to defeat the good counsel of Ahithophel, to the intent that the LORD might bring evil on Absalom. ¹⁵Then said Hushai to Zadok and to Abiathar the priests, Thus and thus did Ahithophel counsel Absalom and the elders of Israel; and thus and thus have I counceled. ¹⁶Now therefore send quickly, and tell David, saying, Lodge not this night in the plains of the wilderness, but speedily pass over; lest the king be swallowed up, and all the people that are with him. ¹⁷Now Jonathan and Ahimaaz stayed by Enrogel; for they might not be seen to come into the city: and a wench went and told them; and they went and told king David. ¹⁸Nevertheless a lad saw them, and told Absalom: but they went both of them away quickly, and came to a man's house in Bahurim, which had a well in his court; where they went down. ¹⁹And the woman took and spread a covering over the well's mouth, and spread ground corn thereon; and the thing was not known. ²⁰And when Absalom's servants came to the woman to the house, they said, Where is Ahimaaz and Jonathan? And the woman said to them, They be gone over the brook of water. And when they had sought and could not find them, they returned to Jerusalem. ²¹And it came to pass, after they were departed, that they came up out of the well, and went and told king David, and said to David, Arise, and pass quickly over the water: for thus has Ahithophel counceled against you. ²²Then David arose, and all the people that were with him, and they passed over Jordan: by the morning light there lacked not one of them that was not gone over Jordan. ²³And when Ahithophel saw that his counsel was not followed, he saddled his ass, and arose, and got him home to his house, to his city, and put his household in order, and hanged himself, and died, and was buried in the sepulcher of his father. ²⁴Then David came to Mahanaim. And Absalom passed over Jordan, he and all the men of Israel with him. ²⁵And Absalom made Amasa captain of the host instead of Joab: which Amasa was a man's son, whose name was Ithra an Israelite, that went in to Abigail the daughter of Nahash, sister to Zeruiah Joab's mother. ²⁶So Israel and Absalom pitched in the land of Gilead. ²⁷And it came to pass, when David was come to Mahanaim, that Shobi the son of Nahash of Rabbah of the children of Ammon, and Machir the son of Ammiel of Lodebar, and Barzillai the Gileadite of Rogelim, ²⁸Brought beds, and basins, and earthen vessels, and wheat, and barley, and flour, and parched corn, and beans, and lentils, and parched vegetables, ²⁹And honey, and butter, and sheep, and cheese of cows, for David, and for the people that were with him, to eat: for they said, The people is hungry, and weary, and thirsty, in the wilderness.

18 ¹And David numbered the people that were with him, and set captains of thousands, and captains of hundreds over them. ²And David sent forth a third part of the people under the hand of Joab, and a third part under the hand of Abishai the son of Zeruiah, Joab's brother, and a third part under the hand of Ittai the Gittite. And the king said to the people, I will surely go forth with you myself also. ³But the people answered, You shall not go forth: for if we flee away, they will not care for us; neither if half of us die, will they care for us: but now you are worth ten thousand of us: therefore now it is better that you succor us out of the city. ⁴And the king said to them, What seems you best I will do. And the king stood by the gate side, and all the people came out by hundreds and by thousands. ⁵And the king commanded Joab and Abishai and Ittai, saying, Deal gently for my sake with the young man, even with Absalom. And all the people heard when the king gave all the captains charge concerning Absalom. ⁶So the people went out into the field against Israel: and the battle was in the wood of Ephraim; ⁷Where the people of Israel were slain before the servants of David, and there was there a great slaughter that day of twenty thousand men. ⁸For the battle was there scattered over the face of all the country: and the wood devoured more people that day than the sword devoured. ⁹And Absalom met the servants of David. And Absalom rode on a mule, and the mule went under the thick boughs of a great oak, and his head caught hold of the oak, and he was taken up between the heaven and the earth; and the mule that was under him went away. ¹⁰And a certain man saw it, and told Joab, and said, Behold, I saw Absalom hanged in an oak. ¹¹And Joab said to the man that told him, And, behold, you saw him, and why did you not smite him there to the ground? and I would have given you ten shekels of silver, and a girdle. ¹²And the man said to Joab, Though I should receive a thousand shekels of silver in my hand, yet would I not put forth my hand against the king's son: for in our hearing the king charged you and Abishai and Ittai, saying, Beware that none touch the young man Absalom. ¹³Otherwise I should have worked falsehood against my own life: for there is no matter hid from the king, and you yourself would have set yourself against me. ¹⁴Then said Joab, I may not tarry thus with you. And he took three darts in his hand, and thrust them through the heart of Absalom, while he was yet alive in the middle of the oak. ¹⁵And ten young men that bore Joab's armor compassed about and smote Absalom, and slew him. ¹⁶And Joab blew the trumpet, and the people returned from pursuing after Israel: for Joab held back the people. ¹⁷And they took Absalom, and cast him into a great pit in the wood, and laid a very great heap of stones on him: and all Israel fled every one to his tent. ¹⁸Now Absalom in his lifetime had taken and reared up for himself a pillar, which is in the king's dale: for he said, I have no son to keep my name in remembrance: and he called the pillar after his own name: and it is called to this day, Absalom's place. ¹⁹Then said Ahimaaz the son of Zadok, Let me now run, and bear the king tidings, how that the LORD has avenged him of his enemies. ²⁰And Joab said to him, You shall not bear tidings this day, but you shall bear tidings another day: but this day you shall bear no tidings, because the king's son is dead. ²¹Then said Joab to Cushi, Go tell the king what you have seen. And Cushi bowed himself to Joab, and ran. ²²Then said Ahimaaz the son of Zadok yet again to Joab, But howsoever, let me, I pray you, also run after Cushi. And Joab said, Why will you run, my son, seeing that you have no tidings ready? ²³But howsoever, said he, let me run. And he said to him, Run. Then Ahimaaz ran by the way of the plain, and overran Cushi. ²⁴And David sat between the two gates: and the watchman went up to the roof over the gate to the wall, and lifted up his eyes, and looked, and behold a man running alone. ²⁵And the watchman cried, and told the king. And the king said, If he be alone, there is tidings in his mouth. And he came apace, and drew near. ²⁶And the watchman saw another man running: and the watchman called to the porter, and said, Behold another man running alone. And the king said, He also brings tidings. ²⁷And the watchman said, Me thinks the running of the foremost is like the running of Ahimaaz the son of Zadok. And the king said, He is a good man, and comes with good tidings. ²⁸And Ahimaaz called, and said to the king, All is well. And he fell down to the earth on his face before the king, and said, Blessed be the LORD your God, which has delivered up the men that lifted up their hand against my lord the king. ²⁹And the king said, Is the young man Absalom safe? And Ahimaaz answered, When Joab sent the king's servant, and me your servant, I saw a great tumult, but

I knew not what it was. ³⁰And the king said to him, Turn aside, and stand here. And he turned aside, and stood still. ³¹And, behold, Cushi came; and Cushi said, Tidings, my lord the king: for the LORD has avenged you this day of all them that rose up against you. ³²And the king said to Cushi, Is the young man Absalom safe? And Cushi answered, The enemies of my lord the king, and all that rise against you to do you hurt, be as that young man is. ³³And the king was much moved, and went up to the chamber over the gate, and wept: and as he went, thus he said, O my son Absalom, my son, my son Absalom! would God I had died for you, O Absalom, my son, my son!

19

¹And it was told Joab, Behold, the king weeps and mourns for Absalom. ²And the victory that day was turned into mourning to all the people: for the people heard say that day how the king was grieved for his son. ³And the people got them by stealth that day into the city, as people being ashamed steal away when they flee in battle. ⁴But the king covered his face, and the king cried with a loud voice, O my son Absalom, O Absalom, my son, my son! ⁵And Joab came into the house to the king, and said, You have shamed this day the faces of all your servants, which this day have saved your life, and the lives of your sons and of your daughters, and the lives of your wives, and the lives of your concubines; ⁶In that you love your enemies, and hate your friends. For you have declared this day, that you regard neither princes nor servants: for this day I perceive, that if Absalom had lived, and all we had died this day, then it had pleased you well. ⁷Now therefore arise, go forth, and speak comfortably to your servants: for I swear by the LORD, if you go not forth, there will not tarry one with you this night: and that will be worse to you than all the evil that befell you from your youth until now. ⁸Then the king arose, and sat in the gate. And they told to all the people, saying, Behold, the king does sit in the gate. And all the people came before the king: for Israel had fled every man to his tent. ⁹And all the people were at strife throughout all the tribes of Israel, saying, The king saved us out of the hand of our enemies, and he delivered us out of the hand of the Philistines; and now he is fled out of the land for Absalom. ¹⁰And Absalom, whom we anointed over us, is dead in battle. Now therefore why speak you not a word of bringing the king back? ¹¹And king David sent to Zadok and to Abiathar the priests, saying, Speak to the elders of Judah, saying, Why are you the last to bring the king back to his house? seeing the speech of all Israel is come to the king, even to his house. ¹²You are my brothers, you are my bones and my flesh: why then are you the last to bring back the king? ¹³And say you to Amasa, Are you not of my bone, and of my flesh? God do so to me, and more also, if you be not captain of the host before me continually in the room of Joab. ¹⁴And he bowed the heart of all the men of Judah, even as the heart of one man; so that they sent this word to the king, Return you, and all your servants. ¹⁵So the king returned, and came to Jordan. And Judah came to Gilgal, to go to meet the king, to conduct the king over Jordan. ¹⁶And Shimei the son of Gera, a Benjamite, which was of Bahurim, hurried and came down with the men of Judah to meet king David. ¹⁷And there were a thousand men of Benjamin with him, and Ziba the servant of the house of Saul, and his fifteen sons and his twenty servants with him; and they went over Jordan before the king. ¹⁸And there went over a ferry boat to carry over the king's household, and to do what he thought good. And Shimei the son of Gera fell down before the king, as he was come over Jordan; ¹⁹And said to the king, Let not my lord impute iniquity to me, neither do you remember that which your servant did perversely the day that my lord the king went out of Jerusalem, that the king should take it to his heart. ²⁰For your servant does know that I have sinned: therefore, behold, I am come the first this day of all the house of Joseph to go down to meet my lord the king. ²¹But Abishai the son of Zeruiah answered and said, Shall not Shimei be put to death for this, because he cursed the LORD's anointed? ²²And David said, What have I to do with you, you sons of Zeruiah, that you should this day be adversaries to me? shall there any man be put to death this day in Israel? for do not I know that I am this day king over Israel? ²³Therefore the king said to Shimei, You shall not die. And the king swore to him. ²⁴And Mephibosheth the son of Saul came down to meet the king, and had neither dressed his feet, nor trimmed his beard, nor washed his clothes, from the day the king departed until the day he came again in peace. ²⁵And it came to pass, when he was come to Jerusalem to meet the king, that the king said to him, Why went not you with me, Mephibosheth? ²⁶And he answered, My lord, O king, my servant deceived me: for your servant said, I will saddle me an ass, that I may ride thereon, and go to the king; because your servant is lame. ²⁷And he has slandered your servant to my lord the king; but my lord the king is as an angel of God: do therefore what is good in your eyes. ²⁸For all of my father's house were but dead men before my lord the king: yet did you set your servant among them that did eat at your own table. What right therefore have I yet to cry any more to the king? ²⁹And the king said to him, Why speak you any more of your matters? I have said, You and Ziba divide the land. ³⁰And Mephibosheth said to the king, Yes, let him take all, for as much as my lord the king is come again in peace to his own house. ³¹And Barzillai the Gileadite came down from Rogelim, and went over Jordan with the king, to conduct him over Jordan. ³²Now Barzillai was a very aged man, even fourscore years old: and he had provided the king of sustenance while he lay at Mahanaim; for he was a very great man. ³³And the king said to Barzillai, Come you over with me, and I will feed you with me in Jerusalem. ³⁴And Barzillai said to the king, How long have I to live, that I should go up with the king to Jerusalem? ³⁵I am this day fourscore years old: and can I discern between good and evil? can your servant taste what I eat or what I drink? can I hear any more the voice of singing men and singing women? why then should your servant be yet a burden to my lord the king? ³⁶Your servant will go a little way over Jordan with the king: and why should the king recompense it me with such a reward? ³⁷Let your servant, I pray you, turn back again, that I may die in my own city, and be buried by the grave of my father and of my mother. But behold your servant Chimham; let him go over with my lord the king; and do to him what shall seem good to you. ³⁸And the king answered, Chimham shall go over with me, and I will do to him that which shall seem good to you: and whatever you shall require of me, that will I do for you. ³⁹And all the

people went over Jordan. And when the king was come over, the king kissed Barzillai, and blessed him; and he returned to his own place. ⁴⁰Then the king went on to Gilgal, and Chimham went on with him: and all the people of Judah conducted the king, and also half the people of Israel. ⁴¹And, behold, all the men of Israel came to the king, and said to the king, Why have our brothers the men of Judah stolen you away, and have brought the king, and his household, and all David's men with him, over Jordan? ⁴²And all the men of Judah answered the men of Israel, Because the king is near of kin to us: why then be you angry for this matter? have we eaten at all of the king's cost? or has he given us any gift? ⁴³And the men of Israel answered the men of Judah, and said, We have ten parts in the king, and we have also more right in David than you: why then did you despise us, that our advice should not be first had in bringing back our king? And the words of the men of Judah were fiercer than the words of the men of Israel.

20 ¹And there happened to be there a man of Belial, whose name was Sheba, the son of Bichri, a Benjamite: and he blew a trumpet, and said, We have no part in David, neither have we inheritance in the son of Jesse: every man to his tents, O Israel. ²So every man of Israel went up from after David, and followed Sheba the son of Bichri: but the men of Judah joined to their king, from Jordan even to Jerusalem. ³And David came to his house at Jerusalem; and the king took the ten women his concubines, whom he had left to keep the house, and put them in ward, and fed them, but went not in to them. So they were shut up to the day of their death, living in widowhood. ⁴Then said the king to Amasa, Assemble me the men of Judah within three days, and be you here present. ⁵So Amasa went to assemble the men of Judah: but he tarried longer than the set time which he had appointed him. ⁶And David said to Abishai, Now shall Sheba the son of Bichri do us more harm than did Absalom: take you your lord's servants, and pursue after him, lest he get him fenced cities, and escape us. ⁷And there went out after him Joab's men, and the Cherethites, and the Pelethites, and all the mighty men: and they went out of Jerusalem, to pursue after Sheba the son of Bichri. ⁸When they were at the great stone which is in Gibeon, Amasa went before them. And Joab's garment that he had put on was girded to him, and on it a girdle with a sword fastened on his loins in the sheath thereof; and as he went forth it fell out. ⁹And Joab said to Amasa, Are you in health, my brother? And Joab took Amasa by the beard with the right hand to kiss him. ¹⁰But Amasa took no heed to the sword that was in Joab's hand: so he smote him therewith in the fifth rib, and shed out his bowels to the ground, and struck him not again; and he died. So Joab and Abishai his brother pursued after Sheba the son of Bichri. ¹¹And one of Joab's men stood by him, and said, He that favors Joab, and he that is for David, let him go after Joab. ¹²And Amasa wallowed in blood in the middle of the highway. And when the man saw that all the people stood still, he removed Amasa out of the highway into the field, and cast a cloth on him, when he saw that every one that came by him stood still. ¹³When he was removed out of the highway, all the people went on after Joab, to pursue after Sheba the son of Bichri. ¹⁴And he went through all the tribes of Israel to Abel, and to Bethmaachah, and all the Berites: and they were gathered together, and went also after him. ¹⁵And they came and besieged him in Abel of Bethmaachah, and they cast up a bank against the city, and it stood in the trench: and all the people that were with Joab battered the wall, to throw it down. ¹⁶Then cried a wise woman out of the city, Hear, hear; say, I pray you, to Joab, Come near here, that I may speak with you. ¹⁷And when he was come near to her, the woman said, Are you Joab? And he answered, I am he. Then she said to him, Hear the words of your handmaid. And he answered, I do hear. ¹⁸Then she spoke, saying, They were wont to speak in old time, saying, They shall surely ask counsel at Abel: and so they ended the matter. ¹⁹I am one of them that are peaceable and faithful in Israel: you seek to destroy a city and a mother in Israel: why will you swallow up the inheritance of the LORD? ²⁰And Joab answered and said, Far be it, far be it from me, that I should swallow up or destroy. ²¹The matter is not so: but a man of mount Ephraim, Sheba the son of Bichri by name, has lifted up his hand against the king, even against David: deliver him only, and I will depart from the city. And the woman said to Joab, Behold, his head shall be thrown to you over the wall. ²²Then the woman went to all the people in her wisdom. And they cut off the head of Sheba the son of Bichri, and cast it out to Joab. And he blew a trumpet, and they retired from the city, every man to his tent. And Joab returned to Jerusalem to the king. ²³Now Joab was over all the host of Israel: and Benaiah the son of Jehoiada was over the Cherethites and over the Pelethites: ²⁴And Adoram was over the tribute: and Jehoshaphat the son of Ahilud was recorder: ²⁵And Sheva was scribe: and Zadok and Abiathar were the priests: ²⁶And Ira also the Jairite was a chief ruler about David.

21 ¹Then there was a famine in the days of David three years, year after year; and David inquired of the LORD. And the LORD answered, It is for Saul, and for his bloody house, because he slew the Gibeonites. ²And the king called the Gibeonites, and said to them; (now the Gibeonites were not of the children of Israel, but of the remnant of the Amorites; and the children of Israel had sworn to them: and Saul sought to slay them in his zeal to the children of Israel and Judah.) ³Why David said to the Gibeonites, What shall I do for you? and with which shall I make the atonement, that you may bless the inheritance of the LORD? ⁴And the Gibeonites said to him, We will have no silver nor gold of Saul, nor of his house; neither for us shall you kill any man in Israel. And he said, What you shall say, that will I do for you. ⁵And they answered the king, The man that consumed us, and that devised against us that we should be destroyed from remaining in any of the coasts of Israel, ⁶Let seven men of his sons be delivered to us, and we will hang them up to the LORD in Gibeah of Saul, whom the LORD did choose. And the king said, I will give them. ⁷But the king spared Mephibosheth, the son of Jonathan the son of Saul, because of the LORD's oath that was between them, between David and Jonathan the son of Saul. ⁸But the king took the two sons of Rizpah the daughter of Aiah, whom she bore to Saul, Armoni and Mephibosheth; and the five sons of Michal the daughter of Saul, whom she brought up for Adriel the son of Barzillai the Meholathite: ⁹And he delivered them into the hands of the Gibeonites, and they hanged them in the hill before the LORD: and they fell all seven together, and were put to death in the days of harvest, in the first days, in the beginning of barley harvest. ¹⁰And Rizpah the daughter of Aiah took sackcloth, and spread it for her on the rock, from the beginning of harvest until water dropped on them out of heaven, and suffered neither the birds of the air to rest on them by day, nor the beasts of the field by night. ¹¹And it was told David what Rizpah the daughter of Aiah, the concubine of Saul, had done. ¹²And David went and took the bones of Saul and the bones of Jonathan his son from the men of Jabeshgilead, which had stolen them from the street of Bethshan, where the Philistines had hanged them, when the Philistines had slain Saul in Gilboa: ¹³And he brought up from there the bones of Saul and the bones of Jonathan his son; and they gathered the bones of them that were hanged. ¹⁴And the bones of Saul and Jonathan his son buried they in the country of Benjamin in Zelah, in the sepulcher of Kish his father: and they performed all that the king commanded. And after that God was entreated for the land. ¹⁵Moreover the Philistines had yet war again with Israel; and David went down, and his servants with him, and fought against the Philistines: and David waxed faint. ¹⁶And Ishbibenob, which was of the sons of the giant, the weight of whose spear weighed three hundred shekels of brass in weight, he being girded with a new sword, thought to have slain David. ¹⁷But Abishai the son of Zeruiah succored him, and smote the Philistine, and killed him. Then the men of David swore to him, saying, You shall go no more out with us to battle, that you quench not the light of Israel. ¹⁸And it came to pass after this, that there was again a battle with the Philistines at Gob: then Sibbechai the Hushathite slew Saph, which was of the sons of the giant. ¹⁹And there was again a battle in Gob with the Philistines, where Elhanan the son of Jaareoregim, a Bethlehemite, slew the brother of Goliath the Gittite, the staff of whose spear was like a weaver's beam. ²⁰And there was yet a battle in Gath, where was a man of great stature, that had on every hand six fingers, and on every foot six toes, four and twenty in number; and he also was born to the giant. ²¹And when he defied Israel, Jonathan the son of Shimeah the brother of David slew him. ²²These four were born to the giant in Gath, and fell by the hand of David, and by the hand of his servants.

22

¹And David spoke to the LORD the words of this song in the day that the LORD had delivered him out of the hand of all his enemies, and out of the hand of Saul: ²And he said, The LORD is my rock, and my fortress, and my deliverer; ³The God of my rock; in him will I trust: he is my shield, and the horn of my salvation, my high tower, and my refuge, my savior; you save me from violence. ⁴I will call on the LORD, who is worthy to be praised: so shall I be saved from my enemies. ⁵When the waves of death compassed me, the floods of ungodly men made me afraid; ⁶The sorrows of hell compassed me about; the snares of death prevented me; ⁷In my distress I called on the LORD, and cried to my God: and he did hear my voice out of his temple, and my cry did enter into his ears. ⁸Then the earth shook and trembled; the foundations of heaven moved and shook, because he was wroth. ⁹There went up a smoke out of his nostrils, and fire out of his mouth devoured: coals were kindled by it. ¹⁰He bowed the heavens also, and came down; and darkness was under his feet. ¹¹And he rode on a cherub, and did fly: and he was seen on the wings of the wind. ¹²And he made darkness pavilions round about him, dark waters, and thick clouds of the skies. ¹³Through the brightness before him were coals of fire kindled. ¹⁴The LORD thundered from heaven, and the most High uttered his voice. ¹⁵And he sent out arrows, and scattered them; lightning, and discomfited them. ¹⁶And the channels of the sea appeared, the foundations of the world were discovered, at the rebuking of the LORD, at the blast of the breath of his nostrils. ¹⁷He sent from above, he took me; he drew me out of many waters; ¹⁸He delivered me from my strong enemy, and from them that hated me: for they were too strong for me. ¹⁹They prevented me in the day of my calamity: but the LORD was my stay. ²⁰He brought me forth also into a large place: he delivered me, because he delighted in me. ²¹The LORD rewarded me according to my righteousness: according to the cleanness of my hands has he recompensed me. ²²For I have kept the ways of the LORD, and have not wickedly departed from my God. ²³For all his judgments were before me: and as for his statutes, I did not depart from them. ²⁴I was also upright before him, and have kept myself from my iniquity. ²⁵Therefore the LORD has recompensed me according to my righteousness; according to my cleanness in his eye sight. ²⁶With the merciful you will show yourself merciful, and with the upright man you will show yourself upright. ²⁷With the pure you will show yourself pure; and with the fraudulent you will show yourself unsavory. ²⁸And the afflicted people you will save: but your eyes are on the haughty, that you may bring them down. ²⁹For you are my lamp, O LORD: and the LORD will lighten my darkness. ³⁰For by you I have run through a troop: by my God have I leaped over a wall. ³¹As for God, his way is perfect; the word of the LORD is tried: he is a buckler to all them that trust in him. ³²For who is God, save the LORD? and who is a rock, save our God? ³³God is my strength and power: and he makes my way perfect. ³⁴He makes my feet like hinds' feet: and sets me on my high places. ³⁵He teaches my hands to war; so that a bow of steel is broken by my arms. ³⁶You have also given me the shield of your salvation: and your gentleness has made me great. ³⁷You have enlarged my steps under me; so that my feet did not slip. ³⁸I have pursued my enemies, and destroyed them; and turned not again until I had consumed them. ³⁹And I have consumed them, and wounded them, that they could not arise: yes, they are fallen under my feet. ⁴⁰For you have girded me with strength to battle: them that rose up against me have you subdued under me. ⁴¹You have also given me the necks of my enemies, that I might destroy them that hate me. ⁴²They looked, but there was none to save; even to the LORD, but he answered them not. ⁴³Then did I beat them as small as the dust of the earth, I did stamp them as the mire of the street, and did spread them abroad. ⁴⁴You also have delivered me from the strivings of my people, you have kept me to be head of the heathen: a people which I knew not shall serve me. ⁴⁵Strangers shall submit themselves to me: as soon as they hear, they shall be obedient to me. ⁴⁶Strangers shall fade away, and they shall be afraid out of their close places. ⁴⁷The LORD lives; and blessed be my rock; and exalted be the God of the rock of my salvation. ⁴⁸It is God

that avenges me, and that brings down the people under me. ⁴⁹And that brings me forth from my enemies: you also have lifted me up on high above them that rose up against me: you have delivered me from the violent man. ⁵⁰Therefore I will give thanks to you, O LORD, among the heathen, and I will sing praises to your name. ⁵¹He is the tower of salvation for his king: and shows mercy to his anointed, to David, and to his seed for ever more.

23

¹Now these be the last words of David. David the son of Jesse said, and the man who was raised up on high, the anointed of the God of Jacob, and the sweet psalmist of Israel, said, ²The Spirit of the LORD spoke by me, and his word was in my tongue. ³The God of Israel said, the Rock of Israel spoke to me, He that rules over men must be just, ruling in the fear of God. ⁴And he shall be as the light of the morning, when the sun rises, even a morning without clouds; as the tender grass springing out of the earth by clear shining after rain. ⁵Although my house be not so with God; yet he has made with me an everlasting covenant, ordered in all things, and sure: for this is all my salvation, and all my desire, although he make it not to grow. ⁶But the sons of Belial shall be all of them as thorns thrust away, because they cannot be taken with hands: ⁷But the man that shall touch them must be fenced with iron and the staff of a spear; and they shall be utterly burned with fire in the same place. ⁸These be the names of the mighty men whom David had: The Tachmonite that sat in the seat, chief among the captains; the same was Adino the Eznite: he lift up his spear against eight hundred, whom he slew at one time. ⁹And after him was Eleazar the son of Dodo the Ahohite, one of the three mighty men with David, when they defied the Philistines that were there gathered together to battle, and the men of Israel were gone away: ¹⁰He arose, and smote the Philistines until his hand was weary, and his hand stuck to the sword: and the LORD worked a great victory that day; and the people returned after him only to spoil. ¹¹And after him was Shammah the son of Agee the Hararite. And the Philistines were gathered together into a troop, where was a piece of ground full of lentils: and the people fled from the Philistines. ¹²But he stood in the middle of the ground, and defended it, and slew the Philistines: and the LORD worked a great victory. ¹³And three of the thirty chief went down, and came to David in the harvest time to the cave of Adullam: and the troop of the Philistines pitched in the valley of Rephaim. ¹⁴And David was then in an hold, and the garrison of the Philistines was then in Bethlehem. ¹⁵And David longed, and said, Oh that one would give me drink of the water of the well of Bethlehem, which is by the gate! ¹⁶And the three mighty men broke through the host of the Philistines, and drew water out of the well of Bethlehem, that was by the gate, and took it, and brought it to David: nevertheless he would not drink thereof, but poured it out to the LORD. ¹⁷And he said, Be it far from me, O LORD, that I should do this: is not this the blood of the men that went in jeopardy of their lives? therefore he would not drink it. These things did these three mighty men. ¹⁸And Abishai, the brother of Joab, the son of Zeruiah, was chief among three. And he lifted up his spear against three hundred, and slew them, and had the name among three. ¹⁹Was he not most honorable of three? therefore he was their captain: however, he attained not to the first three. ²⁰And Benaiah the son of Jehoiada, the son of a valiant man, of Kabzeel, who had done many acts, he slew two lion like men of Moab: he went down also and slew a lion in the middle of a pit in time of snow: ²¹And he slew an Egyptian, a goodly man: and the Egyptian had a spear in his hand; but he went down to him with a staff, and plucked the spear out of the Egyptian's hand, and slew him with his own spear. ²²These things did Benaiah the son of Jehoiada, and had the name among three mighty men. ²³He was more honorable than the thirty, but he attained not to the first three. And David set him over his guard. ²⁴Asahel the brother of Joab was one of the thirty; Elhanan the son of Dodo of Bethlehem; ²⁵Shammah the Harodite, Elika the Harodite, ²⁶Helez the Paltite, Ira the son of Ikkesh the Tekoite, ²⁷Abiezer the Anethothite, Mebunnai the Hushathite, ²⁸Zalmon the Ahohite, Maharai the Netophathite, ²⁹Heleb the son of Baanah, a Netophathite, Ittai the son of Ribai out of Gibeah of the children of Benjamin, ³⁰Benaiah the Pirathonite, Hiddai of the brooks of Gaash, ³¹Abialbon the Arbathite, Azmaveth the Barhumite, ³²Eliahba the Shaalbonite, of the sons of Jashen, Jonathan, ³³Shammah the Hararite, Ahiam the son of Sharar the Hararite, ³⁴Eliphelet the son of Ahasbai, the son of the Maachathite, Eliam the son of Ahithophel the Gilonite, ³⁵Hezrai the Carmelite, Paarai the Arbite, ³⁶Igal the son of Nathan of Zobah, Bani the Gadite, ³⁷Zelek the Ammonite, Nahari the Beerothite, armor bearer to Joab the son of Zeruiah, ³⁸Ira an Ithrite, Gareb an Ithrite, ³⁹Uriah the Hittite: thirty and seven in all.

24

¹And again the anger of the LORD was kindled against Israel, and he moved David against them to say, Go, number Israel and Judah. ²For the king said to Joab the captain of the host, which was with him, Go now through all the tribes of Israel, from Dan even to Beersheba, and number you the people, that I may know the number of the people. ³And Joab said to the king, Now the LORD your God add to the people, how many soever they be, an hundred times, and that the eyes of my lord the king may see it: but why does my lord the king delight in this thing? ⁴Notwithstanding the king's word prevailed against Joab, and against the captains of the host. And Joab and the captains of the host went out from the presence of the king, to number the people of Israel. ⁵And they passed over Jordan, and pitched in Aroer, on the right side of the city that lies in the middle of the river of Gad, and toward Jazer: ⁶Then they came to Gilead, and to the land of Tahtimhodshi; and they came to Danjaan, and about to Zidon, ⁷And came to the strong hold of Tyre, and to all the cities of the Hivites, and of the Canaanites: and they went out to the south of Judah, even to Beersheba. ⁸So when they had gone through all the land, they came to Jerusalem at the end of nine months and twenty days. ⁹And Joab gave up the sum of the number of the people to the king: and there were in Israel eight hundred thousand valiant men that drew the sword; and the men of Judah were five hundred thousand men. ¹⁰And David's heart smote him after that he had numbered the people. And David said to the LORD, I have sinned greatly in that I have done: and now, I beseech you, O LORD, take away the iniquity of your servant; for I have done very foolishly. ¹¹For when David was up in the morning, the word of the LORD

came to the prophet Gad, David's seer, saying, ¹²Go and say to David, Thus says the LORD, I offer you three things; choose you one of them, that I may do it to you. ¹³So Gad came to David, and told him, and said to him, Shall seven years of famine come to you in your land? or will you flee three months before your enemies, while they pursue you? or that there be three days' pestilence in your land? now advise, and see what answer I shall return to him that sent me. ¹⁴And David said to Gad, I am in a great strait: let us fall now into the hand of the LORD; for his mercies are great: and let me not fall into the hand of man. ¹⁵So the LORD sent a pestilence on Israel from the morning even to the time appointed: and there died of the people from Dan even to Beersheba seventy thousand men. ¹⁶And when the angel stretched out his hand on Jerusalem to destroy it, the LORD repented him of the evil, and said to the angel that destroyed the people, It is enough: stay now your hand. And the angel of the LORD was by the threshing place of Araunah the Jebusite. ¹⁷And David spoke to the LORD when he saw the angel that smote the people, and said, See, I have sinned, and I have done wickedly: but these sheep, what have they done? let your hand, I pray you, be against me, and against my father's house. ¹⁸And Gad came that day to David, and said to him, Go up, raise an altar to the LORD in the threshing floor of Araunah the Jebusite. ¹⁹And David, according to the saying of Gad, went up as the LORD commanded. ²⁰And Araunah looked, and saw the king and his servants coming on toward him: and Araunah went out, and bowed himself before the king on his face on the ground. ²¹And Araunah said, Why is my lord the king come to his servant? And David said, To buy the threshing floor of you, to build an altar to the LORD, that the plague may be stayed from the people. ²²And Araunah said to David, Let my lord the king take and offer up what seems good to him: behold, here be oxen for burnt sacrifice, and threshing instruments and other instruments of the oxen for wood. ²³All these things did Araunah, as a king, give to the king. And Araunah said to the king, The LORD your God accept you. ²⁴And the king said to Araunah, No; but I will surely buy it of you at a price: neither will I offer burnt offerings to the LORD my God of that which does cost me nothing. So David bought the threshing floor and the oxen for fifty shekels of silver. ²⁵And David built there an altar to the LORD, and offered burnt offerings and peace offerings. So the LORD was entreated for the land, and the plague was stayed from Israel.

First Kings

1 ¹Now king David was old and stricken in years; and they covered him with clothes, but he got no heat. ²Why his servants said to him, Let there be sought for my lord the king a young virgin: and let her stand before the king, and let her cherish him, and let her lie in your bosom, that my lord the king may get heat. ³So they sought for a fair damsel throughout all the coasts of Israel, and found Abishag a Shunammite, and brought her to the king. ⁴And the damsel was very fair, and cherished the king, and ministered to him: but the king knew her not. ⁵Then Adonijah the son of Haggith exalted himself, saying, I will be king: and he prepared him chariots and horsemen, and fifty men to run before him. ⁶And his father had not displeased him at any time in saying, Why have you done so? and he also was a very goodly man; and his mother bore him after Absalom. ⁷And he conferred with Joab the son of Zeruiah, and with Abiathar the priest: and they following Adonijah helped him. ⁸But Zadok the priest, and Benaiah the son of Jehoiada, and Nathan the prophet, and Shimei, and Rei, and the mighty men which belonged to David, were not with Adonijah. ⁹And Adonijah slew sheep and oxen and fat cattle by the stone of Zoheleth, which is by Enrogel, and called all his brothers the king's sons, and all the men of Judah the king's servants: ¹⁰But Nathan the prophet, and Benaiah, and the mighty men, and Solomon his brother, he called not. ¹¹Why Nathan spoke to Bathsheba the mother of Solomon, saying, Have you not heard that Adonijah the son of Haggith does reign, and David our lord knows it not? ¹²Now therefore come, let me, I pray you, give you counsel, that you may save your own life, and the life of your son Solomon. ¹³Go and get you in to king David, and say to him, Did not you, my lord, O king, swear to your handmaid, saying, Assuredly Solomon your son shall reign after me, and he shall sit on my throne? why then does Adonijah reign? ¹⁴Behold, while you yet talk there with the king, I also will come in after you, and confirm your words. ¹⁵And Bathsheba went in to the king into the chamber: and the king was very old; and Abishag the Shunammite ministered to the king. ¹⁶And Bathsheba bowed, and did obeisance to the king. And the king said, What would you? ¹⁷And she said to him, My lord, you swore by the LORD your God to your handmaid, saying, Assuredly Solomon your son shall reign after me, and he shall sit on my throne. ¹⁸And now, behold, Adonijah reigns; and now, my lord the king, you know it not: ¹⁹And he has slain oxen and fat cattle and sheep in abundance, and has called all the sons of the king, and Abiathar the priest, and Joab the captain of the host: but Solomon your servant has he not called. ²⁰And you, my lord, O king, the eyes of all Israel are on you, that you should tell them who shall sit on the throne of my lord the king after him. ²¹Otherwise it shall come to pass, when my lord the king shall sleep with his fathers, that I and my son Solomon shall be counted offenders. ²²And, see, while she yet talked with the king, Nathan the prophet also came in. ²³And they told the king, saying, Behold Nathan the prophet. And when he was come in before the king, he bowed himself before the king with his face to the ground. ²⁴And Nathan said, My lord, O king, have you said, Adonijah shall reign after me, and he shall sit on my throne? ²⁵For he is gone down this day, and has slain oxen and fat cattle and sheep in abundance, and has called all the king's sons, and the captains of the host, and Abiathar the priest; and, behold, they eat and drink before him, and say, God save king Adonijah. ²⁶But me, even me your servant, and Zadok the priest, and Benaiah the son of Jehoiada, and your servant Solomon, has he not called. ²⁷Is this thing done by my lord the king, and you have not showed it to your servant, who should sit on the throne of my lord the king after him? ²⁸Then king David answered and said, Call me Bathsheba. And she came into the king's presence, and stood before the king. ²⁹And the king swore, and said, As the LORD lives, that has redeemed my soul out of all distress, ³⁰Even as I swore to you by the LORD God of Israel, saying, Assuredly Solomon your son shall reign after me, and he shall sit on my throne in my stead; even so will I certainly do this day. ³¹Then Bathsheba bowed with her face to the earth, and did reverence to the king, and said, Let my lord king David live for ever. ³²And king David said, Call me Zadok the priest, and Nathan the prophet, and Benaiah the son of Jehoiada. And they came before the king. ³³The king also said to them, Take with you the servants of your lord, and cause Solomon my son to ride on my own mule, and bring him down to Gihon: ³⁴And let Zadok the priest and Nathan the prophet anoint him there king over Israel: and blow you with the trumpet, and say, God save king Solomon. ³⁵Then you shall come up after him, that he may come and sit on my throne; for he shall be king in my stead: and I have appointed him to be ruler over Israel and over Judah. ³⁶And Benaiah the son of Jehoiada answered the king, and said, Amen: the LORD God of my lord the king say so too. ³⁷As the LORD has been with my lord the king, even so be he with Solomon, and make his throne greater than the throne of my lord king David. ³⁸So Zadok the priest, and Nathan the prophet, and Benaiah the son of Jehoiada, and the Cherethites, and the Pelethites, went down, and caused Solomon to ride on king David's mule, and brought him to Gihon. ³⁹And Zadok the priest took an horn of oil out of the tabernacle, and anointed Solomon. And they blew the trumpet; and all the people said, God save king Solomon. ⁴⁰And all the people came up after him, and the people piped with pipes, and rejoiced with great joy, so that the earth rent with the sound of them. ⁴¹And Adonijah and all the guests that were with him heard it as they had made an end of eating. And when Joab heard the sound of the trumpet, he said, Why is this noise of the city being in an uproar? ⁴²And while he yet spoke, behold, Jonathan the son of Abiathar the priest came; and Adonijah said to him, Come in; for you are a valiant man, and bring good tidings. ⁴³And Jonathan answered and said to Adonijah, Truly our lord king David has made Solomon king. ⁴⁴And the king has sent with him Zadok the priest, and Nathan the prophet, and Benaiah the son of Jehoiada, and the Cherethites, and the Pelethites, and they have caused him to ride on the king's mule: ⁴⁵And Zadok the priest and Nathan the prophet have anointed him king in Gihon: and they are come up from there rejoicing, so that the city rang again. This is the noise that you have heard. ⁴⁶And also Solomon sits on the throne of the kingdom.

⁴⁷And moreover the king's servants came to bless our lord king David, saying, God make the name of Solomon better than your name, and make his throne greater than your throne. And the king bowed himself on the bed. ⁴⁸And also thus said the king, Blessed be the LORD God of Israel, which has given one to sit on my throne this day, my eyes even seeing it. ⁴⁹And all the guests that were with Adonijah were afraid, and rose up, and went every man his way. ⁵⁰And Adonijah feared because of Solomon, and arose, and went, and caught hold on the horns of the altar. ⁵¹And it was told Solomon, saying, Behold, Adonijah fears king Solomon: for, see, he has caught hold on the horns of the altar, saying, Let king Solomon swear to me today that he will not slay his servant with the sword. ⁵²And Solomon said, If he will show himself a worthy man, there shall not an hair of him fall to the earth: but if wickedness shall be found in him, he shall die. ⁵³So king Solomon sent, and they brought him down from the altar. And he came and bowed himself to king Solomon: and Solomon said to him, Go to your house.

2 ¹Now the days of David drew near that he should die; and he charged Solomon his son, saying, ²I go the way of all the earth: be you strong therefore, and show yourself a man; ³And keep the charge of the LORD your God, to walk in his ways, to keep his statutes, and his commandments, and his judgments, and his testimonies, as it is written in the law of Moses, that you may prosper in all that you do, and wherever you turn yourself: ⁴That the LORD may continue his word which he spoke concerning me, saying, If your children take heed to their way, to walk before me in truth with all their heart and with all their soul, there shall not fail you (said he) a man on the throne of Israel. ⁵Moreover you know also what Joab the son of Zeruiah did to me, and what he did to the two captains of the hosts of Israel, to Abner the son of Ner, and to Amasa the son of Jether, whom he slew, and shed the blood of war in peace, and put the blood of war on his girdle that was about his loins, and in his shoes that were on his feet. ⁶Do therefore according to your wisdom, and let not his hoar head go down to the grave in peace. ⁷But show kindness to the sons of Barzillai the Gileadite, and let them be of those that eat at your table: for so they came to me when I fled because of Absalom your brother. ⁸And, behold, you have with you Shimei the son of Gera, a Benjamite of Bahurim, which cursed me with a grievous curse in the day when I went to Mahanaim: but he came down to meet me at Jordan, and I swore to him by the LORD, saying, I will not put you to death with the sword. ⁹Now therefore hold him not guiltless: for you are a wise man, and know what you ought to do to him; but his hoar head bring you down to the grave with blood. ¹⁰So David slept with his fathers, and was buried in the city of David. ¹¹And the days that David reigned over Israel were forty years: seven years reigned he in Hebron, and thirty and three years reigned he in Jerusalem. ¹²Then sat Solomon on the throne of David his father; and his kingdom was established greatly. ¹³And Adonijah the son of Haggith came to Bathsheba the mother of Solomon. And she said, Come you peaceably? And he said, Peaceably. ¹⁴He said moreover, I have somewhat to say to you. And she said, Say on. ¹⁵And he said, You know that the kingdom was mine, and that all Israel set their faces on me, that I should reign: however, the kingdom is turned about, and is become my brother's: for it was his from the LORD. ¹⁶And now I ask one petition of you, deny me not. And she said to him, Say on. ¹⁷And he said, Speak, I pray you, to Solomon the king, (for he will not say you no,) that he give me Abishag the Shunammite to wife. ¹⁸And Bathsheba said, Well; I will speak for you to the king. ¹⁹Bathsheba therefore went to king Solomon, to speak to him for Adonijah. And the king rose up to meet her, and bowed himself to her, and sat down on his throne, and caused a seat to be set for the king's mother; and she sat on his right hand. ²⁰Then she said, I desire one small petition of you; I pray you, say me not no. And the king said to her, Ask on, my mother: for I will not say you no. ²¹And she said, Let Abishag the Shunammite be given to Adonijah your brother to wife. ²²And king Solomon answered and said to his mother, And why do you ask Abishag the Shunammite for Adonijah? ask for him the kingdom also; for he is my elder brother; even for him, and for Abiathar the priest, and for Joab the son of Zeruiah. ²³Then king Solomon swore by the LORD, saying, God do so to me, and more also, if Adonijah have not spoken this word against his own life. ²⁴Now therefore, as the LORD lives, which has established me, and set me on the throne of David my father, and who has made me an house, as he promised, Adonijah shall be put to death this day. ²⁵And king Solomon sent by the hand of Benaiah the son of Jehoiada; and he fell on him that he died. ²⁶And to Abiathar the priest said the king, Get you to Anathoth, to your own fields; for you are worthy of death: but I will not at this time put you to death, because you bore the ark of the LORD God before David my father, and because you have been afflicted in all wherein my father was afflicted. ²⁷So Solomon thrust out Abiathar from being priest to the LORD; that he might fulfill the word of the LORD, which he spoke concerning the house of Eli in Shiloh. ²⁸Then tidings came to Joab: for Joab had turned after Adonijah, though he turned not after Absalom. And Joab fled to the tabernacle of the LORD, and caught hold on the horns of the altar. ²⁹And it was told king Solomon that Joab was fled to the tabernacle of the LORD; and, behold, he is by the altar. Then Solomon sent Benaiah the son of Jehoiada, saying, Go, fall on him. ³⁰And Benaiah came to the tabernacle of the LORD, and said to him, Thus says the king, Come forth. And he said, No; but I will die here. And Benaiah brought the king word again, saying, Thus said Joab, and thus he answered me. ³¹And the king said to him, Do as he has said, and fall on him, and bury him; that you may take away the innocent blood, which Joab shed, from me, and from the house of my father. ³²And the LORD shall return his blood on his own head, who fell on two men more righteous and better than he, and slew them with the sword, my father David not knowing thereof, to wit, Abner the son of Ner, captain of the host of Israel, and Amasa the son of Jether, captain of the host of Judah. ³³Their blood shall therefore return on the head of Joab, and on the head of his seed for ever: but on David, and on his seed, and on his house, and on his throne, shall there be peace for ever from the LORD. ³⁴So Benaiah the son of Jehoiada went up, and fell on him, and slew him: and he was buried in his own house in the wilderness. ³⁵And the king put Benaiah the son of Jehoiada in his room over the host: and Zadok the priest

did the king put in the room of Abiathar. ³⁶And the king sent and called for Shimei, and said to him, Build you an house in Jerusalem, and dwell there, and go not forth there any where. ³⁷For it shall be, that on the day you go out, and pass over the brook Kidron, you shall know for certain that you shall surely die: your blood shall be on your own head. ³⁸And Shimei said to the king, The saying is good: as my lord the king has said, so will your servant do. And Shimei dwelled in Jerusalem many days. ³⁹And it came to pass at the end of three years, that two of the servants of Shimei ran away to Achish son of Maachah king of Gath. And they told Shimei, saying, Behold, your servants be in Gath. ⁴⁰And Shimei arose, and saddled his ass, and went to Gath to Achish to seek his servants: and Shimei went, and brought his servants from Gath. ⁴¹And it was told Solomon that Shimei had gone from Jerusalem to Gath, and was come again. ⁴²And the king sent and called for Shimei, and said to him, Did I not make you to swear by the LORD, and protested to you, saying, Know for a certain, on the day you go out, and walk abroad any where, that you shall surely die? and you said to me, The word that I have heard is good. ⁴³Why then have you not kept the oath of the LORD, and the commandment that I have charged you with? ⁴⁴The king said moreover to Shimei, You know all the wickedness which your heart is privy to, that you did to David my father: therefore the LORD shall return your wickedness on your own head; ⁴⁵And king Solomon shall be blessed, and the throne of David shall be established before the LORD for ever. ⁴⁶So the king commanded Benaiah the son of Jehoiada; which went out, and fell on him, that he died. And the kingdom was established in the hand of Solomon.

3 ¹And Solomon made affinity with Pharaoh king of Egypt, and took Pharaoh's daughter, and brought her into the city of David, until he had made an end of building his own house, and the house of the LORD, and the wall of Jerusalem round about. ²Only the people sacrificed in high places, because there was no house built to the name of the LORD, until those days. ³And Solomon loved the LORD, walking in the statutes of David his father: only he sacrificed and burnt incense in high places. ⁴And the king went to Gibeon to sacrifice there; for that was the great high place: a thousand burnt offerings did Solomon offer on that altar. ⁵In Gibeon the LORD appeared to Solomon in a dream by night: and God said, Ask what I shall give you. ⁶And Solomon said, You have showed to your servant David my father great mercy, according as he walked before you in truth, and in righteousness, and in uprightness of heart with you; and you have kept for him this great kindness, that you have given him a son to sit on his throne, as it is this day. ⁷And now, O LORD my God, you have made your servant king instead of David my father: and I am but a little child: I know not how to go out or come in. ⁸And your servant is in the middle of your people which you have chosen, a great people, that cannot be numbered nor counted for multitude. ⁹Give therefore your servant an understanding heart to judge your people, that I may discern between good and bad: for who is able to judge this your so great a people? ¹⁰And the speech pleased the LORD, that Solomon had asked this thing. ¹¹And God said to him, Because you have asked this thing, and have not asked for yourself long life; neither have asked riches for yourself, nor have asked the life of your enemies; but have asked for yourself understanding to discern judgment; ¹²Behold, I have done according to your words: see, I have given you a wise and an understanding heart; so that there was none like you before you, neither after you shall any arise like to you. ¹³And I have also given you that which you have not asked, both riches, and honor: so that there shall not be any among the kings like to you all your days. ¹⁴And if you will walk in my ways, to keep my statutes and my commandments, as your father David did walk, then I will lengthen your days. ¹⁵And Solomon awoke; and, behold, it was a dream. And he came to Jerusalem, and stood before the ark of the covenant of the LORD, and offered up burnt offerings, and offered peace offerings, and made a feast to all his servants. ¹⁶Then came there two women, that were harlots, to the king, and stood before him. ¹⁷And the one woman said, O my lord, I and this woman dwell in one house; and I was delivered of a child with her in the house. ¹⁸And it came to pass the third day after that I was delivered, that this woman was delivered also: and we were together; there was no stranger with us in the house, save we two in the house. ¹⁹And this woman's child died in the night; because she overlaid it. ²⁰And she arose at midnight, and took my son from beside me, while your handmaid slept, and laid it in her bosom, and laid her dead child in my bosom. ²¹And when I rose in the morning to give my child suck, behold, it was dead: but when I had considered it in the morning, behold, it was not my son, which I did bear. ²²And the other woman said, No; but the living is my son, and the dead is your son. And this said, No; but the dead is your son, and the living is my son. Thus they spoke before the king. ²³Then said the king, The one says, This is my son that lives, and your son is the dead: and the other says, No; but your son is the dead, and my son is the living. ²⁴And the king said, Bring me a sword. And they brought a sword before the king. ²⁵And the king said, Divide the living child in two, and give half to the one, and half to the other. ²⁶Then spoke the woman whose the living child was to the king, for her bowels yearned on her son, and she said, O my lord, give her the living child, and in no wise slay it. But the other said, Let it be neither my nor yours, but divide it. ²⁷Then the king answered and said, Give her the living child, and in no wise slay it: she is the mother thereof. ²⁸And all Israel heard of the judgment which the king had judged; and they feared the king: for they saw that the wisdom of God was in him, to do judgment.

4 ¹So king Solomon was king over all Israel. ²And these were the princes which he had; Azariah the son of Zadok the priest, ³Elihoreph and Ahiah, the sons of Shisha, scribes; Jehoshaphat the son of Ahilud, the recorder. ⁴And Benaiah the son of Jehoiada was over the host: and Zadok and Abiathar were the priests: ⁵And Azariah the son of Nathan was over the officers: and Zabud the son of Nathan was principal officer, and the king's friend: ⁶And Ahishar was over the household: and Adoniram the son of Abda was over the tribute. ⁷And Solomon had twelve officers over all Israel, which provided victuals for the king and his household: each man his month in a year made provision. ⁸And these are their names: The son of Hur, in mount Ephraim: ⁹The son of Dekar, in Makaz, and in Shaalbim, and

Bethshemesh, and Elonbethhanan: ¹⁰The son of Hesed, in Aruboth; to him pertained Sochoh, and all the land of Hepher: ¹¹The son of Abinadab, in all the region of Dor; which had Taphath the daughter of Solomon to wife: ¹²Baana the son of Ahilud; to him pertained Taanach and Megiddo, and all Bethshean, which is by Zartanah beneath Jezreel, from Bethshean to Abelmeholah, even to the place that is beyond Jokneam: ¹³The son of Geber, in Ramothgilead; to him pertained the towns of Jair the son of Manasseh, which are in Gilead; to him also pertained the region of Argob, which is in Bashan, three score great cities with walls and brazen bars: ¹⁴Ahinadab the son of Iddo had Mahanaim: ¹⁵Ahimaaz was in Naphtali; he also took Basmath the daughter of Solomon to wife: ¹⁶Baanah the son of Hushai was in Asher and in Aloth: ¹⁷Jehoshaphat the son of Paruah, in Issachar: ¹⁸Shimei the son of Elah, in Benjamin: ¹⁹Geber the son of Uri was in the country of Gilead, in the country of Sihon king of the Amorites, and of Og king of Bashan; and he was the only officer which was in the land. ²⁰Judah and Israel were many, as the sand which is by the sea in multitude, eating and drinking, and making merry. ²¹And Solomon reigned over all kingdoms from the river to the land of the Philistines, and to the border of Egypt: they brought presents, and served Solomon all the days of his life. ²²And Solomon's provision for one day was thirty measures of fine flour, and three score measures of meal, ²³Ten fat oxen, and twenty oxen out of the pastures, and an hundred sheep, beside harts, and roebucks, and fallow deer, and fatted fowl. ²⁴For he had dominion over all the region on this side the river, from Tiphsah even to Azzah, over all the kings on this side the river: and he had peace on all sides round about him. ²⁵And Judah and Israel dwelled safely, every man under his vine and under his fig tree, from Dan even to Beersheba, all the days of Solomon. ²⁶And Solomon had forty thousand stalls of horses for his chariots, and twelve thousand horsemen. ²⁷And those officers provided victual for king Solomon, and for all that came to king Solomon's table, every man in his month: they lacked nothing. ²⁸Barley also and straw for the horses and dromedaries brought they to the place where the officers were, every man according to his charge. ²⁹And God gave Solomon wisdom and understanding exceeding much, and largeness of heart, even as the sand that is on the sea shore. ³⁰And Solomon's wisdom excelled the wisdom of all the children of the east country, and all the wisdom of Egypt. ³¹For he was wiser than all men; than Ethan the Ezrahite, and Heman, and Chalcol, and Darda, the sons of Mahol: and his fame was in all nations round about. ³²And he spoke three thousand proverbs: and his songs were a thousand and five. ³³And he spoke of trees, from the cedar tree that is in Lebanon even to the hyssop that springs out of the wall: he spoke also of beasts, and of fowl, and of creeping things, and of fishes. ³⁴And there came of all people to hear the wisdom of Solomon, from all kings of the earth, which had heard of his wisdom.

5

¹And Hiram king of Tyre sent his servants to Solomon; for he had heard that they had anointed him king in the room of his father: for Hiram was ever a lover of David. ²And Solomon sent to Hiram, saying, ³You know how that David my father could not build an house to the name of the LORD his God for the wars which were about him on every side, until the LORD put them under the soles of his feet. ⁴But now the LORD my God has given me rest on every side, so that there is neither adversary nor evil result. ⁵And, behold, I purpose to build an house to the name of the LORD my God, as the LORD spoke to David my father, saying, Your son, whom I will set on your throne in your room, he shall build an house to my name. ⁶Now therefore command you that they hew me cedar trees out of Lebanon; and my servants shall be with your servants: and to you will I give hire for your servants according to all that you shall appoint: for you know that there is not among us any that can skill to hew timber like to the Sidonians. ⁷And it came to pass, when Hiram heard the words of Solomon, that he rejoiced greatly, and said, Blessed be the LORD this day, which has given to David a wise son over this great people. ⁸And Hiram sent to Solomon, saying, I have considered the things which you sent to me for: and I will do all your desire concerning timber of cedar, and concerning timber of fir. ⁹My servants shall bring them down from Lebanon to the sea: and I will convey them by sea in floats to the place that you shall appoint me, and will cause them to be discharged there, and you shall receive them: and you shall accomplish my desire, in giving food for my household. ¹⁰So Hiram gave Solomon cedar trees and fir trees according to all his desire. ¹¹And Solomon gave Hiram twenty thousand measures of wheat for food to his household, and twenty measures of pure oil: thus gave Solomon to Hiram year by year. ¹²And the LORD gave Solomon wisdom, as he promised him: and there was peace between Hiram and Solomon; and they two made a league together. ¹³And king Solomon raised a levy out of all Israel; and the levy was thirty thousand men. ¹⁴And he sent them to Lebanon, ten thousand a month by courses: a month they were in Lebanon, and two months at home: and Adoniram was over the levy. ¹⁵And Solomon had three score and ten thousand that bore burdens, and fourscore thousand hewers in the mountains; ¹⁶Beside the chief of Solomon's officers which were over the work, three thousand and three hundred, which ruled over the people that worked in the work. ¹⁷And the king commanded, and they brought great stones, costly stones, and hewed stones, to lay the foundation of the house. ¹⁸And Solomon's builders and Hiram's builders did hew them, and the stone squarers: so they prepared timber and stones to build the house.

6

¹And it came to pass in the four hundred and eightieth year after the children of Israel were come out of the land of Egypt, in the fourth year of Solomon's reign over Israel, in the month Zif, which is the second month, that he began to build the house of the LORD. ²And the house which king Solomon built for the LORD, the length thereof was three score cubits, and the breadth thereof twenty cubits, and the height thereof thirty cubits. ³And the porch before the temple of the house, twenty cubits was the length thereof, according to the breadth of the house; and ten cubits was the breadth thereof before the house. ⁴And for the house he made windows of narrow lights. ⁵And against the wall of the house he built chambers round about, against the walls of the house round about, both of the temple and of the oracle: and he made chambers round about: ⁶The nethermost chamber was five cubits broad, and the middle was six

cubits broad, and the third was seven cubits broad: for without in the wall of the house he made narrowed rests round about, that the beams should not be fastened in the walls of the house. ⁷And the house, when it was in building, was built of stone made ready before it was brought thither: so that there was neither hammer nor ax nor any tool of iron heard in the house, while it was in building. ⁸The door for the middle chamber was in the right side of the house: and they went up with winding stairs into the middle chamber, and out of the middle into the third. ⁹So he built the house, and finished it; and covered the house with beams and boards of cedar. ¹⁰And then he built chambers against all the house, five cubits high: and they rested on the house with timber of cedar. ¹¹And the word of the LORD came to Solomon, saying, ¹²Concerning this house which you are in building, if you will walk in my statutes, and execute my judgments, and keep all my commandments to walk in them; then will I perform my word with you, which I spoke to David your father: ¹³And I will dwell among the children of Israel, and will not forsake my people Israel. ¹⁴So Solomon built the house, and finished it. ¹⁵And he built the walls of the house within with boards of cedar, both the floor of the house, and the walls of the ceiling: and he covered them on the inside with wood, and covered the floor of the house with planks of fir. ¹⁶And he built twenty cubits on the sides of the house, both the floor and the walls with boards of cedar: he even built them for it within, even for the oracle, even for the most holy place. ¹⁷And the house, that is, the temple before it, was forty cubits long. ¹⁸And the cedar of the house within was carved with knops and open flowers: all was cedar; there was no stone seen. ¹⁹And the oracle he prepared in the house within, to set there the ark of the covenant of the LORD. ²⁰And the oracle in the forepart was twenty cubits in length, and twenty cubits in breadth, and twenty cubits in the height thereof: and he overlaid it with pure gold; and so covered the altar which was of cedar. ²¹So Solomon overlaid the house within with pure gold: and he made a partition by the chains of gold before the oracle; and he overlaid it with gold. ²²And the whole house he overlaid with gold, until he had finished all the house: also the whole altar that was by the oracle he overlaid with gold. ²³And within the oracle he made two cherubim of olive tree, each ten cubits high. ²⁴And five cubits was the one wing of the cherub, and five cubits the other wing of the cherub: from the uttermost part of the one wing to the uttermost part of the other were ten cubits. ²⁵And the other cherub was ten cubits: both the cherubim were of one measure and one size. ²⁶The height of the one cherub was ten cubits, and so was it of the other cherub. ²⁷And he set the cherubim within the inner house: and they stretched forth the wings of the cherubim, so that the wing of the one touched the one wall, and the wing of the other cherub touched the other wall; and their wings touched one another in the middle of the house. ²⁸And he overlaid the cherubim with gold. ²⁹And he carved all the walls of the house round about with carved figures of cherubim and palm trees and open flowers, within and without. ³⁰And the floors of the house he overlaid with gold, within and without. ³¹And for the entering of the oracle he made doors of olive tree: the lintel and side posts were a fifth part of the wall. ³²The two doors also were of olive tree; and he carved on them carvings of cherubim and palm trees and open flowers, and overlaid them with gold, and spread gold on the cherubim, and on the palm trees. ³³So also made he for the door of the temple posts of olive tree, a fourth part of the wall. ³⁴And the two doors were of fir tree: the two leaves of the one door were folding, and the two leaves of the other door were folding. ³⁵And he carved thereon cherubim and palm trees and open flowers: and covered them with gold fitted on the carved work. ³⁶And he built the inner court with three rows of hewed stone, and a row of cedar beams. ³⁷In the fourth year was the foundation of the house of the LORD laid, in the month Zif: ³⁸And in the eleventh year, in the month Bul, which is the eighth month, was the house finished throughout all the parts thereof, and according to all the fashion of it. So was he seven years in building it.

7 ¹But Solomon was building his own house thirteen years, and he finished all his house. ²He built also the house of the forest of Lebanon; the length thereof was an hundred cubits, and the breadth thereof fifty cubits, and the height thereof thirty cubits, on four rows of cedar pillars, with cedar beams on the pillars. ³And it was covered with cedar above on the beams, that lay on forty five pillars, fifteen in a row. ⁴And there were windows in three rows, and light was against light in three ranks. ⁵And all the doors and posts were square, with the windows: and light was against light in three ranks. ⁶And he made a porch of pillars; the length thereof was fifty cubits, and the breadth thereof thirty cubits: and the porch was before them: and the other pillars and the thick beam were before them. ⁷Then he made a porch for the throne where he might judge, even the porch of judgment: and it was covered with cedar from one side of the floor to the other. ⁸And his house where he dwelled had another court within the porch, which was of the like work. Solomon made also an house for Pharaoh's daughter, whom he had taken to wife, like to this porch. ⁹All these were of costly stones, according to the measures of hewed stones, sawed with saws, within and without, even from the foundation to the coping, and so on the outside toward the great court. ¹⁰And the foundation was of costly stones, even great stones, stones of ten cubits, and stones of eight cubits. ¹¹And above were costly stones, after the measures of hewed stones, and cedars. ¹²And the great court round about was with three rows of hewed stones, and a row of cedar beams, both for the inner court of the house of the LORD, and for the porch of the house. ¹³And king Solomon sent and fetched Hiram out of Tyre. ¹⁴He was a widow's son of the tribe of Naphtali, and his father was a man of Tyre, a worker in brass: and he was filled with wisdom, and understanding, and cunning to work all works in brass. And he came to king Solomon, and worked all his work. ¹⁵For he cast two pillars of brass, of eighteen cubits high apiece: and a line of twelve cubits did compass either of them about. ¹⁶And he made two capitals of molten brass, to set on the tops of the pillars: the height of the one capital was five cubits, and the height of the other capital was five cubits: ¹⁷And nets of checker work, and wreaths of chain work, for the capitals which were on the top of the pillars; seven for the one capital, and seven for the other capital. ¹⁸And he made the pillars, and two rows round about on the one network, to cover the capitals that

were on the top, with pomegranates: and so did he for the other capital. ¹⁹And the capitals that were on the top of the pillars were of lily work in the porch, four cubits. ²⁰And the capitals on the two pillars had pomegranates also above, over against the belly which was by the network: and the pomegranates were two hundred in rows round about on the other capital. ²¹And he set up the pillars in the porch of the temple: and he set up the right pillar, and called the name thereof Jachin: and he set up the left pillar, and called the name thereof Boaz. ²²And on the top of the pillars was lily work: so was the work of the pillars finished. ²³And he made a molten sea, ten cubits from the one brim to the other: it was round all about, and his height was five cubits: and a line of thirty cubits did compass it round about. ²⁴And under the brim of it round about there were knops compassing it, ten in a cubit, compassing the sea round about: the knops were cast in two rows, when it was cast. ²⁵It stood on twelve oxen, three looking toward the north, and three looking toward the west, and three looking toward the south, and three looking toward the east: and the sea was set above on them, and all their hinder parts were inward. ²⁶And it was an hand breadth thick, and the brim thereof was worked like the brim of a cup, with flowers of lilies: it contained two thousand baths. ²⁷And he made ten bases of brass; four cubits was the length of one base, and four cubits the breadth thereof, and three cubits the height of it. ²⁸And the work of the bases was on this manner: they had borders, and the borders were between the ledges: ²⁹And on the borders that were between the ledges were lions, oxen, and cherubim: and on the ledges there was a base above: and beneath the lions and oxen were certain additions made of thin work. ³⁰And every base had four brazen wheels, and plates of brass: and the four corners thereof had supports: under the laver were supports molten, at the side of every addition. ³¹And the mouth of it within the capital and above was a cubit: but the mouth thereof was round after the work of the base, a cubit and an half: and also on the mouth of it were engravings with their borders, foursquare, not round. ³²And under the borders were four wheels; and the axletrees of the wheels were joined to the base: and the height of a wheel was a cubit and half a cubit. ³³And the work of the wheels was like the work of a chariot wheel: their axletrees, and their naves, and their felloes, and their spokes, were all molten. ³⁴And there were four supports to the four corners of one base: and the supports were of the very base itself. ³⁵And in the top of the base was there a round compass of half a cubit high: and on the top of the base the ledges thereof and the borders thereof were of the same. ³⁶For on the plates of the ledges thereof, and on the borders thereof, he graved cherubim, lions, and palm trees, according to the proportion of every one, and additions round about. ³⁷After this manner he made the ten bases: all of them had one casting, one measure, and one size. ³⁸Then made he ten lavers of brass: one laver contained forty baths: and every laver was four cubits: and on every one of the ten bases one laver. ³⁹And he put five bases on the right side of the house, and five on the left side of the house: and he set the sea on the right side of the house eastward over against the south. ⁴⁰And Hiram made the lavers, and the shovels, and the basins. So Hiram made an end of doing all the work that he made king Solomon for the house of the LORD: ⁴¹The two pillars, and the two bowls of the capitals that were on the top of the two pillars; and the two networks, to cover the two bowls of the capitals which were on the top of the pillars; ⁴²And four hundred pomegranates for the two networks, even two rows of pomegranates for one network, to cover the two bowls of the capitals that were on the pillars; ⁴³And the ten bases, and ten lavers on the bases; ⁴⁴And one sea, and twelve oxen under the sea; ⁴⁵And the pots, and the shovels, and the basins: and all these vessels, which Hiram made to king Solomon for the house of the LORD, were of bright brass. ⁴⁶In the plain of Jordan did the king cast them, in the clay ground between Succoth and Zarthan. ⁴⁷And Solomon left all the vessels unweighed, because they were exceeding many: neither was the weight of the brass found out. ⁴⁸And Solomon made all the vessels that pertained to the house of the LORD: the altar of gold, and the table of gold, whereupon the show bread was, ⁴⁹And the candlesticks of pure gold, five on the right side, and five on the left, before the oracle, with the flowers, and the lamps, and the tongs of gold, ⁵⁰And the bowls, and the snuffers, and the basins, and the spoons, and the censers of pure gold; and the hinges of gold, both for the doors of the inner house, the most holy place, and for the doors of the house, to wit, of the temple. ⁵¹So was ended all the work that king Solomon made for the house of the LORD. And Solomon brought in the things which David his father had dedicated; even the silver, and the gold, and the vessels, did he put among the treasures of the house of the LORD.

8 ¹Then Solomon assembled the elders of Israel, and all the heads of the tribes, the chief of the fathers of the children of Israel, to king Solomon in Jerusalem, that they might bring up the ark of the covenant of the LORD out of the city of David, which is Zion. ²And all the men of Israel assembled themselves to king Solomon at the feast in the month Ethanim, which is the seventh month. ³And all the elders of Israel came, and the priests took up the ark. ⁴And they brought up the ark of the LORD, and the tabernacle of the congregation, and all the holy vessels that were in the tabernacle, even those did the priests and the Levites bring up. ⁵And king Solomon, and all the congregation of Israel, that were assembled to him, were with him before the ark, sacrificing sheep and oxen, that could not be told nor numbered for multitude. ⁶And the priests brought in the ark of the covenant of the LORD to his place, into the oracle of the house, to the most holy place, even under the wings of the cherubim. ⁷For the cherubim spread forth their two wings over the place of the ark, and the cherubim covered the ark and the staves thereof above. ⁸And they drew out the staves, that the ends of the staves were seen out in the holy place before the oracle, and they were not seen without: and there they are to this day. ⁹There was nothing in the ark save the two tables of stone, which Moses put there at Horeb, when the LORD made a covenant with the children of Israel, when they came out of the land of Egypt. ¹⁰And it came to pass, when the priests were come out of the holy place, that the cloud filled the house of the LORD, ¹¹So that the priests could not stand to minister because of the cloud: for the glory of the LORD had filled the house of the LORD. ¹²Then spoke Solomon, The LORD said that he would dwell in the thick darkness. ¹³I have surely built you an house to dwell in, a settled place for you to abide in for ever. ¹⁴And the king turned his face about, and blessed all the congregation of Israel: (and all the congregation of Israel stood;) ¹⁵And he said, Blessed be the LORD God of Israel, which spoke with his mouth to David my father, and has with his hand fulfilled it, saying, ¹⁶Since the day that I brought forth my people Israel out of Egypt, I chose no city out of all the tribes of Israel to build an house, that my name might be therein; but I chose David to be over my people Israel. ¹⁷And it was in the heart of David my father to build an house for the name of the LORD God of Israel. ¹⁸And the LORD said to David my father, Whereas it was in your heart to build an house to my name, you did well that it was in your heart. ¹⁹Nevertheless you shall not build the house; but your son that shall come forth out of your loins, he shall build the house to my name. ²⁰And the LORD has performed his word that he spoke, and I am risen up in the room of David my father, and sit on the throne of Israel, as the LORD promised, and have built an house for the name of the LORD God of Israel. ²¹And I have set there a place for the ark, wherein is the covenant of the LORD, which he made with our fathers, when he brought them out of the land of Egypt. ²²And Solomon stood before the altar of the LORD in the presence of all the congregation of Israel, and spread forth his hands toward heaven: ²³And he said, LORD God of Israel, there is no God like you, in heaven above, or on earth beneath, who keep covenant and mercy with your servants that walk before you with all their heart: ²⁴Who have kept with your servant David my father that you promised him: you spoke also with your mouth, and have fulfilled it with your hand, as it is this day. ²⁵Therefore now, LORD God of Israel, keep with your servant David my father that you promised him, saying, There shall not fail you a man in my sight to sit on the throne of Israel; so that your children take heed to their way, that they walk before me as you have walked before me. ²⁶And now, O God of Israel, let your word, I pray you, be verified, which you spoke to your servant David my father. ²⁷But will God indeed dwell on the earth? behold, the heaven and heaven of heavens cannot contain you; how much less this house that I have built? ²⁸Yet have you respect to the prayer of your servant, and to his supplication, O LORD my God, to listen to the cry and to the prayer, which your servant prays before you to day: ²⁹That your eyes may be open toward this house night and day, even toward the place of which you have said, My name shall be there: that you may listen to the prayer which your servant shall make toward this place. ³⁰And listen you to the supplication of your servant, and of your people Israel, when they shall pray toward this place: and hear you in heaven your dwelling place: and when you hear, forgive. ³¹If any man trespass against his neighbor, and an oath be laid on him to cause him to swear, and the oath come before your altar in this house: ³²Then hear you in heaven, and do, and judge your servants, condemning the wicked, to bring his way on his head; and justifying the righteous, to give him according to his righteousness. ³³When your people Israel be smitten down before the enemy, because they have sinned against you, and shall turn again to you, and confess your name, and pray, and make supplication to you in this house: ³⁴Then hear you in heaven, and forgive the sin of your people Israel, and bring them again to the land which you gave to their fathers. ³⁵When heaven is shut up, and there is no rain, because they have sinned against you; if they pray toward this place, and confess your name, and turn from their sin, when you afflict them: ³⁶Then hear you in heaven, and forgive the sin of your servants, and of your people Israel, that you teach them the good way wherein they should walk, and give rain on your land, which you have given to your people for an inheritance. ³⁷If there be in the land famine, if there be pestilence, blasting, mildew, locust, or if there be caterpillar; if their enemy besiege them in the land of their cities; whatever plague, whatever sickness there be; ³⁸What prayer and supplication soever be made by any man, or by all your people Israel, which shall know every man the plague of his own heart, and spread forth his hands toward this house: ³⁹Then hear you in heaven your dwelling place, and forgive, and do, and give to every man according to his ways, whose heart you know; (for you, even you only, know the hearts of all the children of men;) ⁴⁰That they may fear you all the days that they live in the land which you gave to our fathers. ⁴¹Moreover concerning a stranger, that is not of your people Israel, but comes out of a far country for your name's sake; ⁴²(For they shall hear of your great name, and of your strong hand, and of your stretched out arm;) when he shall come and pray toward this house; ⁴³Hear you in heaven your dwelling place, and do according to all that the stranger calls to you for: that all people of the earth may know your name, to fear you, as do your people Israel; and that they may know that this house, which I have built, is called by your name. ⁴⁴If your people go out to battle against their enemy, wherever you shall send them, and shall pray to the LORD toward the city which you have chosen, and toward the house that I have built for your name: ⁴⁵Then hear you in heaven their prayer and their supplication, and maintain their cause. ⁴⁶If they sin against you, (for there is no man that sins not,) and you be angry with them, and deliver them to the enemy, so that they carry them away captives to the land of the enemy, far or near; ⁴⁷Yet if they shall bethink themselves in the land where they were carried captives, and repent, and make supplication to you in the land of them that carried them captives, saying, We have sinned, and have done perversely, we have committed wickedness; ⁴⁸And so return to you with all their heart, and with all their soul, in the land of their enemies, which led them away captive, and pray to you toward their land, which you gave to their fathers, the city which you have chosen, and the house which I have built for your name: ⁴⁹Then hear you their prayer and their supplication in heaven your dwelling place, and maintain their cause, ⁵⁰And forgive your people that have sinned against you, and all their transgressions wherein they have transgressed against you, and give them compassion before them who carried them captive, that they may have compassion on them: ⁵¹For they be your people, and your inheritance, which you brought forth out of Egypt, from the middle of the furnace of iron: ⁵²That your eyes may be open to the supplication of your servant, and to the supplication of your people Israel, to listen to them in all that they call for to you. ⁵³For you did separate them from among all the people of the earth, to be your inheritance, as you spoke by the hand of Moses your servant, when you brought our fathers out of Egypt, O LORD God. ⁵⁴And it was so, that when Solomon had made an end of praying all this prayer and supplication to the LORD, he arose from before the altar of the LORD, from kneeling on his knees with his hands spread up to heaven. ⁵⁵And he stood, and blessed all the congregation of Israel with a loud voice, saying, ⁵⁶Blessed be the LORD, that has given rest to his people Israel, according to all that he promised: there has not failed one word of all his good promise, which he promised by the hand of Moses his servant. ⁵⁷The LORD our God be with us, as he was with our fathers: let him not leave us, nor forsake us: ⁵⁸That he may incline our hearts to him, to walk in all his ways, and to keep his commandments, and his statutes, and his judgments, which he commanded our fathers. ⁵⁹And let these my words, with which I have made supplication before the LORD, be near to the LORD our God day and night, that he maintain the cause of his servant, and the cause of his people Israel at all times, as the matter shall require: ⁶⁰That all the people of the earth may know that the LORD is God, and that there is none else. ⁶¹Let your heart therefore be perfect with the LORD our God, to walk in his statutes, and to keep his commandments, as at this day. ⁶²And the king, and all Israel with him, offered sacrifice before the LORD. ⁶³And Solomon offered a sacrifice of peace offerings, which he offered to the LORD, two and twenty thousand oxen, and an hundred and twenty thousand sheep. So the king and all the children of Israel dedicated the house of the LORD. ⁶⁴The same day did the king hallow the middle of the court that was before the house of the LORD: for there he offered burnt offerings, and meat offerings, and the fat of the peace offerings: because the brazen altar that was before the LORD was too little to receive the burnt offerings, and meat offerings, and the fat of the peace offerings. ⁶⁵And at that time Solomon held a feast, and all Israel with him, a great congregation, from the entering in of Hamath to the river of Egypt, before the LORD our God, seven days and seven days, even fourteen days. ⁶⁶On the eighth day he sent the people away: and they blessed the king, and went to their tents joyful and glad of heart for all the goodness that the LORD had done for David his servant, and for Israel his people.

9

¹And it came to pass, when Solomon had finished the building of the house of the LORD, and the king's house, and all Solomon's desire which he was pleased to do, ²That the LORD appeared to Solomon the second time, as he had appeared to him at Gibeon. ³And the LORD said to him, I have heard your prayer and your supplication, that you have made before me: I have hallowed this house, which you have built, to put my name there for ever; and my eyes and my heart shall be there perpetually. ⁴And if you will walk before me, as David your father walked, in integrity of heart, and in uprightness, to do according to all that I have commanded you, and will keep my statutes and my judgments: ⁵Then I will establish the throne of your kingdom on Israel for ever, as I promised to David your father, saying, There shall not fail you a man on the throne of Israel. ⁶But if you shall at all turn from following me, you or your children, and will not keep my commandments and my statutes which I have set before you, but go and serve other gods, and worship them: ⁷Then will I cut off Israel out of the land which I have given them; and this house, which I have hallowed for my name, will I cast out of my sight; and Israel shall be a proverb and a byword among all people: ⁸And at this house, which is high, every one that passes by it shall be astonished, and shall hiss; and they shall say, Why has the LORD done thus to this land, and to this house? ⁹And they shall answer, Because they forsook the LORD their God, who brought forth their fathers out of the land of Egypt, and have taken hold on other gods, and have worshipped them, and served them: therefore has the LORD brought on them all this evil. ¹⁰And it came to pass at the end of twenty years, when Solomon had built the two houses, the house of the LORD, and the king's house, ¹¹(Now Hiram the king of Tyre had furnished Solomon with cedar trees and fir trees, and with gold, according to all his desire,) that then king Solomon gave Hiram twenty cities in the land of Galilee. ¹²And Hiram came out from Tyre to see the cities which Solomon had given him; and they pleased him not. ¹³And he said, What cities are these which you have given me, my brother? And he called them the land of Cabul to this day. ¹⁴And Hiram sent to the king six score talents of gold. ¹⁵And this is the reason of the levy which king Solomon raised; for to build the house of the LORD, and his own house, and Millo, and the wall of Jerusalem, and Hazor, and Megiddo, and Gezer. ¹⁶For Pharaoh king of Egypt had gone up, and taken Gezer, and burnt it with fire, and slain the Canaanites that dwelled in the city, and given it for a present to his daughter, Solomon's wife. ¹⁷And Solomon built Gezer, and Bethhoron the nether, ¹⁸And Baalath, and Tadmor in the wilderness, in the land, ¹⁹And all the cities of store that Solomon had, and cities for his chariots, and cities for his horsemen, and that which Solomon desired to build in Jerusalem, and in Lebanon, and in all the land of his dominion. ²⁰And all the people that were left of the Amorites, Hittites, Perizzites, Hivites, and Jebusites, which were not of the children of Israel, ²¹Their children that were left after them in the land, whom the children of Israel also were not able utterly to destroy, on those did Solomon levy a tribute of slavery to this day. ²²But of the children of Israel did Solomon make no slaves: but they were men of war, and his servants, and his princes, and his captains, and rulers of his chariots, and his horsemen. ²³These were the chief of the officers that were over Solomon's work, five hundred and fifty, which bore rule over the people that worked in the work. ²⁴But Pharaoh's daughter came up out of the city of David to her house which Solomon had built for her: then did he build Millo. ²⁵And three times in a year did Solomon offer burnt offerings and peace offerings on the altar which he built to the LORD, and he burnt incense on the altar that was before the LORD. So he finished the house. ²⁶And king Solomon made a navy of ships in Eziongeber, which is beside Eloth, on the shore of the Red sea, in the land of Edom. ²⁷And Hiram sent in the navy his servants, shipmen that had knowledge of the sea, with the servants of Solomon. ²⁸And they came to Ophir, and fetched from there gold, four hundred and twenty talents, and brought it to king Solomon.

10

¹And when the queen of Sheba heard of the fame of Solomon concerning the name of the LORD, she came to prove him with hard questions. ²And she came to

Jerusalem with a very great train, with camels that bore spices, and very much gold, and precious stones: and when she was come to Solomon, she communed with him of all that was in her heart. ³And Solomon told her all her questions: there was not any thing hid from the king, which he told her not. ⁴And when the queen of Sheba had seen all Solomon's wisdom, and the house that he had built, ⁵And the meat of his table, and the sitting of his servants, and the attendance of his ministers, and their apparel, and his cupbearers, and his ascent by which he went up to the house of the LORD; there was no more spirit in her. ⁶And she said to the king, It was a true report that I heard in my own land of your acts and of your wisdom. ⁷However, I believed not the words, until I came, and my eyes had seen it: and, behold, the half was not told me: your wisdom and prosperity exceeds the fame which I heard. ⁸Happy are your men, happy are these your servants, which stand continually before you, and that hear your wisdom. ⁹Blessed be the LORD your God, which delighted in you, to set you on the throne of Israel: because the LORD loved Israel for ever, therefore made he you king, to do judgment and justice. ¹⁰And she gave the king an hundred and twenty talents of gold, and of spices very great store, and precious stones: there came no more such abundance of spices as these which the queen of Sheba gave to king Solomon. ¹¹And the navy also of Hiram, that brought gold from Ophir, brought in from Ophir great plenty of almug trees, and precious stones. ¹²And the king made of the almug trees pillars for the house of the LORD, and for the king's house, harps also and psalteries for singers: there came no such almug trees, nor were seen to this day. ¹³And king Solomon gave to the queen of Sheba all her desire, whatever she asked, beside that which Solomon gave her of his royal bounty. So she turned and went to her own country, she and her servants. ¹⁴Now the weight of gold that came to Solomon in one year was six hundred three score and six talents of gold, ¹⁵Beside that he had of the merchants, and of the traffic of the spice merchants, and of all the kings of Arabia, and of the governors of the country. ¹⁶And king Solomon made two hundred targets of beaten gold: six hundred shekels of gold went to one target. ¹⁷And he made three hundred shields of beaten gold; three pound of gold went to one shield: and the king put them in the house of the forest of Lebanon. ¹⁸Moreover the king made a great throne of ivory, and overlaid it with the best gold. ¹⁹The throne had six steps, and the top of the throne was round behind: and there were stays on either side on the place of the seat, and two lions stood beside the stays. ²⁰And twelve lions stood there on the one side and on the other on the six steps: there was not the like made in any kingdom. ²¹And all king Solomon's drinking vessels were of gold, and all the vessels of the house of the forest of Lebanon were of pure gold; none were of silver: it was nothing accounted of in the days of Solomon. ²²For the king had at sea a navy of Tharshish with the navy of Hiram: once in three years came the navy of Tharshish, bringing gold, and silver, ivory, and apes, and peacocks. ²³So king Solomon exceeded all the kings of the earth for riches and for wisdom. ²⁴And all the earth sought to Solomon, to hear his wisdom, which God had put in his heart. ²⁵And they brought every man his present, vessels of silver, and vessels of gold, and garments, and armor, and spices, horses, and mules, a rate year by year. ²⁶And Solomon gathered together chariots and horsemen: and he had a thousand and four hundred chariots, and twelve thousand horsemen, whom he bestowed in the cities for chariots, and with the king at Jerusalem. ²⁷And the king made silver to be in Jerusalem as stones, and cedars made he to be as the sycomore trees that are in the vale, for abundance. ²⁸And Solomon had horses brought out of Egypt, and linen yarn: the king's merchants received the linen yarn at a price. ²⁹And a chariot came up and went out of Egypt for six hundred shekels of silver, and an horse for an hundred and fifty: and so for all the kings of the Hittites, and for the kings of Syria, did they bring them out by their means.

11 ¹But king Solomon loved many strange women, together with the daughter of Pharaoh, women of the Moabites, Ammonites, Edomites, Zidonians, and Hittites: ²Of the nations concerning which the LORD said to the children of Israel, You shall not go in to them, neither shall they come in to you: for surely they will turn away your heart after their gods: Solomon joined to these in love. ³And he had seven hundred wives, princesses, and three hundred concubines: and his wives turned away his heart. ⁴For it came to pass, when Solomon was old, that his wives turned away his heart after other gods: and his heart was not perfect with the LORD his God, as was the heart of David his father. ⁵For Solomon went after Ashtoreth the goddess of the Zidonians, and after Milcom the abomination of the Ammonites. ⁶And Solomon did evil in the sight of the LORD, and went not fully after the LORD, as did David his father. ⁷Then did Solomon build an high place for Chemosh, the abomination of Moab, in the hill that is before Jerusalem, and for Molech, the abomination of the children of Ammon. ⁸And likewise did he for all his strange wives, which burnt incense and sacrificed to their gods. ⁹And the LORD was angry with Solomon, because his heart was turned from the LORD God of Israel, which had appeared to him twice, ¹⁰And had commanded him concerning this thing, that he should not go after other gods: but he kept not that which the LORD commanded. ¹¹Why the LORD said to Solomon, For as much as this is done of you, and you have not kept my covenant and my statutes, which I have commanded you, I will surely rend the kingdom from you, and will give it to your servant. ¹²Notwithstanding in your days I will not do it for David your father's sake: but I will rend it out of the hand of your son. ¹³However, I will not rend away all the kingdom; but will give one tribe to your son for David my servant's sake, and for Jerusalem's sake which I have chosen. ¹⁴And the LORD stirred up an adversary to Solomon, Hadad the Edomite: he was of the king's seed in Edom. ¹⁵For it came to pass, when David was in Edom, and Joab the captain of the host was gone up to bury the slain, after he had smitten every male in Edom; ¹⁶(For six months did Joab remain there with all Israel, until he had cut off every male in Edom:) ¹⁷That Hadad fled, he and certain Edomites of his father's servants with him, to go into Egypt; Hadad being yet a little child. ¹⁸And they arose out of Midian, and came to Paran: and they took men with them out of Paran, and they came to Egypt, to Pharaoh king of Egypt; which gave him an house, and appointed him victuals, and gave him land. ¹⁹And Hadad found great favor in the sight of Pharaoh, so that he gave him to wife the sister of his own wife, the sister of Tahpenes the queen. ²⁰And the sister of Tahpenes bore him Genubath his son, whom Tahpenes weaned in Pharaoh's house: and Genubath was in Pharaoh's household among the sons of Pharaoh. ²¹And when Hadad heard in Egypt that David slept with his fathers, and that Joab the captain of the host was dead, Hadad said to Pharaoh, Let me depart, that I may go to my own country. ²²Then Pharaoh said to him, But what have you lacked with me, that, behold, you seek to go to your own country? And he answered, Nothing: however, let me go in any wise. ²³And God stirred him up another adversary, Rezon the son of Eliadah, which fled from his lord Hadadezer king of Zobah: ²⁴And he gathered men to him, and became captain over a band, when David slew them of Zobah: and they went to Damascus, and dwelled therein, and reigned in Damascus. ²⁵And he was an adversary to Israel all the days of Solomon, beside the mischief that Hadad did: and he abhorred Israel, and reigned over Syria. ²⁶And Jeroboam the son of Nebat, an Ephrathite of Zereda, Solomon's servant, whose mother's name was Zeruah, a widow woman, even he lifted up his hand against the king. ²⁷And this was the cause that he lifted up his hand against the king: Solomon built Millo, and repaired the breaches of the city of David his father. ²⁸And the man Jeroboam was a mighty man of valor: and Solomon seeing the young man that he was industrious, he made him ruler over all the charge of the house of Joseph. ²⁹And it came to pass at that time when Jeroboam went out of Jerusalem, that the prophet Ahijah the Shilonite found him in the way; and he had clad himself with a new garment; and they two were alone in the field: ³⁰And Ahijah caught the new garment that was on him, and rent it in twelve pieces: ³¹And he said to Jeroboam, Take you ten pieces: for thus says the LORD, the God of Israel, Behold, I will rend the kingdom out of the hand of Solomon, and will give ten tribes to you: ³²(But he shall have one tribe for my servant David's sake, and for Jerusalem's sake, the city which I have chosen out of all the tribes of Israel:) ³³Because that they have forsaken me, and have worshipped Ashtoreth the goddess of the Zidonians, Chemosh the god of the Moabites, and Milcom the god of the children of Ammon, and have not walked in my ways, to do that which is right in my eyes, and to keep my statutes and my judgments, as did David his father. ³⁴However, I will not take the whole kingdom out of his hand: but I will make him prince all the days of his life for David my servant's sake, whom I chose, because he kept my commandments and my statutes: ³⁵But I will take the kingdom out of his son's hand, and will give it to you, even ten tribes. ³⁶And to his son will I give one tribe, that David my servant may have a light always before me in Jerusalem, the city which I have chosen me to put my name there. ³⁷And I will take you, and you shall reign according to all that your soul desires, and shall be king over Israel. ³⁸And it shall be, if you will listen to all that I command you, and will walk in my ways, and do that is right in my sight, to keep my statutes and my commandments, as David my servant did; that I will be with you, and build you a sure house, as I built for David, and will give Israel to you. ³⁹And I will for this afflict the seed of David, but not for ever. ⁴⁰Solomon sought therefore to kill Jeroboam. And Jeroboam arose, and fled into Egypt, to Shishak king of Egypt, and was in Egypt until the death of Solomon. ⁴¹And the rest of the acts of Solomon, and all that he did, and his wisdom, are they not written in the book of the acts of Solomon? ⁴²And the time that Solomon reigned in Jerusalem over all Israel was forty years. ⁴³And Solomon slept with his fathers, and was buried in the city of David his father: and Rehoboam his son reigned in his stead.

12

¹And Rehoboam went to Shechem: for all Israel were come to Shechem to make him king. ²And it came to pass, when Jeroboam the son of Nebat, who was yet in Egypt, heard of it, (for he was fled from the presence of king Solomon, and Jeroboam dwelled in Egypt;) ³That they sent and called him. And Jeroboam and all the congregation of Israel came, and spoke to Rehoboam, saying, ⁴Your father made our yoke grievous: now therefore make you the grievous service of your father, and his heavy yoke which he put on us, lighter, and we will serve you. ⁵And he said to them, Depart yet for three days, then come again to me. And the people departed. ⁶And king Rehoboam consulted with the old men, that stood before Solomon his father while he yet lived, and said, How do you advise that I may answer this people? ⁷And they spoke to him, saying, If you will be a servant to this people this day, and will serve them, and answer them, and speak good words to them, then they will be your servants for ever. ⁸But he forsook the counsel of the old men, which they had given him, and consulted with the young men that were grown up with him, and which stood before him: ⁹And he said to them, What counsel give you that we may answer this people, who have spoken to me, saying, Make the yoke which your father did put on us lighter? ¹⁰And the young men that were grown up with him spoke to him, saying, Thus shall you speak to this people that spoke to you, saying, Your father made our yoke heavy, but make you it lighter to us; thus shall you say to them, My little finger shall be thicker than my father's loins. ¹¹And now whereas my father did lade you with a heavy yoke, I will add to your yoke: my father has chastised you with whips, but I will chastise you with scorpions. ¹²So Jeroboam and all the people came to Rehoboam the third day, as the king had appointed, saying, Come to me again the third day. ¹³And the king answered the people roughly, and forsook the old men's counsel that they gave him; ¹⁴And spoke to them after the counsel of the young men, saying, My father made your yoke heavy, and I will add to your yoke: my father also chastised you with whips, but I will chastise you with scorpions. ¹⁵Why the king listened not to the people; for the cause was from the LORD, that he might perform his saying, which the LORD spoke by Ahijah the Shilonite to Jeroboam the son of Nebat. ¹⁶So when all Israel saw that the king listened not to them, the people answered the king, saying, What portion have we in David? neither have we inheritance in the son of Jesse: to your tents, O Israel: now see to your own house, David. So Israel departed to their tents. ¹⁷But as for the children of Israel which dwelled in the cities of Judah, Rehoboam reigned over them. ¹⁸Then king Rehoboam sent Adoram, who was over the tribute; and all Israel stoned him with stones, that he died. Therefore king Rehoboam made speed to get him up to his chariot, to flee to

Jerusalem. ¹⁹So Israel rebelled against the house of David to this day. ²⁰And it came to pass, when all Israel heard that Jeroboam was come again, that they sent and called him to the congregation, and made him king over all Israel: there was none that followed the house of David, but the tribe of Judah only. ²¹And when Rehoboam was come to Jerusalem, he assembled all the house of Judah, with the tribe of Benjamin, an hundred and fourscore thousand chosen men, which were warriors, to fight against the house of Israel, to bring the kingdom again to Rehoboam the son of Solomon. ²²But the word of God came to Shemaiah the man of God, saying, ²³Speak to Rehoboam, the son of Solomon, king of Judah, and to all the house of Judah and Benjamin, and to the remnant of the people, saying, ²⁴Thus says the LORD, You shall not go up, nor fight against your brothers the children of Israel: return every man to his house; for this thing is from me. They listened therefore to the word of the LORD, and returned to depart, according to the word of the LORD. ²⁵Then Jeroboam built Shechem in mount Ephraim, and dwelled therein; and went out from there, and built Penuel. ²⁶And Jeroboam said in his heart, Now shall the kingdom return to the house of David: ²⁷If this people go up to do sacrifice in the house of the LORD at Jerusalem, then shall the heart of this people turn again to their lord, even to Rehoboam king of Judah, and they shall kill me, and go again to Rehoboam king of Judah. ²⁸Whereupon the king took counsel, and made two calves of gold, and said to them, It is too much for you to go up to Jerusalem: behold your gods, O Israel, which brought you up out of the land of Egypt. ²⁹And he set the one in Bethel, and the other put he in Dan. ³⁰And this thing became a sin: for the people went to worship before the one, even to Dan. ³¹And he made an house of high places, and made priests of the lowest of the people, which were not of the sons of Levi. ³²And Jeroboam ordained a feast in the eighth month, on the fifteenth day of the month, like to the feast that is in Judah, and he offered on the altar. So did he in Bethel, sacrificing to the calves that he had made: and he placed in Bethel the priests of the high places which he had made. ³³So he offered on the altar which he had made in Bethel the fifteenth day of the eighth month, even in the month which he had devised of his own heart; and ordained a feast to the children of Israel: and he offered on the altar, and burnt incense.

13 ¹And, behold, there came a man of God out of Judah by the word of the LORD to Bethel: and Jeroboam stood by the altar to burn incense. ²And he cried against the altar in the word of the LORD, and said, O altar, altar, thus says the LORD; Behold, a child shall be born to the house of David, Josiah by name; and on you shall he offer the priests of the high places that burn incense on you, and men's bones shall be burnt on you. ³And he gave a sign the same day, saying, This is the sign which the LORD has spoken; Behold, the altar shall be rent, and the ashes that are on it shall be poured out. ⁴And it came to pass, when king Jeroboam heard the saying of the man of God, which had cried against the altar in Bethel, that he put forth his hand from the altar, saying, Lay hold on him. And his hand, which he put forth against him, dried up, so that he could not pull it in again to him. ⁵The altar also was rent, and the ashes poured out from the altar, according to the sign which the man of God had given by the word of the LORD. ⁶And the king answered and said to the man of God, Entreat now the face of the LORD your God, and pray for me, that my hand may be restored me again. And the man of God sought the LORD, and the king's hand was restored him again, and became as it was before. ⁷And the king said to the man of God, Come home with me, and refresh yourself, and I will give you a reward. ⁸And the man of God said to the king, If you will give me half your house, I will not go in with you, neither will I eat bread nor drink water in this place: ⁹For so was it charged me by the word of the LORD, saying, Eat no bread, nor drink water, nor turn again by the same way that you came. ¹⁰So he went another way, and returned not by the way that he came to Bethel. ¹¹Now there dwelled an old prophet in Bethel; and his sons came and told him all the works that the man of God had done that day in Bethel: the words which he had spoken to the king, them they told also to their father. ¹²And their father said to them, What way went he? For his sons had seen what way the man of God went, which came from Judah. ¹³And he said to his sons, Saddle me the ass. So they saddled him the ass: and he rode thereon, ¹⁴And went after the man of God, and found him sitting under an oak: and he said to him, Are you the man of God that came from Judah? And he said, I am. ¹⁵Then he said to him, Come home with me, and eat bread. ¹⁶And he said, I may not return with you, nor go in with you: neither will I eat bread nor drink water with you in this place: ¹⁷For it was said to me by the word of the LORD, You shall eat no bread nor drink water there, nor turn again to go by the way that you came. ¹⁸He said to him, I am a prophet also as you are; and an angel spoke to me by the word of the LORD, saying, Bring him back with you into your house, that he may eat bread and drink water. But he lied to him. ¹⁹So he went back with him, and did eat bread in his house, and drank water. ²⁰And it came to pass, as they sat at the table, that the word of the LORD came to the prophet that brought him back: ²¹And he cried to the man of God that came from Judah, saying, Thus says the LORD, For as much as you have disobeyed the mouth of the LORD, and have not kept the commandment which the LORD your God commanded you, ²²But came back, and have eaten bread and drunk water in the place, of the which the Lord did say to you, Eat no bread, and drink no water; your carcass shall not come to the sepulcher of your fathers. ²³And it came to pass, after he had eaten bread, and after he had drunk, that he saddled for him the ass, to wit, for the prophet whom he had brought back. ²⁴And when he was gone, a lion met him by the way, and slew him: and his carcass was cast in the way, and the ass stood by it, the lion also stood by the carcass. ²⁵And, behold, men passed by, and saw the carcass cast in the way, and the lion standing by the carcass: and they came and told it in the city where the old prophet dwelled. ²⁶And when the prophet that brought him back from the way heard thereof, he said, It is the man of God, who was disobedient to the word of the LORD: therefore the LORD has delivered him to the lion, which has torn him, and slain him, according to the word of the LORD, which he spoke to him. ²⁷And he spoke to his sons, saying, Saddle me the ass. And they saddled him. ²⁸And he went and found his carcass cast in the way, and the ass and the lion standing by the carcass: the lion had not eaten the carcass, nor torn the ass. ²⁹And the prophet took up the carcass of the man of God, and laid it on the ass, and brought it back: and the old prophet came to the city, to mourn and to bury him. ³⁰And he laid his carcass in his own grave; and they mourned over him, saying, Alas, my brother! ³¹And it came to pass, after he had buried him, that he spoke to his sons, saying, When I am dead, then bury me in the sepulcher wherein the man of God is buried; lay my bones beside his bones: ³²For the saying which he cried by the word of the LORD against the altar in Bethel, and against all the houses of the high places which are in the cities of Samaria, shall surely come to pass. ³³After this thing Jeroboam returned not from his evil way, but made again of the lowest of the people priests of the high places: whoever would, he consecrated him, and he became one of the priests of the high places. ³⁴And this thing became sin to the house of Jeroboam, even to cut it off, and to destroy it from off the face of the earth.

14

¹At that time Abijah the son of Jeroboam fell sick. ²And Jeroboam said to his wife, Arise, I pray you, and disguise yourself, that you be not known to be the wife of Jeroboam; and get you to Shiloh: behold, there is Ahijah the prophet, which told me that I should be king over this people. ³And take with you ten loaves, and cracknels, and a cruse of honey, and go to him: he shall tell you what shall become of the child. ⁴And Jeroboam's wife did so, and arose, and went to Shiloh, and came to the house of Ahijah. But Ahijah could not see; for his eyes were set by reason of his age. ⁵And the LORD said to Ahijah, Behold, the wife of Jeroboam comes to ask a thing of you for her son; for he is sick: thus and thus shall you say to her: for it shall be, when she comes in, that she shall feign herself to be another woman. ⁶And it was so, when Ahijah heard the sound of her feet, as she came in at the door, that he said, Come in, you wife of Jeroboam; why feign you yourself to be another? for I am sent to you with heavy tidings. ⁷Go, tell Jeroboam, Thus says the LORD God of Israel, For as much as I exalted you from among the people, and made you prince over my people Israel, ⁸And rent the kingdom away from the house of David, and gave it you: and yet you have not been as my servant David, who kept my commandments, and who followed me with all his heart, to do that only which was right in my eyes; ⁹But have done evil above all that were before you: for you have gone and made you other gods, and molten images, to provoke me to anger, and have cast me behind your back: ¹⁰Therefore, behold, I will bring evil on the house of Jeroboam, and will cut off from Jeroboam him that urinates against the wall, and him that is shut up and left in Israel, and will take away the remnant of the house of Jeroboam, as a man takes away dung, till it be all gone. ¹¹Him that dies of Jeroboam in the city shall the dogs eat; and him that dies in the field shall the fowls of the air eat: for the LORD has spoken it. ¹²Arise you therefore, get you to your own house: and when your feet enter into the city, the child shall die. ¹³And all Israel shall mourn for him, and bury him: for he only of Jeroboam shall come to the grave, because in him there is found some good thing toward the LORD God of Israel in the house of Jeroboam. ¹⁴Moreover the LORD shall raise him up a king over Israel, who shall cut off the house of Jeroboam that day: but what? even now. ¹⁵For the LORD shall smite Israel, as a reed is shaken in the water, and he shall root up Israel out of this good land, which he gave to their fathers, and shall scatter them beyond the river, because they have made their groves, provoking the LORD to anger. ¹⁶And he shall give Israel up because of the sins of Jeroboam, who did sin, and who made Israel to sin. ¹⁷And Jeroboam's wife arose, and departed, and came to Tirzah: and when she came to the threshold of the door, the child died; ¹⁸And they buried him; and all Israel mourned for him, according to the word of the LORD, which he spoke by the hand of his servant Ahijah the prophet. ¹⁹And the rest of the acts of Jeroboam, how he warred, and how he reigned, behold, they are written in the book of the chronicles of the kings of Israel. ²⁰And the days which Jeroboam reigned were two and twenty years: and he slept with his fathers, and Nadab his son reigned in his stead. ²¹And Rehoboam the son of Solomon reigned in Judah. Rehoboam was forty and one years old when he began to reign, and he reigned seventeen years in Jerusalem, the city which the LORD did choose out of all the tribes of Israel, to put his name there. And his mother's name was Naamah an Ammonitess. ²²And Judah did evil in the sight of the LORD, and they provoked him to jealousy with their sins which they had committed, above all that their fathers had done. ²³For they also built them high places, and images, and groves, on every high hill, and under every green tree. ²⁴And there were also sodomites in the land: and they did according to all the abominations of the nations which the LORD cast out before the children of Israel. ²⁵And it came to pass in the fifth year of king Rehoboam, that Shishak king of Egypt came up against Jerusalem: ²⁶And he took away the treasures of the house of the LORD, and the treasures of the king's house; he even took away all: and he took away all the shields of gold which Solomon had made. ²⁷And king Rehoboam made in their stead brazen shields, and committed them to the hands of the chief of the guard, which kept the door of the king's house. ²⁸And it was so, when the king went into the house of the LORD, that the guard bore them, and brought them back into the guard chamber. ²⁹Now the rest of the acts of Rehoboam, and all that he did, are they not written in the book of the chronicles of the kings of Judah? ³⁰And there was war between Rehoboam and Jeroboam all their days. ³¹And Rehoboam slept with his fathers, and was buried with his fathers in the city of David. And his mother's name was Naamah an Ammonitess. And Abijam his son reigned in his stead.

15

¹Now in the eighteenth year of king Jeroboam the son of Nebat reigned Abijam over Judah. ²Three years reigned he in Jerusalem. and his mother's name was Maachah, the daughter of Abishalom. ³And he walked in all the sins of his father, which he had done before him: and his heart was not perfect with the LORD his God, as the heart of David his father. ⁴Nevertheless for David's sake did the LORD his God give him a lamp in Jerusalem, to set up his son after him, and to establish Jerusalem: ⁵Because David did that which was right in the eyes of the LORD, and turned not aside from any thing that he commanded him all the days of his life, save only in the matter of Uriah the Hittite. ⁶And there was war between Rehoboam and Jeroboam all the days of his life. ⁷Now the rest of the acts of

Abijam, and all that he did, are they not written in the book of the chronicles of the kings of Judah? And there was war between Abijam and Jeroboam. ⁸And Abijam slept with his fathers; and they buried him in the city of David: and Asa his son reigned in his stead. ⁹And in the twentieth year of Jeroboam king of Israel reigned Asa over Judah. ¹⁰And forty and one years reigned he in Jerusalem. And his mother's name was Maachah, the daughter of Abishalom. ¹¹And Asa did that which was right in the eyes of the LORD, as did David his father. ¹²And he took away the sodomites out of the land, and removed all the idols that his fathers had made. ¹³And also Maachah his mother, even her he removed from being queen, because she had made an idol in a grove; and Asa destroyed her idol, and burnt it by the brook Kidron. ¹⁴But the high places were not removed: nevertheless Asa's heart was perfect with the LORD all his days. ¹⁵And he brought in the things which his father had dedicated, and the things which himself had dedicated, into the house of the LORD, silver, and gold, and vessels. ¹⁶And there was war between Asa and Baasha king of Israel all their days. ¹⁷And Baasha king of Israel went up against Judah, and built Ramah, that he might not suffer any to go out or come in to Asa king of Judah. ¹⁸Then Asa took all the silver and the gold that were left in the treasures of the house of the LORD, and the treasures of the king's house, and delivered them into the hand of his servants: and king Asa sent them to Benhadad, the son of Tabrimon, the son of Hezion, king of Syria, that dwelled at Damascus, saying, ¹⁹There is a league between me and you, and between my father and your father: behold, I have sent to you a present of silver and gold; come and break your league with Baasha king of Israel, that he may depart from me. ²⁰So Benhadad listened to king Asa, and sent the captains of the hosts which he had against the cities of Israel, and smote Ijon, and Dan, and Abelbethmaachah, and all Cinneroth, with all the land of Naphtali. ²¹And it came to pass, when Baasha heard thereof, that he left off building of Ramah, and dwelled in Tirzah. ²²Then king Asa made a proclamation throughout all Judah; none was exempted: and they took away the stones of Ramah, and the timber thereof, with which Baasha had built; and king Asa built with them Geba of Benjamin, and Mizpah. ²³The rest of all the acts of Asa, and all his might, and all that he did, and the cities which he built, are they not written in the book of the chronicles of the kings of Judah? Nevertheless in the time of his old age he was diseased in his feet. ²⁴And Asa slept with his fathers, and was buried with his fathers in the city of David his father: and Jehoshaphat his son reigned in his stead. ²⁵And Nadab the son of Jeroboam began to reign over Israel in the second year of Asa king of Judah, and reigned over Israel two years. ²⁶And he did evil in the sight of the LORD, and walked in the way of his father, and in his sin with which he made Israel to sin. ²⁷And Baasha the son of Ahijah, of the house of Issachar, conspired against him; and Baasha smote him at Gibbethon, which belonged to the Philistines; for Nadab and all Israel laid siege to Gibbethon. ²⁸Even in the third year of Asa king of Judah did Baasha slay him, and reigned in his stead. ²⁹And it came to pass, when he reigned, that he smote all the house of Jeroboam; he left not to Jeroboam any that breathed, until he had destroyed him, according to the saying of the LORD, which he spoke by his servant Ahijah the Shilonite: ³⁰Because of the sins of Jeroboam which he sinned, and which he made Israel sin, by his provocation with which he provoked the LORD God of Israel to anger. ³¹Now the rest of the acts of Nadab, and all that he did, are they not written in the book of the chronicles of the kings of Israel? ³²And there was war between Asa and Baasha king of Israel all their days. ³³In the third year of Asa king of Judah began Baasha the son of Ahijah to reign over all Israel in Tirzah, twenty and four years. ³⁴And he did evil in the sight of the LORD, and walked in the way of Jeroboam, and in his sin with which he made Israel to sin.

16

¹Then the word of the LORD came to Jehu the son of Hanani against Baasha, saying, ²For as much as I exalted you out of the dust, and made you prince over my people Israel; and you have walked in the way of Jeroboam, and have made my people Israel to sin, to provoke me to anger with their sins; ³Behold, I will take away the posterity of Baasha, and the posterity of his house; and will make your house like the house of Jeroboam the son of Nebat. ⁴Him that dies of Baasha in the city shall the dogs eat; and him that dies of his in the fields shall the fowls of the air eat. ⁵Now the rest of the acts of Baasha, and what he did, and his might, are they not written in the book of the chronicles of the kings of Israel? ⁶So Baasha slept with his fathers, and was buried in Tirzah: and Elah his son reigned in his stead. ⁷And also by the hand of the prophet Jehu the son of Hanani came the word of the LORD against Baasha, and against his house, even for all the evil that he did in the sight of the LORD, in provoking him to anger with the work of his hands, in being like the house of Jeroboam; and because he killed him. ⁸In the twenty and sixth year of Asa king of Judah began Elah the son of Baasha to reign over Israel in Tirzah, two years. ⁹And his servant Zimri, captain of half his chariots, conspired against him, as he was in Tirzah, drinking himself drunk in the house of Arza steward of his house in Tirzah. ¹⁰And Zimri went in and smote him, and killed him, in the twenty and seventh year of Asa king of Judah, and reigned in his stead. ¹¹And it came to pass, when he began to reign, as soon as he sat on his throne, that he slew all the house of Baasha: he left him not one that urinates against a wall, neither of his kinfolks, nor of his friends. ¹²Thus did Zimri destroy all the house of Baasha, according to the word of the LORD, which he spoke against Baasha by Jehu the prophet. ¹³For all the sins of Baasha, and the sins of Elah his son, by which they sinned, and by which they made Israel to sin, in provoking the LORD God of Israel to anger with their vanities. ¹⁴Now the rest of the acts of Elah, and all that he did, are they not written in the book of the chronicles of the kings of Israel? ¹⁵In the twenty and seventh year of Asa king of Judah did Zimri reign seven days in Tirzah. And the people were encamped against Gibbethon, which belonged to the Philistines. ¹⁶And the people that were encamped heard say, Zimri has conspired, and has also slain the king: why all Israel made Omri, the captain of the host, king over Israel that day in the camp. ¹⁷And Omri went up from Gibbethon, and all Israel with him, and they besieged Tirzah. ¹⁸And it came to pass, when Zimri saw that the city was taken, that he went into the palace of the king's house, and burnt the king's house over him with

fire, and died. ¹⁹For his sins which he sinned in doing evil in the sight of the LORD, in walking in the way of Jeroboam, and in his sin which he did, to make Israel to sin. ²⁰Now the rest of the acts of Zimri, and his treason that he worked, are they not written in the book of the chronicles of the kings of Israel? ²¹Then were the people of Israel divided into two parts: half of the people followed Tibni the son of Ginath, to make him king; and half followed Omri. ²²But the people that followed Omri prevailed against the people that followed Tibni the son of Ginath: so Tibni died, and Omri reigned. ²³In the thirty and first year of Asa king of Judah began Omri to reign over Israel, twelve years: six years reigned he in Tirzah. ²⁴And he bought the hill Samaria of Shemer for two talents of silver, and built on the hill, and called the name of the city which he built, after the name of Shemer, owner of the hill, Samaria. ²⁵But Omri worked evil in the eyes of the LORD, and did worse than all that were before him. ²⁶For he walked in all the way of Jeroboam the son of Nebat, and in his sin with which he made Israel to sin, to provoke the LORD God of Israel to anger with their vanities. ²⁷Now the rest of the acts of Omri which he did, and his might that he showed, are they not written in the book of the chronicles of the kings of Israel? ²⁸So Omri slept with his fathers, and was buried in Samaria: and Ahab his son reigned in his stead. ²⁹And in the thirty and eighth year of Asa king of Judah began Ahab the son of Omri to reign over Israel: and Ahab the son of Omri reigned over Israel in Samaria twenty and two years. ³⁰And Ahab the son of Omri did evil in the sight of the LORD above all that were before him. ³¹And it came to pass, as if it had been a light thing for him to walk in the sins of Jeroboam the son of Nebat, that he took to wife Jezebel the daughter of Ethbaal king of the Zidonians, and went and served Baal, and worshipped him. ³²And he reared up an altar for Baal in the house of Baal, which he had built in Samaria. ³³And Ahab made a grove; and Ahab did more to provoke the LORD God of Israel to anger than all the kings of Israel that were before him. ³⁴In his days did Hiel the Bethelite build Jericho: he laid the foundation thereof in Abiram his firstborn, and set up the gates thereof in his youngest son Segub, according to the word of the LORD, which he spoke by Joshua the son of Nun.

17 ¹And Elijah the Tishbite, who was of the inhabitants of Gilead, said to Ahab, As the LORD God of Israel lives, before whom I stand, there shall not be dew nor rain these years, but according to my word. ²And the word of the LORD came to him, saying, ³Get you hence, and turn you eastward, and hide yourself by the brook Cherith, that is before Jordan. ⁴And it shall be, that you shall drink of the brook; and I have commanded the ravens to feed you there. ⁵So he went and did according to the word of the LORD: for he went and dwelled by the brook Cherith, that is before Jordan. ⁶And the ravens brought him bread and flesh in the morning, and bread and flesh in the evening; and he drank of the brook. ⁷And it came to pass after a while, that the brook dried up, because there had been no rain in the land. ⁸And the word of the LORD came to him, saying, ⁹Arise, get you to Zarephath, which belongs to Zidon, and dwell there: behold, I have commanded a widow woman there to sustain you. ¹⁰So he arose and went to Zarephath. And when he came to the gate of the city, behold, the widow woman was there gathering of sticks: and he called to her, and said, Fetch me, I pray you, a little water in a vessel, that I may drink. ¹¹And as she was going to fetch it, he called to her, and said, Bring me, I pray you, a morsel of bread in your hand. ¹²And she said, As the LORD your God lives, I have not a cake, but an handful of meal in a barrel, and a little oil in a cruse: and, behold, I am gathering two sticks, that I may go in and dress it for me and my son, that we may eat it, and die. ¹³And Elijah said to her, Fear not; go and do as you have said: but make me thereof a little cake first, and bring it to me, and after make for you and for your son. ¹⁴For thus says the LORD God of Israel, The barrel of meal shall not waste, neither shall the cruse of oil fail, until the day that the LORD sends rain on the earth. ¹⁵And she went and did according to the saying of Elijah: and she, and he, and her house, did eat many days. ¹⁶And the barrel of meal wasted not, neither did the cruse of oil fail, according to the word of the LORD, which he spoke by Elijah. ¹⁷And it came to pass after these things, that the son of the woman, the mistress of the house, fell sick; and his sickness was so sore, that there was no breath left in him. ¹⁸And she said to Elijah, What have I to do with you, O you man of God? are you come to me to call my sin to remembrance, and to slay my son? ¹⁹And he said to her, Give me your son. And he took him out of her bosom, and carried him up into a loft, where he stayed, and laid him on his own bed. ²⁰And he cried to the LORD, and said, O LORD my God, have you also brought evil on the widow with whom I sojourn, by slaying her son? ²¹And he stretched himself on the child three times, and cried to the LORD, and said, O LORD my God, I pray you, let this child's soul come into him again. ²²And the LORD heard the voice of Elijah; and the soul of the child came into him again, and he revived. ²³And Elijah took the child, and brought him down out of the chamber into the house, and delivered him to his mother: and Elijah said, See, your son lives. ²⁴And the woman said to Elijah, Now by this I know that you are a man of God, and that the word of the LORD in your mouth is truth.

18 ¹And it came to pass after many days, that the word of the LORD came to Elijah in the third year, saying, Go, show yourself to Ahab; and I will send rain on the earth. ²And Elijah went to show himself to Ahab. And there was a sore famine in Samaria. ³And Ahab called Obadiah, which was the governor of his house. (Now Obadiah feared the LORD greatly: ⁴For it was so, when Jezebel cut off the prophets of the LORD, that Obadiah took an hundred prophets, and hid them by fifty in a cave, and fed them with bread and water.) ⁵And Ahab said to Obadiah, Go into the land, to all fountains of water, and to all brooks: peradventure we may find grass to save the horses and mules alive, that we lose not all the beasts. ⁶So they divided the land between them to pass throughout it: Ahab went one way by himself, and Obadiah went another way by himself. ⁷And as Obadiah was in the way, behold, Elijah met him: and he knew him, and fell on his face, and said, Are you that my lord Elijah? ⁸And he answered him, I am: go, tell your lord, Behold, Elijah is here. ⁹And he said, What have I sinned, that you would deliver your servant into the hand of Ahab, to slay me? ¹⁰As the LORD your God lives, there is no nation or kingdom, where my lord has not sent to seek you: and when they said, He is not there; he took an oath of the kingdom and nation, that they found you not. ¹¹And now you say, Go, tell your lord, Behold, Elijah is here. ¹²And it shall come to pass, as soon as I am gone from you, that the Spirit of the LORD shall carry you where I know not; and so when I come and tell Ahab, and he cannot find you, he shall slay me: but I your servant fear the LORD from my youth. ¹³Was it not told my lord what I did when Jezebel slew the prophets of the LORD, how I hid an hundred men of the LORD's prophets by fifty in a cave, and fed them with bread and water? ¹⁴And now you say, Go, tell your lord, Behold, Elijah is here: and he shall slay me. ¹⁵And Elijah said, As the LORD of hosts lives, before whom I stand, I will surely show myself to him to day. ¹⁶So Obadiah went to meet Ahab, and told him: and Ahab went to meet Elijah. ¹⁷And it came to pass, when Ahab saw Elijah, that Ahab said to him, Are you he that troubles Israel? ¹⁸And he answered, I have not troubled Israel; but you, and your father's house, in that you have forsaken the commandments of the LORD, and you have followed Baalim. ¹⁹Now therefore send, and gather to me all Israel to mount Carmel, and the prophets of Baal four hundred and fifty, and the prophets of the groves four hundred, which eat at Jezebel's table. ²⁰So Ahab sent to all the children of Israel, and gathered the prophets together to mount Carmel. ²¹And Elijah came to all the people, and said, How long halt you between two opinions? if the LORD be God, follow him: but if Baal, then follow him. And the people answered him not a word. ²²Then said Elijah to the people, I, even I only, remain a prophet of the LORD; but Baal's prophets are four hundred and fifty men. ²³Let them therefore give us two bullocks; and let them choose one bullock for themselves, and cut it in pieces, and lay it on wood, and put no fire under: and I will dress the other bullock, and lay it on wood, and put no fire under: ²⁴And call you on the name of your gods, and I will call on the name of the LORD: and the God that answers by fire, let him be God. And all the people answered and said, It is well spoken. ²⁵And Elijah said to the prophets of Baal, Choose you one bullock for yourselves, and dress it first; for you are many; and call on the name of your gods, but put no fire under. ²⁶And they took the bullock which was given them, and they dressed it, and called on the name of Baal from morning even until noon, saying, O Baal, hear us. But there was no voice, nor any that answered. And they leaped on the altar which was made. ²⁷And it came to pass at noon, that Elijah mocked them, and said, Cry aloud: for he is a god; either he is talking, or he is pursuing, or he is in a journey, or peradventure he sleeps, and must be awaked. ²⁸And they cried aloud, and cut themselves after their manner with knives and lancets, till the blood gushed out on them. ²⁹And it came to pass, when midday was past, and they prophesied until the time of the offering of the evening sacrifice, that there was neither voice, nor any to answer, nor any that regarded. ³⁰And Elijah said to all the people, Come near to me. And all the people came near to him. And he repaired the altar of the LORD that was broken down. ³¹And Elijah took twelve stones, according to the number of the tribes of the sons of Jacob, to whom the word of the LORD came, saying, Israel shall be your name: ³²And with the stones he built an altar in the name of the LORD: and he made a trench about the altar, as great as would contain two measures of seed. ³³And he put the wood in order, and cut the bullock in pieces, and laid him on the wood, and said, Fill four barrels with water, and pour it on the burnt sacrifice, and on the wood. ³⁴And he said, Do it the second time. And they did it the second time. And he said, Do it the third time. And they did it the third time. ³⁵And the water ran round about the altar; and he filled the trench also with water. ³⁶And it came to pass at the time of the offering of the evening sacrifice, that Elijah the prophet came near, and said, LORD God of Abraham, Isaac, and of Israel, let it be known this day that you are God in Israel, and that I am your servant, and that I have done all these things at your word. ³⁷Hear me, O LORD, hear me, that this people may know that you are the LORD God, and that you have turned their heart back again. ³⁸Then the fire of the LORD fell, and consumed the burnt sacrifice, and the wood, and the stones, and the dust, and licked up the water that was in the trench. ³⁹And when all the people saw it, they fell on their faces: and they said, The LORD, he is the God; the LORD, he is the God. ⁴⁰And Elijah said to them, Take the prophets of Baal; let not one of them escape. And they took them: and Elijah brought them down to the brook Kishon, and slew them there. ⁴¹And Elijah said to Ahab, Get you up, eat and drink; for there is a sound of abundance of rain. ⁴²So Ahab went up to eat and to drink. And Elijah went up to the top of Carmel; and he cast himself down on the earth, and put his face between his knees, ⁴³And said to his servant, Go up now, look toward the sea. And he went up, and looked, and said, There is nothing. And he said, Go again seven times. ⁴⁴And it came to pass at the seventh time, that he said, Behold, there rises a little cloud out of the sea, like a man's hand. And he said, Go up, say to Ahab, Prepare your chariot, and get you down that the rain stop you not. ⁴⁵And it came to pass in the mean while, that the heaven was black with clouds and wind, and there was a great rain. And Ahab rode, and went to Jezreel. ⁴⁶And the hand of the LORD was on Elijah; and he girded up his loins, and ran before Ahab to the entrance of Jezreel.

19 ¹And Ahab told Jezebel all that Elijah had done, and with how he had slain all the prophets with the sword. ²Then Jezebel sent a messenger to Elijah, saying, So let the gods do to me, and more also, if I make not your life as the life of one of them by to morrow about this time. ³And when he saw that, he arose, and went for his life, and came to Beersheba, which belongs to Judah, and left his servant there. ⁴But he himself went a day's journey into the wilderness, and came and sat down under a juniper tree: and he requested for himself that he might die; and said, It is enough; now, O LORD, take away my life; for I am not better than my fathers. ⁵And as he lay and slept under a juniper tree, behold, then an angel touched him, and said to him, Arise and eat. ⁶And he looked, and, behold, there was a cake baked on the coals, and a cruse of water at his head. And he did eat and drink, and laid him down again. ⁷And the angel of the LORD came again the second time, and touched him, and said, Arise and eat; because the journey is too great for you. ⁸And he arose, and did eat and drink, and went in the strength of that meat forty days and forty nights to Horeb the mount of God. ⁹And he came thither to a cave, and lodged there; and, behold, the word of the LORD came to him, and he said to him, What do you here, Elijah? ¹⁰And he said, I have been very jealous for the LORD God of hosts: for the children of Israel have forsaken your covenant, thrown down your altars, and slain your prophets with the sword; and I, even I only, am left; and they seek my life, to take it away. ¹¹And he said, Go forth, and stand on the mount before the LORD. And, behold, the LORD passed by, and a great and strong wind rent the mountains, and broke in pieces the rocks before the LORD; but the LORD was not in the wind: and after the wind an earthquake; but the LORD was not in the earthquake: ¹²And after the earthquake a fire; but the LORD was not in the fire: and after the fire a still small voice. ¹³And it was so, when Elijah heard it, that he wrapped his face in his mantle, and went out, and stood in the entering in of the cave. And, behold, there came a voice to him, and said, What do you here, Elijah? ¹⁴And he said, I have been very jealous for the LORD God of hosts: because the children of Israel have forsaken your covenant, thrown down your altars, and slain your prophets with the sword; and I, even I only, am left; and they seek my life, to take it away. ¹⁵And the LORD said to him, Go, return on your way to the wilderness of Damascus: and when you come, anoint Hazael to be king over Syria: ¹⁶And Jehu the son of Nimshi shall you anoint to be king over Israel: and Elisha the son of Shaphat of Abelmeholah shall you anoint to be prophet in your room. ¹⁷And it shall come to pass, that him that escapes the sword of Hazael shall Jehu slay: and him that escapes from the sword of Jehu shall Elisha slay. ¹⁸Yet I have left me seven thousand in Israel, all the knees which have not bowed to Baal, and every mouth which has not kissed him. ¹⁹So he departed there, and found Elisha the son of Shaphat, who was plowing with twelve yoke of oxen before him, and he with the twelfth: and Elijah passed by him, and cast his mantle on him. ²⁰And he left the oxen, and ran after Elijah, and said, Let me, I pray you, kiss my father and my mother, and then I will follow you. And he said to him, Go back again: for what have I done to you? ²¹And he returned back from him, and took a yoke of oxen, and slew them, and boiled their flesh with the instruments of the oxen, and gave to the people, and they did eat. Then he arose, and went after Elijah, and ministered to him.

20

¹And Benhadad the king of Syria gathered all his host together: and there were thirty and two kings with him, and horses, and chariots; and he went up and besieged Samaria, and warred against it. ²And he sent messengers to Ahab king of Israel into the city, and said to him, Thus says Benhadad, ³Your silver and your gold is mine; your wives also and your children, even the best, are mine. ⁴And the king of Israel answered and said, My lord, O king, according to your saying, I am yours, and all that I have. ⁵And the messengers came again, and said, Thus speaks Benhadad, saying, Although I have sent to you, saying, You shall deliver me your silver, and your gold, and your wives, and your children; ⁶Yet I will send my servants to you to morrow about this time, and they shall search your house, and the houses of your servants; and it shall be, that whatever is pleasant in your eyes, they shall put it in their hand, and take it away. ⁷Then the king of Israel called all the elders of the land, and said, Mark, I pray you, and see how this man seeks mischief: for he sent to me for my wives, and for my children, and for my silver, and for my gold; and I denied him not. ⁸And all the elders and all the people said to him, Listen not to him, nor consent. ⁹Why he said to the messengers of Benhadad, Tell my lord the king, All that you did send for to your servant at the first I will do: but this thing I may not do. And the messengers departed, and brought him word again. ¹⁰And Benhadad sent to him, and said, The gods do so to me, and more also, if the dust of Samaria shall suffice for handfuls for all the people that follow me. ¹¹And the king of Israel answered and said, Tell him, Let not him that girds on his harness boast himself as he that puts it off. ¹²And it came to pass, when Ben-hadad heard this message, as he was drinking, he and the kings in the pavilions, that he said to his servants, Set yourselves in array. And they set themselves in array against the city. ¹³And, behold, there came a prophet to Ahab king of Israel, saying, Thus says the LORD, Have you seen all this great multitude? behold, I will deliver it into your hand this day; and you shall know that I am the LORD. ¹⁴And Ahab said, By whom? And he said, Thus says the LORD, Even by the young men of the princes of the provinces. Then he said, Who shall order the battle? And he answered, You. ¹⁵Then he numbered the young men of the princes of the provinces, and they were two hundred and thirty two: and after them he numbered all the people, even all the children of Israel, being seven thousand. ¹⁶And they went out at noon. But Benhadad was drinking himself drunk in the pavilions, he and the kings, the thirty and two kings that helped him. ¹⁷And the young men of the princes of the provinces went out first; and Benhadad sent out, and they told him, saying, There are men come out of Samaria. ¹⁸And he said, Whether they be come out for peace, take them alive; or whether they be come out for war, take them alive. ¹⁹So these young men of the princes of the provinces came out of the city, and the army which followed them. ²⁰And they slew every one his man: and the Syrians fled; and Israel pursued them: and Benhadad the king of Syria escaped on an horse with the horsemen. ²¹And the king of Israel went out, and smote the horses and chariots, and slew the Syrians with a great slaughter. ²²And the prophet came to the king of Israel, and said to him, Go, strengthen yourself, and mark, and see what you do: for at the return of the year the king of Syria will come up against you. ²³And the servants of the king of Syria said to him, Their gods are gods of the hills; therefore they were stronger than we; but let us fight against them in the plain, and surely we shall be stronger than they. ²⁴And do this thing, Take the kings away, every man out of his place, and put captains in their rooms: ²⁵And number you an army, like the army that you have lost, horse for horse, and chariot for chariot: and we will fight against them in the plain, and surely we shall be stronger than they. And he listened to their voice, and did so. ²⁶And it came to pass at the return of the year, that Benhadad numbered the Syrians, and went up to Aphek, to fight against Israel. ²⁷And the children of Israel were numbered, and were all present, and went against them: and the children of Israel pitched before them like two little flocks of kids; but the Syrians filled the country. ²⁸And there came a man of God, and spoke to the king of Israel,

and said, Thus says the LORD, Because the Syrians have said, The LORD is God of the hills, but he is not God of the valleys, therefore will I deliver all this great multitude into your hand, and you shall know that I am the LORD. [29]And they pitched one over against the other seven days. And so it was, that in the seventh day the battle was joined: and the children of Israel slew of the Syrians an hundred thousand footmen in one day. [30]But the rest fled to Aphek, into the city; and there a wall fell on twenty and seven thousand of the men that were left. And Benhadad fled, and came into the city, into an inner chamber. [31]And his servants said to him, Behold now, we have heard that the kings of the house of Israel are merciful kings: let us, I pray you, put sackcloth on our loins, and ropes on our heads, and go out to the king of Israel: peradventure he will save your life. [32]So they girded sackcloth on their loins, and put ropes on their heads, and came to the king of Israel, and said, Your servant Benhadad says, I pray you, let me live. And he said, Is he yet alive? he is my brother. [33]Now the men did diligently observe whether any thing would come from him, and did hastily catch it: and they said, Your brother Benhadad. Then he said, Go you, bring him. Then Benhadad came forth to him; and he caused him to come up into the chariot. [34]And Ben-hadad said to him, The cities, which my father took from your father, I will restore; and you shall make streets for you in Damascus, as my father made in Samaria. Then said Ahab, I will send you away with this covenant. So he made a covenant with him, and sent him away. [35]And a certain man of the sons of the prophets said to his neighbor in the word of the LORD, Smite me, I pray you. And the man refused to smite him. [36]Then said he to him, Because you have not obeyed the voice of the LORD, behold, as soon as you are departed from me, a lion shall slay you. And as soon as he was departed from him, a lion found him, and slew him. [37]Then he found another man, and said, Smite me, I pray you. And the man smote him, so that in smiting he wounded him. [38]So the prophet departed, and waited for the king by the way, and disguised himself with ashes on his face. [39]And as the king passed by, he cried to the king: and he said, Your servant went out into the middle of the battle; and, behold, a man turned aside, and brought a man to me, and said, Keep this man: if by any means he be missing, then shall your life be for his life, or else you shall pay a talent of silver. [40]And as your servant was busy here and there, he was gone. And the king of Israel said to him, So shall your judgment be; yourself have decided it. [41]And he hurried, and took the ashes away from his face; and the king of Israel discerned him that he was of the prophets. [42]And he said to him, Thus says the LORD, Because you have let go out of your hand a man whom I appointed to utter destruction, therefore your life shall go for his life, and your people for his people. [43]And the king of Israel went to his house heavy and displeased, and came to Samaria.

21

[1]And it came to pass after these things, that Naboth the Jezreelite had a vineyard, which was in Jezreel, hard by the palace of Ahab king of Samaria. [2]And Ahab spoke to Naboth, saying, Give me your vineyard, that I may have it for a garden of herbs, because it is near to my house: and I will give you for it a better vineyard than it; or, if it seem good to you, I will give you the worth of it in money. [3]And Naboth said to Ahab, The LORD forbid it me, that I should give the inheritance of my fathers to you. [4]And Ahab came into his house heavy and displeased because of the word which Naboth the Jezreelite had spoken to him: for he had said, I will not give you the inheritance of my fathers. And he laid him down on his bed, and turned away his face, and would eat no bread. [5]But Jezebel his wife came to him, and said to him, Why is your spirit so sad, that you eat no bread? [6]And he said to her, Because I spoke to Naboth the Jezreelite, and said to him, Give me your vineyard for money; or else, if it please you, I will give you another vineyard for it: and he answered, I will not give you my vineyard. [7]And Jezebel his wife said to him, Do you now govern the kingdom of Israel? arise, and eat bread, and let your heart be merry: I will give you the vineyard of Naboth the Jezreelite. [8]So she wrote letters in Ahab's name, and sealed them with his seal, and sent the letters to the elders and to the nobles that were in his city, dwelling with Naboth. [9]And she wrote in the letters, saying, Proclaim a fast, and set Naboth on high among the people: [10]And set two men, sons of Belial, before him, to bear witness against him, saying, You did blaspheme God and the king. And then carry him out, and stone him, that he may die. [11]And the men of his city, even the elders and the nobles who were the inhabitants in his city, did as Jezebel had sent to them, and as it was written in the letters which she had sent to them. [12]They proclaimed a fast, and set Naboth on high among the people. [13]And there came in two men, children of Belial, and sat before him: and the men of Belial witnessed against him, even against Naboth, in the presence of the people, saying, Naboth did blaspheme God and the king. Then they carried him forth out of the city, and stoned him with stones, that he died. [14]Then they sent to Jezebel, saying, Naboth is stoned, and is dead. [15]And it came to pass, when Jezebel heard that Naboth was stoned, and was dead, that Jezebel said to Ahab, Arise, take possession of the vineyard of Naboth the Jezreelite, which he refused to give you for money: for Naboth is not alive, but dead. [16]And it came to pass, when Ahab heard that Naboth was dead, that Ahab rose up to go down to the vineyard of Naboth the Jezreelite, to take possession of it. [17]And the word of the LORD came to Elijah the Tishbite, saying, [18]Arise, go down to meet Ahab king of Israel, which is in Samaria: behold, he is in the vineyard of Naboth, where he is gone down to possess it. [19]And you shall speak to him, saying, Thus said the LORD, Have you killed, and also taken possession? And you shall speak to him, saying, Thus says the LORD, In the place where dogs licked the blood of Naboth shall dogs lick your blood, even yours. [20]And Ahab said to Elijah, Have you found me, O my enemy? And he answered, I have found you: because you have sold yourself to work evil in the sight of the LORD. [21]Behold, I will bring evil on you, and will take away your posterity, and will cut off from Ahab him that urinates against the wall, and him that is shut up and left in Israel, [22]And will make your house like the house of Jeroboam the son of Nebat, and like the house of Baasha the son of Ahijah, for the provocation with which you have provoked me to anger, and made Israel to sin. [23]And of Jezebel also spoke the LORD, saying, The dogs shall eat Jezebel by the wall of Jezreel. [24]Him that dies of Ahab in the city the dogs

shall eat; and him that dies in the field shall the fowls of the air eat. ²⁵But there was none like to Ahab, which did sell himself to work wickedness in the sight of the LORD, whom Jezebel his wife stirred up. ²⁶And he did very abominably in following idols, according to all things as did the Amorites, whom the LORD cast out before the children of Israel. ²⁷And it came to pass, when Ahab heard those words, that he rent his clothes, and put sackcloth on his flesh, and fasted, and lay in sackcloth, and went softly. ²⁸And the word of the LORD came to Elijah the Tishbite, saying, ²⁹See you how Ahab humbles himself before me? because he humbles himself before me, I will not bring the evil in his days: but in his son's days will I bring the evil on his house.

22 ¹And they continued three years without war between Syria and Israel. ²And it came to pass in the third year, that Jehoshaphat the king of Judah came down to the king of Israel. ³And the king of Israel said to his servants, Know you that Ramoth in Gilead is ours, and we be still, and take it not out of the hand of the king of Syria? ⁴And he said to Jehoshaphat, Will you go with me to battle to Ramothgilead? And Jehoshaphat said to the king of Israel, I am as you are, my people as your people, my horses as your horses. ⁵And Jehoshaphat said to the king of Israel, Inquire, I pray you, at the word of the LORD to day. ⁶Then the king of Israel gathered the prophets together, about four hundred men, and said to them, Shall I go against Ramothgilead to battle, or shall I forbear? And they said, Go up; for the LORD shall deliver it into the hand of the king. ⁷And Jehoshaphat said, Is there not here a prophet of the LORD besides, that we might inquire of him? ⁸And the king of Israel said to Jehoshaphat, There is yet one man, Micaiah the son of Imlah, by whom we may inquire of the LORD: but I hate him; for he does not prophesy good concerning me, but evil. And Jehoshaphat said, Let not the king say so. ⁹Then the king of Israel called an officer, and said, Hasten here Micaiah the son of Imlah. ¹⁰And the king of Israel and Jehoshaphat the king of Judah sat each on his throne, having put on their robes, in a void place in the entrance of the gate of Samaria; and all the prophets prophesied before them. ¹¹And Zedekiah the son of Chenaanah made him horns of iron: and he said, Thus says the LORD, With these shall you push the Syrians, until you have consumed them. ¹²And all the prophets prophesied so, saying, Go up to Ramothgilead, and prosper: for the LORD shall deliver it into the king's hand. ¹³And the messenger that was gone to call Micaiah spoke to him, saying, Behold now, the words of the prophets declare good to the king with one mouth: let your word, I pray you, be like the word of one of them, and speak that which is good. ¹⁴And Micaiah said, As the LORD lives, what the LORD says to me, that will I speak. ¹⁵So he came to the king. And the king said to him, Micaiah, shall we go against Ramothgilead to battle, or shall we forbear? And he answered him, Go, and prosper: for the LORD shall deliver it into the hand of the king. ¹⁶And the king said to him, How many times shall I adjure you that you tell me nothing but that which is true in the name of the LORD? ¹⁷And he said, I saw all Israel scattered on the hills, as sheep that have not a shepherd: and the LORD said, These have no master: let them return every man to his house in peace. ¹⁸And the king of Israel said to Jehoshaphat, Did I not tell you that he would prophesy no good concerning me, but evil? ¹⁹And he said, Hear you therefore the word of the LORD: I saw the LORD sitting on his throne, and all the host of heaven standing by him on his right hand and on his left. ²⁰And the LORD said, Who shall persuade Ahab, that he may go up and fall at Ramothgilead? And one said on this manner, and another said on that manner. ²¹And there came forth a spirit, and stood before the LORD, and said, I will persuade him. ²²And the LORD said to him, With which? And he said, I will go forth, and I will be a lying spirit in the mouth of all his prophets. And he said, You shall persuade him, and prevail also: go forth, and do so. ²³Now therefore, behold, the LORD has put a lying spirit in the mouth of all these your prophets, and the LORD has spoken evil concerning you. ²⁴But Zedekiah the son of Chenaanah went near, and smote Micaiah on the cheek, and said, Which way went the Spirit of the LORD from me to speak to you? ²⁵And Micaiah said, Behold, you shall see in that day, when you shall go into an inner chamber to hide yourself. ²⁶And the king of Israel said, Take Micaiah, and carry him back to Amon the governor of the city, and to Joash the king's son; ²⁷And say, Thus says the king, Put this fellow in the prison, and feed him with bread of affliction and with water of affliction, until I come in peace. ²⁸And Micaiah said, If you return at all in peace, the LORD has not spoken by me. And he said, Listen, O people, every one of you. ²⁹So the king of Israel and Jehoshaphat the king of Judah went up to Ramothgilead. ³⁰And the king of Israel said to Jehoshaphat, I will disguise myself, and enter into the battle; but put you on your robes. And the king of Israel disguised himself, and went into the battle. ³¹But the king of Syria commanded his thirty and two captains that had rule over his chariots, saying, Fight neither with small nor great, save only with the king of Israel. ³²And it came to pass, when the captains of the chariots saw Jehoshaphat, that they said, Surely it is the king of Israel. And they turned aside to fight against him: and Jehoshaphat cried out. ³³And it came to pass, when the captains of the chariots perceived that it was not the king of Israel, that they turned back from pursuing him. ³⁴And a certain man drew a bow at a venture, and smote the king of Israel between the joints of the harness: why he said to the driver of his chariot, Turn your hand, and carry me out of the host; for I am wounded. ³⁵And the battle increased that day: and the king was stayed up in his chariot against the Syrians, and died at even: and the blood ran out of the wound into the middle of the chariot. ³⁶And there went a proclamation throughout the host about the going down of the sun, saying, Every man to his city, and every man to his own country. ³⁷So the king died, and was brought to Samaria; and they buried the king in Samaria. ³⁸And one washed the chariot in the pool of Samaria; and the dogs licked up his blood; and they washed his armor; according to the word of the LORD which he spoke. ³⁹Now the rest of the acts of Ahab, and all that he did, and the ivory house which he made, and all the cities that he built, are they not written in the book of the chronicles of the kings of Israel? ⁴⁰So Ahab slept with his fathers; and Ahaziah his son reigned in his stead. ⁴¹And Jehoshaphat the son of Asa began to reign over Judah in the fourth year of Ahab king of Israel. ⁴²Jehoshaphat was thirty and five years old when he began to reign; and he reigned twenty and five years in Jerusalem. And his mother's name was Azubah the daughter of Shilhi. ⁴³And he walked in all the ways of Asa his father; he turned not aside from it, doing that which was right in the eyes of the LORD: nevertheless the high places were not taken away; for the people offered and burnt incense yet in the high places. ⁴⁴And Jehoshaphat made peace with the king of Israel. ⁴⁵Now the rest of the acts of Jehoshaphat, and his might that he showed, and how he warred, are they not written in the book of the chronicles of the kings of Judah? ⁴⁶And the remnant of the sodomites, which remained in the days of his father Asa, he took out of the land. ⁴⁷There was then no king in Edom: a deputy was king. ⁴⁸Jehoshaphat made ships of Tharshish to go to Ophir for gold: but they went not; for the ships were broken at Eziongeber. ⁴⁹Then said Ahaziah the son of Ahab to Jehoshaphat, Let my servants go with your servants in the ships. But Jehoshaphat would not. ⁵⁰And Jehoshaphat slept with his fathers, and was buried with his fathers in the city of David his father: and Jehoram his son reigned in his stead. ⁵¹Ahaziah the son of Ahab began to reign over Israel in Samaria the seventeenth year of Jehoshaphat king of Judah, and reigned two years over Israel. ⁵²And he did evil in the sight of the LORD, and walked in the way of his father, and in the way of his mother, and in the way of Jeroboam the son of Nebat, who made Israel to sin: ⁵³For he served Baal, and worshipped him, and provoked to anger the LORD God of Israel, according to all that his father had done.

Second Kings

1 ¹Then Moab rebelled against Israel after the death of Ahab. ²And Ahaziah fell down through a lattice in his upper chamber that was in Samaria, and was sick: and he sent messengers, and said to them, Go, inquire of Baalzebub the god of Ekron whether I shall recover of this disease. ³But the angel of the LORD said to Elijah the Tishbite, Arise, go up to meet the messengers of the king of Samaria, and say to them, Is it not because there is not a God in Israel, that you go to inquire of Baalzebub the god of Ekron? ⁴Now therefore thus says the LORD, You shall not come down from that bed on which you are gone up, but shall surely die. And Elijah departed. ⁵And when the messengers turned back to him, he said to them, Why are you now turned back? ⁶And they said to him, There came a man up to meet us, and said to us, Go, turn again to the king that sent you, and say to him, Thus says the LORD, Is it not because there is not a God in Israel, that you send to inquire of Baalzebub the god of Ekron? therefore you shall not come down from that bed on which you are gone up, but shall surely die. ⁷And he said to them, What manner of man was he which came up to meet you, and told you these words? ⁸And they answered him, He was an hairy man, and girt with a girdle of leather about his loins. And he said, It is Elijah the Tishbite. ⁹Then the king sent to him a captain of fifty with his fifty. And he went up to him: and, behold, he sat on the top of an hill. And he spoke to him, You man of God, the king has said, Come down. ¹⁰And Elijah answered and said to the captain of fifty, If I be a man of God, then let fire come down from heaven, and consume you and your fifty. And there came down fire from heaven, and consumed him and his fifty. ¹¹Again also he sent to him another captain of fifty with his fifty. And he answered and said to him, O man of God, thus has the king said, Come down quickly. ¹²And Elijah answered and said to them, If I be a man of God, let fire come down from heaven, and consume you and your fifty. And the fire of God came down from heaven, and consumed him and his fifty. ¹³And he sent again a captain of the third fifty with his fifty. And the third captain of fifty went up, and came and fell on his knees before Elijah, and sought him, and said to him, O man of God, I pray you, let my life, and the life of these fifty your servants, be precious in your sight. ¹⁴Behold, there came fire down from heaven, and burnt up the two captains of the former fifties with their fifties: therefore let my life now be precious in your sight. ¹⁵And the angel of the LORD said to Elijah, Go down with him: be not afraid of him. And he arose, and went down with him to the king. ¹⁶And he said to him, Thus says the LORD, For as much as you have sent messengers to inquire of Baalzebub the god of Ekron, is it not because there is no God in Israel to inquire of his word? therefore you shall not come down off that bed on which you are gone up, but shall surely die. ¹⁷So he died according to the word of the LORD which Elijah had spoken. And Jehoram reigned in his stead in the second year of Jehoram the son of Jehoshaphat king of Judah; because he had no son. ¹⁸Now the rest of the acts of Ahaziah which he did, are they not written in the book of the chronicles of the kings of Israel?

2 ¹And it came to pass, when the LORD would take up Elijah into heaven by a whirlwind, that Elijah went with Elisha from Gilgal. ²And Elijah said to Elisha, Tarry here, I pray you; for the LORD has sent me to Bethel. And Elisha said to him, As the LORD lives, and as your soul lives, I will not leave you. So they went down to Bethel. ³And the sons of the prophets that were at Bethel came forth to Elisha, and said to him, Know you that the LORD will take away your master from your head to day? And he said, Yes, I know it; hold you your peace. ⁴And Elijah said to him, Elisha, tarry here, I pray you; for the LORD has sent me to Jericho. And he said, As the LORD lives, and as your soul lives, I will not leave you. So they came to Jericho. ⁵And the sons of the prophets that were at Jericho came to Elisha, and said to him, Know you that the LORD will take away your master from your head to day? And he answered, Yes, I know it; hold you your peace. ⁶And Elijah said to him, Tarry, I pray you, here; for the LORD has sent me to Jordan. And he said, As the LORD lives, and as your soul lives, I will not leave you. And they two went on. ⁷And fifty men of the sons of the prophets went, and stood to view afar off: and they two stood by Jordan. ⁸And Elijah took his mantle, and wrapped it together, and smote the waters, and they were divided here and thither, so that they two went over on dry ground. ⁹And it came to pass, when they were gone over, that Elijah said to Elisha, Ask what I shall do for you, before I be taken away from you. And Elisha said, I pray you, let a double portion of your spirit be on me. ¹⁰And he said, You have asked a hard thing: nevertheless, if you see me when I am taken from you, it shall be so to you; but if not, it shall not be so. ¹¹And it came to pass, as they still went on, and talked, that, behold, there appeared a chariot of fire, and horses of fire, and parted them both asunder; and Elijah went up by a whirlwind into heaven. ¹²And Elisha saw it, and he cried, My father, my father, the chariot of Israel, and the horsemen thereof. And he saw him no more: and he took hold of his own clothes, and rent them in two pieces. ¹³He took up also the mantle of Elijah that fell from him, and went back, and stood by the bank of Jordan; ¹⁴And he took the mantle of Elijah that fell from him, and smote the waters, and said, Where is the LORD God of Elijah? and when he also had smitten the waters, they parted here and thither: and Elisha went over. ¹⁵And when the sons of the prophets which were to view at Jericho saw him, they said, The spirit of Elijah does rest on Elisha. And they came to meet him, and bowed themselves to the ground before him. ¹⁶And they said to him, Behold now, there be with your servants fifty strong men; let them go, we pray you, and seek your master: lest peradventure the Spirit of the LORD has taken him up, and cast him on some mountain, or into some valley. And he said, You shall not send. ¹⁷And when they urged him till he was ashamed, he said, Send. They sent therefore fifty men; and they sought three days, but found him not. ¹⁸And when they came again to him, (for he tarried at Jericho,) he said to them, Did I not say to you, Go not? ¹⁹And the men of the city said to Elisha, Behold, I pray you, the situation of this city is pleasant, as my lord sees: but the water is naught, and the ground barren. ²⁰And he said, Bring me a new cruse, and put salt therein. And they brought it to him. ²¹And he went forth to the spring of the waters, and cast the salt in there, and said, Thus says the LORD, I have healed these waters; there shall not be from there any more death or barren land. ²²So the waters were healed to this day, according to the saying of Elisha which he spoke. ²³And he went up from there to Bethel: and as he was going up by the way, there came forth little children out of the city, and mocked him, and said to him, Go up, you bald head; go up, you bald head. ²⁴And he turned back, and looked on them, and cursed them in the name of the LORD. And there came forth two she bears out of the wood, and tare forty and two children of them. ²⁵And he went from there to mount Carmel, and from there he returned to Samaria.

3 ¹Now Jehoram the son of Ahab began to reign over Israel in Samaria the eighteenth year of Jehoshaphat king of Judah, and reigned twelve years. ²And he worked evil in the sight of the LORD; but not like his father, and like his mother: for he put away the image of Baal that his father had made. ³Nevertheless he joined to the sins of Jeroboam the son of Nebat, which made Israel to sin; he departed not therefrom. ⁴And Mesha king of Moab was a sheep master, and rendered to the king of Israel an hundred thousand lambs, and an hundred thousand rams, with the wool. ⁵But it came to pass, when Ahab was dead, that the king of Moab rebelled against the king of Israel. ⁶And king Jehoram went out of Samaria the same time, and numbered all Israel. ⁷And he went and sent to Jehoshaphat the king of Judah, saying, The king of Moab has rebelled against me: will you go with me against Moab to battle? And he said, I will go up: I am as you are, my people as your people, and my horses as your horses. ⁸And he said, Which way shall we go up? And he answered, The way through the wilderness of Edom. ⁹So the king of Israel went, and the king of Judah, and the king of Edom: and they fetched a compass of seven days' journey: and there was no water for the host, and for the cattle that followed them. ¹⁰And the king of Israel said, Alas! that the LORD has called these three kings together, to deliver them into the hand of Moab! ¹¹But Jehoshaphat said, Is there not here a prophet of the LORD, that we may inquire of the LORD by him? And one of the king of Israel's servants answered and said, Here is Elisha the son of Shaphat, which poured water on the hands of Elijah. ¹²And Jehoshaphat said, The word of the LORD is with him. So the king of Israel and Jehoshaphat and the king of Edom went down to him. ¹³And Elisha said to the king of Israel, What have I to do with you? get you to the prophets of your father, and to the prophets of your mother. And the king of Israel said to him, No: for the LORD has called these three kings together, to deliver them into the hand of Moab. ¹⁴And Elisha said, As the LORD of hosts lives, before whom I stand, surely, were it not that I regard the presence of Jehoshaphat the king of Judah, I would not look toward you, nor see you. ¹⁵But now bring me a minstrel. And it came to pass, when the minstrel played, that the hand of the LORD came on him. ¹⁶And he said, Thus says the LORD, Make this valley full of ditches. ¹⁷For thus says the LORD, You shall not see wind, neither shall you see rain; yet that valley shall be filled with water, that you may drink, both you, and your cattle, and your beasts. ¹⁸And this is but a light thing in the sight of the LORD: he will deliver the Moabites also into your hand. ¹⁹And you shall smite every fenced city, and every choice city, and shall fell every good tree, and stop all wells of water, and mar every good piece of land with stones. ²⁰And it came to pass in the morning, when the meat offering was offered, that, behold, there came water by the way of Edom, and the country was filled with water. ²¹And when all the Moabites heard that the kings were come up to fight against them, they gathered all that were able to put on armor, and upward, and stood in the border. ²²And they rose up early in the morning, and the sun shone on the water, and the Moabites saw the water on the other side as red as blood: ²³And they said, This is blood: the kings are surely slain, and they have smitten one another: now therefore, Moab, to the spoil. ²⁴And when they came to the camp of Israel, the Israelites rose up and smote the Moabites, so that they fled before them: but they went forward smiting the Moabites, even in their country. ²⁵And they beat down the cities, and on every good piece of land cast every man his stone, and filled it; and they stopped all the wells of water, and felled all the good trees: only in Kirharaseth left they the stones thereof; however, the slingers went about it, and smote it. ²⁶And when the king of Moab saw that the battle was too sore for him, he took with him seven hundred men that drew swords, to break through even to the king of Edom: but they could not. ²⁷Then he took his oldest son that should have reigned in his stead, and offered him for a burnt offering on the wall. And there was great indignation against Israel: and they departed from him, and returned to their own land.

4 ¹Now there cried a certain woman of the wives of the sons of the prophets to Elisha, saying, Your servant my husband is dead; and you know that your servant did fear the LORD: and the creditor is come to take to him my two sons to be slaves. ²And Elisha said to her, What shall I do for you? tell me, what have you in the house? And she said, Your handmaid has not any thing in the house, save a pot of oil. ³Then he said, Go, borrow you vessels abroad of all your neighbors, even empty vessels; borrow not a few. ⁴And when you are come in, you shall shut the door on you and on your sons, and shall pour out into all those vessels, and you shall set aside that which is full. ⁵So she went from him, and shut the door on her and on her sons, who brought the vessels to her; and she poured out. ⁶And it came to pass, when the vessels were full, that she said to her son, Bring me yet a vessel. And he said to her, There is not a vessel more. And the oil stayed. ⁷Then she came and told the man of God. And he said, Go, sell the oil, and pay your debt, and live you and your children of the rest. ⁸And it fell on a day, that Elisha passed to Shunem, where was a great woman; and she constrained him to eat bread. And so it was, that as oft as he passed by, he turned in thither to eat bread. ⁹And she said to her husband, Behold now, I perceive that this is an holy man of God, which passes by us continually. ¹⁰Let us make a little chamber, I pray you, on the wall; and let us set for him there a bed, and a table, and a stool, and a candlestick: and it shall be, when he comes to us, that he shall turn in thither. ¹¹And it fell on a day, that he came thither, and he turned into the chamber, and lay there. ¹²And he said to Gehazi his servant, Call this Shunammite. And when he had called her, she stood before him. ¹³And he said

to him, Say now to her, Behold, you have been careful for us with all this care; what is to be done for you? would you be spoken for to the king, or to the captain of the host? And she answered, I dwell among my own people. ¹⁴And he said, What then is to be done for her? And Gehazi answered, Truly she has no child, and her husband is old. ¹⁵And he said, Call her. And when he had called her, she stood in the door. ¹⁶And he said, About this season, according to the time of life, you shall embrace a son. And she said, No, my lord, you man of God, do not lie to your handmaid. ¹⁷And the woman conceived, and bore a son at that season that Elisha had said to her, according to the time of life. ¹⁸And when the child was grown, it fell on a day, that he went out to his father to the reapers. ¹⁹And he said to his father, My head, my head. And he said to a lad, Carry him to his mother. ²⁰And when he had taken him, and brought him to his mother, he sat on her knees till noon, and then died. ²¹And she went up, and laid him on the bed of the man of God, and shut the door on him, and went out. ²²And she called to her husband, and said, Send me, I pray you, one of the young men, and one of the asses, that I may run to the man of God, and come again. ²³And he said, Why will you go to him to day? it is neither new moon, nor sabbath. And she said, It shall be well. ²⁴Then she saddled an ass, and said to her servant, Drive, and go forward; slack not your riding for me, except I bid you. ²⁵So she went and came to the man of God to mount Carmel. And it came to pass, when the man of God saw her afar off, that he said to Gehazi his servant, Behold, yonder is that Shunammite: ²⁶Run now, I pray you, to meet her, and say to her, Is it well with you? is it well with your husband? is it well with the child? And she answered, It is well: ²⁷And when she came to the man of God to the hill, she caught him by the feet: but Gehazi came near to thrust her away. And the man of God said, Let her alone; for her soul is vexed within her: and the LORD has hid it from me, and has not told me. ²⁸Then she said, Did I desire a son of my lord? did I not say, Do not deceive me? ²⁹Then he said to Gehazi, Gird up your loins, and take my staff in your hand, and go your way: if you meet any man, salute him not; and if any salute you, answer him not again: and lay my staff on the face of the child. ³⁰And the mother of the child said, As the LORD lives, and as your soul lives, I will not leave you. And he arose, and followed her. ³¹And Gehazi passed on before them, and laid the staff on the face of the child; but there was neither voice, nor hearing. Why he went again to meet him, and told him, saying, The child is not awaked. ³²And when Elisha was come into the house, behold, the child was dead, and laid on his bed. ³³He went in therefore, and shut the door on them two, and prayed to the LORD. ³⁴And he went up, and lay on the child, and put his mouth on his mouth, and his eyes on his eyes, and his hands on his hands: and stretched himself on the child; and the flesh of the child waxed warm. ³⁵Then he returned, and walked in the house to and fro; and went up, and stretched himself on him: and the child sneezed seven times, and the child opened his eyes. ³⁶And he called Gehazi, and said, Call this Shunammite. So he called her. And when she was come in to him, he said, Take up your son. ³⁷Then she went in, and fell at his feet, and bowed herself to the ground, and took up her son, and went out. ³⁸And Elisha came again to Gilgal: and there was a dearth in the land; and the sons of the prophets were sitting before him: and he said to his servant, Set on the great pot, and seethe pottage for the sons of the prophets. ³⁹And one went out into the field to gather herbs, and found a wild vine, and gathered thereof wild gourds his lap full, and came and shred them into the pot of pottage: for they knew them not. ⁴⁰So they poured out for the men to eat. And it came to pass, as they were eating of the pottage, that they cried out, and said, O you man of God, there is death in the pot. And they could not eat thereof. ⁴¹But he said, Then bring meal. And he cast it into the pot; and he said, Pour out for the people, that they may eat. And there was no harm in the pot. ⁴²And there came a man from Baalshalisha, and brought the man of God bread of the first fruits, twenty loaves of barley, and full ears of corn in the husk thereof. And he said, Give to the people, that they may eat. ⁴³And his servitor said, What, should I set this before an hundred men? He said again, Give the people, that they may eat: for thus says the LORD, They shall eat, and shall leave thereof. ⁴⁴So he set it before them, and they did eat, and left thereof, according to the word of the LORD.

5 ¹Now Naaman, captain of the host of the king of Syria, was a great man with his master, and honorable, because by him the LORD had given deliverance to Syria: he was also a mighty man in valor, but he was a leper. ²And the Syrians had gone out by companies, and had brought away captive out of the land of Israel a little maid; and she waited on Naaman's wife. ³And she said to her mistress, Would God my lord were with the prophet that is in Samaria! for he would recover him of his leprosy. ⁴And one went in, and told his lord, saying, Thus and thus said the maid that is of the land of Israel. ⁵And the king of Syria said, Go to, go, and I will send a letter to the king of Israel. And he departed, and took with him ten talents of silver, and six thousand pieces of gold, and ten changes of raiment. ⁶And he brought the letter to the king of Israel, saying, Now when this letter is come to you, behold, I have therewith sent Naaman my servant to you, that you may recover him of his leprosy. ⁷And it came to pass, when the king of Israel had read the letter, that he rent his clothes, and said, Am I God, to kill and to make alive, that this man does send to me to recover a man of his leprosy? why consider, I pray you, and see how he seeks a quarrel against me. ⁸And it was so, when Elisha the man of God had heard that the king of Israel had rent his clothes, that he sent to the king, saying, Why have you rent your clothes? let him come now to me, and he shall know that there is a prophet in Israel. ⁹So Naaman came with his horses and with his chariot, and stood at the door of the house of Elisha. ¹⁰And Elisha sent a messenger to him, saying, Go and wash in Jordan seven times, and your flesh shall come again to you, and you shall be clean. ¹¹But Naaman was wroth, and went away, and said, Behold, I thought, He will surely come out to me, and stand, and call on the name of the LORD his God, and strike his hand over the place, and recover the leper. ¹²Are not Abana and Pharpar, rivers of Damascus, better than all the waters of Israel? may I not wash in them, and be clean? So he turned and went away in a rage. ¹³And his servants came near, and spoke to him, and said, My father, if the prophet had bid you do some great thing, would you not have done it? how much rather then, when he says to you, Wash, and be clean? ¹⁴Then went he down, and dipped himself seven times in Jordan, according to the saying of the man of God: and his flesh came again like to the flesh of a little child, and he was clean. ¹⁵And he returned to the man of God, he and all his company, and came, and stood before him: and he said, Behold, now I know that there is no God in all the earth, but in Israel: now therefore, I pray you, take a blessing of your servant. ¹⁶But he said, As the LORD lives, before whom I stand, I will receive none. And he urged him to take it; but he refused. ¹⁷And Naaman said, Shall there not then, I pray you, be given to your servant two mules' burden of earth? for your servant will from now on offer neither burnt offering nor sacrifice to other gods, but to the LORD. ¹⁸In this thing the LORD pardon your servant, that when my master goes into the house of Rimmon to worship there, and he leans on my hand, and I bow myself in the house of Rimmon: when I bow down myself in the house of Rimmon, the LORD pardon your servant in this thing. ¹⁹And he said to him, Go in peace. So he departed from him a little way. ²⁰But Gehazi, the servant of Elisha the man of God, said, Behold, my master has spared Naaman this Syrian, in not receiving at his hands that which he brought: but, as the LORD lives, I will run after him, and take somewhat of him. ²¹So Gehazi followed after Naaman. And when Naaman saw him running after him, he lighted down from the chariot to meet him, and said, Is all well? ²²And he said, All is well. My master has sent me, saying, Behold, even now there be come to me from mount Ephraim two young men of the sons of the prophets: give them, I pray you, a talent of silver, and two changes of garments. ²³And Naaman said, Be content, take two talents. And he urged him, and bound two talents of silver in two bags, with two changes of garments, and laid them on two of his servants; and they bore them before him. ²⁴And when he came to the tower, he took them from their hand, and bestowed them in the house: and he let the men go, and they departed. ²⁵But he went in, and stood before his master. And Elisha said to him, From where come you, Gehazi? And he said, Your servant went no where. ²⁶And he said to him, Went not my heart with you, when the man turned again from his chariot to meet you? Is it a time to receive money, and to receive garments, and olive groves, and vineyards, and sheep, and oxen, and menservants, and maidservants? ²⁷The leprosy therefore of Naaman shall stick to you, and to your seed for ever. And he went out from his presence a leper as white as snow.

6 ¹And the sons of the prophets said to Elisha, Behold now, the place where we dwell with you is too strait for us. ²Let us go, we pray you, to Jordan, and take there every man a beam, and let us make us a place there, where we may dwell. And he answered, Go you. ³And one said, Be content, I pray you, and go with your servants. And he answered, I will go. ⁴So he went with them. And when they came to Jordan, they cut down wood. ⁵But as one was felling a beam, the ax head fell into the water: and he cried, and said, Alas, master! for it was borrowed. ⁶And the man of God said, Where fell it? And he showed him the place. And he cut down a stick, and cast it in thither; and the iron did swim. ⁷Therefore said he, Take it up to you. And he put out his hand, and took it. ⁸Then the king of Syria warred against Israel, and took counsel with his servants, saying, In such and such a place shall be my camp. ⁹And the man of God sent to the king of Israel, saying, Beware that you pass not such a place; for thither the Syrians are come down. ¹⁰And the king of Israel sent to the place which the man of God told him and warned him of, and saved himself there, not once nor twice. ¹¹Therefore the heart of the king of Syria was sore troubled for this thing; and he called his servants, and said to them, Will you not show me which of us is for the king of Israel? ¹²And one of his servants said, None, my lord, O king: but Elisha, the prophet that is in Israel, tells the king of Israel the words that you speak in your bedchamber. ¹³And he said, Go and spy where he is, that I may send and fetch him. And it was told him, saying, Behold, he is in Dothan. ¹⁴Therefore sent he thither horses, and chariots, and a great host: and they came by night, and compassed the city about. ¹⁵And when the servant of the man of God was risen early, and gone forth, behold, an host compassed the city both with horses and chariots. And his servant said to him, Alas, my master! how shall we do? ¹⁶And he answered, Fear not: for they that be with us are more than they that be with them. ¹⁷And Elisha prayed, and said, LORD, I pray you, open his eyes, that he may see. And the LORD opened the eyes of the young man; and he saw: and, behold, the mountain was full of horses and chariots of fire round about Elisha. ¹⁸And when they came down to him, Elisha prayed to the LORD, and said, Smite this people, I pray you, with blindness. And he smote them with blindness according to the word of Elisha. ¹⁹And Elisha said to them, This is not the way, neither is this the city: follow me, and I will bring you to the man whom you seek. But he led them to Samaria. ²⁰And it came to pass, when they were come into Samaria, that Elisha said, LORD, open the eyes of these men, that they may see. And the LORD opened their eyes, and they saw; and, behold, they were in the middle of Samaria. ²¹And the king of Israel said to Elisha, when he saw them, My father, shall I smite them? shall I smite them? ²²And he answered, You shall not smite them: would you smite those whom you have taken captive with your sword and with your bow? set bread and water before them, that they may eat and drink, and go to their master. ²³And he prepared great provision for them: and when they had eaten and drunk, he sent them away, and they went to their master. So the bands of Syria came no more into the land of Israel. ²⁴And it came to pass after this, that Benhadad king of Syria gathered all his host, and went up, and besieged Samaria. ²⁵And there was a great famine in Samaria: and, behold, they besieged it, until an ass's head was sold for fourscore pieces of silver, and the fourth part of a cab of dove's dung for five pieces of silver. ²⁶And as the king of Israel was passing by on the wall, there cried a woman to him, saying, Help, my lord, O king. ²⁷And he said, If the LORD do not help you, from where shall I help you? out of the barn floor, or out of the wine press? ²⁸And the king said to her, What ails you? And she answered, This woman said to me, Give your son, that we may eat him to day, and we will eat my son to morrow. ²⁹So we boiled my son, and did eat him: and I said to her on the next day, Give your son, that we may eat him: and she has hid her son. ³⁰And it came to pass, when the king heard the words of the woman, that he rent his clothes; and he passed by on the wall, and the people looked, and, behold, he had sackcloth within on his flesh. ³¹Then he said, God do so and more also to me, if the head of Elisha the son of Shaphat shall stand on him this day. ³²But Elisha sat in his house, and the elders sat with him; and the king sent a man from before him: but before the messenger came to him, he said to the elders, See you how this son of a murderer has sent to take away my head? look, when the messenger comes, shut the door, and hold him fast at the door: is not the sound of his master's feet behind him? ³³And while he yet talked with them, behold, the messenger came down to him: and he said, Behold, this evil is of the LORD; what should I wait for the LORD any longer?

7 ¹Then Elisha said, Hear you the word of the LORD; Thus says the LORD, To morrow about this time shall a measure of fine flour be sold for a shekel, and two measures of barley for a shekel, in the gate of Samaria. ²Then a lord on whose hand the king leaned answered the man of God, and said, Behold, if the LORD would make windows in heaven, might this thing be? And he said, Behold, you shall see it with your eyes, but shall not eat thereof. ³And there were four leprous men at the entering in of the gate: and they said one to another, Why sit we here until we die? ⁴If we say, We will enter into the city, then the famine is in the city, and we shall die there: and if we sit still here, we die also. Now therefore come, and let us fall to the host of the Syrians: if they save us alive, we shall live; and if they kill us, we shall but die. ⁵And they rose up in the twilight, to go to the camp of the Syrians: and when they were come to the uttermost part of the camp of Syria, behold, there was no man there. ⁶For the LORD had made the host of the Syrians to hear a noise of chariots, and a noise of horses, even the noise of a great host: and they said one to another, See, the king of Israel has hired against us the kings of the Hittites, and the kings of the Egyptians, to come on us. ⁷Why they arose and fled in the twilight, and left their tents, and their horses, and their asses, even the camp as it was, and fled for their life. ⁸And when these lepers came to the uttermost part of the camp, they went into one tent, and did eat and drink, and carried there silver, and gold, and raiment, and went and hid it; and came again, and entered into another tent, and carried there also, and went and hid it. ⁹Then they said one to another, We do not well: this day is a day of good tidings, and we hold our peace: if we tarry till the morning light, some mischief will come on us: now therefore come, that we may go and tell the king's household. ¹⁰So they came and called to the porter of the city: and they told them, saying, We came to the camp of the Syrians, and, behold, there was no man there, neither voice of man, but horses tied, and asses tied, and the tents as they were. ¹¹And he called the porters; and they told it to the king's house within. ¹²And the king arose in the night, and said to his servants, I will now show you what the Syrians have done to us. They know that we be hungry; therefore are they gone out of the camp to hide themselves in the field, saying, When they come out of the city, we shall catch them alive, and get into the city. ¹³And one of his servants answered and said, Let some take, I pray you, five of the horses that remain, which are left in the city, (behold, they are as all the multitude of Israel that are left in it: behold, I say, they are even as all the multitude of the Israelites that are consumed:) and let us send and see. ¹⁴They took therefore two chariot horses; and the king sent after the host of the Syrians, saying, Go and see. ¹⁵And they went after them to Jordan: and, see, all the way was full of garments and vessels, which the Syrians had cast away in their haste. And the messengers returned, and told the king. ¹⁶And the people went out, and spoiled the tents of the Syrians. So a measure of fine flour was sold for a shekel, and two measures of barley for a shekel, according to the word of the LORD. ¹⁷And the king appointed the lord on whose hand he leaned to have the charge of the gate: and the people stepped on him in the gate, and he died, as the man of God had said, who spoke when the king came down to him. ¹⁸And it came to pass as the man of God had spoken to the king, saying, Two measures of barley for a shekel, and a measure of fine flour for a shekel, shall be to morrow about this time in the gate of Samaria: ¹⁹And that lord answered the man of God, and said, Now, behold, if the LORD should make windows in heaven, might such a thing be? And he said, Behold, you shall see it with your eyes, but shall not eat thereof. ²⁰And so it fell out to him: for the people stepped on him in the gate, and he died.

8 ¹Then spoke Elisha to the woman, whose son he had restored to life, saying, Arise, and go you and your household, and sojourn wherever you can sojourn: for the LORD has called for a famine; and it shall also come on the land seven years. ²And the woman arose, and did after the saying of the man of God: and she went with her household, and sojourned in the land of the Philistines seven years. ³And it came to pass at the seven years' end, that the woman returned out of the land of the Philistines: and she went forth to cry to the king for her house and for her land. ⁴And the king talked with Gehazi the servant of the man of God, saying, Tell me, I pray you, all the great things that Elisha has done. ⁵And it came to pass, as he was telling the king how he had restored a dead body to life, that, behold, the woman, whose son he had restored to life, cried to the king for her house and for her land. And Gehazi said, My lord, O king, this is the woman, and this is her son, whom Elisha restored to life. ⁶And when the king asked the woman, she told him. So the king appointed to her a certain officer, saying, Restore all that was hers, and all the fruits of the field since the day that she left the land, even until now. ⁷And Elisha came to Damascus; and Benhadad the king of Syria was sick; and it was told him, saying, The man of God is come here. ⁸And the king said to Hazael, Take a present in your hand, and go, meet the man of God, and inquire of the LORD by him, saying, Shall I recover of this disease? ⁹So Hazael went to meet him, and took a present with him, even of every good thing of Damascus, forty camels' burden, and came and stood before him, and said, Your son Benhadad king of Syria has sent me to you, saying, Shall I recover of this disease? ¹⁰And Elisha said to him, Go, say to him, You may certainly recover: however, the LORD has showed me that he shall surely die. ¹¹And he settled his countenance steadfastly, until he was ashamed: and the man of God wept. ¹²And Hazael said, Why weeps my lord? And he answered, Because I know the evil that you will do to the children of Israel: their strong holds will you set on fire, and their young men will you slay with the sword, and will dash their children, and rip up their women with child. ¹³And Hazael said, But what, is your servant a dog, that he should do this great thing? And Elisha answered, The LORD has showed me that you shall be king over Syria. ¹⁴So he departed from Elisha, and came to his master; who said to him, What said Elisha to you? And he answered, He told me that you should surely recover. ¹⁵And it came to pass on the morrow, that he took a thick cloth, and dipped it in water, and spread it on his face, so that he died: and Hazael reigned in his stead. ¹⁶And in the fifth year of Joram the son of Ahab king of Israel, Jehoshaphat being then king of Judah, Jehoram the son of Je hoshaphat king of Judah began to reign. ¹⁷Thirty and two years old was he when he began to reign; and he reigned eight years in Jerusalem. ¹⁸And he walked in the way of the kings of Israel, as did the house of Ahab: for the daughter of Ahab was his wife: and he did evil in the sight of the LORD. ¹⁹Yet the LORD would not destroy Judah for David his servant's sake, as he promised him to give him always a light, and to his children. ²⁰In his days Edom revolted from under the hand of Judah, and made a king over themselves. ²¹So Joram went over to Zair, and all the chariots with him: and he rose by night, and smote the Edomites which compassed him about, and the captains of the chariots: and the people fled into their tents. ²²Yet Edom revolted from under the hand of Judah to this day. Then Libnah revolted at the same time. ²³And the rest of the acts of Joram, and all that he did, are they not written in the book of the chronicles of the kings of Judah? ²⁴And Joram slept with his fathers, and was buried with his fathers in the city of David: and Ahaziah his son reigned in his stead. ²⁵In the twelfth year of Joram the son of Ahab king of Israel did Ahaziah the son of Jehoram king of Judah begin to reign. ²⁶Two and twenty years old was Ahaziah when he began to reign; and he reigned one year in Jerusalem. And his mother's name was Athaliah, the daughter of Omri king of Israel. ²⁷And he walked in the way of the house of Ahab, and did evil in the sight of the LORD, as did the house of Ahab: for he was the son in law of the house of Ahab. ²⁸And he went with Joram the son of Ahab to the war against Hazael king of Syria in Ramothgilead; and the Syrians wounded Joram. ²⁹And king Joram went back to be healed in Jezreel of the wounds which the Syrians had given him at Ramah, when he fought against Hazael king of Syria. And Ahaziah the son of Jehoram king of Judah went down to see Joram the son of Ahab in Jezreel, because he was sick.

9 ¹And Elisha the prophet called one of the children of the prophets, and said to him, Gird up your loins, and take this box of oil in your hand, and go to Ramothgilead: ²And when you come thither, look out there Jehu the son of Jehoshaphat the son of Nimshi, and go in, and make him arise up from among his brothers, and carry him to an inner chamber; ³Then take the box of oil, and pour it on his head, and say, Thus says the LORD, I have anointed you king over Israel. Then open the door, and flee, and tarry not. ⁴So the young man, even the young man the prophet, went to Ramothgilead. ⁵And when he came, behold, the captains of the host were sitting; and he said, I have an errand to you, O captain. And Jehu said, To which of all us? And he said, To you, O captain. ⁶And he arose, and went into the house; and he poured the oil on his head, and said to him, Thus says the LORD God of Israel, I have anointed you king over the people of the LORD, even over Israel. ⁷And you shall smite the house of Ahab your master, that I may avenge the blood of my servants the prophets, and the blood of all the servants of the LORD, at the hand of Jezebel. ⁸For the whole house of Ahab shall perish: and I will cut off from Ahab him that urinates against the wall, and him that is shut up and left in Israel: ⁹And I will make the house of Ahab like the house of Jeroboam the son of Nebat, and like the house of Baasha the son of Ahijah: ¹⁰And the dogs shall eat Jezebel in the portion of Jezreel, and there shall be none to bury her. And he opened the door, and fled. ¹¹Then Jehu came forth to the servants of his lord: and one said to him, Is all well? why came this mad fellow to you? And he said to them, You know the man, and his communication. ¹²And they said, It is false; tell us now. And he said, Thus and thus spoke he to me, saying, Thus says the LORD, I have anointed you king over Israel. ¹³Then they hurried, and took every man his garment, and put it under him on the top of the stairs, and blew with trumpets, saying, Jehu is king. ¹⁴So Jehu the son of Jehoshaphat the son of Nimshi conspired against Joram. (Now Joram had kept Ramothgilead, he and all Israel, because of Hazael king of Syria. ¹⁵But king Joram was returned to be healed in Jezreel of the wounds which the Syrians had given him, when he fought with Hazael king of Syria.) And Jehu said, If it be your minds, then let none go forth nor escape out of the city to go to tell it in Jezreel. ¹⁶So Jehu rode in a chariot, and went to Jezreel; for Joram lay there. And Ahaziah king of Judah was come down to see Joram. ¹⁷And there stood a watchman on the tower in Jezreel, and he spied the company of Jehu as he came, and said, I see a company. And Joram said, Take an horseman, and send to meet them, and let him say, Is it peace? ¹⁸So there went one on horseback to meet him, and said, Thus says the king, Is it peace? And Jehu said, What have you to do with peace? turn you behind me. And the watchman told, saying, The messenger came to them, but he comes not again. ¹⁹Then he sent out a second on horseback, which came to them, and said, Thus says the king, Is it peace? And Jehu answered, What have you to do with peace? turn you behind me. ²⁰And the watchman told, saying, He came even to them, and comes not again: and the driving is like the driving of Jehu the son of Nimshi; for he drives furiously. ²¹And Joram said, Make ready. And his chariot was made ready. And Joram king of Israel and Ahaziah king of Judah went out, each in his chariot, and they went out against Jehu, and met him in the portion of Naboth the Jezreelite. ²²And it came to pass, when Joram saw Jehu, that he said, Is it peace, Jehu? And he answered, What peace, so long as the prostitutions of your mother Jezebel and her witchcrafts are so many? ²³And Joram turned his hands, and fled, and said to Ahaziah, There is treachery, O Ahaziah. ²⁴And Jehu drew a bow with his full strength, and smote Jehoram between his arms, and the arrow went out at his heart, and he sunk down in his chariot. ²⁵Then said Jehu to Bidkar his captain, Take up, and cast him in the portion of the field of Naboth the Jezreelite: for remember how that, when I and you rode together after Ahab his father, the LORD laid this burden on him; ²⁶Surely I have seen yesterday the blood of Naboth, and the blood of his sons, says the LORD; and I will requite you in this plat, says the LORD. Now therefore take and cast him into the plat of ground, according to the word of the LORD. ²⁷But when Ahaziah the king of Judah saw this, he fled by the way of the garden house. And Jehu followed after him, and said, Smite him also in the chariot. And they did so at the going up to Gur, which is by Ibleam. And he fled to Megiddo, and died there. ²⁸And his servants carried him in a chariot to Jerusalem, and buried him in his sepulcher with his fathers in the city of David. ²⁹And in the eleventh year of Joram the son of Ahab began Ahaziah to reign over Judah. ³⁰And when Jehu was come to Jezreel, Jezebel heard of it; and she painted her face, and tired her head, and looked out at a window. ³¹And as Jehu entered in at the gate, she said, Had Zimri peace, who slew his master? ³²And he lifted up his face to the window, and said, Who is on my side? who? And there looked out to him two or three eunuchs. ³³And he said, Throw her down. So they threw her down: and some of her blood was sprinkled on the wall, and on the horses: and he stepped her under foot. ³⁴And when he was come in, he did eat and drink, and said, Go, see now this cursed woman, and bury her: for she is a king's daughter. ³⁵And they went to bury her: but they found no more of her than the skull, and the feet, and the palms of her hands. ³⁶Why they came again, and told him. And he said, This is the word of the LORD, which he spoke by his servant Elijah the Tishbite, saying, In the portion of Jezreel shall dogs eat the flesh of Jezebel: ³⁷And the carcass of Jezebel shall be as dung on the face of the field in the portion of Jezreel; so that they shall not say, This is Jezebel.

10 ¹And Ahab had seventy sons in Samaria. And Jehu wrote letters, and sent to Samaria, to the rulers of Jezreel, to the elders, and to them that brought up Ahab's children, saying, ²Now as soon as this letter comes to you, seeing your master's sons are with you, and there are with you chariots and horses, a fenced city also, and armor; ³Look even out the best and meet of your master's sons, and set him on his father's throne, and fight for your master's house. ⁴But they were exceedingly afraid, and said, Behold, two kings stood not before him: how then shall we stand? ⁵And he that was over the house, and he that was over the city, the elders also, and the bringers up of the children, sent to Jehu, saying, We are your servants, and will do all that you shall bid us; we will not make any king: do you that which is good in your eyes. ⁶Then he wrote a letter the second time to them, saying, If you be mine, and if you will listen to my voice, take you the heads of the men your master's sons, and come to me to Jezreel by to morrow this time. Now the king's sons, being seventy persons, were with the great men of the city, which brought them up. ⁷And it came to pass, when the letter came to them, that they took the king's sons, and slew seventy persons, and put their heads in baskets, and sent him them to Jezreel. ⁸And there came a messenger, and told him, saying, They have brought the heads of the king's sons. And he said, Lay you them in two heaps at the entering in of the gate until the morning. ⁹And it came to pass in the morning, that he went out, and stood, and said to all the people, You be righteous: behold, I conspired against my master, and slew him: but who slew all these? ¹⁰Know now that there shall fall to the earth nothing of the word of the LORD, which the LORD spoke concerning the house of Ahab: for the LORD has done that which he spoke by his servant Elijah. ¹¹So Jehu slew all that remained of the house of Ahab in Jezreel, and all his great men, and his kinfolks, and his priests, until he left him none remaining. ¹²And he arose and departed, and came to Samaria. And as he was at the shearing house in the way, ¹³Jehu met with the brothers of Ahaziah king of Judah, and said, Who are you? And they answered, We are the brothers of Ahaziah; and we go down to salute the children of the king and the children of the queen. ¹⁴And he said, Take them alive. And they took them alive, and slew them at the pit of the shearing house, even two and forty men; neither left he any of them. ¹⁵And when he was departed there, he lighted on Jehonadab the son of Rechab coming to meet him: and he saluted him, and said to him, Is your heart right, as my heart is with your heart? And Jehonadab answered, It is. If it be, give me your hand. And he gave him his hand; and he took him up to him into the chariot. ¹⁶And he said, Come with me, and see my zeal for the LORD. So they made him ride in his chariot. ¹⁷And when he came to Samaria, he slew all that remained to Ahab in Samaria, till he had destroyed him, according to the saying of the LORD, which he spoke to Elijah. ¹⁸And Jehu gathered all the people together, and said to them, Ahab served Baal a little; but Jehu shall serve him much. ¹⁹Now therefore call to me all the prophets of Baal, all his servants, and all his priests; let none be wanting: for I have a great sacrifice to do to Baal; whoever shall be wanting, he shall not live. But Jehu did it in subtlety, to the intent that he might destroy the worshippers of Baal. ²⁰And Jehu said, Proclaim a solemn assembly for Baal. And they proclaimed it. ²¹And Jehu sent through all Israel: and all the worshippers of Baal came, so that there was not a man left that came not. And they came into the house of Baal; and the house of Baal was full from one end to another. ²²And he said to him that was over the vestry, Bring forth vestments for all the worshippers of Baal. And he brought them forth vestments. ²³And Jehu went, and Jehonadab the son of Rechab, into the house of Baal, and said to the worshippers of Baal, Search, and look that there be here with you none of the servants of the LORD, but the worshippers of Baal only. ²⁴And when they went in to offer sacrifices and burnt offerings, Jehu appointed fourscore men without, and said, If any of the men whom I have brought into your hands escape, he that lets him go, his life shall be for the life of him. ²⁵And it came to pass, as soon as he had made an end of offering the burnt offering, that Jehu said to the guard and to the captains, Go in, and slay them; let none come forth. And they smote them with the edge of the sword; and the guard and the captains cast them out, and went to the city of the house of Baal. ²⁶And they brought forth the images out of the house of Baal, and burned them. ²⁷And they broke down the image of Baal, and broke down the house of Baal, and made it a draught house to this day. ²⁸Thus Jehu destroyed Baal out of Israel. ²⁹However, from the sins of Jeroboam the son of Nebat, who made Israel to sin, Jehu departed not from after them, to wit, the golden calves that were in Bethel, and that were in Dan. ³⁰And the LORD said to Jehu, Because you have done well in executing that which is right in my eyes, and have done to the house of Ahab according to all that was in my heart, your children of the fourth generation shall sit on the throne of Israel. ³¹But

Jehu took no heed to walk in the law of the LORD God of Israel with all his heart: for he departed not from the sins of Jeroboam, which made Israel to sin. ³²In those days the LORD began to cut Israel short: and Hazael smote them in all the coasts of Israel; ³³From Jordan eastward, all the land of Gilead, the Gadites, and the Reubenites, and the Manassites, from Aroer, which is by the river Arnon, even Gilead and Bashan. ³⁴Now the rest of the acts of Jehu, and all that he did, and all his might, are they not written in the book of the chronicles of the kings of Israel? ³⁵And Jehu slept with his fathers: and they buried him in Samaria. And Jehoahaz his son reigned in his stead. ³⁶And the time that Jehu reigned over Israel in Samaria was twenty and eight years.

11 ¹And when Athaliah the mother of Ahaziah saw that her son was dead, she arose and destroyed all the seed royal. ²But Jehosheba, the daughter of king Joram, sister of Ahaziah, took Joash the son of Ahaziah, and stole him from among the king's sons which were slain; and they hid him, even him and his nurse, in the bedchamber from Athaliah, so that he was not slain. ³And he was with her hid in the house of the LORD six years. And Athaliah did reign over the land. ⁴And the seventh year Jehoiada sent and fetched the rulers over hundreds, with the captains and the guard, and brought them to him into the house of the LORD, and made a covenant with them, and took an oath of them in the house of the LORD, and showed them the king's son. ⁵And he commanded them, saying, This is the thing that you shall do; A third part of you that enter in on the sabbath shall even be keepers of the watch of the king's house; ⁶And a third part shall be at the gate of Sur; and a third part at the gate behind the guard: so shall you keep the watch of the house, that it be not broken down. ⁷And two parts of all you that go forth on the sabbath, even they shall keep the watch of the house of the LORD about the king. ⁸And you shall compass the king round about, every man with his weapons in his hand: and he that comes within the ranges, let him be slain: and be you with the king as he goes out and as he comes in. ⁹And the captains over the hundreds did according to all things that Jehoiada the priest commanded: and they took every man his men that were to come in on the sabbath, with them that should go out on the sabbath, and came to Jehoiada the priest. ¹⁰And to the captains over hundreds did the priest give king David's spears and shields, that were in the temple of the LORD. ¹¹And the guard stood, every man with his weapons in his hand, round about the king, from the right corner of the temple to the left corner of the temple, along by the altar and the temple. ¹²And he brought forth the king's son, and put the crown on him, and gave him the testimony; and they made him king, and anointed him; and they clapped their hands, and said, God save the king. ¹³And when Athaliah heard the noise of the guard and of the people, she came to the people into the temple of the LORD. ¹⁴And when she looked, behold, the king stood by a pillar, as the manner was, and the princes and the trumpeters by the king, and all the people of the land rejoiced, and blew with trumpets: and Athaliah rent her clothes, and cried, Treason, Treason. ¹⁵But Jehoiada the priest commanded the captains of the hundreds, the officers of the host, and said to them, Have her forth without the ranges; and him that follows her kill with the sword. For the priest had said, Let her not be slain in the house of the LORD. ¹⁶And they laid hands on her; and she went by the way by the which the horses came into the king's house: and there was she slain. ¹⁷And Jehoiada made a covenant between the LORD and the king and the people, that they should be the LORD's people; between the king also and the people. ¹⁸And all the people of the land went into the house of Baal, and broke it down; his altars and his images broke they in pieces thoroughly, and slew Mattan the priest of Baal before the altars. And the priest appointed officers over the house of the LORD. ¹⁹And he took the rulers over hundreds, and the captains, and the guard, and all the people of the land; and they brought down the king from the house of the LORD, and came by the way of the gate of the guard to the king's house. And he sat on the throne of the kings. ²⁰And all the people of the land rejoiced, and the city was in quiet: and they slew Athaliah with the sword beside the king's house. ²¹Seven years old was Jehoash when he began to reign.

12 ¹In the seventh year of Jehu Jehoash began to reign; and forty years reigned he in Jerusalem. And his mother's name was Zibiah of Beersheba. ²And Jehoash did that which was right in the sight of the LORD all his days wherein Jehoiada the priest instructed him. ³But the high places were not taken away: the people still sacrificed and burnt incense in the high places. ⁴And Jehoash said to the priests, All the money of the dedicated things that is brought into the house of the LORD, even the money of every one that passes the account, the money that every man is set at, and all the money that comes into any man's heart to bring into the house of the LORD, ⁵Let the priests take it to them, every man of his acquaintance: and let them repair the breaches of the house, wherever any breach shall be found. ⁶But it was so, that in the three and twentieth year of king Jehoash the priests had not repaired the breaches of the house. ⁷Then king Jehoash called for Jehoiada the priest, and the other priests, and said to them, Why repair you not the breaches of the house? now therefore receive no more money of your acquaintance, but deliver it for the breaches of the house. ⁸And the priests consented to receive no more money of the people, neither to repair the breaches of the house. ⁹But Jehoiada the priest took a chest, and bored a hole in the lid of it, and set it beside the altar, on the right side as one comes into the house of the LORD: and the priests that kept the door put therein all the money that was brought into the house of the LORD. ¹⁰And it was so, when they saw that there was much money in the chest, that the king's scribe and the high priest came up, and they put up in bags, and told the money that was found in the house of the LORD. ¹¹And they gave the money, being told, into the hands of them that did the work, that had the oversight of the house of the LORD: and they laid it out to the carpenters and builders, that worked on the house of the LORD, ¹²And to masons, and hewers of stone, and to buy timber and hewed stone to repair the breaches of the house of the LORD, and for all that was laid out for the house to repair it. ¹³However, there were not made for the house of the LORD bowls of silver, snuffers, basins, trumpets, any vessels of gold, or vessels of silver, of the money that was brought into the house of the LORD: ¹⁴But they gave that to the workmen,

and repaired therewith the house of the LORD. ¹⁵Moreover they reckoned not with the men, into whose hand they delivered the money to be bestowed on workmen: for they dealt faithfully. ¹⁶The trespass money and sin money was not brought into the house of the LORD: it was the priests'. ¹⁷Then Hazael king of Syria went up, and fought against Gath, and took it: and Hazael set his face to go up to Jerusalem. ¹⁸And Jehoash king of Judah took all the hallowed things that Jehoshaphat, and Jehoram, and Ahaziah, his fathers, kings of Judah, had dedicated, and his own hallowed things, and all the gold that was found in the treasures of the house of the LORD, and in the king's house, and sent it to Hazael king of Syria: and he went away from Jerusalem. ¹⁹And the rest of the acts of Joash, and all that he did, are they not written in the book of the chronicles of the kings of Judah? ²⁰And his servants arose, and made a conspiracy, and slew Joash in the house of Millo, which goes down to Silla. ²¹For Jozachar the son of Shimeath, and Jehozabad the son of Shomer, his servants, smote him, and he died; and they buried him with his fathers in the city of David: and Amaziah his son reigned in his stead.

13 ¹In the three and twentieth year of Joash the son of Ahaziah king of Judah Jehoahaz the son of Jehu began to reign over Israel in Samaria, and reigned seventeen years. ²And he did that which was evil in the sight of the LORD, and followed the sins of Jeroboam the son of Nebat, which made Israel to sin; he departed not therefrom. ³And the anger of the LORD was kindled against Israel, and he delivered them into the hand of Hazael king of Syria, and into the hand of Benhadad the son of Hazael, all their days. ⁴And Jehoahaz sought the LORD, and the LORD listened to him: for he saw the oppression of Israel, because the king of Syria oppressed them. ⁵(And the LORD gave Israel a savior, so that they went out from under the hand of the Syrians: and the children of Israel dwelled in their tents, as beforetime. ⁶Nevertheless they departed not from the sins of the house of Jeroboam, who made Israel sin, but walked therein: and there remained the grove also in Samaria.) ⁷Neither did he leave of the people to Jehoahaz but fifty horsemen, and ten chariots, and ten thousand footmen; for the king of Syria had destroyed them, and had made them like the dust by threshing. ⁸Now the rest of the acts of Jehoahaz, and all that he did, and his might, are they not written in the book of the chronicles of the kings of Israel? ⁹And Jehoahaz slept with his fathers; and they buried him in Samaria: and Joash his son reigned in his stead. ¹⁰In the thirty and seventh year of Joash king of Judah began Jehoash the son of Jehoahaz to reign over Israel in Samaria, and reigned sixteen years. ¹¹And he did that which was evil in the sight of the LORD; he departed not from all the sins of Jeroboam the son of Nebat, who made Israel sin: but he walked therein. ¹²And the rest of the acts of Joash, and all that he did, and his might with which he fought against Amaziah king of Judah, are they not written in the book of the chronicles of the kings of Israel? ¹³And Joash slept with his fathers; and Jeroboam sat on his throne: and Joash was buried in Samaria with the kings of Israel. ¹⁴Now Elisha was fallen sick of his sickness whereof he died. And Joash the king of Israel came down to him, and wept over his face, and said, O my father, my father, the chariot of Israel, and the horsemen thereof. ¹⁵And Elisha said to him, Take bow and arrows. And he took to him bow and arrows. ¹⁶And he said to the king of Israel, Put your hand on the bow. And he put his hand on it: and Elisha put his hands on the king's hands. ¹⁷And he said, Open the window eastward. And he opened it. Then Elisha said, Shoot. And he shot. And he said, The arrow of the LORD's deliverance, and the arrow of deliverance from Syria: for you shall smite the Syrians in Aphek, till you have consumed them. ¹⁸And he said, Take the arrows. And he took them. And he said to the king of Israel, Smite on the ground. And he smote thrice, and stayed. ¹⁹And the man of God was wroth with him, and said, You should have smitten five or six times; then had you smitten Syria till you had consumed it: whereas now you shall smite Syria but thrice. ²⁰And Elisha died, and they buried him. And the bands of the Moabites invaded the land at the coming in of the year. ²¹And it came to pass, as they were burying a man, that, behold, they spied a band of men; and they cast the man into the sepulcher of Elisha: and when the man was let down, and touched the bones of Elisha, he revived, and stood up on his feet. ²²But Hazael king of Syria oppressed Israel all the days of Jehoahaz. ²³And the LORD was gracious to them, and had compassion on them, and had respect to them, because of his covenant with Abraham, Isaac, and Jacob, and would not destroy them, neither cast he them from his presence as yet. ²⁴So Hazael king of Syria died; and Benhadad his son reigned in his stead. ²⁵And Jehoash the son of Jehoahaz took again out of the hand of Benhadad the son of Hazael the cities, which he had taken out of the hand of Jehoahaz his father by war. Three times did Joash beat him, and recovered the cities of Israel.

14 ¹In the second year of Joash son of Jehoahaz king of Israel reigned Amaziah the son of Joash king of Judah. ²He was twenty and five years old when he began to reign, and reigned twenty and nine years in Jerusalem. And his mother's name was Jehoaddan of Jerusalem. ³And he did that which was right in the sight of the LORD, yet not like David his father: he did according to all things as Joash his father did. ⁴However, the high places were not taken away: as yet the people did sacrifice and burnt incense on the high places. ⁵And it came to pass, as soon as the kingdom was confirmed in his hand, that he slew his servants which had slain the king his father. ⁶But the children of the murderers he slew not: according to that which is written in the book of the law of Moses, wherein the LORD commanded, saying, The fathers shall not be put to death for the children, nor the children be put to death for the fathers; but every man shall be put to death for his own sin. ⁷He slew of Edom in the valley of salt ten thousand, and took Selah by war, and called the name of it Joktheel to this day. ⁸Then Amaziah sent messengers to Jehoash, the son of Jehoahaz son of Jehu, king of Israel, saying, Come, let us look one another in the face. ⁹And Jehoash the king of Israel sent to Amaziah king of Judah, saying, The thistle that was in Lebanon sent to the cedar that was in Lebanon, saying, Give your daughter to my son to wife: and there passed by a wild beast that was in Lebanon, and stepped down the thistle. ¹⁰You have indeed smitten Edom, and your heart has lifted you up: glory of this, and tarry at home: for why should you meddle to your hurt, that you should fall, even you, and Judah with you?

¹¹But Amaziah would not hear. Therefore Jehoash king of Israel went up; and he and Amaziah king of Judah looked one another in the face at Bethshemesh, which belongs to Judah. ¹²And Judah was put to the worse before Israel; and they fled every man to their tents. ¹³And Jehoash king of Israel took Amaziah king of Judah, the son of Jehoash the son of Ahaziah, at Bethshemesh, and came to Jerusalem, and broke down the wall of Jerusalem from the gate of Ephraim to the corner gate, four hundred cubits. ¹⁴And he took all the gold and silver, and all the vessels that were found in the house of the LORD, and in the treasures of the king's house, and hostages, and returned to Samaria. ¹⁵Now the rest of the acts of Jehoash which he did, and his might, and how he fought with Amaziah king of Judah, are they not written in the book of the chronicles of the kings of Israel? ¹⁶And Jehoash slept with his fathers, and was buried in Samaria with the kings of Israel; and Jeroboam his son reigned in his stead. ¹⁷And Amaziah the son of Joash king of Judah lived after the death of Jehoash son of Jehoahaz king of Israel fifteen years. ¹⁸And the rest of the acts of Amaziah, are they not written in the book of the chronicles of the kings of Judah? ¹⁹Now they made a conspiracy against him in Jerusalem: and he fled to Lachish; but they sent after him to Lachish, and slew him there. ²⁰And they brought him on horses: and he was buried at Jerusalem with his fathers in the city of David. ²¹And all the people of Judah took Azariah, which was sixteen years old, and made him king instead of his father Amaziah. ²²He built Elath, and restored it to Judah, after that the king slept with his fathers. ²³In the fifteenth year of Amaziah the son of Joash king of Judah Jeroboam the son of Joash king of Israel began to reign in Samaria, and reigned forty and one years. ²⁴And he did that which was evil in the sight of the LORD: he departed not from all the sins of Jeroboam the son of Nebat, who made Israel to sin. ²⁵He restored the coast of Israel from the entering of Hamath to the sea of the plain, according to the word of the LORD God of Israel, which he spoke by the hand of his servant Jonah, the son of Amittai, the prophet, which was of Gathhepher. ²⁶For the LORD saw the affliction of Israel, that it was very bitter: for there was not any shut up, nor any left, nor any helper for Israel. ²⁷And the LORD said not that he would blot out the name of Israel from under heaven: but he saved them by the hand of Jeroboam the son of Joash. ²⁸Now the rest of the acts of Jeroboam, and all that he did, and his might, how he warred, and how he recovered Damascus, and Hamath, which belonged to Judah, for Israel, are they not written in the book of the chronicles of the kings of Israel? ²⁹And Jeroboam slept with his fathers, even with the kings of Israel; and Zachariah his son reigned in his stead.

15

¹In the twenty and seventh year of Jeroboam king of Israel began Azariah son of Amaziah king of Judah to reign. ²Sixteen years old was he when he began to reign, and he reigned two and fifty years in Jerusalem. And his mother's name was Jecholiah of Jerusalem. ³And he did that which was right in the sight of the LORD, according to all that his father Amaziah had done; ⁴Save that the high places were not removed: the people sacrificed and burnt incense still on the high places. ⁵And the LORD smote the king, so that he was a leper to the day of his death, and dwelled in a several house. And Jotham the king's son was over the house, judging the people of the land. ⁶And the rest of the acts of Azariah, and all that he did, are they not written in the book of the chronicles of the kings of Judah? ⁷So Azariah slept with his fathers; and they buried him with his fathers in the city of David: and Jotham his son reigned in his stead. ⁸In the thirty and eighth year of Azariah king of Judah did Zachariah the son of Jeroboam reign over Israel in Samaria six months. ⁹And he did that which was evil in the sight of the LORD, as his fathers had done: he departed not from the sins of Jeroboam the son of Nebat, who made Israel to sin. ¹⁰And Shallum the son of Jabesh conspired against him, and smote him before the people, and slew him, and reigned in his stead. ¹¹And the rest of the acts of Zachariah, behold, they are written in the book of the chronicles of the kings of Israel. ¹²This was the word of the LORD which he spoke to Jehu, saying, Your sons shall sit on the throne of Israel to the fourth generation. And so it came to pass. ¹³Shallum the son of Jabesh began to reign in the nine and thirtieth year of Uzziah king of Judah; and he reigned a full month in Samaria. ¹⁴For Menahem the son of Gadi went up from Tirzah, and came to Samaria, and smote Shallum the son of Jabesh in Samaria, and slew him, and reigned in his stead. ¹⁵And the rest of the acts of Shallum, and his conspiracy which he made, behold, they are written in the book of the chronicles of the kings of Israel. ¹⁶Then Menahem smote Tiphsah, and all that were therein, and the coasts thereof from Tirzah: because they opened not to him, therefore he smote it; and all the women therein that were with child he ripped up. ¹⁷In the nine and thirtieth year of Azariah king of Judah began Menahem the son of Gadi to reign over Israel, and reigned ten years in Samaria. ¹⁸And he did that which was evil in the sight of the LORD: he departed not all his days from the sins of Jeroboam the son of Nebat, who made Israel to sin. ¹⁹And Pul the king of Assyria came against the land: and Menahem gave Pul a thousand talents of silver, that his hand might be with him to confirm the kingdom in his hand. ²⁰And Menahem exacted the money of Israel, even of all the mighty men of wealth, of each man fifty shekels of silver, to give to the king of Assyria. So the king of Assyria turned back, and stayed not there in the land. ²¹And the rest of the acts of Menahem, and all that he did, are they not written in the book of the chronicles of the kings of Israel? ²²And Menahem slept with his fathers; and Pekahiah his son reigned in his stead. ²³In the fiftieth year of Azariah king of Judah Pekahiah the son of Menahem began to reign over Israel in Samaria, and reigned two years. ²⁴And he did that which was evil in the sight of the LORD: he departed not from the sins of Jeroboam the son of Nebat, who made Israel to sin. ²⁵But Pekah the son of Remaliah, a captain of his, conspired against him, and smote him in Samaria, in the palace of the king's house, with Argob and Arieh, and with him fifty men of the Gileadites: and he killed him, and reigned in his room. ²⁶And the rest of the acts of Pekahiah, and all that he did, behold, they are written in the book of the chronicles of the kings of Israel. ²⁷In the two and fiftieth year of Azariah king of Judah Pekah the son of Remaliah began to reign over Israel in Samaria, and reigned twenty years. ²⁸And he did that which was evil in the sight of the LORD: he departed not from the sins of

Jeroboam the son of Nebat, who made Israel to sin. ²⁹In the days of Pekah king of Israel came Tiglathpileser king of Assyria, and took Ijon, and Abelbethmaachah, and Janoah, and Kedesh, and Hazor, and Gilead, and Galilee, all the land of Naphtali, and carried them captive to Assyria. ³⁰And Hoshea the son of Elah made a conspiracy against Pekah the son of Remaliah, and smote him, and slew him, and reigned in his stead, in the twentieth year of Jotham the son of Uzziah. ³¹And the rest of the acts of Pekah, and all that he did, behold, they are written in the book of the chronicles of the kings of Israel. ³²In the second year of Pekah the son of Remaliah king of Israel began Jotham the son of Uzziah king of Judah to reign. ³³Five and twenty years old was he when he began to reign, and he reigned sixteen years in Jerusalem. And his mother's name was Jerusha, the daughter of Zadok. ³⁴And he did that which was right in the sight of the LORD: he did according to all that his father Uzziah had done. ³⁵However, the high places were not removed: the people sacrificed and burned incense still in the high places. He built the higher gate of the house of the LORD. ³⁶Now the rest of the acts of Jotham, and all that he did, are they not written in the book of the chronicles of the kings of Judah? ³⁷In those days the LORD began to send against Judah Rezin the king of Syria, and Pekah the son of Remaliah. ³⁸And Jotham slept with his fathers, and was buried with his fathers in the city of David his father: and Ahaz his son reigned in his stead.

16 ¹In the seventeenth year of Pekah the son of Remaliah Ahaz the son of Jotham king of Judah began to reign. ²Twenty years old was Ahaz when he began to reign, and reigned sixteen years in Jerusalem, and did not that which was right in the sight of the LORD his God, like David his father. ³But he walked in the way of the kings of Israel, yes, and made his son to pass through the fire, according to the abominations of the heathen, whom the LORD cast out from before the children of Israel. ⁴And he sacrificed and burnt incense in the high places, and on the hills, and under every green tree. ⁵Then Rezin king of Syria and Pekah son of Remaliah king of Israel came up to Jerusalem to war: and they besieged Ahaz, but could not overcome him. ⁶At that time Rezin king of Syria recovered Elath to Syria, and drove the Jews from Elath: and the Syrians came to Elath, and dwelled there to this day. ⁷So Ahaz sent messengers to Tiglathpileser king of Assyria, saying, I am your servant and your son: come up, and save me out of the hand of the king of Syria, and out of the hand of the king of Israel, which rise up against me. ⁸And Ahaz took the silver and gold that was found in the house of the LORD, and in the treasures of the king's house, and sent it for a present to the king of Assyria. ⁹And the king of Assyria listened to him: for the king of Assyria went up against Damascus, and took it, and carried the people of it captive to Kir, and slew Rezin. ¹⁰And king Ahaz went to Damascus to meet Tiglathpileser king of Assyria, and saw an altar that was at Damascus: and king Ahaz sent to Urijah the priest the fashion of the altar, and the pattern of it, according to all the workmanship thereof. ¹¹And Urijah the priest built an altar according to all that king Ahaz had sent from Damascus: so Urijah the priest made it against king Ahaz came from Damascus. ¹²And when the king was come from Damascus, the king saw the altar: and the king approached to the altar, and offered thereon. ¹³And he burnt his burnt offering and his meat offering, and poured his drink offering, and sprinkled the blood of his peace offerings, on the altar. ¹⁴And he brought also the brazen altar, which was before the LORD, from the forefront of the house, from between the altar and the house of the LORD, and put it on the north side of the altar. ¹⁵And king Ahaz commanded Urijah the priest, saying, On the great altar burn the morning burnt offering, and the evening meat offering, and the king's burnt sacrifice, and his meat offering, with the burnt offering of all the people of the land, and their meat offering, and their drink offerings; and sprinkle on it all the blood of the burnt offering, and all the blood of the sacrifice: and the brazen altar shall be for me to inquire by. ¹⁶Thus did Urijah the priest, according to all that king Ahaz commanded. ¹⁷And king Ahaz cut off the borders of the bases, and removed the laver from off them; and took down the sea from off the brazen oxen that were under it, and put it on the pavement of stones. ¹⁸And the covert for the sabbath that they had built in the house, and the king's entry without, turned he from the house of the LORD for the king of Assyria. ¹⁹Now the rest of the acts of Ahaz which he did, are they not written in the book of the chronicles of the kings of Judah? ²⁰And Ahaz slept with his fathers, and was buried with his fathers in the city of David: and Hezekiah his son reigned in his stead.

17 ¹In the twelfth year of Ahaz king of Judah began Hoshea the son of Elah to reign in Samaria over Israel nine years. ²And he did that which was evil in the sight of the LORD, but not as the kings of Israel that were before him. ³Against him came up Shalmaneser king of Assyria; and Hoshea became his servant, and gave him presents. ⁴And the king of Assyria found conspiracy in Hoshea: for he had sent messengers to So king of Egypt, and brought no present to the king of Assyria, as he had done year by year: therefore the king of Assyria shut him up, and bound him in prison. ⁵Then the king of Assyria came up throughout all the land, and went up to Samaria, and besieged it three years. ⁶In the ninth year of Hoshea the king of Assyria took Samaria, and carried Israel away into Assyria, and placed them in Halah and in Habor by the river of Gozan, and in the cities of the Medes. ⁷For so it was, that the children of Israel had sinned against the LORD their God, which had brought them up out of the land of Egypt, from under the hand of Pharaoh king of Egypt, and had feared other gods, ⁸And walked in the statutes of the heathen, whom the LORD cast out from before the children of Israel, and of the kings of Israel, which they had made. ⁹And the children of Israel did secretly those things that were not right against the LORD their God, and they built them high places in all their cities, from the tower of the watchmen to the fenced city. ¹⁰And they set them up images and groves in every high hill, and under every green tree: ¹¹And there they burnt incense in all the high places, as did the heathen whom the LORD carried away before them; and worked wicked things to provoke the LORD to anger: ¹²For they served idols, whereof the LORD had said to them, You shall not do this thing. ¹³Yet the LORD testified against Israel, and against Judah, by all the prophets, and by all the seers, saying, Turn you from your evil ways, and keep my commandments and my statutes, according to all the law which I commanded your fathers, and which I sent to you by my servants the prophets. ¹⁴Notwithstanding they would not hear, but hardened their necks, like to the neck of their fathers, that did not believe in the LORD their God. ¹⁵And they rejected his statutes, and his covenant that he made with their fathers, and his testimonies which he testified against them; and they followed vanity, and became vain, and went after the heathen that were round about them, concerning whom the LORD had charged them, that they should not do like them. ¹⁶And they left all the commandments of the LORD their God, and made them molten images, even two calves, and made a grove, and worshipped all the host of heaven, and served Baal. ¹⁷And they caused their sons and their daughters to pass through the fire, and used divination and enchantments, and sold themselves to do evil in the sight of the LORD, to provoke him to anger. ¹⁸Therefore the LORD was very angry with Israel, and removed them out of his sight: there was none left but the tribe of Judah only. ¹⁹Also Judah kept not the commandments of the LORD their God, but walked in the statutes of Israel which they made. ²⁰And the LORD rejected all the seed of Israel, and afflicted them, and delivered them into the hand of spoilers, until he had cast them out of his sight. ²¹For he rent Israel from the house of David; and they made Jeroboam the son of Nebat king: and Jeroboam drove Israel from following the LORD, and made them sin a great sin. ²²For the children of Israel walked in all the sins of Jeroboam which he did; they departed not from them; ²³Until the LORD removed Israel out of his sight, as he had said by all his servants the prophets. So was Israel carried away out of their own land to Assyria to this day. ²⁴And the king of Assyria brought men from Babylon, and from Cuthah, and from Ava, and from Hamath, and from Sepharvaim, and placed them in the cities of Samaria instead of the children of Israel: and they possessed Samaria, and dwelled in the cities thereof. ²⁵And so it was at the beginning of their dwelling there, that they feared not the LORD: therefore the LORD sent lions among them, which slew some of them. ²⁶Why they spoke to the king of Assyria, saying, The nations which you have removed, and placed in the cities of Samaria, know not the manner of the God of the land: therefore he has sent lions among them, and, behold, they slay them, because they know not the manner of the God of the land. ²⁷Then the king of Assyria commanded, saying, Carry thither one of the priests whom you brought from there; and let them go and dwell there, and let him teach them the manner of the God of the land. ²⁸Then one of the priests whom they had carried away from Samaria came and dwelled in Bethel, and taught them how they should fear the LORD. ²⁹However, every nation made gods of their own, and put them in the houses of the high places which the Samaritans had made, every nation in their cities wherein they dwelled. ³⁰And the men of Babylon made Succothbenoth, and the men of Cuth made Nergal, and the men of Hamath made Ashima, ³¹And the Avites made Nibhaz and Tartak, and the Sepharvites burnt their children in fire to Adrammelech and Anammelech, the gods of Sepharvaim. ³²So they feared the LORD, and made to themselves of the lowest of them priests of the high places, which sacrificed for them in the houses of the high places. ³³They feared the LORD, and served their own gods, after the manner of the nations whom they carried away from there. ³⁴To this day they do after the former manners: they fear not the LORD, neither do they after their statutes, or after their ordinances, or after the law and commandment which the LORD commanded the children of Jacob, whom he named Israel; ³⁵With whom the LORD had made a covenant, and charged them, saying, You shall not fear other gods, nor bow yourselves to them, nor serve them, nor sacrifice to them: ³⁶But the LORD, who brought you up out of the land of Egypt with great power and a stretched out arm, him shall you fear, and him shall you worship, and to him shall you do sacrifice. ³⁷And the statutes, and the ordinances, and the law, and the commandment, which he wrote for you, you shall observe to do for ever more; and you shall not fear other gods. ³⁸And the covenant that I have made with you you shall not forget; neither shall you fear other gods. ³⁹But the LORD your God you shall fear; and he shall deliver you out of the hand of all your enemies. ⁴⁰However, they did not listen, but they did after their former manner. ⁴¹So these nations feared the LORD, and served their graven images, both their children, and their children's children: as did their fathers, so do they to this day.

18

¹Now it came to pass in the third year of Hoshea son of Elah king of Israel, that Hezekiah the son of Ahaz king of Judah began to reign. ²Twenty and five years old was he when he began to reign; and he reigned twenty and nine years in Jerusalem. His mother's name also was Abi, the daughter of Zachariah. ³And he did that which was right in the sight of the LORD, according to all that David his father did. ⁴He removed the high places, and broke the images, and cut down the groves, and broke in pieces the brazen serpent that Moses had made: for to those days the children of Israel did burn incense to it: and he called it Nehushtan. ⁵He trusted in the LORD God of Israel; so that after him was none like him among all the kings of Judah, nor any that were before him. ⁶For he held to the LORD, and departed not from following him, but kept his commandments, which the LORD commanded Moses. ⁷And the LORD was with him; and he prospered wherever he went forth: and he rebelled against the king of Assyria, and served him not. ⁸He smote the Philistines, even to Gaza, and the borders thereof, from the tower of the watchmen to the fenced city. ⁹And it came to pass in the fourth year of king Hezekiah, which was the seventh year of Hoshea son of Elah king of Israel, that Shalmaneser king of Assyria came up against Samaria, and besieged it. ¹⁰And at the end of three years they took it: even in the sixth year of Hezekiah, that is in the ninth year of Hoshea king of Israel, Samaria was taken. ¹¹And the king of Assyria did carry away Israel to Assyria, and put them in Halah and in Habor by the river of Gozan, and in the cities of the Medes: ¹²Because they obeyed not the voice of the LORD their God, but transgressed his covenant, and all that Moses the servant of the LORD commanded, and would not hear them, nor do them. ¹³Now in the fourteenth year of king Hezekiah did Sennacherib king of Assyria come up against all the fenced cities of Judah, and took them. ¹⁴And Hezekiah king of Judah sent to the king of Assyria to Lachish, saying, I have offended;

return from me: that which you put on me will I bear. And the king of Assyria appointed to Hezekiah king of Judah three hundred talents of silver and thirty talents of gold. ¹⁵And Hezekiah gave him all the silver that was found in the house of the LORD, and in the treasures of the king's house. ¹⁶At that time did Hezekiah cut off the gold from the doors of the temple of the LORD, and from the pillars which Hezekiah king of Judah had overlaid, and gave it to the king of Assyria. ¹⁷And the king of Assyria sent Tartan and Rabsaris and Rabshakeh from Lachish to king Hezekiah with a great host against Jerusalem. And they went up and came to Jerusalem. And when they were come up, they came and stood by the conduit of the upper pool, which is in the highway of the fuller's field. ¹⁸And when they had called to the king, there came out to them Eliakim the son of Hilkiah, which was over the household, and Shebna the scribe, and Joah the son of Asaph the recorder. ¹⁹And Rabshakeh said to them, Speak you now to Hezekiah, Thus says the great king, the king of Assyria, What confidence is this wherein you trust? ²⁰You say, (but they are but vain words,) I have counsel and strength for the war. Now on whom do you trust, that you rebel against me? ²¹Now, behold, you trust on the staff of this bruised reed, even on Egypt, on which if a man lean, it will go into his hand, and pierce it: so is Pharaoh king of Egypt to all that trust on him. ²²But if you say to me, We trust in the LORD our God: is not that he, whose high places and whose altars Hezekiah has taken away, and has said to Judah and Jerusalem, You shall worship before this altar in Jerusalem? ²³Now therefore, I pray you, give pledges to my lord the king of Assyria, and I will deliver you two thousand horses, if you be able on your part to set riders on them. ²⁴How then will you turn away the face of one captain of the least of my master's servants, and put your trust on Egypt for chariots and for horsemen? ²⁵Am I now come up without the LORD against this place to destroy it? The LORD said to me, Go up against this land, and destroy it. ²⁶Then said Eliakim the son of Hilkiah, and Shebna, and Joah, to Rabshakeh, Speak, I pray you, to your servants in the Syrian language; for we understand it: and talk not with us in the Jews' language in the ears of the people that are on the wall. ²⁷But Rabshakeh said to them, Has my master sent me to your master, and to you, to speak these words? has he not sent me to the men which sit on the wall, that they may eat their own dung, and drink their own urine with you? ²⁸Then Rabshakeh stood and cried with a loud voice in the Jews' language, and spoke, saying, Hear the word of the great king, the king of Assyria: ²⁹Thus says the king, Let not Hezekiah deceive you: for he shall not be able to deliver you out of his hand: ³⁰Neither let Hezekiah make you trust in the LORD, saying, The LORD will surely deliver us, and this city shall not be delivered into the hand of the king of Assyria. ³¹Listen not to Hezekiah: for thus says the king of Assyria, Make an agreement with me by a present, and come out to me, and then eat you every man of his own vine, and every one of his fig tree, and drink you every one the waters of his cistern: ³²Until I come and take you away to a land like your own land, a land of corn and wine, a land of bread and vineyards, a land of oil olive and of honey, that you may live, and not die: and listen not to Hezekiah, when he persuades you, saying, The LORD will deliver us. ³³Has any of the gods of the nations delivered at all his land out of the hand of the king of Assyria? ³⁴Where are the gods of Hamath, and of Arpad? where are the gods of Sepharvaim, Hena, and Ivah? have they delivered Samaria out of my hand? ³⁵Who are they among all the gods of the countries, that have delivered their country out of my hand, that the LORD should deliver Jerusalem out of my hand? ³⁶But the people held their peace, and answered him not a word: for the king's commandment was, saying, Answer him not. ³⁷Then came Eliakim the son of Hilkiah, which was over the household, and Shebna the scribe, and Joah the son of Asaph the recorder, to Hezekiah with their clothes rent, and told him the words of Rabshakeh.

19

¹And it came to pass, when king Hezekiah heard it, that he rent his clothes, and covered himself with sackcloth, and went into the house of the LORD. ²And he sent Eliakim, which was over the household, and Shebna the scribe, and the elders of the priests, covered with sackcloth, to Isaiah the prophet the son of Amoz. ³And they said to him, Thus says Hezekiah, This day is a day of trouble, and of rebuke, and blasphemy; for the children are come to the birth, and there is not strength to bring forth. ⁴It may be the LORD your God will hear all the words of Rabshakeh, whom the king of Assyria his master has sent to reproach the living God; and will reprove the words which the LORD your God has heard: why lift up your prayer for the remnant that are left. ⁵So the servants of king Hezekiah came to Isaiah. ⁶And Isaiah said to them, Thus shall you say to your master, Thus says the LORD, Be not afraid of the words which you have heard, with which the servants of the king of Assyria have blasphemed me. ⁷Behold, I will send a blast on him, and he shall hear a rumor, and shall return to his own land; and I will cause him to fall by the sword in his own land. ⁸So Rabshakeh returned, and found the king of Assyria warring against Libnah: for he had heard that he was departed from Lachish. ⁹And when he heard say of Tirhakah king of Ethiopia, Behold, he is come out to fight against you: he sent messengers again to Hezekiah, saying, ¹⁰Thus shall you speak to Hezekiah king of Judah, saying, Let not your God in whom you trust deceive you, saying, Jerusalem shall not be delivered into the hand of the king of Assyria. ¹¹Behold, you have heard what the kings of Assyria have done to all lands, by destroying them utterly: and shall you be delivered? ¹²Have the gods of the nations delivered them which my fathers have destroyed; as Gozan, and Haran, and Rezeph, and the children of Eden which were in Thelasar? ¹³Where is the king of Hamath, and the king of Arpad, and the king of the city of Sepharvaim, of Hena, and Ivah? ¹⁴And Hezekiah received the letter of the hand of the messengers, and read it: and Hezekiah went up into the house of the LORD, and spread it before the LORD. ¹⁵And Hezekiah prayed before the LORD, and said, O LORD God of Israel, which dwell between the cherubim, you are the God, even you alone, of all the kingdoms of the earth; you have made heaven and earth. ¹⁶LORD, bow down your ear, and hear: open, LORD, your eyes, and see: and hear the words of Sennacherib, which has sent him to reproach the living God. ¹⁷Of a truth, LORD, the kings of Assyria have destroyed the nations and their lands, ¹⁸And have cast their gods into the fire: for they were no gods, but the work of men's hands,

wood and stone: therefore they have destroyed them. ¹⁹Now therefore, O LORD our God, I beseech you, save you us out of his hand, that all the kingdoms of the earth may know that you are the LORD God, even you only. ²⁰Then Isaiah the son of Amoz sent to Hezekiah, saying, Thus says the LORD God of Israel, That which you have prayed to me against Sennacherib king of Assyria I have heard. ²¹This is the word that the LORD has spoken concerning him; The virgin the daughter of Zion has despised you, and laughed you to scorn; the daughter of Jerusalem has shaken her head at you. ²²Whom have you reproached and blasphemed? and against whom have you exalted your voice, and lifted up your eyes on high? even against the Holy One of Israel. ²³By your messengers you have reproached the LORD, and have said, With the multitude of my chariots I am come up to the height of the mountains, to the sides of Lebanon, and will cut down the tall cedar trees thereof, and the choice fir trees thereof: and I will enter into the lodgings of his borders, and into the forest of his Carmel. ²⁴I have dig and drunk strange waters, and with the sole of my feet have I dried up all the rivers of besieged places. ²⁵Have you not heard long ago how I have done it, and of ancient times that I have formed it? now have I brought it to pass, that you should be to lay waste fenced cities into ruinous heaps. ²⁶Therefore their inhabitants were of small power, they were dismayed and confounded; they were as the grass of the field, and as the green herb, as the grass on the house tops, and as corn blasted before it be grown up. ²⁷But I know your stayed, and your going out, and your coming in, and your rage against me. ²⁸Because your rage against me and your tumult is come up into my ears, therefore I will put my hook in your nose, and my bridle in your lips, and I will turn you back by the way by which you came. ²⁹And this shall be a sign to you, You shall eat this year such things as grow of themselves, and in the second year that which springs of the same; and in the third year sow you, and reap, and plant vineyards, and eat the fruits thereof. ³⁰And the remnant that is escaped of the house of Judah shall yet again take root downward, and bear fruit upward. ³¹For out of Jerusalem shall go forth a remnant, and they that escape out of mount Zion: the zeal of the LORD of hosts shall do this. ³²Therefore thus says the LORD concerning the king of Assyria, He shall not come into this city, nor shoot an arrow there, nor come before it with shield, nor cast a bank against it. ³³By the way that he came, by the same shall he return, and shall not come into this city, says the LORD. ³⁴For I will defend this city, to save it, for my own sake, and for my servant David's sake. ³⁵And it came to pass that night, that the angel of the LORD went out, and smote in the camp of the Assyrians an hundred fourscore and five thousand: and when they arose early in the morning, behold, they were all dead corpses. ³⁶So Sennacherib king of Assyria departed, and went and returned, and dwelled at Nineveh. ³⁷And it came to pass, as he was worshipping in the house of Nisroch his god, that Adrammelech and Sharezer his sons smote him with the sword: and they escaped into the land of Armenia. And Esarhaddon his son reigned in his stead.

20 ¹In those days was Hezekiah sick to death. And the prophet Isaiah the son of Amoz came to him, and said to him, Thus says the LORD, Set your house in order; for you shall die, and not live. ²Then he turned his face to the wall, and prayed to the LORD, saying, ³I beseech you, O LORD, remember now how I have walked before you in truth and with a perfect heart, and have done that which is good in your sight. And Hezekiah wept sore. ⁴And it came to pass, before Isaiah was gone out into the middle court, that the word of the LORD came to him, saying, ⁵Turn again, and tell Hezekiah the captain of my people, Thus says the LORD, the God of David your father, I have heard your prayer, I have seen your tears: behold, I will heal you: on the third day you shall go up to the house of the LORD. ⁶And I will add to your days fifteen years; and I will deliver you and this city out of the hand of the king of Assyria; and I will defend this city for my own sake, and for my servant David's sake. ⁷And Isaiah said, Take a lump of figs. And they took and laid it on the boil, and he recovered. ⁸And Hezekiah said to Isaiah, What shall be the sign that the LORD will heal me, and that I shall go up into the house of the LORD the third day? ⁹And Isaiah said, This sign shall you have of the LORD, that the LORD will do the thing that he has spoken: shall the shadow go forward ten degrees, or go back ten degrees? ¹⁰And Hezekiah answered, It is a light thing for the shadow to go down ten degrees: no, but let the shadow return backward ten degrees. ¹¹And Isaiah the prophet cried to the LORD: and he brought the shadow ten degrees backward, by which it had gone down in the dial of Ahaz. ¹²At that time Berodachbaladan, the son of Baladan, king of Babylon, sent letters and a present to Hezekiah: for he had heard that Hezekiah had been sick. ¹³And Hezekiah listened to them, and showed them all the house of his precious things, the silver, and the gold, and the spices, and the precious ointment, and all the house of his armor, and all that was found in his treasures: there was nothing in his house, nor in all his dominion, that Hezekiah showed them not. ¹⁴Then came Isaiah the prophet to king Hezekiah, and said to him, What said these men? and from from where came they to you? And Hezekiah said, They are come from a far country, even from Babylon. ¹⁵And he said, What have they seen in your house? And Hezekiah answered, All the things that are in my house have they seen: there is nothing among my treasures that I have not showed them. ¹⁶And Isaiah said to Hezekiah, Hear the word of the LORD. ¹⁷Behold, the days come, that all that is in your house, and that which your fathers have laid up in store to this day, shall be carried into Babylon: nothing shall be left, says the LORD. ¹⁸And of your sons that shall issue from you, which you shall beget, shall they take away; and they shall be eunuchs in the palace of the king of Babylon. ¹⁹Then said Hezekiah to Isaiah, Good is the word of the LORD which you have spoken. And he said, Is it not good, if peace and truth be in my days? ²⁰And the rest of the acts of Hezekiah, and all his might, and how he made a pool, and a conduit, and brought water into the city, are they not written in the book of the chronicles of the kings of Judah? ²¹And Hezekiah slept with his fathers: and Manasseh his son reigned in his stead.

21 ¹Manasseh was twelve years old when he began to reign, and reigned fifty and five years in Jerusalem. And his mother's name was Hephzibah. ²And he did that which was evil in the sight of the LORD, after the abominations of the heathen, whom the LORD cast out before the children of Israel. ³For he built up again the high places which Hezekiah his father had destroyed; and he reared up altars for Baal, and made a grove, as did Ahab king of Israel; and worshipped all the host of heaven, and served them. ⁴And he built altars in the house of the LORD, of which the LORD said, In Jerusalem will I put my name. ⁵And he built altars for all the host of heaven in the two courts of the house of the LORD. ⁶And he made his son pass through the fire, and observed times, and used enchantments, and dealt with familiar spirits and wizards: he worked much wickedness in the sight of the LORD, to provoke him to anger. ⁷And he set a graven image of the grove that he had made in the house, of which the LORD said to David, and to Solomon his son, In this house, and in Jerusalem, which I have chosen out of all tribes of Israel, will I put my name for ever: ⁸Neither will I make the feet of Israel move any more out of the land which I gave their fathers; only if they will observe to do according to all that I have commanded them, and according to all the law that my servant Moses commanded them. ⁹But they listened not: and Manasseh seduced them to do more evil than did the nations whom the LORD destroyed before the children of Israel. ¹⁰And the LORD spoke by his servants the prophets, saying, ¹¹Because Manasseh king of Judah has done these abominations, and has done wickedly above all that the Amorites did, which were before him, and has made Judah also to sin with his idols: ¹²Therefore thus says the LORD God of Israel, Behold, I am bringing such evil on Jerusalem and Judah, that whoever hears of it, both his ears shall tingle. ¹³And I will stretch over Jerusalem the line of Samaria, and the plummet of the house of Ahab: and I will wipe Jerusalem as a man wipes a dish, wiping it, and turning it upside down. ¹⁴And I will forsake the remnant of my inheritance, and deliver them into the hand of their enemies; and they shall become a prey and a spoil to all their enemies; ¹⁵Because they have done that which was evil in my sight, and have provoked me to anger, since the day their fathers came forth out of Egypt, even to this day. ¹⁶Moreover Manasseh shed innocent blood very much, till he had filled Jerusalem from one end to another; beside his sin with which he made Judah to sin, in doing that which was evil in the sight of the LORD. ¹⁷Now the rest of the acts of Manasseh, and all that he did, and his sin that he sinned, are they not written in the book of the chronicles of the kings of Judah? ¹⁸And Manasseh slept with his fathers, and was buried in the garden of his own house, in the garden of Uzza: and Amon his son reigned in his stead. ¹⁹Amon was twenty and two years old when he began to reign, and he reigned two years in Jerusalem. And his mother's name was Meshullemeth, the daughter of Haruz of Jotbah. ²⁰And he did that which was evil in the sight of the LORD, as his father Manasseh did. ²¹And he walked in all the way that his father walked in, and served the idols that his father served, and worshipped them: ²²And he forsook the LORD God of his fathers, and walked not in the way of the LORD. ²³And the servants of Amon conspired against him, and slew the king in his own house. ²⁴And the people of the land slew all them that had conspired against king Amon; and the people of the land made Josiah his son king in his stead. ²⁵Now the rest of the acts of Amon which he did, are they not written in the book of the chronicles of the kings of Judah? ²⁶And he was buried in his sepulcher in the garden of Uzza: and Josiah his son reigned in his stead.

22

¹Josiah was eight years old when he began to reign, and he reigned thirty and one years in Jerusalem. And his mother's name was Jedidah, the daughter of Adaiah of Boscath. ²And he did that which was right in the sight of the LORD, and walked in all the way of David his father, and turned not aside to the right hand or to the left. ³And it came to pass in the eighteenth year of king Josiah, that the king sent Shaphan the son of Azaliah, the son of Meshullam, the scribe, to the house of the LORD, saying, ⁴Go up to Hilkiah the high priest, that he may sum the silver which is brought into the house of the LORD, which the keepers of the door have gathered of the people: ⁵And let them deliver it into the hand of the doers of the work, that have the oversight of the house of the LORD: and let them give it to the doers of the work which is in the house of the LORD, to repair the breaches of the house, ⁶To carpenters, and builders, and masons, and to buy timber and hewn stone to repair the house. ⁷However, there was no reckoning made with them of the money that was delivered into their hand, because they dealt faithfully. ⁸And Hilkiah the high priest said to Shaphan the scribe, I have found the book of the law in the house of the LORD. And Hilkiah gave the book to Shaphan, and he read it. ⁹And Shaphan the scribe came to the king, and brought the king word again, and said, Your servants have gathered the money that was found in the house, and have delivered it into the hand of them that do the work, that have the oversight of the house of the LORD. ¹⁰And Shaphan the scribe showed the king, saying, Hilkiah the priest has delivered me a book. And Shaphan read it before the king. ¹¹And it came to pass, when the king had heard the words of the book of the law, that he rent his clothes. ¹²And the king commanded Hilkiah the priest, and Ahikam the son of Shaphan, and Achbor the son of Michaiah, and Shaphan the scribe, and Asahiah a servant of the king's, saying, ¹³Go you, inquire of the LORD for me, and for the people, and for all Judah, concerning the words of this book that is found: for great is the wrath of the LORD that is kindled against us, because our fathers have not listened to the words of this book, to do according to all that which is written concerning us. ¹⁴So Hilkiah the priest, and Ahikam, and Achbor, and Shaphan, and Asahiah, went to Huldah the prophetess, the wife of Shallum the son of Tikvah, the son of Harhas, keeper of the wardrobe; (now she dwelled in Jerusalem in the college;) and they communed with her. ¹⁵And she said to them, Thus says the LORD God of Israel, Tell the man that sent you to me, ¹⁶Thus says the LORD, Behold, I will bring evil on this place, and on the inhabitants thereof, even all the words of the book which the king of Judah has read: ¹⁷Because they have forsaken me, and have burned incense to other gods, that they might provoke me to anger with all the works of their hands; therefore my wrath shall be kindled against this place, and shall not be quenched. ¹⁸But to the king of Judah which sent you to inquire of the LORD, thus shall you say to him, Thus says the LORD God of Israel, As touching the words which you have heard; ¹⁹Because your heart was tender, and you

have humbled yourself before the LORD, when you heard what I spoke against this place, and against the inhabitants thereof, that they should become a desolation and a curse, and have rent your clothes, and wept before me; I also have heard you, says the LORD. ²⁰Behold therefore, I will gather you to your fathers, and you shall be gathered into your grave in peace; and your eyes shall not see all the evil which I will bring on this place. And they brought the king word again.

23 ¹And the king sent, and they gathered to him all the elders of Judah and of Jerusalem. ²And the king went up into the house of the LORD, and all the men of Judah and all the inhabitants of Jerusalem with him, and the priests, and the prophets, and all the people, both small and great: and he read in their ears all the words of the book of the covenant which was found in the house of the LORD. ³And the king stood by a pillar, and made a covenant before the LORD, to walk after the LORD, and to keep his commandments and his testimonies and his statutes with all their heart and all their soul, to perform the words of this covenant that were written in this book. And all the people stood to the covenant. ⁴And the king commanded Hilkiah the high priest, and the priests of the second order, and the keepers of the door, to bring forth out of the temple of the LORD all the vessels that were made for Baal, and for the grove, and for all the host of heaven: and he burned them without Jerusalem in the fields of Kidron, and carried the ashes of them to Bethel. ⁵And he put down the idolatrous priests, whom the kings of Judah had ordained to burn incense in the high places in the cities of Judah, and in the places round about Jerusalem; them also that burned incense to Baal, to the sun, and to the moon, and to the planets, and to all the host of heaven. ⁶And he brought out the grove from the house of the LORD, without Jerusalem, to the brook Kidron, and burned it at the brook Kidron, and stamped it small to powder, and cast the powder thereof on the graves of the children of the people. ⁷And he broke down the houses of the sodomites, that were by the house of the LORD, where the women wove hangings for the grove. ⁸And he brought all the priests out of the cities of Judah, and defiled the high places where the priests had burned incense, from Geba to Beersheba, and broke down the high places of the gates that were in the entering in of the gate of Joshua the governor of the city, which were on a man's left hand at the gate of the city. ⁹Nevertheless the priests of the high places came not up to the altar of the LORD in Jerusalem, but they did eat of the unleavened bread among their brothers. ¹⁰And he defiled Topheth, which is in the valley of the children of Hinnom, that no man might make his son or his daughter to pass through the fire to Molech. ¹¹And he took away the horses that the kings of Judah had given to the sun, at the entering in of the house of the LORD, by the chamber of Nathanmelech the chamberlain, which was in the suburbs, and burned the chariots of the sun with fire. ¹²And the altars that were on the top of the upper chamber of Ahaz, which the kings of Judah had made, and the altars which Manasseh had made in the two courts of the house of the LORD, did the king beat down, and broke them down from there, and cast the dust of them into the brook Kidron. ¹³And the high places that were before Jerusalem, which were on the right hand of the mount of corruption, which Solomon the king of Israel had built for Ashtoreth the abomination of the Zidonians, and for Chemosh the abomination of the Moabites, and for Milcom the abomination of the children of Ammon, did the king defile. ¹⁴And he broke in pieces the images, and cut down the groves, and filled their places with the bones of men. ¹⁵Moreover the altar that was at Bethel, and the high place which Jeroboam the son of Nebat, who made Israel to sin, had made, both that altar and the high place he broke down, and burned the high place, and stamped it small to powder, and burned the grove. ¹⁶And as Josiah turned himself, he spied the sepulchers that were there in the mount, and sent, and took the bones out of the sepulchers, and burned them on the altar, and polluted it, according to the word of the LORD which the man of God proclaimed, who proclaimed these words. ¹⁷Then he said, What title is that that I see? And the men of the city told him, It is the sepulcher of the man of God, which came from Judah, and proclaimed these things that you have done against the altar of Bethel. ¹⁸And he said, Let him alone; let no man move his bones. So they let his bones alone, with the bones of the prophet that came out of Samaria. ¹⁹And all the houses also of the high places that were in the cities of Samaria, which the kings of Israel had made to provoke the Lord to anger, Josiah took away, and did to them according to all the acts that he had done in Bethel. ²⁰And he slew all the priests of the high places that were there on the altars, and burned men's bones on them, and returned to Jerusalem. ²¹And the king commanded all the people, saying, Keep the passover to the LORD your God, as it is written in the book of this covenant. ²²Surely there was not held such a passover from the days of the judges that judged Israel, nor in all the days of the kings of Israel, nor of the kings of Judah; ²³But in the eighteenth year of king Josiah, wherein this passover was held to the LORD in Jerusalem. ²⁴Moreover the workers with familiar spirits, and the wizards, and the images, and the idols, and all the abominations that were spied in the land of Judah and in Jerusalem, did Josiah put away, that he might perform the words of the law which were written in the book that Hilkiah the priest found in the house of the LORD. ²⁵And like to him was there no king before him, that turned to the LORD with all his heart, and with all his soul, and with all his might, according to all the law of Moses; neither after him arose there any like him. ²⁶Notwithstanding the LORD turned not from the fierceness of his great wrath, with which his anger was kindled against Judah, because of all the provocations that Manasseh had provoked him with. ²⁷And the LORD said, I will remove Judah also out of my sight, as I have removed Israel, and will cast off this city Jerusalem which I have chosen, and the house of which I said, My name shall be there. ²⁸Now the rest of the acts of Josiah, and all that he did, are they not written in the book of the chronicles of the kings of Judah? ²⁹In his days Pharaohnechoh king of Egypt went up against the king of Assyria to the river Euphrates: and king Josiah went against him; and he slew him at Megiddo, when he had seen him. ³⁰And his servants carried him in a chariot dead from Megiddo, and brought him to Jerusalem, and buried him in his own sepulcher. And the people of the land took Jehoahaz the son of Josiah, and anointed him, and made him king in his father's stead. ³¹Jehoahaz was twenty and three years old when he began to reign; and he reigned three months in Jerusalem. And his mother's name was Hamutal, the daughter of Jeremiah of Libnah. ³²And he did that which was evil in the sight of the LORD, according to all that his fathers had done. ³³And Pharaohnechoh put him in bands at Riblah in the land of Hamath, that he might not reign in Jerusalem; and put the land to a tribute of an hundred talents of silver, and a talent of gold. ³⁴And Pharaohnechoh made Eliakim the son of Josiah king in the room of Josiah his father, and turned his name to Jehoiakim, and took Jehoahaz away: and he came to Egypt, and died there. ³⁵And Jehoiakim gave the silver and the gold to Pharaoh; but he taxed the land to give the money according to the commandment of Pharaoh: he exacted the silver and the gold of the people of the land, of every one according to his taxation, to give it to Pharaohnechoh. ³⁶Jehoiakim was twenty and five years old when he began to reign; and he reigned eleven years in Jerusalem. And his mother's name was Zebudah, the daughter of Pedaiah of Rumah. ³⁷And he did that which was evil in the sight of the LORD, according to all that his fathers had done.

24 ¹In his days Nebuchadnezzar king of Babylon came up, and Jehoiakim became his servant three years: then he turned and rebelled against him. ²And the LORD sent against him bands of the Chaldees, and bands of the Syrians, and bands of the Moabites, and bands of the children of Ammon, and sent them against Judah to destroy it, according to the word of the LORD, which he spoke by his servants the prophets. ³Surely at the commandment of the LORD came this on Judah, to remove them out of his sight, for the sins of Manasseh, according to all that he did; ⁴And also for the innocent blood that he shed: for he filled Jerusalem with innocent blood; which the LORD would not pardon. ⁵Now the rest of the acts of Jehoiakim, and all that he did, are they not written in the book of the chronicles of the kings of Judah? ⁶So Jehoiakim slept with his fathers: and Jehoiachin his son reigned in his stead. ⁷And the king of Egypt came not again any more out of his land: for the king of Babylon had taken from the river of Egypt to the river Euphrates all that pertained to the king of Egypt. ⁸Jehoiachin was eighteen years old when he began to reign, and he reigned in Jerusalem three months. And his mother's name was Nehushta, the daughter of Elnathan of Jerusalem. ⁹And he did that which was evil in the sight of the LORD, according to all that his father had done. ¹⁰At that time the servants of Nebuchadnezzar king of Babylon came up against Jerusalem, and the city was besieged. ¹¹And Nebuchadnezzar king of Babylon came against the city, and his servants did besiege it. ¹²And Jehoiachin the king of Judah went out to the king of Babylon, he, and his mother, and his servants, and his princes, and his officers: and the king of Babylon took him in the eighth year of his reign. ¹³And he carried out there all the treasures of the house of the LORD, and the treasures of the king's house, and cut in pieces all the vessels of gold which Solomon king of Israel had made in the temple of the LORD, as the LORD had said. ¹⁴And he carried away all Jerusalem, and all the princes, and all the mighty men of valor, even ten thousand captives, and all the craftsmen and smiths: none remained, save the poorest sort of the people of the land. ¹⁵And he carried away Jehoiachin to Babylon, and the king's mother, and the king's wives, and his officers, and the mighty of the land, those carried he into captivity from Jerusalem to Babylon. ¹⁶And all the men of might, even seven thousand, and craftsmen and smiths a thousand, all that were strong and apt for war, even them the king of Babylon brought captive to Babylon. ¹⁷And the king of Babylon made Mattaniah his father's brother king in his stead, and changed his name to Zedekiah. ¹⁸Zedekiah was twenty and one years old when he began to reign, and he reigned eleven years in Jerusalem. And his mother's name was Hamutal, the daughter of Jeremiah of Libnah. ¹⁹And he did that which was evil in the sight of the LORD, according to all that Jehoiakim had done. ²⁰For through the anger of the LORD it came to pass in Jerusalem and Judah, until he had cast them out from his presence, that Zedekiah rebelled against the king of Babylon.

25 ¹And it came to pass in the ninth year of his reign, in the tenth month, in the tenth day of the month, that Nebuchadnezzar king of Babylon came, he, and all his host, against Jerusalem, and pitched against it; and they built forts against it round about. ²And the city was besieged to the eleventh year of king Zedekiah. ³And on the ninth day of the fourth month the famine prevailed in the city, and there was no bread for the people of the land. ⁴And the city was broken up, and all the men of war fled by night by the way of the gate between two walls, which is by the king's garden: (now the Chaldees were against the city round about:) and the king went the way toward the plain. ⁵And the army of the Chaldees pursued after the king, and overtook him in the plains of Jericho: and all his army were scattered from him. ⁶So they took the king, and brought him up to the king of Babylon to Riblah; and they gave judgment on him. ⁷And they slew the sons of Zedekiah before his eyes, and put out the eyes of Zedekiah, and bound him with fetters of brass, and carried him to Babylon. ⁸And in the fifth month, on the seventh day of the month, which is the nineteenth year of king Nebuchadnezzar king of Babylon, came Nebuzaradan, captain of the guard, a servant of the king of Babylon, to Jerusalem: ⁹And he burnt the house of the LORD, and the king's house, and all the houses of Jerusalem, and every great man's house burnt he with fire. ¹⁰And all the army of the Chaldees, that were with the captain of the guard, broke down the walls of Jerusalem round about. ¹¹Now the rest of the people that were left in the city, and the fugitives that fell away to the king of Babylon, with the remnant of the multitude, did Nebuzaradan the captain of the guard carry away. ¹²But the captain of the guard left of the door of the poor of the land to be vinedressers and farmers. ¹³And the pillars of brass that were in the house of the LORD, and the bases, and the brazen sea that was in the house of the LORD, did the Chaldees break in pieces, and carried the brass of them to Babylon. ¹⁴And the pots, and the shovels, and the snuffers, and the spoons, and all the vessels of brass with which they ministered, took they away. ¹⁵And the fire pans, and the bowls, and such things as were of gold, in gold, and of silver, in silver, the captain of the guard took away. ¹⁶The two pillars, one sea, and the bases which Solomon had made for the house of the LORD; the brass of

all these vessels was without weight. ¹⁷The height of the one pillar was eighteen cubits, and the capital on it was brass: and the height of the capital three cubits; and the wreathen work, and pomegranates on the capital round about, all of brass: and like to these had the second pillar with wreathen work. ¹⁸And the captain of the guard took Seraiah the chief priest, and Zephaniah the second priest, and the three keepers of the door: ¹⁹And out of the city he took an officer that was set over the men of war, and five men of them that were in the king's presence, which were found in the city, and the principal scribe of the host, which mustered the people of the land, and three score men of the people of the land that were found in the city: ²⁰And Nebuzaradan captain of the guard took these, and brought them to the king of Babylon to Riblah: ²¹And the king of Babylon smote them, and slew them at Riblah in the land of Hamath. So Judah was carried away out of their land. ²²And as for the people that remained in the land of Judah, whom Nebuchadnezzar king of Babylon had left, even over them he made Gedaliah the son of Ahikam, the son of Shaphan, ruler. ²³And when all the captains of the armies, they and their men, heard that the king of Babylon had made Gedaliah governor, there came to Gedaliah to Mizpah, even Ishmael the son of Nethaniah, and Johanan the son of Careah, and Seraiah the son of Tanhumeth the Netophathite, and Jaazaniah the son of a Maachathite, they and their men. ²⁴And Gedaliah swore to them, and to their men, and said to them, Fear not to be the servants of the Chaldees: dwell in the land, and serve the king of Babylon; and it shall be well with you. ²⁵But it came to pass in the seventh month, that Ishmael the son of Nethaniah, the son of Elishama, of the seed royal, came, and ten men with him, and smote Gedaliah, that he died, and the Jews and the Chaldees that were with him at Mizpah. ²⁶And all the people, both small and great, and the captains of the armies, arose, and came to Egypt: for they were afraid of the Chaldees. ²⁷And it came to pass in the seven and thirtieth year of the captivity of Jehoiachin king of Judah, in the twelfth month, on the seven and twentieth day of the month, that Evilmerodach king of Babylon in the year that he began to reign did lift up the head of Jehoiachin king of Judah out of prison; ²⁸And he spoke kindly to him, and set his throne above the throne of the kings that were with him in Babylon; ²⁹And changed his prison garments: and he did eat bread continually before him all the days of his life. ³⁰And his allowance was a continual allowance given him of the king, a daily rate for every day, all the days of his life.

First Chronicles

1 ¹Adam, Sheth, Enosh, ²Kenan, Mahalaleel, Jered, ³Henoch, Methuselah, Lamech, ⁴Noah, Shem, Ham, and Japheth. ⁵The sons of Japheth; Gomer, and Magog, and Madai, and Javan, and Tubal, and Meshech, and Tiras. ⁶And the sons of Gomer; Ashchenaz, and Riphath, and Togarmah. ⁷And the sons of Javan; Elishah, and Tarshish, Kittim, and Dodanim. ⁸The sons of Ham; Cush, and Mizraim, Put, and Canaan. ⁹And the sons of Cush; Seba, and Havilah, and Sabta, and Raamah, and Sabtecha. And the sons of Raamah; Sheba, and Dedan. ¹⁰And Cush begat Nimrod: he began to be mighty on the earth. ¹¹And Mizraim begat Ludim, and Anamim, and Lehabim, and Naphtuhim, ¹²And Pathrusim, and Casluhim, (of whom came the Philistines,) and Caphthorim. ¹³And Canaan begat Zidon his firstborn, and Heth, ¹⁴The Jebusite also, and the Amorite, and the Girgashite, ¹⁵And the Hivite, and the Arkite, and the Sinite, ¹⁶And the Arvadite, and the Zemarite, and the Hamathite. ¹⁷The sons of Shem; Elam, and Asshur, and Arphaxad, and Lud, and Aram, and Uz, and Hul, and Gether, and Meshech. ¹⁸And Arphaxad begat Shelah, and Shelah begat Eber. ¹⁹And to Eber were born two sons: the name of the one was Peleg; because in his days the earth was divided: and his brother's name was Joktan. ²⁰And Joktan begat Almodad, and Sheleph, and Hazarmaveth, and Jerah, ²¹Hadoram also, and Uzal, and Diklah, ²²And Ebal, and Abimael, and Sheba, ²³And Ophir, and Havilah, and Jobab. All these were the sons of Joktan. ²⁴Shem, Arphaxad, Shelah, ²⁵Eber, Peleg, Reu, ²⁶Serug, Nahor, Terah, ²⁷Abram; the same is Abraham. ²⁸The sons of Abraham; Isaac, and Ishmael. ²⁹These are their generations: The firstborn of Ishmael, Nebaioth; then Kedar, and Adbeel, and Mibsam, ³⁰Mishma, and Dumah, Massa, Hadad, and Tema, ³¹Jetur, Naphish, and Kedemah. These are the sons of Ishmael. ³²Now the sons of Keturah, Abraham's concubine: she bore Zimran, and Jokshan, and Medan, and Midian, and Ishbak, and Shuah. And the sons of Jokshan; Sheba, and Dedan. ³³And the sons of Midian; Ephah, and Epher, and Henoch, and Abida, and Eldaah. All these are the sons of Keturah. ³⁴And Abraham begat Isaac. The sons of Isaac; Esau and Israel. ³⁵The sons of Esau; Eliphaz, Reuel, and Jeush, and Jaalam, and Korah. ³⁶The sons of Eliphaz; Teman, and Omar, Zephi, and Gatam, Kenaz, and Timna, and Amalek. ³⁷The sons of Reuel; Nahath, Zerah, Shammah, and Mizzah. ³⁸And the sons of Seir; Lotan, and Shobal, and Zibeon, and Anah, and Dishon, and Ezar, and Dishan. ³⁹And the sons of Lotan; Hori, and Homam: and Timna was Lotan's sister. ⁴⁰The sons of Shobal; Alian, and Manahath, and Ebal, Shephi, and Onam. and the sons of Zibeon; Aiah, and Anah. ⁴¹The sons of Anah; Dishon. And the sons of Dishon; Amram, and Eshban, and Ithran, and Cheran. ⁴²The sons of Ezer; Bilhan, and Zavan, and Jakan. The sons of Dishan; Uz, and Aran. ⁴³Now these are the kings that reigned in the land of Edom before any king reigned over the children of Israel; Bela the son of Beor: and the name of his city was Dinhabah. ⁴⁴And when Bela was dead, Jobab the son of Zerah of Bozrah reigned in his stead. ⁴⁵And when Jobab was dead, Husham of the land of the Temanites reigned in his stead. ⁴⁶And when Husham was dead, Hadad the son of Bedad, which smote Midian in the field of Moab, reigned in his stead: and the name of his city was Avith. ⁴⁷And when Hadad was dead, Samlah of Masrekah reigned in his stead. ⁴⁸And when Samlah was dead, Shaul of Rehoboth by the river reigned in his stead. ⁴⁹And when Shaul was dead, Baalhanan the son of Achbor reigned in his stead. ⁵⁰And when Baalhanan was dead, Hadad reigned in his stead: and the name of his city was Pai; and his wife's name was Mehetabel, the daughter of Matred, the daughter of Mezahab. ⁵¹Hadad died also. And the dukes of Edom were; duke Timnah, duke Aliah, duke Jetheth, ⁵²Duke Aholibamah, duke Elah, duke Pinon, ⁵³Duke Kenaz, duke Teman, duke Mibzar, ⁵⁴Duke Magdiel, duke Iram. These are the dukes of Edom.

2 ¹These are the sons of Israel; Reuben, Simeon, Levi, and Judah, Issachar, and Zebulun, ²Dan, Joseph, and Benjamin, Naphtali, Gad, and Asher. ³The sons of Judah; Er, and Onan, and Shelah: which three were born to him of the daughter of Shua the Canaanitess. And Er, the firstborn of Judah, was evil in the sight of the LORD; and he slew him. ⁴And Tamar his daughter in law bore him Pharez and Zerah. All the sons of Judah were five. ⁵The sons of Pharez; Hezron, and Hamul. ⁶And the sons of Zerah; Zimri, and Ethan, and Heman, and Calcol, and Dara: five of them in all. ⁷And the sons of Carmi; Achar, the troubler of Israel, who transgressed in the thing accursed. ⁸And the sons of Ethan; Azariah. ⁹The sons also of Hezron, that were born to him; Jerahmeel, and Ram, and Chelubai. ¹⁰And Ram begat Amminadab; and Amminadab begat Nahshon, prince of the children of Judah; ¹¹And Nahshon begat Salma, and Salma begat Boaz, ¹²And Boaz begat Obed, and Obed begat Jesse, ¹³And Jesse begat his firstborn Eliab, and Abinadab the second, and Shimma the third, ¹⁴Nethaneel the fourth, Raddai the fifth, ¹⁵Ozem the sixth, David the seventh: ¹⁶Whose sisters were Zeruiah, and Abigail. And the sons of Zeruiah; Abishai, and Joab, and Asahel, three. ¹⁷And Abigail bore Amasa: and the father of Amasa was Jether the Ishmeelite. ¹⁸And Caleb the son of Hezron begat children of Azubah his wife, and of Jerioth: her sons are these; Jesher, and Shobab, and Ardon. ¹⁹And when Azubah was dead, Caleb took to him Ephrath, which bore him Hur. ²⁰And Hur begat Uri, and Uri begat Bezaleel. ²¹And afterward Hezron went in to the daughter of Machir the father of Gilead, whom he married when he was three score years old; and she bore him Segub. ²²And Segub begat Jair, who had three and twenty cities in the land of Gilead. ²³And he took Geshur, and Aram, with the towns of Jair, from them, with Kenath, and the towns thereof, even three score cities. All these belonged to the sons of Machir the father of Gilead. ²⁴And after that Hezron was dead in Calebephratah, then Abiah Hezron's wife bore him Ashur the father of Tekoa. ²⁵And the sons of Jerahmeel the firstborn of Hezron were, Ram the firstborn, and Bunah, and Oren, and Ozem, and Ahijah. ²⁶Jerahmeel had also another wife, whose name was Atarah; she was the mother of Onam. ²⁷And the sons of Ram the firstborn of Jerahmeel were, Maaz, and Jamin, and Eker. ²⁸And the sons of Onam were, Shammai, and Jada. And the sons of Shammai; Nadab and Abishur. ²⁹And the name of the wife of Abishur was Abihail, and she bore him Ahban, and

Molid. ³⁰And the sons of Nadab; Seled, and Appaim: but Seled died without children. ³¹And the sons of Appaim; Ishi. And the sons of Ishi; Sheshan. And the children of Sheshan; Ahlai. ³²And the sons of Jada the brother of Shammai; Jether, and Jonathan: and Jether died without children. ³³And the sons of Jonathan; Peleth, and Zaza. These were the sons of Jerahmeel. ³⁴Now Sheshan had no sons, but daughters. And Sheshan had a servant, an Egyptian, whose name was Jarha. ³⁵And Sheshan gave his daughter to Jarha his servant to wife; and she bore him Attai. ³⁶And Attai begat Nathan, and Nathan begat Zabad, ³⁷And Zabad begat Ephlal, and Ephlal begat Obed, ³⁸And Obed begat Jehu, and Jehu begat Azariah, ³⁹And Azariah begat Helez, and Helez begat Eleasah, ⁴⁰And Eleasah begat Sisamai, and Sisamai begat Shallum, ⁴¹And Shallum begat Jekamiah, and Jekamiah begat Elishama. ⁴²Now the sons of Caleb the brother of Jerahmeel were, Mesha his firstborn, which was the father of Ziph; and the sons of Mareshah the father of Hebron. ⁴³And the sons of Hebron; Korah, and Tappuah, and Rekem, and Shema. ⁴⁴And Shema begat Raham, the father of Jorkoam: and Rekem begat Shammai. ⁴⁵And the son of Shammai was Maon: and Maon was the father of Bethzur. ⁴⁶And Ephah, Caleb's concubine, bore Haran, and Moza, and Gazez: and Haran begat Gazez. ⁴⁷And the sons of Jahdai; Regem, and Jotham, and Gesham, and Pelet, and Ephah, and Shaaph. ⁴⁸Maachah, Caleb's concubine, bore Sheber, and Tirhanah. ⁴⁹She bore also Shaaph the father of Madmannah, Sheva the father of Machbenah, and the father of Gibea: and the daughter of Caleb was Achsa. ⁵⁰These were the sons of Caleb the son of Hur, the firstborn of Ephratah; Shobal the father of Kirjathjearim. ⁵¹Salma the father of Bethlehem, Hareph the father of Bethgader. ⁵²And Shobal the father of Kirjathjearim had sons; Haroeh, and half of the Manahethites. ⁵³And the families of Kirjathjearim; the Ithrites, and the Puhites, and the Shumathites, and the Mishraites; of them came the Zareathites, and the Eshtaulites, ⁵⁴The sons of Salma; Bethlehem, and the Netophathites, Ataroth, the house of Joab, and half of the Manahethites, the Zorites. ⁵⁵And the families of the scribes which dwelled at Jabez; the Tirathites, the Shimeathites, and Suchathites. These are the Kenites that came of Hemath, the father of the house of Rechab.

3 ¹Now these were the sons of David, which were born to him in Hebron; the firstborn Amnon, of Ahinoam the Jezreelitess; the second Daniel, of Abigail the Carmelitess: ²The third, Absalom the son of Maachah the daughter of Talmai king of Geshur: the fourth, Adonijah the son of Haggith: ³The fifth, Shephatiah of Abital: the sixth, Ithream by Eglah his wife. ⁴These six were born to him in Hebron; and there he reigned seven years and six months: and in Jerusalem he reigned thirty and three years. ⁵And these were born to him in Jerusalem; Shimea, and Shobab, and Nathan, and Solomon, four, of Bathshua the daughter of Ammiel: ⁶Ibhar also, and Elishama, and Eliphelet, ⁷And Nogah, and Nepheg, and Japhia, ⁸And Elishama, and Eliada, and Eliphelet, nine. ⁹These were all the sons of David, beside the sons of the concubines, and Tamar their sister. ¹⁰And Solomon's son was Rehoboam, Abia his son, Asa his son, Jehoshaphat his son, ¹¹Joram his son, Ahaziah his son, Joash his son, ¹²Amaziah his son, Azariah his son, Jotham his son, ¹³Ahaz his son, Hezekiah his son, Manasseh his son, ¹⁴Amon his son, Josiah his son. ¹⁵And the sons of Josiah were, the firstborn Johanan, the second Jehoiakim, the third Zedekiah, the fourth Shallum. ¹⁶And the sons of Jehoiakim: Jeconiah his son, Zedekiah his son. ¹⁷And the sons of Jeconiah; Assir, Salathiel his son, ¹⁸Malchiram also, and Pedaiah, and Shenazar, Jecamiah, Hoshama, and Nedabiah. ¹⁹And the sons of Pedaiah were, Zerubbabel, and Shimei: and the sons of Zerubbabel; Meshullam, and Hananiah, and Shelomith their sister: ²⁰And Hashubah, and Ohel, and Berechiah, and Hasadiah, Jushabhesed, five. ²¹And the sons of Hananiah; Pelatiah, and Jesaiah: the sons of Rephaiah, the sons of Arnan, the sons of Obadiah, the sons of Shechaniah. ²²And the sons of Shechaniah; Shemaiah: and the sons of Shemaiah; Hattush, and Igeal, and Bariah, and Neariah, and Shaphat, six. ²³And the sons of Neariah; Elioenai, and Hezekiah, and Azrikam, three. ²⁴And the sons of Elioenai were, Hodaiah, and Eliashib, and Pelaiah, and Akkub, and Johanan, and Dalaiah, and Anani, seven.

4 ¹The sons of Judah; Pharez, Hezron, and Carmi, and Hur, and Shobal. ²And Reaiah the son of Shobal begat Jahath; and Jahath begat Ahumai, and Lahad. These are the families of the Zorathites. ³And these were of the father of Etam; Jezreel, and Ishma, and Idbash: and the name of their sister was Hazelelponi: ⁴And Penuel the father of Gedor, and Ezer the father of Hushah. These are the sons of Hur, the firstborn of Ephratah, the father of Bethlehem. ⁵And Ashur the father of Tekoa had two wives, Helah and Naarah. ⁶And Naarah bore him Ahuzam, and Hepher, and Temeni, and Haahashtari. These were the sons of Naarah. ⁷And the sons of Helah were, Zereth, and Jezoar, and Ethnan. ⁸And Coz begat Anub, and Zobebah, and the families of Aharhel the son of Harum. ⁹And Jabez was more honorable than his brothers: and his mother called his name Jabez, saying, Because I bore him with sorrow. ¹⁰And Jabez called on the God of Israel, saying, Oh that you would bless me indeed, and enlarge my coast, and that your hand might be with me, and that you would keep me from evil, that it may not grieve me! And God granted him that which he requested. ¹¹And Chelub the brother of Shuah begat Mehir, which was the father of Eshton. ¹²And Eshton begat Bethrapha, and Paseah, and Tehinnah the father of Irnahash. These are the men of Rechah. ¹³And the sons of Kenaz; Othniel, and Seraiah: and the sons of Othniel; Hathath. ¹⁴And Meonothai begat Ophrah: and Seraiah begat Joab, the father of the valley of Charashim; for they were craftsmen. ¹⁵And the sons of Caleb the son of Jephunneh; Iru, Elah, and Naam: and the sons of Elah, even Kenaz. ¹⁶And the sons of Jehaleleel; Ziph, and Ziphah, Tiria, and Asareel. ¹⁷And the sons of Ezra were, Jether, and Mered, and Epher, and Jalon: and she bore Miriam, and Shammai, and Ishbah the father of Eshtemoa. ¹⁸And his wife Jehudijah bore Jered the father of Gedor, and Heber the father of Socho, and Jekuthiel the father of Zanoah. And these are the sons of Bithiah the daughter of Pharaoh, which Mered took. ¹⁹And the sons of his wife Hodiah the sister of Naham, the father of Keilah the Garmite, and Eshtemoa the Maachathite. ²⁰And the sons of Shimon were, Amnon, and Rinnah, Benhanan, and Tilon. And the sons of Ishi were, Zoheth, and Benzoheth. ²¹The sons of Shelah the son of Judah were, Er the father of Lecah,

and Laadah the father of Mareshah, and the families of the house of them that worked fine linen, of the house of Ashbea, ²²And Jokim, and the men of Chozeba, and Joash, and Saraph, who had the dominion in Moab, and Jashubilehem. And these are ancient things. ²³These were the potters, and those that dwelled among plants and hedges: there they dwelled with the king for his work. ²⁴The sons of Simeon were, Nemuel, and Jamin, Jarib, Zerah, and Shaul: ²⁵Shallum his son, Mibsam his son, Mishma his son. ²⁶And the sons of Mishma; Hamuel his son, Zacchur his son, Shimei his son. ²⁷And Shimei had sixteen sons and six daughters: but his brothers had not many children, neither did all their family multiply, like to the children of Judah. ²⁸And they dwelled at Beersheba, and Moladah, and Hazarshual, ²⁹And at Bilhah, and at Ezem, and at Tolad, ³⁰And at Bethuel, and at Hormah, and at Ziklag, ³¹And at Bethmarcaboth, and Hazarsusim, and at Bethbirei, and at Shaaraim. These were their cities to the reign of David. ³²And their villages were, Etam, and Ain, Rimmon, and Tochen, and Ashan, five cities: ³³And all their villages that were round about the same cities, to Baal. These were their habitations, and their genealogy. ³⁴And Meshobab, and Jamlech, and Joshah, the son of Amaziah, ³⁵And Joel, and Jehu the son of Josibiah, the son of Seraiah, the son of Asiel, ³⁶And Elioenai, and Jaakobah, and Jeshohaiah, and Asaiah, and Adiel, and Jesimiel, and Benaiah, ³⁷And Ziza the son of Shiphi, the son of Allon, the son of Jedaiah, the son of Shimri, the son of Shemaiah; ³⁸These mentioned by their names were princes in their families: and the house of their fathers increased greatly. ³⁹And they went to the entrance of Gedor, even to the east side of the valley, to seek pasture for their flocks. ⁴⁰And they found fat pasture and good, and the land was wide, and quiet, and peaceable; for they of Ham had dwelled there of old. ⁴¹And these written by name came in the days of Hezekiah king of Judah, and smote their tents, and the habitations that were found there, and destroyed them utterly to this day, and dwelled in their rooms: because there was pasture there for their flocks. ⁴²And some of them, even of the sons of Simeon, five hundred men, went to mount Seir, having for their captains Pelatiah, and Neariah, and Rephaiah, and Uzziel, the sons of Ishi. ⁴³And they smote the rest of the Amalekites that were escaped, and dwelled there to this day.

5 ¹Now the sons of Reuben the firstborn of Israel, (for he was the firstborn; but for as much as he defiled his father's bed, his birthright was given to the sons of Joseph the son of Israel: and the genealogy is not to be reckoned after the birthright. ²For Judah prevailed above his brothers, and of him came the chief ruler; but the birthright was Joseph's:) ³The sons, I say, of Reuben the firstborn of Israel were, Hanoch, and Pallu, Hezron, and Carmi. ⁴The sons of Joel; Shemaiah his son, Gog his son, Shimei his son, ⁵Micah his son, Reaia his son, Baal his son, ⁶Beerah his son, whom Tilgathpilneser king of Assyria carried away captive: he was prince of the Reubenites. ⁷And his brothers by their families, when the genealogy of their generations was reckoned, were the chief, Jeiel, and Zechariah, ⁸And Bela the son of Azaz, the son of Shema, the son of Joel, who dwelled in Aroer, even to Nebo and Baalmeon: ⁹And eastward he inhabited to the entering in of the wilderness from the river Euphrates: because their cattle were multiplied in the land of Gilead. ¹⁰And in the days of Saul they made war with the Hagarites, who fell by their hand: and they dwelled in their tents throughout all the east land of Gilead. ¹¹And the children of Gad dwelled over against them, in the land of Bashan to Salcah: ¹²Joel the chief, and Shapham the next, and Jaanai, and Shaphat in Bashan. ¹³And their brothers of the house of their fathers were, Michael, and Meshullam, and Sheba, and Jorai, and Jachan, and Zia, and Heber, seven. ¹⁴These are the children of Abihail the son of Huri, the son of Jaroah, the son of Gilead, the son of Michael, the son of Jeshishai, the son of Jahdo, the son of Buz; ¹⁵Ahi the son of Abdiel, the son of Guni, chief of the house of their fathers. ¹⁶And they dwelled in Gilead in Bashan, and in her towns, and in all the suburbs of Sharon, on their borders. ¹⁷All these were reckoned by genealogies in the days of Jotham king of Judah, and in the days of Jeroboam king of Israel. ¹⁸The sons of Reuben, and the Gadites, and half the tribe of Manasseh, of valiant men, men able to bear buckler and sword, and to shoot with bow, and skillful in war, were four and forty thousand seven hundred and three score, that went out to the war. ¹⁹And they made war with the Hagarites, with Jetur, and Nephish, and Nodab. ²⁰And they were helped against them, and the Hagarites were delivered into their hand, and all that were with them: for they cried to God in the battle, and he was entreated of them; because they put their trust in him. ²¹And they took away their cattle; of their camels fifty thousand, and of sheep two hundred and fifty thousand, and of asses two thousand, and of men an hundred thousand. ²²For there fell down many slain, because the war was of God. And they dwelled in their steads until the captivity. ²³And the children of the half tribe of Manasseh dwelled in the land: they increased from Bashan to Baalhermon and Senir, and to mount Hermon. ²⁴And these were the heads of the house of their fathers, even Epher, and Ishi, and Eliel, and Azriel, and Jeremiah, and Hodaviah, and Jahdiel, mighty men of valor, famous men, and heads of the house of their fathers. ²⁵And they transgressed against the God of their fathers, and went a whoring after the gods of the people of the land, whom God destroyed before them. ²⁶And the God of Israel stirred up the spirit of Pul king of Assyria, and the spirit of Tilgathpilneser king of Assyria, and he carried them away, even the Reubenites, and the Gadites, and the half tribe of Manasseh, and brought them to Halah, and Habor, and Hara, and to the river Gozan, to this day.

6 ¹The sons of Levi; Gershon, Kohath, and Merari. ²And the sons of Kohath; Amram, Izhar, and Hebron, and Uzziel. ³And the children of Amram; Aaron, and Moses, and Miriam. The sons also of Aaron; Nadab, and Abihu, Eleazar, and Ithamar. ⁴Eleazar begat Phinehas, Phinehas begat Abishua, ⁵And Abishua begat Bukki, and Bukki begat Uzzi, ⁶And Uzzi begat Zerahiah, and Zerahiah begat Meraioth, ⁷Meraioth begat Amariah, and Amariah begat Ahitub, ⁸And Ahitub begat Zadok, and Zadok begat Ahimaaz, ⁹And Ahimaaz begat Azariah, and Azariah begat Johanan, ¹⁰And Johanan begat Azariah, (he it is that executed the priest's office in the temple that Solomon built in Jerusalem:) ¹¹And Azariah begat Amariah, and Amariah begat Ahitub, ¹²And Ahitub begat Zadok, and Zadok begat Shallum, ¹³And Shallum begat Hilkiah, and Hilkiah begat Azariah, ¹⁴And

Azariah begat Seraiah, and Seraiah begat Jehozadak, ¹⁵And Jehozadak went into captivity, when the LORD carried away Judah and Jerusalem by the hand of Nebuchadnezzar. ¹⁶The sons of Levi; Gershom, Kohath, and Merari. ¹⁷And these be the names of the sons of Gershom; Libni, and Shimei. ¹⁸And the sons of Kohath were, Amram, and Izhar, and Hebron, and Uzziel. ¹⁹The sons of Merari; Mahli, and Mushi. And these are the families of the Levites according to their fathers. ²⁰Of Gershom; Libni his son, Jahath his son, Zimmah his son, ²¹Joah his son, Iddo his son, Zerah his son, Jeaterai his son. ²²The sons of Kohath; Amminadab his son, Korah his son, Assir his son, ²³Elkanah his son, and Ebiasaph his son, and Assir his son, ²⁴Tahath his son, Uriel his son, Uzziah his son, and Shaul his son. ²⁵And the sons of Elkanah; Amasai, and Ahimoth. ²⁶As for Elkanah: the sons of Elkanah; Zophai his son, and Nahath his son, ²⁷Eliab his son, Jeroham his son, Elkanah his son. ²⁸And the sons of Samuel; the firstborn Vashni, and Abiah. ²⁹The sons of Merari; Mahli, Libni his son, Shimei his son, Uzza his son, ³⁰Shimea his son, Haggiah his son, Asaiah his son. ³¹And these are they whom David set over the service of song in the house of the LORD, after that the ark had rest. ³²And they ministered before the dwelling place of the tabernacle of the congregation with singing, until Solomon had built the house of the LORD in Jerusalem: and then they waited on their office according to their order. ³³And these are they that waited with their children. Of the sons of the Kohathites: Heman a singer, the son of Joel, the son of Shemuel, ³⁴The son of Elkanah, the son of Jeroham, the son of Eliel, the son of Toah, ³⁵The son of Zuph, the son of Elkanah, the son of Mahath, the son of Amasai, ³⁶The son of Elkanah, the son of Joel, the son of Azariah, the son of Zephaniah, ³⁷The son of Tahath, the son of Assir, the son of Ebiasaph, the son of Korah, ³⁸The son of Izhar, the son of Kohath, the son of Levi, the son of Israel. ³⁹And his brother Asaph, who stood on his right hand, even Asaph the son of Berachiah, the son of Shimea, ⁴⁰The son of Michael, the son of Baaseiah, the son of Malchiah, ⁴¹The son of Ethni, the son of Zerah, the son of Adaiah, ⁴²The son of Ethan, the son of Zimmah, the son of Shimei, ⁴³The son of Jahath, the son of Gershom, the son of Levi. ⁴⁴And their brothers the sons of Merari stood on the left hand: Ethan the son of Kishi, the son of Abdi, the son of Malluch, ⁴⁵The son of Hashabiah, the son of Amaziah, the son of Hilkiah, ⁴⁶The son of Amzi, the son of Bani, the son of Shamer, ⁴⁷The son of Mahli, the son of Mushi, the son of Merari, the son of Levi. ⁴⁸Their brethren also the Levites were appointed to all manner of service of the tabernacle of the house of God. ⁴⁹But Aaron and his sons offered on the altar of the burnt offering, and on the altar of incense, and were appointed for all the work of the place most holy, and to make an atonement for Israel, according to all that Moses the servant of God had commanded. ⁵⁰And these are the sons of Aaron; Eleazar his son, Phinehas his son, Abishua his son, ⁵¹Bukki his son, Uzzi his son, Zerahiah his son, ⁵²Meraioth his son, Amariah his son, Ahitub his son, ⁵³Zadok his son, Ahimaaz his son. ⁵⁴Now these are their dwelling places throughout their castles in their coasts, of the sons of Aaron, of the families of the Kohathites: for theirs was the lot. ⁵⁵And they gave them Hebron in the land of Judah, and the suburbs thereof round about it. ⁵⁶But the fields of the city, and the villages thereof, they gave to Caleb the son of Jephunneh. ⁵⁷And to the sons of Aaron they gave the cities of Judah, namely, Hebron, the city of refuge, and Libnah with her suburbs, and Jattir, and Eshtemoa, with their suburbs, ⁵⁸And Hilen with her suburbs, Debir with her suburbs, ⁵⁹And Ashan with her suburbs, and Bethshemesh with her suburbs: ⁶⁰And out of the tribe of Benjamin; Geba with her suburbs, and Alemeth with her suburbs, and Anathoth with her suburbs. All their cities throughout their families were thirteen cities. ⁶¹And to the sons of Kohath, which were left of the family of that tribe, were cities given out of the half tribe, namely, out of the half tribe of Manasseh, by lot, ten cities. ⁶²And to the sons of Gershom throughout their families out of the tribe of Issachar, and out of the tribe of Asher, and out of the tribe of Naphtali, and out of the tribe of Manasseh in Bashan, thirteen cities. ⁶³To the sons of Merari were given by lot, throughout their families, out of the tribe of Reuben, and out of the tribe of Gad, and out of the tribe of Zebulun, twelve cities. ⁶⁴And the children of Israel gave to the Levites these cities with their suburbs. ⁶⁵And they gave by lot out of the tribe of the children of Judah, and out of the tribe of the children of Simeon, and out of the tribe of the children of Benjamin, these cities, which are called by their names. ⁶⁶And the residue of the families of the sons of Kohath had cities of their coasts out of the tribe of Ephraim. ⁶⁷And they gave to them, of the cities of refuge, Shechem in mount Ephraim with her suburbs; they gave also Gezer with her suburbs, ⁶⁸And Jokmeam with her suburbs, and Bethhoron with her suburbs, ⁶⁹And Aijalon with her suburbs, and Gathrimmon with her suburbs: ⁷⁰And out of the half tribe of Manasseh; Aner with her suburbs, and Bileam with her suburbs, for the family of the remnant of the sons of Kohath. ⁷¹To the sons of Gershom were given out of the family of the half tribe of Manasseh, Golan in Bashan with her suburbs, and Ashtaroth with her suburbs: ⁷²And out of the tribe of Issachar; Kedesh with her suburbs, Daberath with her suburbs, ⁷³And Ramoth with her suburbs, and Anem with her suburbs: ⁷⁴And out of the tribe of Asher; Mashal with her suburbs, and Abdon with her suburbs, ⁷⁵And Hukok with her suburbs, and Rehob with her suburbs: ⁷⁶And out of the tribe of Naphtali; Kedesh in Galilee with her suburbs, and Hammon with her suburbs, and Kirjathaim with her suburbs. ⁷⁷To the rest of the children of Merari were given out of the tribe of Zebulun, Rimmon with her suburbs, Tabor with her suburbs: ⁷⁸And on the other side Jordan by Jericho, on the east side of Jordan, were given them out of the tribe of Reuben, Bezer in the wilderness with her suburbs, and Jahzah with her suburbs, ⁷⁹Kedemoth also with her suburbs, and Mephaath with her suburbs: ⁸⁰And out of the tribe of Gad; Ramoth in Gilead with her suburbs, and Mahanaim with her suburbs, ⁸¹And Heshbon with her suburbs, and Jazer with her suburbs.

7

¹Now the sons of Issachar were, Tola, and Puah, Jashub, and Shimrom, four. ²And the sons of Tola; Uzzi, and Rephaiah, and Jeriel, and Jahmai, and Jibsam, and Shemuel, heads of their father's house, to wit, of Tola: they were valiant men of might in their generations; whose number was in the days of David two and twenty thousand and six hundred. ³And the sons of Uzzi; Izrahiah: and the sons of Izrahiah; Michael, and Obadiah, and Joel, Ishiah, five: all of

them chief men. ⁴And with them, by their generations, after the house of their fathers, were bands of soldiers for war, six and thirty thousand men: for they had many wives and sons. ⁵And their brothers among all the families of Issachar were valiant men of might, reckoned in all by their genealogies fourscore and seven thousand. ⁶The sons of Benjamin; Bela, and Becher, and Jediael, three. ⁷And the sons of Bela; Ezbon, and Uzzi, and Uzziel, and Jerimoth, and Iri, five; heads of the house of their fathers, mighty men of valor; and were reckoned by their genealogies twenty and two thousand and thirty and four. ⁸And the sons of Becher; Zemira, and Joash, and Eliezer, and Elioenai, and Omri, and Jerimoth, and Abiah, and Anathoth, and Alameth. All these are the sons of Becher. ⁹And the number of them, after their genealogy by their generations, heads of the house of their fathers, mighty men of valor, was twenty thousand and two hundred. ¹⁰The sons also of Jediael; Bilhan: and the sons of Bilhan; Jeush, and Benjamin, and Ehud, and Chenaanah, and Zethan, and Tharshish, and Ahishahar. ¹¹All these the sons of Jediael, by the heads of their fathers, mighty men of valor, were seventeen thousand and two hundred soldiers, fit to go out for war and battle. ¹²Shuppim also, and Huppim, the children of Ir, and Hushim, the sons of Aher. ¹³The sons of Naphtali; Jahziel, and Guni, and Jezer, and Shallum, the sons of Bilhah. ¹⁴The sons of Manasseh; Ashriel, whom she bore: (but his concubine the Aramitess bore Machir the father of Gilead: ¹⁵And Machir took to wife the sister of Huppim and Shuppim, whose sister's name was Maachah;) and the name of the second was Zelophehad: and Zelophehad had daughters. ¹⁶And Maachah the wife of Machir bore a son, and she called his name Peresh; and the name of his brother was Sheresh; and his sons were Ulam and Rakem. ¹⁷And the sons of Ulam; Bedan. These were the sons of Gilead, the son of Machir, the son of Manasseh. ¹⁸And his sister Hammoleketh bore Ishod, and Abiezer, and Mahalah. ¹⁹And the sons of Shemidah were, Ahian, and Shechem, and Likhi, and Aniam. ²⁰And the sons of Ephraim; Shuthelah, and Bered his son, and Tahath his son, and Eladah his son, and Tahath his son, ²¹And Zabad his son, and Shuthelah his son, and Ezer, and Elead, whom the men of Gath that were born in that land slew, because they came down to take away their cattle. ²²And Ephraim their father mourned many days, and his brothers came to comfort him. ²³And when he went in to his wife, she conceived, and bore a son, and he called his name Beriah, because it went evil with his house. ²⁴(And his daughter was Sherah, who built Bethhoron the nether, and the upper, and Uzzensherah.) ²⁵And Rephah was his son, also Resheph, and Telah his son, and Tahan his son. ²⁶Laadan his son, Ammihud his son, Elishama his son. ²⁷Non his son, Jehoshuah his son. ²⁸And their possessions and habitations were, Bethel and the towns thereof, and eastward Naaran, and westward Gezer, with the towns thereof; Shechem also and the towns thereof, to Gaza and the towns thereof: ²⁹And by the borders of the children of Manasseh, Bethshean and her towns, Taanach and her towns, Megiddo and her towns, Dor and her towns. In these dwelled the children of Joseph the son of Israel. ³⁰The sons of Asher; Imnah, and Isuah, and Ishuai, and Beriah, and Serah their sister. ³¹And the sons of Beriah; Heber, and Malchiel, who is the father of Birzavith. ³²And Heber begat Japhlet, and Shomer, and Hotham, and Shua their sister. ³³And the sons of Japhlet; Pasach, and Bimhal, and Ashvath. These are the children of Japhlet. ³⁴And the sons of Shamer; Ahi, and Rohgah, Jehubbah, and Aram. ³⁵And the sons of his brother Helem; Zophah, and Imna, and Shelesh, and Amal. ³⁶The sons of Zophah; Suah, and Harnepher, and Shual, and Beri, and Imrah, ³⁷Bezer, and Hod, and Shamma, and Shilshah, and Ithran, and Beera. ³⁸And the sons of Jether; Jephunneh, and Pispah, and Ara. ³⁹And the sons of Ulla; Arah, and Haniel, and Rezia. ⁴⁰All these were the children of Asher, heads of their father's house, choice and mighty men of valor, chief of the princes. And the number throughout the genealogy of them that were apt to the war and to battle was twenty and six thousand men.

8

¹Now Benjamin begat Bela his firstborn, Ashbel the second, and Aharah the third, ²Nohah the fourth, and Rapha the fifth. ³And the sons of Bela were, Addar, and Gera, and Abihud, ⁴And Abishua, and Naaman, and Ahoah, ⁵And Gera, and Shephuphan, and Huram. ⁶And these are the sons of Ehud: these are the heads of the fathers of the inhabitants of Geba, and they removed them to Manahath: ⁷And Naaman, and Ahiah, and Gera, he removed them, and begat Uzza, and Ahihud. ⁸And Shaharaim begat children in the country of Moab, after he had sent them away; Hushim and Baara were his wives. ⁹And he begat of Hodesh his wife, Jobab, and Zibia, and Mesha, and Malcham, ¹⁰And Jeuz, and Shachia, and Mirma. These were his sons, heads of the fathers. ¹¹And of Hushim he begat Abitub, and Elpaal. ¹²The sons of Elpaal; Eber, and Misham, and Shamed, who built Ono, and Lod, with the towns thereof: ¹³Beriah also, and Shema, who were heads of the fathers of the inhabitants of Aijalon, who drove away the inhabitants of Gath: ¹⁴And Ahio, Shashak, and Jeremoth, ¹⁵And Zebadiah, and Arad, and Ader, ¹⁶And Michael, and Ispah, and Joha, the sons of Beriah; ¹⁷And Zebadiah, and Meshullam, and Hezeki, and Heber, ¹⁸Ishmerai also, and Jezliah, and Jobab, the sons of Elpaal; ¹⁹And Jakim, and Zichri, and Zabdi, ²⁰And Elienai, and Zilthai, and Eliel, ²¹And Adaiah, and Beraiah, and Shimrath, the sons of Shimhi; ²²And Ishpan, and Heber, and Eliel, ²³And Abdon, and Zichri, and Hanan, ²⁴And Hananiah, and Elam, and Antothijah, ²⁵And Iphedeiah, and Penuel, the sons of Shashak; ²⁶And Shamsherai, and Shehariah, and Athaliah, ²⁷And Jaresiah, and Eliah, and Zichri, the sons of Jeroham. ²⁸These were heads of the fathers, by their generations, chief men. These dwelled in Jerusalem. ²⁹And at Gibeon dwelled the father of Gibeon; whose wife's name was Maachah: ³⁰And his firstborn son Abdon, and Zur, and Kish, and Baal, and Nadab, ³¹And Gedor, and Ahio, and Zacher. ³²And Mikloth begat Shimeah. And these also dwelled with their brothers in Jerusalem, over against them. ³³And Ner begat Kish, and Kish begat Saul, and Saul begat Jonathan, and Malchishua, and Abinadab, and Eshbaal. ³⁴And the son of Jonathan was Meribbaal; and Meribbaal begat Micah. ³⁵And the sons of Micah were, Pithon, and Melech, and Tarea, and Ahaz. ³⁶And Ahaz begat Jehoadah; and Jehoadah begat Alemeth, and Azmaveth, and Zimri; and Zimri begat Moza, ³⁷And Moza begat Binea: Rapha was his son, Eleasah his son, Azel his son: ³⁸And Azel had six sons, whose names are these, Azrikam, Bocheru, and Ishmael, and Shearjah, and Obadiah, and Hanan. All these were the sons

of Azel. ³⁹And the sons of Eshek his brother were, Ulam his firstborn, Jehush the second, and Eliphelet the third. ⁴⁰And the sons of Ulam were mighty men of valor, archers, and had many sons, and sons' sons, an hundred and fifty. All these are of the sons of Benjamin.

9 ¹So all Israel were reckoned by genealogies; and, behold, they were written in the book of the kings of Israel and Judah, who were carried away to Babylon for their transgression. ²Now the first inhabitants that dwelled in their possessions in their cities were, the Israelites, the priests, Levites, and the Nethinims. ³And in Jerusalem dwelled of the children of Judah, and of the children of Benjamin, and of the children of Ephraim, and Manasseh; ⁴Uthai the son of Ammihud, the son of Omri, the son of Imri, the son of Bani, of the children of Pharez the son of Judah. ⁵And of the Shilonites; Asaiah the firstborn, and his sons. ⁶And of the sons of Zerah; Jeuel, and their brothers, six hundred and ninety. ⁷And of the sons of Benjamin; Sallu the son of Meshullam, the son of Hodaviah, the son of Hasenuah, ⁸And Ibneiah the son of Jeroham, and Elah the son of Uzzi, the son of Michri, and Meshullam the son of Shephathiah, the son of Reuel, the son of Ibnijah; ⁹And their brothers, according to their generations, nine hundred and fifty and six. All these men were chief of the fathers in the house of their fathers. ¹⁰And of the priests; Jedaiah, and Jehoiarib, and Jachin, ¹¹And Azariah the son of Hilkiah, the son of Meshullam, the son of Zadok, the son of Meraioth, the son of Ahitub, the ruler of the house of God; ¹²And Adaiah the son of Jeroham, the son of Pashur, the son of Malchijah, and Maasiai the son of Adiel, the son of Jahzerah, the son of Meshullam, the son of Meshillemith, the son of Immer; ¹³And their brothers, heads of the house of their fathers, a thousand and seven hundred and three score; very able men for the work of the service of the house of God. ¹⁴And of the Levites; Shemaiah the son of Hasshub, the son of Azrikam, the son of Hashabiah, of the sons of Merari; ¹⁵And Bakbakkar, Heresh, and Galal, and Mattaniah the son of Micah, the son of Zichri, the son of Asaph; ¹⁶And Obadiah the son of Shemaiah, the son of Galal, the son of Jeduthun, and Berechiah the son of Asa, the son of Elkanah, that dwelled in the villages of the Netophathites. ¹⁷And the porters were, Shallum, and Akkub, and Talmon, and Ahiman, and their brothers: Shallum was the chief; ¹⁸Who till now waited in the king's gate eastward: they were porters in the companies of the children of Levi. ¹⁹And Shallum the son of Kore, the son of Ebiasaph, the son of Korah, and his brothers, of the house of his father, the Korahites, were over the work of the service, keepers of the gates of the tabernacle: and their fathers, being over the host of the LORD, were keepers of the entry. ²⁰And Phinehas the son of Eleazar was the ruler over them in time past, and the LORD was with him. ²¹And Zechariah the son of Meshelemiah was porter of the door of the tabernacle of the congregation. ²²All these which were chosen to be porters in the gates were two hundred and twelve. These were reckoned by their genealogy in their villages, whom David and Samuel the seer did ordain in their set office. ²³So they and their children had the oversight of the gates of the house of the LORD, namely, the house of the tabernacle, by wards. ²⁴In four quarters were the porters, toward the east, west, north, and south. ²⁵And their brothers, which were in their villages, were to come after seven days from time to time with them. ²⁶For these Levites, the four chief porters, were in their set office, and were over the chambers and treasuries of the house of God. ²⁷And they lodged round about the house of God, because the charge was on them, and the opening thereof every morning pertained to them. ²⁸And certain of them had the charge of the ministering vessels, that they should bring them in and out by tale. ²⁹Some of them also were appointed to oversee the vessels, and all the instruments of the sanctuary, and the fine flour, and the wine, and the oil, and the frankincense, and the spices. ³⁰And some of the sons of the priests made the ointment of the spices. ³¹And Mattithiah, one of the Levites, who was the firstborn of Shallum the Korahite, had the set office over the things that were made in the pans. ³²And other of their brothers, of the sons of the Kohathites, were over the show bread, to prepare it every sabbath. ³³And these are the singers, chief of the fathers of the Levites, who remaining in the chambers were free: for they were employed in that work day and night. ³⁴These chief fathers of the Levites were chief throughout their generations; these dwelled at Jerusalem. ³⁵And in Gibeon dwelled the father of Gibeon, Jehiel, whose wife's name was Maachah: ³⁶And his firstborn son Abdon, then Zur, and Kish, and Baal, and Ner, and Nadab. ³⁷And Gedor, and Ahio, and Zechariah, and Mikloth. ³⁸And Mikloth begat Shimeam. And they also dwelled with their brothers at Jerusalem, over against their brothers. ³⁹And Ner begat Kish; and Kish begat Saul; and Saul begat Jonathan, and Malchishua, and Abinadab, and Eshbaal. ⁴⁰And the son of Jonathan was Meribbaal: and Meribbaal begat Micah. ⁴¹And the sons of Micah were, Pithon, and Melech, and Tahrea, and Ahaz. ⁴²And Ahaz begat Jarah; and Jarah begat Alemeth, and Azmaveth, and Zimri; and Zimri begat Moza; ⁴³And Moza begat Binea; and Rephaiah his son, Eleasah his son, Azel his son. ⁴⁴And Azel had six sons, whose names are these, Azrikam, Bocheru, and Ishmael, and Sheariah, and Obadiah, and Hanan: these were the sons of Azel.

10 ¹Now the Philistines fought against Israel; and the men of Israel fled from before the Philistines, and fell down slain in mount Gilboa. ²And the Philistines followed hard after Saul, and after his sons; and the Philistines slew Jonathan, and Abinadab, and Malchishua, the sons of Saul. ³And the battle went sore against Saul, and the archers hit him, and he was wounded of the archers. ⁴Then said Saul to his armor bearer, Draw your sword, and thrust me through therewith; lest these uncircumcised come and abuse me. But his armor bearer would not; for he was sore afraid. So Saul took a sword, and fell on it. ⁵And when his armor bearer saw that Saul was dead, he fell likewise on the sword, and died. ⁶So Saul died, and his three sons, and all his house died together. ⁷And when all the men of Israel that were in the valley saw that they fled, and that Saul and his sons were dead, then they forsook their cities, and fled: and the Philistines came and dwelled in them. ⁸And it came to pass on the morrow, when the Philistines came to strip the slain, that they found Saul and his sons fallen in mount Gilboa. ⁹And when they had stripped him, they took his head, and his armor, and sent into the land of the Philistines

round about, to carry tidings to their idols, and to the people. ¹⁰And they put his armor in the house of their gods, and fastened his head in the temple of Dagon. ¹¹And when all Jabeshgilead heard all that the Philistines had done to Saul, ¹²They arose, all the valiant men, and took away the body of Saul, and the bodies of his sons, and brought them to Jabesh, and buried their bones under the oak in Jabesh, and fasted seven days. ¹³So Saul died for his transgression which he committed against the LORD, even against the word of the LORD, which he kept not, and also for asking counsel of one that had a familiar spirit, to inquire of it; ¹⁴And inquired not of the LORD: therefore he slew him, and turned the kingdom to David the son of Jesse.

11 ¹Then all Israel gathered themselves to David to Hebron, saying, Behold, we are your bone and your flesh. ²And moreover in time past, even when Saul was king, you were he that led out and brought in Israel: and the LORD your God said to you, You shall feed my people Israel, and you shall be ruler over my people Israel. ³Therefore came all the elders of Israel to the king to Hebron; and David made a covenant with them in Hebron before the LORD; and they anointed David king over Israel, according to the word of the LORD by Samuel. ⁴And David and all Israel went to Jerusalem, which is Jebus; where the Jebusites were, the inhabitants of the land. ⁵And the inhabitants of Jebus said to David, You shall not come here. Nevertheless David took the castle of Zion, which is the city of David. ⁶And David said, Whoever smites the Jebusites first shall be chief and captain. So Joab the son of Zeruiah went first up, and was chief. ⁷And David dwelled in the castle; therefore they called it the city of David. ⁸And he built the city round about, even from Millo round about: and Joab repaired the rest of the city. ⁹So David waxed greater and greater: for the LORD of hosts was with him. ¹⁰These also are the chief of the mighty men whom David had, who strengthened themselves with him in his kingdom, and with all Israel, to make him king, according to the word of the LORD concerning Israel. ¹¹And this is the number of the mighty men whom David had; Jashobeam, an Hachmonite, the chief of the captains: he lifted up his spear against three hundred slain by him at one time. ¹²And after him was Eleazar the son of Dodo, the Ahohite, who was one of the three mighty men. ¹³He was with David at Pasdammim, and there the Philistines were gathered together to battle, where was a parcel of ground full of barley; and the people fled from before the Philistines. ¹⁴And they set themselves in the middle of that parcel, and delivered it, and slew the Philistines; and the LORD saved them by a great deliverance. ¹⁵Now three of the thirty captains went down to the rock to David, into the cave of Adullam; and the host of the Philistines encamped in the valley of Rephaim. ¹⁶And David was then in the hold, and the Philistines' garrison was then at Bethlehem. ¹⁷And David longed, and said, Oh that one would give me drink of the water of the well of Bethlehem, that is at the gate! ¹⁸And the three broke through the host of the Philistines, and drew water out of the well of Bethlehem, that was by the gate, and took it, and brought it to David: but David would not drink of it, but poured it out to the LORD. ¹⁹And said, My God forbid it me, that I should do this thing: shall I drink the blood of these men that have put their lives in jeopardy? for with the jeopardy of their lives they brought it. Therefore he would not drink it. These things did these three mightiest. ²⁰And Abishai the brother of Joab, he was chief of the three: for lifting up his spear against three hundred, he slew them, and had a name among the three. ²¹Of the three, he was more honorable than the two; for he was their captain: however, he attained not to the first three. ²²Benaiah the son of Jehoiada, the son of a valiant man of Kabzeel, who had done many acts; he slew two lion like men of Moab: also he went down and slew a lion in a pit in a snowy day. ²³And he slew an Egyptian, a man of great stature, five cubits high; and in the Egyptian's hand was a spear like a weaver's beam; and he went down to him with a staff, and plucked the spear out of the Egyptian's hand, and slew him with his own spear. ²⁴These things did Benaiah the son of Jehoiada, and had the name among the three mighty men. ²⁵Behold, he was honorable among the thirty, but attained not to the first three: and David set him over his guard. ²⁶Also the valiant men of the armies were, Asahel the brother of Joab, Elhanan the son of Dodo of Bethlehem, ²⁷Shammoth the Harorite, Helez the Pelonite, ²⁸Ira the son of Ikkesh the Tekoite, Abiezer the Antothite, ²⁹Sibbecai the Hushathite, Ilai the Ahohite, ³⁰Maharai the Netophathite, Heled the son of Baanah the Netophathite, ³¹Ithai the son of Ribai of Gibeah, that pertained to the children of Benjamin, Benaiah the Pirathonite, ³²Hurai of the brooks of Gaash, Abiel the Arbathite, ³³Azmaveth the Baharumite, Eliahba the Shaalbonite, ³⁴The sons of Hashem the Gizonite, Jonathan the son of Shage the Hararite, ³⁵Ahiam the son of Sacar the Hararite, Eliphal the son of Ur, ³⁶Hepher the Mecherathite, Ahijah the Pelonite, ³⁷Hezro the Carmelite, Naarai the son of Ezbai, ³⁸Joel the brother of Nathan, Mibhar the son of Haggeri, ³⁹Zelek the Ammonite, Naharai the Berothite, the armor bearer of Joab the son of Zeruiah, ⁴⁰Ira the Ithrite, Gareb the Ithrite, ⁴¹Uriah the Hittite, Zabad the son of Ahlai, ⁴²Adina the son of Shiza the Reubenite, a captain of the Reubenites, and thirty with him, ⁴³Hanan the son of Maachah, and Joshaphat the Mithnite, ⁴⁴Uzzia the Ashterathite, Shama and Jehiel the sons of Hothan the Aroerite, ⁴⁵Jediael the son of Shimri, and Joha his brother, the Tizite, ⁴⁶Eliel the Mahavite, and Jeribai, and Joshaviah, the sons of Elnaam, and Ithmah the Moabite, ⁴⁷Eliel, and Obed, and Jasiel the Mesobaite.

12 ¹Now these are they that came to David to Ziklag, while he yet kept himself close because of Saul the son of Kish: and they were among the mighty men, helpers of the war. ²They were armed with bows, and could use both the right hand and the left in hurling stones and shooting arrows out of a bow, even of Saul's brothers of Benjamin. ³The chief was Ahiezer, then Joash, the sons of Shemaah the Gibeathite; and Jeziel, and Pelet, the sons of Azmaveth; and Berachah, and Jehu the Antothite. ⁴And Ismaiah the Gibeonite, a mighty man among the thirty, and over the thirty; and Jeremiah, and Jahaziel, and Johanan, and Josabad the Gederathite, ⁵Eluzai, and Jerimoth, and Bealiah, and Shemariah, and Shephatiah the Haruphite, ⁶Elkanah, and Jesiah, and Azareel, and Joezer, and Jashobeam, the Korhites, ⁷And Joelah, and Zebadiah, the sons of Jeroham of Gedor. ⁸And of the Gadites there separated themselves to David into the hold to the wilderness men of might, and men of war fit for the battle, that could handle shield and buckler, whose faces were like the faces of lions, and were as swift as the roes on the mountains; ⁹Ezer the first, Obadiah the second, Eliab the third, ¹⁰Mishmannah the fourth, Jeremiah the fifth, ¹¹Attai the sixth, Eliel the seventh, ¹²Johanan the eighth, Elzabad the ninth, ¹³Jeremiah the tenth, Machbanai the eleventh. ¹⁴These were of the sons of Gad, captains of the host: one of the least was over an hundred, and the greatest over a thousand. ¹⁵These are they that went over Jordan in the first month, when it had overflowed all his banks; and they put to flight all them of the valleys, both toward the east, and toward the west. ¹⁶And there came of the children of Benjamin and Judah to the hold to David. ¹⁷And David went out to meet them, and answered and said to them, If you be come peaceably to me to help me, my heart shall be knit to you: but if you be come to betray me to my enemies, seeing there is no wrong in my hands, the God of our fathers look thereon, and rebuke it. ¹⁸Then the spirit came on Amasai, who was chief of the captains, and he said, Your are we, David, and on your side, you son of Jesse: peace, peace be to you, and peace be to your helpers; for your God helps you. Then David received them, and made them captains of the band. ¹⁹And there fell some of Manasseh to David, when he came with the Philistines against Saul to battle: but they helped them not: for the lords of the Philistines on advisement sent him away, saying, He will fall to his master Saul to the jeopardy of our heads. ²⁰As he went to Ziklag, there fell to him of Manasseh, Adnah, and Jozabad, and Jediael, and Michael, and Jozabad, and Elihu, and Zilthai, captains of the thousands that were of Manasseh. ²¹And they helped David against the band of the rovers: for they were all mighty men of valor, and were captains in the host. ²²For at that time day by day there came to David to help him, until it was a great host, like the host of God. ²³And these are the numbers of the bands that were ready armed to the war, and came to David to Hebron, to turn the kingdom of Saul to him, according to the word of the LORD. ²⁴The children of Judah that bore shield and spear were six thousand and eight hundred, ready armed to the war. ²⁵Of the children of Simeon, mighty men of valor for the war, seven thousand and one hundred. ²⁶Of the children of Levi four thousand and six hundred. ²⁷And Jehoiada was the leader of the Aaronites, and with him were three thousand and seven hundred; ²⁸And Zadok, a young man mighty of valor, and of his father's house twenty and two captains. ²⁹And of the children of Benjamin, the kindred of Saul, three thousand: for till now the greatest part of them had kept the ward of the house of Saul. ³⁰And of the children of Ephraim twenty thousand and eight hundred, mighty men of valor, famous throughout the house of their fathers. ³¹And of the half tribe of Manasseh eighteen thousand, which were expressed by name, to come and make David king. ³²And of the children of Issachar, which were men that had understanding of the times, to know what Israel ought to do; the heads of them were two hundred; and all their brothers were at their commandment. ³³Of Zebulun, such as went forth to battle, expert in war, with all instruments of war, fifty thousand, which could keep rank: they were not of double heart. ³⁴And of Naphtali a thousand captains, and with them with shield and spear thirty and seven thousand. ³⁵And of the Danites expert in war twenty and eight thousand and six hundred. ³⁶And of Asher, such as went forth to battle, expert in war, forty thousand. ³⁷And on the other side of Jordan, of the Reubenites, and the Gadites, and of the half tribe of Manasseh, with all manner of instruments of war for the battle, an hundred and twenty thousand. ³⁸All these men of war, that could keep rank, came with a perfect heart to Hebron, to make David king over all Israel: and all the rest also of Israel were of one heart to make David king. ³⁹And there they were with David three days, eating and drinking: for their brothers had prepared for them. ⁴⁰Moreover they that were near them, even to Issachar and Zebulun and Naphtali, brought bread on asses, and on camels, and on mules, and on oxen, and meat, meal, cakes of figs, and bunches of raisins, and wine, and oil, and oxen, and sheep abundantly: for there was joy in Israel.

13 ¹And David consulted with the captains of thousands and hundreds, and with every leader. ²And David said to all the congregation of Israel, If it seem good to you, and that it be of the LORD our God, let us send abroad to our brothers every where, that are left in all the land of Israel, and with them also to the priests and Levites which are in their cities and suburbs, that they may gather themselves to us: ³And let us bring again the ark of our God to us: for we inquired not at it in the days of Saul. ⁴And all the congregation said that they would do so: for the thing was right in the eyes of all the people. ⁵So David gathered all Israel together, from Shihor of Egypt even to the entering of Hemath, to bring the ark of God from Kirjathjearim. ⁶And David went up, and all Israel, to Baalah, that is, to Kirjathjearim, which belonged to Judah, to bring up there the ark of God the LORD, that dwells between the cherubim, whose name is called on it. ⁷And they carried the ark of God in a new cart out of the house of Abinadab: and Uzza and Ahio drove the cart. ⁸And David and all Israel played before God with all their might, and with singing, and with harps, and with psalteries, and with tambourines, and with cymbals, and with trumpets. ⁹And when they came to the threshing floor of Chidon, Uzza put forth his hand to hold the ark; for the oxen stumbled. ¹⁰And the anger of the LORD was kindled against Uzza, and he smote him, because he put his hand to the ark: and there he died before God. ¹¹And David was displeased, because the LORD had made a breach on Uzza: why that place is called Perezuzza to this day. ¹²And David was afraid of God that day, saying, How shall I bring the ark of God home to me? ¹³So David brought not the ark home to himself to the city of David, but carried it aside into the house of Obededom the Gittite. ¹⁴And the ark of God remained with the family of Obededom in his house three months. And the LORD blessed the house of Obededom, and all that he had.

14 ¹Now Hiram king of Tyre sent messengers to David, and timber of cedars, with masons and carpenters, to build him an house. ²And David perceived that the LORD had confirmed him king over Israel, for his kingdom was lifted up on high, because of his people Israel. ³And David took more wives at Jerusalem: and David begat more sons and daughters. ⁴Now these are the names of his children which he had in Jerusalem; Shammua, and Shobab, Nathan, and Solomon, ⁵And Ibhar, and Elishua, and Elpalet, ⁶And Nogah, and Nepheg, and Japhia, ⁷And Elishama, and Beeliada, and Eliphalet. ⁸And when the Philistines heard that David was anointed king over all Israel, all the Philistines went up to seek David. And David heard of it, and went out against them. ⁹And the Philistines came and spread themselves in the valley of Rephaim. ¹⁰And David inquired of God, saying, Shall I go up against the Philistines? And will you deliver them into my hand? And the LORD said to him, Go up; for I will deliver them into your hand. ¹¹So they came up to Baalperazim; and David smote them there. Then David said, God has broken in on my enemies by my hand like the breaking forth of waters: therefore they called the name of that place Baalperazim. ¹²And when they had left their gods there, David gave a commandment, and they were burned with fire. ¹³And the Philistines yet again spread themselves abroad in the valley. ¹⁴Therefore David inquired again of God; and God said to him, Go not up after them; turn away from them, and come on them over against the mulberry trees. ¹⁵And it shall be, when you shall hear a sound of going in the tops of the mulberry trees, that then you shall go out to battle: for God is gone forth before you to smite the host of the Philistines. ¹⁶David therefore did as God commanded him: and they smote the host of the Philistines from Gibeon even to Gazer. ¹⁷And the fame of David went out into all lands; and the LORD brought the fear of him on all nations.

15 ¹And David made him houses in the city of David, and prepared a place for the ark of God, and pitched for it a tent. ²Then David said, None ought to carry the ark of God but the Levites: for them has the LORD chosen to carry the ark of God, and to minister to him for ever. ³And David gathered all Israel together to Jerusalem, to bring up the ark of the LORD to his place, which he had prepared for it. ⁴And David assembled the children of Aaron, and the Levites: ⁵Of the sons of Kohath; Uriel the chief, and his brothers an hundred and twenty: ⁶Of the sons of Merari; Asaiah the chief, and his brothers two hundred and twenty: ⁷Of the sons of Gershom; Joel the chief and his brothers an hundred and thirty: ⁸Of the sons of Elizaphan; Shemaiah the chief, and his brothers two hundred: ⁹Of the sons of Hebron; Eliel the chief, and his brothers fourscore: ¹⁰Of the sons of Uzziel; Amminadab the chief, and his brothers an hundred and twelve. ¹¹And David called for Zadok and Abiathar the priests, and for the Levites, for Uriel, Asaiah, and Joel, Shemaiah, and Eliel, and Amminadab, ¹²And said to them, You are the chief of the fathers of the Levites: sanctify yourselves, both you and your brothers, that you may bring up the ark of the LORD God of Israel to the place that I have prepared for it. ¹³For because you did it not at the first, the LORD our God made a breach on us, for that we sought him not after the due order. ¹⁴So the priests and the Levites sanctified themselves to bring up the ark of the LORD God of Israel. ¹⁵And the children of the Levites bore the ark of God on their shoulders with the staves thereon, as Moses commanded according to the word of the LORD. ¹⁶And David spoke to the chief of the Levites to appoint their brothers to be the singers with instruments of music, psalteries and harps and cymbals, sounding, by lifting up the voice with joy. ¹⁷So the Levites appointed Heman the son of Joel; and of his brothers, Asaph the son of Berechiah; and of the sons of Merari their brothers, Ethan the son of Kushaiah; ¹⁸And with them their brothers of the second degree, Zechariah, Ben, and Jaaziel, and Shemiramoth, and Jehiel, and Unni, Eliab, and Benaiah, and Maaseiah, and Mattithiah, and Elipheleh, and Mikneiah, and Obededom, and Jeiel, the porters. ¹⁹So the singers, Heman, Asaph, and Ethan, were appointed to sound with cymbals of brass; ²⁰And Zechariah, and Aziel, and Shemiramoth, and Jehiel, and Unni, and Eliab, and Maaseiah, and Benaiah, with psalteries on Alamoth; ²¹And Mattithiah, and Elipheleh, and Mikneiah, and Obededom, and Jeiel, and Azaziah, with harps on the Sheminith to excel. ²²And Chenaniah, chief of the Levites, was for song: he instructed about the song, because he was skillful. ²³And Berechiah and Elkanah were doorkeepers for the ark. ²⁴And Shebaniah, and Jehoshaphat, and Nethaneel, and Amasai, and Zechariah, and Benaiah, and Eliezer, the priests, did blow with the trumpets before the ark of God: and Obededom and Jehiah were doorkeepers for the ark. ²⁵So David, and the elders of Israel, and the captains over thousands, went to bring up the ark of the covenant of the LORD out of the house of Obededom with joy. ²⁶And it came to pass, when God helped the Levites that bore the ark of the covenant of the LORD, that they offered seven bullocks and seven rams. ²⁷And David was clothed with a robe of fine linen, and all the Levites that bore the ark, and the singers, and Chenaniah the master of the song with the singers: David also had on him an ephod of linen. ²⁸Thus all Israel brought up the ark of the covenant of the LORD with shouting, and with sound of the cornet, and with trumpets, and with cymbals, making a noise with psalteries and harps. ²⁹And it came to pass, as the ark of the covenant of the LORD came to the city of David, that Michal, the daughter of Saul looking out at a window saw king David dancing and playing: and she despised him in her heart.

16 ¹So they brought the ark of God, and set it in the middle of the tent that David had pitched for it: and they offered burnt sacrifices and peace offerings before God. ²And when David had made an end of offering the burnt offerings and the peace offerings, he blessed the people in the name of the LORD. ³And he dealt to every one of Israel, both man and woman, to every one a loaf of bread, and a good piece of flesh, and a flagon of wine. ⁴And he appointed certain of the Levites to minister before the ark of the LORD, and to record, and to thank and praise the LORD God of Israel: ⁵Asaph the chief, and next to him Zechariah, Jeiel, and Shemiramoth, and Jehiel, and Mattithiah, and Eliab, and Benaiah, and Obededom: and Jeiel with psalteries and with harps; but Asaph made a sound with cymbals; ⁶Benaiah also and Jahaziel the priests with trumpets continually before the ark of the covenant of God. ⁷Then on that day David delivered first this psalm to thank the LORD into the hand of Asaph and his brothers. ⁸Give thanks to the LORD, call on his name, make known his deeds among the people. ⁹Sing to him, sing psalms to him, talk you of all his wondrous works. ¹⁰Glory you in his holy name: let the heart of them rejoice that seek the LORD. ¹¹Seek the LORD and his strength, seek his face continually. ¹²Remember his marvelous works that he has done, his wonders, and the judgments of his mouth; ¹³O you seed of Israel his servant, you children of Jacob, his chosen ones. ¹⁴He is the LORD our God; his judgments are in all the earth. ¹⁵Be you mindful always of his covenant; the word which he commanded to a thousand generations; ¹⁶Even of the covenant which he made with Abraham, and of his oath to Isaac; ¹⁷And has confirmed the same to Jacob for a law, and to Israel for an everlasting covenant, ¹⁸Saying, To you will I give the land of Canaan, the lot of your inheritance; ¹⁹When you were but few, even a few, and strangers in it. ²⁰And when they went from nation to nation, and from one kingdom to another people; ²¹He suffered no man to do them wrong: yes, he reproved kings for their sakes, ²²Saying, Touch not my anointed, and do my prophets no harm. ²³Sing to the LORD, all the earth; show forth from day to day his salvation. ²⁴Declare his glory among the heathen; his marvelous works among all nations. ²⁵For great is the LORD, and greatly to be praised: he also is to be feared above all gods. ²⁶For all the gods of the people are idols: but the LORD made the heavens. ²⁷Glory and honor are in his presence; strength and gladness are in his place. ²⁸Give to the LORD, you kindreds of the people, give to the LORD glory and strength. ²⁹Give to the LORD the glory due to his name: bring an offering, and come before him: worship the LORD in the beauty of holiness. ³⁰Fear before him, all the earth: the world also shall be stable, that it be not moved. ³¹Let the heavens be glad, and let the earth rejoice: and let men say among the nations, The LORD reigns. ³²Let the sea roar, and the fullness thereof: let the fields rejoice, and all that is therein. ³³Then shall the trees of the wood sing out at the presence of the LORD, because he comes to judge the earth. ³⁴O give thanks to the LORD; for he is good; for his mercy endures for ever. ³⁵And say you, Save us, O God of our salvation, and gather us together, and deliver us from the heathen, that we may give thanks to your holy name, and glory in your praise. ³⁶Blessed be the LORD God of Israel for ever and ever. And all the people said, Amen, and praised the LORD. ³⁷So he left there before the ark of the covenant of the LORD Asaph and his brothers, to minister before the ark continually, as every day's work required: ³⁸And Obededom with their brothers, three score and eight; Obededom also the son of Jeduthun and Hosah to be porters: ³⁹And Zadok the priest, and his brothers the priests, before the tabernacle of the LORD in the high place that was at Gibeon, ⁴⁰To offer burnt offerings to the LORD on the altar of the burnt offering continually morning and evening, and to do according to all that is written in the law of the LORD, which he commanded Israel; ⁴¹And with them Heman and Jeduthun, and the rest that were chosen, who were expressed by name, to give thanks to the LORD, because his mercy endures for ever; ⁴²And with them Heman and Jeduthun with trumpets and cymbals for those that should make a sound, and with musical instruments of God. And the sons of Jeduthun were porters. ⁴³And all the people departed every man to his house: and David returned to bless his house.

17

¹Now it came to pass, as David sat in his house, that David said to Nathan the prophet, See, I dwell in an house of cedars, but the ark of the covenant of the LORD remains under curtains. ²Then Nathan said to David, Do all that is in your heart; for God is with you. ³And it came to pass the same night, that the word of God came to Nathan, saying, ⁴Go and tell David my servant, Thus says the LORD, You shall not build me an house to dwell in: ⁵For I have not dwelled in an house since the day that I brought up Israel to this day; but have gone from tent to tent, and from one tabernacle to another. ⁶Wherever I have walked with all Israel, spoke I a word to any of the judges of Israel, whom I commanded to feed my people, saying, Why have you not built me an house of cedars? ⁷Now therefore thus shall you say to my servant David, Thus says the LORD of hosts, I took you from the sheepcote, even from following the sheep, that you should be ruler over my people Israel: ⁸And I have been with you wherever you have walked, and have cut off all your enemies from before you, and have made you a name like the name of the great men that are in the earth. ⁹Also I will ordain a place for my people Israel, and will plant them, and they shall dwell in their place, and shall be moved no more; neither shall the children of wickedness waste them any more, as at the beginning, ¹⁰And since the time that I commanded judges to be over my people Israel. Moreover I will subdue all your enemies. Furthermore I tell you that the LORD will build you an house. ¹¹And it shall come to pass, when your days be expired that you must go to be with your fathers, that I will raise up your seed after you, which shall be of your sons; and I will establish his kingdom. ¹²He shall build me an house, and I will establish his throne for ever. ¹³I will be his father, and he shall be my son: and I will not take my mercy away from him, as I took it from him that was before you: ¹⁴But I will settle him in my house and in my kingdom for ever: and his throne shall be established for ever more. ¹⁵According to all these words, and according to all this vision, so did Nathan speak to David. ¹⁶And David the king came and sat before the LORD, and said, Who am I, O LORD God, and what is my house, that you have brought me till now? ¹⁷And yet this was a small thing in your eyes, O God; for you have also spoken of your servant's house for a great while to come, and have regarded me according to the estate of a man of high degree, O LORD God. ¹⁸What can David speak more to you for the honor of your servant? for you know your servant. ¹⁹O LORD, for your servant's sake, and according to your own heart, have you done all this greatness, in making known all these great things. ²⁰O LORD, there is none like you, neither is there any God beside you, according to all that we have heard with our ears. ²¹And what one nation in the earth is like your people Israel, whom God went to redeem to be his own people, to make you a name of greatness and terribleness, by driving out nations from before your people whom you have redeemed out of Egypt? ²²For your people Israel did you make your own people for ever; and you, LORD, became their God. ²³Therefore now, LORD, let the thing that you have spoken concerning your servant and concerning his house be established for ever, and do as you have said. ²⁴Let it even be established, that your name may be magnified for ever, saying, The LORD of hosts is the God of Israel, even a God to Israel: and let the house of David your servant be established before you. ²⁵For you, O my God, have told your servant that you will build him an house: therefore your servant has found in his heart to pray before you. ²⁶And now, LORD, you are God, and have promised this goodness to your servant: ²⁷Now therefore let

it please you to bless the house of your servant, that it may be before you for ever: for you bless, O LORD, and it shall be blessed for ever.

18 ¹Now after this it came to pass, that David smote the Philistines, and subdued them, and took Gath and her towns out of the hand of the Philistines. ²And he smote Moab; and the Moabites became David's servants, and brought gifts. ³And David smote Hadarezer king of Zobah to Hamath, as he went to establish his dominion by the river Euphrates. ⁴And David took from him a thousand chariots, and seven thousand horsemen, and twenty thousand footmen: David also hamstrung all the chariot horses, but reserved of them an hundred chariots. ⁵And when the Syrians of Damascus came to help Hadarezer king of Zobah, David slew of the Syrians two and twenty thousand men. ⁶Then David put garrisons in Syriadamascus; and the Syrians became David's servants, and brought gifts. Thus the LORD preserved David wherever he went. ⁷And David took the shields of gold that were on the servants of Hadarezer, and brought them to Jerusalem. ⁸Likewise from Tibhath, and from Chun, cities of Hadarezer, brought David very much brass, with which Solomon made the brazen sea, and the pillars, and the vessels of brass. ⁹Now when Tou king of Hamath heard how David had smitten all the host of Hadarezer king of Zobah; ¹⁰He sent Hadoram his son to king David, to inquire of his welfare, and to congratulate him, because he had fought against Hadarezer, and smitten him; (for Hadarezer had war with Tou;) and with him all manner of vessels of gold and silver and brass. ¹¹Them also king David dedicated to the LORD, with the silver and the gold that he brought from all these nations; from Edom, and from Moab, and from the children of Ammon, and from the Philistines, and from Amalek. ¹²Moreover Abishai the son of Zeruiah slew of the Edomites in the valley of salt eighteen thousand. ¹³And he put garrisons in Edom; and all the Edomites became David's servants. Thus the LORD preserved David wherever he went. ¹⁴So David reigned over all Israel, and executed judgment and justice among all his people. ¹⁵And Joab the son of Zeruiah was over the host; and Jehoshaphat the son of Ahilud, recorder. ¹⁶And Zadok the son of Ahitub, and Abimelech the son of Abiathar, were the priests; and Shavsha was scribe; ¹⁷And Benaiah the son of Jehoiada was over the Cherethites and the Pelethites; and the sons of David were chief about the king.

19 ¹Now it came to pass after this, that Nahash the king of the children of Ammon died, and his son reigned in his stead. ²And David said, I will show kindness to Hanun the son of Nahash, because his father showed kindness to me. And David sent messengers to comfort him concerning his father. So the servants of David came into the land of the children of Ammon to Hanun, to comfort him. ³But the princes of the children of Ammon said to Hanun, Think you that David does honor your father, that he has sent comforters to you? are not his servants come to you for to search, and to overthrow, and to spy out the land? ⁴Why Hanun took David's servants, and shaved them, and cut off their garments in the middle hard by their buttocks, and sent them away. ⁵Then there went certain, and told David how the men were served. And he sent to meet them: for the men were greatly ashamed. And the king said, Tarry at Jericho until your beards be grown, and then return. ⁶And when the children of Ammon saw that they had made themselves odious to David, Hanun and the children of Ammon sent a thousand talents of silver to hire them chariots and horsemen out of Mesopotamia, and out of Syriamaachah, and out of Zobah. ⁷So they hired thirty and two thousand chariots, and the king of Maachah and his people; who came and pitched before Medeba. And the children of Ammon gathered themselves together from their cities, and came to battle. ⁸And when David heard of it, he sent Joab, and all the host of the mighty men. ⁹And the children of Ammon came out, and put the battle in array before the gate of the city: and the kings that were come were by themselves in the field. ¹⁰Now when Joab saw that the battle was set against him before and behind, he chose out of all the choice of Israel, and put them in array against the Syrians. ¹¹And the rest of the people he delivered to the hand of Abishai his brother, and they set themselves in array against the children of Ammon. ¹²And he said, If the Syrians be too strong for me, then you shall help me: but if the children of Ammon be too strong for you, then I will help you. ¹³Be of good courage, and let us behave ourselves valiantly for our people, and for the cities of our God: and let the LORD do that which is good in his sight. ¹⁴So Joab and the people that were with him drew near before the Syrians to the battle; and they fled before him. ¹⁵And when the children of Ammon saw that the Syrians were fled, they likewise fled before Abishai his brother, and entered into the city. Then Joab came to Jerusalem. ¹⁶And when the Syrians saw that they were put to the worse before Israel, they sent messengers, and drew forth the Syrians that were beyond the river: and Shophach the captain of the host of Hadarezer went before them. ¹⁷And it was told David; and he gathered all Israel, and passed over Jordan, and came on them, and set the battle in array against them. So when David had put the battle in array against the Syrians, they fought with him. ¹⁸But the Syrians fled before Israel; and David slew of the Syrians seven thousand men which fought in chariots, and forty thousand footmen, and killed Shophach the captain of the host. ¹⁹And when the servants of Hadarezer saw that they were put to the worse before Israel, they made peace with David, and became his servants: neither would the Syrians help the children of Ammon any more.

20 ¹And it came to pass, that after the year was expired, at the time that kings go out to battle, Joab led forth the power of the army, and wasted the country of the children of Ammon, and came and besieged Rabbah. But David tarried at Jerusalem. And Joab smote Rabbah, and destroyed it. ²And David took the crown of their king from off his head, and found it to weigh a talent of gold, and there were precious stones in it; and it was set on David's head: and he brought also exceeding much spoil out of the city. ³And he brought out the people that were in it, and cut them with saws, and with harrows of iron, and with axes. Even so dealt David with all the cities of the children of Ammon. And David and all the people returned to Jerusalem. ⁴And it came to pass after this, that there arose war at Gezer with the Philistines; at which time Sibbechai the Hushathite slew Sippai, that was of the children of the giant: and they were subdued. ⁵And there was war again with the Philistines; and Elhanan the son of Jair slew Lahmi the brother of Goliath the Gittite, whose spear staff was like a weaver's beam. ⁶And yet again there was war at Gath, where was a man of great stature, whose fingers and toes were four and twenty, six on each hand, and six on each foot and he also was the son of the giant. ⁷But when he defied Israel, Jonathan the son of Shimea David's brother slew him. ⁸These were born to the giant in Gath; and they fell by the hand of David, and by the hand of his servants.

21 ¹And Satan stood up against Israel, and provoked David to number Israel. ²And David said to Joab and to the rulers of the people, Go, number Israel from Beersheba even to Dan; and bring the number of them to me, that I may know it. ³And Joab answered, The LORD make his people an hundred times so many more as they be: but, my lord the king, are they not all my lord's servants? why then does my lord require this thing? why will he be a cause of trespass to Israel? ⁴Nevertheless the king's word prevailed against Joab. Why Joab departed, and went throughout all Israel, and came to Jerusalem. ⁵And Joab gave the sum of the number of the people to David. And all they of Israel were a thousand thousand and an hundred thousand men that drew sword: and Judah was four hundred three score and ten thousand men that drew sword. ⁶But Levi and Benjamin counted he not among them: for the king's word was abominable to Joab. ⁷And God was displeased with this thing; therefore he smote Israel. ⁸And David said to God, I have sinned greatly, because I have done this thing: but now, I beseech you, do away the iniquity of your servant; for I have done very foolishly. ⁹And the LORD spoke to Gad, David's seer, saying, ¹⁰Go and tell David, saying, Thus says the LORD, I offer you three things: choose you one of them, that I may do it to you. ¹¹So Gad came to David, and said to him, Thus says the LORD, Choose you ¹²Either three years' famine; or three months to be destroyed before your foes, while that the sword of your enemies overtakes you; or else three days the sword of the LORD, even the pestilence, in the land, and the angel of the LORD destroying throughout all the coasts of Israel. Now therefore advise yourself what word I shall bring again to him that sent me. ¹³And David said to Gad, I am in a great strait: let me fall now into the hand of the LORD; for very great are his mercies: but let me not fall into the hand of man. ¹⁴So the LORD sent pestilence on Israel: and there fell of Israel seventy thousand men. ¹⁵And God sent an angel to Jerusalem to destroy it: and as he was destroying, the LORD beheld, and he repented him of the evil, and said to the angel that destroyed, It is enough, stay now your hand. And the angel of the LORD stood by the threshing floor of Ornan the Jebusite. ¹⁶And David lifted up his eyes, and saw the angel of the LORD stand between the earth and the heaven, having a drawn sword in his hand stretched out over Jerusalem. Then David and the elders of Israel, who were clothed in sackcloth, fell on their faces. ¹⁷And David said to God, Is it not I that commanded the people to be numbered? even I it is that have sinned and done evil indeed; but as for these sheep, what have they done? let your hand, I pray you, O LORD my God, be on me, and on my father's house; but not on your people, that they should be plagued. ¹⁸Then the angel of the LORD commanded Gad to say to David, that David should go up, and set up an altar to the LORD in the threshing floor of Ornan the Jebusite. ¹⁹And David went up at the saying of Gad, which he spoke in the name of the LORD. ²⁰And Ornan turned back, and saw the angel; and his four sons with him hid themselves. Now Ornan was threshing wheat. ²¹And as David came to Ornan, Ornan looked and saw David, and went out of the threshing floor, and bowed himself to David with his face to the ground. ²²Then David said to Ornan, Grant me the place of this threshing floor, that I may build an altar therein to the LORD: you shall grant it me for the full price: that the plague may be stayed from the people. ²³And Ornan said to David, Take it to you, and let my lord the king do that which is good in his eyes: see, I give you the oxen also for burnt offerings, and the threshing instruments for wood, and the wheat for the meat offering; I give it all. ²⁴And king David said to Ornan, No; but I will truly buy it for the full price: for I will not take that which is yours for the LORD, nor offer burnt offerings without cost. ²⁵So David gave to Ornan for the place six hundred shekels of gold by weight. ²⁶And David built there an altar to the LORD, and offered burnt offerings and peace offerings, and called on the LORD; and he answered him from heaven by fire on the altar of burnt offering. ²⁷And the LORD commanded the angel; and he put up his sword again into the sheath thereof. ²⁸At that time when David saw that the LORD had answered him in the threshing floor of Ornan the Jebusite, then he sacrificed there. ²⁹For the tabernacle of the LORD, which Moses made in the wilderness, and the altar of the burnt offering, were at that season in the high place at Gibeon. ³⁰But David could not go before it to inquire of God: for he was afraid because of the sword of the angel of the LORD.

22 ¹Then David said, This is the house of the LORD God, and this is the altar of the burnt offering for Israel. ²And David commanded to gather together the strangers that were in the land of Israel; and he set masons to hew worked stones to build the house of God. ³And David prepared iron in abundance for the nails for the doors of the gates, and for the joinings; and brass in abundance without weight; ⁴Also cedar trees in abundance: for the Zidonians and they of Tyre brought much cedar wood to David. ⁵And David said, Solomon my son is young and tender, and the house that is to be built for the LORD must be exceeding magnificent, of fame and of glory throughout all countries: I will therefore now make preparation for it. So David prepared abundantly before his death. ⁶Then he called for Solomon his son, and charged him to build an house for the LORD God of Israel. ⁷And David said to Solomon, My son, as for me, it was in my mind to build an house to the name of the LORD my God: ⁸But the word of the LORD came to me, saying, You have shed blood abundantly, and have made great wars: you shall not build an house to my name, because you have shed much blood on the earth in my sight. ⁹Behold, a son shall be born to you, who shall be a man of rest; and I will give him rest from all his enemies round about: for his name shall be Solomon, and I will give peace and quietness to Israel in his days. ¹⁰He shall build an house for my name; and he shall be my son, and I will be his father; and I will establish the throne of his kingdom over

Israel for ever. ¹¹Now, my son, the LORD be with you; and prosper you, and build the house of the LORD your God, as he has said of you. ¹²Only the LORD give you wisdom and understanding, and give you charge concerning Israel, that you may keep the law of the LORD your God. ¹³Then shall you prosper, if you take heed to fulfill the statutes and judgments which the LORD charged Moses with concerning Israel: be strong, and of good courage; dread not, nor be dismayed. ¹⁴Now, behold, in my trouble I have prepared for the house of the LORD an hundred thousand talents of gold, and a thousand thousand talents of silver; and of brass and iron without weight; for it is in abundance: timber also and stone have I prepared; and you may add thereto. ¹⁵Moreover there are workmen with you in abundance, hewers and workers of stone and timber, and all manner of cunning men for every manner of work. ¹⁶Of the gold, the silver, and the brass, and the iron, there is no number. Arise therefore, and be doing, and the LORD be with you. ¹⁷David also commanded all the princes of Israel to help Solomon his son, saying, ¹⁸Is not the LORD your God with you? and has he not given you rest on every side? for he has given the inhabitants of the land into my hand; and the land is subdued before the LORD, and before his people. ¹⁹Now set your heart and your soul to seek the LORD your God; arise therefore, and build you the sanctuary of the LORD God, to bring the ark of the covenant of the LORD, and the holy vessels of God, into the house that is to be built to the name of the LORD.

23 ¹So when David was old and full of days, he made Solomon his son king over Israel. ²And he gathered together all the princes of Israel, with the priests and the Levites. ³Now the Levites were numbered from the age of thirty years and upward: and their number by their polls, man by man, was thirty and eight thousand. ⁴Of which, twenty and four thousand were to set forward the work of the house of the LORD; and six thousand were officers and judges: ⁵Moreover four thousand were porters; and four thousand praised the LORD with the instruments which I made, said David, to praise therewith. ⁶And David divided them into courses among the sons of Levi, namely, Gershon, Kohath, and Merari. ⁷Of the Gershonites were, Laadan, and Shimei. ⁸The sons of Laadan; the chief was Jehiel, and Zetham, and Joel, three. ⁹The sons of Shimei; Shelomith, and Haziel, and Haran, three. These were the chief of the fathers of Laadan. ¹⁰And the sons of Shimei were, Jahath, Zina, and Jeush, and Beriah. These four were the sons of Shimei. ¹¹And Jahath was the chief, and Zizah the second: but Jeush and Beriah had not many sons; therefore they were in one reckoning, according to their father's house. ¹²The sons of Kohath; Amram, Izhar, Hebron, and Uzziel, four. ¹³The sons of Amram; Aaron and Moses: and Aaron was separated, that he should sanctify the most holy things, he and his sons for ever, to burn incense before the LORD, to minister to him, and to bless in his name for ever. ¹⁴Now concerning Moses the man of God, his sons were named of the tribe of Levi. ¹⁵The sons of Moses were, Gershom, and Eliezer. ¹⁶Of the sons of Gershom, Shebuel was the chief. ¹⁷And the sons of Eliezer were, Rehabiah the chief. And Eliezer had none other sons; but the sons of Rehabiah were very many. ¹⁸Of the sons of Izhar; Shelomith the chief. ¹⁹Of the sons of Hebron; Jeriah the first, Amariah the second, Jahaziel the third, and Jekameam the fourth. ²⁰Of the sons of Uzziel; Micah the first and Jesiah the second. ²¹The sons of Merari; Mahli, and Mushi. The sons of Mahli; Eleazar, and Kish. ²²And Eleazar died, and had no sons, but daughters: and their brothers the sons of Kish took them. ²³The sons of Mushi; Mahli, and Eder, and Jeremoth, three. ²⁴These were the sons of Levi after the house of their fathers; even the chief of the fathers, as they were counted by number of names by their polls, that did the work for the service of the house of the LORD, from the age of twenty years and upward. ²⁵For David said, The LORD God of Israel has given rest to his people, that they may dwell in Jerusalem for ever: ²⁶And also to the Levites; they shall no more carry the tabernacle, nor any vessels of it for the service thereof. ²⁷For by the last words of David the Levites were numbered from twenty years old and above: ²⁸Because their office was to wait on the sons of Aaron for the service of the house of the LORD, in the courts, and in the chambers, and in the purifying of all holy things, and the work of the service of the house of God; ²⁹Both for the show bread, and for the fine flour for meat offering, and for the unleavened cakes, and for that which is baked in the pan, and for that which is fried, and for all manner of measure and size; ³⁰And to stand every morning to thank and praise the LORD, and likewise at even: ³¹And to offer all burnt sacrifices to the LORD in the sabbaths, in the new moons, and on the set feasts, by number, according to the order commanded to them, continually before the LORD: ³²And that they should keep the charge of the tabernacle of the congregation, and the charge of the holy place, and the charge of the sons of Aaron their brothers, in the service of the house of the LORD.

24 ¹Now these are the divisions of the sons of Aaron. The sons of Aaron; Nadab, and Abihu, Eleazar, and Ithamar. ²But Nadab and Abihu died before their father, and had no children: therefore Eleazar and Ithamar executed the priest's office. ³And David distributed them, both Zadok of the sons of Eleazar, and Ahimelech of the sons of Ithamar, according to their offices in their service. ⁴And there were more chief men found of the sons of Eleazar than of the sons of Ithamar, and thus were they divided. Among the sons of Eleazar there were sixteen chief men of the house of their fathers, and eight among the sons of Ithamar according to the house of their fathers. ⁵Thus were they divided by lot, one sort with another; for the governors of the sanctuary, and governors of the house of God, were of the sons of Eleazar, and of the sons of Ithamar. ⁶And Shemaiah the son of Nethaneel the scribe, one of the Levites, wrote them before the king, and the princes, and Zadok the priest, and Ahimelech the son of Abiathar, and before the chief of the fathers of the priests and Levites: one principal household being taken for Eleazar, and one taken for Ithamar. ⁷Now the first lot came forth to Jehoiarib, the second to Jedaiah, ⁸The third to Harim, the fourth to Seorim, ⁹The fifth to Malchijah, the sixth to Mijamin, ¹⁰The seventh to Hakkoz, the eighth to Abijah, ¹¹The ninth to Jeshuah, the tenth to Shecaniah, ¹²The eleventh to Eliashib, the twelfth to Jakim, ¹³The thirteenth to Huppah, the fourteenth to Jeshebeab, ¹⁴The fifteenth to Bilgah, the sixteenth to Immer, ¹⁵The seventeenth to Hezir, the eighteenth to Aphses, ¹⁶The nineteenth to Pethahiah, the twentieth to Jehezekel, ¹⁷The one and twentieth to Jachin, the two and twentieth to Gamul, ¹⁸The three and twentieth to Delaiah, the four and twentieth to Maaziah. ¹⁹These were the orderings of them in their service to come into the house of the LORD, according to their manner, under Aaron their father, as the LORD God of Israel had commanded him. ²⁰And the rest of the sons of Levi were these: Of the sons of Amram; Shubael: of the sons of Shubael; Jehdeiah. ²¹Concerning Rehabiah: of the sons of Rehabiah, the first was Isshiah. ²²Of the Izharites; Shelomoth: of the sons of Shelomoth; Jahath. ²³And the sons of Hebron; Jeriah the first, Amariah the second, Jahaziel the third, Jekameam the fourth. ²⁴Of the sons of Uzziel; Michah: of the sons of Michah; Shamir. ²⁵The brother of Michah was Isshiah: of the sons of Isshiah; Zechariah. ²⁶The sons of Merari were Mahli and Mushi: the sons of Jaaziah; Beno. ²⁷The sons of Merari by Jaaziah; Beno, and Shoham, and Zaccur, and Ibri. ²⁸Of Mahli came Eleazar, who had no sons. ²⁹Concerning Kish: the son of Kish was Jerahmeel. ³⁰The sons also of Mushi; Mahli, and Eder, and Jerimoth. These were the sons of the Levites after the house of their fathers. ³¹These likewise cast lots over against their brethren the sons of Aaron in the presence of David the king, and Zadok, and Ahimelech, and the chief of the fathers of the priests and Levites, even the principal fathers over against their younger brethren.

25

¹Moreover David and the captains of the host separated to the service of the sons of Asaph, and of Heman, and of Jeduthun, who should prophesy with harps, with psalteries, and with cymbals: and the number of the workmen according to their service was: ²Of the sons of Asaph; Zaccur, and Joseph, and Nethaniah, and Asarelah, the sons of Asaph under the hands of Asaph, which prophesied according to the order of the king. ³Of Jeduthun: the sons of Jeduthun; Gedaliah, and Zeri, and Jeshaiah, Hashabiah, and Mattithiah, six, under the hands of their father Jeduthun, who prophesied with a harp, to give thanks and to praise the LORD. ⁴Of Heman: the sons of Heman: Bukkiah, Mattaniah, Uzziel, Shebuel, and Jerimoth, Hananiah, Hanani, Eliathah, Giddalti, and Romamtiezer, Joshbekashah, Mallothi, Hothir, and Mahazioth: ⁵All these were the sons of Heman the king's seer in the words of God, to lift up the horn. And God gave to Heman fourteen sons and three daughters. ⁶All these were under the hands of their father for song in the house of the LORD, with cymbals, psalteries, and harps, for the service of the house of God, according to the king's order to Asaph, Jeduthun, and Heman. ⁷So the number of them, with their brethren that were instructed in the songs of the LORD, even all that were cunning, was two hundred fourscore and eight. ⁸And they cast lots, ward against ward, as well the small as the great, the teacher as the scholar. ⁹Now the first lot came forth for Asaph to Joseph: the second to Gedaliah, who with his brethren and sons were twelve: ¹⁰The third to Zaccur, he, his sons, and his brethren, were twelve: ¹¹The fourth to Izri, he, his sons, and his brethren, were twelve: ¹²The fifth to Nethaniah, he, his sons, and his brethren, were twelve: ¹³The sixth to Bukkiah, he, his sons, and his brethren, were twelve: ¹⁴The seventh to Jesharelah, he, his sons, and his brethren, were twelve: ¹⁵The eighth to Jeshaiah, he, his sons, and his brethren, were twelve: ¹⁶The ninth to Mattaniah, he, his sons, and his brethren, were twelve: ¹⁷The tenth to Shimei, he, his sons, and his brethren, were twelve: ¹⁸The eleventh to Azareel, he, his sons, and his brethren, were twelve: ¹⁹The twelfth to Hashabiah, he, his sons, and his brethren, were twelve: ²⁰The thirteenth to Shubael, he, his sons, and his brethren, were twelve: ²¹The fourteenth to Mattithiah, he, his sons, and his brethren, were twelve: ²²The fifteenth to Jeremoth, he, his sons, and his brethren, were twelve: ²³The sixteenth to Hananiah, he, his sons, and his brethren, were twelve: ²⁴The seventeenth to Joshbekashah, he, his sons, and his brethren, were twelve: ²⁵The eighteenth to Hanani, he, his sons, and his brethren, were twelve: ²⁶The nineteenth to Mallothi, he, his sons, and his brethren, were twelve: ²⁷The twentieth to Eliathah, he, his sons, and his brethren, were twelve: ²⁸The one and twentieth to Hothir, he, his sons, and his brethren, were twelve: ²⁹The two and twentieth to Giddalti, he, his sons, and his brethren, were twelve: ³⁰The three and twentieth to Mahazioth, he, his sons, and his brethren, were twelve: ³¹The four and twentieth to Romamtiezer, he, his sons, and his brethren, were twelve.

26

¹Concerning the divisions of the porters: Of the Korhites was Meshelemiah the son of Kore, of the sons of Asaph. ²And the sons of Meshelemiah were, Zechariah the firstborn, Jediael the second, Zebadiah the third, Jathniel the fourth, ³Elam the fifth, Jehohanan the sixth, Elioenai the seventh. ⁴Moreover the sons of Obededom were, Shemaiah the firstborn, Jehozabad the second, Joah the third, and Sacar the fourth, and Nethaneel the fifth. ⁵Ammiel the sixth, Issachar the seventh, Peulthai the eighth: for God blessed him. ⁶Also to Shemaiah his son were sons born, that ruled throughout the house of their father: for they were mighty men of valor. ⁷The sons of Shemaiah; Othni, and Rephael, and Obed, Elzabad, whose brethren were strong men, Elihu, and Semachiah. ⁸All these of the sons of Obededom: they and their sons and their brethren, able men for strength for the service, were three score and two of Obededom. ⁹And Meshelemiah had sons and brethren, strong men, eighteen. ¹⁰Also Hosah, of the children of Merari, had sons; Simri the chief, (for though he was not the firstborn, yet his father made him the chief;) ¹¹Hilkiah the second, Tebaliah the third, Zechariah the fourth: all the sons and brethren of Hosah were thirteen. ¹²Among these were the divisions of the porters, even among the chief men, having wards one against another, to minister in the house of the LORD. ¹³And they cast lots, as well the small as the great, according to the house of their fathers, for every gate. ¹⁴And the lot eastward fell to Shelemiah. Then for Zechariah his son, a wise counselor, they cast lots; and his lot came out northward. ¹⁵To Obededom southward; and to his sons the house of Asuppim. ¹⁶To Shuppim and Hosah the lot came forth westward, with the gate Shallecheth, by the causeway of the going up, ward against ward. ¹⁷Eastward were six Levites, northward four a day, southward four a day, and toward Asuppim two and two. ¹⁸At Parbar westward, four at the causeway, and two at Parbar. ¹⁹These are the divisions of the porters among the sons of Kore, and among the sons of Merari. ²⁰And of the Levites, Ahijah was over the treasures of the house of God, and over the treasures of the dedicated things. ²¹As concerning the sons of Laadan; the sons of the Gershonite Laadan, chief fathers,

even of Laadan the Gershonite, were Jehieli. ²²The sons of Jehieli; Zetham, and Joel his brother, which were over the treasures of the house of the LORD. ²³Of the Amramites, and the Izharites, the Hebronites, and the Uzzielites: ²⁴And Shebuel the son of Gershom, the son of Moses, was ruler of the treasures. ²⁵And his brothers by Eliezer; Rehabiah his son, and Jeshaiah his son, and Joram his son, and Zichri his son, and Shelomith his son. ²⁶Which Shelomith and his brothers were over all the treasures of the dedicated things, which David the king, and the chief fathers, the captains over thousands and hundreds, and the captains of the host, had dedicated. ²⁷Out of the spoils won in battles did they dedicate to maintain the house of the LORD. ²⁸And all that Samuel the seer, and Saul the son of Kish, and Abner the son of Ner, and Joab the son of Zeruiah, had dedicated; and whoever had dedicated any thing, it was under the hand of Shelomith, and of his brothers. ²⁹Of the Izharites, Chenaniah and his sons were for the outward business over Israel, for officers and judges. ³⁰And of the Hebronites, Hashabiah and his brothers, men of valor, a thousand and seven hundred, were officers among them of Israel on this side Jordan westward in all the business of the LORD, and in the service of the king. ³¹Among the Hebronites was Jerijah the chief, even among the Hebronites, according to the generations of his fathers. In the fortieth year of the reign of David they were sought for, and there were found among them mighty men of valor at Jazer of Gilead. ³²And his brothers, men of valor, were two thousand and seven hundred chief fathers, whom king David made rulers over the Reubenites, the Gadites, and the half tribe of Manasseh, for every matter pertaining to God, and affairs of the king.

27

¹Now the children of Israel after their number, to wit, the chief fathers and captains of thousands and hundreds, and their officers that served the king in any matter of the courses, which came in and went out month by month throughout all the months of the year, of every course were twenty and four thousand. ²Over the first course for the first month was Jashobeam the son of Zabdiel: and in his course were twenty and four thousand. ³Of the children of Perez was the chief of all the captains of the host for the first month. ⁴And over the course of the second month was Dodai an Ahohite, and of his course was Mikloth also the ruler: in his course likewise were twenty and four thousand. ⁵The third captain of the host for the third month was Benaiah the son of Jehoiada, a chief priest: and in his course were twenty and four thousand. ⁶This is that Benaiah, who was mighty among the thirty, and above the thirty: and in his course was Ammizabad his son. ⁷The fourth captain for the fourth month was Asahel the brother of Joab, and Zebadiah his son after him: and in his course were twenty and four thousand. ⁸The fifth captain for the fifth month was Shamhuth the Izrahite: and in his course were twenty and four thousand. ⁹The sixth captain for the sixth month was Ira the son of Ikkesh the Tekoite: and in his course were twenty and four thousand. ¹⁰The seventh captain for the seventh month was Helez the Pelonite, of the children of Ephraim: and in his course were twenty and four thousand. ¹¹The eighth captain for the eighth month was Sibbecai the Hushathite, of the Zarhites: and in his course were twenty and four thousand. ¹²The ninth captain for the ninth month was Abiezer the Anetothite, of the Benjamites: and in his course were twenty and four thousand. ¹³The tenth captain for the tenth month was Maharai the Netophathite, of the Zarhites: and in his course were twenty and four thousand. ¹⁴The eleventh captain for the eleventh month was Benaiah the Pirathonite, of the children of Ephraim: and in his course were twenty and four thousand. ¹⁵The twelfth captain for the twelfth month was Heldai the Netophathite, of Othniel: and in his course were twenty and four thousand. ¹⁶Furthermore over the tribes of Israel: the ruler of the Reubenites was Eliezer the son of Zichri: of the Simeonites, Shephatiah the son of Maachah: ¹⁷Of the Levites, Hashabiah the son of Kemuel: of the Aaronites, Zadok: ¹⁸Of Judah, Elihu, one of the brothers of David: of Issachar, Omri the son of Michael: ¹⁹Of Zebulun, Ishmaiah the son of Obadiah: of Naphtali, Jerimoth the son of Azriel: ²⁰Of the children of Ephraim, Hoshea the son of Azaziah: of the half tribe of Manasseh, Joel the son of Pedaiah: ²¹Of the half tribe of Manasseh in Gilead, Iddo the son of Zechariah: of Benjamin, Jaasiel the son of Abner: ²²Of Dan, Azareel the son of Jeroham. These were the princes of the tribes of Israel. ²³But David took not the number of them from twenty years old and under: because the LORD had said he would increase Israel like to the stars of the heavens. ²⁴Joab the son of Zeruiah began to number, but he finished not, because there fell wrath for it against Israel; neither was the number put in the account of the chronicles of king David. ²⁵And over the king's treasures was Azmaveth the son of Adiel: and over the storehouses in the fields, in the cities, and in the villages, and in the castles, was Jehonathan the son of Uzziah: ²⁶And over them that did the work of the field for tillage of the ground was Ezri the son of Chelub: ²⁷And over the vineyards was Shimei the Ramathite: over the increase of the vineyards for the wine cellars was Zabdi the Shiphmite: ²⁸And over the olive trees and the sycomore trees that were in the low plains was Baalhanan the Gederite: and over the cellars of oil was Joash: ²⁹And over the herds that fed in Sharon was Shitrai the Sharonite: and over the herds that were in the valleys was Shaphat the son of Adlai: ³⁰Over the camels also was Obil the Ishmaelite: and over the asses was Jehdeiah the Meronothite: ³¹And over the flocks was Jaziz the Hagerite. All these were the rulers of the substance which was king David's. ³²Also Jonathan David's uncle was a counselor, a wise man, and a scribe: and Jehiel the son of Hachmoni was with the king's sons: ³³And Ahithophel was the king's counselor: and Hushai the Archite was the king's companion: ³⁴And after Ahithophel was Jehoiada the son of Benaiah, and Abiathar: and the general of the king's army was Joab.

28

¹And David assembled all the princes of Israel, the princes of the tribes, and the captains of the companies that ministered to the king by course, and the captains over the thousands, and captains over the hundreds, and the stewards over all the substance and possession of the king, and of his sons, with the officers, and with the mighty men, and with all the valiant men, to Jerusalem. ²Then David the king stood up on his feet, and said, Hear me, my brothers, and my people: As for me, I had in my heart to build an house of rest for the ark of the covenant of the LORD, and for the footstool of our God, and had made ready for the building: ³But God said to me, You shall not

build an house for my name, because you have been a man of war, and have shed blood. ⁴However, the LORD God of Israel chose me before all the house of my father to be king over Israel for ever: for he has chosen Judah to be the ruler; and of the house of Judah, the house of my father; and among the sons of my father he liked me to make me king over all Israel: ⁵And of all my sons, (for the LORD has given me many sons,) he has chosen Solomon my son to sit on the throne of the kingdom of the LORD over Israel. ⁶And he said to me, Solomon your son, he shall build my house and my courts: for I have chosen him to be my son, and I will be his father. ⁷Moreover I will establish his kingdom for ever, if he be constant to do my commandments and my judgments, as at this day. ⁸Now therefore in the sight of all Israel the congregation of the LORD, and in the audience of our God, keep and seek for all the commandments of the LORD your God: that you may possess this good land, and leave it for an inheritance for your children after you for ever. ⁹And you, Solomon my son, know you the God of your father, and serve him with a perfect heart and with a willing mind: for the LORD searches all hearts, and understands all the imaginations of the thoughts: if you seek him, he will be found of you; but if you forsake him, he will cast you off for ever. ¹⁰Take heed now; for the LORD has chosen you to build an house for the sanctuary: be strong, and do it. ¹¹Then David gave to Solomon his son the pattern of the porch, and of the houses thereof, and of the treasuries thereof, and of the upper chambers thereof, and of the inner parlors thereof, and of the place of the mercy seat, ¹²And the pattern of all that he had by the spirit, of the courts of the house of the LORD, and of all the chambers round about, of the treasuries of the house of God, and of the treasuries of the dedicated things: ¹³Also for the courses of the priests and the Levites, and for all the work of the service of the house of the LORD, and for all the vessels of service in the house of the LORD. ¹⁴He gave of gold by weight for things of gold, for all instruments of all manner of service; silver also for all instruments of silver by weight, for all instruments of every kind of service: ¹⁵Even the weight for the candlesticks of gold, and for their lamps of gold, by weight for every candlestick, and for the lamps thereof: and for the candlesticks of silver by weight, both for the candlestick, and also for the lamps thereof, according to the use of every candlestick. ¹⁶And by weight he gave gold for the tables of show bread, for every table; and likewise silver for the tables of silver: ¹⁷Also pure gold for the meat hooks, and the bowls, and the cups: and for the golden basins he gave gold by weight for every basin; and likewise silver by weight for every basin of silver: ¹⁸And for the altar of incense refined gold by weight; and gold for the pattern of the chariot of the cherubim, that spread out their wings, and covered the ark of the covenant of the LORD. ¹⁹All this, said David, the LORD made me understand in writing by his hand on me, even all the works of this pattern. ²⁰And David said to Solomon his son, Be strong and of good courage, and do it: fear not, nor be dismayed: for the LORD God, even my God, will be with you; he will not fail you, nor forsake you, until you have finished all the work for the service of the house of the LORD. ²¹And, behold, the courses of the priests and the Levites, even they shall be with you for all the service of the house of God: and there shall be with you for all manner of workmanship every willing skillful man, for any manner of service: also the princes and all the people will be wholly at your commandment.

29

¹Furthermore David the king said to all the congregation, Solomon my son, whom alone God has chosen, is yet young and tender, and the work is great: for the palace is not for man, but for the LORD God. ²Now I have prepared with all my might for the house of my God the gold for things to be made of gold, and the silver for things of silver, and the brass for things of brass, the iron for things of iron, and wood for things of wood; onyx stones, and stones to be set, glistering stones, and of divers colors, and all manner of precious stones, and marble stones in abundance. ³Moreover, because I have set my affection to the house of my God, I have of my own proper good, of gold and silver, which I have given to the house of my God, over and above all that I have prepared for the holy house. ⁴Even three thousand talents of gold, of the gold of Ophir, and seven thousand talents of refined silver, to overlay the walls of the houses with: ⁵The gold for things of gold, and the silver for things of silver, and for all manner of work to be made by the hands of artificers. And who then is willing to consecrate his service this day to the LORD? ⁶Then the chief of the fathers and princes of the tribes of Israel and the captains of thousands and of hundreds, with the rulers of the king's work, offered willingly, ⁷And gave for the service of the house of God of gold five thousand talents and ten thousand drams, and of silver ten thousand talents, and of brass eighteen thousand talents, and one hundred thousand talents of iron. ⁸And they with whom precious stones were found gave them to the treasure of the house of the LORD, by the hand of Jehiel the Gershonite. ⁹Then the people rejoiced, for that they offered willingly, because with perfect heart they offered willingly to the LORD: and David the king also rejoiced with great joy. ¹⁰Why David blessed the LORD before all the congregation: and David said, Blessed be you, LORD God of Israel our father, for ever and ever. ¹¹Yours, O LORD is the greatness, and the power, and the glory, and the victory, and the majesty: for all that is in the heaven and in the earth is yours; your is the kingdom, O LORD, and you are exalted as head above all. ¹²Both riches and honor come of you, and you reign over all; and in your hand is power and might; and in your hand it is to make great, and to give strength to all. ¹³Now therefore, our God, we thank you, and praise your glorious name. ¹⁴But who am I, and what is my people, that we should be able to offer so willingly after this sort? for all things come of you, and of your own have we given you. ¹⁵For we are strangers before you, and sojourners, as were all our fathers: our days on the earth are as a shadow, and there is none abiding. ¹⁶O LORD our God, all this store that we have prepared to build you an house for your holy name comes of your hand, and is all your own. ¹⁷I know also, my God, that you try the heart, and have pleasure in uprightness. As for me, in the uprightness of my heart I have willingly offered all these things: and now have I seen with joy your people, which are present here, to offer willingly to you. ¹⁸O LORD God of Abraham, Isaac, and of Israel, our fathers, keep this for ever in the imagination of the thoughts of the heart of your people, and

prepare their heart to you: [19]And give to Solomon my son a perfect heart, to keep your commandments, your testimonies, and your statutes, and to do all these things, and to build the palace, for the which I have made provision. [20]And David said to all the congregation, Now bless the LORD your God. And all the congregation blessed the LORD God of their fathers, and bowed down their heads, and worshipped the LORD, and the king. [21]And they sacrificed sacrifices to the LORD, and offered burnt offerings to the LORD, on the morrow after that day, even a thousand bullocks, a thousand rams, and a thousand lambs, with their drink offerings, and sacrifices in abundance for all Israel: [22]And did eat and drink before the LORD on that day with great gladness. And they made Solomon the son of David king the second time, and anointed him to the LORD to be the chief governor, and Zadok to be priest. [23]Then Solomon sat on the throne of the LORD as king instead of David his father, and prospered; and all Israel obeyed him. [24]And all the princes, and the mighty men, and all the sons likewise of king David, submitted themselves to Solomon the king. [25]And the LORD magnified Solomon exceedingly in the sight of all Israel, and bestowed on him such royal majesty as had not been on any king before him in Israel. [26]Thus David the son of Jesse reigned over all Israel. [27]And the time that he reigned over Israel was forty years; seven years reigned he in Hebron, and thirty and three years reigned he in Jerusalem. [28]And he died in a good old age, full of days, riches, and honor: and Solomon his son reigned in his stead. [29]Now the acts of David the king, first and last, behold, they are written in the book of Samuel the seer, and in the book of Nathan the prophet, and in the book of Gad the seer, [30]With all his reign and his might, and the times that went over him, and over Israel, and over all the kingdoms of the countries.

Second Chronicles

1 ¹And Solomon the son of David was strengthened in his kingdom, and the LORD his God was with him, and magnified him exceedingly. ²Then Solomon spoke to all Israel, to the captains of thousands and of hundreds, and to the judges, and to every governor in all Israel, the chief of the fathers. ³So Solomon, and all the congregation with him, went to the high place that was at Gibeon; for there was the tabernacle of the congregation of God, which Moses the servant of the LORD had made in the wilderness. ⁴But the ark of God had David brought up from Kirjathjearim to the place which David had prepared for it: for he had pitched a tent for it at Jerusalem. ⁵Moreover the brazen altar, that Bezaleel the son of Uri, the son of Hur, had made, he put before the tabernacle of the LORD: and Solomon and the congregation sought to it. ⁶And Solomon went up thither to the brazen altar before the LORD, which was at the tabernacle of the congregation, and offered a thousand burnt offerings on it. ⁷In that night did God appear to Solomon, and said to him, Ask what I shall give you. ⁸And Solomon said to God, You have showed great mercy to David my father, and have made me to reign in his stead. ⁹Now, O LORD God, let your promise to David my father be established: for you have made me king over a people like the dust of the earth in multitude. ¹⁰Give me now wisdom and knowledge, that I may go out and come in before this people: for who can judge this your people, that is so great? ¹¹And God said to Solomon, Because this was in your heart, and you have not asked riches, wealth, or honor, nor the life of your enemies, neither yet have asked long life; but have asked wisdom and knowledge for yourself, that you may judge my people, over whom I have made you king: ¹²Wisdom and knowledge is granted to you; and I will give you riches, and wealth, and honor, such as none of the kings have had that have been before you, neither shall there any after you have the like. ¹³Then Solomon came from his journey to the high place that was at Gibeon to Jerusalem, from before the tabernacle of the congregation, and reigned over Israel. ¹⁴And Solomon gathered chariots and horsemen: and he had a thousand and four hundred chariots, and twelve thousand horsemen, which he placed in the chariot cities, and with the king at Jerusalem. ¹⁵And the king made silver and gold at Jerusalem as plenteous as stones, and cedar trees made he as the sycomore trees that are in the vale for abundance. ¹⁶And Solomon had horses brought out of Egypt, and linen yarn: the king's merchants received the linen yarn at a price. ¹⁷And they fetched up, and brought forth out of Egypt a chariot for six hundred shekels of silver, and an horse for an hundred and fifty: and so brought they out horses for all the kings of the Hittites, and for the kings of Syria, by their means.

2 ¹And Solomon determined to build an house for the name of the LORD, and an house for his kingdom. ²And Solomon told out three score and ten thousand men to bear burdens, and fourscore thousand to hew in the mountain, and three thousand and six hundred to oversee them. ³And Solomon sent to Huram the king of Tyre, saying, As you did deal with David my father, and did send him cedars to build him an house to dwell therein, even so deal with me. ⁴Behold, I build an house to the name of the LORD my God, to dedicate it to him, and to burn before him sweet incense, and for the continual show bread, and for the burnt offerings morning and evening, on the sabbaths, and on the new moons, and on the solemn feasts of the LORD our God. This is an ordinance for ever to Israel. ⁵And the house which I build is great: for great is our God above all gods. ⁶But who is able to build him an house, seeing the heaven and heaven of heavens cannot contain him? who am I then, that I should build him an house, save only to burn sacrifice before him? ⁷Send me now therefore a man cunning to work in gold, and in silver, and in brass, and in iron, and in purple, and crimson, and blue, and that can skill to grave with the cunning men that are with me in Judah and in Jerusalem, whom David my father did provide. ⁸Send me also cedar trees, fir trees, and algum trees, out of Lebanon: for I know that your servants can skill to cut timber in Lebanon; and, behold, my servants shall be with your servants, ⁹Even to prepare me timber in abundance: for the house which I am about to build shall be wonderful great. ¹⁰And, behold, I will give to your servants, the hewers that cut timber, twenty thousand measures of beaten wheat, and twenty thousand measures of barley, and twenty thousand baths of wine, and twenty thousand baths of oil. ¹¹Then Huram the king of Tyre answered in writing, which he sent to Solomon, Because the LORD has loved his people, he has made you king over them. ¹²Huram said moreover, Blessed be the LORD God of Israel, that made heaven and earth, who has given to David the king a wise son, endued with prudence and understanding, that might build an house for the LORD, and an house for his kingdom. ¹³And now I have sent a cunning man, endued with understanding, of Huram my father's, ¹⁴The son of a woman of the daughters of Dan, and his father was a man of Tyre, skillful to work in gold, and in silver, in brass, in iron, in stone, and in timber, in purple, in blue, and in fine linen, and in crimson; also to grave any manner of engraving, and to find out every device which shall be put to him, with your cunning men, and with the cunning men of my lord David your father. ¹⁵Now therefore the wheat, and the barley, the oil, and the wine, which my lord has spoken of, let him send to his servants: ¹⁶And we will cut wood out of Lebanon, as much as you shall need: and we will bring it to you in floats by sea to Joppa; and you shall carry it up to Jerusalem. ¹⁷And Solomon numbered all the strangers that were in the land of Israel, after the numbering with which David his father had numbered them; and they were found an hundred and fifty thousand and three thousand and six hundred. ¹⁸And he set three score and ten thousand of them to be bearers of burdens, and fourscore thousand to be hewers in the mountain, and three thousand and six hundred overseers to set the people a work.

3 ¹Then Solomon began to build the house of the LORD at Jerusalem in mount Moriah, where the Lord appeared to David his father, in the place that David had prepared in the threshing floor of Ornan the Jebusite. ²And he began to build in the second day of the second month, in the fourth

year of his reign. ³Now these are the things wherein Solomon was instructed for the building of the house of God. The length by cubits after the first measure was three score cubits, and the breadth twenty cubits. ⁴And the porch that was in the front of the house, the length of it was according to the breadth of the house, twenty cubits, and the height was an hundred and twenty: and he overlaid it within with pure gold. ⁵And the greater house he paneled with fir tree, which he overlaid with fine gold, and set thereon palm trees and chains. ⁶And he garnished the house with precious stones for beauty: and the gold was gold of Parvaim. ⁷He overlaid also the house, the beams, the posts, and the walls thereof, and the doors thereof, with gold; and graved cherubim on the walls. ⁸And he made the most holy house, the length whereof was according to the breadth of the house, twenty cubits, and the breadth thereof twenty cubits: and he overlaid it with fine gold, amounting to six hundred talents. ⁹And the weight of the nails was fifty shekels of gold. And he overlaid the upper chambers with gold. ¹⁰And in the most holy house he made two cherubim of image work, and overlaid them with gold. ¹¹And the wings of the cherubim were twenty cubits long: one wing of the one cherub was five cubits, reaching to the wall of the house: and the other wing was likewise five cubits, reaching to the wing of the other cherub. ¹²And one wing of the other cherub was five cubits, reaching to the wall of the house: and the other wing was five cubits also, joining to the wing of the other cherub. ¹³The wings of these cherubim spread themselves forth twenty cubits: and they stood on their feet, and their faces were inward. ¹⁴And he made the veil of blue, and purple, and crimson, and fine linen, and worked cherubim thereon. ¹⁵Also he made before the house two pillars of thirty and five cubits high, and the capital that was on the top of each of them was five cubits. ¹⁶And he made chains, as in the oracle, and put them on the heads of the pillars; and made an hundred pomegranates, and put them on the chains. ¹⁷And he reared up the pillars before the temple, one on the right hand, and the other on the left; and called the name of that on the right hand Jachin, and the name of that on the left Boaz.

4 ¹Moreover he made an altar of brass, twenty cubits the length thereof, and twenty cubits the breadth thereof, and ten cubits the height thereof. ²Also he made a molten sea of ten cubits from brim to brim, round in compass, and five cubits the height thereof; and a line of thirty cubits did compass it round about. ³And under it was the similitude of oxen, which did compass it round about: ten in a cubit, compassing the sea round about. Two rows of oxen were cast, when it was cast. ⁴It stood on twelve oxen, three looking toward the north, and three looking toward the west, and three looking toward the south, and three looking toward the east: and the sea was set above on them, and all their hinder parts were inward. ⁵And the thickness of it was an handbreadth, and the brim of it like the work of the brim of a cup, with flowers of lilies; and it received and held three thousand baths. ⁶He made also ten lavers, and put five on the right hand, and five on the left, to wash in them: such things as they offered for the burnt offering they washed in them; but the sea was for the priests to wash in. ⁷And he made ten candlesticks of gold according to their form, and set them in the temple, five on the right hand, and five on the left. ⁸He made also ten tables, and placed them in the temple, five on the right side, and five on the left. And he made an hundred basins of gold. ⁹Furthermore he made the court of the priests, and the great court, and doors for the court, and overlaid the doors of them with brass. ¹⁰And he set the sea on the right side of the east end, over against the south. ¹¹And Huram made the pots, and the shovels, and the basins. And Huram finished the work that he was to make for king Solomon for the house of God; ¹²To wit, the two pillars, and the pommels, and the capitals which were on the top of the two pillars, and the two wreaths to cover the two pommels of the capitals which were on the top of the pillars; ¹³And four hundred pomegranates on the two wreaths; two rows of pomegranates on each wreath, to cover the two pommels of the capitals which were on the pillars. ¹⁴He made also bases, and lavers made he on the bases; ¹⁵One sea, and twelve oxen under it. ¹⁶The pots also, and the shovels, and the meat hooks, and all their instruments, did Huram his father make to king Solomon for the house of the LORD of bright brass. ¹⁷In the plain of Jordan did the king cast them, in the clay ground between Succoth and Zeredathah. ¹⁸Thus Solomon made all these vessels in great abundance: for the weight of the brass could not be found out. ¹⁹And Solomon made all the vessels that were for the house of God, the golden altar also, and the tables where on the show bread was set; ²⁰Moreover the candlesticks with their lamps, that they should burn after the manner before the oracle, of pure gold; ²¹And the flowers, and the lamps, and the tongs, made he of gold, and that perfect gold; ²²And the snuffers, and the basins, and the spoons, and the censers, of pure gold: and the entry of the house, the inner doors thereof for the most holy place, and the doors of the house of the temple, were of gold.

5 ¹Thus all the work that Solomon made for the house of the LORD was finished: and Solomon brought in all the things that David his father had dedicated; and the silver, and the gold, and all the instruments, put he among the treasures of the house of God. ²Then Solomon assembled the elders of Israel, and all the heads of the tribes, the chief of the fathers of the children of Israel, to Jerusalem, to bring up the ark of the covenant of the LORD out of the city of David, which is Zion. ³Why all the men of Israel assembled themselves to the king in the feast which was in the seventh month. ⁴And all the elders of Israel came; and the Levites took up the ark. ⁵And they brought up the ark, and the tabernacle of the congregation, and all the holy vessels that were in the tabernacle, these did the priests and the Levites bring up. ⁶Also king Solomon, and all the congregation of Israel that were assembled to him before the ark, sacrificed sheep and oxen, which could not be told nor numbered for multitude. ⁷And the priests brought in the ark of the covenant of the LORD to his place, to the oracle of the house, into the most holy place, even under the wings of the cherubim: ⁸For the cherubim spread forth their wings over the place of the ark, and the cherubim covered the ark and the staves thereof above. ⁹And they drew out the staves of the ark, that the ends of the staves were seen from the ark before the oracle; but they were not seen without. And there it is to this day. ¹⁰There was nothing in the ark save the two tables which Moses put therein at Horeb, when the LORD made a covenant with the children of Israel, when they came out of Egypt. ¹¹And it came to pass, when the priests were come out of the holy place: (for all the priests that were present were sanctified, and did not then wait by course: ¹²Also the Levites which were the singers, all of them of Asaph, of Heman, of Jeduthun, with their sons and their brothers, being arrayed in white linen, having cymbals and psalteries and harps, stood at the east end of the altar, and with them an hundred and twenty priests sounding with trumpets:) ¹³It came even to pass, as the trumpeters and singers were as one, to make one sound to be heard in praising and thanking the LORD; and when they lifted up their voice with the trumpets and cymbals and instruments of music, and praised the LORD, saying, For he is good; for his mercy endures for ever: that then the house was filled with a cloud, even the house of the LORD; ¹⁴So that the priests could not stand to minister by reason of the cloud: for the glory of the LORD had filled the house of God.

6 ¹Then said Solomon, The LORD has said that he would dwell in the thick darkness. ²But I have built an house of habitation for you, and a place for your dwelling for ever. ³And the king turned his face, and blessed the whole congregation of Israel: and all the congregation of Israel stood. ⁴And he said, Blessed be the LORD God of Israel, who has with his hands fulfilled that which he spoke with his mouth to my father David, saying, ⁵Since the day that I brought forth my people out of the land of Egypt I chose no city among all the tribes of Israel to build an house in, that my name might be there; neither chose I any man to be a ruler over my people Israel: ⁶But I have chosen Jerusalem, that my name might be there; and have chosen David to be over my people Israel. ⁷Now it was in the heart of David my father to build an house for the name of the LORD God of Israel. ⁸But the LORD said to David my father, For as much as it was in your heart to build an house for my name, you did well in that it was in your heart: ⁹Notwithstanding you shall not build the house; but your son which shall come forth out of your loins, he shall build the house for my name. ¹⁰The LORD therefore has performed his word that he has spoken: for I am risen up in the room of David my father, and am set on the throne of Israel, as the LORD promised, and have built the house for the name of the LORD God of Israel. ¹¹And in it have I put the ark, wherein is the covenant of the LORD, that he made with the children of Israel. ¹²And he stood before the altar of the LORD in the presence of all the congregation of Israel, and spread forth his hands: ¹³For Solomon had made a brazen scaffold of five cubits long, and five cubits broad, and three cubits high, and had set it in the middle of the court: and on it he stood, and kneeled down on his knees before all the congregation of Israel, and spread forth his hands toward heaven. ¹⁴And said, O LORD God of Israel, there is no God like you in the heaven, nor in the earth; which keep covenant, and show mercy to your servants, that walk before you with all their hearts: ¹⁵You which have kept with your servant David my father that which you have promised him; and spoke with your mouth, and have fulfilled it with your hand, as it is this day. ¹⁶Now therefore, O LORD God of Israel, keep with your servant David my father that which you have promised him, saying, There shall not fail you a man in my sight to sit on the throne of Israel; yet so that your children take heed to their way to walk in my law, as you have walked before me. ¹⁷Now then, O LORD God of Israel, let your word be verified, which you have spoken to your servant David. ¹⁸But will God in very deed dwell with men on the earth? behold, heaven and the heaven of heavens cannot contain you; how much less this house which I have built! ¹⁹Have respect therefore to the prayer of your servant, and to his supplication, O LORD my God, to listen to the cry and the prayer which your servant prays before you: ²⁰That your eyes may be open on this house day and night, on the place whereof you have said that you would put your name there; to listen to the prayer which your servant prays toward this place. ²¹Listen therefore to the supplications of your servant, and of your people Israel, which they shall make toward this place: hear you from your dwelling place, even from heaven; and when you hear, forgive. ²²If a man sin against his neighbor, and an oath be laid on him to make him swear, and the oath come before your altar in this house; ²³Then hear you from heaven, and do, and judge your servants, by requiting the wicked, by recompensing his way on his own head; and by justifying the righteous, by giving him according to his righteousness. ²⁴And if your people Israel be put to the worse before the enemy, because they have sinned against you; and shall return and confess your name, and pray and make supplication before you in this house; ²⁵Then hear you from the heavens, and forgive the sin of your people Israel, and bring them again to the land which you gave to them and to their fathers. ²⁶When the heaven is shut up, and there is no rain, because they have sinned against you; yet if they pray toward this place, and confess your name, and turn from their sin, when you do afflict them; ²⁷Then hear you from heaven, and forgive the sin of your servants, and of your people Israel, when you have taught them the good way, wherein they should walk; and send rain on your land, which you have given to your people for an inheritance. ²⁸If there be dearth in the land, if there be pestilence, if there be blasting, or mildew, locusts, or caterpillars; if their enemies besiege them in the cities of their land; whatever sore or whatever sickness there be: ²⁹Then what prayer or what supplication soever shall be made of any man, or of all your people Israel, when every one shall know his own sore and his own grief, and shall spread forth his hands in this house: ³⁰Then hear you from heaven your dwelling place, and forgive, and render to every man according to all his ways, whose heart you know; (for you only know the hearts of the children of men:) ³¹That they may fear you, to walk in your ways, so long as they live in the land which you gave to our fathers. ³²Moreover concerning the stranger, which is not of your people Israel, but is come from a far country for your great name's sake, and your mighty hand, and your stretched out arm; if they come and pray in this house; ³³Then hear you from the heavens, even from your dwelling place, and do according to all that the stranger calls to you for; that all people of the earth may know your name, and fear you, as does your people Israel, and may know that this house which I have built is called by your name. ³⁴If your people go out to war against their enemies by the way that you shall send them, and they pray to you toward this city which you have chosen, and the house which I have built for your name; ³⁵Then hear you from the heavens their prayer and their supplication, and maintain their cause. ³⁶If they sin against you, (for there is no man which sins not,) and you be angry with them, and deliver them over before their enemies, and they carry them away captives to a land far off or near; ³⁷Yet if they bethink themselves in the land where they are carried captive, and turn and pray to you in the land of their captivity, saying, We have sinned, we have done amiss, and have dealt wickedly; ³⁸If they return to you with all their heart and with all their soul in the land of their captivity, where they have carried them captives, and pray toward their land, which you gave to their fathers, and toward the city which you have chosen, and toward the house which I have built for your name; ³⁹Then hear you from the heavens, even from your dwelling place, their prayer and their supplications, and maintain their cause, and forgive your people which have sinned against you. ⁴⁰Now, my God, let, I beseech you, your eyes be open, and let your ears be attentive to the prayer that is made in this place. ⁴¹Now therefore arise, O LORD God, into your resting place, you, and the ark of your strength: let your priests, O LORD God, be clothed with salvation, and let your saints rejoice in goodness. ⁴²O LORD God, turn not away the face of your anointed: remember the mercies of David your servant.

7 ¹Now when Solomon had made an end of praying, the fire came down from heaven, and consumed the burnt offering and the sacrifices; and the glory of the LORD filled the house. ²And the priests could not enter into the house of the LORD, because the glory of the LORD had filled the LORD's house. ³And when all the children of Israel saw how the fire came down, and the glory of the LORD on the house, they bowed themselves with their faces to the ground on the pavement, and worshipped, and praised the LORD, saying, For he is good; for his mercy endures for ever. ⁴Then the king and all the people offered sacrifices before the LORD. ⁵And king Solomon offered a sacrifice of twenty and two thousand oxen, and an hundred and twenty thousand sheep: so the king and all the people dedicated the house of God. ⁶And the priests waited on their offices: the Levites also with instruments of music of the LORD, which David the king had made to praise the LORD, because his mercy endures for ever, when David praised by their ministry; and the priests sounded trumpets before them, and all Israel stood. ⁷Moreover Solomon hallowed the middle of the court that was before the house of the LORD: for there he offered burnt offerings, and the fat of the peace offerings, because the brazen altar which Solomon had made was not able to receive the burnt offerings, and the meat offerings, and the fat. ⁸Also at the same time Solomon kept the feast seven days, and all Israel with him, a very great congregation, from the entering in of Hamath to the river of Egypt. ⁹And in the eighth day they made a solemn assembly: for they kept the dedication of the altar seven days, and the feast seven days. ¹⁰And on the three and twentieth day of the seventh month he sent the people away into their tents, glad and merry in heart for the goodness that the LORD had showed to David, and to Solomon, and to Israel his people. ¹¹Thus Solomon finished the house of the LORD, and the king's house: and all that came into Solomon's heart to make in the house of the LORD, and in his own house, he prosperously effected. ¹²And the LORD appeared to Solomon by night, and said to him, I have heard your prayer, and have chosen this place to myself for an house of sacrifice. ¹³If I shut up heaven that there be no rain, or if I command the locusts to devour the land, or if I send pestilence among my people; ¹⁴If my people, which are called by my name, shall humble themselves, and pray, and seek my face, and turn from their wicked ways; then will I hear from heaven, and will forgive their sin, and will heal their land. ¹⁵Now my eyes shall be open, and my ears attentive to the prayer that is made in this place. ¹⁶For now have I chosen and sanctified this house, that my name may be there for ever: and my eyes and my heart shall be there perpetually. ¹⁷And as for you, if you will walk before me, as David your father walked, and do according to all that I have commanded you, and shall observe my statutes and my judgments; ¹⁸Then will I establish the throne of your kingdom, according as I have covenanted with David your father, saying, There shall not fail you a man to be ruler in Israel. ¹⁹But if you turn away, and forsake my statutes and my commandments, which I have set before you, and shall go and serve other gods, and worship them; ²⁰Then will I pluck them up by the roots out of my land which I have given them; and this house, which I have sanctified for my name, will I cast out of my sight, and will make it to be a proverb and a byword among all nations. ²¹And this house, which is high, shall be an astonishment to every one that passes by it; so that he shall say, Why has the LORD done thus to this land, and to this house? ²²And it shall be answered, Because they forsook the LORD God of their fathers, which brought them forth out of the land of Egypt, and laid hold on other gods, and worshipped them, and served them: therefore has he brought all this evil on them.

8 ¹And it came to pass at the end of twenty years, wherein Solomon had built the house of the LORD, and his own house, ²That the cities which Huram had restored to Solomon, Solomon built them, and caused the children of Israel to dwell there. ³And Solomon went to Hamathzobah, and prevailed against it. ⁴And he built Tadmor in the wilderness, and all the store cities, which he built in Hamath. ⁵Also he built Bethhoron the upper, and Bethhoron the nether, fenced cities, with walls, gates, and bars; ⁶And Baalath, and all the store cities that Solomon had, and all the chariot cities, and the cities of the horsemen, and all that Solomon desired to build in Jerusalem, and in Lebanon, and throughout all the land of his dominion. ⁷As for all the people that were left of the Hittites, and the Amorites, and the Perizzites, and the Hivites, and the Jebusites, which were not of Israel, ⁸But of their children, who were left after them in the land, whom the children of Israel consumed not, them did Solomon make to pay tribute until this day. ⁹But of the children of Israel did Solomon make no servants for his work; but they were men of war, and chief of his captains, and captains of his chariots and horsemen. ¹⁰And these were the chief of king Solomon's officers, even two hundred and fifty, that bore rule over the people. ¹¹And Solomon brought up the daughter of Pharaoh out of the city of David to the house that he had built for her: for he said, My wife shall not

dwell in the house of David king of Israel, because the places are holy, where the ark of the LORD has come. ¹²Then Solomon offered burnt offerings to the LORD on the altar of the LORD, which he had built before the porch, ¹³Even after a certain rate every day, offering according to the commandment of Moses, on the sabbaths, and on the new moons, and on the solemn feasts, three times in the year, even in the feast of unleavened bread, and in the feast of weeks, and in the feast of tabernacles. ¹⁴And he appointed, according to the order of David his father, the courses of the priests to their service, and the Levites to their charges, to praise and minister before the priests, as the duty of every day required: the porters also by their courses at every gate: for so had David the man of God commanded. ¹⁵And they departed not from the commandment of the king to the priests and Levites concerning any matter, or concerning the treasures. ¹⁶Now all the work of Solomon was prepared to the day of the foundation of the house of the LORD, and until it was finished. So the house of the LORD was perfected. ¹⁷Then went Solomon to Eziongeber, and to Eloth, at the sea side in the land of Edom. ¹⁸And Huram sent him by the hands of his servants ships, and servants that had knowledge of the sea; and they went with the servants of Solomon to Ophir, and took there four hundred and fifty talents of gold, and brought them to king Solomon.

9 ¹And when the queen of Sheba heard of the fame of Solomon, she came to prove Solomon with hard questions at Jerusalem, with a very great company, and camels that bore spices, and gold in abundance, and precious stones: and when she was come to Solomon, she communed with him of all that was in her heart. ²And Solomon told her all her questions: and there was nothing hid from Solomon which he told her not. ³And when the queen of Sheba had seen the wisdom of Solomon, and the house that he had built, ⁴And the meat of his table, and the sitting of his servants, and the attendance of his ministers, and their apparel; his cupbearers also, and their apparel; and his ascent by which he went up into the house of the LORD; there was no more spirit in her. ⁵And she said to the king, It was a true report which I heard in my own land of your acts, and of your wisdom: ⁶However, I believed not their words, until I came, and my eyes had seen it: and, behold, the one half of the greatness of your wisdom was not told me: for you exceed the fame that I heard. ⁷Happy are your men, and happy are these your servants, which stand continually before you, and hear your wisdom. ⁸Blessed be the LORD your God, which delighted in you to set you on his throne, to be king for the LORD your God: because your God loved Israel, to establish them for ever, therefore made he you king over them, to do judgment and justice. ⁹And she gave the king an hundred and twenty talents of gold, and of spices great abundance, and precious stones: neither was there any such spice as the queen of Sheba gave king Solomon. ¹⁰And the servants also of Huram, and the servants of Solomon, which brought gold from Ophir, brought algum trees and precious stones. ¹¹And the king made of the algum trees terraces to the house of the LORD, and to the king's palace, and harps and psalteries for singers: and there were none such seen before in the land of Judah. ¹²And king Solomon gave to the queen of Sheba all her desire, whatever she asked, beside that which she had brought to the king. So she turned, and went away to her own land, she and her servants. ¹³Now the weight of gold that came to Solomon in one year was six hundred and three score and six talents of gold; ¹⁴Beside that which chapmen and merchants brought. And all the kings of Arabia and governors of the country brought gold and silver to Solomon. ¹⁵And king Solomon made two hundred targets of beaten gold: six hundred shekels of beaten gold went to one target. ¹⁶And three hundred shields made he of beaten gold: three hundred shekels of gold went to one shield. And the king put them in the house of the forest of Lebanon. ¹⁷Moreover the king made a great throne of ivory, and overlaid it with pure gold. ¹⁸And there were six steps to the throne, with a footstool of gold, which were fastened to the throne, and stays on each side of the sitting place, and two lions standing by the stays: ¹⁹And twelve lions stood there on the one side and on the other on the six steps. There was not the like made in any kingdom. ²⁰And all the drinking vessels of king Solomon were of gold, and all the vessels of the house of the forest of Lebanon were of pure gold: none were of silver; it was not any thing accounted of in the days of Solomon. ²¹For the king's ships went to Tarshish with the servants of Huram: every three years once came the ships of Tarshish bringing gold, and silver, ivory, and apes, and peacocks. ²²And king Solomon passed all the kings of the earth in riches and wisdom. ²³And all the kings of the earth sought the presence of Solomon, to hear his wisdom, that God had put in his heart. ²⁴And they brought every man his present, vessels of silver, and vessels of gold, and raiment, harness, and spices, horses, and mules, a rate year by year. ²⁵And Solomon had four thousand stalls for horses and chariots, and twelve thousand horsemen; whom he bestowed in the chariot cities, and with the king at Jerusalem. ²⁶And he reigned over all the kings from the river even to the land of the Philistines, and to the border of Egypt. ²⁷And the king made silver in Jerusalem as stones, and cedar trees made he as the sycomore trees that are in the low plains in abundance. ²⁸And they brought to Solomon horses out of Egypt, and out of all lands. ²⁹Now the rest of the acts of Solomon, first and last, are they not written in the book of Nathan the prophet, and in the prophecy of Ahijah the Shilonite, and in the visions of Iddo the seer against Jeroboam the son of Nebat? ³⁰And Solomon reigned in Jerusalem over all Israel forty years. ³¹And Solomon slept with his fathers, and he was buried in the city of David his father: and Rehoboam his son reigned in his stead.

10 ¹And Rehoboam went to Shechem: for to Shechem were all Israel come to make him king. ²And it came to pass, when Jeroboam the son of Nebat, who was in Egypt, where he fled from the presence of Solomon the king, heard it, that Jeroboam returned out of Egypt. ³And they sent and called him. So Jeroboam and all Israel came and spoke to Rehoboam, saying, ⁴Your father made our yoke grievous: now therefore ease you somewhat the grievous servitude of your father, and his heavy yoke that he put on us, and we will serve you. ⁵And he said to them, Come again to me after three days. And the people departed. ⁶And king Rehoboam took counsel with the old men that had stood before Solomon his father while he yet lived, saying, What counsel give you me to return answer to this people? ⁷And they spoke to him, saying, If you be kind to this people, and please them, and speak good words to them, they will be your servants for ever. ⁸But he forsook the counsel which the old men gave him, and took counsel with the young men that were brought up with him, that stood before him. ⁹And he said to them, What advice give you that we may return answer to this people, which have spoken to me, saying, Ease somewhat the yoke that your father did put on us? ¹⁰And the young men that were brought up with him spoke to him, saying, Thus shall you answer the people that spoke to you, saying, Your father made our yoke heavy, but make you it somewhat lighter for us; thus shall you say to them, My little finger shall be thicker than my father's loins. ¹¹For whereas my father put a heavy yoke on you, I will put more to your yoke: my father chastised you with whips, but I will chastise you with scorpions. ¹²So Jeroboam and all the people came to Rehoboam on the third day, as the king bade, saying, Come again to me on the third day. ¹³And the king answered them roughly; and king Rehoboam forsook the counsel of the old men, ¹⁴And answered them after the advice of the young men, saying, My father made your yoke heavy, but I will add thereto: my father chastised you with whips, but I will chastise you with scorpions. ¹⁵So the king listened not to the people: for the cause was of God, that the LORD might perform his word, which he spoke by the hand of Ahijah the Shilonite to Jeroboam the son of Nebat. ¹⁶And when all Israel saw that the king would not listen to them, the people answered the king, saying, What portion have we in David? and we have none inheritance in the son of Jesse: every man to your tents, O Israel: and now, David, see to your own house. So all Israel went to their tents. ¹⁷But as for the children of Israel that dwelled in the cities of Judah, Rehoboam reigned over them. ¹⁸Then king Rehoboam sent Hadoram that was over the tribute; and the children of Israel stoned him with stones, that he died. But king Rehoboam made speed to get him up to his chariot, to flee to Jerusalem. ¹⁹And Israel rebelled against the house of David to this day.

11 ¹And when Rehoboam was come to Jerusalem, he gathered of the house of Judah and Benjamin an hundred and fourscore thousand chosen men, which were warriors, to fight against Israel, that he might bring the kingdom again to Rehoboam. ²But the word of the LORD came to Shemaiah the man of God, saying, ³Speak to Rehoboam the son of Solomon, king of Judah, and to all Israel in Judah and Benjamin, saying, ⁴Thus says the LORD, You shall not go up, nor fight against your brothers: return every man to his house: for this thing is done of me. And they obeyed the words of the LORD, and returned from going against Jeroboam. ⁵And Rehoboam dwelled in Jerusalem, and built cities for defense in Judah. ⁶He built even Bethlehem, and Etam, and Tekoa, ⁷And Bethzur, and Shoco, and Adullam, ⁸And Gath, and Mareshah, and Ziph, ⁹And Adoraim, and Lachish, and Azekah, ¹⁰And Zorah, and Aijalon, and Hebron, which are in Judah and in Benjamin fenced cities. ¹¹And he fortified the strong holds, and put captains in them, and store of victual, and of oil and wine. ¹²And in every several city he put shields and spears, and made them exceeding strong, having Judah and Benjamin on his side. ¹³And the priests and the Levites that were in all Israel resorted to him out of all their coasts. ¹⁴For the Levites left their suburbs and their possession, and came to Judah and Jerusalem: for Jeroboam and his sons had cast them off from executing the priest's office to the LORD: ¹⁵And he ordained him priests for the high places, and for the devils, and for the calves which he had made. ¹⁶And after them out of all the tribes of Israel such as set their hearts to seek the LORD God of Israel came to Jerusalem, to sacrifice to the LORD God of their fathers. ¹⁷So they strengthened the kingdom of Judah, and made Rehoboam the son of Solomon strong, three years: for three years they walked in the way of David and Solomon. ¹⁸And Rehoboam took him Mahalath the daughter of Jerimoth the son of David to wife, and Abihail the daughter of Eliab the son of Jesse; ¹⁹Which bore him children; Jeush, and Shamariah, and Zaham. ²⁰And after her he took Maachah the daughter of Absalom; which bore him Abijah, and Attai, and Ziza, and Shelomith. ²¹And Rehoboam loved Maachah the daughter of Absalom above all his wives and his concubines: (for he took eighteen wives, and three score concubines; and begat twenty and eight sons, and three score daughters.) ²²And Rehoboam made Abijah the son of Maachah the chief, to be ruler among his brothers: for he thought to make him king. ²³And he dealt wisely, and dispersed of all his children throughout all the countries of Judah and Benjamin, to every fenced city: and he gave them victual in abundance. And he desired many wives.

12 ¹And it came to pass, when Rehoboam had established the kingdom, and had strengthened himself, he forsook the law of the LORD, and all Israel with him. ²And it came to pass, that in the fifth year of king Rehoboam Shishak king of Egypt came up against Jerusalem, because they had transgressed against the LORD, ³With twelve hundred chariots, and three score thousand horsemen: and the people were without number that came with him out of Egypt; the Lubims, the Sukkiims, and the Ethiopians. ⁴And he took the fenced cities which pertained to Judah, and came to Jerusalem. ⁵Then came Shemaiah the prophet to Rehoboam, and to the princes of Judah, that were gathered together to Jerusalem because of Shishak, and said to them, Thus says the LORD, You have forsaken me, and therefore have I also left you in the hand of Shishak. ⁶Whereupon the princes of Israel and the king humbled themselves; and they said, The LORD is righteous. ⁷And when the LORD saw that they humbled themselves, the word of the LORD came to Shemaiah, saying, They have humbled themselves; therefore I will not destroy them, but I will grant them some deliverance; and my wrath shall not be poured out on Jerusalem by the hand of Shishak. ⁸Nevertheless they shall be his servants; that they may know my service, and the service of the kingdoms of the countries. ⁹So Shishak king of Egypt came up against Jerusalem, and took away the treasures of the house of the LORD, and the treasures of the king's house; he took all: he carried away also the shields of gold which Solomon had made. ¹⁰Instead of which king Rehoboam made shields of brass, and committed them to the hands of the chief of the guard, that kept the entrance of the king's house. ¹¹And when the king entered into the house of the LORD, the guard came and fetched them, and brought them again into the guard chamber. ¹²And when he humbled himself, the wrath of the

LORD turned from him, that he would not destroy him altogether: and also in Judah things went well. ¹³So king Rehoboam strengthened himself in Jerusalem, and reigned: for Rehoboam was one and forty years old when he began to reign, and he reigned seventeen years in Jerusalem, the city which the LORD had chosen out of all the tribes of Israel, to put his name there. And his mother's name was Naamah an Ammonitess. ¹⁴And he did evil, because he prepared not his heart to seek the LORD. ¹⁵Now the acts of Rehoboam, first and last, are they not written in the book of Shemaiah the prophet, and of Iddo the seer concerning genealogies? And there were wars between Rehoboam and Jeroboam continually. ¹⁶And Rehoboam slept with his fathers, and was buried in the city of David: and Abijah his son reigned in his stead.

13 ¹Now in the eighteenth year of king Jeroboam began Abijah to reign over Judah. ²He reigned three years in Jerusalem. His mother's name also was Michaiah the daughter of Uriel of Gibeah. And there was war between Abijah and Jeroboam. ³And Abijah set the battle in array with an army of valiant men of war, even four hundred thousand chosen men: Jeroboam also set the battle in array against him with eight hundred thousand chosen men, being mighty men of valor. ⁴And Abijah stood up on mount Zemaraim, which is in mount Ephraim, and said, Hear me, you Jeroboam, and all Israel; ⁵Ought you not to know that the LORD God of Israel gave the kingdom over Israel to David for ever, even to him and to his sons by a covenant of salt? ⁶Yet Jeroboam the son of Nebat, the servant of Solomon the son of David, is risen up, and has rebelled against his lord. ⁷And there are gathered to him vain men, the children of Belial, and have strengthened themselves against Rehoboam the son of Solomon, when Rehoboam was young and tenderhearted, and could not withstand them. ⁸And now you think to withstand the kingdom of the LORD in the hand of the sons of David; and you be a great multitude, and there are with your golden calves, which Jeroboam made you for gods. ⁹Have you not cast out the priests of the LORD, the sons of Aaron, and the Levites, and have made you priests after the manner of the nations of other lands? so that whoever comes to consecrate himself with a young bullock and seven rams, the same may be a priest of them that are no gods. ¹⁰But as for us, the LORD is our God, and we have not forsaken him; and the priests, which minister to the LORD, are the sons of Aaron, and the Levites wait on their business: ¹¹And they burn to the LORD every morning and every evening burnt sacrifices and sweet incense: the show bread also set they in order on the pure table; and the candlestick of gold with the lamps thereof, to burn every evening: for we keep the charge of the LORD our God; but you have forsaken him. ¹²And, behold, God himself is with us for our captain, and his priests with sounding trumpets to cry alarm against you. O children of Israel, fight you not against the LORD God of your fathers; for you shall not prosper. ¹³But Jeroboam caused an ambush to come about behind them: so they were before Judah, and the ambush was behind them. ¹⁴And when Judah looked back, behold, the battle was before and behind: and they cried to the LORD, and the priests sounded with the trumpets. ¹⁵Then the men of Judah gave a shout: and as the men of Judah shouted, it came to pass, that God smote Jeroboam and all Israel before Abijah and Judah. ¹⁶And the children of Israel fled before Judah: and God delivered them into their hand. ¹⁷And Abijah and his people slew them with a great slaughter: so there fell down slain of Israel five hundred thousand chosen men. ¹⁸Thus the children of Israel were brought under at that time, and the children of Judah prevailed, because they relied on the LORD God of their fathers. ¹⁹And Abijah pursued after Jeroboam, and took cities from him, Bethel with the towns thereof, and Jeshanah with the towns thereof, and Ephraim with the towns thereof. ²⁰Neither did Jeroboam recover strength again in the days of Abijah: and the LORD struck him, and he died. ²¹But Abijah waxed mighty, and married fourteen wives, and begat twenty and two sons, and sixteen daughters. ²²And the rest of the acts of Abijah, and his ways, and his sayings, are written in the story of the prophet Iddo.

14 ¹So Abijah slept with his fathers, and they buried him in the city of David: and Asa his son reigned in his stead. In his days the land was quiet ten years. ²And Asa did that which was good and right in the eyes of the LORD his God: ³For he took away the altars of the strange gods, and the high places, and broke down the images, and cut down the groves: ⁴And commanded Judah to seek the LORD God of their fathers, and to do the law and the commandment. ⁵Also he took away out of all the cities of Judah the high places and the images: and the kingdom was quiet before him. ⁶And he built fenced cities in Judah: for the land had rest, and he had no war in those years; because the LORD had given him rest. ⁷Therefore he said to Judah, Let us build these cities, and make about them walls, and towers, gates, and bars, while the land is yet before us; because we have sought the LORD our God, we have sought him, and he has given us rest on every side. So they built and prospered. ⁸And Asa had an army of men that bore targets and spears, out of Judah three hundred thousand; and out of Benjamin, that bore shields and drew bows, two hundred and fourscore thousand: all these were mighty men of valor. ⁹And there came out against them Zerah the Ethiopian with an host of a thousand thousand, and three hundred chariots; and came to Mareshah. ¹⁰Then Asa went out against him, and they set the battle in array in the valley of Zephathah at Mareshah. ¹¹And Asa cried to the LORD his God, and said, LORD, it is nothing with you to help, whether with many, or with them that have no power: help us, O LORD our God; for we rest on you, and in your name we go against this multitude. O LORD, you are our God; let no man prevail against you. ¹²So the LORD smote the Ethiopians before Asa, and before Judah; and the Ethiopians fled. ¹³And Asa and the people that were with him pursued them to Gerar: and the Ethiopians were overthrown, that they could not recover themselves; for they were destroyed before the LORD, and before his host; and they carried away very much spoil. ¹⁴And they smote all the cities round about Gerar; for the fear of the LORD came on them: and they spoiled all the cities; for there was exceeding much spoil in them. ¹⁵They smote also the tents of cattle, and carried away sheep and camels in abundance, and returned to Jerusalem.

15 ¹And the Spirit of God came on Azariah the son of Oded: ²And he went out to meet Asa, and said to him, Hear you me, Asa, and all Judah and Benjamin; The LORD is with you, while you be with him; and if you seek him, he will be found of you; but if you forsake him, he will forsake you. ³Now for a long season Israel has been without the true God, and without a teaching priest, and without law. ⁴But when they in their trouble did turn to the LORD God of Israel, and sought him, he was found of them. ⁵And in those times there was no peace to him that went out, nor to him that came in, but great vexations were on all the inhabitants of the countries. ⁶And nation was destroyed of nation, and city of city: for God did vex them with all adversity. ⁷Be you strong therefore, and let not your hands be weak: for your work shall be rewarded. ⁸And when Asa heard these words, and the prophecy of Oded the prophet, he took courage, and put away the abominable idols out of all the land of Judah and Benjamin, and out of the cities which he had taken from mount Ephraim, and renewed the altar of the LORD, that was before the porch of the LORD. ⁹And he gathered all Judah and Benjamin, and the strangers with them out of Ephraim and Manasseh, and out of Simeon: for they fell to him out of Israel in abundance, when they saw that the LORD his God was with him. ¹⁰So they gathered themselves together at Jerusalem in the third month, in the fifteenth year of the reign of Asa. ¹¹And they offered to the LORD the same time, of the spoil which they had brought, seven hundred oxen and seven thousand sheep. ¹²And they entered into a covenant to seek the LORD God of their fathers with all their heart and with all their soul; ¹³That whoever would not seek the LORD God of Israel should be put to death, whether small or great, whether man or woman. ¹⁴And they swore to the LORD with a loud voice, and with shouting, and with trumpets, and with cornets. ¹⁵And all Judah rejoiced at the oath: for they had sworn with all their heart, and sought him with their whole desire; and he was found of them: and the LORD gave them rest round about. ¹⁶And also concerning Maachah the mother of Asa the king, he removed her from being queen, because she had made an idol in a grove: and Asa cut down her idol, and stamped it, and burnt it at the brook Kidron. ¹⁷But the high places were not taken away out of Israel: nevertheless the heart of Asa was perfect all his days. ¹⁸And he brought into the house of God the things that his father had dedicated, and that he himself had dedicated, silver, and gold, and vessels. ¹⁹And there was no more war to the five and thirtieth year of the reign of Asa.

16 ¹In the six and thirtieth year of the reign of Asa Baasha king of Israel came up against Judah, and built Ramah, to the intent that he might let none go out or come in to Asa king of Judah. ²Then Asa brought out silver and gold out of the treasures of the house of the LORD and of the king's house, and sent to Benhadad king of Syria, that dwelled at Damascus, saying, ³There is a league between me and you, as there was between my father and your father: behold, I have sent you silver and gold; go, break your league with Baasha king of Israel, that he may depart from me. ⁴And Benhadad listened to king Asa, and sent the captains of his armies against the cities of Israel; and they smote Ijon, and Dan, and Abelmaim, and all the store cities of Naphtali. ⁵And it came to pass, when Baasha heard it, that he left off building of Ramah, and let his work cease. ⁶Then Asa the king took all Judah; and they carried away the stones of Ramah, and the timber thereof, with which Baasha was building; and he built therewith Geba and Mizpah. ⁷And at that time Hanani the seer came to Asa king of Judah, and said to him, Because you have relied on the king of Syria, and not relied on the LORD your God, therefore is the host of the king of Syria escaped out of your hand. ⁸Were not the Ethiopians and the Lubims a huge host, with very many chariots and horsemen? yet, because you did rely on the LORD, he delivered them into your hand. ⁹For the eyes of the LORD run to and fro throughout the whole earth, to show himself strong in the behalf of them whose heart is perfect toward him. Herein you have done foolishly: therefore from now on you shall have wars. ¹⁰Then Asa was wroth with the seer, and put him in a prison house; for he was in a rage with him because of this thing. And Asa oppressed some of the people the same time. ¹¹And, behold, the acts of Asa, first and last, see, they are written in the book of the kings of Judah and Israel. ¹²And Asa in the thirty and ninth year of his reign was diseased in his feet, until his disease was exceeding great: yet in his disease he sought not to the LORD, but to the physicians. ¹³And Asa slept with his fathers, and died in the one and fortieth year of his reign. ¹⁴And they buried him in his own sepulchers, which he had made for himself in the city of David, and laid him in the bed which was filled with sweet odors and divers kinds of spices prepared by the apothecaries' are: and they made a very great burning for him.

17 ¹And Jehoshaphat his son reigned in his stead, and strengthened himself against Israel. ²And he placed forces in all the fenced cities of Judah, and set garrisons in the land of Judah, and in the cities of Ephraim, which Asa his father had taken. ³And the LORD was with Jehoshaphat, because he walked in the first ways of his father David, and sought not to Baalim; ⁴But sought to the Lord God of his father, and walked in his commandments, and not after the doings of Israel. ⁵Therefore the LORD established the kingdom in his hand; and all Judah brought to Jehoshaphat presents; and he had riches and honor in abundance. ⁶And his heart was lifted up in the ways of the LORD: moreover he took away the high places and groves out of Judah. ⁷Also in the third year of his reign he sent to his princes, even to Benhail, and to Obadiah, and to Zechariah, and to Nethaneel, and to Michaiah, to teach in the cities of Judah. ⁸And with them he sent Levites, even Shemaiah, and Nethaniah, and Zebadiah, and Asahel, and Shemiramoth, and Jehonathan, and Adonijah, and Tobijah, and Tobadonijah, Levites; and with them Elishama and Jehoram, priests. ⁹And they taught in Judah, and had the book of the law of the LORD with them, and went about throughout all the cities of Judah, and taught the people. ¹⁰And the fear of the LORD fell on all the kingdoms of the lands that were round about Judah, so that they made no war against Jehoshaphat. ¹¹Also some of the Philistines brought Jehoshaphat presents, and tribute silver; and the Arabians brought him flocks, seven thousand and seven hundred rams, and seven thousand and seven hundred he goats. ¹²And Jehoshaphat waxed great exceedingly; and he built in Judah castles, and cities of store. ¹³And he had much business in the cities of Judah: and the men of war, mighty men of valor, were in Jerusalem. ¹⁴And these are the numbers of them according to the house of their fathers: Of Judah, the captains of thousands; Adnah the chief, and with him mighty men of valor three hundred thousand. ¹⁵And next to him was Jehohanan the captain, and with him two hundred and fourscore thousand. ¹⁶And next him was Amasiah the son of Zichri, who willingly offered himself to the LORD; and with him two hundred thousand mighty men of valor. ¹⁷And of Benjamin; Eliada a mighty man of valor, and with him armed men with bow and shield two hundred thousand. ¹⁸And next him was Jehozabad, and with him an hundred and fourscore thousand ready prepared for the war. ¹⁹These waited on the king, beside those whom the king put in the fenced cities throughout all Judah.

18

¹Now Jehoshaphat had riches and honor in abundance, and joined affinity with Ahab. ²And after certain years he went down to Ahab to Samaria. And Ahab killed sheep and oxen for him in abundance, and for the people that he had with him, and persuaded him to go up with him to Ramothgilead. ³And Ahab king of Israel said to Jehoshaphat king of Judah, Will you go with me to Ramothgilead? And he answered him, I am as you are, and my people as your people; and we will be with you in the war. ⁴And Jehoshaphat said to the king of Israel, Inquire, I pray you, at the word of the LORD to day. ⁵Therefore the king of Israel gathered together of prophets four hundred men, and said to them, Shall we go to Ramothgilead to battle, or shall I forbear? And they said, Go up; for God will deliver it into the king's hand. ⁶But Jehoshaphat said, Is there not here a prophet of the LORD besides, that we might inquire of him? ⁷And the king of Israel said to Jehoshaphat, There is yet one man, by whom we may inquire of the LORD: but I hate him; for he never prophesied good to me, but always evil: the same is Micaiah the son of Imla. And Jehoshaphat said, Let not the king say so. ⁸And the king of Israel called for one of his officers, and said, Fetch quickly Micaiah the son of Imla. ⁹And the king of Israel and Jehoshaphat king of Judah sat either of them on his throne, clothed in their robes, and they sat in a void place at the entering in of the gate of Samaria; and all the prophets prophesied before them. ¹⁰And Zedekiah the son of Chenaanah had made him horns of iron, and said, Thus says the LORD, With these you shall push Syria until they be consumed. ¹¹And all the prophets prophesied so, saying, Go up to Ramothgilead, and prosper: for the LORD shall deliver it into the hand of the king. ¹²And the messenger that went to call Micaiah spoke to him, saying, Behold, the words of the prophets declare good to the king with one assent; let your word therefore, I pray you, be like one of theirs, and speak you good. ¹³And Micaiah said, As the LORD lives, even what my God says, that will I speak. ¹⁴And when he was come to the king, the king said to him, Micaiah, shall we go to Ramothgilead to battle, or shall I forbear? And he said, Go you up, and prosper, and they shall be delivered into your hand. ¹⁵And the king said to him, How many times shall I adjure you that you say nothing but the truth to me in the name of the LORD? ¹⁶Then he said, I did see all Israel scattered on the mountains, as sheep that have no shepherd: and the LORD said, These have no master; let them return therefore every man to his house in peace. ¹⁷And the king of Israel said to Jehoshaphat, Did I not tell you that he would not prophesy good to me, but evil? ¹⁸Again he said, Therefore hear the word of the LORD; I saw the LORD sitting on his throne, and all the host of heaven standing on his right hand and on his left. ¹⁹And the LORD said, Who shall entice Ahab king of Israel, that he may go up and fall at Ramothgilead? And one spoke saying after this manner, and another saying after that manner. ²⁰Then there came out a spirit, and stood before the LORD, and said, I will entice him. And the LORD said to him, With which? ²¹And he said, I will go out, and be a lying spirit in the mouth of all his prophets. And the Lord said, You shall entice him, and you shall also prevail: go out, and do even so. ²²Now therefore, behold, the LORD has put a lying spirit in the mouth of these your prophets, and the LORD has spoken evil against you. ²³Then Zedekiah the son of Chenaanah came near, and smote Micaiah on the cheek, and said, Which way went the Spirit of the LORD from me to speak to you? ²⁴And Micaiah said, Behold, you shall see on that day when you shall go into an inner chamber to hide yourself. ²⁵Then the king of Israel said, Take you Micaiah, and carry him back to Amon the governor of the city, and to Joash the king's son; ²⁶And say, Thus says the king, Put this fellow in the prison, and feed him with bread of affliction and with water of affliction, until I return in peace. ²⁷And Micaiah said, If you certainly return in peace, then has not the LORD spoken by me. And he said, Listen, all you people. ²⁸So the king of Israel and Jehoshaphat the king of Judah went up to Ramothgilead. ²⁹And the king of Israel said to Jehoshaphat, I will disguise myself, and I will go to the battle; but put you on your robes. So the king of Israel disguised himself; and they went to the battle. ³⁰Now the king of Syria had commanded the captains of the chariots that were with him, saying, Fight you not with small or great, save only with the king of Israel. ³¹And it came to pass, when the captains of the chariots saw Jehoshaphat, that they said, It is the king of Israel. Therefore they compassed about him to fight: but Jehoshaphat cried out, and the LORD helped him; and God moved them to depart from him. ³²For it came to pass, that, when the captains of the chariots perceived that it was not the king of Israel, they turned back again from pursuing him. ³³And a certain man drew a bow at a venture, and smote the king of Israel between the joints of the harness: therefore he said to his chariot man, Turn your hand, that you may carry me out of the host; for I am wounded. ³⁴And the battle increased that day: however, the king of Israel stayed himself up in his chariot against the Syrians until the even: and about the time of the sun going down he died.

19

¹And Jehoshaphat the king of Judah returned to his house in peace to Jerusalem. ²And Jehu the son of Hanani the seer went out to meet him, and said to king Jehoshaphat, Should you help the ungodly, and love them that hate the LORD? therefore is wrath on you from before the LORD. ³Nevertheless there are good things found in you, in that you have taken away the groves out of the land, and have prepared your heart to seek God. ⁴And Jehoshaphat dwelled at Jerusalem: and he went out again through the people from Beersheba to mount Ephraim, and brought them

back to the LORD God of their fathers. ⁵And he set judges in the land throughout all the fenced cities of Judah, city by city, ⁶And said to the judges, Take heed what you do: for you judge not for man, but for the LORD, who is with you in the judgment. ⁷Why now let the fear of the LORD be on you; take heed and do it: for there is no iniquity with the LORD our God, nor respect of persons, nor taking of gifts. ⁸Moreover in Jerusalem did Jehoshaphat set of the Levites, and of the priests, and of the chief of the fathers of Israel, for the judgment of the LORD, and for controversies, when they returned to Jerusalem. ⁹And he charged them, saying, Thus shall you do in the fear of the LORD, faithfully, and with a perfect heart. ¹⁰And what cause soever shall come to you of your brothers that dwell in your cities, between blood and blood, between law and commandment, statutes and judgments, you shall even warn them that they trespass not against the LORD, and so wrath come on you, and on your brothers: this do, and you shall not trespass. ¹¹And, behold, Amariah the chief priest is over you in all matters of the LORD; and Zebadiah the son of Ishmael, the ruler of the house of Judah, for all the king's matters: also the Levites shall be officers before you. Deal courageously, and the LORD shall be with the good.

20

¹It came to pass after this also, that the children of Moab, and the children of Ammon, and with them other beside the Ammonites, came against Jehoshaphat to battle. ²Then there came some that told Jehoshaphat, saying, There comes a great multitude against you from beyond the sea on this side Syria; and, behold, they be in Hazazontamar, which is Engedi. ³And Jehoshaphat feared, and set himself to seek the LORD, and proclaimed a fast throughout all Judah. ⁴And Judah gathered themselves together, to ask help of the LORD: even out of all the cities of Judah they came to seek the LORD. ⁵And Jehoshaphat stood in the congregation of Judah and Jerusalem, in the house of the LORD, before the new court, ⁶And said, O LORD God of our fathers, are not you God in heaven? and rule not you over all the kingdoms of the heathen? and in your hand is there not power and might, so that none is able to withstand you? ⁷Are not you our God, who did drive out the inhabitants of this land before your people Israel, and gave it to the seed of Abraham your friend for ever? ⁸And they dwelled therein, and have built you a sanctuary therein for your name, saying, ⁹If, when evil comes on us, as the sword, judgment, or pestilence, or famine, we stand before this house, and in your presence, (for your name is in this house,) and cry to you in our affliction, then you will hear and help. ¹⁰And now, behold, the children of Ammon and Moab and mount Seir, whom you would not let Israel invade, when they came out of the land of Egypt, but they turned from them, and destroyed them not; ¹¹Behold, I say, how they reward us, to come to cast us out of your possession, which you have given us to inherit. ¹²O our God, will you not judge them? for we have no might against this great company that comes against us; neither know we what to do: but our eyes are on you. ¹³And all Judah stood before the LORD, with their little ones, their wives, and their children. ¹⁴Then on Jahaziel the son of Zechariah, the son of Benaiah, the son of Jeiel, the son of Mattaniah, a Levite of the sons of Asaph, came the Spirit of the LORD in the middle of the congregation; ¹⁵And he said, Listen you, all Judah, and you inhabitants of Jerusalem, and you king Jehoshaphat, Thus says the LORD to you, Be not afraid nor dismayed by reason of this great multitude; for the battle is not yours, but God's. ¹⁶To morrow go you down against them: behold, they come up by the cliff of Ziz; and you shall find them at the end of the brook, before the wilderness of Jeruel. ¹⁷You shall not need to fight in this battle: set yourselves, stand you still, and see the salvation of the LORD with you, O Judah and Jerusalem: fear not, nor be dismayed; to morrow go out against them: for the LORD will be with you. ¹⁸And Jehoshaphat bowed his head with his face to the ground: and all Judah and the inhabitants of Jerusalem fell before the LORD, worshipping the LORD. ¹⁹And the Levites, of the children of the Kohathites, and of the children of the Korhites, stood up to praise the LORD God of Israel with a loud voice on high. ²⁰And they rose early in the morning, and went forth into the wilderness of Tekoa: and as they went forth, Jehoshaphat stood and said, Hear me, O Judah, and you inhabitants of Jerusalem; Believe in the LORD your God, so shall you be established; believe his prophets, so shall you prosper. ²¹And when he had consulted with the people, he appointed singers to the LORD, and that should praise the beauty of holiness, as they went out before the army, and to say, Praise the LORD; for his mercy endures for ever. ²²And when they began to sing and to praise, the LORD set ambushes against the children of Ammon, Moab, and mount Seir, which were come against Judah; and they were smitten. ²³For the children of Ammon and Moab stood up against the inhabitants of mount Seir, utterly to slay and destroy them: and when they had made an end of the inhabitants of Seir, every one helped to destroy another. ²⁴And when Judah came toward the watch tower in the wilderness, they looked to the multitude, and, behold, they were dead bodies fallen to the earth, and none escaped. ²⁵And when Jehoshaphat and his people came to take away the spoil of them, they found among them in abundance both riches with the dead bodies, and precious jewels, which they stripped off for themselves, more than they could carry away: and they were three days in gathering of the spoil, it was so much. ²⁶And on the fourth day they assembled themselves in the valley of Berachah; for there they blessed the LORD: therefore the name of the same place was called, The valley of Berachah, to this day. ²⁷Then they returned, every man of Judah and Jerusalem, and Jehoshaphat in the forefront of them, to go again to Jerusalem with joy; for the LORD had made them to rejoice over their enemies. ²⁸And they came to Jerusalem with psalteries and harps and trumpets to the house of the LORD. ²⁹And the fear of God was on all the kingdoms of those countries, when they had heard that the LORD fought against the enemies of Israel. ³⁰So the realm of Jehoshaphat was quiet: for his God gave him rest round about. ³¹And Jehoshaphat reigned over Judah: he was thirty and five years old when he began to reign, and he reigned twenty and five years in Jerusalem. And his mother's name was Azubah the daughter of Shilhi. ³²And he walked in the way of Asa his father, and departed not from it, doing that which was right in the sight of the LORD. ³³However, the high places were not taken away: for as yet the people had not prepared their hearts to the God of their fathers. ³⁴Now the rest of the acts

of Jehoshaphat, first and last, behold, they are written in the book of Jehu the son of Hanani, who is mentioned in the book of the kings of Israel. ³⁵And after this did Jehoshaphat king of Judah join himself with Ahaziah king of Israel, who did very wickedly: ³⁶And he joined himself with him to make ships to go to Tarshish: and they made the ships in Eziongaber. ³⁷Then Eliezer the son of Dodavah of Mareshah prophesied against Jehoshaphat, saying, Because you have joined yourself with Ahaziah, the LORD has broken your works. And the ships were broken, that they were not able to go to Tarshish.

21

¹Now Jehoshaphat slept with his fathers, and was buried with his fathers in the city of David. And Jehoram his son reigned in his stead. ²And he had brothers the sons of Jehoshaphat, Azariah, and Jehiel, and Zechariah, and Azariah, and Michael, and Shephatiah: all these were the sons of Jehoshaphat king of Israel. ³And their father gave them great gifts of silver, and of gold, and of precious things, with fenced cities in Judah: but the kingdom gave he to Jehoram; because he was the firstborn. ⁴Now when Jehoram was risen up to the kingdom of his father, he strengthened himself, and slew all his brothers with the sword, and divers also of the princes of Israel. ⁵Jehoram was thirty and two years old when he began to reign, and he reigned eight years in Jerusalem. ⁶And he walked in the way of the kings of Israel, like as did the house of Ahab: for he had the daughter of Ahab to wife: and he worked that which was evil in the eyes of the LORD. ⁷However, the LORD would not destroy the house of David, because of the covenant that he had made with David, and as he promised to give a light to him and to his sons for ever. ⁸In his days the Edomites revolted from under the dominion of Judah, and made themselves a king. ⁹Then Jehoram went forth with his princes, and all his chariots with him: and he rose up by night, and smote the Edomites which compassed him in, and the captains of the chariots. ¹⁰So the Edomites revolted from under the hand of Judah to this day. The same time also did Libnah revolt from under his hand; because he had forsaken the LORD God of his fathers. ¹¹Moreover he made high places in the mountains of Judah and caused the inhabitants of Jerusalem to commit fornication, and compelled Judah thereto. ¹²And there came a writing to him from Elijah the prophet, saying, Thus says the LORD God of David your father, Because you have not walked in the ways of Jehoshaphat your father, nor in the ways of Asa king of Judah, ¹³But have walked in the way of the kings of Israel, and have made Judah and the inhabitants of Jerusalem to go a whoring, like to the prostitutions of the house of Ahab, and also have slain your brothers of your father's house, which were better than yourself: ¹⁴Behold, with a great plague will the LORD smite your people, and your children, and your wives, and all your goods: ¹⁵And you shall have great sickness by disease of your bowels, until your bowels fall out by reason of the sickness day by day. ¹⁶Moreover the LORD stirred up against Jehoram the spirit of the Philistines, and of the Arabians, that were near the Ethiopians: ¹⁷And they came up into Judah, and broke into it, and carried away all the substance that was found in the king's house, and his sons also, and his wives; so that there was never a son left him, save Jehoahaz, the youngest of his sons. ¹⁸And after all this the LORD smote him in his bowels with an incurable disease. ¹⁹And it came to pass, that in process of time, after the end of two years, his bowels fell out by reason of his sickness: so he died of sore diseases. And his people made no burning for him, like the burning of his fathers. ²⁰Thirty and two years old was he when he began to reign, and he reigned in Jerusalem eight years, and departed without being desired. However, they buried him in the city of David, but not in the sepulchers of the kings.

22

¹And the inhabitants of Jerusalem made Ahaziah his youngest son king in his stead: for the band of men that came with the Arabians to the camp had slain all the oldest. So Ahaziah the son of Jehoram king of Judah reigned. ²Forty and two years old was Ahaziah when he began to reign, and he reigned one year in Jerusalem. His mother's name also was Athaliah the daughter of Omri. ³He also walked in the ways of the house of Ahab: for his mother was his counselor to do wickedly. ⁴Why he did evil in the sight of the LORD like the house of Ahab: for they were his counsellors after the death of his father to his destruction. ⁵He walked also after their counsel, and went with Jehoram the son of Ahab king of Israel to war against Hazael king of Syria at Ramothgilead: and the Syrians smote Joram. ⁶And he returned to be healed in Jezreel because of the wounds which were given him at Ramah, when he fought with Hazael king of Syria. And Azariah the son of Jehoram king of Judah went down to see Jehoram the son of Ahab at Jezreel, because he was sick. ⁷And the destruction of Ahaziah was of God by coming to Joram: for when he was come, he went out with Jehoram against Jehu the son of Nimshi, whom the LORD had anointed to cut off the house of Ahab. ⁸And it came to pass, that, when Jehu was executing judgment on the house of Ahab, and found the princes of Judah, and the sons of the brothers of Ahaziah, that ministered to Ahaziah, he slew them. ⁹And he sought Ahaziah: and they caught him, (for he was hid in Samaria,) and brought him to Jehu: and when they had slain him, they buried him: Because, said they, he is the son of Jehoshaphat, who sought the LORD with all his heart. So the house of Ahaziah had no power to keep still the kingdom. ¹⁰But when Athaliah the mother of Ahaziah saw that her son was dead, she arose and destroyed all the seed royal of the house of Judah. ¹¹But Jehoshabeath, the daughter of the king, took Joash the son of Ahaziah, and stole him from among the king's sons that were slain, and put him and his nurse in a bedchamber. So Jehoshabeath, the daughter of king Jehoram, the wife of Jehoiada the priest, (for she was the sister of Ahaziah,) hid him from Athaliah, so that she slew him not. ¹²And he was with them hid in the house of God six years: and Athaliah reigned over the land.

23

¹And in the seventh year Jehoiada strengthened himself, and took the captains of hundreds, Azariah the son of Jeroham, and Ishmael the son of Jehohanan, and Azariah the son of Obed, and Maaseiah the son of Adaiah, and Elishaphat the son of Zichri, into covenant with him. ²And they went about in Judah, and gathered the Levites out of all the cities of Judah, and the chief of the fathers of Israel, and they came to Jerusalem. ³And all the congregation made a covenant with the king in the house of

God. And he said to them, Behold, the king's son shall reign, as the LORD has said of the sons of David. ⁴This is the thing that you shall do; A third part of you entering on the sabbath, of the priests and of the Levites, shall be porters of the doors; ⁵And a third part shall be at the king's house; and a third part at the gate of the foundation: and all the people shall be in the courts of the house of the LORD. ⁶But let none come into the house of the LORD, save the priests, and they that minister of the Levites; they shall go in, for they are holy: but all the people shall keep the watch of the LORD. ⁷And the Levites shall compass the king round about, every man with his weapons in his hand; and whoever else comes into the house, he shall be put to death: but be you with the king when he comes in, and when he goes out. ⁸So the Levites and all Judah did according to all things that Jehoiada the priest had commanded, and took every man his men that were to come in on the sabbath, with them that were to go out on the sabbath: for Jehoiada the priest dismissed not the courses. ⁹Moreover Jehoiada the priest delivered to the captains of hundreds spears, and bucklers, and shields, that had been king David's, which were in the house of God. ¹⁰And he set all the people, every man having his weapon in his hand, from the right side of the temple to the left side of the temple, along by the altar and the temple, by the king round about. ¹¹Then they brought out the king's son, and put on him the crown, and gave him the testimony, and made him king. And Jehoiada and his sons anointed him, and said, God save the king. ¹²Now when Athaliah heard the noise of the people running and praising the king, she came to the people into the house of the LORD: ¹³And she looked, and, behold, the king stood at his pillar at the entering in, and the princes and the trumpets by the king: and all the people of the land rejoiced, and sounded with trumpets, also the singers with instruments of music, and such as taught to sing praise. Then Athaliah rent her clothes, and said, Treason, Treason. ¹⁴Then Jehoiada the priest brought out the captains of hundreds that were set over the host, and said to them, Have her forth of the ranges: and whoever follows her, let him be slain with the sword. For the priest said, Slay her not in the house of the LORD. ¹⁵So they laid hands on her; and when she was come to the entering of the horse gate by the king's house, they slew her there. ¹⁶And Jehoiada made a covenant between him, and between all the people, and between the king, that they should be the LORD's people. ¹⁷Then all the people went to the house of Baal, and broke it down, and broke his altars and his images in pieces, and slew Mattan the priest of Baal before the altars. ¹⁸Also Jehoiada appointed the offices of the house of the LORD by the hand of the priests the Levites, whom David had distributed in the house of the LORD, to offer the burnt offerings of the LORD, as it is written in the law of Moses, with rejoicing and with singing, as it was ordained by David. ¹⁹And he set the porters at the gates of the house of the LORD, that none which was unclean in any thing should enter in. ²⁰And he took the captains of hundreds, and the nobles, and the governors of the people, and all the people of the land, and brought down the king from the house of the LORD: and they came through the high gate into the king's house, and set the king on the throne of the kingdom. ²¹And all the people of the land rejoiced: and the city was quiet, after that they had slain Athaliah with the sword.

24

¹Joash was seven years old when he began to reign, and he reigned forty years in Jerusalem. His mother's name also was Zibiah of Beersheba. ²And Joash did that which was right in the sight of the LORD all the days of Jehoiada the priest. ³And Jehoiada took for him two wives; and he begat sons and daughters. ⁴And it came to pass after this, that Joash was minded to repair the house of the LORD. ⁵And he gathered together the priests and the Levites, and said to them, Go out to the cities of Judah, and gather of all Israel money to repair the house of your God from year to year, and see that you hasten the matter. However, the Levites hastened it not. ⁶And the king called for Jehoiada the chief, and said to him, Why have you not required of the Levites to bring in out of Judah and out of Jerusalem the collection, according to the commandment of Moses the servant of the LORD, and of the congregation of Israel, for the tabernacle of witness? ⁷For the sons of Athaliah, that wicked woman, had broken up the house of God; and also all the dedicated things of the house of the LORD did they bestow on Baalim. ⁸And at the king's commandment they made a chest, and set it without at the gate of the house of the LORD. ⁹And they made a proclamation through Judah and Jerusalem, to bring in to the LORD the collection that Moses the servant of God laid on Israel in the wilderness. ¹⁰And all the princes and all the people rejoiced, and brought in, and cast into the chest, until they had made an end. ¹¹Now it came to pass, that at what time the chest was brought to the king's office by the hand of the Levites, and when they saw that there was much money, the king's scribe and the high priest's officer came and emptied the chest, and took it, and carried it to his place again. Thus they did day by day, and gathered money in abundance. ¹²And the king and Jehoiada gave it to such as did the work of the service of the house of the LORD, and hired masons and carpenters to repair the house of the LORD, and also such as worked iron and brass to mend the house of the LORD. ¹³So the workmen worked, and the work was perfected by them, and they set the house of God in his state, and strengthened it. ¹⁴And when they had finished it, they brought the rest of the money before the king and Jehoiada, whereof were made vessels for the house of the LORD, even vessels to minister, and to offer with, and spoons, and vessels of gold and silver. And they offered burnt offerings in the house of the LORD continually all the days of Jehoiada. ¹⁵But Jehoiada waxed old, and was full of days when he died; an hundred and thirty years old was he when he died. ¹⁶And they buried him in the city of David among the kings, because he had done good in Israel, both toward God, and toward his house. ¹⁷Now after the death of Jehoiada came the princes of Judah, and made obeisance to the king. Then the king listened to them. ¹⁸And they left the house of the LORD God of their fathers, and served groves and idols: and wrath came on Judah and Jerusalem for this their trespass. ¹⁹Yet he sent prophets to them, to bring them again to the LORD; and they testified against them: but they would not give ear. ²⁰And the Spirit of God came on Zechariah the son of Jehoiada the priest, which stood above the people, and said to them, Thus says God, Why transgress

you the commandments of the LORD, that you cannot prosper? because you have forsaken the LORD, he has also forsaken you. ²¹And they conspired against him, and stoned him with stones at the commandment of the king in the court of the house of the LORD. ²²Thus Joash the king remembered not the kindness which Jehoiada his father had done to him, but slew his son. And when he died, he said, The LORD look on it, and require it. ²³And it came to pass at the end of the year, that the host of Syria came up against him: and they came to Judah and Jerusalem, and destroyed all the princes of the people from among the people, and sent all the spoil of them to the king of Damascus. ²⁴For the army of the Syrians came with a small company of men, and the LORD delivered a very great host into their hand, because they had forsaken the LORD God of their fathers. So they executed judgment against Joash. ²⁵And when they were departed from him, (for they left him in great diseases,) his own servants conspired against him for the blood of the sons of Jehoiada the priest, and slew him on his bed, and he died: and they buried him in the city of David, but they buried him not in the sepulchers of the kings. ²⁶And these are they that conspired against him; Zabad the son of Shimeath an Ammonitess, and Jehozabad the son of Shimrith a Moabitess. ²⁷Now concerning his sons, and the greatness of the burdens laid on him, and the repairing of the house of God, behold, they are written in the story of the book of the kings. And Amaziah his son reigned in his stead.

25

¹Amaziah was twenty and five years old when he began to reign, and he reigned twenty and nine years in Jerusalem. And his mother's name was Jehoaddan of Jerusalem. ²And he did that which was right in the sight of the LORD, but not with a perfect heart. ³Now it came to pass, when the kingdom was established to him, that he slew his servants that had killed the king his father. ⁴But he slew not their children, but did as it is written in the law in the book of Moses, where the LORD commanded, saying, The fathers shall not die for the children, neither shall the children die for the fathers, but every man shall die for his own sin. ⁵Moreover Amaziah gathered Judah together, and made them captains over thousands, and captains over hundreds, according to the houses of their fathers, throughout all Judah and Benjamin: and he numbered them from twenty years old and above, and found them three hundred thousand choice men, able to go forth to war, that could handle spear and shield. ⁶He hired also an hundred thousand mighty men of valor out of Israel for an hundred talents of silver. ⁷But there came a man of God to him, saying, O king, let not the army of Israel go with you; for the LORD is not with Israel, to wit, with all the children of Ephraim. ⁸But if you will go, do it; be strong for the battle: God shall make you fall before the enemy: for God has power to help, and to cast down. ⁹And Amaziah said to the man of God, But what shall we do for the hundred talents which I have given to the army of Israel? And the man of God answered, The LORD is able to give you much more than this. ¹⁰Then Amaziah separated them, to wit, the army that was come to him out of Ephraim, to go home again: why their anger was greatly kindled against Judah, and they returned home in great anger. ¹¹And Amaziah strengthened himself, and led forth his people, and went to the valley of salt, and smote of the children of Seir ten thousand. ¹²And other ten thousand left alive did the children of Judah carry away captive, and brought them to the top of the rock, and cast them down from the top of the rock, that they all were broken in pieces. ¹³But the soldiers of the army which Amaziah sent back, that they should not go with him to battle, fell on the cities of Judah, from Samaria even to Bethhoron, and smote three thousand of them, and took much spoil. ¹⁴Now it came to pass, after that Amaziah was come from the slaughter of the Edomites, that he brought the gods of the children of Seir, and set them up to be his gods, and bowed down himself before them, and burned incense to them. ¹⁵Why the anger of the LORD was kindled against Amaziah, and he sent to him a prophet, which said to him, Why have you sought after the gods of the people, which could not deliver their own people out of your hand? ¹⁶And it came to pass, as he talked with him, that the king said to him, Are you made of the king's counsel? forbear; why should you be smitten? Then the prophet declined, and said, I know that God has determined to destroy you, because you have done this, and have not listened to my counsel. ¹⁷Then Amaziah king of Judah took advice, and sent to Joash, the son of Jehoahaz, the son of Jehu, king of Israel, saying, Come, let us see one another in the face. ¹⁸And Joash king of Israel sent to Amaziah king of Judah, saying, The thistle that was in Lebanon sent to the cedar that was in Lebanon, saying, Give your daughter to my son to wife: and there passed by a wild beast that was in Lebanon, and stepped down the thistle. ¹⁹You say, See, you have smitten the Edomites; and your heart lifts you up to boast: abide now at home; why should you meddle to your hurt, that you should fall, even you, and Judah with you? ²⁰But Amaziah would not hear; for it came of God, that he might deliver them into the hand of their enemies, because they sought after the gods of Edom. ²¹So Joash the king of Israel went up; and they saw one another in the face, both he and Amaziah king of Judah, at Bethshemesh, which belongs to Judah. ²²And Judah was put to the worse before Israel, and they fled every man to his tent. ²³And Joash the king of Israel took Amaziah king of Judah, the son of Joash, the son of Jehoahaz, at Bethshemesh, and brought him to Jerusalem, and broke down the wall of Jerusalem from the gate of Ephraim to the corner gate, four hundred cubits. ²⁴And he took all the gold and the silver, and all the vessels that were found in the house of God with Obededom, and the treasures of the king's house, the hostages also, and returned to Samaria. ²⁵And Amaziah the son of Joash king of Judah lived after the death of Joash son of Jehoahaz king of Israel fifteen years. ²⁶Now the rest of the acts of Amaziah, first and last, behold, are they not written in the book of the kings of Judah and Israel? ²⁷Now after the time that Amaziah did turn away from following the LORD they made a conspiracy against him in Jerusalem; and he fled to Lachish: but they sent to Lachish after him, and slew him there. ²⁸And they brought him on horses, and buried him with his fathers in the city of Judah.

26

¹Then all the people of Judah took Uzziah, who was sixteen years old, and made him king in the room of his father Amaziah. ²He built Eloth, and restored it to Judah, after that the king slept with his fathers. ³Sixteen years old

was Uzziah when he began to reign, and he reigned fifty and two years in Jerusalem. His mother's name also was Jecoliah of Jerusalem. ⁴And he did that which was right in the sight of the LORD, according to all that his father Amaziah did. ⁵And he sought God in the days of Zechariah, who had understanding in the visions of God: and as long as he sought the LORD, God made him to prosper. ⁶And he went forth and warred against the Philistines, and broke down the wall of Gath, and the wall of Jabneh, and the wall of Ashdod, and built cities about Ashdod, and among the Philistines. ⁷And God helped him against the Philistines, and against the Arabians that dwelled in Gurbaal, and the Mehunims. ⁸And the Ammonites gave gifts to Uzziah: and his name spread abroad even to the entering in of Egypt; for he strengthened himself exceedingly. ⁹Moreover Uzziah built towers in Jerusalem at the corner gate, and at the valley gate, and at the turning of the wall, and fortified them. ¹⁰Also he built towers in the desert, and dig many wells: for he had much cattle, both in the low country, and in the plains: farmers also, and vine dressers in the mountains, and in Carmel: for he loved husbandry. ¹¹Moreover Uzziah had an host of fighting men, that went out to war by bands, according to the number of their account by the hand of Jeiel the scribe and Maaseiah the ruler, under the hand of Hananiah, one of the king's captains. ¹²The whole number of the chief of the fathers of the mighty men of valor were two thousand and six hundred. ¹³And under their hand was an army, three hundred thousand and seven thousand and five hundred, that made war with mighty power, to help the king against the enemy. ¹⁴And Uzziah prepared for them throughout all the host shields, and spears, and helmets, and habergeons, and bows, and slings to cast stones. ¹⁵And he made in Jerusalem engines, invented by cunning men, to be on the towers and on the bulwarks, to shoot arrows and great stones with. And his name spread far abroad; for he was marvelously helped, till he was strong. ¹⁶But when he was strong, his heart was lifted up to his destruction: for he transgressed against the LORD his God, and went into the temple of the LORD to burn incense on the altar of incense. ¹⁷And Azariah the priest went in after him, and with him fourscore priests of the LORD, that were valiant men: ¹⁸And they withstood Uzziah the king, and said to him, It appertains not to you, Uzziah, to burn incense to the LORD, but to the priests the sons of Aaron, that are consecrated to burn incense: go out of the sanctuary; for you have trespassed; neither shall it be for your honor from the LORD God. ¹⁹Then Uzziah was wroth, and had a censer in his hand to burn incense: and while he was wroth with the priests, the leprosy even rose up in his forehead before the priests in the house of the LORD, from beside the incense altar. ²⁰And Azariah the chief priest, and all the priests, looked on him, and, behold, he was leprous in his forehead, and they thrust him out from there; yes, himself hurried also to go out, because the LORD had smitten him. ²¹And Uzziah the king was a leper to the day of his death, and dwelled in a several house, being a leper; for he was cut off from the house of the LORD: and Jotham his son was over the king's house, judging the people of the land. ²²Now the rest of the acts of Uzziah, first and last, did Isaiah the prophet, the son of Amoz, write. ²³So Uzziah slept with his fathers, and they buried him with his fathers in the field of the burial which belonged to the kings; for they said, He is a leper: and Jotham his son reigned in his stead.

27

¹Jotham was twenty and five years old when he began to reign, and he reigned sixteen years in Jerusalem. His mother's name also was Jerushah, the daughter of Zadok. ²And he did that which was right in the sight of the LORD, according to all that his father Uzziah did: however, he entered not into the temple of the LORD. And the people did yet corruptly. ³He built the high gate of the house of the LORD, and on the wall of Ophel he built much. ⁴Moreover he built cities in the mountains of Judah, and in the forests he built castles and towers. ⁵He fought also with the king of the Ammonites, and prevailed against them. And the children of Ammon gave him the same year an hundred talents of silver, and ten thousand measures of wheat, and ten thousand of barley. So much did the children of Ammon pay to him, both the second year, and the third. ⁶So Jotham became mighty, because he prepared his ways before the LORD his God. ⁷Now the rest of the acts of Jotham, and all his wars, and his ways, see, they are written in the book of the kings of Israel and Judah. ⁸He was five and twenty years old when he began to reign, and reigned sixteen years in Jerusalem. ⁹And Jotham slept with his fathers, and they buried him in the city of David: and Ahaz his son reigned in his stead.

28

¹Ahaz was twenty years old when he began to reign, and he reigned sixteen years in Jerusalem: but he did not that which was right in the sight of the LORD, like David his father: ²For he walked in the ways of the kings of Israel, and made also molten images for Baalim. ³Moreover he burnt incense in the valley of the son of Hinnom, and burnt his children in the fire, after the abominations of the heathen whom the LORD had cast out before the children of Israel. ⁴He sacrificed also and burnt incense in the high places, and on the hills, and under every green tree. ⁵Why the LORD his God delivered him into the hand of the king of Syria; and they smote him, and carried away a great multitude of them captives, and brought them to Damascus. And he was also delivered into the hand of the king of Israel, who smote him with a great slaughter. ⁶For Pekah the son of Remaliah slew in Judah an hundred and twenty thousand in one day, which were all valiant men; because they had forsaken the LORD God of their fathers. ⁷And Zichri, a mighty man of Ephraim, slew Maaseiah the king's son, and Azrikam the governor of the house, and Elkanah that was next to the king. ⁸And the children of Israel carried away captive of their brothers two hundred thousand, women, sons, and daughters, and took also away much spoil from them, and brought the spoil to Samaria. ⁹But a prophet of the LORD was there, whose name was Oded: and he went out before the host that came to Samaria, and said to them, Behold, because the LORD God of your fathers was wroth with Judah, he has delivered them into your hand, and you have slain them in a rage that reaches up to heaven. ¹⁰And now you purpose to keep under the children of Judah and Jerusalem for slaves and bondwomen to you: but are there not with you, even with you, sins against the LORD your God? ¹¹Now hear me therefore, and deliver the captives

again, which you have taken captive of your brothers: for the fierce wrath of the LORD is on you. ¹²Then certain of the heads of the children of Ephraim, Azariah the son of Johanan, Berechiah the son of Meshillemoth, and Jehizkiah the son of Shallum, and Amasa the son of Hadlai, stood up against them that came from the war, ¹³And said to them, You shall not bring in the captives here: for whereas we have offended against the LORD already, you intend to add more to our sins and to our trespass: for our trespass is great, and there is fierce wrath against Israel. ¹⁴So the armed men left the captives and the spoil before the princes and all the congregation. ¹⁵And the men which were expressed by name rose up, and took the captives, and with the spoil clothed all that were naked among them, and arrayed them, and shod them, and gave them to eat and to drink, and anointed them, and carried all the feeble of them on asses, and brought them to Jericho, the city of palm trees, to their brothers: then they returned to Samaria. ¹⁶At that time did king Ahaz send to the kings of Assyria to help him. ¹⁷For again the Edomites had come and smitten Judah, and carried away captives. ¹⁸The Philistines also had invaded the cities of the low country, and of the south of Judah, and had taken Bethshemesh, and Ajalon, and Gederoth, and Shocho with the villages thereof, and Timnah with the villages thereof, Gimzo also and the villages thereof: and they dwelled there. ¹⁹For the LORD brought Judah low because of Ahaz king of Israel; for he made Judah naked, and transgressed sore against the LORD. ²⁰And Tilgathpilneser king of Assyria came to him, and distressed him, but strengthened him not. ²¹For Ahaz took away a portion out of the house of the LORD, and out of the house of the king, and of the princes, and gave it to the king of Assyria: but he helped him not. ²²And in the time of his distress did he trespass yet more against the LORD: this is that king Ahaz. ²³For he sacrificed to the gods of Damascus, which smote him: and he said, Because the gods of the kings of Syria help them, therefore will I sacrifice to them, that they may help me. But they were the ruin of him, and of all Israel. ²⁴And Ahaz gathered together the vessels of the house of God, and cut in pieces the vessels of the house of God, and shut up the doors of the house of the LORD, and he made him altars in every corner of Jerusalem. ²⁵And in every several city of Judah he made high places to burn incense to other gods, and provoked to anger the LORD God of his fathers. ²⁶Now the rest of his acts and of all his ways, first and last, behold, they are written in the book of the kings of Judah and Israel. ²⁷And Ahaz slept with his fathers, and they buried him in the city, even in Jerusalem: but they brought him not into the sepulchers of the kings of Israel: and Hezekiah his son reigned in his stead.

29

¹Hezekiah began to reign when he was five and twenty years old, and he reigned nine and twenty years in Jerusalem. And his mother's name was Abijah, the daughter of Zechariah. ²And he did that which was right in the sight of the LORD, according to all that David his father had done. ³He in the first year of his reign, in the first month, opened the doors of the house of the LORD, and repaired them. ⁴And he brought in the priests and the Levites, and gathered them together into the east street, ⁵And said to them, Hear me, you Levites, sanctify now yourselves, and sanctify the house of the LORD God of your fathers, and carry forth the filthiness out of the holy place. ⁶For our fathers have trespassed, and done that which was evil in the eyes of the LORD our God, and have forsaken him, and have turned away their faces from the habitation of the LORD, and turned their backs. ⁷Also they have shut up the doors of the porch, and put out the lamps, and have not burned incense nor offered burnt offerings in the holy place to the God of Israel. ⁸Why the wrath of the LORD was on Judah and Jerusalem, and he has delivered them to trouble, to astonishment, and to hissing, as you see with your eyes. ⁹For, see, our fathers have fallen by the sword, and our sons and our daughters and our wives are in captivity for this. ¹⁰Now it is in my heart to make a covenant with the LORD God of Israel, that his fierce wrath may turn away from us. ¹¹My sons, be not now negligent: for the LORD has chosen you to stand before him, to serve him, and that you should minister to him, and burn incense. ¹²Then the Levites arose, Mahath the son of Amasai, and Joel the son of Azariah, of the sons of the Kohathites: and of the sons of Merari, Kish the son of Abdi, and Azariah the son of Jehalelel: and of the Gershonites; Joah the son of Zimmah, and Eden the son of Joah: ¹³And of the sons of Elizaphan; Shimri, and Jeiel: and of the sons of Asaph; Zechariah, and Mattaniah: ¹⁴And of the sons of Heman; Jehiel, and Shimei: and of the sons of Jeduthun; Shemaiah, and Uzziel. ¹⁵And they gathered their brothers, and sanctified themselves, and came, according to the commandment of the king, by the words of the LORD, to cleanse the house of the LORD. ¹⁶And the priests went into the inner part of the house of the LORD, to cleanse it, and brought out all the uncleanness that they found in the temple of the LORD into the court of the house of the LORD. And the Levites took it, to carry it out abroad into the brook Kidron. ¹⁷Now they began on the first day of the first month to sanctify, and on the eighth day of the month came they to the porch of the LORD: so they sanctified the house of the LORD in eight days; and in the sixteenth day of the first month they made an end. ¹⁸Then they went in to Hezekiah the king, and said, We have cleansed all the house of the LORD, and the altar of burnt offering, with all the vessels thereof, and the show bread table, with all the vessels thereof. ¹⁹Moreover all the vessels, which king Ahaz in his reign did cast away in his transgression, have we prepared and sanctified, and, behold, they are before the altar of the LORD. ²⁰Then Hezekiah the king rose early, and gathered the rulers of the city, and went up to the house of the LORD. ²¹And they brought seven bullocks, and seven rams, and seven lambs, and seven he goats, for a sin offering for the kingdom, and for the sanctuary, and for Judah. And he commanded the priests the sons of Aaron to offer them on the altar of the LORD. ²²So they killed the bullocks, and the priests received the blood, and sprinkled it on the altar: likewise, when they had killed the rams, they sprinkled the blood on the altar: they killed also the lambs, and they sprinkled the blood on the altar. ²³And they brought forth the he goats for the sin offering before the king and the congregation; and they laid their hands on them: ²⁴And the priests killed them, and they made reconciliation with their blood on the altar, to make an atonement for all Israel: for the king commanded that the burnt offering and the sin offering should be made for all Israel. ²⁵And he set the

Levites in the house of the LORD with cymbals, with psalteries, and with harps, according to the commandment of David, and of Gad the king's seer, and Nathan the prophet: for so was the commandment of the LORD by his prophets. ²⁶And the Levites stood with the instruments of David, and the priests with the trumpets. ²⁷And Hezekiah commanded to offer the burnt offering on the altar. And when the burnt offering began, the song of the LORD began also with the trumpets, and with the instruments ordained by David king of Israel. ²⁸And all the congregation worshipped, and the singers sang, and the trumpeters sounded: and all this continued until the burnt offering was finished. ²⁹And when they had made an end of offering, the king and all that were present with him bowed themselves, and worshipped. ³⁰Moreover Hezekiah the king and the princes commanded the Levites to sing praise to the LORD with the words of David, and of Asaph the seer. And they sang praises with gladness, and they bowed their heads and worshipped. ³¹Then Hezekiah answered and said, Now you have consecrated yourselves to the LORD, come near and bring sacrifices and thank offerings into the house of the LORD. And the congregation brought in sacrifices and thank offerings; and as many as were of a free heart burnt offerings. ³²And the number of the burnt offerings, which the congregation brought, was three score and ten bullocks, an hundred rams, and two hundred lambs: all these were for a burnt offering to the LORD. ³³And the consecrated things were six hundred oxen and three thousand sheep. ³⁴But the priests were too few, so that they could not flay all the burnt offerings: why their brothers the Levites did help them, till the work was ended, and until the other priests had sanctified themselves: for the Levites were more upright in heart to sanctify themselves than the priests. ³⁵And also the burnt offerings were in abundance, with the fat of the peace offerings, and the drink offerings for every burnt offering. So the service of the house of the LORD was set in order. ³⁶And Hezekiah rejoiced, and all the people, that God had prepared the people: for the thing was done suddenly.

30 ¹And Hezekiah sent to all Israel and Judah, and wrote letters also to Ephraim and Manasseh, that they should come to the house of the LORD at Jerusalem, to keep the passover to the LORD God of Israel. ²For the king had taken counsel, and his princes, and all the congregation in Jerusalem, to keep the passover in the second month. ³For they could not keep it at that time, because the priests had not sanctified themselves sufficiently, neither had the people gathered themselves together to Jerusalem. ⁴And the thing pleased the king and all the congregation. ⁵So they established a decree to make proclamation throughout all Israel, from Beersheba even to Dan, that they should come to keep the passover to the LORD God of Israel at Jerusalem: for they had not done it of a long time in such sort as it was written. ⁶So the posts went with the letters from the king and his princes throughout all Israel and Judah, and according to the commandment of the king, saying, You children of Israel, turn again to the LORD God of Abraham, Isaac, and Israel, and he will return to the remnant of you, that are escaped out of the hand of the kings of Assyria. ⁷And be not you like your fathers, and like your brothers, which trespassed against the LORD God of their fathers, who therefore gave them up to desolation, as you see. ⁸Now be you not stiff necked, as your fathers were, but yield yourselves to the LORD, and enter into his sanctuary, which he has sanctified for ever: and serve the LORD your God, that the fierceness of his wrath may turn away from you. ⁹For if you turn again to the LORD, your brothers and your children shall find compassion before them that lead them captive, so that they shall come again into this land: for the LORD your God is gracious and merciful, and will not turn away his face from you, if you return to him. ¹⁰So the posts passed from city to city through the country of Ephraim and Manasseh even to Zebulun: but they laughed them to scorn, and mocked them. ¹¹Nevertheless divers of Asher and Manasseh and of Zebulun humbled themselves, and came to Jerusalem. ¹²Also in Judah the hand of God was to give them one heart to do the commandment of the king and of the princes, by the word of the LORD. ¹³And there assembled at Jerusalem much people to keep the feast of unleavened bread in the second month, a very great congregation. ¹⁴And they arose and took away the altars that were in Jerusalem, and all the altars for incense took they away, and cast them into the brook Kidron. ¹⁵Then they killed the passover on the fourteenth day of the second month: and the priests and the Levites were ashamed, and sanctified themselves, and brought in the burnt offerings into the house of the LORD. ¹⁶And they stood in their place after their manner, according to the law of Moses the man of God: the priests sprinkled the blood, which they received of the hand of the Levites. ¹⁷For there were many in the congregation that were not sanctified: therefore the Levites had the charge of the killing of the passovers for every one that was not clean, to sanctify them to the LORD. ¹⁸For a multitude of the people, even many of Ephraim, and Manasseh, Issachar, and Zebulun, had not cleansed themselves, yet did they eat the passover otherwise than it was written. But Hezekiah prayed for them, saying, The good LORD pardon every one ¹⁹That prepares his heart to seek God, the LORD God of his fathers, though he be not cleansed according to the purification of the sanctuary. ²⁰And the LORD listened to Hezekiah, and healed the people. ²¹And the children of Israel that were present at Jerusalem kept the feast of unleavened bread seven days with great gladness: and the Levites and the priests praised the LORD day by day, singing with loud instruments to the LORD. ²²And Hezekiah spoke comfortably to all the Levites that taught the good knowledge of the LORD: and they did eat throughout the feast seven days, offering peace offerings, and making confession to the LORD God of their fathers. ²³And the whole assembly took counsel to keep other seven days: and they kept other seven days with gladness. ²⁴For Hezekiah king of Judah did give to the congregation a thousand bullocks and seven thousand sheep; and the princes gave to the congregation a thousand bullocks and ten thousand sheep: and a great number of priests sanctified themselves. ²⁵And all the congregation of Judah, with the priests and the Levites, and all the congregation that came out of Israel, and the strangers that came out of the land of Israel, and that dwelled in Judah, rejoiced. ²⁶So there was great joy in Jerusalem: for since the time of Solomon the son of David king of Israel there was not the like in Jerusalem.

²⁷Then the priests the Levites arose and blessed the people: and their voice was heard, and their prayer came up to his holy dwelling place, even to heaven.

31

¹Now when all this was finished, all Israel that were present went out to the cities of Judah, and broke the images in pieces, and cut down the groves, and threw down the high places and the altars out of all Judah and Benjamin, in Ephraim also and Manasseh, until they had utterly destroyed them all. Then all the children of Israel returned, every man to his possession, into their own cities. ²And Hezekiah appointed the courses of the priests and the Levites after their courses, every man according to his service, the priests and Levites for burnt offerings and for peace offerings, to minister, and to give thanks, and to praise in the gates of the tents of the LORD. ³He appointed also the king's portion of his substance for the burnt offerings, to wit, for the morning and evening burnt offerings, and the burnt offerings for the sabbaths, and for the new moons, and for the set feasts, as it is written in the law of the LORD. ⁴Moreover he commanded the people that dwelled in Jerusalem to give the portion of the priests and the Levites, that they might be encouraged in the law of the LORD. ⁵And as soon as the commandment came abroad, the children of Israel brought in abundance the first fruits of corn, wine, and oil, and honey, and of all the increase of the field; and the tithe of all things brought they in abundantly. ⁶And concerning the children of Israel and Judah, that dwelled in the cities of Judah, they also brought in the tithe of oxen and sheep, and the tithe of holy things which were consecrated to the LORD their God, and laid them by heaps. ⁷In the third month they began to lay the foundation of the heaps, and finished them in the seventh month. ⁸And when Hezekiah and the princes came and saw the heaps, they blessed the LORD, and his people Israel. ⁹Then Hezekiah questioned with the priests and the Levites concerning the heaps. ¹⁰And Azariah the chief priest of the house of Zadok answered him, and said, Since the people began to bring the offerings into the house of the LORD, we have had enough to eat, and have left plenty: for the LORD has blessed his people; and that which is left is this great store. ¹¹Then Hezekiah commanded to prepare chambers in the house of the LORD; and they prepared them, ¹²And brought in the offerings and the tithes and the dedicated things faithfully: over which Cononiah the Levite was ruler, and Shimei his brother was the next. ¹³And Jehiel, and Azaziah, and Nahath, and Asahel, and Jerimoth, and Jozabad, and Eliel, and Ismachiah, and Mahath, and Benaiah, were overseers under the hand of Cononiah and Shimei his brother, at the commandment of Hezekiah the king, and Azariah the ruler of the house of God. ¹⁴And Kore the son of Imnah the Levite, the porter toward the east, was over the freewill offerings of God, to distribute the oblations of the LORD, and the most holy things. ¹⁵And next him were Eden, and Miniamin, and Jeshua, and Shemaiah, Amariah, and Shecaniah, in the cities of the priests, in their set office, to give to their brothers by courses, as well to the great as to the small: ¹⁶Beside their genealogy of males, from three years old and upward, even to every one that enters into the house of the LORD, his daily portion for their service in their charges according to their courses; ¹⁷Both to the genealogy of the priests by the house of their fathers, and the Levites from twenty years old and upward, in their charges by their courses; ¹⁸And to the genealogy of all their little ones, their wives, and their sons, and their daughters, through all the congregation: for in their set office they sanctified themselves in holiness: ¹⁹Also of the sons of Aaron the priests, which were in the fields of the suburbs of their cities, in every several city, the men that were expressed by name, to give portions to all the males among the priests, and to all that were reckoned by genealogies among the Levites. ²⁰And thus did Hezekiah throughout all Judah, and worked that which was good and right and truth before the LORD his God. ²¹And in every work that he began in the service of the house of God, and in the law, and in the commandments, to seek his God, he did it with all his heart, and prospered.

32

¹After these things, and the establishment thereof, Sennacherib king of Assyria came, and entered into Judah, and encamped against the fenced cities, and thought to win them for himself. ²And when Hezekiah saw that Sennacherib was come, and that he was purposed to fight against Jerusalem, ³He took counsel with his princes and his mighty men to stop the waters of the fountains which were without the city: and they did help him. ⁴So there was gathered much people together, who stopped all the fountains, and the brook that ran through the middle of the land, saying, Why should the kings of Assyria come, and find much water? ⁵Also he strengthened himself, and built up all the wall that was broken, and raised it up to the towers, and another wall without, and repaired Millo in the city of David, and made darts and shields in abundance. ⁶And he set captains of war over the people, and gathered them together to him in the street of the gate of the city, and spoke comfortably to them, saying, ⁷Be strong and courageous, be not afraid nor dismayed for the king of Assyria, nor for all the multitude that is with him: for there be more with us than with him: ⁸With him is an arm of flesh; but with us is the LORD our God to help us, and to fight our battles. And the people rested themselves on the words of Hezekiah king of Judah. ⁹After this did Sennacherib king of Assyria send his servants to Jerusalem, (but he himself laid siege against Lachish, and all his power with him,) to Hezekiah king of Judah, and to all Judah that were at Jerusalem, saying, ¹⁰Thus says Sennacherib king of Assyria, Where on do you trust, that you abide in the siege in Jerusalem? ¹¹Does not Hezekiah persuade you to give over yourselves to die by famine and by thirst, saying, The LORD our God shall deliver us out of the hand of the king of Assyria? ¹²Has not the same Hezekiah taken away his high places and his altars, and commanded Judah and Jerusalem, saying, You shall worship before one altar, and burn incense on it? ¹³Know you not what I and my fathers have done to all the people of other lands? were the gods of the nations of those lands any ways able to deliver their lands out of my hand? ¹⁴Who was there among all the gods of those nations that my fathers utterly destroyed, that could deliver his people out of my hand, that your God should be able to deliver you out of my hand? ¹⁵Now therefore let not Hezekiah deceive you, nor persuade you on this manner, neither yet believe him: for no god of any nation or kingdom was able to deliver his people out of my hand, and out of the

hand of my fathers: how much less shall your God deliver you out of my hand? ¹⁶And his servants spoke yet more against the LORD God, and against his servant Hezekiah. ¹⁷He wrote also letters to rail on the LORD God of Israel, and to speak against him, saying, As the gods of the nations of other lands have not delivered their people out of my hand, so shall not the God of Hezekiah deliver his people out of my hand. ¹⁸Then they cried with a loud voice in the Jews' speech to the people of Jerusalem that were on the wall, to affright them, and to trouble them; that they might take the city. ¹⁹And they spoke against the God of Jerusalem, as against the gods of the people of the earth, which were the work of the hands of man. ²⁰And for this cause Hezekiah the king, and the prophet Isaiah the son of Amoz, prayed and cried to heaven. ²¹And the LORD sent an angel, which cut off all the mighty men of valor, and the leaders and captains in the camp of the king of Assyria. So he returned with shame of face to his own land. And when he was come into the house of his god, they that came forth of his own bowels slew him there with the sword. ²²Thus the LORD saved Hezekiah and the inhabitants of Jerusalem from the hand of Sennacherib the king of Assyria, and from the hand of all other, and guided them on every side. ²³And many brought gifts to the LORD to Jerusalem, and presents to Hezekiah king of Judah: so that he was magnified in the sight of all nations from thereafter. ²⁴In those days Hezekiah was sick to the death, and prayed to the LORD: and he spoke to him, and he gave him a sign. ²⁵But Hezekiah rendered not again according to the benefit done to him; for his heart was lifted up: therefore there was wrath on him, and on Judah and Jerusalem. ²⁶Notwithstanding Hezekiah humbled himself for the pride of his heart, both he and the inhabitants of Jerusalem, so that the wrath of the LORD came not on them in the days of Hezekiah. ²⁷And Hezekiah had exceeding much riches and honor: and he made himself treasuries for silver, and for gold, and for precious stones, and for spices, and for shields, and for all manner of pleasant jewels; ²⁸Storehouses also for the increase of corn, and wine, and oil; and stalls for all manner of beasts, and cotes for flocks. ²⁹Moreover he provided him cities, and possessions of flocks and herds in abundance: for God had given him substance very much. ³⁰This same Hezekiah also stopped the upper watercourse of Gihon, and brought it straight down to the west side of the city of David. And Hezekiah prospered in all his works. ³¹However, in the business of the ambassadors of the princes of Babylon, who sent to him to inquire of the wonder that was done in the land, God left him, to try him, that he might know all that was in his heart. ³²Now the rest of the acts of Hezekiah, and his goodness, behold, they are written in the vision of Isaiah the prophet, the son of Amoz, and in the book of the kings of Judah and Israel. ³³And Hezekiah slept with his fathers, and they buried him in the most chief of the sepulchers of the sons of David: and all Judah and the inhabitants of Jerusalem did him honor at his death. And Manasseh his son reigned in his stead.

33

¹Manasseh was twelve years old when he began to reign, and he reigned fifty and five years in Jerusalem: ²But did that which was evil in the sight of the LORD, like to the abominations of the heathen, whom the LORD had cast out before the children of Israel. ³For he built again the high places which Hezekiah his father had broken down, and he reared up altars for Baalim, and made groves, and worshipped all the host of heaven, and served them. ⁴Also he built altars in the house of the LORD, whereof the LORD had said, In Jerusalem shall my name be for ever. ⁵And he built altars for all the host of heaven in the two courts of the house of the LORD. ⁶And he caused his children to pass through the fire in the valley of the son of Hinnom: also he observed times, and used enchantments, and used witchcraft, and dealt with a familiar spirit, and with wizards: he worked much evil in the sight of the LORD, to provoke him to anger. ⁷And he set a carved image, the idol which he had made, in the house of God, of which God had said to David and to Solomon his son, In this house, and in Jerusalem, which I have chosen before all the tribes of Israel, will I put my name for ever: ⁸Neither will I any more remove the foot of Israel from out of the land which I have appointed for your fathers; so that they will take heed to do all that I have commanded them, according to the whole law and the statutes and the ordinances by the hand of Moses. ⁹So Manasseh made Judah and the inhabitants of Jerusalem to err, and to do worse than the heathen, whom the LORD had destroyed before the children of Israel. ¹⁰And the LORD spoke to Manasseh, and to his people: but they would not listen. ¹¹Why the LORD brought on them the captains of the host of the king of Assyria, which took Manasseh among the thorns, and bound him with fetters, and carried him to Babylon. ¹²And when he was in affliction, he sought the LORD his God, and humbled himself greatly before the God of his fathers, ¹³And prayed to him: and he was entreated of him, and heard his supplication, and brought him again to Jerusalem into his kingdom. Then Manasseh knew that the LORD he was God. ¹⁴Now after this he built a wall without the city of David, on the west side of Gihon, in the valley, even to the entering in at the fish gate, and compassed about Ophel, and raised it up a very great height, and put captains of war in all the fenced cities of Judah. ¹⁵And he took away the strange gods, and the idol out of the house of the LORD, and all the altars that he had built in the mount of the house of the LORD, and in Jerusalem, and cast them out of the city. ¹⁶And he repaired the altar of the LORD, and sacrificed thereon peace offerings and thank offerings, and commanded Judah to serve the LORD God of Israel. ¹⁷Nevertheless the people did sacrifice still in the high places, yet to the LORD their God only. ¹⁸Now the rest of the acts of Manasseh, and his prayer to his God, and the words of the seers that spoke to him in the name of the LORD God of Israel, behold, they are written in the book of the kings of Israel. ¹⁹His prayer also, and how God was entreated of him, and all his sins, and his trespass, and the places wherein he built high places, and set up groves and graven images, before he was humbled: behold, they are written among the sayings of the seers. ²⁰So Manasseh slept with his fathers, and they buried him in his own house: and Amon his son reigned in his stead. ²¹Amon was two and twenty years old when he began to reign, and reigned two years in Jerusalem. ²²But he did that which was evil in the sight of the LORD, as did Manasseh his father: for Amon sacrificed to all the carved images which Manasseh his father had made, and

served them; ²³And humbled not himself before the LORD, as Manasseh his father had humbled himself; but Amon trespassed more and more. ²⁴And his servants conspired against him, and slew him in his own house. ²⁵But the people of the land slew all them that had conspired against king Amon; and the people of the land made Josiah his son king in his stead.

34 ¹Josiah was eight years old when he began to reign, and he reigned in Jerusalem one and thirty years. ²And he did that which was right in the sight of the LORD, and walked in the ways of David his father, and declined neither to the right hand, nor to the left. ³For in the eighth year of his reign, while he was yet young, he began to seek after the God of David his father: and in the twelfth year he began to purge Judah and Jerusalem from the high places, and the groves, and the carved images, and the molten images. ⁴And they broke down the altars of Baalim in his presence; and the images, that were on high above them, he cut down; and the groves, and the carved images, and the molten images, he broke in pieces, and made dust of them, and strewed it on the graves of them that had sacrificed to them. ⁵And he burnt the bones of the priests on their altars, and cleansed Judah and Jerusalem. ⁶And so did he in the cities of Manasseh, and Ephraim, and Simeon, even to Naphtali, with their mattocks round about. ⁷And when he had broken down the altars and the groves, and had beaten the graven images into powder, and cut down all the idols throughout all the land of Israel, he returned to Jerusalem. ⁸Now in the eighteenth year of his reign, when he had purged the land, and the house, he sent Shaphan the son of Azaliah, and Maaseiah the governor of the city, and Joah the son of Joahaz the recorder, to repair the house of the LORD his God. ⁹And when they came to Hilkiah the high priest, they delivered the money that was brought into the house of God, which the Levites that kept the doors had gathered of the hand of Manasseh and Ephraim, and of all the remnant of Israel, and of all Judah and Benjamin; and they returned to Jerusalem. ¹⁰And they put it in the hand of the workmen that had the oversight of the house of the LORD, and they gave it to the workmen that worked in the house of the LORD, to repair and amend the house: ¹¹Even to the artificers and builders gave they it, to buy hewn stone, and timber for couplings, and to floor the houses which the kings of Judah had destroyed. ¹²And the men did the work faithfully: and the overseers of them were Jahath and Obadiah, the Levites, of the sons of Merari; and Zechariah and Meshullam, of the sons of the Kohathites, to set it forward; and other of the Levites, all that could skill of instruments of music. ¹³Also they were over the bearers of burdens, and were overseers of all that worked the work in any manner of service: and of the Levites there were scribes, and officers, and porters. ¹⁴And when they brought out the money that was brought into the house of the LORD, Hilkiah the priest found a book of the law of the LORD given by Moses. ¹⁵And Hilkiah answered and said to Shaphan the scribe, I have found the book of the law in the house of the LORD. And Hilkiah delivered the book to Shaphan. ¹⁶And Shaphan carried the book to the king, and brought the king word back again, saying, All that was committed to your servants, they do it. ¹⁷And they have gathered together the money that was found in the house of the LORD, and have delivered it into the hand of the overseers, and to the hand of the workmen. ¹⁸Then Shaphan the scribe told the king, saying, Hilkiah the priest has given me a book. And Shaphan read it before the king. ¹⁹And it came to pass, when the king had heard the words of the law, that he rent his clothes. ²⁰And the king commanded Hilkiah, and Ahikam the son of Shaphan, and Abdon the son of Micah, and Shaphan the scribe, and Asaiah a servant of the king's, saying, ²¹Go, inquire of the LORD for me, and for them that are left in Israel and in Judah, concerning the words of the book that is found: for great is the wrath of the LORD that is poured out on us, because our fathers have not kept the word of the LORD, to do after all that is written in this book. ²²And Hilkiah, and they that the king had appointed, went to Huldah the prophetess, the wife of Shallum the son of Tikvath, the son of Hasrah, keeper of the wardrobe; (now she dwelled in Jerusalem in the college:) and they spoke to her to that effect. ²³And she answered them, Thus says the LORD God of Israel, Tell you the man that sent you to me, ²⁴Thus says the LORD, Behold, I will bring evil on this place, and on the inhabitants thereof, even all the curses that are written in the book which they have read before the king of Judah: ²⁵Because they have forsaken me, and have burned incense to other gods, that they might provoke me to anger with all the works of their hands; therefore my wrath shall be poured out on this place, and shall not be quenched. ²⁶And as for the king of Judah, who sent you to inquire of the LORD, so shall you say to him, Thus says the LORD God of Israel concerning the words which you have heard; ²⁷Because your heart was tender, and you did humble yourself before God, when you heard his words against this place, and against the inhabitants thereof, and humbled yourself before me, and did rend your clothes, and weep before me; I have even heard you also, says the LORD. ²⁸Behold, I will gather you to your fathers, and you shall be gathered to your grave in peace, neither shall your eyes see all the evil that I will bring on this place, and on the inhabitants of the same. So they brought the king word again. ²⁹Then the king sent and gathered together all the elders of Judah and Jerusalem. ³⁰And the king went up into the house of the LORD, and all the men of Judah, and the inhabitants of Jerusalem, and the priests, and the Levites, and all the people, great and small: and he read in their ears all the words of the book of the covenant that was found in the house of the LORD. ³¹And the king stood in his place, and made a covenant before the LORD, to walk after the LORD, and to keep his commandments, and his testimonies, and his statutes, with all his heart, and with all his soul, to perform the words of the covenant which are written in this book. ³²And he caused all that were present in Jerusalem and Benjamin to stand to it. And the inhabitants of Jerusalem did according to the covenant of God, the God of their fathers. ³³And Josiah took away all the abominations out of all the countries that pertained to the children of Israel, and made all that were present in Israel to serve, even to serve the LORD their God. And all his days they departed not from following the LORD, the God of their fathers.

35 ¹Moreover Josiah kept a passover to the LORD in Jerusalem: and they killed the passover on the fourteenth day of the first month. ²And he set the priests in their charges, and encouraged them to the service of the house of the LORD, ³And said to the Levites that taught all Israel, which were holy to the LORD, Put the holy ark in the house which Solomon the son of David king of Israel did build; it shall not be a burden on your shoulders: serve now the LORD your God, and his people Israel, ⁴And prepare yourselves by the houses of your fathers, after your courses, according to the writing of David king of Israel, and according to the writing of Solomon his son. ⁵And stand in the holy place according to the divisions of the families of the fathers of your brothers the people, and after the division of the families of the Levites. ⁶So kill the passover, and sanctify yourselves, and prepare your brothers, that they may do according to the word of the LORD by the hand of Moses. ⁷And Josiah gave to the people, of the flock, lambs and kids, all for the passover offerings, for all that were present, to the number of thirty thousand, and three thousand bullocks: these were of the king's substance. ⁸And his princes gave willingly to the people, to the priests, and to the Levites: Hilkiah and Zechariah and Jehiel, rulers of the house of God, gave to the priests for the passover offerings two thousand and six hundred small cattle and three hundred oxen. ⁹Conaniah also, and Shemaiah and Nethaneel, his brothers, and Hashabiah and Jeiel and Jozabad, chief of the Levites, gave to the Levites for passover offerings five thousand small cattle, and five hundred oxen. ¹⁰So the service was prepared, and the priests stood in their place, and the Levites in their courses, according to the king's commandment. ¹¹And they killed the passover, and the priests sprinkled the blood from their hands, and the Levites flayed them. ¹²And they removed the burnt offerings, that they might give according to the divisions of the families of the people, to offer to the LORD, as it is written in the book of Moses. And so did they with the oxen. ¹³And they roasted the passover with fire according to the ordinance: but the other holy offerings sod they in pots, and in caldrons, and in pans, and divided them speedily among all the people. ¹⁴And afterward they made ready for themselves, and for the priests: because the priests the sons of Aaron were busied in offering of burnt offerings and the fat until night; therefore the Levites prepared for themselves, and for the priests the sons of Aaron. ¹⁵And the singers the sons of Asaph were in their place, according to the commandment of David, and Asaph, and Heman, and Jeduthun the king's seer; and the porters waited at every gate; they might not depart from their service; for their brothers the Levites prepared for them. ¹⁶So all the service of the LORD was prepared the same day, to keep the passover, and to offer burnt offerings on the altar of the LORD, according to the commandment of king Josiah. ¹⁷And the children of Israel that were present kept the passover at that time, and the feast of unleavened bread seven days. ¹⁸And there was no passover like to that kept in Israel from the days of Samuel the prophet; neither did all the kings of Israel keep such a passover as Josiah kept, and the priests, and the Levites, and all Judah and Israel that were present, and the inhabitants of Jerusalem. ¹⁹In the eighteenth year of the reign of Josiah was this passover kept. ²⁰After all this, when Josiah had prepared the temple, Necho king of Egypt came up to fight against Charchemish by Euphrates: and Josiah went out against him. ²¹But he sent ambassadors to him, saying, What have I to do with you, you king of Judah? I come not against you this day, but against the house with which I have war: for God commanded me to make haste: forbear you from meddling with God, who is with me, that he destroy you not. ²²Nevertheless Josiah would not turn his face from him, but disguised himself, that he might fight with him, and listened not to the words of Necho from the mouth of God, and came to fight in the valley of Megiddo. ²³And the archers shot at king Josiah; and the king said to his servants, Have me away; for I am sore wounded. ²⁴His servants therefore took him out of that chariot, and put him in the second chariot that he had; and they brought him to Jerusalem, and he died, and was buried in one of the sepulchers of his fathers. And all Judah and Jerusalem mourned for Josiah. ²⁵And Jeremiah lamented for Josiah: and all the singing men and the singing women spoke of Josiah in their lamentations to this day, and made them an ordinance in Israel: and, behold, they are written in the lamentations. ²⁶Now the rest of the acts of Josiah, and his goodness, according to that which was written in the law of the LORD, ²⁷And his deeds, first and last, behold, they are written in the book of the kings of Israel and Judah.

36

¹Then the people of the land took Jehoahaz the son of Josiah, and made him king in his father's stead in Jerusalem. ²Jehoahaz was twenty and three years old when he began to reign, and he reigned three months in Jerusalem. ³And the king of Egypt put him down at Jerusalem, and condemned the land in an hundred talents of silver and a talent of gold. ⁴And the king of Egypt made Eliakim his brother king over Judah and Jerusalem, and turned his name to Jehoiakim. And Necho took Jehoahaz his brother, and carried him to Egypt. ⁵Jehoiakim was twenty and five years old when he began to reign, and he reigned eleven years in Jerusalem: and he did that which was evil in the sight of the LORD his God. ⁶Against him came up Nebuchadnezzar king of Babylon, and bound him in fetters, to carry him to Babylon. ⁷Nebuchadnezzar also carried of the vessels of the house of the LORD to Babylon, and put them in his temple at Babylon. ⁸Now the rest of the acts of Jehoiakim, and his abominations which he did, and that which was found in him, behold, they are written in the book of the kings of Israel and Judah: and Jehoiachin his son reigned in his stead. ⁹Jehoiachin was eight years old when he began to reign, and he reigned three months and ten days in Jerusalem: and he did that which was evil in the sight of the LORD. ¹⁰And when the year was expired, king Nebuchadnezzar sent, and brought him to Babylon, with the goodly vessels of the house of the LORD, and made Zedekiah his brother king over Judah and Jerusalem. ¹¹Zedekiah was one and twenty years old when he began to reign, and reigned eleven years in Jerusalem. ¹²And he did that which was evil in the sight of the LORD his God, and humbled not himself before Jeremiah the prophet speaking from the mouth of the LORD. ¹³And he also rebelled against king Nebuchadnezzar, who had made him swear by God: but he stiffened his neck, and hardened his heart from turning to the LORD God of Israel. ¹⁴Moreover all the chief of the priests, and the people, transgressed very much after all the abominations of the

heathen; and polluted the house of the LORD which he had hallowed in Jerusalem. ¹⁵And the LORD God of their fathers sent to them by his messengers, rising up betimes, and sending; because he had compassion on his people, and on his dwelling place: ¹⁶But they mocked the messengers of God, and despised his words, and misused his prophets, until the wrath of the LORD arose against his people, till there was no remedy. ¹⁷Therefore he brought on them the king of the Chaldees, who slew their young men with the sword in the house of their sanctuary, and had no compassion on young man or maiden, old man, or him that stooped for age: he gave them all into his hand. ¹⁸And all the vessels of the house of God, great and small, and the treasures of the house of the LORD, and the treasures of the king, and of his princes; all these he brought to Babylon. ¹⁹And they burnt the house of God, and broke down the wall of Jerusalem, and burnt all the palaces thereof with fire, and destroyed all the goodly vessels thereof. ²⁰And them that had escaped from the sword carried he away to Babylon; where they were servants to him and his sons until the reign of the kingdom of Persia: ²¹To fulfill the word of the LORD by the mouth of Jeremiah, until the land had enjoyed her sabbaths: for as long as she lay desolate she kept sabbath, to fulfill three score and ten years. ²²Now in the first year of Cyrus king of Persia, that the word of the LORD spoken by the mouth of Jeremiah might be accomplished, the LORD stirred up the spirit of Cyrus king of Persia, that he made a proclamation throughout all his kingdom, and put it also in writing, saying, ²³Thus says Cyrus king of Persia, All the kingdoms of the earth has the LORD God of heaven given me; and he has charged me to build him an house in Jerusalem, which is in Judah. Who is there among you of all his people? The LORD his God be with him, and let him go up.

Ezra

1 ¹Now in the first year of Cyrus king of Persia, that the word of the LORD by the mouth of Jeremiah might be fulfilled, the LORD stirred up the spirit of Cyrus king of Persia, that he made a proclamation throughout all his kingdom, and put it also in writing, saying, ²Thus says Cyrus king of Persia, The LORD God of heaven has given me all the kingdoms of the earth; and he has charged me to build him an house at Jerusalem, which is in Judah. ³Who is there among you of all his people? his God be with him, and let him go up to Jerusalem, which is in Judah, and build the house of the LORD God of Israel, (he is the God,) which is in Jerusalem. ⁴And whoever remains in any place where he sojourns, let the men of his place help him with silver, and with gold, and with goods, and with beasts, beside the freewill offering for the house of God that is in Jerusalem. ⁵Then rose up the chief of the fathers of Judah and Benjamin, and the priests, and the Levites, with all them whose spirit God had raised, to go up to build the house of the LORD which is in Jerusalem. ⁶And all they that were about them strengthened their hands with vessels of silver, with gold, with goods, and with beasts, and with precious things, beside all that was willingly offered. ⁷Also Cyrus the king brought forth the vessels of the house of the LORD, which Nebuchadnezzar had brought forth out of Jerusalem, and had put them in the house of his gods; ⁸Even those did Cyrus king of Persia bring forth by the hand of Mithredath the treasurer, and numbered them to Sheshbazzar, the prince of Judah. ⁹And this is the number of them: thirty chargers of gold, a thousand chargers of silver, nine and twenty knives, ¹⁰Thirty basins of gold, silver basins of a second sort four hundred and ten, and other vessels a thousand. ¹¹All the vessels of gold and of silver were five thousand and four hundred. All these did Sheshbazzar bring up with them of the captivity that were brought up from Babylon to Jerusalem.

2 ¹Now these are the children of the province that went up out of the captivity, of those which had been carried away, whom Nebuchadnezzar the king of Babylon had carried away to Babylon, and came again to Jerusalem and Judah, every one to his city; ²Which came with Zerubbabel: Jeshua, Nehemiah, Seraiah, Reelaiah, Mordecai, Bilshan, Mizpar, Bigvai, Rehum, Baanah. The number of the men of the people of Israel: ³The children of Parosh, two thousand an hundred seventy and two. ⁴The children of Shephatiah, three hundred seventy and two. ⁵The children of Arah, seven hundred seventy and five. ⁶The children of Pahathmoab, of the children of Jeshua and Joab, two thousand eight hundred and twelve. ⁷The children of Elam, a thousand two hundred fifty and four. ⁸The children of Zattu, nine hundred forty and five. ⁹The children of Zaccai, seven hundred and three score. ¹⁰The children of Bani, six hundred forty and two. ¹¹The children of Bebai, six hundred twenty and three. ¹²The children of Azgad, a thousand two hundred twenty and two. ¹³The children of Adonikam, six hundred sixty and six. ¹⁴The children of Bigvai, two thousand fifty and six. ¹⁵The children of Adin, four hundred fifty and four. ¹⁶The children of Ater of Hezekiah, ninety and eight. ¹⁷The children of Bezai, three hundred twenty and three. ¹⁸The children of Jorah, an hundred and twelve. ¹⁹The children of Hashum, two hundred twenty and three. ²⁰The children of Gibbar, ninety and five. ²¹The children of Bethlehem, an hundred twenty and three. ²²The men of Netophah, fifty and six. ²³The men of Anathoth, an hundred twenty and eight. ²⁴The children of Azmaveth, forty and two. ²⁵The children of Kirjatharim, Chephirah, and Beeroth, seven hundred and forty and three. ²⁶The children of Ramah and Gaba, six hundred twenty and one. ²⁷The men of Michmas, an hundred twenty and two. ²⁸The men of Bethel and Ai, two hundred twenty and three. ²⁹The children of Nebo, fifty and two. ³⁰The children of Magbish, an hundred fifty and six. ³¹The children of the other Elam, a thousand two hundred fifty and four. ³²The children of Harim, three hundred and twenty. ³³The children of Lod, Hadid, and Ono, seven hundred twenty and five. ³⁴The children of Jericho, three hundred forty and five. ³⁵The children of Senaah, three thousand and six hundred and thirty. ³⁶The priests: the children of Jedaiah, of the house of Jeshua, nine hundred seventy and three. ³⁷The children of Immer, a thousand fifty and two. ³⁸The children of Pashur, a thousand two hundred forty and seven. ³⁹The children of Harim, a thousand and seventeen. ⁴⁰The Levites: the children of Jeshua and Kadmiel, of the children of Hodaviah, seventy and four. ⁴¹The singers: the children of Asaph, an hundred twenty and eight. ⁴²The children of the porters: the children of Shallum, the children of Ater, the children of Talmon, the children of Akkub, the children of Hatita, the children of Shobai, in all an hundred thirty and nine. ⁴³The Nethinims: the children of Ziha, the children of Hasupha, the children of Tabbaoth, ⁴⁴The children of Keros, the children of Siaha, the children of Padon, ⁴⁵The children of Lebanah, the children of Hagabah, the children of Akkub, ⁴⁶The children of Hagab, the children of Shalmai, the children of Hanan, ⁴⁷The children of Giddel, the children of Gahar, the children of Reaiah, ⁴⁸The children of Rezin, the children of Nekoda, the children of Gazzam, ⁴⁹The children of Uzza, the children of Paseah, the children of Besai, ⁵⁰The children of Asnah, the children of Mehunim, the children of Nephusim, ⁵¹The children of Bakbuk, the children of Hakupha, the children of Harhur, ⁵²The children of Bazluth, the children of Mehida, the children of Harsha, ⁵³The children of Barkos, the children of Sisera, the children of Thamah, ⁵⁴The children of Neziah, the children of Hatipha. ⁵⁵The children of Solomon's servants: the children of Sotai, the children of Sophereth, the children of Peruda, ⁵⁶The children of Jaalah, the children of Darkon, the children of Giddel, ⁵⁷The children of Shephatiah, the children of Hattil, the children of Pochereth of Zebaim, the children of Ami. ⁵⁸All the Nethinims, and the children of Solomon's servants, were three hundred ninety and two. ⁵⁹And these were they which went up from Telmelah, Telharsa, Cherub, Addan, and Immer: but they could not show their father's house, and their seed, whether they were of Israel: ⁶⁰The children of Delaiah, the children of Tobiah, the children of Nekoda, six hundred fifty and two. ⁶¹And of the children of the priests: the children of Habaiah, the children of Koz, the children of Barzillai; which took a wife of the daughters of Barzillai the Gileadite, and was called after their name: ⁶²These sought their register among those that were reckoned by genealogy, but they were not found: therefore were they, as polluted, put from the priesthood. ⁶³And the Tirshatha said to them, that they should not eat of the most holy things, till there stood up a priest with Urim and with Thummim. ⁶⁴The whole congregation together was forty and two thousand three hundred and three score, ⁶⁵Beside their servants and their maids, of whom there were seven thousand three hundred thirty and seven: and there were among them two hundred singing men and singing women. ⁶⁶Their horses were seven hundred thirty and six; their mules, two hundred forty and five; ⁶⁷Their camels, four hundred thirty and five; their asses, six thousand seven hundred and twenty. ⁶⁸And some of the chief of the fathers, when they came to the house of the LORD which is at Jerusalem, offered freely for the house of God to set it up in his place: ⁶⁹They gave after their ability to the treasure of the work three score and one thousand drams of gold, and five thousand pound of silver, and one hundred priests' garments. ⁷⁰So the priests, and the Levites, and some of the people, and the singers, and the porters, and the Nethinims, dwelled in their cities, and all Israel in their cities.

3 ¹And when the seventh month was come, and the children of Israel were in the cities, the people gathered themselves together as one man to Jerusalem. ²Then stood up Jeshua the son of Jozadak, and his brothers the priests, and Zerubbabel the son of Shealtiel, and his brothers, and built the altar of the God of Israel, to offer burnt offerings thereon, as it is written in the law of Moses the man of God. ³And they set the altar on his bases; for fear was on them because of the people of those countries: and they offered burnt offerings thereon to the LORD, even burnt offerings morning and evening. ⁴They kept also the feast of tabernacles, as it is written, and offered the daily burnt offerings by number, according to the custom, as the duty of every day required; ⁵And afterward offered the continual burnt offering, both of the new moons, and of all the set feasts of the LORD that were consecrated, and of every one that willingly offered a freewill offering to the LORD. ⁶From the first day of the seventh month began they to offer burnt offerings to the LORD. But the foundation of the temple of the LORD was not yet laid. ⁷They gave money also to the masons, and to the carpenters; and meat, and drink, and oil, to them of Zidon, and to them of Tyre, to bring cedar trees from Lebanon to the sea of Joppa, according to the grant that they had of Cyrus king of Persia. ⁸Now in the second year of their coming to the house of God at Jerusalem, in the second month, began Zerubbabel the son of Shealtiel, and Jeshua the son of Jozadak, and the remnant of their brothers the priests and the Levites, and all they that were come out of the captivity to Jerusalem; and appointed the Levites, from twenty years old and upward, to set forward the work of the house of the LORD. ⁹Then stood Jeshua with his sons and his brothers, Kadmiel and his sons, the sons of Judah, together, to set forward the workmen in the house of God: the sons of Henadad, with their sons and their brothers the Levites. ¹⁰And when the builders laid the foundation of the temple of the LORD, they set the priests in their apparel with trumpets, and the Levites the sons of Asaph with cymbals, to praise the LORD, after the ordinance of David king of Israel. ¹¹And they sang together by course in praising and giving thanks to the LORD; because he is good, for his mercy endures for ever toward Israel. And all the people shouted with a great shout, when they praised the LORD, because the foundation of the house of the LORD was laid. ¹²But many of the priests and Levites and chief of the fathers, who were ancient men, that had seen the first house, when the foundation of this house was laid before their eyes, wept with a loud voice; and many shouted aloud for joy: ¹³So that the people could not discern the noise of the shout of joy from the noise of the weeping of the people: for the people shouted with a loud shout, and the noise was heard afar off.

4 ¹Now when the adversaries of Judah and Benjamin heard that the children of the captivity built the temple to the LORD God of Israel; ²Then they came to Zerubbabel, and to the chief of the fathers, and said to them, Let us build with you: for we seek your God, as you do; and we do sacrifice to him since the days of Esarhaddon king of Assur, which brought us up here. ³But Zerubbabel, and Jeshua, and the rest of the chief of the fathers of Israel, said to them, You have nothing to do with us to build an house to our God; but we ourselves together will build to the LORD God of Israel, as king Cyrus the king of Persia has commanded us. ⁴Then the people of the land weakened the hands of the people of Judah, and troubled them in building, ⁵And hired counsellors against them, to frustrate their purpose, all the days of Cyrus king of Persia, even until the reign of Darius king of Persia. ⁶And in the reign of Ahasuerus, in the beginning of his reign, wrote they to him an accusation against the inhabitants of Judah and Jerusalem. ⁷And in the days of Artaxerxes wrote Bishlam, Mithredath, Tabeel, and the rest of their companions, to Artaxerxes king of Persia; and the writing of the letter was written in the Syrian tongue, and interpreted in the Syrian tongue. ⁸Rehum the chancellor and Shimshai the scribe wrote a letter against Jerusalem to Artaxerxes the king in this sort: ⁹Then wrote Rehum the chancellor, and Shimshai the scribe, and the rest of their companions; the Dinaites, the Apharsathchites, the Tarpelites, the Apharsites, the Archevites, the Babylonians, the Susanchites, the Dehavites, and the Elamites, ¹⁰And the rest of the nations whom the great and noble Asnapper brought over, and set in the cities of Samaria, and the rest that are on this side the river, and at such a time. ¹¹This is the copy of the letter that they sent to him, even to Artaxerxes the king; Your servants the men on this side the river, and at such a time. ¹²Be it known to the king, that the Jews which came up from you to us are come to Jerusalem, building the rebellious and the bad city, and have set up the walls thereof, and joined the foundations. ¹³Be it known now to the king, that, if this city be built, and the walls set up again, then will they not pay toll, tribute, and custom, and so you shall damage the revenue of the kings. ¹⁴Now because we have maintenance from the king's palace, and it was not meet for us to see the king's dishonor, therefore have we sent and certified the king; ¹⁵That search may be made in the book of the records of your fathers: so shall you find in the book of the records, and know that this city is a rebellious city, and hurtful to kings and provinces, and that they have moved sedition within the same of old time: for which cause was this city destroyed. ¹⁶We certify the king that, if this city be built again, and the walls thereof set up, by this means you shall have no portion on this side the river. ¹⁷Then sent the king an answer to Rehum the chancellor, and to Shimshai the scribe, and to the rest of their companions that dwell in Samaria, and to the rest beyond the river, Peace, and at such a time. ¹⁸The letter which you sent to us has been plainly read before me. ¹⁹And I commanded, and search has been made, and it is found that this city of old time has made insurrection against kings, and that rebellion and sedition have been made therein. ²⁰There have been mighty kings also over Jerusalem, which have ruled over all countries beyond the river; and toll, tribute, and custom, was paid to them. ²¹Give you now commandment to cause these men to cease, and that this city be not built, until another commandment shall be given from me. ²²Take heed now that you fail not to do this: why should damage grow to the hurt of the kings? ²³Now when the copy of king Artaxerxes' letter was read before Rehum, and Shimshai the scribe, and their companions, they went up in haste to Jerusalem to the Jews, and made them to cease by force and power. ²⁴Then ceased the work of the house of God which is at Jerusalem. So it ceased to the second year of the reign of Darius king of Persia.

5 ¹Then the prophets, Haggai the prophet, and Zechariah the son of Iddo, prophesied to the Jews that were in Judah and Jerusalem in the name of the God of Israel, even to them. ²Then rose up Zerubbabel the son of Shealtiel, and Jeshua the son of Jozadak, and began to build the house of God which is at Jerusalem: and with them were the prophets of God helping them. ³At the same time came to them Tatnai, governor on this side the river, and Shetharboznai and their companions, and said thus to them, Who has commanded you to build this house, and to make up this wall? ⁴Then said we to them after this manner, What are the names of the men that make this building? ⁵But the eye of their God was on the elders of the Jews, that they could not cause them to cease, till the matter came to Darius: and then they returned answer by letter concerning this matter. ⁶The copy of the letter that Tatnai, governor on this side the river, and Shetharboznai and his companions the Apharsachites, which were on this side the river, sent to Darius the king: ⁷They sent a letter to him, wherein was written thus; To Darius the king, all peace. ⁸Be it known to the king, that we went into the province of Judea, to the house of the great God, which is built with great stones, and timber is laid in the walls, and this work goes fast on, and prospers in their hands. ⁹Then asked we those elders, and said to them thus, Who commanded you to build this house, and to make up these walls? ¹⁰We asked their names also, to certify you, that we might write the names of the men that were the chief of them. ¹¹And thus they returned us answer, saying, We are the servants of the God of heaven and earth, and build the house that was built these many years ago, which a great king of Israel built and set up. ¹²But after that our fathers had provoked the God of heaven to wrath, he gave them into the hand of Nebuchadnezzar the king of Babylon, the Chaldean, who destroyed this house, and carried the people away into Babylon. ¹³But in the first year of Cyrus the king of Babylon the same king Cyrus made a decree to build this house of God. ¹⁴And the vessels also of gold and silver of the house of God, which Nebuchadnezzar took out of the temple that was in Jerusalem, and brought them into the temple of Babylon, those did Cyrus the king take out of the temple of Babylon, and they were delivered to one, whose name was Sheshbazzar, whom he had made governor; ¹⁵And said to him, Take these vessels, go, carry them into the temple that is in Jerusalem, and let the house of God be built in his place. ¹⁶Then came the same Sheshbazzar, and laid the foundation of the house of God which is in Jerusalem: and since that time even until now has it been in building, and yet it is not finished. ¹⁷Now therefore, if it seem good to the king, let there be search made in the king's treasure house, which is there at Babylon, whether it be so, that a decree was made of Cyrus the king to build this house of God at Jerusalem, and let the king send his pleasure to us concerning this matter.

6 ¹Then Darius the king made a decree, and search was made in the house of the rolls, where the treasures were laid up in Babylon. ²And there was found at Achmetha, in the palace that is in the province of the Medes, a roll, and therein was a record thus written: ³In the first year of Cyrus the king the same Cyrus the king made a decree concerning the house of God at Jerusalem, Let the house be built, the place where they offered sacrifices, and let the foundations thereof be strongly laid; the height thereof three score cubits, and the breadth thereof three score cubits; ⁴With three rows of great stones, and a row of new timber: and let the expenses be given out of the king's house: ⁵And also let the golden and silver vessels of the house of God, which Nebuchadnezzar took forth out of the temple which is at Jerusalem, and brought to Babylon, be restored, and brought again to the temple which is at Jerusalem, every one to his place, and place them in the house of God. ⁶Now therefore, Tatnai, governor beyond the river, Shetharboznai, and your companions the Apharsachites, which are beyond the river, be you far from there: ⁷Let the work of this house of God alone; let the governor of the Jews and the elders of the Jews build this house of God in his place. ⁸Moreover I make a decree what you shall do to the elders of these Jews for the building of this house of God: that of the king's goods, even of the tribute beyond the river, immediately expenses be given to these men, that they be not hindered. ⁹And that which they have need of, both young bullocks, and rams, and lambs, for the burnt offerings of the God of heaven, wheat, salt, wine, and oil, according to the appointment of the priests which are at Jerusalem, let it be given them day by day without fail: ¹⁰That they may offer sacrifices of sweet smells to the God of heaven, and pray for the life of the king, and of his sons. ¹¹Also I have made a decree, that whoever shall alter this word, let timber be pulled down from his house, and being set up, let him be hanged thereon; and let his house be made a dunghill for this. ¹²And the God that has caused his name to dwell there destroy all kings and people, that shall put to their hand to alter and to destroy this house of God which is at Jerusalem. I Darius have made a decree; let it be done with speed. ¹³Then Tatnai, governor on this side the river, Shetharboznai, and their companions, according to that which Darius the king had sent, so they did speedily. ¹⁴And the elders of the Jews built, and they prospered through the prophesying of Haggai the prophet and Zechariah the son of Iddo. And they built, and finished it, according to the commandment of the God of Israel, and according to the commandment of Cyrus, and Darius, and Artaxerxes king of Persia. ¹⁵And this house was finished on the third day of the month Adar, which was in the sixth year of the reign of Darius the king. ¹⁶And the children of Israel, the priests, and the Levites, and the rest of the children of the captivity, kept the dedication of this house of God with joy. ¹⁷And offered at the dedication of this house of God an hundred bullocks, two hundred rams, four hundred lambs; and for a sin offering for all Israel, twelve he goats, according to the number of the tribes of Israel. ¹⁸And they set the priests in their divisions, and the Levites in their courses, for the service of God, which is at Jerusalem; as it is written in the book of Moses. ¹⁹And the children of the captivity kept the passover on the fourteenth day of the first month. ²⁰For the priests and the Levites were purified together, all of them were pure, and killed the passover for all the children of the captivity, and for their brothers the priests, and for themselves. ²¹And the children of Israel, which were come again out of captivity, and all such as had separated themselves to them from the filthiness of the heathen of the land, to seek the LORD God of Israel, did eat, ²²And kept the feast of unleavened bread seven days with joy: for the LORD had made them joyful, and turned the heart of the king of Assyria to them, to strengthen their hands in the work of the house of God, the God of Israel.

7 ¹Now after these things, in the reign of Artaxerxes king of Persia, Ezra the son of Seraiah, the son of Azariah, the son of Hilkiah, ²The son of Shallum, the son of Zadok, the son of Ahitub, ³The son of Amariah, the son of Azariah, the son of Meraioth, ⁴The son of Zerahiah, the son of Uzzi, the son of Bukki, ⁵The son of Abishua, the son of Phinehas, the son of Eleazar, the son of Aaron the chief priest: ⁶This Ezra went up from Babylon; and he was a ready scribe in the law of Moses, which the LORD God of Israel had given: and the king granted him all his request, according to the hand of the LORD his God on him. ⁷And there went up some of the children of Israel, and of the priests, and the Levites, and the singers, and the porters, and the Nethinims, to Jerusalem, in the seventh year of Artaxerxes the king. ⁸And he came to Jerusalem in the fifth month, which was in the seventh year of the king. ⁹For on the first day of the first month began he to go up from Babylon, and on the first day of the fifth month came he to Jerusalem, according to the good hand of his God on him. ¹⁰For Ezra had prepared his heart to seek the law of the LORD, and to do it, and to teach in Israel statutes and judgments. ¹¹Now this is the copy of the letter that the king Artaxerxes gave to Ezra the priest, the scribe, even a scribe of the words of the commandments of the LORD, and of his statutes to Israel. ¹²Artaxerxes, king of kings, to Ezra the priest, a scribe of the law of the God of heaven, perfect peace, and at such a time. ¹³I make a decree, that all they of the people of Israel, and of his priests and Levites, in my realm, which are minded of their own freewill to go up to Jerusalem, go with you. ¹⁴For as much as you are sent of the king, and of his seven counsellors, to inquire concerning Judah and Jerusalem, according to the law of your God which is in your hand; ¹⁵And to carry the silver and gold, which the king and his counsellors have freely offered to the God of Israel, whose habitation is in Jerusalem, ¹⁶And all the silver and gold that you can find in all the province of Babylon, with the freewill offering of the people, and of the priests, offering willingly for the house of their God which is in Jerusalem: ¹⁷That you may buy speedily with this money bullocks, rams, lambs, with their meat offerings and their drink offerings, and offer them on the altar of the house of your God which is in Jerusalem. ¹⁸And whatever shall seem good to you, and to your brothers, to do with the rest of the silver and the gold, that do after the will of your God. ¹⁹The vessels also that are given you for the service of the house of your God, those deliver you before the God of Jerusalem. ²⁰And whatever more shall be needful for the house of your God, which you shall have occasion to bestow, bestow it out of the king's treasure house. ²¹And I, even I Artaxerxes the king, do make a decree to all the treasurers which are beyond the river, that whatever Ezra the priest, the scribe of the law of the God of heaven, shall require of you, it be done speedily, ²²To an hundred talents of silver, and to an hundred measures of wheat, and to an hundred baths of wine, and to an hundred baths of oil, and salt without prescribing how much. ²³Whatever is commanded by the God of heaven, let it be diligently done for the house of the God of heaven: for why should there be wrath against the realm of the king and his sons? ²⁴Also we certify you, that touching any of the priests and Levites, singers, porters, Nethinims, or ministers of this house of God, it shall not be lawful to impose toll, tribute, or custom, on them. ²⁵And you, Ezra, after the wisdom of your God, that is in your hand, set magistrates and judges, which may judge all the people that are beyond the river, all such as know the laws of your God; and teach you them that know them not. ²⁶And whoever will not do the law of your God, and the law of the king, let judgment be executed speedily on him, whether it be to death, or to banishment, or to confiscation of goods, or to imprisonment. ²⁷Blessed be the LORD God of our fathers, which has put such a thing as this in the king's heart, to beautify the house of the LORD which is in Jerusalem: ²⁸And has extended mercy to me before the king, and his counsellors, and before all the king's mighty princes. And I was strengthened as the hand of the LORD my God was on me, and I gathered together out of Israel chief men to go up with me.

8 ¹These are now the chief of their fathers, and this is the genealogy of them that went up with me from Babylon, in the reign of Artaxerxes the king. ²Of the sons of Phinehas; Gershom: of the sons of Ithamar; Daniel: of the sons of David; Hattush. ³Of the sons of Shechaniah, of the sons of Pharosh; Zechariah: and with him were reckoned by genealogy of the males an hundred and fifty. ⁴Of the sons of Pahathmoab; Elihoenai the son of Zerahiah, and with him two hundred males. ⁵Of the sons of Shechaniah; the son of Jahaziel, and with him three hundred males. ⁶Of the sons also of Adin; Ebed the son of Jonathan, and with him fifty males. ⁷And of the sons of Elam; Jeshaiah the son of Athaliah, and with him seventy males. ⁸And of the sons of Shephatiah; Zebadiah the son of Michael, and with him fourscore males. ⁹Of the sons of Joab; Obadiah the son of Jehiel, and with him two hundred and eighteen males. ¹⁰And of the sons of Shelomith; the son of Josiphiah, and with him an hundred and three score males. ¹¹And of the sons of

Bebai; Zechariah the son of Bebai, and with him twenty and eight males. ¹²And of the sons of Azgad; Johanan the son of Hakkatan, and with him an hundred and ten males. ¹³And of the last sons of Adonikam, whose names are these, Eliphelet, Jeiel, and Shemaiah, and with them three score males. ¹⁴Of the sons also of Bigvai; Uthai, and Zabbud, and with them seventy males. ¹⁵And I gathered them together to the river that runs to Ahava; and there stayed we in tents three days: and I viewed the people, and the priests, and found there none of the sons of Levi. ¹⁶Then sent I for Eliezer, for Ariel, for Shemaiah, and for Elnathan, and for Jarib, and for Elnathan, and for Nathan, and for Zechariah, and for Meshullam, chief men; also for Joiarib, and for Elnathan, men of understanding. ¹⁷And I sent them with commandment to Iddo the chief at the place Casiphia, and I told them what they should say to Iddo, and to his brothers the Nethinims, at the place Casiphia, that they should bring to us ministers for the house of our God. ¹⁸And by the good hand of our God on us they brought us a man of understanding, of the sons of Mahli, the son of Levi, the son of Israel; and Sherebiah, with his sons and his brothers, eighteen; ¹⁹And Hashabiah, and with him Jeshaiah of the sons of Merari, his brothers and their sons, twenty; ²⁰Also of the Nethinims, whom David and the princes had appointed for the service of the Levites, two hundred and twenty Nethinims: all of them were expressed by name. ²¹Then I proclaimed a fast there, at the river of Ahava, that we might afflict ourselves before our God, to seek of him a right way for us, and for our little ones, and for all our substance. ²²For I was ashamed to require of the king a band of soldiers and horsemen to help us against the enemy in the way: because we had spoken to the king, saying, The hand of our God is on all them for good that seek him; but his power and his wrath is against all them that forsake him. ²³So we fasted and sought our God for this: and he was entreated of us. ²⁴Then I separated twelve of the chief of the priests, Sherebiah, Hashabiah, and ten of their brothers with them, ²⁵And weighed to them the silver, and the gold, and the vessels, even the offering of the house of our God, which the king, and his counsellors, and his lords, and all Israel there present, had offered: ²⁶I even weighed to their hand six hundred and fifty talents of silver, and silver vessels an hundred talents, and of gold an hundred talents; ²⁷Also twenty basins of gold, of a thousand drams; and two vessels of fine copper, precious as gold. ²⁸And I said to them, You are holy to the LORD; the vessels are holy also; and the silver and the gold are a freewill offering to the LORD God of your fathers. ²⁹Watch you, and keep them, until you weigh them before the chief of the priests and the Levites, and chief of the fathers of Israel, at Jerusalem, in the chambers of the house of the LORD. ³⁰So took the priests and the Levites the weight of the silver, and the gold, and the vessels, to bring them to Jerusalem to the house of our God. ³¹Then we departed from the river of Ahava on the twelfth day of the first month, to go to Jerusalem: and the hand of our God was on us, and he delivered us from the hand of the enemy, and of such as lay in wait by the way. ³²And we came to Jerusalem, and stayed there three days. ³³Now on the fourth day was the silver and the gold and the vessels weighed in the house of our God by the hand of Meremoth the son of Uriah the priest; and with him was Eleazar the son of Phinehas; and with them was Jozabad the son of Jeshua, and Noadiah the son of Binnui, Levites; ³⁴By number and by weight of every one: and all the weight was written at that time. ³⁵Also the children of those that had been carried away, which were come out of the captivity, offered burnt offerings to the God of Israel, twelve bullocks for all Israel, ninety and six rams, seventy and seven lambs, twelve he goats for a sin offering: all this was a burnt offering to the LORD. ³⁶And they delivered the king's commissions to the king's lieutenants, and to the governors on this side the river: and they furthered the people, and the house of God.

9

¹Now when these things were done, the princes came to me, saying, The people of Israel, and the priests, and the Levites, have not separated themselves from the people of the lands, doing according to their abominations, even of the Canaanites, the Hittites, the Perizzites, the Jebusites, the Ammonites, the Moabites, the Egyptians, and the Amorites. ²For they have taken of their daughters for themselves, and for their sons: so that the holy seed have mingled themselves with the people of those lands: yes, the hand of the princes and rulers has been chief in this trespass. ³And when I heard this thing, I rent my garment and my mantle, and plucked off the hair of my head and of my beard, and sat down astonished. ⁴Then were assembled to me every one that trembled at the words of the God of Israel, because of the transgression of those that had been carried away; and I sat astonished until the evening sacrifice. ⁵And at the evening sacrifice I arose up from my heaviness; and having rent my garment and my mantle, I fell on my knees, and spread out my hands to the LORD my God, ⁶And said, O my God, I am ashamed and blush to lift up my face to you, my God: for our iniquities are increased over our head, and our trespass is grown up to the heavens. ⁷Since the days of our fathers have we been in a great trespass to this day; and for our iniquities have we, our kings, and our priests, been delivered into the hand of the kings of the lands, to the sword, to captivity, and to a spoil, and to confusion of face, as it is this day. ⁸And now for a little space grace has been showed from the LORD our God, to leave us a remnant to escape, and to give us a nail in his holy place, that our God may lighten our eyes, and give us a little reviving in our bondage. ⁹For we were slaves; yet our God has not forsaken us in our bondage, but has extended mercy to us in the sight of the kings of Persia, to give us a reviving, to set up the house of our God, and to repair the desolations thereof, and to give us a wall in Judah and in Jerusalem. ¹⁰And now, O our God, what shall we say after this? for we have forsaken your commandments, ¹¹Which you have commanded by your servants the prophets, saying, The land, to which you go to possess it, is an unclean land with the filthiness of the people of the lands, with their abominations, which have filled it from one end to another with their uncleanness. ¹²Now therefore give not your daughters to their sons, neither take their daughters to your sons, nor seek their peace or their wealth for ever: that you may be strong, and eat the good of the land, and leave it for an inheritance to your children for ever. ¹³And after all that is come on us for our evil deeds, and for our great trespass, seeing that you our God have punished us less than our iniquities deserve, and have given

us such deliverance as this; ¹⁴Should we again break your commandments, and join in affinity with the people of these abominations? would not you be angry with us till you had consumed us, so that there should be no remnant nor escaping? ¹⁵O LORD God of Israel, you are righteous: for we remain yet escaped, as it is this day: behold, we are before you in our trespasses: for we cannot stand before you because of this.

10

¹Now when Ezra had prayed, and when he had confessed, weeping and casting himself down before the house of God, there assembled to him out of Israel a very great congregation of men and women and children: for the people wept very sore. ²And Shechaniah the son of Jehiel, one of the sons of Elam, answered and said to Ezra, We have trespassed against our God, and have taken strange wives of the people of the land: yet now there is hope in Israel concerning this thing. ³Now therefore let us make a covenant with our God to put away all the wives, and such as are born of them, according to the counsel of my lord, and of those that tremble at the commandment of our God; and let it be done according to the law. ⁴Arise; for this matter belongs to you: we also will be with you: be of good courage, and do it. ⁵Then arose Ezra, and made the chief priests, the Levites, and all Israel, to swear that they should do according to this word. And they swore. ⁶Then Ezra rose up from before the house of God, and went into the chamber of Johanan the son of Eliashib: and when he came thither, he did eat no bread, nor drink water: for he mourned because of the transgression of them that had been carried away. ⁷And they made proclamation throughout Judah and Jerusalem to all the children of the captivity, that they should gather themselves together to Jerusalem; ⁸And that whoever would not come within three days, according to the counsel of the princes and the elders, all his substance should be forfeited, and himself separated from the congregation of those that had been carried away. ⁹Then all the men of Judah and Benjamin gathered themselves together to Jerusalem within three days. It was the ninth month, on the twentieth day of the month; and all the people sat in the street of the house of God, trembling because of this matter, and for the great rain. ¹⁰And Ezra the priest stood up, and said to them, You have transgressed, and have taken strange wives, to increase the trespass of Israel. ¹¹Now therefore make confession to the LORD God of your fathers, and do his pleasure: and separate yourselves from the people of the land, and from the strange wives. ¹²Then all the congregation answered and said with a loud voice, As you have said, so must we do. ¹³But the people are many, and it is a time of much rain, and we are not able to stand without, neither is this a work of one day or two: for we are many that have transgressed in this thing. ¹⁴Let now our rulers of all the congregation stand, and let all them which have taken strange wives in our cities come at appointed times, and with them the elders of every city, and the judges thereof, until the fierce wrath of our God for this matter be turned from us. ¹⁵Only Jonathan the son of Asahel and Jahaziah the son of Tikvah were employed about this matter: and Meshullam and Shabbethai the Levite helped them. ¹⁶And the children of the captivity did so. And Ezra the priest, with certain chief of the fathers, after the house of their fathers, and all of them by their names, were separated, and sat down in the first day of the tenth month to examine the matter. ¹⁷And they made an end with all the men that had taken strange wives by the first day of the first month. ¹⁸And among the sons of the priests there were found that had taken strange wives: namely, of the sons of Jeshua the son of Jozadak, and his brothers; Maaseiah, and Eliezer, and Jarib, and Gedaliah. ¹⁹And they gave their hands that they would put away their wives; and being guilty, they offered a ram of the flock for their trespass. ²⁰And of the sons of Immer; Hanani, and Zebadiah. ²¹And of the sons of Harim; Maaseiah, and Elijah, and Shemaiah, and Jehiel, and Uzziah. ²²And of the sons of Pashur; Elioenai, Maaseiah, Ishmael, Nethaneel, Jozabad, and Elasah. ²³Also of the Levites; Jozabad, and Shimei, and Kelaiah, (the same is Kelita,) Pethahiah, Judah, and Eliezer. ²⁴Of the singers also; Eliashib: and of the porters; Shallum, and Telem, and Uri. ²⁵Moreover of Israel: of the sons of Parosh; Ramiah, and Jeziah, and Malchiah, and Miamin, and Eleazar, and Malchijah, and Benaiah. ²⁶And of the sons of Elam; Mattaniah, Zechariah, and Jehiel, and Abdi, and Jeremoth, and Eliah. ²⁷And of the sons of Zattu; Elioenai, Eliashib, Mattaniah, and Jeremoth, and Zabad, and Aziza. ²⁸Of the sons also of Bebai; Jehohanan, Hananiah, Zabbai, and Athlai. ²⁹And of the sons of Bani; Meshullam, Malluch, and Adaiah, Jashub, and Sheal, and Ramoth. ³⁰And of the sons of Pahathmoab; Adna, and Chelal, Benaiah, Maaseiah, Mattaniah, Bezaleel, and Binnui, and Manasseh. ³¹And of the sons of Harim; Eliezer, Ishijah, Malchiah, Shemaiah, Shimeon, ³²Benjamin, Malluch, and Shemariah. ³³Of the sons of Hashum; Mattenai, Mattathah, Zabad, Eliphelet, Jeremai, Manasseh, and Shimei. ³⁴Of the sons of Bani; Maadai, Amram, and Uel, ³⁵Benaiah, Bedeiah, Chelluh, ³⁶Vaniah, Meremoth, Eliashib, ³⁷Mattaniah, Mattenai, and Jaasau, ³⁸And Bani, and Binnui, Shimei, ³⁹And Shelemiah, and Nathan, and Adaiah, ⁴⁰Machnadebai, Shashai, Sharai, ⁴¹Azareel, and Shelemiah, Shemariah, ⁴²Shallum, Amariah, and Joseph. ⁴³Of the sons of Nebo; Jeiel, Mattithiah, Zabad, Zebina, Jadau, and Joel, Benaiah. ⁴⁴All these had taken strange wives: and some of them had wives by whom they had children.

Nehemiah

1 ¹The words of Nehemiah the son of Hachaliah. And it came to pass in the month Chisleu, in the twentieth year, as I was in Shushan the palace, ²That Hanani, one of my brothers, came, he and certain men of Judah; and I asked them concerning the Jews that had escaped, which were left of the captivity, and concerning Jerusalem. ³And they said to me, The remnant that are left of the captivity there in the province are in great affliction and reproach: the wall of Jerusalem also is broken down, and the gates thereof are burned with fire. ⁴And it came to pass, when I heard these words, that I sat down and wept, and mourned certain days, and fasted, and prayed before the God of heaven, ⁵And said, I beseech you, O LORD God of heaven, the great and terrible God, that keeps covenant and mercy for them that love him and observe his commandments: ⁶Let your ear now be attentive, and your eyes open, that you may hear the prayer of your servant, which I pray before you now, day and night, for the children of Israel your servants, and confess the sins of the children of Israel, which we have sinned against you: both I and my father's house have sinned. ⁷We have dealt very corruptly against you, and have not kept the commandments, nor the statutes, nor the judgments, which you commanded your servant Moses. ⁸Remember, I beseech you, the word that you commanded your servant Moses, saying, If you transgress, I will scatter you abroad among the nations: ⁹But if you turn to me, and keep my commandments, and do them; though there were of you cast out to the uttermost part of the heaven, yet will I gather them from there, and will bring them to the place that I have chosen to set my name there. ¹⁰Now these are your servants and your people, whom you have redeemed by your great power, and by your strong hand. ¹¹O LORD, I beseech you, let now your ear be attentive to the prayer of your servant, and to the prayer of your servants, who desire to fear your name: and prosper, I pray you, your servant this day, and grant him mercy in the sight of this man. For I was the king's cupbearer.

2 ¹And it came to pass in the month Nisan, in the twentieth year of Artaxerxes the king, that wine was before him: and I took up the wine, and gave it to the king. Now I had not been beforetime sad in his presence. ²Why the king said to me, Why is your countenance sad, seeing you are not sick? this is nothing else but sorrow of heart. Then I was very sore afraid, ³And said to the king, Let the king live for ever: why should not my countenance be sad, when the city, the place of my fathers' sepulchers, lies waste, and the gates thereof are consumed with fire? ⁴Then the king said to me, For what do you make request? So I prayed to the God of heaven. ⁵And I said to the king, If it please the king, and if your servant have found favor in your sight, that you would send me to Judah, to the city of my fathers' sepulchers, that I may build it. ⁶And the king said to me, (the queen also sitting by him,) For how long shall your journey be? and when will you return? So it pleased the king to send me; and I set him a time. ⁷Moreover I said to the king, If it please the king, let letters be given me to the governors beyond the river, that they may convey me over till I come into Judah; ⁸And a letter to Asaph the keeper of the king's forest, that he may give me timber to make beams for the gates of the palace which appertained to the house, and for the wall of the city, and for the house that I shall enter into. And the king granted me, according to the good hand of my God on me. ⁹Then I came to the governors beyond the river, and gave them the king's letters. Now the king had sent captains of the army and horsemen with me. ¹⁰When Sanballat the Horonite, and Tobiah the servant, the Ammonite, heard of it, it grieved them exceedingly that there was come a man to seek the welfare of the children of Israel. ¹¹So I came to Jerusalem, and was there three days. ¹²And I arose in the night, I and some few men with me; neither told I any man what my God had put in my heart to do at Jerusalem: neither was there any beast with me, save the beast that I rode on. ¹³And I went out by night by the gate of the valley, even before the dragon well, and to the dung port, and viewed the walls of Jerusalem, which were broken down, and the gates thereof were consumed with fire. ¹⁴Then I went on to the gate of the fountain, and to the king's pool: but there was no place for the beast that was under me to pass. ¹⁵Then went I up in the night by the brook, and viewed the wall, and turned back, and entered by the gate of the valley, and so returned. ¹⁶And the rulers knew not where I went, or what I did; neither had I as yet told it to the Jews, nor to the priests, nor to the nobles, nor to the rulers, nor to the rest that did the work. ¹⁷Then said I to them, You see the distress that we are in, how Jerusalem lies waste, and the gates thereof are burned with fire: come, and let us build up the wall of Jerusalem, that we be no more a reproach. ¹⁸Then I told them of the hand of my God which was good on me; as also the king's words that he had spoken to me. And they said, Let us rise up and build. So they strengthened their hands for this good work. ¹⁹But when Sanballat the Horonite, and Tobiah the servant, the Ammonite, and Geshem the Arabian, heard it, they laughed us to scorn, and despised us, and said, What is this thing that you do? will you rebel against the king? ²⁰Then answered I them, and said to them, The God of heaven, he will prosper us; therefore we his servants will arise and build: but you have no portion, nor right, nor memorial, in Jerusalem.

3 ¹Then Eliashib the high priest rose up with his brothers the priests, and they built the sheep gate; they sanctified it, and set up the doors of it; even to the tower of Meah they sanctified it, to the tower of Hananeel. ²And next to him built the men of Jericho. And next to them built Zaccur the son of Imri. ³But the fish gate did the sons of Hassenaah build, who also laid the beams thereof, and set up the doors thereof, the locks thereof, and the bars thereof. ⁴And next to them repaired Meremoth the son of Urijah, the son of Koz. And next to them repaired Meshullam the son of Berechiah, the son of Meshezabeel. And next to them repaired Zadok the son of Baana. ⁵And next to them the Tekoites repaired; but their nobles put not their necks to the work of their LORD. ⁶Moreover the old gate repaired Jehoiada the son of Paseah, and Meshullam the son of Besodeiah; they laid the beams thereof, and set up the doors thereof, and the locks thereof, and the bars thereof. ⁷And next to them repaired Melatiah the Gibeonite, and Jadon the Meronothite, the men of Gibeon, and of Mizpah, to the throne of the governor on this side the river. ⁸Next to him repaired Uzziel the son of Harhaiah, of the goldsmiths. Next to him also repaired Hananiah the son of one of the apothecaries, and they fortified Jerusalem to the broad wall. ⁹And next to them repaired Rephaiah the son of Hur, the ruler of the half part of Jerusalem. ¹⁰And next to them repaired Jedaiah the son of Harumaph, even over against his house. And next to him repaired Hattush the son of Hashabniah. ¹¹Malchijah the son of Harim, and Hashub the son of Pahathmoab, repaired the other piece, and the tower of the furnaces. ¹²And next to him repaired Shallum the son of Halohesh, the ruler of the half part of Jerusalem, he and his daughters. ¹³The valley gate repaired Hanun, and the inhabitants of Zanoah; they built it, and set up the doors thereof, the locks thereof, and the bars thereof, and a thousand cubits on the wall to the dung gate. ¹⁴But the dung gate repaired Malchiah the son of Rechab, the ruler of part of Bethhaccerem; he built it, and set up the doors thereof, the locks thereof, and the bars thereof. ¹⁵But the gate of the fountain repaired Shallun the son of Colhozeh, the ruler of part of Mizpah; he built it, and covered it, and set up the doors thereof, the locks thereof, and the bars thereof, and the wall of the pool of Siloah by the king's garden, and to the stairs that go down from the city of David. ¹⁶After him repaired Nehemiah the son of Azbuk, the ruler of the half part of Bethzur, to the place over against the sepulchers of David, and to the pool that was made, and to the house of the mighty. ¹⁷After him repaired the Levites, Rehum the son of Bani. Next to him repaired Hashabiah, the ruler of the half part of Keilah, in his part. ¹⁸After him repaired their brothers, Bavai the son of Henadad, the ruler of the half part of Keilah. ¹⁹And next to him repaired Ezer the son of Jeshua, the ruler of Mizpah, another piece over against the going up to the armory at the turning of the wall. ²⁰After him Baruch the son of Zabbai earnestly repaired the other piece, from the turning of the wall to the door of the house of Eliashib the high priest. ²¹After him repaired Meremoth the son of Urijah the son of Koz another piece, from the door of the house of Eliashib even to the end of the house of Eliashib. ²²And after him repaired the priests, the men of the plain. ²³After him repaired Benjamin and Hashub over against their house. After him repaired Azariah the son of Maaseiah the son of Ananiah by his house. ²⁴After him repaired Binnui the son of Henadad another piece, from the house of Azariah to the turning of the wall, even to the corner. ²⁵Palal the son of Uzai, over against the turning of the wall, and the tower which lies out from the king's high house, that was by the court of the prison. After him Pedaiah the son of Parosh. ²⁶Moreover the Nethinims dwelled in Ophel, to the place over against the water gate toward the east, and the tower that lies out. ²⁷After them the Tekoites repaired another piece, over against the great tower that lies out, even to the wall of Ophel. ²⁸From above the horse gate repaired the priests, every one over against his house. ²⁹After them repaired Zadok the son of Immer over against his house. After him repaired also Shemaiah the son of Shechaniah, the keeper of the east gate. ³⁰After him repaired Hananiah the son of Shelemiah, and Hanun the sixth son of Zalaph, another piece. After him repaired Meshullam the son of Berechiah over against his chamber. ³¹After him repaired Malchiah the goldsmith's son to the place of the Nethinims, and of the merchants, over against the gate Miphkad, and to the going up of the corner. ³²And between the going up of the corner to the sheep gate repaired the goldsmiths and the merchants.

4 ¹But it came to pass, that when Sanballat heard that we built the wall, he was wroth, and took great indignation, and mocked the Jews. ²And he spoke before his brothers and the army of Samaria, and said, What do these feeble Jews? will they fortify themselves? will they sacrifice? will they make an end in a day? will they revive the stones out of the heaps of the rubbish which are burned? ³Now Tobiah the Ammonite was by him, and he said, Even that which they build, if a fox go up, he shall even break down their stone wall. ⁴Hear, O our God; for we are despised: and turn their reproach on their own head, and give them for a prey in the land of captivity: ⁵And cover not their iniquity, and let not their sin be blotted out from before you: for they have provoked you to anger before the builders. ⁶So built we the wall; and all the wall was joined together to the half thereof: for the people had a mind to work. ⁷But it came to pass, that when Sanballat, and Tobiah, and the Arabians, and the Ammonites, and the Ashdodites, heard that the walls of Jerusalem were made up, and that the breaches began to be stopped, then they were very wroth, ⁸And conspired all of them together to come and to fight against Jerusalem, and to hinder it. ⁹Nevertheless we made our prayer to our God, and set a watch against them day and night, because of them. ¹⁰And Judah said, The strength of the bearers of burdens is decayed, and there is much rubbish; so that we are not able to build the wall. ¹¹And our adversaries said, They shall not know, neither see, till we come in the middle among them, and slay them, and cause the work to cease. ¹²And it came to pass, that when the Jews which dwelled by them came, they said to us ten times, From all places from where you shall return to us they will be on you. ¹³Therefore set I in the lower places behind the wall, and on the higher places, I even set the people after their families with their swords, their spears, and their bows. ¹⁴And I looked, and rose up, and said to the nobles, and to the rulers, and to the rest of the people, Be not you afraid of them: remember the LORD, which is great and terrible, and fight for your brothers, your sons, and your daughters, your wives, and your houses. ¹⁵And it came to pass, when our enemies heard that it was known to us, and God had brought their counsel to nothing, that we returned all of us to the wall, every one to his work. ¹⁶And it came to pass from that time forth, that the half of my servants worked in the work, and the other half of them held both the spears, the shields, and the bows, and the habergeons; and the rulers were behind all the house of Judah. ¹⁷They which built on the wall, and they that bore burdens, with those that laded, every one with one of his hands worked in the work, and with the other hand held a weapon. ¹⁸For the builders, every one had his sword girded by his side, and so built. And he that sounded the trumpet was by me. ¹⁹And I said to the nobles, and to the rulers, and to the rest of the people, The work is great and large, and we are separated on the wall, one far from another. ²⁰In what place therefore you hear the sound of the trumpet, resort you thither to us: our God

shall fight for us. ²¹So we labored in the work: and half of them held the spears from the rising of the morning till the stars appeared. ²²Likewise at the same time said I to the people, Let every one with his servant lodge within Jerusalem, that in the night they may be a guard to us, and labor on the day. ²³So neither I, nor my brothers, nor my servants, nor the men of the guard which followed me, none of us put off our clothes, saving that every one put them off for washing.

5 ¹And there was a great cry of the people and of their wives against their brothers the Jews. ²For there were that said, We, our sons, and our daughters, are many: therefore we take up corn for them, that we may eat, and live. ³Some also there were that said, We have mortgaged our lands, vineyards, and houses, that we might buy corn, because of the dearth. ⁴There were also that said, We have borrowed money for the king's tribute, and that on our lands and vineyards. ⁵Yet now our flesh is as the flesh of our brothers, our children as their children: and, see, we bring into bondage our sons and our daughters to be servants, and some of our daughters are brought to bondage already: neither is it in our power to redeem them; for other men have our lands and vineyards. ⁶And I was very angry when I heard their cry and these words. ⁷Then I consulted with myself, and I rebuked the nobles, and the rulers, and said to them, You exact usury, every one of his brother. And I set a great assembly against them. ⁸And I said to them, We after our ability have redeemed our brothers the Jews, which were sold to the heathen; and will you even sell your brothers? or shall they be sold to us? Then held they their peace, and found nothing to answer. ⁹Also I said, It is not good that you do: should you not to walk in the fear of our God because of the reproach of the heathen our enemies? ¹⁰I likewise, and my brothers, and my servants, might exact of them money and corn: I pray you, let us leave off this usury. ¹¹Restore, I pray you, to them, even this day, their lands, their vineyards, their olive groves, and their houses, also the hundredth part of the money, and of the corn, the wine, and the oil, that you exact of them. ¹²Then said they, We will restore them, and will require nothing of them; so will we do as you say. Then I called the priests, and took an oath of them, that they should do according to this promise. ¹³Also I shook my lap, and said, So God shake out every man from his house, and from his labor, that performs not this promise, even thus be he shaken out, and emptied. And all the congregation said, Amen, and praised the LORD. And the people did according to this promise. ¹⁴Moreover from the time that I was appointed to be their governor in the land of Judah, from the twentieth year even to the two and thirtieth year of Artaxerxes the king, that is, twelve years, I and my brothers have not eaten the bread of the governor. ¹⁵But the former governors that had been before me were chargeable to the people, and had taken of them bread and wine, beside forty shekels of silver; yes, even their servants bore rule over the people: but so did not I, because of the fear of God. ¹⁶Yes, also I continued in the work of this wall, neither bought we any land: and all my servants were gathered thither to the work. ¹⁷Moreover there were at my table an hundred and fifty of the Jews and rulers, beside those that came to us from among the heathen that are about us. ¹⁸Now that which was prepared for me daily was one ox and six choice sheep; also fowls were prepared for me, and once in ten days store of all sorts of wine: yet for all this required not I the bread of the governor, because the bondage was heavy on this people. ¹⁹Think on me, my God, for good, according to all that I have done for this people.

6 ¹Now it came to pass when Sanballat, and Tobiah, and Geshem the Arabian, and the rest of our enemies, heard that I had built the wall, and that there was no breach left therein; (though at that time I had not set up the doors on the gates;) ²That Sanballat and Geshem sent to me, saying, Come, let us meet together in some one of the villages in the plain of Ono. But they thought to do me mischief. ³And I sent messengers to them, saying, I am doing a great work, so that I cannot come down: why should the work cease, whilst I leave it, and come down to you? ⁴Yet they sent to me four times after this sort; and I answered them after the same manner. ⁵Then sent Sanballat his servant to me in like manner the fifth time with an open letter in his hand; ⁶Wherein was written, It is reported among the heathen, and Gashmu says it, that you and the Jews think to rebel: for which cause you build the wall, that you may be their king, according to these words. ⁷And you have also appointed prophets to preach of you at Jerusalem, saying, There is a king in Judah: and now shall it be reported to the king according to these words. Come now therefore, and let us take counsel together. ⁸Then I sent to him, saying, There are no such things done as you say, but you feign them out of your own heart. ⁹For they all made us afraid, saying, Their hands shall be weakened from the work, that it be not done. Now therefore, O God, strengthen my hands. ¹⁰Afterward I came to the house of Shemaiah the son of Delaiah the son of Mehetabeel, who was shut up; and he said, Let us meet together in the house of God, within the temple, and let us shut the doors of the temple: for they will come to slay you; yes, in the night will they come to slay you. ¹¹And I said, Should such a man as I flee? and who is there, that, being as I am, would go into the temple to save his life? I will not go in. ¹²And, see, I perceived that God had not sent him; but that he pronounced this prophecy against me: for Tobiah and Sanballat had hired him. ¹³Therefore was he hired, that I should be afraid, and do so, and sin, and that they might have matter for an evil report, that they might reproach me. ¹⁴My God, think you on Tobiah and Sanballat according to these their works, and on the prophetess Noadiah, and the rest of the prophets, that would have put me in fear. ¹⁵So the wall was finished in the twenty and fifth day of the month Elul, in fifty and two days. ¹⁶And it came to pass, that when all our enemies heard thereof, and all the heathen that were about us saw these things, they were much cast down in their own eyes: for they perceived that this work was worked of our God. ¹⁷Moreover in those days the nobles of Judah sent many letters to Tobiah, and the letters of Tobiah came to them. ¹⁸For there were many in Judah sworn to him, because he was the son in law of Shechaniah the son of Arah; and his son Johanan had taken the daughter of Meshullam the son of Berechiah. ¹⁹Also they reported his good deeds before me, and uttered my words to him. And Tobiah sent letters to put me in fear.

7 ¹Now it came to pass, when the wall was built, and I had set up the doors, and the porters and the singers and the Levites were appointed, ²That I gave my brother Hanani, and Hananiah the ruler of the palace, charge over Jerusalem: for he was a faithful man, and feared God above many. ³And I said to them, Let not the gates of Jerusalem be opened until the sun be hot; and while they stand by, let them shut the doors, and bar them: and appoint watches of the inhabitants of Jerusalem, every one in his watch, and every one to be over against his house. ⁴Now the city was large and great: but the people were few therein, and the houses were not built. ⁵And my God put into my heart to gather together the nobles, and the rulers, and the people, that they might be reckoned by genealogy. And I found a register of the genealogy of them which came up at the first, and found written therein, ⁶These are the children of the province, that went up out of the captivity, of those that had been carried away, whom Nebuchadnezzar the king of Babylon had carried away, and came again to Jerusalem and to Judah, every one to his city; ⁷Who came with Zerubbabel, Jeshua, Nehemiah, Azariah, Raamiah, Nahamani, Mordecai, Bilshan, Mispereth, Bigvai, Nehum, Baanah. The number, I say, of the men of the people of Israel was this; ⁸The children of Parosh, two thousand an hundred seventy and two. ⁹The children of Shephatiah, three hundred seventy and two. ¹⁰The children of Arah, six hundred fifty and two. ¹¹The children of Pahathmoab, of the children of Jeshua and Joab, two thousand and eight hundred and eighteen. ¹²The children of Elam, a thousand two hundred fifty and four. ¹³The children of Zattu, eight hundred forty and five. ¹⁴The children of Zaccai, seven hundred and three score. ¹⁵The children of Binnui, six hundred forty and eight. ¹⁶The children of Bebai, six hundred twenty and eight. ¹⁷The children of Azgad, two thousand three hundred twenty and two. ¹⁸The children of Adonikam, six hundred three score and seven. ¹⁹The children of Bigvai, two thousand three score and seven. ²⁰The children of Adin, six hundred fifty and five. ²¹The children of Ater of Hezekiah, ninety and eight. ²²The children of Hashum, three hundred twenty and eight. ²³The children of Bezai, three hundred twenty and four. ²⁴The children of Hariph, an hundred and twelve. ²⁵The children of Gibeon, ninety and five. ²⁶The men of Bethlehem and Netophah, an hundred fourscore and eight. ²⁷The men of Anathoth, an hundred twenty and eight. ²⁸The men of Bethazmaveth, forty and two. ²⁹The men of Kirjathjearim, Chephirah, and Beeroth, seven hundred forty and three. ³⁰The men of Ramah and Gaba, six hundred twenty and one. ³¹The men of Michmas, an hundred and twenty and two. ³²The men of Bethel and Ai, an hundred twenty and three. ³³The men of the other Nebo, fifty and two. ³⁴The children of the other Elam, a thousand two hundred fifty and four. ³⁵The children of Harim, three hundred and twenty. ³⁶The children of Jericho, three hundred forty and five. ³⁷The children of Lod, Hadid, and Ono, seven hundred twenty and one. ³⁸The children of Senaah, three thousand nine hundred and thirty. ³⁹The priests: the children of Jedaiah, of the house of Jeshua, nine hundred seventy and three. ⁴⁰The children of Immer, a thousand fifty and two. ⁴¹The children of Pashur, a thousand two hundred forty and seven. ⁴²The children of Harim, a thousand and seventeen. ⁴³The Levites: the children of Jeshua, of Kadmiel, and of the children of Hodevah, seventy and four. ⁴⁴The singers: the children of Asaph, an hundred forty and eight. ⁴⁵The porters: the children of Shallum, the children of Ater, the children of Talmon, the children of Akkub, the children of Hatita, the children of Shobai, an hundred thirty and eight. ⁴⁶The Nethinims: the children of Ziha, the children of Hashupha, the children of Tabbaoth, ⁴⁷The children of Keros, the children of Sia, the children of Padon, ⁴⁸The children of Lebana, the children of Hagaba, the children of Shalmai, ⁴⁹The children of Hanan, the children of Giddel, the children of Gahar, ⁵⁰The children of Reaiah, the children of Rezin, the children of Nekoda, ⁵¹The children of Gazzam, the children of Uzza, the children of Phaseah, ⁵²The children of Besai, the children of Meunim, the children of Nephishesim, ⁵³The children of Bakbuk, the children of Hakupha, the children of Harhur, ⁵⁴The children of Bazlith, the children of Mehida, the children of Harsha, ⁵⁵The children of Barkos, the children of Sisera, the children of Tamah, ⁵⁶The children of Neziah, the children of Hatipha. ⁵⁷The children of Solomon's servants: the children of Sotai, the children of Sophereth, the children of Perida, ⁵⁸The children of Jaala, the children of Darkon, the children of Giddel, ⁵⁹The children of Shephatiah, the children of Hattil, the children of Pochereth of Zebaim, the children of Amon. ⁶⁰All the Nethinims, and the children of Solomon's servants, were three hundred ninety and two. ⁶¹And these were they which went up also from Telmelah, Telharesha, Cherub, Addon, and Immer: but they could not show their father's house, nor their seed, whether they were of Israel. ⁶²The children of Delaiah, the children of Tobiah, the children of Nekoda, six hundred forty and two. ⁶³And of the priests: the children of Habaiah, the children of Koz, the children of Barzillai, which took one of the daughters of Barzillai the Gileadite to wife, and was called after their name. ⁶⁴These sought their register among those that were reckoned by genealogy, but it was not found: therefore were they, as polluted, put from the priesthood. ⁶⁵And the Tirshatha said to them, that they should not eat of the most holy things, till there stood up a priest with Urim and Thummim. ⁶⁶The whole congregation together was forty and two thousand three hundred and three score, ⁶⁷Beside their manservants and their maidservants, of whom there were seven thousand three hundred thirty and seven: and they had two hundred forty and five singing men and singing women. ⁶⁸Their horses, seven hundred thirty and six: their mules, two hundred forty and five: ⁶⁹Their camels, four hundred thirty and five: six thousand seven hundred and twenty asses. ⁷⁰And some of the chief of the fathers gave to the work. The Tirshatha gave to the treasure a thousand drams of gold, fifty basins, five hundred and thirty priests' garments. ⁷¹And some of the chief of the fathers gave to the treasure of the work twenty thousand drams of gold, and two thousand and two hundred pound of silver. ⁷²And that which the rest of the people gave was twenty thousand drams of gold, and two thousand pound of silver, and three score and seven priests' garments. ⁷³So the priests, and the Levites, and the porters, and the singers, and some of the people, and the Nethinims, and all Israel, dwelled in their cities; and when the seventh month came, the children of Israel were in their cities.

8 ¹And all the people gathered themselves together as one man into the street that was before the water gate; and they spoke to Ezra the scribe to bring the book of the law of Moses, which the LORD had commanded to Israel. ²And Ezra the priest brought the law before the congregation both of men and women, and all that could hear with understanding, on the first day of the seventh month. ³And he read therein before the street that was before the water gate from the morning until midday, before the men and the women, and those that could understand; and the ears of all the people were attentive to the book of the law. ⁴And Ezra the scribe stood on a pulpit of wood, which they had made for the purpose; and beside him stood Mattithiah, and Shema, and Anaiah, and Urijah, and Hilkiah, and Maaseiah, on his right hand; and on his left hand, Pedaiah, and Mishael, and Malchiah, and Hashum, and Hashbadana, Zechariah, and Meshullam. ⁵And Ezra opened the book in the sight of all the people; (for he was above all the people;) and when he opened it, all the people stood up: ⁶And Ezra blessed the LORD, the great God. And all the people answered, Amen, Amen, with lifting up their hands: and they bowed their heads, and worshipped the LORD with their faces to the ground. ⁷Also Jeshua, and Bani, and Sherebiah, Jamin, Akkub, Shabbethai, Hodijah, Maaseiah, Kelita, Azariah, Jozabad, Hanan, Pelaiah, and the Levites, caused the people to understand the law: and the people stood in their place. ⁸So they read in the book in the law of God distinctly, and gave the sense, and caused them to understand the reading. ⁹And Nehemiah, which is the Tirshatha, and Ezra the priest the scribe, and the Levites that taught the people, said to all the people, This day is holy to the LORD your God; mourn not, nor weep. For all the people wept, when they heard the words of the law. ¹⁰Then he said to them, Go your way, eat the fat, and drink the sweet, and send portions to them for whom nothing is prepared: for this day is holy to our LORD: neither be you sorry; for the joy of the LORD is your strength. ¹¹So the Levites stilled all the people, saying, Hold your peace, for the day is holy; neither be you grieved. ¹²And all the people went their way to eat, and to drink, and to send portions, and to make great mirth, because they had understood the words that were declared to them. ¹³And on the second day were gathered together the chief of the fathers of all the people, the priests, and the Levites, to Ezra the scribe, even to understand the words of the law. ¹⁴And they found written in the law which the LORD had commanded by Moses, that the children of Israel should dwell in booths in the feast of the seventh month: ¹⁵And that they should publish and proclaim in all their cities, and in Jerusalem, saying, Go forth to the mount, and fetch olive branches, and pine branches, and myrtle branches, and palm branches, and branches of thick trees, to make booths, as it is written. ¹⁶So the people went forth, and brought them, and made themselves booths, every one on the roof of his house, and in their courts, and in the courts of the house of God, and in the street of the water gate, and in the street of the gate of Ephraim. ¹⁷And all the congregation of them that were come again out of the captivity made booths, and sat under the booths: for since the days of Jeshua the son of Nun to that day had not the children of Israel done so. And there was very great gladness. ¹⁸Also day by day, from the first day to the last day, he read in the book of the law of God. And they kept the feast seven days; and on the eighth day was a solemn assembly, according to the manner.

9 ¹Now in the twenty and fourth day of this month the children of Israel were assembled with fasting, and with sackcloths, and earth on them. ²And the seed of Israel separated themselves from all strangers, and stood and confessed their sins, and the iniquities of their fathers. ³And they stood up in their place, and read in the book of the law of the LORD their God one fourth part of the day; and another fourth part they confessed, and worshipped the LORD their God. ⁴Then stood up on the stairs, of the Levites, Jeshua, and Bani, Kadmiel, Shebaniah, Bunni, Sherebiah, Bani, and Chenani, and cried with a loud voice to the LORD their God. ⁵Then the Levites, Jeshua, and Kadmiel, Bani, Hashabniah, Sherebiah, Hodijah, Shebaniah, and Pethahiah, said, Stand up and bless the LORD your God for ever and ever: and blessed be your glorious name, which is exalted above all blessing and praise. ⁶You, even you, are LORD alone; you have made heaven, the heaven of heavens, with all their host, the earth, and all things that are therein, the seas, and all that is therein, and you preserve them all; and the host of heaven worships you. ⁷You are the LORD the God, who did choose Abram, and brought him forth out of Ur of the Chaldees, and gave him the name of Abraham; ⁸And found his heart faithful before you, and made a covenant with him to give the land of the Canaanites, the Hittites, the Amorites, and the Perizzites, and the Jebusites, and the Girgashites, to give it, I say, to his seed, and have performed your words; for you are righteous: ⁹And did see the affliction of our fathers in Egypt, and heard their cry by the Red sea; ¹⁰And showed signs and wonders on Pharaoh, and on all his servants, and on all the people of his land: for you knew that they dealt proudly against them. So did you get you a name, as it is this day. ¹¹And you did divide the sea before them, so that they went through the middle of the sea on the dry land; and their persecutors you threw into the deeps, as a stone into the mighty waters. ¹²Moreover you led them in the day by a cloudy pillar; and in the night by a pillar of fire, to give them light in the way wherein they should go. ¹³You came down also on mount Sinai, and spoke with them from heaven, and gave them right judgments, and true laws, good statutes and commandments: ¹⁴And made known to them your holy sabbath, and commanded them precepts, statutes, and laws, by the hand of Moses your servant: ¹⁵And gave them bread from heaven for their hunger, and brought forth water for them out of the rock for their thirst, and promised them that they should go in to possess the land which you had sworn to give them. ¹⁶But they and our fathers dealt proudly, and hardened their necks, and listened not to your commandments, ¹⁷And refused to obey, neither were mindful of your wonders that you did among them; but hardened their necks, and in their rebellion appointed a captain to return to their bondage: but you are a God ready to pardon, gracious and merciful, slow to anger, and of great kindness, and forsook them not. ¹⁸Yes, when they had made them a molten calf, and said, This is your God that brought you up out of Egypt, and had worked great provocations; ¹⁹Yet you in your manifold mercies forsook them not in the wilderness: the pillar of the cloud departed not from them by day, to lead them in the way; neither the pillar of fire by night, to show them light, and the way wherein they should go. ²⁰You gave also your good spirit to instruct them, and withheld not your manna from their mouth, and gave them water for their thirst. ²¹Yes, forty years did you sustain them in the wilderness, so that they lacked nothing; their clothes waxed not old, and their feet swelled not. ²²Moreover you gave them kingdoms and nations, and did divide them into corners: so they possessed the land of Sihon, and the land of the king of Heshbon, and the land of Og king of Bashan. ²³Their children also multiplied you as the stars of heaven, and brought them into the land, concerning which you had promised to their fathers, that they should go in to possess it. ²⁴So the children went in and possessed the land, and you subdued before them the inhabitants of the land, the Canaanites, and gave them into their hands, with their kings, and the people of the land, that they might do with them as they would. ²⁵And they took strong cities, and a fat land, and possessed houses full of all goods, wells dig, vineyards, and olive groves, and fruit trees in abundance: so they did eat, and were filled, and became fat, and delighted themselves in your great goodness. ²⁶Nevertheless they were disobedient, and rebelled against you, and cast your law behind their backs, and slew your prophets which testified against them to turn them to you, and they worked great provocations. ²⁷Therefore you delivered them into the hand of their enemies, who vexed them: and in the time of their trouble, when they cried to you, you heard them from heaven; and according to your manifold mercies you gave them saviors, who saved them out of the hand of their enemies. ²⁸But after they had rest, they did evil again before you: therefore left you them in the land of their enemies, so that they had the dominion over them: yet when they returned, and cried to you, you heard them from heaven; and many times did you deliver them according to your mercies; ²⁹And testified against them, that you might bring them again to your law: yet they dealt proudly, and listened not to your commandments, but sinned against your judgments, (which if a man do, he shall live in them;) and withdrew the shoulder, and hardened their neck, and would not hear. ³⁰Yet many years did you forbear them, and testified against them by your spirit in your prophets: yet would they not give ear: therefore gave you them into the hand of the people of the lands. ³¹Nevertheless for your great mercies' sake you did not utterly consume them, nor forsake them; for you are a gracious and merciful God. ³²Now therefore, our God, the great, the mighty, and the terrible God, who keep covenant and mercy, let not all the trouble seem little before you, that has come on us, on our kings, on our princes, and on our priests, and on our prophets, and on our fathers, and on all your people, since the time of the kings of Assyria to this day. ³³However, you are just in all that is brought on us; for you have done right, but we have done wickedly: ³⁴Neither have our kings, our princes, our priests, nor our fathers, kept your law, nor listened to your commandments and your testimonies, with which you did testify against them. ³⁵For they have not served you in their kingdom, and in your great goodness that you gave them, and in the large and fat land which you gave before them, neither turned they from their wicked works. ³⁶Behold, we are servants this day, and for the land that you gave to our fathers to eat the fruit thereof and the good thereof, behold, we are servants in it: ³⁷And it yields much increase to the kings whom you have set over us because of our sins: also they have dominion over our bodies, and over our cattle, at their pleasure, and we are in great distress. ³⁸And because of all this we make a sure covenant, and write it; and our princes, Levites, and priests, seal to it.

10

¹Now those that sealed were, Nehemiah, the Tirshatha, the son of Hachaliah, and Zidkijah, ²Seraiah, Azariah, Jeremiah, ³Pashur, Amariah, Malchijah, ⁴Hattush, Shebaniah, Malluch, ⁵Harim, Meremoth, Obadiah, ⁶Daniel, Ginnethon, Baruch, ⁷Meshullam, Abijah, Mijamin, ⁸Maaziah, Bilgai, Shemaiah: these were the priests. ⁹And the Levites: both Jeshua the son of Azaniah, Binnui of the sons of Henadad, Kadmiel; ¹⁰And their brothers, Shebaniah, Hodijah, Kelita, Pelaiah, Hanan, ¹¹Micha, Rehob, Hashabiah, ¹²Zaccur, Sherebiah, Shebaniah, ¹³Hodijah, Bani, Beninu. ¹⁴The chief of the people; Parosh, Pahathmoab, Elam, Zatthu, Bani, ¹⁵Bunni, Azgad, Bebai, ¹⁶Adonijah, Bigvai, Adin, ¹⁷Ater, Hizkijah, Azzur, ¹⁸Hodijah, Hashum, Bezai, ¹⁹Hariph, Anathoth, Nebai, ²⁰Magpiash, Meshullam, Hezir, ²¹Meshezabeel, Zadok, Jaddua, ²²Pelatiah, Hanan, Anaiah, ²³Hoshea, Hananiah, Hashub, ²⁴Hallohesh, Pileha, Shobek, ²⁵Rehum, Hashabnah, Maaseiah, ²⁶And Ahijah, Hanan, Anan, ²⁷Malluch, Harim, Baanah. ²⁸And the rest of the people, the priests, the Levites, the porters, the singers, the Nethinims, and all they that had separated themselves from the people of the lands to the law of God, their wives, their sons, and their daughters, every one having knowledge, and having understanding; ²⁹They joined to their brothers, their nobles, and entered into a curse, and into an oath, to walk in God's law, which was given by Moses the servant of God, and to observe and do all the commandments of the LORD our Lord, and his judgments and his statutes; ³⁰And that we would not give our daughters to the people of the land, not take their daughters for our sons: ³¹And if the people of the land bring ware or any victuals on the sabbath day to sell, that we would not buy it of them on the sabbath, or on the holy day: and that we would leave the seventh year, and the exaction of every debt. ³²Also we made ordinances for us, to charge ourselves yearly with the third part of a shekel for the service of the house of our God; ³³For the show bread, and for the continual meat offering, and for the continual burnt offering, of the sabbaths, of the new moons, for the set feasts, and for the holy things, and for the sin offerings to make an atonement for Israel, and for all the work of the house of our God. ³⁴And we cast the lots among the priests, the Levites, and the people, for the wood offering, to bring it into the house of our God, after the houses of our fathers, at times appointed year by year, to burn on the altar of the LORD our God, as it is written in the law: ³⁵And to bring the first fruits of our ground, and the first fruits of all fruit of all trees, year by year, to the house of the LORD: ³⁶Also the firstborn of our sons, and of our cattle, as it is written in the law, and the firstborn of our herds and of our flocks, to bring to the house of our God, to the priests that minister in the house of our God: ³⁷And that we should bring the first fruits

of our dough, and our offerings, and the fruit of all manner of trees, of wine and of oil, to the priests, to the chambers of the house of our God; and the tithes of our ground to the Levites, that the same Levites might have the tithes in all the cities of our tillage. ³⁸And the priest the son of Aaron shall be with the Levites, when the Levites take tithes: and the Levites shall bring up the tithe of the tithes to the house of our God, to the chambers, into the treasure house. ³⁹For the children of Israel and the children of Levi shall bring the offering of the corn, of the new wine, and the oil, to the chambers, where are the vessels of the sanctuary, and the priests that minister, and the porters, and the singers: and we will not forsake the house of our God.

11 ¹And the rulers of the people dwelled at Jerusalem: the rest of the people also cast lots, to bring one of ten to dwell in Jerusalem the holy city, and nine parts to dwell in other cities. ²And the people blessed all the men, that willingly offered themselves to dwell at Jerusalem. ³Now these are the chief of the province that dwelled in Jerusalem: but in the cities of Judah dwelled every one in his possession in their cities, to wit, Israel, the priests, and the Levites, and the Nethinims, and the children of Solomon's servants. ⁴And at Jerusalem dwelled certain of the children of Judah, and of the children of Benjamin. Of the children of Judah; Athaiah the son of Uzziah, the son of Zechariah, the son of Amariah, the son of Shephatiah, the son of Mahalaleel, of the children of Perez; ⁵And Maaseiah the son of Baruch, the son of Colhozeh, the son of Hazaiah, the son of Adaiah, the son of Joiarib, the son of Zechariah, the son of Shiloni. ⁶All the sons of Perez that dwelled at Jerusalem were four hundred three score and eight valiant men. ⁷And these are the sons of Benjamin; Sallu the son of Meshullam, the son of Joed, the son of Pedaiah, the son of Kolaiah, the son of Maaseiah, the son of Ithiel, the son of Jesaiah. ⁸And after him Gabbai, Sallai, nine hundred twenty and eight. ⁹And Joel the son of Zichri was their overseer: and Judah the son of Senuah was second over the city. ¹⁰Of the priests: Jedaiah the son of Joiarib, Jachin. ¹¹Seraiah the son of Hilkiah, the son of Meshullam, the son of Zadok, the son of Meraioth, the son of Ahitub, was the ruler of the house of God. ¹²And their brothers that did the work of the house were eight hundred twenty and two: and Adaiah the son of Jeroham, the son of Pelaliah, the son of Amzi, the son of Zechariah, the son of Pashur, the son of Malchiah. ¹³And his brothers, chief of the fathers, two hundred forty and two: and Amashai the son of Azareel, the son of Ahasai, the son of Meshillemoth, the son of Immer, ¹⁴And their brothers, mighty men of valor, an hundred twenty and eight: and their overseer was Zabdiel, the son of one of the great men. ¹⁵Also of the Levites: Shemaiah the son of Hashub, the son of Azrikam, the son of Hashabiah, the son of Bunni, ¹⁶And Shabbethai and Jozabad, of the chief of the Levites, had the oversight of the outward business of the house of God. ¹⁷And Mattaniah the son of Micha, the son of Zabdi, the son of Asaph, was the principal to begin the thanksgiving in prayer: and Bakbukiah the second among his brothers, and Abda the son of Shammua, the son of Galal, the son of Jeduthun. ¹⁸All the Levites in the holy city were two hundred fourscore and four. ¹⁹Moreover the porters, Akkub, Talmon, and their brothers that kept the gates, were an hundred seventy and two. ²⁰And the residue of Israel, of the priests, and the Levites, were in all the cities of Judah, every one in his inheritance. ²¹But the Nethinims dwelled in Ophel: and Ziha and Gispa were over the Nethinims. ²²The overseer also of the Levites at Jerusalem was Uzzi the son of Bani, the son of Hashabiah, the son of Mattaniah, the son of Micha. Of the sons of Asaph, the singers were over the business of the house of God. ²³For it was the king's commandment concerning them, that a certain portion should be for the singers, due for every day. ²⁴And Pethahiah the son of Meshezabeel, of the children of Zerah the son of Judah, was at the king's hand in all matters concerning the people. ²⁵And for the villages, with their fields, some of the children of Judah dwelled at Kirjatharba, and in the villages thereof, and at Dibon, and in the villages thereof, and at Jekabzeel, and in the villages thereof, ²⁶And at Jeshua, and at Moladah, and at Bethphelet, ²⁷And at Hazarshual, and at Beersheba, and in the villages thereof, ²⁸And at Ziklag, and at Mekonah, and in the villages thereof, ²⁹And at Enrimmon, and at Zareah, and at Jarmuth, ³⁰Zanoah, Adullam, and in their villages, at Lachish, and the fields thereof, at Azekah, and in the villages thereof. And they dwelled from Beersheba to the valley of Hinnom. ³¹The children also of Benjamin from Geba dwelled at Michmash, and Aija, and Bethel, and in their villages. ³²And at Anathoth, Nob, Ananiah, ³³Hazor, Ramah, Gittaim, ³⁴Hadid, Zeboim, Neballat, ³⁵Lod, and Ono, the valley of craftsmen. ³⁶And of the Levites were divisions in Judah, and in Benjamin.

12 ¹Now these are the priests and the Levites that went up with Zerubbabel the son of Shealtiel, and Jeshua: Seraiah, Jeremiah, Ezra, ²Amariah, Malluch, Hattush, ³Shechaniah, Rehum, Meremoth, ⁴Iddo, Ginnetho, Abijah, ⁵Miamin, Maadiah, Bilgah, ⁶Shemaiah, and Joiarib, Jedaiah, ⁷Sallu, Amok, Hilkiah, Jedaiah. These were the chief of the priests and of their brothers in the days of Jeshua. ⁸Moreover the Levites: Jeshua, Binnui, Kadmiel, Sherebiah, Judah, and Mattaniah, which was over the thanksgiving, he and his brothers. ⁹Also Bakbukiah and Unni, their brothers, were over against them in the watches. ¹⁰And Jeshua begat Joiakim, Joiakim also begat Eliashib, and Eliashib begat Joiada, ¹¹And Joiada begat Jonathan, and Jonathan begat Jaddua. ¹²And in the days of Joiakim were priests, the chief of the fathers: of Seraiah, Meraiah; of Jeremiah, Hananiah; ¹³Of Ezra, Meshullam; of Amariah, Jehohanan; ¹⁴Of Melicu, Jonathan; of Shebaniah, Joseph; ¹⁵Of Harim, Adna; of Meraioth, Helkai; ¹⁶Of Iddo, Zechariah; of Ginnethon, Meshullam; ¹⁷Of Abijah, Zichri; of Miniamin, of Moadiah, Piltai: ¹⁸Of Bilgah, Shammua; of Shemaiah, Jehonathan; ¹⁹And of Joiarib, Mattenai; of Jedaiah, Uzzi; ²⁰Of Sallai, Kallai; of Amok, Eber; ²¹Of Hilkiah, Hashabiah; of Jedaiah, Nethaneel. ²²The Levites in the days of Eliashib, Joiada, and Johanan, and Jaddua, were recorded chief of the fathers: also the priests, to the reign of Darius the Persian. ²³The sons of Levi, the chief of the fathers, were written in the book of the chronicles, even until the days of Johanan the son of Eliashib. ²⁴And the chief of the Levites: Hashabiah, Sherebiah, and Jeshua the son of Kadmiel, with their brothers over against them, to praise and to give thanks, according to the commandment of David the man of God, ward over against ward. ²⁵Mattaniah, and Bakbukiah,

Obadiah, Meshullam, Talmon, Akkub, were porters keeping the ward at the thresholds of the gates. ²⁶These were in the days of Joiakim the son of Jeshua, the son of Jozadak, and in the days of Nehemiah the governor, and of Ezra the priest, the scribe. ²⁷And at the dedication of the wall of Jerusalem they sought the Levites out of all their places, to bring them to Jerusalem, to keep the dedication with gladness, both with thanksgivings, and with singing, with cymbals, psalteries, and with harps. ²⁸And the sons of the singers gathered themselves together, both out of the plain country round about Jerusalem, and from the villages of Netophathi; ²⁹Also from the house of Gilgal, and out of the fields of Geba and Azmaveth: for the singers had built them villages round about Jerusalem. ³⁰And the priests and the Levites purified themselves, and purified the people, and the gates, and the wall. ³¹Then I brought up the princes of Judah on the wall, and appointed two great companies of them that gave thanks, whereof one went on the right hand on the wall toward the dung gate: ³²And after them went Hoshaiah, and half of the princes of Judah, ³³And Azariah, Ezra, and Meshullam, ³⁴Judah, and Benjamin, and Shemaiah, and Jeremiah, ³⁵And certain of the priests' sons with trumpets; namely, Zechariah the son of Jonathan, the son of Shemaiah, the son of Mattaniah, the son of Michaiah, the son of Zaccur, the son of Asaph: ³⁶And his brothers, Shemaiah, and Azarael, Milalai, Gilalai, Maai, Nethaneel, and Judah, Hanani, with the musical instruments of David the man of God, and Ezra the scribe before them. ³⁷And at the fountain gate, which was over against them, they went up by the stairs of the city of David, at the going up of the wall, above the house of David, even to the water gate eastward. ³⁸And the other company of them that gave thanks went over against them, and I after them, and the half of the people on the wall, from beyond the tower of the furnaces even to the broad wall; ³⁹And from above the gate of Ephraim, and above the old gate, and above the fish gate, and the tower of Hananeel, and the tower of Meah, even to the sheep gate: and they stood still in the prison gate. ⁴⁰So stood the two companies of them that gave thanks in the house of God, and I, and the half of the rulers with me: ⁴¹And the priests; Eliakim, Maaseiah, Miniamin, Michaiah, Elioenai, Zechariah, and Hananiah, with trumpets; ⁴²And Maaseiah, and Shemaiah, and Eleazar, and Uzzi, and Jehohanan, and Malchijah, and Elam, and Ezer. And the singers sang loud, with Jezrahiah their overseer. ⁴³Also that day they offered great sacrifices, and rejoiced: for God had made them rejoice with great joy: the wives also and the children rejoiced: so that the joy of Jerusalem was heard even afar off. ⁴⁴And at that time were some appointed over the chambers for the treasures, for the offerings, for the first fruits, and for the tithes, to gather into them out of the fields of the cities the portions of the law for the priests and Levites: for Judah rejoiced for the priests and for the Levites that waited. ⁴⁵And both the singers and the porters kept the ward of their God, and the ward of the purification, according to the commandment of David, and of Solomon his son. ⁴⁶For in the days of David and Asaph of old there were chief of the singers, and songs of praise and thanksgiving to God. ⁴⁷And all Israel in the days of Zerubbabel, and in the days of Nehemiah, gave the portions of the singers and the porters, every day his portion: and they sanctified holy things to the Levites; and the Levites sanctified them to the children of Aaron.

13 ¹On that day they read in the book of Moses in the audience of the people; and therein was found written, that the Ammonite and the Moabite should not come into the congregation of God for ever; ²Because they met not the children of Israel with bread and with water, but hired Balaam against them, that he should curse them: however, our God turned the curse into a blessing. ³Now it came to pass, when they had heard the law, that they separated from Israel all the mixed multitude. ⁴And before this, Eliashib the priest, having the oversight of the chamber of the house of our God, was allied to Tobiah: ⁵And he had prepared for him a great chamber, where aforetime they laid the meat offerings, the frankincense, and the vessels, and the tithes of the corn, the new wine, and the oil, which was commanded to be given to the Levites, and the singers, and the porters; and the offerings of the priests. ⁶But in all this time was not I at Jerusalem: for in the two and thirtieth year of Artaxerxes king of Babylon came I to the king, and after certain days obtained I leave of the king: ⁷And I came to Jerusalem, and understood of the evil that Eliashib did for Tobiah, in preparing him a chamber in the courts of the house of God. ⁸And it grieved me sore: therefore I cast forth all the household stuff to Tobiah out of the chamber. ⁹Then I commanded, and they cleansed the chambers: and thither brought I again the vessels of the house of God, with the meat offering and the frankincense. ¹⁰And I perceived that the portions of the Levites had not been given them: for the Levites and the singers, that did the work, were fled every one to his field. ¹¹Then contended I with the rulers, and said, Why is the house of God forsaken? And I gathered them together, and set them in their place. ¹²Then brought all Judah the tithe of the corn and the new wine and the oil to the treasuries. ¹³And I made treasurers over the treasuries, Shelemiah the priest, and Zadok the scribe, and of the Levites, Pedaiah: and next to them was Hanan the son of Zaccur, the son of Mattaniah: for they were counted faithful, and their office was to distribute to their brothers. ¹⁴Remember me, O my God, concerning this, and wipe not out my good deeds that I have done for the house of my God, and for the offices thereof. ¹⁵In those days saw I in Judah some treading wine presses on the sabbath, and bringing in sheaves, and lading asses; as also wine, grapes, and figs, and all manner of burdens, which they brought into Jerusalem on the sabbath day: and I testified against them in the day wherein they sold victuals. ¹⁶There dwelled men of Tyre also therein, which brought fish, and all manner of ware, and sold on the sabbath to the children of Judah, and in Jerusalem. ¹⁷Then I contended with the nobles of Judah, and said to them, What evil thing is this that you do, and profane the sabbath day? ¹⁸Did not your fathers thus, and did not our God bring all this evil on us, and on this city? yet you bring more wrath on Israel by profaning the sabbath. ¹⁹And it came to pass, that when the gates of Jerusalem began to be dark before the sabbath, I commanded that the gates should be shut, and charged that they should not be opened till after the sabbath: and some of my servants set I at the gates, that there should no burden be brought in on the sabbath day. ²⁰So the merchants and sellers of all kind of ware lodged without Jerusalem once or twice. ²¹Then I testified against them, and said to them, Why lodge you about the wall? if you do so again, I will lay hands on you. From that time forth came they no more on the sabbath. ²²And I commanded the Levites that they should cleanse themselves, and that they should come and keep the gates, to sanctify the sabbath day. Remember me, O my God, concerning this also, and spare me according to the greatness of your mercy. ²³In those days also saw I Jews that had married wives of Ashdod, of Ammon, and of Moab: ²⁴And their children spoke half in the speech of Ashdod, and could not speak in the Jews' language, but according to the language of each people. ²⁵And I contended with them, and cursed them, and smote certain of them, and plucked off their hair, and made them swear by God, saying, You shall not give your daughters to their sons, nor take their daughters to your sons, or for yourselves. ²⁶Did not Solomon king of Israel sin by these things? yet among many nations was there no king like him, who was beloved of his God, and God made him king over all Israel: nevertheless even him did outlandish women cause to sin. ²⁷Shall we then listen to you to do all this great evil, to transgress against our God in marrying strange wives? ²⁸And one of the sons of Joiada, the son of Eliashib the high priest, was son in law to Sanballat the Horonite: therefore I chased him from me. ²⁹Remember them, O my God, because they have defiled the priesthood, and the covenant of the priesthood, and of the Levites. ³⁰Thus cleansed I them from all strangers, and appointed the wards of the priests and the Levites, every one in his business; ³¹And for the wood offering, at times appointed, and for the first fruits. Remember me, O my God, for good.

Esther

1 ¹Now it came to pass in the days of Ahasuerus, (this is Ahasuerus which reigned, from India even to Ethiopia, over an hundred and seven and twenty provinces:) ²That in those days, when the king Ahasuerus sat on the throne of his kingdom, which was in Shushan the palace, ³In the third year of his reign, he made a feast to all his princes and his servants; the power of Persia and Media, the nobles and princes of the provinces, being before him: ⁴When he showed the riches of his glorious kingdom and the honor of his excellent majesty many days, even an hundred and fourscore days. ⁵And when these days were expired, the king made a feast to all the people that were present in Shushan the palace, both to great and small, seven days, in the court of the garden of the king's palace; ⁶Where were white, green, and blue, hangings, fastened with cords of fine linen and purple to silver rings and pillars of marble: the beds were of gold and silver, on a pavement of red, and blue, and white, and black, marble. ⁷And they gave them drink in vessels of gold, (the vessels being diverse one from another,) and royal wine in abundance, according to the state of the king. ⁸And the drinking was according to the law; none did compel: for so the king had appointed to all the officers of his house, that they should do according to every man's pleasure. ⁹Also Vashti the queen made a feast for the women in the royal house which belonged to king Ahasuerus. ¹⁰On the seventh day, when the heart of the king was merry with wine, he commanded Mehuman, Biztha, Harbona, Bigtha, and Abagtha, Zethar, and Carcas, the seven chamberlains that served in the presence of Ahasuerus the king, ¹¹To bring Vashti the queen before the king with the crown royal, to show the people and the princes her beauty: for she was fair to look on. ¹²But the queen Vashti refused to come at the king's commandment by his chamberlains: therefore was the king very wroth, and his anger burned in him. ¹³Then the king said to the wise men, which knew the times, (for so was the king's manner toward all that knew law and judgment: ¹⁴And the next to him was Carshena, Shethar, Admatha, Tarshish, Meres, Marsena, and Memucan, the seven princes of Persia and Media, which saw the king's face, and which sat the first in the kingdom;) ¹⁵What shall we do to the queen Vashti according to law, because she has not performed the commandment of the king Ahasuerus by the chamberlains? ¹⁶And Memucan answered before the king and the princes, Vashti the queen has not done wrong to the king only, but also to all the princes, and to all the people that are in all the provinces of the king Ahasuerus. ¹⁷For this deed of the queen shall come abroad to all women, so that they shall despise their husbands in their eyes, when it shall be reported, The king Ahasuerus commanded Vashti the queen to be brought in before him, but she came not. ¹⁸Likewise shall the ladies of Persia and Media say this day to all the king's princes, which have heard of the deed of the queen. Thus shall there arise too much contempt and wrath. ¹⁹If it please the king, let there go a royal commandment from him, and let it be written among the laws of the Persians and the Medes, that it be not altered, That Vashti come no more before king Ahasuerus; and let the king give her royal estate to another that is better than she. ²⁰And when the king's decree which he shall make shall be published throughout all his empire, (for it is great,) all the wives shall give to their husbands honor, both to great and small. ²¹And the saying pleased the king and the princes; and the king did according to the word of Memucan: ²²For he sent letters into all the king's provinces, into every province according to the writing thereof, and to every people after their language, that every man should bear rule in his own house, and that it should be published according to the language of every people.

2 ¹After these things, when the wrath of king Ahasuerus was appeased, he remembered Vashti, and what she had done, and what was decreed against her. ²Then said the king's servants that ministered to him, Let there be fair young virgins sought for the king: ³And let the king appoint officers in all the provinces of his kingdom, that they may gather together all the fair young virgins to Shushan the palace, to the house of the women, to the custody of Hege the king's chamberlain, keeper of the women; and let their things for purification be given them: ⁴And let the maiden which pleases the king be queen instead of Vashti. And the thing pleased the king; and he did so. ⁵Now in Shushan the palace there was a certain Jew, whose name was Mordecai, the son of Jair, the son of Shimei, the son of Kish, a Benjamite; ⁶Who had been carried away from Jerusalem with the captivity which had been carried away with Jeconiah king of Judah, whom Nebuchadnezzar the king of Babylon had carried away. ⁷And he brought up Hadassah, that is, Esther, his uncle's daughter: for she had neither father nor mother, and the maid was fair and beautiful; whom Mordecai, when her father and mother were dead, took for his own daughter. ⁸So it came to pass, when the king's commandment and his decree was heard, and when many maidens were gathered together to Shushan the palace, to the custody of Hegai, that Esther was brought also to the king's house, to the custody of Hegai, keeper of the women. ⁹And the maiden pleased him, and she obtained kindness of him; and he speedily gave her her things for purification, with such things as belonged to her, and seven maidens, which were meet to be given her, out of the king's house: and he preferred her and her maids to the best place of the house of the women. ¹⁰Esther had not showed her people nor her kindred: for Mordecai had charged her that she should not show it. ¹¹And Mordecai walked every day before the court of the women's house, to know how Esther did, and what should become of her. ¹²Now when every maid's turn was come to go in to king Ahasuerus, after that she had been twelve months, according to the manner of the women, (for so were the days of their purifications accomplished, to wit, six months with oil of myrrh, and six months with sweet odors, and with other things for the purifying of the women;) ¹³Then thus came every maiden to the king; whatever she desired was given her to go with her out of the house of the women to the king's house. ¹⁴In the evening she went, and on the morrow she returned into the second house of the women, to the custody of Shaashgaz, the king's chamberlain, which kept the concubines: she came in to the king no more, except the king delighted in her, and that she were called by name. ¹⁵Now when the turn of Esther, the daughter of Abihail the uncle of Mordecai, who had taken her for his daughter, was come to go in to the king, she required nothing but what Hegai the king's chamberlain, the keeper of the women, appointed. And Esther obtained favor in the sight of all them that looked on her. ¹⁶So Esther was taken to king Ahasuerus into his house royal in the tenth month, which is the month Tebeth, in the seventh year of his reign. ¹⁷And the king loved Esther above all the women, and she obtained grace and favor in his sight more than all the virgins; so that he set the royal crown on her head, and made her queen instead of Vashti. ¹⁸Then the king made a great feast to all his princes and his servants, even Esther's feast; and he made a release to the provinces, and gave gifts, according to the state of the king. ¹⁹And when the virgins were gathered together the second time, then Mordecai sat in the king's gate. ²⁰Esther had not yet showed her kindred nor her people; as Mordecai had charged her: for Esther did the commandment of Mordecai, like as when she was brought up with him. ²¹In those days, while Mordecai sat in the king's gate, two of the king's chamberlains, Bigthan and Teresh, of those which kept the door, were wroth, and sought to lay hands on the king Ahasuerus. ²²And the thing was known to Mordecai, who told it to Esther the queen; and Esther certified the king thereof in Mordecai's name. ²³And when inquisition was made of the matter, it was found out; therefore they were both hanged on a tree: and it was written in the book of the chronicles before the king.

3 ¹After these things did king Ahasuerus promote Haman the son of Hammedatha the Agagite, and advanced him, and set his seat above all the princes that were with him. ²And all the king's servants, that were in the king's gate, bowed, and reverenced Haman: for the king had so commanded concerning him. But Mordecai bowed not, nor did him reverence. ³Then the king's servants, which were in the king's gate, said to Mordecai, Why transgress you the king's commandment? ⁴Now it came to pass, when they spoke daily to him, and he listened not to them, that they told Haman, to see whether Mordecai's matters would stand: for he had told them that he was a Jew. ⁵And when Haman saw that Mordecai bowed not, nor did him reverence, then was Haman full of wrath. ⁶And he thought scorn to lay hands on Mordecai alone; for they had showed him the people of Mordecai: why Haman sought to destroy all the Jews that were throughout the whole kingdom of Ahasuerus, even the people of Mordecai. ⁷In the first month, that is, the month Nisan, in the twelfth year of king Ahasuerus, they cast Pur, that is, the lot, before Haman from day to day, and from month to month, to the twelfth month, that is, the month Adar. ⁸And Haman said to king Ahasuerus, There is a certain people scattered abroad and dispersed among the people in all the provinces of your kingdom; and their laws are diverse from all people; neither keep they the king's laws: therefore it is not for the king's profit to suffer them. ⁹If it please the king, let it be written that they may be destroyed: and I will pay ten thousand talents of silver to the hands of those that have the charge of the business, to bring it into the king's treasuries. ¹⁰And the king took his ring from his hand, and gave it to Haman the son of Hammedatha the Agagite, the Jews' enemy. ¹¹And the king said to Haman, The silver is given to you, the people also, to do with them as it seems good to you. ¹²Then were the king's scribes called on the thirteenth day of the first month, and there was written according to all that Haman had commanded to the king's lieutenants, and to the governors that were over every province, and to the rulers of every people of every province according to the writing thereof, and to every people after their language; in the name of king Ahasuerus was it written, and sealed with the king's ring. ¹³And the letters were sent by posts into all the king's provinces, to destroy, to kill, and to cause to perish, all Jews, both young and old, little children and women, in one day, even on the thirteenth day of the twelfth month, which is the month Adar, and to take the spoil of them for a prey. ¹⁴The copy of the writing for a commandment to be given in every province was published to all people, that they should be ready against that day. ¹⁵The posts went out, being hastened by the king's commandment, and the decree was given in Shushan the palace. And the king and Haman sat down to drink; but the city Shushan was perplexed.

4 ¹When Mordecai perceived all that was done, Mordecai rent his clothes, and put on sackcloth with ashes, and went out into the middle of the city, and cried with a loud and a bitter cry; ²And came even before the king's gate: for none might enter into the king's gate clothed with sackcloth. ³And in every province, wherever the king's commandment and his decree came, there was great mourning among the Jews, and fasting, and weeping, and wailing; and many lay in sackcloth and ashes. ⁴So Esther's maids and her chamberlains came and told it her. Then was the queen exceedingly grieved; and she sent raiment to clothe Mordecai, and to take away his sackcloth from him: but he received it not. ⁵Then called Esther for Hatach, one of the king's chamberlains, whom he had appointed to attend on her, and gave him a commandment to Mordecai, to know what it was, and why it was. ⁶So Hatach went forth to Mordecai to the street of the city, which was before the king's gate. ⁷And Mordecai told him of all that had happened to him, and of the sum of the money that Haman had promised to pay to the king's treasuries for the Jews, to destroy them. ⁸Also he gave him the copy of the writing of the decree that was given at Shushan to destroy them, to show it to Esther, and to declare it to her, and to charge her that she should go in to the king, to make supplication to him, and to make request before him for her people. ⁹And Hatach came and told Esther the words of Mordecai. ¹⁰Again Esther spoke to Hatach, and gave him commandment to Mordecai; ¹¹All the king's servants, and the people of the king's provinces, do know, that whoever, whether man or women, shall come to the king into the inner court, who is not called, there is one law of his to put him to death, except such to whom the king shall hold out the golden scepter, that he may live: but I have not been called to come in to the king these thirty days. ¹²And they told to Mordecai Esther's words. ¹³Then Mordecai commanded to answer Esther, Think not with yourself that you shall escape in the king's house, more than all the Jews. ¹⁴For if you altogether hold your peace at this time, then shall there enlargement and deliverance arise to the Jews from another place; but you and your father's house shall be destroyed: and who knows whether you are come to the kingdom for such a time as this? ¹⁵Then Esther bade them return Mordecai this answer, ¹⁶Go, gather together all the Jews that are present in Shushan, and fast you for me, and neither eat nor drink three days, night or day: I also and my maidens will fast likewise; and so will I go in to the king, which is not according to the law: and if I perish, I perish. ¹⁷So Mordecai went his way, and did according to all that Esther had commanded him.

5 ¹Now it came to pass on the third day, that Esther put on her royal apparel, and stood in the inner court of the king's house, over against the king's house: and the king sat on his royal throne in the royal house, over against the gate of the house. ²And it was so, when the king saw Esther the queen standing in the court, that she obtained favor in his sight: and the king held out to Esther the golden scepter that was in his hand. So Esther drew near, and touched the top of the scepter. ³Then said the king to her, What will you, queen Esther? and what is your request? it shall be even given you to the half of the kingdom. ⁴And Esther answered, If it seem good to the king, let the king and Haman come this day to the banquet that I have prepared for him. ⁵Then the king said, Cause Haman to make haste, that he may do as Esther has said. So the king and Haman came to the banquet that Esther had prepared. ⁶And the king said to Esther at the banquet of wine, What is your petition? and it shall be granted you: and what is your request? even to the half of the kingdom it shall be performed. ⁷Then answered Esther, and said, My petition and my request is; ⁸If I have found favor in the sight of the king, and if it please the king to grant my petition, and to perform my request, let the king and Haman come to the banquet that I shall prepare for them, and I will do to morrow as the king has said. ⁹Then went Haman forth that day joyful and with a glad heart: but when Haman saw Mordecai in the king's gate, that he stood not up, nor moved for him, he was full of indignation against Mordecai. ¹⁰Nevertheless Haman refrained himself: and when he came home, he sent and called for his friends, and Zeresh his wife. ¹¹And Haman told them of the glory of his riches, and the multitude of his children, and all the things wherein the king had promoted him, and how he had advanced him above the princes and servants of the king. ¹²Haman said moreover, Yes, Esther the queen did let no man come in with the king to the banquet that she had prepared but myself; and to morrow am I invited to her also with the king. ¹³Yet all this avails me nothing, so long as I see Mordecai the Jew sitting at the king's gate. ¹⁴Then said Zeresh his wife and all his friends to him, Let a gallows be made of fifty cubits high, and to morrow speak you to the king that Mordecai may be hanged thereon: then go you in merrily with the king to the banquet. And the thing pleased Haman; and he caused the gallows to be made.

6 ¹On that night could not the king sleep, and he commanded to bring the book of records of the chronicles; and they were read before the king. ²And it was found written, that Mordecai had told of Bigthana and Teresh, two of the king's chamberlains, the keepers of the door, who sought to lay hand on the king Ahasuerus. ³And the king said, What honor and dignity has been done to Mordecai for this? Then said the king's servants that ministered to him, There is nothing done for him. ⁴And the king said, Who is in the court? Now Haman was come into the outward court of the king's house, to speak to the king to hang Mordecai on the gallows that he had prepared for him. ⁵And the king's servants said to him, Behold, Haman stands in the court. And the king said, Let him come in. ⁶So Haman came in. And the king said to him, What shall be done to the man whom the king delights to honor? Now Haman thought in his heart, To whom would the king delight to do honor more than to myself? ⁷And Haman answered the king, For the man whom the king delights to honor, ⁸Let the royal apparel be brought which the king uses to wear, and the horse that the king rides on, and the crown royal which is set on his head: ⁹And let this apparel and horse be delivered to the hand of one of the king's most noble princes, that they may array the man with whom the king delights to honor, and bring him on horseback through the street of the city, and proclaim before him, Thus shall it be done to the man whom the king delights to honor. ¹⁰Then the king said to Haman, Make haste, and take the apparel and the horse, as you have said, and do even so to Mordecai the Jew, that sits at the king's gate: let nothing fail of all that you have spoken. ¹¹Then took Haman the apparel and the horse, and arrayed Mordecai, and brought him on horseback through the street of the city, and proclaimed before him, Thus shall it be done to the man whom the king delights to honor. ¹²And Mordecai came again to the king's gate. But Haman hurried to his house mourning, and having his head covered. ¹³And Haman told Zeresh his wife and all his friends every thing that had befallen him. Then said his wise men and Zeresh his wife to him, If Mordecai be of the seed of the Jews, before whom you have begun to fall, you shall not prevail against him, but shall surely fall before him. ¹⁴And while they were yet talking with him, came the king's chamberlains, and hurried to bring Haman to the banquet that Esther had prepared.

7 ¹So the king and Haman came to banquet with Esther the queen. ²And the king said again to Esther on the second day at the banquet of wine, What is your petition, queen Esther? and it shall be granted you: and what is your request? and it shall be performed, even to the half of the kingdom. ³Then Esther the queen answered and said, If I have found favor in your sight, O king, and if it please the king, let my life be given me at my petition, and my people at my request: ⁴For we are sold, I and my people, to be destroyed, to be slain, and to perish. But if we had been sold for slaves and bondwomen, I had held my tongue, although the enemy could not countervail the king's damage. ⁵Then the king Ahasuerus answered and said to Esther the queen, Who is he, and where is he, that dared presume in his heart to do so? ⁶And Esther said, The adversary and enemy is this wicked Haman. Then Haman was afraid before the king and the queen. ⁷And the king arising from the banquet of wine in his wrath went into the palace garden: and Haman stood up to make request for his life to Esther the queen; for he saw that there was evil determined against him by the king. ⁸Then the king returned out of the palace garden into the place of the banquet of wine; and Haman was fallen on the bed where on Esther was. Then said the king, Will he force the queen also before me in the house? As the word went out of king's mouth, they covered Haman's face. ⁹And Harbonah,

one of the chamberlains, said before the king, Behold also, the gallows fifty cubits high, which Haman had made for Mordecai, who spoken good for the king, stands in the house of Haman. Then the king said, Hang him thereon. ¹⁰So they hanged Haman on the gallows that he had prepared for Mordecai. Then was the king's wrath pacified.

8 ¹On that day did the king Ahasuerus give the house of Haman the Jews' enemy to Esther the queen. And Mordecai came before the king; for Esther had told what he was to her. ²And the king took off his ring, which he had taken from Haman, and gave it to Mordecai. And Esther set Mordecai over the house of Haman. ³And Esther spoke yet again before the king, and fell down at his feet, and sought him with tears to put away the mischief of Haman the Agagite, and his device that he had devised against the Jews. ⁴Then the king held out the golden scepter toward Esther. So Esther arose, and stood before the king, ⁵And said, If it please the king, and if I have favor in his sight, and the thing seem right before the king, and I be pleasing in his eyes, let it be written to reverse the letters devised by Haman the son of Hammedatha the Agagite, which he wrote to destroy the Jews which are in all the king's provinces: ⁶For how can I endure to see the evil that shall come to my people? or how can I endure to see the destruction of my kindred? ⁷Then the king Ahasuerus said to Esther the queen and to Mordecai the Jew, Behold, I have given Esther the house of Haman, and him they have hanged on the gallows, because he laid his hand on the Jews. ⁸Write you also for the Jews, as it likes you, in the king's name, and seal it with the king's ring: for the writing which is written in the king's name, and sealed with the king's ring, may no man reverse. ⁹Then were the king's scribes called at that time in the third month, that is, the month Sivan, on the three and twentieth day thereof; and it was written according to all that Mordecai commanded to the Jews, and to the lieutenants, and the deputies and rulers of the provinces which are from India to Ethiopia, an hundred twenty and seven provinces, to every province according to the writing thereof, and to every people after their language, and to the Jews according to their writing, and according to their language. ¹⁰And he wrote in the king Ahasuerus' name, and sealed it with the king's ring, and sent letters by posts on horseback, and riders on mules, camels, and young dromedaries: ¹¹Wherein the king granted the Jews which were in every city to gather themselves together, and to stand for their life, to destroy, to slay and to cause to perish, all the power of the people and province that would assault them, both little ones and women, and to take the spoil of them for a prey, ¹²On one day in all the provinces of king Ahasuerus, namely, on the thirteenth day of the twelfth month, which is the month Adar. ¹³The copy of the writing for a commandment to be given in every province was published to all people, and that the Jews should be ready against that day to avenge themselves on their enemies. ¹⁴So the posts that rode on mules and camels went out, being hastened and pressed on by the king's commandment. And the decree was given at Shushan the palace. ¹⁵And Mordecai went out from the presence of the king in royal apparel of blue and white, and with a great crown of gold, and with a garment of fine linen and purple: and the city of Shushan rejoiced and was glad. ¹⁶The Jews had light, and gladness, and joy, and honor. ¹⁷And in every province, and in every city, wherever the king's commandment and his decree came, the Jews had joy and gladness, a feast and a good day. And many of the people of the land became Jews; for the fear of the Jews fell on them.

9 ¹Now in the twelfth month, that is, the month Adar, on the thirteenth day of the same, when the king's commandment and his decree drew near to be put in execution, in the day that the enemies of the Jews hoped to have power over them, (though it was turned to the contrary, that the Jews had rule over them that hated them;) ²The Jews gathered themselves together in their cities throughout all the provinces of the king Ahasuerus, to lay hand on such as sought their hurt: and no man could withstand them; for the fear of them fell on all people. ³And all the rulers of the provinces, and the lieutenants, and the deputies, and officers of the king, helped the Jews; because the fear of Mordecai fell on them. ⁴For Mordecai was great in the king's house, and his fame went out throughout all the provinces: for this man Mordecai waxed greater and greater. ⁵Thus the Jews smote all their enemies with the stroke of the sword, and slaughter, and destruction, and did what they would to those that hated them. ⁶And in Shushan the palace the Jews slew and destroyed five hundred men. ⁷And Parshandatha, and Dalphon, and Aspatha, ⁸And Poratha, and Adalia, and Aridatha, ⁹And Parmashta, and Arisai, and Aridai, and Vajezatha, ¹⁰The ten sons of Haman the son of Hammedatha, the enemy of the Jews, slew they; but on the spoil laid they not their hand. ¹¹On that day the number of those that were slain in Shushan the palace was brought before the king. ¹²And the king said to Esther the queen, The Jews have slain and destroyed five hundred men in Shushan the palace, and the ten sons of Haman; what have they done in the rest of the king's provinces? now what is your petition? and it shall be granted you: or what is your request further? and it shall be done. ¹³Then said Esther, If it please the king, let it be granted to the Jews which are in Shushan to do to morrow also according to this day's decree, and let Haman's ten sons be hanged on the gallows. ¹⁴And the king commanded it so to be done: and the decree was given at Shushan; and they hanged Haman's ten sons. ¹⁵For the Jews that were in Shushan gathered themselves together on the fourteenth day also of the month Adar, and slew three hundred men at Shushan; but on the prey they laid not their hand. ¹⁶But the other Jews that were in the king's provinces gathered themselves together, and stood for their lives, and had rest from their enemies, and slew of their foes seventy and five thousand, but they laid not their hands on the prey, ¹⁷On the thirteenth day of the month Adar; and on the fourteenth day of the same rested they, and made it a day of feasting and gladness. ¹⁸But the Jews that were at Shushan assembled together on the thirteenth day thereof, and on the fourteenth thereof; and on the fifteenth day of the same they rested, and made it a day of feasting and gladness. ¹⁹Therefore the Jews of the villages, that dwelled in the unwalled towns, made the fourteenth day of the month Adar a day of gladness and feasting, and a good day, and of sending portions one to another. ²⁰And Mordecai wrote these things, and sent letters to all the Jews that were in all the provinces of the king Ahasuerus, both near and far, ²¹To establish this among them, that they should keep the fourteenth day of the month Adar, and the fifteenth day of the same, yearly, ²²As the days wherein the Jews rested from their enemies, and the month which was turned to them from sorrow to joy, and from mourning into a good day: that they should make them days of feasting and joy, and of sending portions one to another, and gifts to the poor. ²³And the Jews undertook to do as they had begun, and as Mordecai had written to them; ²⁴Because Haman the son of Hammedatha, the Agagite, the enemy of all the Jews, had devised against the Jews to destroy them, and had cast Pur, that is, the lot, to consume them, and to destroy them; ²⁵But when Esther came before the king, he commanded by letters that his wicked device, which he devised against the Jews, should return on his own head, and that he and his sons should be hanged on the gallows. ²⁶Why they called these days Purim after the name of Pur. Therefore for all the words of this letter, and of that which they had seen concerning this matter, and which had come to them, ²⁷The Jews ordained, and took on them, and on their seed, and on all such as joined themselves to them, so as it should not fail, that they would keep these two days according to their writing, and according to their appointed time every year; ²⁸And that these days should be remembered and kept throughout every generation, every family, every province, and every city; and that these days of Purim should not fail from among the Jews, nor the memorial of them perish from their seed. ²⁹Then Esther the queen, the daughter of Abihail, and Mordecai the Jew, wrote with all authority, to confirm this second letter of Purim. ³⁰And he sent the letters to all the Jews, to the hundred twenty and seven provinces of the kingdom of Ahasuerus, with words of peace and truth, ³¹To confirm these days of Purim in their times appointed, according as Mordecai the Jew and Esther the queen had enjoined them, and as they had decreed for themselves and for their seed, the matters of the fastings and their cry. ³²And the decree of Esther confirmed these matters of Purim; and it was written in the book.

10 ¹And the king Ahasuerus laid a tribute on the land, and on the isles of the sea. ²And all the acts of his power and of his might, and the declaration of the greatness of Mordecai, which the king advanced him, are they not written in the book of the chronicles of the kings of Media and Persia? ³For Mordecai the Jew was next to king Ahasuerus, and great among the Jews, and accepted of the multitude of his brothers, seeking the wealth of his people, and speaking peace to all his seed.

Job

1 ¹There was a man in the land of Uz, whose name was Job; and that man was perfect and upright, and one that feared God, and eschewed evil. ²And there were born to him seven sons and three daughters. ³His substance also was seven thousand sheep, and three thousand camels, and five hundred yoke of oxen, and five hundred she asses, and a very great household; so that this man was the greatest of all the men of the east. ⁴And his sons went and feasted in their houses, every one his day; and sent and called for their three sisters to eat and to drink with them. ⁵And it was so, when the days of their feasting were gone about, that Job sent and sanctified them, and rose up early in the morning, and offered burnt offerings according to the number of them all: for Job said, It may be that my sons have sinned, and cursed God in their hearts. Thus did Job continually. ⁶Now there was a day when the sons of God came to present themselves before the LORD, and Satan came also among them. ⁷And the LORD said to Satan, From where come you? Then Satan answered the LORD, and said, From going to and fro in the earth, and from walking up and down in it. ⁸And the LORD said to Satan, Have you considered my servant Job, that there is none like him in the earth, a perfect and an upright man, one that fears God, and eschews evil? ⁹Then Satan answered the LORD, and said, Does Job fear God for nothing? ¹⁰Have not you made an hedge about him, and about his house, and about all that he has on every side? you have blessed the work of his hands, and his substance is increased in the land. ¹¹But put forth your hand now, and touch all that he has, and he will curse you to your face. ¹²And the LORD said to Satan, Behold, all that he has is in your power; only on himself put not forth your hand. So Satan went forth from the presence of the LORD. ¹³And there was a day when his sons and his daughters were eating and drinking wine in their oldest brother's house: ¹⁴And there came a messenger to Job, and said, The oxen were plowing, and the asses feeding beside them: ¹⁵And the Sabeans fell on them, and took them away; yes, they have slain the servants with the edge of the sword; and I only am escaped alone to tell you. ¹⁶While he was yet speaking, there came also another, and said, The fire of God is fallen from heaven, and has burned up the sheep, and the servants, and consumed them; and I only am escaped alone to tell you. ¹⁷While he was yet speaking, there came also another, and said, The Chaldeans made out three bands, and fell on the camels, and have carried them away, yes, and slain the servants with the edge of the sword; and I only am escaped alone to tell you. ¹⁸While he was yet speaking, there came also another, and said, Your sons and your daughters were eating and drinking wine in their oldest brother's house: ¹⁹And, behold, there came a great wind from the wilderness, and smote the four corners of the house, and it fell on the young men, and they are dead; and I only am escaped alone to tell you. ²⁰Then Job arose, and rent his mantle, and shaved his head, and fell down on the ground, and worshipped, ²¹And said, Naked came I out of my mother's womb, and naked shall I return thither: the LORD gave, and the LORD has taken away; blessed be the name of the LORD. ²²In all this Job sinned not, nor charged God foolishly.

2 ¹Again there was a day when the sons of God came to present themselves before the LORD, and Satan came also among them to present himself before the LORD. ²And the LORD said to Satan, From where come you? And Satan answered the LORD, and said, From going to and fro in the earth, and from walking up and down in it. ³And the LORD said to Satan, Have you considered my servant Job, that there is none like him in the earth, a perfect and an upright man, one that fears God, and eschews evil? and still he holds fast his integrity, although you moved me against him, to destroy him without cause. ⁴And Satan answered the LORD, and said, Skin for skin, yes, all that a man has will he give for his life. ⁵But put forth your hand now, and touch his bone and his flesh, and he will curse you to your face. ⁶And the LORD said to Satan, Behold, he is in your hand; but save his life. ⁷So went Satan forth from the presence of the LORD, and smote Job with sore boils from the sole of his foot to his crown. ⁸And he took him a potsherd to scrape himself with; and he sat down among the ashes. ⁹Then said his wife to him, Do you still retain your integrity? curse God, and die. ¹⁰But he said to her, You speak as one of the foolish women speaks. What? shall we receive good at the hand of God, and shall we not receive evil? In all this did not Job sin with his lips. ¹¹Now when Job's three friends heard of all this evil that was come on him, they came every one from his own place; Eliphaz the Temanite, and Bildad the Shuhite, and Zophar the Naamathite: for they had made an appointment together to come to mourn with him and to comfort him. ¹²And when they lifted up their eyes afar off, and knew him not, they lifted up their voice, and wept; and they rent every one his mantle, and sprinkled dust on their heads toward heaven. ¹³So they sat down with him on the ground seven days and seven nights, and none spoke a word to him: for they saw that his grief was very great.

3 ¹After this opened Job his mouth, and cursed his day. ²And Job spoke, and said, ³Let the day perish wherein I was born, and the night in which it was said, There is a man child conceived. ⁴Let that day be darkness; let not God regard it from above, neither let the light shine on it. ⁵Let darkness and the shadow of death stain it; let a cloud dwell on it; let the blackness of the day terrify it. ⁶As for that night, let darkness seize on it; let it not be joined to the days of the year, let it not come into the number of the months. ⁷See, let that night be solitary, let no joyful voice come therein. ⁸Let them curse it that curse the day, who are ready to raise up their mourning. ⁹Let the stars of the twilight thereof be dark; let it look for light, but have none; neither let it see the dawning of the day: ¹⁰Because it shut not up the doors of my mother's womb, nor hid sorrow from my eyes. ¹¹Why died I not from the womb? why did I not give up the ghost when I came out of the belly? ¹²Why did the knees prevent me? or why the breasts that I should suck? ¹³For now should I have lain still and been quiet, I should have slept: then had I been at rest, ¹⁴With kings and counsellors of the earth, which build desolate places for themselves; ¹⁵Or with princes that had gold, who filled their houses with silver: ¹⁶Or as an hidden untimely birth I had not been; as infants which never saw light. ⁱ⁷There the wicked cease from troubling; and there the weary be at rest. ¹⁸There the prisoners rest together; they hear not the voice of the oppressor. ¹⁹The small and great are there; and the servant is free from his master. ²⁰Why is light given to him that is in misery, and life to the bitter in soul; ²¹Which long for death, but it comes not; and dig for it more than for hid treasures; ²²Which rejoice exceedingly, and are glad, when they can find the grave? ²³Why is light given to a man whose way is hid, and whom God has hedged in? ²⁴For my sighing comes before I eat, and my roarings are poured out like the waters. ²⁵For the thing which I greatly feared is come on me, and that which I was afraid of is come to me. ²⁶I was not in safety, neither had I rest, neither was I quiet; yet trouble came.

4 ¹Then Eliphaz the Temanite answered and said, ²If we assay to commune with you, will you be grieved? but who can withhold himself from speaking? ³Behold, you have instructed many, and you have strengthened the weak hands. ⁴Your words have upheld him that was falling, and you have strengthened the feeble knees. ⁵But now it is come on you, and you faint; it touches you, and you are troubled. ⁶Is not this your fear, your confidence, your hope, and the uprightness of your ways? ⁷Remember, I pray you, who ever perished, being innocent? or where were the righteous cut off? ⁸Even as I have seen, they that plow iniquity, and sow wickedness, reap the same. ⁹By the blast of God they perish, and by the breath of his nostrils are they consumed. ¹⁰The roaring of the lion, and the voice of the fierce lion, and the teeth of the young lions, are broken. ¹¹The old lion perishes for lack of prey, and the stout lion's whelps are scattered abroad. ¹²Now a thing was secretly brought to me, and my ear received a little thereof. ¹³In thoughts from the visions of the night, when deep sleep falls on men, ¹⁴Fear came on me, and trembling, which made all my bones to shake. ¹⁵Then a spirit passed before my face; the hair of my flesh stood up: ¹⁶It stood still, but I could not discern the form thereof: an image was before my eyes, there was silence, and I heard a voice, saying, ¹⁷Shall mortal man be more just than God? shall a man be more pure than his maker? ¹⁸Behold, he put no trust in his servants; and his angels he charged with folly: ¹⁹How much less in them that dwell in houses of clay, whose foundation is in the dust, which are crushed before the moth? ²⁰They are destroyed from morning to evening: they perish for ever without any regarding it. ²¹Does not their excellency which is in them go away? they die, even without wisdom.

5 ¹Call now, if there be any that will answer you; and to which of the saints will you turn? ²For wrath kills the foolish man, and envy slays the silly one. ³I have seen the foolish taking root: but suddenly I cursed his habitation. ⁴His children are far from safety, and they are crushed in the gate, neither is there any to deliver them. ⁵Whose harvest the hungry eats up, and takes it even out of the thorns, and the robber swallows up their substance. ⁶Although affliction comes not forth of the dust, neither does trouble spring out of the ground; ⁷Yet man is born to trouble, as the sparks fly upward. ⁸I would seek to God, and to God would I commit my cause: ⁹Which does great things and unsearchable; marvelous things without number: ¹⁰Who gives rain on the earth, and sends waters on the fields: ¹¹To set up on high those that be low; that those which mourn may be exalted to safety. ¹²He disappoints the devices of the crafty, so that their hands cannot perform their enterprise. ¹³He takes the wise in their own craftiness: and the counsel of the fraudulent is carried headlong. ¹⁴They meet with darkness in the day time, and grope in the noonday as in the night. ¹⁵But he saves the poor from the sword, from their mouth, and from the hand of the mighty. ¹⁶So the poor has hope, and iniquity stops her mouth. ¹⁷Behold, happy is the man whom God corrects: therefore despise not you the chastening of the Almighty: ¹⁸For he makes sore, and binds up: he wounds, and his hands make whole. ¹⁹He shall deliver you in six troubles: yes, in seven there shall no evil touch you. ²⁰In famine he shall redeem you from death: and in war from the power of the sword. ²¹You shall be hid from the whip of the tongue: neither shall you be afraid of destruction when it comes. ²²At destruction and famine you shall laugh: neither shall you be afraid of the beasts of the earth. ²³For you shall be in league with the stones of the field: and the beasts of the field shall be at peace with you. ²⁴And you shall know that your tabernacle shall be in peace; and you shall visit your habitation, and shall not sin. ²⁵You shall know also that your seed shall be great, and your offspring as the grass of the earth. ²⁶You shall come to your grave in a full age, like as a shock of corn comes in in his season. ²⁷See this, we have searched it, so it is; hear it, and know you it for your good.

6 ¹But Job answered and said, ²Oh that my grief were thoroughly weighed, and my calamity laid in the balances together! ³For now it would be heavier than the sand of the sea: therefore my words are swallowed up. ⁴For the arrows of the Almighty are within me, the poison whereof drinks up my spirit: the terrors of God do set themselves in array against me. ⁵Does the wild ass bray when he has grass? or lows the ox over his fodder? ⁶Can that which is unsavory be eaten without salt? or is there any taste in the white of an egg? ⁷The things that my soul refused to touch are as my sorrowful meat. ⁸Oh that I might have my request; and that God would grant me the thing that I long for! ⁹Even that it would please God to destroy me; that he would let loose his hand, and cut me off! ¹⁰Then should I yet have comfort; yes, I would harden myself in sorrow: let him not spare; for I have not concealed the words of the Holy One. ¹¹What is my strength, that I should hope? and what is my end, that I should prolong my life? ¹²Is my strength the strength of stones? or is my flesh of brass? ¹³Is not my help in me? and is wisdom driven quite from me? ¹⁴To him that is afflicted pity should be showed from his friend; but he forsakes the fear of the Almighty. ¹⁵My brothers have dealt deceitfully as a brook, and as the stream of brooks they pass away; ¹⁶Which are blackish by reason of the ice, and wherein the snow is hid: ¹⁷What time they wax warm, they vanish: when it is hot, they are consumed out of their place. ¹⁸The paths of their way are turned aside; they go to nothing, and perish. ¹⁹The troops of Tema looked, the companies of Sheba waited for them. ²⁰They were confounded because they had hoped; they came thither, and were ashamed. ²¹For now you are nothing; you see my casting down, and are afraid. ²²Did I say, Bring to me? or, Give a reward for me of your substance? ²³Or, Deliver me from the enemy's hand? or,

Redeem me from the hand of the mighty? ²⁴Teach me, and I will hold my tongue: and cause me to understand wherein I have erred. ²⁵How forcible are right words! but what does your arguing reprove? ²⁶Do you imagine to reprove words, and the speeches of one that is desperate, which are as wind? ²⁷Yes, you overwhelm the fatherless, and you dig a pit for your friend. ²⁸Now therefore be content, look on me; for it is evident to you if I lie. ²⁹Return, I pray you, let it not be iniquity; yes, return again, my righteousness is in it. ³⁰Is there iniquity in my tongue? cannot my taste discern perverse things?

7 ¹Is there not an appointed time to man on earth? are not his days also like the days of an hireling? ²As a servant earnestly desires the shadow, and as an hireling looks for the reward of his work: ³So am I made to possess months of vanity, and wearisome nights are appointed to me. ⁴When I lie down, I say, When shall I arise, and the night be gone? and I am full of tossings to and fro to the dawning of the day. ⁵My flesh is clothed with worms and clods of dust; my skin is broken, and become loathsome. ⁶My days are swifter than a weaver's shuttle, and are spent without hope. ⁷O remember that my life is wind: my eye shall no more see good. ⁸The eye of him that has seen me shall see me no more: your eyes are on me, and I am not. ⁹As the cloud is consumed and vanishes away: so he that goes down to the grave shall come up no more. ¹⁰He shall return no more to his house, neither shall his place know him any more. ¹¹Therefore I will not refrain my mouth; I will speak in the anguish of my spirit; I will complain in the bitterness of my soul. ¹²Am I a sea, or a whale, that you set a watch over me? ¹³When I say, My bed shall comfort me, my couch shall ease my complaints; ¹⁴Then you scare me with dreams, and terrify me through visions: ¹⁵So that my soul chooses strangling, and death rather than my life. ¹⁶I loathe it; I would not live always: let me alone; for my days are vanity. ¹⁷What is man, that you should magnify him? and that you should set your heart on him? ¹⁸And that you should visit him every morning, and try him every moment? ¹⁹How long will you not depart from me, nor let me alone till I swallow down my spittle? ²⁰I have sinned; what shall I do to you, O you preserver of men? why have you set me as a mark against you, so that I am a burden to myself? ²¹And why do you not pardon my transgression, and take away my iniquity? for now shall I sleep in the dust; and you shall seek me in the morning, but I shall not be.

8 ¹Then answered Bildad the Shuhite, and said, ²How long will you speak these things? and how long shall the words of your mouth be like a strong wind? ³Does God pervert judgment? or does the Almighty pervert justice? ⁴If your children have sinned against him, and he have cast them away for their transgression; ⁵If you would seek to God betimes, and make your supplication to the Almighty; ⁶If you were pure and upright; surely now he would awake for you, and make the habitation of your righteousness prosperous. ⁷Though your beginning was small, yet your latter end should greatly increase. ⁸For inquire, I pray you, of the former age, and prepare yourself to the search of their fathers: ⁹(For we are but of yesterday, and know nothing, because our days on earth are a shadow:) ¹⁰Shall not they teach you, and tell you, and utter words out of their heart? ¹¹Can the rush grow up without mire? can the flag grow without water? ¹²Whilst it is yet in his greenness, and not cut down, it wither before any other herb. ¹³So are the paths of all that forget God; and the hypocrite's hope shall perish: ¹⁴Whose hope shall be cut off, and whose trust shall be a spider's web. ¹⁵He shall lean on his house, but it shall not stand: he shall hold it fast, but it shall not endure. ¹⁶He is green before the sun, and his branch shoots forth in his garden. ¹⁷His roots are wrapped about the heap, and sees the place of stones. ¹⁸If he destroy him from his place, then it shall deny him, saying, I have not seen you. ¹⁹Behold, this is the joy of his way, and out of the earth shall others grow. ²⁰Behold, God will not cast away a perfect man, neither will he help the evil doers: ²¹Till he fill your mouth with laughing, and your lips with rejoicing. ²²They that hate you shall be clothed with shame; and the dwelling place of the wicked shall come to nothing.

9 ¹Then Job answered and said, ²I know it is so of a truth: but how should man be just with God? ³If he will contend with him, he cannot answer him one of a thousand. ⁴He is wise in heart, and mighty in strength: who has hardened himself against him, and has prospered? ⁵Which removes the mountains, and they know not: which overturns them in his anger. ⁶Which shakes the earth out of her place, and the pillars thereof tremble. ⁷Which commands the sun, and it rises not; and seals up the stars. ⁸Which alone spreads out the heavens, and treads on the waves of the sea. ⁹Which makes Arcturus, Orion, and Pleiades, and the chambers of the south. ¹⁰Which does great things past finding out; yes, and wonders without number. ¹¹See, he goes by me, and I see him not: he passes on also, but I perceive him not. ¹²Behold, he takes away, who can hinder him? who will say to him, What do you? ¹³If God will not withdraw his anger, the proud helpers do stoop under him. ¹⁴How much less shall I answer him, and choose out my words to reason with him? ¹⁵Whom, though I were righteous, yet would I not answer, but I would make supplication to my judge. ¹⁶If I had called, and he had answered me; yet would I not believe that he had listened to my voice. ¹⁷For he breaks me with a tempest, and multiplies my wounds without cause. ¹⁸He will not suffer me to take my breath, but fills me with bitterness. ¹⁹If I speak of strength, see, he is strong: and if of judgment, who shall set me a time to plead? ²⁰If I justify myself, my own mouth shall condemn me: if I say, I am perfect, it shall also prove me perverse. ²¹Though I were perfect, yet would I not know my soul: I would despise my life. ²²This is one thing, therefore I said it, He destroys the perfect and the wicked. ²³If the whip slay suddenly, he will laugh at the trial of the innocent. ²⁴The earth is given into the hand of the wicked: he covers the faces of the judges thereof; if not, where, and who is he? ²⁵Now my days are swifter than a post: they flee away, they see no good. ²⁶They are passed away as the swift ships: as the eagle that hastens to the prey. ²⁷If I say, I will forget my complaint, I will leave off my heaviness, and comfort myself: ²⁸I am afraid of all my sorrows, I know that you will not hold me innocent. ²⁹If I be wicked, why then labor I in vain? ³⁰If I wash myself with snow water, and make my hands never so clean; ³¹Yet shall you plunge me in the ditch, and my own clothes shall abhor me. ³²For he is not a man, as

I am, that I should answer him, and we should come together in judgment. ³³Neither is there any judge between us, that might lay his hand on us both. ³⁴Let him take his rod away from me, and let not his fear terrify me: ³⁵Then would I speak, and not fear him; but it is not so with me.

10 ¹My soul is weary of my life; I will leave my complaint on myself; I will speak in the bitterness of my soul. ²I will say to God, Do not condemn me; show me why you contend with me. ³Is it good to you that you should oppress, that you should despise the work of your hands, and shine on the counsel of the wicked? ⁴Have you eyes of flesh? or see you as man sees? ⁵Are your days as the days of man? are your years as man's days, ⁶That you enquire after my iniquity, and search after my sin? ⁷You know that I am not wicked; and there is none that can deliver out of your hand. ⁸Your hands have made me and fashioned me together round about; yet you do destroy me. ⁹Remember, I beseech you, that you have made me as the clay; and will you bring me into dust again? ¹⁰Have you not poured me out as milk, and curdled me like cheese? ¹¹You have clothed me with skin and flesh, and have fenced me with bones and sinews. ¹²You have granted me life and favor, and your visitation has preserved my spirit. ¹³And these things have you hid in your heart: I know that this is with you. ¹⁴If I sin, then you mark me, and you will not acquit me from my iniquity. ¹⁵If I be wicked, woe to me; and if I be righteous, yet will I not lift up my head. I am full of confusion; therefore see you my affliction; ¹⁶For it increases. You hunt me as a fierce lion: and again you show yourself marvelous on me. ¹⁷You renew your witnesses against me, and increase your indignation on me; changes and war are against me. ¹⁸Why then have you brought me forth out of the womb? Oh that I had given up the ghost, and no eye had seen me! ¹⁹I should have been as though I had not been; I should have been carried from the womb to the grave. ²⁰Are not my days few? cease then, and let me alone, that I may take comfort a little, ²¹Before I go from where I shall not return, even to the land of darkness and the shadow of death; ²²A land of darkness, as darkness itself; and of the shadow of death, without any order, and where the light is as darkness.

11 ¹Then answered Zophar the Naamathite, and said, ²Should not the multitude of words be answered? and should a man full of talk be justified? ³Should your lies make men hold their peace? and when you mock, shall no man make you ashamed? ⁴For you have said, My doctrine is pure, and I am clean in your eyes. ⁵But oh that God would speak, and open his lips against you; ⁶And that he would show you the secrets of wisdom, that they are double to that which is! Know therefore that God exacts of you less than your iniquity deserves. ⁷Can you by searching find out God? can you find out the Almighty to perfection? ⁸It is as high as heaven; what can you do? deeper than hell; what can you know? ⁹The measure thereof is longer than the earth, and broader than the sea. ¹⁰If he cut off, and shut up, or gather together, then who can hinder him? ¹¹For he knows vain men: he sees wickedness also; will he not then consider it? ¹²For vain men would be wise, though man be born like a wild ass's colt. ¹³If you prepare your heart, and stretch out your hands toward him; ¹⁴If iniquity be in your hand, put it far away, and let not wickedness dwell in your tabernacles. ¹⁵For then shall you lift up your face without spot; yes, you shall be steadfast, and shall not fear: ¹⁶Because you shall forget your misery, and remember it as waters that pass away: ¹⁷And your age shall be clearer than the noonday: you shall shine forth, you shall be as the morning. ¹⁸And you shall be secure, because there is hope; yes, you shall dig about you, and you shall take your rest in safety. ¹⁹Also you shall lie down, and none shall make you afraid; yes, many shall make suit to you. ²⁰But the eyes of the wicked shall fail, and they shall not escape, and their hope shall be as the giving up of the ghost.

12 ¹And Job answered and said, ²No doubt but you are the people, and wisdom shall die with you. ³But I have understanding as well as you; I am not inferior to you: yes, who knows not such things as these? ⁴I am as one mocked of his neighbor, who calls on God, and he answers him: the just upright man is laughed to scorn. ⁵He that is ready to slip with his feet is as a lamp despised in the thought of him that is at ease. ⁶The tabernacles of robbers prosper, and they that provoke God are secure; into whose hand God brings abundantly. ⁷But ask now the beasts, and they shall teach you; and the fowls of the air, and they shall tell you: ⁸Or speak to the earth, and it shall teach you: and the fishes of the sea shall declare to you. ⁹Who knows not in all these that the hand of the LORD has worked this? ¹⁰In whose hand is the soul of every living thing, and the breath of all mankind. ¹¹Does not the ear try words? and the mouth taste his meat? ¹²With the ancient is wisdom; and in length of days understanding. ¹³With him is wisdom and strength, he has counsel and understanding. ¹⁴Behold, he breaks down, and it cannot be built again: he shuts up a man, and there can be no opening. ¹⁵Behold, he withholds the waters, and they dry up: also he sends them out, and they overturn the earth. ¹⁶With him is strength and wisdom: the deceived and the deceiver are his. ¹⁷He leads counsellors away spoiled, and makes the judges fools. ¹⁸He looses the bond of kings, and girds their loins with a girdle. ¹⁹He leads princes away spoiled, and overthrows the mighty. ²⁰He removes away the speech of the trusty, and takes away the understanding of the aged. ²¹He pours contempt on princes, and weakens the strength of the mighty. ²²He discovers deep things out of darkness, and brings out to light the shadow of death. ²³He increases the nations, and destroys them: he enlarges the nations, and straitens them again. ²⁴He takes away the heart of the chief of the people of the earth, and causes them to wander in a wilderness where there is no way. ²⁵They grope in the dark without light, and he makes them to stagger like a drunken man.

13 ¹See, my eye has seen all this, my ear has heard and understood it. ²What you know, the same do I know also: I am not inferior to you. ³Surely I would speak to the Almighty, and I desire to reason with God. ⁴But you are forgers of lies, you are all physicians of no value. ⁵O that you would altogether hold your peace! and it should be your wisdom. ⁶Hear now my reasoning, and listen to the pleadings of my lips. ⁷Will you speak wickedly for God? and talk deceitfully for him? ⁸Will you accept his person? will you contend for God? ⁹Is it good that he should search you out? or as one man mocks another, do you so mock him? ¹⁰He will surely reprove you, if you do secretly accept persons. ¹¹Shall not his excellency make you afraid? and his dread fall on you? ¹²Your remembrances are like to ashes, your bodies to bodies of clay. ¹³Hold your peace, let me alone, that I may speak, and let come on me what will. ¹⁴Why do I take my flesh in my teeth, and put my life in my hand? ¹⁵Though he slay me, yet will I trust in him: but I will maintain my own ways before him. ¹⁶He also shall be my salvation: for an hypocrite shall not come before him. ¹⁷Hear diligently my speech, and my declaration with your ears. ¹⁸Behold now, I have ordered my cause; I know that I shall be justified. ¹⁹Who is he that will plead with me? for now, if I hold my tongue, I shall give up the ghost. ²⁰Only do not two things to me: then will I not hide myself from you. ²¹Withdraw your hand far from me: and let not your dread make me afraid. ²²Then call you, and I will answer: or let me speak, and answer you me. ²³How many are my iniquities and sins? make me to know my transgression and my sin. ²⁴Why hide you your face, and hold me for your enemy? ²⁵Will you break a leaf driven to and fro? and will you pursue the dry stubble? ²⁶For you write bitter things against me, and make me to possess the iniquities of my youth. ²⁷You put my feet also in the stocks, and look narrowly to all my paths; you set a print on the heels of my feet. ²⁸And he, as a rotten thing, consumes, as a garment that is moth eaten.

14 ¹Man that is born of a woman is of few days and full of trouble. ²He comes forth like a flower, and is cut down: he flees also as a shadow, and continues not. ³And does you open your eyes on such an one, and bring me into judgment with you? ⁴Who can bring a clean thing out of an unclean? not one. ⁵Seeing his days are determined, the number of his months are with you, you have appointed his bounds that he cannot pass; ⁶Turn from him, that he may rest, till he shall accomplish, as an hireling, his day. ⁷For there is hope of a tree, if it be cut down, that it will sprout again, and that the tender branch thereof will not cease. ⁸Though the root thereof wax old in the earth, and the stock thereof die in the ground; ⁹Yet through the scent of water it will bud, and bring forth boughs like a plant. ¹⁰But man dies, and wastes away: yes, man gives up the ghost, and where is he? ¹¹As the waters fail from the sea, and the flood decays and dries up: ¹²So man lies down, and rises not: till the heavens be no more, they shall not awake, nor be raised out of their sleep. ¹³O that you would hide me in the grave, that you would keep me secret, until your wrath be past, that you would appoint me a set time, and remember me! ¹⁴If a man die, shall he live again? all the days of my appointed time will I wait, till my change come. ¹⁵You shall call, and I will answer you: you will have a desire to the work of your hands. ¹⁶For now you number my steps: do you not watch over my sin? ¹⁷My transgression is sealed up in a bag, and you sew up my iniquity. ¹⁸And surely the mountains falling comes to nothing, and the rock is removed out of his place. ¹⁹The waters wear the stones: you wash away the things which grow out of the dust of the earth; and you destroy the hope of man. ²⁰You prevail for ever against him, and he passes: you change his countenance, and send him away. ²¹His sons come to honor, and he knows it not; and they are brought low, but he perceives it not of them. ²²But his flesh on him shall have pain, and his soul within him shall mourn.

15 ¹Then answered Eliphaz the Temanite, and said, ²Should a wise man utter vain knowledge, and fill his belly with the east wind? ³Should he reason with unprofitable talk? or with speeches with which he can do no good? ⁴Yes, you cast off fear, and restrain prayer before God. ⁵For your mouth utters your iniquity, and you choose the tongue of the crafty. ⁶Your own mouth condemns you, and not I: yes, your own lips testify against you. ⁷Are you the first man that was born? or were you made before the hills? ⁸Have you heard the secret of God? and do you restrain wisdom to yourself? ⁹What know you, that we know not? what understand you, which is not in us? ¹⁰With us are both the gray headed and very aged men, much elder than your father. ¹¹Are the consolations of God small with you? is there any secret thing with you? ¹²Why does your heart carry you away? and what do your eyes wink at, ¹³That you turn your spirit against God, and let such words go out of your mouth? ¹⁴What is man, that he should be clean? and he which is born of a woman, that he should be righteous? ¹⁵Behold, he puts no trust in his saints; yes, the heavens are not clean in his sight. ¹⁶How much more abominable and filthy is man, which drinks iniquity like water? ¹⁷I will show you, hear me; and that which I have seen I will declare; ¹⁸Which wise men have told from their fathers, and have not hid it: ¹⁹To whom alone the earth was given, and no stranger passed among them. ²⁰The wicked man travails with pain all his days, and the number of years is hidden to the oppressor. ²¹A dreadful sound is in his ears: in prosperity the destroyer shall come on him. ²²He believes not that he shall return out of darkness, and he is waited for of the sword. ²³He wanders abroad for bread, saying, Where is it? he knows that the day of darkness is ready at his hand. ²⁴Trouble and anguish shall make him afraid; they shall prevail against him, as a king ready to the battle. ²⁵For he stretches out his hand against God, and strengthens himself against the Almighty. ²⁶He runs on him, even on his neck, on the thick bosses of his bucklers: ²⁷Because he covers his face with his fatness, and makes bulges of fat on his flanks. ²⁸And he dwells in desolate cities, and in houses which no man inhabits, which are ready to become heaps. ²⁹He shall not be rich, neither shall his substance continue, neither shall he prolong the perfection thereof on the earth. ³⁰He shall not depart out of darkness; the flame shall dry up his branches, and by the breath of his mouth shall he go away. ³¹Let not him that is deceived trust in vanity: for vanity shall be his recompense. ³²It shall be accomplished before his time, and his branch shall not be green. ³³He shall shake off his unripe grape as the vine, and shall cast off his flower as the olive. ³⁴For the congregation of hypocrites shall be desolate, and fire shall consume the tabernacles of bribery. ³⁵They conceive mischief, and bring forth vanity, and their belly prepares deceit.

16 ¹Then Job answered and said, ²I have heard many such things: miserable comforters are you all. ³Shall vain words have an end? or what emboldens you that you answer? ⁴I also could speak as you do: if your soul were in my soul's stead, I could heap up words against you, and shake my head at you. ⁵But I would strengthen you with my mouth, and the moving of my lips should assuage your grief. ⁶Though I speak, my grief is not assuaged: and though I forbear, what am I eased? ⁷But now he has made me weary: you have made desolate all my company. ⁸And you have filled me with wrinkles, which is a witness against me: and my leanness rising up in me bears witness to my face. ⁹He tears me in his wrath, who hates me: he gnashes on me with his teeth; my enemy sharpens his eyes on me. ¹⁰They have gaped on me with their mouth; they have smitten me on the cheek reproachfully; they have gathered themselves together against me. ¹¹God has delivered me to the ungodly, and turned me over into the hands of the wicked. ¹²I was at ease, but he has broken me asunder: he has also taken me by my neck, and shaken me to pieces, and set me up for his mark. ¹³His archers compass me round about, he splits my reins asunder, and does not spare; he pours out my gall on the ground. ¹⁴He breaks me with breach on breach, he runs on me like a giant. ¹⁵I have sewed sackcloth on my skin, and defiled my horn in the dust. ¹⁶My face is foul with weeping, and on my eyelids is the shadow of death; ¹⁷Not for any injustice in my hands: also my prayer is pure. ¹⁸O earth, cover not you my blood, and let my cry have no place. ¹⁹Also now, behold, my witness is in heaven, and my record is on high. ²⁰My friends scorn me: but my eye pours out tears to God. ²¹O that one might plead for a man with God, as a man pleads for his neighbor! ²²When a few years are come, then I shall go the way from where I shall not return.

17 ¹My breath is corrupt, my days are extinct, the graves are ready for me. ²Are there not mockers with me? and does not my eye continue in their provocation? ³Lay down now, put me in a surety with you; who is he that will strike hands with me? ⁴For you have hid their heart from understanding: therefore shall you not exalt them. ⁵He that speaks flattery to his friends, even the eyes of his children shall fail. ⁶He has made me also a byword of the people; and aforetime I was as a tabret. ⁷My eye also is dim by reason of sorrow, and all my members are as a shadow. ⁸Upright men shall be astonished at this, and the innocent shall stir up himself against the hypocrite. ⁹The righteous also shall hold on his way, and he that has clean hands shall be stronger and stronger. ¹⁰But as for you all, do you return, and come now: for I cannot find one wise man among you. ¹¹My days are past, my purposes are broken off, even the thoughts of my heart. ¹²They change the night into day: the light is short because of darkness. ¹³If I wait, the grave is my house: I have made my bed in the darkness. ¹⁴I have said to corruption, You are my father: to the worm, You are my mother, and my sister. ¹⁵And where is now my hope? as for my hope, who shall see it? ¹⁶They shall go down to the bars of the pit, when our rest together is in the dust.

18 ¹Then answered Bildad the Shuhite, and said, ²How long will it be before you make an end of words? mark, and afterwards we will speak. ³Why are we counted as beasts, and reputed vile in your sight? ⁴He tears himself in his anger: shall the earth be forsaken for you? and shall the rock be removed out of his place? ⁵Yes, the light of the wicked shall be put out, and the spark of his fire shall not shine. ⁶The light shall be dark in his tabernacle, and his candle shall be put out with him. ⁷The steps of his strength shall be straitened, and his own counsel shall cast him down. ⁸For he is cast into a net by his own feet, and he walks on a snare. ⁹The gin shall take him by the heel, and the robber shall prevail against him. ¹⁰The snare is laid for him in the ground, and a trap for him in the way. ¹¹Terrors shall make him afraid on every side, and shall drive him to his feet. ¹²His strength shall be extremely hungry, and destruction shall be ready at his side. ¹³It shall devour the strength of his skin: even the firstborn of death shall devour his strength. ¹⁴His confidence shall be rooted out of his tabernacle, and it shall bring him to the king of terrors. ¹⁵It shall dwell in his tabernacle, because it is none of his: brimstone shall be scattered on his habitation. ¹⁶His roots shall be dried up beneath, and above shall his branch be cut off. ¹⁷His remembrance shall perish from the earth, and he shall have no name in the street. ¹⁸He shall be driven from light into darkness, and chased out of the world. ¹⁹He shall neither have son nor nephew among his people, nor any remaining in his dwellings. ²⁰They that come after him shall be astonished in his day, as they that went before were affrighted. ²¹Surely such are the dwellings of the wicked, and this is the place of him that knows not God.

19 ¹Then Job answered and said, ²How long will you vex my soul, and break me in pieces with words? ³These ten times have you reproached me: you are not ashamed that you make yourselves strange to me. ⁴And be it indeed that I have erred, my error remains with myself. ⁵If indeed you will magnify yourselves against me, and plead against me my reproach: ⁶Know now that God has overthrown me, and has compassed me with his net. ⁷Behold, I cry out of wrong, but I am not heard: I cry aloud, but there is no judgment. ⁸He has fenced up my way that I cannot pass, and he has set darkness in my paths. ⁹He has stripped me of my glory, and taken the crown from my head. ¹⁰He has destroyed me on every side, and I am gone: and my hope has he removed like a tree. ¹¹He has also kindled his wrath against me, and he counts me to him as one of his enemies. ¹²His troops come together, and raise up their way against me, and encamp round about my tabernacle. ¹³He has put my brothers far from me, and my acquaintance are truly estranged from me. ¹⁴My kinsfolk have failed, and my familiar friends have forgotten me. ¹⁵They that dwell in my house, and my maids, count me for a stranger: I am an alien in their sight. ¹⁶I called my servant, and he gave me no answer; I entreated him with my mouth. ¹⁷My breath is strange to my wife, though I entreated for the children's sake of my own body. ¹⁸Yes, young children despised me; I arose, and they spoke against me. ¹⁹All my inward friends abhorred me: and they whom I loved are turned against me. ²⁰My bone sticks to my skin and to my flesh, and I am escaped with the skin of my teeth. ²¹Have pity on me, have pity on me, O you my friends; for the hand of God has touched me. ²²Why do you persecute me as God, and are not satisfied with my flesh? ²³Oh that my words were now written! oh that they were printed in a book! ²⁴That they were graven with an iron pen and lead in the rock for ever! ²⁵For I know that my redeemer lives, and that he shall stand at the latter day on the earth: ²⁶And though after my skin worms destroy this body, yet in my flesh shall I see God: ²⁷Whom I shall see for myself, and my eyes shall behold, and not another; though my reins be consumed within me. ²⁸But you should say, Why persecute we him, seeing the root of the matter is found in me? ²⁹Be you afraid of the sword: for wrath brings the punishments of the sword, that you may know there is a judgment.

20 ¹Then answered Zophar the Naamathite, and said, ²Therefore do my thoughts cause me to answer, and for this I make haste. ³I have heard the check of my reproach, and the spirit of my understanding causes me to answer. ⁴Know you not this of old, since man was placed on earth, ⁵That the triumphing of the wicked is short, and the joy of the hypocrite but for a moment? ⁶Though his excellency mount up to the heavens, and his head reach to the clouds; ⁷Yet he shall perish for ever like his own dung: they which have seen him shall say, Where is he? ⁸He shall fly away as a dream, and shall not be found: yes, he shall be chased away as a vision of the night. ⁹The eye also which saw him shall see him no more; neither shall his place any more behold him. ¹⁰His children shall seek to please the poor, and his hands shall restore their goods. ¹¹His bones are full of the sin of his youth, which shall lie down with him in the dust. ¹²Though wickedness be sweet in his mouth, though he hide it under his tongue; ¹³Though he spare it, and forsake it not; but keep it still within his mouth: ¹⁴Yet his meat in his bowels is turned, it is the gall of asps within him. ¹⁵He has swallowed down riches, and he shall vomit them up again: God shall cast them out of his belly. ¹⁶He shall suck the poison of asps: the viper's tongue shall slay him. ¹⁷He shall not see the rivers, the floods, the brooks of honey and butter. ¹⁸That which he labored for shall he restore, and shall not swallow it down: according to his substance shall the restitution be, and he shall not rejoice therein. ¹⁹Because he has oppressed and has forsaken the poor; because he has violently taken away an house which he built not; ²⁰Surely he shall not feel quietness in his belly, he shall not save of that which he desired. ²¹There shall none of his meat be left; therefore shall no man look for his goods. ²²In the fullness of his sufficiency he shall be in straits: every hand of the wicked shall come on him. ²³When he is about to fill his belly, God shall cast the fury of his wrath on him, and shall rain it on him while he is eating. ²⁴He shall flee from the iron weapon, and the bow of steel shall strike him through. ²⁵It is drawn, and comes out of the body; yes, the glittering sword comes out of his gall: terrors are on him. ²⁶All darkness shall be hid in his secret places: a fire not blown shall consume him; it shall go ill with him that is left in his tabernacle. ²⁷The heaven shall reveal his iniquity; and the earth shall rise up against him. ²⁸The increase of his house shall depart, and his goods shall flow away in the day of his wrath. ²⁹This is the portion of a wicked man from God, and the heritage appointed to him by God.

21 ¹But Job answered and said, ²Hear diligently my speech, and let this be your consolations. ³Suffer me that I may speak; and after that I have spoken, mock on. ⁴As for me, is my complaint to man? and if it were so, why should not my spirit be troubled? ⁵Mark me, and be astonished, and lay your hand on your mouth. ⁶Even when I remember I am afraid, and trembling takes hold on my flesh. ⁷Why do the wicked live, become old, yes, are mighty in power? ⁸Their seed is established in their sight with them, and their offspring before their eyes. ⁹Their houses are safe from fear, neither is the rod of God on them. ¹⁰Their bull engenders, and fails not; their cow calves, and casts not her calf. ¹¹They send forth their little ones like a flock, and their children dance. ¹²They take the tambourine and harp, and rejoice at the sound of the organ. ¹³They spend their days in wealth, and in a moment go down to the grave. ¹⁴Therefore they say to God, Depart from us; for we desire not the knowledge of your ways. ¹⁵What is the Almighty, that we should serve him? and what profit should we have, if we pray to him? ¹⁶See, their good is not in their hand: the counsel of the wicked is far from me. ¹⁷How oft is the candle of the wicked put out! and how oft comes their destruction on them! God distributes sorrows in his anger. ¹⁸They are as stubble before the wind, and as chaff that the storm carries away. ¹⁹God lays up his iniquity for his children: he rewards him, and he shall know it. ²⁰His eyes shall see his destruction, and he shall drink of the wrath of the Almighty. ²¹For what pleasure has he in his house after him, when the number of his months is cut off in the middle? ²²Shall any teach God knowledge? seeing he judges those that are high. ²³One dies in his full strength, being wholly at ease and quiet. ²⁴His breasts are full of milk, and his bones are moistened with marrow. ²⁵And another dies in the bitterness of his soul, and never eats with pleasure. ²⁶They shall lie down alike in the dust, and the worms shall cover them. ²⁷Behold, I know your thoughts, and the devices which you wrongfully imagine against me. ²⁸For you say, Where is the house of the prince? and where are the dwelling places of the wicked? ²⁹Have you not asked them that go by by the way? and do you not know their tokens, ³⁰That the wicked is reserved to the day of destruction? they shall be brought forth to the day of wrath. ³¹Who shall declare his way to his face? and who shall repay him what he has done? ³²Yet shall he be brought to the grave, and shall remain in the tomb. ³³The clods of the valley shall be sweet to him, and every man shall draw after him, as there are innumerable before him. ³⁴How then comfort you me in vain, seeing in your answers there remains falsehood?

22 ¹Then Eliphaz the Temanite answered and said, ²Can a man be profitable to God, as he that is wise may be profitable to himself? ³Is it any pleasure to the Almighty, that you are righteous? or is it gain to him, that you make your ways perfect? ⁴Will he reprove you for fear of you? will he enter with you into judgment? ⁵Is not your wickedness great? and your iniquities infinite? ⁶For you have taken a pledge from your brother for nothing, and stripped the naked of their clothing. ⁷You have not given water to the weary to drink, and you have withheld bread from the hungry. ⁸But as for the mighty man, he had the earth; and the honorable man dwelled in it. ⁹You have sent widows away empty, and the arms of the fatherless have been broken. ¹⁰Therefore snares are round about you, and sudden fear troubles you; ¹¹Or darkness, that you can not see; and abundance of waters cover you. ¹²Is not God in the height of heaven? and behold the height of the stars, how high they are! ¹³And you say, How does God know? can he judge through the dark cloud? ¹⁴Thick clouds are a covering to him, that he sees not; and he walks in the circuit of heaven. ¹⁵Have you marked the old way which wicked men have trodden? ¹⁶Which were cut down out of time, whose foundation was overflowed with a flood: ¹⁷Which said to God, Depart from us: and what can the Almighty do for them? ¹⁸Yet he filled their houses with good things: but the counsel of the wicked is far from me. ¹⁹The righteous see it, and are glad: and the innocent laugh them to scorn. ²⁰Whereas our substance is not cut down, but the remnant of them the fire consumes. ²¹Acquaint now yourself with him, and be at peace: thereby good shall come to you. ²²Receive, I pray you, the law from his mouth, and lay up his words in your heart. ²³If you return to the Almighty, you shall be built up, you shall put away iniquity far from your tabernacles. ²⁴Then shall you lay up gold as dust, and the gold of Ophir as the stones of the brooks. ²⁵Yes, the Almighty shall be your defense, and you shall have plenty of silver. ²⁶For then shall you have your delight in the Almighty, and shall lift up your face to God. ²⁷You shall make your prayer to him, and he shall hear you, and you shall pay your vows. ²⁸You shall also decree a thing, and it shall be established to you: and the light shall shine on your ways. ²⁹When men are cast down, then you shall say, There is lifting up; and he shall save the humble person. ³⁰He shall deliver the island of the innocent: and it is delivered by the pureness of your hands.

23

¹Then Job answered and said, ²Even to day is my complaint bitter: my stroke is heavier than my groaning. ³Oh that I knew where I might find him! that I might come even to his seat! ⁴I would order my cause before him, and fill my mouth with arguments. ⁵I would know the words which he would answer me, and understand what he would say to me. ⁶Will he plead against me with his great power? No; but he would put strength in me. ⁷There the righteous might dispute with him; so should I be delivered for ever from my judge. ⁸Behold, I go forward, but he is not there; and backward, but I cannot perceive him: ⁹On the left hand, where he does work, but I cannot behold him: he hides himself on the right hand, that I cannot see him: ¹⁰But he knows the way that I take: when he has tried me, I shall come forth as gold. ¹¹My foot has held his steps, his way have I kept, and not declined. ¹²Neither have I gone back from the commandment of his lips; I have esteemed the words of his mouth more than my necessary food. ¹³But he is in one mind, and who can turn him? and what his soul desires, even that he does. ¹⁴For he performs the thing that is appointed for me: and many such things are with him. ¹⁵Therefore am I troubled at his presence: when I consider, I am afraid of him. ¹⁶For God makes my heart soft, and the Almighty troubles me: ¹⁷Because I was not cut off before the darkness, neither has he covered the darkness from my face.

24

¹Why, seeing times are not hidden from the Almighty, do they that know him not see his days? ²Some remove the landmarks; they violently take away flocks, and feed thereof. ³They drive away the ass of the fatherless, they take the widow's ox for a pledge. ⁴They turn the needy out of the way: the poor of the earth hide themselves together. ⁵Behold, as wild asses in the desert, go they forth to their work; rising betimes for a prey: the wilderness yields food for them and for their children. ⁶They reap every one his corn in the field: and they gather the vintage of the wicked. ⁷They cause the naked to lodge without clothing, that they have no covering in the cold. ⁸They are wet with the showers of the mountains, and embrace the rock for want of a shelter. ⁹They pluck the fatherless from the breast, and take a pledge of the poor. ¹⁰They cause him to go naked without clothing, and they take away the sheaf from the hungry; ¹¹Which make oil within their walls, and tread their winepresses, and suffer thirst. ¹²Men groan from out of the city, and the soul of the wounded cries out: yet God lays not folly to them. ¹³They are of those that rebel against the light; they know not the ways thereof, nor abide in the paths thereof. ¹⁴The murderer rising with the light kills the poor and needy, and in the night is as a thief. ¹⁵The eye also of the adulterer waits for the twilight, saying, No eye shall see me: and disguises his face. ¹⁶In the dark they dig through houses, which they had marked for themselves in the daytime: they know not the light. ¹⁷For the morning is to them even as the shadow of death: if one know them, they are in the terrors of the shadow of death. ¹⁸He is swift as the waters; their portion is cursed in the earth: he beholds not the way of the vineyards. ¹⁹Drought and heat consume the snow waters: so does the grave those which have sinned. ²⁰The womb shall forget him; the worm shall feed sweetly on him; he shall be no more remembered; and wickedness shall be broken as a tree. ²¹He evil entreats the barren that bears not: and does not good to the widow. ²²He draws also the mighty with his power: he rises up, and no man is sure of life. ²³Though it be given him to be in safety, where on he rests; yet his eyes are on their ways. ²⁴They are exalted for a little while, but are gone and brought low; they are taken out of the way as all other, and cut off as the tops of the ears of corn. ²⁵And if it be not so now, who will make me a liar, and make my speech nothing worth?

25

¹Then answered Bildad the Shuhite, and said, ²Dominion and fear are with him, he makes peace in his high places. ³Is there any number of his armies? and on whom does not his light arise? ⁴How then can man be justified with God? or how can he be clean that is born of a woman? ⁵Behold even to the moon, and it shines not; yes, the stars are not pure in his sight. ⁶How much less man, that is a worm? and the son of man, which is a worm?

26

¹But Job answered and said, ²How have you helped him that is without power? how save you the arm that has no strength? ³How have you counceled him that has no wisdom? and how have you plentifully declared the thing as it is? ⁴To whom have you uttered words? and whose spirit came from you? ⁵Dead things are formed from under the waters, and the inhabitants thereof. ⁶Hell is naked before him, and destruction has no covering. ⁷He stretches out the north over the empty place, and hangs the earth on nothing. ⁸He binds up the waters in his thick clouds; and the cloud is not rent under them. ⁹He holds back the face of his throne, and spreads his cloud on it. ¹⁰He has compassed the waters with bounds, until the day and night come to an end. ¹¹The pillars of heaven tremble and are astonished at his reproof. ¹²He divides the sea with his power, and by his understanding he smites through the proud. ¹³By his spirit he has garnished the heavens; his hand has formed the crooked

serpent. ¹⁴See, these are parts of his ways: but how little a portion is heard of him? but the thunder of his power who can understand?

27 ¹Moreover Job continued his parable, and said, ²As God lives, who has taken away my judgment; and the Almighty, who has vexed my soul; ³All the while my breath is in me, and the spirit of God is in my nostrils; ⁴My lips shall not speak wickedness, nor my tongue utter deceit. ⁵God forbid that I should justify you: till I die I will not remove my integrity from me. ⁶My righteousness I hold fast, and will not let it go: my heart shall not reproach me so long as I live. ⁷Let my enemy be as the wicked, and he that rises up against me as the unrighteous. ⁸For what is the hope of the hypocrite, though he has gained, when God takes away his soul? ⁹Will God hear his cry when trouble comes on him? ¹⁰Will he delight himself in the Almighty? will he always call on God? ¹¹I will teach you by the hand of God: that which is with the Almighty will I not conceal. ¹²Behold, all you yourselves have seen it; why then are you thus altogether vain? ¹³This is the portion of a wicked man with God, and the heritage of oppressors, which they shall receive of the Almighty. ¹⁴If his children be multiplied, it is for the sword: and his offspring shall not be satisfied with bread. ¹⁵Those that remain of him shall be buried in death: and his widows shall not weep. ¹⁶Though he heap up silver as the dust, and prepare raiment as the clay; ¹⁷He may prepare it, but the just shall put it on, and the innocent shall divide the silver. ¹⁸He builds his house as a moth, and as a booth that the keeper makes. ¹⁹The rich man shall lie down, but he shall not be gathered: he opens his eyes, and he is not. ²⁰Terrors take hold on him as waters, a tempest steals him away in the night. ²¹The east wind carries him away, and he departs: and as a storm hurls him out of his place. ²²For God shall cast on him, and not spare: he would fain flee out of his hand. ²³Men shall clap their hands at him, and shall hiss him out of his place.

28 ¹Surely there is a vein for the silver, and a place for gold where they fine it. ²Iron is taken out of the earth, and brass is molten out of the stone. ³He sets an end to darkness, and searches out all perfection: the stones of darkness, and the shadow of death. ⁴The flood breaks out from the inhabitant; even the waters forgotten of the foot: they are dried up, they are gone away from men. ⁵As for the earth, out of it comes bread: and under it is turned up as it were fire. ⁶The stones of it are the place of sapphires: and it has dust of gold. ⁷There is a path which no fowl knows, and which the vulture's eye has not seen: ⁸The lion's whelps have not trodden it, nor the fierce lion passed by it. ⁹He puts forth his hand on the rock; he overturns the mountains by the roots. ¹⁰He cuts out rivers among the rocks; and his eye sees every precious thing. ¹¹He binds the floods from overflowing; and the thing that is hid brings he forth to light. ¹²But where shall wisdom be found? and where is the place of understanding? ¹³Man knows not the price thereof; neither is it found in the land of the living. ¹⁴The depth says, It is not in me: and the sea said, It is not with me. ¹⁵It cannot be gotten for gold, neither shall silver be weighed for the price thereof. ¹⁶It cannot be valued with the gold of Ophir, with the precious onyx, or the sapphire. ¹⁷The gold and the crystal cannot equal it: and the exchange of it shall not be for jewels of fine gold. ¹⁸No mention shall be made of coral, or of pearls: for the price of wisdom is above rubies. ¹⁹The topaz of Ethiopia shall not equal it, neither shall it be valued with pure gold. ²⁰From where then comes wisdom? and where is the place of understanding? ²¹Seeing it is hid from the eyes of all living, and kept close from the fowls of the air. ²²Destruction and death say, We have heard the fame thereof with our ears. ²³God understands the way thereof, and he knows the place thereof. ²⁴For he looks to the ends of the earth, and sees under the whole heaven; ²⁵To make the weight for the winds; and he weighs the waters by measure. ²⁶When he made a decree for the rain, and a way for the lightning of the thunder: ²⁷Then did he see it, and declare it; he prepared it, yes, and searched it out. ²⁸And to man he said, Behold, the fear of the LORD, that is wisdom; and to depart from evil is understanding.

29 ¹Moreover Job continued his parable, and said, ²Oh that I were as in months past, as in the days when God preserved me; ³When his candle shined on my head, and when by his light I walked through darkness; ⁴As I was in the days of my youth, when the secret of God was on my tabernacle; ⁵When the Almighty was yet with me, when my children were about me; ⁶When I washed my steps with butter, and the rock poured me out rivers of oil; ⁷When I went out to the gate through the city, when I prepared my seat in the street! ⁸The young men saw me, and hid themselves: and the aged arose, and stood up. ⁹The princes refrained talking, and laid their hand on their mouth. ¹⁰The nobles held their peace, and their tongue stuck to the roof of their mouth. ¹¹When the ear heard me, then it blessed me; and when the eye saw me, it gave witness to me: ¹²Because I delivered the poor that cried, and the fatherless, and him that had none to help him. ¹³The blessing of him that was ready to perish came on me: and I caused the widow's heart to sing for joy. ¹⁴I put on righteousness, and it clothed me: my judgment was as a robe and a diadem. ¹⁵I was eyes to the blind, and feet was I to the lame. ¹⁶I was a father to the poor: and the cause which I knew not I searched out. ¹⁷And I broke the jaws of the wicked, and plucked the spoil out of his teeth. ¹⁸Then I said, I shall die in my nest, and I shall multiply my days as the sand. ¹⁹My root was spread out by the waters, and the dew lay all night on my branch. ²⁰My glory was fresh in me, and my bow was renewed in my hand. ²¹To me men gave ear, and waited, and kept silence at my counsel. ²²After my words they spoke not again; and my speech dropped on them. ²³And they waited for me as for the rain; and they opened their mouth wide as for the latter rain. ²⁴If I laughed on them, they believed it not; and the light of my countenance they cast not down. ²⁵I chose out their way, and sat chief, and dwelled as a king in the army, as one that comforts the mourners.

30 ¹But now they that are younger than I have me in derision, whose fathers I would have disdained to have set with the dogs of my flock. ²Yes, whereto might the strength of their hands profit me, in whom old age was perished? ³For want and famine they were solitary; fleeing into the wilderness in former time desolate and waste. ⁴Who cut up mallows by the bushes, and juniper roots for their meat. ⁵They were driven forth from among men, (they cried after them as after a thief;) ⁶To dwell in the cliffs of the valleys, in caves of the earth, and in the rocks. ⁷Among the bushes they brayed; under the nettles they were gathered together. ⁸They were children of fools, yes, children of base men: they were viler than the earth. ⁹And now am I their song, yes, I am their byword. ¹⁰They abhor me, they flee far from me, and spare not to spit in my face. ¹¹Because he has loosed my cord, and afflicted me, they have also let loose the bridle before me. ¹²On my right hand rise the youth; they push away my feet, and they raise up against me the ways of their destruction. ¹³They mar my path, they set forward my calamity, they have no helper. ¹⁴They came on me as a wide breaking in of waters: in the desolation they rolled themselves on me. ¹⁵Terrors are turned on me: they pursue my soul as the wind: and my welfare passes away as a cloud. ¹⁶And now my soul is poured out on me; the days of affliction have taken hold on me. ¹⁷My bones are pierced in me in the night season: and my sinews take no rest. ¹⁸By the great force of my disease is my garment changed: it binds me about as the collar of my coat. ¹⁹He has cast me into the mire, and I am become like dust and ashes. ²⁰I cry to you, and you do not hear me: I stand up, and you regard me not. ²¹You are become cruel to me: with your strong hand you oppose yourself against me. ²²You lift me up to the wind; you cause me to ride on it, and dissolve my substance. ²³For I know that you will bring me to death, and to the house appointed for all living. ²⁴However, he will not stretch out his hand to the grave, though they cry in his destruction. ²⁵Did not I weep for him that was in trouble? was not my soul grieved for the poor? ²⁶When I looked for good, then evil came to me: and when I waited for light, there came darkness. ²⁷My bowels boiled, and rested not: the days of affliction prevented me. ²⁸I went mourning without the sun: I stood up, and I cried in the congregation. ²⁹I am a brother to dragons, and a companion to owls. ³⁰My skin is black on me, and my bones are burned with heat. ³¹My harp also is turned to mourning, and my organ into the voice of them that weep.

31 ¹I made a covenant with my eyes; why then should I think on a maid? ²For what portion of God is there from above? and what inheritance of the Almighty from on high? ³Is not destruction to the wicked? and a strange punishment to the workers of iniquity? ⁴Does not he see my ways, and count all my steps? ⁵If I have walked with vanity, or if my foot has hurried to deceit; ⁶Let me be weighed in an even balance that God may know my integrity. ⁷If my step has turned out of the way, and my heart walked after my eyes, and if any blot has stuck to my hands; ⁸Then let me sow, and let another eat; yes, let my offspring be rooted out. ⁹If my heart have been deceived by a woman, or if I have laid wait at my neighbor's door; ¹⁰Then let my wife grind to another, and let others bow down on her. ¹¹For this is an heinous crime; yes, it is an iniquity to be punished by the judges. ¹²For it is a fire that consumes to destruction, and would root out all my increase. ¹³If I did despise the cause of my manservant or of my maidservant, when they contended with me; ¹⁴What then shall I do when God rises up? and when he visits, what shall I answer him? ¹⁵Did not he that made me in the womb make him? and did not one fashion us in the womb? ¹⁶If I have withheld the poor from their desire, or have caused the eyes of the widow to fail; ¹⁷Or have eaten my morsel myself alone, and the fatherless has not eaten thereof; ¹⁸(For from my youth he was brought up with me, as with a father, and I have guided her from my mother's womb;) ¹⁹If I have seen any perish for want of clothing, or any poor without covering; ²⁰If his loins have not blessed me, and if he were not warmed with the fleece of my sheep; ²¹If I have lifted up my hand against the fatherless, when I saw my help in the gate: ²²Then let my arm fall from my shoulder blade, and my arm be broken from the bone. ²³For destruction from God was a terror to me, and by reason of his highness I could not endure. ²⁴If I have made gold my hope, or have said to the fine gold, You are my confidence; ²⁵If I rejoice because my wealth was great, and because my hand had gotten much; ²⁶If I beheld the sun when it shined, or the moon walking in brightness; ²⁷And my heart has been secretly enticed, or my mouth has kissed my hand: ²⁸This also were an iniquity to be punished by the judge: for I should have denied the God that is above. ²⁹If I rejoice at the destruction of him that hated me, or lifted up myself when evil found him: ³⁰Neither have I suffered my mouth to sin by wishing a curse to his soul. ³¹If the men of my tabernacle said not, Oh that we had of his flesh! we cannot be satisfied. ³²The stranger did not lodge in the street: but I opened my doors to the travelers. ³³If I covered my transgressions as Adam, by hiding my iniquity in my bosom: ³⁴Did I fear a great multitude, or did the contempt of families terrify me, that I kept silence, and went not out of the door? ³⁵Oh that one would hear me! behold, my desire is, that the Almighty would answer me, and that my adversary had written a book. ³⁶Surely I would take it on my shoulder, and bind it as a crown to me. ³⁷I would declare to him the number of my steps; as a prince would I go near to him. ³⁸If my land cry against me, or that the furrows likewise thereof complain; ³⁹If I have eaten the fruits thereof without money, or have caused the owners thereof to lose their life: ⁴⁰Let thistles grow instead of wheat, and cockle instead of barley. The words of Job are ended.

32 ¹So these three men ceased to answer Job, because he was righteous in his own eyes. ²Then was kindled the wrath of Elihu the son of Barachel the Buzite, of the kindred of Ram: against Job was his wrath kindled, because he justified himself rather than God. ³Also against his three friends was his wrath kindled, because they had found no answer, and yet had condemned Job. ⁴Now Elihu had waited till Job had spoken, because they were elder than he. ⁵When Elihu saw that there was no answer in the mouth of these three men, then his wrath was kindled. ⁶And Elihu the son of Barachel the Buzite answered and said, I am young, and you are very old; why I was afraid, and dared not show you my opinion. ⁷I said, Days should speak, and multitude of years should teach wisdom. ⁸But there is a spirit in man: and the inspiration of the Almighty gives them understanding. ⁹Great men are not always wise: neither do the aged understand judgment. ¹⁰Therefore I said, Listen to me; I also will show my opinion. ¹¹Behold, I waited for your words; I gave ear to your reasons, whilst you searched out what to say. ¹²Yes, I attended to you, and, behold, there was none of you that convinced Job, or that answered his words: ¹³Lest you should say, We have found out wisdom: God thrusts him down, not man. ¹⁴Now he has not directed his words against me: neither will I answer him with your speeches. ¹⁵They were amazed, they answered no more: they left off speaking. ¹⁶When I had waited, (for they spoke not, but stood still, and answered no more;) ¹⁷I said, I will answer also my part, I also will show my opinion. ¹⁸For I am full of matter, the spirit within me constrains me. ¹⁹Behold, my belly is as wine which has no vent; it is ready to burst like new bottles. ²⁰I will speak, that I may be refreshed: I will open my lips and answer. ²¹Let me not, I pray you, accept any man's person, neither let me give flattering titles to man. ²²For I know not to give flattering titles; in so doing my maker would soon take me away.

33 ¹Why, Job, I pray you, hear my speeches, and listen to all my words. ²Behold, now I have opened my mouth, my tongue has spoken in my mouth. ³My words shall be of the uprightness of my heart: and my lips shall utter knowledge clearly. ⁴The spirit of God has made me, and the breath of the Almighty has given me life. ⁵If you can answer me, set your words in order before me, stand up. ⁶Behold, I am according to your wish in God's stead: I also am formed out of the clay. ⁷Behold, my terror shall not make you afraid, neither shall my hand be heavy on you. ⁸Surely you have spoken in my hearing, and I have heard the voice of your words, saying, ⁹I am clean without transgression, I am innocent; neither is there iniquity in me. ¹⁰Behold, he finds occasions against me, he counts me for his enemy, ¹¹He puts my feet in the stocks, he marks all my paths. ¹²Behold, in this you are not just: I will answer you, that God is greater than man. ¹³Why do you strive against him? for he gives not account of any of his matters. ¹⁴For God speaks once, yes twice, yet man perceives it not. ¹⁵In a dream, in a vision of the night, when deep sleep falls on men, in slumberings on the bed; ¹⁶Then he opens the ears of men, and seals their instruction, ¹⁷That he may withdraw man from his purpose, and hide pride from man. ¹⁸He keeps back his soul from the pit, and his life from perishing by the sword. ¹⁹He is chastened also with pain on his bed, and the multitude of his bones with strong pain: ²⁰So that his life abhors bread, and his soul dainty meat. ²¹His flesh is consumed away, that it cannot be seen; and his bones that were not seen stick out. ²²Yes, his soul draws near to the grave, and his life to the destroyers. ²³If there be a messenger with him, an interpreter, one among a thousand, to show to man his uprightness: ²⁴Then he is gracious to him, and says, Deliver him from going down to the pit: I have found a ransom. ²⁵His flesh shall be fresher than a child's: he shall return to the days of his youth: ²⁶He shall pray to God, and he will be favorable to him: and he shall see his face with joy: for he will render to man his righteousness. ²⁷He looks on men, and if any say, I have sinned, and perverted that which was right, and it profited me not; ²⁸He will deliver his soul from going into the pit, and his life shall see the light. ²⁹See, all these things works God oftentimes with man, ³⁰To bring back his soul from the pit, to be enlightened with the light of the living. ³¹Mark well, O Job, listen to me: hold your peace, and I will speak. ³²If you have anything to say, answer me: speak, for I desire to justify you. ³³If not, listen to me: hold your peace, and I shall teach you wisdom.

34 ¹Furthermore Elihu answered and said, ²Hear my words, O you wise men; and give ear to me, you that have knowledge. ³For the ear tries words, as the mouth tastes meat. ⁴Let us choose to us judgment: let us know among ourselves what is good. ⁵For Job has said, I am righteous: and God has taken away my judgment. ⁶Should I lie against my right? my wound is incurable without transgression. ⁷What man is like Job, who drinks up scorning like water? ⁸Which goes in company with the workers of iniquity, and walks with wicked men. ⁹For he has said, It profits a man nothing that he should delight himself with God. ¹⁰Therefore listen to me you men of understanding: far be it from God, that he should do wickedness; and from the Almighty, that he should commit iniquity. ¹¹For the work of a man shall he render to him, and cause every man to find according to his ways. ¹²Yes, surely God will not do wickedly, neither will the Almighty pervert judgment. ¹³Who has given him a charge over the earth? or who has disposed the whole world? ¹⁴If he set his heart on man, if he gather to himself his spirit and his breath; ¹⁵All flesh shall perish together, and man shall turn again to dust. ¹⁶If now you have understanding, hear this: listen to the voice of my words. ¹⁷Shall even he that hates right govern? and will you condemn him that is most just? ¹⁸Is it fit to say to a king, You are wicked? and to princes, You are ungodly? ¹⁹How much less to him that accepts not the persons of princes, nor regards the rich more than the poor? for they all are the work of his hands. ²⁰In a moment shall they die, and the people shall be troubled at midnight, and pass away: and the mighty shall be taken away without hand. ²¹For his eyes are on the ways of man, and he sees all his goings. ²²There is no darkness, nor shadow of death, where the workers of iniquity may hide themselves. ²³For he will not lay on man more than right; that he should enter into judgment with God. ²⁴He shall break in pieces mighty men without number, and set others in their stead. ²⁵Therefore he knows their works, and he overturns them in the night, so that they are destroyed. ²⁶He strikes them as wicked men in the open sight of others; ²⁷Because they turned back from him, and would not consider any of his ways: ²⁸So that they cause the cry of the poor to come to him, and he hears the cry of the afflicted. ²⁹When he gives quietness, who then can make trouble? and when he hides his face, who then can behold him? whether it be done against a nation, or against a man only: ³⁰That the hypocrite reign not, lest the people be ensnared. ³¹Surely it is meet to be said to God, I have borne chastisement, I will not offend any more: ³²That which I see not teach you me: if I have done iniquity, I will do no more. ³³Should it be according to your mind? he will recompense it, whether you refuse, or whether you choose; and not I: therefore speak what you know. ³⁴Let men of understanding tell me, and let a wise man listen to me. ³⁵Job has spoken without knowledge, and his words were without wisdom. ³⁶My desire is that Job may be tried to the end because of his answers for wicked men. ³⁷For he adds rebellion to his sin, he claps his hands among us, and multiplies his words against God.

35 ¹Elihu spoke moreover, and said, ²Think you this to be right, that you said, My righteousness is more than God's? ³For you said, What advantage will it be to you?

and, What profit shall I have, if I be cleansed from my sin? ⁴I will answer you, and your companions with you. ⁵Look to the heavens, and see; and behold the clouds which are higher than you. ⁶If you sin, what do you against him? or if your transgressions be multiplied, what do you to him? ⁷If you be righteous, what give you him? or what receives he of your hand? ⁸Your wickedness may hurt a man as you are; and your righteousness may profit the son of man. ⁹By reason of the multitude of oppressions they make the oppressed to cry: they cry out by reason of the arm of the mighty. ¹⁰But none says, Where is God my maker, who gives songs in the night; ¹¹Who teaches us more than the beasts of the earth, and makes us wiser than the fowls of heaven? ¹²There they cry, but none gives answer, because of the pride of evil men. ¹³Surely God will not hear vanity, neither will the Almighty regard it. ¹⁴Although you say you shall not see him, yet judgment is before him; therefore trust you in him. ¹⁵But now, because it is not so, he has visited in his anger; yet he knows it not in great extremity: ¹⁶Therefore does Job open his mouth in vain; he multiplies words without knowledge.

36 ¹Elihu also proceeded, and said, ²Suffer me a little, and I will show you that I have yet to speak on God's behalf. ³I will fetch my knowledge from afar, and will ascribe righteousness to my Maker. ⁴For truly my words shall not be false: he that is perfect in knowledge is with you. ⁵Behold, God is mighty, and despises not any: he is mighty in strength and wisdom. ⁶He preserves not the life of the wicked: but gives right to the poor. ⁷He withdraws not his eyes from the righteous: but with kings are they on the throne; yes, he does establish them for ever, and they are exalted. ⁸And if they be bound in fetters, and be held in cords of affliction; ⁹Then he shows them their work, and their transgressions that they have exceeded. ¹⁰He opens also their ear to discipline, and commands that they return from iniquity. ¹¹If they obey and serve him, they shall spend their days in prosperity, and their years in pleasures. ¹²But if they obey not, they shall perish by the sword, and they shall die without knowledge. ¹³But the hypocrites in heart heap up wrath: they cry not when he binds them. ¹⁴They die in youth, and their life is among the unclean. ¹⁵He delivers the poor in his affliction, and opens their ears in oppression. ¹⁶Even so would he have removed you out of the strait into a broad place, where there is no narrow place; and that which should be set on your table should be full of fatness. ¹⁷But you have fulfilled the judgment of the wicked: judgment and justice take hold on you. ¹⁸Because there is wrath, beware lest he take you away with his stroke: then a great ransom cannot deliver you. ¹⁹Will he esteem your riches? no, not gold, nor all the forces of strength. ²⁰Desire not the night, when people are cut off in their place. ²¹Take heed, regard not iniquity: for this have you chosen rather than affliction. ²²Behold, God exalts by his power: who teaches like him? ²³Who has enjoined him his way? or who can say, You have worked iniquity? ²⁴Remember that you magnify his work, which men behold. ²⁵Every man may see it; man may behold it afar off. ²⁶Behold, God is great, and we know him not, neither can the number of his years be searched out. ²⁷For he makes small the drops of water: they pour down rain according to the vapor thereof: ²⁸Which the clouds do drop and distil on man abundantly. ²⁹Also can any understand the spreading of the clouds, or the noise of his tabernacle? ³⁰Behold, he spreads his light on it, and covers the bottom of the sea. ³¹For by them judges he the people; he gives meat in abundance. ³²With clouds he covers the light; and commands it not to shine by the cloud that comes between. ³³The noise thereof shows concerning it, the cattle also concerning the vapor.

37 ¹At this also my heart trembles, and is moved out of his place. ²Hear attentively the noise of his voice, and the sound that goes out of his mouth. ³He directs it under the whole heaven, and his lightning to the ends of the earth. ⁴After it a voice roars: he thunders with the voice of his excellency; and he will not stay them when his voice is heard. ⁵God thunders marvelously with his voice; great things does he, which we cannot comprehend. ⁶For he says to the snow, Be you on the earth; likewise to the small rain, and to the great rain of his strength. ⁷He seals up the hand of every man; that all men may know his work. ⁸Then the beasts go into dens, and remain in their places. ⁹Out of the south comes the whirlwind: and cold out of the north. ¹⁰By the breath of God frost is given: and the breadth of the waters is straitened. ¹¹Also by watering he wearies the thick cloud: he scatters his bright cloud: ¹²And it is turned round about by his counsels: that they may do whatever he commands them on the face of the world in the earth. ¹³He causes it to come, whether for correction, or for his land, or for mercy. ¹⁴Listen to this, O Job: stand still, and consider the wondrous works of God. ¹⁵Do you know when God disposed them, and caused the light of his cloud to shine? ¹⁶Do you know the balancing of the clouds, the wondrous works of him which is perfect in knowledge? ¹⁷How your garments are warm, when he quiets the earth by the south wind? ¹⁸Have you with him spread out the sky, which is strong, and as a molten looking glass? ¹⁹Teach us what we shall say to him; for we cannot order our speech by reason of darkness. ²⁰Shall it be told him that I speak? if a man speak, surely he shall be swallowed up. ²¹And now men see not the bright light which is in the clouds: but the wind passes, and cleans them. ²²Fair weather comes out of the north: with God is terrible majesty. ²³Touching the Almighty, we cannot find him out: he is excellent in power, and in judgment, and in plenty of justice: he will not afflict. ²⁴Men do therefore fear him: he respects not any that are wise of heart.

38 ¹Then the LORD answered Job out of the whirlwind, and said, ²Who is this that darkens counsel by words without knowledge? ³Gird up now your loins like a man; for I will demand of you, and answer you me. ⁴Where were you when I laid the foundations of the earth? declare, if you have understanding. ⁵Who has laid the measures thereof, if you know? or who has stretched the line on it? ⁶Whereupon are the foundations thereof fastened? or who laid the corner stone thereof; ⁷When the morning stars sang together, and all the sons of God shouted for joy? ⁸Or who shut up the sea with doors, when it broke forth, as if it had issued out of the womb? ⁹When I made the cloud the garment thereof, and thick darkness a swaddling cloth for it, ¹⁰And broke up for it my decreed place, and set bars and doors, ¹¹And said, Till now shall you come, but no further: and here shall your proud waves be stayed? ¹²Have you commanded the morning since your days; and caused the dayspring to know his place; ¹³That it might take hold of the ends of the earth, that the wicked might be shaken out of it? ¹⁴It is turned as clay to the seal; and they stand as a garment. ¹⁵And from the wicked their light is withheld, and the high arm shall be broken. ¹⁶Have you entered into the springs of the sea? or have you walked in the search of the depth? ¹⁷Have the gates of death been opened to you? or have you seen the doors of the shadow of death? ¹⁸Have you perceived the breadth of the earth? declare if you know it all. ¹⁹Where is the way where light dwells? and as for darkness, where is the place thereof, ²⁰That you should take it to the bound thereof, and that you should know the paths to the house thereof? ²¹Know you it, because you were then born? or because the number of your days is great? ²²Have you entered into the treasures of the snow? or have you seen the treasures of the hail, ²³Which I have reserved against the time of trouble, against the day of battle and war? ²⁴By what way is the light parted, which scatters the east wind on the earth? ²⁵Who has divided a watercourse for the overflowing of waters, or a way for the lightning of thunder; ²⁶To cause it to rain on the earth, where no man is; on the wilderness, wherein there is no man; ²⁷To satisfy the desolate and waste ground; and to cause the bud of the tender herb to spring forth? ²⁸Has the rain a father? or who has begotten the drops of dew? ²⁹Out of whose womb came the ice? and the hoary frost of heaven, who has gendered it? ³⁰The waters are hid as with a stone, and the face of the deep is frozen. ³¹Can you bind the sweet influences of Pleiades, or loose the bands of Orion? ³²Can you bring forth Mazzaroth in his season? or can you guide Arcturus with his sons? ³³Know you the ordinances of heaven? can you set the dominion thereof in the earth? ³⁴Can you lift up your voice to the clouds, that abundance of waters may cover you? ³⁵Can you send lightning, that they may go and say to you, Here we are? ³⁶Who has put wisdom in the inward parts? or who has given understanding to the heart? ³⁷Who can number the clouds in wisdom? or who can stay the bottles of heaven, ³⁸When the dust grows into hardness, and the clods stuck fast together? ³⁹Will you hunt the prey for the lion? or fill the appetite of the young lions, ⁴⁰When they couch in their dens, and abide in the covert to lie in wait? ⁴¹Who provides for the raven his food? when his young ones cry to God, they wander for lack of meat.

39

¹Know you the time when the wild goats of the rock bring forth? or can you mark when the hinds do calve? ²Can you number the months that they fulfill? or know you the time when they bring forth? ³They bow themselves, they bring forth their young ones, they cast out their sorrows. ⁴Their young ones are in good liking, they grow up with corn; they go forth, and return not to them. ⁵Who has sent out the wild ass free? or who has loosed the bands of the wild ass? ⁶Whose house I have made the wilderness, and the barren land his dwellings. ⁷He scorns the multitude of the city, neither regards he the crying of the driver. ⁸The range of the mountains is his pasture, and he searches after every green thing. ⁹Will the unicorn be willing to serve you, or abide by your crib? ¹⁰Can you bind the unicorn with his band in the furrow? or will he harrow the valleys after you? ¹¹Will you trust him, because his strength is great? or will you leave your labor to him? ¹²Will you believe him, that he will bring home your seed, and gather it into your barn? ¹³Gave you the goodly wings to the peacocks? or wings and feathers to the ostrich? ¹⁴Which leaves her eggs in the earth, and warms them in dust, ¹⁵And forgets that the foot may crush them, or that the wild beast may break them. ¹⁶She is hardened against her young ones, as though they were not her's: her labor is in vain without fear; ¹⁷Because God has deprived her of wisdom, neither has he imparted to her understanding. ¹⁸What time she lifts up herself on high, she scorns the horse and his rider. ¹⁹Have you given the horse strength? have you clothed his neck with thunder? ²⁰Can you make him afraid as a grasshopper? the glory of his nostrils is terrible. ²¹He paws in the valley, and rejoices in his strength: he goes on to meet the armed men. ²²He mocks at fear, and is not affrighted; neither turns he back from the sword. ²³The quiver rattles against him, the glittering spear and the shield. ²⁴He swallows the ground with fierceness and rage: neither believes he that it is the sound of the trumpet. ²⁵He says among the trumpets, Ha, ha; and he smells the battle afar off, the thunder of the captains, and the shouting. ²⁶Does the hawk fly by your wisdom, and stretch her wings toward the south? ²⁷Does the eagle mount up at your command, and make her nest on high? ²⁸She dwells and stays on the rock, on the crag of the rock, and the strong place. ²⁹From there she seeks the prey, and her eyes behold afar off. ³⁰Her young ones also suck up blood: and where the slain are, there is she.

40

¹Moreover the LORD answered Job, and said, ²Shall he that contends with the Almighty instruct him? he that reproves God, let him answer it. ³Then Job answered the LORD, and said, ⁴Behold, I am vile; what shall I answer you? I will lay my hand on my mouth. ⁵Once have I spoken; but I will not answer: yes, twice; but I will proceed no further. ⁶Then answered the LORD to Job out of the whirlwind, and said, ⁷Gird up your loins now like a man: I will demand of you, and declare you to me. ⁸Will you also cancel my judgment? will you condemn me, that you may be righteous? ⁹Have you an arm like God? or can you thunder with a voice like him? ¹⁰Deck yourself now with majesty and excellency; and array yourself with glory and beauty. ¹¹Cast abroad the rage of your wrath: and behold every one that is proud, and abase him. ¹²Look on every one that is proud, and bring him low; and tread down the wicked in their place. ¹³Hide them in the dust together; and bind their faces in secret. ¹⁴Then will I also confess to you that your own right hand can save you. ¹⁵Behold now behemoth, which I made with you; he eats grass as an ox. ¹⁶See now, his strength is in his loins, and his force is in the navel of his belly. ¹⁷He moves his tail like a cedar: the sinews of his stones are wrapped together. ¹⁸His bones are as strong pieces of brass; his bones are like bars of iron. ¹⁹He is the chief of the ways of God: he that made him can make his sword to approach to him. ²⁰Surely the mountains bring him forth food, where all the beasts of the field play. ²¹He lies under the shady trees, in the covert of the reed, and fens. ²²The shady trees cover him with their shadow; the willows of the brook compass him about. ²³Behold, he drinks up a river, and hastens not: he trusts that he can draw up Jordan into his

mouth. ²⁴He takes it with his eyes: his nose pierces through snares.

41 ¹Can you draw out leviathan with an hook? or his tongue with a cord which you let down? ²Can you put an hook into his nose? or bore his jaw through with a thorn? ³Will he make many supplications to you? will he speak soft words to you? ⁴Will he make a covenant with you? will you take him for a servant for ever? ⁵Will you play with him as with a bird? or will you bind him for your maidens? ⁶Shall the companions make a banquet of him? shall they part him among the merchants? ⁷Can you fill his skin with barbed irons? or his head with fish spears? ⁸Lay your hand on him, remember the battle, do no more. ⁹Behold, the hope of him is in vain: shall not one be cast down even at the sight of him? ¹⁰None is so fierce that dare stir him up: who then is able to stand before me? ¹¹Who has prevented me, that I should repay him? whatever is under the whole heaven is mine. ¹²I will not conceal his parts, nor his power, nor his comely proportion. ¹³Who can discover the face of his garment? or who can come to him with his double bridle? ¹⁴Who can open the doors of his face? his teeth are terrible round about. ¹⁵His scales are his pride, shut up together as with a close seal. ¹⁶One is so near to another, that no air can come between them. ¹⁷They are joined one to another, they stick together, that they cannot be sundered. ¹⁸By his neesings a light does shine, and his eyes are like the eyelids of the morning. ¹⁹Out of his mouth go burning lamps, and sparks of fire leap out. ²⁰Out of his nostrils goes smoke, as out of a seething pot or caldron. ²¹His breath kindles coals, and a flame goes out of his mouth. ²²In his neck remains strength, and sorrow is turned into joy before him. ²³The flakes of his flesh are joined together: they are firm in themselves; they cannot be moved. ²⁴His heart is as firm as a stone; yes, as hard as a piece of the nether millstone. ²⁵When he raises up himself, the mighty are afraid: by reason of breakings they purify themselves. ²⁶The sword of him that lays at him cannot hold: the spear, the dart, nor the habergeon. ²⁷He esteems iron as straw, and brass as rotten wood. ²⁸The arrow cannot make him flee: sling stones are turned with him into stubble. ²⁹Darts are counted as stubble: he laughs at the shaking of a spear. ³⁰Sharp stones are under him: he spreads sharp pointed things on the mire. ³¹He makes the deep to boil like a pot: he makes the sea like a pot of ointment. ³²He makes a path to shine after him; one would think the deep to be hoary. ³³On earth there is not his like, who is made without fear. ³⁴He beholds all high things: he is a king over all the children of pride.

42 ¹Then Job answered the LORD, and said, ²I know that you can do every thing, and that no thought can be withheld from you. ³Who is he that hides counsel without knowledge? therefore have I uttered that I understood not; things too wonderful for me, which I knew not. ⁴Hear, I beseech you, and I will speak: I will demand of you, and declare you to me. ⁵I have heard of you by the hearing of the ear: but now my eye sees you. ⁶Why I abhor myself, and repent in dust and ashes. ⁷And it was so, that after the LORD had spoken these words to Job, the LORD said to Eliphaz the Temanite, My wrath is kindled against you, and against your two friends: for you have not spoken of me the thing that is right, as my servant Job has. ⁸Therefore take to you now seven bullocks and seven rams, and go to my servant Job, and offer up for yourselves a burnt offering; and my servant Job shall pray for you: for him will I accept: lest I deal with you after your folly, in that you have not spoken of me the thing which is right, like my servant Job. ⁹So Eliphaz the Temanite and Bildad the Shuhite and Zophar the Naamathite went, and did according as the LORD commanded them: the LORD also accepted Job. ¹⁰And the LORD turned the captivity of Job, when he prayed for his friends: also the LORD gave Job twice as much as he had before. ¹¹Then came there to him all his brothers, and all his sisters, and all they that had been of his acquaintance before, and did eat bread with him in his house: and they bemoaned him, and comforted him over all the evil that the LORD had brought on him: every man also gave him a piece of money, and every one an earring of gold. ¹²So the LORD blessed the latter end of Job more than his beginning: for he had fourteen thousand sheep, and six thousand camels, and a thousand yoke of oxen, and a thousand she asses. ¹³He had also seven sons and three daughters. ¹⁴And he called the name of the first, Jemima; and the name of the second, Kezia; and the name of the third, Kerenhappuch. ¹⁵And in all the land were no women found so fair as the daughters of Job: and their father gave them inheritance among their brothers. ¹⁶After this lived Job an hundred and forty years, and saw his sons, and his sons' sons, even four generations. ¹⁷So Job died, being old and full of days.

Psalms

1 ¹Blessed is the man that walks not in the counsel of the ungodly, nor stands in the way of sinners, nor sits in the seat of the scornful. ²But his delight is in the law of the LORD; and in his law does he meditate day and night. ³And he shall be like a tree planted by the rivers of water, that brings forth his fruit in his season; his leaf also shall not wither; and whatever he does shall prosper. ⁴The ungodly are not so: but are like the chaff which the wind drives away. ⁵Therefore the ungodly shall not stand in the judgment, nor sinners in the congregation of the righteous. ⁶For the LORD knows the way of the righteous: but the way of the ungodly shall perish.

2 ¹Why do the heathen rage, and the people imagine a vain thing? ²The kings of the earth set themselves, and the rulers take counsel together, against the LORD, and against his anointed, saying, ³Let us break their bands asunder, and cast away their cords from us. ⁴He that sits in the heavens shall laugh: the LORD shall have them in derision. ⁵Then shall he speak to them in his wrath, and vex them in his sore displeasure. ⁶Yet have I set my king on my holy hill of Zion. ⁷I will declare the decree: the LORD has said to me, You are my Son; this day have I begotten you. ⁸Ask of me, and I shall give you the heathen for your inheritance, and the uttermost parts of the earth for your possession. ⁹You shall break them with a rod of iron; you shall dash them in pieces like a potter's vessel. ¹⁰Be wise now therefore, O you kings: be instructed, you judges of the earth. ¹¹Serve the LORD with fear, and rejoice with trembling. ¹²Kiss the Son, lest he be angry, and you perish from the way, when his wrath is kindled but a little. Blessed are all they that put their trust in him.

3 ¹Lord, how are they increased that trouble me! many are they that rise up against me. ²Many there be which say of my soul, There is no help for him in God. Selah. ³But you, O LORD, are a shield for me; my glory, and the lifter up of my head. ⁴I cried to the LORD with my voice, and he heard me out of his holy hill. Selah. ⁵I laid me down and slept; I awaked; for the LORD sustained me. ⁶I will not be afraid of ten thousands of people, that have set themselves against me round about. ⁷Arise, O LORD; save me, O my God: for you have smitten all my enemies on the cheek bone; you have broken the teeth of the ungodly. ⁸Salvation belongs to the LORD: your blessing is on your people. Selah.

4 ¹Hear me when I call, O God of my righteousness: you have enlarged me when I was in distress; have mercy on me, and hear my prayer. ²O you sons of men, how long will you turn my glory into shame? how long will you love vanity, and seek after leasing? Selah. ³But know that the LORD has set apart him that is godly for himself: the LORD will hear when I call to him. ⁴Stand in awe, and sin not: commune with your own heart on your bed, and be still. Selah. ⁵Offer the sacrifices of righteousness, and put your trust in the LORD. ⁶There be many that say, Who will show us any good? LORD, lift you up the light of your countenance on us. ⁷You have put gladness in my heart, more than in the time that their corn and their wine increased. ⁸I will both lay me down in peace, and sleep: for you, LORD, only make me dwell in safety.

5 ¹Give ear to my words, O LORD, consider my meditation. ²Listen to the voice of my cry, my King, and my God: for to you will I pray. ³My voice shall you hear in the morning, O LORD; in the morning will I direct my prayer to you, and will look up. ⁴For you are not a God that has pleasure in wickedness: neither shall evil dwell with you. ⁵The foolish shall not stand in your sight: you hate all workers of iniquity. ⁶You shall destroy them that speak leasing: the LORD will abhor the bloody and deceitful man. ⁷But as for me, I will come into your house in the multitude of your mercy: and in your fear will I worship toward your holy temple. ⁸Lead me, O LORD, in your righteousness because of my enemies; make your way straight before my face. ⁹For there is no faithfulness in their mouth; their inward part is very wickedness; their throat is an open sepulcher; they flatter with their tongue. ¹⁰Destroy you them, O God; let them fall by their own counsels; cast them out in the multitude of their transgressions; for they have rebelled against you. ¹¹But let all those that put their trust in you rejoice: let them ever shout for joy, because you defend them: let them also that love your name be joyful in you. ¹²For you, LORD, will bless the righteous; with favor will you compass him as with a shield.

6 ¹O LORD, rebuke me not in your anger, neither chasten me in your hot displeasure. ²Have mercy on me, O LORD; for I am weak: O LORD, heal me; for my bones are vexed. ³My soul is also sore vexed: but you, O LORD, how long? ⁴Return, O LORD, deliver my soul: oh save me for your mercies' sake. ⁵For in death there is no remembrance of you: in the grave who shall give you thanks? ⁶I am weary with my groaning; all the night make I my bed to swim; I water my couch with my tears. ⁷My eye is consumed because of grief; it waxes old because of all my enemies. ⁸Depart from me, all you workers of iniquity; for the LORD has heard the voice of my weeping. ⁹The LORD has heard my supplication; the LORD will receive my prayer. ¹⁰Let all my enemies be ashamed and sore vexed: let them return and be ashamed suddenly.

7 ¹O LORD my God, in you do I put my trust: save me from all them that persecute me, and deliver me: ²Lest he tear my soul like a lion, rending it in pieces, while there is none to deliver. ³O LORD my God, If I have done this; if there be iniquity in my hands; ⁴If I have rewarded evil to him that was at peace with me; (yes, I have delivered him that without cause is my enemy:) ⁵Let the enemy persecute my soul, and take it; yes, let him tread down my life on the earth, and lay my honor in the dust. Selah. ⁶Arise, O LORD, in your anger, lift up yourself because of the rage of my enemies: and awake for me to the judgment that you have commanded. ⁷So shall the congregation of the people compass you about: for their sakes therefore return you on high. ⁸The LORD shall judge the people: judge me, O LORD, according to my righteousness, and according to my integrity that is in me. ⁹Oh let the wickedness of the wicked come to an end; but establish the just: for the righteous God

tries the hearts and reins. ¹⁰My defense is of God, which saves the upright in heart. ¹¹God judges the righteous, and God is angry with the wicked every day. ¹²If he turn not, he will whet his sword; he has bent his bow, and made it ready. ¹³He has also prepared for him the instruments of death; he ordains his arrows against the persecutors. ¹⁴Behold, he travails with iniquity, and has conceived mischief, and brought forth falsehood. ¹⁵He made a pit, and dig it, and is fallen into the ditch which he made. ¹⁶His mischief shall return on his own head, and his violent dealing shall come down on his own pate. ¹⁷I will praise the LORD according to his righteousness: and will sing praise to the name of the LORD most high.

8 ¹O LORD, our Lord, how excellent is your name in all the earth! who have set your glory above the heavens. ²Out of the mouth of babes and sucklings have you ordained strength because of your enemies, that you might still the enemy and the avenger. ³When I consider your heavens, the work of your fingers, the moon and the stars, which you have ordained; ⁴What is man, that you are mindful of him? and the son of man, that you visit him? ⁵For you have made him a little lower than the angels, and have crowned him with glory and honor. ⁶You made him to have dominion over the works of your hands; you have put all things under his feet: ⁷All sheep and oxen, yes, and the beasts of the field; ⁸The fowl of the air, and the fish of the sea, and whatever passes through the paths of the seas. ⁹O LORD our Lord, how excellent is your name in all the earth!

9 ¹I will praise you, O LORD, with my whole heart; I will show forth all your marvelous works. ²I will be glad and rejoice in you: I will sing praise to your name, O you most High. ³When my enemies are turned back, they shall fall and perish at your presence. ⁴For you have maintained my right and my cause; you sat in the throne judging right. ⁵You have rebuked the heathen, you have destroyed the wicked, you have put out their name for ever and ever. ⁶O you enemy, destructions are come to a perpetual end: and you have destroyed cities; their memorial is perished with them. ⁷But the LORD shall endure for ever: he has prepared his throne for judgment. ⁸And he shall judge the world in righteousness, he shall minister judgment to the people in uprightness. ⁹The LORD also will be a refuge for the oppressed, a refuge in times of trouble. ¹⁰And they that know your name will put their trust in you: for you, LORD, have not forsaken them that seek you. ¹¹Sing praises to the LORD, which dwells in Zion: declare among the people his doings. ¹²When he makes inquisition for blood, he remembers them: he forgets not the cry of the humble. ¹³Have mercy on me, O LORD; consider my trouble which I suffer of them that hate me, you that lift me up from the gates of death: ¹⁴That I may show forth all your praise in the gates of the daughter of Zion: I will rejoice in your salvation. ¹⁵The heathen are sunk down in the pit that they made: in the net which they hid is their own foot taken. ¹⁶The LORD is known by the judgment which he executes: the wicked is snared in the work of his own hands. Higgaion. Selah. ¹⁷The wicked shall be turned into hell, and all the nations that forget God. ¹⁸For the needy shall not always be forgotten: the expectation of the poor shall not perish for ever. ¹⁹Arise, O LORD; let not man prevail: let the heathen be judged in your sight. ²⁰Put them in fear, O LORD: that the nations may know themselves to be but men. Selah.

10 ¹Why stand you afar off, O LORD? why hide you yourself in times of trouble? ²The wicked in his pride does persecute the poor: let them be taken in the devices that they have imagined. ³For the wicked boasts of his heart's desire, and blesses the covetous, whom the LORD abhors. ⁴The wicked, through the pride of his countenance, will not seek after God: God is not in all his thoughts. ⁵His ways are always grievous; your judgments are far above out of his sight: as for all his enemies, he puffs at them. ⁶He has said in his heart, I shall not be moved: for I shall never be in adversity. ⁷His mouth is full of cursing and deceit and fraud: under his tongue is mischief and vanity. ⁸He sits in the lurking places of the villages: in the secret places does he murder the innocent: his eyes are privately set against the poor. ⁹He lies in wait secretly as a lion in his den: he lies in wait to catch the poor: he does catch the poor, when he draws him into his net. ¹⁰He crouches, and humbles himself, that the poor may fall by his strong ones. ¹¹He has said in his heart, God has forgotten: he hides his face; he will never see it. ¹²Arise, O LORD; O God, lift up your hand: forget not the humble. ¹³Why does the wicked scorn God? he has said in his heart, You will not require it. ¹⁴You have seen it; for you behold mischief and spite, to requite it with your hand: the poor commits himself to you; you are the helper of the fatherless. ¹⁵Break you the arm of the wicked and the evil man: seek out his wickedness till you find none. ¹⁶The LORD is King for ever and ever: the heathen are perished out of his land. ¹⁷LORD, you have heard the desire of the humble: you will prepare their heart, you will cause your ear to hear: ¹⁸To judge the fatherless and the oppressed, that the man of the earth may no more oppress.

11 ¹In the LORD put I my trust: how say you to my soul, Flee as a bird to your mountain? ²For, see, the wicked bend their bow, they make ready their arrow on the string, that they may privately shoot at the upright in heart. ³If the foundations be destroyed, what can the righteous do? ⁴The LORD is in his holy temple, the LORD's throne is in heaven: his eyes behold, his eyelids try, the children of men. ⁵The LORD tries the righteous: but the wicked and him that loves violence his soul hates. ⁶On the wicked he shall rain snares, fire and brimstone, and an horrible tempest: this shall be the portion of their cup. ⁷For the righteous LORD loves righteousness; his countenance does behold the upright.

12 ¹Help, LORD; for the godly man ceases; for the faithful fail from among the children of men. ²They speak vanity every one with his neighbor: with flattering lips and with a double heart do they speak. ³The LORD shall cut off all flattering lips, and the tongue that speaks proud things: ⁴Who have said, With our tongue will we prevail; our lips are our own: who is lord over us? ⁵For the oppression of the poor, for the sighing of the needy, now will I arise, says the LORD; I will set him in safety from him that puffs at him. ⁶The words of the LORD are pure words: as silver tried in a furnace of earth, purified seven times. ⁷You shall keep them, O LORD, you shall preserve them from this generation for ever. ⁸The wicked walk on every side, when the vilest men are exalted.

13 ¹How long will you forget me, O LORD? for ever? how long will you hide your face from me? ²How long shall I take counsel in my soul, having sorrow in my heart daily? how long shall my enemy be exalted over me? ³Consider and hear me, O LORD my God: lighten my eyes, lest I sleep the sleep of death; ⁴Lest my enemy say, I have prevailed against him; and those that trouble me rejoice when I am moved. ⁵But I have trusted in your mercy; my heart shall rejoice in your salvation. ⁶I will sing to the LORD, because he has dealt bountifully with me.

14 ¹The fool has said in his heart, There is no God. They are corrupt, they have done abominable works, there is none that does good. ²The LORD looked down from heaven on the children of men, to see if there were any that did understand, and seek God. ³They are all gone aside, they are all together become filthy: there is none that does good, no, not one. ⁴Have all the workers of iniquity no knowledge? who eat up my people as they eat bread, and call not on the LORD. ⁵There were they in great fear: for God is in the generation of the righteous. ⁶You have shamed the counsel of the poor, because the LORD is his refuge. ⁷Oh that the salvation of Israel were come out of Zion! when the LORD brings back the captivity of his people, Jacob shall rejoice, and Israel shall be glad.

15 ¹Lord, who shall abide in your tabernacle? who shall dwell in your holy hill? ²He that walks uprightly, and works righteousness, and speaks the truth in his heart. ³He that backbites not with his tongue, nor does evil to his neighbor, nor takes up a reproach against his neighbor. ⁴In whose eyes a vile person is scorned; but he honors them that fear the LORD. He that swears to his own hurt, and changes not. ⁵He that puts not out his money to usury, nor takes reward against the innocent. He that does these things shall never be moved.

16 ¹Preserve me, O God: for in you do I put my trust. ²O my soul, you have said to the LORD, You are my Lord: my goodness extends not to you; ³But to the saints that are in the earth, and to the excellent, in whom is all my delight. ⁴Their sorrows shall be multiplied that hasten after another god: their drink offerings of blood will I not offer, nor take up their names into my lips. ⁵The LORD is the portion of my inheritance and of my cup: you maintain my lot. ⁶The lines are fallen to me in pleasant places; yes, I have a goodly heritage. ⁷I will bless the LORD, who has given me counsel: my reins also instruct me in the night seasons. ⁸I have set the LORD always before me: because he is at my right hand, I shall not be moved. ⁹Therefore my heart is glad, and my glory rejoices: my flesh also shall rest in hope. ¹⁰For you will not leave my soul in hell; neither will you suffer your Holy One to see corruption. ¹¹You will show me the path of life: in your presence is fullness of joy; at your right hand there are pleasures for ever more.

17 ¹Hear the right, O LORD, attend to my cry, give ear to my prayer, that goes not out of feigned lips. ²Let my sentence come forth from your presence; let your eyes behold the things that are equal. ³You have proved my heart; you have visited me in the night; you have tried me, and shall find nothing; I am purposed that my mouth shall not transgress. ⁴Concerning the works of men, by the word of your lips I have kept me from the paths of the destroyer. ⁵Hold up my goings in your paths, that my footsteps slip not. ⁶I have called on you, for you will hear me, O God: incline your ear to me, and hear my speech. ⁷Show your marvelous loving kindness, O you that save by your right hand them which put their trust in you from those that rise up against them. ⁸Keep me as the apple of the eye, hide me under the shadow of your wings, ⁹From the wicked that oppress me, from my deadly enemies, who compass me about. ¹⁰They are enclosed in their own fat: with their mouth they speak proudly. ¹¹They have now compassed us in our steps: they have set their eyes bowing down to the earth; ¹²Like as a lion that is greedy of his prey, and as it were a young lion lurking in secret places. ¹³Arise, O LORD, disappoint him, cast him down: deliver my soul from the wicked, which is your sword: ¹⁴From men which are your hand, O LORD, from men of the world, which have their portion in this life, and whose belly you fill with your hid treasure: they are full of children, and leave the rest of their substance to their babes. ¹⁵As for me, I will behold your face in righteousness: I shall be satisfied, when I awake, with your likeness.

18 ¹I will love you, O LORD, my strength. ²The LORD is my rock, and my fortress, and my deliverer; my God, my strength, in whom I will trust; my buckler, and the horn of my salvation, and my high tower. ³I will call on the LORD, who is worthy to be praised: so shall I be saved from my enemies. ⁴The sorrows of death compassed me, and the floods of ungodly men made me afraid. ⁵The sorrows of hell compassed me about: the snares of death prevented me. ⁶In my distress I called on the LORD, and cried to my God: he heard my voice out of his temple, and my cry came before him, even into his ears. ⁷Then the earth shook and trembled; the foundations also of the hills moved and were shaken, because he was wroth. ⁸There went up a smoke out of his nostrils, and fire out of his mouth devoured: coals were kindled by it. ⁹He bowed the heavens also, and came down: and darkness was under his feet. ¹⁰And he rode on a cherub, and did fly: yes, he did fly on the wings of the wind. ¹¹He made darkness his secret place; his pavilion round about him were dark waters and thick clouds of the skies. ¹²At the brightness that was before him his thick clouds passed, hail stones and coals of fire. ¹³The LORD also thundered in the heavens, and the Highest gave his voice; hail stones and coals of fire. ¹⁴Yes, he sent out his arrows, and scattered them; and he shot out lightning, and discomfited them. ¹⁵Then the channels of waters were seen, and the foundations of the world were discovered at your rebuke, O LORD, at the blast of the breath of your nostrils. ¹⁶He sent from above, he took me, he drew me out of many waters. ¹⁷He delivered me from my strong enemy, and from them which hated me: for they were too strong for me. ¹⁸They prevented me in the day of my calamity: but the LORD was my stay. ¹⁹He brought me forth also into a large place; he delivered me, because he delighted in me. ²⁰The LORD rewarded me according to my righteousness; according to the cleanness of my hands has he recompensed me. ²¹For I have kept the ways of the LORD, and have not wickedly departed from my God. ²²For all his judgments were before me, and I did not put away his statutes from me. ²³I was also upright before him, and I kept myself from my iniquity. ²⁴Therefore has the LORD recompensed me according to my righteousness, according to the cleanness of my hands in his eyesight. ²⁵With the merciful you will show yourself merciful; with an upright man you will show yourself upright; ²⁶With the pure you will show yourself pure; and with the fraudulent you will show yourself devious. ²⁷For you will save the afflicted people; but will bring down high looks. ²⁸For you will light my candle: the LORD my God will enlighten my darkness. ²⁹For by you I have run through a troop; and by my God have I leaped over a wall. ³⁰As for God, his way is perfect: the word of the LORD is tried: he is a buckler to all those that trust in him. ³¹For who is God save the LORD? or who is a rock save our God? ³²It is God that girds me with strength, and makes my way perfect. ³³He makes my feet like hinds' feet, and sets me on my high places. ³⁴He teaches my hands to war, so that a bow of steel is broken by my arms. ³⁵You have also given me the shield of your salvation: and your right hand has held me up, and your gentleness has made me great. ³⁶You have enlarged my steps under me, that my feet did not slip. ³⁷I have pursued my enemies, and overtaken them: neither did I turn again till they were consumed. ³⁸I have wounded them that they were not able to rise: they are fallen under my feet. ³⁹For you have girded me with strength to the battle: you have subdued under me those that rose up against me. ⁴⁰You have also given me the necks of my enemies; that I might destroy them that hate me. ⁴¹They cried, but there was none to save them: even to the LORD, but he answered them not. ⁴²Then did I beat them small as the dust before the wind: I did cast them out as the dirt in the streets. ⁴³You have delivered me from the strivings of the people; and you have made me the head of the heathen: a people whom I have not known shall serve me. ⁴⁴As soon as they hear of me, they shall obey me: the strangers shall submit themselves to me. ⁴⁵The strangers shall fade away, and be afraid out of their close places. ⁴⁶The LORD lives; and blessed be my rock; and let the God of my salvation be exalted. ⁴⁷It is God that avenges me, and subdues the people under me. ⁴⁸He delivers me from my enemies: yes, you lift me up above those that rise up against me: you have delivered me from the violent man. ⁴⁹Therefore will I give thanks to you, O LORD, among the heathen, and sing praises to your name. ⁵⁰Great deliverance gives he to his king; and shows mercy to his anointed, to David, and to his seed for ever more.

19 ¹The heavens declare the glory of God; and the firmament shows his handiwork. ²Day to day utters speech, and night to night shows knowledge. ³There is no speech nor language, where their voice is not heard. ⁴Their line is gone out through all the earth, and their words to the end of the world. In them has he set a tabernacle for the sun, ⁵Which is as a bridegroom coming out of his chamber, and rejoices as a strong man to run a race. ⁶His going forth is from the end of the heaven, and his circuit to the ends of it: and there is nothing hid from the heat thereof. ⁷The law of the LORD is perfect, converting the soul: the testimony of the LORD is sure, making wise the simple. ⁸The statutes of the LORD are right, rejoicing the heart: the commandment of the LORD is pure, enlightening the eyes. ⁹The fear of the LORD is clean, enduring for ever: the judgments of the LORD are true and righteous altogether. ¹⁰More to be desired are they than gold, yes, than much fine gold: sweeter also than honey and the honeycomb. ¹¹Moreover by them is your servant warned: and in keeping of them there is great reward. ¹²Who can understand his errors? cleanse you me from secret faults. ¹³Keep back your servant also from presumptuous sins; let them not have dominion over me: then shall I be upright, and I shall be innocent from the great transgression. ¹⁴Let the words of my mouth, and the meditation of my heart, be acceptable in your sight, O LORD, my strength, and my redeemer.

20 ¹The LORD hear you in the day of trouble; the name of the God of Jacob defend you; ²Send you help from the sanctuary, and strengthen you out of Zion; ³Remember all your offerings, and accept your burnt sacrifice; Selah. ⁴Grant you according to your own heart, and fulfill all your counsel. ⁵We will rejoice in your salvation, and in the name of our God we will set up our banners: the LORD fulfill all your petitions. ⁶Now know I that the LORD saves his anointed; he will hear him from his holy heaven with the saving strength of his right hand. ⁷Some trust in chariots, and some in horses: but we will remember the name of the LORD our God. ⁸They are brought down and fallen: but we are risen, and stand upright. ⁹Save, LORD: let the king hear us when we call.

21 ¹The king shall joy in your strength, O LORD; and in your salvation how greatly shall he rejoice! ²You have given him his heart's desire, and have not withheld the request of his lips. Selah. ³For you prevent him with the blessings of goodness: you set a crown of pure gold on his head. ⁴He asked life of you, and you gave it him, even length of days for ever and ever. ⁵His glory is great in your salvation: honor and majesty have you laid on him. ⁶For you have made him most blessed for ever: you have made him exceeding glad with your countenance. ⁷For the king trusts in the LORD, and through the mercy of the most High he shall not be moved. ⁸Your hand shall find out all your enemies: your right hand shall find out those that hate you. ⁹You shall make them as a fiery oven in the time of your anger: the LORD shall swallow them up in his wrath, and the fire shall devour them. ¹⁰Their fruit shall you destroy from the earth, and their seed from among the children of men. ¹¹For they intended evil against you: they imagined a mischievous device, which they are not able to perform. ¹²Therefore shall you make them turn their back, when you shall make ready your arrows on your strings against the face of them. ¹³Be you exalted, LORD, in your own strength: so will we sing and praise your power.

22 ¹My God, my God, why have you forsaken me? why are you so far from helping me, and from the words of my roaring? ²O my God, I cry in the day time, but you hear not; and in the night season, and am not silent. ³But you are holy, O you that inhabit the praises of Israel. ⁴Our fathers trusted in you: they trusted, and you did deliver them. ⁵They cried to you, and were delivered: they trusted in you, and were not confounded. ⁶But I am a worm, and no man; a reproach of men, and despised of the people. ⁷All they that see me laugh me to scorn: they shoot out the lip, they shake the head, saying, ⁸He trusted on the LORD that he would deliver him: let him deliver him, seeing he delighted in him. ⁹But you are he that took me out of the womb: you did make me hope when I was on my mother's breasts. ¹⁰I was cast on you from the womb: you are my God from my mother's belly. ¹¹Be not far from me; for trouble is near; for there is none to help. ¹²Many bulls have compassed me: strong bulls of Bashan have beset me round. ¹³They gaped on me with their mouths, as a ravening and a roaring lion. ¹⁴I am poured out like water, and all my bones are out of joint: my heart is like wax; it is melted in the middle of my bowels. ¹⁵My strength is dried up like a potsherd; and my tongue sticks to my jaws; and you have brought me into the dust of death. ¹⁶For dogs have compassed me: the assembly of the wicked have enclosed me: they pierced my hands and my feet. ¹⁷I may tell all my bones: they look and stare on me. ¹⁸They part my garments among them, and cast lots on my clothing. ¹⁹But be not you far from me, O LORD: O my strength, haste you to help me. ²⁰Deliver my soul from the sword; my darling from the power of the dog. ²¹Save me from the lion's mouth: for you have heard me from the horns of the unicorns. ²²I will declare your name to my brothers: in the middle of the congregation will I praise you. ²³You that fear the LORD, praise him; all you the seed of Jacob, glorify him; and fear him, all you the seed of Israel. ²⁴For he has not despised nor abhorred the affliction of the afflicted; neither has he hid his face from him; but when he cried to him, he heard. ²⁵My praise shall be of you in the great congregation: I will pay my vows before them that fear him. ²⁶The meek shall eat and be satisfied: they shall praise the LORD that seek him: your heart shall live for ever. ²⁷All the ends of the world shall remember and turn to the LORD: and all the kindreds of the nations shall worship before you. ²⁸For the kingdom is the LORD's: and he is the governor among the nations. ²⁹All they that be fat on earth shall eat and worship: all they that go down to the dust shall bow before him: and none can keep alive his own soul. ³⁰A seed shall serve him; it shall be accounted to the Lord for a generation. ³¹They shall come, and shall declare his righteousness to a people that shall be born, that he has done this.

23

¹The LORD is my shepherd; I shall not want. ²He makes me to lie down in green pastures: he leads me beside the still waters. ³He restores my soul: he leads me in the paths of righteousness for his name's sake. ⁴Yes, though I walk through the valley of the shadow of death, I will fear no evil: for you are with me; your rod and your staff they comfort me. ⁵You prepare a table before me in the presence of my enemies: you anoint my head with oil; my cup runs over. ⁶Surely goodness and mercy shall follow me all the days of my life: and I will dwell in the house of the LORD for ever.

24

¹The earth is the LORD's, and the fullness thereof; the world, and they that dwell therein. ²For he has founded it on the seas, and established it on the floods. ³Who shall ascend into the hill of the LORD? or who shall stand in his holy place? ⁴He that has clean hands, and a pure heart; who has not lifted up his soul to vanity, nor sworn deceitfully. ⁵He shall receive the blessing from the LORD, and righteousness from the God of his salvation. ⁶This is the generation of them that seek him, that seek your face, O Jacob. Selah. ⁷Lift up your heads, O you gates; and be you lift up, you everlasting doors; and the King of glory shall come in. ⁸Who is this King of glory? The LORD strong and mighty, the LORD mighty in battle. ⁹Lift up your heads, O you gates; even lift them up, you everlasting doors; and the King of glory shall come in. ¹⁰Who is this King of glory? The LORD of hosts, he is the King of glory. Selah.

25

¹To you, O LORD, do I lift up my soul. ²O my God, I trust in you: let me not be ashamed, let not my enemies triumph over me. ³Yes, let none that wait on you be ashamed: let them be ashamed which transgress without cause. ⁴Show me your ways, O LORD; teach me your paths. ⁵Lead me in your truth, and teach me: for you are the God of my salvation; on you do I wait all the day. ⁶Remember, O LORD, your tender mercies and your loving kindnesses; for they have been ever of old. ⁷Remember not the sins of my youth, nor my transgressions: according to your mercy remember you me for your goodness' sake, O LORD. ⁸Good and upright is the LORD: therefore will he teach sinners in the way. ⁹The meek will he guide in judgment: and the meek will he teach his way. ¹⁰All the paths of the LORD are mercy and truth to such as keep his covenant and his testimonies. ¹¹For your name's sake, O LORD, pardon my iniquity; for it is great. ¹²What man is he that fears the LORD? him shall he teach in the way that he shall choose. ¹³His soul shall dwell at ease; and his seed shall inherit the earth. ¹⁴The secret of the LORD is with them that fear him; and he will show them his covenant. ¹⁵My eyes are ever toward the LORD; for he shall pluck my feet out of the net. ¹⁶Turn you to me, and have mercy on me; for I am desolate and afflicted. ¹⁷The troubles of my heart are enlarged: O bring you me out of my distresses. ¹⁸Look on my affliction and my pain; and forgive all my sins. ¹⁹Consider my enemies; for they are many; and they hate me with cruel hatred. ²⁰O keep my soul, and deliver me: let me not be ashamed; for I put my trust in you. ²¹Let integrity and uprightness preserve me; for I wait on you. ²²Redeem Israel, O God, out of all his troubles.

26

¹Judge me, O LORD; for I have walked in my integrity: I have trusted also in the LORD; therefore I shall not slide. ²Examine me, O LORD, and prove me; try my reins and my heart. ³For your loving kindness is before my eyes: and I have walked in your truth. ⁴I have not sat with vain persons, neither will I go in with dissemblers. ⁵I have hated the congregation of evil doers; and will not sit with the wicked. ⁶I will wash my hands in innocence: so will I compass your altar, O LORD: ⁷That I may publish with the voice of thanksgiving, and tell of all your wondrous works. ⁸LORD, I have loved the habitation of your house, and the place where your honor dwells. ⁹Gather not my soul with sinners, nor my life with bloody men: ¹⁰In whose hands is mischief, and their right hand is full of bribes. ¹¹But as for me, I will walk in my integrity: redeem me, and be merciful to me. ¹²My foot stands in an even place: in the congregations will I bless the LORD.

27

¹The LORD is my light and my salvation; whom shall I fear? the LORD is the strength of my life; of whom shall I be afraid? ²When the wicked, even my enemies

and my foes, came on me to eat up my flesh, they stumbled and fell. ³Though an host should encamp against me, my heart shall not fear: though war should rise against me, in this will I be confident. ⁴One thing have I desired of the LORD, that will I seek after; that I may dwell in the house of the LORD all the days of my life, to behold the beauty of the LORD, and to inquire in his temple. ⁵For in the time of trouble he shall hide me in his pavilion: in the secret of his tabernacle shall he hide me; he shall set me up on a rock. ⁶And now shall my head be lifted up above my enemies round about me: therefore will I offer in his tabernacle sacrifices of joy; I will sing, yes, I will sing praises to the LORD. ⁷Hear, O LORD, when I cry with my voice: have mercy also on me, and answer me. ⁸When you said, Seek you my face; my heart said to you, Your face, LORD, will I seek. ⁹Hide not your face far from me; put not your servant away in anger: you have been my help; leave me not, neither forsake me, O God of my salvation. ¹⁰When my father and my mother forsake me, then the LORD will take me up. ¹¹Teach me your way, O LORD, and lead me in a plain path, because of my enemies. ¹²Deliver me not over to the will of my enemies: for false witnesses are risen up against me, and such as breathe out cruelty. ¹³I had fainted, unless I had believed to see the goodness of the LORD in the land of the living. ¹⁴Wait on the LORD: be of good courage, and he shall strengthen your heart: wait, I say, on the LORD.

28

¹To you will I cry, O LORD my rock; be not silent to me: lest, if you be silent to me, I become like them that go down into the pit. ²Hear the voice of my supplications, when I cry to you, when I lift up my hands toward your holy oracle. ³Draw me not away with the wicked, and with the workers of iniquity, which speak peace to their neighbors, but mischief is in their hearts. ⁴Give them according to their deeds, and according to the wickedness of their endeavors: give them after the work of their hands; render to them their desert. ⁵Because they regard not the works of the LORD, nor the operation of his hands, he shall destroy them, and not build them up. ⁶Blessed be the LORD, because he has heard the voice of my supplications. ⁷The LORD is my strength and my shield; my heart trusted in him, and I am helped: therefore my heart greatly rejoices; and with my song will I praise him. ⁸The LORD is their strength, and he is the saving strength of his anointed. ⁹Save your people, and bless your inheritance: feed them also, and lift them up for ever.

29

¹Give to the LORD, O you mighty, give to the LORD glory and strength. ²Give to the LORD the glory due to his name; worship the LORD in the beauty of holiness. ³The voice of the LORD is on the waters: the God of glory thunders: the LORD is on many waters. ⁴The voice of the LORD is powerful; the voice of the LORD is full of majesty. ⁵The voice of the LORD breaks the cedars; yes, the LORD breaks the cedars of Lebanon. ⁶He makes them also to skip like a calf; Lebanon and Sirion like a young unicorn. ⁷The voice of the LORD divides the flames of fire. ⁸The voice of the LORD shakes the wilderness; the LORD shakes the wilderness of Kadesh. ⁹The voice of the LORD makes the hinds to calve, and discovers the forests: and in his temple does every one speak of his glory. ¹⁰The LORD sits on the flood; yes, the LORD sits King for ever. ¹¹The LORD will give strength to his people; the LORD will bless his people with peace.

30

¹I will extol you, O LORD; for you have lifted me up, and have not made my foes to rejoice over me. ²O LORD my God, I cried to you, and you have healed me. ³O LORD, you have brought up my soul from the grave: you have kept me alive, that I should not go down to the pit. ⁴Sing to the LORD, O you saints of his, and give thanks at the remembrance of his holiness. ⁵For his anger endures but a moment; in his favor is life: weeping may endure for a night, but joy comes in the morning. ⁶And in my prosperity I said, I shall never be moved. ⁷LORD, by your favor you have made my mountain to stand strong: you did hide your face, and I was troubled. ⁸I cried to you, O LORD; and to the LORD I made supplication. ⁹What profit is there in my blood, when I go down to the pit? Shall the dust praise you? shall it declare your truth? ¹⁰Hear, O LORD, and have mercy on me: LORD, be you my helper. ¹¹You have turned for me my mourning into dancing: you have put off my sackcloth, and girded me with gladness; ¹²To the end that my glory may sing praise to you, and not be silent. O LORD my God, I will give thanks to you for ever.

31

¹In you, O LORD, do I put my trust; let me never be ashamed: deliver me in your righteousness. ²Bow down your ear to me; deliver me speedily: be you my strong rock, for an house of defense to save me. ³For you are my rock and my fortress; therefore for your name's sake lead me, and guide me. ⁴Pull me out of the net that they have laid privately for me: for you are my strength. ⁵Into your hand I commit my spirit: you have redeemed me, O LORD God of truth. ⁶I have hated them that regard lying vanities: but I trust in the LORD. ⁷I will be glad and rejoice in your mercy: for you have considered my trouble; you have known my soul in adversities; ⁸And have not shut me up into the hand of the enemy: you have set my feet in a large room. ⁹Have mercy on me, O LORD, for I am in trouble: my eye is consumed with grief, yes, my soul and my belly. ¹⁰For my life is spent with grief, and my years with sighing: my strength fails because of my iniquity, and my bones are consumed. ¹¹I was a reproach among all my enemies, but especially among my neighbors, and a fear to my acquaintance: they that did see me without fled from me. ¹²I am forgotten as a dead man out of mind: I am like a broken vessel. ¹³For I have heard the slander of many: fear was on every side: while they took counsel together against me, they devised to take away my life. ¹⁴But I trusted in you, O LORD: I said, You are my God. ¹⁵My times are in your hand: deliver me from the hand of my enemies, and from them that persecute me. ¹⁶Make your face to shine on your servant: save me for your mercies' sake. ¹⁷Let me not be ashamed, O LORD; for I have called on you: let the wicked be ashamed, and let them be silent in the grave. ¹⁸Let the lying lips be put to silence; which speak grievous things proudly and contemptuously against the righteous. ¹⁹Oh how great is your goodness, which you have laid up for them that fear you; which you have worked for them that trust in you before the sons of men! ²⁰You shall hide them in the secret of your presence from the pride of man: you shall keep them secretly in a

pavilion from the strife of tongues. ²¹Blessed be the LORD: for he has showed me his marvelous kindness in a strong city. ²²For I said in my haste, I am cut off from before your eyes: nevertheless you heard the voice of my supplications when I cried to you. ²³O love the LORD, all you his saints: for the LORD preserves the faithful, and plentifully rewards the proud doer. ²⁴Be of good courage, and he shall strengthen your heart, all you that hope in the LORD.

32 ¹Blessed is he whose transgression is forgiven, whose sin is covered. ²Blessed is the man to whom the LORD imputes not iniquity, and in whose spirit there is no guile. ³When I kept silence, my bones waxed old through my roaring all the day long. ⁴For day and night your hand was heavy on me: my moisture is turned into the drought of summer. Selah. ⁵I acknowledge my sin to you, and my iniquity have I not hid. I said, I will confess my transgressions to the LORD; and you forgave the iniquity of my sin. Selah. ⁶For this shall every one that is godly pray to you in a time when you may be found: surely in the floods of great waters they shall not come near to him. ⁷You are my hiding place; you shall preserve me from trouble; you shall compass me about with songs of deliverance. Selah. ⁸I will instruct you and teach you in the way which you shall go: I will guide you with my eye. ⁹Be you not as the horse, or as the mule, which have no understanding: whose mouth must be held in with bit and bridle, lest they come near to you. ¹⁰Many sorrows shall be to the wicked: but he that trusts in the LORD, mercy shall compass him about. ¹¹Be glad in the LORD, and rejoice, you righteous: and shout for joy, all you that are upright in heart.

33 ¹Rejoice in the LORD, O you righteous: for praise is comely for the upright. ²Praise the LORD with harp: sing to him with the psaltery and an instrument of ten strings. ³Sing to him a new song; play skillfully with a loud noise. ⁴For the word of the LORD is right; and all his works are done in truth. ⁵He loves righteousness and judgment: the earth is full of the goodness of the LORD. ⁶By the word of the LORD were the heavens made; and all the host of them by the breath of his mouth. ⁷He gathers the waters of the sea together as an heap: he lays up the depth in storehouses. ⁸Let all the earth fear the LORD: let all the inhabitants of the world stand in awe of him. ⁹For he spoke, and it was done; he commanded, and it stood fast. ¹⁰The LORD brings the counsel of the heathen to nothing: he makes the devices of the people of none effect. ¹¹The counsel of the LORD stands for ever, the thoughts of his heart to all generations. ¹²Blessed is the nation whose God is the LORD; and the people whom he has chosen for his own inheritance. ¹³The LORD looks from heaven; he beholds all the sons of men. ¹⁴From the place of his habitation he looks on all the inhabitants of the earth. ¹⁵He fashions their hearts alike; he considers all their works. ¹⁶There is no king saved by the multitude of an host: a mighty man is not delivered by much strength. ¹⁷An horse is a vain thing for safety: neither shall he deliver any by his great strength. ¹⁸Behold, the eye of the LORD is on them that fear him, on them that hope in his mercy; ¹⁹To deliver their soul from death, and to keep them alive in famine. ²⁰Our soul waits for the LORD: he is our help and our shield. ²¹For our heart shall rejoice in him, because we have trusted in his holy name. ²²Let your mercy, O LORD, be on us, according as we hope in you.

34 ¹I will bless the LORD at all times: his praise shall continually be in my mouth. ²My soul shall make her boast in the LORD: the humble shall hear thereof, and be glad. ³O magnify the LORD with me, and let us exalt his name together. ⁴I sought the LORD, and he heard me, and delivered me from all my fears. ⁵They looked to him, and were lightened: and their faces were not ashamed. ⁶This poor man cried, and the LORD heard him, and saved him out of all his troubles. ⁷The angel of the LORD encamps round about them that fear him, and delivers them. ⁸O taste and see that the LORD is good: blessed is the man that trusts in him. ⁹O fear the LORD, you his saints: for there is no want to them that fear him. ¹⁰The young lions do lack, and suffer hunger: but they that seek the LORD shall not want any good thing. ¹¹Come, you children, listen to me: I will teach you the fear of the LORD. ¹²What man is he that desires life, and loves many days, that he may see good? ¹³Keep your tongue from evil, and your lips from speaking guile. ¹⁴Depart from evil, and do good; seek peace, and pursue it. ¹⁵The eyes of the LORD are on the righteous, and his ears are open to their cry. ¹⁶The face of the LORD is against them that do evil, to cut off the remembrance of them from the earth. ¹⁷The righteous cry, and the LORD hears, and delivers them out of all their troubles. ¹⁸The LORD is near to them that are of a broken heart; and saves such as be of a contrite spirit. ¹⁹Many are the afflictions of the righteous: but the LORD delivers him out of them all. ²⁰He keeps all his bones: not one of them is broken. ²¹Evil shall slay the wicked: and they that hate the righteous shall be desolate. ²²The LORD redeems the soul of his servants: and none of them that trust in him shall be desolate.

35 ¹Plead my cause, O LORD, with them that strive with me: fight against them that fight against me. ²Take hold of shield and buckler, and stand up for my help. ³Draw out also the spear, and stop the way against them that persecute me: say to my soul, I am your salvation. ⁴Let them be confounded and put to shame that seek after my soul: let them be turned back and brought to confusion that devise my hurt. ⁵Let them be as chaff before the wind: and let the angel of the LORD chase them. ⁶Let their way be dark and slippery: and let the angel of the LORD persecute them. ⁷For without cause have they hid for me their net in a pit, which without cause they have dig for my soul. ⁸Let destruction come on him at unawares; and let his net that he has hid catch himself: into that very destruction let him fall. ⁹And my soul shall be joyful in the LORD: it shall rejoice in his salvation. ¹⁰All my bones shall say, LORD, who is like to you, which deliver the poor from him that is too strong for him, yes, the poor and the needy from him that spoils him? ¹¹False witnesses did rise up; they laid to my charge things that I knew not. ¹²They rewarded me evil for good to the spoiling of my soul. ¹³But as for me, when they were sick, my clothing was sackcloth: I humbled my soul with fasting; and my prayer returned into my own bosom. ¹⁴I behaved myself as though he had been my friend or brother: I bowed down heavily, as one that mourns for his mother. ¹⁵But in my adversity they rejoiced, and gathered themselves together:

yes, the attackers gathered themselves together against me, and I knew it not; they did tear me, and ceased not: ⁱ⁶With hypocritical mockers in feasts, they gnashed on me with their teeth. ¹⁷Lord, how long will you look on? rescue my soul from their destructions, my darling from the lions. ¹⁸I will give you thanks in the great congregation: I will praise you among much people. ¹⁹Let not them that are my enemies wrongfully rejoice over me: neither let them wink with the eye that hate me without a cause. ²⁰For they speak not peace: but they devise deceitful matters against them that are quiet in the land. ²¹Yes, they opened their mouth wide against me, and said, Aha, aha, our eye has seen it. ²²This you have seen, O LORD: keep not silence: O Lord, be not far from me. ²³Stir up yourself, and awake to my judgment, even to my cause, my God and my Lord. ²⁴Judge me, O LORD my God, according to your righteousness; and let them not rejoice over me. ²⁵Let them not say in their hearts, Ah, so would we have it: let them not say, We have swallowed him up. ²⁶Let them be ashamed and brought to confusion together that rejoice at my hurt: let them be clothed with shame and dishonor that magnify themselves against me. ²⁷Let them shout for joy, and be glad, that favor my righteous cause: yes, let them say continually, Let the LORD be magnified, which has pleasure in the prosperity of his servant. ²⁸And my tongue shall speak of your righteousness and of your praise all the day long.

36

¹The transgression of the wicked says within my heart, that there is no fear of God before his eyes. ²For he flatters himself in his own eyes, until his iniquity be found to be hateful. ³The words of his mouth are iniquity and deceit: he has left off to be wise, and to do good. ⁴He devises mischief on his bed; he sets himself in a way that is not good; he abhors not evil. ⁵Your mercy, O LORD, is in the heavens; and your faithfulness reaches to the clouds. ⁶Your righteousness is like the great mountains; your judgments are a great deep: O LORD, you preserve man and beast. ⁷How excellent is your loving kindness, O God! therefore the children of men put their trust under the shadow of your wings. ⁸They shall be abundantly satisfied with the fatness of your house; and you shall make them drink of the river of your pleasures. ⁹For with you is the fountain of life: in your light shall we see light. ¹⁰O continue your loving kindness to them that know you; and your righteousness to the upright in heart. ¹¹Let not the foot of pride come against me, and let not the hand of the wicked remove me. ¹²There are the workers of iniquity fallen: they are cast down, and shall not be able to rise.

37

¹Fret not yourself because of evildoers, neither be you envious against the workers of iniquity. ²For they shall soon be cut down like the grass, and wither as the green herb. ³Trust in the LORD, and do good; so shall you dwell in the land, and truly you shall be fed. ⁴Delight yourself also in the LORD: and he shall give you the desires of your heart. ⁵Commit your way to the LORD; trust also in him; and he shall bring it to pass. ⁶And he shall bring forth your righteousness as the light, and your judgment as the noonday. ⁷Rest in the LORD, and wait patiently for him: fret not yourself because of him who prospers in his way, because of the man who brings wicked devices to pass. ⁸Cease from anger, and forsake wrath: fret not yourself in any wise to do evil. ⁹For evildoers shall be cut off: but those that wait on the LORD, they shall inherit the earth. ¹⁰For yet a little while, and the wicked shall not be: yes, you shall diligently consider his place, and it shall not be. ¹¹But the meek shall inherit the earth; and shall delight themselves in the abundance of peace. ¹²The wicked plots against the just, and gnashes on him with his teeth. ¹³The LORD shall laugh at him: for he sees that his day is coming. ¹⁴The wicked have drawn out the sword, and have bent their bow, to cast down the poor and needy, and to slay such as be of upright conversation. ¹⁵Their sword shall enter into their own heart, and their bows shall be broken. ¹⁶A little that a righteous man has is better than the riches of many wicked. ¹⁷For the arms of the wicked shall be broken: but the LORD upholds the righteous. ¹⁸The LORD knows the days of the upright: and their inheritance shall be for ever. ¹⁹They shall not be ashamed in the evil time: and in the days of famine they shall be satisfied. ²⁰But the wicked shall perish, and the enemies of the LORD shall be as the fat of lambs: they shall consume; into smoke shall they consume away. ²¹The wicked borrows, and pays not again: but the righteous shows mercy, and gives. ²²For such as be blessed of him shall inherit the earth; and they that be cursed of him shall be cut off. ²³The steps of a good man are ordered by the LORD: and he delights in his way. ²⁴Though he fall, he shall not be utterly cast down: for the LORD upholds him with his hand. ²⁵I have been young, and now am old; yet have I not seen the righteous forsaken, nor his seed begging bread. ²⁶He is ever merciful, and lends; and his seed is blessed. ²⁷Depart from evil, and do good; and dwell for ever more. ²⁸For the LORD loves judgment, and forsakes not his saints; they are preserved for ever: but the seed of the wicked shall be cut off. ²⁹The righteous shall inherit the land, and dwell therein for ever. ³⁰The mouth of the righteous speaks wisdom, and his tongue talks of judgment. ³¹The law of his God is in his heart; none of his steps shall slide. ³²The wicked watches the righteous, and seeks to slay him. ³³The LORD will not leave him in his hand, nor condemn him when he is judged. ³⁴Wait on the LORD, and keep his way, and he shall exalt you to inherit the land: when the wicked are cut off, you shall see it. ³⁵I have seen the wicked in great power, and spreading himself like a green bay tree. ³⁶Yet he passed away, and, see, he was not: yes, I sought him, but he could not be found. ³⁷Mark the perfect man, and behold the upright: for the end of that man is peace. ³⁸But the transgressors shall be destroyed together: the end of the wicked shall be cut off. ³⁹But the salvation of the righteous is of the LORD: he is their strength in the time of trouble. ⁴⁰And the LORD shall help them, and deliver them: he shall deliver them from the wicked, and save them, because they trust in him.

38

¹O lord, rebuke me not in your wrath: neither chasten me in your hot displeasure. ²For your arrows stick fast in me, and your hand presses me sore. ³There is no soundness in my flesh because of your anger; neither is there any rest in my bones because of my sin. ⁴For my iniquities are gone over my head: as an heavy burden they are too heavy for me. ⁵My wounds stink and are corrupt because of my foolishness. ⁶I am troubled; I am bowed down greatly; I go mourning all the day long. ⁷For my loins are filled with a

loathsome disease: and there is no soundness in my flesh. ⁸I am feeble and sore broken: I have roared by reason of the disquietness of my heart. ⁹Lord, all my desire is before you; and my groaning is not hid from you. ¹⁰My heart pants, my strength fails me: as for the light of my eyes, it also is gone from me. ¹¹My lovers and my friends stand aloof from my sore; and my kinsmen stand afar off. ¹²They also that seek after my life lay snares for me: and they that seek my hurt speak mischievous things, and imagine deceits all the day long. ¹³But I, as a deaf man, heard not; and I was as a dumb man that opens not his mouth. ¹⁴Thus I was as a man that hears not, and in whose mouth are no reproofs. ¹⁵For in you, O LORD, do I hope: you will hear, O Lord my God. ¹⁶For I said, Hear me, lest otherwise they should rejoice over me: when my foot slips, they magnify themselves against me. ¹⁷For I am ready to halt, and my sorrow is continually before me. ¹⁸For I will declare my iniquity; I will be sorry for my sin. ¹⁹But my enemies are lively, and they are strong: and they that hate me wrongfully are multiplied. ²⁰They also that render evil for good are my adversaries; because I follow the thing that good is. ²¹Forsake me not, O LORD: O my God, be not far from me. ²²Make haste to help me, O Lord my salvation.

39

¹I said, I will take heed to my ways, that I sin not with my tongue: I will keep my mouth with a bridle, while the wicked is before me. ²I was dumb with silence, I held my peace, even from good; and my sorrow was stirred. ³My heart was hot within me, while I was musing the fire burned: then spoke I with my tongue, ⁴LORD, make me to know my end, and the measure of my days, what it is: that I may know how frail I am. ⁵Behold, you have made my days as an handbreadth; and my age is as nothing before you: truly every man at his best state is altogether vanity. Selah. ⁶Surely every man walks in a vain show: surely they are disquieted in vain: he heaps up riches, and knows not who shall gather them. ⁷And now, Lord, what wait I for? my hope is in you. ⁸Deliver me from all my transgressions: make me not the reproach of the foolish. ⁹I was dumb, I opened not my mouth; because you did it. ¹⁰Remove your stroke away from me: I am consumed by the blow of your hand. ¹¹When you with rebukes do correct man for iniquity, you make his beauty to consume away like a moth: surely every man is vanity. Selah. ¹²Hear my prayer, O LORD, and give ear to my cry; hold not your peace at my tears: for I am a stranger with you, and a sojourner, as all my fathers were. ¹³O spare me, that I may recover strength, before I go hence, and be no more.

40

¹I waited patiently for the LORD; and he inclined to me, and heard my cry. ²He brought me up also out of an horrible pit, out of the miry clay, and set my feet on a rock, and established my goings. ³And he has put a new song in my mouth, even praise to our God: many shall see it, and fear, and shall trust in the LORD. ⁴Blessed is that man that makes the LORD his trust, and respects not the proud, nor such as turn aside to lies. ⁵Many, O LORD my God, are your wonderful works which you have done, and your thoughts which are to us-ward: they cannot be reckoned up in order to you: if I would declare and speak of them, they are more than can be numbered. ⁶Sacrifice and offering you did not desire; my ears have you opened: burnt offering and sin offering have you not required. ⁷Then said I, See, I come: in the volume of the book it is written of me, ⁸I delight to do your will, O my God: yes, your law is within my heart. ⁹I have preached righteousness in the great congregation: see, I have not refrained my lips, O LORD, you know. ¹⁰I have not hid your righteousness within my heart; I have declared your faithfulness and your salvation: I have not concealed your loving kindness and your truth from the great congregation. ¹¹Withhold not you your tender mercies from me, O LORD: let your loving kindness and your truth continually preserve me. ¹²For innumerable evils have compassed me about: my iniquities have taken hold on me, so that I am not able to look up; they are more than the hairs of my head: therefore my heart fails me. ¹³Be pleased, O LORD, to deliver me: O LORD, make haste to help me. ¹⁴Let them be ashamed and confounded together that seek after my soul to destroy it; let them be driven backward and put to shame that wish me evil. ¹⁵Let them be desolate for a reward of their shame that say to me, Aha, aha. ¹⁶Let all those that seek you rejoice and be glad in you: let such as love your salvation say continually, The LORD be magnified. ¹⁷But I am poor and needy; yet the Lord thinks on me: you are my help and my deliverer; make no tarrying, O my God.

41

¹Blessed is he that considers the poor: the LORD will deliver him in time of trouble. ²The LORD will preserve him, and keep him alive; and he shall be blessed on the earth: and you will not deliver him to the will of his enemies. ³The LORD will strengthen him on the bed of languishing: you will make all his bed in his sickness. ⁴I said, LORD, be merciful to me: heal my soul; for I have sinned against you. ⁵My enemies speak evil of me, When shall he die, and his name perish? ⁶And if he come to see me, he speaks vanity: his heart gathers iniquity to itself; when he goes abroad, he tells it. ⁷All that hate me whisper together against me: against me do they devise my hurt. ⁸An evil disease, say they, sticks fast to him: and now that he lies he shall rise up no more. ⁹Yes, my own familiar friend, in whom I trusted, which did eat of my bread, has lifted up his heel against me. ¹⁰But you, O LORD, be merciful to me, and raise me up, that I may requite them. ¹¹By this I know that you favor me, because my enemy does not triumph over me. ¹²And as for me, you uphold me in my integrity, and set me before your face for ever. ¹³Blessed be the LORD God of Israel from everlasting, and to everlasting. Amen, and Amen.

42

¹As the hart pants after the water brooks, so pants my soul after you, O God. ²My soul thirsts for God, for the living God: when shall I come and appear before God? ³My tears have been my meat day and night, while they continually say to me, Where is your God? ⁴When I remember these things, I pour out my soul in me: for I had gone with the multitude, I went with them to the house of God, with the voice of joy and praise, with a multitude that kept holy day. ⁵Why are you cast down, O my soul? and why are you disquieted in me? hope you in God: for I shall yet praise him for the help of his countenance. ⁶O my God, my soul is cast down within me: therefore will I remember you from the land of Jordan, and of the Hermonites, from the hill

Mizar. ⁷Deep calls to deep at the noise of your waterspouts: all your waves and your billows are gone over me. ⁸Yet the LORD will command his loving kindness in the day time, and in the night his song shall be with me, and my prayer to the God of my life. ⁹I will say to God my rock, Why have you forgotten me? why go I mourning because of the oppression of the enemy? ¹⁰As with a sword in my bones, my enemies reproach me; while they say daily to me, Where is your God? ¹¹Why are you cast down, O my soul? and why are you disquieted within me? hope you in God: for I shall yet praise him, who is the health of my countenance, and my God.

43 ¹Judge me, O God, and plead my cause against an ungodly nation: O deliver me from the deceitful and unjust man. ²For you are the God of my strength: why do you cast me off? why go I mourning because of the oppression of the enemy? ³O send out your light and your truth: let them lead me; let them bring me to your holy hill, and to your tabernacles. ⁴Then will I go to the altar of God, to God my exceeding joy: yes, on the harp will I praise you, O God my God. ⁵Why are you cast down, O my soul? and why are you disquieted within me? hope in God: for I shall yet praise him, who is the health of my countenance, and my God.

44 ¹We have heard with our ears, O God, our fathers have told us, what work you did in their days, in the times of old. ²How you did drive out the heathen with your hand, and planted them; how you did afflict the people, and cast them out. ³For they got not the land in possession by their own sword, neither did their own arm save them: but your right hand, and your arm, and the light of your countenance, because you had a favor to them. ⁴You are my King, O God: command deliverances for Jacob. ⁵Through you will we push down our enemies: through your name will we tread them under that rise up against us. ⁶For I will not trust in my bow, neither shall my sword save me. ⁷But you have saved us from our enemies, and have put them to shame that hated us. ⁸In God we boast all the day long, and praise your name for ever. Selah. ⁹But you have cast off, and put us to shame; and go not forth with our armies. ¹⁰You make us to turn back from the enemy: and they which hate us spoil for themselves. ¹¹You have given us like sheep appointed for meat; and have scattered us among the heathen. ¹²You sell your people for nothing, and do not increase your wealth by their price. ¹³You make us a reproach to our neighbors, a scorn and a derision to them that are round about us. ¹⁴You make us a byword among the heathen, a shaking of the head among the people. ¹⁵My confusion is continually before me, and the shame of my face has covered me, ¹⁶For the voice of him that reproaches and blasphemes; by reason of the enemy and avenger. ¹⁷All this is come on us; yet have we not forgotten you, neither have we dealt falsely in your covenant. ¹⁸Our heart is not turned back, neither have our steps declined from your way; ¹⁹Though you have sore broken us in the place of dragons, and covered us with the shadow of death. ²⁰If we have forgotten the name of our God, or stretched out our hands to a strange god; ²¹Shall not God search this out? for he knows the secrets of the heart. ²²Yes, for your sake are we killed all the day long; we are counted as sheep for the slaughter. ²³Awake, why sleep you, O Lord? arise, cast us not off for ever. ²⁴Why hide you your face, and forget our affliction and our oppression? ²⁵For our soul is bowed down to the dust: our belly sticks to the earth. ²⁶Arise for our help, and redeem us for your mercies' sake.

45 ¹My heart is gushing a good matter: I speak of the things which I have made touching the king: my tongue is the pen of a ready writer. ²You are fairer than the children of men: grace is poured into your lips: therefore God has blessed you for ever. ³Gird your sword on your thigh, O most mighty, with your glory and your majesty. ⁴And in your majesty ride prosperously because of truth and meekness and righteousness; and your right hand shall teach you terrible things. ⁵Your arrows are sharp in the heart of the king's enemies; whereby the people fall under you. ⁶Your throne, O God, is for ever and ever: the scepter of your kingdom is a right scepter. ⁷You love righteousness, and hate wickedness: therefore God, your God, has anointed you with the oil of gladness above your fellows. ⁸All your garments smell of myrrh, and aloes, and cassia, out of the ivory palaces, whereby they have made you glad. ⁹Kings' daughters were among your honorable women: on your right hand did stand the queen in gold of Ophir. ¹⁰Listen, O daughter, and consider, and incline your ear; forget also your own people, and your father's house; ¹¹So shall the king greatly desire your beauty: for he is your Lord; and worship you him. ¹²And the daughter of Tyre shall be there with a gift; even the rich among the people shall entreat your favor. ¹³The king's daughter is all glorious within: her clothing is of worked gold. ¹⁴She shall be brought to the king in raiment of needlework: the virgins her companions that follow her shall be brought to you. ¹⁵With gladness and rejoicing shall they be brought: they shall enter into the king's palace. ¹⁶Instead of your fathers shall be your children, whom you may make princes in all the earth. ¹⁷I will make your name to be remembered in all generations: therefore shall the people praise you for ever and ever.

46 ¹God is our refuge and strength, a very present help in trouble. ²Therefore will not we fear, though the earth be removed, and though the mountains be carried into the middle of the sea; ³Though the waters thereof roar and be troubled, though the mountains shake with the swelling thereof. Selah. ⁴There is a river, the streams whereof shall make glad the city of God, the holy place of the tabernacles of the most High. ⁵God is in the middle of her; she shall not be moved: God shall help her, and that right early. ⁶The heathen raged, the kingdoms were moved: he uttered his voice, the earth melted. ⁷The LORD of hosts is with us; the God of Jacob is our refuge. Selah. ⁸Come, behold the works of the LORD, what desolations he has made in the earth. ⁹He makes wars to cease to the end of the earth; he breaks the bow, and cuts the spear in sunder; he burns the chariot in the fire. ¹⁰Be still, and know that I am God: I will be exalted among the heathen, I will be exalted in the earth. ¹¹The LORD of hosts is with us; the God of Jacob is our refuge. Selah.

47 ¹O clap your hands, all you people; shout to God with the voice of triumph. ²For the LORD most high is terrible; he is a great King over all the earth. ³He shall subdue the people under us, and the nations under our feet. ⁴He shall choose our inheritance for us, the excellency of Jacob whom he loved. Selah. ⁵God is gone up with a shout, the LORD with the sound of a trumpet. ⁶Sing praises to God, sing praises: sing praises to our King, sing praises. ⁷For God is the King of all the earth: sing you praises with understanding. ⁸God reigns over the heathen: God sits on the throne of his holiness. ⁹The princes of the people are gathered together, even the people of the God of Abraham: for the shields of the earth belong to God: he is greatly exalted.

48 ¹Great is the LORD, and greatly to be praised in the city of our God, in the mountain of his holiness. ²Beautiful for situation, the joy of the whole earth, is mount Zion, on the sides of the north, the city of the great King. ³God is known in her palaces for a refuge. ⁴For, see, the kings were assembled, they passed by together. ⁵They saw it, and so they marveled; they were troubled, and hurried away. ⁶Fear took hold on them there, and pain, as of a woman in travail. ⁷You break the ships of Tarshish with an east wind. ⁸As we have heard, so have we seen in the city of the LORD of hosts, in the city of our God: God will establish it for ever. Selah. ⁹We have thought of your loving kindness, O God, in the middle of your temple. ¹⁰According to your name, O God, so is your praise to the ends of the earth: your right hand is full of righteousness. ¹¹Let mount Zion rejoice, let the daughters of Judah be glad, because of your judgments. ¹²Walk about Zion, and go round about her: tell the towers thereof. ¹³Mark you well her bulwarks, consider her palaces; that you may tell it to the generation following. ¹⁴For this God is our God for ever and ever: he will be our guide even to death.

49 ¹Hear this, all you people; give ear, all you inhabitants of the world: ²Both low and high, rich and poor, together. ³My mouth shall speak of wisdom; and the meditation of my heart shall be of understanding. ⁴I will incline my ear to a parable: I will open my dark saying on the harp. ⁵Why should I fear in the days of evil, when the iniquity of my heels shall compass me about? ⁶They that trust in their wealth, and boast themselves in the multitude of their riches; ⁷None of them can by any means redeem his brother, nor give to God a ransom for him: ⁸(For the redemption of their soul is precious, and it ceases for ever:) ⁹That he should still live for ever, and not see corruption. ¹⁰For he sees that wise men die, likewise the fool and the brutish person perish, and leave their wealth to others. ¹¹Their inward thought is, that their houses shall continue for ever, and their dwelling places to all generations; they call their lands after their own names. ¹²Nevertheless man being in honor stays not: he is like the beasts that perish. ¹³This their way is their folly: yet their posterity approve their sayings. Selah. ¹⁴Like sheep they are laid in the grave; death shall feed on them; and the upright shall have dominion over them in the morning; and their beauty shall consume in the grave from their dwelling. ¹⁵But God will redeem my soul from the power of the grave: for he shall receive me. Selah. ¹⁶Be not you afraid when one is made rich, when the glory of his house is increased; ¹⁷For when he dies he shall carry nothing away: his glory shall not descend after him. ¹⁸Though while he lived he blessed his soul: and men will praise you, when you do well to yourself. ¹⁹He shall go to the generation of his fathers; they shall never see light. ²⁰Man that is in honor, and understands not, is like the beasts that perish.

50 ¹The mighty God, even the LORD, has spoken, and called the earth from the rising of the sun to the going down thereof. ²Out of Zion, the perfection of beauty, God has shined. ³Our God shall come, and shall not keep silence: a fire shall devour before him, and it shall be very tempestuous round about him. ⁴He shall call to the heavens from above, and to the earth, that he may judge his people. ⁵Gather my saints together to me; those that have made a covenant with me by sacrifice. ⁶And the heavens shall declare his righteousness: for God is judge himself. Selah. ⁷Hear, O my people, and I will speak; O Israel, and I will testify against you: I am God, even your God. ⁸I will not reprove you for your sacrifices or your burnt offerings, to have been continually before me. ⁹I will take no bullock out of your house, nor he goats out of your folds. ¹⁰For every beast of the forest is mine, and the cattle on a thousand hills. ¹¹I know all the fowls of the mountains: and the wild beasts of the field are mine. ¹²If I were hungry, I would not tell you: for the world is mine, and the fullness thereof. ¹³Will I eat the flesh of bulls, or drink the blood of goats? ¹⁴Offer to God thanksgiving; and pay your vows to the most High: ¹⁵And call on me in the day of trouble: I will deliver you, and you shall glorify me. ¹⁶But to the wicked God says, What have you to do to declare my statutes, or that you should take my covenant in your mouth? ¹⁷Seeing you hate instruction, and casts my words behind you. ¹⁸When you saw a thief, then you consented with him, and have been partaker with adulterers. ¹⁹You give your mouth to evil, and your tongue frames deceit. ²⁰You sit and speak against your brother; you slander your own mother's son. ²¹These things have you done, and I kept silence; you thought that I was altogether such an one as yourself: but I will reprove you, and set them in order before your eyes. ²²Now consider this, you that forget God, lest I tear you in pieces, and there be none to deliver. ²³Whoever offers praise glorifies me: and to him that orders his conversation aright will I show the salvation of God.

51 ¹Have mercy on me, O God, according to your loving kindness: according to the multitude of your tender mercies blot out my transgressions. ²Wash me thoroughly from my iniquity, and cleanse me from my sin. ³For I acknowledge my transgressions: and my sin is ever before me. ⁴Against you, you only, have I sinned, and done this evil in your sight: that you might be justified when you speak, and be clear when you judge. ⁵Behold, I was shaped in iniquity; and in sin did my mother conceive me. ⁶Behold, you desire truth in the inward parts: and in the hidden part you shall make me to know wisdom. ⁷Purge me with hyssop, and I shall be clean: wash me, and I shall be whiter than snow. ⁸Make me to hear joy and gladness; that the bones which you have broken may rejoice. ⁹Hide your face from my sins, and blot out all my iniquities. ¹⁰Create in me a clean heart, O God; and renew a right spirit within me. ¹¹Cast me not away from your presence; and take not your holy spirit from me. ¹²Restore to me the joy of your salvation; and uphold me with your free spirit. ¹³Then will I teach transgressors your ways; and sinners shall be converted to you. ¹⁴Deliver me from bloodguiltiness, O God, you God of my salvation: and my tongue shall sing aloud of your righteousness. ¹⁵O Lord, open you my lips; and my mouth shall show forth your praise. ¹⁶For you desire not sacrifice; else would I give it: you delight not in burnt offering. ¹⁷The sacrifices of God are a broken spirit: a broken and a contrite heart, O God, you will not despise. ¹⁸Do good in your good pleasure to Zion: build you the walls of Jerusalem. ¹⁹Then shall you be pleased with the sacrifices of righteousness, with burnt offering and whole burnt offering: then shall they offer bullocks on your altar.

52

¹Why boast you yourself in mischief, O mighty man? the goodness of God endures continually. ²The tongue devises mischiefs; like a sharp razor, working deceitfully. ³You love evil more than good; and lying rather than to speak righteousness. Selah. ⁴You love all devouring words, O you deceitful tongue. ⁵God shall likewise destroy you for ever, he shall take you away, and pluck you out of your dwelling place, and root you out of the land of the living. Selah. ⁶The righteous also shall see, and fear, and shall laugh at him: ⁷See, this is the man that made not God his strength; but trusted in the abundance of his riches, and strengthened himself in his wickedness. ⁸But I am like a green olive tree in the house of God: I trust in the mercy of God for ever and ever. ⁹I will praise you for ever, because you have done it: and I will wait on your name; for it is good before your saints.

53

¹The fool has said in his heart, There is no God. Corrupt are they, and have done abominable iniquity: there is none that does good. ²God looked down from heaven on the children of men, to see if there were any that did understand, that did seek God. ³Every one of them is gone back: they are altogether become filthy; there is none that does good, no, not one. ⁴Have the workers of iniquity no knowledge? who eat up my people as they eat bread: they have not called on God. ⁵There were they in great fear, where no fear was: for God has scattered the bones of him that encamps against you: you have put them to shame, because God has despised them. ⁶Oh that the salvation of Israel were come out of Zion! When God brings back the captivity of his people, Jacob shall rejoice, and Israel shall be glad.

54

¹Save me, O God, by your name, and judge me by your strength. ²Hear my prayer, O God; give ear to the words of my mouth. ³For strangers are risen up against me, and oppressors seek after my soul: they have not set God before them. Selah. ⁴Behold, God is my helper: the Lord is with them that uphold my soul. ⁵He shall reward evil to my enemies: cut them off in your truth. ⁶I will freely sacrifice to you: I will praise your name, O LORD; for it is good. ⁷For he has delivered me out of all trouble: and my eye has seen his desire on my enemies.

55

¹Give ear to my prayer, O God; and hide not yourself from my supplication. ²Attend to me, and hear me: I mourn in my complaint, and make a noise; ³Because of the voice of the enemy, because of the oppression of the wicked: for they cast iniquity on me, and in wrath they hate me. ⁴My heart is sore pained within me: and the terrors of death are fallen on me. ⁵Fearfulness and trembling are come on me, and horror has overwhelmed me. ⁶And I said, Oh that I had wings like a dove! for then would I fly away, and be at rest. ⁷See, then would I wander far off, and remain in the wilderness. Selah. ⁸I would hasten my escape from the windy storm and tempest. ⁹Destroy, O Lord, and divide their tongues: for I have seen violence and strife in the city. ¹⁰Day and night they go about it on the walls thereof: mischief also and sorrow are in the middle of it. ¹¹Wickedness is in the middle thereof: deceit and guile depart not from her streets. ¹²For it was not an enemy that reproached me; then I could have borne it: neither was it he that hated me that did magnify himself against me; then I would have hid myself from him: ¹³But it was you, a man my equal, my guide, and my acquaintance. ¹⁴We took sweet counsel together, and walked to the house of God in company. ¹⁵Let death seize on them, and let them go down quick into hell: for wickedness is in their dwellings, and among them. ¹⁶As for me, I will call on God; and the LORD shall save me. ¹⁷Evening, and morning, and at noon, will I pray, and cry aloud: and he shall hear my voice. ¹⁸He has delivered my soul in peace from the battle that was against me: for there were many with me. ¹⁹God shall hear, and afflict them, even he that stays of old. Selah. Because they have no changes, therefore they fear not God. ²⁰He has put forth his hands against such as be at peace with him: he has broken his covenant. ²¹The words of his mouth were smoother than butter, but war was in his heart: his words were softer than oil, yet were they drawn swords. ²²Cast your burden on the LORD, and he shall sustain you: he shall never suffer the righteous to be moved. ²³But you, O God, shall bring them down into the pit of destruction: bloody and deceitful men shall not live out half their days; but I will trust in you.

56

¹Be merciful to me, O God: for man would swallow me up; he fighting daily oppresses me. ²My enemies would daily swallow me up: for they be many that fight against me, O you most High. ³What time I am afraid, I will trust in you. ⁴In God I will praise his word, in God I have put my trust; I will not fear what flesh can do to me. ⁵Every day they wrest my words: all their thoughts are against me for evil. ⁶They gather themselves together, they hide themselves, they mark my steps, when they wait for my soul. ⁷Shall they escape by iniquity? in your anger cast down the people, O God. ⁸You tell my wanderings: put you my tears into your bottle: are they not in your book? ⁹When I cry to you, then shall my enemies turn back: this I know; for God is for me. ¹⁰In God will I praise his word: in the LORD will I praise his word. ¹¹In God have I put my trust: I will not be afraid what man can do to me. ¹²Your vows are on me, O God: I will render praises to you. ¹³For you have delivered my soul from death: will not you deliver my feet from falling, that I may walk before God in the light of the living?

57

¹Be merciful to me, O God, be merciful to me: for my soul trusts in you: yes, in the shadow of your

wings will I make my refuge, until these calamities be over. ²I will cry to God most high; to God that performs all things for me. ³He shall send from heaven, and save me from the reproach of him that would swallow me up. Selah. God shall send forth his mercy and his truth. ⁴My soul is among lions: and I lie even among them that are set on fire, even the sons of men, whose teeth are spears and arrows, and their tongue a sharp sword. ⁵Be you exalted, O God, above the heavens; let your glory be above all the earth. ⁶They have prepared a net for my steps; my soul is bowed down: they have dig a pit before me, into the middle whereof they are fallen themselves. Selah. ⁷My heart is fixed, O God, my heart is fixed: I will sing and give praise. ⁸Awake up, my glory; awake, psaltery and harp: I myself will awake early. ⁹I will praise you, O Lord, among the people: I will sing to you among the nations. ¹⁰For your mercy is great to the heavens, and your truth to the clouds. ¹¹Be you exalted, O God, above the heavens: let your glory be above all the earth.

58 ¹Do you indeed speak righteousness, O congregation? do you judge uprightly, O you sons of men? ²Yes, in heart you work wickedness; you weigh the violence of your hands in the earth. ³The wicked are estranged from the womb: they go astray as soon as they be born, speaking lies. ⁴Their poison is like the poison of a serpent: they are like the deaf adder that stops her ear; ⁵Which will not listen to the voice of charmers, charming never so wisely. ⁶Break their teeth, O God, in their mouth: break out the great teeth of the young lions, O LORD. ⁷Let them melt away as waters which run continually: when he bends his bow to shoot his arrows, let them be as cut in pieces. ⁸As a snail which melts, let every one of them pass away: like the untimely birth of a woman, that they may not see the sun. ⁹Before your pots can feel the thorns, he shall take them away as with a whirlwind, both living, and in his wrath. ¹⁰The righteous shall rejoice when he sees the vengeance: he shall wash his feet in the blood of the wicked. ¹¹So that a man shall say, Truly there is a reward for the righteous: truly he is a God that judges in the earth.

59 ¹Deliver me from my enemies, O my God: defend me from them that rise up against me. ²Deliver me from the workers of iniquity, and save me from bloody men. ³For, see, they lie in wait for my soul: the mighty are gathered against me; not for my transgression, nor for my sin, O LORD. ⁴They run and prepare themselves without my fault: awake to help me, and behold. ⁵You therefore, O LORD God of hosts, the God of Israel, awake to visit all the heathen: be not merciful to any wicked transgressors. Selah. ⁶They return at evening: they make a noise like a dog, and go round about the city. ⁷Behold, they belch out with their mouth: swords are in their lips: for who, say they, does hear? ⁸But you, O LORD, shall laugh at them; you shall have all the heathen in derision. ⁹Because of his strength will I wait on you: for God is my defense. ¹⁰The God of my mercy shall prevent me: God shall let me see my desire on my enemies. ¹¹Slay them not, lest my people forget: scatter them by your power; and bring them down, O Lord our shield. ¹²For the sin of their mouth and the words of their lips let them even be taken in their pride: and for cursing and lying which they speak. ¹³Consume them in wrath, consume them, that they may not be: and let them know that God rules in Jacob to the ends of the earth. Selah. ¹⁴And at evening let them return; and let them make a noise like a dog, and go round about the city. ¹⁵Let them wander up and down for meat, and grudge if they be not satisfied. ¹⁶But I will sing of your power; yes, I will sing aloud of your mercy in the morning: for you have been my defense and refuge in the day of my trouble. ¹⁷To you, O my strength, will I sing: for God is my defense, and the God of my mercy.

60 ¹O God, you have cast us off, you have scattered us, you have been displeased; O turn yourself to us again. ²You have made the earth to tremble; you have broken it: heal the breaches thereof; for it shakes. ³You have showed your people hard things: you have made us to drink the wine of astonishment. ⁴You have given a banner to them that fear you, that it may be displayed because of the truth. Selah. ⁵That your beloved may be delivered; save with your right hand, and hear me. ⁶God has spoken in his holiness; I will rejoice, I will divide Shechem, and mete out the valley of Succoth. ⁷Gilead is mine, and Manasseh is mine; Ephraim also is the strength of my head; Judah is my lawgiver; ⁸Moab is my wash pot; over Edom will I cast out my shoe: Philistia, triumph you because of me. ⁹Who will bring me into the strong city? who will lead me into Edom? ¹⁰Will not you, O God, which had cast us off? and you, O God, which did not go out with our armies? ¹¹Give us help from trouble: for vain is the help of man. ¹²Through God we shall do valiantly: for he it is that shall tread down our enemies.

61 ¹Hear my cry, O God; attend to my prayer. ²From the end of the earth will I cry to you, when my heart is overwhelmed: lead me to the rock that is higher than I. ³For you have been a shelter for me, and a strong tower from the enemy. ⁴I will abide in your tabernacle for ever: I will trust in the covert of your wings. Selah. ⁵For you, O God, have heard my vows: you have given me the heritage of those that fear your name. ⁶You will prolong the king's life: and his years as many generations. ⁷He shall abide before God for ever: O prepare mercy and truth, which may preserve him. ⁸So will I sing praise to your name for ever, that I may daily perform my vows.

62 ¹Truly my soul waits on God: from him comes my salvation. ²He only is my rock and my salvation; he is my defense; I shall not be greatly moved. ³How long will you imagine mischief against a man? you shall be slain all of you: as a bowing wall shall you be, and as a tottering fence. ⁴They only consult to cast him down from his excellency: they delight in lies: they bless with their mouth, but they curse inwardly. Selah. ⁵My soul, wait you only on God; for my expectation is from him. ⁶He only is my rock and my salvation: he is my defense; I shall not be moved. ⁷In God is my salvation and my glory: the rock of my strength, and my refuge, is in God. ⁸Trust in him at all times; you people, pour out your heart before him: God is a refuge for us. Selah. ⁹Surely men of low degree are vanity, and men of high degree are a lie: to be laid in the balance, they are altogether lighter than vanity. ¹⁰Trust not in oppression, and become not vain in robbery: if riches increase, set not your heart on them. ¹¹God has spoken once; twice have I heard this; that power belongs to God. ¹²Also to you, O Lord, belongs mercy: for you render to every man according to his work.

63 ¹O God, you are my God; early will I seek you: my soul thirsts for you, my flesh longs for you in a dry and thirsty land, where no water is; ²To see your power and your glory, so as I have seen you in the sanctuary. ³Because your loving kindness is better than life, my lips shall praise you. ⁴Thus will I bless you while I live: I will lift up my hands in your name. ⁵My soul shall be satisfied as with marrow and fatness; and my mouth shall praise you with joyful lips: ⁶When I remember you on my bed, and meditate on you in the night watches. ⁷Because you have been my help, therefore in the shadow of your wings will I rejoice. ⁸My soul follows hard after you: your right hand upholds me. ⁹But those that seek my soul, to destroy it, shall go into the lower parts of the earth. ¹⁰They shall fall by the sword: they shall be a portion for foxes. ¹¹But the king shall rejoice in God; every one that swears by him shall glory: but the mouth of them that speak lies shall be stopped.

64 ¹Hear my voice, O God, in my prayer: preserve my life from fear of the enemy. ²Hide me from the secret counsel of the wicked; from the insurrection of the workers of iniquity: ³Who whet their tongue like a sword, and bend their bows to shoot their arrows, even bitter words: ⁴That they may shoot in secret at the perfect: suddenly do they shoot at him, and fear not. ⁵They encourage themselves in an evil matter: they commune of laying snares privately; they say, Who shall see them? ⁶They search out iniquities; they accomplish a diligent search: both the inward thought of every one of them, and the heart, is deep. ⁷But God shall shoot at them with an arrow; suddenly shall they be wounded. ⁸So they shall make their own tongue to fall on themselves: all that see them shall flee away. ⁹And all men shall fear, and shall declare the work of God; for they shall wisely consider of his doing. ¹⁰The righteous shall be glad in the LORD, and shall trust in him; and all the upright in heart shall glory.

65 ¹Praise waits for you, O God, in Sion: and to you shall the vow be performed. ²O you that hear prayer, to you shall all flesh come. ³Iniquities prevail against me: as for our transgressions, you shall purge them away. ⁴Blessed is the man whom you choose, and cause to approach to you, that he may dwell in your courts: we shall be satisfied with the goodness of your house, even of your holy temple. ⁵By terrible things in righteousness will you answer us, O God of our salvation; who are the confidence of all the ends of the earth, and of them that are afar off on the sea: ⁶Which by his strength sets fast the mountains; being girded with power: ⁷Which stills the noise of the seas, the noise of their waves, and the tumult of the people. ⁸They also that dwell in the uttermost parts are afraid at your tokens: you make the outgoings of the morning and evening to rejoice. ⁹You visit the earth, and water it: you greatly enrich it with the river of God, which is full of water: you prepare them corn, when you have so provided for it. ¹⁰You water the ridges thereof abundantly: you settle the furrows thereof: you make it soft with showers: you bless the springing thereof. ¹¹You crown the year with your goodness; and your paths drop fatness. ¹²They drop on the pastures of the wilderness: and the little hills rejoice on every side. ¹³The pastures are clothed with flocks; the valleys also are covered over with corn; they shout for joy, they also sing.

66 ¹Make a joyful noise to God, all you lands: ²Sing forth the honor of his name: make his praise glorious. ³Say to God, How terrible are you in your works! through the greatness of your power shall your enemies submit themselves to you. ⁴All the earth shall worship you, and shall sing to you; they shall sing to your name. Selah. ⁵Come and see the works of God: he is terrible in his doing toward the children of men. ⁶He turned the sea into dry land: they went through the flood on foot: there did we rejoice in him. ⁷He rules by his power for ever; his eyes behold the nations: let not the rebellious exalt themselves. Selah. ⁸O bless our God, you people, and make the voice of his praise to be heard: ⁹Which holds our soul in life, and suffers not our feet to be moved. ¹⁰For you, O God, have proved us: you have tried us, as silver is tried. ¹¹You brought us into the net; you laid affliction on our loins. ¹²You have caused men to ride over our heads; we went through fire and through water: but you brought us out into a wealthy place. ¹³I will go into your house with burnt offerings: I will pay you my vows, ¹⁴Which my lips have uttered, and my mouth has spoken, when I was in trouble. ¹⁵I will offer to you burnt sacrifices of fatted calves, with the incense of rams; I will offer bullocks with goats. Selah. ¹⁶Come and hear, all you that fear God, and I will declare what he has done for my soul. ¹⁷I cried to him with my mouth, and he was extolled with my tongue. ¹⁸If I regard iniquity in my heart, the Lord will not hear me: ¹⁹But truly God has heard me; he has attended to the voice of my prayer. ²⁰Blessed be God, which has not turned away my prayer, nor his mercy from me.

67 ¹God be merciful to us, and bless us; and cause his face to shine on us; Selah. ²That your way may be known on earth, your saving health among all nations. ³Let the people praise you, O God; let all the people praise you. ⁴O let the nations be glad and sing for joy: for you shall judge the people righteously, and govern the nations on earth. Selah. ⁵Let the people praise you, O God; let all the people praise you. ⁶Then shall the earth yield her increase; and God, even our own God, shall bless us. ⁷God shall bless us; and all the ends of the earth shall fear him.

68 ¹Let God arise, let his enemies be scattered: let them also that hate him flee before him. ²As smoke is driven away, so drive them away: as wax melts before the fire, so let the wicked perish at the presence of God. ³But let the righteous be glad; let them rejoice before God: yes, let them exceedingly rejoice. ⁴Sing to God, sing praises to his name: extol him that rides on the heavens by his name JAH, and rejoice before him. ⁵A father of the fatherless, and a judge of the widows, is God in his holy habitation. ⁶God sets the solitary in families: he brings out those which are bound with chains: but the rebellious dwell in a dry land. ⁷O God, when you went forth before your people, when you did march through the wilderness; Selah: ⁸The earth shook, the heavens also dropped at the presence of God: even Sinai itself was moved at the presence of God, the God of Israel. ⁹You, O God, did send a plentiful rain, whereby you did confirm your inheritance, when it was weary. ¹⁰Your congregation has dwelled therein: you, O God, have prepared of your goodness for the poor. ¹¹The Lord gave the word: great was the company of those that published it. ¹²Kings of armies did flee apace: and she that tarried at home divided the spoil. ¹³Though you have lien among the pots, yet shall you be as the wings of a dove covered with silver, and her feathers with yellow gold. ¹⁴When the Almighty scattered kings in it, it was white as snow in Salmon. ¹⁵The hill of God is as the hill of Bashan; an high hill as the hill of Bashan. ¹⁶Why leap you, you high hills? this is the hill which God desires to dwell in; yes, the LORD will dwell in it for ever. ¹⁷The chariots of God are twenty thousand, even thousands of angels: the Lord is among them, as in Sinai, in the holy place. ¹⁸You have ascended on high, you have led captivity captive: you have received gifts for men; yes, for the rebellious also, that the LORD God might dwell among them. ¹⁹Blessed be the Lord, who daily loads us with benefits, even the God of our salvation. Selah. ²⁰He that is our God is the God of salvation; and to GOD the Lord belong the issues from death. ²¹But God shall wound the head of his enemies, and the hairy scalp of such an one as goes on still in his trespasses. ²²The Lord said, I will bring again from Bashan, I will bring my people again from the depths of the sea: ²³That your foot may be dipped in the blood of your enemies, and the tongue of your dogs in the same. ²⁴They have seen your goings, O God; even the goings of my God, my King, in the sanctuary. ²⁵The singers went before, the players on instruments followed after; among them were the damsels playing with tambourines. ²⁶Bless you God in the congregations, even the Lord, from the fountain of Israel. ²⁷There is little Benjamin with their ruler, the princes of Judah and their council, the princes of Zebulun, and the princes of Naphtali. ²⁸Your God has commanded your strength: strengthen, O God, that which you have worked for us. ²⁹Because of your temple at Jerusalem shall kings bring presents to you. ³⁰Rebuke the company of spearmen, the multitude of the bulls, with the calves of the people, till every one submit himself with pieces of silver: scatter you the people that delight in war. ³¹Princes shall come out of Egypt; Ethiopia shall soon stretch out her hands to God. ³²Sing to God, you kingdoms of the earth; O sing praises to the Lord; Selah: ³³To him that rides on the heavens of heavens, which were of old; see, he does send out his voice, and that a mighty voice. ³⁴Ascribe you strength to God: his excellency is over Israel, and his strength is in the clouds. ³⁵O God, you are terrible out of your holy places: the God of Israel is he that gives strength and power to his people. Blessed be God.

69 ¹Save me, O God; for the waters are come in to my soul. ²I sink in deep mire, where there is no standing: I am come into deep waters, where the floods overflow me. ³I am weary of my crying: my throat is dried: my eyes fail while I wait for my God. ⁴They that hate me without a cause are more than the hairs of my head: they that would destroy me, being my enemies wrongfully, are mighty: then I restored that which I took not away. ⁵O God, you know my foolishness; and my sins are not hid from you. ⁶Let not them that wait on you, O Lord GOD of hosts, be ashamed for my sake: let not those that seek you be confounded for my sake, O God of Israel. ⁷Because for your sake I have borne reproach; shame has covered my face. ⁸I am become a stranger to my brothers, and an alien to my mother's children. ⁹For the zeal of your house has eaten me up; and the reproaches of them that reproached you are fallen on me. ¹⁰When I wept, and chastened my soul with fasting, that was to my reproach. ¹¹I made sackcloth also my garment; and I became a proverb to them. ¹²They that sit in the gate speak against me; and I was the song of the drunkards. ¹³But as for me, my prayer is to you, O LORD, in an acceptable time: O God, in the multitude of your mercy hear me, in the truth of your salvation. ¹⁴Deliver me out of the mire, and let me not sink: let me be delivered from them that hate me, and out of the deep waters. ¹⁵Let not the flood overflow me, neither let the deep swallow me up, and let not the pit shut her mouth on me. ¹⁶Hear me, O LORD; for your loving kindness is good: turn to me according to the multitude of your tender mercies. ¹⁷And hide not your face from your servant; for I am in trouble: hear me speedily. ¹⁸Draw near to my soul, and redeem it: deliver me because of my enemies. ¹⁹You have known my reproach, and my shame, and my dishonor: my adversaries are all before you. ²⁰Reproach has broken my heart; and I am full of heaviness: and I looked for some to take pity, but there was none; and for comforters, but I found none. ²¹They gave me also gall for my meat; and in my thirst they gave me vinegar to drink. ²²Let their table become a snare before them: and that which should have been for their welfare, let it become a trap. ²³Let their eyes be darkened, that they see not; and make their loins continually to shake. ²⁴Pour out your indignation on them, and let your wrathful anger take hold of them. ²⁵Let their habitation be desolate; and let none dwell in their tents. ²⁶For they persecute him whom you have smitten; and they talk to the grief of those whom you have wounded. ²⁷Add iniquity to their iniquity: and let them not come into your righteousness. ²⁸Let them be blotted out of the book of the living, and not be written with the righteous. ²⁹But I am poor and sorrowful: let your salvation, O God, set me up on high. ³⁰I will praise the name of God with a song, and will magnify him with thanksgiving. ³¹This also shall please the LORD better than an ox or bullock that has horns and hoofs. ³²The humble shall see this, and be glad: and your heart shall live that seek God. ³³For the LORD hears the poor, and despises not his prisoners. ³⁴Let the heaven and earth praise him, the seas, and every thing that moves therein. ³⁵For God will save Zion, and will build the cities of Judah: that they may dwell there, and have it in possession. ³⁶The seed also of his servants shall inherit it: and they that love his name shall dwell therein.

70 ¹MAKE HASTE, O GOD, TO DELIVER ME; MAKE HASTE TO HELP ME, O LORD. ²Let them be ashamed and confounded that seek after my soul: let them be turned backward, and put to confusion, that desire my hurt. ³Let them be turned back for a reward of their shame that say, Aha, aha. ⁴Let all those that seek you rejoice and be glad in you: and let such as love your salvation say continually, Let God be magnified. ⁵But I am poor and needy: make haste to me, O God: you are my help and my deliverer; O LORD, make no tarrying.

71

¹In you, O LORD, do I put my trust: let me never be put to confusion. ²Deliver me in your righteousness, and cause me to escape: incline your ear to me, and save me. ³Be you my strong habitation, where I may continually resort: you have given commandment to save me; for you are my rock and my fortress. ⁴Deliver me, O my God, out of the hand of the wicked, out of the hand of the unrighteous and cruel man. ⁵For you are my hope, O Lord GOD: you are my trust from my youth. ⁶By you have I been held up from the womb: you are he that took me out of my mother's bowels: my praise shall be continually of you. ⁷I am as a wonder to many; but you are my strong refuge. ⁸Let my mouth be filled with your praise and with your honor all the day. ⁹Cast me not off in the time of old age; forsake me not when my strength fails. ¹⁰For my enemies speak against me; and they that lay wait for my soul take counsel together, ¹¹Saying, God has forsaken him: persecute and take him; for there is none to deliver him. ¹²O God, be not far from me: O my God, make haste for my help. ¹³Let them be confounded and consumed that are adversaries to my soul; let them be covered with reproach and dishonor that seek my hurt. ¹⁴But I will hope continually, and will yet praise you more and more. ¹⁵My mouth shall show forth your righteousness and your salvation all the day; for I know not the numbers thereof. ¹⁶I will go in the strength of the Lord GOD: I will make mention of your righteousness, even of your only. ¹⁷O God, you have taught me from my youth: and till now have I declared your wondrous works. ¹⁸Now also when I am old and gray headed, O God, forsake me not; until I have showed your strength to this generation, and your power to every one that is to come. ¹⁹Your righteousness also, O God, is very high, who have done great things: O God, who is like to you! ²⁰You, which have showed me great and sore troubles, shall quicken me again, and shall bring me up again from the depths of the earth. ²¹You shall increase my greatness, and comfort me on every side. ²²I will also praise you with the psaltery, even your truth, O my God: to you will I sing with the harp, O you Holy One of Israel. ²³My lips shall greatly rejoice when I sing to you; and my soul, which you have redeemed. ²⁴My tongue also shall talk of your righteousness all the day long: for they are confounded, for they are brought to shame, that seek my hurt.

72

¹Give the king your judgments, O God, and your righteousness to the king's son. ²He shall judge your people with righteousness, and your poor with judgment. ³The mountains shall bring peace to the people, and the little hills, by righteousness. ⁴He shall judge the poor of the people, he shall save the children of the needy, and shall break in pieces the oppressor. ⁵They shall fear you as long as the sun and moon endure, throughout all generations. ⁶He shall come down like rain on the mown grass: as showers that water the earth. ⁷In his days shall the righteous flourish; and abundance of peace so long as the moon endures. ⁸He shall have dominion also from sea to sea, and from the river to the ends of the earth. ⁹They that dwell in the wilderness shall bow before him; and his enemies shall lick the dust. ¹⁰The kings of Tarshish and of the isles shall bring presents: the kings of Sheba and Seba shall offer gifts. ¹¹Yes, all kings shall fall down before him: all nations shall serve him. ¹²For he shall deliver the needy when he cries; the poor also, and him that has no helper. ¹³He shall spare the poor and needy, and shall save the souls of the needy. ¹⁴He shall redeem their soul from deceit and violence: and precious shall their blood be in his sight. ¹⁵And he shall live, and to him shall be given of the gold of Sheba: prayer also shall be made for him continually; and daily shall he be praised. ¹⁶There shall be an handful of corn in the earth on the top of the mountains; the fruit thereof shall shake like Lebanon: and they of the city shall flourish like grass of the earth. ¹⁷His name shall endure for ever: his name shall be continued as long as the sun: and men shall be blessed in him: all nations shall call him blessed. ¹⁸Blessed be the LORD God, the God of Israel, who only does wondrous things. ¹⁹And blessed be his glorious name for ever: and let the whole earth be filled with his glory; Amen, and Amen. ²⁰The prayers of David the son of Jesse are ended.

73

¹Truly God is good to Israel, even to such as are of a clean heart. ²But as for me, my feet were almost gone; my steps had well near slipped. ³For I was envious at the foolish, when I saw the prosperity of the wicked. ⁴For there are no bands in their death: but their strength is firm. ⁵They are not in trouble as other men; neither are they plagued like other men. ⁶Therefore pride compasses them about as a chain; violence covers them as a garment. ⁷Their eyes stand out with fatness: they have more than heart could wish. ⁸They are corrupt, and speak wickedly concerning oppression: they speak loftily. ⁹They set their mouth against the heavens, and their tongue walks through the earth. ¹⁰Therefore his people return here: and waters of a full cup are wrung out to them. ¹¹And they say, How does God know? and is there knowledge in the most High? ¹²Behold, these are the ungodly, who prosper in the world; they increase in riches. ¹³Truly I have cleansed my heart in vain, and washed my hands in innocence. ¹⁴For all the day long have I been plagued, and chastened every morning. ¹⁵If I say, I will speak thus; behold, I should offend against the generation of your children. ¹⁶When I thought to know this, it was too painful for me; ¹⁷Until I went into the sanctuary of God; then understood I their end. ¹⁸Surely you did set them in slippery places: you cast them down into destruction. ¹⁹How are they brought into desolation, as in a moment! they are utterly consumed with terrors. ²⁰As a dream when one wakes; so, O Lord, when you wake, you shall despise their image. ²¹Thus my heart was grieved, and I was pricked in my reins. ²²So foolish was I, and ignorant: I was as a beast before you. ²³Nevertheless I am continually with you: you have held me by my right hand. ²⁴You shall guide me with your counsel, and afterward receive me to glory. ²⁵Whom have I in heaven but you? and there is none on earth that I desire beside you. ²⁶My flesh and my heart fails: but God is the strength of my heart, and my portion for ever. ²⁷For, see, they that are far from you shall perish: you have destroyed all them that go a whoring from you. ²⁸But it is good for me to draw near to God: I have put my trust in the Lord GOD, that I may declare all your works.

74

¹O God, why have you cast us off for ever? why does your anger smoke against the sheep of your pasture? ²Remember your congregation, which you have purchased of old; the rod of your inheritance, which you

have redeemed; this mount Zion, wherein you have dwelled. ³Lift up your feet to the perpetual desolations; even all that the enemy has done wickedly in the sanctuary. ⁴Your enemies roar in the middle of your congregations; they set up their ensigns for signs. ⁵A man was famous according as he had lifted up axes on the thick trees. ⁶But now they break down the carved work thereof at once with axes and hammers. ⁷They have cast fire into your sanctuary, they have defiled by casting down the dwelling place of your name to the ground. ⁸They said in their hearts, Let us destroy them together: they have burned up all the synagogues of God in the land. ⁹We see not our signs: there is no more any prophet: neither is there among us any that knows how long. ¹⁰O God, how long shall the adversary reproach? shall the enemy blaspheme your name for ever? ¹¹Why withdraw you your hand, even your right hand? pluck it out of your bosom. ¹²For God is my King of old, working salvation in the middle of the earth. ¹³You did divide the sea by your strength: you brake the heads of the dragons in the waters. ¹⁴You brake the heads of leviathan in pieces, and gave him to be meat to the people inhabiting the wilderness. ¹⁵You did split the fountain and the flood: you dried up mighty rivers. ¹⁶The day is yours, the night also is yours: you have prepared the light and the sun. ¹⁷You have set all the borders of the earth: you have made summer and winter. ¹⁸Remember this, that the enemy has reproached, O LORD, and that the foolish people have blasphemed your name. ¹⁹O deliver not the soul of your turtledove to the multitude of the wicked: forget not the congregation of your poor for ever. ²⁰Have respect to the covenant: for the dark places of the earth are full of the habitations of cruelty. ²¹O let not the oppressed return ashamed: let the poor and needy praise your name. ²²Arise, O God, plead your own cause: remember how the foolish man reproaches you daily. ²³Forget not the voice of your enemies: the tumult of those that rise up against you increases continually.

75

¹To you, O God, do we give thanks, to you do we give thanks: for that your name is near your wondrous works declare. ²When I shall receive the congregation I will judge uprightly. ³The earth and all the inhabitants thereof are dissolved: I bear up the pillars of it. Selah. ⁴I said to the fools, Deal not foolishly: and to the wicked, Lift not up the horn: ⁵Lift not up your horn on high: speak not with a stiff neck. ⁶For promotion comes neither from the east, nor from the west, nor from the south. ⁷But God is the judge: he puts down one, and sets up another. ⁸For in the hand of the LORD there is a cup, and the wine is red; it is full of mixture; and he pours out of the same: but the dregs thereof, all the wicked of the earth shall wring them out, and drink them. ⁹But I will declare for ever; I will sing praises to the God of Jacob. ¹⁰All the horns of the wicked also will I cut off; but the horns of the righteous shall be exalted.

76

¹In Judah is God known: his name is great in Israel. ²In Salem also is his tabernacle, and his dwelling place in Zion. ³There broke he the arrows of the bow, the shield, and the sword, and the battle. Selah. ⁴You are more glorious and excellent than the mountains of prey. ⁵The stouthearted are spoiled, they have slept their sleep: and none of the men of might have found their hands. ⁶At your rebuke, O God of Jacob, both the chariot and horse are cast into a dead sleep. ⁷You, even you, are to be feared: and who may stand in your sight when once you are angry? ⁸You did cause judgment to be heard from heaven; the earth feared, and was still, ⁹When God arose to judgment, to save all the meek of the earth. Selah. ¹⁰Surely the wrath of man shall praise you: the remainder of wrath shall you restrain. ¹¹Vow, and pay to the LORD your God: let all that be round about him bring presents to him that ought to be feared. ¹²He shall cut off the spirit of princes: he is terrible to the kings of the earth.

77

¹I cried to God with my voice, even to God with my voice; and he gave ear to me. ²In the day of my trouble I sought the Lord: my sore ran in the night, and ceased not: my soul refused to be comforted. ³I remembered God, and was troubled: I complained, and my spirit was overwhelmed. Selah. ⁴You hold my eyes waking: I am so troubled that I cannot speak. ⁵I have considered the days of old, the years of ancient times. ⁶I call to remembrance my song in the night: I commune with my own heart: and my spirit made diligent search. ⁷Will the Lord cast off for ever? and will he be favorable no more? ⁸Is his mercy clean gone for ever? does his promise fail for ever more? ⁹Has God forgotten to be gracious? has he in anger shut up his tender mercies? Selah. ¹⁰And I said, This is my infirmity: but I will remember the years of the right hand of the most High. ¹¹I will remember the works of the LORD: surely I will remember your wonders of old. ¹²I will meditate also of all your work, and talk of your doings. ¹³Your way, O God, is in the sanctuary: who is so great a God as our God? ¹⁴You are the God that do wonders: you have declared your strength among the people. ¹⁵You have with your arm redeemed your people, the sons of Jacob and Joseph. Selah. ¹⁶The waters saw you, O God, the waters saw you; they were afraid: the depths also were troubled. ¹⁷The clouds poured out water: the skies sent out a sound: your arrows also went abroad. ¹⁸The voice of your thunder was in the heaven: the lightning lightened the world: the earth trembled and shook. ¹⁹Your way is in the sea, and your path in the great waters, and your footsteps are not known. ²⁰You led your people like a flock by the hand of Moses and Aaron.

78

¹Give ear, O my people, to my law: incline your ears to the words of my mouth. ²I will open my mouth in a parable: I will utter dark sayings of old: ³Which we have heard and known, and our fathers have told us. ⁴We will not hide them from their children, showing to the generation to come the praises of the LORD, and his strength, and his wonderful works that he has done. ⁵For he established a testimony in Jacob, and appointed a law in Israel, which he commanded our fathers, that they should make them known to their children: ⁶That the generation to come might know them, even the children which should be born; who should arise and declare them to their children: ⁷That they might set their hope in God, and not forget the works of God, but keep his commandments: ⁸And might not be as their fathers, a stubborn and rebellious generation; a generation that set not their heart aright, and whose spirit was not steadfast with God. ⁹The children of Ephraim, being armed, and carrying

bows, turned back in the day of battle. ¹⁰They kept not the covenant of God, and refused to walk in his law; ¹¹And forgot his works, and his wonders that he had showed them. ¹²Marvelous things did he in the sight of their fathers, in the land of Egypt, in the field of Zoan. ¹³He divided the sea, and caused them to pass through; and he made the waters to stand as an heap. ¹⁴In the daytime also he led them with a cloud, and all the night with a light of fire. ¹⁵He split the rocks in the wilderness, and gave them drink as out of the great depths. ¹⁶He brought streams also out of the rock, and caused waters to run down like rivers. ¹⁷And they sinned yet more against him by provoking the most High in the wilderness. ¹⁸And they tempted God in their heart by asking meat for their lust. ¹⁹Yes, they spoke against God; they said, Can God furnish a table in the wilderness? ²⁰Behold, he smote the rock, that the waters gushed out, and the streams overflowed; can he give bread also? can he provide flesh for his people? ²¹Therefore the LORD heard this, and was wroth: so a fire was kindled against Jacob, and anger also came up against Israel; ²²Because they believed not in God, and trusted not in his salvation: ²³Though he had commanded the clouds from above, and opened the doors of heaven, ²⁴And had rained down manna on them to eat, and had given them of the corn of heaven. ²⁵Man did eat angels' food: he sent them meat to the full. ²⁶He caused an east wind to blow in the heaven: and by his power he brought in the south wind. ²⁷He rained flesh also on them as dust, and feathered fowls like as the sand of the sea: ²⁸And he let it fall in the middle of their camp, round about their habitations. ²⁹So they did eat, and were well filled: for he gave them their own desire; ³⁰They were not estranged from their lust. But while their meat was yet in their mouths, ³¹The wrath of God came on them, and slew the fattest of them, and smote down the chosen men of Israel. ³²For all this they sinned still, and believed not for his wondrous works. ³³Therefore their days did he consume in vanity, and their years in trouble. ³⁴When he slew them, then they sought him: and they returned and inquired early after God. ³⁵And they remembered that God was their rock, and the high God their redeemer. ³⁶Nevertheless they did flatter him with their mouth, and they lied to him with their tongues. ³⁷For their heart was not right with him, neither were they steadfast in his covenant. ³⁸But he, being full of compassion, forgave their iniquity, and destroyed them not: yes, many a time turned he his anger away, and did not stir up all his wrath. ³⁹For he remembered that they were but flesh; a wind that passes away, and comes not again. ⁴⁰How oft did they provoke him in the wilderness, and grieve him in the desert! ⁴¹Yes, they turned back and tempted God, and limited the Holy One of Israel. ⁴²They remembered not his hand, nor the day when he delivered them from the enemy. ⁴³How he had worked his signs in Egypt, and his wonders in the field of Zoan. ⁴⁴And had turned their rivers into blood; and their floods, that they could not drink. ⁴⁵He sent divers sorts of flies among them, which devoured them; and frogs, which destroyed them. ⁴⁶He gave also their increase to the caterpillar, and their labor to the locust. ⁴⁷He destroyed their vines with hail, and their sycomore trees with frost. ⁴⁸He gave up their cattle also to the hail, and their flocks to hot thunderbolts. ⁴⁹He cast on them the fierceness of his anger, wrath, and indignation, and trouble, by sending evil angels among them. ⁵⁰He made a way to his anger; he spared not their soul from death, but gave their life over to the pestilence; ⁵¹And smote all the firstborn in Egypt; the chief of their strength in the tabernacles of Ham: ⁵²But made his own people to go forth like sheep, and guided them in the wilderness like a flock. ⁵³And he led them on safely, so that they feared not: but the sea overwhelmed their enemies. ⁵⁴And he brought them to the border of his sanctuary, even to this mountain, which his right hand had purchased. ⁵⁵He cast out the heathen also before them, and divided them an inheritance by line, and made the tribes of Israel to dwell in their tents. ⁵⁶Yet they tempted and provoked the most high God, and kept not his testimonies: ⁵⁷But turned back, and dealt unfaithfully like their fathers: they were turned aside like a deceitful bow. ⁵⁸For they provoked him to anger with their high places, and moved him to jealousy with their graven images. ⁵⁹When God heard this, he was wroth, and greatly abhorred Israel: ⁶⁰So that he forsook the tabernacle of Shiloh, the tent which he placed among men; ⁶¹And delivered his strength into captivity, and his glory into the enemy's hand. ⁶²He gave his people over also to the sword; and was wroth with his inheritance. ⁶³The fire consumed their young men; and their maidens were not given to marriage. ⁶⁴Their priests fell by the sword; and their widows made no lamentation. ⁶⁵Then the LORD awaked as one out of sleep, and like a mighty man that shouts by reason of wine. ⁶⁶And he smote his enemies in the hinder parts: he put them to a perpetual reproach. ⁶⁷Moreover he refused the tabernacle of Joseph, and chose not the tribe of Ephraim: ⁶⁸But chose the tribe of Judah, the mount Zion which he loved. ⁶⁹And he built his sanctuary like high palaces, like the earth which he has established for ever. ⁷⁰He chose David also his servant, and took him from the sheepfolds: ⁷¹From following the ewes great with young he brought him to feed Jacob his people, and Israel his inheritance. ⁷²So he fed them according to the integrity of his heart; and guided them by the skillfulness of his hands.

79

¹O God, the heathen are come into your inheritance; your holy temple have they defiled; they have laid Jerusalem on heaps. ²The dead bodies of your servants have they given to be meat to the fowls of the heaven, the flesh of your saints to the beasts of the earth. ³Their blood have they shed like water round about Jerusalem; and there was none to bury them. ⁴We are become a reproach to our neighbors, a scorn and derision to them that are round about us. ⁵How long, LORD? will you be angry for ever? shall your jealousy burn like fire? ⁶Pour out your wrath on the heathen that have not known you, and on the kingdoms that have not called on your name. ⁷For they have devoured Jacob, and laid waste his dwelling place. ⁸O remember not against us former iniquities: let your tender mercies speedily prevent us: for we are brought very low. ⁹Help us, O God of our salvation, for the glory of your name: and deliver us, and purge away our sins, for your name's sake. ¹⁰Why should the heathen say, Where is their God? let him be known among the heathen in our sight by the revenging of the blood of your servants which is shed. ¹¹Let the sighing of the prisoner come before you; according to the greatness of your power preserve you those that are appointed to die; ¹²And render to our neighbors

sevenfold into their bosom their reproach, with which they have reproached you, O Lord. ¹³So we your people and sheep of your pasture will give you thanks for ever: we will show forth your praise to all generations.

80

¹Give ear, O Shepherd of Israel, you that lead Joseph like a flock; you that dwell between the cherubim, shine forth. ²Before Ephraim and Benjamin and Manasseh stir up your strength, and come and save us. ³Turn us again, O God, and cause your face to shine; and we shall be saved. ⁴O LORD God of hosts, how long will you be angry against the prayer of your people? ⁵You feed them with the bread of tears; and give them tears to drink in great measure. ⁶You make us a strife to our neighbors: and our enemies laugh among themselves. ⁷Turn us again, O God of hosts, and cause your face to shine; and we shall be saved. ⁸You have brought a vine out of Egypt: you have cast out the heathen, and planted it. ⁹You prepared room before it, and did cause it to take deep root, and it filled the land. ¹⁰The hills were covered with the shadow of it, and the boughs thereof were like the goodly cedars. ¹¹She sent out her boughs to the sea, and her branches to the river. ¹²Why have you then broken down her hedges, so that all they which pass by the way do pluck her? ¹³The boar out of the wood does waste it, and the wild beast of the field does devour it. ¹⁴Return, we beseech you, O God of hosts: look down from heaven, and behold, and visit this vine; ¹⁵And the vineyard which your right hand has planted, and the branch that you made strong for yourself. ¹⁶It is burned with fire, it is cut down: they perish at the rebuke of your countenance. ¹⁷Let your hand be on the man of your right hand, on the son of man whom you made strong for yourself. ¹⁸So will not we go back from you: quicken us, and we will call on your name. ¹⁹Turn us again, O LORD God of hosts, cause your face to shine; and we shall be saved.

81

¹Sing aloud to God our strength: make a joyful noise to the God of Jacob. ²Take a psalm, and bring here the tambourine, the pleasant harp with the psaltery. ³Blow up the trumpet in the new moon, in the time appointed, on our solemn feast day. ⁴For this was a statute for Israel, and a law of the God of Jacob. ⁵This he ordained in Joseph for a testimony, when he went out through the land of Egypt: where I heard a language that I understood not. ⁶I removed his shoulder from the burden: his hands were delivered from the pots. ⁷You called in trouble, and I delivered you; I answered you in the secret place of thunder: I proved you at the waters of Meribah. Selah. ⁸Hear, O my people, and I will testify to you: O Israel, if you will listen to me; ⁹There shall no strange god be in you; neither shall you worship any strange god. ¹⁰I am the LORD your God, which brought you out of the land of Egypt: open your mouth wide, and I will fill it. ¹¹But my people would not listen to my voice; and Israel would none of me. ¹²So I gave them up to their own hearts' lust: and they walked in their own counsels. ¹³Oh that my people had listened to me, and Israel had walked in my ways! ¹⁴I should soon have subdued their enemies, and turned my hand against their adversaries. ¹⁵The haters of the LORD should have submitted themselves to him: but their time should have endured for ever. ¹⁶He should have fed them also with the finest of the wheat: and with honey out of the rock should I have satisfied you.

82

¹God stands in the congregation of the mighty; he judges among the gods. ²How long will you judge unjustly, and accept the persons of the wicked? Selah. ³Defend the poor and fatherless: do justice to the afflicted and needy. ⁴Deliver the poor and needy: rid them out of the hand of the wicked. ⁵They know not, neither will they understand; they walk on in darkness: all the foundations of the earth are out of course. ⁶I have said, You are gods; and all of you are children of the most High. ⁷But you shall die like men, and fall like one of the princes. ⁸Arise, O God, judge the earth: for you shall inherit all nations.

83

¹Keep not you silence, O God: hold not your peace, and be not still, O God. ²For, see, your enemies make a tumult: and they that hate you have lifted up the head. ³They have taken crafty counsel against your people, and consulted against your hidden ones. ⁴They have said, Come, and let us cut them off from being a nation; that the name of Israel may be no more in remembrance. ⁵For they have consulted together with one consent: they are confederate against you: ⁶The tabernacles of Edom, and the Ishmaelites; of Moab, and the Hagarenes; ⁷Gebal, and Ammon, and Amalek; the Philistines with the inhabitants of Tyre; ⁸Assur also is joined with them: they have helped the children of Lot. Selah. ⁹Do to them as to the Midianites; as to Sisera, as to Jabin, at the brook of Kison: ¹⁰Which perished at Endor: they became as dung for the earth. ¹¹Make their nobles like Oreb, and like Zeeb: yes, all their princes as Zebah, and as Zalmunna: ¹²Who said, Let us take to ourselves the houses of God in possession. ¹³O my God, make them like a wheel; as the stubble before the wind. ¹⁴As the fire burns a wood, and as the flame sets the mountains on fire; ¹⁵So persecute them with your tempest, and make them afraid with your storm. ¹⁶Fill their faces with shame; that they may seek your name, O LORD. ¹⁷Let them be confounded and troubled for ever; yes, let them be put to shame, and perish: ¹⁸That men may know that you, whose name alone is JEHOVAH, are the most high over all the earth.

84

¹How amiable are your tabernacles, O LORD of hosts! ²My soul longs, yes, even faints for the courts of the LORD: my heart and my flesh cries out for the living God. ³Yes, the sparrow has found an house, and the swallow a nest for herself, where she may lay her young, even your altars, O LORD of hosts, my King, and my God. ⁴Blessed are they that dwell in your house: they will be still praising you. Selah. ⁵Blessed is the man whose strength is in you; in whose heart are the ways of them. ⁶Who passing through the valley of Baca make it a well; the rain also fills the pools. ⁷They go from strength to strength, every one of them in Zion appears before God. ⁸O LORD God of hosts, hear my prayer: give ear, O God of Jacob. Selah. ⁹Behold, O God our shield, and look on the face of your anointed. ¹⁰For a day in your courts is better than a thousand. I had rather be a doorkeeper in the house of my God, than to dwell in the tents of wickedness. ¹¹For the LORD God is a sun and shield: the LORD will give grace and glory: no good thing

will he withhold from them that walk uprightly. ¹²O LORD of hosts, blessed is the man that trusts in you.

85 ¹Lord, you have been favorable to your land: you have brought back the captivity of Jacob. ²You have forgiven the iniquity of your people, you have covered all their sin. Selah. ³You have taken away all your wrath: you have turned yourself from the fierceness of your anger. ⁴Turn us, O God of our salvation, and cause your anger toward us to cease. ⁵Will you be angry with us for ever? will you draw out your anger to all generations? ⁶Will you not revive us again: that your people may rejoice in you? ⁷Show us your mercy, O LORD, and grant us your salvation. ⁸I will hear what God the LORD will speak: for he will speak peace to his people, and to his saints: but let them not turn again to folly. ⁹Surely his salvation is near them that fear him; that glory may dwell in our land. ¹⁰Mercy and truth are met together; righteousness and peace have kissed each other. ¹¹Truth shall spring out of the earth; and righteousness shall look down from heaven. ¹²Yes, the LORD shall give that which is good; and our land shall yield her increase. ¹³Righteousness shall go before him; and shall set us in the way of his steps.

86 ¹Bow down your ear, O LORD, hear me: for I am poor and needy. ²Preserve my soul; for I am holy: O you my God, save your servant that trusts in you. ³Be merciful to me, O Lord: for I cry to you daily. ⁴Rejoice the soul of your servant: for to you, O Lord, do I lift up my soul. ⁵For you, Lord, are good, and ready to forgive; and plenteous in mercy to all them that call on you. ⁶Give ear, O LORD, to my prayer; and attend to the voice of my supplications. ⁷In the day of my trouble I will call on you: for you will answer me. ⁸Among the gods there is none like to you, O Lord; neither are there any works like to your works. ⁹All nations whom you have made shall come and worship before you, O Lord; and shall glorify your name. ¹⁰For you are great, and do wondrous things: you are God alone. ¹¹Teach me your way, O LORD; I will walk in your truth: unite my heart to fear your name. ¹²I will praise you, O Lord my God, with all my heart: and I will glorify your name for ever more. ¹³For great is your mercy toward me: and you have delivered my soul from the lowest hell. ¹⁴O God, the proud are risen against me, and the assemblies of violent men have sought after my soul; and have not set you before them. ¹⁵But you, O Lord, are a God full of compassion, and gracious, long suffering, and plenteous in mercy and truth. ¹⁶O turn to me, and have mercy on me; give your strength to your servant, and save the son of your handmaid. ¹⁷Show me a token for good; that they which hate me may see it, and be ashamed: because you, LORD, have helped me, and comforted me.

87 ¹His foundation is in the holy mountains. ²The LORD loves the gates of Zion more than all the dwellings of Jacob. ³Glorious things are spoken of you, O city of God. Selah. ⁴I will make mention of Rahab and Babylon to them that know me: behold Philistia, and Tyre, with Ethiopia; this man was born there. ⁵And of Zion it shall be said, This and that man was born in her: and the highest himself shall establish her. ⁶The LORD shall count, when he writes up the people, that this man was born there. Selah. ⁷As well the singers as the players on instruments shall be there: all my springs are in you.

88 ¹O lord God of my salvation, I have cried day and night before you: ²Let my prayer come before you: incline your ear to my cry; ³For my soul is full of troubles: and my life draws near to the grave. ⁴I am counted with them that go down into the pit: I am as a man that has no strength: ⁵Free among the dead, like the slain that lie in the grave, whom you remember no more: and they are cut off from your hand. ⁶You have laid me in the lowest pit, in darkness, in the deeps. ⁷Your wrath lies hard on me, and you have afflicted me with all your waves. Selah. ⁸You have put away my acquaintance far from me; you have made me an abomination to them: I am shut up, and I cannot come forth. ⁹My eye mourns by reason of affliction: LORD, I have called daily on you, I have stretched out my hands to you. ¹⁰Will you show wonders to the dead? shall the dead arise and praise you? Selah. ¹¹Shall your loving kindness be declared in the grave? or your faithfulness in destruction? ¹²Shall your wonders be known in the dark? and your righteousness in the land of forgetfulness? ¹³But to you have I cried, O LORD; and in the morning shall my prayer prevent you. ¹⁴LORD, why cast you off my soul? why hide you your face from me? ¹⁵I am afflicted and ready to die from my youth up: while I suffer your terrors I am distracted. ¹⁶Your fierce wrath goes over me; your terrors have cut me off. ¹⁷They came round about me daily like water; they compassed me about together. ¹⁸Lover and friend have you put far from me, and my acquaintance into darkness.

89 ¹I will sing of the mercies of the LORD for ever: with my mouth will I make known your faithfulness to all generations. ²For I have said, Mercy shall be built up for ever: your faithfulness shall you establish in the very heavens. ³I have made a covenant with my chosen, I have sworn to David my servant, ⁴Your seed will I establish for ever, and build up your throne to all generations. Selah. ⁵And the heavens shall praise your wonders, O LORD: your faithfulness also in the congregation of the saints. ⁶For who in the heaven can be compared to the LORD? who among the sons of the mighty can be likened to the LORD? ⁷God is greatly to be feared in the assembly of the saints, and to be had in reverence of all them that are about him. ⁸O LORD God of hosts, who is a strong LORD like to you? or to your faithfulness round about you? ⁹You rule the raging of the sea: when the waves thereof arise, you still them. ¹⁰You have broken Rahab in pieces, as one that is slain; you have scattered your enemies with your strong arm. ¹¹The heavens are yours, the earth also is yours: as for the world and the fullness thereof, you have founded them. ¹²The north and the south you have created them: Tabor and Hermon shall rejoice in your name. ¹³You have a mighty arm: strong is your hand, and high is your right hand. ¹⁴Justice and judgment are the habitation of your throne: mercy and truth shall go before your face. ¹⁵Blessed is the people that know the joyful sound: they shall walk, O LORD, in the light of your countenance. ¹⁶In your name shall they rejoice all the day: and in your righteousness shall they be exalted. ¹⁷For you are the glory of their strength: and in your favor our horn shall be exalted. ¹⁸For the LORD is our defense; and the Holy One of Israel is our king. ¹⁹Then you spoke in vision to your holy one, and said, I have laid help on one that is mighty; I have exalted one chosen out of the people. ²⁰I have found David my servant; with my holy oil have I anointed him: ²¹With whom my hand shall be established: my arm also shall strengthen him. ²²The enemy shall not exact on him; nor the son of wickedness afflict him. ²³And I will beat down his foes before his face, and plague them that hate him. ²⁴But my faithfulness and my mercy shall be with him: and in my name shall his horn be exalted. ²⁵I will set his hand also in the sea, and his right hand in the rivers. ²⁶He shall cry to me, You are my father, my God, and the rock of my salvation. ²⁷Also I will make him my firstborn, higher than the kings of the earth. ²⁸My mercy will I keep for him for ever more, and my covenant shall stand fast with him. ²⁹His seed also will I make to endure for ever, and his throne as the days of heaven. ³⁰If his children forsake my law, and walk not in my judgments; ³¹If they break my statutes, and keep not my commandments; ³²Then will I visit their transgression with the rod, and their iniquity with stripes. ³³Nevertheless my loving kindness will I not utterly take from him, nor suffer my faithfulness to fail. ³⁴My covenant will I not break, nor alter the thing that is gone out of my lips. ³⁵Once have I sworn by my holiness that I will not lie to David. ³⁶His seed shall endure for ever, and his throne as the sun before me. ³⁷It shall be established for ever as the moon, and as a faithful witness in heaven. Selah. ³⁸But you have cast off and abhorred, you have been wroth with your anointed. ³⁹You have made void the covenant of your servant: you have profaned his crown by casting it to the ground. ⁴⁰You have broken down all his hedges; you have brought his strong holds to ruin. ⁴¹All that pass by the way spoil him: he is a reproach to his neighbors. ⁴²You have set up the right hand of his adversaries; you have made all his enemies to rejoice. ⁴³You have also turned the edge of his sword, and have not made him to stand in the battle. ⁴⁴You have made his glory to cease, and cast his throne down to the ground. ⁴⁵The days of his youth have you shortened: you have covered him with shame. Selah. ⁴⁶How long, LORD? will you hide yourself for ever? shall your wrath burn like fire? ⁴⁷Remember how short my time is: why have you made all men in vain? ⁴⁸What man is he that lives, and shall not see death? shall he deliver his soul from the hand of the grave? Selah. ⁴⁹Lord, where are your former loving kindnesses, which you swore to David in your truth? ⁵⁰Remember, Lord, the reproach of your servants; how I do bear in my bosom the reproach of all the mighty people; ⁵¹With which your enemies have reproached, O LORD; with which they have reproached the footsteps of your anointed. ⁵²Blessed be the LORD for ever more. Amen, and Amen.

90

¹Lord, you have been our dwelling place in all generations. ²Before the mountains were brought forth, or ever you had formed the earth and the world, even from everlasting to everlasting, you are God. ³You turn man to destruction; and say, Return, you children of men. ⁴For a thousand years in your sight are but as yesterday when it is past, and as a watch in the night. ⁵You carry them away as with a flood; they are as a sleep: in the morning they are like grass which grows up. ⁶In the morning it flourishes, and grows up; in the evening it is cut down, and wither. ⁷For we are consumed by your anger, and by your wrath are we troubled. ⁸You have set our iniquities before you, our secret sins in the light of your countenance. ⁹For all our days are passed away in your wrath: we spend our years as a tale that is told. ¹⁰The days of our years are three score years and ten; and if by reason of strength they be fourscore years, yet is their strength labor and sorrow; for it is soon cut off, and we fly away. ¹¹Who knows the power of your anger? even according to your fear, so is your wrath. ¹²So teach us to number our days, that we may apply our hearts to wisdom. ¹³Return, O LORD, how long? and let it repent you concerning your servants. ¹⁴O satisfy us early with your mercy; that we may rejoice and be glad all our days. ¹⁵Make us glad according to the days wherein you have afflicted us, and the years wherein we have seen evil. ¹⁶Let your work appear to your servants, and your glory to their children. ¹⁷And let the beauty of the LORD our God be on us: and establish you the work of our hands on us; yes, the work of our hands establish you it.

91

¹He that dwells in the secret place of the most High shall abide under the shadow of the Almighty. ²I will say of the LORD, He is my refuge and my fortress: my God; in him will I trust. ³Surely he shall deliver you from the snare of the fowler, and from the noisome pestilence. ⁴He shall cover you with his feathers, and under his wings shall you trust: his truth shall be your shield and buckler. ⁵You shall not be afraid for the terror by night; nor for the arrow that flies by day; ⁶Nor for the pestilence that walks in darkness; nor for the destruction that wastes at noonday. ⁷A thousand shall fall at your side, and ten thousand at your right hand; but it shall not come near you. ⁸Only with your eyes shall you behold and see the reward of the wicked. ⁹Because you have made the LORD, which is my refuge, even the most High, your habitation; ¹⁰There shall no evil befall you, neither shall any plague come near your dwelling. ¹¹For he shall give his angels charge over you, to keep you in all your ways. ¹²They shall bear you up in their hands, lest you dash your foot against a stone. ¹³You shall tread on the lion and adder: the young lion and the dragon shall you trample under feet. ¹⁴Because he has set his love on me, therefore will I deliver him: I will set him on high, because he has known my name. ¹⁵He shall call on me, and I will answer him: I will be with him in trouble; I will deliver him, and honor him. ¹⁶With long life will I satisfy him, and show him my salvation.

92

¹IT IS A GOOD THING TO GIVE THANKS UNTO THE LORD, AND TO SING PRAISES UNTO THY NAME, O MOST HIGH: ²To show forth your loving kindness in the morning, and your faithfulness every night, ³On an instrument of ten strings, and on the psaltery; on the harp with a solemn sound. ⁴For you, LORD, have made me glad through your work: I will triumph in the works of your hands. ⁵O LORD, how great are your works! and your thoughts are very deep. ⁶A brutish man knows not; neither does a fool understand this. ⁷When the wicked spring as the grass, and when all the workers of iniquity do flourish; it is that they shall be destroyed for ever: ⁸But you, LORD, are most high for ever more. ⁹For, see, your enemies,

O LORD, for, see, your enemies shall perish; all the workers of iniquity shall be scattered. ¹⁰But my horn shall you exalt like the horn of an unicorn: I shall be anointed with fresh oil. ¹¹My eye also shall see my desire on my enemies, and my ears shall hear my desire of the wicked that rise up against me. ¹²The righteous shall flourish like the palm tree: he shall grow like a cedar in Lebanon. ¹³Those that be planted in the house of the LORD shall flourish in the courts of our God. ¹⁴They shall still bring forth fruit in old age; they shall be fat and flourishing; ¹⁵To show that the LORD is upright: he is my rock, and there is no unrighteousness in him.

93 ¹The LORD reigns, he is clothed with majesty; the LORD is clothed with strength, with which he has girded himself: the world also is established, that it cannot be moved. ²Your throne is established of old: you are from everlasting. ³The floods have lifted up, O LORD, the floods have lifted up their voice; the floods lift up their waves. ⁴The LORD on high is mightier than the noise of many waters, yes, than the mighty waves of the sea. ⁵Your testimonies are very sure: holiness becomes your house, O LORD, for ever.

94 ¹O Lord God, to whom vengeance belongs; O God, to whom vengeance belongs, show yourself. ²Lift up yourself, you judge of the earth: render a reward to the proud. ³LORD, how long shall the wicked, how long shall the wicked triumph? ⁴How long shall they utter and speak hard things? and all the workers of iniquity boast themselves? ⁵They break in pieces your people, O LORD, and afflict your heritage. ⁶They slay the widow and the stranger, and murder the fatherless. ⁷Yet they say, The LORD shall not see, neither shall the God of Jacob regard it. ⁸Understand, you brutish among the people: and you fools, when will you be wise? ⁹He that planted the ear, shall he not hear? he that formed the eye, shall he not see? ¹⁰He that chastises the heathen, shall not he correct? he that teaches man knowledge, shall not he know? ¹¹The LORD knows the thoughts of man, that they are vanity. ¹²Blessed is the man whom you chasten, O LORD, and teach him out of your law; ¹³That you may give him rest from the days of adversity, until the pit be dig for the wicked. ¹⁴For the LORD will not cast off his people, neither will he forsake his inheritance. ¹⁵But judgment shall return to righteousness: and all the upright in heart shall follow it. ¹⁶Who will rise up for me against the evildoers? or who will stand up for me against the workers of iniquity? ¹⁷Unless the LORD had been my help, my soul had almost dwelled in silence. ¹⁸When I said, My foot slips; your mercy, O LORD, held me up. ¹⁹In the multitude of my thoughts within me your comforts delight my soul. ²⁰Shall the throne of iniquity have fellowship with you, which frames mischief by a law? ²¹They gather themselves together against the soul of the righteous, and condemn the innocent blood. ²²But the LORD is my defense; and my God is the rock of my refuge. ²³And he shall bring on them their own iniquity, and shall cut them off in their own wickedness; yes, the LORD our God shall cut them off.

95 ¹O come, let us sing to the LORD: let us make a joyful noise to the rock of our salvation. ²Let us come before his presence with thanksgiving, and make a joyful noise to him with psalms. ³For the LORD is a great God, and a great King above all gods. ⁴In his hand are the deep places of the earth: the strength of the hills is his also. ⁵The sea is his, and he made it: and his hands formed the dry land. ⁶O come, let us worship and bow down: let us kneel before the LORD our maker. ⁷For he is our God; and we are the people of his pasture, and the sheep of his hand. To day if you will hear his voice, ⁸Harden not your heart, as in the provocation, and as in the day of temptation in the wilderness: ⁹When your fathers tempted me, proved me, and saw my work. ¹⁰Forty years long was I grieved with this generation, and said, It is a people that do err in their heart, and they have not known my ways: ¹¹To whom I swore in my wrath that they should not enter into my rest.

96 ¹O sing to the LORD a new song: sing to the LORD, all the earth. ²Sing to the LORD, bless his name; show forth his salvation from day to day. ³Declare his glory among the heathen, his wonders among all people. ⁴For the LORD is great, and greatly to be praised: he is to be feared above all gods. ⁵For all the gods of the nations are idols: but the LORD made the heavens. ⁶Honor and majesty are before him: strength and beauty are in his sanctuary. ⁷Give to the LORD, O you kindreds of the people, give to the LORD glory and strength. ⁸Give to the LORD the glory due to his name: bring an offering, and come into his courts. ⁹O worship the LORD in the beauty of holiness: fear before him, all the earth. ¹⁰Say among the heathen that the LORD reigns: the world also shall be established that it shall not be moved: he shall judge the people righteously. ¹¹Let the heavens rejoice, and let the earth be glad; let the sea roar, and the fullness thereof. ¹²Let the field be joyful, and all that is therein: then shall all the trees of the wood rejoice ¹³Before the LORD: for he comes, for he comes to judge the earth: he shall judge the world with righteousness, and the people with his truth.

97 ¹The LORD reigns; let the earth rejoice; let the multitude of isles be glad thereof. ²Clouds and darkness are round about him: righteousness and judgment are the habitation of his throne. ³A fire goes before him, and burns up his enemies round about. ⁴His lightning enlightened the world: the earth saw, and trembled. ⁵The hills melted like wax at the presence of the LORD, at the presence of the Lord of the whole earth. ⁶The heavens declare his righteousness, and all the people see his glory. ⁷Confounded be all they that serve graven images, that boast themselves of idols: worship him, all you gods. ⁸Zion heard, and was glad; and the daughters of Judah rejoiced because of your judgments, O LORD. ⁹For you, LORD, are high above all the earth: you are exalted far above all gods. ¹⁰You that love the LORD, hate evil: he preserves the souls of his saints; he delivers them out of the hand of the wicked. ¹¹Light is sown for the righteous, and gladness for the upright in heart. ¹²Rejoice in the LORD, you righteous; and give thanks at the remembrance of his holiness.

98 ¹O sing to the LORD a new song; for he has done marvelous things: his right hand, and his holy arm, has gotten him the victory. ²The LORD has made known his salvation: his righteousness has he openly showed in the sight of the heathen. ³He has remembered his mercy and his truth toward the house of Israel: all the ends of the earth have seen the salvation of our God. ⁴Make a joyful noise to the LORD, all the earth: make a loud noise, and rejoice, and sing praise. ⁵Sing to the LORD with the harp; with the harp, and the voice of a psalm. ⁶With trumpets and sound of cornet make a joyful noise before the LORD, the King. ⁷Let the sea roar, and the fullness thereof; the world, and they that dwell therein. ⁸Let the floods clap their hands: let the hills be joyful together ⁹Before the LORD; for he comes to judge the earth: with righteousness shall he judge the world, and the people with equity.

99

¹The LORD reigns; let the people tremble: he sits between the cherubim; let the earth be moved. ²The LORD is great in Zion; and he is high above all the people. ³Let them praise your great and terrible name; for it is holy. ⁴The king's strength also loves judgment; you do establish equity, you execute judgment and righteousness in Jacob. ⁵Exalt you the LORD our God, and worship at his footstool; for he is holy. ⁶Moses and Aaron among his priests, and Samuel among them that call on his name; they called on the LORD, and he answered them. ⁷He spoke to them in the cloudy pillar: they kept his testimonies, and the ordinance that he gave them. ⁸You answered them, O LORD our God: you were a God that forgave them, though you took vengeance of their inventions. ⁹Exalt the LORD our God, and worship at his holy hill; for the LORD our God is holy.

100

¹Make a joyful noise to the LORD, all you lands. ²Serve the LORD with gladness: come before his presence with singing. ³Know you that the LORD he is God: it is he that has made us, and not we ourselves; we are his people, and the sheep of his pasture. ⁴Enter into his gates with thanksgiving, and into his courts with praise: be thankful to him, and bless his name. ⁵For the LORD is good; his mercy is everlasting; and his truth endures to all generations.

101

¹I will sing of mercy and judgment: to you, O LORD, will I sing. ²I will behave myself wisely in a perfect way. O when will you come to me? I will walk within my house with a perfect heart. ³I will set no wicked thing before my eyes: I hate the work of them that turn aside; it shall not stick to me. ⁴A fraudulent heart shall depart from me: I will not know a wicked person. ⁵Whoever privately slanders his neighbor, him will I cut off: him that has an high look and a proud heart will not I suffer. ⁶My eyes shall be on the faithful of the land, that they may dwell with me: he that walks in a perfect way, he shall serve me. ⁷He that works deceit shall not dwell within my house: he that tells lies shall not tarry in my sight. ⁸I will early destroy all the wicked of the land; that I may cut off all wicked doers from the city of the LORD.

102

¹Hear my prayer, O LORD, and let my cry come to you. ²Hide not your face from me in the day when I am in trouble; incline your ear to me: in the day when I call answer me speedily. ³For my days are consumed like smoke, and my bones are burned as an hearth. ⁴My heart is smitten, and withered like grass; so that I forget to eat my bread. ⁵By reason of the voice of my groaning my bones stick to my skin. ⁶I am like a pelican of the wilderness: I am like an owl of the desert. ⁷I watch, and am as a sparrow alone on the house top. ⁸My enemies reproach me all the day; and they that are mad against me are sworn against me. ⁹For I have eaten ashes like bread, and mingled my drink with weeping. ¹⁰Because of your indignation and your wrath: for you have lifted me up, and cast me down. ¹¹My days are like a shadow that declines; and I am withered like grass. ¹²But you, O LORD, shall endure for ever; and your remembrance to all generations. ¹³You shall arise, and have mercy on Zion: for the time to favor her, yes, the set time, is come. ¹⁴For your servants take pleasure in her stones, and favor the dust thereof. ¹⁵So the heathen shall fear the name of the LORD, and all the kings of the earth your glory. ¹⁶When the LORD shall build up Zion, he shall appear in his glory. ¹⁷He will regard the prayer of the destitute, and not despise their prayer. ¹⁸This shall be written for the generation to come: and the people which shall be created shall praise the LORD. ¹⁹For he has looked down from the height of his sanctuary; from heaven did the LORD behold the earth; ²⁰To hear the groaning of the prisoner; to loose those that are appointed to death; ²¹To declare the name of the LORD in Zion, and his praise in Jerusalem; ²²When the people are gathered together, and the kingdoms, to serve the LORD. ²³He weakened my strength in the way; he shortened my days. ²⁴I said, O my God, take me not away in the middle of my days: your years are throughout all generations. ²⁵Of old have you laid the foundation of the earth: and the heavens are the work of your hands. ²⁶They shall perish, but you shall endure: yes, all of them shall wax old like a garment; as a clothing shall you change them, and they shall be changed: ²⁷But you are the same, and your years shall have no end. ²⁸The children of your servants shall continue, and their seed shall be established before you.

103

¹Bless the LORD, O my soul: and all that is within me, bless his holy name. ²Bless the LORD, O my soul, and forget not all his benefits: ³Who forgives all your iniquities; who heals all your diseases; ⁴Who redeems your life from destruction; who crowns you with loving kindness and tender mercies; ⁵Who satisfies your mouth with good things; so that your youth is renewed like the eagle's. ⁶The LORD executes righteousness and judgment for all that are oppressed. ⁷He made known his ways to Moses, his acts to the children of Israel. ⁸The LORD is merciful and gracious, slow to anger, and plenteous in mercy. ⁹He will not always chide: neither will he keep his anger for ever. ¹⁰He has not dealt with us after our sins; nor rewarded us according to our iniquities. ¹¹For as the heaven is high above the earth, so great is his mercy toward them that fear him. ¹²As far as the east is from the west, so far has he removed our transgressions from us. ¹³Like as a father pities his children, so the LORD pities them that fear him. ¹⁴For he knows our frame; he remembers that we are dust. ¹⁵As for man, his days are as grass: as a flower of the field, so he flourishes. ¹⁶For the wind passes over it, and it is gone; and the place thereof shall know it no more. ¹⁷But the mercy of the LORD is from everlasting to everlasting on them that fear him, and his righteousness to children's children; ¹⁸To such as keep his covenant, and to those that remember his commandments to do them. ¹⁹The LORD has prepared his throne in the heavens; and his kingdom rules over all. ²⁰Bless the LORD, you his angels, that excel in strength, that do his

commandments, hearkening to the voice of his word. ²¹Bless you the LORD, all you his hosts; you ministers of his, that do his pleasure. ²²Bless the LORD, all his works in all places of his dominion: bless the LORD, O my soul.

104

¹Bless the LORD, O my soul. O LORD my God, you are very great; you are clothed with honor and majesty. ²Who cover yourself with light as with a garment: who stretch out the heavens like a curtain: ³Who lays the beams of his chambers in the waters: who makes the clouds his chariot: who walks on the wings of the wind: ⁴Who makes his angels spirits; his ministers a flaming fire: ⁵Who laid the foundations of the earth, that it should not be removed for ever. ⁶You covered it with the deep as with a garment: the waters stood above the mountains. ⁷At your rebuke they fled; at the voice of your thunder they hurried away. ⁸They go up by the mountains; they go down by the valleys to the place which you have founded for them. ⁹You have set a bound that they may not pass over; that they turn not again to cover the earth. ¹⁰He sends the springs into the valleys, which run among the hills. ¹¹They give drink to every beast of the field: the wild asses quench their thirst. ¹²By them shall the fowls of the heaven have their habitation, which sing among the branches. ¹³He waters the hills from his chambers: the earth is satisfied with the fruit of your works. ¹⁴He causes the grass to grow for the cattle, and herb for the service of man: that he may bring forth food out of the earth; ¹⁵And wine that makes glad the heart of man, and oil to make his face to shine, and bread which strengthens man's heart. ¹⁶The trees of the LORD are full of sap; the cedars of Lebanon, which he has planted; ¹⁷Where the birds make their nests: as for the stork, the fir trees are her house. ¹⁸The high hills are a refuge for the wild goats; and the rocks for the conies. ¹⁹He appointed the moon for seasons: the sun knows his going down. ²⁰You make darkness, and it is night: wherein all the beasts of the forest do creep forth. ²¹The young lions roar after their prey, and seek their meat from God. ²²The sun rises, they gather themselves together, and lay them down in their dens. ²³Man goes forth to his work and to his labor until the evening. ²⁴O LORD, how manifold are your works! in wisdom have you made them all: the earth is full of your riches. ²⁵So is this great and wide sea, wherein are things creeping innumerable, both small and great beasts. ²⁶There go the ships: there is that leviathan, whom you have made to play therein. ²⁷These wait all on you; that you may give them their meat in due season. ²⁸That you give them they gather: you open your hand, they are filled with good. ²⁹You hide your face, they are troubled: you take away their breath, they die, and return to their dust. ³⁰You send forth your spirit, they are created: and you renew the face of the earth. ³¹The glory of the LORD shall endure for ever: the LORD shall rejoice in his works. ³²He looks on the earth, and it trembles: he touches the hills, and they smoke. ³³I will sing to the LORD as long as I live: I will sing praise to my God while I have my being. ³⁴My meditation of him shall be sweet: I will be glad in the LORD. ³⁵Let the sinners be consumed out of the earth, and let the wicked be no more. Bless you the LORD, O my soul. Praise you the LORD.

105

¹O give thanks to the LORD; call on his name: make known his deeds among the people. ²Sing to him, sing psalms to him: talk you of all his wondrous works. ³Glory you in his holy name: let the heart of them rejoice that seek the LORD. ⁴Seek the LORD, and his strength: seek his face ever more. ⁵Remember his marvelous works that he has done; his wonders, and the judgments of his mouth; ⁶O you seed of Abraham his servant, you children of Jacob his chosen. ⁷He is the LORD our God: his judgments are in all the earth. ⁸He has remembered his covenant for ever, the word which he commanded to a thousand generations. ⁹Which covenant he made with Abraham, and his oath to Isaac; ¹⁰And confirmed the same to Jacob for a law, and to Israel for an everlasting covenant: ¹¹Saying, To you will I give the land of Canaan, the lot of your inheritance: ¹²When they were but a few men in number; yes, very few, and strangers in it. ¹³When they went from one nation to another, from one kingdom to another people; ¹⁴He suffered no man to do them wrong: yes, he reproved kings for their sakes; ¹⁵Saying, Touch not my anointed, and do my prophets no harm. ¹⁶Moreover he called for a famine on the land: he broke the whole staff of bread. ¹⁷He sent a man before them, even Joseph, who was sold for a servant: ¹⁸Whose feet they hurt with fetters: he was laid in iron: ¹⁹Until the time that his word came: the word of the LORD tried him. ²⁰The king sent and loosed him; even the ruler of the people, and let him go free. ²¹He made him lord of his house, and ruler of all his substance: ²²To bind his princes at his pleasure; and teach his senators wisdom. ²³Israel also came into Egypt; and Jacob sojourned in the land of Ham. ²⁴And he increased his people greatly; and made them stronger than their enemies. ²⁵He turned their heart to hate his people, to deal subtly with his servants. ²⁶He sent Moses his servant; and Aaron whom he had chosen. ²⁷They showed his signs among them, and wonders in the land of Ham. ²⁸He sent darkness, and made it dark; and they rebelled not against his word. ²⁹He turned their waters into blood, and slew their fish. ³⁰Their land brought forth frogs in abundance, in the chambers of their kings. ³¹He spoke, and there came divers sorts of flies, and lice in all their coasts. ³²He gave them hail for rain, and flaming fire in their land. ³³He smote their vines also and their fig trees; and broke the trees of their coasts. ³⁴He spoke, and the locusts came, and caterpillars, and that without number, ³⁵And did eat up all the herbs in their land, and devoured the fruit of their ground. ³⁶He smote also all the firstborn in their land, the chief of all their strength. ³⁷He brought them forth also with silver and gold: and there was not one feeble person among their tribes. ³⁸Egypt was glad when they departed: for the fear of them fell on them. ³⁹He spread a cloud for a covering; and fire to give light in the night. ⁴⁰The people asked, and he brought quails, and satisfied them with the bread of heaven. ⁴¹He opened the rock, and the waters gushed out; they ran in the dry places like a river. ⁴²For he remembered his holy promise, and Abraham his servant. ⁴³And he brought forth his people with joy, and his chosen with gladness: ⁴⁴And gave them the lands of the heathen: and they inherited the labor of the people; ⁴⁵That they might observe his statutes, and keep his laws. Praise you the LORD.

106 ¹Praise you the LORD. O give thanks to the LORD; for he is good: for his mercy endures for ever. ²Who can utter the mighty acts of the LORD? who can show forth all his praise? ³Blessed are they that keep judgment, and he that does righteousness at all times. ⁴Remember me, O LORD, with the favor that you bore to your people: O visit me with your salvation; ⁵That I may see the good of your chosen, that I may rejoice in the gladness of your nation, that I may glory with your inheritance. ⁶We have sinned with our fathers, we have committed iniquity, we have done wickedly. ⁷Our fathers understood not your wonders in Egypt; they remembered not the multitude of your mercies; but provoked him at the sea, even at the Red sea. ⁸Nevertheless he saved them for his name's sake, that he might make his mighty power to be known. ⁹He rebuked the Red sea also, and it was dried up: so he led them through the depths, as through the wilderness. ¹⁰And he saved them from the hand of him that hated them, and redeemed them from the hand of the enemy. ¹¹And the waters covered their enemies: there was not one of them left. ¹²Then believed they his words; they sang his praise. ¹³They soon forgot his works; they waited not for his counsel: ¹⁴But lusted exceedingly in the wilderness, and tempted God in the desert. ¹⁵And he gave them their request; but sent leanness into their soul. ¹⁶They envied Moses also in the camp, and Aaron the saint of the LORD. ¹⁷The earth opened and swallowed up Dathan and covered the company of Abiram. ¹⁸And a fire was kindled in their company; the flame burned up the wicked. ¹⁹They made a calf in Horeb, and worshiped the molten image. ²⁰Thus they changed their glory into the similitude of an ox that eats grass. ²¹They forgot God their savior, which had done great things in Egypt; ²²Wondrous works in the land of Ham, and terrible things by the Red sea. ²³Therefore he said that he would destroy them, had not Moses his chosen stood before him in the breach, to turn away his wrath, lest he should destroy them. ²⁴Yes, they despised the pleasant land, they believed not his word: ²⁵But murmured in their tents, and listened not to the voice of the LORD. ²⁶Therefore he lifted up his hand against them, to overthrow them in the wilderness: ²⁷To overthrow their seed also among the nations, and to scatter them in the lands. ²⁸They joined themselves also to Baalpeor, and ate the sacrifices of the dead. ²⁹Thus they provoked him to anger with their inventions: and the plague broke in on them. ³⁰Then stood up Phinehas, and executed judgment: and so the plague was stayed. ³¹And that was counted to him for righteousness to all generations for ever more. ³²They angered him also at the waters of strife, so that it went ill with Moses for their sakes: ³³Because they provoked his spirit, so that he spoke unadvisedly with his lips. ³⁴They did not destroy the nations, concerning whom the LORD commanded them: ³⁵But were mingled among the heathen, and learned their works. ³⁶And they served their idols: which were a snare to them. ³⁷Yes, they sacrificed their sons and their daughters to devils, ³⁸And shed innocent blood, even the blood of their sons and of their daughters, whom they sacrificed to the idols of Canaan: and the land was polluted with blood. ³⁹Thus were they defiled with their own works, and went a whoring with their own inventions. ⁴⁰Therefore was the wrath of the LORD kindled against his people, so that he abhorred his own inheritance. ⁴¹And he gave them into the hand of the heathen; and they that hated them ruled over them. ⁴²Their enemies also oppressed them, and they were brought into subjection under their hand. ⁴³Many times did he deliver them; but they provoked him with their counsel, and were brought low for their iniquity. ⁴⁴Nevertheless he regarded their affliction, when he heard their cry: ⁴⁵And he remembered for them his covenant, and repented according to the multitude of his mercies. ⁴⁶He made them also to be pitied of all those that carried them captives. ⁴⁷Save us, O LORD our God, and gather us from among the heathen, to give thanks to your holy name, and to triumph in your praise. ⁴⁸Blessed be the LORD God of Israel from everlasting to everlasting: and let all the people say, Amen. Praise you the LORD.

107 ¹O give thanks to the LORD, for he is good: for his mercy endures for ever. ²Let the redeemed of the LORD say so, whom he has redeemed from the hand of the enemy; ³And gathered them out of the lands, from the east, and from the west, from the north, and from the south. ⁴They wandered in the wilderness in a solitary way; they found no city to dwell in. ⁵Hungry and thirsty, their soul fainted in them. ⁶Then they cried to the LORD in their trouble, and he delivered them out of their distresses. ⁷And he led them forth by the right way, that they might go to a city of habitation. ⁸Oh that men would praise the LORD for his goodness, and for his wonderful works to the children of men! ⁹For he satisfies the longing soul, and fills the hungry soul with goodness. ¹⁰Such as sit in darkness and in the shadow of death, being bound in affliction and iron; ¹¹Because they rebelled against the words of God, and scorned the counsel of the most High: ¹²Therefore he brought down their heart with labor; they fell down, and there was none to help. ¹³Then they cried to the LORD in their trouble, and he saved them out of their distresses. ¹⁴He brought them out of darkness and the shadow of death, and broke their bands in sunder. ¹⁵Oh that men would praise the LORD for his goodness, and for his wonderful works to the children of men! ¹⁶For he has broken the gates of brass, and cut the bars of iron in sunder. ¹⁷Fools because of their transgression, and because of their iniquities, are afflicted. ¹⁸Their soul abhors all manner of meat; and they draw near to the gates of death. ¹⁹Then they cry to the LORD in their trouble, and he saves them out of their distresses. ²⁰He sent his word, and healed them, and delivered them from their destructions. ²¹Oh that men would praise the LORD for his goodness, and for his wonderful works to the children of men! ²²And let them sacrifice the sacrifices of thanksgiving, and declare his works with rejoicing. ²³They that go down to the sea in ships, that do business in great waters; ²⁴These see the works of the LORD, and his wonders in the deep. ²⁵For he commands, and raises the stormy wind, which lifts up the waves thereof. ²⁶They mount up to the heaven, they go down again to the depths: their soul is melted because of trouble. ²⁷They reel to and fro, and stagger like a drunken man, and are at their wit's end. ²⁸Then they cry to the LORD in their trouble, and he brings them out of their distresses. ²⁹He makes the storm a calm, so that the waves thereof are still. ³⁰Then are they glad because they be quiet; so he brings them to their desired haven. ³¹Oh that men would praise the LORD for his goodness, and for his wonderful works to the children of men! ³²Let them exalt him also in the congregation of the people, and praise him in the assembly of the elders. ³³He turns rivers into a wilderness, and the springs into dry ground; ³⁴A fruitful land into barrenness, for the wickedness of them that dwell therein. ³⁵He turns the wilderness into a standing water, and dry ground into springs. ³⁶And there he makes the hungry to dwell, that they may prepare a city for habitation; ³⁷And sow the fields, and plant vineyards, which may yield fruits of increase. ³⁸He blesses them also, so that they are multiplied greatly; and suffers not their cattle to decrease. ³⁹Again, they are diminished and brought low through oppression, affliction, and sorrow. ⁴⁰He pours contempt on princes, and causes them to wander in the wilderness, where there is no way. ⁴¹Yet sets he the poor on high from affliction, and makes him families like a flock. ⁴²The righteous shall see it, and rejoice: and all iniquity shall stop her mouth. ⁴³Whoever is wise, and will observe these things, even they shall understand the loving kindness of the LORD.

108 ¹O god, my heart is fixed; I will sing and give praise, even with my glory. ²Awake, psaltery and harp: I myself will awake early. ³I will praise you, O LORD, among the people: and I will sing praises to you among the nations. ⁴For your mercy is great above the heavens: and your truth reaches to the clouds. ⁵Be you exalted, O God, above the heavens: and your glory above all the earth; ⁶That your beloved may be delivered: save with your right hand, and answer me. ⁷God has spoken in his holiness; I will rejoice, I will divide Shechem, and mete out the valley of Succoth. ⁸Gilead is mine; Manasseh is mine; Ephraim also is the strength of my head; Judah is my lawgiver; ⁹Moab is my wash pot; over Edom will I cast out my shoe; over Philistia will I triumph. ¹⁰Who will bring me into the strong city? who will lead me into Edom? ¹¹Will not you, O God, who have cast us off? and will not you, O God, go forth with our hosts? ¹²Give us help from trouble: for vain is the help of man. ¹³Through God we shall do valiantly: for he it is that shall tread down our enemies.

109 ¹Hold not your peace, O God of my praise; ²For the mouth of the wicked and the mouth of the deceitful are opened against me: they have spoken against me with a lying tongue. ³They compassed me about also with words of hatred; and fought against me without a cause. ⁴For my love they are my adversaries: but I give myself to prayer. ⁵And they have rewarded me evil for good, and hatred for my love. ⁶Set you a wicked man over him: and let Satan stand at his right hand. ⁷When he shall be judged, let him be condemned: and let his prayer become sin. ⁸Let his days be few; and let another take his office. ⁹Let his children be fatherless, and his wife a widow. ¹⁰Let his children be continually vagabonds, and beg: let them seek their bread also out of their desolate places. ¹¹Let the extortionist catch all that he has; and let the strangers spoil his labor. ¹²Let there be none to extend mercy to him: neither let there be any to favor his fatherless children. ¹³Let his posterity be cut off; and in the generation following let their name be blotted out. ¹⁴Let the iniquity of his fathers be remembered with the LORD; and let not the sin of his mother be blotted out. ¹⁵Let them be before the LORD continually, that he may cut off the memory of them from the earth. ¹⁶Because that he remembered not to show mercy, but persecuted the poor and needy man, that he might even slay the broken in heart. ¹⁷As he loved cursing, so let it come to him: as he delighted not in blessing, so let it be far from him. ¹⁸As he clothed himself with cursing like as with his garment, so let it come into his bowels like water, and like oil into his bones. ¹⁹Let it be to him as the garment which covers him, and for a girdle with which he is girded continually. ²⁰Let this be the reward of my adversaries from the LORD, and of them that speak evil against my soul. ²¹But do you for me, O GOD the Lord, for your name's sake: because your mercy is good, deliver you me. ²²For I am poor and needy, and my heart is wounded within me. ²³I am gone like the shadow when it declines: I am tossed up and down as the locust. ²⁴My knees are weak through fasting; and my flesh fails of fatness. ²⁵I became also a reproach to them: when they looked on me they shook their heads. ²⁶Help me, O LORD my God: O save me according to your mercy: ²⁷That they may know that this is your hand; that you, LORD, have done it. ²⁸Let them curse, but bless you: when they arise, let them be ashamed; but let your servant rejoice. ²⁹Let my adversaries be clothed with shame, and let them cover themselves with their own confusion, as with a mantle. ³⁰I will greatly praise the LORD with my mouth; yes, I will praise him among the multitude. ³¹For he shall stand at the right hand of the poor, to save him from those that condemn his soul.

110 ¹The LORD said to my Lord, Sit you at my right hand, until I make your enemies your footstool. ²The LORD shall send the rod of your strength out of Zion: rule you in the middle of your enemies. ³Your people shall be willing in the day of your power, in the beauties of holiness from the womb of the morning: you have the dew of your youth. ⁴The LORD has sworn, and will not repent, You are a priest for ever after the order of Melchizedek. ⁵The Lord at your right hand shall strike through kings in the day of his wrath. ⁶He shall judge among the heathen, he shall fill the places with the dead bodies; he shall wound the heads over many countries. ⁷He shall drink of the brook in the way: therefore shall he lift up the head.

111 ¹Praise you the LORD. I will praise the LORD with my whole heart, in the assembly of the upright, and in the congregation. ²The works of the LORD are great, sought out of all them that have pleasure therein. ³His work is honorable and glorious: and his righteousness endures for ever. ⁴He has made his wonderful works to be remembered: the LORD is gracious and full of compassion. ⁵He has given meat to them that fear him: he will ever be mindful of his covenant. ⁶He has showed his people the power of his works, that he may give them the heritage of the heathen. ⁷The works of his hands are verity and judgment; all his commandments are sure. ⁸They stand fast for ever and ever, and are done in truth and uprightness. ⁹He sent redemption to his people: he has commanded his covenant for ever: holy and reverend is his name. ¹⁰The fear of the LORD is the beginning of wisdom: a good understanding have all they that do his commandments: his praise endures for ever.

112
¹Praise you the LORD. Blessed is the man that fears the LORD, that delights greatly in his commandments. ²His seed shall be mighty on earth: the generation of the upright shall be blessed. ³Wealth and riches shall be in his house: and his righteousness endures for ever. ⁴To the upright there rises light in the darkness: he is gracious, and full of compassion, and righteous. ⁵A good man shows favor, and lends: he will guide his affairs with discretion. ⁶Surely he shall not be moved for ever: the righteous shall be in everlasting remembrance. ⁷He shall not be afraid of evil tidings: his heart is fixed, trusting in the LORD. ⁸His heart is established, he shall not be afraid, until he see his desire on his enemies. ⁹He has dispersed, he has given to the poor; his righteousness endures for ever; his horn shall be exalted with honor. ¹⁰The wicked shall see it, and be grieved; he shall gnash with his teeth, and melt away: the desire of the wicked shall perish.

113
¹Praise you the LORD. Praise, O you servants of the LORD, praise the name of the LORD. ²Blessed be the name of the LORD from this time forth and for ever more. ³From the rising of the sun to the going down of the same the LORD's name is to be praised. ⁴The LORD is high above all nations, and his glory above the heavens. ⁵Who is like to the LORD our God, who dwells on high, ⁶Who humbles himself to behold the things that are in heaven, and in the earth! ⁷He raises up the poor out of the dust, and lifts the needy out of the dunghill; ⁸That he may set him with princes, even with the princes of his people. ⁹He makes the barren woman to keep house, and to be a joyful mother of children. Praise you the LORD.

114
¹When Israel went out of Egypt, the house of Jacob from a people of strange language; ²Judah was his sanctuary, and Israel his dominion. ³The sea saw it, and fled: Jordan was driven back. ⁴The mountains skipped like rams, and the little hills like lambs. ⁵What ailed you, O you sea, that you fled? you Jordan, that you were driven back? ⁶You mountains, that you skipped like rams; and you little hills, like lambs? ⁷Tremble, you earth, at the presence of the Lord, at the presence of the God of Jacob; ⁸Which turned the rock into a standing water, the flint into a fountain of waters.

115
¹Not to us, O LORD, not to us, but to your name give glory, for your mercy, and for your truth's sake. ²Why should the heathen say, Where is now their God? ³But our God is in the heavens: he has done whatever he has pleased. ⁴Their idols are silver and gold, the work of men's hands. ⁵They have mouths, but they speak not: eyes have they, but they see not: ⁶They have ears, but they hear not: noses have they, but they smell not: ⁷They have hands, but they handle not: feet have they, but they walk not: neither speak they through their throat. ⁸They that make them are like to them; so is every one that trusts in them. ⁹O Israel, trust you in the LORD: he is their help and their shield. ¹⁰O house of Aaron, trust in the LORD: he is their help and their shield. ¹¹You that fear the LORD, trust in the LORD: he is their help and their shield. ¹²The LORD has been mindful of us: he will bless us; he will bless the house of Israel; he will bless the house of Aaron. ¹³He will bless them that fear the LORD, both small and great. ¹⁴The LORD shall increase you more and more, you and your children. ¹⁵You are blessed of the LORD which made heaven and earth. ¹⁶The heaven, even the heavens, are the LORD's: but the earth has he given to the children of men. ¹⁷The dead praise not the LORD, neither any that go down into silence. ¹⁸But we will bless the LORD from this time forth and for ever more. Praise the LORD.

116
¹I love the LORD, because he has heard my voice and my supplications. ²Because he has inclined his ear to me, therefore will I call on him as long as I live. ³The sorrows of death compassed me, and the pains of hell got hold on me: I found trouble and sorrow. ⁴Then called I on the name of the LORD; O LORD, I beseech you, deliver my soul. ⁵Gracious is the LORD, and righteous; yes, our God is merciful. ⁶The LORD preserves the simple: I was brought low, and he helped me. ⁷Return to your rest, O my soul; for the LORD has dealt bountifully with you. ⁸For you have delivered my soul from death, my eyes from tears, and my feet from falling. ⁹I will walk before the LORD in the land of the living. ¹⁰I believed, therefore have I spoken: I was greatly afflicted: ¹¹I said in my haste, All men are liars. ¹²What shall I render to the LORD for all his benefits toward me? ¹³I will take the cup of salvation, and call on the name of the LORD. ¹⁴I will pay my vows to the LORD now in the presence of all his people. ¹⁵Precious in the sight of the LORD is the death of his saints. ¹⁶O LORD, truly I am your servant; I am your servant, and the son of your handmaid: you have loosed my bonds. ¹⁷I will offer to you the sacrifice of thanksgiving, and will call on the name of the LORD. ¹⁸I will pay my vows to the LORD now in the presence of all his people. ¹⁹In the courts of the LORD's house, in the middle of you, O Jerusalem. Praise you the LORD.

117
¹O praise the LORD, all you nations: praise him, all you people. ²For his merciful kindness is great toward us: and the truth of the LORD endures for ever. Praise you the LORD.

118
¹O give thanks to the LORD; for he is good: because his mercy endures for ever. ²Let Israel now say, that his mercy endures for ever. ³Let the house of Aaron now say, that his mercy endures for ever. ⁴Let them now that fear the LORD say, that his mercy endures for ever. ⁵I called on the LORD in distress: the LORD answered me, and set me in a large place. ⁶The LORD is on my side; I will not fear: what can man do to me? ⁷The LORD takes my part with them that help me: therefore shall I see my desire on them that hate me. ⁸It is better to trust in the LORD than to put confidence in man. ⁹It is better to trust in the LORD than to put confidence in princes. ¹⁰All nations compassed me about: but in the name of the LORD will I destroy them. ¹¹They compassed me about; yes, they compassed me about: but in the name of the LORD I will destroy them. ¹²They compassed me about like bees: they are quenched as the fire of thorns: for in the name of the LORD I will destroy them. ¹³You have thrust sore at me that I might fall: but the LORD helped me. ¹⁴The LORD is my strength and song, and is become my salvation. ¹⁵The voice of rejoicing and salvation is in the tabernacles of the righteous: the right hand of the

LORD does valiantly. ¹⁶The right hand of the LORD is exalted: the right hand of the LORD does valiantly. ¹⁷I shall not die, but live, and declare the works of the LORD. ¹⁸The LORD has chastened me sore: but he has not given me over to death. ¹⁹Open to me the gates of righteousness: I will go into them, and I will praise the LORD: ²⁰This gate of the LORD, into which the righteous shall enter. ²¹I will praise you: for you have heard me, and are become my salvation. ²²The stone which the builders refused is become the head stone of the corner. ²³This is the LORD's doing; it is marvelous in our eyes. ²⁴This is the day which the LORD has made; we will rejoice and be glad in it. ²⁵Save now, I beseech you, O LORD: O LORD, I beseech you, send now prosperity. ²⁶Blessed be he that comes in the name of the LORD: we have blessed you out of the house of the LORD. ²⁷God is the LORD, which has showed us light: bind the sacrifice with cords, even to the horns of the altar. ²⁸You are my God, and I will praise you: you are my God, I will exalt you. ²⁹O give thanks to the LORD; for he is good: for his mercy endures for ever.

119 ¹Blessed are the undefiled in the way, who walk in the law of the LORD. ²Blessed are they that keep his testimonies, and that seek him with the whole heart. ³They also do no iniquity: they walk in his ways. ⁴You have commanded us to keep your precepts diligently. ⁵O that my ways were directed to keep your statutes! ⁶Then shall I not be ashamed, when I have respect to all your commandments. ⁷I will praise you with uprightness of heart, when I shall have learned your righteous judgments. ⁸I will keep your statutes: O forsake me not utterly. ⁹Wherewithal shall a young man cleanse his way? by taking heed thereto according to your word. ¹⁰With my whole heart have I sought you: O let me not wander from your commandments. ¹¹Your word have I hid in my heart, that I might not sin against you. ¹²Blessed are you, O LORD: teach me your statutes. ¹³With my lips have I declared all the judgments of your mouth. ¹⁴I have rejoiced in the way of your testimonies, as much as in all riches. ¹⁵I will meditate in your precepts, and have respect to your ways. ¹⁶I will delight myself in your statutes: I will not forget your word. ¹⁷Deal bountifully with your servant, that I may live, and keep your word. ¹⁸Open you my eyes, that I may behold wondrous things out of your law. ¹⁹I am a stranger in the earth: hide not your commandments from me. ²⁰My soul breaks for the longing that it has to your judgments at all times. ²¹You have rebuked the proud that are cursed, which do err from your commandments. ²²Remove from me reproach and contempt; for I have kept your testimonies. ²³Princes also did sit and speak against me: but your servant did meditate in your statutes. ²⁴Your testimonies also are my delight and my counsellors. ²⁵My soul sticks to the dust: quicken you me according to your word. ²⁶I have declared my ways, and you heard me: teach me your statutes. ²⁷Make me to understand the way of your precepts: so shall I talk of your wondrous works. ²⁸My soul melts for heaviness: strengthen you me according to your word. ²⁹Remove from me the way of lying: and grant me your law graciously. ³⁰I have chosen the way of truth: your judgments have I laid before me. ³¹I have stuck to your testimonies: O LORD, put me not to shame. ³²I will run the way of your commandments, when you shall enlarge my heart. ³³Teach me, O LORD, the way of your statutes; and I shall keep it to the end. ³⁴Give me understanding, and I shall keep your law; yes, I shall observe it with my whole heart. ³⁵Make me to go in the path of your commandments; for therein do I delight. ³⁶Incline my heart to your testimonies, and not to covetousness. ³⁷Turn away my eyes from beholding vanity; and quicken you me in your way. ³⁸Establish your word to your servant, who is devoted to your fear. ³⁹Turn away my reproach which I fear: for your judgments are good. ⁴⁰Behold, I have longed after your precepts: quicken me in your righteousness. ⁴¹Let your mercies come also to me, O LORD, even your salvation, according to your word. ⁴²So shall I have with which to answer him that reproaches me: for I trust in your word. ⁴³And take not the word of truth utterly out of my mouth; for I have hoped in your judgments. ⁴⁴So shall I keep your law continually for ever and ever. ⁴⁵And I will walk at liberty: for I seek your precepts. ⁴⁶I will speak of your testimonies also before kings, and will not be ashamed. ⁴⁷And I will delight myself in your commandments, which I have loved. ⁴⁸My hands also will I lift up to your commandments, which I have loved; and I will meditate in your statutes. ⁴⁹Remember the word to your servant, on which you have caused me to hope. ⁵⁰This is my comfort in my affliction: for your word has quickened me. ⁵¹The proud have had me greatly in derision: yet have I not declined from your law. ⁵²I remembered your judgments of old, O LORD; and have comforted myself. ⁵³Horror has taken hold on me because of the wicked that forsake your law. ⁵⁴Your statutes have been my songs in the house of my pilgrimage. ⁵⁵I have remembered your name, O LORD, in the night, and have kept your law. ⁵⁶This I had, because I kept your precepts. ⁵⁷You are my portion, O LORD: I have said that I would keep your words. ⁵⁸I entreated your favor with my whole heart: be merciful to me according to your word. ⁵⁹I thought on my ways, and turned my feet to your testimonies. ⁶⁰I made haste, and delayed not to keep your commandments. ⁶¹The bands of the wicked have robbed me: but I have not forgotten your law. ⁶²At midnight I will rise to give thanks to you because of your righteous judgments. ⁶³I am a companion of all them that fear you, and of them that keep your precepts. ⁶⁴The earth, O LORD, is full of your mercy: teach me your statutes. ⁶⁵You have dealt well with your servant, O LORD, according to your word. ⁶⁶Teach me good judgment and knowledge: for I have believed your commandments. ⁶⁷Before I was afflicted I went astray: but now have I kept your word. ⁶⁸You are good, and do good; teach me your statutes. ⁶⁹The proud have forged a lie against me: but I will keep your precepts with my whole heart. ⁷⁰Their heart is as fat as grease; but I delight in your law. ⁷¹It is good for me that I have been afflicted; that I might learn your statutes. ⁷²The law of your mouth is better to me than thousands of gold and silver. ⁷³Your hands have made me and fashioned me: give me understanding, that I may learn your commandments. ⁷⁴They that fear you will be glad when they see me; because I have hoped in your word. ⁷⁵I know, O LORD, that your judgments are right, and that you in faithfulness have afflicted me. ⁷⁶Let, I pray you, your merciful kindness be for my comfort, according to your word to your servant. ⁷⁷Let your tender mercies come to me,

that I may live: for your law is my delight. ⁷⁸Let the proud be ashamed; for they dealt perversely with me without a cause: but I will meditate in your precepts. ⁷⁹Let those that fear you turn to me, and those that have known your testimonies. ⁸⁰Let my heart be sound in your statutes; that I be not ashamed. ⁸¹My soul faints for your salvation: but I hope in your word. ⁸²My eyes fail for your word, saying, When will you comfort me? ⁸³For I am become like a bottle in the smoke; yet do I not forget your statutes. ⁸⁴How many are the days of your servant? when will you execute judgment on them that persecute me? ⁸⁵The proud have dig pits for me, which are not after your law. ⁸⁶All your commandments are faithful: they persecute me wrongfully; help you me. ⁸⁷They had almost consumed me on earth; but I forsook not your precepts. ⁸⁸Quicken me after your loving kindness; so shall I keep the testimony of your mouth. ⁸⁹For ever, O LORD, your word is settled in heaven. ⁹⁰Your faithfulness is to all generations: you have established the earth, and it stays. ⁹¹They continue this day according to your ordinances: for all are your servants. ⁹²Unless your law had been my delights, I should then have perished in my affliction. ⁹³I will never forget your precepts: for with them you have quickened me. ⁹⁴I am yours, save me: for I have sought your precepts. ⁹⁵The wicked have waited for me to destroy me: but I will consider your testimonies. ⁹⁶I have seen an end of all perfection: but your commandment is exceeding broad. ⁹⁷O how I love your law! it is my meditation all the day. ⁹⁸You through your commandments have made me wiser than my enemies: for they are ever with me. ⁹⁹I have more understanding than all my teachers: for your testimonies are my meditation. ¹⁰⁰I understand more than the ancients, because I keep your precepts. ¹⁰¹I have refrained my feet from every evil way, that I might keep your word. ¹⁰²I have not departed from your judgments: for you have taught me. ¹⁰³How sweet are your words to my taste! yes, sweeter than honey to my mouth! ¹⁰⁴Through your precepts I get understanding: therefore I hate every false way. ¹⁰⁵Your word is a lamp to my feet, and a light to my path. ¹⁰⁶I have sworn, and I will perform it, that I will keep your righteous judgments. ¹⁰⁷I am afflicted very much: quicken me, O LORD, according to your word. ¹⁰⁸Accept, I beseech you, the freewill offerings of my mouth, O LORD, and teach me your judgments. ¹⁰⁹My soul is continually in my hand: yet do I not forget your law. ¹¹⁰The wicked have laid a snare for me: yet I erred not from your precepts. ¹¹¹Your testimonies have I taken as an heritage for ever: for they are the rejoicing of my heart. ¹¹²I have inclined my heart to perform your statutes always, even to the end. ¹¹³I hate vain thoughts: but your law do I love. ¹¹⁴You are my hiding place and my shield: I hope in your word. ¹¹⁵Depart from me, you evildoers: for I will keep the commandments of my God. ¹¹⁶Uphold me according to your word, that I may live: and let me not be ashamed of my hope. ¹¹⁷Hold you me up, and I shall be safe: and I will have respect to your statutes continually. ¹¹⁸You have trodden down all them that err from your statutes: for their deceit is falsehood. ¹¹⁹You put away all the wicked of the earth like dross: therefore I love your testimonies. ¹²⁰My flesh trembles for fear of you; and I am afraid of your judgments. ¹²¹I have done judgment and justice: leave me not to my oppressors. ¹²²Be surety for your servant for good: let not the proud oppress me. ¹²³My eyes fail for your salvation, and for the word of your righteousness. ¹²⁴Deal with your servant according to your mercy, and teach me your statutes. ¹²⁵I am your servant; give me understanding, that I may know your testimonies. ¹²⁶It is time for you, LORD, to work: for they have made void your law. ¹²⁷Therefore I love your commandments above gold; yes, above fine gold. ¹²⁸Therefore I esteem all your precepts concerning all things to be right; and I hate every false way. ¹²⁹Your testimonies are wonderful: therefore does my soul keep them. ¹³⁰The entrance of your words gives light; it gives understanding to the simple. ¹³¹I opened my mouth, and panted: for I longed for your commandments. ¹³²Look you on me, and be merciful to me, as you use to do to those that love your name. ¹³³Order my steps in your word: and let not any iniquity have dominion over me. ¹³⁴Deliver me from the oppression of man: so will I keep your precepts. ¹³⁵Make your face to shine on your servant; and teach me your statutes. ¹³⁶Rivers of waters run down my eyes, because they keep not your law. ¹³⁷Righteous are you, O LORD, and upright are your judgments. ¹³⁸Your testimonies that you have commanded are righteous and very faithful. ¹³⁹My zeal has consumed me, because my enemies have forgotten your words. ¹⁴⁰Your word is very pure: therefore your servant loves it. ¹⁴¹I am small and despised: yet do not I forget your precepts. ¹⁴²Your righteousness is an everlasting righteousness, and your law is the truth. ¹⁴³Trouble and anguish have taken hold on me: yet your commandments are my delights. ¹⁴⁴The righteousness of your testimonies is everlasting: give me understanding, and I shall live. ¹⁴⁵I cried with my whole heart; hear me, O LORD: I will keep your statutes. ¹⁴⁶I cried to you; save me, and I shall keep your testimonies. ¹⁴⁷I prevented the dawning of the morning, and cried: I hoped in your word. ¹⁴⁸My eyes prevent the night watches, that I might meditate in your word. ¹⁴⁹Hear my voice according to your loving kindness: O LORD, quicken me according to your judgment. ¹⁵⁰They draw near that follow after mischief: they are far from your law. ¹⁵¹You are near, O LORD; and all your commandments are truth. ¹⁵²Concerning your testimonies, I have known of old that you have founded them for ever. ¹⁵³Consider my affliction, and deliver me: for I do not forget your law. ¹⁵⁴Plead my cause, and deliver me: quicken me according to your word. ¹⁵⁵Salvation is far from the wicked: for they seek not your statutes. ¹⁵⁶Great are your tender mercies, O LORD: quicken me according to your judgments. ¹⁵⁷Many are my persecutors and my enemies; yet do I not decline from your testimonies. ¹⁵⁸I beheld the transgressors, and was grieved; because they kept not your word. ¹⁵⁹Consider how I love your precepts: quicken me, O LORD, according to your loving kindness. ¹⁶⁰Your word is true from the beginning: and every one of your righteous judgments endures for ever. ¹⁶¹Princes have persecuted me without a cause: but my heart stands in awe of your word. ¹⁶²I rejoice at your word, as one that finds great spoil. ¹⁶³I hate and abhor lying: but your law do I love. ¹⁶⁴Seven times a day do I praise you because of your righteous judgments. ¹⁶⁵Great peace have they which love your law: and nothing shall offend them. ¹⁶⁶LORD, I have hoped for your salvation, and done your commandments. ¹⁶⁷My soul has kept your testimonies; and I love them exceedingly. ¹⁶⁸I have kept your precepts and your testimonies: for all my ways are before you. ¹⁶⁹Let my cry come near before you, O LORD: give me understanding according to your word. ¹⁷⁰Let my supplication come before you: deliver me according to your word. ¹⁷¹My lips shall utter praise, when you have taught me your statutes. ¹⁷²My tongue shall speak of your word: for all your commandments are righteousness. ¹⁷³Let your hand help me; for I have chosen your precepts. ¹⁷⁴I have longed for your salvation, O LORD; and your law is my delight. ¹⁷⁵Let my soul live, and it shall praise you; and let your judgments help me. ¹⁷⁶I have gone astray like a lost sheep; seek your servant; for I do not forget your commandments.

120 ¹In my distress I cried to the LORD, and he heard me. ²Deliver my soul, O LORD, from lying lips, and from a deceitful tongue. ³What shall be given to you? or what shall be done to you, you false tongue? ⁴Sharp arrows of the mighty, with coals of juniper. ⁵Woe is me, that I sojourn in Mesech, that I dwell in the tents of Kedar! ⁶My soul has long dwelled with him that hates peace. ⁷I am for peace: but when I speak, they are for war.

121 ¹I will lift up my eyes to the hills, from where comes my help. ²My help comes from the LORD, which made heaven and earth. ³He will not suffer your foot to be moved: he that keeps you will not slumber. ⁴Behold, he that keeps Israel shall neither slumber nor sleep. ⁵The LORD is your keeper: the LORD is your shade on your right hand. ⁶The sun shall not smite you by day, nor the moon by night. ⁷The LORD shall preserve you from all evil: he shall preserve your soul. ⁸The LORD shall preserve your going out and your coming in from this time forth, and even for ever more.

122 ¹I was glad when they said to me, Let us go into the house of the LORD. ²Our feet shall stand within your gates, O Jerusalem. ³Jerusalem is built as a city that is compact together: ⁴Where the tribes go up, the tribes of the LORD, to the testimony of Israel, to give thanks to the name of the LORD. ⁵For there are set thrones of judgment, the thrones of the house of David. ⁶Pray for the peace of Jerusalem: they shall prosper that love you. ⁷Peace be within your walls, and prosperity within your palaces. ⁸For my brothers and companions' sakes, I will now say, Peace be within you. ⁹Because of the house of the LORD our God I will seek your good.

123 ¹To you lift I up my eyes, O you that dwell in the heavens. ²Behold, as the eyes of servants look to the hand of their masters, and as the eyes of a maiden to the hand of her mistress; so our eyes wait on the LORD our God, until that he have mercy on us. ³Have mercy on us, O LORD, have mercy on us: for we are exceedingly filled with contempt. ⁴Our soul is exceedingly filled with the scorning of those that are at ease, and with the contempt of the proud.

124 ¹If it had not been the LORD who was on our side, now may Israel say; ²If it had not been the LORD who was on our side, when men rose up against us: ³Then they had swallowed us up quick, when their wrath was kindled against us: ⁴Then the waters had overwhelmed us, the stream had gone over our soul: ⁵Then the proud waters had gone over our soul. ⁶Blessed be the LORD, who has not given us as a prey to their teeth. ⁷Our soul is escaped as a bird out of the snare of the fowlers: the snare is broken, and we are escaped. ⁸Our help is in the name of the LORD, who made heaven and earth.

125 ¹They that trust in the LORD shall be as mount Zion, which cannot be removed, but stays for ever. ²As the mountains are round about Jerusalem, so the LORD is round about his people from now on even for ever. ³For the rod of the wicked shall not rest on the lot of the righteous; lest the righteous put forth their hands to iniquity. ⁴Do good, O LORD, to those that be good, and to them that are upright in their hearts. ⁵As for such as turn aside to their crooked ways, the LORD shall lead them forth with the workers of iniquity: but peace shall be on Israel.

126 ¹When the LORD turned again the captivity of Zion, we were like them that dream. ²Then was our mouth filled with laughter, and our tongue with singing: then said they among the heathen, The LORD has done great things for them. ³The LORD has done great things for us; whereof we are glad. ⁴Turn again our captivity, O LORD, as the streams in the south. ⁵They that sow in tears shall reap in joy. ⁶He that goes forth and weeps, bearing precious seed, shall doubtless come again with rejoicing, bringing his sheaves with him.

127 ¹Except the LORD build the house, they labor in vain that build it: except the LORD keep the city, the watchman wakes but in vain. ²It is vain for you to rise up early, to sit up late, to eat the bread of sorrows: for so he gives his beloved sleep. ³See, children are an heritage of the LORD: and the fruit of the womb is his reward. ⁴As arrows are in the hand of a mighty man; so are children of the youth. ⁵Happy is the man that has his quiver full of them: they shall not be ashamed, but they shall speak with the enemies in the gate.

128 ¹Blessed is every one that fears the LORD; that walks in his ways. ²For you shall eat the labor of your hands: happy shall you be, and it shall be well with you. ³Your wife shall be as a fruitful vine by the sides of your house: your children like olive plants round about your table. ⁴Behold, that thus shall the man be blessed that fears the LORD. ⁵The LORD shall bless you out of Zion: and you shall see the good of Jerusalem all the days of your life. ⁶Yes, you shall see your children's children, and peace on Israel.

129 ¹Many a time have they afflicted me from my youth, may Israel now say: ²Many a time have they afflicted me from my youth: yet they have not prevailed against me. ³The plowers plowed on my back: they made long their furrows. ⁴The LORD is righteous: he has cut asunder the cords of the wicked. ⁵Let them all be confounded and turned back that hate Zion. ⁶Let them be as the grass on the housetops, which wither before it grows up: ⁷With which the mower fills not his hand; nor he that binds sheaves his bosom. ⁸Neither do they which go by say, The blessing of the LORD be on you: we bless you in the name of the LORD.

130 ¹Out of the depths have I cried to you, O LORD. ²Lord, hear my voice: let your ears be attentive to the voice of my supplications. ³If you, LORD, should mark iniquities, O Lord, who shall stand? ⁴But there is forgiveness with you, that you may be feared. ⁵I wait for the LORD, my soul does wait, and in his word do I hope. ⁶My soul waits for the Lord more than they that watch for the morning: I say, more than they that watch for the morning. ⁷Let Israel hope in the LORD: for with the LORD there is mercy, and with him is plenteous redemption. ⁸And he shall redeem Israel from all his iniquities.

131 ¹Lord, my heart is not haughty, nor my eyes lofty: neither do I exercise myself in great matters, or in things too high for me. ²Surely I have behaved and quieted myself, as a child that is weaned of his mother: my soul is even as a weaned child. ³Let Israel hope in the LORD from now on and for ever.

132 ¹Lord, remember David, and all his afflictions: ²How he swore to the LORD, and vowed to the mighty God of Jacob; ³Surely I will not come into the tabernacle of my house, nor go up into my bed; ⁴I will not give sleep to my eyes, or slumber to my eyelids, ⁵Until I find out a place for the LORD, an habitation for the mighty God of Jacob. ⁶See, we heard of it at Ephratah: we found it in the fields of the wood. ⁷We will go into his tabernacles: we will worship at his footstool. ⁸Arise, O LORD, into your rest; you, and the ark of your strength. ⁹Let your priests be clothed with righteousness; and let your saints shout for joy. ¹⁰For your servant David's sake turn not away the face of your anointed. ¹¹The LORD has sworn in truth to David; he will not turn from it; Of the fruit of your body will I set on your throne. ¹²If your children will keep my covenant and my testimony that I shall teach them, their children shall also sit on your throne for ever more. ¹³For the LORD has chosen Zion; he has desired it for his habitation. ¹⁴This is my rest for ever: here will I dwell; for I have desired it. ¹⁵I will abundantly bless her provision: I will satisfy her poor with bread. ¹⁶I will also clothe her priests with salvation: and her saints shall shout aloud for joy. ¹⁷There will I make the horn of David to bud: I have ordained a lamp for my anointed. ¹⁸His enemies will I clothe with shame: but on himself shall his crown flourish.

133 ¹Behold, how good and how pleasant it is for brothers to dwell together in unity! ²It is like the precious ointment on the head, that ran down on the beard, even Aaron's beard: that went down to the skirts of his garments; ³As the dew of Hermon, and as the dew that descended on the mountains of Zion: for there the LORD commanded the blessing, even life for ever more.

134 ¹Behold, bless you the LORD, all you servants of the LORD, which by night stand in the house of the LORD. ²Lift up your hands in the sanctuary, and bless the LORD. ³The LORD that made heaven and earth bless you out of Zion.

135 ¹Praise you the LORD. Praise you the name of the LORD; praise him, O you servants of the LORD. ²You that stand in the house of the LORD, in the courts of the house of our God. ³Praise the LORD; for the LORD is good: sing praises to his name; for it is pleasant. ⁴For the LORD has chosen Jacob to himself, and Israel for his peculiar treasure. ⁵For I know that the LORD is great, and that our Lord is above all gods. ⁶Whatever the LORD pleased, that did he in heaven, and in earth, in the seas, and all deep places. ⁷He causes the vapors to ascend from the ends of the earth; he makes lightning for the rain; he brings the wind out of his treasuries. ⁸Who smote the firstborn of Egypt, both of man and beast. ⁹Who sent tokens and wonders into the middle of you, O Egypt, on Pharaoh, and on all his servants. ¹⁰Who smote great nations, and slew mighty kings; ¹¹Sihon king of the Amorites, and Og king of Bashan, and all the kingdoms of Canaan: ¹²And gave their land for an heritage, an heritage to Israel his people. ¹³Your name, O LORD, endures for ever; and your memorial, O LORD, throughout all generations. ¹⁴For the LORD will judge his people, and he will repent himself concerning his servants. ¹⁵The idols of the heathen are silver and gold, the work of men's hands. ¹⁶They have mouths, but they speak not; eyes have they, but they see not; ¹⁷They have ears, but they hear not; neither is there any breath in their mouths. ¹⁸They that make them are like to them: so is every one that trusts in them. ¹⁹Bless the LORD, O house of Israel: bless the LORD, O house of Aaron: ²⁰Bless the LORD, O house of Levi: you that fear the LORD, bless the LORD. ²¹Blessed be the LORD out of Zion, which dwells at Jerusalem. Praise you the LORD.

136 ¹O give thanks to the LORD; for he is good: for his mercy endures for ever. ²O give thanks to the God of gods: for his mercy endures for ever. ³O give thanks to the Lord of lords: for his mercy endures for ever. ⁴To him who alone does great wonders: for his mercy endures for ever. ⁵To him that by wisdom made the heavens: for his mercy endures for ever. ⁶To him that stretched out the earth above the waters: for his mercy endures for ever. ⁷To him that made great lights: for his mercy endures for ever: ⁸The sun to rule by day: for his mercy endures for ever: ⁹The moon and stars to rule by night: for his mercy endures for ever. ¹⁰To him that smote Egypt in their firstborn: for his mercy endures for ever: ¹¹And brought out Israel from among them: for his mercy endures for ever: ¹²With a strong hand, and with a stretched out arm: for his mercy endures for ever. ¹³To him which divided the Red sea into parts: for his mercy endures for ever: ¹⁴And made Israel to pass through the middle of it: for his mercy endures for ever: ¹⁵But overthrew Pharaoh and his host in the Red sea: for his mercy endures for ever. ¹⁶To him which led his people through the wilderness: for his mercy endures for ever. ¹⁷To him which smote great kings: for his mercy endures for ever: ¹⁸And slew famous kings: for his mercy endures for ever: ¹⁹Sihon king of the Amorites: for his mercy endures for ever: ²⁰And Og the king of Bashan: for his mercy endures for ever: ²¹And gave their land for an heritage: for his mercy endures for ever: ²²Even an heritage to Israel his servant: for his mercy endures for ever. ²³Who remembered us in our low estate: for his mercy endures for ever: ²⁴And has redeemed us from our enemies: for his mercy endures for ever. ²⁵Who gives food to all flesh: for his mercy endures for ever. ²⁶O give thanks to the God of heaven: for his mercy endures for ever.

137 ¹By the rivers of Babylon, there we sat down, yes, we wept, when we remembered Zion. ²We hanged our harps on the willows in the middle thereof. ³For there they that carried us away captive required of us a song; and they that wasted us required of us mirth, saying, Sing us one of the songs of Zion. ⁴How shall we sing the LORD's song in a strange land? ⁵If I forget you, O Jerusalem, let my right hand forget her cunning. ⁶If I do not remember you, let my tongue stick to the roof of my mouth; if I prefer not Jerusalem above my chief joy. ⁷Remember, O LORD, the children of Edom in the day of Jerusalem; who said, Raze it, raze it, even to the foundation thereof. ⁸O daughter of Babylon, who are to be destroyed; happy shall he be, that rewards you as you have served us. ⁹Happy shall he be, that takes and dashes your little ones against the stones.

138 ¹I will praise you with my whole heart: before the gods will I sing praise to you. ²I will worship toward your holy temple, and praise your name for your loving kindness and for your truth: for you have magnified your word above all your name. ³In the day when I cried you answered me, and strengthened me with strength in my soul. ⁴All the kings of the earth shall praise you, O LORD, when they hear the words of your mouth. ⁵Yes, they shall sing in the ways of the LORD: for great is the glory of the LORD. ⁶Though the LORD be high, yet has he respect to the lowly: but the proud he knows afar off. ⁷Though I walk in the middle of trouble, you will revive me: you shall stretch forth your hand against the wrath of my enemies, and your right hand shall save me. ⁸The LORD will perfect that which concerns me: your mercy, O LORD, endures for ever: forsake not the works of your own hands.

139 ¹O lord, you have searched me, and known me. ²You know my sitting down and my rising up, you understand my thought afar off. ³You compass my path and my lying down, and are acquainted with all my ways. ⁴For there is not a word in my tongue, but, see, O LORD, you know it altogether. ⁵You have beset me behind and before, and laid your hand on me. ⁶Such knowledge is too wonderful for me; it is high, I cannot attain to it. ⁷Where shall I go from your spirit? or where shall I flee from your presence? ⁸If I ascend up into heaven, you are there: if I make my bed in hell, behold, you are there. ⁹If I take the wings of the morning, and dwell in the uttermost parts of the sea; ¹⁰Even there shall your hand lead me, and your right hand shall hold me. ¹¹If I say, Surely the darkness shall cover me; even the night shall be light about me. ¹²Yes, the darkness hides not from you; but the night shines as the day: the darkness and the light are both alike to you. ¹³For you have possessed my reins: you have covered me in my mother's womb. ¹⁴I will praise you; for I am fearfully and wonderfully made: marvelous are your works; and that my soul knows right well. ¹⁵My substance was not hid from you, when I was made in secret, and curiously worked in the lowest parts of the earth. ¹⁶Your eyes did see my substance, yet being imperfect; and in your book all my members were written, which in continuance were fashioned, when as yet there was none of them. ¹⁷How precious also are your thoughts to me, O God! how great is the sum of them! ¹⁸If I should count them, they are more in number than the sand: when I awake, I am still with you. ¹⁹Surely you will slay the wicked, O God: depart from me therefore, you bloody men. ²⁰For they speak against you wickedly, and your enemies take your name in vain. ²¹Do not I hate them, O LORD, that hate you? and am not I grieved with those that rise up against you? ²²I hate them with perfect hatred: I count them my enemies. ²³Search me, O God, and know my heart: try me, and know my thoughts: ²⁴And see if there be any wicked way in me, and lead me in the way everlasting.

140 ¹Deliver me, O LORD, from the evil man: preserve me from the violent man; ²Which imagine mischiefs in their heart; continually are they gathered together for war. ³They have sharpened their tongues like a serpent; adders' poison is under their lips. Selah. ⁴Keep me, O LORD, from the hands of the wicked; preserve me from the violent man; who have purposed to overthrow my goings. ⁵The proud have hid a snare for me, and cords; they have spread a net by the wayside; they have set gins for me. Selah. ⁶I said to the LORD, You are my God: hear the voice of my supplications, O LORD. ⁷O GOD the Lord, the strength of my salvation, you have covered my head in the day of battle. ⁸Grant not, O LORD, the desires of the wicked: further not his wicked device; lest they exalt themselves. Selah. ⁹As for the head of those that compass me about, let the mischief of their own lips cover them. ¹⁰Let burning coals fall on them: let them be cast into the fire; into deep pits, that they rise not up again. ¹¹Let not an evil speaker be established in the earth: evil shall hunt the violent man to overthrow him. ¹²I know that the LORD will maintain the cause of the afflicted, and the right of the poor. ¹³Surely the righteous shall give thanks to your name: the upright shall dwell in your presence.

141 ¹Lord, I cry to you: make haste to me; give ear to my voice, when I cry to you. ²Let my prayer be set forth before you as incense; and the lifting up of my hands as the evening sacrifice. ³Set a watch, O LORD, before my mouth; keep the door of my lips. ⁴Incline not my heart to any evil thing, to practice wicked works with men that work iniquity: and let me not eat of their dainties. ⁵Let the righteous smite me; it shall be a kindness: and let him reprove me; it shall be an excellent oil, which shall not break my head: for yet my prayer also shall be in their calamities. ⁶When their judges are overthrown in stony places, they shall hear my words; for they are sweet. ⁷Our bones are scattered at the grave's mouth, as when one cuts and splits wood on the earth. ⁸But my eyes are to you, O GOD the Lord: in you is my trust; leave not my soul destitute. ⁹Keep me from the snares which they have laid for me, and the gins of the workers of iniquity. ¹⁰Let the wicked fall into their own nets, whilst that I with escape.

142 ¹I cried to the LORD with my voice; with my voice to the LORD did I make my supplication. ²I poured out my complaint before him; I showed before him my trouble. ³When my spirit was overwhelmed within me, then you knew my path. In the way wherein I walked have they privately laid a snare for me. ⁴I looked on my right hand, and beheld, but there was no man that would know me: refuge failed me; no man cared for my soul. ⁵I cried to you, O LORD: I said, You are my refuge and my portion in the land of the living. ⁶Attend to my cry; for I am brought very low: deliver me from my persecutors; for they are stronger than I. ⁷Bring my soul out of prison, that I may praise your name: the righteous shall compass me about; for you shall deal bountifully with me.

143 ¹Hear my prayer, O LORD, give ear to my supplications: in your faithfulness answer me, and in your righteousness. ²And enter not into judgment with your servant: for in your sight shall no man living be justified. ³For the enemy has persecuted my soul; he has smitten my life down to the ground; he has made me to dwell in darkness, as those that have been long dead. ⁴Therefore is my spirit overwhelmed within me; my heart within me is desolate. ⁵I remember the days of old; I meditate on all your works; I muse on the work of your hands. ⁶I stretch forth my hands to you: my soul thirsts after you, as a thirsty land. Selah. ⁷Hear me speedily, O LORD: my spirit fails: hide not your face from me, lest I be like to them that go down into the pit. ⁸Cause me to hear your loving kindness in the morning; for in you do I trust: cause me to know the way wherein I should walk; for I lift up my soul to you. ⁹Deliver me, O LORD, from my enemies: I flee to you to hide me. ¹⁰Teach me to do your will; for you are my God: your spirit is good; lead me into the land of uprightness. ¹¹Quicken me, O LORD, for your name's sake: for your righteousness' sake bring my soul out of trouble. ¹²And of your mercy cut off my enemies, and destroy all them that afflict my soul: for I am your servant.

144 ¹Blessed be the LORD my strength which teaches my hands to war, and my fingers to fight: ²My goodness, and my fortress; my high tower, and my deliverer; my shield, and he in whom I trust; who subdues my people under me. ³LORD, what is man, that you take knowledge of him! or the son of man, that you make account of him! ⁴Man is like to vanity: his days are as a shadow that passes away. ⁵Bow your heavens, O LORD, and come down: touch the mountains, and they shall smoke. ⁶Cast forth lightning, and scatter them: shoot out your arrows, and destroy them. ⁷Send your hand from above; rid me, and deliver me out of great waters, from the hand of strange children; ⁸Whose mouth speaks vanity, and their right hand is a right hand of falsehood. ⁹I will sing a new song to you, O God: on a psaltery and an instrument of ten strings will I sing praises to you. ¹⁰It is he that gives salvation to kings: who delivers David his servant from the hurtful sword. ¹¹Rid me, and deliver me from the hand of strange children, whose mouth speaks vanity, and their right hand is a right hand of falsehood: ¹²That our sons may be as plants grown up in their youth; that our daughters may be as corner stones, polished after the similitude of a palace: ¹³That our garners may be full, affording all manner of store: that our sheep may bring forth thousands and ten thousands in our streets: ¹⁴That our oxen may be strong to labor; that there be no breaking in, nor going out; that there be no complaining in our streets. ¹⁵Happy is that people, that is in such a case: yes, happy is that people, whose God is the LORD.

145 ¹I will extol you, my God, O king; and I will bless your name for ever and ever. ²Every day will I bless you; and I will praise your name for ever and ever. ³Great is the LORD, and greatly to be praised; and his greatness is unsearchable. ⁴One generation shall praise your works to another, and shall declare your mighty acts. ⁵I will speak of the glorious honor of your majesty, and of your wondrous works. ⁶And men shall speak of the might of your terrible acts: and I will declare your greatness. ⁷They shall abundantly utter the memory of your great goodness, and shall sing of your righteousness. ⁸The LORD is gracious, and full of compassion; slow to anger, and of great mercy. ⁹The LORD is good to all: and his tender mercies are over all his works. ¹⁰All your works shall praise you, O LORD; and your saints shall bless you. ¹¹They shall speak of the glory of your kingdom, and talk of your power; ¹²To make known to the sons of men his mighty acts, and the glorious majesty of his kingdom. ¹³Your kingdom is an everlasting kingdom, and your dominion endures throughout all generations. ¹⁴The LORD upholds all that fall, and raises up all those that be bowed down. ¹⁵The eyes of all wait on you; and you give them their meat in due season. ¹⁶You open your hand, and satisfy the desire of every living thing. ¹⁷The LORD is righteous in all his ways, and holy in all his works. ¹⁸The LORD is near to all them that call on him, to all that call on him in truth. ¹⁹He will fulfill the desire of them that fear him: he also will hear their cry, and will save them. ²⁰The LORD preserves all them that love him: but all the wicked will he destroy. ²¹My mouth shall speak the praise of the LORD: and let all flesh bless his holy name for ever and ever.

146 ¹Praise you the LORD. Praise the LORD, O my soul. ²While I live will I praise the LORD: I will sing praises to my God while I have any being. ³Put not your trust in princes, nor in the son of man, in whom there is no help. ⁴His breath goes forth, he returns to his earth; in that very day his thoughts perish. ⁵Happy is he that has the God of Jacob for his help, whose hope is in the LORD his God: ⁶Which made heaven, and earth, the sea, and all that therein is: which keeps truth for ever: ⁷Which executes judgment for the oppressed: which gives food to the hungry. The LORD looses the prisoners: ⁸The LORD opens the eyes of the blind: the LORD raises them that are bowed down: the LORD loves the righteous: ⁹The LORD preserves the strangers; he relieves the fatherless and widow: but the way of the wicked he turns upside down. ¹⁰The LORD shall reign for ever, even your God, O Zion, to all generations. Praise you the LORD.

147 ¹Praise you the LORD: for it is good to sing praises to our God; for it is pleasant; and praise is comely. ²The LORD does build up Jerusalem: he gathers together the outcasts of Israel. ³He heals the broken in heart, and binds up their wounds. ⁴He tells the number of the stars; he calls them all by their names. ⁵Great is our Lord, and of great power: his understanding is infinite. ⁶The LORD lifts up the meek: he casts the wicked down to the ground. ⁷Sing to the LORD with thanksgiving; sing praise on the harp to our God: ⁸Who covers the heaven with clouds, who prepares rain for the earth, who makes grass to grow on the mountains. ⁹He gives to the beast his food, and to the young ravens which cry. ¹⁰He delights not in the strength of the horse: he takes not pleasure in the legs of a man. ¹¹The

LORD takes pleasure in them that fear him, in those that hope in his mercy. ¹²Praise the LORD, O Jerusalem; praise your God, O Zion. ¹³For he has strengthened the bars of your gates; he has blessed your children within you. ¹⁴He makes peace in your borders, and fills you with the finest of the wheat. ¹⁵He sends forth his commandment on earth: his word runs very swiftly. ¹⁶He gives snow like wool: he scatters the hoarfrost like ashes. ¹⁷He casts forth his ice like morsels: who can stand before his cold? ¹⁸He sends out his word, and melts them: he causes his wind to blow, and the waters flow. ¹⁹He shows his word to Jacob, his statutes and his judgments to Israel. ²⁰He has not dealt so with any nation: and as for his judgments, they have not known them. Praise you the LORD.

148 ¹Praise you the LORD. Praise you the LORD from the heavens: praise him in the heights. ²Praise you him, all his angels: praise you him, all his hosts. ³Praise you him, sun and moon: praise him, all you stars of light. ⁴Praise him, you heavens of heavens, and you waters that be above the heavens. ⁵Let them praise the name of the LORD: for he commanded, and they were created. ⁶He has also established them for ever and ever: he has made a decree which shall not pass. ⁷Praise the LORD from the earth, you dragons, and all deeps: ⁸Fire, and hail; snow, and vapors; stormy wind fulfilling his word: ⁹Mountains, and all hills; fruitful trees, and all cedars: ¹⁰Beasts, and all cattle; creeping things, and flying fowl: ¹¹Kings of the earth, and all people; princes, and all judges of the earth: ¹²Both young men, and maidens; old men, and children: ¹³Let them praise the name of the LORD: for his name alone is excellent; his glory is above the earth and heaven. ¹⁴He also exalts the horn of his people, the praise of all his saints; even of the children of Israel, a people near to him. Praise you the LORD.

149 ¹Praise you the LORD. Sing to the LORD a new song, and his praise in the congregation of saints. ²Let Israel rejoice in him that made him: let the children of Zion be joyful in their King. ³Let them praise his name in the dance: let them sing praises to him with the tambourine and harp. ⁴For the LORD takes pleasure in his people: he will beautify the meek with salvation. ⁵Let the saints be joyful in glory: let them sing aloud on their beds. ⁶Let the high praises of God be in their mouth, and a two-edged sword in their hand; ⁷To execute vengeance on the heathen, and punishments on the people; ⁸To bind their kings with chains, and their nobles with fetters of iron; ⁹To execute on them the judgment written: this honor have all his saints. Praise you the LORD.

150 ¹Praise you the LORD. Praise God in his sanctuary: praise him in the firmament of his power. ²Praise him for his mighty acts: praise him according to his excellent greatness. ³Praise him with the sound of the trumpet: praise him with the psaltery and harp. ⁴Praise him with the tambourine and dance: praise him with stringed instruments and organs. ⁵Praise him on the loud cymbals: praise him on the high sounding cymbals. ⁶Let every thing that has breath praise the LORD. Praise you the LORD.

Proverbs

1 ¹The proverbs of Solomon the son of David, king of Israel; ²To know wisdom and instruction; to perceive the words of understanding; ³To receive the instruction of wisdom, justice, and judgment, and equity; ⁴To give subtlety to the simple, to the young man knowledge and discretion. ⁵A wise man will hear, and will increase learning; and a man of understanding shall attain to wise counsels: ⁶To understand a proverb, and the interpretation; the words of the wise, and their dark sayings. ⁷The fear of the LORD is the beginning of knowledge: but fools despise wisdom and instruction. ⁸My son, hear the instruction of your father, and forsake not the law of your mother: ⁹For they shall be an ornament of grace to your head, and chains about your neck. ¹⁰My son, if sinners entice you, consent you not. ¹¹If they say, Come with us, let us lay wait for blood, let us lurk privately for the innocent without cause: ¹²Let us swallow them up alive as the grave; and whole, as those that go down into the pit: ¹³We shall find all precious substance, we shall fill our houses with spoil: ¹⁴Cast in your lot among us; let us all have one purse: ¹⁵My son, walk not you in the way with them; refrain your foot from their path: ¹⁶For their feet run to evil, and make haste to shed blood. ¹⁷Surely in vain the net is spread in the sight of any bird. ¹⁸And they lay wait for their own blood; they lurk privately for their own lives. ¹⁹So are the ways of every one that is greedy of gain; which takes away the life of the owners thereof. ²⁰Wisdom cries without; she utters her voice in the streets: ²¹She cries in the chief place of concourse, in the openings of the gates: in the city she utters her words, saying, ²²How long, you simple ones, will you love simplicity? and the scorners delight in their scorning, and fools hate knowledge? ²³Turn you at my reproof: behold, I will pour out my spirit to you, I will make known my words to you. ²⁴Because I have called, and you refused; I have stretched out my hand, and no man regarded; ²⁵But you have set at nothing all my counsel, and would none of my reproof: ²⁶I also will laugh at your calamity; I will mock when your fear comes; ²⁷When your fear comes as desolation, and your destruction comes as a whirlwind; when distress and anguish comes on you. ²⁸Then shall they call on me, but I will not answer; they shall seek me early, but they shall not find me: ²⁹For that they hated knowledge, and did not choose the fear of the LORD: ³⁰They would none of my counsel: they despised all my reproof. ³¹Therefore shall they eat of the fruit of their own way, and be filled with their own devices. ³²For the turning away of the simple shall slay them, and the prosperity of fools shall destroy them. ³³But whoever listens to me shall dwell safely, and shall be quiet from fear of evil.

2 ¹My son, if you will receive my words, and hide my commandments with you; ²So that you incline your ear to wisdom, and apply your heart to understanding; ³Yes, if you cry after knowledge, and lift up your voice for understanding; ⁴If you seek her as silver, and search for her as for hid treasures; ⁵Then shall you understand the fear of the LORD, and find the knowledge of God. ⁶For the LORD gives wisdom: out of his mouth comes knowledge and understanding. ⁷He lays up sound wisdom for the righteous: he is a buckler to them that walk uprightly. ⁸He keeps the paths of judgment, and preserves the way of his saints. ⁹Then shall you understand righteousness, and judgment, and equity; yes, every good path. ¹⁰When wisdom enters into your heart, and knowledge is pleasant to your soul; ¹¹Discretion shall preserve you, understanding shall keep you: ¹²To deliver you from the way of the evil man, from the man that speaks fraudulent things; ¹³Who leave the paths of uprightness, to walk in the ways of darkness; ¹⁴Who rejoice to do evil, and delight in the frowardness of the wicked; ¹⁵Whose ways are crooked, and they fraudulent in their paths: ¹⁶To deliver you from the strange woman, even from the stranger which flatters with her words; ¹⁷Which forsakes the guide of her youth, and forgets the covenant of her God. ¹⁸For her house inclines to death, and her paths to the dead. ¹⁹None that go to her return again, neither take they hold of the paths of life. ²⁰That you may walk in the way of good men, and keep the paths of the righteous. ²¹For the upright shall dwell in the land, and the perfect shall remain in it. ²²But the wicked shall be cut off from the earth, and the transgressors shall be rooted out of it.

3 ¹My son, forget not my law; but let your heart keep my commandments: ²For length of days, and long life, and peace, shall they add to you. ³Let not mercy and truth forsake you: bind them about your neck; write them on the table of your heart: ⁴So shall you find favor and good understanding in the sight of God and man. ⁵Trust in the LORD with all your heart; and lean not to your own understanding. ⁶In all your ways acknowledge him, and he shall direct your paths. ⁷Be not wise in your own eyes: fear the LORD, and depart from evil. ⁸It shall be health to your navel, and marrow to your bones. ⁹Honor the LORD with your substance, and with the first fruits of all your increase: ¹⁰So shall your barns be filled with plenty, and your presses shall burst out with new wine. ¹¹My son, despise not the chastening of the LORD; neither be weary of his correction: ¹²For whom the LORD loves he corrects; even as a father the son in whom he delights. ¹³Happy is the man that finds wisdom, and the man that gets understanding. ¹⁴For the merchandise of it is better than the merchandise of silver, and the gain thereof than fine gold. ¹⁵She is more precious than rubies: and all the things you can desire are not to be compared to her. ¹⁶Length of days is in her right hand; and in her left hand riches and honor. ¹⁷Her ways are ways of pleasantness, and all her paths are peace. ¹⁸She is a tree of life to them that lay hold on her: and happy is every one that retains her. ¹⁹The LORD by wisdom has founded the earth; by understanding has he established the heavens. ²⁰By his knowledge the depths are broken up, and the clouds drop down the dew. ²¹My son, let not them depart from your eyes: keep sound wisdom and discretion: ²²So shall they be life to your soul, and grace to your neck. ²³Then shall you walk in your way safely, and your foot shall not stumble. ²⁴When you lie down, you shall not be afraid: yes, you shall lie down, and your sleep shall be sweet. ²⁵Be not afraid of sudden fear, neither of the desolation of the wicked, when it comes. ²⁶For the LORD shall be your confidence, and shall keep your foot from being taken. ²⁷Withhold not good from them to whom it is due, when it is in the power of your hand to do it. ²⁸Say not to your neighbor, Go, and come again, and to morrow I will give; when you have it by you. ²⁹Devise not evil against your neighbor, seeing he dwells securely by you. ³⁰Strive not with a man without cause, if he have done you no harm. ³¹Envy you not the oppressor, and choose none of his ways. ³²For the fraudulent is abomination to the LORD: but his secret is with the righteous. ³³The curse of the LORD is in the house of the wicked: but he blesses the habitation of the just. ³⁴Surely he scorns the scorners: but he gives grace to the lowly. ³⁵The wise shall inherit glory: but shame shall be the promotion of fools.

4 ¹Hear, you children, the instruction of a father, and attend to know understanding. ²For I give you good doctrine, forsake you not my law. ³For I was my father's son, tender and only beloved in the sight of my mother. ⁴He taught me also, and said to me, Let your heart retain my words: keep my commandments, and live. ⁵Get wisdom, get understanding: forget it not; neither decline from the words of my mouth. ⁶Forsake her not, and she shall preserve you: love her, and she shall keep you. ⁷Wisdom is the principal thing; therefore get wisdom: and with all your getting get understanding. ⁸Exalt her, and she shall promote you: she shall bring you to honor, when you do embrace her. ⁹She shall give to your head an ornament of grace: a crown of glory shall she deliver to you. ¹⁰Hear, O my son, and receive my sayings; and the years of your life shall be many. ¹¹I have taught you in the way of wisdom; I have led you in right paths. ¹²When you go, your steps shall not be straitened; and when you run, you shall not stumble. ¹³Take fast hold of instruction; let her not go: keep her; for she is your life. ¹⁴Enter not into the path of the wicked, and go not in the way of evil men. ¹⁵Avoid it, pass not by it, turn from it, and pass away. ¹⁶For they sleep not, except they have done mischief; and their sleep is taken away, unless they cause some to fall. ¹⁷For they eat the bread of wickedness, and drink the wine of violence. ¹⁸But the path of the just is as the shining light, that shines more and more to the perfect day. ¹⁹The way of the wicked is as darkness: they know not at what they stumble. ²⁰My son, attend to my words; incline your ear to my sayings. ²¹Let them not depart from your eyes; keep them in the middle of your heart. ²²For they are life to those that find them, and health to all their flesh. ²³Keep your heart with all diligence; for out of it are the issues of life. ²⁴Put away from you a fraudulent mouth, and perverse lips put far from you. ²⁵Let your eyes look right on, and let your eyelids look straight before you. ²⁶Ponder the path of your feet, and let all your ways be established. ²⁷Turn not to the right hand nor to the left: remove your foot from evil.

5 ¹My son, attend to my wisdom, and bow your ear to my understanding: ²That you may regard discretion, and that your lips may keep knowledge. ³For the lips of a strange woman drop as an honeycomb, and her mouth is smoother than oil: ⁴But her end is bitter as wormwood, sharp as a two-edged sword. ⁵Her feet go down to death; her steps take hold on hell. ⁶Lest you should ponder the path of life, her ways are moveable, that you can not know them. ⁷Hear me now therefore, O you children, and depart not from the words of my mouth. ⁸Remove your way far from her, and come not near the door of her house: ⁹Lest you give your honor to others, and your years to the cruel: ¹⁰Lest strangers be filled with your wealth; and your labors be in the house of a stranger; ¹¹And you mourn at the last, when your flesh and your body are consumed, ¹²And say, How have I hated instruction, and my heart despised reproof; ¹³And have not obeyed the voice of my teachers, nor inclined my ear to them that instructed me! ¹⁴I was almost in all evil in the middle of the congregation and assembly. ¹⁵Drink waters out of your own cistern, and running waters out of your own well. ¹⁶Let your fountains be dispersed abroad, and rivers of waters in the streets. ¹⁷Let them be only your own, and not strangers' with you. ¹⁸Let your fountain be blessed: and rejoice with the wife of your youth. ¹⁹Let her be as the loving hind and pleasant roe; let her breasts satisfy you at all times; and be you ravished always with her love. ²⁰And why will you, my son, be ravished with a strange woman, and embrace the bosom of a stranger? ²¹For the ways of man are before the eyes of the LORD, and he ponders all his goings. ²²His own iniquities shall take the wicked himself, and he shall be held with the cords of his sins. ²³He shall die without instruction; and in the greatness of his folly he shall go astray.

6 ¹My son, if you be surety for your friend, if you have stricken your hand with a stranger, ²You are snared with the words of your mouth, you are taken with the words of your mouth. ³Do this now, my son, and deliver yourself, when you are come into the hand of your friend; go, humble yourself, and make sure your friend. ⁴Give not sleep to your eyes, nor slumber to your eyelids. ⁵Deliver yourself as a roe from the hand of the hunter, and as a bird from the hand of the fowler. ⁶Go to the ant, you sluggard; consider her ways, and be wise: ⁷Which having no guide, overseer, or ruler, ⁸Provides her meat in the summer, and gathers her food in the harvest. ⁹How long will you sleep, O sluggard? when will you arise out of your sleep? ¹⁰Yet a little sleep, a little slumber, a little folding of the hands to sleep: ¹¹So shall your poverty come as one that travels, and your want as an armed man. ¹²A naughty person, a wicked man, walks with a fraudulent mouth. ¹³He winks with his eyes, he speaks with his feet, he teaches with his fingers; ¹⁴Frowardness is in his heart, he devises mischief continually; he sows discord. ¹⁵Therefore shall his calamity come suddenly; suddenly shall he be broken without remedy. ¹⁶These six things does the LORD hate: yes, seven are an abomination to him: ¹⁷A proud look, a lying tongue, and hands that shed innocent blood, ¹⁸An heart that devises wicked imaginations, feet that be swift in running to mischief, ¹⁹A false witness that speaks lies, and he that sows discord among brothers. ²⁰My son, keep your father's commandment, and forsake not the law of your mother: ²¹Bind them continually on your heart, and tie them about your neck. ²²When you go, it shall lead you; when you sleep, it shall keep you; and when you wake, it shall talk with you. ²³For the commandment is a lamp; and the law is light; and reproofs of instruction are the way of life: ²⁴To keep you from the evil woman, from the flattery of the tongue of a strange woman. ²⁵Lust not after her beauty in your heart; neither let her take you with her eyelids. ²⁶For by means of a whorish woman a man is brought to a piece of bread: and the adulteress will hunt for the precious life. ²⁷Can a man take fire in his bosom, and his clothes not be

burned? ²⁸Can one go on hot coals, and his feet not be burned? ²⁹So he that goes in to his neighbor's wife; whoever touches her shall not be innocent. ³⁰Men do not despise a thief, if he steal to satisfy his soul when he is hungry; ³¹But if he be found, he shall restore sevenfold; he shall give all the substance of his house. ³²But whoever commits adultery with a woman lacks understanding: he that does it destroys his own soul. ³³A wound and dishonor shall he get; and his reproach shall not be wiped away. ³⁴For jealousy is the rage of a man: therefore he will not spare in the day of vengeance. ³⁵He will not regard any ransom; neither will he rest content, though you give many gifts.

7 ¹My son, keep my words, and lay up my commandments with you. ²Keep my commandments, and live; and my law as the apple of your eye. ³Bind them on your fingers, write them on the table of your heart. ⁴Say to wisdom, You are my sister; and call understanding your kinswoman: ⁵That they may keep you from the strange woman, from the stranger which flatters with her words. ⁶For at the window of my house I looked through my casement, ⁷And beheld among the simple ones, I discerned among the youths, a young man void of understanding, ⁸Passing through the street near her corner; and he went the way to her house, ⁹In the twilight, in the evening, in the black and dark night: ¹⁰And, behold, there met him a woman with the attire of an harlot, and subtle of heart. ¹¹(She is loud and stubborn; her feet abide not in her house: ¹²Now is she without, now in the streets, and lies in wait at every corner.) ¹³So she caught him, and kissed him, and with an impudent face said to him, ¹⁴I have peace offerings with me; this day have I paid my vows. ¹⁵Therefore came I forth to meet you, diligently to seek your face, and I have found you. ¹⁶I have decked my bed with coverings of tapestry, with carved works, with fine linen of Egypt. ¹⁷I have perfumed my bed with myrrh, aloes, and cinnamon. ¹⁸Come, let us take our fill of love until the morning: let us solace ourselves with loves. ¹⁹For the manager is not at home, he is gone a long journey: ²⁰He has taken a bag of money with him, and will come home at the day appointed. ²¹With her much fair speech she caused him to yield, with the flattering of her lips she forced him. ²²He goes after her straightway, as an ox goes to the slaughter, or as a fool to the correction of the stocks; ²³Till a dart strike through his liver; as a bird hastens to the snare, and knows not that it is for his life. ²⁴Listen to me now therefore, O you children, and attend to the words of my mouth. ²⁵Let not your heart decline to her ways, go not astray in her paths. ²⁶For she has cast down many wounded: yes, many strong men have been slain by her. ²⁷Her house is the way to hell, going down to the chambers of death.

8 ¹Does not wisdom cry? and understanding put forth her voice? ²She stands in the top of high places, by the way in the places of the paths. ³She cries at the gates, at the entry of the city, at the coming in at the doors. ⁴To you, O men, I call; and my voice is to the sons of man. ⁵O you simple, understand wisdom: and, you fools, be you of an understanding heart. ⁶Hear; for I will speak of excellent things; and the opening of my lips shall be right things. ⁷For my mouth shall speak truth; and wickedness is an abomination to my lips. ⁸All the words of my mouth are in righteousness; there is nothing fraudulent or perverse in them. ⁹They are all plain to him that understands, and right to them that find knowledge. ¹⁰Receive my instruction, and not silver; and knowledge rather than choice gold. ¹¹For wisdom is better than rubies; and all the things that may be desired are not to be compared to it. ¹²I wisdom dwell with prudence, and find out knowledge of witty inventions. ¹³The fear of the LORD is to hate evil: pride, and arrogance, and the evil way, and the fraudulent mouth, do I hate. ¹⁴Counsel is mine, and sound wisdom: I am understanding; I have strength. ¹⁵By me kings reign, and princes decree justice. ¹⁶By me princes rule, and nobles, even all the judges of the earth. ¹⁷I love them that love me; and those that seek me early shall find me. ¹⁸Riches and honor are with me; yes, durable riches and righteousness. ¹⁹My fruit is better than gold, yes, than fine gold; and my revenue than choice silver. ²⁰I lead in the way of righteousness, in the middle of the paths of judgment: ²¹That I may cause those that love me to inherit substance; and I will fill their treasures. ²²The LORD possessed me in the beginning of his way, before his works of old. ²³I was set up from everlasting, from the beginning, or ever the earth was. ²⁴When there were no depths, I was brought forth; when there were no fountains abounding with water. ²⁵Before the mountains were settled, before the hills was I brought forth: ²⁶While as yet he had not made the earth, nor the fields, nor the highest part of the dust of the world. ²⁷When he prepared the heavens, I was there: when he set a compass on the face of the depth: ²⁸When he established the clouds above: when he strengthened the fountains of the deep: ²⁹When he gave to the sea his decree, that the waters should not pass his commandment: when he appointed the foundations of the earth: ³⁰Then I was by him, as one brought up with him: and I was daily his delight, rejoicing always before him; ³¹Rejoicing in the habitable part of his earth; and my delights were with the sons of men. ³²Now therefore listen to me, O you children: for blessed are they that keep my ways. ³³Hear instruction, and be wise, and refuse it not. ³⁴Blessed is the man that hears me, watching daily at my gates, waiting at the posts of my doors. ³⁵For whoever finds me finds life, and shall obtain favor of the LORD. ³⁶But he that sins against me wrongs his own soul: all they that hate me love death.

9 ¹Wisdom has built her house, she has hewn out her seven pillars: ²She has killed her beasts; she has mingled her wine; she has also furnished her table. ³She has sent forth her maidens: she cries on the highest places of the city, ⁴Whoever is simple, let him turn in here: as for him that wants understanding, she says to him, ⁵Come, eat of my bread, and drink of the wine which I have mingled. ⁶Forsake the foolish, and live; and go in the way of understanding. ⁷He that reproves a scorner gets to himself shame: and he that rebukes a wicked man gets himself a blot. ⁸Reprove not a scorner, lest he hate you: rebuke a wise man, and he will love you. ⁹Give instruction to a wise man, and he will be yet wiser: teach a just man, and he will increase in learning. ¹⁰The fear of the LORD is the beginning of wisdom: and the knowledge of the holy is understanding. ¹¹For by me your days shall be multiplied, and the years of your life shall be increased. ¹²If you be wise, you shall be wise for yourself: but if you scorn, you alone shall bear it. ¹³A foolish woman

is clamorous: she is simple, and knows nothing. ¹⁴For she sits at the door of her house, on a seat in the high places of the city, ¹⁵To call passengers who go right on their ways: ¹⁶Whoever is simple, let him turn in here: and as for him that wants understanding, she says to him, ¹⁷Stolen waters are sweet, and bread eaten in secret is pleasant. ¹⁸But he knows not that the dead are there; and that her guests are in the depths of hell.

10 ¹The proverbs of Solomon. A wise son makes a glad father: but a foolish son is the heaviness of his mother. ²Treasures of wickedness profit nothing: but righteousness delivers from death. ³The LORD will not suffer the soul of the righteous to famish: but he casts away the substance of the wicked. ⁴He becomes poor that deals with a slack hand: but the hand of the diligent makes rich. ⁵He that gathers in summer is a wise son: but he that sleeps in harvest is a son that causes shame. ⁶Blessings are on the head of the just: but violence covers the mouth of the wicked. ⁷The memory of the just is blessed: but the name of the wicked shall rot. ⁸The wise in heart will receive commandments: but a prating fool shall fall. ⁹He that walks uprightly walks surely: but he that perverts his ways shall be known. ¹⁰He that winks with the eye causes sorrow: but a prating fool shall fall. ¹¹The mouth of a righteous man is a well of life: but violence covers the mouth of the wicked. ¹²Hatred stirs up strifes: but love covers all sins. ¹³In the lips of him that has understanding wisdom is found: but a rod is for the back of him that is void of understanding. ¹⁴Wise men lay up knowledge: but the mouth of the foolish is near destruction. ¹⁵The rich man's wealth is his strong city: the destruction of the poor is their poverty. ¹⁶The labor of the righteous tends to life: the fruit of the wicked to sin. ¹⁷He is in the way of life that keeps instruction: but he that refuses reproof errs. ¹⁸He that hides hatred with lying lips, and he that utters a slander, is a fool. ¹⁹In the multitude of words there wants not sin: but he that refrains his lips is wise. ²⁰The tongue of the just is as choice silver: the heart of the wicked is little worth. ²¹The lips of the righteous feed many: but fools die for want of wisdom. ²²The blessing of the LORD, it makes rich, and he adds no sorrow with it. ²³It is as sport to a fool to do mischief: but a man of understanding has wisdom. ²⁴The fear of the wicked, it shall come on him: but the desire of the righteous shall be granted. ²⁵As the whirlwind passes, so is the wicked no more: but the righteous is an everlasting foundation. ²⁶As vinegar to the teeth, and as smoke to the eyes, so is the sluggard to them that send him. ²⁷The fear of the LORD prolongs days: but the years of the wicked shall be shortened. ²⁸The hope of the righteous shall be gladness: but the expectation of the wicked shall perish. ²⁹The way of the LORD is strength to the upright: but destruction shall be to the workers of iniquity. ³⁰The righteous shall never be removed: but the wicked shall not inhabit the earth. ³¹The mouth of the just brings forth wisdom: but the fraudulent tongue shall be cut out. ³²The lips of the righteous know what is acceptable: but the mouth of the wicked speaks frowardness.

11 ¹A false balance is abomination to the LORD: but a just weight is his delight. ²When pride comes, then comes shame: but with the lowly is wisdom. ³The integrity of the upright shall guide them: but the perverseness of transgressors shall destroy them. ⁴Riches profit not in the day of wrath: but righteousness delivers from death. ⁵The righteousness of the perfect shall direct his way: but the wicked shall fall by his own wickedness. ⁶The righteousness of the upright shall deliver them: but transgressors shall be taken in their own naughtiness. ⁷When a wicked man dies, his expectation shall perish: and the hope of unjust men perishes. ⁸The righteous is delivered out of trouble, and the wicked comes in his stead. ⁹An hypocrite with his mouth destroys his neighbor: but through knowledge shall the just be delivered. ¹⁰When it goes well with the righteous, the city rejoices: and when the wicked perish, there is shouting. ¹¹By the blessing of the upright the city is exalted: but it is overthrown by the mouth of the wicked. ¹²He that is void of wisdom despises his neighbor: but a man of understanding holds his peace. ¹³A talebearer reveals secrets: but he that is of a faithful spirit conceals the matter. ¹⁴Where no counsel is, the people fall: but in the multitude of counsellors there is safety. ¹⁵He that is surety for a stranger shall smart for it: and he that hates indebtedness is sure. ¹⁶A gracious woman retains honor: and strong men retain riches. ¹⁷The merciful man does good to his own soul: but he that is cruel troubles his own flesh. ¹⁸The wicked works a deceitful work: but to him that sows righteousness shall be a sure reward. ¹⁹As righteousness tends to life: so he that pursues evil pursues it to his own death. ²⁰They that are of a fraudulent heart are abomination to the LORD: but such as are upright in their way are his delight. ²¹Though hand join in hand, the wicked shall not be unpunished: but the seed of the righteous shall be delivered. ²²As a jewel of gold in a swine's snout, so is a fair woman which is without discretion. ²³The desire of the righteous is only good: but the expectation of the wicked is wrath. ²⁴There is that scatters, and yet increases; and there is that withholds more than is meet, but it tends to poverty. ²⁵The liberal soul shall be made fat: and he that waters shall be watered also himself. ²⁶He that withholds corn, the people shall curse him: but blessing shall be on the head of him that sells it. ²⁷He that diligently seeks good procures favor: but he that seeks mischief, it shall come to him. ²⁸He that trusts in his riches shall fall; but the righteous shall flourish as a branch. ²⁹He that troubles his own house shall inherit the wind: and the fool shall be servant to the wise of heart. ³⁰The fruit of the righteous is a tree of life; and he that wins souls is wise. ³¹Behold, the righteous shall be recompensed in the earth: much more the wicked and the sinner.

12 ¹Whoever loves instruction loves knowledge: but he that hates reproof is brutish. ²A good man obtains favor of the LORD: but a man of wicked devices will he condemn. ³A man shall not be established by wickedness: but the root of the righteous shall not be moved. ⁴A virtuous woman is a crown to her husband: but she that makes ashamed is as rottenness in his bones. ⁵The thoughts of the righteous are right: but the counsels of the wicked are deceit. ⁶The words of the wicked are to lie in wait for blood: but the mouth of the upright shall deliver them. ⁷The wicked are overthrown, and are not: but the house of the righteous shall stand. ⁸A man shall be commended according to his wisdom: but he that is of a perverse heart shall be despised. ⁹He that is despised, and has a servant, is better than he that honors

himself, and lacks bread. ¹⁰A righteous man regards the life of his beast: but the tender mercies of the wicked are cruel. ¹¹He that tills his land shall be satisfied with bread: but he that follows vain persons is void of understanding. ¹²The wicked desires the net of evil men: but the root of the righteous yields fruit. ¹³The wicked is snared by the transgression of his lips: but the just shall come out of trouble. ¹⁴A man shall be satisfied with good by the fruit of his mouth: and the recompense of a man's hands shall be rendered to him. ¹⁵The way of a fool is right in his own eyes: but he that listens to counsel is wise. ¹⁶A fool's wrath is presently known: but a prudent man covers shame. ¹⁷He that speaks truth shows forth righteousness: but a false witness deceit. ¹⁸There is that speaks like the piercings of a sword: but the tongue of the wise is health. ¹⁹The lip of truth shall be established for ever: but a lying tongue is but for a moment. ²⁰Deceit is in the heart of them that imagine evil: but to the counsellors of peace is joy. ²¹There shall no evil happen to the just: but the wicked shall be filled with mischief. ²²Lying lips are abomination to the LORD: but they that deal truly are his delight. ²³A prudent man conceals knowledge: but the heart of fools proclaims foolishness. ²⁴The hand of the diligent shall bear rule: but the slothful shall be under tribute. ²⁵Heaviness in the heart of man makes it stoop: but a good word makes it glad. ²⁶The righteous is more excellent than his neighbor: but the way of the wicked seduces them. ²⁷The slothful man roasts not that which he took in hunting: but the substance of a diligent man is precious. ²⁸In the way of righteousness is life: and in the pathway thereof there is no death.

13 ¹A wise son hears his father's instruction: but a scorner hears not rebuke. ²A man shall eat good by the fruit of his mouth: but the soul of the transgressors shall eat violence. ³He that keeps his mouth keeps his life: but he that opens wide his lips shall have destruction. ⁴The soul of the sluggard desires, and has nothing: but the soul of the diligent shall be made fat. ⁵A righteous man hates lying: but a wicked man is loathsome, and comes to shame. ⁶Righteousness keeps him that is upright in the way: but wickedness overthrows the sinner. ⁷There is that makes himself rich, yet has nothing: there is that makes himself poor, yet has great riches. ⁸The ransom of a man's life are his riches: but the poor hears not rebuke. ⁹The light of the righteous rejoices: but the lamp of the wicked shall be put out. ¹⁰Only by pride comes contention: but with the well advised is wisdom. ¹¹Wealth gotten by vanity shall be diminished: but he that gathers by labor shall increase. ¹²Hope deferred makes the heart sick: but when the desire comes, it is a tree of life. ¹³Whoever despises the word shall be destroyed: but he that fears the commandment shall be rewarded. ¹⁴The law of the wise is a fountain of life, to depart from the snares of death. ¹⁵Good understanding gives favor: but the way of transgressors is hard. ¹⁶Every prudent man deals with knowledge: but a fool lays open his folly. ¹⁷A wicked messenger falls into mischief: but a faithful ambassador is health. ¹⁸Poverty and shame shall be to him that refuses instruction: but he that regards reproof shall be honored. ¹⁹The desire accomplished is sweet to the soul: but it is abomination to fools to depart from evil. ²⁰He that walks with wise men shall be wise: but a companion of fools shall be destroyed. ²¹Evil pursues sinners: but to the righteous good shall be repaid. ²²A good man leaves an inheritance to his children's children: and the wealth of the sinner is laid up for the just. ²³Much food is in the tillage of the poor: but there is that is destroyed for want of judgment. ²⁴He that spares his rod hates his son: but he that loves him chastens him betimes. ²⁵The righteous eats to the satisfying of his soul: but the belly of the wicked shall want.

14 ¹Every wise woman builds her house: but the foolish plucks it down with her hands. ²He that walks in his uprightness fears the LORD: but he that is perverse in his ways despises him. ³In the mouth of the foolish is a rod of pride: but the lips of the wise shall preserve them. ⁴Where no oxen are, the crib is clean: but much increase is by the strength of the ox. ⁵A faithful witness will not lie: but a false witness will utter lies. ⁶A scorner seeks wisdom, and finds it not: but knowledge is easy to him that understands. ⁷Go from the presence of a foolish man, when you perceive not in him the lips of knowledge. ⁸The wisdom of the prudent is to understand his way: but the folly of fools is deceit. ⁹Fools make a mock at sin: but among the righteous there is favor. ¹⁰The heart knows his own bitterness; and a stranger does not intermeddle with his joy. ¹¹The house of the wicked shall be overthrown: but the tabernacle of the upright shall flourish. ¹²There is a way which seems right to a man, but the end thereof are the ways of death. ¹³Even in laughter the heart is sorrowful; and the end of that mirth is heaviness. ¹⁴The backslider in heart shall be filled with his own ways: and a good man shall be satisfied from himself. ¹⁵The simple believes every word: but the prudent man looks well to his going. ¹⁶A wise man fears, and departs from evil: but the fool rages, and is confident. ¹⁷He that is soon angry deals foolishly: and a man of wicked devices is hated. ¹⁸The simple inherit folly: but the prudent are crowned with knowledge. ¹⁹The evil bow before the good; and the wicked at the gates of the righteous. ²⁰The poor is hated even of his own neighbor: but the rich has many friends. ²¹He that despises his neighbor sins: but he that has mercy on the poor, happy is he. ²²Do they not err that devise evil? but mercy and truth shall be to them that devise good. ²³In all labor there is profit: but the talk of the lips tends only to penury. ²⁴The crown of the wise is their riches: but the foolishness of fools is folly. ²⁵A true witness delivers souls: but a deceitful witness speaks lies. ²⁶In the fear of the LORD is strong confidence: and his children shall have a place of refuge. ²⁷The fear of the LORD is a fountain of life, to depart from the snares of death. ²⁸In the multitude of people is the king's honor: but in the want of people is the destruction of the prince. ²⁹He that is slow to wrath is of great understanding: but he that is hasty of spirit exalts folly. ³⁰A sound heart is the life of the flesh: but envy the rottenness of the bones. ³¹He that oppresses the poor reproaches his Maker: but he that honors him has mercy on the poor. ³²The wicked is driven away in his wickedness: but the righteous has hope in his death. ³³Wisdom rests in the heart of him that has understanding: but that which is in the middle of fools is made known. ³⁴Righteousness exalts a nation: but sin is a reproach to any people. ³⁵The king's favor is toward a wise servant: but his wrath is against him that causes shame.

15 ¹A soft answer turns away wrath: but grievous words stir up anger. ²The tongue of the wise uses knowledge aright: but the mouth of fools pours out foolishness. ³The eyes of the LORD are in every place, beholding the evil and the good. ⁴A wholesome tongue is a tree of life: but perverseness therein is a breach in the spirit. ⁵A fool despises his father's instruction: but he that regards reproof is prudent. ⁶In the house of the righteous is much treasure: but in the revenues of the wicked is trouble. ⁷The lips of the wise disperse knowledge: but the heart of the foolish does not so. ⁸The sacrifice of the wicked is an abomination to the LORD: but the prayer of the upright is his delight. ⁹The way of the wicked is an abomination to the LORD: but he loves him that follows after righteousness. ¹⁰Correction is grievous to him that forsakes the way: and he that hates reproof shall die. ¹¹Hell and destruction are before the LORD: how much more then the hearts of the children of men? ¹²A scorner loves not one that reproves him: neither will he go to the wise. ¹³A merry heart makes a cheerful countenance: but by sorrow of the heart the spirit is broken. ¹⁴The heart of him that has understanding seeks knowledge: but the mouth of fools feeds on foolishness. ¹⁵All the days of the afflicted are evil: but he that is of a merry heart has a continual feast. ¹⁶Better is little with the fear of the LORD than great treasure and trouble therewith. ¹⁷Better is a dinner of herbs where love is, than a stalled ox and hatred therewith. ¹⁸A wrathful man stirs up strife: but he that is slow to anger appeases strife. ¹⁹The way of the slothful man is as an hedge of thorns: but the way of the righteous is made plain. ²⁰A wise son makes a glad father: but a foolish man despises his mother. ²¹Folly is joy to him that is destitute of wisdom: but a man of understanding walks uprightly. ²²Without counsel purposes are disappointed: but in the multitude of counsellors they are established. ²³A man has joy by the answer of his mouth: and a word spoken in due season, how good is it! ²⁴The way of life is above to the wise, that he may depart from hell beneath. ²⁵The LORD will destroy the house of the proud: but he will establish the border of the widow. ²⁶The thoughts of the wicked are an abomination to the LORD: but the words of the pure are pleasant words. ²⁷He that is greedy of gain troubles his own house; but he that hates gifts shall live. ²⁸The heart of the righteous studies to answer: but the mouth of the wicked pours out evil things. ²⁹The LORD is far from the wicked: but he hears the prayer of the righteous. ³⁰The light of the eyes rejoices the heart: and a good report makes the bones fat. ³¹The ear that hears the reproof of life stays among the wise. ³²He that refuses instruction despises his own soul: but he that hears reproof gets understanding. ³³The fear of the LORD is the instruction of wisdom; and before honor is humility.

16 ¹The preparations of the heart in man, and the answer of the tongue, is from the LORD. ²All the ways of a man are clean in his own eyes; but the LORD weighs the spirits. ³Commit your works to the LORD, and your thoughts shall be established. ⁴The LORD has made all things for himself: yes, even the wicked for the day of evil. ⁵Every one that is proud in heart is an abomination to the LORD: though hand join in hand, he shall not be unpunished. ⁶By mercy and truth iniquity is purged: and by the fear of the LORD men depart from evil. ⁷When a man's ways please the LORD, he makes even his enemies to be at peace with him. ⁸Better is a little with righteousness than great revenues without right. ⁹A man's heart devises his way: but the LORD directs his steps. ¹⁰A divine sentence is in the lips of the king: his mouth transgresses not in judgment. ¹¹A just weight and balance are the LORD's: all the weights of the bag are his work. ¹²It is an abomination to kings to commit wickedness: for the throne is established by righteousness. ¹³Righteous lips are the delight of kings; and they love him that speaks right. ¹⁴The wrath of a king is as messengers of death: but a wise man will pacify it. ¹⁵In the light of the king's countenance is life; and his favor is as a cloud of the latter rain. ¹⁶How much better is it to get wisdom than gold! and to get understanding rather to be chosen than silver! ¹⁷The highway of the upright is to depart from evil: he that keeps his way preserves his soul. ¹⁸Pride goes before destruction, and an haughty spirit before a fall. ¹⁹Better it is to be of an humble spirit with the lowly, than to divide the spoil with the proud. ²⁰He that handles a matter wisely shall find good: and whoever trusts in the LORD, happy is he. ²¹The wise in heart shall be called prudent: and the sweetness of the lips increases learning. ²²Understanding is a wellspring of life to him that has it: but the instruction of fools is folly. ²³The heart of the wise teaches his mouth, and adds learning to his lips. ²⁴Pleasant words are as an honeycomb, sweet to the soul, and health to the bones. ²⁵There is a way that seems right to a man, but the end thereof are the ways of death. ²⁶He that labors labors for himself; for his mouth craves it of him. ²⁷An ungodly man digs up evil: and in his lips there is as a burning fire. ²⁸A fraudulent man sows strife: and a whisperer separates chief friends. ²⁹A violent man entices his neighbor, and leads him into the way that is not good. ³⁰He shuts his eyes to devise fraudulent things: moving his lips he brings evil to pass. ³¹The hoary head is a crown of glory, if it be found in the way of righteousness. ³²He that is slow to anger is better than the mighty; and he that rules his spirit than he that takes a city. ³³The lot is cast into the lap; but the whole disposing thereof is of the LORD.

17 ¹Better is a dry morsel, and quietness therewith, than an house full of sacrifices with strife. ²A wise servant shall have rule over a son that causes shame, and shall have part of the inheritance among the brothers. ³The fining pot is for silver, and the furnace for gold: but the LORD tries the hearts. ⁴A wicked doer gives heed to false lips; and a liar gives ear to a naughty tongue. ⁵Whoever mocks the poor reproaches his Maker: and he that is glad at calamities shall not be unpunished. ⁶Children's children are the crown of old men; and the glory of children are their fathers. ⁷Excellent speech becomes not a fool: much less do lying lips a prince. ⁸A gift is as a precious stone in the eyes of him that has it: wherever it turns, it prospers. ⁹He that covers a transgression seeks love; but he that repeats a matter separates very friends. ¹⁰A reproof enters more into a wise man than an hundred stripes into a fool. ¹¹An evil man seeks only rebellion: therefore a cruel messenger shall be sent against him. ¹²Let a bear robbed of her whelps meet a man, rather than a fool in his folly. ¹³Whoever rewards evil for good, evil shall not depart from his house. ¹⁴The beginning of strife is as when one lets out water: therefore leave off contention, before it be meddled with. ¹⁵He that justifies the wicked, and he that condemns the just, even they both are abomination to the LORD. ¹⁶Why is there a price in the hand of a fool to get wisdom, seeing he has no heart to it? ¹⁷A friend loves at all times, and a brother is born for adversity. ¹⁸A man void of understanding strikes hands, and becomes surety in the presence of his friend. ¹⁹He loves transgression that loves strife: and he that exalts his gate seeks destruction. ²⁰He that has a fraudulent heart finds no good: and he that has a perverse tongue falls into mischief. ²¹He that begets a fool does it to his sorrow: and the father of a fool has no joy. ²²A merry heart does good like a medicine: but a broken spirit dries the bones. ²³A wicked man takes a gift out of the bosom to pervert the ways of judgment. ²⁴Wisdom is before him that has understanding; but the eyes of a fool are in the ends of the earth. ²⁵A foolish son is a grief to his father, and bitterness to her that bore him. ²⁶Also to punish the just is not good, nor to strike princes for equity. ²⁷He that has knowledge spares his words: and a man of understanding is of an excellent spirit. ²⁸Even a fool, when he holds his peace, is counted wise: and he that shuts his lips is esteemed a man of understanding.

18 ¹Through desire a man, having separated himself, seeks and intermeddles with all wisdom. ²A fool has no delight in understanding, but that his heart may discover itself. ³When the wicked comes, then comes also contempt, and with ignominy reproach. ⁴The words of a man's mouth are as deep waters, and the wellspring of wisdom as a flowing brook. ⁵It is not good to accept the person of the wicked, to overthrow the righteous in judgment. ⁶A fool's lips enter into contention, and his mouth calls for strokes. ⁷A fool's mouth is his destruction, and his lips are the snare of his soul. ⁸The words of a talebearer are as wounds, and they go down into the innermost parts of the belly. ⁹He also that is slothful in his work is brother to him that is a great waster. ¹⁰The name of the LORD is a strong tower: the righteous runs into it, and is safe. ¹¹The rich man's wealth is his strong city, and as an high wall in his own conceit. ¹²Before destruction the heart of man is haughty, and before honor is humility. ¹³He that answers a matter before he hears it, it is folly and shame to him. ¹⁴The spirit of a man will sustain his infirmity; but a wounded spirit who can bear? ¹⁵The heart of the prudent gets knowledge; and the ear of the wise seeks knowledge. ¹⁶A man's gift makes room for him, and brings him before great men. ¹⁷He that is first in his own cause seems just; but his neighbor comes and searches him. ¹⁸The lot causes contentions to cease, and parts between the mighty. ¹⁹A brother offended is harder to be won than a strong city: and their contentions are like the bars of a castle. ²⁰A man's belly shall be satisfied with the fruit of his mouth; and with the increase of his lips shall he be filled. ²¹Death and life are in the power of the tongue: and they that love it shall eat the fruit thereof. ²²Whoever finds a wife finds a good thing, and obtains favor of the LORD. ²³The poor uses entreaties; but the rich answers roughly. ²⁴A man that has friends must show himself friendly: and there is a friend that sticks closer than a brother.

19 ¹Better is the poor that walks in his integrity, than he that is perverse in his lips, and is a fool. ²Also, that the soul be without knowledge, it is not good; and he that hastens with his feet sins. ³The foolishness of man perverts his way: and his heart frets against the LORD. ⁴Wealth makes many friends; but the poor is separated from his neighbor. ⁵A false witness shall not be unpunished, and he that speaks lies shall not escape. ⁶Many will entreat the favor of the prince: and every man is a friend to him that gives gifts. ⁷All the brothers of the poor do hate him: how much more do his friends go far from him? he pursues them with words, yet they are wanting to him. ⁸He that gets wisdom loves his own soul: he that keeps understanding shall find good. ⁹A false witness shall not be unpunished, and he that speaks lies shall perish. ¹⁰Delight is not seemly for a fool; much less for a servant to have rule over princes. ¹¹The discretion of a man defers his anger; and it is his glory to pass over a transgression. ¹²The king's wrath is as the roaring of a lion; but his favor is as dew on the grass. ¹³A foolish son is the calamity of his father: and the contentions of a wife are a continual dropping. ¹⁴House and riches are the inheritance of fathers: and a prudent wife is from the LORD. ¹⁵Slothfulness casts into a deep sleep; and an idle soul shall suffer hunger. ¹⁶He that keeps the commandment keeps his own soul; but he that despises his ways shall die. ¹⁷He that has pity on the poor lends to the LORD; and that which he has given will he pay him again. ¹⁸Chasten your son while there is hope, and let not your soul spare for his crying. ¹⁹A man of great wrath shall suffer punishment: for if you deliver him, yet you must do it again. ²⁰Hear counsel, and receive instruction, that you may be wise in your latter end. ²¹There are many devices in a man's heart; nevertheless the counsel of the LORD, that shall stand. ²²The desire of a man is his kindness: and a poor man is better than a liar. ²³The fear of the LORD tends to life: and he that has it shall abide satisfied; he shall not be visited with evil. ²⁴A slothful man hides his hand in his bosom, and will not so much as bring it to his mouth again. ²⁵Smite a scorner, and the simple will beware: and reprove one that has understanding, and he will understand knowledge. ²⁶He that wastes his father, and chases away his mother, is a son that causes shame, and brings reproach. ²⁷Cease, my son, to hear the instruction that causes to err from the words of knowledge. ²⁸An ungodly witness scorns judgment: and the mouth of the wicked devours iniquity. ²⁹Judgments are prepared for scorners, and stripes for the back of fools.

20 ¹Wine is a mocker, strong drink is raging: and whoever is deceived thereby is not wise. ²The fear of a king is as the roaring of a lion: whoever provokes him to anger sins against his own soul. ³It is an honor for a man to cease from strife: but every fool will be meddling. ⁴The sluggard will not plow by reason of the cold; therefore shall he beg in harvest, and have nothing. ⁵Counsel in the heart of man is like deep water; but a man of understanding will draw it out. ⁶Most men will proclaim every one his own goodness: but a faithful man who can find? ⁷The just man walks in his integrity: his children are blessed after him. ⁸A king that sits in the throne of judgment scatters away all evil with his eyes. ⁹Who can say, I have made my heart clean, I am pure from my sin? ¹⁰Divers weights, and divers measures, both of them are alike abomination to the LORD. ¹¹Even a child is known by his doings, whether his work be pure, and whether it be right. ¹²The hearing ear, and the seeing eye, the LORD has made even both of them. ¹³Love not sleep, lest you come to poverty; open your eyes, and you shall be satisfied with bread. ¹⁴It is naught, it is naught, says the buyer: but when he is gone his way, then he boasts. ¹⁵There is gold, and a multitude of rubies: but the lips of knowledge are a precious jewel. ¹⁶Take his garment that is surety for a stranger: and take a pledge of him for a strange woman. ¹⁷Bread of deceit is sweet to a man; but afterwards his mouth shall be filled with gravel. ¹⁸Every purpose is established by counsel: and with good advice make war. ¹⁹He that goes about as a talebearer reveals secrets: therefore meddle not with him that flatters with his lips. ²⁰Whoever curses his father or his mother, his lamp shall be put out in obscure darkness. ²¹An inheritance may be gotten hastily at the beginning; but the end thereof shall not be blessed. ²²Say not you, I will recompense evil; but wait on the LORD, and he shall save you. ²³Divers weights are an abomination to the LORD; and a false balance is not good. ²⁴Man's goings are of the LORD; how can a man then understand his own way? ²⁵It is a snare to the man who devours that which is holy, and after vows to make enquiry. ²⁶A wise king scatters the wicked, and brings the wheel over them. ²⁷The spirit of man is the candle of the LORD, searching all the inward parts of the belly. ²⁸Mercy and truth preserve the king: and his throne is upheld by mercy. ²⁹The glory of young men is their strength: and the beauty of old men is the grey head. ³⁰The blueness of a wound cleans away evil: so do stripes the inward parts of the belly.

21

¹The king's heart is in the hand of the LORD, as the rivers of water: he turns it wherever he will. ²Every way of a man is right in his own eyes: but the LORD ponders the hearts. ³To do justice and judgment is more acceptable to the LORD than sacrifice. ⁴An high look, and a proud heart, and the plowing of the wicked, is sin. ⁵The thoughts of the diligent tend only to plenty; but of every one that is hasty only to want. ⁶The getting of treasures by a lying tongue is a vanity tossed to and fro of them that seek death. ⁷The robbery of the wicked shall destroy them; because they refuse to do judgment. ⁸The way of man is fraudulent and strange: but as for the pure, his work is right. ⁹It is better to dwell in a corner of the housetop, than with a brawling woman in a wide house. ¹⁰The soul of the wicked desires evil: his neighbor finds no favor in his eyes. ¹¹When the scorner is punished, the simple is made wise: and when the wise is instructed, he receives knowledge. ¹²The righteous man wisely considers the house of the wicked: but God overthrows the wicked for their wickedness. ¹³Whoever stops his ears at the cry of the poor, he also shall cry himself, but shall not be heard. ¹⁴A gift in secret pacifies anger: and a reward in the bosom strong wrath. ¹⁵It is joy to the just to do judgment: but destruction shall be to the workers of iniquity. ¹⁶The man that wanders out of the way of understanding shall remain in the congregation of the dead. ¹⁷He that loves pleasure shall be a poor man: he that loves wine and oil shall not be rich. ¹⁸The wicked shall be a ransom for the righteous, and the transgressor for the upright. ¹⁹It is better to dwell in the wilderness, than with a contentious and an angry woman. ²⁰There is treasure to be desired and oil in the dwelling of the wise; but a foolish man spends it up. ²¹He that follows after righteousness and mercy finds life, righteousness, and honor. ²²A wise man scales the city of the mighty, and casts down the strength of the confidence thereof. ²³Whoever keeps his mouth and his tongue keeps his soul from troubles. ²⁴Proud and haughty scorner is his name, who deals in proud wrath. ²⁵The desire of the slothful kills him; for his hands refuse to labor. ²⁶He covets greedily all the day long: but the righteous gives and spares not. ²⁷The sacrifice of the wicked is abomination: how much more, when he brings it with a wicked mind? ²⁸A false witness shall perish: but the man that hears speaks constantly. ²⁹A wicked man hardens his face: but as for the upright, he directs his way. ³⁰There is no wisdom nor understanding nor counsel against the LORD. ³¹The horse is prepared against the day of battle: but safety is of the LORD.

22

¹A GOOD name is rather to be chosen than great riches, and loving favor rather than silver and gold. ²The rich and poor meet together: the LORD is the maker of them all. ³A prudent man foresees the evil, and hides himself: but the simple pass on, and are punished. ⁴By humility and the fear of the LORD are riches, and honor, and life. ⁵Thorns and snares are in the way of the fraudulent: he that does keep his soul shall be far from them. ⁶Train up a child in the way he should go: and when he is old, he will not depart from it. ⁷The rich rules over the poor, and the borrower is servant to the lender. ⁸He that sows iniquity shall reap vanity: and the rod of his anger shall fail. ⁹He that has a bountiful eye shall be blessed; for he gives of his bread to the poor. ¹⁰Cast out the scorner, and contention shall go out; yes, strife and reproach shall cease. ¹¹He that loves pureness of heart, for the grace of his lips the king shall be his friend. ¹²The eyes of the LORD preserve knowledge, and he overthrows the words of the transgressor. ¹³The slothful man says, There is a lion without, I shall be slain in the streets. ¹⁴The mouth of strange women is a deep pit: he that is abhorred of the LORD shall fall therein. ¹⁵Foolishness is bound in the heart of a child; but the rod of correction shall drive it far from him. ¹⁶He that oppresses the poor to increase his riches, and he that gives to the rich, shall surely come to want. ¹⁷Bow down your ear, and hear the words of the wise, and apply your heart to my knowledge. ¹⁸For it is a pleasant thing if you keep them within you; they shall with be fitted in your lips. ¹⁹That your trust may be in the LORD, I have made known to you this day, even to you. ²⁰Have not I written to you excellent things in counsels and knowledge, ²¹That I might make you know the certainty of the words of truth; that you might answer the words of truth to them that send to you? ²²Rob not the poor, because he is poor: neither oppress the afflicted in the gate: ²³For the LORD will plead their cause, and spoil the soul of those that spoiled them. ²⁴Make no friendship with an angry man; and with a furious man you shall not go: ²⁵Lest you learn his ways, and get a snare to your soul. ²⁶Be not you one of them that strike hands, or of them that are sureties for debts. ²⁷If you have nothing to pay, why should he take away your bed from under you? ²⁸Remove not the ancient landmark, which your fathers have set. ²⁹See you a man diligent in his business? he

shall stand before kings; he shall not stand before mean men.

23
¹When you sit to eat with a ruler, consider diligently what is before you: ²And put a knife to your throat, if you be a man given to appetite. ³Be not desirous of his dainties: for they are deceitful meat. ⁴Labor not to be rich: cease from your own wisdom. ⁵Will you set your eyes on that which is not? for riches certainly make themselves wings; they fly away as an eagle toward heaven. ⁶Eat you not the bread of him that has an evil eye, neither desire you his dainty meats: ⁷For as he thinks in his heart, so is he: Eat and drink, says he to you; but his heart is not with you. ⁸The morsel which you have eaten shall you vomit up, and lose your sweet words. ⁹Speak not in the ears of a fool: for he will despise the wisdom of your words. ¹⁰Remove not the old landmark; and enter not into the fields of the fatherless: ¹¹For their redeemer is mighty; he shall plead their cause with you. ¹²Apply your heart to instruction, and your ears to the words of knowledge. ¹³Withhold not correction from the child: for if you beat him with the rod, he shall not die. ¹⁴You shall beat him with the rod, and shall deliver his soul from hell. ¹⁵My son, if your heart be wise, my heart shall rejoice, even mine. ¹⁶Yes, my reins shall rejoice, when your lips speak right things. ¹⁷Let not your heart envy sinners: but be you in the fear of the LORD all the day long. ¹⁸For surely there is an end; and your expectation shall not be cut off. ¹⁹Hear you, my son, and be wise, and guide your heart in the way. ²⁰Be not among winebibbers; among riotous eaters of flesh: ²¹For the drunkard and the glutton shall come to poverty: and drowsiness shall clothe a man with rags. ²²Listen to your father that begat you, and despise not your mother when she is old. ²³Buy the truth, and sell it not; also wisdom, and instruction, and understanding. ²⁴The father of the righteous shall greatly rejoice: and he that begets a wise child shall have joy of him. ²⁵Your father and your mother shall be glad, and she that bore you shall rejoice. ²⁶My son, give me your heart, and let your eyes observe my ways. ²⁷For a whore is a deep ditch; and a strange woman is a narrow pit. ²⁸She also lies in wait as for a prey, and increases the transgressors among men. ²⁹Who has woe? who has sorrow? who has contentions? who has babbling? who has wounds without cause? who has redness of eyes? ³⁰They that tarry long at the wine; they that go to seek mixed wine. ³¹Look not you on the wine when it is red, when it gives his color in the cup, when it moves itself aright. ³²At the last it bites like a serpent, and stings like an adder. ³³Your eyes shall behold strange women, and your heart shall utter perverse things. ³⁴Yes, you shall be as he that lies down in the middle of the sea, or as he that lies on the top of a mast. ³⁵They have stricken me, shall you say, and I was not sick; they have beaten me, and I felt it not: when shall I awake? I will seek it yet again.

24
¹Be not you envious against evil men, neither desire to be with them. ²For their heart studies destruction, and their lips talk of mischief. ³Through wisdom is an house built; and by understanding it is established: ⁴And by knowledge shall the chambers be filled with all precious and pleasant riches. ⁵A wise man is strong; yes, a man of knowledge increases strength. ⁶For by wise counsel you shall make your war: and in multitude of counsellors there is safety. ⁷Wisdom is too high for a fool: he opens not his mouth in the gate. ⁸He that devises to do evil shall be called a mischievous person. ⁹The thought of foolishness is sin: and the scorner is an abomination to men. ¹⁰If you faint in the day of adversity, your strength is small. ¹¹If you forbear to deliver them that are drawn to death, and those that are ready to be slain; ¹²If you say, Behold, we knew it not; does not he that ponders the heart consider it? and he that keeps your soul, does not he know it? and shall not he render to every man according to his works? ¹³My son, eat you honey, because it is good; and the honeycomb, which is sweet to your taste: ¹⁴So shall the knowledge of wisdom be to your soul: when you have found it, then there shall be a reward, and your expectation shall not be cut off. ¹⁵Lay not wait, O wicked man, against the dwelling of the righteous; spoil not his resting place: ¹⁶For a just man falls seven times, and rises up again: but the wicked shall fall into mischief. ¹⁷Rejoice not when your enemy falls, and let not your heart be glad when he stumbles: ¹⁸Lest the LORD see it, and it displease him, and he turn away his wrath from him. ¹⁹Fret not yourself because of evil men, neither be you envious at the wicked: ²⁰For there shall be no reward to the evil man; the candle of the wicked shall be put out. ²¹My son, fear you the LORD and the king: and meddle not with them that are given to change: ²²For their calamity shall rise suddenly; and who knows the ruin of them both? ²³These things also belong to the wise. It is not good to have respect of persons in judgment. ²⁴He that says to the wicked, You are righteous; him shall the people curse, nations shall abhor him: ²⁵But to them that rebuke him shall be delight, and a good blessing shall come on them. ²⁶Every man shall kiss his lips that gives a right answer. ²⁷Prepare your work without, and make it fit for yourself in the field; and afterwards build your house. ²⁸Be not a witness against your neighbor without cause; and deceive not with your lips. ²⁹Say not, I will do so to him as he has done to me: I will render to the man according to his work. ³⁰I went by the field of the slothful, and by the vineyard of the man void of understanding; ³¹And, see, it was all grown over with thorns, and nettles had covered the face thereof, and the stone wall thereof was broken down. ³²Then I saw, and considered it well: I looked on it, and received instruction. ³³Yet a little sleep, a little slumber, a little folding of the hands to sleep: ³⁴So shall your poverty come as one that travels; and your want as an armed man.

25
¹These are also proverbs of Solomon, which the men of Hezekiah king of Judah copied out. ²It is the glory of God to conceal a thing: but the honor of kings is to search out a matter. ³The heaven for height, and the earth for depth, and the heart of kings is unsearchable. ⁴Take away the dross from the silver, and there shall come forth a vessel for the finer. ⁵Take away the wicked from before the king, and his throne shall be established in righteousness. ⁶Put not forth yourself in the presence of the king, and stand not in the place of great men: ⁷For better it is that it be said to you, Come up here; than that you should be put lower in the presence of the prince whom your eyes have seen. ⁸Go not forth hastily to strive, lest you know not what to do in the end thereof, when your neighbor has put you to shame. ⁹Debate your cause with your neighbor himself; and discover

not a secret to another: ¹⁰Lest he that hears it put you to shame, and your infamy turn not away. ¹¹A word fitly spoken is like apples of gold in pictures of silver. ¹²As an earring of gold, and an ornament of fine gold, so is a wise reprover on an obedient ear. ¹³As the cold of snow in the time of harvest, so is a faithful messenger to them that send him: for he refreshes the soul of his masters. ¹⁴Whoever boasts himself of a false gift is like clouds and wind without rain. ¹⁵By long forbearing is a prince persuaded, and a soft tongue breaks the bone. ¹⁶Have you found honey? eat so much as is sufficient for you, lest you be filled therewith, and vomit it. ¹⁷Withdraw your foot from your neighbor's house; lest he be weary of you, and so hate you. ¹⁸A man that bears false witness against his neighbor is a maul, and a sword, and a sharp arrow. ¹⁹Confidence in an unfaithful man in time of trouble is like a broken tooth, and a foot out of joint. ²⁰As he that takes away a garment in cold weather, and as vinegar on nitre, so is he that singes songs to an heavy heart. ²¹If your enemy be hungry, give him bread to eat; and if he be thirsty, give him water to drink: ²²For you shall heap coals of fire on his head, and the LORD shall reward you. ²³The north wind drives away rain: so does an angry countenance a backbiting tongue. ²⁴It is better to dwell in the corner of the housetop, than with a brawling woman and in a wide house. ²⁵As cold waters to a thirsty soul, so is good news from a far country. ²⁶A righteous man falling down before the wicked is as a troubled fountain, and a corrupt spring. ²⁷It is not good to eat much honey: so for men to search their own glory is not glory. ²⁸He that has no rule over his own spirit is like a city that is broken down, and without walls.

26 ¹As snow in summer, and as rain in harvest, so honor is not seemly for a fool. ²As the bird by wandering, as the swallow by flying, so the curse causeless shall not come. ³A whip for the horse, a bridle for the ass, and a rod for the fool's back. ⁴Answer not a fool according to his folly, lest you also be like to him. ⁵Answer a fool according to his folly, lest he be wise in his own conceit. ⁶He that sends a message by the hand of a fool cuts off the feet, and drinks damage. ⁷The legs of the lame are not equal: so is a parable in the mouth of fools. ⁸As he that binds a stone in a sling, so is he that gives honor to a fool. ⁹As a thorn goes up into the hand of a drunkard, so is a parable in the mouths of fools. ¹⁰The great God that formed all things both rewards the fool, and rewards transgressors. ¹¹As a dog returns to his vomit, so a fool returns to his folly. ¹²See you a man wise in his own conceit? there is more hope of a fool than of him. ¹³The slothful man says, There is a lion in the way; a lion is in the streets. ¹⁴As the door turns on his hinges, so does the slothful on his bed. ¹⁵The slothful hides his hand in his bosom; it grieves him to bring it again to his mouth. ¹⁶The sluggard is wiser in his own conceit than seven men that can render a reason. ¹⁷He that passes by, and meddles with strife belonging not to him, is like one that takes a dog by the ears. ¹⁸As a mad man who casts firebrands, arrows, and death, ¹⁹So is the man that deceives his neighbor, and says, Am not I in sport? ²⁰Where no wood is, there the fire goes out: so where there is no talebearer, the strife ceases. ²¹As coals are to burning coals, and wood to fire; so is a contentious man to kindle strife. ²²The words of a talebearer are as wounds, and they go down into the innermost parts of the belly. ²³Burning lips and a wicked heart are like a potsherd covered with silver dross. ²⁴He that hates dissembles with his lips, and lays up deceit within him; ²⁵When he speaks fair, believe him not: for there are seven abominations in his heart. ²⁶Whose hatred is covered by deceit, his wickedness shall be showed before the whole congregation. ²⁷Whoever digs a pit shall fall therein: and he that rolls a stone, it will return on him. ²⁸A lying tongue hates those that are afflicted by it; and a flattering mouth works ruin.

27 ¹Boast not yourself of to morrow; for you know not what a day may bring forth. ²Let another man praise you, and not your own mouth; a stranger, and not your own lips. ³A stone is heavy, and the sand weighty; but a fool's wrath is heavier than them both. ⁴Wrath is cruel, and anger is outrageous; but who is able to stand before envy? ⁵Open rebuke is better than secret love. ⁶Faithful are the wounds of a friend; but the kisses of an enemy are deceitful. ⁷The full soul loathes an honeycomb; but to the hungry soul every bitter thing is sweet. ⁸As a bird that wanders from her nest, so is a man that wanders from his place. ⁹Ointment and perfume rejoice the heart: so does the sweetness of a man's friend by hearty counsel. ¹⁰Your own friend, and your father's friend, forsake not; neither go into your brother's house in the day of your calamity: for better is a neighbor that is near than a brother far off. ¹¹My son, be wise, and make my heart glad, that I may answer him that reproaches me. ¹²A prudent man foresees the evil, and hides himself; but the simple pass on, and are punished. ¹³Take his garment that is surety for a stranger, and take a pledge of him for a strange woman. ¹⁴He that blesses his friend with a loud voice, rising early in the morning, it shall be counted a curse to him. ¹⁵A continual dropping in a very rainy day and a contentious woman are alike. ¹⁶Whoever hides her hides the wind, and the ointment of his right hand, which denudes itself. ¹⁷Iron sharpens iron; so a man sharpens the countenance of his friend. ¹⁸Whoever keeps the fig tree shall eat the fruit thereof: so he that waits on his master shall be honored. ¹⁹As in water face answers to face, so the heart of man to man. ²⁰Hell and destruction are never full; so the eyes of man are never satisfied. ²¹As the fining pot for silver, and the furnace for gold; so is a man to his praise. ²²Though you should bray a fool in a mortar among wheat with a pestle, yet will not his foolishness depart from him. ²³Be you diligent to know the state of your flocks, and look well to your herds. ²⁴For riches are not for ever: and does the crown endure to every generation? ²⁵The hay appears, and the tender grass shows itself, and herbs of the mountains are gathered. ²⁶The lambs are for your clothing, and the goats are the price of the field. ²⁷And you shall have goats' milk enough for your food, for the food of your household, and for the maintenance for your maidens.

28 ¹The wicked flee when no man pursues: but the righteous are bold as a lion. ²For the transgression of a land many are the princes thereof: but by a man of understanding and knowledge the state thereof shall be prolonged. ³A poor man that oppresses the poor is like a sweeping rain which leaves no food. ⁴They that forsake the law praise the wicked: but such as keep the law contend with them. ⁵Evil men understand not judgment: but they that seek the LORD understand all things. ⁶Better is the poor that walks in his uprightness, than he that is perverse in his ways, though he be rich. ⁷Whoever keeps the law is a wise son: but he that is a companion of riotous men shames his father. ⁸He that by usury and unjust gain increases his substance, he shall gather it for him that will pity the poor. ⁹He that turns away his ear from hearing the law, even his prayer shall be abomination. ¹⁰Whoever causes the righteous to go astray in an evil way, he shall fall himself into his own pit: but the upright shall have good things in possession. ¹¹The rich man is wise in his own conceit; but the poor that has understanding searches him out. ¹²When righteous men do rejoice, there is great glory: but when the wicked rise, a man is hidden. ¹³He that covers his sins shall not prosper: but whoever confesses and forsakes them shall have mercy. ¹⁴Happy is the man that fears always: but he that hardens his heart shall fall into mischief. ¹⁵As a roaring lion, and a ranging bear; so is a wicked ruler over the poor people. ¹⁶The prince that wants understanding is also a great oppressor: but he that hates covetousness shall prolong his days. ¹⁷A man that does violence to the blood of any person shall flee to the pit; let no man stay him. ¹⁸Whoever walks uprightly shall be saved: but he that is perverse in his ways shall fall at once. ¹⁹He that tills his land shall have plenty of bread: but he that follows after vain persons shall have poverty enough. ²⁰A faithful man shall abound with blessings: but he that makes haste to be rich shall not be innocent. ²¹To have respect of persons is not good: for for a piece of bread that man will transgress. ²²He that hastens to be rich has an evil eye, and considers not that poverty shall come on him. ²³He that rebukes a man afterwards shall find more favor than he that flatters with the tongue. ²⁴Whoever robs his father or his mother, and says, It is no transgression; the same is the companion of a destroyer. ²⁵He that is of a proud heart stirs up strife: but he that puts his trust in the LORD shall be made fat. ²⁶He that trusts in his own heart is a fool: but whoever walks wisely, he shall be delivered. ²⁷He that gives to the poor shall not lack: but he that hides his eyes shall have many a curse. ²⁸When the wicked rise, men hide themselves: but when they perish, the righteous increase.

29 ¹He, that being often reproved hardens his neck, shall suddenly be destroyed, and that without remedy. ²When the righteous are in authority, the people rejoice: but when the wicked bears rule, the people mourn. ³Whoever loves wisdom rejoices his father: but he that keeps company with harlots spends his substance. ⁴The king by judgment establishes the land: but he that receives gifts overthrows it. ⁵A man that flatters his neighbor spreads a net for his feet. ⁶In the transgression of an evil man there is a snare: but the righteous does sing and rejoice. ⁷The righteous considers the cause of the poor: but the wicked regards not to know it. ⁸Scornful men bring a city into a snare: but wise men turn away wrath. ⁹If a wise man contends with a foolish man, whether he rage or laugh, there is no rest. ¹⁰The bloodthirsty hate the upright: but the just seek his soul. ¹¹A fool utters all his mind: but a wise man keeps it in till afterwards. ¹²If a ruler listen to lies, all his servants are wicked. ¹³The poor and the deceitful man meet together: the LORD lightens both their eyes. ¹⁴The king that faithfully judges the poor, his throne shall be established for ever. ¹⁵The rod and reproof give wisdom: but a child left to himself brings his mother to shame. ¹⁶When the wicked are multiplied, transgression increases: but the righteous shall see their fall. ¹⁷Correct your son, and he shall give you rest; yes, he shall give delight to your soul. ¹⁸Where there is no vision, the people perish: but he that keeps the law, happy is he. ¹⁹A servant will not be corrected by words: for though he understand he will not answer. ²⁰See you a man that is hasty in his words? there is more hope of a fool than of him. ²¹He that delicately brings up his servant from a child shall have him become his son at the length. ²²An angry man stirs up strife, and a furious man abounds in transgression. ²³A man's pride shall bring him low: but honor shall uphold the humble in spirit. ²⁴Whoever is partner with a thief hates his own soul: he hears cursing, and denudes it not. ²⁵The fear of man brings a snare: but whoever puts his trust in the LORD shall be safe. ²⁶Many seek the ruler's favor; but every man's judgment comes from the LORD. ²⁷An unjust man is an abomination to the just: and he that is upright in the way is abomination to the wicked.

30 ¹The words of Agur the son of Jakeh, even the prophecy: the man spoke to Ithiel, even to Ithiel and Ucal, ²Surely I am more brutish than any man, and have not the understanding of a man. ³I neither learned wisdom, nor have the knowledge of the holy. ⁴Who has ascended up into heaven, or descended? who has gathered the wind in his fists? who has bound the waters in a garment? who has established all the ends of the earth? what is his name, and what is his son's name, if you can tell? ⁵Every word of God is pure: he is a shield to them that put their trust in him. ⁶Add you not to his words, lest he reprove you, and you be found a liar. ⁷Two things have I required of you; deny me them not before I die: ⁸Remove far from me vanity and lies: give me neither poverty nor riches; feed me with food convenient for me: ⁹Lest I be full, and deny you, and say, Who is the LORD? or lest I be poor, and steal, and take the name of my God in vain. ¹⁰Accuse not a servant to his master, lest he curse you, and you be found guilty. ¹¹There is a generation that curses their father, and does not bless their mother. ¹²There is a generation that are pure in their own eyes, and yet is not washed from their filthiness. ¹³There is a generation, O how lofty are their eyes! and their eyelids are lifted up. ¹⁴There is a generation, whose teeth are as swords, and their jaw teeth as knives, to devour the poor from off the earth, and the needy from among men. ¹⁵The horse leach has two daughters, crying, Give, give. There are three things that are never satisfied, yes, four things say not, It is enough: ¹⁶The grave; and the barren womb; the earth that is not filled with water; and the fire that says not, It is enough. ¹⁷The eye that mocks at his father, and despises to obey his mother, the ravens of the valley shall pick it out, and the young eagles shall eat it. ¹⁸There be three things which are too wonderful for me, yes, four which I know not: ¹⁹The way of an eagle in the air; the way of a serpent on a rock; the way of a ship in the middle of the sea; and the way of a man with a maid. ²⁰Such is the way of an adulterous woman; she eats, and wipes her mouth, and says, I have done no wickedness. ²¹For three things the earth is disquieted, and for four which it cannot bear: ²²For a servant when he reigns; and a fool when he is filled with meat; ²³For an odious woman when she is married; and an handmaid that is heir to her mistress. ²⁴There be four things which are little on the earth, but they are exceeding wise: ²⁵The ants are a people not strong, yet they prepare their meat in the summer; ²⁶The conies are but a feeble folk, yet make they their houses in the rocks; ²⁷The locusts have no king, yet go they forth all of them by bands; ²⁸The spider takes hold with her hands, and is in kings' palaces. ²⁹There be three things which go well, yes, four are comely in going: ³⁰A lion which is strongest among beasts, and turns not away for any; ³¹A greyhound; an he goat also; and a king, against whom there is no rising up. ³²If you have done foolishly in lifting up yourself, or if you have thought evil, lay your hand on your mouth. ³³Surely the churning of milk brings forth butter, and the wringing of the nose brings forth blood: so the forcing of wrath brings forth strife.

31

¹The words of king Lemuel, the prophecy that his mother taught him. ²What, my son? and what, the son of my womb? and what, the son of my vows? ³Give not your strength to women, nor your ways to that which destroys kings. ⁴It is not for kings, O Lemuel, it is not for kings to drink wine; nor for princes strong drink: ⁵Lest they drink, and forget the law, and pervert the judgment of any of the afflicted. ⁶Give strong drink to him that is ready to perish, and wine to those that be of heavy hearts. ⁷Let him drink, and forget his poverty, and remember his misery no more. ⁸Open your mouth for the dumb in the cause of all such as are appointed to destruction. ⁹Open your mouth, judge righteously, and plead the cause of the poor and needy. ¹⁰Who can find a virtuous woman? for her price is far above rubies. ¹¹The heart of her husband does safely trust in her, so that he shall have no need of spoil. ¹²She will do him good and not evil all the days of her life. ¹³She seeks wool, and flax, and works willingly with her hands. ¹⁴She is like the merchants' ships; she brings her food from afar. ¹⁵She rises also while it is yet night, and gives meat to her household, and a portion to her maidens. ¹⁶She considers a field, and buys it: with the fruit of her hands she plants a vineyard. ¹⁷She girds her loins with strength, and strengthens her arms. ¹⁸She perceives that her merchandise is good: her candle goes not out by night. ¹⁹She lays her hands to the spindle, and her hands hold the distaff. ²⁰She stretches out her hand to the poor; yes, she reaches forth her hands to the needy. ²¹She is not afraid of the snow for her household: for all her household are clothed with scarlet. ²²She makes herself coverings of tapestry; her clothing is silk and purple. ²³Her husband is known in the gates, when he sits among the elders of the land. ²⁴She makes fine linen, and sells it; and delivers girdles to the merchant. ²⁵Strength and honor are her clothing; and she shall rejoice in time to come. ²⁶She opens her mouth with wisdom; and in her tongue is the law of kindness. ²⁷She looks well to the ways of her household, and eats not the bread of idleness. ²⁸Her children arise up, and call her blessed; her husband also, and he praises her. ²⁹Many daughters have done virtuously, but you excel them all. ³⁰Favor is deceitful, and beauty is vain: but a woman that fears the LORD, she shall be praised. ³¹Give her of the fruit of her hands; and let her own works praise her in the gates.

Ecclesiastes

1 ¹The words of the Preacher, the son of David, king in Jerusalem. ²Vanity of vanities, says the Preacher, vanity of vanities; all is vanity. ³What profit has a man of all his labor which he takes under the sun? ⁴One generation passes away, and another generation comes: but the earth stays for ever. ⁵The sun also rises, and the sun goes down, and hastens to his place where he arose. ⁶The wind goes toward the south, and turns about to the north; it whirls about continually, and the wind returns again according to his circuits. ⁷All the rivers run into the sea; yet the sea is not full; to the place from where the rivers come, thither they return again. ⁸All things are full of labor; man cannot utter it: the eye is not satisfied with seeing, nor the ear filled with hearing. ⁹The thing that has been, it is that which shall be; and that which is done is that which shall be done: and there is no new thing under the sun. ¹⁰Is there any thing whereof it may be said, See, this is new? it has been already of old time, which was before us. ¹¹There is no remembrance of former things; neither shall there be any remembrance of things that are to come with those that shall come after. ¹²I the Preacher was king over Israel in Jerusalem. ¹³And I gave my heart to seek and search out by wisdom concerning all things that are done under heaven: this sore travail has God given to the sons of man to be exercised therewith. ¹⁴I have seen all the works that are done under the sun; and, behold, all is vanity and vexation of spirit. ¹⁵That which is crooked cannot be made straight: and that which is wanting cannot be numbered. ¹⁶I communed with my own heart, saying, See, I am come to great estate, and have gotten more wisdom than all they that have been before me in Jerusalem: yes, my heart had great experience of wisdom and knowledge. ¹⁷And I gave my heart to know wisdom, and to know madness and folly: I perceived that this also is vexation of spirit. ¹⁸For in much wisdom is much grief: and he that increases knowledge increases sorrow.

2 ¹I said in my heart, Go to now, I will prove you with mirth, therefore enjoy pleasure: and, behold, this also is vanity. ²I said of laughter, It is mad: and of mirth, What does it? ³I sought in my heart to give myself to wine, yet acquainting my heart with wisdom; and to lay hold on folly, till I might see what was that good for the sons of men, which they should do under the heaven all the days of their life. ⁴I made me great works; I built me houses; I planted me vineyards: ⁵I made me gardens and orchards, and I planted trees in them of all kind of fruits: ⁶I made me pools of water, to water therewith the wood that brings forth trees: ⁷I got me servants and maidens, and had servants born in my house; also I had great possessions of great and small cattle above all that were in Jerusalem before me: ⁸I gathered me also silver and gold, and the peculiar treasure of kings and of the provinces: I got me men singers and women singers, and the delights of the sons of men, as musical instruments, and that of all sorts. ⁹So I was great, and increased more than all that were before me in Jerusalem: also my wisdom remained with me. ¹⁰And whatever my eyes desired I kept not from them, I withheld not my heart from any joy; for my heart rejoiced in all my labor: and this was my portion of all my labor. ¹¹Then I looked on all the works that my hands had worked, and on the labor that I had labored to do: and, behold, all was vanity and vexation of spirit, and there was no profit under the sun. ¹²And I turned myself to behold wisdom, and madness, and folly: for what can the man do that comes after the king? even that which has been already done. ¹³Then I saw that wisdom excels folly, as far as light excels darkness. ¹⁴The wise man's eyes are in his head; but the fool walks in darkness: and I myself perceived also that one event happens to them all. ¹⁵Then said I in my heart, As it happens to the fool, so it happens even to me; and why was I then more wise? Then I said in my heart, that this also is vanity. ¹⁶For there is no remembrance of the wise more than of the fool for ever; seeing that which now is in the days to come shall all be forgotten. And how dies the wise man? as the fool. ¹⁷Therefore I hated life; because the work that is worked under the sun is grievous to me: for all is vanity and vexation of spirit. ¹⁸Yes, I hated all my labor which I had taken under the sun: because I should leave it to the man that shall be after me. ¹⁹And who knows whether he shall be a wise man or a fool? yet shall he have rule over all my labor wherein I have labored, and wherein I have showed myself wise under the sun. This is also vanity. ²⁰Therefore I went about to cause my heart to despair of all the labor which I took under the sun. ²¹For there is a man whose labor is in wisdom, and in knowledge, and in equity; yet to a man that has not labored therein shall he leave it for his portion. This also is vanity and a great evil. ²²For what has man of all his labor, and of the vexation of his heart, wherein he has labored under the sun? ²³For all his days are sorrows, and his travail grief; yes, his heart takes not rest in the night. This is also vanity. ²⁴There is nothing better for a man, than that he should eat and drink, and that he should make his soul enjoy good in his labor. This also I saw, that it was from the hand of God. ²⁵For who can eat, or who else can hasten hereunto, more than I? ²⁶For God gives to a man that is good in his sight wisdom, and knowledge, and joy: but to the sinner he gives travail, to gather and to heap up, that he may give to him that is good before God. This also is vanity and vexation of spirit.

3 ¹To every thing there is a season, and a time to every purpose under the heaven: ²A time to be born, and a time to die; a time to plant, and a time to pluck up that which is planted; ³A time to kill, and a time to heal; a time to break down, and a time to build up; ⁴A time to weep, and a time to laugh; a time to mourn, and a time to dance; ⁵A time to cast away stones, and a time to gather stones together; a time to embrace, and a time to refrain from embracing; ⁶A time to get, and a time to lose; a time to keep, and a time to cast away; ⁷A time to rend, and a time to sew; a time to keep silence, and a time to speak; ⁸A time to love, and a time to hate; a time of war, and a time of peace. ⁹What profit has he that works in that wherein he labors? ¹⁰I have seen the travail, which God has given to the sons of men to be exercised in it. ¹¹He has made every thing beautiful in his time: also he has set the world in their heart, so that no man can find out the work that God makes from the beginning to the end. ¹²I know that there is no good in them, but for a man to rejoice, and to do good in his life. ¹³And also that every man should eat and drink, and enjoy the good of all his labor, it is the gift of God. ¹⁴I know that, whatever God does, it shall be for ever: nothing can be put to it, nor any thing taken from it: and God does it, that men should fear before him. ¹⁵That which has been is now; and that which is to be has already been; and God requires that which is past. ¹⁶And moreover I saw under the sun the place of judgment, that wickedness was there; and the place of righteousness, that iniquity was there. ¹⁷I said in my heart, God shall judge the righteous and the wicked: for there is a time there for every purpose and for every work. ¹⁸I said in my heart concerning the estate of the sons of men, that God might manifest them, and that they might see that they themselves are beasts. ¹⁹For that which befalls the sons of men befalls beasts; even one thing befalls them: as the one dies, so dies the other; yes, they have all one breath; so that a man has no preeminence above a beast: for all is vanity. ²⁰All go to one place; all are of the dust, and all turn to dust again. ²¹Who knows the spirit of man that goes upward, and the spirit of the beast that goes downward to the earth? ²²Why I perceive that there is nothing better, than that a man should rejoice in his own works; for that is his portion: for who shall bring him to see what shall be after him?

4 ¹So I returned, and considered all the oppressions that are done under the sun: and behold the tears of such as were oppressed, and they had no comforter; and on the side of their oppressors there was power; but they had no comforter. ²Why I praised the dead which are already dead more than the living which are yet alive. ³Yes, better is he than both they, which has not yet been, who has not seen the evil work that is done under the sun. ⁴Again, I considered all travail, and every right work, that for this a man is envied of his neighbor. This is also vanity and vexation of spirit. ⁵The fool folds his hands together, and eats his own flesh. ⁶Better is an handful with quietness, than both the hands full with travail and vexation of spirit. ⁷Then I returned, and I saw vanity under the sun. ⁸There is one alone, and there is not a second; yes, he has neither child nor brother: yet is there no end of all his labor; neither is his eye satisfied with riches; neither says he, For whom do I labor, and bereave my soul of good? This is also vanity, yes, it is a sore travail. ⁹Two are better than one; because they have a good reward for their labor. ¹⁰For if they fall, the one will lift up his fellow: but woe to him that is alone when he falls; for he has not another to help him up. ¹¹Again, if two lie together, then they have heat: but how can one be warm alone? ¹²And if one prevail against him, two shall withstand him; and a threefold cord is not quickly broken. ¹³Better is a poor and a wise child than an old and foolish king, who will no more be admonished. ¹⁴For out of prison he comes to reign; whereas also he that is born in his kingdom becomes poor. ¹⁵I considered all the living which walk under the sun, with the second child that shall stand up in his stead. ¹⁶There is no end of all the people, even of all that have been before them: they also that come after shall not rejoice in him. Surely this also is vanity and vexation of spirit.

5 ¹Keep your foot when you go to the house of God, and be more ready to hear, than to give the sacrifice of fools: for they consider not that they do evil. ²Be not rash with your mouth, and let not your heart be hasty to utter any thing before God: for God is in heaven, and you on earth: therefore let your words be few. ³For a dream comes through the multitude of business; and a fool's voice is known by multitude of words. ⁴When you vow a vow to God, defer not to pay it; for he has no pleasure in fools: pay that which you have vowed. ⁵Better is it that you should not vow, than that you should vow and not pay. ⁶Suffer not your mouth to cause your flesh to sin; neither say you before the angel, that it was an error: why should God be angry at your voice, and destroy the work of your hands? ⁷For in the multitude of dreams and many words there are also divers vanities: but fear you God. ⁸If you see the oppression of the poor, and violent perverting of judgment and justice in a province, marvel not at the matter: for he that is higher than the highest regards; and there be higher than they. ⁹Moreover the profit of the earth is for all: the king himself is served by the field. ¹⁰He that loves silver shall not be satisfied with silver; nor he that loves abundance with increase: this is also vanity. ¹¹When goods increase, they are increased that eat them: and what good is there to the owners thereof, saving the beholding of them with their eyes? ¹²The sleep of a laboring man is sweet, whether he eat little or much: but the abundance of the rich will not suffer him to sleep. ¹³There is a sore evil which I have seen under the sun, namely, riches kept for the owners thereof to their hurt. ¹⁴But those riches perish by evil travail: and he begets a son, and there is nothing in his hand. ¹⁵As he came forth of his mother's womb, naked shall he return to go as he came, and shall take nothing of his labor, which he may carry away in his hand. ¹⁶And this also is a sore evil, that in all points as he came, so shall he go: and what profit has he that has labored for the wind? ¹⁷All his days also he eats in darkness, and he has much sorrow and wrath with his sickness. ¹⁸Behold that which I have seen: it is good and comely for one to eat and to drink, and to enjoy the good of all his labor that he takes under the sun all the days of his life, which God gives him: for it is his portion. ¹⁹Every man also to whom God has given riches and wealth, and has given him power to eat thereof, and to take his portion, and to rejoice in his labor; this is the gift of God. ²⁰For he shall not much remember the days of his life; because God answers him in the joy of his heart.

6 ¹There is an evil which I have seen under the sun, and it is common among men: ²A man to whom God has given riches, wealth, and honor, so that he wants nothing for his soul of all that he desires, yet God gives him not power to eat thereof, but a stranger eats it: this is vanity, and it is an evil disease. ³If a man beget an hundred children, and live many years, so that the days of his years be many, and his soul be not filled with good, and also that he have no burial; I say, that an untimely birth is better than he. ⁴For he comes in with vanity, and departs in darkness, and his name shall be covered with darkness. ⁵Moreover he has not seen the sun, nor known any thing: this has more rest than the other. ⁶Yes, though he live a thousand years twice told, yet has he seen no good: do not all go to one place? ⁷All the labor of man is for his mouth, and yet the appetite is not filled. ⁸For what has the wise more than the fool? what has the poor, that knows to walk before the living? ⁹Better is the sight of

the eyes than the wandering of the desire: this is also vanity and vexation of spirit. ¹⁰That which has been is named already, and it is known that it is man: neither may he contend with him that is mightier than he. ¹¹Seeing there be many things that increase vanity, what is man the better? ¹²For who knows what is good for man in this life, all the days of his vain life which he spends as a shadow? for who can tell a man what shall be after him under the sun?

7 ¹A good name is better than precious ointment; and the day of death than the day of one's birth. ²It is better to go to the house of mourning, than to go to the house of feasting: for that is the end of all men; and the living will lay it to his heart. ³Sorrow is better than laughter: for by the sadness of the countenance the heart is made better. ⁴The heart of the wise is in the house of mourning; but the heart of fools is in the house of mirth. ⁵It is better to hear the rebuke of the wise, than for a man to hear the song of fools. ⁶For as the crackling of thorns under a pot, so is the laughter of the fool: this also is vanity. ⁷Surely oppression makes a wise man mad; and a gift destroys the heart. ⁸Better is the end of a thing than the beginning thereof: and the patient in spirit is better than the proud in spirit. ⁹Be not hasty in your spirit to be angry: for anger rests in the bosom of fools. ¹⁰Say not you, What is the cause that the former days were better than these? for you do not inquire wisely concerning this. ¹¹Wisdom is good with an inheritance: and by it there is profit to them that see the sun. ¹²For wisdom is a defense, and money is a defense: but the excellency of knowledge is, that wisdom gives life to them that have it. ¹³Consider the work of God: for who can make that straight, which he has made crooked? ¹⁴In the day of prosperity be joyful, but in the day of adversity consider: God also has set the one over against the other, to the end that man should find nothing after him. ¹⁵All things have I seen in the days of my vanity: there is a just man that perishes in his righteousness, and there is a wicked man that prolongs his life in his wickedness. ¹⁶Be not righteous over much; neither make yourself over wise: why should you destroy yourself? ¹⁷Be not over much wicked, neither be you foolish: why should you die before your time? ¹⁸It is good that you should take hold of this; yes, also from this withdraw not your hand: for he that fears God shall come forth of them all. ¹⁹Wisdom strengthens the wise more than ten mighty men which are in the city. ²⁰For there is not a just man on earth, that does good, and sins not. ²¹Also take no heed to all words that are spoken; lest you hear your servant curse you: ²²For oftentimes also your own heart knows that you yourself likewise have cursed others. ²³All this have I proved by wisdom: I said, I will be wise; but it was far from me. ²⁴That which is far off, and exceeding deep, who can find it out? ²⁵I applied my heart to know, and to search, and to seek out wisdom, and the reason of things, and to know the wickedness of folly, even of foolishness and madness: ²⁶And I find more bitter than death the woman, whose heart is snares and nets, and her hands as bands: whoever pleases God shall escape from her; but the sinner shall be taken by her. ²⁷Behold, this have I found, says the preacher, counting one by one, to find out the account: ²⁸Which yet my soul seeks, but I find not: one man among a thousand have I found; but a woman among all those have I not found. ²⁹See, this only have I found, that God has made man upright; but they have sought out many inventions.

8 ¹Who is as the wise man? and who knows the interpretation of a thing? a man's wisdom makes his face to shine, and the boldness of his face shall be changed. ²I counsel you to keep the king's commandment, and that in regard of the oath of God. ³Be not hasty to go out of his sight: stand not in an evil thing; for he does whatever pleases him. ⁴Where the word of a king is, there is power: and who may say to him, What do you? ⁵Whoever keeps the commandment shall feel no evil thing: and a wise man's heart discerns both time and judgment. ⁶Because to every purpose there is time and judgment, therefore the misery of man is great on him. ⁷For he knows not that which shall be: for who can tell him when it shall be? ⁸There is no man that has power over the spirit to retain the spirit; neither has he power in the day of death: and there is no discharge in that war; neither shall wickedness deliver those that are given to it. ⁹All this have I seen, and applied my heart to every work that is done under the sun: there is a time wherein one man rules over another to his own hurt. ¹⁰And so I saw the wicked buried, who had come and gone from the place of the holy, and they were forgotten in the city where they had so done: this is also vanity. ¹¹Because sentence against an evil work is not executed speedily, therefore the heart of the sons of men is fully set in them to do evil. ¹²Though a sinner do evil an hundred times, and his days be prolonged, yet surely I know that it shall be well with them that fear God, which fear before him: ¹³But it shall not be well with the wicked, neither shall he prolong his days, which are as a shadow; because he fears not before God. ¹⁴There is a vanity which is done on the earth; that there be just men, to whom it happens according to the work of the wicked; again, there be wicked men, to whom it happens according to the work of the righteous: I said that this also is vanity. ¹⁵Then I commended mirth, because a man has no better thing under the sun, than to eat, and to drink, and to be merry: for that shall abide with him of his labor the days of his life, which God gives him under the sun. ¹⁶When I applied my heart to know wisdom, and to see the business that is done on the earth: (for also there is that neither day nor night sees sleep with his eyes:) ¹⁷Then I beheld all the work of God, that a man cannot find out the work that is done under the sun: because though a man labor to seek it out, yet he shall not find it; yes farther; though a wise man think to know it, yet shall he not be able to find it.

9 ¹For all this I considered in my heart even to declare all this, that the righteous, and the wise, and their works, are in the hand of God: no man knows either love or hatred by all that is before them. ²All things come alike to all: there is one event to the righteous, and to the wicked; to the good and to the clean, and to the unclean; to him that sacrifices, and to him that sacrifices not: as is the good, so is the sinner; and he that swears, as he that fears an oath. ³This is an evil among all things that are done under the sun, that there is one event to all: yes, also the heart of the sons of men is full of evil, and madness is in their heart while they live, and after that they go to the dead. ⁴For to him that is joined to all the living there is hope: for a living dog is better than a dead

lion. ⁵For the living know that they shall die: but the dead know not any thing, neither have they any more a reward; for the memory of them is forgotten. ⁶Also their love, and their hatred, and their envy, is now perished; neither have they any more a portion for ever in any thing that is done under the sun. ⁷Go your way, eat your bread with joy, and drink your wine with a merry heart; for God now accepts your works. ⁸Let your garments be always white; and let your head lack no ointment. ⁹Live joyfully with the wife whom you love all the days of the life of your vanity, which he has given you under the sun, all the days of your vanity: for that is your portion in this life, and in your labor which you take under the sun. ¹⁰Whatever your hand finds to do, do it with your might; for there is no work, nor device, nor knowledge, nor wisdom, in the grave, where you go. ¹¹I returned, and saw under the sun, that the race is not to the swift, nor the battle to the strong, neither yet bread to the wise, nor yet riches to men of understanding, nor yet favor to men of skill; but time and chance happens to them all. ¹²For man also knows not his time: as the fishes that are taken in an evil net, and as the birds that are caught in the snare; so are the sons of men snared in an evil time, when it falls suddenly on them. ¹³This wisdom have I seen also under the sun, and it seemed great to me: ¹⁴There was a little city, and few men within it; and there came a great king against it, and besieged it, and built great bulwarks against it: ¹⁵Now there was found in it a poor wise man, and he by his wisdom delivered the city; yet no man remembered that same poor man. ¹⁶Then said I, Wisdom is better than strength: nevertheless the poor man's wisdom is despised, and his words are not heard. ¹⁷The words of wise men are heard in quiet more than the cry of him that rules among fools. ¹⁸Wisdom is better than weapons of war: but one sinner destroys much good.

10 ¹Dead flies cause the ointment of the apothecary to send forth a stinking smell: so does a little folly him that is in reputation for wisdom and honor. ²A wise man's heart is at his right hand; but a fool's heart at his left. ³Yes also, when he that is a fool walks by the way, his wisdom fails him, and he says to every one that he is a fool. ⁴If the spirit of the ruler rise up against you, leave not your place; for yielding pacifies great offenses. ⁵There is an evil which I have seen under the sun, as an error which proceeds from the ruler: ⁶Folly is set in great dignity, and the rich sit in low place. ⁷I have seen servants on horses, and princes walking as servants on the earth. ⁸He that digs a pit shall fall into it; and whoever breaks an hedge, a serpent shall bite him. ⁹Whoever removes stones shall be hurt therewith; and he that splits wood shall be endangered thereby. ¹⁰If the iron be blunt, and he do not whet the edge, then must he put to more strength: but wisdom is profitable to direct. ¹¹Surely the serpent will bite without enchantment; and a babbler is no better. ¹²The words of a wise man's mouth are gracious; but the lips of a fool will swallow up himself. ¹³The beginning of the words of his mouth is foolishness: and the end of his talk is mischievous madness. ¹⁴A fool also is full of words: a man cannot tell what shall be; and what shall be after him, who can tell him? ¹⁵The labor of the foolish wearies every one of them, because he knows not how to go to the city. ¹⁶Woe to you, O land, when your king is a child, and your princes eat in the morning! ¹⁷Blessed are you, O land, when your king is the son of nobles, and your princes eat in due season, for strength, and not for drunkenness! ¹⁸By much slothfulness the building decays; and through idleness of the hands the house drops through. ¹⁹A feast is made for laughter, and wine makes merry: but money answers all things. ²⁰Curse not the king, no not in your thought; and curse not the rich in your bedchamber: for a bird of the air shall carry the voice, and that which has wings shall tell the matter.

11 ¹Cast your bread on the waters: for you shall find it after many days. ²Give a portion to seven, and also to eight; for you know not what evil shall be on the earth. ³If the clouds be full of rain, they empty themselves on the earth: and if the tree fall toward the south, or toward the north, in the place where the tree falls, there it shall be. ⁴He that observes the wind shall not sow; and he that regards the clouds shall not reap. ⁵As you know not what is the way of the spirit, nor how the bones do grow in the womb of her that is with child: even so you know not the works of God who makes all. ⁶In the morning sow your seed, and in the evening withhold not your hand: for you know not whether shall prosper, either this or that, or whether they both shall be alike good. ⁷Truly the light is sweet, and a pleasant thing it is for the eyes to behold the sun: ⁸But if a man live many years, and rejoice in them all; yet let him remember the days of darkness; for they shall be many. All that comes is vanity. ⁹Rejoice, O young man, in your youth; and let your heart cheer you in the days of your youth, and walk in the ways of your heart, and in the sight of your eyes: but know you, that for all these things God will bring you into judgment. ¹⁰Therefore remove sorrow from your heart, and put away evil from your flesh: for childhood and youth are vanity.

12 ¹Remember now your Creator in the days of your youth, while the evil days come not, nor the years draw near, when you shall say, I have no pleasure in them; ²While the sun, or the light, or the moon, or the stars, be not darkened, nor the clouds return after the rain: ³In the day when the keepers of the house shall tremble, and the strong men shall bow themselves, and the grinders cease because they are few, and those that look out of the windows be darkened, ⁴And the doors shall be shut in the streets, when the sound of the grinding is low, and he shall rise up at the voice of the bird, and all the daughters of music shall be brought low; ⁵Also when they shall be afraid of that which is high, and fears shall be in the way, and the almond tree shall flourish, and the grasshopper shall be a burden, and desire shall fail: because man goes to his long home, and the mourners go about the streets: ⁶Or ever the silver cord be loosed, or the golden bowl be broken, or the pitcher be broken at the fountain, or the wheel broken at the cistern. ⁷Then shall the dust return to the earth as it was: and the spirit shall return to God who gave it. ⁸Vanity of vanities, says the preacher; all is vanity. ⁹And moreover, because the preacher was wise, he still taught the people knowledge; yes, he gave good heed, and sought out, and set in order many proverbs. ¹⁰The preacher sought to find out acceptable words: and that which was written was upright, even words of truth. ¹¹The words of the wise are as goads, and as nails fastened by the masters of assemblies, which are given from one shepherd. ¹²And further, by these, my son, be admonished: of making many books there is no end; and much study is a weariness of the flesh. ¹³Let us hear the conclusion of the whole matter: Fear God, and keep his commandments: for this is the whole duty of man. ¹⁴For God shall bring every work into judgment, with every secret thing, whether it be good, or whether it be evil.

Song of Solomon

1 ¹The song of songs, which is Solomon's. ²Let him kiss me with the kisses of his mouth: for your love is better than wine. ³Because of the smell of your good ointments your name is as ointment poured forth, therefore do the virgins love you. ⁴Draw me, we will run after you: the king has brought me into his chambers: we will be glad and rejoice in you, we will remember your love more than wine: the upright love you. ⁵I am black, but comely, O you daughters of Jerusalem, as the tents of Kedar, as the curtains of Solomon. ⁶Look not on me, because I am black, because the sun has looked on me: my mother's children were angry with me; they made me the keeper of the vineyards; but my own vineyard have I not kept. ⁷Tell me, O you whom my soul loves, where you feed, where you make your flock to rest at noon: for why should I be as one that turns aside by the flocks of your companions? ⁸If you know not, O you fairest among women, go your way forth by the footsteps of the flock, and feed your kids beside the shepherds' tents. ⁹I have compared you, O my love, to a company of horses in Pharaoh's chariots. ¹⁰Your cheeks are comely with rows of jewels, your neck with chains of gold. ¹¹We will make you borders of gold with studs of silver. ¹²While the king sits at his table, my spikenard sends forth the smell thereof. ¹³A bundle of myrrh is my well-beloved to me; he shall lie all night between my breasts. ¹⁴My beloved is to me as a cluster of camphire in the vineyards of Engedi. ¹⁵Behold, you are fair, my love; behold, you are fair; you have doves' eyes. ¹⁶Behold, you are fair, my beloved, yes, pleasant: also our bed is green. ¹⁷The beams of our house are cedar, and our rafters of fir.

2 ¹I am the rose of Sharon, and the lily of the valleys. ²As the lily among thorns, so is my love among the daughters. ³As the apple tree among the trees of the wood, so is my beloved among the sons. I sat down under his shadow with great delight, and his fruit was sweet to my taste. ⁴He brought me to the banqueting house, and his banner over me was love. ⁵Stay me with flagons, comfort me with apples: for I am sick of love. ⁶His left hand is under my head, and his right hand does embrace me. ⁷I charge you, O you daughters of Jerusalem, by the roes, and by the hinds of the field, that you stir not up, nor awake my love, till he please. ⁸The voice of my beloved! behold, he comes leaping on the mountains, skipping on the hills. ⁹My beloved is like a roe or a young hart: behold, he stands behind our wall, he looks forth at the windows, showing himself through the lattice. ¹⁰My beloved spoke, and said to me, Rise up, my love, my fair one, and come away. ¹¹For, see, the winter is past, the rain is over and gone; ¹²The flowers appear on the earth; the time of the singing of birds is come, and the voice of the turtle is heard in our land; ¹³The fig tree puts forth her green figs, and the vines with the tender grape give a good smell. Arise, my love, my fair one, and come away. ¹⁴O my dove, that are in the clefts of the rock, in the secret places of the stairs, let me see your countenance, let me hear your voice; for sweet is your voice, and your countenance is comely. ¹⁵Take us the foxes, the little foxes, that spoil the vines: for our vines have tender grapes. ¹⁶My beloved is mine, and I am his: he feeds among the lilies. ¹⁷Until the day break, and the shadows flee away, turn, my beloved, and be you like a roe or a young hart on the mountains of Bether.

3 ¹By night on my bed I sought him whom my soul loves: I sought him, but I found him not. ²I will rise now, and go about the city in the streets, and in the broad ways I will seek him whom my soul loves: I sought him, but I found him not. ³The watchmen that go about the city found me: to whom I said, Saw you him whom my soul loves? ⁴It was but a little that I passed from them, but I found him whom my soul loves: I held him, and would not let him go, until I had brought him into my mother's house, and into the chamber of her that conceived me. ⁵I charge you, O you daughters of Jerusalem, by the roes, and by the hinds of the field, that you stir not up, nor awake my love, till he please. ⁶Who is this that comes out of the wilderness like pillars of smoke, perfumed with myrrh and frankincense, with all powders of the merchant? ⁷Behold his bed, which is Solomon's; three score valiant men are about it, of the valiant of Israel. ⁸They all hold swords, being expert in war: every man has his sword on his thigh because of fear in the night. ⁹King Solomon made himself a chariot of the wood of Lebanon. ¹⁰He made the pillars thereof of silver, the bottom thereof of gold, the covering of it of purple, the middle thereof being paved with love, for the daughters of Jerusalem. ¹¹Go forth, O you daughters of Zion, and behold king Solomon with the crown with which his mother crowned him in the day of his espousals, and in the day of the gladness of his heart.

4 ¹Behold, you are fair, my love; behold, you are fair; you have doves' eyes within your locks: your hair is as a flock of goats, that appear from mount Gilead. ²Your teeth are like a flock of sheep that are even shorn, which came up from the washing; whereof every one bear twins, and none is barren among them. ³Your lips are like a thread of scarlet, and your speech is comely: your temples are like a piece of a pomegranate within your locks. ⁴Your neck is like the tower of David built for an armory, where on there hang a thousand bucklers, all shields of mighty men. ⁵Your two breasts are like two young roes that are twins, which feed among the lilies. ⁶Until the day break, and the shadows flee away, I will get me to the mountain of myrrh, and to the hill of frankincense. ⁷You are all fair, my love; there is no spot in you. ⁸Come with me from Lebanon, my spouse, with me from Lebanon: look from the top of Amana, from the top of Shenir and Hermon, from the lions' dens, from the mountains of the leopards. ⁹You have ravished my heart, my sister, my spouse; you have ravished my heart with one of your eyes, with one chain of your neck. ¹⁰How fair is your love, my sister, my spouse! how much better is your love than wine! and the smell of your ointments than all spices! ¹¹Your lips, O my spouse, drop as the honeycomb: honey and milk are under your tongue; and the smell of your garments is like the smell of Lebanon. ¹²A garden enclosed is my sister, my spouse; a spring shut up, a fountain sealed. ¹³Your plants are an orchard of pomegranates, with pleasant fruits; camphire, with spikenard, ¹⁴Spikenard and saffron; calamus and cinnamon, with all trees of frankincense; myrrh and aloes, with all the chief spices: ¹⁵A fountain of gardens, a well of living waters, and streams from Lebanon. ¹⁶Awake, O north wind; and come, you south; blow on my garden, that the spices thereof may flow out. Let my beloved come into his garden, and eat his pleasant fruits.

5 ¹I am come into my garden, my sister, my spouse: I have gathered my myrrh with my spice; I have eaten my honeycomb with my honey; I have drunk my wine with my milk: eat, O friends; drink, yes, drink abundantly, O beloved. ²I sleep, but my heart wakes: it is the voice of my beloved that knocks, saying, Open to me, my sister, my love, my dove, my undefiled: for my head is filled with dew, and my locks with the drops of the night. ³I have put off my coat; how shall I put it on? I have washed my feet; how shall I defile them? ⁴My beloved put in his hand by the hole of the door, and my bowels were moved for him. ⁵I rose up to open to my beloved; and my hands dropped with myrrh, and my fingers with sweet smelling myrrh, on the handles of the lock. ⁶I opened to my beloved; but my beloved had withdrawn himself, and was gone: my soul failed when he spoke: I sought him, but I could not find him; I called him, but he gave me no answer. ⁷The watchmen that went about the city found me, they smote me, they wounded me; the keepers of the walls took away my veil from me. ⁸I charge you, O daughters of Jerusalem, if you find my beloved, that you tell him, that I am sick of love. ⁹What is your beloved more than another beloved, O you fairest among women? what is your beloved more than another beloved, that you do so charge us? ¹⁰My beloved is white and ruddy, the most chief among ten thousand. ¹¹His head is as the most fine gold, his locks are bushy, and black as a raven. ¹²His eyes are as the eyes of doves by the rivers of waters, washed with milk, and fitly set. ¹³His cheeks are as a bed of spices, as sweet flowers: his lips like lilies, dropping sweet smelling myrrh. ¹⁴His hands are as gold rings set with the beryl: his belly is as bright ivory overlaid with sapphires. ¹⁵His legs are as pillars of marble, set on sockets of fine gold: his countenance is as Lebanon, excellent as the cedars. ¹⁶His mouth is most sweet: yes, he is altogether lovely. This is my beloved, and this is my friend, O daughters of Jerusalem.

6 ¹Where is your beloved gone, O you fairest among women? where is your beloved turned aside? that we may seek him with you. ²My beloved is gone down into his garden, to the beds of spices, to feed in the gardens, and to gather lilies. ³I am my beloved's, and my beloved is mine: he feeds among the lilies. ⁴You are beautiful, O my love, as Tirzah, comely as Jerusalem, terrible as an army with banners. ⁵Turn away your eyes from me, for they have overcome me: your hair is as a flock of goats that appear from Gilead. ⁶Your teeth are as a flock of sheep which go up from the washing, whereof every one bears twins, and there is not one barren among them. ⁷As a piece of a pomegranate are your temples within your locks. ⁸There are three score queens, and fourscore concubines, and virgins without number. ⁹My dove, my undefiled is but one; she is the only one of her mother, she is the choice one of her that bore her. The daughters saw her, and blessed her; yes, the queens and the concubines, and they praised her. ¹⁰Who is she that looks forth as the morning, fair as the moon, clear as the sun, and terrible as an army with banners? ¹¹I went down into the garden of nuts to see the fruits of the valley, and to see whether the vine flourished and the pomegranates budded. ¹²Or ever I was aware, my soul made me like the chariots of Amminadib. ¹³Return, return, O Shulamite; return, return, that we may look on you. What will you see in the Shulamite? As it were the company of two armies.

7 ¹How beautiful are your feet with shoes, O prince's daughter! the joints of your thighs are like jewels, the work of the hands of a cunning workman. ²Your navel is like a round goblet, which wants not liquor: your belly is like an heap of wheat set about with lilies. ³Your two breasts are like two young roes that are twins. ⁴Your neck is as a tower of ivory; your eyes like the fish pools in Heshbon, by the gate of Bathrabbim: your nose is as the tower of Lebanon which looks toward Damascus. ⁵Your head on you is like Carmel, and the hair of your head like purple; the king is held in the galleries. ⁶How fair and how pleasant are you, O love, for delights! ⁷This your stature is like to a palm tree, and your breasts to clusters of grapes. ⁸I said, I will go up to the palm tree, I will take hold of the boughs thereof: now also your breasts shall be as clusters of the vine, and the smell of your nose like apples; ⁹And the roof of your mouth like the best wine for my beloved, that goes down sweetly, causing the lips of those that are asleep to speak. ¹⁰I am my beloved's, and his desire is toward me. ¹¹Come, my beloved, let us go forth into the field; let us lodge in the villages. ¹²Let us get up early to the vineyards; let us see if the vine flourish, whether the tender grape appear, and the pomegranates bud forth: there will I give you my loves. ¹³The mandrakes give a smell, and at our gates are all manner of pleasant fruits, new and old, which I have laid up for you, O my beloved.

8 ¹O that you were as my brother, that sucked the breasts of my mother! when I should find you without, I would kiss you; yes, I should not be despised. ²I would lead you, and bring you into my mother's house, who would instruct me: I would cause you to drink of spiced wine of the juice of my pomegranate. ³His left hand should be under my head, and his right hand should embrace me. ⁴I charge you, O daughters of Jerusalem, that you stir not up, nor awake my love, until he please. ⁵Who is this that comes up from the wilderness, leaning on her beloved? I raised you up under the apple tree: there your mother brought you forth: there she brought you forth that bore you. ⁶Set me as a seal on your heart, as a seal on your arm: for love is strong as death; jealousy is cruel as the grave: the coals thereof are coals of fire, which has a most vehement flame. ⁷Many waters cannot quench love, neither can the floods drown it: if a man would give all the substance of his house for love, it would utterly be scorned. ⁸We have a little sister, and she has no breasts: what shall we do for our sister in the day when she shall be spoken for? ⁹If she be a wall, we will build on her a palace of silver: and if she be a door, we will enclose her with boards of cedar. ¹⁰I am a wall, and my breasts like towers: then was I in his eyes as one that found favor. ¹¹Solomon had a vineyard at Baalhamon; he let out the vineyard to keepers; every one for the fruit thereof was to bring a thousand pieces of silver. ¹²My vineyard, which is mine, is before me: you, O Solomon, must have a thousand, and those that keep the fruit

thereof two hundred. ¹³You that dwell in the gardens, the companions listen to your voice: cause me to hear it. ¹⁴Make haste, my beloved, and be you like to a roe or to a young hart on the mountains of spices.

Isaiah

1 ¹The vision of Isaiah the son of Amoz, which he saw concerning Judah and Jerusalem in the days of Uzziah, Jotham, Ahaz, and Hezekiah, kings of Judah. ²Hear, O heavens, and give ear, O earth: for the LORD has spoken, I have nourished and brought up children, and they have rebelled against me. ³The ox knows his owner, and the ass his master's crib: but Israel does not know, my people does not consider. ⁴Ah sinful nation, a people laden with iniquity, a seed of evildoers, children that are corrupters: they have forsaken the LORD, they have provoked the Holy One of Israel to anger, they are gone away backward. ⁵Why should you be stricken any more? you will revolt more and more: the whole head is sick, and the whole heart faint. ⁶From the sole of the foot even to the head there is no soundness in it; but wounds, and bruises, and putrefying sores: they have not been closed, neither bound up, neither mollified with ointment. ⁷Your country is desolate, your cities are burned with fire: your land, strangers devour it in your presence, and it is desolate, as overthrown by strangers. ⁸And the daughter of Zion is left as a cottage in a vineyard, as a lodge in a garden of cucumbers, as a besieged city. ⁹Except the LORD of hosts had left to us a very small remnant, we should have been as Sodom, and we should have been like to Gomorrah. ¹⁰Hear the word of the LORD, you rulers of Sodom; give ear to the law of our God, you people of Gomorrah. ¹¹To what purpose is the multitude of your sacrifices to me? says the LORD: I am full of the burnt offerings of rams, and the fat of fed beasts; and I delight not in the blood of bullocks, or of lambs, or of he goats. ¹²When you come to appear before me, who has required this at your hand, to tread my courts? ¹³Bring no more vain oblations; incense is an abomination to me; the new moons and sabbaths, the calling of assemblies, I cannot away with; it is iniquity, even the solemn meeting. ¹⁴Your new moons and your appointed feasts my soul hates: they are a trouble to me; I am weary to bear them. ¹⁵And when you spread forth your hands, I will hide my eyes from you: yes, when you make many prayers, I will not hear: your hands are full of blood. ¹⁶Wash you, make you clean; put away the evil of your doings from before my eyes; cease to do evil; ¹⁷Learn to do well; seek judgment, relieve the oppressed, judge the fatherless, plead for the widow. ¹⁸Come now, and let us reason together, says the LORD: though your sins be as scarlet, they shall be as white as snow; though they be red like crimson, they shall be as wool. ¹⁹If you be willing and obedient, you shall eat the good of the land: ²⁰But if you refuse and rebel, you shall be devoured with the sword: for the mouth of the LORD has spoken it. ²¹How is the faithful city become an harlot! it was full of judgment; righteousness lodged in it; but now murderers. ²²Your silver is become dross, your wine mixed with water: ²³Your princes are rebellious, and companions of thieves: every one loves gifts, and follows after rewards: they judge not the fatherless, neither does the cause of the widow come to them. ²⁴Therefore says the LORD, the LORD of hosts, the mighty One of Israel, Ah, I will ease me of my adversaries, and avenge me of my enemies: ²⁵And I will turn my hand on you, and purely purge away your dross, and take away all your tin: ²⁶And I will restore your judges as at the first, and your counsellors as at the beginning: afterward you shall be called, The city of righteousness, the faithful city. ²⁷Zion shall be redeemed with judgment, and her converts with righteousness. ²⁸And the destruction of the transgressors and of the sinners shall be together, and they that forsake the LORD shall be consumed. ²⁹For they shall be ashamed of the oaks which you have desired, and you shall be confounded for the gardens that you have chosen. ³⁰For you shall be as an oak whose leaf fades, and as a garden that has no water. ³¹And the strong shall be as wick, and the maker of it as a spark, and they shall both burn together, and none shall quench them.

2 ¹The word that Isaiah the son of Amoz saw concerning Judah and Jerusalem. ²And it shall come to pass in the last days, that the mountain of the LORD's house shall be established in the top of the mountains, and shall be exalted above the hills; and all nations shall flow to it. ³And many people shall go and say, Come you, and let us go up to the mountain of the LORD, to the house of the God of Jacob; and he will teach us of his ways, and we will walk in his paths: for out of Zion shall go forth the law, and the word of the LORD from Jerusalem. ⁴And he shall judge among the nations, and shall rebuke many people: and they shall beat their swords into plowshares, and their spears into pruning hooks: nation shall not lift up sword against nation, neither shall they learn war any more. ⁵O house of Jacob, come you, and let us walk in the light of the LORD. ⁶Therefore you have forsaken your people the house of Jacob, because they be replenished from the east, and are soothsayers like the Philistines, and they please themselves in the children of strangers. ⁷Their land also is full of silver and gold, neither is there any end of their treasures; their land is also full of horses, neither is there any end of their chariots: ⁸Their land also is full of idols; they worship the work of their own hands, that which their own fingers have made: ⁹And the mean man bows down, and the great man humbles himself: therefore forgive them not. ¹⁰Enter into the rock, and hide you in the dust, for fear of the LORD, and for the glory of his majesty. ¹¹The lofty looks of man shall be humbled, and the haughtiness of men shall be bowed down, and the LORD alone shall be exalted in that day. ¹²For the day of the LORD of hosts shall be on every one that is proud and lofty, and on every one that is lifted up; and he shall be brought low: ¹³And on all the cedars of Lebanon, that are high and lifted up, and on all the oaks of Bashan, ¹⁴And on all the high mountains, and on all the hills that are lifted up, ¹⁵And on every high tower, and on every fenced wall, ¹⁶And on all the ships of Tarshish, and on all pleasant pictures. ¹⁷And the loftiness of man shall be bowed down, and the haughtiness of men shall be made low: and the LORD alone shall be exalted in that day. ¹⁸And the idols he shall utterly abolish. ¹⁹And they shall go into the holes of the rocks, and into the caves of the earth, for fear of the LORD, and for the glory of his majesty, when he rises to shake terribly the earth. ²⁰In that day a man shall cast his idols of silver, and his idols of gold, which they made each one for himself to worship, to the moles and to the bats; ²¹To go into the clefts of the rocks, and into the tops of the ragged rocks, for fear of the LORD, and for the glory of his majesty, when he rises to shake terribly the earth. ²²Cease you from man, whose breath is in his nostrils: for wherein is he to be accounted of?

3 ¹For, behold, the Lord, the LORD of hosts, does take away from Jerusalem and from Judah the stay and the staff, the whole stay of bread, and the whole stay of water. ²The mighty man, and the man of war, the judge, and the prophet, and the prudent, and the ancient, ³The captain of fifty, and the honorable man, and the counselor, and the cunning artificer, and the eloquent orator. ⁴And I will give children to be their princes, and babes shall rule over them. ⁵And the people shall be oppressed, every one by another, and every one by his neighbor: the child shall behave himself proudly against the ancient, and the base against the honorable. ⁶When a man shall take hold of his brother of the house of his father, saying, You have clothing, be you our ruler, and let this ruin be under your hand: ⁷In that day shall he swear, saying, I will not be an healer; for in my house is neither bread nor clothing: make me not a ruler of the people. ⁸For Jerusalem is ruined, and Judah is fallen: because their tongue and their doings are against the LORD, to provoke the eyes of his glory. ⁹The show of their countenance does witness against them; and they declare their sin as Sodom, they hide it not. Woe to their soul! for they have rewarded evil to themselves. ¹⁰Say you to the righteous, that it shall be well with him: for they shall eat the fruit of their doings. ¹¹Woe to the wicked! it shall be ill with him: for the reward of his hands shall be given him. ¹²As for my people, children are their oppressors, and women rule over them. O my people, they which lead you cause you to err, and destroy the way of your paths. ¹³The LORD stands up to plead, and stands to judge the people. ¹⁴The LORD will enter into judgment with the ancients of his people, and the princes thereof: for you have eaten up the vineyard; the spoil of the poor is in your houses. ¹⁵What mean you that you beat my people to pieces, and grind the faces of the poor? says the Lord GOD of hosts. ¹⁶Moreover the LORD says, Because the daughters of Zion are haughty, and walk with stretched forth necks and wanton eyes, walking and mincing as they go, and making a tinkling with their feet: ¹⁷Therefore the LORD will smite with a scab the crown of the head of the daughters of Zion, and the LORD will discover their secret parts. ¹⁸In that day the Lord will take away the bravery of their tinkling ornaments about their feet, and their cauls, and their round tires like the moon, ¹⁹The chains, and the bracelets, and the mufflers, ²⁰The bonnets, and the ornaments of the legs, and the headbands, and the tablets, and the earrings, ²¹The rings, and nose jewels, ²²The changeable suits of apparel, and the mantles, and the wimples, and the crisping pins, ²³The glasses, and the fine linen, and the hoods, and the veils. ²⁴And it shall come to pass, that instead of sweet smell there shall be stink; and instead of a girdle a rent; and instead of well set hair baldness; and instead of a stomacher a girding of sackcloth; and burning instead of beauty. ²⁵Your men shall fall by the sword, and your mighty in the war. ²⁶And her gates shall lament and mourn; and she being desolate shall sit on the ground.

4 ¹And in that day seven women shall take hold of one man, saying, We will eat our own bread, and wear our own apparel: only let us be called by your name, to take away our reproach. ²In that day shall the branch of the LORD be beautiful and glorious, and the fruit of the earth shall be excellent and comely for them that are escaped of Israel. ³And it shall come to pass, that he that is left in Zion, and he that remains in Jerusalem, shall be called holy, even every one that is written among the living in Jerusalem: ⁴When the Lord shall have washed away the filth of the daughters of Zion, and shall have purged the blood of Jerusalem from the middle thereof by the spirit of judgment, and by the spirit of burning. ⁵And the LORD will create on every dwelling place of mount Zion, and on her assemblies, a cloud and smoke by day, and the shining of a flaming fire by night: for on all the glory shall be a defense. ⁶And there shall be a tabernacle for a shadow in the day time from the heat, and for a place of refuge, and for a covert from storm and from rain.

5 ¹Now will I sing to my well beloved a song of my beloved touching his vineyard. My well beloved has a vineyard in a very fruitful hill: ²And he fenced it, and gathered out the stones thereof, and planted it with the choicest vine, and built a tower in the middle of it, and also made a wine press therein: and he looked that it should bring forth grapes, and it brought forth wild grapes. ³And now, O inhabitants of Jerusalem, and men of Judah, judge, I pray you, between me and my vineyard. ⁴What could have been done more to my vineyard, that I have not done in it? why, when I looked that it should bring forth grapes, brought it forth wild grapes? ⁵And now go to; I will tell you what I will do to my vineyard: I will take away the hedge thereof, and it shall be eaten up; and break down the wall thereof, and it shall be trodden down: ⁶And I will lay it waste: it shall not be pruned, nor dig; but there shall come up briers and thorns: I will also command the clouds that they rain no rain on it. ⁷For the vineyard of the LORD of hosts is the house of Israel, and the men of Judah his pleasant plant: and he looked for judgment, but behold oppression; for righteousness, but behold a cry. ⁸Woe to them that join house to house, that lay field to field, till there be no place, that they may be placed alone in the middle of the earth! ⁹In my ears said the LORD of hosts, Of a truth many houses shall be desolate, even great and fair, without inhabitant. ¹⁰Yes, ten acres of vineyard shall yield one bath, and the seed of an homer shall yield an ephah. ¹¹Woe to them that rise up early in the morning, that they may follow strong drink; that continue until night, till wine inflame them! ¹²And the harp, and the viol, the tabret, and pipe, and wine, are in their feasts: but they regard not the work of the LORD, neither consider the operation of his hands. ¹³Therefore my people are gone into captivity, because they have no knowledge: and their honorable men are famished, and their multitude dried up with thirst. ¹⁴Therefore hell has enlarged herself, and opened her mouth without measure: and their glory, and their multitude, and their pomp, and he that rejoices, shall descend into it. ¹⁵And the mean man shall be brought down, and the mighty man shall be humbled, and the eyes of the lofty shall be humbled: ¹⁶But the LORD of hosts shall be exalted in judgment, and God that is holy shall be sanctified in righteousness. ¹⁷Then shall the lambs feed after their manner, and the waste places of the fat ones shall strangers eat. ¹⁸Woe to them that draw iniquity with cords of vanity, and sin as it were with a cart rope: ¹⁹That say, Let him make speed, and hasten his work, that we may see it: and let the counsel of the Holy One of Israel draw near and come, that we may know it! ²⁰Woe to them that call evil good, and good evil; that put darkness for light, and light for darkness; that put bitter for sweet, and sweet for bitter! ²¹Woe to them that are wise in their own eyes, and prudent in their own sight! ²²Woe to them that are mighty to drink wine, and men of strength to mingle strong drink: ²³Which justify the wicked for reward, and take away the righteousness of the righteous from him! ²⁴Therefore as the fire devours the stubble, and the flame consumes the chaff, so their root shall be as rottenness, and their blossom shall go up as dust: because they have cast away the law of the LORD of hosts, and despised the word of the Holy One of Israel. ²⁵Therefore is the anger of the LORD kindled against his people, and he has stretched forth his hand against them, and has smitten them: and the hills did tremble, and their carcasses were torn in the middle of the streets. For all this his anger is not turned away, but his hand is stretched out still. ²⁶And he will lift up an ensign to the nations from far, and will hiss to them from the end of the earth: and, behold, they shall come with speed swiftly: ²⁷None shall be weary nor stumble among them; none shall slumber nor sleep; neither shall the girdle of their loins be loosed, nor the lace of their shoes be broken: ²⁸Whose arrows are sharp, and all their bows bent, their horses' hoofs shall be counted like flint, and their wheels like a whirlwind: ²⁹Their roaring shall be like a lion, they shall roar like young lions: yes, they shall roar, and lay hold of the prey, and shall carry it away safe, and none shall deliver it. ³⁰And in that day they shall roar against them like the roaring of the sea: and if one look to the land, behold darkness and sorrow, and the light is darkened in the heavens thereof.

6 ¹In the year that king Uzziah died I saw also the LORD sitting on a throne, high and lifted up, and his train filled the temple. ²Above it stood the seraphim: each one had six wings; with two he covered his face, and with two he covered his feet, and with two he did fly. ³And one cried to another, and said, Holy, holy, holy, is the LORD of hosts: the whole earth is full of his glory. ⁴And the posts of the door moved at the voice of him that cried, and the house was filled with smoke. ⁵Then said I, Woe is me! for I am undone; because I am a man of unclean lips, and I dwell in the middle of a people of unclean lips: for my eyes have seen the King, the LORD of hosts. ⁶Then flew one of the seraphim to me, having a live coal in his hand, which he had taken with the tongs from off the altar: ⁷And he laid it on my mouth, and said, See, this has touched your lips; and your iniquity is taken away, and your sin purged. ⁸Also I heard the voice of the Lord, saying, Whom shall I send, and who will go for us? Then said I, Here am I; send me. ⁹And he said, Go, and tell this people, Hear you indeed, but understand not; and see you indeed, but perceive not. ¹⁰Make the heart of this people fat, and make their ears heavy, and shut their eyes; lest they see with their eyes, and hear with their ears, and understand with their heart, and convert, and be healed. ¹¹Then said I, Lord, how long? And he answered, Until the cities be wasted without inhabitant, and the houses without man, and the land be utterly desolate, ¹²And the LORD have removed men far away, and there be a great forsaking in the middle of the land. ¹³But yet in it shall be a tenth, and it shall return, and shall be eaten: as a teil tree, and as an oak, whose substance is in them, when they cast their leaves: so the holy seed shall be the substance thereof.

7 ¹And it came to pass in the days of Ahaz the son of Jotham, the son of Uzziah, king of Judah, that Rezin the king of Syria, and Pekah the son of Remaliah, king of Israel, went up toward Jerusalem to war against it, but could not prevail against it. ²And it was told the house of David, saying, Syria is confederate with Ephraim. And his heart was moved, and the heart of his people, as the trees of the wood are moved with the wind. ³Then said the LORD to Isaiah, Go forth now to meet Ahaz, you, and Shearjashub your son, at the end of the conduit of the upper pool in the highway of the fuller's field; ⁴And say to him, Take heed, and be quiet; fear not, neither be fainthearted for the two tails of these smoking firebrands, for the fierce anger of Rezin with Syria, and of the son of Remaliah. ⁵Because Syria, Ephraim, and the son of Remaliah, have taken evil counsel against you, saying, ⁶Let us go up against Judah, and vex it, and let us make a breach therein for us, and set a king in the middle of it, even the son of Tabeal: ⁷Thus says the Lord GOD, It shall not stand, neither shall it come to pass. ⁸For the head of Syria is Damascus, and the head of Damascus is Rezin; and within three score and five years shall Ephraim be broken, that it be not a people. ⁹And the head of Ephraim is Samaria, and the head of Samaria is Remaliah's son. If you will not believe, surely you shall not be established. ¹⁰Moreover the LORD spoke again to Ahaz, saying, ¹¹Ask you a sign of the LORD your God; ask it either in the depth, or in the height above. ¹²But Ahaz said, I will not ask, neither will I tempt the LORD. ¹³And he said, Hear you now, O house of David; Is it a small thing for you to weary men, but will you weary my God also? ¹⁴Therefore the Lord himself shall give you a sign; Behold, a virgin shall conceive, and bear a son, and shall call his name Immanuel. ¹⁵Butter and honey shall he eat, that he may know to refuse the evil, and choose the good. ¹⁶For before the child shall know to refuse the evil, and choose the good, the land that you abhor shall be forsaken of both her kings. ¹⁷The LORD shall bring on you, and on your people, and on your father's house, days that have not come, from the day that Ephraim departed from Judah; even the king of Assyria. ¹⁸And it shall come to pass in that day, that the LORD shall hiss for the fly that is in the uttermost part of the rivers of Egypt, and for the bee that is in the land of Assyria. ¹⁹And they shall come, and shall rest all of them in the desolate valleys, and in the holes of the rocks, and on all thorns, and on all bushes. ²⁰In the same day shall the Lord shave with a razor that is hired, namely, by them beyond the river, by the king of Assyria, the head, and the hair of the feet: and it shall also consume the beard. ²¹And it shall come to pass in that day, that a man shall nourish a young cow, and two sheep; ²²And it shall come to pass, for the abundance of milk that they shall give he shall eat butter: for butter and honey shall every one eat that is left in the land. ²³And it shall come to pass in that day,

that every place shall be, where there were a thousand vines at a thousand sliver coins, it shall even be for briers and thorns. ²⁴With arrows and with bows shall men come thither; because all the land shall become briers and thorns. ²⁵And on all hills that shall be dig with the mattock, there shall not come thither the fear of briers and thorns: but it shall be for the sending forth of oxen, and for the treading of lesser cattle.

8 ¹Moreover the LORD said to me, Take you a great roll, and write in it with a man's pen concerning Mahershalalhashbaz. ²And I took to me faithful witnesses to record, Uriah the priest, and Zechariah the son of Jeberechiah. ³And I went to the prophetess; and she conceived, and bore a son. Then said the LORD to me, Call his name Mahershalalhashbaz. ⁴For before the child shall have knowledge to cry, My father, and my mother, the riches of Damascus and the spoil of Samaria shall be taken away before the king of Assyria. ⁵The LORD spoke also to me again, saying, ⁶For as much as this people refuses the waters of Shiloah that go softly, and rejoice in Rezin and Remaliah's son; ⁷Now therefore, behold, the Lord brings up on them the waters of the river, strong and many, even the king of Assyria, and all his glory: and he shall come up over all his channels, and go over all his banks: ⁸And he shall pass through Judah; he shall overflow and go over, he shall reach even to the neck; and the stretching out of his wings shall fill the breadth of your land, O Immanuel. ⁹Associate yourselves, O you people, and you shall be broken in pieces; and give ear, all you of far countries: gird yourselves, and you shall be broken in pieces; gird yourselves, and you shall be broken in pieces. ¹⁰Take counsel together, and it shall come to nothing; speak the word, and it shall not stand: for God is with us. ¹¹For the LORD spoke thus to me with a strong hand, and instructed me that I should not walk in the way of this people, saying, ¹²Say you not, A confederacy, to all them to whom this people shall say, A confederacy; neither fear you their fear, nor be afraid. ¹³Sanctify the LORD of hosts himself; and let him be your fear, and let him be your dread. ¹⁴And he shall be for a sanctuary; but for a stone of stumbling and for a rock of offense to both the houses of Israel, for a gin and for a snare to the inhabitants of Jerusalem. ¹⁵And many among them shall stumble, and fall, and be broken, and be snared, and be taken. ¹⁶Bind up the testimony, seal the law among my disciples. ¹⁷And I will wait on the LORD, that hides his face from the house of Jacob, and I will look for him. ¹⁸Behold, I and the children whom the LORD has given me are for signs and for wonders in Israel from the LORD of hosts, which dwells in mount Zion. ¹⁹And when they shall say to you, Seek to them that have familiar spirits, and to wizards that peep, and that mutter: should not a people seek to their God? for the living to the dead? ²⁰To the law and to the testimony: if they speak not according to this word, it is because there is no light in them. ²¹And they shall pass through it, hardly bestead and hungry: and it shall come to pass, that when they shall be hungry, they shall fret themselves, and curse their king and their God, and look upward. ²²And they shall look to the earth; and behold trouble and darkness, dimness of anguish; and they shall be driven to darkness.

9 ¹Nevertheless the dimness shall not be such as was in her vexation, when at the first he lightly afflicted the land of Zebulun and the land of Naphtali, and afterward did more grievously afflict her by the way of the sea, beyond Jordan, in Galilee of the nations. ²The people that walked in darkness have seen a great light: they that dwell in the land of the shadow of death, on them has the light shined. ³You have multiplied the nation, and not increased the joy: they joy before you according to the joy in harvest, and as men rejoice when they divide the spoil. ⁴For you have broken the yoke of his burden, and the staff of his shoulder, the rod of his oppressor, as in the day of Midian. ⁵For every battle of the warrior is with confused noise, and garments rolled in blood; but this shall be with burning and fuel of fire. ⁶For to us a child is born, to us a son is given: and the government shall be on his shoulder: and his name shall be called Wonderful, Counselor, The mighty God, The everlasting Father, The Prince of Peace. ⁷Of the increase of his government and peace there shall be no end, on the throne of David, and on his kingdom, to order it, and to establish it with judgment and with justice from now on even for ever. The zeal of the LORD of hosts will perform this. ⁸The Lord sent a word into Jacob, and it has lighted on Israel. ⁹And all the people shall know, even Ephraim and the inhabitant of Samaria, that say in the pride and stoutness of heart, ¹⁰The bricks are fallen down, but we will build with hewn stones: the sycomores are cut down, but we will change them into cedars. ¹¹Therefore the LORD shall set up the adversaries of Rezin against him, and join his enemies together; ¹²The Syrians before, and the Philistines behind; and they shall devour Israel with open mouth. For all this his anger is not turned away, but his hand is stretched out still. ¹³For the people turns not to him that smites them, neither do they seek the LORD of hosts. ¹⁴Therefore the LORD will cut off from Israel head and tail, branch and rush, in one day. ¹⁵The ancient and honorable, he is the head; and the prophet that teaches lies, he is the tail. ¹⁶For the leaders of this people cause them to err; and they that are led of them are destroyed. ¹⁷Therefore the LORD shall have no joy in their young men, neither shall have mercy on their fatherless and widows: for every one is an hypocrite and an evildoer, and every mouth speaks folly. For all this his anger is not turned away, but his hand is stretched out still. ¹⁸For wickedness burns as the fire: it shall devour the briers and thorns, and shall kindle in the thickets of the forest, and they shall mount up like the lifting up of smoke. ¹⁹Through the wrath of the LORD of hosts is the land darkened, and the people shall be as the fuel of the fire: no man shall spare his brother. ²⁰And he shall snatch on the right hand, and be hungry; and he shall eat on the left hand, and they shall not be satisfied: they shall eat every man the flesh of his own arm: ²¹Manasseh, Ephraim; and Ephraim, Manasseh: and they together shall be against Judah. For all this his anger is not turned away, but his hand is stretched out still.

10 ¹Woe to them that decree unrighteous decrees, and that write grievousness which they have prescribed; ²To turn aside the needy from judgment, and to take away the right from the poor of my people, that widows may be their prey, and that they may rob the fatherless! ³And what will you do in the day of visitation, and in the desolation

which shall come from far? to whom will you flee for help? and where will you leave your glory? ⁴Without me they shall bow down under the prisoners, and they shall fall under the slain. For all this his anger is not turned away, but his hand is stretched out still. ⁵O Assyrian, the rod of my anger, and the staff in their hand is my indignation. ⁶I will send him against an hypocritical nation, and against the people of my wrath will I give him a charge, to take the spoil, and to take the prey, and to tread them down like the mire of the streets. ⁷However, he means not so, neither does his heart think so; but it is in his heart to destroy and cut off nations not a few. ⁸For he says, Are not my princes altogether kings? ⁹Is not Calno as Carchemish? is not Hamath as Arpad? is not Samaria as Damascus? ¹⁰As my hand has found the kingdoms of the idols, and whose graven images did excel them of Jerusalem and of Samaria; ¹¹Shall I not, as I have done to Samaria and her idols, so do to Jerusalem and her idols? ¹²Why it shall come to pass, that when the Lord has performed his whole work on mount Zion and on Jerusalem, I will punish the fruit of the stout heart of the king of Assyria, and the glory of his high looks. ¹³For he says, By the strength of my hand I have done it, and by my wisdom; for I am prudent: and I have removed the bounds of the people, and have robbed their treasures, and I have put down the inhabitants like a valiant man: ¹⁴And my hand has found as a nest the riches of the people: and as one gathers eggs that are left, have I gathered all the earth; and there was none that moved the wing, or opened the mouth, or peeped. ¹⁵Shall the ax boast itself against him that hews therewith? or shall the saw magnify itself against him that shakes it? as if the rod should shake itself against them that lift it up, or as if the staff should lift up itself, as if it were no wood. ¹⁶Therefore shall the Lord, the Lord of hosts, send among his fat ones leanness; and under his glory he shall kindle a burning like the burning of a fire. ¹⁷And the light of Israel shall be for a fire, and his Holy One for a flame: and it shall burn and devour his thorns and his briers in one day; ¹⁸And shall consume the glory of his forest, and of his fruitful field, both soul and body: and they shall be as when a standard-bearer faints. ¹⁹And the rest of the trees of his forest shall be few, that a child may write them. ²⁰And it shall come to pass in that day, that the remnant of Israel, and such as are escaped of the house of Jacob, shall no more again stay on him that smote them; but shall stay on the LORD, the Holy One of Israel, in truth. ²¹The remnant shall return, even the remnant of Jacob, to the mighty God. ²²For though your people Israel be as the sand of the sea, yet a remnant of them shall return: the consumption decreed shall overflow with righteousness. ²³For the Lord GOD of hosts shall make a consumption, even determined, in the middle of all the land. ²⁴Therefore thus says the Lord GOD of hosts, O my people that dwell in Zion, be not afraid of the Assyrian: he shall smite you with a rod, and shall lift up his staff against you, after the manner of Egypt. ²⁵For yet a very little while, and the indignation shall cease, and my anger in their destruction. ²⁶And the LORD of hosts shall stir up a whip for him according to the slaughter of Midian at the rock of Oreb: and as his rod was on the sea, so shall he lift it up after the manner of Egypt. ²⁷And it shall come to pass in that day, that his burden shall be taken away from off your shoulder, and his yoke from off your neck, and the yoke shall be destroyed because of the anointing. ²⁸He is come to Aiath, he is passed to Migron; at Michmash he has laid up his carriages: ²⁹They are gone over the passage: they have taken up their lodging at Geba; Ramah is afraid; Gibeah of Saul is fled. ³⁰Lift up your voice, O daughter of Gallim: cause it to be heard to Laish, O poor Anathoth. ³¹Madmenah is removed; the inhabitants of Gebim gather themselves to flee. ³²As yet shall he remain at Nob that day: he shall shake his hand against the mount of the daughter of Zion, the hill of Jerusalem. ³³Behold, the Lord, the LORD of hosts, shall lop the bough with terror: and the high ones of stature shall be hewn down, and the haughty shall be humbled. ³⁴And he shall cut down the thickets of the forest with iron, and Lebanon shall fall by a mighty one.

11

¹And there shall come forth a rod out of the stem of Jesse, and a Branch shall grow out of his roots: ²And the spirit of the LORD shall rest on him, the spirit of wisdom and understanding, the spirit of counsel and might, the spirit of knowledge and of the fear of the LORD; ³And shall make him of quick understanding in the fear of the LORD: and he shall not judge after the sight of his eyes, neither reprove after the hearing of his ears: ⁴But with righteousness shall he judge the poor, and reprove with equity for the meek of the earth: and he shall smite the earth: with the rod of his mouth, and with the breath of his lips shall he slay the wicked. ⁵And righteousness shall be the girdle of his loins, and faithfulness the girdle of his reins. ⁶The wolf also shall dwell with the lamb, and the leopard shall lie down with the kid; and the calf and the young lion and the fatted calf together; and a little child shall lead them. ⁷And the cow and the bear shall feed; their young ones shall lie down together: and the lion shall eat straw like the ox. ⁸And the sucking child shall play on the hole of the asp, and the weaned child shall put his hand on the cockatrice' den. ⁹They shall not hurt nor destroy in all my holy mountain: for the earth shall be full of the knowledge of the LORD, as the waters cover the sea. ¹⁰And in that day there shall be a root of Jesse, which shall stand for an ensign of the people; to it shall the Gentiles seek: and his rest shall be glorious. ¹¹And it shall come to pass in that day, that the Lord shall set his hand again the second time to recover the remnant of his people, which shall be left, from Assyria, and from Egypt, and from Pathros, and from Cush, and from Elam, and from Shinar, and from Hamath, and from the islands of the sea. ¹²And he shall set up an ensign for the nations, and shall assemble the outcasts of Israel, and gather together the dispersed of Judah from the four corners of the earth. ¹³The envy also of Ephraim shall depart, and the adversaries of Judah shall be cut off: Ephraim shall not envy Judah, and Judah shall not vex Ephraim. ¹⁴But they shall fly on the shoulders of the Philistines toward the west; they shall spoil them of the east together: they shall lay their hand on Edom and Moab; and the children of Ammon shall obey them. ¹⁵And the LORD shall utterly destroy the tongue of the Egyptian sea; and with his mighty wind shall he shake his hand over the river, and shall smite it in the seven streams, and make men go over with dry sandals. ¹⁶And there shall be an highway for the remnant of his people, which shall be left, from Assyria; like as it was to Israel in the day that he came up out of the land of Egypt.

12

¹And in that day you shall say, O LORD, I will praise you: though you were angry with me, your anger is turned away, and you comforted me. ²Behold, God is my salvation; I will trust, and not be afraid: for the LORD JEHOVAH is my strength and my song; he also is become my salvation. ³Therefore with joy shall you draw water out of the wells of salvation. ⁴And in that day shall you say, Praise the LORD, call on his name, declare his doings among the people, make mention that his name is exalted. ⁵Sing to the LORD; for he has done excellent things: this is known in all the earth. ⁶Cry out and shout, you inhabitant of Zion: for great is the Holy One of Israel in the middle of you.

13

¹The burden of Babylon, which Isaiah the son of Amoz did see. ²Lift you up a banner on the high mountain, exalt the voice to them, shake the hand, that they may go into the gates of the nobles. ³I have commanded my sanctified ones, I have also called my mighty ones for my anger, even them that rejoice in my highness. ⁴The noise of a multitude in the mountains, like as of a great people; a tumultuous noise of the kingdoms of nations gathered together: the LORD of hosts musters the host of the battle. ⁵They come from a far country, from the end of heaven, even the LORD, and the weapons of his indignation, to destroy the whole land. ⁶Howl you; for the day of the LORD is at hand; it shall come as a destruction from the Almighty. ⁷Therefore shall all hands be faint, and every man's heart shall melt: ⁸And they shall be afraid: pangs and sorrows shall take hold of them; they shall be in pain as a woman that travails: they shall be amazed one at another; their faces shall be as flames. ⁹Behold, the day of the LORD comes, cruel both with wrath and fierce anger, to lay the land desolate: and he shall destroy the sinners thereof out of it. ¹⁰For the stars of heaven and the constellations thereof shall not give their light: the sun shall be darkened in his going forth, and the moon shall not cause her light to shine. ¹¹And I will punish the world for their evil, and the wicked for their iniquity; and I will cause the arrogance of the proud to cease, and will lay low the haughtiness of the terrible. ¹²I will make a man more precious than fine gold; even a man than the golden wedge of Ophir. ¹³Therefore I will shake the heavens, and the earth shall remove out of her place, in the wrath of the LORD of hosts, and in the day of his fierce anger. ¹⁴And it shall be as the chased roe, and as a sheep that no man takes up: they shall every man turn to his own people, and flee every one into his own land. ¹⁵Every one that is found shall be thrust through; and every one that is joined to them shall fall by the sword. ¹⁶Their children also shall be dashed to pieces before their eyes; their houses shall be spoiled, and their wives ravished. ¹⁷Behold, I will stir up the Medes against them, which shall not regard silver; and as for gold, they shall not delight in it. ¹⁸Their bows also shall dash the young men to pieces; and they shall have no pity on the fruit of the womb; their eyes shall not spare children. ¹⁹And Babylon, the glory of kingdoms, the beauty of the Chaldees' excellency, shall be as when God overthrew Sodom and Gomorrah. ²⁰It shall never be inhabited, neither shall be dwelled in from generation to generation: neither shall the Arabian pitch tent there; neither shall the shepherds make their fold there. ²¹But wild beasts of the desert shall lie there; and their houses shall be full of doleful creatures; and owls shall dwell there, and satyrs shall dance there. ²²And the wild beasts of the islands shall cry in their desolate houses, and dragons in their pleasant palaces: and her time is near to come, and her days shall not be prolonged.

14

¹For the LORD will have mercy on Jacob, and will yet choose Israel, and set them in their own land: and the strangers shall be joined with them, and they shall join to the house of Jacob. ²And the people shall take them, and bring them to their place: and the house of Israel shall possess them in the land of the LORD for servants and handmaids: and they shall take them captives, whose captives they were; and they shall rule over their oppressors. ³And it shall come to pass in the day that the LORD shall give you rest from your sorrow, and from your fear, and from the hard bondage wherein you were made to serve, ⁴That you shall take up this proverb against the king of Babylon, and say, How has the oppressor ceased! the golden city ceased! ⁵The LORD has broken the staff of the wicked, and the scepter of the rulers. ⁶He who smote the people in wrath with a continual stroke, he that ruled the nations in anger, is persecuted, and none hinders. ⁷The whole earth is at rest, and is quiet: they break forth into singing. ⁸Yes, the fir trees rejoice at you, and the cedars of Lebanon, saying, Since you are laid down, no feller is come up against us. ⁹Hell from beneath is moved for you to meet you at your coming: it stirs up the dead for you, even all the chief ones of the earth; it has raised up from their thrones all the kings of the nations. ¹⁰All they shall speak and say to you, Are you also become weak as we? are you become like to us? ¹¹Your pomp is brought down to the grave, and the noise of your viols: the worm is spread under you, and the worms cover you. ¹²How are you fallen from heaven, O Lucifer, son of the morning! how are you cut down to the ground, which did weaken the nations! ¹³For you have said in your heart, I will ascend into heaven, I will exalt my throne above the stars of God: I will sit also on the mount of the congregation, in the sides of the north: ¹⁴I will ascend above the heights of the clouds; I will be like the most High. ¹⁵Yet you shall be brought down to hell, to the sides of the pit. ¹⁶They that see you shall narrowly look on you, and consider you, saying, Is this the man that made the earth to tremble, that did shake kingdoms; ¹⁷That made the world as a wilderness, and destroyed the cities thereof; that opened not the house of his prisoners? ¹⁸All the kings of the nations, even all of them, lie in glory, every one in his own house. ¹⁹But you are cast out of your grave like an abominable branch, and as the raiment of those that are slain, thrust through with a sword, that go down to the stones of the pit; as a carcass trodden under feet. ²⁰You shall not be joined with them in burial, because you have destroyed your land, and slain your people: the seed of evildoers shall never be renowned. ²¹Prepare slaughter for his children for the iniquity of their fathers; that they do not rise, nor possess the land, nor fill the face of the world with cities. ²²For I will rise up against them, says the LORD of hosts, and cut off from Babylon the name, and remnant, and son, and nephew, says the LORD. ²³I will also make it a possession for the bittern, and pools of water: and I will sweep it with the besom of destruction, says the LORD of hosts. ²⁴The LORD of hosts has sworn, saying, Surely as I

have thought, so shall it come to pass; and as I have purposed, so shall it stand: ²⁵That I will break the Assyrian in my land, and on my mountains tread him under foot: then shall his yoke depart from off them, and his burden depart from off their shoulders. ²⁶This is the purpose that is purposed on the whole earth: and this is the hand that is stretched out on all the nations. ²⁷For the LORD of hosts has purposed, and who shall cancel it? and his hand is stretched out, and who shall turn it back? ²⁸In the year that king Ahaz died was this burden. ²⁹Rejoice not you, whole Palestina, because the rod of him that smote you is broken: for out of the serpent's root shall come forth a cockatrice, and his fruit shall be a fiery flying serpent. ³⁰And the firstborn of the poor shall feed, and the needy shall lie down in safety: and I will kill your root with famine, and he shall slay your remnant. ³¹Howl, O gate; cry, O city; you, whole Palestina, are dissolved: for there shall come from the north a smoke, and none shall be alone in his appointed times. ³²What shall one then answer the messengers of the nation? That the LORD has founded Zion, and the poor of his people shall trust in it.

15 ¹The burden of Moab. Because in the night Ar of Moab is laid waste, and brought to silence; because in the night Kir of Moab is laid waste, and brought to silence; ²He is gone up to Bajith, and to Dibon, the high places, to weep: Moab shall howl over Nebo, and over Medeba: on all their heads shall be baldness, and every beard cut off. ³In their streets they shall gird themselves with sackcloth: on the tops of their houses, and in their streets, every one shall howl, weeping abundantly. ⁴And Heshbon shall cry, and Elealeh: their voice shall be heard even to Jahaz: therefore the armed soldiers of Moab shall cry out; his life shall be grievous to him. ⁵My heart shall cry out for Moab; his fugitives shall flee to Zoar, an heifer of three years old: for by the mounting up of Luhith with weeping shall they go it up; for in the way of Horonaim they shall raise up a cry of destruction. ⁶For the waters of Nimrim shall be desolate: for the hay is withered away, the grass fails, there is no green thing. ⁷Therefore the abundance they have gotten, and that which they have laid up, shall they carry away to the brook of the willows. ⁸For the cry is gone round about the borders of Moab; the howling thereof to Eglaim, and the howling thereof to Beerelim. ⁹For the waters of Dimon shall be full of blood: for I will bring more on Dimon, lions on him that escapes of Moab, and on the remnant of the land.

16 ¹Send you the lamb to the ruler of the land from Sela to the wilderness, to the mount of the daughter of Zion. ²For it shall be, that, as a wandering bird cast out of the nest, so the daughters of Moab shall be at the fords of Arnon. ³Take counsel, execute judgment; make your shadow as the night in the middle of the noonday; hide the outcasts; denude not him that wanders. ⁴Let my outcasts dwell with you, Moab; be you a covert to them from the face of the spoiler: for the extortionist is at an end, the spoiler ceases, the oppressors are consumed out of the land. ⁵And in mercy shall the throne be established: and he shall sit on it in truth in the tabernacle of David, judging, and seeking judgment, and hastening righteousness. ⁶We have heard of the pride of Moab; he is very proud: even of his haughtiness, and his pride, and his wrath: but his lies shall not be so. ⁷Therefore shall Moab howl for Moab, every one shall howl: for the foundations of Kirhareseth shall you mourn; surely they are stricken. ⁸For the fields of Heshbon languish, and the vine of Sibmah: the lords of the heathen have broken down the principal plants thereof, they are come even to Jazer, they wandered through the wilderness: her branches are stretched out, they are gone over the sea. ⁹Therefore I will mourn with the weeping of Jazer the vine of Sibmah: I will water you with my tears, O Heshbon, and Elealeh: for the shouting for your summer fruits and for your harvest is fallen. ¹⁰And gladness is taken away, and joy out of the plentiful field; and in the vineyards there shall be no singing, neither shall there be shouting: the treaders shall tread out no wine in their presses; I have made their vintage shouting to cease. ¹¹Why my bowels shall sound like an harp for Moab, and my inward parts for Kirharesh. ¹²And it shall come to pass, when it is seen that Moab is weary on the high place, that he shall come to his sanctuary to pray; but he shall not prevail. ¹³This is the word that the LORD has spoken concerning Moab since that time. ¹⁴But now the LORD has spoken, saying, Within three years, as the years of an hireling, and the glory of Moab shall be scorned, with all that great multitude; and the remnant shall be very small and feeble.

17 ¹The burden of Damascus. Behold, Damascus is taken away from being a city, and it shall be a ruinous heap. ²The cities of Aroer are forsaken: they shall be for flocks, which shall lie down, and none shall make them afraid. ³The fortress also shall cease from Ephraim, and the kingdom from Damascus, and the remnant of Syria: they shall be as the glory of the children of Israel, says the LORD of hosts. ⁴And in that day it shall come to pass, that the glory of Jacob shall be made thin, and the fatness of his flesh shall wax lean. ⁵And it shall be as when the harvestman gathers the corn, and reaps the ears with his arm; and it shall be as he that gathers ears in the valley of Rephaim. ⁶Yet gleaning grapes shall be left in it, as the shaking of an olive tree, two or three berries in the top of the uppermost bough, four or five in the outmost fruitful branches thereof, says the LORD God of Israel. ⁷At that day shall a man look to his Maker, and his eyes shall have respect to the Holy One of Israel. ⁸And he shall not look to the altars, the work of his hands, neither shall respect that which his fingers have made, either the groves, or the images. ⁹In that day shall his strong cities be as a forsaken bough, and an uppermost branch, which they left because of the children of Israel: and there shall be desolation. ¹⁰Because you have forgotten the God of your salvation, and have not been mindful of the rock of your strength, therefore shall you plant pleasant plants, and shall set it with strange slips: ¹¹In the day shall you make your plant to grow, and in the morning shall you make your seed to flourish: but the harvest shall be a heap in the day of grief and of desperate sorrow. ¹²Woe to the multitude of many people, which make a noise like the noise of the seas; and to the rushing of nations, that make a rushing like the rushing of mighty waters! ¹³The nations shall rush like the rushing of many waters: but God shall rebuke them, and they shall flee far off, and shall be chased as the chaff of the mountains before the wind, and like a rolling thing before the whirlwind. ¹⁴And behold at evening trouble; and before the

morning he is not. This is the portion of them that spoil us, and the lot of them that rob us.

18 ¹Woe to the land shadowing with wings, which is beyond the rivers of Ethiopia: ²That sends ambassadors by the sea, even in vessels of bulrushes on the waters, saying, Go, you swift messengers, to a nation scattered and peeled, to a people terrible from their beginning till now; a nation meted out and trodden down, whose land the rivers have spoiled! ³All you inhabitants of the world, and dwellers on the earth, see you, when he lifts up an ensign on the mountains; and when he blows a trumpet, hear you. ⁴For so the LORD said to me, I will take my rest, and I will consider in my dwelling place like a clear heat on herbs, and like a cloud of dew in the heat of harvest. ⁵For before the harvest, when the bud is perfect, and the sour grape is ripening in the flower, he shall both cut off the sprigs with pruning hooks, and take away and cut down the branches. ⁶They shall be left together to the fowls of the mountains, and to the beasts of the earth: and the fowls shall summer on them, and all the beasts of the earth shall winter on them. ⁷In that time shall the present be brought to the LORD of hosts of a people scattered and peeled, and from a people terrible from their beginning till now; a nation meted out and trodden under foot, whose land the rivers have spoiled, to the place of the name of the LORD of hosts, the mount Zion.

19 ¹The burden of Egypt. Behold, the LORD rides on a swift cloud, and shall come into Egypt: and the idols of Egypt shall be moved at his presence, and the heart of Egypt shall melt in the middle of it. ²And I will set the Egyptians against the Egyptians: and they shall fight every one against his brother, and every one against his neighbor; city against city, and kingdom against kingdom. ³And the spirit of Egypt shall fail in the middle thereof; and I will destroy the counsel thereof: and they shall seek to the idols, and to the charmers, and to them that have familiar spirits, and to the wizards. ⁴And the Egyptians will I give over into the hand of a cruel lord; and a fierce king shall rule over them, says the Lord, the LORD of hosts. ⁵And the waters shall fail from the sea, and the river shall be wasted and dried up. ⁶And they shall turn the rivers far away; and the brooks of defense shall be emptied and dried up: the reeds and flags shall wither. ⁷The paper reeds by the brooks, by the mouth of the brooks, and every thing sown by the brooks, shall wither, be driven away, and be no more. ⁸The fishers also shall mourn, and all they that cast angle into the brooks shall lament, and they that spread nets on the waters shall languish. ⁹Moreover they that work in fine flax, and they that weave networks, shall be confounded. ¹⁰And they shall be broken in the purposes thereof, all that make sluices and ponds for fish. ¹¹Surely the princes of Zoan are fools, the counsel of the wise counsellors of Pharaoh is become brutish: how say you to Pharaoh, I am the son of the wise, the son of ancient kings? ¹²Where are they? where are your wise men? and let them tell you now, and let them know what the LORD of hosts has purposed on Egypt. ¹³The princes of Zoan are become fools, the princes of Noph are deceived; they have also seduced Egypt, even they that are the stay of the tribes thereof. ¹⁴The LORD has mingled a perverse spirit in the middle thereof: and they have caused Egypt to err in every work thereof, as a drunken man staggers in his vomit. ¹⁵Neither shall there be any work for Egypt, which the head or tail, branch or rush, may do. ¹⁶In that day shall Egypt be like to women: and it shall be afraid and fear because of the shaking of the hand of the LORD of hosts, which he shakes over it. ¹⁷And the land of Judah shall be a terror to Egypt, every one that makes mention thereof shall be afraid in himself, because of the counsel of the LORD of hosts, which he has determined against it. ¹⁸In that day shall five cities in the land of Egypt speak the language of Canaan, and swear to the LORD of hosts; one shall be called, The city of destruction. ¹⁹In that day shall there be an altar to the LORD in the middle of the land of Egypt, and a pillar at the border thereof to the LORD. ²⁰And it shall be for a sign and for a witness to the LORD of hosts in the land of Egypt: for they shall cry to the LORD because of the oppressors, and he shall send them a savior, and a great one, and he shall deliver them. ²¹And the LORD shall be known to Egypt, and the Egyptians shall know the LORD in that day, and shall do sacrifice and oblation; yes, they shall vow a vow to the LORD, and perform it. ²²And the LORD shall smite Egypt: he shall smite and heal it: and they shall return even to the LORD, and he shall be entreated of them, and shall heal them. ²³In that day shall there be a highway out of Egypt to Assyria, and the Assyrian shall come into Egypt, and the Egyptian into Assyria, and the Egyptians shall serve with the Assyrians. ²⁴In that day shall Israel be the third with Egypt and with Assyria, even a blessing in the middle of the land: ²⁵Whom the LORD of hosts shall bless, saying, Blessed be Egypt my people, and Assyria the work of my hands, and Israel my inheritance.

20 ¹In the year that Tartan came to Ashdod, (when Sargon the king of Assyria sent him,) and fought against Ashdod, and took it; ²At the same time spoke the LORD by Isaiah the son of Amoz, saying, Go and loose the sackcloth from off your loins, and put off your shoe from your foot. And he did so, walking naked and barefoot. ³And the LORD said, Like as my servant Isaiah has walked naked and barefoot three years for a sign and wonder on Egypt and on Ethiopia; ⁴So shall the king of Assyria lead away the Egyptians prisoners, and the Ethiopians captives, young and old, naked and barefoot, even with their buttocks uncovered, to the shame of Egypt. ⁵And they shall be afraid and ashamed of Ethiopia their expectation, and of Egypt their glory. ⁶And the inhabitant of this isle shall say in that day, Behold, such is our expectation, where we flee for help to be delivered from the king of Assyria: and how shall we escape?

21 ¹The burden of the desert of the sea. As whirlwinds in the south pass through; so it comes from the desert, from a terrible land. ²A grievous vision is declared to me; the treacherous dealer deals treacherously, and the spoiler spoils. Go up, O Elam: besiege, O Media; all the sighing thereof have I made to cease. ³Therefore are my loins filled with pain: pangs have taken hold on me, as the pangs of a woman that travails: I was bowed down at the hearing of it; I was dismayed at the seeing of it. ⁴My heart panted, fearfulness affrighted me: the night of my pleasure has he turned into fear to me. ⁵Prepare the table, watch in the watchtower, eat, drink: arise, you princes, and anoint the shield. ⁶For thus has the LORD said to me, Go, set a watchman, let him declare what he sees. ⁷And he saw a chariot with a couple of horsemen, a chariot of asses, and a chariot of camels; and he listened diligently with much heed: ⁸And he cried, A lion: My lord, I stand continually on the watchtower in the daytime, and I am set in my ward whole nights: ⁹And, behold, here comes a chariot of men, with a couple of horsemen. And he answered and said, Babylon is fallen, is fallen; and all the graven images of her gods he has broken to the ground. ¹⁰O my threshing, and the corn of my floor: that which I have heard of the LORD of hosts, the God of Israel, have I declared to you. ¹¹The burden of Dumah. He calls to me out of Seir, Watchman, what of the night? Watchman, what of the night? ¹²The watchman said, The morning comes, and also the night: if you will inquire, inquire you: return, come. ¹³The burden on Arabia. In the forest in Arabia shall you lodge, O you traveling companies of Dedanim. ¹⁴The inhabitants of the land of Tema brought water to him that was thirsty, they prevented with their bread him that fled. ¹⁵For they fled from the swords, from the drawn sword, and from the bent bow, and from the grievousness of war. ¹⁶For thus has the LORD said to me, Within a year, according to the years of an hireling, and all the glory of Kedar shall fail: ¹⁷And the residue of the number of archers, the mighty men of the children of Kedar, shall be diminished: for the LORD God of Israel has spoken it.

22 ¹The burden of the valley of vision. What ails you now, that you are wholly gone up to the housetops? ²You that are full of stirs, a tumultuous city, joyous city: your slain men are not slain with the sword, nor dead in battle. ³All your rulers are fled together, they are bound by the archers: all that are found in you are bound together, which have fled from far. ⁴Therefore said I, Look away from me; I will weep bitterly, labor not to comfort me, because of the spoiling of the daughter of my people. ⁵For it is a day of trouble, and of treading down, and of perplexity by the Lord GOD of hosts in the valley of vision, breaking down the walls, and of crying to the mountains. ⁶And Elam bore the quiver with chariots of men and horsemen, and Kir uncovered the shield. ⁷And it shall come to pass, that your choicest valleys shall be full of chariots, and the horsemen shall set themselves in array at the gate. ⁸And he discovered the covering of Judah, and you did look in that day to the armor of the house of the forest. ⁹You have seen also the breaches of the city of David, that they are many: and you gathered together the waters of the lower pool. ¹⁰And you have numbered the houses of Jerusalem, and the houses have you broken down to fortify the wall. ¹¹You made also a ditch between the two walls for the water of the old pool: but you have not looked to the maker thereof, neither had respect to him that fashioned it long ago. ¹²And in that day did the Lord GOD of hosts call to weeping, and to mourning, and to baldness, and to girding with sackcloth: ¹³And behold joy and gladness, slaying oxen, and killing sheep, eating flesh, and drinking wine: let us eat and drink; for to morrow we shall die. ¹⁴And it was revealed in my ears by the LORD of hosts, Surely this iniquity shall not be purged from you till you die, says the Lord GOD of hosts. ¹⁵Thus says the Lord GOD of hosts, Go, get you to this treasurer, even to Shebna, which is over the house, and say, ¹⁶What have you here? and whom have you here, that you have hewed you out a sepulcher here, as he that hews him out a sepulcher on high, and that engraves an habitation for himself in a rock? ¹⁷Behold, the LORD will carry you away with a mighty captivity, and will surely cover you. ¹⁸He will surely violently turn and toss you like a ball into a large country: there shall you die, and there the chariots of your glory shall be the shame of your lord's house. ¹⁹And I will drive you from your station, and from your state shall he pull you down. ²⁰And it shall come to pass in that day, that I will call my servant Eliakim the son of Hilkiah: ²¹And I will clothe him with your robe, and strengthen him with your girdle, and I will commit your government into his hand: and he shall be a father to the inhabitants of Jerusalem, and to the house of Judah. ²²And the key of the house of David will I lay on his shoulder; so he shall open, and none shall shut; and he shall shut, and none shall open. ²³And I will fasten him as a nail in a sure place; and he shall be for a glorious throne to his father's house. ²⁴And they shall hang on him all the glory of his father's house, the offspring and the issue, all vessels of small quantity, from the vessels of cups, even to all the vessels of flagons. ²⁵In that day, says the LORD of hosts, shall the nail that is fastened in the sure place be removed, and be cut down, and fall; and the burden that was on it shall be cut off: for the LORD has spoken it.

23 ¹The burden of Tyre. Howl, you ships of Tarshish; for it is laid waste, so that there is no house, no entering in: from the land of Chittim it is revealed to them. ²Be still, you inhabitants of the isle; you whom the merchants of Zidon, that pass over the sea, have replenished. ³And by great waters the seed of Sihor, the harvest of the river, is her revenue; and she is a mart of nations. ⁴Be you ashamed, O Zidon: for the sea has spoken, even the strength of the sea, saying, I travail not, nor bring forth children, neither do I nourish up young men, nor bring up virgins. ⁵As at the report concerning Egypt, so shall they be sorely pained at the report of Tyre. ⁶Pass you over to Tarshish; howl, you inhabitants of the isle. ⁷Is this your joyous city, whose antiquity is of ancient days? her own feet shall carry her afar off to sojourn. ⁸Who has taken this counsel against Tyre, the crowning city, whose merchants are princes, whose traffickers are the honorable of the earth? ⁹The LORD of hosts has purposed it, to stain the pride of all glory, and to bring into contempt all the honorable of the earth. ¹⁰Pass through your land as a river, O daughter of Tarshish: there is no more strength. ¹¹He stretched out his hand over the sea, he shook the kingdoms: the LORD has given a commandment against the merchant city, to destroy the strong holds thereof. ¹²And he said, You shall no more rejoice, O you oppressed virgin, daughter of Zidon: arise, pass over to Chittim; there also shall you have no rest. ¹³Behold the land of the Chaldeans; this people was not, till the Assyrian founded it for them that dwell in the wilderness: they set up the towers thereof, they raised up the palaces thereof; and he brought it to ruin. ¹⁴Howl, you ships of Tarshish: for your strength is laid waste. ¹⁵And it shall come to pass in that day, that Tyre shall be forgotten seventy years, according to the days of one king: after the end of seventy years shall Tyre sing as an harlot. ⁱ⁶Take an harp, go about the city, you harlot that have been forgotten; make sweet melody, sing many songs, that you may be remembered. ¹⁷And it shall come to pass after the end of seventy years, that the LORD will visit Tyre, and she shall turn to her hire, and shall commit fornication with all the kingdoms of the world on the face of the earth. ¹⁸And her merchandise and her hire shall be holiness to the LORD: it shall not be treasured nor laid up; for her merchandise shall be for them that dwell before the LORD, to eat sufficiently, and for durable clothing.

24 ¹Behold, the LORD makes the earth empty, and makes it waste, and turns it upside down, and scatters abroad the inhabitants thereof. ²And it shall be, as with the people, so with the priest; as with the servant, so with his master; as with the maid, so with her mistress; as with the buyer, so with the seller; as with the lender, so with the borrower; as with the taker of usury, so with the giver of usury to him. ³The land shall be utterly emptied, and utterly spoiled: for the LORD has spoken this word. ⁴The earth mourns and fades away, the world languishes and fades away, the haughty people of the earth do languish. ⁵The earth also is defiled under the inhabitants thereof; because they have transgressed the laws, changed the ordinance, broken the everlasting covenant. ⁶Therefore has the curse devoured the earth, and they that dwell therein are desolate: therefore the inhabitants of the earth are burned, and few men left. ⁷The new wine mourns, the vine languishes, all the merry hearted do sigh. ⁸The mirth of tabrets ceases, the noise of them that rejoice ends, the joy of the harp ceases. ⁹They shall not drink wine with a song; strong drink shall be bitter to them that drink it. ¹⁰The city of confusion is broken down: every house is shut up, that no man may come in. ¹¹There is a crying for wine in the streets; all joy is darkened, the mirth of the land is gone. ¹²In the city is left desolation, and the gate is smitten with destruction. ¹³When thus it shall be in the middle of the land among the people, there shall be as the shaking of an olive tree, and as the gleaning grapes when the vintage is done. ¹⁴They shall lift up their voice, they shall sing for the majesty of the LORD, they shall cry aloud from the sea. ¹⁵Why glorify you the LORD in the fires, even the name of the LORD God of Israel in the isles of the sea. ¹⁶From the uttermost part of the earth have we heard songs, even glory to the righteous. But I said, My leanness, my leanness, woe to me! the treacherous dealers have dealt treacherously; yes, the treacherous dealers have dealt very treacherously. ¹⁷Fear, and the pit, and the snare, are on you, O inhabitant of the earth. ¹⁸And it shall come to pass, that he who flees from the noise of the fear shall fall into the pit; and he that comes up out of the middle of the pit shall be taken in the snare: for the windows from on high are open, and the foundations of the earth do shake. ¹⁹The earth is utterly broken down, the earth is clean dissolved, the earth is moved exceedingly. ²⁰The earth shall reel to and fro like a drunkard, and shall be removed like a cottage; and the transgression thereof shall be heavy on it; and it shall fall, and not rise again. ²¹And it shall come to pass in that day, that the LORD shall punish the host of the high ones that are on high, and the kings of the earth on the earth. ²²And they shall be gathered together, as prisoners are gathered in the pit, and shall be shut up in the prison, and after many days shall they be visited. ²³Then the moon shall be confounded, and the sun ashamed, when the LORD of hosts shall reign in mount Zion, and in Jerusalem, and before his ancients gloriously.

25 ¹O Lord, you are my God; I will exalt you, I will praise your name; for you have done wonderful things; your counsels of old are faithfulness and truth. ²For you have made of a city an heap; of a defended city a ruin: a palace of strangers to be no city; it shall never be built. ³Therefore shall the strong people glorify you, the city of the terrible nations shall fear you. ⁴For you have been a strength to the poor, a strength to the needy in his distress, a refuge from the storm, a shadow from the heat, when the blast of the terrible ones is as a storm against the wall. ⁵You shall bring down the noise of strangers, as the heat in a dry place; even the heat with the shadow of a cloud: the branch of the terrible ones shall be brought low. ⁶And in this mountain shall the LORD of hosts make to all people a feast of fat things, a feast of wines on the lees, of fat things full of marrow, of wines on the lees well refined. ⁷And he will destroy in this mountain the face of the covering cast over all people, and the veil that is spread over all nations. ⁸He will swallow up death in victory; and the Lord GOD will wipe away tears from off all faces; and the rebuke of his people shall he take away from off all the earth: for the LORD has spoken it. ⁹And it shall be said in that day, See, this is our God; we have waited for him, and he will save us: this is the LORD; we have waited for him, we will be glad and rejoice in his salvation. ¹⁰For in this mountain shall the hand of the LORD rest, and Moab shall be trodden down under him, even as straw is trodden down for the dunghill. ¹¹And he shall spread forth his hands in the middle of them, as he that swims spreads forth his hands to swim: and he shall bring down their pride together with the spoils of their hands. ¹²And the fortress of the high fort of your walls shall he bring down, lay low, and bring to the ground, even to the dust.

26 ¹In that day shall this song be sung in the land of Judah; We have a strong city; salvation will God appoint for walls and bulwarks. ²Open you the gates, that the righteous nation which keeps the truth may enter in. ³You will keep him in perfect peace, whose mind is stayed on you: because he trusts in you. ⁴Trust you in the LORD for ever: for in the LORD JEHOVAH is everlasting strength: ⁵For he brings down them that dwell on high; the lofty city, he lays it low; he lays it low, even to the ground; he brings it even to the dust. ⁶The foot shall tread it down, even the feet of the poor, and the steps of the needy. ⁷The way of the just is uprightness: you, most upright, do weigh the path of the just. ⁸Yes, in the way of your judgments, O LORD, have we waited for you; the desire of our soul is to your name, and to the remembrance of you. ⁹With my soul have I desired you in the night; yes, with my spirit within me will I seek you early: for when your judgments are in the earth, the inhabitants of the world will learn righteousness. ¹⁰Let favor be showed to the wicked, yet will he not learn righteousness: in the land of uprightness will he deal unjustly, and will not behold the majesty of the LORD. ¹¹LORD, when your hand is lifted up, they will not see: but they shall see, and be ashamed for their envy at the people; yes, the fire of your enemies shall devour them. ¹²LORD, you will ordain peace for us: for you also have worked all our works in us. ¹³O LORD our God, other lords beside you have had dominion over us: but by you only will we make mention of your name. ¹⁴They are dead, they shall not live; they are deceased, they shall not rise: therefore have you visited and destroyed them, and made all their memory to perish. ¹⁵You have increased the nation, O LORD, you have increased the nation: you are glorified: you have removed it far to all the ends of the earth. ¹⁶LORD, in trouble have they visited you, they poured out a prayer when your chastening was on them. ¹⁷Like as a woman with child, that draws near the time of her delivery, is in pain, and cries out in her pangs; so have we been in your sight, O LORD. ¹⁸We have been with child, we have been in pain, we have as it were brought forth wind; we have not worked any deliverance in the earth; neither have the inhabitants of the world fallen. ¹⁹Your dead men shall live, together with my dead body shall they arise. Awake and sing, you that dwell in dust: for your dew is as the dew of herbs, and the earth shall cast out the dead. ²⁰Come, my people, enter you into your chambers, and shut your doors about you: hide yourself as it were for a little moment, until the indignation be over. ²¹For, behold, the LORD comes out of his place to punish the inhabitants of the earth for their iniquity: the earth also shall disclose her blood, and shall no more cover her slain.

27

¹In that day the LORD with his sore and great and strong sword shall punish leviathan the piercing serpent, even leviathan that crooked serpent; and he shall slay the dragon that is in the sea. ²In that day sing you to her, A vineyard of red wine. ³I the LORD do keep it; I will water it every moment: lest any hurt it, I will keep it night and day. ⁴Fury is not in me: who would set the briers and thorns against me in battle? I would go through them, I would burn them together. ⁵Or let him take hold of my strength, that he may make peace with me; and he shall make peace with me. ⁶He shall cause them that come of Jacob to take root: Israel shall blossom and bud, and fill the face of the world with fruit. ⁷Has he smitten him, as he smote those that smote him? or is he slain according to the slaughter of them that are slain by him? ⁸In measure, when it shoots forth, you will debate with it: he stays his rough wind in the day of the east wind. ⁹By this therefore shall the iniquity of Jacob be purged; and this is all the fruit to take away his sin; when he makes all the stones of the altar as chalkstones that are beaten in sunder, the groves and images shall not stand up. ¹⁰Yet the defended city shall be desolate, and the habitation forsaken, and left like a wilderness: there shall the calf feed, and there shall he lie down, and consume the branches thereof. ¹¹When the boughs thereof are withered, they shall be broken off: the women come, and set them on fire: for it is a people of no understanding: therefore he that made them will not have mercy on them, and he that formed them will show them no favor. ¹²And it shall come to pass in that day, that the LORD shall beat off from the channel of the river to the stream of Egypt, and you shall be gathered one by one, O you children of Israel. ¹³And it shall come to pass in that day, that the great trumpet shall be blown, and they shall come which were ready to perish in the land of Assyria, and the outcasts in the land of Egypt, and shall worship the LORD in the holy mount at Jerusalem.

28

¹Woe to the crown of pride, to the drunkards of Ephraim, whose glorious beauty is a fading flower, which are on the head of the fat valleys of them that are overcome with wine! ²Behold, the Lord has a mighty and strong one, which as a tempest of hail and a destroying storm, as a flood of mighty waters overflowing, shall cast down to the earth with the hand. ³The crown of pride, the drunkards of Ephraim, shall be trodden under feet: ⁴And the glorious beauty, which is on the head of the fat valley, shall be a fading flower, and as the hasty fruit before the summer; which when he that looks on it sees, while it is yet in his hand he eats it up. ⁵In that day shall the LORD of hosts be for a crown of glory, and for a diadem of beauty, to the residue of his people, ⁶And for a spirit of judgment to him that sits in judgment, and for strength to them that turn the battle to the gate. ⁷But they also have erred through wine, and through strong drink are out of the way; the priest and the prophet have erred through strong drink, they are swallowed up of wine, they are out of the way through strong drink; they err in vision, they stumble in judgment. ⁸For all tables are full of vomit and filthiness, so that there is no place clean. ⁹Whom shall he teach knowledge? and whom shall he make to understand doctrine? them that are weaned from the milk, and drawn from the breasts. ¹⁰For precept must be on precept, precept on precept; line on line, line on line; here a little, and there a little: ¹¹For with stammering lips and another tongue will he speak to this people. ¹²To whom he said, This is the rest with which you may cause the weary to rest; and this is the refreshing: yet they would not hear. ¹³But the word of the LORD was to them precept on precept, precept on precept; line on line, line on line; here a little, and there a little; that they might go, and fall backward, and be broken, and snared, and taken. ¹⁴Why hear the word of the LORD, you scornful men, that rule this people which is in Jerusalem. ¹⁵Because you have said, We have made a covenant with death, and with hell are we at agreement; when the overflowing whip shall pass through, it shall not come to us: for we have made lies our refuge, and under falsehood have we hid ourselves: ¹⁶Therefore thus says the Lord GOD, Behold, I lay in Zion for a foundation a stone, a tried stone, a precious corner stone, a sure foundation: he that believes shall not make haste. ¹⁷Judgment also will I lay to the line, and righteousness to the plummet: and the hail shall sweep away the refuge of lies, and the waters shall overflow the hiding place. ¹⁸And your covenant with death shall be disannulled, and your agreement with hell shall not stand; when the overflowing whip shall pass through, then you shall be trodden down by it. ¹⁹From the time that it goes forth it shall take you: for morning by morning shall it pass over, by day and by night: and it shall be a vexation only to understand the report. ²⁰For the bed is shorter than that a man can stretch himself on it: and the covering narrower than that he can wrap himself in it. ²¹For the LORD shall rise up as in mount Perazim, he shall be wroth as in the valley of Gibeon, that he may do his work, his strange work; and bring to pass his act, his strange act.

²²Now therefore be you not mockers, lest your bands be made strong: for I have heard from the Lord GOD of hosts a consumption, even determined on the whole earth. ²³Give you ear, and hear my voice; listen, and hear my speech. ²⁴Does the plowman plow all day to sow? does he open and break the clods of his ground? ²⁵When he has made plain the face thereof, does he not cast abroad the fitches, and scatter the cummin, and cast in the principal wheat and the appointed barley and the rye in their place? ²⁶For his God does instruct him to discretion, and does teach him. ²⁷For the fitches are not threshed with a threshing instrument, neither is a cart wheel turned about on the cummin; but the fitches are beaten out with a staff, and the cummin with a rod. ²⁸Bread corn is bruised; because he will not ever be threshing it, nor break it with the wheel of his cart, nor bruise it with his horsemen. ²⁹This also comes forth from the LORD of hosts, which is wonderful in counsel, and excellent in working.

29 ¹Woe to Ariel, to Ariel, the city where David dwelled! add you year to year; let them kill sacrifices. ²Yet I will distress Ariel, and there shall be heaviness and sorrow: and it shall be to me as Ariel. ³And I will camp against you round about, and will lay siege against you with a mount, and I will raise forts against you. ⁴And you shall be brought down, and shall speak out of the ground, and your speech shall be low out of the dust, and your voice shall be, as of one that has a familiar spirit, out of the ground, and your speech shall whisper out of the dust. ⁵Moreover the multitude of your strangers shall be like small dust, and the multitude of the terrible ones shall be as chaff that passes away: yes, it shall be at an instant suddenly. ⁶You shall be visited of the LORD of hosts with thunder, and with earthquake, and great noise, with storm and tempest, and the flame of devouring fire. ⁷And the multitude of all the nations that fight against Ariel, even all that fight against her and her fortification, and that distress her, shall be as a dream of a night vision. ⁸It shall even be as when an hungry man dreams, and, behold, he eats; but he wakes, and his soul is empty: or as when a thirsty man dreams, and, behold, he drinks; but he wakes, and, behold, he is faint, and his soul has appetite: so shall the multitude of all the nations be, that fight against mount Zion. ⁹Stay yourselves, and wonder; cry you out, and cry: they are drunken, but not with wine; they stagger, but not with strong drink. ¹⁰For the LORD has poured out on you the spirit of deep sleep, and has closed your eyes: the prophets and your rulers, the seers has he covered. ¹¹And the vision of all is become to you as the words of a book that is sealed, which men deliver to one that is learned, saying, Read this, I pray you: and he says, I cannot; for it is sealed: ¹²And the book is delivered to him that is not learned, saying, Read this, I pray you: and he says, I am not learned. ¹³Why the Lord said, For as much as this people draw near me with their mouth, and with their lips do honor me, but have removed their heart far from me, and their fear toward me is taught by the precept of men: ¹⁴Therefore, behold, I will proceed to do a marvelous work among this people, even a marvelous work and a wonder: for the wisdom of their wise men shall perish, and the understanding of their prudent men shall be hid. ¹⁵Woe to them that seek deep to hide their counsel from the LORD, and their works are in the dark, and they say, Who sees us? and who knows us? ¹⁶Surely your turning of things upside down shall be esteemed as the potter's clay: for shall the work say of him that made it, He made me not? or shall the thing framed say of him that framed it, He had no understanding? ¹⁷Is it not yet a very little while, and Lebanon shall be turned into a fruitful field, and the fruitful field shall be esteemed as a forest? ¹⁸And in that day shall the deaf hear the words of the book, and the eyes of the blind shall see out of obscurity, and out of darkness. ¹⁹The meek also shall increase their joy in the LORD, and the poor among men shall rejoice in the Holy One of Israel. ²⁰For the terrible one is brought to nothing, and the scorner is consumed, and all that watch for iniquity are cut off: ²¹That make a man an offender for a word, and lay a snare for him that reproves in the gate, and turn aside the just for a thing of nothing. ²²Therefore thus says the LORD, who redeemed Abraham, concerning the house of Jacob, Jacob shall not now be ashamed, neither shall his face now wax pale. ²³But when he sees his children, the work of my hands, in the middle of him, they shall sanctify my name, and sanctify the Holy One of Jacob, and shall fear the God of Israel. ²⁴They also that erred in spirit shall come to understanding, and they that murmured shall learn doctrine.

30 ¹Woe to the rebellious children, says the LORD, that take counsel, but not of me; and that cover with a covering, but not of my spirit, that they may add sin to sin: ²That walk to go down into Egypt, and have not asked at my mouth; to strengthen themselves in the strength of Pharaoh, and to trust in the shadow of Egypt! ³Therefore shall the strength of Pharaoh be your shame, and the trust in the shadow of Egypt your confusion. ⁴For his princes were at Zoan, and his ambassadors came to Hanes. ⁵They were all ashamed of a people that could not profit them, nor be an help nor profit, but a shame, and also a reproach. ⁶The burden of the beasts of the south: into the land of trouble and anguish, from where come the young and old lion, the viper and fiery flying serpent, they will carry their riches on the shoulders of young asses, and their treasures on the bunches of camels, to a people that shall not profit them. ⁷For the Egyptians shall help in vain, and to no purpose: therefore have I cried concerning this, Their strength is to sit still. ⁸Now go, write it before them in a table, and note it in a book, that it may be for the time to come for ever and ever: ⁹That this is a rebellious people, lying children, children that will not hear the law of the LORD: ¹⁰Which say to the seers, See not; and to the prophets, Prophesy not to us right things, speak to us smooth things, prophesy deceits: ¹¹Get you out of the way, turn aside out of the path, cause the Holy One of Israel to cease from before us. ¹²Why thus says the Holy One of Israel, Because you despise this word, and trust in oppression and perverseness, and stay thereon: ¹³Therefore this iniquity shall be to you as a breach ready to fall, swelling out in a high wall, whose breaking comes suddenly at an instant. ¹⁴And he shall break it as the breaking of the potters' vessel that is broken in pieces; he shall not spare: so that there shall not be found in the bursting of it a shard to take fire from the hearth, or to take water with out of the pit. ¹⁵For thus says the Lord GOD, the Holy One of Israel; In returning and rest shall you be saved; in quietness and in confidence shall be your strength: and you would not. ¹⁶But you said, No; for we will flee on horses; therefore shall you flee: and, We will ride on the swift; therefore shall they that pursue you be swift. ¹⁷One thousand shall flee at the rebuke of one; at the rebuke of five shall you flee: till you be left as a beacon on the top of a mountain, and as an ensign on an hill. ¹⁸And therefore will the LORD wait, that he may be gracious to you, and therefore will he be exalted, that he may have mercy on you: for the LORD is a God of judgment: blessed are all they that wait for him. ¹⁹For the people shall dwell in Zion at Jerusalem: you shall weep no more: he will be very gracious to you at the voice of your cry; when he shall hear it, he will answer you. ²⁰And though the Lord give you the bread of adversity, and the water of affliction, yet shall not your teachers be removed into a corner any more, but your eyes shall see your teachers: ²¹And your ears shall hear a word behind you, saying, This is the way, walk you in it, when you turn to the right hand, and when you turn to the left. ²²You shall defile also the covering of your graven images of silver, and the ornament of your molten images of gold: you shall cast them away as a menstruous cloth; you shall say to it, Get you hence. ²³Then shall he give the rain of your seed, that you shall sow the ground with; and bread of the increase of the earth, and it shall be fat and plenteous: in that day shall your cattle feed in large pastures. ²⁴The oxen likewise and the young asses that ear the ground shall eat clean provender, which has been winnowed with the shovel and with the fan. ²⁵And there shall be on every high mountain, and on every high hill, rivers and streams of waters in the day of the great slaughter, when the towers fall. ²⁶Moreover the light of the moon shall be as the light of the sun, and the light of the sun shall be sevenfold, as the light of seven days, in the day that the LORD binds up the breach of his people, and heals the stroke of their wound. ²⁷Behold, the name of the LORD comes from far, burning with his anger, and the burden thereof is heavy: his lips are full of indignation, and his tongue as a devouring fire: ²⁸And his breath, as an overflowing stream, shall reach to the middle of the neck, to sift the nations with the sieve of vanity: and there shall be a bridle in the jaws of the people, causing them to err. ²⁹You shall have a song, as in the night when a holy solemnity is kept; and gladness of heart, as when one goes with a pipe to come into the mountain of the LORD, to the mighty One of Israel. ³⁰And the LORD shall cause his glorious voice to be heard, and shall show the lighting down of his arm, with the indignation of his anger, and with the flame of a devouring fire, with scattering, and tempest, and hailstones. ³¹For through the voice of the LORD shall the Assyrian be beaten down, which smote with a rod. ³²And in every place where the grounded staff shall pass, which the LORD shall lay on him, it shall be with tabrets and harps: and in battles of shaking will he fight with it. ³³For Tophet is ordained of old; yes, for the king it is prepared; he has made it deep and large: the pile thereof is fire and much wood; the breath of the LORD, like a stream of brimstone, does kindle it.

31

¹Woe to them that go down to Egypt for help; and stay on horses, and trust in chariots, because they are many; and in horsemen, because they are very strong; but they look not to the Holy One of Israel, neither seek the LORD! ²Yet he also is wise, and will bring evil, and will not call back his words: but will arise against the house of the evildoers, and against the help of them that work iniquity. ³Now the Egyptians are men, and not God; and their horses flesh, and not spirit. When the LORD shall stretch out his hand, both he that helps shall fall, and he that is helped shall fall down, and they all shall fail together. ⁴For thus has the LORD spoken to me, Like as the lion and the young lion roaring on his prey, when a multitude of shepherds is called forth against him, he will not be afraid of their voice, nor abase himself for the noise of them: so shall the LORD of hosts come down to fight for mount Zion, and for the hill thereof. ⁵As birds flying, so will the LORD of hosts defend Jerusalem; defending also he will deliver it; and passing over he will preserve it. ⁶Turn you to him from whom the children of Israel have deeply revolted. ⁷For in that day every man shall cast away his idols of silver, and his idols of gold, which your own hands have made to you for a sin. ⁸Then shall the Assyrian fall with the sword, not of a mighty man; and the sword, not of a mean man, shall devour him: but he shall flee from the sword, and his young men shall be discomfited. ⁹And he shall pass over to his strong hold for fear, and his princes shall be afraid of the ensign, says the LORD, whose fire is in Zion, and his furnace in Jerusalem.

32

¹Behold, a king shall reign in righteousness, and princes shall rule in judgment. ²And a man shall be as an hiding place from the wind, and a covert from the tempest; as rivers of water in a dry place, as the shadow of a great rock in a weary land. ³And the eyes of them that see shall not be dim, and the ears of them that hear shall listen. ⁴The heart also of the rash shall understand knowledge, and the tongue of the stammerers shall be ready to speak plainly. ⁵The vile person shall be no more called liberal, nor the churl said to be bountiful. ⁶For the vile person will speak villainy, and his heart will work iniquity, to practice hypocrisy, and to utter error against the LORD, to make empty the soul of the hungry, and he will cause the drink of the thirsty to fail. ⁷The instruments also of the churl are evil: he devises wicked devices to destroy the poor with lying words, even when the needy speaks right. ⁸But the liberal devises liberal things; and by liberal things shall he stand. ⁹Rise up, you women that are at ease; hear my voice, you careless daughters; give ear to my speech. ¹⁰Many days and years shall you be troubled, you careless women: for the vintage shall fail, the gathering shall not come. ¹¹Tremble, you women that are at ease; be troubled, you careless ones: strip you, and make you bore, and gird sackcloth on your loins. ¹²They shall lament for the teats, for the pleasant fields, for the fruitful vine. ¹³On the land of my people shall come up thorns and briers; yes, on all the houses of joy in the joyous city: ¹⁴Because the palaces shall be forsaken; the multitude of the city shall be left; the forts and towers shall be for dens for ever, a joy of wild asses, a pasture of flocks; ¹⁵Until the spirit be poured on us from on high, and the wilderness be a fruitful field, and the fruitful field be counted for a forest. ¹⁶Then judgment shall dwell in the wilderness, and righteousness remain in the fruitful field. ¹⁷And the work of righteousness shall be peace; and the effect of righteousness quietness and assurance for ever. ¹⁸And my people shall dwell in a peaceable habitation, and in sure dwellings, and in

quiet resting places; ¹⁹When it shall hail, coming down on the forest; and the city shall be low in a low place. ²⁰Blessed are you that sow beside all waters, that send forth thither the feet of the ox and the ass.

33 ¹Woe to you that spoil, and you were not spoiled; and deal treacherously, and they dealt not treacherously with you! when you shall cease to spoil, you shall be spoiled; and when you shall make an end to deal treacherously, they shall deal treacherously with you. ²O LORD, be gracious to us; we have waited for you: be you their arm every morning, our salvation also in the time of trouble. ³At the noise of the tumult the people fled; at the lifting up of yourself the nations were scattered. ⁴And your spoil shall be gathered like the gathering of the caterpillar: as the running to and fro of locusts shall he run on them. ⁵The LORD is exalted; for he dwells on high: he has filled Zion with judgment and righteousness. ⁶And wisdom and knowledge shall be the stability of your times, and strength of salvation: the fear of the LORD is his treasure. ⁷Behold, their valiant ones shall cry without: the ambassadors of peace shall weep bitterly. ⁸The highways lie waste, the wayfaring man ceases: he has broken the covenant, he has despised the cities, he regards no man. ⁹The earth mourns and languishes: Lebanon is ashamed and hewn down: Sharon is like a wilderness; and Bashan and Carmel shake off their fruits. ¹⁰Now will I rise, says the LORD; now will I be exalted; now will I lift up myself. ¹¹You shall conceive chaff, you shall bring forth stubble: your breath, as fire, shall devour you. ¹²And the people shall be as the burnings of lime: as thorns cut up shall they be burned in the fire. ¹³Hear, you that are far off, what I have done; and, you that are near, acknowledge my might. ¹⁴The sinners in Zion are afraid; fearfulness has surprised the hypocrites. Who among us shall dwell with the devouring fire? who among us shall dwell with everlasting burnings? ¹⁵He that walks righteously, and speaks uprightly; he that despises the gain of oppressions, that shakes his hands from holding of bribes, that stops his ears from hearing of blood, and shuts his eyes from seeing evil; ¹⁶He shall dwell on high: his place of defense shall be the munitions of rocks: bread shall be given him; his waters shall be sure. ¹⁷Your eyes shall see the king in his beauty: they shall behold the land that is very far off. ¹⁸Your heart shall meditate terror. Where is the scribe? where is the receiver? where is he that counted the towers? ¹⁹You shall not see a fierce people, a people of a deeper speech than you can perceive; of a stammering tongue, that you can not understand. ²⁰Look on Zion, the city of our solemnities: your eyes shall see Jerusalem a quiet habitation, a tabernacle that shall not be taken down; not one of the stakes thereof shall ever be removed, neither shall any of the cords thereof be broken. ²¹But there the glorious LORD will be to us a place of broad rivers and streams; wherein shall go no galley with oars, neither shall gallant ship pass thereby. ²²For the LORD is our judge, the LORD is our lawgiver, the LORD is our king; he will save us. ²³Your tacklings are loosed; they could not well strengthen their mast, they could not spread the sail: then is the prey of a great spoil divided; the lame take the prey. ²⁴And the inhabitant shall not say, I am sick: the people that dwell therein shall be forgiven their iniquity.

34 ¹Come near, you nations, to hear; and listen, you people: let the earth hear, and all that is therein; the world, and all things that come forth of it. ²For the indignation of the LORD is on all nations, and his fury on all their armies: he has utterly destroyed them, he has delivered them to the slaughter. ³Their slain also shall be cast out, and their stink shall come up out of their carcasses, and the mountains shall be melted with their blood. ⁴And all the host of heaven shall be dissolved, and the heavens shall be rolled together as a scroll: and all their host shall fall down, as the leaf falls off from the vine, and as a falling fig from the fig tree. ⁵For my sword shall be bathed in heaven: behold, it shall come down on Idumea, and on the people of my curse, to judgment. ⁶The sword of the LORD is filled with blood, it is made fat with fatness, and with the blood of lambs and goats, with the fat of the kidneys of rams: for the LORD has a sacrifice in Bozrah, and a great slaughter in the land of Idumea. ⁷And the unicorns shall come down with them, and the bullocks with the bulls; and their land shall be soaked with blood, and their dust made fat with fatness. ⁸For it is the day of the LORD's vengeance, and the year of recompenses for the controversy of Zion. ⁹And the streams thereof shall be turned into pitch, and the dust thereof into brimstone, and the land thereof shall become burning pitch. ¹⁰It shall not be quenched night nor day; the smoke thereof shall go up for ever: from generation to generation it shall lie waste; none shall pass through it for ever and ever. ¹¹But the cormorant and the bittern shall possess it; the owl also and the raven shall dwell in it: and he shall stretch out on it the line of confusion, and the stones of emptiness. ¹²They shall call the nobles thereof to the kingdom, but none shall be there, and all her princes shall be nothing. ¹³And thorns shall come up in her palaces, nettles and brambles in the fortresses thereof: and it shall be an habitation of dragons, and a court for owls. ¹⁴The wild beasts of the desert shall also meet with the wild beasts of the island, and the satyr shall cry to his fellow; the screech owl also shall rest there, and find for herself a place of rest. ¹⁵There shall the great owl make her nest, and lay, and hatch, and gather under her shadow: there shall the vultures also be gathered, every one with her mate. ¹⁶Seek you out of the book of the LORD, and read: no one of these shall fail, none shall want her mate: for my mouth it has commanded, and his spirit it has gathered them. ¹⁷And he has cast the lot for them, and his hand has divided it to them by line: they shall possess it for ever, from generation to generation shall they dwell therein.

35 ¹The wilderness and the solitary place shall be glad for them; and the desert shall rejoice, and blossom as the rose. ²It shall blossom abundantly, and rejoice even with joy and singing: the glory of Lebanon shall be given to it, the excellency of Carmel and Sharon, they shall see the glory of the LORD, and the excellency of our God. ³Strengthen you the weak hands, and confirm the feeble knees. ⁴Say to them that are of a fearful heart, Be strong, fear not: behold, your God will come with vengeance, even God with a recompense; he will come and save you. ⁵Then the eyes of the blind shall be opened, and the ears of the deaf shall be unstopped. ⁶Then shall the lame man leap as an hart, and the tongue of the dumb sing: for in the wilderness shall waters break out, and streams in the desert. ⁷And the parched ground shall become a pool, and the thirsty land springs of water: in the habitation of dragons, where each lay, shall be grass with reeds and rushes. ⁸And an highway shall be there, and a way, and it shall be called The way of holiness; the unclean shall not pass over it; but it shall be for those: the wayfaring men, though fools, shall not err therein. ⁹No lion shall be there, nor any ravenous beast shall go up thereon, it shall not be found there; but the redeemed shall walk there: ¹⁰And the ransomed of the LORD shall return, and come to Zion with songs and everlasting joy on their heads: they shall obtain joy and gladness, and sorrow and sighing shall flee away.

36 ¹Now it came to pass in the fourteenth year of king Hezekiah, that Sennacherib king of Assyria came up against all the defended cities of Judah, and took them. ²And the king of Assyria sent Rabshakeh from Lachish to Jerusalem to king Hezekiah with a great army. And he stood by the conduit of the upper pool in the highway of the fuller's field. ³Then came forth to him Eliakim, Hilkiah's son, which was over the house, and Shebna the scribe, and Joah, Asaph's son, the recorder. ⁴And Rabshakeh said to them, Say you now to Hezekiah, Thus says the great king, the king of Assyria, What confidence is this wherein you trust? ⁵I say, say you, (but they are but vain words) I have counsel and strength for war: now on whom do you trust, that you rebel against me? ⁶See, you trust in the staff of this broken reed, on Egypt; where on if a man lean, it will go into his hand, and pierce it: so is Pharaoh king of Egypt to all that trust in him. ⁷But if you say to me, We trust in the LORD our God: is it not he, whose high places and whose altars Hezekiah has taken away, and said to Judah and to Jerusalem, You shall worship before this altar? ⁸Now therefore give pledges, I pray you, to my master the king of Assyria, and I will give you two thousand horses, if you be able on your part to set riders on them. ⁹How then will you turn away the face of one captain of the least of my master's servants, and put your trust on Egypt for chariots and for horsemen? ¹⁰And am I now come up without the LORD against this land to destroy it? the LORD said to me, Go up against this land, and destroy it. ¹¹Then said Eliakim and Shebna and Joah to Rabshakeh, Speak, I pray you, to your servants in the Syrian language; for we understand it: and speak not to us in the Jews' language, in the ears of the people that are on the wall. ¹²But Rabshakeh said, Has my master sent me to your master and to you to speak these words? has he not sent me to the men that sit on the wall, that they may eat their own dung, and drink their own urine with you? ¹³Then Rabshakeh stood, and cried with a loud voice in the Jews' language, and said, Hear you the words of the great king, the king of Assyria. ¹⁴Thus says the king, Let not Hezekiah deceive you: for he shall not be able to deliver you. ¹⁵Neither let Hezekiah make you trust in the LORD, saying, The LORD will surely deliver us: this city shall not be delivered into the hand of the king of Assyria. ¹⁶Listen not to Hezekiah: for thus says the king of Assyria, Make an agreement with me by a present, and come out to me: and eat you every one of his vine, and every one of his fig tree, and drink you every one the waters of his own cistern; ¹⁷Until I come and take you away to a land like your own land, a land of corn and wine, a land of bread and vineyards. ¹⁸Beware lest Hezekiah persuade you, saying, the LORD will deliver us. Has any of the gods of the nations delivered his land out of the hand of the king of Assyria? ¹⁹Where are the gods of Hamath and Arphad? where are the gods of Sepharvaim? and have they delivered Samaria out of my hand? ²⁰Who are they among all the gods of these lands, that have delivered their land out of my hand, that the LORD should deliver Jerusalem out of my hand? ²¹But they held their peace, and answered him not a word: for the king's commandment was, saying, Answer him not. ²²Then came Eliakim, the son of Hilkiah, that was over the household, and Shebna the scribe, and Joah, the son of Asaph, the recorder, to Hezekiah with their clothes rent, and told him the words of Rabshakeh.

37 ¹And it came to pass, when king Hezekiah heard it, that he rent his clothes, and covered himself with sackcloth, and went into the house of the LORD. ²And he sent Eliakim, who was over the household, and Shebna the scribe, and the elders of the priests covered with sackcloth, to Isaiah the prophet the son of Amoz. ³And they said to him, Thus says Hezekiah, This day is a day of trouble, and of rebuke, and of blasphemy: for the children are come to the birth, and there is not strength to bring forth. ⁴It may be the LORD your God will hear the words of Rabshakeh, whom the king of Assyria his master has sent to reproach the living God, and will reprove the words which the LORD your God has heard: why lift up your prayer for the remnant that is left. ⁵So the servants of king Hezekiah came to Isaiah. ⁶And Isaiah said to them, Thus shall you say to your master, Thus says the LORD, Be not afraid of the words that you have heard, with which the servants of the king of Assyria have blasphemed me. ⁷Behold, I will send a blast on him, and he shall hear a rumor, and return to his own land; and I will cause him to fall by the sword in his own land. ⁸So Rabshakeh returned, and found the king of Assyria warring against Libnah: for he had heard that he was departed from Lachish. ⁹And he heard say concerning Tirhakah king of Ethiopia, He is come forth to make war with you. And when he heard it, he sent messengers to Hezekiah, saying, ¹⁰Thus shall you speak to Hezekiah king of Judah, saying, Let not your God, in whom you trust, deceive you, saying, Jerusalem shall not be given into the hand of the king of Assyria. ¹¹Behold, you have heard what the kings of Assyria have done to all lands by destroying them utterly; and shall you be delivered? ¹²Have the gods of the nations delivered them which my fathers have destroyed, as Gozan, and Haran, and Rezeph, and the children of Eden which were in Telassar? ¹³Where is the king of Hamath, and the king of Arphad, and the king of the city of Sepharvaim, Hena, and Ivah? ¹⁴And Hezekiah received the letter from the hand of the messengers, and read it: and Hezekiah went up to the house of the LORD, and spread it before the LORD. ¹⁵And Hezekiah prayed to the LORD, saying, ¹⁶O LORD of hosts, God of Israel, that dwell between the cherubim, you are the God, even you alone, of all the kingdoms of the earth: you have made heaven and earth. ¹⁷Incline your ear, O LORD, and hear; open your eyes, O LORD, and see: and hear all the words of Sennacherib, which has sent to reproach the living God. ¹⁸Of a truth, LORD, the kings of Assyria have laid waste all the nations, and their countries, ¹⁹And have cast their gods into the fire: for they were no gods, but the work of men's hands, wood and stone: therefore they have destroyed them. ²⁰Now therefore, O LORD our God, save us from his hand, that all the kingdoms of the earth may know that you are the LORD, even you only. ²¹Then Isaiah the son of Amoz sent to Hezekiah, saying, Thus says the LORD God of Israel, Whereas you have prayed to me against Sennacherib king of Assyria: ²²This is the word which the LORD has spoken concerning him; The virgin, the daughter of Zion, has despised you, and laughed you to scorn; the daughter of Jerusalem has shaken her head at you. ²³Whom have you reproached and blasphemed? and against whom have you exalted your voice, and lifted up your eyes on high? even against the Holy One of Israel. ²⁴By your servants have you reproached the Lord, and have said, By the multitude of my chariots am I come up to the height of the mountains, to the sides of Lebanon; and I will cut down the tall cedars thereof, and the choice fir trees thereof: and I will enter into the height of his border, and the forest of his Carmel. ²⁵I have dig, and drunk water; and with the sole of my feet have I dried up all the rivers of the besieged places. ²⁶Have you not heard long ago, how I have done it; and of ancient times, that I have formed it? now have I brought it to pass, that you should be to lay waste defended cities into ruinous heaps. ²⁷Therefore their inhabitants were of small power, they were dismayed and confounded: they were as the grass of the field, and as the green herb, as the grass on the housetops, and as corn blasted before it be grown up. ²⁸But I know your stayed, and your going out, and your coming in, and your rage against me. ²⁹Because your rage against me, and your tumult, is come up into my ears, therefore will I put my hook in your nose, and my bridle in your lips, and I will turn you back by the way by which you came. ³⁰And this shall be a sign to you, You shall eat this year such as grows of itself; and the second year that which springs of the same: and in the third year sow you, and reap, and plant vineyards, and eat the fruit thereof. ³¹And the remnant that is escaped of the house of Judah shall again take root downward, and bear fruit upward: ³²For out of Jerusalem shall go forth a remnant, and they that escape out of mount Zion: the zeal of the LORD of hosts shall do this. ³³Therefore thus says the LORD concerning the king of Assyria, He shall not come into this city, nor shoot an arrow there, nor come before it with shields, nor cast a bank against it. ³⁴By the way that he came, by the same shall he return, and shall not come into this city, says the LORD. ³⁵For I will defend this city to save it for my own sake, and for my servant David's sake. ³⁶Then the angel of the LORD went forth, and smote in the camp of the Assyrians a hundred and fourscore and five thousand: and when they arose early in the morning, behold, they were all dead corpses. ³⁷So Sennacherib king of Assyria departed, and went and returned, and dwelled at Nineveh. ³⁸And it came to pass, as he was worshipping in the house of Nisroch his god, that Adrammelech and Sharezer his sons smote him with the sword; and they escaped into the land of Armenia: and Esarhaddon his son reigned in his stead.

38 ¹In those days was Hezekiah sick to death. And Isaiah the prophet the son of Amoz came to him, and said to him, Thus says the LORD, Set your house in order: for you shall die, and not live. ²Then Hezekiah turned his face toward the wall, and prayed to the LORD, ³And said, Remember now, O LORD, I beseech you, how I have walked before you in truth and with a perfect heart, and have done that which is good in your sight. And Hezekiah wept sore. ⁴Then came the word of the LORD to Isaiah, saying, ⁵Go, and say to Hezekiah, Thus says the LORD, the God of David your father, I have heard your prayer, I have seen your tears: behold, I will add to your days fifteen years. ⁶And I will deliver you and this city out of the hand of the king of Assyria: and I will defend this city. ⁷And this shall be a sign to you from the LORD, that the LORD will do this thing that he has spoken; ⁸Behold, I will bring again the shadow of the degrees, which is gone down in the sun dial of Ahaz, ten degrees backward. So the sun returned ten degrees, by which degrees it was gone down. ⁹The writing of Hezekiah king of Judah, when he had been sick, and was recovered of his sickness: ¹⁰I said in the cutting off of my days, I shall go to the gates of the grave: I am deprived of the residue of my years. ¹¹I said, I shall not see the LORD, even the LORD, in the land of the living: I shall behold man no more with the inhabitants of the world. ¹²My age is departed, and is removed from me as a shepherd's tent: I have cut off like a weaver my life: he will cut me off with pining sickness: from day even to night will you make an end of me. ¹³I reckoned till morning, that, as a lion, so will he break all my bones: from day even to night will you make an end of me. ¹⁴Like a crane or a swallow, so did I chatter: I did mourn as a dove: my eyes fail with looking upward: O LORD, I am oppressed; undertake for me. ¹⁵What shall I say? he has both spoken to me, and himself has done it: I shall go softly all my years in the bitterness of my soul. ¹⁶O LORD, by these things men live, and in all these things is the life of my spirit: so will you recover me, and make me to live. ¹⁷Behold, for peace I had great bitterness: but you have in love to my soul delivered it from the pit of corruption: for you have cast all my sins behind your back. ¹⁸For the grave cannot praise you, death can not celebrate you: they that go down into the pit cannot hope for your truth. ¹⁹The living, the living, he shall praise you, as I do this day: the father to the children shall make known your truth. ²⁰The LORD was ready to save me: therefore we will sing my songs to the stringed instruments all the days of our life in the house of the LORD. ²¹For Isaiah had said, Let them take a lump of figs, and lay it for a plaster on the boil, and he shall recover. ²²Hezekiah also had said, What is the sign that I shall go up to the house of the LORD?

39 ¹At that time Merodachbaladan, the son of Baladan, king of Babylon, sent letters and a present to Hezekiah: for he had heard that he had been sick, and was recovered. ²And Hezekiah was glad of them, and showed them the house of his precious things, the silver, and the gold, and the spices, and the precious ointment, and all the house of his armor, and all that was found in his treasures: there was nothing in his house, nor in all his dominion, that Hezekiah showed them not. ³Then came Isaiah the prophet to king Hezekiah, and said to him, What said these men? and from where came they to you? And Hezekiah said, They are come from a far country to me, even from Babylon. ⁴Then said he, What have they seen in your house? And Hezekiah answered, All that is in my house have they seen:

there is nothing among my treasures that I have not showed them. ⁵Then said Isaiah to Hezekiah, Hear the word of the LORD of hosts: ⁶Behold, the days come, that all that is in your house, and that which your fathers have laid up in store until this day, shall be carried to Babylon: nothing shall be left, says the LORD. ⁷And of your sons that shall issue from you, which you shall beget, shall they take away; and they shall be eunuchs in the palace of the king of Babylon. ⁸Then said Hezekiah to Isaiah, Good is the word of the LORD which you have spoken. He said moreover, For there shall be peace and truth in my days.

40

¹Comfort you, comfort you my people, says your God. ²Speak you comfortably to Jerusalem, and cry to her, that her warfare is accomplished, that her iniquity is pardoned: for she has received of the LORD's hand double for all her sins. ³The voice of him that cries in the wilderness, Prepare you the way of the LORD, make straight in the desert a highway for our God. ⁴Every valley shall be exalted, and every mountain and hill shall be made low: and the crooked shall be made straight, and the rough places plain: ⁵And the glory of the LORD shall be revealed, and all flesh shall see it together: for the mouth of the LORD has spoken it. ⁶The voice said, Cry. And he said, What shall I cry? All flesh is grass, and all the goodliness thereof is as the flower of the field: ⁷The grass wither, the flower fades: because the spirit of the LORD blows on it: surely the people is grass. ⁸The grass wither, the flower fades: but the word of our God shall stand for ever. ⁹O Zion, that bring good tidings, get you up into the high mountain; O Jerusalem, that bring good tidings, lift up your voice with strength; lift it up, be not afraid; say to the cities of Judah, Behold your God! ¹⁰Behold, the Lord GOD will come with strong hand, and his arm shall rule for him: behold, his reward is with him, and his work before him. ¹¹He shall feed his flock like a shepherd: he shall gather the lambs with his arm, and carry them in his bosom, and shall gently lead those that are with young. ¹²Who has measured the waters in the hollow of his hand, and meted out heaven with the span, and comprehended the dust of the earth in a measure, and weighed the mountains in scales, and the hills in a balance? ¹³Who has directed the Spirit of the LORD, or being his counselor has taught him? ¹⁴With whom took he counsel, and who instructed him, and taught him in the path of judgment, and taught him knowledge, and showed to him the way of understanding? ¹⁵Behold, the nations are as a drop of a bucket, and are counted as the small dust of the balance: behold, he takes up the isles as a very little thing. ¹⁶And Lebanon is not sufficient to burn, nor the beasts thereof sufficient for a burnt offering. ¹⁷All nations before him are as nothing; and they are counted to him less than nothing, and vanity. ¹⁸To whom then will you liken God? or what likeness will you compare to him? ¹⁹The workman melts a graven image, and the goldsmith spreads it over with gold, and casts silver chains. ²⁰He that is so impoverished that he has no oblation chooses a tree that will not rot; he seeks to him a cunning workman to prepare a graven image, that shall not be moved. ²¹Have you not known? have you not heard? has it not been told you from the beginning? have you not understood from the foundations of the earth? ²²It is he that sits on the circle of the earth, and the inhabitants thereof are as grasshoppers; that stretches out the heavens as a curtain, and spreads them out as a tent to dwell in: ²³That brings the princes to nothing; he makes the judges of the earth as vanity. ²⁴Yes, they shall not be planted; yes, they shall not be sown: yes, their stock shall not take root in the earth: and he shall also blow on them, and they shall wither, and the whirlwind shall take them away as stubble. ²⁵To whom then will you liken me, or shall I be equal? says the Holy One. ²⁶Lift up your eyes on high, and behold who has created these things, that brings out their host by number: he calls them all by names by the greatness of his might, for that he is strong in power; not one fails. ²⁷Why say you, O Jacob, and speak, O Israel, My way is hid from the LORD, and my judgment is passed over from my God? ²⁸Have you not known? have you not heard, that the everlasting God, the LORD, the Creator of the ends of the earth, faints not, neither is weary? there is no searching of his understanding. ²⁹He gives power to the faint; and to them that have no might he increases strength. ³⁰Even the youths shall faint and be weary, and the young men shall utterly fall: ³¹But they that wait on the LORD shall renew their strength; they shall mount up with wings as eagles; they shall run, and not be weary; and they shall walk, and not faint.

41

¹Keep silence before me, O islands; and let the people renew their strength: let them come near; then let them speak: let us come near together to judgment. ²Who raised up the righteous man from the east, called him to his foot, gave the nations before him, and made him rule over kings? he gave them as the dust to his sword, and as driven stubble to his bow. ³He pursued them, and passed safely; even by the way that he had not gone with his feet. ⁴Who has worked and done it, calling the generations from the beginning? I the LORD, the first, and with the last; I am he. ⁵The isles saw it, and feared; the ends of the earth were afraid, drew near, and came. ⁶They helped every one his neighbor; and every one said to his brother, Be of good courage. ⁷So the carpenter encouraged the goldsmith, and he that smoothes with the hammer him that smote the anvil, saying, It is ready for the soldering: and he fastened it with nails, that it should not be moved. ⁸But you, Israel, are my servant, Jacob whom I have chosen, the seed of Abraham my friend. ⁹You whom I have taken from the ends of the earth, and called you from the chief men thereof, and said to you, You are my servant; I have chosen you, and not cast you away. ¹⁰Fear you not; for I am with you: be not dismayed; for I am your God: I will strengthen you; yes, I will help you; yes, I will uphold you with the right hand of my righteousness. ¹¹Behold, all they that were incensed against you shall be ashamed and confounded: they shall be as nothing; and they that strive with you shall perish. ¹²You shall seek them, and shall not find them, even them that contended with you: they that war against you shall be as nothing, and as a thing of nothing. ¹³For I the LORD your God will hold your right hand, saying to you, Fear not; I will help you. ¹⁴Fear not, you worm Jacob, and you men of Israel; I will help you, says the LORD, and your redeemer, the Holy One of Israel. ¹⁵Behold, I will make you a new sharp threshing instrument having teeth: you shall thresh the mountains, and beat them small, and shall make the hills as chaff. ¹⁶You shall fan them, and the wind shall carry them

away, and the whirlwind shall scatter them: and you shall rejoice in the LORD, and shall glory in the Holy One of Israel. ¹⁷When the poor and needy seek water, and there is none, and their tongue fails for thirst, I the LORD will hear them, I the God of Israel will not forsake them. ¹⁸I will open rivers in high places, and fountains in the middle of the valleys: I will make the wilderness a pool of water, and the dry land springs of water. ¹⁹I will plant in the wilderness the cedar, the shittah tree, and the myrtle, and the oil tree; I will set in the desert the fir tree, and the pine, and the box tree together: ²⁰That they may see, and know, and consider, and understand together, that the hand of the LORD has done this, and the Holy One of Israel has created it. ²¹Produce your cause, says the LORD; bring forth your strong reasons, says the King of Jacob. ²²Let them bring them forth, and show us what shall happen: let them show the former things, what they be, that we may consider them, and know the latter end of them; or declare us things for to come. ²³Show the things that are to come hereafter, that we may know that you are gods: yes, do good, or do evil, that we may be dismayed, and behold it together. ²⁴Behold, you are of nothing, and your work of nothing: an abomination is he that chooses you. ²⁵I have raised up one from the north, and he shall come: from the rising of the sun shall he call on my name: and he shall come on princes as on mortar, and as the potter treads clay. ²⁶Who has declared from the beginning, that we may know? and beforetime, that we may say, He is righteous? yes, there is none that shows, yes, there is none that declares, yes, there is none that hears your words. ²⁷The first shall say to Zion, Behold, behold them: and I will give to Jerusalem one that brings good tidings. ²⁸For I beheld, and there was no man; even among them, and there was no counselor, that, when I asked of them, could answer a word. ²⁹Behold, they are all vanity; their works are nothing: their molten images are wind and confusion.

42 ¹Behold my servant, whom I uphold; my elect, in whom my soul delights; I have put my spirit on him: he shall bring forth judgment to the Gentiles. ²He shall not cry, nor lift up, nor cause his voice to be heard in the street. ³A bruised reed shall he not break, and the smoking flax shall he not quench: he shall bring forth judgment to truth. ⁴He shall not fail nor be discouraged, till he have set judgment in the earth: and the isles shall wait for his law. ⁵Thus says God the LORD, he that created the heavens, and stretched them out; he that spread forth the earth, and that which comes out of it; he that gives breath to the people on it, and spirit to them that walk therein: ⁶I the LORD have called you in righteousness, and will hold your hand, and will keep you, and give you for a covenant of the people, for a light of the Gentiles; ⁷To open the blind eyes, to bring out the prisoners from the prison, and them that sit in darkness out of the prison house. ⁸I am the LORD: that is my name: and my glory will I not give to another, neither my praise to graven images. ⁹Behold, the former things are come to pass, and new things do I declare: before they spring forth I tell you of them. ¹⁰Sing to the LORD a new song, and his praise from the end of the earth, you that go down to the sea, and all that is therein; the isles, and the inhabitants thereof. ¹¹Let the wilderness and the cities thereof lift up their voice, the villages that Kedar does inhabit: let the inhabitants of the rock sing, let them shout from the top of the mountains. ¹²Let them give glory to the LORD, and declare his praise in the islands. ¹³The LORD shall go forth as a mighty man, he shall stir up jealousy like a man of war: he shall cry, yes, roar; he shall prevail against his enemies. ¹⁴I have long time held my peace; I have been still, and refrained myself: now will I cry like a travailing woman; I will destroy and devour at once. ¹⁵I will make waste mountains and hills, and dry up all their herbs; and I will make the rivers islands, and I will dry up the pools. ¹⁶And I will bring the blind by a way that they knew not; I will lead them in paths that they have not known: I will make darkness light before them, and crooked things straight. These things will I do to them, and not forsake them. ¹⁷They shall be turned back, they shall be greatly ashamed, that trust in graven images, that say to the molten images, You are our gods. ¹⁸Hear, you deaf; and look, you blind, that you may see. ¹⁹Who is blind, but my servant? or deaf, as my messenger that I sent? who is blind as he that is perfect, and blind as the LORD's servant? ²⁰Seeing many things, but you observe not; opening the ears, but he hears not. ²¹The LORD is well pleased for his righteousness' sake; he will magnify the law, and make it honorable. ²²But this is a people robbed and spoiled; they are all of them snared in holes, and they are hid in prison houses: they are for a prey, and none delivers; for a spoil, and none says, Restore. ²³Who among you will give ear to this? who will listen and hear for the time to come? ²⁴Who gave Jacob for a spoil, and Israel to the robbers? did not the LORD, he against whom we have sinned? for they would not walk in his ways, neither were they obedient to his law. ²⁵Therefore he has poured on him the fury of his anger, and the strength of battle: and it has set him on fire round about, yet he knew not; and it burned him, yet he laid it not to heart.

43 ¹But now thus says the LORD that created you, O Jacob, and he that formed you, O Israel, Fear not: for I have redeemed you, I have called you by your name; you are mine. ²When you pass through the waters, I will be with you; and through the rivers, they shall not overflow you: when you walk through the fire, you shall not be burned; neither shall the flame kindle on you. ³For I am the LORD your God, the Holy One of Israel, your Savior: I gave Egypt for your ransom, Ethiopia and Seba for you. ⁴Since you were precious in my sight, you have been honorable, and I have loved you: therefore will I give men for you, and people for your life. ⁵Fear not: for I am with you: I will bring your seed from the east, and gather you from the west; ⁶I will say to the north, Give up; and to the south, Keep not back: bring my sons from far, and my daughters from the ends of the earth; ⁷Even every one that is called by my name: for I have created him for my glory, I have formed him; yes, I have made him. ⁸Bring forth the blind people that have eyes, and the deaf that have ears. ⁹Let all the nations be gathered together, and let the people be assembled: who among them can declare this, and show us former things? let them bring forth their witnesses, that they may be justified: or let them hear, and say, It is truth. ¹⁰You are my witnesses, says the LORD, and my servant whom I have chosen: that you may know and believe me, and understand that I am he: before me there was no God formed, neither shall there be after me. ¹¹I, even I, am the

LORD; and beside me there is no savior. ¹²I have declared, and have saved, and I have showed, when there was no strange god among you: therefore you are my witnesses, says the LORD, that I am God. ¹³Yes, before the day was I am he; and there is none that can deliver out of my hand: I will work, and who shall let it? ¹⁴Thus says the LORD, your redeemer, the Holy One of Israel; For your sake I have sent to Babylon, and have brought down all their nobles, and the Chaldeans, whose cry is in the ships. ¹⁵I am the LORD, your Holy One, the creator of Israel, your King. ¹⁶Thus says the LORD, which makes a way in the sea, and a path in the mighty waters; ¹⁷Which brings forth the chariot and horse, the army and the power; they shall lie down together, they shall not rise: they are extinct, they are quenched as wick. ¹⁸Remember you not the former things, neither consider the things of old. ¹⁹Behold, I will do a new thing; now it shall spring forth; shall you not know it? I will even make a way in the wilderness, and rivers in the desert. ²⁰The beast of the field shall honor me, the dragons and the owls: because I give waters in the wilderness, and rivers in the desert, to give drink to my people, my chosen. ²¹This people have I formed for myself; they shall show forth my praise. ²²But you have not called on me, O Jacob; but you have been weary of me, O Israel. ²³You have not brought me the small cattle of your burnt offerings; neither have you honored me with your sacrifices. I have not caused you to serve with an offering, nor wearied you with incense. ²⁴You have bought me no sweet cane with money, neither have you filled me with the fat of your sacrifices: but you have made me to serve with your sins, you have wearied me with your iniquities. ²⁵I, even I, am he that blots out your transgressions for my own sake, and will not remember your sins. ²⁶Put me in remembrance: let us plead together: declare you, that you may be justified. ²⁷Your first father has sinned, and your teachers have transgressed against me. ²⁸Therefore I have profaned the princes of the sanctuary, and have given Jacob to the curse, and Israel to reproaches.

44

¹Yet now hear, O Jacob my servant; and Israel, whom I have chosen: ²Thus says the LORD that made you, and formed you from the womb, which will help you; Fear not, O Jacob, my servant; and you, Jesurun, whom I have chosen. ³For I will pour water on him that is thirsty, and floods on the dry ground: I will pour my spirit on your seed, and my blessing on your offspring: ⁴And they shall spring up as among the grass, as willows by the water courses. ⁵One shall say, I am the LORD's; and another shall call himself by the name of Jacob; and another shall subscribe with his hand to the LORD, and surname himself by the name of Israel. ⁶Thus says the LORD the King of Israel, and his redeemer the LORD of hosts; I am the first, and I am the last; and beside me there is no God. ⁷And who, as I, shall call, and shall declare it, and set it in order for me, since I appointed the ancient people? and the things that are coming, and shall come, let them show to them. ⁸Fear not, neither be afraid: have not I told you from that time, and have declared it? you are even my witnesses. Is there a God beside me? yes, there is no God; I know not any. ⁹They that make a graven image are all of them vanity; and their delectable things shall not profit; and they are their own witnesses; they see not, nor know; that they may be ashamed. ¹⁰Who has formed a god, or molten a graven image that is profitable for nothing? ¹¹Behold, all his fellows shall be ashamed: and the workmen, they are of men: let them all be gathered together, let them stand up; yet they shall fear, and they shall be ashamed together. ¹²The smith with the tongs both works in the coals, and fashions it with hammers, and works it with the strength of his arms: yes, he is hungry, and his strength fails: he drinks no water, and is faint. ¹³The carpenter stretches out his rule; he marks it out with a line; he fits it with planes, and he marks it out with the compass, and makes it after the figure of a man, according to the beauty of a man; that it may remain in the house. ¹⁴He hews him down cedars, and takes the cypress and the oak, which he strengthens for himself among the trees of the forest: he plants an ash, and the rain does nourish it. ¹⁵Then shall it be for a man to burn: for he will take thereof, and warm himself; yes, he kindles it, and bakes bread; yes, he makes a god, and worships it; he makes it a graven image, and falls down thereto. ¹⁶He burns part thereof in the fire; with part thereof he eats flesh; he roasts roast, and is satisfied: yes, he warms himself, and says, Aha, I am warm, I have seen the fire: ¹⁷And the residue thereof he makes a god, even his graven image: he falls down to it, and worships it, and prays to it, and says, Deliver me; for you are my god. ¹⁸They have not known nor understood: for he has shut their eyes, that they cannot see; and their hearts, that they cannot understand. ¹⁹And none considers in his heart, neither is there knowledge nor understanding to say, I have burned part of it in the fire; yes, also I have baked bread on the coals thereof; I have roasted flesh, and eaten it: and shall I make the residue thereof an abomination? shall I fall down to the stock of a tree? ²⁰He feeds on ashes: a deceived heart has turned him aside, that he cannot deliver his soul, nor say, Is there not a lie in my right hand? ²¹Remember these, O Jacob and Israel; for you are my servant: I have formed you; you are my servant: O Israel, you shall not be forgotten of me. ²²I have blotted out, as a thick cloud, your transgressions, and, as a cloud, your sins: return to me; for I have redeemed you. ²³Sing, O you heavens; for the LORD has done it: shout, you lower parts of the earth: break forth into singing, you mountains, O forest, and every tree therein: for the LORD has redeemed Jacob, and glorified himself in Israel. ²⁴Thus says the LORD, your redeemer, and he that formed you from the womb, I am the LORD that makes all things; that stretches forth the heavens alone; that spreads abroad the earth by myself; ²⁵That frustrates the tokens of the liars, and makes diviners mad; that turns wise men backward, and makes their knowledge foolish; ²⁶That confirms the word of his servant, and performs the counsel of his messengers; that says to Jerusalem, You shall be inhabited; and to the cities of Judah, You shall be built, and I will raise up the decayed places thereof: ²⁷That says to the deep, Be dry, and I will dry up your rivers: ²⁸That says of Cyrus, He is my shepherd, and shall perform all my pleasure: even saying to Jerusalem, You shall be built; and to the temple, Your foundation shall be laid.

45

¹Thus says the LORD to his anointed, to Cyrus, whose right hand I have held, to subdue nations before him; and I will loose the loins of kings, to open before him the two leaved gates; and the gates shall not be

shut; ²I will go before you, and make the crooked places straight: I will break in pieces the gates of brass, and cut in sunder the bars of iron: ³And I will give you the treasures of darkness, and hidden riches of secret places, that you may know that I, the LORD, which call you by your name, am the God of Israel. ⁴For Jacob my servant's sake, and Israel my elect, I have even called you by your name: I have surnamed you, though you have not known me. ⁵I am the LORD, and there is none else, there is no God beside me: I girded you, though you have not known me: ⁶That they may know from the rising of the sun, and from the west, that there is none beside me. I am the LORD, and there is none else. ⁷I form the light, and create darkness: I make peace, and create evil: I the LORD do all these things. ⁸Drop down, you heavens, from above, and let the skies pour down righteousness: let the earth open, and let them bring forth salvation, and let righteousness spring up together; I the LORD have created it. ⁹Woe to him that strives with his Maker! Let the potsherd strive with the potsherds of the earth. Shall the clay say to him that fashions it, What make you? or your work, He has no hands? ¹⁰Woe to him that says to his father, What beget you? or to the woman, What have you brought forth? ¹¹Thus says the LORD, the Holy One of Israel, and his Maker, Ask me of things to come concerning my sons, and concerning the work of my hands command you me. ¹²I have made the earth, and created man on it: I, even my hands, have stretched out the heavens, and all their host have I commanded. ¹³I have raised him up in righteousness, and I will direct all his ways: he shall build my city, and he shall let go my captives, not for price nor reward, says the LORD of hosts. ¹⁴Thus says the LORD, The labor of Egypt, and merchandise of Ethiopia and of the Sabeans, men of stature, shall come over to you, and they shall be yours: they shall come after you; in chains they shall come over, and they shall fall down to you, they shall make supplication to you, saying, Surely God is in you; and there is none else, there is no God. ¹⁵Truly you are a God that hide yourself, O God of Israel, the Savior. ¹⁶They shall be ashamed, and also confounded, all of them: they shall go to confusion together that are makers of idols. ¹⁷But Israel shall be saved in the LORD with an everlasting salvation: you shall not be ashamed nor confounded world without end. ¹⁸For thus says the LORD that created the heavens; God himself that formed the earth and made it; he has established it, he created it not in vain, he formed it to be inhabited: I am the LORD; and there is none else. ¹⁹I have not spoken in secret, in a dark place of the earth: I said not to the seed of Jacob, Seek you me in vain: I the LORD speak righteousness, I declare things that are right. ²⁰Assemble yourselves and come; draw near together, you that are escaped of the nations: they have no knowledge that set up the wood of their graven image, and pray to a god that cannot save. ²¹Tell you, and bring them near; yes, let them take counsel together: who has declared this from ancient time? who has told it from that time? have not I the LORD? and there is no God else beside me; a just God and a Savior; there is none beside me. ²²Look to me, and be you saved, all the ends of the earth: for I am God, and there is none else. ²³I have sworn by myself, the word is gone out of my mouth in righteousness, and shall not return, That to me every knee shall bow, every tongue shall swear. ²⁴Surely, shall one say, in the LORD have I righteousness and strength: even to him shall men come; and all that are incensed against him shall be ashamed. ²⁵In the LORD shall all the seed of Israel be justified, and shall glory.

46 ¹Bel bows down, Nebo stoops, their idols were on the beasts, and on the cattle: your carriages were heavy laden; they are a burden to the weary beast. ²They stoop, they bow down together; they could not deliver the burden, but themselves are gone into captivity. ³Listen to me, O house of Jacob, and all the remnant of the house of Israel, which are borne by me from the belly, which are carried from the womb: ⁴And even to your old age I am he; and even to hoar hairs will I carry you: I have made, and I will bear; even I will carry, and will deliver you. ⁵To whom will you liken me, and make me equal, and compare me, that we may be like? ⁶They lavish gold out of the bag, and weigh silver in the balance, and hire a goldsmith; and he makes it a god: they fall down, yes, they worship. ⁷They bear him on the shoulder, they carry him, and set him in his place, and he stands; from his place shall he not remove: yes, one shall cry to him, yet can he not answer, nor save him out of his trouble. ⁸Remember this, and show yourselves men: bring it again to mind, O you transgressors. ⁹Remember the former things of old: for I am God, and there is none else; I am God, and there is none like me, ¹⁰Declaring the end from the beginning, and from ancient times the things that are not yet done, saying, My counsel shall stand, and I will do all my pleasure: ¹¹Calling a ravenous bird from the east, the man that executes my counsel from a far country: yes, I have spoken it, I will also bring it to pass; I have purposed it, I will also do it. ¹²Listen to me, you stouthearted, that are far from righteousness: ¹³I bring near my righteousness; it shall not be far off, and my salvation shall not tarry: and I will place salvation in Zion for Israel my glory.

47 ¹Come down, and sit in the dust, O virgin daughter of Babylon, sit on the ground: there is no throne, O daughter of the Chaldeans: for you shall no more be called tender and delicate. ²Take the millstones, and grind meal: uncover your locks, make bore the leg, uncover the thigh, pass over the rivers. ³Your nakedness shall be uncovered, yes, your shame shall be seen: I will take vengeance, and I will not meet you as a man. ⁴As for our redeemer, the LORD of hosts is his name, the Holy One of Israel. ⁵Sit you silent, and get you into darkness, O daughter of the Chaldeans: for you shall no more be called, The lady of kingdoms. ⁶I was wroth with my people, I have polluted my inheritance, and given them into your hand: you did show them no mercy; on the ancient have you very heavily laid your yoke. ⁷And you said, I shall be a lady for ever: so that you did not lay these things to your heart, neither did remember the latter end of it. ⁸Therefore hear now this, you that are given to pleasures, that dwell carelessly, that say in your heart, I am, and none else beside me; I shall not sit as a widow, neither shall I know the loss of children: ⁹But these two things shall come to you in a moment in one day, the loss of children, and widowhood: they shall come on you in their perfection for the multitude of your sorceries, and for the great abundance of your enchantments. ¹⁰For you have trusted in your wickedness: you have said, None sees me. Your wisdom and your knowledge, it has perverted you; and you have said in your heart, I am, and none else beside me. ¹¹Therefore shall evil come on you; you shall not know from where it rises: and mischief shall fall on you; you shall not be able to put it off: and desolation shall come on you suddenly, which you shall not know. ¹²Stand now with your enchantments, and with the multitude of your sorceries, wherein you have labored from your youth; if so be you shall be able to profit, if so be you may prevail. ¹³You are wearied in the multitude of your counsels. Let now the astrologers, the stargazers, the monthly prognosticators, stand up, and save you from these things that shall come on you. ¹⁴Behold, they shall be as stubble; the fire shall burn them; they shall not deliver themselves from the power of the flame: there shall not be a coal to warm at, nor fire to sit before it. ¹⁵Thus shall they be to you with whom you have labored, even your merchants, from your youth: they shall wander every one to his quarter; none shall save you.

48 ¹Hear you this, O house of Jacob, which are called by the name of Israel, and are come forth out of the waters of Judah, which swear by the name of the LORD, and make mention of the God of Israel, but not in truth, nor in righteousness. ²For they call themselves of the holy city, and stay themselves on the God of Israel; The LORD of hosts is his name. ³I have declared the former things from the beginning; and they went forth out of my mouth, and I showed them; I did them suddenly, and they came to pass. ⁴Because I knew that you are obstinate, and your neck is an iron sinew, and your brow brass; ⁵I have even from the beginning declared it to you; before it came to pass I showed it you: lest you should say, My idol has done them, and my graven image, and my molten image, has commanded them. ⁶You have heard, see all this; and will not you declare it? I have showed you new things from this time, even hidden things, and you did not know them. ⁷They are created now, and not from the beginning; even before the day when you heard them not; lest you should say, Behold, I knew them. ⁸Yes, you heard not; yes, you knew not; yes, from that time that your ear was not opened: for I knew that you would deal very treacherously, and were called a transgressor from the womb. ⁹For my name's sake will I defer my anger, and for my praise will I refrain for you, that I cut you not off. ¹⁰Behold, I have refined you, but not with silver; I have chosen you in the furnace of affliction. ¹¹For my own sake, even for my own sake, will I do it: for how should my name be polluted? and I will not give my glory to another. ¹²Listen to me, O Jacob and Israel, my called; I am he; I am the first, I also am the last. ¹³My hand also has laid the foundation of the earth, and my right hand has spanned the heavens: when I call to them, they stand up together. ¹⁴All you, assemble yourselves, and hear; which among them has declared these things? The LORD has loved him: he will do his pleasure on Babylon, and his arm shall be on the Chaldeans. ¹⁵I, even I, have spoken; yes, I have called him: I have brought him, and he shall make his way prosperous. ¹⁶Come you near to me, hear you this; I have not spoken in secret from the beginning; from the time that it was, there am I: and now the Lord GOD, and his Spirit, has sent me. ¹⁷Thus says the LORD, your Redeemer, the Holy One of Israel; I am the LORD your God which teaches you to profit, which leads you by the way that you should go. ¹⁸O that you had listened to my commandments! then had your peace been as a river, and your righteousness as the waves of the sea: ¹⁹Your seed also had been as the sand, and the offspring of your bowels like the gravel thereof; his name should not have been cut off nor destroyed from before me. ²⁰Go you forth of Babylon, flee you from the Chaldeans, with a voice of singing declare you, tell this, utter it even to the end of the earth; say you, The LORD has redeemed his servant Jacob. ²¹And they thirsted not when he led them through the deserts: he caused the waters to flow out of the rock for them: he split the rock also, and the waters gushed out. ²²There is no peace, says the LORD, to the wicked.

49 ¹Listen, O isles, to me; and listen, you people, from far; The LORD has called me from the womb; from the bowels of my mother has he made mention of my name. ²And he has made my mouth like a sharp sword; in the shadow of his hand has he hid me, and made me a polished shaft; in his quiver has he hid me; ³And said to me, You are my servant, O Israel, in whom I will be glorified. ⁴Then I said, I have labored in vain, I have spent my strength for nothing, and in vain: yet surely my judgment is with the LORD, and my work with my God. ⁵And now, says the LORD that formed me from the womb to be his servant, to bring Jacob again to him, Though Israel be not gathered, yet shall I be glorious in the eyes of the LORD, and my God shall be my strength. ⁶And he said, It is a light thing that you should be my servant to raise up the tribes of Jacob, and to restore the preserved of Israel: I will also give you for a light to the Gentiles, that you may be my salvation to the end of the earth. ⁷Thus says the LORD, the Redeemer of Israel, and his Holy One, to him whom man despises, to him whom the nation abhors, to a servant of rulers, Kings shall see and arise, princes also shall worship, because of the LORD that is faithful, and the Holy One of Israel, and he shall choose you. ⁸Thus says the LORD, In an acceptable time have I heard you, and in a day of salvation have I helped you: and I will preserve you, and give you for a covenant of the people, to establish the earth, to cause to inherit the desolate heritages; ⁹That you may say to the prisoners, Go forth; to them that are in darkness, Show yourselves. They shall feed in the ways, and their pastures shall be in all high places. ¹⁰They shall not hunger nor thirst; neither shall the heat nor sun smite them: for he that has mercy on them shall lead them, even by the springs of water shall he guide them. ¹¹And I will make all my mountains a way, and my highways shall be exalted. ¹²Behold, these shall come from far: and, see, these from the north and from the west; and these from the land of Sinim. ¹³Sing, O heavens; and be joyful, O earth; and break forth into singing, O mountains: for the LORD has comforted his people, and will have mercy on his afflicted. ¹⁴But Zion said, The LORD has forsaken me, and my Lord has forgotten me. ¹⁵Can a woman forget her sucking child, that she should not have compassion on the son of her womb? yes, they may forget, yet will I not forget you. ¹⁶Behold, I have graven you on the palms of my hands; your walls are continually before me. ¹⁷Your children shall make haste; your destroyers and they that made you waste shall go forth of you. ¹⁸Lift up your eyes round about, and behold: all these gather themselves together, and come to you. As I live, says the LORD, you shall surely clothe you with them all, as with an ornament, and bind them on you, as a bride does. ¹⁹For your waste and your desolate places, and the land of your destruction, shall even now be too narrow by reason of the inhabitants, and they that swallowed you up shall be far away. ²⁰The children which you shall have, after you have lost the other, shall say again in your ears, The place is too strait for me: give place to me that I may dwell. ²¹Then shall you say in your heart, Who has begotten me these, seeing I have lost my children, and am desolate, a captive, and removing to and fro? and who has brought up these? Behold, I was left alone; these, where had they been? ²²Thus says the Lord GOD, Behold, I will lift up my hand to the Gentiles, and set up my standard to the people: and they shall bring your sons in their arms, and your daughters shall be carried on their shoulders. ²³And kings shall be your nursing fathers, and their queens your nursing mothers: they shall bow down to you with their face toward the earth, and lick up the dust of your feet; and you shall know that I am the LORD: for they shall not be ashamed that wait for me. ²⁴Shall the prey be taken from the mighty, or the lawful captive delivered? ²⁵But thus says the LORD, Even the captives of the mighty shall be taken away, and the prey of the terrible shall be delivered: for I will contend with him that contends with you, and I will save your children. ²⁶And I will feed them that oppress you with their own flesh; and they shall be drunken with their own blood, as with sweet wine: and all flesh shall know that I the LORD am your Savior and your Redeemer, the mighty One of Jacob.

50 ¹Thus says the LORD, Where is the bill of your mother's divorce, whom I have put away? or which of my creditors is it to whom I have sold you? Behold, for your iniquities have you sold yourselves, and for your transgressions is your mother put away. ²Why, when I came, was there no man? when I called, was there none to answer? Is my hand shortened at all, that it cannot redeem? or have I no power to deliver? behold, at my rebuke I dry up the sea, I make the rivers a wilderness: their fish stinks, because there is no water, and dies for thirst. ³I clothe the heavens with blackness, and I make sackcloth their covering. ⁴The Lord GOD has given me the tongue of the learned, that I should know how to speak a word in season to him that is weary: he wakens morning by morning, he wakens my ear to hear as the learned. ⁵The Lord GOD has opened my ear, and I was not rebellious, neither turned away back. ⁶I gave my back to the smiters, and my cheeks to them that plucked off the hair: I hid not my face from shame and spitting. ⁷For the Lord GOD will help me; therefore shall I not be confounded: therefore have I set my face like a flint, and I know that I shall not be ashamed. ⁸He is near that justifies me; who will contend with me? let us stand together: who is my adversary? let him come near to me. ⁹Behold, the Lord GOD will help me; who is he that shall condemn me? see, they all shall wax old as a garment; the moth shall eat them up. ¹⁰Who is among you that fears the LORD, that obeys the voice of his servant, that walks in darkness, and has no light? let him trust in the name of the LORD, and stay on his God. ¹¹Behold, all you that kindle a fire, that compass yourselves about with sparks: walk in the light of your fire, and in the sparks that you have kindled. This shall you have of my hand; you shall lie down in sorrow.

51 ¹Listen to me, you that follow after righteousness, you that seek the LORD: look to the rock from where you are hewn, and to the hole of the pit from where you are dig. ²Look to Abraham your father, and to Sarah that bore you: for I called him alone, and blessed him, and increased him. ³For the LORD shall comfort Zion: he will comfort all her waste places; and he will make her wilderness like Eden, and her desert like the garden of the LORD; joy and gladness shall be found therein, thanksgiving, and the voice of melody. ⁴Listen to me, my people; and give ear to me, O my nation: for a law shall proceed from me, and I will make my judgment to rest for a light of the people. ⁵My righteousness is near; my salvation is gone forth, and my arms shall judge the people; the isles shall wait on me, and on my arm shall they trust. ⁶Lift up your eyes to the heavens, and look on the earth beneath: for the heavens shall vanish away like smoke, and the earth shall wax old like a garment, and they that dwell therein shall die in like manner: but my salvation shall be for ever, and my righteousness shall not be abolished. ⁷Listen to me, you that know righteousness, the people in whose heart is my law; fear you not the reproach of men, neither be you afraid of their revilings. ⁸For the moth shall eat them up like a garment, and the worm shall eat them like wool: but my righteousness shall be for ever, and my salvation from generation to generation. ⁹Awake, awake, put on strength, O arm of the LORD; awake, as in the ancient days, in the generations of old. Are you not it that has cut Rahab, and wounded the dragon? ¹⁰Are you not it which has dried the sea, the waters of the great deep; that has made the depths of the sea a way for the ransomed to pass over? ¹¹Therefore the redeemed of the LORD shall return, and come with singing to Zion; and everlasting joy shall be on their head: they shall obtain gladness and joy; and sorrow and mourning shall flee away. ¹²I, even I, am he that comforts you: who are you, that you should be afraid of a man that shall die, and of the son of man which shall be made as grass; ¹³And forget the LORD your maker, that has stretched forth the heavens, and laid the foundations of the earth; and have feared continually every day because of the fury of the oppressor, as if he were ready to destroy? and where is the fury of the oppressor? ¹⁴The captive exile hastens that he may be loosed, and that he should not die in the pit, nor that his bread should fail. ¹⁵But I am the LORD your God, that divided the sea, whose waves roared: The LORD of hosts is his name. ¹⁶And I have put my words in your mouth, and I have covered you in the shadow of my hand, that I may plant the heavens, and lay the foundations of the earth, and say to Zion, You are my people. ¹⁷Awake, awake, stand up, O Jerusalem, which have drunk at the hand of the LORD the cup of his fury; you have drunken the dregs of the cup of trembling, and wrung them out. ¹⁸There is none to guide her among all the sons whom she has brought forth; neither is there any that takes her by the hand of all the sons that she has brought up. ¹⁹These two things are come to you; who shall be sorry for you? desolation, and destruction, and the famine, and the sword: by whom shall I comfort you? ²⁰Your sons have fainted, they lie at the head of all the streets, as a wild bull in a net: they are full of the fury of the LORD, the rebuke of your God. ²¹Therefore hear now this, you afflicted, and drunken, but not with wine: ²²Thus says your Lord the LORD, and your God that pleads the cause of his people, Behold, I have taken out of your hand the cup of trembling, even the dregs of the cup of my fury; you shall no more drink it again: ²³But I will put it into the hand of them that afflict you; which have said to your soul, Bow down, that we may go over: and you have laid your body as the ground, and as the street, to them that went over.

52 ¹Awake, awake; put on your strength, O Zion; put on your beautiful garments, O Jerusalem, the holy city: for from now on there shall no more come into you the uncircumcised and the unclean. ²Shake yourself from the dust; arise, and sit down, O Jerusalem: loose yourself from the bands of your neck, O captive daughter of Zion. ³For thus says the LORD, You have sold yourselves for nothing; and you shall be redeemed without money. ⁴For thus says the Lord GOD, My people went down aforetime into Egypt to sojourn there; and the Assyrian oppressed them without cause. ⁵Now therefore, what have I here, says the LORD, that my people is taken away for nothing? they that rule over them make them to howl, said the LORD; and my name continually every day is blasphemed. ⁶Therefore my people shall know my name: therefore they shall know in that day that I am he that does speak: behold, it is I. ⁷How beautiful on the mountains are the feet of him that brings good tidings, that publishes peace; that brings good tidings of good, that publishes salvation; that said to Zion, Your God reigns! ⁸Your watchmen shall lift up the voice; with the voice together shall they sing: for they shall see eye to eye, when the LORD shall bring again Zion. ⁹Break forth into joy, sing together, you waste places of Jerusalem: for the LORD has comforted his people, he has redeemed Jerusalem. ¹⁰The LORD has made bore his holy arm in the eyes of all the nations; and all the ends of the earth shall see the salvation of our God. ¹¹Depart you, depart you, go you out from there, touch no unclean thing; go you out of the middle of her; be you clean, that bear the vessels of the LORD. ¹²For you shall not go out with haste, nor go by flight: for the LORD will go before you; and the God of Israel will be your rear guard. ¹³Behold, my servant shall deal prudently, he shall be exalted and extolled, and be very high. ¹⁴As many were astonished at you; his visage was so marred more than any man, and his form more than the sons of men: ¹⁵So shall he sprinkle many nations; the kings shall shut their mouths at him: for that which had not been told them shall they see; and that which they had not heard shall they consider.

53 ¹Who has believed our report? and to whom is the arm of the LORD revealed? ²For he shall grow up before him as a tender plant, and as a root out of a dry ground: he has no form nor comeliness; and when we shall see him, there is no beauty that we should desire him. ³He is despised and rejected of men; a man of sorrows, and acquainted with grief: and we hid as it were our faces from him; he was despised, and we esteemed him not. ⁴Surely he has borne our griefs, and carried our sorrows: yet we did esteem him stricken, smitten of God, and afflicted. ⁵But he was wounded for our transgressions, he was bruised for our iniquities: the chastisement of our peace was on him; and with his stripes we are healed. ⁶All we like sheep have gone astray; we have turned every one to his own way; and the LORD has laid on him the iniquity of us all. ⁷He was oppressed, and he was afflicted, yet he opened not his mouth: he is brought as a lamb to the slaughter, and as a sheep before her shearers is dumb, so he opens not his mouth. ⁸He was taken from prison and from judgment: and who shall declare his generation? for he was cut off out of the land of the living: for the transgression of my people was he stricken. ⁹And he made his grave with the wicked, and with the rich in his death; because he had done no violence, neither was any deceit in his mouth. ¹⁰Yet it pleased the LORD to bruise him; he has put him to grief: when you shall make his soul an offering for sin, he shall see his seed, he shall prolong his days, and the pleasure of the LORD shall prosper in his hand. ¹¹He shall see of the travail of his soul, and shall be satisfied: by his knowledge shall my righteous servant justify many; for he shall bear their iniquities. ¹²Therefore will I divide him a portion with the great, and he shall divide the spoil with the strong; because he has poured out his soul to death: and he was numbered with the transgressors; and he bore the sin of many, and made intercession for the transgressors.

54 ¹Sing, O barren, you that did not bear; break forth into singing, and cry aloud, you that did not travail with child: for more are the children of the desolate than the children of the married wife, says the LORD. ²Enlarge the place of your tent, and let them stretch forth the curtains of your habitations: spare not, lengthen your cords, and strengthen your stakes; ³For you shall break forth on the right hand and on the left; and your seed shall inherit the Gentiles, and make the desolate cities to be inhabited. ⁴Fear not; for you shall not be ashamed: neither be you confounded; for you shall not be put to shame: for you shall forget the shame of your youth, and shall not remember the reproach of your widowhood any more. ⁵For your Maker is your husband; the LORD of hosts is his name; and your Redeemer the Holy One of Israel; The God of the whole earth shall he be called. ⁶For the LORD has called you as a woman forsaken and grieved in spirit, and a wife of youth, when you were refused, says your God. ⁷For a small moment have I forsaken you; but with great mercies will I gather you. ⁸In a little wrath I hid my face from you for a moment; but with everlasting kindness will I have mercy on you, says the LORD your Redeemer. ⁹For this is as the waters of Noah to me: for as I have sworn that the waters of Noah should no more go over the earth; so have I sworn that I would not be wroth with you, nor rebuke you. ¹⁰For the mountains shall depart, and the hills be removed; but my kindness shall not depart from you, neither shall the covenant of my peace be removed, says the LORD that has mercy on you. ¹¹O you afflicted, tossed with tempest, and not comforted, behold, I will lay your stones with fair colors, and lay your foundations with sapphires. ¹²And I will make your windows of agates, and your gates of carbuncles, and all your borders of pleasant stones. ¹³And all your children shall be taught of the LORD; and great shall be the peace of your children. ¹⁴In righteousness shall you be established: you shall be far from oppression; for you shall not fear: and from terror; for it shall not come near you. ¹⁵Behold, they shall surely gather together, but not by me: whoever shall gather together against you shall fall for your sake. ¹⁶Behold, I have created the smith that blows the coals in the fire, and that brings forth an instrument for his work; and I have created the waster to destroy. ¹⁷No weapon that is formed against you shall prosper; and every tongue that shall rise against you in judgment you shall condemn. This is the heritage of the servants of the LORD, and their righteousness is of me, says the LORD.

55

¹Ho, every one that thirsts, come you to the waters, and he that has no money; come you, buy, and eat; yes, come, buy wine and milk without money and without price. ²Why do you spend money for that which is not bread? and your labor for that which satisfies not? listen diligently to me, and eat you that which is good, and let your soul delight itself in fatness. ³Incline your ear, and come to me: hear, and your soul shall live; and I will make an everlasting covenant with you, even the sure mercies of David. ⁴Behold, I have given him for a witness to the people, a leader and commander to the people. ⁵Behold, you shall call a nation that you know not, and nations that knew not you shall run to you because of the LORD your God, and for the Holy One of Israel; for he has glorified you. ⁶Seek you the LORD while he may be found, call you on him while he is near: ⁷Let the wicked forsake his way, and the unrighteous man his thoughts: and let him return to the LORD, and he will have mercy on him; and to our God, for he will abundantly pardon. ⁸For my thoughts are not your thoughts, neither are your ways my ways, says the LORD. ⁹For as the heavens are higher than the earth, so are my ways higher than your ways, and my thoughts than your thoughts. ¹⁰For as the rain comes down, and the snow from heaven, and returns not thither, but waters the earth, and makes it bring forth and bud, that it may give seed to the sower, and bread to the eater; ¹¹So shall my word be that goes forth out of my mouth: it shall not return to me void, but it shall accomplish that which I please, and it shall prosper in the thing whereto I sent it. ¹²For you shall go out with joy, and be led forth with peace: the mountains and the hills shall break forth before you into singing, and all the trees of the field shall clap their hands. ¹³Instead of the thorn shall come up the fir tree, and instead of the brier shall come up the myrtle tree: and it shall be to the LORD for a name, for an everlasting sign that shall not be cut off.

56

¹Thus says the LORD, Keep you judgment, and do justice: for my salvation is near to come, and my righteousness to be revealed. ²Blessed is the man that does this, and the son of man that lays hold on it; that keeps the sabbath from polluting it, and keeps his hand from doing any evil. ³Neither let the son of the stranger, that has joined himself to the LORD, speak, saying, The LORD has utterly separated me from his people: neither let the eunuch say, Behold, I am a dry tree. ⁴For thus says the LORD to the eunuchs that keep my sabbaths, and choose the things that please me, and take hold of my covenant; ⁵Even to them will I give in my house and within my walls a place and a name better than of sons and of daughters: I will give them an everlasting name, that shall not be cut off. ⁶Also the sons of the stranger, that join themselves to the LORD, to serve him, and to love the name of the LORD, to be his servants, every one that keeps the sabbath from polluting it, and takes hold of my covenant; ⁷Even them will I bring to my holy mountain, and make them joyful in my house of prayer: their burnt offerings and their sacrifices shall be accepted on my altar; for my house shall be called an house of prayer for all people. ⁸The Lord GOD, which gathers the outcasts of Israel says, Yet will I gather others to him, beside those that are gathered to him. ⁹All you beasts of the field, come to devour, yes, all you beasts in the forest. ¹⁰His watchmen are blind: they are all ignorant, they are all dumb dogs, they cannot bark; sleeping, lying down, loving to slumber. ¹¹Yes, they are greedy dogs which can never have enough, and they are shepherds that cannot understand: they all look to their own way, every one for his gain, from his quarter. ¹²Come you, say they, I will fetch wine, and we will fill ourselves with strong drink; and to morrow shall be as this day, and much more abundant.

57

¹The righteous perishes, and no man lays it to heart: and merciful men are taken away, none considering that the righteous is taken away from the evil to come. ²He shall enter into peace: they shall rest in their beds, each one walking in his uprightness. ³But draw near here, you sons of the sorceress, the seed of the adulterer and the whore. ⁴Against whom do you sport yourselves? against whom make you a wide mouth, and draw out the tongue? are you not children of transgression, a seed of falsehood. ⁵Enflaming yourselves with idols under every green tree, slaying the children in the valleys under the clefts of the rocks? ⁶Among the smooth stones of the stream is your portion; they, they are your lot: even to them have you poured a drink offering, you have offered a meat offering. Should I receive comfort in these? ⁷On a lofty and high mountain have you set your bed: even thither went you up to offer sacrifice. ⁸Behind the doors also and the posts have you set up your remembrance: for you have discovered yourself to another than me, and are gone up; you have enlarged your bed, and made you a covenant with them; you loved their bed where you saw it. ⁹And you went to the king with ointment, and did increase your perfumes, and did send your messengers far off, and did debase yourself even to hell. ¹⁰You are wearied in the greatness of your way; yet said you not, There is no hope: you have found the life of your hand; therefore you were not grieved. ¹¹And of whom have you been afraid or feared, that you have lied, and have not remembered me, nor laid it to your heart? have not I held my peace even of old, and you fear me not? ¹²I will declare your righteousness, and your works; for they shall not profit you. ¹³When you cry, let your companies deliver you; but the wind shall carry them all away; vanity shall take them: but he that puts his trust in me shall possess the land, and shall inherit my holy mountain; ¹⁴And shall say, Cast you up, cast you up, prepare the way, take up the stumbling block out of the way of my people. ¹⁵For thus says the high and lofty One that inhabits eternity, whose name is Holy; I dwell in the high and holy place, with him also that is of a contrite and humble spirit, to revive the spirit of the humble, and to

revive the heart of the contrite ones. ¹⁶For I will not contend for ever, neither will I be always wroth: for the spirit should fail before me, and the souls which I have made. ¹⁷For the iniquity of his covetousness was I wroth, and smote him: I hid me, and was wroth, and he went on frowardly in the way of his heart. ¹⁸I have seen his ways, and will heal him: I will lead him also, and restore comforts to him and to his mourners. ¹⁹I create the fruit of the lips; Peace, peace to him that is far off, and to him that is near, says the LORD; and I will heal him. ²⁰But the wicked are like the troubled sea, when it cannot rest, whose waters cast up mire and dirt. ²¹There is no peace, says my God, to the wicked.

58

¹Cry aloud, spare not, lift up your voice like a trumpet, and show my people their transgression, and the house of Jacob their sins. ²Yet they seek me daily, and delight to know my ways, as a nation that did righteousness, and forsook not the ordinance of their God: they ask of me the ordinances of justice; they take delight in approaching to God. ³Why have we fasted, say they, and you see not? why have we afflicted our soul, and you take no knowledge? Behold, in the day of your fast you find pleasure, and exact all your labors. ⁴Behold, you fast for strife and debate, and to smite with the fist of wickedness: you shall not fast as you do this day, to make your voice to be heard on high. ⁵Is it such a fast that I have chosen? a day for a man to afflict his soul? is it to bow down his head as a bulrush, and to spread sackcloth and ashes under him? will you call this a fast, and an acceptable day to the LORD? ⁶Is not this the fast that I have chosen? to loose the bands of wickedness, to undo the heavy burdens, and to let the oppressed go free, and that you break every yoke? ⁷Is it not to deal your bread to the hungry, and that you bring the poor that are cast out to your house? when you see the naked, that you cover him; and that you hide not yourself from your own flesh? ⁸Then shall your light break forth as the morning, and your health shall spring forth speedily: and your righteousness shall go before you; the glory of the LORD shall be your rear guard. ⁹Then shall you call, and the LORD shall answer; you shall cry, and he shall say, Here I am. If you take away from the middle of you the yoke, the putting forth of the finger, and speaking vanity; ¹⁰And if you draw out your soul to the hungry, and satisfy the afflicted soul; then shall your light rise in obscurity, and your darkness be as the noon day: ¹¹And the LORD shall guide you continually, and satisfy your soul in drought, and make fat your bones: and you shall be like a watered garden, and like a spring of water, whose waters fail not. ¹²And they that shall be of you shall build the old waste places: you shall raise up the foundations of many generations; and you shall be called, The repairer of the breach, The restorer of paths to dwell in. ¹³If you turn away your foot from the sabbath, from doing your pleasure on my holy day; and call the sabbath a delight, the holy of the LORD, honorable; and shall honor him, not doing your own ways, nor finding your own pleasure, nor speaking your own words: ¹⁴Then shall you delight yourself in the LORD; and I will cause you to ride on the high places of the earth, and feed you with the heritage of Jacob your father: for the mouth of the LORD has spoken it.

59

¹Behold, the LORD's hand is not shortened, that it cannot save; neither his ear heavy, that it cannot hear: ²But your iniquities have separated between you and your God, and your sins have hid his face from you, that he will not hear. ³For your hands are defiled with blood, and your fingers with iniquity; your lips have spoken lies, your tongue has muttered perverseness. ⁴None calls for justice, nor any pleads for truth: they trust in vanity, and speak lies; they conceive mischief, and bring forth iniquity. ⁵They hatch cockatrice' eggs, and weave the spider's web: he that eats of their eggs dies, and that which is crushed breaks out into a viper. ⁶Their webs shall not become garments, neither shall they cover themselves with their works: their works are works of iniquity, and the act of violence is in their hands. ⁷Their feet run to evil, and they make haste to shed innocent blood: their thoughts are thoughts of iniquity; wasting and destruction are in their paths. ⁸The way of peace they know not; and there is no judgment in their goings: they have made them crooked paths: whoever goes therein shall not know peace. ⁹Therefore is judgment far from us, neither does justice overtake us: we wait for light, but behold obscurity; for brightness, but we walk in darkness. ¹⁰We grope for the wall like the blind, and we grope as if we had no eyes: we stumble at noon day as in the night; we are in desolate places as dead men. ¹¹We roar all like bears, and mourn sore like doves: we look for judgment, but there is none; for salvation, but it is far off from us. ¹²For our transgressions are multiplied before you, and our sins testify against us: for our transgressions are with us; and as for our iniquities, we know them; ¹³In transgressing and lying against the LORD, and departing away from our God, speaking oppression and revolt, conceiving and uttering from the heart words of falsehood. ¹⁴And judgment is turned away backward, and justice stands afar off: for truth is fallen in the street, and equity cannot enter. ¹⁵Yes, truth fails; and he that departs from evil makes himself a prey: and the LORD saw it, and it displeased him that there was no judgment. ¹⁶And he saw that there was no man, and wondered that there was no intercessor: therefore his arm brought salvation to him; and his righteousness, it sustained him. ¹⁷For he put on righteousness as a breastplate, and an helmet of salvation on his head; and he put on the garments of vengeance for clothing, and was clad with zeal as a cloak. ¹⁸According to their deeds, accordingly he will repay, fury to his adversaries, recompense to his enemies; to the islands he will repay recompense. ¹⁹So shall they fear the name of the LORD from the west, and his glory from the rising of the sun. When the enemy shall come in like a flood, the Spirit of the LORD shall lift up a standard against him. ²⁰And the Redeemer shall come to Zion, and to them that turn from transgression in Jacob, says the LORD. ²¹As for me, this is my covenant with them, says the LORD; My spirit that is on you, and my words which I have put in your mouth, shall not depart out of your mouth, nor out of the mouth of your seed, nor out of the mouth of your seed's seed, says the LORD, from now on and for ever.

60

¹Arise, shine; for your light is come, and the glory of the LORD is risen on you. ²For, behold, the darkness shall cover the earth, and gross darkness the people: but the LORD shall arise on you, and his glory shall

be seen on you. ³And the Gentiles shall come to your light, and kings to the brightness of your rising. ⁴Lift up your eyes round about, and see: all they gather themselves together, they come to you: your sons shall come from far, and your daughters shall be nursed at your side. ⁵Then you shall see, and flow together, and your heart shall fear, and be enlarged; because the abundance of the sea shall be converted to you, the forces of the Gentiles shall come to you. ⁶The multitude of camels shall cover you, the dromedaries of Midian and Ephah; all they from Sheba shall come: they shall bring gold and incense; and they shall show forth the praises of the LORD. ⁷All the flocks of Kedar shall be gathered together to you, the rams of Nebaioth shall minister to you: they shall come up with acceptance on my altar, and I will glorify the house of my glory. ⁸Who are these that fly as a cloud, and as the doves to their windows? ⁹Surely the isles shall wait for me, and the ships of Tarshish first, to bring your sons from far, their silver and their gold with them, to the name of the LORD your God, and to the Holy One of Israel, because he has glorified you. ¹⁰And the sons of strangers shall build up your walls, and their kings shall minister to you: for in my wrath I smote you, but in my favor have I had mercy on you. ¹¹Therefore your gates shall be open continually; they shall not be shut day nor night; that men may bring to you the forces of the Gentiles, and that their kings may be brought. ¹²For the nation and kingdom that will not serve you shall perish; yes, those nations shall be utterly wasted. ¹³The glory of Lebanon shall come to you, the fir tree, the pine tree, and the box together, to beautify the place of my sanctuary; and I will make the place of my feet glorious. ¹⁴The sons also of them that afflicted you shall come bending to you; and all they that despised you shall bow themselves down at the soles of your feet; and they shall call you; The city of the LORD, The Zion of the Holy One of Israel. ¹⁵Whereas you has been forsaken and hated, so that no man went through you, I will make you an eternal excellency, a joy of many generations. ¹⁶You shall also suck the milk of the Gentiles, and shall suck the breast of kings: and you shall know that I the LORD am your Savior and your Redeemer, the mighty One of Jacob. ¹⁷For brass I will bring gold, and for iron I will bring silver, and for wood brass, and for stones iron: I will also make your officers peace, and your exactors righteousness. ¹⁸Violence shall no more be heard in your land, wasting nor destruction within your borders; but you shall call your walls Salvation, and your gates Praise. ¹⁹The sun shall be no more your light by day; neither for brightness shall the moon give light to you: but the LORD shall be to you an everlasting light, and your God your glory. ²⁰Your sun shall no more go down; neither shall your moon withdraw itself: for the LORD shall be your everlasting light, and the days of your mourning shall be ended. ²¹Your people also shall be all righteous: they shall inherit the land for ever, the branch of my planting, the work of my hands, that I may be glorified. ²²A little one shall become a thousand, and a small one a strong nation: I the LORD will hasten it in his time.

61 ¹The Spirit of the Lord GOD is on me; because the LORD has anointed me to preach good tidings to the meek; he has sent me to bind up the brokenhearted, to proclaim liberty to the captives, and the opening of the prison to them that are bound; ²To proclaim the acceptable year of the LORD, and the day of vengeance of our God; to comfort all that mourn; ³To appoint to them that mourn in Zion, to give to them beauty for ashes, the oil of joy for mourning, the garment of praise for the spirit of heaviness; that they might be called trees of righteousness, the planting of the LORD, that he might be glorified. ⁴And they shall build the old wastes, they shall raise up the former desolations, and they shall repair the waste cities, the desolations of many generations. ⁵And strangers shall stand and feed your flocks, and the sons of the alien shall be your plowmen and your vinedressers. ⁶But you shall be named the Priests of the LORD: men shall call you the Ministers of our God: you shall eat the riches of the Gentiles, and in their glory shall you boast yourselves. ⁷For your shame you shall have double; and for confusion they shall rejoice in their portion: therefore in their land they shall possess the double: everlasting joy shall be to them. ⁸For I the LORD love judgment, I hate robbery for burnt offering; and I will direct their work in truth, and I will make an everlasting covenant with them. ⁹And their seed shall be known among the Gentiles, and their offspring among the people: all that see them shall acknowledge them, that they are the seed which the LORD has blessed. ¹⁰I will greatly rejoice in the LORD, my soul shall be joyful in my God; for he has clothed me with the garments of salvation, he has covered me with the robe of righteousness, as a bridegroom decks himself with ornaments, and as a bride adorns herself with her jewels. ¹¹For as the earth brings forth her bud, and as the garden causes the things that are sown in it to spring forth; so the Lord GOD will cause righteousness and praise to spring forth before all the nations.

62 ¹For Zion's sake will I not hold my peace, and for Jerusalem's sake I will not rest, until the righteousness thereof go forth as brightness, and the salvation thereof as a lamp that burns. ²And the Gentiles shall see your righteousness, and all kings your glory: and you shall be called by a new name, which the mouth of the LORD shall name. ³You shall also be a crown of glory in the hand of the LORD, and a royal diadem in the hand of your God. ⁴You shall no more be termed Forsaken; neither shall your land any more be termed Desolate: but you shall be called Hephzibah, and your land Beulah: for the LORD delights in you, and your land shall be married. ⁵For as a young man marries a virgin, so shall your sons marry you: and as the bridegroom rejoices over the bride, so shall your God rejoice over you. ⁶I have set watchmen on your walls, O Jerusalem, which shall never hold their peace day nor night: you that make mention of the LORD, keep not silence, ⁷And give him no rest, till he establish, and till he make Jerusalem a praise in the earth. ⁸The LORD has sworn by his right hand, and by the arm of his strength, Surely I will no more give your corn to be meat for your enemies; and the sons of the stranger shall not drink your wine, for the which you have labored: ⁹But they that have gathered it shall eat it, and praise the LORD; and they that have brought it together shall drink it in the courts of my holiness. ¹⁰Go through, go through the gates; prepare you the way of the people; cast up, cast up the highway; gather out the stones; lift up a standard for the people. ¹¹Behold, the LORD has proclaimed to the end of the world, Say you to the daughter of Zion, Behold, your salvation comes; behold, his reward is with him, and his work before him. ¹²And they shall call them, The holy people, The redeemed of the LORD: and you shall be called, Sought out, A city not forsaken.

63

¹Who is this that comes from Edom, with dyed garments from Bozrah? this that is glorious in his apparel, traveling in the greatness of his strength? I that speak in righteousness, mighty to save. ²Why are you red in your apparel, and your garments like him that treads in the winefat? ³I have trodden the wine press alone; and of the people there was none with me: for I will tread them in my anger, and trample them in my fury; and their blood shall be sprinkled on my garments, and I will stain all my raiment. ⁴For the day of vengeance is in my heart, and the year of my redeemed is come. ⁵And I looked, and there was none to help; and I wondered that there was none to uphold: therefore my own arm brought salvation to me; and my fury, it upheld me. ⁶And I will tread down the people in my anger, and make them drunk in my fury, and I will bring down their strength to the earth. ⁷I will mention the loving kindnesses of the LORD, and the praises of the LORD, according to all that the LORD has bestowed on us, and the great goodness toward the house of Israel, which he has bestowed on them according to his mercies, and according to the multitude of his loving kindnesses. ⁸For he said, Surely they are my people, children that will not lie: so he was their Savior. ⁹In all their affliction he was afflicted, and the angel of his presence saved them: in his love and in his pity he redeemed them; and he bore them, and carried them all the days of old. ¹⁰But they rebelled, and vexed his holy Spirit: therefore he was turned to be their enemy, and he fought against them. ¹¹Then he remembered the days of old, Moses, and his people, saying, Where is he that brought them up out of the sea with the shepherd of his flock? where is he that put his holy Spirit within him? ¹²That led them by the right hand of Moses with his glorious arm, dividing the water before them, to make himself an everlasting name? ¹³That led them through the deep, as an horse in the wilderness, that they should not stumble? ¹⁴As a beast goes down into the valley, the Spirit of the LORD caused him to rest: so did you lead your people, to make yourself a glorious name. ¹⁵Look down from heaven, and behold from the habitation of your holiness and of your glory: where is your zeal and your strength, the sounding of your bowels and of your mercies toward me? are they restrained? ¹⁶Doubtless you are our father, though Abraham be ignorant of us, and Israel acknowledge us not: you, O LORD, are our father, our redeemer; your name is from everlasting. ¹⁷O LORD, why have you made us to err from your ways, and hardened our heart from your fear? Return for your servants' sake, the tribes of your inheritance. ¹⁸The people of your holiness have possessed it but a little while: our adversaries have trodden down your sanctuary. ¹⁹We are yours: you never bore rule over them; they were not called by your name.

64

¹Oh that you would rend the heavens, that you would come down, that the mountains might flow down at your presence, ²As when the melting fire burns, the fire causes the waters to boil, to make your name known to your adversaries, that the nations may tremble at your presence! ³When you did terrible things which we looked not for, you came down, the mountains flowed down at your presence. ⁴For since the beginning of the world men have not heard, nor perceived by the ear, neither has the eye seen, O God, beside you, what he has prepared for him that waits for him. ⁵You meet him that rejoices and works righteousness, those that remember you in your ways: behold, you are wroth; for we have sinned: in those is continuance, and we shall be saved. ⁶But we are all as an unclean thing, and all our righteousnesses are as filthy rags; and we all do fade as a leaf; and our iniquities, like the wind, have taken us away. ⁷And there is none that calls on your name, that stirs up himself to take hold of you: for you have hid your face from us, and have consumed us, because of our iniquities. ⁸But now, O LORD, you are our father; we are the clay, and you our potter; and we all are the work of your hand. ⁹Be not wroth very sore, O LORD, neither remember iniquity for ever: behold, see, we beseech you, we are all your people. ¹⁰Your holy cities are a wilderness, Zion is a wilderness, Jerusalem a desolation. ¹¹Our holy and our beautiful house, where our fathers praised you, is burned up with fire: and all our pleasant things are laid waste. ¹²Will you refrain yourself for these things, O LORD? will you hold your peace, and afflict us very sore?

65

¹I am sought of them that asked not for me; I am found of them that sought me not: I said, Behold me, behold me, to a nation that was not called by my name. ²I have spread out my hands all the day to a rebellious people, which walks in a way that was not good, after their own thoughts; ³A people that provokes me to anger continually to my face; that sacrifices in gardens, and burns incense on altars of brick; ⁴Which remain among the graves, and lodge in the monuments, which eat swine's flesh, and broth of abominable things is in their vessels; ⁵Which say, Stand by yourself, come not near to me; for I am holier than you. These are a smoke in my nose, a fire that burns all the day. ⁶Behold, it is written before me: I will not keep silence, but will recompense, even recompense into their bosom, ⁷Your iniquities, and the iniquities of your fathers together, says the LORD, which have burned incense on the mountains, and blasphemed me on the hills: therefore will I measure their former work into their bosom. ⁸Thus says the LORD, As the new wine is found in the cluster, and one said, Destroy it not; for a blessing is in it: so will I do for my servants' sakes, that I may not destroy them all. ⁹And I will bring forth a seed out of Jacob, and out of Judah an inheritor of my mountains: and my elect shall inherit it, and my servants shall dwell there. ¹⁰And Sharon shall be a fold of flocks, and the valley of Achor a place for the herds to lie down in, for my people that have sought me. ¹¹But you are they that forsake the LORD, that forget my holy mountain, that prepare a table for that troop, and that furnish the drink offering to that number. ¹²Therefore will I number you to the sword, and you shall all bow down to the slaughter: because when I called, you did not answer; when I spoke, you did not hear; but did evil before my eyes, and did choose that wherein I delighted not. ¹³Therefore thus says the Lord GOD, Behold, my servants shall eat, but you shall be

hungry: behold, my servants shall drink, but you shall be thirsty: behold, my servants shall rejoice, but you shall be ashamed: ¹⁴Behold, my servants shall sing for joy of heart, but you shall cry for sorrow of heart, and shall howl for vexation of spirit. ¹⁵And you shall leave your name for a curse to my chosen: for the Lord GOD shall slay you, and call his servants by another name: ¹⁶That he who blesses himself in the earth shall bless himself in the God of truth; and he that swears in the earth shall swear by the God of truth; because the former troubles are forgotten, and because they are hid from my eyes. ¹⁷For, behold, I create new heavens and a new earth: and the former shall not be remembered, nor come into mind. ¹⁸But be you glad and rejoice for ever in that which I create: for, behold, I create Jerusalem a rejoicing, and her people a joy. ¹⁹And I will rejoice in Jerusalem, and joy in my people: and the voice of weeping shall be no more heard in her, nor the voice of crying. ²⁰There shall be no more there an infant of days, nor an old man that has not filled his days: for the child shall die an hundred years old; but the sinner being an hundred years old shall be accursed. ²¹And they shall build houses, and inhabit them; and they shall plant vineyards, and eat the fruit of them. ²²They shall not build, and another inhabit; they shall not plant, and another eat: for as the days of a tree are the days of my people, and my elect shall long enjoy the work of their hands. ²³They shall not labor in vain, nor bring forth for trouble; for they are the seed of the blessed of the LORD, and their offspring with them. ²⁴And it shall come to pass, that before they call, I will answer; and while they are yet speaking, I will hear. ²⁵The wolf and the lamb shall feed together, and the lion shall eat straw like the bullock: and dust shall be the serpent's meat. They shall not hurt nor destroy in all my holy mountain, says the LORD.

66

¹Thus says the LORD, The heaven is my throne, and the earth is my footstool: where is the house that you build to me? and where is the place of my rest? ²For all those things has my hand made, and all those things have been, says the LORD: but to this man will I look, even to him that is poor and of a contrite spirit, and trembles at my word. ³He that kills an ox is as if he slew a man; he that sacrifices a lamb, as if he cut off a dog's neck; he that offers an oblation, as if he offered swine's blood; he that burns incense, as if he blessed an idol. Yes, they have chosen their own ways, and their soul delights in their abominations. ⁴I also will choose their delusions, and will bring their fears on them; because when I called, none did answer; when I spoke, they did not hear: but they did evil before my eyes, and chose that in which I delighted not. ⁵Hear the word of the LORD, you that tremble at his word; Your brothers that hated you, that cast you out for my name's sake, said, Let the LORD be glorified: but he shall appear to your joy, and they shall be ashamed. ⁶A voice of noise from the city, a voice from the temple, a voice of the LORD that renders recompense to his enemies. ⁷Before she travailed, she brought forth; before her pain came, she was delivered of a man child. ⁸Who has heard such a thing? who has seen such things? Shall the earth be made to bring forth in one day? or shall a nation be born at once? for as soon as Zion travailed, she brought forth her children. ⁹Shall I bring to the birth, and not cause to bring forth? says the LORD: shall I cause to bring forth, and shut the womb? said your God. ¹⁰Rejoice you with Jerusalem, and be glad with her, all you that love her: rejoice for joy with her, all you that mourn for her: ¹¹That you may suck, and be satisfied with the breasts of her consolations; that you may milk out, and be delighted with the abundance of her glory. ¹²For thus says the LORD, Behold, I will extend peace to her like a river, and the glory of the Gentiles like a flowing stream: then shall you suck, you shall be borne on her sides, and be dandled on her knees. ¹³As one whom his mother comforts, so will I comfort you; and you shall be comforted in Jerusalem. ¹⁴And when you see this, your heart shall rejoice, and your bones shall flourish like an herb: and the hand of the LORD shall be known toward his servants, and his indignation toward his enemies. ¹⁵For, behold, the LORD will come with fire, and with his chariots like a whirlwind, to render his anger with fury, and his rebuke with flames of fire. ¹⁶For by fire and by his sword will the LORD plead with all flesh: and the slain of the LORD shall be many. ¹⁷They that sanctify themselves, and purify themselves in the gardens behind one tree in the middle, eating swine's flesh, and the abomination, and the mouse, shall be consumed together, says the LORD. ¹⁸For I know their works and their thoughts: it shall come, that I will gather all nations and tongues; and they shall come, and see my glory. ¹⁹And I will set a sign among them, and I will send those that escape of them to the nations, to Tarshish, Pul, and Lud, that draw the bow, to Tubal, and Javan, to the isles afar off, that have not heard my fame, neither have seen my glory; and they shall declare my glory among the Gentiles. ²⁰And they shall bring all your brothers for an offering to the LORD out of all nations on horses, and in chariots, and in litters, and on mules, and on swift beasts, to my holy mountain Jerusalem, said the LORD, as the children of Israel bring an offering in a clean vessel into the house of the LORD. ²¹And I will also take of them for priests and for Levites, says the LORD. ²²For as the new heavens and the new earth, which I will make, shall remain before me, says the LORD, so shall your seed and your name remain. ²³And it shall come to pass, that from one new moon to another, and from one sabbath to another, shall all flesh come to worship before me, says the LORD. ²⁴And they shall go forth, and look on the carcasses of the men that have transgressed against me: for their worm shall not die, neither shall their fire be quenched; and they shall be an abhorring to all flesh.

Jeremiah

1 ¹The words of Jeremiah the son of Hilkiah, of the priests that were in Anathoth in the land of Benjamin: ²To whom the word of the LORD came in the days of Josiah the son of Amon king of Judah, in the thirteenth year of his reign. ³It came also in the days of Jehoiakim the son of Josiah king of Judah, to the end of the eleventh year of Zedekiah the son of Josiah king of Judah, to the carrying away of Jerusalem captive in the fifth month. ⁴Then the word of the LORD came to me, saying, ⁵Before I formed you in the belly I knew you; and before you came forth out of the womb I sanctified you, and I ordained you a prophet to the nations. ⁶Then said I, Ah, Lord GOD! behold, I cannot speak: for I am a child. ⁷But the LORD said to me, Say not, I am a child: for you shall go to all that I shall send you, and whatever I command you you shall speak. ⁸Be not afraid of their faces: for I am with you to deliver you, says the LORD. ⁹Then the LORD put forth his hand, and touched my mouth. And the LORD said to me, Behold, I have put my words in your mouth. ¹⁰See, I have this day set you over the nations and over the kingdoms, to root out, and to pull down, and to destroy, and to throw down, to build, and to plant. ¹¹Moreover the word of the LORD came to me, saying, Jeremiah, what see you? And I said, I see a rod of an almond tree. ¹²Then said the LORD to me, You have well seen: for I will hasten my word to perform it. ¹³And the word of the LORD came to me the second time, saying, What see you? And I said, I see a seething pot; and the face thereof is toward the north. ¹⁴Then the LORD said to me, Out of the north an evil shall break forth on all the inhabitants of the land. ¹⁵For, see, I will call all the families of the kingdoms of the north, says the LORD; and they shall come, and they shall set every one his throne at the entering of the gates of Jerusalem, and against all the walls thereof round about, and against all the cities of Judah. ¹⁶And I will utter my judgments against them touching all their wickedness, who have forsaken me, and have burned incense to other gods, and worshipped the works of their own hands. ¹⁷You therefore gird up your loins, and arise, and speak to them all that I command you: be not dismayed at their faces, lest I confound you before them. ¹⁸For, behold, I have made you this day a defended city, and an iron pillar, and brazen walls against the whole land, against the kings of Judah, against the princes thereof, against the priests thereof, and against the people of the land. ¹⁹And they shall fight against you; but they shall not prevail against you; for I am with you, says the LORD, to deliver you.

2 ¹Moreover the word of the LORD came to me, saying, ²Go and cry in the ears of Jerusalem, saying, Thus says the LORD; I remember you, the kindness of your youth, the love of your espousals, when you went after me in the wilderness, in a land that was not sown. ³Israel was holiness to the LORD, and the first fruits of his increase: all that devour him shall offend; evil shall come on them, says the LORD. ⁴Hear you the word of the LORD, O house of Jacob, and all the families of the house of Israel: ⁵Thus says the LORD, What iniquity have your fathers found in me, that they are gone far from me, and have walked after vanity, and are become vain? ⁶Neither said they, Where is the LORD that brought us up out of the land of Egypt, that led us through the wilderness, through a land of deserts and of pits, through a land of drought, and of the shadow of death, through a land that no man passed through, and where no man dwelled? ⁷And I brought you into a plentiful country, to eat the fruit thereof and the goodness thereof; but when you entered, you defiled my land, and made my heritage an abomination. ⁸The priests said not, Where is the LORD? and they that handle the law knew me not: the pastors also transgressed against me, and the prophets prophesied by Baal, and walked after things that do not profit. ⁹Why I will yet plead with you, says the LORD, and with your children's children will I plead. ¹⁰For pass over the isles of Chittim, and see; and send to Kedar, and consider diligently, and see if there be such a thing. ¹¹Has a nation changed their gods, which are yet no gods? but my people have changed their glory for that which does not profit. ¹²Be astonished, O you heavens, at this, and be horribly afraid, be you very desolate, says the LORD. ¹³For my people have committed two evils; they have forsaken me the fountain of living waters, and hewed them out cisterns, broken cisterns, that can hold no water. ¹⁴Is Israel a servant? is he a home born slave? why is he spoiled? ¹⁵The young lions roared on him, and yelled, and they made his land waste: his cities are burned without inhabitant. ¹⁶Also the children of Noph and Tahapanes have broken the crown of your head. ¹⁷Have you not procured this to yourself, in that you have forsaken the LORD your God, when he led you by the way? ¹⁸And now what have you to do in the way of Egypt, to drink the waters of Sihor? or what have you to do in the way of Assyria, to drink the waters of the river? ¹⁹Your own wickedness shall correct you, and your backslidings shall reprove you: know therefore and see that it is an evil thing and bitter, that you have forsaken the LORD your God, and that my fear is not in you, says the Lord GOD of hosts. ²⁰For of old time I have broken your yoke, and burst your bands; and you said, I will not transgress; when on every high hill and under every green tree you wander, playing the harlot. ²¹Yet I had planted you a noble vine, wholly a right seed: how then are you turned into the degenerate plant of a strange vine to me? ²²For though you wash you with nitre, and take you much soap, yet your iniquity is marked before me, says the Lord GOD. ²³How can you say, I am not polluted, I have not gone after Baalim? see your way in the valley, know what you have done: you are a swift dromedary traversing her ways; ²⁴A wild ass used to the wilderness, that snuffs up the wind at her pleasure; in her occasion who can turn her away? all they that seek her will not weary themselves; in her month they shall find her. ²⁵Withhold your foot from being unshod, and your throat from thirst: but you said, There is no hope: no; for I have loved strangers, and after them will I go. ²⁶As the thief is ashamed when he is found, so is the house of Israel ashamed; they, their kings, their princes, and their priests, and their prophets. ²⁷Saying to a stock, You are my father; and to a stone, You have brought me forth: for they have turned their back to me, and not their face: but in the time of their trouble they will say, Arise, and save us. ²⁸But where are your gods that you have made you? let them arise, if they can save you in the time of your trouble: for according to the number of your cities are your gods, O Judah. ²⁹Why will you plead with me? you all have transgressed against me, says the LORD. ³⁰In vain have I smitten your children; they received no correction: your own sword has devoured your prophets, like a destroying lion. ³¹O generation, see you the word of the LORD. Have I been a wilderness to Israel? a land of darkness? why say my people, We are lords; we will come no more to you? ³²Can a maid forget her ornaments, or a bride her attire? yet my people have forgotten me days without number. ³³Why trim you your way to seek love? therefore have you also taught the wicked ones your ways. ³⁴Also in your skirts is found the blood of the souls of the poor innocents: I have not found it by secret search, but on all these. ³⁵Yet you say, Because I am innocent, surely his anger shall turn from me. Behold, I will plead with you, because you say, I have not sinned. ³⁶Why gad you about so much to change your way? you also shall be ashamed of Egypt, as you were ashamed of Assyria. ³⁷Yes, you shall go forth from him, and your hands on your head: for the LORD has rejected your confidences, and you shall not prosper in them.

3 ¹They say, If a man put away his wife, and she go from him, and become another man's, shall he return to her again? shall not that land be greatly polluted? but you have played the harlot with many lovers; yet return again to me, says the LORD. ²Lift up your eyes to the high places, and see where you have not been lien with. In the ways have you sat for them, as the Arabian in the wilderness; and you have polluted the land with your prostitutions and with your wickedness. ³Therefore the showers have been withheld, and there has been no latter rain; and you had a whore's forehead, you refused to be ashamed. ⁴Will you not from this time cry to me, My father, you are the guide of my youth? ⁵Will he reserve his anger for ever? will he keep it to the end? Behold, you have spoken and done evil things as you could. ⁶The LORD said also to me in the days of Josiah the king, Have you seen that which backsliding Israel has done? she is gone up on every high mountain and under every green tree, and there has played the harlot. ⁷And I said after she had done all these things, Turn you to me. But she returned not. And her treacherous sister Judah saw it. ⁸And I saw, when for all the causes whereby backsliding Israel committed adultery I had put her away, and given her a bill of divorce; yet her treacherous sister Judah feared not, but went and played the harlot also. ⁹And it came to pass through the lightness of her prostitution, that she defiled the land, and committed adultery with stones and with stocks. ¹⁰And yet for all this her treacherous sister Judah has not turned to me with her whole heart, but feignedly, says the LORD. ¹¹And the LORD said to me, The backsliding Israel has justified herself more than treacherous Judah. ¹²Go and proclaim these words toward the north, and say, Return, you backsliding Israel, says the LORD; and I will not cause my anger to fall on you: for I am merciful, said the LORD, and I will not keep anger for ever. ¹³Only acknowledge your iniquity, that you have transgressed against the LORD your God, and have scattered your ways to the strangers under every green tree, and you have not obeyed my voice, says the LORD. ¹⁴Turn, O backsliding children, says the LORD; for I am married to you: and I will take you one of a city, and two of a family, and I will bring you to Zion: ¹⁵And I will give you pastors according to my heart, which shall feed you with knowledge and understanding. ¹⁶And it shall come to pass, when you be multiplied and increased in the land, in those days, says the LORD, they shall say no more, The ark of the covenant of the LORD: neither shall it come to mind: neither shall they remember it; neither shall they visit it; neither shall that be done any more. ¹⁷At that time they shall call Jerusalem the throne of the LORD; and all the nations shall be gathered to it, to the name of the LORD, to Jerusalem: neither shall they walk any more after the imagination of their evil heart. ¹⁸In those days the house of Judah shall walk with the house of Israel, and they shall come together out of the land of the north to the land that I have given for an inheritance to your fathers. ¹⁹But I said, How shall I put you among the children, and give you a pleasant land, a goodly heritage of the hosts of nations? and I said, You shall call me, My father; and shall not turn away from me. ²⁰Surely as a wife treacherously departs from her husband, so have you dealt treacherously with me, O house of Israel, says the LORD. ²¹A voice was heard on the high places, weeping and supplications of the children of Israel: for they have perverted their way, and they have forgotten the LORD their God. ²²Return, you backsliding children, and I will heal your backslidings. Behold, we come to you; for you are the LORD our God. ²³Truly in vain is salvation hoped for from the hills, and from the multitude of mountains: truly in the LORD our God is the salvation of Israel. ²⁴For shame has devoured the labor of our fathers from our youth; their flocks and their herds, their sons and their daughters. ²⁵We lie down in our shame, and our confusion covers us: for we have sinned against the LORD our God, we and our fathers, from our youth even to this day, and have not obeyed the voice of the LORD our God.

4 ¹If you will return, O Israel, says the LORD, return to me: and if you will put away your abominations out of my sight, then shall you not remove. ²And you shall swear, The LORD lives, in truth, in judgment, and in righteousness; and the nations shall bless themselves in him, and in him shall they glory. ³For thus says the LORD to the men of Judah and Jerusalem, Break up your fallow ground, and sow not among thorns. ⁴Circumcise yourselves to the LORD, and take away the foreskins of your heart, you men of Judah and inhabitants of Jerusalem: lest my fury come forth like fire, and burn that none can quench it, because of the evil of your doings. ⁵Declare you in Judah, and publish in Jerusalem; and say, Blow you the trumpet in the land: cry, gather together, and say, Assemble yourselves, and let us go into the defended cities. ⁶Set up the standard toward Zion: retire, stay not: for I will bring evil from the north, and a great destruction. ⁷The lion is come up from his thicket, and the destroyer of the Gentiles is on his way; he is gone forth from his place to make your land desolate; and your cities shall be laid waste, without an inhabitant. ⁸For this gird you with sackcloth, lament and howl: for the fierce anger of the LORD is not turned back from us. ⁹And it shall come to pass at that day, says the LORD, that the heart of the king shall perish, and the heart of the princes; and the priests shall be astonished, and the prophets shall wonder. ¹⁰Then said I, Ah,

Lord GOD! surely you have greatly deceived this people and Jerusalem, saying, You shall have peace; whereas the sword reaches to the soul. ¹¹At that time shall it be said to this people and to Jerusalem, A dry wind of the high places in the wilderness toward the daughter of my people, not to fan, nor to cleanse, ¹²Even a full wind from those places shall come to me: now also will I give sentence against them. ¹³Behold, he shall come up as clouds, and his chariots shall be as a whirlwind: his horses are swifter than eagles. Woe to us! for we are spoiled. ¹⁴O Jerusalem, wash your heart from wickedness, that you may be saved. How long shall your vain thoughts lodge within you? ¹⁵For a voice declares from Dan, and publishes affliction from mount Ephraim. ¹⁶Make you mention to the nations; behold, publish against Jerusalem, that watchers come from a far country, and give out their voice against the cities of Judah. ¹⁷As keepers of a field, are they against her round about; because she has been rebellious against me, says the LORD. ¹⁸Your way and your doings have procured these things to you; this is your wickedness, because it is bitter, because it reaches to your heart. ¹⁹My bowels, my bowels! I am pained at my very heart; my heart makes a noise in me; I cannot hold my peace, because you have heard, O my soul, the sound of the trumpet, the alarm of war. ²⁰Destruction on destruction is cried; for the whole land is spoiled: suddenly are my tents spoiled, and my curtains in a moment. ²¹How long shall I see the standard, and hear the sound of the trumpet? ²²For my people is foolish, they have not known me; they are silly children, and they have none understanding: they are wise to do evil, but to do good they have no knowledge. ²³I beheld the earth, and, see, it was without form, and void; and the heavens, and they had no light. ²⁴I beheld the mountains, and, see, they trembled, and all the hills moved lightly. ²⁵I beheld, and, see, there was no man, and all the birds of the heavens were fled. ²⁶I beheld, and, see, the fruitful place was a wilderness, and all the cities thereof were broken down at the presence of the LORD, and by his fierce anger. ²⁷For thus has the LORD said, The whole land shall be desolate; yet will I not make a full end. ²⁸For this shall the earth mourn, and the heavens above be black; because I have spoken it, I have purposed it, and will not repent, neither will I turn back from it. ²⁹The whole city shall flee for the noise of the horsemen and bowmen; they shall go into thickets, and climb up on the rocks: every city shall be forsaken, and not a man dwell therein. ³⁰And when you are spoiled, what will you do? Though you clothe yourself with crimson, though you deck you with ornaments of gold, though you rend your face with painting, in vain shall you make yourself fair; your lovers will despise you, they will seek your life. ³¹For I have heard a voice as of a woman in travail, and the anguish as of her that brings forth her first child, the voice of the daughter of Zion, that mourns herself, that spreads her hands, saying, Woe is me now! for my soul is wearied because of murderers.

5 ¹Run you to and fro through the streets of Jerusalem, and see now, and know, and seek in the broad places thereof, if you can find a man, if there be any that executes judgment, that seeks the truth; and I will pardon it. ²And though they say, The LORD lives; surely they swear falsely. ³O LORD, are not your eyes on the truth? you have stricken them, but they have not grieved; you have consumed them, but they have refused to receive correction: they have made their faces harder than a rock; they have refused to return. ⁴Therefore I said, Surely these are poor; they are foolish: for they know not the way of the LORD, nor the judgment of their God. ⁵I will get me to the great men, and will speak to them; for they have known the way of the LORD, and the judgment of their God: but these have altogether broken the yoke, and burst the bonds. ⁶Why a lion out of the forest shall slay them, and a wolf of the evenings shall spoil them, a leopard shall watch over their cities: every one that goes out there shall be torn in pieces: because their transgressions are many, and their backslidings are increased. ⁷How shall I pardon you for this? your children have forsaken me, and sworn by them that are no gods: when I had fed them to the full, they then committed adultery, and assembled themselves by troops in the harlots' houses. ⁸They were as fed horses in the morning: every one neighed after his neighbor's wife. ⁹Shall I not visit for these things? says the LORD: and shall not my soul be avenged on such a nation as this? ¹⁰Go you up on her walls, and destroy; but make not a full end: take away her battlements; for they are not the LORD's. ¹¹For the house of Israel and the house of Judah have dealt very treacherously against me, says the LORD. ¹²They have belied the LORD, and said, It is not he; neither shall evil come on us; neither shall we see sword nor famine: ¹³And the prophets shall become wind, and the word is not in them: thus shall it be done to them. ¹⁴Why thus says the LORD God of hosts, Because you speak this word, behold, I will make my words in your mouth fire, and this people wood, and it shall devour them. ¹⁵See, I will bring a nation on you from far, O house of Israel, says the LORD: it is a mighty nation, it is an ancient nation, a nation whose language you know not, neither understand what they say. ¹⁶Their quiver is as an open sepulcher, they are all mighty men. ¹⁷And they shall eat up your harvest, and your bread, which your sons and your daughters should eat: they shall eat up your flocks and your herds: they shall eat up your vines and your fig trees: they shall impoverish your fenced cities, wherein you trusted, with the sword. ¹⁸Nevertheless in those days, says the LORD, I will not make a full end with you. ¹⁹And it shall come to pass, when you shall say, Why does the LORD our God all these things to us? then shall you answer them, Like as you have forsaken me, and served strange gods in your land, so shall you serve strangers in a land that is not yours. ²⁰Declare this in the house of Jacob, and publish it in Judah, saying, ²¹Hear now this, O foolish people, and without understanding; which have eyes, and see not; which have ears, and hear not: ²²Fear you not me? says the LORD: will you not tremble at my presence, which have placed the sand for the bound of the sea by a perpetual decree, that it cannot pass it: and though the waves thereof toss themselves, yet can they not prevail; though they roar, yet can they not pass over it? ²³But this people has a revolting and a rebellious heart; they are revolted and gone. ²⁴Neither say they in their heart, Let us now fear the LORD our God, that gives rain, both the former and the latter, in his season: he reserves to us the appointed weeks of the harvest. ²⁵Your iniquities have turned away these things, and your sins have withheld good things from you. ²⁶For among my people are found wicked men: they lay wait, as he that sets snares; they set a trap, they catch men. ²⁷As a cage is full of birds, so are their houses full of deceit: therefore they are become great, and waxen rich. ²⁸They are waxen fat, they shine: yes, they overpass the deeds of the wicked: they judge not the cause, the cause of the fatherless, yet they prosper; and the right of the needy do they not judge. ²⁹Shall I not visit for these things? says the LORD: shall not my soul be avenged on such a nation as this? ³⁰A wonderful and horrible thing is committed in the land; ³¹The prophets prophesy falsely, and the priests bear rule by their means; and my people love to have it so: and what will you do in the end thereof?

6 ¹O you children of Benjamin, gather yourselves to flee out of the middle of Jerusalem, and blow the trumpet in Tekoa, and set up a sign of fire in Bethhaccerem: for evil appears out of the north, and great destruction. ²I have likened the daughter of Zion to a comely and delicate woman. ³The shepherds with their flocks shall come to her; they shall pitch their tents against her round about; they shall feed every one in his place. ⁴Prepare you war against her; arise, and let us go up at noon. Woe to us! for the day goes away, for the shadows of the evening are stretched out. ⁵Arise, and let us go by night, and let us destroy her palaces. ⁶For thus has the LORD of hosts said, Hew you down trees, and cast a mount against Jerusalem: this is the city to be visited; she is wholly oppression in the middle of her. ⁷As a fountain casts out her waters, so she casts out her wickedness: violence and spoil is heard in her; before me continually is grief and wounds. ⁸Be you instructed, O Jerusalem, lest my soul depart from you; lest I make you desolate, a land not inhabited. ⁹Thus says the LORD of hosts, They shall thoroughly glean the remnant of Israel as a vine: turn back your hand as a grape gatherer into the baskets. ¹⁰To whom shall I speak, and give warning, that they may hear? behold, their ear is uncircumcised, and they cannot listen: behold, the word of the LORD is to them a reproach; they have no delight in it. ¹¹Therefore I am full of the fury of the LORD; I am weary with holding in: I will pour it out on the children abroad, and on the assembly of young men together: for even the husband with the wife shall be taken, the aged with him that is full of days. ¹²And their houses shall be turned to others, with their fields and wives together: for I will stretch out my hand on the inhabitants of the land, says the LORD. ¹³For from the least of them even to the greatest of them every one is given to covetousness; and from the prophet even to the priest every one deals falsely. ¹⁴They have healed also the hurt of the daughter of my people slightly, saying, Peace, peace; when there is no peace. ¹⁵Were they ashamed when they had committed abomination? no, they were not at all ashamed, neither could they blush: therefore they shall fall among them that fall: at the time that I visit them they shall be cast down, says the LORD. ¹⁶Thus says the LORD, Stand you in the ways, and see, and ask for the old paths, where is the good way, and walk therein, and you shall find rest for your souls. But they said, We will not walk therein. ¹⁷Also I set watchmen over you, saying, Listen to the sound of the trumpet. But they said, We will not listen. ¹⁸Therefore hear, you nations, and know, O congregation, what is among them. ¹⁹Hear, O earth: behold, I will bring evil on this people, even the fruit of their thoughts, because they have not listened to my words, nor to my law, but rejected it. ²⁰To what purpose comes there to me incense from Sheba, and the sweet cane from a far country? your burnt offerings are not acceptable, nor your sacrifices sweet to me. ²¹Therefore thus says the LORD, Behold, I will lay stumbling blocks before this people, and the fathers and the sons together shall fall on them; the neighbor and his friend shall perish. ²²Thus says the LORD, Behold, a people comes from the north country, and a great nation shall be raised from the sides of the earth. ²³They shall lay hold on bow and spear; they are cruel, and have no mercy; their voice roars like the sea; and they ride on horses, set in array as men for war against you, O daughter of Zion. ²⁴We have heard the fame thereof: our hands wax feeble: anguish has taken hold of us, and pain, as of a woman in travail. ²⁵Go not forth into the field, nor walk by the way; for the sword of the enemy and fear is on every side. ²⁶O daughter of my people, gird you with sackcloth, and wallow yourself in ashes: make you mourning, as for an only son, most bitter lamentation: for the spoiler shall suddenly come on us. ²⁷I have set you for a tower and a fortress among my people, that you may know and try their way. ²⁸They are all grievous rebels, walking with slanders: they are brass and iron; they are all corrupters. ²⁹The bellows are burned, the lead is consumed of the fire; the founder melts in vain: for the wicked are not plucked away. ³⁰Reprobate silver shall men call them, because the LORD has rejected them.

7 ¹The word that came to Jeremiah from the LORD, saying, ²Stand in the gate of the LORD's house, and proclaim there this word, and say, Hear the word of the LORD, all you of Judah, that enter in at these gates to worship the LORD. ³Thus says the LORD of hosts, the God of Israel, Amend your ways and your doings, and I will cause you to dwell in this place. ⁴Trust you not in lying words, saying, The temple of the LORD, The temple of the LORD, The temple of the LORD, are these. ⁵For if you thoroughly amend your ways and your doings; if you thoroughly execute judgment between a man and his neighbor; ⁶If you oppress not the stranger, the fatherless, and the widow, and shed not innocent blood in this place, neither walk after other gods to your hurt: ⁷Then will I cause you to dwell in this place, in the land that I gave to your fathers, for ever and ever. ⁸Behold, you trust in lying words, that cannot profit. ⁹Will you steal, murder, and commit adultery, and swear falsely, and burn incense to Baal, and walk after other gods whom you know not; ¹⁰And come and stand before me in this house, which is called by my name, and say, We are delivered to do all these abominations? ¹¹Is this house, which is called by my name, become a den of robbers in your eyes? Behold, even I have seen it, says the LORD. ¹²But go you now to my place which was in Shiloh, where I set my name at the first, and see what I did to it for the wickedness of my people Israel. ¹³And now, because you have done all these works, says the LORD, and I spoke to you, rising up early and speaking, but you heard not; and I called you, but you answered not; ¹⁴Therefore will I do to this house, which is called by my name, wherein you trust, and to the place which I gave to you and to your fathers, as I have done to

Shiloh. ¹⁵And I will cast you out of my sight, as I have cast out all your brothers, even the whole seed of Ephraim. ¹⁶Therefore pray not you for this people, neither lift up cry nor prayer for them, neither make intercession to me: for I will not hear you. ¹⁷See you not what they do in the cities of Judah and in the streets of Jerusalem? ¹⁸The children gather wood, and the fathers kindle the fire, and the women knead their dough, to make cakes to the queen of heaven, and to pour out drink offerings to other gods, that they may provoke me to anger. ¹⁹Do they provoke me to anger? says the LORD: do they not provoke themselves to the confusion of their own faces? ²⁰Therefore thus says the Lord GOD; Behold, my anger and my fury shall be poured out on this place, on man, and on beast, and on the trees of the field, and on the fruit of the ground; and it shall burn, and shall not be quenched. ²¹Thus says the LORD of hosts, the God of Israel; Put your burnt offerings to your sacrifices, and eat flesh. ²²For I spoke not to your fathers, nor commanded them in the day that I brought them out of the land of Egypt, concerning burnt offerings or sacrifices: ²³But this thing commanded I them, saying, Obey my voice, and I will be your God, and you shall be my people: and walk you in all the ways that I have commanded you, that it may be well to you. ²⁴But they listened not, nor inclined their ear, but walked in the counsels and in the imagination of their evil heart, and went backward, and not forward. ²⁵Since the day that your fathers came forth out of the land of Egypt to this day I have even sent to you all my servants the prophets, daily rising up early and sending them: ²⁶Yet they listened not to me, nor inclined their ear, but hardened their neck: they did worse than their fathers. ²⁷Therefore you shall speak all these words to them; but they will not listen to you: you shall also call to them; but they will not answer you. ²⁸But you shall say to them, This is a nation that obeys not the voice of the LORD their God, nor receives correction: truth is perished, and is cut off from their mouth. ²⁹Cut off your hair, O Jerusalem, and cast it away, and take up a lamentation on high places; for the LORD has rejected and forsaken the generation of his wrath. ³⁰For the children of Judah have done evil in my sight, says the LORD: they have set their abominations in the house which is called by my name, to pollute it. ³¹And they have built the high places of Tophet, which is in the valley of the son of Hinnom, to burn their sons and their daughters in the fire; which I commanded them not, neither came it into my heart. ³²Therefore, behold, the days come, says the LORD, that it shall no more be called Tophet, nor the valley of the son of Hinnom, but the valley of slaughter: for they shall bury in Tophet, till there be no place. ³³And the carcasses of this people shall be meat for the fowls of the heaven, and for the beasts of the earth; and none shall fray them away. ³⁴Then will I cause to cease from the cities of Judah, and from the streets of Jerusalem, the voice of mirth, and the voice of gladness, the voice of the bridegroom, and the voice of the bride: for the land shall be desolate.

8 ¹At that time, says the LORD, they shall bring out the bones of the kings of Judah, and the bones of his princes, and the bones of the priests, and the bones of the prophets, and the bones of the inhabitants of Jerusalem, out of their graves: ²And they shall spread them before the sun, and the moon, and all the host of heaven, whom they have loved, and whom they have served, and after whom they have walked, and whom they have sought, and whom they have worshipped: they shall not be gathered, nor be buried; they shall be for dung on the face of the earth. ³And death shall be chosen rather than life by all the residue of them that remain of this evil family, which remain in all the places where I have driven them, says the LORD of hosts. ⁴Moreover you shall say to them, Thus says the LORD; Shall they fall, and not arise? shall he turn away, and not return? ⁵Why then is this people of Jerusalem slid back by a perpetual backsliding? they hold fast deceit, they refuse to return. ⁶I listened and heard, but they spoke not aright: no man repented him of his wickedness, saying, What have I done? every one turned to his course, as the horse rushes into the battle. ⁷Yes, the stork in the heaven knows her appointed times; and the turtle and the crane and the swallow observe the time of their coming; but my people know not the judgment of the LORD. ⁸How do you say, We are wise, and the law of the LORD is with us? See, certainly in vain made he it; the pen of the scribes is in vain. ⁹The wise men are ashamed, they are dismayed and taken: see, they have rejected the word of the LORD; and what wisdom is in them? ¹⁰Therefore will I give their wives to others, and their fields to them that shall inherit them: for every one from the least even to the greatest is given to covetousness, from the prophet even to the priest every one deals falsely. ¹¹For they have healed the hurt of the daughter of my people slightly, saying, Peace, peace; when there is no peace. ¹²Were they ashamed when they had committed abomination? no, they were not at all ashamed, neither could they blush: therefore shall they fall among them that fall: in the time of their visitation they shall be cast down, says the LORD. ¹³I will surely consume them, says the LORD: there shall be no grapes on the vine, nor figs on the fig tree, and the leaf shall fade; and the things that I have given them shall pass away from them. ¹⁴Why do we sit still? assemble yourselves, and let us enter into the defended cities, and let us be silent there: for the LORD our God has put us to silence, and given us water of gall to drink, because we have sinned against the LORD. ¹⁵We looked for peace, but no good came; and for a time of health, and behold trouble! ¹⁶The snorting of his horses was heard from Dan: the whole land trembled at the sound of the neighing of his strong ones; for they are come, and have devoured the land, and all that is in it; the city, and those that dwell therein. ¹⁷For, behold, I will send serpents, cockatrices, among you, which will not be charmed, and they shall bite you, says the LORD. ¹⁸When I would comfort myself against sorrow, my heart is faint in me. ¹⁹Behold the voice of the cry of the daughter of my people because of them that dwell in a far country: Is not the LORD in Zion? is not her king in her? Why have they provoked me to anger with their graven images, and with strange vanities? ²⁰The harvest is past, the summer is ended, and we are not saved. ²¹For the hurt of the daughter of my people am I hurt; I am black; astonishment has taken hold on me. ²²Is there no balm in Gilead; is there no physician there? why then is not the health of the daughter of my people recovered?

9

¹Oh that my head were waters, and my eyes a fountain of tears, that I might weep day and night for the slain of the daughter of my people! ²Oh that I had in the wilderness a lodging place of wayfaring men; that I might leave my people, and go from them! for they be all adulterers, an assembly of treacherous men. ³And they bend their tongues like their bow for lies: but they are not valiant for the truth on the earth; for they proceed from evil to evil, and they know not me, says the LORD. ⁴Take you heed every one of his neighbor, and trust you not in any brother: for every brother will utterly supplant, and every neighbor will walk with slanders. ⁵And they will deceive every one his neighbor, and will not speak the truth: they have taught their tongue to speak lies, and weary themselves to commit iniquity. ⁶Your habitation is in the middle of deceit; through deceit they refuse to know me, says the LORD. ⁷Therefore thus says the LORD of hosts, Behold, I will melt them, and try them; for how shall I do for the daughter of my people? ⁸Their tongue is as an arrow shot out; it speaks deceit: one speaks peaceably to his neighbor with his mouth, but in heart he lays his wait. ⁹Shall I not visit them for these things? says the LORD: shall not my soul be avenged on such a nation as this? ¹⁰For the mountains will I take up a weeping and wailing, and for the habitations of the wilderness a lamentation, because they are burned up, so that none can pass through them; neither can men hear the voice of the cattle; both the fowl of the heavens and the beast are fled; they are gone. ¹¹And I will make Jerusalem heaps, and a den of dragons; and I will make the cities of Judah desolate, without an inhabitant. ¹²Who is the wise man, that may understand this? and who is he to whom the mouth of the LORD has spoken, that he may declare it, for what the land perishes and is burned up like a wilderness, that none passes through? ¹³And the LORD says, Because they have forsaken my law which I set before them, and have not obeyed my voice, neither walked therein; ¹⁴But have walked after the imagination of their own heart, and after Baalim, which their fathers taught them: ¹⁵Therefore thus says the LORD of hosts, the God of Israel; Behold, I will feed them, even this people, with wormwood, and give them water of gall to drink. ¹⁶I will scatter them also among the heathen, whom neither they nor their fathers have known: and I will send a sword after them, till I have consumed them. ¹⁷Thus says the LORD of hosts, Consider you, and call for the mourning women, that they may come; and send for cunning women, that they may come: ¹⁸And let them make haste, and take up a wailing for us, that our eyes may run down with tears, and our eyelids gush out with waters. ¹⁹For a voice of wailing is heard out of Zion, How are we spoiled! we are greatly confounded, because we have forsaken the land, because our dwellings have cast us out. ²⁰Yet hear the word of the LORD, O you women, and let your ear receive the word of his mouth, and teach your daughters wailing, and every one her neighbor lamentation. ²¹For death is come up into our windows, and is entered into our palaces, to cut off the children from without, and the young men from the streets. ²²Speak, Thus says the LORD, Even the carcasses of men shall fall as dung on the open field, and as the handful after the harvestman, and none shall gather them. ²³Thus says the LORD, Let not the wise man glory in his wisdom, neither let the mighty man glory in his might, let not the rich man glory in his riches: ²⁴But let him that glories glory in this, that he understands and knows me, that I am the LORD which exercise loving kindness, judgment, and righteousness, in the earth: for in these things I delight, says the LORD. ²⁵Behold, the days come, says the LORD, that I will punish all them which are circumcised with the uncircumcised; ²⁶Egypt, and Judah, and Edom, and the children of Ammon, and Moab, and all that are in the utmost corners, that dwell in the wilderness: for all these nations are uncircumcised, and all the house of Israel are uncircumcised in the heart.

10

¹Hear you the word which the LORD speaks to you, O house of Israel: ²Thus says the LORD, Learn not the way of the heathen, and be not dismayed at the signs of heaven; for the heathen are dismayed at them. ³For the customs of the people are vain: for one cuts a tree out of the forest, the work of the hands of the workman, with the ax. ⁴They deck it with silver and with gold; they fasten it with nails and with hammers, that it move not. ⁵They are upright as the palm tree, but speak not: they must needs be borne, because they cannot go. Be not afraid of them; for they cannot do evil, neither also is it in them to do good. ⁶For as much as there is none like to you, O LORD; you are great, and your name is great in might. ⁷Who would not fear you, O King of nations? for to you does it appertain: for as much as among all the wise men of the nations, and in all their kingdoms, there is none like to you. ⁸But they are altogether brutish and foolish: the stock is a doctrine of vanities. ⁹Silver spread into plates is brought from Tarshish, and gold from Uphaz, the work of the workman, and of the hands of the founder: blue and purple is their clothing: they are all the work of cunning men. ¹⁰But the LORD is the true God, he is the living God, and an everlasting king: at his wrath the earth shall tremble, and the nations shall not be able to abide his indignation. ¹¹Thus shall you say to them, The gods that have not made the heavens and the earth, even they shall perish from the earth, and from under these heavens. ¹²He has made the earth by his power, he has established the world by his wisdom, and has stretched out the heavens by his discretion. ¹³When he utters his voice, there is a multitude of waters in the heavens, and he causes the vapors to ascend from the ends of the earth; he makes lightning with rain, and brings forth the wind out of his treasures. ¹⁴Every man is brutish in his knowledge: every founder is confounded by the graven image: for his molten image is falsehood, and there is no breath in them. ¹⁵They are vanity, and the work of errors: in the time of their visitation they shall perish. ¹⁶The portion of Jacob is not like them: for he is the former of all things; and Israel is the rod of his inheritance: The LORD of hosts is his name. ¹⁷Gather up your wares out of the land, O inhabitant of the fortress. ¹⁸For thus says the LORD, Behold, I will sling out the inhabitants of the land at this once, and will distress them, that they may find it so. ¹⁹Woe is me for my hurt! my wound is grievous; but I said, Truly this is a grief, and I must bear it. ²⁰My tabernacle is spoiled, and all my cords are broken: my children are gone forth of me, and they are not: there is none to stretch forth my tent any more, and to set up my curtains. ²¹For the pastors are become brutish, and have not sought the LORD: therefore they shall

not prosper, and all their flocks shall be scattered. ²²Behold, the noise of the bruit is come, and a great commotion out of the north country, to make the cities of Judah desolate, and a den of dragons. ²³O LORD, I know that the way of man is not in himself: it is not in man that walks to direct his steps. ²⁴O LORD, correct me, but with judgment; not in your anger, lest you bring me to nothing. ²⁵Pour out your fury on the heathen that know you not, and on the families that call not on your name: for they have eaten up Jacob, and devoured him, and consumed him, and have made his habitation desolate.

11 ¹The word that came to Jeremiah from the LORD saying, ²Hear you the words of this covenant, and speak to the men of Judah, and to the inhabitants of Jerusalem; ³And say you to them, Thus says the LORD God of Israel; Cursed be the man that obeys not the words of this covenant, ⁴Which I commanded your fathers in the day that I brought them forth out of the land of Egypt, from the iron furnace, saying, Obey my voice, and do them, according to all which I command you: so shall you be my people, and I will be your God: ⁵That I may perform the oath which I have sworn to your fathers, to give them a land flowing with milk and honey, as it is this day. Then answered I, and said, So be it, O LORD. ⁶Then the LORD said to me, Proclaim all these words in the cities of Judah, and in the streets of Jerusalem, saying, Hear you the words of this covenant, and do them. ⁷For I earnestly protested to your fathers in the day that I brought them up out of the land of Egypt, even to this day, rising early and protesting, saying, Obey my voice. ⁸Yet they obeyed not, nor inclined their ear, but walked every one in the imagination of their evil heart: therefore I will bring on them all the words of this covenant, which I commanded them to do: but they did them not. ⁹And the LORD said to me, A conspiracy is found among the men of Judah, and among the inhabitants of Jerusalem. ¹⁰They are turned back to the iniquities of their forefathers, which refused to hear my words; and they went after other gods to serve them: the house of Israel and the house of Judah have broken my covenant which I made with their fathers. ¹¹Therefore thus says the LORD, Behold, I will bring evil on them, which they shall not be able to escape; and though they shall cry to me, I will not listen to them. ¹²Then shall the cities of Judah and inhabitants of Jerusalem go, and cry to the gods to whom they offer incense: but they shall not save them at all in the time of their trouble. ¹³For according to the number of your cities were your gods, O Judah; and according to the number of the streets of Jerusalem have you set up altars to that shameful thing, even altars to burn incense to Baal. ¹⁴Therefore pray not you for this people, neither lift up a cry or prayer for them: for I will not hear them in the time that they cry to me for their trouble. ¹⁵What has my beloved to do in my house, seeing she has worked lewdness with many, and the holy flesh is passed from you? when you do evil, then you rejoice. ¹⁶The LORD called your name, A green olive tree, fair, and of goodly fruit: with the noise of a great tumult he has kindled fire on it, and the branches of it are broken. ¹⁷For the LORD of hosts, that planted you, has pronounced evil against you, for the evil of the house of Israel and of the house of Judah, which they have done against themselves to provoke me to anger in offering incense to Baal. ¹⁸And the LORD has given me knowledge of it, and I know it: then you showed me their doings. ¹⁹But I was like a lamb or an ox that is brought to the slaughter; and I knew not that they had devised devices against me, saying, Let us destroy the tree with the fruit thereof, and let us cut him off from the land of the living, that his name may be no more remembered. ²⁰But, O LORD of hosts, that judge righteously, that try the reins and the heart, let me see your vengeance on them: for to you have I revealed my cause. ²¹Therefore thus says the LORD of the men of Anathoth, that seek your life, saying, Prophesy not in the name of the LORD, that you die not by our hand: ²²Therefore thus says the LORD of hosts, Behold, I will punish them: the young men shall die by the sword; their sons and their daughters shall die by famine: ²³And there shall be no remnant of them: for I will bring evil on the men of Anathoth, even the year of their visitation.

12 ¹Righteous are you, O LORD, when I plead with you: yet let me talk with you of your judgments: Why does the way of the wicked prosper? why are all they happy that deal very treacherously? ²You have planted them, yes, they have taken root: they grow, yes, they bring forth fruit: you are near in their mouth, and far from their reins. ³But you, O LORD, know me: you have seen me, and tried my heart toward you: pull them out like sheep for the slaughter, and prepare them for the day of slaughter. ⁴How long shall the land mourn, and the herbs of every field wither, for the wickedness of them that dwell therein? the beasts are consumed, and the birds; because they said, He shall not see our last end. ⁵If you have run with the footmen, and they have wearied you, then how can you contend with horses? and if in the land of peace, wherein you trusted, they wearied you, then how will you do in the swelling of Jordan? ⁶For even your brothers, and the house of your father, even they have dealt treacherously with you; yes, they have called a multitude after you: believe them not, though they speak fair words to you. ⁷I have forsaken my house, I have left my heritage; I have given the dearly beloved of my soul into the hand of her enemies. ⁸My heritage is to me as a lion in the forest; it cries out against me: therefore have I hated it. ⁹My heritage is to me as a speckled bird, the birds round about are against her; come you, assemble all the beasts of the field, come to devour. ¹⁰Many pastors have destroyed my vineyard, they have trodden my portion under foot, they have made my pleasant portion a desolate wilderness. ¹¹They have made it desolate, and being desolate it mourns to me; the whole land is made desolate, because no man lays it to heart. ¹²The spoilers are come on all high places through the wilderness: for the sword of the LORD shall devour from the one end of the land even to the other end of the land: no flesh shall have peace. ¹³They have sown wheat, but shall reap thorns: they have put themselves to pain, but shall not profit: and they shall be ashamed of your revenues because of the fierce anger of the LORD. ¹⁴Thus says the LORD against all my evil neighbors, that touch the inheritance which I have caused my people Israel to inherit; Behold, I will pluck them out of their land, and pluck out the house of Judah from among them. ¹⁵And it shall come to pass, after that I have plucked them out I will return, and have compassion on them, and will bring them again, every man to his heritage, and every man to his land. ¹⁶And it shall come to pass, if they will diligently learn the ways of my people, to swear by my name, The LORD lives; as they taught my people to swear by Baal; then shall they be built in the middle of my people. ¹⁷But if they will not obey, I will utterly pluck up and destroy that nation, says the LORD.

13 ¹Thus says the LORD to me, Go and get you a linen girdle, and put it on your loins, and put it not in water. ²So I got a girdle according to the word of the LORD, and put it on my loins. ³And the word of the LORD came to me the second time, saying, ⁴Take the girdle that you have got, which is on your loins, and arise, go to Euphrates, and hide it there in a hole of the rock. ⁵So I went, and hid it by Euphrates, as the LORD commanded me. ⁶And it came to pass after many days, that the LORD said to me, Arise, go to Euphrates, and take the girdle from there, which I commanded you to hide there. ⁷Then I went to Euphrates, and dig, and took the girdle from the place where I had hid it: and, behold, the girdle was marred, it was profitable for nothing. ⁸Then the word of the LORD came to me, saying, ⁹Thus says the LORD, After this manner will I mar the pride of Judah, and the great pride of Jerusalem. ¹⁰This evil people, which refuse to hear my words, which walk in the imagination of their heart, and walk after other gods, to serve them, and to worship them, shall even be as this girdle, which is good for nothing. ¹¹For as the girdle sticks to the loins of a man, so have I caused to stick to me the whole house of Israel and the whole house of Judah, says the LORD; that they might be to me for a people, and for a name, and for a praise, and for a glory: but they would not hear. ¹²Therefore you shall speak to them this word; Thus says the LORD God of Israel, Every bottle shall be filled with wine: and they shall say to you, Do we not certainly know that every bottle shall be filled with wine? ¹³Then shall you say to them, Thus says the LORD, Behold, I will fill all the inhabitants of this land, even the kings that sit on David's throne, and the priests, and the prophets, and all the inhabitants of Jerusalem, with drunkenness. ¹⁴And I will dash them one against another, even the fathers and the sons together, says the LORD: I will not pity, nor spare, nor have mercy, but destroy them. ¹⁵Hear you, and give ear; be not proud: for the LORD has spoken. ¹⁶Give glory to the LORD your God, before he cause darkness, and before your feet stumble on the dark mountains, and, while you look for light, he turn it into the shadow of death, and make it gross darkness. ¹⁷But if you will not hear it, my soul shall weep in secret places for your pride; and my eye shall weep sore, and run down with tears, because the LORD's flock is carried away captive. ¹⁸Say to the king and to the queen, Humble yourselves, sit down: for your principalities shall come down, even the crown of your glory. ¹⁹The cities of the south shall be shut up, and none shall open them: Judah shall be carried away captive all of it, it shall be wholly carried away captive. ²⁰Lift up your eyes, and behold them that come from the north: where is the flock that was given you, your beautiful flock? ²¹What will you say when he shall punish you? for you have taught them to be captains, and as chief over you: shall not sorrows take you, as a woman in travail? ²²And if you say in your heart, Why come these things on me? For the greatness of your iniquity are your skirts discovered, and your heels made bore. ²³Can the Ethiopian change his skin, or the leopard his spots? then may you also do good, that are accustomed to do evil. ²⁴Therefore will I scatter them as the stubble that passes away by the wind of the wilderness. ²⁵This is your lot, the portion of your measures from me, says the LORD; because you have forgotten me, and trusted in falsehood. ²⁶Therefore will I discover your skirts on your face, that your shame may appear. ²⁷I have seen your adulteries, and your neighings, the lewdness of your prostitution, and your abominations on the hills in the fields. Woe to you, O Jerusalem! will you not be made clean? when shall it once be?

14 ¹The word of the LORD that came to Jeremiah concerning the dearth. ²Judah mourns, and the gates thereof languish; they are black to the ground; and the cry of Jerusalem is gone up. ³And their nobles have sent their little ones to the waters: they came to the pits, and found no water; they returned with their vessels empty; they were ashamed and confounded, and covered their heads. ⁴Because the ground is beat down, for there was no rain in the earth, the plowmen were ashamed, they covered their heads. ⁵Yes, the hind also calved in the field, and forsook it, because there was no grass. ⁶And the wild asses did stand in the high places, they snuffed up the wind like dragons; their eyes did fail, because there was no grass. ⁷O LORD, though our iniquities testify against us, do you it for your name's sake: for our backslidings are many; we have sinned against you. ⁸O the hope of Israel, the savior thereof in time of trouble, why should you be as a stranger in the land, and as a wayfaring man that turns aside to tarry for a night? ⁹Why should you be as a man astonished, as a mighty man that cannot save? yet you, O LORD, are in the middle of us, and we are called by your name; leave us not. ¹⁰Thus says the LORD to this people, Thus have they loved to wander, they have not refrained their feet, therefore the LORD does not accept them; he will now remember their iniquity, and visit their sins. ¹¹Then said the LORD to me, Pray not for this people for their good. ¹²When they fast, I will not hear their cry; and when they offer burnt offering and an oblation, I will not accept them: but I will consume them by the sword, and by the famine, and by the pestilence. ¹³Then said I, Ah, Lord GOD! behold, the prophets say to them, You shall not see the sword, neither shall you have famine; but I will give you assured peace in this place. ¹⁴Then the LORD said to me, The prophets prophesy lies in my name: I sent them not, neither have I commanded them, neither spoke to them: they prophesy to you a false vision and divination, and a thing of nothing, and the deceit of their heart. ¹⁵Therefore thus says the LORD concerning the prophets that prophesy in my name, and I sent them not, yet they say, Sword and famine shall not be in this land; By sword and famine shall those prophets be consumed. ¹⁶And the people to whom they prophesy shall be cast out in the streets of Jerusalem because of the famine and the sword; and they shall have none to bury them, them, their wives, nor their sons, nor their daughters: for I will pour their wickedness on them. ¹⁷Therefore you shall say this word to them; Let my eyes run down with tears night and day, and let them not cease: for the virgin daughter of my people is broken with a great breach, with a very grievous blow. ¹⁸If I go forth into the field, then behold the slain with the sword! and if I enter into the city, then behold them that are sick with famine! yes, both the prophet and the priest go about into a land that they know not. ¹⁹Have you utterly rejected Judah? has your soul loathed Zion? why have you smitten us, and there is no healing for us? we looked for peace, and there is no good; and for the time of healing, and behold trouble! ²⁰We acknowledge, O LORD, our wickedness, and the iniquity of our fathers: for we have sinned against you. ²¹Do not abhor us, for your name's sake, do not disgrace the throne of your glory: remember, break not your covenant with us. ²²Are there any among the vanities of the Gentiles that can cause rain? or can the heavens give showers? are not you he, O LORD our God? therefore we will wait on you: for you have made all these things.

15 ¹Then said the LORD to me, Though Moses and Samuel stood before me, yet my mind could not be toward this people: cast them out of my sight, and let them go forth. ²And it shall come to pass, if they say to you, Where shall we go forth? then you shall tell them, Thus says the LORD; Such as are for death, to death; and such as are for the sword, to the sword; and such as are for the famine, to the famine; and such as are for the captivity, to the captivity. ³And I will appoint over them four kinds, says the LORD: the sword to slay, and the dogs to tear, and the fowls of the heaven, and the beasts of the earth, to devour and destroy. ⁴And I will cause them to be removed into all kingdoms of the earth, because of Manasseh the son of Hezekiah king of Judah, for that which he did in Jerusalem. ⁵For who shall have pity on you, O Jerusalem? or who shall bemoan you? or who shall go aside to ask how you do? ⁶You have forsaken me, says the LORD, you are gone backward: therefore will I stretch out my hand against you, and destroy you; I am weary with repenting. ⁷And I will fan them with a fan in the gates of the land; I will bereave them of children, I will destroy my people since they return not from their ways. ⁸Their widows are increased to me above the sand of the seas: I have brought on them against the mother of the young men a spoiler at noonday: I have caused him to fall on it suddenly, and terrors on the city. ⁹She that has borne seven languishes: she has given up the ghost; her sun is gone down while it was yet day: she has been ashamed and confounded: and the residue of them will I deliver to the sword before their enemies, says the LORD. ¹⁰Woe is me, my mother, that you have borne me a man of strife and a man of contention to the whole earth! I have neither lent on usury, nor men have lent to me on usury; yet every one of them does curse me. ¹¹The LORD said, Truly it shall be well with your remnant; truly I will cause the enemy to entreat you well in the time of evil and in the time of affliction. ¹²Shall iron break the northern iron and the steel? ¹³Your substance and your treasures will I give to the spoil without price, and that for all your sins, even in all your borders. ¹⁴And I will make you to pass with your enemies into a land which you know not: for a fire is kindled in my anger, which shall burn on you. ¹⁵O LORD, you know: remember me, and visit me, and revenge me of my persecutors; take me not away in your long-suffering: know that for your sake I have suffered rebuke. ¹⁶Your words were found, and I did eat them; and your word was to me the joy and rejoicing of my heart: for I am called by your name, O LORD God of hosts. ¹⁷I sat not in the assembly of the mockers, nor rejoiced; I sat alone because of your hand: for you have filled me with indignation. ¹⁸Why is my pain perpetual, and my wound incurable, which refuses to be healed? will you be altogether to me as a liar, and as waters that fail? ¹⁹Therefore thus says the LORD, If you return, then will I bring you again, and you shall stand before me: and if you take forth the precious from the vile, you shall be as my mouth: let them return to you; but return not you to them. ²⁰And I will make you to this people a fenced brazen wall: and they shall fight against you, but they shall not prevail against you: for I am with you to save you and to deliver you, says the LORD. ²¹And I will deliver you out of the hand of the wicked, and I will redeem you out of the hand of the terrible.

16 ¹The word of the LORD came also to me, saying, ²You shall not take you a wife, neither shall you have sons or daughters in this place. ³For thus says the LORD concerning the sons and concerning the daughters that are born in this place, and concerning their mothers that bore them, and concerning their fathers that begat them in this land; ⁴They shall die of grievous deaths; they shall not be lamented; neither shall they be buried; but they shall be as dung on the face of the earth: and they shall be consumed by the sword, and by famine; and their carcasses shall be meat for the fowls of heaven, and for the beasts of the earth. ⁵For thus says the LORD, Enter not into the house of mourning, neither go to lament nor bemoan them: for I have taken away my peace from this people, said the LORD, even loving kindness and mercies. ⁶Both the great and the small shall die in this land: they shall not be buried, neither shall men lament for them, nor cut themselves, nor make themselves bald for them: ⁷Neither shall men tear themselves for them in mourning, to comfort them for the dead; neither shall men give them the cup of consolation to drink for their father or for their mother. ⁸You shall not also go into the house of feasting, to sit with them to eat and to drink. ⁹For thus says the LORD of hosts, the God of Israel; Behold, I will cause to cease out of this place in your eyes, and in your days, the voice of mirth, and the voice of gladness, the voice of the bridegroom, and the voice of the bride. ¹⁰And it shall come to pass, when you shall show this people all these words, and they shall say to you, Why has the LORD pronounced all this great evil against us? or what is our iniquity? or what is our sin that we have committed against the LORD our God? ¹¹Then shall you say to them, Because your fathers have forsaken me, says the LORD, and have walked after other gods, and have served them, and have worshipped them, and have forsaken me, and have not kept my law; ¹²And you have done worse than your fathers; for, behold, you walk every one after the imagination of his evil heart, that they may not listen to me: ¹³Therefore will I cast you out of this land into a land that you know not, neither you nor your fathers; and there shall you serve other gods day and night; where I will not show you favor. ¹⁴Therefore, behold, the days come, says the LORD, that it shall no more be said, The LORD lives, that brought up the children of Israel out of the land of Egypt; ¹⁵But, The LORD lives, that brought up the children of Israel from the land of the north, and from all the lands where he had driven them: and I will bring them again into their land that I gave to their fathers. ¹⁶Behold, I will send for many fishers, says the LORD, and they shall fish them; and after will I send for many hunters, and they shall hunt them from every mountain, and from every hill, and out of the holes of the rocks. ¹⁷For my eyes are on all their ways: they are not hid from my face, neither is their iniquity hid from my eyes. ¹⁸And first I will recompense their iniquity and their sin double; because they have defiled my land, they have filled my inheritance with the carcasses of their detestable and abominable things. ¹⁹O LORD, my strength, and my fortress, and my refuge in the day of affliction, the Gentiles shall come to you from the ends of the earth, and shall say, Surely our fathers have inherited lies, vanity, and things wherein there is no profit. ²⁰Shall a man make gods to himself, and they are no gods? ²¹Therefore, behold, I will this once cause them to know, I will cause them to know my hand and my might; and they shall know that my name is The LORD.

17 ¹The sin of Judah is written with a pen of iron, and with the point of a diamond: it is graven on the table of their heart, and on the horns of your altars; ²Whilst their children remember their altars and their groves by the green trees on the high hills. ³O my mountain in the field, I will give your substance and all your treasures to the spoil, and your high places for sin, throughout all your borders. ⁴And you, even yourself, shall discontinue from your heritage that I gave you; and I will cause you to serve your enemies in the land which you know not: for you have kindled a fire in my anger, which shall burn for ever. ⁵Thus says the LORD; Cursed be the man that trusts in man, and makes flesh his arm, and whose heart departs from the LORD. ⁶For he shall be like the heath in the desert, and shall not see when good comes; but shall inhabit the parched places in the wilderness, in a salt land and not inhabited. ⁷Blessed is the man that trusts in the LORD, and whose hope the LORD is. ⁸For he shall be as a tree planted by the waters, and that spreads out her roots by the river, and shall not see when heat comes, but her leaf shall be green; and shall not be careful in the year of drought, neither shall cease from yielding fruit. ⁹The heart is deceitful above all things, and desperately wicked: who can know it? ¹⁰I the LORD search the heart, I try the reins, even to give every man according to his ways, and according to the fruit of his doings. ¹¹As the partridge sits on eggs, and hatches them not; so he that gets riches, and not by right, shall leave them in the middle of his days, and at his end shall be a fool. ¹²A glorious high throne from the beginning is the place of our sanctuary. ¹³O LORD, the hope of Israel, all that forsake you shall be ashamed, and they that depart from me shall be written in the earth, because they have forsaken the LORD, the fountain of living waters. ¹⁴Heal me, O LORD, and I shall be healed; save me, and I shall be saved: for you are my praise. ¹⁵Behold, they say to me, Where is the word of the LORD? let it come now. ¹⁶As for me, I have not hastened from being a pastor to follow you: neither have I desired the woeful day; you know: that which came out of my lips was right before you. ¹⁷Be not a terror to me: you are my hope in the day of evil. ¹⁸Let them be confounded that persecute me, but let not me be confounded: let them be dismayed, but let not me be dismayed: bring on them the day of evil, and destroy them with double destruction. ¹⁹Thus said the LORD to me; Go and stand in the gate of the children of the people, whereby the kings of Judah come in, and by the which they go out, and in all the gates of Jerusalem; ²⁰And say to them, Hear you the word of the LORD, you kings of Judah, and all Judah, and all the inhabitants of Jerusalem, that enter in by these gates: ²¹Thus says the LORD; Take heed to yourselves, and bear no burden on the sabbath day, nor bring it in by the gates of Jerusalem; ²²Neither carry forth a burden out of your houses on the sabbath day, neither do you any work, but hallow you the sabbath day, as I commanded your fathers. ²³But they obeyed not, neither inclined their ear, but made their neck stiff, that they might not hear, nor receive instruction. ²⁴And it shall come to pass, if you diligently listen to me, says the LORD, to bring in no burden through the gates of this city on the sabbath day, but hallow the sabbath day, to do no work therein; ²⁵Then shall there enter into the gates of this city kings and princes sitting on the throne of David, riding in chariots and on horses, they, and their princes, the men of Judah, and the inhabitants of Jerusalem: and this city shall remain for ever. ²⁶And they shall come from the cities of Judah, and from the places about Jerusalem, and from the land of Benjamin, and from the plain, and from the mountains, and from the south, bringing burnt offerings, and sacrifices, and meat offerings, and incense, and bringing sacrifices of praise, to the house of the LORD. ²⁷But if you will not listen to me to hallow the sabbath day, and not to bear a burden, even entering in at the gates of Jerusalem on the sabbath day; then will I kindle a fire in the gates thereof, and it shall devour the palaces of Jerusalem, and it shall not be quenched.

18 ¹The word which came to Jeremiah from the LORD, saying, ²Arise, and go down to the potter's house, and there I will cause you to hear my words. ³Then I went down to the potter's house, and, behold, he worked a work on the wheels. ⁴And the vessel that he made of clay was marred in the hand of the potter: so he made it again another vessel, as seemed good to the potter to make it. ⁵Then the word of the LORD came to me, saying, ⁶O house of Israel, cannot I do with you as this potter? says the LORD. Behold, as the clay is in the potter's hand, so are you in my hand, O house of Israel. ⁷At what instant I shall speak concerning a nation, and concerning a kingdom, to pluck up, and to pull down, and to destroy it; ⁸If that nation, against whom I have pronounced, turn from their evil, I will repent of the evil that I thought to do to them. ⁹And at what instant I shall speak concerning a nation, and concerning a kingdom, to build and to plant it; ¹⁰If it do evil in my sight, that it obey not my voice, then I will repent of the good, with which I said I would benefit them. ¹¹Now therefore go to, speak to the men of Judah, and to the inhabitants of Jerusalem, saying, Thus says the LORD; Behold, I frame evil against you, and devise a device against you: return you now every one from his evil way, and make your ways and your doings good. ¹²And they said, There is no hope: but we will walk after our own devices, and we will every one do the imagination of his evil heart. ¹³Therefore thus says the LORD; Ask you now among the heathen, who has heard such things: the virgin of Israel has done a very horrible thing. ¹⁴Will a man leave the snow of Lebanon which comes from the rock of the field? or shall the cold flowing waters that come from another place be forsaken? ¹⁵Because my people has forgotten me, they have burned incense to vanity, and they have caused them to stumble in their ways from the ancient paths, to walk in paths, in a way not cast up; ¹⁶To make their land desolate, and a perpetual hissing; every one that passes thereby shall be astonished, and wag his head. ¹⁷I will scatter them as with an east wind before the enemy; I will show them the back, and not the face, in the day of their calamity. ¹⁸Then said they, Come and let us devise devices against Jeremiah; for the law shall not perish from the priest, nor counsel from the wise, nor the word from the prophet. Come, and let us smite him with the tongue, and let us not give heed to any of his words. ¹⁹Give heed to me, O LORD, and listen to the voice of them that contend with me. ²⁰Shall evil be recompensed for good? for they have dig a pit for my soul. Remember that I stood before you to speak good for them, and to turn away your wrath from them. ²¹Therefore deliver up their children to the famine, and pour out their blood by the force of the sword; and let their wives be bereaved of their children, and be widows; and let their men be put to death; let their young men be slain by the sword in battle. ²²Let a cry be heard from their houses, when you shall bring a troop suddenly on them: for they have dig a pit to take me, and hid snares for my feet. ²³Yet, LORD, you know all their counsel against me to slay me: forgive not their iniquity, neither blot out their sin from your sight, but let them be overthrown before you; deal thus with them in the time of your anger.

19 ¹Thus says the LORD, Go and get a potter's earthen bottle, and take of the ancients of the people, and of the ancients of the priests; ²And go forth to the valley of the son of Hinnom, which is by the entry of the east gate, and proclaim there the words that I shall tell you, ³And say, Hear you the word of the LORD, O kings of Judah, and inhabitants of Jerusalem; Thus says the LORD of hosts, the God of Israel; Behold, I will bring evil on this place, the which whoever hears, his ears shall tingle. ⁴Because they have forsaken me, and have estranged this place, and have burned incense in it to other gods, whom neither they nor their fathers have known, nor the kings of Judah, and have filled this place with the blood of innocents; ⁵They have built also the high places of Baal, to burn their sons with fire for burnt offerings to Baal, which I commanded not, nor spoke it, neither came it into my mind: ⁶Therefore, behold, the days come, says the LORD, that this place shall no more be called Tophet, nor The valley of the son of Hinnom, but The valley of slaughter. ⁷And I will make void the counsel of Judah and Jerusalem in this place; and I will cause them to fall by the sword before their enemies, and by the hands of them that seek their lives: and their carcasses will I give to be meat for the fowls of the heaven, and for the beasts of the earth. ⁸And I will make this city desolate, and an hissing; every one that passes thereby shall be astonished and hiss because of all the plagues thereof. ⁹And I will cause them to eat the flesh of their sons and the flesh of their daughters, and they shall eat every one the flesh of his friend in the siege and narrow place, with which their enemies, and they that seek their lives, shall straiten them. ¹⁰Then shall you break the bottle in the sight of the men that go with you, ¹¹And shall say to them, Thus says the LORD of hosts; Even so will I break this people and this city, as one breaks a potter's vessel, that cannot be made whole again: and they shall bury them in Tophet, till there be no place to bury. ¹²Thus will I do to this place, says the LORD, and to the inhabitants thereof, and even make this city as Tophet: ¹³And the houses of Jerusalem, and the houses of the kings of Judah, shall be defiled as the place of Tophet, because of all the houses on whose roofs they have burned incense to all the host of heaven, and have poured out drink offerings to other gods. ¹⁴Then came Jeremiah from Tophet, where the LORD had sent him to prophesy; and he stood in the court of the LORD's house; and said to all the people, ¹⁵Thus says the LORD of hosts, the God of Israel; Behold, I will bring on this city and on all her towns all the evil that I have pronounced against it, because they have hardened their necks, that they might not hear my words.

20 ¹Now Pashur the son of Immer the priest, who was also chief governor in the house of the LORD, heard that Jeremiah prophesied these things. ²Then Pashur smote Jeremiah the prophet, and put him in the stocks that were in the high gate of Benjamin, which was by the house of the LORD. ³And it came to pass on the morrow, that Pashur brought forth Jeremiah out of the stocks. Then said Jeremiah to him, The LORD has not called your name Pashur, but Magormissabib. ⁴For thus says the LORD, Behold, I will make you a terror to yourself, and to all your friends: and they shall fall by the sword of their enemies, and your eyes shall behold it: and I will give all Judah into the hand of the king of Babylon, and he shall carry them captive into Babylon, and shall slay them with the sword. ⁵Moreover I will deliver all the strength of this city, and all the labors thereof, and all the precious things thereof, and all the treasures of the kings of Judah will I give into the hand of their enemies, which shall spoil them, and take them, and carry them to Babylon. ⁶And you, Pashur, and all that dwell in your house shall go into captivity: and you shall come to Babylon, and there you shall die, and shall be buried there, you, and all your friends, to whom you have prophesied lies. ⁷O LORD, you have deceived me, and I was deceived; you are stronger than I, and have prevailed: I am in derision daily, every one mocks me. ⁸For since I spoke, I cried out, I cried violence and spoil; because the word of the LORD was made a reproach to me, and a derision, daily. ⁹Then I said, I will not make mention of him, nor speak any more in his name. But his word was in my heart as a burning fire shut up in my bones, and I was weary with forbearing, and I could not stay. ¹⁰For I heard the defaming of many, fear on every side. Report, say they, and we will report it. All my familiars watched for my halting, saying, Peradventure he will be enticed, and we shall prevail against him, and we shall take our revenge on him. ¹¹But the LORD is with me as a mighty terrible one: therefore my persecutors shall stumble, and they shall not prevail: they shall be greatly ashamed; for they shall not prosper: their everlasting confusion shall never be forgotten. ¹²But, O LORD of hosts, that try the righteous, and see the reins and the heart, let me see your vengeance on them: for to you have I opened my cause. ¹³Sing to the LORD, praise you the LORD: for he has delivered the soul of the poor from the hand of evildoers.

¹⁴Cursed be the day wherein I was born: let not the day wherein my mother bore me be blessed. ¹⁵Cursed be the man who brought tidings to my father, saying, A man child is born to you; making him very glad. ¹⁶And let that man be as the cities which the LORD overthrew, and repented not: and let him hear the cry in the morning, and the shouting at noontide; ¹⁷Because he slew me not from the womb; or that my mother might have been my grave, and her womb to be always great with me. ¹⁸Why came I forth out of the womb to see labor and sorrow, that my days should be consumed with shame?

21

¹The word which came to Jeremiah from the LORD, when king Zedekiah sent to him Pashur the son of Melchiah, and Zephaniah the son of Maaseiah the priest, saying, ²Inquire, I pray you, of the LORD for us; for Nebuchadrezzar king of Babylon makes war against us; if so be that the LORD will deal with us according to all his wondrous works, that he may go up from us. ³Then said Jeremiah to them, Thus shall you say to Zedekiah: ⁴Thus says the LORD God of Israel; Behold, I will turn back the weapons of war that are in your hands, with which you fight against the king of Babylon, and against the Chaldeans, which besiege you without the walls, and I will assemble them into the middle of this city. ⁵And I myself will fight against you with an outstretched hand and with a strong arm, even in anger, and in fury, and in great wrath. ⁶And I will smite the inhabitants of this city, both man and beast: they shall die of a great pestilence. ⁷And afterward, says the LORD, I will deliver Zedekiah king of Judah, and his servants, and the people, and such as are left in this city from the pestilence, from the sword, and from the famine, into the hand of Nebuchadrezzar king of Babylon, and into the hand of their enemies, and into the hand of those that seek their life: and he shall smite them with the edge of the sword; he shall not spare them, neither have pity, nor have mercy. ⁸And to this people you shall say, Thus says the LORD; Behold, I set before you the way of life, and the way of death. ⁹He that stays in this city shall die by the sword, and by the famine, and by the pestilence: but he that goes out, and falls to the Chaldeans that besiege you, he shall live, and his life shall be to him for a prey. ¹⁰For I have set my face against this city for evil, and not for good, says the LORD: it shall be given into the hand of the king of Babylon, and he shall burn it with fire. ¹¹And touching the house of the king of Judah, say, Hear you the word of the LORD; ¹²O house of David, thus says the LORD; Execute judgment in the morning, and deliver him that is spoiled out of the hand of the oppressor, lest my fury go out like fire, and burn that none can quench it, because of the evil of your doings. ¹³Behold, I am against you, O inhabitant of the valley, and rock of the plain, says the LORD; which say, Who shall come down against us? or who shall enter into our habitations? ¹⁴But I will punish you according to the fruit of your doings, says the LORD: and I will kindle a fire in the forest thereof, and it shall devour all things round about it.

22

¹Thus says the LORD; Go down to the house of the king of Judah, and speak there this word, ²And say, Hear the word of the LORD, O king of Judah, that sit on the throne of David, you, and your servants, and your people that enter in by these gates: ³Thus says the LORD; Execute you judgment and righteousness, and deliver the spoiled out of the hand of the oppressor: and do no wrong, do no violence to the stranger, the fatherless, nor the widow, neither shed innocent blood in this place. ⁴For if you do this thing indeed, then shall there enter in by the gates of this house kings sitting on the throne of David, riding in chariots and on horses, he, and his servants, and his people. ⁵But if you will not hear these words, I swear by myself, says the LORD, that this house shall become a desolation. ⁶For thus says the LORD to the king's house of Judah; You are Gilead to me, and the head of Lebanon: yet surely I will make you a wilderness, and cities which are not inhabited. ⁷And I will prepare destroyers against you, every one with his weapons: and they shall cut down your choice cedars, and cast them into the fire. ⁸And many nations shall pass by this city, and they shall say every man to his neighbor, Why has the LORD done thus to this great city? ⁹Then they shall answer, Because they have forsaken the covenant of the LORD their God, and worshipped other gods, and served them. ¹⁰Weep you not for the dead, neither bemoan him: but weep sore for him that goes away: for he shall return no more, nor see his native country. ¹¹For thus says the LORD touching Shallum the son of Josiah king of Judah, which reigned instead of Josiah his father, which went forth out of this place; He shall not return thither any more: ¹²But he shall die in the place where they have led him captive, and shall see this land no more. ¹³Woe to him that builds his house by unrighteousness, and his chambers by wrong; that uses his neighbor's service without wages, and gives him not for his work; ¹⁴That says, I will build me a wide house and large chambers, and cuts him out windows; and it is paneled with cedar, and painted with vermilion. ¹⁵Shall you reign, because you close yourself in cedar? did not your father eat and drink, and do judgment and justice, and then it was well with him? ¹⁶He judged the cause of the poor and needy; then it was well with him: was not this to know me? says the LORD. ¹⁷But your eyes and your heart are not but for your covetousness, and for to shed innocent blood, and for oppression, and for violence, to do it. ¹⁸Therefore thus says the LORD concerning Jehoiakim the son of Josiah king of Judah; They shall not lament for him, saying, Ah my brother! or, Ah sister! they shall not lament for him, saying, Ah lord! or, Ah his glory! ¹⁹He shall be buried with the burial of an ass, drawn and cast forth beyond the gates of Jerusalem. ²⁰Go up to Lebanon, and cry; and lift up your voice in Bashan, and cry from the passages: for all your lovers are destroyed. ²¹I spoke to you in your prosperity; but you said, I will not hear. This has been your manner from your youth, that you obeyed not my voice. ²²The wind shall eat up all your pastors, and your lovers shall go into captivity: surely then shall you be ashamed and confounded for all your wickedness. ²³O inhabitant of Lebanon, that make your nest in the cedars, how gracious shall you be when pangs come on you, the pain as of a woman in travail! ²⁴As I live, says the LORD, though Coniah the son of Jehoiakim king of Judah were the signet on my right hand, yet would I pluck you there; ²⁵And I will give you into the hand of them that seek your life, and into the hand of them whose face you fear, even into the hand of

Nebuchadrezzar king of Babylon, and into the hand of the Chaldeans. ²⁶And I will cast you out, and your mother that bore you, into another country, where you were not born; and there shall you die. ²⁷But to the land where they desire to return, thither shall they not return. ²⁸Is this man Coniah a despised broken idol? is he a vessel wherein is no pleasure? why are they cast out, he and his seed, and are cast into a land which they know not? ²⁹O earth, earth, earth, hear the word of the LORD. ³⁰Thus says the LORD, Write you this man childless, a man that shall not prosper in his days: for no man of his seed shall prosper, sitting on the throne of David, and ruling any more in Judah.

23 ¹Woe be to the pastors that destroy and scatter the sheep of my pasture! says the LORD. ²Therefore thus said the LORD God of Israel against the pastors that feed my people; You have scattered my flock, and driven them away, and have not visited them: behold, I will visit on you the evil of your doings, says the LORD. ³And I will gather the remnant of my flock out of all countries where I have driven them, and will bring them again to their folds; and they shall be fruitful and increase. ⁴And I will set up shepherds over them which shall feed them: and they shall fear no more, nor be dismayed, neither shall they be lacking, says the LORD. ⁵Behold, the days come, says the LORD, that I will raise to David a righteous Branch, and a King shall reign and prosper, and shall execute judgment and justice in the earth. ⁶In his days Judah shall be saved, and Israel shall dwell safely: and this is his name whereby he shall be called, THE LORD OUR RIGHTEOUSNESS. ⁷Therefore, behold, the days come, says the LORD, that they shall no more say, The LORD lives, which brought up the children of Israel out of the land of Egypt; ⁸But, The LORD lives, which brought up and which led the seed of the house of Israel out of the north country, and from all countries where I had driven them; and they shall dwell in their own land. ⁹My heart within me is broken because of the prophets; all my bones shake; I am like a drunken man, and like a man whom wine has overcome, because of the LORD, and because of the words of his holiness. ¹⁰For the land is full of adulterers; for because of swearing the land mourns; the pleasant places of the wilderness are dried up, and their course is evil, and their force is not right. ¹¹For both prophet and priest are profane; yes, in my house have I found their wickedness, says the LORD. ¹²Why their way shall be to them as slippery ways in the darkness: they shall be driven on, and fall therein: for I will bring evil on them, even the year of their visitation, says the LORD. ¹³And I have seen folly in the prophets of Samaria; they prophesied in Baal, and caused my people Israel to err. ¹⁴I have seen also in the prophets of Jerusalem an horrible thing: they commit adultery, and walk in lies: they strengthen also the hands of evildoers, that none does return from his wickedness; they are all of them to me as Sodom, and the inhabitants thereof as Gomorrah. ¹⁵Therefore thus says the LORD of hosts concerning the prophets; Behold, I will feed them with wormwood, and make them drink the water of gall: for from the prophets of Jerusalem is profaneness gone forth into all the land. ¹⁶Thus says the LORD of hosts, Listen not to the words of the prophets that prophesy to you: they make you vain: they speak a vision of their own heart, and not out of the mouth of the LORD. ¹⁷They say still to them that despise me, The LORD has said, You shall have peace; and they say to every one that walks after the imagination of his own heart, No evil shall come on you. ¹⁸For who has stood in the counsel of the LORD, and has perceived and heard his word? who has marked his word, and heard it? ¹⁹Behold, a whirlwind of the LORD is gone forth in fury, even a grievous whirlwind: it shall fall grievously on the head of the wicked. ²⁰The anger of the LORD shall not return, until he have executed, and till he have performed the thoughts of his heart: in the latter days you shall consider it perfectly. ²¹I have not sent these prophets, yet they ran: I have not spoken to them, yet they prophesied. ²²But if they had stood in my counsel, and had caused my people to hear my words, then they should have turned them from their evil way, and from the evil of their doings. ²³Am I a God at hand, says the LORD, and not a God afar off? ²⁴Can any hide himself in secret places that I shall not see him? says the LORD. Do not I fill heaven and earth? said the LORD. ²⁵I have heard what the prophets said, that prophesy lies in my name, saying, I have dreamed, I have dreamed. ²⁶How long shall this be in the heart of the prophets that prophesy lies? yes, they are prophets of the deceit of their own heart; ²⁷Which think to cause my people to forget my name by their dreams which they tell every man to his neighbor, as their fathers have forgotten my name for Baal. ²⁸The prophet that has a dream, let him tell a dream; and he that has my word, let him speak my word faithfully. What is the chaff to the wheat? says the LORD. ²⁹Is not my word like as a fire? says the LORD; and like a hammer that breaks the rock in pieces? ³⁰Therefore, behold, I am against the prophets, says the LORD, that steal my words every one from his neighbor. ³¹Behold, I am against the prophets, says the LORD, that use their tongues, and says, He said. ³²Behold, I am against them that prophesy false dreams, says the LORD, and do tell them, and cause my people to err by their lies, and by their lightness; yet I sent them not, nor commanded them: therefore they shall not profit this people at all, says the LORD. ³³And when this people, or the prophet, or a priest, shall ask you, saying, What is the burden of the LORD? you shall then say to them, What burden? I will even forsake you, says the LORD. ³⁴And as for the prophet, and the priest, and the people, that shall say, The burden of the LORD, I will even punish that man and his house. ³⁵Thus shall you say every one to his neighbor, and every one to his brother, What has the LORD answered? and, What has the LORD spoken? ³⁶And the burden of the LORD shall you mention no more: for every man's word shall be his burden; for you have perverted the words of the living God, of the LORD of hosts our God. ³⁷Thus shall you say to the prophet, What has the LORD answered you? and, What has the LORD spoken? ³⁸But since you say, The burden of the LORD; therefore thus says the LORD; Because you say this word, The burden of the LORD, and I have sent to you, saying, You shall not say, The burden of the LORD; ³⁹Therefore, behold, I, even I, will utterly forget you, and I will forsake you, and the city that I gave you and your fathers, and cast you out of my presence: ⁴⁰And I will bring an everlasting reproach on you, and a perpetual shame, which shall not be forgotten.

24 ¹The LORD showed me, and, behold, two baskets of figs were set before the temple of the LORD, after that Nebuchadrezzar king of Babylon had carried away captive Jeconiah the son of Jehoiakim king of Judah, and the princes of Judah, with the carpenters and smiths, from Jerusalem, and had brought them to Babylon. ²One basket had very good figs, even like the figs that are first ripe: and the other basket had very naughty figs, which could not be eaten, they were so bad. ³Then said the LORD to me, What see you, Jeremiah? And I said, Figs; the good figs, very good; and the evil, very evil, that cannot be eaten, they are so evil. ⁴Again the word of the LORD came to me, saying, ⁵Thus says the LORD, the God of Israel; Like these good figs, so will I acknowledge them that are carried away captive of Judah, whom I have sent out of this place into the land of the Chaldeans for their good. ⁶For I will set my eyes on them for good, and I will bring them again to this land: and I will build them, and not pull them down; and I will plant them, and not pluck them up. ⁷And I will give them an heart to know me, that I am the LORD: and they shall be my people, and I will be their God: for they shall return to me with their whole heart. ⁸And as the evil figs, which cannot be eaten, they are so evil; surely thus says the LORD, So will I give Zedekiah the king of Judah, and his princes, and the residue of Jerusalem, that remain in this land, and them that dwell in the land of Egypt: ⁹And I will deliver them to be removed into all the kingdoms of the earth for their hurt, to be a reproach and a proverb, a taunt and a curse, in all places where I shall drive them. ¹⁰And I will send the sword, the famine, and the pestilence, among them, till they be consumed from off the land that I gave to them and to their fathers.

25 ¹The word that came to Jeremiah concerning all the people of Judah in the fourth year of Jehoiakim the son of Josiah king of Judah, that was the first year of Nebuchadrezzar king of Babylon; ²The which Jeremiah the prophet spoke to all the people of Judah, and to all the inhabitants of Jerusalem, saying, ³From the thirteenth year of Josiah the son of Amon king of Judah, even to this day, that is the three and twentieth year, the word of the LORD has come to me, and I have spoken to you, rising early and speaking; but you have not listened. ⁴And the LORD has sent to you all his servants the prophets, rising early and sending them; but you have not listened, nor inclined your ear to hear. ⁵They said, Turn you again now every one from his evil way, and from the evil of your doings, and dwell in the land that the LORD has given to you and to your fathers for ever and ever: ⁶And go not after other gods to serve them, and to worship them, and provoke me not to anger with the works of your hands; and I will do you no hurt. ⁷Yet you have not listened to me, says the LORD; that you might provoke me to anger with the works of your hands to your own hurt. ⁸Therefore thus says the LORD of hosts; Because you have not heard my words, ⁹Behold, I will send and take all the families of the north, says the LORD, and Nebuchadrezzar the king of Babylon, my servant, and will bring them against this land, and against the inhabitants thereof, and against all these nations round about, and will utterly destroy them, and make them an astonishment, and an hissing, and perpetual desolations. ¹⁰Moreover I will take from them the voice of mirth, and the voice of gladness, the voice of the bridegroom, and the voice of the bride, the sound of the millstones, and the light of the candle. ¹¹And this whole land shall be a desolation, and an astonishment; and these nations shall serve the king of Babylon seventy years. ¹²And it shall come to pass, when seventy years are accomplished, that I will punish the king of Babylon, and that nation, says the LORD, for their iniquity, and the land of the Chaldeans, and will make it perpetual desolations. ¹³And I will bring on that land all my words which I have pronounced against it, even all that is written in this book, which Jeremiah has prophesied against all the nations. ¹⁴For many nations and great kings shall serve themselves of them also: and I will recompense them according to their deeds, and according to the works of their own hands. ¹⁵For thus says the LORD God of Israel to me; Take the wine cup of this fury at my hand, and cause all the nations, to whom I send you, to drink it. ¹⁶And they shall drink, and be moved, and be mad, because of the sword that I will send among them. ¹⁷Then took I the cup at the LORD's hand, and made all the nations to drink, to whom the LORD had sent me: ¹⁸To wit, Jerusalem, and the cities of Judah, and the kings thereof, and the princes thereof, to make them a desolation, an astonishment, an hissing, and a curse; as it is this day; ¹⁹Pharaoh king of Egypt, and his servants, and his princes, and all his people; ²⁰And all the mingled people, and all the kings of the land of Uz, and all the kings of the land of the Philistines, and Ashkelon, and Azzah, and Ekron, and the remnant of Ashdod, ²¹Edom, and Moab, and the children of Ammon, ²²And all the kings of Tyrus, and all the kings of Zidon, and the kings of the isles which are beyond the sea, ²³Dedan, and Tema, and Buz, and all that are in the utmost corners, ²⁴And all the kings of Arabia, and all the kings of the mingled people that dwell in the desert, ²⁵And all the kings of Zimri, and all the kings of Elam, and all the kings of the Medes, ²⁶And all the kings of the north, far and near, one with another, and all the kingdoms of the world, which are on the face of the earth: and the king of Sheshach shall drink after them. ²⁷Therefore you shall say to them, Thus says the LORD of hosts, the God of Israel; Drink you, and be drunken, and spew, and fall, and rise no more, because of the sword which I will send among you. ²⁸And it shall be, if they refuse to take the cup at your hand to drink, then shall you say to them, Thus says the LORD of hosts; You shall certainly drink. ²⁹For, see, I begin to bring evil on the city which is called by my name, and should you be utterly unpunished? You shall not be unpunished: for I will call for a sword on all the inhabitants of the earth, says the LORD of hosts. ³⁰Therefore prophesy you against them all these words, and say to them, The LORD shall roar from on high, and utter his voice from his holy habitation; he shall mightily roar on his habitation; he shall give a shout, as they that tread the grapes, against all the inhabitants of the earth. ³¹A noise shall come even to the ends of the earth; for the LORD has a controversy with the nations, he will plead with all flesh; he will give them that are wicked to the sword, says the LORD. ³²Thus says the LORD of hosts, Behold, evil shall go forth from nation to nation, and a great whirlwind shall be raised up from the coasts of the earth. ³³And the slain of the LORD shall be at that day from one end of the earth even to the other end of the earth: they shall not be lamented, neither gathered, nor buried; they shall be dung on the ground. ³⁴Howl, you shepherds, and cry; and wallow yourselves in the ashes, you principal of the flock: for the days of your slaughter and of your dispersions are accomplished; and you shall fall like a pleasant vessel. ³⁵And the shepherds shall have no way to flee, nor the principal of the flock to escape. ³⁶A voice of the cry of the shepherds, and an howling of the principal of the flock, shall be heard: for the LORD has spoiled their pasture. ³⁷And the peaceable habitations are cut down because of the fierce anger of the LORD. ³⁸He has forsaken his covert, as the lion: for their land is desolate because of the fierceness of the oppressor, and because of his fierce anger.

26 ¹In the beginning of the reign of Jehoiakim the son of Josiah king of Judah came this word from the LORD, saying, ²Thus says the LORD; Stand in the court of the LORD's house, and speak to all the cities of Judah, which come to worship in the LORD's house, all the words that I command you to speak to them; diminish not a word: ³If so be they will listen, and turn every man from his evil way, that I may repent me of the evil, which I purpose to do to them because of the evil of their doings. ⁴And you shall say to them, Thus says the LORD; If you will not listen to me, to walk in my law, which I have set before you, ⁵To listen to the words of my servants the prophets, whom I sent to you, both rising up early, and sending them, but you have not listened; ⁶Then will I make this house like Shiloh, and will make this city a curse to all the nations of the earth. ⁷So the priests and the prophets and all the people heard Jeremiah speaking these words in the house of the LORD. ⁸Now it came to pass, when Jeremiah had made an end of speaking all that the LORD had commanded him to speak to all the people, that the priests and the prophets and all the people took him, saying, You shall surely die. ⁹Why have you prophesied in the name of the LORD, saying, This house shall be like Shiloh, and this city shall be desolate without an inhabitant? And all the people were gathered against Jeremiah in the house of the LORD. ¹⁰When the princes of Judah heard these things, then they came up from the king's house to the house of the LORD, and sat down in the entry of the new gate of the LORD's house. ¹¹Then spoke the priests and the prophets to the princes and to all the people, saying, This man is worthy to die; for he has prophesied against this city, as you have heard with your ears. ¹²Then spoke Jeremiah to all the princes and to all the people, saying, The LORD sent me to prophesy against this house and against this city all the words that you have heard. ¹³Therefore now amend your ways and your doings, and obey the voice of the LORD your God; and the LORD will repent him of the evil that he has pronounced against you. ¹⁴As for me, behold, I am in your hand: do with me as seems good and meet to you. ¹⁵But know you for certain, that if you put me to death, you shall surely bring innocent blood on yourselves, and on this city, and on the inhabitants thereof: for of a truth the LORD has sent me to you to speak all these words in your ears. ¹⁶Then said the princes and all the people to the priests and to the prophets; This man is not worthy to die: for he has spoken to us in the name of the LORD our God. ¹⁷Then rose up certain of the elders of the land, and spoke to all the assembly of the people, saying, ¹⁸Micah the Morasthite prophesied in the days of Hezekiah king of Judah, and spoke to all the people of Judah, saying, Thus says the LORD of hosts; Zion shall be plowed like a field, and Jerusalem shall become heaps, and the mountain of the house as the high places of a forest. ¹⁹Did Hezekiah king of Judah and all Judah put him at all to death? did he not fear the LORD, and sought the LORD, and the LORD repented him of the evil which he had pronounced against them? Thus might we procure great evil against our souls. ²⁰And there was also a man that prophesied in the name of the LORD, Urijah the son of Shemaiah of Kirjathjearim, who prophesied against this city and against this land according to all the words of Jeremiah. ²¹And when Jehoiakim the king, with all his mighty men, and all the princes, heard his words, the king sought to put him to death: but when Urijah heard it, he was afraid, and fled, and went into Egypt; ²²And Jehoiakim the king sent men into Egypt, namely, Elnathan the son of Achbor, and certain men with him into Egypt. ²³And they fetched forth Urijah out of Egypt, and brought him to Jehoiakim the king; who slew him with the sword, and cast his dead body into the graves of the common people. ²⁴Nevertheless the hand of Ahikam the son of Shaphan was with Jeremiah, that they should not give him into the hand of the people to put him to death.

27 ¹In the beginning of the reign of Jehoiakim the son of Josiah king of Judah came this word to Jeremiah from the LORD, saying, ²Thus says the LORD to me; Make you bonds and yokes, and put them on your neck, ³And send them to the king of Edom, and to the king of Moab, and to the king of the Ammonites, and to the king of Tyrus, and to the king of Zidon, by the hand of the messengers which come to Jerusalem to Zedekiah king of Judah; ⁴And command them to say to their masters, Thus says the LORD of hosts, the God of Israel; Thus shall you say to your masters; ⁵I have made the earth, the man and the beast that are on the ground, by my great power and by my outstretched arm, and have given it to whom it seemed meet to me. ⁶And now have I given all these lands into the hand of Nebuchadnezzar the king of Babylon, my servant; and the beasts of the field have I given him also to serve him. ⁷And all nations shall serve him, and his son, and his son's son, until the very time of his land come: and then many nations and great kings shall serve themselves of him. ⁸And it shall come to pass, that the nation and kingdom which will not serve the same Nebuchadnezzar the king of Babylon, and that will not put their neck under the yoke of the king of Babylon, that nation will I punish, says the LORD, with the sword, and with the famine, and with the pestilence, until I have consumed them by his hand. ⁹Therefore listen not you to your prophets, nor to your diviners, nor to your dreamers, nor to your enchanters, nor to your sorcerers, which speak to you, saying, You shall not serve the king of Babylon: ¹⁰For they prophesy a lie to you, to remove you far from your land; and that I should drive you out, and you should perish. ¹¹But the nations that bring their neck under the yoke of the king of Babylon, and serve him, those will I let remain still in their own land, says the LORD; and they shall till it, and dwell therein. ¹²I spoke also to Zedekiah king of Judah according to all these words, saying, Bring your necks under the yoke of the king of Babylon, and serve him and his people, and live. ¹³Why will you die, you and your people, by the sword, by the famine, and by the pestilence, as the LORD has spoken against the nation that will not serve the king of Babylon? ¹⁴Therefore listen not to the words of the prophets that speak to you, saying, You shall not serve the king of Babylon: for they prophesy a lie to you. ¹⁵For I have not sent them, says the LORD, yet they prophesy a lie in my name; that I might drive you out, and that you might perish, you, and the prophets that prophesy to you. ¹⁶Also I spoke to the priests and to all this people, saying, Thus says the LORD; Listen not to the words of your prophets that prophesy to you, saying, Behold, the vessels of the LORD's house shall now shortly be brought again from Babylon: for they prophesy a lie to you. ¹⁷Listen not to them; serve the king of Babylon, and live: why should this city be laid waste? ¹⁸But if they be prophets, and if the word of the LORD be with them, let them now make intercession to the LORD of hosts, that the vessels which are left in the house of the LORD, and in the house of the king of Judah, and at Jerusalem, go not to Babylon. ¹⁹For thus says the LORD of hosts concerning the pillars, and concerning the sea, and concerning the bases, and concerning the residue of the vessels that remain in this city. ²⁰Which Nebuchadnezzar king of Babylon took not, when he carried away captive Jeconiah the son of Jehoiakim king of Judah from Jerusalem to Babylon, and all the nobles of Judah and Jerusalem; ²¹Yes, thus says the LORD of hosts, the God of Israel, concerning the vessels that remain in the house of the LORD, and in the house of the king of Judah and of Jerusalem; ²²They shall be carried to Babylon, and there shall they be until the day that I visit them, says the LORD; then will I bring them up, and restore them to this place.

28 ¹And it came to pass the same year, in the beginning of the reign of Zedekiah king of Judah, in the fourth year, and in the fifth month, that Hananiah the son of Azur the prophet, which was of Gibeon, spoke to me in the house of the LORD, in the presence of the priests and of all the people, saying, ²Thus speaks the LORD of hosts, the God of Israel, saying, I have broken the yoke of the king of Babylon. ³Within two full years will I bring again into this place all the vessels of the LORD's house, that Nebuchadnezzar king of Babylon took away from this place, and carried them to Babylon: ⁴And I will bring again to this place Jeconiah the son of Jehoiakim king of Judah, with all the captives of Judah, that went into Babylon, says the LORD: for I will break the yoke of the king of Babylon. ⁵Then the prophet Jeremiah said to the prophet Hananiah in the presence of the priests, and in the presence of all the people that stood in the house of the LORD, ⁶Even the prophet Jeremiah said, Amen: the LORD do so: the LORD perform your words which you have prophesied, to bring again the vessels of the LORD's house, and all that is carried away captive, from Babylon into this place. ⁷Nevertheless hear you now this word that I speak in your ears, and in the ears of all the people; ⁸The prophets that have been before me and before you of old prophesied both against many countries, and against great kingdoms, of war, and of evil, and of pestilence. ⁹The prophet which prophesies of peace, when the word of the prophet shall come to pass, then shall the prophet be known, that the LORD has truly sent him. ¹⁰Then Hananiah the prophet took the yoke from off the prophet Jeremiah's neck, and broke it. ¹¹And Hananiah spoke in the presence of all the people, saying, Thus says the LORD; Even so will I break the yoke of Nebuchadnezzar king of Babylon from the neck of all nations within the space of two full years. And the prophet Jeremiah went his way. ¹²Then the word of the LORD came to Jeremiah the prophet, after that Hananiah the prophet had broken the yoke from off the neck of the prophet Jeremiah, saying, ¹³Go and tell Hananiah, saying, Thus says the LORD; You have broken the yokes of wood; but you shall make for them yokes of iron. ¹⁴For thus says the LORD of hosts, the God of Israel; I have put a yoke of iron on the neck of all these nations, that they may serve Nebuchadnezzar king of Babylon; and they shall serve him: and I have given him the beasts of the field also. ¹⁵Then said the prophet Jeremiah to Hananiah the prophet, Hear now, Hananiah; The LORD has not sent you; but you make this people to trust in a lie. ¹⁶Therefore thus says the LORD; Behold, I will cast you from off the face of the earth: this year you shall die, because you have taught rebellion against the LORD. ¹⁷So Hananiah the prophet died the same year in the seventh month.

29 ¹Now these are the words of the letter that Jeremiah the prophet sent from Jerusalem to the residue of the elders which were carried away captives, and to the priests, and to the prophets, and to all the people whom Nebuchadnezzar had carried away captive from Jerusalem to Babylon; ²(After that Jeconiah the king, and the queen, and the eunuchs, the princes of Judah and Jerusalem, and the carpenters, and the smiths, were departed from Jerusalem;) ³By the hand of Elasah the son of Shaphan, and Gemariah the son of Hilkiah, (whom Zedekiah king of Judah sent to Babylon to Nebuchadnezzar king of Babylon) saying, ⁴Thus says the LORD of hosts, the God of Israel, to all that are carried away captives, whom I have caused to be carried away from Jerusalem to Babylon; ⁵Build you houses, and dwell in them; and plant gardens, and eat the fruit of them; ⁶Take you wives, and beget sons and daughters; and take wives for your sons, and give your daughters to husbands, that they may bear sons and daughters; that you may be increased there, and not diminished. ⁷And seek the peace of the city where I have caused you to be carried away captives, and pray to the LORD for it: for in the peace thereof shall you have peace. ⁸For thus says the LORD of hosts, the God of Israel; Let not your prophets and your diviners, that be in the middle of you, deceive you, neither listen to your dreams which you cause to be dreamed. ⁹For they prophesy falsely to you in my name: I have not sent them, says the LORD. ¹⁰For thus says the LORD, That after seventy years be accomplished at Babylon I will visit you, and perform my good word toward you, in causing you to return to this place. ¹¹For I know the thoughts that I think toward you, says the LORD, thoughts of peace, and not of evil, to give you an expected end. ¹²Then shall you call on me, and you shall go and pray to me, and I will listen to you. ¹³And you shall seek me, and find me, when you shall search for me with all your heart. ¹⁴And I will be found of you, said the LORD: and I will turn away your captivity, and I will gather you from all the nations, and from all the places where I have driven you, says the LORD; and I will bring you again into the place from where I caused you to be carried away captive. ¹⁵Because you have said, The LORD has raised us up prophets in Babylon; ¹⁶Know that thus says the LORD of the king that sits on the throne of David, and of all the people that dwells in this city, and of your brothers that are not gone forth with you into captivity; ¹⁷Thus says the LORD of hosts; Behold, I will send on them the sword, the famine, and the pestilence, and will make them like vile figs, that cannot be eaten, they are so evil. ¹⁸And I will persecute them with the sword, with the famine, and with the pestilence, and will deliver them to be removed to all the kingdoms of the earth, to be a curse, and an astonishment, and an hissing, and a reproach, among all the nations where I have driven them: ¹⁹Because they have not listened to my words, says the LORD, which I sent to them by my servants the prophets, rising up early and sending them; but you would not hear, said the LORD. ²⁰Hear you therefore the word of the LORD, all you of the captivity, whom I have sent from Jerusalem to Babylon: ²¹Thus says the LORD of hosts, the God of Israel, of Ahab the son of Kolaiah, and of Zedekiah the son of Maaseiah, which prophesy a lie to you in my name; Behold, I will deliver them into the hand of Nebuchadrezzar king of Babylon; and he shall slay them before your eyes; ²²And of them shall be taken up a curse by all the captivity of Judah which are in Babylon, saying, The LORD make you like Zedekiah and like Ahab, whom the king of Babylon roasted in the fire; ²³Because they have committed villainy in Israel, and have committed adultery with their neighbors' wives, and have spoken lying words in my name, which I have not commanded them; even I know, and am a witness, says the LORD. ²⁴Thus shall you also speak to Shemaiah the Nehelamite, saying, ²⁵Thus speaks the LORD of hosts, the God of Israel, saying, Because you have sent letters in your name to all the people that are at Jerusalem, and to Zephaniah the son of Maaseiah the priest, and to all the priests, saying, ²⁶The LORD has made you priest in the stead of Jehoiada the priest, that you should be officers in the house of the LORD, for every man that is mad, and makes himself a prophet, that you should put him in prison, and in the stocks. ²⁷Now therefore why have you not reproved Jeremiah of Anathoth, which makes himself a prophet to you? ²⁸For therefore he sent to us in Babylon, saying, This captivity is long: build you houses, and dwell in them; and plant gardens, and eat the fruit of them. ²⁹And Zephaniah the priest read this letter in the ears of Jeremiah the prophet. ³⁰Then came the word of the LORD to Jeremiah, saying, ³¹Send to all them of the captivity, saying, Thus says the LORD concerning Shemaiah the Nehelamite; Because that Shemaiah has prophesied to you, and I sent him not, and he caused you to trust in a lie; ³²Therefore thus says the LORD; Behold, I will punish Shemaiah the Nehelamite, and his seed: he shall not have a man to dwell among this people; neither shall he behold the good that I will do for my people, said the LORD; because he has taught rebellion against the LORD.

30

¹The word that came to Jeremiah from the LORD, saying, ²Thus speaks the LORD God of Israel, saying, Write you all the words that I have spoken to you in a book. ³For, see, the days come, says the LORD, that I will bring again the captivity of my people Israel and Judah, said the LORD: and I will cause them to return to the land that I gave to their fathers, and they shall possess it. ⁴And these are the words that the LORD spoke concerning Israel and concerning Judah. ⁵For thus says the LORD; We have heard a voice of trembling, of fear, and not of peace. ⁶Ask you now, and see whether a man does travail with child? why do I see every man with his hands on his loins, as a woman in travail, and all faces are turned into paleness? ⁷Alas! for that day is great, so that none is like it: it is even the time of Jacob's trouble, but he shall be saved out of it. ⁸For it shall come to pass in that day, says the LORD of hosts, that I will break his yoke from off your neck, and will burst your bonds, and strangers shall no more serve themselves of him: ⁹But they shall serve the LORD their God, and David their king, whom I will raise up to them. ¹⁰Therefore fear you not, O my servant Jacob, says the LORD; neither be dismayed, O Israel: for, see, I will save you from afar, and your seed from the land of their captivity; and Jacob shall return, and shall be in rest, and be quiet, and none shall make him afraid. ¹¹For I am with you, says the LORD, to save you: though I make a full end of all nations where I have scattered you, yet I will not make a full end of you: but I will correct you in measure, and will not leave you altogether unpunished. ¹²For thus says the LORD, Your bruise is incurable, and your wound is grievous. ¹³There is none to plead your cause, that you may be bound up: you have no healing medicines. ¹⁴All your lovers have forgotten you; they seek you not; for I have wounded you with the wound of an enemy, with the chastisement of a cruel one, for the multitude of your iniquity; because your sins were increased. ¹⁵Why cry you for your affliction? your sorrow is incurable for the multitude of your iniquity: because your sins were increased, I have done these things to you. ¹⁶Therefore all they that devour you shall be devoured; and all your adversaries, every one of them, shall go into captivity; and they that spoil you shall be a spoil, and all that prey on you will I give for a prey. ¹⁷For I will restore health to you, and I will heal you of your wounds, says the LORD; because they called you an Outcast, saying, This is Zion, whom no man seeks after. ¹⁸Thus says the LORD; Behold, I will bring again the captivity of Jacob's tents, and have mercy on his dwelling places; and the city shall be built on her own heap, and the palace shall remain after the manner thereof. ¹⁹And out of them shall proceed thanksgiving and the voice of them that make merry: and I will multiply them, and they shall not be few; I will also glorify them, and they shall not be small. ²⁰Their children also shall be as aforetime, and their congregation shall be established before me, and I will punish all that oppress them. ²¹And their nobles shall be of themselves, and their governor shall proceed from the middle of them; and I will cause him to draw near, and he shall approach to me: for who is this that engaged his heart to approach to me? says the LORD. ²²And you shall be my people, and I will be your God. ²³Behold, the whirlwind of the LORD goes forth with fury, a continuing whirlwind: it shall fall with pain on the head of the wicked. ²⁴The fierce anger of the LORD shall not return, until he has done it, and

until he have performed the intents of his heart: in the latter days you shall consider it.

31

¹At the same time, says the LORD, will I be the God of all the families of Israel, and they shall be my people. ²Thus says the LORD, The people which were left of the sword found grace in the wilderness; even Israel, when I went to cause him to rest. ³The LORD has appeared of old to me, saying, Yes, I have loved you with an everlasting love: therefore with loving kindness have I drawn you. ⁴Again I will build you, and you shall be built, O virgin of Israel: you shall again be adorned with your tabrets, and shall go forth in the dances of them that make merry. ⁵You shall yet plant vines on the mountains of Samaria: the planters shall plant, and shall eat them as common things. ⁶For there shall be a day, that the watchmen on the mount Ephraim shall cry, Arise you, and let us go up to Zion to the LORD our God. ⁷For thus says the LORD; Sing with gladness for Jacob, and shout among the chief of the nations: publish you, praise you, and say, O LORD, save your people, the remnant of Israel. ⁸Behold, I will bring them from the north country, and gather them from the coasts of the earth, and with them the blind and the lame, the woman with child and her that travails with child together: a great company shall return thither. ⁹They shall come with weeping, and with supplications will I lead them: I will cause them to walk by the rivers of waters in a straight way, wherein they shall not stumble: for I am a father to Israel, and Ephraim is my firstborn. ¹⁰Hear the word of the LORD, O you nations, and declare it in the isles afar off, and say, He that scattered Israel will gather him, and keep him, as a shepherd does his flock. ¹¹For the LORD has redeemed Jacob, and ransomed him from the hand of him that was stronger than he. ¹²Therefore they shall come and sing in the height of Zion, and shall flow together to the goodness of the LORD, for wheat, and for wine, and for oil, and for the young of the flock and of the herd: and their soul shall be as a watered garden; and they shall not sorrow any more at all. ¹³Then shall the virgin rejoice in the dance, both young men and old together: for I will turn their mourning into joy, and will comfort them, and make them rejoice from their sorrow. ¹⁴And I will satiate the soul of the priests with fatness, and my people shall be satisfied with my goodness, says the LORD. ¹⁵Thus says the LORD; A voice was heard in Ramah, lamentation, and bitter weeping; Rahel weeping for her children refused to be comforted for her children, because they were not. ¹⁶Thus says the LORD; Refrain your voice from weeping, and your eyes from tears: for your work shall be rewarded, said the LORD; and they shall come again from the land of the enemy. ¹⁷And there is hope in your end, says the LORD, that your children shall come again to their own border. ¹⁸I have surely heard Ephraim bemoaning himself thus; You have chastised me, and I was chastised, as a bullock unaccustomed to the yoke: turn you me, and I shall be turned; for you are the LORD my God. ¹⁹Surely after that I was turned, I repented; and after that I was instructed, I smote on my thigh: I was ashamed, yes, even confounded, because I did bear the reproach of my youth. ²⁰Is Ephraim my dear son? is he a pleasant child? for since I spoke against him, I do earnestly remember him still: therefore my bowels are troubled for him; I will surely have mercy on him, says the LORD. ²¹Set you up markers, make you high heaps: set your heart toward the highway, even the way which you went: turn again, O virgin of Israel, turn again to these your cities. ²²How long will you go about, O you backsliding daughter? for the LORD has created a new thing in the earth, A woman shall compass a man. ²³Thus says the LORD of hosts, the God of Israel; As yet they shall use this speech in the land of Judah and in the cities thereof, when I shall bring again their captivity; The LORD bless you, O habitation of justice, and mountain of holiness. ²⁴And there shall dwell in Judah itself, and in all the cities thereof together, farmers, and they that go forth with flocks. ²⁵For I have satiated the weary soul, and I have replenished every sorrowful soul. ²⁶On this I awaked, and beheld; and my sleep was sweet to me. ²⁷Behold, the days come, says the LORD, that I will sow the house of Israel and the house of Judah with the seed of man, and with the seed of beast. ²⁸And it shall come to pass, that like as I have watched over them, to pluck up, and to break down, and to throw down, and to destroy, and to afflict; so will I watch over them, to build, and to plant, says the LORD. ²⁹In those days they shall say no more, The fathers have eaten a sour grape, and the children's teeth are set on edge. ³⁰But every one shall die for his own iniquity: every man that eats the sour grape, his teeth shall be set on edge. ³¹Behold, the days come, says the LORD, that I will make a new covenant with the house of Israel, and with the house of Judah: ³²Not according to the covenant that I made with their fathers in the day that I took them by the hand to bring them out of the land of Egypt; which my covenant they broke, although I was an husband to them, says the LORD: ³³But this shall be the covenant that I will make with the house of Israel; After those days, says the LORD, I will put my law in their inward parts, and write it in their hearts; and will be their God, and they shall be my people. ³⁴And they shall teach no more every man his neighbor, and every man his brother, saying, Know the LORD: for they shall all know me, from the least of them to the greatest of them, says the LORD: for I will forgive their iniquity, and I will remember their sin no more. ³⁵Thus says the LORD, which gives the sun for a light by day, and the ordinances of the moon and of the stars for a light by night, which divides the sea when the waves thereof roar; The LORD of hosts is his name: ³⁶If those ordinances depart from before me, says the LORD, then the seed of Israel also shall cease from being a nation before me for ever. ³⁷Thus says the LORD; If heaven above can be measured, and the foundations of the earth searched out beneath, I will also cast off all the seed of Israel for all that they have done, says the LORD. ³⁸Behold, the days come, says the LORD, that the city shall be built to the LORD from the tower of Hananeel to the gate of the corner. ³⁹And the measuring line shall yet go forth over against it on the hill Gareb, and shall compass about to Goath. ⁴⁰And the whole valley of the dead bodies, and of the ashes, and all the fields to the brook of Kidron, to the corner of the horse gate toward the east, shall be holy to the LORD; it shall not be plucked up, nor thrown down any more for ever.

32

¹The word that came to Jeremiah from the LORD in the tenth year of Zedekiah king of Judah, which was the eighteenth year of Nebuchadrezzar. ²For then the king of

Babylon's army besieged Jerusalem: and Jeremiah the prophet was shut up in the court of the prison, which was in the king of Judah's house. ³For Zedekiah king of Judah had shut him up, saying, Why do you prophesy, and say, Thus says the LORD, Behold, I will give this city into the hand of the king of Babylon, and he shall take it; ⁴And Zedekiah king of Judah shall not escape out of the hand of the Chaldeans, but shall surely be delivered into the hand of the king of Babylon, and shall speak with him mouth to mouth, and his eyes shall behold his eyes; ⁵And he shall lead Zedekiah to Babylon, and there shall he be until I visit him, says the LORD: though you fight with the Chaldeans, you shall not prosper. ⁶And Jeremiah said, The word of the LORD came to me, saying, ⁷Behold, Hanameel the son of Shallum your uncle shall come to you saying, Buy you my field that is in Anathoth: for the right of redemption is your to buy it. ⁸So Hanameel my uncle's son came to me in the court of the prison according to the word of the LORD, and said to me, Buy my field, I pray you, that is in Anathoth, which is in the country of Benjamin: for the right of inheritance is yours, and the redemption is yours; buy it for yourself. Then I knew that this was the word of the LORD. ⁹And I bought the field of Hanameel my uncle's son, that was in Anathoth, and weighed him the money, even seventeen shekels of silver. ¹⁰And I subscribed the evidence, and sealed it, and took witnesses, and weighed him the money in the balances. ¹¹So I took the evidence of the purchase, both that which was sealed according to the law and custom, and that which was open: ¹²And I gave the evidence of the purchase to Baruch the son of Neriah, the son of Maaseiah, in the sight of Hanameel my uncle's son, and in the presence of the witnesses that subscribed the book of the purchase, before all the Jews that sat in the court of the prison. ¹³And I charged Baruch before them, saying, ¹⁴Thus says the LORD of hosts, the God of Israel; Take these evidences, this evidence of the purchase, both which is sealed, and this evidence which is open; and put them in an earthen vessel, that they may continue many days. ¹⁵For thus says the LORD of hosts, the God of Israel; Houses and fields and vineyards shall be possessed again in this land. ¹⁶Now when I had delivered the evidence of the purchase to Baruch the son of Neriah, I prayed to the LORD, saying, ¹⁷Ah Lord GOD! behold, you have made the heaven and the earth by your great power and stretched out arm, and there is nothing too hard for you: ¹⁸You show loving kindness to thousands, and recompense the iniquity of the fathers into the bosom of their children after them: the Great, the Mighty God, the LORD of hosts, is his name, ¹⁹Great in counsel, and mighty in work: for your eyes are open on all the ways of the sons of men: to give every one according to his ways, and according to the fruit of his doings: ²⁰Which have set signs and wonders in the land of Egypt, even to this day, and in Israel, and among other men; and have made you a name, as at this day; ²¹And have brought forth your people Israel out of the land of Egypt with signs, and with wonders, and with a strong hand, and with a stretched out arm, and with great terror; ²²And have given them this land, which you did swear to their fathers to give them, a land flowing with milk and honey; ²³And they came in, and possessed it; but they obeyed not your voice, neither walked in your law; they have done nothing of all that you commanded them to do: therefore you have caused all this evil to come on them: ²⁴Behold the mounts, they are come to the city to take it; and the city is given into the hand of the Chaldeans, that fight against it, because of the sword, and of the famine, and of the pestilence: and what you have spoken is come to pass; and, behold, you see it. ²⁵And you have said to me, O Lord GOD, Buy you the field for money, and take witnesses; for the city is given into the hand of the Chaldeans. ²⁶Then came the word of the LORD to Jeremiah, saying, ²⁷Behold, I am the LORD, the God of all flesh: is there any thing too hard for me? ²⁸Therefore thus says the LORD; Behold, I will give this city into the hand of the Chaldeans, and into the hand of Nebuchadrezzar king of Babylon, and he shall take it: ²⁹And the Chaldeans, that fight against this city, shall come and set fire on this city, and burn it with the houses, on whose roofs they have offered incense to Baal, and poured out drink offerings to other gods, to provoke me to anger. ³⁰For the children of Israel and the children of Judah have only done evil before me from their youth: for the children of Israel have only provoked me to anger with the work of their hands, says the LORD. ³¹For this city has been to me as a provocation of my anger and of my fury from the day that they built it even to this day; that I should remove it from before my face, ³²Because of all the evil of the children of Israel and of the children of Judah, which they have done to provoke me to anger, they, their kings, their princes, their priests, and their prophets, and the men of Judah, and the inhabitants of Jerusalem. ³³And they have turned to me the back, and not the face: though I taught them, rising up early and teaching them, yet they have not listened to receive instruction. ³⁴But they set their abominations in the house, which is called by my name, to defile it. ³⁵And they built the high places of Baal, which are in the valley of the son of Hinnom, to cause their sons and their daughters to pass through the fire to Molech; which I commanded them not, neither came it into my mind, that they should do this abomination, to cause Judah to sin. ³⁶And now therefore thus says the LORD, the God of Israel, concerning this city, whereof you say, It shall be delivered into the hand of the king of Babylon by the sword, and by the famine, and by the pestilence; ³⁷Behold, I will gather them out of all countries, where I have driven them in my anger, and in my fury, and in great wrath; and I will bring them again to this place, and I will cause them to dwell safely: ³⁸And they shall be my people, and I will be their God: ³⁹And I will give them one heart, and one way, that they may fear me for ever, for the good of them, and of their children after them: ⁴⁰And I will make an everlasting covenant with them, that I will not turn away from them, to do them good; but I will put my fear in their hearts, that they shall not depart from me. ⁴¹Yes, I will rejoice over them to do them good, and I will plant them in this land assuredly with my whole heart and with my whole soul. ⁴²For thus says the LORD; Like as I have brought all this great evil on this people, so will I bring on them all the good that I have promised them. ⁴³And fields shall be bought in this land, whereof you say, It is desolate without man or beast; it is given into the hand of the Chaldeans. ⁴⁴Men shall buy fields for money, and subscribe evidences, and seal them, and take witnesses in the land of Benjamin, and in the places about Jerusalem, and in the cities of Judah, and in the cities of the mountains, and in the cities of the valley, and in the cities of the south: for I will cause their captivity to return, says the LORD.

33

¹Moreover the word of the LORD came to Jeremiah the second time, while he was yet shut up in the court of the prison, saying, ²Thus says the LORD the maker thereof, the LORD that formed it, to establish it; the LORD is his name; ³Call to me, and I will answer you, and show you great and mighty things, which you know not. ⁴For thus says the LORD, the God of Israel, concerning the houses of this city, and concerning the houses of the kings of Judah, which are thrown down by the mounts, and by the sword; ⁵They come to fight with the Chaldeans, but it is to fill them with the dead bodies of men, whom I have slain in my anger and in my fury, and for all whose wickedness I have hid my face from this city. ⁶Behold, I will bring it health and cure, and I will cure them, and will reveal to them the abundance of peace and truth. ⁷And I will cause the captivity of Judah and the captivity of Israel to return, and will build them, as at the first. ⁸And I will cleanse them from all their iniquity, whereby they have sinned against me; and I will pardon all their iniquities, whereby they have sinned, and whereby they have transgressed against me. ⁹And it shall be to me a name of joy, a praise and an honor before all the nations of the earth, which shall hear all the good that I do to them: and they shall fear and tremble for all the goodness and for all the prosperity that I procure to it. ¹⁰Thus says the LORD; Again there shall be heard in this place, which you say shall be desolate without man and without beast, even in the cities of Judah, and in the streets of Jerusalem, that are desolate, without man, and without inhabitant, and without beast, ¹¹The voice of joy, and the voice of gladness, the voice of the bridegroom, and the voice of the bride, the voice of them that shall say, Praise the LORD of hosts: for the LORD is good; for his mercy endures for ever: and of them that shall bring the sacrifice of praise into the house of the LORD. For I will cause to return the captivity of the land, as at the first, says the LORD. ¹²Thus says the LORD of hosts; Again in this place, which is desolate without man and without beast, and in all the cities thereof, shall be an habitation of shepherds causing their flocks to lie down. ¹³In the cities of the mountains, in the cities of the vale, and in the cities of the south, and in the land of Benjamin, and in the places about Jerusalem, and in the cities of Judah, shall the flocks pass again under the hands of him that tells them, says the LORD. ¹⁴Behold, the days come, says the LORD, that I will perform that good thing which I have promised to the house of Israel and to the house of Judah. ¹⁵In those days, and at that time, will I cause the Branch of righteousness to grow up to David; and he shall execute judgment and righteousness in the land. ¹⁶In those days shall Judah be saved, and Jerusalem shall dwell safely: and this is the name with which she shall be called, The LORD our righteousness. ¹⁷For thus says the LORD; David shall never want a man to sit on the throne of the house of Israel; ¹⁸Neither shall the priests the Levites want a man before me to offer burnt offerings, and to kindle meat offerings, and to do sacrifice continually. ¹⁹And the word of the LORD came to Jeremiah, saying, ²⁰Thus says the LORD; If you can break my covenant of the day, and my covenant of the night, and that there should not be day and night in their season; ²¹Then may also my covenant be broken with David my servant, that he should not have a son to reign on his throne; and with the Levites the priests, my ministers. ²²As the host of heaven cannot be numbered, neither the sand of the sea measured: so will I multiply the seed of David my servant, and the Levites that minister to me. ²³Moreover the word of the LORD came to Jeremiah, saying, ²⁴Consider you not what this people have spoken, saying, The two families which the LORD has chosen, he has even cast them off? thus they have despised my people, that they should be no more a nation before them. ²⁵Thus says the LORD; If my covenant be not with day and night, and if I have not appointed the ordinances of heaven and earth; ²⁶Then will I cast away the seed of Jacob and David my servant, so that I will not take any of his seed to be rulers over the seed of Abraham, Isaac, and Jacob: for I will cause their captivity to return, and have mercy on them.

34

¹The word which came to Jeremiah from the LORD, when Nebuchadnezzar king of Babylon, and all his army, and all the kingdoms of the earth of his dominion, and all the people, fought against Jerusalem, and against all the cities thereof, saying, ²Thus says the LORD, the God of Israel; Go and speak to Zedekiah king of Judah, and tell him, Thus said the LORD; Behold, I will give this city into the hand of the king of Babylon, and he shall burn it with fire: ³And you shall not escape out of his hand, but shall surely be taken, and delivered into his hand; and your eyes shall behold the eyes of the king of Babylon, and he shall speak with you mouth to mouth, and you shall go to Babylon. ⁴Yet hear the word of the LORD, O Zedekiah king of Judah; Thus says the LORD of you, You shall not die by the sword: ⁵But you shall die in peace: and with the burnings of your fathers, the former kings which were before you, so shall they burn odors for you; and they will lament you, saying, Ah lord! for I have pronounced the word, says the LORD. ⁶Then Jeremiah the prophet spoke all these words to Zedekiah king of Judah in Jerusalem, ⁷When the king of Babylon's army fought against Jerusalem, and against all the cities of Judah that were left, against Lachish, and against Azekah: for these defended cities remained of the cities of Judah. ⁸This is the word that came to Jeremiah from the LORD, after that the king Zedekiah had made a covenant with all the people which were at Jerusalem, to proclaim liberty to them; ⁹That every man should let his manservant, and every man his maidservant, being an Hebrew or an Hebrewess, go free; that none should serve himself of them, to wit, of a Jew his brother. ¹⁰Now when all the princes, and all the people, which had entered into the covenant, heard that every one should let his manservant, and every one his maidservant, go free, that none should serve themselves of them any more, then they obeyed, and let them go. ¹¹But afterward they turned, and caused the servants and the handmaids, whom they had let go free, to return, and brought them into subjection for servants and for handmaids. ¹²Therefore the word of the LORD came to Jeremiah from the LORD, saying, ¹³Thus says the LORD, the God of Israel; I made a covenant with your fathers in the day that I brought them forth out of the land of Egypt, out of

the house of slaves, saying, ¹⁴At the end of seven years let you go every man his brother an Hebrew, which has been sold to you; and when he has served you six years, you shall let him go free from you: but your fathers listened not to me, neither inclined their ear. ¹⁵And you were now turned, and had done right in my sight, in proclaiming liberty every man to his neighbor; and you had made a covenant before me in the house which is called by my name: ¹⁶But you turned and polluted my name, and caused every man his servant, and every man his handmaid, whom he had set at liberty at their pleasure, to return, and brought them into subjection, to be to you for servants and for handmaids. ¹⁷Therefore thus says the LORD; You have not listened to me, in proclaiming liberty, every one to his brother, and every man to his neighbor: behold, I proclaim a liberty for you, said the LORD, to the sword, to the pestilence, and to the famine; and I will make you to be removed into all the kingdoms of the earth. ¹⁸And I will give the men that have transgressed my covenant, which have not performed the words of the covenant which they had made before me, when they cut the calf in two, and passed between the parts thereof, ¹⁹The princes of Judah, and the princes of Jerusalem, the eunuchs, and the priests, and all the people of the land, which passed between the parts of the calf; ²⁰I will even give them into the hand of their enemies, and into the hand of them that seek their life: and their dead bodies shall be for meat to the fowls of the heaven, and to the beasts of the earth. ²¹And Zedekiah king of Judah and his princes will I give into the hand of their enemies, and into the hand of them that seek their life, and into the hand of the king of Babylon's army, which are gone up from you. ²²Behold, I will command, says the LORD, and cause them to return to this city; and they shall fight against it, and take it, and burn it with fire: and I will make the cities of Judah a desolation without an inhabitant.

35 ¹The word which came to Jeremiah from the LORD in the days of Jehoiakim the son of Josiah king of Judah, saying, ²Go to the house of the Rechabites, and speak to them, and bring them into the house of the LORD, into one of the chambers, and give them wine to drink. ³Then I took Jaazaniah the son of Jeremiah, the son of Habaziniah, and his brothers, and all his sons, and the whole house of the Rechabites; ⁴And I brought them into the house of the LORD, into the chamber of the sons of Hanan, the son of Igdaliah, a man of God, which was by the chamber of the princes, which was above the chamber of Maaseiah the son of Shallum, the keeper of the door: ⁵And I set before the sons of the house of the Rechabites pots full of wine, and cups, and I said to them, Drink you wine. ⁶But they said, We will drink no wine: for Jonadab the son of Rechab our father commanded us, saying, You shall drink no wine, neither you, nor your sons for ever: ⁷Neither shall you build house, nor sow seed, nor plant vineyard, nor have any: but all your days you shall dwell in tents; that you may live many days in the land where you be strangers. ⁸Thus have we obeyed the voice of Jonadab the son of Rechab our father in all that he has charged us, to drink no wine all our days, we, our wives, our sons, nor our daughters; ⁹Nor to build houses for us to dwell in: neither have we vineyard, nor field, nor seed: ¹⁰But we have dwelled in tents, and have obeyed, and done according to all that Jonadab our father commanded us. ¹¹But it came to pass, when Nebuchadrezzar king of Babylon came up into the land, that we said, Come, and let us go to Jerusalem for fear of the army of the Chaldeans, and for fear of the army of the Syrians: so we dwell at Jerusalem. ¹²Then came the word of the LORD to Jeremiah, saying, ¹³Thus says the LORD of hosts, the God of Israel; Go and tell the men of Judah and the inhabitants of Jerusalem, Will you not receive instruction to listen to my words? said the LORD. ¹⁴The words of Jonadab the son of Rechab, that he commanded his sons not to drink wine, are performed; for to this day they drink none, but obey their father's commandment: notwithstanding I have spoken to you, rising early and speaking; but you listened not to me. ¹⁵I have sent also to you all my servants the prophets, rising up early and sending them, saying, Return you now every man from his evil way, and amend your doings, and go not after other gods to serve them, and you shall dwell in the land which I have given to you and to your fathers: but you have not inclined your ear, nor listened to me. ¹⁶Because the sons of Jonadab the son of Rechab have performed the commandment of their father, which he commanded them; but this people has not listened to me: ¹⁷Therefore thus says the LORD God of hosts, the God of Israel; Behold, I will bring on Judah and on all the inhabitants of Jerusalem all the evil that I have pronounced against them: because I have spoken to them, but they have not heard; and I have called to them, but they have not answered. ¹⁸And Jeremiah said to the house of the Rechabites, Thus says the LORD of hosts, the God of Israel; Because you have obeyed the commandment of Jonadab your father, and kept all his precepts, and done according to all that he has commanded you: ¹⁹Therefore thus says the LORD of hosts, the God of Israel; Jonadab the son of Rechab shall not want a man to stand before me for ever.

36 ¹And it came to pass in the fourth year of Jehoiakim the son of Josiah king of Judah, that this word came to Jeremiah from the LORD, saying, ²Take you a roll of a book, and write therein all the words that I have spoken to you against Israel, and against Judah, and against all the nations, from the day I spoke to you, from the days of Josiah, even to this day. ³It may be that the house of Judah will hear all the evil which I purpose to do to them; that they may return every man from his evil way; that I may forgive their iniquity and their sin. ⁴Then Jeremiah called Baruch the son of Neriah: and Baruch wrote from the mouth of Jeremiah all the words of the LORD, which he had spoken to him, on a roll of a book. ⁵And Jeremiah commanded Baruch, saying, I am shut up; I cannot go into the house of the LORD: ⁶Therefore go you, and read in the roll, which you have written from my mouth, the words of the LORD in the ears of the people in the LORD's house on the fasting day: and also you shall read them in the ears of all Judah that come out of their cities. ⁷It may be they will present their supplication before the LORD, and will return every one from his evil way: for great is the anger and the fury that the LORD has pronounced against this people. ⁸And Baruch the son of Neriah did according to all that Jeremiah the prophet commanded him, reading in the book the words of the LORD in the LORD's house. ⁹And it came to pass in the fifth year of Jehoiakim the son of Josiah king of Judah, in the ninth month, that they proclaimed a fast before the

LORD to all the people in Jerusalem, and to all the people that came from the cities of Judah to Jerusalem. ¹⁰Then read Baruch in the book the words of Jeremiah in the house of the LORD, in the chamber of Gemariah the son of Shaphan the scribe, in the higher court, at the entry of the new gate of the LORD's house, in the ears of all the people. ¹¹When Michaiah the son of Gemariah, the son of Shaphan, had heard out of the book all the words of the LORD, ¹²Then he went down into the king's house, into the scribe's chamber: and, see, all the princes sat there, even Elishama the scribe, and Delaiah the son of Shemaiah, and Elnathan the son of Achbor, and Gemariah the son of Shaphan, and Zedekiah the son of Hananiah, and all the princes. ¹³Then Michaiah declared to them all the words that he had heard, when Baruch read the book in the ears of the people. ¹⁴Therefore all the princes sent Jehudi the son of Nethaniah, the son of Shelemiah, the son of Cushi, to Baruch, saying, Take in your hand the roll wherein you have read in the ears of the people, and come. So Baruch the son of Neriah took the roll in his hand, and came to them. ¹⁵And they said to him, Sit down now, and read it in our ears. So Baruch read it in their ears. ¹⁶Now it came to pass, when they had heard all the words, they were afraid both one and other, and said to Baruch, We will surely tell the king of all these words. ¹⁷And they asked Baruch, saying, Tell us now, How did you write all these words at his mouth? ¹⁸Then Baruch answered them, He pronounced all these words to me with his mouth, and I wrote them with ink in the book. ¹⁹Then said the princes to Baruch, Go, hide you, you and Jeremiah; and let no man know where you be. ²⁰And they went in to the king into the court, but they laid up the roll in the chamber of Elishama the scribe, and told all the words in the ears of the king. ²¹So the king sent Jehudi to fetch the roll: and he took it out of Elishama the scribe's chamber. And Jehudi read it in the ears of the king, and in the ears of all the princes which stood beside the king. ²²Now the king sat in the winter house in the ninth month: and there was a fire on the hearth burning before him. ²³And it came to pass, that when Jehudi had read three or four leaves, he cut it with the penknife, and cast it into the fire that was on the hearth, until all the roll was consumed in the fire that was on the hearth. ²⁴Yet they were not afraid, nor rent their garments, neither the king, nor any of his servants that heard all these words. ²⁵Nevertheless Elnathan and Delaiah and Gemariah had made intercession to the king that he would not burn the roll: but he would not hear them. ²⁶But the king commanded Jerahmeel the son of Hammelech, and Seraiah the son of Azriel, and Shelemiah the son of Abdeel, to take Baruch the scribe and Jeremiah the prophet: but the LORD hid them. ²⁷Then the word of the LORD came to Jeremiah, after that the king had burned the roll, and the words which Baruch wrote at the mouth of Jeremiah, saying, ²⁸Take you again another roll, and write in it all the former words that were in the first roll, which Jehoiakim the king of Judah has burned. ²⁹And you shall say to Jehoiakim king of Judah, Thus says the LORD; You have burned this roll, saying, Why have you written therein, saying, The king of Babylon shall certainly come and destroy this land, and shall cause to cease from there man and beast? ³⁰Therefore thus says the LORD of Jehoiakim king of Judah; He shall have none to sit on the throne of David: and his dead body shall be cast out in the day to the heat, and in the night to the frost. ³¹And I will punish him and his seed and his servants for their iniquity; and I will bring on them, and on the inhabitants of Jerusalem, and on the men of Judah, all the evil that I have pronounced against them; but they listened not. ³²Then took Jeremiah another roll, and gave it to Baruch the scribe, the son of Neriah; who wrote therein from the mouth of Jeremiah all the words of the book which Jehoiakim king of Judah had burned in the fire: and there were added besides to them many like words.

37 ¹And king Zedekiah the son of Josiah reigned instead of Coniah the son of Jehoiakim, whom Nebuchadrezzar king of Babylon made king in the land of Judah. ²But neither he, nor his servants, nor the people of the land, did listen to the words of the LORD, which he spoke by the prophet Jeremiah. ³And Zedekiah the king sent Jehucal the son of Shelemiah and Zephaniah the son of Maaseiah the priest to the prophet Jeremiah, saying, Pray now to the LORD our God for us. ⁴Now Jeremiah came in and went out among the people: for they had not put him into prison. ⁵Then Pharaoh's army was come forth out of Egypt: and when the Chaldeans that besieged Jerusalem heard tidings of them, they departed from Jerusalem. ⁶Then came the word of the LORD to the prophet Jeremiah saying, ⁷Thus says the LORD, the God of Israel; Thus shall you say to the king of Judah, that sent you to me to inquire of me; Behold, Pharaoh's army, which is come forth to help you, shall return to Egypt into their own land. ⁸And the Chaldeans shall come again, and fight against this city, and take it, and burn it with fire. ⁹Thus says the LORD; Deceive not yourselves, saying, The Chaldeans shall surely depart from us: for they shall not depart. ¹⁰For though you had smitten the whole army of the Chaldeans that fight against you, and there remained but wounded men among them, yet should they rise up every man in his tent, and burn this city with fire. ¹¹And it came to pass, that when the army of the Chaldeans was broken up from Jerusalem for fear of Pharaoh's army, ¹²Then Jeremiah went forth out of Jerusalem to go into the land of Benjamin, to separate himself there in the middle of the people. ¹³And when he was in the gate of Benjamin, a captain of the ward was there, whose name was Irijah, the son of Shelemiah, the son of Hananiah; and he took Jeremiah the prophet, saying, You fall away to the Chaldeans. ¹⁴Then said Jeremiah, It is false; I fall not away to the Chaldeans. But he listened not to him: so Irijah took Jeremiah, and brought him to the princes. ¹⁵Why the princes were wroth with Jeremiah, and smote him, and put him in prison in the house of Jonathan the scribe: for they had made that the prison. ¹⁶When Jeremiah was entered into the dungeon, and into the cabins, and Jeremiah had remained there many days; ¹⁷Then Zedekiah the king sent, and took him out: and the king asked him secretly in his house, and said, Is there any word from the LORD? And Jeremiah said, There is: for, said he, you shall be delivered into the hand of the king of Babylon. ¹⁸Moreover Jeremiah said to king Zedekiah, What have I offended against you, or against your servants, or against this people, that you have put me in prison? ¹⁹Where are now your prophets which prophesied to you, saying, The king of Babylon shall not come against you, nor against this land? ²⁰Therefore hear now, I pray you,

O my lord the king: let my supplication, I pray you, be accepted before you; that you cause me not to return to the house of Jonathan the scribe, lest I die there. ²¹Then Zedekiah the king commanded that they should commit Jeremiah into the court of the prison, and that they should give him daily a piece of bread out of the bakers' street, until all the bread in the city were spent. Thus Jeremiah remained in the court of the prison.

38 ¹Then Shephatiah the son of Mattan, and Gedaliah the son of Pashur, and Jucal the son of Shelemiah, and Pashur the son of Malchiah, heard the words that Jeremiah had spoken to all the people, saying, ²Thus says the LORD, He that remains in this city shall die by the sword, by the famine, and by the pestilence: but he that goes forth to the Chaldeans shall live; for he shall have his life for a prey, and shall live. ³Thus says the LORD, This city shall surely be given into the hand of the king of Babylon's army, which shall take it. ⁴Therefore the princes said to the king, We beseech you, let this man be put to death: for thus he weakens the hands of the men of war that remain in this city, and the hands of all the people, in speaking such words to them: for this man seeks not the welfare of this people, but the hurt. ⁵Then Zedekiah the king said, Behold, he is in your hand: for the king is not he that can do any thing against you. ⁶Then took they Jeremiah, and cast him into the dungeon of Malchiah the son of Hammelech, that was in the court of the prison: and they let down Jeremiah with cords. And in the dungeon there was no water, but mire: so Jeremiah sunk in the mire. ⁷Now when Ebedmelech the Ethiopian, one of the eunuchs which was in the king's house, heard that they had put Jeremiah in the dungeon; the king then sitting in the gate of Benjamin; ⁸Ebedmelech went forth out of the king's house, and spoke to the king saying, ⁹My lord the king, these men have done evil in all that they have done to Jeremiah the prophet, whom they have cast into the dungeon; and he is like to die for hunger in the place where he is: for there is no more bread in the city. ¹⁰Then the king commanded Ebedmelech the Ethiopian, saying, Take from hence thirty men with you, and take up Jeremiah the prophet out of the dungeon, before he die. ¹¹So Ebedmelech took the men with him, and went into the house of the king under the treasury, and took there old cast clouts and old rotten rags, and let them down by cords into the dungeon to Jeremiah. ¹²And Ebedmelech the Ethiopian said to Jeremiah, Put now these old cast clouts and rotten rags under your armholes under the cords. And Jeremiah did so. ¹³So they drew up Jeremiah with cords, and took him up out of the dungeon: and Jeremiah remained in the court of the prison. ¹⁴Then Zedekiah the king sent, and took Jeremiah the prophet to him into the third entry that is in the house of the LORD: and the king said to Jeremiah, I will ask you a thing; hide nothing from me. ¹⁵Then Jeremiah said to Zedekiah, If I declare it to you, will you not surely put me to death? and if I give you counsel, will you not listen to me? ¹⁶So Zedekiah the king swore secretly to Jeremiah, saying, As the LORD lives, that made us this soul, I will not put you to death, neither will I give you into the hand of these men that seek your life. ¹⁷Then said Jeremiah to Zedekiah, Thus says the LORD, the God of hosts, the God of Israel; If you will assuredly go forth to the king of Babylon's princes, then your soul shall live, and this city shall not be burned with fire; and you shall live, and your house: ¹⁸But if you will not go forth to the king of Babylon's princes, then shall this city be given into the hand of the Chaldeans, and they shall burn it with fire, and you shall not escape out of their hand. ¹⁹And Zedekiah the king said to Jeremiah, I am afraid of the Jews that are fallen to the Chaldeans, lest they deliver me into their hand, and they mock me. ²⁰But Jeremiah said, They shall not deliver you. Obey, I beseech you, the voice of the LORD, which I speak to you: so it shall be well to you, and your soul shall live. ²¹But if you refuse to go forth, this is the word that the LORD has showed me: ²²And, behold, all the women that are left in the king of Judah's house shall be brought forth to the king of Babylon's princes, and those women shall say, Your friends have set you on, and have prevailed against you: your feet are sunk in the mire, and they are turned away back. ²³So they shall bring out all your wives and your children to the Chaldeans: and you shall not escape out of their hand, but shall be taken by the hand of the king of Babylon: and you shall cause this city to be burned with fire. ²⁴Then said Zedekiah to Jeremiah, Let no man know of these words, and you shall not die. ²⁵But if the princes hear that I have talked with you, and they come to you, and say to you, Declare to us now what you have said to the king, hide it not from us, and we will not put you to death; also what the king said to you: ²⁶Then you shall say to them, I presented my supplication before the king, that he would not cause me to return to Jonathan's house, to die there. ²⁷Then came all the princes to Jeremiah, and asked him: and he told them according to all these words that the king had commanded. So they left off speaking with him; for the matter was not perceived. ²⁸So Jeremiah stayed in the court of the prison until the day that Jerusalem was taken: and he was there when Jerusalem was taken.

39 ¹In the ninth year of Zedekiah king of Judah, in the tenth month, came Nebuchadrezzar king of Babylon and all his army against Jerusalem, and they besieged it. ²And in the eleventh year of Zedekiah, in the fourth month, the ninth day of the month, the city was broken up. ³And all the princes of the king of Babylon came in, and sat in the middle gate, even Nergalsharezer, Samgarnebo, Sarsechim, Rabsaris, Nergalsharezer, Rabmag, with all the residue of the princes of the king of Babylon. ⁴And it came to pass, that when Zedekiah the king of Judah saw them, and all the men of war, then they fled, and went forth out of the city by night, by the way of the king's garden, by the gate between the two walls: and he went out the way of the plain. ⁵But the Chaldeans' army pursued after them, and overtook Zedekiah in the plains of Jericho: and when they had taken him, they brought him up to Nebuchadnezzar king of Babylon to Riblah in the land of Hamath, where he gave judgment on him. ⁶Then the king of Babylon slew the sons of Zedekiah in Riblah before his eyes: also the king of Babylon slew all the nobles of Judah. ⁷Moreover he put out Zedekiah's eyes, and bound him with chains, to carry him to Babylon. ⁸And the Chaldeans burned the king's house, and the houses of the people, with fire, and broke down the walls of Jerusalem. ⁹Then Nebuzaradan the captain of the guard carried away captive into Babylon the remnant of the people that remained in the city, and those that fell away, that fell to him, with the rest of the people that remained. ¹⁰But Nebuzaradan the captain of the guard left of the poor of the people, which had nothing, in the land of Judah, and gave them vineyards and fields at the same time. ¹¹Now Nebuchadrezzar king of Babylon gave charge concerning Jeremiah to Nebuzaradan the captain of the guard, saying, ¹²Take him, and look well to him, and do him no harm; but do to him even as he shall say to you. ¹³So Nebuzaradan the captain of the guard sent, and Nebushasban, Rabsaris, and Nergalsharezer, Rabmag, and all the king of Babylon's princes; ¹⁴Even they sent, and took Jeremiah out of the court of the prison, and committed him to Gedaliah the son of Ahikam the son of Shaphan, that he should carry him home: so he dwelled among the people. ¹⁵Now the word of the LORD came to Jeremiah, while he was shut up in the court of the prison, saying, ¹⁶Go and speak to Ebedmelech the Ethiopian, saying, Thus says the LORD of hosts, the God of Israel; Behold, I will bring my words on this city for evil, and not for good; and they shall be accomplished in that day before you. ¹⁷But I will deliver you in that day, says the LORD: and you shall not be given into the hand of the men of whom you are afraid. ¹⁸For I will surely deliver you, and you shall not fall by the sword, but your life shall be for a prey to you: because you have put your trust in me, says the LORD.

40 ¹The word that came to Jeremiah from the LORD, after that Nebuzaradan the captain of the guard had let him go from Ramah, when he had taken him being bound in chains among all that were carried away captive of Jerusalem and Judah, which were carried away captive to Babylon. ²And the captain of the guard took Jeremiah, and said to him, The LORD your God has pronounced this evil on this place. ³Now the LORD has brought it, and done according as he has said: because you have sinned against the LORD, and have not obeyed his voice, therefore this thing is come on you. ⁴And now, behold, I loose you this day from the chains which were on your hand. If it seem good to you to come with me into Babylon, come; and I will look well to you: but if it seem ill to you to come with me into Babylon, forbear: behold, all the land is before you: where it seems good and convenient for you to go, thither go. ⁵Now while he was not yet gone back, he said, Go back also to Gedaliah the son of Ahikam the son of Shaphan, whom the king of Babylon has made governor over the cities of Judah, and dwell with him among the people: or go wherever it seems convenient to you to go. So the captain of the guard gave him victuals and a reward, and let him go. ⁶Then went Jeremiah to Gedaliah the son of Ahikam to Mizpah; and dwelled with him among the people that were left in the land. ⁷Now when all the captains of the forces which were in the fields, even they and their men, heard that the king of Babylon had made Gedaliah the son of Ahikam governor in the land, and had committed to him men, and women, and children, and of the poor of the land, of them that were not carried away captive to Babylon; ⁸Then they came to Gedaliah to Mizpah, even Ishmael the son of Nethaniah, and Johanan and Jonathan the sons of Kareah, and Seraiah the son of Tanhumeth, and the sons of Ephai the Netophathite, and Jezaniah the son of a Maachathite, they and their men. ⁹And Gedaliah the son of Ahikam the son of Shaphan swore to them and to their men, saying, Fear not to serve the Chaldeans: dwell in the land, and serve the king of Babylon, and it shall be well with you. ¹⁰As for me, behold, I will dwell at Mizpah, to serve the Chaldeans, which will come to us: but you, gather you wine, and summer fruits, and oil, and put them in your vessels, and dwell in your cities that you have taken. ¹¹Likewise when all the Jews that were in Moab, and among the Ammonites, and in Edom, and that were in all the countries, heard that the king of Babylon had left a remnant of Judah, and that he had set over them Gedaliah the son of Ahikam the son of Shaphan; ¹²Even all the Jews returned out of all places where they were driven, and came to the land of Judah, to Gedaliah, to Mizpah, and gathered wine and summer fruits very much. ¹³Moreover Johanan the son of Kareah, and all the captains of the forces that were in the fields, came to Gedaliah to Mizpah, ¹⁴And said to him, Do you certainly know that Baalis the king of the Ammonites has sent Ishmael the son of Nethaniah to slay you? But Gedaliah the son of Ahikam believed them not. ¹⁵Then Johanan the son of Kareah spoke to Gedaliah in Mizpah secretly saying, Let me go, I pray you, and I will slay Ishmael the son of Nethaniah, and no man shall know it: why should he slay you, that all the Jews which are gathered to you should be scattered, and the remnant in Judah perish? ¹⁶But Gedaliah the son of Ahikam said to Johanan the son of Kareah, You shall not do this thing: for you speak falsely of Ishmael.

41 ¹Now it came to pass in the seventh month, that Ishmael the son of Nethaniah the son of Elishama, of the seed royal, and the princes of the king, even ten men with him, came to Gedaliah the son of Ahikam to Mizpah; and there they did eat bread together in Mizpah. ²Then arose Ishmael the son of Nethaniah, and the ten men that were with him, and smote Gedaliah the son of Ahikam the son of Shaphan with the sword, and slew him, whom the king of Babylon had made governor over the land. ³Ishmael also slew all the Jews that were with him, even with Gedaliah, at Mizpah, and the Chaldeans that were found there, and the men of war. ⁴And it came to pass the second day after he had slain Gedaliah, and no man knew it, ⁵That there came certain from Shechem, from Shiloh, and from Samaria, even fourscore men, having their beards shaven, and their clothes rent, and having cut themselves, with offerings and incense in their hand, to bring them to the house of the LORD. ⁶And Ishmael the son of Nethaniah went forth from Mizpah to meet them, weeping all along as he went: and it came to pass, as he met them, he said to them, Come to Gedaliah the son of Ahikam. ⁷And it was so, when they came into the middle of the city, that Ishmael the son of Nethaniah slew them, and cast them into the middle of the pit, he, and the men that were with him. ⁸But ten men were found among them that said to Ishmael, Slay us not: for we have treasures in the field, of wheat, and of barley, and of oil, and of honey. So he declined, and slew them not among their brothers. ⁹Now the pit wherein Ishmael had cast all the dead bodies of the men, whom he had slain because of Gedaliah, was it which Asa the king had made for fear of Baasha king of Israel: and Ishmael the son of Nethaniah filled it with them that were slain. ¹⁰Then Ishmael carried away captive all the residue of the people that were in Mizpah, even the king's daughters, and all the people that remained in Mizpah, whom Nebuzaradan the captain of the guard had committed to Gedaliah the son of Ahikam: and Ishmael the son of Nethaniah carried them away captive, and departed to go over to the Ammonites. ¹¹But when Johanan the son of Kareah, and all the captains of the forces that were with him, heard of all the evil that Ishmael the son of Nethaniah had done, ¹²Then they took all the men, and went to fight with Ishmael the son of Nethaniah, and found him by the great waters that are in Gibeon. ¹³Now it came to pass, that when all the people which were with Ishmael saw Johanan the son of Kareah, and all the captains of the forces that were with him, then they were glad. ¹⁴So all the people that Ishmael had carried away captive from Mizpah cast about and returned, and went to Johanan the son of Kareah. ¹⁵But Ishmael the son of Nethaniah escaped from Johanan with eight men, and went to the Ammonites. ¹⁶Then took Johanan the son of Kareah, and all the captains of the forces that were with him, all the remnant of the people whom he had recovered from Ishmael the son of Nethaniah, from Mizpah, after that he had slain Gedaliah the son of Ahikam, even mighty men of war, and the women, and the children, and the eunuchs, whom he had brought again from Gibeon: ¹⁷And they departed, and dwelled in the habitation of Chimham, which is by Bethlehem, to go to enter into Egypt, ¹⁸Because of the Chaldeans: for they were afraid of them, because Ishmael the son of Nethaniah had slain Gedaliah the son of Ahikam, whom the king of Babylon made governor in the land.

42

¹Then all the captains of the forces, and Johanan the son of Kareah, and Jezaniah the son of Hoshaiah, and all the people from the least even to the greatest, came near, ²And said to Jeremiah the prophet, Let, we beseech you, our supplication be accepted before you, and pray for us to the LORD your God, even for all this remnant; (for we are left but a few of many, as your eyes do behold us:) ³That the LORD your God may show us the way wherein we may walk, and the thing that we may do. ⁴Then Jeremiah the prophet said to them, I have heard you; behold, I will pray to the LORD your God according to your words; and it shall come to pass, that whatever thing the LORD shall answer you, I will declare it to you; I will keep nothing back from you. ⁵Then they said to Jeremiah, The LORD be a true and faithful witness between us, if we do not even according to all things for the which the LORD your God shall send you to us. ⁶Whether it be good, or whether it be evil, we will obey the voice of the LORD our God, to whom we send you; that it may be well with us, when we obey the voice of the LORD our God. ⁷And it came to pass after ten days, that the word of the LORD came to Jeremiah. ⁸Then called he Johanan the son of Kareah, and all the captains of the forces which were with him, and all the people from the least even to the greatest, ⁹And said to them, Thus says the LORD, the God of Israel, to whom you sent me to present your supplication before him; ¹⁰If you will still abide in this land, then will I build you, and not pull you down, and I will plant you, and not pluck you up: for I repent me of the evil that I have done to you. ¹¹Be not afraid of the king of Babylon, of whom you are afraid; be not afraid of him, says the LORD: for I am with you to save you, and to deliver you from his hand. ¹²And I will show mercies to you, that he may have mercy on you, and cause you to return to your own land. ¹³But if you say, We will not dwell in this land, neither obey the voice of the LORD your God, ¹⁴Saying, No; but we will go into the land of Egypt, where we shall see no war, nor hear the sound of the trumpet, nor have hunger of bread; and there will we dwell: ¹⁵And now therefore hear the word of the LORD, you remnant of Judah; Thus says the LORD of hosts, the God of Israel; If you wholly set your faces to enter into Egypt, and go to sojourn there; ¹⁶Then it shall come to pass, that the sword, which you feared, shall overtake you there in the land of Egypt, and the famine, whereof you were afraid, shall follow close after you there in Egypt; and there you shall die. ¹⁷So shall it be with all the men that set their faces to go into Egypt to sojourn there; they shall die by the sword, by the famine, and by the pestilence: and none of them shall remain or escape from the evil that I will bring on them. ¹⁸For thus says the LORD of hosts, the God of Israel; As my anger and my fury has been poured forth on the inhabitants of Jerusalem; so shall my fury be poured forth on you, when you shall enter into Egypt: and you shall be an execration, and an astonishment, and a curse, and a reproach; and you shall see this place no more. ¹⁹The LORD has said concerning you, O you remnant of Judah; Go you not into Egypt: know certainly that I have admonished you this day. ²⁰For you dissembled in your hearts, when you sent me to the LORD your God, saying, Pray for us to the LORD our God; and according to all that the LORD our God shall say, so declare to us, and we will do it. ²¹And now I have this day declared it to you; but you have not obeyed the voice of the LORD your God, nor any thing for the which he has sent me to you. ²²Now therefore know certainly that you shall die by the sword, by the famine, and by the pestilence, in the place where you desire to go and to sojourn.

43

¹And it came to pass, that when Jeremiah had made an end of speaking to all the people all the words of the LORD their God, for which the LORD their God had sent him to them, even all these words, ²Then spoke Azariah the son of Hoshaiah, and Johanan the son of Kareah, and all the proud men, saying to Jeremiah, You speak falsely: the LORD our God has not sent you to say, Go not into Egypt to sojourn there: ³But Baruch the son of Neriah sets you on against us, for to deliver us into the hand of the Chaldeans, that they might put us to death, and carry us away captives into Babylon. ⁴So Johanan the son of Kareah, and all the captains of the forces, and all the people, obeyed not the voice of the LORD, to dwell in the land of Judah. ⁵But Johanan the son of Kareah, and all the captains of the forces, took all the remnant of Judah, that were returned from all nations, where they had been driven, to dwell in the land of Judah; ⁶Even men, and women, and children, and the king's daughters, and every person that Nebuzaradan the captain of the guard had left with Gedaliah the son of Ahikam the son of Shaphan, and Jeremiah the prophet, and Baruch the son of Neriah. ⁷So they came into the land of Egypt: for they obeyed not the voice of the LORD: thus came they even to Tahpanhes. ⁸Then came the word of the LORD to Jeremiah in Tahpanhes, saying, ⁹Take great stones in your hand, and hide them in the clay in the brick kiln, which is at the entry of Pharaoh's house in Tahpanhes, in the sight of the men of

Judah; ¹⁰And say to them, Thus says the LORD of hosts, the God of Israel; Behold, I will send and take Nebuchadrezzar the king of Babylon, my servant, and will set his throne on these stones that I have hid; and he shall spread his royal pavilion over them. ¹¹And when he comes, he shall smite the land of Egypt, and deliver such as are for death to death; and such as are for captivity to captivity; and such as are for the sword to the sword. ¹²And I will kindle a fire in the houses of the gods of Egypt; and he shall burn them, and carry them away captives: and he shall array himself with the land of Egypt, as a shepherd puts on his garment; and he shall go forth from there in peace. ¹³He shall break also the images of Bethshemesh, that is in the land of Egypt; and the houses of the gods of the Egyptians shall he burn with fire.

44 ¹The word that came to Jeremiah concerning all the Jews which dwell in the land of Egypt, which dwell at Migdol, and at Tahpanhes, and at Noph, and in the country of Pathros, saying, ²Thus says the LORD of hosts, the God of Israel; You have seen all the evil that I have brought on Jerusalem, and on all the cities of Judah; and, behold, this day they are a desolation, and no man dwells therein, ³Because of their wickedness which they have committed to provoke me to anger, in that they went to burn incense, and to serve other gods, whom they knew not, neither they, you, nor your fathers. ⁴However, I sent to you all my servants the prophets, rising early and sending them, saying, Oh, do not this abominable thing that I hate. ⁵But they listened not, nor inclined their ear to turn from their wickedness, to burn no incense to other gods. ⁶Why my fury and my anger was poured forth, and was kindled in the cities of Judah and in the streets of Jerusalem; and they are wasted and desolate, as at this day. ⁷Therefore now thus says the LORD, the God of hosts, the God of Israel; Why commit you this great evil against your souls, to cut off from you man and woman, child and suckling, out of Judah, to leave you none to remain; ⁸In that you provoke me to wrath with the works of your hands, burning incense to other gods in the land of Egypt, where you be gone to dwell, that you might cut yourselves off, and that you might be a curse and a reproach among all the nations of the earth? ⁹Have you forgotten the wickedness of your fathers, and the wickedness of the kings of Judah, and the wickedness of their wives, and your own wickedness, and the wickedness of your wives, which they have committed in the land of Judah, and in the streets of Jerusalem? ¹⁰They are not humbled even to this day, neither have they feared, nor walked in my law, nor in my statutes, that I set before you and before your fathers. ¹¹Therefore thus says the LORD of hosts, the God of Israel; Behold, I will set my face against you for evil, and to cut off all Judah. ¹²And I will take the remnant of Judah, that have set their faces to go into the land of Egypt to sojourn there, and they shall all be consumed, and fall in the land of Egypt; they shall even be consumed by the sword and by the famine: they shall die, from the least even to the greatest, by the sword and by the famine: and they shall be an execration, and an astonishment, and a curse, and a reproach. ¹³For I will punish them that dwell in the land of Egypt, as I have punished Jerusalem, by the sword, by the famine, and by the pestilence: ¹⁴So that none of the remnant of Judah, which are gone into the land of Egypt to sojourn there, shall escape or remain, that they should return into the land of Judah, to the which they have a desire to return to dwell there: for none shall return but such as shall escape. ¹⁵Then all the men which knew that their wives had burned incense to other gods, and all the women that stood by, a great multitude, even all the people that dwelled in the land of Egypt, in Pathros, answered Jeremiah, saying, ¹⁶As for the word that you have spoken to us in the name of the LORD, we will not listen to you. ¹⁷But we will certainly do whatever thing goes forth out of our own mouth, to burn incense to the queen of heaven, and to pour out drink offerings to her, as we have done, we, and our fathers, our kings, and our princes, in the cities of Judah, and in the streets of Jerusalem: for then had we plenty of victuals, and were well, and saw no evil. ¹⁸But since we left off to burn incense to the queen of heaven, and to pour out drink offerings to her, we have wanted all things, and have been consumed by the sword and by the famine. ¹⁹And when we burned incense to the queen of heaven, and poured out drink offerings to her, did we make her cakes to worship her, and pour out drink offerings to her, without our men? ²⁰Then Jeremiah said to all the people, to the men, and to the women, and to all the people which had given him that answer, saying, ²¹The incense that you burned in the cities of Judah, and in the streets of Jerusalem, you, and your fathers, your kings, and your princes, and the people of the land, did not the LORD remember them, and came it not into his mind? ²²So that the LORD could no longer bear, because of the evil of your doings, and because of the abominations which you have committed; therefore is your land a desolation, and an astonishment, and a curse, without an inhabitant, as at this day. ²³Because you have burned incense, and because you have sinned against the LORD, and have not obeyed the voice of the LORD, nor walked in his law, nor in his statutes, nor in his testimonies; therefore this evil is happened to you, as at this day. ²⁴Moreover Jeremiah said to all the people, and to all the women, Hear the word of the LORD, all Judah that are in the land of Egypt: ²⁵Thus says the LORD of hosts, the God of Israel, saying; You and your wives have both spoken with your mouths, and fulfilled with your hand, saying, We will surely perform our vows that we have vowed, to burn incense to the queen of heaven, and to pour out drink offerings to her: you will surely accomplish your vows, and surely perform your vows. ²⁶Therefore hear you the word of the LORD, all Judah that dwell in the land of Egypt; Behold, I have sworn by my great name, says the LORD, that my name shall no more be named in the mouth of any man of Judah in all the land of Egypt, saying, The Lord GOD lives. ²⁷Behold, I will watch over them for evil, and not for good: and all the men of Judah that are in the land of Egypt shall be consumed by the sword and by the famine, until there be an end of them. ²⁸Yet a small number that escape the sword shall return out of the land of Egypt into the land of Judah, and all the remnant of Judah, that are gone into the land of Egypt to sojourn there, shall know whose words shall stand, mine, or theirs. ²⁹And this shall be a sign to you, says the LORD, that I will punish you in this place, that you may know that my words shall surely stand against you for evil: ³⁰Thus says the LORD; Behold, I will give pharaoh Hophra king of Egypt into the hand of his enemies, and into the hand of them that seek his life; as I gave Zedekiah king of Judah into the hand of Nebuchadrezzar king of Babylon, his enemy, and that sought his life.

45

¹The word that Jeremiah the prophet spoke to Baruch the son of Neriah, when he had written these words in a book at the mouth of Jeremiah, in the fourth year of Jehoiakim the son of Josiah king of Judah, saying, ²Thus says the LORD, the God of Israel, to you, O Baruch: ³You did say, Woe is me now! for the LORD has added grief to my sorrow; I fainted in my sighing, and I find no rest. ⁴Thus shall you say to him, The LORD says thus; Behold, that which I have built will I break down, and that which I have planted I will pluck up, even this whole land. ⁵And seek you great things for yourself? seek them not: for, behold, I will bring evil on all flesh, says the LORD: but your life will I give to you for a prey in all places where you go.

46

¹The word of the LORD which came to Jeremiah the prophet against the Gentiles; ²Against Egypt, against the army of Pharaohnecho king of Egypt, which was by the river Euphrates in Carchemish, which Nebuchadrezzar king of Babylon smote in the fourth year of Jehoiakim the son of Josiah king of Judah. ³Order you the buckler and shield, and draw near to battle. ⁴Harness the horses; and get up, you horsemen, and stand forth with your helmets; furbish the spears, and put on the brigandines. ⁵Why have I seen them dismayed and turned away back? and their mighty ones are beaten down, and are fled apace, and look not back: for fear was round about, says the LORD. ⁶Let not the swift flee away, nor the mighty man escape; they shall stumble, and fall toward the north by the river Euphrates. ⁷Who is this that comes up as a flood, whose waters are moved as the rivers? ⁸Egypt rises up like a flood, and his waters are moved like the rivers; and he says, I will go up, and will cover the earth; I will destroy the city and the inhabitants thereof. ⁹Come up, you horses; and rage, you chariots; and let the mighty men come forth; the Ethiopians and the Libyans, that handle the shield; and the Lydians, that handle and bend the bow. ¹⁰For this is the day of the Lord GOD of hosts, a day of vengeance, that he may avenge him of his adversaries: and the sword shall devour, and it shall be satiate and made drunk with their blood: for the Lord GOD of hosts has a sacrifice in the north country by the river Euphrates. ¹¹Go up into Gilead, and take balm, O virgin, the daughter of Egypt: in vain shall you use many medicines; for you shall not be cured. ¹²The nations have heard of your shame, and your cry has filled the land: for the mighty man has stumbled against the mighty, and they are fallen both together. ¹³The word that the LORD spoke to Jeremiah the prophet, how Nebuchadrezzar king of Babylon should come and smite the land of Egypt. ¹⁴Declare you in Egypt, and publish in Migdol, and publish in Noph and in Tahpanhes: say you, Stand fast, and prepare you; for the sword shall devour round about you. ¹⁵Why are your valiant men swept away? they stood not, because the LORD did drive them. ¹⁶He made many to fall, yes, one fell on another: and they said, Arise, and let us go again to our own people, and to the land of our nativity, from the oppressing sword. ¹⁷They did cry there, Pharaoh king of Egypt is but a noise; he has passed the time appointed. ¹⁸As I live, says the King, whose name is the LORD of hosts, Surely as Tabor is among the mountains, and as Carmel by the sea, so shall he come. ¹⁹O you daughter dwelling in Egypt, furnish yourself to go into captivity: for Noph shall be waste and desolate without an inhabitant. ²⁰Egypt is like a very fair heifer, but destruction comes; it comes out of the north. ²¹Also her hired men are in the middle of her like fatted bullocks; for they also are turned back, and are fled away together: they did not stand, because the day of their calamity was come on them, and the time of their visitation. ²²The voice thereof shall go like a serpent; for they shall march with an army, and come against her with axes, as hewers of wood. ²³They shall cut down her forest, says the LORD, though it cannot be searched; because they are more than the grasshoppers, and are innumerable. ²⁴The daughter of Egypt shall be confounded; she shall be delivered into the hand of the people of the north. ²⁵The LORD of hosts, the God of Israel, says; Behold, I will punish the multitude of No, and Pharaoh, and Egypt, with their gods, and their kings; even Pharaoh, and all them that trust in him: ²⁶And I will deliver them into the hand of those that seek their lives, and into the hand of Nebuchadrezzar king of Babylon, and into the hand of his servants: and afterward it shall be inhabited, as in the days of old, says the LORD. ²⁷But fear not you, O my servant Jacob, and be not dismayed, O Israel: for, behold, I will save you from afar off, and your seed from the land of their captivity; and Jacob shall return, and be in rest and at ease, and none shall make him afraid. ²⁸Fear you not, O Jacob my servant, says the LORD: for I am with you; for I will make a full end of all the nations where I have driven you: but I will not make a full end of you, but correct you in measure; yet will I not leave you wholly unpunished.

47

¹The word of the LORD that came to Jeremiah the prophet against the Philistines, before that Pharaoh smote Gaza. ²Thus says the LORD; Behold, waters rise up out of the north, and shall be an overflowing flood, and shall overflow the land, and all that is therein; the city, and them that dwell therein: then the men shall cry, and all the inhabitants of the land shall howl. ³At the noise of the stamping of the hoofs of his strong horses, at the rushing of his chariots, and at the rumbling of his wheels, the fathers shall not look back to their children for feebleness of hands; ⁴Because of the day that comes to spoil all the Philistines, and to cut off from Tyrus and Zidon every helper that remains: for the LORD will spoil the Philistines, the remnant of the country of Caphtor. ⁵Baldness is come on Gaza; Ashkelon is cut off with the remnant of their valley: how long will you cut yourself? ⁶O you sword of the LORD, how long will it be before you be quiet? put up yourself into your scabbard, rest, and be still. ⁷How can it be quiet, seeing the LORD has given it a charge against Ashkelon, and against the sea shore? there has he appointed it.

48

¹Against Moab thus says the LORD of hosts, the God of Israel; Woe to Nebo! for it is spoiled: Kiriathaim is confounded and taken: Misgab is confounded and dismayed. ²There shall be no more praise of Moab: in Heshbon they have devised evil against it; come, and let us cut it off from being a nation. Also you shall be cut down, O

Madmen; the sword shall pursue you. ³A voice of crying shall be from Horonaim, spoiling and great destruction. ⁴Moab is destroyed; her little ones have caused a cry to be heard. ⁵For in the going up of Luhith continual weeping shall go up; for in the going down of Horonaim the enemies have heard a cry of destruction. ⁶Flee, save your lives, and be like the heath in the wilderness. ⁷For because you have trusted in your works and in your treasures, you shall also be taken: and Chemosh shall go forth into captivity with his priests and his princes together. ⁸And the spoiler shall come on every city, and no city shall escape: the valley also shall perish, and the plain shall be destroyed, as the LORD has spoken. ⁹Give wings to Moab, that it may flee and get away: for the cities thereof shall be desolate, without any to dwell therein. ¹⁰Cursed be he that does the work of the LORD deceitfully, and cursed be he that keeps back his sword from blood. ¹¹Moab has been at ease from his youth, and he has settled on his lees, and has not been emptied from vessel to vessel, neither has he gone into captivity: therefore his taste remained in him, and his scent is not changed. ¹²Therefore, behold, the days come, says the LORD, that I will send to him wanderers, that shall cause him to wander, and shall empty his vessels, and break their bottles. ¹³And Moab shall be ashamed of Chemosh, as the house of Israel was ashamed of Bethel their confidence. ¹⁴How say you, We are mighty and strong men for the war? ¹⁵Moab is spoiled, and gone up out of her cities, and his chosen young men are gone down to the slaughter, says the King, whose name is the LORD of hosts. ¹⁶The calamity of Moab is near to come, and his affliction hastens fast. ¹⁷All you that are about him, bemoan him; and all you that know his name, say, How is the strong staff broken, and the beautiful rod! ¹⁸You daughter that do inhabit Dibon, come down from your glory, and sit in thirst; for the spoiler of Moab shall come on you, and he shall destroy your strong holds. ¹⁹O inhabitant of Aroer, stand by the way, and espy; ask him that flees, and her that escapes, and say, What is done? ²⁰Moab is confounded; for it is broken down: howl and cry; tell you it in Arnon, that Moab is spoiled, ²¹And judgment is come on the plain country; on Holon, and on Jahazah, and on Mephaath, ²²And on Dibon, and on Nebo, and on Bethdiblathaim, ²³And on Kiriathaim, and on Bethgamul, and on Bethmeon, ²⁴And on Kerioth, and on Bozrah, and on all the cities of the land of Moab, far or near. ²⁵The horn of Moab is cut off, and his arm is broken, says the LORD. ²⁶Make you him drunken: for he magnified himself against the LORD: Moab also shall wallow in his vomit, and he also shall be in derision. ²⁷For was not Israel a derision to you? was he found among thieves? for since you spoke of him, you skipped for joy. ²⁸O you that dwell in Moab, leave the cities, and dwell in the rock, and be like the dove that makes her nest in the sides of the hole's mouth. ²⁹We have heard the pride of Moab, (he is exceeding proud) his loftiness, and his arrogance, and his pride, and the haughtiness of his heart. ³⁰I know his wrath, says the LORD; but it shall not be so; his lies shall not so effect it. ³¹Therefore will I howl for Moab, and I will cry out for all Moab; my heart shall mourn for the men of Kirheres. ³²O vine of Sibmah, I will weep for you with the weeping of Jazer: your plants are gone over the sea, they reach even to the sea of Jazer: the spoiler is fallen on your summer fruits and on your vintage. ³³And joy and gladness is taken from the plentiful field, and from the land of Moab, and I have caused wine to fail from the winepresses: none shall tread with shouting; their shouting shall be no shouting. ³⁴From the cry of Heshbon even to Elealeh, and even to Jahaz, have they uttered their voice, from Zoar even to Horonaim, as an heifer of three years old: for the waters also of Nimrim shall be desolate. ³⁵Moreover I will cause to cease in Moab, says the LORD, him that offers in the high places, and him that burns incense to his gods. ³⁶Therefore my heart shall sound for Moab like pipes, and my heart shall sound like pipes for the men of Kirheres: because the riches that he has gotten are perished. ³⁷For every head shall be bald, and every beard clipped: on all the hands shall be cuttings, and on the loins sackcloth. ³⁸There shall be lamentation generally on all the housetops of Moab, and in the streets thereof: for I have broken Moab like a vessel wherein is no pleasure, says the LORD. ³⁹They shall howl, saying, How is it broken down! how has Moab turned the back with shame! so shall Moab be a derision and a dismaying to all them about him. ⁴⁰For thus says the LORD; Behold, he shall fly as an eagle, and shall spread his wings over Moab. ⁴¹Kerioth is taken, and the strong holds are surprised, and the mighty men's hearts in Moab at that day shall be as the heart of a woman in her pangs. ⁴²And Moab shall be destroyed from being a people, because he has magnified himself against the LORD. ⁴³Fear, and the pit, and the snare, shall be on you, O inhabitant of Moab, says the LORD. ⁴⁴He that flees from the fear shall fall into the pit; and he that gets up out of the pit shall be taken in the snare: for I will bring on it, even on Moab, the year of their visitation, says the LORD. ⁴⁵They that fled stood under the shadow of Heshbon because of the force: but a fire shall come forth out of Heshbon, and a flame from the middle of Sihon, and shall devour the corner of Moab, and the crown of the head of the tumultuous ones. ⁴⁶Woe be to you, O Moab! the people of Chemosh perishes: for your sons are taken captives, and your daughters captives. ⁴⁷Yet will I bring again the captivity of Moab in the latter days, says the LORD. Thus far is the judgment of Moab.

49 ¹Concerning the Ammonites, thus says the LORD; Has Israel no sons? has he no heir? why then does their king inherit Gad, and his people dwell in his cities? ²Therefore, behold, the days come, says the LORD, that I will cause an alarm of war to be heard in Rabbah of the Ammonites; and it shall be a desolate heap, and her daughters shall be burned with fire: then shall Israel be heir to them that were his heirs, said the LORD. ³Howl, O Heshbon, for Ai is spoiled: cry, you daughters of Rabbah, gird you with sackcloth; lament, and run to and fro by the hedges; for their king shall go into captivity, and his priests and his princes together. ⁴Why glory you in the valleys, your flowing valley, O backsliding daughter? that trusted in her treasures, saying, Who shall come to me? ⁵Behold, I will bring a fear on you, says the Lord GOD of hosts, from all those that be about you; and you shall be driven out every man right forth; and none shall gather up him that wanders. ⁶And afterward I will bring again the captivity of the children of Ammon, says the LORD. ⁷Concerning Edom, thus says the LORD of hosts; Is wisdom no more in Teman? is counsel perished from the prudent? is their wisdom vanished? ⁸Flee you, turn back, dwell deep, O inhabitants of Dedan; for I will bring the calamity of Esau on him, the time that I will visit him. ⁹If grape gatherers come to you, would they not leave some gleaning grapes? if thieves by night, they will destroy till they have enough. ¹⁰But I have made Esau bore, I have uncovered his secret places, and he shall not be able to hide himself: his seed is spoiled, and his brothers, and his neighbors, and he is not. ¹¹Leave your fatherless children, I will preserve them alive; and let your widows trust in me. ¹²For thus says the LORD; Behold, they whose judgment was not to drink of the cup have assuredly drunken; and are you he that shall altogether go unpunished? you shall not go unpunished, but you shall surely drink of it. ¹³For I have sworn by myself, says the LORD, that Bozrah shall become a desolation, a reproach, a waste, and a curse; and all the cities thereof shall be perpetual wastes. ¹⁴I have heard a rumor from the LORD, and an ambassador is sent to the heathen, saying, Gather you together, and come against her, and rise up to the battle. ¹⁵For, see, I will make you small among the heathen, and despised among men. ¹⁶Your terribleness has deceived you, and the pride of your heart, O you that dwell in the clefts of the rock, that hold the height of the hill: though you should make your nest as high as the eagle, I will bring you down from there, says the LORD. ¹⁷Also Edom shall be a desolation: every one that goes by it shall be astonished, and shall hiss at all the plagues thereof. ¹⁸As in the overthrow of Sodom and Gomorrah and the neighbor cities thereof, says the LORD, no man shall abide there, neither shall a son of man dwell in it. ¹⁹Behold, he shall come up like a lion from the swelling of Jordan against the habitation of the strong: but I will suddenly make him run away from her: and who is a chosen man, that I may appoint over her? for who is like me? and who will appoint me the time? and who is that shepherd that will stand before me? ²⁰Therefore hear the counsel of the LORD, that he has taken against Edom; and his purposes, that he has purposed against the inhabitants of Teman: Surely the least of the flock shall draw them out: surely he shall make their habitations desolate with them. ²¹The earth is moved at the noise of their fall, at the cry the noise thereof was heard in the Red sea. ²²Behold, he shall come up and fly as the eagle, and spread his wings over Bozrah: and at that day shall the heart of the mighty men of Edom be as the heart of a woman in her pangs. ²³Concerning Damascus. Hamath is confounded, and Arpad: for they have heard evil tidings: they are fainthearted; there is sorrow on the sea; it cannot be quiet. ²⁴Damascus is waxed feeble, and turns herself to flee, and fear has seized on her: anguish and sorrows have taken her, as a woman in travail. ²⁵How is the city of praise not left, the city of my joy! ²⁶Therefore her young men shall fall in her streets, and all the men of war shall be cut off in that day, says the LORD of hosts. ²⁷And I will kindle a fire in the wall of Damascus, and it shall consume the palaces of Benhadad. ²⁸Concerning Kedar, and concerning the kingdoms of Hazor, which Nebuchadrezzar king of Babylon shall smite, thus says the LORD; Arise you, go up to Kedar, and spoil the men of the east. ²⁹Their tents and their flocks shall they take away: they shall take to themselves their curtains, and all their vessels, and their camels; and they shall cry to them, Fear is on every side. ³⁰Flee, get you far off, dwell deep, O you inhabitants of Hazor, says the LORD; for Nebuchadrezzar king of Babylon has taken counsel against you, and has conceived a purpose against you. ³¹Arise, get you up to the wealthy nation, that dwells without care, says the LORD, which have neither gates nor bars, which dwell alone. ³²And their camels shall be a booty, and the multitude of their cattle a spoil: and I will scatter into all winds them that are in the utmost corners; and I will bring their calamity from all sides thereof, says the LORD. ³³And Hazor shall be a dwelling for dragons, and a desolation for ever: there shall no man abide there, nor any son of man dwell in it. ³⁴The word of the LORD that came to Jeremiah the prophet against Elam in the beginning of the reign of Zedekiah king of Judah, saying, ³⁵Thus says the LORD of hosts; Behold, I will break the bow of Elam, the chief of their might. ³⁶And on Elam will I bring the four winds from the four quarters of heaven, and will scatter them toward all those winds; and there shall be no nation where the outcasts of Elam shall not come. ³⁷For I will cause Elam to be dismayed before their enemies, and before them that seek their life: and I will bring evil on them, even my fierce anger, says the LORD; and I will send the sword after them, till I have consumed them: ³⁸And I will set my throne in Elam, and will destroy from there the king and the princes, says the LORD. ³⁹But it shall come to pass in the latter days, that I will bring again the captivity of Elam, says the LORD.

50 ¹The word that the LORD spoke against Babylon and against the land of the Chaldeans by Jeremiah the prophet. ²Declare you among the nations, and publish, and set up a standard; publish, and conceal not: say, Babylon is taken, Bel is confounded, Merodach is broken in pieces; her idols are confounded, her images are broken in pieces. ³For out of the north there comes up a nation against her, which shall make her land desolate, and none shall dwell therein: they shall remove, they shall depart, both man and beast. ⁴In those days, and in that time, says the LORD, the children of Israel shall come, they and the children of Judah together, going and weeping: they shall go, and seek the LORD their God. ⁵They shall ask the way to Zion with their faces thitherward, saying, Come, and let us join ourselves to the LORD in a perpetual covenant that shall not be forgotten. ⁶My people has been lost sheep: their shepherds have caused them to go astray, they have turned them away on the mountains: they have gone from mountain to hill, they have forgotten their resting place. ⁷All that found them have devoured them: and their adversaries said, We offend not, because they have sinned against the LORD, the habitation of justice, even the LORD, the hope of their fathers. ⁸Remove out of the middle of Babylon, and go forth out of the land of the Chaldeans, and be as the he goats before the flocks. ⁹For, see, I will raise and cause to come up against Babylon an assembly of great nations from the north country: and they shall set themselves in array against her; from there she shall be taken: their arrows shall be as of a mighty expert man; none shall return in vain. ¹⁰And Chaldea shall be a spoil: all that spoil her shall be satisfied, says the LORD. ¹¹Because you were glad, because you rejoiced, O you destroyers of my heritage, because you are grown fat as the heifer at grass, and bellow as bulls; ¹²Your mother shall be sore confounded; she that bore you shall be ashamed:

behold, the last of the nations shall be a wilderness, a dry land, and a desert. ¹³Because of the wrath of the LORD it shall not be inhabited, but it shall be wholly desolate: every one that goes by Babylon shall be astonished, and hiss at all her plagues. ¹⁴Put yourselves in array against Babylon round about: all you that bend the bow, shoot at her, spare no arrows: for she has sinned against the LORD. ¹⁵Shout against her round about: she has given her hand: her foundations are fallen, her walls are thrown down: for it is the vengeance of the LORD: take vengeance on her; as she has done, do to her. ¹⁶Cut off the sower from Babylon, and him that handles the sickle in the time of harvest: for fear of the oppressing sword they shall turn every one to his people, and they shall flee every one to his own land. ¹⁷Israel is a scattered sheep; the lions have driven him away: first the king of Assyria has devoured him; and last this Nebuchadrezzar king of Babylon has broken his bones. ¹⁸Therefore thus says the LORD of hosts, the God of Israel; Behold, I will punish the king of Babylon and his land, as I have punished the king of Assyria. ¹⁹And I will bring Israel again to his habitation, and he shall feed on Carmel and Bashan, and his soul shall be satisfied on mount Ephraim and Gilead. ²⁰In those days, and in that time, says the LORD, the iniquity of Israel shall be sought for, and there shall be none; and the sins of Judah, and they shall not be found: for I will pardon them whom I reserve. ²¹Go up against the land of Merathaim, even against it, and against the inhabitants of Pekod: waste and utterly destroy after them, says the LORD, and do according to all that I have commanded you. ²²A sound of battle is in the land, and of great destruction. ²³How is the hammer of the whole earth cut asunder and broken! how is Babylon become a desolation among the nations! ²⁴I have laid a snare for you, and you are also taken, O Babylon, and you were not aware: you are found, and also caught, because you have striven against the LORD. ²⁵The LORD has opened his armory, and has brought forth the weapons of his indignation: for this is the work of the Lord GOD of hosts in the land of the Chaldeans. ²⁶Come against her from the utmost border, open her storehouses: cast her up as heaps, and destroy her utterly: let nothing of her be left. ²⁷Slay all her bullocks; let them go down to the slaughter: woe to them! for their day is come, the time of their visitation. ²⁸The voice of them that flee and escape out of the land of Babylon, to declare in Zion the vengeance of the LORD our God, the vengeance of his temple. ²⁹Call together the archers against Babylon: all you that bend the bow, camp against it round about; let none thereof escape: recompense her according to her work; according to all that she has done, do to her: for she has been proud against the LORD, against the Holy One of Israel. ³⁰Therefore shall her young men fall in the streets, and all her men of war shall be cut off in that day, says the LORD. ³¹Behold, I am against you, O you most proud, says the Lord GOD of hosts: for your day is come, the time that I will visit you. ³²And the most proud shall stumble and fall, and none shall raise him up: and I will kindle a fire in his cities, and it shall devour all round about him. ³³Thus says the LORD of hosts; The children of Israel and the children of Judah were oppressed together: and all that took them captives held them fast; they refused to let them go. ³⁴Their Redeemer is strong; the LORD of hosts is his name: he shall thoroughly plead their cause, that he may give rest to the land, and disquiet the inhabitants of Babylon. ³⁵A sword is on the Chaldeans, says the LORD, and on the inhabitants of Babylon, and on her princes, and on her wise men. ³⁶A sword is on the liars; and they shall dote: a sword is on her mighty men; and they shall be dismayed. ³⁷A sword is on their horses, and on their chariots, and on all the mingled people that are in the middle of her; and they shall become as women: a sword is on her treasures; and they shall be robbed. ³⁸A drought is on her waters; and they shall be dried up: for it is the land of graven images, and they are mad on their idols. ³⁹Therefore the wild beasts of the desert with the wild beasts of the islands shall dwell there, and the owls shall dwell therein: and it shall be no more inhabited for ever; neither shall it be dwelled in from generation to generation. ⁴⁰As God overthrew Sodom and Gomorrah and the neighbor cities thereof, says the LORD; so shall no man abide there, neither shall any son of man dwell therein. ⁴¹Behold, a people shall come from the north, and a great nation, and many kings shall be raised up from the coasts of the earth. ⁴²They shall hold the bow and the lance: they are cruel, and will not show mercy: their voice shall roar like the sea, and they shall ride on horses, every one put in array, like a man to the battle, against you, O daughter of Babylon. ⁴³The king of Babylon has heard the report of them, and his hands waxed feeble: anguish took hold of him, and pangs as of a woman in travail. ⁴⁴Behold, he shall come up like a lion from the swelling of Jordan to the habitation of the strong: but I will make them suddenly run away from her: and who is a chosen man, that I may appoint over her? for who is like me? and who will appoint me the time? and who is that shepherd that will stand before me? ⁴⁵Therefore hear you the counsel of the LORD, that he has taken against Babylon; and his purposes, that he has purposed against the land of the Chaldeans: Surely the least of the flock shall draw them out: surely he shall make their habitation desolate with them. ⁴⁶At the noise of the taking of Babylon the earth is moved, and the cry is heard among the nations.

51

¹Thus says the LORD; Behold, I will raise up against Babylon, and against them that dwell in the middle of them that rise up against me, a destroying wind; ²And will send to Babylon fanners, that shall fan her, and shall empty her land: for in the day of trouble they shall be against her round about. ³Against him that bends let the archer bend his bow, and against him that lifts himself up in his brigandine: and spare you not her young men; destroy you utterly all her host. ⁴Thus the slain shall fall in the land of the Chaldeans, and they that are thrust through in her streets. ⁵For Israel has not been forsaken, nor Judah of his God, of the LORD of hosts; though their land was filled with sin against the Holy One of Israel. ⁶Flee out of the middle of Babylon, and deliver every man his soul: be not cut off in her iniquity; for this is the time of the LORD's vengeance; he will render to her a recompense. ⁷Babylon has been a golden cup in the LORD's hand, that made all the earth drunken: the nations have drunken of her wine; therefore the nations are mad. ⁸Babylon is suddenly fallen and destroyed: howl for her; take balm for her pain, if so be she may be healed. ⁹We would have healed Babylon, but she is not healed: forsake her, and let us go every one into his

own country: for her judgment reaches to heaven, and is lifted up even to the skies. ¹⁰The LORD has brought forth our righteousness: come, and let us declare in Zion the work of the LORD our God. ¹¹Make bright the arrows; gather the shields: the LORD has raised up the spirit of the kings of the Medes: for his device is against Babylon, to destroy it; because it is the vengeance of the LORD, the vengeance of his temple. ¹²Set up the standard on the walls of Babylon, make the watch strong, set up the watchmen, prepare the ambushes: for the LORD has both devised and done that which he spoke against the inhabitants of Babylon. ¹³O you that dwell on many waters, abundant in treasures, your end is come, and the measure of your covetousness. ¹⁴The LORD of hosts has sworn by himself, saying, Surely I will fill you with men, as with caterpillars; and they shall lift up a shout against you. ¹⁵He has made the earth by his power, he has established the world by his wisdom, and has stretched out the heaven by his understanding. ¹⁶When he utters his voice, there is a multitude of waters in the heavens; and he causes the vapors to ascend from the ends of the earth: he makes lightning with rain, and brings forth the wind out of his treasures. ¹⁷Every man is brutish by his knowledge; every founder is confounded by the graven image: for his molten image is falsehood, and there is no breath in them. ¹⁸They are vanity, the work of errors: in the time of their visitation they shall perish. ¹⁹The portion of Jacob is not like them; for he is the former of all things: and Israel is the rod of his inheritance: the LORD of hosts is his name. ²⁰You are my battle ax and weapons of war: for with you will I break in pieces the nations, and with you will I destroy kingdoms; ²¹And with you will I break in pieces the horse and his rider; and with you will I break in pieces the chariot and his rider; ²²With you also will I break in pieces man and woman; and with you will I break in pieces old and young; and with you will I break in pieces the young man and the maid; ²³I will also break in pieces with you the shepherd and his flock; and with you will I break in pieces the farmer and his yoke of oxen; and with you will I break in pieces captains and rulers. ²⁴And I will render to Babylon and to all the inhabitants of Chaldea all their evil that they have done in Zion in your sight, says the LORD. ²⁵Behold, I am against you, O destroying mountain, says the LORD, which destroy all the earth: and I will stretch out my hand on you, and roll you down from the rocks, and will make you a burnt mountain. ²⁶And they shall not take of you a stone for a corner, nor a stone for foundations; but you shall be desolate for ever, says the LORD. ²⁷Set you up a standard in the land, blow the trumpet among the nations, prepare the nations against her, call together against her the kingdoms of Ararat, Minni, and Ashchenaz; appoint a captain against her; cause the horses to come up as the rough caterpillars. ²⁸Prepare against her the nations with the kings of the Medes, the captains thereof, and all the rulers thereof, and all the land of his dominion. ²⁹And the land shall tremble and sorrow: for every purpose of the LORD shall be performed against Babylon, to make the land of Babylon a desolation without an inhabitant. ³⁰The mighty men of Babylon have declined to fight, they have remained in their holds: their might has failed; they became as women: they have burned her dwelling places; her bars are broken. ³¹One post shall run to meet another, and one messenger to meet another, to show the king of Babylon that his city is taken at one end, ³²And that the passages are stopped, and the reeds they have burned with fire, and the men of war are affrighted. ³³For thus says the LORD of hosts, the God of Israel; The daughter of Babylon is like a threshing floor, it is time to thresh her: yet a little while, and the time of her harvest shall come. ³⁴Nebuchadrezzar the king of Babylon has devoured me, he has crushed me, he has made me an empty vessel, he has swallowed me up like a dragon, he has filled his belly with my delicates, he has cast me out. ³⁵The violence done to me and to my flesh be on Babylon, shall the inhabitant of Zion say; and my blood on the inhabitants of Chaldea, shall Jerusalem say. ³⁶Therefore thus says the LORD; Behold, I will plead your cause, and take vengeance for you; and I will dry up her sea, and make her springs dry. ³⁷And Babylon shall become heaps, a dwelling place for dragons, an astonishment, and an hissing, without an inhabitant. ³⁸They shall roar together like lions: they shall yell as lions' whelps. ³⁹In their heat I will make their feasts, and I will make them drunken, that they may rejoice, and sleep a perpetual sleep, and not wake, says the LORD. ⁴⁰I will bring them down like lambs to the slaughter, like rams with he goats. ⁴¹How is Sheshach taken! and how is the praise of the whole earth surprised! how is Babylon become an astonishment among the nations! ⁴²The sea is come up on Babylon: she is covered with the multitude of the waves thereof. ⁴³Her cities are a desolation, a dry land, and a wilderness, a land wherein no man dwells, neither does any son of man pass thereby. ⁴⁴And I will punish Bel in Babylon, and I will bring forth out of his mouth that which he has swallowed up: and the nations shall not flow together any more to him: yes, the wall of Babylon shall fall. ⁴⁵My people, go you out of the middle of her, and deliver you every man his soul from the fierce anger of the LORD. ⁴⁶And lest your heart faint, and you fear for the rumor that shall be heard in the land; a rumor shall both come one year, and after that in another year shall come a rumor, and violence in the land, ruler against ruler. ⁴⁷Therefore, behold, the days come, that I will do judgment on the graven images of Babylon: and her whole land shall be confounded, and all her slain shall fall in the middle of her. ⁴⁸Then the heaven and the earth, and all that is therein, shall sing for Babylon: for the spoilers shall come to her from the north, says the LORD. ⁴⁹As Babylon has caused the slain of Israel to fall, so at Babylon shall fall the slain of all the earth. ⁵⁰You that have escaped the sword, go away, stand not still: remember the LORD afar off, and let Jerusalem come into your mind. ⁵¹We are confounded, because we have heard reproach: shame has covered our faces: for strangers are come into the sanctuaries of the LORD's house. ⁵²Why, behold, the days come, says the LORD, that I will do judgment on her graven images: and through all her land the wounded shall groan. ⁵³Though Babylon should mount up to heaven, and though she should fortify the height of her strength, yet from me shall spoilers come to her, says the LORD. ⁵⁴A sound of a cry comes from Babylon, and great destruction from the land of the Chaldeans: ⁵⁵Because the LORD has spoiled Babylon, and destroyed out of her the great voice; when her waves do roar like great waters, a noise of their voice is uttered: ⁵⁶Because the spoiler is come on her, even on

Babylon, and her mighty men are taken, every one of their bows is broken: for the LORD God of recompenses shall surely requite. ⁵⁷And I will make drunk her princes, and her wise men, her captains, and her rulers, and her mighty men: and they shall sleep a perpetual sleep, and not wake, says the King, whose name is the LORD of hosts. ⁵⁸Thus says the LORD of hosts; The broad walls of Babylon shall be utterly broken, and her high gates shall be burned with fire; and the people shall labor in vain, and the folk in the fire, and they shall be weary. ⁵⁹The word which Jeremiah the prophet commanded Seraiah the son of Neriah, the son of Maaseiah, when he went with Zedekiah the king of Judah into Babylon in the fourth year of his reign. And this Seraiah was a quiet prince. ⁶⁰So Jeremiah wrote in a book all the evil that should come on Babylon, even all these words that are written against Babylon. ⁶¹And Jeremiah said to Seraiah, When you come to Babylon, and shall see, and shall read all these words; ⁶²Then shall you say, O LORD, you have spoken against this place, to cut it off, that none shall remain in it, neither man nor beast, but that it shall be desolate for ever. ⁶³And it shall be, when you have made an end of reading this book, that you shall bind a stone to it, and cast it into the middle of Euphrates: ⁶⁴And you shall say, Thus shall Babylon sink, and shall not rise from the evil that I will bring on her: and they shall be weary. Thus far are the words of Jeremiah.

52 ¹Zedekiah was one and twenty years old when he began to reign, and he reigned eleven years in Jerusalem. And his mother's name was Hamutal the daughter of Jeremiah of Libnah. ²And he did that which was evil in the eyes of the LORD, according to all that Jehoiakim had done. ³For through the anger of the LORD it came to pass in Jerusalem and Judah, till he had cast them out from his presence, that Zedekiah rebelled against the king of Babylon. ⁴And it came to pass in the ninth year of his reign, in the tenth month, in the tenth day of the month, that Nebuchadrezzar king of Babylon came, he and all his army, against Jerusalem, and pitched against it, and built forts against it round about. ⁵So the city was besieged to the eleventh year of king Zedekiah. ⁶And in the fourth month, in the ninth day of the month, the famine was sore in the city, so that there was no bread for the people of the land. ⁷Then the city was broken up, and all the men of war fled, and went forth out of the city by night by the way of the gate between the two walls, which was by the king's garden; (now the Chaldeans were by the city round about:) and they went by the way of the plain. ⁸But the army of the Chaldeans pursued after the king, and overtook Zedekiah in the plains of Jericho; and all his army was scattered from him. ⁹Then they took the king, and carried him up to the king of Babylon to Riblah in the land of Hamath; where he gave judgment on him. ¹⁰And the king of Babylon slew the sons of Zedekiah before his eyes: he slew also all the princes of Judah in Riblah. ¹¹Then he put out the eyes of Zedekiah; and the king of Babylon bound him in chains, and carried him to Babylon, and put him in prison till the day of his death. ¹²Now in the fifth month, in the tenth day of the month, which was the nineteenth year of Nebuchadrezzar king of Babylon, came Nebuzaradan, captain of the guard, which served the king of Babylon, into Jerusalem, ¹³And burned the house of the LORD, and the king's house; and all the houses of Jerusalem, and all the houses of the great men, burned he with fire: ¹⁴And all the army of the Chaldeans, that were with the captain of the guard, broke down all the walls of Jerusalem round about. ¹⁵Then Nebuzaradan the captain of the guard carried away captive certain of the poor of the people, and the residue of the people that remained in the city, and those that fell away, that fell to the king of Babylon, and the rest of the multitude. ¹⁶But Nebuzaradan the captain of the guard left certain of the poor of the land for vinedressers and for farmers. ¹⁷Also the pillars of brass that were in the house of the LORD, and the bases, and the brazen sea that was in the house of the LORD, the Chaldeans broke, and carried all the brass of them to Babylon. ¹⁸The caldrons also, and the shovels, and the snuffers, and the bowls, and the spoons, and all the vessels of brass with which they ministered, took they away. ¹⁹And the basins, and the fire pans, and the bowls, and the caldrons, and the candlesticks, and the spoons, and the cups; that which was of gold in gold, and that which was of silver in silver, took the captain of the guard away. ²⁰The two pillars, one sea, and twelve brazen bulls that were under the bases, which king Solomon had made in the house of the LORD: the brass of all these vessels was without weight. ²¹And concerning the pillars, the height of one pillar was eighteen cubits; and a fillet of twelve cubits did compass it; and the thickness thereof was four fingers: it was hollow. ²²And a capital of brass was on it; and the height of one capital was five cubits, with network and pomegranates on the capitals round about, all of brass. The second pillar also and the pomegranates were like to these. ²³And there were ninety and six pomegranates on a side; and all the pomegranates on the network were an hundred round about. ²⁴And the captain of the guard took Seraiah the chief priest, and Zephaniah the second priest, and the three keepers of the door: ²⁵He took also out of the city an eunuch, which had the charge of the men of war; and seven men of them that were near the king's person, which were found in the city; and the principal scribe of the host, who mustered the people of the land; and three score men of the people of the land, that were found in the middle of the city. ²⁶So Nebuzaradan the captain of the guard took them, and brought them to the king of Babylon to Riblah. ²⁷And the king of Babylon smote them, and put them to death in Riblah in the land of Hamath. Thus Judah was carried away captive out of his own land. ²⁸This is the people whom Nebuchadrezzar carried away captive: in the seventh year three thousand Jews and three and twenty: ²⁹In the eighteenth year of Nebuchadrezzar he carried away captive from Jerusalem eight hundred thirty and two persons: ³⁰In the three and twentieth year of Nebuchadrezzar Nebuzaradan the captain of the guard carried away captive of the Jews seven hundred forty and five persons: all the persons were four thousand and six hundred. ³¹And it came to pass in the seven and thirtieth year of the captivity of Jehoiachin king of Judah, in the twelfth month, in the five and twentieth day of the month, that Evilmerodach king of Babylon in the first year of his reign lifted up the head of Jehoiachin king of Judah, and brought him forth out of prison. ³²And spoke kindly to him, and set his throne above the throne of the kings that were with him in Babylon, ³³And changed his prison garments: and he did continually eat bread before him all the days of his life. ³⁴And for his diet, there was a continual diet given him of the king of Babylon, every day a portion until the day of his death, all the days of his life.

Lamentations

1 ¹How does the city sit solitary, that was full of people! how is she become as a widow! she that was great among the nations, and princess among the provinces, how is she become tributary! ²She weeps sore in the night, and her tears are on her cheeks: among all her lovers she has none to comfort her: all her friends have dealt treacherously with her, they are become her enemies. ³Judah is gone into captivity because of affliction, and because of great servitude: she dwells among the heathen, she finds no rest: all her persecutors overtook her between the straits. ⁴The ways of Zion do mourn, because none come to the solemn feasts: all her gates are desolate: her priests sigh, her virgins are afflicted, and she is in bitterness. ⁵Her adversaries are the chief, her enemies prosper; for the LORD has afflicted her for the multitude of her transgressions: her children are gone into captivity before the enemy. ⁶And from the daughter of Zion all her beauty is departed: her princes are become like harts that find no pasture, and they are gone without strength before the pursuer. ⁷Jerusalem remembered in the days of her affliction and of her miseries all her pleasant things that she had in the days of old, when her people fell into the hand of the enemy, and none did help her: the adversaries saw her, and did mock at her sabbaths. ⁸Jerusalem has grievously sinned; therefore she is removed: all that honored her despise her, because they have seen her nakedness: yes, she sighs, and turns backward. ⁹Her filthiness is in her skirts; she remembers not her last end; therefore she came down wonderfully: she had no comforter. O LORD, behold my affliction: for the enemy has magnified himself. ¹⁰The adversary has spread out his hand on all her pleasant things: for she has seen that the heathen entered into her sanctuary, whom you did command that they should not enter into your congregation. ¹¹All her people sigh, they seek bread; they have given their pleasant things for meat to relieve the soul: see, O LORD, and consider; for I am become vile. ¹²Is it nothing to you, all you that pass by? behold, and see if there be any sorrow like to my sorrow, which is done to me, with which the LORD has afflicted me in the day of his fierce anger. ¹³From above has he sent fire into my bones, and it prevails against them: he has spread a net for my feet, he has turned me back: he has made me desolate and faint all the day. ¹⁴The yoke of my transgressions is bound by his hand: they are wreathed, and come up on my neck: he has made my strength to fall, the LORD has delivered me into their hands, from whom I am not able to rise up. ¹⁵The LORD has trodden under foot all my mighty men in the middle of me: he has called an assembly against me to crush my young men: the LORD has trodden the virgin, the daughter of Judah, as in a wine press. ¹⁶For these things I weep; my eye, my eye runs down with water, because the comforter that should relieve my soul is far from me: my children are desolate, because the enemy prevailed. ¹⁷Zion spreads forth her hands, and there is none to comfort her: the LORD has commanded concerning Jacob, that his adversaries should be round about him: Jerusalem is as a menstruous woman among them. ¹⁸The LORD is righteous; for I have rebelled against his commandment: hear, I pray you, all people, and behold my sorrow: my virgins and my young men are gone into captivity. ¹⁹I called for my lovers, but they deceived me: my priests and my elders gave up the ghost in the city, while they sought their meat to relieve their souls. ²⁰Behold, O LORD; for I am in distress: my bowels are troubled; my heart is turned within me; for I have grievously rebelled: abroad the sword bereaves, at home there is as death. ²¹They have heard that I sigh: there is none to comfort me: all my enemies have heard of my trouble; they are glad that you have done it: you will bring the day that you have called, and they shall be like to me. ²²Let all their wickedness come before you; and do to them, as you have done to me for all my transgressions: for my sighs are many, and my heart is faint.

2 ¹How has the LORD covered the daughter of Zion with a cloud in his anger, and cast down from heaven to the earth the beauty of Israel, and remembered not his footstool in the day of his anger! ²The LORD has swallowed up all the habitations of Jacob, and has not pitied: he has thrown down in his wrath the strong holds of the daughter of Judah; he has brought them down to the ground: he has polluted the kingdom and the princes thereof. ³He has cut off in his fierce anger all the horn of Israel: he has drawn back his right hand from before the enemy, and he burned against Jacob like a flaming fire, which devours round about. ⁴He has bent his bow like an enemy: he stood with his right hand as an adversary, and slew all that were pleasant to the eye in the tabernacle of the daughter of Zion: he poured out his fury like fire. ⁵The LORD was as an enemy: he has swallowed up Israel, he has swallowed up all her palaces: he has destroyed his strong holds, and has increased in the daughter of Judah mourning and lamentation. ⁶And he has violently taken away his tabernacle, as if it were of a garden: he has destroyed his places of the assembly: the LORD has caused the solemn feasts and sabbaths to be forgotten in Zion, and has despised in the indignation of his anger the king and the priest. ⁷The LORD has cast off his altar, he has abhorred his sanctuary, he has given up into the hand of the enemy the walls of her palaces; they have made a noise in the house of the LORD, as in the day of a solemn feast. ⁸The LORD has purposed to destroy the wall of the daughter of Zion: he has stretched out a line, he has not withdrawn his hand from destroying: therefore he made the rampart and the wall to lament; they languished together. ⁹Her gates are sunk into the ground; he has destroyed and broken her bars: her king and her princes are among the Gentiles: the law is no more; her prophets also find no vision from the LORD. ¹⁰The elders of the daughter of Zion sit on the ground, and keep silence: they have cast up dust on their heads; they have girded themselves with sackcloth: the virgins of Jerusalem hang down their heads to the ground. ¹¹My eyes do fail with tears, my bowels are troubled, my liver is poured on the earth, for the destruction of the daughter of my people; because the children and the sucklings swoon in the streets of the city. ¹²They say to their mothers, Where is corn and wine? when they swooned as the wounded in the streets of the city, when their soul was poured out into their mothers' bosom. ¹³What thing shall I take to witness for you? what thing shall I liken to you, O daughter of Jerusalem? what shall I equal to you, that I may comfort you, O virgin daughter of Zion? for your breach is great like the sea: who can heal you? ¹⁴Your prophets have seen vain and foolish things for you: and they have not discovered your iniquity, to turn away your captivity; but have seen for you false burdens and causes of banishment. ¹⁵All that pass by clap their hands at you; they hiss and wag their head at the daughter of Jerusalem, saying, Is this the city that men call The perfection of beauty, The joy of the whole earth? ¹⁶All your enemies have opened their mouth against you: they hiss and gnash the teeth: they say, We have swallowed her up: certainly this is the day that we looked for; we have found, we have seen it. ¹⁷The LORD has done that which he had devised; he has fulfilled his word that he had commanded in the days of old: he has thrown down, and has not pitied: and he has caused your enemy to rejoice over you, he has set up the horn of your adversaries. ¹⁸Their heart cried to the LORD, O wall of the daughter of Zion, let tears run down like a river day and night: give yourself no rest; let not the apple of your eye cease. ¹⁹Arise, cry out in the night: in the beginning of the watches pour out your heart like water before the face of the LORD: lift up your hands toward him for the life of your young children, that faint for hunger in the top of every street. ²⁰Behold, O LORD, and consider to whom you have done this. Shall the women eat their fruit, and children of a span long? shall the priest and the prophet be slain in the sanctuary of the Lord? ²¹The young and the old lie on the ground in the streets: my virgins and my young men are fallen by the sword; you have slain them in the day of your anger; you have killed, and not pitied. ²²You have called as in a solemn day my terrors round about, so that in the day of the LORD's anger none escaped nor remained: those that I have swaddled and brought up has my enemy consumed.

3 ¹I AM the man that has seen affliction by the rod of his wrath. ²He has led me, and brought me into darkness, but not into light. ³Surely against me is he turned; he turns his hand against me all the day. ⁴My flesh and my skin has he made old; he has broken my bones. ⁵He has built against me, and compassed me with gall and travail. ⁶He has set me in dark places, as they that be dead of old. ⁷He has hedged me about, that I cannot get out: he has made my chain heavy. ⁸Also when I cry and shout, he shuts out my prayer. ⁹He has enclosed my ways with hewn stone, he has made my paths crooked. ¹⁰He was to me as a bear lying in wait, and as a lion in secret places. ¹¹He has turned aside my ways, and pulled me in pieces: he has made me desolate. ¹²He has bent his bow, and set me as a mark for the arrow. ¹³He has caused the arrows of his quiver to enter into my reins. ¹⁴I was a derision to all my people; and their song all the day. ¹⁵He has filled me with bitterness, he has made me drunken with wormwood. ¹⁶He has also broken my teeth with gravel stones, he has covered me with ashes. ¹⁷And you have removed my soul far off from peace: I forgot prosperity. ¹⁸And I said, My strength and my hope is perished from the LORD: ¹⁹Remembering my affliction and my misery, the wormwood and the gall. ²⁰My soul has them still in remembrance, and is humbled in me. ²¹This I recall to my mind, therefore have I hope. ²²It is of the LORD's mercies that we are not consumed, because his compassions fail not. ²³They are new every morning: great is your faithfulness. ²⁴The LORD is my portion, says my soul; therefore will I hope in him. ²⁵The LORD is good to them that wait for him, to the soul that seeks him. ²⁶It is good that a man should both hope and quietly wait for the salvation of the LORD. ²⁷It is good for a man that he bear the yoke of his youth. ²⁸He sits alone and keeps silence, because he has borne it on him. ²⁹He puts his mouth in the dust; if so be there may be hope. ³⁰He gives his cheek to him that smites him: he is filled full with reproach. ³¹For the LORD will not cast off for ever: ³²But though he cause grief, yet will he have compassion according to the multitude of his mercies. ³³For he does not afflict willingly nor grieve the children of men. ³⁴To crush under his feet all the prisoners of the earth. ³⁵To turn aside the right of a man before the face of the most High, ³⁶To subvert a man in his cause, the LORD approves not. ³⁷Who is he that says, and it comes to pass, when the Lord commands it not? ³⁸Out of the mouth of the most High proceeds not evil and good? ³⁹Why does a living man complain, a man for the punishment of his sins? ⁴⁰Let us search and try our ways, and turn again to the LORD. ⁴¹Let us lift up our heart with our hands to God in the heavens. ⁴²We have transgressed and have rebelled: you have not pardoned. ⁴³You have covered with anger, and persecuted us: you have slain, you have not pitied. ⁴⁴You have covered yourself with a cloud, that our prayer should not pass through. ⁴⁵You have made us as the offscouring and refuse in the middle of the people. ⁴⁶All our enemies have opened their mouths against us. ⁴⁷Fear and a snare is come on us, desolation and destruction. ⁴⁸My eye runs down with rivers of water for the destruction of the daughter of my people. ⁴⁹My eye trickles down, and ceases not, without any intermission. ⁵⁰Till the LORD look down, and behold from heaven. ⁵¹My eye affects my heart because of all the daughters of my city. ⁵²My enemies chased me sore, like a bird, without cause. ⁵³They have cut off my life in the dungeon, and cast a stone on me. ⁵⁴Waters flowed over my head; then I said, I am cut off. ⁵⁵I called on your name, O LORD, out of the low dungeon. ⁵⁶You have heard my voice: hide not your ear at my breathing, at my cry. ⁵⁷You drew near in the day that I called on you: you said, Fear not. ⁵⁸O LORD, you have pleaded the causes of my soul; you have redeemed my life. ⁵⁹O LORD, you have seen my wrong: judge you my cause. ⁶⁰You have seen all their vengeance and all their imaginations against me. ⁶¹You have heard their reproach, O LORD, and all their imaginations against me; ⁶²The lips of those that rose up against me, and their device against me all the day. ⁶³Behold their sitting down, and their rising up; I am their music. ⁶⁴Render to them a recompense, O LORD, according to the work of their hands. ⁶⁵Give them sorrow of heart, your curse to them. ⁶⁶Persecute and destroy them in anger from under the heavens of the LORD.

4 ¹How is the gold become dim! how is the most fine gold changed! the stones of the sanctuary are poured out in the top of every street. ²The precious sons of Zion, comparable to fine gold, how are they esteemed as earthen pitchers, the work of the hands of the potter! ³Even the sea monsters draw out the breast, they give suck to their young ones: the daughter of my people is become cruel, like the ostriches in the wilderness. ⁴The tongue of the sucking child sticks to the roof of his mouth for thirst: the young children ask bread, and no man breaks it to them. ⁵They that did feed

delicately are desolate in the streets: they that were brought up in scarlet embrace dunghills. ⁶For the punishment of the iniquity of the daughter of my people is greater than the punishment of the sin of Sodom, that was overthrown as in a moment, and no hands stayed on her. ⁷Her Nazarites were purer than snow, they were whiter than milk, they were more ruddy in body than rubies, their polishing was of sapphire: ⁸Their visage is blacker than a coal; they are not known in the streets: their skin sticks to their bones; it is withered, it is become like a stick. ⁹They that be slain with the sword are better than they that be slain with hunger: for these pine away, stricken through for want of the fruits of the field. ¹⁰The hands of the pitiful women have sodden their own children: they were their meat in the destruction of the daughter of my people. ¹¹The LORD has accomplished his fury; he has poured out his fierce anger, and has kindled a fire in Zion, and it has devoured the foundations thereof. ¹²The kings of the earth, and all the inhabitants of the world, would not have believed that the adversary and the enemy should have entered into the gates of Jerusalem. ¹³For the sins of her prophets, and the iniquities of her priests, that have shed the blood of the just in the middle of her, ¹⁴They have wandered as blind men in the streets, they have polluted themselves with blood, so that men could not touch their garments. ¹⁵They cried to them, Depart you; it is unclean; depart, depart, touch not: when they fled away and wandered, they said among the heathen, They shall no more sojourn there. ¹⁶The anger of the LORD has divided them; he will no more regard them: they respected not the persons of the priests, they favored not the elders. ¹⁷As for us, our eyes as yet failed for our vain help: in our watching we have watched for a nation that could not save us. ¹⁸They hunt our steps, that we cannot go in our streets: our end is near, our days are fulfilled; for our end is come. ¹⁹Our persecutors are swifter than the eagles of the heaven: they pursued us on the mountains, they laid wait for us in the wilderness. ²⁰The breath of our nostrils, the anointed of the LORD, was taken in their pits, of whom we said, Under his shadow we shall live among the heathen. ²¹Rejoice and be glad, O daughter of Edom, that dwell in the land of Uz; the cup also shall pass through to you: you shall be drunken, and shall make yourself naked. ²²The punishment of your iniquity is accomplished, O daughter of Zion; he will no more carry you away into captivity: he will visit your iniquity, O daughter of Edom; he will discover your sins.

5 ¹Remember, O LORD, what is come on us: consider, and behold our reproach. ²Our inheritance is turned to strangers, our houses to aliens. ³We are orphans and fatherless, our mothers are as widows. ⁴We have drunken our water for money; our wood is sold to us. ⁵Our necks are under persecution: we labor, and have no rest. ⁶We have given the hand to the Egyptians, and to the Assyrians, to be satisfied with bread. ⁷Our fathers have sinned, and are not; and we have borne their iniquities. ⁸Servants have ruled over us: there is none that does deliver us out of their hand. ⁹We got our bread with the peril of our lives because of the sword of the wilderness. ¹⁰Our skin was black like an oven because of the terrible famine. ¹¹They ravished the women in Zion, and the maids in the cities of Judah. ¹²Princes are hanged up by their hand: the faces of elders were not honored. ¹³They took the young men to grind, and the children fell under the wood. ¹⁴The elders have ceased from the gate, the young men from their music. ¹⁵The joy of our heart is ceased; our dance is turned into mourning. ¹⁶The crown is fallen from our head: woe to us, that we have sinned! ¹⁷For this our heart is faint; for these things our eyes are dim. ¹⁸Because of the mountain of Zion, which is desolate, the foxes walk on it. ¹⁹You, O LORD, remain for ever; your throne from generation to generation. ²⁰Why do you forget us for ever, and forsake us so long time? ²¹Turn you us to you, O LORD, and we shall be turned; renew our days as of old. ²²But you have utterly rejected us; you are very wroth against us.

Ezekiel

1 ¹Now it came to pass in the thirtieth year, in the fourth month, in the fifth day of the month, as I was among the captives by the river of Chebar, that the heavens were opened, and I saw visions of God. ²In the fifth day of the month, which was the fifth year of king Jehoiachin's captivity, ³The word of the LORD came expressly to Ezekiel the priest, the son of Buzi, in the land of the Chaldeans by the river Chebar; and the hand of the LORD was there on him. ⁴And I looked, and, behold, a whirlwind came out of the north, a great cloud, and a fire enfolding itself, and a brightness was about it, and out of the middle thereof as the color of amber, out of the middle of the fire. ⁵Also out of the middle thereof came the likeness of four living creatures. And this was their appearance; they had the likeness of a man. ⁶And every one had four faces, and every one had four wings. ⁷And their feet were straight feet; and the sole of their feet was like the sole of a calf's foot: and they sparkled like the color of burnished brass. ⁸And they had the hands of a man under their wings on their four sides; and they four had their faces and their wings. ⁹Their wings were joined one to another; they turned not when they went; they went every one straight forward. ¹⁰As for the likeness of their faces, they four had the face of a man, and the face of a lion, on the right side: and they four had the face of an ox on the left side; they four also had the face of an eagle. ¹¹Thus were their faces: and their wings were stretched upward; two wings of every one were joined one to another, and two covered their bodies. ¹²And they went every one straight forward: where the spirit was to go, they went; and they turned not when they went. ¹³As for the likeness of the living creatures, their appearance was like burning coals of fire, and like the appearance of lamps: it went up and down among the living creatures; and the fire was bright, and out of the fire went forth lightning. ¹⁴And the living creatures ran and returned as the appearance of a flash of lightning. ¹⁵Now as I beheld the living creatures, behold one wheel on the earth by the living creatures, with his four faces. ¹⁶The appearance of the wheels and their work was like to the color of a beryl: and they four had one likeness: and their appearance and their work was as it were a wheel in the middle of a wheel. ¹⁷When they went, they went on their four sides: and they turned not when they went. ¹⁸As for their rings, they were so high that they were dreadful; and their rings were full of eyes round about them four. ¹⁹And when the living creatures went, the wheels went by them: and when the living creatures were lifted up from the earth, the wheels were lifted up. ²⁰Wherever the spirit was to go, they went, thither was their spirit to go; and the wheels were lifted up over against them: for the spirit of the living creature was in the wheels. ²¹When those went, these went; and when those stood, these stood; and when those were lifted up from the earth, the wheels were lifted up over against them: for the spirit of the living creature was in the wheels. ²²And the likeness of the firmament on the heads of the living creature was as the color of the terrible crystal, stretched forth over their heads above. ²³And under the firmament were their wings straight, the one toward the other: every one had two, which covered on this side, and every one had two, which covered on that side, their bodies. ²⁴And when they went, I heard the noise of their wings, like the noise of great waters, as the voice of the Almighty, the voice of speech, as the noise of an host: when they stood, they let down their wings. ²⁵And there was a voice from the firmament that was over their heads, when they stood, and had let down their wings. ²⁶And above the firmament that was over their heads was the likeness of a throne, as the appearance of a sapphire stone: and on the likeness of the throne was the likeness as the appearance of a man above on it. ²⁷And I saw as the color of amber, as the appearance of fire round about within it, from the appearance of his loins even upward, and from the appearance of his loins even downward, I saw as it were the appearance of fire, and it had brightness round about. ²⁸As the appearance of the bow that is in the cloud in the day of rain, so was the appearance of the brightness round about. This was the appearance of the likeness of the glory of the LORD. And when I saw it, I fell on my face, and I heard a voice of one that spoke.

2 ¹And he said to me, Son of man, stand on your feet, and I will speak to you. ²And the spirit entered into me when he spoke to me, and set me on my feet, that I heard him that spoke to me. ³And he said to me, Son of man, I send you to the children of Israel, to a rebellious nation that has rebelled against me: they and their fathers have transgressed against me, even to this very day. ⁴For they are impudent children and stiff hearted. I do send you to them; and you shall say to them, Thus says the Lord GOD. ⁵And they, whether they will hear, or whether they will forbear, (for they are a rebellious house,) yet shall know that there has been a prophet among them. ⁶And you, son of man, be not afraid of them, neither be afraid of their words, though briers and thorns be with you, and you do dwell among scorpions: be not afraid of their words, nor be dismayed at their looks, though they be a rebellious house. ⁷And you shall speak my words to them, whether they will hear, or whether they will forbear: for they are most rebellious. ⁸But you, son of man, hear what I say to you; Be not you rebellious like that rebellious house: open your mouth, and eat that I give you. ⁹And when I looked, behold, an hand was sent to me; and, see, a roll of a book was therein; ¹⁰And he spread it before me; and it was written within and without: and there was written therein lamentations, and mourning, and woe.

3 ¹Moreover he said to me, Son of man, eat that you find; eat this roll, and go speak to the house of Israel. ²So I opened my mouth, and he caused me to eat that roll. ³And he said to me, Son of man, cause your belly to eat, and fill your bowels with this roll that I give you. Then did I eat it; and it was in my mouth as honey for sweetness. ⁴And he said to me, Son of man, go, get you to the house of Israel, and speak with my words to them. ⁵For you are not sent to a people of a strange speech and of an hard language, but to the house of Israel; ⁶Not to many people of a strange speech and of an hard language, whose words you can not understand. Surely, had I sent you to them, they would have listened to you. ⁷But the house of Israel will not listen to you; for they will not listen to me: for all the house of Israel are impudent and hardhearted. ⁸Behold, I have made your face strong against their faces, and your forehead strong against their foreheads. ⁹As an adamant harder than flint have I made your forehead: fear them not, neither be dismayed at their looks, though they be a rebellious house. ¹⁰Moreover he said to me, Son of man, all my words that I shall speak to you receive in your heart, and hear with your ears. ¹¹And go, get you to them of the captivity, to the children of your people, and speak to them, and tell them, Thus says the Lord GOD; whether they will hear, or whether they will forbear. ¹²Then the spirit took me up, and I heard behind me a voice of a great rushing, saying, Blessed be the glory of the LORD from his place. ¹³I heard also the noise of the wings of the living creatures that touched one another, and the noise of the wheels over against them, and a noise of a great rushing. ¹⁴So the spirit lifted me up, and took me away, and I went in bitterness, in the heat of my spirit; but the hand of the LORD was strong on me. ¹⁵Then I came to them of the captivity at Telabib, that dwelled by the river of Chebar, and I sat where they sat, and remained there astonished among them seven days. ¹⁶And it came to pass at the end of seven days, that the word of the LORD came to me, saying, ¹⁷Son of man, I have made you a watchman to the house of Israel: therefore hear the word at my mouth, and give them warning from me. ¹⁸When I say to the wicked, You shall surely die; and you give him not warning, nor speak to warn the wicked from his wicked way, to save his life; the same wicked man shall die in his iniquity; but his blood will I require at your hand. ¹⁹Yet if you warn the wicked, and he turn not from his wickedness, nor from his wicked way, he shall die in his iniquity; but you have delivered your soul. ²⁰Again, When a righteous man does turn from his righteousness, and commit iniquity, and I lay a stumbling-block before him, he shall die: because you have not given him warning, he shall die in his sin, and his righteousness which he has done shall not be remembered; but his blood will I require at your hand. ²¹Nevertheless if you warn the righteous man, that the righteous sin not, and he does not sin, he shall surely live, because he is warned; also you have delivered your soul. ²²And the hand of the LORD was there on me; and he said to me, Arise, go forth into the plain, and I will there talk with you. ²³Then I arose, and went forth into the plain: and, behold, the glory of the LORD stood there, as the glory which I saw by the river of Chebar: and I fell on my face. ²⁴Then the spirit entered into me, and set me on my feet, and spoke with me, and said to me, Go, shut yourself within your house. ²⁵But you, O son of man, behold, they shall put bands on you, and shall bind you with them, and you shall not go out among them: ²⁶And I will make your tongue sticks to the roof of your mouth, that you shall be dumb, and shall not be to them a reprover: for they are a rebellious house. ²⁷But when I speak with you, I will open your mouth, and you shall say to them, Thus says the Lord GOD; He that hears, let him hear; and he that declines, let him forbear: for they are a rebellious house.

4 ¹You also, son of man, take you a tile, and lay it before you, and portray on it the city, even Jerusalem: ²And lay siege against it, and build a fort against it, and cast a mount against it; set the camp also against it, and set battering rams against it round about. ³Moreover take you to you an iron pan, and set it for a wall of iron between you and the city: and set your face against it, and it shall be besieged, and you shall lay siege against it. This shall be a sign to the house of Israel. ⁴Lie you also on your left side, and lay the iniquity of the house of Israel on it: according to the number of the days that you shall lie on it you shall bear their iniquity. ⁵For I have laid on you the years of their iniquity, according to the number of the days, three hundred and ninety days: so shall you bear the iniquity of the house of Israel. ⁶And when you have accomplished them, lie again on your right side, and you shall bear the iniquity of the house of Judah forty days: I have appointed you each day for a year. ⁷Therefore you shall set your face toward the siege of Jerusalem, and your arm shall be uncovered, and you shall prophesy against it. ⁸And, behold, I will lay bands on you, and you shall not turn you from one side to another, till you have ended the days of your siege. ⁹Take you also to you wheat, and barley, and beans, and lentils, and millet, and fitches, and put them in one vessel, and make you bread thereof, according to the number of the days that you shall lie on your side, three hundred and ninety days shall you eat thereof. ¹⁰And your meat which you shall eat shall be by weight, twenty shekels a day: from time to time shall you eat it. ¹¹You shall drink also water by measure, the sixth part of an hin: from time to time shall you drink. ¹²And you shall eat it as barley cakes, and you shall bake it with dung that comes out of man, in their sight. ¹³And the LORD said, Even thus shall the children of Israel eat their defiled bread among the Gentiles, where I will drive them. ¹⁴Then said I, Ah Lord GOD! behold, my soul has not been polluted: for from my youth up even till now have I not eaten of that which dies of itself, or is torn in pieces; neither came there abominable flesh into my mouth. ¹⁵Then he said to me, See, I have given you cow's dung for man's dung, and you shall prepare your bread therewith. ¹⁶Moreover he said to me, Son of man, behold, I will break the staff of bread in Jerusalem: and they shall eat bread by weight, and with care; and they shall drink water by measure, and with astonishment: ¹⁷That they may want bread and water, and be astonished one with another, and consume away for their iniquity.

5 ¹And you, son of man, take you a sharp knife, take you a barber's razor, and cause it to pass on your head and on your beard: then take you balances to weigh, and divide the hair. ²You shall burn with fire a third part in the middle of the city, when the days of the siege are fulfilled: and you shall take a third part, and smite about it with a knife: and a third part you shall scatter in the wind; and I will draw out a sword after them. ³You shall also take thereof a few in number, and bind them in your skirts. ⁴Then take of them again, and cast them into the middle of the fire, and burn them in the fire; for thereof shall a fire come forth into all the house of Israel. ⁵Thus says the Lord GOD; This is Jerusalem: I have set it in the middle of the nations and countries that are round about her. ⁶And she has changed my judgments into wickedness more than the nations, and my statutes more than the countries that are round about her: for they have refused my judgments and my statutes, they have not walked in them. ⁷Therefore thus says the Lord GOD;

Because you multiplied more than the nations that are round about you, and have not walked in my statutes, neither have kept my judgments, neither have done according to the judgments of the nations that are round about you; ⁸Therefore thus says the Lord GOD; Behold, I, even I, am against you, and will execute judgments in the middle of you in the sight of the nations. ⁹And I will do in you that which I have not done, and which I will not do any more the like, because of all your abominations. ¹⁰Therefore the fathers shall eat the sons in the middle of you, and the sons shall eat their fathers; and I will execute judgments in you, and the whole remnant of you will I scatter into all the winds. ¹¹Why, as I live, says the Lord GOD; Surely, because you have defiled my sanctuary with all your detestable things, and with all your abominations, therefore will I also diminish you; neither shall my eye spare, neither will I have any pity. ¹²A third part of you shall die with the pestilence, and with famine shall they be consumed in the middle of you: and a third part shall fall by the sword round about you; and I will scatter a third part into all the winds, and I will draw out a sword after them. ¹³Thus shall my anger be accomplished, and I will cause my fury to rest on them, and I will be comforted: and they shall know that I the LORD have spoken it in my zeal, when I have accomplished my fury in them. ¹⁴Moreover I will make you waste, and a reproach among the nations that are round about you, in the sight of all that pass by. ¹⁵So it shall be a reproach and a taunt, an instruction and an astonishment to the nations that are round about you, when I shall execute judgments in you in anger and in fury and in furious rebukes. I the LORD have spoken it. ¹⁶When I shall send on them the evil arrows of famine, which shall be for their destruction, and which I will send to destroy you: and I will increase the famine on you, and will break your staff of bread: ¹⁷So will I send on you famine and evil beasts, and they shall bereave you: and pestilence and blood shall pass through you; and I will bring the sword on you. I the LORD have spoken it.

6 ¹And the word of the LORD came to me, saying, ²Son of man, set your face toward the mountains of Israel, and prophesy against them, ³And say, You mountains of Israel, hear the word of the Lord GOD; Thus says the Lord GOD to the mountains, and to the hills, to the rivers, and to the valleys; Behold, I, even I, will bring a sword on you, and I will destroy your high places. ⁴And your altars shall be desolate, and your images shall be broken: and I will cast down your slain men before your idols. ⁵And I will lay the dead carcasses of the children of Israel before their idols; and I will scatter your bones round about your altars. ⁶In all your dwelling places the cities shall be laid waste, and the high places shall be desolate; that your altars may be laid waste and made desolate, and your idols may be broken and cease, and your images may be cut down, and your works may be abolished. ⁷And the slain shall fall in the middle of you, and you shall know that I am the LORD. ⁸Yet will I leave a remnant, that you may have some that shall escape the sword among the nations, when you shall be scattered through the countries. ⁹And they that escape of you shall remember me among the nations where they shall be carried captives, because I am broken with their whorish heart, which has departed from me, and with their eyes, which go a whoring after their idols: and they shall loathe themselves for the evils which they have committed in all their abominations. ¹⁰And they shall know that I am the LORD, and that I have not said in vain that I would do this evil to them. ¹¹Thus says the Lord GOD; Smite with your hand, and stamp with your foot, and say, Alas for all the evil abominations of the house of Israel! for they shall fall by the sword, by the famine, and by the pestilence. ¹²He that is far off shall die of the pestilence; and he that is near shall fall by the sword; and he that remains and is besieged shall die by the famine: thus will I accomplish my fury on them. ¹³Then shall you know that I am the LORD, when their slain men shall be among their idols round about their altars, on every high hill, in all the tops of the mountains, and under every green tree, and under every thick oak, the place where they did offer sweet smell to all their idols. ¹⁴So will I stretch out my hand on them, and make the land desolate, yes, more desolate than the wilderness toward Diblath, in all their habitations: and they shall know that I am the LORD.

7 ¹Moreover the word of the LORD came to me, saying, ²Also, you son of man, thus says the Lord GOD to the land of Israel; An end, the end is come on the four corners of the land. ³Now is the end come on you, and I will send my anger on you, and will judge you according to your ways, and will recompense on you all your abominations. ⁴And my eye shall not spare you, neither will I have pity: but I will recompense your ways on you, and your abominations shall be in the middle of you: and you shall know that I am the LORD. ⁵Thus says the Lord GOD; An evil, an only evil, behold, is come. ⁶An end is come, the end is come: it watches for you; behold, it is come. ⁷The morning is come to you, O you that dwell in the land: the time is come, the day of trouble is near, and not the sounding again of the mountains. ⁸Now will I shortly pour out my fury on you, and accomplish my anger on you: and I will judge you according to your ways, and will recompense you for all your abominations. ⁹And my eye shall not spare, neither will I have pity: I will recompense you according to your ways and your abominations that are in the middle of you; and you shall know that I am the LORD that smites. ¹⁰Behold the day, behold, it is come: the morning is gone forth; the rod has blossomed, pride has budded. ¹¹Violence is risen up into a rod of wickedness: none of them shall remain, nor of their multitude, nor of any of theirs: neither shall there be wailing for them. ¹²The time is come, the day draws near: let not the buyer rejoice, nor the seller mourn: for wrath is on all the multitude thereof. ¹³For the seller shall not return to that which is sold, although they were yet alive: for the vision is touching the whole multitude thereof, which shall not return; neither shall any strengthen himself in the iniquity of his life. ¹⁴They have blown the trumpet, even to make all ready; but none goes to the battle: for my wrath is on all the multitude thereof. ¹⁵The sword is without, and the pestilence and the famine within: he that is in the field shall die with the sword; and he that is in the city, famine and pestilence shall devour him. ¹⁶But they that escape of them shall escape, and shall be on the mountains like doves of the valleys, all of them mourning, every one for his iniquity. ¹⁷All hands shall be feeble, and all knees shall be weak as water. ¹⁸They shall also gird themselves with sackcloth, and horror shall cover them; and shame shall be on all faces, and baldness on all their heads. ¹⁹They shall cast their silver in the streets, and their gold shall be removed: their silver and their gold shall not be able to deliver them in the day of the wrath of the LORD: they shall not satisfy their souls, neither fill their bowels: because it is the stumbling block of their iniquity. ²⁰As for the beauty of his ornament, he set it in majesty: but they made the images of their abominations and of their detestable things therein: therefore have I set it far from them. ²¹And I will give it into the hands of the strangers for a prey, and to the wicked of the earth for a spoil; and they shall pollute it. ²²My face will I turn also from them, and they shall pollute my secret place: for the robbers shall enter into it, and defile it. ²³Make a chain: for the land is full of bloody crimes, and the city is full of violence. ²⁴Why I will bring the worst of the heathen, and they shall possess their houses: I will also make the pomp of the strong to cease; and their holy places shall be defiled. ²⁵Destruction comes; and they shall seek peace, and there shall be none. ²⁶Mischief shall come on mischief, and rumor shall be on rumor; then shall they seek a vision of the prophet; but the law shall perish from the priest, and counsel from the ancients. ²⁷The king shall mourn, and the prince shall be clothed with desolation, and the hands of the people of the land shall be troubled: I will do to them after their way, and according to their deserts will I judge them; and they shall know that I am the LORD.

8 ¹And it came to pass in the sixth year, in the sixth month, in the fifth day of the month, as I sat in my house, and the elders of Judah sat before me, that the hand of the Lord GOD fell there on me. ²Then I beheld, and see a likeness as the appearance of fire: from the appearance of his loins even downward, fire; and from his loins even upward, as the appearance of brightness, as the color of amber. ³And he put forth the form of an hand, and took me by a lock of my head; and the spirit lifted me up between the earth and the heaven, and brought me in the visions of God to Jerusalem, to the door of the inner gate that looks toward the north; where was the seat of the image of jealousy, which provokes to jealousy. ⁴And, behold, the glory of the God of Israel was there, according to the vision that I saw in the plain. ⁵Then said he to me, Son of man, lift up your eyes now the way toward the north. So I lifted up my eyes the way toward the north, and behold northward at the gate of the altar this image of jealousy in the entry. ⁶He said furthermore to me, Son of man, see you what they do? even the great abominations that the house of Israel commits here, that I should go far off from my sanctuary? but turn you yet again, and you shall see greater abominations. ⁷And he brought me to the door of the court; and when I looked, behold a hole in the wall. ⁸Then said he to me, Son of man, dig now in the wall: and when I had dig in the wall, behold a door. ⁹And he said to me, Go in, and behold the wicked abominations that they do here. ¹⁰So I went in and saw; and behold every form of creeping things, and abominable beasts, and all the idols of the house of Israel, portrayed on the wall round about. ¹¹And there stood before them seventy men of the ancients of the house of Israel, and in the middle of them stood Jaazaniah the son of Shaphan, with every man his censer in his hand; and a thick cloud of incense went up.

¹²Then said he to me, Son of man, have you seen what the ancients of the house of Israel do in the dark, every man in the chambers of his imagery? for they say, the LORD sees us not; the LORD has forsaken the earth. ¹³He said also to me, Turn you yet again, and you shall see greater abominations that they do. ¹⁴Then he brought me to the door of the gate of the LORD's house which was toward the north; and, behold, there sat women weeping for Tammuz. ¹⁵Then said he to me, Have you seen this, O son of man? turn you yet again, and you shall see greater abominations than these. ¹⁶And he brought me into the inner court of the LORD's house, and, behold, at the door of the temple of the LORD, between the porch and the altar, were about five and twenty men, with their backs toward the temple of the LORD, and their faces toward the east; and they worshipped the sun toward the east. ¹⁷Then he said to me, Have you seen this, O son of man? Is it a light thing to the house of Judah that they commit the abominations which they commit here? for they have filled the land with violence, and have returned to provoke me to anger: and, see, they put the branch to their nose. ¹⁸Therefore will I also deal in fury: my eye shall not spare, neither will I have pity: and though they cry in my ears with a loud voice, yet will I not hear them.

9 ¹He cried also in my ears with a loud voice, saying, Cause them that have charge over the city to draw near, even every man with his destroying weapon in his hand. ²And, behold, six men came from the way of the higher gate, which lies toward the north, and every man a slaughter weapon in his hand; and one man among them was clothed with linen, with a writer's inkhorn by his side: and they went in, and stood beside the brazen altar. ³And the glory of the God of Israel was gone up from the cherub, whereupon he was, to the threshold of the house. And he called to the man clothed with linen, which had the writer's inkhorn by his side; ⁴And the LORD said to him, Go through the middle of the city, through the middle of Jerusalem, and set a mark on the foreheads of the men that sigh and that cry for all the abominations that be done in the middle thereof. ⁵And to the others he said in my hearing, Go you after him through the city, and smite: let not your eye spare, neither have you pity: ⁶Slay utterly old and young, both maids, and little children, and women: but come not near any man on whom is the mark; and begin at my sanctuary. Then they began at the ancient men which were before the house. ⁷And he said to them, Defile the house, and fill the courts with the slain: go you forth. And they went forth, and slew in the city. ⁸And it came to pass, while they were slaying them, and I was left, that I fell on my face, and cried, and said, Ah Lord GOD! will you destroy all the residue of Israel in your pouring out of your fury on Jerusalem? ⁹Then said he to me, The iniquity of the house of Israel and Judah is exceeding great, and the land is full of blood, and the city full of perverseness: for they say, The LORD has forsaken the earth, and the LORD sees not. ¹⁰And as for me also, my eye shall not spare, neither will I have pity, but I will recompense their way on their head. ¹¹And, behold, the man clothed with linen, which had the inkhorn by his side, reported the matter, saying, I have done as you have commanded me.

10 ¹Then I looked, and, behold, in the firmament that was above the head of the cherubim there appeared over them as it were a sapphire stone, as the appearance of the likeness of a throne. ²And he spoke to the man clothed with linen, and said, Go in between the wheels, even under the cherub, and fill your hand with coals of fire from between the cherubim, and scatter them over the city. And he went in in my sight. ³Now the cherubim stood on the right side of the house, when the man went in; and the cloud filled the inner court. ⁴Then the glory of the LORD went up from the cherub, and stood over the threshold of the house; and the house was filled with the cloud, and the court was full of the brightness of the LORD's glory. ⁵And the sound of the cherubims' wings was heard even to the outer court, as the voice of the Almighty God when he speaks. ⁶And it came to pass, that when he had commanded the man clothed with linen, saying, Take fire from between the wheels, from between the cherubim; then he went in, and stood beside the wheels. ⁷And one cherub stretched forth his hand from between the cherubim to the fire that was between the cherubim, and took thereof, and put it into the hands of him that was clothed with linen: who took it, and went out. ⁸And there appeared in the cherubim the form of a man's hand under their wings. ⁹And when I looked, behold the four wheels by the cherubim, one wheel by one cherub, and another wheel by another cherub: and the appearance of the wheels was as the color of a beryl stone. ¹⁰And as for their appearances, they four had one likeness, as if a wheel had been in the middle of a wheel. ¹¹When they went, they went on their four sides; they turned not as they went, but to the place where the head looked they followed it; they turned not as they went. ¹²And their whole body, and their backs, and their hands, and their wings, and the wheels, were full of eyes round about, even the wheels that they four had. ¹³As for the wheels, it was cried to them in my hearing, O wheel. ¹⁴And every one had four faces: the first face was the face of a cherub, and the second face was the face of a man, and the third the face of a lion, and the fourth the face of an eagle. ¹⁵And the cherubim were lifted up. This is the living creature that I saw by the river of Chebar. ¹⁶And when the cherubim went, the wheels went by them: and when the cherubim lifted up their wings to mount up from the earth, the same wheels also turned not from beside them. ¹⁷When they stood, these stood; and when they were lifted up, these lifted up themselves also: for the spirit of the living creature was in them. ¹⁸Then the glory of the LORD departed from off the threshold of the house, and stood over the cherubim. ¹⁹And the cherubim lifted up their wings, and mounted up from the earth in my sight: when they went out, the wheels also were beside them, and every one stood at the door of the east gate of the LORD's house; and the glory of the God of Israel was over them above. ²⁰This is the living creature that I saw under the God of Israel by the river of Chebar; and I knew that they were the cherubim. ²¹Every one had four faces apiece, and every one four wings; and the likeness of the hands of a man was under their wings. ²²And the likeness of their faces was the same faces which I saw by the river of Chebar, their appearances and themselves: they went every one straight forward.

11 ¹Moreover the spirit lifted me up, and brought me to the east gate of the LORD's house, which looks eastward: and behold at the door of the gate five and twenty men; among whom I saw Jaazaniah the son of Azur, and Pelatiah the son of Benaiah, princes of the people. ²Then said he to me, Son of man, these are the men that devise mischief, and give wicked counsel in this city: ³Which say, It is not near; let us build houses: this city is the caldron, and we be the flesh. ⁴Therefore prophesy against them, prophesy, O son of man. ⁵And the Spirit of the LORD fell on me, and said to me, Speak; Thus says the LORD; Thus have you said, O house of Israel: for I know the things that come into your mind, every one of them. ⁶You have multiplied your slain in this city, and you have filled the streets thereof with the slain. ⁷Therefore thus says the Lord GOD; Your slain whom you have laid in the middle of it, they are the flesh, and this city is the caldron: but I will bring you forth out of the middle of it. ⁸You have feared the sword; and I will bring a sword on you, says the Lord GOD. ⁹And I will bring you out of the middle thereof, and deliver you into the hands of strangers, and will execute judgments among you. ¹⁰You shall fall by the sword; I will judge you in the border of Israel; and you shall know that I am the LORD. ¹¹This city shall not be your caldron, neither shall you be the flesh in the middle thereof; but I will judge you in the border of Israel: ¹²And you shall know that I am the LORD: for you have not walked in my statutes, neither executed my judgments, but have done after the manners of the heathen that are round about you. ¹³And it came to pass, when I prophesied, that Pelatiah the son of Benaiah died. Then fell I down on my face, and cried with a loud voice, and said, Ah Lord GOD! will you make a full end of the remnant of Israel? ¹⁴Again the word of the LORD came to me, saying, ¹⁵Son of man, your brothers, even your brothers, the men of your kindred, and all the house of Israel wholly, are they to whom the inhabitants of Jerusalem have said, Get you far from the LORD: to us is this land given in possession. ¹⁶Therefore say, Thus says the Lord GOD; Although I have cast them far off among the heathen, and although I have scattered them among the countries, yet will I be to them as a little sanctuary in the countries where they shall come. ¹⁷Therefore say, Thus says the Lord GOD; I will even gather you from the people, and assemble you out of the countries where you have been scattered, and I will give you the land of Israel. ¹⁸And they shall come thither, and they shall take away all the detestable things thereof and all the abominations thereof from there. ¹⁹And I will give them one heart, and I will put a new spirit within you; and I will take the stony heart out of their flesh, and will give them an heart of flesh: ²⁰That they may walk in my statutes, and keep my ordinances, and do them: and they shall be my people, and I will be their God. ²¹But as for them whose heart walks after the heart of their detestable things and their abominations, I will recompense their way on their own heads, says the Lord GOD. ²²Then did the cherubim lift up their wings, and the wheels beside them; and the glory of the God of Israel was over them above. ²³And the glory of the LORD went up from the middle of the city, and stood on the mountain which is on the east side of the city. ²⁴Afterwards the spirit took me up, and brought me in a vision by the Spirit of God into

Chaldea, to them of the captivity. So the vision that I had seen went up from me. ²⁵Then I spoke to them of the captivity all the things that the LORD had showed me.

12 ¹The word of the LORD also came to me, saying, ²Son of man, you dwell in the middle of a rebellious house, which have eyes to see, and see not; they have ears to hear, and hear not: for they are a rebellious house. ³Therefore, you son of man, prepare you stuff for removing, and remove by day in their sight; and you shall remove from your place to another place in their sight: it may be they will consider, though they be a rebellious house. ⁴Then shall you bring forth your stuff by day in their sight, as stuff for removing: and you shall go forth at even in their sight, as they that go forth into captivity. ⁵Dig you through the wall in their sight, and carry out thereby. ⁶In their sight shall you bear it on your shoulders, and carry it forth in the twilight: you shall cover your face, that you see not the ground: for I have set you for a sign to the house of Israel. ⁷And I did so as I was commanded: I brought forth my stuff by day, as stuff for captivity, and in the even I dig through the wall with my hand; I brought it forth in the twilight, and I bore it on my shoulder in their sight. ⁸And in the morning came the word of the LORD to me, saying, ⁹Son of man, has not the house of Israel, the rebellious house, said to you, What do you? ¹⁰Say you to them, Thus says the Lord GOD; This burden concerns the prince in Jerusalem, and all the house of Israel that are among them. ¹¹Say, I am your sign: like as I have done, so shall it be done to them: they shall remove and go into captivity. ¹²And the prince that is among them shall bear on his shoulder in the twilight, and shall go forth: they shall dig through the wall to carry out thereby: he shall cover his face, that he see not the ground with his eyes. ¹³My net also will I spread on him, and he shall be taken in my snare: and I will bring him to Babylon to the land of the Chaldeans; yet shall he not see it, though he shall die there. ¹⁴And I will scatter toward every wind all that are about him to help him, and all his bands; and I will draw out the sword after them. ¹⁵And they shall know that I am the LORD, when I shall scatter them among the nations, and disperse them in the countries. ¹⁶But I will leave a few men of them from the sword, from the famine, and from the pestilence; that they may declare all their abominations among the heathen where they come; and they shall know that I am the LORD. ¹⁷Moreover the word of the LORD came to me, saying, ¹⁸Son of man, eat your bread with quaking, and drink your water with trembling and with carefulness; ¹⁹And say to the people of the land, Thus says the Lord GOD of the inhabitants of Jerusalem, and of the land of Israel; They shall eat their bread with carefulness, and drink their water with astonishment, that her land may be desolate from all that is therein, because of the violence of all them that dwell therein. ²⁰And the cities that are inhabited shall be laid waste, and the land shall be desolate; and you shall know that I am the LORD. ²¹And the word of the LORD came to me, saying, ²²Son of man, what is that proverb that you have in the land of Israel, saying, The days are prolonged, and every vision fails? ²³Tell them therefore, Thus says the Lord GOD; I will make this proverb to cease, and they shall no more use it as a proverb in Israel; but say to them, The days are at hand, and the effect of every vision. ²⁴For there shall be no more any vain vision nor flattering divination within the house of Israel. ²⁵For I am the LORD: I will speak, and the word that I shall speak shall come to pass; it shall be no more prolonged: for in your days, O rebellious house, will I say the word, and will perform it, says the Lord GOD. ²⁶Again the word of the LORD came to me, saying. ²⁷Son of man, behold, they of the house of Israel say, The vision that he sees is for many days to come, and he prophesies of the times that are far off. ²⁸Therefore say to them, Thus says the Lord GOD; There shall none of my words be prolonged any more, but the word which I have spoken shall be done, says the Lord GOD.

13 ¹And the word of the LORD came to me, saying, ²Son of man, prophesy against the prophets of Israel that prophesy, and say you to them that prophesy out of their own hearts, Hear you the word of the LORD; ³Thus says the Lord GOD; Woe to the foolish prophets, that follow their own spirit, and have seen nothing! ⁴O Israel, your prophets are like the foxes in the deserts. ⁵You have not gone up into the gaps, neither made up the hedge for the house of Israel to stand in the battle in the day of the LORD. ⁶They have seen vanity and lying divination, saying, The LORD says: and the LORD has not sent them: and they have made others to hope that they would confirm the word. ⁷Have you not seen a vain vision, and have you not spoken a lying divination, whereas you say, The LORD says it; albeit I have not spoken? ⁸Therefore thus says the Lord GOD; Because you have spoken vanity, and seen lies, therefore, behold, I am against you, says the Lord GOD. ⁹And my hand shall be on the prophets that see vanity, and that divine lies: they shall not be in the assembly of my people, neither shall they be written in the writing of the house of Israel, neither shall they enter into the land of Israel; and you shall know that I am the Lord GOD. ¹⁰Because, even because they have seduced my people, saying, Peace; and there was no peace; and one built up a wall, and, see, others daubed it with untempered mortar: ¹¹Say to them which daub it with untempered mortar, that it shall fall: there shall be an overflowing shower; and you, O great hailstones, shall fall; and a stormy wind shall rend it. ¹²See, when the wall is fallen, shall it not be said to you, Where is the daubing with which you have daubed it? ¹³Therefore thus says the Lord GOD; I will even rend it with a stormy wind in my fury; and there shall be an overflowing shower in my anger, and great hailstones in my fury to consume it. ¹⁴So will I break down the wall that you have daubed with untempered mortar, and bring it down to the ground, so that the foundation thereof shall be discovered, and it shall fall, and you shall be consumed in the middle thereof: and you shall know that I am the LORD. ¹⁵Thus will I accomplish my wrath on the wall, and on them that have daubed it with untempered mortar, and will say to you, The wall is no more, neither they that daubed it; ¹⁶To wit, the prophets of Israel which prophesy concerning Jerusalem, and which see visions of peace for her, and there is no peace, says the Lord GOD. ¹⁷Likewise, you son of man, set your face against the daughters of your people, which prophesy out of their own heart; and prophesy you against them, ¹⁸And say, Thus says the Lord GOD; Woe to the women that sew pillows to all armholes, and make kerchiefs on the head of every stature to hunt souls! Will you hunt the souls of my people, and will you save the souls alive that come to you? ¹⁹And will you pollute me among my people for handfuls of barley and for pieces of bread, to slay the souls that should not die, and to save the souls alive that should not live, by your lying to my people that hear your lies? ²⁰Why thus says the Lord GOD; Behold, I am against your pillows, with which you there hunt the souls to make them fly, and I will tear them from your arms, and will let the souls go, even the souls that you hunt to make them fly. ²¹Your kerchiefs also will I tear, and deliver my people out of your hand, and they shall be no more in your hand to be hunted; and you shall know that I am the LORD. ²²Because with lies you have made the heart of the righteous sad, whom I have not made sad; and strengthened the hands of the wicked, that he should not return from his wicked way, by promising him life: ²³Therefore you shall see no more vanity, nor divine divinations: for I will deliver my people out of your hand: and you shall know that I am the LORD.

14

¹Then came certain of the elders of Israel to me, and sat before me. ²And the word of the LORD came to me, saying, ³Son of man, these men have set up their idols in their heart, and put the stumbling block of their iniquity before their face: should I be inquired of at all by them? ⁴Therefore speak to them, and say to them, Thus says the Lord GOD; Every man of the house of Israel that sets up his idols in his heart, and puts the stumbling block of his iniquity before his face, and comes to the prophet; I the LORD will answer him that comes according to the multitude of his idols; ⁵That I may take the house of Israel in their own heart, because they are all estranged from me through their idols. ⁶Therefore say to the house of Israel, Thus says the Lord GOD; Repent, and turn yourselves from your idols; and turn away your faces from all your abominations. ⁷For every one of the house of Israel, or of the stranger that sojourns in Israel, which separates himself from me, and sets up his idols in his heart, and puts the stumbling block of his iniquity before his face, and comes to a prophet to inquire of him concerning me; I the LORD will answer him by myself: ⁸And I will set my face against that man, and will make him a sign and a proverb, and I will cut him off from the middle of my people; and you shall know that I am the LORD. ⁹And if the prophet be deceived when he has spoken a thing, I the LORD have deceived that prophet, and I will stretch out my hand on him, and will destroy him from the middle of my people Israel. ¹⁰And they shall bear the punishment of their iniquity: the punishment of the prophet shall be even as the punishment of him that seeks to him; ¹¹That the house of Israel may go no more astray from me, neither be polluted any more with all their transgressions; but that they may be my people, and I may be their God, says the Lord GOD. ¹²The word of the LORD came again to me, saying, ¹³Son of man, when the land sins against me by trespassing grievously, then will I stretch out my hand on it, and will break the staff of the bread thereof, and will send famine on it, and will cut off man and beast from it: ¹⁴Though these three men, Noah, Daniel, and Job, were in it, they should deliver but their own souls by their righteousness, says the Lord GOD. ¹⁵If I cause noisome beasts to pass through the land, and they spoil it, so that it be desolate, that no man may pass through because of the beasts: ¹⁶Though these three men were in it, as I live, says the Lord GOD, they shall deliver neither sons nor daughters; they only shall be delivered, but the land shall be desolate. ¹⁷Or if I bring a sword on that land, and say, Sword, go through the land; so that I cut off man and beast from it: ¹⁸Though these three men were in it, as I live, says the Lord GOD, they shall deliver neither sons nor daughters, but they only shall be delivered themselves. ¹⁹Or if I send a pestilence into that land, and pour out my fury on it in blood, to cut off from it man and beast: ²⁰Though Noah, Daniel, and Job were in it, as I live, says the Lord GOD, they shall deliver neither son nor daughter; they shall but deliver their own souls by their righteousness. ²¹For thus says the Lord GOD; How much more when I send my four sore judgments on Jerusalem, the sword, and the famine, and the noisome beast, and the pestilence, to cut off from it man and beast? ²²Yet, behold, therein shall be left a remnant that shall be brought forth, both sons and daughters: behold, they shall come forth to you, and you shall see their way and their doings: and you shall be comforted concerning the evil that I have brought on Jerusalem, even concerning all that I have brought on it. ²³And they shall comfort you, when you see their ways and their doings: and you shall know that I have not done without cause all that I have done in it, says the Lord GOD.

15

¹And the word of the LORD came to me, saying, ²Son of man, what is the vine tree more than any tree, or than a branch which is among the trees of the forest? ³Shall wood be taken thereof to do any work? or will men take a pin of it to hang any vessel thereon? ⁴Behold, it is cast into the fire for fuel; the fire devours both the ends of it, and the middle of it is burned. Is it meet for any work? ⁵Behold, when it was whole, it was meet for no work: how much less shall it be meet yet for any work, when the fire has devoured it, and it is burned? ⁶Therefore thus says the Lord GOD; As the vine tree among the trees of the forest, which I have given to the fire for fuel, so will I give the inhabitants of Jerusalem. ⁷And I will set my face against them; they shall go out from one fire, and another fire shall devour them; and you shall know that I am the LORD, when I set my face against them. ⁸And I will make the land desolate, because they have committed a trespass, says the Lord GOD.

16

¹Again the word of the LORD came to me, saying, ²Son of man, cause Jerusalem to know her abominations, ³And say, Thus says the Lord GOD to Jerusalem; Your birth and your nativity is of the land of Canaan; your father was an Amorite, and your mother an Hittite. ⁴And as for your nativity, in the day you were born your navel was not cut, neither were you washed in water to supple you; you were not salted at all, nor swaddled at all. ⁵None eye pitied you, to do any of these to you, to have compassion on you; but you were cast out in the open field, to the loathing of your person, in the day that you were born. ⁶And when I passed by you, and saw you polluted in your own blood, I said to you when you were in your blood, Live; yes, I said to you when you were in your blood, Live. ⁷I have caused you to multiply as the bud of the field, and you have increased and waxen great, and you are come to excellent

ornaments: your breasts are fashioned, and your hair is grown, whereas you were naked and bore. ⁸Now when I passed by you, and looked on you, behold, your time was the time of love; and I spread my skirt over you, and covered your nakedness: yes, I swore to you, and entered into a covenant with you, says the Lord GOD, and you became mine. ⁹Then washed I you with water; yes, I thoroughly washed away your blood from you, and I anointed you with oil. ¹⁰I clothed you also with broidered work, and shod you with badgers' skin, and I girded you about with fine linen, and I covered you with silk. ¹¹I decked you also with ornaments, and I put bracelets on your hands, and a chain on your neck. ¹²And I put a jewel on your forehead, and earrings in your ears, and a beautiful crown on your head. ¹³Thus were you decked with gold and silver; and your raiment was of fine linen, and silk, and broidered work; you did eat fine flour, and honey, and oil: and you were exceeding beautiful, and you did prosper into a kingdom. ¹⁴And your renown went forth among the heathen for your beauty: for it was perfect through my comeliness, which I had put on you, says the Lord GOD. ¹⁵But you did trust in your own beauty, and played the harlot because of your renown, and poured out your fornications on every one that passed by; his it was. ¹⁶And of your garments you did take, and decked your high places with divers colors, and played the harlot thereupon: the like things shall not come, neither shall it be so. ¹⁷You have also taken your fair jewels of my gold and of my silver, which I had given you, and made to yourself images of men, and did commit prostitution with them, ¹⁸And took your broidered garments, and covered them: and you have set my oil and my incense before them. ¹⁹My meat also which I gave you, fine flour, and oil, and honey, with which I fed you, you have even set it before them for a sweet smell: and thus it was, says the Lord GOD. ²⁰Moreover you have taken your sons and your daughters, whom you have borne to me, and these have you sacrificed to them to be devoured. Is this of your prostitutions a small matter, ²¹That you have slain my children, and delivered them to cause them to pass through the fire for them? ²²And in all your abominations and your prostitutions you have not remembered the days of your youth, when you were naked and bore, and were polluted in your blood. ²³And it came to pass after all your wickedness, (woe, woe to you! says the LORD GOD;) ²⁴That you have also built to you an eminent place, and have made you an high place in every street. ²⁵You have built your high place at every head of the way, and have made your beauty to be abhorred, and have opened your feet to every one that passed by, and multiplied your prostitutions. ²⁶You have also committed fornication with the Egyptians your neighbors, great of flesh; and have increased your prostitutions, to provoke me to anger. ²⁷Behold, therefore I have stretched out my hand over you, and have diminished your ordinary food, and delivered you to the will of them that hate you, the daughters of the Philistines, which are ashamed of your lewd way. ²⁸You have played the whore also with the Assyrians, because you were insatiable; yes, you have played the harlot with them, and yet could not be satisfied. ²⁹You have moreover multiplied your fornication in the land of Canaan to Chaldea; and yet you were not satisfied therewith. ³⁰How weak is your heart, says the LORD GOD, seeing you do all these things, the work of an imperious whorish woman; ³¹In that you build your eminent place in the head of every way, and make your high place in every street; and have not been as an harlot, in that you scorn hire; ³²But as a wife that commits adultery, which takes strangers instead of her husband! ³³They give gifts to all whores: but you give your gifts to all your lovers, and hire them, that they may come to you on every side for your prostitution. ³⁴And the contrary is in you from other women in your prostitutions, whereas none follows you to commit prostitutions: and in that you give a reward, and no reward is given to you, therefore you are contrary. ³⁵Why, O harlot, hear the word of the LORD: ³⁶Thus says the Lord GOD; Because your filthiness was poured out, and your nakedness discovered through your prostitutions with your lovers, and with all the idols of your abominations, and by the blood of your children, which you did give to them; ³⁷Behold, therefore I will gather all your lovers, with whom you have taken pleasure, and all them that you have loved, with all them that you have hated; I will even gather them round about against you, and will discover your nakedness to them, that they may see all your nakedness. ³⁸And I will judge you, as women that break wedlock and shed blood are judged; and I will give you blood in fury and jealousy. ³⁹And I will also give you into their hand, and they shall throw down your eminent place, and shall break down your high places: they shall strip you also of your clothes, and shall take your fair jewels, and leave you naked and bore. ⁴⁰They shall also bring up a company against you, and they shall stone you with stones, and thrust you through with their swords. ⁴¹And they shall burn your houses with fire, and execute judgments on you in the sight of many women: and I will cause you to cease from playing the harlot, and you also shall give no hire any more. ⁴²So will I make my fury toward you to rest, and my jealousy shall depart from you, and I will be quiet, and will be no more angry. ⁴³Because you have not remembered the days of your youth, but have fretted me in all these things; behold, therefore I also will recompense your way on your head, says the Lord GOD: and you shall not commit this lewdness above all your abominations. ⁴⁴Behold, every one that uses proverbs shall use this proverb against you, saying, As is the mother, so is her daughter. ⁴⁵You are your mother's daughter, that lothes her husband and her children; and you are the sister of your sisters, which loathed their husbands and their children: your mother was an Hittite, and your father an Amorite. ⁴⁶And your elder sister is Samaria, she and her daughters that dwell at your left hand: and your younger sister, that dwells at your right hand, is Sodom and her daughters. ⁴⁷Yet have you not walked after their ways, nor done after their abominations: but, as if that were a very little thing, you were corrupted more than they in all your ways. ⁴⁸As I live, says the Lord GOD, Sodom your sister has not done, she nor her daughters, as you have done, you and your daughters. ⁴⁹Behold, this was the iniquity of your sister Sodom, pride, fullness of bread, and abundance of idleness was in her and in her daughters, neither did she strengthen the hand of the poor and needy. ⁵⁰And they were haughty, and committed abomination before me: therefore I took them away as I saw good. ⁵¹Neither has Samaria committed half of your sins; but you have multiplied your abominations more than they, and have justified your sisters in all your abominations which you have done. ⁵²You also, which have judged your sisters, bear your own shame for your sins that you have committed more abominable than they: they are more righteous than you: yes, be you confounded also, and bear your shame, in that you have justified your sisters. ⁵³When I shall bring again their captivity, the captivity of Sodom and her daughters, and the captivity of Samaria and her daughters, then will I bring again the captivity of your captives in the middle of them: ⁵⁴That you may bear your own shame, and may be confounded in all that you have done, in that you are a comfort to them. ⁵⁵When your sisters, Sodom and her daughters, shall return to their former estate, and Samaria and her daughters shall return to their former estate, then you and your daughters shall return to your former estate. ⁵⁶For your sister Sodom was not mentioned by your mouth in the day of your pride, ⁵⁷Before your wickedness was discovered, as at the time of your reproach of the daughters of Syria, and all that are round about her, the daughters of the Philistines, which despise you round about. ⁵⁸You have borne your lewdness and your abominations, says the LORD. ⁵⁹For thus says the Lord GOD; I will even deal with you as you have done, which have despised the oath in breaking the covenant. ⁶⁰Nevertheless I will remember my covenant with you in the days of your youth, and I will establish to you an everlasting covenant. ⁶¹Then you shall remember your ways, and be ashamed, when you shall receive your sisters, your elder and your younger: and I will give them to you for daughters, but not by your covenant. ⁶²And I will establish my covenant with you; and you shall know that I am the LORD: ⁶³That you may remember, and be confounded, and never open your mouth any more because of your shame, when I am pacified toward you for all that you have done, says the Lord GOD.

17 ¹And the word of the LORD came to me, saying, ²Son of man, put forth a riddle, and speak a parable to the house of Israel; ³And say, Thus says the Lord GOD; A great eagle with great wings, long winged, full of feathers, which had divers colors, came to Lebanon, and took the highest branch of the cedar: ⁴He cropped off the top of his young twigs, and carried it into a land of traffic; he set it in a city of merchants. ⁵He took also of the seed of the land, and planted it in a fruitful field; he placed it by great waters, and set it as a willow tree. ⁶And it grew, and became a spreading vine of low stature, whose branches turned toward him, and the roots thereof were under him: so it became a vine, and brought forth branches, and shot forth sprigs. ⁷There was also another great eagle with great wings and many feathers: and, behold, this vine did bend her roots toward him, and shot forth her branches toward him, that he might water it by the furrows of her plantation. ⁸It was planted in a good soil by great waters, that it might bring forth branches, and that it might bear fruit, that it might be a goodly vine. ⁹Say you, Thus says the Lord GOD; Shall it prosper? shall he not pull up the roots thereof, and cut off the fruit thereof, that it wither? it shall wither in all the leaves of her spring, even without great power or many people to pluck it up by the roots thereof. ¹⁰Yes, behold, being planted, shall it prosper? shall it not utterly wither, when the east wind touches it? it shall wither in the furrows where it grew. ¹¹Moreover the word of the LORD came to me, saying, ¹²Say now to the rebellious house, Know you not what these things mean? tell them, Behold, the king of Babylon is come to Jerusalem, and has taken the king thereof, and the princes thereof, and led them with him to Babylon; ¹³And has taken of the king's seed, and made a covenant with him, and has taken an oath of him: he has also taken the mighty of the land: ¹⁴That the kingdom might be base, that it might not lift itself up, but that by keeping of his covenant it might stand. ¹⁵But he rebelled against him in sending his ambassadors into Egypt, that they might give him horses and much people. Shall he prosper? shall he escape that does such things? or shall he break the covenant, and be delivered? ¹⁶As I live, says the Lord GOD, surely in the place where the king dwells that made him king, whose oath he despised, and whose covenant he broke, even with him in the middle of Babylon he shall die. ¹⁷Neither shall Pharaoh with his mighty army and great company make for him in the war, by casting up mounts, and building forts, to cut off many persons: ¹⁸Seeing he despised the oath by breaking the covenant, when, see, he had given his hand, and has done all these things, he shall not escape. ¹⁹Therefore thus says the Lord GOD; As I live, surely my oath that he has despised, and my covenant that he has broken, even it will I recompense on his own head. ²⁰And I will spread my net on him, and he shall be taken in my snare, and I will bring him to Babylon, and will plead with him there for his trespass that he has trespassed against me. ²¹And all his fugitives with all his bands shall fall by the sword, and they that remain shall be scattered toward all winds: and you shall know that I the LORD have spoken it. ²²Thus says the Lord GOD; I will also take of the highest branch of the high cedar, and will set it; I will crop off from the top of his young twigs a tender one, and will plant it on an high mountain and eminent: ²³In the mountain of the height of Israel will I plant it: and it shall bring forth boughs, and bear fruit, and be a goodly cedar: and under it shall dwell all fowl of every wing; in the shadow of the branches thereof shall they dwell. ²⁴And all the trees of the field shall know that I the LORD have brought down the high tree, have exalted the low tree, have dried up the green tree, and have made the dry tree to flourish: I the LORD have spoken and have done it.

18 ¹The word of the LORD came to me again, saying, ²What mean you, that you use this proverb concerning the land of Israel, saying, The fathers have eaten sour grapes, and the children's teeth are set on edge? ³As I live, says the Lord GOD, you shall not have occasion any more to use this proverb in Israel. ⁴Behold, all souls are mine; as the soul of the father, so also the soul of the son is mine: the soul that sins, it shall die. ⁵But if a man be just, and do that which is lawful and right, ⁶And has not eaten on the mountains, neither has lifted up his eyes to the idols of the house of Israel, neither has defiled his neighbor's wife, neither has come near to a menstruous woman, ⁷And has not oppressed any, but has restored to the debtor his pledge, has spoiled none by violence, has given his bread to the hungry, and has covered the naked with a garment; ⁸He that has not given forth on usury, neither has taken any increase, that has withdrawn his hand from iniquity, has executed true judgment between man and man, ⁹Has walked in my statutes, and has kept my judgments, to deal truly; he is just, he shall surely live, says the Lord GOD. ¹⁰If he beget a son that is a robber, a shedder of blood, and that does the like to any one of these things, ¹¹And that does not any of those duties, but even has eaten on the mountains, and defiled his neighbor's wife, ¹²Has oppressed the poor and needy, has spoiled by violence, has not restored the pledge, and has lifted up his eyes to the idols, has committed abomination, ¹³Has given forth on usury, and has taken increase: shall he then live? he shall not live: he has done all these abominations; he shall surely die; his blood shall be on him. ¹⁴Now, see, if he beget a son, that sees all his father's sins which he has done, and considers, and does not such like, ¹⁵That has not eaten on the mountains, neither has lifted up his eyes to the idols of the house of Israel, has not defiled his neighbor's wife, ¹⁶Neither has oppressed any, has not withheld the pledge, neither has spoiled by violence, but has given his bread to the hungry, and has covered the naked with a garment, ¹⁷That has taken off his hand from the poor, that has not received usury nor increase, has executed my judgments, has walked in my statutes; he shall not die for the iniquity of his father, he shall surely live. ¹⁸As for his father, because he cruelly oppressed, spoiled his brother by violence, and did that which is not good among his people, see, even he shall die in his iniquity. ¹⁹Yet say you, Why? does not the son bear the iniquity of the father? When the son has done that which is lawful and right, and has kept all my statutes, and has done them, he shall surely live. ²⁰The soul that sins, it shall die. The son shall not bear the iniquity of the father, neither shall the father bear the iniquity of the son: the righteousness of the righteous shall be on him, and the wickedness of the wicked shall be on him. ²¹But if the wicked will turn from all his sins that he has committed, and keep all my statutes, and do that which is lawful and right, he shall surely live, he shall not die. ²²All his transgressions that he has committed, they shall not be mentioned to him: in his righteousness that he has done he shall live. ²³Have I any pleasure at all that the wicked should die? says the Lord GOD: and not that he should return from his ways, and live? ²⁴But when the righteous turns away from his righteousness, and commits iniquity, and does according to all the abominations that the wicked man does, shall he live? All his righteousness that he has done shall not be mentioned: in his trespass that he has trespassed, and in his sin that he has sinned, in them shall he die. ²⁵Yet you say, The way of the LORD is not equal. Hear now, O house of Israel; Is not my way equal? are not your ways unequal? ²⁶When a righteous man turns away from his righteousness, and commits iniquity, and dies in them; for his iniquity that he has done shall he die. ²⁷Again, when the wicked man turns away from his wickedness that he has committed, and does that which is lawful and right, he shall save his soul alive. ²⁸Because he considers, and turns away from all his transgressions that he has committed, he shall surely live, he shall not die. ²⁹Yet says the house of Israel, The way of the LORD is not equal. O house of Israel, are not my ways equal? are not your ways unequal? ³⁰Therefore I will judge you, O house of Israel, every one according to his ways, says the Lord GOD. Repent, and turn yourselves from all your transgressions; so iniquity shall not be your ruin. ³¹Cast away from you all your transgressions, whereby you have transgressed; and make you a new heart and a new spirit: for why will you die, O house of Israel? ³²For I have no pleasure in the death of him that dies, says the Lord GOD: why turn yourselves, and live you.

19

¹Moreover take you up a lamentation for the princes of Israel, ²And say, What is your mother? A lioness: she lay down among lions, she nourished her whelps among young lions. ³And she brought up one of her whelps: it became a young lion, and it learned to catch the prey; it devoured men. ⁴The nations also heard of him; he was taken in their pit, and they brought him with chains to the land of Egypt. ⁵Now when she saw that she had waited, and her hope was lost, then she took another of her whelps, and made him a young lion. ⁶And he went up and down among the lions, he became a young lion, and learned to catch the prey, and devoured men. ⁷And he knew their desolate palaces, and he laid waste their cities; and the land was desolate, and the fullness thereof, by the noise of his roaring. ⁸Then the nations set against him on every side from the provinces, and spread their net over him: he was taken in their pit. ⁹And they put him in ward in chains, and brought him to the king of Babylon: they brought him into holds, that his voice should no more be heard on the mountains of Israel. ¹⁰Your mother is like a vine in your blood, planted by the waters: she was fruitful and full of branches by reason of many waters. ¹¹And she had strong rods for the scepters of them that bore rule, and her stature was exalted among the thick branches, and she appeared in her height with the multitude of her branches. ¹²But she was plucked up in fury, she was cast down to the ground, and the east wind dried up her fruit: her strong rods were broken and withered; the fire consumed them. ¹³And now she is planted in the wilderness, in a dry and thirsty ground. ¹⁴And fire is gone out of a rod of her branches, which has devoured her fruit, so that she has no strong rod to be a scepter to rule. This is a lamentation, and shall be for a lamentation.

20

¹And it came to pass in the seventh year, in the fifth month, the tenth day of the month, that certain of the elders of Israel came to inquire of the LORD, and sat before me. ²Then came the word of the LORD to me, saying, ³Son of man, speak to the elders of Israel, and say to them, Thus says the Lord GOD; Are you come to inquire of me? As I live, said the Lord GOD, I will not be inquired of by you. ⁴Will you judge them, son of man, will you judge them? cause them to know the abominations of their fathers: ⁵And say to them, Thus says the Lord GOD; In the day when I chose Israel, and lifted up my hand to the seed of the house of Jacob, and made myself known to them in the land of Egypt, when I lifted up my hand to them, saying, I am the LORD your God; ⁶In the day that I lifted up my hand to them, to bring them forth of the land of Egypt into a land that I had espied for them, flowing with milk and honey, which is the glory of all lands: ⁷Then said I to them, Cast you away every man the abominations of his eyes, and defile not yourselves with the idols of Egypt: I am the LORD your God. ⁸But they rebelled against me, and would not listen to me: they did not every man cast away the

abominations of their eyes, neither did they forsake the idols of Egypt: then I said, I will pour out my fury on them, to accomplish my anger against them in the middle of the land of Egypt. ⁹But I worked for my name's sake, that it should not be polluted before the heathen, among whom they were, in whose sight I made myself known to them, in bringing them forth out of the land of Egypt. ¹⁰Why I caused them to go forth out of the land of Egypt, and brought them into the wilderness. ¹¹And I gave them my statutes, and showed them my judgments, which if a man do, he shall even live in them. ¹²Moreover also I gave them my sabbaths, to be a sign between me and them, that they might know that I am the LORD that sanctify them. ¹³But the house of Israel rebelled against me in the wilderness: they walked not in my statutes, and they despised my judgments, which if a man do, he shall even live in them; and my sabbaths they greatly polluted: then I said, I would pour out my fury on them in the wilderness, to consume them. ¹⁴But I worked for my name's sake, that it should not be polluted before the heathen, in whose sight I brought them out. ¹⁵Yet also I lifted up my hand to them in the wilderness, that I would not bring them into the land which I had given them, flowing with milk and honey, which is the glory of all lands; ¹⁶Because they despised my judgments, and walked not in my statutes, but polluted my sabbaths: for their heart went after their idols. ¹⁷Nevertheless my eye spared them from destroying them, neither did I make an end of them in the wilderness. ¹⁸But I said to their children in the wilderness, Walk you not in the statutes of your fathers, neither observe their judgments, nor defile yourselves with their idols: ¹⁹I am the LORD your God; walk in my statutes, and keep my judgments, and do them; ²⁰And hallow my sabbaths; and they shall be a sign between me and you, that you may know that I am the LORD your God. ²¹Notwithstanding the children rebelled against me: they walked not in my statutes, neither kept my judgments to do them, which if a man do, he shall even live in them; they polluted my sabbaths: then I said, I would pour out my fury on them, to accomplish my anger against them in the wilderness. ²²Nevertheless I withdrew my hand, and worked for my name's sake, that it should not be polluted in the sight of the heathen, in whose sight I brought them forth. ²³I lifted up my hand to them also in the wilderness, that I would scatter them among the heathen, and disperse them through the countries; ²⁴Because they had not executed my judgments, but had despised my statutes, and had polluted my sabbaths, and their eyes were after their fathers' idols. ²⁵Why I gave them also statutes that were not good, and judgments whereby they should not live; ²⁶And I polluted them in their own gifts, in that they caused to pass through the fire all that opens the womb, that I might make them desolate, to the end that they might know that I am the LORD. ²⁷Therefore, son of man, speak to the house of Israel, and say to them, Thus says the Lord GOD; Yet in this your fathers have blasphemed me, in that they have committed a trespass against me. ²⁸For when I had brought them into the land, for the which I lifted up my hand to give it to them, then they saw every high hill, and all the thick trees, and they offered there their sacrifices, and there they presented the provocation of their offering: there also they made their sweet smell, and poured out there their drink offerings. ²⁹Then I said to them, What is the high place where you go? And the name whereof is called Bamah to this day. ³⁰Why say to the house of Israel, Thus says the Lord GOD; Are you polluted after the manner of your fathers? and commit you prostitution after their abominations? ³¹For when you offer your gifts, when you make your sons to pass through the fire, you pollute yourselves with all your idols, even to this day: and shall I be inquired of by you, O house of Israel? As I live, says the Lord GOD, I will not be inquired of by you. ³²And that which comes into your mind shall not be at all, that you say, We will be as the heathen, as the families of the countries, to serve wood and stone. ³³As I live, says the Lord GOD, surely with a mighty hand, and with a stretched out arm, and with fury poured out, will I rule over you: ³⁴And I will bring you out from the people, and will gather you out of the countries wherein you are scattered, with a mighty hand, and with a stretched out arm, and with fury poured out. ³⁵And I will bring you into the wilderness of the people, and there will I plead with you face to face. ³⁶Like as I pleaded with your fathers in the wilderness of the land of Egypt, so will I plead with you, says the Lord GOD. ³⁷And I will cause you to pass under the rod, and I will bring you into the bond of the covenant: ³⁸And I will purge out from among you the rebels, and them that transgress against me: I will bring them forth out of the country where they sojourn, and they shall not enter into the land of Israel: and you shall know that I am the LORD. ³⁹As for you, O house of Israel, thus says the Lord GOD; Go you, serve you every one his idols, and hereafter also, if you will not listen to me: but pollute you my holy name no more with your gifts, and with your idols. ⁴⁰For in my holy mountain, in the mountain of the height of Israel, says the Lord GOD, there shall all the house of Israel, all of them in the land, serve me: there will I accept them, and there will I require your offerings, and the first fruits of your oblations, with all your holy things. ⁴¹I will accept you with your sweet smell, when I bring you out from the people, and gather you out of the countries wherein you have been scattered; and I will be sanctified in you before the heathen. ⁴²And you shall know that I am the LORD, when I shall bring you into the land of Israel, into the country for the which I lifted up my hand to give it to your fathers. ⁴³And there shall you remember your ways, and all your doings, wherein you have been defiled; and you shall loathe yourselves in your own sight for all your evils that you have committed. ⁴⁴And you shall know that I am the LORD when I have worked with you for my name's sake, not according to your wicked ways, nor according to your corrupt doings, O you house of Israel, says the Lord GOD. ⁴⁵Moreover the word of the LORD came to me, saying, ⁴⁶Son of man, set your face toward the south, and drop your word toward the south, and prophesy against the forest of the south field; ⁴⁷And say to the forest of the south, Hear the word of the LORD; Thus says the Lord GOD; Behold, I will kindle a fire in you, and it shall devour every green tree in you, and every dry tree: the flaming flame shall not be quenched, and all faces from the south to the north shall be burned therein. ⁴⁸And all flesh shall see that I the LORD have kindled it: it shall not be quenched. ⁴⁹Then said I, Ah Lord GOD! they say of me, Does he not speak parables?

21 ¹And the word of the LORD came to me, saying, ²Son of man, set your face toward Jerusalem, and drop your word toward the holy places, and prophesy against the land of Israel, ³And say to the land of Israel, Thus says the LORD; Behold, I am against you, and will draw forth my sword out of his sheath, and will cut off from you the righteous and the wicked. ⁴Seeing then that I will cut off from you the righteous and the wicked, therefore shall my sword go forth out of his sheath against all flesh from the south to the north: ⁵That all flesh may know that I the LORD have drawn forth my sword out of his sheath: it shall not return any more. ⁶Sigh therefore, you son of man, with the breaking of your loins; and with bitterness sigh before their eyes. ⁷And it shall be, when they say to you, Why sigh you? that you shall answer, For the tidings; because it comes: and every heart shall melt, and all hands shall be feeble, and every spirit shall faint, and all knees shall be weak as water: behold, it comes, and shall be brought to pass, says the Lord GOD. ⁸Again the word of the LORD came to me, saying, ⁹Son of man, prophesy, and say, Thus says the LORD; Say, A sword, a sword is sharpened, and also furbished: ¹⁰It is sharpened to make a sore slaughter; it is furbished that it may glitter: should we then make mirth? it scorns the rod of my son, as every tree. ¹¹And he has given it to be furbished, that it may be handled: this sword is sharpened, and it is furbished, to give it into the hand of the slayer. ¹²Cry and howl, son of man: for it shall be on my people, it shall be on all the princes of Israel: terrors by reason of the sword shall be on my people: smite therefore on your thigh. ¹³Because it is a trial, and what if the sword scorn even the rod? it shall be no more, says the Lord GOD. ¹⁴You therefore, son of man, prophesy, and smite your hands together. and let the sword be doubled the third time, the sword of the slain: it is the sword of the great men that are slain, which enters into their privy chambers. ¹⁵I have set the point of the sword against all their gates, that their heart may faint, and their ruins be multiplied: ah! it is made bright, it is wrapped up for the slaughter. ¹⁶Go you one way or other, either on the right hand, or on the left, wherever your face is set. ¹⁷I will also smite my hands together, and I will cause my fury to rest: I the LORD have said it. ¹⁸The word of the LORD came to me again, saying, ¹⁹Also, you son of man, appoint you two ways, that the sword of the king of Babylon may come: both two shall come forth out of one land: and choose you a place, choose it at the head of the way to the city. ²⁰Appoint a way, that the sword may come to Rabbath of the Ammonites, and to Judah in Jerusalem the defended. ²¹For the king of Babylon stood at the parting of the way, at the head of the two ways, to use divination: he made his arrows bright, he consulted with images, he looked in the liver. ²²At his right hand was the divination for Jerusalem, to appoint captains, to open the mouth in the slaughter, to lift up the voice with shouting, to appoint battering rams against the gates, to cast a mount, and to build a fort. ²³And it shall be to them as a false divination in their sight, to them that have sworn oaths: but he will call to remembrance the iniquity, that they may be taken. ²⁴Therefore thus says the Lord GOD; Because you have made your iniquity to be remembered, in that your transgressions are discovered, so that in all your doings your sins do appear; because, I say, that you are come to remembrance, you shall be taken with the hand. ²⁵And you, profane wicked prince of Israel, whose day is come, when iniquity shall have an end, ²⁶Thus says the Lord GOD; Remove the diadem, and take off the crown: this shall not be the same: exalt him that is low, and abase him that is high. ²⁷I will overturn, overturn, overturn, it: and it shall be no more, until he come whose right it is; and I will give it him. ²⁸And you, son of man, prophesy and say, Thus says the Lord GOD concerning the Ammonites, and concerning their reproach; even say you, The sword, the sword is drawn: for the slaughter it is furbished, to consume because of the glittering: ²⁹Whiles they see vanity to you, whiles they divine a lie to you, to bring you on the necks of them that are slain, of the wicked, whose day is come, when their iniquity shall have an end. ³⁰Shall I cause it to return into his sheath? I will judge you in the place where you were created, in the land of your nativity. ³¹And I will pour out my indignation on you, I will blow against you in the fire of my wrath, and deliver you into the hand of brutish men, and skillful to destroy. ³²You shall be for fuel to the fire; your blood shall be in the middle of the land; you shall be no more remembered: for I the LORD have spoken it.

22 ¹Moreover the word of the LORD came to me, saying, ²Now, you son of man, will you judge, will you judge the bloody city? yes, you shall show her all her abominations. ³Then say you, Thus says the Lord GOD, The city sheds blood in the middle of it, that her time may come, and makes idols against herself to defile herself. ⁴You are become guilty in your blood that you have shed; and have defiled yourself in your idols which you have made; and you have caused your days to draw near, and are come even to your years: therefore have I made you a reproach to the heathen, and a mocking to all countries. ⁵Those that be near, and those that be far from you, shall mock you, which are infamous and much vexed. ⁶Behold, the princes of Israel, every one were in you to their power to shed blood. ⁷In you have they set light by father and mother: in the middle of you have they dealt by oppression with the stranger: in you have they vexed the fatherless and the widow. ⁸You have despised my holy things, and have profaned my sabbaths. ⁹In you are men that carry tales to shed blood: and in you they eat on the mountains: in the middle of you they commit lewdness. ¹⁰In you have they discovered their fathers' nakedness: in you have they humbled her that was set apart for pollution. ¹¹And one has committed abomination with his neighbor's wife; and another has lewdly defiled his daughter in law; and another in you has humbled his sister, his father's daughter. ¹²In you have they taken gifts to shed blood; you have taken usury and increase, and you have greedily gained of your neighbors by extortion, and have forgotten me, says the Lord GOD. ¹³Behold, therefore I have smitten my hand at your dishonest gain which you have made, and at your blood which has been in the middle of you. ¹⁴Can your heart endure, or can your hands be strong, in the days that I shall deal with you? I the LORD have spoken it, and will do it. ¹⁵And I will scatter you among the heathen, and disperse you in the countries, and will consume your filthiness out of you. ¹⁶And you shall take your inheritance in yourself in the sight of the heathen, and you shall know that I am the LORD. ¹⁷And the word of the LORD came to me, saying, ¹⁸Son of man, the house of Israel is to me become dross: all they are brass, and tin, and iron, and lead, in the middle of the furnace; they are even the dross of silver. ¹⁹Therefore thus says the Lord GOD; Because you are all become dross, behold, therefore I will gather you into the middle of Jerusalem. ²⁰As they gather silver, and brass, and iron, and lead, and tin, into the middle of the furnace, to blow the fire on it, to melt it; so will I gather you in my anger and in my fury, and I will leave you there, and melt you. ²¹Yes, I will gather you, and blow on you in the fire of my wrath, and you shall be melted in the middle therof. ²²As silver is melted in the middle of the furnace, so shall you be melted in the middle thereof; and you shall know that I the LORD have poured out my fury on you. ²³And the word of the LORD came to me, saying, ²⁴Son of man, say to her, You are the land that is not cleansed, nor rained on in the day of indignation. ²⁵There is a conspiracy of her prophets in the middle thereof, like a roaring lion ravening the prey; they have devoured souls; they have taken the treasure and precious things; they have made her many widows in the middle thereof. ²⁶Her priests have violated my law, and have profaned my holy things: they have put no difference between the holy and profane, neither have they showed difference between the unclean and the clean, and have hid their eyes from my sabbaths, and I am profaned among them. ²⁷Her princes in the middle thereof are like wolves ravening the prey, to shed blood, and to destroy souls, to get dishonest gain. ²⁸And her prophets have daubed them with untempered mortar, seeing vanity, and divining lies to them, saying, Thus says the Lord GOD, when the LORD has not spoken. ²⁹The people of the land have used oppression, and exercised robbery, and have vexed the poor and needy: yes, they have oppressed the stranger wrongfully. ³⁰And I sought for a man among them, that should make up the hedge, and stand in the gap before me for the land, that I should not destroy it: but I found none. ³¹Therefore have I poured out my indignation on them; I have consumed them with the fire of my wrath: their own way have I recompensed on their heads, says the Lord GOD.

23 ¹The word of the LORD came again to me, saying, ²Son of man, there were two women, the daughters of one mother: ³And they committed prostitutions in Egypt; they committed prostitutions in their youth: there were their breasts pressed, and there they bruised the teats of their virginity. ⁴And the names of them were Aholah the elder, and Aholibah her sister: and they were mine, and they bore sons and daughters. Thus were their names; Samaria is Aholah, and Jerusalem Aholibah. ⁵And Aholah played the harlot when she was mine; and she doted on her lovers, on the Assyrians her neighbors, ⁶Which were clothed with blue, captains and rulers, all of them desirable young men, horsemen riding on horses. ⁷Thus she committed her prostitutions with them, with all them that were the chosen men of Assyria, and with all on whom she doted: with all their idols she defiled herself. ⁸Neither left she her prostitutions brought from Egypt: for in her youth they lay with her, and they bruised the breasts of her virginity, and poured their prostitution on her. ⁹Why I have delivered her into the hand of her lovers, into the hand of the Assyrians, on whom she doted. ¹⁰These discovered her nakedness: they took her sons and her daughters, and slew her with the sword: and she became famous among women; for they had executed judgment on her. ¹¹And when her sister Aholibah saw this, she was more corrupt in her inordinate love than she, and in her prostitutions more than her sister in her prostitutions. ¹²She doted on the Assyrians her neighbors, captains and rulers clothed most gorgeously, horsemen riding on horses, all of them desirable young men. ¹³Then I saw that she was defiled, that they took both one way, ¹⁴And that she increased her prostitutions: for when she saw men portrayed on the wall, the images of the Chaldeans portrayed with vermilion, ¹⁵Girded with girdles on their loins, exceeding in dyed attire on their heads, all of them princes to look to, after the manner of the Babylonians of Chaldea, the land of their nativity: ¹⁶And as soon as she saw them with her eyes, she doted on them, and sent messengers to them into Chaldea. ¹⁷And the Babylonians came to her into the bed of love, and they defiled her with their prostitution, and she was polluted with them, and her mind was alienated from them. ¹⁸So she discovered her prostitutions, and discovered her nakedness: then my mind was alienated from her, like as my mind was alienated from her sister. ¹⁹Yet she multiplied her prostitutions, in calling to remembrance the days of her youth, wherein she had played the harlot in the land of Egypt. ²⁰For she doted on their paramours, whose flesh is as the flesh of asses, and whose issue is like the issue of horses. ²¹Thus you called to remembrance the lewdness of your youth, in bruising your teats by the Egyptians for the breasts of your youth. ²²Therefore, O Aholibah, thus says the Lord GOD; Behold, I will raise up your lovers against you, from whom your mind is alienated, and I will bring them against you on every side; ²³The Babylonians, and all the Chaldeans, Pekod, and Shoa, and Koa, and all the Assyrians with them: all of them desirable young men, captains and rulers, great lords and renowned, all of them riding on horses. ²⁴And they shall come against you with chariots, wagons, and wheels, and with an assembly of people, which shall set against you buckler and shield and helmet round about: and I will set judgment before them, and they shall judge you according to their judgments. ²⁵And I will set my jealousy against you, and they shall deal furiously with you: they shall take away your nose and your ears; and your remnant shall fall by the sword: they shall take your sons and your daughters; and your residue shall be devoured by the fire. ²⁶They shall also strip you out of your clothes, and take away your fair jewels. ²⁷Thus will I make your lewdness to cease from you, and your prostitution brought from the land of Egypt: so that you shall not lift up your eyes to them, nor remember Egypt any more. ²⁸For thus says the Lord GOD; Behold, I will deliver you into the hand of them whom you hate, into the hand of them from whom your mind is alienated: ²⁹And they shall deal with you hatefully, and shall take away all your labor, and shall leave you naked and bore: and the nakedness of your prostitutions shall be discovered, both your lewdness and your prostitutions. ³⁰I will do these things to you, because you have gone a whoring after the heathen, and because you are polluted with their idols. ³¹You have walked in the way of your sister; therefore will I give her cup into your hand. ³²Thus says the Lord GOD; You shall drink of your sister's cup deep and large: you shall be laughed to scorn and had in derision; it contains much. ³³You shall be filled with drunkenness and sorrow, with the cup of astonishment and desolation, with the cup of your sister Samaria. ³⁴You shall even drink it and suck it out, and you shall break the shards thereof, and pluck off your own breasts: for I have spoken it, says the Lord GOD. ³⁵Therefore thus says the Lord GOD; Because you have forgotten me, and cast me behind your back, therefore bear you also your lewdness and your prostitutions. ³⁶The LORD said moreover to me; Son of man, will you judge Aholah and Aholibah? yes, declare to them their abominations; ³⁷That they have committed adultery, and blood is in their hands, and with their idols have they committed adultery, and have also caused their sons, whom they bore to me, to pass for them through the fire, to devour them. ³⁸Moreover this they have done to me: they have defiled my sanctuary in the same day, and have profaned my sabbaths. ³⁹For when they had slain their children to their idols, then they came the same day into my sanctuary to profane it; and, see, thus have they done in the middle of my house. ⁴⁰And furthermore, that you have sent for men to come from far, to whom a messenger was sent; and, see, they came: for whom you did wash yourself, painted your eyes, and decked yourself with ornaments, ⁴¹And sat on a stately bed, and a table prepared before it, whereupon you have set my incense and my oil. ⁴²And a voice of a multitude being at ease was with her: and with the men of the common sort were brought Sabeans from the wilderness, which put bracelets on their hands, and beautiful crowns on their heads. ⁴³Then said I to her that was old in adulteries, Will they now commit prostitutions with her, and she with them? ⁴⁴Yet they went in to her, as they go in to a woman that plays the harlot: so went they in to Aholah and to Aholibah, the lewd women. ⁴⁵And the righteous men, they shall judge them after the manner of adulteresses, and after the manner of women that shed blood; because they are adulteresses, and blood is in their hands. ⁴⁶For thus says the Lord GOD; I will bring up a company on them, and will give them to be removed and spoiled. ⁴⁷And the company shall stone them with stones, and dispatch them with their swords; they shall slay their sons and their daughters, and burn up their houses with fire. ⁴⁸Thus will I cause lewdness to cease out of the land, that all women may be taught not to do after your lewdness. ⁴⁹And they shall recompense your lewdness on you, and you shall bear the sins of your idols: and you shall know that I am the Lord GOD.

24

¹Again in the ninth year, in the tenth month, in the tenth day of the month, the word of the LORD came to me, saying, ²Son of man, write you the name of the day, even of this same day: the king of Babylon set himself against Jerusalem this same day. ³And utter a parable to the rebellious house, and say to them, Thus says the Lord GOD; Set on a pot, set it on, and also pour water into it: ⁴Gather the pieces thereof into it, even every good piece, the thigh, and the shoulder; fill it with the choice bones. ⁵Take the choice of the flock, and burn also the bones under it, and make it boil well, and let them seethe the bones of it therein. ⁶Why thus says the Lord GOD; Woe to the bloody city, to the pot whose scum is therein, and whose scum is not gone out of it! bring it out piece by piece; let no lot fall on it. ⁷For her blood is in the middle of her; she set it on the top of a rock; she poured it not on the ground, to cover it with dust; ⁸That it might cause fury to come up to take vengeance; I have set her blood on the top of a rock, that it should not be covered. ⁹Therefore thus says the Lord GOD; Woe to the bloody city! I will even make the pile for fire great. ¹⁰Heap on wood, kindle the fire, consume the flesh, and spice it well, and let the bones be burned. ¹¹Then set it empty on the coals thereof, that the brass of it may be hot, and may burn, and that the filthiness of it may be molten in it, that the scum of it may be consumed. ¹²She has wearied herself with lies, and her great scum went not forth out of her: her scum shall be in the fire. ¹³In your filthiness is lewdness: because I have purged you, and you were not purged, you shall not be purged from your filthiness any more, till I have caused my fury to rest on you. ¹⁴I the LORD have spoken it: it shall come to pass, and I will do it; I will not go back, neither will I spare, neither will I repent; according to your ways, and according to your doings, shall they judge you, says the Lord GOD. ¹⁵Also the word of the LORD came to me, saying, ¹⁶Son of man, behold, I take away from you the desire of your eyes with a stroke: yet neither shall you mourn nor weep, neither shall your tears run down. ¹⁷Forbear to cry, make no mourning for the dead, bind the tire of your head on you, and put on your shoes on your feet, and cover not your lips, and eat not the bread of men. ¹⁸So I spoke to the people in the morning: and at even my wife died; and I did in the morning as I was commanded. ¹⁹And the people said to me, Will you not tell us what these things are to us, that you do so? ²⁰Then I answered them, The word of the LORD came to me, saying, ²¹Speak to the house of Israel, Thus says the Lord GOD; Behold, I will profane my sanctuary, the excellency of your strength, the desire of your eyes, and that which your soul pities; and your sons and your daughters whom you have left shall fall by the sword. ²²And you shall do as I have done: you shall not cover your lips, nor eat the bread of men. ²³And your tires shall be on your heads, and your shoes on your feet: you shall not mourn nor weep; but you shall pine away for your iniquities, and mourn one toward another. ²⁴Thus Ezekiel is to you a sign: according to all that he has done shall you do: and when this comes, you shall know that I am the Lord GOD. ²⁵Also, you son of man, shall it not be in the day when I take from them their strength, the joy of their glory, the desire of their eyes, and that whereupon they set their minds, their sons and their daughters, ²⁶That he that escapes in that day shall come to you, to cause you to hear it with your ears? ²⁷In that day shall your mouth be opened to him which is escaped, and you shall speak, and be no more dumb: and you shall be a sign to them; and they shall know that I am the LORD.

25

¹The word of the LORD came again to me, saying, ²Son of man, set your face against the Ammonites, and prophesy against them; ³And say to the Ammonites, Hear the word of the Lord GOD; Thus says the Lord GOD; Because you said, Aha, against my sanctuary, when it was profaned; and against the land of Israel, when it was desolate; and against the house of Judah, when they went into captivity; ⁴Behold, therefore I will deliver you to the men of the east for a possession, and they shall set their

palaces in you, and make their dwellings in you: they shall eat your fruit, and they shall drink your milk. ⁵And I will make Rabbah a stable for camels, and the Ammonites a couching place for flocks: and you shall know that I am the LORD. ⁶For thus says the Lord GOD; Because you have clapped your hands, and stamped with the feet, and rejoiced in heart with all your despite against the land of Israel; ⁷Behold, therefore I will stretch out my hand on you, and will deliver you for a spoil to the heathen; and I will cut you off from the people, and I will cause you to perish out of the countries: I will destroy you; and you shall know that I am the LORD. ⁸Thus says the Lord GOD; Because that Moab and Seir do say, Behold, the house of Judah is like to all the heathen; ⁹Therefore, behold, I will open the side of Moab from the cities, from his cities which are on his frontiers, the glory of the country, Bethjeshimoth, Baalmeon, and Kiriathaim, ¹⁰To the men of the east with the Ammonites, and will give them in possession, that the Ammonites may not be remembered among the nations. ¹¹And I will execute judgments on Moab; and they shall know that I am the LORD. ¹²Thus says the Lord GOD; Because that Edom has dealt against the house of Judah by taking vengeance, and has greatly offended, and revenged himself on them; ¹³Therefore thus says the Lord GOD; I will also stretch out my hand on Edom, and will cut off man and beast from it; and I will make it desolate from Teman; and they of Dedan shall fall by the sword. ¹⁴And I will lay my vengeance on Edom by the hand of my people Israel: and they shall do in Edom according to my anger and according to my fury; and they shall know my vengeance, says the Lord GOD. ¹⁵Thus says the Lord GOD; Because the Philistines have dealt by revenge, and have taken vengeance with a despiteful heart, to destroy it for the old hatred; ¹⁶Therefore thus says the Lord GOD; Behold, I will stretch out my hand on the Philistines, and I will cut off the Cherethims, and destroy the remnant of the sea coast. ¹⁷And I will execute great vengeance on them with furious rebukes; and they shall know that I am the LORD, when I shall lay my vengeance on them.

26 ¹And it came to pass in the eleventh year, in the first day of the month, that the word of the LORD came to me, saying, ²Son of man, because that Tyrus has said against Jerusalem, Aha, she is broken that was the gates of the people: she is turned to me: I shall be replenished, now she is laid waste: ³Therefore thus says the Lord GOD; Behold, I am against you, O Tyrus, and will cause many nations to come up against you, as the sea causes his waves to come up. ⁴And they shall destroy the walls of Tyrus, and break down her towers: I will also scrape her dust from her, and make her like the top of a rock. ⁵It shall be a place for the spreading of nets in the middle of the sea: for I have spoken it, says the Lord GOD: and it shall become a spoil to the nations. ⁶And her daughters which are in the field shall be slain by the sword; and they shall know that I am the LORD. ⁷For thus says the Lord GOD; Behold, I will bring on Tyrus Nebuchadrezzar king of Babylon, a king of kings, from the north, with horses, and with chariots, and with horsemen, and companies, and much people. ⁸He shall slay with the sword your daughters in the field: and he shall make a fort against you, and cast a mount against you, and lift up the buckler against you. ⁹And he shall set engines of war against your walls, and with his axes he shall break down your towers. ¹⁰By reason of the abundance of his horses their dust shall cover you: your walls shall shake at the noise of the horsemen, and of the wheels, and of the chariots, when he shall enter into your gates, as men enter into a city wherein is made a breach. ¹¹With the hoofs of his horses shall he tread down all your streets: he shall slay your people by the sword, and your strong garrisons shall go down to the ground. ¹²And they shall make a spoil of your riches, and make a prey of your merchandise: and they shall break down your walls, and destroy your pleasant houses: and they shall lay your stones and your timber and your dust in the middle of the water. ¹³And I will cause the noise of your songs to cease; and the sound of your harps shall be no more heard. ¹⁴And I will make you like the top of a rock: you shall be a place to spread nets on; you shall be built no more: for I the LORD have spoken it, says the Lord GOD. ¹⁵Thus says the Lord GOD to Tyrus; Shall not the isles shake at the sound of your fall, when the wounded cry, when the slaughter is made in the middle of you? ¹⁶Then all the princes of the sea shall come down from their thrones, and lay away their robes, and put off their broidered garments: they shall clothe themselves with trembling; they shall sit on the ground, and shall tremble at every moment, and be astonished at you. ¹⁷And they shall take up a lamentation for you, and say to you, How are you destroyed, that were inhabited of seafaring men, the renowned city, which were strong in the sea, she and her inhabitants, which cause their terror to be on all that haunt it! ¹⁸Now shall the isles tremble in the day of your fall; yes, the isles that are in the sea shall be troubled at your departure. ¹⁹For thus says the Lord GOD; When I shall make you a desolate city, like the cities that are not inhabited; when I shall bring up the deep on you, and great waters shall cover you; ²⁰When I shall bring you down with them that descend into the pit, with the people of old time, and shall set you in the low parts of the earth, in places desolate of old, with them that go down to the pit, that you be not inhabited; and I shall set glory in the land of the living; ²¹I will make you a terror, and you shall be no more: though you be sought for, yet shall you never be found again, says the Lord GOD.

27 ¹The word of the LORD came again to me, saying, ²Now, you son of man, take up a lamentation for Tyrus; ³And say to Tyrus, O you that are situate at the entry of the sea, which are a merchant of the people for many isles, Thus says the Lord GOD; O Tyrus, you have said, I am of perfect beauty. ⁴Your borders are in the middle of the seas, your builders have perfected your beauty. ⁵They have made all your ship boards of fir trees of Senir: they have taken cedars from Lebanon to make masts for you. ⁶Of the oaks of Bashan have they made your oars; the company of the Ashurites have made your benches of ivory, brought out of the isles of Chittim. ⁷Fine linen with broidered work from Egypt was that which you spread forth to be your sail; blue and purple from the isles of Elishah was that which covered you. ⁸The inhabitants of Zidon and Arvad were your mariners: your wise men, O Tyrus, that were in you, were your pilots. ⁹The ancients of Gebal and the wise men thereof were in you your caulkers: all the ships of the sea with their mariners were in you to occupy your merchandise. ¹⁰They of Persia and of Lud and of Phut were in your army, your men of war: they hanged the shield and helmet in you; they set forth your comeliness. ¹¹The men of Arvad with your army were on your walls round about, and the Gammadims were in your towers: they hanged their shields on your walls round about; they have made your beauty perfect. ¹²Tarshish was your merchant by reason of the multitude of all kind of riches; with silver, iron, tin, and lead, they traded in your fairs. ¹³Javan, Tubal, and Meshech, they were your merchants: they traded the persons of men and vessels of brass in your market. ¹⁴They of the house of Togarmah traded in your fairs with horses and horsemen and mules. ¹⁵The men of Dedan were your merchants; many isles were the merchandise of your hand: they brought you for a present horns of ivory and ebony. ¹⁶Syria was your merchant by reason of the multitude of the wares of your making: they occupied in your fairs with emeralds, purple, and broidered work, and fine linen, and coral, and agate. ¹⁷Judah, and the land of Israel, they were your merchants: they traded in your market wheat of Minnith, and Pannag, and honey, and oil, and balm. ¹⁸Damascus was your merchant in the multitude of the wares of your making, for the multitude of all riches; in the wine of Helbon, and white wool. ¹⁹Dan also and Javan going to and fro occupied in your fairs: bright iron, cassia, and calamus, were in your market. ²⁰Dedan was your merchant in precious clothes for chariots. ²¹Arabia, and all the princes of Kedar, they occupied with you in lambs, and rams, and goats: in these were they your merchants. ²²The merchants of Sheba and Raamah, they were your merchants: they occupied in your fairs with chief of all spices, and with all precious stones, and gold. ²³Haran, and Canneh, and Eden, the merchants of Sheba, Asshur, and Chilmad, were your merchants. ²⁴These were your merchants in all sorts of things, in blue clothes, and broidered work, and in chests of rich apparel, bound with cords, and made of cedar, among your merchandise. ²⁵The ships of Tarshish did sing of you in your market: and you were replenished, and made very glorious in the middle of the seas. ²⁶Your rowers have brought you into great waters: the east wind has broken you in the middle of the seas. ²⁷Your riches, and your fairs, your merchandise, your mariners, and your pilots, your caulkers, and the occupiers of your merchandise, and all your men of war, that are in you, and in all your company which is in the middle of you, shall fall into the middle of the seas in the day of your ruin. ²⁸The suburbs shall shake at the sound of the cry of your pilots. ²⁹And all that handle the oar, the mariners, and all the pilots of the sea, shall come down from their ships, they shall stand on the land; ³⁰And shall cause their voice to be heard against you, and shall cry bitterly, and shall cast up dust on their heads, they shall wallow themselves in the ashes: ³¹And they shall make themselves utterly bald for you, and gird them with sackcloth, and they shall weep for you with bitterness of heart and bitter wailing. ³²And in their wailing they shall take up a lamentation for you, and lament over you, saying, What city is like Tyrus, like the destroyed in the middle of the sea? ³³When your wares went forth out of the seas, you filled many people; you did enrich the kings of the earth with the multitude of your riches and of your merchandise. ³⁴In the time when you shall be broken by the seas in the depths of the waters your merchandise and all your company in the middle of you shall fall. ³⁵All the inhabitants of the isles shall be astonished at you, and their kings shall be sore afraid, they shall be troubled in their countenance. ³⁶The merchants among the people shall hiss at you; you shall be a terror, and never shall be any more.

28

¹The word of the LORD came again to me, saying, ²Son of man, say to the prince of Tyrus, Thus says the Lord GOD; Because your heart is lifted up, and you have said, I am a God, I sit in the seat of God, in the middle of the seas; yet you are a man, and not God, though you set your heart as the heart of God: ³Behold, you are wiser than Daniel; there is no secret that they can hide from you: ⁴With your wisdom and with your understanding you have gotten you riches, and have gotten gold and silver into your treasures: ⁵By your great wisdom and by your traffic have you increased your riches, and your heart is lifted up because of your riches: ⁶Therefore thus says the Lord GOD; Because you have set your heart as the heart of God; ⁷Behold, therefore I will bring strangers on you, the terrible of the nations: and they shall draw their swords against the beauty of your wisdom, and they shall defile your brightness. ⁸They shall bring you down to the pit, and you shall die the deaths of them that are slain in the middle of the seas. ⁹Will you yet say before him that slays you, I am God? but you shall be a man, and no God, in the hand of him that slays you. ¹⁰You shall die the deaths of the uncircumcised by the hand of strangers: for I have spoken it, says the Lord GOD. ¹¹Moreover the word of the LORD came to me, saying, ¹²Son of man, take up a lamentation on the king of Tyrus, and say to him, Thus says the Lord GOD; You seal up the sum, full of wisdom, and perfect in beauty. ¹³You have been in Eden the garden of God; every precious stone was your covering, the sardius, topaz, and the diamond, the beryl, the onyx, and the jasper, the sapphire, the emerald, and the carbuncle, and gold: the workmanship of your tabrets and of your pipes was prepared in you in the day that you were created. ¹⁴You are the anointed cherub that covers; and I have set you so: you were on the holy mountain of God; you have walked up and down in the middle of the stones of fire. ¹⁵You were perfect in your ways from the day that you were created, till iniquity was found in you. ¹⁶By the multitude of your merchandise they have filled the middle of you with violence, and you have sinned: therefore I will cast you as profane out of the mountain of God: and I will destroy you, O covering cherub, from the middle of the stones of fire. ¹⁷Your heart was lifted up because of your beauty, you have corrupted your wisdom by reason of your brightness: I will cast you to the ground, I will lay you before kings, that they may behold you. ¹⁸You have defiled your sanctuaries by the multitude of your iniquities, by the iniquity of your traffic; therefore will I bring forth a fire from the middle of you, it shall devour you, and I will bring you to ashes on the earth in the sight of all them that behold you. ¹⁹All they that know you among the people shall be astonished at you: you shall be a terror, and never shall you be any more. ²⁰Again the word of the LORD came to me, saying, ²¹Son of man, set your face against Zidon, and prophesy against it, ²²And say, Thus says the

Lord GOD; Behold, I am against you, O Zidon; and I will be glorified in the middle of you: and they shall know that I am the LORD, when I shall have executed judgments in her, and shall be sanctified in her. ²³For I will send into her pestilence, and blood into her streets; and the wounded shall be judged in the middle of her by the sword on her on every side; and they shall know that I am the LORD. ²⁴And there shall be no more a pricking brier to the house of Israel, nor any grieving thorn of all that are round about them, that despised them; and they shall know that I am the Lord GOD. ²⁵Thus says the Lord GOD; When I shall have gathered the house of Israel from the people among whom they are scattered, and shall be sanctified in them in the sight of the heathen, then shall they dwell in their land that I have given to my servant Jacob. ²⁶And they shall dwell safely therein, and shall build houses, and plant vineyards; yes, they shall dwell with confidence, when I have executed judgments on all those that despise them round about them; and they shall know that I am the LORD their God.

29

¹In the tenth year, in the tenth month, in the twelfth day of the month, the word of the LORD came to me, saying, ²Son of man, set your face against Pharaoh king of Egypt, and prophesy against him, and against all Egypt: ³Speak, and say, Thus says the Lord GOD; Behold, I am against you, Pharaoh king of Egypt, the great dragon that lies in the middle of his rivers, which has said, My river is my own, and I have made it for myself. ⁴But I will put hooks in your jaws, and I will cause the fish of your rivers to stick to your scales, and I will bring you up out of the middle of your rivers, and all the fish of your rivers shall stick to your scales. ⁵And I will leave you thrown into the wilderness, you and all the fish of your rivers: you shall fall on the open fields; you shall not be brought together, nor gathered: I have given you for meat to the beasts of the field and to the fowls of the heaven. ⁶And all the inhabitants of Egypt shall know that I am the LORD, because they have been a staff of reed to the house of Israel. ⁷When they took hold of you by your hand, you did break, and rend all their shoulder: and when they leaned on you, you brake, and made all their loins to be at a stand. ⁸Therefore thus says the Lord GOD; Behold, I will bring a sword on you, and cut off man and beast out of you. ⁹And the land of Egypt shall be desolate and waste; and they shall know that I am the LORD: because he has said, The river is mine, and I have made it. ¹⁰Behold, therefore I am against you, and against your rivers, and I will make the land of Egypt utterly waste and desolate, from the tower of Syene even to the border of Ethiopia. ¹¹No foot of man shall pass through it, nor foot of beast shall pass through it, neither shall it be inhabited forty years. ¹²And I will make the land of Egypt desolate in the middle of the countries that are desolate, and her cities among the cities that are laid waste shall be desolate forty years: and I will scatter the Egyptians among the nations, and will disperse them through the countries. ¹³Yet thus says the Lord GOD; At the end of forty years will I gather the Egyptians from the people where they were scattered: ¹⁴And I will bring again the captivity of Egypt, and will cause them to return into the land of Pathros, into the land of their habitation; and they shall be there a base kingdom. ¹⁵It shall be the basest of the kingdoms; neither shall it exalt itself any more above the nations: for I will diminish them, that they shall no more rule over the nations. ¹⁶And it shall be no more the confidence of the house of Israel, which brings their iniquity to remembrance, when they shall look after them: but they shall know that I am the Lord GOD. ¹⁷And it came to pass in the seven and twentieth year, in the first month, in the first day of the month, the word of the LORD came to me, saying, ¹⁸Son of man, Nebuchadrezzar king of Babylon caused his army to serve a great service against Tyrus: every head was made bald, and every shoulder was peeled: yet had he no wages, nor his army, for Tyrus, for the service that he had served against it: ¹⁹Therefore thus says the Lord GOD; Behold, I will give the land of Egypt to Nebuchadrezzar king of Babylon; and he shall take her multitude, and take her spoil, and take her prey; and it shall be the wages for his army. ²⁰I have given him the land of Egypt for his labor with which he served against it, because they worked for me, says the Lord GOD. ²¹In that day will I cause the horn of the house of Israel to bud forth, and I will give you the opening of the mouth in the middle of them; and they shall know that I am the LORD.

30

¹The word of the LORD came again to me, saying, ²Son of man, prophesy and say, Thus says the Lord GOD; Howl you, Woe worth the day! ³For the day is near, even the day of the LORD is near, a cloudy day; it shall be the time of the heathen. ⁴And the sword shall come on Egypt, and great pain shall be in Ethiopia, when the slain shall fall in Egypt, and they shall take away her multitude, and her foundations shall be broken down. ⁵Ethiopia, and Libya, and Lydia, and all the mingled people, and Chub, and the men of the land that is in league, shall fall with them by the sword. ⁶Thus says the LORD; They also that uphold Egypt shall fall; and the pride of her power shall come down: from the tower of Syene shall they fall in it by the sword, said the Lord GOD. ⁷And they shall be desolate in the middle of the countries that are desolate, and her cities shall be in the middle of the cities that are wasted. ⁸And they shall know that I am the LORD, when I have set a fire in Egypt, and when all her helpers shall be destroyed. ⁹In that day shall messengers go forth from me in ships to make the careless Ethiopians afraid, and great pain shall come on them, as in the day of Egypt: for, see, it comes. ¹⁰Thus says the Lord GOD; I will also make the multitude of Egypt to cease by the hand of Nebuchadrezzar king of Babylon. ¹¹He and his people with him, the terrible of the nations, shall be brought to destroy the land: and they shall draw their swords against Egypt, and fill the land with the slain. ¹²And I will make the rivers dry, and sell the land into the hand of the wicked: and I will make the land waste, and all that is therein, by the hand of strangers: I the LORD have spoken it. ¹³Thus says the Lord GOD; I will also destroy the idols, and I will cause their images to cease out of Noph; and there shall be no more a prince of the land of Egypt: and I will put a fear in the land of Egypt. ¹⁴And I will make Pathros desolate, and will set fire in Zoan, and will execute judgments in No. ¹⁵And I will pour my fury on Sin, the strength of Egypt; and I will cut off the multitude of No. ¹⁶And I will set fire in Egypt: Sin shall have great pain, and No shall be rent asunder, and Noph shall have distresses daily. ¹⁷The young men of Aven and of Pibeseth shall fall by

the sword: and these cities shall go into captivity. ⁱ⁸At Tehaphnehes also the day shall be darkened, when I shall break there the yokes of Egypt: and the pomp of her strength shall cease in her: as for her, a cloud shall cover her, and her daughters shall go into captivity. ¹⁹Thus will I execute judgments in Egypt: and they shall know that I am the LORD. ²⁰And it came to pass in the eleventh year, in the first month, in the seventh day of the month, that the word of the LORD came to me, saying, ²¹Son of man, I have broken the arm of Pharaoh king of Egypt; and, see, it shall not be bound up to be healed, to put a roller to bind it, to make it strong to hold the sword. ²²Therefore thus says the Lord GOD; Behold, I am against Pharaoh king of Egypt, and will break his arms, the strong, and that which was broken; and I will cause the sword to fall out of his hand. ²³And I will scatter the Egyptians among the nations, and will disperse them through the countries. ²⁴And I will strengthen the arms of the king of Babylon, and put my sword in his hand: but I will break Pharaoh's arms, and he shall groan before him with the groanings of a deadly wounded man. ²⁵But I will strengthen the arms of the king of Babylon, and the arms of Pharaoh shall fall down; and they shall know that I am the LORD, when I shall put my sword into the hand of the king of Babylon, and he shall stretch it out on the land of Egypt. ²⁶And I will scatter the Egyptians among the nations, and disperse them among the countries; and they shall know that I am the LORD.

31 ¹And it came to pass in the eleventh year, in the third month, in the first day of the month, that the word of the LORD came to me, saying, ²Son of man, speak to Pharaoh king of Egypt, and to his multitude; Whom are you like in your greatness? ³Behold, the Assyrian was a cedar in Lebanon with fair branches, and with a shadowing shroud, and of an high stature; and his top was among the thick boughs. ⁴The waters made him great, the deep set him up on high with her rivers running round about his plants, and sent her little rivers to all the trees of the field. ⁵Therefore his height was exalted above all the trees of the field, and his boughs were multiplied, and his branches became long because of the multitude of waters, when he shot forth. ⁶All the fowls of heaven made their nests in his boughs, and under his branches did all the beasts of the field bring forth their young, and under his shadow dwelled all great nations. ⁷Thus was he fair in his greatness, in the length of his branches: for his root was by great waters. ⁸The cedars in the garden of God could not hide him: the fir trees were not like his boughs, and the chestnut trees were not like his branches; nor any tree in the garden of God was like to him in his beauty. ⁹I have made him fair by the multitude of his branches: so that all the trees of Eden, that were in the garden of God, envied him. ¹⁰Therefore thus says the Lord GOD; Because you have lifted up yourself in height, and he has shot up his top among the thick boughs, and his heart is lifted up in his height; ¹¹I have therefore delivered him into the hand of the mighty one of the heathen; he shall surely deal with him: I have driven him out for his wickedness. ¹²And strangers, the terrible of the nations, have cut him off, and have left him: on the mountains and in all the valleys his branches are fallen, and his boughs are broken by all the rivers of the land; and all the people of the earth are gone down from his shadow, and have left him. ¹³On his ruin shall all the fowls of the heaven remain, and all the beasts of the field shall be on his branches: ¹⁴To the end that none of all the trees by the waters exalt themselves for their height, neither shoot up their top among the thick boughs, neither their trees stand up in their height, all that drink water: for they are all delivered to death, to the nether parts of the earth, in the middle of the children of men, with them that go down to the pit. ¹⁵Thus says the Lord GOD; In the day when he went down to the grave I caused a mourning: I covered the deep for him, and I restrained the floods thereof, and the great waters were stayed: and I caused Lebanon to mourn for him, and all the trees of the field fainted for him. ¹⁶I made the nations to shake at the sound of his fall, when I cast him down to hell with them that descend into the pit: and all the trees of Eden, the choice and best of Lebanon, all that drink water, shall be comforted in the nether parts of the earth. ¹⁷They also went down into hell with him to them that be slain with the sword; and they that were his arm, that dwelled under his shadow in the middle of the heathen. ¹⁸To whom are you thus like in glory and in greatness among the trees of Eden? yet shall you be brought down with the trees of Eden to the nether parts of the earth: you shall lie in the middle of the uncircumcised with them that be slain by the sword. This is Pharaoh and all his multitude, says the Lord GOD.

32 ¹And it came to pass in the twelfth year, in the twelfth month, in the first day of the month, that the word of the LORD came to me, saying, ²Son of man, take up a lamentation for Pharaoh king of Egypt, and say to him, You are like a young lion of the nations, and you are as a whale in the seas: and you came forth with your rivers, and troubled the waters with your feet, and fouled their rivers. ³Thus says the Lord GOD; I will therefore spread out my net over you with a company of many people; and they shall bring you up in my net. ⁴Then will I leave you on the land, I will cast you forth on the open field, and will cause all the fowls of the heaven to remain on you, and I will fill the beasts of the whole earth with you. ⁵And I will lay your flesh on the mountains, and fill the valleys with your height. ⁶I will also water with your blood the land wherein you swim, even to the mountains; and the rivers shall be full of you. ⁷And when I shall put you out, I will cover the heaven, and make the stars thereof dark; I will cover the sun with a cloud, and the moon shall not give her light. ⁸All the bright lights of heaven will I make dark over you, and set darkness on your land, says the Lord GOD. ⁹I will also vex the hearts of many people, when I shall bring your destruction among the nations, into the countries which you have not known. ¹⁰Yes, I will make many people amazed at you, and their kings shall be horribly afraid for you, when I shall brandish my sword before them; and they shall tremble at every moment, every man for his own life, in the day of your fall. ¹¹For thus says the Lord GOD; The sword of the king of Babylon shall come on you. ¹²By the swords of the mighty will I cause your multitude to fall, the terrible of the nations, all of them: and they shall spoil the pomp of Egypt, and all the multitude thereof shall be destroyed. ¹³I will destroy also all the beasts thereof from beside the great waters; neither shall the foot of man trouble them any more, nor the hoofs of beasts trouble them. ¹⁴Then will I make their waters deep, and cause their rivers to run like oil, says the Lord GOD. ¹⁵When I shall make the land of Egypt desolate, and the country shall be destitute of that whereof it was full, when I shall smite all them that dwell therein, then shall they know that I am the LORD. ¹⁶This is the lamentation with which they shall lament her: the daughters of the nations shall lament her: they shall lament for her, even for Egypt, and for all her multitude, says the Lord GOD. ¹⁷It came to pass also in the twelfth year, in the fifteenth day of the month, that the word of the LORD came to me, saying, ¹⁸Son of man, wail for the multitude of Egypt, and cast them down, even her, and the daughters of the famous nations, to the nether parts of the earth, with them that go down into the pit. ¹⁹Whom do you pass in beauty? go down, and be you laid with the uncircumcised. ²⁰They shall fall in the middle of them that are slain by the sword: she is delivered to the sword: draw her and all her multitudes. ²¹The strong among the mighty shall speak to him out of the middle of hell with them that help him: they are gone down, they lie uncircumcised, slain by the sword. ²²Asshur is there and all her company: his graves are about him: all of them slain, fallen by the sword: ²³Whose graves are set in the sides of the pit, and her company is round about her grave: all of them slain, fallen by the sword, which caused terror in the land of the living. ²⁴There is Elam and all her multitude round about her grave, all of them slain, fallen by the sword, which are gone down uncircumcised into the nether parts of the earth, which caused their terror in the land of the living; yet have they borne their shame with them that go down to the pit. ²⁵They have set her a bed in the middle of the slain with all her multitude: her graves are round about him: all of them uncircumcised, slain by the sword: though their terror was caused in the land of the living, yet have they borne their shame with them that go down to the pit: he is put in the middle of them that be slain. ²⁶There is Meshech, Tubal, and all her multitude: her graves are round about him: all of them uncircumcised, slain by the sword, though they caused their terror in the land of the living. ²⁷And they shall not lie with the mighty that are fallen of the uncircumcised, which are gone down to hell with their weapons of war: and they have laid their swords under their heads, but their iniquities shall be on their bones, though they were the terror of the mighty in the land of the living. ²⁸Yes, you shall be broken in the middle of the uncircumcised, and shall lie with them that are slain with the sword. ²⁹There is Edom, her kings, and all her princes, which with their might are laid by them that were slain by the sword: they shall lie with the uncircumcised, and with them that go down to the pit. ³⁰There be the princes of the north, all of them, and all the Zidonians, which are gone down with the slain; with their terror they are ashamed of their might; and they lie uncircumcised with them that be slain by the sword, and bear their shame with them that go down to the pit. ³¹Pharaoh shall see them, and shall be comforted over all his multitude, even Pharaoh and all his army slain by the sword, says the Lord GOD. ³²For I have caused my terror in the land of the living: and he shall be laid in the middle of the uncircumcised with them that are slain with the sword, even Pharaoh and all his multitude, says the Lord GOD.

33 ¹Again the word of the LORD came to me, saying, ²Son of man, speak to the children of your people, and say to them, When I bring the sword on a land, if the people of the land take a man of their coasts, and set him for their watchman: ³If when he sees the sword come on the land, he blow the trumpet, and warn the people; ⁴Then whoever hears the sound of the trumpet, and takes not warning; if the sword come, and take him away, his blood shall be on his own head. ⁵He heard the sound of the trumpet, and took not warning; his blood shall be on him. But he that takes warning shall deliver his soul. ⁶But if the watchman see the sword come, and blow not the trumpet, and the people be not warned; if the sword come, and take any person from among them, he is taken away in his iniquity; but his blood will I require at the watchman's hand. ⁷So you, O son of man, I have set you a watchman to the house of Israel; therefore you shall hear the word at my mouth, and warn them from me. ⁸When I say to the wicked, O wicked man, you shall surely die; if you do not speak to warn the wicked from his way, that wicked man shall die in his iniquity; but his blood will I require at your hand. ⁹Nevertheless, if you warn the wicked of his way to turn from it; if he do not turn from his way, he shall die in his iniquity; but you have delivered your soul. ¹⁰Therefore, O you son of man, speak to the house of Israel; Thus you speak, saying, If our transgressions and our sins be on us, and we pine away in them, how should we then live? ¹¹Say to them, As I live, says the Lord GOD, I have no pleasure in the death of the wicked; but that the wicked turn from his way and live: turn you, turn you from your evil ways; for why will you die, O house of Israel? ¹²Therefore, you son of man, say to the children of your people, The righteousness of the righteous shall not deliver him in the day of his transgression: as for the wickedness of the wicked, he shall not fall thereby in the day that he turns from his wickedness; neither shall the righteous be able to live for his righteousness in the day that he sins. ¹³When I shall say to the righteous, that he shall surely live; if he trust to his own righteousness, and commit iniquity, all his righteousnesses shall not be remembered; but for his iniquity that he has committed, he shall die for it. ¹⁴Again, when I say to the wicked, You shall surely die; if he turn from his sin, and do that which is lawful and right; ¹⁵If the wicked restore the pledge, give again that he had robbed, walk in the statutes of life, without committing iniquity; he shall surely live, he shall not die. ¹⁶None of his sins that he has committed shall be mentioned to him: he has done that which is lawful and right; he shall surely live. ¹⁷Yet the children of your people say, The way of the Lord is not equal: but as for them, their way is not equal. ¹⁸When the righteous turns from his righteousness, and commits iniquity, he shall even die thereby. ¹⁹But if the wicked turn from his wickedness, and do that which is lawful and right, he shall live thereby. ²⁰Yet you say, The way of the Lord is not equal. O you house of Israel, I will judge you every one after his ways. ²¹And it came to pass in the twelfth year of our captivity, in the tenth month, in the fifth day of the month, that one that had escaped out of Jerusalem came to me, saying, The city is smitten. ²²Now the hand of the LORD was on me in the evening, before he that was escaped came; and had opened

my mouth, until he came to me in the morning; and my mouth was opened, and I was no more dumb. ²³Then the word of the LORD came to me, saying, ²⁴Son of man, they that inhabit those wastes of the land of Israel speak, saying, Abraham was one, and he inherited the land: but we are many; the land is given us for inheritance. ²⁵Why say to them, Thus says the Lord GOD; You eat with the blood, and lift up your eyes toward your idols, and shed blood: and shall you possess the land? ²⁶You stand on your sword, you work abomination, and you defile every one his neighbor's wife: and shall you possess the land? ²⁷Say you thus to them, Thus says the Lord GOD; As I live, surely they that are in the wastes shall fall by the sword, and him that is in the open field will I give to the beasts to be devoured, and they that be in the forts and in the caves shall die of the pestilence. ²⁸For I will lay the land most desolate, and the pomp of her strength shall cease; and the mountains of Israel shall be desolate, that none shall pass through. ²⁹Then shall they know that I am the LORD, when I have laid the land most desolate because of all their abominations which they have committed. ³⁰Also, you son of man, the children of your people still are talking against you by the walls and in the doors of the houses, and speak one to another, every one to his brother, saying, Come, I pray you, and hear what is the word that comes forth from the LORD. ³¹And they come to you as the people comes, and they sit before you as my people, and they hear your words, but they will not do them: for with their mouth they show much love, but their heart goes after their covetousness. ³²And, see, you are to them as a very lovely song of one that has a pleasant voice, and can play well on an instrument: for they hear your words, but they do them not. ³³And when this comes to pass, (see, it will come,) then shall they know that a prophet has been among them.

34

¹And the word of the LORD came to me, saying, ²Son of man, prophesy against the shepherds of Israel, prophesy, and say to them, Thus says the Lord GOD to the shepherds; Woe be to the shepherds of Israel that do feed themselves! should not the shepherds feed the flocks? ³You eat the fat, and you clothe you with the wool, you kill them that are fed: but you feed not the flock. ⁴The diseased have you not strengthened, neither have you healed that which was sick, neither have you bound up that which was broken, neither have you brought again that which was driven away, neither have you sought that which was lost; but with force and with cruelty have you ruled them. ⁵And they were scattered, because there is no shepherd: and they became meat to all the beasts of the field, when they were scattered. ⁶My sheep wandered through all the mountains, and on every high hill: yes, my flock was scattered on all the face of the earth, and none did search or seek after them. ⁷Therefore, you shepherds, hear the word of the LORD; ⁸As I live, says the Lord GOD, surely because my flock became a prey, and my flock became meat to every beast of the field, because there was no shepherd, neither did my shepherds search for my flock, but the shepherds fed themselves, and fed not my flock; ⁹Therefore, O you shepherds, hear the word of the LORD; ¹⁰Thus says the Lord GOD; Behold, I am against the shepherds; and I will require my flock at their hand, and cause them to cease from feeding the flock; neither shall the shepherds feed themselves any more; for I will deliver my flock from their mouth, that they may not be meat for them. ¹¹For thus says the Lord GOD; Behold, I, even I, will both search my sheep, and seek them out. ¹²As a shepherd seeks out his flock in the day that he is among his sheep that are scattered; so will I seek out my sheep, and will deliver them out of all places where they have been scattered in the cloudy and dark day. ¹³And I will bring them out from the people, and gather them from the countries, and will bring them to their own land, and feed them on the mountains of Israel by the rivers, and in all the inhabited places of the country. ¹⁴I will feed them in a good pasture, and on the high mountains of Israel shall their fold be: there shall they lie in a good fold, and in a fat pasture shall they feed on the mountains of Israel. ¹⁵I will feed my flock, and I will cause them to lie down, says the Lord GOD. ¹⁶I will seek that which was lost, and bring again that which was driven away, and will bind up that which was broken, and will strengthen that which was sick: but I will destroy the fat and the strong; I will feed them with judgment. ¹⁷And as for you, O my flock, thus says the Lord GOD; Behold, I judge between cattle and cattle, between the rams and the he goats. ¹⁸Seems it a small thing to you to have eaten up the good pasture, but you must tread down with your feet the residue of your pastures? and to have drunk of the deep waters, but you must foul the residue with your feet? ¹⁹And as for my flock, they eat that which you have trodden with your feet; and they drink that which you have fouled with your feet. ²⁰Therefore thus says the Lord GOD to them; Behold, I, even I, will judge between the fat cattle and between the lean cattle. ²¹Because you have thrust with side and with shoulder, and pushed all the diseased with your horns, till you have scattered them abroad; ²²Therefore will I save my flock, and they shall no more be a prey; and I will judge between cattle and cattle. ²³And I will set up one shepherd over them, and he shall feed them, even my servant David; he shall feed them, and he shall be their shepherd. ²⁴And I the LORD will be their God, and my servant David a prince among them; I the LORD have spoken it. ²⁵And I will make with them a covenant of peace, and will cause the evil beasts to cease out of the land: and they shall dwell safely in the wilderness, and sleep in the woods. ²⁶And I will make them and the places round about my hill a blessing; and I will cause the shower to come down in his season; there shall be showers of blessing. ²⁷And the tree of the field shall yield her fruit, and the earth shall yield her increase, and they shall be safe in their land, and shall know that I am the LORD, when I have broken the bands of their yoke, and delivered them out of the hand of those that served themselves of them. ²⁸And they shall no more be a prey to the heathen, neither shall the beast of the land devour them; but they shall dwell safely, and none shall make them afraid. ²⁹And I will raise up for them a plant of renown, and they shall be no more consumed with hunger in the land, neither bear the shame of the heathen any more. ³⁰Thus shall they know that I the LORD their God am with them, and that they, even the house of Israel, are my people, says the Lord GOD. ³¹And you my flock, the flock of my pasture, are men, and I am your God, says the Lord GOD.

35

¹Moreover the word of the LORD came to me, saying, ²Son of man, set your face against mount Seir, and prophesy against it, ³And say to it, Thus says the Lord GOD; Behold, O mount Seir, I am against you, and I will stretch out my hand against you, and I will make you most desolate. ⁴I will lay your cities waste, and you shall be desolate, and you shall know that I am the LORD. ⁵Because you have had a perpetual hatred, and have shed the blood of the children of Israel by the force of the sword in the time of their calamity, in the time that their iniquity had an end: ⁶Therefore, as I live, says the Lord GOD, I will prepare you to blood, and blood shall pursue you: since you have not hated blood, even blood shall pursue you. ⁷Thus will I make mount Seir most desolate, and cut off from it him that passes out and him that returns. ⁸And I will fill his mountains with his slain men: in your hills, and in your valleys, and in all your rivers, shall they fall that are slain with the sword. ⁹I will make you perpetual desolations, and your cities shall not return: and you shall know that I am the LORD. ¹⁰Because you have said, These two nations and these two countries shall be mine, and we will possess it; whereas the LORD was there: ¹¹Therefore, as I live, says the Lord GOD, I will even do according to your anger, and according to your envy which you have used out of your hatred against them; and I will make myself known among them, when I have judged you. ¹²And you shall know that I am the LORD, and that I have heard all your blasphemies which you have spoken against the mountains of Israel, saying, They are laid desolate, they are given us to consume. ¹³Thus with your mouth you have boasted against me, and have multiplied your words against me: I have heard them. ¹⁴Thus says the Lord GOD; When the whole earth rejoices, I will make you desolate. ¹⁵As you did rejoice at the inheritance of the house of Israel, because it was desolate, so will I do to you: you shall be desolate, O mount Seir, and all Idumea, even all of it: and they shall know that I am the LORD.

36

¹Also, you son of man, prophesy to the mountains of Israel, and say, You mountains of Israel, hear the word of the LORD: ²Thus says the Lord GOD; Because the enemy has said against you, Aha, even the ancient high places are ours in possession: ³Therefore prophesy and say, Thus says the Lord GOD; Because they have made you desolate, and swallowed you up on every side, that you might be a possession to the residue of the heathen, and you are taken up in the lips of talkers, and are an infamy of the people: ⁴Therefore, you mountains of Israel, hear the word of the Lord GOD; Thus says the Lord GOD to the mountains, and to the hills, to the rivers, and to the valleys, to the desolate wastes, and to the cities that are forsaken, which became a prey and derision to the residue of the heathen that are round about; ⁵Therefore thus says the Lord GOD; Surely in the fire of my jealousy have I spoken against the residue of the heathen, and against all Idumea, which have appointed my land into their possession with the joy of all their heart, with despiteful minds, to cast it out for a prey. ⁶Prophesy therefore concerning the land of Israel, and say to the mountains, and to the hills, to the rivers, and to the valleys, Thus says the Lord GOD; Behold, I have spoken in my jealousy and in my fury, because you have borne the shame of the heathen: ⁷Therefore thus says the Lord GOD; I have lifted up my hand, Surely the heathen that are about you, they shall bear their shame. ⁸But you, O mountains of Israel, you shall shoot forth your branches, and yield your fruit to my people of Israel; for they are at hand to come. ⁹For, behold, I am for you, and I will turn to you, and you shall be tilled and sown: ¹⁰And I will multiply men on you, all the house of Israel, even all of it: and the cities shall be inhabited, and the wastes shall be built: ¹¹And I will multiply on you man and beast; and they shall increase and bring fruit: and I will settle you after your old estates, and will do better to you than at your beginnings: and you shall know that I am the LORD. ¹²Yes, I will cause men to walk on you, even my people Israel; and they shall possess you, and you shall be their inheritance, and you shall no more from now on bereave them of men. ¹³Thus says the Lord GOD; Because they say to you, You land devour up men, and have bereaved your nations: ¹⁴Therefore you shall devour men no more, neither bereave your nations any more, says the Lord GOD. ¹⁵Neither will I cause men to hear in you the shame of the heathen any more, neither shall you bear the reproach of the people any more, neither shall you cause your nations to fall any more, says the Lord GOD. ¹⁶Moreover the word of the LORD came to me, saying, ¹⁷Son of man, when the house of Israel dwelled in their own land, they defiled it by their own way and by their doings: their way was before me as the uncleanness of a removed woman. ¹⁸Why I poured my fury on them for the blood that they had shed on the land, and for their idols with which they had polluted it: ¹⁹And I scattered them among the heathen, and they were dispersed through the countries: according to their way and according to their doings I judged them. ²⁰And when they entered to the heathen, where they went, they profaned my holy name, when they said to them, These are the people of the LORD, and are gone forth out of his land. ²¹But I had pity for my holy name, which the house of Israel had profaned among the heathen, where they went. ²²Therefore say to the house of Israel, thus says the Lord GOD; I do not this for your sakes, O house of Israel, but for my holy name's sake, which you have profaned among the heathen, where you went. ²³And I will sanctify my great name, which was profaned among the heathen, which you have profaned in the middle of them; and the heathen shall know that I am the LORD, says the Lord GOD, when I shall be sanctified in you before their eyes. ²⁴For I will take you from among the heathen, and gather you out of all countries, and will bring you into your own land. ²⁵Then will I sprinkle clean water on you, and you shall be clean: from all your filthiness, and from all your idols, will I cleanse you. ²⁶A new heart also will I give you, and a new spirit will I put within you: and I will take away the stony heart out of your flesh, and I will give you an heart of flesh. ²⁷And I will put my spirit within you, and cause you to walk in my statutes, and you shall keep my judgments, and do them. ²⁸And you shall dwell in the land that I gave to your fathers; and you shall be my people, and I will be your God. ²⁹I will also save you from all your uncleannesses: and I will call for the corn, and will increase it, and lay no famine on you. ³⁰And I will multiply the fruit of the tree, and the increase of the field, that you shall receive no more reproach of famine among the heathen. ³¹Then shall you remember your own evil ways, and

your doings that were not good, and shall loathe yourselves in your own sight for your iniquities and for your abominations. ³²Not for your sakes do I this, says the Lord GOD, be it known to you: be ashamed and confounded for your own ways, O house of Israel. ³³Thus says the Lord GOD; In the day that I shall have cleansed you from all your iniquities I will also cause you to dwell in the cities, and the wastes shall be built. ³⁴And the desolate land shall be tilled, whereas it lay desolate in the sight of all that passed by. ³⁵And they shall say, This land that was desolate is become like the garden of Eden; and the waste and desolate and ruined cities are become fenced, and are inhabited. ³⁶Then the heathen that are left round about you shall know that I the LORD build the ruined places, and plant that that was desolate: I the LORD have spoken it, and I will do it. ³⁷Thus says the Lord GOD; I will yet for this be inquired of by the house of Israel, to do it for them; I will increase them with men like a flock. ³⁸As the holy flock, as the flock of Jerusalem in her solemn feasts; so shall the waste cities be filled with flocks of men: and they shall know that I am the LORD.

37 ¹The hand of the LORD was on me, and carried me out in the spirit of the LORD, and set me down in the middle of the valley which was full of bones, ²And caused me to pass by them round about: and, behold, there were very many in the open valley; and, see, they were very dry. ³And he said to me, Son of man, can these bones live? And I answered, O Lord GOD, you know. ⁴Again he said to me, Prophesy on these bones, and say to them, O you dry bones, hear the word of the LORD. ⁵Thus says the Lord GOD to these bones; Behold, I will cause breath to enter into you, and you shall live: ⁶And I will lay sinews on you, and will bring up flesh on you, and cover you with skin, and put breath in you, and you shall live; and you shall know that I am the LORD. ⁷So I prophesied as I was commanded: and as I prophesied, there was a noise, and behold a shaking, and the bones came together, bone to his bone. ⁸And when I beheld, see, the sinews and the flesh came up on them, and the skin covered them above: but there was no breath in them. ⁹Then said he to me, Prophesy to the wind, prophesy, son of man, and say to the wind, Thus says the Lord GOD; Come from the four winds, O breath, and breathe on these slain, that they may live. ¹⁰So I prophesied as he commanded me, and the breath came into them, and they lived, and stood up on their feet, an exceeding great army. ¹¹Then he said to me, Son of man, these bones are the whole house of Israel: behold, they say, Our bones are dried, and our hope is lost: we are cut off for our parts. ¹²Therefore prophesy and say to them, Thus says the Lord GOD; Behold, O my people, I will open your graves, and cause you to come up out of your graves, and bring you into the land of Israel. ¹³And you shall know that I am the LORD, when I have opened your graves, O my people, and brought you up out of your graves, ¹⁴And shall put my spirit in you, and you shall live, and I shall place you in your own land: then shall you know that I the LORD have spoken it, and performed it, says the LORD. ¹⁵The word of the LORD came again to me, saying, ¹⁶Moreover, you son of man, take you one stick, and write on it, For Judah, and for the children of Israel his companions: then take another stick, and write on it, For Joseph, the stick of Ephraim and for all the house of Israel his companions: ¹⁷And join them one to another into one stick; and they shall become one in your hand. ¹⁸And when the children of your people shall speak to you, saying, Will you not show us what you mean by these? ¹⁹Say to them, Thus says the Lord GOD; Behold, I will take the stick of Joseph, which is in the hand of Ephraim, and the tribes of Israel his fellows, and will put them with him, even with the stick of Judah, and make them one stick, and they shall be one in my hand. ²⁰And the sticks where on you write shall be in your hand before their eyes. ²¹And say to them, Thus says the Lord GOD; Behold, I will take the children of Israel from among the heathen, where they be gone, and will gather them on every side, and bring them into their own land: ²²And I will make them one nation in the land on the mountains of Israel; and one king shall be king to them all: and they shall be no more two nations, neither shall they be divided into two kingdoms any more at all. ²³Neither shall they defile themselves any more with their idols, nor with their detestable things, nor with any of their transgressions: but I will save them out of all their dwelling places, wherein they have sinned, and will cleanse them: so shall they be my people, and I will be their God. ²⁴And David my servant shall be king over them; and they all shall have one shepherd: they shall also walk in my judgments, and observe my statutes, and do them. ²⁵And they shall dwell in the land that I have given to Jacob my servant, wherein your fathers have dwelled; and they shall dwell therein, even they, and their children, and their children's children for ever: and my servant David shall be their prince for ever. ²⁶Moreover I will make a covenant of peace with them; it shall be an everlasting covenant with them: and I will place them, and multiply them, and will set my sanctuary in the middle of them for ever more. ²⁷My tabernacle also shall be with them: yes, I will be their God, and they shall be my people. ²⁸And the heathen shall know that I the LORD do sanctify Israel, when my sanctuary shall be in the middle of them for ever more.

38 ¹And the word of the LORD came to me, saying, ²Son of man, set your face against Gog, the land of Magog, the chief prince of Meshech and Tubal, and prophesy against him, ³And say, Thus says the Lord GOD; Behold, I am against you, O Gog, the chief prince of Meshech and Tubal: ⁴And I will turn you back, and put hooks into your jaws, and I will bring you forth, and all your army, horses and horsemen, all of them clothed with all sorts of armor, even a great company with bucklers and shields, all of them handling swords: ⁵Persia, Ethiopia, and Libya with them; all of them with shield and helmet: ⁶Gomer, and all his bands; the house of Togarmah of the north quarters, and all his bands: and many people with you. ⁷Be you prepared, and prepare for yourself, you, and all your company that are assembled to you, and be you a guard to them. ⁸After many days you shall be visited: in the latter years you shall come into the land that is brought back from the sword, and is gathered out of many people, against the mountains of Israel, which have been always waste: but it is brought forth out of the nations, and they shall dwell safely all of them. ⁹You shall ascend and come like a storm, you shall be like a cloud to cover the land, you, and all your bands, and many people with you. ¹⁰Thus says the Lord GOD; It shall also come to pass, that at the same time shall things come into your mind, and you shall think an evil thought; ¹¹And you shall say, I will go up to the land of unwalled villages; I will go to them that are at rest, that dwell safely, all of them dwelling without walls, and having neither bars nor gates, ¹²To take a spoil, and to take a prey; to turn your hand on the desolate places that are now inhabited, and on the people that are gathered out of the nations, which have gotten cattle and goods, that dwell in the middle of the land. ¹³Sheba, and Dedan, and the merchants of Tarshish, with all the young lions thereof, shall say to you, Are you come to take a spoil? have you gathered your company to take a prey? to carry away silver and gold, to take away cattle and goods, to take a great spoil? ¹⁴Therefore, son of man, prophesy and say to Gog, Thus says the Lord GOD; In that day when my people of Israel dwells safely, shall you not know it? ¹⁵And you shall come from your place out of the north parts, you, and many people with you, all of them riding on horses, a great company, and a mighty army: ¹⁶And you shall come up against my people of Israel, as a cloud to cover the land; it shall be in the latter days, and I will bring you against my land, that the heathen may know me, when I shall be sanctified in you, O Gog, before their eyes. ¹⁷Thus says the Lord GOD; Are you he of whom I have spoken in old time by my servants the prophets of Israel, which prophesied in those days many years that I would bring you against them? ¹⁸And it shall come to pass at the same time when Gog shall come against the land of Israel, says the Lord GOD, that my fury shall come up in my face. ¹⁹For in my jealousy and in the fire of my wrath have I spoken, Surely in that day there shall be a great shaking in the land of Israel; ²⁰So that the fishes of the sea, and the fowls of the heaven, and the beasts of the field, and all creeping things that creep on the earth, and all the men that are on the face of the earth, shall shake at my presence, and the mountains shall be thrown down, and the steep places shall fall, and every wall shall fall to the ground. ²¹And I will call for a sword against him throughout all my mountains, says the Lord GOD: every man's sword shall be against his brother. ²²And I will plead against him with pestilence and with blood; and I will rain on him, and on his bands, and on the many people that are with him, an overflowing rain, and great hailstones, fire, and brimstone. ²³Thus will I magnify myself, and sanctify myself; and I will be known in the eyes of many nations, and they shall know that I am the LORD.

39

¹Therefore, you son of man, prophesy against Gog, and say, Thus says the Lord GOD; Behold, I am against you, O Gog, the chief prince of Meshech and Tubal: ²And I will turn you back, and leave but the sixth part of you, and will cause you to come up from the north parts, and will bring you on the mountains of Israel: ³And I will smite your bow out of your left hand, and will cause your arrows to fall out of your right hand. ⁴You shall fall on the mountains of Israel, you, and all your bands, and the people that is with you: I will give you to the ravenous birds of every sort, and to the beasts of the field to be devoured. ⁵You shall fall on the open field: for I have spoken it, says the Lord GOD. ⁶And I will send a fire on Magog, and among them that dwell carelessly in the isles: and they shall know that I am the LORD. ⁷So will I make my holy name known in the middle of my people Israel; and I will not let them pollute my holy name any more: and the heathen shall know that I am the LORD, the Holy One in Israel. ⁸Behold, it is come, and it is done, says the Lord GOD; this is the day whereof I have spoken. ⁹And they that dwell in the cities of Israel shall go forth, and shall set on fire and burn the weapons, both the shields and the bucklers, the bows and the arrows, and the hand staves, and the spears, and they shall burn them with fire seven years: ¹⁰So that they shall take no wood out of the field, neither cut down any out of the forests; for they shall burn the weapons with fire: and they shall spoil those that spoiled them, and rob those that robbed them, says the Lord GOD. ¹¹And it shall come to pass in that day, that I will give to Gog a place there of graves in Israel, the valley of the passengers on the east of the sea: and it shall stop the noses of the passengers: and there shall they bury Gog and all his multitude: and they shall call it The valley of Hamongog. ¹²And seven months shall the house of Israel be burying of them, that they may cleanse the land. ¹³Yes, all the people of the land shall bury them; and it shall be to them a renown the day that I shall be glorified, says the Lord GOD. ¹⁴And they shall sever out men of continual employment, passing through the land to bury with the passengers those that remain on the face of the earth, to cleanse it: after the end of seven months shall they search. ¹⁵And the passengers that pass through the land, when any sees a man's bone, then shall he set up a sign by it, till the buriers have buried it in the valley of Hamongog. ¹⁶And also the name of the city shall be Hamonah. Thus shall they cleanse the land. ¹⁷And, you son of man, thus says the Lord GOD; Speak to every feathered fowl, and to every beast of the field, Assemble yourselves, and come; gather yourselves on every side to my sacrifice that I do sacrifice for you, even a great sacrifice on the mountains of Israel, that you may eat flesh, and drink blood. ¹⁸You shall eat the flesh of the mighty, and drink the blood of the princes of the earth, of rams, of lambs, and of goats, of bullocks, all of them fatted calves of Bashan. ¹⁹And you shall eat fat till you be full, and drink blood till you be drunken, of my sacrifice which I have sacrificed for you. ²⁰Thus you shall be filled at my table with horses and chariots, with mighty men, and with all men of war, says the Lord GOD. ²¹And I will set my glory among the heathen, and all the heathen shall see my judgment that I have executed, and my hand that I have laid on them. ²²So the house of Israel shall know that I am the LORD their God from that day and forward. ²³And the heathen shall know that the house of Israel went into captivity for their iniquity: because they trespassed against me, therefore hid I my face from them, and gave them into the hand of their enemies: so fell they all by the sword. ²⁴According to their uncleanness and according to their transgressions have I done to them, and hid my face from them. ²⁵Therefore thus says the Lord GOD; Now will I bring again the captivity of Jacob, and have mercy on the whole house of Israel, and will be jealous for my holy name; ²⁶After that they have borne their shame, and all their trespasses whereby they have trespassed against me, when they dwelled safely in their land, and none made them afraid. ²⁷When I have brought them again from the people, and gathered them out of their enemies' lands, and

am sanctified in them in the sight of many nations; ²⁸Then shall they know that I am the LORD their God, which caused them to be led into captivity among the heathen: but I have gathered them to their own land, and have left none of them any more there. ²⁹Neither will I hide my face any more from them: for I have poured out my spirit on the house of Israel, says the Lord GOD.

40

¹In the five and twentieth year of our captivity, in the beginning of the year, in the tenth day of the month, in the fourteenth year after that the city was smitten, in the selfsame day the hand of the LORD was on me, and brought me thither. ²In the visions of God brought he me into the land of Israel, and set me on a very high mountain, by which was as the frame of a city on the south. ³And he brought me thither, and, behold, there was a man, whose appearance was like the appearance of brass, with a line of flax in his hand, and a measuring reed; and he stood in the gate. ⁴And the man said to me, Son of man, behold with your eyes, and hear with your ears, and set your heart on all that I shall show you; for to the intent that I might show them to you are you brought here: declare all that you see to the house of Israel. ⁵And behold a wall on the outside of the house round about, and in the man's hand a measuring reed of six cubits long by the cubit and an hand breadth: so he measured the breadth of the building, one reed; and the height, one reed. ⁶Then came he to the gate which looks toward the east, and went up the stairs thereof, and measured the threshold of the gate, which was one reed broad; and the other threshold of the gate, which was one reed broad. ⁷And every little chamber was one reed long, and one reed broad; and between the little chambers were five cubits; and the threshold of the gate by the porch of the gate within was one reed. ⁸He measured also the porch of the gate within, one reed. ⁹Then measured he the porch of the gate, eight cubits; and the posts thereof, two cubits; and the porch of the gate was inward. ¹⁰And the little chambers of the gate eastward were three on this side, and three on that side; they three were of one measure: and the posts had one measure on this side and on that side. ¹¹And he measured the breadth of the entry of the gate, ten cubits; and the length of the gate, thirteen cubits. ¹²The space also before the little chambers was one cubit on this side, and the space was one cubit on that side: and the little chambers were six cubits on this side, and six cubits on that side. ¹³He measured then the gate from the roof of one little chamber to the roof of another: the breadth was five and twenty cubits, door against door. ¹⁴He made also posts of three score cubits, even to the post of the court round about the gate. ¹⁵And from the face of the gate of the entrance to the face of the porch of the inner gate were fifty cubits. ¹⁶And there were narrow windows to the little chambers, and to their posts within the gate round about, and likewise to the arches: and windows were round about inward: and on each post were palm trees. ¹⁷Then brought he me into the outward court, and, see, there were chambers, and a pavement made for the court round about: thirty chambers were on the pavement. ¹⁸And the pavement by the side of the gates over against the length of the gates was the lower pavement. ¹⁹Then he measured the breadth from the forefront of the lower gate to the forefront of the inner court without, an hundred cubits eastward and northward. ²⁰And the gate of the outward court that looked toward the north, he measured the length thereof, and the breadth thereof. ²¹And the little chambers thereof were three on this side and three on that side; and the posts thereof and the arches thereof were after the measure of the first gate: the length thereof was fifty cubits, and the breadth five and twenty cubits. ²²And their windows, and their arches, and their palm trees, were after the measure of the gate that looks toward the east; and they went up to it by seven steps; and the arches thereof were before them. ²³And the gate of the inner court was over against the gate toward the north, and toward the east; and he measured from gate to gate an hundred cubits. ²⁴After that he brought me toward the south, and behold a gate toward the south: and he measured the posts thereof and the arches thereof according to these measures. ²⁵And there were windows in it and in the arches thereof round about, like those windows: the length was fifty cubits, and the breadth five and twenty cubits. ²⁶And there were seven steps to go up to it, and the arches thereof were before them: and it had palm trees, one on this side, and another on that side, on the posts thereof. ²⁷And there was a gate in the inner court toward the south: and he measured from gate to gate toward the south an hundred cubits. ²⁸And he brought me to the inner court by the south gate: and he measured the south gate according to these measures; ²⁹And the little chambers thereof, and the posts thereof, and the arches thereof, according to these measures: and there were windows in it and in the arches thereof round about: it was fifty cubits long, and five and twenty cubits broad. ³⁰And the arches round about were five and twenty cubits long, and five cubits broad. ³¹And the arches thereof were toward the utter court; and palm trees were on the posts thereof: and the going up to it had eight steps. ³²And he brought me into the inner court toward the east: and he measured the gate according to these measures. ³³And the little chambers thereof, and the posts thereof, and the arches thereof, were according to these measures: and there were windows therein and in the arches thereof round about: it was fifty cubits long, and five and twenty cubits broad. ³⁴And the arches thereof were toward the outward court; and palm trees were on the posts thereof, on this side, and on that side: and the going up to it had eight steps. ³⁵And he brought me to the north gate, and measured it according to these measures; ³⁶The little chambers thereof, the posts thereof, and the arches thereof, and the windows to it round about: the length was fifty cubits, and the breadth five and twenty cubits. ³⁷And the posts thereof were toward the utter court; and palm trees were on the posts thereof, on this side, and on that side: and the going up to it had eight steps. ³⁸And the chambers and the entries thereof were by the posts of the gates, where they washed the burnt offering. ³⁹And in the porch of the gate were two tables on this side, and two tables on that side, to slay thereon the burnt offering and the sin offering and the trespass offering. ⁴⁰And at the side without, as one goes up to the entry of the north gate, were two tables; and on the other side, which was at the porch of the gate, were two tables. ⁴¹Four tables were on this side, and four tables on that side, by the side of the gate; eight tables, whereupon they slew their sacrifices. ⁴²And the four tables were of hewn stone for the burnt offering, of a cubit and an

half long, and a cubit and an half broad, and one cubit high: whereupon also they laid the instruments with which they slew the burnt offering and the sacrifice. ⁴³And within were hooks, an hand broad, fastened round about: and on the tables was the flesh of the offering. ⁴⁴And without the inner gate were the chambers of the singers in the inner court, which was at the side of the north gate; and their prospect was toward the south: one at the side of the east gate having the prospect toward the north. ⁴⁵And he said to me, This chamber, whose prospect is toward the south, is for the priests, the keepers of the charge of the house. ⁴⁶And the chamber whose prospect is toward the north is for the priests, the keepers of the charge of the altar: these are the sons of Zadok among the sons of Levi, which come near to the LORD to minister to him. ⁴⁷So he measured the court, an hundred cubits long, and an hundred cubits broad, foursquare; and the altar that was before the house. ⁴⁸And he brought me to the porch of the house, and measured each post of the porch, five cubits on this side, and five cubits on that side: and the breadth of the gate was three cubits on this side, and three cubits on that side. ⁴⁹The length of the porch was twenty cubits, and the breadth eleven cubits, and he brought me by the steps whereby they went up to it: and there were pillars by the posts, one on this side, and another on that side.

41

¹Afterward he brought me to the temple, and measured the posts, six cubits broad on the one side, and six cubits broad on the other side, which was the breadth of the tabernacle. ²And the breadth of the door was ten cubits; and the sides of the door were five cubits on the one side, and five cubits on the other side: and he measured the length thereof, forty cubits: and the breadth, twenty cubits. ³Then went he inward, and measured the post of the door, two cubits; and the door, six cubits; and the breadth of the door, seven cubits. ⁴So he measured the length thereof, twenty cubits; and the breadth, twenty cubits, before the temple: and he said to me, This is the most holy place. ⁵After he measured the wall of the house, six cubits; and the breadth of every side chamber, four cubits, round about the house on every side. ⁶And the side chambers were three, one over another, and thirty in order; and they entered into the wall which was of the house for the side chambers round about, that they might have hold, but they had not hold in the wall of the house. ⁷And there was an enlarging, and a winding about still upward to the side chambers: for the winding about of the house went still upward round about the house: therefore the breadth of the house was still upward, and so increased from the lowest chamber to the highest by the middle. ⁸I saw also the height of the house round about: the foundations of the side chambers were a full reed of six great cubits. ⁹The thickness of the wall, which was for the side chamber without, was five cubits: and that which was left was the place of the side chambers that were within. ¹⁰And between the chambers was the wideness of twenty cubits round about the house on every side. ¹¹And the doors of the side chambers were toward the place that was left, one door toward the north, and another door toward the south: and the breadth of the place that was left was five cubits round about. ¹²Now the building that was before the separate place at the end toward the west was seventy cubits broad; and the wall of the building was five cubits thick round about, and the length thereof ninety cubits. ¹³So he measured the house, an hundred cubits long; and the separate place, and the building, with the walls thereof, an hundred cubits long; ¹⁴Also the breadth of the face of the house, and of the separate place toward the east, an hundred cubits. ¹⁵And he measured the length of the building over against the separate place which was behind it, and the galleries thereof on the one side and on the other side, an hundred cubits, with the inner temple, and the porches of the court; ¹⁶The door posts, and the narrow windows, and the galleries round about on their three stories, over against the door, paneled with wood round about, and from the ground up to the windows, and the windows were covered; ¹⁷To that above the door, even to the inner house, and without, and by all the wall round about within and without, by measure. ¹⁸And it was made with cherubim and palm trees, so that a palm tree was between a cherub and a cherub; and every cherub had two faces; ¹⁹So that the face of a man was toward the palm tree on the one side, and the face of a young lion toward the palm tree on the other side: it was made through all the house round about. ²⁰From the ground to above the door were cherubim and palm trees made, and on the wall of the temple. ²¹The posts of the temple were squared, and the face of the sanctuary; the appearance of the one as the appearance of the other. ²²The altar of wood was three cubits high, and the length thereof two cubits; and the corners thereof, and the length thereof, and the walls thereof, were of wood: and he said to me, This is the table that is before the LORD. ²³And the temple and the sanctuary had two doors. ²⁴And the doors had two leaves apiece, two turning leaves; two leaves for the one door, and two leaves for the other door. ²⁵And there were made on them, on the doors of the temple, cherubim and palm trees, like as were made on the walls; and there were thick planks on the face of the porch without. ²⁶And there were narrow windows and palm trees on the one side and on the other side, on the sides of the porch, and on the side chambers of the house, and thick planks.

42

¹Then he brought me forth into the utter court, the way toward the north: and he brought me into the chamber that was over against the separate place, and which was before the building toward the north. ²Before the length of an hundred cubits was the north door, and the breadth was fifty cubits. ³Over against the twenty cubits which were for the inner court, and over against the pavement which was for the utter court, was gallery against gallery in three stories. ⁴And before the chambers was a walk to ten cubits breadth inward, a way of one cubit; and their doors toward the north. ⁵Now the upper chambers were shorter: for the galleries were higher than these, than the lower, and than the middlemost of the building. ⁶For they were in three stories, but had not pillars as the pillars of the courts: therefore the building was straitened more than the lowest and the middlemost from the ground. ⁷And the wall that was without over against the chambers, toward the utter court on the forepart of the chambers, the length thereof was fifty cubits. ⁸For the length of the chambers that were in the utter court was fifty cubits: and, see, before the temple were an hundred cubits. ⁹And from under these chambers was the entry on the

east side, as one goes into them from the utter court. ¹⁰The chambers were in the thickness of the wall of the court toward the east, over against the separate place, and over against the building. ¹¹And the way before them was like the appearance of the chambers which were toward the north, as long as they, and as broad as they: and all their goings out were both according to their fashions, and according to their doors. ¹²And according to the doors of the chambers that were toward the south was a door in the head of the way, even the way directly before the wall toward the east, as one enters into them. ¹³Then said he to me, The north chambers and the south chambers, which are before the separate place, they be holy chambers, where the priests that approach to the LORD shall eat the most holy things: there shall they lay the most holy things, and the meat offering, and the sin offering, and the trespass offering; for the place is holy. ¹⁴When the priests enter therein, then shall they not go out of the holy place into the utter court, but there they shall lay their garments wherein they minister; for they are holy; and shall put on other garments, and shall approach to those things which are for the people. ¹⁵Now when he had made an end of measuring the inner house, he brought me forth toward the gate whose prospect is toward the east, and measured it round about. ¹⁶He measured the east side with the measuring reed, five hundred reeds, with the measuring reed round about. ¹⁷He measured the north side, five hundred reeds, with the measuring reed round about. ¹⁸He measured the south side, five hundred reeds, with the measuring reed. ¹⁹He turned about to the west side, and measured five hundred reeds with the measuring reed. ²⁰He measured it by the four sides: it had a wall round about, five hundred reeds long, and five hundred broad, to make a separation between the sanctuary and the profane place.

43

¹Afterward he brought me to the gate, even the gate that looks toward the east: ²And, behold, the glory of the God of Israel came from the way of the east: and his voice was like a noise of many waters: and the earth shined with his glory. ³And it was according to the appearance of the vision which I saw, even according to the vision that I saw when I came to destroy the city: and the visions were like the vision that I saw by the river Chebar; and I fell on my face. ⁴And the glory of the LORD came into the house by the way of the gate whose prospect is toward the east. ⁵So the spirit took me up, and brought me into the inner court; and, behold, the glory of the LORD filled the house. ⁶And I heard him speaking to me out of the house; and the man stood by me. ⁷And he said to me, Son of man, the place of my throne, and the place of the soles of my feet, where I will dwell in the middle of the children of Israel for ever, and my holy name, shall the house of Israel no more defile, neither they, nor their kings, by their prostitution, nor by the carcasses of their kings in their high places. ⁸In their setting of their threshold by my thresholds, and their post by my posts, and the wall between me and them, they have even defiled my holy name by their abominations that they have committed: why I have consumed them in my anger. ⁹Now let them put away their prostitution, and the carcasses of their kings, far from me, and I will dwell in the middle of them for ever. ¹⁰You son of man, show the house to the house of Israel, that they may be ashamed of their iniquities: and let them measure the pattern. ¹¹And if they be ashamed of all that they have done, show them the form of the house, and the fashion thereof, and the goings out thereof, and the comings in thereof, and all the forms thereof, and all the ordinances thereof, and all the forms thereof, and all the laws thereof: and write it in their sight, that they may keep the whole form thereof, and all the ordinances thereof, and do them. ¹²This is the law of the house; On the top of the mountain the whole limit thereof round about shall be most holy. Behold, this is the law of the house. ¹³And these are the measures of the altar after the cubits: The cubit is a cubit and an hand breadth; even the bottom shall be a cubit, and the breadth a cubit, and the border thereof by the edge thereof round about shall be a span: and this shall be the higher place of the altar. ¹⁴And from the bottom on the ground even to the lower settle shall be two cubits, and the breadth one cubit; and from the lesser settle even to the greater settle shall be four cubits, and the breadth one cubit. ¹⁵So the altar shall be four cubits; and from the altar and upward shall be four horns. ¹⁶And the altar shall be twelve cubits long, twelve broad, square in the four squares thereof. ¹⁷And the settle shall be fourteen cubits long and fourteen broad in the four squares thereof; and the border about it shall be half a cubit; and the bottom thereof shall be a cubit about; and his stairs shall look toward the east. ¹⁸And he said to me, Son of man, thus says the Lord GOD; These are the ordinances of the altar in the day when they shall make it, to offer burnt offerings thereon, and to sprinkle blood thereon. ¹⁹And you shall give to the priests the Levites that be of the seed of Zadok, which approach to me, to minister to me, says the Lord GOD, a young bullock for a sin offering. ²⁰And you shall take of the blood thereof, and put it on the four horns of it, and on the four corners of the settle, and on the border round about: thus shall you cleanse and purge it. ²¹You shall take the bullock also of the sin offering, and he shall burn it in the appointed place of the house, without the sanctuary. ²²And on the second day you shall offer a kid of the goats without blemish for a sin offering; and they shall cleanse the altar, as they did cleanse it with the bullock. ²³When you have made an end of cleansing it, you shall offer a young bullock without blemish, and a ram out of the flock without blemish. ²⁴And you shall offer them before the LORD, and the priests shall cast salt on them, and they shall offer them up for a burnt offering to the LORD. ²⁵Seven days shall you prepare every day a goat for a sin offering: they shall also prepare a young bullock, and a ram out of the flock, without blemish. ²⁶Seven days shall they purge the altar and purify it; and they shall consecrate themselves. ²⁷And when these days are expired, it shall be, that on the eighth day, and so forward, the priests shall make your burnt offerings on the altar, and your peace offerings; and I will accept you, says the Lord GOD.

44

¹Then he brought me back the way of the gate of the outward sanctuary which looks toward the east; and it was shut. ²Then said the LORD to me; This gate shall be shut, it shall not be opened, and no man shall enter in by it; because the LORD, the God of Israel, has entered in by it, therefore it shall be shut. ³It is for the prince; the prince, he shall sit in it to eat bread before the LORD; he shall enter by the way of the porch of that gate, and shall go out by the

way of the same. ⁴Then brought he me the way of the north gate before the house: and I looked, and, behold, the glory of the LORD filled the house of the LORD: and I fell on my face. ⁵And the LORD said to me, Son of man, mark well, and behold with your eyes, and hear with your ears all that I say to you concerning all the ordinances of the house of the LORD, and all the laws thereof; and mark well the entering in of the house, with every going forth of the sanctuary. ⁶And you shall say to the rebellious, even to the house of Israel, Thus says the Lord GOD; O you house of Israel, let it suffice you of all your abominations, ⁷In that you have brought into my sanctuary strangers, uncircumcised in heart, and uncircumcised in flesh, to be in my sanctuary, to pollute it, even my house, when you offer my bread, the fat and the blood, and they have broken my covenant because of all your abominations. ⁸And you have not kept the charge of my holy things: but you have set keepers of my charge in my sanctuary for yourselves. ⁹Thus says the Lord GOD; No stranger, uncircumcised in heart, nor uncircumcised in flesh, shall enter into my sanctuary, of any stranger that is among the children of Israel. ¹⁰And the Levites that are gone away far from me, when Israel went astray, which went astray away from me after their idols; they shall even bear their iniquity. ¹¹Yet they shall be ministers in my sanctuary, having charge at the gates of the house, and ministering to the house: they shall slay the burnt offering and the sacrifice for the people, and they shall stand before them to minister to them. ¹²Because they ministered to them before their idols, and caused the house of Israel to fall into iniquity; therefore have I lifted up my hand against them, says the Lord GOD, and they shall bear their iniquity. ¹³And they shall not come near to me, to do the office of a priest to me, nor to come near to any of my holy things, in the most holy place: but they shall bear their shame, and their abominations which they have committed. ¹⁴But I will make them keepers of the charge of the house, for all the service thereof, and for all that shall be done therein. ¹⁵But the priests the Levites, the sons of Zadok, that kept the charge of my sanctuary when the children of Israel went astray from me, they shall come near to me to minister to me, and they shall stand before me to offer to me the fat and the blood, says the Lord GOD: ¹⁶They shall enter into my sanctuary, and they shall come near to my table, to minister to me, and they shall keep my charge. ¹⁷And it shall come to pass, that when they enter in at the gates of the inner court, they shall be clothed with linen garments; and no wool shall come on them, whiles they minister in the gates of the inner court, and within. ¹⁸They shall have linen bonnets on their heads, and shall have linen breeches on their loins; they shall not gird themselves with any thing that causes sweat. ¹⁹And when they go forth into the utter court, even into the utter court to the people, they shall put off their garments wherein they ministered, and lay them in the holy chambers, and they shall put on other garments; and they shall not sanctify the people with their garments. ²⁰Neither shall they shave their heads, nor suffer their locks to grow long; they shall only poll their heads. ²¹Neither shall any priest drink wine, when they enter into the inner court. ²²Neither shall they take for their wives a widow, nor her that is put away: but they shall take maidens of the seed of the house of Israel, or a widow that had a priest before. ²³And they shall teach my people the difference between the holy and profane, and cause them to discern between the unclean and the clean. ²⁴And in controversy they shall stand in judgment; and they shall judge it according to my judgments: and they shall keep my laws and my statutes in all my assemblies; and they shall hallow my sabbaths. ²⁵And they shall come at no dead person to defile themselves: but for father, or for mother, or for son, or for daughter, for brother, or for sister that has had no husband, they may defile themselves. ²⁶And after he is cleansed, they shall reckon to him seven days. ²⁷And in the day that he goes into the sanctuary, to the inner court, to minister in the sanctuary, he shall offer his sin offering, says the Lord GOD. ²⁸And it shall be to them for an inheritance: I am their inheritance: and you shall give them no possession in Israel: I am their possession. ²⁹They shall eat the meat offering, and the sin offering, and the trespass offering: and every dedicated thing in Israel shall be theirs. ³⁰And the first of all the first fruits of all things, and every oblation of all, of every sort of your oblations, shall be the priest's: you shall also give to the priest the first of your dough, that he may cause the blessing to rest in your house. ³¹The priests shall not eat of any thing that is dead of itself, or torn, whether it be fowl or beast.

45

¹Moreover, when you shall divide by lot the land for inheritance, you shall offer an oblation to the LORD, an holy portion of the land: the length shall be the length of five and twenty thousand reeds, and the breadth shall be ten thousand. This shall be holy in all the borders thereof round about. ²Of this there shall be for the sanctuary five hundred in length, with five hundred in breadth, square round about; and fifty cubits round about for the suburbs thereof. ³And of this measure shall you measure the length of five and twenty thousand, and the breadth of ten thousand: and in it shall be the sanctuary and the most holy place. ⁴The holy portion of the land shall be for the priests the ministers of the sanctuary, which shall come near to minister to the LORD: and it shall be a place for their houses, and an holy place for the sanctuary. ⁵And the five and twenty thousand of length, and the ten thousand of breadth shall also the Levites, the ministers of the house, have for themselves, for a possession for twenty chambers. ⁶And you shall appoint the possession of the city five thousand broad, and five and twenty thousand long, over against the oblation of the holy portion: it shall be for the whole house of Israel. ⁷And a portion shall be for the prince on the one side and on the other side of the oblation of the holy portion, and of the possession of the city, before the oblation of the holy portion, and before the possession of the city, from the west side westward, and from the east side eastward: and the length shall be over against one of the portions, from the west border to the east border. ⁸In the land shall be his possession in Israel: and my princes shall no more oppress my people; and the rest of the land shall they give to the house of Israel according to their tribes. ⁹Thus says the Lord GOD; Let it suffice you, O princes of Israel: remove violence and spoil, and execute judgment and justice, take away your exactions from my people, said the Lord GOD. ¹⁰You shall have just balances, and a just ephah, and a just bath. ¹¹The ephah and the bath shall be of one

measure, that the bath may contain the tenth part of an homer, and the ephah the tenth part of an homer: the measure thereof shall be after the homer. ¹²And the shekel shall be twenty gerahs: twenty shekels, five and twenty shekels, fifteen shekels, shall be your maneh. ¹³This is the oblation that you shall offer; the sixth part of an ephah of an homer of wheat, and you shall give the sixth part of an ephah of an homer of barley: ¹⁴Concerning the ordinance of oil, the bath of oil, you shall offer the tenth part of a bath out of the cor, which is an homer of ten baths; for ten baths are an homer: ¹⁵And one lamb out of the flock, out of two hundred, out of the fat pastures of Israel; for a meat offering, and for a burnt offering, and for peace offerings, to make reconciliation for them, says the Lord GOD. ¹⁶All the people of the land shall give this oblation for the prince in Israel. ¹⁷And it shall be the prince's part to give burnt offerings, and meat offerings, and drink offerings, in the feasts, and in the new moons, and in the sabbaths, in all solemnities of the house of Israel: he shall prepare the sin offering, and the meat offering, and the burnt offering, and the peace offerings, to make reconciliation for the house of Israel. ¹⁸Thus says the Lord GOD; In the first month, in the first day of the month, you shall take a young bullock without blemish, and cleanse the sanctuary: ¹⁹And the priest shall take of the blood of the sin offering, and put it on the posts of the house, and on the four corners of the settle of the altar, and on the posts of the gate of the inner court. ²⁰And so you shall do the seventh day of the month for every one that errs, and for him that is simple: so shall you reconcile the house. ²¹In the first month, in the fourteenth day of the month, you shall have the passover, a feast of seven days; unleavened bread shall be eaten. ²²And on that day shall the prince prepare for himself and for all the people of the land a bullock for a sin offering. ²³And seven days of the feast he shall prepare a burnt offering to the LORD, seven bullocks and seven rams without blemish daily the seven days; and a kid of the goats daily for a sin offering. ²⁴And he shall prepare a meat offering of an ephah for a bullock, and an ephah for a ram, and an hin of oil for an ephah. ²⁵In the seventh month, in the fifteenth day of the month, shall he do the like in the feast of the seven days, according to the sin offering, according to the burnt offering, and according to the meat offering, and according to the oil.

46

¹Thus says the Lord GOD; The gate of the inner court that looks toward the east shall be shut the six working days; but on the sabbath it shall be opened, and in the day of the new moon it shall be opened. ²And the prince shall enter by the way of the porch of that gate without, and shall stand by the post of the gate, and the priests shall prepare his burnt offering and his peace offerings, and he shall worship at the threshold of the gate: then he shall go forth; but the gate shall not be shut until the evening. ³Likewise the people of the land shall worship at the door of this gate before the LORD in the sabbaths and in the new moons. ⁴And the burnt offering that the prince shall offer to the LORD in the sabbath day shall be six lambs without blemish, and a ram without blemish. ⁵And the meat offering shall be an ephah for a ram, and the meat offering for the lambs as he shall be able to give, and an hin of oil to an ephah. ⁶And in the day of the new moon it shall be a young bullock without blemish, and six lambs, and a ram: they shall be without blemish. ⁷And he shall prepare a meat offering, an ephah for a bullock, and an ephah for a ram, and for the lambs according as his hand shall attain to, and an hin of oil to an ephah. ⁸And when the prince shall enter, he shall go in by the way of the porch of that gate, and he shall go forth by the way thereof. ⁹But when the people of the land shall come before the LORD in the solemn feasts, he that enters in by the way of the north gate to worship shall go out by the way of the south gate; and he that enters by the way of the south gate shall go forth by the way of the north gate: he shall not return by the way of the gate whereby he came in, but shall go forth over against it. ¹⁰And the prince in the middle of them, when they go in, shall go in; and when they go forth, shall go forth. ¹¹And in the feasts and in the solemnities the meat offering shall be an ephah to a bullock, and an ephah to a ram, and to the lambs as he is able to give, and an hin of oil to an ephah. ¹²Now when the prince shall prepare a voluntary burnt offering or peace offerings voluntarily to the LORD, one shall then open him the gate that looks toward the east, and he shall prepare his burnt offering and his peace offerings, as he did on the sabbath day: then he shall go forth; and after his going forth one shall shut the gate. ¹³You shall daily prepare a burnt offering to the LORD of a lamb of the first year without blemish: you shall prepare it every morning. ¹⁴And you shall prepare a meat offering for it every morning, the sixth part of an ephah, and the third part of an hin of oil, to temper with the fine flour; a meat offering continually by a perpetual ordinance to the LORD. ¹⁵Thus shall they prepare the lamb, and the meat offering, and the oil, every morning for a continual burnt offering. ¹⁶Thus says the Lord GOD; If the prince give a gift to any of his sons, the inheritance thereof shall be his sons'; it shall be their possession by inheritance. ¹⁷But if he give a gift of his inheritance to one of his servants, then it shall be his to the year of liberty; after it shall return to the prince: but his inheritance shall be his sons' for them. ¹⁸Moreover the prince shall not take of the people's inheritance by oppression, to thrust them out of their possession; but he shall give his sons inheritance out of his own possession: that my people be not scattered every man from his possession. ¹⁹After he brought me through the entry, which was at the side of the gate, into the holy chambers of the priests, which looked toward the north: and, behold, there was a place on the two sides westward. ²⁰Then said he to me, This is the place where the priests shall boil the trespass offering and the sin offering, where they shall bake the meat offering; that they bear them not out into the utter court, to sanctify the people. ²¹Then he brought me forth into the utter court, and caused me to pass by the four corners of the court; and, behold, in every corner of the court there was a court. ²²In the four corners of the court there were courts joined of forty cubits long and thirty broad: these four corners were of one measure. ²³And there was a row of building round about in them, round about them four, and it was made with boiling places under the rows round about. ²⁴Then said he to me, These are the places of them that boil, where the ministers of the house shall boil the sacrifice of the people.

47

¹Afterward he brought me again to the door of the house; and, behold, waters issued out from under the threshold of the house eastward: for the forefront of the house stood toward the east, and the waters came down from under from the right side of the house, at the south side of the altar. ²Then brought he me out of the way of the gate northward, and led me about the way without to the utter gate by the way that looks eastward; and, behold, there ran out waters on the right side. ³And when the man that had the line in his hand went forth eastward, he measured a thousand cubits, and he brought me through the waters; the waters were to the ankles. ⁴Again he measured a thousand, and brought me through the waters; the waters were to the knees. Again he measured a thousand, and brought me through; the waters were to the loins. ⁵Afterward he measured a thousand; and it was a river that I could not pass over: for the waters were risen, waters to swim in, a river that could not be passed over. ⁶And he said to me, Son of man, have you seen this? Then he brought me, and caused me to return to the brink of the river. ⁷Now when I had returned, behold, at the bank of the river were very many trees on the one side and on the other. ⁸Then said he to me, These waters issue out toward the east country, and go down into the desert, and go into the sea: which being brought forth into the sea, the waters shall be healed. ⁹And it shall come to pass, that every thing that lives, which moves, wherever the rivers shall come, shall live: and there shall be a very great multitude of fish, because these waters shall come thither: for they shall be healed; and every thing shall live where the river comes. ¹⁰And it shall come to pass, that the fishers shall stand on it from Engedi even to Eneglaim; they shall be a place to spread forth nets; their fish shall be according to their kinds, as the fish of the great sea, exceeding many. ¹¹But the miry places thereof and the marshes thereof shall not be healed; they shall be given to salt. ¹²And by the river on the bank thereof, on this side and on that side, shall grow all trees for meat, whose leaf shall not fade, neither shall the fruit thereof be consumed: it shall bring forth new fruit according to his months, because their waters they issued out of the sanctuary: and the fruit thereof shall be for meat, and the leaf thereof for medicine. ¹³Thus says the Lord GOD; This shall be the border, whereby you shall inherit the land according to the twelve tribes of Israel: Joseph shall have two portions. ¹⁴And you shall inherit it, one as well as another: concerning the which I lifted up my hand to give it to your fathers: and this land shall fall to you for inheritance. ¹⁵And this shall be the border of the land toward the north side, from the great sea, the way of Hethlon, as men go to Zedad; ¹⁶Hamath, Berothah, Sibraim, which is between the border of Damascus and the border of Hamath; Hazarhatticon, which is by the coast of Hauran. ¹⁷And the border from the sea shall be Hazarenan, the border of Damascus, and the north northward, and the border of Hamath. And this is the north side. ¹⁸And the east side you shall measure from Hauran, and from Damascus, and from Gilead, and from the land of Israel by Jordan, from the border to the east sea. And this is the east side. ¹⁹And the south side southward, from Tamar even to the waters of strife in Kadesh, the river to the great sea. And this is the south side southward. ²⁰The west side also shall be the great sea from the border, till a man come over against Hamath. This is the west side. ²¹So shall you divide this land to you according to the tribes of Israel. ²²And it shall come to pass, that you shall divide it by lot for an inheritance to you, and to the strangers that sojourn among you, which shall beget children among you: and they shall be to you as born in the country among the children of Israel; they shall have inheritance with you among the tribes of Israel. ²³And it shall come to pass, that in what tribe the stranger sojourns, there shall you give him his inheritance, says the Lord GOD.

48

¹Now these are the names of the tribes. From the north end to the coast of the way of Hethlon, as one goes to Hamath, Hazarenan, the border of Damascus northward, to the coast of Hamath; for these are his sides east and west; a portion for Dan. ²And by the border of Dan, from the east side to the west side, a portion for Asher. ³And by the border of Asher, from the east side even to the west side, a portion for Naphtali. ⁴And by the border of Naphtali, from the east side to the west side, a portion for Manasseh. ⁵And by the border of Manasseh, from the east side to the west side, a portion for Ephraim. ⁶And by the border of Ephraim, from the east side even to the west side, a portion for Reuben. ⁷And by the border of Reuben, from the east side to the west side, a portion for Judah. ⁸And by the border of Judah, from the east side to the west side, shall be the offering which you shall offer of five and twenty thousand reeds in breadth, and in length as one of the other parts, from the east side to the west side: and the sanctuary shall be in the middle of it. ⁹The oblation that you shall offer to the LORD shall be of five and twenty thousand in length, and of ten thousand in breadth. ¹⁰And for them, even for the priests, shall be this holy oblation; toward the north five and twenty thousand in length, and toward the west ten thousand in breadth, and toward the east ten thousand in breadth, and toward the south five and twenty thousand in length: and the sanctuary of the LORD shall be in the middle thereof. ¹¹It shall be for the priests that are sanctified of the sons of Zadok; which have kept my charge, which went not astray when the children of Israel went astray, as the Levites went astray. ¹²And this oblation of the land that is offered shall be to them a thing most holy by the border of the Levites. ¹³And over against the border of the priests the Levites shall have five and twenty thousand in length, and ten thousand in breadth: all the length shall be five and twenty thousand, and the breadth ten thousand. ¹⁴And they shall not sell of it, neither exchange, nor alienate the first fruits of the land: for it is holy to the LORD. ¹⁵And the five thousand, that are left in the breadth over against the five and twenty thousand, shall be a profane place for the city, for dwelling, and for suburbs: and the city shall be in the middle thereof. ¹⁶And these shall be the measures thereof; the north side four thousand and five hundred, and the south side four thousand and five hundred, and on the east side four thousand and five hundred, and the west side four thousand and five hundred. ¹⁷And the suburbs of the city shall be toward the north two hundred and fifty, and toward the south two hundred and fifty, and toward the east two hundred and fifty, and toward the west two hundred and fifty. ¹⁸And the residue in length over against the oblation of the holy portion shall be ten thousand eastward, and ten thousand westward: and it shall

be over against the oblation of the holy portion; and the increase thereof shall be for food to them that serve the city. ¹⁹And they that serve the city shall serve it out of all the tribes of Israel. ²⁰All the oblation shall be five and twenty thousand by five and twenty thousand: you shall offer the holy oblation foursquare, with the possession of the city. ²¹And the residue shall be for the prince, on the one side and on the other of the holy oblation, and of the possession of the city, over against the five and twenty thousand of the oblation toward the east border, and westward over against the five and twenty thousand toward the west border, over against the portions for the prince: and it shall be the holy oblation; and the sanctuary of the house shall be in the middle thereof. ²²Moreover from the possession of the Levites, and from the possession of the city, being in the middle of that which is the prince's, between the border of Judah and the border of Benjamin, shall be for the prince. ²³As for the rest of the tribes, from the east side to the west side, Benjamin shall have a portion. ²⁴And by the border of Benjamin, from the east side to the west side, Simeon shall have a portion. ²⁵And by the border of Simeon, from the east side to the west side, Issachar a portion. ²⁶And by the border of Issachar, from the east side to the west side, Zebulun a portion. ²⁷And by the border of Zebulun, from the east side to the west side, Gad a portion. ²⁸And by the border of Gad, at the south side southward, the border shall be even from Tamar to the waters of strife in Kadesh, and to the river toward the great sea. ²⁹This is the land which you shall divide by lot to the tribes of Israel for inheritance, and these are their portions, says the Lord GOD. ³⁰And these are the goings out of the city on the north side, four thousand and five hundred measures. ³¹And the gates of the city shall be after the names of the tribes of Israel: three gates northward; one gate of Reuben, one gate of Judah, one gate of Levi. ³²And at the east side four thousand and five hundred: and three gates; and one gate of Joseph, one gate of Benjamin, one gate of Dan. ³³And at the south side four thousand and five hundred measures: and three gates; one gate of Simeon, one gate of Issachar, one gate of Zebulun. ³⁴At the west side four thousand and five hundred, with their three gates; one gate of Gad, one gate of Asher, one gate of Naphtali. ³⁵It was round about eighteen thousand measures: and the name of the city from that day shall be, The LORD is there.

Daniel

1 ¹In the third year of the reign of Jehoiakim king of Judah came Nebuchadnezzar king of Babylon to Jerusalem, and besieged it. ²And the Lord gave Jehoiakim king of Judah into his hand, with part of the vessels of the house of God: which he carried into the land of Shinar to the house of his god; and he brought the vessels into the treasure house of his god. ³And the king spoke to Ashpenaz the master of his eunuchs, that he should bring certain of the children of Israel, and of the king's seed, and of the princes; ⁴Children in whom was no blemish, but well favored, and skillful in all wisdom, and cunning in knowledge, and understanding science, and such as had ability in them to stand in the king's palace, and whom they might teach the learning and the tongue of the Chaldeans. ⁵And the king appointed them a daily provision of the king's meat, and of the wine which he drank: so nourishing them three years, that at the end thereof they might stand before the king. ⁶Now among these were of the children of Judah, Daniel, Hananiah, Mishael, and Azariah: ⁷To whom the prince of the eunuchs gave names: for he gave to Daniel the name of Belteshazzar; and to Hananiah, of Shadrach; and to Mishael, of Meshach; and to Azariah, of Abednego. ⁸But Daniel purposed in his heart that he would not defile himself with the portion of the king's meat, nor with the wine which he drank: therefore he requested of the prince of the eunuchs that he might not defile himself. ⁹Now God had brought Daniel into favor and tender love with the prince of the eunuchs. ¹⁰And the prince of the eunuchs said to Daniel, I fear my lord the king, who has appointed your meat and your drink: for why should he see your faces worse liking than the children which are of your sort? then shall you make me endanger my head to the king. ¹¹Then said Daniel to Melzar, whom the prince of the eunuchs had set over Daniel, Hananiah, Mishael, and Azariah, ¹²Prove your servants, I beseech you, ten days; and let them give us vegetables to eat, and water to drink. ¹³Then let our countenances be looked on before you, and the countenance of the children that eat of the portion of the king's meat: and as you see, deal with your servants. ¹⁴So he consented to them in this matter, and proved them ten days. ¹⁵And at the end of ten days their countenances appeared fairer and fatter in flesh than all the children which did eat the portion of the king's meat. ¹⁶Thus Melzar took away the portion of their meat, and the wine that they should drink; and gave them vegetables. ¹⁷As for these four children, God gave them knowledge and skill in all learning and wisdom: and Daniel had understanding in all visions and dreams. ¹⁸Now at the end of the days that the king had said he should bring them in, then the prince of the eunuchs brought them in before Nebuchadnezzar. ¹⁹And the king communed with them; and among them all was found none like Daniel, Hananiah, Mishael, and Azariah: therefore stood they before the king. ²⁰And in all matters of wisdom and understanding, that the king inquired of them, he found them ten times better than all the magicians and astrologers that were in all his realm. ²¹And Daniel continued even to the first year of king Cyrus.

2 ¹And in the second year of the reign of Nebuchadnezzar Nebuchadnezzar dreamed dreams, with which his spirit was troubled, and his sleep broke from him. ²Then the king commanded to call the magicians, and the astrologers, and the sorcerers, and the Chaldeans, for to show the king his dreams. So they came and stood before the king. ³And the king said to them, I have dreamed a dream, and my spirit was troubled to know the dream. ⁴Then spoke the Chaldeans to the king in Syriack, O king, live for ever: tell your servants the dream, and we will show the interpretation. ⁵The king answered and said to the Chaldeans, The thing is gone from me: if you will not make known to me the dream, with the interpretation thereof, you shall be cut in pieces, and your houses shall be made a dunghill. ⁶But if you show the dream, and the interpretation thereof, you shall receive of me gifts and rewards and great honor: therefore show me the dream, and the interpretation thereof. ⁷They answered again and said, Let the king tell his servants the dream, and we will show the interpretation of it. ⁸The king answered and said, I know of certainty that you would gain the time, because you see the thing is gone from me. ⁹But if you will not make known to me the dream, there is but one decree for you: for you have prepared lying and corrupt words to speak before me, till the time be changed: therefore tell me the dream, and I shall know that you can show me the interpretation thereof. ¹⁰The Chaldeans answered before the king, and said, There is not a man on the earth that can show the king's matter: therefore there is no king, lord, nor ruler, that asked such things at any magician, or astrologer, or Chaldean. ¹¹And it is a rare thing that the king requires, and there is none other that can show it before the king, except the gods, whose dwelling is not with flesh. ¹²For this cause the king was angry and very furious, and commanded to destroy all the wise men of Babylon. ¹³And the decree went forth that the wise men should be slain; and they sought Daniel and his fellows to be slain. ¹⁴Then Daniel answered with counsel and wisdom to Arioch the captain of the king's guard, which was gone forth to slay the wise men of Babylon: ¹⁵He answered and said to Arioch the king's captain, Why is the decree so hasty from the king? Then Arioch made the thing known to Daniel. ¹⁶Then Daniel went in, and desired of the king that he would give him time, and that he would show the king the interpretation. ¹⁷Then Daniel went to his house, and made the thing known to Hananiah, Mishael, and Azariah, his companions: ¹⁸That they would desire mercies of the God of heaven concerning this secret; that Daniel and his fellows should not perish with the rest of the wise men of Babylon. ¹⁹Then was the secret revealed to Daniel in a night vision. Then Daniel blessed the God of heaven. ²⁰Daniel answered and said, Blessed be the name of God for ever and ever: for wisdom and might are his: ²¹And he changes the times and the seasons: he removes kings, and sets up kings: he gives wisdom to the wise, and knowledge to them that know understanding: ²²He reveals the deep and secret things: he knows what is in the darkness, and the light dwells with him. ²³I thank you, and praise you, O you God of my fathers, who have given me wisdom and might, and have made known to me now what we desired of you: for you have now made known to us the king's matter. ²⁴Therefore Daniel went in to Arioch, whom the king had ordained to

destroy the wise men of Babylon: he went and said thus to him; Destroy not the wise men of Babylon: bring me in before the king, and I will show to the king the interpretation. ²⁵Then Arioch brought in Daniel before the king in haste, and said thus to him, I have found a man of the captives of Judah, that will make known to the king the interpretation. ²⁶The king answered and said to Daniel, whose name was Belteshazzar, Are you able to make known to me the dream which I have seen, and the interpretation thereof? ²⁷Daniel answered in the presence of the king, and said, The secret which the king has demanded cannot the wise men, the astrologers, the magicians, the soothsayers, show to the king; ²⁸But there is a God in heaven that reveals secrets, and makes known to the king Nebuchadnezzar what shall be in the latter days. Your dream, and the visions of your head on your bed, are these; ²⁹As for you, O king, your thoughts came into your mind on your bed, what should come to pass hereafter: and he that reveals secrets makes known to you what shall come to pass. ³⁰But as for me, this secret is not revealed to me for any wisdom that I have more than any living, but for their sakes that shall make known the interpretation to the king, and that you might know the thoughts of your heart. ³¹You, O king, saw, and behold a great image. This great image, whose brightness was excellent, stood before you; and the form thereof was terrible. ³²This image's head was of fine gold, his breast and his arms of silver, his belly and his thighs of brass, ³³His legs of iron, his feet part of iron and part of clay. ³⁴You saw till that a stone was cut out without hands, which smote the image on his feet that were of iron and clay, and broke them to pieces. ³⁵Then was the iron, the clay, the brass, the silver, and the gold, broken to pieces together, and became like the chaff of the summer threshing floors; and the wind carried them away, that no place was found for them: and the stone that smote the image became a great mountain, and filled the whole earth. ³⁶This is the dream; and we will tell the interpretation thereof before the king. ³⁷You, O king, are a king of kings: for the God of heaven has given you a kingdom, power, and strength, and glory. ³⁸And wherever the children of men dwell, the beasts of the field and the fowls of the heaven has he given into your hand, and has made you ruler over them all. You are this head of gold. ³⁹And after you shall arise another kingdom inferior to you, and another third kingdom of brass, which shall bear rule over all the earth. ⁴⁰And the fourth kingdom shall be strong as iron: for as much as iron breaks in pieces and subdues all things: and as iron that breaks all these, shall it break in pieces and bruise. ⁴¹And whereas you saw the feet and toes, part of potters' clay, and part of iron, the kingdom shall be divided; but there shall be in it of the strength of the iron, for as much as you saw the iron mixed with miry clay. ⁴²And as the toes of the feet were part of iron, and part of clay, so the kingdom shall be partly strong, and partly broken. ⁴³And whereas you saw iron mixed with miry clay, they shall mingle themselves with the seed of men: but they shall not join one to another, even as iron is not mixed with clay. ⁴⁴And in the days of these kings shall the God of heaven set up a kingdom, which shall never be destroyed: and the kingdom shall not be left to other people, but it shall break in pieces and consume all these kingdoms, and it shall stand for ever. ⁴⁵For as much as you saw that the stone was cut out of the mountain without hands, and that it broke in pieces the iron, the brass, the clay, the silver, and the gold; the great God has made known to the king what shall come to pass hereafter: and the dream is certain, and the interpretation thereof sure. ⁴⁶Then the king Nebuchadnezzar fell on his face, and worshipped Daniel, and commanded that they should offer an oblation and sweet odors to him. ⁴⁷The king answered to Daniel, and said, Of a truth it is, that your God is a God of gods, and a Lord of kings, and a revealer of secrets, seeing you could reveal this secret. ⁴⁸Then the king made Daniel a great man, and gave him many great gifts, and made him ruler over the whole province of Babylon, and chief of the governors over all the wise men of Babylon. ⁴⁹Then Daniel requested of the king, and he set Shadrach, Meshach, and Abednego, over the affairs of the province of Babylon: but Daniel sat in the gate of the king.

3 ¹Nebuchadnezzar the king made an image of gold, whose height was three score cubits, and the breadth thereof six cubits: he set it up in the plain of Dura, in the province of Babylon. ²Then Nebuchadnezzar the king sent to gather together the princes, the governors, and the captains, the judges, the treasurers, the counsellors, the sheriffs, and all the rulers of the provinces, to come to the dedication of the image which Nebuchadnezzar the king had set up. ³Then the princes, the governors, and captains, the judges, the treasurers, the counsellors, the sheriffs, and all the rulers of the provinces, were gathered together to the dedication of the image that Nebuchadnezzar the king had set up; and they stood before the image that Nebuchadnezzar had set up. ⁴Then an herald cried aloud, To you it is commanded, O people, nations, and languages, ⁵That at what time you hear the sound of the cornet, flute, harp, sackbut, psaltery, dulcimer, and all kinds of music, you fall down and worship the golden image that Nebuchadnezzar the king has set up: ⁶And whoever falls not down and worships shall the same hour be cast into the middle of a burning fiery furnace. ⁷Therefore at that time, when all the people heard the sound of the cornet, flute, harp, sackbut, psaltery, and all kinds of music, all the people, the nations, and the languages, fell down and worshipped the golden image that Nebuchadnezzar the king had set up. ⁸Why at that time certain Chaldeans came near, and accused the Jews. ⁹They spoke and said to the king Nebuchadnezzar, O king, live for ever. ¹⁰You, O king, have made a decree, that every man that shall hear the sound of the cornet, flute, harp, sackbut, psaltery, and dulcimer, and all kinds of music, shall fall down and worship the golden image: ¹¹And whoever falls not down and worships, that he should be cast into the middle of a burning fiery furnace. ¹²There are certain Jews whom you have set over the affairs of the province of Babylon, Shadrach, Meshach, and Abednego; these men, O king, have not regarded you: they serve not your gods, nor worship the golden image which you have set up. ¹³Then Nebuchadnezzar in his rage and fury commanded to bring Shadrach, Meshach, and Abednego. Then they brought these men before the king. ¹⁴Nebuchadnezzar spoke and said to them, Is it true, O Shadrach, Meshach, and Abednego, do not you serve my gods, nor worship the golden image which I have set up? ¹⁵Now if you be ready that at what time you hear the sound of the cornet, flute, harp, sackbut, psaltery, and dulcimer, and all kinds of music, you fall down and worship the image which I have made; well: but if you worship not, you shall be cast the same hour into the middle of a burning fiery furnace; and who is that God that shall deliver you out of my hands? ¹⁶Shadrach, Meshach, and Abednego, answered and said to the king, O Nebuchadnezzar, we are not careful to answer you in this matter. ¹⁷If it be so, our God whom we serve is able to deliver us from the burning fiery furnace, and he will deliver us out of your hand, O king. ¹⁸But if not, be it known to you, O king, that we will not serve your gods, nor worship the golden image which you have set up. ¹⁹Then was Nebuchadnezzar full of fury, and the form of his visage was changed against Shadrach, Meshach, and Abednego: therefore he spoke, and commanded that they should heat the furnace one seven times more than it was wont to be heated. ²⁰And he commanded the most mighty men that were in his army to bind Shadrach, Meshach, and Abednego, and to cast them into the burning fiery furnace. ²¹Then these men were bound in their coats, their hosen, and their hats, and their other garments, and were cast into the middle of the burning fiery furnace. ²²Therefore because the king's commandment was urgent, and the furnace exceeding hot, the flames of the fire slew those men that took up Shadrach, Meshach, and Abednego. ²³And these three men, Shadrach, Meshach, and Abednego, fell down bound into the middle of the burning fiery furnace. ²⁴Then Nebuchadnezzar the king was astonished, and rose up in haste, and spoke, and said to his counsellors, Did not we cast three men bound into the middle of the fire? They answered and said to the king, True, O king. ²⁵He answered and said, See, I see four men loose, walking in the middle of the fire, and they have no hurt; and the form of the fourth is like the Son of God. ²⁶Then Nebuchadnezzar came near to the mouth of the burning fiery furnace, and spoke, and said, Shadrach, Meshach, and Abednego, you servants of the most high God, come forth, and come here. Then Shadrach, Meshach, and Abednego, came forth of the middle of the fire. ²⁷And the princes, governors, and captains, and the king's counsellors, being gathered together, saw these men, on whose bodies the fire had no power, nor was an hair of their head singed, neither were their coats changed, nor the smell of fire had passed on them. ²⁸Then Nebuchadnezzar spoke, and said, Blessed be the God of Shadrach, Meshach, and Abednego, who has sent his angel, and delivered his servants that trusted in him, and have changed the king's word, and yielded their bodies, that they might not serve nor worship any god, except their own God. ²⁹Therefore I make a decree, That every people, nation, and language, which speak any thing amiss against the God of Shadrach, Meshach, and Abednego, shall be cut in pieces, and their houses shall be made a dunghill: because there is no other God that can deliver after this sort. ³⁰Then the king promoted Shadrach, Meshach, and Abednego, in the province of Babylon.

4 ¹Nebuchadnezzar the king, to all people, nations, and languages, that dwell in all the earth; Peace be multiplied to you. ²I thought it good to show the signs and wonders that the high God has worked toward me. ³How great are his signs! and how mighty are his wonders! his kingdom is an everlasting kingdom, and his dominion is from generation to generation. ⁴I Nebuchadnezzar was at rest in my house, and flourishing in my palace: ⁵I saw a dream which made me afraid, and the thoughts on my bed and the visions of my head troubled me. ⁶Therefore made I a decree to bring in all the wise men of Babylon before me, that they might make known to me the interpretation of the dream. ⁷Then came in the magicians, the astrologers, the Chaldeans, and the soothsayers: and I told the dream before them; but they did not make known to me the interpretation thereof. ⁸But at the last Daniel came in before me, whose name was Belteshazzar, according to the name of my God, and in whom is the spirit of the holy gods: and before him I told the dream, saying, ⁹O Belteshazzar, master of the magicians, because I know that the spirit of the holy gods is in you, and no secret troubles you, tell me the visions of my dream that I have seen, and the interpretation thereof. ¹⁰Thus were the visions of my head in my bed; I saw, and behold a tree in the middle of the earth, and the height thereof was great. ¹¹The tree grew, and was strong, and the height thereof reached to heaven, and the sight thereof to the end of all the earth: ¹²The leaves thereof were fair, and the fruit thereof much, and in it was meat for all: the beasts of the field had shadow under it, and the fowls of the heaven dwelled in the boughs thereof, and all flesh was fed of it. ¹³I saw in the visions of my head on my bed, and, behold, a watcher and an holy one came down from heaven; ¹⁴He cried aloud, and said thus, Hew down the tree, and cut off his branches, shake off his leaves, and scatter his fruit: let the beasts get away from under it, and the fowls from his branches: ¹⁵Nevertheless leave the stump of his roots in the earth, even with a band of iron and brass, in the tender grass of the field; and let it be wet with the dew of heaven, and let his portion be with the beasts in the grass of the earth: ¹⁶Let his heart be changed from man's, and let a beast's heart be given to him; and let seven times pass over him. ¹⁷This matter is by the decree of the watchers, and the demand by the word of the holy ones: to the intent that the living may know that the most High rules in the kingdom of men, and gives it to whomsoever he will, and sets up over it the basest of men. ¹⁸This dream I king Nebuchadnezzar have seen. Now you, O Belteshazzar, declare the interpretation thereof, for as much as all the wise men of my kingdom are not able to make known to me the interpretation: but you are able; for the spirit of the holy gods is in you. ¹⁹Then Daniel, whose name was Belteshazzar, was astonished for one hour, and his thoughts troubled him. The king spoke, and said, Belteshazzar, let not the dream, or the interpretation thereof, trouble you. Belteshazzar answered and said, My lord, the dream be to them that hate you, and the interpretation thereof to your enemies. ²⁰The tree that you saw, which grew, and was strong, whose height reached to the heaven, and the sight thereof to all the earth; ²¹Whose leaves were fair, and the fruit thereof much, and in it was meat for all; under which the beasts of the field dwelled, and on whose branches the fowls of the heaven had their habitation: ²²It is you, O king, that are grown and become strong: for your greatness is grown, and reaches to heaven, and your dominion to the end of the earth. ²³And whereas the king saw a watcher and an holy one coming

down from heaven, and saying, Hew the tree down, and destroy it; yet leave the stump of the roots thereof in the earth, even with a band of iron and brass, in the tender grass of the field; and let it be wet with the dew of heaven, and let his portion be with the beasts of the field, till seven times pass over him; ²⁴This is the interpretation, O king, and this is the decree of the most High, which is come on my lord the king: ²⁵That they shall drive you from men, and your dwelling shall be with the beasts of the field, and they shall make you to eat grass as oxen, and they shall wet you with the dew of heaven, and seven times shall pass over you, till you know that the most High rules in the kingdom of men, and gives it to whomsoever he will. ²⁶And whereas they commanded to leave the stump of the tree roots; your kingdom shall be sure to you, after that you shall have known that the heavens do rule. ²⁷Why, O king, let my counsel be acceptable to you, and break off your sins by righteousness, and your iniquities by showing mercy to the poor; if it may be a lengthening of your tranquility. ²⁸All this came on the king Nebuchadnezzar. ²⁹At the end of twelve months he walked in the palace of the kingdom of Babylon. ³⁰The king spoke, and said, Is not this great Babylon, that I have built for the house of the kingdom by the might of my power, and for the honor of my majesty? ³¹While the word was in the king's mouth, there fell a voice from heaven, saying, O king Nebuchadnezzar, to you it is spoken; The kingdom is departed from you. ³²And they shall drive you from men, and your dwelling shall be with the beasts of the field: they shall make you to eat grass as oxen, and seven times shall pass over you, until you know that the most High rules in the kingdom of men, and gives it to whomsoever he will. ³³The same hour was the thing fulfilled on Nebuchadnezzar: and he was driven from men, and did eat grass as oxen, and his body was wet with the dew of heaven, till his hairs were grown like eagles' feathers, and his nails like birds' claws. ³⁴And at the end of the days I Nebuchadnezzar lifted up my eyes to heaven, and my understanding returned to me, and I blessed the most High, and I praised and honored him that lives for ever, whose dominion is an everlasting dominion, and his kingdom is from generation to generation: ³⁵And all the inhabitants of the earth are reputed as nothing: and he does according to his will in the army of heaven, and among the inhabitants of the earth: and none can stay his hand, or say to him, What do you? ³⁶At the same time my reason returned to me; and for the glory of my kingdom, my honor and brightness returned to me; and my counsellors and my lords sought to me; and I was established in my kingdom, and excellent majesty was added to me. ³⁷Now I Nebuchadnezzar praise and extol and honor the King of heaven, all whose works are truth, and his ways judgment: and those that walk in pride he is able to abase.

5 ¹Belshazzar the king made a great feast to a thousand of his lords, and drank wine before the thousand. ²Belshazzar, whiles he tasted the wine, commanded to bring the golden and silver vessels which his father Nebuchadnezzar had taken out of the temple which was in Jerusalem; that the king, and his princes, his wives, and his concubines, might drink therein. ³Then they brought the golden vessels that were taken out of the temple of the house of God which was at Jerusalem; and the king, and his princes, his wives, and his concubines, drank in them. ⁴They drank wine, and praised the gods of gold, and of silver, of brass, of iron, of wood, and of stone. ⁵In the same hour came forth fingers of a man's hand, and wrote over against the candlestick on the plaster of the wall of the king's palace: and the king saw the part of the hand that wrote. ⁶Then the king's countenance was changed, and his thoughts troubled him, so that the joints of his loins were loosed, and his knees smote one against another. ⁷The king cried aloud to bring in the astrologers, the Chaldeans, and the soothsayers. And the king spoke, and said to the wise men of Babylon, Whoever shall read this writing, and show me the interpretation thereof, shall be clothed with scarlet, and have a chain of gold about his neck, and shall be the third ruler in the kingdom. ⁸Then came in all the king's wise men: but they could not read the writing, nor make known to the king the interpretation thereof. ⁹Then was king Belshazzar greatly troubled, and his countenance was changed in him, and his lords were astonished. ¹⁰Now the queen by reason of the words of the king and his lords came into the banquet house: and the queen spoke and said, O king, live for ever: let not your thoughts trouble you, nor let your countenance be changed: ¹¹There is a man in your kingdom, in whom is the spirit of the holy gods; and in the days of your father light and understanding and wisdom, like the wisdom of the gods, was found in him; whom the king Nebuchadnezzar your father, the king, I say, your father, made master of the magicians, astrologers, Chaldeans, and soothsayers; ¹²For as much as an excellent spirit, and knowledge, and understanding, interpreting of dreams, and showing of hard sentences, and dissolving of doubts, were found in the same Daniel, whom the king named Belteshazzar: now let Daniel be called, and he will show the interpretation. ¹³Then was Daniel brought in before the king. And the king spoke and said to Daniel, Are you that Daniel, which are of the children of the captivity of Judah, whom the king my father brought out of Jewry? ¹⁴I have even heard of you, that the spirit of the gods is in you, and that light and understanding and excellent wisdom is found in you. ¹⁵And now the wise men, the astrologers, have been brought in before me, that they should read this writing, and make known to me the interpretation thereof: but they could not show the interpretation of the thing: ¹⁶And I have heard of you, that you can make interpretations, and dissolve doubts: now if you can read the writing, and make known to me the interpretation thereof, you shall be clothed with scarlet, and have a chain of gold about your neck, and shall be the third ruler in the kingdom. ¹⁷Then Daniel answered and said before the king, Let your gifts be to yourself, and give your rewards to another; yet I will read the writing to the king, and make known to him the interpretation. ¹⁸O you king, the most high God gave Nebuchadnezzar your father a kingdom, and majesty, and glory, and honor: ¹⁹And for the majesty that he gave him, all people, nations, and languages, trembled and feared before him: whom he would he slew; and whom he would he kept alive; and whom he would he set up; and whom he would he put down. ²⁰But when his heart was lifted up, and his mind hardened in pride, he was deposed from his kingly throne, and they took his glory from him: ²¹And he was driven from the sons of men; and his heart was made like the beasts, and his dwelling was with the wild asses: they fed him with grass like oxen, and his body was wet with the dew of heaven; till he knew that the most high God ruled in the kingdom of men, and that he appoints over it whomsoever he will. ²²And you his son, O Belshazzar, have not humbled your heart, though you knew all this; ²³But have lifted up yourself against the Lord of heaven; and they have brought the vessels of his house before you, and you, and your lords, your wives, and your concubines, have drunk wine in them; and you have praised the gods of silver, and gold, of brass, iron, wood, and stone, which see not, nor hear, nor know: and the God in whose hand your breath is, and whose are all your ways, have you not glorified: ²⁴Then was the part of the hand sent from him; and this writing was written. ²⁵And this is the writing that was written, MENE, MENE, TEKEL, UPHARSIN. ²⁶This is the interpretation of the thing: MENE; God has numbered your kingdom, and finished it. ²⁷TEKEL; You are weighed in the balances, and are found wanting. ²⁸PERES; Your kingdom is divided, and given to the Medes and Persians. ²⁹Then commanded Belshazzar, and they clothed Daniel with scarlet, and put a chain of gold about his neck, and made a proclamation concerning him, that he should be the third ruler in the kingdom. ³⁰In that night was Belshazzar the king of the Chaldeans slain. ³¹And Darius the Median took the kingdom, being about three score and two years old.

6 ¹It pleased Darius to set over the kingdom an hundred and twenty princes, which should be over the whole kingdom; ²And over these three presidents; of whom Daniel was first: that the princes might give accounts to them, and the king should have no damage. ³Then this Daniel was preferred above the presidents and princes, because an excellent spirit was in him; and the king thought to set him over the whole realm. ⁴Then the presidents and princes sought to find occasion against Daniel concerning the kingdom; but they could find none occasion nor fault; for as much as he was faithful, neither was there any error or fault found in him. ⁵Then said these men, We shall not find any occasion against this Daniel, except we find it against him concerning the law of his God. ⁶Then these presidents and princes assembled together to the king, and said thus to him, King Darius, live for ever. ⁷All the presidents of the kingdom, the governors, and the princes, the counsellors, and the captains, have consulted together to establish a royal statute, and to make a firm decree, that whoever shall ask a petition of any God or man for thirty days, save of you, O king, he shall be cast into the den of lions. ⁸Now, O king, establish the decree, and sign the writing, that it be not changed, according to the law of the Medes and Persians, which alters not. ⁹Why king Darius signed the writing and the decree. ¹⁰Now when Daniel knew that the writing was signed, he went into his house; and his windows being open in his chamber toward Jerusalem, he kneeled on his knees three times a day, and prayed, and gave thanks before his God, as he did aforetime. ¹¹Then these men assembled, and found Daniel praying and making supplication before his God. ¹²Then they came near, and spoke before the king concerning the king's decree; Have you not signed a decree, that every man that shall ask a petition of any God or man within thirty days, save of you, O king, shall be cast into the den of lions? The king answered and said, The thing is true, according to the law of the Medes and Persians, which alters not. ¹³Then answered they and said before the king, That Daniel, which is of the children of the captivity of Judah, regards not you, O king, nor the decree that you have signed, but makes his petition three times a day. ¹⁴Then the king, when he heard these words, was sore displeased with himself, and set his heart on Daniel to deliver him: and he labored till the going down of the sun to deliver him. ¹⁵Then these men assembled to the king, and said to the king, Know, O king, that the law of the Medes and Persians is, That no decree nor statute which the king establishes may be changed. ¹⁶Then the king commanded, and they brought Daniel, and cast him into the den of lions. Now the king spoke and said to Daniel, Your God whom you serve continually, he will deliver you. ¹⁷And a stone was brought, and laid on the mouth of the den; and the king sealed it with his own signet, and with the signet of his lords; that the purpose might not be changed concerning Daniel. ¹⁸Then the king went to his palace, and passed the night fasting: neither were instruments of music brought before him: and his sleep went from him. ¹⁹Then the king arose very early in the morning, and went in haste to the den of lions. ²⁰And when he came to the den, he cried with a lamentable voice to Daniel: and the king spoke and said to Daniel, O Daniel, servant of the living God, is your God, whom you serve continually, able to deliver you from the lions? ²¹Then said Daniel to the king, O king, live for ever. ²²My God has sent his angel, and has shut the lions' mouths, that they have not hurt me: for as much as before him innocence was found in me; and also before you, O king, have I done no hurt. ²³Then was the king exceedingly glad for him, and commanded that they should take Daniel up out of the den. So Daniel was taken up out of the den, and no manner of hurt was found on him, because he believed in his God. ²⁴And the king commanded, and they brought those men which had accused Daniel, and they cast them into the den of lions, them, their children, and their wives; and the lions had the mastery of them, and broke all their bones in pieces or ever they came at the bottom of the den. ²⁵Then king Darius wrote to all people, nations, and languages, that dwell in all the earth; Peace be multiplied to you. ²⁶I make a decree, That in every dominion of my kingdom men tremble and fear before the God of Daniel: for he is the living God, and steadfast for ever, and his kingdom that which shall not be destroyed, and his dominion shall be even to the end. ²⁷He delivers and rescues, and he works signs and wonders in heaven and in earth, who has delivered Daniel from the power of the lions. ²⁸So this Daniel prospered in the reign of Darius, and in the reign of Cyrus the Persian.

7 ¹In the first year of Belshazzar king of Babylon Daniel had a dream and visions of his head on his bed: then he wrote the dream, and told the sum of the matters. ²Daniel spoke and said, I saw in my vision by night, and, behold, the four winds of the heaven strove on the great sea. ³And four great beasts came up from the sea, diverse one from another. ⁴The first was like a lion, and had eagle's wings: I beheld till the wings thereof were plucked, and it was lifted up from the earth, and made stand on the feet as a man, and a man's heart

was given to it. ⁵And behold another beast, a second, like to a bear, and it raised up itself on one side, and it had three ribs in the mouth of it between the teeth of it: and they said thus to it, Arise, devour much flesh. ⁶After this I beheld, and see another, like a leopard, which had on the back of it four wings of a fowl; the beast had also four heads; and dominion was given to it. ⁷After this I saw in the night visions, and behold a fourth beast, dreadful and terrible, and strong exceedingly; and it had great iron teeth: it devoured and broke in pieces, and stamped the residue with the feet of it: and it was diverse from all the beasts that were before it; and it had ten horns. ⁸I considered the horns, and, behold, there came up among them another little horn, before whom there were three of the first horns plucked up by the roots: and, behold, in this horn were eyes like the eyes of man, and a mouth speaking great things. ⁹I beheld till the thrones were cast down, and the Ancient of days did sit, whose garment was white as snow, and the hair of his head like the pure wool: his throne was like the fiery flame, and his wheels as burning fire. ¹⁰A fiery stream issued and came forth from before him: thousand thousands ministered to him, and ten thousand times ten thousand stood before him: the judgment was set, and the books were opened. ¹¹I beheld then because of the voice of the great words which the horn spoke: I beheld even till the beast was slain, and his body destroyed, and given to the burning flame. ¹²As concerning the rest of the beasts, they had their dominion taken away: yet their lives were prolonged for a season and time. ¹³I saw in the night visions, and, behold, one like the Son of man came with the clouds of heaven, and came to the Ancient of days, and they brought him near before him. ¹⁴And there was given him dominion, and glory, and a kingdom, that all people, nations, and languages, should serve him: his dominion is an everlasting dominion, which shall not pass away, and his kingdom that which shall not be destroyed. ¹⁵I Daniel was grieved in my spirit in the middle of my body, and the visions of my head troubled me. ¹⁶I came near to one of them that stood by, and asked him the truth of all this. So he told me, and made me know the interpretation of the things. ¹⁷These great beasts, which are four, are four kings, which shall arise out of the earth. ¹⁸But the saints of the most High shall take the kingdom, and possess the kingdom for ever, even for ever and ever. ¹⁹Then I would know the truth of the fourth beast, which was diverse from all the others, exceeding dreadful, whose teeth were of iron, and his nails of brass; which devoured, broke in pieces, and stamped the residue with his feet; ²⁰And of the ten horns that were in his head, and of the other which came up, and before whom three fell; even of that horn that had eyes, and a mouth that spoke very great things, whose look was more stout than his fellows. ²¹I beheld, and the same horn made war with the saints, and prevailed against them; ²²Until the Ancient of days came, and judgment was given to the saints of the most High; and the time came that the saints possessed the kingdom. ²³Thus he said, The fourth beast shall be the fourth kingdom on earth, which shall be diverse from all kingdoms, and shall devour the whole earth, and shall tread it down, and break it in pieces. ²⁴And the ten horns out of this kingdom are ten kings that shall arise: and another shall rise after them; and he shall be diverse from the first, and he shall subdue three kings. ²⁵And he shall speak great words against the most High, and shall wear out the saints of the most High, and think to change times and laws: and they shall be given into his hand until a time and times and the dividing of time. ²⁶But the judgment shall sit, and they shall take away his dominion, to consume and to destroy it to the end. ²⁷And the kingdom and dominion, and the greatness of the kingdom under the whole heaven, shall be given to the people of the saints of the most High, whose kingdom is an everlasting kingdom, and all dominions shall serve and obey him. ²⁸Till now is the end of the matter. As for me Daniel, my cogitations much troubled me, and my countenance changed in me: but I kept the matter in my heart.

8

¹In the third year of the reign of king Belshazzar a vision appeared to me, even to me Daniel, after that which appeared to me at the first. ²And I saw in a vision; and it came to pass, when I saw, that I was at Shushan in the palace, which is in the province of Elam; and I saw in a vision, and I was by the river of Ulai. ³Then I lifted up my eyes, and saw, and, behold, there stood before the river a ram which had two horns: and the two horns were high; but one was higher than the other, and the higher came up last. ⁴I saw the ram pushing westward, and northward, and southward; so that no beasts might stand before him, neither was there any that could deliver out of his hand; but he did according to his will, and became great. ⁵And as I was considering, behold, an he goat came from the west on the face of the whole earth, and touched not the ground: and the goat had a notable horn between his eyes. ⁶And he came to the ram that had two horns, which I had seen standing before the river, and ran to him in the fury of his power. ⁷And I saw him come close to the ram, and he was moved with choler against him, and smote the ram, and broke his two horns: and there was no power in the ram to stand before him, but he cast him down to the ground, and stamped on him: and there was none that could deliver the ram out of his hand. ⁸Therefore the he goat waxed very great: and when he was strong, the great horn was broken; and for it came up four notable ones toward the four winds of heaven. ⁹And out of one of them came forth a little horn, which waxed exceeding great, toward the south, and toward the east, and toward the pleasant land. ¹⁰And it waxed great, even to the host of heaven; and it cast down some of the host and of the stars to the ground, and stamped on them. ¹¹Yes, he magnified himself even to the prince of the host, and by him the daily sacrifice was taken away, and the place of the sanctuary was cast down. ¹²And an host was given him against the daily sacrifice by reason of transgression, and it cast down the truth to the ground; and it practiced, and prospered. ¹³Then I heard one saint speaking, and another saint said to that certain saint which spoke, How long shall be the vision concerning the daily sacrifice, and the transgression of desolation, to give both the sanctuary and the host to be trodden under foot? ¹⁴And he said to me, To two thousand and three hundred days; then shall the sanctuary be cleansed. ¹⁵And it came to pass, when I, even I Daniel, had seen the vision, and sought for the meaning, then, behold, there stood before me as the appearance of a man. ¹⁶And I heard a man's voice between the banks of Ulai, which called, and said, Gabriel, make this man to understand the vision. ¹⁷So he

came near where I stood: and when he came, I was afraid, and fell on my face: but he said to me, Understand, O son of man: for at the time of the end shall be the vision. ¹⁸Now as he was speaking with me, I was in a deep sleep on my face toward the ground: but he touched me, and set me upright. ¹⁹And he said, Behold, I will make you know what shall be in the last end of the indignation: for at the time appointed the end shall be. ²⁰The ram which you saw having two horns are the kings of Media and Persia. ²¹And the rough goat is the king of Grecia: and the great horn that is between his eyes is the first king. ²²Now that being broken, whereas four stood up for it, four kingdoms shall stand up out of the nation, but not in his power. ²³And in the latter time of their kingdom, when the transgressors are come to the full, a king of fierce countenance, and understanding dark sentences, shall stand up. ²⁴And his power shall be mighty, but not by his own power: and he shall destroy wonderfully, and shall prosper, and practice, and shall destroy the mighty and the holy people. ²⁵And through his policy also he shall cause craft to prosper in his hand; and he shall magnify himself in his heart, and by peace shall destroy many: he shall also stand up against the Prince of princes; but he shall be broken without hand. ²⁶And the vision of the evening and the morning which was told is true: why shut you up the vision; for it shall be for many days. ²⁷And I Daniel fainted, and was sick certain days; afterward I rose up, and did the king's business; and I was astonished at the vision, but none understood it.

9 ¹In the first year of Darius the son of Ahasuerus, of the seed of the Medes, which was made king over the realm of the Chaldeans; ²In the first year of his reign I Daniel understood by books the number of the years, whereof the word of the LORD came to Jeremiah the prophet, that he would accomplish seventy years in the desolations of Jerusalem. ³And I set my face to the Lord God, to seek by prayer and supplications, with fasting, and sackcloth, and ashes: ⁴And I prayed to the LORD my God, and made my confession, and said, O Lord, the great and dreadful God, keeping the covenant and mercy to them that love him, and to them that keep his commandments; ⁵We have sinned, and have committed iniquity, and have done wickedly, and have rebelled, even by departing from your precepts and from your judgments: ⁶Neither have we listened to your servants the prophets, which spoke in your name to our kings, our princes, and our fathers, and to all the people of the land. ⁷O LORD, righteousness belongs to you, but to us confusion of faces, as at this day; to the men of Judah, and to the inhabitants of Jerusalem, and to all Israel, that are near, and that are far off, through all the countries where you have driven them, because of their trespass that they have trespassed against you. ⁸O Lord, to us belongs confusion of face, to our kings, to our princes, and to our fathers, because we have sinned against you. ⁹To the Lord our God belong mercies and forgivenesses, though we have rebelled against him; ¹⁰Neither have we obeyed the voice of the LORD our God, to walk in his laws, which he set before us by his servants the prophets. ¹¹Yes, all Israel have transgressed your law, even by departing, that they might not obey your voice; therefore the curse is poured on us, and the oath that is written in the law of Moses the servant of God, because we have sinned against him. ¹²And he has confirmed his words, which he spoke against us, and against our judges that judged us, by bringing on us a great evil: for under the whole heaven has not been done as has been done on Jerusalem. ¹³As it is written in the law of Moses, all this evil is come on us: yet made we not our prayer before the LORD our God, that we might turn from our iniquities, and understand your truth. ¹⁴Therefore has the LORD watched on the evil, and brought it on us: for the LORD our God is righteous in all his works which he does: for we obeyed not his voice. ¹⁵And now, O Lord our God, that have brought your people forth out of the land of Egypt with a mighty hand, and have gotten you renown, as at this day; we have sinned, we have done wickedly. ¹⁶O LORD, according to all your righteousness, I beseech you, let your anger and your fury be turned away from your city Jerusalem, your holy mountain: because for our sins, and for the iniquities of our fathers, Jerusalem and your people are become a reproach to all that are about us. ¹⁷Now therefore, O our God, hear the prayer of your servant, and his supplications, and cause your face to shine on your sanctuary that is desolate, for the Lord's sake. ¹⁸O my God, incline your ear, and hear; open your eyes, and behold our desolations, and the city which is called by your name: for we do not present our supplications before you for our righteousnesses, but for your great mercies. ¹⁹O Lord, hear; O Lord, forgive; O Lord, listen and do; defer not, for your own sake, O my God: for your city and your people are called by your name. ²⁰And whiles I was speaking, and praying, and confessing my sin and the sin of my people Israel, and presenting my supplication before the LORD my God for the holy mountain of my God; ²¹Yes, whiles I was speaking in prayer, even the man Gabriel, whom I had seen in the vision at the beginning, being caused to fly swiftly, touched me about the time of the evening oblation. ²²And he informed me, and talked with me, and said, O Daniel, I am now come forth to give you skill and understanding. ²³At the beginning of your supplications the commandment came forth, and I am come to show you; for you are greatly beloved: therefore understand the matter, and consider the vision. ²⁴Seventy weeks are determined on your people and on your holy city, to finish the transgression, and to make an end of sins, and to make reconciliation for iniquity, and to bring in everlasting righteousness, and to seal up the vision and prophecy, and to anoint the most Holy. ²⁵Know therefore and understand, that from the going forth of the commandment to restore and to build Jerusalem to the Messiah the Prince shall be seven weeks, and three score and two weeks: the street shall be built again, and the wall, even in troublous times. ²⁶And after three score and two weeks shall Messiah be cut off, but not for himself: and the people of the prince that shall come shall destroy the city and the sanctuary; and the end thereof shall be with a flood, and to the end of the war desolations are determined. ²⁷And he shall confirm the covenant with many for one week: and in the middle of the week he shall cause the sacrifice and the oblation to cease, and for the overspreading of abominations he shall make it desolate, even until the consummation, and that determined shall be poured on the desolate.

10 ¹In the third year of Cyrus king of Persia a thing was revealed to Daniel, whose name was called Belteshazzar; and the thing was true, but the time appointed was long: and he understood the thing, and had understanding of the vision. ²In those days I Daniel was mourning three full weeks. ³I ate no pleasant bread, neither came flesh nor wine in my mouth, neither did I anoint myself at all, till three whole weeks were fulfilled. ⁴And in the four and twentieth day of the first month, as I was by the side of the great river, which is Hiddekel; ⁵Then I lifted up my eyes, and looked, and behold a certain man clothed in linen, whose loins were girded with fine gold of Uphaz: ⁶His body also was like the beryl, and his face as the appearance of lightning, and his eyes as lamps of fire, and his arms and his feet like in color to polished brass, and the voice of his words like the voice of a multitude. ⁷And I Daniel alone saw the vision: for the men that were with me saw not the vision; but a great quaking fell on them, so that they fled to hide themselves. ⁸Therefore I was left alone, and saw this great vision, and there remained no strength in me: for my comeliness was turned in me into corruption, and I retained no strength. ⁹Yet heard I the voice of his words: and when I heard the voice of his words, then was I in a deep sleep on my face, and my face toward the ground. ¹⁰And, behold, an hand touched me, which set me on my knees and on the palms of my hands. ¹¹And he said to me, O Daniel, a man greatly beloved, understand the words that I speak to you, and stand upright: for to you am I now sent. And when he had spoken this word to me, I stood trembling. ¹²Then said he to me, Fear not, Daniel: for from the first day that you did set your heart to understand, and to chasten yourself before your God, your words were heard, and I am come for your words. ¹³But the prince of the kingdom of Persia withstood me one and twenty days: but, see, Michael, one of the chief princes, came to help me; and I remained there with the kings of Persia. ¹⁴Now I am come to make you understand what shall befall your people in the latter days: for yet the vision is for many days. ¹⁵And when he had spoken such words to me, I set my face toward the ground, and I became dumb. ¹⁶And, behold, one like the similitude of the sons of men touched my lips: then I opened my mouth, and spoke, and said to him that stood before me, O my lord, by the vision my sorrows are turned on me, and I have retained no strength. ¹⁷For how can the servant of this my lord talk with this my lord? for as for me, straightway there remained no strength in me, neither is there breath left in me. ¹⁸Then there came again and touched me one like the appearance of a man, and he strengthened me, ¹⁹And said, O man greatly beloved, fear not: peace be to you, be strong, yes, be strong. And when he had spoken to me, I was strengthened, and said, Let my lord speak; for you have strengthened me. ²⁰Then said he, Know you why I come to you? and now will I return to fight with the prince of Persia: and when I am gone forth, see, the prince of Grecia shall come. ²¹But I will show you that which is noted in the scripture of truth: and there is none that holds with me in these things, but Michael your prince.

11 ¹Also I in the first year of Darius the Mede, even I, stood to confirm and to strengthen him. ²And now will I show you the truth. Behold, there shall stand up yet three kings in Persia; and the fourth shall be far richer than they all: and by his strength through his riches he shall stir up all against the realm of Grecia. ³And a mighty king shall stand up, that shall rule with great dominion, and do according to his will. ⁴And when he shall stand up, his kingdom shall be broken, and shall be divided toward the four winds of heaven; and not to his posterity, nor according to his dominion which he ruled: for his kingdom shall be plucked up, even for others beside those. ⁵And the king of the south shall be strong, and one of his princes; and he shall be strong above him, and have dominion; his dominion shall be a great dominion. ⁶And in the end of years they shall join themselves together; for the king's daughter of the south shall come to the king of the north to make an agreement: but she shall not retain the power of the arm; neither shall he stand, nor his arm: but she shall be given up, and they that brought her, and he that begat her, and he that strengthened her in these times. ⁷But out of a branch of her roots shall one stand up in his estate, which shall come with an army, and shall enter into the fortress of the king of the north, and shall deal against them, and shall prevail: ⁸And shall also carry captives into Egypt their gods, with their princes, and with their precious vessels of silver and of gold; and he shall continue more years than the king of the north. ⁹So the king of the south shall come into his kingdom, and shall return into his own land. ¹⁰But his sons shall be stirred up, and shall assemble a multitude of great forces: and one shall certainly come, and overflow, and pass through: then shall he return, and be stirred up, even to his fortress. ¹¹And the king of the south shall be moved with choler, and shall come forth and fight with him, even with the king of the north: and he shall set forth a great multitude; but the multitude shall be given into his hand. ¹²And when he has taken away the multitude, his heart shall be lifted up; and he shall cast down many ten thousands: but he shall not be strengthened by it. ¹³For the king of the north shall return, and shall set forth a multitude greater than the former, and shall certainly come after certain years with a great army and with much riches. ¹⁴And in those times there shall many stand up against the king of the south: also the robbers of your people shall exalt themselves to establish the vision; but they shall fall. ¹⁵So the king of the north shall come, and cast up a mount, and take the most fenced cities: and the arms of the south shall not withstand, neither his chosen people, neither shall there be any strength to withstand. ¹⁶But he that comes against him shall do according to his own will, and none shall stand before him: and he shall stand in the glorious land, which by his hand shall be consumed. ¹⁷He shall also set his face to enter with the strength of his whole kingdom, and upright ones with him; thus shall he do: and he shall give him the daughter of women, corrupting her: but she shall not stand on his side, neither be for him. ¹⁸After this shall he turn his face to the isles, and shall take many: but a prince for his own behalf shall cause the reproach offered by him to cease; without his own reproach he shall cause it to turn on him. ¹⁹Then he shall turn his face toward the fort of his own land: but he shall stumble and fall, and not be found. ²⁰Then shall stand up in his estate a raiser of taxes in the glory of the kingdom: but within few days he shall be destroyed, neither in anger, nor in battle. ²¹And in his estate shall stand up a vile person, to whom they shall not give the honor of the kingdom: but he shall come in peaceably, and obtain the kingdom by flatteries. ²²And with the arms of a flood shall they be overflowed from before him, and shall be broken; yes, also the prince of the covenant. ²³And after the league made with him he shall work deceitfully: for he shall come up, and shall become strong with a small people. ²⁴He shall enter peaceably even on the fattest places of the province; and he shall do that which his fathers have not done, nor his fathers' fathers; he shall scatter among them the prey, and spoil, and riches: yes, and he shall forecast his devices against the strong holds, even for a time. ²⁵And he shall stir up his power and his courage against the king of the south with a great army; and the king of the south shall be stirred up to battle with a very great and mighty army; but he shall not stand: for they shall forecast devices against him. ²⁶Yes, they that feed of the portion of his meat shall destroy him, and his army shall overflow: and many shall fall down slain. ²⁷And both of these kings' hearts shall be to do mischief, and they shall speak lies at one table; but it shall not prosper: for yet the end shall be at the time appointed. ²⁸Then shall he return into his land with great riches; and his heart shall be against the holy covenant; and he shall do exploits, and return to his own land. ²⁹At the time appointed he shall return, and come toward the south; but it shall not be as the former, or as the latter. ³⁰For the ships of Chittim shall come against him: therefore he shall be grieved, and return, and have indignation against the holy covenant: so shall he do; he shall even return, and have intelligence with them that forsake the holy covenant. ³¹And arms shall stand on his part, and they shall pollute the sanctuary of strength, and shall take away the daily sacrifice, and they shall place the abomination that makes desolate. ³²And such as do wickedly against the covenant shall he corrupt by flatteries: but the people that do know their God shall be strong, and do exploits. ³³And they that understand among the people shall instruct many: yet they shall fall by the sword, and by flame, by captivity, and by spoil, many days. ³⁴Now when they shall fall, they shall be helped with a little help: but many shall join to them with flatteries. ³⁵And some of them of understanding shall fall, to try them, and to purge, and to make them white, even to the time of the end: because it is yet for a time appointed. ³⁶And the king shall do according to his will; and he shall exalt himself, and magnify himself above every god, and shall speak marvelous things against the God of gods, and shall prosper till the indignation be accomplished: for that that is determined shall be done. ³⁷Neither shall he regard the God of his fathers, nor the desire of women, nor regard any god: for he shall magnify himself above all. ³⁸But in his estate shall he honor the God of forces: and a god whom his fathers knew not shall he honor with gold, and silver, and with precious stones, and pleasant things. ³⁹Thus shall he do in the most strong holds with a strange god, whom he shall acknowledge and increase with glory: and he shall cause them to rule over many, and shall divide the land for gain. ⁴⁰And at the time of the end shall the king of the south push at him: and the king of the north shall come against him like a whirlwind, with chariots, and with horsemen, and with many ships; and he shall enter into the countries, and shall overflow and pass over. ⁴¹He shall enter also into the glorious land, and many countries shall be overthrown: but these shall escape out of his hand, even Edom, and Moab, and the chief of the children of Ammon. ⁴²He shall stretch forth his hand also on the countries: and the land of Egypt shall not escape. ⁴³But he shall have power over the treasures of gold and of silver, and over all the precious things of Egypt: and the Libyans and the Ethiopians shall be at his steps. ⁴⁴But tidings out of the east and out of the north shall trouble him: therefore he shall go forth with great fury to destroy, and utterly to make away many. ⁴⁵And he shall plant the tabernacles of his palace between the seas in the glorious holy mountain; yet he shall come to his end, and none shall help him.

12

¹And at that time shall Michael stand up, the great prince which stands for the children of your people: and there shall be a time of trouble, such as never was since there was a nation even to that same time: and at that time your people shall be delivered, every one that shall be found written in the book. ²And many of them that sleep in the dust of the earth shall awake, some to everlasting life, and some to shame and everlasting contempt. ³And they that be wise shall shine as the brightness of the firmament; and they that turn many to righteousness as the stars for ever and ever. ⁴But you, O Daniel, shut up the words, and seal the book, even to the time of the end: many shall run to and fro, and knowledge shall be increased. ⁵Then I Daniel looked, and, behold, there stood other two, the one on this side of the bank of the river, and the other on that side of the bank of the river. ⁶And one said to the man clothed in linen, which was on the waters of the river, How long shall it be to the end of these wonders? ⁷And I heard the man clothed in linen, which was on the waters of the river, when he held up his right hand and his left hand to heaven, and swore by him that lives for ever that it shall be for a time, times, and an half; and when he shall have accomplished to scatter the power of the holy people, all these things shall be finished. ⁸And I heard, but I understood not: then said I, O my Lord, what shall be the end of these things? ⁹And he said, Go your way, Daniel: for the words are closed up and sealed till the time of the end. ¹⁰Many shall be purified, and made white, and tried; but the wicked shall do wickedly: and none of the wicked shall understand; but the wise shall understand. ¹¹And from the time that the daily sacrifice shall be taken away, and the abomination that makes desolate set up, there shall be a thousand two hundred and ninety days. ¹²Blessed is he that waits, and comes to the thousand three hundred and five and thirty days. ¹³But go you your way till the end be: for you shall rest, and stand in your lot at the end of the days.

Hosea

1 ¹The word of the LORD that came to Hosea, the son of Beeri, in the days of Uzziah, Jotham, Ahaz, and Hezekiah, kings of Judah, and in the days of Jeroboam the son of Joash, king of Israel. ²The beginning of the word of the LORD by Hosea. And the LORD said to Hosea, Go, take to you a wife of prostitutions and children of prostitutions: for the land has committed great prostitution, departing from the LORD. ³So he went and took Gomer the daughter of Diblaim; which conceived, and bore him a son. ⁴And the LORD said to him, Call his name Jezreel; for yet a little while, and I will avenge the blood of Jezreel on the house of Jehu, and will cause to cease the kingdom of the house of Israel. ⁵And it shall come to pass at that day, that I will break the bow of Israel, in the valley of Jezreel. ⁶And she conceived again, and bore a daughter. And God said to him, Call her name Loruhamah: for I will no more have mercy on the house of Israel; but I will utterly take them away. ⁷But I will have mercy on the house of Judah, and will save them by the LORD their God, and will not save them by bow, nor by sword, nor by battle, by horses, nor by horsemen. ⁸Now when she had weaned Loruhamah, she conceived, and bore a son. ⁹Then said God, Call his name Loammi: for you are not my people, and I will not be your God. ¹⁰Yet the number of the children of Israel shall be as the sand of the sea, which cannot be measured nor numbered; and it shall come to pass, that in the place where it was said to them, You are not my people, there it shall be said to them, You are the sons of the living God. ¹¹Then shall the children of Judah and the children of Israel be gathered together, and appoint themselves one head, and they shall come up out of the land: for great shall be the day of Jezreel.

2 ¹Say you to your brothers, Ammi; and to your sisters, Ruhamah. ²Plead with your mother, plead: for she is not my wife, neither am I her husband: let her therefore put away her prostitutions out of her sight, and her adulteries from between her breasts; ³Lest I strip her naked, and set her as in the day that she was born, and make her as a wilderness, and set her like a dry land, and slay her with thirst. ⁴And I will not have mercy on her children; for they be the children of prostitutions. ⁵For their mother has played the harlot: she that conceived them has done shamefully: for she said, I will go after my lovers, that give me my bread and my water, my wool and my flax, my oil and my drink. ⁶Therefore, behold, I will hedge up your way with thorns, and make a wall, that she shall not find her paths. ⁷And she shall follow after her lovers, but she shall not overtake them; and she shall seek them, but shall not find them: then shall she say, I will go and return to my first husband; for then was it better with me than now. ⁸For she did not know that I gave her corn, and wine, and oil, and multiplied her silver and gold, which they prepared for Baal. ⁹Therefore will I return, and take away my corn in the time thereof, and my wine in the season thereof, and will recover my wool and my flax given to cover her nakedness. ¹⁰And now will I discover her lewdness in the sight of her lovers, and none shall deliver her out of my hand. ¹¹I will also cause all her mirth to cease, her feast days, her new moons, and her sabbaths, and all her solemn feasts. ¹²And I will destroy her vines and her fig trees, whereof she has said, These are my rewards that my lovers have given me: and I will make them a forest, and the beasts of the field shall eat them. ¹³And I will visit on her the days of Baalim, wherein she burned incense to them, and she decked herself with her earrings and her jewels, and she went after her lovers, and forgot me, says the LORD. ¹⁴Therefore, behold, I will allure her, and bring her into the wilderness, and speak comfortably to her. ¹⁵And I will give her her vineyards from there, and the valley of Achor for a door of hope: and she shall sing there, as in the days of her youth, and as in the day when she came up out of the land of Egypt. ¹⁶And it shall be at that day, says the LORD, that you shall call me Ishi; and shall call me no more Baali. ¹⁷For I will take away the names of Baalim out of her mouth, and they shall no more be remembered by their name. ¹⁸And in that day will I make a covenant for them with the beasts of the field and with the fowls of heaven, and with the creeping things of the ground: and I will break the bow and the sword and the battle out of the earth, and will make them to lie down safely. ¹⁹And I will betroth you to me for ever; yes, I will betroth you to me in righteousness, and in judgment, and in loving kindness, and in mercies. ²⁰I will even betroth you to me in faithfulness: and you shall know the LORD. ²¹And it shall come to pass in that day, I will hear, says the LORD, I will hear the heavens, and they shall hear the earth; ²²And the earth shall hear the corn, and the wine, and the oil; and they shall hear Jezreel. ²³And I will sow her to me in the earth; and I will have mercy on her that had not obtained mercy; and I will say to them which were not my people, You are my people; and they shall say, You are my God.

3 ¹Then said the LORD to me, Go yet, love a woman beloved of her friend, yet an adulteress, according to the love of the LORD toward the children of Israel, who look to other gods, and love flagons of wine. ²So I bought her to me for fifteen pieces of silver, and for an homer of barley, and an half homer of barley: ³And I said to her, You shall abide for me many days; you shall not play the harlot, and you shall not be for another man: so will I also be for you. ⁴For the children of Israel shall abide many days without a king, and without a prince, and without a sacrifice, and without an image, and without an ephod, and without teraphim: ⁵Afterward shall the children of Israel return, and seek the LORD their God, and David their king; and shall fear the LORD and his goodness in the latter days.

4 ¹Hear the word of the LORD, you children of Israel: for the LORD has a controversy with the inhabitants of the land, because there is no truth, nor mercy, nor knowledge of God in the land. ²By swearing, and lying, and killing, and stealing, and committing adultery, they break out, and blood touches blood. ³Therefore shall the land mourn, and every one that dwells therein shall languish, with the beasts of the field, and with the fowls of heaven; yes, the fishes of the sea also shall be taken away. ⁴Yet let no man strive, nor reprove another: for your people are as they that strive with the priest. ⁵Therefore shall you fall in the day, and the prophet

also shall fall with you in the night, and I will destroy your mother. ⁶My people are destroyed for lack of knowledge: because you have rejected knowledge, I will also reject you, that you shall be no priest to me: seeing you have forgotten the law of your God, I will also forget your children. ⁷As they were increased, so they sinned against me: therefore will I change their glory into shame. ⁸They eat up the sin of my people, and they set their heart on their iniquity. ⁹And there shall be, like people, like priest: and I will punish them for their ways, and reward them their doings. ¹⁰For they shall eat, and not have enough: they shall commit prostitution, and shall not increase: because they have left off to take heed to the LORD. ¹¹Prostitution and wine and new wine take away the heart. ¹²My people ask counsel at their stocks, and their staff declares to them: for the spirit of prostitutions has caused them to err, and they have gone a whoring from under their God. ¹³They sacrifice on the tops of the mountains, and burn incense on the hills, under oaks and poplars and elms, because the shadow thereof is good: therefore your daughters shall commit prostitution, and your spouses shall commit adultery. ¹⁴I will not punish your daughters when they commit prostitution, nor your spouses when they commit adultery: for themselves are separated with whores, and they sacrifice with harlots: therefore the people that does not understand shall fall. ¹⁵Though you, Israel, play the harlot, yet let not Judah offend; and come not you to Gilgal, neither go you up to Bethaven, nor swear, The LORD lives. ¹⁶For Israel slides back as a backsliding heifer: now the LORD will feed them as a lamb in a large place. ¹⁷Ephraim is joined to idols: let him alone. ¹⁸Their drink is sour: they have committed prostitution continually: her rulers with shame do love, Give you. ¹⁹The wind has bound her up in her wings, and they shall be ashamed because of their sacrifices.

5 ¹Hear you this, O priests; and listen, you house of Israel; and give you ear, O house of the king; for judgment is toward you, because you have been a snare on Mizpah, and a net spread on Tabor. ²And the rebels are profound to make slaughter, though I have been a rebuker of them all. ³I know Ephraim, and Israel is not hid from me: for now, O Ephraim, you commit prostitution, and Israel is defiled. ⁴They will not frame their doings to turn to their God: for the spirit of prostitutions is in the middle of them, and they have not known the LORD. ⁵And the pride of Israel does testify to his face: therefore shall Israel and Ephraim fall in their iniquity: Judah also shall fall with them. ⁶They shall go with their flocks and with their herds to seek the LORD; but they shall not find him; he has withdrawn himself from them. ⁷They have dealt treacherously against the LORD: for they have begotten strange children: now shall a month devour them with their portions. ⁸Blow you the cornet in Gibeah, and the trumpet in Ramah: cry aloud at Bethaven, after you, O Benjamin. ⁹Ephraim shall be desolate in the day of rebuke: among the tribes of Israel have I made known that which shall surely be. ¹⁰The princes of Judah were like them that remove the bound: therefore I will pour out my wrath on them like water. ¹¹Ephraim is oppressed and broken in judgment, because he willingly walked after the commandment. ¹²Therefore will I be to Ephraim as a moth, and to the house of Judah as rottenness. ¹³When Ephraim saw his sickness, and Judah saw his wound, then went Ephraim to the Assyrian, and sent to king Jareb: yet could he not heal you, nor cure you of your wound. ¹⁴For I will be to Ephraim as a lion, and as a young lion to the house of Judah: I, even I, will tear and go away; I will take away, and none shall rescue him. ¹⁵I will go and return to my place, till they acknowledge their offense, and seek my face: in their affliction they will seek me early.

6 ¹Come, and let us return to the LORD: for he has torn, and he will heal us; he has smitten, and he will bind us up. ²After two days will he revive us: in the third day he will raise us up, and we shall live in his sight. ³Then shall we know, if we follow on to know the LORD: his going forth is prepared as the morning; and he shall come to us as the rain, as the latter and former rain to the earth. ⁴O Ephraim, what shall I do to you? O Judah, what shall I do to you? for your goodness is as a morning cloud, and as the early dew it goes away. ⁵Therefore have I hewed them by the prophets; I have slain them by the words of my mouth: and your judgments are as the light that goes forth. ⁶For I desired mercy, and not sacrifice; and the knowledge of God more than burnt offerings. ⁷But they like men have transgressed the covenant: there have they dealt treacherously against me. ⁸Gilead is a city of them that work iniquity, and is polluted with blood. ⁹And as troops of robbers wait for a man, so the company of priests murder in the way by consent: for they commit lewdness. ¹⁰I have seen an horrible thing in the house of Israel: there is the prostitution of Ephraim, Israel is defiled. ¹¹Also, O Judah, he has set an harvest for you, when I returned the captivity of my people.

7 ¹When I would have healed Israel, then the iniquity of Ephraim was discovered, and the wickedness of Samaria: for they commit falsehood; and the thief comes in, and the troop of robbers spoils without. ²And they consider not in their hearts that I remember all their wickedness: now their own doings have beset them about; they are before my face. ³They make the king glad with their wickedness, and the princes with their lies. ⁴They are all adulterers, as an oven heated by the baker, who ceases from raising after he has kneaded the dough, until it be leavened. ⁵In the day of our king the princes have made him sick with bottles of wine; he stretched out his hand with scorners. ⁶For they have made ready their heart like an oven, whiles they lie in wait: their baker sleeps all the night; in the morning it burns as a flaming fire. ⁷They are all hot as an oven, and have devoured their judges; all their kings are fallen: there is none among them that calls to me. ⁸Ephraim, he has mixed himself among the people; Ephraim is a cake not turned. ⁹Strangers have devoured his strength, and he knows it not: yes, gray hairs are here and there on him, yet he knows not. ¹⁰And the pride of Israel testifies to his face: and they do not return to the LORD their God, nor seek him for all this. ¹¹Ephraim also is like a silly dove without heart: they call to Egypt, they go to Assyria. ¹²When they shall go, I will spread my net on them; I will bring them down as the fowls of the heaven; I will chastise them, as their congregation has heard. ¹³Woe to them! for they have fled from me: destruction to them! because they have transgressed against me: though I have redeemed them, yet they have spoken lies against me.

[14] And they have not cried to me with their heart, when they howled on their beds: they assemble themselves for corn and wine, and they rebel against me. [15] Though I have bound and strengthened their arms, yet do they imagine mischief against me. [16] They return, but not to the most High: they are like a deceitful bow: their princes shall fall by the sword for the rage of their tongue: this shall be their derision in the land of Egypt.

8 [1] Set the trumpet to your mouth. He shall come as an eagle against the house of the LORD, because they have transgressed my covenant, and trespassed against my law. [2] Israel shall cry to me, My God, we know you. [3] Israel has cast off the thing that is good: the enemy shall pursue him. [4] They have set up kings, but not by me: they have made princes, and I knew it not: of their silver and their gold have they made them idols, that they may be cut off. [5] Your calf, O Samaria, has cast you off; my anger is kindled against them: how long will it be before they attain to innocence? [6] For from Israel was it also: the workman made it; therefore it is not God: but the calf of Samaria shall be broken in pieces. [7] For they have sown the wind, and they shall reap the whirlwind: it has no stalk; the bud shall yield no meal: if so be it yield, the strangers shall swallow it up. [8] Israel is swallowed up: now shall they be among the Gentiles as a vessel wherein is no pleasure. [9] For they are gone up to Assyria, a wild ass alone by himself: Ephraim has hired lovers. [10] Yes, though they have hired among the nations, now will I gather them, and they shall sorrow a little for the burden of the king of princes. [11] Because Ephraim has made many altars to sin, altars shall be to him to sin. [12] I have written to him the great things of my law, but they were counted as a strange thing. [13] They sacrifice flesh for the sacrifices of my offerings, and eat it; but the LORD accepts them not; now will he remember their iniquity, and visit their sins: they shall return to Egypt. [14] For Israel has forgotten his Maker, and builds temples; and Judah has multiplied fenced cities: but I will send a fire on his cities, and it shall devour the palaces thereof.

9 [1] Rejoice not, O Israel, for joy, as other people: for you have gone a whoring from your God, you have loved a reward on every corn floor. [2] The floor and the wine press shall not feed them, and the new wine shall fail in her. [3] They shall not dwell in the LORD's land; but Ephraim shall return to Egypt, and they shall eat unclean things in Assyria. [4] They shall not offer wine offerings to the LORD, neither shall they be pleasing to him: their sacrifices shall be to them as the bread of mourners; all that eat thereof shall be polluted: for their bread for their soul shall not come into the house of the LORD. [5] What will you do in the solemn day, and in the day of the feast of the LORD? [6] For, see, they are gone because of destruction: Egypt shall gather them up, Memphis shall bury them: the pleasant places for their silver, nettles shall possess them: thorns shall be in their tabernacles. [7] The days of visitation are come, the days of recompense are come; Israel shall know it: the prophet is a fool, the spiritual man is mad, for the multitude of your iniquity, and the great hatred. [8] The watchman of Ephraim was with my God: but the prophet is a snare of a fowler in all his ways, and hatred in the house of his God. [9] They have deeply corrupted themselves, as in the days of Gibeah: therefore he will remember their iniquity, he will visit their sins. [10] I found Israel like grapes in the wilderness; I saw your fathers as the first ripe in the fig tree at her first time: but they went to Baalpeor, and separated themselves to that shame; and their abominations were according as they loved. [11] As for Ephraim, their glory shall fly away like a bird, from the birth, and from the womb, and from the conception. [12] Though they bring up their children, yet will I bereave them, that there shall not be a man left: yes, woe also to them when I depart from them! [13] Ephraim, as I saw Tyrus, is planted in a pleasant place: but Ephraim shall bring forth his children to the murderer. [14] Give them, O LORD: what will you give? give them a miscarrying womb and dry breasts. [15] All their wickedness is in Gilgal: for there I hated them: for the wickedness of their doings I will drive them out of my house, I will love them no more: all their princes are rebels. [16] Ephraim is smitten, their root is dried up, they shall bear no fruit: yes, though they bring forth, yet will I slay even the beloved fruit of their womb. [17] My God will cast them away, because they did not listen to him: and they shall be wanderers among the nations.

10 [1] Israel is an empty vine, he brings forth fruit to himself: according to the multitude of his fruit he has increased the altars; according to the goodness of his land they have made goodly images. [2] Their heart is divided; now shall they be found faulty: he shall break down their altars, he shall spoil their images. [3] For now they shall say, We have no king, because we feared not the LORD; what then should a king do to us? [4] They have spoken words, swearing falsely in making a covenant: thus judgment springs up as hemlock in the furrows of the field. [5] The inhabitants of Samaria shall fear because of the calves of Bethaven: for the people thereof shall mourn over it, and the priests thereof that rejoiced on it, for the glory thereof, because it is departed from it. [6] It shall be also carried to Assyria for a present to king Jareb: Ephraim shall receive shame, and Israel shall be ashamed of his own counsel. [7] As for Samaria, her king is cut off as the foam on the water. [8] The high places also of Aven, the sin of Israel, shall be destroyed: the thorn and the thistle shall come up on their altars; and they shall say to the mountains, Cover us; and to the hills, Fall on us. [9] O Israel, you have sinned from the days of Gibeah: there they stood: the battle in Gibeah against the children of iniquity did not overtake them. [10] It is in my desire that I should chastise them; and the people shall be gathered against them, when they shall bind themselves in their two furrows. [11] And Ephraim is as an heifer that is taught, and loves to tread out the corn; but I passed over on her fair neck: I will make Ephraim to ride; Judah shall plow, and Jacob shall break his clods. [12] Sow to yourselves in righteousness, reap in mercy; break up your fallow ground: for it is time to seek the LORD, till he come and rain righteousness on you. [13] You have plowed wickedness, you have reaped iniquity; you have eaten the fruit of lies: because you did trust in your way, in the multitude of your mighty men. [14] Therefore shall a tumult arise among your people, and all your fortresses shall be spoiled, as Shalman spoiled Betharbel in the day of battle: the mother was dashed in pieces on her children. [15] So shall Bethel do to you because of your great wickedness: in a morning shall the king of Israel utterly be cut off.

11

¹When Israel was a child, then I loved him, and called my son out of Egypt. ²As they called them, so they went from them: they sacrificed to Baalim, and burned incense to graven images. ³I taught Ephraim also to go, taking them by their arms; but they knew not that I healed them. ⁴I drew them with cords of a man, with bands of love: and I was to them as they that take off the yoke on their jaws, and I laid meat to them. ⁵He shall not return into the land of Egypt, and the Assyrian shall be his king, because they refused to return. ⁶And the sword shall abide on his cities, and shall consume his branches, and devour them, because of their own counsels. ⁷And my people are bent to backsliding from me: though they called them to the most High, none at all would exalt him. ⁸How shall I give you up, Ephraim? how shall I deliver you, Israel? how shall I make you as Admah? how shall I set you as Zeboim? my heart is turned within me, my repentings are kindled together. ⁹I will not execute the fierceness of my anger, I will not return to destroy Ephraim: for I am God, and not man; the Holy One in the middle of you: and I will not enter into the city. ¹⁰They shall walk after the LORD: he shall roar like a lion: when he shall roar, then the children shall tremble from the west. ¹¹They shall tremble as a bird out of Egypt, and as a dove out of the land of Assyria: and I will place them in their houses, says the LORD. ¹²Ephraim compasses me about with lies, and the house of Israel with deceit: but Judah yet rules with God, and is faithful with the saints.

12

¹Ephraim feeds on wind, and follows after the east wind: he daily increases lies and desolation; and they do make a covenant with the Assyrians, and oil is carried into Egypt. ²The LORD has also a controversy with Judah, and will punish Jacob according to his ways; according to his doings will he recompense him. ³He took his brother by the heel in the womb, and by his strength he had power with God: ⁴Yes, he had power over the angel, and prevailed: he wept, and made supplication to him: he found him in Bethel, and there he spoke with us; ⁵Even the LORD God of hosts; the LORD is his memorial. ⁶Therefore turn you to your God: keep mercy and judgment and wait on your God continually. ⁷He is a merchant, the balances of deceit are in his hand: he loves to oppress. ⁸And Ephraim said, Yet I am become rich, I have found me out substance: in all my labors they shall find none iniquity in me that were sin. ⁹And I that am the LORD your God from the land of Egypt will yet make you to dwell in tabernacles, as in the days of the solemn feast. ¹⁰I have also spoken by the prophets, and I have multiplied visions, and used similitudes, by the ministry of the prophets. ¹¹Is there iniquity in Gilead? surely they are vanity: they sacrifice bullocks in Gilgal; yes, their altars are as heaps in the furrows of the fields. ¹²And Jacob fled into the country of Syria, and Israel served for a wife, and for a wife he kept sheep. ¹³And by a prophet the LORD brought Israel out of Egypt, and by a prophet was he preserved. ¹⁴Ephraim provoked him to anger most bitterly: therefore shall he leave his blood on him, and his reproach shall his LORD return to him.

13

¹When Ephraim spoke trembling, he exalted himself in Israel; but when he offended in Baal, he died. ²And now they sin more and more, and have made them molten images of their silver, and idols according to their own understanding, all of it the work of the craftsmen: they say of them, Let the men that sacrifice kiss the calves. ³Therefore they shall be as the morning cloud and as the early dew that passes away, as the chaff that is driven with the whirlwind out of the floor, and as the smoke out of the chimney. ⁴Yet I am the LORD your God from the land of Egypt, and you shall know no god but me: for there is no savior beside me. ⁵I did know you in the wilderness, in the land of great drought. ⁶According to their pasture, so were they filled; they were filled, and their heart was exalted; therefore have they forgotten me. ⁷Therefore I will be to them as a lion: as a leopard by the way will I observe them: ⁸I will meet them as a bear that is bereaved of her whelps, and will rend the lobe of their heart, and there will I devour them like a lion: the wild beast shall tear them. ⁹O Israel, you have destroyed yourself; but in me is your help. ¹⁰I will be your king: where is any other that may save you in all your cities? and your judges of whom you said, Give me a king and princes? ¹¹I gave you a king in my anger, and took him away in my wrath. ¹²The iniquity of Ephraim is bound up; his sin is hid. ¹³The sorrows of a travailing woman shall come on him: he is an unwise son; for he should not stay long in the place of the breaking forth of children. ¹⁴I will ransom them from the power of the grave; I will redeem them from death: O death, I will be your plagues; O grave, I will be your destruction: repentance shall be hid from my eyes. ¹⁵Though he be fruitful among his brothers, an east wind shall come, the wind of the LORD shall come up from the wilderness, and his spring shall become dry, and his fountain shall be dried up: he shall spoil the treasure of all pleasant vessels. ¹⁶Samaria shall become desolate; for she has rebelled against her God: they shall fall by the sword: their infants shall be dashed in pieces, and their women with child shall be ripped up.

14

¹O Israel, return to the LORD your God; for you have fallen by your iniquity. ²Take with you words, and turn to the LORD: say to him, Take away all iniquity, and receive us graciously: so will we render the calves of our lips. ³Asshur shall not save us; we will not ride on horses: neither will we say any more to the work of our hands, You are our gods: for in you the fatherless finds mercy. ⁴I will heal their backsliding, I will love them freely: for my anger is turned away from him. ⁵I will be as the dew to Israel: he shall grow as the lily, and cast forth his roots as Lebanon. ⁶His branches shall spread, and his beauty shall be as the olive tree, and his smell as Lebanon. ⁷They that dwell under his shadow shall return; they shall revive as the corn, and grow as the vine: the scent thereof shall be as the wine of Lebanon. ⁸Ephraim shall say, What have I to do any more with idols? I have heard him, and observed him: I am like a green fir tree. From me is your fruit found. ⁹Who is wise, and he shall understand these things? prudent, and he shall know them? for the ways of the LORD are right, and the just shall walk in them: but the transgressors shall fall therein.

Joel

1 ¹The word of the LORD that came to Joel the son of Pethuel. ²Hear this, you old men, and give ear, all you inhabitants of the land. Has this been in your days, or even in the days of your fathers? ³Tell you your children of it, and let your children tell their children, and their children another generation. ⁴That which the palmerworm has left has the locust eaten; and that which the locust has left has the cankerworm eaten; and that which the cankerworm has left has the caterpillar eaten. ⁵Awake, you drunkards, and weep; and howl, all you drinkers of wine, because of the new wine; for it is cut off from your mouth. ⁶For a nation is come up on my land, strong, and without number, whose teeth are the teeth of a lion, and he has the cheek teeth of a great lion. ⁷He has laid my vine waste, and barked my fig tree: he has made it clean bore, and cast it away; the branches thereof are made white. ⁸Lament like a virgin girded with sackcloth for the husband of her youth. ⁹The meat offering and the drink offering is cut off from the house of the LORD; the priests, the LORD's ministers, mourn. ¹⁰The field is wasted, the land mourns; for the corn is wasted: the new wine is dried up, the oil languishes. ¹¹Be you ashamed, O you farmers; howl, O you vinedressers, for the wheat and for the barley; because the harvest of the field is perished. ¹²The vine is dried up, and the fig tree languishes; the pomegranate tree, the palm tree also, and the apple tree, even all the trees of the field, are withered: because joy is withered away from the sons of men. ¹³Gird yourselves, and lament, you priests: howl, you ministers of the altar: come, lie all night in sackcloth, you ministers of my God: for the meat offering and the drink offering is withheld from the house of your God. ¹⁴Sanctify you a fast, call a solemn assembly, gather the elders and all the inhabitants of the land into the house of the LORD your God, and cry to the LORD, ¹⁵Alas for the day! for the day of the LORD is at hand, and as a destruction from the Almighty shall it come. ¹⁶Is not the meat cut off before our eyes, yes, joy and gladness from the house of our God? ¹⁷The seed is rotten under their clods, the garners are laid desolate, the barns are broken down; for the corn is withered. ¹⁸How do the beasts groan! the herds of cattle are perplexed, because they have no pasture; yes, the flocks of sheep are made desolate. ¹⁹O LORD, to you will I cry: for the fire has devoured the pastures of the wilderness, and the flame has burned all the trees of the field. ²⁰The beasts of the field cry also to you: for the rivers of waters are dried up, and the fire has devoured the pastures of the wilderness.

2 ¹Blow you the trumpet in Zion, and sound an alarm in my holy mountain: let all the inhabitants of the land tremble: for the day of the LORD comes, for it is near at hand; ²A day of darkness and of gloominess, a day of clouds and of thick darkness, as the morning spread on the mountains: a great people and a strong; there has not been ever the like, neither shall be any more after it, even to the years of many generations. ³A fire devours before them; and behind them a flame burns: the land is as the garden of Eden before them, and behind them a desolate wilderness; yes, and nothing shall escape them. ⁴The appearance of them is as the appearance of horses; and as horsemen, so shall they run. ⁵Like the noise of chariots on the tops of mountains shall they leap, like the noise of a flame of fire that devours the stubble, as a strong people set in battle array. ⁶Before their face the people shall be much pained: all faces shall gather blackness. ⁷They shall run like mighty men; they shall climb the wall like men of war; and they shall march every one on his ways, and they shall not break their ranks: ⁸Neither shall one thrust another; they shall walk every one in his path: and when they fall on the sword, they shall not be wounded. ⁹They shall run to and fro in the city; they shall run on the wall, they shall climb up on the houses; they shall enter in at the windows like a thief. ¹⁰The earth shall quake before them; the heavens shall tremble: the sun and the moon shall be dark, and the stars shall withdraw their shining: ¹¹And the LORD shall utter his voice before his army: for his camp is very great: for he is strong that executes his word: for the day of the LORD is great and very terrible; and who can abide it? ¹²Therefore also now, says the LORD, turn you even to me with all your heart, and with fasting, and with weeping, and with mourning: ¹³And rend your heart, and not your garments, and turn to the LORD your God: for he is gracious and merciful, slow to anger, and of great kindness, and repents him of the evil. ¹⁴Who knows if he will return and repent, and leave a blessing behind him; even a meat offering and a drink offering to the LORD your God? ¹⁵Blow the trumpet in Zion, sanctify a fast, call a solemn assembly: ¹⁶Gather the people, sanctify the congregation, assemble the elders, gather the children, and those that suck the breasts: let the bridegroom go forth of his chamber, and the bride out of her closet. ¹⁷Let the priests, the ministers of the LORD, weep between the porch and the altar, and let them say, Spare your people, O LORD, and give not your heritage to reproach, that the heathen should rule over them: why should they say among the people, Where is their God? ¹⁸Then will the LORD be jealous for his land, and pity his people. ¹⁹Yes, the LORD will answer and say to his people, Behold, I will send you corn, and wine, and oil, and you shall be satisfied therewith: and I will no more make you a reproach among the heathen: ²⁰But I will remove far off from you the northern army, and will drive him into a land barren and desolate, with his face toward the east sea, and his hinder part toward the utmost sea, and his stink shall come up, and his ill smell shall come up, because he has done great things. ²¹Fear not, O land; be glad and rejoice: for the LORD will do great things. ²²Be not afraid, you beasts of the field: for the pastures of the wilderness do spring, for the tree bears her fruit, the fig tree and the vine do yield their strength. ²³Be glad then, you children of Zion, and rejoice in the LORD your God: for he has given you the former rain moderately, and he will cause to come down for you the rain, the former rain, and the latter rain in the first month. ²⁴And the floors shall be full of wheat, and the vats shall overflow with wine and oil. ²⁵And I will restore to you the years that the locust has eaten, the cankerworm, and the caterpillar, and the palmerworm, my great army which I sent among you. ²⁶And you shall eat in plenty, and be satisfied, and praise the name of the LORD your God, that has dealt wondrously with you: and my people shall never be ashamed. ²⁷And you shall know that I am in the middle of Israel, and that I am the LORD your God, and none else: and my people shall never be ashamed. ²⁸And it shall come to pass afterward, that I will pour out my spirit on all flesh; and your sons and your daughters shall prophesy, your old men shall dream dreams, your young men shall see visions: ²⁹And also on the servants and on the handmaids in those days will I pour out my spirit. ³⁰And I will show wonders in the heavens and in the earth, blood, and fire, and pillars of smoke. ³¹The sun shall be turned into darkness, and the moon into blood, before the great and terrible day of the LORD come. ³²And it shall come to pass, that whoever shall call on the name of the LORD shall be delivered: for in mount Zion and in Jerusalem shall be deliverance, as the LORD has said, and in the remnant whom the LORD shall call.

3 ¹For, behold, in those days, and in that time, when I shall bring again the captivity of Judah and Jerusalem, ²I will also gather all nations, and will bring them down into the valley of Jehoshaphat, and will plead with them there for my people and for my heritage Israel, whom they have scattered among the nations, and parted my land. ³And they have cast lots for my people; and have given a boy for an harlot, and sold a girl for wine, that they might drink. ⁴Yes, and what have you to do with me, O Tyre, and Zidon, and all the coasts of Palestine? will you render me a recompense? and if you recompense me, swiftly and speedily will I return your recompense on your own head; ⁵Because you have taken my silver and my gold, and have carried into your temples my goodly pleasant things: ⁶The children also of Judah and the children of Jerusalem have you sold to the Grecians, that you might remove them far from their border. ⁷Behold, I will raise them out of the place where you have sold them, and will return your recompense on your own head: ⁸And I will sell your sons and your daughters into the hand of the children of Judah, and they shall sell them to the Sabeans, to a people far off: for the LORD has spoken it. ⁹Proclaim you this among the Gentiles; Prepare war, wake up the mighty men, let all the men of war draw near; let them come up: ¹⁰Beat your plowshares into swords and your pruning hooks into spears: let the weak say, I am strong. ¹¹Assemble yourselves, and come, all you heathen, and gather yourselves together round about: thither cause your mighty ones to come down, O LORD. ¹²Let the heathen be wakened, and come up to the valley of Jehoshaphat: for there will I sit to judge all the heathen round about. ¹³Put you in the sickle, for the harvest is ripe: come, get you down; for the press is full, the fats overflow; for their wickedness is great. ¹⁴Multitudes, multitudes in the valley of decision: for the day of the LORD is near in the valley of decision. ¹⁵The sun and the moon shall be darkened, and the stars shall withdraw their shining. ¹⁶The LORD also shall roar out of Zion, and utter his voice from Jerusalem; and the heavens and the earth shall shake: but the LORD will be the hope of his people, and the strength of the children of Israel. ¹⁷So shall you know that I am the LORD your God dwelling in Zion, my holy mountain: then shall Jerusalem be holy, and there shall no strangers pass through her any more. ¹⁸And it shall come to pass in that day, that the mountains shall drop down new wine, and the hills shall flow with milk, and all the rivers of Judah shall flow with waters, and a fountain shall come forth out of the house of the LORD, and shall water the valley of Shittim. ¹⁹Egypt shall be a desolation, and Edom shall be a desolate wilderness, for the violence against the children of Judah, because they have shed innocent blood in their land. ²⁰But Judah shall dwell for ever, and Jerusalem from generation to generation. ²¹For I will cleanse their blood that I have not cleansed: for the LORD dwells in Zion.

Amos

1 ¹The words of Amos, who was among the herdsmen of Tekoa, which he saw concerning Israel in the days of Uzziah king of Judah, and in the days of Jeroboam the son of Joash king of Israel, two years before the earthquake. ²And he said, The LORD will roar from Zion, and utter his voice from Jerusalem; and the habitations of the shepherds shall mourn, and the top of Carmel shall wither. ³Thus says the LORD; For three transgressions of Damascus, and for four, I will not turn away the punishment thereof; because they have threshed Gilead with threshing instruments of iron: ⁴But I will send a fire into the house of Hazael, which shall devour the palaces of Benhadad. ⁵I will break also the bar of Damascus, and cut off the inhabitant from the plain of Aven, and him that holds the scepter from the house of Eden: and the people of Syria shall go into captivity to Kir, says the LORD. ⁶Thus says the LORD; For three transgressions of Gaza, and for four, I will not turn away the punishment thereof; because they carried away captive the whole captivity, to deliver them up to Edom: ⁷But I will send a fire on the wall of Gaza, which shall devour the palaces thereof: ⁸And I will cut off the inhabitant from Ashdod, and him that holds the scepter from Ashkelon, and I will turn my hand against Ekron: and the remnant of the Philistines shall perish, says the Lord GOD. ⁹Thus says the LORD; For three transgressions of Tyrus, and for four, I will not turn away the punishment thereof; because they delivered up the whole captivity to Edom, and remembered not the brotherly covenant: ¹⁰But I will send a fire on the wall of Tyrus, which shall devour the palaces thereof. ¹¹Thus says the LORD; For three transgressions of Edom, and for four, I will not turn away the punishment thereof; because he did pursue his brother with the sword, and did cast off all pity, and his anger did tear perpetually, and he kept his wrath for ever: ¹²But I will send a fire on Teman, which shall devour the palaces of Bozrah. ¹³Thus says the LORD; For three transgressions of the children of Ammon, and for four, I will not turn away the punishment thereof; because they have ripped up the women with child of Gilead, that they might enlarge their border: ¹⁴But I will kindle a fire in the wall of Rabbah, and it shall devour the palaces thereof, with shouting in the day of battle, with a tempest in the day of the whirlwind: ¹⁵And their king shall go into captivity, he and his princes together, said the LORD.

2 ¹Thus says the LORD; For three transgressions of Moab, and for four, I will not turn away the punishment thereof; because he burned the bones of the king of Edom into lime: ²But I will send a fire on Moab, and it shall devour the palaces of Kirioth: and Moab shall die with tumult, with shouting, and with the sound of the trumpet: ³And I will cut off the judge from the middle thereof, and will slay all the princes thereof with him, says the LORD. ⁴Thus says the LORD; For three transgressions of Judah, and for four, I will not turn away the punishment thereof; because they have despised the law of the LORD, and have not kept his commandments, and their lies caused them to err, after the which their fathers have walked: ⁵But I will send a fire on Judah, and it shall devour the palaces of Jerusalem. ⁶Thus says the LORD; For three transgressions of Israel, and for four, I will not turn away the punishment thereof; because they sold the righteous for silver, and the poor for a pair of shoes; ⁷That pant after the dust of the earth on the head of the poor, and turn aside the way of the meek: and a man and his father will go in to the same maid, to profane my holy name: ⁸And they lay themselves down on clothes laid to pledge by every altar, and they drink the wine of the condemned in the house of their god. ⁹Yet destroyed I the Amorite before them, whose height was like the height of the cedars, and he was strong as the oaks; yet I destroyed his fruit from above, and his roots from beneath. ¹⁰Also I brought you up from the land of Egypt, and led you forty years through the wilderness, to possess the land of the Amorite. ¹¹And I raised up of your sons for prophets, and of your young men for Nazarites. Is it not even thus, O you children of Israel? says the LORD. ¹²But you gave the Nazarites wine to drink; and commanded the prophets, saying, Prophesy not. ¹³Behold, I am pressed under you, as a cart is pressed that is full of sheaves. ¹⁴Therefore the flight shall perish from the swift, and the strong shall not strengthen his force, neither shall the mighty deliver himself: ¹⁵Neither shall he stand that handles the bow; and he that is swift of foot shall not deliver himself: neither shall he that rides the horse deliver himself. ¹⁶And he that is courageous among the mighty shall flee away naked in that day, says the LORD.

3 ¹Hear this word that the LORD has spoken against you, O children of Israel, against the whole family which I brought up from the land of Egypt, saying, ²You only have I known of all the families of the earth: therefore I will punish you for all your iniquities. ³Can two walk together, except they be agreed? ⁴Will a lion roar in the forest, when he has no prey? will a young lion cry out of his den, if he have taken nothing? ⁵Can a bird fall in a snare on the earth, where no gin is for him? shall one take up a snare from the earth, and have taken nothing at all? ⁶Shall a trumpet be blown in the city, and the people not be afraid? shall there be evil in a city, and the LORD has not done it? ⁷Surely the Lord GOD will do nothing, but he reveals his secret to his servants the prophets. ⁸The lion has roared, who will not fear? the Lord GOD has spoken, who can but prophesy? ⁹Publish in the palaces at Ashdod, and in the palaces in the land of Egypt, and say, Assemble yourselves on the mountains of Samaria, and behold the great tumults in the middle thereof, and the oppressed in the middle thereof. ¹⁰For they know not to do right, says the LORD, who store up violence and robbery in their palaces. ¹¹Therefore thus says the Lord GOD; An adversary there shall be even round about the land; and he shall bring down your strength from you, and your palaces shall be spoiled. ¹²Thus says the LORD; As the shepherd takes out of the mouth of the lion two legs, or a piece of an ear; so shall the children of Israel be taken out that dwell in Samaria in the corner of a bed, and in Damascus in a couch. ¹³Hear you, and testify in the house of Jacob, says the Lord GOD, the God of hosts, ¹⁴That in the day that I shall visit the transgressions of Israel on him I will also visit the altars of Bethel: and the horns of the altar shall be cut off, and fall to the ground. ¹⁵And I will smite the winter house with the summer house; and the houses of ivory shall perish, and the great houses shall have an end, says the LORD.

4 ¹Hear this word, you cows of Bashan, that are in the mountain of Samaria, which oppress the poor, which crush the needy, which say to their masters, Bring, and let us drink. ²The Lord GOD has sworn by his holiness, that, see, the days shall come on you, that he will take you away with hooks, and your posterity with fishhooks. ³And you shall go out at the breaches, every cow at that which is before her; and you shall cast them into the palace, says the LORD. ⁴Come to Bethel, and transgress; at Gilgal multiply transgression; and bring your sacrifices every morning, and your tithes after three years: ⁵And offer a sacrifice of thanksgiving with leaven, and proclaim and publish the free offerings: for this likes you, O you children of Israel, says the Lord GOD. ⁶And I also have given you cleanness of teeth in all your cities, and want of bread in all your places: yet have you not returned to me, says the LORD. ⁷And also I have withheld the rain from you, when there were yet three months to the harvest: and I caused it to rain on one city, and caused it not to rain on another city: one piece was rained on, and the piece whereupon it rained not withered. ⁸So two or three cities wandered to one city, to drink water; but they were not satisfied: yet have you not returned to me, says the LORD. ⁹I have smitten you with blasting and mildew: when your gardens and your vineyards and your fig trees and your olive trees increased, the palmerworm devoured them: yet have you not returned to me, says the LORD. ¹⁰I have sent among you the pestilence after the manner of Egypt: your young men have I slain with the sword, and have taken away your horses; and I have made the stink of your camps to come up to your nostrils: yet have you not returned to me, says the LORD. ¹¹I have overthrown some of you, as God overthrew Sodom and Gomorrah, and you were as a firebrand plucked out of the burning: yet have you not returned to me, says the LORD. ¹²Therefore thus will I do to you, O Israel: and because I will do this to you, prepare to meet your God, O Israel. ¹³For, see, he that forms the mountains, and creates the wind, and declares to man what is his thought, that makes the morning darkness, and treads on the high places of the earth, The LORD, The God of hosts, is his name.

5 ¹Hear you this word which I take up against you, even a lamentation, O house of Israel. ²The virgin of Israel is fallen; she shall no more rise: she is forsaken on her land; there is none to raise her up. ³For thus says the Lord GOD; The city that went out by a thousand shall leave an hundred, and that which went forth by an hundred shall leave ten, to the house of Israel. ⁴For thus says the LORD to the house of Israel, Seek you me, and you shall live: ⁵But seek not Bethel, nor enter into Gilgal, and pass not to Beersheba: for Gilgal shall surely go into captivity, and Bethel shall come to nothing. ⁶Seek the LORD, and you shall live; lest he break out like fire in the house of Joseph, and devour it, and there be none to quench it in Bethel. ⁷You who turn judgment to wormwood, and leave off righteousness in the earth, ⁸Seek him that makes the seven stars and Orion, and turns the shadow of death into the morning, and makes the day dark with night: that calls for the waters of the sea, and pours them out on the face of the earth: The LORD is his name: ⁹That strengthens the spoiled against the strong, so that the spoiled shall come against the fortress. ¹⁰They hate him that rebukes in the gate, and they abhor him that speaks uprightly. ¹¹For as much therefore as your treading is on the poor, and you take from him burdens of wheat: you have built houses of hewn stone, but you shall not dwell in them; you have planted pleasant vineyards, but you shall not drink wine of them. ¹²For I know your manifold transgressions and your mighty sins: they afflict the just, they take a bribe, and they turn aside the poor in the gate from their right. ¹³Therefore the prudent shall keep silence in that time; for it is an evil time. ¹⁴Seek good, and not evil, that you may live: and so the LORD, the God of hosts, shall be with you, as you have spoken. ¹⁵Hate the evil, and love the good, and establish judgment in the gate: it may be that the LORD God of hosts will be gracious to the remnant of Joseph. ¹⁶Therefore the LORD, the God of hosts, the LORD, says thus; Wailing shall be in all streets; and they shall say in all the highways, Alas! alas! and they shall call the farmer to mourning, and such as are skillful of lamentation to wailing. ¹⁷And in all vineyards shall be wailing: for I will pass through you, says the LORD. ¹⁸Woe to you that desire the day of the LORD! to what end is it for you? the day of the LORD is darkness, and not light. ¹⁹As if a man did flee from a lion, and a bear met him; or went into the house, and leaned his hand on the wall, and a serpent bit him. ²⁰Shall not the day of the LORD be darkness, and not light? even very dark, and no brightness in it? ²¹I hate, I despise your feast days, and I will not smell in your solemn assemblies. ²²Though you offer me burnt offerings and your meat offerings, I will not accept them: neither will I regard the peace offerings of your fat beasts. ²³Take you away from me the noise of your songs; for I will not hear the melody of your viols. ²⁴But let judgment run down as waters, and righteousness as a mighty stream. ²⁵Have you offered to me sacrifices and offerings in the wilderness forty years, O house of Israel? ²⁶But you have borne the tabernacle of your Moloch and Chiun your images, the star of your god, which you made to yourselves. ²⁷Therefore will I cause you to go into captivity beyond Damascus, says the LORD, whose name is The God of hosts.

6 ¹Woe to them that are at ease in Zion, and trust in the mountain of Samaria, which are named chief of the nations, to whom the house of Israel came! ²Pass you to Calneh, and see; and from there go you to Hamath the great: then go down to Gath of the Philistines: be they better than these kingdoms? or their border greater than your border? ³You that put far away the evil day, and cause the seat of violence to come near; ⁴That lie on beds of ivory, and stretch themselves on their couches, and eat the lambs out of the flock, and the calves out of the middle of the stall; ⁵That chant to the sound of the viol, and invent to themselves instruments of music, like David; ⁶That drink wine in bowls, and anoint themselves with the chief ointments: but they are not grieved for the affliction of Joseph. ⁷Therefore now shall they go captive with the first that go captive, and the banquet of them that stretched themselves shall be removed. ⁸The Lord GOD has sworn by himself, says the LORD the God of hosts, I abhor the excellency of Jacob, and hate his palaces: therefore will I deliver up the city with all that is therein. ⁹And it shall come to pass, if there remain ten men in one house, that they shall die. ¹⁰And a man's uncle shall take him up, and he that burns him, to bring out the bones out of the house, and shall say to him that is by the sides of the house, Is there yet any with you? and he shall say, No. Then shall he say, Hold your tongue: for we may not make mention of the name of the LORD. ¹¹For, behold, the LORD commands, and he will smite the great house with breaches, and the little house with clefts. ¹²Shall horses run on the rock? will one plow there with oxen? for you have turned judgment into gall, and the fruit of righteousness into hemlock: ¹³You which rejoice in a thing of nothing, which say, Have we not taken to us horns by our own strength? ¹⁴But, behold, I will raise up against you a nation, O house of Israel, says the LORD the God of hosts; and they shall afflict you from the entering in of Hemath to the river of the wilderness.

7 ¹Thus has the Lord GOD showed to me; and, behold, he formed grasshoppers in the beginning of the shooting up of the latter growth; and, see, it was the latter growth after the king's mowings. ²And it came to pass, that when they had made an end of eating the grass of the land, then I said, O Lord GOD, forgive, I beseech you: by whom shall Jacob arise? for he is small. ³The LORD repented for this: It shall not be, says the LORD. ⁴Thus has the Lord GOD showed to me: and, behold, the Lord GOD called to contend by fire, and it devoured the great deep, and did eat up a part. ⁵Then said I, O Lord GOD, cease, I beseech you: by whom shall Jacob arise? for he is small. ⁶The LORD repented for this: This also shall not be, says the Lord GOD. ⁷Thus he showed me: and, behold, the LORD stood on a wall made by a plumb line, with a plumb line in his hand. ⁸And the LORD said to me, Amos, what see you? And I said, A plumb line. Then said the LORD, Behold, I will set a plumb line in the middle of my people Israel: I will not again pass by them any more: ⁹And the high places of Isaac shall be desolate, and the sanctuaries of Israel shall be laid waste; and I will rise against the house of Jeroboam with the sword. ¹⁰Then Amaziah the priest of Bethel sent to Jeroboam king of Israel, saying, Amos has conspired against you in the middle of the house of Israel: the land is not able to bear all his words. ¹¹For thus Amos says, Jeroboam shall die by the sword, and Israel shall surely be led away captive out of their own land. ¹²Also Amaziah said to Amos, O you seer, go, flee you away into the land of Judah, and there eat bread, and prophesy there: ¹³But prophesy not again any more at Bethel: for it is the king's chapel, and it is the king's court. ¹⁴Then answered Amos, and said to Amaziah, I was no prophet, neither was I a prophet's son; but I was an herdsman, and a gatherer of sycomore fruit: ¹⁵And the LORD took me as I followed the flock, and the LORD said to me, Go, prophesy to my people Israel. ¹⁶Now therefore hear you the word of the LORD: You say, Prophesy not against Israel, and drop not your word against the house of Isaac. ¹⁷Therefore thus says the LORD; Your wife shall be an harlot in the city, and your sons and your daughters shall fall by the sword, and your land shall be divided by line; and you shall die in a polluted land: and Israel shall surely go into captivity forth of his land.

8 ¹Thus has the Lord GOD showed to me: and behold a basket of summer fruit. ²And he said, Amos, what see you? And I said, A basket of summer fruit. Then said the LORD to me, The end is come on my people of Israel; I will not again pass by them any more. ³And the songs of the temple shall be howlings in that day, says the Lord GOD: there shall be many dead bodies in every place; they shall cast them forth with silence. ⁴Hear this, O you that swallow up the needy, even to make the poor of the land to fail, ⁵Saying, When will the new moon be gone, that we may sell corn? and the sabbath, that we may set forth wheat, making the ephah small, and the shekel great, and falsifying the balances by deceit? ⁶That we may buy the poor for silver, and the needy for a pair of shoes; yes, and sell the refuse of the wheat? ⁷The LORD has sworn by the excellency of Jacob, Surely I will never forget any of their works. ⁸Shall not the land tremble for this, and every one mourn that dwells therein? and it shall rise up wholly as a flood; and it shall be cast out and drowned, as by the flood of Egypt. ⁹And it shall come to pass in that day, says the Lord GOD, that I will cause the sun to go down at noon, and I will darken the earth in the clear day: ¹⁰And I will turn your feasts into mourning, and all your songs into lamentation; and I will bring up sackcloth on all loins, and baldness on every head; and I will make it as the mourning of an only son, and the end thereof as a bitter day. ¹¹Behold, the days come, says the Lord GOD, that I will send a famine in the land, not a famine of bread, nor a thirst for water, but of hearing the words of the LORD: ¹²And they shall wander from sea to sea, and from the north even to the east, they shall run to and fro to seek the word of the LORD, and shall not find it. ¹³In that day shall the fair virgins and young men faint for thirst. ¹⁴They that swear by the sin of Samaria, and say, Your god, O Dan, lives; and, The manner of Beersheba lives; even they shall fall, and never rise up again.

9 ¹I saw the LORD standing on the altar: and he said, Smite the lintel of the door, that the posts may shake: and cut them in the head, all of them; and I will slay the last of them with the sword: he that flees of them shall not flee away, and he that escapes of them shall not be delivered. ²Though they dig into hell, there shall my hand take them; though they climb up to heaven, there will I bring them down: ³And though they hide themselves in the top of Carmel, I will search and take them out there; and though they be hid from my sight in the bottom of the sea, there will I command the serpent, and he shall bite them: ⁴And though they go into captivity before their enemies, there will I command the sword, and it shall slay them: and I will set my eyes on them for evil, and not for good. ⁵And the Lord GOD of hosts is he that touches the land, and it shall melt, and all that dwell therein shall mourn: and it shall rise up wholly like a flood; and shall be drowned, as by the flood of Egypt. ⁶It is he that builds his stories in the heaven, and has founded his troop in the earth; he that calls for the waters of the sea, and pours them out on the face of the earth: The LORD is his name. ⁷Are you not as children of the Ethiopians to me, O children of Israel? says the LORD. Have not I brought up Israel out of the land of Egypt? and the Philistines from Caphtor, and the Syrians from Kir? ⁸Behold, the eyes of the Lord GOD are on the sinful kingdom, and I will destroy it from off the face of the earth; saving that I will not utterly destroy the house of Jacob, says the LORD. ⁹For, see, I will command, and I will sift the house of Israel among all nations, like as corn is sifted in a sieve, yet shall not the least grain fall on the earth. ¹⁰All the sinners of my people shall die by the sword, which say, The evil shall not overtake nor prevent us. ¹¹In that day will I raise up the tabernacle of David that is fallen, and close up the breaches thereof; and I will raise up his ruins, and I will build it as in the days of old: ¹²That they may possess the remnant of Edom, and of all the heathen, which are called by my name, says the LORD that does this. ¹³Behold, the days come, says the LORD, that the plowman shall overtake the reaper, and the treader of grapes him that sows seed; and the mountains shall drop sweet wine, and all the hills shall melt. ¹⁴And I will bring again the captivity of my people of Israel, and they shall build the waste cities, and inhabit them; and they shall plant vineyards, and drink the wine thereof; they shall also make gardens, and eat the fruit of them. ¹⁵And I will plant them on their land, and they shall no more be pulled up out of their land which I have given them, says the LORD your God.

Obadiah

1 ¹The vision of Obadiah. Thus says the Lord GOD concerning Edom; We have heard a rumor from the LORD, and an ambassador is sent among the heathen, Arise you, and let us rise up against her in battle. ²Behold, I have made you small among the heathen: you are greatly despised. ³The pride of your heart has deceived you, you that dwell in the clefts of the rock, whose habitation is high; that says in his heart, Who shall bring me down to the ground? ⁴Though you exalt yourself as the eagle, and though you set your nest among the stars, there will I bring you down, says the LORD. ⁵If thieves came to you, if robbers by night, (how are you cut off!) would they not have stolen till they had enough? if the grape gatherers came to you, would they not leave some grapes? ⁶How are the things of Esau searched out! how are his hidden things sought up! ⁷All the men of your confederacy have brought you even to the border: the men that were at peace with you have deceived you, and prevailed against you; that they eat your bread have laid a wound under you: there is none understanding in him. ⁸Shall I not in that day, says the LORD, even destroy the wise men out of Edom, and understanding out of the mount of Esau? ⁹And your mighty men, O Teman, shall be dismayed, to the end that every one of the mount of Esau may be cut off by slaughter. ¹⁰For your violence against your brother Jacob shame shall cover you, and you shall be cut off for ever. ¹¹In the day that you stood on the other side, in the day that the strangers carried away captive his forces, and foreigners entered into his gates, and cast lots on Jerusalem, even you were as one of them. ¹²But you should not have looked on the day of your brother in the day that he became a stranger; neither should you have rejoiced over the children of Judah in the day of their destruction; neither should you have spoken proudly in the day of distress. ¹³You should not have entered into the gate of my people in the day of their calamity; yes, you should not have looked on their affliction in the day of their calamity, nor have laid hands on their substance in the day of their calamity; ¹⁴Neither should you have stood in the crossway, to cut off those of his that did escape; neither should you have delivered up those of his that did remain in the day of distress. ¹⁵For the day of the LORD is near on all the heathen: as you have done, it shall be done to you: your reward shall return on your own head. ¹⁶For as you have drunk on my holy mountain, so shall all the heathen drink continually, yes, they shall drink, and they shall swallow down, and they shall be as though they had not been. ¹⁷But on mount Zion shall be deliverance, and there shall be holiness; and the house of Jacob shall possess their possessions. ¹⁸And the house of Jacob shall be a fire, and the house of Joseph a flame, and the house of Esau for stubble, and they shall kindle in them, and devour them; and there shall not be any remaining of the house of Esau; for the LORD has spoken it. ¹⁹And they of the south shall possess the mount of Esau; and they of the plain the Philistines: and they shall possess the fields of Ephraim, and the fields of Samaria: and Benjamin shall possess Gilead. ²⁰And the captivity of this host of the children of Israel shall possess that of the Canaanites, even to Zarephath; and the captivity of Jerusalem, which is in Sepharad, shall possess the cities of the south. ²¹And saviors shall come up on mount Zion to judge the mount of Esau; and the kingdom shall be the LORD's.

Jonah

1 ¹Now the word of the LORD came to Jonah the son of Amittai, saying, ²Arise, go to Nineveh, that great city, and cry against it; for their wickedness is come up before me. ³But Jonah rose up to flee to Tarshish from the presence of the LORD, and went down to Joppa; and he found a ship going to Tarshish: so he paid the fare thereof, and went down into it, to go with them to Tarshish from the presence of the LORD. ⁴But the LORD sent out a great wind into the sea, and there was a mighty tempest in the sea, so that the ship was like to be broken. ⁵Then the mariners were afraid, and cried every man to his god, and cast forth the wares that were in the ship into the sea, to lighten it of them. But Jonah was gone down into the sides of the ship; and he lay, and was fast asleep. ⁶So the shipmaster came to him, and said to him, What mean you, O sleeper? arise, call on your God, if so be that God will think on us, that we perish not. ⁷And they said every one to his fellow, Come, and let us cast lots, that we may know for whose cause this evil is on us. So they cast lots, and the lot fell on Jonah. ⁸Then said they to him, Tell us, we pray you, for whose cause this evil is on us; What is your occupation? and from where come you? what is your country? and of what people are you? ⁹And he said to them, I am an Hebrew; and I fear the LORD, the God of heaven, which has made the sea and the dry land. ¹⁰Then were the men exceedingly afraid, and said to him, Why have you done this? For the men knew that he fled from the presence of the LORD, because he had told them. ¹¹Then said they to him, What shall we do to you, that the sea may be calm to us? for the sea worked, and was tempestuous. ¹²And he said to them, Take me up, and cast me forth into the sea; so shall the sea be calm to you: for I know that for my sake this great tempest is on you. ¹³Nevertheless the men rowed hard to bring it to the land; but they could not: for the sea worked, and was tempestuous against them. ¹⁴Why they cried to the LORD, and said, We beseech you, O LORD, we beseech you, let us not perish for this man's life, and lay not on us innocent blood: for you, O LORD, have done as it pleased you. ¹⁵So they look up Jonah, and cast him forth into the sea: and the sea ceased from her raging. ¹⁶Then the men feared the LORD exceedingly, and offered a sacrifice to the LORD, and made vows. ¹⁷Now the LORD had prepared a great fish to swallow up Jonah. And Jonah was in the belly of the fish three days and three nights.

2 ¹Then Jonah prayed to the LORD his God out of the fish's belly, ²And said, I cried by reason of my affliction to the LORD, and he heard me; out of the belly of hell cried I, and you heard my voice. ³For you had cast me into the deep, in the middle of the seas; and the floods compassed me about: all your billows and your waves passed over me. ⁴Then I said, I am cast out of your sight; yet I will look again toward your holy temple. ⁵The waters compassed me about, even to the soul: the depth closed me round about, the weeds were wrapped about my head. ⁶I went down to the bottoms of the mountains; the earth with her bars was about me for ever: yet have you brought up my life from corruption, O LORD my God. ⁷When my soul fainted within me I remembered the LORD: and my prayer came in to you, into your holy temple. ⁸They that observe lying vanities forsake their own mercy. ⁹But I will sacrifice to you with the voice of thanksgiving; I will pay that that I have vowed. Salvation is of the LORD. ¹⁰And the LORD spoke to the fish, and it vomited out Jonah on the dry land.

3 ¹And the word of the LORD came to Jonah the second time, saying, ²Arise, go to Nineveh, that great city, and preach to it the preaching that I bid you. ³So Jonah arose, and went to Nineveh, according to the word of the LORD. Now Nineveh was an exceeding great city of three days' journey. ⁴And Jonah began to enter into the city a day's journey, and he cried, and said, Yet forty days, and Nineveh shall be overthrown. ⁵So the people of Nineveh believed God, and proclaimed a fast, and put on sackcloth, from the greatest of them even to the least of them. ⁶For word came to the king of Nineveh, and he arose from his throne, and he laid his robe from him, and covered him with sackcloth, and sat in ashes. ⁷And he caused it to be proclaimed and published through Nineveh by the decree of the king and his nobles, saying, Let neither man nor beast, herd nor flock, taste any thing: let them not feed, nor drink water: ⁸But let man and beast be covered with sackcloth, and cry mightily to God: yes, let them turn every one from his evil way, and from the violence that is in their hands. ⁹Who can tell if God will turn and repent, and turn away from his fierce anger, that we perish not? ¹⁰And God saw their works, that they turned from their evil way; and God repented of the evil, that he had said that he would do to them; and he did it not.

4 ¹But it displeased Jonah exceedingly, and he was very angry. ²And he prayed to the LORD, and said, I pray you, O LORD, was not this my saying, when I was yet in my country? Therefore I fled before to Tarshish: for I knew that you are a gracious God, and merciful, slow to anger, and of great kindness, and repent you of the evil. ³Therefore now, O LORD, take, I beseech you, my life from me; for it is better for me to die than to live. ⁴Then said the LORD, Do you well to be angry? ⁵So Jonah went out of the city, and sat on the east side of the city, and there made him a booth, and sat under it in the shadow, till he might see what would become of the city. ⁶And the LORD God prepared a gourd, and made it to come up over Jonah, that it might be a shadow over his head, to deliver him from his grief. So Jonah was exceeding glad of the gourd. ⁷But God prepared a worm when the morning rose the next day, and it smote the gourd that it withered. ⁸And it came to pass, when the sun did arise, that God prepared a vehement east wind; and the sun beat on the head of Jonah, that he fainted, and wished in himself to die, and said, It is better for me to die than to live. ⁹And God said to Jonah, Do you well to be angry for the gourd? And he said, I do well to be angry, even to death. ¹⁰Then said the LORD, You have had pity on the gourd, for the which you have not labored, neither made it grow; which came up in a night, and perished in a night: ¹¹And should not I spare Nineveh, that great city, wherein are more then six score thousand persons that cannot discern between their right hand and their left hand; and also much cattle?

Micah

1 ¹The word of the LORD that came to Micah the Morasthite in the days of Jotham, Ahaz, and Hezekiah, kings of Judah, which he saw concerning Samaria and Jerusalem. ²Hear, all you people; listen, O earth, and all that therein is: and let the Lord GOD be witness against you, the LORD from his holy temple. ³For, behold, the LORD comes forth out of his place, and will come down, and tread on the high places of the earth. ⁴And the mountains shall be molten under him, and the valleys shall be cleft, as wax before the fire, and as the waters that are poured down a steep place. ⁵For the transgression of Jacob is all this, and for the sins of the house of Israel. What is the transgression of Jacob? is it not Samaria? and what are the high places of Judah? are they not Jerusalem? ⁶Therefore I will make Samaria as an heap of the field, and as plantings of a vineyard: and I will pour down the stones thereof into the valley, and I will discover the foundations thereof. ⁷And all the graven images thereof shall be beaten to pieces, and all the hires thereof shall be burned with the fire, and all the idols thereof will I lay desolate: for she gathered it of the hire of an harlot, and they shall return to the hire of an harlot. ⁸Therefore I will wail and howl, I will go stripped and naked: I will make a wailing like the dragons, and mourning as the owls. ⁹For her wound is incurable; for it is come to Judah; he is come to the gate of my people, even to Jerusalem. ¹⁰Declare you it not at Gath, weep you not at all: in the house of Aphrah roll yourself in the dust. ¹¹Pass you away, you inhabitant of Saphir, having your shame naked: the inhabitant of Zaanan came not forth in the mourning of Bethezel; he shall receive of you his standing. ¹²For the inhabitant of Maroth waited carefully for good: but evil came down from the LORD to the gate of Jerusalem. ¹³O you inhabitant of Lachish, bind the chariot to the swift beast: she is the beginning of the sin to the daughter of Zion: for the transgressions of Israel were found in you. ¹⁴Therefore shall you give presents to Moreshethgath: the houses of Achzib shall be a lie to the kings of Israel. ¹⁵Yet will I bring an heir to you, O inhabitant of Mareshah: he shall come to Adullam the glory of Israel. ¹⁶Make you bald, and poll you for your delicate children; enlarge your baldness as the eagle; for they are gone into captivity from you.

2 ¹Woe to them that devise iniquity, and work evil on their beds! when the morning is light, they practice it, because it is in the power of their hand. ²And they covet fields, and take them by violence; and houses, and take them away: so they oppress a man and his house, even a man and his heritage. ³Therefore thus says the LORD; Behold, against this family do I devise an evil, from which you shall not remove your necks; neither shall you go haughtily: for this time is evil. ⁴In that day shall one take up a parable against you, and lament with a doleful lamentation, and say, We be utterly spoiled: he has changed the portion of my people: how has he removed it from me! turning away he has divided our fields. ⁵Therefore you shall have none that shall cast a cord by lot in the congregation of the LORD. ⁶Prophesy you not, say they to them that prophesy: they shall not prophesy to them, that they shall not take shame. ⁷O you that are named the house of Jacob, is the spirit of the LORD straitened? are these his doings? do not my words do good to him that walks uprightly? ⁸Even of late my people is risen up as an enemy: you pull off the robe with the garment from them that pass by securely as men averse from war. ⁹The women of my people have you cast out from their pleasant houses; from their children have you taken away my glory for ever. ¹⁰Arise you, and depart; for this is not your rest: because it is polluted, it shall destroy you, even with a sore destruction. ¹¹If a man walking in the spirit and falsehood do lie, saying, I will prophesy to you of wine and of strong drink; he shall even be the prophet of this people. ¹²I will surely assemble, O Jacob, all of you; I will surely gather the remnant of Israel; I will put them together as the sheep of Bozrah, as the flock in the middle of their fold: they shall make great noise by reason of the multitude of men. ¹³The breaker is come up before them: they have broken up, and have passed through the gate, and are gone out by it: and their king shall pass before them, and the LORD on the head of them.

3 ¹And I said, Hear, I pray you, O heads of Jacob, and you princes of the house of Israel; Is it not for you to know judgment? ²Who hate the good, and love the evil; who pluck off their skin from off them, and their flesh from off their bones; ³Who also eat the flesh of my people, and flay their skin from off them; and they break their bones, and chop them in pieces, as for the pot, and as flesh within the caldron. ⁴Then shall they cry to the LORD, but he will not hear them: he will even hide his face from them at that time, as they have behaved themselves ill in their doings. ⁵Thus says the LORD concerning the prophets that make my people err, that bite with their teeth, and cry, Peace; and he that puts not into their mouths, they even prepare war against him. ⁶Therefore night shall be to you, that you shall not have a vision; and it shall be dark to you, that you shall not divine; and the sun shall go down over the prophets, and the day shall be dark over them. ⁷Then shall the seers be ashamed, and the diviners confounded: yes, they shall all cover their lips; for there is no answer of God. ⁸But truly I am full of power by the spirit of the LORD, and of judgment, and of might, to declare to Jacob his transgression, and to Israel his sin. ⁹Hear this, I pray you, you heads of the house of Jacob, and princes of the house of Israel, that abhor judgment, and pervert all equity. ¹⁰They build up Zion with blood, and Jerusalem with iniquity. ¹¹The heads thereof judge for reward, and the priests thereof teach for hire, and the prophets thereof divine for money: yet will they lean on the LORD, and say, Is not the LORD among us? none evil can come on us. ¹²Therefore shall Zion for your sake be plowed as a field, and Jerusalem shall become heaps, and the mountain of the house as the high places of the forest.

4 ¹But in the last days it shall come to pass, that the mountain of the house of the LORD shall be established in the top of the mountains, and it shall be exalted above the hills; and people shall flow to it. ²And many nations shall come, and say, Come, and let us go up to the mountain of the LORD, and to the house of the God of Jacob; and he will teach us of his ways, and we will walk in his paths: for the law shall go forth of Zion, and the word of the LORD from Jerusalem. ³And he shall judge among many people, and rebuke strong nations afar off; and they shall beat their swords into plowshares, and their spears into pruning hooks: nation shall not lift up a sword against nation, neither shall they learn war any more. ⁴But they shall sit every man under his vine and under his fig tree; and none shall make them afraid: for the mouth of the LORD of hosts has spoken it. ⁵For all people will walk every one in the name of his god, and we will walk in the name of the LORD our God for ever and ever. ⁶In that day, says the LORD, will I assemble her that halts, and I will gather her that is driven out, and her that I have afflicted; ⁷And I will make her that halted a remnant, and her that was cast far off a strong nation: and the LORD shall reign over them in mount Zion from now on, even for ever. ⁸And you, O tower of the flock, the strong hold of the daughter of Zion, to you shall it come, even the first dominion; the kingdom shall come to the daughter of Jerusalem. ⁹Now why do you cry out aloud? is there no king in you? is your counselor perished? for pangs have taken you as a woman in travail. ¹⁰Be in pain, and labor to bring forth, O daughter of Zion, like a woman in travail: for now shall you go forth out of the city, and you shall dwell in the field, and you shall go even to Babylon; there shall you be delivered; there the LORD shall redeem you from the hand of your enemies. ¹¹Now also many nations are gathered against you, that say, Let her be defiled, and let our eye look on Zion. ¹²But they know not the thoughts of the LORD, neither understand they his counsel: for he shall gather them as the sheaves into the floor. ¹³Arise and thresh, O daughter of Zion: for I will make your horn iron, and I will make your hoofs brass: and you shall beat in pieces many people: and I will consecrate their gain to the LORD, and their substance to the Lord of the whole earth.

5 ¹Now gather yourself in troops, O daughter of troops: he has laid siege against us: they shall smite the judge of Israel with a rod on the cheek. ²But you, Bethlehem Ephratah, though you be little among the thousands of Judah, yet out of you shall he come forth to me that is to be ruler in Israel; whose goings forth have been from of old, from everlasting. ³Therefore will he give them up, until the time that she which travails has brought forth: then the remnant of his brothers shall return to the children of Israel. ⁴And he shall stand and feed in the strength of the LORD, in the majesty of the name of the LORD his God; and they shall abide: for now shall he be great to the ends of the earth. ⁵And this man shall be the peace, when the Assyrian shall come into our land: and when he shall tread in our palaces, then shall we raise against him seven shepherds, and eight principal men. ⁶And they shall waste the land of Assyria with the sword, and the land of Nimrod in the entrances thereof: thus shall he deliver us from the Assyrian, when he comes into our land, and when he treads within our borders. ⁷And the remnant of Jacob shall be in the middle of many people as a dew from the LORD, as the showers on the grass, that tarries not for man, nor waits for the sons of men. ⁸And the remnant of Jacob shall be among the Gentiles in the middle of many people as a lion among the beasts of the forest, as a young lion among the flocks of sheep: who, if he go through, both treads down, and tears in pieces, and none can deliver. ⁹Your hand shall be lifted up on your adversaries, and all your enemies shall be cut off. ¹⁰And it shall come to pass in that day, says the LORD, that I will cut off your horses out of the middle of you, and I will destroy your chariots: ¹¹And I will cut off the cities of your land, and throw down all your strong holds: ¹²And I will cut off witchcrafts out of your hand; and you shall have no more soothsayers: ¹³Your graven images also will I cut off, and your standing images out of the middle of you; and you shall no more worship the work of your hands. ¹⁴And I will pluck up your groves out of the middle of you: so will I destroy your cities. ¹⁵And I will execute vengeance in anger and fury on the heathen, such as they have not heard.

6 ¹Hear you now what the LORD says; Arise, contend you before the mountains, and let the hills hear your voice. ²Hear you, O mountains, the LORD's controversy, and you strong foundations of the earth: for the LORD has a controversy with his people, and he will plead with Israel. ³O my people, what have I done to you? and wherein have I wearied you? testify against me. ⁴For I brought you up out of the land of Egypt, and redeemed you out of the house of servants; and I sent before you Moses, Aaron, and Miriam. ⁵O my people, remember now what Balak king of Moab consulted, and what Balaam the son of Beor answered him from Shittim to Gilgal; that you may know the righteousness of the LORD. ⁶With which shall I come before the LORD, and bow myself before the high God? shall I come before him with burnt offerings, with calves of a year old? ⁷Will the LORD be pleased with thousands of rams, or with ten thousands of rivers of oil? shall I give my firstborn for my transgression, the fruit of my body for the sin of my soul? ⁸He has showed you, O man, what is good; and what does the LORD require of you, but to do justly, and to love mercy, and to walk humbly with your God? ⁹The LORD's voice cries to the city, and the man of wisdom shall see your name: hear you the rod, and who has appointed it. ¹⁰Are there yet the treasures of wickedness in the house of the wicked, and the scant measure that is abominable? ¹¹Shall I count them pure with the wicked balances, and with the bag of deceitful weights? ¹²For the rich men thereof are full of violence, and the inhabitants thereof have spoken lies, and their tongue is deceitful in their mouth. ¹³Therefore also will I make you sick in smiting you, in making you desolate because of your sins. ¹⁴You shall eat, but not be satisfied; and your casting down shall be in the middle of you; and you shall take hold, but shall not deliver; and that which you deliver will I give up to the sword. ¹⁵You shall sow, but you shall not reap; you shall tread the olives, but you shall not anoint you with oil; and sweet wine, but shall not drink wine. ¹⁶For the statutes of Omri are kept, and all the works of the house of Ahab, and you walk in their counsels; that I should make you a desolation, and the inhabitants thereof an hissing: therefore you shall bear the reproach of my people.

7 ¹Woe is me! for I am as when they have gathered the summer fruits, as the grape gleanings of the vintage: there is no cluster to eat: my soul desired the first ripe fruit. ²The good man is perished out of the earth: and there is none upright among men: they all lie in wait for blood; they hunt

every man his brother with a net. ³That they may do evil with both hands earnestly, the prince asks, and the judge asks for a reward; and the great man, he utters his mischievous desire: so they wrap it up. ⁴The best of them is as a brier: the most upright is sharper than a thorn hedge: the day of your watchmen and your visitation comes; now shall be their perplexity. ⁵Trust you not in a friend, put you not confidence in a guide: keep the doors of your mouth from her that lies in your bosom. ⁶For the son dishonors the father, the daughter rises up against her mother, the daughter in law against her mother in law; a man's enemies are the men of his own house. ⁷Therefore I will look to the LORD; I will wait for the God of my salvation: my God will hear me. ⁸Rejoice not against me, O my enemy: when I fall, I shall arise; when I sit in darkness, the LORD shall be a light to me. ⁹I will bear the indignation of the LORD, because I have sinned against him, until he plead my cause, and execute judgment for me: he will bring me forth to the light, and I shall behold his righteousness. ¹⁰Then she that is my enemy shall see it, and shame shall cover her which said to me, Where is the LORD your God? my eyes shall behold her: now shall she be trodden down as the mire of the streets. ¹¹In the day that your walls are to be built, in that day shall the decree be far removed. ¹²In that day also he shall come even to you from Assyria, and from the fortified cities, and from the fortress even to the river, and from sea to sea, and from mountain to mountain. ¹³Notwithstanding the land shall be desolate because of them that dwell therein, for the fruit of their doings. ¹⁴Feed your people with your rod, the flock of your heritage, which dwell solitarily in the wood, in the middle of Carmel: let them feed in Bashan and Gilead, as in the days of old. ¹⁵According to the days of your coming out of the land of Egypt will I show to him marvelous things. ¹⁶The nations shall see and be confounded at all their might: they shall lay their hand on their mouth, their ears shall be deaf. ¹⁷They shall lick the dust like a serpent, they shall move out of their holes like worms of the earth: they shall be afraid of the LORD our God, and shall fear because of you. ¹⁸Who is a God like to you, that pardons iniquity, and passes by the transgression of the remnant of his heritage? he retains not his anger for ever, because he delights in mercy. ¹⁹He will turn again, he will have compassion on us; he will subdue our iniquities; and you will cast all their sins into the depths of the sea. ²⁰You will perform the truth to Jacob, and the mercy to Abraham, which you have sworn to our fathers from the days of old.

Nahum

1 ¹The burden of Nineveh. The book of the vision of Nahum the Elkoshite. ²God is jealous, and the LORD revenges; the LORD revenges, and is furious; the LORD will take vengeance on his adversaries, and he reserves wrath for his enemies. ³The LORD is slow to anger, and great in power, and will not at all acquit the wicked: the LORD has his way in the whirlwind and in the storm, and the clouds are the dust of his feet. ⁴He rebukes the sea, and makes it dry, and dries up all the rivers: Bashan languishes, and Carmel, and the flower of Lebanon languishes. ⁵The mountains quake at him, and the hills melt, and the earth is burned at his presence, yes, the world, and all that dwell therein. ⁶Who can stand before his indignation? and who can abide in the fierceness of his anger? his fury is poured out like fire, and the rocks are thrown down by him. ⁷The LORD is good, a strong hold in the day of trouble; and he knows them that trust in him. ⁸But with an overrunning flood he will make an utter end of the place thereof, and darkness shall pursue his enemies. ⁹What do you imagine against the LORD? he will make an utter end: affliction shall not rise up the second time. ¹⁰For while they be entwined together as thorns, and while they are drunken as drunkards, they shall be devoured as stubble fully dry. ¹¹There is one come out of you, that imagines evil against the LORD, a wicked counselor. ¹²Thus says the LORD; Though they be quiet, and likewise many, yet thus shall they be cut down, when he shall pass through. Though I have afflicted you, I will afflict you no more. ¹³For now will I break his yoke from off you, and will burst your bonds in sunder. ¹⁴And the LORD has given a commandment concerning you, that no more of your name be sown: out of the house of your gods will I cut off the graven image and the molten image: I will make your grave; for you are vile. ¹⁵Behold on the mountains the feet of him that brings good tidings, that publishes peace! O Judah, keep your solemn feasts, perform your vows: for the wicked shall no more pass through you; he is utterly cut off.

2 ¹He that dashes in pieces is come up before your face: keep the fortification, watch the way, make your loins strong, fortify your power mightily. ²For the LORD has turned away the excellency of Jacob, as the excellency of Israel: for the emptiers have emptied them out, and marred their vine branches. ³The shield of his mighty men is made red, the valiant men are in scarlet: the chariots shall be with flaming torches in the day of his preparation, and the fir trees shall be terribly shaken. ⁴The chariots shall rage in the streets, they shall jostle one against another in the broad ways: they shall seem like torches, they shall run like the lightning. ⁵He shall recount his worthies: they shall stumble in their walk; they shall make haste to the wall thereof, and the defense shall be prepared. ⁶The gates of the rivers shall be opened, and the palace shall be dissolved. ⁷And Huzzab shall be led away captive, she shall be brought up, and her maids shall lead her as with the voice of doves, beating on their breasts. ⁸But Nineveh is of old like a pool of water: yet they shall flee away. Stand, stand, shall they cry; but none shall look back. ⁹Take you the spoil of silver, take the spoil of gold: for there is none end of the store and glory out of all the pleasant furniture. ¹⁰She is empty, and void, and waste: and the heart melts, and the knees smite together, and much pain is in all loins, and the faces of them all gather blackness. ¹¹Where is the dwelling of the lions, and the feeding place of the young lions, where the lion, even the old lion, walked, and the lion's whelp, and none made them afraid? ¹²The lion did tear in pieces enough for his whelps, and strangled for his lionesses, and filled his holes with prey, and his dens with shred. ¹³Behold, I am against you, says the LORD of hosts, and I will burn her chariots in the smoke, and the sword shall devour your young lions: and I will cut off your prey from the earth, and the voice of your messengers shall no more be heard.

3 ¹Woe to the bloody city! it is all full of lies and robbery; the prey departs not; ²The noise of a whip, and the noise of the rattling of the wheels, and of the prancing horses, and of the jumping chariots. ³The horseman lifts up both the bright sword and the glittering spear: and there is a multitude of slain, and a great number of carcasses; and there is none end of their corpses; they stumble on their corpses: ⁴Because of the multitude of the prostitutions of the well favored harlot, the mistress of witchcrafts, that sells nations through her prostitutions, and families through her witchcrafts. ⁵Behold, I am against you, says the LORD of hosts; and I will discover your skirts on your face, and I will show the nations your nakedness, and the kingdoms your shame. ⁶And I will cast abominable filth on you, and make you vile, and will set you as a spectacle. ⁷And it shall come to pass, that all they that look on you shall flee from you, and say, Nineveh is laid waste: who will bemoan her? from where shall I seek comforters for you? ⁸Are you better than populous No, that was situate among the rivers, that had the waters round about it, whose rampart was the sea, and her wall was from the sea? ⁹Ethiopia and Egypt were her strength, and it was infinite; Put and Lubim were your helpers. ¹⁰Yet was she carried away, she went into captivity: her young children also were dashed in pieces at the top of all the streets: and they cast lots for her honorable men, and all her great men were bound in chains. ¹¹You also shall be drunken: you shall be hid, you also shall seek strength because of the enemy. ¹²All your strong holds shall be like fig trees with the first ripe figs: if they be shaken, they shall even fall into the mouth of the eater. ¹³Behold, your people in the middle of you are women: the gates of your land shall be set wide open to your enemies: the fire shall devour your bars. ¹⁴Draw you waters for the siege, fortify your strong holds: go into clay, and tread the mortar, make strong the brick kiln. ¹⁵There shall the fire devour you; the sword shall cut you off, it shall eat you up like the cankerworm: make yourself many as the cankerworm, make yourself many as the locusts. ¹⁶You have multiplied your merchants above the stars of heaven: the cankerworm spoils, and flees away. ¹⁷Your crowned are as the locusts, and your captains as the great grasshoppers, which camp in the hedges in the cold day, but when the sun rises they flee away, and their place is not known where they are. ¹⁸Your shepherds slumber, O king of Assyria: your nobles shall dwell in the dust: your people is scattered on the mountains, and no man gathers them. ¹⁹There is no healing of your bruise; your wound is grievous:

all that hear the bruit of you shall clap the hands over you:
for on whom has not your wickedness passed continually?

Habakkuk

1 ¹The burden which Habakkuk the prophet did see. ²O LORD, how long shall I cry, and you will not hear! even cry out to you of violence, and you will not save! ³Why do you show me iniquity, and cause me to behold grievance? for spoiling and violence are before me: and there are that raise up strife and contention. ⁴Therefore the law is slacked, and judgment does never go forth: for the wicked does compass about the righteous; therefore wrong judgment proceeds. ⁵Behold you among the heathen, and regard, and wonder marvelously: for I will work a work in your days which you will not believe, though it be told you. ⁶For, see, I raise up the Chaldeans, that bitter and hasty nation, which shall march through the breadth of the land, to possess the dwelling places that are not theirs. ⁷They are terrible and dreadful: their judgment and their dignity shall proceed of themselves. ⁸Their horses also are swifter than the leopards, and are more fierce than the evening wolves: and their horsemen shall spread themselves, and their horsemen shall come from far; they shall fly as the eagle that hastens to eat. ⁹They shall come all for violence: their faces shall sup up as the east wind, and they shall gather the captivity as the sand. ¹⁰And they shall scoff at the kings, and the princes shall be a scorn to them: they shall deride every strong hold; for they shall heap dust, and take it. ¹¹Then shall his mind change, and he shall pass over, and offend, imputing this his power to his god. ¹²Are you not from everlasting, O LORD my God, my Holy One? we shall not die. O LORD, you have ordained them for judgment; and, O mighty God, you have established them for correction. ¹³You are of purer eyes than to behold evil, and can not look on iniquity: why look you on them that deal treacherously, and hold your tongue when the wicked devours the man that is more righteous than he? ¹⁴And make men as the fishes of the sea, as the creeping things, that have no ruler over them? ¹⁵They take up all of them with the angle, they catch them in their net, and gather them in their drag: therefore they rejoice and are glad. ¹⁶Therefore they sacrifice to their net, and burn incense to their drag; because by them their portion is fat, and their meat plenteous. ¹⁷Shall they therefore empty their net, and not spare continually to slay the nations?

2 ¹I will stand on my watch, and set me on the tower, and will watch to see what he will say to me, and what I shall answer when I am reproved. ²And the LORD answered me, and said, Write the vision, and make it plain on tables, that he may run that reads it. ³For the vision is yet for an appointed time, but at the end it shall speak, and not lie: though it tarry, wait for it; because it will surely come, it will not tarry. ⁴Behold, his soul which is lifted up is not upright in him: but the just shall live by his faith. ⁵Yes also, because he transgresses by wine, he is a proud man, neither keeps at home, who enlarges his desire as hell, and is as death, and cannot be satisfied, but gathers to him all nations, and heaps to him all people: ⁶Shall not all these take up a parable against him, and a taunting proverb against him, and say, Woe to him that increases that which is not his! how long? and to him that lades himself with thick clay! ⁷Shall they not rise up suddenly that shall bite you, and awake that shall vex you, and you shall be for booties to them? ⁸Because you have spoiled many nations, all the remnant of the people shall spoil you; because of men's blood, and for the violence of the land, of the city, and of all that dwell therein. ⁹Woe to him that covets an evil covetousness to his house, that he may set his nest on high, that he may be delivered from the power of evil! ¹⁰You have consulted shame to your house by cutting off many people, and have sinned against your soul. ¹¹For the stone shall cry out of the wall, and the beam out of the timber shall answer it. ¹²Woe to him that builds a town with blood, and establishes a city by iniquity! ¹³Behold, is it not of the LORD of hosts that the people shall labor in the very fire, and the people shall weary themselves for very vanity? ¹⁴For the earth shall be filled with the knowledge of the glory of the LORD, as the waters cover the sea. ¹⁵Woe to him that gives his neighbor drink, that put your bottle to him, and make him drunken also, that you may look on their nakedness! ¹⁶You are filled with shame for glory: drink you also, and let your foreskin be uncovered: the cup of the LORD's right hand shall be turned to you, and shameful spewing shall be on your glory. ¹⁷For the violence of Lebanon shall cover you, and the spoil of beasts, which made them afraid, because of men's blood, and for the violence of the land, of the city, and of all that dwell therein. ¹⁸What profits the graven image that the maker thereof has graven it; the molten image, and a teacher of lies, that the maker of his work trusts therein, to make dumb idols? ¹⁹Woe to him that says to the wood, Awake; to the dumb stone, Arise, it shall teach! Behold, it is laid over with gold and silver, and there is no breath at all in the middle of it. ²⁰But the LORD is in his holy temple: let all the earth keep silence before him.

3 ¹A prayer of Habakkuk the prophet on Shigionoth. ²O LORD, I have heard your speech, and was afraid: O LORD, revive your work in the middle of the years, in the middle of the years make known; in wrath remember mercy. ³God came from Teman, and the Holy One from mount Paran. Selah. His glory covered the heavens, and the earth was full of his praise. ⁴And his brightness was as the light; he had horns coming out of his hand: and there was the hiding of his power. ⁵Before him went the pestilence, and burning coals went forth at his feet. ⁶He stood, and measured the earth: he beheld, and drove asunder the nations; and the everlasting mountains were scattered, the perpetual hills did bow: his ways are everlasting. ⁷I saw the tents of Cushan in affliction: and the curtains of the land of Midian did tremble. ⁸Was the LORD displeased against the rivers? was your anger against the rivers? was your wrath against the sea, that you did ride on your horses and your chariots of salvation? ⁹Your bow was made quite naked, according to the oaths of the tribes, even your word. Selah. You did split the earth with rivers. ¹⁰The mountains saw you, and they trembled: the overflowing of the water passed by: the deep uttered his voice, and lifted up his hands on high. ¹¹The sun and moon stood still in their habitation: at the light of your arrows they went, and at the shining of your glittering spear. ¹²You did march through the land in indignation, you did thresh the heathen in anger. ¹³You went forth for the salvation of your people, even for salvation with your anointed; you wounded the head out of the house of the wicked, by discovering the foundation to the neck. Selah. [14]You did strike through with his staves the head of his villages: they came out as a whirlwind to scatter me: their rejoicing was as to devour the poor secretly. [15]You did walk through the sea with your horses, through the heap of great waters. [16]When I heard, my belly trembled; my lips quivered at the voice: rottenness entered into my bones, and I trembled in myself, that I might rest in the day of trouble: when he comes up to the people, he will invade them with his troops. [17]Although the fig tree shall not blossom, neither shall fruit be in the vines; the labor of the olive shall fail, and the fields shall yield no meat; the flock shall be cut off from the fold, and there shall be no herd in the stalls: [18]Yet I will rejoice in the LORD, I will joy in the God of my salvation. [19]The LORD God is my strength, and he will make my feet like hinds' feet, and he will make me to walk on my high places. To the chief singer on my stringed instruments.

Zephaniah

1 ¹The word of the LORD which came to Zephaniah the son of Cushi, the son of Gedaliah, the son of Amariah, the son of Hizkiah, in the days of Josiah the son of Amon, king of Judah. ²I will utterly consume all things from off the land, says the LORD. ³I will consume man and beast; I will consume the fowls of the heaven, and the fishes of the sea, and the stumbling blocks with the wicked: and I will cut off man from off the land, says the LORD. ⁴I will also stretch out my hand on Judah, and on all the inhabitants of Jerusalem; and I will cut off the remnant of Baal from this place, and the name of the Chemarims with the priests; ⁵And them that worship the host of heaven on the housetops; and them that worship and that swear by the LORD, and that swear by Malcham; ⁶And them that are turned back from the LORD; and those that have not sought the LORD, nor inquired for him. ⁷Hold your peace at the presence of the Lord GOD: for the day of the LORD is at hand: for the LORD has prepared a sacrifice, he has bid his guests. ⁸And it shall come to pass in the day of the LORD's sacrifice, that I will punish the princes, and the king's children, and all such as are clothed with strange apparel. ⁹In the same day also will I punish all those that leap on the threshold, which fill their masters' houses with violence and deceit. ¹⁰And it shall come to pass in that day, says the LORD, that there shall be the noise of a cry from the fish gate, and an howling from the second, and a great crashing from the hills. ¹¹Howl, you inhabitants of Maktesh, for all the merchant people are cut down; all they that bear silver are cut off. ¹²And it shall come to pass at that time, that I will search Jerusalem with candles, and punish the men that are settled on their lees: that say in their heart, The LORD will not do good, neither will he do evil. ¹³Therefore their goods shall become a booty, and their houses a desolation: they shall also build houses, but not inhabit them; and they shall plant vineyards, but not drink the wine thereof. ¹⁴The great day of the LORD is near, it is near, and hastens greatly, even the voice of the day of the LORD: the mighty man shall cry there bitterly. ¹⁵That day is a day of wrath, a day of trouble and distress, a day of devastation and desolation, a day of darkness and gloominess, a day of clouds and thick darkness, ¹⁶A day of the trumpet and alarm against the fenced cities, and against the high towers. ¹⁷And I will bring distress on men, that they shall walk like blind men, because they have sinned against the LORD: and their blood shall be poured out as dust, and their flesh as the dung. ¹⁸Neither their silver nor their gold shall be able to deliver them in the day of the LORD's wrath; but the whole land shall be devoured by the fire of his jealousy: for he shall make even a speedy riddance of all them that dwell in the land.

2 ¹Gather yourselves together, yes, gather together, O nation not desired; ²Before the decree bring forth, before the day pass as the chaff, before the fierce anger of the LORD come on you, before the day of the LORD's anger come on you. ³Seek you the LORD, all you meek of the earth, which have worked his judgment; seek righteousness, seek meekness: it may be you shall be hid in the day of the LORD's anger. ⁴For Gaza shall be forsaken, and Ashkelon a desolation: they shall drive out Ashdod at the noon day, and Ekron shall be rooted up. ⁵Woe to the inhabitants of the sea coast, the nation of the Cherethites! the word of the LORD is against you; O Canaan, the land of the Philistines, I will even destroy you, that there shall be no inhabitant. ⁶And the sea coast shall be dwellings and cottages for shepherds, and folds for flocks. ⁷And the coast shall be for the remnant of the house of Judah; they shall feed thereupon: in the houses of Ashkelon shall they lie down in the evening: for the LORD their God shall visit them, and turn away their captivity. ⁸I have heard the reproach of Moab, and the revilings of the children of Ammon, whereby they have reproached my people, and magnified themselves against their border. ⁹Therefore as I live, says the LORD of hosts, the God of Israel, Surely Moab shall be as Sodom, and the children of Ammon as Gomorrah, even the breeding of nettles, and salt pits, and a perpetual desolation: the residue of my people shall spoil them, and the remnant of my people shall possess them. ¹⁰This shall they have for their pride, because they have reproached and magnified themselves against the people of the LORD of hosts. ¹¹The LORD will be terrible to them: for he will famish all the gods of the earth; and men shall worship him, every one from his place, even all the isles of the heathen. ¹²You Ethiopians also, you shall be slain by my sword. ¹³And he will stretch out his hand against the north, and destroy Assyria; and will make Nineveh a desolation, and dry like a wilderness. ¹⁴And flocks shall lie down in the middle of her, all the beasts of the nations: both the cormorant and the bittern shall lodge in the upper lintels of it; their voice shall sing in the windows; desolation shall be in the thresholds; for he shall uncover the cedar work. ¹⁵This is the rejoicing city that dwelled carelessly, that said in her heart, I am, and there is none beside me: how is she become a desolation, a place for beasts to lie down in! every one that passes by her shall hiss, and wag his hand.

3 ¹Woe to her that is filthy and polluted, to the oppressing city! ²She obeyed not the voice; she received not correction; she trusted not in the LORD; she drew not near to her God. ³Her princes within her are roaring lions; her judges are evening wolves; they gnaw not the bones till the morrow. ⁴Her prophets are light and treacherous persons: her priests have polluted the sanctuary, they have done violence to the law. ⁵The just LORD is in the middle thereof; he will not do iniquity: every morning does he bring his judgment to light, he fails not; but the unjust knows no shame. ⁶I have cut off the nations: their towers are desolate; I made their streets waste, that none passes by: their cities are destroyed, so that there is no man, that there is none inhabitant. ⁷I said, Surely you will fear me, you will receive instruction; so their dwelling should not be cut off, howsoever I punished them: but they rose early, and corrupted all their doings. ⁸Therefore wait you on me, says the LORD, until the day that I rise up to the prey: for my determination is to gather the nations, that I may assemble the kingdoms, to pour on them my indignation, even all my fierce anger: for all the earth shall be devoured with the fire of my jealousy. ⁹For then will I turn to the people a pure language, that they may all call on the name of the LORD, to serve him with one consent.

¹⁰From beyond the rivers of Ethiopia my suppliants, even the daughter of my dispersed, shall bring my offering. ¹¹In that day shall you not be ashamed for all your doings, wherein you have transgressed against me: for then I will take away out of the middle of you them that rejoice in your pride, and you shall no more be haughty because of my holy mountain. ¹²I will also leave in the middle of you an afflicted and poor people, and they shall trust in the name of the LORD. ¹³The remnant of Israel shall not do iniquity, nor speak lies; neither shall a deceitful tongue be found in their mouth: for they shall feed and lie down, and none shall make them afraid. ¹⁴Sing, O daughter of Zion; shout, O Israel; be glad and rejoice with all the heart, O daughter of Jerusalem. ¹⁵The LORD has taken away your judgments, he has cast out your enemy: the king of Israel, even the LORD, is in the middle of you: you shall not see evil any more. ¹⁶In that day it shall be said to Jerusalem, Fear you not: and to Zion, Let not your hands be slack. ¹⁷The LORD your God in the middle of you is mighty; he will save, he will rejoice over you with joy; he will rest in his love, he will joy over you with singing. ¹⁸I will gather them that are sorrowful for the solemn assembly, who are of you, to whom the reproach of it was a burden. ¹⁹Behold, at that time I will undo all that afflict you: and I will save her that halts, and gather her that was driven out; and I will get them praise and fame in every land where they have been put to shame. ²⁰At that time will I bring you again, even in the time that I gather you: for I will make you a name and a praise among all people of the earth, when I turn back your captivity before your eyes, said the LORD.

Haggai

1 ¹In the second year of Darius the king, in the sixth month, in the first day of the month, came the word of the LORD by Haggai the prophet to Zerubbabel the son of Shealtiel, governor of Judah, and to Joshua the son of Josedech, the high priest, saying, ²Thus speaks the LORD of hosts, saying, This people say, The time is not come, the time that the LORD's house should be built. ³Then came the word of the LORD by Haggai the prophet, saying, ⁴Is it time for you, O you, to dwell in your paneled houses, and this house lie waste? ⁵Now therefore thus says the LORD of hosts; Consider your ways. ⁶You have sown much, and bring in little; you eat, but you have not enough; you drink, but you are not filled with drink; you clothe you, but there is none warm; and he that earns wages earns wages to put it into a bag with holes. ⁷Thus says the LORD of hosts; Consider your ways. ⁸Go up to the mountain, and bring wood, and build the house; and I will take pleasure in it, and I will be glorified, says the LORD. ⁹You looked for much, and, see it came to little; and when you brought it home, I did blow on it. Why? says the LORD of hosts. Because of my house that is waste, and you run every man to his own house. ¹⁰Therefore the heaven over you is stayed from dew, and the earth is stayed from her fruit. ¹¹And I called for a drought on the land, and on the mountains, and on the corn, and on the new wine, and on the oil, and on that which the ground brings forth, and on men, and on cattle, and on all the labor of the hands. ¹²Then Zerubbabel the son of Shealtiel, and Joshua the son of Josedech, the high priest, with all the remnant of the people, obeyed the voice of the LORD their God, and the words of Haggai the prophet, as the LORD their God had sent him, and the people did fear before the LORD. ¹³Then spoke Haggai the LORD's messenger in the LORD's message to the people, saying, I am with you, says the LORD. ¹⁴And the LORD stirred up the spirit of Zerubbabel the son of Shealtiel, governor of Judah, and the spirit of Joshua the son of Josedech, the high priest, and the spirit of all the remnant of the people; and they came and did work in the house of the LORD of hosts, their God, ¹⁵In the four and twentieth day of the sixth month, in the second year of Darius the king.

2 ¹In the seventh month, in the one and twentieth day of the month, came the word of the LORD by the prophet Haggai, saying, ²Speak now to Zerubbabel the son of Shealtiel, governor of Judah, and to Joshua the son of Josedech, the high priest, and to the residue of the people, saying, ³Who is left among you that saw this house in her first glory? and how do you see it now? is it not in your eyes in comparison of it as nothing? ⁴Yet now be strong, O Zerubbabel, says the LORD; and be strong, O Joshua, son of Josedech, the high priest; and be strong, all you people of the land, says the LORD, and work: for I am with you, says the LORD of hosts: ⁵According to the word that I covenanted with you when you came out of Egypt, so my spirit remains among you: fear you not. ⁶For thus says the LORD of hosts; Yet once, it is a little while, and I will shake the heavens, and the earth, and the sea, and the dry land; ⁷And I will shake all nations, and the desire of all nations shall come: and I will fill this house with glory, says the LORD of hosts. ⁸The silver is mine, and the gold is mine, says the LORD of hosts. ⁹The glory of this latter house shall be greater than of the former, says the LORD of hosts: and in this place will I give peace, says the LORD of hosts. ¹⁰In the four and twentieth day of the ninth month, in the second year of Darius, came the word of the LORD by Haggai the prophet, saying, ¹¹Thus says the LORD of hosts; Ask now the priests concerning the law, saying, ¹²If one bear holy flesh in the skirt of his garment, and with his skirt do touch bread, or pottage, or wine, or oil, or any meat, shall it be holy? And the priests answered and said, No. ¹³Then said Haggai, If one that is unclean by a dead body touch any of these, shall it be unclean? And the priests answered and said, It shall be unclean. ¹⁴Then answered Haggai, and said, So is this people, and so is this nation before me, says the LORD; and so is every work of their hands; and that which they offer there is unclean. ¹⁵And now, I pray you, consider from this day and upward, from before a stone was laid on a stone in the temple of the LORD: ¹⁶Since those days were, when one came to an heap of twenty measures, there were but ten: when one came to the fat press for to draw out fifty vessels out of the press, there were but twenty. ¹⁷I smote you with blasting and with mildew and with hail in all the labors of your hands; yet you turned not to me, says the LORD. ¹⁸Consider now from this day and upward, from the four and twentieth day of the ninth month, even from the day that the foundation of the LORD's temple was laid, consider it. ¹⁹Is the seed yet in the barn? yes, as yet the vine, and the fig tree, and the pomegranate, and the olive tree, has not brought forth: from this day will I bless you. ²⁰And again the word of the LORD came to Haggai in the four and twentieth day of the month, saying, ²¹Speak to Zerubbabel, governor of Judah, saying, I will shake the heavens and the earth; ²²And I will overthrow the throne of kingdoms, and I will destroy the strength of the kingdoms of the heathen; and I will overthrow the chariots, and those that ride in them; and the horses and their riders shall come down, every one by the sword of his brother. ²³In that day, says the LORD of hosts, will I take you, O Zerubbabel, my servant, the son of Shealtiel, said the LORD, and will make you as a signet: for I have chosen you, says the LORD of hosts.

Zechariah

1 ¹In the eighth month, in the second year of Darius, came the word of the LORD to Zechariah, the son of Berechiah, the son of Iddo the prophet, saying, ²The LORD has been sore displeased with your fathers. ³Therefore say you to them, Thus says the LORD of hosts; Turn you to me, says the LORD of hosts, and I will turn to you, says the LORD of hosts. ⁴Be you not as your fathers, to whom the former prophets have cried, saying, Thus says the LORD of hosts; Turn you now from your evil ways, and from your evil doings: but they did not hear, nor listen to me, says the LORD. ⁵Your fathers, where are they? and the prophets, do they live for ever? ⁶But my words and my statutes, which I commanded my servants the prophets, did they not take hold of your fathers? and they returned and said, Like as the LORD of hosts thought to do to us, according to our ways, and according to our doings, so has he dealt with us. ⁷On the four and twentieth day of the eleventh month, which is the month Sebat, in the second year of Darius, came the word of the LORD to Zechariah, the son of Berechiah, the son of Iddo the prophet, saying, ⁸I saw by night, and behold a man riding on a red horse, and he stood among the myrtle trees that were in the bottom; and behind him were there red horses, speckled, and white. ⁹Then said I, O my lord, what are these? And the angel that talked with me said to me, I will show you what these be. ¹⁰And the man that stood among the myrtle trees answered and said, These are they whom the LORD has sent to walk to and fro through the earth. ¹¹And they answered the angel of the LORD that stood among the myrtle trees, and said, We have walked to and fro through the earth, and, behold, all the earth sits still, and is at rest. ¹²Then the angel of the LORD answered and said, O LORD of hosts, how long will you not have mercy on Jerusalem and on the cities of Judah, against which you have had indignation these three score and ten years? ¹³And the LORD answered the angel that talked with me with good words and comfortable words. ¹⁴So the angel that communed with me said to me, Cry you, saying, Thus says the LORD of hosts; I am jealous for Jerusalem and for Zion with a great jealousy. ¹⁵And I am very sore displeased with the heathen that are at ease: for I was but a little displeased, and they helped forward the affliction. ¹⁶Therefore thus says the LORD; I am returned to Jerusalem with mercies: my house shall be built in it, says the LORD of hosts, and a line shall be stretched forth on Jerusalem. ¹⁷Cry yet, saying, Thus says the LORD of hosts; My cities through prosperity shall yet be spread abroad; and the LORD shall yet comfort Zion, and shall yet choose Jerusalem. ¹⁸Then lifted I up my eyes, and saw, and behold four horns. ¹⁹And I said to the angel that talked with me, What be these? And he answered me, These are the horns which have scattered Judah, Israel, and Jerusalem. ²⁰And the LORD showed me four carpenters. ²¹Then said I, What come these to do? And he spoke, saying, These are the horns which have scattered Judah, so that no man did lift up his head: but these are come to fray them, to cast out the horns of the Gentiles, which lifted up their horn over the land of Judah to scatter it.

2 ¹I lifted up my eyes again, and looked, and behold a man with a measuring line in his hand. ²Then said I, Where go you? And he said to me, To measure Jerusalem, to see what is the breadth thereof, and what is the length thereof. ³And, behold, the angel that talked with me went forth, and another angel went out to meet him, ⁴And said to him, Run, speak to this young man, saying, Jerusalem shall be inhabited as towns without walls for the multitude of men and cattle therein: ⁵For I, says the LORD, will be to her a wall of fire round about, and will be the glory in the middle of her. ⁶Ho, ho, come forth, and flee from the land of the north, says the LORD: for I have spread you abroad as the four winds of the heaven, said the LORD. ⁷Deliver yourself, O Zion, that dwell with the daughter of Babylon. ⁸For thus says the LORD of hosts; After the glory has he sent me to the nations which spoiled you: for he that touches you touches the apple of his eye. ⁹For, behold, I will shake my hand on them, and they shall be a spoil to their servants: and you shall know that the LORD of hosts has sent me. ¹⁰Sing and rejoice, O daughter of Zion: for, see, I come, and I will dwell in the middle of you, says the LORD. ¹¹And many nations shall be joined to the LORD in that day, and shall be my people: and I will dwell in the middle of you, and you shall know that the LORD of hosts has sent me to you. ¹²And the LORD shall inherit Judah his portion in the holy land, and shall choose Jerusalem again. ¹³Be silent, O all flesh, before the LORD: for he is raised up out of his holy habitation.

3 ¹And he showed me Joshua the high priest standing before the angel of the LORD, and Satan standing at his right hand to resist him. ²And the LORD said to Satan, The LORD rebuke you, O Satan; even the LORD that has chosen Jerusalem rebuke you: is not this a brand plucked out of the fire? ³Now Joshua was clothed with filthy garments, and stood before the angel. ⁴And he answered and spoke to those that stood before him, saying, Take away the filthy garments from him. And to him he said, Behold, I have caused your iniquity to pass from you, and I will clothe you with change of raiment. ⁵And I said, Let them set a fair turban on his head. So they set a fair turban on his head, and clothed him with garments. And the angel of the LORD stood by. ⁶And the angel of the LORD protested to Joshua, saying, ⁷Thus says the LORD of hosts; If you will walk in my ways, and if you will keep my charge, then you shall also judge my house, and shall also keep my courts, and I will give you places to walk among these that stand by. ⁸Hear now, O Joshua the high priest, you, and your fellows that sit before you: for they are men wondered at: for, behold, I will bring forth my servant the BRANCH. ⁹For behold the stone that I have laid before Joshua; on one stone shall be seven eyes: behold, I will engrave the engraving thereof, says the LORD of hosts, and I will remove the iniquity of that land in one day. ¹⁰In that day, says the LORD of hosts, shall you call every man his neighbor under the vine and under the fig tree.

4 ¹And the angel that talked with me came again, and waked me, as a man that is wakened out of his sleep. ²And said to me, What see you? And I said, I have looked, and behold a candlestick all of gold, with a bowl on the top of it, and his seven lamps thereon, and seven pipes to the seven lamps, which are on the top thereof: ³And two olive trees by it, one on the right side of the bowl, and the other on the left side thereof. ⁴So I answered and spoke to the angel that talked with me, saying, What are these, my lord? ⁵Then the angel that talked with me answered and said to me, Know you not what these be? And I said, No, my lord. ⁶Then he answered and spoke to me, saying, This is the word of the LORD to Zerubbabel, saying, Not by might, nor by power, but by my spirit, says the LORD of hosts. ⁷Who are you, O great mountain? before Zerubbabel you shall become a plain: and he shall bring forth the headstone thereof with shoutings, crying, Grace, grace to it. ⁸Moreover the word of the LORD came to me, saying, ⁹The hands of Zerubbabel have laid the foundation of this house; his hands shall also finish it; and you shall know that the LORD of hosts has sent me to you. ¹⁰For who has despised the day of small things? for they shall rejoice, and shall see the plummet in the hand of Zerubbabel with those seven; they are the eyes of the LORD, which run to and fro through the whole earth. ¹¹Then answered I, and said to him, What are these two olive trees on the right side of the candlestick and on the left side thereof? ¹²And I answered again, and said to him, What be these two olive branches which through the two golden pipes empty the golden oil out of themselves? ¹³And he answered me and said, Know you not what these be? And I said, No, my lord. ¹⁴Then said he, These are the two anointed ones, that stand by the LORD of the whole earth.

5 ¹Then I turned, and lifted up my eyes, and looked, and behold a flying roll. ²And he said to me, What see you? And I answered, I see a flying roll; the length thereof is twenty cubits, and the breadth thereof ten cubits. ³Then said he to me, This is the curse that goes forth over the face of the whole earth: for every one that steals shall be cut off as on this side according to it; and every one that swears shall be cut off as on that side according to it. ⁴I will bring it forth, says the LORD of hosts, and it shall enter into the house of the thief, and into the house of him that swears falsely by my name: and it shall remain in the middle of his house, and shall consume it with the timber thereof and the stones thereof. ⁵Then the angel that talked with me went forth, and said to me, Lift up now your eyes, and see what is this that goes forth. ⁶And I said, What is it? And he said, This is an ephah that goes forth. He said moreover, This is their resemblance through all the earth. ⁷And, behold, there was lifted up a talent of lead: and this is a woman that sits in the middle of the ephah. ⁸And he said, This is wickedness. And he cast it into the middle of the ephah; and he cast the weight of lead on the mouth thereof. ⁹Then lifted I up my eyes, and looked, and, behold, there came out two women, and the wind was in their wings; for they had wings like the wings of a stork: and they lifted up the ephah between the earth and the heaven. ¹⁰Then said I to the angel that talked with me, Where do these bear the ephah? ¹¹And he said to me, To build it an house in the land of Shinar: and it shall be established, and set there on her own base.

6 ¹And I turned, and lifted up my eyes, and looked, and, behold, there came four chariots out from between two mountains; and the mountains were mountains of brass. ²In the first chariot were red horses; and in the second chariot black horses; ³And in the third chariot white horses; and in the fourth chariot spotted and bay horses. ⁴Then I answered and said to the angel that talked with me, What are these, my lord? ⁵And the angel answered and said to me, These are the four spirits of the heavens, which go forth from standing before the LORD of all the earth. ⁶The black horses which are therein go forth into the north country; and the white go forth after them; and the spotted go forth toward the south country. ⁷And the bay went forth, and sought to go that they might walk to and fro through the earth: and he said, Get you hence, walk to and fro through the earth. So they walked to and fro through the earth. ⁸Then cried he on me, and spoke to me, saying, Behold, these that go toward the north country have quieted my spirit in the north country. ⁹And the word of the LORD came to me, saying, ¹⁰Take of them of the captivity, even of Heldai, of Tobijah, and of Jedaiah, which are come from Babylon, and come you the same day, and go into the house of Josiah the son of Zephaniah; ¹¹Then take silver and gold, and make crowns, and set them on the head of Joshua the son of Josedech, the high priest; ¹²And speak to him, saying, Thus speaks the LORD of hosts, saying, Behold the man whose name is The BRANCH; and he shall grow up out of his place, and he shall build the temple of the LORD: ¹³Even he shall build the temple of the LORD; and he shall bear the glory, and shall sit and rule on his throne; and he shall be a priest on his throne: and the counsel of peace shall be between them both. ¹⁴And the crowns shall be to Helem, and to Tobijah, and to Jedaiah, and to Hen the son of Zephaniah, for a memorial in the temple of the LORD. ¹⁵And they that are far off shall come and build in the temple of the LORD, and you shall know that the LORD of hosts has sent me to you. And this shall come to pass, if you will diligently obey the voice of the LORD your God.

7 ¹And it came to pass in the fourth year of king Darius, that the word of the LORD came to Zechariah in the fourth day of the ninth month, even in Chisleu; ²When they had sent to the house of God Sherezer and Regemmelech, and their men, to pray before the LORD, ³And to speak to the priests which were in the house of the LORD of hosts, and to the prophets, saying, Should I weep in the fifth month, separating myself, as I have done these so many years? ⁴Then came the word of the LORD of hosts to me, saying, ⁵Speak to all the people of the land, and to the priests, saying, When you fasted and mourned in the fifth and seventh month, even those seventy years, did you at all fast to me, even to me? ⁶And when you did eat, and when you did drink, did not you eat for yourselves, and drink for yourselves? ⁷Should you not hear the words which the LORD has cried by the former prophets, when Jerusalem was inhabited and in prosperity, and the cities thereof round about her, when men inhabited the south and the plain? ⁸And the word of the LORD came to Zechariah, saying, ⁹Thus speaks the LORD of hosts, saying, Execute true judgment, and show mercy and compassions every man to his brother: ¹⁰And oppress not the widow, nor the fatherless, the stranger, nor the poor; and let none of you imagine evil against his brother in your heart. ¹¹But they refused to listen, and pulled away the shoulder, and stopped their ears, that they should

not hear. ¹²Yes, they made their hearts as an adamant stone, lest they should hear the law, and the words which the LORD of hosts has sent in his spirit by the former prophets: therefore came a great wrath from the LORD of hosts. ¹³Therefore it is come to pass, that as he cried, and they would not hear; so they cried, and I would not hear, says the LORD of hosts: ¹⁴But I scattered them with a whirlwind among all the nations whom they knew not. Thus the land was desolate after them, that no man passed through nor returned: for they laid the pleasant land desolate.

8 ¹Again the word of the LORD of hosts came to me, saying, ²Thus says the LORD of hosts; I was jealous for Zion with great jealousy, and I was jealous for her with great fury. ³Thus says the LORD; I am returned to Zion, and will dwell in the middle of Jerusalem: and Jerusalem shall be called a city of truth; and the mountain of the LORD of hosts the holy mountain. ⁴Thus says the LORD of hosts; There shall yet old men and old women dwell in the streets of Jerusalem, and every man with his staff in his hand for very age. ⁵And the streets of the city shall be full of boys and girls playing in the streets thereof. ⁶Thus says the LORD of hosts; If it be marvelous in the eyes of the remnant of this people in these days, should it also be marvelous in my eyes? says the LORD of hosts. ⁷Thus said the LORD of hosts; Behold, I will save my people from the east country, and from the west country; ⁸And I will bring them, and they shall dwell in the middle of Jerusalem: and they shall be my people, and I will be their God, in truth and in righteousness. ⁹Thus says the LORD of hosts; Let your hands be strong, you that hear in these days these words by the mouth of the prophets, which were in the day that the foundation of the house of the LORD of hosts was laid, that the temple might be built. ¹⁰For before these days there was no hire for man, nor any hire for beast; neither was there any peace to him that went out or came in because of the affliction: for I set all men every one against his neighbor. ¹¹But now I will not be to the residue of this people as in the former days, says the LORD of hosts. ¹²For the seed shall be prosperous; the vine shall give her fruit, and the ground shall give her increase, and the heavens shall give their dew; and I will cause the remnant of this people to possess all these things. ¹³And it shall come to pass, that as you were a curse among the heathen, O house of Judah, and house of Israel; so will I save you, and you shall be a blessing: fear not, but let your hands be strong. ¹⁴For thus says the LORD of hosts; As I thought to punish you, when your fathers provoked me to wrath, said the LORD of hosts, and I repented not: ¹⁵So again have I thought in these days to do well to Jerusalem and to the house of Judah: fear you not. ¹⁶These are the things that you shall do; Speak you every man the truth to his neighbor; execute the judgment of truth and peace in your gates: ¹⁷And let none of you imagine evil in your hearts against his neighbor; and love no false oath: for all these are things that I hate, says the LORD. ¹⁸And the word of the LORD of hosts came to me, saying, ¹⁹Thus says the LORD of hosts; The fast of the fourth month, and the fast of the fifth, and the fast of the seventh, and the fast of the tenth, shall be to the house of Judah joy and gladness, and cheerful feasts; therefore love the truth and peace. ²⁰Thus says the LORD of hosts; It shall yet come to pass, that there shall come people, and the inhabitants of many cities: ²¹And the inhabitants of one city shall go to another, saying, Let us go speedily to pray before the LORD, and to seek the LORD of hosts: I will go also. ²²Yes, many people and strong nations shall come to seek the LORD of hosts in Jerusalem, and to pray before the LORD. ²³Thus says the LORD of hosts; In those days it shall come to pass, that ten men shall take hold out of all languages of the nations, even shall take hold of the skirt of him that is a Jew, saying, We will go with you: for we have heard that God is with you.

9 ¹The burden of the word of the LORD in the land of Hadrach, and Damascus shall be the rest thereof: when the eyes of man, as of all the tribes of Israel, shall be toward the LORD. ²And Hamath also shall border thereby; Tyrus, and Zidon, though it be very wise. ³And Tyrus did build herself a strong hold, and heaped up silver as the dust, and fine gold as the mire of the streets. ⁴Behold, the LORD will cast her out, and he will smite her power in the sea; and she shall be devoured with fire. ⁵Ashkelon shall see it, and fear; Gaza also shall see it, and be very sorrowful, and Ekron; for her expectation shall be ashamed; and the king shall perish from Gaza, and Ashkelon shall not be inhabited. ⁶And a bastard shall dwell in Ashdod, and I will cut off the pride of the Philistines. ⁷And I will take away his blood out of his mouth, and his abominations from between his teeth: but he that remains, even he, shall be for our God, and he shall be as a governor in Judah, and Ekron as a Jebusite. ⁸And I will encamp about my house because of the army, because of him that passes by, and because of him that returns: and no oppressor shall pass through them any more: for now have I seen with my eyes. ⁹Rejoice greatly, O daughter of Zion; shout, O daughter of Jerusalem: behold, your King comes to you: he is just, and having salvation; lowly, and riding on an ass, and on a colt the foal of an ass. ¹⁰And I will cut off the chariot from Ephraim, and the horse from Jerusalem, and the battle bow shall be cut off: and he shall speak peace to the heathen: and his dominion shall be from sea even to sea, and from the river even to the ends of the earth. ¹¹As for you also, by the blood of your covenant I have sent forth your prisoners out of the pit wherein is no water. ¹²Turn you to the strong hold, you prisoners of hope: even to day do I declare that I will render double to you; ¹³When I have bent Judah for me, filled the bow with Ephraim, and raised up your sons, O Zion, against your sons, O Greece, and made you as the sword of a mighty man. ¹⁴And the LORD shall be seen over them, and his arrow shall go forth as the lightning: and the LORD God shall blow the trumpet, and shall go with whirlwinds of the south. ¹⁵The LORD of hosts shall defend them; and they shall devour, and subdue with sling stones; and they shall drink, and make a noise as through wine; and they shall be filled like bowls, and as the corners of the altar. ¹⁶And the LORD their God shall save them in that day as the flock of his people: for they shall be as the stones of a crown, lifted up as an ensign on his land. ¹⁷For how great is his goodness, and how great is his beauty! corn shall make the young men cheerful, and new wine the maids.

10 ¹Ask you of the LORD rain in the time of the latter rain; so the LORD shall make bright clouds, and give them showers of rain, to every one grass in the field.

²For the idols have spoken vanity, and the diviners have seen a lie, and have told false dreams; they comfort in vain: therefore they went their way as a flock, they were troubled, because there was no shepherd. ³My anger was kindled against the shepherds, and I punished the goats: for the LORD of hosts has visited his flock the house of Judah, and has made them as his goodly horse in the battle. ⁴Out of him came forth the corner, out of him the nail, out of him the battle bow, out of him every oppressor together. ⁵And they shall be as mighty men, which tread down their enemies in the mire of the streets in the battle: and they shall fight, because the LORD is with them, and the riders on horses shall be confounded. ⁶And I will strengthen the house of Judah, and I will save the house of Joseph, and I will bring them again to place them; for I have mercy on them: and they shall be as though I had not cast them off: for I am the LORD their God, and will hear them. ⁷And they of Ephraim shall be like a mighty man, and their heart shall rejoice as through wine: yes, their children shall see it, and be glad; their heart shall rejoice in the LORD. ⁸I will hiss for them, and gather them; for I have redeemed them: and they shall increase as they have increased. ⁹And I will sow them among the people: and they shall remember me in far countries; and they shall live with their children, and turn again. ¹⁰I will bring them again also out of the land of Egypt, and gather them out of Assyria; and I will bring them into the land of Gilead and Lebanon; and place shall not be found for them. ¹¹And he shall pass through the sea with affliction, and shall smite the waves in the sea, and all the deeps of the river shall dry up: and the pride of Assyria shall be brought down, and the scepter of Egypt shall depart away. ¹²And I will strengthen them in the LORD; and they shall walk up and down in his name, says the LORD.

11

¹Open your doors, O Lebanon, that the fire may devour your cedars. ²Howl, fir tree; for the cedar is fallen; because the mighty are spoiled: howl, O you oaks of Bashan; for the forest of the vintage is come down. ³There is a voice of the howling of the shepherds; for their glory is spoiled: a voice of the roaring of young lions; for the pride of Jordan is spoiled. ⁴Thus says the LORD my God; Feed the flock of the slaughter; ⁵Whose possessors slay them, and hold themselves not guilty: and they that sell them say, Blessed be the LORD; for I am rich: and their own shepherds pity them not. ⁶For I will no more pity the inhabitants of the land, says the LORD: but, see, I will deliver the men every one into his neighbor's hand, and into the hand of his king: and they shall smite the land, and out of their hand I will not deliver them. ⁷And I will feed the flock of slaughter, even you, O poor of the flock. And I took to me two staves; the one I called Beauty, and the other I called Bands; and I fed the flock. ⁸Three shepherds also I cut off in one month; and my soul loathed them, and their soul also abhorred me. ⁹Then said I, I will not feed you: that that dies, let it die; and that that is to be cut off, let it be cut off; and let the rest eat every one the flesh of another. ¹⁰And I took my staff, even Beauty, and cut it asunder, that I might break my covenant which I had made with all the people. ¹¹And it was broken in that day: and so the poor of the flock that waited on me knew that it was the word of the LORD. ¹²And I said to them, If you think good, give me my price; and if not, forbear. So they weighed for my price thirty pieces of silver. ¹³And the LORD said to me, Cast it to the potter: a goodly price that I was priced at of them. And I took the thirty pieces of silver, and cast them to the potter in the house of the LORD. ¹⁴Then I cut asunder my other staff, even Bands, that I might break the brotherhood between Judah and Israel. ¹⁵And the LORD said to me, Take to you yet the instruments of a foolish shepherd. ¹⁶For, see, I will raise up a shepherd in the land, which shall not visit those that be cut off, neither shall seek the young one, nor heal that that is broken, nor feed that that stands still: but he shall eat the flesh of the fat, and tear their claws in pieces. ¹⁷Woe to the idol shepherd that leaves the flock! the sword shall be on his arm, and on his right eye: his arm shall be clean dried up, and his right eye shall be utterly darkened.

12

¹The burden of the word of the LORD for Israel, says the LORD, which stretches forth the heavens, and lays the foundation of the earth, and forms the spirit of man within him. ²Behold, I will make Jerusalem a cup of trembling to all the people round about, when they shall be in the siege both against Judah and against Jerusalem. ³And in that day will I make Jerusalem a burdensome stone for all people: all that burden themselves with it shall be cut in pieces, though all the people of the earth be gathered together against it. ⁴In that day, says the LORD, I will smite every horse with astonishment, and his rider with madness: and I will open my eyes on the house of Judah, and will smite every horse of the people with blindness. ⁵And the governors of Judah shall say in their heart, The inhabitants of Jerusalem shall be my strength in the LORD of hosts their God. ⁶In that day will I make the governors of Judah like an hearth of fire among the wood, and like a torch of fire in a sheaf; and they shall devour all the people round about, on the right hand and on the left: and Jerusalem shall be inhabited again in her own place, even in Jerusalem. ⁷The LORD also shall save the tents of Judah first, that the glory of the house of David and the glory of the inhabitants of Jerusalem do not magnify themselves against Judah. ⁸In that day shall the LORD defend the inhabitants of Jerusalem; and he that is feeble among them at that day shall be as David; and the house of David shall be as God, as the angel of the LORD before them. ⁹And it shall come to pass in that day, that I will seek to destroy all the nations that come against Jerusalem. ¹⁰And I will pour on the house of David, and on the inhabitants of Jerusalem, the spirit of grace and of supplications: and they shall look on me whom they have pierced, and they shall mourn for him, as one mourns for his only son, and shall be in bitterness for him, as one that is in bitterness for his firstborn. ¹¹In that day shall there be a great mourning in Jerusalem, as the mourning of Hadadrimmon in the valley of Megiddon. ¹²And the land shall mourn, every family apart; the family of the house of David apart, and their wives apart; the family of the house of Nathan apart, and their wives apart; ¹³The family of the house of Levi apart, and their wives apart; the family of Shimei apart, and their wives apart; ¹⁴All the families that remain, every family apart, and their wives apart.

13

¹In that day there shall be a fountain opened to the house of David and to the inhabitants of Jerusalem

for sin and for uncleanness. ²And it shall come to pass in that day, says the LORD of hosts, that I will cut off the names of the idols out of the land, and they shall no more be remembered: and also I will cause the prophets and the unclean spirit to pass out of the land. ³And it shall come to pass, that when any shall yet prophesy, then his father and his mother that begat him shall say to him, You shall not live; for you speak lies in the name of the LORD: and his father and his mother that begat him shall thrust him through when he prophesies. ⁴And it shall come to pass in that day, that the prophets shall be ashamed every one of his vision, when he has prophesied; neither shall they wear a rough garment to deceive: ⁵But he shall say, I am no prophet, I am an farmer; for man taught me to keep cattle from my youth. ⁶And one shall say to him, What are these wounds in your hands? Then he shall answer, Those with which I was wounded in the house of my friends. ⁷Awake, O sword, against my shepherd, and against the man that is my fellow, says the LORD of hosts: smite the shepherd, and the sheep shall be scattered: and I will turn my hand on the little ones. ⁸And it shall come to pass, that in all the land, says the LORD, two parts therein shall be cut off and die; but the third shall be left therein. ⁹And I will bring the third part through the fire, and will refine them as silver is refined, and will try them as gold is tried: they shall call on my name, and I will hear them: I will say, It is my people: and they shall say, The LORD is my God.

14 ¹Behold, the day of the LORD comes, and your spoil shall be divided in the middle of you. ²For I will gather all nations against Jerusalem to battle; and the city shall be taken, and the houses rifled, and the women ravished; and half of the city shall go forth into captivity, and the residue of the people shall not be cut off from the city. ³Then shall the LORD go forth, and fight against those nations, as when he fought in the day of battle. ⁴And his feet shall stand in that day on the mount of Olives, which is before Jerusalem on the east, and the mount of Olives shall split in the middle thereof toward the east and toward the west, and there shall be a very great valley; and half of the mountain shall remove toward the north, and half of it toward the south. ⁵And you shall flee to the valley of the mountains; for the valley of the mountains shall reach to Azal: yes, you shall flee, like as you fled from before the earthquake in the days of Uzziah king of Judah: and the LORD my God shall come, and all the saints with you. ⁶And it shall come to pass in that day, that the light shall not be clear, nor dark: ⁷But it shall be one day which shall be known to the LORD, not day, nor night: but it shall come to pass, that at evening time it shall be light. ⁸And it shall be in that day, that living waters shall go out from Jerusalem; half of them toward the former sea, and half of them toward the hinder sea: in summer and in winter shall it be. ⁹And the LORD shall be king over all the earth: in that day shall there be one LORD, and his name one. ¹⁰All the land shall be turned as a plain from Geba to Rimmon south of Jerusalem: and it shall be lifted up, and inhabited in her place, from Benjamin's gate to the place of the first gate, to the corner gate, and from the tower of Hananeel to the king's winepresses. ¹¹And men shall dwell in it, and there shall be no more utter destruction; but Jerusalem shall be safely inhabited. ¹²And this shall be the plague with which the LORD will smite all the people that have fought against Jerusalem; Their flesh shall consume away while they stand on their feet, and their eyes shall consume away in their holes, and their tongue shall consume away in their mouth. ¹³And it shall come to pass in that day, that a great tumult from the LORD shall be among them; and they shall lay hold every one on the hand of his neighbor, and his hand shall rise up against the hand of his neighbor. ¹⁴And Judah also shall fight at Jerusalem; and the wealth of all the heathen round about shall be gathered together, gold, and silver, and apparel, in great abundance. ¹⁵And so shall be the plague of the horse, of the mule, of the camel, and of the ass, and of all the beasts that shall be in these tents, as this plague. ¹⁶And it shall come to pass, that every one that is left of all the nations which came against Jerusalem shall even go up from year to year to worship the King, the LORD of hosts, and to keep the feast of tabernacles. ¹⁷And it shall be, that whoever will not come up of all the families of the earth to Jerusalem to worship the King, the LORD of hosts, even on them shall be no rain. ¹⁸And if the family of Egypt go not up, and come not, that have no rain; there shall be the plague, with which the LORD will smite the heathen that come not up to keep the feast of tabernacles. ¹⁹This shall be the punishment of Egypt, and the punishment of all nations that come not up to keep the feast of tabernacles. ²⁰In that day shall there be on the bells of the horses, HOLINESS UNTO THE LORD; and the pots in the LORD's house shall be like the bowls before the altar. ²¹Yes, every pot in Jerusalem and in Judah shall be holiness to the LORD of hosts: and all they that sacrifice shall come and take of them, and seethe therein: and in that day there shall be no more the Canaanite in the house of the LORD of hosts.

Malachi

1 ¹The burden of the word of the LORD to Israel by Malachi. ²I have loved you, says the LORD. Yet you say, Wherein have you loved us? Was not Esau Jacob's brother? says the LORD: yet I loved Jacob, ³And I hated Esau, and laid his mountains and his heritage waste for the dragons of the wilderness. ⁴Whereas Edom said, We are impoverished, but we will return and build the desolate places; thus says the LORD of hosts, They shall build, but I will throw down; and they shall call them, The border of wickedness, and, The people against whom the LORD has indignation for ever. ⁵And your eyes shall see, and you shall say, The LORD will be magnified from the border of Israel. ⁶A son honors his father, and a servant his master: if then I be a father, where is my honor? and if I be a master, where is my fear? says the LORD of hosts to you, O priests, that despise my name. And you say, Wherein have we despised your name? ⁷You offer polluted bread on my altar; and you say, Wherein have we polluted you? In that you say, The table of the LORD is contemptible. ⁸And if you offer the blind for sacrifice, is it not evil? and if you offer the lame and sick, is it not evil? offer it now to your governor; will he be pleased with you, or accept your person? says the LORD of hosts. ⁹And now, I pray you, beseech God that he will be gracious to us: this has been by your means: will he regard your persons? says the LORD of hosts. ¹⁰Who is there even among you that would shut the doors for nothing? neither do you kindle fire on my altar for nothing. I have no pleasure in you, says the LORD of hosts, neither will I accept an offering at your hand. ¹¹For from the rising of the sun even to the going down of the same my name shall be great among the Gentiles; and in every place incense shall be offered to my name, and a pure offering: for my name shall be great among the heathen, says the LORD of hosts. ¹²But you have profaned it, in that you say, The table of the LORD is polluted; and the fruit thereof, even his meat, is contemptible. ¹³You said also, Behold, what a weariness is it! and you have snuffed at it, says the LORD of hosts; and you brought that which was torn, and the lame, and the sick; thus you brought an offering: should I accept this of your hand? says the LORD. ¹⁴But cursed be the deceiver, which has in his flock a male, and vows, and sacrifices to the LORD a corrupt thing: for I am a great King, says the LORD of hosts, and my name is dreadful among the heathen.

2 ¹And now, O you priests, this commandment is for you. ²If you will not hear, and if you will not lay it to heart, to give glory to my name, says the LORD of hosts, I will even send a curse on you, and I will curse your blessings: yes, I have cursed them already, because you do not lay it to heart. ³Behold, I will corrupt your seed, and spread dung on your faces, even the dung of your solemn feasts; and one shall take you away with it. ⁴And you shall know that I have sent this commandment to you, that my covenant might be with Levi, says the LORD of hosts. ⁵My covenant was with him of life and peace; and I gave them to him for the fear with which he feared me, and was afraid before my name. ⁶The law of truth was in his mouth, and iniquity was not found in his lips: he walked with me in peace and equity, and did turn many away from iniquity. ⁷For the priest's lips should keep knowledge, and they should seek the law at his mouth: for he is the messenger of the LORD of hosts. ⁸But you are departed out of the way; you have caused many to stumble at the law; you have corrupted the covenant of Levi, says the LORD of hosts. ⁹Therefore have I also made you contemptible and base before all the people, according as you have not kept my ways, but have been partial in the law. ¹⁰Have we not all one father? has not one God created us? why do we deal treacherously every man against his brother, by profaning the covenant of our fathers? ¹¹Judah has dealt treacherously, and an abomination is committed in Israel and in Jerusalem; for Judah has profaned the holiness of the LORD which he loved, and has married the daughter of a strange god. ¹²The LORD will cut off the man that does this, the master and the scholar, out of the tabernacles of Jacob, and him that offers an offering to the LORD of hosts. ¹³And this have you done again, covering the altar of the LORD with tears, with weeping, and with crying out, so that he regards not the offering any more, or receives it with good will at your hand. ¹⁴Yet you say, Why? Because the LORD has been witness between you and the wife of your youth, against whom you have dealt treacherously: yet is she your companion, and the wife of your covenant. ¹⁵And did not he make one? Yet had he the residue of the spirit. And why one? That he might seek a godly seed. Therefore take heed to your spirit, and let none deal treacherously against the wife of his youth. ¹⁶For the LORD, the God of Israel, says that he hates putting away: for one covers violence with his garment, says the LORD of hosts: therefore take heed to your spirit, that you deal not treacherously. ¹⁷You have wearied the LORD with your words. Yet you say, Wherein have we wearied him? When you say, Every one that does evil is good in the sight of the LORD, and he delights in them; or, Where is the God of judgment?

3 ¹Behold, I will send my messenger, and he shall prepare the way before me: and the LORD, whom you seek, shall suddenly come to his temple, even the messenger of the covenant, whom you delight in: behold, he shall come, says the LORD of hosts. ²But who may abide the day of his coming? and who shall stand when he appears? for he is like a refiner's fire, and like fullers' soap: ³And he shall sit as a refiner and purifier of silver: and he shall purify the sons of Levi, and purge them as gold and silver, that they may offer to the LORD an offering in righteousness. ⁴Then shall the offering of Judah and Jerusalem be pleasant to the LORD, as in the days of old, and as in former years. ⁵And I will come near to you to judgment; and I will be a swift witness against the sorcerers, and against the adulterers, and against false swearers, and against those that oppress the hireling in his wages, the widow, and the fatherless, and that turn aside the stranger from his right, and fear not me, says the LORD of hosts. ⁶For I am the LORD, I change not; therefore you sons of Jacob are not consumed. ⁷Even from the days of your fathers you are gone away from my ordinances, and have not kept them. Return to me, and I will return to you, says the LORD of hosts. But you said, Wherein shall we return? ⁸Will a man rob God? Yet you have robbed me. But you say,

Wherein have we robbed you? In tithes and offerings. ⁹You are cursed with a curse: for you have robbed me, even this whole nation. ¹⁰Bring you all the tithes into the storehouse, that there may be meat in my house, and prove me now herewith, says the LORD of hosts, if I will not open you the windows of heaven, and pour you out a blessing, that there shall not be room enough to receive it. ¹¹And I will rebuke the devourer for your sakes, and he shall not destroy the fruits of your ground; neither shall your vine cast her fruit before the time in the field, says the LORD of hosts. ¹²And all nations shall call you blessed: for you shall be a delightsome land, says the LORD of hosts. ¹³Your words have been stout against me, says the LORD. Yet you say, What have we spoken so much against you? ¹⁴You have said, It is vain to serve God: and what profit is it that we have kept his ordinance, and that we have walked mournfully before the LORD of hosts? ¹⁵And now we call the proud happy; yes, they that work wickedness are set up; yes, they that tempt God are even delivered. ¹⁶Then they that feared the LORD spoke often one to another: and the LORD listened, and heard it, and a book of remembrance was written before him for them that feared the LORD, and that thought on his name. ¹⁷And they shall be mine, says the LORD of hosts, in that day when I make up my jewels; and I will spare them, as a man spares his own son that serves him. ¹⁸Then shall you return, and discern between the righteous and the wicked, between him that serves God and him that serves him not.

4 ¹For, behold, the day comes, that shall burn as an oven; and all the proud, yes, and all that do wickedly, shall be stubble: and the day that comes shall burn them up, says the LORD of hosts, that it shall leave them neither root nor branch. ²But to you that fear my name shall the Sun of righteousness arise with healing in his wings; and you shall go forth, and grow up as calves of the stall. ³And you shall tread down the wicked; for they shall be ashes under the soles of your feet in the day that I shall do this, says the LORD of hosts. ⁴Remember you the law of Moses my servant, which I commanded to him in Horeb for all Israel, with the statutes and judgments. ⁵Behold, I will send you Elijah the prophet before the coming of the great and dreadful day of the LORD: ⁶And he shall turn the heart of the fathers to the children, and the heart of the children to their fathers, lest I come and smite the earth with a curse.

New Testament

Matthew

1 ¹The book of the generation of Jesus Christ, the son of David, the son of Abraham. ²Abraham was the father of Isaac; and Isaac was the father of Jacob; and Jacob was the father of Judas and his brothers; ³And Judas was the father of Phares and Zara of Thamar; and Phares was the father of Esrom; and Esrom was the father of Aram; ⁴And Aram was the father of Aminadab; and Aminadab was the father of Naasson; and Naasson was the father of Salmon; ⁵And Salmon was the father of Booz of Rachab; and Booz was the father of Obed of Ruth; and Obed was the father of Jesse; ⁶And Jesse was the father of David the king; and David the king was the father of Solomon of her that had been the wife of Urias; ⁷And Solomon was the father of Roboam; and Roboam was the father of Abia; and Abia was the father of Asa; ⁸And Asa was the father of Josaphat; and Josaphat was the father of Joram; and Joram was the father of Ozias; ⁹And Ozias was the father of Joatham; and Joatham was the father of Achaz; and Achaz was the father of Ezekias; ¹⁰And Ezekias was the father of Manasses; and Manasses was the father of Amon; and Amon was the father of Josias; ¹¹And Josias was the father of Jechonias and his brothers, about the time they were carried away to Babylon: ¹²And after they were brought to Babylon, Jechonias was the father of Salathiel; and Salathiel was the father of Zorobabel; ¹³And Zorobabel was the father of Abiud; and Abiud was the father of Eliakim; and Eliakim was the father of Azor; ¹⁴And Azor was the father of Sadoc; and Sadoc was the father of Achim; and Achim was the father of Eliud; ¹⁵And Eliud was the father of Eleazar; and Eleazar was the father of Matthan; and Matthan was the father of Jacob; ¹⁶And Jacob was the father of Joseph the husband of Mary, of whom was born Jesus, who is called Christ. ¹⁷So all the generations from Abraham to David are fourteen generations; and from David until the carrying away into Babylon are fourteen generations; and from the carrying away into Babylon to Christ are fourteen generations. ¹⁸Now the birth of Jesus Christ was on this wise: When as his mother Mary was espoused to Joseph, before they came together, she was found with child of the Holy Ghost. ¹⁹Then Joseph her husband, being a just man, and not willing to make her a public example, was minded to put her away privately. ²⁰But while he thought on these things, behold, the angel of the LORD appeared to him in a dream, saying, Joseph, you son of David, fear not to take to you Mary your wife: for that which is conceived in her is of the Holy Ghost. ²¹And she shall bring forth a son, and you shall call his name JESUS: for he shall save his people from their sins. ²²Now all this was done, that it might be fulfilled which was spoken of the Lord by the prophet, saying, ²³Behold, a virgin shall be with child, and shall bring forth a son, and they shall call his name Emmanuel, which being interpreted is, God with us. ²⁴Then Joseph being raised from sleep did as the angel of the Lord had bidden him, and took to him his wife: ²⁵And knew her not till she had brought forth her firstborn son: and he called his name JESUS.

2 ¹Now when Jesus was born in Bethlehem of Judaea in the days of Herod the king, behold, there came wise men from the east to Jerusalem, ²Saying, Where is he that is born King of the Jews? for we have seen his star in the east, and are come to worship him. ³When Herod the king had heard these things, he was troubled, and all Jerusalem with him. ⁴And when he had gathered all the chief priests and scribes of the people together, he demanded of them where Christ should be born. ⁵And they said to him, In Bethlehem of Judaea: for thus it is written by the prophet, ⁶And you Bethlehem, in the land of Juda, are not the least among the princes of Juda: for out of you shall come a Governor, that shall rule my people Israel. ⁷Then Herod, when he had privately called the wise men, inquired of them diligently what time the star appeared. ⁸And he sent them to Bethlehem, and said, Go and search diligently for the young child; and when you have found him, bring me word again, that I may come and worship him also. ⁹When they had heard the king, they departed; and, see, the star, which they saw in the east, went before them, till it came and stood over where the young child was. ¹⁰When they saw the star, they rejoiced with exceeding great joy. ¹¹And when they were come into the house, they saw the young child with Mary his mother, and fell down, and worshipped him: and when they had opened their treasures, they presented to him gifts; gold, and frankincense and myrrh. ¹²And being warned of God in a dream that they should not return to Herod, they departed into their own country another way. ¹³And when they were departed, behold, the angel of the Lord appears to Joseph in a dream, saying, Arise, and take the young child and his mother, and flee into Egypt, and be you there until I bring you word: for Herod will seek the young child to destroy him. ¹⁴When he arose, he took the young child and his mother by night, and departed into Egypt: ¹⁵And was there until the death of Herod: that it might be fulfilled which was spoken of the Lord by the prophet, saying, Out of Egypt have I called my son. ¹⁶Then Herod, when he saw that he was mocked of the wise men, was exceeding wroth, and sent forth, and slew all the children that were in Bethlehem, and in all the coasts thereof, from two years old and under, according to the time which he had diligently inquired of the wise men. ¹⁷Then was fulfilled that which was spoken by Jeremy the prophet, saying, ¹⁸In Rama was there a voice heard, lamentation, and weeping, and great mourning, Rachel weeping for her children, and would not be comforted, because they are not. ¹⁹But when Herod was dead, behold, an angel of the Lord appears in a dream to Joseph in Egypt, ²⁰Saying, Arise, and take the young child and his mother, and go into the land of Israel: for they are dead which sought the young child's life. ²¹And he arose, and took the young child and his mother, and came into the land of Israel. ²²But when he heard that Archelaus did reign in Judaea in the room of his father Herod, he was afraid to go thither: notwithstanding, being warned of God in a dream, he turned aside into the parts of Galilee: ²³And he came and dwelled in a city called Nazareth: that it might be fulfilled which was spoken by the prophets, He shall be called a Nazarene.

3 ¹In those days came John the Baptist, preaching in the wilderness of Judaea, ²And saying, Repent you: for the kingdom of heaven is at hand. ³For this is he that was spoken of by the prophet Isaiah, saying, The voice of one crying in the wilderness, Prepare you the way of the Lord, make his paths straight. ⁴And the same John had his raiment of camel's hair, and a leather girdle about his loins; and his meat was locusts and wild honey. ⁵Then went out to him Jerusalem, and all Judaea, and all the region round about Jordan, ⁶And were baptized of him in Jordan, confessing their sins. ⁷But when he saw many of the Pharisees and Sadducees come to his baptism, he said to them, O generation of vipers, who has warned you to flee from the wrath to come? ⁸Bring forth therefore fruits meet for repentance: ⁹And think not to say within yourselves, We have Abraham to our father: for I say to you, that God is able of these stones to raise up children to Abraham. ¹⁰And now also the ax is laid to the root of the trees: therefore every tree which brings not forth good fruit is hewn down, and cast into the fire. ¹¹I indeed baptize you with water to repentance. but he that comes after me is mightier than I, whose shoes I am not worthy to bear: he shall baptize you with the Holy Ghost, and with fire: ¹²Whose fan is in his hand, and he will thoroughly purge his floor, and gather his wheat into the garner; but he will burn up the chaff with unquenchable fire. ¹³Then comes Jesus from Galilee to Jordan to John, to be baptized of him. ¹⁴But John forbade him, saying, I have need to be baptized of you, and come you to me? ¹⁵And Jesus answering said to him, Suffer it to be so now: for thus it becomes us to fulfill all righteousness. Then he suffered him. ¹⁶And Jesus, when he was baptized, went up straightway out of the water: and, see, the heavens were opened to him, and he saw the Spirit of God descending like a dove, and lighting on him: ¹⁷And see a voice from heaven, saying, This is my beloved Son, in whom I am well pleased.

4 ¹Then was Jesus led up of the spirit into the wilderness to be tempted of the devil. ²And when he had fasted forty days and forty nights, he was afterward an hungered. ³And when the tempter came to him, he said, If you be the Son of God, command that these stones be made bread. ⁴But he answered and said, It is written, Man shall not live by bread alone, but by every word that proceeds out of the mouth of God. ⁵Then the devil takes him up into the holy city, and sets him on a pinnacle of the temple, ⁶And says to him, If you be the Son of God, cast yourself down: for it is written, He shall give his angels charge concerning you: and in their hands they shall bear you up, lest at any time you dash your foot against a stone. ⁷Jesus said to him, It is written again, You shall not tempt the Lord your God. ⁸Again, the devil takes him up into an exceeding high mountain, and shows him all the kingdoms of the world, and the glory of them; ⁹And says to him, All these things will I give you, if you will fall down and worship me. ¹⁰Then says Jesus to him, Get you hence, Satan: for it is written, You shall worship the Lord your God, and him only shall you serve. ¹¹Then the devil leaves him, and, behold, angels came and ministered to him. ¹²Now when Jesus had heard that John was cast into prison, he departed into Galilee; ¹³And leaving Nazareth, he came and dwelled in Capernaum, which is on the sea coast, in the borders of Zabulon and Nephthalim: ¹⁴That it might be fulfilled which was spoken by Isaiah the prophet, saying, ¹⁵The land of Zabulon, and the land of Nephthalim, by the way of the sea, beyond Jordan, Galilee of the Gentiles; ¹⁶The people which sat in darkness saw great light; and to them which sat in the region and shadow of death light is sprung up. ¹⁷From that time Jesus began to preach, and to say, Repent: for the kingdom of heaven is at hand. ¹⁸And Jesus, walking by the sea of Galilee, saw two brothers, Simon called Peter, and Andrew his brother, casting a net into the sea: for they were fishers. ¹⁹And he says to them, Follow me, and I will make you fishers of men. ²⁰And they straightway left their nets, and followed him. ²¹And going on from there, he saw other two brothers, James the son of Zebedee, and John his brother, in a ship with Zebedee their father, mending their nets; and he called them. ²²And they immediately left the ship and their father, and followed him. ²³And Jesus went about all Galilee, teaching in their synagogues, and preaching the gospel of the kingdom, and healing all manner of sickness and all manner of disease among the people. ²⁴And his fame went throughout all Syria: and they brought to him all sick people that were taken with divers diseases and torments, and those which were possessed with devils, and those which were lunatic, and those that had the palsy; and he healed them. ²⁵And there followed him great multitudes of people from Galilee, and from Decapolis, and from Jerusalem, and from Judaea, and from beyond Jordan.

5 ¹And seeing the multitudes, he went up into a mountain: and when he was set, his disciples came to him: ²And he opened his mouth, and taught them, saying, ³Blessed are the poor in spirit: for theirs is the kingdom of heaven. ⁴Blessed are they that mourn: for they shall be comforted. ⁵Blessed are the meek: for they shall inherit the earth. ⁶Blessed are they which do hunger and thirst after righteousness: for they shall be filled. ⁷Blessed are the merciful: for they shall obtain mercy. ⁸Blessed are the pure in heart: for they shall see God. ⁹Blessed are the peacemakers: for they shall be called the children of God. ¹⁰Blessed are they which are persecuted for righteousness' sake: for theirs is the kingdom of heaven. ¹¹Blessed are you, when men shall revile you, and persecute you, and shall say all manner of evil against you falsely, for my sake. ¹²Rejoice, and be exceeding glad: for great is your reward in heaven: for so persecuted they the prophets which were before you. ¹³You are the salt of the earth: but if the salt have lost his flavor, with which shall it be salted? it is thereafter good for nothing, but to be cast out, and to be trodden under foot of men. ¹⁴You are the light of the world. A city that is set on an hill cannot be hid. ¹⁵Neither do men light a candle, and put it under a bushel, but on a candlestick; and it gives light to all that are in the house. ¹⁶Let your light so shine before men, that they may see your good works, and glorify your Father which is in heaven. ¹⁷Think not that I am come to destroy the law, or the prophets: I am not come to destroy, but to fulfill. ¹⁸For truly I say to you, Till heaven and earth pass, one stroke or one pronunciation mark shall in no wise pass from the law, till

all be fulfilled. ¹⁹Whoever therefore shall break one of these least commandments, and shall teach men so, he shall be called the least in the kingdom of heaven: but whoever shall do and teach them, the same shall be called great in the kingdom of heaven. ²⁰For I say to you, That except your righteousness shall exceed the righteousness of the scribes and Pharisees, you shall in no case enter into the kingdom of heaven. ²¹You have heard that it was said of them of old time, You shall not kill; and whoever shall kill shall be in danger of the judgment: ²²But I say to you, That whoever is angry with his brother without a cause shall be in danger of the judgment: and whoever shall say to his brother, Raca, shall be in danger of the council: but whoever shall say, You fool, shall be in danger of hell fire. ²³Therefore if you bring your gift to the altar, and there remember that your brother has something against you; ²⁴Leave there your gift before the altar, and go your way; first be reconciled to your brother, and then come and offer your gift. ²⁵Agree with your adversary quickly, whiles you are in the way with him; lest at any time the adversary deliver you to the judge, and the judge deliver you to the officer, and you be cast into prison. ²⁶Truly I say to you, You shall by no means come out there, till you have paid the uttermost farthing. ²⁷You have heard that it was said by them of old time, You shall not commit adultery: ²⁸But I say to you, That whoever looks on a woman to lust after her has committed adultery with her already in his heart. ²⁹And if your right eye offend you, pluck it out, and cast it from you: for it is profitable for you that one of your members should perish, and not that your whole body should be cast into hell. ³⁰And if your right hand offend you, cut it off, and cast it from you: for it is profitable for you that one of your members should perish, and not that your whole body should be cast into hell. ³¹It has been said, Whoever shall put away his wife, let him give her a writing of divorce: ³²But I say to you, That whoever shall put away his wife, saving for the cause of fornication, causes her to commit adultery: and whoever shall marry her that is divorced commits adultery. ³³Again, you have heard that it has been said by them of old time, You shall not forswear yourself, but shall perform to the Lord your oaths: ³⁴But I say to you, Swear not at all; neither by heaven; for it is God's throne: ³⁵Nor by the earth; for it is his footstool: neither by Jerusalem; for it is the city of the great King. ³⁶Neither shall you swear by your head, because you can not make one hair white or black. ³⁷But let your communication be, Yes, yes; No, no: for whatever is more than these comes of evil. ³⁸You have heard that it has been said, An eye for an eye, and a tooth for a tooth: ³⁹But I say to you, That you resist not evil: but whoever shall smite you on your right cheek, turn to him the other also. ⁴⁰And if any man will sue you at the law, and take away your coat, let him have your cloak also. ⁴¹And whoever shall compel you to go a mile, go with him two. ⁴²Give to him that asks you, and from him that would borrow of you turn not you away. ⁴³You have heard that it has been said, You shall love your neighbor, and hate your enemy. ⁴⁴But I say to you, Love your enemies, bless them that curse you, do good to them that hate you, and pray for them which spitefully use you, and persecute you; ⁴⁵That you may be the children of your Father which is in heaven: for he makes his sun to rise on the evil and on the good, and sends rain on the just and on the unjust. ⁴⁶For if you love them which love you, what reward have you? do not even the publicans the same? ⁴⁷And if you salute your brothers only, what do you more than others? do not even the publicans so? ⁴⁸Be you therefore perfect, even as your Father which is in heaven is perfect.

6 ¹Take heed that you do not your alms before men, to be seen of them: otherwise you have no reward of your Father which is in heaven. ²Therefore when you do your alms, do not sound a trumpet before you, as the hypocrites do in the synagogues and in the streets, that they may have glory of men. Truly I say to you, They have their reward. ³But when you do alms, let not your left hand know what your right hand does: ⁴That your alms may be in secret: and your Father which sees in secret himself shall reward you openly. ⁵And when you pray, you shall not be as the hypocrites are: for they love to pray standing in the synagogues and in the corners of the streets, that they may be seen of men. Truly I say to you, They have their reward. ⁶But you, when you pray, enter into your closet, and when you have shut your door, pray to your Father which is in secret; and your Father which sees in secret shall reward you openly. ⁷But when you pray, use not vain repetitions, as the heathen do: for they think that they shall be heard for their much speaking. ⁸Be not you therefore like to them: for your Father knows what things you have need of, before you ask him. ⁹After this manner therefore pray you: Our Father which are in heaven, Hallowed be your name. ¹⁰Your kingdom come, Your will be done in earth, as it is in heaven. ¹¹Give us this day our daily bread. ¹²And forgive us our debts, as we forgive our debtors. ¹³And lead us not into temptation, but deliver us from evil: For your is the kingdom, and the power, and the glory, for ever. Amen. ¹⁴For if you forgive men their trespasses, your heavenly Father will also forgive you: ¹⁵But if you forgive not men their trespasses, neither will your Father forgive your trespasses. ¹⁶Moreover when you fast, be not, as the hypocrites, of a sad countenance: for they disfigure their faces, that they may appear to men to fast. Truly I say to you, They have their reward. ¹⁷But you, when you fast, anoint your head, and wash your face; ¹⁸That you appear not to men to fast, but to your Father which is in secret: and your Father, which sees in secret, shall reward you openly. ¹⁹Lay not up for yourselves treasures on earth, where moth and rust does corrupt, and where thieves break through and steal: ²⁰But lay up for yourselves treasures in heaven, where neither moth nor rust does corrupt, and where thieves do not break through nor steal: ²¹For where your treasure is, there will your heart be also. ²²The light of the body is the eye: if therefore your eye be single, your whole body shall be full of light. ²³But if your eye be evil, your whole body shall be full of darkness. If therefore the light that is in you be darkness, how great is that darkness! ²⁴No man can serve two masters: for either he will hate the one, and love the other; or else he will hold to the one, and despise the other. You cannot serve God and mammon. ²⁵Therefore I say to you, Take no thought for your life, what you shall eat, or what you shall drink; nor yet for your body, what you shall put on. Is not the life more than meat, and the body than raiment? ²⁶Behold the fowls of the air: for they sow not, neither do they reap, nor gather into barns; yet your heavenly Father feeds them. Are you not much better than they? ²⁷Which of you by taking thought can add one cubit to his stature? ²⁸And why take you thought for raiment? Consider the lilies of the field, how they grow; they toil not, neither do they spin; ²⁹And yet I say to you, That even Solomon in all his glory was not arrayed like one of these. ³⁰Why, if God so clothe the grass of the field, which to day is, and to morrow is cast into the oven, shall he not much more clothe you, O you of little faith? ³¹Therefore take no thought, saying, What shall we eat? or, What shall we drink? or, Wherewithal shall we be clothed? ³²(For after all these things do the Gentiles seek:) for your heavenly Father knows that you have need of all these things. ³³But seek you first the kingdom of God, and his righteousness; and all these things shall be added to you. ³⁴Take therefore no thought for the morrow: for the morrow shall take thought for the things of itself. Sufficient to the day is the evil thereof.

7 ¹Judge not, that you be not judged. ²For with what judgment you judge, you shall be judged: and with what measure you mete, it shall be measured to you again. ³And why behold you the mote that is in your brother's eye, but consider not the beam that is in your own eye? ⁴Or how will you say to your brother, Let me pull out the mote out of your eye; and, behold, a beam is in your own eye? ⁵You hypocrite, first cast out the beam out of your own eye; and then shall you see clearly to cast out the mote out of your brother's eye. ⁶Give not that which is holy to the dogs, neither cast you your pearls before swine, lest they trample them under their feet, and turn again and rend you. ⁷Ask, and it shall be given you; seek, and you shall find; knock, and it shall be opened to you: ⁸For every one that asks receives; and he that seeks finds; and to him that knocks it shall be opened. ⁹Or what man is there of you, whom if his son ask bread, will he give him a stone? ¹⁰Or if he ask a fish, will he give him a serpent? ¹¹If you then, being evil, know how to give good gifts to your children, how much more shall your Father which is in heaven give good things to them that ask him? ¹²Therefore all things whatever you would that men should do to you, do you even so to them: for this is the law and the prophets. ¹³Enter you in at the strait gate: for wide is the gate, and broad is the way, that leads to destruction, and many there be which go in thereat: ¹⁴Because strait is the gate, and narrow is the way, which leads to life, and few there be that find it. ¹⁵Beware of false prophets, which come to you in sheep's clothing, but inwardly they are ravening wolves. ¹⁶You shall know them by their fruits. Do men gather grapes of thorns, or figs of thistles? ¹⁷Even so every good tree brings forth good fruit; but a corrupt tree brings forth evil fruit. ¹⁸A good tree cannot bring forth evil fruit, neither can a corrupt tree bring forth good fruit. ¹⁹Every tree that brings not forth good fruit is hewn down, and cast into the fire. ²⁰Why by their fruits you shall know them. ²¹Not every one that says to me, Lord, Lord, shall enter into the kingdom of heaven; but he that does the will of my Father which is in heaven. ²²Many will say to me in that day, Lord, Lord, have we not prophesied in your name? and in your name have cast out devils? and in your name done many wonderful works? ²³And then will I profess to them, I never knew you: depart from me, you that work iniquity. ²⁴Therefore whoever hears these sayings of mine, and does them, I will liken him to a wise man, which built his house on a rock: ²⁵And the rain descended, and the floods came, and the winds blew, and beat on that house; and it fell not: for it was founded on a rock. ²⁶And every one that hears these sayings of mine, and does them not, shall be likened to a foolish man, which built his house on the sand: ²⁷And the rain descended, and the floods came, and the winds blew, and beat on that house; and it fell: and great was the fall of it. ²⁸And it came to pass, when Jesus had ended these sayings, the people were astonished at his doctrine: ²⁹For he taught them as one having authority, and not as the scribes.

8 ¹When he was come down from the mountain, great multitudes followed him. ²And, behold, there came a leper and worshipped him, saying, Lord, if you will, you can make me clean. ³And Jesus put forth his hand, and touched him, saying, I will; be you clean. And immediately his leprosy was cleansed. ⁴And Jesus says to him, See you tell no man; but go your way, show yourself to the priest, and offer the gift that Moses commanded, for a testimony to them. ⁵And when Jesus was entered into Capernaum, there came to him a centurion, beseeching him, ⁶And saying, Lord, my servant lies at home sick of the palsy, grievously tormented. ⁷And Jesus says to him, I will come and heal him. ⁸The centurion answered and said, Lord, I am not worthy that you should come under my roof: but speak the word only, and my servant shall be healed. ⁹For I am a man under authority, having soldiers under me: and I say to this man, Go, and he goes; and to another, Come, and he comes; and to my servant, Do this, and he does it. ¹⁰When Jesus heard it, he marveled, and said to them that followed, Truly I say to you, I have not found so great faith, no, not in Israel. ¹¹And I say to you, That many shall come from the east and west, and shall sit down with Abraham, and Isaac, and Jacob, in the kingdom of heaven. ¹²But the children of the kingdom shall be cast out into outer darkness: there shall be weeping and gnashing of teeth. ¹³And Jesus said to the centurion, Go your way; and as you have believed, so be it done to you. And his servant was healed in the selfsame hour. ¹⁴And when Jesus was come into Peter's house, he saw his wife's mother laid, and sick of a fever. ¹⁵And he touched her hand, and the fever left her: and she arose, and ministered to them. ¹⁶When the even was come, they brought to him many that were possessed with devils: and he cast out the spirits with his word, and healed all that were sick: ¹⁷That it might be fulfilled which was spoken by Isaiah the prophet, saying, Himself took our infirmities, and bore our sicknesses. ¹⁸Now when Jesus saw great multitudes about him, he gave commandment to depart to the other side. ¹⁹And a certain scribe came, and said to him, Master, I will follow you wherever you go. ²⁰And Jesus says to him, The foxes have holes, and the birds of the air have nests; but the Son of man has not where to lay his head. ²¹And another of his disciples said to him, Lord, suffer me first to go and bury my father. ²²But Jesus said to him, Follow me; and let the dead bury their dead. ²³And when he was entered into a ship, his disciples followed him. ²⁴And, behold, there arose a great tempest in the sea, so that the ship was covered with the waves: but he was asleep. ²⁵And his disciples came to him, and awoke him, saying, Lord, save us: we perish. ²⁶And he says to them, Why are you fearful, O you of little faith? Then he arose, and rebuked the winds and the sea; and there was a great calm. ²⁷But the men marveled, saying, What manner of man is this, that even the winds and the sea obey him! ²⁸And when he was come to the other side into the country of the Gergesenes, there met him two possessed with devils, coming out of the tombs, exceeding fierce, so that no man might pass by that way. ²⁹And, behold, they cried out, saying, What have we to do with you, Jesus, you Son of God? are you come here to torment us before the time? ³⁰And there was a good way off from them an herd of many swine feeding. ³¹So the devils sought him, saying, If you cast us out, suffer us to go away into the herd of swine. ³²And he said to them, Go. And when they were come out, they went into the herd of swine: and, behold, the whole herd of swine ran violently down a steep place into the sea, and perished in the waters. ³³And they that kept them fled, and went their ways into the city, and told every thing, and what was befallen to the possessed of the devils. ³⁴And, behold, the whole city came out to meet Jesus: and when they saw him, they sought him that he would depart out of their coasts.

9 ¹And he entered into a ship, and passed over, and came into his own city. ²And, behold, they brought to him a man sick of the palsy, lying on a bed: and Jesus seeing their faith said to the sick of the palsy; Son, be of good cheer; your sins be forgiven you. ³And, behold, certain of the scribes said within themselves, This man blasphemes. ⁴And Jesus knowing their thoughts said, Why think you evil in your hearts? ⁵For whether is easier, to say, Your sins be forgiven you; or to say, Arise, and walk? ⁶But that you may know that the Son of man has power on earth to forgive sins, (then says he to the sick of the palsy,) Arise, take up your bed, and go to your house. ⁷And he arose, and departed to his house. ⁸But when the multitudes saw it, they marveled, and glorified God, which had given such power to men. ⁹And as Jesus passed forth from there, he saw a man, named Matthew, sitting at the receipt of custom: and he says to him, Follow me. And he arose, and followed him. ¹⁰And it came to pass, as Jesus sat at meat in the house, behold, many publicans and sinners came and sat down with him and his disciples. ¹¹And when the Pharisees saw it, they said to his disciples, Why eats your Master with publicans and sinners? ¹²But when Jesus heard that, he said to them, They that be whole need not a physician, but they that are sick. ¹³But go you and learn what that means, I will have mercy, and not sacrifice: for I am not come to call the righteous, but sinners to repentance. ¹⁴Then came to him the disciples of John, saying, Why do we and the Pharisees fast oft, but your disciples fast not? ¹⁵And Jesus said to them, Can the children of the bridal chamber mourn, as long as the bridegroom is with them? but the days will come, when the bridegroom shall be taken from them, and then shall they fast. ¹⁶No man puts a piece of new cloth to an old garment, for that which is put in to fill it up takes from the garment, and the rent is made worse. ¹⁷Neither do men put new wine into old bottles: else the bottles break, and the wine runs out, and the bottles perish: but they put new wine into new bottles, and both are preserved. ¹⁸While he spoke these things to them, behold, there came a certain ruler, and worshipped him, saying, My daughter is even now dead: but come and lay your hand on her, and she shall live. ¹⁹And Jesus arose, and followed him, and so did his disciples. ²⁰And, behold, a woman, which was diseased with an issue of blood twelve years, came behind him, and touched the hem of his garment: ²¹For she said within herself, If I may but touch his garment, I shall be whole. ²²But Jesus turned him about, and when he saw her, he said, Daughter, be of good comfort; your faith has made you whole. And the woman was made whole from that hour. ²³And when Jesus came into the ruler's house, and saw the minstrels and the people making a noise, ²⁴He said to them, Give place: for the maid is not dead, but sleeps. And they laughed him to scorn. ²⁵But when the people were put forth, he went in, and took her by the hand, and the maid arose. ²⁶And the fame hereof went abroad into all that land. ²⁷And when Jesus departed there, two blind men followed him, crying, and saying, You son of David, have mercy on us. ²⁸And when he was come into the house, the blind men came to him: and Jesus says to them, Believe you that I am able to do this? They said to him, Yes, Lord. ²⁹Then touched he their eyes, saying, According to your faith be it to you. ³⁰And their eyes were opened; and Jesus straightly charged them, saying, See that no man know it. ³¹But they, when they were departed, spread abroad his fame in all that country. ³²As they went out, behold, they brought to him a dumb man possessed with a devil. ³³And when the devil was cast out, the dumb spoke: and the multitudes marveled, saying, It was never so seen in Israel. ³⁴But the Pharisees said, He casts out devils through the prince of the devils. ³⁵And Jesus went about all the cities and villages, teaching in their synagogues, and preaching the gospel of the kingdom, and healing every sickness and every disease among the people. ³⁶But when he saw the multitudes, he was moved with compassion on them, because they fainted, and were scattered abroad, as sheep having no shepherd. ³⁷Then says he to his disciples, The harvest truly is plenteous, but the laborers are few; ³⁸Pray you therefore the Lord of the harvest, that he will send forth laborers into his harvest.

10 ¹And when he had called to him his twelve disciples, he gave them power against unclean spirits, to cast them out, and to heal all manner of sickness and all manner of disease. ²Now the names of the twelve apostles are these; The first, Simon, who is called Peter, and Andrew his brother; James the son of Zebedee, and John his brother; ³Philip, and Bartholomew; Thomas, and Matthew the publican; James the son of Alphaeus, and Lebbaeus, whose surname was Thaddaeus; ⁴Simon the Canaanite, and Judas Iscariot, who also betrayed him. ⁵These twelve Jesus sent forth, and commanded them, saying, Go not into the way of the Gentiles, and into any city of the Samaritans enter you not: ⁶But go rather to the lost sheep of the house of Israel. ⁷And as you go, preach, saying, The kingdom of heaven is at hand. ⁸Heal the sick, cleanse the lepers, raise the dead, cast out devils: freely you have received, freely give.

⁹Provide neither gold, nor silver, nor brass in your purses, ¹⁰Nor money for your journey, neither two coats, neither shoes, nor yet staves: for the workman is worthy of his meat. ¹¹And into whatever city or town you shall enter, inquire who in it is worthy; and there abide till you go there. ¹²And when you come into an house, salute it. ¹³And if the house be worthy, let your peace come on it: but if it be not worthy, let your peace return to you. ¹⁴And whoever shall not receive you, nor hear your words, when you depart out of that house or city, shake off the dust of your feet. ¹⁵Truly I say to you, It shall be more tolerable for the land of Sodom and Gomorrha in the day of judgment, than for that city. ¹⁶Behold, I send you forth as sheep in the middle of wolves: be you therefore wise as serpents, and harmless as doves. ¹⁷But beware of men: for they will deliver you up to the councils, and they will whip you in their synagogues; ¹⁸And you shall be brought before governors and kings for my sake, for a testimony against them and the Gentiles. ¹⁹But when they deliver you up, take no thought how or what you shall speak: for it shall be given you in that same hour what you shall speak. ²⁰For it is not you that speak, but the Spirit of your Father which speaks in you. ²¹And the brother shall deliver up the brother to death, and the father the child: and the children shall rise up against their parents, and cause them to be put to death. ²²And you shall be hated of all men for my name's sake: but he that endures to the end shall be saved. ²³But when they persecute you in this city, flee you into another: for truly I say to you, You shall not have gone over the cities of Israel, till the Son of man be come. ²⁴The disciple is not above his master, nor the servant above his lord. ²⁵It is enough for the disciple that he be as his master, and the servant as his lord. If they have called the master of the house Beelzebub, how much more shall they call them of his household? ²⁶Fear them not therefore: for there is nothing covered, that shall not be revealed; and hid, that shall not be known. ²⁷What I tell you in darkness, that speak you in light: and what you hear in the ear, that preach you on the housetops. ²⁸And fear not them which kill the body, but are not able to kill the soul: but rather fear him which is able to destroy both soul and body in hell. ²⁹Are not two sparrows sold for a farthing? and one of them shall not fall on the ground without your Father. ³⁰But the very hairs of your head are all numbered. ³¹Fear you not therefore, you are of more value than many sparrows. ³²Whoever therefore shall confess me before men, him will I confess also before my Father which is in heaven. ³³But whoever shall deny me before men, him will I also deny before my Father which is in heaven. ³⁴Think not that I am come to send peace on earth: I came not to send peace, but a sword. ³⁵For I am come to set a man at variance against his father, and the daughter against her mother, and the daughter in law against her mother in law. ³⁶And a man's foes shall be they of his own household. ³⁷He that loves father or mother more than me is not worthy of me: and he that loves son or daughter more than me is not worthy of me. ³⁸And he that takes not his cross, and follows after me, is not worthy of me. ³⁹He that finds his life shall lose it: and he that loses his life for my sake shall find it. ⁴⁰He that receives you receives me, and he that receives me receives him that sent me. ⁴¹He that receives a prophet in the name of a prophet shall receive a prophet's reward; and he that receives a righteous man in the name of a righteous man shall receive a righteous man's reward. ⁴²And whoever shall give to drink to one of these little ones a cup of cold water only in the name of a disciple, truly I say to you, he shall in no wise lose his reward.

11 ¹And it came to pass, when Jesus had made an end of commanding his twelve disciples, he departed there to teach and to preach in their cities. ²Now when John had heard in the prison the works of Christ, he sent two of his disciples, ³And said to him, Are you he that should come, or do we look for another? ⁴Jesus answered and said to them, Go and show John again those things which you do hear and see: ⁵The blind receive their sight, and the lame walk, the lepers are cleansed, and the deaf hear, the dead are raised up, and the poor have the gospel preached to them. ⁶And blessed is he, whoever shall not be offended in me. ⁷And as they departed, Jesus began to say to the multitudes concerning John, What went you out into the wilderness to see? A reed shaken with the wind? ⁸But what went you out for to see? A man clothed in soft raiment? behold, they that wear soft clothing are in kings' houses. ⁹But what went you out for to see? A prophet? yes, I say to you, and more than a prophet. ¹⁰For this is he, of whom it is written, Behold, I send my messenger before your face, which shall prepare your way before you. ¹¹Truly I say to you, Among them that are born of women there has not risen a greater than John the Baptist: notwithstanding he that is least in the kingdom of heaven is greater than he. ¹²And from the days of John the Baptist until now the kingdom of heaven suffers violence, and the violent take it by force. ¹³For all the prophets and the law prophesied until John. ¹⁴And if you will receive it, this is Elias, which was for to come. ¹⁵He that has ears to hear, let him hear. ¹⁶But to what shall I liken this generation? It is like to children sitting in the markets, and calling to their fellows, ¹⁷And saying, We have piped to you, and you have not danced; we have mourned to you, and you have not lamented. ¹⁸For John came neither eating nor drinking, and they say, He has a devil. ¹⁹The Son of man came eating and drinking, and they say, Behold a man gluttonous, and a drunkard, a friend of publicans and sinners. But wisdom is justified of her children. ²⁰Then began he to upbraid the cities wherein most of his mighty works were done, because they repented not: ²¹Woe to you, Chorazin! woe to you, Bethsaida! for if the mighty works, which were done in you, had been done in Tyre and Sidon, they would have repented long ago in sackcloth and ashes. ²²But I say to you, It shall be more tolerable for Tyre and Sidon at the day of judgment, than for you. ²³And you, Capernaum, which are exalted to heaven, shall be brought down to hell: for if the mighty works, which have been done in you, had been done in Sodom, it would have remained until this day. ²⁴But I say to you, That it shall be more tolerable for the land of Sodom in the day of judgment, than for you. ²⁵At that time Jesus answered and said, I thank you, O Father, Lord of heaven and earth, because you have hid these things from the wise and prudent, and have revealed them to babes. ²⁶Even so, Father: for so it seemed good in your sight. ²⁷All things are delivered to me of my Father: and no man knows the Son,

but the Father; neither knows any man the Father, save the Son, and he to whomsoever the Son will reveal him. ²⁸Come to me, all you that labor and are heavy laden, and I will give you rest. ²⁹Take my yoke on you, and learn of me; for I am meek and lowly in heart: and you shall find rest to your souls. ³⁰For my yoke is easy, and my burden is light.

12 ¹At that time Jesus went on the sabbath day through the corn; and his disciples were an hungered, and began to pluck the ears of corn and to eat. ²But when the Pharisees saw it, they said to him, Behold, your disciples do that which is not lawful to do on the sabbath day. ³But he said to them, Have you not read what David did, when he was an hungered, and they that were with him; ⁴How he entered into the house of God, and did eat the show bread, which was not lawful for him to eat, neither for them which were with him, but only for the priests? ⁵Or have you not read in the law, how that on the sabbath days the priests in the temple profane the sabbath, and are blameless? ⁶But I say to you, That in this place is one greater than the temple. ⁷But if you had known what this means, I will have mercy, and not sacrifice, you would not have condemned the guiltless. ⁸For the Son of man is Lord even of the sabbath day. ⁹And when he was departed there, he went into their synagogue: ¹⁰And, behold, there was a man which had his hand withered. And they asked him, saying, Is it lawful to heal on the sabbath days? that they might accuse him. ¹¹And he said to them, What man shall there be among you, that shall have one sheep, and if it fall into a pit on the sabbath day, will he not lay hold on it, and lift it out? ¹²How much then is a man better than a sheep? Why it is lawful to do well on the sabbath days. ¹³Then says he to the man, Stretch forth your hand. And he stretched it forth; and it was restored whole, like as the other. ¹⁴Then the Pharisees went out, and held a council against him, how they might destroy him. ¹⁵But when Jesus knew it, he withdrew himself from there: and great multitudes followed him, and he healed them all; ¹⁶And charged them that they should not make him known: ¹⁷That it might be fulfilled which was spoken by Isaiah the prophet, saying, ¹⁸Behold my servant, whom I have chosen; my beloved, in whom my soul is well pleased: I will put my spirit on him, and he shall show judgment to the Gentiles. ¹⁹He shall not strive, nor cry; neither shall any man hear his voice in the streets. ²⁰A bruised reed shall he not break, and smoking flax shall he not quench, till he send forth judgment to victory. ²¹And in his name shall the Gentiles trust. ²²Then was brought to him one possessed with a devil, blind, and dumb: and he healed him, so that the blind and dumb both spoke and saw. ²³And all the people were amazed, and said, Is not this the son of David? ²⁴But when the Pharisees heard it, they said, This fellow does not cast out devils, but by Beelzebub the prince of the devils. ²⁵And Jesus knew their thoughts, and said to them, Every kingdom divided against itself is brought to desolation; and every city or house divided against itself shall not stand: ²⁶And if Satan cast out Satan, he is divided against himself; how shall then his kingdom stand? ²⁷And if I by Beelzebub cast out devils, by whom do your children cast them out? therefore they shall be your judges. ²⁸But if I cast out devils by the Spirit of God, then the kingdom of God is come to you. ²⁹Or else how can one enter into a strong man's house, and spoil his goods, except he first bind the strong man? and then he will spoil his house. ³⁰He that is not with me is against me; and he that gathers not with me scatters abroad. ³¹Why I say to you, All manner of sin and blasphemy shall be forgiven to men: but the blasphemy against the Holy Ghost shall not be forgiven to men. ³²And whoever speaks a word against the Son of man, it shall be forgiven him: but whoever speaks against the Holy Ghost, it shall not be forgiven him, neither in this world, neither in the world to come. ³³Either make the tree good, and his fruit good; or else make the tree corrupt, and his fruit corrupt: for the tree is known by his fruit. ³⁴O generation of vipers, how can you, being evil, speak good things? for out of the abundance of the heart the mouth speaks. ³⁵A good man out of the good treasure of the heart brings forth good things: and an evil man out of the evil treasure brings forth evil things. ³⁶But I say to you, That every idle word that men shall speak, they shall give account thereof in the day of judgment. ³⁷For by your words you shall be justified, and by your words you shall be condemned. ³⁸Then certain of the scribes and of the Pharisees answered, saying, Master, we would see a sign from you. ³⁹But he answered and said to them, An evil and adulterous generation seeks after a sign; and there shall no sign be given to it, but the sign of the prophet Jonas: ⁴⁰For as Jonas was three days and three nights in the whale's belly; so shall the Son of man be three days and three nights in the heart of the earth. ⁴¹The men of Nineveh shall rise in judgment with this generation, and shall condemn it: because they repented at the preaching of Jonas; and, behold, a greater than Jonas is here. ⁴²The queen of the south shall rise up in the judgment with this generation, and shall condemn it: for she came from the uttermost parts of the earth to hear the wisdom of Solomon; and, behold, a greater than Solomon is here. ⁴³When the unclean spirit is gone out of a man, he walks through dry places, seeking rest, and finds none. ⁴⁴Then he says, I will return into my house from where I came out; and when he is come, he finds it empty, swept, and garnished. ⁴⁵Then goes he, and takes with himself seven other spirits more wicked than himself, and they enter in and dwell there: and the last state of that man is worse than the first. Even so shall it be also to this wicked generation. ⁴⁶While he yet talked to the people, behold, his mother and his brothers stood without, desiring to speak with him. ⁴⁷Then one said to him, Behold, your mother and your brothers stand without, desiring to speak with you. ⁴⁸But he answered and said to him that told him, Who is my mother? and who are my brothers? ⁴⁹And he stretched forth his hand toward his disciples, and said, Behold my mother and my brothers! ⁵⁰For whoever shall do the will of my Father which is in heaven, the same is my brother, and sister, and mother.

13 ¹The same day went Jesus out of the house, and sat by the sea side. ²And great multitudes were gathered together to him, so that he went into a ship, and sat; and the whole multitude stood on the shore. ³And he spoke many things to them in parables, saying, Behold, a sower went forth to sow; ⁴And when he sowed, some seeds fell by the way side, and the fowls came and devoured them up:

⁵Some fell on stony places, where they had not much earth: and immediately they sprung up, because they had no deepness of earth: ⁶And when the sun was up, they were scorched; and because they had no root, they withered away. ⁷And some fell among thorns; and the thorns sprung up, and choked them: ⁸But other fell into good ground, and brought forth fruit, some an hundred times, some sixty times, some thirty times. ⁹Who has ears to hear, let him hear. ¹⁰And the disciples came, and said to him, Why speak you to them in parables? ¹¹He answered and said to them, Because it is given to you to know the mysteries of the kingdom of heaven, but to them it is not given. ¹²For whoever has, to him shall be given, and he shall have more abundance: but whoever has not, from him shall be taken away even that he has. ¹³Therefore speak I to them in parables: because they seeing see not; and hearing they hear not, neither do they understand. ¹⁴And in them is fulfilled the prophecy of Isaiah, which says, By hearing you shall hear, and shall not understand; and seeing you shall see, and shall not perceive: ¹⁵For this people's heart is waxed gross, and their ears are dull of hearing, and their eyes they have closed; lest at any time they should see with their eyes and hear with their ears, and should understand with their heart, and should be converted, and I should heal them. ¹⁶But blessed are your eyes, for they see: and your ears, for they hear. ¹⁷For truly I say to you, That many prophets and righteous men have desired to see those things which you see, and have not seen them; and to hear those things which you hear, and have not heard them. ¹⁸Hear you therefore the parable of the sower. ¹⁹When any one hears the word of the kingdom, and understands it not, then comes the wicked one, and catches away that which was sown in his heart. This is he which received seed by the way side. ²⁰But he that received the seed into stony places, the same is he that hears the word, and immediately with joy receives it; ²¹Yet has he not root in himself, but endures for a while: for when tribulation or persecution rises because of the word, by and by he is offended. ²²He also that received seed among the thorns is he that hears the word; and the care of this world, and the deceitfulness of riches, choke the word, and he becomes unfruitful. ²³But he that received seed into the good ground is he that hears the word, and understands it; which also bears fruit, and brings forth, some an hundred times, some sixty, some thirty. ²⁴Another parable put he forth to them, saying, The kingdom of heaven is likened to a man which sowed good seed in his field: ²⁵But while men slept, his enemy came and sowed tares among the wheat, and went his way. ²⁶But when the blade was sprung up, and brought forth fruit, then appeared the tares also. ²⁷So the servants of the householder came and said to him, Sir, did not you sow good seed in your field? from where then has it tares? ²⁸He said to them, An enemy has done this. The servants said to him, Will you then that we go and gather them up? ²⁹But he said, No; lest while you gather up the tares, you root up also the wheat with them. ³⁰Let both grow together until the harvest: and in the time of harvest I will say to the reapers, Gather you together first the tares, and bind them in bundles to burn them: but gather the wheat into my barn. ³¹Another parable put he forth to them, saying, The kingdom of heaven is like to a grain of mustard seed, which a man took, and sowed in his field: ³²Which indeed is the least of all seeds: but when it is grown, it is the greatest among herbs, and becomes a tree, so that the birds of the air come and lodge in the branches thereof. ³³Another parable spoke he to them; The kingdom of heaven is like to leaven, which a woman took, and hid in three measures of meal, till the whole was leavened. ³⁴All these things spoke Jesus to the multitude in parables; and without a parable spoke he not to them: ³⁵That it might be fulfilled which was spoken by the prophet, saying, I will open my mouth in parables; I will utter things which have been kept secret from the foundation of the world. ³⁶Then Jesus sent the multitude away, and went into the house: and his disciples came to him, saying, Declare to us the parable of the tares of the field. ³⁷He answered and said to them, He that sows the good seed is the Son of man; ³⁸The field is the world; the good seed are the children of the kingdom; but the tares are the children of the wicked one; ³⁹The enemy that sowed them is the devil; the harvest is the end of the world; and the reapers are the angels. ⁴⁰As therefore the tares are gathered and burned in the fire; so shall it be in the end of this world. ⁴¹The Son of man shall send forth his angels, and they shall gather out of his kingdom all things that offend, and them which do iniquity; ⁴²And shall cast them into a furnace of fire: there shall be wailing and gnashing of teeth. ⁴³Then shall the righteous shine forth as the sun in the kingdom of their Father. Who has ears to hear, let him hear. ⁴⁴Again, the kingdom of heaven is like to treasure hid in a field; the which when a man has found, he hides, and for joy thereof goes and sells all that he has, and buys that field. ⁴⁵Again, the kingdom of heaven is like to a merchant man, seeking goodly pearls: ⁴⁶Who, when he had found one pearl of great price, went and sold all that he had, and bought it. ⁴⁷Again, the kingdom of heaven is like to a net, that was cast into the sea, and gathered of every kind: ⁴⁸Which, when it was full, they drew to shore, and sat down, and gathered the good into vessels, but cast the bad away. ⁴⁹So shall it be at the end of the world: the angels shall come forth, and sever the wicked from among the just, ⁵⁰And shall cast them into the furnace of fire: there shall be wailing and gnashing of teeth. ⁵¹Jesus says to them, Have you understood all these things? They say to him, Yes, Lord. ⁵²Then said he to them, Therefore every scribe which is instructed to the kingdom of heaven is like to a man that is an householder, which brings forth out of his treasure things new and old. ⁵³And it came to pass, that when Jesus had finished these parables, he departed there. ⁵⁴And when he was come into his own country, he taught them in their synagogue, so that they were astonished, and said, From where has this man this wisdom, and these mighty works? ⁵⁵Is not this the carpenter's son? is not his mother called Mary? and his brothers, James, and Joses, and Simon, and Judas? ⁵⁶And his sisters, are they not all with us? From where then has this man all these things? ⁵⁷And they were offended in him. But Jesus said to them, A prophet is not without honor, save in his own country, and in his own house. ⁵⁸And he did not many mighty works there because of their unbelief.

14 ¹At that time Herod the tetrarch heard of the fame of Jesus, ²And said to his servants, This is John the

Baptist; he is risen from the dead; and therefore mighty works do show forth themselves in him. ³For Herod had laid hold on John, and bound him, and put him in prison for Herodias' sake, his brother Philip's wife. ⁴For John said to him, It is not lawful for you to have her. ⁵And when he would have put him to death, he feared the multitude, because they counted him as a prophet. ⁶But when Herod's birthday was kept, the daughter of Herodias danced before them, and pleased Herod. ⁷Whereupon he promised with an oath to give her whatever she would ask. ⁸And she, being before instructed of her mother, said, Give me here John Baptist's head in a charger. ⁹And the king was sorry: nevertheless for the oath's sake, and them which sat with him at meat, he commanded it to be given her. ¹⁰And he sent, and beheaded John in the prison. ¹¹And his head was brought in a charger, and given to the damsel: and she brought it to her mother. ¹²And his disciples came, and took up the body, and buried it, and went and told Jesus. ¹³When Jesus heard of it, he departed there by ship into a desert place apart: and when the people had heard thereof, they followed him on foot out of the cities. ¹⁴And Jesus went forth, and saw a great multitude, and was moved with compassion toward them, and he healed their sick. ¹⁵And when it was evening, his disciples came to him, saying, This is a desert place, and the time is now past; send the multitude away, that they may go into the villages, and buy themselves victuals. ¹⁶But Jesus said to them, They need not depart; give you them to eat. ¹⁷And they say to him, We have here but five loaves, and two fishes. ¹⁸He said, Bring them here to me. ¹⁹And he commanded the multitude to sit down on the grass, and took the five loaves, and the two fishes, and looking up to heaven, he blessed, and broke, and gave the loaves to his disciples, and the disciples to the multitude. ²⁰And they did all eat, and were filled: and they took up of the fragments that remained twelve baskets full. ²¹And they that had eaten were about five thousand men, beside women and children. ²²And straightway Jesus constrained his disciples to get into a ship, and to go before him to the other side, while he sent the multitudes away. ²³And when he had sent the multitudes away, he went up into a mountain apart to pray: and when the evening was come, he was there alone. ²⁴But the ship was now in the middle of the sea, tossed with waves: for the wind was contrary. ²⁵And in the fourth watch of the night Jesus went to them, walking on the sea. ²⁶And when the disciples saw him walking on the sea, they were troubled, saying, It is a spirit; and they cried out for fear. ²⁷But straightway Jesus spoke to them, saying, Be of good cheer; it is I; be not afraid. ²⁸And Peter answered him and said, Lord, if it be you, bid me come to you on the water. ²⁹And he said, Come. And when Peter was come down out of the ship, he walked on the water, to go to Jesus. ³⁰But when he saw the wind boisterous, he was afraid; and beginning to sink, he cried, saying, Lord, save me. ³¹And immediately Jesus stretched forth his hand, and caught him, and said to him, O you of little faith, why did you doubt? ³²And when they were come into the ship, the wind ceased. ³³Then they that were in the ship came and worshipped him, saying, Of a truth you are the Son of God. ³⁴And when they were gone over, they came into the land of Gennesaret.

³⁵And when the men of that place had knowledge of him, they sent out into all that country round about, and brought to him all that were diseased; ³⁶And sought him that they might only touch the hem of his garment: and as many as touched were made perfectly whole.

15

¹Then came to Jesus scribes and Pharisees, which were of Jerusalem, saying, ²Why do your disciples transgress the tradition of the elders? for they wash not their hands when they eat bread. ³But he answered and said to them, Why do you also transgress the commandment of God by your tradition? ⁴For God commanded, saying, Honor your father and mother: and, He that curses father or mother, let him die the death. ⁵But you say, Whoever shall say to his father or his mother, It is a gift, by whatever you might be profited by me; ⁶And honor not his father or his mother, he shall be free. Thus have you made the commandment of God of none effect by your tradition. ⁷You hypocrites, well did Isaiah prophesy of you, saying, ⁸This people draws near to me with their mouth, and honors me with their lips; but their heart is far from me. ⁹But in vain they do worship me, teaching for doctrines the commandments of men. ¹⁰And he called the multitude, and said to them, Hear, and understand: ¹¹Not that which goes into the mouth defiles a man; but that which comes out of the mouth, this defiles a man. ¹²Then came his disciples, and said to him, Know you that the Pharisees were offended, after they heard this saying? ¹³But he answered and said, Every plant, which my heavenly Father has not planted, shall be rooted up. ¹⁴Let them alone: they be blind leaders of the blind. And if the blind lead the blind, both shall fall into the ditch. ¹⁵Then answered Peter and said to him, Declare to us this parable. ¹⁶And Jesus said, Are you also yet without understanding? ¹⁷Do not you yet understand, that whatever enters in at the mouth goes into the belly, and is cast out into the draught? ¹⁸But those things which proceed out of the mouth come forth from the heart; and they defile the man. ¹⁹For out of the heart proceed evil thoughts, murders, adulteries, fornications, thefts, false witness, blasphemies: ²⁰These are the things which defile a man: but to eat with unwashed hands defiles not a man. ²¹Then Jesus went there, and departed into the coasts of Tyre and Sidon. ²²And, behold, a woman of Canaan came out of the same coasts, and cried to him, saying, Have mercy on me, O Lord, you son of David; my daughter is grievously vexed with a devil. ²³But he answered her not a word. And his disciples came and sought him, saying, Send her away; for she cries after us. ²⁴But he answered and said, I am not sent but to the lost sheep of the house of Israel. ²⁵Then came she and worshipped him, saying, Lord, help me. ²⁶But he answered and said, It is not meet to take the children's bread, and to cast it to dogs. ²⁷And she said, Truth, Lord: yet the dogs eat of the crumbs which fall from their masters' table. ²⁸Then Jesus answered and said to her, O woman, great is your faith: be it to you even as you will. And her daughter was made whole from that very hour. ²⁹And Jesus departed from there, and came near to the sea of Galilee; and went up into a mountain, and sat down there. ³⁰And great multitudes came to him, having with them those that were lame, blind, dumb, maimed, and many others, and cast them down at Jesus' feet; and he healed them: ³¹So that the multitude

wondered, when they saw the dumb to speak, the maimed to be whole, the lame to walk, and the blind to see: and they glorified the God of Israel. ³²Then Jesus called his disciples to him, and said, I have compassion on the multitude, because they continue with me now three days, and have nothing to eat: and I will not send them away fasting, lest they faint in the way. ³³And his disciples say to him, From where should we have so much bread in the wilderness, as to fill so great a multitude? ³⁴And Jesus says to them, How many loaves have you? And they said, Seven, and a few little fishes. ³⁵And he commanded the multitude to sit down on the ground. ³⁶And he took the seven loaves and the fishes, and gave thanks, and broke them, and gave to his disciples, and the disciples to the multitude. ³⁷And they did all eat, and were filled: and they took up of the broken meat that was left seven baskets full. ³⁸And they that did eat were four thousand men, beside women and children. ³⁹And he sent away the multitude, and took ship, and came into the coasts of Magdala.

16 ¹The Pharisees also with the Sadducees came, and tempting desired him that he would show them a sign from heaven. ²He answered and said to them, When it is evening, you say, It will be fair weather: for the sky is red. ³And in the morning, It will be foul weather to day: for the sky is red and lowering. O you hypocrites, you can discern the face of the sky; but can you not discern the signs of the times? ⁴A wicked and adulterous generation seeks after a sign; and there shall no sign be given to it, but the sign of the prophet Jonas. And he left them, and departed. ⁵And when his disciples were come to the other side, they had forgotten to take bread. ⁶Then Jesus said to them, Take heed and beware of the leaven of the Pharisees and of the Sadducees. ⁷And they reasoned among themselves, saying, It is because we have taken no bread. ⁸Which when Jesus perceived, he said to them, O you of little faith, why reason you among yourselves, because you have brought no bread? ⁹Do you not yet understand, neither remember the five loaves of the five thousand, and how many baskets you took up? ¹⁰Neither the seven loaves of the four thousand, and how many baskets you took up? ¹¹How is it that you do not understand that I spoke it not to you concerning bread, that you should beware of the leaven of the Pharisees and of the Sadducees? ¹²Then understood they how that he bade them not beware of the leaven of bread, but of the doctrine of the Pharisees and of the Sadducees. ¹³When Jesus came into the coasts of Caesarea Philippi, he asked his disciples, saying, Whom do men say that I the Son of man am? ¹⁴And they said, Some say that you are John the Baptist: some, Elias; and others, Jeremias, or one of the prophets. ¹⁵He says to them, But whom say you that I am? ¹⁶And Simon Peter answered and said, You are the Christ, the Son of the living God. ¹⁷And Jesus answered and said to him, Blessed are you, Simon Barjona: for flesh and blood has not revealed it to you, but my Father which is in heaven. ¹⁸And I say also to you, That you are Peter, and on this rock I will build my church; and the gates of hell shall not prevail against it. ¹⁹And I will give to you the keys of the kingdom of heaven: and whatever you shall bind on earth shall be bound in heaven; and whatever you shall loose on earth shall be loosed in heaven. ²⁰Then charged he his disciples that they should tell no man that he was Jesus the Christ. ²¹From that time forth began Jesus to show to his disciples, how that he must go to Jerusalem, and suffer many things of the elders and chief priests and scribes, and be killed, and be raised again the third day. ²²Then Peter took him, and began to rebuke him, saying, Be it far from you, Lord: this shall not be to you. ²³But he turned, and said to Peter, Get you behind me, Satan: you are an offense to me: for you mind not the things that be of God, but those that be of men. ²⁴Then said Jesus to his disciples, If any man will come after me, let him deny himself, and take up his cross, and follow me. ²⁵For whoever will save his life shall lose it: and whoever will lose his life for my sake shall find it. ²⁶For what is a man profited, if he shall gain the whole world, and lose his own soul? or what shall a man give in exchange for his soul? ²⁷For the Son of man shall come in the glory of his Father with his angels; and then he shall reward every man according to his works. ²⁸Truly I say to you, There be some standing here, which shall not taste of death, till they see the Son of man coming in his kingdom.

17 ¹And after six days Jesus takes Peter, James, and John his brother, and brings them up into an high mountain apart, ²And was transfigured before them: and his face did shine as the sun, and his raiment was white as the light. ³And, behold, there appeared to them Moses and Elias talking with him. ⁴Then answered Peter, and said to Jesus, Lord, it is good for us to be here: if you will, let us make here three tabernacles; one for you, and one for Moses, and one for Elias. ⁵While he yet spoke, behold, a bright cloud overshadowed them: and behold a voice out of the cloud, which said, This is my beloved Son, in whom I am well pleased; hear you him. ⁶And when the disciples heard it, they fell on their face, and were sore afraid. ⁷And Jesus came and touched them, and said, Arise, and be not afraid. ⁸And when they had lifted up their eyes, they saw no man, save Jesus only. ⁹And as they came down from the mountain, Jesus charged them, saying, Tell the vision to no man, until the Son of man be risen again from the dead. ¹⁰And his disciples asked him, saying, Why then say the scribes that Elias must first come? ¹¹And Jesus answered and said to them, Elias truly shall first come, and restore all things. ¹²But I say to you, That Elias is come already, and they knew him not, but have done to him whatever they listed. Likewise shall also the Son of man suffer of them. ¹³Then the disciples understood that he spoke to them of John the Baptist. ¹⁴And when they were come to the multitude, there came to him a certain man, kneeling down to him, and saying, ¹⁵Lord, have mercy on my son: for he is lunatic, and sore vexed: for often he falls into the fire, and oft into the water. ¹⁶And I brought him to your disciples, and they could not cure him. ¹⁷Then Jesus answered and said, O faithless and perverse generation, how long shall I be with you? how long shall I suffer you? bring him here to me. ¹⁸And Jesus rebuked the devil; and he departed out of him: and the child was cured from that very hour. ¹⁹Then came the disciples to Jesus apart, and said, Why could not we cast him out? ²⁰And Jesus said to them, Because of your unbelief: for truly I say to you, If you have faith as a grain of mustard seed, you shall say to this mountain, Remove hence to yonder place; and it shall remove; and nothing shall be impossible to you. ²¹However, this kind goes not out but by prayer and fasting. ²²And while they stayed in Galilee, Jesus said to them, The Son of man shall be betrayed into the hands of men: ²³And they shall kill him, and the third day he shall be raised again. And they were exceeding sorry. ²⁴And when they were come to Capernaum, they that received tribute money came to Peter, and said, Does not your master pay tribute? ²⁵He says, Yes. And when he was come into the house, Jesus prevented him, saying, What think you, Simon? of whom do the kings of the earth take custom or tribute? of their own children, or of strangers? ²⁶Peter says to him, Of strangers. Jesus says to him, Then are the children free. ²⁷Notwithstanding, lest we should offend them, go you to the sea, and cast an hook, and take up the fish that first comes up; and when you have opened his mouth, you shall find a piece of money: that take, and give to them for me and you.

18 ¹At the same time came the disciples to Jesus, saying, Who is the greatest in the kingdom of heaven? ²And Jesus called a little child to him, and set him in the middle of them, ³And said, Truly I say to you, Except you be converted, and become as little children, you shall not enter into the kingdom of heaven. ⁴Whoever therefore shall humble himself as this little child, the same is greatest in the kingdom of heaven. ⁵And whoever shall receive one such little child in my name receives me. ⁶But whoever shall offend one of these little ones which believe in me, it were better for him that a millstone were hanged about his neck, and that he were drowned in the depth of the sea. ⁷Woe to the world because of offenses! for it must needs be that offenses come; but woe to that man by whom the offense comes! ⁸Why if your hand or your foot offend you, cut them off, and cast them from you: it is better for you to enter into life halt or maimed, rather than having two hands or two feet to be cast into everlasting fire. ⁹And if your eye offend you, pluck it out, and cast it from you: it is better for you to enter into life with one eye, rather than having two eyes to be cast into hell fire. ¹⁰Take heed that you despise not one of these little ones; for I say to you, That in heaven their angels do always behold the face of my Father which is in heaven. ¹¹For the Son of man is come to save that which was lost. ¹²How think you? if a man have an hundred sheep, and one of them be gone astray, does he not leave the ninety and nine, and goes into the mountains, and seeks that which is gone astray? ¹³And if so be that he find it, truly I say to you, he rejoices more of that sheep, than of the ninety and nine which went not astray. ¹⁴Even so it is not the will of your Father which is in heaven, that one of these little ones should perish. ¹⁵Moreover if your brother shall trespass against you, go and tell him his fault between you and him alone: if he shall hear you, you have gained your brother. ¹⁶But if he will not hear you, then take with you one or two more, that in the mouth of two or three witnesses every word may be established. ¹⁷And if he shall neglect to hear them, tell it to the church: but if he neglect to hear the church, let him be to you as an heathen man and a publican. ¹⁸Truly I say to you, Whatever you shall bind on earth shall be bound in heaven: and whatever you shall loose on earth shall be loosed in heaven. ¹⁹Again I say to you, That if two of you shall agree on earth as touching any thing that they shall ask, it shall be done for them of my Father which is in heaven. ²⁰For where two or three are gathered together in my name, there am I in the middle of them. ²¹Then came Peter to him, and said, Lord, how oft shall my brother sin against me, and I forgive him? till seven times? ²²Jesus says to him, I say not to you, Until seven times: but, Until seventy times seven. ²³Therefore is the kingdom of heaven likened to a certain king, which would take account of his servants. ²⁴And when he had begun to reckon, one was brought to him, which owed him ten thousand talents. ²⁵But for as much as he had not to pay, his lord commanded him to be sold, and his wife, and children, and all that he had, and payment to be made. ²⁶The servant therefore fell down, and worshipped him, saying, Lord, have patience with me, and I will pay you all. ²⁷Then the lord of that servant was moved with compassion, and loosed him, and forgave him the debt. ²⁸But the same servant went out, and found one of his fellow servants, which owed him an hundred pence: and he laid hands on him, and took him by the throat, saying, Pay me that you owe. ²⁹And his fellow servant fell down at his feet, and sought him, saying, Have patience with me, and I will pay you all. ³⁰And he would not: but went and cast him into prison, till he should pay the debt. ³¹So when his fellow servants saw what was done, they were very sorry, and came and told to their lord all that was done. ³²Then his lord, after that he had called him, said to him, O you wicked servant, I forgave you all that debt, because you desired me: ³³Should not you also have had compassion on your fellow servant, even as I had pity on you? ³⁴And his lord was wroth, and delivered him to the tormentors, till he should pay all that was due to him. ³⁵So likewise shall my heavenly Father do also to you, if you from your hearts forgive not every one his brother their trespasses.

19 ¹And it came to pass, that when Jesus had finished these sayings, he departed from Galilee, and came into the coasts of Judaea beyond Jordan; ²And great multitudes followed him; and he healed them there. ³The Pharisees also came to him, tempting him, and saying to him, Is it lawful for a man to put away his wife for every cause? ⁴And he answered and said to them, Have you not read, that he which made them at the beginning made them male and female, ⁵And said, For this cause shall a man leave father and mother, and shall join to his wife: and they two shall be one flesh? ⁶Why they are no more two, but one flesh. What therefore God has joined together, let not man put asunder. ⁷They say to him, Why did Moses then command to give a writing of divorce, and to put her away? ⁸He says to them, Moses because of the hardness of your hearts suffered you to put away your wives: but from the beginning it was not so. ⁹And I say to you, Whoever shall put away his wife, except it be for fornication, and shall marry another, commits adultery: and whoever marries her which is put away does commit adultery. ¹⁰His disciples say to him, If the case of the man be so with his wife, it is not good to marry. ¹¹But he said to them, All men cannot receive this saying, save they to whom it is given. ¹²For there are some eunuchs, which were so born from their mother's womb: and there are some eunuchs, which were made eunuchs of men: and there be eunuchs, which have made themselves eunuchs for the kingdom of heaven's sake. He that is able to receive it, let him receive it. [13]Then were there brought to him little children, that he should put his hands on them, and pray: and the disciples rebuked them. [14]But Jesus said, Suffer little children, and forbid them not, to come to me: for of such is the kingdom of heaven. [15]And he laid his hands on them, and departed there. [16]And, behold, one came and said to him, Good Master, what good thing shall I do, that I may have eternal life? [17]And he said to him, Why call you me good? there is none good but one, that is, God: but if you will enter into life, keep the commandments. [18]He says to him, Which? Jesus said, You shall do no murder, You shall not commit adultery, You shall not steal, You shall not bear false witness, [19]Honor your father and your mother: and, You shall love your neighbor as yourself. [20]The young man says to him, All these things have I kept from my youth up: what lack I yet? [21]Jesus said to him, If you will be perfect, go and sell that you have, and give to the poor, and you shall have treasure in heaven: and come and follow me. [22]But when the young man heard that saying, he went away sorrowful: for he had great possessions. [23]Then said Jesus to his disciples, Truly I say to you, That a rich man shall hardly enter into the kingdom of heaven. [24]And again I say to you, It is easier for a camel to go through the eye of a needle, than for a rich man to enter into the kingdom of God. [25]When his disciples heard it, they were exceedingly amazed, saying, Who then can be saved? [26]But Jesus beheld them, and said to them, With men this is impossible; but with God all things are possible. [27]Then answered Peter and said to him, Behold, we have forsaken all, and followed you; what shall we have therefore? [28]And Jesus said to them, Truly I say to you, That you which have followed me, in the regeneration when the Son of man shall sit in the throne of his glory, you also shall sit on twelve thrones, judging the twelve tribes of Israel. [29]And every one that has forsaken houses, or brothers, or sisters, or father, or mother, or wife, or children, or lands, for my name's sake, shall receive an hundred times, and shall inherit everlasting life. [30]But many that are first shall be last; and the last shall be first.

20 [1]For the kingdom of heaven is like to a man that is an householder, which went out early in the morning to hire laborers into his vineyard. [2]And when he had agreed with the laborers for a penny a day, he sent them into his vineyard. [3]And he went out about the third hour, and saw others standing idle in the marketplace, [4]And said to them; Go you also into the vineyard, and whatever is right I will give you. And they went their way. [5]Again he went out about the sixth and ninth hour, and did likewise. [6]And about the eleventh hour he went out, and found others standing idle, and says to them, Why stand you here all the day idle? [7]They say to him, Because no man has hired us. He says to them, Go you also into the vineyard; and whatever is right, that shall you receive. [8]So when even was come, the lord of the vineyard says to his steward, Call the laborers, and give them their hire, beginning from the last to the first. [9]And when they came that were hired about the eleventh hour, they received every man a penny. [10]But when the first came, they supposed that they should have received more; and they likewise received every man a penny. [11]And when they had received it, they murmured against the manager of the house, [12]Saying, These last have worked but one hour, and you have made them equal to us, which have borne the burden and heat of the day. [13]But he answered one of them, and said, Friend, I do you no wrong: did not you agree with me for a penny? [14]Take that your is, and go your way: I will give to this last, even as to you. [15]Is it not lawful for me to do what I will with my own? Is your eye evil, because I am good? [16]So the last shall be first, and the first last: for many be called, but few chosen. [17]And Jesus going up to Jerusalem took the twelve disciples apart in the way, and said to them, [18]Behold, we go up to Jerusalem; and the Son of man shall be betrayed to the chief priests and to the scribes, and they shall condemn him to death, [19]And shall deliver him to the Gentiles to mock, and to whip, and to crucify him: and the third day he shall rise again. [20]Then came to him the mother of Zebedees children with her sons, worshipping him, and desiring a certain thing of him. [21]And he said to her, What will you? She says to him, Grant that these my two sons may sit, the one on your right hand, and the other on the left, in your kingdom. [22]But Jesus answered and said, You know not what you ask. Are you able to drink of the cup that I shall drink of, and to be baptized with the baptism that I am baptized with? They say to him, We are able. [23]And he says to them, You shall drink indeed of my cup, and be baptized with the baptism that I am baptized with: but to sit on my right hand, and on my left, is not my to give, but it shall be given to them for whom it is prepared of my Father. [24]And when the ten heard it, they were moved with indignation against the two brothers. [25]But Jesus called them to him, and said, You know that the princes of the Gentiles exercise dominion over them, and they that are great exercise authority on them. [26]But it shall not be so among you: but whoever will be great among you, let him be your minister; [27]And whoever will be chief among you, let him be your servant: [28]Even as the Son of man came not to be ministered to, but to minister, and to give his life a ransom for many. [29]And as they departed from Jericho, a great multitude followed him. [30]And, behold, two blind men sitting by the way side, when they heard that Jesus passed by, cried out, saying, Have mercy on us, O Lord, you son of David. [31]And the multitude rebuked them, because they should hold their peace: but they cried the more, saying, Have mercy on us, O Lord, you son of David. [32]And Jesus stood still, and called them, and said, What will you that I shall do to you? [33]They say to him, Lord, that our eyes may be opened. [34]So Jesus had compassion on them, and touched their eyes: and immediately their eyes received sight, and they followed him.

21 [1]And when they drew near to Jerusalem, and were come to Bethphage, to the mount of Olives, then sent Jesus two disciples, [2]Saying to them, Go into the village over against you, and straightway you shall find an ass tied, and a colt with her: loose them, and bring them to me. [3]And if any man say something to you, you shall say, The Lord has need of them; and straightway he will send them. [4]All this was done, that it might be fulfilled which was spoken by the prophet, saying, ⁵Tell you the daughter of Sion, Behold, your King comes to you, meek, and sitting on an ass, and a colt the foal of an ass. ⁶And the disciples went, and did as Jesus commanded them, ⁷And brought the ass, and the colt, and put on them their clothes, and they set him thereon. ⁸And a very great multitude spread their garments in the way; others cut down branches from the trees, and strewed them in the way. ⁹And the multitudes that went before, and that followed, cried, saying, Hosanna to the son of David: Blessed is he that comes in the name of the Lord; Hosanna in the highest. ¹⁰And when he was come into Jerusalem, all the city was moved, saying, Who is this? ¹¹And the multitude said, This is Jesus the prophet of Nazareth of Galilee. ¹²And Jesus went into the temple of God, and cast out all them that sold and bought in the temple, and overthrew the tables of the moneychangers, and the seats of them that sold doves, ¹³And said to them, It is written, My house shall be called the house of prayer; but you have made it a den of thieves. ¹⁴And the blind and the lame came to him in the temple; and he healed them. ¹⁵And when the chief priests and scribes saw the wonderful things that he did, and the children crying in the temple, and saying, Hosanna to the son of David; they were sore displeased, ¹⁶And said to him, Hear you what these say? And Jesus says to them, Yes; have you never read, Out of the mouth of babes and sucklings you have perfected praise? ¹⁷And he left them, and went out of the city into Bethany; and he lodged there. ¹⁸Now in the morning as he returned into the city, he hungry. ¹⁹And when he saw a fig tree in the way, he came to it, and found nothing thereon, but leaves only, and said to it, Let no fruit grow on you henceforward for ever. And presently the fig tree withered away. ²⁰And when the disciples saw it, they marveled, saying, How soon is the fig tree withered away! ²¹Jesus answered and said to them, Truly I say to you, If you have faith, and doubt not, you shall not only do this which is done to the fig tree, but also if you shall say to this mountain, Be you removed, and be you cast into the sea; it shall be done. ²²And all things, whatever you shall ask in prayer, believing, you shall receive. ²³And when he was come into the temple, the chief priests and the elders of the people came to him as he was teaching, and said, By what authority do you these things? and who gave you this authority? ²⁴And Jesus answered and said to them, I also will ask you one thing, which if you tell me, I in like wise will tell you by what authority I do these things. ²⁵The baptism of John, from where was it? from heaven, or of men? And they reasoned with themselves, saying, If we shall say, From heaven; he will say to us, Why did you not then believe him? ²⁶But if we shall say, Of men; we fear the people; for all hold John as a prophet. ²⁷And they answered Jesus, and said, We cannot tell. And he said to them, Neither tell I you by what authority I do these things. ²⁸But what think you? A certain man had two sons; and he came to the first, and said, Son, go work to day in my vineyard. ²⁹He answered and said, I will not: but afterward he repented, and went. ³⁰And he came to the second, and said likewise. And he answered and said, I go, sir: and went not. ³¹Whether of them two did the will of his father? They say to him, The first. Jesus says to them, Truly I say to you, That the publicans and the harlots go into the kingdom of God before you. ³²For John came to you in the way of righteousness, and you believed him not: but the publicans and the harlots believed him: and you, when you had seen it, repented not afterward, that you might believe him. ³³Hear another parable: There was a certain householder, which planted a vineyard, and hedged it round about, and dig a wine press in it, and built a tower, and let it out to farmers, and went into a far country: ³⁴And when the time of the fruit drew near, he sent his servants to the farmers, that they might receive the fruits of it. ³⁵And the farmers took his servants, and beat one, and killed another, and stoned another. ³⁶Again, he sent other servants more than the first: and they did to them likewise. ³⁷But last of all he sent to them his son, saying, They will reverence my son. ³⁸But when the farmers saw the son, they said among themselves, This is the heir; come, let us kill him, and let us seize on his inheritance. ³⁹And they caught him, and cast him out of the vineyard, and slew him. ⁴⁰When the lord therefore of the vineyard comes, what will he do to those farmers? ⁴¹They say to him, He will miserably destroy those wicked men, and will let out his vineyard to other farmers, which shall render him the fruits in their seasons. ⁴²Jesus says to them, Did you never read in the scriptures, The stone which the builders rejected, the same is become the head of the corner: this is the Lord's doing, and it is marvelous in our eyes? ⁴³Therefore say I to you, The kingdom of God shall be taken from you, and given to a nation bringing forth the fruits thereof. ⁴⁴And whoever shall fall on this stone shall be broken: but on whomsoever it shall fall, it will grind him to powder. ⁴⁵And when the chief priests and Pharisees had heard his parables, they perceived that he spoke of them. ⁴⁶But when they sought to lay hands on him, they feared the multitude, because they took him for a prophet.

22 ¹And Jesus answered and spoke to them again by parables, and said, ²The kingdom of heaven is like to a certain king, which made a marriage for his son, ³And sent forth his servants to call them that were bidden to the wedding: and they would not come. ⁴Again, he sent forth other servants, saying, Tell them which are bidden, Behold, I have prepared my dinner: my oxen and my fatted calves are killed, and all things are ready: come to the marriage. ⁵But they made light of it, and went their ways, one to his farm, another to his merchandise: ⁶And the remnant took his servants, and entreated them spitefully, and slew them. ⁷But when the king heard thereof, he was wroth: and he sent forth his armies, and destroyed those murderers, and burned up their city. ⁸Then says he to his servants, The wedding is ready, but they which were bidden were not worthy. ⁹Go you therefore into the highways, and as many as you shall find, bid to the marriage. ¹⁰So those servants went out into the highways, and gathered together all as many as they found, both bad and good: and the wedding was furnished with guests. ¹¹And when the king came in to see the guests, he saw there a man which had not on a wedding garment: ¹²And he says to him, Friend, how came you in here not having a wedding garment? And he was speechless. ¹³Then said the king to the servants, Bind him hand and foot, and take him away, and cast him into outer darkness, there shall be weeping and gnashing of teeth. ¹⁴For many are called, but few are chosen. ¹⁵Then went the Pharisees, and took counsel how they might entangle him in his talk. ¹⁶And they sent out to him their disciples with the Herodians, saying, Master, we know that you are true, and teach the way of God in truth, neither care you for any man: for you regard not the person of men. ¹⁷Tell us therefore, What think you? Is it lawful to give tribute to Caesar, or not? ¹⁸But Jesus perceived their wickedness, and said, Why tempt you me, you hypocrites? ¹⁹Show me the tribute money. And they brought to him a penny. ²⁰And he says to them, Whose is this image and superscription? ²¹They say to him, Caesar's. Then says he to them, Render therefore to Caesar the things which are Caesar's; and to God the things that are God's. ²²When they had heard these words, they marveled, and left him, and went their way. ²³The same day came to him the Sadducees, which say that there is no resurrection, and asked him, ²⁴Saying, Master, Moses said, If a man die, having no children, his brother shall marry his wife, and raise up seed to his brother. ²⁵Now there were with us seven brothers: and the first, when he had married a wife, deceased, and, having no issue, left his wife to his brother: ²⁶Likewise the second also, and the third, to the seventh. ²⁷And last of all the woman died also. ²⁸Therefore in the resurrection whose wife shall she be of the seven? for they all had her. ²⁹Jesus answered and said to them, You do err, not knowing the scriptures, nor the power of God. ³⁰For in the resurrection they neither marry, nor are given in marriage, but are as the angels of God in heaven. ³¹But as touching the resurrection of the dead, have you not read that which was spoken to you by God, saying, ³²I am the God of Abraham, and the God of Isaac, and the God of Jacob? God is not the God of the dead, but of the living. ³³And when the multitude heard this, they were astonished at his doctrine. ³⁴But when the Pharisees had heard that he had put the Sadducees to silence, they were gathered together. ³⁵Then one of them, which was a lawyer, asked him a question, tempting him, and saying, ³⁶Master, which is the great commandment in the law? ³⁷Jesus said to him, You shall love the Lord your God with all your heart, and with all your soul, and with all your mind. ³⁸This is the first and great commandment. ³⁹And the second is like to it, You shall love your neighbor as yourself. ⁴⁰On these two commandments hang all the law and the prophets. ⁴¹While the Pharisees were gathered together, Jesus asked them, ⁴²Saying, What think you of Christ? whose son is he? They say to him, The son of David. ⁴³He says to them, How then does David in spirit call him Lord, saying, ⁴⁴The LORD said to my Lord, Sit you on my right hand, till I make your enemies your footstool? ⁴⁵If David then call him Lord, how is he his son? ⁴⁶And no man was able to answer him a word, neither dared any man from that day forth ask him any more questions.

23 ¹Then spoke Jesus to the multitude, and to his disciples, ²Saying The scribes and the Pharisees sit in Moses' seat: ³All therefore whatever they bid you observe, that observe and do; but do not you after their works: for they say, and do not. ⁴For they bind heavy burdens and grievous to be borne, and lay them on men's shoulders; but they themselves will not move them with one of their fingers. ⁵But all their works they do for to be seen of men: they make broad their phylacteries, and enlarge the borders of their garments, ⁶And love the uppermost rooms at feasts, and the chief seats in the synagogues, ⁷And greetings in the markets, and to be called of men, Rabbi, Rabbi. ⁸But be not you called Rabbi: for one is your Master, even Christ; and all you are brothers. ⁹And call no man your father on the earth: for one is your Father, which is in heaven. ¹⁰Neither be you called masters: for one is your Master, even Christ. ¹¹But he that is greatest among you shall be your servant. ¹²And whoever shall exalt himself shall be abased; and he that shall humble himself shall be exalted. ¹³But woe to you, scribes and Pharisees, hypocrites! for you shut up the kingdom of heaven against men: for you neither go in yourselves, neither suffer you them that are entering to go in. ¹⁴Woe to you, scribes and Pharisees, hypocrites! for you devour widows' houses, and for a pretense make long prayer: therefore you shall receive the greater damnation. ¹⁵Woe to you, scribes and Pharisees, hypocrites! for you compass sea and land to make one proselyte, and when he is made, you make him twofold more the child of hell than yourselves. ¹⁶Woe to you, you blind guides, which say, Whoever shall swear by the temple, it is nothing; but whoever shall swear by the gold of the temple, he is a debtor! ¹⁷You fools and blind: for whether is greater, the gold, or the temple that sanctifies the gold? ¹⁸And, Whoever shall swear by the altar, it is nothing; but whoever swears by the gift that is on it, he is guilty. ¹⁹You fools and blind: for whether is greater, the gift, or the altar that sanctifies the gift? ²⁰Whoever therefore shall swear by the altar, swears by it, and by all things thereon. ²¹And whoever shall swear by the temple, swears by it, and by him that dwells therein. ²²And he that shall swear by heaven, swears by the throne of God, and by him that sits thereon. ²³Woe to you, scribes and Pharisees, hypocrites! for you pay tithe of mint and anise and cummin, and have omitted the weightier matters of the law, judgment, mercy, and faith: these you should have done, and not to leave the other undone. ²⁴You blind guides, which strain at a gnat, and swallow a camel. ²⁵Woe to you, scribes and Pharisees, hypocrites! for you make clean the outside of the cup and of the platter, but within they are full of extortion and excess. ²⁶You blind Pharisee, cleanse first that which is within the cup and platter, that the outside of them may be clean also. ²⁷Woe to you, scribes and Pharisees, hypocrites! for you are like to white washed sepulchers, which indeed appear beautiful outward, but are within full of dead men's bones, and of all uncleanness. ²⁸Even so you also outwardly appear righteous to men, but within you are full of hypocrisy and iniquity. ²⁹Woe to you, scribes and Pharisees, hypocrites! because you build the tombs of the prophets, and garnish the sepulchers of the righteous, ³⁰And say, If we had been in the days of our fathers, we would not have been partakers with them in the blood of the prophets. ³¹Why you be witnesses to yourselves, that you are the children of them which killed the prophets. ³²Fill you up then the measure of your fathers. ³³You serpents, generation of vipers, how can you escape the damnation of hell? ³⁴Why, behold, I send to you prophets, and wise men, and scribes: and some of them you shall kill and crucify; and some of them shall you whip in your synagogues, and persecute them from city to city: ³⁵That on you may come all the righteous blood shed on the earth, from the blood of righteous Abel to the blood of Zacharias son of Barachias, whom you slew between the temple and the altar. ³⁶Truly I say to you, All these things shall come on this generation. ³⁷O Jerusalem, Jerusalem, you that kill the prophets, and stone them which are sent to you, how often would I have gathered your children together, even as a hen gathers her chickens under her wings, and you would not! ³⁸Behold, your house is left to you desolate. ³⁹For I say to you, You shall not see me from now on, till you shall say, Blessed is he that comes in the name of the Lord.

24

¹And Jesus went out, and departed from the temple: and his disciples came to him for to show him the buildings of the temple. ²And Jesus said to them, See you not all these things? truly I say to you, There shall not be left here one stone on another, that shall not be thrown down. ³And as he sat on the mount of Olives, the disciples came to him privately, saying, Tell us, when shall these things be? and what shall be the sign of your coming, and of the end of the world? ⁴And Jesus answered and said to them, Take heed that no man deceive you. ⁵For many shall come in my name, saying, I am Christ; and shall deceive many. ⁶And you shall hear of wars and rumors of wars: see that you be not troubled: for all these things must come to pass, but the end is not yet. ⁷For nation shall rise against nation, and kingdom against kingdom: and there shall be famines, and pestilences, and earthquakes, in divers places. ⁸All these are the beginning of sorrows. ⁹Then shall they deliver you up to be afflicted, and shall kill you: and you shall be hated of all nations for my name's sake. ¹⁰And then shall many be offended, and shall betray one another, and shall hate one another. ¹¹And many false prophets shall rise, and shall deceive many. ¹²And because iniquity shall abound, the love of many shall wax cold. ¹³But he that shall endure to the end, the same shall be saved. ¹⁴And this gospel of the kingdom shall be preached in all the world for a witness to all nations; and then shall the end come. ¹⁵When you therefore shall see the abomination of desolation, spoken of by Daniel the prophet, stand in the holy place, (whoever reads, let him understand:) ¹⁶Then let them which be in Judaea flee into the mountains: ¹⁷Let him which is on the housetop not come down to take any thing out of his house: ¹⁸Neither let him which is in the field return back to take his clothes. ¹⁹And woe to them that are with child, and to them that give suck in those days! ²⁰But pray you that your flight be not in the winter, neither on the sabbath day: ²¹For then shall be great tribulation, such as was not since the beginning of the world to this time, no, nor ever shall be. ²²And except those days should be shortened, there should no flesh be saved: but for the elect's sake those days shall be shortened. ²³Then if any man shall say to you, See, here is Christ, or there; believe it not. ²⁴For there shall arise false Christs, and false prophets, and shall show great signs and wonders; so that, if it were possible, they shall deceive the very elect. ²⁵Behold, I have told you before. ²⁶Why if they shall say to you, Behold, he is in the desert; go not forth: behold, he is in the secret chambers; believe it not. ²⁷For as the lightning comes out of the east, and shines even to the west; so shall also the coming of the Son of man be. ²⁸For wherever the carcass is, there will the eagles be gathered together. ²⁹Immediately after the tribulation of those days shall the sun be darkened, and the moon shall not give her light, and the stars shall fall from heaven, and the powers of the heavens shall be shaken: ³⁰And then shall appear the sign of the Son of man in heaven: and then shall all the tribes of the earth mourn, and they shall see the Son of man coming in the clouds of heaven with power and great glory. ³¹And he shall send his angels with a great sound of a trumpet, and they shall gather together his elect from the four winds, from one end of heaven to the other. ³²Now learn a parable of the fig tree; When his branch is yet tender, and puts forth leaves, you know that summer is near: ³³So likewise you, when you shall see all these things, know that it is near, even at the doors. ³⁴Truly I say to you, This generation shall not pass, till all these things be fulfilled. ³⁵Heaven and earth shall pass away, but my words shall not pass away. ³⁶But of that day and hour knows no man, no, not the angels of heaven, but my Father only. ³⁷But as the days of Noe were, so shall also the coming of the Son of man be. ³⁸For as in the days that were before the flood they were eating and drinking, marrying and giving in marriage, until the day that Noe entered into the ark, ³⁹And knew not until the flood came, and took them all away; so shall also the coming of the Son of man be. ⁴⁰Then shall two be in the field; the one shall be taken, and the other left. ⁴¹Two women shall be grinding at the mill; the one shall be taken, and the other left. ⁴²Watch therefore: for you know not what hour your Lord does come. ⁴³But know this, that if the manager of the house had known in what watch the thief would come, he would have watched, and would not have suffered his house to be broken up. ⁴⁴Therefore be you also ready: for in such an hour as you think not the Son of man comes. ⁴⁵Who then is a faithful and wise servant, whom his lord has made ruler over his household, to give them meat in due season? ⁴⁶Blessed is that servant, whom his lord when he comes shall find so doing. ⁴⁷Truly I say to you, That he shall make him ruler over all his goods. ⁴⁸But and if that evil servant shall say in his heart, My lord delays his coming; ⁴⁹And shall begin to smite his fellow servants, and to eat and drink with the drunken; ⁵⁰The lord of that servant shall come in a day when he looks not for him, and in an hour that he is not aware of, ⁵¹And shall cut him asunder, and appoint him his portion with the hypocrites: there shall be weeping and gnashing of teeth.

25

¹Then shall the kingdom of heaven be likened to ten virgins, which took their lamps, and went forth to meet the bridegroom. ²And five of them were wise, and five were foolish. ³They that were foolish took their lamps, and took no oil with them: ⁴But the wise took oil in their vessels with their lamps. ⁵While the bridegroom tarried, they all slumbered and slept. ⁶And at midnight there was a cry made, Behold, the bridegroom comes; go you out to meet him. ⁷Then all those virgins arose, and trimmed their lamps. ⁸And the foolish said to the wise, Give us of your oil; for our lamps are gone out. ⁹But the wise answered, saying, Not so; lest there be not enough for us and you: but go you rather to them that sell, and buy for yourselves. ¹⁰And while they went to buy, the bridegroom came; and they that were ready

went in with him to the marriage: and the door was shut. ¹¹Afterward came also the other virgins, saying, Lord, Lord, open to us. ¹²But he answered and said, Truly I say to you, I know you not. ¹³Watch therefore, for you know neither the day nor the hour wherein the Son of man comes. ¹⁴For the kingdom of heaven is as a man traveling into a far country, who called his own servants, and delivered to them his goods. ¹⁵And to one he gave five talents, to another two, and to another one; to every man according to his several ability; and straightway took his journey. ¹⁶Then he that had received the five talents went and traded with the same, and made them other five talents. ¹⁷And likewise he that had received two, he also gained other two. ¹⁸But he that had received one went and dig in the earth, and hid his lord's money. ¹⁹After a long time the lord of those servants comes, and reckons with them. ²⁰And so he that had received five talents came and brought other five talents, saying, Lord, you delivered to me five talents: behold, I have gained beside them five talents more. ²¹His lord said to him, Well done, you good and faithful servant: you have been faithful over a few things, I will make you ruler over many things: enter you into the joy of your lord. ²²He also that had received two talents came and said, Lord, you delivered to me two talents: behold, I have gained two other talents beside them. ²³His lord said to him, Well done, good and faithful servant; you have been faithful over a few things, I will make you ruler over many things: enter you into the joy of your lord. ²⁴Then he which had received the one talent came and said, Lord, I knew you that you are an hard man, reaping where you have not sown, and gathering where you have not strewed: ²⁵And I was afraid, and went and hid your talent in the earth: see, there you have that is yours. ²⁶His lord answered and said to him, You wicked and slothful servant, you knew that I reap where I sowed not, and gather where I have not strewed: ²⁷You should therefore to have put my money to the exchangers, and then at my coming I should have received my own with usury. ²⁸Take therefore the talent from him, and give it to him which has ten talents. ²⁹For to every one that has shall be given, and he shall have abundance: but from him that has not shall be taken away even that which he has. ³⁰And cast you the unprofitable servant into outer darkness: there shall be weeping and gnashing of teeth. ³¹When the Son of man shall come in his glory, and all the holy angels with him, then shall he sit on the throne of his glory: ³²And before him shall be gathered all nations: and he shall separate them one from another, as a shepherd divides his sheep from the goats: ³³And he shall set the sheep on his right hand, but the goats on the left. ³⁴Then shall the King say to them on his right hand, Come, you blessed of my Father, inherit the kingdom prepared for you from the foundation of the world: ³⁵For I was an hungered, and you gave me meat: I was thirsty, and you gave me drink: I was a stranger, and you took me in: ³⁶Naked, and you clothed me: I was sick, and you visited me: I was in prison, and you came to me. ³⁷Then shall the righteous answer him, saying, Lord, when saw we you an hungered, and fed you? or thirsty, and gave you drink? ³⁸When saw we you a stranger, and took you in? or naked, and clothed you? ³⁹Or when saw we you sick, or in prison, and came to you?

⁴⁰And the King shall answer and say to them, Truly I say to you, Inasmuch as you have done it to one of the least of these my brothers, you have done it to me. ⁴¹Then shall he say also to them on the left hand, Depart from me, you cursed, into everlasting fire, prepared for the devil and his angels: ⁴²For I was an hungered, and you gave me no meat: I was thirsty, and you gave me no drink: ⁴³I was a stranger, and you took me not in: naked, and you clothed me not: sick, and in prison, and you visited me not. ⁴⁴Then shall they also answer him, saying, Lord, when saw we you an hungered, or thirsty, or a stranger, or naked, or sick, or in prison, and did not minister to you? ⁴⁵Then shall he answer them, saying, Truly I say to you, Inasmuch as you did it not to one of the least of these, you did it not to me. ⁴⁶And these shall go away into everlasting punishment: but the righteous into life eternal.

26

¹And it came to pass, when Jesus had finished all these sayings, he said to his disciples, ²You know that after two days is the feast of the passover, and the Son of man is betrayed to be crucified. ³Then assembled together the chief priests, and the scribes, and the elders of the people, to the palace of the high priest, who was called Caiaphas, ⁴And consulted that they might take Jesus by subtlety, and kill him. ⁵But they said, Not on the feast day, lest there be an uproar among the people. ⁶Now when Jesus was in Bethany, in the house of Simon the leper, ⁷There came to him a woman having an alabaster box of very precious ointment, and poured it on his head, as he sat at meat. ⁸But when his disciples saw it, they had indignation, saying, To what purpose is this waste? ⁹For this ointment might have been sold for much, and given to the poor. ¹⁰When Jesus understood it, he said to them, Why trouble you the woman? for she has worked a good work on me. ¹¹For you have the poor always with you; but me you have not always. ¹²For in that she has poured this ointment on my body, she did it for my burial. ¹³Truly I say to you, Wherever this gospel shall be preached in the whole world, there shall also this, that this woman has done, be told for a memorial of her. ¹⁴Then one of the twelve, called Judas Iscariot, went to the chief priests, ¹⁵And said to them, What will you give me, and I will deliver him to you? And they covenanted with him for thirty pieces of silver. ¹⁶And from that time he sought opportunity to betray him. ¹⁷Now the first day of the feast of unleavened bread the disciples came to Jesus, saying to him, Where will you that we prepare for you to eat the passover? ¹⁸And he says, Go into the city to such a man, and say to him, The Master said, My time is at hand; I will keep the passover at your house with my disciples. ¹⁹And the disciples did as Jesus had appointed them; and they made ready the passover. ²⁰Now when the even was come, he sat down with the twelve. ²¹And as they did eat, he said, Truly I say to you, that one of you shall betray me. ²²And they were exceeding sorrowful, and began every one of them to say to him, Lord, is it I? ²³And he answered and said, He that dips his hand with me in the dish, the same shall betray me. ²⁴The Son of man goes as it is written of him: but woe to that man by whom the Son of man is betrayed! it had been good for that man if he had not been born. ²⁵Then Judas, which betrayed him, answered and said, Master, is it I? He said to

him, You have said. ²⁶And as they were eating, Jesus took bread, and blessed it, and broke it, and gave it to the disciples, and said, Take, eat; this is my body. ²⁷And he took the cup, and gave thanks, and gave it to them, saying, Drink you all of it; ²⁸For this is my blood of the new testament, which is shed for many for the remission of sins. ²⁹But I say to you, I will not drink from now on of this fruit of the vine, until that day when I drink it new with you in my Father's kingdom. ³⁰And when they had sung an hymn, they went out into the mount of Olives. ³¹Then says Jesus to them, All you shall be offended because of me this night: for it is written, I will smite the shepherd, and the sheep of the flock shall be scattered abroad. ³²But after I am risen again, I will go before you into Galilee. ³³Peter answered and said to him, Though all men shall be offended because of you, yet will I never be offended. ³⁴Jesus said to him, Truly I say to you, That this night, before the cock crow, you shall deny me thrice. ³⁵Peter said to him, Though I should die with you, yet will I not deny you. Likewise also said all the disciples. ³⁶Then comes Jesus with them to a place called Gethsemane, and says to the disciples, Sit you here, while I go and pray yonder. ³⁷And he took with him Peter and the two sons of Zebedee, and began to be sorrowful and very heavy. ³⁸Then says he to them, My soul is exceeding sorrowful, even to death: tarry you here, and watch with me. ³⁹And he went a little farther, and fell on his face, and prayed, saying, O my Father, if it be possible, let this cup pass from me: nevertheless not as I will, but as you will. ⁴⁰And he comes to the disciples, and finds them asleep, and says to Peter, What, could you not watch with me one hour? ⁴¹Watch and pray, that you enter not into temptation: the spirit indeed is willing, but the flesh is weak. ⁴²He went away again the second time, and prayed, saying, O my Father, if this cup may not pass away from me, except I drink it, your will be done. ⁴³And he came and found them asleep again: for their eyes were heavy. ⁴⁴And he left them, and went away again, and prayed the third time, saying the same words. ⁴⁵Then comes he to his disciples, and says to them, Sleep on now, and take your rest: behold, the hour is at hand, and the Son of man is betrayed into the hands of sinners. ⁴⁶Rise, let us be going: behold, he is at hand that does betray me. ⁴⁷And while he yet spoke, see, Judas, one of the twelve, came, and with him a great multitude with swords and staves, from the chief priests and elders of the people. ⁴⁸Now he that betrayed him gave them a sign, saying, Whomsoever I shall kiss, that same is he: hold him fast. ⁴⁹And immediately he came to Jesus, and said, Hail, master; and kissed him. ⁵⁰And Jesus said to him, Friend, why are you come? Then came they, and laid hands on Jesus and took him. ⁵¹And, behold, one of them which were with Jesus stretched out his hand, and drew his sword, and struck a servant of the high priest's, and smote off his ear. ⁵²Then said Jesus to him, Put up again your sword into his place: for all they that take the sword shall perish with the sword. ⁵³Think you that I cannot now pray to my Father, and he shall presently give me more than twelve legions of angels? ⁵⁴But how then shall the scriptures be fulfilled, that thus it must be? ⁵⁵In that same hour said Jesus to the multitudes, Are you come out as against a thief with swords and staves for to take me? I sat daily with you teaching in the temple, and you laid no hold on me. ⁵⁶But all this was done, that the scriptures of the prophets might be fulfilled. Then all the disciples forsook him, and fled. ⁵⁷And they that had laid hold on Jesus led him away to Caiaphas the high priest, where the scribes and the elders were assembled. ⁵⁸But Peter followed him afar off to the high priest's palace, and went in, and sat with the servants, to see the end. ⁵⁹Now the chief priests, and elders, and all the council, sought false witness against Jesus, to put him to death; ⁶⁰But found none: yes, though many false witnesses came, yet found they none. At the last came two false witnesses, ⁶¹And said, This fellow said, I am able to destroy the temple of God, and to build it in three days. ⁶²And the high priest arose, and said to him, Answer you nothing? what is it which these witness against you? ⁶³But Jesus held his peace, And the high priest answered and said to him, I adjure you by the living God, that you tell us whether you be the Christ, the Son of God. ⁶⁴Jesus says to him, You have said: nevertheless I say to you, Hereafter shall you see the Son of man sitting on the right hand of power, and coming in the clouds of heaven. ⁶⁵Then the high priest rent his clothes, saying, He has spoken blasphemy; what further need have we of witnesses? behold, now you have heard his blasphemy. ⁶⁶What think you? They answered and said, He is guilty of death. ⁶⁷Then did they spit in his face, and buffeted him; and others smote him with the palms of their hands, ⁶⁸Saying, Prophesy to us, you Christ, Who is he that smote you? ⁶⁹Now Peter sat without in the palace: and a damsel came to him, saying, You also were with Jesus of Galilee. ⁷⁰But he denied before them all, saying, I know not what you say. ⁷¹And when he was gone out into the porch, another maid saw him, and said to them that were there, This fellow was also with Jesus of Nazareth. ⁷²And again he denied with an oath, I do not know the man. ⁷³And after a while came to him they that stood by, and said to Peter, Surely you also are one of them; for your speech denudes you. ⁷⁴Then began he to curse and to swear, saying, I know not the man. And immediately the cock crew. ⁷⁵And Peter remembered the word of Jesus, which said to him, Before the cock crow, you shall deny me thrice. And he went out, and wept bitterly.

27 ¹When the morning was come, all the chief priests and elders of the people took counsel against Jesus to put him to death: ²And when they had bound him, they led him away, and delivered him to Pontius Pilate the governor. ³Then Judas, which had betrayed him, when he saw that he was condemned, repented himself, and brought again the thirty pieces of silver to the chief priests and elders, ⁴Saying, I have sinned in that I have betrayed the innocent blood. And they said, What is that to us? see you to that. ⁵And he cast down the pieces of silver in the temple, and departed, and went and hanged himself. ⁶And the chief priests took the silver pieces, and said, It is not lawful for to put them into the treasury, because it is the price of blood. ⁷And they took counsel, and bought with them the potter's field, to bury strangers in. ⁸Why that field was called, The field of blood, to this day. ⁹Then was fulfilled that which was spoken by Jeremy the prophet, saying, And they took the thirty pieces of silver, the price of him that was valued, whom they of the children of Israel did value; ¹⁰And gave them for the potter's field, as the Lord appointed me. ¹¹And Jesus stood before the governor: and the governor asked him, saying, Are you the King of the Jews? And Jesus said to him, You say. ¹²And when he was accused of the chief priests and elders, he answered nothing. ¹³Then said Pilate to him, Hear you not how many things they witness against you? ¹⁴And he answered him to never a word; so that the governor marveled greatly. ¹⁵Now at that feast the governor was wont to release to the people a prisoner, whom they would. ¹⁶And they had then a notable prisoner, called Barabbas. ¹⁷Therefore when they were gathered together, Pilate said to them, Whom will you that I release to you? Barabbas, or Jesus which is called Christ? ¹⁸For he knew that for envy they had delivered him. ¹⁹When he was set down on the judgment seat, his wife sent to him, saying, Have you nothing to do with that just man: for I have suffered many things this day in a dream because of him. ²⁰But the chief priests and elders persuaded the multitude that they should ask Barabbas, and destroy Jesus. ²¹The governor answered and said to them, Whether of the two will you that I release to you? They said, Barabbas. ²²Pilate says to them, What shall I do then with Jesus which is called Christ? They all say to him, Let him be crucified. ²³And the governor said, Why, what evil has he done? But they cried out the more, saying, Let him be crucified. ²⁴When Pilate saw that he could prevail nothing, but that rather a tumult was made, he took water, and washed his hands before the multitude, saying, I am innocent of the blood of this just person: see you to it. ²⁵Then answered all the people, and said, His blood be on us, and on our children. ²⁶Then released he Barabbas to them: and when he had scourged Jesus, he delivered him to be crucified. ²⁷Then the soldiers of the governor took Jesus into the common hall, and gathered to him the whole band of soldiers. ²⁸And they stripped him, and put on him a scarlet robe. ²⁹And when they had platted a crown of thorns, they put it on his head, and a reed in his right hand: and they bowed the knee before him, and mocked him, saying, Hail, King of the Jews! ³⁰And they spit on him, and took the reed, and smote him on the head. ³¹And after that they had mocked him, they took the robe off from him, and put his own raiment on him, and led him away to crucify him. ³²And as they came out, they found a man of Cyrene, Simon by name: him they compelled to bear his cross. ³³And when they were come to a place called Golgotha, that is to say, a place of a skull, ³⁴They gave him vinegar to drink mingled with gall: and when he had tasted thereof, he would not drink. ³⁵And they crucified him, and parted his garments, casting lots: that it might be fulfilled which was spoken by the prophet, They parted my garments among them, and on my clothing did they cast lots. ³⁶And sitting down they watched him there; ³⁷And set up over his head his accusation written, THIS IS JESUS THE KING OF THE JEWS. ³⁸Then were there two thieves crucified with him, one on the right hand, and another on the left. ³⁹And they that passed by reviled him, wagging their heads, ⁴⁰And saying, You that destroy the temple, and build it in three days, save yourself. If you be the Son of God, come down from the cross. ⁴¹Likewise also the chief priests mocking him, with the scribes and elders, said, ⁴²He saved others; himself he cannot save. If he be the King of Israel, let him now come down from the cross, and we will believe him. ⁴³He trusted in God; let him deliver him now, if he will have him: for he said, I am the Son of God. ⁴⁴The thieves also, which were crucified with him, cast the same in his teeth. ⁴⁵Now from the sixth hour there was darkness over all the land to the ninth hour. ⁴⁶And about the ninth hour Jesus cried with a loud voice, saying, Eli, Eli, lama sabachthani? that is to say, My God, my God, why have you forsaken me? ⁴⁷Some of them that stood there, when they heard that, said, This man calls for Elias. ⁴⁸And straightway one of them ran, and took a sponge, and filled it with vinegar, and put it on a reed, and gave him to drink. ⁴⁹The rest said, Let be, let us see whether Elias will come to save him. ⁵⁰Jesus, when he had cried again with a loud voice, yielded up the ghost. ⁵¹And, behold, the veil of the temple was rent in two from the top to the bottom; and the earth did quake, and the rocks rent; ⁵²And the graves were opened; and many bodies of the saints which slept arose, ⁵³And came out of the graves after his resurrection, and went into the holy city, and appeared to many. ⁵⁴Now when the centurion, and they that were with him, watching Jesus, saw the earthquake, and those things that were done, they feared greatly, saying, Truly this was the Son of God. ⁵⁵And many women were there beholding afar off, which followed Jesus from Galilee, ministering to him: ⁵⁶Among which was Mary Magdalene, and Mary the mother of James and Joses, and the mother of Zebedees children. ⁵⁷When the even was come, there came a rich man of Arimathaea, named Joseph, who also himself was Jesus' disciple: ⁵⁸He went to Pilate, and begged the body of Jesus. Then Pilate commanded the body to be delivered. ⁵⁹And when Joseph had taken the body, he wrapped it in a clean linen cloth, ⁶⁰And laid it in his own new tomb, which he had hewn out in the rock: and he rolled a great stone to the door of the sepulcher, and departed. ⁶¹And there was Mary Magdalene, and the other Mary, sitting over against the sepulcher. ⁶²Now the next day, that followed the day of the preparation, the chief priests and Pharisees came together to Pilate, ⁶³Saying, Sir, we remember that that deceiver said, while he was yet alive, After three days I will rise again. ⁶⁴Command therefore that the sepulcher be made sure until the third day, lest his disciples come by night, and steal him away, and say to the people, He is risen from the dead: so the last error shall be worse than the first. ⁶⁵Pilate said to them, You have a watch: go your way, make it as sure as you can. ⁶⁶So they went, and made the sepulcher sure, sealing the stone, and setting a watch.

28

¹In the end of the sabbath, as it began to dawn toward the first day of the week, came Mary Magdalene and the other Mary to see the sepulcher. ²And, behold, there was a great earthquake: for the angel of the Lord descended from heaven, and came and rolled back the stone from the door, and sat on it. ³His countenance was like lightning, and his raiment white as snow: ⁴And for fear of him the keepers did shake, and became as dead men. ⁵And the angel answered and said to the women, Fear not you: for I know that you seek Jesus, which was crucified. ⁶He is not here: for he is risen, as he said. Come, see the place where

the Lord lay. ⁷And go quickly, and tell his disciples that he is risen from the dead; and, behold, he goes before you into Galilee; there shall you see him: see, I have told you. ⁸And they departed quickly from the sepulcher with fear and great joy; and did run to bring his disciples word. ⁹And as they went to tell his disciples, behold, Jesus met them, saying, All hail. And they came and held him by the feet, and worshipped him. ¹⁰Then said Jesus to them, Be not afraid: go tell my brothers that they go into Galilee, and there shall they see me. ¹¹Now when they were going, behold, some of the watch came into the city, and showed to the chief priests all the things that were done. ¹²And when they were assembled with the elders, and had taken counsel, they gave large money to the soldiers, ¹³Saying, Say you, His disciples came by night, and stole him away while we slept. ¹⁴And if this come to the governor's ears, we will persuade him, and secure you. ¹⁵So they took the money, and did as they were taught: and this saying is commonly reported among the Jews until this day. ¹⁶Then the eleven disciples went away into Galilee, into a mountain where Jesus had appointed them. ¹⁷And when they saw him, they worshipped him: but some doubted. ¹⁸And Jesus came and spoke to them, saying, All power is given to me in heaven and in earth. ¹⁹Go you therefore, and teach all nations, baptizing them in the name of the Father, and of the Son, and of the Holy Ghost: ²⁰Teaching them to observe all things whatever I have commanded you: and, see, I am with you always, even to the end of the world. Amen.

Mark

1 ¹The beginning of the gospel of Jesus Christ, the Son of God; ²As it is written in the prophets, Behold, I send my messenger before your face, which shall prepare your way before you. ³The voice of one crying in the wilderness, Prepare you the way of the Lord, make his paths straight. ⁴John did baptize in the wilderness, and preach the baptism of repentance for the remission of sins. ⁵And there went out to him all the land of Judaea, and they of Jerusalem, and were all baptized of him in the river of Jordan, confessing their sins. ⁶And John was clothed with camel's hair, and with a girdle of a skin about his loins; and he did eat locusts and wild honey; ⁷And preached, saying, There comes one mightier than I after me, the lace of whose shoes I am not worthy to stoop down and unloose. ⁸I indeed have baptized you with water: but he shall baptize you with the Holy Ghost. ⁹And it came to pass in those days, that Jesus came from Nazareth of Galilee, and was baptized of John in Jordan. ¹⁰And straightway coming up out of the water, he saw the heavens opened, and the Spirit like a dove descending on him: ¹¹And there came a voice from heaven, saying, You are my beloved Son, in whom I am well pleased. ¹²And immediately the spirit drives him into the wilderness. ¹³And he was there in the wilderness forty days, tempted of Satan; and was with the wild beasts; and the angels ministered to him. ¹⁴Now after that John was put in prison, Jesus came into Galilee, preaching the gospel of the kingdom of God, ¹⁵And saying, The time is fulfilled, and the kingdom of God is at hand: repent you, and believe the gospel. ¹⁶Now as he walked by the sea of Galilee, he saw Simon and Andrew his brother casting a net into the sea: for they were fishers. ¹⁷And Jesus said to them, Come you after me, and I will make you to become fishers of men. ¹⁸And straightway they forsook their nets, and followed him. ¹⁹And when he had gone a little farther there, he saw James the son of Zebedee, and John his brother, who also were in the ship mending their nets. ²⁰And straightway he called them: and they left their father Zebedee in the ship with the hired servants, and went after him. ²¹And they went into Capernaum; and straightway on the sabbath day he entered into the synagogue, and taught. ²²And they were astonished at his doctrine: for he taught them as one that had authority, and not as the scribes. ²³And there was in their synagogue a man with an unclean spirit; and he cried out, ²⁴Saying, Let us alone; what have we to do with you, you Jesus of Nazareth? are you come to destroy us? I know you who you are, the Holy One of God. ²⁵And Jesus rebuked him, saying, Hold your peace, and come out of him. ²⁶And when the unclean spirit had torn him, and cried with a loud voice, he came out of him. ²⁷And they were all amazed, so that they questioned among themselves, saying, What thing is this? what new doctrine is this? for with authority commands he even the unclean spirits, and they do obey him. ²⁸And immediately his fame spread abroad throughout all the region round about Galilee. ²⁹And immediately, when they were come out of the synagogue, they entered into the house of Simon and Andrew, with James and John. ³⁰But Simon's wife's mother lay sick of a fever, and immediately they tell him of her. ³¹And he came and took her by the hand, and lifted her up; and immediately the fever left her, and she ministered to them. ³²And at even, when the sun did set, they brought to him all that were diseased, and them that were possessed with devils. ³³And all the city was gathered together at the door. ³⁴And he healed many that were sick of divers diseases, and cast out many devils; and suffered not the devils to speak, because they knew him. ³⁵And in the morning, rising up a great while before day, he went out, and departed into a solitary place, and there prayed. ³⁶And Simon and they that were with him followed after him. ³⁷And when they had found him, they said to him, All men seek for you. ³⁸And he said to them, Let us go into the next towns, that I may preach there also: for therefore came I forth. ³⁹And he preached in their synagogues throughout all Galilee, and cast out devils. ⁴⁰And there came a leper to him, beseeching him, and kneeling down to him, and saying to him, If you will, you can make me clean. ⁴¹And Jesus, moved with compassion, put forth his hand, and touched him, and says to him, I will; be you clean. ⁴²And as soon as he had spoken, immediately the leprosy departed from him, and he was cleansed. ⁴³And he straightly charged him, and immediately sent him away; ⁴⁴And says to him, See you say nothing to any man: but go your way, show yourself to the priest, and offer for your cleansing those things which Moses commanded, for a testimony to them. ⁴⁵But he went out, and began to publish it much, and to blaze abroad the matter, so that Jesus could no more openly enter into the city, but was without in desert places: and they came to him from every quarter.

2 ¹And again he entered into Capernaum after some days; and it was noised that he was in the house. ²And straightway many were gathered together, so that there was no room to receive them, no, not so much as about the door: and he preached the word to them. ³And they come to him, bringing one sick of the palsy, which was borne of four. ⁴And when they could not come near to him for the press, they uncovered the roof where he was: and when they had broken it up, they let down the bed wherein the sick of the palsy lay. ⁵When Jesus saw their faith, he said to the sick of the palsy, Son, your sins be forgiven you. ⁶But there was certain of the scribes sitting there, and reasoning in their hearts, ⁷Why does this man thus speak blasphemies? who can forgive sins but God only? ⁸And immediately when Jesus perceived in his spirit that they so reasoned within themselves, he said to them, Why reason you these things in your hearts? ⁹Whether is it easier to say to the sick of the palsy, Your sins be forgiven you; or to say, Arise, and take up your bed, and walk? ¹⁰But that you may know that the Son of man has power on earth to forgive sins, (he says to the sick of the palsy,) ¹¹I say to you, Arise, and take up your bed, and go your way into your house. ¹²And immediately he arose, took up the bed, and went forth before them all; so that they were all amazed, and glorified God, saying, We never saw it on this fashion. ¹³And he went forth again by the sea side; and all the multitude resorted to him, and taught them. ¹⁴And as he passed by, he saw Levi the son of

Alphaeus sitting at the receipt of custom, and said to him, Follow me. And he arose and followed him. ¹⁵And it came to pass, that, as Jesus sat at meat in his house, many publicans and sinners sat also together with Jesus and his disciples: for there were many, and they followed him. ¹⁶And when the scribes and Pharisees saw him eat with publicans and sinners, they said to his disciples, How is it that he eats and drinks with publicans and sinners? ¹⁷When Jesus heard it, he says to them, They that are whole have no need of the physician, but they that are sick: I came not to call the righteous, but sinners to repentance. ¹⁸And the disciples of John and of the Pharisees used to fast: and they come and say to him, Why do the disciples of John and of the Pharisees fast, but your disciples fast not? ¹⁹And Jesus said to them, Can the children of the bridal chamber fast, while the bridegroom is with them? as long as they have the bridegroom with them, they cannot fast. ²⁰But the days will come, when the bridegroom shall be taken away from them, and then shall they fast in those days. ²¹No man also sews a piece of new cloth on an old garment: else the new piece that filled it up takes away from the old, and the rent is made worse. ²²And no man puts new wine into old bottles: else the new wine does burst the bottles, and the wine is spilled, and the bottles will be marred: but new wine must be put into new bottles. ²³And it came to pass, that he went through the corn fields on the sabbath day; and his disciples began, as they went, to pluck the ears of corn. ²⁴And the Pharisees said to him, Behold, why do they on the sabbath day that which is not lawful? ²⁵And he said to them, Have you never read what David did, when he had need, and was an hungered, he, and they that were with him? ²⁶How he went into the house of God in the days of Abiathar the high priest, and did eat the show bread, which is not lawful to eat but for the priests, and gave also to them which were with him? ²⁷And he said to them, The sabbath was made for man, and not man for the sabbath: ²⁸Therefore the Son of man is Lord also of the sabbath.

3 ¹And he entered again into the synagogue; and there was a man there which had a withered hand. ²And they watched him, whether he would heal him on the sabbath day; that they might accuse him. ³And he says to the man which had the withered hand, Stand forth. ⁴And he says to them, Is it lawful to do good on the sabbath days, or to do evil? to save life, or to kill? But they held their peace. ⁵And when he had looked round about on them with anger, being grieved for the hardness of their hearts, he says to the man, Stretch forth your hand. And he stretched it out: and his hand was restored whole as the other. ⁶And the Pharisees went forth, and straightway took counsel with the Herodians against him, how they might destroy him. ⁷But Jesus withdrew himself with his disciples to the sea: and a great multitude from Galilee followed him, and from Judaea, ⁸And from Jerusalem, and from Idumaea, and from beyond Jordan; and they about Tyre and Sidon, a great multitude, when they had heard what great things he did, came to him. ⁹And he spoke to his disciples, that a small ship should wait on him because of the multitude, lest they should throng him. ¹⁰For he had healed many; so that they pressed on him for to touch him, as many as had plagues. ¹¹And unclean spirits, when they saw him, fell down before him, and cried, saying, You are the Son of God. ¹²And he straightly charged them that they should not make him known. ¹³And he goes up into a mountain, and calls to him whom he would: and they came to him. ¹⁴And he ordained twelve, that they should be with him, and that he might send them forth to preach, ¹⁵And to have power to heal sicknesses, and to cast out devils: ¹⁶And Simon he surnamed Peter; ¹⁷And James the son of Zebedee, and John the brother of James; and he surnamed them Boanerges, which is, The sons of thunder: ¹⁸And Andrew, and Philip, and Bartholomew, and Matthew, and Thomas, and James the son of Alphaeus, and Thaddaeus, and Simon the Canaanite, ¹⁹And Judas Iscariot, which also betrayed him: and they went into an house. ²⁰And the multitude comes together again, so that they could not so much as eat bread. ²¹And when his friends heard of it, they went out to lay hold on him: for they said, He is beside himself. ²²And the scribes which came down from Jerusalem said, He has Beelzebub, and by the prince of the devils casts he out devils. ²³And he called them to him, and said to them in parables, How can Satan cast out Satan? ²⁴And if a kingdom be divided against itself, that kingdom cannot stand. ²⁵And if a house be divided against itself, that house cannot stand. ²⁶And if Satan rise up against himself, and be divided, he cannot stand, but has an end. ²⁷No man can enter into a strong man's house, and spoil his goods, except he will first bind the strong man; and then he will spoil his house. ²⁸Truly I say to you, All sins shall be forgiven to the sons of men, and blasphemies with which soever they shall blaspheme: ²⁹But he that shall blaspheme against the Holy Ghost has never forgiveness, but is in danger of eternal damnation. ³⁰Because they said, He has an unclean spirit. ³¹There came then his brothers and his mother, and, standing without, sent to him, calling him. ³²And the multitude sat about him, and they said to him, Behold, your mother and your brothers without seek for you. ³³And he answered them, saying, Who is my mother, or my brothers? ³⁴And he looked round about on them which sat about him, and said, Behold my mother and my brothers! ³⁵For whoever shall do the will of God, the same is my brother, and my sister, and mother.

4 ¹And he began again to teach by the sea side: and there was gathered to him a great multitude, so that he entered into a ship, and sat in the sea; and the whole multitude was by the sea on the land. ²And he taught them many things by parables, and said to them in his doctrine, ³Listen; Behold, there went out a sower to sow: ⁴And it came to pass, as he sowed, some fell by the way side, and the fowls of the air came and devoured it up. ⁵And some fell on stony ground, where it had not much earth; and immediately it sprang up, because it had no depth of earth: ⁶But when the sun was up, it was scorched; and because it had no root, it withered away. ⁷And some fell among thorns, and the thorns grew up, and choked it, and it yielded no fruit. ⁸And other fell on good ground, and did yield fruit that sprang up and increased; and brought forth, some thirty, and some sixty, and some an hundred. ⁹And he said to them, He that has ears to hear, let him hear. ¹⁰And when he was alone, they that were about him with the twelve asked of him the parable. ¹¹And he said to them, To you it is given to know the mystery of the kingdom of God: but to them that are without, all these things are done in parables: ¹²That seeing they may see, and not perceive; and hearing they may hear, and not understand; lest at any time they should be converted, and their sins should be forgiven them. ¹³And he said to them, Know you not this parable? and how then will you know all parables? ¹⁴The sower sows the word. ¹⁵And these are they by the way side, where the word is sown; but when they have heard, Satan comes immediately, and takes away the word that was sown in their hearts. ¹⁶And these are they likewise which are sown on stony ground; who, when they have heard the word, immediately receive it with gladness; ¹⁷And have no root in themselves, and so endure but for a time: afterward, when affliction or persecution rises for the word's sake, immediately they are offended. ¹⁸And these are they which are sown among thorns; such as hear the word, ¹⁹And the cares of this world, and the deceitfulness of riches, and the lusts of other things entering in, choke the word, and it becomes unfruitful. ²⁰And these are they which are sown on good ground; such as hear the word, and receive it, and bring forth fruit, some thirty times, some sixty, and some an hundred. ²¹And he said to them, Is a candle brought to be put under a bushel, or under a bed? and not to be set on a candlestick? ²²For there is nothing hid, which shall not be manifested; neither was any thing kept secret, but that it should come abroad. ²³If any man have ears to hear, let him hear. ²⁴And he said to them, Take heed what you hear: with what measure you mete, it shall be measured to you: and to you that hear shall more be given. ²⁵For he that has, to him shall be given: and he that has not, from him shall be taken even that which he has. ²⁶And he said, So is the kingdom of God, as if a man should cast seed into the ground; ²⁷And should sleep, and rise night and day, and the seed should spring and grow up, he knows not how. ²⁸For the earth brings forth fruit of herself; first the blade, then the ear, after that the full corn in the ear. ²⁹But when the fruit is brought forth, immediately he puts in the sickle, because the harvest is come. ³⁰And he said, To what shall we liken the kingdom of God? or with what comparison shall we compare it? ³¹It is like a grain of mustard seed, which, when it is sown in the earth, is less than all the seeds that be in the earth: ³²But when it is sown, it grows up, and becomes greater than all herbs, and shoots out great branches; so that the fowls of the air may lodge under the shadow of it. ³³And with many such parables spoke he the word to them, as they were able to hear it. ³⁴But without a parable spoke he not to them: and when they were alone, he expounded all things to his disciples. ³⁵And the same day, when the even was come, he says to them, Let us pass over to the other side. ³⁶And when they had sent away the multitude, they took him even as he was in the ship. And there were also with him other little ships. ³⁷And there arose a great storm of wind, and the waves beat into the ship, so that it was now full. ³⁸And he was in the hinder part of the ship, asleep on a pillow: and they awake him, and say to him, Master, care you not that we perish? ³⁹And he arose, and rebuked the wind, and said to the sea, Peace, be still. And the wind ceased, and there was a great calm. ⁴⁰And he said to them, Why are you so fearful? how is it that you have no faith? ⁴¹And they feared exceedingly, and said one to another, What manner of man is this, that even the wind and the sea obey him?

5 ¹And they came over to the other side of the sea, into the country of the Gadarenes. ²And when he was come out of the ship, immediately there met him out of the tombs a man with an unclean spirit, ³Who had his dwelling among the tombs; and no man could bind him, no, not with chains: ⁴Because that he had been often bound with fetters and chains, and the chains had been plucked asunder by him, and the fetters broken in pieces: neither could any man tame him. ⁵And always, night and day, he was in the mountains, and in the tombs, crying, and cutting himself with stones. ⁶But when he saw Jesus afar off, he ran and worshipped him, ⁷And cried with a loud voice, and said, What have I to do with you, Jesus, you Son of the most high God? I adjure you by God, that you torment me not. ⁸For he said to him, Come out of the man, you unclean spirit. ⁹And he asked him, What is your name? And he answered, saying, My name is Legion: for we are many. ¹⁰And he sought him much that he would not send them away out of the country. ¹¹Now there was there near to the mountains a great herd of swine feeding. ¹²And all the devils sought him, saying, Send us into the swine, that we may enter into them. ¹³And immediately Jesus gave them leave. And the unclean spirits went out, and entered into the swine: and the herd ran violently down a steep place into the sea, (they were about two thousand;) and were choked in the sea. ¹⁴And they that fed the swine fled, and told it in the city, and in the country. And they went out to see what it was that was done. ¹⁵And they come to Jesus, and see him that was possessed with the devil, and had the legion, sitting, and clothed, and in his right mind: and they were afraid. ¹⁶And they that saw it told them how it befell to him that was possessed with the devil, and also concerning the swine. ¹⁷And they began to pray him to depart out of their coasts. ¹⁸And when he was come into the ship, he that had been possessed with the devil prayed him that he might be with him. ¹⁹However, Jesus suffered him not, but says to him, Go home to your friends, and tell them how great things the Lord has done for you, and has had compassion on you. ²⁰And he departed, and began to publish in Decapolis how great things Jesus had done for him: and all men did marvel. ²¹And when Jesus was passed over again by ship to the other side, much people gathered to him: and he was near to the sea. ²²And, behold, there comes one of the rulers of the synagogue, Jairus by name; and when he saw him, he fell at his feet, ²³And sought him greatly, saying, My little daughter lies at the point of death: I pray you, come and lay your hands on her, that she may be healed; and she shall live. ²⁴And Jesus went with him; and much people followed him, and thronged him. ²⁵And a certain woman, which had an issue of blood twelve years, ²⁶And had suffered many things of many physicians, and had spent all that she had, and was nothing bettered, but rather grew worse, ²⁷When she had heard of Jesus, came in the press behind, and touched his garment. ²⁸For she said, If I may touch but his clothes, I shall be whole. ²⁹And straightway the fountain of her blood was dried up; and she felt in her body that she was healed of that plague. ³⁰And Jesus, immediately knowing in himself that virtue had gone

out of him, turned him about in the press, and said, Who touched my clothes? ³¹And his disciples said to him, You see the multitude thronging you, and say you, Who touched me? ³²And he looked round about to see her that had done this thing. ³³But the woman fearing and trembling, knowing what was done in her, came and fell down before him, and told him all the truth. ³⁴And he said to her, Daughter, your faith has made you whole; go in peace, and be whole of your plague. ³⁵While he yet spoke, there came from the ruler of the synagogue's house certain which said, Your daughter is dead: why trouble you the Master any further? ³⁶As soon as Jesus heard the word that was spoken, he says to the ruler of the synagogue, Be not afraid, only believe. ³⁷And he suffered no man to follow him, save Peter, and James, and John the brother of James. ³⁸And he comes to the house of the ruler of the synagogue, and sees the tumult, and them that wept and wailed greatly. ³⁹And when he was come in, he says to them, Why make you this ado, and weep? the damsel is not dead, but sleeps. ⁴⁰And they laughed him to scorn. But when he had put them all out, he takes the father and the mother of the damsel, and them that were with him, and enters in where the damsel was lying. ⁴¹And he took the damsel by the hand, and said to her, Talitha cumi; which is, being interpreted, Damsel, I say to you, arise. ⁴²And straightway the damsel arose, and walked; for she was of the age of twelve years. And they were astonished with a great astonishment. ⁴³And he charged them straightly that no man should know it; and commanded that something should be given her to eat.

6 ¹And he went out from there, and came into his own country; and his disciples follow him. ²And when the sabbath day was come, he began to teach in the synagogue: and many hearing him were astonished, saying, From where has this man these things? and what wisdom is this which is given to him, that even such mighty works are worked by his hands? ³Is not this the carpenter, the son of Mary, the brother of James, and Joses, and of Juda, and Simon? and are not his sisters here with us? And they were offended at him. ⁴But Jesus, said to them, A prophet is not without honor, but in his own country, and among his own kin, and in his own house. ⁵And he could there do no mighty work, save that he laid his hands on a few sick folk, and healed them. ⁶And he marveled because of their unbelief. And he went round about the villages, teaching. ⁷And he called to him the twelve, and began to send them forth by two and two; and gave them power over unclean spirits; ⁸And commanded them that they should take nothing for their journey, save a staff only; no money, no bread, no money in their purse: ⁹But be shod with sandals; and not put on two coats. ¹⁰And he said to them, In what place soever you enter into an house, there abide till you depart from that place. ¹¹And whoever shall not receive you, nor hear you, when you depart there, shake off the dust under your feet for a testimony against them. Truly I say to you, It shall be more tolerable for Sodom and Gomorrha in the day of judgment, than for that city. ¹²And they went out, and preached that men should repent. ¹³And they cast out many devils, and anointed with oil many that were sick, and healed them. ¹⁴And king Herod heard of him; (for his name was spread abroad:) and he said, That John the Baptist was risen from the dead, and therefore mighty works do show forth themselves in him. ¹⁵Others said, That it is Elias. And others said, That it is a prophet, or as one of the prophets. ¹⁶But when Herod heard thereof, he said, It is John, whom I beheaded: he is risen from the dead. ¹⁷For Herod himself had sent forth and laid hold on John, and bound him in prison for Herodias' sake, his brother Philip's wife: for he had married her. ¹⁸For John had said to Herod, It is not lawful for you to have your brother's wife. ¹⁹Therefore Herodias had a quarrel against him, and would have killed him; but she could not: ²⁰For Herod feared John, knowing that he was a just man and an holy, and observed him; and when he heard him, he did many things, and heard him gladly. ²¹And when a convenient day was come, that Herod on his birthday made a supper to his lords, high captains, and chief estates of Galilee; ²²And when the daughter of the said Herodias came in, and danced, and pleased Herod and them that sat with him, the king said to the damsel, Ask of me whatever you will, and I will give it you. ²³And he swore to her, Whatever you shall ask of me, I will give it you, to the half of my kingdom. ²⁴And she went forth, and said to her mother, What shall I ask? And she said, The head of John the Baptist. ²⁵And she came in straightway with haste to the king, and asked, saying, I will that you give me by and by in a charger the head of John the Baptist. ²⁶And the king was exceeding sorry; yet for his oath's sake, and for their sakes which sat with him, he would not reject her. ²⁷And immediately the king sent an executioner, and commanded his head to be brought: and he went and beheaded him in the prison, ²⁸And brought his head in a charger, and gave it to the damsel: and the damsel gave it to her mother. ²⁹And when his disciples heard of it, they came and took up his corpse, and laid it in a tomb. ³⁰And the apostles gathered themselves together to Jesus, and told him all things, both what they had done, and what they had taught. ³¹And he said to them, Come you yourselves apart into a desert place, and rest a while: for there were many coming and going, and they had no leisure so much as to eat. ³²And they departed into a desert place by ship privately. ³³And the people saw them departing, and many knew him, and ran afoot thither out of all cities, and preceded them, and came together to him. ³⁴And Jesus, when he came out, saw much people, and was moved with compassion toward them, because they were as sheep not having a shepherd: and he began to teach them many things. ³⁵And when the day was now far spent, his disciples came to him, and said, This is a desert place, and now the time is far passed: ³⁶Send them away, that they may go into the country round about, and into the villages, and buy themselves bread: for they have nothing to eat. ³⁷He answered and said to them, Give you them to eat. And they say to him, Shall we go and buy two hundred pennyworth of bread, and give them to eat? ³⁸He says to them, How many loaves have you? go and see. And when they knew, they say, Five, and two fishes. ³⁹And he commanded them to make all sit down by companies on the green grass. ⁴⁰And they sat down in ranks, by hundreds, and by fifties. ⁴¹And when he had taken the five loaves and the two fishes, he looked up to heaven, and blessed, and broke the loaves, and gave them to his disciples to set before them; and the two

fishes divided he among them all. ⁴²And they did all eat, and were filled. ⁴³And they took up twelve baskets full of the fragments, and of the fishes. ⁴⁴And they that did eat of the loaves were about five thousand men. ⁴⁵And straightway he constrained his disciples to get into the ship, and to go to the other side before to Bethsaida, while he sent away the people. ⁴⁶And when he had sent them away, he departed into a mountain to pray. ⁴⁷And when even was come, the ship was in the middle of the sea, and he alone on the land. ⁴⁸And he saw them toiling in rowing; for the wind was contrary to them: and about the fourth watch of the night he comes to them, walking on the sea, and would have passed by them. ⁴⁹But when they saw him walking on the sea, they supposed it had been a spirit, and cried out: ⁵⁰For they all saw him, and were troubled. And immediately he talked with them, and says to them, Be of good cheer: it is I; be not afraid. ⁵¹And he went up to them into the ship; and the wind ceased: and they were sore amazed in themselves beyond measure, and wondered. ⁵²For they considered not the miracle of the loaves: for their heart was hardened. ⁵³And when they had passed over, they came into the land of Gennesaret, and drew to the shore. ⁵⁴And when they were come out of the ship, straightway they knew him, ⁵⁵And ran through that whole region round about, and began to carry about in beds those that were sick, where they heard he was. ⁵⁶And wherever he entered, into villages, or cities, or country, they laid the sick in the streets, and sought him that they might touch if it were but the border of his garment: and as many as touched him were made whole.

7 ¹Then came together to him the Pharisees, and certain of the scribes, which came from Jerusalem. ²And when they saw some of his disciples eat bread with defiled, that is to say, with unwashed, hands, they found fault. ³For the Pharisees, and all the Jews, except they wash their hands oft, eat not, holding the tradition of the elders. ⁴And when they come from the market, except they wash, they eat not. And many other things there be, which they have received to hold, as the washing of cups, and pots, brazen vessels, and of tables. ⁵Then the Pharisees and scribes asked him, Why walk not your disciples according to the tradition of the elders, but eat bread with unwashed hands? ⁶He answered and said to them, Well has Isaiah prophesied of you hypocrites, as it is written, This people honors me with their lips, but their heart is far from me. ⁷However, in vain do they worship me, teaching for doctrines the commandments of men. ⁸For laying aside the commandment of God, you hold the tradition of men, as the washing of pots and cups: and many other such like things you do. ⁹And he said to them, Full well you reject the commandment of God, that you may keep your own tradition. ¹⁰For Moses said, Honor your father and your mother; and, Whoever curses father or mother, let him die the death: ¹¹But you say, If a man shall say to his father or mother, It is Corban, that is to say, a gift, by whatever you might be profited by me; he shall be free. ¹²And you suffer him no more to do something for his father or his mother; ¹³Making the word of God of none effect through your tradition, which you have delivered: and many such like things do you. ¹⁴And when he had called all the people to him, he said to them, Listen to me every one of you, and understand: ¹⁵There is nothing from without a man, that entering into him can defile him: but the things which come out of him, those are they that defile the man. ¹⁶If any man have ears to hear, let him hear. ¹⁷And when he was entered into the house from the people, his disciples asked him concerning the parable. ¹⁸And he says to them, Are you so without understanding also? Do you not perceive, that whatever thing from without enters into the man, it cannot defile him; ¹⁹Because it enters not into his heart, but into the belly, and goes out into the draught, purging all meats? ²⁰And he said, That which comes out of the man, that defiles the man. ²¹For from within, out of the heart of men, proceed evil thoughts, adulteries, fornications, murders, ²²Thefts, covetousness, wickedness, deceit, lasciviousness, an evil eye, blasphemy, pride, foolishness: ²³All these evil things come from within, and defile the man. ²⁴And from there he arose, and went into the borders of Tyre and Sidon, and entered into an house, and would have no man know it: but he could not be hid. ²⁵For a certain woman, whose young daughter had an unclean spirit, heard of him, and came and fell at his feet: ²⁶The woman was a Greek, a Syrophenician by nation; and she sought him that he would cast forth the devil out of her daughter. ²⁷But Jesus said to her, Let the children first be filled: for it is not meet to take the children's bread, and to cast it to the dogs. ²⁸And she answered and said to him, Yes, Lord: yet the dogs under the table eat of the children's crumbs. ²⁹And he said to her, For this saying go your way; the devil is gone out of your daughter. ³⁰And when she was come to her house, she found the devil gone out, and her daughter laid on the bed. ³¹And again, departing from the coasts of Tyre and Sidon, he came to the sea of Galilee, through the middle of the coasts of Decapolis. ³²And they bring to him one that was deaf, and had an impediment in his speech; and they beseech him to put his hand on him. ³³And he took him aside from the multitude, and put his fingers into his ears, and he spit, and touched his tongue; ³⁴And looking up to heaven, he sighed, and says to him, Ephphatha, that is, Be opened. ³⁵And straightway his ears were opened, and the string of his tongue was loosed, and he spoke plain. ³⁶And he charged them that they should tell no man: but the more he charged them, so much the more a great deal they published it; ³⁷And were beyond measure astonished, saying, He has done all things well: he makes both the deaf to hear, and the dumb to speak.

8 ¹In those days the multitude being very great, and having nothing to eat, Jesus called his disciples to him, and says to them, ²I have compassion on the multitude, because they have now been with me three days, and have nothing to eat: ³And if I send them away fasting to their own houses, they will faint by the way: for divers of them came from far. ⁴And his disciples answered him, From where can a man satisfy these men with bread here in the wilderness? ⁵And he asked them, How many loaves have you? And they said, Seven. ⁶And he commanded the people to sit down on the ground: and he took the seven loaves, and gave thanks, and broke, and gave to his disciples to set before them; and they did set them before the people. ⁷And they had a few small fishes: and he blessed, and commanded to set them also before them. ⁸So they did eat, and were filled: and they

took up of the broken meat that was left seven baskets. ⁹And they that had eaten were about four thousand: and he sent them away. ¹⁰And straightway he entered into a ship with his disciples, and came into the parts of Dalmanutha. ¹¹And the Pharisees came forth, and began to question with him, seeking of him a sign from heaven, tempting him. ¹²And he sighed deeply in his spirit, and says, Why does this generation seek after a sign? truly I say to you, There shall no sign be given to this generation. ¹³And he left them, and entering into the ship again departed to the other side. ¹⁴Now the disciples had forgotten to take bread, neither had they in the ship with them more than one loaf. ¹⁵And he charged them, saying, Take heed, beware of the leaven of the Pharisees, and of the leaven of Herod. ¹⁶And they reasoned among themselves, saying, It is because we have no bread. ¹⁷And when Jesus knew it, he says to them, Why reason you, because you have no bread? perceive you not yet, neither understand? have you your heart yet hardened? ¹⁸Having eyes, see you not? and having ears, hear you not? and do you not remember? ¹⁹When I broke the five loaves among five thousand, how many baskets full of fragments took you up? They say to him, Twelve. ²⁰And when the seven among four thousand, how many baskets full of fragments took you up? And they said, Seven. ²¹And he said to them, How is it that you do not understand? ²²And he comes to Bethsaida; and they bring a blind man to him, and sought him to touch him. ²³And he took the blind man by the hand, and led him out of the town; and when he had spit on his eyes, and put his hands on him, he asked him if he saw something. ²⁴And he looked up, and said, I see men as trees, walking. ²⁵After that he put his hands again on his eyes, and made him look up: and he was restored, and saw every man clearly. ²⁶And he sent him away to his house, saying, Neither go into the town, nor tell it to any in the town. ²⁷And Jesus went out, and his disciples, into the towns of Caesarea Philippi: and by the way he asked his disciples, saying to them, Whom do men say that I am? ²⁸And they answered, John the Baptist; but some say, Elias; and others, One of the prophets. ²⁹And he says to them, But whom say you that I am? And Peter answers and said to him, You are the Christ. ³⁰And he charged them that they should tell no man of him. ³¹And he began to teach them, that the Son of man must suffer many things, and be rejected of the elders, and of the chief priests, and scribes, and be killed, and after three days rise again. ³²And he spoke that saying openly. And Peter took him, and began to rebuke him. ³³But when he had turned about and looked on his disciples, he rebuked Peter, saying, Get you behind me, Satan: for you mind not the things that be of God, but the things that be of men. ³⁴And when he had called the people to him with his disciples also, he said to them, Whoever will come after me, let him deny himself, and take up his cross, and follow me. ³⁵For whoever will save his life shall lose it; but whoever shall lose his life for my sake and the gospel's, the same shall save it. ³⁶For what shall it profit a man, if he shall gain the whole world, and lose his own soul? ³⁷Or what shall a man give in exchange for his soul? ³⁸Whoever therefore shall be ashamed of me and of my words in this adulterous and sinful generation; of him also shall the Son of man be ashamed, when he comes in the glory of his Father with the holy angels.

9

¹And he said to them, Truly I say to you, That there be some of them that stand here, which shall not taste of death, till they have seen the kingdom of God come with power. ²And after six days Jesus takes with him Peter, and James, and John, and leads them up into an high mountain apart by themselves: and he was transfigured before them. ³And his raiment became shining, exceeding white as snow; so as no fuller on earth can white them. ⁴And there appeared to them Elias with Moses: and they were talking with Jesus. ⁵And Peter answered and said to Jesus, Master, it is good for us to be here: and let us make three tabernacles; one for you, and one for Moses, and one for Elias. ⁶For he knew not what to say; for they were sore afraid. ⁷And there was a cloud that overshadowed them: and a voice came out of the cloud, saying, This is my beloved Son: hear him. ⁸And suddenly, when they had looked round about, they saw no man any more, save Jesus only with themselves. ⁹And as they came down from the mountain, he charged them that they should tell no man what things they had seen, till the Son of man were risen from the dead. ¹⁰And they kept that saying with themselves, questioning one with another what the rising from the dead should mean. ¹¹And they asked him, saying, Why say the scribes that Elias must first come? ¹²And he answered and told them, Elias truly comes first, and restores all things; and how it is written of the Son of man, that he must suffer many things, and be set at nothing. ¹³But I say to you, That Elias is indeed come, and they have done to him whatever they listed, as it is written of him. ¹⁴And when he came to his disciples, he saw a great multitude about them, and the scribes questioning with them. ¹⁵And straightway all the people, when they beheld him, were greatly amazed, and running to him saluted him. ¹⁶And he asked the scribes, What question you with them? ¹⁷And one of the multitude answered and said, Master, I have brought to you my son, which has a dumb spirit; ¹⁸And wherever he takes him, he tears him: and he foams, and gnashes with his teeth, and pines away: and I spoke to your disciples that they should cast him out; and they could not. ¹⁹He answers him, and says, O faithless generation, how long shall I be with you? how long shall I suffer you? bring him to me. ²⁰And they brought him to him: and when he saw him, straightway the spirit tare him; and he fell on the ground, and wallowed foaming. ²¹And he asked his father, How long is it ago since this came to him? And he said, Of a child. ²²And often it has cast him into the fire, and into the waters, to destroy him: but if you can do any thing, have compassion on us, and help us. ²³Jesus said to him, If you can believe, all things are possible to him that believes. ²⁴And straightway the father of the child cried out, and said with tears, Lord, I believe; help you my unbelief. ²⁵When Jesus saw that the people came running together, he rebuked the foul spirit, saying to him, You dumb and deaf spirit, I charge you, come out of him, and enter no more into him. ²⁶And the spirit cried, and rent him sore, and came out of him: and he was as one dead; so that many said, He is dead. ²⁷But Jesus took him by the hand, and lifted him up; and he arose. ²⁸And when he was come into the house, his disciples asked him privately, Why

could not we cast him out? ²⁹And he said to them, This kind can come forth by nothing, but by prayer and fasting. ³⁰And they departed there, and passed through Galilee; and he would not that any man should know it. ³¹For he taught his disciples, and said to them, The Son of man is delivered into the hands of men, and they shall kill him; and after that he is killed, he shall rise the third day. ³²But they understood not that saying, and were afraid to ask him. ³³And he came to Capernaum: and being in the house he asked them, What was it that you disputed among yourselves by the way? ³⁴But they held their peace: for by the way they had disputed among themselves, who should be the greatest. ³⁵And he sat down, and called the twelve, and says to them, If any man desire to be first, the same shall be last of all, and servant of all. ³⁶And he took a child, and set him in the middle of them: and when he had taken him in his arms, he said to them, ³⁷Whoever shall receive one of such children in my name, receives me: and whoever shall receive me, receives not me, but him that sent me. ³⁸And John answered him, saying, Master, we saw one casting out devils in your name, and he follows not us: and we forbade him, because he follows not us. ³⁹But Jesus said, Forbid him not: for there is no man which shall do a miracle in my name, that can lightly speak evil of me. ⁴⁰For he that is not against us is on our part. ⁴¹For whoever shall give you a cup of water to drink in my name, because you belong to Christ, truly I say to you, he shall not lose his reward. ⁴²And whoever shall offend one of these little ones that believe in me, it is better for him that a millstone were hanged about his neck, and he were cast into the sea. ⁴³And if your hand offend you, cut it off: it is better for you to enter into life maimed, than having two hands to go into hell, into the fire that never shall be quenched: ⁴⁴Where their worm dies not, and the fire is not quenched. ⁴⁵And if your foot offend you, cut it off: it is better for you to enter halt into life, than having two feet to be cast into hell, into the fire that never shall be quenched: ⁴⁶Where their worm dies not, and the fire is not quenched. ⁴⁷And if your eye offend you, pluck it out: it is better for you to enter into the kingdom of God with one eye, than having two eyes to be cast into hell fire: ⁴⁸Where their worm dies not, and the fire is not quenched. ⁴⁹For every one shall be salted with fire, and every sacrifice shall be salted with salt. ⁵⁰Salt is good: but if the salt have lost his saltiness, with which will you season it? Have salt in yourselves, and have peace one with another.

10

¹And he arose from there, and comes into the coasts of Judaea by the farther side of Jordan: and the people resort to him again; and, as he was wont, he taught them again. ²And the Pharisees came to him, and asked him, Is it lawful for a man to put away his wife? tempting him. ³And he answered and said to them, What did Moses command you? ⁴And they said, Moses suffered to write a bill of divorce, and to put her away. ⁵And Jesus answered and said to them, For the hardness of your heart he wrote you this precept. ⁶But from the beginning of the creation God made them male and female. ⁷For this cause shall a man leave his father and mother, and join to his wife; ⁸And they two shall be one flesh: so then they are no more two, but one flesh. ⁹What therefore God has joined together, let not man put asunder. ¹⁰And in the house his disciples asked him again of the same matter. ¹¹And he says to them, Whoever shall put away his wife, and marry another, commits adultery against her. ¹²And if a woman shall put away her husband, and be married to another, she commits adultery. ¹³And they brought young children to him, that he should touch them: and his disciples rebuked those that brought them. ¹⁴But when Jesus saw it, he was much displeased, and said to them, Suffer the little children to come to me, and forbid them not: for of such is the kingdom of God. ¹⁵Truly I say to you, Whoever shall not receive the kingdom of God as a little child, he shall not enter therein. ¹⁶And he took them up in his arms, put his hands on them, and blessed them. ¹⁷And when he was gone forth into the way, there came one running, and kneeled to him, and asked him, Good Master, what shall I do that I may inherit eternal life? ¹⁸And Jesus said to him, Why call you me good? there is none good but one, that is, God. ¹⁹You know the commandments, Do not commit adultery, Do not kill, Do not steal, Do not bear false witness, Defraud not, Honor your father and mother. ²⁰And he answered and said to him, Master, all these have I observed from my youth. ²¹Then Jesus beholding him loved him, and said to him, One thing you lack: go your way, sell whatever you have, and give to the poor, and you shall have treasure in heaven: and come, take up the cross, and follow me. ²²And he was sad at that saying, and went away grieved: for he had great possessions. ²³And Jesus looked round about, and says to his disciples, How hardly shall they that have riches enter into the kingdom of God! ²⁴And the disciples were astonished at his words. But Jesus answers again, and says to them, Children, how hard is it for them that trust in riches to enter into the kingdom of God! ²⁵It is easier for a camel to go through the eye of a needle, than for a rich man to enter into the kingdom of God. ²⁶And they were astonished out of measure, saying among themselves, Who then can be saved? ²⁷And Jesus looking on them says, With men it is impossible, but not with God: for with God all things are possible. ²⁸Then Peter began to say to him, See, we have left all, and have followed you. ²⁹And Jesus answered and said, Truly I say to you, There is no man that has left house, or brothers, or sisters, or father, or mother, or wife, or children, or lands, for my sake, and the gospel's, ³⁰But he shall receive an hundred times now in this time, houses, and brothers, and sisters, and mothers, and children, and lands, with persecutions; and in the world to come eternal life. ³¹But many that are first shall be last; and the last first. ³²And they were in the way going up to Jerusalem; and Jesus went before them: and they were amazed; and as they followed, they were afraid. And he took again the twelve, and began to tell them what things should happen to him, ³³Saying, Behold, we go up to Jerusalem; and the Son of man shall be delivered to the chief priests, and to the scribes; and they shall condemn him to death, and shall deliver him to the Gentiles: ³⁴And they shall mock him, and shall whip him, and shall spit on him, and shall kill him: and the third day he shall rise again. ³⁵And James and John, the sons of Zebedee, come to him, saying, Master, we would that you should do for us whatever we shall desire. ³⁶And he said to them, What would you that I

should do for you? ³⁷They said to him, Grant to us that we may sit, one on your right hand, and the other on your left hand, in your glory. ³⁸But Jesus said to them, You know not what you ask: can you drink of the cup that I drink of? and be baptized with the baptism that I am baptized with? ³⁹And they said to him, We can. And Jesus said to them, You shall indeed drink of the cup that I drink of; and with the baptism that I am baptized with shall you be baptized: ⁴⁰But to sit on my right hand and on my left hand is not my to give; but it shall be given to them for whom it is prepared. ⁴¹And when the ten heard it, they began to be much displeased with James and John. ⁴²But Jesus called them to him, and says to them, You know that they which are accounted to rule over the Gentiles exercise lordship over them; and their great ones exercise authority on them. ⁴³But so shall it not be among you: but whoever will be great among you, shall be your minister: ⁴⁴And whoever of you will be the most chief, shall be servant of all. ⁴⁵For even the Son of man came not to be ministered to, but to minister, and to give his life a ransom for many. ⁴⁶And they came to Jericho: and as he went out of Jericho with his disciples and a great number of people, blind Bartimaeus, the son of Timaeus, sat by the highway side begging. ⁴⁷And when he heard that it was Jesus of Nazareth, he began to cry out, and say, Jesus, you son of David, have mercy on me. ⁴⁸And many charged him that he should hold his peace: but he cried the more a great deal, You son of David, have mercy on me. ⁴⁹And Jesus stood still, and commanded him to be called. And they call the blind man, saying to him, Be of good comfort, rise; he calls you. ⁵⁰And he, casting away his garment, rose, and came to Jesus. ⁵¹And Jesus answered and said to him, What will you that I should do to you? The blind man said to him, Lord, that I might receive my sight. ⁵²And Jesus said to him, Go your way; your faith has made you whole. And immediately he received his sight, and followed Jesus in the way.

11 ¹And when they came near to Jerusalem, to Bethphage and Bethany, at the mount of Olives, he sends forth two of his disciples, ²And says to them, Go your way into the village over against you: and as soon as you be entered into it, you shall find a colt tied, where on never man sat; loose him, and bring him. ³And if any man say to you, Why do you this? say you that the Lord has need of him; and straightway he will send him here. ⁴And they went their way, and found the colt tied by the door without in a place where two ways met; and they loose him. ⁵And certain of them that stood there said to them, What do you, loosing the colt? ⁶And they said to them even as Jesus had commanded: and they let them go. ⁷And they brought the colt to Jesus, and cast their garments on him; and he sat on him. ⁸And many spread their garments in the way: and others cut down branches off the trees, and strewed them in the way. ⁹And they that went before, and they that followed, cried, saying, Hosanna; Blessed is he that comes in the name of the Lord: ¹⁰Blessed be the kingdom of our father David, that comes in the name of the Lord: Hosanna in the highest. ¹¹And Jesus entered into Jerusalem, and into the temple: and when he had looked round about on all things, and now the eventide was come, he went out to Bethany with the twelve. ¹²And on the morrow, when they were come from Bethany, he was hungry: ¹³And seeing a fig tree afar off having leaves, he came, if haply he might find any thing thereon: and when he came to it, he found nothing but leaves; for the time of figs was not yet. ¹⁴And Jesus answered and said to it, No man eat fruit of you hereafter for ever. And his disciples heard it. ¹⁵And they come to Jerusalem: and Jesus went into the temple, and began to cast out them that sold and bought in the temple, and overthrew the tables of the moneychangers, and the seats of them that sold doves; ¹⁶And would not suffer that any man should carry any vessel through the temple. ¹⁷And he taught, saying to them, Is it not written, My house shall be called of all nations the house of prayer? but you have made it a den of thieves. ¹⁸And the scribes and chief priests heard it, and sought how they might destroy him: for they feared him, because all the people was astonished at his doctrine. ¹⁹And when even was come, he went out of the city. ²⁰And in the morning, as they passed by, they saw the fig tree dried up from the roots. ²¹And Peter calling to remembrance says to him, Master, behold, the fig tree which you cursed is withered away. ²²And Jesus answering says to them, Have faith in God. ²³For truly I say to you, That whoever shall say to this mountain, Be you removed, and be you cast into the sea; and shall not doubt in his heart, but shall believe that those things which he says shall come to pass; he shall have whatever he says. ²⁴Therefore I say to you, What things soever you desire, when you pray, believe that you receive them, and you shall have them. ²⁵And when you stand praying, forgive, if you have something against any: that your Father also which is in heaven may forgive you your trespasses. ²⁶But if you do not forgive, neither will your Father which is in heaven forgive your trespasses. ²⁷And they come again to Jerusalem: and as he was walking in the temple, there come to him the chief priests, and the scribes, and the elders, ²⁸And say to him, By what authority do you these things? and who gave you this authority to do these things? ²⁹And Jesus answered and said to them, I will also ask of you one question, and answer me, and I will tell you by what authority I do these things. ³⁰The baptism of John, was it from heaven, or of men? answer me. ³¹And they reasoned with themselves, saying, If we shall say, From heaven; he will say, Why then did you not believe him? ³²But if we shall say, Of men; they feared the people: for all men counted John, that he was a prophet indeed. ³³And they answered and said to Jesus, We cannot tell. And Jesus answering says to them, Neither do I tell you by what authority I do these things.

12 ¹And he began to speak to them by parables. A certain man planted a vineyard, and set an hedge about it, and dig a place for the winefat, and built a tower, and let it out to farmers, and went into a far country. ²And at the season he sent to the farmers a servant, that he might receive from the farmers of the fruit of the vineyard. ³And they caught him, and beat him, and sent him away empty. ⁴And again he sent to them another servant; and at him they cast stones, and wounded him in the head, and sent him away shamefully handled. ⁵And again he sent another; and him they killed, and many others; beating some, and killing some. ⁶Having yet therefore one son, his well beloved, he sent him also last to them, saying, They will reverence my son. ⁷But those farmers said among themselves, This is the heir; come, let us kill him, and the inheritance shall be ours. ⁸And they took him, and killed him, and cast him out of the vineyard. ⁹What shall therefore the lord of the vineyard do? he will come and destroy the farmers, and will give the vineyard to others. ¹⁰And have you not read this scripture; The stone which the builders rejected is become the head of the corner: ¹¹This was the Lord's doing, and it is marvelous in our eyes? ¹²And they sought to lay hold on him, but feared the people: for they knew that he had spoken the parable against them: and they left him, and went their way. ¹³And they send to him certain of the Pharisees and of the Herodians, to catch him in his words. ¹⁴And when they were come, they say to him, Master, we know that you are true, and care for no man: for you regard not the person of men, but teach the way of God in truth: Is it lawful to give tribute to Caesar, or not? ¹⁵Shall we give, or shall we not give? But he, knowing their hypocrisy, said to them, Why tempt you me? bring me a penny, that I may see it. ¹⁶And they brought it. And he says to them, Whose is this image and superscription? And they said to him, Caesar's. ¹⁷And Jesus answering said to them, Render to Caesar the things that are Caesar's, and to God the things that are God's. And they marveled at him. ¹⁸Then come to him the Sadducees, which say there is no resurrection; and they asked him, saying, ¹⁹Master, Moses wrote to us, If a man's brother die, and leave his wife behind him, and leave no children, that his brother should take his wife, and raise up seed to his brother. ²⁰Now there were seven brothers: and the first took a wife, and dying left no seed. ²¹And the second took her, and died, neither left he any seed: and the third likewise. ²²And the seven had her, and left no seed: last of all the woman died also. ²³In the resurrection therefore, when they shall rise, whose wife shall she be of them? for the seven had her to wife. ²⁴And Jesus answering said to them, Do you not therefore err, because you know not the scriptures, neither the power of God? ²⁵For when they shall rise from the dead, they neither marry, nor are given in marriage; but are as the angels which are in heaven. ²⁶And as touching the dead, that they rise: have you not read in the book of Moses, how in the bush God spoke to him, saying, I am the God of Abraham, and the God of Isaac, and the God of Jacob? ²⁷He is not the God of the dead, but the God of the living: you therefore do greatly err. ²⁸And one of the scribes came, and having heard them reasoning together, and perceiving that he had answered them well, asked him, Which is the first commandment of all? ²⁹And Jesus answered him, The first of all the commandments is, Hear, O Israel; The Lord our God is one Lord: ³⁰And you shall love the Lord your God with all your heart, and with all your soul, and with all your mind, and with all your strength: this is the first commandment. ³¹And the second is like, namely this, You shall love your neighbor as yourself. There is none other commandment greater than these. ³²And the scribe said to him, Well, Master, you have said the truth: for there is one God; and there is none other but he: ³³And to love him with all the heart, and with all the understanding, and with all the soul, and with all the strength, and to love his neighbor as himself, is more than all whole burnt offerings and sacrifices. ³⁴And when Jesus saw that he answered discreetly, he said to him, You are not far from the kingdom of God. And no man after that dared ask him any question. ³⁵And Jesus answered and said, while he taught in the temple, How say the scribes that Christ is the son of David? ³⁶For David himself said by the Holy Ghost, The LORD said to my Lord, Sit you on my right hand, till I make your enemies your footstool. ³⁷David therefore himself calls him Lord; and from where is he then his son? And the common people heard him gladly. ³⁸And he said to them in his doctrine, Beware of the scribes, which love to go in long clothing, and love salutations in the marketplaces, ³⁹And the chief seats in the synagogues, and the uppermost rooms at feasts: ⁴⁰Which devour widows' houses, and for a pretense make long prayers: these shall receive greater damnation. ⁴¹And Jesus sat over against the treasury, and beheld how the people cast money into the treasury: and many that were rich cast in much. ⁴²And there came a certain poor widow, and she threw in two mites, which make a farthing. ⁴³And he called to him his disciples, and says to them, Truly I say to you, That this poor widow has cast more in, than all they which have cast into the treasury: ⁴⁴For all they did cast in of their abundance; but she of her want did cast in all that she had, even all her living.

13

¹And as he went out of the temple, one of his disciples says to him, Master, see what manner of stones and what buildings are here! ²And Jesus answering said to him, See you these great buildings? there shall not be left one stone on another, that shall not be thrown down. ³And as he sat on the mount of Olives over against the temple, Peter and James and John and Andrew asked him privately, ⁴Tell us, when shall these things be? and what shall be the sign when all these things shall be fulfilled? ⁵And Jesus answering them began to say, Take heed lest any man deceive you: ⁶For many shall come in my name, saying, I am Christ; and shall deceive many. ⁷And when you shall hear of wars and rumors of wars, be you not troubled: for such things must needs be; but the end shall not be yet. ⁸For nation shall rise against nation, and kingdom against kingdom: and there shall be earthquakes in divers places, and there shall be famines and troubles: these are the beginnings of sorrows. ⁹But take heed to yourselves: for they shall deliver you up to councils; and in the synagogues you shall be beaten: and you shall be brought before rulers and kings for my sake, for a testimony against them. ¹⁰And the gospel must first be published among all nations. ¹¹But when they shall lead you, and deliver you up, take no thought beforehand what you shall speak, neither do you premeditate: but whatever shall be given you in that hour, that speak you: for it is not you that speak, but the Holy Ghost. ¹²Now the brother shall betray the brother to death, and the father the son; and children shall rise up against their parents, and shall cause them to be put to death. ¹³And you shall be hated of all men for my name's sake: but he that shall endure to the end, the same shall be saved. ¹⁴But when you shall see the abomination of desolation, spoken of by Daniel the prophet, standing where it should not, (let him that reads understand,) then let them that be in Judaea flee to the mountains: ¹⁵And let him that is on the housetop not go

down into the house, neither enter therein, to take any thing out of his house: ¹⁶And let him that is in the field not turn back again for to take up his garment. ¹⁷But woe to them that are with child, and to them that give suck in those days! ¹⁸And pray you that your flight be not in the winter. ¹⁹For in those days shall be affliction, such as was not from the beginning of the creation which God created to this time, neither shall be. ²⁰And except that the Lord had shortened those days, no flesh should be saved: but for the elect's sake, whom he has chosen, he has shortened the days. ²¹And then if any man shall say to you, See, here is Christ; or, see, he is there; believe him not: ²²For false Christs and false prophets shall rise, and shall show signs and wonders, to seduce, if it were possible, even the elect. ²³But take you heed: behold, I have foretold you all things. ²⁴But in those days, after that tribulation, the sun shall be darkened, and the moon shall not give her light, ²⁵And the stars of heaven shall fall, and the powers that are in heaven shall be shaken. ²⁶And then shall they see the Son of man coming in the clouds with great power and glory. ²⁷And then shall he send his angels, and shall gather together his elect from the four winds, from the uttermost part of the earth to the uttermost part of heaven. ²⁸Now learn a parable of the fig tree; When her branch is yet tender, and puts forth leaves, you know that summer is near: ²⁹So you in like manner, when you shall see these things come to pass, know that it is near, even at the doors. ³⁰Truly I say to you, that this generation shall not pass, till all these things be done. ³¹Heaven and earth shall pass away: but my words shall not pass away. ³²But of that day and that hour knows no man, no, not the angels which are in heaven, neither the Son, but the Father. ³³Take you heed, watch and pray: for you know not when the time is. ³⁴For the Son of Man is as a man taking a far journey, who left his house, and gave authority to his servants, and to every man his work, and commanded the porter to watch. ³⁵Watch you therefore: for you know not when the master of the house comes, at even, or at midnight, or at the cock-crowing, or in the morning: ³⁶Lest coming suddenly he find you sleeping. ³⁷And what I say to you I say to all, Watch.

14 ¹After two days was the feast of the passover, and of unleavened bread: and the chief priests and the scribes sought how they might take him by craft, and put him to death. ²But they said, Not on the feast day, lest there be an uproar of the people. ³And being in Bethany in the house of Simon the leper, as he sat at meat, there came a woman having an alabaster box of ointment of spikenard very precious; and she broke the box, and poured it on his head. ⁴And there were some that had indignation within themselves, and said, Why was this waste of the ointment made? ⁵For it might have been sold for more than three hundred pence, and have been given to the poor. And they murmured against her. ⁶And Jesus said, Let her alone; why trouble you her? she has worked a good work on me. ⁷For you have the poor with you always, and whenever you will you may do them good: but me you have not always. ⁸She has done what she could: she is come beforehand to anoint my body to the burying. ⁹Truly I say to you, Wherever this gospel shall be preached throughout the whole world, this also that she has done shall be spoken of for a memorial of her. ¹⁰And Judas Iscariot, one of the twelve, went to the chief priests, to betray him to them. ¹¹And when they heard it, they were glad, and promised to give him money. And he sought how he might conveniently betray him. ¹²And the first day of unleavened bread, when they killed the passover, his disciples said to him, Where will you that we go and prepare that you may eat the passover? ¹³And he sends forth two of his disciples, and says to them, Go you into the city, and there shall meet you a man bearing a pitcher of water: follow him. ¹⁴And wherever he shall go in, say you to the manager of the house, The Master says, Where is the guest room, where I shall eat the passover with my disciples? ¹⁵And he will show you a large upper room furnished and prepared: there make ready for us. ¹⁶And his disciples went forth, and came into the city, and found as he had said to them: and they made ready the passover. ¹⁷And in the evening he comes with the twelve. ¹⁸And as they sat and did eat, Jesus said, Truly I say to you, One of you which eats with me shall betray me. ¹⁹And they began to be sorrowful, and to say to him one by one, Is it I? and another said, Is it I? ²⁰And he answered and said to them, It is one of the twelve, that dips with me in the dish. ²¹The Son of man indeed goes, as it is written of him: but woe to that man by whom the Son of man is betrayed! good were it for that man if he had never been born. ²²And as they did eat, Jesus took bread, and blessed, and broke it, and gave to them, and said, Take, eat: this is my body. ²³And he took the cup, and when he had given thanks, he gave it to them: and they all drank of it. ²⁴And he said to them, This is my blood of the new testament, which is shed for many. ²⁵Truly I say to you, I will drink no more of the fruit of the vine, until that day that I drink it new in the kingdom of God. ²⁶And when they had sung an hymn, they went out into the mount of Olives. ²⁷And Jesus says to them, All you shall be offended because of me this night: for it is written, I will smite the shepherd, and the sheep shall be scattered. ²⁸But after that I am risen, I will go before you into Galilee. ²⁹But Peter said to him, Although all shall be offended, yet will not I. ³⁰And Jesus says to him, Truly I say to you, That this day, even in this night, before the cock crow twice, you shall deny me thrice. ³¹But he spoke the more vehemently, If I should die with you, I will not deny you in any wise. Likewise also said they all. ³²And they came to a place which was named Gethsemane: and he says to his disciples, Sit you here, while I shall pray. ³³And he takes with him Peter and James and John, and began to be sore amazed, and to be very heavy; ³⁴And says to them, My soul is exceeding sorrowful to death: tarry you here, and watch. ³⁵And he went forward a little, and fell on the ground, and prayed that, if it were possible, the hour might pass from him. ³⁶And he said, Abba, Father, all things are possible to you; take away this cup from me: nevertheless not what I will, but what you will. ³⁷And he comes, and finds them sleeping, and says to Peter, Simon, sleep you? could not you watch one hour? ³⁸Watch you and pray, lest you enter into temptation. The spirit truly is ready, but the flesh is weak. ³⁹And again he went away, and prayed, and spoke the same words. ⁴⁰And when he returned, he found them asleep again, (for their eyes were heavy,) neither knew they what to answer him. ⁴¹And he comes the third time, and says to them, Sleep on now, and take your rest: it is enough, the hour is come; behold, the Son of man is betrayed into the hands of sinners. ⁴²Rise up, let us go; see, he that betrays me is at hand. ⁴³And immediately, while he yet spoke, comes Judas, one of the twelve, and with him a great multitude with swords and staves, from the chief priests and the scribes and the elders. ⁴⁴And he that betrayed him had given them a token, saying, Whomsoever I shall kiss, that same is he; take him, and lead him away safely. ⁴⁵And as soon as he was come, he goes straightway to him, and says, Master, master; and kissed him. ⁴⁶And they laid their hands on him, and took him. ⁴⁷And one of them that stood by drew a sword, and smote a servant of the high priest, and cut off his ear. ⁴⁸And Jesus answered and said to them, Are you come out, as against a thief, with swords and with staves to take me? ⁴⁹I was daily with you in the temple teaching, and you took me not: but the scriptures must be fulfilled. ⁵⁰And they all forsook him, and fled. ⁵¹And there followed him a certain young man, having a linen cloth cast about his naked body; and the young men laid hold on him: ⁵²And he left the linen cloth, and fled from them naked. ⁵³And they led Jesus away to the high priest: and with him were assembled all the chief priests and the elders and the scribes. ⁵⁴And Peter followed him afar off, even into the palace of the high priest: and he sat with the servants, and warmed himself at the fire. ⁵⁵And the chief priests and all the council sought for witness against Jesus to put him to death; and found none. ⁵⁶For many bore false witness against him, but their witness agreed not together. ⁵⁷And there arose certain, and bore false witness against him, saying, ⁵⁸We heard him say, I will destroy this temple that is made with hands, and within three days I will build another made without hands. ⁵⁹But neither so did their witness agree together. ⁶⁰And the high priest stood up in the middle, and asked Jesus, saying, Answer you nothing? what is it which these witness against you? ⁶¹But he held his peace, and answered nothing. Again the high priest asked him, and said to him, Are you the Christ, the Son of the Blessed? ⁶²And Jesus said, I am: and you shall see the Son of man sitting on the right hand of power, and coming in the clouds of heaven. ⁶³Then the high priest rent his clothes, and says, What need we any further witnesses? ⁶⁴You have heard the blasphemy: what think you? And they all condemned him to be guilty of death. ⁶⁵And some began to spit on him, and to cover his face, and to buffet him, and to say to him, Prophesy: and the servants did strike him with the palms of their hands. ⁶⁶And as Peter was beneath in the palace, there comes one of the maids of the high priest: ⁶⁷And when she saw Peter warming himself, she looked on him, and said, And you also were with Jesus of Nazareth. ⁶⁸But he denied, saying, I know not, neither understand I what you say. And he went out into the porch; and the cock crew. ⁶⁹And a maid saw him again, and began to say to them that stood by, This is one of them. ⁷⁰And he denied it again. And a little after, they that stood by said again to Peter, Surely you are one of them: for you are a Galilaean, and your speech agrees thereto. ⁷¹But he began to curse and to swear, saying, I know not this man of whom you speak. ⁷²And the second time the cock crew. And Peter called to mind the word that Jesus said to him, Before the cock crow twice, you shall deny me thrice. And when he thought thereon, he wept.

15

¹And straightway in the morning the chief priests held a consultation with the elders and scribes and the whole council, and bound Jesus, and carried him away, and delivered him to Pilate. ²And Pilate asked him, Are you the King of the Jews? And he answering said to them, You say it. ³And the chief priests accused him of many things: but he answered nothing. ⁴And Pilate asked him again, saying, Answer you nothing? behold how many things they witness against you. ⁵But Jesus yet answered nothing; so that Pilate marveled. ⁶Now at that feast he released to them one prisoner, whomsoever they desired. ⁷And there was one named Barabbas, which lay bound with them that had made insurrection with him, who had committed murder in the insurrection. ⁸And the multitude crying aloud began to desire him to do as he had ever done to them. ⁹But Pilate answered them, saying, Will you that I release to you the King of the Jews? ¹⁰For he knew that the chief priests had delivered him for envy. ¹¹But the chief priests moved the people, that he should rather release Barabbas to them. ¹²And Pilate answered and said again to them, What will you then that I shall do to him whom you call the King of the Jews? ¹³And they cried out again, Crucify him. ¹⁴Then Pilate said to them, Why, what evil has he done? And they cried out the more exceedingly, Crucify him. ¹⁵And so Pilate, willing to content the people, released Barabbas to them, and delivered Jesus, when he had scourged him, to be crucified. ¹⁶And the soldiers led him away into the hall, called Praetorium; and they call together the whole band. ¹⁷And they clothed him with purple, and platted a crown of thorns, and put it about his head, ¹⁸And began to salute him, Hail, King of the Jews! ¹⁹And they smote him on the head with a reed, and did spit on him, and bowing their knees worshipped him. ²⁰And when they had mocked him, they took off the purple from him, and put his own clothes on him, and led him out to crucify him. ²¹And they compel one Simon a Cyrenian, who passed by, coming out of the country, the father of Alexander and Rufus, to bear his cross. ²²And they bring him to the place Golgotha, which is, being interpreted, The place of a skull. ²³And they gave him to drink wine mingled with myrrh: but he received it not. ²⁴And when they had crucified him, they parted his garments, casting lots on them, what every man should take. ²⁵And it was the third hour, and they crucified him. ²⁶And the superscription of his accusation was written over, THE KING OF THE JEWS. ²⁷And with him they crucify two thieves; the one on his right hand, and the other on his left. ²⁸And the scripture was fulfilled, which says, And he was numbered with the transgressors. ²⁹And they that passed by railed on him, wagging their heads, and saying, Ah, you that destroy the temple, and build it in three days, ³⁰Save yourself, and come down from the cross. ³¹Likewise also the chief priests mocking said among themselves with the scribes, He saved others; himself he cannot save. ³²Let Christ the King of Israel descend now from the cross, that we may see and believe. And they that were crucified with him reviled him. ³³And when the sixth hour was come, there was darkness over the whole land until the ninth hour. ³⁴And

at the ninth hour Jesus cried with a loud voice, saying, Eloi, Eloi, lama sabachthani? which is, being interpreted, My God, my God, why have you forsaken me? ³⁵And some of them that stood by, when they heard it, said, Behold, he calls Elias. ³⁶And one ran and filled a sponge full of vinegar, and put it on a reed, and gave him to drink, saying, Let alone; let us see whether Elias will come to take him down. ³⁷And Jesus cried with a loud voice, and gave up the ghost. ³⁸And the veil of the temple was rent in two from the top to the bottom. ³⁹And when the centurion, which stood over against him, saw that he so cried out, and gave up the ghost, he said, Truly this man was the Son of God. ⁴⁰There were also women looking on afar off: among whom was Mary Magdalene, and Mary the mother of James the less and of Joses, and Salome; ⁴¹(Who also, when he was in Galilee, followed him, and ministered to him;) and many other women which came up with him to Jerusalem. ⁴²And now when the even was come, because it was the preparation, that is, the day before the sabbath, ⁴³Joseph of Arimathaea, an honorable counselor, which also waited for the kingdom of God, came, and went in boldly to Pilate, and craved the body of Jesus. ⁴⁴And Pilate marveled if he were already dead: and calling to him the centurion, he asked him whether he had been any while dead. ⁴⁵And when he knew it of the centurion, he gave the body to Joseph. ⁴⁶And he bought fine linen, and took him down, and wrapped him in the linen, and laid him in a sepulcher which was hewn out of a rock, and rolled a stone to the door of the sepulcher. ⁴⁷And Mary Magdalene and Mary the mother of Joses beheld where he was laid.

16 ¹And when the sabbath was past, Mary Magdalene, and Mary the mother of James, and Salome, had bought sweet spices, that they might come and anoint him. ²And very early in the morning the first day of the week, they came to the sepulcher at the rising of the sun. ³And they said among themselves, Who shall roll us away the stone from the door of the sepulcher? ⁴And when they looked, they saw that the stone was rolled away: for it was very great. ⁵And entering into the sepulcher, they saw a young man sitting on the right side, clothed in a long white garment; and they were affrighted. ⁶And he says to them, Be not affrighted: You seek Jesus of Nazareth, which was crucified: he is risen; he is not here: behold the place where they laid him. ⁷But go your way, tell his disciples and Peter that he goes before you into Galilee: there shall you see him, as he said to you. ⁸And they went out quickly, and fled from the sepulcher; for they trembled and were amazed: neither said they any thing to any man; for they were afraid. ⁹Now when Jesus was risen early the first day of the week, he appeared first to Mary Magdalene, out of whom he had cast seven devils. ¹⁰And she went and told them that had been with him, as they mourned and wept. ¹¹And they, when they had heard that he was alive, and had been seen of her, believed not. ¹²After that he appeared in another form to two of them, as they walked, and went into the country. ¹³And they went and told it to the residue: neither believed they them. ¹⁴Afterward he appeared to the eleven as they sat at meat, and upbraided them with their unbelief and hardness of heart, because they believed not them which had seen him after he was risen. ¹⁵And he said to them, Go you into all the world, and preach the gospel to every creature. ¹⁶He that believes and is baptized shall be saved; but he that believes not shall be damned. ¹⁷And these signs shall follow them that believe; In my name shall they cast out devils; they shall speak with new tongues; ¹⁸They shall take up serpents; and if they drink any deadly thing, it shall not hurt them; they shall lay hands on the sick, and they shall recover. ¹⁹So then after the Lord had spoken to them, he was received up into heaven, and sat on the right hand of God. ²⁰And they went forth, and preached every where, the Lord working with them, and confirming the word with signs following. Amen.

Luke

1 ¹For as much as many have taken in hand to set forth in order a declaration of those things which are most surely believed among us, ²Even as they delivered them to us, which from the beginning were eyewitnesses, and ministers of the word; ³It seemed good to me also, having had perfect understanding of all things from the very first, to write to you in order, most excellent Theophilus, ⁴That you might know the certainty of those things, wherein you have been instructed. ⁵THERE was in the days of Herod, the king of Judaea, a certain priest named Zacharias, of the course of Abia: and his wife was of the daughters of Aaron, and her name was Elisabeth. ⁶And they were both righteous before God, walking in all the commandments and ordinances of the Lord blameless. ⁷And they had no child, because that Elisabeth was barren, and they both were now well stricken in years. ⁸And it came to pass, that while he executed the priest's office before God in the order of his course, ⁹According to the custom of the priest's office, his lot was to burn incense when he went into the temple of the Lord. ¹⁰And the whole multitude of the people were praying without at the time of incense. ¹¹And there appeared to him an angel of the Lord standing on the right side of the altar of incense. ¹²And when Zacharias saw him, he was troubled, and fear fell on him. ¹³But the angel said to him, Fear not, Zacharias: for your prayer is heard; and your wife Elisabeth shall bear you a son, and you shall call his name John. ¹⁴And you shall have joy and gladness; and many shall rejoice at his birth. ¹⁵For he shall be great in the sight of the Lord, and shall drink neither wine nor strong drink; and he shall be filled with the Holy Ghost, even from his mother's womb. ¹⁶And many of the children of Israel shall he turn to the Lord their God. ¹⁷And he shall go before him in the spirit and power of Elias, to turn the hearts of the fathers to the children, and the disobedient to the wisdom of the just; to make ready a people prepared for the Lord. ¹⁸And Zacharias said to the angel, Whereby shall I know this? for I am an old man, and my wife well stricken in years. ¹⁹And the angel answering said to him, I am Gabriel, that stand in the presence of God; and am sent to speak to you, and to show you these glad tidings. ²⁰And, behold, you shall be dumb, and not able to speak, until the day that these things shall be performed, because you believe not my words, which shall be fulfilled in their season. ²¹And the people waited for Zacharias, and marveled that he tarried so long in the temple. ²²And when he came out, he could not speak to them: and they perceived that he had seen a vision in the temple: for he beckoned to them, and remained speechless. ²³And it came to pass, that, as soon as the days of his ministration were accomplished, he departed to his own house. ²⁴And after those days his wife Elisabeth conceived, and hid herself five months, saying, ²⁵Thus has the Lord dealt with me in the days wherein he looked on me, to take away my reproach among men. ²⁶And in the sixth month the angel Gabriel was sent from God to a city of Galilee, named Nazareth, ²⁷To a virgin espoused to a man whose name was Joseph, of the house of David; and the virgin's name was Mary. ²⁸And the angel came in to her, and said, Hail, you that are highly favored, the Lord is with you: blessed are you among women. ²⁹And when she saw him, she was troubled at his saying, and cast in her mind what manner of salutation this should be. ³⁰And the angel said to her, Fear not, Mary: for you have found favor with God. ³¹And, behold, you shall conceive in your womb, and bring forth a son, and shall call his name JESUS. ³²He shall be great, and shall be called the Son of the Highest: and the Lord God shall give to him the throne of his father David: ³³And he shall reign over the house of Jacob for ever; and of his kingdom there shall be no end. ³⁴Then said Mary to the angel, How shall this be, seeing I know not a man? ³⁵And the angel answered and said to her, The Holy Ghost shall come on you, and the power of the Highest shall overshadow you: therefore also that holy thing which shall be born of you shall be called the Son of God. ³⁶And, behold, your cousin Elisabeth, she has also conceived a son in her old age: and this is the sixth month with her, who was called barren. ³⁷For with God nothing shall be impossible. ³⁸And Mary said, Behold the handmaid of the Lord; be it to me according to your word. And the angel departed from her. ³⁹And Mary arose in those days, and went into the hill country with haste, into a city of Juda; ⁴⁰And entered into the house of Zacharias, and saluted Elisabeth. ⁴¹And it came to pass, that, when Elisabeth heard the salutation of Mary, the babe leaped in her womb; and Elisabeth was filled with the Holy Ghost: ⁴²And she spoke out with a loud voice, and said, Blessed are you among women, and blessed is the fruit of your womb. ⁴³And what is this to me, that the mother of my Lord should come to me? ⁴⁴For, see, as soon as the voice of your salutation sounded in my ears, the babe leaped in my womb for joy. ⁴⁵And blessed is she that believed: for there shall be a performance of those things which were told her from the Lord. ⁴⁶And Mary said, My soul does magnify the Lord, ⁴⁷And my spirit has rejoiced in God my Savior. ⁴⁸For he has regarded the low estate of his handmaiden: for, behold, from now on all generations shall call me blessed. ⁴⁹For he that is mighty has done to me great things; and holy is his name. ⁵⁰And his mercy is on them that fear him from generation to generation. ⁵¹He has showed strength with his arm; he has scattered the proud in the imagination of their hearts. ⁵²He has put down the mighty from their seats, and exalted them of low degree. ⁵³He has filled the hungry with good things; and the rich he has sent empty away. ⁵⁴He has helped his servant Israel, in remembrance of his mercy; ⁵⁵As he spoke to our fathers, to Abraham, and to his seed for ever. ⁵⁶And Mary stayed with her about three months, and returned to her own house. ⁵⁷Now Elisabeth's full time came that she should be delivered; and she brought forth a son. ⁵⁸And her neighbors and her cousins heard how the Lord had showed great mercy on her; and they rejoiced with her. ⁵⁹And it came to pass, that on the eighth day they came to circumcise the child; and they called him Zacharias, after the name of his father. ⁶⁰And his mother answered and said, Not so; but he shall be called John. ⁶¹And they said to her, There is none of your kindred that is called by this name. ⁶²And they made signs to his father, how he would have him called. ⁶³And he asked for a writing table, and wrote, saying, His name is John. And they marveled all. ⁶⁴And his mouth was opened immediately, and his tongue loosed, and he spoke, and praised God. ⁶⁵And fear came on all that dwelled round about them: and all these sayings were noised abroad throughout all the hill country of Judaea. ⁶⁶And all they that heard them laid them up in their hearts, saying, What manner of child shall this be! And the hand of the Lord was with him. ⁶⁷And his father Zacharias was filled with the Holy Ghost, and prophesied, saying, ⁶⁸Blessed be the Lord God of Israel; for he has visited and redeemed his people, ⁶⁹And has raised up an horn of salvation for us in the house of his servant David; ⁷⁰As he spoke by the mouth of his holy prophets, which have been since the world began: ⁷¹That we should be saved from our enemies, and from the hand of all that hate us; ⁷²To perform the mercy promised to our fathers, and to remember his holy covenant; ⁷³The oath which he swore to our father Abraham, ⁷⁴That he would grant to us, that we being delivered out of the hand of our enemies might serve him without fear, ⁷⁵In holiness and righteousness before him, all the days of our life. ⁷⁶And you, child, shall be called the prophet of the Highest: for you shall go before the face of the Lord to prepare his ways; ⁷⁷To give knowledge of salvation to his people by the remission of their sins, ⁷⁸Through the tender mercy of our God; whereby the dayspring from on high has visited us, ⁷⁹To give light to them that sit in darkness and in the shadow of death, to guide our feet into the way of peace. ⁸⁰And the child grew, and waxed strong in spirit, and was in the deserts till the day of his showing to Israel.

2 ¹And it came to pass in those days, that there went out a decree from Caesar Augustus that all the world should be taxed. ²(And this taxing was first made when Cyrenius was governor of Syria.) ³And all went to be taxed, every one into his own city. ⁴And Joseph also went up from Galilee, out of the city of Nazareth, into Judaea, to the city of David, which is called Bethlehem; (because he was of the house and lineage of David:) ⁵To be taxed with Mary his espoused wife, being great with child. ⁶And so it was, that, while they were there, the days were accomplished that she should be delivered. ⁷And she brought forth her firstborn son, and wrapped him in swaddling clothes, and laid him in a manger; because there was no room for them in the inn. ⁸And there were in the same country shepherds abiding in the field, keeping watch over their flock by night. ⁹And, see, the angel of the Lord came on them, and the glory of the Lord shone round about them: and they were sore afraid. ¹⁰And the angel said to them, Fear not: for, behold, I bring you good tidings of great joy, which shall be to all people. ¹¹For to you is born this day in the city of David a Savior, which is Christ the Lord. ¹²And this shall be a sign to you; You shall find the babe wrapped in swaddling clothes, lying in a manger. ¹³And suddenly there was with the angel a multitude of the heavenly host praising God, and saying, ¹⁴Glory to God in the highest, and on earth peace, good will toward men. ¹⁵And it came to pass, as the angels were gone away from them into heaven, the shepherds said one to another, Let us now go even to Bethlehem, and see this thing which is come to pass, which the Lord has made known to us. ¹⁶And they came with haste, and found Mary, and Joseph, and the babe lying in a manger. ¹⁷And when they had seen it, they made known abroad the saying which was told them concerning this child. ¹⁸And all they that heard it wondered at those things which were told them by the shepherds. ¹⁹But Mary kept all these things, and pondered them in her heart. ²⁰And the shepherds returned, glorifying and praising God for all the things that they had heard and seen, as it was told to them. ²¹And when eight days were accomplished for the circumcising of the child, his name was called JESUS, which was so named of the angel before he was conceived in the womb. ²²And when the days of her purification according to the law of Moses were accomplished, they brought him to Jerusalem, to present him to the Lord; ²³(As it is written in the law of the LORD, Every male that opens the womb shall be called holy to the Lord;) ²⁴And to offer a sacrifice according to that which is said in the law of the Lord, A pair of turtledoves, or two young pigeons. ²⁵And, behold, there was a man in Jerusalem, whose name was Simeon; and the same man was just and devout, waiting for the consolation of Israel: and the Holy Ghost was on him. ²⁶And it was revealed to him by the Holy Ghost, that he should not see death, before he had seen the Lord's Christ. ²⁷And he came by the Spirit into the temple: and when the parents brought in the child Jesus, to do for him after the custom of the law, ²⁸Then took he him up in his arms, and blessed God, and said, ²⁹Lord, now let you your servant depart in peace, according to your word: ³⁰For my eyes have seen your salvation, ³¹Which you have prepared before the face of all people; ³²A light to lighten the Gentiles, and the glory of your people Israel. ³³And Joseph and his mother marveled at those things which were spoken of him. ³⁴And Simeon blessed them, and said to Mary his mother, Behold, this child is set for the fall and rising again of many in Israel; and for a sign which shall be spoken against; ³⁵(Yes, a sword shall pierce through your own soul also,) that the thoughts of many hearts may be revealed. ³⁶And there was one Anna, a prophetess, the daughter of Phanuel, of the tribe of Aser: she was of a great age, and had lived with an husband seven years from her virginity; ³⁷And she was a widow of about fourscore and four years, which departed not from the temple, but served God with fastings and prayers night and day. ³⁸And she coming in that instant gave thanks likewise to the Lord, and spoke of him to all them that looked for redemption in Jerusalem. ³⁹And when they had performed all things according to the law of the Lord, they returned into Galilee, to their own city Nazareth. ⁴⁰And the child grew, and waxed strong in spirit, filled with wisdom: and the grace of God was on him. ⁴¹Now his parents went to Jerusalem every year at the feast of the passover. ⁴²And when he was twelve years old, they went up to Jerusalem after the custom of the feast. ⁴³And when they had fulfilled the days, as they returned, the child Jesus tarried behind in Jerusalem; and Joseph and his mother knew not of it. ⁴⁴But they, supposing him to have been in the company, went a day's journey; and they sought him among their kinsfolk and acquaintance. ⁴⁵And when they found him not, they turned back again to Jerusalem, seeking him. ⁴⁶And it came to pass, that after three days they found him in the temple, sitting in the middle of the doctors, both hearing

them, and asking them questions. ⁴⁷And all that heard him were astonished at his understanding and answers. ⁴⁸And when they saw him, they were amazed: and his mother said to him, Son, why have you thus dealt with us? behold, your father and I have sought you sorrowing. ⁴⁹And he said to them, How is it that you sought me? knew you not that I must be about my Father's business? ⁵⁰And they understood not the saying which he spoke to them. ⁵¹And he went down with them, and came to Nazareth, and was subject to them: but his mother kept all these sayings in her heart. ⁵²And Jesus increased in wisdom and stature, and in favor with God and man.

3 ¹Now in the fifteenth year of the reign of Tiberius Caesar, Pontius Pilate being governor of Judaea, and Herod being tetrarch of Galilee, and his brother Philip tetrarch of Ituraea and of the region of Trachonitis, and Lysanias the tetrarch of Abilene, ²Annas and Caiaphas being the high priests, the word of God came to John the son of Zacharias in the wilderness. ³And he came into all the country about Jordan, preaching the baptism of repentance for the remission of sins; ⁴As it is written in the book of the words of Isaiah the prophet, saying, The voice of one crying in the wilderness, Prepare you the way of the Lord, make his paths straight. ⁵Every valley shall be filled, and every mountain and hill shall be brought low; and the crooked shall be made straight, and the rough ways shall be made smooth; ⁶And all flesh shall see the salvation of God. ⁷Then said he to the multitude that came forth to be baptized of him, O generation of vipers, who has warned you to flee from the wrath to come? ⁸Bring forth therefore fruits worthy of repentance, and begin not to say within yourselves, We have Abraham to our father: for I say to you, That God is able of these stones to raise up children to Abraham. ⁹And now also the ax is laid to the root of the trees: every tree therefore which brings not forth good fruit is hewn down, and cast into the fire. ¹⁰And the people asked him, saying, What shall we do then? ¹¹He answers and says to them, He that has two coats, let him impart to him that has none; and he that has meat, let him do likewise. ¹²Then came also publicans to be baptized, and said to him, Master, what shall we do? ¹³And he said to them, Exact no more than that which is appointed you. ¹⁴And the soldiers likewise demanded of him, saying, And what shall we do? And he said to them, Do violence to no man, neither accuse any falsely; and be content with your wages. ¹⁵And as the people were in expectation, and all men mused in their hearts of John, whether he were the Christ, or not; ¹⁶John answered, saying to them all, I indeed baptize you with water; but one mightier than I comes, the lace of whose shoes I am not worthy to unloose: he shall baptize you with the Holy Ghost and with fire: ¹⁷Whose fan is in his hand, and he will thoroughly purge his floor, and will gather the wheat into his garner; but the chaff he will burn with fire unquenchable. ¹⁸And many other things in his exhortation preached he to the people. ¹⁹But Herod the tetrarch, being reproved by him for Herodias his brother Philip's wife, and for all the evils which Herod had done, ²⁰Added yet this above all, that he shut up John in prison. ²¹Now when all the people were baptized, it came to pass, that Jesus also being baptized, and praying, the heaven was opened, ²²And the Holy Ghost descended in a bodily shape like a dove on him, and a voice came from heaven, which said, You are my beloved Son; in you I am well pleased. ²³And Jesus himself began to be about thirty years of age, being (as was supposed) the son of Joseph, which was the son of Heli, ²⁴Which was the son of Matthat, which was the son of Levi, which was the son of Melchi, which was the son of Janna, which was the son of Joseph, ²⁵Which was the son of Mattathias, which was the son of Amos, which was the son of Naum, which was the son of Esli, which was the son of Nagge, ²⁶Which was the son of Maath, which was the son of Mattathias, which was the son of Semei, which was the son of Joseph, which was the son of Juda, ²⁷Which was the son of Joanna, which was the son of Rhesa, which was the son of Zorobabel, which was the son of Salathiel, which was the son of Neri, ²⁸Which was the son of Melchi, which was the son of Addi, which was the son of Cosam, which was the son of Elmodam, which was the son of Er, ²⁹Which was the son of Jose, which was the son of Eliezer, which was the son of Jorim, which was the son of Matthat, which was the son of Levi, ³⁰Which was the son of Simeon, which was the son of Juda, which was the son of Joseph, which was the son of Jonan, which was the son of Eliakim, ³¹Which was the son of Melea, which was the son of Menan, which was the son of Mattatha, which was the son of Nathan, which was the son of David, ³²Which was the son of Jesse, which was the son of Obed, which was the son of Booz, which was the son of Salmon, which was the son of Naasson, ³³Which was the son of Aminadab, which was the son of Aram, which was the son of Esrom, which was the son of Phares, which was the son of Juda, ³⁴Which was the son of Jacob, which was the son of Isaac, which was the son of Abraham, which was the son of Thara, which was the son of Nachor, ³⁵Which was the son of Saruch, which was the son of Ragau, which was the son of Phalec, which was the son of Heber, which was the son of Sala, ³⁶Which was the son of Cainan, which was the son of Arphaxad, which was the son of Sem, which was the son of Noe, which was the son of Lamech, ³⁷Which was the son of Mathusala, which was the son of Enoch, which was the son of Jared, which was the son of Maleleel, which was the son of Cainan, ³⁸Which was the son of Enos, which was the son of Seth, which was the son of Adam, which was the son of God.

4 ¹And Jesus being full of the Holy Ghost returned from Jordan, and was led by the Spirit into the wilderness, ²Being forty days tempted of the devil. And in those days he did eat nothing: and when they were ended, he afterward hungry. ³And the devil said to him, If you be the Son of God, command this stone that it be made bread. ⁴And Jesus answered him, saying, It is written, That man shall not live by bread alone, but by every word of God. ⁵And the devil, taking him up into an high mountain, showed to him all the kingdoms of the world in a moment of time. ⁶And the devil said to him, All this power will I give you, and the glory of them: for that is delivered to me; and to whomsoever I will I give it. ⁷If you therefore will worship me, all shall be yours. ⁸And Jesus answered and said to him, Get you behind me, Satan: for it is written, You shall worship the Lord your

God, and him only shall you serve. ⁹And he brought him to Jerusalem, and set him on a pinnacle of the temple, and said to him, If you be the Son of God, cast yourself down from hence: ¹⁰For it is written, He shall give his angels charge over you, to keep you: ¹¹And in their hands they shall bear you up, lest at any time you dash your foot against a stone. ¹²And Jesus answering said to him, It is said, You shall not tempt the Lord your God. ¹³And when the devil had ended all the temptation, he departed from him for a season. ¹⁴And Jesus returned in the power of the Spirit into Galilee: and there went out a fame of him through all the region round about. ¹⁵And he taught in their synagogues, being glorified of all. ¹⁶And he came to Nazareth, where he had been brought up: and, as his custom was, he went into the synagogue on the sabbath day, and stood up for to read. ¹⁷And there was delivered to him the book of the prophet Isaiah. And when he had opened the book, he found the place where it was written, ¹⁸The Spirit of the Lord is on me, because he has anointed me to preach the gospel to the poor; he has sent me to heal the brokenhearted, to preach deliverance to the captives, and recovering of sight to the blind, to set at liberty them that are bruised, ¹⁹To preach the acceptable year of the Lord. ²⁰And he closed the book, and he gave it again to the minister, and sat down. And the eyes of all them that were in the synagogue were fastened on him. ²¹And he began to say to them, This day is this scripture fulfilled in your ears. ²²And all bore him witness, and wondered at the gracious words which proceeded out of his mouth. And they said, Is not this Joseph's son? ²³And he said to them, You will surely say to me this proverb, Physician, heal yourself: whatever we have heard done in Capernaum, do also here in your country. ²⁴And he said, Truly I say to you, No prophet is accepted in his own country. ²⁵But I tell you of a truth, many widows were in Israel in the days of Elias, when the heaven was shut up three years and six months, when great famine was throughout all the land; ²⁶But to none of them was Elias sent, save to Sarepta, a city of Sidon, to a woman that was a widow. ²⁷And many lepers were in Israel in the time of Eliseus the prophet; and none of them was cleansed, saving Naaman the Syrian. ²⁸And all they in the synagogue, when they heard these things, were filled with wrath, ²⁹And rose up, and thrust him out of the city, and led him to the brow of the hill where on their city was built, that they might cast him down headlong. ³⁰But he passing through the middle of them went his way, ³¹And came down to Capernaum, a city of Galilee, and taught them on the sabbath days. ³²And they were astonished at his doctrine: for his word was with power. ³³And in the synagogue there was a man, which had a spirit of an unclean devil, and cried out with a loud voice, ³⁴Saying, Let us alone; what have we to do with you, you Jesus of Nazareth? are you come to destroy us? I know you who you are; the Holy One of God. ³⁵And Jesus rebuked him, saying, Hold your peace, and come out of him. And when the devil had thrown him in the middle, he came out of him, and hurt him not. ³⁶And they were all amazed, and spoke among themselves, saying, What a word is this! for with authority and power he commands the unclean spirits, and they come out. ³⁷And the fame of him went out into every place of the country round about. ³⁸And he arose out of the synagogue, and entered into Simon's house. And Simon's wife's mother was taken with a great fever; and they sought him for her. ³⁹And he stood over her, and rebuked the fever; and it left her: and immediately she arose and ministered to them. ⁴⁰Now when the sun was setting, all they that had any sick with divers diseases brought them to him; and he laid his hands on every one of them, and healed them. ⁴¹And devils also came out of many, crying out, and saying, You are Christ the Son of God. And he rebuking them suffered them not to speak: for they knew that he was Christ. ⁴²And when it was day, he departed and went into a desert place: and the people sought him, and came to him, and stayed him, that he should not depart from them. ⁴³And he said to them, I must preach the kingdom of God to other cities also: for therefore am I sent. ⁴⁴And he preached in the synagogues of Galilee.

5 ¹And it came to pass, that, as the people pressed on him to hear the word of God, he stood by the lake of Gennesaret, ²And saw two ships standing by the lake: but the fishermen were gone out of them, and were washing their nets. ³And he entered into one of the ships, which was Simon's, and prayed him that he would thrust out a little from the land. And he sat down, and taught the people out of the ship. ⁴Now when he had left speaking, he said to Simon, Launch out into the deep, and let down your nets for a draught. ⁵And Simon answering said to him, Master, we have toiled all the night, and have taken nothing: nevertheless at your word I will let down the net. ⁶And when they had this done, they enclosed a great multitude of fishes: and their net broke. ⁷And they beckoned to their partners, which were in the other ship, that they should come and help them. And they came, and filled both the ships, so that they began to sink. ⁸When Simon Peter saw it, he fell down at Jesus' knees, saying, Depart from me; for I am a sinful man, O Lord. ⁹For he was astonished, and all that were with him, at the draught of the fishes which they had taken: ¹⁰And so was also James, and John, the sons of Zebedee, which were partners with Simon. And Jesus said to Simon, Fear not; from now on you shall catch men. ¹¹And when they had brought their ships to land, they forsook all, and followed him. ¹²And it came to pass, when he was in a certain city, behold a man full of leprosy: who seeing Jesus fell on his face, and sought him, saying, Lord, if you will, you can make me clean. ¹³And he put forth his hand, and touched him, saying, I will: be you clean. And immediately the leprosy departed from him. ¹⁴And he charged him to tell no man: but go, and show yourself to the priest, and offer for your cleansing, according as Moses commanded, for a testimony to them. ¹⁵But so much the more went there a fame abroad of him: and great multitudes came together to hear, and to be healed by him of their infirmities. ¹⁶And he withdrew himself into the wilderness, and prayed. ¹⁷And it came to pass on a certain day, as he was teaching, that there were Pharisees and doctors of the law sitting by, which were come out of every town of Galilee, and Judaea, and Jerusalem: and the power of the Lord was present to heal them. ¹⁸And, behold, men brought in a bed a man which was taken with a palsy: and they sought means to bring him in, and to lay him before him. ¹⁹And when they could not find by what way they might bring him in because of the multitude, they went on the housetop, and let him down through the tiling with his couch into the middle before Jesus. [20]And when he saw their faith, he said to him, Man, your sins are forgiven you. [21]And the scribes and the Pharisees began to reason, saying, Who is this which speaks blasphemies? Who can forgive sins, but God alone? [22]But when Jesus perceived their thoughts, he answering said to them, What reason you in your hearts? [23]Whether is easier, to say, Your sins be forgiven you; or to say, Rise up and walk? [24]But that you may know that the Son of man has power on earth to forgive sins, (he said to the sick of the palsy,) I say to you, Arise, and take up your couch, and go into your house. [25]And immediately he rose up before them, and took up that where on he lay, and departed to his own house, glorifying God. [26]And they were all amazed, and they glorified God, and were filled with fear, saying, We have seen strange things to day. [27]And after these things he went forth, and saw a publican, named Levi, sitting at the receipt of custom: and he said to him, Follow me. [28]And he left all, rose up, and followed him. [29]And Levi made him a great feast in his own house: and there was a great company of publicans and of others that sat down with them. [30]But their scribes and Pharisees murmured against his disciples, saying, Why do you eat and drink with publicans and sinners? [31]And Jesus answering said to them, They that are whole need not a physician; but they that are sick. [32]I came not to call the righteous, but sinners to repentance. [33]And they said to him, Why do the disciples of John fast often, and make prayers, and likewise the disciples of the Pharisees; but your eat and drink? [34]And he said to them, Can you make the children of the bridal chamber fast, while the bridegroom is with them? [35]But the days will come, when the bridegroom shall be taken away from them, and then shall they fast in those days. [36]And he spoke also a parable to them; No man puts a piece of a new garment on an old; if otherwise, then both the new makes a rent, and the piece that was taken out of the new agrees not with the old. [37]And no man puts new wine into old bottles; else the new wine will burst the bottles, and be spilled, and the bottles shall perish. [38]But new wine must be put into new bottles; and both are preserved. [39]No man also having drunk old wine straightway desires new: for he says, The old is better.

6 [1]And it came to pass on the second sabbath after the first, that he went through the corn fields; and his disciples plucked the ears of corn, and did eat, rubbing them in their hands. [2]And certain of the Pharisees said to them, Why do you that which is not lawful to do on the sabbath days? [3]And Jesus answering them said, Have you not read so much as this, what David did, when himself was an hungered, and they which were with him; [4]How he went into the house of God, and did take and eat the show bread, and gave also to them that were with him; which it is not lawful to eat but for the priests alone? [5]And he said to them, That the Son of man is Lord also of the sabbath. [6]And it came to pass also on another sabbath, that he entered into the synagogue and taught: and there was a man whose right hand was withered. [7]And the scribes and Pharisees watched him, whether he would heal on the sabbath day; that they might find an accusation against him. [8]But he knew their thoughts, and said to the man which had the withered hand, Rise up, and stand forth in the middle. And he arose and stood forth. [9]Then said Jesus to them, I will ask you one thing; Is it lawful on the sabbath days to do good, or to do evil? to save life, or to destroy it? [10]And looking round about on them all, he said to the man, Stretch forth your hand. And he did so: and his hand was restored whole as the other. [11]And they were filled with madness; and communed one with another what they might do to Jesus. [12]And it came to pass in those days, that he went out into a mountain to pray, and continued all night in prayer to God. [13]And when it was day, he called to him his disciples: and of them he chose twelve, whom also he named apostles; [14]Simon, (whom he also named Peter,) and Andrew his brother, James and John, Philip and Bartholomew, [15]Matthew and Thomas, James the son of Alphaeus, and Simon called Zelotes, [16]And Judas the brother of James, and Judas Iscariot, which also was the traitor. [17]And he came down with them, and stood in the plain, and the company of his disciples, and a great multitude of people out of all Judaea and Jerusalem, and from the sea coast of Tyre and Sidon, which came to hear him, and to be healed of their diseases; [18]And they that were vexed with unclean spirits: and they were healed. [19]And the whole multitude sought to touch him: for there went virtue out of him, and healed them all. [20]And he lifted up his eyes on his disciples, and said, Blessed be you poor: for yours is the kingdom of God. [21]Blessed are you that hunger now: for you shall be filled. Blessed are you that weep now: for you shall laugh. [22]Blessed are you, when men shall hate you, and when they shall separate you from their company, and shall reproach you, and cast out your name as evil, for the Son of man's sake. [23]Rejoice you in that day, and leap for joy: for, behold, your reward is great in heaven: for in the like manner did their fathers to the prophets. [24]But woe to you that are rich! for you have received your consolation. [25]Woe to you that are full! for you shall hunger. Woe to you that laugh now! for you shall mourn and weep. [26]Woe to you, when all men shall speak well of you! for so did their fathers to the false prophets. [27]But I say to you which hear, Love your enemies, do good to them which hate you, [28]Bless them that curse you, and pray for them which spitefully use you. [29]And to him that smites you on the one cheek offer also the other; and him that takes away your cloak forbid not to take your coat also. [30]Give to every man that asks of you; and of him that takes away your goods ask them not again. [31]And as you would that men should do to you, do you also to them likewise. [32]For if you love them which love you, what thank have you? for sinners also love those that love them. [33]And if you do good to them which do good to you, what thank have you? for sinners also do even the same. [34]And if you lend to them of whom you hope to receive, what thank have you? for sinners also lend to sinners, to receive as much again. [35]But love you your enemies, and do good, and lend, hoping for nothing again; and your reward shall be great, and you shall be the children of the Highest: for he is kind to the unthankful and to the evil. [36]Be you therefore merciful, as your Father also is merciful. [37]Judge not, and you shall not be judged: condemn not, and you shall not be condemned:

forgive, and you shall be forgiven: ³⁸Give, and it shall be given to you; good measure, pressed down, and shaken together, and running over, shall men give into your bosom. For with the same measure that you mete with it shall be measured to you again. ³⁹And he spoke a parable to them, Can the blind lead the blind? shall they not both fall into the ditch? ⁴⁰The disciple is not above his master: but every one that is perfect shall be as his master. ⁴¹And why behold you the mote that is in your brother's eye, but perceive not the beam that is in your own eye? ⁴²Either how can you say to your brother, Brother, let me pull out the mote that is in your eye, when you yourself behold not the beam that is in your own eye? You hypocrite, cast out first the beam out of your own eye, and then shall you see clearly to pull out the mote that is in your brother's eye. ⁴³For a good tree brings not forth corrupt fruit; neither does a corrupt tree bring forth good fruit. ⁴⁴For every tree is known by his own fruit. For of thorns men do not gather figs, nor of a bramble bush gather they grapes. ⁴⁵A good man out of the good treasure of his heart brings forth that which is good; and an evil man out of the evil treasure of his heart brings forth that which is evil: for of the abundance of the heart his mouth speaks. ⁴⁶And why call you me, Lord, Lord, and do not the things which I say? ⁴⁷Whoever comes to me, and hears my sayings, and does them, I will show you to whom he is like: ⁴⁸He is like a man which built an house, and dig deep, and laid the foundation on a rock: and when the flood arose, the stream beat vehemently on that house, and could not shake it: for it was founded on a rock. ⁴⁹But he that hears, and does not, is like a man that without a foundation built an house on the earth; against which the stream did beat vehemently, and immediately it fell; and the ruin of that house was great.

7 ¹Now when he had ended all his sayings in the audience of the people, he entered into Capernaum. ²And a certain centurion's servant, who was dear to him, was sick, and ready to die. ³And when he heard of Jesus, he sent to him the elders of the Jews, beseeching him that he would come and heal his servant. ⁴And when they came to Jesus, they sought him instantly, saying, That he was worthy for whom he should do this: ⁵For he loves our nation, and he has built us a synagogue. ⁶Then Jesus went with them. And when he was now not far from the house, the centurion sent friends to him, saying to him, Lord, trouble not yourself: for I am not worthy that you should enter under my roof: ⁷Why neither thought I myself worthy to come to you: but say in a word, and my servant shall be healed. ⁸For I also am a man set under authority, having under me soldiers, and I say to one, Go, and he goes; and to another, Come, and he comes; and to my servant, Do this, and he does it. ⁹When Jesus heard these things, he marveled at him, and turned him about, and said to the people that followed him, I say to you, I have not found so great faith, no, not in Israel. ¹⁰And they that were sent, returning to the house, found the servant whole that had been sick. ¹¹And it came to pass the day after, that he went into a city called Nain; and many of his disciples went with him, and much people. ¹²Now when he came near to the gate of the city, behold, there was a dead man carried out, the only son of his mother, and she was a widow: and much people of the city was with her. ¹³And when the Lord saw her, he had compassion on her, and said to her, Weep not. ¹⁴And he came and touched the bier: and they that bore him stood still. And he said, Young man, I say to you, Arise. ¹⁵And he that was dead sat up, and began to speak. And he delivered him to his mother. ¹⁶And there came a fear on all: and they glorified God, saying, That a great prophet is risen up among us; and, That God has visited his people. ¹⁷And this rumor of him went forth throughout all Judaea, and throughout all the region round about. ¹⁸And the disciples of John showed him of all these things. ¹⁹And John calling to him two of his disciples sent them to Jesus, saying, Are you he that should come? or look we for another? ²⁰When the men were come to him, they said, John Baptist has sent us to you, saying, Are you he that should come? or look we for another? ²¹And in that same hour he cured many of their infirmities and plagues, and of evil spirits; and to many that were blind he gave sight. ²²Then Jesus answering said to them, Go your way, and tell John what things you have seen and heard; how that the blind see, the lame walk, the lepers are cleansed, the deaf hear, the dead are raised, to the poor the gospel is preached. ²³And blessed is he, whoever shall not be offended in me. ²⁴And when the messengers of John were departed, he began to speak to the people concerning John, What went you out into the wilderness for to see? A reed shaken with the wind? ²⁵But what went you out for to see? A man clothed in soft raiment? Behold, they which are gorgeously appareled, and live delicately, are in kings' courts. ²⁶But what went you out for to see? A prophet? Yes, I say to you, and much more than a prophet. ²⁷This is he, of whom it is written, Behold, I send my messenger before your face, which shall prepare your way before you. ²⁸For I say to you, Among those that are born of women there is not a greater prophet than John the Baptist: but he that is least in the kingdom of God is greater than he. ²⁹And all the people that heard him, and the publicans, justified God, being baptized with the baptism of John. ³⁰But the Pharisees and lawyers rejected the counsel of God against themselves, being not baptized of him. ³¹And the Lord said, To what then shall I liken the men of this generation? and to what are they like? ³²They are like to children sitting in the marketplace, and calling one to another, and saying, We have piped to you, and you have not danced; we have mourned to you, and you have not wept. ³³For John the Baptist came neither eating bread nor drinking wine; and you say, He has a devil. ³⁴The Son of man is come eating and drinking; and you say, Behold a gluttonous man, and a drunkard, a friend of publicans and sinners! ³⁵But wisdom is justified of all her children. ³⁶And one of the Pharisees desired him that he would eat with him. And he went into the Pharisee's house, and sat down to meat. ³⁷And, behold, a woman in the city, which was a sinner, when she knew that Jesus sat at meat in the Pharisee's house, brought an alabaster box of ointment, ³⁸And stood at his feet behind him weeping, and began to wash his feet with tears, and did wipe them with the hairs of her head, and kissed his feet, and anointed them with the ointment. ³⁹Now when the Pharisee which had bidden him saw it, he spoke within himself, saying, This man, if he were a prophet, would have known who and what manner of woman this is that touches him: for she is a sinner. ⁴⁰And

Jesus answering said to him, Simon, I have somewhat to say to you. And he says, Master, say on. ⁴¹There was a certain creditor which had two debtors: the one owed five hundred pence, and the other fifty. ⁴²And when they had nothing to pay, he frankly forgave them both. Tell me therefore, which of them will love him most? ⁴³Simon answered and said, I suppose that he, to whom he forgave most. And he said to him, You have rightly judged. ⁴⁴And he turned to the woman, and said to Simon, See you this woman? I entered into your house, you gave me no water for my feet: but she has washed my feet with tears, and wiped them with the hairs of her head. ⁴⁵You gave me no kiss: but this woman since the time I came in has not ceased to kiss my feet. ⁴⁶My head with oil you did not anoint: but this woman has anointed my feet with ointment. ⁴⁷Why I say to you, Her sins, which are many, are forgiven; for she loved much: but to whom little is forgiven, the same loves little. ⁴⁸And he said to her, Your sins are forgiven. ⁴⁹And they that sat at meat with him began to say within themselves, Who is this that forgives sins also? ⁵⁰And he said to the woman, Your faith has saved you; go in peace.

8 ¹And it came to pass afterward, that he went throughout every city and village, preaching and showing the glad tidings of the kingdom of God: and the twelve were with him, ²And certain women, which had been healed of evil spirits and infirmities, Mary called Magdalene, out of whom went seven devils, ³And Joanna the wife of Chuza Herod's steward, and Susanna, and many others, which ministered to him of their substance. ⁴And when much people were gathered together, and were come to him out of every city, he spoke by a parable: ⁵A sower went out to sow his seed: and as he sowed, some fell by the way side; and it was trodden down, and the fowls of the air devoured it. ⁶And some fell on a rock; and as soon as it was sprung up, it withered away, because it lacked moisture. ⁷And some fell among thorns; and the thorns sprang up with it, and choked it. ⁸And other fell on good ground, and sprang up, and bore fruit an hundred times. And when he had said these things, he cried, He that has ears to hear, let him hear. ⁹And his disciples asked him, saying, What might this parable be? ¹⁰And he said, To you it is given to know the mysteries of the kingdom of God: but to others in parables; that seeing they might not see, and hearing they might not understand. ¹¹Now the parable is this: The seed is the word of God. ¹²Those by the way side are they that hear; then comes the devil, and takes away the word out of their hearts, lest they should believe and be saved. ¹³They on the rock are they, which, when they hear, receive the word with joy; and these have no root, which for a while believe, and in time of temptation fall away. ¹⁴And that which fell among thorns are they, which, when they have heard, go forth, and are choked with cares and riches and pleasures of this life, and bring no fruit to perfection. ¹⁵But that on the good ground are they, which in an honest and good heart, having heard the word, keep it, and bring forth fruit with patience. ¹⁶No man, when he has lighted a candle, covers it with a vessel, or puts it under a bed; but sets it on a candlestick, that they which enter in may see the light. ¹⁷For nothing is secret, that shall not be made manifest; neither any thing hid, that shall not be known and come abroad. ¹⁸Take heed therefore how you hear: for whoever has, to him shall be given; and whoever has not, from him shall be taken even that which he seems to have. ¹⁹Then came to him his mother and his brothers, and could not come at him for the press. ²⁰And it was told him by certain which said, Your mother and your brothers stand without, desiring to see you. ²¹And he answered and said to them, My mother and my brothers are these which hear the word of God, and do it. ²²Now it came to pass on a certain day, that he went into a ship with his disciples: and he said to them, Let us go over to the other side of the lake. And they launched forth. ²³But as they sailed he fell asleep: and there came down a storm of wind on the lake; and they were filled with water, and were in jeopardy. ²⁴And they came to him, and awoke him, saying, Master, master, we perish. Then he arose, and rebuked the wind and the raging of the water: and they ceased, and there was a calm. ²⁵And he said to them, Where is your faith? And they being afraid wondered, saying one to another, What manner of man is this! for he commands even the winds and water, and they obey him. ²⁶And they arrived at the country of the Gadarenes, which is over against Galilee. ²⁷And when he went forth to land, there met him out of the city a certain man, which had devils long time, and ware no clothes, neither stayed in any house, but in the tombs. ²⁸When he saw Jesus, he cried out, and fell down before him, and with a loud voice said, What have I to do with you, Jesus, you Son of God most high? I beseech you, torment me not. ²⁹(For he had commanded the unclean spirit to come out of the man. For oftentimes it had caught him: and he was kept bound with chains and in fetters; and he broke the bands, and was driven of the devil into the wilderness.) ³⁰And Jesus asked him, saying, What is your name? And he said, Legion: because many devils were entered into him. ³¹And they sought him that he would not command them to go out into the deep. ³²And there was there an herd of many swine feeding on the mountain: and they sought him that he would suffer them to enter into them. And he suffered them. ³³Then went the devils out of the man, and entered into the swine: and the herd ran violently down a steep place into the lake, and were choked. ³⁴When they that fed them saw what was done, they fled, and went and told it in the city and in the country. ³⁵Then they went out to see what was done; and came to Jesus, and found the man, out of whom the devils were departed, sitting at the feet of Jesus, clothed, and in his right mind: and they were afraid. ³⁶They also which saw it told them by what means he that was possessed of the devils was healed. ³⁷Then the whole multitude of the country of the Gadarenes round about sought him to depart from them; for they were taken with great fear: and he went up into the ship, and returned back again. ³⁸Now the man out of whom the devils were departed sought him that he might be with him: but Jesus sent him away, saying, ³⁹Return to your own house, and show how great things God has done to you. And he went his way, and published throughout the whole city how great things Jesus had done to him. ⁴⁰And it came to pass, that, when Jesus was returned, the people gladly received him: for they were all waiting for him. ⁴¹And, behold, there came a man named Jairus, and he was a ruler of the synagogue: and he fell down at Jesus' feet, and sought him that he would come into his house: ⁴²For he had one only daughter, about twelve years of age, and she lay a dying. But as he went the people thronged him. ⁴³And a woman having an issue of blood twelve years, which had spent all her living on physicians, neither could be healed of any, ⁴⁴Came behind him, and touched the border of his garment: and immediately her issue of blood stanched. ⁴⁵And Jesus said, Who touched me? When all denied, Peter and they that were with him said, Master, the multitude throng you and press you, and say you, Who touched me? ⁴⁶And Jesus said, Somebody has touched me: for I perceive that virtue is gone out of me. ⁴⁷And when the woman saw that she was not hid, she came trembling, and falling down before him, she declared to him before all the people for what cause she had touched him, and how she was healed immediately. ⁴⁸And he said to her, Daughter, be of good comfort: your faith has made you whole; go in peace. ⁴⁹While he yet spoke, there comes one from the ruler of the synagogue's house, saying to him, Your daughter is dead; trouble not the Master. ⁵⁰But when Jesus heard it, he answered him, saying, Fear not: believe only, and she shall be made whole. ⁵¹And when he came into the house, he suffered no man to go in, save Peter, and James, and John, and the father and the mother of the maiden. ⁵²And all wept, and bewailed her: but he said, Weep not; she is not dead, but sleeps. ⁵³And they laughed him to scorn, knowing that she was dead. ⁵⁴And he put them all out, and took her by the hand, and called, saying, Maid, arise. ⁵⁵And her spirit came again, and she arose straightway: and he commanded to give her meat. ⁵⁶And her parents were astonished: but he charged them that they should tell no man what was done.

9 ¹Then he called his twelve disciples together, and gave them power and authority over all devils, and to cure diseases. ²And he sent them to preach the kingdom of God, and to heal the sick. ³And he said to them, Take nothing for your journey, neither staves, nor money, neither bread, neither money; neither have two coats apiece. ⁴And whatever house you enter into, there abide, and there depart. ⁵And whoever will not receive you, when you go out of that city, shake off the very dust from your feet for a testimony against them. ⁶And they departed, and went through the towns, preaching the gospel, and healing every where. ⁷Now Herod the tetrarch heard of all that was done by him: and he was perplexed, because that it was said of some, that John was risen from the dead; ⁸And of some, that Elias had appeared; and of others, that one of the old prophets was risen again. ⁹And Herod said, John have I beheaded: but who is this, of whom I hear such things? And he desired to see him. ¹⁰And the apostles, when they were returned, told him all that they had done. And he took them, and went aside privately into a desert place belonging to the city called Bethsaida. ¹¹And the people, when they knew it, followed him: and he received them, and spoke to them of the kingdom of God, and healed them that had need of healing. ¹²And when the day began to wear away, then came the twelve, and said to him, Send the multitude away, that they may go into the towns and country round about, and lodge, and get victuals: for we are here in a desert place. ¹³But he said to them, Give you them to eat. And they said, We have no more but five loaves and two fishes; except we should go and buy meat for all this people. ¹⁴For they were about five thousand men. And he said to his disciples, Make them sit down by fifties in a company. ¹⁵And they did so, and made them all sit down. ¹⁶Then he took the five loaves and the two fishes, and looking up to heaven, he blessed them, and broke, and gave to the disciples to set before the multitude. ¹⁷And they did eat, and were all filled: and there was taken up of fragments that remained to them twelve baskets. ¹⁸And it came to pass, as he was alone praying, his disciples were with him: and he asked them, saying, Whom say the people that I am? ¹⁹They answering said, John the Baptist; but some say, Elias; and others say, that one of the old prophets is risen again. ²⁰He said to them, But whom say you that I am? Peter answering said, The Christ of God. ²¹And he straightly charged them, and commanded them to tell no man that thing; ²²Saying, The Son of man must suffer many things, and be rejected of the elders and chief priests and scribes, and be slain, and be raised the third day. ²³And he said to them all, If any man will come after me, let him deny himself, and take up his cross daily, and follow me. ²⁴For whoever will save his life shall lose it: but whoever will lose his life for my sake, the same shall save it. ²⁵For what is a man advantaged, if he gain the whole world, and lose himself, or be cast away? ²⁶For whoever shall be ashamed of me and of my words, of him shall the Son of man be ashamed, when he shall come in his own glory, and in his Father's, and of the holy angels. ²⁷But I tell you of a truth, there be some standing here, which shall not taste of death, till they see the kingdom of God. ²⁸And it came to pass about an eight days after these sayings, he took Peter and John and James, and went up into a mountain to pray. ²⁹And as he prayed, the fashion of his countenance was altered, and his raiment was white and glistering. ³⁰And, behold, there talked with him two men, which were Moses and Elias: ³¹Who appeared in glory, and spoke of his decease which he should accomplish at Jerusalem. ³²But Peter and they that were with him were heavy with sleep: and when they were awake, they saw his glory, and the two men that stood with him. ³³And it came to pass, as they departed from him, Peter said to Jesus, Master, it is good for us to be here: and let us make three tabernacles; one for you, and one for Moses, and one for Elias: not knowing what he said. ³⁴While he thus spoke, there came a cloud, and overshadowed them: and they feared as they entered into the cloud. ³⁵And there came a voice out of the cloud, saying, This is my beloved Son: hear him. ³⁶And when the voice was past, Jesus was found alone. And they kept it close, and told no man in those days any of those things which they had seen. ³⁷And it came to pass, that on the next day, when they were come down from the hill, much people met him. ³⁸And, behold, a man of the company cried out, saying, Master, I beseech you, look on my son: for he is my only child. ³⁹And, see, a spirit takes him, and he suddenly cries out; and it tears him that he foams again, and bruising him hardly departs from him. ⁴⁰And I sought your disciples to cast him out; and they could not. ⁴¹And Jesus answering said, O faithless and perverse generation, how long shall I be with you, and suffer you? Bring your son here. ⁴²And as he was yet a coming, the devil threw him down, and tare him. And Jesus rebuked the unclean spirit, and healed the child, and delivered him again to his father. ⁴³And they were all amazed at the mighty power of God. But while they wondered every one at all things which Jesus did, he said to his disciples, ⁴⁴Let these sayings sink down into your ears: for the Son of man shall be delivered into the hands of men. ⁴⁵But they understood not this saying, and it was hid from them, that they perceived it not: and they feared to ask him of that saying. ⁴⁶Then there arose a reasoning among them, which of them should be greatest. ⁴⁷And Jesus, perceiving the thought of their heart, took a child, and set him by him, ⁴⁸And said to them, Whoever shall receive this child in my name receives me: and whoever shall receive me receives him that sent me: for he that is least among you all, the same shall be great. ⁴⁹And John answered and said, Master, we saw one casting out devils in your name; and we forbade him, because he follows not with us. ⁵⁰And Jesus said to him, Forbid him not: for he that is not against us is for us. ⁵¹And it came to pass, when the time was come that he should be received up, he steadfastly set his face to go to Jerusalem, ⁵²And sent messengers before his face: and they went, and entered into a village of the Samaritans, to make ready for him. ⁵³And they did not receive him, because his face was as though he would go to Jerusalem. ⁵⁴And when his disciples James and John saw this, they said, Lord, will you that we command fire to come down from heaven, and consume them, even as Elias did? ⁵⁵But he turned, and rebuked them, and said, You know not what manner of spirit you are of. ⁵⁶For the Son of man is not come to destroy men's lives, but to save them. And they went to another village. ⁵⁷And it came to pass, that, as they went in the way, a certain man said to him, Lord, I will follow you wherever you go. ⁵⁸And Jesus said to him, Foxes have holes, and birds of the air have nests; but the Son of man has not where to lay his head. ⁵⁹And he said to another, Follow me. But he said, Lord, suffer me first to go and bury my father. ⁶⁰Jesus said to him, Let the dead bury their dead: but go you and preach the kingdom of God. ⁶¹And another also said, Lord, I will follow you; but let me first go bid them farewell, which are at home at my house. ⁶²And Jesus said to him, No man, having put his hand to the plough, and looking back, is fit for the kingdom of God.

10 ¹After these things the LORD appointed other seventy also, and sent them two and two before his face into every city and place, where he himself would come. ²Therefore said he to them, The harvest truly is great, but the laborers are few: pray you therefore the Lord of the harvest, that he would send forth laborers into his harvest. ³Go your ways: behold, I send you forth as lambs among wolves. ⁴Carry neither purse, nor money, nor shoes: and salute no man by the way. ⁵And into whatever house you enter, first say, Peace be to this house. ⁶And if the son of peace be there, your peace shall rest on it: if not, it shall turn to you again. ⁷And in the same house remain, eating and drinking such things as they give: for the laborer is worthy of his hire. Go not from house to house. ⁸And into whatever city you enter, and they receive you, eat such things as are set before you: ⁹And heal the sick that are therein, and say to them, The kingdom of God is come near to you. ¹⁰But into whatever city you enter, and they receive you not, go your ways out into the streets of the same, and say, ¹¹Even the very dust of your city, which sticks on us, we do wipe off against you: notwithstanding be you sure of this, that the kingdom of God is come near to you. ¹²But I say to you, that it shall be more tolerable in that day for Sodom, than for that city. ¹³Woe to you, Chorazin! woe to you, Bethsaida! for if the mighty works had been done in Tyre and Sidon, which have been done in you, they had a great while ago repented, sitting in sackcloth and ashes. ¹⁴But it shall be more tolerable for Tyre and Sidon at the judgment, than for you. ¹⁵And you, Capernaum, which are exalted to heaven, shall be thrust down to hell. ¹⁶He that hears you hears me; and he that despises you despises me; and he that despises me despises him that sent me. ¹⁷And the seventy returned again with joy, saying, Lord, even the devils are subject to us through your name. ¹⁸And he said to them, I beheld Satan as lightning fall from heaven. ¹⁹Behold, I give to you power to tread on serpents and scorpions, and over all the power of the enemy: and nothing shall by any means hurt you. ²⁰Notwithstanding in this rejoice not, that the spirits are subject to you; but rather rejoice, because your names are written in heaven. ²¹In that hour Jesus rejoiced in spirit, and said, I thank you, O Father, Lord of heaven and earth, that you have hid these things from the wise and prudent, and have revealed them to babes: even so, Father; for so it seemed good in your sight. ²²All things are delivered to me of my Father: and no man knows who the Son is, but the Father; and who the Father is, but the Son, and he to whom the Son will reveal him. ²³And he turned him to his disciples, and said privately, Blessed are the eyes which see the things that you see: ²⁴For I tell you, that many prophets and kings have desired to see those things which you see, and have not seen them; and to hear those things which you hear, and have not heard them. ²⁵And, behold, a certain lawyer stood up, and tempted him, saying, Master, what shall I do to inherit eternal life? ²⁶He said to him, What is written in the law? how read you? ²⁷And he answering said, You shall love the Lord your God with all your heart, and with all your soul, and with all your strength, and with all your mind; and your neighbor as yourself. ²⁸And he said to him, You have answered right: this do, and you shall live. ²⁹But he, willing to justify himself, said to Jesus, And who is my neighbor? ³⁰And Jesus answering said, A certain man went down from Jerusalem to Jericho, and fell among thieves, which stripped him of his raiment, and wounded him, and departed, leaving him half dead. ³¹And by chance there came down a certain priest that way: and when he saw him, he passed by on the other side. ³²And likewise a Levite, when he was at the place, came and looked on him, and passed by on the other side. ³³But a certain Samaritan, as he journeyed, came where he was: and when he saw him, he had compassion on him, ³⁴And went to him, and bound up his wounds, pouring in oil and wine, and set him on his own beast, and brought him to an inn, and took care of him. ³⁵And on the morrow when he departed, he took out two pence, and gave them to the host, and said to him, Take care of him; and whatever you spend more, when I come again, I will repay you. ³⁶Which now of these three, think you, was neighbor to him that fell among the thieves? ³⁷And he said, He that showed mercy on him. Then said

Jesus to him, Go, and do you likewise. ³⁸Now it came to pass, as they went, that he entered into a certain village: and a certain woman named Martha received him into her house. ³⁹And she had a sister called Mary, which also sat at Jesus' feet, and heard his word. ⁴⁰But Martha was encumbered about much serving, and came to him, and said, Lord, do you not care that my sister has left me to serve alone? bid her therefore that she help me. ⁴¹And Jesus answered and said to her, Martha, Martha, you are careful and troubled about many things: ⁴²But one thing is needful: and Mary has chosen that good part, which shall not be taken away from her.

11 ¹And it came to pass, that, as he was praying in a certain place, when he ceased, one of his disciples said to him, Lord, teach us to pray, as John also taught his disciples. ²And he said to them, When you pray, say, Our Father which are in heaven, Hallowed be your name. Your kingdom come. Your will be done, as in heaven, so in earth. ³Give us day by day our daily bread. ⁴And forgive us our sins; for we also forgive every one that is indebted to us. And lead us not into temptation; but deliver us from evil. ⁵And he said to them, Which of you shall have a friend, and shall go to him at midnight, and say to him, Friend, lend me three loaves; ⁶For a friend of my in his journey is come to me, and I have nothing to set before him? ⁷And he from within shall answer and say, Trouble me not: the door is now shut, and my children are with me in bed; I cannot rise and give you. ⁸I say to you, Though he will not rise and give him, because he is his friend, yet because of his importunity he will rise and give him as many as he needs. ⁹And I say to you, Ask, and it shall be given you; seek, and you shall find; knock, and it shall be opened to you. ¹⁰For every one that asks receives; and he that seeks finds; and to him that knocks it shall be opened. ¹¹If a son shall ask bread of any of you that is a father, will he give him a stone? or if he ask a fish, will he for a fish give him a serpent? ¹²Or if he shall ask an egg, will he offer him a scorpion? ¹³If you then, being evil, know how to give good gifts to your children: how much more shall your heavenly Father give the Holy Spirit to them that ask him? ¹⁴And he was casting out a devil, and it was dumb. And it came to pass, when the devil was gone out, the dumb spoke; and the people wondered. ¹⁵But some of them said, He casts out devils through Beelzebub the chief of the devils. ¹⁶And others, tempting him, sought of him a sign from heaven. ¹⁷But he, knowing their thoughts, said to them, Every kingdom divided against itself is brought to desolation; and a house divided against a house falls. ¹⁸If Satan also be divided against himself, how shall his kingdom stand? because you say that I cast out devils through Beelzebub. ¹⁹And if I by Beelzebub cast out devils, by whom do your sons cast them out? therefore shall they be your judges. ²⁰But if I with the finger of God cast out devils, no doubt the kingdom of God is come on you. ²¹When a strong man armed keeps his palace, his goods are in peace: ²²But when a stronger than he shall come on him, and overcome him, he takes from him all his armor wherein he trusted, and divides his spoils. ²³He that is not with me is against me: and he that gathers not with me scatters. ²⁴When the unclean spirit is gone out of a man, he walks through dry places, seeking rest; and finding none, he says, I will return to my house from where I came out. ²⁵And when he comes, he finds it swept and garnished. ²⁶Then goes he, and takes to him seven other spirits more wicked than himself; and they enter in, and dwell there: and the last state of that man is worse than the first. ²⁷And it came to pass, as he spoke these things, a certain woman of the company lifted up her voice, and said to him, Blessed is the womb that bore you, and the breasts which you have sucked. ²⁸But he said, Yes rather, blessed are they that hear the word of God, and keep it. ²⁹And when the people were gathered thick together, he began to say, This is an evil generation: they seek a sign; and there shall no sign be given it, but the sign of Jonas the prophet. ³⁰For as Jonas was a sign to the Ninevites, so shall also the Son of man be to this generation. ³¹The queen of the south shall rise up in the judgment with the men of this generation, and condemn them: for she came from the utmost parts of the earth to hear the wisdom of Solomon; and, behold, a greater than Solomon is here. ³²The men of Nineve shall rise up in the judgment with this generation, and shall condemn it: for they repented at the preaching of Jonas; and, behold, a greater than Jonas is here. ³³No man, when he has lighted a candle, puts it in a secret place, neither under a bushel, but on a candlestick, that they which come in may see the light. ³⁴The light of the body is the eye: therefore when your eye is single, your whole body also is full of light; but when your eye is evil, your body also is full of darkness. ³⁵Take heed therefore that the light which is in you be not darkness. ³⁶If your whole body therefore be full of light, having no part dark, the whole shall be full of light, as when the bright shining of a candle does give you light. ³⁷And as he spoke, a certain Pharisee sought him to dine with him: and he went in, and sat down to meat. ³⁸And when the Pharisee saw it, he marveled that he had not first washed before dinner. ³⁹And the Lord said to him, Now do you Pharisees make clean the outside of the cup and the platter; but your inward part is full of ravening and wickedness. ⁴⁰You fools, did not he that made that which is without make that which is within also? ⁴¹But rather give alms of such things as you have; and, behold, all things are clean to you. ⁴²But woe to you, Pharisees! for you tithe mint and rue and all manner of herbs, and pass over judgment and the love of God: these you should have done, and not to leave the other undone. ⁴³Woe to you, Pharisees! for you love the uppermost seats in the synagogues, and greetings in the markets. ⁴⁴Woe to you, scribes and Pharisees, hypocrites! for you are as graves which appear not, and the men that walk over them are not aware of them. ⁴⁵Then answered one of the lawyers, and said to him, Master, thus saying you reproach us also. ⁴⁶And he said, Woe to you also, you lawyers! for you lade men with burdens grievous to be borne, and you yourselves touch not the burdens with one of your fingers. ⁴⁷Woe to you! for you build the sepulchers of the prophets, and your fathers killed them. ⁴⁸Truly you bear witness that you allow the deeds of your fathers: for they indeed killed them, and you build their sepulchers. ⁴⁹Therefore also said the wisdom of God, I will send them prophets and apostles, and some of them they shall slay and persecute: ⁵⁰That the blood of all the prophets, which was shed from the foundation of the world, may be required of this generation; ⁵¹From the blood

of Abel to the blood of Zacharias which perished between the altar and the temple: truly I say to you, It shall be required of this generation. ⁵²Woe to you, lawyers! for you have taken away the key of knowledge: you entered not in yourselves, and them that were entering in you hindered. ⁵³And as he said these things to them, the scribes and the Pharisees began to urge him vehemently, and to provoke him to speak of many things: ⁵⁴Laying wait for him, and seeking to catch something out of his mouth, that they might accuse him.

12 ¹In the mean time, when there were gathered together an innumerable multitude of people, so that they stepped one on another, he began to say to his disciples first of all, Beware you of the leaven of the Pharisees, which is hypocrisy. ²For there is nothing covered, that shall not be revealed; neither hid, that shall not be known. ³Therefore whatever you have spoken in darkness shall be heard in the light; and that which you have spoken in the ear in closets shall be proclaimed on the housetops. ⁴And I say to you my friends, Be not afraid of them that kill the body, and after that have no more that they can do. ⁵But I will forewarn you whom you shall fear: Fear him, which after he has killed has power to cast into hell; yes, I say to you, Fear him. ⁶Are not five sparrows sold for two farthings, and not one of them is forgotten before God? ⁷But even the very hairs of your head are all numbered. Fear not therefore: you are of more value than many sparrows. ⁸Also I say to you, Whoever shall confess me before men, him shall the Son of man also confess before the angels of God: ⁹But he that denies me before men shall be denied before the angels of God. ¹⁰And whoever shall speak a word against the Son of man, it shall be forgiven him: but to him that blasphemes against the Holy Ghost it shall not be forgiven. ¹¹And when they bring you to the synagogues, and to magistrates, and powers, take you no thought how or what thing you shall answer, or what you shall say: ¹²For the Holy Ghost shall teach you in the same hour what you ought to say. ¹³And one of the company said to him, Master, speak to my brother, that he divide the inheritance with me. ¹⁴And he said to him, Man, who made me a judge or a divider over you? ¹⁵And he said to them, Take heed, and beware of covetousness: for a man's life consists not in the abundance of the things which he possesses. ¹⁶And he spoke a parable to them, saying, The ground of a certain rich man brought forth plentifully: ¹⁷And he thought within himself, saying, What shall I do, because I have no room where to bestow my fruits? ¹⁸And he said, This will I do: I will pull down my barns, and build greater; and there will I bestow all my fruits and my goods. ¹⁹And I will say to my soul, Soul, you have much goods laid up for many years; take your ease, eat, drink, and be merry. ²⁰But God said to him, You fool, this night your soul shall be required of you: then whose shall those things be, which you have provided? ²¹So is he that lays up treasure for himself, and is not rich toward God. ²²And he said to his disciples, Therefore I say to you, Take no thought for your life, what you shall eat; neither for the body, what you shall put on. ²³The life is more than meat, and the body is more than raiment. ²⁴Consider the ravens: for they neither sow nor reap; which neither have storehouse nor barn; and God feeds them: how much more are you better than the fowls? ²⁵And which of you with taking thought can add to his stature one cubit? ²⁶If you then be not able to do that thing which is least, why take you thought for the rest? ²⁷Consider the lilies how they grow: they toil not, they spin not; and yet I say to you, that Solomon in all his glory was not arrayed like one of these. ²⁸If then God so clothe the grass, which is to day in the field, and to morrow is cast into the oven; how much more will he clothe you, O you of little faith? ²⁹And seek not you what you shall eat, or what you shall drink, neither be you of doubtful mind. ³⁰For all these things do the nations of the world seek after: and your Father knows that you have need of these things. ³¹But rather seek you the kingdom of God; and all these things shall be added to you. ³²Fear not, little flock; for it is your Father's good pleasure to give you the kingdom. ³³Sell that you have, and give alms; provide yourselves bags which wax not old, a treasure in the heavens that fails not, where no thief approaches, neither moth corrupts. ³⁴For where your treasure is, there will your heart be also. ³⁵Let your loins be girded about, and your lights burning; ³⁶And you yourselves like to men that wait for their lord, when he will return from the wedding; that when he comes and knocks, they may open to him immediately. ³⁷Blessed are those servants, whom the lord when he comes shall find watching: truly I say to you, that he shall gird himself, and make them to sit down to meat, and will come forth and serve them. ³⁸And if he shall come in the second watch, or come in the third watch, and find them so, blessed are those servants. ³⁹And this know, that if the manager of the house had known what hour the thief would come, he would have watched, and not have suffered his house to be broken through. ⁴⁰Be you therefore ready also: for the Son of man comes at an hour when you think not. ⁴¹Then Peter said to him, Lord, speak you this parable to us, or even to all? ⁴²And the Lord said, Who then is that faithful and wise steward, whom his lord shall make ruler over his household, to give them their portion of meat in due season? ⁴³Blessed is that servant, whom his lord when he comes shall find so doing. ⁴⁴Of a truth I say to you, that he will make him ruler over all that he has. ⁴⁵But and if that servant say in his heart, My lord delays his coming; and shall begin to beat the menservants and maidens, and to eat and drink, and to be drunken; ⁴⁶The lord of that servant will come in a day when he looks not for him, and at an hour when he is not aware, and will cut him in sunder, and will appoint him his portion with the unbelievers. ⁴⁷And that servant, which knew his lord's will, and prepared not himself, neither did according to his will, shall be beaten with many stripes. ⁴⁸But he that knew not, and did commit things worthy of stripes, shall be beaten with few stripes. For to whomsoever much is given, of him shall be much required: and to whom men have committed much, of him they will ask the more. ⁴⁹I am come to send fire on the earth; and what will I, if it be already kindled? ⁵⁰But I have a baptism to be baptized with; and how am I straitened till it be accomplished! ⁵¹Suppose you that I am come to give peace on earth? I tell you, No; but rather division: ⁵²For from now on there shall be five in one house divided, three against two, and two against three. ⁵³The father shall be divided against the son, and the son against the father; the mother against the daughter, and the daughter against the mother; the mother in law against her daughter in law, and the daughter in law against her mother in law. ⁵⁴And he said also to the people, When you see a cloud rise out of the west, straightway you say, There comes a shower; and so it is. ⁵⁵And when you see the south wind blow, you say, There will be heat; and it comes to pass. ⁵⁶You hypocrites, you can discern the face of the sky and of the earth; but how is it that you do not discern this time? ⁵⁷Yes, and why even of yourselves judge you not what is right? ⁵⁸When you go with your adversary to the magistrate, as you are in the way, give diligence that you may be delivered from him; lest he hale you to the judge, and the judge deliver you to the officer, and the officer cast you into prison. ⁵⁹I tell you, you shall not depart there, till you have paid the very last mite.

13 ¹There were present at that season some that told him of the Galilaeans, whose blood Pilate had mingled with their sacrifices. ²And Jesus answering said to them, Suppose you that these Galilaeans were sinners above all the Galilaeans, because they suffered such things? ³I tell you, No: but, except you repent, you shall all likewise perish. ⁴Or those eighteen, on whom the tower in Siloam fell, and slew them, think you that they were sinners above all men that dwelled in Jerusalem? ⁵I tell you, No: but, except you repent, you shall all likewise perish. ⁶He spoke also this parable; A certain man had a fig tree planted in his vineyard; and he came and sought fruit thereon, and found none. ⁷Then said he to the dresser of his vineyard, Behold, these three years I come seeking fruit on this fig tree, and find none: cut it down; why encumbers it the ground? ⁸And he answering said to him, Lord, let it alone this year also, till I shall dig about it, and dung it: ⁹And if it bear fruit, well: and if not, then after that you shall cut it down. ¹⁰And he was teaching in one of the synagogues on the sabbath. ¹¹And, behold, there was a woman which had a spirit of infirmity eighteen years, and was bowed together, and could in no wise lift up herself. ¹²And when Jesus saw her, he called her to him, and said to her, Woman, you are loosed from your infirmity. ¹³And he laid his hands on her: and immediately she was made straight, and glorified God. ¹⁴And the ruler of the synagogue answered with indignation, because that Jesus had healed on the sabbath day, and said to the people, There are six days in which men ought to work: in them therefore come and be healed, and not on the sabbath day. ¹⁵The Lord then answered him, and said, You hypocrite, does not each one of you on the sabbath loose his ox or his ass from the stall, and lead him away to watering? ¹⁶And should not this woman, being a daughter of Abraham, whom Satan has bound, see, these eighteen years, be loosed from this bond on the sabbath day? ¹⁷And when he had said these things, all his adversaries were ashamed: and all the people rejoiced for all the glorious things that were done by him. ¹⁸Then said he, To what is the kingdom of God like? and to what shall I resemble it? ¹⁹It is like a grain of mustard seed, which a man took, and cast into his garden; and it grew, and waxed a great tree; and the fowls of the air lodged in the branches of it. ²⁰And again he said, Whereunto shall I liken the kingdom of God? ²¹It is like leaven, which a woman took and hid in three measures of meal, till the whole was leavened. ²²And he went through the cities and villages, teaching, and journeying toward Jerusalem. ²³Then said one to him, Lord, are there few that be saved? And he said to them, ²⁴Strive to enter in at the strait gate: for many, I say to you, will seek to enter in, and shall not be able. ²⁵When once the master of the house is risen up, and has shut to the door, and you begin to stand without, and to knock at the door, saying, Lord, Lord, open to us; and he shall answer and say to you, I know you not from where you are: ²⁶Then shall you begin to say, We have eaten and drunk in your presence, and you have taught in our streets. ²⁷But he shall say, I tell you, I know you not from where you are; depart from me, all you workers of iniquity. ²⁸There shall be weeping and gnashing of teeth, when you shall see Abraham, and Isaac, and Jacob, and all the prophets, in the kingdom of God, and you yourselves thrust out. ²⁹And they shall come from the east, and from the west, and from the north, and from the south, and shall sit down in the kingdom of God. ³⁰And, behold, there are last which shall be first, and there are first which shall be last. ³¹The same day there came certain of the Pharisees, saying to him, Get you out, and depart hence: for Herod will kill you. ³²And he said to them, Go you, and tell that fox, Behold, I cast out devils, and I do cures to day and to morrow, and the third day I shall be perfected. ³³Nevertheless I must walk to day, and to morrow, and the day following: for it cannot be that a prophet perish out of Jerusalem. ³⁴O Jerusalem, Jerusalem, which kill the prophets, and stone them that are sent to you; how often would I have gathered your children together, as a hen does gather her brood under her wings, and you would not! ³⁵Behold, your house is left to you desolate: and truly I say to you, You shall not see me, until the time come when you shall say, Blessed is he that comes in the name of the Lord.

14 ¹And it came to pass, as he went into the house of one of the chief Pharisees to eat bread on the sabbath day, that they watched him. ²And, behold, there was a certain man before him which had the dropsy. ³And Jesus answering spoke to the lawyers and Pharisees, saying, Is it lawful to heal on the sabbath day? ⁴And they held their peace. And he took him, and healed him, and let him go; ⁵And answered them, saying, Which of you shall have an ass or an ox fallen into a pit, and will not straightway pull him out on the sabbath day? ⁶And they could not answer him again to these things. ⁷And he put forth a parable to those which were bidden, when he marked how they chose out the chief rooms; saying to them, ⁸When you are bidden of any man to a wedding, sit not down in the highest room; lest a more honorable man than you be bidden of him; ⁹And he that bade you and him come and say to you, Give this man place; and you begin with shame to take the lowest room. ¹⁰But when you are bidden, go and sit down in the lowest room; that when he that bade you comes, he may say to you, Friend, go up higher: then shall you have worship in the presence of them that sit at meat with you. ¹¹For whoever exalts himself shall be abased; and he that humbles himself shall be exalted. ¹²Then said he also to him that bade him, When you make a dinner or a supper, call not your friends, nor your brothers, neither your kinsmen, nor your rich neighbors; lest they also bid you again, and a recompense be made you. ¹³But when you make a feast, call the poor, the maimed, the lame, the blind: ¹⁴And you shall be blessed; for they cannot recompense you: for you shall be recompensed at the resurrection of the just. ¹⁵And when one of them that sat at meat with him heard these things, he said to him, Blessed is he that shall eat bread in the kingdom of God. ¹⁶Then said he to him, A certain man made a great supper, and bade many: ¹⁷And sent his servant at supper time to say to them that were bidden, Come; for all things are now ready. ¹⁸And they all with one consent began to make excuse. The first said to him, I have bought a piece of ground, and I must needs go and see it: I pray you have me excused. ¹⁹And another said, I have bought five yoke of oxen, and I go to prove them: I pray you have me excused. ²⁰And another said, I have married a wife, and therefore I cannot come. ²¹So that servant came, and showed his lord these things. Then the master of the house being angry said to his servant, Go out quickly into the streets and lanes of the city, and bring in here the poor, and the maimed, and the halt, and the blind. ²²And the servant said, Lord, it is done as you have commanded, and yet there is room. ²³And the lord said to the servant, Go out into the highways and hedges, and compel them to come in, that my house may be filled. ²⁴For I say to you, That none of those men which were bidden shall taste of my supper. ²⁵And there went great multitudes with him: and he turned, and said to them, ²⁶If any man come to me, and hate not his father, and mother, and wife, and children, and brothers, and sisters, yes, and his own life also, he cannot be my disciple. ²⁷And whoever does not bear his cross, and come after me, cannot be my disciple. ²⁸For which of you, intending to build a tower, sits not down first, and counts the cost, whether he have sufficient to finish it? ²⁹Lest haply, after he has laid the foundation, and is not able to finish it, all that behold it begin to mock him, ³⁰Saying, This man began to build, and was not able to finish. ³¹Or what king, going to make war against another king, sits not down first, and consults whether he be able with ten thousand to meet him that comes against him with twenty thousand? ³²Or else, while the other is yet a great way off, he sends an ambassador, and desires conditions of peace. ³³So likewise, whoever he be of you that forsakes not all that he has, he cannot be my disciple. ³⁴Salt is good: but if the salt have lost his flavor, with which shall it be seasoned? ³⁵It is neither fit for the land, nor yet for the dunghill; but men cast it out. He that has ears to hear, let him hear.

15

¹Then drew near to him all the publicans and sinners for to hear him. ²And the Pharisees and scribes murmured, saying, This man receives sinners, and eats with them. ³And he spoke this parable to them, saying, ⁴What man of you, having an hundred sheep, if he lose one of them, does not leave the ninety and nine in the wilderness, and go after that which is lost, until he find it? ⁵And when he has found it, he lays it on his shoulders, rejoicing. ⁶And when he comes home, he calls together his friends and neighbors, saying to them, Rejoice with me; for I have found my sheep which was lost. ⁷I say to you, that likewise joy shall be in heaven over one sinner that repents, more than over ninety and nine just persons, which need no repentance. ⁸Either what woman having ten pieces of silver, if she lose one piece, does not light a candle, and sweep the house, and seek diligently till she find it? ⁹And when she has found it, she calls her friends and her neighbors together, saying, Rejoice with me; for I have found the piece which I had lost. ¹⁰Likewise, I say to you, there is joy in the presence of the angels of God over one sinner that repents. ¹¹And he said, A certain man had two sons: ¹²And the younger of them said to his father, Father, give me the portion of goods that falls to me. And he divided to them his living. ¹³And not many days after the younger son gathered all together, and took his journey into a far country, and there wasted his substance with riotous living. ¹⁴And when he had spent all, there arose a mighty famine in that land; and he began to be in want. ¹⁵And he went and joined himself to a citizen of that country; and he sent him into his fields to feed swine. ¹⁶And he would fain have filled his belly with the husks that the swine did eat: and no man gave to him. ¹⁷And when he came to himself, he said, How many hired servants of my father's have bread enough and to spare, and I perish with hunger! ¹⁸I will arise and go to my father, and will say to him, Father, I have sinned against heaven, and before you, ¹⁹And am no more worthy to be called your son: make me as one of your hired servants. ²⁰And he arose, and came to his father. But when he was yet a great way off, his father saw him, and had compassion, and ran, and fell on his neck, and kissed him. ²¹And the son said to him, Father, I have sinned against heaven, and in your sight, and am no more worthy to be called your son. ²²But the father said to his servants, Bring forth the best robe, and put it on him; and put a ring on his hand, and shoes on his feet: ²³And bring here the fatted calf, and kill it; and let us eat, and be merry: ²⁴For this my son was dead, and is alive again; he was lost, and is found. And they began to be merry. ²⁵Now his elder son was in the field: and as he came and drew near to the house, he heard music and dancing. ²⁶And he called one of the servants, and asked what these things meant. ²⁷And he said to him, Your brother is come; and your father has killed the fatted calf, because he has received him safe and sound. ²⁸And he was angry, and would not go in: therefore came his father out, and entreated him. ²⁹And he answering said to his father, See, these many years do I serve you, neither transgressed I at any time your commandment: and yet you never gave me a kid, that I might make merry with my friends: ³⁰But as soon as this your son was come, which has devoured your living with harlots, you have killed for him the fatted calf. ³¹And he said to him, Son, you are ever with me, and all that I have is yours. ³²It was meet that we should make merry, and be glad: for this your brother was dead, and is alive again; and was lost, and is found.

16

¹And he said also to his disciples, There was a certain rich man, which had a steward; and the same was accused to him that he had wasted his goods. ²And he called him, and said to him, How is it that I hear this of you? give an account of your stewardship; for you may be no longer steward. ³Then the steward said within himself, What shall I do? for my lord takes away from me the stewardship: I cannot dig; to beg I am ashamed. ⁴I am resolved what to

do, that, when I am put out of the stewardship, they may receive me into their houses. ⁵So he called every one of his lord's debtors to him, and said to the first, How much owe you to my lord? ⁶And he said, An hundred measures of oil. And he said to him, Take your bill, and sit down quickly, and write fifty. ⁷Then said he to another, And how much owe you? And he said, An hundred measures of wheat. And he said to him, Take your bill, and write fourscore. ⁸And the lord commended the unjust steward, because he had done wisely: for the children of this world are in their generation wiser than the children of light. ⁹And I say to you, Make to yourselves friends of the mammon of unrighteousness; that, when you fail, they may receive you into everlasting habitations. ¹⁰He that is faithful in that which is least is faithful also in much: and he that is unjust in the least is unjust also in much. ¹¹If therefore you have not been faithful in the unrighteous mammon, who will commit to your trust the true riches? ¹²And if you have not been faithful in that which is another man's, who shall give you that which is your own? ¹³No servant can serve two masters: for either he will hate the one, and love the other; or else he will hold to the one, and despise the other. You cannot serve God and mammon. ¹⁴And the Pharisees also, who were covetous, heard all these things: and they derided him. ¹⁵And he said to them, You are they which justify yourselves before men; but God knows your hearts: for that which is highly esteemed among men is abomination in the sight of God. ¹⁶The law and the prophets were until John: since that time the kingdom of God is preached, and every man presses into it. ¹⁷And it is easier for heaven and earth to pass, than one pronunciation mark of the law to fail. ¹⁸Whoever puts away his wife, and marries another, commits adultery: and whoever marries her that is put away from her husband commits adultery. ¹⁹There was a certain rich man, which was clothed in purple and fine linen, and fared sumptuously every day: ²⁰And there was a certain beggar named Lazarus, which was laid at his gate, full of sores, ²¹And desiring to be fed with the crumbs which fell from the rich man's table: moreover the dogs came and licked his sores. ²²And it came to pass, that the beggar died, and was carried by the angels into Abraham's bosom: the rich man also died, and was buried; ²³And in hell he lift up his eyes, being in torments, and sees Abraham afar off, and Lazarus in his bosom. ²⁴And he cried and said, Father Abraham, have mercy on me, and send Lazarus, that he may dip the tip of his finger in water, and cool my tongue; for I am tormented in this flame. ²⁵But Abraham said, Son, remember that you in your lifetime received your good things, and likewise Lazarus evil things: but now he is comforted, and you are tormented. ²⁶And beside all this, between us and you there is a great gulf fixed: so that they which would pass from hence to you cannot; neither can they pass to us, that would come from there. ²⁷Then he said, I pray you therefore, father, that you would send him to my father's house: ²⁸For I have five brothers; that he may testify to them, lest they also come into this place of torment. ²⁹Abraham says to him, They have Moses and the prophets; let them hear them. ³⁰And he said, No, father Abraham: but if one went to them from the dead, they will repent. ³¹And he said to him, If they hear not Moses and the prophets, neither will they be persuaded, though one rose from the dead.

17

¹Then said he to the disciples, It is impossible but that offenses will come: but woe to him, through whom they come! ²It were better for him that a millstone were hanged about his neck, and he cast into the sea, than that he should offend one of these little ones. ³Take heed to yourselves: If your brother trespass against you, rebuke him; and if he repent, forgive him. ⁴And if he trespass against you seven times in a day, and seven times in a day turn again to you, saying, I repent; you shall forgive him. ⁵And the apostles said to the Lord, Increase our faith. ⁶And the Lord said, If you had faith as a grain of mustard seed, you might say to this sycamine tree, Be you plucked up by the root, and be you planted in the sea; and it should obey you. ⁷But which of you, having a servant plowing or feeding cattle, will say to him by and by, when he is come from the field, Go and sit down to meat? ⁸And will not rather say to him, Make ready with which I may sup, and gird yourself, and serve me, till I have eaten and drunken; and afterward you shall eat and drink? ⁹Does he thank that servant because he did the things that were commanded him? I trow not. ¹⁰So likewise you, when you shall have done all those things which are commanded you, say, We are unprofitable servants: we have done that which was our duty to do. ¹¹And it came to pass, as he went to Jerusalem, that he passed through the middle of Samaria and Galilee. ¹²And as he entered into a certain village, there met him ten men that were lepers, which stood afar off: ¹³And they lifted up their voices, and said, Jesus, Master, have mercy on us. ¹⁴And when he saw them, he said to them, Go show yourselves to the priests. And it came to pass, that, as they went, they were cleansed. ¹⁵And one of them, when he saw that he was healed, turned back, and with a loud voice glorified God, ¹⁶And fell down on his face at his feet, giving him thanks: and he was a Samaritan. ¹⁷And Jesus answering said, Were there not ten cleansed? but where are the nine? ¹⁸There are not found that returned to give glory to God, save this stranger. ¹⁹And he said to him, Arise, go your way: your faith has made you whole. ²⁰And when he was demanded of the Pharisees, when the kingdom of God should come, he answered them and said, The kingdom of God comes not with observation: ²¹Neither shall they say, See here! or, see there! for, behold, the kingdom of God is within you. ²²And he said to the disciples, The days will come, when you shall desire to see one of the days of the Son of man, and you shall not see it. ²³And they shall say to you, See here; or, see there: go not after them, nor follow them. ²⁴For as the lightning, that lightens out of the one part under heaven, shines to the other part under heaven; so shall also the Son of man be in his day. ²⁵But first must he suffer many things, and be rejected of this generation. ²⁶And as it was in the days of Noe, so shall it be also in the days of the Son of man. ²⁷They did eat, they drank, they married wives, they were given in marriage, until the day that Noe entered into the ark, and the flood came, and destroyed them all. ²⁸Likewise also as it was in the days of Lot; they did eat, they drank, they bought, they sold, they planted, they built; ²⁹But the same day that Lot went out of Sodom it rained fire and

brimstone from heaven, and destroyed them all. ³⁰Even thus shall it be in the day when the Son of man is revealed. ³¹In that day, he which shall be on the housetop, and his stuff in the house, let him not come down to take it away: and he that is in the field, let him likewise not return back. ³²Remember Lot's wife. ³³Whoever shall seek to save his life shall lose it; and whoever shall lose his life shall preserve it. ³⁴I tell you, in that night there shall be two men in one bed; the one shall be taken, and the other shall be left. ³⁵Two women shall be grinding together; the one shall be taken, and the other left. ³⁶Two men shall be in the field; the one shall be taken, and the other left. ³⁷And they answered and said to him, Where, Lord? And he said to them, Wherever the body is, thither will the eagles be gathered together.

18 ¹And he spoke a parable to them to this end, that men should always to pray, and not to faint; ²Saying, There was in a city a judge, which feared not God, neither regarded man; ³And there was a widow in that city; and she came to him, saying, Avenge me of my adversary. ⁴And he would not for a while: but afterward he said within himself, Though I fear not God, nor regard man; ⁵Yet because this widow troubles me, I will avenge her, lest by her continual coming she weary me. ⁶And the Lord said, Hear what the unjust judge says. ⁷And shall not God avenge his own elect, which cry day and night to him, though he bear long with them? ⁸I tell you that he will avenge them speedily. Nevertheless when the Son of man comes, shall he find faith on the earth? ⁹And he spoke this parable to certain which trusted in themselves that they were righteous, and despised others: ¹⁰Two men went up into the temple to pray; the one a Pharisee, and the other a publican. ¹¹The Pharisee stood and prayed thus with himself, God, I thank you, that I am not as other men are, extortionists, unjust, adulterers, or even as this publican. ¹²I fast twice in the week, I give tithes of all that I possess. ¹³And the publican, standing afar off, would not lift up so much as his eyes to heaven, but smote on his breast, saying, God be merciful to me a sinner. ¹⁴I tell you, this man went down to his house justified rather than the other: for every one that exalts himself shall be abased; and he that humbles himself shall be exalted. ¹⁵And they brought to him also infants, that he would touch them: but when his disciples saw it, they rebuked them. ¹⁶But Jesus called them to him, and said, Suffer little children to come to me, and forbid them not: for of such is the kingdom of God. ¹⁷Truly I say to you, Whoever shall not receive the kingdom of God as a little child shall in no wise enter therein. ¹⁸And a certain ruler asked him, saying, Good Master, what shall I do to inherit eternal life? ¹⁹And Jesus said to him, Why call you me good? none is good, save one, that is, God. ²⁰You know the commandments, Do not commit adultery, Do not kill, Do not steal, Do not bear false witness, Honor your father and your mother. ²¹And he said, All these have I kept from my youth up. ²²Now when Jesus heard these things, he said to him, Yet lack you one thing: sell all that you have, and distribute to the poor, and you shall have treasure in heaven: and come, follow me. ²³And when he heard this, he was very sorrowful: for he was very rich. ²⁴And when Jesus saw that he was very sorrowful, he said, How hardly shall they that have riches enter into the kingdom of God! ²⁵For it is easier for a camel to go through a needle's eye, than for a rich man to enter into the kingdom of God. ²⁶And they that heard it said, Who then can be saved? ²⁷And he said, The things which are impossible with men are possible with God. ²⁸Then Peter said, See, we have left all, and followed you. ²⁹And he said to them, Truly I say to you, There is no man that has left house, or parents, or brothers, or wife, or children, for the kingdom of God's sake, ³⁰Who shall not receive manifold more in this present time, and in the world to come life everlasting. ³¹Then he took to him the twelve, and said to them, Behold, we go up to Jerusalem, and all things that are written by the prophets concerning the Son of man shall be accomplished. ³²For he shall be delivered to the Gentiles, and shall be mocked, and spitefully entreated, and spitted on: ³³And they shall whip him, and put him to death: and the third day he shall rise again. ³⁴And they understood none of these things: and this saying was hid from them, neither knew they the things which were spoken. ³⁵And it came to pass, that as he was come near to Jericho, a certain blind man sat by the way side begging: ³⁶And hearing the multitude pass by, he asked what it meant. ³⁷And they told him, that Jesus of Nazareth passes by. ³⁸And he cried, saying, Jesus, you son of David, have mercy on me. ³⁹And they which went before rebuked him, that he should hold his peace: but he cried so much the more, You son of David, have mercy on me. ⁴⁰And Jesus stood, and commanded him to be brought to him: and when he was come near, he asked him, ⁴¹Saying, What will you that I shall do to you? And he said, Lord, that I may receive my sight. ⁴²And Jesus said to him, Receive your sight: your faith has saved you. ⁴³And immediately he received his sight, and followed him, glorifying God: and all the people, when they saw it, gave praise to God.

19 ¹And Jesus entered and passed through Jericho. ²And, behold, there was a man named Zacchaeus, which was the chief among the publicans, and he was rich. ³And he sought to see Jesus who he was; and could not for the press, because he was little of stature. ⁴And he ran before, and climbed up into a sycamore tree to see him: for he was to pass that way. ⁵And when Jesus came to the place, he looked up, and saw him, and said to him, Zacchaeus, make haste, and come down; for to day I must abide at your house. ⁶And he made haste, and came down, and received him joyfully. ⁷And when they saw it, they all murmured, saying, That he was gone to be guest with a man that is a sinner. ⁸And Zacchaeus stood, and said to the Lord: Behold, Lord, the half of my goods I give to the poor; and if I have taken any thing from any man by false accusation, I restore him fourfold. ⁹And Jesus said to him, This day is salvation come to this house, as much as he also is a son of Abraham. ¹⁰For the Son of man is come to seek and to save that which was lost. ¹¹And as they heard these things, he added and spoke a parable, because he was near to Jerusalem, and because they thought that the kingdom of God should immediately appear. ¹²He said therefore, A certain nobleman went into a far country to receive for himself a kingdom, and to return. ¹³And he called his ten servants, and delivered them ten pounds, and said to them, Occupy till I come. ¹⁴But his citizens hated him, and sent a message after him, saying,

We will not have this man to reign over us. ¹⁵And it came to pass, that when he was returned, having received the kingdom, then he commanded these servants to be called to him, to whom he had given the money, that he might know how much every man had gained by trading. ¹⁶Then came the first, saying, Lord, your pound has gained ten pounds. ¹⁷And he said to him, Well, you good servant: because you have been faithful in a very little, have you authority over ten cities. ¹⁸And the second came, saying, Lord, your pound has gained five pounds. ¹⁹And he said likewise to him, Be you also over five cities. ²⁰And another came, saying, Lord, behold, here is your pound, which I have kept laid up in a napkin: ²¹For I feared you, because you are an austere man: you take up that you layed not down, and reap that you did not sow. ²²And he says to him, Out of your own mouth will I judge you, you wicked servant. You knew that I was an austere man, taking up that I laid not down, and reaping that I did not sow: ²³Why then gave not you my money into the bank, that at my coming I might have required my own with usury? ²⁴And he said to them that stood by, Take from him the pound, and give it to him that has ten pounds. ²⁵(And they said to him, Lord, he has ten pounds.) ²⁶For I say to you, That to every one which has shall be given; and from him that has not, even that he has shall be taken away from him. ²⁷But those my enemies, which would not that I should reign over them, bring here, and slay them before me. ²⁸And when he had thus spoken, he went before, ascending up to Jerusalem. ²⁹And it came to pass, when he was come near to Bethphage and Bethany, at the mount called the mount of Olives, he sent two of his disciples, ³⁰Saying, Go you into the village over against you; in the which at your entering you shall find a colt tied, where on yet never man sat: loose him, and bring him here. ³¹And if any man ask you, Why do you loose him? thus shall you say to him, Because the Lord has need of him. ³²And they that were sent went their way, and found even as he had said to them. ³³And as they were loosing the colt, the owners thereof said to them, Why loose you the colt? ³⁴And they said, The Lord has need of him. ³⁵And they brought him to Jesus: and they cast their garments on the colt, and they set Jesus thereon. ³⁶And as he went, they spread their clothes in the way. ³⁷And when he was come near, even now at the descent of the mount of Olives, the whole multitude of the disciples began to rejoice and praise God with a loud voice for all the mighty works that they had seen; ³⁸Saying, Blessed be the King that comes in the name of the Lord: peace in heaven, and glory in the highest. ³⁹And some of the Pharisees from among the multitude said to him, Master, rebuke your disciples. ⁴⁰And he answered and said to them, I tell you that, if these should hold their peace, the stones would immediately cry out. ⁴¹And when he was come near, he beheld the city, and wept over it, ⁴²Saying, If you had known, even you, at least in this your day, the things which belong to your peace! but now they are hid from your eyes. ⁴³For the days shall come on you, that your enemies shall cast a trench about you, and compass you round, and keep you in on every side, ⁴⁴And shall lay you even with the ground, and your children within you; and they shall not leave in you one stone on another; because you knew not the time of your visitation. ⁴⁵And he went into the temple, and began to cast out them that sold therein, and them that bought; ⁴⁶Saying to them, It is written, My house is the house of prayer: but you have made it a den of thieves. ⁴⁷And he taught daily in the temple. But the chief priests and the scribes and the chief of the people sought to destroy him, ⁴⁸And could not find what they might do: for all the people were very attentive to hear him.

20

¹And it came to pass, that on one of those days, as he taught the people in the temple, and preached the gospel, the chief priests and the scribes came on him with the elders, ²And spoke to him, saying, Tell us, by what authority do you these things? or who is he that gave you this authority? ³And he answered and said to them, I will also ask you one thing; and answer me: ⁴The baptism of John, was it from heaven, or of men? ⁵And they reasoned with themselves, saying, If we shall say, From heaven; he will say, Why then believed you him not? ⁶But and if we say, Of men; all the people will stone us: for they be persuaded that John was a prophet. ⁷And they answered, that they could not tell from where it was. ⁸And Jesus said to them, Neither tell I you by what authority I do these things. ⁹Then began he to speak to the people this parable; A certain man planted a vineyard, and let it forth to farmers, and went into a far country for a long time. ¹⁰And at the season he sent a servant to the farmers, that they should give him of the fruit of the vineyard: but the farmers beat him, and sent him away empty. ¹¹And again he sent another servant: and they beat him also, and entreated him shamefully, and sent him away empty. ¹²And again he sent a third: and they wounded him also, and cast him out. ¹³Then said the lord of the vineyard, What shall I do? I will send my beloved son: it may be they will reverence him when they see him. ¹⁴But when the farmers saw him, they reasoned among themselves, saying, This is the heir: come, let us kill him, that the inheritance may be ours. ¹⁵So they cast him out of the vineyard, and killed him. What therefore shall the lord of the vineyard do to them? ¹⁶He shall come and destroy these farmers, and shall give the vineyard to others. And when they heard it, they said, God forbid. ¹⁷And he beheld them, and said, What is this then that is written, The stone which the builders rejected, the same is become the head of the corner? ¹⁸Whoever shall fall on that stone shall be broken; but on whomsoever it shall fall, it will grind him to powder. ¹⁹And the chief priests and the scribes the same hour sought to lay hands on him; and they feared the people: for they perceived that he had spoken this parable against them. ²⁰And they watched him, and sent forth spies, which should feign themselves just men, that they might take hold of his words, that so they might deliver him to the power and authority of the governor. ²¹And they asked him, saying, Master, we know that you say and teach rightly, neither accept you the person of any, but teach the way of God truly: ²²Is it lawful for us to give tribute to Caesar, or no? ²³But he perceived their craftiness, and said to them, Why tempt you me? ²⁴Show me a penny. Whose image and superscription has it? They answered and said, Caesar's. ²⁵And he said to them, Render therefore to Caesar the things which be Caesar's, and to God the things which be God's. ²⁶And they could not take hold of his words before the

people: and they marveled at his answer, and held their peace. ²⁷Then came to him certain of the Sadducees, which deny that there is any resurrection; and they asked him, ²⁸Saying, Master, Moses wrote to us, If any man's brother die, having a wife, and he die without children, that his brother should take his wife, and raise up seed to his brother. ²⁹There were therefore seven brothers: and the first took a wife, and died without children. ³⁰And the second took her to wife, and he died childless. ³¹And the third took her; and in like manner the seven also: and they left no children, and died. ³²Last of all the woman died also. ³³Therefore in the resurrection whose wife of them is she? for seven had her to wife. ³⁴And Jesus answering said to them, The children of this world marry, and are given in marriage: ³⁵But they which shall be accounted worthy to obtain that world, and the resurrection from the dead, neither marry, nor are given in marriage: ³⁶Neither can they die any more: for they are equal to the angels; and are the children of God, being the children of the resurrection. ³⁷Now that the dead are raised, even Moses showed at the bush, when he calls the Lord the God of Abraham, and the God of Isaac, and the God of Jacob. ³⁸For he is not a God of the dead, but of the living: for all live to him. ³⁹Then certain of the scribes answering said, Master, you have well said. ⁴⁰And after that they dared not ask him any question at all. ⁴¹And he said to them, How say they that Christ is David's son? ⁴²And David himself says in the book of Psalms, The LORD said to my Lord, Sit you on my right hand, ⁴³Till I make your enemies your footstool. ⁴⁴David therefore calls him Lord, how is he then his son? ⁴⁵Then in the audience of all the people he said to his disciples, ⁴⁶Beware of the scribes, which desire to walk in long robes, and love greetings in the markets, and the highest seats in the synagogues, and the chief rooms at feasts; ⁴⁷Which devour widows' houses, and for a show make long prayers: the same shall receive greater damnation.

21

¹And he looked up, and saw the rich men casting their gifts into the treasury. ²And he saw also a certain poor widow casting in thither two mites. ³And he said, Of a truth I say to you, that this poor widow has cast in more than they all: ⁴For all these have of their abundance cast in to the offerings of God: but she of her penury has cast in all the living that she had. ⁵And as some spoke of the temple, how it was adorned with goodly stones and gifts, he said, ⁶As for these things which you behold, the days will come, in the which there shall not be left one stone on another, that shall not be thrown down. ⁷And they asked him, saying, Master, but when shall these things be? and what sign will there be when these things shall come to pass? ⁸And he said, Take heed that you be not deceived: for many shall come in my name, saying, I am Christ; and the time draws near: go you not therefore after them. ⁹But when you shall hear of wars and commotions, be not terrified: for these things must first come to pass; but the end is not by and by. ¹⁰Then said he to them, Nation shall rise against nation, and kingdom against kingdom: ¹¹And great earthquakes shall be in divers places, and famines, and pestilences; and fearful sights and great signs shall there be from heaven. ¹²But before all these, they shall lay their hands on you, and persecute you, delivering you up to the synagogues, and into prisons, being brought before kings and rulers for my name's sake. ¹³And it shall turn to you for a testimony. ¹⁴Settle it therefore in your hearts, not to meditate before what you shall answer: ¹⁵For I will give you a mouth and wisdom, which all your adversaries shall not be able to gainsay nor resist. ¹⁶And you shall be betrayed both by parents, and brothers, and kinfolks, and friends; and some of you shall they cause to be put to death. ¹⁷And you shall be hated of all men for my name's sake. ¹⁸But there shall not an hair of your head perish. ¹⁹In your patience possess you your souls. ²⁰And when you shall see Jerusalem compassed with armies, then know that the desolation thereof is near. ²¹Then let them which be in Judaea flee to the mountains; and let them which are in the middle of it depart out; and let not them that are in the countries enter thereinto. ²²For these be the days of vengeance, that all things which are written may be fulfilled. ²³But woe to them that are with child, and to them that give suck, in those days! for there shall be great distress in the land, and wrath on this people. ²⁴And they shall fall by the edge of the sword, and shall be led away captive into all nations: and Jerusalem shall be trodden down of the Gentiles, until the times of the Gentiles be fulfilled. ²⁵And there shall be signs in the sun, and in the moon, and in the stars; and on the earth distress of nations, with perplexity; the sea and the waves roaring; ²⁶Men's hearts failing them for fear, and for looking after those things which are coming on the earth: for the powers of heaven shall be shaken. ²⁷And then shall they see the Son of man coming in a cloud with power and great glory. ²⁸And when these things begin to come to pass, then look up, and lift up your heads; for your redemption draws near. ²⁹And he spoke to them a parable; Behold the fig tree, and all the trees; ³⁰When they now shoot forth, you see and know of your own selves that summer is now near at hand. ³¹So likewise you, when you see these things come to pass, know you that the kingdom of God is near at hand. ³²Truly I say to you, This generation shall not pass away, till all be fulfilled. ³³Heaven and earth shall pass away: but my words shall not pass away. ³⁴And take heed to yourselves, lest at any time your hearts be overcharged with surfeiting, and drunkenness, and cares of this life, and so that day come on you unawares. ³⁵For as a snare shall it come on all them that dwell on the face of the whole earth. ³⁶Watch you therefore, and pray always, that you may be accounted worthy to escape all these things that shall come to pass, and to stand before the Son of man. ³⁷And in the day time he was teaching in the temple; and at night he went out, and stayed in the mount that is called the mount of Olives. ³⁸And all the people came early in the morning to him in the temple, for to hear him.

22

¹Now the feast of unleavened bread drew near, which is called the Passover. ²And the chief priests and scribes sought how they might kill him; for they feared the people. ³Then entered Satan into Judas surnamed Iscariot, being of the number of the twelve. ⁴And he went his way, and communed with the chief priests and captains, how he might betray him to them. ⁵And they were glad, and covenanted to give him money. ⁶And he promised, and

sought opportunity to betray him to them in the absence of the multitude. ⁷Then came the day of unleavened bread, when the passover must be killed. ⁸And he sent Peter and John, saying, Go and prepare us the passover, that we may eat. ⁹And they said to him, Where will you that we prepare? ¹⁰And he said to them, Behold, when you are entered into the city, there shall a man meet you, bearing a pitcher of water; follow him into the house where he enters in. ¹¹And you shall say to the manager of the house, The Master says to you, Where is the guest room, where I shall eat the passover with my disciples? ¹²And he shall show you a large upper room furnished: there make ready. ¹³And they went, and found as he had said to them: and they made ready the passover. ¹⁴And when the hour was come, he sat down, and the twelve apostles with him. ¹⁵And he said to them, With desire I have desired to eat this passover with you before I suffer: ¹⁶For I say to you, I will not any more eat thereof, until it be fulfilled in the kingdom of God. ¹⁷And he took the cup, and gave thanks, and said, Take this, and divide it among yourselves: ¹⁸For I say to you, I will not drink of the fruit of the vine, until the kingdom of God shall come. ¹⁹And he took bread, and gave thanks, and broke it, and gave to them, saying, This is my body which is given for you: this do in remembrance of me. ²⁰Likewise also the cup after supper, saying, This cup is the new testament in my blood, which is shed for you. ²¹But, behold, the hand of him that betrays me is with me on the table. ²²And truly the Son of man goes, as it was determined: but woe to that man by whom he is betrayed! ²³And they began to inquire among themselves, which of them it was that should do this thing. ²⁴And there was also a strife among them, which of them should be accounted the greatest. ²⁵And he said to them, The kings of the Gentiles exercise lordship over them; and they that exercise authority on them are called benefactors. ²⁶But you shall not be so: but he that is greatest among you, let him be as the younger; and he that is chief, as he that does serve. ²⁷For whether is greater, he that sits at meat, or he that serves? is not he that sits at meat? but I am among you as he that serves. ²⁸You are they which have continued with me in my temptations. ²⁹And I appoint to you a kingdom, as my Father has appointed to me; ³⁰That you may eat and drink at my table in my kingdom, and sit on thrones judging the twelve tribes of Israel. ³¹And the Lord said, Simon, Simon, behold, Satan has desired to have you, that he may sift you as wheat: ³²But I have prayed for you, that your faith fail not: and when you are converted, strengthen your brothers. ³³And he said to him, Lord, I am ready to go with you, both into prison, and to death. ³⁴And he said, I tell you, Peter, the cock shall not crow this day, before that you shall thrice deny that you know me. ³⁵And he said to them, When I sent you without purse, and money, and shoes, lacked you any thing? And they said, Nothing. ³⁶Then said he to them, But now, he that has a purse, let him take it, and likewise his money; and he that has no sword, let him sell his garment, and buy one. ³⁷For I say to you, that this that is written must yet be accomplished in me, And he was reckoned among the transgressors: for the things concerning me have an end. ³⁸And they said, Lord, behold, here are two swords. And he said to them, It is enough. ³⁹And he came out, and went, as he was wont, to the mount of Olives; and his disciples also followed him. ⁴⁰And when he was at the place, he said to them, Pray that you enter not into temptation. ⁴¹And he was withdrawn from them about a stone's cast, and kneeled down, and prayed, ⁴²Saying, Father, if you be willing, remove this cup from me: nevertheless not my will, but yours, be done. ⁴³And there appeared an angel to him from heaven, strengthening him. ⁴⁴And being in an agony he prayed more earnestly: and his sweat was as it were great drops of blood falling down to the ground. ⁴⁵And when he rose up from prayer, and was come to his disciples, he found them sleeping for sorrow, ⁴⁶And said to them, Why sleep you? rise and pray, lest you enter into temptation. ⁴⁷And while he yet spoke, behold a multitude, and he that was called Judas, one of the twelve, went before them, and drew near to Jesus to kiss him. ⁴⁸But Jesus said to him, Judas, betray you the Son of man with a kiss? ⁴⁹When they which were about him saw what would follow, they said to him, Lord, shall we smite with the sword? ⁵⁰And one of them smote the servant of the high priest, and cut off his right ear. ⁵¹And Jesus answered and said, Suffer you thus far. And he touched his ear, and healed him. ⁵²Then Jesus said to the chief priests, and captains of the temple, and the elders, which were come to him, Be you come out, as against a thief, with swords and staves? ⁵³When I was daily with you in the temple, you stretched forth no hands against me: but this is your hour, and the power of darkness. ⁵⁴Then took they him, and led him, and brought him into the high priest's house. And Peter followed afar off. ⁵⁵And when they had kindled a fire in the middle of the hall, and were set down together, Peter sat down among them. ⁵⁶But a certain maid beheld him as he sat by the fire, and earnestly looked on him, and said, This man was also with him. ⁵⁷And he denied him, saying, Woman, I know him not. ⁵⁸And after a little while another saw him, and said, You are also of them. And Peter said, Man, I am not. ⁵⁹And about the space of one hour after another confidently affirmed, saying, Of a truth this fellow also was with him: for he is a Galilaean. ⁶⁰And Peter said, Man, I know not what you say. And immediately, while he yet spoke, the cock crew. ⁶¹And the Lord turned, and looked on Peter. And Peter remembered the word of the Lord, how he had said to him, Before the cock crow, you shall deny me thrice. ⁶²And Peter went out, and wept bitterly. ⁶³And the men that held Jesus mocked him, and smote him. ⁶⁴And when they had blindfolded him, they struck him on the face, and asked him, saying, Prophesy, who is it that smote you? ⁶⁵And many other things blasphemously spoke they against him. ⁶⁶And as soon as it was day, the elders of the people and the chief priests and the scribes came together, and led him into their council, saying, ⁶⁷Are you the Christ? tell us. And he said to them, If I tell you, you will not believe: ⁶⁸And if I also ask you, you will not answer me, nor let me go. ⁶⁹Hereafter shall the Son of man sit on the right hand of the power of God. ⁷⁰Then said they all, Are you then the Son of God? And he said to them, You say that I am. ⁷¹And they said, What need we any further witness? for we ourselves have heard of his own mouth.

23 ¹And the whole multitude of them arose, and led him to Pilate. ²And they began to accuse him, saying, We found this fellow perverting the nation, and forbidding to give tribute to Caesar, saying that he himself is Christ a King. ³And Pilate asked him, saying, Are you the King of the Jews? And he answered him and said, You say it. ⁴Then said Pilate to the chief priests and to the people, I find no fault in this man. ⁵And they were the more fierce, saying, He stirs up the people, teaching throughout all Jewry, beginning from Galilee to this place. ⁶When Pilate heard of Galilee, he asked whether the man were a Galilaean. ⁷And as soon as he knew that he belonged to Herod's jurisdiction, he sent him to Herod, who himself also was at Jerusalem at that time. ⁸And when Herod saw Jesus, he was exceeding glad: for he was desirous to see him of a long season, because he had heard many things of him; and he hoped to have seen some miracle done by him. ⁹Then he questioned with him in many words; but he answered him nothing. ¹⁰And the chief priests and scribes stood and vehemently accused him. ¹¹And Herod with his men of war set him at nothing, and mocked him, and arrayed him in a gorgeous robe, and sent him again to Pilate. ¹²And the same day Pilate and Herod were made friends together: for before they were at enmity between themselves. ¹³And Pilate, when he had called together the chief priests and the rulers and the people, ¹⁴Said to them, You have brought this man to me, as one that perverts the people: and, behold, I, having examined him before you, have found no fault in this man touching those things whereof you accuse him: ¹⁵No, nor yet Herod: for I sent you to him; and, see, nothing worthy of death is done to him. ¹⁶I will therefore chastise him, and release him. ¹⁷(For of necessity he must release one to them at the feast.) ¹⁸And they cried out all at once, saying, Away with this man, and release to us Barabbas: ¹⁹(Who for a certain sedition made in the city, and for murder, was cast into prison.) ²⁰Pilate therefore, willing to release Jesus, spoke again to them. ²¹But they cried, saying, Crucify him, crucify him. ²²And he said to them the third time, Why, what evil has he done? I have found no cause of death in him: I will therefore chastise him, and let him go. ²³And they were instant with loud voices, requiring that he might be crucified. And the voices of them and of the chief priests prevailed. ²⁴And Pilate gave sentence that it should be as they required. ²⁵And he released to them him that for sedition and murder was cast into prison, whom they had desired; but he delivered Jesus to their will. ²⁶And as they led him away, they laid hold on one Simon, a Cyrenian, coming out of the country, and on him they laid the cross, that he might bear it after Jesus. ²⁷And there followed him a great company of people, and of women, which also bewailed and lamented him. ²⁸But Jesus turning to them said, Daughters of Jerusalem, weep not for me, but weep for yourselves, and for your children. ²⁹For, behold, the days are coming, in the which they shall say, Blessed are the barren, and the wombs that never bore, and the breasts which never gave suck. ³⁰Then shall they begin to say to the mountains, Fall on us; and to the hills, Cover us. ³¹For if they do these things in a green tree, what shall be done in the dry? ³²And there were also two other, malefactors, led with him to be put to death. ³³And when they were come to the place, which is called Calvary, there they crucified him, and the malefactors, one on the right hand, and the other on the left. ³⁴Then said Jesus, Father, forgive them; for they know not what they do. And they parted his raiment, and cast lots. ³⁵And the people stood beholding. And the rulers also with them derided him, saying, He saved others; let him save himself, if he be Christ, the chosen of God. ³⁶And the soldiers also mocked him, coming to him, and offering him vinegar, ³⁷And saying, If you be the king of the Jews, save yourself. ³⁸And a superscription also was written over him in letters of Greek, and Latin, and Hebrew, THIS IS THE KING OF THE JEWS. ³⁹And one of the malefactors which were hanged railed on him, saying, If you be Christ, save yourself and us. ⁴⁰But the other answering rebuked him, saying, Do not you fear God, seeing you are in the same condemnation? ⁴¹And we indeed justly; for we receive the due reward of our deeds: but this man has done nothing amiss. ⁴²And he said to Jesus, Lord, remember me when you come into your kingdom. ⁴³And Jesus said to him, Truly I say to you, To day shall you be with me in paradise. ⁴⁴And it was about the sixth hour, and there was a darkness over all the earth until the ninth hour. ⁴⁵And the sun was darkened, and the veil of the temple was rent in the middle. ⁴⁶And when Jesus had cried with a loud voice, he said, Father, into your hands I commend my spirit: and having said thus, he gave up the ghost. ⁴⁷Now when the centurion saw what was done, he glorified God, saying, Certainly this was a righteous man. ⁴⁸And all the people that came together to that sight, beholding the things which were done, smote their breasts, and returned. ⁴⁹And all his acquaintance, and the women that followed him from Galilee, stood afar off, beholding these things. ⁵⁰And, behold, there was a man named Joseph, a counselor; and he was a good man, and a just: ⁵¹(The same had not consented to the counsel and deed of them;) he was of Arimathaea, a city of the Jews: who also himself waited for the kingdom of God. ⁵²This man went to Pilate, and begged the body of Jesus. ⁵³And he took it down, and wrapped it in linen, and laid it in a sepulcher that was hewn in stone, wherein never man before was laid. ⁵⁴And that day was the preparation, and the sabbath drew on. ⁵⁵And the women also, which came with him from Galilee, followed after, and beheld the sepulcher, and how his body was laid. ⁵⁶And they returned, and prepared spices and ointments; and rested the sabbath day according to the commandment.

24 ¹Now on the first day of the week, very early in the morning, they came to the sepulcher, bringing the spices which they had prepared, and certain others with them. ²And they found the stone rolled away from the sepulcher. ³And they entered in, and found not the body of the Lord Jesus. ⁴And it came to pass, as they were much perplexed thereabout, behold, two men stood by them in shining garments: ⁵And as they were afraid, and bowed down their faces to the earth, they said to them, Why seek you the living among the dead? ⁶He is not here, but is risen: remember how he spoke to you when he was yet in Galilee, ⁷Saying, The Son of man must be delivered into the hands of sinful men, and be crucified, and the third day rise again.

⁸And they remembered his words, ⁹And returned from the sepulcher, and told all these things to the eleven, and to all the rest. ¹⁰It was Mary Magdalene and Joanna, and Mary the mother of James, and other women that were with them, which told these things to the apostles. ¹¹And their words seemed to them as idle tales, and they believed them not. ¹²Then arose Peter, and ran to the sepulcher; and stooping down, he beheld the linen clothes laid by themselves, and departed, wondering in himself at that which was come to pass. ¹³And, behold, two of them went that same day to a village called Emmaus, which was from Jerusalem about three score furlongs. ¹⁴And they talked together of all these things which had happened. ¹⁵And it came to pass, that, while they communed together and reasoned, Jesus himself drew near, and went with them. ¹⁶But their eyes were held that they should not know him. ¹⁷And he said to them, What manner of communications are these that you have one to another, as you walk, and are sad? ¹⁸And the one of them, whose name was Cleopas, answering said to him, Are you only a stranger in Jerusalem, and have not known the things which are come to pass there in these days? ¹⁹And he said to them, What things? And they said to him, Concerning Jesus of Nazareth, which was a prophet mighty in deed and word before God and all the people: ²⁰And how the chief priests and our rulers delivered him to be condemned to death, and have crucified him. ²¹But we trusted that it had been he which should have redeemed Israel: and beside all this, to day is the third day since these things were done. ²²Yes, and certain women also of our company made us astonished, which were early at the sepulcher; ²³And when they found not his body, they came, saying, that they had also seen a vision of angels, which said that he was alive. ²⁴And certain of them which were with us went to the sepulcher, and found it even so as the women had said: but him they saw not. ²⁵Then he said to them, O fools, and slow of heart to believe all that the prophets have spoken: ²⁶Ought not Christ to have suffered these things, and to enter into his glory? ²⁷And beginning at Moses and all the prophets, he expounded to them in all the scriptures the things concerning himself. ²⁸And they drew near to the village, where they went: and he made as though he would have gone further. ²⁹But they constrained him, saying, Abide with us: for it is toward evening, and the day is far spent. And he went in to tarry with them. ³⁰And it came to pass, as he sat at meat with them, he took bread, and blessed it, and broke, and gave to them. ³¹And their eyes were opened, and they knew him; and he vanished out of their sight. ³²And they said one to another, Did not our heart burn within us, while he talked with us by the way, and while he opened to us the scriptures? ³³And they rose up the same hour, and returned to Jerusalem, and found the eleven gathered together, and them that were with them, ³⁴Saying, The Lord is risen indeed, and has appeared to Simon. ³⁵And they told what things were done in the way, and how he was known of them in breaking of bread. ³⁶And as they thus spoke, Jesus himself stood in the middle of them, and says to them, Peace be to you. ³⁷But they were terrified and affrighted, and supposed that they had seen a spirit. ³⁸And he said to them, Why are you troubled? and why do thoughts arise in your hearts? ³⁹Behold my hands and my feet, that it is I myself: handle me, and see; for a spirit has not flesh and bones, as you see me have. ⁴⁰And when he had thus spoken, he showed them his hands and his feet. ⁴¹And while they yet believed not for joy, and wondered, he said to them, Have you here any meat? ⁴²And they gave him a piece of a broiled fish, and of an honeycomb. ⁴³And he took it, and did eat before them. ⁴⁴And he said to them, These are the words which I spoke to you, while I was yet with you, that all things must be fulfilled, which were written in the law of Moses, and in the prophets, and in the psalms, concerning me. ⁴⁵Then opened he their understanding, that they might understand the scriptures, ⁴⁶And said to them, Thus it is written, and thus it behooved Christ to suffer, and to rise from the dead the third day: ⁴⁷And that repentance and remission of sins should be preached in his name among all nations, beginning at Jerusalem. ⁴⁸And you are witnesses of these things. ⁴⁹And, behold, I send the promise of my Father on you: but tarry you in the city of Jerusalem, until you be endued with power from on high. ⁵⁰And he led them out as far as to Bethany, and he lifted up his hands, and blessed them. ⁵¹And it came to pass, while he blessed them, he was parted from them, and carried up into heaven. ⁵²And they worshipped him, and returned to Jerusalem with great joy: ⁵³And were continually in the temple, praising and blessing God. Amen.

John

1 ¹In the beginning was the Word, and the Word was with God, and the Word was God. ²The same was in the beginning with God. ³All things were made by him; and without him was not any thing made that was made. ⁴In him was life; and the life was the light of men. ⁵And the light shines in darkness; and the darkness comprehended it not. ⁶There was a man sent from God, whose name was John. ⁷The same came for a witness, to bear witness of the Light, that all men through him might believe. ⁸He was not that Light, but was sent to bear witness of that Light. ⁹That was the true Light, which lights every man that comes into the world. ¹⁰He was in the world, and the world was made by him, and the world knew him not. ¹¹He came to his own, and his own received him not. ¹²But as many as received him, to them gave he power to become the sons of God, even to them that believe on his name: ¹³Which were born, not of blood, nor of the will of the flesh, nor of the will of man, but of God. ¹⁴And the Word was made flesh, and dwelled among us, (and we beheld his glory, the glory as of the only begotten of the Father,) full of grace and truth. ¹⁵John bore witness of him, and cried, saying, This was he of whom I spoke, He that comes after me is preferred before me: for he was before me. ¹⁶And of his fullness have all we received, and grace for grace. ¹⁷For the law was given by Moses, but grace and truth came by Jesus Christ. ¹⁸No man has seen God at any time, the only begotten Son, which is in the bosom of the Father, he has declared him. ¹⁹And this is the record of John, when the Jews sent priests and Levites from Jerusalem to ask him, Who are you? ²⁰And he confessed, and denied not; but confessed, I am not the Christ. ²¹And they asked him, What then? Are you Elias? And he says, I am not. Are you that prophet? And he answered, No. ²²Then said they to him, Who are you? that we may give an answer to them that sent us. What say you of yourself? ²³He said, I am the voice of one crying in the wilderness, Make straight the way of the Lord, as said the prophet Isaiah. ²⁴And they which were sent were of the Pharisees. ²⁵And they asked him, and said to him, Why baptize you then, if you be not that Christ, nor Elias, neither that prophet? ²⁶John answered them, saying, I baptize with water: but there stands one among you, whom you know not; ²⁷He it is, who coming after me is preferred before me, whose shoe's lace I am not worthy to unloose. ²⁸These things were done in Bethabara beyond Jordan, where John was baptizing. ²⁹The next day John sees Jesus coming to him, and says, Behold the Lamb of God, which takes away the sin of the world. ³⁰This is he of whom I said, After me comes a man which is preferred before me: for he was before me. ³¹And I knew him not: but that he should be made manifest to Israel, therefore am I come baptizing with water. ³²And John bore record, saying, I saw the Spirit descending from heaven like a dove, and it stayed on him. ³³And I knew him not: but he that sent me to baptize with water, the same said to me, On whom you shall see the Spirit descending, and remaining on him, the same is he which baptizes with the Holy Ghost. ³⁴And I saw, and bore record that this is the Son of God. ³⁵Again the next day after John stood, and two of his disciples; ³⁶And looking on Jesus as he walked, he says, Behold the Lamb of God! ³⁷And the two disciples heard him speak, and they followed Jesus. ³⁸Then Jesus turned, and saw them following, and says to them, What seek you? They said to him, Rabbi, (which is to say, being interpreted, Master,) where dwell you? ³⁹He says to them, Come and see. They came and saw where he dwelled, and stayed with him that day: for it was about the tenth hour. ⁴⁰One of the two which heard John speak, and followed him, was Andrew, Simon Peter's brother. ⁴¹He first finds his own brother Simon, and says to him, We have found the Messias, which is, being interpreted, the Christ. ⁴²And he brought him to Jesus. And when Jesus beheld him, he said, You are Simon the son of Jona: you shall be called Cephas, which is by interpretation, A stone. ⁴³The day following Jesus would go forth into Galilee, and finds Philip, and says to him, Follow me. ⁴⁴Now Philip was of Bethsaida, the city of Andrew and Peter. ⁴⁵Philip finds Nathanael, and says to him, We have found him, of whom Moses in the law, and the prophets, did write, Jesus of Nazareth, the son of Joseph. ⁴⁶And Nathanael says to him, Can there any good thing come out of Nazareth? Philip said to him, Come and see. ⁴⁷Jesus saw Nathanael coming to him, and says of him, Behold an Israelite indeed, in whom is no guile! ⁴⁸Nathanael says to him, From where know you me? Jesus answered and said to him, Before that Philip called you, when you were under the fig tree, I saw you. ⁴⁹Nathanael answered and says to him, Rabbi, you are the Son of God; you are the King of Israel. ⁵⁰Jesus answered and said to him, Because I said to you, I saw you under the fig tree, believe you? you shall see greater things than these. ⁵¹And he says to him, Truly, truly, I say to you, Hereafter you shall see heaven open, and the angels of God ascending and descending on the Son of man.

2 ¹And the third day there was a marriage in Cana of Galilee; and the mother of Jesus was there: ²And both Jesus was called, and his disciples, to the marriage. ³And when they wanted wine, the mother of Jesus says to him, They have no wine. ⁴Jesus says to her, Woman, what have I to do with you? my hour is not yet come. ⁵His mother says to the servants, Whatever he said to you, do it. ⁶And there were set there six water pots of stone, after the manner of the purifying of the Jews, containing two or three firkins apiece. ⁷Jesus says to them, Fill the water pots with water. And they filled them up to the brim. ⁸And he says to them, Draw out now, and bear to the governor of the feast. And they bore it. ⁹When the ruler of the feast had tasted the water that was made wine, and knew not from where it was: (but the servants which drew the water knew;) the governor of the feast called the bridegroom, ¹⁰And says to him, Every man at the beginning does set forth good wine; and when men have well drunk, then that which is worse: but you have kept the good wine until now. ¹¹This beginning of miracles did Jesus in Cana of Galilee, and manifested forth his glory; and his disciples believed on him. ¹²After this he went down to Capernaum, he, and his mother, and his brothers, and his disciples: and they continued there not many days. ¹³And the Jews' passover was at hand, and Jesus went up to Jerusalem.

¹⁴And found in the temple those that sold oxen and sheep and doves, and the changers of money sitting: ¹⁵And when he had made a whip of small cords, he drove them all out of the temple, and the sheep, and the oxen; and poured out the changers' money, and overthrew the tables; ¹⁶And said to them that sold doves, Take these things hence; make not my Father's house an house of merchandise. ¹⁷And his disciples remembered that it was written, The zeal of your house has eaten me up. ¹⁸Then answered the Jews and said to him, What sign show you to us, seeing that you do these things? ¹⁹Jesus answered and said to them, Destroy this temple, and in three days I will raise it up. ²⁰Then said the Jews, Forty and six years was this temple in building, and will you raise it up in three days? ²¹But he spoke of the temple of his body. ²²When therefore he was risen from the dead, his disciples remembered that he had said this to them; and they believed the scripture, and the word which Jesus had said. ²³Now when he was in Jerusalem at the passover, in the feast day, many believed in his name, when they saw the miracles which he did. ²⁴But Jesus did not commit himself to them, because he knew all men, ²⁵And needed not that any should testify of man: for he knew what was in man.

3 ¹There was a man of the Pharisees, named Nicodemus, a ruler of the Jews: ²The same came to Jesus by night, and said to him, Rabbi, we know that you are a teacher come from God: for no man can do these miracles that you do, except God be with him. ³Jesus answered and said to him, Truly, truly, I say to you, Except a man be born again, he cannot see the kingdom of God. ⁴Nicodemus says to him, How can a man be born when he is old? can he enter the second time into his mother's womb, and be born? ⁵Jesus answered, Truly, truly, I say to you, Except a man be born of water and of the Spirit, he cannot enter into the kingdom of God. ⁶That which is born of the flesh is flesh; and that which is born of the Spirit is spirit. ⁷Marvel not that I said to you, You must be born again. ⁸The wind blows where it wants, and you hear the sound thereof, but can not tell from where it comes, and where it goes: so is every one that is born of the Spirit. ⁹Nicodemus answered and said to him, How can these things be? ¹⁰Jesus answered and said to him, Are you a master of Israel, and know not these things? ¹¹Truly, truly, I say to you, We speak that we do know, and testify that we have seen; and you receive not our witness. ¹²If I have told you earthly things, and you believe not, how shall you believe, if I tell you of heavenly things? ¹³And no man has ascended up to heaven, but he that came down from heaven, even the Son of man which is in heaven. ¹⁴And as Moses lifted up the serpent in the wilderness, even so must the Son of man be lifted up: ¹⁵That whoever believes in him should not perish, but have eternal life. ¹⁶For God so loved the world, that he gave his only begotten Son, that whoever believes in him should not perish, but have everlasting life. ¹⁷For God sent not his Son into the world to condemn the world; but that the world through him might be saved. ¹⁸He that believes on him is not condemned: but he that believes not is condemned already, because he has not believed in the name of the only begotten Son of God. ¹⁹And this is the condemnation, that light is come into the world, and men loved darkness rather than light, because their deeds were evil. ²⁰For every one that does evil hates the light, neither comes to the light, lest his deeds should be reproved. ²¹But he that does truth comes to the light, that his deeds may be made manifest, that they are worked in God. ²²After these things came Jesus and his disciples into the land of Judaea; and there he tarried with them, and baptized. ²³And John also was baptizing in Aenon near to Salim, because there was much water there: and they came, and were baptized. ²⁴For John was not yet cast into prison. ²⁵Then there arose a question between some of John's disciples and the Jews about purifying. ²⁶And they came to John, and said to him, Rabbi, he that was with you beyond Jordan, to whom you bore witness, behold, the same baptizes, and all men come to him. ²⁷John answered and said, A man can receive nothing, except it be given him from heaven. ²⁸You yourselves bear me witness, that I said, I am not the Christ, but that I am sent before him. ²⁹He that has the bride is the bridegroom: but the friend of the bridegroom, which stands and hears him, rejoices greatly because of the bridegroom's voice: this my joy therefore is fulfilled. ³⁰He must increase, but I must decrease. ³¹He that comes from above is above all: he that is of the earth is earthly, and speaks of the earth: he that comes from heaven is above all. ³²And what he has seen and heard, that he testifies; and no man receives his testimony. ³³He that has received his testimony has set to his seal that God is true. ³⁴For he whom God has sent speaks the words of God: for God gives not the Spirit by measure to him. ³⁵The Father loves the Son, and has given all things into his hand. ³⁶He that believes on the Son has everlasting life: and he that believes not the Son shall not see life; but the wrath of God stays on him.

4 ¹When therefore the LORD knew how the Pharisees had heard that Jesus made and baptized more disciples than John, ²(Though Jesus himself baptized not, but his disciples,) ³He left Judaea, and departed again into Galilee. ⁴And he must needs go through Samaria. ⁵Then comes he to a city of Samaria, which is called Sychar, near to the parcel of ground that Jacob gave to his son Joseph. ⁶Now Jacob's well was there. Jesus therefore, being wearied with his journey, sat thus on the well: and it was about the sixth hour. ⁷There comes a woman of Samaria to draw water: Jesus says to her, Give me to drink. ⁸(For his disciples were gone away to the city to buy meat.) ⁹Then says the woman of Samaria to him, How is it that you, being a Jew, ask drink of me, which am a woman of Samaria? for the Jews have no dealings with the Samaritans. ¹⁰Jesus answered and said to her, If you knew the gift of God, and who it is that says to you, Give me to drink; you would have asked of him, and he would have given you living water. ¹¹The woman says to him, Sir, you have nothing to draw with, and the well is deep: from where then have you that living water? ¹²Are you greater than our father Jacob, which gave us the well, and drank thereof himself, and his children, and his cattle? ¹³Jesus answered and said to her, Whoever drinks of this water shall thirst again: ¹⁴But whoever drinks of the water that I shall give him shall never thirst; but the water that I shall give him shall be in him a well of water springing up into everlasting life. ¹⁵The woman says to him, Sir, give me this water, that I thirst not, neither come here to draw.

¹⁶Jesus says to her, Go, call your husband, and come here. ¹⁷The woman answered and said, I have no husband. Jesus said to her, You have well said, I have no husband: ¹⁸For you have had five husbands; and he whom you now have is not your husband: in that said you truly. ¹⁹The woman says to him, Sir, I perceive that you are a prophet. ²⁰Our fathers worshipped in this mountain; and you say, that in Jerusalem is the place where men ought to worship. ²¹Jesus says to her, Woman, believe me, the hour comes, when you shall neither in this mountain, nor yet at Jerusalem, worship the Father. ²²You worship you know not what: we know what we worship: for salvation is of the Jews. ²³But the hour comes, and now is, when the true worshippers shall worship the Father in spirit and in truth: for the Father seeks such to worship him. ²⁴God is a Spirit: and they that worship him must worship him in spirit and in truth. ²⁵The woman says to him, I know that Messias comes, which is called Christ: when he is come, he will tell us all things. ²⁶Jesus says to her, I that speak to you am he. ²⁷And on this came his disciples, and marveled that he talked with the woman: yet no man said, What seek you? or, Why talk you with her? ²⁸The woman then left her water pot, and went her way into the city, and says to the men, ²⁹Come, see a man, which told me all things that ever I did: is not this the Christ? ³⁰Then they went out of the city, and came to him. ³¹In the mean while his disciples prayed him, saying, Master, eat. ³²But he said to them, I have meat to eat that you know not of. ³³Therefore says the disciples one to another, Has any man brought him something to eat? ³⁴Jesus said to them, My meat is to do the will of him that sent me, and to finish his work. ³⁵Say not you, There are yet four months, and then comes harvest? behold, I say to you, Lift up your eyes, and look on the fields; for they are white already to harvest. ³⁶And he that reaps receives wages, and gathers fruit to life eternal: that both he that sows and he that reaps may rejoice together. ³⁷And herein is that saying true, One sows, and another reaps. ³⁸I sent you to reap that where on you bestowed no labor: other men labored, and you are entered into their labors. ³⁹And many of the Samaritans of that city believed on him for the saying of the woman, which testified, He told me all that ever I did. ⁴⁰So when the Samaritans were come to him, they sought him that he would tarry with them: and he stayed there two days. ⁴¹And many more believed because of his own word; ⁴²And said to the woman, Now we believe, not because of your saying: for we have heard him ourselves, and know that this is indeed the Christ, the Savior of the world. ⁴³Now after two days he departed there, and went into Galilee. ⁴⁴For Jesus himself testified, that a prophet has no honor in his own country. ⁴⁵Then when he was come into Galilee, the Galilaeans received him, having seen all the things that he did at Jerusalem at the feast: for they also went to the feast. ⁴⁶So Jesus came again into Cana of Galilee, where he made the water wine. And there was a certain nobleman, whose son was sick at Capernaum. ⁴⁷When he heard that Jesus was come out of Judaea into Galilee, he went to him, and sought him that he would come down, and heal his son: for he was at the point of death. ⁴⁸Then said Jesus to him, Except you see signs and wonders, you will not believe. ⁴⁹The nobleman says to him, Sir, come down before my child dies. ⁵⁰Jesus says to him, Go your way; your son lives. And the man believed the word that Jesus had spoken to him, and he went his way. ⁵¹And as he was now going down, his servants met him, and told him, saying, Your son lives. ⁵²Then inquired he of them the hour when he began to amend. And they said to him, Yesterday at the seventh hour the fever left him. ⁵³So the father knew that it was at the same hour, in the which Jesus said to him, Your son lives: and himself believed, and his whole house. ⁵⁴This is again the second miracle that Jesus did, when he was come out of Judaea into Galilee.

5 ¹After this there was a feast of the Jews; and Jesus went up to Jerusalem. ²Now there is at Jerusalem by the sheep market a pool, which is called in the Hebrew tongue Bethesda, having five porches. ³In these lay a great multitude of weak folk, of blind, halt, withered, waiting for the moving of the water. ⁴For an angel went down at a certain season into the pool, and troubled the water: whoever then first after the troubling of the water stepped in was made whole of whatever disease he had. ⁵And a certain man was there, which had an infirmity thirty and eight years. ⁶When Jesus saw him lie, and knew that he had been now a long time in that case, he says to him, Will you be made whole? ⁷The weak man answered him, Sir, I have no man, when the water is troubled, to put me into the pool: but while I am coming, another steps down before me. ⁸Jesus says to him, Rise, take up your bed, and walk. ⁹And immediately the man was made whole, and took up his bed, and walked: and on the same day was the sabbath. ¹⁰The Jews therefore said to him that was cured, It is the sabbath day: it is not lawful for you to carry your bed. ¹¹He answered them, He that made me whole, the same said to me, Take up your bed, and walk. ¹²Then asked they him, What man is that which said to you, Take up your bed, and walk? ¹³And he that was healed knew not who it was: for Jesus had conveyed himself away, a multitude being in that place. ¹⁴Afterward Jesus finds him in the temple, and said to him, Behold, you are made whole: sin no more, lest a worse thing come to you. ¹⁵The man departed, and told the Jews that it was Jesus, which had made him whole. ¹⁶And therefore did the Jews persecute Jesus, and sought to slay him, because he had done these things on the sabbath day. ¹⁷But Jesus answered them, My Father works till now, and I work. ¹⁸Therefore the Jews sought the more to kill him, because he not only had broken the sabbath, but said also that God was his Father, making himself equal with God. ¹⁹Then answered Jesus and said to them, Truly, truly, I say to you, The Son can do nothing of himself, but what he sees the Father do: for what things soever he does, these also does the Son likewise. ²⁰For the Father loves the Son, and shows him all things that himself does: and he will show him greater works than these, that you may marvel. ²¹For as the Father raises up the dead, and vivifies them; even so the Son vivifies whom he will. ²²For the Father judges no man, but has committed all judgment to the Son: ²³That all men should honor the Son, even as they honor the Father. He that honors not the Son honors not the Father which has sent him. ²⁴Truly, truly, I say to you, He that hears my word, and believes on him that sent me, has everlasting life, and shall not come into

condemnation; but is passed from death to life. ²⁵Truly, truly, I say to you, The hour is coming, and now is, when the dead shall hear the voice of the Son of God: and they that hear shall live. ²⁶For as the Father has life in himself; so has he given to the Son to have life in himself; ²⁷And has given him authority to execute judgment also, because he is the Son of man. ²⁸Marvel not at this: for the hour is coming, in the which all that are in the graves shall hear his voice, ²⁹And shall come forth; they that have done good, to the resurrection of life; and they that have done evil, to the resurrection of damnation. ³⁰I can of my own self do nothing: as I hear, I judge: and my judgment is just; because I seek not my own will, but the will of the Father which has sent me. ³¹If I bear witness of myself, my witness is not true. ³²There is another that bears witness of me; and I know that the witness which he witnesses of me is true. ³³You sent to John, and he bore witness to the truth. ³⁴But I receive not testimony from man: but these things I say, that you might be saved. ³⁵He was a burning and a shining light: and you were willing for a season to rejoice in his light. ³⁶But I have greater witness than that of John: for the works which the Father has given me to finish, the same works that I do, bear witness of me, that the Father has sent me. ³⁷And the Father himself, which has sent me, has borne witness of me. You have neither heard his voice at any time, nor seen his shape. ³⁸And you have not his word abiding in you: for whom he has sent, him you believe not. ³⁹Search the scriptures; for in them you think you have eternal life: and they are they which testify of me. ⁴⁰And you will not come to me, that you might have life. ⁴¹I receive not honor from men. ⁴²But I know you, that you have not the love of God in you. ⁴³I am come in my Father's name, and you receive me not: if another shall come in his own name, him you will receive. ⁴⁴How can you believe, which receive honor one of another, and seek not the honor that comes from God only? ⁴⁵Do not think that I will accuse you to the Father: there is one that accuses you, even Moses, in whom you trust. ⁴⁶For had you believed Moses, you would have believed me; for he wrote of me. ⁴⁷But if you believe not his writings, how shall you believe my words?

6 ¹After these things Jesus went over the sea of Galilee, which is the sea of Tiberias. ²And a great multitude followed him, because they saw his miracles which he did on them that were diseased. ³And Jesus went up into a mountain, and there he sat with his disciples. ⁴And the passover, a feast of the Jews, was near. ⁵When Jesus then lifted up his eyes, and saw a great company come to him, he says to Philip, From where shall we buy bread, that these may eat? ⁶And this he said to prove him: for he himself knew what he would do. ⁷Philip answered him, Two hundred pennyworth of bread is not sufficient for them, that every one of them may take a little. ⁸One of his disciples, Andrew, Simon Peter's brother, says to him, ⁹There is a lad here, which has five barley loaves, and two small fishes: but what are they among so many? ¹⁰And Jesus said, Make the men sit down. Now there was much grass in the place. So the men sat down, in number about five thousand. ¹¹And Jesus took the loaves; and when he had given thanks, he distributed to the disciples, and the disciples to them that were set down; and likewise of the fishes as much as they would. ¹²When they were filled, he said to his disciples, Gather up the fragments that remain, that nothing be lost. ¹³Therefore they gathered them together, and filled twelve baskets with the fragments of the five barley loaves, which remained over and above to them that had eaten. ¹⁴Then those men, when they had seen the miracle that Jesus did, said, This is of a truth that prophet that should come into the world. ¹⁵When Jesus therefore perceived that they would come and take him by force, to make him a king, he departed again into a mountain himself alone. ¹⁶And when even was now come, his disciples went down to the sea, ¹⁷And entered into a ship, and went over the sea toward Capernaum. And it was now dark, and Jesus was not come to them. ¹⁸And the sea arose by reason of a great wind that blew. ¹⁹So when they had rowed about five and twenty or thirty furlongs, they see Jesus walking on the sea, and drawing near to the ship: and they were afraid. ²⁰But he says to them, It is I; be not afraid. ²¹Then they willingly received him into the ship: and immediately the ship was at the land where they went. ²²The day following, when the people which stood on the other side of the sea saw that there was none other boat there, save that one into where his disciples were entered, and that Jesus went not with his disciples into the boat, but that his disciples were gone away alone; ²³(However, there came other boats from Tiberias near to the place where they did eat bread, after that the Lord had given thanks:) ²⁴When the people therefore saw that Jesus was not there, neither his disciples, they also took shipping, and came to Capernaum, seeking for Jesus. ²⁵And when they had found him on the other side of the sea, they said to him, Rabbi, when came you here? ²⁶Jesus answered them and said, Truly, truly, I say to you, You seek me, not because you saw the miracles, but because you did eat of the loaves, and were filled. ²⁷Labor not for the meat which perishes, but for that meat which endures to everlasting life, which the Son of man shall give to you: for him has God the Father sealed. ²⁸Then said they to him, What shall we do, that we might work the works of God? ²⁹Jesus answered and said to them, This is the work of God, that you believe on him whom he has sent. ³⁰They said therefore to him, What sign show you then, that we may see, and believe you? what do you work? ³¹Our fathers did eat manna in the desert; as it is written, He gave them bread from heaven to eat. ³²Then Jesus said to them, Truly, truly, I say to you, Moses gave you not that bread from heaven; but my Father gives you the true bread from heaven. ³³For the bread of God is he which comes down from heaven, and gives life to the world. ³⁴Then said they to him, Lord, ever more give us this bread. ³⁵And Jesus said to them, I am the bread of life: he that comes to me shall never hunger; and he that believes on me shall never thirst. ³⁶But I said to you, That you also have seen me, and believe not. ³⁷All that the Father gives me shall come to me; and him that comes to me I will in no wise cast out. ³⁸For I came down from heaven, not to do my own will, but the will of him that sent me. ³⁹And this is the Father's will which has sent me, that of all which he has given me I should lose nothing, but should raise it up again at the last day. ⁴⁰And this is the will of him that sent me, that every one which sees the Son, and believes on him, may have everlasting life: and I will raise him up at the last day. ⁴¹The Jews then murmured at him, because he said, I am the bread which came down from heaven. ⁴²And they said, Is not this Jesus, the son of Joseph, whose father and mother we know? how is it then that he says, I came down from heaven? ⁴³Jesus therefore answered and said to them, Murmur not among yourselves. ⁴⁴No man can come to me, except the Father which has sent me draw him: and I will raise him up at the last day. ⁴⁵It is written in the prophets, And they shall be all taught of God. Every man therefore that has heard, and has learned of the Father, comes to me. ⁴⁶Not that any man has seen the Father, save he which is of God, he has seen the Father. ⁴⁷Truly, truly, I say to you, He that believes on me has everlasting life. ⁴⁸I am that bread of life. ⁴⁹Your fathers did eat manna in the wilderness, and are dead. ⁵⁰This is the bread which comes down from heaven, that a man may eat thereof, and not die. ⁵¹I am the living bread which came down from heaven: if any man eat of this bread, he shall live for ever: and the bread that I will give is my flesh, which I will give for the life of the world. ⁵²The Jews therefore strove among themselves, saying, How can this man give us his flesh to eat? ⁵³Then Jesus said to them, Truly, truly, I say to you, Except you eat the flesh of the Son of man, and drink his blood, you have no life in you. ⁵⁴Whoever eats my flesh, and drinks my blood, has eternal life; and I will raise him up at the last day. ⁵⁵For my flesh is meat indeed, and my blood is drink indeed. ⁵⁶He that eats my flesh, and drinks my blood, dwells in me, and I in him. ⁵⁷As the living Father has sent me, and I live by the Father: so he that eats me, even he shall live by me. ⁵⁸This is that bread which came down from heaven: not as your fathers did eat manna, and are dead: he that eats of this bread shall live for ever. ⁵⁹These things said he in the synagogue, as he taught in Capernaum. ⁶⁰Many therefore of his disciples, when they had heard this, said, This is an hard saying; who can hear it? ⁶¹When Jesus knew in himself that his disciples murmured at it, he said to them, Does this offend you? ⁶²What and if you shall see the Son of man ascend up where he was before? ⁶³It is the spirit that vivifies; the flesh profits nothing: the words that I speak to you, they are spirit, and they are life. ⁶⁴But there are some of you that believe not. For Jesus knew from the beginning who they were that believed not, and who should betray him. ⁶⁵And he said, Therefore said I to you, that no man can come to me, except it were given to him of my Father. ⁶⁶From that time many of his disciples went back, and walked no more with him. ⁶⁷Then said Jesus to the twelve, Will you also go away? ⁶⁸Then Simon Peter answered him, Lord, to whom shall we go? you have the words of eternal life. ⁶⁹And we believe and are sure that you are that Christ, the Son of the living God. ⁷⁰Jesus answered them, Have not I chosen you twelve, and one of you is a devil? ⁷¹He spoke of Judas Iscariot the son of Simon: for he it was that should betray him, being one of the twelve.

7 ¹After these things Jesus walked in Galilee: for he would not walk in Jewry, because the Jews sought to kill him. ²Now the Jew's feast of tabernacles was at hand. ³His brothers therefore said to him, Depart hence, and go into Judaea, that your disciples also may see the works that you do. ⁴For there is no man that does any thing in secret, and he himself seeks to be known openly. If you do these things, show yourself to the world. ⁵For neither did his brothers believe in him. ⁶Then Jesus said to them, My time is not yet come: but your time is always ready. ⁷The world cannot hate you; but me it hates, because I testify of it, that the works thereof are evil. ⁸Go you up to this feast: I go not up yet to this feast: for my time is not yet full come. ⁹When he had said these words to them, he stayed still in Galilee. ¹⁰But when his brothers were gone up, then went he also up to the feast, not openly, but as it were in secret. ¹¹Then the Jews sought him at the feast, and said, Where is he? ¹²And there was much murmuring among the people concerning him: for some said, He is a good man: others said, No; but he deceives the people. ¹³However, no man spoke openly of him for fear of the Jews. ¹⁴Now about the middle of the feast Jesus went up into the temple, and taught. ¹⁵And the Jews marveled, saying, How knows this man letters, having never learned? ¹⁶Jesus answered them, and said, My doctrine is not mine, but his that sent me. ¹⁷If any man will do his will, he shall know of the doctrine, whether it be of God, or whether I speak of myself. ¹⁸He that speaks of himself seeks his own glory: but he that seeks his glory that sent him, the same is true, and no unrighteousness is in him. ¹⁹Did not Moses give you the law, and yet none of you keeps the law? Why go you about to kill me? ²⁰The people answered and said, You have a devil: who goes about to kill you? ²¹Jesus answered and said to them, I have done one work, and you all marvel. ²²Moses therefore gave to you circumcision; (not because it is of Moses, but of the fathers;) and you on the sabbath day circumcise a man. ²³If a man on the sabbath day receive circumcision, that the law of Moses should not be broken; are you angry at me, because I have made a man every whit whole on the sabbath day? ²⁴Judge not according to the appearance, but judge righteous judgment. ²⁵Then said some of them of Jerusalem, Is not this he, whom they seek to kill? ²⁶But, see, he speaks boldly, and they say nothing to him. Do the rulers know indeed that this is the very Christ? ²⁷However, we know this man from where he is: but when Christ comes, no man knows from where he is. ²⁸Then cried Jesus in the temple as he taught, saying, You both know me, and you know from where I am: and I am not come of myself, but he that sent me is true, whom you know not. ²⁹But I know him: for I am from him, and he has sent me. ³⁰Then they sought to take him: but no man laid hands on him, because his hour was not yet come. ³¹And many of the people believed on him, and said, When Christ comes, will he do more miracles than these which this man has done? ³²The Pharisees heard that the people murmured such things concerning him; and the Pharisees and the chief priests sent officers to take him. ³³Then said Jesus to them, Yet a little while am I with you, and then I go to him that sent me. ³⁴You shall seek me, and shall not find me: and where I am, thither you cannot come. ³⁵Then said the Jews among themselves, Where will he go, that we shall not find him? will he go to the dispersed among the Gentiles, and teach the Gentiles? ³⁶What manner of saying is this that he said, You shall seek me, and shall not find me: and where I am, thither you cannot come? ³⁷In the last day, that great day of the feast, Jesus stood and cried, saying, If any man thirst, let him come to me, and drink. ³⁸He that believes on me, as the scripture has said, out of his belly shall flow rivers of living water. ³⁹(But this spoke he of the Spirit, which they that believe on him should receive: for the Holy Ghost was not yet given; because that Jesus was not yet glorified.) ⁴⁰Many of the people therefore, when they heard this saying, said, Of a truth this is the Prophet. ⁴¹Others said, This is the Christ. But some said, Shall Christ come out of Galilee? ⁴²Has not the scripture said, That Christ comes of the seed of David, and out of the town of Bethlehem, where David was? ⁴³So there was a division among the people because of him. ⁴⁴And some of them would have taken him; but no man laid hands on him. ⁴⁵Then came the officers to the chief priests and Pharisees; and they said to them, Why have you not brought him? ⁴⁶The officers answered, Never man spoke like this man. ⁴⁷Then answered them the Pharisees, Are you also deceived? ⁴⁸Have any of the rulers or of the Pharisees believed on him? ⁴⁹But this people who knows not the law are cursed. ⁵⁰Nicodemus says to them, (he that came to Jesus by night, being one of them,) ⁵¹Does our law judge any man, before it hear him, and know what he does? ⁵²They answered and said to him, Are you also of Galilee? Search, and look: for out of Galilee rises no prophet. ⁵³And every man went to his own house.

8 ¹Jesus went to the mount of Olives. ²And early in the morning he came again into the temple, and all the people came to him; and he sat down, and taught them. ³And the scribes and Pharisees brought to him a woman taken in adultery; and when they had set her in the middle, ⁴They say to him, Master, this woman was taken in adultery, in the very act. ⁵Now Moses in the law commanded us, that such should be stoned: but what say you? ⁶This they said, tempting him, that they might have to accuse him. But Jesus stooped down, and with his finger wrote on the ground, as though he heard them not. ⁷So when they continued asking him, he lifted up himself, and said to them, He that is without sin among you, let him first cast a stone at her. ⁸And again he stooped down, and wrote on the ground. ⁹And they which heard it, being convicted by their own conscience, went out one by one, beginning at the oldest, even to the last: and Jesus was left alone, and the woman standing in the middle. ¹⁰When Jesus had lifted up himself, and saw none but the woman, he said to her, Woman, where are those your accusers? has no man condemned you? ¹¹She said, No man, Lord. And Jesus said to her, Neither do I condemn you: go, and sin no more. ¹²Then spoke Jesus again to them, saying, I am the light of the world: he that follows me shall not walk in darkness, but shall have the light of life. ¹³The Pharisees therefore said to him, You bore record of yourself; your record is not true. ¹⁴Jesus answered and said to them, Though I bear record of myself, yet my record is true: for I know from where I came, and where I go; but you cannot tell from where I come, and where I go. ¹⁵You judge after the flesh; I judge no man. ¹⁶And yet if I judge, my judgment is true: for I am not alone, but I and the Father that sent me. ¹⁷It is also written in your law, that the testimony of two men is true. ¹⁸I am one that bear witness of myself, and the Father that sent me bears witness of me. ¹⁹Then said they to him, Where is your Father? Jesus answered, You neither know me, nor my Father: if you had known me, you should have known my Father also. ²⁰These words spoke Jesus in the treasury, as he taught in the temple: and no man laid hands on him; for his hour was not yet come. ²¹Then said Jesus again to them, I go my way, and you shall seek me, and shall die in your sins: where I go, you cannot come. ²²Then said the Jews, Will he kill himself? because he says, Where I go, you cannot come. ²³And he said to them, You are from beneath; I am from above: you are of this world; I am not of this world. ²⁴I said therefore to you, that you shall die in your sins: for if you believe not that I am he, you shall die in your sins. ²⁵Then said they to him, Who are you? And Jesus says to them, Even the same that I said to you from the beginning. ²⁶I have many things to say and to judge of you: but he that sent me is true; and I speak to the world those things which I have heard of him. ²⁷They understood not that he spoke to them of the Father. ²⁸Then said Jesus to them, When you have lifted up the Son of man, then shall you know that I am he, and that I do nothing of myself; but as my Father has taught me, I speak these things. ²⁹And he that sent me is with me: the Father has not left me alone; for I do always those things that please him. ³⁰As he spoke these words, many believed on him. ³¹Then said Jesus to those Jews which believed on him, If you continue in my word, then are you my disciples indeed; ³²And you shall know the truth, and the truth shall make you free. ³³They answered him, We be Abraham's seed, and were never in bondage to any man: how say you, You shall be made free? ³⁴Jesus answered them, Truly, truly, I say to you, Whoever commits sin is the servant of sin. ³⁵And the servant stays not in the house for ever: but the Son stays ever. ³⁶If the Son therefore shall make you free, you shall be free indeed. ³⁷I know that you are Abraham's seed; but you seek to kill me, because my word has no place in you. ³⁸I speak that which I have seen with my Father: and you do that which you have seen with your father. ³⁹They answered and said to him, Abraham is our father. Jesus says to them, If you were Abraham's children, you would do the works of Abraham. ⁴⁰But now you seek to kill me, a man that has told you the truth, which I have heard of God: this did not Abraham. ⁴¹You do the deeds of your father. Then said they to him, We be not born of fornication; we have one Father, even God. ⁴²Jesus said to them, If God were your Father, you would love me: for I proceeded forth and came from God; neither came I of myself, but he sent me. ⁴³Why do you not understand my speech? even because you cannot hear my word. ⁴⁴You are of your father the devil, and the lusts of your father you will do. He was a murderer from the beginning, and stayed not in the truth, because there is no truth in him. When he speaks a lie, he speaks of his own: for he is a liar, and the father of it. ⁴⁵And because I tell you the truth, you believe me not. ⁴⁶Which of you convinces me of sin? And if I say the truth, why do you not believe me? ⁴⁷He that is of God hears God's words: you therefore hear them not, because you are not of God. ⁴⁸Then answered the Jews, and said to him, Say we not well that you are a Samaritan, and have a devil? ⁴⁹Jesus answered, I have not a devil; but I honor my Father, and you do dishonor me. ⁵⁰And I seek not my own glory: there is one that seeks and judges. ⁵¹Truly, truly, I say to you, If a man keep my saying, he shall never see death. ⁵²Then said the Jews to him, Now we know that you have a devil. Abraham is dead, and the prophets; and you say, If a man keep my saying, he shall never taste of death. ⁵³Are you greater than our father Abraham, which is dead? and the prophets are dead: whom make you yourself? ⁵⁴Jesus answered, If I honor myself, my honor is nothing: it is my Father that honors me; of whom you say, that he is your God: ⁵⁵Yet you have not known him; but I know him: and if I should say, I know him not, I shall be a liar like to you: but I know him, and keep his saying. ⁵⁶Your father Abraham rejoiced to see my day: and he saw it, and was glad. ⁵⁷Then said the Jews to him, You are not yet fifty years old, and have you seen Abraham? ⁵⁸Jesus said to them, Truly, truly, I say to you, Before Abraham was, I am. ⁵⁹Then took they up stones to cast at him: but Jesus hid himself, and went out of the temple, going through the middle of them, and so passed by.

9 ¹And as Jesus passed by, he saw a man which was blind from his birth. ²And his disciples asked him, saying, Master, who did sin, this man, or his parents, that he was born blind? ³Jesus answered, Neither has this man sinned, nor his parents: but that the works of God should be made manifest in him. ⁴I must work the works of him that sent me, while it is day: the night comes, when no man can work. ⁵As long as I am in the world, I am the light of the world. ⁶When he had thus spoken, he spat on the ground, and made clay of the spittle, and he anointed the eyes of the blind man with the clay, ⁷And said to him, Go, wash in the pool of Siloam, (which is by interpretation, Sent.) He went his way therefore, and washed, and came seeing. ⁸The neighbors therefore, and they which before had seen him that he was blind, said, Is not this he that sat and begged? ⁹Some said, This is he: others said, He is like him: but he said, I am he. ¹⁰Therefore said they to him, How were your eyes opened? ¹¹He answered and said, A man that is called Jesus made clay, and anointed my eyes, and said to me, Go to the pool of Siloam, and wash: and I went and washed, and I received sight. ¹²Then said they to him, Where is he? He said, I know not. ¹³They brought to the Pharisees him that aforetime was blind. ¹⁴And it was the sabbath day when Jesus made the clay, and opened his eyes. ¹⁵Then again the Pharisees also asked him how he had received his sight. He said to them, He put clay on my eyes, and I washed, and do see. ¹⁶Therefore said some of the Pharisees, This man is not of God, because he keeps not the sabbath day. Others said, How can a man that is a sinner do such miracles? And there was a division among them. ¹⁷They say to the blind man again, What say you of him, that he has opened your eyes? He said, He is a prophet. ¹⁸But the Jews did not believe concerning him, that he had been blind, and received his sight, until they called the parents of him that had received his sight. ¹⁹And they asked them, saying, Is this your son, who you say was born blind? how then does he now see? ²⁰His parents answered them and said, We know that this is our son, and that he was born blind: ²¹But by what means he now sees, we know not; or who has opened his eyes, we know not: he is of age; ask him: he shall speak for himself. ²²These words spoke his parents, because they feared the Jews: for the Jews had agreed already, that if any man did confess that he was Christ, he should be put out of the synagogue. ²³Therefore said his parents, He is of age; ask him. ²⁴Then again called they the man that was blind, and says to him, Give God the praise: we know that this man is a sinner. ²⁵He answered and said, Whether he be a sinner or no, I know not: one thing I know, that, whereas I was blind, now I see. ²⁶Then said they to him again, What did he to you? how opened he your eyes? ²⁷He answered them, I have told you already, and you did not hear: why would you hear it again? will you also be his disciples? ²⁸Then they reviled him, and said, You are his disciple; but we are Moses' disciples. ²⁹We know that God spoke to Moses: as for this fellow, we know not from where he is. ³⁰The man answered and said to them, Why herein is a marvelous thing, that you know not from where he is, and yet he has opened my eyes. ³¹Now we know that God hears not sinners: but if any man be a worshipper of God, and does his will, him he hears. ³²Since the world began was it not heard that any man opened the eyes of one that was born blind. ³³If this man were not of God, he could do nothing. ³⁴They answered and said to him, You were altogether born in sins, and do you teach us? And they cast him out. ³⁵Jesus heard that they had cast him out; and when he had found him, he said to him, Do you believe on the Son of God? ³⁶He answered and said, Who is he, Lord, that I might believe on him? ³⁷And Jesus said to him, You have both seen him, and it is he that talks with you. ³⁸And he said, Lord, I believe. And he worshipped him. ³⁹And Jesus said, For judgment I am come into this world, that they which see not might see; and that they which see might be made blind. ⁴⁰And some of the Pharisees which were with him heard these words, and said to him, Are we blind also? ⁴¹Jesus said to them, If you were blind, you should have no sin: but now you say, We see; therefore your sin remains.

10 ¹Truly, truly, I say to you, He that enters not by the door into the sheepfold, but climbs up some other way, the same is a thief and a robber. ²But he that enters in by the door is the shepherd of the sheep. ³To him the porter opens; and the sheep hear his voice: and he calls his own sheep by name, and leads them out. ⁴And when he puts forth his own sheep, he goes before them, and the sheep follow him: for they know his voice. ⁵And a stranger will they not follow, but will flee from him: for they know not the voice of strangers. ⁶This parable spoke Jesus to them: but they understood not what things they were which he spoke to them. ⁷Then said Jesus to them again, Truly, truly, I say to you, I am the door of the sheep. ⁸All that ever came before me are thieves and robbers: but the sheep did not hear them. ⁹I am the door: by me if any man enter in, he shall be saved, and shall go in and out, and find pasture. ¹⁰The thief comes not, but for to steal, and to kill, and to destroy: I am come that they might have life, and that they might have it more abundantly. ¹¹I am the good shepherd: the good shepherd gives his life for the sheep. ¹²But he that is an hireling, and not the shepherd, whose own the sheep are not, sees the wolf coming, and leaves the sheep, and flees: and the wolf catches them, and scatters the sheep. ¹³The hireling flees, because he is an hireling, and cares not for the sheep. ¹⁴I am

the good shepherd, and know my sheep, and am known of mine. ¹⁵As the Father knows me, even so know I the Father: and I lay down my life for the sheep. ¹⁶And other sheep I have, which are not of this fold: them also I must bring, and they shall hear my voice; and there shall be one fold, and one shepherd. ¹⁷Therefore does my Father love me, because I lay down my life, that I might take it again. ¹⁸No man takes it from me, but I lay it down of myself. I have power to lay it down, and I have power to take it again. This commandment have I received of my Father. ¹⁹There was a division therefore again among the Jews for these sayings. ²⁰And many of them said, He has a devil, and is mad; why hear you him? ²¹Others said, These are not the words of him that has a devil. Can a devil open the eyes of the blind? ²²And it was at Jerusalem the feast of the dedication, and it was winter. ²³And Jesus walked in the temple in Solomon's porch. ²⁴Then came the Jews round about him, and said to him, How long do you make us to doubt? If you be the Christ, tell us plainly. ²⁵Jesus answered them, I told you, and you believed not: the works that I do in my Father's name, they bear witness of me. ²⁶But you believe not, because you are not of my sheep, as I said to you. ²⁷My sheep hear my voice, and I know them, and they follow me: ²⁸And I give to them eternal life; and they shall never perish, neither shall any man pluck them out of my hand. ²⁹My Father, which gave them me, is greater than all; and no man is able to pluck them out of my Father's hand. ³⁰I and my Father are one. ³¹Then the Jews took up stones again to stone him. ³²Jesus answered them, Many good works have I showed you from my Father; for which of those works do you stone me? ³³The Jews answered him, saying, For a good work we stone you not; but for blasphemy; and because that you, being a man, make yourself God. ³⁴Jesus answered them, Is it not written in your law, I said, You are gods? ³⁵If he called them gods, to whom the word of God came, and the scripture cannot be broken; ³⁶Say you of him, whom the Father has sanctified, and sent into the world, You blaspheme; because I said, I am the Son of God? ³⁷If I do not the works of my Father, believe me not. ³⁸But if I do, though you believe not me, believe the works: that you may know, and believe, that the Father is in me, and I in him. ³⁹Therefore they sought again to take him: but he escaped out of their hand, ⁴⁰And went away again beyond Jordan into the place where John at first baptized; and there he stayed. ⁴¹And many resorted to him, and said, John did no miracle: but all things that John spoke of this man were true. ⁴²And many believed on him there.

11 ¹Now a certain man was sick, named Lazarus, of Bethany, the town of Mary and her sister Martha. ²(It was that Mary which anointed the Lord with ointment, and wiped his feet with her hair, whose brother Lazarus was sick.) ³Therefore his sisters sent to him, saying, Lord, behold, he whom you love is sick. ⁴When Jesus heard that, he said, This sickness is not to death, but for the glory of God, that the Son of God might be glorified thereby. ⁵Now Jesus loved Martha, and her sister, and Lazarus. ⁶When he had heard therefore that he was sick, he stayed two days still in the same place where he was. ⁷Then after that says he to his disciples, Let us go into Judaea again. ⁸His disciples say to him, Master, the Jews of late sought to stone you; and go you thither again? ⁹Jesus answered, Are there not twelve hours in the day? If any man walk in the day, he stumbles not, because he sees the light of this world. ¹⁰But if a man walk in the night, he stumbles, because there is no light in him. ¹¹These things said he: and after that he says to them, Our friend Lazarus sleeps; but I go, that I may awake him out of sleep. ¹²Then said his disciples, Lord, if he sleep, he shall do well. ¹³However, Jesus spoke of his death: but they thought that he had spoken of taking of rest in sleep. ¹⁴Then said Jesus to them plainly, Lazarus is dead. ¹⁵And I am glad for your sakes that I was not there, to the intent you may believe; nevertheless let us go to him. ¹⁶Then said Thomas, which is called Didymus, to his fellow disciples, Let us also go, that we may die with him. ¹⁷Then when Jesus came, he found that he had lain in the grave four days already. ¹⁸Now Bethany was near to Jerusalem, about fifteen furlongs off: ¹⁹And many of the Jews came to Martha and Mary, to comfort them concerning their brother. ²⁰Then Martha, as soon as she heard that Jesus was coming, went and met him: but Mary sat still in the house. ²¹Then said Martha to Jesus, Lord, if you had been here, my brother had not died. ²²But I know, that even now, whatever you will ask of God, God will give it you. ²³Jesus says to her, Your brother shall rise again. ²⁴Martha says to him, I know that he shall rise again in the resurrection at the last day. ²⁵Jesus said to her, I am the resurrection, and the life: he that believes in me, though he were dead, yet shall he live: ²⁶And whoever lives and believes in me shall never die. Believe you this? ²⁷She says to him, Yes, Lord: I believe that you are the Christ, the Son of God, which should come into the world. ²⁸And when she had so said, she went her way, and called Mary her sister secretly, saying, The Master is come, and calls for you. ²⁹As soon as she heard that, she arose quickly, and came to him. ³⁰Now Jesus was not yet come into the town, but was in that place where Martha met him. ³¹The Jews then which were with her in the house, and comforted her, when they saw Mary, that she rose up hastily and went out, followed her, saying, She goes to the grave to weep there. ³²Then when Mary was come where Jesus was, and saw him, she fell down at his feet, saying to him, Lord, if you had been here, my brother had not died. ³³When Jesus therefore saw her weeping, and the Jews also weeping which came with her, he groaned in the spirit, and was troubled. ³⁴And said, Where have you laid him? They said to him, Lord, come and see. ³⁵Jesus wept. ³⁶Then said the Jews, Behold how he loved him! ³⁷And some of them said, Could not this man, which opened the eyes of the blind, have caused that even this man should not have died? ³⁸Jesus therefore again groaning in himself comes to the grave. It was a cave, and a stone lay on it. ³⁹Jesus says, Take you away the stone. Martha, the sister of him that was dead, said to him, Lord, by this time he stinks: for he has been dead four days. ⁴⁰Jesus says to her, Said I not to you, that, if you would believe, you should see the glory of God? ⁴¹Then they took away the stone from the place where the dead was laid. And Jesus lifted up his eyes, and said, Father, I thank you that you have heard me. ⁴²And I knew that you hear me always: but because of the people which stand by I said it, that they may believe that you have sent me. ⁴³And when he thus had spoken, he cried with a loud voice, Lazarus, come forth. ⁴⁴And he that was dead came forth, bound hand and foot with grave clothes: and his face was bound about with a napkin. Jesus says to them, Loose him, and let him go. ⁴⁵Then many of the Jews which came to Mary, and had seen the things which Jesus did, believed on him. ⁴⁶But some of them went their ways to the Pharisees, and told them what things Jesus had done. ⁴⁷Then gathered the chief priests and the Pharisees a council, and said, What do we? for this man does many miracles. ⁴⁸If we let him thus alone, all men will believe on him: and the Romans shall come and take away both our place and nation. ⁴⁹And one of them, named Caiaphas, being the high priest that same year, said to them, You know nothing at all, ⁵⁰Nor consider that it is expedient for us, that one man should die for the people, and that the whole nation perish not. ⁵¹And this spoke he not of himself: but being high priest that year, he prophesied that Jesus should die for that nation; ⁵²And not for that nation only, but that also he should gather together in one the children of God that were scattered abroad. ⁵³Then from that day forth they took counsel together for to put him to death. ⁵⁴Jesus therefore walked no more openly among the Jews; but went there to a country near to the wilderness, into a city called Ephraim, and there continued with his disciples. ⁵⁵And the Jews' passover was near at hand: and many went out of the country up to Jerusalem before the passover, to purify themselves. ⁵⁶Then sought they for Jesus, and spoke among themselves, as they stood in the temple, What think you, that he will not come to the feast? ⁵⁷Now both the chief priests and the Pharisees had given a commandment, that, if any man knew where he were, he should show it, that they might take him.

12 ¹Then Jesus six days before the passover came to Bethany, where Lazarus was, which had been dead, whom he raised from the dead. ²There they made him a supper; and Martha served: but Lazarus was one of them that sat at the table with him. ³Then took Mary a pound of ointment of spikenard, very costly, and anointed the feet of Jesus, and wiped his feet with her hair: and the house was filled with the odor of the ointment. ⁴Then says one of his disciples, Judas Iscariot, Simon's son, which should betray him, ⁵Why was not this ointment sold for three hundred pence, and given to the poor? ⁶This he said, not that he cared for the poor; but because he was a thief, and had the bag, and bore what was put therein. ⁷Then said Jesus, Let her alone: against the day of my burying has she kept this. ⁸For the poor always you have with you; but me you have not always. ⁹Much people of the Jews therefore knew that he was there: and they came not for Jesus' sake only, but that they might see Lazarus also, whom he had raised from the dead. ¹⁰But the chief priests consulted that they might put Lazarus also to death; ¹¹Because that by reason of him many of the Jews went away, and believed on Jesus. ¹²On the next day much people that were come to the feast, when they heard that Jesus was coming to Jerusalem, ¹³Took branches of palm trees, and went forth to meet him, and cried, Hosanna: Blessed is the King of Israel that comes in the name of the Lord. ¹⁴And Jesus, when he had found a young ass, sat thereon; as it is written, ¹⁵Fear not, daughter of Sion: behold, your King comes, sitting on an ass's colt. ¹⁶These things understood not his disciples at the first: but when Jesus was glorified, then remembered they that these things were written of him, and that they had done these things to him. ¹⁷The people therefore that was with him when he called Lazarus out of his grave, and raised him from the dead, bore record. ¹⁸For this cause the people also met him, for that they heard that he had done this miracle. ¹⁹The Pharisees therefore said among themselves, Perceive you how you prevail nothing? behold, the world is gone after him. ²⁰And there were certain Greeks among them that came up to worship at the feast: ²¹The same came therefore to Philip, which was of Bethsaida of Galilee, and desired him, saying, Sir, we would see Jesus. ²²Philip comes and tells Andrew: and again Andrew and Philip tell Jesus. ²³And Jesus answered them, saying, The hour is come, that the Son of man should be glorified. ²⁴Truly, truly, I say to you, Except a corn of wheat fall into the ground and die, it stays alone: but if it die, it brings forth much fruit. ²⁵He that loves his life shall lose it; and he that hates his life in this world shall keep it to life eternal. ²⁶If any man serve me, let him follow me; and where I am, there shall also my servant be: if any man serve me, him will my Father honor. ²⁷Now is my soul troubled; and what shall I say? Father, save me from this hour: but for this cause came I to this hour. ²⁸Father, glorify your name. Then came there a voice from heaven, saying, I have both glorified it, and will glorify it again. ²⁹The people therefore, that stood by, and heard it, said that it thundered: others said, An angel spoke to him. ³⁰Jesus answered and said, This voice came not because of me, but for your sakes. ³¹Now is the judgment of this world: now shall the prince of this world be cast out. ³²And I, if I be lifted up from the earth, will draw all men to me. ³³This he said, signifying what death he should die. ³⁴The people answered him, We have heard out of the law that Christ stays for ever: and how say you, The Son of man must be lifted up? who is this Son of man? ³⁵Then Jesus said to them, Yet a little while is the light with you. Walk while you have the light, lest darkness come on you: for he that walks in darkness knows not where he goes. ³⁶While you have light, believe in the light, that you may be the children of light. These things spoke Jesus, and departed, and did hide himself from them. ³⁷But though he had done so many miracles before them, yet they believed not on him: ³⁸That the saying of Isaiah the prophet might be fulfilled, which he spoke, Lord, who has believed our report? and to whom has the arm of the Lord been revealed? ³⁹Therefore they could not believe, because that Isaiah said again, ⁴⁰He has blinded their eyes, and hardened their heart; that they should not see with their eyes, nor understand with their heart, and be converted, and I should heal them. ⁴¹These things said Isaiah, when he saw his glory, and spoke of him. ⁴²Nevertheless among the chief rulers also many believed on him; but because of the Pharisees they did not confess him, lest they should be put out of the synagogue: ⁴³For they loved the praise of men more than the praise of God. ⁴⁴Jesus cried and said, He that believes on me, believes not on me, but on him that sent me. ⁴⁵And he that sees me sees him that sent me. ⁴⁶I am come a light into the world, that whoever believes on me should not abide in darkness. ⁴⁷And if any man hear my words, and believe not, I judge him not: for I came not to judge the world, but to save the world. ⁴⁸He that rejects me, and receives not my words, has one that judges him: the word that I have spoken, the same shall judge him in the last day. ⁴⁹For I have not spoken of myself; but the Father which sent me, he gave me a commandment, what I should say, and what I should speak. ⁵⁰And I know that his commandment is life everlasting: whatever I speak therefore, even as the Father said to me, so I speak.

13 ¹Now before the feast of the passover, when Jesus knew that his hour was come that he should depart out of this world to the Father, having loved his own which were in the world, he loved them to the end. ²And supper being ended, the devil having now put into the heart of Judas Iscariot, Simon's son, to betray him; ³Jesus knowing that the Father had given all things into his hands, and that he was come from God, and went to God; ⁴He rises from supper, and laid aside his garments; and took a towel, and girded himself. ⁵After that he pours water into a basin, and began to wash the disciples' feet, and to wipe them with the towel with which he was girded. ⁶Then comes he to Simon Peter: and Peter says to him, Lord, do you wash my feet? ⁷Jesus answered and said to him, What I do you know not now; but you shall know hereafter. ⁸Peter says to him, You shall never wash my feet. Jesus answered him, If I wash you not, you have no part with me. ⁹Simon Peter says to him, Lord, not my feet only, but also my hands and my head. ¹⁰Jesus says to him, He that is washed needs not save to wash his feet, but is clean every whit: and you are clean, but not all. ¹¹For he knew who should betray him; therefore said he, You are not all clean. ¹²So after he had washed their feet, and had taken his garments, and was set down again, he said to them, Know you what I have done to you? ¹³You call me Master and Lord: and you say well; for so I am. ¹⁴If I then, your Lord and Master, have washed your feet; you also ought to wash one another's feet. ¹⁵For I have given you an example, that you should do as I have done to you. ¹⁶Truly, truly, I say to you, The servant is not greater than his lord; neither he that is sent greater than he that sent him. ¹⁷If you know these things, happy are you if you do them. ¹⁸I speak not of you all: I know whom I have chosen: but that the scripture may be fulfilled, He that eats bread with me has lifted up his heel against me. ¹⁹Now I tell you before it come, that, when it is come to pass, you may believe that I am he. ²⁰Truly, truly, I say to you, He that receives whomsoever I send receives me; and he that receives me receives him that sent me. ²¹When Jesus had thus said, he was troubled in spirit, and testified, and said, Truly, truly, I say to you, that one of you shall betray me. ²²Then the disciples looked one on another, doubting of whom he spoke. ²³Now there was leaning on Jesus' bosom one of his disciples, whom Jesus loved. ²⁴Simon Peter therefore beckoned to him, that he should ask who it should be of whom he spoke. ²⁵He then lying on Jesus' breast says to him, Lord, who is it? ²⁶Jesus answered, He it is, to whom I shall give a sop, when I have dipped it. And when he had dipped the sop, he gave it to Judas Iscariot, the son of Simon. ²⁷And after the sop Satan entered into him. Then said Jesus to him, That you do, do quickly. ²⁸Now no man at the table knew for what intent he spoke this to him. ²⁹For some of them thought, because Judas had the bag, that Jesus had said to him, Buy those things that we have need of against the feast; or, that he should give something to the poor. ³⁰He then having received the sop went immediately out: and it was night. ³¹Therefore, when he was gone out, Jesus said, Now is the Son of man glorified, and God is glorified in him. ³²If God be glorified in him, God shall also glorify him in himself, and shall straightway glorify him. ³³Little children, yet a little while I am with you. You shall seek me: and as I said to the Jews, Where I go, you cannot come; so now I say to you. ³⁴A new commandment I give to you, That you love one another; as I have loved you, that you also love one another. ³⁵By this shall all men know that you are my disciples, if you have love one to another. ³⁶Simon Peter said to him, Lord, where go you? Jesus answered him, Where I go, you can not follow me now; but you shall follow me afterwards. ³⁷Peter said to him, Lord, why cannot I follow you now? I will lay down my life for your sake. ³⁸Jesus answered him, Will you lay down your life for my sake? Truly, truly, I say to you, The cock shall not crow, till you have denied me thrice.

14 ¹Let not your heart be troubled: you believe in God, believe also in me. ²In my Father's house are many mansions: if it were not so, I would have told you. I go to prepare a place for you. ³And if I go and prepare a place for you, I will come again, and receive you to myself; that where I am, there you may be also. ⁴And where I go you know, and the way you know. ⁵Thomas says to him, Lord, we know not where you go; and how can we know the way? ⁶Jesus says to him, I am the way, the truth, and the life: no man comes to the Father, but by me. ⁷If you had known me, you should have known my Father also: and from now on you know him, and have seen him. ⁸Philip says to him, Lord, show us the Father, and it suffices us. ⁹Jesus says to him, Have I been so long time with you, and yet have you not known me, Philip? he that has seen me has seen the Father; and how say you then, Show us the Father? ¹⁰Believe you not that I am in the Father, and the Father in me? the words that I speak to you I speak not of myself: but the Father that dwells in me, he does the works. ¹¹Believe me that I am in the Father, and the Father in me: or else believe me for the very works' sake. ¹²Truly, truly, I say to you, He that believes on me, the works that I do shall he do also; and greater works than these shall he do; because I go to my Father. ¹³And whatever you shall ask in my name, that will I do, that the Father may be glorified in the Son. ¹⁴If you shall ask any thing in my name, I will do it. ¹⁵If you love me, keep my commandments. ¹⁶And I will pray the Father, and he shall give you another Comforter, that he may abide with you for ever; ¹⁷Even the Spirit of truth; whom the world cannot receive, because it sees him not, neither knows him: but you know him; for he dwells with you, and shall be in you. ¹⁸I will not leave you comfortless: I will come to you. ¹⁹Yet a little while, and the world sees me no more; but you see me: because I live, you shall live also. ²⁰At that day you shall know that I am in my Father, and you in me, and I in you. ²¹He that has my commandments, and keeps them, he it is that loves me: and he that loves me shall be loved of my

Father, and I will love him, and will manifest myself to him. ²²Judas says to him, not Iscariot, Lord, how is it that you will manifest yourself to us, and not to the world? ²³Jesus answered and said to him, If a man love me, he will keep my words: and my Father will love him, and we will come to him, and make our stayed with him. ²⁴He that loves me not keeps not my sayings: and the word which you hear is not mine, but the Father's which sent me. ²⁵These things have I spoken to you, being yet present with you. ²⁶But the Comforter, which is the Holy Ghost, whom the Father will send in my name, he shall teach you all things, and bring all things to your remembrance, whatever I have said to you. ²⁷Peace I leave with you, my peace I give to you: not as the world gives, give I to you. Let not your heart be troubled, neither let it be afraid. ²⁸You have heard how I said to you, I go away, and come again to you. If you loved me, you would rejoice, because I said, I go to the Father: for my Father is greater than I. ²⁹And now I have told you before it come to pass, that, when it is come to pass, you might believe. ³⁰Hereafter I will not talk much with you: for the prince of this world comes, and has nothing in me. ³¹But that the world may know that I love the Father; and as the Father gave me commandment, even so I do. Arise, let us go hence.

15

¹I am the true vine, and my Father is the farmer. ²Every branch in me that bears not fruit he takes away: and every branch that bears fruit, he purges it, that it may bring forth more fruit. ³Now you are clean through the word which I have spoken to you. ⁴Abide in me, and I in you. As the branch cannot bear fruit of itself, except it abide in the vine; no more can you, except you abide in me. ⁵I am the vine, you are the branches: He that stays in me, and I in him, the same brings forth much fruit: for without me you can do nothing. ⁶If a man abide not in me, he is cast forth as a branch, and is withered; and men gather them, and cast them into the fire, and they are burned. ⁷If you abide in me, and my words abide in you, you shall ask what you will, and it shall be done to you. ⁸Herein is my Father glorified, that you bear much fruit; so shall you be my disciples. ⁹As the Father has loved me, so have I loved you: continue you in my love. ¹⁰If you keep my commandments, you shall abide in my love; even as I have kept my Father's commandments, and abide in his love. ¹¹These things have I spoken to you, that my joy might remain in you, and that your joy might be full. ¹²This is my commandment, That you love one another, as I have loved you. ¹³Greater love has no man than this, that a man lay down his life for his friends. ¹⁴You are my friends, if you do whatever I command you. ¹⁵From now on I call you not servants; for the servant knows not what his lord does: but I have called you friends; for all things that I have heard of my Father I have made known to you. ¹⁶You have not chosen me, but I have chosen you, and ordained you, that you should go and bring forth fruit, and that your fruit should remain: that whatever you shall ask of the Father in my name, he may give it you. ¹⁷These things I command you, that you love one another. ¹⁸If the world hate you, you know that it hated me before it hated you. ¹⁹If you were of the world, the world would love his own: but because you are not of the world, but I have chosen you out of the world, therefore the world hates you. ²⁰Remember the word that I said to you, The servant is not greater than his lord. If they have persecuted me, they will also persecute you; if they have kept my saying, they will keep yours also. ²¹But all these things will they do to you for my name's sake, because they know not him that sent me. ²²If I had not come and spoken to them, they had not had sin: but now they have no cloak for their sin. ²³He that hates me hates my Father also. ²⁴If I had not done among them the works which none other man did, they had not had sin: but now have they both seen and hated both me and my Father. ²⁵But this comes to pass, that the word might be fulfilled that is written in their law, They hated me without a cause. ²⁶But when the Comforter is come, whom I will send to you from the Father, even the Spirit of truth, which proceeds from the Father, he shall testify of me: ²⁷And you also shall bear witness, because you have been with me from the beginning.

16

¹These things have I spoken to you, that you should not be offended. ²They shall put you out of the synagogues: yes, the time comes, that whoever kills you will think that he does God service. ³And these things will they do to you, because they have not known the Father, nor me. ⁴But these things have I told you, that when the time shall come, you may remember that I told you of them. And these things I said not to you at the beginning, because I was with you. ⁵But now I go my way to him that sent me; and none of you asks me, Where go you? ⁶But because I have said these things to you, sorrow has filled your heart. ⁷Nevertheless I tell you the truth; It is expedient for you that I go away: for if I go not away, the Comforter will not come to you; but if I depart, I will send him to you. ⁸And when he is come, he will reprove the world of sin, and of righteousness, and of judgment: ⁹Of sin, because they believe not on me; ¹⁰Of righteousness, because I go to my Father, and you see me no more; ¹¹Of judgment, because the prince of this world is judged. ¹²I have yet many things to say to you, but you cannot bear them now. ¹³However, when he, the Spirit of truth, is come, he will guide you into all truth: for he shall not speak of himself; but whatever he shall hear, that shall he speak: and he will show you things to come. ¹⁴He shall glorify me: for he shall receive of mine, and shall show it to you. ¹⁵All things that the Father has are mine: therefore said I, that he shall take of mine, and shall show it to you. ¹⁶A little while, and you shall not see me: and again, a little while, and you shall see me, because I go to the Father. ¹⁷Then said some of his disciples among themselves, What is this that he says to us, A little while, and you shall not see me: and again, a little while, and you shall see me: and, Because I go to the Father? ¹⁸They said therefore, What is this that he says, A little while? we cannot tell what he said. ¹⁹Now Jesus knew that they were desirous to ask him, and said to them, Do you inquire among yourselves of that I said, A little while, and you shall not see me: and again, a little while, and you shall see me? ²⁰Truly, truly, I say to you, That you shall weep and lament, but the world shall rejoice: and you shall be sorrowful, but your sorrow shall be turned into joy. ²¹A woman when she is in travail has sorrow, because her hour is come: but as soon as she is delivered of the child, she remembers no more the anguish, for joy that a man is born into the world. ²²And you now

therefore have sorrow: but I will see you again, and your heart shall rejoice, and your joy no man takes from you. ²³And in that day you shall ask me nothing. Truly, truly, I say to you, Whatever you shall ask the Father in my name, he will give it you. ²⁴Till now have you asked nothing in my name: ask, and you shall receive, that your joy may be full. ²⁵These things have I spoken to you in proverbs: but the time comes, when I shall no more speak to you in proverbs, but I shall show you plainly of the Father. ²⁶At that day you shall ask in my name: and I say not to you, that I will pray the Father for you: ²⁷For the Father himself loves you, because you have loved me, and have believed that I came out from God. ²⁸I came forth from the Father, and am come into the world: again, I leave the world, and go to the Father. ²⁹His disciples said to him, See, now speak you plainly, and speak no proverb. ³⁰Now are we sure that you know all things, and need not that any man should ask you: by this we believe that you came forth from God. ³¹Jesus answered them, Do you now believe? ³²Behold, the hour comes, yes, is now come, that you shall be scattered, every man to his own, and shall leave me alone: and yet I am not alone, because the Father is with me. ³³These things I have spoken to you, that in me you might have peace. In the world you shall have tribulation: but be of good cheer; I have overcome the world.

17 ¹These words spoke Jesus, and lifted up his eyes to heaven, and said, Father, the hour is come; glorify your Son, that your Son also may glorify you: ²As you have given him power over all flesh, that he should give eternal life to as many as you have given him. ³And this is life eternal, that they might know you the only true God, and Jesus Christ, whom you have sent. ⁴I have glorified you on the earth: I have finished the work which you gave me to do. ⁵And now, O Father, glorify you me with your own self with the glory which I had with you before the world was. ⁶I have manifested your name to the men which you gave me out of the world: your they were, and you gave them me; and they have kept your word. ⁷Now they have known that all things whatever you have given me are of you. ⁸For I have given to them the words which you gave me; and they have received them, and have known surely that I came out from you, and they have believed that you did send me. ⁹I pray for them: I pray not for the world, but for them which you have given me; for they are yours. ¹⁰And all my are yours, and your are mine; and I am glorified in them. ¹¹And now I am no more in the world, but these are in the world, and I come to you. Holy Father, keep through your own name those whom you have given me, that they may be one, as we are. ¹²While I was with them in the world, I kept them in your name: those that you gave me I have kept, and none of them is lost, but the son of perdition; that the scripture might be fulfilled. ¹³And now come I to you; and these things I speak in the world, that they might have my joy fulfilled in themselves. ¹⁴I have given them your word; and the world has hated them, because they are not of the world, even as I am not of the world. ¹⁵I pray not that you should take them out of the world, but that you should keep them from the evil. ¹⁶They are not of the world, even as I am not of the world. ¹⁷Sanctify them through your truth: your word is truth. ¹⁸As you have sent me into the world, even so have I also sent them into the world. ¹⁹And for their sakes I sanctify myself, that they also might be sanctified through the truth. ²⁰Neither pray I for these alone, but for them also which shall believe on me through their word; ²¹That they all may be one; as you, Father, are in me, and I in you, that they also may be one in us: that the world may believe that you have sent me. ²²And the glory which you gave me I have given them; that they may be one, even as we are one: ²³I in them, and you in me, that they may be made perfect in one; and that the world may know that you have sent me, and have loved them, as you have loved me. ²⁴Father, I will that they also, whom you have given me, be with me where I am; that they may behold my glory, which you have given me: for you loved me before the foundation of the world. ²⁵O righteous Father, the world has not known you: but I have known you, and these have known that you have sent me. ²⁶And I have declared to them your name, and will declare it: that the love with which you have loved me may be in them, and I in them.

18 ¹When Jesus had spoken these words, he went forth with his disciples over the brook Cedron, where was a garden, into the which he entered, and his disciples. ²And Judas also, which betrayed him, knew the place: for Jesus often resorted thither with his disciples. ³Judas then, having received a band of men and officers from the chief priests and Pharisees, comes thither with lanterns and torches and weapons. ⁴Jesus therefore, knowing all things that should come on him, went forth, and said to them, Whom seek you? ⁵They answered him, Jesus of Nazareth. Jesus says to them, I am he. And Judas also, which betrayed him, stood with them. ⁶As soon then as he had said to them, I am he, they went backward, and fell to the ground. ⁷Then asked he them again, Whom seek you? And they said, Jesus of Nazareth. ⁸Jesus answered, I have told you that I am he: if therefore you seek me, let these go their way: ⁹That the saying might be fulfilled, which he spoke, Of them which you gave me have I lost none. ¹⁰Then Simon Peter having a sword drew it, and smote the high priest's servant, and cut off his right ear. The servant's name was Malchus. ¹¹Then said Jesus to Peter, Put up your sword into the sheath: the cup which my Father has given me, shall I not drink it? ¹²Then the band and the captain and officers of the Jews took Jesus, and bound him, ¹³And led him away to Annas first; for he was father in law to Caiaphas, which was the high priest that same year. ¹⁴Now Caiaphas was he, which gave counsel to the Jews, that it was expedient that one man should die for the people. ¹⁵And Simon Peter followed Jesus, and so did another disciple: that disciple was known to the high priest, and went in with Jesus into the palace of the high priest. ¹⁶But Peter stood at the door without. Then went out that other disciple, which was known to the high priest, and spoke to her that kept the door, and brought in Peter. ¹⁷Then says the damsel that kept the door to Peter, Are not you also one of this man's disciples? He says, I am not. ¹⁸And the servants and officers stood there, who had made a fire of coals; for it was cold: and they warmed themselves: and Peter stood with them, and warmed himself. ¹⁹The high priest then asked Jesus of his disciples, and of his doctrine. ²⁰Jesus answered him, I spoke openly to the world; I ever taught in the synagogue, and in the temple, where the Jews always resort; and in secret have I said nothing. ²¹Why ask you me? ask them which heard me, what I have said to them: behold, they know what I said. ²²And when he had thus spoken, one of the officers which stood by struck Jesus with the palm of his hand, saying, Answer you the high priest so? ²³Jesus answered him, If I have spoken evil, bear witness of the evil: but if well, why smite you me? ²⁴Now Annas had sent him bound to Caiaphas the high priest. ²⁵And Simon Peter stood and warmed himself. They said therefore to him, Are not you also one of his disciples? He denied it, and said, I am not. ²⁶One of the servants of the high priest, being his kinsman whose ear Peter cut off, says, Did not I see you in the garden with him? ²⁷Peter then denied again: and immediately the cock crew. ²⁸Then led they Jesus from Caiaphas to the hall of judgment: and it was early; and they themselves went not into the judgment hall, lest they should be defiled; but that they might eat the passover. ²⁹Pilate then went out to them, and said, What accusation bring you against this man? ³⁰They answered and said to him, If he were not a malefactor, we would not have delivered him up to you. ³¹Then said Pilate to them, Take you him, and judge him according to your law. The Jews therefore said to him, It is not lawful for us to put any man to death: ³²That the saying of Jesus might be fulfilled, which he spoke, signifying what death he should die. ³³Then Pilate entered into the judgment hall again, and called Jesus, and said to him, Are you the King of the Jews? ³⁴Jesus answered him, Say you this thing of yourself, or did others tell it you of me? ³⁵Pilate answered, Am I a Jew? Your own nation and the chief priests have delivered you to me: what have you done? ³⁶Jesus answered, My kingdom is not of this world: if my kingdom were of this world, then would my servants fight, that I should not be delivered to the Jews: but now is my kingdom not from hence. ³⁷Pilate therefore said to him, Are you a king then? Jesus answered, You say that I am a king. To this end was I born, and for this cause came I into the world, that I should bear witness to the truth. Every one that is of the truth hears my voice. ³⁸Pilate says to him, What is truth? And when he had said this, he went out again to the Jews, and said to them, I find in him no fault at all. ³⁹But you have a custom, that I should release to you one at the passover: will you therefore that I release to you the King of the Jews? ⁴⁰Then cried they all again, saying, Not this man, but Barabbas. Now Barabbas was a robber.

19

¹Then Pilate therefore took Jesus, and scourged him. ²And the soldiers platted a crown of thorns, and put it on his head, and they put on him a purple robe, ³And said, Hail, King of the Jews! and they smote him with their hands. ⁴Pilate therefore went forth again, and says to them, Behold, I bring him forth to you, that you may know that I find no fault in him. ⁵Then came Jesus forth, wearing the crown of thorns, and the purple robe. And Pilate says to them, Behold the man! ⁶When the chief priests therefore and officers saw him, they cried out, saying, Crucify him, crucify him. Pilate says to them, Take you him, and crucify him: for I find no fault in him. ⁷The Jews answered him, We have a law, and by our law he ought to die, because he made himself the Son of God. ⁸When Pilate therefore heard that saying, he was the more afraid; ⁹And went again into the judgment hall, and says to Jesus, From where are you? But Jesus gave him no answer. ¹⁰Then says Pilate to him, Speak you not to me? know you not that I have power to crucify you, and have power to release you? ¹¹Jesus answered, You could have no power at all against me, except it were given you from above: therefore he that delivered me to you has the greater sin. ¹²And from thereafter Pilate sought to release him: but the Jews cried out, saying, If you let this man go, you are not Caesar's friend: whoever makes himself a king speaks against Caesar. ¹³When Pilate therefore heard that saying, he brought Jesus forth, and sat down in the judgment seat in a place that is called the Pavement, but in the Hebrew, Gabbatha. ¹⁴And it was the preparation of the passover, and about the sixth hour: and he says to the Jews, Behold your King! ¹⁵But they cried out, Away with him, away with him, crucify him. Pilate says to them, Shall I crucify your King? The chief priests answered, We have no king but Caesar. ¹⁶Then delivered he him therefore to them to be crucified. And they took Jesus, and led him away. ¹⁷And he bearing his cross went forth into a place called the place of a skull, which is called in the Hebrew Golgotha: ¹⁸Where they crucified him, and two other with him, on either side one, and Jesus in the middle. ¹⁹And Pilate wrote a title, and put it on the cross. And the writing was JESUS OF NAZARETH THE KING OF THE JEWS. ²⁰This title then read many of the Jews: for the place where Jesus was crucified was near to the city: and it was written in Hebrew, and Greek, and Latin. ²¹Then said the chief priests of the Jews to Pilate, Write not, The King of the Jews; but that he said, I am King of the Jews. ²²Pilate answered, What I have written I have written. ²³Then the soldiers, when they had crucified Jesus, took his garments, and made four parts, to every soldier a part; and also his coat: now the coat was without seam, woven from the top throughout. ²⁴They said therefore among themselves, Let us not rend it, but cast lots for it, whose it shall be: that the scripture might be fulfilled, which says, They parted my raiment among them, and for my clothing they did cast lots. These things therefore the soldiers did. ²⁵Now there stood by the cross of Jesus his mother, and his mother's sister, Mary the wife of Cleophas, and Mary Magdalene. ²⁶When Jesus therefore saw his mother, and the disciple standing by, whom he loved, he says to his mother, Woman, behold your son! ²⁷Then says he to the disciple, Behold your mother! And from that hour that disciple took her to his own home. ²⁸After this, Jesus knowing that all things were now accomplished, that the scripture might be fulfilled, says, I thirst. ²⁹Now there was set a vessel full of vinegar: and they filled a sponge with vinegar, and put it on hyssop, and put it to his mouth. ³⁰When Jesus therefore had received the vinegar, he said, It is finished: and he bowed his head, and gave up the ghost. ³¹The Jews therefore, because it was the preparation, that the bodies should not remain on the cross on the sabbath day, (for that sabbath day was an high day,) sought Pilate that their legs might be broken, and that they might be taken away. ³²Then came the soldiers, and broke the legs of the first, and of the other which was crucified with him. ³³But when they came to Jesus, and saw that he was dead already,

they broke not his legs: ³⁴But one of the soldiers with a spear pierced his side, and immediately came there out blood and water. ³⁵And he that saw it bore record, and his record is true: and he knows that he says true, that you might believe. ³⁶For these things were done, that the scripture should be fulfilled, A bone of him shall not be broken. ³⁷And again another scripture says, They shall look on him whom they pierced. ³⁸And after this Joseph of Arimathaea, being a disciple of Jesus, but secretly for fear of the Jews, sought Pilate that he might take away the body of Jesus: and Pilate gave him leave. He came therefore, and took the body of Jesus. ³⁹And there came also Nicodemus, which at the first came to Jesus by night, and brought a mixture of myrrh and aloes, about an hundred pound weight. ⁴⁰Then took they the body of Jesus, and wound it in linen clothes with the spices, as the manner of the Jews is to bury. ⁴¹Now in the place where he was crucified there was a garden; and in the garden a new sepulcher, wherein was never man yet laid. ⁴²There laid they Jesus therefore because of the Jews' preparation day; for the sepulcher was near at hand.

20 ¹The first day of the week comes Mary Magdalene early, when it was yet dark, to the sepulcher, and sees the stone taken away from the sepulcher. ²Then she runs, and comes to Simon Peter, and to the other disciple, whom Jesus loved, and says to them, They have taken away the LORD out of the sepulcher, and we know not where they have laid him. ³Peter therefore went forth, and that other disciple, and came to the sepulcher. ⁴So they ran both together: and the other disciple did outrun Peter, and came first to the sepulcher. ⁵And he stooping down, and looking in, saw the linen clothes lying; yet went he not in. ⁶Then comes Simon Peter following him, and went into the sepulcher, and sees the linen clothes lie, ⁷And the napkin, that was about his head, not lying with the linen clothes, but wrapped together in a place by itself. ⁸Then went in also that other disciple, which came first to the sepulcher, and he saw, and believed. ⁹For as yet they knew not the scripture, that he must rise again from the dead. ¹⁰Then the disciples went away again to their own home. ¹¹But Mary stood without at the sepulcher weeping: and as she wept, she stooped down, and looked into the sepulcher, ¹²And sees two angels in white sitting, the one at the head, and the other at the feet, where the body of Jesus had lain. ¹³And they say to her, Woman, why weep you? She says to them, Because they have taken away my LORD, and I know not where they have laid him. ¹⁴And when she had thus said, she turned herself back, and saw Jesus standing, and knew not that it was Jesus. ¹⁵Jesus says to her, Woman, why weep you? whom seek you? She, supposing him to be the gardener, says to him, Sir, if you have borne him hence, tell me where you have laid him, and I will take him away. ¹⁶Jesus says to her, Mary. She turned herself, and says to him, Rabboni; which is to say, Master. ¹⁷Jesus says to her, Touch me not; for I am not yet ascended to my Father: but go to my brothers, and say to them, I ascend to my Father, and your Father; and to my God, and your God. ¹⁸Mary Magdalene came and told the disciples that she had seen the LORD, and that he had spoken these things to her. ¹⁹Then the same day at evening, being the first day of the week, when the doors were shut where the disciples were assembled for fear of the Jews, came Jesus and stood in the middle, and says to them, Peace be to you. ²⁰And when he had so said, he showed to them his hands and his side. Then were the disciples glad, when they saw the LORD. ²¹Then said Jesus to them again, Peace be to you: as my Father has sent me, even so send I you. ²²And when he had said this, he breathed on them, and says to them, Receive you the Holy Ghost: ²³Whose soever sins you remit, they are remitted to them; and whose soever sins you retain, they are retained. ²⁴But Thomas, one of the twelve, called Didymus, was not with them when Jesus came. ²⁵The other disciples therefore said to him, We have seen the LORD. But he said to them, Except I shall see in his hands the print of the nails, and put my finger into the print of the nails, and thrust my hand into his side, I will not believe. ²⁶And after eight days again his disciples were within, and Thomas with them: then came Jesus, the doors being shut, and stood in the middle, and said, Peace be to you. ²⁷Then says he to Thomas, Reach here your finger, and behold my hands; and reach here your hand, and thrust it into my side: and be not faithless, but believing. ²⁸And Thomas answered and said to him, My LORD and my God. ²⁹Jesus says to him, Thomas, because you have seen me, you have believed: blessed are they that have not seen, and yet have believed. ³⁰And many other signs truly did Jesus in the presence of his disciples, which are not written in this book: ³¹But these are written, that you might believe that Jesus is the Christ, the Son of God; and that believing you might have life through his name.

21 ¹After these things Jesus showed himself again to the disciples at the sea of Tiberias; and on this wise showed he himself. ²There were together Simon Peter, and Thomas called Didymus, and Nathanael of Cana in Galilee, and the sons of Zebedee, and two other of his disciples. ³Simon Peter says to them, I go a fishing. They say to him, We also go with you. They went forth, and entered into a ship immediately; and that night they caught nothing. ⁴But when the morning was now come, Jesus stood on the shore: but the disciples knew not that it was Jesus. ⁵Then Jesus says to them, Children, have you any meat? They answered him, No. ⁶And he said to them, Cast the net on the right side of the ship, and you shall find. They cast therefore, and now they were not able to draw it for the multitude of fishes. ⁷Therefore that disciple whom Jesus loved says to Peter, It is the Lord. Now when Simon Peter heard that it was the Lord, he girt his fisher's coat to him, (for he was naked,) and did cast himself into the sea. ⁸And the other disciples came in a little ship; (for they were not far from land, but as it were two hundred cubits,) dragging the net with fishes. ⁹As soon then as they were come to land, they saw a fire of coals there, and fish laid thereon, and bread. ¹⁰Jesus says to them, Bring of the fish which you have now caught. ¹¹Simon Peter went up, and drew the net to land full of great fishes, an hundred and fifty and three: and for all there were so many, yet was not the net broken. ¹²Jesus says to them, Come and dine. And none of the disciples dared ask him, Who are you? knowing that it was the Lord. ¹³Jesus then comes, and takes bread, and gives them, and fish likewise. ¹⁴This is now the third time that Jesus showed himself to his disciples, after that he was risen from the dead. ¹⁵So when they had dined, Jesus says to Simon Peter, Simon, son of Jonas, love you me more than these? He says to him, Yes, Lord; you know that I love you. He said to him, Feed my lambs. ¹⁶He says to him again the second time, Simon, son of Jonas, love you me? He says to him, Yes, Lord; you know that I love you. He said to him, Feed my sheep. ¹⁷He says to him the third time, Simon, son of Jonas, love you me? Peter was grieved because he said to him the third time, Love you me? And he said to him, Lord, you know all things; you know that I love you. Jesus says to him, Feed my sheep. ¹⁸Truly, truly, I say to you, When you were young, you gird yourself, and walked where you would: but when you shall be old, you shall stretch forth your hands, and another shall gird you, and carry you where you would not. ¹⁹This spoke he, signifying by what death he should glorify God. And when he had spoken this, he says to him, Follow me. ²⁰Then Peter, turning about, sees the disciple whom Jesus loved following; which also leaned on his breast at supper, and said, Lord, which is he that betrays you? ²¹Peter seeing him says to Jesus, Lord, and what shall this man do? ²²Jesus says to him, If I will that he tarry till I come, what is that to you? follow you me. ²³Then went this saying abroad among the brothers, that that disciple should not die: yet Jesus said not to him, He shall not die; but, If I will that he tarry till I come, what is that to you? ²⁴This is the disciple which testifies of these things, and wrote these things: and we know that his testimony is true. ²⁵And there are also many other things which Jesus did, the which, if they should be written every one, I suppose that even the world itself could not contain the books that should be written. Amen.

Acts

1 ¹The former treatise have I made, O Theophilus, of all that Jesus began both to do and teach, ²Until the day in which he was taken up, after that he through the Holy Ghost had given commandments to the apostles whom he had chosen: ³To whom also he showed himself alive after his passion by many infallible proofs, being seen of them forty days, and speaking of the things pertaining to the kingdom of God: ⁴And, being assembled together with them, commanded them that they should not depart from Jerusalem, but wait for the promise of the Father, which, says he, you have heard of me. ⁵For John truly baptized with water; but you shall be baptized with the Holy Ghost not many days hence. ⁶When they therefore were come together, they asked of him, saying, Lord, will you at this time restore again the kingdom to Israel? ⁷And he said to them, It is not for you to know the times or the seasons, which the Father has put in his own power. ⁸But you shall receive power, after that the Holy Ghost is come on you: and you shall be witnesses to me both in Jerusalem, and in all Judaea, and in Samaria, and to the uttermost part of the earth. ⁹And when he had spoken these things, while they beheld, he was taken up; and a cloud received him out of their sight. ¹⁰And while they looked steadfastly toward heaven as he went up, behold, two men stood by them in white apparel; ¹¹Which also said, You men of Galilee, why stand you gazing up into heaven? this same Jesus, which is taken up from you into heaven, shall so come in like manner as you have seen him go into heaven. ¹²Then returned they to Jerusalem from the mount called Olivet, which is from Jerusalem a sabbath day's journey. ¹³And when they were come in, they went up into an upper room, where stayed both Peter, and James, and John, and Andrew, Philip, and Thomas, Bartholomew, and Matthew, James the son of Alphaeus, and Simon Zelotes, and Judas the brother of James. ¹⁴These all continued with one accord in prayer and supplication, with the women, and Mary the mother of Jesus, and with his brothers. ¹⁵And in those days Peter stood up in the middle of the disciples, and said, (the number of names together were about an hundred and twenty,) ¹⁶Men and brothers, this scripture must needs have been fulfilled, which the Holy Ghost by the mouth of David spoke before concerning Judas, which was guide to them that took Jesus. ¹⁷For he was numbered with us, and had obtained part of this ministry. ¹⁸Now this man purchased a field with the reward of iniquity; and falling headlong, he burst asunder in the middle, and all his bowels gushed out. ¹⁹And it was known to all the dwellers at Jerusalem; so as that field is called in their proper tongue, Aceldama, that is to say, The field of blood. ²⁰For it is written in the book of Psalms, Let his habitation be desolate, and let no man dwell therein: and his position as bishop let another take. ²¹Why of these men which have companied with us all the time that the Lord Jesus went in and out among us, ²²Beginning from the baptism of John, to that same day that he was taken up from us, must one be ordained to be a witness with us of his resurrection. ²³And they appointed two, Joseph called Barsabas, who was surnamed Justus, and Matthias. ²⁴And they prayed, and said, You, Lord, which know the hearts of all men, show whether of these two you have chosen, ²⁵That he may take part of this ministry and apostleship, from which Judas by transgression fell, that he might go to his own place. ²⁶And they gave forth their lots; and the lot fell on Matthias; and he was numbered with the eleven apostles.

2 ¹And when the day of Pentecost was fully come, they were all with one accord in one place. ²And suddenly there came a sound from heaven as of a rushing mighty wind, and it filled all the house where they were sitting. ³And there appeared to them cloven tongues like as of fire, and it sat on each of them. ⁴And they were all filled with the Holy Ghost, and began to speak with other tongues, as the Spirit gave them utterance. ⁵And there were dwelling at Jerusalem Jews, devout men, out of every nation under heaven. ⁶Now when this was noised abroad, the multitude came together, and were confounded, because that every man heard them speak in his own language. ⁷And they were all amazed and marveled, saying one to another, Behold, are not all these which speak Galilaeans? ⁸And how hear we every man in our own tongue, wherein we were born? ⁹Parthians, and Medes, and Elamites, and the dwellers in Mesopotamia, and in Judaea, and Cappadocia, in Pontus, and Asia, ¹⁰Phrygia, and Pamphylia, in Egypt, and in the parts of Libya about Cyrene, and strangers of Rome, Jews and proselytes, ¹¹Cretes and Arabians, we do hear them speak in our tongues the wonderful works of God. ¹²And they were all amazed, and were in doubt, saying one to another, What means this? ¹³Others mocking said, These men are full of new wine. ¹⁴But Peter, standing up with the eleven, lifted up his voice, and said to them, You men of Judaea, and all you that dwell at Jerusalem, be this known to you, and listen to my words: ¹⁵For these are not drunken, as you suppose, seeing it is but the third hour of the day. ¹⁶But this is that which was spoken by the prophet Joel; ¹⁷And it shall come to pass in the last days, says God, I will pour out of my Spirit on all flesh: and your sons and your daughters shall prophesy, and your young men shall see visions, and your old men shall dream dreams: ¹⁸And on my servants and on my handmaidens I will pour out in those days of my Spirit; and they shall prophesy: ¹⁹And I will show wonders in heaven above, and signs in the earth beneath; blood, and fire, and vapor of smoke: ²⁰The sun shall be turned into darkness, and the moon into blood, before the great and notable day of the Lord come: ²¹And it shall come to pass, that whoever shall call on the name of the Lord shall be saved. ²²You men of Israel, hear these words; Jesus of Nazareth, a man approved of God among you by miracles and wonders and signs, which God did by him in the middle of you, as you yourselves also know: ²³Him, being delivered by the determinate counsel and foreknowledge of God, you have taken, and by wicked hands have crucified and slain: ²⁴Whom God has raised up, having loosed the pains of death: because it was not possible that he should be held of it. ²⁵For David speaks concerning him, I foresaw the Lord always before my face, for he is on my right hand, that I should not be moved: ²⁶Therefore did my heart rejoice, and my tongue was glad; moreover also my flesh shall rest in hope: ²⁷Because you will not leave my soul in hell, neither will you suffer your Holy One to see corruption. ²⁸You have made known to me the ways of life; you shall make me full of joy with your countenance. ²⁹Men and brothers, let me freely speak to you of the patriarch David, that he is both dead and buried, and his sepulcher is with us to this day. ³⁰Therefore being a prophet, and knowing that God had sworn with an oath to him, that of the fruit of his loins, according to the flesh, he would raise up Christ to sit on his throne; ³¹He seeing this before spoke of the resurrection of Christ, that his soul was not left in hell, neither his flesh did see corruption. ³²This Jesus has God raised up, whereof we all are witnesses. ³³Therefore being by the right hand of God exalted, and having received of the Father the promise of the Holy Ghost, he has shed forth this, which you now see and hear. ³⁴For David is not ascended into the heavens: but he says himself, The Lord said to my Lord, Sit you on my right hand, ³⁵Until I make your foes your footstool. ³⁶Therefore let all the house of Israel know assuredly, that God has made the same Jesus, whom you have crucified, both Lord and Christ. ³⁷Now when they heard this, they were pricked in their heart, and said to Peter and to the rest of the apostles, Men and brothers, what shall we do? ³⁸Then Peter said to them, Repent, and be baptized every one of you in the name of Jesus Christ for the remission of sins, and you shall receive the gift of the Holy Ghost. ³⁹For the promise is to you, and to your children, and to all that are afar off, even as many as the LORD our God shall call. ⁴⁰And with many other words did he testify and exhort, saying, Save yourselves from this untoward generation. ⁴¹Then they that gladly received his word were baptized: and the same day there were added to them about three thousand souls. ⁴²And they continued steadfastly in the apostles' doctrine and fellowship, and in breaking of bread, and in prayers. ⁴³And fear came on every soul: and many wonders and signs were done by the apostles. ⁴⁴And all that believed were together, and had all things common; ⁴⁵And sold their possessions and goods, and parted them to all men, as every man had need. ⁴⁶And they, continuing daily with one accord in the temple, and breaking bread from house to house, did eat their meat with gladness and singleness of heart, ⁴⁷Praising God, and having favor with all the people. And the Lord added to the church daily such as should be saved.

3 ¹Now Peter and John went up together into the temple at the hour of prayer, being the ninth hour. ²And a certain man lame from his mother's womb was carried, whom they laid daily at the gate of the temple which is called Beautiful, to ask alms of them that entered into the temple; ³Who seeing Peter and John about to go into the temple asked an alms. ⁴And Peter, fastening his eyes on him with John, said, Look on us. ⁵And he gave heed to them, expecting to receive something of them. ⁶Then Peter said, Silver and gold have I none; but such as I have give I you: In the name of Jesus Christ of Nazareth rise up and walk. ⁷And he took him by the right hand, and lifted him up: and immediately his feet and ankle bones received strength. ⁸And he leaping up stood, and walked, and entered with them into the temple, walking, and leaping, and praising God. ⁹And all the people saw him walking and praising God: ¹⁰And they knew that it was he which sat for alms at the Beautiful gate of the temple: and they were filled with wonder and amazement at that which had happened to him. ¹¹And as the lame man which was healed held Peter and John, all the people ran together to them in the porch that is called Solomon's, greatly wondering. ¹²And when Peter saw it, he answered to the people, You men of Israel, why marvel you at this? or why look you so earnestly on us, as though by our own power or holiness we had made this man to walk? ¹³The God of Abraham, and of Isaac, and of Jacob, the God of our fathers, has glorified his Son Jesus; whom you delivered up, and denied him in the presence of Pilate, when he was determined to let him go. ¹⁴But you denied the Holy One and the Just, and desired a murderer to be granted to you; ¹⁵And killed the Prince of life, whom God has raised from the dead; whereof we are witnesses. ¹⁶And his name through faith in his name has made this man strong, whom you see and know: yes, the faith which is by him has given him this perfect soundness in the presence of you all. ¹⁷And now, brothers, I know that through ignorance you did it, as did also your rulers. ¹⁸But those things, which God before had showed by the mouth of all his prophets, that Christ should suffer, he has so fulfilled. ¹⁹Repent you therefore, and be converted, that your sins may be blotted out, when the times of refreshing shall come from the presence of the Lord. ²⁰And he shall send Jesus Christ, which before was preached to you: ²¹Whom the heaven must receive until the times of restitution of all things, which God has spoken by the mouth of all his holy prophets since the world began. ²²For Moses truly said to the fathers, A prophet shall the Lord your God raise up to you of your brothers, like to me; him shall you hear in all things whatever he shall say to you. ²³And it shall come to pass, that every soul, which will not hear that prophet, shall be destroyed from among the people. ²⁴Yes, and all the prophets from Samuel and those that follow after, as many as have spoken, have likewise foretold of these days. ²⁵You are the children of the prophets, and of the covenant which God made with our fathers, saying to Abraham, And in your seed shall all the kindreds of the earth be blessed. ²⁶To you first God, having raised up his Son Jesus, sent him to bless you, in turning away every one of you from his iniquities.

4 ¹And as they spoke to the people, the priests, and the captain of the temple, and the Sadducees, came on them, ²Being grieved that they taught the people, and preached through Jesus the resurrection from the dead. ³And they laid hands on them, and put them in hold to the next day: for it was now eventide. ⁴However, many of them which heard the word believed; and the number of the men was about five thousand. ⁵And it came to pass on the morrow, that their rulers, and elders, and scribes, ⁶And Annas the high priest, and Caiaphas, and John, and Alexander, and as many as were of the kindred of the high priest, were gathered together at Jerusalem. ⁷And when they had set them in the middle, they asked, By what power, or by what name, have you done this? ⁸Then Peter, filled with the Holy Ghost, said to them, You rulers of the people, and elders of Israel, ⁹If we this day be examined of the good deed done to the weak man, by what means he is made whole; ¹⁰Be it known to you all, and to all the people of

Israel, that by the name of Jesus Christ of Nazareth, whom you crucified, whom God raised from the dead, even by him does this man stand here before you whole. ¹¹This is the stone which was set at nothing of you builders, which is become the head of the corner. ¹²Neither is there salvation in any other: for there is none other name under heaven given among men, whereby we must be saved. ¹³Now when they saw the boldness of Peter and John, and perceived that they were unlearned and ignorant men, they marveled; and they took knowledge of them, that they had been with Jesus. ¹⁴And beholding the man which was healed standing with them, they could say nothing against it. ¹⁵But when they had commanded them to go aside out of the council, they conferred among themselves, ¹⁶Saying, What shall we do to these men? for that indeed a notable miracle has been done by them is manifest to all them that dwell in Jerusalem; and we cannot deny it. ¹⁷But that it spread no further among the people, let us straightly threaten them, that they speak from now on to no man in this name. ¹⁸And they called them, and commanded them not to speak at all nor teach in the name of Jesus. ¹⁹But Peter and John answered and said to them, Whether it be right in the sight of God to listen to you more than to God, judge you. ²⁰For we cannot but speak the things which we have seen and heard. ²¹So when they had further threatened them, they let them go, finding nothing how they might punish them, because of the people: for all men glorified God for that which was done. ²²For the man was above forty years old, on whom this miracle of healing was showed. ²³And being let go, they went to their own company, and reported all that the chief priests and elders had said to them. ²⁴And when they heard that, they lifted up their voice to God with one accord, and said, Lord, you are God, which have made heaven, and earth, and the sea, and all that in them is: ²⁵Who by the mouth of your servant David have said, Why did the heathen rage, and the people imagine vain things? ²⁶The kings of the earth stood up, and the rulers were gathered together against the Lord, and against his Christ. ²⁷For of a truth against your holy child Jesus, whom you have anointed, both Herod, and Pontius Pilate, with the Gentiles, and the people of Israel, were gathered together, ²⁸For to do whatever your hand and your counsel determined before to be done. ²⁹And now, Lord, behold their threatenings: and grant to your servants, that with all boldness they may speak your word, ³⁰By stretching forth your hand to heal; and that signs and wonders may be done by the name of your holy child Jesus. ³¹And when they had prayed, the place was shaken where they were assembled together; and they were all filled with the Holy Ghost, and they spoke the word of God with boldness. ³²And the multitude of them that believed were of one heart and of one soul: neither said any of them that something of the things which he possessed was his own; but they had all things common. ³³And with great power gave the apostles witness of the resurrection of the Lord Jesus: and great grace was on them all. ³⁴Neither was there any among them that lacked: for as many as were possessors of lands or houses sold them, and brought the prices of the things that were sold, ³⁵And laid them down at the apostles' feet: and distribution was made to every man according as he had need. ³⁶And Joses, who by the apostles was surnamed Barnabas, (which is, being interpreted, The son of consolation,) a Levite, and of the country of Cyprus, ³⁷Having land, sold it, and brought the money, and laid it at the apostles' feet.

5 ¹But a certain man named Ananias, with Sapphira his wife, sold a possession, ²And kept back part of the price, his wife also being privy to it, and brought a certain part, and laid it at the apostles' feet. ³But Peter said, Ananias, why has Satan filled your heart to lie to the Holy Ghost, and to keep back part of the price of the land? ⁴Whiles it remained, was it not your own? and after it was sold, was it not in your own power? why have you conceived this thing in your heart? you have not lied to men, but to God. ⁵And Ananias hearing these words fell down, and gave up the ghost: and great fear came on all them that heard these things. ⁶And the young men arose, wound him up, and carried him out, and buried him. ⁷And it was about the space of three hours after, when his wife, not knowing what was done, came in. ⁸And Peter answered to her, Tell me whether you sold the land for so much? And she said, Yes, for so much. ⁹Then Peter said to her, How is it that you have agreed together to tempt the Spirit of the Lord? behold, the feet of them which have buried your husband are at the door, and shall carry you out. ¹⁰Then fell she down straightway at his feet, and yielded up the ghost: and the young men came in, and found her dead, and, carrying her forth, buried her by her husband. ¹¹And great fear came on all the church, and on as many as heard these things. ¹²And by the hands of the apostles were many signs and wonders worked among the people; (and they were all with one accord in Solomon's porch. ¹³And of the rest dared no man join himself to them: but the people magnified them. ¹⁴And believers were the more added to the Lord, multitudes both of men and women.) ¹⁵So that they brought forth the sick into the streets, and laid them on beds and couches, that at the least the shadow of Peter passing by might overshadow some of them. ¹⁶There came also a multitude out of the cities round about to Jerusalem, bringing sick folks, and them which were vexed with unclean spirits: and they were healed every one. ¹⁷Then the high priest rose up, and all they that were with him, (which is the sect of the Sadducees,) and were filled with indignation, ¹⁸And laid their hands on the apostles, and put them in the common prison. ¹⁹But the angel of the Lord by night opened the prison doors, and brought them forth, and said, ²⁰Go, stand and speak in the temple to the people all the words of this life. ²¹And when they heard that, they entered into the temple early in the morning, and taught. But the high priest came, and they that were with him, and called the council together, and all the senate of the children of Israel, and sent to the prison to have them brought. ²²But when the officers came, and found them not in the prison, they returned and told, ²³Saying, The prison truly found we shut with all safety, and the keepers standing without before the doors: but when we had opened, we found no man within. ²⁴Now when the high priest and the captain of the temple and the chief priests heard these things, they doubted of them to what this would grow. ²⁵Then came one and told them, saying, Behold, the men whom you put in prison are standing in the temple, and

teaching the people. ²⁶Then went the captain with the officers, and brought them without violence: for they feared the people, lest they should have been stoned. ²⁷And when they had brought them, they set them before the council: and the high priest asked them, ²⁸Saying, Did not we straightly command you that you should not teach in this name? and, behold, you have filled Jerusalem with your doctrine, and intend to bring this man's blood on us. ²⁹Then Peter and the other apostles answered and said, We ought to obey God rather than men. ³⁰The God of our fathers raised up Jesus, whom you slew and hanged on a tree. ³¹Him has God exalted with his right hand to be a Prince and a Savior, for to give repentance to Israel, and forgiveness of sins. ³²And we are his witnesses of these things; and so is also the Holy Ghost, whom God has given to them that obey him. ³³When they heard that, they were cut to the heart, and took counsel to slay them. ³⁴Then stood there up one in the council, a Pharisee, named Gamaliel, a doctor of the law, had in reputation among all the people, and commanded to put the apostles forth a little space; ³⁵And said to them, You men of Israel, take heed to yourselves what you intend to do as touching these men. ³⁶For before these days rose up Theudas, boasting himself to be somebody; to whom a number of men, about four hundred, joined themselves: who was slain; and all, as many as obeyed him, were scattered, and brought to nothing. ³⁷After this man rose up Judas of Galilee in the days of the taxing, and drew away much people after him: he also perished; and all, even as many as obeyed him, were dispersed. ³⁸And now I say to you, Refrain from these men, and let them alone: for if this counsel or this work be of men, it will come to nothing: ³⁹But if it be of God, you cannot overthrow it; lest haply you be found even to fight against God. ⁴⁰And to him they agreed: and when they had called the apostles, and beaten them, they commanded that they should not speak in the name of Jesus, and let them go. ⁴¹And they departed from the presence of the council, rejoicing that they were counted worthy to suffer shame for his name. ⁴²And daily in the temple, and in every house, they ceased not to teach and preach Jesus Christ.

6 ¹And in those days, when the number of the disciples was multiplied, there arose a murmuring of the Grecians against the Hebrews, because their widows were neglected in the daily ministration. ²Then the twelve called the multitude of the disciples to them, and said, It is not reason that we should leave the word of God, and serve tables. ³Why, brothers, look you out among you seven men of honest report, full of the Holy Ghost and wisdom, whom we may appoint over this business. ⁴But we will give ourselves continually to prayer, and to the ministry of the word. ⁵And the saying pleased the whole multitude: and they chose Stephen, a man full of faith and of the Holy Ghost, and Philip, and Prochorus, and Nicanor, and Timon, and Parmenas, and Nicolas a proselyte of Antioch: ⁶Whom they set before the apostles: and when they had prayed, they laid their hands on them. ⁷And the word of God increased; and the number of the disciples multiplied in Jerusalem greatly; and a great company of the priests were obedient to the faith. ⁸And Stephen, full of faith and power, did great wonders and miracles among the people. ⁹Then there arose certain of the synagogue, which is called the synagogue of the Libertines, and Cyrenians, and Alexandrians, and of them of Cilicia and of Asia, disputing with Stephen. ¹⁰And they were not able to resist the wisdom and the spirit by which he spoke. ¹¹Then they suborned men, which said, We have heard him speak blasphemous words against Moses, and against God. ¹²And they stirred up the people, and the elders, and the scribes, and came on him, and caught him, and brought him to the council, ¹³And set up false witnesses, which said, This man ceases not to speak blasphemous words against this holy place, and the law: ¹⁴For we have heard him say, that this Jesus of Nazareth shall destroy this place, and shall change the customs which Moses delivered us. ¹⁵And all that sat in the council, looking steadfastly on him, saw his face as it had been the face of an angel.

7 ¹Then said the high priest, Are these things so? ²And he said, Men, brothers, and fathers, listen; The God of glory appeared to our father Abraham, when he was in Mesopotamia, before he dwelled in Charran, ³And said to him, Get you out of your country, and from your kindred, and come into the land which I shall show you. ⁴Then came he out of the land of the Chaldaeans, and dwelled in Charran: and from there, when his father was dead, he removed him into this land, wherein you now dwell. ⁵And he gave him none inheritance in it, no, not so much as to set his foot on: yet he promised that he would give it to him for a possession, and to his seed after him, when as yet he had no child. ⁶And God spoke on this wise, That his seed should sojourn in a strange land; and that they should bring them into bondage, and entreat them evil four hundred years. ⁷And the nation to whom they shall be in bondage will I judge, said God: and after that shall they come forth, and serve me in this place. ⁸And he gave him the covenant of circumcision: and so Abraham was the father of Isaac, and circumcised him the eighth day; and Isaac was the father of Jacob; and Jacob was the father of the twelve patriarchs. ⁹And the patriarchs, moved with envy, sold Joseph into Egypt: but God was with him, ¹⁰And delivered him out of all his afflictions, and gave him favor and wisdom in the sight of Pharaoh king of Egypt; and he made him governor over Egypt and all his house. ¹¹Now there came a dearth over all the land of Egypt and Chanaan, and great affliction: and our fathers found no sustenance. ¹²But when Jacob heard that there was corn in Egypt, he sent out our fathers first. ¹³And at the second time Joseph was made known to his brothers; and Joseph's kindred was made known to Pharaoh. ¹⁴Then sent Joseph, and called his father Jacob to him, and all his kindred, three score and fifteen souls. ¹⁵So Jacob went down into Egypt, and died, he, and our fathers, ¹⁶And were carried over into Sychem, and laid in the sepulcher that Abraham bought for a sum of money of the sons of Emmor the father of Sychem. ¹⁷But when the time of the promise drew near, which God had sworn to Abraham, the people grew and multiplied in Egypt, ¹⁸Till another king arose, which knew not Joseph. ¹⁹The same dealt subtly with our kindred, and evil entreated our fathers, so that they cast out their young children, to the end they might not live. ²⁰In which time Moses was born, and was exceeding fair, and nourished up in his father's house three months: ²¹And when he was cast out, Pharaoh's daughter took him up, and nourished him for her own son. ²²And Moses was learned in all the wisdom of the Egyptians, and was mighty in words and in deeds. ²³And when he was full forty years old, it came into his heart to visit his brothers the children of Israel. ²⁴And seeing one of them suffer wrong, he defended him, and avenged him that was oppressed, and smote the Egyptian: ²⁵For he supposed his brothers would have understood how that God by his hand would deliver them: but they understood not. ²⁶And the next day he showed himself to them as they strove, and would have set them at one again, saying, Sirs, you are brothers; why do you wrong one to another? ²⁷But he that did his neighbor wrong thrust him away, saying, Who made you a ruler and a judge over us? ²⁸Will you kill me, as you did the Egyptian yesterday? ²⁹Then fled Moses at this saying, and was a stranger in the land of Madian, where he was the father of two sons. ³⁰And when forty years were expired, there appeared to him in the wilderness of mount Sina an angel of the Lord in a flame of fire in a bush. ³¹When Moses saw it, he wondered at the sight: and as he drew near to behold it, the voice of the LORD came to him, ³²Saying, I am the God of your fathers, the God of Abraham, and the God of Isaac, and the God of Jacob. Then Moses trembled, and dared not behold. ³³Then said the Lord to him, Put off your shoes from your feet: for the place where you stand is holy ground. ³⁴I have seen, I have seen the affliction of my people which is in Egypt, and I have heard their groaning, and am come down to deliver them. And now come, I will send you into Egypt. ³⁵This Moses whom they refused, saying, Who made you a ruler and a judge? the same did God send to be a ruler and a deliverer by the hand of the angel which appeared to him in the bush. ³⁶He brought them out, after that he had showed wonders and signs in the land of Egypt, and in the Red sea, and in the wilderness forty years. ³⁷This is that Moses, which said to the children of Israel, A prophet shall the Lord your God raise up to you of your brothers, like to me; him shall you hear. ³⁸This is he, that was in the church in the wilderness with the angel which spoke to him in the mount Sina, and with our fathers: who received the lively oracles to give to us: ³⁹To whom our fathers would not obey, but thrust him from them, and in their hearts turned back again into Egypt, ⁴⁰Saying to Aaron, Make us gods to go before us: for as for this Moses, which brought us out of the land of Egypt, we know not what is become of him. ⁴¹And they made a calf in those days, and offered sacrifice to the idol, and rejoiced in the works of their own hands. ⁴²Then God turned, and gave them up to worship the host of heaven; as it is written in the book of the prophets, O you house of Israel, have you offered to me slain beasts and sacrifices by the space of forty years in the wilderness? ⁴³Yes, you took up the tabernacle of Moloch, and the star of your god Remphan, figures which you made to worship them: and I will carry you away beyond Babylon. ⁴⁴Our fathers had the tabernacle of witness in the wilderness, as he had appointed, speaking to Moses, that he should make it according to the fashion that he had seen. ⁴⁵Which also our fathers that came after brought in with Jesus into the possession of the Gentiles, whom God drove out before the face of our fathers, to the days of David; ⁴⁶Who found favor before God, and desired to find a tabernacle for the God of Jacob. ⁴⁷But Solomon built him an house. ⁴⁸However, the most High dwells not in temples made with hands; as says the prophet, ⁴⁹Heaven is my throne, and earth is my footstool: what house will you build me? says the Lord: or what is the place of my rest? ⁵⁰Has not my hand made all these things? ⁵¹You stiff necked and uncircumcised in heart and ears, you do always resist the Holy Ghost: as your fathers did, so do you. ⁵²Which of the prophets have not your fathers persecuted? and they have slain them which showed before of the coming of the Just One; of whom you have been now the betrayers and murderers: ⁵³Who have received the law by the disposition of angels, and have not kept it. ⁵⁴When they heard these things, they were cut to the heart, and they gnashed on him with their teeth. ⁵⁵But he, being full of the Holy Ghost, looked up steadfastly into heaven, and saw the glory of God, and Jesus standing on the right hand of God, ⁵⁶And said, Behold, I see the heavens opened, and the Son of man standing on the right hand of God. ⁵⁷Then they cried out with a loud voice, and stopped their ears, and ran on him with one accord, ⁵⁸And cast him out of the city, and stoned him: and the witnesses laid down their clothes at a young man's feet, whose name was Saul. ⁵⁹And they stoned Stephen, calling on God, and saying, Lord Jesus, receive my spirit. ⁶⁰And he kneeled down, and cried with a loud voice, Lord, lay not this sin to their charge. And when he had said this, he fell asleep.

8 ¹And Saul was consenting to his death. And at that time there was a great persecution against the church which was at Jerusalem; and they were all scattered abroad throughout the regions of Judaea and Samaria, except the apostles. ²And devout men carried Stephen to his burial, and made great lamentation over him. ³As for Saul, he made havoc of the church, entering into every house, and haling men and women committed them to prison. ⁴Therefore they that were scattered abroad went every where preaching the word. ⁵Then Philip went down to the city of Samaria, and preached Christ to them. ⁶And the people with one accord gave heed to those things which Philip spoke, hearing and seeing the miracles which he did. ⁷For unclean spirits, crying with loud voice, came out of many that were possessed with them: and many taken with palsies, and that were lame, were healed. ⁸And there was great joy in that city. ⁹But there was a certain man, called Simon, which beforetime in the same city used sorcery, and bewitched the people of Samaria, giving out that himself was some great one: ¹⁰To whom they all gave heed, from the least to the greatest, saying, This man is the great power of God. ¹¹And to him they had regard, because that of long time he had bewitched them with sorceries. ¹²But when they believed Philip preaching the things concerning the kingdom of God, and the name of Jesus Christ, they were baptized, both men and women. ¹³Then Simon himself believed also: and when he was baptized, he continued with Philip, and wondered, beholding the miracles and signs which were done. ¹⁴Now when the apostles which were at Jerusalem heard that Samaria had received the word of God, they sent to them Peter and John: ¹⁵Who, when they were come down, prayed for them, that they might receive the Holy Ghost: ¹⁶(For as yet he was fallen on none of them: only they were baptized in the name of the Lord Jesus.) ¹⁷Then laid they their hands on them, and they received the Holy Ghost. ¹⁸And when Simon saw that through laying on of the apostles' hands the Holy Ghost was given, he offered them money, ¹⁹Saying, Give me also this power, that on whomsoever I lay hands, he may receive the Holy Ghost. ²⁰But Peter said to him, Your money perish with you, because you have thought that the gift of God may be purchased with money. ²¹You have neither part nor lot in this matter: for your heart is not right in the sight of God. ²²Repent therefore of this your wickedness, and pray God, if perhaps the thought of your heart may be forgiven you. ²³For I perceive that you are in the gall of bitterness, and in the bond of iniquity. ²⁴Then answered Simon, and said, Pray you to the LORD for me, that none of these things which you have spoken come on me. ²⁵And they, when they had testified and preached the word of the Lord, returned to Jerusalem, and preached the gospel in many villages of the Samaritans. ²⁶And the angel of the Lord spoke to Philip, saying, Arise, and go toward the south to the way that goes down from Jerusalem to Gaza, which is desert. ²⁷And he arose and went: and, behold, a man of Ethiopia, an eunuch of great authority under Candace queen of the Ethiopians, who had the charge of all her treasure, and had come to Jerusalem for to worship, ²⁸Was returning, and sitting in his chariot read Isaiah the prophet. ²⁹Then the Spirit said to Philip, Go near, and join yourself to this chariot. ³⁰And Philip ran thither to him, and heard him read the prophet Isaiah, and said, Understand you what you read? ³¹And he said, How can I, except some man should guide me? And he desired Philip that he would come up and sit with him. ³²The place of the scripture which he read was this, He was led as a sheep to the slaughter; and like a lamb dumb before his shearer, so opened he not his mouth: ³³In his humiliation his judgment was taken away: and who shall declare his generation? for his life is taken from the earth. ³⁴And the eunuch answered Philip, and said, I pray you, of whom speaks the prophet this? of himself, or of some other man? ³⁵Then Philip opened his mouth, and began at the same scripture, and preached to him Jesus. ³⁶And as they went on their way, they came to a certain water: and the eunuch said, See, here is water; what does hinder me to be baptized? ³⁷And Philip said, If you believe with all your heart, you may. And he answered and said, I believe that Jesus Christ is the Son of God. ³⁸And he commanded the chariot to stand still: and they went down both into the water, both Philip and the eunuch; and he baptized him. ³⁹And when they were come up out of the water, the Spirit of the Lord caught away Philip, that the eunuch saw him no more: and he went on his way rejoicing. ⁴⁰But Philip was found at Azotus: and passing through he preached in all the cities, till he came to Caesarea.

9 ¹And Saul, yet breathing out threatenings and slaughter against the disciples of the Lord, went to the high priest, ²And desired of him letters to Damascus to the synagogues, that if he found any of this way, whether they were men or women, he might bring them bound to Jerusalem. ³And as he journeyed, he came near Damascus: and suddenly there shined round about him a light from heaven: ⁴And he fell to the earth, and heard a voice saying to him, Saul, Saul, why persecute you me? ⁵And he said, Who are you, Lord? And the Lord said, I am Jesus whom you persecute: it is hard for you to kick against the pricks. ⁶And he trembling and astonished said, Lord, what will you have me to do? And the Lord said to him, Arise, and go into the city, and it shall be told you what you must do. ⁷And the men which journeyed with him stood speechless, hearing a voice, but seeing no man. ⁸And Saul arose from the earth; and when his eyes were opened, he saw no man: but they led him by the hand, and brought him into Damascus. ⁹And he was three days without sight, and neither did eat nor drink. ¹⁰And there was a certain disciple at Damascus, named Ananias; and to him said the Lord in a vision, Ananias. And he said, Behold, I am here, Lord. ¹¹And the Lord said to him, Arise, and go into the street which is called Straight, and inquire in the house of Judas for one called Saul, of Tarsus: for, behold, he prays, ¹²And has seen in a vision a man named Ananias coming in, and putting his hand on him, that he might receive his sight. ¹³Then Ananias answered, Lord, I have heard by many of this man, how much evil he has done to your saints at Jerusalem: ¹⁴And here he has authority from the chief priests to bind all that call on your name. ¹⁵But the Lord said to him, Go your way: for he is a chosen vessel to me, to bear my name before the Gentiles, and kings, and the children of Israel: ¹⁶For I will show him how great things he must suffer for my name's sake. ¹⁷And Ananias went his way, and entered into the house; and putting his hands on him said, Brother Saul, the Lord, even Jesus, that appeared to you in the way as you came, has sent me, that you might receive your sight, and be filled with the Holy Ghost. ¹⁸And immediately there fell from his eyes as it had been scales: and he received sight immediately, and arose, and was baptized. ¹⁹And when he had received meat, he was strengthened. Then was Saul certain days with the disciples which were at Damascus. ²⁰And straightway he preached Christ in the synagogues, that he is the Son of God. ²¹But all that heard him were amazed, and said; Is not this he that destroyed them which called on this name in Jerusalem, and came here for that intent, that he might bring them bound to the chief priests? ²²But Saul increased the more in strength, and confounded the Jews which dwelled at Damascus, proving that this is very Christ. ²³And after that many days were fulfilled, the Jews took counsel to kill him: ²⁴But their laying await was known of Saul. And they watched the gates day and night to kill him. ²⁵Then the disciples took him by night, and let him down by the wall in a basket. ²⁶And when Saul was come to Jerusalem, he assayed to join himself to the disciples: but they were all afraid of him, and believed not that he was a disciple. ²⁷But Barnabas took him, and brought him to the apostles, and declared to them how he had seen the Lord in the way, and that he had spoken to him, and how he had preached boldly at Damascus in the name of Jesus. ²⁸And he was with them coming in and going out at Jerusalem. ²⁹And he spoke boldly in the name of the Lord Jesus, and disputed against the Grecians: but they went about to slay him. ³⁰Which when the brothers knew, they brought him down to Caesarea, and sent him forth to Tarsus. ³¹Then had the churches rest throughout all Judaea and Galilee and Samaria, and were edified; and walking in the fear of the Lord, and in the comfort of the Holy Ghost, were multiplied. ³²And it came to pass, as Peter passed throughout all quarters, he came down also to the saints which dwelled at Lydda. ³³And there he found a certain man named Aeneas, which had kept his bed eight years, and was sick of the palsy. ³⁴And Peter said to him, Aeneas, Jesus Christ makes you whole: arise, and make your bed. And he arose immediately. ³⁵And all that dwelled at Lydda and Saron saw him, and turned to the Lord. ³⁶Now there was at Joppa a certain disciple named Tabitha, which by interpretation is called Dorcas: this woman was full of good works and giving of alms which she did. ³⁷And it came to pass in those days, that she was sick, and died: whom when they had washed, they laid her in an upper chamber. ³⁸And for as much as Lydda was near to Joppa, and the disciples had heard that Peter was there, they sent to him two men, desiring him that he would not delay to come to them. ³⁹Then Peter arose and went with them. When he was come, they brought him into the upper chamber: and all the widows stood by him weeping, and showing the coats and garments which Dorcas made, while she was with them. ⁴⁰But Peter put them all forth, and kneeled down, and prayed; and turning him to the body said, Tabitha, arise. And she opened her eyes: and when she saw Peter, she sat up. ⁴¹And he gave her his hand, and lifted her up, and when he had called the saints and widows, presented her alive. ⁴²And it was known throughout all Joppa; and many believed in the Lord. ⁴³And it came to pass, that he tarried many days in Joppa with one Simon a tanner.

10

¹There was a certain man in Caesarea called Cornelius, a centurion of the band called the Italian band, ²A devout man, and one that feared God with all his house, which gave much alms to the people, and prayed to God always. ³He saw in a vision evidently about the ninth hour of the day an angel of God coming in to him, and saying to him, Cornelius. ⁴And when he looked on him, he was afraid, and said, What is it, Lord? And he said to him, Your prayers and your alms are come up for a memorial before God. ⁵And now send men to Joppa, and call for one Simon, whose surname is Peter: ⁶He lodges with one Simon a tanner, whose house is by the sea side: he shall tell you what you ought to do. ⁷And when the angel which spoke to Cornelius was departed, he called two of his household servants, and a devout soldier of them that waited on him continually; ⁸And when he had declared all these things to them, he sent them to Joppa. ⁹On the morrow, as they went on their journey, and drew near to the city, Peter went up on the housetop to pray about the sixth hour: ¹⁰And he became very hungry, and would have eaten: but while they made ready, he fell into a trance, ¹¹And saw heaven opened, and a certain vessel descending on him, as it had been a great sheet knit at the four corners, and let down to the earth: ¹²Wherein were all manner of four footed beasts of the earth, and wild beasts, and creeping things, and fowls of the air. ¹³And there came a voice to him, Rise, Peter; kill, and eat. ¹⁴But Peter said, Not so, Lord; for I have never eaten any thing that is common or unclean. ¹⁵And the voice spoke to him again the second time, What God has cleansed, call not you common. ¹⁶This was done thrice: and the vessel was received up again into heaven. ¹⁷Now while Peter doubted in himself what this vision which he had seen should mean, behold, the men which were sent from Cornelius had made inquiry for Simon's house, and stood before the gate, ¹⁸And called, and asked whether Simon, which was surnamed Peter, were lodged there. ¹⁹While Peter thought on the vision, the Spirit said to him, Behold, three men seek you. ²⁰Arise therefore, and get you down, and go with them, doubting nothing: for I have sent them. ²¹Then Peter went down to the men which were sent to him from Cornelius; and said, Behold, I am he whom you seek: what is the cause why you are come? ²²And they said, Cornelius the centurion, a just man, and one that fears God, and of good report among all the nation of the Jews, was warned from God by an holy angel to send for you into his house, and to hear words of you. ²³Then called he them in, and lodged them. And on the morrow Peter went away with them, and certain brothers from Joppa accompanied him. ²⁴And the morrow after they entered into Caesarea. And Cornelius waited for them, and he had called together his kinsmen and near friends. ²⁵And as Peter was coming in, Cornelius met him, and fell down at his feet, and worshipped him. ²⁶But Peter took him up, saying, Stand up; I myself also am a man. ²⁷And as he talked with him, he went in, and found many that were come together. ²⁸And he said to them, You know how that it is an unlawful thing for a man that is a Jew to keep company, or come to one of another nation; but God has showed me that I should not call any man common or unclean. ²⁹Therefore came I to you without gainsaying, as soon as I was sent for: I ask therefore for what intent you have sent for me? ³⁰And Cornelius said, Four days ago I was fasting until this hour; and at the ninth hour I prayed in my house, and, behold, a man stood before me in bright clothing, ³¹And said, Cornelius, your prayer is heard, and your alms are had in remembrance in the sight of God. ³²Send therefore to Joppa, and call here Simon, whose surname is Peter; he is lodged in the house of one Simon a tanner by the sea side: who, when he comes, shall speak to you. ³³Immediately therefore I sent to you; and you have well done that you are come. Now therefore are we all here present before God, to hear all things that are commanded you of God. ³⁴Then Peter opened his mouth, and said, Of a truth I perceive that God is no respecter of persons: ³⁵But in every nation he that fears him, and works righteousness, is accepted with him. ³⁶The word which God sent to the children of Israel, preaching peace by Jesus Christ: (he is Lord of all:) ³⁷That word, I say, you know, which was published throughout all Judaea, and began from Galilee, after the baptism which John preached; ³⁸How God anointed Jesus of Nazareth with the Holy Ghost and with power: who went about doing good, and healing all that were oppressed of the devil; for God was with him. ³⁹And we are witnesses of all things which he did both in the land of the Jews, and in Jerusalem; whom they slew and hanged on a tree: ⁴⁰Him God raised up the third day, and showed him openly; ⁴¹Not to all the people, but to witnesses chosen before God, even to us, who did eat and drink with him after he rose from the dead. ⁴²And he commanded us to preach to the people, and to testify that it is he which was ordained of God to be the Judge of quick and dead. ⁴³To him give all the prophets

witness, that through his name whoever believes in him shall receive remission of sins. ⁴⁴While Peter yet spoke these words, the Holy Ghost fell on all them which heard the word. ⁴⁵And they of the circumcision which believed were astonished, as many as came with Peter, because that on the Gentiles also was poured out the gift of the Holy Ghost. ⁴⁶For they heard them speak with tongues, and magnify God. Then answered Peter, ⁴⁷Can any man forbid water, that these should not be baptized, which have received the Holy Ghost as well as we? ⁴⁸And he commanded them to be baptized in the name of the Lord. Then prayed they him to tarry certain days.

11 ¹And the apostles and brothers that were in Judaea heard that the Gentiles had also received the word of God. ²And when Peter was come up to Jerusalem, they that were of the circumcision contended with him, ³Saying, You went in to men uncircumcised, and did eat with them. ⁴But Peter rehearsed the matter from the beginning, and expounded it by order to them, saying, ⁵I was in the city of Joppa praying: and in a trance I saw a vision, A certain vessel descend, as it had been a great sheet, let down from heaven by four corners; and it came even to me: ⁶On the which when I had fastened my eyes, I considered, and saw four footed beasts of the earth, and wild beasts, and creeping things, and fowls of the air. ⁷And I heard a voice saying to me, Arise, Peter; slay and eat. ⁸But I said, Not so, Lord: for nothing common or unclean has at any time entered into my mouth. ⁹But the voice answered me again from heaven, What God has cleansed, that call not you common. ¹⁰And this was done three times: and all were drawn up again into heaven. ¹¹And, behold, immediately there were three men already come to the house where I was, sent from Caesarea to me. ¹²And the Spirit bade me go with them, nothing doubting. Moreover these six brothers accompanied me, and we entered into the man's house: ¹³And he showed us how he had seen an angel in his house, which stood and said to him, Send men to Joppa, and call for Simon, whose surname is Peter; ¹⁴Who shall tell you words, whereby you and all your house shall be saved. ¹⁵And as I began to speak, the Holy Ghost fell on them, as on us at the beginning. ¹⁶Then remembered I the word of the Lord, how that he said, John indeed baptized with water; but you shall be baptized with the Holy Ghost. ¹⁷For as much then as God gave them the like gift as he did to us, who believed on the Lord Jesus Christ; what was I, that I could withstand God? ¹⁸When they heard these things, they held their peace, and glorified God, saying, Then has God also to the Gentiles granted repentance to life. ¹⁹Now they which were scattered abroad on the persecution that arose about Stephen traveled as far as Phenice, and Cyprus, and Antioch, preaching the word to none but to the Jews only. ²⁰And some of them were men of Cyprus and Cyrene, which, when they were come to Antioch, spoke to the Grecians, preaching the LORD Jesus. ²¹And the hand of the Lord was with them: and a great number believed, and turned to the Lord. ²²Then tidings of these things came to the ears of the church which was in Jerusalem: and they sent forth Barnabas, that he should go as far as Antioch. ²³Who, when he came, and had seen the grace of God, was glad, and exhorted them all, that with purpose of heart they would hold to the Lord. ²⁴For he was a good man, and full of the Holy Ghost and of faith: and much people was added to the Lord. ²⁵Then departed Barnabas to Tarsus, for to seek Saul: ²⁶And when he had found him, he brought him to Antioch. And it came to pass, that a whole year they assembled themselves with the church, and taught much people. And the disciples were called Christians first in Antioch. ²⁷And in these days came prophets from Jerusalem to Antioch. ²⁸And there stood up one of them named Agabus, and signified by the Spirit that there should be great dearth throughout all the world: which came to pass in the days of Claudius Caesar. ²⁹Then the disciples, every man according to his ability, determined to send relief to the brothers which dwelled in Judaea: ³⁰Which also they did, and sent it to the elders by the hands of Barnabas and Saul.

12 ¹Now about that time Herod the king stretched forth his hands to vex certain of the church. ²And he killed James the brother of John with the sword. ³And because he saw it pleased the Jews, he proceeded further to take Peter also. (Then were the days of unleavened bread.) ⁴And when he had apprehended him, he put him in prison, and delivered him to four squads of soldiers to keep him; intending after Easter to bring him forth to the people. ⁵Peter therefore was kept in prison: but prayer was made without ceasing of the church to God for him. ⁶And when Herod would have brought him forth, the same night Peter was sleeping between two soldiers, bound with two chains: and the keepers before the door kept the prison. ⁷And, behold, the angel of the Lord came on him, and a light shined in the prison: and he smote Peter on the side, and raised him up, saying, Arise up quickly. And his chains fell off from his hands. ⁸And the angel said to him, Gird yourself, and bind on your sandals. And so he did. And he says to him, Cast your garment about you, and follow me. ⁹And he went out, and followed him; and knew not that it was true which was done by the angel; but thought he saw a vision. ¹⁰When they were past the first and the second ward, they came to the iron gate that leads to the city; which opened to them of his own accord: and they went out, and passed on through one street; and immediately the angel departed from him. ¹¹And when Peter was come to himself, he said, Now I know of a surety, that the LORD has sent his angel, and has delivered me out of the hand of Herod, and from all the expectation of the people of the Jews. ¹²And when he had considered the thing, he came to the house of Mary the mother of John, whose surname was Mark; where many were gathered together praying. ¹³And as Peter knocked at the door of the gate, a damsel came to listen, named Rhoda. ¹⁴And when she knew Peter's voice, she opened not the gate for gladness, but ran in, and told how Peter stood before the gate. ¹⁵And they said to her, You are mad. But she constantly affirmed that it was even so. Then said they, It is his angel. ¹⁶But Peter continued knocking: and when they had opened the door, and saw him, they were astonished. ¹⁷But he, beckoning to them with the hand to hold their peace, declared to them how the Lord had brought him out of the prison. And he said, Go show these things to James, and to the brothers. And he departed, and went into another place. ¹⁸Now as soon as it was day, there was no small stir among the soldiers, what was become of Peter. ¹⁹And when Herod had sought for him, and found him not, he examined the keepers, and commanded that they should be put to death. And he went down from Judaea to Caesarea, and there stayed. ²⁰And Herod was highly displeased with them of Tyre and Sidon: but they came with one accord to him, and, having made Blastus the king's chamberlain their friend, desired peace; because their country was nourished by the king's country. ²¹And on a set day Herod, arrayed in royal apparel, sat on his throne, and made an oration to them. ²²And the people gave a shout, saying, It is the voice of a god, and not of a man. ²³And immediately the angel of the Lord smote him, because he gave not God the glory: and he was eaten of worms, and gave up the ghost. ²⁴But the word of God grew and multiplied. ²⁵And Barnabas and Saul returned from Jerusalem, when they had fulfilled their ministry, and took with them John, whose surname was Mark.

13 ¹Now there were in the church that was at Antioch certain prophets and teachers; as Barnabas, and Simeon that was called Niger, and Lucius of Cyrene, and Manaen, which had been brought up with Herod the tetrarch, and Saul. ²As they ministered to the Lord, and fasted, the Holy Ghost said, Separate me Barnabas and Saul for the work to which I have called them. ³And when they had fasted and prayed, and laid their hands on them, they sent them away. ⁴So they, being sent forth by the Holy Ghost, departed to Seleucia; and from there they sailed to Cyprus. ⁵And when they were at Salamis, they preached the word of God in the synagogues of the Jews: and they had also John to their minister. ⁶And when they had gone through the isle to Paphos, they found a certain sorcerer, a false prophet, a Jew, whose name was Barjesus: ⁷Which was with the deputy of the country, Sergius Paulus, a prudent man; who called for Barnabas and Saul, and desired to hear the word of God. ⁸But Elymas the sorcerer (for so is his name by interpretation) withstood them, seeking to turn away the deputy from the faith. ⁹Then Saul, (who also is called Paul,) filled with the Holy Ghost, set his eyes on him. ¹⁰And said, O full of all subtlety and all mischief, you child of the devil, you enemy of all righteousness, will you not cease to pervert the right ways of the Lord? ¹¹And now, behold, the hand of the Lord is on you, and you shall be blind, not seeing the sun for a season. And immediately there fell on him a mist and a darkness; and he went about seeking some to lead him by the hand. ¹²Then the deputy, when he saw what was done, believed, being astonished at the doctrine of the Lord. ¹³Now when Paul and his company loosed from Paphos, they came to Perga in Pamphylia: and John departing from them returned to Jerusalem. ¹⁴But when they departed from Perga, they came to Antioch in Pisidia, and went into the synagogue on the sabbath day, and sat down. ¹⁵And after the reading of the law and the prophets the rulers of the synagogue sent to them, saying, You men and brothers, if you have any word of exhortation for the people, say on. ¹⁶Then Paul stood up, and beckoning with his hand said, Men of Israel, and you that fear God, give audience. ¹⁷The God of this people of Israel chose our fathers, and exalted the people when they dwelled as strangers in the land of Egypt, and with an high arm brought he them out of it. ¹⁸And about the time of forty years suffered he their manners in the wilderness. ¹⁹And when he had destroyed seven nations in the land of Chanaan, he divided their land to them by lot. ²⁰And after that he gave to them judges about the space of four hundred and fifty years, until Samuel the prophet. ²¹And afterward they desired a king: and God gave to them Saul the son of Cis, a man of the tribe of Benjamin, by the space of forty years. ²²And when he had removed him, he raised up to them David to be their king; to whom also he gave their testimony, and said, I have found David the son of Jesse, a man after my own heart, which shall fulfill all my will. ²³Of this man's seed has God according to his promise raised to Israel a Savior, Jesus: ²⁴When John had first preached before his coming the baptism of repentance to all the people of Israel. ²⁵And as John fulfilled his course, he said, Whom think you that I am? I am not he. But, behold, there comes one after me, whose shoes of his feet I am not worthy to loose. ²⁶Men and brothers, children of the stock of Abraham, and whoever among you fears God, to you is the word of this salvation sent. ²⁷For they that dwell at Jerusalem, and their rulers, because they knew him not, nor yet the voices of the prophets which are read every sabbath day, they have fulfilled them in condemning him. ²⁸And though they found no cause of death in him, yet desired they Pilate that he should be slain. ²⁹And when they had fulfilled all that was written of him, they took him down from the tree, and laid him in a sepulcher. ³⁰But God raised him from the dead: ³¹And he was seen many days of them which came up with him from Galilee to Jerusalem, who are his witnesses to the people. ³²And we declare to you glad tidings, how that the promise which was made to the fathers, ³³God has fulfilled the same to us their children, in that he has raised up Jesus again; as it is also written in the second psalm, You are my Son, this day have I begotten you. ³⁴And as concerning that he raised him up from the dead, now no more to return to corruption, he said on this wise, I will give you the sure mercies of David. ³⁵Why he says also in another psalm, You shall not suffer your Holy One to see corruption. ³⁶For David, after he had served his own generation by the will of God, fell on sleep, and was laid to his fathers, and saw corruption: ³⁷But he, whom God raised again, saw no corruption. ³⁸Be it known to you therefore, men and brothers, that through this man is preached to you the forgiveness of sins: ³⁹And by him all that believe are justified from all things, from which you could not be justified by the law of Moses. ⁴⁰Beware therefore, lest that come on you, which is spoken of in the prophets; ⁴¹Behold, you despisers, and wonder, and perish: for I work a work in your days, a work which you shall in no wise believe, though a man declare it to you. ⁴²And when the Jews were gone out of the synagogue, the Gentiles sought that these words might be preached to them the next sabbath. ⁴³Now when the congregation was broken up, many of the Jews and religious proselytes followed Paul and Barnabas: who, speaking to them, persuaded them to continue in the grace of God. ⁴⁴And the next sabbath day came almost the whole city together to hear the word of God. ⁴⁵But when the Jews saw the multitudes, they were filled with envy, and spoke against those things which were spoken by Paul, contradicting and blaspheming. ⁴⁶Then Paul and Barnabas waxed bold, and said, It was necessary that the word of God should first have been spoken to you: but seeing you put it from you, and judge yourselves unworthy of everlasting life, see, we turn to the Gentiles. ⁴⁷For so has the Lord commanded us, saying, I have set you to be a light of the Gentiles, that you should be for salvation to the ends of the earth. ⁴⁸And when the Gentiles heard this, they were glad, and glorified the word of the Lord: and as many as were ordained to eternal life believed. ⁴⁹And the word of the Lord was published throughout all the region. ⁵⁰But the Jews stirred up the devout and honorable women, and the chief men of the city, and raised persecution against Paul and Barnabas, and expelled them out of their coasts. ⁵¹But they shook off the dust of their feet against them, and came to Iconium. ⁵²And the disciples were filled with joy, and with the Holy Ghost.

14 ¹And it came to pass in Iconium, that they went both together into the synagogue of the Jews, and so spoke, that a great multitude both of the Jews and also of the Greeks believed. ²But the unbelieving Jews stirred up the Gentiles, and made their minds evil affected against the brothers. ³Long time therefore stayed they speaking boldly in the Lord, which gave testimony to the word of his grace, and granted signs and wonders to be done by their hands. ⁴But the multitude of the city was divided: and part held with the Jews, and part with the apostles. ⁵And when there was an assault made both of the Gentiles, and also of the Jews with their rulers, to use them spitefully, and to stone them, ⁶They were ware of it, and fled to Lystra and Derbe, cities of Lycaonia, and to the region that lies round about: ⁷And there they preached the gospel. ⁸And there sat a certain man at Lystra, weak in his feet, being a cripple from his mother's womb, who never had walked: ⁹The same heard Paul speak: who steadfastly beholding him, and perceiving that he had faith to be healed, ¹⁰Said with a loud voice, Stand upright on your feet. And he leaped and walked. ¹¹And when the people saw what Paul had done, they lifted up their voices, saying in the speech of Lycaonia, The gods are come down to us in the likeness of men. ¹²And they called Barnabas, Jupiter; and Paul, Mercurius, because he was the chief speaker. ¹³Then the priest of Jupiter, which was before their city, brought oxen and garlands to the gates, and would have done sacrifice with the people. ¹⁴Which when the apostles, Barnabas and Paul, heard of, they rent their clothes, and ran in among the people, crying out, ¹⁵And saying, Sirs, why do you these things? We also are men of like passions with you, and preach to you that you should turn from these vanities to the living God, which made heaven, and earth, and the sea, and all things that are therein: ¹⁶Who in times past suffered all nations to walk in their own ways. ¹⁷Nevertheless he left not himself without witness, in that he did good, and gave us rain from heaven, and fruitful seasons, filling our hearts with food and gladness. ¹⁸And with these sayings scarce restrained they the people, that they had not done sacrifice to them. ¹⁹And there came thither certain Jews from Antioch and Iconium, who persuaded the people, and having stoned Paul, drew him out of the city, supposing he had been dead. ²⁰However,, as the disciples stood round about him, he rose up, and came into the city: and the next day he departed with Barnabas to Derbe. ²¹And when they had preached the gospel to that city, and had taught many, they returned again to Lystra, and to Iconium, and Antioch, ²²Confirming the souls of the disciples, and exhorting them to continue in the faith, and that we must through much tribulation enter into the kingdom of God. ²³And when they had ordained them elders in every church, and had prayed with fasting, they commended them to the Lord, on whom they believed. ²⁴And after they had passed throughout Pisidia, they came to Pamphylia. ²⁵And when they had preached the word in Perga, they went down into Attalia: ²⁶And there sailed to Antioch, from where they had been recommended to the grace of God for the work which they fulfilled. ²⁷And when they were come, and had gathered the church together, they rehearsed all that God had done with them, and how he had opened the door of faith to the Gentiles. ²⁸And there they stayed long time with the disciples.

15 ¹And certain men which came down from Judaea taught the brothers, and said, Except you be circumcised after the manner of Moses, you cannot be saved. ²When therefore Paul and Barnabas had no small dissension and disputation with them, they determined that Paul and Barnabas, and certain other of them, should go up to Jerusalem to the apostles and elders about this question. ³And being brought on their way by the church, they passed through Phenice and Samaria, declaring the conversion of the Gentiles: and they caused great joy to all the brothers. ⁴And when they were come to Jerusalem, they were received of the church, and of the apostles and elders, and they declared all things that God had done with them. ⁵But there rose up certain of the sect of the Pharisees which believed, saying, That it was needful to circumcise them, and to command them to keep the law of Moses. ⁶And the apostles and elders came together for to consider of this matter. ⁷And when there had been much disputing, Peter rose up, and said to them, Men and brothers, you know how that a good while ago God made choice among us, that the Gentiles by my mouth should hear the word of the gospel, and believe. ⁸And God, which knows the hearts, bore them witness, giving them the Holy Ghost, even as he did to us; ⁹And put no difference between us and them, purifying their hearts by faith. ¹⁰Now therefore why tempt you God, to put a yoke on the neck of the disciples, which neither our fathers nor we were able to bear? ¹¹But we believe that through the grace of the LORD Jesus Christ we shall be saved, even as they. ¹²Then all the multitude kept silence, and gave audience to Barnabas and Paul, declaring what miracles and wonders God had worked among the Gentiles by them. ¹³And after they had held their peace, James answered, saying, Men and brothers, listen to me: ¹⁴Simeon has declared how God at the first did visit the Gentiles, to take out of them a people for his name. ¹⁵And to this agree the words of the prophets; as it is written, ¹⁶After this I will return, and will build again the tabernacle of David, which is fallen down; and I will build again the ruins thereof, and I will set it up: ¹⁷That the residue of men might seek after the Lord, and all the Gentiles, on whom my name is called, says the Lord, who does all these

things. ¹⁸Known to God are all his works from the beginning of the world. ¹⁹Why my sentence is, that we trouble not them, which from among the Gentiles are turned to God: ²⁰But that we write to them, that they abstain from pollutions of idols, and from fornication, and from things strangled, and from blood. ²¹For Moses of old time has in every city them that preach him, being read in the synagogues every sabbath day. ²²Then pleased it the apostles and elders with the whole church, to send chosen men of their own company to Antioch with Paul and Barnabas; namely, Judas surnamed Barsabas and Silas, chief men among the brothers: ²³And they wrote letters by them after this manner; The apostles and elders and brothers send greeting to the brothers which are of the Gentiles in Antioch and Syria and Cilicia. ²⁴For as much as we have heard, that certain which went out from us have troubled you with words, subverting your souls, saying, You must be circumcised, and keep the law: to whom we gave no such commandment: ²⁵It seemed good to us, being assembled with one accord, to send chosen men to you with our beloved Barnabas and Paul, ²⁶Men that have hazarded their lives for the name of our Lord Jesus Christ. ²⁷We have sent therefore Judas and Silas, who shall also tell you the same things by mouth. ²⁸For it seemed good to the Holy Ghost, and to us, to lay on you no greater burden than these necessary things; ²⁹That you abstain from meats offered to idols, and from blood, and from things strangled, and from fornication: from which if you keep yourselves, you shall do well. Fare you well. ³⁰So when they were dismissed, they came to Antioch: and when they had gathered the multitude together, they delivered the letter: ³¹Which when they had read, they rejoiced for the consolation. ³²And Judas and Silas, being prophets also themselves, exhorted the brothers with many words, and confirmed them. ³³And after they had tarried there a space, they were let go in peace from the brothers to the apostles. ³⁴Notwithstanding it pleased Silas to abide there still. ³⁵Paul also and Barnabas continued in Antioch, teaching and preaching the word of the Lord, with many others also. ³⁶And some days after Paul said to Barnabas, Let us go again and visit our brothers in every city where we have preached the word of the LORD, and see how they do. ³⁷And Barnabas determined to take with them John, whose surname was Mark. ³⁸But Paul thought not good to take him with them, who departed from them from Pamphylia, and went not with them to the work. ³⁹And the contention was so sharp between them, that they departed asunder one from the other: and so Barnabas took Mark, and sailed to Cyprus; ⁴⁰And Paul chose Silas, and departed, being recommended by the brothers to the grace of God. ⁴¹And he went through Syria and Cilicia, confirming the churches.

16

¹Then came he to Derbe and Lystra: and, behold, a certain disciple was there, named Timotheus, the son of a certain woman, which was a Jewess, and believed; but his father was a Greek: ²Which was well reported of by the brothers that were at Lystra and Iconium. ³Him would Paul have to go forth with him; and took and circumcised him because of the Jews which were in those quarters: for they knew all that his father was a Greek. ⁴And as they went through the cities, they delivered them the decrees for to keep, that were ordained of the apostles and elders which were at Jerusalem. ⁵And so were the churches established in the faith, and increased in number daily. ⁶Now when they had gone throughout Phrygia and the region of Galatia, and were forbidden of the Holy Ghost to preach the word in Asia, ⁷After they were come to Mysia, they assayed to go into Bithynia: but the Spirit suffered them not. ⁸And they passing by Mysia came down to Troas. ⁹And a vision appeared to Paul in the night; There stood a man of Macedonia, and prayed him, saying, Come over into Macedonia, and help us. ¹⁰And after he had seen the vision, immediately we endeavored to go into Macedonia, assuredly gathering that the Lord had called us for to preach the gospel to them. ¹¹Therefore loosing from Troas, we came with a straight course to Samothracia, and the next day to Neapolis; ¹²And from there to Philippi, which is the chief city of that part of Macedonia, and a colony: and we were in that city abiding certain days. ¹³And on the sabbath we went out of the city by a river side, where prayer was wont to be made; and we sat down, and spoke to the women which resorted thither. ¹⁴And a certain woman named Lydia, a seller of purple, of the city of Thyatira, which worshipped God, heard us: whose heart the Lord opened, that she attended to the things which were spoken of Paul. ¹⁵And when she was baptized, and her household, she sought us, saying, If you have judged me to be faithful to the Lord, come into my house, and abide there. And she constrained us. ¹⁶And it came to pass, as we went to prayer, a certain damsel possessed with a spirit of divination met us, which brought her masters much gain by soothsaying: ¹⁷The same followed Paul and us, and cried, saying, These men are the servants of the most high God, which show to us the way of salvation. ¹⁸And this did she many days. But Paul, being grieved, turned and said to the spirit, I command you in the name of Jesus Christ to come out of her. And he came out the same hour. ¹⁹And when her masters saw that the hope of their gains was gone, they caught Paul and Silas, and drew them into the marketplace to the rulers, ²⁰And brought them to the magistrates, saying, These men, being Jews, do exceedingly trouble our city, ²¹And teach customs, which are not lawful for us to receive, neither to observe, being Romans. ²²And the multitude rose up together against them: and the magistrates rent off their clothes, and commanded to beat them. ²³And when they had laid many stripes on them, they cast them into prison, charging the jailor to keep them safely: ²⁴Who, having received such a charge, thrust them into the inner prison, and made their feet fast in the stocks. ²⁵And at midnight Paul and Silas prayed, and sang praises to God: and the prisoners heard them. ²⁶And suddenly there was a great earthquake, so that the foundations of the prison were shaken: and immediately all the doors were opened, and every one's bands were loosed. ²⁷And the keeper of the prison awaking out of his sleep, and seeing the prison doors open, he drew out his sword, and would have killed himself, supposing that the prisoners had been fled. ²⁸But Paul cried with a loud voice, saying, Do yourself no harm: for we are all here. ²⁹Then he called for a light, and sprang in, and came trembling, and fell down before Paul and Silas, ³⁰And brought them out, and said, Sirs, what must I do to be saved? ³¹And they said, Believe on the Lord Jesus Christ,

and you shall be saved, and your house. ³²And they spoke to him the word of the Lord, and to all that were in his house. ³³And he took them the same hour of the night, and washed their stripes; and was baptized, he and all his, straightway. ³⁴And when he had brought them into his house, he set meat before them, and rejoiced, believing in God with all his house. ³⁵And when it was day, the magistrates sent the sergeants, saying, Let those men go. ³⁶And the keeper of the prison told this saying to Paul, The magistrates have sent to let you go: now therefore depart, and go in peace. ³⁷But Paul said to them, They have beaten us openly uncondemned, being Romans, and have cast us into prison; and now do they thrust us out privately? no truly; but let them come themselves and fetch us out. ³⁸And the sergeants told these words to the magistrates: and they feared, when they heard that they were Romans. ³⁹And they came and sought them, and brought them out, and desired them to depart out of the city. ⁴⁰And they went out of the prison, and entered into the house of Lydia: and when they had seen the brothers, they comforted them, and departed.

17 ¹Now when they had passed through Amphipolis and Apollonia, they came to Thessalonica, where was a synagogue of the Jews: ²And Paul, as his manner was, went in to them, and three sabbath days reasoned with them out of the scriptures, ³Opening and alleging, that Christ must needs have suffered, and risen again from the dead; and that this Jesus, whom I preach to you, is Christ. ⁴And some of them believed, and consorted with Paul and Silas; and of the devout Greeks a great multitude, and of the chief women not a few. ⁵But the Jews which believed not, moved with envy, took to them certain lewd fellows of the baser sort, and gathered a company, and set all the city on an uproar, and assaulted the house of Jason, and sought to bring them out to the people. ⁶And when they found them not, they drew Jason and certain brothers to the rulers of the city, crying, These that have turned the world upside down are come here also; ⁷Whom Jason has received: and these all do contrary to the decrees of Caesar, saying that there is another king, one Jesus. ⁸And they troubled the people and the rulers of the city, when they heard these things. ⁹And when they had taken security of Jason, and of the other, they let them go. ¹⁰And the brothers immediately sent away Paul and Silas by night to Berea: who coming thither went into the synagogue of the Jews. ¹¹These were more noble than those in Thessalonica, in that they received the word with all readiness of mind, and searched the scriptures daily, whether those things were so. ¹²Therefore many of them believed; also of honorable women which were Greeks, and of men, not a few. ¹³But when the Jews of Thessalonica had knowledge that the word of God was preached of Paul at Berea, they came thither also, and stirred up the people. ¹⁴And then immediately the brothers sent away Paul to go as it were to the sea: but Silas and Timotheus stayed there still. ¹⁵And they that conducted Paul brought him to Athens: and receiving a commandment to Silas and Timotheus for to come to him with all speed, they departed. ¹⁶Now while Paul waited for them at Athens, his spirit was stirred in him, when he saw the city wholly given to idolatry. ¹⁷Therefore disputed he in the synagogue with the Jews, and with the devout persons, and in the market daily with them that met with him. ¹⁸Then certain philosophers of the Epicureans, and of the Stoicks, encountered him. And some said, What will this babbler say? other some, He seems to be a setter forth of strange gods: because he preached to them Jesus, and the resurrection. ¹⁹And they took him, and brought him to Areopagus, saying, May we know what this new doctrine, whereof you speak, is? ²⁰For you bring certain strange things to our ears: we would know therefore what these things mean. ²¹(For all the Athenians and strangers which were there spent their time in nothing else, but either to tell, or to hear some new thing.) ²²Then Paul stood in the middle of Mars' hill, and said, You men of Athens, I perceive that in all things you are too superstitious. ²³For as I passed by, and beheld your devotions, I found an altar with this inscription, TO THE UNKNOWN GOD. Whom therefore you ignorantly worship, him declare I to you. ²⁴God that made the world and all things therein, seeing that he is Lord of heaven and earth, dwells not in temples made with hands; ²⁵Neither is worshipped with men's hands, as though he needed any thing, seeing he gives to all life, and breath, and all things; ²⁶And has made of one blood all nations of men for to dwell on all the face of the earth, and has determined the times before appointed, and the bounds of their habitation; ²⁷That they should seek the Lord, if haply they might feel after him, and find him, though he be not far from every one of us: ²⁸For in him we live, and move, and have our being; as certain also of your own poets have said, For we are also his offspring. ²⁹For as much then as we are the offspring of God, we ought not to think that the Godhead is like to gold, or silver, or stone, graven by are and man's device. ³⁰And the times of this ignorance God winked at; but now commands all men every where to repent: ³¹Because he has appointed a day, in the which he will judge the world in righteousness by that man whom he has ordained; whereof he has given assurance to all men, in that he has raised him from the dead. ³²And when they heard of the resurrection of the dead, some mocked: and others said, We will hear you again of this matter. ³³So Paul departed from among them. ³⁴However, certain men joined to him, and believed: among the which was Dionysius the Areopagite, and a woman named Damaris, and others with them.

18 ¹After these things Paul departed from Athens, and came to Corinth; ²And found a certain Jew named Aquila, born in Pontus, lately come from Italy, with his wife Priscilla; (because that Claudius had commanded all Jews to depart from Rome:) and came to them. ³And because he was of the same craft, he stayed with them, and worked: for by their occupation they were tentmakers. ⁴And he reasoned in the synagogue every sabbath, and persuaded the Jews and the Greeks. ⁵And when Silas and Timotheus were come from Macedonia, Paul was pressed in the spirit, and testified to the Jews that Jesus was Christ. ⁶And when they opposed themselves, and blasphemed, he shook his raiment, and said to them, Your blood be on your own heads; I am clean; from now on I will go to the Gentiles. ⁷And he departed there, and entered into a certain man's house, named Justus, one that worshipped God, whose house joined hard to the synagogue. ⁸And Crispus, the chief ruler of the synagogue, believed on the Lord with all his house; and many of the Corinthians hearing believed, and were baptized. ⁹Then spoke the Lord to Paul in the night by a vision, Be not afraid, but speak, and hold not your peace: ¹⁰For I am with you, and no man shall set on you to hurt you: for I have much people in this city. ¹¹And he continued there a year and six months, teaching the word of God among them. ¹²And when Gallio was the deputy of Achaia, the Jews made insurrection with one accord against Paul, and brought him to the judgment seat, ¹³Saying, This fellow persuades men to worship God contrary to the law. ¹⁴And when Paul was now about to open his mouth, Gallio said to the Jews, If it were a matter of wrong or wicked lewdness, O you Jews, reason would that I should bear with you: ¹⁵But if it be a question of words and names, and of your law, look you to it; for I will be no judge of such matters. ¹⁶And he drove them from the judgment seat. ¹⁷Then all the Greeks took Sosthenes, the chief ruler of the synagogue, and beat him before the judgment seat. And Gallio cared for none of those things. ¹⁸And Paul after this tarried there yet a good while, and then took his leave of the brothers, and sailed there into Syria, and with him Priscilla and Aquila; having shorn his head in Cenchrea: for he had a vow. ¹⁹And he came to Ephesus, and left them there: but he himself entered into the synagogue, and reasoned with the Jews. ²⁰When they desired him to tarry longer time with them, he consented not; ²¹But bade them farewell, saying, I must by all means keep this feast that comes in Jerusalem: but I will return again to you, if God will. And he sailed from Ephesus. ²²And when he had landed at Caesarea, and gone up, and saluted the church, he went down to Antioch. ²³And after he had spent some time there, he departed, and went over all the country of Galatia and Phrygia in order, strengthening all the disciples. ²⁴And a certain Jew named Apollos, born at Alexandria, an eloquent man, and mighty in the scriptures, came to Ephesus. ²⁵This man was instructed in the way of the Lord; and being fervent in the spirit, he spoke and taught diligently the things of the Lord, knowing only the baptism of John. ²⁶And he began to speak boldly in the synagogue: whom when Aquila and Priscilla had heard, they took him to them, and expounded to him the way of God more perfectly. ²⁷And when he was disposed to pass into Achaia, the brothers wrote, exhorting the disciples to receive him: who, when he was come, helped them much which had believed through grace: ²⁸For he mightily convinced the Jews, and that publicly, showing by the scriptures that Jesus was Christ.

19
¹And it came to pass, that, while Apollos was at Corinth, Paul having passed through the upper coasts came to Ephesus: and finding certain disciples, ²He said to them, Have you received the Holy Ghost since you believed? And they said to him, We have not so much as heard whether there be any Holy Ghost. ³And he said to them, To what then were you baptized? And they said, To John's baptism. ⁴Then said Paul, John truly baptized with the baptism of repentance, saying to the people, that they should believe on him which should come after him, that is, on Christ Jesus. ⁵When they heard this, they were baptized in the name of the Lord Jesus. ⁶And when Paul had laid his hands on them, the Holy Ghost came on them; and they spoke with tongues, and prophesied. ⁷And all the men were about twelve. ⁸And he went into the synagogue, and spoke boldly for the space of three months, disputing and persuading the things concerning the kingdom of God. ⁹But when divers were hardened, and believed not, but spoke evil of that way before the multitude, he departed from them, and separated the disciples, disputing daily in the school of one Tyrannus. ¹⁰And this continued by the space of two years; so that all they which dwelled in Asia heard the word of the Lord Jesus, both Jews and Greeks. ¹¹And God worked special miracles by the hands of Paul: ¹²So that from his body were brought to the sick handkerchiefs or aprons, and the diseases departed from them, and the evil spirits went out of them. ¹³Then certain of the vagabond Jews, exorcists, took on them to call over them which had evil spirits the name of the LORD Jesus, saying, We adjure you by Jesus whom Paul preaches. ¹⁴And there were seven sons of one Sceva, a Jew, and chief of the priests, which did so. ¹⁵And the evil spirit answered and said, Jesus I know, and Paul I know; but who are you? ¹⁶And the man in whom the evil spirit was leaped on them, and overcame them, and prevailed against them, so that they fled out of that house naked and wounded. ¹⁷And this was known to all the Jews and Greeks also dwelling at Ephesus; and fear fell on them all, and the name of the Lord Jesus was magnified. ¹⁸And many that believed came, and confessed, and showed their deeds. ¹⁹Many of them also which used curious arts brought their books together, and burned them before all men: and they counted the price of them, and found it fifty thousand pieces of silver. ²⁰So mightily grew the word of God and prevailed. ²¹After these things were ended, Paul purposed in the spirit, when he had passed through Macedonia and Achaia, to go to Jerusalem, saying, After I have been there, I must also see Rome. ²²So he sent into Macedonia two of them that ministered to him, Timotheus and Erastus; but he himself stayed in Asia for a season. ²³And the same time there arose no small stir about that way. ²⁴For a certain man named Demetrius, a silversmith, which made silver shrines for Diana, brought no small gain to the craftsmen; ²⁵Whom he called together with the workmen of like occupation, and said, Sirs, you know that by this craft we have our wealth. ²⁶Moreover you see and hear, that not alone at Ephesus, but almost throughout all Asia, this Paul has persuaded and turned away much people, saying that they be no gods, which are made with hands: ²⁷So that not only this our craft is in danger to be set at nothing; but also that the temple of the great goddess Diana should be despised, and her magnificence should be destroyed, whom all Asia and the world worships. ²⁸And when they heard these sayings, they were full of wrath, and cried out, saying, Great is Diana of the Ephesians. ²⁹And the whole city was filled with confusion: and having caught Gaius and Aristarchus, men of Macedonia, Paul's companions in travel, they rushed with one accord into the theatre. ³⁰And when Paul would have entered in to the people, the disciples suffered him not. ³¹And certain of the chief of Asia, which were his friends, sent to him, desiring him that he would not adventure himself into the theatre. ³²Some therefore cried one thing, and some another: for the assembly was confused: and the more part knew not why they were come together. ³³And

they drew Alexander out of the multitude, the Jews putting him forward. And Alexander beckoned with the hand, and would have made his defense to the people. ³⁴But when they knew that he was a Jew, all with one voice about the space of two hours cried out, Great is Diana of the Ephesians. ³⁵And when the town cleark had appeased the people, he said, You men of Ephesus, what man is there that knows not how that the city of the Ephesians is a worshipper of the great goddess Diana, and of the image which fell down from Jupiter? ³⁶Seeing then that these things cannot be spoken against, you ought to be quiet, and to do nothing rashly. ³⁷For you have brought here these men, which are neither robbers of churches, nor yet blasphemers of your goddess. ³⁸Why if Demetrius, and the craftsmen which are with him, have a matter against any man, the law is open, and there are deputies: let them accuse one another. ³⁹But if you inquire any thing concerning other matters, it shall be determined in a lawful assembly. ⁴⁰For we are in danger to be called in question for this day's uproar, there being no cause whereby we may give an account of this concourse. ⁴¹And when he had thus spoken, he dismissed the assembly.

20 ¹And after the uproar was ceased, Paul called to him the disciples, and embraced them, and departed for to go into Macedonia. ²And when he had gone over those parts, and had given them much exhortation, he came into Greece, ³And there stayed three months. And when the Jews laid wait for him, as he was about to sail into Syria, he purposed to return through Macedonia. ⁴And there accompanied him into Asia Sopater of Berea; and of the Thessalonians, Aristarchus and Secundus; and Gaius of Derbe, and Timotheus; and of Asia, Tychicus and Trophimus. ⁵These going before tarried for us at Troas. ⁶And we sailed away from Philippi after the days of unleavened bread, and came to them to Troas in five days; where we stayed seven days. ⁷And on the first day of the week, when the disciples came together to break bread, Paul preached to them, ready to depart on the morrow; and continued his speech until midnight. ⁸And there were many lights in the upper chamber, where they were gathered together. ⁹And there sat in a window a certain young man named Eutychus, being fallen into a deep sleep: and as Paul was long preaching, he sunk down with sleep, and fell down from the third loft, and was taken up dead. ¹⁰And Paul went down, and fell on him, and embracing him said, Trouble not yourselves; for his life is in him. ¹¹When he therefore was come up again, and had broken bread, and eaten, and talked a long while, even till break of day, so he departed. ¹²And they brought the young man alive, and were not a little comforted. ¹³And we went before to ship, and sailed to Assos, there intending to take in Paul: for so had he appointed, minding himself to go afoot. ¹⁴And when he met with us at Assos, we took him in, and came to Mitylene. ¹⁵And we sailed there, and came the next day over against Chios; and the next day we arrived at Samos, and tarried at Trogyllium; and the next day we came to Miletus. ¹⁶For Paul had determined to sail by Ephesus, because he would not spend the time in Asia: for he hurried, if it were possible for him, to be at Jerusalem the day of Pentecost. ¹⁷And from Miletus he sent to Ephesus, and called the elders of the church. ¹⁸And when they were come to him, he said to them, You know, from the first day that I came into Asia, after what manner I have been with you at all seasons, ¹⁹Serving the LORD with all humility of mind, and with many tears, and temptations, which befell me by the lying in wait of the Jews: ²⁰And how I kept back nothing that was profitable to you, but have showed you, and have taught you publicly, and from house to house, ²¹Testifying both to the Jews, and also to the Greeks, repentance toward God, and faith toward our Lord Jesus Christ. ²²And now, behold, I go bound in the spirit to Jerusalem, not knowing the things that shall befall me there: ²³Save that the Holy Ghost witnesses in every city, saying that bonds and afflictions abide me. ²⁴But none of these things move me, neither count I my life dear to myself, so that I might finish my course with joy, and the ministry, which I have received of the Lord Jesus, to testify the gospel of the grace of God. ²⁵And now, behold, I know that you all, among whom I have gone preaching the kingdom of God, shall see my face no more. ²⁶Why I take you to record this day, that I am pure from the blood of all men. ²⁷For I have not shunned to declare to you all the counsel of God. ²⁸Take heed therefore to yourselves, and to all the flock, over the which the Holy Ghost has made you overseers, to feed the church of God, which he has purchased with his own blood. ²⁹For I know this, that after my departing shall grievous wolves enter in among you, not sparing the flock. ³⁰Also of your own selves shall men arise, speaking perverse things, to draw away disciples after them. ³¹Therefore watch, and remember, that by the space of three years I ceased not to warn every one night and day with tears. ³²And now, brothers, I commend you to God, and to the word of his grace, which is able to build you up, and to give you an inheritance among all them which are sanctified. ³³I have coveted no man's silver, or gold, or apparel. ³⁴Yes, you yourselves know, that these hands have ministered to my necessities, and to them that were with me. ³⁵I have showed you all things, how that so laboring you ought to support the weak, and to remember the words of the Lord Jesus, how he said, It is more blessed to give than to receive. ³⁶And when he had thus spoken, he kneeled down, and prayed with them all. ³⁷And they all wept sore, and fell on Paul's neck, and kissed him, ³⁸Sorrowing most of all for the words which he spoke, that they should see his face no more. And they accompanied him to the ship.

21 ¹And it came to pass, that after we were gotten from them, and had launched, we came with a straight course to Coos, and the day following to Rhodes, and from there to Patara: ²And finding a ship sailing over to Phenicia, we went aboard, and set forth. ³Now when we had discovered Cyprus, we left it on the left hand, and sailed into Syria, and landed at Tyre: for there the ship was to unlade her burden. ⁴And finding disciples, we tarried there seven days: who said to Paul through the Spirit, that he should not go up to Jerusalem. ⁵And when we had accomplished those days, we departed and went our way; and they all brought us on our way, with wives and children, till we were out of the city: and we kneeled down on the shore, and prayed. ⁶And when we had taken our leave one of another, we took ship; and they returned home again. ⁷And when we had finished our course from Tyre, we came to Ptolemais, and saluted the brothers, and stayed with them one day. ⁸And the next day we that were of Paul's company departed, and came to Caesarea: and we entered into the house of Philip the evangelist, which was one of the seven; and stayed with him. ⁹And the same man had four daughters, virgins, which did prophesy. ¹⁰And as we tarried there many days, there came down from Judaea a certain prophet, named Agabus. ¹¹And when he was come to us, he took Paul's girdle, and bound his own hands and feet, and said, Thus says the Holy Ghost, So shall the Jews at Jerusalem bind the man that owns this girdle, and shall deliver him into the hands of the Gentiles. ¹²And when we heard these things, both we, and they of that place, sought him not to go up to Jerusalem. ¹³Then Paul answered, What mean you to weep and to break my heart? for I am ready not to be bound only, but also to die at Jerusalem for the name of the Lord Jesus. ¹⁴And when he would not be persuaded, we ceased, saying, The will of the Lord be done. ¹⁵And after those days we took up our carriages, and went up to Jerusalem. ¹⁶There went with us also certain of the disciples of Caesarea, and brought with them one Mnason of Cyprus, an old disciple, with whom we should lodge. ¹⁷And when we were come to Jerusalem, the brothers received us gladly. ¹⁸And the day following Paul went in with us to James; and all the elders were present. ¹⁹And when he had saluted them, he declared particularly what things God had worked among the Gentiles by his ministry. ²⁰And when they heard it, they glorified the Lord, and said to him, You see, brother, how many thousands of Jews there are which believe; and they are all zealous of the law: ²¹And they are informed of you, that you teach all the Jews which are among the Gentiles to forsake Moses, saying that they ought not to circumcise their children, neither to walk after the customs. ²²What is it therefore? the multitude must needs come together: for they will hear that you are come. ²³Do therefore this that we say to you: We have four men which have a vow on them; ²⁴Them take, and purify yourself with them, and be at charges with them, that they may shave their heads: and all may know that those things, whereof they were informed concerning you, are nothing; but that you yourself also walk orderly, and keep the law. ²⁵As touching the Gentiles which believe, we have written and concluded that they observe no such thing, save only that they keep themselves from things offered to idols, and from blood, and from strangled, and from fornication. ²⁶Then Paul took the men, and the next day purifying himself with them entered into the temple, to signify the accomplishment of the days of purification, until that an offering should be offered for every one of them. ²⁷And when the seven days were almost ended, the Jews which were of Asia, when they saw him in the temple, stirred up all the people, and laid hands on him, ²⁸Crying out, Men of Israel, help: This is the man, that teaches all men every where against the people, and the law, and this place: and further brought Greeks also into the temple, and has polluted this holy place. ²⁹(For they had seen before with him in the city Trophimus an Ephesian, whom they supposed that Paul had brought into the temple.) ³⁰And all the city was moved, and the people ran together: and they took Paul, and drew him out of the temple: and immediately the doors were shut. ³¹And as they went about to kill him, tidings came to the chief captain of the band, that all Jerusalem was in an uproar. ³²Who immediately took soldiers and centurions, and ran down to them: and when they saw the chief captain and the soldiers, they left beating of Paul. ³³Then the chief captain came near, and took him, and commanded him to be bound with two chains; and demanded who he was, and what he had done. ³⁴And some cried one thing, some another, among the multitude: and when he could not know the certainty for the tumult, he commanded him to be carried into the castle. ³⁵And when he came on the stairs, so it was, that he was borne of the soldiers for the violence of the people. ³⁶For the multitude of the people followed after, crying, Away with him. ³⁷And as Paul was to be led into the castle, he said to the chief captain, May I speak to you? Who said, Can you speak Greek? ³⁸Are not you that Egyptian, which before these days made an uproar, and led out into the wilderness four thousand men that were murderers? ³⁹But Paul said, I am a man which am a Jew of Tarsus, a city in Cilicia, a citizen of no mean city: and, I beseech you, suffer me to speak to the people. ⁴⁰And when he had given him license, Paul stood on the stairs, and beckoned with the hand to the people. And when there was made a great silence, he spoke to them in the Hebrew tongue, saying,

22

¹Men, brothers, and fathers, hear you my defense which I make now to you. ²(And when they heard that he spoke in the Hebrew tongue to them, they kept the more silence: and he says,) ³I am truly a man which am a Jew, born in Tarsus, a city in Cilicia, yet brought up in this city at the feet of Gamaliel, and taught according to the perfect manner of the law of the fathers, and was zealous toward God, as you all are this day. ⁴And I persecuted this way to the death, binding and delivering into prisons both men and women. ⁵As also the high priest does bear me witness, and all the estate of the elders: from whom also I received letters to the brothers, and went to Damascus, to bring them which were there bound to Jerusalem, for to be punished. ⁶And it came to pass, that, as I made my journey, and was come near to Damascus about noon, suddenly there shone from heaven a great light round about me. ⁷And I fell to the ground, and heard a voice saying to me, Saul, Saul, why persecute you me? ⁸And I answered, Who are you, Lord? And he said to me, I am Jesus of Nazareth, whom you persecute. ⁹And they that were with me saw indeed the light, and were afraid; but they heard not the voice of him that spoke to me. ¹⁰And I said, What shall I do, LORD? And the Lord said to me, Arise, and go into Damascus; and there it shall be told you of all things which are appointed for you to do. ¹¹And when I could not see for the glory of that light, being led by the hand of them that were with me, I came into Damascus. ¹²And one Ananias, a devout man according to the law, having a good report of all the Jews which dwelled there, ¹³Came to me, and stood, and said to me, Brother Saul, receive your sight. And the same hour I looked up on him. ¹⁴And he said, The God of our fathers has chosen you, that you should know his will, and see that Just One, and should hear the voice of his mouth. ¹⁵For you shall be his witness to all men of what you have seen and heard. ¹⁶And now why tarry you? arise, and be baptized, and wash away

your sins, calling on the name of the Lord. ¹⁷And it came to pass, that, when I was come again to Jerusalem, even while I prayed in the temple, I was in a trance; ¹⁸And saw him saying to me, Make haste, and get you quickly out of Jerusalem: for they will not receive your testimony concerning me. ¹⁹And I said, Lord, they know that I imprisoned and beat in every synagogue them that believed on you: ²⁰And when the blood of your martyr Stephen was shed, I also was standing by, and consenting to his death, and kept the raiment of them that slew him. ²¹And he said to me, Depart: for I will send you far hence to the Gentiles. ²²And they gave him audience to this word, and then lifted up their voices, and said, Away with such a fellow from the earth: for it is not fit that he should live. ²³And as they cried out, and cast off their clothes, and threw dust into the air, ²⁴The chief captain commanded him to be brought into the castle, and bade that he should be examined by scourging; that he might know why they cried so against him. ²⁵And as they bound him with thongs, Paul said to the centurion that stood by, Is it lawful for you to whip a man that is a Roman, and uncondemned? ²⁶When the centurion heard that, he went and told the chief captain, saying, Take heed what you do: for this man is a Roman. ²⁷Then the chief captain came, and said to him, Tell me, are you a Roman? He said, Yes. ²⁸And the chief captain answered, With a great sum obtained I this freedom. And Paul said, But I was free born. ²⁹Then straightway they departed from him which should have examined him: and the chief captain also was afraid, after he knew that he was a Roman, and because he had bound him. ³⁰On the morrow, because he would have known the certainty why he was accused of the Jews, he loosed him from his bands, and commanded the chief priests and all their council to appear, and brought Paul down, and set him before them.

23

¹And Paul, earnestly beholding the council, said, Men and brothers, I have lived in all good conscience before God until this day. ²And the high priest Ananias commanded them that stood by him to smite him on the mouth. ³Then said Paul to him, God shall smite you, you white washed wall: for sit you to judge me after the law, and command me to be smitten contrary to the law? ⁴And they that stood by said, Revile you God's high priest? ⁵Then said Paul, I knew not, brothers, that he was the high priest: for it is written, You shall not speak evil of the ruler of your people. ⁶But when Paul perceived that the one part were Sadducees, and the other Pharisees, he cried out in the council, Men and brothers, I am a Pharisee, the son of a Pharisee: of the hope and resurrection of the dead I am called in question. ⁷And when he had so said, there arose a dissension between the Pharisees and the Sadducees: and the multitude was divided. ⁸For the Sadducees say that there is no resurrection, neither angel, nor spirit: but the Pharisees confess both. ⁹And there arose a great cry: and the scribes that were of the Pharisees' part arose, and strove, saying, We find no evil in this man: but if a spirit or an angel has spoken to him, let us not fight against God. ¹⁰And when there arose a great dissension, the chief captain, fearing lest Paul should have been pulled in pieces of them, commanded the soldiers to go down, and to take him by force from among them, and to bring him into the castle. ¹¹And the night following the Lord stood by him, and said, Be of good cheer, Paul: for as you have testified of me in Jerusalem, so must you bear witness also at Rome. ¹²And when it was day, certain of the Jews banded together, and bound themselves under a curse, saying that they would neither eat nor drink till they had killed Paul. ¹³And they were more than forty which had made this conspiracy. ¹⁴And they came to the chief priests and elders, and said, We have bound ourselves under a great curse, that we will eat nothing until we have slain Paul. ¹⁵Now therefore you with the council signify to the chief captain that he bring him down to you to morrow, as though you would inquire something more perfectly concerning him: and we, or ever he come near, are ready to kill him. ¹⁶And when Paul's sister's son heard of their lying in wait, he went and entered into the castle, and told Paul. ¹⁷Then Paul called one of the centurions to him, and said, Bring this young man to the chief captain: for he has a certain thing to tell him. ¹⁸So he took him, and brought him to the chief captain, and said, Paul the prisoner called me to him, and prayed me to bring this young man to you, who has something to say to you. ¹⁹Then the chief captain took him by the hand, and went with him aside privately, and asked him, What is that you have to tell me? ²⁰And he said, The Jews have agreed to desire you that you would bring down Paul to morrow into the council, as though they would inquire somewhat of him more perfectly. ²¹But do not you yield to them: for there lie in wait for him of them more than forty men, which have bound themselves with an oath, that they will neither eat nor drink till they have killed him: and now are they ready, looking for a promise from you. ²²So the chief captain then let the young man depart, and charged him, See you tell no man that you have showed these things to me. ²³And he called to him two centurions, saying, Make ready two hundred soldiers to go to Caesarea, and horsemen three score and ten, and spearmen two hundred, at the third hour of the night; ²⁴And provide them beasts, that they may set Paul on, and bring him safe to Felix the governor. ²⁵And he wrote a letter after this manner: ²⁶Claudius Lysias to the most excellent governor Felix sends greeting. ²⁷This man was taken of the Jews, and should have been killed of them: then came I with an army, and rescued him, having understood that he was a Roman. ²⁸And when I would have known the cause why they accused him, I brought him forth into their council: ²⁹Whom I perceived to be accused of questions of their law, but to have nothing laid to his charge worthy of death or of bonds. ³⁰And when it was told me how that the Jews laid wait for the man, I sent straightway to you, and gave commandment to his accusers also to say before you what they had against him. Farewell. ³¹Then the soldiers, as it was commanded them, took Paul, and brought him by night to Antipatris. ³²On the morrow they left the horsemen to go with him, and returned to the castle: ³³Who, when they came to Caesarea and delivered the letter to the governor, presented Paul also before him. ³⁴And when the governor had read the letter, he asked of what province he was. And when he understood that he was of Cilicia; ³⁵I will hear you, said he, when your accusers are also come. And he commanded him to be kept in Herod's judgment hall.

24

¹And after five days Ananias the high priest descended with the elders, and with a certain orator named Tertullus, who informed the governor against Paul. ²And when he was called forth, Tertullus began to accuse him, saying, Seeing that by you we enjoy great quietness, and that very worthy deeds are done to this nation by your providence, ³We accept it always, and in all places, most noble Felix, with all thankfulness. ⁴Notwithstanding, that I be not further tedious to you, I pray you that you would hear us of your clemency a few words. ⁵For we have found this man a pestilent fellow, and a mover of sedition among all the Jews throughout the world, and a ringleader of the sect of the Nazarenes: ⁶Who also has gone about to profane the temple: whom we took, and would have judged according to our law. ⁷But the chief captain Lysias came on us, and with great violence took him away out of our hands, ⁸Commanding his accusers to come to you: by examining of whom yourself may take knowledge of all these things, whereof we accuse him. ⁹And the Jews also assented, saying that these things were so. ¹⁰Then Paul, after that the governor had beckoned to him to speak, answered, For as much as I know that you have been of many years a judge to this nation, I do the more cheerfully answer for myself: ¹¹Because that you may understand, that there are yet but twelve days since I went up to Jerusalem for to worship. ¹²And they neither found me in the temple disputing with any man, neither raising up the people, neither in the synagogues, nor in the city: ¹³Neither can they prove the things whereof they now accuse me. ¹⁴But this I confess to you, that after the way which they call heresy, so worship I the God of my fathers, believing all things which are written in the law and in the prophets: ¹⁵And have hope toward God, which they themselves also allow, that there shall be a resurrection of the dead, both of the just and unjust. ¹⁶And herein do I exercise myself, to have always a conscience void to offense toward God, and toward men. ¹⁷Now after many years I came to bring alms to my nation, and offerings. ¹⁸Whereupon certain Jews from Asia found me purified in the temple, neither with multitude, nor with tumult. ¹⁹Who ought to have been here before you, and object, if they had something against me. ²⁰Or else let these same here say, if they have found any evil doing in me, while I stood before the council, ²¹Except it be for this one voice, that I cried standing among them, Touching the resurrection of the dead I am called in question by you this day. ²²And when Felix heard these things, having more perfect knowledge of that way, he deferred them, and said, When Lysias the chief captain shall come down, I will know the uttermost of your matter. ²³And he commanded a centurion to keep Paul, and to let him have liberty, and that he should forbid none of his acquaintance to minister or come to him. ²⁴And after certain days, when Felix came with his wife Drusilla, which was a Jewess, he sent for Paul, and heard him concerning the faith in Christ. ²⁵And as he reasoned of righteousness, temperance, and judgment to come, Felix trembled, and answered, Go your way for this time; when I have a convenient season, I will call for you. ²⁶He hoped also that money should have been given him of Paul, that he might loose him: why he sent for him the oftener, and communed with him. ²⁷But after two years Porcius Festus came into Felix' room: and Felix, willing to show the Jews a pleasure, left Paul bound.

25

¹Now when Festus was come into the province, after three days he ascended from Caesarea to Jerusalem. ²Then the high priest and the chief of the Jews informed him against Paul, and sought him, ³And desired favor against him, that he would send for him to Jerusalem, laying wait in the way to kill him. ⁴But Festus answered, that Paul should be kept at Caesarea, and that he himself would depart shortly thither. ⁵Let them therefore, said he, which among you are able, go down with me, and accuse this man, if there be any wickedness in him. ⁶And when he had tarried among them more than ten days, he went down to Caesarea; and the next day sitting on the judgment seat commanded Paul to be brought. ⁷And when he was come, the Jews which came down from Jerusalem stood round about, and laid many and grievous complaints against Paul, which they could not prove. ⁸While he answered for himself, Neither against the law of the Jews, neither against the temple, nor yet against Caesar, have I offended any thing at all. ⁹But Festus, willing to do the Jews a pleasure, answered Paul, and said, Will you go up to Jerusalem, and there be judged of these things before me? ¹⁰Then said Paul, I stand at Caesar's judgment seat, where I ought to be judged: to the Jews have I done no wrong, as you very well know. ¹¹For if I be an offender, or have committed any thing worthy of death, I refuse not to die: but if there be none of these things whereof these accuse me, no man may deliver me to them. I appeal to Caesar. ¹²Then Festus, when he had conferred with the council, answered, Have you appealed to Caesar? to Caesar shall you go. ¹³And after certain days king Agrippa and Bernice came to Caesarea to salute Festus. ¹⁴And when they had been there many days, Festus declared Paul's cause to the king, saying, There is a certain man left in bonds by Felix: ¹⁵About whom, when I was at Jerusalem, the chief priests and the elders of the Jews informed me, desiring to have judgment against him. ¹⁶To whom I answered, It is not the manner of the Romans to deliver any man to die, before that he which is accused have the accusers face to face, and have license to answer for himself concerning the crime laid against him. ¹⁷Therefore, when they were come here, without any delay on the morrow I sat on the judgment seat, and commanded the man to be brought forth. ¹⁸Against whom when the accusers stood up, they brought none accusation of such things as I supposed: ¹⁹But had certain questions against him of their own superstition, and of one Jesus, which was dead, whom Paul affirmed to be alive. ²⁰And because I doubted of such manner of questions, I asked him whether he would go to Jerusalem, and there be judged of these matters. ²¹But when Paul had appealed to be reserved to the hearing of Augustus, I commanded him to be kept till I might send him to Caesar. ²²Then Agrippa said to Festus, I would also hear the man myself. To morrow, said he, you shall hear him. ²³And on the morrow, when Agrippa was come, and Bernice, with great pomp, and was entered into the place of hearing, with the chief captains, and principal men of the city, at Festus' commandment Paul was brought forth. ²⁴And Festus said, King Agrippa, and all men which are here present with us, you see this man, about

whom all the multitude of the Jews have dealt with me, both at Jerusalem, and also here, crying that he ought not to live any longer. ²⁵But when I found that he had committed nothing worthy of death, and that he himself has appealed to Augustus, I have determined to send him. ²⁶Of whom I have no certain thing to write to my lord. Why I have brought him forth before you, and specially before you, O king Agrippa, that, after examination had, I might have somewhat to write. ²⁷For it seems to me unreasonable to send a prisoner, and not with to signify the crimes laid against him.

26 ¹Then Agrippa said to Paul, You are permitted to speak for yourself. Then Paul stretched forth the hand, and answered for himself: ²I think myself happy, king Agrippa, because I shall answer for myself this day before you touching all the things whereof I am accused of the Jews: ³Especially because I know you to be expert in all customs and questions which are among the Jews: why I beseech you to hear me patiently. ⁴My manner of life from my youth, which was at the first among my own nation at Jerusalem, know all the Jews; ⁵Which knew me from the beginning, if they would testify, that after the most strait sect of our religion I lived a Pharisee. ⁶And now I stand and am judged for the hope of the promise made of God, to our fathers: ⁷To which promise our twelve tribes, instantly serving God day and night, hope to come. For which hope's sake, king Agrippa, I am accused of the Jews. ⁸Why should it be thought a thing incredible with you, that God should raise the dead? ⁹I truly thought with myself, that I ought to do many things contrary to the name of Jesus of Nazareth. ¹⁰Which thing I also did in Jerusalem: and many of the saints did I shut up in prison, having received authority from the chief priests; and when they were put to death, I gave my voice against them. ¹¹And I punished them oft in every synagogue, and compelled them to blaspheme; and being exceedingly mad against them, I persecuted them even to strange cities. ¹²Whereupon as I went to Damascus with authority and commission from the chief priests, ¹³At midday, O king, I saw in the way a light from heaven, above the brightness of the sun, shining round about me and them which journeyed with me. ¹⁴And when we were all fallen to the earth, I heard a voice speaking to me, and saying in the Hebrew tongue, Saul, Saul, why persecute you me? it is hard for you to kick against the pricks. ¹⁵And I said, Who are you, Lord? And he said, I am Jesus whom you persecute. ¹⁶But rise, and stand on your feet: for I have appeared to you for this purpose, to make you a minister and a witness both of these things which you have seen, and of those things in the which I will appear to you; ¹⁷Delivering you from the people, and from the Gentiles, to whom now I send you, ¹⁸To open their eyes, and to turn them from darkness to light, and from the power of Satan to God, that they may receive forgiveness of sins, and inheritance among them which are sanctified by faith that is in me. ¹⁹Whereupon, O king Agrippa, I was not disobedient to the heavenly vision: ²⁰But showed first to them of Damascus, and at Jerusalem, and throughout all the coasts of Judaea, and then to the Gentiles, that they should repent and turn to God, and do works meet for repentance. ²¹For these causes the Jews caught me in the temple, and went about to kill me. ²²Having therefore obtained help of God, I continue to this day, witnessing both to small and great, saying none other things than those which the prophets and Moses did say should come: ²³That Christ should suffer, and that he should be the first that should rise from the dead, and should show light to the people, and to the Gentiles. ²⁴And as he thus spoke for himself, Festus said with a loud voice, Paul, you are beside yourself; much learning does make you mad. ²⁵But he said, I am not mad, most noble Festus; but speak forth the words of truth and soberness. ²⁶For the king knows of these things, before whom also I speak freely: for I am persuaded that none of these things are hidden from him; for this thing was not done in a corner. ²⁷King Agrippa, believe you the prophets? I know that you believe. ²⁸Then Agrippa said to Paul, Almost you persuade me to be a Christian. ²⁹And Paul said, I would to God, that not only you, but also all that hear me this day, were both almost, and altogether such as I am, except these bonds. ³⁰And when he had thus spoken, the king rose up, and the governor, and Bernice, and they that sat with them: ³¹And when they were gone aside, they talked between themselves, saying, This man does nothing worthy of death or of bonds. ³²Then said Agrippa to Festus, This man might have been set at liberty, if he had not appealed to Caesar.

27 ¹And when it was determined that we should sail into Italy, they delivered Paul and certain other prisoners to one named Julius, a centurion of Augustus' band. ²And entering into a ship of Adramyttium, we launched, meaning to sail by the coasts of Asia; one Aristarchus, a Macedonian of Thessalonica, being with us. ³And the next day we touched at Sidon. And Julius courteously entreated Paul, and gave him liberty to go to his friends to refresh himself. ⁴And when we had launched from there, we sailed under Cyprus, because the winds were contrary. ⁵And when we had sailed over the sea of Cilicia and Pamphylia, we came to Myra, a city of Lycia. ⁶And there the centurion found a ship of Alexandria sailing into Italy; and he put us therein. ⁷And when we had sailed slowly many days, and scarce were come over against Cnidus, the wind not suffering us, we sailed under Crete, over against Salmone; ⁸And, hardly passing it, came to a place which is called The fair havens; near to where was the city of Lasea. ⁹Now when much time was spent, and when sailing was now dangerous, because the fast was now already past, Paul admonished them, ¹⁰And said to them, Sirs, I perceive that this voyage will be with hurt and much damage, not only of the lading and ship, but also of our lives. ¹¹Nevertheless the centurion believed the master and the owner of the ship, more than those things which were spoken by Paul. ¹²And because the haven was not commodious to winter in, the more part advised to depart there also, if by any means they might attain to Phenice, and there to winter; which is an haven of Crete, and lies toward the south west and north west. ¹³And when the south wind blew softly, supposing that they had obtained their purpose, loosing there, they sailed close by Crete. ¹⁴But not long after there arose against it a tempestuous wind, called Euroclydon. ¹⁵And when the ship was caught, and could not bear up into the wind, we let her drive. ¹⁶And running under a certain island which is called

Clauda, we had much work to come by the boat: ¹⁷Which when they had taken up, they used helps, under girding the ship; and, fearing lest they should fall into the quicksands, struck sail, and so were driven. ¹⁸And we being exceedingly tossed with a tempest, the next day they lightened the ship; ¹⁹And the third day we cast out with our own hands the tackling of the ship. ²⁰And when neither sun nor stars in many days appeared, and no small tempest lay on us, all hope that we should be saved was then taken away. ²¹But after long abstinence Paul stood forth in the middle of them, and said, Sirs, you should have listened to me, and not have loosed from Crete, and to have gained this harm and loss. ²²And now I exhort you to be of good cheer: for there shall be no loss of any man's life among you, but of the ship. ²³For there stood by me this night the angel of God, whose I am, and whom I serve, ²⁴Saying, Fear not, Paul; you must be brought before Caesar: and, see, God has given you all them that sail with you. ²⁵Why, sirs, be of good cheer: for I believe God, that it shall be even as it was told me. ²⁶However, we must be cast on a certain island. ²⁷But when the fourteenth night was come, as we were driven up and down in Adria, about midnight the shipmen deemed that they drew near to some country; ²⁸And sounded, and found it twenty fathoms: and when they had gone a little further, they sounded again, and found it fifteen fathoms. ²⁹Then fearing lest we should have fallen on rocks, they cast four anchors out of the stern, and wished for the day. ³⁰And as the shipmen were about to flee out of the ship, when they had let down the boat into the sea, under color as though they would have cast anchors out of the bow, ³¹Paul said to the centurion and to the soldiers, Except these abide in the ship, you cannot be saved. ³²Then the soldiers cut off the ropes of the boat, and let her fall off. ³³And while the day was coming on, Paul sought them all to take meat, saying, This day is the fourteenth day that you have tarried and continued fasting, having taken nothing. ³⁴Why I pray you to take some meat: for this is for your health: for there shall not an hair fall from the head of any of you. ³⁵And when he had thus spoken, he took bread, and gave thanks to God in presence of them all: and when he had broken it, he began to eat. ³⁶Then were they all of good cheer, and they also took some meat. ³⁷And we were in all in the ship two hundred three score and sixteen souls. ³⁸And when they had eaten enough, they lightened the ship, and cast out the wheat into the sea. ³⁹And when it was day, they knew not the land: but they discovered a certain creek with a shore, into the which they were minded, if it were possible, to thrust in the ship. ⁴⁰And when they had taken up the anchors, they committed themselves to the sea, and loosed the rudder bands, and hoisted up the mainsail to the wind, and made toward shore. ⁴¹And falling into a place where two seas met, they ran the ship aground; and the forepart stuck fast, and remained unmovable, but the hinder part was broken with the violence of the waves. ⁴²And the soldiers' counsel was to kill the prisoners, lest any of them should swim out, and escape. ⁴³But the centurion, willing to save Paul, kept them from their purpose; and commanded that they which could swim should cast themselves first into the sea, and get to land: ⁴⁴And the rest, some on boards, and some on broken pieces of the ship. And so it came to pass, that they escaped all safe to land.

28

¹And when they were escaped, then they knew that the island was called Melita. ²And the barbarous people showed us no little kindness: for they kindled a fire, and received us every one, because of the present rain, and because of the cold. ³And when Paul had gathered a bundle of sticks, and laid them on the fire, there came a viper out of the heat, and fastened on his hand. ⁴And when the barbarians saw the venomous beast hang on his hand, they said among themselves, No doubt this man is a murderer, whom, though he has escaped the sea, yet vengeance suffers not to live. ⁵And he shook off the beast into the fire, and felt no harm. ⁶However, they looked when he should have swollen, or fallen down dead suddenly: but after they had looked a great while, and saw no harm come to him, they changed their minds, and said that he was a god. ⁷In the same quarters were possessions of the chief man of the island, whose name was Publius; who received us, and lodged us three days courteously. ⁸And it came to pass, that the father of Publius lay sick of a fever and of a bloody flux: to whom Paul entered in, and prayed, and laid his hands on him, and healed him. ⁹So when this was done, others also, which had diseases in the island, came, and were healed: ¹⁰Who also honored us with many honors; and when we departed, they laded us with such things as were necessary. ¹¹And after three months we departed in a ship of Alexandria, which had wintered in the isle, whose sign was Castor and Pollux. ¹²And landing at Syracuse, we tarried there three days. ¹³And from there we fetched a compass, and came to Rhegium: and after one day the south wind blew, and we came the next day to Puteoli: ¹⁴Where we found brothers, and were desired to tarry with them seven days: and so we went toward Rome. ¹⁵And from there, when the brothers heard of us, they came to meet us as far as Appii forum, and The three taverns: whom when Paul saw, he thanked God, and took courage. ¹⁶And when we came to Rome, the centurion delivered the prisoners to the captain of the guard: but Paul was suffered to dwell by himself with a soldier that kept him. ¹⁷And it came to pass, that after three days Paul called the chief of the Jews together: and when they were come together, he said to them, Men and brothers, though I have committed nothing against the people, or customs of our fathers, yet was I delivered prisoner from Jerusalem into the hands of the Romans. ¹⁸Who, when they had examined me, would have let me go, because there was no cause of death in me. ¹⁹But when the Jews spoke against it, I was constrained to appeal to Caesar; not that I had something to accuse my nation of. ²⁰For this cause therefore have I called for you, to see you, and to speak with you: because that for the hope of Israel I am bound with this chain. ²¹And they said to him, We neither received letters out of Judaea concerning you, neither any of the brothers that came showed or spoke any harm of you. ²²But we desire to hear of you what you think: for as concerning this sect, we know that every where it is spoken against. ²³And when they had appointed him a day, there came many to him into his lodging; to whom he expounded and testified the kingdom of God, persuading them concerning Jesus, both out of the

law of Moses, and out of the prophets, from morning till evening. ²⁴And some believed the things which were spoken, and some believed not. ²⁵And when they agreed not among themselves, they departed, after that Paul had spoken one word, Well spoke the Holy Ghost by Isaiah the prophet to our fathers, ²⁶Saying, Go to this people, and say, Hearing you shall hear, and shall not understand; and seeing you shall see, and not perceive: ²⁷For the heart of this people is waxed gross, and their ears are dull of hearing, and their eyes have they closed; lest they should see with their eyes, and hear with their ears, and understand with their heart, and should be converted, and I should heal them. ²⁸Be it known therefore to you, that the salvation of God is sent to the Gentiles, and that they will hear it. ²⁹And when he had said these words, the Jews departed, and had great reasoning among themselves. ³⁰And Paul dwelled two whole years in his own hired house, and received all that came in to him, ³¹Preaching the kingdom of God, and teaching those things which concern the Lord Jesus Christ, with all confidence, no man forbidding him.

Romans

1 ¹Paul, a servant of Jesus Christ, called to be an apostle, separated to the gospel of God, ²(Which he had promised before by his prophets in the holy scriptures,) ³Concerning his Son Jesus Christ our Lord, which was made of the seed of David according to the flesh; ⁴And declared to be the Son of God with power, according to the spirit of holiness, by the resurrection from the dead: ⁵By whom we have received grace and apostleship, for obedience to the faith among all nations, for his name: ⁶Among whom are you also the called of Jesus Christ: ⁷To all that be in Rome, beloved of God, called to be saints: Grace to you and peace from God our Father, and the Lord Jesus Christ. ⁸First, I thank my God through Jesus Christ for you all, that your faith is spoken of throughout the whole world. ⁹For God is my witness, whom I serve with my spirit in the gospel of his Son, that without ceasing I make mention of you always in my prayers; ¹⁰Making request, if by any means now at length I might have a prosperous journey by the will of God to come to you. ¹¹For I long to see you, that I may impart to you some spiritual gift, to the end you may be established; ¹²That is, that I may be comforted together with you by the mutual faith both of you and me. ¹³Now I would not have you ignorant, brothers, that oftentimes I purposed to come to you, (but was let till now,) that I might have some fruit among you also, even as among other Gentiles. ¹⁴I am debtor both to the Greeks, and to the Barbarians; both to the wise, and to the unwise. ¹⁵So, as much as in me is, I am ready to preach the gospel to you that are at Rome also. ¹⁶For I am not ashamed of the gospel of Christ: for it is the power of God to salvation to every one that believes; to the Jew first, and also to the Greek. ¹⁷For therein is the righteousness of God revealed from faith to faith: as it is written, The just shall live by faith. ¹⁸For the wrath of God is revealed from heaven against all ungodliness and unrighteousness of men, who hold the truth in unrighteousness; ¹⁹Because that which may be known of God is manifest in them; for God has showed it to them. ²⁰For the invisible things of him from the creation of the world are clearly seen, being understood by the things that are made, even his eternal power and Godhead; so that they are without excuse: ²¹Because that, when they knew God, they glorified him not as God, neither were thankful; but became vain in their imaginations, and their foolish heart was darkened. ²²Professing themselves to be wise, they became fools, ²³And changed the glory of the incorruptible God into an image made like to corruptible man, and to birds, and four footed beasts, and creeping things. ²⁴Why God also gave them up to uncleanness through the lusts of their own hearts, to dishonor their own bodies between themselves: ²⁵Who changed the truth of God into a lie, and worshipped and served the creature more than the Creator, who is blessed for ever. Amen. ²⁶For this cause God gave them up to vile affections: for even their women did change the natural use into that which is against nature: ²⁷And likewise also the men, leaving the natural use of the woman, burned in their lust one toward another; men with men working that which is unseemly, and receiving in themselves that recompense of their error which was meet. ²⁸And even as they did not like to retain God in their knowledge, God gave them over to a reprobate mind, to do those things which are not convenient; ²⁹Being filled with all unrighteousness, fornication, wickedness, covetousness, maliciousness; full of envy, murder, debate, deceit, malignity; whisperers, ³⁰Backbiters, haters of God, despiteful, proud, boasters, inventors of evil things, disobedient to parents, ³¹Without understanding, covenant breakers, without natural affection, implacable, unmerciful: ³²Who knowing the judgment of God, that they which commit such things are worthy of death, not only do the same, but have pleasure in them that do them.

2 ¹Therefore you are inexcusable, O man, whoever you are that judge: for wherein you judge another, you condemn yourself; for you that judge do the same things. ²But we are sure that the judgment of God is according to truth against them which commit such things. ³And think you this, O man, that judge them which do such things, and do the same, that you shall escape the judgment of God? ⁴Or despise you the riches of his goodness and forbearance and long-suffering; not knowing that the goodness of God leads you to repentance? ⁵But after your hardness and impenitent heart treasure up to yourself wrath against the day of wrath and revelation of the righteous judgment of God; ⁶Who will render to every man according to his deeds: ⁷To them who by patient continuance in well doing seek for glory and honor and immortality, eternal life: ⁸But to them that are contentious, and do not obey the truth, but obey unrighteousness, indignation and wrath, ⁹Tribulation and anguish, on every soul of man that does evil, of the Jew first, and also of the Gentile; ¹⁰But glory, honor, and peace, to every man that works good, to the Jew first, and also to the Gentile: ¹¹For there is no respect of persons with God. ¹²For as many as have sinned without law shall also perish without law: and as many as have sinned in the law shall be judged by the law; ¹³(For not the hearers of the law are just before God, but the doers of the law shall be justified. ¹⁴For when the Gentiles, which have not the law, do by nature the things contained in the law, these, having not the law, are a law to themselves: ¹⁵Which show the work of the law written in their hearts, their conscience also bearing witness, and their thoughts the mean while accusing or else excusing one another;) ¹⁶In the day when God shall judge the secrets of men by Jesus Christ according to my gospel. ¹⁷Behold, you are called a Jew, and rest in the law, and make your boast of God, ¹⁸And know his will, and approve the things that are more excellent, being instructed out of the law; ¹⁹And are confident that you yourself are a guide of the blind, a light of them which are in darkness, ²⁰An instructor of the foolish, a teacher of babes, which have the form of knowledge and of the truth in the law. ²¹You therefore which teach another, teach you not yourself? you that preach a man should not steal, do you steal? ²²You that say a man should not commit adultery, do you commit adultery? you that abhor idols, do you commit sacrilege? ²³You that make your boast of the law, through breaking the law dishonor you God? ²⁴For the name of God is blasphemed among the Gentiles through

you, as it is written. ²⁵For circumcision truly profits, if you keep the law: but if you be a breaker of the law, your circumcision is made uncircumcision. ²⁶Therefore if the uncircumcision keep the righteousness of the law, shall not his uncircumcision be counted for circumcision? ²⁷And shall not uncircumcision which is by nature, if it fulfill the law, judge you, who by the letter and circumcision do transgress the law? ²⁸For he is not a Jew, which is one outwardly; neither is that circumcision, which is outward in the flesh: ²⁹But he is a Jew, which is one inwardly; and circumcision is that of the heart, in the spirit, and not in the letter; whose praise is not of men, but of God.

3 ¹What advantage then has the Jew? or what profit is there of circumcision? ²Much every way: chiefly, because that to them were committed the oracles of God. ³For what if some did not believe? shall their unbelief make the faith of God without effect? ⁴God forbid: yes, let God be true, but every man a liar; as it is written, That you might be justified in your sayings, and might overcome when you are judged. ⁵But if our unrighteousness commend the righteousness of God, what shall we say? Is God unrighteous who takes vengeance? (I speak as a man) ⁶God forbid: for then how shall God judge the world? ⁷For if the truth of God has more abounded through my lie to his glory; why yet am I also judged as a sinner? ⁸And not rather, (as we be slanderously reported, and as some affirm that we say,) Let us do evil, that good may come? whose damnation is just. ⁹What then? are we better than they? No, in no wise: for we have before proved both Jews and Gentiles, that they are all under sin; ¹⁰As it is written, There is none righteous, no, not one; ¹¹There is none that understands, there is none that seeks after God. ¹²They are all gone out of the way, they are together become unprofitable; there is none that does good, no, not one. ¹³Their throat is an open sepulcher; with their tongues they have used deceit; the poison of asps is under their lips: ¹⁴Whose mouth is full of cursing and bitterness: ¹⁵Their feet are swift to shed blood: ¹⁶Destruction and misery are in their ways: ¹⁷And the way of peace have they not known: ¹⁸There is no fear of God before their eyes. ¹⁹Now we know that what things soever the law said, it says to them who are under the law: that every mouth may be stopped, and all the world may become guilty before God. ²⁰Therefore by the deeds of the law there shall no flesh be justified in his sight: for by the law is the knowledge of sin. ²¹But now the righteousness of God without the law is manifested, being witnessed by the law and the prophets; ²²Even the righteousness of God which is by faith of Jesus Christ to all and on all them that believe: for there is no difference: ²³For all have sinned, and come short of the glory of God; ²⁴Being justified freely by his grace through the redemption that is in Christ Jesus: ²⁵Whom God has set forth to be a propitiation through faith in his blood, to declare his righteousness for the remission of sins that are past, through the forbearance of God; ²⁶To declare, I say, at this time his righteousness: that he might be just, and the justifier of him which believes in Jesus. ²⁷Where is boasting then? It is excluded. By what law? of works? No: but by the law of faith. ²⁸Therefore we conclude that a man is justified by faith without the deeds of the law. ²⁹Is he the God of the Jews only? is he not also of the Gentiles? Yes, of the Gentiles also: ³⁰Seeing it is one God, which shall justify the circumcision by faith, and uncircumcision through faith. ³¹Do we then make void the law through faith? God forbid: yes, we establish the law.

4 ¹What shall we say then that Abraham our father, as pertaining to the flesh, has found? ²For if Abraham were justified by works, he has whereof to glory; but not before God. ³For what says the scripture? Abraham believed God, and it was counted to him for righteousness. ⁴Now to him that works is the reward not reckoned of grace, but of debt. ⁵But to him that works not, but believes on him that justifies the ungodly, his faith is counted for righteousness. ⁶Even as David also describes the blessedness of the man, to whom God imputes righteousness without works, ⁷Saying, Blessed are they whose iniquities are forgiven, and whose sins are covered. ⁸Blessed is the man to whom the Lord will not impute sin. ⁹Comes this blessedness then on the circumcision only, or on the uncircumcision also? for we say that faith was reckoned to Abraham for righteousness. ¹⁰How was it then reckoned? when he was in circumcision, or in uncircumcision? Not in circumcision, but in uncircumcision. ¹¹And he received the sign of circumcision, a seal of the righteousness of the faith which he had yet being uncircumcised: that he might be the father of all them that believe, though they be not circumcised; that righteousness might be imputed to them also: ¹²And the father of circumcision to them who are not of the circumcision only, but who also walk in the steps of that faith of our father Abraham, which he had being yet uncircumcised. ¹³For the promise, that he should be the heir of the world, was not to Abraham, or to his seed, through the law, but through the righteousness of faith. ¹⁴For if they which are of the law be heirs, faith is made void, and the promise made of none effect: ¹⁵Because the law works wrath: for where no law is, there is no transgression. ¹⁶Therefore it is of faith, that it might be by grace; to the end the promise might be sure to all the seed; not to that only which is of the law, but to that also which is of the faith of Abraham; who is the father of us all, ¹⁷(As it is written, I have made you a father of many nations,) before him whom he believed, even God, who vivifies the dead, and calls those things which be not as though they were. ¹⁸Who against hope believed in hope, that he might become the father of many nations, according to that which was spoken, So shall your seed be. ¹⁹And being not weak in faith, he considered not his own body now dead, when he was about an hundred years old, neither yet the deadness of Sarah's womb: ²⁰He staggered not at the promise of God through unbelief; but was strong in faith, giving glory to God; ²¹And being fully persuaded that, what he had promised, he was able also to perform. ²²And therefore it was imputed to him for righteousness. ²³Now it was not written for his sake alone, that it was imputed to him; ²⁴But for us also, to whom it shall be imputed, if we believe on him that raised up Jesus our Lord from the dead; ²⁵Who was delivered for our offenses, and was raised again for our justification.

5 ¹Therefore being justified by faith, we have peace with God through our Lord Jesus Christ; ²By whom also we have access by faith into this grace wherein we stand, and rejoice in hope of the glory of God. ³And not only so, but we glory in tribulations also: knowing that tribulation works patience; ⁴And patience, experience; and experience, hope: ⁵And hope makes not ashamed; because the love of God is shed abroad in our hearts by the Holy Ghost which is given to us. ⁶For when we were yet without strength, in due time Christ died for the ungodly. ⁷For scarcely for a righteous man will one die: yet peradventure for a good man some would even dare to die. ⁸But God commends his love toward us, in that, while we were yet sinners, Christ died for us. ⁹Much more then, being now justified by his blood, we shall be saved from wrath through him. ¹⁰For if, when we were enemies, we were reconciled to God by the death of his Son, much more, being reconciled, we shall be saved by his life. ¹¹And not only so, but we also joy in God through our Lord Jesus Christ, by whom we have now received the atonement. ¹²Why, as by one man sin entered into the world, and death by sin; and so death passed on all men, for that all have sinned: ¹³(For until the law sin was in the world: but sin is not imputed when there is no law. ¹⁴Nevertheless death reigned from Adam to Moses, even over them that had not sinned after the similitude of Adam's transgression, who is the figure of him that was to come. ¹⁵But not as the offense, so also is the free gift. For if through the offense of one many be dead, much more the grace of God, and the gift by grace, which is by one man, Jesus Christ, has abounded to many. ¹⁶And not as it was by one that sinned, so is the gift: for the judgment was by one to condemnation, but the free gift is of many offenses to justification. ¹⁷For if by one man's offense death reigned by one; much more they which receive abundance of grace and of the gift of righteousness shall reign in life by one, Jesus Christ.) ¹⁸Therefore as by the offense of one judgment came on all men to condemnation; even so by the righteousness of one the free gift came on all men to justification of life. ¹⁹For as by one man's disobedience many were made sinners, so by the obedience of one shall many be made righteous. ²⁰Moreover the law entered, that the offense might abound. But where sin abounded, grace did much more abound: ²¹That as sin has reigned to death, even so might grace reign through righteousness to eternal life by Jesus Christ our Lord.

6 ¹What shall we say then? Shall we continue in sin, that grace may abound? ²God forbid. How shall we, that are dead to sin, live any longer therein? ³Know you not, that so many of us as were baptized into Jesus Christ were baptized into his death? ⁴Therefore we are buried with him by baptism into death: that like as Christ was raised up from the dead by the glory of the Father, even so we also should walk in newness of life. ⁵For if we have been planted together in the likeness of his death, we shall be also in the likeness of his resurrection: ⁶Knowing this, that our old man is crucified with him, that the body of sin might be destroyed, that from now on we should not serve sin. ⁷For he that is dead is freed from sin. ⁸Now if we be dead with Christ, we believe that we shall also live with him: ⁹Knowing that Christ being raised from the dead dies no more; death has no more dominion over him. ¹⁰For in that he died, he died to sin once: but in that he lives, he lives to God. ¹¹Likewise reckon you also yourselves to be dead indeed to sin, but alive to God through Jesus Christ our Lord. ¹²Let not sin therefore reign in your mortal body, that you should obey it in the lusts thereof. ¹³Neither yield you your members as instruments of unrighteousness to sin: but yield yourselves to God, as those that are alive from the dead, and your members as instruments of righteousness to God. ¹⁴For sin shall not have dominion over you: for you are not under the law, but under grace. ¹⁵What then? shall we sin, because we are not under the law, but under grace? God forbid. ¹⁶Know you not, that to whom you yield yourselves servants to obey, his servants you are to whom you obey; whether of sin to death, or of obedience to righteousness? ¹⁷But God be thanked, that you were the servants of sin, but you have obeyed from the heart that form of doctrine which was delivered you. ¹⁸Being then made free from sin, you became the servants of righteousness. ¹⁹I speak after the manner of men because of the infirmity of your flesh: for as you have yielded your members servants to uncleanness and to iniquity to iniquity; even so now yield your members servants to righteousness to holiness. ²⁰For when you were the servants of sin, you were free from righteousness. ²¹What fruit had you then in those things whereof you are now ashamed? for the end of those things is death. ²²But now being made free from sin, and become servants to God, you have your fruit to holiness, and the end everlasting life. ²³For the wages of sin is death; but the gift of God is eternal life through Jesus Christ our Lord.

7 ¹Know you not, brothers, (for I speak to them that know the law,) how that the law has dominion over a man as long as he lives? ²For the woman which has an husband is bound by the law to her husband so long as he lives; but if the husband be dead, she is loosed from the law of her husband. ³So then if, while her husband lives, she be married to another man, she shall be called an adulteress: but if her husband be dead, she is free from that law; so that she is no adulteress, though she be married to another man. ⁴Why, my brothers, you also are become dead to the law by the body of Christ; that you should be married to another, even to him who is raised from the dead, that we should bring forth fruit to God. ⁵For when we were in the flesh, the motions of sins, which were by the law, did work in our members to bring forth fruit to death. ⁶But now we are delivered from the law, that being dead wherein we were held; that we should serve in newness of spirit, and not in the oldness of the letter. ⁷What shall we say then? Is the law sin? God forbid. No, I had not known sin, but by the law: for I had not known lust, except the law had said, You shall not covet. ⁸But sin, taking occasion by the commandment, worked in me all manner of concupiscence. For without the law sin was dead. ⁹For I was alive without the law once: but when the commandment came, sin revived, and I died. ¹⁰And the commandment, which was ordained to life, I found to be to death. ¹¹For sin, taking occasion by the commandment, deceived me, and by it slew me. ¹²Why the law is holy, and the commandment holy, and just, and good. ¹³Was then that which is good made death to me? God forbid. But sin, that it might appear sin, working death in me by that which is good; that sin by the commandment might become exceeding sinful. ¹⁴For we know that the law is spiritual: but I am carnal, sold under sin. ¹⁵For that which I do I allow not: for what I would, that do I not; but what I hate, that do I. ¹⁶If then I do that which I would not, I consent to the law that it is good. ¹⁷Now then it is no more I that do it, but sin that dwells in me. ¹⁸For I know that in me (that is, in my flesh,) dwells no good thing: for to will is present with me; but how to perform that which is good I find not. ¹⁹For the good that I would I do not: but the evil which I would not, that I do. ²⁰Now if I do that I would not, it is no more I that do it, but sin that dwells in me. ²¹I find then a law, that, when I would do good, evil is present with me. ²²For I delight in the law of God after the inward man: ²³But I see another law in my members, warring against the law of my mind, and bringing me into captivity to the law of sin which is in my members. ²⁴O wretched man that I am! who shall deliver me from the body of this death? ²⁵I thank God through Jesus Christ our Lord. So then with the mind I myself serve the law of God; but with the flesh the law of sin.

8 ¹There is therefore now no condemnation to them which are in Christ Jesus, who walk not after the flesh, but after the Spirit. ²For the law of the Spirit of life in Christ Jesus has made me free from the law of sin and death. ³For what the law could not do, in that it was weak through the flesh, God sending his own Son in the likeness of sinful flesh, and for sin, condemned sin in the flesh: ⁴That the righteousness of the law might be fulfilled in us, who walk not after the flesh, but after the Spirit. ⁵For they that are after the flesh do mind the things of the flesh; but they that are after the Spirit the things of the Spirit. ⁶For to be carnally minded is death; but to be spiritually minded is life and peace. ⁷Because the carnal mind is enmity against God: for it is not subject to the law of God, neither indeed can be. ⁸So then they that are in the flesh cannot please God. ⁹But you are not in the flesh, but in the Spirit, if so be that the Spirit of God dwell in you. Now if any man have not the Spirit of Christ, he is none of his. ¹⁰And if Christ be in you, the body is dead because of sin; but the Spirit is life because of righteousness. ¹¹But if the Spirit of him that raised up Jesus from the dead dwell in you, he that raised up Christ from the dead shall also quicken your mortal bodies by his Spirit that dwells in you. ¹²Therefore, brothers, we are debtors, not to the flesh, to live after the flesh. ¹³For if you live after the flesh, you shall die: but if you through the Spirit do mortify the deeds of the body, you shall live. ¹⁴For as many as are led by the Spirit of God, they are the sons of God. ¹⁵For you have not received the spirit of bondage again to fear; but you have received the Spirit of adoption, whereby we cry, Abba, Father. ¹⁶The Spirit itself bears witness with our spirit, that we are the children of God: ¹⁷And if children, then heirs; heirs of God, and joint-heirs with Christ; if so be that we suffer with him, that we may be also glorified together. ¹⁸For I reckon that the sufferings of this present time are not worthy to be compared with the glory which shall be revealed in us. ¹⁹For the earnest expectation of the creature waits for the manifestation of the sons of God. ²⁰For the creature was made subject to vanity, not willingly, but by reason of him who has subjected the same in hope, ²¹Because the creature itself also shall be delivered from the bondage of corruption into the glorious liberty of the children of God. ²²For we know that the whole creation groans and travails in pain together until now. ²³And not only they, but ourselves also, which have the first fruits of the Spirit, even we ourselves groan within ourselves, waiting for the adoption, to wit, the redemption of our body. ²⁴For we are saved by hope: but hope that is seen is not hope: for what a man sees, why does he yet hope for? ²⁵But if we hope for that we see not, then do we with patience wait for it. ²⁶Likewise the Spirit also helps our infirmities: for we know not what we should pray for as we should: but the Spirit itself makes intercession for us with groanings which cannot be uttered. ²⁷And he that searches the hearts knows what is the mind of the Spirit, because he makes intercession for the saints according to the will of God. ²⁸And we know that all things work together for good to them that love God, to them who are the called according to his purpose. ²⁹For whom he did foreknow, he also did predestinate to be conformed to the image of his Son, that he might be the firstborn among many brothers. ³⁰Moreover whom he did predestinate, them he also called: and whom he called, them he also justified: and whom he justified, them he also glorified. ³¹What shall we then say to these things? If God be for us, who can be against us? ³²He that spared not his own Son, but delivered him up for us all, how shall he not with him also freely give us all things? ³³Who shall lay any thing to the charge of God's elect? It is God that justifies. ³⁴Who is he that condemns? It is Christ that died, yes rather, that is risen again, who is even at the right hand of God, who also makes intercession for us. ³⁵Who shall separate us from the love of Christ? shall tribulation, or distress, or persecution, or famine, or nakedness, or peril, or sword? ³⁶As it is written, For your sake we are killed all the day long; we are accounted as sheep for the slaughter. ³⁷No, in all these things we are more than conquerors through him that loved us. ³⁸For I am persuaded, that neither death, nor life, nor angels, nor principalities, nor powers, nor things present, nor things to come, ³⁹Nor height, nor depth, nor any other creature, shall be able to separate us from the love of God, which is in Christ Jesus our Lord.

9 ¹I say the truth in Christ, I lie not, my conscience also bearing me witness in the Holy Ghost, ²That I have great heaviness and continual sorrow in my heart. ³For I could wish that myself were accursed from Christ for my brothers, my kinsmen according to the flesh: ⁴Who are Israelites; to whom pertains the adoption, and the glory, and the covenants, and the giving of the law, and the service of God, and the promises; ⁵Whose are the fathers, and of whom as concerning the flesh Christ came, who is over all, God blessed for ever. Amen. ⁶Not as though the word of God has taken none effect. For they are not all Israel, which are of Israel: ⁷Neither, because they are the seed of Abraham, are they all children: but, In Isaac shall your seed be called. ⁸That is, They which are the children of the flesh, these are not the children of God: but the children of the promise are counted for the seed. ⁹For this is the word of promise, At this time will I come, and Sarah shall have a son. ¹⁰And not only this; but when Rebecca also had conceived by one, even by our father Isaac; ¹¹(For the children being not yet born, neither having done any good or evil, that the purpose of God according to election might stand, not of works, but of him that calls;) ¹²It was said to her, The elder shall serve the younger. ¹³As it is written, Jacob have I loved, but Esau have I hated. ¹⁴What shall we say then? Is there unrighteousness with God? God forbid. ¹⁵For he says to Moses, I will have mercy on whom I will have mercy, and I will have compassion on whom I will have compassion. ¹⁶So then it is not of him that wills, nor of him that runs, but of God that shows mercy. ¹⁷For the scripture says to Pharaoh, Even for this same purpose have I raised you up, that I might show my power in you, and that my name might be declared throughout all the earth. ¹⁸Therefore has he mercy on whom he will have mercy, and whom he will he hardens. ¹⁹You will say then to me, Why does he yet find fault? For who has resisted his will? ²⁰No but, O man, who are you that reply against God? Shall the thing formed say to him that formed it, Why have you made me thus? ²¹Has not the potter power over the clay, of the same lump to make one vessel to honor, and another to dishonor? ²²What if God, willing to show his wrath, and to make his power known, endured with much long-suffering the vessels of wrath fitted to destruction: ²³And that he might make known the riches of his glory on the vessels of mercy, which he had before prepared to glory, ²⁴Even us, whom he has called, not of the Jews only, but also of the Gentiles? ²⁵As he says also in Hosea, I will call them my people, which were not my people; and her beloved, which was not beloved. ²⁶And it shall come to pass, that in the place where it was said to them, You are not my people; there shall they be called the children of the living God. ²⁷Isaiah also cries concerning Israel, Though the number of the children of Israel be as the sand of the sea, a remnant shall be saved: ²⁸For he will finish the work, and cut it short in righteousness: because a short work will the Lord make on the earth. ²⁹And as Isaiah said before, Except the Lord of Sabaoth had left us a seed, we had been as Sodoma, and been made like to Gomorrha. ³⁰What shall we say then? That the Gentiles, which followed not after righteousness, have attained to righteousness, even the righteousness which is of faith. ³¹But Israel, which followed after the law of righteousness, has not attained to the law of righteousness. ³²Why? Because they sought it not by faith, but as it were by the works of the law. For they stumbled at that stumbling stone; ³³As it is written, Behold, I lay in Sion a stumbling stone and rock of offense: and whoever believes on him shall not be ashamed.

10 ¹Brothers, my heart's desire and prayer to God for Israel is, that they might be saved. ²For I bear them record that they have a zeal of God, but not according to knowledge. ³For they being ignorant of God's righteousness, and going about to establish their own righteousness, have not submitted themselves to the righteousness of God. ⁴For Christ is the end of the law for righteousness to every one that believes. ⁵For Moses describes the righteousness which is of the law, That the man which does those things shall live by them. ⁶But the righteousness which is of faith speaks on this wise, Say not in your heart, Who shall ascend into heaven? (that is, to bring Christ down from above:) ⁷Or, Who shall descend into the deep? (that is, to bring up Christ again from the dead.) ⁸But what says it? The word is near you, even in your mouth, and in your heart: that is, the word of faith, which we preach; ⁹That if you shall confess with your mouth the Lord Jesus, and shall believe in your heart that God has raised him from the dead, you shall be saved. ¹⁰For with the heart man believes to righteousness; and with the mouth confession is made to salvation. ¹¹For the scripture says, Whoever believes on him shall not be ashamed. ¹²For there is no difference between the Jew and the Greek: for the same Lord over all is rich to all that call on him. ¹³For whoever shall call on the name of the Lord shall be saved. ¹⁴How then shall they call on him in whom they have not believed? and how shall they believe in him of whom they have not heard? and how shall they hear without a preacher? ¹⁵And how shall they preach, except they be sent? as it is written, How beautiful are the feet of them that preach the gospel of peace, and bring glad tidings of good things! ¹⁶But they have not all obeyed the gospel. For Isaiah says, Lord, who has believed our report? ¹⁷So then faith comes by hearing, and hearing by the word of God. ¹⁸But I say, Have they not heard? Yes truly, their sound went into all the earth, and their words to the ends of the world. ¹⁹But I say, Did not Israel know? First Moses says, I will provoke you to jealousy by them that are no people, and by a foolish nation I will anger you. ²⁰But Isaiah is very bold, and said, I was found of them that sought me not; I was made manifest to them that asked not after me. ²¹But to Israel he says, All day long I have stretched forth my hands to a disobedient and gainsaying people.

11 ¹I say then, Has God cast away his people? God forbid. For I also am an Israelite, of the seed of Abraham, of the tribe of Benjamin. ²God has not cast away his people which he foreknew. Know you not what the scripture says of Elijah? how he makes intercession to God against Israel saying, ³Lord, they have killed your prophets, and dig down your altars; and I am left alone, and they seek my life. ⁴But what says the answer of God to him? I have reserved to myself seven thousand men, who have not bowed the knee to the image of Baal. ⁵Even so then at this present time also there is a remnant according to the election of grace. ⁶And if by grace, then is it no more of works: otherwise grace is no more grace. But if it be of works, then it is no more grace: otherwise work is no more work. ⁷What then? Israel has not obtained that which he seeks for; but the election has obtained it, and the rest were blinded. ⁸(According as it is written, God has given them the spirit of slumber, eyes that they should not see, and ears that they should not hear;) to this day. ⁹And David says, Let their table be made a snare, and a trap, and a stumbling block, and a recompense to them: ¹⁰Let their eyes be darkened, that they may not see, and bow down their back always. ¹¹I say then, Have they stumbled that they should fall? God forbid: but rather through their fall salvation is come to the Gentiles, for to provoke them to jealousy. ¹²Now if the fall of them be the riches of the world, and the diminishing of them the riches of the Gentiles; how much more their fullness? ¹³For I speak to you Gentiles, inasmuch as I am the apostle of the

Gentiles, I magnify my office: ¹⁴If by any means I may provoke to emulation them which are my flesh, and might save some of them. ¹⁵For if the casting away of them be the reconciling of the world, what shall the receiving of them be, but life from the dead? ¹⁶For if the first fruit be holy, the lump is also holy: and if the root be holy, so are the branches. ¹⁷And if some of the branches be broken off, and you, being a wild olive tree, were grafted in among them, and with them partake of the root and fatness of the olive tree; ¹⁸Boast not against the branches. But if you boast, you bore not the root, but the root you. ¹⁹You will say then, The branches were broken off, that I might be grafted in. ²⁰Well; because of unbelief they were broken off, and you stand by faith. Be not high minded, but fear: ²¹For if God spared not the natural branches, take heed lest he also spare not you. ²²Behold therefore the goodness and severity of God: on them which fell, severity; but toward you, goodness, if you continue in his goodness: otherwise you also shall be cut off. ²³And they also, if they abide not still in unbelief, shall be grafted in: for God is able to graft them in again. ²⁴For if you were cut out of the olive tree which is wild by nature, and were grafted contrary to nature into a good olive tree: how much more shall these, which be the natural branches, be grafted into their own olive tree? ²⁵For I would not, brothers, that you should be ignorant of this mystery, lest you should be wise in your own conceits; that blindness in part is happened to Israel, until the fullness of the Gentiles be come in. ²⁶And so all Israel shall be saved: as it is written, There shall come out of Sion the Deliverer, and shall turn away ungodliness from Jacob: ²⁷For this is my covenant to them, when I shall take away their sins. ²⁸As concerning the gospel, they are enemies for your sakes: but as touching the election, they are beloved for the father's sakes. ²⁹For the gifts and calling of God are without repentance. ³⁰For as you in times past have not believed God, yet have now obtained mercy through their unbelief: ³¹Even so have these also now not believed, that through your mercy they also may obtain mercy. ³²For God has concluded them all in unbelief, that he might have mercy on all. ³³O the depth of the riches both of the wisdom and knowledge of God! how unsearchable are his judgments, and his ways past finding out! ³⁴For who has known the mind of the Lord? or who has been his counselor? ³⁵Or who has first given to him, and it shall be recompensed to him again? ³⁶For of him, and through him, and to him, are all things: to whom be glory for ever. Amen.

12 ¹I beseech you therefore, brothers, by the mercies of God, that you present your bodies a living sacrifice, holy, acceptable to God, which is your reasonable service. ²And be not conformed to this world: but be you transformed by the renewing of your mind, that you may prove what is that good, and acceptable, and perfect, will of God. ³For I say, through the grace given to me, to every man that is among you, not to think of himself more highly than he ought to think; but to think soberly, according as God has dealt to every man the measure of faith. ⁴For as we have many members in one body, and all members have not the same office: ⁵So we, being many, are one body in Christ, and every one members one of another. ⁶Having then gifts differing according to the grace that is given to us, whether prophecy, let us prophesy according to the proportion of faith; ⁷Or ministry, let us wait on our ministering: or he that teaches, on teaching; ⁸Or he that exhorts, on exhortation: he that gives, let him do it with simplicity; he that rules, with diligence; he that shows mercy, with cheerfulness. ⁹Let love be without dissimulation. Abhor that which is evil; hold to that which is good. ¹⁰Be kindly affectionate one to another with brotherly love; in honor preferring one another; ¹¹Not slothful in business; fervent in spirit; serving the Lord; ¹²Rejoicing in hope; patient in tribulation; continuing instant in prayer; ¹³Distributing to the necessity of saints; given to hospitality. ¹⁴Bless them which persecute you: bless, and curse not. ¹⁵Rejoice with them that do rejoice, and weep with them that weep. ¹⁶Be of the same mind one toward another. Mind not high things, but condescend to men of low estate. Be not wise in your own conceits. ¹⁷Recompense to no man evil for evil. Provide things honest in the sight of all men. ¹⁸If it be possible, as much as lies in you, live peaceably with all men. ¹⁹Dearly beloved, avenge not yourselves, but rather give place to wrath: for it is written, Vengeance is mine; I will repay, says the Lord. ²⁰Therefore if your enemy hunger, feed him; if he thirst, give him drink: for in so doing you shall heap coals of fire on his head. ²¹Be not overcome of evil, but overcome evil with good.

13 ¹Let every soul be subject to the higher powers. For there is no power but of God: the powers that be are ordained of God. ²Whoever therefore resists the power, resists the ordinance of God: and they that resist shall receive to themselves damnation. ³For rulers are not a terror to good works, but to the evil. Will you then not be afraid of the power? do that which is good, and you shall have praise of the same: ⁴For he is the minister of God to you for good. But if you do that which is evil, be afraid; for he bears not the sword in vain: for he is the minister of God, a revenger to execute wrath on him that does evil. ⁵Why you must needs be subject, not only for wrath, but also for conscience sake. ⁶For for this cause pay you tribute also: for they are God's ministers, attending continually on this very thing. ⁷Render therefore to all their dues: tribute to whom tribute is due; custom to whom custom; fear to whom fear; honor to whom honor. ⁸Owe no man any thing, but to love one another: for he that loves another has fulfilled the law. ⁹For this, You shall not commit adultery, You shall not kill, You shall not steal, You shall not bear false witness, You shall not covet; and if there be any other commandment, it is briefly comprehended in this saying, namely, You shall love your neighbor as yourself. ¹⁰Love works no ill to his neighbor: therefore love is the fulfilling of the law. ¹¹And that, knowing the time, that now it is high time to awake out of sleep: for now is our salvation nearer than when we believed. ¹²The night is far spent, the day is at hand: let us therefore cast off the works of darkness, and let us put on the armor of light. ¹³Let us walk honestly, as in the day; not in rioting and drunkenness, not in chambering and wantonness, not in strife and envying. ¹⁴But put you on the Lord Jesus Christ, and make not provision for the flesh, to fulfill the lusts thereof.

14 ¹Him that is weak in the faith receive you, but not to doubtful disputations. ²For one believes that he may eat all things: another, who is weak, eats herbs. ³Let not him that eats despise him that eats not; and let not him which eats not judge him that eats: for God has received him. ⁴Who are you that judge another man's servant? to his own master he stands or falls. Yes, he shall be held up: for God is able to make him stand. ⁵One man esteems one day above another: another esteems every day alike. Let every man be fully persuaded in his own mind. ⁶He that regards the day, regards it to the Lord; and he that regards not the day, to the Lord he does not regard it. He that eats, eats to the Lord, for he gives God thanks; and he that eats not, to the Lord he eats not, and gives God thanks. ⁷For none of us lives to himself, and no man dies to himself. ⁸For whether we live, we live to the Lord; and whether we die, we die to the Lord: whether we live therefore, or die, we are the Lord's. ⁹For to this end Christ both died, and rose, and revived, that he might be Lord both of the dead and living. ¹⁰But why do you judge your brother? or why do you set at nothing your brother? for we shall all stand before the judgment seat of Christ. ¹¹For it is written, As I live, says the Lord, every knee shall bow to me, and every tongue shall confess to God. ¹²So then every one of us shall give account of himself to God. ¹³Let us not therefore judge one another any more: but judge this rather, that no man put a stumbling block or an occasion to fall in his brother's way. ¹⁴I know, and am persuaded by the Lord Jesus, that there is nothing unclean of itself: but to him that esteems any thing to be unclean, to him it is unclean. ¹⁵But if your brother be grieved with your meat, now walk you not charitably. Destroy not him with your meat, for whom Christ died. ¹⁶Let not then your good be evil spoken of: ¹⁷For the kingdom of God is not meat and drink; but righteousness, and peace, and joy in the Holy Ghost. ¹⁸For he that in these things serves Christ is acceptable to God, and approved of men. ¹⁹Let us therefore follow after the things which make for peace, and things with which one may edify another. ²⁰For meat destroy not the work of God. All things indeed are pure; but it is evil for that man who eats with offense. ²¹It is good neither to eat flesh, nor to drink wine, nor any thing whereby your brother stumbles, or is offended, or is made weak. ²²Have you faith? have it to yourself before God. Happy is he that condemns not himself in that thing which he allows. ²³And he that doubts is damned if he eat, because he eats not of faith: for whatever is not of faith is sin.

15 ¹We then that are strong ought to bear the infirmities of the weak, and not to please ourselves. ²Let every one of us please his neighbor for his good to edification. ³For even Christ pleased not himself; but, as it is written, The reproaches of them that reproached you fell on me. ⁴For whatever things were written aforetime were written for our learning, that we through patience and comfort of the scriptures might have hope. ⁵Now the God of patience and consolation grant you to be like minded one toward another according to Christ Jesus: ⁶That you may with one mind and one mouth glorify God, even the Father of our Lord Jesus Christ. ⁷Why receive you one another, as Christ also received us to the glory of God. ⁸Now I say that Jesus Christ was a minister of the circumcision for the truth of God, to confirm the promises made to the fathers: ⁹And that the Gentiles might glorify God for his mercy; as it is written, For this cause I will confess to you among the Gentiles, and sing to your name. ¹⁰And again he says, Rejoice, you Gentiles, with his people. ¹¹And again, Praise the Lord, all you Gentiles; and laud him, all you people. ¹²And again, Isaiah says, There shall be a root of Jesse, and he that shall rise to reign over the Gentiles; in him shall the Gentiles trust. ¹³Now the God of hope fill you with all joy and peace in believing, that you may abound in hope, through the power of the Holy Ghost. ¹⁴And I myself also am persuaded of you, my brothers, that you also are full of goodness, filled with all knowledge, able also to admonish one another. ¹⁵Nevertheless, brothers, I have written the more boldly to you in some sort, as putting you in mind, because of the grace that is given to me of God, ¹⁶That I should be the minister of Jesus Christ to the Gentiles, ministering the gospel of God, that the offering up of the Gentiles might be acceptable, being sanctified by the Holy Ghost. ¹⁷I have therefore whereof I may glory through Jesus Christ in those things which pertain to God. ¹⁸For I will not dare to speak of any of those things which Christ has not worked by me, to make the Gentiles obedient, by word and deed, ¹⁹Through mighty signs and wonders, by the power of the Spirit of God; so that from Jerusalem, and round about to Illyricum, I have fully preached the gospel of Christ. ²⁰Yes, so have I strived to preach the gospel, not where Christ was named, lest I should build on another man's foundation: ²¹But as it is written, To whom he was not spoken of, they shall see: and they that have not heard shall understand. ²²For which cause also I have been much hindered from coming to you. ²³But now having no more place in these parts, and having a great desire these many years to come to you; ²⁴Whenever I take my journey into Spain, I will come to you: for I trust to see you in my journey, and to be brought on my way thitherward by you, if first I be somewhat filled with your company. ²⁵But now I go to Jerusalem to minister to the saints. ²⁶For it has pleased them of Macedonia and Achaia to make a certain contribution for the poor saints which are at Jerusalem. ²⁷It has pleased them truly; and their debtors they are. For if the Gentiles have been made partakers of their spiritual things, their duty is also to minister to them in carnal things. ²⁸When therefore I have performed this, and have sealed to them this fruit, I will come by you into Spain. ²⁹And I am sure that, when I come to you, I shall come in the fullness of the blessing of the gospel of Christ. ³⁰Now I beseech you, brothers, for the Lord Jesus Christ's sake, and for the love of the Spirit, that you strive together with me in your prayers to God for me; ³¹That I may be delivered from them that do not believe in Judaea; and that my service which I have for Jerusalem may be accepted of the saints; ³²That I may come to you with joy by the will of God, and may with you be refreshed. ³³Now the God of peace be with you all. Amen.

16 ¹I commend to you Phebe our sister, which is a servant of the church which is at Cenchrea: ²That you receive her in the Lord, as becomes saints, and that you assist her in whatever business she has need of you: for she has been a succorer of many, and of myself also. ³Greet Priscilla and Aquila my helpers in Christ Jesus: ⁴Who have for my life laid down their own necks: to whom not only I give thanks, but also all the churches of the Gentiles. ⁵Likewise greet the church that is in their house. Salute my well-beloved Epaenetus, who is the first fruits of Achaia to Christ. ⁶Greet Mary, who bestowed much labor on us. ⁷Salute Andronicus and Junia, my kinsmen, and my fellow-prisoners, who are of note among the apostles, who also were in Christ before me. ⁸Greet Amplias my beloved in the Lord. ⁹Salute Urbane, our helper in Christ, and Stachys my beloved. ¹⁰Salute Apelles approved in Christ. Salute them which are of Aristobulus' household. ¹¹Salute Herodion my kinsman. Greet them that be of the household of Narcissus, which are in the Lord. ¹²Salute Tryphena and Tryphosa, who labor in the Lord. Salute the beloved Persis, which labored much in the Lord. ¹³Salute Rufus chosen in the Lord, and his mother and mine. ¹⁴Salute Asyncritus, Phlegon, Hermas, Patrobas, Hermes, and the brothers which are with them. ¹⁵Salute Philologus, and Julia, Nereus, and his sister, and Olympas, and all the saints which are with them. ¹⁶Salute one another with an holy kiss. The churches of Christ salute you. ¹⁷Now I beseech you, brothers, mark them which cause divisions and offenses contrary to the doctrine which you have learned; and avoid them. ¹⁸For they that are such serve not our Lord Jesus Christ, but their own belly; and by good words and fair speeches deceive the hearts of the simple. ¹⁹For your obedience is come abroad to all men. I am glad therefore on your behalf: but yet I would have you wise to that which is good, and simple concerning evil. ²⁰And the God of peace shall bruise Satan under your feet shortly. The grace of our Lord Jesus Christ be with you. Amen. ²¹Timotheus my workfellow, and Lucius, and Jason, and Sosipater, my kinsmen, salute you. ²²I Tertius, who wrote this letter, salute you in the Lord. ²³Gaius my host, and of the whole church, salutes you. Erastus the chamberlain of the city salutes you, and Quartus a brother. ²⁴The grace of our Lord Jesus Christ be with you all. Amen. ²⁵Now to him that is of power to establish you according to my gospel, and the preaching of Jesus Christ, according to the revelation of the mystery, which was kept secret since the world began, ²⁶But now is made manifest, and by the scriptures of the prophets, according to the commandment of the everlasting God, made known to all nations for the obedience of faith: ²⁷To God only wise, be glory through Jesus Christ for ever. Amen.

First Corinthians

1 ¹Paul called to be an apostle of Jesus Christ through the will of God, and Sosthenes our brother, ²To the church of God which is at Corinth, to them that are sanctified in Christ Jesus, called to be saints, with all that in every place call on the name of Jesus Christ our Lord, both theirs and ours: ³Grace be to you, and peace, from God our Father, and from the Lord Jesus Christ. ⁴I thank my God always on your behalf, for the grace of God which is given you by Jesus Christ; ⁵That in every thing you are enriched by him, in all utterance, and in all knowledge; ⁶Even as the testimony of Christ was confirmed in you: ⁷So that you come behind in no gift; waiting for the coming of our Lord Jesus Christ: ⁸Who shall also confirm you to the end, that you may be blameless in the day of our Lord Jesus Christ. ⁹God is faithful, by whom you were called to the fellowship of his Son Jesus Christ our Lord. ¹⁰Now I beseech you, brothers, by the name of our Lord Jesus Christ, that you all speak the same thing, and that there be no divisions among you; but that you be perfectly joined together in the same mind and in the same judgment. ¹¹For it has been declared to me of you, my brothers, by them which are of the house of Chloe, that there are contentions among you. ¹²Now this I say, that every one of you says, I am of Paul; and I of Apollos; and I of Cephas; and I of Christ. ¹³Is Christ divided? was Paul crucified for you? or were you baptized in the name of Paul? ¹⁴I thank God that I baptized none of you, but Crispus and Gaius; ¹⁵Lest any should say that I had baptized in my own name. ¹⁶And I baptized also the household of Stephanas: besides, I know not whether I baptized any other. ¹⁷For Christ sent me not to baptize, but to preach the gospel: not with wisdom of words, lest the cross of Christ should be made of none effect. ¹⁸For the preaching of the cross is to them that perish foolishness; but to us which are saved it is the power of God. ¹⁹For it is written, I will destroy the wisdom of the wise, and will bring to nothing the understanding of the prudent. ²⁰Where is the wise? where is the scribe? where is the disputer of this world? has not God made foolish the wisdom of this world? ²¹For after that in the wisdom of God the world by wisdom knew not God, it pleased God by the foolishness of preaching to save them that believe. ²²For the Jews require a sign, and the Greeks seek after wisdom: ²³But we preach Christ crucified, to the Jews a stumbling block, and to the Greeks foolishness; ²⁴But to them which are called, both Jews and Greeks, Christ the power of God, and the wisdom of God. ²⁵Because the foolishness of God is wiser than men; and the weakness of God is stronger than men. ²⁶For you see your calling, brothers, how that not many wise men after the flesh, not many mighty, not many noble, are called: ²⁷But God has chosen the foolish things of the world to confound the wise; and God has chosen the weak things of the world to confound the things which are mighty; ²⁸And base things of the world, and things which are despised, has God chosen, yes, and things which are not, to bring to nothing things that are: ²⁹That no flesh should glory in his presence. ³⁰But of him are you in Christ Jesus, who of God is made to us wisdom, and righteousness, and sanctification, and redemption: ³¹That, according as it is written, He that glories, let him glory in the Lord.

2 ¹And I, brothers, when I came to you, came not with excellency of speech or of wisdom, declaring to you the testimony of God. ²For I determined not to know any thing among you, save Jesus Christ, and him crucified. ³And I was with you in weakness, and in fear, and in much trembling. ⁴And my speech and my preaching was not with enticing words of man's wisdom, but in demonstration of the Spirit and of power: ⁵That your faith should not stand in the wisdom of men, but in the power of God. ⁶However, we speak wisdom among them that are perfect: yet not the wisdom of this world, nor of the princes of this world, that come to nothing: ⁷But we speak the wisdom of God in a mystery, even the hidden wisdom, which God ordained before the world to our glory: ⁸Which none of the princes of this world knew: for had they known it, they would not have crucified the Lord of glory. ⁹But as it is written, Eye has not seen, nor ear heard, neither have entered into the heart of man, the things which God has prepared for them that love him. ¹⁰But God has revealed them to us by his Spirit: for the Spirit searches all things, yes, the deep things of God. ¹¹For what man knows the things of a man, save the spirit of man which is in him? even so the things of God knows no man, but the Spirit of God. ¹²Now we have received, not the spirit of the world, but the spirit which is of God; that we might know the things that are freely given to us of God. ¹³Which things also we speak, not in the words which man's wisdom teaches, but which the Holy Ghost teaches; comparing spiritual things with spiritual. ¹⁴But the natural man receives not the things of the Spirit of God: for they are foolishness to him: neither can he know them, because they are spiritually discerned. ¹⁵But he that is spiritual judges all things, yet he himself is judged of no man. ¹⁶For who has known the mind of the Lord, that he may instruct him? But we have the mind of Christ.

3 ¹And I, brothers, could not speak to you as to spiritual, but as to carnal, even as to babes in Christ. ²I have fed you with milk, and not with meat: for till now you were not able to bear it, neither yet now are you able. ³For you are yet carnal: for whereas there is among you envying, and strife, and divisions, are you not carnal, and walk as men? ⁴For while one says, I am of Paul; and another, I am of Apollos; are you not carnal? ⁵Who then is Paul, and who is Apollos, but ministers by whom you believed, even as the Lord gave to every man? ⁶I have planted, Apollos watered; but God gave the increase. ⁷So then neither is he that plants any thing, neither he that waters; but God that gives the increase. ⁸Now he that plants and he that waters are one: and every man shall receive his own reward according to his own labor. ⁹For we are laborers together with God: you are God's husbandry, you are God's building. ¹⁰According to the grace of God which is given to me, as a wise master builder, I have laid the foundation, and another builds thereon. But let every man take heed how he builds thereupon. ¹¹For other foundation can no man lay than that is laid, which is Jesus Christ. ¹²Now if any man build on this foundation gold,

silver, precious stones, wood, hay, stubble; ¹³Every man's work shall be made manifest: for the day shall declare it, because it shall be revealed by fire; and the fire shall try every man's work of what sort it is. ¹⁴If any man's work abide which he has built thereupon, he shall receive a reward. ¹⁵If any man's work shall be burned, he shall suffer loss: but he himself shall be saved; yet so as by fire. ¹⁶Know you not that you are the temple of God, and that the Spirit of God dwells in you? ¹⁷If any man defile the temple of God, him shall God destroy; for the temple of God is holy, which temple you are. ¹⁸Let no man deceive himself. If any man among you seems to be wise in this world, let him become a fool, that he may be wise. ¹⁹For the wisdom of this world is foolishness with God. For it is written, He takes the wise in their own craftiness. ²⁰And again, The Lord knows the thoughts of the wise, that they are vain. ²¹Therefore let no man glory in men. For all things are yours; ²²Whether Paul, or Apollos, or Cephas, or the world, or life, or death, or things present, or things to come; all are yours; ²³And you are Christ's; and Christ is God's.

4 ¹Let a man so account of us, as of the ministers of Christ, and stewards of the mysteries of God. ²Moreover it is required in stewards, that a man be found faithful. ³But with me it is a very small thing that I should be judged of you, or of man's judgment: yes, I judge not my own self. ⁴For I know nothing by myself; yet am I not hereby justified: but he that judges me is the Lord. ⁵Therefore judge nothing before the time, until the Lord come, who both will bring to light the hidden things of darkness, and will make manifest the counsels of the hearts: and then shall every man have praise of God. ⁶And these things, brothers, I have in a figure transferred to myself and to Apollos for your sakes; that you might learn in us not to think of men above that which is written, that no one of you be puffed up for one against another. ⁷For who makes you to differ from another? and what have you that you did not receive? now if you did receive it, why do you glory, as if you had not received it? ⁸Now you are full, now you are rich, you have reigned as kings without us: and I would to God you did reign, that we also might reign with you. ⁹For I think that God has set forth us the apostles last, as it were appointed to death: for we are made a spectacle to the world, and to angels, and to men. ¹⁰We are fools for Christ's sake, but you are wise in Christ; we are weak, but you are strong; you are honorable, but we are despised. ¹¹Even to this present hour we both hunger, and thirst, and are naked, and are buffeted, and have no certain dwelling place; ¹²And labor, working with our own hands: being reviled, we bless; being persecuted, we suffer it: ¹³Being defamed, we entreat: we are made as the filth of the world, and are the offscouring of all things to this day. ¹⁴I write not these things to shame you, but as my beloved sons I warn you. ¹⁵For though you have ten thousand instructors in Christ, yet have you not many fathers: for in Christ Jesus I have begotten you through the gospel. ¹⁶Why I beseech you, be you followers of me. ¹⁷For this cause have I sent to you Timotheus, who is my beloved son, and faithful in the Lord, who shall bring you into remembrance of my ways which be in Christ, as I teach every where in every church. ¹⁸Now some are puffed up, as though I would not come to you. ¹⁹But I will come to you shortly, if the Lord will, and will know, not the speech of them which are puffed up, but the power. ²⁰For the kingdom of God is not in word, but in power. ²¹What will you? shall I come to you with a rod, or in love, and in the spirit of meekness?

5 ¹It is reported commonly that there is fornication among you, and such fornication as is not so much as named among the Gentiles, that one should have his father's wife. ²And you are puffed up, and have not rather mourned, that he that has done this deed might be taken away from among you. ³For I truly, as absent in body, but present in spirit, have judged already, as though I were present, concerning him that has so done this deed, ⁴In the name of our Lord Jesus Christ, when you are gathered together, and my spirit, with the power of our Lord Jesus Christ, ⁵To deliver such an one to Satan for the destruction of the flesh, that the spirit may be saved in the day of the Lord Jesus. ⁶Your glorying is not good. Know you not that a little leaven leavens the whole lump? ⁷Purge out therefore the old leaven, that you may be a new lump, as you are unleavened. For even Christ our passover is sacrificed for us: ⁸Therefore let us keep the feast, not with old leaven, neither with the leaven of malice and wickedness; but with the unleavened bread of sincerity and truth. ⁹I wrote to you in an letter not to company with fornicators: ¹⁰Yet not altogether with the fornicators of this world, or with the covetous, or extortionists, or with idolaters; for then must you needs go out of the world. ¹¹But now I have written to you not to keep company, if any man that is called a brother be a fornicator, or covetous, or an idolater, or a reviler, or a drunkard, or an extortionist; with such an one no not to eat. ¹²For what have I to do to judge them also that are without? do not you judge them that are within? ¹³But them that are without God judges. Therefore put away from among yourselves that wicked person.

6 ¹Dare any of you, having a matter against another, go to law before the unjust, and not before the saints? ²Do you not know that the saints shall judge the world? and if the world shall be judged by you, are you unworthy to judge the smallest matters? ³Know you not that we shall judge angels? how much more things that pertain to this life? ⁴If then you have judgments of things pertaining to this life, set them to judge who are least esteemed in the church. ⁵I speak to your shame. Is it so, that there is not a wise man among you? no, not one that shall be able to judge between his brothers? ⁶But brother goes to law with brother, and that before the unbelievers. ⁷Now therefore there is utterly a fault among you, because you go to law one with another. Why do you not rather take wrong? why do you not rather suffer yourselves to be defrauded? ⁸No, you do wrong, and defraud, and that your brothers. ⁹Know you not that the unrighteous shall not inherit the kingdom of God? Be not deceived: neither fornicators, nor idolaters, nor adulterers, nor effeminate, nor abusers of themselves with mankind, ¹⁰Nor thieves, nor covetous, nor drunkards, nor revilers, nor extortionists, shall inherit the kingdom of God. ¹¹And such were some of you: but you are washed, but you are sanctified, but you are justified in the name of the Lord Jesus, and by the Spirit of our God. ¹²All things are lawful to me, but all things are not expedient: all things are lawful for me, but I will not be brought under the power of any. ¹³Meats for the belly, and the belly for meats: but God shall destroy both it and them. Now the body is not for fornication, but for the Lord; and the Lord for the body. ¹⁴And God has both raised up the Lord, and will also raise up us by his own power. ¹⁵Know you not that your bodies are the members of Christ? shall I then take the members of Christ, and make them the members of an harlot? God forbid. ¹⁶What? know you not that he which is joined to an harlot is one body? for two, says he, shall be one flesh. ¹⁷But he that is joined to the Lord is one spirit. ¹⁸Flee fornication. Every sin that a man does is without the body; but he that commits fornication sins against his own body. ¹⁹What? know you not that your body is the temple of the Holy Ghost which is in you, which you have of God, and you are not your own? ²⁰For you are bought with a price: therefore glorify God in your body, and in your spirit, which are God's.

7 ¹Now concerning the things whereof you wrote to me: It is good for a man not to touch a woman. ²Nevertheless, to avoid fornication, let every man have his own wife, and let every woman have her own husband. ³Let the husband render to the wife due benevolence: and likewise also the wife to the husband. ⁴The wife has not power of her own body, but the husband: and likewise also the husband has not power of his own body, but the wife. ⁵Defraud you not one the other, except it be with consent for a time, that you may give yourselves to fasting and prayer; and come together again, that Satan tempt you not for your incontinency. ⁶But I speak this by permission, and not of commandment. ⁷For I would that all men were even as I myself. But every man has his proper gift of God, one after this manner, and another after that. ⁸I say therefore to the unmarried and widows, It is good for them if they abide even as I. ⁹But if they cannot contain, let them marry: for it is better to marry than to burn. ¹⁰And to the married I command, yet not I, but the Lord, Let not the wife depart from her husband: ¹¹But and if she depart, let her remain unmarried or be reconciled to her husband: and let not the husband put away his wife. ¹²But to the rest speak I, not the Lord: If any brother has a wife that believes not, and she be pleased to dwell with him, let him not put her away. ¹³And the woman which has an husband that believes not, and if he be pleased to dwell with her, let her not leave him. ¹⁴For the unbelieving husband is sanctified by the wife, and the unbelieving wife is sanctified by the husband: else were your children unclean; but now are they holy. ¹⁵But if the unbelieving depart, let him depart. A brother or a sister is not under bondage in such cases: but God has called us to peace. ¹⁶For what know you, O wife, whether you shall save your husband? or how know you, O man, whether you shall save your wife? ¹⁷But as God has distributed to every man, as the Lord has called every one, so let him walk. And so ordain I in all churches. ¹⁸Is any man called being circumcised? let him not become uncircumcised. Is any called in uncircumcision? let him not be circumcised. ¹⁹Circumcision is nothing, and uncircumcision is nothing, but the keeping of the commandments of God. ²⁰Let every man abide in the same calling wherein he was called. ²¹Are you called being a servant? care not for it: but if you may be made free, use it rather. ²²For he that is called in the Lord, being a servant, is the Lord's freeman: likewise also he that is called, being free, is Christ's servant. ²³You are bought with a price; be not you the servants of men. ²⁴Brothers, let every man, wherein he is called, therein abide with God. ²⁵Now concerning virgins I have no commandment of the Lord: yet I give my judgment, as one that has obtained mercy of the Lord to be faithful. ²⁶I suppose therefore that this is good for the present distress, I say, that it is good for a man so to be. ²⁷Are you bound to a wife? seek not to be loosed. Are you loosed from a wife? seek not a wife. ²⁸But and if you marry, you have not sinned; and if a virgin marry, she has not sinned. Nevertheless such shall have trouble in the flesh: but I spare you. ²⁹But this I say, brothers, the time is short: it remains, that both they that have wives be as though they had none; ³⁰And they that weep, as though they wept not; and they that rejoice, as though they rejoiced not; and they that buy, as though they possessed not; ³¹And they that use this world, as not abusing it: for the fashion of this world passes away. ³²But I would have you without carefulness. He that is unmarried cares for the things that belong to the Lord, how he may please the Lord: ³³But he that is married cares for the things that are of the world, how he may please his wife. ³⁴There is difference also between a wife and a virgin. The unmarried woman cares for the things of the Lord, that she may be holy both in body and in spirit: but she that is married cares for the things of the world, how she may please her husband. ³⁵And this I speak for your own profit; not that I may cast a snare on you, but for that which is comely, and that you may attend on the Lord without distraction. ³⁶But if any man think that he behaves himself uncomely toward his virgin, if she pass the flower of her age, and need so require, let him do what he will, he sins not: let them marry. ³⁷Nevertheless he that stands steadfast in his heart, having no necessity, but has power over his own will, and has so decreed in his heart that he will keep his virgin, does well. ³⁸So then he that gives her in marriage does well; but he that gives her not in marriage does better. ³⁹The wife is bound by the law as long as her husband lives; but if her husband be dead, she is at liberty to be married to whom she will; only in the Lord. ⁴⁰But she is happier if she so abide, after my judgment: and I think also that I have the Spirit of God.

8 ¹Now as touching things offered to idols, we know that we all have knowledge. Knowledge puffs up, but charity edifies. ²And if any man think that he knows any thing, he knows nothing yet as he ought to know. ³But if any man love God, the same is known of him. ⁴As concerning therefore the eating of those things that are offered in sacrifice to idols, we know that an idol is nothing in the world, and that there is none other God but one. ⁵For though there be that are called gods, whether in heaven or in earth, (as there be gods many, and lords many,) ⁶But to us there is but one God, the Father, of whom are all things, and we in him; and one Lord Jesus Christ, by whom are all things, and we by him. ⁷However, there is not in every man that knowledge: for some with conscience of the idol to this hour eat it as a thing offered to an idol; and their conscience being weak is defiled. ⁸But meat commends us not to God: for neither, if we eat, are we the better; neither, if we eat not, are we the worse. ⁹But take heed lest by any means this liberty of yours become a stumbling block to them that are weak. ¹⁰For if any man see you which have knowledge sit at meat in the idol's temple, shall not the conscience of him which is weak be emboldened to eat those things which are offered to idols; ¹¹And through your knowledge shall the weak brother perish, for whom Christ died? ¹²But when you sin so against the brothers, and wound their weak conscience, you sin against Christ. ¹³Why, if meat make my brother to offend, I will eat no flesh while the world stands, lest I make my brother to offend.

9 ¹Am I not an apostle? am I not free? have I not seen Jesus Christ our Lord? are not you my work in the Lord? ²If I be not an apostle to others, yet doubtless I am to you: for the seal of my apostleship are you in the Lord. ³My answer to them that do examine me is this, ⁴Have we not power to eat and to drink? ⁵Have we not power to lead about a sister, a wife, as well as other apostles, and as the brothers of the Lord, and Cephas? ⁶Or I only and Barnabas, have not we power to forbear working? ⁷Who goes a warfare any time at his own charges? who plants a vineyard, and eats not of the fruit thereof? or who feeds a flock, and eats not of the milk of the flock? ⁸Say I these things as a man? or says not the law the same also? ⁹For it is written in the law of Moses, You shall not muzzle the mouth of the ox that treads out the corn. Does God take care for oxen? ¹⁰Or says he it altogether for our sakes? For our sakes, no doubt, this is written: that he that plows should plow in hope; and that he that threshes in hope should be partaker of his hope. ¹¹If we have sown to you spiritual things, is it a great thing if we shall reap your carnal things? ¹²If others be partakers of this power over you, are not we rather? Nevertheless we have not used this power; but suffer all things, lest we should hinder the gospel of Christ. ¹³Do you not know that they which minister about holy things live of the things of the temple? and they which wait at the altar are partakers with the altar? ¹⁴Even so has the Lord ordained that they which preach the gospel should live of the gospel. ¹⁵But I have used none of these things: neither have I written these things, that it should be so done to me: for it were better for me to die, than that any man should make my glorying void. ¹⁶For though I preach the gospel, I have nothing to glory of: for necessity is laid on me; yes, woe is to me, if I preach not the gospel! ¹⁷For if I do this thing willingly, I have a reward: but if against my will, a dispensation of the gospel is committed to me. ¹⁸What is my reward then? Truly that, when I preach the gospel, I may make the gospel of Christ without charge, that I abuse not my power in the gospel. ¹⁹For though I be free from all men, yet have I made myself servant to all, that I might gain the more. ²⁰And to the Jews I became as a Jew, that I might gain the Jews; to them that are under the law, as under the law, that I might gain them that are under the law; ²¹To them that are without law, as without law, (being not without law to God, but under the law to Christ,) that I might gain them that are without law. ²²To the weak became I as weak, that I might gain the weak: I am made all things to all men, that I might by all means save some. ²³And this I do for the gospel's sake, that I might be partaker thereof with you. ²⁴Know you not that they which run in a race run all, but one receives the prize? So run, that you may obtain. ²⁵And every man that strives for the mastery is temperate in all things. Now they do it to obtain a corruptible crown; but we an incorruptible. ²⁶I therefore so run, not as uncertainly; so fight I, not as one that beats the air: ²⁷But I keep under my body, and bring it into subjection: lest that by any means, when I have preached to others, I myself should be a castaway.

10 ¹Moreover, brothers, I would not that you should be ignorant, how that all our fathers were under the cloud, and all passed through the sea; ²And were all baptized to Moses in the cloud and in the sea; ³And did all eat the same spiritual meat; ⁴And did all drink the same spiritual drink: for they drank of that spiritual Rock that followed them: and that Rock was Christ. ⁵But with many of them God was not well pleased: for they were overthrown in the wilderness. ⁶Now these things were our examples, to the intent we should not lust after evil things, as they also lusted. ⁷Neither be you idolaters, as were some of them; as it is written, The people sat down to eat and drink, and rose up to play. ⁸Neither let us commit fornication, as some of them committed, and fell in one day three and twenty thousand. ⁹Neither let us tempt Christ, as some of them also tempted, and were destroyed of serpents. ¹⁰Neither murmur you, as some of them also murmured, and were destroyed of the destroyer. ¹¹Now all these things happened to them for ensamples: and they are written for our admonition, on whom the ends of the world are come. ¹²Why let him that thinks he stands take heed lest he fall. ¹³There has no temptation taken you but such as is common to man: but God is faithful, who will not suffer you to be tempted above that you are able; but will with the temptation also make a way to escape, that you may be able to bear it. ¹⁴Why, my dearly beloved, flee from idolatry. ¹⁵I speak as to wise men; judge you what I say. ¹⁶The cup of blessing which we bless, is it not the communion of the blood of Christ? The bread which we break, is it not the communion of the body of Christ? ¹⁷For we being many are one bread, and one body: for we are all partakers of that one bread. ¹⁸Behold Israel after the flesh: are not they which eat of the sacrifices partakers of the altar? ¹⁹What say I then? that the idol is any thing, or that which is offered in sacrifice to idols is any thing? ²⁰But I say, that the things which the Gentiles sacrifice, they sacrifice to devils, and not to God: and I would not that you should have fellowship with devils. ²¹You cannot drink the cup of the Lord, and the cup of devils: you cannot be partakers of the Lord's table, and of the table of devils. ²²Do we provoke the Lord to jealousy? are we stronger than he? ²³All things are lawful for me, but all things are not expedient: all things are lawful for me, but all things edify not. ²⁴Let no man seek his own, but every man another's wealth. ²⁵Whatever is sold in the shambles, that eat, asking no question for conscience sake: ²⁶For the earth is the Lord's, and the fullness thereof. ²⁷If any of them that believe not bid you to a feast, and you be disposed to go; whatever is set before you, eat, asking no question for conscience sake. ²⁸But if any man say to you, This is offered in sacrifice to idols, eat not for his sake that showed it, and for conscience sake: for the earth is the Lord's, and the fullness thereof: [29]Conscience, I say, not your own, but of the other: for why is my liberty judged of another man's conscience? [30]For if I by grace be a partaker, why am I evil spoken of for that for which I give thanks? [31]Whether therefore you eat, or drink, or whatever you do, do all to the glory of God. [32]Give none offense, neither to the Jews, nor to the Gentiles, nor to the church of God: [33]Even as I please all men in all things, not seeking my own profit, but the profit of many, that they may be saved.

11 [1]Be you followers of me, even as I also am of Christ. [2]Now I praise you, brothers, that you remember me in all things, and keep the ordinances, as I delivered them to you. [3]But I would have you know, that the head of every man is Christ; and the head of the woman is the man; and the head of Christ is God. [4]Every man praying or prophesying, having his head covered, dishonors his head. [5]But every woman that prays or prophesies with her head uncovered dishonors her head: for that is even all one as if she were shaven. [6]For if the woman be not covered, let her also be shorn: but if it be a shame for a woman to be shorn or shaven, let her be covered. [7]For a man indeed ought not to cover his head, for as much as he is the image and glory of God: but the woman is the glory of the man. [8]For the man is not of the woman: but the woman of the man. [9]Neither was the man created for the woman; but the woman for the man. [10]For this cause ought the woman to have power on her head because of the angels. [11]Nevertheless neither is the man without the woman, neither the woman without the man, in the Lord. [12]For as the woman is of the man, even so is the man also by the woman; but all things of God. [13]Judge in yourselves: is it comely that a woman pray to God uncovered? [14]Does not even nature itself teach you, that, if a man have long hair, it is a shame to him? [15]But if a woman have long hair, it is a glory to her: for her hair is given her for a covering. [16]But if any man seem to be contentious, we have no such custom, neither the churches of God. [17]Now in this that I declare to you I praise you not, that you come together not for the better, but for the worse. [18]For first of all, when you come together in the church, I hear that there be divisions among you; and I partly believe it. [19]For there must be also heresies among you, that they which are approved may be made manifest among you. [20]When you come together therefore into one place, this is not to eat the Lord's supper. [21]For in eating every one takes before other his own supper: and one is hungry, and another is drunken. [22]What? have you not houses to eat and to drink in? or despise you the church of God, and shame them that have not? What shall I say to you? shall I praise you in this? I praise you not. [23]For I have received of the Lord that which also I delivered to you, That the Lord Jesus the same night in which he was betrayed took bread: [24]And when he had given thanks, he broke it, and said, Take, eat: this is my body, which is broken for you: this do in remembrance of me. [25]After the same manner also he took the cup, when he had supped, saying, This cup is the new testament in my blood: this do you, as oft as you drink it, in remembrance of me. [26]For as often as you eat this bread, and drink this cup, you do show the Lord's death till he come. [27]Why whoever shall eat this bread, and drink this cup of the Lord, unworthily, shall be guilty of the body and blood of the Lord. [28]But let a man examine himself, and so let him eat of that bread, and drink of that cup. [29]For he that eats and drinks unworthily, eats and drinks damnation to himself, not discerning the Lord's body. [30]For this cause many are weak and sickly among you, and many sleep. [31]For if we would judge ourselves, we should not be judged. [32]But when we are judged, we are chastened of the Lord, that we should not be condemned with the world. [33]Why, my brothers, when you come together to eat, tarry one for another. [34]And if any man hunger, let him eat at home; that you come not together to condemnation. And the rest will I set in order when I come.

12 [1]Now concerning spiritual gifts, brothers, I would not have you ignorant. [2]You know that you were Gentiles, carried away to these dumb idols, even as you were led. [3]Why I give you to understand, that no man speaking by the Spirit of God calls Jesus accursed: and that no man can say that Jesus is the Lord, but by the Holy Ghost. [4]Now there are diversities of gifts, but the same Spirit. [5]And there are differences of administrations, but the same Lord. [6]And there are diversities of operations, but it is the same God which works all in all. [7]But the manifestation of the Spirit is given to every man to profit with. [8]For to one is given by the Spirit the word of wisdom; to another the word of knowledge by the same Spirit; [9]To another faith by the same Spirit; to another the gifts of healing by the same Spirit; [10]To another the working of miracles; to another prophecy; to another discerning of spirits; to another divers kinds of tongues; to another the interpretation of tongues: [11]But all these works that one and the selfsame Spirit, dividing to every man severally as he will. [12]For as the body is one, and has many members, and all the members of that one body, being many, are one body: so also is Christ. [13]For by one Spirit are we all baptized into one body, whether we be Jews or Gentiles, whether we be bond or free; and have been all made to drink into one Spirit. [14]For the body is not one member, but many. [15]If the foot shall say, Because I am not the hand, I am not of the body; is it therefore not of the body? [16]And if the ear shall say, Because I am not the eye, I am not of the body; is it therefore not of the body? [17]If the whole body were an eye, where were the hearing? If the whole were hearing, where were the smelling? [18]But now has God set the members every one of them in the body, as it has pleased him. [19]And if they were all one member, where were the body? [20]But now are they many members, yet but one body. [21]And the eye cannot say to the hand, I have no need of you: nor again the head to the feet, I have no need of you. [22]No, much more those members of the body, which seem to be more feeble, are necessary: [23]And those members of the body, which we think to be less honorable, on these we bestow more abundant honor; and our uncomely parts have more abundant comeliness. [24]For our comely parts have no need: but God has tempered the body together, having given more abundant honor to that part which lacked. [25]That there should be no schism in the body; but that the members should have the same care one for another. [26]And whether one member suffer, all the members suffer with it; or one member be honored, all the members rejoice with it. ²⁷Now you are the body of Christ, and members in particular. ²⁸And God has set some in the church, first apostles, secondarily prophets, thirdly teachers, after that miracles, then gifts of healings, helps, governments, diversities of tongues. ²⁹Are all apostles? are all prophets? are all teachers? are all workers of miracles? ³⁰Have all the gifts of healing? do all speak with tongues? do all interpret? ³¹But covet earnestly the best gifts: and yet show I to you a more excellent way.

13

¹Though I speak with the tongues of men and of angels, and have not charity, I am become as sounding brass, or a tinkling cymbal. ²And though I have the gift of prophecy, and understand all mysteries, and all knowledge; and though I have all faith, so that I could remove mountains, and have not charity, I am nothing. ³And though I bestow all my goods to feed the poor, and though I give my body to be burned, and have not charity, it profits me nothing. ⁴Charity suffers long, and is kind; charity envies not; charity brags not itself, is not puffed up, ⁵Does not behave itself unseemly, seeks not her own, is not easily provoked, thinks no evil; ⁶Rejoices not in iniquity, but rejoices in the truth; ⁷Bears all things, believes all things, hopes all things, endures all things. ⁸Charity never fails: but whether there be prophecies, they shall fail; whether there be tongues, they shall cease; whether there be knowledge, it shall vanish away. ⁹For we know in part, and we prophesy in part. ¹⁰But when that which is perfect is come, then that which is in part shall be done away. ¹¹When I was a child, I spoke as a child, I understood as a child, I thought as a child: but when I became a man, I put away childish things. ¹²For now we see through a glass, darkly; but then face to face: now I know in part; but then shall I know even as also I am known. ¹³And now stays faith, hope, charity, these three; but the greatest of these is charity.

14

¹Follow after charity, and desire spiritual gifts, but rather that you may prophesy. ²For he that speaks in an unknown tongue speaks not to men, but to God: for no man understands him; however, in the spirit he speaks mysteries. ³But he that prophesies speaks to men to edification, and exhortation, and comfort. ⁴He that speaks in an unknown tongue edifies himself; but he that prophesies edifies the church. ⁵I would that you all spoke with tongues but rather that you prophesied: for greater is he that prophesies than he that speaks with tongues, except he interpret, that the church may receive edifying. ⁶Now, brothers, if I come to you speaking with tongues, what shall I profit you, except I shall speak to you either by revelation, or by knowledge, or by prophesying, or by doctrine? ⁷And even things without life giving sound, whether pipe or harp, except they give a distinction in the sounds, how shall it be known what is piped or harped? ⁸For if the trumpet give an uncertain sound, who shall prepare himself to the battle? ⁹So likewise you, except you utter by the tongue words easy to be understood, how shall it be known what is spoken? for you shall speak into the air. ¹⁰There are, it may be, so many kinds of voices in the world, and none of them is without signification. ¹¹Therefore if I know not the meaning of the voice, I shall be to him that speaks a barbarian, and he that speaks shall be a barbarian to me. ¹²Even so you, for as much as you are zealous of spiritual gifts, seek that you may excel to the edifying of the church. ¹³Why let him that speaks in an unknown tongue pray that he may interpret. ¹⁴For if I pray in an unknown tongue, my spirit prays, but my understanding is unfruitful. ¹⁵What is it then? I will pray with the spirit, and I will pray with the understanding also: I will sing with the spirit, and I will sing with the understanding also. ¹⁶Else when you shall bless with the spirit, how shall he that occupies the room of the unlearned say Amen at your giving of thanks, seeing he understands not what you say? ¹⁷For you truly give thanks well, but the other is not edified. ¹⁸I thank my God, I speak with tongues more than you all: ¹⁹Yet in the church I had rather speak five words with my understanding, that by my voice I might teach others also, than ten thousand words in an unknown tongue. ²⁰Brothers, be not children in understanding: however, in malice be you children, but in understanding be men. ²¹In the law it is written, With men of other tongues and other lips will I speak to this people; and yet for all that will they not hear me, says the LORD. ²²Why tongues are for a sign, not to them that believe, but to them that believe not: but prophesying serves not for them that believe not, but for them which believe. ²³If therefore the whole church be come together into one place, and all speak with tongues, and there come in those that are unlearned, or unbelievers, will they not say that you are mad? ²⁴But if all prophesy, and there come in one that believes not, or one unlearned, he is convinced of all, he is judged of all: ²⁵And thus are the secrets of his heart made manifest; and so falling down on his face he will worship God, and report that God is in you of a truth. ²⁶How is it then, brothers? when you come together, every one of you has a psalm, has a doctrine, has a tongue, has a revelation, has an interpretation. Let all things be done to edifying. ²⁷If any man speak in an unknown tongue, let it be by two, or at the most by three, and that by course; and let one interpret. ²⁸But if there be no interpreter, let him keep silence in the church; and let him speak to himself, and to God. ²⁹Let the prophets speak two or three, and let the other judge. ³⁰If any thing be revealed to another that sits by, let the first hold his peace. ³¹For you may all prophesy one by one, that all may learn, and all may be comforted. ³²And the spirits of the prophets are subject to the prophets. ³³For God is not the author of confusion, but of peace, as in all churches of the saints. ³⁴Let your women keep silence in the churches: for it is not permitted to them to speak; but they are commanded to be under obedience as also says the law. ³⁵And if they will learn any thing, let them ask their husbands at home: for it is a shame for women to speak in the church. ³⁶What? came the word of God out from you? or came it to you only? ³⁷If any man think himself to be a prophet, or spiritual, let him acknowledge that the things that I write to you are the commandments of the Lord. ³⁸But if any man be ignorant, let him be ignorant. ³⁹Why, brothers, covet to prophesy, and forbid not to speak with tongues. ⁴⁰Let all things be done decently and in order.

15

¹Moreover, brothers, I declare to you the gospel which I preached to you, which also you have

received, and wherein you stand; ²By which also you are saved, if you keep in memory what I preached to you, unless you have believed in vain. ³For I delivered to you first of all that which I also received, how that Christ died for our sins according to the scriptures; ⁴And that he was buried, and that he rose again the third day according to the scriptures: ⁵And that he was seen of Cephas, then of the twelve: ⁶After that, he was seen of above five hundred brothers at once; of whom the greater part remain to this present, but some are fallen asleep. ⁷After that, he was seen of James; then of all the apostles. ⁸And last of all he was seen of me also, as of one born out of due time. ⁹For I am the least of the apostles, that am not meet to be called an apostle, because I persecuted the church of God. ¹⁰But by the grace of God I am what I am: and his grace which was bestowed on me was not in vain; but I labored more abundantly than they all: yet not I, but the grace of God which was with me. ¹¹Therefore whether it were I or they, so we preach, and so you believed. ¹²Now if Christ be preached that he rose from the dead, how say some among you that there is no resurrection of the dead? ¹³But if there be no resurrection of the dead, then is Christ not risen: ¹⁴And if Christ be not risen, then is our preaching vain, and your faith is also vain. ¹⁵Yes, and we are found false witnesses of God; because we have testified of God that he raised up Christ: whom he raised not up, if so be that the dead rise not. ¹⁶For if the dead rise not, then is not Christ raised: ¹⁷And if Christ be not raised, your faith is vain; you are yet in your sins. ¹⁸Then they also which are fallen asleep in Christ are perished. ¹⁹If in this life only we have hope in Christ, we are of all men most miserable. ²⁰But now is Christ risen from the dead, and become the first fruits of them that slept. ²¹For since by man came death, by man came also the resurrection of the dead. ²²For as in Adam all die, even so in Christ shall all be made alive. ²³But every man in his own order: Christ the first fruits; afterward they that are Christ's at his coming. ²⁴Then comes the end, when he shall have delivered up the kingdom to God, even the Father; when he shall have put down all rule and all authority and power. ²⁵For he must reign, till he has put all enemies under his feet. ²⁶The last enemy that shall be destroyed is death. ²⁷For he has put all things under his feet. But when he says all things are put under him, it is manifest that he is excepted, which did put all things under him. ²⁸And when all things shall be subdued to him, then shall the Son also himself be subject to him that put all things under him, that God may be all in all. ²⁹Else what shall they do which are baptized for the dead, if the dead rise not at all? why are they then baptized for the dead? ³⁰And why stand we in jeopardy every hour? ³¹I protest by your rejoicing which I have in Christ Jesus our LORD, I die daily. ³²If after the manner of men I have fought with beasts at Ephesus, what advantages it me, if the dead rise not? let us eat and drink; for to morrow we die. ³³Be not deceived: evil communications corrupt good manners. ³⁴Awake to righteousness, and sin not; for some have not the knowledge of God: I speak this to your shame. ³⁵But some man will say, How are the dead raised up? and with what body do they come? ³⁶You fool, that which you sow is not quickened, except it die: ³⁷And that which you sow, you sow not that body that shall be, but bore grain, it may chance of wheat, or of some other grain: ³⁸But God gives it a body as it has pleased him, and to every seed his own body. ³⁹All flesh is not the same flesh: but there is one kind of flesh of men, another flesh of beasts, another of fishes, and another of birds. ⁴⁰There are also celestial bodies, and bodies terrestrial: but the glory of the celestial is one, and the glory of the terrestrial is another. ⁴¹There is one glory of the sun, and another glory of the moon, and another glory of the stars: for one star differs from another star in glory. ⁴²So also is the resurrection of the dead. It is sown in corruption; it is raised in incorruption: ⁴³It is sown in dishonor; it is raised in glory: it is sown in weakness; it is raised in power: ⁴⁴It is sown a natural body; it is raised a spiritual body. There is a natural body, and there is a spiritual body. ⁴⁵And so it is written, The first man Adam was made a living soul; the last Adam was made a quickening spirit. ⁴⁶However, that was not first which is spiritual, but that which is natural; and afterward that which is spiritual. ⁴⁷The first man is of the earth, earthy; the second man is the Lord from heaven. ⁴⁸As is the earthy, such are they also that are earthy: and as is the heavenly, such are they also that are heavenly. ⁴⁹And as we have borne the image of the earthy, we shall also bear the image of the heavenly. ⁵⁰Now this I say, brothers, that flesh and blood cannot inherit the kingdom of God; neither does corruption inherit incorruption. ⁵¹Behold, I show you a mystery; We shall not all sleep, but we shall all be changed, ⁵²In a moment, in the twinkling of an eye, at the last trump: for the trumpet shall sound, and the dead shall be raised incorruptible, and we shall be changed. ⁵³For this corruptible must put on incorruption, and this mortal must put on immortality. ⁵⁴So when this corruptible shall have put on incorruption, and this mortal shall have put on immortality, then shall be brought to pass the saying that is written, Death is swallowed up in victory. ⁵⁵O death, where is your sting? O grave, where is your victory? ⁵⁶The sting of death is sin; and the strength of sin is the law. ⁵⁷But thanks be to God, which gives us the victory through our Lord Jesus Christ. ⁵⁸Therefore, my beloved brothers, be you steadfast, unmovable, always abounding in the work of the Lord, for as much as you know that your labor is not in vain in the Lord.

16 ¹Now concerning the collection for the saints, as I have given order to the churches of Galatia, even so do you. ²On the first day of the week let every one of you lay by him in store, as God has prospered him, that there be no gatherings when I come. ³And when I come, whomsoever you shall approve by your letters, them will I send to bring your liberality to Jerusalem. ⁴And if it be meet that I go also, they shall go with me. ⁵Now I will come to you, when I shall pass through Macedonia: for I do pass through Macedonia. ⁶And it may be that I will abide, yes, and winter with you, that you may bring me on my journey wherever I go. ⁷For I will not see you now by the way; but I trust to tarry a while with you, if the Lord permit. ⁸But I will tarry at Ephesus until Pentecost. ⁹For a great door and effectual is opened to me, and there are many adversaries. ¹⁰Now if Timotheus come, see that he may be with you without fear: for he works the work of the Lord, as I also do. ¹¹Let no man therefore despise him: but conduct him forth in peace, that he may come to me: for I look for him with the brothers. [12]As touching our brother Apollos, I greatly desired him to come to you with the brothers: but his will was not at all to come at this time; but he will come when he shall have convenient time. [13]Watch you, stand fast in the faith, quit you like men, be strong. [14]Let all your things be done with charity. [15]I beseech you, brothers, (you know the house of Stephanas, that it is the first fruits of Achaia, and that they have addicted themselves to the ministry of the saints,) [16]That you submit yourselves to such, and to every one that helps with us, and labors. [17]I am glad of the coming of Stephanas and Fortunatus and Achaicus: for that which was lacking on your part they have supplied. [18]For they have refreshed my spirit and yours: therefore acknowledge you them that are such. [19]The churches of Asia salute you. Aquila and Priscilla salute you much in the Lord, with the church that is in their house. [20]All the brothers greet you. Greet you one another with an holy kiss. [21]The salutation of me Paul with my own hand. [22]If any man love not the Lord Jesus Christ, let him be Anathema Maranatha. [23]The grace of our Lord Jesus Christ be with you. [24]My love be with you all in Christ Jesus. Amen.

Second Corinthians

1 ¹Paul, an apostle of Jesus Christ by the will of God, and Timothy our brother, to the church of God which is at Corinth, with all the saints which are in all Achaia: ²Grace be to you and peace from God our Father, and from the Lord Jesus Christ. ³Blessed be God, even the Father of our Lord Jesus Christ, the Father of mercies, and the God of all comfort; ⁴Who comforts us in all our tribulation, that we may be able to comfort them which are in any trouble, by the comfort with which we ourselves are comforted of God. ⁵For as the sufferings of Christ abound in us, so our consolation also abounds by Christ. ⁶And whether we be afflicted, it is for your consolation and salvation, which is effectual in the enduring of the same sufferings which we also suffer: or whether we be comforted, it is for your consolation and salvation. ⁷And our hope of you is steadfast, knowing, that as you are partakers of the sufferings, so shall you be also of the consolation. ⁸For we would not, brothers, have you ignorant of our trouble which came to us in Asia, that we were pressed out of measure, above strength, so that we despaired even of life: ⁹But we had the sentence of death in ourselves, that we should not trust in ourselves, but in God which raises the dead: ¹⁰Who delivered us from so great a death, and does deliver: in whom we trust that he will yet deliver us; ¹¹You also helping together by prayer for us, that for the gift bestowed on us by the means of many persons thanks may be given by many on our behalf. ¹²For our rejoicing is this, the testimony of our conscience, that in simplicity and godly sincerity, not with fleshly wisdom, but by the grace of God, we have had our conversation in the world, and more abundantly to you-ward. ¹³For we write none other things to you, than what you read or acknowledge; and I trust you shall acknowledge even to the end; ¹⁴As also you have acknowledged us in part, that we are your rejoicing, even as you also are ours in the day of the Lord Jesus. ¹⁵And in this confidence I was minded to come to you before, that you might have a second benefit; ¹⁶And to pass by you into Macedonia, and to come again out of Macedonia to you, and of you to be brought on my way toward Judaea. ¹⁷When I therefore was thus minded, did I use lightness? or the things that I purpose, do I purpose according to the flesh, that with me there should be yes yes, and no no? ¹⁸But as God is true, our word toward you was not yes and no. ¹⁹For the Son of God, Jesus Christ, who was preached among you by us, even by me and Silvanus and Timotheus, was not yes and no, but in him was yes. ²⁰For all the promises of God in him are yes, and in him Amen, to the glory of God by us. ²¹Now he which establishes us with you in Christ, and has anointed us, is God; ²²Who has also sealed us, and given the earnest of the Spirit in our hearts. ²³Moreover I call God for a record on my soul, that to spare you I came not as yet to Corinth. ²⁴Not for that we have dominion over your faith, but are helpers of your joy: for by faith you stand.

2 ¹But I determined this with myself, that I would not come again to you in heaviness. ²For if I make you sorry, who is he then that makes me glad, but the same which is made sorry by me? ³And I wrote this same to you, lest, when I came, I should have sorrow from them of whom I ought to rejoice; having confidence in you all, that my joy is the joy of you all. ⁴For out of much affliction and anguish of heart I wrote to you with many tears; not that you should be grieved, but that you might know the love which I have more abundantly to you. ⁵But if any have caused grief, he has not grieved me, but in part: that I may not overcharge you all. ⁶Sufficient to such a man is this punishment, which was inflicted of many. ⁷So that contrariwise you ought rather to forgive him, and comfort him, lest perhaps such a one should be swallowed up with overmuch sorrow. ⁸Why I beseech you that you would confirm your love toward him. ⁹For to this end also did I write, that I might know the proof of you, whether you be obedient in all things. ¹⁰To whom you forgive any thing, I forgive also: for if I forgave any thing, to whom I forgave it, for your sakes forgave I it in the person of Christ; ¹¹Lest Satan should get an advantage of us: for we are not ignorant of his devices. ¹²Furthermore, when I came to Troas to preach Christ's gospel, and a door was opened to me of the Lord, ¹³I had no rest in my spirit, because I found not Titus my brother: but taking my leave of them, I went from there into Macedonia. ¹⁴Now thanks be to God, which always causes us to triumph in Christ, and makes manifest the aroma of his knowledge by us in every place. ¹⁵For we are to God a sweet smell of Christ, in them that are saved, and in them that perish: ¹⁶To the one we are the smell of death to death; and to the other the smell of life to life. And who is sufficient for these things? ¹⁷For we are not as many, which corrupt the word of God: but as of sincerity, but as of God, in the sight of God speak we in Christ.

3 ¹Do we begin again to commend ourselves? or need we, as some others, letters of commendation to you, or letters of commendation from you? ²You are our letter written in our hearts, known and read of all men: ³For as much as you are manifestly declared to be the letter of Christ ministered by us, written not with ink, but with the Spirit of the living God; not in tables of stone, but in fleshy tables of the heart. ⁴And such trust have we through Christ to God-ward: ⁵Not that we are sufficient of ourselves to think any thing as of ourselves; but our sufficiency is of God; ⁶Who also has made us able ministers of the new testament; not of the letter, but of the spirit: for the letter kills, but the spirit gives life. ⁷But if the ministration of death, written and engraved in stones, was glorious, so that the children of Israel could not steadfastly behold the face of Moses for the glory of his countenance; which glory was to be done away: ⁸How shall not the ministration of the spirit be rather glorious? ⁹For if the ministration of condemnation be glory, much more does the ministration of righteousness exceed in glory. ¹⁰For even that which was made glorious had no glory in this respect, by reason of the glory that excels. ¹¹For if that which is done away was glorious, much more that which remains is glorious. ¹²Seeing then that we have such hope, we use great plainness of speech: ¹³And not as Moses, which put a veil over his face, that the children of Israel could not steadfastly look to the end of that which is abolished: ¹⁴But their minds were blinded: for until this day remains the same veil not taken away in the reading of the old testament; which veil is done away in Christ. ¹⁵But even to this day, when Moses is read, the veil is on their heart. ¹⁶Nevertheless when it shall turn to the Lord, the veil shall be taken away. ¹⁷Now the Lord is that Spirit: and where the Spirit of the Lord is, there is liberty. ¹⁸But we all, with open face beholding as in a glass the glory of the Lord, are changed into the same image from glory to glory, even as by the Spirit of the LORD.

4 ¹Therefore seeing we have this ministry, as we have received mercy, we faint not; ²But have renounced the hidden things of dishonesty, not walking in craftiness, nor handling the word of God deceitfully; but by manifestation of the truth commending ourselves to every man's conscience in the sight of God. ³But if our gospel be hid, it is hid to them that are lost: ⁴In whom the god of this world has blinded the minds of them which believe not, lest the light of the glorious gospel of Christ, who is the image of God, should shine to them. ⁵For we preach not ourselves, but Christ Jesus the Lord; and ourselves your servants for Jesus' sake. ⁶For God, who commanded the light to shine out of darkness, has shined in our hearts, to give the light of the knowledge of the glory of God in the face of Jesus Christ. ⁷But we have this treasure in earthen vessels, that the excellency of the power may be of God, and not of us. ⁸We are troubled on every side, yet not distressed; we are perplexed, but not in despair; ⁹Persecuted, but not forsaken; cast down, but not destroyed; ¹⁰Always bearing about in the body the dying of the Lord Jesus, that the life also of Jesus might be made manifest in our body. ¹¹For we which live are always delivered to death for Jesus' sake, that the life also of Jesus might be made manifest in our mortal flesh. ¹²So then death works in us, but life in you. ¹³We having the same spirit of faith, according as it is written, I believed, and therefore have I spoken; we also believe, and therefore speak; ¹⁴Knowing that he which raised up the Lord Jesus shall raise up us also by Jesus, and shall present us with you. ¹⁵For all things are for your sakes, that the abundant grace might through the thanksgiving of many redound to the glory of God. ¹⁶For which cause we faint not; but though our outward man perish, yet the inward man is renewed day by day. ¹⁷For our light affliction, which is but for a moment, works for us a far more exceeding and eternal weight of glory; ¹⁸While we look not at the things which are seen, but at the things which are not seen: for the things which are seen are temporal; but the things which are not seen are eternal.

5 ¹For we know that if our earthly house of this tabernacle were dissolved, we have a building of God, an house not made with hands, eternal in the heavens. ²For in this we groan, earnestly desiring to be clothed on with our house which is from heaven: ³If so be that being clothed we shall not be found naked. ⁴For we that are in this tabernacle do groan, being burdened: not for that we would be unclothed, but clothed on, that mortality might be swallowed up of life. ⁵Now he that has worked us for the selfsame thing is God, who also has given to us the earnest of the Spirit. ⁶Therefore we are always confident, knowing that, whilst we are at home in the body, we are absent from the Lord: ⁷(For we walk by faith, not by sight:) ⁸We are confident, I say, and willing rather to be absent from the body, and to be present with the Lord. ⁹Why we labor, that, whether present or absent, we may be accepted of him. ¹⁰For we must all appear before the judgment seat of Christ; that every one may receive the things done in his body, according to that he has done, whether it be good or bad. ¹¹Knowing therefore the terror of the Lord, we persuade men; but we are made manifest to God; and I trust also are made manifest in your consciences. ¹²For we commend not ourselves again to you, but give you occasion to glory on our behalf, that you may have somewhat to answer them which glory in appearance, and not in heart. ¹³For whether we be beside ourselves, it is to God: or whether we be sober, it is for your cause. ¹⁴For the love of Christ constrains us; because we thus judge, that if one died for all, then were all dead: ¹⁵And that he died for all, that they which live should not from now on live to themselves, but to him which died for them, and rose again. ¹⁶Why from now on know we no man after the flesh: yes, though we have known Christ after the flesh, yet now from now on know we him no more. ¹⁷Therefore if any man be in Christ, he is a new creature: old things are passed away; behold, all things are become new. ¹⁸And all things are of God, who has reconciled us to himself by Jesus Christ, and has given to us the ministry of reconciliation; ¹⁹To wit, that God was in Christ, reconciling the world to himself, not imputing their trespasses to them; and has committed to us the word of reconciliation. ²⁰Now then we are ambassadors for Christ, as though God did beseech you by us: we pray you in Christ's stead, be you reconciled to God. ²¹For he has made him to be sin for us, who knew no sin; that we might be made the righteousness of God in him.

6 ¹We then, as workers together with him, beseech you also that you receive not the grace of God in vain. ²(For he says, I have heard you in a time accepted, and in the day of salvation have I succored you: behold, now is the accepted time; behold, now is the day of salvation.) ³Giving no offense in any thing, that the ministry be not blamed: ⁴But in all things approving ourselves as the ministers of God, in much patience, in afflictions, in necessities, in distresses, ⁵In stripes, in imprisonments, in tumults, in labors, in watchings, in fastings; ⁶By pureness, by knowledge, by long-suffering, by kindness, by the Holy Ghost, by love unfeigned, ⁷By the word of truth, by the power of God, by the armor of righteousness on the right hand and on the left, ⁸By honor and dishonor, by evil report and good report: as deceivers, and yet true; ⁹As unknown, and yet well known; as dying, and, behold, we live; as chastened, and not killed; ¹⁰As sorrowful, yet always rejoicing; as poor, yet making many rich; as having nothing, and yet possessing all things. ¹¹O you Corinthians, our mouth is open to you, our heart is enlarged. ¹²You are not straitened in us, but you are straitened in your own bowels. ¹³Now for a recompense in the same, (I speak as to my children,) be you also enlarged. ¹⁴Be you not unequally yoked together with unbelievers: for what fellowship has righteousness with unrighteousness? and what communion has light with darkness? ¹⁵And what concord has Christ with

Belial? or what part has he that believes with an infidel? ¹⁶And what agreement has the temple of God with idols? for you are the temple of the living God; as God has said, I will dwell in them, and walk in them; and I will be their God, and they shall be my people. ¹⁷Why come out from among them, and be you separate, says the Lord, and touch not the unclean thing; and I will receive you. ¹⁸And will be a Father to you, and you shall be my sons and daughters, says the Lord Almighty.

7 ¹Having therefore these promises, dearly beloved, let us cleanse ourselves from all filthiness of the flesh and spirit, perfecting holiness in the fear of God. ²Receive us; we have wronged no man, we have corrupted no man, we have defrauded no man. ³I speak not this to condemn you: for I have said before, that you are in our hearts to die and live with you. ⁴Great is my boldness of speech toward you, great is my glorying of you: I am filled with comfort, I am exceeding joyful in all our tribulation. ⁵For, when we were come into Macedonia, our flesh had no rest, but we were troubled on every side; without were fights, within were fears. ⁶Nevertheless God, that comforts those that are cast down, comforted us by the coming of Titus; ⁷And not by his coming only, but by the consolation with which he was comforted in you, when he told us your earnest desire, your mourning, your fervent mind toward me; so that I rejoiced the more. ⁸For though I made you sorry with a letter, I do not repent, though I did repent: for I perceive that the same letter has made you sorry, though it were but for a season. ⁹Now I rejoice, not that you were made sorry, but that you sorrowed to repentance: for you were made sorry after a godly manner, that you might receive damage by us in nothing. ¹⁰For godly sorrow works repentance to salvation not to be repented of: but the sorrow of the world works death. ¹¹For behold this selfsame thing, that you sorrowed after a godly sort, what carefulness it worked in you, yes, what clearing of yourselves, yes, what indignation, yes, what fear, yes, what vehement desire, yes, what zeal, yes, what revenge! In all things you have approved yourselves to be clear in this matter. ¹²Why, though I wrote to you, I did it not for his cause that had done the wrong, nor for his cause that suffered wrong, but that our care for you in the sight of God might appear to you. ¹³Therefore we were comforted in your comfort: yes, and exceedingly the more joyed we for the joy of Titus, because his spirit was refreshed by you all. ¹⁴For if I have boasted any thing to him of you, I am not ashamed; but as we spoke all things to you in truth, even so our boasting, which I made before Titus, is found a truth. ¹⁵And his inward affection is more abundant toward you, whilst he remembers the obedience of you all, how with fear and trembling you received him. ¹⁶I rejoice therefore that I have confidence in you in all things.

8 ¹Moreover, brothers, we do you to wit of the grace of God bestowed on the churches of Macedonia; ²How that in a great trial of affliction the abundance of their joy and their deep poverty abounded to the riches of their liberality. ³For to their power, I bear record, yes, and beyond their power they were willing of themselves; ⁴Praying us with much entreaty that we would receive the gift, and take on us the fellowship of the ministering to the saints. ⁵And this they did, not as we hoped, but first gave their own selves to the Lord, and to us by the will of God. ⁶So that we desired Titus, that as he had begun, so he would also finish in you the same grace also. ⁷Therefore, as you abound in every thing, in faith, and utterance, and knowledge, and in all diligence, and in your love to us, see that you abound in this grace also. ⁸I speak not by commandment, but by occasion of the forwardness of others, and to prove the sincerity of your love. ⁹For you know the grace of our Lord Jesus Christ, that, though he was rich, yet for your sakes he became poor, that you through his poverty might be rich. ¹⁰And herein I give my advice: for this is expedient for you, who have begun before, not only to do, but also to be forward a year ago. ¹¹Now therefore perform the doing of it; that as there was a readiness to will, so there may be a performance also out of that which you have. ¹²For if there be first a willing mind, it is accepted according to that a man has, and not according to that he has not. ¹³For I mean not that other men be eased, and you burdened: ¹⁴But by an equality, that now at this time your abundance may be a supply for their want, that their abundance also may be a supply for your want: that there may be equality: ¹⁵As it is written, He that had gathered much had nothing over; and he that had gathered little had no lack. ¹⁶But thanks be to God, which put the same earnest care into the heart of Titus for you. ¹⁷For indeed he accepted the exhortation; but being more forward, of his own accord he went to you. ¹⁸And we have sent with him the brother, whose praise is in the gospel throughout all the churches; ¹⁹And not that only, but who was also chosen of the churches to travel with us with this grace, which is administered by us to the glory of the same Lord, and declaration of your ready mind: ²⁰Avoiding this, that no man should blame us in this abundance which is administered by us: ²¹Providing for honest things, not only in the sight of the Lord, but also in the sight of men. ²²And we have sent with them our brother, whom we have oftentimes proved diligent in many things, but now much more diligent, on the great confidence which I have in you. ²³Whether any do inquire of Titus, he is my partner and fellow helper concerning you: or our brothers be inquired of, they are the messengers of the churches, and the glory of Christ. ²⁴Why show you to them, and before the churches, the proof of your love, and of our boasting on your behalf.

9 ¹For as touching the ministering to the saints, it is superfluous for me to write to you: ²For I know the forwardness of your mind, for which I boast of you to them of Macedonia, that Achaia was ready a year ago; and your zeal has provoked very many. ³Yet have I sent the brothers, lest our boasting of you should be in vain in this behalf; that, as I said, you may be ready: ⁴Lest haply if they of Macedonia come with me, and find you unprepared, we (that we say not, you) should be ashamed in this same confident boasting. ⁵Therefore I thought it necessary to exhort the brothers, that they would go before to you, and make up beforehand your bounty, whereof you had notice before, that the same might be ready, as a matter of bounty, and not as of covetousness. ⁶But this I say, He which sows sparingly shall reap also sparingly; and he which sows bountifully shall reap also bountifully. ⁷Every man according as he purposes in his heart, so let him give; not grudgingly, or of necessity: for God loves a cheerful giver. ⁸And God is able to make all grace abound toward you; that you, always having all sufficiency in all things, may abound to every good work: ⁹(As it is written, He has dispersed abroad; he has given to the poor: his righteousness remains for ever. ¹⁰Now he that ministers seed to the sower both minister bread for your food, and multiply your seed sown, and increase the fruits of your righteousness;) ¹¹Being enriched in every thing to all bountifulness, which causes through us thanksgiving to God. ¹²For the administration of this service not only supplies the want of the saints, but is abundant also by many thanksgivings to God; ¹³Whiles by the experiment of this ministration they glorify God for your professed subjection to the gospel of Christ, and for your liberal distribution to them, and to all men; ¹⁴And by their prayer for you, which long after you for the exceeding grace of God in you. ¹⁵Thanks be to God for his unspeakable gift.

10 ¹Now I Paul myself beseech you by the meekness and gentleness of Christ, who in presence am base among you, but being absent am bold toward you: ²But I beseech you, that I may not be bold when I am present with that confidence, with which I think to be bold against some, which think of us as if we walked according to the flesh. ³For though we walk in the flesh, we do not war after the flesh: ⁴(For the weapons of our warfare are not carnal, but mighty through God to the pulling down of strong holds;) ⁵Casting down imaginations, and every high thing that exalts itself against the knowledge of God, and bringing into captivity every thought to the obedience of Christ; ⁶And having in a readiness to revenge all disobedience, when your obedience is fulfilled. ⁷Do you look on things after the outward appearance? If any man trust to himself that he is Christ's, let him of himself think this again, that, as he is Christ's, even so are we Christ's. ⁸For though I should boast somewhat more of our authority, which the Lord has given us for edification, and not for your destruction, I should not be ashamed: ⁹That I may not seem as if I would terrify you by letters. ¹⁰For his letters, say they, are weighty and powerful; but his bodily presence is weak, and his speech contemptible. ¹¹Let such an one think this, that, such as we are in word by letters when we are absent, such will we be also in deed when we are present. ¹²For we dare not make ourselves of the number, or compare ourselves with some that commend themselves: but they measuring themselves by themselves, and comparing themselves among themselves, are not wise. ¹³But we will not boast of things without our measure, but according to the measure of the rule which God has distributed to us, a measure to reach even to you. ¹⁴For we stretch not ourselves beyond our measure, as though we reached not to you: for we are come as far as to you also in preaching the gospel of Christ: ¹⁵Not boasting of things without our measure, that is, of other men's labors; but having hope, when your faith is increased, that we shall be enlarged by you according to our rule abundantly, ¹⁶To preach the gospel in the regions beyond you, and not to boast in another man's line of things made ready to our hand. ¹⁷But he that glories, let him glory in the Lord. ¹⁸For not he that commends himself is approved, but whom the Lord commends.

11 ¹Would to God you could bear with me a little in my folly: and indeed bear with me. ²For I am jealous over you with godly jealousy: for I have espoused you to one husband, that I may present you as a chaste virgin to Christ. ³But I fear, lest by any means, as the serpent beguiled Eve through his subtlety, so your minds should be corrupted from the simplicity that is in Christ. ⁴For if he that comes preaches another Jesus, whom we have not preached, or if you receive another spirit, which you have not received, or another gospel, which you have not accepted, you might well bear with him. ⁵For I suppose I was not a whit behind the very most chief apostles. ⁶But though I be rude in speech, yet not in knowledge; but we have been thoroughly made manifest among you in all things. ⁷Have I committed an offense in abasing myself that you might be exalted, because I have preached to you the gospel of God freely? ⁸I robbed other churches, taking wages of them, to do you service. ⁹And when I was present with you, and wanted, I was chargeable to no man: for that which was lacking to me the brothers which came from Macedonia supplied: and in all things I have kept myself from being burdensome to you, and so will I keep myself. ¹⁰As the truth of Christ is in me, no man shall stop me of this boasting in the regions of Achaia. ¹¹Why? because I love you not? God knows. ¹²But what I do, that I will do, that I may cut off occasion from them which desire occasion; that wherein they glory, they may be found even as we. ¹³For such are false apostles, deceitful workers, transforming themselves into the apostles of Christ. ¹⁴And no marvel; for Satan himself is transformed into an angel of light. ¹⁵Therefore it is no great thing if his ministers also be transformed as the ministers of righteousness; whose end shall be according to their works. ¹⁶I say again, Let no man think me a fool; if otherwise, yet as a fool receive me, that I may boast myself a little. ¹⁷That which I speak, I speak it not after the Lord, but as it were foolishly, in this confidence of boasting. ¹⁸Seeing that many glory after the flesh, I will glory also. ¹⁹For you suffer fools gladly, seeing you yourselves are wise. ²⁰For you suffer, if a man bring you into bondage, if a man devour you, if a man take of you, if a man exalt himself, if a man smite you on the face. ²¹I speak as concerning reproach, as though we had been weak. However, when ever any is bold, (I speak foolishly,) I am bold also. ²²Are they Hebrews? so am I. Are they Israelites? so am I. Are they the seed of Abraham? so am I. ²³Are they ministers of Christ? (I speak as a fool) I am more; in labors more abundant, in stripes above measure, in prisons more frequent, in deaths oft. ²⁴Of the Jews five times received I forty stripes save one. ²⁵Thrice was I beaten with rods, once was I stoned, thrice I suffered shipwreck, a night and a day I have been in the deep; ²⁶In journeys often, in perils of waters, in perils of robbers, in perils by my own countrymen, in perils by the heathen, in perils in the city, in perils in the wilderness, in perils in the sea, in perils among false brothers; ²⁷In weariness and painfulness, in watchings often, in hunger and thirst, in fastings often, in cold and nakedness. ²⁸Beside those things that are without, that which comes on me daily, the care of all the churches. ²⁹Who is weak, and I am not weak? who is offended, and I burn not? ³⁰If I must needs glory, I will glory of the things which concern my infirmities. ³¹The God and Father of our Lord Jesus Christ, which is blessed for ever more, knows that I lie not. ³²In Damascus the governor under Aretas the king kept the city of the Damascenes with a garrison, desirous to apprehend me: ³³And through a window in a basket was I let down by the wall, and escaped his hands.

12 ¹It is not expedient for me doubtless to glory. I will come to visions and revelations of the Lord. ²I knew a man in Christ above fourteen years ago, (whether in the body, I cannot tell; or whether out of the body, I cannot tell: God knows;) such an one caught up to the third heaven. ³And I knew such a man, (whether in the body, or out of the body, I cannot tell: God knows;) ⁴How that he was caught up into paradise, and heard unspeakable words, which it is not lawful for a man to utter. ⁵Of such an one will I glory: yet of myself I will not glory, but in my infirmities. ⁶For though I would desire to glory, I shall not be a fool; for I will say the truth: but now I forbear, lest any man should think of me above that which he sees me to be, or that he hears of me. ⁷And lest I should be exalted above measure through the abundance of the revelations, there was given to me a thorn in the flesh, the messenger of Satan to buffet me, lest I should be exalted above measure. ⁸For this thing I sought the Lord thrice, that it might depart from me. ⁹And he said to me, My grace is sufficient for you: for my strength is made perfect in weakness. Most gladly therefore will I rather glory in my infirmities, that the power of Christ may rest on me. ¹⁰Therefore I take pleasure in infirmities, in reproaches, in necessities, in persecutions, in distresses for Christ's sake: for when I am weak, then am I strong. ¹¹I am become a fool in glorying; you have compelled me: for I ought to have been commended of you: for in nothing am I behind the very most chief apostles, though I be nothing. ¹²Truly the signs of an apostle were worked among you in all patience, in signs, and wonders, and mighty deeds. ¹³For what is it wherein you were inferior to other churches, except it be that I myself was not burdensome to you? forgive me this wrong. ¹⁴Behold, the third time I am ready to come to you; and I will not be burdensome to you: for I seek not yours but you: for the children ought not to lay up for the parents, but the parents for the children. ¹⁵And I will very gladly spend and be spent for you; though the more abundantly I love you, the less I be loved. ¹⁶But be it so, I did not burden you: nevertheless, being crafty, I caught you with guile. ¹⁷Did I make a gain of you by any of them whom I sent to you? ¹⁸I desired Titus, and with him I sent a brother. Did Titus make a gain of you? walked we not in the same spirit? walked we not in the same steps? ¹⁹Again, think you that we excuse ourselves to you? we speak before God in Christ: but we do all things, dearly beloved, for your edifying. ²⁰For I fear, lest, when I come, I shall not find you such as I would, and that I shall be found to you such as you would not: lest there be debates, contentions, wraths, strifes, backbitings, whisperings, arrogance, tumults: ²¹And lest, when I come again, my God will humble me among you, and that I shall mourn many which have sinned already, and have not repented of the uncleanness and fornication and lasciviousness which they have committed.

13 ¹This is the third time I am coming to you. In the mouth of two or three witnesses shall every word be established. ²I told you before, and foretell you, as if I were present, the second time; and being absent now I write to them which heretofore have sinned, and to all other, that, if I come again, I will not spare: ³Since you seek a proof of Christ speaking in me, which to you-ward is not weak, but is mighty in you. ⁴For though he was crucified through weakness, yet he lives by the power of God. For we also are weak in him, but we shall live with him by the power of God toward you. ⁵Examine yourselves, whether you be in the faith; prove your own selves. Know you not your own selves, how that Jesus Christ is in you, except you be reprobates? ⁶But I trust that you shall know that we are not reprobates. ⁷Now I pray to God that you do no evil; not that we should appear approved, but that you should do that which is honest, though we be as reprobates. ⁸For we can do nothing against the truth, but for the truth. ⁹For we are glad, when we are weak, and you are strong: and this also we wish, even your perfection. ¹⁰Therefore I write these things being absent, lest being present I should use sharpness, according to the power which the Lord has given me to edification, and not to destruction. ¹¹Finally, brothers, farewell. Be perfect, be of good comfort, be of one mind, live in peace; and the God of love and peace shall be with you. ¹²Greet one another with an holy kiss. ¹³All the saints salute you. ¹⁴The grace of the Lord Jesus Christ, and the love of God, and the communion of the Holy Ghost, be with you all. Amen.

Galatians

1 ¹Paul, an apostle, (not of men, neither by man, but by Jesus Christ, and God the Father, who raised him from the dead;) ²And all the brothers which are with me, to the churches of Galatia: ³Grace be to you and peace from God the Father, and from our Lord Jesus Christ, ⁴Who gave himself for our sins, that he might deliver us from this present evil world, according to the will of God and our Father: ⁵To whom be glory for ever and ever. Amen. ⁶I marvel that you are so soon removed from him that called you into the grace of Christ to another gospel: ⁷Which is not another; but there be some that trouble you, and would pervert the gospel of Christ. ⁸But though we, or an angel from heaven, preach any other gospel to you than that which we have preached to you, let him be accursed. ⁹As we said before, so say I now again, if any man preach any other gospel to you than that you have received, let him be accursed. ¹⁰For do I now persuade men, or God? or do I seek to please men? for if I yet pleased men, I should not be the servant of Christ. ¹¹But I certify you, brothers, that the gospel which was preached of me is not after man. ¹²For I neither received it of man, neither was I taught it, but by the revelation of Jesus Christ. ¹³For you have heard of my conversation in time past in the Jews' religion, how that beyond measure I persecuted the church of God, and wasted it: ¹⁴And profited in the Jews' religion above many my equals in my own nation, being more exceedingly zealous of the traditions of my fathers. ¹⁵But when it pleased God, who separated me from my mother's womb, and called me by his grace, ¹⁶To reveal his Son in me, that I might preach him among the heathen; immediately I conferred not with flesh and blood: ¹⁷Neither went I up to Jerusalem to them which were apostles before me; but I went into Arabia, and returned again to Damascus. ¹⁸Then after three years I went up to Jerusalem to see Peter, and stayed with him fifteen days. ¹⁹But other of the apostles saw I none, save James the Lord's brother. ²⁰Now the things which I write to you, behold, before God, I lie not. ²¹Afterwards I came into the regions of Syria and Cilicia; ²²And was unknown by face to the churches of Judaea which were in Christ: ²³But they had heard only, That he which persecuted us in times past now preaches the faith which once he destroyed. ²⁴And they glorified God in me.

2 ¹Then fourteen years after I went up again to Jerusalem with Barnabas, and took Titus with me also. ²And I went up by revelation, and communicated to them that gospel which I preach among the Gentiles, but privately to them which were of reputation, lest by any means I should run, or had run, in vain. ³But neither Titus, who was with me, being a Greek, was compelled to be circumcised: ⁴And that because of false brothers unawares brought in, who came in privately to spy out our liberty which we have in Christ Jesus, that they might bring us into bondage: ⁵To whom we gave place by subjection, no, not for an hour; that the truth of the gospel might continue with you. ⁶But of these who seemed to be somewhat, (whatever they were, it makes no matter to me: God accepts no man's person:) for they who seemed to be somewhat in conference added nothing to me: ⁷But contrariwise, when they saw that the gospel of the uncircumcision was committed to me, as the gospel of the circumcision was to Peter; ⁸(For he that worked effectually in Peter to the apostleship of the circumcision, the same was mighty in me toward the Gentiles:) ⁹And when James, Cephas, and John, who seemed to be pillars, perceived the grace that was given to me, they gave to me and Barnabas the right hands of fellowship; that we should go to the heathen, and they to the circumcision. ¹⁰Only they would that we should remember the poor; the same which I also was forward to do. ¹¹But when Peter was come to Antioch, I withstood him to the face, because he was to be blamed. ¹²For before that certain came from James, he did eat with the Gentiles: but when they were come, he withdrew and separated himself, fearing them which were of the circumcision. ¹³And the other Jews dissembled likewise with him; so that Barnabas also was carried away with their dissimulation. ¹⁴But when I saw that they walked not uprightly according to the truth of the gospel, I said to Peter before them all, If you, being a Jew, live after the manner of Gentiles, and not as do the Jews, why compel you the Gentiles to live as do the Jews? ¹⁵We who are Jews by nature, and not sinners of the Gentiles, ¹⁶Knowing that a man is not justified by the works of the law, but by the faith of Jesus Christ, even we have believed in Jesus Christ, that we might be justified by the faith of Christ, and not by the works of the law: for by the works of the law shall no flesh be justified. ¹⁷But if, while we seek to be justified by Christ, we ourselves also are found sinners, is therefore Christ the minister of sin? God forbid. ¹⁸For if I build again the things which I destroyed, I make myself a transgressor. ¹⁹For I through the law am dead to the law, that I might live to God. ²⁰I am crucified with Christ: nevertheless I live; yet not I, but Christ lives in me: and the life which I now live in the flesh I live by the faith of the Son of God, who loved me, and gave himself for me. ²¹I do not frustrate the grace of God: for if righteousness come by the law, then Christ is dead in vain.

3 ¹O foolish Galatians, who has bewitched you, that you should not obey the truth, before whose eyes Jesus Christ has been evidently set forth, crucified among you? ²This only would I learn of you, Received you the Spirit by the works of the law, or by the hearing of faith? ³Are you so foolish? having begun in the Spirit, are you now made perfect by the flesh? ⁴Have you suffered so many things in vain? if it be yet in vain. ⁵He therefore that ministers to you the Spirit, and works miracles among you, does he it by the works of the law, or by the hearing of faith? ⁶Even as Abraham believed God, and it was accounted to him for righteousness. ⁷Know you therefore that they which are of faith, the same are the children of Abraham. ⁸And the scripture, foreseeing that God would justify the heathen through faith, preached before the gospel to Abraham, saying, In you shall all nations be blessed. ⁹So then they which be of faith are blessed with faithful Abraham. ¹⁰For as many as are of the works of the law are under the curse: for it is written, Cursed is every one that continues not in all things which are written in the book of the law to do them. ¹¹But that no man is justified by the law in the sight of God, it is evident: for, The just shall live by faith. ¹²And the law is not of faith: but, The man that does them shall live in them. ¹³Christ has redeemed us from the curse of the law, being made a curse for us: for it is written, Cursed is every one that hangs on a tree: ¹⁴That the blessing of Abraham might come on the Gentiles through Jesus Christ; that we might receive the promise of the Spirit through faith. ¹⁵Brothers, I speak after the manner of men; Though it be but a man's covenant, yet if it be confirmed, no man cancels, or adds thereto. ¹⁶Now to Abraham and his seed were the promises made. He says not, And to seeds, as of many; but as of one, And to your seed, which is Christ. ¹⁷And this I say, that the covenant, that was confirmed before of God in Christ, the law, which was four hundred and thirty years after, cannot cancel, that it should make the promise of none effect. ¹⁸For if the inheritance be of the law, it is no more of promise: but God gave it to Abraham by promise. ¹⁹Why then serves the law? It was added because of transgressions, till the seed should come to whom the promise was made; and it was ordained by angels in the hand of a mediator. ²⁰Now a mediator is not a mediator of one, but God is one. ²¹Is the law then against the promises of God? God forbid: for if there had been a law given which could have given life, truly righteousness should have been by the law. ²²But the scripture has concluded all under sin, that the promise by faith of Jesus Christ might be given to them that believe. ²³But before faith came, we were kept under the law, shut up to the faith which should afterwards be revealed. ²⁴Why the law was our schoolmaster to bring us to Christ, that we might be justified by faith. ²⁵But after that faith is come, we are no longer under a schoolmaster. ²⁶For you are all the children of God by faith in Christ Jesus. ²⁷For as many of you as have been baptized into Christ have put on Christ. ²⁸There is neither Jew nor Greek, there is neither bond nor free, there is neither male nor female: for you are all one in Christ Jesus. ²⁹And if you be Christ's, then are you Abraham's seed, and heirs according to the promise.

4 ¹Now I say, That the heir, as long as he is a child, differs nothing from a servant, though he be lord of all; ²But is under tutors and governors until the time appointed of the father. ³Even so we, when we were children, were in bondage under the elements of the world: ⁴But when the fullness of the time was come, God sent forth his Son, made of a woman, made under the law, ⁵To redeem them that were under the law, that we might receive the adoption of sons. ⁶And because you are sons, God has sent forth the Spirit of his Son into your hearts, crying, Abba, Father. ⁷Why you are no more a servant, but a son; and if a son, then an heir of God through Christ. ⁸However, then, when you knew not God, you did service to them which by nature are no gods. ⁹But now, after that you have known God, or rather are known of God, how turn you again to the weak and beggarly elements, to which you desire again to be in bondage? ¹⁰You observe days, and months, and times, and years. ¹¹I am afraid of you, lest I have bestowed on you labor in vain. ¹²Brothers, I beseech you, be as I am; for I am as you are: you have not injured me at all. ¹³You know how through infirmity of the flesh I preached the gospel to you at the first. ¹⁴And my temptation which was in my flesh you despised not, nor rejected; but received me as an angel of God, even as Christ Jesus. ¹⁵Where is then the blessedness you spoke of? for I bear you record, that, if it had been possible, you would have plucked out your own eyes, and have given them to me. ¹⁶Am I therefore become your enemy, because I tell you the truth? ¹⁷They zealously affect you, but not well; yes, they would exclude you, that you might affect them. ¹⁸But it is good to be zealously affected always in a good thing, and not only when I am present with you. ¹⁹My little children, of whom I travail in birth again until Christ be formed in you, ²⁰I desire to be present with you now, and to change my voice; for I stand in doubt of you. ²¹Tell me, you that desire to be under the law, do you not hear the law? ²²For it is written, that Abraham had two sons, the one by a female slave, the other by a free woman. ²³But he who was of the female slave was born after the flesh; but he of the free woman was by promise. ²⁴Which things are an allegory: for these are the two covenants; the one from the mount Sinai, which engenders to bondage, which is Agar. ²⁵For this Agar is mount Sinai in Arabia, and answers to Jerusalem which now is, and is in bondage with her children. ²⁶But Jerusalem which is above is free, which is the mother of us all. ²⁷For it is written, Rejoice, you barren that bore not; break forth and cry, you that travail not: for the desolate has many more children than she which has an husband. ²⁸Now we, brothers, as Isaac was, are the children of promise. ²⁹But as then he that was born after the flesh persecuted him that was born after the Spirit, even so it is now. ³⁰Nevertheless what says the scripture? Cast out the female slave and her son: for the son of the female slave shall not be heir with the son of the free woman. ³¹So then, brothers, we are not children of the female slave, but of the free.

5 ¹Stand fast therefore in the liberty with which Christ has made us free, and be not entangled again with the yoke of bondage. ²Behold, I Paul say to you, that if you be circumcised, Christ shall profit you nothing. ³For I testify again to every man that is circumcised, that he is a debtor to do the whole law. ⁴Christ is become of no effect to you, whoever of you are justified by the law; you are fallen from grace. ⁵For we through the Spirit wait for the hope of righteousness by faith. ⁶For in Jesus Christ neither circumcision avails any thing, nor uncircumcision; but faith which works by love. ⁷You did run well; who did hinder you that you should not obey the truth? ⁸This persuasion comes not of him that calls you. ⁹A little leaven leavens the whole lump. ¹⁰I have confidence in you through the Lord, that you will be none otherwise minded: but he that troubles you shall bear his judgment, whoever he be. ¹¹And I, brothers, if I yet preach circumcision, why do I yet suffer persecution? then is the offense of the cross ceased. ¹²I would they were even cut off which trouble you. ¹³For, brothers, you have been called to liberty; only use not liberty for an occasion to the flesh, but by love serve one another. ¹⁴For all the law is fulfilled in one word, even in this; You shall love your neighbor as yourself. ¹⁵But if you bite and devour one another, take heed that you be not consumed one of another.

[16] This I say then, Walk in the Spirit, and you shall not fulfill the lust of the flesh. [17] For the flesh lusts against the Spirit, and the Spirit against the flesh: and these are contrary the one to the other: so that you cannot do the things that you would. [18] But if you be led of the Spirit, you are not under the law. [19] Now the works of the flesh are manifest, which are these; Adultery, fornication, uncleanness, lasciviousness, [20] Idolatry, witchcraft, hatred, variance, jealousies, wrath, strife, seditions, heresies, [21] Contentions, murders, drunkenness, revelings, and such like: of the which I tell you before, as I have also told you in time past, that they which do such things shall not inherit the kingdom of God. [22] But the fruit of the Spirit is love, joy, peace, long-suffering, gentleness, goodness, faith, [23] Meekness, temperance: against such there is no law. [24] And they that are Christ's have crucified the flesh with the affections and lusts. [25] If we live in the Spirit, let us also walk in the Spirit. [26] Let us not be desirous of vain glory, provoking one another, envying one another.

6

[1] Brothers, if a man be overtaken in a fault, you which are spiritual, restore such an one in the spirit of meekness; considering yourself, lest you also be tempted. [2] Bear you one another's burdens, and so fulfill the law of Christ. [3] For if a man think himself to be something, when he is nothing, he deceives himself. [4] But let every man prove his own work, and then shall he have rejoicing in himself alone, and not in another. [5] For every man shall bear his own burden. [6] Let him that is taught in the word communicate to him that teaches in all good things. [7] Be not deceived; God is not mocked: for whatever a man sows, that shall he also reap. [8] For he that sows to his flesh shall of the flesh reap corruption; but he that sows to the Spirit shall of the Spirit reap life everlasting. [9] And let us not be weary in well doing: for in due season we shall reap, if we faint not. [10] As we have therefore opportunity, let us do good to all men, especially to them who are of the household of faith. [11] You see how large a letter I have written to you with my own hand. [12] As many as desire to make a fair show in the flesh, they constrain you to be circumcised; only lest they should suffer persecution for the cross of Christ. [13] For neither they themselves who are circumcised keep the law; but desire to have you circumcised, that they may glory in your flesh. [14] But God forbid that I should glory, save in the cross of our Lord Jesus Christ, by whom the world is crucified to me, and I to the world. [15] For in Christ Jesus neither circumcision avails any thing, nor uncircumcision, but a new creature. [16] And as many as walk according to this rule, peace be on them, and mercy, and on the Israel of God. [17] From now on let no man trouble me: for I bear in my body the marks of the Lord Jesus. [18] Brothers, the grace of our Lord Jesus Christ be with your spirit. Amen.

Ephesians

1 ¹Paul, an apostle of Jesus Christ by the will of God, to the saints which are at Ephesus, and to the faithful in Christ Jesus: ²Grace be to you, and peace, from God our Father, and from the Lord Jesus Christ. ³Blessed be the God and Father of our Lord Jesus Christ, who has blessed us with all spiritual blessings in heavenly places in Christ: ⁴According as he has chosen us in him before the foundation of the world, that we should be holy and without blame before him in love: ⁵Having predestinated us to the adoption of children by Jesus Christ to himself, according to the good pleasure of his will, ⁶To the praise of the glory of his grace, wherein he has made us accepted in the beloved. ⁷In whom we have redemption through his blood, the forgiveness of sins, according to the riches of his grace; ⁸Wherein he has abounded toward us in all wisdom and prudence; ⁹Having made known to us the mystery of his will, according to his good pleasure which he has purposed in himself: ¹⁰That in the dispensation of the fullness of times he might gather together in one all things in Christ, both which are in heaven, and which are on earth; even in him: ¹¹In whom also we have obtained an inheritance, being predestinated according to the purpose of him who works all things after the counsel of his own will: ¹²That we should be to the praise of his glory, who first trusted in Christ. ¹³In whom you also trusted, after that you heard the word of truth, the gospel of your salvation: in whom also after that you believed, you were sealed with that holy Spirit of promise, ¹⁴Which is the earnest of our inheritance until the redemption of the purchased possession, to the praise of his glory. ¹⁵Why I also, after I heard of your faith in the Lord Jesus, and love to all the saints, ¹⁶Cease not to give thanks for you, making mention of you in my prayers; ¹⁷That the God of our Lord Jesus Christ, the Father of glory, may give to you the spirit of wisdom and revelation in the knowledge of him: ¹⁸The eyes of your understanding being enlightened; that you may know what is the hope of his calling, and what the riches of the glory of his inheritance in the saints, ¹⁹And what is the exceeding greatness of his power to us-ward who believe, according to the working of his mighty power, ²⁰Which he worked in Christ, when he raised him from the dead, and set him at his own right hand in the heavenly places, ²¹Far above all principality, and power, and might, and dominion, and every name that is named, not only in this world, but also in that which is to come: ²²And has put all things under his feet, and gave him to be the head over all things to the church, ²³Which is his body, the fullness of him that fills all in all.

2 ¹And you has he quickened, who were dead in trespasses and sins; ²Wherein in time past you walked according to the course of this world, according to the prince of the power of the air, the spirit that now works in the children of disobedience: ³Among whom also we all had our conversation in times past in the lusts of our flesh, fulfilling the desires of the flesh and of the mind; and were by nature the children of wrath, even as others. ⁴But God, who is rich in mercy, for his great love with which he loved us, ⁵Even when we were dead in sins, has quickened us together with Christ, (by grace you are saved;) ⁶And has raised us up together, and made us sit together in heavenly places in Christ Jesus: ⁷That in the ages to come he might show the exceeding riches of his grace in his kindness toward us through Christ Jesus. ⁸For by grace are you saved through faith; and that not of yourselves: it is the gift of God: ⁹Not of works, lest any man should boast. ¹⁰For we are his workmanship, created in Christ Jesus to good works, which God has before ordained that we should walk in them. ¹¹Why remember, that you being in time past Gentiles in the flesh, who are called Uncircumcision by that which is called the Circumcision in the flesh made by hands; ¹²That at that time you were without Christ, being aliens from the commonwealth of Israel, and strangers from the covenants of promise, having no hope, and without God in the world: ¹³But now in Christ Jesus you who sometimes were far off are made near by the blood of Christ. ¹⁴For he is our peace, who has made both one, and has broken down the middle wall of partition between us; ¹⁵Having abolished in his flesh the enmity, even the law of commandments contained in ordinances; for to make in himself of two one new man, so making peace; ¹⁶And that he might reconcile both to God in one body by the cross, having slain the enmity thereby: ¹⁷And came and preached peace to you which were afar off, and to them that were near. ¹⁸For through him we both have access by one Spirit to the Father. ¹⁹Now therefore you are no more strangers and foreigners, but fellow citizens with the saints, and of the household of God; ²⁰And are built on the foundation of the apostles and prophets, Jesus Christ himself being the chief corner stone; ²¹In whom all the building fitly framed together grows to an holy temple in the Lord: ²²In whom you also are built together for an habitation of God through the Spirit.

3 ¹For this cause I Paul, the prisoner of Jesus Christ for you Gentiles, ²If you have heard of the dispensation of the grace of God which is given me to you-ward: ³How that by revelation he made known to me the mystery; (as I wrote before in few words, ⁴Whereby, when you read, you may understand my knowledge in the mystery of Christ) ⁵Which in other ages was not made known to the sons of men, as it is now revealed to his holy apostles and prophets by the Spirit; ⁶That the Gentiles should be fellow heirs, and of the same body, and partakers of his promise in Christ by the gospel: ⁷Whereof I was made a minister, according to the gift of the grace of God given to me by the effectual working of his power. ⁸To me, who am less than the least of all saints, is this grace given, that I should preach among the Gentiles the unsearchable riches of Christ; ⁹And to make all men see what is the fellowship of the mystery, which from the beginning of the world has been hid in God, who created all things by Jesus Christ: ¹⁰To the intent that now to the principalities and powers in heavenly places might be known by the church the manifold wisdom of God, ¹¹According to the eternal purpose which he purposed in Christ Jesus our Lord: ¹²In whom we have boldness and access with confidence by the faith of him. ¹³Why I desire that you faint not at my tribulations for you, which is your

glory. ¹⁴For this cause I bow my knees to the Father of our Lord Jesus Christ, ¹⁵Of whom the whole family in heaven and earth is named, ¹⁶That he would grant you, according to the riches of his glory, to be strengthened with might by his Spirit in the inner man; ¹⁷That Christ may dwell in your hearts by faith; that you, being rooted and grounded in love, ¹⁸May be able to comprehend with all saints what is the breadth, and length, and depth, and height; ¹⁹And to know the love of Christ, which passes knowledge, that you might be filled with all the fullness of God. ²⁰Now to him that is able to do exceeding abundantly above all that we ask or think, according to the power that works in us, ²¹To him be glory in the church by Christ Jesus throughout all ages, world without end. Amen.

4 ¹I therefore, the prisoner of the Lord, beseech you that you walk worthy of the vocation with which you are called, ²With all lowliness and meekness, with longsuffering, forbearing one another in love; ³Endeavoring to keep the unity of the Spirit in the bond of peace. ⁴There is one body, and one Spirit, even as you are called in one hope of your calling; ⁵One Lord, one faith, one baptism, ⁶One God and Father of all, who is above all, and through all, and in you all. ⁷But to every one of us is given grace according to the measure of the gift of Christ. ⁸Why he says, When he ascended up on high, he led captivity captive, and gave gifts to men. ⁹(Now that he ascended, what is it but that he also descended first into the lower parts of the earth? ¹⁰He that descended is the same also that ascended up far above all heavens, that he might fill all things.) ¹¹And he gave some, apostles; and some, prophets; and some, evangelists; and some, pastors and teachers; ¹²For the perfecting of the saints, for the work of the ministry, for the edifying of the body of Christ: ¹³Till we all come in the unity of the faith, and of the knowledge of the Son of God, to a perfect man, to the measure of the stature of the fullness of Christ: ¹⁴That we from now on be no more children, tossed to and fro, and carried about with every wind of doctrine, by the sleight of men, and cunning craftiness, whereby they lie in wait to deceive; ¹⁵But speaking the truth in love, may grow up into him in all things, which is the head, even Christ: ¹⁶From whom the whole body fitly joined together and compacted by that which every joint supplies, according to the effectual working in the measure of every part, makes increase of the body to the edifying of itself in love. ¹⁷This I say therefore, and testify in the Lord, that you from now on walk not as other Gentiles walk, in the vanity of their mind, ¹⁸Having the understanding darkened, being alienated from the life of God through the ignorance that is in them, because of the blindness of their heart: ¹⁹Who being past feeling have given themselves over to lasciviousness, to work all uncleanness with greediness. ²⁰But you have not so learned Christ; ²¹If so be that you have heard him, and have been taught by him, as the truth is in Jesus: ²²That you put off concerning the former conversation the old man, which is corrupt according to the deceitful lusts; ²³And be renewed in the spirit of your mind; ²⁴And that you put on the new man, which after God is created in righteousness and true holiness. ²⁵Why putting away lying, speak every man truth with his neighbor: for we are members one of another. ²⁶Be you angry, and sin not: let not the sun go down on your wrath: ²⁷Neither give place to the devil. ²⁸Let him that stole steal no more: but rather let him labor, working with his hands the thing which is good, that he may have to give to him that needs. ²⁹Let no corrupt communication proceed out of your mouth, but that which is good to the use of edifying, that it may minister grace to the hearers. ³⁰And grieve not the holy Spirit of God, whereby you are sealed to the day of redemption. ³¹Let all bitterness, and wrath, and anger, and clamor, and evil speaking, be put away from you, with all malice: ³²And be you kind one to another, tenderhearted, forgiving one another, even as God for Christ's sake has forgiven you.

5 ¹Be you therefore followers of God, as dear children; ²And walk in love, as Christ also has loved us, and has given himself for us an offering and a sacrifice to God for a sweet smelling smell. ³But fornication, and all uncleanness, or covetousness, let it not be once named among you, as becomes saints; ⁴Neither filthiness, nor foolish talking, nor jesting, which are not convenient: but rather giving of thanks. ⁵For this you know, that no fornicator, nor unclean person, nor covetous man, who is an idolater, has any inheritance in the kingdom of Christ and of God. ⁶Let no man deceive you with vain words: for because of these things comes the wrath of God on the children of disobedience. ⁷Be not you therefore partakers with them. ⁸For you were sometimes darkness, but now are you light in the Lord: walk as children of light: ⁹(For the fruit of the Spirit is in all goodness and righteousness and truth;) ¹⁰Proving what is acceptable to the Lord. ¹¹And have no fellowship with the unfruitful works of darkness, but rather reprove them. ¹²For it is a shame even to speak of those things which are done of them in secret. ¹³But all things that are reproved are made manifest by the light: for whatever does make manifest is light. ¹⁴Why he says, Awake you that sleep, and arise from the dead, and Christ shall give you light. ¹⁵See then that you walk circumspectly, not as fools, but as wise, ¹⁶Redeeming the time, because the days are evil. ¹⁷Why be you not unwise, but understanding what the will of the Lord is. ¹⁸And be not drunk with wine, wherein is excess; but be filled with the Spirit; ¹⁹Speaking to yourselves in psalms and hymns and spiritual songs, singing and making melody in your heart to the Lord; ²⁰Giving thanks always for all things to God and the Father in the name of our Lord Jesus Christ; ²¹Submitting yourselves one to another in the fear of God. ²²Wives, submit yourselves to your own husbands, as to the Lord. ²³For the husband is the head of the wife, even as Christ is the head of the church: and he is the savior of the body. ²⁴Therefore as the church is subject to Christ, so let the wives be to their own husbands in every thing. ²⁵Husbands, love your wives, even as Christ also loved the church, and gave himself for it; ²⁶That he might sanctify and cleanse it with the washing of water by the word, ²⁷That he might present it to himself a glorious church, not having spot, or wrinkle, or any such thing; but that it should be holy and without blemish. ²⁸So ought men to love their wives as their own bodies. He that loves his wife loves himself. ²⁹For no man ever yet hated his own flesh; but nourishes and cherishes it, even as the Lord the church: ³⁰For we are members of his body, of his flesh, and of his bones. ³¹For this cause shall a man leave his father and mother, and shall be joined to his wife, and they two shall be one flesh. ³²This is a great mystery: but I speak concerning Christ and the church. ³³Nevertheless let every one of you in particular so love his wife even as himself; and the wife see that she reverence her husband.

6 ¹Children, obey your parents in the Lord: for this is right. ²Honor your father and mother; which is the first commandment with promise; ³That it may be well with you, and you may live long on the earth. ⁴And, you fathers, provoke not your children to wrath: but bring them up in the nurture and admonition of the Lord. ⁵Servants, be obedient to them that are your masters according to the flesh, with fear and trembling, in singleness of your heart, as to Christ; ⁶Not with eye-service, as men pleasers; but as the servants of Christ, doing the will of God from the heart; ⁷With good will doing service, as to the Lord, and not to men: ⁸Knowing that whatever good thing any man does, the same shall he receive of the Lord, whether he be bond or free. ⁹And, you masters, do the same things to them, forbearing threatening: knowing that your Master also is in heaven; neither is there respect of persons with him. ¹⁰Finally, my brothers, be strong in the Lord, and in the power of his might. ¹¹Put on the whole armor of God, that you may be able to stand against the wiles of the devil. ¹²For we wrestle not against flesh and blood, but against principalities, against powers, against the rulers of the darkness of this world, against spiritual wickedness in high places. ¹³Why take to you the whole armor of God, that you may be able to withstand in the evil day, and having done all, to stand. ¹⁴Stand therefore, having your loins girt about with truth, and having on the breastplate of righteousness; ¹⁵And your feet shod with the preparation of the gospel of peace; ¹⁶Above all, taking the shield of faith, with which you shall be able to quench all the fiery darts of the wicked. ¹⁷And take the helmet of salvation, and the sword of the Spirit, which is the word of God: ¹⁸Praying always with all prayer and supplication in the Spirit, and watching thereunto with all perseverance and supplication for all saints; ¹⁹And for me, that utterance may be given to me, that I may open my mouth boldly, to make known the mystery of the gospel, ²⁰For which I am an ambassador in bonds: that therein I may speak boldly, as I ought to speak. ²¹But that you also may know my affairs, and how I do, Tychicus, a beloved brother and faithful minister in the Lord, shall make known to you all things: ²²Whom I have sent to you for the same purpose, that you might know our affairs, and that he might comfort your hearts. ²³Peace be to the brothers, and love with faith, from God the Father and the Lord Jesus Christ. ²⁴Grace be with all them that love our Lord Jesus Christ in sincerity. Amen.

Philippians

1 ¹Paul and Timotheus, the servants of Jesus Christ, to all the saints in Christ Jesus which are at Philippi, with the bishops and deacons: ²Grace be to you, and peace, from God our Father, and from the Lord Jesus Christ. ³I thank my God on every remembrance of you, ⁴Always in every prayer of my for you all making request with joy, ⁵For your fellowship in the gospel from the first day until now; ⁶Being confident of this very thing, that he which has begun a good work in you will perform it until the day of Jesus Christ: ⁷Even as it is meet for me to think this of you all, because I have you in my heart; inasmuch as both in my bonds, and in the defense and confirmation of the gospel, you all are partakers of my grace. ⁸For God is my record, how greatly I long after you all in the bowels of Jesus Christ. ⁹And this I pray, that your love may abound yet more and more in knowledge and in all judgment; ¹⁰That you may approve things that are excellent; that you may be sincere and without offense till the day of Christ. ¹¹Being filled with the fruits of righteousness, which are by Jesus Christ, to the glory and praise of God. ¹²But I would you should understand, brothers, that the things which happened to me have fallen out rather to the furtherance of the gospel; ¹³So that my bonds in Christ are manifest in all the palace, and in all other places; ¹⁴And many of the brothers in the Lord, waxing confident by my bonds, are much more bold to speak the word without fear. ¹⁵Some indeed preach Christ even of envy and strife; and some also of good will: ¹⁶The one preach Christ of contention, not sincerely, supposing to add affliction to my bonds: ¹⁷But the other of love, knowing that I am set for the defense of the gospel. ¹⁸What then? notwithstanding, every way, whether in pretense, or in truth, Christ is preached; and I therein do rejoice, yes, and will rejoice. ¹⁹For I know that this shall turn to my salvation through your prayer, and the supply of the Spirit of Jesus Christ, ²⁰According to my earnest expectation and my hope, that in nothing I shall be ashamed, but that with all boldness, as always, so now also Christ shall be magnified in my body, whether it be by life, or by death. ²¹For to me to live is Christ, and to die is gain. ²²But if I live in the flesh, this is the fruit of my labor: yet what I shall choose I know not. ²³For I am in a strait between two, having a desire to depart, and to be with Christ; which is far better: ²⁴Nevertheless to abide in the flesh is more needful for you. ²⁵And having this confidence, I know that I shall abide and continue with you all for your furtherance and joy of faith; ²⁶That your rejoicing may be more abundant in Jesus Christ for me by my coming to you again. ²⁷Only let your conversation be as it becomes the gospel of Christ: that whether I come and see you, or else be absent, I may hear of your affairs, that you stand fast in one spirit, with one mind striving together for the faith of the gospel; ²⁸And in nothing terrified by your adversaries: which is to them an evident token of perdition, but to you of salvation, and that of God. ²⁹For to you it is given in the behalf of Christ, not only to believe on him, but also to suffer for his sake; ³⁰Having the same conflict which you saw in me, and now hear to be in me.

2 ¹If there be therefore any consolation in Christ, if any comfort of love, if any fellowship of the Spirit, if any bowels and mercies, ²Fulfill you my joy, that you be like minded, having the same love, being of one accord, of one mind. ³Let nothing be done through strife or vainglory; but in lowliness of mind let each esteem other better than themselves. ⁴Look not every man on his own things, but every man also on the things of others. ⁵Let this mind be in you, which was also in Christ Jesus: ⁶Who, being in the form of God, thought it not robbery to be equal with God: ⁷But made himself of no reputation, and took on him the form of a servant, and was made in the likeness of men: ⁸And being found in fashion as a man, he humbled himself, and became obedient to death, even the death of the cross. ⁹Why God also has highly exalted him, and given him a name which is above every name: ¹⁰That at the name of Jesus every knee should bow, of things in heaven, and things in earth, and things under the earth; ¹¹And that every tongue should confess that Jesus Christ is Lord, to the glory of God the Father. ¹²Why, my beloved, as you have always obeyed, not as in my presence only, but now much more in my absence, work out your own salvation with fear and trembling. ¹³For it is God which works in you both to will and to do of his good pleasure. ¹⁴Do all things without murmurings and disputings: ¹⁵That you may be blameless and harmless, the sons of God, without rebuke, in the middle of a crooked and perverse nation, among whom you shine as lights in the world; ¹⁶Holding forth the word of life; that I may rejoice in the day of Christ, that I have not run in vain, neither labored in vain. ¹⁷Yes, and if I be offered on the sacrifice and service of your faith, I joy, and rejoice with you all. ¹⁸For the same cause also do you joy, and rejoice with me. ¹⁹But I trust in the Lord Jesus to send Timotheus shortly to you, that I also may be of good comfort, when I know your state. ²⁰For I have no man like minded, who will naturally care for your state. ²¹For all seek their own, not the things which are Jesus Christ's. ²²But you know the proof of him, that, as a son with the father, he has served with me in the gospel. ²³Him therefore I hope to send presently, so soon as I shall see how it will go with me. ²⁴But I trust in the Lord that I also myself shall come shortly. ²⁵Yet I supposed it necessary to send to you Epaphroditus, my brother, and companion in labor, and fellow soldier, but your messenger, and he that ministered to my wants. ²⁶For he longed after you all, and was full of heaviness, because that you had heard that he had been sick. ²⁷For indeed he was sick near to death: but God had mercy on him; and not on him only, but on me also, lest I should have sorrow on sorrow. ²⁸I sent him therefore the more carefully, that, when you see him again, you may rejoice, and that I may be the less sorrowful. ²⁹Receive him therefore in the Lord with all gladness; and hold such in reputation: ³⁰Because for the work of Christ he was near to death, not regarding his life, to supply your lack of service toward me.

3 ¹Finally, my brothers, rejoice in the Lord. To write the same things to you, to me indeed is not grievous, but for you it is safe. ²Beware of dogs, beware of evil workers,

beware of the concision. ³For we are the circumcision, which worship God in the spirit, and rejoice in Christ Jesus, and have no confidence in the flesh. ⁴Though I might also have confidence in the flesh. If any other man thinks that he has whereof he might trust in the flesh, I more: ⁵Circumcised the eighth day, of the stock of Israel, of the tribe of Benjamin, an Hebrew of the Hebrews; as touching the law, a Pharisee; ⁶Concerning zeal, persecuting the church; touching the righteousness which is in the law, blameless. ⁷But what things were gain to me, those I counted loss for Christ. ⁸Yes doubtless, and I count all things but loss for the excellency of the knowledge of Christ Jesus my Lord: for whom I have suffered the loss of all things, and do count them but dung, that I may win Christ, ⁹And be found in him, not having my own righteousness, which is of the law, but that which is through the faith of Christ, the righteousness which is of God by faith: ¹⁰That I may know him, and the power of his resurrection, and the fellowship of his sufferings, being made conformable to his death; ¹¹If by any means I might attain to the resurrection of the dead. ¹²Not as though I had already attained, either were already perfect: but I follow after, if that I may apprehend that for which also I am apprehended of Christ Jesus. ¹³Brothers, I count not myself to have apprehended: but this one thing I do, forgetting those things which are behind, and reaching forth to those things which are before, ¹⁴I press toward the mark for the prize of the high calling of God in Christ Jesus. ¹⁵Let us therefore, as many as be perfect, be thus minded: and if in any thing you be otherwise minded, God shall reveal even this to you. ¹⁶Nevertheless, whereto we have already attained, let us walk by the same rule, let us mind the same thing. ¹⁷Brothers, be followers together of me, and mark them which walk so as you have us for an ensample. ¹⁸(For many walk, of whom I have told you often, and now tell you even weeping, that they are the enemies of the cross of Christ: ¹⁹Whose end is destruction, whose God is their belly, and whose glory is in their shame, who mind earthly things.) ²⁰For our conversation is in heaven; from where also we look for the Savior, the Lord Jesus Christ: ²¹Who shall change our vile body, that it may be fashioned like to his glorious body, according to the working whereby he is able even to subdue all things to himself.

4 ¹Therefore, my brothers dearly beloved and longed for, my joy and crown, so stand fast in the Lord, my dearly beloved. ²I beseech Euodias, and beseech Syntyche, that they be of the same mind in the Lord. ³And I entreat you also, true yoke fellow, help those women which labored with me in the gospel, with Clement also, and with other my fellow laborers, whose names are in the book of life. ⁴Rejoice in the Lord always: and again I say, Rejoice. ⁵Let your moderation be known to all men. The Lord is at hand. ⁶Be careful for nothing; but in every thing by prayer and supplication with thanksgiving let your requests be made known to God. ⁷And the peace of God, which passes all understanding, shall keep your hearts and minds through Christ Jesus. ⁸Finally, brothers, whatever things are true, whatever things are honest, whatever things are just, whatever things are pure, whatever things are lovely, whatever things are of good report; if there be any virtue, and if there be any praise, think on these things. ⁹Those things, which you have both learned, and received, and heard, and seen in me, do: and the God of peace shall be with you. ¹⁰But I rejoiced in the Lord greatly, that now at the last your care of me has flourished again; wherein you were also careful, but you lacked opportunity. ¹¹Not that I speak in respect of want: for I have learned, in whatever state I am, therewith to be content. ¹²I know both how to be abased, and I know how to abound: every where and in all things I am instructed both to be full and to be hungry, both to abound and to suffer need. ¹³I can do all things through Christ which strengthens me. ¹⁴Notwithstanding you have well done, that you did communicate with my affliction. ¹⁵Now you Philippians know also, that in the beginning of the gospel, when I departed from Macedonia, no church communicated with me as concerning giving and receiving, but you only. ¹⁶For even in Thessalonica you sent once and again to my necessity. ¹⁷Not because I desire a gift: but I desire fruit that may abound to your account. ¹⁸But I have all, and abound: I am full, having received of Epaphroditus the things which were sent from you, an odor of a sweet smell, a sacrifice acceptable, well pleasing to God. ¹⁹But my God shall supply all your need according to his riches in glory by Christ Jesus. ²⁰Now to God and our Father be glory for ever and ever. Amen. ²¹Salute every saint in Christ Jesus. The brothers which are with me greet you. ²²All the saints salute you, chiefly they that are of Caesar's household. ²³The grace of our Lord Jesus Christ be with you all. Amen.

Colossians

1 ¹Paul, an apostle of Jesus Christ by the will of God, and Timotheus our brother, ²To the saints and faithful brothers in Christ which are at Colosse: Grace be to you, and peace, from God our Father and the Lord Jesus Christ. ³We give thanks to God and the Father of our Lord Jesus Christ, praying always for you, ⁴Since we heard of your faith in Christ Jesus, and of the love which you have to all the saints, ⁵For the hope which is laid up for you in heaven, whereof you heard before in the word of the truth of the gospel; ⁶Which is come to you, as it is in all the world; and brings forth fruit, as it does also in you, since the day you heard of it, and knew the grace of God in truth: ⁷As you also learned of Epaphras our dear fellow servant, who is for you a faithful minister of Christ; ⁸Who also declared to us your love in the Spirit. ⁹For this cause we also, since the day we heard it, do not cease to pray for you, and to desire that you might be filled with the knowledge of his will in all wisdom and spiritual understanding; ¹⁰That you might walk worthy of the Lord to all pleasing, being fruitful in every good work, and increasing in the knowledge of God; ¹¹Strengthened with all might, according to his glorious power, to all patience and long-suffering with joyfulness; ¹²Giving thanks to the Father, which has made us meet to be partakers of the inheritance of the saints in light: ¹³Who has delivered us from the power of darkness, and has translated us into the kingdom of his dear Son: ¹⁴In whom we have redemption through his blood, even the forgiveness of sins: ¹⁵Who is the image of the invisible God, the firstborn of every creature: ¹⁶For by him were all things created, that are in heaven, and that are in earth, visible and invisible, whether they be thrones, or dominions, or principalities, or powers: all things were created by him, and for him: ¹⁷And he is before all things, and by him all things consist. ¹⁸And he is the head of the body, the church: who is the beginning, the firstborn from the dead; that in all things he might have the preeminence. ¹⁹For it pleased the Father that in him should all fullness dwell; ²⁰And, having made peace through the blood of his cross, by him to reconcile all things to himself; by him, I say, whether they be things in earth, or things in heaven. ²¹And you, that were sometime alienated and enemies in your mind by wicked works, yet now has he reconciled ²²In the body of his flesh through death, to present you holy and blameless and unreproveable in his sight: ²³If you continue in the faith grounded and settled, and be not moved away from the hope of the gospel, which you have heard, and which was preached to every creature which is under heaven; whereof I Paul am made a minister; ²⁴Who now rejoice in my sufferings for you, and fill up that which is behind of the afflictions of Christ in my flesh for his body's sake, which is the church: ²⁵Whereof I am made a minister, according to the dispensation of God which is given to me for you, to fulfill the word of God; ²⁶Even the mystery which has been hid from ages and from generations, but now is made manifest to his saints: ²⁷To whom God would make known what is the riches of the glory of this mystery among the Gentiles; which is Christ in you, the hope of glory: ²⁸Whom we preach, warning every man, and teaching every man in all wisdom; that we may present every man perfect in Christ Jesus: ²⁹Whereunto I also labor, striving according to his working, which works in me mightily.

2 ¹For I would that you knew what great conflict I have for you, and for them at Laodicea, and for as many as have not seen my face in the flesh; ²That their hearts might be comforted, being knit together in love, and to all riches of the full assurance of understanding, to the acknowledgment of the mystery of God, and of the Father, and of Christ; ³In whom are hid all the treasures of wisdom and knowledge. ⁴And this I say, lest any man should beguile you with enticing words. ⁵For though I be absent in the flesh, yet am I with you in the spirit, rejoicing and beholding your order, and the steadfastness of your faith in Christ. ⁶As you have therefore received Christ Jesus the Lord, so walk you in him: ⁷Rooted and built up in him, and established in the faith, as you have been taught, abounding therein with thanksgiving. ⁸Beware lest any man spoil you through philosophy and vain deceit, after the tradition of men, after the rudiments of the world, and not after Christ. ⁹For in him dwells all the fullness of the Godhead bodily. ¹⁰And you are complete in him, which is the head of all principality and power: ¹¹In whom also you are circumcised with the circumcision made without hands, in putting off the body of the sins of the flesh by the circumcision of Christ: ¹²Buried with him in baptism, wherein also you are risen with him through the faith of the operation of God, who has raised him from the dead. ¹³And you, being dead in your sins and the uncircumcision of your flesh, has he quickened together with him, having forgiven you all trespasses; ¹⁴Blotting out the handwriting of ordinances that was against us, which was contrary to us, and took it out of the way, nailing it to his cross; ¹⁵And having spoiled principalities and powers, he made a show of them openly, triumphing over them in it. ¹⁶Let no man therefore judge you in meat, or in drink, or in respect of an holy day, or of the new moon, or of the sabbath days: ¹⁷Which are a shadow of things to come; but the body is of Christ. ¹⁸Let no man beguile you of your reward in a voluntary humility and worshiping of angels, intruding into those things which he has not seen, vainly puffed up by his fleshly mind, ¹⁹And not holding the Head, from which all the body by joints and bands having nourishment ministered, and knit together, increases with the increase of God. ²⁰Why if you be dead with Christ from the rudiments of the world, why, as though living in the world, are you subject to ordinances, ²¹(Touch not; taste not; handle not; ²²Which all are to perish with the using;) after the commandments and doctrines of men? ²³Which things have indeed a show of wisdom in will worship, and humility, and neglecting of the body: not in any honor to the satisfying of the flesh.

3 ¹If you then be risen with Christ, seek those things which are above, where Christ sits on the right hand of God. ²Set your affection on things above, not on things on the earth. ³For you are dead, and your life is hid with Christ in God. ⁴When Christ, who is our life, shall appear, then shall you also appear with him in glory. ⁵Mortify therefore your members which are on the earth; fornication, uncleanness, inordinate affection, evil concupiscence, and covetousness, which is idolatry: ⁶For which things' sake the wrath of God comes on the children of disobedience: ⁷In the which you also walked some time, when you lived in them. ⁸But now you also put off all these; anger, wrath, malice, blasphemy, filthy communication out of your mouth. ⁹Lie not one to another, seeing that you have put off the old man with his deeds; ¹⁰And have put on the new man, which is renewed in knowledge after the image of him that created him: ¹¹Where there is neither Greek nor Jew, circumcision nor uncircumcision, Barbarian, Scythian, bond nor free: but Christ is all, and in all. ¹²Put on therefore, as the elect of God, holy and beloved, bowels of mercies, kindness, humbleness of mind, meekness, long-suffering; ¹³Forbearing one another, and forgiving one another, if any man have a quarrel against any: even as Christ forgave you, so also do you. ¹⁴And above all these things put on charity, which is the bond of perfection. ¹⁵And let the peace of God rule in your hearts, to the which also you are called in one body; and be you thankful. ¹⁶Let the word of Christ dwell in you richly in all wisdom; teaching and admonishing one another in psalms and hymns and spiritual songs, singing with grace in your hearts to the Lord. ¹⁷And whatever you do in word or deed, do all in the name of the Lord Jesus, giving thanks to God and the Father by him. ¹⁸Wives, submit yourselves to your own husbands, as it is fit in the Lord. ¹⁹Husbands, love your wives, and be not bitter against them. ²⁰Children, obey your parents in all things: for this is well pleasing to the Lord. ²¹Fathers, provoke not your children to anger, lest they be discouraged. ²²Servants, obey in all things your masters according to the flesh; not with eye-service, as men pleasers; but in singleness of heart, fearing God; ²³And whatever you do, do it heartily, as to the Lord, and not to men; ²⁴Knowing that of the Lord you shall receive the reward of the inheritance: for you serve the Lord Christ. ²⁵But he that does wrong shall receive for the wrong which he has done: and there is no respect of persons.

4 ¹Masters, give to your servants that which is just and equal; knowing that you also have a Master in heaven. ²Continue in prayer, and watch in the same with thanksgiving; ³With praying also for us, that God would open to us a door of utterance, to speak the mystery of Christ, for which I am also in bonds: ⁴That I may make it manifest, as I ought to speak. ⁵Walk in wisdom toward them that are without, redeeming the time. ⁶Let your speech be always with grace, seasoned with salt, that you may know how you ought to answer every man. ⁷All my state shall Tychicus declare to you, who is a beloved brother, and a faithful minister and fellow servant in the Lord: ⁸Whom I have sent to you for the same purpose, that he might know your estate, and comfort your hearts; ⁹With Onesimus, a faithful and beloved brother, who is one of you. They shall make known to you all things which are done here. ¹⁰Aristarchus my fellow prisoner salutes you, and Marcus, sister's son to Barnabas, (touching whom you received commandments: if he come to you, receive him;) ¹¹And Jesus, which is called Justus, who are of the circumcision. These only are my fellow workers to the kingdom of God, which have been a comfort to me. ¹²Epaphras, who is one of you, a servant of Christ, salutes you, always laboring fervently for you in prayers, that you may stand perfect and complete in all the will of God. ¹³For I bear him record, that he has a great zeal for you, and them that are in Laodicea, and them in Hierapolis. ¹⁴Luke, the beloved physician, and Demas, greet you. ¹⁵Salute the brothers which are in Laodicea, and Nymphas, and the church which is in his house. ¹⁶And when this letter is read among you, cause that it be read also in the church of the Laodiceans; and that you likewise read the letter from Laodicea. ¹⁷And say to Archippus, Take heed to the ministry which you have received in the Lord, that you fulfill it. ¹⁸The salutation by the hand of me Paul. Remember my bonds. Grace be with you. Amen.

First Thessalonians

1 ¹Paul, and Silvanus, and Timotheus, to the church of the Thessalonians which is in God the Father and in the Lord Jesus Christ: Grace be to you, and peace, from God our Father, and the Lord Jesus Christ. ²We give thanks to God always for you all, making mention of you in our prayers; ³Remembering without ceasing your work of faith, and labor of love, and patience of hope in our Lord Jesus Christ, in the sight of God and our Father; ⁴Knowing, brothers beloved, your election of God. ⁵For our gospel came not to you in word only, but also in power, and in the Holy Ghost, and in much assurance; as you know what manner of men we were among you for your sake. ⁶And you became followers of us, and of the Lord, having received the word in much affliction, with joy of the Holy Ghost. ⁷So that you were ensamples to all that believe in Macedonia and Achaia. ⁸For from you sounded out the word of the Lord not only in Macedonia and Achaia, but also in every place your faith to God-ward is spread abroad; so that we need not to speak any thing. ⁹For they themselves show of us what manner of entering in we had to you, and how you turned to God from idols to serve the living and true God; ¹⁰And to wait for his Son from heaven, whom he raised from the dead, even Jesus, which delivered us from the wrath to come.

2 ¹For yourselves, brothers, know our entrance in to you, that it was not in vain: ²But even after that we had suffered before, and were shamefully entreated, as you know, at Philippi, we were bold in our God to speak to you the gospel of God with much contention. ³For our exhortation was not of deceit, nor of uncleanness, nor in guile: ⁴But as we were allowed of God to be put in trust with the gospel, even so we speak; not as pleasing men, but God, which tries our hearts. ⁵For neither at any time used we flattering words, as you know, nor a cloak of covetousness; God is witness: ⁶Nor of men sought we glory, neither of you, nor yet of others, when we might have been burdensome, as the apostles of Christ. ⁷But we were gentle among you, even as a nurse cherishes her children: ⁸So being affectionately desirous of you, we were willing to have imparted to you, not the gospel of God only, but also our own souls, because you were dear to us. ⁹For you remember, brothers, our labor and travail: for laboring night and day, because we would not be chargeable to any of you, we preached to you the gospel of God. ¹⁰You are witnesses, and God also, how piously and justly and blamelessly we behaved ourselves among you that believe: ¹¹As you know how we exhorted and comforted and charged every one of you, as a father does his children, ¹²That you would walk worthy of God, who has called you to his kingdom and glory. ¹³For this cause also thank we God without ceasing, because, when you received the word of God which you heard of us, you received it not as the word of men, but as it is in truth, the word of God, which effectually works also in you that believe. ¹⁴For you, brothers, became followers of the churches of God which in Judaea are in Christ Jesus: for you also have suffered like things of your own countrymen, even as they have of the Jews: ¹⁵Who both killed the Lord Jesus, and their own prophets, and have persecuted us; and they please not God, and are contrary to all men: ¹⁶Forbidding us to speak to the Gentiles that they might be saved, to fill up their sins always: for the wrath is come on them to the uttermost. ¹⁷But we, brothers, being taken from you for a short time in presence, not in heart, endeavored the more abundantly to see your face with great desire. ¹⁸Why we would have come to you, even I Paul, once and again; but Satan hindered us. ¹⁹For what is our hope, or joy, or crown of rejoicing? Are not even you in the presence of our Lord Jesus Christ at his coming? ²⁰For you are our glory and joy.

3 ¹Why when we could no longer forbear, we thought it good to be left at Athens alone; ²And sent Timotheus, our brother, and minister of God, and our fellow laborer in the gospel of Christ, to establish you, and to comfort you concerning your faith: ³That no man should be moved by these afflictions: for yourselves know that we are appointed thereunto. ⁴For truly, when we were with you, we told you before that we should suffer tribulation; even as it came to pass, and you know. ⁵For this cause, when I could no longer forbear, I sent to know your faith, lest by some means the tempter have tempted you, and our labor be in vain. ⁶But now when Timotheus came from you to us, and brought us good tidings of your faith and charity, and that you have good remembrance of us always, desiring greatly to see us, as we also to see you: ⁷Therefore, brothers, we were comforted over you in all our affliction and distress by your faith: ⁸For now we live, if you stand fast in the Lord. ⁹For what thanks can we render to God again for you, for all the joy with which we joy for your sakes before our God; ¹⁰Night and day praying exceedingly that we might see your face, and might perfect that which is lacking in your faith? ¹¹Now God himself and our Father, and our Lord Jesus Christ, direct our way to you. ¹²And the Lord make you to increase and abound in love one toward another, and toward all men, even as we do toward you: ¹³To the end he may establish your hearts blameless in holiness before God, even our Father, at the coming of our Lord Jesus Christ with all his saints.

4 ¹Furthermore then we beseech you, brothers, and exhort you by the Lord Jesus, that as you have received of us how you ought to walk and to please God, so you would abound more and more. ²For you know what commandments we gave you by the Lord Jesus. ³For this is the will of God, even your sanctification, that you should abstain from fornication: ⁴That every one of you should know how to possess his vessel in sanctification and honor; ⁵Not in the lust of concupiscence, even as the Gentiles which know not God: ⁶That no man go beyond and defraud his brother in any matter: because that the Lord is the avenger of all such, as we also have forewarned you and testified. ⁷For God has not called us to uncleanness, but to holiness. ⁸He therefore that despises, despises not man, but God, who has also given to us his holy Spirit. ⁹But as touching brotherly love you need not that I write to you: for you yourselves are taught of God to love one another. ¹⁰And indeed you do it toward all the brothers which are in all Macedonia: but we beseech you, brothers, that you increase more and more; ¹¹And that you study to be quiet, and to do your own business, and to work with your own hands, as we commanded you; ¹²That you may walk honestly toward them that are without, and that you may have lack of nothing. ¹³But I would not have you to be ignorant, brothers, concerning them which are asleep, that you sorrow not, even as others which have no hope. ¹⁴For if we believe that Jesus died and rose again, even so them also which sleep in Jesus will God bring with him. ¹⁵For this we say to you by the word of the Lord, that we which are alive and remain to the coming of the Lord shall not prevent them which are asleep. ¹⁶For the Lord himself shall descend from heaven with a shout, with the voice of the archangel, and with the trump of God: and the dead in Christ shall rise first: ¹⁷Then we which are alive and remain shall be caught up together with them in the clouds, to meet the Lord in the air: and so shall we ever be with the Lord. ¹⁸Why comfort one another with these words.

5 ¹But of the times and the seasons, brothers, you have no need that I write to you. ²For yourselves know perfectly that the day of the Lord so comes as a thief in the night. ³For when they shall say, Peace and safety; then sudden destruction comes on them, as travail on a woman with child; and they shall not escape. ⁴But you, brothers, are not in darkness, that that day should overtake you as a thief. ⁵You are all the children of light, and the children of the day: we are not of the night, nor of darkness. ⁶Therefore let us not sleep, as do others; but let us watch and be sober. ⁷For they that sleep sleep in the night; and they that be drunken are drunken in the night. ⁸But let us, who are of the day, be sober, putting on the breastplate of faith and love; and for an helmet, the hope of salvation. ⁹For God has not appointed us to wrath, but to obtain salvation by our Lord Jesus Christ, ¹⁰Who died for us, that, whether we wake or sleep, we should live together with him. ¹¹Why comfort yourselves together, and edify one another, even as also you do. ¹²And we beseech you, brothers, to know them which labor among you, and are over you in the Lord, and admonish you; ¹³And to esteem them very highly in love for their work's sake. And be at peace among yourselves. ¹⁴Now we exhort you, brothers, warn them that are unruly, comfort the feebleminded, support the weak, be patient toward all men. ¹⁵See that none render evil for evil to any man; but ever follow that which is good, both among yourselves, and to all men. ¹⁶Rejoice ever more. ¹⁷Pray without ceasing. ¹⁸In every thing give thanks: for this is the will of God in Christ Jesus concerning you. ¹⁹Quench not the Spirit. ²⁰Despise not prophesyings. ²¹Prove all things; hold fast that which is good. ²²Abstain from all appearance of evil. ²³And the very God of peace sanctify you wholly; and I pray God your whole spirit and soul and body be preserved blameless to the coming of our Lord Jesus Christ. ²⁴Faithful is he that calls you, who also will do it. ²⁵Brothers, pray for us. ²⁶Greet all the brothers with an holy kiss. ²⁷I charge you by the Lord that this letter be read to all the holy brothers. ²⁸The grace of our Lord Jesus Christ be with you. Amen.

Second Thessalonians

1 ¹Paul, and Silvanus, and Timotheus, to the church of the Thessalonians in God our Father and the Lord Jesus Christ: ²Grace to you, and peace, from God our Father and the Lord Jesus Christ. ³We are bound to thank God always for you, brothers, as it is meet, because that your faith grows exceedingly, and the charity of every one of you all toward each other abounds; ⁴So that we ourselves glory in you in the churches of God for your patience and faith in all your persecutions and tribulations that you endure: ⁵Which is a manifest token of the righteous judgment of God, that you may be counted worthy of the kingdom of God, for which you also suffer: ⁶Seeing it is a righteous thing with God to recompense tribulation to them that trouble you; ⁷And to you who are troubled rest with us, when the Lord Jesus shall be revealed from heaven with his mighty angels, ⁸In flaming fire taking vengeance on them that know not God, and that obey not the gospel of our Lord Jesus Christ: ⁹Who shall be punished with everlasting destruction from the presence of the Lord, and from the glory of his power; ¹⁰When he shall come to be glorified in his saints, and to be admired in all them that believe (because our testimony among you was believed) in that day. ¹¹Why also we pray always for you, that our God would count you worthy of this calling, and fulfill all the good pleasure of his goodness, and the work of faith with power: ¹²That the name of our Lord Jesus Christ may be glorified in you, and you in him, according to the grace of our God and the Lord Jesus Christ.

2 ¹Now we beseech you, brothers, by the coming of our Lord Jesus Christ, and by our gathering together to him, ²That you be not soon shaken in mind, or be troubled, neither by spirit, nor by word, nor by letter as from us, as that the day of Christ is at hand. ³Let no man deceive you by any means: for that day shall not come, except there come a falling away first, and that man of sin be revealed, the son of perdition; ⁴Who opposes and exalts himself above all that is called God, or that is worshipped; so that he as God sits in the temple of God, showing himself that he is God. ⁵Remember you not, that, when I was yet with you, I told you these things? ⁶And now you know what withholds that he might be revealed in his time. ⁷For the mystery of iniquity does already work: only he who now lets will let, until he be taken out of the way. ⁸And then shall that Wicked be revealed, whom the Lord shall consume with the spirit of his mouth, and shall destroy with the brightness of his coming: ⁹Even him, whose coming is after the working of Satan with all power and signs and lying wonders, ¹⁰And with all delusion of unrighteousness in them that perish; because they received not the love of the truth, that they might be saved. ¹¹And for this cause God shall send them strong delusion, that they should believe a lie: ¹²That they all might be damned who believed not the truth, but had pleasure in unrighteousness. ¹³But we are bound to give thanks always to God for you, brothers beloved of the Lord, because God has from the beginning chosen you to salvation through sanctification of the Spirit and belief of the truth: ¹⁴Whereunto he called you by our gospel, to the obtaining of the glory of our Lord Jesus Christ. ¹⁵Therefore, brothers, stand fast, and hold the traditions which you have been taught, whether by word, or our letter. ¹⁶Now our Lord Jesus Christ himself, and God, even our Father, which has loved us, and has given us everlasting consolation and good hope through grace, ¹⁷Comfort your hearts, and establish you in every good word and work.

3 ¹Finally, brothers, pray for us, that the word of the Lord may have free course, and be glorified, even as it is with you: ²And that we may be delivered from unreasonable and wicked men: for all men have not faith. ³But the Lord is faithful, who shall establish you, and keep you from evil. ⁴And we have confidence in the Lord touching you, that you both do and will do the things which we command you. ⁵And the Lord direct your hearts into the love of God, and into the patient waiting for Christ. ⁶Now we command you, brothers, in the name of our Lord Jesus Christ, that you withdraw yourselves from every brother that walks disorderly, and not after the tradition which he received of us. ⁷For yourselves know how you ought to follow us: for we behaved not ourselves disorderly among you; ⁸Neither did we eat any man's bread for nothing; but worked with labor and travail night and day, that we might not be chargeable to any of you: ⁹Not because we have not power, but to make ourselves an ensample to you to follow us. ¹⁰For even when we were with you, this we commanded you, that if any would not work, neither should he eat. ¹¹For we hear that there are some which walk among you disorderly, working not at all, but are busybodies. ¹²Now them that are such we command and exhort by our Lord Jesus Christ, that with quietness they work, and eat their own bread. ¹³But you, brothers, be not weary in well doing. ¹⁴And if any man obey not our word by this letter, note that man, and have no company with him, that he may be ashamed. ¹⁵Yet count him not as an enemy, but admonish him as a brother. ¹⁶Now the Lord of peace himself give you peace always by all means. The Lord be with you all. ¹⁷The salutation of Paul with my own hand, which is the token in every letter: so I write. ¹⁸The grace of our Lord Jesus Christ be with you all. Amen.

First Timothy

1 ¹Paul, an apostle of Jesus Christ by the commandment of God our Savior, and Lord Jesus Christ, which is our hope; ²To Timothy, my own son in the faith: Grace, mercy, and peace, from God our Father and Jesus Christ our Lord. ³As I sought you to abide still at Ephesus, when I went into Macedonia, that you might charge some that they teach no other doctrine, ⁴Neither give heed to fables and endless genealogies, which minister questions, rather than godly edifying which is in faith: so do. ⁵Now the end of the commandment is charity out of a pure heart, and of a good conscience, and of faith unfeigned: ⁶From which some having swerved have turned aside to vain jangling; ⁷Desiring to be teachers of the law; understanding neither what they say, nor whereof they affirm. ⁸But we know that the law is good, if a man use it lawfully; ⁹Knowing this, that the law is not made for a righteous man, but for the lawless and disobedient, for the ungodly and for sinners, for unholy and profane, for murderers of fathers and murderers of mothers, for murderers, ¹⁰For fornicators, for them that defile themselves with mankind, for enslavers, for liars, for perjured persons, and if there be any other thing that is contrary to sound doctrine; ¹¹According to the glorious gospel of the blessed God, which was committed to my trust. ¹²And I thank Christ Jesus our Lord, who has enabled me, for that he counted me faithful, putting me into the ministry; ¹³Who was before a blasphemer, and a persecutor, and injurious: but I obtained mercy, because I did it ignorantly in unbelief. ¹⁴And the grace of our Lord was exceeding abundant with faith and love which is in Christ Jesus. ¹⁵This is a faithful saying, and worthy of all acceptation, that Christ Jesus came into the world to save sinners; of whom I am chief. ¹⁶However, for this cause I obtained mercy, that in me first Jesus Christ might show forth all long-suffering, for a pattern to them which should hereafter believe on him to life everlasting. ¹⁷Now to the King eternal, immortal, invisible, the only wise God, be honor and glory for ever and ever. Amen. ¹⁸This charge I commit to you, son Timothy, according to the prophecies which went before on you, that you by them might war a good warfare; ¹⁹Holding faith, and a good conscience; which some having put away concerning faith have made shipwreck: ²⁰Of whom is Hymenaeus and Alexander; whom I have delivered to Satan, that they may learn not to blaspheme.

2 ¹I exhort therefore, that, first of all, supplications, prayers, intercessions, and giving of thanks, be made for all men; ²For kings, and for all that are in authority; that we may lead a quiet and peaceable life in all godliness and honesty. ³For this is good and acceptable in the sight of God our Savior; ⁴Who will have all men to be saved, and to come to the knowledge of the truth. ⁵For there is one God, and one mediator between God and men, the man Christ Jesus; ⁶Who gave himself a ransom for all, to be testified in due time. ⁷Whereunto I am ordained a preacher, and an apostle, (I speak the truth in Christ, and lie not;) a teacher of the Gentiles in faith and verity. ⁸I will therefore that men pray every where, lifting up holy hands, without wrath and doubting. ⁹In like manner also, that women adorn themselves in modest apparel, with modesty and sobriety; not with braided hair, or gold, or pearls, or costly array; ¹⁰But (which becomes women professing godliness) with good works. ¹¹Let the woman learn in silence with all subjection. ¹²But I suffer not a woman to teach, nor to usurp authority over the man, but to be in silence. ¹³For Adam was first formed, then Eve. ¹⁴And Adam was not deceived, but the woman being deceived was in the transgression. ¹⁵Notwithstanding she shall be saved in childbearing, if they continue in faith and charity and holiness with sobriety.

3 ¹This is a true saying, If a man desire the office of a bishop, he desires a good work. ²A bishop then must be blameless, the husband of one wife, vigilant, sober, of good behavior, given to hospitality, apt to teach; ³Not given to wine, no striker, not greedy of filthy lucre; but patient, not a brawler, not covetous; ⁴One that rules well his own house, having his children in subjection with all gravity; ⁵(For if a man know not how to rule his own house, how shall he take care of the church of God?) ⁶Not a novice, lest being lifted up with pride he fall into the condemnation of the devil. ⁷Moreover he must have a good report of them which are without; lest he fall into reproach and the snare of the devil. ⁸Likewise must the deacons be grave, not double-tongued, not given to much wine, not greedy of filthy lucre; ⁹Holding the mystery of the faith in a pure conscience. ¹⁰And let these also first be proved; then let them use the office of a deacon, being found blameless. ¹¹Even so must their wives be grave, not slanderers, sober, faithful in all things. ¹²Let the deacons be the husbands of one wife, ruling their children and their own houses well. ¹³For they that have used the office of a deacon well purchase to themselves a good degree, and great boldness in the faith which is in Christ Jesus. ¹⁴These things write I to you, hoping to come to you shortly: ¹⁵But if I tarry long, that you may know how you ought to behave yourself in the house of God, which is the church of the living God, the pillar and ground of the truth. ¹⁶And without controversy great is the mystery of godliness: God was manifest in the flesh, justified in the Spirit, seen of angels, preached to the Gentiles, believed on in the world, received up into glory.

4 ¹Now the Spirit speaks expressly, that in the latter times some shall depart from the faith, giving heed to seducing spirits, and doctrines of devils; ²Speaking lies in hypocrisy; having their conscience seared with a hot iron; ³Forbidding to marry, and commanding to abstain from meats, which God has created to be received with thanksgiving of them which believe and know the truth. ⁴For every creature of God is good, and nothing to be refused, if it be received with thanksgiving: ⁵For it is sanctified by the word of God and prayer. ⁶If you put the brothers in remembrance of these things, you shall be a good minister of Jesus Christ, nourished up in the words of faith and of good doctrine, to which you have attained. ⁷But refuse profane and old wives' fables, and exercise yourself rather to godliness. ⁸For bodily exercise profits little: but godliness is profitable to all things, having promise of the life that now is, and of that which is to come. ⁹This is a faithful saying and worthy of all acceptation. ¹⁰For therefore we both labor and suffer reproach, because we trust in the living God, who is the Savior of all men, specially of those that believe. ¹¹These things command and teach. ¹²Let no man despise your youth; but be you an example of the believers, in word, in conversation, in charity, in spirit, in faith, in purity. ¹³Till I come, give attendance to reading, to exhortation, to doctrine. ¹⁴Neglect not the gift that is in you, which was given you by prophecy, with the laying on of the hands of the presbytery. ¹⁵Meditate on these things; give yourself wholly to them; that your profiting may appear to all. ¹⁶Take heed to yourself, and to the doctrine; continue in them: for in doing this you shall both save yourself, and them that hear you.

5 ¹Rebuke not an elder, but entreat him as a father; and the younger men as brothers; ²The elder women as mothers; the younger as sisters, with all purity. ³Honor widows that are widows indeed. ⁴But if any widow have children or nephews, let them learn first to show piety at home, and to requite their parents: for that is good and acceptable before God. ⁵Now she that is a widow indeed, and desolate, trusts in God, and continues in supplications and prayers night and day. ⁶But she that lives in pleasure is dead while she lives. ⁷And these things give in charge, that they may be blameless. ⁸But if any provide not for his own, and specially for those of his own house, he has denied the faith, and is worse than an infidel. ⁹Let not a widow be taken into the number under three score years old, having been the wife of one man. ¹⁰Well reported of for good works; if she have brought up children, if she have lodged strangers, if she have washed the saints' feet, if she have relieved the afflicted, if she have diligently followed every good work. ¹¹But the younger widows refuse: for when they have begun to wax wanton against Christ, they will marry; ¹²Having damnation, because they have cast off their first faith. ¹³And with they learn to be idle, wandering about from house to house; and not only idle, but tattlers also and busybodies, speaking things which they should not. ¹⁴I will therefore that the younger women marry, bear children, guide the house, give none occasion to the adversary to speak reproachfully. ¹⁵For some are already turned aside after Satan. ¹⁶If any man or woman that believes have widows, let them relieve them, and let not the church be charged; that it may relieve them that are widows indeed. ¹⁷Let the elders that rule well be counted worthy of double honor, especially they who labor in the word and doctrine. ¹⁸For the scripture says, You shall not muzzle the ox that treads out the corn. And, The laborer is worthy of his reward. ¹⁹Against an elder receive not an accusation, but before two or three witnesses. ²⁰Them that sin rebuke before all, that others also may fear. ²¹I charge you before God, and the Lord Jesus Christ, and the elect angels, that you observe these things without preferring one before another, doing nothing by partiality. ²²Lay hands suddenly on no man, neither be partaker of other men's sins: keep yourself pure. ²³Drink no longer water, but use a little wine for your stomach's sake and your often infirmities. ²⁴Some men's sins are open beforehand, going before to judgment; and some men they follow after. ²⁵Likewise also the good works of some are manifest beforehand; and they that are otherwise cannot be hid.

6 ¹Let as many servants as are under the yoke count their own masters worthy of all honor, that the name of God and his doctrine be not blasphemed. ²And they that have believing masters, let them not despise them, because they are brothers; but rather do them service, because they are faithful and beloved, partakers of the benefit. These things teach and exhort. ³If any man teach otherwise, and consent not to wholesome words, even the words of our Lord Jesus Christ, and to the doctrine which is according to godliness; ⁴He is proud, knowing nothing, but doting about questions and strifes of words, whereof comes envy, strife, railings, evil surmisings, ⁵Perverse disputings of men of corrupt minds, and destitute of the truth, supposing that gain is godliness: from such withdraw yourself. ⁶But godliness with contentment is great gain. ⁷For we brought nothing into this world, and it is certain we can carry nothing out. ⁸And having food and raiment let us be therewith content. ⁹But they that will be rich fall into temptation and a snare, and into many foolish and hurtful lusts, which drown men in destruction and perdition. ¹⁰For the love of money is the root of all evil: which while some coveted after, they have erred from the faith, and pierced themselves through with many sorrows. ¹¹But you, O man of God, flee these things; and follow after righteousness, godliness, faith, love, patience, meekness. ¹²Fight the good fight of faith, lay hold on eternal life, to which you are also called, and have professed a good profession before many witnesses. ¹³I give you charge in the sight of God, who vivifies all things, and before Christ Jesus, who before Pontius Pilate witnessed a good confession; ¹⁴That you keep this commandment without spot, unrebukable, until the appearing of our Lord Jesus Christ: ¹⁵Which in his times he shall show, who is the blessed and only Potentate, the King of kings, and Lord of lords; ¹⁶Who only has immortality, dwelling in the light which no man can approach to; whom no man has seen, nor can see: to whom be honor and power everlasting. Amen. ¹⁷Charge them that are rich in this world, that they be not high minded, nor trust in uncertain riches, but in the living God, who gives us richly all things to enjoy; ¹⁸That they do good, that they be rich in good works, ready to distribute, willing to communicate; ¹⁹Laying up in store for themselves a good foundation against the time to come, that they may lay hold on eternal life. ²⁰O Timothy, keep that which is committed to your trust, avoiding profane and vain babblings, and oppositions of science falsely so called: ²¹Which some professing have erred concerning the faith. Grace be with you. Amen.

Second Timothy

1 ¹Paul, an apostle of Jesus Christ by the will of God, according to the promise of life which is in Christ Jesus, ²To Timothy, my dearly beloved son: Grace, mercy, and peace, from God the Father and Christ Jesus our Lord. ³I thank God, whom I serve from my forefathers with pure conscience, that without ceasing I have remembrance of you in my prayers night and day; ⁴Greatly desiring to see you, being mindful of your tears, that I may be filled with joy; ⁵When I call to remembrance the unfeigned faith that is in you, which dwelled first in your grandmother Lois, and your mother Eunice; and I am persuaded that in you also. ⁶Why I put you in remembrance that you stir up the gift of God, which is in you by the putting on of my hands. ⁷For God has not given us the spirit of fear; but of power, and of love, and of a sound mind. ⁸Be not you therefore ashamed of the testimony of our Lord, nor of me his prisoner: but be you partaker of the afflictions of the gospel according to the power of God; ⁹Who has saved us, and called us with an holy calling, not according to our works, but according to his own purpose and grace, which was given us in Christ Jesus before the world began, ¹⁰But is now made manifest by the appearing of our Savior Jesus Christ, who has abolished death, and has brought life and immortality to light through the gospel: ¹¹Whereunto I am appointed a preacher, and an apostle, and a teacher of the Gentiles. ¹²For the which cause I also suffer these things: nevertheless I am not ashamed: for I know whom I have believed, and am persuaded that he is able to keep that which I have committed to him against that day. ¹³Hold fast the form of sound words, which you have heard of me, in faith and love which is in Christ Jesus. ¹⁴That good thing which was committed to you keep by the Holy Ghost which dwells in us. ¹⁵This you know, that all they which are in Asia be turned away from me; of whom are Phygellus and Hermogenes. ¹⁶The Lord give mercy to the house of Onesiphorus; for he oft refreshed me, and was not ashamed of my chain: ¹⁷But, when he was in Rome, he sought me out very diligently, and found me. ¹⁸The Lord grant to him that he may find mercy of the Lord in that day: and in how many things he ministered to me at Ephesus, you know very well.

2 ¹You therefore, my son, be strong in the grace that is in Christ Jesus. ²And the things that you have heard of me among many witnesses, the same commit you to faithful men, who shall be able to teach others also. ³You therefore endure hardness, as a good soldier of Jesus Christ. ⁴No man that wars entangles himself with the affairs of this life; that he may please him who has chosen him to be a soldier. ⁵And if a man also strive for masteries, yet is he not crowned, except he strive lawfully. ⁶The farmer that labors must be first partaker of the fruits. ⁷Consider what I say; and the Lord give you understanding in all things. ⁸Remember that Jesus Christ of the seed of David was raised from the dead according to my gospel: ⁹Wherein I suffer trouble, as an evil doer, even to bonds; but the word of God is not bound. ¹⁰Therefore I endure all things for the elect's sakes, that they may also obtain the salvation which is in Christ Jesus with eternal glory. ¹¹It is a faithful saying: For if we be dead with him, we shall also live with him: ¹²If we suffer, we shall also reign with him: if we deny him, he also will deny us: ¹³If we believe not, yet he stays faithful: he cannot deny himself. ¹⁴Of these things put them in remembrance, charging them before the Lord that they strive not about words to no profit, but to the subverting of the hearers. ¹⁵Study to show yourself approved to God, a workman that needs not to be ashamed, rightly dividing the word of truth. ¹⁶But shun profane and vain babblings: for they will increase to more ungodliness. ¹⁷And their word will eat as does a canker: of whom is Hymenaeus and Philetus; ¹⁸Who concerning the truth have erred, saying that the resurrection is past already; and overthrow the faith of some. ¹⁹Nevertheless the foundation of God stands sure, having this seal, The Lord knows them that are his. And, Let every one that names the name of Christ depart from iniquity. ²⁰But in a great house there are not only vessels of gold and of silver, but also of wood and of earth; and some to honor, and some to dishonor. ²¹If a man therefore purge himself from these, he shall be a vessel to honor, sanctified, and meet for the master's use, and prepared to every good work. ²²Flee also youthful lusts: but follow righteousness, faith, charity, peace, with them that call on the Lord out of a pure heart. ²³But foolish and unlearned questions avoid, knowing that they do engender strifes. ²⁴And the servant of the Lord must not strive; but be gentle to all men, apt to teach, patient, ²⁵In meekness instructing those that oppose themselves; if God peradventure will give them repentance to the acknowledging of the truth; ²⁶And that they may recover themselves out of the snare of the devil, who are taken captive by him at his will.

3 ¹This know also, that in the last days perilous times shall come. ²For men shall be lovers of their own selves, covetous, boasters, proud, blasphemers, disobedient to parents, unthankful, unholy, ³Without natural affection, truce breakers, false accusers, incontinent, fierce, despisers of those that are good, ⁴Traitors, heady, high minded, lovers of pleasures more than lovers of God; ⁵Having a form of godliness, but denying the power thereof: from such turn away. ⁶For of this sort are they which creep into houses, and lead captive silly women laden with sins, led away with divers lusts, ⁷Ever learning, and never able to come to the knowledge of the truth. ⁸Now as Jannes and Jambres withstood Moses, so do these also resist the truth: men of corrupt minds, reprobate concerning the faith. ⁹But they shall proceed no further: for their folly shall be manifest to all men, as theirs also was. ¹⁰But you have fully known my doctrine, manner of life, purpose, faith, long-suffering, charity, patience, ¹¹Persecutions, afflictions, which came to me at Antioch, at Iconium, at Lystra; what persecutions I endured: but out of them all the Lord delivered me. ¹²Yes, and all that will live godly in Christ Jesus shall suffer persecution. ¹³But evil men and seducers shall wax worse and worse, deceiving, and being deceived. ¹⁴But continue you in the things which you have learned and have been assured of, knowing of whom you have learned them; ¹⁵And that from a child you have known the holy scriptures, which are able to make you wise to salvation through faith which is in Christ Jesus. ¹⁶All scripture is given by inspiration of God, and is profitable for doctrine, for reproof, for correction, for instruction in righteousness: ¹⁷That the man of God may be perfect, thoroughly furnished to all good works.

4 ¹I charge you therefore before God, and the Lord Jesus Christ, who shall judge the quick and the dead at his appearing and his kingdom; ²Preach the word; be instant in season, out of season; reprove, rebuke, exhort with all longsuffering and doctrine. ³For the time will come when they will not endure sound doctrine; but after their own lusts shall they heap to themselves teachers, having itching ears; ⁴And they shall turn away their ears from the truth, and shall be turned to fables. ⁵But watch you in all things, endure afflictions, do the work of an evangelist, make full proof of your ministry. ⁶For I am now ready to be offered, and the time of my departure is at hand. ⁷I have fought a good fight, I have finished my course, I have kept the faith: ⁸From now on there is laid up for me a crown of righteousness, which the Lord, the righteous judge, shall give me at that day: and not to me only, but to all them also that love his appearing. ⁹Do your diligence to come shortly to me: ¹⁰For Demas has forsaken me, having loved this present world, and is departed to Thessalonica; Crescens to Galatia, Titus to Dalmatia. ¹¹Only Luke is with me. Take Mark, and bring him with you: for he is profitable to me for the ministry. ¹²And Tychicus have I sent to Ephesus. ¹³The cloak that I left at Troas with Carpus, when you come, bring with you, and the books, but especially the parchments. ¹⁴Alexander the coppersmith did me much evil: the Lord reward him according to his works: ¹⁵Of whom be you ware also; for he has greatly withstood our words. ¹⁶At my first answer no man stood with me, but all men forsook me: I pray God that it may not be laid to their charge. ¹⁷Notwithstanding the Lord stood with me, and strengthened me; that by me the preaching might be fully known, and that all the Gentiles might hear: and I was delivered out of the mouth of the lion. ¹⁸And the Lord shall deliver me from every evil work, and will preserve me to his heavenly kingdom: to whom be glory for ever and ever. Amen. ¹⁹Salute Prisca and Aquila, and the household of Onesiphorus. ²⁰Erastus stayed at Corinth: but Trophimus have I left at Miletum sick. ²¹Do your diligence to come before winter. Eubulus greets you, and Pudens, and Linus, and Claudia, and all the brothers. ²²The Lord Jesus Christ be with your spirit. Grace be with you. Amen.

Titus

1 ¹Paul, a servant of God, and an apostle of Jesus Christ, according to the faith of God's elect, and the acknowledging of the truth which is after godliness; ²In hope of eternal life, which God, that cannot lie, promised before the world began; ³But has in due times manifested his word through preaching, which is committed to me according to the commandment of God our Savior; ⁴To Titus, my own son after the common faith: Grace, mercy, and peace, from God the Father and the Lord Jesus Christ our Savior. ⁵For this cause left I you in Crete, that you should set in order the things that are wanting, and ordain elders in every city, as I had appointed you: ⁶If any be blameless, the husband of one wife, having faithful children not accused of riot or unruly. ⁷For a bishop must be blameless, as the steward of God; not self-willed, not soon angry, not given to wine, no striker, not given to filthy lucre; ⁸But a lover of hospitality, a lover of good men, sober, just, holy, temperate; ⁹Holding fast the faithful word as he has been taught, that he may be able by sound doctrine both to exhort and to convince the disputers. ¹⁰For there are many unruly and vain talkers and deceivers, specially they of the circumcision: ¹¹Whose mouths must be stopped, who subvert whole houses, teaching things which they should not, for filthy lucre's sake. ¹²One of themselves, even a prophet of their own, said, The Cretians are always liars, evil beasts, slow bellies. ¹³This witness is true. Why rebuke them sharply, that they may be sound in the faith; ¹⁴Not giving heed to Jewish fables, and commandments of men, that turn from the truth. ¹⁵To the pure all things are pure: but to them that are defiled and unbelieving is nothing pure; but even their mind and conscience is defiled. ¹⁶They profess that they know God; but in works they deny him, being abominable, and disobedient, and to every good work reprobate.

2 ¹But speak you the things which become sound doctrine: ²That the aged men be sober, grave, temperate, sound in faith, in charity, in patience. ³The aged women likewise, that they be in behavior as becomes holiness, not false accusers, not given to much wine, teachers of good things; ⁴That they may teach the young women to be sober, to love their husbands, to love their children, ⁵To be discreet, chaste, keepers at home, good, obedient to their own husbands, that the word of God be not blasphemed. ⁶Young men likewise exhort to be sober minded. ⁷In all things showing yourself a pattern of good works: in doctrine showing soundness, gravity, sincerity, ⁸Sound speech, that cannot be condemned; that he that is of the contrary part may be ashamed, having no evil thing to say of you. ⁹Exhort servants to be obedient to their own masters, and to please them well in all things; not answering again; ¹⁰Not purloining, but showing all good fidelity; that they may adorn the doctrine of God our Savior in all things. ¹¹For the grace of God that brings salvation has appeared to all men, ¹²Teaching us that, denying ungodliness and worldly lusts, we should live soberly, righteously, and godly, in this present world; ¹³Looking for that blessed hope, and the glorious appearing of the great God and our Savior Jesus Christ; ¹⁴Who gave himself for us, that he might redeem us from all iniquity, and purify to himself a peculiar people, zealous of good works. ¹⁵These things speak, and exhort, and rebuke with all authority. Let no man despise you.

3 ¹Put them in mind to be subject to principalities and powers, to obey magistrates, to be ready to every good work, ²To speak evil of no man, to be no brawlers, but gentle, showing all meekness to all men. ³For we ourselves also were sometimes foolish, disobedient, deceived, serving divers lusts and pleasures, living in malice and envy, hateful, and hating one another. ⁴But after that the kindness and love of God our Savior toward man appeared, ⁵Not by works of righteousness which we have done, but according to his mercy he saved us, by the washing of regeneration, and renewing of the Holy Ghost; ⁶Which he shed on us abundantly through Jesus Christ our Savior; ⁷That being justified by his grace, we should be made heirs according to the hope of eternal life. ⁸This is a faithful saying, and these things I will that you affirm constantly, that they which have believed in God might be careful to maintain good works. These things are good and profitable to men. ⁹But avoid foolish questions, and genealogies, and contentions, and strivings about the law; for they are unprofitable and vain. ¹⁰A man that is an heretic after the first and second admonition reject; ¹¹Knowing that he that is such is subverted, and sins, being condemned of himself. ¹²When I shall send Artemas to you, or Tychicus, be diligent to come to me to Nicopolis: for I have determined there to winter. ¹³Bring Zenas the lawyer and Apollos on their journey diligently, that nothing be wanting to them. ¹⁴And let ours also learn to maintain good works for necessary uses, that they be not unfruitful. ¹⁵All that are with me salute you. Greet them that love us in the faith. Grace be with you all. Amen.

Philemon

1 ¹Paul, a prisoner of Jesus Christ, and Timothy our brother, to Philemon our dearly beloved, and fellow laborer, ²And to our beloved Apphia, and Archippus our fellow soldier, and to the church in your house: ³Grace to you, and peace, from God our Father and the Lord Jesus Christ. ⁴I thank my God, making mention of you always in my prayers, ⁵Hearing of your love and faith, which you have toward the Lord Jesus, and toward all saints; ⁶That the communication of your faith may become effectual by the acknowledging of every good thing which is in you in Christ Jesus. ⁷For we have great joy and consolation in your love, because the bowels of the saints are refreshed by you, brother. ⁸Why, though I might be much bold in Christ to enjoin you that which is convenient, ⁹Yet for love's sake I rather beseech you, being such an one as Paul the aged, and now also a prisoner of Jesus Christ. ¹⁰I beseech you for my son Onesimus, whom I have begotten in my bonds: ¹¹Which in time past was to you unprofitable, but now profitable to you and to me: ¹²Whom I have sent again: you therefore receive him, that is, my own bowels: ¹³Whom I would have retained with me, that in your stead he might have ministered to me in the bonds of the gospel: ¹⁴But without your mind would I do nothing; that your benefit should not be as it were of necessity, but willingly. ¹⁵For perhaps he therefore departed for a season, that you should receive him for ever; ¹⁶Not now as a servant, but above a servant, a brother beloved, specially to me, but how much more to you, both in the flesh, and in the Lord? ¹⁷If you count me therefore a partner, receive him as myself. ¹⁸If he has wronged you, or owes you something, put that on my account; ¹⁹I Paul have written it with my own hand, I will repay it: albeit I do not say to you how you owe to me even your own self besides. ²⁰Yes, brother, let me have joy of you in the Lord: refresh my bowels in the Lord. ²¹Having confidence in your obedience I wrote to you, knowing that you will also do more than I say. ²²But with prepare me also a lodging: for I trust that through your prayers I shall be given to you. ²³There salute you Epaphras, my fellow prisoner in Christ Jesus; ²⁴Marcus, Aristarchus, Demas, Lucas, my fellow laborers. ²⁵The grace of our Lord Jesus Christ be with your spirit. Amen.

Hebrews

1 ¹God, who at sundry times and in divers manners spoke in time past to the fathers by the prophets, ²Has in these last days spoken to us by his Son, whom he has appointed heir of all things, by whom also he made the worlds; ³Who being the brightness of his glory, and the express image of his person, and upholding all things by the word of his power, when he had by himself purged our sins, sat down on the right hand of the Majesty on high: ⁴Being made so much better than the angels, as he has by inheritance obtained a more excellent name than they. ⁵For to which of the angels said he at any time, You are my Son, this day have I begotten you? And again, I will be to him a Father, and he shall be to me a Son? ⁶And again, when he brings in the first-begotten into the world, he says, And let all the angels of God worship him. ⁷And of the angels he says, Who makes his angels spirits, and his ministers a flame of fire. ⁸But to the Son he says, Your throne, O God, is for ever and ever: a scepter of righteousness is the scepter of your kingdom. ⁹You have loved righteousness, and hated iniquity; therefore God, even your God, has anointed you with the oil of gladness above your fellows. ¹⁰And, You, Lord, in the beginning have laid the foundation of the earth; and the heavens are the works of your hands: ¹¹They shall perish; but you remain; and they all shall wax old as does a garment; ¹²And as a clothing shall you fold them up, and they shall be changed: but you are the same, and your years shall not fail. ¹³But to which of the angels said he at any time, Sit on my right hand, until I make your enemies your footstool? ¹⁴Are they not all ministering spirits, sent forth to minister for them who shall be heirs of salvation?

2 ¹Therefore we ought to give the more earnest heed to the things which we have heard, lest at any time we should let them slip. ²For if the word spoken by angels was steadfast, and every transgression and disobedience received a just recompense of reward; ³How shall we escape, if we neglect so great salvation; which at the first began to be spoken by the Lord, and was confirmed to us by them that heard him; ⁴God also bearing them witness, both with signs and wonders, and with divers miracles, and gifts of the Holy Ghost, according to his own will? ⁵For to the angels has he not put in subjection the world to come, whereof we speak. ⁶But one in a certain place testified, saying, What is man, that you are mindful of him? or the son of man that you visit him? ⁷You made him a little lower than the angels; you crowned him with glory and honor, and did set him over the works of your hands: ⁸You have put all things in subjection under his feet. For in that he put all in subjection under him, he left nothing that is not put under him. But now we see not yet all things put under him. ⁹But we see Jesus, who was made a little lower than the angels for the suffering of death, crowned with glory and honor; that he by the grace of God should taste death for every man. ¹⁰For it became him, for whom are all things, and by whom are all things, in bringing many sons to glory, to make the captain of their salvation perfect through sufferings. ¹¹For both he that sanctifies and they who are sanctified are all of one: for which cause he is not ashamed to call them brothers, ¹²Saying, I will declare your name to my brothers, in the middle of the church will I sing praise to you. ¹³And again, I will put my trust in him. And again, Behold I and the children which God has given me. ¹⁴For as much then as the children are partakers of flesh and blood, he also himself likewise took part of the same; that through death he might destroy him that had the power of death, that is, the devil; ¹⁵And deliver them who through fear of death were all their lifetime subject to bondage. ¹⁶For truly he took not on him the nature of angels; but he took on him the seed of Abraham. ¹⁷Why in all things it behooved him to be made like to his brothers, that he might be a merciful and faithful high priest in things pertaining to God, to make reconciliation for the sins of the people. ¹⁸For in that he himself has suffered being tempted, he is able to succor them that are tempted.

3 ¹Why, holy brothers, partakers of the heavenly calling, consider the Apostle and High Priest of our profession, Christ Jesus; ²Who was faithful to him that appointed him, as also Moses was faithful in all his house. ³For this man was counted worthy of more glory than Moses, inasmuch as he who has built the house has more honor than the house. ⁴For every house is built by some man; but he that built all things is God. ⁵And Moses truly was faithful in all his house, as a servant, for a testimony of those things which were to be spoken after; ⁶But Christ as a son over his own house; whose house are we, if we hold fast the confidence and the rejoicing of the hope firm to the end. ⁷Why (as the Holy Ghost says, To day if you will hear his voice, ⁸Harden not your hearts, as in the provocation, in the day of temptation in the wilderness: ⁹When your fathers tempted me, proved me, and saw my works forty years. ¹⁰Why I was grieved with that generation, and said, They do always err in their heart; and they have not known my ways. ¹¹So I swore in my wrath, They shall not enter into my rest.) ¹²Take heed, brothers, lest there be in any of you an evil heart of unbelief, in departing from the living God. ¹³But exhort one another daily, while it is called To day; lest any of you be hardened through the deceitfulness of sin. ¹⁴For we are made partakers of Christ, if we hold the beginning of our confidence steadfast to the end; ¹⁵While it is said, To day if you will hear his voice, harden not your hearts, as in the provocation. ¹⁶For some, when they had heard, did provoke: however, not all that came out of Egypt by Moses. ¹⁷But with whom was he grieved forty years? was it not with them that had sinned, whose carcasses fell in the wilderness? ¹⁸And to whom swore he that they should not enter into his rest, but to them that believed not? ¹⁹So we see that they could not enter in because of unbelief.

4 ¹Let us therefore fear, lest, a promise being left us of entering into his rest, any of you should seem to come short of it. ²For to us was the gospel preached, as well as to them: but the word preached did not profit them, not being mixed with faith in them that heard it. ³For we which have believed do enter into rest, as he said, As I have sworn in my wrath, if they shall enter into my rest: although the works were finished from the foundation of the world. ⁴For he

spoke in a certain place of the seventh day on this wise, And God did rest the seventh day from all his works. ⁵And in this place again, If they shall enter into my rest. ⁶Seeing therefore it remains that some must enter therein, and they to whom it was first preached entered not in because of unbelief: ⁷Again, he limits a certain day, saying in David, To day, after so long a time; as it is said, To day if you will hear his voice, harden not your hearts. ⁸For if Jesus had given them rest, then would he not afterward have spoken of another day. ⁹There remains therefore a rest to the people of God. ¹⁰For he that is entered into his rest, he also has ceased from his own works, as God did from his. ¹¹Let us labor therefore to enter into that rest, lest any man fall after the same example of unbelief. ¹²For the word of God is quick, and powerful, and sharper than any two edged sword, piercing even to the dividing asunder of soul and spirit, and of the joints and marrow, and is a discerner of the thoughts and intents of the heart. ¹³Neither is there any creature that is not manifest in his sight: but all things are naked and opened to the eyes of him with whom we have to do. ¹⁴Seeing then that we have a great high priest, that is passed into the heavens, Jesus the Son of God, let us hold fast our profession. ¹⁵For we have not an high priest which cannot be touched with the feeling of our infirmities; but was in all points tempted like as we are, yet without sin. ¹⁶Let us therefore come boldly to the throne of grace, that we may obtain mercy, and find grace to help in time of need.

5 ¹For every high priest taken from among men is ordained for men in things pertaining to God, that he may offer both gifts and sacrifices for sins: ²Who can have compassion on the ignorant, and on them that are out of the way; for that he himself also is compassed with infirmity. ³And by reason hereof he ought, as for the people, so also for himself, to offer for sins. ⁴And no man takes this honor to himself, but he that is called of God, as was Aaron. ⁵So also Christ glorified not himself to be made an high priest; but he that said to him, You are my Son, to day have I begotten you. ⁶As he says also in another place, You are a priest for ever after the order of Melchisedec. ⁷Who in the days of his flesh, when he had offered up prayers and supplications with strong crying and tears to him that was able to save him from death, and was heard in that he feared; ⁸Though he were a Son, yet learned he obedience by the things which he suffered; ⁹And being made perfect, he became the author of eternal salvation to all them that obey him; ¹⁰Called of God an high priest after the order of Melchisedec. ¹¹Of whom we have many things to say, and hard to be uttered, seeing you are dull of hearing. ¹²For when for the time you ought to be teachers, you have need that one teach you again which be the first principles of the oracles of God; and are become such as have need of milk, and not of strong meat. ¹³For every one that uses milk is unskillful in the word of righteousness: for he is a babe. ¹⁴But strong meat belongs to them that are of full age, even those who by reason of use have their senses exercised to discern both good and evil.

6 ¹Therefore leaving the principles of the doctrine of Christ, let us go on to perfection; not laying again the foundation of repentance from dead works, and of faith toward God, ²Of the doctrine of baptisms, and of laying on of hands, and of resurrection of the dead, and of eternal judgment. ³And this will we do, if God permit. ⁴For it is impossible for those who were once enlightened, and have tasted of the heavenly gift, and were made partakers of the Holy Ghost, ⁵And have tasted the good word of God, and the powers of the world to come, ⁶If they shall fall away, to renew them again to repentance; seeing they crucify to themselves the Son of God afresh, and put him to an open shame. ⁷For the earth which drinks in the rain that comes oft on it, and brings forth herbs meet for them by whom it is dressed, receives blessing from God: ⁸But that which bears thorns and briers is rejected, and is near to cursing; whose end is to be burned. ⁹But, beloved, we are persuaded better things of you, and things that accompany salvation, though we thus speak. ¹⁰For God is not unrighteous to forget your work and labor of love, which you have showed toward his name, in that you have ministered to the saints, and do minister. ¹¹And we desire that every one of you do show the same diligence to the full assurance of hope to the end: ¹²That you be not slothful, but followers of them who through faith and patience inherit the promises. ¹³For when God made promise to Abraham, because he could swear by no greater, he swore by himself, ¹⁴Saying, Surely blessing I will bless you, and multiplying I will multiply you. ¹⁵And so, after he had patiently endured, he obtained the promise. ¹⁶For men truly swear by the greater: and an oath for confirmation is to them an end of all strife. ¹⁷Wherein God, willing more abundantly to show to the heirs of promise the immutability of his counsel, confirmed it by an oath: ¹⁸That by two immutable things, in which it was impossible for God to lie, we might have a strong consolation, who have fled for refuge to lay hold on the hope set before us: ¹⁹Which hope we have as an anchor of the soul, both sure and steadfast, and which enters into that within the veil; ²⁰Where the forerunner is for us entered, even Jesus, made an high priest for ever after the order of Melchisedec.

7 ¹For this Melchisedec, king of Salem, priest of the most high God, who met Abraham returning from the slaughter of the kings, and blessed him; ²To whom also Abraham gave a tenth part of all; first being by interpretation King of righteousness, and after that also King of Salem, which is, King of peace; ³Without father, without mother, without descent, having neither beginning of days, nor end of life; but made like to the Son of God; stays a priest continually. ⁴Now consider how great this man was, to whom even the patriarch Abraham gave the tenth of the spoils. ⁵And truly they that are of the sons of Levi, who receive the office of the priesthood, have a commandment to take tithes of the people according to the law, that is, of their brothers, though they come out of the loins of Abraham: ⁶But he whose descent is not counted from them received tithes of Abraham, and blessed him that had the promises. ⁷And without all contradiction the less is blessed of the better. ⁸And here men that die receive tithes; but there he receives them, of whom it is witnessed that he lives. ⁹And as I may so say, Levi also, who receives tithes, paid tithes in Abraham. ¹⁰For he was yet in the loins of his father, when Melchisedec met him. ¹¹If therefore perfection were by the

Levitical priesthood, (for under it the people received the law,) what further need was there that another priest should rise after the order of Melchisedec, and not be called after the order of Aaron? ¹²For the priesthood being changed, there is made of necessity a change also of the law. ¹³For he of whom these things are spoken pertains to another tribe, of which no man gave attendance at the altar. ¹⁴For it is evident that our Lord sprang out of Juda; of which tribe Moses spoke nothing concerning priesthood. ¹⁵And it is yet far more evident: for that after the similitude of Melchisedec there rises another priest, ¹⁶Who is made, not after the law of a carnal commandment, but after the power of an endless life. ¹⁷For he testifies, You are a priest for ever after the order of Melchisedec. ¹⁸For there is truly a cancellation of the commandment going before for the weakness and unprofitableness thereof. ¹⁹For the law made nothing perfect, but the bringing in of a better hope did; by the which we draw near to God. ²⁰And inasmuch as not without an oath he was made priest: ²¹(For those priests were made without an oath; but this with an oath by him that said to him, The Lord swore and will not repent, You are a priest for ever after the order of Melchisedec:) ²²By so much was Jesus made a surety of a better testament. ²³And they truly were many priests, because they were not suffered to continue by reason of death: ²⁴But this man, because he continues ever, has an unchangeable priesthood. ²⁵Why he is able also to save them to the uttermost that come to God by him, seeing he ever lives to make intercession for them. ²⁶For such an high priest became us, who is holy, harmless, undefiled, separate from sinners, and made higher than the heavens; ²⁷Who needs not daily, as those high priests, to offer up sacrifice, first for his own sins, and then for the people's: for this he did once, when he offered up himself. ²⁸For the law makes men high priests which have infirmity; but the word of the oath, which was since the law, makes the Son, who is consecrated for ever more.

8 ¹Now of the things which we have spoken this is the sum: We have such an high priest, who is set on the right hand of the throne of the Majesty in the heavens; ²A minister of the sanctuary, and of the true tabernacle, which the Lord pitched, and not man. ³For every high priest is ordained to offer gifts and sacrifices: why it is of necessity that this man have somewhat also to offer. ⁴For if he were on earth, he should not be a priest, seeing that there are priests that offer gifts according to the law: ⁵Who serve to the example and shadow of heavenly things, as Moses was admonished of God when he was about to make the tabernacle: for, See, says he, that you make all things according to the pattern showed to you in the mount. ⁶But now has he obtained a more excellent ministry, by how much also he is the mediator of a better covenant, which was established on better promises. ⁷For if that first covenant had been faultless, then should no place have been sought for the second. ⁸For finding fault with them, he says, Behold, the days come, says the Lord, when I will make a new covenant with the house of Israel and with the house of Judah: ⁹Not according to the covenant that I made with their fathers in the day when I took them by the hand to lead them out of the land of Egypt; because they continued not in my covenant, and I regarded them not, says the Lord. ¹⁰For this is the covenant that I will make with the house of Israel after those days, says the Lord; I will put my laws into their mind, and write them in their hearts: and I will be to them a God, and they shall be to me a people: ¹¹And they shall not teach every man his neighbor, and every man his brother, saying, Know the Lord: for all shall know me, from the least to the greatest. ¹²For I will be merciful to their unrighteousness, and their sins and their iniquities will I remember no more. ¹³In that he says, A new covenant, he has made the first old. Now that which decays and waxes old is ready to vanish away.

9 ¹Then truly the first covenant had also ordinances of divine service, and a worldly sanctuary. ²For there was a tabernacle made; the first, wherein was the candlestick, and the table, and the show bread; which is called the sanctuary. ³And after the second veil, the tabernacle which is called the Holiest of all; ⁴Which had the golden censer, and the ark of the covenant overlaid round about with gold, wherein was the golden pot that had manna, and Aaron's rod that budded, and the tables of the covenant; ⁵And over it the cherubim of glory shadowing the mercy seat; of which we cannot now speak particularly. ⁶Now when these things were thus ordained, the priests went always into the first tabernacle, accomplishing the service of God. ⁷But into the second went the high priest alone once every year, not without blood, which he offered for himself, and for the errors of the people: ⁸The Holy Ghost this signifying, that the way into the holiest of all was not yet made manifest, while as the first tabernacle was yet standing: ⁹Which was a figure for the time then present, in which were offered both gifts and sacrifices, that could not make him that did the service perfect, as pertaining to the conscience; ¹⁰Which stood only in meats and drinks, and divers washings, and carnal ordinances, imposed on them until the time of reformation. ¹¹But Christ being come an high priest of good things to come, by a greater and more perfect tabernacle, not made with hands, that is to say, not of this building; ¹²Neither by the blood of goats and calves, but by his own blood he entered in once into the holy place, having obtained eternal redemption for us. ¹³For if the blood of bulls and of goats, and the ashes of an heifer sprinkling the unclean, sanctifies to the purifying of the flesh: ¹⁴How much more shall the blood of Christ, who through the eternal Spirit offered himself without spot to God, purge your conscience from dead works to serve the living God? ¹⁵And for this cause he is the mediator of the new testament, that by means of death, for the redemption of the transgressions that were under the first testament, they which are called might receive the promise of eternal inheritance. ¹⁶For where a testament is, there must also of necessity be the death of the testator. ¹⁷For a testament is of force after men are dead: otherwise it is of no strength at all while the testator lives. ¹⁸Whereupon neither the first testament was dedicated without blood. ¹⁹For when Moses had spoken every precept to all the people according to the law, he took the blood of calves and of goats, with water, and scarlet wool, and hyssop, and sprinkled both the book, and all the people, ²⁰Saying, This is the blood of the testament which God has enjoined to you. ²¹Moreover he sprinkled with blood both the tabernacle, and all the vessels of the ministry. ²²And almost all things are by the law purged with blood; and without shedding of blood is no remission. ²³It was therefore necessary that the patterns of things in the heavens should be purified with these; but the heavenly things themselves with better sacrifices than these. ²⁴For Christ is not entered into the holy places made with hands, which are the figures of the true; but into heaven itself, now to appear in the presence of God for us: ²⁵Nor yet that he should offer himself often, as the high priest enters into the holy place every year with blood of others; ²⁶For then must he often have suffered since the foundation of the world: but now once in the end of the world has he appeared to put away sin by the sacrifice of himself. ²⁷And as it is appointed to men once to die, but after this the judgment: ²⁸So Christ was once offered to bear the sins of many; and to them that look for him shall he appear the second time without sin to salvation.

10 ¹For the law having a shadow of good things to come, and not the very image of the things, can never with those sacrifices which they offered year by year continually make the comers thereunto perfect. ²For then would they not have ceased to be offered? because that the worshippers once purged should have had no more conscience of sins. ³But in those sacrifices there is a remembrance again made of sins every year. ⁴For it is not possible that the blood of bulls and of goats should take away sins. ⁵Why when he comes into the world, he says, Sacrifice and offering you would not, but a body have you prepared me: ⁶In burnt offerings and sacrifices for sin you have had no pleasure. ⁷Then said I, See, I come (in the volume of the book it is written of me,) to do your will, O God. ⁸Above when he said, Sacrifice and offering and burnt offerings and offering for sin you would not, neither had pleasure therein; which are offered by the law; ⁹Then said he, See, I come to do your will, O God. He takes away the first, that he may establish the second. ¹⁰By the which will we are sanctified through the offering of the body of Jesus Christ once for all. ¹¹And every priest stands daily ministering and offering oftentimes the same sacrifices, which can never take away sins: ¹²But this man, after he had offered one sacrifice for sins for ever, sat down on the right hand of God; ¹³From now on expecting till his enemies be made his footstool. ¹⁴For by one offering he has perfected for ever them that are sanctified. ¹⁵Whereof the Holy Ghost also is a witness to us: for after that he had said before, ¹⁶This is the covenant that I will make with them after those days, says the Lord, I will put my laws into their hearts, and in their minds will I write them; ¹⁷And their sins and iniquities will I remember no more. ¹⁸Now where remission of these is, there is no more offering for sin. ¹⁹Having therefore, brothers, boldness to enter into the holiest by the blood of Jesus, ²⁰By a new and living way, which he has consecrated for us, through the veil, that is to say, his flesh; ²¹And having an high priest over the house of God; ²²Let us draw near with a true heart in full assurance of faith, having our hearts sprinkled from an evil conscience, and our bodies washed with pure water. ²³Let us hold fast the profession of our faith without wavering; (for he is faithful that promised;) ²⁴And let us consider one another to provoke to love and to good works: ²⁵Not forsaking the assembling of ourselves together, as the manner of some is; but exhorting one another: and so much the more, as you see the day approaching. ²⁶For if we sin willfully after that we have received the knowledge of the truth, there remains no more sacrifice for sins, ²⁷But a certain fearful looking for of judgment and fiery indignation, which shall devour the adversaries. ²⁸He that despised Moses' law died without mercy under two or three witnesses: ²⁹Of how much sorer punishment, suppose you, shall he be thought worthy, who has trodden under foot the Son of God, and has counted the blood of the covenant, with which he was sanctified, an unholy thing, and has done despite to the Spirit of grace? ³⁰For we know him that has says, Vengeance belongs to me, I will recompense, said the Lord. And again, The Lord shall judge his people. ³¹It is a fearful thing to fall into the hands of the living God. ³²But call to remembrance the former days, in which, after you were illuminated, you endured a great fight of afflictions; ³³Partly, whilst you were made a spectacle both by reproaches and afflictions; and partly, whilst you became companions of them that were so used. ³⁴For you had compassion of me in my bonds, and took joyfully the spoiling of your goods, knowing in yourselves that you have in heaven a better and an enduring substance. ³⁵Cast not away therefore your confidence, which has great recompense of reward. ³⁶For you have need of patience, that, after you have done the will of God, you might receive the promise. ³⁷For yet a little while, and he that shall come will come, and will not tarry. ³⁸Now the just shall live by faith: but if any man draw back, my soul shall have no pleasure in him. ³⁹But we are not of them who draw back to perdition; but of them that believe to the saving of the soul.

11 ¹Now faith is the substance of things hoped for, the evidence of things not seen. ²For by it the elders obtained a good report. ³Through faith we understand that the worlds were framed by the word of God, so that things which are seen were not made of things which do appear. ⁴By faith Abel offered to God a more excellent sacrifice than Cain, by which he obtained witness that he was righteous, God testifying of his gifts: and by it he being dead yet speaks. ⁵By faith Enoch was translated that he should not see death; and was not found, because God had translated him: for before his translation he had this testimony, that he pleased God. ⁶But without faith it is impossible to please him: for he that comes to God must believe that he is, and that he is a rewarder of them that diligently seek him. ⁷By faith Noah, being warned of God of things not seen as yet, moved with fear, prepared an ark to the saving of his house; by the which he condemned the world, and became heir of the righteousness which is by faith. ⁸By faith Abraham, when he was called to go out into a place which he should after receive for an inheritance, obeyed; and he went out, not knowing where he went. ⁹By faith he sojourned in the land of promise, as in a strange country, dwelling in tabernacles with Isaac and Jacob, the heirs with him of the same promise: ¹⁰For he looked for a city which has foundations, whose builder and maker is God. ¹¹Through faith also Sara herself received strength to conceive seed, and was delivered of a child when she was past age, because she judged him faithful who had promised. ¹²Therefore sprang there even of one, and him as good as dead, so many as the stars of the sky in multitude, and as the sand which is by the sea shore innumerable. ¹³These all died in faith, not having received the promises, but having seen them afar off, and were persuaded of them, and embraced them, and confessed that they were strangers and pilgrims on the earth. ¹⁴For they that say such things declare plainly that they seek a country. ¹⁵And truly, if they had been mindful of that country from where they came out, they might have had opportunity to have returned. ¹⁶But now they desire a better country, that is, an heavenly: why God is not ashamed to be called their God: for he has prepared for them a city. ¹⁷By faith Abraham, when he was tried, offered up Isaac: and he that had received the promises offered up his only begotten son, ¹⁸Of whom it was said, That in Isaac shall your seed be called: ¹⁹Accounting that God was able to raise him up, even from the dead; from where also he received him in a figure. ²⁰By faith Isaac blessed Jacob and Esau concerning things to come. ²¹By faith Jacob, when he was a dying, blessed both the sons of Joseph; and worshipped, leaning on the top of his staff. ²²By faith Joseph, when he died, made mention of the departing of the children of Israel; and gave commandment concerning his bones. ²³By faith Moses, when he was born, was hid three months of his parents, because they saw he was a proper child; and they were not afraid of the king's commandment. ²⁴By faith Moses, when he was come to years, refused to be called the son of Pharaoh's daughter; ²⁵Choosing rather to suffer affliction with the people of God, than to enjoy the pleasures of sin for a season; ²⁶Esteeming the reproach of Christ greater riches than the treasures in Egypt: for he had respect to the recompense of the reward. ²⁷By faith he forsook Egypt, not fearing the wrath of the king: for he endured, as seeing him who is invisible. ²⁸Through faith he kept the passover, and the sprinkling of blood, lest he that destroyed the firstborn should touch them. ²⁹By faith they passed through the Red sea as by dry land: which the Egyptians assaying to do were drowned. ³⁰By faith the walls of Jericho fell down, after they were compassed about seven days. ³¹By faith the harlot Rahab perished not with them that believed not, when she had received the spies with peace. ³²And what shall I more say? for the time would fail me to tell of Gedeon, and of Barak, and of Samson, and of Jephthae; of David also, and Samuel, and of the prophets: ³³Who through faith subdued kingdoms, worked righteousness, obtained promises, stopped the mouths of lions. ³⁴Quenched the violence of fire, escaped the edge of the sword, out of weakness were made strong, waxed valiant in fight, turned to flight the armies of the aliens. ³⁵Women received their dead raised to life again: and others were tortured, not accepting deliverance; that they might obtain a better resurrection: ³⁶And others had trial of cruel mockings and scourgings, yes, moreover of bonds and imprisonment: ³⁷They were stoned, they were sawn asunder, were tempted, were slain with the sword: they wandered about in sheepskins and goatskins; being destitute, afflicted, tormented; ³⁸(Of whom the world was not worthy:) they wandered in deserts, and in mountains, and in dens and caves of the earth. ³⁹And these all, having obtained a good report through faith, received not the promise: ⁴⁰God having provided some better thing for us, that they without us should not be made perfect.

12

¹Why seeing we also are compassed about with so great a cloud of witnesses, let us lay aside every weight, and the sin which does so easily beset us, and let us run with patience the race that is set before us, ²Looking to Jesus the author and finisher of our faith; who for the joy that was set before him endured the cross, despising the shame, and is set down at the right hand of the throne of God. ³For consider him that endured such contradiction of sinners against himself, lest you be wearied and faint in your minds. ⁴You have not yet resisted to blood, striving against sin. ⁵And you have forgotten the exhortation which speaks to you as to children, My son, despise not you the chastening of the Lord, nor faint when you are rebuked of him: ⁶For whom the Lord loves he chastens, and whips every son whom he receives. ⁷If you endure chastening, God deals with you as with sons; for what son is he whom the father chastens not? ⁸But if you be without chastisement, whereof all are partakers, then are you bastards, and not sons. ⁹Furthermore we have had fathers of our flesh which corrected us, and we gave them reverence: shall we not much rather be in subjection to the Father of spirits, and live? ¹⁰For they truly for a few days chastened us after their own pleasure; but he for our profit, that we might be partakers of his holiness. ¹¹Now no chastening for the present seems to be joyous, but grievous: nevertheless afterward it yields the peaceable fruit of righteousness to them which are exercised thereby. ¹²Why lift up the hands which hang down, and the feeble knees; ¹³And make straight paths for your feet, lest that which is lame be turned out of the way; but let it rather be healed. ¹⁴Follow peace with all men, and holiness, without which no man shall see the Lord: ¹⁵Looking diligently lest any man fail of the grace of God; lest any root of bitterness springing up trouble you, and thereby many be defiled; ¹⁶Lest there be any fornicator, or profane person, as Esau, who for one morsel of meat sold his birthright. ¹⁷For you know how that afterward, when he would have inherited the blessing, he was rejected: for he found no place of repentance, though he sought it carefully with tears. ¹⁸For you are not come to the mount that might be touched, and that burned with fire, nor to blackness, and darkness, and tempest, ¹⁹And the sound of a trumpet, and the voice of words; which voice they that heard entreated that the word should not be spoken to them any more: ²⁰(For they could not endure that which was commanded, And if so much as a beast touch the mountain, it shall be stoned, or thrust through with a dart: ²¹And so terrible was the sight, that Moses said, I exceedingly fear and quake:) ²²But you are come to mount Sion, and to the city of the living God, the heavenly Jerusalem, and to an innumerable company of angels, ²³To the general assembly and church of the firstborn, which are written in heaven, and to God the Judge of all, and to the spirits of just men made perfect, ²⁴And to Jesus the mediator of the new covenant, and to the blood of sprinkling, that speaks better things that that of Abel. ²⁵See that you refuse not him that speaks. For if they escaped not

who refused him that spoke on earth, much more shall not we escape, if we turn away from him that speaks from heaven: ²⁶Whose voice then shook the earth: but now he has promised, saying, Yet once more I shake not the earth only, but also heaven. ²⁷And this word, Yet once more, signifies the removing of those things that are shaken, as of things that are made, that those things which cannot be shaken may remain. ²⁸Why we receiving a kingdom which cannot be moved, let us have grace, whereby we may serve God acceptably with reverence and godly fear: ²⁹For our God is a consuming fire.

13 ¹Let brotherly love continue. ²Be not forgetful to entertain strangers: for thereby some have entertained angels unawares. ³Remember them that are in bonds, as bound with them; and them which suffer adversity, as being yourselves also in the body. ⁴Marriage is honorable in all, and the bed undefiled: but fornicators and adulterers God will judge. ⁵Let your conversation be without covetousness; and be content with such things as you have: for he has said, I will never leave you, nor forsake you. ⁶So that we may boldly say, The Lord is my helper, and I will not fear what man shall do to me. ⁷Remember them which have the rule over you, who have spoken to you the word of God: whose faith follow, considering the end of their conversation. ⁸Jesus Christ the same yesterday, and to day, and for ever. ⁹Be not carried about with divers and strange doctrines. For it is a good thing that the heart be established with grace; not with meats, which have not profited them that have been occupied therein. ¹⁰We have an altar, whereof they have no right to eat which serve the tabernacle. ¹¹For the bodies of those beasts, whose blood is brought into the sanctuary by the high priest for sin, are burned without the camp. ¹²Why Jesus also, that he might sanctify the people with his own blood, suffered without the gate. ¹³Let us go forth therefore to him without the camp, bearing his reproach. ¹⁴For here have we no continuing city, but we seek one to come. ¹⁵By him therefore let us offer the sacrifice of praise to God continually, that is, the fruit of our lips giving thanks to his name. ¹⁶But to do good and to communicate forget not: for with such sacrifices God is well pleased. ¹⁷Obey them that have the rule over you, and submit yourselves: for they watch for your souls, as they that must give account, that they may do it with joy, and not with grief: for that is unprofitable for you. ¹⁸Pray for us: for we trust we have a good conscience, in all things willing to live honestly. ¹⁹But I beseech you the rather to do this, that I may be restored to you the sooner. ²⁰Now the God of peace, that brought again from the dead our Lord Jesus, that great shepherd of the sheep, through the blood of the everlasting covenant, ²¹Make you perfect in every good work to do his will, working in you that which is well pleasing in his sight, through Jesus Christ; to whom be glory for ever and ever. Amen. ²²And I beseech you, brothers, suffer the word of exhortation: for I have written a letter to you in few words. ²³Know you that our brother Timothy is set at liberty; with whom, if he come shortly, I will see you. ²⁴Salute all them that have the rule over you, and all the saints. They of Italy salute you. ²⁵Grace be with you all. Amen.

James

1 ¹James, a servant of God and of the Lord Jesus Christ, to the twelve tribes which are scattered abroad, greeting. ²My brothers, count it all joy when you fall into divers temptations; ³Knowing this, that the trying of your faith works patience. ⁴But let patience have her perfect work, that you may be perfect and entire, wanting nothing. ⁵If any of you lack wisdom, let him ask of God, that gives to all men liberally, and upbraids not; and it shall be given him. ⁶But let him ask in faith, nothing wavering. For he that wavers is like a wave of the sea driven with the wind and tossed. ⁷For let not that man think that he shall receive any thing of the Lord. ⁸A double minded man is unstable in all his ways. ⁹Let the brother of low degree rejoice in that he is exalted: ¹⁰But the rich, in that he is made low: because as the flower of the grass he shall pass away. ¹¹For the sun is no sooner risen with a burning heat, but it wither the grass, and the flower thereof falls, and the grace of the fashion of it perishes: so also shall the rich man fade away in his ways. ¹²Blessed is the man that endures temptation: for when he is tried, he shall receive the crown of life, which the Lord has promised to them that love him. ¹³Let no man say when he is tempted, I am tempted of God: for God cannot be tempted with evil, neither tempts he any man: ¹⁴But every man is tempted, when he is drawn away of his own lust, and enticed. ¹⁵Then when lust has conceived, it brings forth sin: and sin, when it is finished, brings forth death. ¹⁶Do not err, my beloved brothers. ¹⁷Every good gift and every perfect gift is from above, and comes down from the Father of lights, with whom is no ficklenss, neither shadow of turning. ¹⁸Of his own will fathered he us with the word of truth, that we should be a kind of first fruits of his creatures. ¹⁹Why, my beloved brothers, let every man be swift to hear, slow to speak, slow to wrath: ²⁰For the wrath of man works not the righteousness of God. ²¹Why lay apart all filthiness and superfluity of naughtiness, and receive with meekness the engrafted word, which is able to save your souls. ²²But be you doers of the word, and not hearers only, deceiving your own selves. ²³For if any be a hearer of the word, and not a doer, he is like to a man beholding his natural face in a glass: ²⁴For he beholds himself, and goes his way, and straightway forgets what manner of man he was. ²⁵But whoever looks into the perfect law of liberty, and continues therein, he being not a forgetful hearer, but a doer of the work, this man shall be blessed in his deed. ²⁶If any man among you seem to be religious, and bridles not his tongue, but deceives his own heart, this man's religion is vain. ²⁷Pure religion and undefiled before God and the Father is this, To visit the fatherless and widows in their affliction, and to keep himself unspotted from the world.

2 ¹My brothers, have not the faith of our Lord Jesus Christ, the Lord of glory, with respect of persons. ²For if there come to your assembly a man with a gold ring, in goodly apparel, and there come in also a poor man in vile raiment; ³And you have respect to him that wears the gay clothing, and say to him, Sit you here in a good place; and say to the poor, Stand you there, or sit here under my footstool: ⁴Are you not then partial in yourselves, and are become judges of evil thoughts? ⁵Listen, my beloved brothers, Has not God chosen the poor of this world rich in faith, and heirs of the kingdom which he has promised to them that love him? ⁶But you have despised the poor. Do not rich men oppress you, and draw you before the judgment seats? ⁷Do not they blaspheme that worthy name by the which you are called? ⁸If you fulfill the royal law according to the scripture, You shall love your neighbor as yourself, you do well: ⁹But if you have respect to persons, you commit sin, and are convinced of the law as transgressors. ¹⁰For whoever shall keep the whole law, and yet offend in one point, he is guilty of all. ¹¹For he that said, Do not commit adultery, said also, Do not kill. Now if you commit no adultery, yet if you kill, you are become a transgressor of the law. ¹²So speak you, and so do, as they that shall be judged by the law of liberty. ¹³For he shall have judgment without mercy, that has showed no mercy; and mercy rejoices against judgment. ¹⁴What does it profit, my brothers, though a man say he has faith, and have not works? can faith save him? ¹⁵If a brother or sister be naked, and destitute of daily food, ¹⁶And one of you say to them, Depart in peace, be you warmed and filled; notwithstanding you give them not those things which are needful to the body; what does it profit? ¹⁷Even so faith, if it has not works, is dead, being alone. ¹⁸Yes, a man may say, You have faith, and I have works: show me your faith without your works, and I will show you my faith by my works. ¹⁹You believe that there is one God; you do well: the devils also believe, and tremble. ²⁰But will you know, O vain man, that faith without works is dead? ²¹Was not Abraham our father justified by works, when he had offered Isaac his son on the altar? ²²See you how faith worked with his works, and by works was faith made perfect? ²³And the scripture was fulfilled which says, Abraham believed God, and it was imputed to him for righteousness: and he was called the Friend of God. ²⁴You see then how that by works a man is justified, and not by faith only. ²⁵Likewise also was not Rahab the harlot justified by works, when she had received the messengers, and had sent them out another way? ²⁶For as the body without the spirit is dead, so faith without works is dead also.

3 ¹My brothers, be not many masters, knowing that we shall receive the greater condemnation. ²For in many things we offend all. If any man offend not in word, the same is a perfect man, and able also to bridle the whole body. ³Behold, we put bits in the horses' mouths, that they may obey us; and we turn about their whole body. ⁴Behold also the ships, which though they be so great, and are driven of fierce winds, yet are they turned about with a very small helm, wherever the governor wants. ⁵Even so the tongue is a little member, and boasts great things. Behold, how great a matter a little fire kindles! ⁶And the tongue is a fire, a world of iniquity: so is the tongue among our members, that it defiles the whole body, and sets on fire the course of nature; and it is set on fire of hell. ⁷For every kind of beasts, and of birds, and of serpents, and of things in the sea, is tamed, and has been tamed of mankind: ⁸But the tongue can no man tame; it is an unruly evil, full of deadly poison. ⁹Therewith bless we God, even the Father; and therewith curse we men, which are made after the similitude of God. ¹⁰Out of the same mouth proceeds blessing and cursing. My brothers, these things ought not so to be. ¹¹Does a fountain send forth at the same place sweet water and bitter? ¹²Can the fig tree, my brothers, bear olive berries? either a vine, figs? so can no fountain both yield salt water and fresh. ¹³Who is a wise man and endued with knowledge among you? let him show out of a good conversation his works with meekness of wisdom. ¹⁴But if you have bitter envying and strife in your hearts, glory not, and lie not against the truth. ¹⁵This wisdom descends not from above, but is earthly, sensual, devilish. ¹⁶For where envying and strife is, there is confusion and every evil work. ¹⁷But the wisdom that is from above is first pure, then peaceable, gentle, and easy to be entreated, full of mercy and good fruits, without partiality, and without hypocrisy. ¹⁸And the fruit of righteousness is sown in peace of them that make peace.

4 ¹From where come wars and fights among you? come they not hence, even of your lusts that war in your members? ²You lust, and have not: you kill, and desire to have, and cannot obtain: you fight and war, yet you have not, because you ask not. ³You ask, and receive not, because you ask amiss, that you may consume it on your lusts. ⁴You adulterers and adulteresses, know you not that the friendship of the world is enmity with God? whoever therefore will be a friend of the world is the enemy of God. ⁵Do you think that the scripture says in vain, The spirit that dwells in us lusts to envy? ⁶But he gives more grace. Why he says, God resists the proud, but gives grace to the humble. ⁷Submit yourselves therefore to God. Resist the devil, and he will flee from you. ⁸Draw near to God, and he will draw near to you. Cleanse your hands, you sinners; and purify your hearts, you double minded. ⁹Be afflicted, and mourn, and weep: let your laughter be turned to mourning, and your joy to heaviness. ¹⁰Humble yourselves in the sight of the Lord, and he shall lift you up. ¹¹Speak not evil one of another, brothers. He that speaks evil of his brother, and judges his brother, speaks evil of the law, and judges the law: but if you judge the law, you are not a doer of the law, but a judge. ¹²There is one lawgiver, who is able to save and to destroy: who are you that judge another? ¹³Go to now, you that say, To day or to morrow we will go into such a city, and continue there a year, and buy and sell, and get gain: ¹⁴Whereas you know not what shall be on the morrow. For what is your life? It is even a vapor, that appears for a little time, and then vanishes away. ¹⁵For that you ought to say, If the Lord will, we shall live, and do this, or that. ¹⁶But now you rejoice in your boastings: all such rejoicing is evil. ¹⁷Therefore to him that knows to do good, and does it not, to him it is sin.

5 ¹Go to now, you rich men, weep and howl for your miseries that shall come on you. ²Your riches are corrupted, and your garments are moth-eaten. ³Your gold and silver is corroded; and the rust of them shall be a witness against you, and shall eat your flesh as it were fire. You have heaped treasure together for the last days. ⁴Behold, the hire of the laborers who have reaped down your fields, which is of you kept back by fraud, cries: and the cries of them which have reaped are entered into the ears of the Lord of sabaoth. ⁵You have lived in pleasure on the earth, and been wanton; you have nourished your hearts, as in a day of slaughter. ⁶You have condemned and killed the just; and he does not resist you. ⁷Be patient therefore, brothers, to the coming of the Lord. Behold, the farmer waits for the precious fruit of the earth, and has long patience for it, until he receive the early and latter rain. ⁸Be you also patient; establish your hearts: for the coming of the Lord draws near. ⁹Grudge not one against another, brothers, lest you be condemned: behold, the judge stands before the door. ¹⁰Take, my brothers, the prophets, who have spoken in the name of the Lord, for an example of suffering affliction, and of patience. ¹¹Behold, we count them happy which endure. You have heard of the patience of Job, and have seen the end of the Lord; that the Lord is very pitiful, and of tender mercy. ¹²But above all things, my brothers, swear not, neither by heaven, neither by the earth, neither by any other oath: but let your yes be yes; and your no, no; lest you fall into condemnation. ¹³Is any among you afflicted? let him pray. Is any merry? let him sing psalms. ¹⁴Is any sick among you? let him call for the elders of the church; and let them pray over him, anointing him with oil in the name of the Lord: ¹⁵And the prayer of faith shall save the sick, and the Lord shall raise him up; and if he have committed sins, they shall be forgiven him. ¹⁶Confess your faults one to another, and pray one for another, that you may be healed. The effectual fervent prayer of a righteous man avails much. ¹⁷Elias was a man subject to like passions as we are, and he prayed earnestly that it might not rain: and it rained not on the earth by the space of three years and six months. ¹⁸And he prayed again, and the heaven gave rain, and the earth brought forth her fruit. ¹⁹Brothers, if any of you do err from the truth, and one convert him; ²⁰Let him know, that he which converts the sinner from the error of his way shall save a soul from death, and shall hide a multitude of sins.

First Peter

1 ¹Peter, an apostle of Jesus Christ, to the strangers scattered throughout Pontus, Galatia, Cappadocia, Asia, and Bithynia, ²Elect according to the foreknowledge of God the Father, through sanctification of the Spirit, to obedience and sprinkling of the blood of Jesus Christ: Grace to you, and peace, be multiplied. ³Blessed be the God and Father of our Lord Jesus Christ, which according to his abundant mercy has begotten us again to a lively hope by the resurrection of Jesus Christ from the dead, ⁴To an inheritance incorruptible, and undefiled, and that fades not away, reserved in heaven for you, ⁵Who are kept by the power of God through faith to salvation ready to be revealed in the last time. ⁶Wherein you greatly rejoice, though now for a season, if need be, you are in heaviness through manifold temptations: ⁷That the trial of your faith, being much more precious than of gold that perishes, though it be tried with fire, might be found to praise and honor and glory at the appearing of Jesus Christ: ⁸Whom having not seen, you love; in whom, though now you see him not, yet believing, you rejoice with joy unspeakable and full of glory: ⁹Receiving the end of your faith, even the salvation of your souls. ¹⁰Of which salvation the prophets have inquired and searched diligently, who prophesied of the grace that should come to you: ¹¹Searching what, or what manner of time the Spirit of Christ which was in them did signify, when it testified beforehand the sufferings of Christ, and the glory that should follow. ¹²To whom it was revealed, that not to themselves, but to us they did minister the things, which are now reported to you by them that have preached the gospel to you with the Holy Ghost sent down from heaven; which things the angels desire to look into. ¹³Why gird up the loins of your mind, be sober, and hope to the end for the grace that is to be brought to you at the revelation of Jesus Christ; ¹⁴As obedient children, not fashioning yourselves according to the former lusts in your ignorance: ¹⁵But as he which has called you is holy, so be you holy in all manner of conversation; ¹⁶Because it is written, Be you holy; for I am holy. ¹⁷And if you call on the Father, who without respect of persons judges according to every man's work, pass the time of your sojourning here in fear: ¹⁸For as much as you know that you were not redeemed with corruptible things, as silver and gold, from your vain conversation received by tradition from your fathers; ¹⁹But with the precious blood of Christ, as of a lamb without blemish and without spot: ²⁰Who truly was foreordained before the foundation of the world, but was manifest in these last times for you, ²¹Who by him do believe in God, that raised him up from the dead, and gave him glory; that your faith and hope might be in God. ²²Seeing you have purified your souls in obeying the truth through the Spirit to unfeigned love of the brothers, see that you love one another with a pure heart fervently: ²³Being born again, not of corruptible seed, but of incorruptible, by the word of God, which lives and stays for ever. ²⁴For all flesh is as grass, and all the glory of man as the flower of grass. The grass wither, and the flower thereof falls away: ²⁵But the word of the Lord endures for ever. And this is the word which by the gospel is preached to you.

2 ¹Why laying aside all malice, and all guile, and hypocrisies, and envies, all evil speakings, ²As newborn babes, desire the sincere milk of the word, that you may grow thereby: ³If so be you have tasted that the Lord is gracious. ⁴To whom coming, as to a living stone, disallowed indeed of men, but chosen of God, and precious, ⁵You also, as lively stones, are built up a spiritual house, an holy priesthood, to offer up spiritual sacrifices, acceptable to God by Jesus Christ. ⁶Why also it is contained in the scripture, Behold, I lay in Sion a chief corner stone, elect, precious: and he that believes on him shall not be confounded. ⁷To you therefore which believe he is precious: but to them which be disobedient, the stone which the builders disallowed, the same is made the head of the corner, ⁸And a stone of stumbling, and a rock of offense, even to them which stumble at the word, being disobedient: to which also they were appointed. ⁹But you are a chosen generation, a royal priesthood, an holy nation, a peculiar people; that you should show forth the praises of him who has called you out of darkness into his marvelous light; ¹⁰Which in time past were not a people, but are now the people of God: which had not obtained mercy, but now have obtained mercy. ¹¹Dearly beloved, I beseech you as strangers and pilgrims, abstain from fleshly lusts, which war against the soul; ¹²Having your conversation honest among the Gentiles: that, whereas they speak against you as evildoers, they may by your good works, which they shall behold, glorify God in the day of visitation. ¹³Submit yourselves to every ordinance of man for the Lord's sake: whether it be to the king, as supreme; ¹⁴Or to governors, as to them that are sent by him for the punishment of evildoers, and for the praise of them that do well. ¹⁵For so is the will of God, that with well doing you may put to silence the ignorance of foolish men: ¹⁶As free, and not using your liberty for a cloak of maliciousness, but as the servants of God. ¹⁷Honor all men. Love the brotherhood. Fear God. Honor the king. ¹⁸Servants, be subject to your masters with all fear; not only to the good and gentle, but also to the fraudulent. ¹⁹For this is thank worthy, if a man for conscience toward God endure grief, suffering wrongfully. ²⁰For what glory is it, if, when you be buffeted for your faults, you shall take it patiently? but if, when you do well, and suffer for it, you take it patiently, this is acceptable with God. ²¹For even hereunto were you called: because Christ also suffered for us, leaving us an example, that you should follow his steps: ²²Who did no sin, neither was guile found in his mouth: ²³Who, when he was reviled, reviled not again; when he suffered, he threatened not; but committed himself to him that judges righteously: ²⁴Who his own self bore our sins in his own body on the tree, that we, being dead to sins, should live to righteousness: by whose stripes you were healed. ²⁵For you were as sheep going astray; but are now returned to the Shepherd and Bishop of your souls.

3 ¹Likewise, you wives, be in subjection to your own husbands; that, if any obey not the word, they also may without the word be won by the conversation of the wives; ²While they behold your chaste conversation coupled with

fear. ³Whose adorning let it not be that outward adorning of plaiting the hair, and of wearing of gold, or of putting on of apparel; ⁴But let it be the hidden man of the heart, in that which is not corruptible, even the ornament of a meek and quiet spirit, which is in the sight of God of great price. ⁵For after this manner in the old time the holy women also, who trusted in God, adorned themselves, being in subjection to their own husbands: ⁶Even as Sara obeyed Abraham, calling him lord: whose daughters you are, as long as you do well, and are not afraid with any amazement. ⁷Likewise, you husbands, dwell with them according to knowledge, giving honor to the wife, as to the weaker vessel, and as being heirs together of the grace of life; that your prayers be not hindered. ⁸Finally, be you all of one mind, having compassion one of another, love as brothers, be pitiful, be courteous: ⁹Not rendering evil for evil, or railing for railing: but contrariwise blessing; knowing that you are thereunto called, that you should inherit a blessing. ¹⁰For he that will love life, and see good days, let him refrain his tongue from evil, and his lips that they speak no guile: ¹¹Let him eschew evil, and do good; let him seek peace, and ensue it. ¹²For the eyes of the Lord are over the righteous, and his ears are open to their prayers: but the face of the Lord is against them that do evil. ¹³And who is he that will harm you, if you be followers of that which is good? ¹⁴But and if you suffer for righteousness' sake, happy are you: and be not afraid of their terror, neither be troubled; ¹⁵But sanctify the Lord God in your hearts: and be ready always to give an answer to every man that asks you a reason of the hope that is in you with meekness and fear: ¹⁶Having a good conscience; that, whereas they speak evil of you, as of evildoers, they may be ashamed that falsely accuse your good conversation in Christ. ¹⁷For it is better, if the will of God be so, that you suffer for well doing, than for evil doing. ¹⁸For Christ also has once suffered for sins, the just for the unjust, that he might bring us to God, being put to death in the flesh, but quickened by the Spirit: ¹⁹By which also he went and preached to the spirits in prison; ²⁰Which sometime were disobedient, when once the long-suffering of God waited in the days of Noah, while the ark was a preparing, wherein few, that is, eight souls were saved by water. ²¹The like figure to which even baptism does also now save us (not the putting away of the filth of the flesh, but the answer of a good conscience toward God,) by the resurrection of Jesus Christ: ²²Who is gone into heaven, and is on the right hand of God; angels and authorities and powers being made subject to him.

4 ¹For as much then as Christ has suffered for us in the flesh, arm yourselves likewise with the same mind: for he that has suffered in the flesh has ceased from sin; ²That he no longer should live the rest of his time in the flesh to the lusts of men, but to the will of God. ³For the time past of our life may suffice us to have worked the will of the Gentiles, when we walked in lasciviousness, lusts, excess of wine, revelings, parties, and abominable idolatries: ⁴Wherein they think it strange that you run not with them to the same excess of riot, speaking evil of you: ⁵Who shall give account to him that is ready to judge the quick and the dead. ⁶For for this cause was the gospel preached also to them that are dead, that they might be judged according to men in the flesh, but live according to God in the spirit. ⁷But the end of all things is at hand: be you therefore sober, and watch to prayer. ⁸And above all things have fervent charity among yourselves: for charity shall cover the multitude of sins. ⁹Use hospitality one to another without grudging. ¹⁰As every man has received the gift, even so minister the same one to another, as good stewards of the manifold grace of God. ¹¹If any man speak, let him speak as the oracles of God; if any man minister, let him do it as of the ability which God gives: that God in all things may be glorified through Jesus Christ, to whom be praise and dominion for ever and ever. Amen. ¹²Beloved, think it not strange concerning the fiery trial which is to try you, as though some strange thing happened to you: ¹³But rejoice, inasmuch as you are partakers of Christ's sufferings; that, when his glory shall be revealed, you may be glad also with exceeding joy. ¹⁴If you be reproached for the name of Christ, happy are you; for the spirit of glory and of God rests on you: on their part he is evil spoken of, but on your part he is glorified. ¹⁵But let none of you suffer as a murderer, or as a thief, or as an evildoer, or as a busybody in other men's matters. ¹⁶Yet if any man suffer as a Christian, let him not be ashamed; but let him glorify God on this behalf. ¹⁷For the time is come that judgment must begin at the house of God: and if it first begin at us, what shall the end be of them that obey not the gospel of God? ¹⁸And if the righteous scarcely be saved, where shall the ungodly and the sinner appear? ¹⁹Why let them that suffer according to the will of God commit the keeping of their souls to him in well doing, as to a faithful Creator.

5 ¹The elders which are among you I exhort, who am also an elder, and a witness of the sufferings of Christ, and also a partaker of the glory that shall be revealed: ²Feed the flock of God which is among you, taking the oversight thereof, not by constraint, but willingly; not for filthy lucre, but of a ready mind; ³Neither as being lords over God's heritage, but being ensamples to the flock. ⁴And when the chief Shepherd shall appear, you shall receive a crown of glory that fades not away. ⁵Likewise, you younger, submit yourselves to the elder. Yes, all of you be subject one to another, and be clothed with humility: for God resists the proud, and gives grace to the humble. ⁶Humble yourselves therefore under the mighty hand of God, that he may exalt you in due time: ⁷Casting all your care on him; for he cares for you. ⁸Be sober, be vigilant; because your adversary the devil, as a roaring lion, walks about, seeking whom he may devour: ⁹Whom resist steadfast in the faith, knowing that the same afflictions are accomplished in your brothers that are in the world. ¹⁰But the God of all grace, who has called us to his eternal glory by Christ Jesus, after that you have suffered a while, make you perfect, establish, strengthen, settle you. ¹¹To him be glory and dominion for ever and ever. Amen. ¹²By Silvanus, a faithful brother to you, as I suppose, I have written briefly, exhorting, and testifying that this is the true grace of God wherein you stand. ¹³The church that is at Babylon, elected together with you, salutes you; and so does Marcus my son. ¹⁴Greet you one another with a kiss of charity. Peace be with you all that are in Christ Jesus. Amen.

Second Peter

1 ¹Simon Peter, a servant and an apostle of Jesus Christ, to them that have obtained like precious faith with us through the righteousness of God and our Savior Jesus Christ: ²Grace and peace be multiplied to you through the knowledge of God, and of Jesus our Lord, ³According as his divine power has given to us all things that pertain to life and godliness, through the knowledge of him that has called us to glory and virtue: ⁴Whereby are given to us exceeding great and precious promises: that by these you might be partakers of the divine nature, having escaped the corruption that is in the world through lust. ⁵And beside this, giving all diligence, add to your faith virtue; and to virtue knowledge; ⁶And to knowledge temperance; and to temperance patience; and to patience godliness; ⁷And to godliness brotherly kindness; and to brotherly kindness charity. ⁸For if these things be in you, and abound, they make you that you shall neither be barren nor unfruitful in the knowledge of our Lord Jesus Christ. ⁹But he that lacks these things is blind, and cannot see afar off, and has forgotten that he was purged from his old sins. ¹⁰Why the rather, brothers, give diligence to make your calling and election sure: for if you do these things, you shall never fall: ¹¹For so an entrance shall be ministered to you abundantly into the everlasting kingdom of our Lord and Savior Jesus Christ. ¹²Why I will not be negligent to put you always in remembrance of these things, though you know them, and be established in the present truth. ¹³Yes, I think it meet, as long as I am in this tabernacle, to stir you up by putting you in remembrance; ¹⁴Knowing that shortly I must put off this my tabernacle, even as our Lord Jesus Christ has showed me. ¹⁵Moreover I will endeavor that you may be able after my decease to have these things always in remembrance. ¹⁶For we have not followed cunningly devised fables, when we made known to you the power and coming of our Lord Jesus Christ, but were eyewitnesses of his majesty. ¹⁷For he received from God the Father honor and glory, when there came such a voice to him from the excellent glory, This is my beloved Son, in whom I am well pleased. ¹⁸And this voice which came from heaven we heard, when we were with him in the holy mount. ¹⁹We have also a more sure word of prophecy; to which you do well that you take heed, as to a light that shines in a dark place, until the day dawn, and the day star arise in your hearts: ²⁰Knowing this first, that no prophecy of the scripture is of any private interpretation. ²¹For the prophecy came not in old time by the will of man: but holy men of God spoke as they were moved by the Holy Ghost.

2 ¹But there were false prophets also among the people, even as there shall be false teachers among you, who privately shall bring in damnable heresies, even denying the Lord that bought them, and bring on themselves swift destruction. ²And many shall follow their pernicious ways; by reason of whom the way of truth shall be evil spoken of. ³And through covetousness shall they with feigned words make merchandise of you: whose judgment now of a long time lingers not, and their damnation slumbers not. ⁴For if God spared not the angels that sinned, but cast them down to hell, and delivered them into chains of darkness, to be reserved to judgment; ⁵And spared not the old world, but saved Noah the eighth person, a preacher of righteousness, bringing in the flood on the world of the ungodly; ⁶And turning the cities of Sodom and Gomorrha into ashes condemned them with an overthrow, making them an ensample to those that after should live ungodly; ⁷And delivered just Lot, vexed with the filthy conversation of the wicked: ⁸(For that righteous man dwelling among them, in seeing and hearing, vexed his righteous soul from day to day with their unlawful deeds;) ⁹The Lord knows how to deliver the godly out of temptations, and to reserve the unjust to the day of judgment to be punished: ¹⁰But chiefly them that walk after the flesh in the lust of uncleanness, and despise government. Presumptuous are they, self-willed, they are not afraid to speak evil of dignities. ¹¹Whereas angels, which are greater in power and might, bring not railing accusation against them before the Lord. ¹²But these, as natural brute beasts, made to be taken and destroyed, speak evil of the things that they understand not; and shall utterly perish in their own corruption; ¹³And shall receive the reward of unrighteousness, as they that count it pleasure to riot in the day time. Spots they are and blemishes, sporting themselves with their own deceivings while they feast with you; ¹⁴Having eyes full of adultery, and that cannot cease from sin; beguiling unstable souls: an heart they have exercised with covetous practices; cursed children: ¹⁵Which have forsaken the right way, and are gone astray, following the way of Balaam the son of Bosor, who loved the wages of unrighteousness; ¹⁶But was rebuked for his iniquity: the dumb ass speaking with man's voice forbade the madness of the prophet. ¹⁷These are wells without water, clouds that are carried with a tempest; to whom the mist of darkness is reserved for ever. ¹⁸For when they speak great swelling words of vanity, they allure through the lusts of the flesh, through much wantonness, those that were clean escaped from them who live in error. ¹⁹While they promise them liberty, they themselves are the servants of corruption: for of whom a man is overcome, of the same is he brought in bondage. ²⁰For if after they have escaped the pollutions of the world through the knowledge of the Lord and Savior Jesus Christ, they are again entangled therein, and overcome, the latter end is worse with them than the beginning. ²¹For it had been better for them not to have known the way of righteousness, than, after they have known it, to turn from the holy commandment delivered to them. ²²But it is happened to them according to the true proverb, The dog is turned to his own vomit again; and the sow that was washed to her wallowing in the mire.

3 ¹This second letter, beloved, I now write to you; in both which I stir up your pure minds by way of remembrance: ²That you may be mindful of the words which were spoken before by the holy prophets, and of the commandment of us the apostles of the Lord and Savior: ³Knowing this first, that there shall come in the last days scoffers, walking after their own lusts, ⁴And saying, Where

is the promise of his coming? for since the fathers fell asleep, all things continue as they were from the beginning of the creation. ⁵For this they willingly are ignorant of, that by the word of God the heavens were of old, and the earth standing out of the water and in the water: ⁶Whereby the world that then was, being overflowed with water, perished: ⁷But the heavens and the earth, which are now, by the same word are kept in store, reserved to fire against the day of judgment and perdition of ungodly men. ⁸But, beloved, be not ignorant of this one thing, that one day is with the Lord as a thousand years, and a thousand years as one day. ⁹The Lord is not slack concerning his promise, as some men count slackness; but is long-suffering to us-ward, not willing that any should perish, but that all should come to repentance. ¹⁰But the day of the Lord will come as a thief in the night; in the which the heavens shall pass away with a great noise, and the elements shall melt with fervent heat, the earth also and the works that are therein shall be burned up. ¹¹Seeing then that all these things shall be dissolved, what manner of persons ought you to be in all holy conversation and godliness, ¹²Looking for and hastening to the coming of the day of God, wherein the heavens being on fire shall be dissolved, and the elements shall melt with fervent heat? ¹³Nevertheless we, according to his promise, look for new heavens and a new earth, wherein dwells righteousness. ¹⁴Why, beloved, seeing that you look for such things, be diligent that you may be found of him in peace, without spot, and blameless. ¹⁵And account that the long-suffering of our Lord is salvation; even as our beloved brother Paul also according to the wisdom given to him has written to you; ¹⁶As also in all his letters, speaking in them of these things; in which are some things hard to be understood, which they that are unlearned and unstable wrest, as they do also the other scriptures, to their own destruction. ¹⁷You therefore, beloved, seeing you know these things before, beware lest you also, being led away with the error of the wicked, fall from your own steadfastness. ¹⁸But grow in grace, and in the knowledge of our Lord and Savior Jesus Christ. To him be glory both now and for ever. Amen.

First John

1 ¹That which was from the beginning, which we have heard, which we have seen with our eyes, which we have looked on, and our hands have handled, of the Word of life; ²(For the life was manifested, and we have seen it, and bear witness, and show to you that eternal life, which was with the Father, and was manifested to us;) ³That which we have seen and heard declare we to you, that you also may have fellowship with us: and truly our fellowship is with the Father, and with his Son Jesus Christ. ⁴And these things write we to you, that your joy may be full. ⁵This then is the message which we have heard of him, and declare to you, that God is light, and in him is no darkness at all. ⁶If we say that we have fellowship with him, and walk in darkness, we lie, and do not the truth: ⁷But if we walk in the light, as he is in the light, we have fellowship one with another, and the blood of Jesus Christ his Son cleans us from all sin. ⁸If we say that we have no sin, we deceive ourselves, and the truth is not in us. ⁹If we confess our sins, he is faithful and just to forgive us our sins, and to cleanse us from all unrighteousness. ¹⁰If we say that we have not sinned, we make him a liar, and his word is not in us.

2 ¹My little children, these things write I to you, that you sin not. And if any man sin, we have an advocate with the Father, Jesus Christ the righteous: ²And he is the propitiation for our sins: and not for ours only, but also for the sins of the whole world. ³And hereby we do know that we know him, if we keep his commandments. ⁴He that says, I know him, and keeps not his commandments, is a liar, and the truth is not in him. ⁵But whoever keeps his word, in him truly is the love of God perfected: hereby know we that we are in him. ⁶He that says he stays in him ought himself also so to walk, even as he walked. ⁷Brothers, I write no new commandment to you, but an old commandment which you had from the beginning. The old commandment is the word which you have heard from the beginning. ⁸Again, a new commandment I write to you, which thing is true in him and in you: because the darkness is past, and the true light now shines. ⁹He that says he is in the light, and hates his brother, is in darkness even until now. ¹⁰He that loves his brother stays in the light, and there is none occasion of stumbling in him. ¹¹But he that hates his brother is in darkness, and walks in darkness, and knows not where he goes, because that darkness has blinded his eyes. ¹²I write to you, little children, because your sins are forgiven you for his name's sake. ¹³I write to you, fathers, because you have known him that is from the beginning. I write to you, young men, because you have overcome the wicked one. I write to you, little children, because you have known the Father. ¹⁴I have written to you, fathers, because you have known him that is from the beginning. I have written to you, young men, because you are strong, and the word of God stays in you, and you have overcome the wicked one. ¹⁵Love not the world, neither the things that are in the world. If any man love the world, the love of the Father is not in him. ¹⁶For all that is in the world, the lust of the flesh, and the lust of the eyes, and the pride of life, is not of the Father, but is of the world. ¹⁷And the world passes away, and the lust thereof: but he that does the will of God stays for ever. ¹⁸Little children, it is the last time: and as you have heard that antichrist shall come, even now are there many antichrists; whereby we know that it is the last time. ¹⁹They went out from us, but they were not of us; for if they had been of us, they would no doubt have continued with us: but they went out, that they might be made manifest that they were not all of us. ²⁰But you have an unction from the Holy One, and you know all things. ²¹I have not written to you because you know not the truth, but because you know it, and that no lie is of the truth. ²²Who is a liar but he that denies that Jesus is the Christ? He is antichrist, that denies the Father and the Son. ²³Whoever denies the Son, the same has not the Father: he that acknowledges the Son has the Father also. ²⁴Let that therefore abide in you, which you have heard from the beginning. If that which you have heard from the beginning shall remain in you, you also shall continue in the Son, and in the Father. ²⁵And this is the promise that he has promised us, even eternal life. ²⁶These things have I written to you concerning them that seduce you. ²⁷But the anointing which you have received of him stays in you, and you need not that any man teach you: but as the same anointing teaches you of all things, and is truth, and is no lie, and even as it has taught you, you shall abide in him. ²⁸And now, little children, abide in him; that, when he shall appear, we may have confidence, and not be ashamed before him at his coming. ²⁹If you know that he is righteous, you know that every one that does righteousness is born of him.

3 ¹Behold, what manner of love the Father has bestowed on us, that we should be called the sons of God: therefore the world knows us not, because it knew him not. ²Beloved, now are we the sons of God, and it does not yet appear what we shall be: but we know that, when he shall appear, we shall be like him; for we shall see him as he is. ³And every man that has this hope in him purifies himself, even as he is pure. ⁴Whoever commits sin transgresses also the law: for sin is the transgression of the law. ⁵And you know that he was manifested to take away our sins; and in him is no sin. ⁶Whoever stays in him sins not: whoever sins has not seen him, neither known him. ⁷Little children, let no man deceive you: he that does righteousness is righteous, even as he is righteous. ⁸He that commits sin is of the devil; for the devil sins from the beginning. For this purpose the Son of God was manifested, that he might destroy the works of the devil. ⁹Whoever is born of God does not commit sin; for his seed remains in him: and he cannot sin, because he is born of God. ¹⁰In this the children of God are manifest, and the children of the devil: whoever does not righteousness is not of God, neither he that loves not his brother. ¹¹For this is the message that you heard from the beginning, that we should love one another. ¹²Not as Cain, who was of that wicked one, and slew his brother. And why slew he him? Because his own works were evil, and his brother's righteous. ¹³Marvel not, my brothers, if the world hate you. ¹⁴We know that we have passed from death to life, because we love the brothers. He that loves not his brother stays in death. ¹⁵Whoever hates his brother is a murderer: and you know that no murderer has eternal life abiding in him. ¹⁶Hereby perceive we the love of God, because he laid down his life for us: and we ought to lay down our lives for the brothers. ¹⁷But whoever has this world's good, and sees his brother have need, and shuts up his bowels of compassion from him, how dwells the love of God in him? ¹⁸My little children, let us not love in word, neither in tongue; but in deed and in truth. ¹⁹And hereby we know that we are of the truth, and shall assure our hearts before him. ²⁰For if our heart condemn us, God is greater than our heart, and knows all things. ²¹Beloved, if our heart condemn us not, then have we confidence toward God. ²²And whatever we ask, we receive of him, because we keep his commandments, and do those things that are pleasing in his sight. ²³And this is his commandment, That we should believe on the name of his Son Jesus Christ, and love one another, as he gave us commandment. ²⁴And he that keeps his commandments dwells in him, and he in him. And hereby we know that he stays in us, by the Spirit which he has given us.

4 ¹Beloved, believe not every spirit, but try the spirits whether they are of God: because many false prophets are gone out into the world. ²Hereby know you the Spirit of God: Every spirit that confesses that Jesus Christ is come in the flesh is of God: ³And every spirit that confesses not that Jesus Christ is come in the flesh is not of God: and this is that spirit of antichrist, whereof you have heard that it should come; and even now already is it in the world. ⁴You are of God, little children, and have overcome them: because greater is he that is in you, than he that is in the world. ⁵They are of the world: therefore speak they of the world, and the world hears them. ⁶We are of God: he that knows God hears us; he that is not of God hears not us. Hereby know we the spirit of truth, and the spirit of error. ⁷Beloved, let us love one another: for love is of God; and every one that loves is born of God, and knows God. ⁸He that loves not knows not God; for God is love. ⁹In this was manifested the love of God toward us, because that God sent his only begotten Son into the world, that we might live through him. ¹⁰Herein is love, not that we loved God, but that he loved us, and sent his Son to be the propitiation for our sins. ¹¹Beloved, if God so loved us, we ought also to love one another. ¹²No man has seen God at any time. If we love one another, God dwells in us, and his love is perfected in us. ¹³Hereby know we that we dwell in him, and he in us, because he has given us of his Spirit. ¹⁴And we have seen and do testify that the Father sent the Son to be the Savior of the world. ¹⁵Whoever shall confess that Jesus is the Son of God, God dwells in him, and he in God. ¹⁶And we have known and believed the love that God has to us. God is love; and he that dwells in love dwells in God, and God in him. ¹⁷Herein is our love made perfect, that we may have boldness in the day of judgment: because as he is, so are we in this world. ¹⁸There is no fear in love; but perfect love casts out fear: because fear has torment. He that fears is not made perfect in love. ¹⁹We love him, because he first loved us. ²⁰If a man say, I love God, and hates his brother, he is a liar: for he that loves not his brother whom he has seen, how can he love God whom he has not seen? ²¹And this commandment have we from him, That he who loves God love his brother also.

5 ¹Whoever believes that Jesus is the Christ is born of God: and every one that loves him that fathered loves him also that is begotten of him. ²By this we know that we love the children of God, when we love God, and keep his commandments. ³For this is the love of God, that we keep his commandments: and his commandments are not grievous. ⁴For whatever is born of God overcomes the world: and this is the victory that overcomes the world, even our faith. ⁵Who is he that overcomes the world, but he that believes that Jesus is the Son of God? ⁶This is he that came by water and blood, even Jesus Christ; not by water only, but by water and blood. And it is the Spirit that bears witness, because the Spirit is truth. ⁷For there are three that bear record in heaven, the Father, the Word, and the Holy Ghost: and these three are one. ⁸And there are three that bear witness in earth, the Spirit, and the water, and the blood: and these three agree in one. ⁹If we receive the witness of men, the witness of God is greater: for this is the witness of God which he has testified of his Son. ¹⁰He that believes on the Son of God has the witness in himself: he that believes not God has made him a liar; because he believes not the record that God gave of his Son. ¹¹And this is the record, that God has given to us eternal life, and this life is in his Son. ¹²He that has the Son has life; and he that has not the Son of God has not life. ¹³These things have I written to you that believe on the name of the Son of God; that you may know that you have eternal life, and that you may believe on the name of the Son of God. ¹⁴And this is the confidence that we have in him, that, if we ask any thing according to his will, he hears us: ¹⁵And if we know that he hear us, whatever we ask, we know that we have the petitions that we desired of him. ¹⁶If any man see his brother sin a sin which is not to death, he shall ask, and he shall give him life for them that sin not to death. There is a sin to death: I do not say that he shall pray for it. ¹⁷All unrighteousness is sin: and there is a sin not to death. ¹⁸We know that whoever is born of God sins not; but he that is begotten of God keeps himself, and that wicked one touches him not. ¹⁹And we know that we are of God, and the whole world lies in wickedness. ²⁰And we know that the Son of God is come, and has given us an understanding, that we may know him that is true, and we are in him that is true, even in his Son Jesus Christ. This is the true God, and eternal life. ²¹Little children, keep yourselves from idols. Amen.

Second John

1 ¹The elder to the elect lady and her children, whom I love in the truth; and not I only, but also all they that have known the truth; ²For the truth's sake, which dwells in us, and shall be with us for ever. ³Grace be with you, mercy, and peace, from God the Father, and from the Lord Jesus Christ, the Son of the Father, in truth and love. ⁴I rejoiced greatly that I found of your children walking in truth, as we have received a commandment from the Father. ⁵And now I beseech you, lady, not as though I wrote a new commandment to you, but that which we had from the beginning, that we love one another. ⁶And this is love, that we walk after his commandments. This is the commandment, That, as you have heard from the beginning, you should walk in it. ⁷For many deceivers are entered into the world, who confess not that Jesus Christ is come in the flesh. This is a deceiver and an antichrist. ⁸Look to yourselves, that we lose not those things which we have worked, but that we receive a full reward. ⁹Whoever transgresses, and stays not in the doctrine of Christ, has not God. He that stays in the doctrine of Christ, he has both the Father and the Son. ¹⁰If there come any to you, and bring not this doctrine, receive him not into your house, neither bid him God speed: ¹¹For he that bids him God speed is partaker of his evil deeds. ¹²Having many things to write to you, I would not write with paper and ink: but I trust to come to you, and speak face to face, that our joy may be full. ¹³The children of your elect sister greet you. Amen.

Third John

1 ¹The elder to the well beloved Gaius, whom I love in the truth. ²Beloved, I wish above all things that you may prosper and be in health, even as your soul prospers. ³For I rejoiced greatly, when the brothers came and testified of the truth that is in you, even as you walk in the truth. ⁴I have no greater joy than to hear that my children walk in truth. ⁵Beloved, you do faithfully whatever you do to the brothers, and to strangers; ⁶Which have borne witness of your charity before the church: whom if you bring forward on their journey after a godly sort, you shall do well: ⁷Because that for his name's sake they went forth, taking nothing of the Gentiles. ⁸We therefore ought to receive such, that we might be fellow helpers to the truth. ⁹I wrote to the church: but Diotrephes, who loves to have the preeminence among them, receives us not. ¹⁰Why, if I come, I will remember his deeds which he does, prating against us with malicious words: and not content therewith, neither does he himself receive the brothers, and forbids them that would, and casts them out of the church. ¹¹Beloved, follow not that which is evil, but that which is good. He that does good is of God: but he that does evil has not seen God. ¹²Demetrius has good report of all men, and of the truth itself: yes, and we also bear record; and you know that our record is true. ¹³I had many things to write, but I will not with ink and pen write to you: ¹⁴But I trust I shall shortly see you, and we shall speak face to face. Peace be to you. Our friends salute you. Greet the friends by name.

Jude

1 ¹Jude, the servant of Jesus Christ, and brother of James, to them that are sanctified by God the Father, and preserved in Jesus Christ, and called: ²Mercy to you, and peace, and love, be multiplied. ³Beloved, when I gave all diligence to write to you of the common salvation, it was needful for me to write to you, and exhort you that you should earnestly contend for the faith which was once delivered to the saints. ⁴For there are certain men crept in unawares, who were before of old ordained to this condemnation, ungodly men, turning the grace of our God into lasciviousness, and denying the only Lord God, and our Lord Jesus Christ. ⁵I will therefore put you in remembrance, though you once knew this, how that the Lord, having saved the people out of the land of Egypt, afterward destroyed them that believed not. ⁶And the angels which kept not their first estate, but left their own habitation, he has reserved in everlasting chains under darkness to the judgment of the great day. ⁷Even as Sodom and Gomorrha, and the cities about them in like manner, giving themselves over to fornication, and going after strange flesh, are set forth for an example, suffering the vengeance of eternal fire. ⁸Likewise also these filthy dreamers defile the flesh, despise dominion, and speak evil of dignities. ⁹Yet Michael the archangel, when contending with the devil he disputed about the body of Moses, dared not bring against him a railing accusation, but said, The Lord rebuke you. ¹⁰But these speak evil of those things which they know not: but what they know naturally, as brute beasts, in those things they corrupt themselves. ¹¹Woe to them! for they have gone in the way of Cain, and ran greedily after the error of Balaam for reward, and perished in the gainsaying of Core. ¹²These are spots in your feasts of charity, when they feast with you, feeding themselves without fear: clouds they are without water, carried about of winds; trees whose fruit wither, without fruit, twice dead, plucked up by the roots; ¹³Raging waves of the sea, foaming out their own shame; wandering stars, to whom is reserved the blackness of darkness for ever. ¹⁴And Enoch also, the seventh from Adam, prophesied of these, saying, Behold, the Lord comes with ten thousands of his saints, ¹⁵To execute judgment on all, and to convince all that are ungodly among them of all their ungodly deeds which they have ungodly committed, and of all their hard speeches which ungodly sinners have spoken against him. ¹⁶These are murmurers, complainers, walking after their own lusts; and their mouth speaks great swelling words, having men's persons in admiration because of advantage. ¹⁷But, beloved, remember you the words which were spoken before of the apostles of our Lord Jesus Christ; ¹⁸How that they told you there should be mockers in the last time, who should walk after their own ungodly lusts. ¹⁹These be they who separate themselves, sensual, having not the Spirit. ²⁰But you, beloved, building up yourselves on your most holy faith, praying in the Holy Ghost, ²¹Keep yourselves in the love of God, looking for the mercy of our Lord Jesus Christ to eternal life. ²²And of some have compassion, making a difference: ²³And others save with fear, pulling them out of the fire; hating even the garment spotted by the flesh. ²⁴Now to him that is able to keep you from falling, and to present you faultless before the presence of his glory with exceeding joy, ²⁵To the only wise God our Savior, be glory and majesty, dominion and power, both now and ever. Amen.

Revelation

1 ¹The Revelation of Jesus Christ, which God gave to him, to show to his servants things which must shortly come to pass; and he sent and signified it by his angel to his servant John: ²Who bore record of the word of God, and of the testimony of Jesus Christ, and of all things that he saw. ³Blessed is he that reads, and they that hear the words of this prophecy, and keep those things which are written therein: for the time is at hand. ⁴John to the seven churches which are in Asia: Grace be to you, and peace, from him which is, and which was, and which is to come; and from the seven Spirits which are before his throne; ⁵And from Jesus Christ, who is the faithful witness, and the first begotten of the dead, and the prince of the kings of the earth. To him that loved us, and washed us from our sins in his own blood, ⁶And has made us kings and priests to God and his Father; to him be glory and dominion for ever and ever. Amen. ⁷Behold, he comes with clouds; and every eye shall see him, and they also which pierced him: and all kindreds of the earth shall wail because of him. Even so, Amen. ⁸I am Alpha and Omega, the beginning and the ending, says the Lord, which is, and which was, and which is to come, the Almighty. ⁹I John, who also am your brother, and companion in tribulation, and in the kingdom and patience of Jesus Christ, was in the isle that is called Patmos, for the word of God, and for the testimony of Jesus Christ. ¹⁰I was in the Spirit on the Lord's day, and heard behind me a great voice, as of a trumpet, ¹¹Saying, I am Alpha and Omega, the first and the last: and, What you see, write in a book, and send it to the seven churches which are in Asia; to Ephesus, and to Smyrna, and to Pergamos, and to Thyatira, and to Sardis, and to Philadelphia, and to Laodicea. ¹²And I turned to see the voice that spoke with me. And being turned, I saw seven golden candlesticks; ¹³And in the middle of the seven candlesticks one like to the Son of man, clothed with a garment down to the foot, and girt about the breasts with a golden girdle. ¹⁴His head and his hairs were white like wool, as white as snow; and his eyes were as a flame of fire; ¹⁵And his feet like to fine brass, as if they burned in a furnace; and his voice as the sound of many waters. ¹⁶And he had in his right hand seven stars: and out of his mouth went a sharp two edged sword: and his countenance was as the sun shines in his strength. ¹⁷And when I saw him, I fell at his feet as dead. And he laid his right hand on me, saying to me, Fear not; I am the first and the last: ¹⁸I am he that lives, and was dead; and, behold, I am alive for ever more, Amen; and have the keys of hell and of death. ¹⁹Write the things which you have seen, and the things which are, and the things which shall be hereafter; ²⁰The mystery of the seven stars which you saw in my right hand, and the seven golden candlesticks. The seven stars are the angels of the seven churches: and the seven candlesticks which you saw are the seven churches.

2 ¹To the angel of the church of Ephesus write; These things says he that holds the seven stars in his right hand, who walks in the middle of the seven golden candlesticks; ²I know your works, and your labor, and your patience, and how you can not bear them which are evil: and you have tried them which say they are apostles, and are not, and have found them liars: ³And have borne, and have patience, and for my name's sake have labored, and have not fainted. ⁴Nevertheless I have somewhat against you, because you have left your first love. ⁵Remember therefore from where you are fallen, and repent, and do the first works; or else I will come to you quickly, and will remove your candlestick out of his place, except you repent. ⁶But this you have, that you hate the deeds of the Nicolaitanes, which I also hate. ⁷He that has an ear, let him hear what the Spirit says to the churches; To him that overcomes will I give to eat of the tree of life, which is in the middle of the paradise of God. ⁸And to the angel of the church in Smyrna write; These things says the first and the last, which was dead, and is alive; ⁹I know your works, and tribulation, and poverty, (but you are rich) and I know the blasphemy of them which say they are Jews, and are not, but are the synagogue of Satan. ¹⁰Fear none of those things which you shall suffer: behold, the devil shall cast some of you into prison, that you may be tried; and you shall have tribulation ten days: be you faithful to death, and I will give you a crown of life. ¹¹He that has an ear, let him hear what the Spirit says to the churches; He that overcomes shall not be hurt of the second death. ¹²And to the angel of the church in Pergamos write; These things says he which has the sharp sword with two edges; ¹³I know your works, and where you dwell, even where Satan's seat is: and you hold fast my name, and have not denied my faith, even in those days wherein Antipas was my faithful martyr, who was slain among you, where Satan dwells. ¹⁴But I have a few things against you, because you have there them that hold the doctrine of Balaam, who taught Balac to cast a stumbling block before the children of Israel, to eat things sacrificed to idols, and to commit fornication. ¹⁵So have you also them that hold the doctrine of the Nicolaitanes, which thing I hate. ¹⁶Repent; or else I will come to you quickly, and will fight against them with the sword of my mouth. ¹⁷He that has an ear, let him hear what the Spirit says to the churches; To him that overcomes will I give to eat of the hidden manna, and will give him a white stone, and in the stone a new name written, which no man knows saving he that receives it. ¹⁸And to the angel of the church in Thyatira write; These things says the Son of God, who has his eyes like to a flame of fire, and his feet are like fine brass; ¹⁹I know your works, and charity, and service, and faith, and your patience, and your works; and the last to be more than the first. ²⁰Notwithstanding I have a few things against you, because you suffer that woman Jezebel, which calls herself a prophetess, to teach and to seduce my servants to commit fornication, and to eat things sacrificed to idols. ²¹And I gave her space to repent of her fornication; and she repented not. ²²Behold, I will cast her into a bed, and them that commit adultery with her into great tribulation, except they repent of their deeds. ²³And I will kill her children with death; and all the churches shall know that I am he which searches the reins and hearts: and I will give to every one of you according to your works. ²⁴But to you I say, and to the rest in Thyatira, as many as have not this doctrine, and which have not known the depths of Satan, as they speak; I will put on you none other burden. ^{25}But that which you have already hold fast till I come. ^{26}And he that overcomes, and keeps my works to the end, to him will I give power over the nations: ^{27}And he shall rule them with a rod of iron; as the vessels of a potter shall they be broken to shivers: even as I received of my Father. ^{28}And I will give him the morning star. ^{29}He that has an ear, let him hear what the Spirit says to the churches.

3 ^{1}And to the angel of the church in Sardis write; These things says he that has the seven Spirits of God, and the seven stars; I know your works, that you have a name that you live, and are dead. ^{2}Be watchful, and strengthen the things which remain, that are ready to die: for I have not found your works perfect before God. ^{3}Remember therefore how you have received and heard, and hold fast, and repent. If therefore you shall not watch, I will come on you as a thief, and you shall not know what hour I will come on you. ^{4}You have a few names even in Sardis which have not defiled their garments; and they shall walk with me in white: for they are worthy. ^{5}He that overcomes, the same shall be clothed in white raiment; and I will not blot out his name out of the book of life, but I will confess his name before my Father, and before his angels. ^{6}He that has an ear, let him hear what the Spirit says to the churches. ^{7}And to the angel of the church in Philadelphia write; These things says he that is holy, he that is true, he that has the key of David, he that opens, and no man shuts; and shuts, and no man opens; ^{8}I know your works: behold, I have set before you an open door, and no man can shut it: for you have a little strength, and have kept my word, and have not denied my name. ^{9}Behold, I will make them of the synagogue of Satan, which say they are Jews, and are not, but do lie; behold, I will make them to come and worship before your feet, and to know that I have loved you. ^{10}Because you have kept the word of my patience, I also will keep you from the hour of temptation, which shall come on all the world, to try them that dwell on the earth. ^{11}Behold, I come quickly: hold that fast which you have, that no man take your crown. ^{12}Him that overcomes will I make a pillar in the temple of my God, and he shall go no more out: and I will write on him the name of my God, and the name of the city of my God, which is new Jerusalem, which comes down out of heaven from my God: and I will write on him my new name. ^{13}He that has an ear, let him hear what the Spirit says to the churches. ^{14}And to the angel of the church of the Laodiceans write; These things says the Amen, the faithful and true witness, the beginning of the creation of God; ^{15}I know your works, that you are neither cold nor hot: I would you were cold or hot. ^{16}So then because you are lukewarm, and neither cold nor hot, I will spew you out of my mouth. ^{17}Because you say, I am rich, and increased with goods, and have need of nothing; and know not that you are wretched, and miserable, and poor, and blind, and naked: ^{18}I counsel you to buy of me gold tried in the fire, that you may be rich; and white raiment, that you may be clothed, and that the shame of your nakedness do not appear; and anoint your eyes with eye salve, that you may see. ^{19}As many as I love, I rebuke and chasten: be zealous therefore, and repent. ^{20}Behold, I stand at the door, and knock; if any man hear my voice, and open the door, I will come in to him, and will sup with him, and he with me. ^{21}To him that overcomes will I grant to sit with me in my throne, even as I also overcame, and am set down with my Father in his throne. ^{22}He that has an ear, let him hear what the Spirit says to the churches.

4 ^{1}After this I looked, and, behold, a door was opened in heaven: and the first voice which I heard was as it were of a trumpet talking with me; which said, Come up here, and I will show you things which must be hereafter. ^{2}And immediately I was in the spirit: and, behold, a throne was set in heaven, and one sat on the throne. ^{3}And he that sat was to look on like a jasper and a sardine stone: and there was a rainbow round about the throne, in sight like to an emerald. ^{4}And round about the throne were four and twenty seats: and on the seats I saw four and twenty elders sitting, clothed in white raiment; and they had on their heads crowns of gold. ^{5}And out of the throne proceeded lightning and thunder and voices: and there were seven lamps of fire burning before the throne, which are the seven Spirits of God. ^{6}And before the throne there was a sea of glass like to crystal: and in the middle of the throne, and round about the throne, were four beasts full of eyes before and behind. ^{7}And the first beast was like a lion, and the second beast like a calf, and the third beast had a face as a man, and the fourth beast was like a flying eagle. ^{8}And the four beasts had each of them six wings about him; and they were full of eyes within: and they rest not day and night, saying, Holy, holy, holy, LORD God Almighty, which was, and is, and is to come. ^{9}And when those beasts give glory and honor and thanks to him that sat on the throne, who lives for ever and ever, ^{10}The four and twenty elders fall down before him that sat on the throne, and worship him that lives for ever and ever, and cast their crowns before the throne, saying, ^{11}You are worthy, O Lord, to receive glory and honor and power: for you have created all things, and for your pleasure they are and were created.

5 ^{1}And I saw in the right hand of him that sat on the throne a book written within and on the backside, sealed with seven seals. ^{2}And I saw a strong angel proclaiming with a loud voice, Who is worthy to open the book, and to loose the seals thereof? ^{3}And no man in heaven, nor in earth, neither under the earth, was able to open the book, neither to look thereon. ^{4}And I wept much, because no man was found worthy to open and to read the book, neither to look thereon. ^{5}And one of the elders says to me, Weep not: behold, the Lion of the tribe of Juda, the Root of David, has prevailed to open the book, and to loose the seven seals thereof. ^{6}And I beheld, and, see, in the middle of the throne and of the four beasts, and in the middle of the elders, stood a Lamb as it had been slain, having seven horns and seven eyes, which are the seven Spirits of God sent forth into all the earth. ^{7}And he came and took the book out of the right hand of him that sat on the throne. ^{8}And when he had taken the book, the four beasts and four and twenty elders fell down before the Lamb, having every one of them harps, and golden vials full of odors, which are the prayers of saints. ^{9}And they sung a new song, saying, You are worthy to take the book, and to open the seals thereof: for you were slain, and have redeemed us to God by your blood out of every kindred, and tongue, and people, and nation; ^{10}And have made us to our God kings and priests: and we shall reign on the earth. ¹¹And I beheld, and I heard the voice of many angels round about the throne and the beasts and the elders: and the number of them was ten thousand times ten thousand, and thousands of thousands; ¹²Saying with a loud voice, Worthy is the Lamb that was slain to receive power, and riches, and wisdom, and strength, and honor, and glory, and blessing. ¹³And every creature which is in heaven, and on the earth, and under the earth, and such as are in the sea, and all that are in them, heard I saying, Blessing, and honor, and glory, and power, be to him that sits on the throne, and to the Lamb for ever and ever. ¹⁴And the four beasts said, Amen. And the four and twenty elders fell down and worshipped him that lives for ever and ever.

6 ¹And I saw when the Lamb opened one of the seals, and I heard, as it were the noise of thunder, one of the four beasts saying, Come and see. ²And I saw, and behold a white horse: and he that sat on him had a bow; and a crown was given to him: and he went forth conquering, and to conquer. ³And when he had opened the second seal, I heard the second beast say, Come and see. ⁴And there went out another horse that was red: and power was given to him that sat thereon to take peace from the earth, and that they should kill one another: and there was given to him a great sword. ⁵And when he had opened the third seal, I heard the third beast say, Come and see. And I beheld, and see a black horse; and he that sat on him had a pair of balances in his hand. ⁶And I heard a voice in the middle of the four beasts say, A measure of wheat for a penny, and three measures of barley for a penny; and see you hurt not the oil and the wine. ⁷And when he had opened the fourth seal, I heard the voice of the fourth beast say, Come and see. ⁸And I looked, and behold a pale horse: and his name that sat on him was Death, and Hell followed with him. And power was given to them over the fourth part of the earth, to kill with sword, and with hunger, and with death, and with the beasts of the earth. ⁹And when he had opened the fifth seal, I saw under the altar the souls of them that were slain for the word of God, and for the testimony which they held: ¹⁰And they cried with a loud voice, saying, How long, O Lord, holy and true, do you not judge and avenge our blood on them that dwell on the earth? ¹¹And white robes were given to every one of them; and it was said to them, that they should rest yet for a little season, until their fellow servants also and their brothers, that should be killed as they were, should be fulfilled. ¹²And I beheld when he had opened the sixth seal, and, see, there was a great earthquake; and the sun became black as sackcloth of hair, and the moon became as blood; ¹³And the stars of heaven fell to the earth, even as a fig tree casts her untimely figs, when she is shaken of a mighty wind. ¹⁴And the heaven departed as a scroll when it is rolled together; and every mountain and island were moved out of their places. ¹⁵And the kings of the earth, and the great men, and the rich men, and the chief captains, and the mighty men, and every slave, and every free man, hid themselves in the dens and in the rocks of the mountains; ¹⁶And said to the mountains and rocks, Fall on us, and hide us from the face of him that sits on the throne, and from the wrath of the Lamb: ¹⁷For the great day of his wrath is come; and who shall be able to stand?

7 ¹And after these things I saw four angels standing on the four corners of the earth, holding the four winds of the earth, that the wind should not blow on the earth, nor on the sea, nor on any tree. ²And I saw another angel ascending from the east, having the seal of the living God: and he cried with a loud voice to the four angels, to whom it was given to hurt the earth and the sea, ³Saying, Hurt not the earth, neither the sea, nor the trees, till we have sealed the servants of our God in their foreheads. ⁴And I heard the number of them which were sealed: and there were sealed an hundred and forty and four thousand of all the tribes of the children of Israel. ⁵Of the tribe of Juda were sealed twelve thousand. Of the tribe of Reuben were sealed twelve thousand. Of the tribe of Gad were sealed twelve thousand. ⁶Of the tribe of Aser were sealed twelve thousand. Of the tribe of Nephthalim were sealed twelve thousand. Of the tribe of Manasses were sealed twelve thousand. ⁷Of the tribe of Simeon were sealed twelve thousand. Of the tribe of Levi were sealed twelve thousand. Of the tribe of Issachar were sealed twelve thousand. ⁸Of the tribe of Zabulon were sealed twelve thousand. Of the tribe of Joseph were sealed twelve thousand. Of the tribe of Benjamin were sealed twelve thousand. ⁹After this I beheld, and, see, a great multitude, which no man could number, of all nations, and kindreds, and people, and tongues, stood before the throne, and before the Lamb, clothed with white robes, and palms in their hands; ¹⁰And cried with a loud voice, saying, Salvation to our God which sits on the throne, and to the Lamb. ¹¹And all the angels stood round about the throne, and about the elders and the four beasts, and fell before the throne on their faces, and worshipped God, ¹²Saying, Amen: Blessing, and glory, and wisdom, and thanksgiving, and honor, and power, and might, be to our God for ever and ever. Amen. ¹³And one of the elders answered, saying to me, What are these which are arrayed in white robes? and from where came they? ¹⁴And I said to him, Sir, you know. And he said to me, These are they which came out of great tribulation, and have washed their robes, and made them white in the blood of the Lamb. ¹⁵Therefore are they before the throne of God, and serve him day and night in his temple: and he that sits on the throne shall dwell among them. ¹⁶They shall hunger no more, neither thirst any more; neither shall the sun light on them, nor any heat. ¹⁷For the Lamb which is in the middle of the throne shall feed them, and shall lead them to living fountains of waters: and God shall wipe away all tears from their eyes.

8 ¹And when he had opened the seventh seal, there was silence in heaven about the space of half an hour. ²And I saw the seven angels which stood before God; and to them were given seven trumpets. ³And another angel came and stood at the altar, having a golden censer; and there was given to him much incense, that he should offer it with the prayers of all saints on the golden altar which was before the throne. ⁴And the smoke of the incense, which came with the prayers of the saints, ascended up before God out of the angel's hand. ⁵And the angel took the censer, and filled it with fire of the altar, and cast it into the earth: and there

were voices, and thunder, and lightning, and an earthquake. ⁶And the seven angels which had the seven trumpets prepared themselves to sound. ⁷The first angel sounded, and there followed hail and fire mingled with blood, and they were cast on the earth: and the third part of trees was burnt up, and all green grass was burnt up. ⁸And the second angel sounded, and as it were a great mountain burning with fire was cast into the sea: and the third part of the sea became blood; ⁹And the third part of the creatures which were in the sea, and had life, died; and the third part of the ships were destroyed. ¹⁰And the third angel sounded, and there fell a great star from heaven, burning as it were a lamp, and it fell on the third part of the rivers, and on the fountains of waters; ¹¹And the name of the star is called Wormwood: and the third part of the waters became wormwood; and many men died of the waters, because they were made bitter. ¹²And the fourth angel sounded, and the third part of the sun was smitten, and the third part of the moon, and the third part of the stars; so as the third part of them was darkened, and the day shone not for a third part of it, and the night likewise. ¹³And I beheld, and heard an angel flying through the middle of heaven, saying with a loud voice, Woe, woe, woe, to the inhabitants of the earth by reason of the other voices of the trumpet of the three angels, which are yet to sound!

9 ¹And the fifth angel sounded, and I saw a star fall from heaven to the earth: and to him was given the key of the bottomless pit. ²And he opened the bottomless pit; and there arose a smoke out of the pit, as the smoke of a great furnace; and the sun and the air were darkened by reason of the smoke of the pit. ³And there came out of the smoke locusts on the earth: and to them was given power, as the scorpions of the earth have power. ⁴And it was commanded them that they should not hurt the grass of the earth, neither any green thing, neither any tree; but only those men which have not the seal of God in their foreheads. ⁵And to them it was given that they should not kill them, but that they should be tormented five months: and their torment was as the torment of a scorpion, when he strikes a man. ⁶And in those days shall men seek death, and shall not find it; and shall desire to die, and death shall flee from them. ⁷And the shapes of the locusts were like to horses prepared to battle; and on their heads were as it were crowns like gold, and their faces were as the faces of men. ⁸And they had hair as the hair of women, and their teeth were as the teeth of lions. ⁹And they had breastplates, as it were breastplates of iron; and the sound of their wings was as the sound of chariots of many horses running to battle. ¹⁰And they had tails like to scorpions, and there were stings in their tails: and their power was to hurt men five months. ¹¹And they had a king over them, which is the angel of the bottomless pit, whose name in the Hebrew tongue is Abaddon, but in the Greek tongue has his name Apollyon. ¹²One woe is past; and, behold, there come two woes more hereafter. ¹³And the sixth angel sounded, and I heard a voice from the four horns of the golden altar which is before God, ¹⁴Saying to the sixth angel which had the trumpet, Loose the four angels which are bound in the great river Euphrates. ¹⁵And the four angels were loosed, which were prepared for an hour, and a day, and a month, and a year, for to slay the third part of men.

¹⁶And the number of the army of the horsemen were two hundred thousand thousand: and I heard the number of them. ¹⁷And thus I saw the horses in the vision, and them that sat on them, having breastplates of fire, and of jacinth, and brimstone: and the heads of the horses were as the heads of lions; and out of their mouths issued fire and smoke and brimstone. ¹⁸By these three was the third part of men killed, by the fire, and by the smoke, and by the brimstone, which issued out of their mouths. ¹⁹For their power is in their mouth, and in their tails: for their tails were like to serpents, and had heads, and with them they do hurt. ²⁰And the rest of the men which were not killed by these plagues yet repented not of the works of their hands, that they should not worship devils, and idols of gold, and silver, and brass, and stone, and of wood: which neither can see, nor hear, nor walk: ²¹Neither repented they of their murders, nor of their sorceries, nor of their fornication, nor of their thefts.

10 ¹And I saw another mighty angel come down from heaven, clothed with a cloud: and a rainbow was on his head, and his face was as it were the sun, and his feet as pillars of fire: ²And he had in his hand a little book open: and he set his right foot on the sea, and his left foot on the earth, ³And cried with a loud voice, as when a lion roars: and when he had cried, seven thunders uttered their voices. ⁴And when the seven thunders had uttered their voices, I was about to write: and I heard a voice from heaven saying to me, Seal up those things which the seven thunders uttered, and write them not. ⁵And the angel which I saw stand on the sea and on the earth lifted up his hand to heaven, ⁶And swore by him that lives for ever and ever, who created heaven, and the things that therein are, and the earth, and the things that therein are, and the sea, and the things which are therein, that there should be time no longer: ⁷But in the days of the voice of the seventh angel, when he shall begin to sound, the mystery of God should be finished, as he has declared to his servants the prophets. ⁸And the voice which I heard from heaven spoke to me again, and said, Go and take the little book which is open in the hand of the angel which stands on the sea and on the earth. ⁹And I went to the angel, and said to him, Give me the little book. And he said to me, Take it, and eat it up; and it shall make your belly bitter, but it shall be in your mouth sweet as honey. ¹⁰And I took the little book out of the angel's hand, and ate it up; and it was in my mouth sweet as honey: and as soon as I had eaten it, my belly was bitter. ¹¹And he said to me, You must prophesy again before many peoples, and nations, and tongues, and kings.

11 ¹And there was given me a reed like to a rod: and the angel stood, saying, Rise, and measure the temple of God, and the altar, and them that worship therein. ²But the court which is without the temple leave out, and measure it not; for it is given to the Gentiles: and the holy city shall they tread under foot forty and two months. ³And I will give power to my two witnesses, and they shall prophesy a thousand two hundred and three score days, clothed in sackcloth. ⁴These are the two olive trees, and the two candlesticks standing before the God of the earth. ⁵And if any man will hurt them, fire proceeds out of their mouth, and devours their enemies: and if any man will hurt them, he must in this manner be killed. ⁶These have power to shut heaven, that it rain not in the days of their prophecy: and have power over waters to turn them to blood, and to smite the earth with all plagues, as often as they will. ⁷And when they shall have finished their testimony, the beast that ascends out of the bottomless pit shall make war against them, and shall overcome them, and kill them. ⁸And their dead bodies shall lie in the street of the great city, which spiritually is called Sodom and Egypt, where also our Lord was crucified. ⁹And they of the people and kindreds and tongues and nations shall see their dead bodies three days and an half, and shall not suffer their dead bodies to be put in graves. ¹⁰And they that dwell on the earth shall rejoice over them, and make merry, and shall send gifts one to another; because these two prophets tormented them that dwelled on the earth. ¹¹And after three days and an half the spirit of life from God entered into them, and they stood on their feet; and great fear fell on them which saw them. ¹²And they heard a great voice from heaven saying to them, Come up here. And they ascended up to heaven in a cloud; and their enemies beheld them. ¹³And the same hour was there a great earthquake, and the tenth part of the city fell, and in the earthquake were slain of men seven thousand: and the remnant were affrighted, and gave glory to the God of heaven. ¹⁴The second woe is past; and, behold, the third woe comes quickly. ¹⁵And the seventh angel sounded; and there were great voices in heaven, saying, The kingdoms of this world are become the kingdoms of our Lord, and of his Christ; and he shall reign for ever and ever. ¹⁶And the four and twenty elders, which sat before God on their seats, fell on their faces, and worshipped God, ¹⁷Saying, We give you thanks, O LORD God Almighty, which are, and were, and are to come; because you have taken to you your great power, and have reigned. ¹⁸And the nations were angry, and your wrath is come, and the time of the dead, that they should be judged, and that you should give reward to your servants the prophets, and to the saints, and them that fear your name, small and great; and should destroy them which destroy the earth. ¹⁹And the temple of God was opened in heaven, and there was seen in his temple the ark of his testament: and there were lightning, and voices, and thunder, and an earthquake, and great hail.

12

¹And there appeared a great wonder in heaven; a woman clothed with the sun, and the moon under her feet, and on her head a crown of twelve stars: ²And she being with child cried, travailing in birth, and pained to be delivered. ³And there appeared another wonder in heaven; and behold a great red dragon, having seven heads and ten horns, and seven crowns on his heads. ⁴And his tail drew the third part of the stars of heaven, and did cast them to the earth: and the dragon stood before the woman which was ready to be delivered, for to devour her child as soon as it was born. ⁵And she brought forth a man child, who was to rule all nations with a rod of iron: and her child was caught up to God, and to his throne. ⁶And the woman fled into the wilderness, where she has a place prepared of God, that they should feed her there a thousand two hundred and three score days. ⁷And there was war in heaven: Michael and his angels fought against the dragon; and the dragon fought and his angels, ⁸And prevailed not; neither was their place found any more in heaven. ⁹And the great dragon was cast out, that old serpent, called the Devil, and Satan, which deceives the whole world: he was cast out into the earth, and his angels were cast out with him. ¹⁰And I heard a loud voice saying in heaven, Now is come salvation, and strength, and the kingdom of our God, and the power of his Christ: for the accuser of our brothers is cast down, which accused them before our God day and night. ¹¹And they overcame him by the blood of the Lamb, and by the word of their testimony; and they loved not their lives to the death. ¹²Therefore rejoice, you heavens, and you that dwell in them. Woe to the inhabitants of the earth and of the sea! for the devil is come down to you, having great wrath, because he knows that he has but a short time. ¹³And when the dragon saw that he was cast to the earth, he persecuted the woman which brought forth the man child. ¹⁴And to the woman were given two wings of a great eagle, that she might fly into the wilderness, into her place, where she is nourished for a time, and times, and half a time, from the face of the serpent. ¹⁵And the serpent cast out of his mouth water as a flood after the woman, that he might cause her to be carried away of the flood. ¹⁶And the earth helped the woman, and the earth opened her mouth, and swallowed up the flood which the dragon cast out of his mouth. ¹⁷And the dragon was wroth with the woman, and went to make war with the remnant of her seed, which keep the commandments of God, and have the testimony of Jesus Christ.

13

¹And I stood on the sand of the sea, and saw a beast rise up out of the sea, having seven heads and ten horns, and on his horns ten crowns, and on his heads the name of blasphemy. ²And the beast which I saw was like to a leopard, and his feet were as the feet of a bear, and his mouth as the mouth of a lion: and the dragon gave him his power, and his seat, and great authority. ³And I saw one of his heads as it were wounded to death; and his deadly wound was healed: and all the world wondered after the beast. ⁴And they worshipped the dragon which gave power to the beast: and they worshipped the beast, saying, Who is like to the beast? who is able to make war with him? ⁵And there was given to him a mouth speaking great things and blasphemies; and power was given to him to continue forty and two months. ⁶And he opened his mouth in blasphemy against God, to blaspheme his name, and his tabernacle, and them that dwell in heaven. ⁷And it was given to him to make war with the saints, and to overcome them: and power was given him over all kindreds, and tongues, and nations. ⁸And all that dwell on the earth shall worship him, whose names are not written in the book of life of the Lamb slain from the foundation of the world. ⁹If any man have an ear, let him hear. ¹⁰He that leads into captivity shall go into captivity: he that kills with the sword must be killed with the sword. Here is the patience and the faith of the saints. ¹¹And I beheld another beast coming up out of the earth; and he had two horns like a lamb, and he spoke as a dragon. ¹²And he exercises all the power of the first beast before him, and causes the earth and them which dwell therein to worship the first beast, whose deadly wound was healed. ¹³And he does great wonders, so that he makes fire come down from

heaven on the earth in the sight of men, ¹⁴And deceives them that dwell on the earth by the means of those miracles which he had power to do in the sight of the beast; saying to them that dwell on the earth, that they should make an image to the beast, which had the wound by a sword, and did live. ¹⁵And he had power to give life to the image of the beast, that the image of the beast should both speak, and cause that as many as would not worship the image of the beast should be killed. ¹⁶And he causes all, both small and great, rich and poor, free and bond, to receive a mark in their right hand, or in their foreheads: ¹⁷And that no man might buy or sell, save he that had the mark, or the name of the beast, or the number of his name. ¹⁸Here is wisdom. Let him that has understanding count the number of the beast: for it is the number of a man; and his number is Six hundred three score and six.

14 ¹And I looked, and, see, a Lamb stood on the mount Sion, and with him an hundred forty and four thousand, having his Father's name written in their foreheads. ²And I heard a voice from heaven, as the voice of many waters, and as the voice of a great thunder: and I heard the voice of harpers harping with their harps: ³And they sung as it were a new song before the throne, and before the four beasts, and the elders: and no man could learn that song but the hundred and forty and four thousand, which were redeemed from the earth. ⁴These are they which were not defiled with women; for they are virgins. These are they which follow the Lamb wherever he goes. These were redeemed from among men, being the first fruits to God and to the Lamb. ⁵And in their mouth was found no guile: for they are without fault before the throne of God. ⁶And I saw another angel fly in the middle of heaven, having the everlasting gospel to preach to them that dwell on the earth, and to every nation, and kindred, and tongue, and people, ⁷Saying with a loud voice, Fear God, and give glory to him; for the hour of his judgment is come: and worship him that made heaven, and earth, and the sea, and the fountains of waters. ⁸And there followed another angel, saying, Babylon is fallen, is fallen, that great city, because she made all nations drink of the wine of the wrath of her fornication. ⁹And the third angel followed them, saying with a loud voice, If any man worship the beast and his image, and receive his mark in his forehead, or in his hand, ¹⁰The same shall drink of the wine of the wrath of God, which is poured out without mixture into the cup of his indignation; and he shall be tormented with fire and brimstone in the presence of the holy angels, and in the presence of the Lamb: ¹¹And the smoke of their torment ascends up for ever and ever: and they have no rest day nor night, who worship the beast and his image, and whoever receives the mark of his name. ¹²Here is the patience of the saints: here are they that keep the commandments of God, and the faith of Jesus. ¹³And I heard a voice from heaven saying to me, Write, Blessed are the dead which die in the Lord from now on: Yes, says the Spirit, that they may rest from their labors; and their works do follow them. ¹⁴And I looked, and behold a white cloud, and on the cloud one sat like to the Son of man, having on his head a golden crown, and in his hand a sharp sickle. ¹⁵And another angel came out of the temple, crying with a loud voice to him that sat on the cloud, Thrust in your sickle, and reap: for the time is come for you to reap; for the harvest of the earth is ripe. ¹⁶And he that sat on the cloud thrust in his sickle on the earth; and the earth was reaped. ¹⁷And another angel came out of the temple which is in heaven, he also having a sharp sickle. ¹⁸And another angel came out from the altar, which had power over fire; and cried with a loud cry to him that had the sharp sickle, saying, Thrust in your sharp sickle, and gather the clusters of the vine of the earth; for her grapes are fully ripe. ¹⁹And the angel thrust in his sickle into the earth, and gathered the vine of the earth, and cast it into the great wine press of the wrath of God. ²⁰And the wine press was trodden without the city, and blood came out of the wine press, even to the horse bridles, by the space of a thousand and six hundred furlongs.

15 ¹And I saw another sign in heaven, great and marvelous, seven angels having the seven last plagues; for in them is filled up the wrath of God. ²And I saw as it were a sea of glass mingled with fire: and them that had gotten the victory over the beast, and over his image, and over his mark, and over the number of his name, stand on the sea of glass, having the harps of God. ³And they sing the song of Moses the servant of God, and the song of the Lamb, saying, Great and marvelous are your works, Lord God Almighty; just and true are your ways, you King of saints. ⁴Who shall not fear you, O Lord, and glorify your name? for you only are holy: for all nations shall come and worship before you; for your judgments are made manifest. ⁵And after that I looked, and, behold, the temple of the tabernacle of the testimony in heaven was opened: ⁶And the seven angels came out of the temple, having the seven plagues, clothed in pure and white linen, and having their breasts girded with golden girdles. ⁷And one of the four beasts gave to the seven angels seven golden vials full of the wrath of God, who lives for ever and ever. ⁸And the temple was filled with smoke from the glory of God, and from his power; and no man was able to enter into the temple, till the seven plagues of the seven angels were fulfilled.

16 ¹And I heard a great voice out of the temple saying to the seven angels, Go your ways, and pour out the vials of the wrath of God on the earth. ²And the first went, and poured out his vial on the earth; and there fell a noisome and grievous sore on the men which had the mark of the beast, and on them which worshipped his image. ³And the second angel poured out his vial on the sea; and it became as the blood of a dead man: and every living soul died in the sea. ⁴And the third angel poured out his vial on the rivers and fountains of waters; and they became blood. ⁵And I heard the angel of the waters say, You are righteous, O Lord, which are, and were, and shall be, because you have judged thus. ⁶For they have shed the blood of saints and prophets, and you have given them blood to drink; for they are worthy. ⁷And I heard another out of the altar say, Even so, Lord God Almighty, true and righteous are your judgments. ⁸And the fourth angel poured out his vial on the sun; and power was given to him to scorch men with fire. ⁹And men were scorched with great heat, and blasphemed the name of God, which has power over these plagues: and they repented not to give him glory. ¹⁰And the fifth angel poured out his vial on the seat of the beast; and his kingdom was full of darkness; and they gnawed their tongues for pain, ¹¹And blasphemed the God of heaven because of their pains and their sores, and repented not of their deeds. ¹²And the sixth angel poured out his vial on the great river Euphrates; and the water thereof was dried up, that the way of the kings of the east might be prepared. ¹³And I saw three unclean spirits like frogs come out of the mouth of the dragon, and out of the mouth of the beast, and out of the mouth of the false prophet. ¹⁴For they are the spirits of devils, working miracles, which go forth to the kings of the earth and of the whole world, to gather them to the battle of that great day of God Almighty. ¹⁵Behold, I come as a thief. Blessed is he that watches, and keeps his garments, lest he walk naked, and they see his shame. ¹⁶And he gathered them together into a place called in the Hebrew tongue Armageddon. ¹⁷And the seventh angel poured out his vial into the air; and there came a great voice out of the temple of heaven, from the throne, saying, It is done. ¹⁸And there were voices, and thunders, and lightning; and there was a great earthquake, such as was not since men were on the earth, so mighty an earthquake, and so great. ¹⁹And the great city was divided into three parts, and the cities of the nations fell: and great Babylon came in remembrance before God, to give to her the cup of the wine of the fierceness of his wrath. ²⁰And every island fled away, and the mountains were not found. ²¹And there fell on men a great hail out of heaven, every stone about the weight of a talent: and men blasphemed God because of the plague of the hail; for the plague thereof was exceeding great.

17

¹And there came one of the seven angels which had the seven vials, and talked with me, saying to me, Come here; I will show to you the judgment of the great whore that sits on many waters: ²With whom the kings of the earth have committed fornication, and the inhabitants of the earth have been made drunk with the wine of her fornication. ³So he carried me away in the spirit into the wilderness: and I saw a woman sit on a scarlet colored beast, full of names of blasphemy, having seven heads and ten horns. ⁴And the woman was arrayed in purple and scarlet color, and decked with gold and precious stones and pearls, having a golden cup in her hand full of abominations and filthiness of her fornication: ⁵And on her forehead was a name written, MYSTERY, BABYLON THE GREAT, THE MOTHER OF HARLOTS AND ABOMINATIONS OF THE EARTH. ⁶And I saw the woman drunken with the blood of the saints, and with the blood of the martyrs of Jesus: and when I saw her, I wondered with great admiration. ⁷And the angel said to me, Why did you marvel? I will tell you the mystery of the woman, and of the beast that carries her, which has the seven heads and ten horns. ⁸The beast that you saw was, and is not; and shall ascend out of the bottomless pit, and go into perdition: and they that dwell on the earth shall wonder, whose names were not written in the book of life from the foundation of the world, when they behold the beast that was, and is not, and yet is. ⁹And here is the mind which has wisdom. The seven heads are seven mountains, on which the woman sits. ¹⁰And there are seven kings: five are fallen, and one is, and the other is not yet come; and when he comes, he must continue a short space. ¹¹And the beast that was, and is not, even he is the eighth, and is of the seven, and goes into perdition. ¹²And the ten horns which you saw are ten kings, which have received no kingdom as yet; but receive power as kings one hour with the beast. ¹³These have one mind, and shall give their power and strength to the beast. ¹⁴These shall make war with the Lamb, and the Lamb shall overcome them: for he is Lord of lords, and King of kings: and they that are with him are called, and chosen, and faithful. ¹⁵And he says to me, The waters which you saw, where the whore sits, are peoples, and multitudes, and nations, and tongues. ¹⁶And the ten horns which you saw on the beast, these shall hate the whore, and shall make her desolate and naked, and shall eat her flesh, and burn her with fire. ¹⁷For God has put in their hearts to fulfill his will, and to agree, and give their kingdom to the beast, until the words of God shall be fulfilled. ¹⁸And the woman which you saw is that great city, which reigns over the kings of the earth.

18

¹And after these things I saw another angel come down from heaven, having great power; and the earth was lightened with his glory. ²And he cried mightily with a strong voice, saying, Babylon the great is fallen, is fallen, and is become the habitation of devils, and the hold of every foul spirit, and a cage of every unclean and hateful bird. ³For all nations have drunk of the wine of the wrath of her fornication, and the kings of the earth have committed fornication with her, and the merchants of the earth are waxed rich through the abundance of her delicacies. ⁴And I heard another voice from heaven, saying, Come out of her, my people, that you be not partakers of her sins, and that you receive not of her plagues. ⁵For her sins have reached to heaven, and God has remembered her iniquities. ⁶Reward her even as she rewarded you, and double to her double according to her works: in the cup which she has filled fill to her double. ⁷How much she has glorified herself, and lived deliciously, so much torment and sorrow give her: for she says in her heart, I sit a queen, and am no widow, and shall see no sorrow. ⁸Therefore shall her plagues come in one day, death, and mourning, and famine; and she shall be utterly burned with fire: for strong is the Lord God who judges her. ⁹And the kings of the earth, who have committed fornication and lived deliciously with her, shall mourn her, and lament for her, when they shall see the smoke of her burning, ¹⁰Standing afar off for the fear of her torment, saying, Alas, alas that great city Babylon, that mighty city! for in one hour is your judgment come. ¹¹And the merchants of the earth shall weep and mourn over her; for no man buys their merchandise any more: ¹²The merchandise of gold, and silver, and precious stones, and of pearls, and fine linen, and purple, and silk, and scarlet, and all thyine wood, and all manner vessels of ivory, and all manner vessels of most precious wood, and of brass, and iron, and marble, ¹³And cinnamon, and odors, and ointments, and frankincense, and wine, and oil, and fine flour, and wheat, and beasts, and sheep, and horses, and chariots, and slaves, and souls of men. ¹⁴And the fruits that your soul lusted after are departed from you, and all things which were dainty and goodly are departed from you, and you shall find them no more at all.

¹⁵The merchants of these things, which were made rich by her, shall stand afar off for the fear of her torment, weeping and wailing, ¹⁶And saying, Alas, alas that great city, that was clothed in fine linen, and purple, and scarlet, and decked with gold, and precious stones, and pearls! ¹⁷For in one hour so great riches is come to nothing. And every shipmaster, and all the company in ships, and sailors, and as many as trade by sea, stood afar off, ¹⁸And cried when they saw the smoke of her burning, saying, What city is like to this great city! ¹⁹And they cast dust on their heads, and cried, weeping and wailing, saying, Alas, alas that great city, wherein were made rich all that had ships in the sea by reason of her costliness! for in one hour is she made desolate. ²⁰Rejoice over her, you heaven, and you holy apostles and prophets; for God has avenged you on her. ²¹And a mighty angel took up a stone like a great millstone, and cast it into the sea, saying, Thus with violence shall that great city Babylon be thrown down, and shall be found no more at all. ²²And the voice of harpers, and musicians, and of pipers, and trumpeters, shall be heard no more at all in you; and no craftsman, of whatever craft he be, shall be found any more in you; and the sound of a millstone shall be heard no more at all in you; ²³And the light of a candle shall shine no more at all in you; and the voice of the bridegroom and of the bride shall be heard no more at all in you: for your merchants were the great men of the earth; for by your sorceries were all nations deceived. ²⁴And in her was found the blood of prophets, and of saints, and of all that were slain on the earth.

19 ¹And after these things I heard a great voice of much people in heaven, saying, Alleluia; Salvation, and glory, and honor, and power, to the Lord our God: ²For true and righteous are his judgments: for he has judged the great whore, which did corrupt the earth with her fornication, and has avenged the blood of his servants at her hand. ³And again they said, Alleluia And her smoke rose up for ever and ever. ⁴And the four and twenty elders and the four beasts fell down and worshipped God that sat on the throne, saying, Amen; Alleluia. ⁵And a voice came out of the throne, saying, Praise our God, all you his servants, and you that fear him, both small and great. ⁶And I heard as it were the voice of a great multitude, and as the voice of many waters, and as the voice of mighty thunder, saying, Alleluia: for the Lord God omnipotent reigns. ⁷Let us be glad and rejoice, and give honor to him: for the marriage of the Lamb is come, and his wife has made herself ready. ⁸And to her was granted that she should be arrayed in fine linen, clean and white: for the fine linen is the righteousness of saints. ⁹And he says to me, Write, Blessed are they which are called to the marriage supper of the Lamb. And he says to me, These are the true sayings of God. ¹⁰And I fell at his feet to worship him. And he said to me, See you do it not: I am your fellow servant, and of your brothers that have the testimony of Jesus: worship God: for the testimony of Jesus is the spirit of prophecy. ¹¹And I saw heaven opened, and behold a white horse; and he that sat on him was called Faithful and True, and in righteousness he does judge and make war. ¹²His eyes were as a flame of fire, and on his head were many crowns; and he had a name written, that no man knew, but he himself. ¹³And he was clothed with a clothing dipped in blood: and his name is called The Word of God. ¹⁴And the armies which were in heaven followed him on white horses, clothed in fine linen, white and clean. ¹⁵And out of his mouth goes a sharp sword, that with it he should smite the nations: and he shall rule them with a rod of iron: and he treads the wine press of the fierceness and wrath of Almighty God. ¹⁶And he has on his clothing and on his thigh a name written, KING OF KINGS, AND LORD OF LORDS. ¹⁷And I saw an angel standing in the sun; and he cried with a loud voice, saying to all the fowls that fly in the middle of heaven, Come and gather yourselves together to the supper of the great God; ¹⁸That you may eat the flesh of kings, and the flesh of captains, and the flesh of mighty men, and the flesh of horses, and of them that sit on them, and the flesh of all men, both free and bond, both small and great. ¹⁹And I saw the beast, and the kings of the earth, and their armies, gathered together to make war against him that sat on the horse, and against his army. ²⁰And the beast was taken, and with him the false prophet that worked miracles before him, with which he deceived them that had received the mark of the beast, and them that worshipped his image. These both were cast alive into a lake of fire burning with brimstone. ²¹And the remnant were slain with the sword of him that sat on the horse, which sword proceeded out of his mouth: and all the fowls were filled with their flesh.

20 ¹And I saw an angel come down from heaven, having the key of the bottomless pit and a great chain in his hand. ²And he laid hold on the dragon, that old serpent, which is the Devil, and Satan, and bound him a thousand years, ³And cast him into the bottomless pit, and shut him up, and set a seal on him, that he should deceive the nations no more, till the thousand years should be fulfilled: and after that he must be loosed a little season. ⁴And I saw thrones, and they sat on them, and judgment was given to them: and I saw the souls of them that were beheaded for the witness of Jesus, and for the word of God, and which had not worshipped the beast, neither his image, neither had received his mark on their foreheads, or in their hands; and they lived and reigned with Christ a thousand years. ⁵But the rest of the dead lived not again until the thousand years were finished. This is the first resurrection. ⁶Blessed and holy is he that has part in the first resurrection: on such the second death has no power, but they shall be priests of God and of Christ, and shall reign with him a thousand years. ⁷And when the thousand years are expired, Satan shall be loosed out of his prison, ⁸And shall go out to deceive the nations which are in the four quarters of the earth, Gog, and Magog, to gather them together to battle: the number of whom is as the sand of the sea. ⁹And they went up on the breadth of the earth, and compassed the camp of the saints about, and the beloved city: and fire came down from God out of heaven, and devoured them. ¹⁰And the devil that deceived them was cast into the lake of fire and brimstone, where the beast and the false prophet are, and shall be tormented day and night for ever and ever. ¹¹And I saw a great white throne, and him that sat on it, from whose face the earth and the heaven fled away; and there was found no place for them. ¹²And I saw the dead, small and great, stand before God; and the books were opened: and another book was opened, which is the book of life: and the dead were judged out of those things which were written in the books, according to their works. ¹³And the sea gave up the dead which were in it; and death and hell delivered up the dead which were in them: and they were judged every man according to their works. ¹⁴And death and hell were cast into the lake of fire. This is the second death. ¹⁵And whoever was not found written in the book of life was cast into the lake of fire.

21

¹And I saw a new heaven and a new earth: for the first heaven and the first earth were passed away; and there was no more sea. ²And I John saw the holy city, new Jerusalem, coming down from God out of heaven, prepared as a bride adorned for her husband. ³And I heard a great voice out of heaven saying, Behold, the tabernacle of God is with men, and he will dwell with them, and they shall be his people, and God himself shall be with them, and be their God. ⁴And God shall wipe away all tears from their eyes; and there shall be no more death, neither sorrow, nor crying, neither shall there be any more pain: for the former things are passed away. ⁵And he that sat on the throne said, Behold, I make all things new. And he said to me, Write: for these words are true and faithful. ⁶And he said to me, It is done. I am Alpha and Omega, the beginning and the end. I will give to him that is thirsty of the fountain of the water of life freely. ⁷He that overcomes shall inherit all things; and I will be his God, and he shall be my son. ⁸But the fearful, and unbelieving, and the abominable, and murderers, and fornicators, and sorcerers, and idolaters, and all liars, shall have their part in the lake which burns with fire and brimstone: which is the second death. ⁹And there came to me one of the seven angels which had the seven vials full of the seven last plagues, and talked with me, saying, Come here, I will show you the bride, the Lamb's wife. ¹⁰And he carried me away in the spirit to a great and high mountain, and showed me that great city, the holy Jerusalem, descending out of heaven from God, ¹¹Having the glory of God: and her light was like to a stone most precious, even like a jasper stone, clear as crystal; ¹²And had a wall great and high, and had twelve gates, and at the gates twelve angels, and names written thereon, which are the names of the twelve tribes of the children of Israel: ¹³On the east three gates; on the north three gates; on the south three gates; and on the west three gates. ¹⁴And the wall of the city had twelve foundations, and in them the names of the twelve apostles of the Lamb. ¹⁵And he that talked with me had a golden reed to measure the city, and the gates thereof, and the wall thereof. ¹⁶And the city lies foursquare, and the length is as large as the breadth: and he measured the city with the reed, twelve thousand furlongs. The length and the breadth and the height of it are equal. ¹⁷And he measured the wall thereof, an hundred and forty and four cubits, according to the measure of a man, that is, of the angel. ¹⁸And the building of the wall of it was of jasper: and the city was pure gold, like to clear glass. ¹⁹And the foundations of the wall of the city were garnished with all manner of precious stones. The first foundation was jasper; the second, sapphire; the third, a chalcedony; the fourth, an emerald; ²⁰The fifth, sardonyx; the sixth, sardius; the seventh, chrysolyte; the eighth, beryl; the ninth, a topaz; the tenth, a chrysoprasus; the eleventh, a jacinth; the twelfth, an amethyst. ²¹And the twelve gates were twelve pearls: every several gate was of one pearl: and the street of the city was pure gold, as it were transparent glass. ²²And I saw no temple therein: for the Lord God Almighty and the Lamb are the temple of it. ²³And the city had no need of the sun, neither of the moon, to shine in it: for the glory of God did lighten it, and the Lamb is the light thereof. ²⁴And the nations of them which are saved shall walk in the light of it: and the kings of the earth do bring their glory and honor into it. ²⁵And the gates of it shall not be shut at all by day: for there shall be no night there. ²⁶And they shall bring the glory and honor of the nations into it. ²⁷And there shall in no wise enter into it any thing that defiles, neither whatever works abomination, or makes a lie: but they which are written in the Lamb's book of life.

22

¹And he showed me a pure river of water of life, clear as crystal, proceeding out of the throne of God and of the Lamb. ²In the middle of the street of it, and on either side of the river, was there the tree of life, which bore twelve manner of fruits, and yielded her fruit every month: and the leaves of the tree were for the healing of the nations. ³And there shall be no more curse: but the throne of God and of the Lamb shall be in it; and his servants shall serve him: ⁴And they shall see his face; and his name shall be in their foreheads. ⁵And there shall be no night there; and they need no candle, neither light of the sun; for the Lord God gives them light: and they shall reign for ever and ever. ⁶And he said to me, These sayings are faithful and true: and the Lord God of the holy prophets sent his angel to show to his servants the things which must shortly be done. ⁷Behold, I come quickly: blessed is he that keeps the sayings of the prophecy of this book. ⁸And I John saw these things, and heard them. And when I had heard and seen, I fell down to worship before the feet of the angel which showed me these things. ⁹Then says he to me, See you do it not: for I am your fellow servant, and of your brothers the prophets, and of them which keep the sayings of this book: worship God. ¹⁰And he says to me, Seal not the sayings of the prophecy of this book: for the time is at hand. ¹¹He that is unjust, let him be unjust still: and he which is filthy, let him be filthy still: and he that is righteous, let him be righteous still: and he that is holy, let him be holy still. ¹²And, behold, I come quickly; and my reward is with me, to give every man according as his work shall be. ¹³I am Alpha and Omega, the beginning and the end, the first and the last. ¹⁴Blessed are they that do his commandments, that they may have right to the tree of life, and may enter in through the gates into the city. ¹⁵For without are dogs, and sorcerers, and fornicators, and murderers, and idolaters, and whoever loves and makes a lie. ¹⁶I Jesus have sent my angel to testify to you these things in the churches. I am the root and the offspring of David, and the bright and morning star. ¹⁷And the Spirit and the bride say, Come. And let him that hears say, Come. And let him that is thirsty come. And whoever will, let him take the water of life freely. ¹⁸For I testify to every man that hears the words of the prophecy of this book, If any man shall add to these things, God shall add to him the plagues that are

written in this book: [19]And if any man shall take away from the words of the book of this prophecy, God shall take away his part out of the book of life, and out of the holy city, and from the things which are written in this book. [20]He which testifies these things says, Surely I come quickly. Amen. Even so, come, Lord Jesus. [21]The grace of our Lord Jesus Christ be with you all. Amen.

Appendix

List of archaic KJV words and modern words in AKJV.

A

abhorrest, abhor
abhorreth, abhors
abideth, stays
abode, stayed
abodest, stayed
aboundeth, abounds
acceptest, accept
accepteth, accepts
accuseth, accuses
acknowledgeth, acknowledges
addeth, adds
adorneth, adorns
advantageth, advantages
affecteth, affects
afflictest, afflict
aforehand, beforehand
agreeth, agrees
aileth, ails
alloweth, allows
altereth, alters
alway, always
amongst, among
anointedst, anointed
anointest, anoint
anon, immediately
answeredst, answered
answerest, answer
answereth, answers
appeareth, appears
appeaseth, appeases
appertaineth, appertains
appointeth, appoints
approacheth, approaches
approvest, approve
approveth, approves
ariseth, rises
art, are
ascendeth, ascends
askest, ask
asketh, asks
asswaged, assuaged
athirst, thirsty
availeth, avails
avangeth, avenges
avengest, avenge
awakest, wake
awaketh, wakes
axe, ax

B

backbiteth, backbites
badest, bade
baketh, bakes
baptizest, baptize
baptizeth, baptizes
bare, bear
barest, bear
bearest, bear
beareth, bears
beatest, beat
beateth, beats
becamest, became
becometh, becomes
befalleth, befalls
begat, was the father of/fathered
begettest, beget
begetteth, begets
beginnest, begin
behaveth, behaves
beheld, saw
beholdest, behold
beholdeth, beholds
believest, believe
believeth, believes
belongest, belong
belongeth, belongs
bendeth, bends
bereaveth, bereaves
besought, sought
betrayes, betrays
betrayest, betray
betrayeth, betrays
bewaileth, bewails
bewrayeth, betrays
biddeth, bids
bindeth, binds
biteth, bites
blasphemest, blaspheme
blasphemeth, blasphemes
bleseth, blesses
blessest, bless
blesseth, blesses
blindeth, blinds
blotteth, blots
bloweth, blows
boastest, boast
boasteth, boasts
borroweth, borrows
boweth, bows
brakest, brake
brasen, brazen
breakest, break
breaketh, breaks
breatheth, breathes
bridechamber, bride chamber
bridleth, bridles
bringest, bring
bringeth, brings
broughtest, brought
builded, built
buildedst, built
buildest, build
buildeth, builds
burneth, burns
buyest, buy
buyeth, buys

C

calledst, called
callest, call
calleth, calls
calveth, calves
camest, came
canst, can
carcase, carcass
carcases, carcasses
carest, care
careth, cares
carriest, carry
carrieth, carries
castedst, cast
castest, cast
casteth, casts
catcheth, catches
causest, cause
causeth, causes
ceaseth, ceases
challengeth, challenges
chanceth, chances
changest, change
changeth, changes
chargedst, charged
chargest, charge
chaseth, chases
chastenest, chasten
chasteneth, chastens
chastiseth, chastises
cheereth, cheers
cherisheth, cherishes
cheweth, chews
chiefest, most chief
choosest, choose
chooseth, chooses
clappeth, claps
clave, cut

cleanseth, cleans
cleaveth, cleaves
climbeth, climbs
closest, close
clothest, clothe
cockcrowing, cock-crowing
comest, come
cometh, comes
comfortedst, comforted
comforteth, comforts
commandedst, commanded
commandest, command
commandeth, commands
commendest, commend
commendeth, commends
committest, commit
committeth, commits
compassest, compass
compasseth, compasses
compellest, compel
compoundeth, compounds
concealeth, conceals
concerneth, concerns
condemnest, condemn
condemneth, condemns
confesseth, confesses
confirmeth, confirms
consentedst, consented
considerest, consider
considereth, considers
consisteth, consists
constraineth, constrains
consulteth, consults
consumeth, consumes
containeth, contains
contemn, scorn
contemned, scorned
contemneth, scorns
contendest, contend
contendeth, contends
continueth, continues
converteth, converts
convinceth, convinces
correcteth, corrects
corrupteth, corrupts
coucheth, couches
couldest, could
counsellor, counselor
counteth, counts
coupleth, couples
coveredst, covered
coverest, cover
covereth, covers
coveteth, covets
craveth, craves
createth, creates
creepeth, creeps
criest, cry
crieth, cries
croucheth, crouches

crownedst, crowned
crownest, crown
crowneth, crowns
cumber, encumber
cumbered, encumbered
cumbereth, encumbers
cursedst, cursed
cursest, curse
curseth, curses
cuttest, cut
cutteth, cuts

D

darkeneth, darkens
dasheth, dashes
dealest, deal
dealeth, deals
decayeth, decays
deceiveth, deceives
deckedst, decked
deckest, deck
decketh, decks
declareth, declares
declineth, declines
defendest, defend
deferreth, defers
defiledst, defiled
defileth, defiles
delayeth, delays
delightest, delight
delighteth, delights
deliveredst, delivered
deliverest, deliver
delivereth, delivers
denieth, denies
departeth, departs
descendeth, descends
describeth, describes
deserveth, deserves
desiredest, desired
desiredst, desired
desirest, desire
desireth, desires
despisest, despise
despiseth, despises
despitefully, spitefully
destroyest, destroy
destroyeth, destroys
deviseth, devises
devourest, devour
devoureth, devours
diddest, did
didst, did
diest, die
dieth, dies
differeth, differs
digged, dig
diggedst, digged
diggeth, digs

dippeth, dips
directeth, directs
disannulleth, disannuls
disappointeth, disappoints
discerneth, discerns
discovereth, discovers
disguiseth, disguises
dishonourest, dishonour
dishonoureth, dishonours
dissembleth, dissembles
dissolvest, dissolve
distributeth, distributes
divideth, divides
divineth, divines
divorcement, divorce
doest, do
doeth, does
dost, do
doth, does
doubteth, doubts
draweth, draws
dreameth, dreams
dresseth, dresses
drewest, drew
driedst, dried
drieth, dries
drinketh, drinks
driveth, drives
droppeth, drops
dureth, endures
durst, dared
dweeleth, dwells
dwellest, dwell
dwelleth, dwells
dwelt, dwelled

E

earneth, earns
eatest, eat
eateth, eats
eateth, eats
edifieth, edifies
eldest, oldest
Elias, Elijah
emboldeneth, emboldens
encampeth, encamps
endeth, ends
endureth, endures
enlargeth, enlarges
enquire, inquire
enquired, inquired
enquirest, inquire
enquiry, inquiry
enrichest, enrich
entangleth, entangles
entereth, enters
enticeth, entices
entreateth, entreats
enviest, envy

envieth, envies
ere, before
erreth, errs
Esaias, Isaiah
escapeth, escapes
escheweth, eschews
establisheth, establishes
esteemeth, esteems
exacteth, exacts
exaltest, exalt
exalteth, exalts
exceedest, exceed
exceedeth, exceeds
excellest, excel
excelleth, excels
executedst, executed
executest, execute
executeth, executes
exerciseth, exercises
exhorteth, exhorts
extendeth, extends

F

fadeth, fades
faileth, fails
faintest, faint
fainteth, faints
fallest, fall
falleth, falls
fashioneth, fashions
fastest, fast
fatling, fatted calf
fatlings, fatted calves
favour, favor
favoured, favored
favourest, favor
favoureth, favors
fearest, fear
feareth, fears
feedest, feed
feedeth, feeds
feignest, feign
fellest, fell
fellowservant, fellow servant
fellowservants, fellow servants
fetcheth, fetches
fetcht, fetched
fighteth, fights
filledst, filled
fillest, fill
filleth, fills
findest, find
findeth, finds
firbiddeth, forbids
firstling, firstborn
firstlings, firstborns
fitteth, fits
flattereth, flatters
fleddest, fled

fleeth, flees
flieth, flies
flourisheth, flourishes
floweth, flows
fluttereth, flutters
foameth, foams
foldest, fold
foldeth, folds
followedest, followed
followedst, followed
followeth, follows
forasmuch, for as much
forbad, forbade
forbeareth, forbears
forbiddeth, forbids
foregivest, forgive
foregiveth, forgives
foreseeth, foresees
forgat, forgot
forgavest, forgave
forgettest, forget
forgetteth, forgets
forgiveth, forgives
formeth, forms
forsaketh, forsakes
forsookest, forsook
forthwith, immediately
fouledst, fouled
foundest, found
frameth, frames
fretteth, frets
frustrateth, frustrates
fulfil, fulfill
fulness, fullness

G

gaddest, gad
gat, got
gatherest, gather
gathereth, gathers
gavest, gave
gendereth, genders
getteth, gets
girdedst, girded
girdest, gird
girdeth, girds
givest, give
giveth, gives
gloriest, glory
glorieth, glories
glorifieth, glorifies
gnasheth, gnashes
goest, go
goeth, goes
goodliest, best
goodman, manager
graveth, carved
greeteth, greets
grieveth, grieves

groaneth, groans
gropeth, gropes
groweth, grows
guestchamber, guest room

H

hadst, had
halteth, halts
handleth, handles
hangeth, hangs
happeneth, happens
hardeneth, hardens
hast, have
hasted, hurried
hasteneth, hastens
hasteth, hastes
hatcheth, hatches
hatest, hates
hateth, hate
hath, has
healeth, heals
heapeth, heaps
heardest, heard
hearest, hear
heareth, hears
hearken, listen
hearkened, listened
hearkenedst, listened
hearkeneth, hearkens
helpeth, helps
hence, away
henceforth, now on
herdmen, herdsmen
heweth, hews
hidest, hide
hideth, hides
hindereth, hinders
hirest, hire
hither, here
hitherto, till now
holdest, hold
holdeth, holds
holpen, helped
honour, honor
honourable, honorable
honourest, honour
honoureth, honours
honours, honors
hopest, hope
hopeth, hopes
howbeit, how is it
humbledst, humbled
humbleth, humbles
hundredfold, hundred times
hungered, hungry
hungred, hungered
huntest, hunt

hunteth, hunts
hurleth, hurls (2018)
husbandman, manager
husbandmen, managers

I

imagineth, imagines
impotent, weak
imputeth, imputes
inclineth, inclines
increasest, increase
increaseth, increases
inhabitest, inhabit
inhabiteth, inhabits
inheriteth, inherits
innocency, innocence
insomuch, so much
instructer, instructor
intendest, intend
intermeddleth, intermeddles
intreat, entreat
intreated, entreated

J

judgest, judge
judgeth, judges
justifieth, justifies

K

keepest, keep
keepeth, keeps
killedst, killed
killest, kill
killeth, kills
kindleth, kindles
kine, cows
knewest, knew
knocketh, knocks
knowest, know
knoweth, knows

L

labour, labor
labourers, laborers
laboureth, labours
lackest, lack
lacketh, lacks
ladeth, covers
laidst, laid
languisheth, languishes
lappeth, laps
latchet, lace
laugheth, laughs
layedst, layed
layest, lay
layeth, lays

leadest, lead
leadeth, leads
leaneth, leans
leathern, leather
leaveneth, leavens
leaveth, leaves
leddest, led
leftest, left
lendeth, lends
lettest, let
letteth, lets
licketh, licks
liest, lie
lieth, lies
liftest, lift
lifteth, lifts
lighteneth, lightens
lightest, light
lighteth, lights
liketh, likes
limiteth, limits
lingereth, lingers
listeth, wants
livest, live
liveth, lives
loadeth, loads
loatheth, loathes
lodgest, lodge
lodgeth, lodges
longedst, longed
longeth, longs
lookest, look
looketh, looks
looseth, looses
loseth, loses
lotheth, loathes
lovedst, loved
lovest, love
loveth, loves
loweth, lows
lunatick, lunatic
lusteth, lusts

M

madest, made
maintainest, maintain
makest, make
maketh, makes
marchedst, marched
markest, mark
marketh, marks
marrieth, marries
marvelled, marveled
marvellous, marvelous
mayest, may
meanest, mean
meaneth, means
meddleth, meddles
meetest, meet

meeteth, meets
melteth, melts
messias, messiah
midst, middle
mightest, might
milch, milk
ministereth, ministers
mnameth, names
mockest, mock
mocketh, mocks
morter, mortar
mourneth, mourns
movedst, moved
moveth, moves
multipliedst, multiplied
multiplieth, multiplies
mustereth, musters

N

nameth, names
needest, need
needeth, needs
neighbour, neighbor
neighbours, neighbors
Noe, Noah
nought, nothing
nourisheth, nourishes
numberest, number

O

obeyedst, obeyed
obeyeth, obeys
observest, observe
observeth, observes
obtaineth, obtains
occupieth, occupies
offence, offense
offences, offenses
offereth, offers
oftimes, often
openest, open
openeth, opens
opposest, oppose
opposeth, opposes
oppresseth, oppresses
ordaineth, ordains
ordereth, orders
Osee, Hosea
ought, any(thing)/some(thing)/should
oughtest, ought
our's, ours
outwent, preceded
overcometh, overcomes
overfloweth, overflows
overtaketh, overtakes
overthroweth, overthrows
overturneth, overturns
owest, owe

oweth, owes
owneth, owns

P

pacifieth, pacifies
paintedst, painted
panteth, pants
pardoneth, pardons
partakest, partake
parteth, parts
passedst, passed
passest, pass
passeth, passes
paweth, paws
payeth, pays
perceivest, perceive
perceiveth, perceives
performeth, performs (2018)
perisheth, perishes
persecutest, persecute
persuadest, persuade
persuadeth, persuades
pertaineth, pertains
perverteth, perverts
pharaoh-hophra, pharaoh Hophra
pierceth, pierces
pineth, pines
piss, urine
pisseth, urinates
pitieth, pities
plantedst, planted
planteth, plants
playedst, played
playeth, plays
pleadeth, pleads
pleaseth, pleases
plenteousness, plenty
plotteth, plots
ploweth, plows
plucketh, plucks
pluckt, plucked
pondereth, ponders
possessest, possess
possesseth, possesses
pouredst, poured
poureth, pours
praiseth, praises
prayest, pray
prayeth, prays
preachest, preach
preacheth, preaches
preparedst, prepared
preparest, prepare
prepareth, prepares
preservest, preserve
preserveth, preserves
presseth, presses
pretence, pretense
prevailest, prevail

prevaileth, prevails
preventest, prevent
privily, privately
proceedeth, proceeds
proclaimeth, proclaims
procureth, procures
profaneth, profanes
profiteth, profits
prolongeth, prolongs
promisedst, promised
prophesieth, prophesies
prospereth, prospers
proveth, proves
provideth, provides
provokedst, provoked
provoketh, provokes
publick, public
publisheth, publishes
puffeth, puffs
purgeth, purges
purifieth, purifies
purposeth, purposes
pursueth, pursues
puttest, puts
putteth, puts

Q

quickeneth, revives
quieteth, quiets

R

rageth, rages
raiseth, raises
rattleth, rattles
reacheth, reaches
readest, read
readeth, reads
reapest, reap
reapeth, reaps
rebellest, rebel
rebuketh, rebukes
receivedst, received
receiveth, receives
reckoneth, reckons
recompensest, recompense
redeemedst, redeemed
redeemeth, redeems
refraineth, refrains
refresheth, refreshes
refusedst, refused
refuseth, refuses
regardest, regard
regardeth, regards
reignest, reign
reigneth, reigns
rejecteth, rejects
rejoicest, rejoice

rejoiceth, rejoices
relieveth, relieves
remainest, remain
remaineth, remains
remaineth, remains
rememberest, remember
remembereth, remembers
removeth, removes
renderest, render
rendereth, renders
renewest, renew
rentest, cover
repayeth, repays
repeateth, repeats
repentest, repent
repenteth, repents
repliest, reply
reproachest, reproach
reproacheth, reproaches
reproveth, reproves
requirest, require
requireth, requires
rescueth, rescues
reserveth, reserves
resisteth, resists
respecteth, respects
restest, rest
resteth, rests
restoreth, restores
restrainest, restrain
retaineth, retains
returneth, returns
revealeth, reveals
revengeth, revenges
revilest, revile
rewardeth, rewards
rideth, rides
rigour, rigor
risest, rise
riseth, rises
roareth, roars
roasteth, roasts
robbeth, robs
rolleth, rolls
rulest, rule
ruleth, rules
rumours, rumors
runnest, run
runneth, runs
rusheth, rushes

S

sacrificedst, sacrificed
sacrificeth, sacrifices
saidst, said
saith, says (2018)
saltines, saltiness
saluteth, salutes
sanctifieth, sanctifies

satest, sate
satisfiest, satisfy
satisfieth, satisfies
savest, save
saveth, saves
saviour, savior
savourest, savor
savours, savors
sawest, saw
sayest, say
scaleth, scales
scarest, scare
scattereth, scatters
scornest, scorn
scorneth, scorns
scourge, whip
scourgeth, scourges
scrip, money
sealest, seal
sealeth, seals
searchest, search
searcheth, searches
seduceth, seduces
seekest, seek
seeketh, seeks
seemeth, seems
seest, see
seeth, sees
selfwill, self-will
sellest, sell
selleth, sells
sendest, send
sendeth, sends
sentest, sent
separateth, separates
septre, scepter
sepulchre, sepulcher
sepulchres, sepulchers
servedst, served
servest, serve
serveth, serves
settest, set
setteth, sets
settlest, settle
sewest, sew
seweth, sews
shaketh, shakes
shalt, will
shameth, shames
sharpeneth, sharpens
sheddeth, sheds
sheepshearers, sheep shearers
shew, show
shewbread, show-bread
shewed, showed
shewedst, showed
shewest, show
sheweth, shows
shewing, showing
shineth, shines

shooteth, shoots
shouldest, should
shouteth, shouts
shutteth, shuts
sighest, sigh
sigheth, sighs
signifieth, signifies
singeth, singes
sinnest, sin
sinneth, sins
sittest, sit
sitteth, sits
sixtyfold, sixty times
skippedst, skipped
slanderest, slander
slandereth, slanders
slayeth, slays
sleepest, sleep
sleepeth, sleeps
slewest, slew
slideth, slides
slimepits, slime pits
slippeth, slips
slumbereth, slumbers
smellest, smell
smelleth, smells
smitest, smite
smiteth, smites
smootheth, smoothes
smotest, smote
snuffeth, snuffs
sojourneth, sojourns (2018)
sorroweth, sorrows
soundeth, sounds
sowedst, sowed
sowest, sow
soweth, sows
spake, spoke
spakest, spoke
spareth, spares
speakest, speak
speaketh, speaks
spendest, spend
spendeth, spends
spicery, spices
spoilest, spoil
spoileth, spoils
spreadest, spread
spreadeth, spreads
springeth, springs
sprinkleth, sprinkles
spunge, sponge
spunges, sponges
stablisheth, establishes
staggereth, staggers
standest, stand
standeth, stands
stayeth, stays
stealeth, steals
steppeth, steps

sticketh, sticks
stillest, still
stilleth, stills
stingeth, stings
stinketh, stinks
stirreth, stirs
stonest, stone
stoodest, stood
stoopeth, stoops
stoppeth, stops
straightly, sternly
straiteneth, straitens
straitest, strait
straitly, straightly
strawed, strewed
strengthenedst, strengthened
strengtheneth, strengthens
stretchedst, stretched
stretchest, stretch
stretcheth, stretches
striketh, strikes
stript, stripped
strivest, strive
striveth, strives
studieth, studies
stumbleth, stumbles
subduedst, subdued
subdueth, subdues
subtil, subtle
subtilty, subtlety
succeedest, succeed
sufferest, suffer
suffereth, suffers
sufficeth, suffices
supplieth, supplies
swalloweth, swallows
sware, swore
swarest, sware
swareth, swears
sweareth, swears
swimmest, swim
swimmeth, swims

T

takest, take
taketh, takes
talkest, talk
talketh, talks
tarriest, tarry
tarrieth, tarries
tasteth, tastes
teachest, teach
teacheth, teaches
teareth, tears
tellest, tell
telleth, tells
tempteth, tempts
tendeth, tends
terrifiest, terrify

testifiedst, testified
testifieth, testifies
thee, you
their's, theirs
thence, there
thenceforth, thereafter
thereof, there
thinkest, think
thinketh, thinks
thirsteth, thirsts
thirtyfold, thirty times
thou, you
thoughtest, thought
thresheth, threshes
threwest, threw
throughly, thoroughly
thrusteth, thrusts
thundereth, thunders
thy, your
thyself, yourself
tillest, till
tilleth, tills
tookest, took
toucheth, touches
transgressest, transgress
transgresseth, transgresses
travailest, travail
travaileth, travails
travelleth, travels
travelling, traveling
treadeth, treads
treasurest, treasure
trembleth, trembles
trickleth, trickles
triest, try
trieth, tries
trimmest, trim
troubledst, troubled
troublest, trouble
troubleth, troubles
trustedst, trusted
trustest, trust
trusteth, trusts
turnest, turn
turneth, turns
twain, two

U

uncovereth, uncovers
understandest, understand
understandeth, understands
unsavoury, unsavory
unto, to
unwashen, unwashed
upbraideth, upbraids (2018)
upholdest, uphold
upholdeth, upholds
upon, on
usest, use

useth, uses
uttereth, utters

V

valuest, value
vanisheth, vanish
vaunteth, brags (2018)
verily, truly
vesture, clothing
visitest, visit
visiteth, visits
vomiteth, vomits
vowedst, vowed
vowest, vow
voweth, vows

W

waiteth, waits
wakeneth, wakens
waketh, wakes
walkedst, walked
walkest, walk
walketh, walks
wanderest, wander
wandereth, wanders
wanteth, wants
warmeth, warms
warreth, wars
washest, wash
wast, were
wasteth, wastes
watcheth, watches
wateredst, watered
waterest, water
watereth, waters
wavereth, wavers
waxeth, waxes
weakeneth, weakens
weareth, wears
wearieth, wearies
weavest, weave
weepeth, weeps
weepest, weep
weepeth, weeps
weigheth, weighs
weighteth, weights
wellbeloved, well-beloved
wentest, went
whatsoever, whatever
whence, where
whensoever, whenever
whereon, which
wheresoever, wherever
whereunto, to what/which/where
wherewith, with which
whirleth, whirls
whither, where
whithersoever, wherever

whoso, whoever
whosoever, whoever
willeth, wills
winebibber, drunkard
winefat, wine vat
winepress, wine press
winketh, winks
winneth, wins
winnoweth, winnows
wipeth, wipes
wist, knew
withal, therewith
withdrawest, withdraw
withdraweth, withdraws
withereth, withers
withheldest, withheld
withholdeth, withholds
witnesseth, witnesses
worketh, works
worshippeth, worships
wot, know
wouldest, would
woundedst, wounded
woundeth, wounds
writest, write
writeth, writes
wrongeth, wrongs
wrought, worked
wroughtest, worked

Y

ye, you
yesternight, last night
yieldeth, yields
your's, yours

FOUNDING DOCUMENTS

The Declaration of Independence

In Congress, July 4, 1776

The unanimous Declaration of the thirteen united States of America, When in the Course of human events, it becomes necessary for one people to dissolve the political bands which have connected them with another, and to assume among the powers of the earth, the separate and equal station to which the Laws of Nature and of Nature's God entitle them, a decent respect to the opinions of mankind requires that they should declare the causes which impel them to the separation.

We hold these truths to be self-evident, that all men are created equal, that they are endowed by their Creator with certain unalienable Rights, that among these are Life, Liberty and the pursuit of Happiness.--That to secure these rights, Governments are instituted among Men, deriving their just powers from the consent of the governed, --That whenever any Form of Government becomes destructive of these ends, it is the Right of the People to alter or to abolish it, and to institute new Government, laying its foundation on such principles and organizing its powers in such form, as to them shall seem most likely to effect their Safety and Happiness. Prudence, indeed, will dictate that Governments long established should not be changed for light and transient causes; and accordingly all experience hath shewn, that mankind are more disposed to suffer, while evils are sufferable, than to right themselves by abolishing the forms to which they are accustomed. But when a long train of abuses and usurpations, pursuing invariably the same Object evinces a design to reduce them under absolute Despotism, it is their right, it is their duty, to throw off such Government, and to provide new Guards for their future security.--Such has been the patient sufferance of these Colonies; and such is now the necessity which constrains them to alter their former Systems of Government. The history of the present King of Great Britain is a history of repeated injuries and usurpations, all having in direct object the establishment of an absolute Tyranny over these States. To prove this, let Facts be submitted to a candid world.

He has refused his Assent to Laws, the most wholesome and necessary for the public good.

He has forbidden his Governors to pass Laws of immediate and pressing importance, unless suspended in their operation till his Assent should be obtained; and when so suspended, he has utterly neglected to attend to them.

He has refused to pass other Laws for the accommodation of large districts of people, unless those people would relinquish the right of Representation in the Legislature, a right inestimable to them and formidable to tyrants only.

He has called together legislative bodies at places unusual, uncomfortable, and distant from the depository of their public Records, for the sole purpose of fatiguing them into compliance with his measures.

He has dissolved Representative Houses repeatedly, for opposing with manly firmness his invasions on the rights of the people.

He has refused for a long time, after such dissolutions, to cause others to be elected; whereby the Legislative powers, incapable of Annihilation, have returned to the People at large for their exercise; the State remaining in the mean time exposed to all the dangers of invasion from without, and convulsions within.

He has endeavoured to prevent the population of these States; for that purpose obstructing the Laws for Naturalization of Foreigners; refusing to pass others to encourage their migrations hither, and raising the conditions of new Appropriations of Lands.

He has obstructed the Administration of Justice, by refusing his Assent to Laws for establishing Judiciary powers.

He has made Judges dependent on his Will alone, for the tenure of their offices, and the amount and payment of their salaries.

He has erected a multitude of New Offices, and sent hither swarms of Officers to harrass our people, and eat out their substance.

He has kept among us, in times of peace, Standing Armies without the Consent of our legislatures.

He has affected to render the Military independent of and superior to the Civil power.

He has combined with others to subject us to a jurisdiction foreign to our constitution, and unacknowledged by our laws; giving his Assent to their Acts of pretended Legislation:

For Quartering large bodies of armed troops among us:

For protecting them, by a mock Trial, from punishment for any Murders which they should commit on the Inhabitants of these States:

For cutting off our Trade with all parts of the world:

For imposing Taxes on us without our Consent:

For depriving us in many cases, of the benefits of Trial by Jury:

For transporting us beyond Seas to be tried for pretended offences:

For abolishing the free System of English Laws in a neighbouring Province, establishing therein an Arbitrary government, and enlarging its Boundaries so as to render it at once an example and fit instrument for introducing the same absolute rule into these Colonies:

For taking away our Charters, abolishing our most valuable Laws, and altering fundamentally the Forms of our Governments:

For suspending our own Legislatures, and declaring themselves invested with power to legislate for us in all cases whatsoever.

He has abdicated Government here, by declaring us out of his Protection and waging War against us.

He has plundered our seas, ravaged our Coasts, burnt our towns, and destroyed the lives of our people.

He is at this time transporting large Armies of foreign Mercenaries to compleat the works of death, desolation and tyranny, already begun with circumstances of Cruelty & perfidy scarcely paralleled in the most barbarous ages, and totally unworthy the Head of a civilized nation.

He has constrained our fellow Citizens taken Captive on the high Seas to bear Arms against their Country, to become the executioners of their friends and Brethren, or to fall themselves by their Hands.

He has excited domestic insurrections amongst us, and has endeavoured to bring on the inhabitants of our frontiers, the merciless Indian Savages, whose known rule of warfare, is an undistinguished destruction of all ages, sexes and conditions.

In every stage of these Oppressions We have Petitioned for Redress in the most humble terms: Our repeated Petitions have been answered only by repeated injury. A Prince whose character is thus marked by every act which may define a Tyrant, is unfit to be the ruler of a free people.

Nor have We been wanting in attentions to our Brittish brethren. We have warned them from time to time of attempts by their legislature to extend an unwarrantable jurisdiction over us. We have reminded them of the circumstances of our emigration and settlement here. We have appealed to their native justice and magnanimity, and we have conjured them by the ties of our common kindred to disavow these usurpations, which, would inevitably interrupt our connections and correspondence. They too have been deaf to the voice of justice and of consanguinity. We must, therefore, acquiesce in the necessity, which denounces our Separation, and hold them, as we hold the rest of mankind, Enemies in War, in Peace Friends.

We, therefore, the Representatives of the united States of America, in General Congress, Assembled, appealing to the Supreme Judge of the world for the rectitude of our intentions, do, in the Name, and by Authority of the good People of these Colonies, solemnly publish and declare, That these United Colonies are, and of Right ought to be Free and Independent States; that they are Absolved from all Allegiance to the British Crown, and that all political connection between them and the State of Great Britain, is and ought to be totally dissolved; and that as Free and Independent States, they have full Power to levy War, conclude Peace, contract Alliances, establish Commerce, and to do all other Acts and Things which Independent States may of right do. And for the support of this Declaration, with a firm reliance on the protection of divine Providence, we mutually pledge to each other our Lives, our Fortunes and our sacred Honor.

Georgia

Button Gwinnett

Lyman Hall

George Walton

North Carolina

William Hooper

Joseph Hewes

John Penn

South Carolina

Edward Rutledge

Thomas Heyward, Jr.

Thomas Lynch, Jr.

Arthur Middleton

Massachusetts

John Hancock

Maryland

Samuel Chase

William Paca

Thomas Stone

Charles Carroll of Carrollton

Virginia

George Wythe

Richard Henry Lee

Thomas Jefferson

Benjamin Harrison

Thomas Nelson, Jr.

Francis Lightfoot Lee

Carter Braxton

Pennsylvania

Robert Morris

Benjamin Rush

Benjamin Franklin

Pennsylvania (cont.)
John Morton
George Clymer
James Smith
George Taylor
James Wilson
George Ross

Delaware
Caesar Rodney
George Read
Thomas McKean

New York
William Floyd
Philip Livingston
Francis Lewis
Lewis Morris

New Jersey
Richard Stockton
John Witherspoon
Francis Hopkinson
John Hart
Abraham Clark

New Hampshire
Josiah Bartlett
William Whipple

Massachusetts
Samuel Adams
John Adams
Robert Treat Paine
Elbridge Gerry

Rhode Island
Stephen Hopkins
William Ellery

Connecticut
Roger Sherman
Samuel Huntington
William Williams
Oliver Wolcott

New Hampshire
Matthew Thornton

The Constitution of the United States

We the People of the United States, in Order to form a more perfect Union, establish Justice, insure domestic Tranquility, provide for the common defence, promote the general Welfare, and secure the Blessings of Liberty to ourselves and our Posterity, do ordain and establish this Constitution for the United States of America.

Article. I.

Section. 1.

All legislative Powers herein granted shall be vested in a Congress of the United States, which shall consist of a Senate and House of Representatives.

Section. 2.

The House of Representatives shall be composed of Members chosen every second Year by the People of the several States, and the Electors in each State shall have the Qualifications requisite for Electors of the most numerous Branch of the State Legislature.

No Person shall be a Representative who shall not have attained to the Age of twenty five Years, and been seven Years a Citizen of the United States, and who shall not, when elected, be an Inhabitant of that State in which he shall be chosen.

Representatives and direct Taxes shall be apportioned among the several States which may be included within this Union, according to their respective Numbers, which shall be determined by adding to the whole Number of free Persons, including those bound to Service for a Term of Years, and excluding Indians not taxed, three fifths of all other Persons. The actual Enumeration shall be made within three Years after the first Meeting of the Congress of the United States, and within every subsequent Term of ten Years, in such Manner as they shall by Law direct. The Number of Representatives shall not exceed one for every thirty Thousand, but each State shall have at Least one Representative; and until such enumeration shall be made, the State of New Hampshire shall be entitled to chuse three, Massachusetts eight, Rhode-Island and Providence Plantations one, Connecticut five, New-York six, New Jersey four, Pennsylvania eight, Delaware one, Maryland six, Virginia ten, North Carolina five, South Carolina five, and Georgia three.

When vacancies happen in the Representation from any State, the Executive Authority thereof shall issue Writs of Election to fill such Vacancies.

The House of Representatives shall chuse their Speaker and other Officers; and shall have the sole Power of Impeachment.

Section. 3.

The Senate of the United States shall be composed of two Senators from each State, chosen by the Legislature thereof, for six Years; and each Senator shall have one Vote.

Immediately after they shall be assembled in Consequence of the first Election, they shall be divided as equally as may be into three Classes. The Seats of the Senators of the first Class shall be vacated at the Expiration of the second Year, of the second Class at the Expiration of the fourth Year, and of the third Class at the Expiration of the sixth Year, so that one third may be chosen every second Year; and if Vacancies happen by Resignation, or otherwise, during the Recess of the Legislature of any State, the Executive thereof may make temporary Appointments until the next Meeting of the Legislature, which shall then fill such Vacancies.

No Person shall be a Senator who shall not have attained to the Age of thirty Years, and been nine Years a Citizen of the United States, and who shall not, when elected, be an Inhabitant of that State for which he shall be chosen.

The Vice President of the United States shall be President of the Senate, but shall have no Vote, unless they be equally divided.

The Senate shall chuse their other Officers, and also a President pro tempore, in the Absence of the Vice President, or when he shall exercise the Office of President of the United States.

The Senate shall have the sole Power to try all Impeachments. When sitting for that Purpose, they shall be on Oath or Affirmation. When the President of the United States is tried, the Chief Justice shall preside: And no Person shall be convicted without the Concurrence of two thirds of the Members present.

Judgment in Cases of Impeachment shall not extend further than to removal from Office, and disqualification to hold and enjoy any Office of honor, Trust or Profit under the United States: but the Party convicted shall nevertheless be liable and subject to Indictment, Trial, Judgment and Punishment, according to Law.

Section. 4.

The Times, Places and Manner of holding Elections for Senators and Representatives, shall be prescribed in each State by the Legislature thereof; but the Congress may at any time by Law make or alter such Regulations, except as to the Places of chusing Senators.

The Congress shall assemble at least once in every Year, and such Meeting shall be on the first Monday in December, unless they shall by Law appoint a different Day.

Section. 5.

Each House shall be the Judge of the Elections, Returns and Qualifications of its own Members, and a Majority of each shall constitute a Quorum to do Business; but a smaller Number may adjourn from day to day, and may be authorized to compel the Attendance of absent Members, in such Manner, and under such Penalties as each House may provide.

Each House may determine the Rules of its Proceedings, punish its Members for disorderly Behaviour, and, with the Concurrence of two thirds, expel a Member.

Each House shall keep a Journal of its Proceedings, and from time to time publish the same, excepting such Parts as may in their Judgment require Secrecy; and the Yeas and Nays of the Members of either House on any question shall, at the Desire of one fifth of those Present, be entered on the Journal.

Neither House, during the Session of Congress, shall, without the Consent of the other, adjourn for more than three days, nor to any other Place than that in which the two Houses shall be sitting.

Section. 6.

The Senators and Representatives shall receive a Compensation for their Services, to be ascertained by Law, and paid out of the Treasury of the United States. They shall in all Cases, except Treason, Felony and Breach of the Peace, be privileged from Arrest during their Attendance at the Session of their respective Houses, and in going to and returning from the same; and for any Speech or Debate in either House, they shall not be questioned in any other Place.

No Senator or Representative shall, during the Time for which he was elected, be appointed to any civil Office under the Authority of the United States, which shall have been created, or the Emoluments whereof shall have been encreased during such time; and no Person holding any Office under the United States, shall be a Member of either House during his Continuance in Office.

Section. 7.

All Bills for raising Revenue shall originate in the House of Representatives; but the Senate may propose or concur with Amendments as on other Bills.

Every Bill which shall have passed the House of Representatives and the Senate, shall, before it become a Law, be presented to the President of the United States; If he approve he shall sign it, but if not he shall return it, with his Objections to that House in which it shall have originated, who shall enter the Objections at large on their Journal, and proceed to reconsider it. If after such Reconsideration two thirds of that House shall agree to pass the Bill, it shall be sent, together with the Objections, to the other House, by which it shall likewise be reconsidered, and if approved by two thirds of that House, it shall become a Law. But in all such Cases the Votes of both Houses shall be determined by yeas and Nays, and the Names of the Persons voting for and against the Bill shall be entered on the Journal of each House respectively. If any Bill shall not be returned by the President within ten Days (Sundays excepted) after it shall have been presented to him, the Same shall be a Law, in like Manner as if he had signed it, unless the Congress by their Adjournment prevent its Return, in which Case it shall not be a Law.

Every Order, Resolution, or Vote to which the Concurrence of the Senate and House of Representatives may be necessary (except on a question of Adjournment) shall be presented to the President of the United States; and before the Same shall take Effect, shall be approved by him, or being disapproved by him, shall be repassed by two thirds of the Senate and House of Representatives, according to the Rules and Limitations prescribed in the Case of a Bill.

Section. 8.

The Congress shall have Power To lay and collect Taxes, Duties, Imposts and Excises, to pay the Debts and provide for the common Defence and general Welfare of the United States; but all Duties, Imposts and Excises shall be uniform throughout the United States;

To borrow Money on the credit of the United States;

To regulate Commerce with foreign Nations, and among the several States, and with the Indian Tribes;

To establish an uniform Rule of Naturalization, and uniform Laws on the subject of Bankruptcies throughout the United States;

To coin Money, regulate the Value thereof, and of foreign Coin, and fix the Standard of Weights and Measures;

To provide for the Punishment of counterfeiting the Securities and current Coin of the United States;

To establish Post Offices and post Roads;

To promote the Progress of Science and useful Arts, by securing for limited Times to Authors and Inventors the exclusive Right to their respective Writings and Discoveries;

To constitute Tribunals inferior to the supreme Court;

To define and punish Piracies and Felonies committed on the high Seas, and Offences against the Law of Nations;

To declare War, grant Letters of Marque and Reprisal, and make Rules concerning Captures on Land and Water;

To raise and support Armies, but no Appropriation of Money to that Use shall be for a longer Term than two Years;

To provide and maintain a Navy;

To make Rules for the Government and Regulation of the land and naval Forces;

To provide for calling forth the Militia to execute the Laws of the Union, suppress Insurrections and repel Invasions;

To provide for organizing, arming, and disciplining, the Militia, and for governing such Part of them as may be employed in the Service of the United States, reserving to the States respectively, the Appointment of the Officers, and the Authority of training the Militia according to the discipline prescribed by Congress;

To exercise exclusive Legislation in all Cases whatsoever, over such District (not exceeding ten Miles square) as may, by Cession of particular States, and the Acceptance of Congress, become the Seat of the Government of the United States, and to exercise like Authority over all Places purchased by the Consent of the Legislature of the State in which the Same shall be, for the Erection of Forts, Magazines, Arsenals, dock-Yards, and other needful Buildings;—And

To make all Laws which shall be necessary and proper for carrying into Execution the foregoing Powers, and all other Powers vested by this Constitution in the Government of the United States, or in any Department or Officer thereof.

Section. 9.

The Migration or Importation of such Persons as any of the States now existing shall think proper to admit, shall not be prohibited by the Congress prior to the Year one thousand eight hundred and eight, but a Tax or duty may be imposed on such Importation, not exceeding ten dollars for each Person.

The Privilege of the Writ of Habeas Corpus shall not be suspended, unless when in Cases of Rebellion or Invasion the public Safety may require it.

No Bill of Attainder or ex post facto Law shall be passed.

No Capitation, or other direct, Tax shall be laid, unless in Proportion to the Census or enumeration herein before directed to be taken.

No Tax or Duty shall be laid on Articles exported from any State.

No Preference shall be given by any Regulation of Commerce or Revenue to the Ports of one State over those of another: nor shall Vessels bound to, or from, one State, be obliged to enter, clear, or pay Duties in another.

No Money shall be drawn from the Treasury, but in Consequence of Appropriations made by Law; and a regular Statement and Account of the Receipts and Expenditures of all public Money shall be published from time to time.

No Title of Nobility shall be granted by the United States: And no Person holding any Office of Profit or Trust under them, shall, without the Consent of the Congress, accept of any present, Emolument, Office, or Title, of any kind whatever, from any King, Prince, or foreign State.

Section. 10.

No State shall enter into any Treaty, Alliance, or Confederation; grant Letters of Marque and Reprisal; coin Money; emit Bills of Credit; make any Thing but gold and silver Coin a Tender in Payment of Debts; pass any Bill of Attainder, ex post facto Law, or Law impairing the Obligation of Contracts, or grant any Title of Nobility.

No State shall, without the Consent of the Congress, lay any Imposts or Duties on Imports or Exports, except what may be absolutely necessary for executing it's inspection Laws: and the net Produce of all Duties and Imposts, laid by any State on Imports or Exports, shall be for the Use of the Treasury of the United States; and all such Laws shall be subject to the Revision and Controul of the Congress.

No State shall, without the Consent of Congress, lay any Duty of Tonnage, keep Troops, or Ships of War in time of Peace, enter into any Agreement or Compact with another State, or with a foreign Power, or engage in War, unless actually invaded, or in such imminent Danger as will not admit of delay.

Article. II.

Section. 1.

The executive Power shall be vested in a President of the United States of America. He shall hold his Office during the Term of four Years, and, together with the Vice President, chosen for the same Term, be elected, as follows

Each State shall appoint, in such Manner as the Legislature thereof may direct, a Number of Electors, equal to the whole Number of Senators and Representatives to which the State may be entitled in the Congress: but no Senator or Representative, or Person holding an Office of Trust or Profit under the United States, shall be appointed an Elector.

The Electors shall meet in their respective States, and vote by Ballot for two Persons, of whom one at least shall not be an Inhabitant of the same State with themselves. And they shall make a List of all the Persons voted for, and of the Number of Votes for each; which List they shall sign and certify, and transmit sealed to the Seat of the Government of the United States, directed to the President of the Senate. The President of the Senate shall, in the Presence of the Senate and House of Representatives, open all the Certificates, and the Votes shall then be counted. The Person having the greatest Number of Votes shall be the President, if such Number be a Majority of the whole Number of Electors appointed; and if there be more than one who have such Majority, and have an equal Number of Votes, then the House of Representatives shall immediately chuse by Ballot one of them for President; and if no Person have a Majority, then from the five highest on the List the said House shall in like Manner chuse the President. But in chusing the President, the Votes shall be taken by States, the Representation from each State having one Vote; A quorum for this Purpose shall consist of a Member or Members from two thirds of the States, and a Majority of all the States shall be necessary to a Choice. In every Case, after the Choice of the President, the Person having the greatest Number of Votes of the Electors shall be the Vice President. But if there should remain two or more who have equal Votes, the Senate shall chuse from them by Ballot the Vice President.

The Congress may determine the Time of chusing the Electors, and the Day on which they shall give their Votes; which Day shall be the same throughout the United States.

No Person except a natural born Citizen, or a Citizen of the United States, at the time of the Adoption of this Constitution, shall be eligible to the Office of President; neither shall any Person be eligible to that Office who shall not have attained to the Age of thirty five Years, and been fourteen Years a Resident within the United States.

In Case of the Removal of the President from Office, or of his Death, Resignation, or Inability to discharge the Powers and Duties of the said Office, the Same shall devolve on the Vice President, and the Congress may by Law provide for the Case of Removal, Death, Resignation or Inability, both of the President and Vice President, declaring what Officer shall then act as President, and such Officer shall act accordingly, until the Disability be removed, or a President shall be elected.

The President shall, at stated Times, receive for his Services, a Compensation, which shall neither be encreased nor diminished during the Period for which he shall have been elected, and he shall not receive within that Period any other Emolument from the United States, or any of them.

Before he enter on the Execution of his Office, he shall take the following Oath or Affirmation:—"I do solemnly swear (or affirm) that I will faithfully execute the Office of President of the United States, and will to the best of my Ability, preserve, protect and defend the Constitution of the United States."

Section. 2.

The President shall be Commander in Chief of the Army and Navy of the United States, and of the Militia of the several States, when called into the actual Service of the United States; he may require the Opinion, in writing, of the principal Officer in each of the executive Departments, upon any Subject relating to the Duties of their respective Offices, and he shall have Power to grant Reprieves and Pardons for Offences against the United States, except in Cases of Impeachment.

He shall have Power, by and with the Advice and Consent of the Senate, to make Treaties, provided two thirds of the Senators present concur; and he shall nominate, and by and with the Advice and Consent of the Senate, shall appoint Ambassadors, other public Ministers and Consuls, Judges of the supreme Court, and all other Officers of the United States, whose Appointments are not herein otherwise provided for, and which shall be established by Law: but the Congress may by Law vest the Appointment of such inferior Officers, as they think proper, in the President alone, in the Courts of Law, or in the Heads of Departments.

The President shall have Power to fill up all Vacancies that may happen during the Recess of the Senate, by granting Commissions which shall expire at the End of their next Session.

Section. 3.

He shall from time to time give to the Congress Information of the State of the Union, and recommend to their Consideration such Measures as he shall judge necessary and expedient; he may, on extraordinary Occasions, convene both Houses, or either of them, and in Case of Disagreement between them, with Respect to the Time of Adjournment, he may adjourn them to such Time as he shall think proper; he shall receive Ambassadors and other public Ministers; he shall take Care that the Laws be faithfully executed, and shall Commission all the Officers of the United States.

Section. 4.

The President, Vice President and all civil Officers of the United States, shall be removed from Office on Impeachment for, and Conviction of, Treason, Bribery, or other high Crimes and Misdemeanors.

Article. III.

Section. 1.

The judicial Power of the United States, shall be vested in one supreme Court, and in such inferior Courts as the Congress may from time to time ordain and establish. The Judges, both of the supreme and inferior Courts, shall hold their Offices during good Behaviour, and shall, at stated Times, receive for their Services, a Compensation, which shall not be diminished during their Continuance in Office.

Section. 2.

The judicial Power shall extend to all Cases, in Law and Equity, arising under this Constitution, the Laws of the United States, and Treaties made, or which shall be made, under their Authority;—to all Cases affecting Ambassadors, other public Ministers and Consuls;—to all Cases of admiralty and maritime Jurisdiction;—to Controversies to which the United States shall be a Party;—to Controversies between two or more States;—between a State and Citizens of another State,—between Citizens of different States,—between Citizens of the same State claiming Lands under Grants of different States, and between a State, or the Citizens thereof, and foreign States, Citizens or Subjects.

In all Cases affecting Ambassadors, other public Ministers and Consuls, and those in which a State shall be Party, the supreme Court shall have original Jurisdiction. In all the other Cases before mentioned, the supreme Court shall have appellate Jurisdiction, both as to Law and Fact, with such Exceptions, and under such Regulations as the Congress shall make.

The Trial of all Crimes, except in Cases of Impeachment, shall be by Jury; and such Trial shall be held in the State where the said Crimes shall have been committed; but when not committed within any State, the Trial shall be at such Place or Places as the Congress may by Law have directed.

Section. 3.

Treason against the United States, shall consist only in levying War against them, or in adhering to their Enemies, giving them Aid and Comfort. No Person shall be convicted of Treason unless on the Testimony of two Witnesses to the same overt Act, or on Confession in open Court.

The Congress shall have Power to declare the Punishment of Treason, but no Attainder of Treason shall work Corruption of Blood, or Forfeiture except during the Life of the Person attainted.

Article. IV.

Section. 1.

Full Faith and Credit shall be given in each State to the public Acts, Records, and judicial Proceedings of every other State. And the Congress may by general Laws prescribe the Manner in which such Acts, Records and Proceedings shall be proved, and the Effect thereof.

Section. 2.

The Citizens of each State shall be entitled to all Privileges and Immunities of Citizens in the several States.

A Person charged in any State with Treason, Felony, or other Crime, who shall flee from Justice, and be found in another State, shall on Demand of the executive Authority of the State from which he fled, be delivered up, to be removed to the State having Jurisdiction of the Crime.

No Person held to Service or Labour in one State, under the Laws thereof, escaping into another, shall, in Consequence of any Law or Regulation therein, be discharged from such Service or Labour, but shall be delivered up on Claim of the Party to whom such Service or Labour may be due.

Section. 3.

New States may be admitted by the Congress into this Union; but no new State shall be formed or erected within the Jurisdiction of any other State; nor any State be formed by the Junction of two or more States, or Parts of States, without the Consent of the Legislatures of the States concerned as well as of the Congress.

The Congress shall have Power to dispose of and make all needful Rules and Regulations respecting the Territory or other Property belonging to the United States; and nothing in this Constitution shall be so construed as to Prejudice any Claims of the United States, or of any particular State.

Section. 4.

The United States shall guarantee to every State in this Union a Republican Form of Government, and shall protect each of them against Invasion; and on Application of the Legislature, or of the Executive (when the Legislature cannot be convened) against domestic Violence.

Article. V.

The Congress, whenever two thirds of both Houses shall deem it necessary, shall propose Amendments to this Constitution, or, on the Application of the Legislatures of two thirds of the several States, shall call a Convention for proposing Amendments, which, in either Case, shall be valid to all Intents and Purposes, as Part of this Constitution, when ratified by the Legislatures of three fourths of the several States, or by Conventions in three fourths thereof, as the one or the other Mode of Ratification may be proposed by the Congress; Provided that no Amendment which may be made prior to the Year One thousand eight hundred and eight shall in any Manner affect the first and fourth Clauses in the Ninth Section of the first Article; and that no State, without its Consent, shall be deprived of its equal Suffrage in the Senate.

Article. VI.

All Debts contracted and Engagements entered into, before the Adoption of this Constitution, shall be as valid against the United States under this Constitution, as under the Confederation.

This Constitution, and the Laws of the United States which shall be made in Pursuance thereof; and all Treaties made, or which shall be made, under the Authority of the United States, shall be the supreme Law of the Land; and the Judges in every State shall be bound thereby, any Thing in the Constitution or Laws of any State to the Contrary notwithstanding.

The Senators and Representatives before mentioned, and the Members of the several State Legislatures, and all executive and judicial Officers, both of the United States and of the several States, shall be bound by Oath or Affirmation, to support this Constitution; but no religious Test shall ever be required as a Qualification to any Office or public Trust under the United States.

Article. VII.

The Ratification of the Conventions of nine States, shall be sufficient for the Establishment of this Constitution between the States so ratifying the Same.

The Word, "the," being interlined between the seventh and eighth Lines of the first Page, The Word "Thirty" being partly written on an Erazure in the fifteenth Line of the first Page, The Words "is tried" being interlined between the thirty second and thirty third Lines of the first Page and the Word "the" being interlined between the forty third and forty fourth Lines of the second Page.

Attest William Jackson Secretary

done in Convention by the Unanimous Consent of the States present the Seventeenth Day of September in the Year of our Lord one thousand seven hundred and Eighty seven and of the Independance of the United States of America the Twelfth In witness whereof We have hereunto subscribed our Names,

G°. Washington
Presidt and deputy from Virginia

Delaware
Geo: Read
Gunning Bedford jun
John Dickinson
Richard Bassett
Jaco: Broom

Maryland
James McHenry
Dan of St Thos. Jenifer
Danl. Carroll

Virginia
John Blair
James Madison Jr.

North Carolina
Wm. Blount
Richd. Dobbs Spaight
Hu Williamson

South Carolina
J. Rutledge
Charles Cotesworth Pinckney
Charles Pinckney
Pierce Butler

Georgia
William Few
Abr Baldwin

New Hampshire
John Langdon
Nicholas Gilman

Massachusetts
Nathaniel Gorham
Rufus King

Connecticut
Wm. Saml. Johnson
Roger Sherman

New York
Alexander Hamilton

New Jersey
Wil: Livingston
David Brearley
Wm. Paterson
Jona: Dayton

Pennsylvania
B Franklin
Thomas Mifflin
Robt. Morris
Geo. Clymer
Thos. FitzSimons
Jared Ingersoll
James Wilson
Gouv Morris

The U. S. Bill of Rights

Amendment I

Congress shall make no law respecting an establishment of religion, or prohibiting the free exercise thereof; or abridging the freedom of speech, or of the press; or the right of the people peaceably to assemble, and to petition the Government for a redress of grievances.

Amendment II

A well regulated Militia, being necessary to the security of a free State, the right of the people to keep and bear Arms, shall not be infringed.

Amendment III

No Soldier shall, in time of peace be quartered in any house, without the consent of the Owner, nor in time of war, but in a manner to be prescribed by law.

Amendment IV

The right of the people to be secure in their persons, houses, papers, and effects, against unreasonable searches and seizures, shall not be violated, and no Warrants shall issue, but upon probable cause, supported by Oath or affirmation, and particularly describing the place to be searched, and the persons or things to be seized.

Amendment V

No person shall be held to answer for a capital, or otherwise infamous crime, unless on a presentment or indictment of a Grand Jury, except in cases arising in the land or naval forces, or in the Militia, when in actual service in time of War or public danger; nor shall any person be subject for the same offence to be twice put in jeopardy of life or limb; nor shall be compelled in any criminal case to be a witness against himself, nor be deprived of life, liberty, or property, without due process of law; nor shall private property be taken for public use, without just compensation.

Amendment VI

In all criminal prosecutions, the accused shall enjoy the right to a speedy and public trial, by an impartial jury of the State and district wherein the crime shall have been committed, which district shall have been previously ascertained by law, and to be informed of the nature and cause of the accusation; to be confronted with the witnesses against him; to have compulsory process for obtaining witnesses in his favor, and to have the Assistance of Counsel for his defence.

Amendment VII

In Suits at common law, where the value in controversy shall exceed twenty dollars, the right of trial by jury shall be preserved, and no fact tried by a jury, shall be otherwise re-examined in any Court of the United States, than according to the rules of the common law.

Amendment VIII

Excessive bail shall not be required, nor excessive fines imposed, nor cruel and unusual punishments inflicted.

Amendment IX

The enumeration in the Constitution, of certain rights, shall not be construed to deny or disparage others retained by the people.

Amendment X

The powers not delegated to the United States by the Constitution, nor prohibited by it to the States, are reserved to the States respectively, or to the people.

The United States Pledge of Allegiance

I pledge allegiance to the flag of the United States of America,
and to the republic for which it stands,
one nation under God, indivisible,
with liberty and justice for all.

FOUNDERS' DOCUMENTS AND QUOTES

The Great Awakening and Sermons Sparked the American Revolution

The Great Awakening not only brought tens of thousands to new life in Jesus Christ; it also rekindled the Biblical foundation of submission to King Jesus and resistance to evil authorities. This was in opposition to the Church of England (called Anglican in America) who taught submission to all authorities, and an obligation to suffer under oppressive rulers (tyrants). One of the early battle flags of the War of Independence had the motto formerly used by persecuted Christians in Europe: "Resistance to tyrants is obedience to God". The great spiritual awakening to freedom in Christ caused a great political awakening to have freedom from oppression.

Jonathan Mayhew preached civil and religious liberties were ordained by God. His sermon *Discourse Concerning Unlimited Submission and Non-Resistance to the Higher Powers* (1750) answered the Anglican argument that Christians were obliged to suffer under an oppressive ruler with a resounding "No." From Romans 13:1-7 he taught that Christians were obligated to obey godly authorities who punished evil and rewarded good while equally obligated to resist authorities who punished good and rewarded evil. Jonathan Mayhew wrote, "If it be our duty, for example, to obey our king, merely for this reason, that he rules for the public welfare, (which is the only argument the apostle makes use of) it follows, by a parity of reason, that when he turns tyrant, and makes his subjects his prey to devour and to destroy, instead of his charge to defend and cherish, we are bound to throw off our allegiance to him, and to resist; and that according to the tenor of the apostle's argument in this passage."

John Adams wrote regarding Jonathan Mayhew's printed sermon that "It was read by everybody; celebrated by friends, and abused by enemies....It spread an universal alarm against the authority of Parliament. It excited a general and just apprehension, that bishops, and dioceses, and churches, and priests, and tithes, were to be imposed on us by Parliament."

In 1761 patriot James Otis spoke for five hours *Against the Writs of Assistance* which allowed the British to search anyone or anything for suspected smuggled goods. This was contrary to British common law. Young John Adams made the following note of his speech: "He asserted that every man, merely natural, was an independent sovereign, subject to no law but the law written on his heart and revealed to him by his Maker, in the constitution of his nature and the inspiration of his understanding and his conscience. His right to his life, his liberty, no created being could rightfully contest. Nor was his right to his property less incontestable...When general councils and deliberations commenced, the objects could be no other than the mutual defense and security of every individual for his life, his liberty, and his property."

["Life, liberty and property" was a reference to Adam and Eve being given life, free will, and dominion over the Earth by their Creator first published by Englishman John Locke in 1690, and upheld by the colonists.]

Samuel Adams, leader of the Sons of Liberty and signer of the *Declaration of Independence* wrote in the *Rights of Colonists* (1772) that "The rights of the colonists as Christians... may be best understood by reading and carefully studying the institutes of the Great Law Giver and Head of the Christian Church, which are to be found clearly written and promulgated in the New Testament." [Many of the ideas in the *Declaration of Independence* are found in his report.]

About the time of the Boston Tea Party in 1774, a report of the Crown-appointed Governor of Boston, Massachusetts, sent to the Board of Trade in England, stated, "If you ask an American, who is his master? He will tell you he has none, nor any governor but Jesus Christ." The Committees of Correspondence and the people began crying out across the Colonies: "No King but King Jesus!" (Peter Powers' Election Sermon entitled *Jesus Christ the King* Newburyport, 1778).

Patrick Henry stated: "Bad men cannot make good citizens. It is impossible that a nation of infidels or idolaters should be a nation of free-men. It is when a people forget God, that tyrants forge their chains. A vitiated state of morals, a corrupted public conscience, is incompatible with freedom."

Elias Boudinot was president of the Continental Congress in 1783 and a founder of the American Bible Society. (He was baptized by George Whitefield during the Great Awakening.) He stated, "If the Moral character of a people degenerate, their political character must follow. These considerations should lead to an attentive solicitude to be religiously careful in our choice of all public officers...and judge of the tree by its fruits." (This is a reference to Matthew 7: 15-20.)

Gouverneur Morris spoke more often during the Constitutional Convention than any other delegate, and he wrote the final draft and signed the Constitution. [Gouverneur was his first name, he was not a governor.] He stated, "Religion is the only solid basis of good morals; therefore education should teach the precepts of religion, and the duties of man towards God."

John Adams wrote the following to Thomas Jefferson on June 28th, 1813: "The general Principles, on which the Fathers Achieved Independence, were the only Principles in which that beautiful Assembly of young Gentlemen could Unite, and these Principles only could be intended by them in their Address, or by me in my Answer. And what were these general Principles? I answer, the general Principles of Christianity, in which all those Sects were united: And the general Principles of English and American Liberty, in which all those young Men United, and which had United all Parties in America, in Majorities sufficient to assert and maintain her Independence."

Henry Laurens stated, "I had the honor of being one who framed that Constitution. In order effectually to accomplish these great ends set forth in the Constitution, it is especially the duty of those who bear rule to promote and encourage respect for God and virtue and to discourage every degree of vice and immorality."

Patrick Henry championed religious freedom

In 1768, Patrick Henry rode several miles on horseback to a trial where three Baptist ministers were being tried for having preached without the sanction of the Episcopalian Church. He interrupted the proceedings, saying, "May it please your lordships, what did I hear read? Did I hear an expression that these men, whom you worships are about to try for misdemeanor, are charged with preaching the gospel of the Son of God?"

Patrick Henry was Commander in Chief of the Virginia Militia and a member of the Virginia General Assembly and House of Burgesses. The House of Burgesses was the only elected assembly in colonial Virginia, established from the beginning in 1619. On the reverse of The Stamp Act Resolves, passed in the House of Burgesses, May 1765, Patrick Henry wrote and signed the following note: "This brought on the war which finally separated the two countries and gave independence to ours. Whether this will prove a blessing or a curse, will depend upon the use our people make of the blessings, which a gracious God hath bestowed on us. If they are wise, they will be great and happy. If they are of a contrary character, they will be miserable. Righteousness alone can exalt them as a nation. Reader! Whoever thou art, remember this, and in thy sphere practice virtue thyself, and encourage it in others."

During the Second Virginia Convention in 1775, Patrick Henry stated: "It is only in this way that we can hope to arrive at truth, and fulfill the great responsibility which we hold to God and our country....Our petitions have been slighted; our remonstrances have produced additional violence and insult; our supplications have been disregarded; and we have been spurned, with contempt....An appeal to arms and to the God of Hosts is all that is left us!...Besides, sir, we shall not fight our battle alone. There is a just God who presides over the destines of nations; and who will raise up friends to fight our battle for us....Is life so dear, or peace so sweet, as to be purchased at the price of chains and slavery? Forbid it, Almighty God! I know not what course others may take; but as for me, give me liberty or give me death!"

In 1784, Patrick Henry supported a bill establishing a "Provision for Teachers of the Christian Religion": "The general diffusion of Christian knowledge hath a natural tendency to correct the morals of men, restrain their vices, and preserve the peace of society..."

The following are quotes from Patrick Henry's speech to the Virginia Convention in 1788 which were later printed in *The Anti-Federalist Papers*: "...liberty ought to be the direct end of your Government.... will submit to your recollection whether liberty has been destroyed most often by the licentiousness of the people, or by the tyranny or rulers...the preservation of our liberty depends on the single chance of men being virtuous enough to make laws to punish themselves....In this scheme of energetic Government, the people will find two sets of tax-gatherers: the State and the Federal Sheriffs. This it seems to me will produce such dreadful oppression, as the people cannot possibly bear."

Samuel Adams, father of the Revolution

As members were signing the *Declaration of Independence*, Samuel Adams, the father of the Revolution, said, "We have this day restored the Sovereign to Whom all men ought to be obedient. He reigns in heaven and from the rising to the setting of the sun, let His kingdom come." After the public reading of the *Declaration of Independence*, Samuel Adams noted, "The people, I am told, recognize the resolution as though it were a decree promulgated from heaven."

Samuel Adams wrote to John Scollay of Boston on April 30, 1776: "Our grateful acknowledgements are to the Supreme Being who has not been regardless of the multiplied oppressions which the inhabitants of that city have suffered....Revelation assures us that 'Righteousness exalteth a nation.' Communities are dealt with in this world by the wise and just Ruler of the Universe. He rewards or punishes them according to their general character. The diminution of public virtue is usually attended with that of public happiness, and the public liberty will not long survive the total extinction of morals....Could I be assured that America would remain virtuous, I would venture to defy the utmost efforts of enemies to subjugate her." (Proverbs 14:34 states: "Righteousness exalteth a nation: but sin is a reproach to any people.")

Samuel Adams addressed the Continental Congress on August 1, 1776: "Countrymen and brethren...This day, I trust, the reign of political protestantism will commence. We have explored the temple of royalty, and found that the idol we have bowed down to, has eyes which see not, ears that hear not our prayers, and a heart like the nether millstone. We have this day restored the Sovereign, to whom alone all men ought to be obedient. He reigns in Heaven, and with a propitious eye beholds his subjects assuming that freedom of thought, and dignity of self-direction which He bestowed on them...."

"We are now on this continent to the astonishment of the world three millions of souls united in one common cause. We have large armies, well disciplined and appointed, with commanders inferior to none in military skill, and superior in activity and zeal. We are furnished with arsenals and stores beyond our most sanguine expectations, and foreign nations are waiting to crown our success by their alliances. There are instances of, I would say, an almost astonishing Providence in our favor; our success has staggered our enemies, and almost given faith to infidels; so that we may truly say it is not our own arm which has saved us. The hand of Heaven appears to have led us on to be, perhaps, humble instruments and means in the great Providential dispensation which is completing. We have fled from the political Sodom; let us not look back, lest we perish and become a monument of infamy and derision to the world!"

"...if it was ever granted to mortals to trace the designs of Providence, and interpret its manifestations in favor of their cause, we may, with humility of soul, cry out, 'Not unto us, not unto us, but to thy Name be the praise.'...The time at which this attempt on our liberties was made, when we were ripened into maturity, had acquired a knowledge of war, and were free from the incursions of enemies in this country, the gradual advances of our oppressors enabling us to prepare for our defence, the unusual fertility of our lands and clemency of the seasons, the success which at first attended our feeble arms, producing unanimity among our friends and reducing our internal foes to acquiescence —Theses are all strong and palpable marks and assurances, that Providence is yet gracious unto Zion, that it will turn away the captivity of Jacob."

"Our glorious reformers, when they broke through the fetters of superstition, effected more than could be expected from an age so darkened. But they left much to be done by their posterity. They lopped off, indeed, some of the branches...but they left the root and stock when they left us under the domination of human systems and decisions, usurping the infallibility which can be attributed to Revelation alone. They dethroned one usurper only to raise up another....And if we now cast our eyes over the nations of the earth we shall find, that instead of possessing the pure religion of the gospel, they may be divided either into infidels who deny the truth, or politicians who make religion a stalking horse for their ambition, of professors, who walk in the trammels of orthodoxy, and are more attentive to traditions and ordinances of men than to the oracles of truth."

"Thus by the beneficence of Providence, we shall behold our empire arising, founded on justice and the voluntary consent of the people, and giving full scope to the exercise of those faculties and rights which most ennoble our species. Besides the advantages of liberty and the most equal constitution, Heaven has given us a country with every variety of climate and soil, pouring forth in abundance whatever is necessary for the support, comfort, and strength of a nation. Within our own borders we possess all the means of sustenance, defence, and commerce; at the same time, these advantages are so distributed among the different States of this continent, as if nature had in view to proclaim to us — be united among yourselves, and you will want nothing from the rest of the world....Go on, then, in your generous enterprise, with gratitude to Heaven for past success, and confidence of it in the future."

ALL EDUCATION IS RELIGIOUS

Samuel Adams wrote a letter on October 4, 1790 to his cousin John Adams, who was vice president of the United States: "Let divines and philosophers, statesmen and patriots, unite their endeavors to renovate the age, by impressing the minds of men with the importance of educating their little boys and girls, of inculcating in the minds of youth the fear and love of the Deity and universal philanthropy, and in subordination to these great principles, the love of their country; of instructing them in the art of self-government... in short, of leading them in the study and practice of the exalted virtues of the Christian system. Knowledge apart from God and His truth is little better than complete ignorance, because the most important aspect of education is the imbuing of moral principles. All education is religious — it imparts a basic set of principles and ideals, a worldview. How the youth are educated today will determine the course a nation takes in the future."

Governor Samuel Adams addressed the Massachusetts Legislature on January 17, 1794: "Human laws excite fears and apprehensions, lest crimes committed be detected and punished; But a virtuous education is calculated to reach and influence the heart, and to prevent crimes....Such an education, which leads the youth beyond mere outside show, will impress their minds with a profound reverence of the Deity, universal benevolence, and a warm attachment and affection towards their country. It will excite in them a just regard to Divine Revelation, which informs them of the original character and dignity of man; and it will inspire them with a sense of true honor."

Governor Samuel Adams of Massachusetts, addressed the State Legislature in 1794: "In the supposed state of nature, all men are equally bound by the laws of nature, or to speak more properly, the laws of the Creator: They are imprinted by the finger of God on the heart of man. Thou shall do no injury to thy neighbor, is the voice of nature and reason, and it is confirmed by written revelation."

On March 20, 1797, in a Proclamation of a Day of Fast, Massachusetts Governor Samuel Adams stated: "And as it is our duty to extend our wishes to the happiness of the great family of man, I conceive that we cannot better express ourselves than by humbly supplicating the Supreme Ruler of the world that the rod of tyrants may be broken to pieces, and the oppressed made free again; that wars may cease in all the earth, and that the confusions that are and have been among nations may be overruled by promoting and speedily bringing on that holy and happy period when the kingdom of our Lord and Saviour Jesus Christ may be everywhere established, and all people everywhere willingly bow to the sceptre of Him who is Prince of Peace."

Definitions

A Christian is someone who believes and confesses Jesus Christ, the sinless Son of God, physically died for his/her sins, was buried, rose again the third day according to the Scriptures, and was seen by hundreds of people after His resurrection (1 Corinthians 15:1-6 and 1 John 4:1-3).

A deist is someone who believes God created the world which thereafter operates only by natural and self-sustaining laws of the Creator without His miraculous intervention. A deist does not believe the divinity of Christ in His claim, "I and the Father are one" (John 10:30), because they don't believe in the divine inspiration of the Bible. Observations of nature and reason are his/her only guides in doctrine and practice.

An infidel is someone who does not believe in the existence of a God who will reward or punish people in this world or that which is to come, and who does not recognize the inspiration of or obligation to the Bible. Most of the founding fathers were Christians; none of them were infidels or strict deists.

Since a deist only believes in a Creator-God and does not believe Jesus Christ is that Creator-God in the flesh, a deist can not be a Christian. Since a Christian does believe God the Father sent His Son Jesus Christ to save people from their sins, a Christian can not be a deist. An infidel does not believe in a God who judges peoples' actions nor in the Bible that dictates which actions are good and bad, so that they can live how they please. An atheist doesn't believe God even exists.

Benjamin Franklin wrote the following in *Information to Those Who Would Remove to America*: "...that serious Religion, under its various Denominations, is not only tolerated, but respected and practised. Atheism is unknown there; infidelity rare and secret; so that persons may live to a great Age in that Country, without having their Piety shocked by meeting with either an Atheist or an Infidel."

Deists wrongly claimed founding fathers among them very early

In a letter to his daughter in 1796, Patrick Henry wrote: "Amongst other strange things said of me, I hear it is said by the deists that I am one of their number; and, indeed, that some good people think I am no Christian. This thought gives me much more pain than the appellation of Tory; because I think religion of infinitely higher importance than politics; and I find much cause to reproach myself that I have lived so long and have given no decided and public proofs of my being a Christian. But, indeed, my dear child, this is the character which I prize far above all this world has, or can boast." (Just because a religious group claims someone is a member does not make him a member.)

Benjamin Franklin and Thomas Jefferson were not Christians, but they weren't very good deists either. Their writings denied the divinity of Christ, but they proposed Biblical miracles for the great seal of the United States. (Deists don't believe in miracles or divine inspiration of the Bible.) Jefferson first recommended the "Children of Israel in the wilderness, led by a cloud by day, and a pillar of fire by night." Franklin proposed "Moses lifting up his wand, and dividing the red sea, and pharaoh in his chariot overwhelmed with the waters. This motto: 'Rebellion to tyrants is obedience to God.'" Then they combined the two. Franklin and Jefferson were among the most theologically liberal of the Founders, yet they often referred to the Bible in the course of their governmental duties.

John Jay told atheists he believed in Christ

John Jay served as the President of the Continental Congress from 1778-1779. He wrote five articles in the Federalist Papers. In a letter to John Bristed, April 23, 1811, Jay recounted a conversation he had with several atheists while in France for the signing of the Treaty of Paris: "I was at a large party, of which were several of that description. They spoke freely and contemptuously of religion. I took no part in the conversation. In the course of it, one of them asked me if I believed in Christ. I answered that I did, and that I thanked God that I did....I frequently observed him drawing the conversation towards religion, and I constantly gave it another direction. He, nevertheless, during one of his visits, very abruptly remarked that there was no God, and he hoped the time would come when there would be no religion in the world. I very concisely remarked that if there was no God there could be no moral obligations, and I did not see how society could subsist without them."

John Jay was also the first Secretary of State and first chief justice of the United States. Jay wrote "Let us therefore persevere steadfastly in distributing the Scriptures far and near, and without note or comment. We are assured that they 'are profitable for doctrine, for reproof, for correction, for instruction in righteousness (2 Tim. 3:16).'"

Alexander Hamilton could prove the truth of Christianity

Alexander Hamilton was an author of the Federalist Papers and the first Secretary of the Treasury. He stated, "I have carefully examined the evidences of the Christian religion, and if I was sitting as a juror upon its authenticity I would unhesitatingly give my verdict in its favor. I can prove its truth as clearly as any proposition ever submitted to the mind of man." Robert Troup, his roommate at King's College described Alexander Hamilton as: "Attentive to public worship and in the habit of praying upon his knees both night and morning....I have lived in the same room with him for some time, and I have often been powerfully affected by the fervor and eloquence of his prayers. He had read many of the polemical writers on religious subjects, and he was a zealous believer in the fundamental doctrines of Christianity....I confess that the arguments with which he was accustomed to justify his belief, have tended in no small degree to confirm my own faith in revealed religion."

John Adams believed in miracles and was not a deist

In 1756, Adams made this diary entry: "The great and Almighty author of nature, who at first established those rules which regulate the world, can as easily suspend those laws whenever his providence sees sufficient reason for such suspension. This can be no objection, then, to the miracles of Jesus Christ. Although some very thoughtful and contemplative men among the heathen attained a strong persuasion of the great principles of religion, yet the far greater number, having little time for speculation, gradually sunk into the grossest opinions and the grossest practices. These...could not be made to embrace the true religion till their attention was roused by some astonishing and miraculous appearances. The reasoning of philosophers...could not overcome the force of prejudice, custom, passion, and bigotry. But when wise and virtuous men commissioned from heaven, by miracles awakened men's attention to their reasonings, the force of truth made its way with ease to their minds." On October 11, 1798, President John Adams told the militia of Massachusetts, "We have no government armed in power capable of contending in human passions unbridled by morality and religion. Avarice, ambition, revenge, or gallantry, would break the strongest cords of our Constitution as a whale goes through a net. Our constitution was made only for a moral and religious people. It is wholly inadequate for the government of any other."

Bible's Importance

James Madison, the fourth President, studied his Bible and took notes
The following are some of the notes James Madison made in his personal Bible: "Christ's Divinity appears by St. John -- 'And Thomas answered and said unto Him, My Lord and my God!' Resurrection testified to and witnessed by the Apostles -- 'And with great power gave the apostles witness of the resurrection of the Lord Jesus, and great grace was upon them all.' Apostles did greater Miracles than Christ, in the matter, not manner. Grace, it is the free gift of God. Jesus is an Hebrew name and signifies a Saviour. Christ is a Greek name and signifies Anointed. Christ did by the power of his Godhead purify our nature from all the pollution of our Ancestors."

Continental Congress relieved Bible shortage
On Sept. 11, 1777 Continental Congress approved the importation of 20,000 copies of the Holy Bible, in response to the shortage caused by the Revolutionary War. "The use of the Bible is so universal and its importance so great that your committee refers the above to the consideration of Congress, and if Congress shall not think it expedient to order the importation of types and paper, the Committee recommends that Congress will order the Committee of Commerce to import 20,000 Bibles from Holland, Scotland, or elsewhere, into the different parts of the States of the Union. Whereupon it was resolved accordingly to direct said Committee of Commerce to import 20,000 copies of the Bible."

Signers of Constitution founded Bible societies
Several signers of the Constitution founded Bible societies and publicly practiced their Christian faith. Charles Pinckney and John Langdon were founders of the American Bible Society. James McHenry was a founder of the Baltimore Bible Society. Rufus King helped found a Bible society for Anglicans. Abraham Baldwin was renown for his piety and devotion to his duties as a chaplain in the army during the War of Independence. James Wilson and William Paterson had prayer over juries as U. S. Supreme Court Justices. Roger Sherman, William Samuel Johnson, John Dickinson, and Jacob Broom were Christian theological authors.

Northwest Ordinance decreed religion and morality to be taught in public schools
In 1787 Congress debated regulations for settling the new northwestern lands, resulting in the Northwest Ordinance. Its third article states, "Religion, morality, and knowledge, being necessary to good government and the happiness of mankind, schools and the means of education shall forever be encouraged." Congress passed the same ordinance again and George Washington signed it into law in 1789 during the same time period the First Amendment was being debated. There was no objection to government support of religious education according to those debating the First Amendment. For Ohio to become a state, Thomas Jefferson wrote on April 30, 1802 that it should "not be repugnant to the \[Northwest\] Ordinance."

Bible and Christian religion to be taught in public schools
Signer of the Declaration of Independence and "father of public schools," Dr. Benjamin Rush stated, "Let the children... be carefully instructed in the principles and obligations of the Christian religion. This is the most essential part of education. The great enemy of the salvation of man, in my opinion, never invented a more effectual means of extirpating [removing] Christianity from the world than by persuading mankind that it was improper to read the Bible at schools. The Bible should be read at our schools in preference to all other books."

Dr. Benjamin Rush wrote in 1798, "In contemplating the political institutions of the United States, I lament that we waste so much time and money in punishing crimes and take so little pains to prevent them. We profess to be republicans, and yet we neglect the only means of establishing and perpetuating our republican forms of government, that is, the universal education of our youth in the principles of Christianity by the means of the Bible. For this Divine book, above all others, favors that equality among mankind, that respect for just laws, and those sober and frugal virtues, which constitute the soul of republicanism." Dr. Benjamin Rush later stated, "Without religion, I believe that learning does real mischief to the morals and principles of mankind."

Fisher Ames argued in the Sept. 20, 1789 issue of Palladium magazine, "We have a dangerous trend beginning to take place in our education. We're starting to put more and more textbooks into our schools....We've become accustomed of late of putting little books into the hands of children containing fables and moral lessons.... We are spending less time in the classroom on the Bible, which should be the principle text in our schools.... The Bible states these great moral lessons better than any other manmade book." Twenty years later the 'dangerous trend' of Bible reading being squeezed out by textbooks had become worse. In his 1809 book, Fisher Ames wrote, "Should not the Bible regain the place it once held as a schoolbook? Its morals are pure, its examples are captivating and noble.... In no Book is there so good English, so pure and so elegant, and by teaching all the same they will speak alike, and the Bible will justly remain the standard of language as well as of faith."

Presbyterian Minister John Witherspoon preached from Psalm 76 (1776)
Continental Congress declared a National Day of Fasting, Humiliation and Prayer on May 17, 1776 for God's guidance in the war. That same day Reverend John Witherspoon delivered a sermon on Psalm 76 at Princeton University entitled *The Dominion of Providence over the Passions of Men*, in which he stated: "While we give praise to God, the Supreme Disposer

of all events, for His interposition on our behalf, let us guard against the dangerous error of trusting in, or boasting of, an arm of flesh....If your cause is just, if your principles are pure, and if your conduct is prudent, you need not fear the multitude of opposing hosts. What follows from this? That he is the best friend to American liberty, who is most sincere and active in promoting true and undefiled religion, and who sets himself with the greatest firmness to bear down profanity and immorality of every kind. Whoever is an avowed enemy of God, I scruple not to call him an enemy of his country."

Witherspoon used the example of how the wrath of people against the Son of God crucified Jesus, but led to His resurrection; thus "the wrath of man shall praise thee" (Psalm 76:10a). He spoke of how the fears of war can open the conscience to "the arrows of conviction," saying, "Have you assembled together willingly to hear what shall be said on public affairs, and to join in imploring the blessing of God on the counsels and arms of the United Colonies, and can you be unconcerned what shall become of you for ever..."and reminded them "now is the day of salvation."

Witherspoon referred to England's *Declaratory Act* in his sermon stating, "I call this claim unjust, of making laws to bind us 'in all cases whatsoever'." His 1776 sermon continued: "If your cause is just, you may look with confidence to the Lord, and intreat him to plead it as his own....the cause in which america is now in arms, is the cause of justice, of liberty, and of human nature. so far as we have hitherto proceeded, I am satisfied that the confederacy of the colonies has not been the effect of pride, resentment, or sedition, but of a deep and general conviction that our civil and religious liberties, and consequently in a great measure the temporal and eternal happiness of us and our posterity, depended on the issue. ...There is not a single instance in history, in which civil liberty was lost, and religious liberty preserved entire. If therefore we yield up our temporal property, we at the same time deliver the conscience into bondage."

Witherspoon's 1776 sermon further stated, "Nothing is more certain than that a general profligacy and corruption of manners make a people ripe for destruction. A good form of government may hold the rotten materials together for some time, but beyond a certain pitch, even the best constitution will be ineffectual, and slavery must ensue. On the other hand, when the manners of a nation are pure, when true religion and internal principles maintain their vigour, the attempts of the most powerful enemies to oppress them are commonly baffled and disappointed."

Dr. John Witherspoon became an American 3 months after his arrival from Scotland. He signed the *Declaration of Independence* and the *Articles of Confederation*. He championed separation of powers insisting on inclusions to check and balance the power of government. He served on over 120 Congressional committees, including: the Board of War, Committee on Secret Correspondence, Foreign Affairs, and Committee on Clothing for the Army.

Witherspoon taught the men who shaped America

As president of Princeton University, 1768-94, Dr. John Witherspoon graduated 469 students who directly shaped America. He physically taught them in small classes: 114 became ministers, 13 became presidents of universities in eight different states, 6 men were members of the Continental Congress, 9 of his students were appointed to Cabinet positions, 12 were chosen as Governors of states, and at least 60 became Senators or Representatives in Congress. One of his students, James Madison, served eight years as Secretary of State and eight years as U.S. President. Two honorary doctorates were given during his tenure; one to Thomas Jefferson and one to Alexander Hamilton. Many of Witherspoon's former students left New Jersey to fill academic positions on the frontier of emerging America. Although Witherspoon did not attend the Constitutional Convention himself, one-sixth of its 55 delegates were graduates of Princeton University: Gunning Bedford Jr. of Delaware; David Brearley of New Jersey; William Richardson Davie of North Carolina; Jonathan Dayton of New Jersey; William Churchill Houston of New Jersey; James Madison of Virginia; Alexander Martin of North Carolina; Luther Martin of Maryland; and William Paterson of New Jersey.

"It is in the man of piety an inward principle that we may expect to find the uncorrupted patriot, the useful citizen, and the invincible soldier. God grant in America true religion and civil liberty may be inseparable and the unjust attempts to destroy the one, may in the issue tend to the support and establishment of both." (*Works of John Witherspoon*, 1802)

Lex Rex ("law is king") was written by Samuel Rutherford in 1644. The Scottish minister answered 44 questions about the relationship between God and civil government. Rutherford concluded that church and state were to be two separate governments under God, and that the only King of the Church is King Jesus. The book so demolished the doctrine of the divine right of kings that it was against the law to own a copy of it. Between 1715 and 1776 about 250,000 Scottish immigrants arrived in the colonies. Most were Presbyterians who fled religious persecution. By 1776 almost a sixth of Americans were Scots or of immediate Scottish descent. John Witherspoon beseeched Scotsmen to insist on their "ancient rights" against Britain and circulated a letter urging ministers to support independence.

Adam Smith studied at the University of Glasgow in Scotland. Smith published his first book *Theory of Moral Sentiments* in 1759, in which he states, "The happiness of mankind, as well as of all other rational creatures, seems to have been the original purpose of the Author of Nature." But it is Smith's second book *The Wealth of Nations* published in 1776 from which Americans gained his Scottish notions of money management and a free market economy. Smith argued that freeing of producers and consumers from any regulation by government would almost automatically produce wealth. "The natural effort of every individual to better his own condition, when suffered to exert itself with freedom and security, is so powerful a principle, that it is alone, and without any assistance, not only capable of carrying on the society to wealth and prosperity, but of surmounting a hundred impertinent obstructions with which the folly of human laws too often encumbers its operations..."

John Adams, the first Vice-President and second President

In 1765, John Adams published his *Essay on the Canon and Feudal Law*. It informed colonists of how their ancestors escaped persecution but retained their rights and privileges. In conclusion, Adams exclaims, "let the pulpit resound with the doctrines and sentiments of religious liberty. Let us hear the danger of thralldom to our consciences, from ignorance, extreme poverty and dependence, in short, from civil and political slavery. Let us see delineated before us, the true map of man – let us hear the dignity of his nature, and the noble rank he holds among the works of God! that consenting to slavery is a sacrilegious breach of trust, as offensive in the sight of God, as it is derogatory from our own honour, or interest, of happiness; and that God Almighty has promulgated from heaven, liberty, peace, and good will to man."

John Adams wrote to his wife regarding the opening session of the First Congress: "When the Congress met, Mr. Cushing made a motion that it should be opened with Prayer. It was opposed by Mr. Jay of New York, and Mr. Rutledge of South Carolina because we were so divided in religious sentiments...that we could not join in the same act of worship. Mr. Samuel Adams arose and said that he was no bigot, and could hear a Prayer from any gentleman of Piety and virtue, who was at the same time a friend to his Country....Accordingly, next morning [Reverend Mr. Duche'] ...read several prayers...and read...the thirty-fifth Psalm. You must remember, this was the next morning after we heard the horrible rumor of the cannonade of Boston. ...After this, Mr. Duche', unexpectedly to every body, struck out into an extemporary prayer, which filled the bosom of every man present. ...It has had an excellent effect upon everybody here. I must beg you to read that Psalm."

On June 21, 1776, John Adams wrote: "Statesmen, my dear Sir, may plan and speculate for liberty, but it is Religion and Morality alone, which can establish the Principles upon which Freedom can securely stand. The only foundation of a free Constitution is pure Virtue, and if this cannot be inspired into our People in a greater Measure, than they have it now, they may change their Rulers and the forms of Government, but they will not obtain a lasting liberty."

The day following Congressional approval of the Declaration of Independence, John Adams wrote his wife: "The second day of July, 1776, will be the most memorable epoch in the history of America. I am apt to believe that it will be celebrated by succeeding generations as the great anniversary Festival. It ought to be commemorated, as the Day of Deliverance, by solemn acts of devotion to God Almighty. It ought to be solemnized with pomp and parade, with shows, games, sports, guns, bells, bonfires and illuminations, from one end of this continent to the other, from this time forward forever....I am well aware of the toil and blood and treasure that it will cost to maintain this Declaration, and support and defend these States. Yet through all the gloom I can see the rays of ravishing light and glory. I can see that the end is worth more than all the means; that posterity will triumph in that day's transaction, even though we may regret it, which I trust in God we shall not."

John Adams was Vice-President under George Washington from 1789 to 1797. On August 14, 1796, he made this diary entry: "One great advantage of the Christian religion is that it brings the great principle of the law of nature and nations -- Love your neighbor as yourself and do to others as you would that others should do to you, -- to the knowledge, belief, and veneration of the whole people....No other institution for education, no kind of political discipline, could diffuse this kind of necessary information, so universally among all ranks and descriptions of citizens. The duties and rights of the man and the citizen are thus taught from early infancy to every creature. The sanctions of a future life are thus added to the observance of civil and political, as well as domestic and private duties. Prudence, justice, temperance, and fortitude, are thus taught to be the means and conditions of future as well as present happiness."

John Adams wrote the following in a letter to Dr. Benjamin Rush on January 21, 1810: "The Christian Religion, as I understand it, is the brightest of the glory and the express portrait of the eternal, self-evident, independent, benevolent, all-powerful and all-merciful Creator, Preserver and Father of the Universe, the first good, first perfect, and first fair. It will last as long as the world. Neither savage nor civilized man could ever have discovered or invented it. Ask me not then whether I am a Catholic or Protestant, Calvinist or Arminian. As far as they are Christians, I wish to be a fellow disciple of them all.

John Adams wrote the following to Thomas Jefferson on June 28th, 1813 regarding the founders: "Who composed that Army of fine young Fellows that was then before my Eyes? There were among them, Roman Catholicks, English Episcopalians, Scotch and American Presbyterians, Methodists, Moravians, Anababtists, German Lutherans, German Calvinists Universalists, Arians, Priestleyans, Socinians, Independents, Congregationalists, Horse Protestants and House Protestants, Deists and Atheists; and "Protestans qui ne croyent rien ("Protestants who believe nothing")." Very few however of several of these Species. Nevertheless all Educated in the general Principles of Christianity: and the general Principles of English and American Liberty." [Horse Protestants traveled by horse to different towns to preach. House Protestants held home Bible studies.]

John Adams was the second President of the United States (1797-1801)

In John Adams' inaugural address, he stated: "...the representatives of this nation...not only broke to pieces the chains which were forging and the rod of iron that was lifted up, but frankly cut asunder the ties which had bound them... With humble reverence, I feel it to be my duty to add, if a veneration for the religion of a people who profess and call themselves Christians, and a fixed resolution to consider a decent respect for Christianity among the best recommendations for the public service, can enable me in any degree to comply with your wishes, it shall be my strenuous endeavor that this sagacious injunction of the two Houses shall not be without effect....And may that Being who is supreme over all, the Patron of Order, the Fountain of Justice, and the Protector in all ages of the world of virtuous liberty, continue His blessings upon this nation and its Government and give it all possible success and duration consistent with the ends of His Providence."

Wars and treaties with Muslims (1783-1817): Was America a Christian nation or not?

Muslim Barbary Powers (Tunis, Morocco, Algiers, Tripoli, and Turkey) were warring against the "Christian" nations (England, France, Spain, Denmark, and the US) in retaliation for Crusades of previous centuries. From about 1783 to 1817 these "Barbary pirates" attacked undefended American merchant ships and enslaved "Christian" seamen. In exchange for "tribute", American envoys negotiated numerous treaties with the Barbary nations to ensure "protection" of American merchant ships in the Mediterranean Sea. Upon receipt of such tribute, one Barbary ruler said, "To speak truly and candidly...we must acknowledge to you that we have never received articles of the kind of so excellent a quality from any Christian nation." The 1797 Treaty of Tripoli cost America "...forty thousand Spanish dollars, thirteen watches of gold, silver & pinsbach, five rings, of which three of diamonds, one of sapphire and one with a watch in it, One hundred & forty piques of cloth, and four caftans of brocade."

The Muslims warred with the United States because we were a Christian nation, but to prevent escalation of a "Holy War", Article 11 of the 1797 Treaty of Tripoli stated: "As the government of the United States of America is not in any sense founded on the Christian religion as it has in itself no character of enmity against the laws, religion or tranquility of Musselmen (Muslims) and as the said States (America) have never entered into any war or act of hostility against any Mahometan nation, it is declared by the parties that no pretext arising from religious opinions shall ever produce an interruption of the harmony existing between the two countries." (Article 11 was dropped eight years later.)

While discussing the Barbary conflict with Thomas Jefferson, President John Adams declared: "The policy of Christendom has made cowards of all their sailors before the standard of Mahomet. It would be heroical and glorious in us to restore courage to ours." **President John Adams, along with Congress, ratified the Treaty of Tripoli in 1797. The treaty of Tripoli remained on the books for eight years, at which time the treaty was renegotiated, and Article 11 was dropped.**

President John Adams appointed General William Eaton as "Consul to Tunis", and he later led military expeditions against Tripoli. Eaton's official correspondence during his service confirms that the conflict was a Muslim war against a Christian America. Eaton apprised the Secretary of State as to why the Muslims would be such fearsome foes: "Taught by revelation that war with the Christians will guarantee the salvation of their souls, and finding so great secular advantages in the observance of this religious duty [the secular advantage of keeping captured cargoes], their inducements to desperate fighting are very powerful." To a new Secretary of State, Eaton wrote: "It is a maxim of the Barbary States, that "The Christians who would be on good terms with them must fight well or pay well."

When General Eaton ended his military action against Tripoli, he noted in his personal journal: "April 8th. We find it almost impossible to inspire these wild bigots with confidence in us or to persuade them that, being Christians, we can be otherwise than enemies to Musselmen. We have a difficult undertaking!...May 23rd. Hassien Bey, the commander in chief of the enemy's forces, has offered by private insinuation for my head six thousand dollars and double the sum for me a prisoner; and $30 per head for Christians."

In a letter to Thomas Jefferson on June 28, 1813, John Adams wrote: "The general principles, on which the Fathers achieved independence, were the only Principles in which that beautiful Assembly of young Gentlemen could Unite....And what were these general Principles? I answer, the general Principles of Christianity, in which all these Sects were United: And the general Principles of English and American Liberty, in which all those young Men United, and which had United all Parties in America, in Majorities sufficient to assert and maintain her Independence. Now I will avow, that I then believe, and now believe, that those general Principles of Christianity, are as eternal and immutable, as the Existence and Attributes of God; and that those Principles of Liberty, are as unalterable as human Nature and our terrestrial, mundane System."

In a letter to Judge F.A. Van der Kemp on January 13, 1815, John Adams stated: "I have searched after truth by every means and by every opportunity in my power, and with a sincerity and impartiality, for which I can appeal to God, my adored Maker. My religion is founded on the love of God and my neighbor; in the hope of pardon for my offenses; upon contrition; upon the duty as well as the necessity of supporting with patience the inevitable evils of life; in the duty of doing no wrong, but all the good I can, to the creation, of which I am but an infinitesimal part. I believe, too, in a future state of rewards and punishments..."

John Adams wrote, "The Bible contains the most profound philosophy, the most perfect morality, and the most refined policy that ever was conceived upon earth."

In his 1848 book, *Signers of the Declaration of Independence*, B. J. Lossing wrote regarding John Adams: "In the Spring of 1826 his physical powers rapidly declined, and on the fourth of July of that year he expired, in the ninety-second year of his age. On the very same day, and at nearly the same hour, his fellow committee-man in drawing up the *Declaration of Independence*, Thomas Jefferson, also died. It was the fiftieth anniversary of that glorious act and the coincidence made a deep impression upon the public mind."

James Madison, 4th U. S. President (1809-1817)

Madison wrote to William Bradford, Jr., one of his friends from Princeton, in November of 1772: " A watchful eye must be kept on ourselves lest while we are building ideal monuments of Renown and Bliss here we neglect to have our names enrolled in the Annals of Heaven. As for myself, I am too dull and infirm now to look out for any extraordinary things in this world, for I think my sensations for many months past have intimated to me not to expect a long and healthy life ... though it may be better with me after some time, [but] I hardly dare expect it, and therefore have little spirit and to set about anything that is difficult in acquiring and useless in possessing after one has exchanged time for eternity." [Note: He outlived all others who signed the U.S. Constitution.]

James Madison wrote again to William Bradford in September of 1773: "My advice is... that you would always keep the Ministry obliquely in View whatever your profession be....I have sometimes thought there could not be a stronger testimony in favor of Religion or against temporal Enjoyments even the most rational and manly than for men who occupy the most honorable and gainful departments and are rising in reputation and wealth, publicly to declare their unsatisfactoriness by becoming fervent Advocates in the cause of Christ, & I wish you may give in your Evidence in this way."

Madison disapproved of Virginia's religious persecution

Madison was baptized and raised in the Anglican faith, the established religion of the colony of Virginia. His strong position of defending religious freedom began when he stood with his father outside a jail and listened to several Baptists preach from their cell windows, having been imprisoned for their faith. Madison disapproved of this to his friend William Bradford in January of 1774: "There are at this [time] in the adjacent County not less than 5 or 6 well meaning men in close Goal [jail] for publishing their religious Sentiments which in the main are very orthodox."

Madison framed Virginia's constitution

Madison was elected to the Virginia Constitutional Convention in April, 1776 where he framed its constitution. Accompanying the new state constitution, a *Declaration of Rights* was drafted by George Mason with a significant amendment by young James Madison that "all men are equally entitled to the free exercise of religion, according to the dictates of conscience." Madison later referred to Virginia's *Declaration of Rights* as "the basis and foundation of government."

Madison, the architect of the U. S. Constitution

James Madison and Alexander Hamilton called for a constitutional convention. Madison sent an outline of his Virginia Plan to Washington, urging his attendance. The governor of Virginia, Edmund Randolph, presented the Virginia Plan to the assembly, but Madison spoke 161 times during the debates. William Pierce, a delegate from Georgia, wrote: "Mr. Maddison is a character who has long been in public life; and what is very remarkable every Person seems to acknowledge his greatness. He blends together the profound politician, with the Scholar. In the management of every great question he evidently took the lead in the Convention, and tho' he cannot be called an Orator, he is a most agreeable, eloquent and convincing Speaker. From a spirit of industry and application which he possesses in a most eminent degree, he always comes forward the best informed Man of any point in debate...Mr. Maddison is about 37 years of age, a Gentleman of great modesty, – with a remarkable sweet temper."

James Madison was one of the primary authors of *The Federalist Papers* which helped to ratify the *U. S. Constitution*. As a member of Congress, he also authored nine of the ten accepted articles in the Bill of Rights, excluding the first. He also assisted in organizing the executive department and creating a system of federal taxation. In opposition to Hamilton's policies, he and Jefferson founded the Democratic-Republican Party.

Marbury v. Madison: the beginning of Judicial Review (1803)

As Jefferson's new Secretary of State, Madison refused to deliver the remaining commissions to judges appointed by former President Adams, including William Marbury's. Marbury sued, and the Supreme Court sided with him. Madison supported judicial review of state actions, but he didn't believe the Supreme Court had the constitutional authority to "review" his actions. So Madison refused to deliver the commission to Marbury. Madison had his decision to ignore the Judiciary Act of 1789 overturned by the Supreme Court; yet that Act exceeded the authority allotted the Court under Article 3 of the Constitution. Because Congress did not remove or reprimand those judges for "bad behavior", it set precedent for judicial activism today.

In Madison's first inaugural address of 1809, he concluded, saying, "...we have all been encouraged to feel in the guardianship and guidance of that Almighty Being whose power regulates the destiny of nations, whose blessings have been so conspicuously dispensed to this rising Republic, and to whom we are bound to address our devout gratitude for the past, as well as our fervent supplications and best hopes for the future."

Virginia Statute of Religious Freedom

An act for establishing religious Freedom.

Whereas, Almighty God hath created the mind free;

That all attempts to influence it by temporal punishments or burthens, or by civil incapacitations tend only to beget habits of hypocrisy and meanness, and therefore are a departure from the plan of the holy author of our religion, who being Lord, both of body and mind yet chose not to propagate it by coercions on either, as was in his Almighty power to do,

That the impious presumption of legislators and rulers, civil as well as ecclesiastical, who, being themselves but fallible and uninspired men have assumed dominion over the faith of others, setting up their own opinions and modes of thinking as the only true and infallible, and as such endeavouring to impose them on others, hath established and maintained false religions over the greatest part of the world and through all time;

That to compel a man to furnish contributions of money for the propagation of opinions, which he disbelieves is sinful and tyrannical;

That even the forcing him to support this or that teacher of his own religious persuasion is depriving him of the comfortable liberty of giving his contributions to the particular pastor, whose morals he would make his pattern, and whose powers he feels most persuasive to righteousness, and is withdrawing from the Ministry those temporary rewards, which, proceeding from an approbation of their personal conduct are an additional incitement to earnest and unremitting labours for the instruction of mankind;

That our civil rights have no dependence on our religious opinions any more than our opinions in physics or geometry,

That therefore the proscribing any citizen as unworthy the public confidence, by laying upon him an incapacity of being called to offices of trust and emolument, unless he profess or renounce this or that religious opinion, is depriving him injuriously of those privileges and advantages, to which, in common with his fellow citizens, he has a natural right,

That it tends only to corrupt the principles of that very Religion it is meant to encourage, by bribing with a monopoly of worldly honours and emoluments those who will externally profess and conform to it;

That though indeed, these are criminal who do not withstand such temptation, yet neither are those innocent who lay the bait in their way;

That to suffer the civil magistrate to intrude his powers into the field of opinion and to restrain the profession or propagation of principles on supposition of their ill tendency is a dangerous fallacy which at once destroys all religious liberty because he being of course judge of that tendency will make his opinions the rule of judgment and approve or condemn the sentiments of others only as they shall square with or differ from his own;

That it is time enough for the rightful purposes of civil government, for its officers to interfere when principles break out into overt acts against peace and good order;

And finally, that Truth is great, and will prevail if left to herself, that she is the proper and sufficient antagonist to error, and has nothing to fear from the conflict, unless by human interposition disarmed of her natural weapons free argument and debate, errors ceasing to be dangerous when it is permitted freely to contradict them:

Be it enacted by General Assembly that no man shall be compelled to frequent or support any religious worship, place, or ministry whatsoever, nor shall be enforced, restrained, molested, or burthened in his body or goods, nor shall otherwise suffer on account of his religious opinions or belief, but that all men shall be free to profess, and by argument to maintain, their opinions in matters of Religion, and that the same shall in no wise diminish, enlarge or affect their civil capacities. And though we well know that this Assembly elected by the people for the ordinary purposes of Legislation only, have no power to restrain the acts of succeeding Assemblies constituted with powers equal to our own, and that therefore to declare this act irrevocable would be of no effect in law; yet we are free to declare, and do declare that the rights hereby asserted, are of the natural rights of mankind, and that if any act shall be hereafter passed to repeal the present or to narrow its operation, such act will be an infringement of natural right.

[Thomas Jefferson drafted the Virginia Statue of Religious Freedom in 1777, but it was not passed into law until 1786 when James Madison proposed it.]

"I think by far the most important bill in our whole code is that for the diffusion of knowlege among the people. no other sure foundation can be devised for the preservation of freedom, and happiness." (Jefferson to George Wythe August 13, 1786)

First Amendment prohibited establishment of one Christian denomination

George Mason proposed the First Amendment be worded, "All men have an equal, natural and unalienable right to the free exercise of religion, according to the dictates of conscience; and that no particular sect or society of Christians ought to be favored or established by law in preference to others." Roger Sherman was also on the committee which decided the wording of the First Amendment. He opposed the First Amendment at first, since Congress had no authority delegated from the Constitution in such areas, he deemed it unnecessary. The final wording came from Fisher Ames, "Congress shall make no law respecting an establishment of religion, or prohibiting the free exercise thereof; or abridging the freedom of speech, or of the press; or the right of the people peaceably to assemble, and to petition the government for a redress of grievances."

Joseph Story was the son of one of the Boston Tea Party "Indians", a US Representative from 1808 to 1809, and was appointed as a Justice on the US Supreme Court in 1811 by President James Madison. In his work, *A Familiar Exposition of the Constitution of the United States* (1840), Justice Joseph Story, stated: "We are not to attribute this prohibition of a national religious establishment (First Amendment) to an indifference to religion in general, and especially to Christianity (which none could hold in more reverence than the framers of the Constitution)....The real object of the First Amendment was not to countenance, much less to advance Mohammedanism, or Judaism, or infidelity, by prostrating Christianity, but to exclude all rivalry among Christian sects and to prevent any national ecclesiastical establishment which should give to a hierarchy the exclusive patronage of the national government."

President Jefferson's "Wall of Separation" Draft

To messers Nehemiah Dodge, Ephraim Robbins, & Stephen S. Nelson, a committee of the Danbury Baptist association in the state of Connecticut.

Gentlemen

The affectionate sentiments of esteem & approbation which you are so good as to express towards me, on behalf of the Danbury Baptist association, give me the highest satisfaction. my duties dictate a faithful & zealous pursuit of the interests of my constituents, and, in proportion as they are persuaded of my fidelity to those duties, the discharge of them becomes more & more pleasing.

Believing with you that religion is a matter which lies solely between man & his god, that he owes account to none other for his faith or his worship, that <u>the legitimate powers of government reach actions only and not opinions</u>, I contemplate with sovereign reverence that act of the whole American people which declared that their legislature should "<u>make no law respecting an establishment of religion, or prohibiting the free exercise thereof;</u>" thus building a wall of eternal separation between Church & State. Congress thus inhibited from acts respecting religion, and the Executive authorised only to execute their acts, I have refrained from prescribing even those occasional performances of devotion, practiced indeed by the Executive of another nation as the legal head of its church, but subject here, as religious exercises only to the voluntary regulations and discipline of each respective sect,

[Jefferson first wrote: "*confining myself therefore to the duties of my station, which are merely temporal, <u>be assured that your religious rights shall never be infringed by any act of mine</u> and that.*" These lines he crossed out and then wrote: "*concurring with*"; having crossed out these two words, he wrote: "*Adhering to this great act of national legislation in behalf of the rights of conscience*"; next he crossed out these words and wrote: "*Adhering to this expression of the supreme will of the nation in behalf of the rights of conscience I shall see with friendly dispositions the progress of those sentiments which tend to restore to man all his natural rights, convinced that he has no natural rights in opposition to his social duties.*"]

I reciprocate your kind prayers for the protection & blessing of the common father and creator of man, and tender you for yourselves & the Danbury Baptist [your religious] association assurances of my high respect & esteem.

Th Jefferson
Jan. 1. 1802.

(<u>emphasis</u> added)

[President Thomas Jefferson's plan of education for the schools in the District of Washington was adopted. His plan required the Bible and Isaac Watt's *Hymnal* as the primary books to teach reading.]

Signers from Northern Colonies/States

The Northern colonies consisted of Massachusetts, Connecticut, New Hampshire, and Rhode Island. They had strong Puritan (Congregationalist) roots often typified in public days of fasting and prayer. The following proclamation was issued by John Langdon, governor of New Hampshire, in 1786: "Vain is the acknowledgment of a Supreme Ruler of the Universe, unless such acknowledgments influence our practice, and call forth those expressions of homage and adoration that are due to his character and providential government... It having been the laudable practice of this State... to set apart a day... [to] penitently confess their manifold sins and transgressions, and fervently implore the divine benediction... that we may all be disposed to lead quiet and peaceable lives, in all godliness and honesty... and above all, that he would rain down righteousness upon the earth, revive religion, and spread abroad the knowledge of the true GOD, the Saviour of man, throughout the world."

The delegates of Massachusetts who signed the Declaration of Independence were Elbridge Gerry (Episcopalian), Robert Treat Paine (Congregationalist), John Adams (Congregationalist), Samuel Adams (Congregationalist), and John Hancock (Congregationalist). Elbridge Gerry, Samuel Adams, and John Hancock also signed the Articles of Confederation, as did Francis Dana, James Lovell, and Samuel Holten. Rufus King (Episcopalian), and Nathaniel Gorham (Congregationalist) signed the US Constitution. After graduating from Harvard, Robert Treat Paine took a voyage to Europe. Upon returning, he studied theology and confirmed his belief in the truth of Christianity. In 1755, he served as chaplain to an expedition to the north, and afterwards preached a few times in several places.

John Hancock befriended righteous government (1774)
On the event of the Boston Massacre, John Hancock gave the following speech in Boston: "Some boast of being 'friends to government': I am a friend to 'righteous' government, to a government founded upon the principles of reason and justice.... And let us play the man for our GOD, and for the cities of our GOD; while we are using the means in our power, let us humbly commit our righteous cause to the great LORD of the universe, who loveth righteousness and hateth inequity. -- And having secured the approbation of our hearts, by a faithful and unwearied discharge of our duty to our country, let us joyfully leave her important concerns in the hands of HIM who raiseth up and putteth down empires and kingdoms of the world as HE pleases; and with cheerful submission to HIS sovereign will, devoutly say, 'Although the fig-tree shall not blossom... we will joy in the GOD of our salvation.'(Habakkuk 3:17-18)"

As President of the Massachusetts Provincial Congress, John Hancock encouraged the people of his colony to repent: "We think it is encumbent upon this people to humble themselves before God on account of their sins, for He hath been pleased in His righteous judgment to suffer a great calamity to befall us, as the present controversy between Great Britain and the Colonies. [And] also implore the Divine Blessing upon us, that by the assistance of His grace, we may be enabled to reform whatever is amiss among us, so that God may be pleased to continue to us the blessings we enjoy, and remove the tokens of His displeasure, by causing harmony and union to be restored between Great Britain and these Colonies."

CONNECTICUT
Roger Sherman (Congregationalist) signed all three of America's founding documents. William Williams (Congregationalist) only signed the *Declaration of Independence*. Titus Hosmer and Andrew Adams signed the *Articles of Confederation*. Samuel Huntington (Christian) and Oliver Wolcott (Christian) signed both early documents. William Samuel Johnson (Episcopalian) signed the *U. S. Constitution*, but Oliver Ellsworth (Congregationalist) left the convention before signing it. Roger Sherman's support of a national Thanksgiving holiday was recorded in the Annals of Congress: "Mr. Sherman justified the practice of thanksgiving, on any signal event, not only as a laudable one in itself, but as warranted by a number of precedents in Holy Writ: for instance, the solemn thanksgivings and rejoicings which took place in the time of Solomon, after the building of the temple, was a case in point. This example, he thought, worthy of Christian imitation on the present occasion."

Samuel Huntington was a member of the Continental Congress, and its president from 1779-1781. B. J. Lossing wrote in 1848, "His integrity and patriotism were stern and unbending; and so conspicuous became his sound judgment and untiring industry, that in 1779 he was appointed President of Congress, then the highest office in the nation." He was governor of Connecticut from 1786-1796. Mr. Lossing wrote, "Governor Huntinton lived the life of the irreproachable and sincere Christian, and those who knew him most intimately, loved him the most affectionately....Hence as a devoted Christian and a true patriot, he never swerved from duty, or looked back after he placed his hand to the work."

Oliver Elsworth wrote, "The primary objects of government are the peace, order, and prosperity of society. To the promotion of these objects, good morals are essential. Institutions for the promotion of good morals are therefore objects of legislative provision and support; and among these, religious institutions are imminently useful and important."

Oliver Wolcott was a member of the Continental Congress and fought during the War of Independence. He became Governor of Connecticut in 1796. B. J. Lossing's 1848 book, *Signers of the Declaration of Independence*, described Wolcott: "As a patriot and statesman, a christian and a man, Governor Wolcott presented a bright example; for inflexibility, virtue, piety and integrity, were his prominent characteristics."

William Samuel Johnson was president of Columbia University from 1787-1800. The following was his speech to the first graduating class after the Revolutionary War: "You this day, gentlemen, assume new characters, enter into new relations, and consequently incur new duties. You have, by the favor of Providence and the attention of friends, received a public education, the purpose whereof hath been to qualify you the better to serve your Creator and your country....Your first great duties...are those you owe to Heaven, to your Creator and Redeemer. Remember... that you are bought with a price... of the precious blood of the Son of God....Love, fear, and serve Him as your Creator, Redeemer, and Sanctifier....Make Him your friend and protector and your felicity is secured both here and hereafter. And with respect to particular duties to Him, it is your happiness that you are well assured that he best serves his Maker, who does most good to his country and to mankind."

Roger Sherman's Connecticut Compromise
A heated dispute erupted during the Constitutional Convention concerning State representation in Congress. After Ben Franklin's call for prayer, Roger Sherman suggested that state representation in the Senate be equal and that state representation in the House be based on population; this proposal came to be called the "Connecticut Compromise," and was adopted. He also served on a committee responsible for creating instructions for representatives headed for Canada, which stated: "You are further to declare that we hold sacred the rights of conscience, and may promise to the whole people, solemnly in our name, the free and undisturbed exercise of their religion. And...that all civil rights and the right to hold office were to be extended to persons of any Christian denomination."

NEW HAMPSHIRE
The following delegates of New Hampshire signed the *Declaration on Independence*: Matthew Thornton (Christian), William Whipple (Congregationalist), and Josiah Bartlett (Congregationalist). Josiah Bartlett also signed the Articles of Confederation, as did John Wentworth, Jr.. John Langdon and Nicholas Gilman, both Congregationalists, signed the *U. S. Constitution*.

Regarding Matthew Thornton, in his 1848 book, *Signers of the Declaration of Independence*, B. J. Lossing wrote, "Dr. Thornton was greatly beloved by all who knew him, and to the close of his long life he was a consistent and zealous Christian. He always enjoyed remarkably good health, and, by practice of those hygeian virtues, temperance and cheerfulness, he attained a patriarchal age (p. 89)."

John Langdon supplied arms and money to the Continental Army, and also fought as a colonel in the militia. He considered laziness the same as infidelity, stating before Congress: "There was evidence in New Hampshire of an "infidel age" in which the indolent, extravagant and wicked may divide the blessings of life with the industrious, the prudent and the virtuous." John Langdon was also the first president of the New Hampshire Bible Society, whose goal was to place a Bible into every home in New Hampshire.
As governor of New Hampshire, John Langdon made a Proclamation for a General Thanksgiving in 1785: "It therefore becomes our indispensable Duty, not only to acknowledge... our dependence on the Supreme Ruler of the Universe, but as a People peculiarly favoured, to testify our Gratitude to the Author of all our Mercies, in the most solemn and public manner....to celebrate the Praises of our divine Benefactor; to acknowledge our own Unworthiness, confess our manifold Transgressions, implore his Forgiveness, and intreat the continuance of those Favours which he had been graciously pleased to bestow upon us; that he would inspire our Rulers with Wisdom, prosper our Trade and Commerce, smile upon our Husbandry, bless our Seminaries of Learning, and spread the Gospel of his Grace over all the Earth. And all servile Labour is forbidden on said Day."

RHODE ISLAND
As delegates of Rhode Island, Elbridge Gerry (Episcopalian), Stephen Hopkins (Christian) and William Ellery (Congregationalist) signed the *Declaration of Independence*. William Ellery also signed the *Articles of Confederation*, as did Henry Marchant and John Collins. As the smallest State, Rhode Island refused to send delegates to the Constitutional Convention, expecting only larger States would control its outcome. Rhode Island rejected the Constitution in 1788, and they were the last State to ratify it in 1790.

In his 1848 book, *Signers of the Declaration of Independence*, B. J. Lossing wrote regarding William Ellery: "In connection with Rufus King, of New York, he made strong efforts in 1785, to have slavery in the United States abolished. After the new constitution was adopted in 1788, and the new government was put in operation, he was appointed collector for the port of Newport, which office he retained until his death, which occurred on the fifteenth of February, 1820, in the seventy-third year of his age. As a patriot and a Christian, his name will ever be revered."

In his 1848 book, *Signers of the Declaration of Independence*, B. J. Lossing wrote regarding Stephen Hopkins: "The life of Mr. Hopkins exhibits a fine example of the rewards of honest, persevering industry. Although his early education was limited, yet he became a distinguished mathematician and filled almost every public station in the gift of the people, with singular ability. He was a sincere and consistent Christian, and the impress of his profession [of faith] was upon all his deeds."

Signers from Middle Colonies/States

The middle colonies consisted of Pennsylvania, New York, New Jersey, and Delaware. They were mostly Quaker and Dutch Reformed. The dominant denominations of the middle colonies were Quaker and Dutch Reformed. Quakers were members of the Religious Society of Friends who were known for their pacifism. The Dutch Reformed Church was founded in New York in 1628, and was renamed the Reformed Church of America in 1867.

John Dickinson was a politician and an attorney from Delaware and Pennsylvania, and also a wealthy farmer with 37 slaves. He earned his epithet "penman of the Revolution" after his *Letters from a Farmer in Pennsylvania* were published throughout the Colonies (1767-1768) and Europe (1770). He was a member of the First and Second Continental Congresses. He wrote most of the 1774 Petition to the King and the 1775 Olive Branch Petition, and the final draft of the 1775 Declaration of the Causes and Necessity of Taking Up Arms.

John Dickinson did not sign the *Declaration of Independence* because he thought the Colonies should establish foreign allies who would support them first; but he did free his slaves after it was signed. He was one of the few members among the Founders who actually fought in the Revolutionary War. Dickinson was elected president of the 1786 Annapolis Convention which called for the Constitutional Convention to be held the following year. Dickinson signed the *U. S. Constitution* as a delegate from Delaware.

PENNSYLVANIA

Pennsylvanian Robert Morris (Episcopalian), the financier of the Revolution, signed all three founding documents. The delegates of Pennsylvania who signed the *Declaration of Independence* were Dr. Benjamin Rush (Presbyterian), John Morton (attended St. James Church), James Smith (Presbyterian), George Taylor (Presbyterian), George Ross, and James Wilson (Episcopalian); and George Clymer (Quaker/Lutheran) and Benjamin Franklin (Deist who had a pew at Christ Church) who also signed the *U. S. Constitution*. The signers of the *Articles of Confederation* were Daniel Roberdeau, Jonathan Bayard Smith, and William Clingan. The other signers of the *U. S. Constitution* were Thomas Mifflin (Quaker/Lutheran), Thomas Fitzsimons (Roman Catholic) and Jared Ingersoll, Jr. (Presbyterian); James Wilson supported it but left the Convention before signing.

Dr. Benjamin Rush

Dr. Benjamin Rush wrote *Essays, Literary, Moral, and Philosophical* (1798), in which he wrote the following referring to public education: "I know there is an objection among many people to teaching children doctrines of any kind, because they are liable to be controverted. But let us not be wiser than our Maker. If moral precepts alone could have reformed mankind, the mission of the Son of God into all the world would have been unnecessary. The perfect morality of the Gospel rests upon the doctrine which, though often controverted has never been refuted: I mean the vicarious life and death of the Son of God." Rush also wrote, "The Bible contains more truths than any other book in the world."

James Wilson

As the first Law Professor of the University of Philadelphia, James Wilson explained that all law comes from God, stating: "That law, which God has made for man in his present state; that law, which is communicated to us by reason and conscience, the divine monitors within us, and by the sacred oracles, the divine monitors without us....As promulgated by reason and the moral sense it has been called natural; as promulgated by the holy scriptures, it has been called revealed law. As addressed to men, it has been denominated the law of nature; as addressed to political societies, it has been denominated the law of nations. But it should always be remembered, that this law, natural or revealed, made for men or for nations, flows from the same divine source; it is the law of God....Human law must rest its authority, ultimately, upon the authority of that law, which is divine."

George Clymer

B.J. Lossing wrote the following regarding George Clymer in his 1848 book *Signers of the Declaration of Independence*: "...the remainder of his days were spent in acts of private usefulness, and a personal preparation for another world. He died on the twenty-fourth day of January, 1813, in the seventy-fourth year of his age. His long life was an active and useful one, and not a single moral stain marked its manifested purity."

NEW JERSEY

The following delegates of New Jersey signed the *Declaration of Independence*: Francis Hopkinson (Episcopalian), John Hart (Presbyterian), Abraham Clark (Presbyterian), and Richard Stockton (Presbyterian); and Rev. John Witherspoon (Presbyterian) who also signed the *Articles of Confederation*. Nathaniel Scudder also signed the *Articles*. Those from New Jersey who signed the *U. S. Constitution* were William Livingston (Presbyterian), David Brearly (Episcopalian), William Paterson (Presbyterian), and Jonathan Dayton (Episcopalian); William Churchill Houston (Presbyterian) attended the Convention for two weeks and left before signing. Jonathan Dayton was the youngest signer of the *Constitution of the United States*. The city of Dayton, Ohio, was named after him.

Richard Stockton
In his Last Will and Testament, Richard Stockton wrote: "As my children will have frequent occasion of perusing this instrument, and may probably be peculiarly impressed with the last words of their father, I think proper here, not only to subscribe to the entire belief of the great leading doctrine of the Christian religion... but also in the heart of a father's affection, to charge and exhort them to remember "that the fear of the Lord is the beginning of wisdom.""

David Brearly
David Brearly was instructed by Rev. John Witherspoon at Princeton University. Brearly became a lawyer in 1767 and was such an outspoken patriot that he was arrested for "high treason" against Britain. David Brearly was also "...a warden of St. Michael's Church....a compiler of the Protestant Episcopal Prayer Book and a delegate to the Episcopal General Convention in 1786."

William Livingston
William Livingston was a member of the First and Second Continental Congresses. He also served as the first Governor of New Jersey, and was re-elected for 14 years.

He published articles defending his faith, such as No. 46: "I believe the Scriptures of the Old and New Testaments, without any foreign comments or human explanations....I believe that he who feareth God and worketh righteousness will be accepted of Him....I believe that the virulence of some...proceeds not from their affection to Christianity, which is founded on too firm a basis to be shaken by the freest inquiry, and the Divine authority of which I sincerely believe without receiving a farthing for saying so."

William Patterson
William Patterson was Governor of New Jersey after Governor Livingston died. He also served as a U.S. Supreme Court Justice appointed by President George Washington. On May 24, 1800, William Patterson stated: "Religion and morality...[are] necessary to good government, good order, and good laws, for 'when the righteous are in authority, the people rejoice."

NEW YORK
The following delegates of New York signed the *Declaration of Independence*, with the exception of Robert R. Livingston (Christian): William Floyd (Presbyterian), Phillip Livingston (Presbyterian), and Lewis Morris; and Francis Lewis who also signed the *Articles of Confederation*. The other New York delegates who signed the *Articles of Confederation* were James Duane (Episcopalian), William Duer, and Gouverneur Morris (Episcopalian). Although New York sent three delegates to the Constitutional Convention only Alexander Hamilton (Episcopalian) signed it, because the other two, Robert Yates (Dutch Reformed) and John Lansing (Dutch Reformed), were Anti-Federalists.

Robert R. Livingston
Robert R. Livingston may have withheld his signature from the *Declaration* because of a strong commitment to his New York constituents. He later helped frame New York's *Constitution*, and he was the first Chancellor (governor) to administrate New York according to it. He applied to New York for navigation rights on the Hudson for river boats "propelled by fire or steam" in 1798, but his experiments were unsuccessful. He later teamed up with Robert Fulton to produce a successful steamboat in 1807. In *Signers of the Declaration of Independence* (1848) author B. J. Lossing described the life of Robert R. Livingston as follows: "And to all of his eminent virtues and attainments he added that of a sincere and devoted Christian, the crowning attribute in the character of a good and great man."

Gouverneur Morris
In 1785, Morris stated the following in the Pennsylvania State Assembly: "How can we hope for public peace and national prosperity, if the faith of governments so solemnly pledged can be so lightly infringed? Destroy this prop, which once gave us support, and where will you turn in the hour of distress? To whom will you look for succor? By what promise or vows can you hope to obtain confidence? This hour of distress will come. It comes to all, and the moment of affliction is known to Him alone, whose Divine Providence exalts or depresses states and kingdoms. Not by the blind dictates of arbitrary will. Not by a tyrannous and despotic mandate. But in proportion to their obedience or disobedience of His just and holy laws. It is He who commands us that we abstain from wrong. It is He who tells you, "do unto others as ye would that they would do unto you."

Alexander Hamilton's Christian Constitutional Society
Alexander Hamilton helped the adoption of the *Constitution* by writing 52 of the 85 essays in *The Federalist Papers*, and by conducting a ratification campaign in reluctant New York. After the Constitutional Convention, Alexander Hamilton stated: "For my own part, I sincerely esteem it a system which without the finger of God, never could have been suggested and agreed upon by such a diversity of interests."He wrote to James Bayard: "In my opinion, the present constitution is the standard to which we are to cling. Under its banner *bona fide* must we combat our political foes, rejecting all changes but through the channel itself provided for amendments. By these general views of the subject have my reflections been guided.

I now offer you the outline of the plan they have suggested. Let an association be formed to be denominated "The Christian Constitutional Society," its object to be first: The support of the Christian religion. second: The support of the United States."

Alexander Hamilton's death from dueling with Aaron Burr
On July 11, 1804, Hamilton was fatally shot by Aaron Burr. The Episcopalian Reverend Benjamin Moore ministered the last rites to him. He recorded Hamilton's last words: "I have a tender reliance on the mercy of the Almighty, through the merits of the Lord Jesus Christ. I am a sinner. I look to Him for mercy; pray for me." In his eulogy, Alexander Hamilton was quoted as stating: "Mortals hastening to the tomb, and once the companions of my pilgrimage, take warning, and avoid my errors. Cultivate the virtues I have recommended. Choose the Saviour I have chosen'. Live disinterestedly, and would you rescue anything from final dissolution, lay it up in God."

DELAWARE
Delaware's delegates who signed the *Declaration of Independence* were Caesar Rodney (Episcopalian) and Thomas McKean (Presbyterian). Thomas McKean also signed the *Articles of Confederation* along with Nicholas Van Dyke (Episcopalian); and John Dickinson (Quaker/Episcopalian) who also signed the *U. S. Constitution*. The other delegates who signed the *U. S. Constitution* were George Read (Episcopalian), Gunning Bedford (Presbyterian), Richard Bassett (Methodist), and Jacob Broom (Lutheran). Delaware's State motto is "Liberty and Independence".

George Read
George Read was known as "the Father of Delaware," for writing "the first edition of her laws," and the *Constitution of the State*. Delaware's 1776 requirements, for holding office included: "Every person who shall be chosen a member of either house, or appointed to any office or place of trust...shall...make and subscribe the following declaration, to wit: "I, _____, do profess faith in God the Father, and in Jesus Christ His only Son, and in the Holy Ghost, one God, blessed for evermore; and I do acknowledge the holy scriptures of the Old and New Testament to be given by divine inspiration."

John Dickinson
John Dickinson, "The Penman of the Revolution," wrote pamphlets including Petition to the King, 1771; The Declaration and Resolves of the First Continental Congress, 1774; and The Declaration of the Cause of Taking Up Arms, 1775. His most famous were the Letters from a Farmer in Pennsylvania, 1767-68: "But, above all, let us implore the protection of that infinitely good and gracious Being 'by whom kings reign, and princes decree justice.'(Proverbs 8:15) '...that they should sit every man under his vine, and under his fig-tree, and NONE SHOULD MAKE THEM AFRAID.'(Micah 4:4) But whatever kind of minister he is, that attempts to innovate a single iota in the privileges of these colonies, him I hope you will undauntedly oppose; and that you will never suffer yourselves to be cheated or frightened into any unworthy obsequiousness. On such emergencies you may surely, without presumption, believe that ALMIGHTY GOD himself will look upon your righteous contest with gracious approbation."

Richard Bassett
John Wesley was one of the preachers of the Great Awakening. He also introduced a new "method" of worship, and those who followed this method came to be called Methodists. Captain Richard Bassett converted to Methodism during the Revolutionary War. He personally contributed half the cost of building the First Methodist Church in Dover. He emancipated his slaves and then paid them as hired labor. He held Methodist campmeetings on his own plantation, and would joyfully sing with his former slaves.

Jacob Broom
Jacob Broom was described in the *Official Papers of Delaware* (1909), as follows: "A fair example of the product of a sturdy, energetic, sagacious ancestry and evangelical Swedish orthodoxy, co-operating amid the trying environments of a struggling colony in an undeveloped land....He lived in one of the potential crises of history, in which and for which the sublime visions and words of prophets and apostles had developed and inspired a stalwart manhood....As it is an accepted fact that "the foundation of all permanent prosperity is a right regard for the Divine Being", it is proper to say that Jacob Broom was a God-fearing man."

Signers from Southern Colonies/States

VIRGINIA
The following delegates of Virginia signed the *Declaration of Independence*: Thomas Jefferson ("freethinker" who called himself a Christian), Benjamin Harrison, Thomas Nelson, Jr., Carter Braxton, and George Wythe (Episcopalian); and Christians Francis Lightfoot Lee and Richard Henry Lee who also signed the *Articles of Confederation*. Other Virginia delegates who signed the *Articles of Confederation* included John Banister, Thomas Adams, and John Harvie. Episcopalians John Blair, Jr., James Madison, Jr., and George Washington signed the *U. S. Constitution*. George Wythe and James McClurg left before signing, and George Mason (Episcopalian) and Edmund Randolph (Episcopalian) refused to sign the *Constitution* without a bill of rights. Virginia was an Anglican colony whose religious order was ruled by England. During the Revolution, Virginian's maintained the same form of worship, but chose their own bishops to govern the new American Episcopal Church.

George Mason
George Mason stated before the General Court of Virginia: "The laws of nature are the laws of God, whose authority can be superseded by no power on earth." George Mason was the author of the *Virginia Constitution* and the *Virginia Bill of Rights*. He refused to sign the United States Constitution because it did not abolish slavery and did not keep the Federal Government's power from infringing on the States. George Mason later insisted that Congress add a bill of rights. On August 22, 1787, George Mason addressed the Continental Congress, saying, "Every master of slaves is born a petty tyrant. They bring the judgment of heaven upon a country. As nations cannot be rewarded or punished in the next world, they must be in this. By an inevitable chain of causes and effects, Providence punishes national sins, by national calamities."

Edmund Randolph
After Benjamin Franklin's appeal for prayer during the Constitutional Convention, Edmund Randolph moved "That a sermon be preached at the request of the convention on the 4th of July, the anniversary of Independence; & thenceforward prayers be used in ye Convention every morning." Congress has opened with prayers ever since. On the 4th of July all the members of the Constitutional Convention assembled in the Reformed Calvinistic Church to hear a sermon by Rev. William Rogers.

Richard Henry Lee
According to B.J. Lossing's *Signers of the Declaration of Independence* (1848), "Mr. Lee was a sincere practical Christian, a kind and affectionate husband and parent, a generous neighbor, a constant friend, and in all the relations of life, he maintained a character above reproach. 'His hospitable door,' says Sanderson, 'was open to all; the poor and destitute frequented it for relief, and consolation...'"

Francis Lightfoot Lee
B.J. Lossing described Francis Lightfoot Lee in *Signers of the Declaration of Independence* (1848): "Possessed of ample wealth, he used it like a philosopher and a Christian in dispensing its blessings for the benefit of his country and his fellow men."

John Blair, Jr.
John Blair, Jr. wrote a letter to his sister upon her husband's death, in which he quotes Hebrews 9:27 and I Corinthians 2:9: "...it being appointed for all men once to die...Let us seek for comfort where alone it may be found...now as our Holy Religion teaches we may contemplate him translated to a better Life and ineffably enjoying all that variety of Bliss which Eye hath not seen nor Ear heard nor the Heart conceived. May the Celestial vision forever preserve you from the Gloominess of Grief and reconcile you to all the Dispensations of Him who cannot err. My situation both with Respect to my Family and Fortune (all being in the Power of the Enemy and much in their possession) is bad enough. But I trust for a happy issue and for power to bear all His appointments as I ought."

MARYLAND
The following delegates of Maryland signed the *Declaration of Independence*: Samuel Chase (Episcopalian), Thomas Stone, William Paca (Christian), and Charles Carroll of Carrollton (Roman Catholic). John Hanson and Daniel Carroll (Roman Catholic, who also signed the *U. S. Constitution*) signed the *Articles of Confederation*. James McHenry (Presbyterian) and Daniel of St Thomas Jenifer (Episcopalian) signed the *U. S. Constitution*, but Episcopalians Luther Martin and John Francis Mercer left early. Named for Catholic Queen Mary, Maryland had a high Catholic population, which was represented by two delegates.

Samuel Chase
Samuel Chase was appointed by George Washington as a U.S. Supreme Court Justice, 1796-1811. Justice Chase gave the court's opinion in Runkel v. Winemiller (1799): "Religion is of general and public concern, and on its support depend, in great measure, the peace and good order of government, the safety and happiness of the people. By our form of government, the Christian religion is the established religion; and all sects and denominations of Christians are placed upon the same equal footing, and are equally entitled to protection in their religious liberty."

William Paca
B.J. Lossing describe William Paca in *Signers of the Declaration of Independence* (1848): He was a pure and active patriot, a consistent Christian, and a valuable citizen, in every sense of the word. His death was mourned as a public calamity; and his life, pure and spotless, active and useful, exhibited a bright exemplar for the imitation of the young men of America."

Charles Carroll
Charles Carroll, a Roman Catholic, wrote to Charles W. Wharton on September 27, 1825: "On the mercy of my Redeemer I rely for salvation and on His merits not on the works I have done in obedience to His precepts." He wrote to Rev. John Stanford on October 9, 1827, stating: "To obtain religious as well as civil liberty I entered jealously into the Revolution, and observing the Christian religion divided into many sects, I founded the hope that no one would be so predominant as to become the religion of the State. That hope was thus early entertained, because all of them joined in the same cause, with few exceptions of individuals." Roman Catholics believe that church traditions and Papal decrees are equal to the Bible in authority.

Luther Martin
Luther Martin proposed the "electoral college" system for selecting the President that we still use today. Individuals vote for Presidential candidates in November, and then each state's members of the electoral college vote in December; therefore it is possible for a Presidential candidate to win the popular vote but lose the election for lack of electoral college votes.

He strongly opposed a central government which would usurp State authority. Luther Martin described himself as being devoted to "The sacred truths of the Christian religion."

James McHenry
Doctor James McHenry served with distinction under General Washington. As president of the first Bible society in Baltimore, Maryland, he sought funds for distributing Bibles to the public: "In vain, without the Bible, we increase penal laws and draw intrenchments around our institutions. Bibles are strong intrenchments. Where they abound, men cannot pursue wicked courses, and at the same time enjoy quiet conscience....It is a book of councils and directions, fitted to every situation in which man can be placed. It is an oracle which reveals to mortals the secrets of heavens and the hidden will of the Almighty....It is an estate, whose title is guaranteed by Christ, whose delicious fruits ripen every season, survive the worm, and keep through eternity. It is for the purpose of distributing this divine book more effectually and extensively among the multitudes, whose circumstances render such a donation necessary, that your cooperation is most earnestly requested."

NORTH CAROLINA
The following delegates of North Carolina signed the *Declaration of Independence*: William Hooper (Episcopalian) and Joseph Hewes (Episcopalian); and John Penn who also signed the *Articles of Confederation*. Cornelius Harnett, Jr. (Episcopalian/Deist) and John Williams also signed the *Articles of Confederation*. William Blount (Presbyterian), Richard Dobbs Spaight, Jr. (Episcopalian), and Hugh Williamson (Presbyterian) signed the *U. S. Constitution*, but Alexander Martin (Presbyterian/Episcopalian) and William Richardson Davie (Presbyterian) left the convention early. Presbyterians had no tie to the Anglican Church, whereas the Episcopalian Church was derived from the Anglican Church. Presbyterians were Protestants who primarily followed John Calvin's reformed theology.

Hugh Williamson
Hugh Williamson studied for the ministry, visiting and praying for the sick in his neighborhood. "In 1759 he went to Connecticut, where he pursued his theological studies and was licensed to preach. After returning from Connecticut, he was admitted to membership in the Presbytery of Philadelphia...[and there] preached nearly two years." Hugh Williamson's book, *Observations of the Climate in Different Parts of America*, provided scientific explanations for Noah's flood and the miracles of the exodus.

SOUTH CAROLINA
The following delegates of South Carolina signed the *Declaration of Independence*: Arthur Middleton, Thomas Lynch, Jr., and Edward Rutledge (Anglican); and Thomas Heyward, Jr. who also signed the Articles of Confederation. Other delegates who signed the *Articles of Confederation* were Henry Laurens (Huguenot), William Henry Drayton, John Mathews, and Richard Hutson (Presbyterian). Episcopalians John Ruteledge, Charles Cotesworth Pinckney, Charles Pinckney III, and Pierce Butler signed the *U. S. Constitution*. Huguenots were French Protestants who referred to themselves as reformers who followed the teachings of John Calvin. They suffered tremendous persecution in France for their beliefs.

Charles Cotesworth Pinckney
Charles Cotesworth Pinckney learned "to love Christ and the Church." As the first president of the Charleston Bible Society, he distributed Bibles to Negroes, and laid aside finances to evangelize the slaves and teach them to read the Bible.

Henry Laurens
Henry Laurens stated, "I had the honor of being one who framed that *Constitution*. In order effectually to accomplish these great ends set forth in the *Constitution*, it is especially the duty of those who bear rule to promote and encourage respect for God and virtue and to discourage every degree of vice and immorality."

GEORGIA
The following delegates of Georgia signed the *Declaration of Independence*: Button Gwinnett (Episcopalian), Lyman Hall (Congregationalist), and George Walton (Anglican). John Walton, Edward Telfair, and Edward Langworthy (Episcopalian) signed the *Articles of Confederation*. William Few (Methodist) and Abraham Baldwin (Congregationalist) signed the *U. S. Constitution*, but Episcopalians William Leigh Pierce and William Houstoun left the convention before signing. Georgia had a large Baptist population at the time. Baptists believe in salvation by faith in Jesus Christ sealed by immersion, and unable to be changed, leading to the phrase "once saved, always saved".

Lyman Hall
Lyman Hall's epitaph reads as follows: "Beneath this stone rest the remains of the Hon. Lyman Hall, Formerly Governor of this State, who departed this life the 19th of Oct., 1790, in the 67th year of his age." "In the cause of America he was uniformly a patriot. In the incumbent duties of a husband and a father he acquitted himself with affection and tenderness. But, reader, above all, know from this inscription that he left the probationary scene as a true Christian and an honest man."

George Washington

George Washington was a vestryman at Pohick Church from 1762 to 1784. A plaque at Pohick Church contains his Prayer for America. "Almighty God; We make our earnest prayer that Thou wilt keep the United States in Thy Holy protection; and Thou wilt incline the hearts of the Citizens to cultivate a spirit of subordination and obedience to Government; and entertain a brotherly affection and love for one another and for their fellow Citizens of the United States at large, and particularly for their brethren who have served in the Field. And finally that Thou wilt most graciously be pleased to dispose us all to do justice, to love mercy, and to demean ourselves with that Charity, humility, and pacific temper of mind which were the Characteristics of the Divine Author of our blessed Religion, and without a humble imitation of whose example in these things we can never hope to be a happy nation. Grant our supplication, we beseech Thee, through Jesus Christ our Lord. Amen."

[Roger Sherman served on the committee which produced the 1st Amendment in 1789. He encouraged President Washington to declare a national Thanksgiving Day, stating so during a session of Congress:]

"Mr. [Roger] Sherman justified the practice of **thanksgiving**, on any signal event, not only as a laudable one in itself but as warranted by a number of precedents in Holy Writ: for instance, the solemn thanksgivings and rejoicings which took place in the time of Solomon after the building of the temple was a case in point. This example he thought worthy of Christian imitation on the present occasion; and he would agree with the gentleman who moved the resolution."

[This proclamation for a national day of thanks regarding God's provision of Americans prior to the Revolution, His aid to them in achieving independence, and His wisdom in establishing a constitutional government follows:]

By the President of the United States of America, a Proclamation.

Whereas it is the duty of all Nations to acknowledge the providence of Almighty God, to obey his will, to be grateful for his benefits, and humbly to implore his protection and favor− and whereas both Houses of Congress have by their joint Committee requested me to recommend to the People of the United States a day of public thanksgiving and prayer to be observed by acknowledging with grateful hearts the many signal favors of Almighty God especially by affording them an opportunity peaceably to establish a form of government for their safety and happiness.

Now therefore I do recommend and assign Thursday the 26th day of November next to be devoted by the People of these States to the service of that great and glorious Being, who is the beneficent Author of all the good that was, that is, or that will be-- That we may then all unite in rendering unto him our sincere and humble thanks−for his kind care and protection of the People of this Country previous to their becoming a Nation−for the signal and manifold mercies, and the favorable interpositions of his Providence which we experienced in the course and conclusion of the late war−for the great degree of tranquility, union, and plenty, which we have since enjoyed--for the peaceable and rational manner, in which we have been enabled to establish constitutions of government for our safety and happiness, and particularly the national One now lately instituted−for the civil and religious liberty with which we are blessed; and the means we have of acquiring and diffusing useful knowledge; and in general for all the great and various favors which he hath been pleased to confer upon us.

and also that we may then unite in most humbly offering our prayers and supplications to the great Lord and Ruler of Nations and beseech him to pardon our national and other transgressions−to enable us all, whether in public or private stations, to perform our several and relative duties properly and punctually−to render our national government a blessing to all the people, by constantly being a Government of wise, just, and constitutional laws, discreetly and faithfully executed and obeyed−to protect and guide all Sovereigns and Nations (especially such as have shewn kindness unto us) and to bless them with good government, peace, and concord−To promote the knowledge and practice of true religion and virtue, and the encrease of science among them and us−and generally to grant unto all Mankind such a degree of temporal prosperity as he alone knows to be best.

Given under my hand at the City of New York the third day of October in the year of our Lord 1789.

Go: Washington

Washington's Farewell Address

Madison and Hamilton shaped President Washington's notes into the address he sought.

September 17, 1796

Friends and Fellow Citizens:

The period for a new election of a citizen to administer the Executive Government of the United States being not far distant, and the time actually arrived when your thoughts must be employed in designating the person who is to be clothed with that important trust, it appears to me proper, especially as it may conduce to a more distinct expression of the public voice, that I should now apprise you of the resolution I have formed to decline being considered among the number of those out of whom a choice is to be made.

I beg you at the same time to do me the justice to be assured that this resolution has not been taken without a strict regard to all the considerations appertaining to the relation which binds a dutiful citizen to his country; and that in withdrawing the tender of service, which silence in my situation might imply, I am influenced by no diminution of zeal for your future interest, no deficiency of grateful respect for your past kindness, but am supported by a full conviction that the step is compatible with both.

The acceptance of and continuance hitherto in the office to which your suffrages have twice called me have been a uniform sacrifice of inclination to the opinion of duty and to a deference for what appeared to be your desire. I constantly hoped that it would have been much earlier in my power, consistently with motives which I was not at liberty to disregard, to return to that retirement from which I had been reluctantly drawn. The strength of my inclination to do this previous to the last election had even led to the preparation of an address to declare it to you; but mature reflection on the then perplexed and critical posture of our affairs with foreign nations and the unanimous advice of persons entitled to my confidence impelled me to abandon the idea. I rejoice that the state of your concerns, external as well as internal, no longer renders the pursuit of inclination incompatible with the sentiment of duty or propriety, and am persuaded, whatever partiality may be retained for my services, that in the present circumstances of our country you will not disapprove my determination to retire.

The impressions with which I first undertook the arduous trust were explained on the proper occasion. In the discharge of this trust I will only say that I have, with good intentions, contributed toward the organization and administration of the Government the best exertions of which a very fallible judgment was capable, Not unconscious in the outset of the inferiority of my qualifications, experience in my own eyes, perhaps still more in the eyes of others, has strengthened the motives to diffidence of myself; and every day the increasing weight of years admonishes me more and more that the shade of retirement is as necessary to me as it will be welcome. Satisfied that if any circumstances have given peculiar value to my services they were temporary, I have the consolation to believe that, while choice and prudence invite me to quit the political scene, patriotism does not forbid it.

In looking forward to the moment which is intended to terminate the career of my political life my feelings do not permit me to suspend the deep acknowledgment of that debt of gratitude which I owe to my beloved country for the many honors it has conferred upon me; still more for the steadfast confidence with which it has supported me, and for the opportunities I have thence enjoyed of manifesting my inviolable attachment by services faithful and persevering, though in usefulness unequal to my zeal. If benefits have resulted to our country from these services, let it always be remembered to your praise and as an instructive example in our annals that under circumstances in which the passions, agitated in every direction, were liable to mislead; amidst appearances sometimes dubious; vicissitudes of fortune often discouraging; in situations in which not unfrequently want of success has countenanced the spirit of criticism, the constancy of your support was the essential prop of the efforts and a guaranty of the plans by which they were effected. Profoundly penetrated with this idea, I shall carry it with me to my grave as a strong incitement to unceasing vows that Heaven may continue to you the choicest tokens of its beneficence; that your union and brotherly affection may be perpetual; that the free Constitution which is the work of your hands may be sacredly maintained; that its administration in every department may be stamped with wisdom and virtue; that, in fine, the happiness of the people of these States, under the auspices of liberty, may be made complete by so careful a preservation and so prudent a use of this blessing as will acquire to them the glory of recommending it to the applause, the affection, and adoption of every nation which is yet a stranger to it.

Here, perhaps, I ought to stop. But a solicitude for your welfare which can not end but with my life, and the apprehension of danger natural to that solicitude, urge me on an occasion like the present to offer to your solemn contemplation and to recommend to your frequent review some sentiments which are the result of much reflection, of no inconsiderable observation, and which appear to me all important to the permanency of your felicity as a people. These will be offered to you with the more freedom as you can only see in them the disinterested warnings of a parting friend, who can possibly have no personal motive to bias his counsel. Nor can I forget as an encouragement to it your indulgent reception of my sentiments on a former and not dissimilar occasion.

Interwoven as is the love of liberty with every ligament of your hearts, no recommendation of mine is necessary to fortify or confirm the attachment.

The unity of government which constitutes you one people is also now dear to you. It is justly so, for it is a main pillar in the edifice of your real independence, the support of your tranquillity at home, your peace abroad, of your safety, of your prosperity, of that very liberty which you so highly prize. But as it is easy to foresee that from different causes and from different quarters much pains will be taken, many artifices employed, to weaken in your minds the conviction of this truth, as this is the point in your political fortress against which the batteries of internal and external enemies will be most constantly and actively (though often covertly and insidiously) directed, it is of infinite moment that you should properly estimate the immense value of your national union to your collective and individual happiness; that you should cherish a cordial, habitual, and immovable attachment to it; accustoming yourselves to think and speak of it as of the palladium of your political safety and prosperity; watching for its preservation with jealous anxiety; discountenancing whatever may suggest even a suspicion that it can in any event be abandoned, and indignantly frowning upon the first dawning of every attempt to alienate any portion of our country from the rest or to enfeeble the sacred ties which now link together the various parts.

For this you have every inducement of sympathy and interest. Citizens by birth or choice of a common country, that country has a right to concentrate your affections. The name of American, which belongs to you in your national capacity, must always exalt the just pride of patriotism more than any appellation derived from local discriminations. With slight shades of difference, you have the same religion, manners, habits, and political principles. You have in a common cause fought and triumphed together. The independence and liberty you possess are the work of joint councils and joint efforts, of common dangers, sufferings, and successes.

But these considerations, however powerfully they address themselves to your sensibility, are greatly outweighed by those which apply more immediately to your interest. Here every portion of our country finds the most commanding motives for carefully guarding and preserving the union of the whole.

The *North*, in an unrestrained intercourse with the *South*, protected by the equal laws of a common government, finds in the productions of the latter great additional resources of maritime and commercial enterprise and precious materials of manufacturing industry. The *South*, in the same intercourse, benefiting by the same agency of the *North*, sees its agriculture grow and its commerce expand. Turning partly into its own channels the seamen of the *North*, it finds its particular navigation invigorated; and while it contributes in different ways to nourish and increase the general mass of the national navigation, it looks forward to the protection of a maritime strength to which itself is unequally adapted. The *East*, in a like intercourse with the *West*, already finds, and in the progressive improvement of interior communications by land and water will more and more find, a valuable vent for the commodities which it brings from abroad or manufactures at home. The *West* derives from the *East* supplies requisite to its growth and comfort, and what is perhaps of still greater consequence, it must of necessity owe the *secure* enjoyment of indispensable *outlets* for its own productions to the weight, influence, and the future maritime strength of the Atlantic side of the Union, directed by an indissoluble community of interest as *one nation*. Any other tenure by which the *West* can hold this essential advantage, whether derived from its own separate strength or from an apostate and unnatural connection with any foreign power, must be intrinsically precarious.

While, then, every part of our country thus feels an immediate and particular interest in union, all the parts combined can not fail to find in the united mass of means and efforts greater strength, greater resource, proportionably greater security from external danger, a less frequent interruption of their peace by foreign nations, and what is of inestimable value, they must derive from union an exemption from those broils and wars between themselves which so frequently afflict neighboring countries not tied together by the same governments, which their own rivalships alone would be sufficient to produce, but which opposite foreign alliances, attachments, and intrigues would stimulate and imbitter. Hence, likewise, they will avoid the necessity of those overgrown military establishments which, under any form of government, are inauspicious to liberty, and which are to be regarded as particularly hostile to republican liberty. In this sense it is that your union ought to be considered as a main prop of your liberty, and that the love of the one ought to endear to you the preservation of the other.

These considerations speak a persuasive language to every reflecting and virtuous mind, and exhibit the continuance of the union as a primary object of patriotic desire. Is there a doubt whether a common government can embrace so large a sphere? Let experience solve it. To listen to mere speculation in such a case were criminal. We are authorized to hope that a proper organization of the whole, with the auxiliary agency of governments for the respective subdivisions, will afford a happy issue to the experiment. It is well worth a fair and full experiment. With such powerful and obvious motives to union affecting all parts of our country, while experience shall not have demonstrated its impracticability, there will always be reason to distrust the patriotism of those who in any quarter may endeavor to weaken its bands.

In contemplating the causes which may disturb our union it occurs as matter of serious concern that any ground should have been furnished for characterizing parties by *geographical discriminations--Northern* and *Southern, Atlantic* and *Western-- whence* designing men may endeavor to excite a belief that there is a real difference of local interests and views. One of the expedients of party to acquire influence within particular districts is to misrepresent the opinions and aims of other districts. You can not shield yourselves too much against the jealousies and heartburnings which spring from these misrepresentations; they tend to render alien to each other those who ought to be bound together by fraternal affection. The inhabitants of our Western country have lately had a useful lesson on this head. They have seen in the negotiation by the Executive and in the unanimous ratification by the Senate of the treaty with Spain, and in the universal satisfaction at that event throughout the

United States, a decisive proof how unfounded were the suspicions propagated among them of a policy in the General Government and in the Atlantic States unfriendly to their interests in regard to the Mississippi. They have been witnesses to the formation of two treaties that with Great Britain and that with Spain--which secure to them everything they could desire in respect to our foreign relations toward confirming their prosperity. Will it not be their wisdom to rely for the preservation of these advantages on the union by which they were procured? Will they not henceforth be deaf to those advisers, if such there are, who would sever them from their brethren and connect them with aliens?

To the efficacy and permanency of your union a government for the whole is indispensable. No alliances, however strict, between the parts can be an adequate substitute. They must inevitably experience the infractions and interruptions which all alliances in all times have experienced. Sensible of this momentous truth, you have improved upon your first essay by the adoption of a Constitution of Government better calculated than your former for an intimate union and for the efficacious management of your common concerns. This Government, the offspring of our own choice, uninfluenced and unawed, adopted upon full investigation and mature deliberation, completely free in its principles, in the distribution of its powers, uniting security with energy, and containing within itself a provision for its own amendment, has a just claim to your confidence and your support. Respect for its authority, compliance with its laws, acquiescence in its measures, are duties enjoined by the fundamental maxims of true liberty. The basis of our political systems is the right of the people to make and to alter their constitutions of government. But the constitution which at any time exists till changed by an explicit and authentic act of the whole people is sacredly obligatory upon all. The very idea of the power and the right of the people to establish government presupposes the duty of every individual to obey the established government.

All obstructions to the execution of the laws, all combinations and associations, under whatever plausible character, with the real design to direct, control, counteract, or awe the regular deliberation and action of the constituted authorities, are destructive of this fundamental principle and of fatal tendency. They serve to organize faction; to give it an artificial and extraordinary force; to put in the place of the delegated will of the nation the will of a party, often a small but artful and enterprising minority of the community, and, according to the alternate triumphs of different parties, to make the public administration the mirror of the ill-concerted and incongruous projects of faction rather than the organ of consistent and wholesome plans, digested by common counsels and modified by mutual interests.

However combinations or associations of the above description may now and then answer popular ends, they are likely in the course of time and things to become potent engines by which cunning, ambitious, and unprincipled men will be enabled to subvert the power of the people, and to usurp for themselves the reins of government, destroying afterwards the very engines which have lifted them to unjust dominion.

Toward the preservation of your Government and the permanency of your present happy state, it is requisite not only that you steadily discountenance irregular oppositions to its acknowledged authority, but also that you resist with care the spirit of innovation upon its principles, however specious the pretexts. One method of assault may be to effect in the forms of the Constitution alterations which will impair the energy of the system, and thus to undermine what can not be directly overthrown. In all the changes to which you may be invited remember that time and habit are at least as necessary to fix the true character of governments as of other human institutions; that experience is the surest standard by which to test the real tendency of the existing constitution of a country; that facility in changes upon the credit of mere hypothesis and opinion exposes to perpetual change, from the endless variety of hypothesis and opinion; and remember especially that for the efficient management of your common interests in a country so extensive as ours a government of as much vigor as is consistent with the perfect security of liberty is indispensable. Liberty itself will find in such a government, with powers properly distributed and adjusted, its surest guardian. It is, indeed, little else than a name where the government is too feeble to withstand the enterprises of faction, to confine each member of the society within the limits prescribed by the laws, and to maintain all in the secure and tranquil enjoyment of the rights of person and property.

I have already intimated to you the danger of parties in the State, with particular reference to the founding of them on geographical discriminations. Let me now take a more comprehensive view, and warn you in the most solemn manner against the baneful effects of the spirit of party generally.

This spirit, unfortunately, is inseparable from our nature, having its root in the strongest passions of the human mind. It exists under different shapes in all governments, more or less stifled, controlled, or repressed; but in those of the popular form it is seen in its greatest rankness and is truly their worst enemy.

The alternate domination of one faction over another, sharpened by the spirit of revenge natural to party dissension, which in different ages and countries has perpetrated the most horrid enormities, is itself a frightful despotism. But this leads at length to a more formal and permanent despotism. The disorders and miseries which result gradually incline the minds of men to seek security and repose in the absolute power of an individual, and sooner or later the chief of some prevailing faction, more able or more fortunate than his competitors, turns this disposition to the purposes of his own elevation on the ruins of public liberty.

Without looking forward to an extremity of this kind (which nevertheless ought not to be entirely out of sight), the common and continual mischiefs of the spirit of party are sufficient to make it the interest and duty of a wise people to discourage and restrain it.

It serves always to distract the public councils and enfeeble the public administration. It agitates the community with ill-founded jealousies and false alarms; kindles the animosity of one part against another; foments occasionally riot and insurrection. It opens the door to foreign influence and corruption, which find a facilitated access to the government itself through the channels of party passion. Thus the policy and the will of one country are subjected to the policy and will of another.

There is an opinion that parties in free countries are useful checks upon the administration of the government, and serve to keep alive the spirit of liberty. This within certain limits is probably true; and in governments of a monarchical cast patriotism may look with indulgence, if not with favor, upon the spirit of party. But in those of the popular character, in governments purely elective, it is a spirit not to be encouraged. From their natural tendency it is certain there will always be enough of that spirit for every salutary purpose; and there being constant danger of excess, the effort ought to be by force of public opinion to mitigate and assuage it. A fire not to be quenched, it demands a uniform vigilance to prevent its bursting into a flame, lest, instead of warming, it should consume.

It is important, likewise, that the habits of thinking in a free country should inspire caution in those intrusted with its administration to confine themselves within their respective constitutional spheres, avoiding in the exercise of the powers of one department to encroach upon another. The spirit of encroachment tends to consolidate the powers of all the departments in one, and thus to create, whatever the form of government, a real despotism. A just estimate of that love of power and proneness to abuse it which predominates in the human heart is sufficient to satisfy us of the truth of this position. The necessity of reciprocal checks in the exercise of political power, by dividing and distributing it into different depositories, and constituting each the guardian of the public weal against invasions by the others, has been evinced by experiments ancient and modern, some of them in our country and under our own eyes. To preserve them must be as necessary as to institute them. If in the opinion of the people the distribution or modification of the constitutional powers be in any particular wrong, let it be corrected by an amendment in the way which the Constitution designates. But let there be no change by usurpation; for though this in one instance may be the instrument of good, it is the customary weapon by which free governments are destroyed. The precedent must always greatly overbalance in permanent evil any partial or transient benefit which the use can at any time yield.

Of all the dispositions and habits which lead to political prosperity, religion and morality are indispensable supports. In vain would that man claim the tribute of patriotism who should labor to subvert these great pillars of human happiness--these firmest props of the duties of men and citizens. The mere politician, equally with the pious man, ought to respect and to cherish them. A volume could not trace all their connections with private and public felicity. Let it simply be asked, Where is the security for property, for reputation, for life, if the sense of religious obligation *desert* the oaths which are the instruments of investigation in courts of justice? And let us with caution indulge the supposition that morality can be maintained without religion. Whatever may be conceded to the influence of refined education on minds of peculiar structure, reason and experience both forbid us to expect that national morality can prevail in exclusion of religious principle.

It is substantially true that virtue or morality is a necessary spring of popular government. The rule indeed extends with more or less force to every species of free government. Who that is a sincere friend to it can look with indifference upon attempts to shake the foundation of the fabric? Promote, then, as an object of primary importance, institutions 'for the general diffusion of knowledge. In proportion as the structure of a government gives force to public opinion, it is essential that public opinion should be enlightened.

As a very important source of strength and security, cherish public credit. One method of preserving it is to use it as sparingly as possible, avoiding occasions of expense by cultivating peace, but remembering also that timely disbursements to prepare for danger frequently prevent much greater disbursements to repel it; avoiding likewise the accumulation of debt, not only by shunning occasions of expense, but by vigorous exertions in time of peace to discharge the debts which unavoidable wars have occasioned, not ungenerously throwing upon posterity the burthen which we ourselves ought to bear. The execution of these maxims belongs to your representatives; but it is necessary that public opinion should cooperate. To facilitate to them the performance of their duty it is essential that you should practically bear in mind that toward the payment of debts there must be revenue; that to have revenue there must be taxes; that no taxes can be devised which are not more or less inconvenient and unpleasant; that thee intrinsic embarrassment inseparable from the selection of the proper objects (which is always a choice of difficulties), ought to be a decisive motive for a candid construction of the conduct of the Government in making it, and for a spirit of acquiescence in the measures for obtaining revenue which the public exigencies may at any time dictate.

Observe good faith and justice toward all nations. Cultivate peace and harmony with all. Religion and morality enjoin this conduct. And can it be that good policy does not equally enjoin it? It will be worthy of a free, enlightened, and at no distant period a great nation to give to mankind the magnanimous and too novel example of a people always guided by an exalted justice and benevolence. Who can doubt that in the course of time and things the fruits of such a plan would richly repay any temporary advantages which might be lost by a steady adherence to it? Can it be that Providence has not connected the permanent felicity of a nation with its virtue? The experiment, at least, is recommended by every sentiment which ennobles human nature. Alas! is it rendered impossible by its vices?

In the execution of such a plan nothing is more essential than that permanent, inveterate antipathies against particular nations and passionate attachments for others should be excluded, and that in place of them just and amicable feelings toward all should be cultivated. The nation which indulges toward another an habitual hatred or an habitual fondness is in some degree a slave. It is a slave to its animosity or to its affection, either of which is sufficient to lead it astray from its duty and its interest. Antipathy in one nation against another disposes each more readily to offer insult and injury, to lay hold of slight causes of umbrage, and to be haughty and intractable when accidental or trifling occasions of dispute occur.

Hence frequent collisions, obstinate, envenomed, and bloody contests. The nation prompted by ill will and resentment sometimes impels to war the government contrary to the best calculations of policy. The government sometimes participates in the national propensity, and adopts through passion what reason would reject. At other times it makes the animosity of the nation subservient to projects of hostility, instigated by pride, ambition, and other sinister and pernicious motives. The peace often, sometimes perhaps the liberty, of nations has been the victim.

So, likewise, a passionate attachment of one nation for another produces a variety of evils. Sympathy for the favorite nation, facilitating the illusion of an imaginary common interest in cases where no real common interest exists, and infusing into one the enmities of the other, betrays the former into a participation in the quarrels and wars of the latter without adequate inducement or justification. It leads also to concessions to the favorite nation of privileges denied to others, which is apt doubly to injure the nation making the concessions by unnecessarily parting with what ought to have been retained, and by exciting jealousy, ill will, and a disposition to retaliate in the parties from whom equal privileges are withheld; and it gives to ambitious, corrupted, or deluded citizens (who devote themselves to the favorite nation) facility to betray or sacrifice the interests of their own country without odium, sometimes even with popularity, gilding with the appearances of a virtuous sense of obligation, a commendable deference for public opinion, or a laudable zeal for public good the base or foolish compliances of ambition, corruption, or infatuation.

As avenues to foreign influence in innumerable ways, such attachments are particularly alarming to the truly enlightened and independent patriot. How many opportunities do they afford to tamper with domestic factions, to practice the arts of seduction, to mislead public opinion, to influence or awe the public councils! Such an attachment of a small or weak toward a great and powerful nation dooms the former to be the satellite of the latter. Against the insidious wiles of foreign influence (I conjure you to believe me, fellow-citizens) the jealousy of a free people ought to be *constantly* awake, since history and experience prove that foreign influence is one of the most baneful foes of republican government. But that jealousy, to be useful, must be impartial, else it becomes the instrument of the very influence to be avoided, instead of a defense against it. Excessive partiality for one foreign nation and excessive dislike of another cause those whom they actuate to see danger only on one side, and serve to veil and even second the arts of influence on the other. Real patriots who may resist the intrigues of the favorite are liable to become suspected and odious, while its tools and dupes usurp the applause and confidence of the people to surrender their interests.

The great rule of conduct for us in regard to foreign nations is, in extending our commercial relations to have with them as little political connection as possible. So far as we have already formed engagements let them be fulfilled with perfect good faith. Here let us stop.

Europe has a set of primary interests which to us have none or a very remote relation. Hence she must be engaged in frequent controversies, the causes of which are essentially foreign to our concerns. Hence, therefore, it must be unwise in us to implicate ourselves by artificial ties in the ordinary vicissitudes of her politics or the ordinary combinations and collisions of her friendships or enmities.

Our detached and distant situation invites and enables us to pursue a different course. If we remain one people, under an efficient government, the period is not far off when we may defy material injury from external annoyance; when we may take such an attitude as will cause the neutrality we may at any time resolve upon to be scrupulously respected; when belligerent nations, under the impossibility of making acquisitions upon us, will not lightly hazard the giving us provocation; when we may choose peace or war, as our interest, guided by justice, shall counsel.

Why forego the advantages of so peculiar a situation? Why quit our own to stand upon foreign ground? Why, by interweaving our destiny with that of any part of Europe, entangle our peace and prosperity in the toils of European ambition, rivalship, interest, humor, or caprice?

It is our true policy to steer clear of permanent alliances with any portion of the foreign world, so far, I mean, as we are now at liberty to do it; for let me not be understood as capable of patronizing infidelity to existing engagements. I hold the maxim no less applicable to public than to private affairs that honesty is always the best policy. I repeat, therefore, let those engagements be observed in their genuine sense. But in my opinion it is unnecessary and would be unwise to extend them.

Taking care always to keep ourselves by suitable establishments on a respectable defensive posture, we may safely trust to temporary alliances for extraordinary emergencies.

Harmony, liberal intercourse with all nations are recommended by policy, humanity, and interest. But even our commercial policy should hold an equal and impartial hand, neither seeking nor granting exclusive favors or preferences; consulting the natural course of things; diffusing and diversifying by gentle means the streams of commerce, but forcing nothing; establishing with powers so disposed, in order to give trade a stable course, to define the rights of our merchants, and to enable the Government to support them, conventional rules of intercourse, the best that present circumstances and mutual opinion will permit, but temporary and liable to be from time to time abandoned or varied as experience and circumstances shall dictate; constantly keeping in view that it is folly in one nation to look for disinterested favors from another; that it must pay with a portion of its independence for whatever it may accept under that character; that by such acceptance it may place itself in the condition of having given equivalents for nominal favors, and yet of being reproached with ingratitude for not giving more. There can be no greater error than to expect or calculate upon real favors from nation to nation. It is an illusion which experience must cure, which a just pride ought to discard.

In offering to you, my countrymen, these counsels of an old and affectionate friend I dare not hope they will make the strong and lasting impression I could wish--that they will control the usual current of the passions or prevent our nation from running the course which has hitherto marked the destiny of nations. But if I may even flatter myself that they may be productive of some partial benefit, some occasional good--that they may now and then recur to moderate the fury of party spirit, to warn against the mischiefs of foreign intrigue, to guard against the impostures of pretended patriotism-- this hope will be a full recompense for the solicitude for your welfare by which they have been dictated.

How far in the discharge of my official duties I have been guided by the principles which have been delineated the public records and other evidences of my conduct must witness to you and to the world. To myself, the assurance of my own conscience is that I have at least believed myself to be guided by them.

In relation to the still subsisting war in Europe my proclamation of the 22d of April, 1793, is the index to my plan. Sanctioned by your approving voice and by that of your representatives in both Houses of Congress, the spirit of that measure has continually governed me, uninfluenced by any attempts to deter or divert me from it.

After deliberate examination, with the aid of the best lights I could obtain, I was well satisfied that our country, under all the circumstances of the case, had a right to take, and was bound in duty and interest to take, a neutral position. Having taken it, I determined as far as should depend upon me to maintain it with moderation, perseverance, and firmness.

The considerations which respect the right to hold this conduct it is not necessary on this occasion to detail. I will only observe that, according to my understanding of the matter, that right, so far from being denied by any of the belligerent powers, has been virtually admitted by all.

The duty of holding a neutral conduct may be inferred, without anything more, from the obligation which justice and humanity impose on every nation, in cases in which it is free to act, to maintain inviolate the relations of peace and amity toward other nations.

The inducements of interest for observing that conduct will best be referred to your own reflections and experience. With me a predominant motive has been to endeavor to gain time to our country to settle and mature its yet recent institutions, and to progress without interruption to that degree of strength and consistency which is necessary to give it, humanly speaking, the command of its own fortunes.

Though in reviewing the incidents of my Administration I am unconscious of intentional error, I am nevertheless too sensible of my defects not to think it probable that I may have committed many errors. Whatever they may be, I fervently beseech the Almighty to avert or mitigate the evils to which they may tend. I shall also carry with me the hope that my country will never cease to view them with indulgence, and that, after forty-five years of my life dedicated to its service with an upright zeal, the faults of incompetent abilities will be consigned to oblivion, as myself must soon be to the mansions of rest.

Relying on its kindness in this as in other things, and actuated by that fervent love toward it which is so natural to a man who views in it the native soil of himself and his progenitors for several generations, I anticipate with pleasing expectation that retreat in which I promise myself to realize without alloy the sweet enjoyment of partaking in the midst of my fellow-citizens the benign influence of good laws under a free government--the ever-favorite object of my heart, and the happy reward, as I trust, of our mutual cares, labors, and dangers.

GO. WASHINGTON.

Benjamin Franklin

On June 28, 1787 Benjamin Franklin motioned for Congress to be opened with prayer, and it still does today.

Mr. President:

The small progress we have made after 4 or five weeks close attendance & continual reasonings with each other -- our different sentiments on almost every question, several of the last producing as many noes as ays, is methinks a melancholy proof of the imperfection of the Human Understanding. We indeed seem to feel our own want of political wisdom, since we have been running about in search of it. We have gone back to ancient history for models of government, and examined the different forms of those Republics which having been formed with the seeds of their own dissolution now no longer exist. And we have viewed Modern States all round Europe, but find none of their Constitutions suitable to our circumstances.

In this situation of this Assembly groping as it were in the dark to find political truth, and scarce able to distinguish it when presented to us, how has it happened, Sir, that we have not hitherto once thought of humbly applying to the Father of lights to illuminate our understandings? In the beginning of the contest with G. Britain, when we were sensible of danger we had daily prayer in this room for the Divine Protection. -- Our prayers, Sir, were heard, and they were graciously answered. All of us who were engaged in the struggle must have observed frequent instances of a Superintending providence in our favor. To that kind providence we owe this happy opportunity of consulting in peace on the means of establishing our future national felicity. And have we now forgotten that powerful [F]riend? Or do we imagine that we no longer need His assistance.

I have lived, Sir, a long time and the longer I live, the more convincing proofs I see of this truth -- that **God** *governs in the affairs of men*. And if a sparrow cannot fall to the ground without [H]is notice, is it probable that an empire can rise without [H]is aid? We have been assured, Sir, in the sacred writings that "except the Lord build they labor in vain that build it." I firmly believe this; and I also believe that without [H]is concurring aid we shall succeed in this political building no better than the Builders of Babel: We shall be divided by our little partial local interests; our projects will be confounded, and we ourselves shall be become a reproach and a bye word down to future age. And what is worse, mankind may hereafter from this unfortunate instance, despair of establishing Governments by Human Wisdom, and leave it to chance, war, and conquest.

I therefore beg leave to move -- that henceforth prayers imploring the assistance of Heaven, and its blessings on our deliberations, be held in this Assembly every morning before we proceed to business, and that one or more of the Clergy of this City be requested to officiate in that service.

www.ingramcontent.com/pod-product-compliance
Lightning Source LLC
Chambersburg PA
CBHW081837230426
43669CB00018B/2733